500 Guide

Standard & Poor's 500 Guide

2007 Edition

Standard & Poor's

McGraw-Hill

New York Chicago San Francisco
Lisbon London Madrid Mexico City
Milan New Delhi San Juan Seoul
Singapore Sydney Toronto

FOR STANDARD & POOR'S
Vice President, Index Products & Services: Robert Barriera
Publisher: Frank LoVaglio

The McGraw-Hill Companies

1 2 3 4 5 6 7 8 9 0 CUS/CUS 0 9 8 7 6

ISBN-13 978-0-07-147906-6
ISBN-10 0-07-147906-6

This book is printed on acid-free paper.

The companies contained in this handbook represented the components of the S&P 500 Index as of November 1, 2006.
Additions to or deletions from the Index will cause its composition to change over time. Company additions and company deletions from the Standard & Poor's equity indexes do not in any way reflect an opinion on the investment merits of the company.

ABOUT THE AUTHOR

Standard & Poor's, a division of The McGraw-Hill Companies, Inc., is the nation's leading securities information company. It provides a broad range of financial services, including the respected Standard & Poor's ratings and stock rankings, advisory services, data guides, and the most closely watched and widely reported gauges of stock market activity—the S&P 500, S&P MidCap 400, S&P SmallCap 600, and the S&P Composite 1500 stock price indexes. Standard & Poor's products are marketed around the world and used extensively by financial professionals and individual investors.

Introduction

by Alan J. Miller, C.F.A.

While he was getting dressed one morning, Art Jones heard a news report on the radio saying that the Dow Jones Industrial Average had risen nine points on the previous day. Later he read in his morning newspaper that more stocks had declined than advanced. "How could that be?" he wondered. "Had the market gone up or down?"

Jenny Martin had been interviewing investment advisors to find someone to manage her stock portfolio and it seemed that everyone she spoke to claimed to have outperformed the market. That struck her as hard to believe and, in fact, all the managers she spoke to did seem to be comparing their results to different benchmarks. How could she tell how well those managers really had done?

"I think the market is really going to take off," Mark Johnson thought, "and I'd like to participate. But I'm afraid that even if I'm right, I could end up buying the wrong stocks and the ones I buy could go down while everything else goes up. I can't afford to diversify by buying 1,000 different companies. I just wish there were some way I could buy the whole market. Is there anything I can do?"

Mary Carter had a question for her accountant. "I'd like to invest in a few high-quality, well-established companies that are selling at reasonable prices," she said. "But with thousands and thousands of different companies around—including many that I just wouldn't be interested in because they're too new or too small—I just wouldn't know where to begin. Is there some way I could cut that number down to manageable size and know that the universe I'm looking at consists only of large capitalization, established companies?"

Andrew Perez is the marketing manager for a nationwide computer company whose products and services are used by many of the largest corporations in the country—and he's always on the lookout for even more customers. What he's really looking for are established companies that are in good financial shape and growing, so that they'll be responsive to his suggestions for upgrading their hardware, purchasing additional software, or engaging in more sophisticated networking—and will have the funds to carry out those plans if he convinces them of their value. But where can he find the names of those companies and the information about them which he requires?

Sally Kennedy is the founder and president of a small company in an industry dominated by a dozen or so major competitors. She'd really like to find out how well those larger companies in her industry are doing. Where can she look?

Six different questions, all leading to the same answer: Turn to the Standard & Poor's 500 Index.

What Is the S&P 500?

For sheer longevity, no other stock market indicators compare with the Dow Jones Industrial Average, which was first published in 1896, and the Standard & Poor's 500 Composite Stock Price Index, which was first introduced in 1923. Over the decades, both indicators have been consistently and widely cited as benchmarks of market performance.

Historically, the two indicators were viewed as complementary measures—but in recent years, the key differences between the DJIA and the S&P 500 Index have come into sharper focus. Today, sophisticated investors realize that the DJIA and the S&P 500 Index cannot be used interchangeably: based on different universes and methodologies, they provide very different pictures of market activity.

The DJIA tracks the stock performance of 30 "blue chip" companies, allowing equal weight to a one point move in each stock, notwithstanding substantial differences in stock prices and company capitalizations. As a result, a 5% move, say, in a $200 stock would have ten times the weight of a 5% move in a $20 stock and companies with larger equity capitalizations would not necessarily be weighted any more heavily than companies with smaller capitalizations. Despite these methodological shortcomings, the DJIA has generally been accepted as a reasonable indicator for the "blue chip" market but, because it contains nothing but "blue chip" stocks, by no stretch of the imagination could it be considered representative of the *overall* market.

The S&P 500, on the other hand, covers a far larger and more varied universe of companies, and hence is a more accurate barometer of the overall stock market.

Standard & Poor's 500 composite stock-price index is widely regarded as the most accurate proxy for the stock market and is used by virtually all professional consultants as the benchmark against which to measure money managers' performance. The index contains a representative sample of common stocks that trade on the New York Stock Exchange as well as on the Nasdaq Stock Market (those issues that are part of the Nasdaq National Market). Moreover, because the companies chosen for inclusion in the S&P 500 tend to be top companies in the United States, the S&P 500 Index became a component of the U.S. Department of Commerce's Index of Leading Economic Indicators in 1968. Now published by the Conference Board, a private research organization, that widely followed measure is used to signal potential turning points in the U.S. economy. Also, more than $1 trillion in passive index funds are currently indexed to the S&P 500.

As the name indicates, the S&P 500 consists of 500 U.S. companies, which represent about 77% of the total market value of American stocks. Although these are not necessarily the 500 largest companies in the United States, most of the largest companies are included. All of these stocks are widely held and the total market value of the "500" is over $12.7 trillion.

Approximately 85% (424 issues representing 85% of the market value) of the issues in the index are listed on the New York Stock Exchange. The remaining 15% (76 issues accounting for about 15% of the market value) are traded on the Nasdaq Stock Market.

But let's take another look at the half-dozen questions raised at the beginning of this introduction.

The Six Questions...Answered

1. Art Jones

If the Dow Jones Industrial Average rose nine points but more stocks declined than advanced, had the market really gone up or down?

In a sense, there really is no one answer to that question because it all depends on how you choose to define "the market." But in another sense, it is probably fair to say that the S&P 500 Index provides as good a picture of what the market "really" does as any index around. It is, after all, an average of 500 companies, not just 30, which makes it a better proxy for the overall market than the DJIA. And since, unlike advance-decline indices, the 500 stocks are *capitalization* weighted, it wouldn't be distorted by declines in a large number of small companies which might actually have been more than offset (in terms of total dollars gained or lost by investors) by increases in a smaller number of large companies. So if Art wants to know how the market "really" did, he ought to take a look at the S&P 500.

2. Jenny Martin

If all the investment advisors she talks to claim to have outperformed the market (by comparing their results to different benchmarks), how can she tell how well they've truly done?

Now this question turns out to be somewhat easier than it appeared to be at first blush. For if the S&P 500 really is the best proxy for the overall stock market, then an investment advisor who invests in common stocks can reasonably be measured by comparing his performance to that index. Of course, if the advisor invests only in international stocks, or small capitalization stocks, or long-term bonds, or some other mix of assets, a different benchmark would have to be developed to measure his performance fairly. But for the typical common stock manager, the best benchmark probably is the S&P 500.

3. Mark Johnson

How can he invest in the overall market without taking the risk of investing in the stocks of individual companies?

Consider the alternatives. First, Mark might just invest in an actively managed common stock mutual fund which is broadly diversified among hundreds of companies. If the diversification is broad enough, and if the securities owned are selected at random, the law of averages would suggest that the fund's results would approximate those of the overall market (as measured by the S&P 500).

Unfortunately, however, most funds *aren't* that diversified. They might own a couple of hundred stocks, but probably not 500. And for that reason alone, this approach might not work.

But there is another even more important reason why this approach would not work. It is because the portfolios of *actively managed* funds, by definition, are *not* randomized, but rather are consciously structured by their managers to reflect those managers' best judgments regarding the relative attractiveness of alternative investment vehicles. Thus, those managers *intentionally* overweight some companies (which the fund managers expect to be stellar performers) and underweight others (which they expect to fare relatively poorly).

Now, if the fund managers' judgments turn out to be right, terrific. But suppose they're not? In that case, the fund, despite its being broadly diversified, still may perform substantially worse than the market (as measured by the S&P 500). And remember, that risk—the chance of performing poorly as a result of picking the wrong stocks, even though the market on average did well—is precisely the risk that Mark is seeking to avoid.

No, selecting an *actively* managed fund *wouldn't* solve Mark's problem. But suppose Mark could invest in a *passively* managed fund—one whose managers simply tried to replicate the performance of the market as a whole, without trying to add value (and thereby running the risk of subtracting value instead) through individual stock selection. Would that satisfy Mark's need?

In fact, it would. And, fortunately for Mark, *passively* managed mutual funds which merely seek to replicate the performance of the S&P 500 Index (commonly known as index funds) abound. Indeed, these funds have grown in popularity (in large part because, strange as it may seem, stock market indices actually have tended to *outperform* a majority of mutual funds and pension plans actively managed by professionals). For those investors seeking intraday trading flexibility, exchange-traded funds (ETFs), such as Standard & Poor's Depository Receipts (SPDRs) and iShares, are listed securities representing a basket of equities that mirror the underlying index's performance.

But passively managed index funds and ETFs are not the only options open to Mark. He may make an even more direct bet on the direction of the market by investing in "stock index futures" themselves—or, if he is even more speculatively inclined, in *options* on stock index futures.

Stock index futures are, in effect, futures contracts on the value of the theoretical basket of securities which comprise a stock index. Indices on which futures contracts may be written include the New York Stock Exchange Composite Index (traded on the New York Futures Exchange), the Value Line Composite Index (traded on the Kansas City Board of Trade), and, of course, the Standard & Poor's 500 Index and Standard & Poor's MidCap 400 Index (both traded on the Chicago Mercantile Exchange). Since investors in such indices obviously can't deliver an index of stocks to a futures buyer, settlement of such contracts is in cash.

The Chicago Mercantile Exchange also trades options on Standard & Poor's 500 and MidCap 400 futures contracts. Exercise of one of those options establishes a position in the underlying futures contract. Options on the Standard & Poor's 500 Index are traded on the Chicago Board Options Exchange, and options on the Standard & Poor's MidCap 400 Index are traded on the American Stock Exchange. Unlike options on futures contracts, options on stock indices are settled in cash.

Of course, if Mark thought that the market was likely to decline rather than advance, but didn't want to incur the risk of going short the wrong stocks (those that might turn out to rise even in a falling market), trading in Standard & Poor's 500 Index futures contracts and options on those contracts could serve his purposes too. In that event, he would sell short futures contracts or call options on futures contracts or buy put options on futures contracts, rather than buying futures contracts or call options.

Finally, if Mark discovered a stock which he believed would outperform the market substantially but thought that the overall market itself was just as likely to decline as to rise, the futures contracts and options markets could help him too. In that event, he could buy the stock and short the market (by shorting futures contracts or calls on futures contracts on the S&P 500 Composite Index). If he turned out to be right and the stock did substantially outperform the market, he would do well whether the stock market itself rose or fell: if the stock market rose, the stock would rise even more (on a percentage basis), so he'd make more money on his long position in the stock than he would lose on his short positions in the futures or options markets. On the other hand, if the stock market declined, the stock would decline less (or maybe even rise) and he'd make more money on his short positions in futures contracts or options than he'd lose on the stock itself (or maybe, if he got really lucky, even make money on both).

4. Mary Carter

How can she find individual high-quality, well-established companies from which to select, for investment purposes, those that are selling at reasonable prices?

The components of the S&P 500 Composite Index are just what Mary is looking for. Indeed, the "average" S&P 500 company boasts a market value of $25.5 billion.

What Mary should do is to turn to the pages of this book, which include extensive data on all 500 companies in the S&P 500 Composite Index. But before doing so, she should be sure to read the final sections of this introduction—"What You'll Find in This Book" and "How to Use This Book to Select Investments"—in order to learn just how to extract the most value from that data.

5. Andrew Perez

How can Andrew find established companies that are in good financial shape, growing, and have the funds to acquire the hardware or software he'll be recommending to them?

The companies in the S&P 500 Composite Index should be Andrew's starting point, too, and the pages of this book are where he'll find the information on those companies which he requires. But before thumbing through these pages, Andrew, like Mary, would be well advised to refer first to the section titled "What You'll Find in This Book," which appears below.

6. Sally Kennedy

How can Sally find out how her major competitors, the larger companies in her industry, are doing?

You guessed it: A good place for Sally to start would be with the companies in this book. If Sally's industry is dominated by a number of large competitors, there is little doubt that most, if not all, will show up here. And here's where she's likely to find a lot of the information on those companies too.

But we're at the point now where we really must try to provide Mary, Andrew, and Sally with more guidance. Art, Jenny, and Mark, you will recall, were primarily concerned with using the Standard & Poor's 500

Composite Index in the aggregate, in order to find out how the market's "really" doing (Art), to measure investment managers' performance (Jenny), or to invest in the market as a whole or hedge individual stock positions (Mark). And we've explained all that.

Mary, Andrew, and Sally, however, are primarily interested in the *components* of the S&P 500, in their quest for companies which might represent good individual investments (Mary), or companies which could turn out to be good potential clients (Andrew), or companies which are important business competitors (Sally). And it is those individual companies which most of this book is about. So it's time to show Mary, Andrew, Sally—and you. . . .

What You'll Find in This Book

In the pages that follow you will find an array of text and statistical data on 500 different companies spanning 147 sub-industries. This information, dealing with everything from the nature of these companies' basic businesses, recent corporate developments, current outlooks, and select financial information relating to revenues, earnings, dividends, margins, capitalization, and so forth, might initially seem overwhelming. However, it's not that difficult. Just take a few moments to familiarize yourself with what you'll find on these pages.

Following is a glossary of terms and definitions used throughout this book. Please refer to this section as you encounter terms which need further clarification.

Glossary

S&P STARS -Since January 1, 1987, Standard and Poor's Equity Research Services has ranked a universe of common stocks based on a given stock's potential for future performance. Under proprietary STARS (STock Appreciation Ranking System), S&P equity analysts rank stocks according to their individual forecast of a stock's future total return potential versus the expected total return of a relevant benchmark (e.g., a regional index (S&P Asia 50 Index, S&P Europe 350 Index or S&P 500 Index)), based on a 12-month time horizon. STARS was designed to meet the needs of investors looking to put their investment decisions in perspective.

S&P 12-Month Target Price -The S&P equity analyst's projection of the market price a given security will command 12 months hence, based on a combination of intrinsic, relative, and private market valuation metrics.

Investment Style Classification - Characterizes the stock as either a growth- or value-oriented investment, and, indicates the market value (size) of the company as large-cap, mid-cap or small-cap. Growth stocks typically have a higher price-to-earnings and price-to-cash flow ratio, that represents the premium that is being paid for the expected higher growth. Value stocks typically have higher dividends and more moderate price-to-earnings ratios consistent with their current return policies.

Qualitative Risk Assessment - The S&P equity analyst's view of a given company's operational risk, or the risk of a firm's ability to continue as an ongoing concern. The Qualitative Risk Assessment is a relative ranking to the S&P U.S. STARS universe, and should be reflective of risk factors related to a company's operations, as opposed to risk and volatility measures associated with share prices.

Quantitative Evaluations - In contrast to our qualitative STARS recommendations, which are assigned by S&P analysts, the quantitative evaluations described below are derived from proprietary arithmetic models. These computer-driven evaluations may at times contradict an analyst's qualitative assessment of a stock. One primary reason for this is that different measures are used to determine each. For instance, when designating STARS, S&P analysts assess many factors that cannot be reflected in a model, such as risks and opportunities, management changes, recent competitive shifts, patent expiration, litigation risk, etc.

S&P Quality Rankings (also known as **S&P Earnings & Dividend Rankings**) - Growth and stability of earnings and dividends are deemed key elements in establishing S&P's Quality Rankings for common stocks, which are designed to capsulize the nature of this record in a single symbol. It should be noted, however, that the process also takes into consideration certain adjustments and modifications deemed desirable in establishing such rankings. The final score for each stock is measured against a scoring matrix determined by analysis of the scores of a large and representative sample of stocks. The range of scores in the array of this sample has been aligned with the following ladder of rankings:

A+	Highest	B-	Lower
A	High	C	Lowest
A-	Above Average	D	In Reorganization
B+	Average	NR	Not Ranked
B	Below Average		

S&P Fair Value Rank - Using S&P's exclusive proprietary quantitative model, stocks are ranked in one of five groups, ranging from Group 5, listing the most undervalued stocks, to Group 1, the most overvalued issues. Group 5 stocks are expected to generally outperform all others. A positive (+) or negative (-) Timing Index is placed next to the Fair Value ranking to further aid the selection process. A stock with a (+) added to the Fair Value Rank simply means that this stock has a somewhat better chance to outperform other stocks with the same Fair Value Rank. A stock with a (-) has a somewhat lesser chance to outperform other stocks with the same Fair Value Rank. The Fair Value rankings imply the following: 5-Stock is significantly undervalued; 4-Stock is moderately undervalued; 3-Stock is fairly valued; 2-Stock is modestly overvalued; 1-Stock is significantly overvalued.

S&P Fair Value Calculation - The price at which a stock should trade at, according to S&P's proprietary quantitative model that incorporates both actual and estimated variables (as opposed to only actual variables in the case of S&P Quality Ranking). Relying heavily on a company's actual return on equity, the S&P Fair Value model places a value on a security based on placing a formula-derived price-to-book multiple on a company's consensus earnings per share estimate.

Insider Activity - Gives an insight as to insider sentiment by showing whether directors, officers and key employees who have proprietary information not available to the general public, are buying or selling the company's stock during the most recent six months.

Investability Quotient (IQ) - The IQ is a measure of investment desirability. It serves as an indicator of potential medium-to-long term return and as a caution against downside risk. The measure takes into account variables such as technical indicators, earnings estimates, liquidity, financial ratios and selected S&P proprietary measures.

Volatility - Rates the volatility of the stock's price over the past year.

Technical Evaluation - In researching the past market history of prices and trading volume for each company, S&P's computer models apply special technical methods and formulas to identify and project price trends for the stock.

Relative Strength Rank - Shows, on a scale of 1 to 99, how the stock has performed versus all other companies in S&P's universe on a rolling 13-week basis.

Global Industry Classification Standard (GICS) - An industry classification standard, developed by Standard & Poor's in collaboration with Morgan Stanley Capital International (MSCI). GICS is currently comprised of 10 Sectors, 24 Industry Groups, 67 Industries, and 147 Sub-Industries.

S&P Core Earnings - Standard & Poor's Core Earnings is a uniform methodology for adjusting operating earnings by focusing on a company's after-tax earnings generated from its principal businesses. Included in the Standard & Poor's definition are employee stock option grant expenses, pension costs, restructuring charges from ongoing operations, write-downs of depreciable or amortizable operating assets, purchased research and development, M&A related expenses and unrealized gains/losses from hedging activities. Excluded from the definition are pension gains, impairment of goodwill charges, gains or losses from asset sales, reversal of prior-year charges and provision from litigation or insurance settlements.

S&P Issuer Credit Rating - A Standard & Poor's Issuer Credit Rating is a current opinion of an obligor's overall financial capacity (its creditworthiness) to pay its financial obligations. This opinion focuses on the obligor's capacity and willingness to meet its financial commitments as they come due. It does not apply to any specific financial obligation, as it does not take into account the nature of and provisions of the obligation, its standing in bankruptcy or liquidation, statutory preferences, or the legality and enforceability of the obligation. In addition, it does not take into account the creditworthiness of the guarantors, insurers, or other forms of credit enhancement on the obligation. The Issuer Credit Rating is not a recommendation to purchase, sell, or hold a financial obligation issued by an obligor, as it does not comment on market price or suitability for a particular investor. Issuer Credit Ratings are based on current information furnished by obligors or obtained by Standard & Poor's from other sources it considers reliable. Standard & Poor's does not perform an audit in connection with any Issuer Credit Rating and may, on occasion, rely on unaudited financial information. Issuer Credit Ratings may be changed, suspended, or withdrawn as a result of changes in, or unavailability of, such information, or based on other circumstances.

S&P Equity Research Services - Standard & Poor's Equity Research Services U.S. includes Standard & Poor's Investment Advisory Services LLC; Standard & Poor's Equity Research Services Europe includes Standard & Poor's LLC-London and Standard & Poor's AB (Sweden); Standard & Poor's Equity Research Services Asia includes Standard & Poor's LLC's offices in Hong Kong, Singapore and Tokyo, Standard & Poor's Malaysia Sdn Bhd, and Standard & Poor's Information Services (Australia) Pty Ltd.

Required Disclosures

S&P Global STARS Distribution
In the U.S.:
As of September 30, 2006, research analysts at Standard & Poor's Equity Research Services U.S. have recommended 33.9% of issuers with buy recommendations, 56.6% with hold recommendations and 9.5% with sell recommendations.

In Europe:
As of September 30, 2006, research analysts at Standard & Poor's Equity Research Services Europe have recommended 43.8% of issuers with buy recommendations, 40.5% with hold recommendations and 15.7% with sell recommendations.

In Asia:
As of September 30, 2006, research analysts at Standard & Poor's Equity Research Services Asia have recommended 31.2% of issuers with buy recommendations, 59.6% with hold recommendations and 9.2% with sell recommendations.

Globally:
As of September 30, 2006, research analysts at Standard & Poor's Equity Research Services globally have recommended 34.7% of issuers with buy recommendations, 55.2% with hold recommendations and 10.1% with sell recommendations.

5-STARS (Strong Buy): Total return is expected to outperform the total return of a relevant benchmark, by a wide margin over the coming 12 months, with shares rising in price on an absolute basis.

4-STARS (Buy): Total return is expected to outperform the total return of a relevant benchmark over the coming 12 months, with shares rising in price on an absolute basis.

3-STARS (Hold): Total return is expected to closely approximate the total return of a relevant benchmark over the coming 12 months, with shares generally rising in price on an absolute basis.

2-STARS (Sell): Total return is expected to underperform the total return of a relevant benchmark over the coming 12 months, and the share price not anticipated to show a gain.

1-STAR (Strong Sell): Total return is expected to underperform the total return of a relevant benchmark by a wide margin over the coming 12 months, with shares falling in price on an absolute basis.

Relevant benchmarks: In the U.S. the relevant benchmark is the S&P 500 Index, in Europe and in Asia, the relevant benchmarks are generally the S&P Europe 350 Index and the S&P Asia 50 Index.

For All Regions:
All of the views expressed in this research report accurately reflect the research analyst's personal views regarding any and all of the subject securities or issuers. No part of analyst compensation was, is, or will be directly or indirectly, related to the specific recommendations or views expressed in this research report.

Additional information is available upon request.

Other Disclosures

This report has been prepared and issued by Standard & Poor's and/or one of its affiliates. In the United States, research reports are prepared by Standard & Poor's Investment Advisory Services LLC ("SPIAS"). In the United States, research reports are issued by Standard & Poor's ("S&P"); in the United Kingdom by Standard & Poor's LLC ("S&P LLC"), which is authorized and regulated by the Financial Services Authority; in Hong Kong by Standard & Poor's LLC which is regulated by the Hong Kong Securities Futures Commission; in Singapore by Standard & Poor's LLC, which is regulated by the Monetary Authority of Singapore; in Japan by Standard & Poor's LLC, which is regulated by the Kanto Financial Bureau; in Sweden by Standard & Poor's AB ("S&P AB"); in Malaysia by Standard & Poor's Malaysia Sdn Bhd ("S&PM") which is regulated by the Securities Commission; in Australia by Standard & Poor's Information Services (Australia) Pty Ltd ("SPIS"), which is regulated by the Australian Securities & Investments Commission; and in Korea by SPIAS, which is also registered in Korea as a cross-border investment advisory company.

The research and analytical services performed by SPIAS, S&P LLC, S&P AB, S&PM, and SPIS are each conducted separately from any other analytical activity of Standard & Poor's.

Standard & Poor's or an affiliate may license certain intellectual property or provide pricing or other services to, or otherwise have a financial interest in, certain issuers of securities, including exchange-traded funds whose investment objective is to substantially replicate the returns of a proprietary Standard & Poor's index, such as the S&P 500. In cases where Standard & Poor's or an affiliate is paid fees that are tied to the amount of assets that are invested in the fund or the volume of trading activity in the fund, investment in the fund will generally result in Standard & Poor's or an affiliate earning compensation in addition to the subscription fees or other compensation for services rendered by Standard & Poor's.

For a list of companies mentioned in this report with whom Standard & Poor's and/or one of its affiliates has had business relationships within the past year, please go to:

http://www2.standardandpoors.com/servlet/Satellite?pagename=sp/sp_article/ArticleTemplate&c=sp_article&cid=1145719622102

Disclaimers

This material is based upon information that we consider to be reliable, but neither S&P nor its affiliates warrant its completeness, accuracy or adequacy and it should not be relied upon as such. With respect to reports issued by S&P LLC-Japan and in the case of inconsistencies between the English and Japanese version of a report, the English version prevails. Neither S&P LLC nor S&P guarantees the accuracy of the translation. Assumptions, opinions and estimates constitute our judgment as of the date of this material and are subject to change without notice. Neither S&P nor its affiliates are responsible for any errors or omissions or for results obtained from the use of this information. Past performance is not necessarily indicative of future results. This material is not intended as an offer or solicitation for the purchase or sale of any security or other financial instrument. Securities, financial instruments or strategies mentioned herein may not be suitable for all investors. Any opinions expressed herein are given in good faith, are subject to change without notice, and are only correct as of the stated date of their issue. Prices, values, or income from any securities or investments mentioned in this report may fall against the interests of the investor and the investor may get back less than the amount invested. Where an investment is described as being likely to yield income, please note that the amount of income that the investor will receive from such an investment may fluctuate. Where an investment or security is denominated in a different currency to the investor's currency of reference, changes in rates of exchange may have an adverse effect on the value, price or income of or from that investment to the investor. The information contained in this report does not constitute advice on the tax consequences of making any particular investment decision. This material does not take into account your particular investment objectives, financial situations or needs and is not intended as a recommendation of particular securities, financial instruments or strategies to you. Before acting on any recommendation in this material, you should consider whether it is suitable for your particular circumstances and, if necessary, seek professional advice.

For residents of the U.K. - this report is only directed at and should only be relied on by persons outside of the United Kingdom or persons who are inside the United Kingdom and who have professional experience in matters relating to investments or who are high net worth persons, as defined in Article 19(5) or Article 49(2) (a) to (d) of the Financial Services and Markets Act 2000 (Financial Promotion) Order 2001, respectively.

For residents of Malaysia, all queries in relation to this report should be referred to Alexander Chia, Lee Leng Hoe, or Ching Wah Tam.

This investment analysis was prepared from the following sources: S&P MarketScope, S&P Compustat, S&P Industry Reports, I/B/E/S International, Inc.; Standard & Poor's, 55 Water St., New York, NY 10041.

Key Stock Statistics

Market Cap.—The stock price multiplied by number of shares outstanding, based on market value calculated at the issue level.

Value of $10,000 Invested 5 years ago—The value today of a $10,000 investment in the stock made 5 years ago, assuming year-end reinvestment of dividends.

Beta—The beta coefficient is a measure of the volatility of a stock's price relative to the S&P 500 Index (a proxy for the overall market). An issue with a beta of 1.5 for example, tends to move 50% more than the overall market, in the same direction. An issue with a beta of 0.5 tends to move 50% less. If a stock moved exactly as the market moved, it would have a beta of 1.0. A stock with a negative beta tends to move in a direction opposite to that of the overall market.

Per Share Data ($) Tables

Cash Flow—Net income plus depreciation, depletion, and amortization, divided by shares used to calculate earnings per common share. (See also: "Cash Flow" under Industrial Companies.)

Earnings—The amount a company reports as having been earned for the year on its common stock based on generally accepted accounting standards. Earnings per share are presented on a "diluted" basis pursuant to FASB 128, which became effective December 15, 1997, and are generally reported from continuing operations, before extraordinary items. This reflects a change from previously reported *primary earnings per share.* Insurance companies report *operating earnings* before gains/losses on security transactions and *earnings* after such transactions.

Dividends—Generally total cash payments per share based on the ex-dividend dates over a 12-month period. May also be reported on a declared basis where this has been established to be a company's payout policy.

Net Asset Value—Appears on investment company reports and reflects the market value of stocks, bonds, and net cash divided by outstanding shares. The % difference indicates the percentage premium or discount of the market price over the net asset value.

Payout Ratio—Indicates the percentage of earnings paid out in dividends. It is calculated by dividing the annual dividend by the earnings. For insurance companies, *earnings* after gains/losses on security transactions are used.

P/E Ratio High/Low—The ratio of market price to earnings—essentially indicates the valuation investors place on a company's earnings. Obtained by dividing the annual earnings into the high and low market price for the year. For insurance companies, *operating earnings* before gains/losses on security transactions are used.

Portfolio Turnover—Appears on investment company reports and indicates percentage of total security purchases and sales for the year to overall investment assets. Primarily mirrors trading aggressiveness.

Prices High/Low—Shows the calendar year high and low of a stock's market price.

Tangible Book Value; Book Value (See also: "Common Equity" under Industrial Companies)—Indicates the theoretical dollar amount per common share one might expect to receive from a company's tangible "book" assets should liquidation take place. Generally, book value is determined by adding the stated value of the common stock, paid-in capital and retained earnings and then subtracting intangible assets (excess cost over equity of acquired companies, goodwill, and patents), preferred stock at liquidating value and unamortized debt discount. Divide that amount by the outstanding shares to get book value per common share.

Income/Balance Sheet Data Tables

Banks

Cash—Mainly vault cash, interest-bearing deposits placed with banks, reserves required by the Federal Reserve, and items in the process of collection—generally referred to as float.

Commercial Loans—Commercial, industrial, financial, agricultural loans and leases, gross.

Common Equity—Includes common/capital surplus, undivided profits, reserve for contingencies and other capital reserves.

Deposits—Primarily classified as either *demand* (payable at any time upon demand of depositor) or *time* (not payable within 30 days).

Deposits/Capital Funds—Average deposits divided by average capital funds. Capital funds include capital notes/debentures, other long-term debt, capital stock, surplus, and undivided profits. May be used as a "leverage" measure.

Earning Assets—Assets on which interest is earned.

Effective Tax Rate—Actual income tax expense divided by net before taxes.

Gains/Losses on Securities Transactions—Realized losses on sales of securities, usually bonds.

Government Securities—Includes United States Treasury securities and securities of other U.S. government agencies at book or carrying value. A bank's major "liquid asset."

Investment Securities—Federal, state, and local government bonds and other securities.

Loan Loss Provision—Amount charged to operating expenses to provide an adequate reserve to cover anticipated losses in the loan portfolio.

Loans—All domestic and foreign loans (excluding leases), less unearned discount and reserve for possible losses. Generally considered a bank's principal asset.

Long-Term Debt—Total borrowings for terms beyond one year including notes payable, mortgages, debentures, term loans, and capitalized lease obligations.

Money Market Assets—Interest-bearing interbank deposits, federal funds sold, trading account securities.

Net Before Taxes—Amount remaining after operating expenses are deducted from income, including gains or losses on security transactions.

Net Income—The final profit before dividends (common/preferred) from all sources after deduction of expenses, taxes, and fixed charges, but before any discontinued operations or extraordinary items.

Net Interest Income—Interest and dividend income, minus interest expense.

Net Interest Margin—A percentage computed by dividing net interest income, on a taxable equivalent basis, by average earning assets. Used as an analytical tool to measure profit margins from providing credit services.

Noninterest Income—Service fees, trading, and other income, excluding gains/losses on securities transactions.

Other Loans—Gross consumer, real estate and foreign loans.

% Equity to Assets—Average common equity divided by average total assets. Used as a measure of capital adequacy.

% Equity to Loans—Average common equity divided by average loans. Reflects the degree of equity coverage to loans outstanding.

% Expenses/Op. Revenues—Noninterest expense as a percentage of taxable equivalent net interest income plus noninterest income (before securities gains/losses). A measure of cost control.

% Loan Loss Reserve—Contra-account to loan assets, built through provisions for loan losses, which serves as a cushion for possible future loan charge-offs.

% Loans/Deposits—Proportion of loans funded by deposits. A measure of liquidity and an indication of bank's ability to write more loans.

% Return on Assets—Net income divided by average total assets. An analytical measure of asset-use efficiency and industry comparison.

% Return on Equity—Net income (minus preferred dividend requirements) divided by average common equity. Generally used to measure performance.

% Return on Revenues—Net income divided by gross revenues.

State and Municipal Securities—State and municipal securities owned at book value.

Taxable Equivalent Adjustment—Increase to render income from tax-exempt loans and securities comparable to fully taxed income.

Total Assets—Includes interest-earning financial instruments—principally commercial, real estate, consumer loans and leases; investment securities/trading accounts; cash/money market investments; other owned assets.

Industrial Companies

Following data is based on Form 10K Annual Report data as filed with SEC.

Capital Expenditures—The sum of additions at cost to property, plant and equipment, and leaseholds, generally excluding amounts arising from acquisitions.

Cash—Includes all cash and government and other marketable securities.

Cash Flow—Net income (before extraordinary items and discontinued operations, and after preferred dividends) plus depreciation, depletion, and amortization.

Common Equity [See also "Tangible Book Value" under Per Share Data($) Tables]—Common stock plus capital surplus and retained earnings, less any difference between the carrying value and liquidating value of preferred stock.

Current Assets—Those assets expected to be realized in cash or used up in the production of revenue within one year.

Current Liabilities—Generally includes all debts/obligations falling due within one year.

Current Ratio—Current assets divided by current liabilities. A measure of liquidity.

Depreciation—Includes noncash charges for obsolescence, wear on property, current portion of capitalized expenses (intangibles), and depletion charges.

Effective Tax Rate—Actual income tax charges divided by net before taxes.

Interest Expense—Includes all interest expense on short/long-term debt, amortization of debt discount/premium, and deferred expenses (e.g., financing costs).

Long-Term Debt—Debts/obligations due after one year. Includes bonds, notes payable, mortgages, lease obligations, and industrial revenue bonds. Other long-term debt, when reported as a separate account, is excluded. This account generally includes pension and retirement benefits.

Net Before Taxes—Includes operating and nonoperating revenues (including extraordinary items not net of taxes), less all operating and nonoperating expenses, except income taxes and minority interest, but including equity in nonconsolidated subsidiaries.

Net Income—Profits derived from all sources after deduction of expenses, taxes, and fixed charges, but before any discontinued operations, extraordinary items, and dividends (preferred/common).

Operating Income—Net sales and operating revenues less cost of goods sold and operating expenses (including research and development, profit sharing, exploration and bad debt, but excluding depreciation and amortization).

% Long-Term Debt of Invested Capital—Long-term debt divided by total invested capital. Indicates how highly "leveraged" a business might be.

% Operating Income of Revenues—Net sales and operating revenues divided into operating income. Used as a measure of operating profitability.

% Net Income of Revenues—Net income divided by sales/operating revenues.

% Return on Assets—Net income divided by average total assets on a per common share basis. Used in industry analysis and as a measure of asset-use efficiency.

% Return on Equity—Net income less preferred dividend requirements divided by average common shareholders' equity on a per common share basis. Generally used to measure performance and industry comparisons.

Revenues—Net sales and other operating revenues. Includes franchise/leased department income for retailers, and royalties for publishers and oil and mining companies. Excludes excise taxes for tobacco, liquor, and oil companies.

Total Assets—Current assets plus net plant and other noncurrent assets (intangibles and deferred items).

Total Invested Capital—The sum of stockholders' equity plus long-term debt, capital lease obligations, deferred income taxes, investment credits, and minority interest.

Utilities

Capital Expenditures—Represents the amounts spent on capital improvements to plant and funds for construction programs.

Capitalization Ratios—Reflect the percentage of each type of debt/equity issues outstanding to total capitalization. % DEBT is obtained by dividing total debt by the sum of debt, preferred, common, paid-in capital and retained earnings. % PREFERRED is obtained by dividing the preferred stocks outstanding by total capitalization. % COMMON, divide the sum of common stocks, paid-in capital and retained earnings by total capitalization.

Construction Credits—Credits for interest charged to the cost of constructing new plant. A combination of allowance for equity funds used during construction and allowance for borrowed funds used during construction—credit.

Depreciation—Amounts charged to income to compensate for the decline in useful value of plant and equipment.

Effective Tax Rate—Actual income tax expense divided by the total of net income and actual income tax expense.

Fixed Charges Coverage—The number of times income before interest charges (operating income plus other income) after taxes covers total interest charges and preferred dividend requirements.

Gross Property—Includes utility plant at cost, plant work in progress, and nuclear fuel.

Long-Term Debt—Debt obligations due beyond one year from balance sheet date.

Maintenance—Amounts spent to keep plants in good operating condition.

Net Income—Amount of earnings for the year which is available for preferred and common dividend payments.

Net Property—Includes items in gross property less provision for depreciation.

Operating Revenues—Represents the amount billed to customers by the utility.

Operating Ratio—Ratio of operating costs to operating revenues or the proportion of revenues absorbed by expenses. Obtained by dividing operating expenses including depreciation, maintenance, and taxes by revenues.

% Earned on Net Property—Percentage obtained by dividing operating income by average net property for the year. A measure of plant efficiency.

% Return on Common Equity—Percentage obtained by dividing income available for common stock (net income less preferred dividend requirements) by average common equity.

% Return on Invested Capital—Percentage obtained by dividing income available for fixed charges by average total invested capital.

% Return on Revenues—Obtained by dividing net income for the year by revenues.

Total Capitalization—Combined sum of total common equity, preferred stock and long-term debt.

Total Invested Capital—Sum of total capitalization (common-preferred-debt), accumulated deferred income taxes, accumulated investment tax credits, minority interest, contingency reserves, and contributions in aid of construction.

Finally, at the very bottom of the right-hand page, you'll find general information about the company: its address and telephone number, the names of its senior executive officers and directors (usually including the name of the investor contact), and the state in which the company is incorporated.

How to Use This Book to Select Investments

And so, at last, we come to the $64,000 question: Given this vast array of data, how might a businesswoman seeking to find out about her competition, the marketing manager looking for clients, a job seeker, and the investor use it to best serve their respective purposes?

If you are like one of the first three of these individuals—a businesswoman, the marketing manager, or the job seeker—your task will be arduous, to be sure, but this book will provide you with an excellent starting point and your payoff can make it all worthwhile. You will have to go through this book page by page, looking for those companies that are in the industries in which you are interested, that are of the size and financial strength that appeal to you, that are located geographically in your territory or where you're willing to relocate, that have been profitable and growing, and so forth. And then you will have to read about just what's going on at those companies by referring to the appropriate "Highlights" and "Business Summary" comments in these reports.

Of course, this book won't do it *all* for you. It is, after all, just a starting point, not a conclusive summary of everything you might need to know. It is designed to educate, not to render advice or provide recommendations. But it will get you pointed in the right direction.

Finally, what about the investor who wants to use this book to find good individual investments from among the 500 stocks in the S&P 500 Index? If you fall into that category, what should you do?

Well, you can approach your quest the same way that the businesswoman looking for information about her competitors, the marketing manager, and the job seeker approached theirs—by thumbing through this book page by page, looking for companies with high historic growth rates, generous dividend payout policies, wide profit margins, A+ Standard & Poor's Quality Rankings, or whatever other characteristics you consider desirable in stocks in which you might invest. In this case, however, we have made your job just a little bit easier.

We have already prescreened the 500 companies in this book for several of the stock characteristics in which investors generally are most interested, including Standard & Poor's Quality Rankings, growth records, and dividend payment histories, and we're pleased to present on the next four pages lists of those companies which score highest on the bases of these criteria. So if you, like most investors, find these characteristics important in potential investments, you might want to turn first to the companies on these lists in your search for attractive investments.

Good luck and happy investment returns!

Companies With Five Consecutive Years of Earnings Increases

This table, compiled from a computer screen of the stocks in this handbook, shows companies that have recorded rising per-share earnings for five consecutive years, have a minimum 10% five-year EPS growth rate based on trailing 12-month earnings, have estimated 2006 EPS at least 10% above those reported for 2005, pay dividends, and have Standard & Poor's Quality Rankings of A– or better.

Company	Business	Fiscal Year End	5 Yr EPS Growth Rate %	EPS $ 2005 Act.	EPS $ 2006 Est.	S&P Quality Rank	Price	P/E on 2006 Est.	% Yield
Capital One Financial	Bank card issuer/svcs	Dec	20	6.73	8.12	A+	80.65	10.4	0.1
Bank of America	Comm'l bkg:Southeast,N.C.,CA	Dec	14	4.04	4.60	A-	53.43	11.4	4.2
Bear Stearns Cos	Investment bank'g,brokerage	Nov	22	10.31	13.48	A	153.80	11.4	0.7
Amer Intl Group	Major int'l insur hldg co	Dec	12	3.99	5.55	A+	66.70	11.6	1.0
Home Depot	Bldg mtls,home improv strs	Jan+	18	2.72	3.02	A+	36.50	12.3	1.6
Merrill Lynch	Investment,finance,insurance	Dec	50	5.16	7.03	A-	86.08	13.1	1.2
Sherwin-Williams	Large paint & varnish mfr	Dec	18	3.28	4.12	A	58.26	14.1	1.7
Wells Fargo	Comm'l banking,Minneapolis	Dec	17	2.25	2.51	A	36.45	14.6	3.1
VF Corp	Apparel mfr:intimate,leisure	Dec	26	4.54	5.10	A-	74.74	14.8	2.9
Lowe's Cos	Dstr bldg mtls: consum'r gds	Jan+	24	1.73	2.01	A+	30.45	15.3	0.7
Illinois Tool Works	Fasteners,tools, plastic items	Dec	18	2.60	3.03	A+	46.96	15.5	1.8
Compass Bancshares	Commercial bkg,Alabama,TX	Dec	10	3.18	3.55	A+	55.70	15.8	2.8
Synovus Financial	Commercial bkg,Georgia	Dec	11	1.64	1.85	A+	29.54	15.9	2.6
Burlington Northn Santa Fe	Railroad sys operations U.S.	Dec	20	4.01	4.99	A-	79.35	16.0	1.3
Johnson Controls	Auto interior sys/bldg ctrls	Sep	13	4.68	5.30	A+	84.35	16.2	1.3
UnitedHealth Group	Manages health maint svcs	Dec	32	2.48	2.80	A+	49.84	16.8	0.1
NIKE, Inc'B'	Athletic footwear	May#	18	4.48	5.28	A+	91.13	17.3	1.4
United Technologies	Aerospace,climate ctrl sys	Dec	13	3.12	3.70	A+	65.12	17.6	1.6
Harley-Davidson	Manufactures motorcycles	Dec	21	3.41	3.92	A+	69.59	17.9	1.2
TJX Companies	Off-price specialty stores	Jan+	10	1.41	1.58	A+	29.56	18.6	0.9
Emerson Electric	Mfr electric/electronic prdts	Sep	11	3.40	4.38	A	84.72	19.3	2.1
Darden Restaurants	Oper family style restaurants	May#	13	1.78	2.16	A	41.84	19.4	1.1
Praxair Inc	Ind'l gases/spcl coatings	Dec	12	2.22	2.87	A	59.50	20.4	1.7
Omnicom Group	Major int'l advertising co	Dec	11	4.36	5.02	A+	101.07	20.5	1.0
Biomet, Inc	Mfr surgical implant devices	May#	13	1.38	1.63	A	35.69	21.9	0.8
Danaher Corp	Mfr hand tools,auto parts	Dec	25	2.76	3.24	A+	70.88	22.0	0.1
Walgreen Co	Major retail drug chain	Aug#	15	1.52	1.72	A+	43.87	25.5	0.7
Ecolab Inc	Comm'l cleaning&sanitizing	Dec	13	1.23	1.42	A	44.86	31.4	0.9
Paychex Inc	Computer payroll acctg svcs	May#	13	0.97	1.22	A+	39.65	32.5	2.1

+ Actual 2006 EPS & estimated 2007 EPS; P/E based on estimated 2007 EPS. #Actual 2006 EPS; P/E based on actual 2006 EPS.
Chart based on October 24, 2006 prices and data.
NOTE: All earnings estimates are Standard & Poor's projections.

Stocks With A+ Rankings

Based on the issues in this handbook, this screen shows stocks of all companies with Standard & Poor's Quality Rankings of A+.

Company	Business	Company	Business
Alberto-Culver	Hair care,health,beauty aids,	Illinois Tool Works	Fasteners,tools, plastic items
Altria Group	Cigarettes,food prod,brew'g	Johnson Controls	Auto interior sys/bldg ctrls
Ambac Financial Group	Muni bond insurance co	Johnson & Johnson	Health care products
Amer Intl Group	Major int'l insur hldg co	Kimco Realty	Real estate investment trust
Anheuser-Busch Cos	Largest U.S. brewer:baking	Lowe's Cos	Dstr bldg mtls: consum'r gds
Automatic Data Proc	Computer services	M&T Bank	Comm'l bkg,Buffalo,New York
Capital One Financial	Bank card issuer/svcs	McCormick & Co	Spices, flavoring, tea, mixes
Cardinal Health	Wholesale dstr drug,hlth prod	NIKE, Inc'B'	Athletic footwear
Carnival Corp	Cruise ships,hotel,casino	Omnicom Group	Major int'l advertising co
Centex Corp	Home bldg,constr'n prd,S & L	Paychex Inc	Computer payroll acctg svcs
Cintas Corp	Sales & rental of uniforms	PepsiCo Inc	Soft drink:snack foods
Citigroup Inc	Diversified financial svcs	Pulte Homes	Homebuilding/fin'l services
Colgate-Palmolive	Household & personal care	Sigma-Aldrich	Specialty chem prod
Commerce Bancorp	Commercial banking, NJ	SunTrust Banks	Comm'l bkg,Georgia,FL,Tenn
Compass Bancshares	Commercial bkg,Alabama,TX	Synovus Financial	Commercial bkg,Georgia
D.R.Horton	Single-family home constr'n	Sysco Corp	Food distr & service systems
Danaher Corp	Mfr hand tools,auto parts	Target Corp	Depart/disc/spec stores
Dollar General	Self-service discount stores	TJX Companies	Off-price specialty stores
Family Dollar Stores	Self-service retail stores	United Technologies	Aerospace,climate ctrl sys
Fifth Third Bancorp	Comm'l bkg,Cincinnati,Ohio	UnitedHealth Group	Manages health maint svcs
First Horizon Natl	Comm'l bkg,Tennessee	Wal-Mart Stores	Operates discount stores
Genl Electric	Consumer/ind'l prod,broad'cst	Walgreen Co	Major retail drug chain
Harley-Davidson	Manufactures motorcycles	Wrigley, (Wm) Jr	Major chewing gum producer
Home Depot	Bldg mtls,home improv strs		

Table based on October 24, 2006 prices and data.

Rapid Growth Stocks

The stocks listed below have shown strong and consistent earnings growth. Issues of rapidly growing companies tend to carry high price-earnings ratios and offer potential for substantial appreciation. At the same time, though, the stocks are subject to strong selling pressures should growth in earnings slow. Five-year earnings growth rates have been calculated for fiscal years 2001 through 2005 and the most current 12-month earnings.

Company	Business	S&P Quality Ranking	Fiscal Year End	— EPS $ — 2005 Act.	2006 Est.	5 Yr. EPS% Growth	Price	P/E on 2006 Est.	% Yield
Amer Intl Group	Major int'l insur hldg co	A+	Dec	3.99	5.55	12	66.70	11.6	1.0
Capital One Financial	Bank card issuer/svcs	A+	Dec	6.73	8.12	20	80.65	10.4	0.1
Coventry Health Care	Hlth benefit svcs/oper HMO's	B	Dec	3.10	3.52	42	50.01	14.3	0.0
Darden Restaurants	Oper family style restaurants	A	May#	1.78	2.16	13	41.84	19.4	1.1
Harley-Davidson	Manufactures motorcycles	A+	Dec	3.41	3.92	21	69.59	17.9	1.2
Home Depot	Bldg mtls,home improv strs	A+	Jan+	2.72	3.02	18	36.50	12.3	1.6
Humana Inc	Provides managed hlth plans	B	Dec	1.87	2.88	22	65.72	23.4	0.0
Kohl's Corp	Oper family oriented dept strs	B+	Jan+	2.43	3.20	12	73.48	23.1	0.0
L-3 Communications Hldgs	Communication systems/pds	NF	Dec	4.20	5.02	21	76.82	18.2	1.0
Laboratory Corp Amer Hldgs	Clinical lab svcs in U.S.	B	Dec	2.71	3.19	17	68.87	21.9	0.0
Lowe's Cos	Dstr bldg mtls: consum'r gds	A+	Jan+	1.73	2.01	24	30.45	15.3	0.7
Quest Diagnostics	Clinical laboratory test svcs	B	Dec	2.66	3.06	22	50.47	16.2	0.8
Rockwell Collins	Aviation/communic elec tr'ns	NF	Sep	2.20	2.67	26	58.40	21.6	1.1
Starbucks Corp	Retails high-quality coffees	B+	Sep	0.61	0.74	27	38.2[illegible]	52.3	0.0
Stryker Corp	Specialty medical devices	B+	Dec	1.64	2.02	22	53.92	26.7	0.2
United Technologies	Aerospace,climate ctrl sys	A+	Dec	3.12	3.70	13	65.12	17.6	1.6
UnitedHealth Group	Manages health maint svcs	A+	Dec	2.48	2.80	32	49.84	16.8	0.1
Walgreen Co	Major retail drug chain	A+	Aug#	1.52	1.72	15	43.87	25.5	0.7
WellPoint Inc	Operate HMO svcs	NF	Dec	3.94	4.76	20	78.62	16.5	0.0

– Actual 2006 EPS & estimated 2007 EPS; P/E based on estimated 2007 EPS. # Actual 2006 EPS; P/E based on actual 2006 EPS.
Chart based on October 24, 2006 prices and data.
NOTE: All earnings estimates are Standard & Poor's projections.

Fast-Rising Dividends

Based on the issues in this handbook, the companies below were chosen on the basis of their five-year annual growth rate in dividends from 2000 to the current 12-month indicated rate. All have increased their dividend payments each calendar year from 2001 to their current 12-month indicated rate and have a minimum yield of 1.5%.

Company	-- $ Divd. --- Paid 2001	Paid 2005	†Ind. Divd. Rate	* Divd. Growth Rate %	Price	% Yield
Kinder Morgan	0.20	2.90	3.50	86.60	105.98	3.3
D.R.Horton	0.07	0.34	0.60	53.57	23.58	2.5
Countrywide Financial	0.10	0.59	0.60	52.54	37.33	1.6
McDonald's Corp	0.23	0.67	1.00	36.61	42.25	2.4
SLM Corp	0.24	0.85	1.00	35.45	47.31	2.1
Federated Investors 'B'	0.17	0.57	0.72	34.32	33.88	2.1
Linear Technology Cp	0.15	0.40	0.60	31.17	30.56	2.0
Citigroup Inc	0.60	1.76	1.96	29.54	50.47	3.9
AFLAC Inc	0.19	0.44	0.74	29.01	44.61	1.7
Home Depot	0.17	0.40	0.60	27.35	36.50	1.6
Norfolk Southern	0.24	0.48	0.72	24.82	48.80	1.5
Praxair Inc	0.34	0.72	1.00	24.19	59.50	1.7
Wachovia Corp	0.96	1.94	2.24	20.44	55.96	4.0
Washington Mutual	0.90	1.90	2.12	19.62	43.11	4.9
United Technologies	0.45	0.88	1.06	19.55	65.12	1.6
M&T Bank	1.00	1.75	2.40	19.37	121.74	2.0
Sysco Corp	0.28	0.60	0.68	19.16	34.04	2.0
Federal Home Loan	0.80	1.52	1.88	18.89	68.20	2.8
Wells Fargo	0.50	1.00	1.12	18.84	36.45	3.1
U.S. Bancorp	0.56	1.20	1.32	17.88	33.78	3.9
PepsiCo Inc	0.57	0.98	1.20	16.93	63.20	1.9
MBIA Inc	0.59	1.08	1.24	16.68	61.30	2.0
Johnson & Johnson	0.70	1.27	1.50	16.67	68.75	2.2
United Parcel'B'	0.74	1.27	1.52	16.60	76.06	2.0
Pfizer, Inc	0.44	0.76	0.96	15.90	27.26	3.5
ConocoPhillips	0.70	1.18	1.44	15.69	61.40	2.3
Fifth Third Bancorp	0.78	1.43	1.60	15.18	39.44	4.1
Avon Products	0.38	0.66	0.70	14.85	30.00	2.3
Paychex Inc	0.38	0.55	0.84	14.44	39.65	2.1
VF Corp	0.93	1.10	2.20	14.44	74.74	2.9

Company	-- $ Divd. --- Paid 2001	Paid 2005	†Ind. Divd. Rate	* Divd. Growth Rate %	Price	% Yield
Constellation Energy Grp	0.78	1.29	1.51	14.30	62.56	2.4
PPL Corp	0.53	0.92	1.10	14.17	35.12	3.1
Allstate Corp	0.74	1.24	1.40	14.05	61.74	2.3
Colgate-Palmolive	0.68	1.11	1.28	13.92	60.47	2.1
Marshall & Ilsley	0.57	0.93	1.08	13.90	47.87	2.3
Illinois Tool Works	0.41	0.58	0.84	13.65	46.96	1.8
Hershey Co	0.58	0.93	1.08	13.40	51.55	2.1
McCormick & Co	0.40	0.64	0.72	13.39	36.88	2.0
Air Products & Chem	0.78	1.25	1.36	12.79	69.07	2.0
Cincinnati Financial	0.74	1.16	1.34	12.77	46.90	2.9
Kimberly-Clark	1.11	1.75	1.96	12.68	65.33	3.0
North Fork Bancorp	0.54	0.88	1.00	12.44	29.06	3.4
Automatic Data Proc	0.41	0.62	0.74	12.11	47.80	1.5
ACE Limited	0.56	0.88	1.00	11.98	57.69	1.7
H & R Block	0.30	0.46	0.54	11.86	21.83	2.5
Coca-Cola Co	0.72	1.12	1.24	11.64	47.03	2.6
Hartford Finl Svcs Gp	1.00	1.16	2.00	11.56	89.15	2.2
Compass Bancshares	0.91	1.36	1.56	11.45	55.70	2.8
Masco Corp	0.53	0.78	0.88	11.43	28.00	3.1
Brown-Forman'B'	0.66	0.98	1.12	11.40	71.29	1.6
Sherwin-Williams	0.58	0.82	1.00	11.32	58.26	1.7
Anheuser-Busch Cos	0.69	1.03	1.18	11.30	46.89	2.5
Procter & Gamble	0.73	1.09	1.24	11.27	62.88	2.0
Caterpillar Inc	0.69	0.91	1.20	10.99	60.93	2.0
Wrigley, (Wm) Jr	0.60	0.86	1.02	10.96	53.14	1.9
BB&T Corp	0.98	1.46	1.68	10.95	43.08	3.9
Regions Financial	0.90	1.36	1.40	10.84	38.08	3.7
Rohm & Haas	0.80	1.12	1.32	10.71	51.22	2.6
Fortune Brands	0.97	1.38	1.56	10.15	75.49	2.1
Grainger (W.W.)	0.69	0.92	1.16	10.15	73.10	1.6

†12-month indicated rate. *Five-year annual compounded growth rate. Chart based on October 24, 2006 prices and data.

Stock Reports

In using the Stock Reports in this handbook, please pay particular attention to the dates attached to each evaluation, recommendation, or analysis section. Opinions rendered are as of that date and may change often. It is strongly suggested that before investing in any security you should obtain the current analysis on that issue.

To order the latest Standard & Poor's Stock Report on a company, for as little as $3.00 per report, please call:

S&P Reports On-Demand at 1-800-292-0808.

STANDARD &POOR'S

Abbott Laboratories

S&P Recommendation BUY ★★★★★

Price $47.67 (as of Oct 27, 2006)

12-Mo. Target Price $56.00

Investment Style Large-Cap Growth

GICS Sector Health Care
Sub-Industry Pharmaceuticals

Comment This diversified life science company is a leading maker of drugs, nutritional products, diabetes monitoring devices, and diagnostics.

Key Stock Statistics (Source S&P, Vickers, company reports)

52-Wk Range	$49.87–37.50	S&P Oper. EPS 2006E	2.52	P/E on S&P Oper. EPS 2006E	18.9	Dividend Rate/Share	$1.18
Trailing 12-Month EPS	$2.06	S&P Oper. EPS 2007E	2.86	Common Shares Outstg. (M)	1,527.8	Yield (%)	2.48
Trailing 12-Month P/E	23.1	S&P Core EPS 2006E	2.52	Market Capitalization(B)	$72.831	Beta	0.37
$10K Invested 5 Yrs Ago	$10,562	S&P Core EPS 2007E	2.86	Institutional Ownership (%)	63	S&P Credit Rating	AA

Price Performance

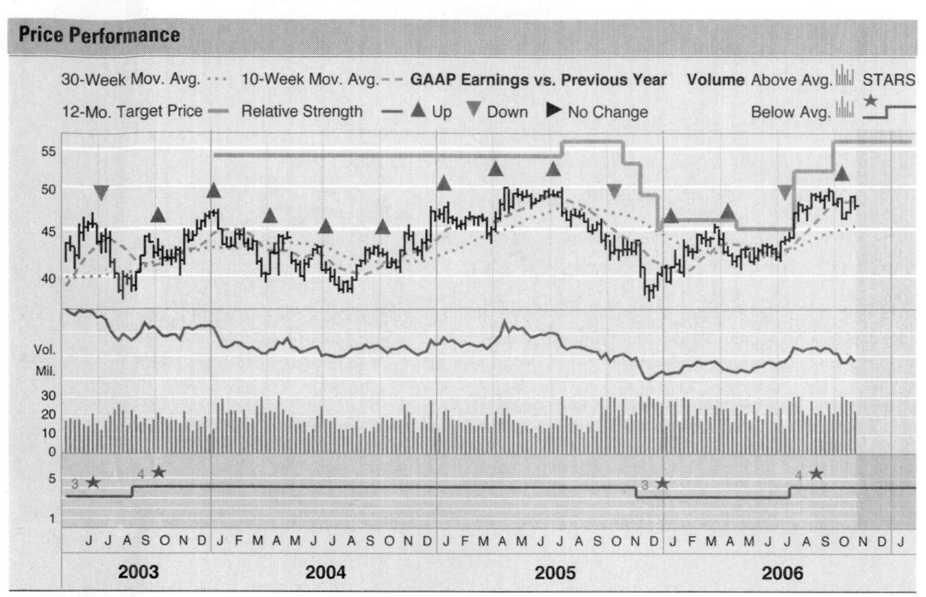

Options: ASE, CBOE, P, Ph

Analysis prepared by **Robert M. Gold** on October 26, 2006, when the stock traded at **$ 47.89**.

Highlights

- We believe 2007 revenues will approximate $25 billion, up from a projected $22.5 billion in 2006, driven by an expected 10% gain in the pharmaceutical segment, 5% in nutritionals ,and 9% in diagnostics. We think the vascular intervention business will add about $1.6 billion to 2007 sales, up from a projected $1.1 billion in 2006. Beyond 2007, we believe a successful U.S. launch of the company's Xience drug coated coronary stent will be a critical driver of sales growth. The launch is expected to occur during early 2008.

- In April 2006, ABT completed its acquisition of Guidant's vascular business from Boston Scientific for about $4.1 billion and potential milestones for its Xience drug-eluting stent, if approved. We estimate that sales were about $1 billion in 2005.

- We expect that gross margin expansion will persist through 2009, aided by a more favorable sales mix, with 2006 gross margins alone boosted by a change in accounting for certain low-margined products. We look for R&D spending to consume 9.5% to 10.0% of sales through 2009. Our stock option-inclusive operating EPS estimate for 2006 is $2.52, rising to $2.86 in 2007.

Investment Rationale/Risk

- In our opinion, the stock is attractive at current levels, and we see several potential catalysts on the horizon. We remain positive on both the short-term and long-term prospects for Humira, and consider the drug to have an advantage over Enbrel in the dermatology space. During the first nine months of 2006, sales of Humira rose nearly 58% in the U.S., and 52% overseas (excluding a negative impact of 3.6% from currency fluctuations). We think revenue growth in 2007 and 2008 will further benefit from increased sales in the vascular intervention area.

- Risks to our recommendation and target price include disappointing product sales (notably for Humira), new generic competition to Synthroid and Biaxin, pipeline disappointments, and a lack of cost savings from planned restructurings.

- The stock's P/E to growth (PEG) ratio, based on our 2006 EPS estimate, is 1.5X, in line with pharma and device peers. Our annualized projected EPS growth rate for ABT is 13%. Assuming ABT shares trade at a PEG ratio of 1.5X our 2007 EPS estimate, our 12-month target price is $56.

Qualitative Risk Assessment

LOW | MEDIUM | HIGH

Abbott operates in competitive markets and is exposed to the potential for generic competition. However, we believe the company has a relatively strong new product pipeline, with potentially significant launches in both the medical device and pharmaceutical areas. In our opinion, the company is financially sound, with a strong balance sheet. It also has an S&P Quality Ranking of A.

Quantitative Evaluations

S&P Quality Ranking A

D | C | B- | B | B+ | A- | A | A+

Relative Strength Rank MODERATE

37

LOWEST = 1 HIGHEST = 99

Revenue/Earnings Data

Revenue (Million $)

	1Q	2Q	3Q	4Q	Year
2006	5,183	5,501	5,574	--	--
2005	5,383	5,524	5,384	6,047	22,338
2004	4,641	4,703	4,682	5,654	19,680
2003	4,580	4,724	4,846	5,531	19,681
2002	4,189	4,315	4,342	4,839	17,685
2001	3,560	4,099	4,181	4,445	16,285

Earnings Per Share ($)

2006	0.56	0.40	0.46	E0.75	E2.52
2005	0.53	0.56	0.44	0.63	2.16
2004	0.52	0.40	0.51	0.62	2.02
2003	0.51	0.16	0.48	0.60	1.75
2002	0.54	0.38	0.46	0.40	1.78
2001	-0.14	0.34	0.40	0.39	0.99

Fiscal year ended Dec. 31. Next earnings report expected: Late January. EPS Estimates based on S&P Operating Earnings; historical GAAP earnings are as reported.

Dividend Data (Dates: mm/dd Payment Date: mm/dd/yy)

Amount ($)	Date Decl.	Ex-Div. Date	Stk. of Record	Payment Date
0.275	12/09	01/11	01/13	02/15/06
0.295	02/17	04/11	04/13	05/15/06
0.295	06/16	07/12	07/14	08/15/06
0.295	09/08	10/11	10/13	11/15/06

Dividends have been paid since 1926. Source: Company reports.

Abbott Laboratories

Business Summary October 26, 2006

CORPORATE OVERVIEW. Abbott Laboratories (ABT) is a leading player in several growing health care markets. Through acquisitions, product diversification and R&D programs, ABT offers a wide range of prescription pharmaceuticals, infant and adult nutritionals, diagnostics, and medical devices.

Pharmaceuticals accounted for 59% of operating revenues in 2005, nutritionals 20%, diagnostics 17%, and other 4%.

ABT's Pharmaceutical Products Group markets a wide array of human therapeutics. Major products include: Humira to treat rheumatoid arthritis and psoriatic arthritis ($1.4 billion in 2005 sales, up sharply from sales of $852 million in 2004); Biaxin and Biaxin XL ($1.07 billion, down 9.9%), a major class of broad-spectrum antibiotics used for a wide variety of infections, including h-pylori (associated with duodenal ulcers); Depakote ($1.1 billion, up 6.7%), a leading antiepileptic and bipolar disorder drug; Kaletra, an antiHIV medication ($1 billion, up 12.2%), and cholesterol treatment TriCor ($927 million, up 18.9%). In May 2005, the FDA approved oral Zemplar for secondary hyperparathyroidism in predialysis patients.

Nutritionals fall under U.S.-based Ross Products and Abbott Nutrition International. Products include leading infant formulas sold under the Similac and Isomil names, as well as adult nutritionals, such as Ensure and ProSure for patients with special dietary needs, including cancer and diabetes patients. ABT also markets enteral feeding items.

Abbott Diabetes Care markets the Precision and FreeStyle lines of hand-held glucose monitors for diabetes patients. This division also markets data management and point-of-care systems, insulin pumps and syringes, and Glucerna shakes and nutrition bars tailored for diabetics.

Abbott Vascular markets coronary and carotid stents, catheters and guide wires, and products used for surgical closure. In April 2006, Abbott acquired Guidant's vascular business from Boston Scientific for approximately $4.1 billion. Boston Scientific is also entitled to milestones if the Xience V stent is approved in the U.S. or Japan. Sales from Guidant's vascular unit were about $1 billion in 2005.

Company Financials

Per Share Data ($) Year Ended Dec. 31	**2005**	**2004**	**2003**	**2002**	**2001**	**2000**	**1999**	**1998**	**1997**	**1996**
Tangible Book Value	2.89	2.22	2.90	1.93	1.14	4.54	3.78	2.88	2.55	2.48
Cash Flow	3.02	2.84	2.56	2.52	1.74	2.31	2.10	2.02	1.81	1.65
Earnings	2.16	2.02	1.75	1.78	0.99	1.78	1.57	1.51	1.34	1.21
S&P Core Earnings	2.01	1.90	1.95	1.62	0.77	NA	NA	NA	NA	NA
Dividends	1.09	1.03	0.97	0.92	0.82	0.74	0.66	0.58	0.52	0.47
Payout Ratio	50%	51%	55%	51%	83%	42%	42%	39%	39%	39%
Prices:High	50.00	47.63	47.15	58.00	57.17	56.25	53.31	50.06	34.88	28.69
Prices:Low	37.50	38.26	33.75	29.80	42.00	29.38	33.00	32.53	24.88	19.06
P/E Ratio:High	23	24	27	33	58	32	34	33	26	24
P/E Ratio:Low	17	19	19	17	42	16	21	22	19	16
Income Statement Analysis (Million $)										
Revenue	22,338	19,680	19,681	17,685	16,285	13,746	13,178	12,478	11,883	11,013
Operating Income	5,738	5,187	4,597	4,815	3,062	4,228	3,977	3,902	3,578	3,303
Depreciation	1,359	1,289	1,274	1,177	1,168	827	828	784	728	686
Interest Expense	241	200	146	239	307	114	81.8	160	135	95.0
Pretax Income	4,620	4,126	3,734	3,673	1,883	3,816	3,397	3,241	2,949	2,670
Effective Tax Rate	27.0%	23.0%	26.3%	23.9%	17.7%	27.0%	28.0%	28.0%	29.0%	29.5%
Net Income	3,372	3,176	2,753	2,794	1,550	2,786	2,446	2,333	2,094	1,882
S&P Core Earnings	3,158	2,972	2,971	2,561	1,233	NA	NA	NA	NA	NA
Balance Sheet & Other Financial Data (Million $)										
Cash	2,894	1,226	995	704	657	914	608	383	230	123
Current Assets	11,386	10,734	10,290	9,122	8,419	7,376	6,420	5,553	5,038	4,481
Total Assets	29,141	28,767	26,715	24,259	23,296	15,283	14,471	13,216	12,061	11,126
Current Liabilities	7,416	6,826	7,640	7,002	7,927	4,298	4,517	4,962	5,034	4,344
Long Term Debt	4,572	4,788	3,452	4,274	4,335	1,076	1,337	1,340	938	933
Common Equity	14,415	14,326	13,072	10,665	9,059	8,571	7,428	5,714	4,999	4,820
Total Capital	19,570	19,334	16,525	14,939	13,395	9,647	9,046	7,163	6,074	5,906
Capital Expenditures	1,207	1,292	1,247	1,296	1,164	1,036	217	991	1,007	949
Cash Flow	4,731	4,465	4,027	3,971	2,718	3,613	3,274	3,117	2,822	2,568
Current Ratio	1.5	1.6	1.3	1.3	1.1	1.7	1.4	1.1	1.0	1.0
% Long Term Debt of Capitalization	23.4	24.8	20.9	28.6	32.4	11.2	14.8	18.7	15.4	15.8
% Net Income of Revenue	15.1	16.1	14.0	15.8	9.5	20.3	18.6	18.7	17.6	17.1
% Return on Assets	11.6	11.6	10.8	11.7	8.0	18.7	17.6	18.5	18.1	18.3
% Return on Equity	23.5	23.2	23.2	28.3	17.6	34.8	37.2	43.6	42.7	40.8

Data as orig reptd.; bef. results of disc opers/spec. items. Per share data adj. for stk. divs.; EPS diluted. E-Estimated. NA-Not Available. NM-Not Meaningful. NR-Not Ranked. UR-Under Review.

Office: 100 Abbott Park Road, Abbott Park, IL 60064-6400.
Telephone: 847-937-6100.
Website: http://www.abbott.com
Chrmn & CEO: M.D. White

Pres & COO: R.A. Gonzalez
EVP & CFO: T.C. Freyman
SVP, Secy & General Counsel: L.J. Schumacher
VP & Cntlr: G. Linder

Board of Directors: R. S. Austin, W. Daley, W. J. Farrell, H. L. Fuller, R. A. Gonzalez, J. M. Greenberg, J. M. Leiden, D. Owen, B. Powell, Jr., W. A. Reynolds, R. S. Roberts, W. D. Smithburg, J. R. Walter, M. D. White

Founded: 1888
Domicile: Illinois
Employees: 59,735

ACE Ltd

STANDARD &POOR'S

S&P Recommendation BUY ★★★★★

Price $57.77 (as of Oct 27, 2006)

12-Mo. Target Price $67.00

Investment Style Large-Cap Value

GICS Sector Financials
Sub-Industry Property & Casualty Insurance

Comment This Bermuda-based Cayman Islands company provides insurance and reinsurance for a diverse group of international clients.

Key Stock Statistics (Source S&P, Vickers, company reports)

52-Wk Range	$59.24–47.81	S&P Oper. EPS 2006E	6.60	P/E on S&P Oper. EPS 2006E	8.8	Dividend Rate/Share	$1.00
Trailing 12-Month EPS	$5.60	S&P Oper. EPS 2007E	6.70	Common Shares Outstg. (M)	325.6	Yield (%)	1.73
Trailing 12-Month P/E	10.3	S&P Core EPS 2006E	6.27	Market Capitalization(B)	$18.807	Beta	0.95
$10K Invested 5 Yrs Ago	$17,354	S&P Core EPS 2007E	6.36	Institutional Ownership (%)	92	S&P Credit Rating	BBB+

Price Performance

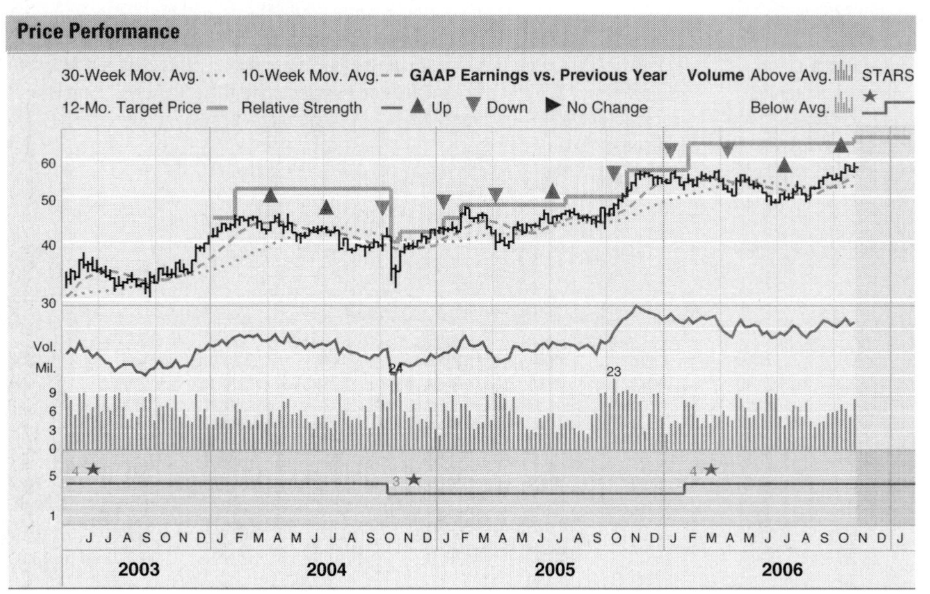

Options: ASE, CBOE, P, Ph

Highlights

- The 12-month target price for ACE has recently been changed to $67.00 from $65.00. The Highlights section of this Stock Report will be updated accordingly.

Investment Rationale/Risk

- The Investment Rationale/Risk section of this Stock Report will be updated shortly. For the latest News story on ACE from MarketScope, see below.

- 10/25/06 10:11 am EDT... S&P MAINTAINS BUY RECOMMENDATION ON SHARES OF ACE LIMITED (ACE 58.64****): Q3 operating EPS of $1.96, vs. $0.70 year-ago loss, beat our $1.50 estimate. Results were driven by sharply lower catastrophe losses, at $0.01 per share vs. $2.56, and some improvement in underlying claim trends. Although 9 months net written premiums were flat, we note the core US line posted a 6.3% rise, above that of many peers. We are raising our '06 EPS estimate by $0.30 to $6.60 to reflect these results, and '07's by $0.05 to $6.70. Our $67 target price, raised by $2 today, assumes ACE trades at 10X our '07 estimate, still a nearly 20% discount to peers. /C.Seifert

Qualitative Risk Assessment

LOW | **MEDIUM** | HIGH

Our risk assessment reflects our view of ACE as an opportunistic underwriter, partially offset by its exposure to catastrophe claims and concerns we have over reserve levels in certain lines of business.

Quantitative Evaluations

S&P Quality Ranking B

D | C | B- | **B** | B+ | A- | A | A+

Relative Strength Rank MODERATE

66

LOWEST = 1 HIGHEST = 99

Revenue/Earnings Data

Revenue (Million $)

	1Q	2Q	3Q	4Q	Year
2006	3,181	3,289	--	--	--
2005	3,148	3,258	3,494	3,188	13,088
2004	2,887	3,067	3,073	3,293	12,320
2003	2,256	2,710	2,690	3,236	10,892
2002	--	--	--	--	7,227
2001	--	--	--	--	6,784

Earnings Per Share ($)

2006	1.45	1.72	1.73	E1.47	E6.60
2005	1.48	1.58	-0.43	0.69	3.31
2004	1.53	1.44	-0.03	0.93	3.88
2003	0.96	1.42	1.21	1.61	5.25
2002	--	--	--	--	0.27
2001	--	--	--	--	-0.88

Fiscal year ended Dec. 31. Next earnings report expected: Early February. EPS Estimates based on S&P Operating Earnings; historical GAAP earnings are as reported.

Dividend Data (Dates: mm/dd Payment Date: mm/dd/yy)

Amount ($)	Date Decl.	Ex-Div. Date	Stk. of Record	Payment Date
0.230	11/17	12/28	12/30	01/12/06
0.230	02/23	03/29	03/31	04/13/06
0.250	05/18	06/28	06/30	07/14/06
0.250	08/18	09/27	09/30	10/13/06

Dividends have been paid since 1993. Source: Company reports.

ACE Ltd

Business Summary September 29, 2006

ACE Ltd. underwrites an array of insurance and reinsurance; and also provides funds to support underwriting capacity for Lloyd's syndicates managed by Lloyd's managing agencies. Net earned premiums totaled $11.7 billion in 2005 (up 5.4% from $11.1 billion in 2004), with North American Insurance operations accounting for 45%, Overseas General Insurance for 36%, Global Reinsurance for 13%, and Financial Services and Other for 6%. Underwriting deteriorated slightly in 2005 amid higher catastrophe claims, and the combined ratio ended 2005 at 99.6%, versus 96.4% in 2004.

Insurance - North America provides property and casualty insurance and reinsurance coverage, including excess liability, professional lines, satellite, excess property and political risk, to a diverse group of industrial, commercial and other enterprises.

Insurance - Overseas General includes the operations of ACE International, which provides property and casualty insurance, accident and health insurance and consumer-oriented products to individuals, mid-sized firms and large commercial clients. It also provides customized and comprehensive insurance policies and services to multinational companies and their cross-border subsidiaries. In addition, the segment includes the insurance operations of ACE Global Markets, which mainly encompasses operations in the Lloyd's market.

Global Reinsurance includes the operations of ACE Tempest Re and several other subsidiaries that mainly provide property catastrophe reinsurance worldwide to insurers of commercial and personal property.

Financial Products includes the financial guaranty business of ACE Guaranty Re and ACE Capital Re International (ACE Financial Services). ACE Financial Services provides value-added reinsurance products in several specialty insurance markets. On April 28, 2004, ACE sold approximately 65% of Assured Guaranty Ltd. in an initial public offering that netted ACE about $835 million.

Company Financials

Per Share Data ($) Year Ended Dec. 31	2005	2004	2003	2002	2001	2000	1999	1998	1997	1996
Tangible Book Value	28.17	25.11	21.52	13.20	12.13	10.35	7.49	16.40	14.60	11.70
Operating Earnings	NA	NA	NA	NA	NA	NA	1.63	1.96	1.93	1.57
Earnings	3.31	3.88	5.25	0.27	-0.88	2.19	1.85	2.96	2.67	1.94
Dividends	0.90	0.82	0.74	0.66	0.58	0.48	0.40	0.50	0.27	0.21
Payout Ratio	27%	21%	14%	NM	NM	22%	22%	17%	10%	11%
Prices:High	56.85	45.98	42.80	44.98	43.19	43.94	35.25	43.00	33.69	20.08
Prices:Low	38.36	31.80	23.59	22.01	18.10	14.06	15.50	24.38	18.71	12.58
P/E Ratio:High	17	NM	NM	NM	NM	NM	19	15	13	10
P/E Ratio:Low	12	NM	NM	NM	NM	NM	8	8	7	6

Income Statement Analysis (Million $)										
Premium Income	11,748	11,110	9,727	6,905	6,039	4,539	2,486	894	645	587
Net Investment Income	1,264	1,013	901	812	803	781	493	325	238	207
Other Revenue	76.0	198	265	-489	-58.0	-39.0	38.0	188	128	55.0
Total Revenue	13,088	12,320	10,892	7,227	6,784	5,281	3,017	1,407	1,011	849
Pretax Income	1,317	1,439	1,794	-11.7	-247	598	394	580	NA	NA
Net Operating Income	NA	NA	NA	NA	NA	NA	323	372	333	235
Net Income	1,028	1,153	1,482	100	-158	517	365	560	461	290

Balance Sheet & Other Financial Data (Million $)										
Cash & Equivalent	850	807	817	NA	NA	NA	771	318	147	96.0
Premiums Due	3,343	3,255	2,823	2,654	NA	NA	2,019	377	136	85.0
Investment Assets:Bonds	27,361	22,891	19,312	NA	NA	NA	9,850	5,057	3,290	3,390
Investment Assets:Stocks	1,507	1,266	562	NA	NA	NA	933	190	635	323
Investment Assets:Loans	Nil	Nil	Nil	NA	NA	NA	Nil	Nil	Nil	Nil
Investment Assets:Total	34,521	26,925	22,555	17,555	15,197	13,064	12,276	5,883	4,475	4,102
Deferred Policy Costs	930	944	1,005	832	679	573	514	76.4	NA	NA
Total Assets	62,440	56,183	49,317	43,874	37,186	31,837	30,123	8,789	5,002	4,574
Debt	2,120	2,261	1,824	2,224	2,224	2,299	1,999	250	Nil	Nil
Common Equity	11,810	9,843	8,821	6,269	6,010	5,358	4,450	3,714	2,619	2,244
Property & Casualty:Loss Ratio	74.5	70.6	64.6	73.7	83.9	65.6	66.0	57.8	60.4	68.8
Property & Casualty:Expense Ratio	25.1	25.8	26.4	27.5	28.5	30.8	33.5	30.4	19.0	18.3
Property & Casualty Combined Ratio	99.6	96.4	91.0	101.2	112.4	96.4	99.5	88.2	79.4	87.1
% Return on Revenue	7.9	9.4	13.6	1.4	NM	9.8	12.1	39.8	45.6	34.1
% Return on Equity	9.5	11.9	19.2	1.2	NM	NA	8.7	17.7	19.0	7.4

Data as orig reptd.; bef. results of disc opers/spec. items. Per share data adj. for stk. divs.; EPS diluted. 2004-2000 data restated based on 2004 SEC Form 10-K/A. E-Estimated. NA-Not Available. NM-Not Meaningful. NR-Not Ranked. UR-Under Review.

Office: 17 Woodbourne Avenue, Hamilton, Bermuda HM 08.
Telephone: 441-295-5200.
Email: investorrelations@ace.bm
Website: http://www.acelimited.com

Chrmn: B. Duperreault
Pres & CEO: E.G. Greenberg
CFO: P.V. Bancroft
Chief Acctg Officer: P. Medini

Secy & General Counsel: R.F. Cusumano
Investor Contact: H.M. Wilson (441-299-9283)
Board of Directors: M. G. Atieh, M. A. Cirillo, B. L. Crockett, B. Duperreault, E. G. Greenberg, R. M. Hernandez, J. A. Krol, P. Menikoff, T. J. Neff, R. Ripp, D. F. Smurfit, G. M. Stuart

Founded: 1985
Domicile: Cayman Islands
Employees: 10,061

STANDARD & POOR'S

ADC Telecommunications Inc

S&P Recommendation BUY ★★★★★	**Price** $14.09 (as of Oct 27, 2006)	**12-Mo. Target Price** $18.00	**Investment Style** Mid-Cap Value

GICS Sector Information Technology
Sub-Industry Communications Equipment

Comment This company is a leading global supplier of fiber optics, network equipment, software and integration services for broadband and multiservice networks.

Key Stock Statistics (Source S&P, Vickers, company reports)

52-Wk Range	**$27.90–11.81**	S&P Oper. EPS 2006**E**	**0.79**	P/E on S&P Oper. EPS 2006**E**	**17.8**	Dividend Rate/Share	**Nil**
Trailing 12-Month EPS	**$0.29**	S&P Oper. EPS 2007**E**	**1.10**	Common Shares Outstg. (M)	**117.2**	Yield (%)	**Nil**
Trailing 12-Month P/E	**48.6**	S&P Core EPS 2006**E**	**0.79**	Market Capitalization(B)	**$1.652**	Beta	**2.61**
$10K Invested 5 Yrs Ago	**$3,962**	S&P Core EPS 2007**E**	**1.10**	Institutional Ownership (%)	**80**	S&P Credit Rating	**NA**

Price Performance

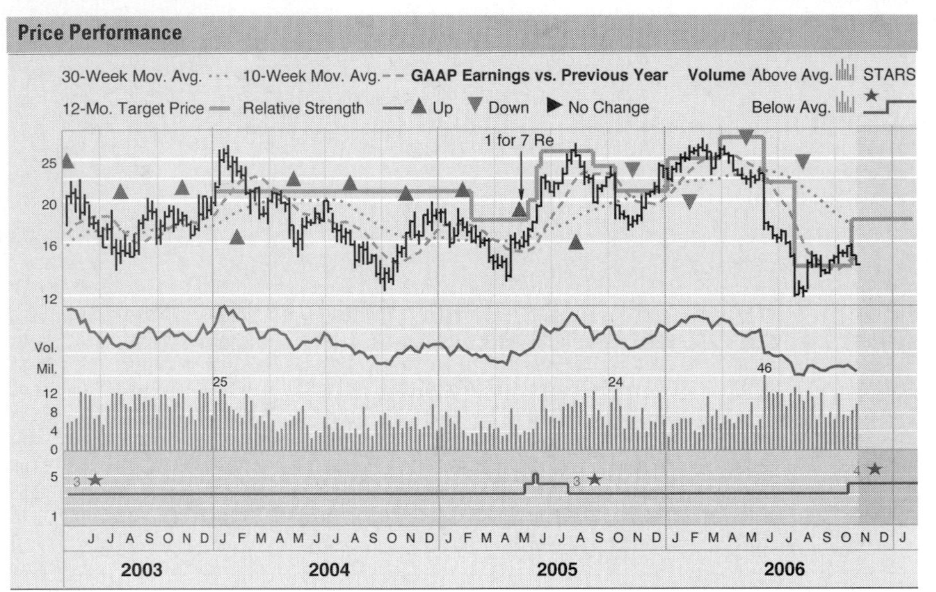

Options: ASE, CBOE, P, Ph

Analysis prepared by **Ari Bensinger** on October 19, 2006, when the stock traded at **$ 15.00**.

Highlights

- Following an 11% sales increase we estimate for FY 06 (Oct.), we look for sales to advance 8% in FY 07, driven by solid carrier and enterprise spending on broadband connectivity products. We are particularly optimistic about the growth opportunities available to ADCT in the fiber connectivity segment (30% of total sales). We see continued strong product demand in the company's enterprise structured cabling segment (15%).
- Based largely on improved manufacturing efficiencies, mainly reflecting product redesign and manufacturing relocation initiatives, we expect FY 07 gross margins to widen roughly 300 basis points, to 35%. Operating expenses as a percentage of sales should decline on higher sales volume, despite increased FTTP (fiber-to-the-premise) development costs.
- After minimal taxes, due to loss carryovers, we project FY 07 EPS of $1.10, up sharply from the $0.79 that we estimate for FY 06. Both fiscal years include $0.08 of projected stock option expense.

Investment Rationale/Risk

- While its failure to acquire Andrew Corp. was disappointing, we think ADCT remains well positioned to benefit from an ongoing spending shift toward broadband connectivity, particularly for FTTP and wireless products. Based on the significant leverage that we see inherent in the company's operating model, we believe ADCT should post earnings growth well above peers during FY 07.
- Risks to our recommendation and target price include lower telecom spending, slower than expected acceptance of the FTTP technology, increased acceptance of competing technologies, and the loss of a major customer.
- Our 12-month target price of $18 is primarily based on 16X our FY 07 EPS estimate, below peers to account for our view of poor sales visibility related to the uneven nature of telecom network spending. Our discounted cash flow model, assuming a weighted average cost of capital of 12% and a terminal growth rate for free cash flow of 3%, also indicates an intrinsic value of about $18.

Qualitative Risk Assessment

LOW | MEDIUM | **HIGH**

Our risk assessment reflects the highly competitive nature of the industry in which ADCT operates, significant pricing pressure on communications equipment due to strong customer buying power, and our view of ADCT's dependence on telecom carrier spending, which tends to be uneven because of the uncertain timing of new network build-outs and upgrades.

Quantitative Evaluations

S&P Quality Ranking **B**

D | C | B- | **B** | B+ | A- | A | A+

Relative Strength Rank **WEAK**

15

LOWEST = 1 HIGHEST = 99

Revenue/Earnings Data

Revenue (Million $)

	1Q	2Q	3Q	4Q	Year
2006	280.2	365.6	343.6	--	--
2005	240.6	312.4	314.6	301.6	1,169
2004	136.7	153.6	227.7	266.3	784.3
2003	199.9	191.9	188.5	192.9	773.2
2002	293.5	298.4	235.1	220.7	1,048
2001	811.3	652.4	547.5	391.6	2,403

Earnings Per Share ($)

	1Q	2Q	3Q	4Q	Year
2006	-0.02	0.19	0.20	**E**0.18	**E**0.79
2005	0.12	0.28	0.28	0.02	0.72
2004	Nil	-0.21	Nil	0.35	0.28
2003	-0.35	-0.28	-0.14	0.07	-0.70
2002	-0.42	-0.77	-5.53	-3.36	-10.08
2001	-0.07	-9.31	-0.49	-1.54	-11.48

Fiscal year ended Oct. 31. Next earnings report expected: Mid December. EPS Estimates based on S&P Operating Earnings; historical GAAP earnings are as reported.

Dividend Data

No cash dividends have been paid.

ADC Telecommunications Inc

Business Summary October 19, 2006

CORPORATE OVERVIEW. ADC Telecommunications is a global supplier of broadband network equipment, software, and systems integration services that enable communications service providers to deliver high-speed Internet, data, video and voice services. Product offerings are focused on increasing the speed and efficiency of the last mile portion of communications networks, that is, the network equipment that connects the service provider offices to end user homes and businesses. The company reports sales in two principal product segments: broadband infrastructure and access and integrated solutions.

The broadband infrastructure and access segment, which accounted for 81% of sales in FY 05 (Oct.), focuses on network infrastructure connectivity and component products for wireline, wireless, cable, broadcast and enterprise network applications. The professional services (19%) segment provides integration services for broadband communications. International sales accounted for 45% of total sales in FY 05, up from 40% in FY 04.

MARKET PROFILE. Increased use of the Internet has fueled demand for broadband access technologies such as digital subscriber line (DSL) and cable modem. Outside of the U.S., a lack of cable TV infrastructure contributes to DSL's dominant position as the leading global broadband access technology. With a focus on DSL technology, the majority of ADCT's sales are made to telecommunications service providers, with the four major U.S. incumbent local exchange carriers combined accounting for approximately 26% of revenue during FY 05.

Broadband equipment suppliers like ADCT should continue to benefit from the increasingly competitive environment between cable and telecom operators for new high-speed access subscribers, in our view. Independent research firm Ovum-RHK sees the broadband access equipment market at over $13 billion in 2006, with DSL network equipment accounting for 70% of the total market.

Company Financials

Per Share Data ($) Year Ended Oct. 31	**2005**	**2004**	**2003**	**2002**	**2001**	**2000**	**1999**	**1998**	**1997**	**1996**
Tangible Book Value	3.16	3.36	5.46	6.37	14.84	21.77	23.59	11.87	8.26	6.72
Cash Flow	1.16	0.63	-0.15	-9.11	-9.69	9.22	4.34	2.72	2.10	1.66
Earnings	0.72	0.28	-0.70	-10.08	-11.48	7.91	0.98	1.89	1.45	1.19
S&P Core Earnings	0.49	-0.07	-1.05	-10.43	-5.25	NA	NA	NA	NA	NA
Dividends	Nil	Nil	Nil	Nil	Nil	Nil	Nil	Nil	Nil	Nil
Payout Ratio	Nil	Nil	Nil	Nil	Nil	Nil	Nil	Nil	Nil	Nil
Prices:High	27.14	26.95	22.47	40.32	152.70	343.02	132.57	73.50	78.75	70.44
Prices:Low	12.88	12.25	13.70	7.14	18.41	106.76	60.16	27.56	37.19	24.94
P/E Ratio:High	38	96	NM	NM	NM	43	NM	39	54	59
P/E Ratio:Low	18	44	NM	NM	NM	13	NM	15	26	21
Income Statement Analysis (Million $)										
Revenue	1,169	784	773	1,048	2,403	3,288	1,927	1,380	1,165	828
Operating Income	155	78.2	19.9	-206	-136	670	414	291	238	167
Depreciation	67.2	41.7	59.2	105	198	146	102	65.1	49.8	33.8
Interest Expense	11.2	Nil	Nil	Nil	Nil	Nil	7.62	0.61	0.39	0.40
Pretax Income	92.7	33.2	-82.1	-882	-1,921	1,460	160	226	170	137
Effective Tax Rate	7.77%	5.72%	NM	NM	NM	40.6%	45.4%	35.0%	36.0%	36.0%
Net Income	85.5	31.3	-76.7	-1,145	-1,288	868	87.6	147	109	87.5
S&P Core Earnings	54.8	-8.12	-124	-1,188	-595	NA	NA	NA	NA	NA
Balance Sheet & Other Financial Data (Million $)										
Cash	110	66.2	740	456	349	217	144	288	110	183
Current Assets	853	836	1,006	686	1,305	2,651	1,029	863	550	500
Total Assets	1,535	1,428	1,297	1,144	2,500	3,971	1,673	1,301	936	769
Current Liabilities	287	302	266	398	599	1,041	413	383	182	142
Long Term Debt	400	400	400	10.8	3.00	16.5	11.0	2.77	3.10	6.90
Common Equity	774	659	628	732	1,893	2,913	1,249	914	751	617
Total Capital	1,174	1,059	1,028	743	1,896	2,929	1,260	917	754	627
Capital Expenditures	30.2	10.3	69.5	25.6	241	375	105	94.5	119	69.1
Cash Flow	153	73.0	-17.5	-1,040	-1,090	1,014	190	212	159	121
Current Ratio	3.0	2.8	3.8	1.7	2.2	2.5	2.5	2.3	3.0	3.5
% Long Term Debt of Capitalization	34.1	37.8	38.9	1.5	0.2	0.6	0.9	0.3	0.0	1.1
% Net Income of Revenue	7.3	4.0	NM	NM	NM	26.4	4.5	10.6	9.3	10.6
% Return on Assets	5.8	2.3	NM	NM	NM	28.8	5.6	13.1	12.8	12.8
% Return on Equity	11.9	4.9	NM	NM	NM	38.5	7.6	17.6	15.9	15.5

Data as orig reptd.; bef. results of disc opers/spec. items. Per share data adj. for stk. divs.; EPS diluted. E-Estimated. NA-Not Available. NM-Not Meaningful. NR-Not Ranked. UR-Under Review.

Office: 13625 Technology Drive, Eden Prairie, MN 55344.
Telephone: 952-938-8080.
Email: investor@adc.com
Website: http://www.adc.com

Chrmn: J.A. Blanchard, III
Pres & CEO: R.E. Switz
VP & CFO: G.V. Hemmady
VP, Secy & General Counsel: J.D. Pflaum

VP & Cntlr: J. Mathews
Investor Contact: M.P. Borman (952-917-0590)
Board of Directors: J. A. Blanchard, III, J. J. Boyle, III, J. C. Castle, M. P. Foret, K. Gilligan, L. M. Martin, J. E. Rehfeld, J. Rosso, W. Spivey, R. E. Switz, L. Wangberg, J. D. Wunsch

Founded: 1935
Domicile: Minnesota
Employees: 8,200

Adobe Systems Inc

STANDARD &POOR'S

S&P Recommendation HOLD ★★★★★	**Price** $38.57 (as of Oct 27, 2006)	**12-Mo. Target Price** $38.00	**Investment Style** Large-Cap Growth

GICS Sector Information Technology
Sub-Industry Application Software

Comment ADBE provides software for multimedia content creation, distribution, and management.

Key Stock Statistics (Source S&P, Vickers, company reports)

52-Wk Range	**$40.85–25.98**	S&P Oper. EPS 2006**E**	**1.14**	P/E on S&P Oper. EPS 2006**E**	**33.8**	Dividend Rate/Share	**Nil**
Trailing 12-Month EPS	**$0.84**	S&P Oper. EPS 2007**E**	**1.36**	Common Shares Outstg. (M)	**583.3**	Yield (%)	**Nil**
Trailing 12-Month P/E	**45.9**	S&P Core EPS 2006**E**	**1.14**	Market Capitalization(B)	**$22.500**	Beta	**1.91**
$10K Invested 5 Yrs Ago	**$23,721**	S&P Core EPS 2007**E**	**1.36**	Institutional Ownership (%)	**85**	S&P Credit Rating	**NA**

Price Performance

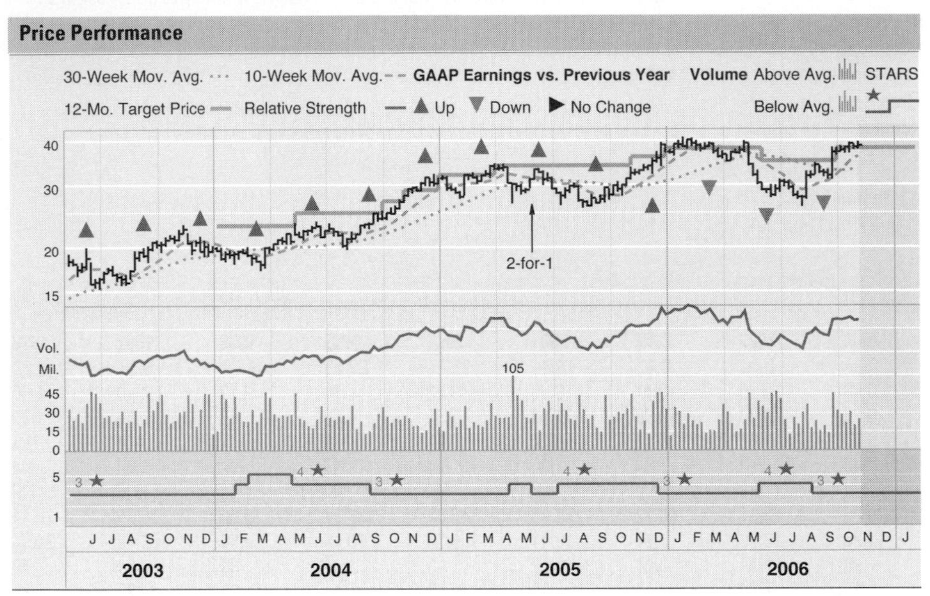

Options: ASE, CBOE, P, Ph

Analysis prepared by **Scott H. Kessler** on September 18, 2006, when the stock traded at **$ 37.00**.

Highlights

- We project that revenues will increase 30% in FY 06 (Nov.), reflecting the December 2005 acquisition of Macromedia. We believe ADBE's FY 06 revenues have been adversely impacted by anticipated transitions to the "Mactel" platform. We foresee 16% revenue growth in FY 07, reflecting releases of Acrobat and Creative Suite offerings expected by spring 2007.
- We project a gross margin of 95% and an operating margin of 34% for FY 06, reflecting the positive impact of restructuring efforts and operating efficiencies, offset somewhat by the aforementioned transitions. We expect higher annual gross and operating margins in FY 07, aided by new product introductions.
- In December 2005, ADBE acquired content software company Macromedia in a deal valued at $3.4 billion in stock. In April 2005, ADBE announced a stock repurchase program of $1 billion, which began following the consummation of the Macromedia merger. We believe the buyback, which was announced as completed in September 2006, aided EPS. Our estimates include per-share anticipated stock option expenses of $0.13 in FY 06 and $0.15 in FY 07.

Investment Rationale/Risk

- We believe ADBE is well positioned to participate in the continuing growth and usage of the Internet, particularly related to documents and forms. We also think Macromedia has enhanced ADBE's technology and products.
- Risks to our recommendation and target price include weaker demand than we expect for ADBE's Creative Suite offerings (the latest of which was announced in April 2005), uncertainties related to the acquisition of Macromedia (including integration matters and potential employee retention issues), and heightened competition for the Acrobat franchise.
- ADBE's calendar year 2006 P/E and P/E-to-growth (PEG) ratios were recently well above those of the S&P 500 Software Industry. However, our discounted cash flow analysis (with assumptions including a discount rate of 11.0% and annual free cash flow growth averaging 16% from FY 06 to FY 10) yields an intrinsic value of $35. Allowing for a premium, due to what we see as ADBE's market leadership and strong execution record, our 12-month target price is $38.

Qualitative Risk Assessment

LOW | **MEDIUM** | HIGH

Our risk assessment reflects our view of ADBE's size and market leadership, consistent operating history, and a strong balance sheet, as well as the regularly changing nature of the software industry.

Quantitative Evaluations

S&P Quality Ranking **B+**

D | C | B- | B | **B+** | A- | A | A+

Relative Strength Rank **STRONG**

80

LOWEST = 1 HIGHEST = 99

Revenue/Earnings Data

Revenue (Million $)

	1Q	2Q	3Q	4Q	Year
2006	655.5	635.5	602.2	--	--
2005	472.9	496.0	487.0	510.4	1,966
2004	423.3	410.1	403.7	429.5	1,667
2003	296.9	320.2	319.1	358.6	1,295
2002	267.9	317.4	284.9	294.7	1,165
2001	329.0	344.1	292.1	264.5	1,230

Earnings Per Share ($)

2006	0.17	0.20	0.16	**E**0.31	**E**1.14
2005	0.30	0.29	0.29	0.31	1.19
2004	0.25	0.22	0.21	0.23	0.91
2003	0.12	0.14	0.14	0.17	0.55
2002	0.10	0.11	0.10	0.09	0.40
2001	0.14	0.13	0.08	0.07	0.42

Fiscal year ended Nov. 30. Next earnings report expected: Mid December. EPS Estimates based on S&P Operating Earnings; historical GAAP earnings are as reported.

Dividend Data

No cash dividends have been paid since 2005.

Adobe Systems Inc

Business Summary September 18, 2006

CORPORATE OVERVIEW. Adobe Systems is one of the world's largest software companies. It offers creative, business, and mobile software and services used by consumers, creative professionals, designers, knowledge workers, original equipment manufacturers, developers, and enterprises for creating, managing, delivering and experiencing content across multiple operating systems, devices and media. Its cornerstone products include Acrobat (for document creation, distribution and management), Illustrator (to create graphic artwork), and Photoshop (for photo design, enhancement, and editing). In December 2005, ADBE acquired Macromedia, a leading developer of software that enables the creation and consumption of digital content, for $4.3 billion in stock. We believe this was an extremely important transaction for the company. Macromedia's important products include Dreamweaver (for Web development) and Flash (which provides an environment to create dynamic digital content).

CORPORATE STRATEGY. ADBE's indicated strategy is to address the needs of a variety of customers with offerings that support industry standards and can be deployed in a variety of contexts. We believe ADBE is focused on leveraging its market leading software franchises with bundles and enhancements. Selling multiple products together has enabled ADBE to gain market share, increase penetration with existing customers, and expand its overall customer base, in our view. The Creative Suite is the company's flagship bundled offering. Macromedia was acquired to further this strategy, and bundles of legacy Adobe and Macromedia software were released just days after their combination was completed.

We believe the purchase of Macromedia was an excellent strategic move for ADBE because it contributed technologies and products that have achieved notable adoption in the areas of dynamic digital content creation, and mobile platforms. In our opinion, ADBE's offerings in these segments were previously somewhat lacking and Macromedia will bolster these businesses. However, we think that ADBE may have overpaid for Macromedia, and that the integration of management and other personnel could prove to be challenging. There has already been notable announced executive turnover.

Company Financials

Per Share Data ($) Year Ended Nov. 30	**2005**	**2004**	**2003**	**2002**	**2001**	**2000**	**1999**	**1998**	**1997**	**1996**
Tangible Book Value	3.54	2.68	2.08	1.24	1.23	1.45	1.01	1.03	1.35	1.19
Cash Flow	1.31	1.03	0.65	0.52	0.53	0.65	0.56	0.30	0.41	0.35
Earnings	1.19	0.91	0.55	0.40	0.42	0.57	0.46	0.19	0.32	0.26
S&P Core Earnings	1.01	0.69	0.18	0.05	0.11	NA	NA	NA	NA	NA
Dividends	0.01	0.03	0.03	0.03	0.03	0.03	0.03	0.03	0.03	0.03
Payout Ratio	1%	3%	5%	6%	6%	6%	5%	13%	8%	10%
Prices:High	39.48	32.24	23.19	21.66	30.81	43.66	19.75	6.48	6.64	8.03
Prices:Low	25.80	17.15	12.29	8.25	11.10	13.36	4.71	2.05	4.00	3.50
P/E Ratio:High	33	35	42	55	74	77	43	33	21	31
P/E Ratio:Low	22	19	22	21	27	24	10	15	13	14

Income Statement Analysis (Million $)	2005	2004	2003	2002	2001	2000	1999	1998	1997	1996
Revenue	1,966	1,667	1,295	1,165	1,230	1,266	1,015	895	912	787
Operating Income	793	653	428	368	447	457	337	220	296	229
Depreciation	64.3	60.8	49.0	63.5	56.6	43.3	50.8	56.3	59.4	55.6
Interest Expense	Nil	Nil	Nil	Nil	Nil	Nil	Nil	Nil	Nil	Nil
Pretax Income	766	609	380	285	307	444	374	168	296	245
Effective Tax Rate	21.3%	26.0%	30.0%	32.8%	33.0%	35.1%	36.5%	37.3%	36.9%	37.4%
Net Income	603	450	266	191	206	288	238	105	187	153
S&P Core Earnings	515	343	86.7	20.6	51.7	NA	NA	NA	NA	NA

Balance Sheet & Other Financial Data (Million $)	2005	2004	2003	2002	2001	2000	1999	1998	1997	1996
Cash	421	376	190	184	219	237	171	111	268	111
Current Assets	2,009	1,551	1,329	814	767	878	623	456	679	737
Total Assets	2,440	1,959	1,555	1,052	931	1,069	804	767	940	1,012
Current Liabilities	480	451	437	377	314	315	268	251	225	231
Long Term Debt	Nil	Nil	Nil	Nil	Nil	Nil	Nil	Nil	Nil	Nil
Common Equity	1,864	1,423	1,101	674	617	753	512	516	715	707
Total Capital	1,943	1,502	1,119	674	617	755	536	516	715	710
Capital Expenditures	48.9	63.2	39.5	31.6	46.6	29.8	42.2	59.7	33.9	45.9
Cash Flow	667	511	315	255	262	331	289	161	246	209
Current Ratio	4.2	3.4	3.0	2.2	2.4	2.8	2.3	1.8	3.0	3.2
% Long Term Debt of Capitalization	Nil	Nil	Nil	Nil	Nil	Nil	Nil	Nil	Nil	Nil
% Net Income of Revenue	30.7	27.0	20.6	16.4	16.7	22.7	23.4	11.8	20.5	19.4
% Return on Assets	27.4	25.6	20.4	19.3	20.6	30.7	30.3	12.3	19.1	16.2
% Return on Equity	36.7	35.7	30.0	29.6	30.0	45.5	46.2	17.1	26.3	21.8

Data as orig reptd.; bef. results of disc opers/spec. items. Per share data adj. for stk. divs.; EPS diluted. E-Estimated. NA-Not Available. NM-Not Meaningful. NR-Not Ranked. UR-Under Review.

Office: 345 Park Avenue, San Jose, CA, USA 95110-2704.
Telephone: 408-536-6000.
Email: ir@adobe.com
Website: http://www.adobe.com

Co-Chrmn: J.E. Warnock
Co-Chrmn: C.M. Geschke
Pres & COO: S. Narayen
CEO: B.R. Chizen

EVP & CFO: R. Furr
Auditor: KPMG, Mountain View, CA
Board of Directors: E. W. Barnholt, R. Burgess, M. Cannon, B. R. Chizen, J. Daley, C. M. Geschke, C. Mills, C. M. Pouliot, R. Sedgewick, J. E. Warnock, D. W. Yocam

Founded: 1983
Domicile: Delaware
Employees: 4,285

Advanced Micro Devices Inc.

STANDARD &POOR'S

S&P Recommendation HOLD ★★★★★

Price $20.86 (as of Oct 27, 2006)

12-Mo. Target Price $28.00

Investment Style Large-Cap Value

GICS Sector Information Technology
Sub-Industry Semiconductors

Comment AMD is a leading producer of semiconductors that are used principally by the computer and telecommunications industries.

Key Stock Statistics (Source S&P, Vickers, company reports)

52-Wk Range	**$42.70–16.90**	S&P Oper. EPS 2006**E**	**1.13**	P/E on S&P Oper. EPS 2006**E**	**18.5**	Dividend Rate/Share	**Nil**
Trailing 12-Month EPS	**$1.05**	S&P Oper. EPS 2007**E**	**1.57**	Common Shares Outstg. (M)	**2,542.4**	Yield (%)	**Nil**
Trailing 12-Month P/E	**19.9**	S&P Core EPS 2006**E**	**1.13**	Market Capitalization(B)	**$53.035**	Beta	**3.72**
$10K Invested 5 Yrs Ago	**$20,174**	S&P Core EPS 2007**E**	**1.60**	Institutional Ownership (%)	**82**	S&P Credit Rating	**B+**

Price Performance

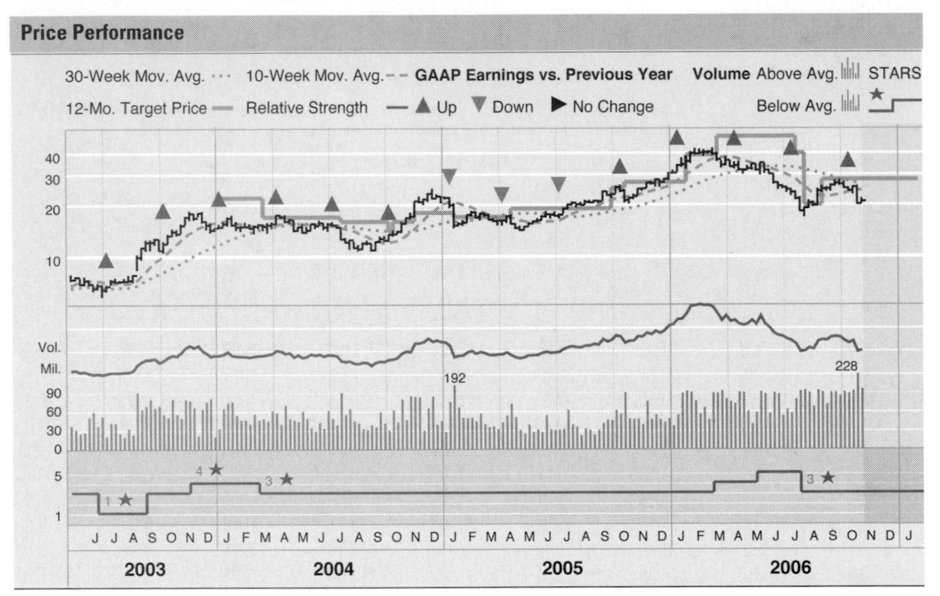

Options: ASE, CBOE, P, Ph

Analysis prepared by **Clyde Montevirgen** on October 24, 2006, when the stock traded at **$ 20.32**.

Highlights

- We expect sales to decrease 9.0% in 2006, followed by an 11% rise in 2007. AMD's 2006 top-line comparison with 2005 suffers from the absence of revenue from memory operations that were spun off in an IPO late in the fourth quarter of 2005. Memory operations represented about 33% of AMD's 2005 sales. Although we estimate that AMD will increase unit sales of processors briskly, we expect average selling prices (ASPs) to be weak through the fourth quarter of 2006 as prime rival Intel tries to regain market share.
- We estimate gross margins of 55% for 2006, compared to 41% in 2005, which included the memory operations. However, we see narrowing gross margins heading into the last quarter of 2006 as ASPs for desktop PCs deteriorate. On July 24, AMD agreed to acquire ATI Technologies, a fabless graphics processor maker based near Toronto, Canada, for about $5.4 billion in cash and stock. Subject to customary approvals, AMD expects the proposed deal to close in the 2006 fourth quarter.
- We project operating EPS of $1.13 for 2006 and $1.57 for 2007, including projected stock option expense.

Investment Rationale/Risk

- Although we currently see a challenging pricing and demand environment for microprocessors, we expect longer term profitability to be enhanced by an improving market position in PC and server processors. In the near term, however, we think Intel's relatively high levels of finished goods inventory may lead to future price wars, posing substantial risks to AMD's profitability. The shares may appear attractive on some valuation measures, but we view unfavorably the risk-reward payoff in light of Intel's aggressive new product campaigns.
- Risks to our opinion and target price include demand for computers and semiconductors turning lower than we expect, and that the market share gains we project might not be achieved.
- Our blended 12-month target price of $28 is derived partly by applying a price-to-sales ratio of 2.4X, at the high end of the historical range but low among peers, to our 2007 sales per share estimate of $11.85, indicating a value of $28. Applying a peer-group target P/E multiple of 24.5X to our forward 12-month EPS estimate of $1.14 also indicates a $28 value.

Qualitative Risk Assessment

LOW | MEDIUM | **HIGH**

AMD is subject to the cyclical swings of the semiconductor industry, demand fluctuations for computer end-products, fluctuations in average selling prices for chips, and strong competition from Intel, which is a much larger rival in microprocessors.

Quantitative Evaluations

S&P Quality Ranking **B-**

D | C | **B-** | B | B+ | A- | A | A+

Relative Strength Rank **WEAK**

7

LOWEST = 1 HIGHEST = 99

Revenue/Earnings Data

Revenue (Million $)

	1Q	2Q	3Q	4Q	Year
2006	1,332	1,216	1,328	--	--
2005	1,227	1,260	1,523	1,838	5,848
2004	1,236	1,262	1,239	1,264	5,001
2003	714.6	645.3	953.8	1,206	3,519
2002	902.1	600.3	508.2	686.4	2,697
2001	1,189	985.0	765.9	951.9	3,892

Earnings Per Share ($)

	1Q	2Q	3Q	4Q	Year
2006	0.38	0.18	0.27	**E**0.38	**E**1.13
2005	-0.04	0.03	0.18	0.21	0.40
2004	0.12	0.09	0.12	-0.08	0.25
2003	-0.42	-0.40	-0.09	0.12	-0.79
2002	-0.03	-0.54	-0.74	-2.49	-3.81
2001	0.37	0.05	-0.54	-0.05	-0.18

Fiscal year ended Dec. 31. Next earnings report expected: Mid January. EPS Estimates based on S&P Operating Earnings; historical GAAP earnings are as reported.

Dividend Data

Except for a special payment of $0.01 a share in 1995, no cash dividends have been paid.

Advanced Micro Devices Inc.

Business Summary October 24, 2006

Advanced Micro Devices makes digital integrated circuits, including microprocessors for computers, embedded microprocessors for personal connectivity devices and, until late 2005, flash memory devices. It is the prime competitor of dominant player Intel Corp. in the PC microprocessor market, and occasionally has captured over 20% market share. According to market research firm Mercury Research, AMD's market share in desktops rose 5.1% in 2005 to hit 24.3%.

The largest portion of the company's revenues (64% in 2005, 51% in 2004) comes from the Computation Products Group. AMD's processor brands for desktop PCs consist of the Athlon 64, Athlon 64 FX, and Sempron processors. In 2003, the company introduced its Athlon 64 microprocessor, the first Windows-compatible, x86 architecture-based 64-bit PC processor. Athlon 64 processors, which allow the simultaneous use of both 32-bit and 64-bit software applications, are designed for enterprises and sophisticated PC users that seek to access large amounts of data and memory. Simultaneously with the introduction of the Athlon 64, AMD introduced the Athlon 64 FX processor, designed specifically for gamers, PC enthusiasts, and digital content creators that require products that can perform graphic-intensive tasks. Sempron processors, introduced in July 2004, are designed for value-conscious consumers of desktop and notebook PCs. The company also sells chipsets that support its processors, as well as motherboard reference design kits.

In 2005, Hewlett-Packard accounted for 12% of total sales and Fujitsu accounted for 15%. Hewlett-Packard sales were mainly from the Computation segment and Fujitsu mainly distributed Spansion flash memory products. Some 79% of sales came from outside the U.S. in both 2005 and 2004.

AMD's microprocessors for the mobile computing market include AMD Turion 64 mobile technology, introduced in March 2005, and AMD Athlon 64 processors and mobile AMD Sempron processors.

Company Financials

Per Share Data ($) Year Ended Dec. 31	**2005**	**2004**	**2003**	**2002**	**2001**	**2000**	**1999**	**1998**	**1997**	**1996**
Tangible Book Value	7.70	7.68	6.96	7.16	10.64	10.09	6.66	6.89	7.11	7.34
Cash Flow	3.14	3.54	2.08	-1.60	1.69	4.53	1.45	1.27	1.33	0.97
Earnings	0.40	0.25	-0.79	-3.81	-0.18	2.95	-0.30	-0.36	-0.08	-0.26
S&P Core Earnings	0.38	-0.19	-1.08	-4.24	-0.49	NA	NA	NA	NA	NA
Dividends	Nil	Nil	Nil	Nil	Nil	Nil	Nil	Nil	Nil	Nil
Payout Ratio	Nil	Nil	Nil	Nil	Nil	Nil	Nil	Nil	Nil	Nil
Prices:High	31.84	24.95	18.50	20.60	34.65	48.50	16.50	16.38	24.25	14.19
Prices:Low	14.08	10.76	4.78	3.10	7.69	13.56	7.28	6.38	8.56	5.13
P/E Ratio:High	80	NM	NM	NM	NM	16	NM	NM	NM	NM
P/E Ratio:Low	35	NM	NM	NM	NM	5	NM	NM	NM	NM
Income Statement Analysis (Million $)										
Revenue	5,848	5,001	3,519	2,697	3,892	4,644	2,858	2,542	2,356	1,953
Operating Income	1,451	1,452	748	-139	654	1,468	233	304	304	79.3
Depreciation	1,219	1,224	996	756	623	579	516	468	394	333
Interest Expense	105	112	110	71.3	61.4	60.0	69.3	66.5	45.3	32.5
Pretax Income	33.7	116	-316	-1,258	-75.0	1,263	78.4	-196	-76.2	-209
Effective Tax Rate	NM	5.05%	NM	NM	NM	20.3%	NM	NM	NM	NM
Net Income	165	91.2	-274	-1,303	-60.6	1,006	-88.9	-104	-21.1	-69.0
S&P Core Earnings	155	-68.2	-373	-1,450	-161	NA	NA	NA	NA	NA
Balance Sheet & Other Financial Data (Million $)										
Cash	633	918	968	429	427	591	294	362	241	386
Current Assets	3,559	3,228	2,900	2,020	2,353	2,658	1,410	1,562	1,175	1,029
Total Assets	7,288	7,844	7,094	5,619	5,647	5,768	4,378	4,253	3,515	3,145
Current Liabilities	1,822	1,846	1,452	1,372	1,314	1,224	911	841	727	583
Long Term Debt	1,327	1,628	1,900	1,780	673	1,168	1,427	1,372	663	445
Common Equity	3,352	3,010	2,438	2,467	3,555	3,172	1,979	2,005	2,030	2,022
Total Capital	5,006	5,583	5,213	4,247	4,333	4,544	3,467	3,412	2,789	2,562
Capital Expenditures	1,513	1,440	570	705	679	805	620	996	685	485
Cash Flow	1,385	1,315	721	-547	562	1,585	427	364	373	264
Current Ratio	2.0	1.7	2.0	1.5	1.8	2.2	1.5	1.9	1.6	1.8
% Long Term Debt of Capitalization	26.5	29.2	36.4	41.9	15.5	25.7	41.2	40.2	23.8	17.4
% Net Income of Revenue	2.8	1.8	NM	NM	NM	21.7	NM	NM	NM	NM
% Return on Assets	2.2	1.2	NM	NM	NM	19.8	NM	NM	NM	NM
% Return on Equity	5.2	3.3	NM	NM	NM	39.1	NM	NM	NM	NM

Data as orig reptd.; bef. results of disc opers/spec. items. Per share data adj. for stk. divs.; EPS diluted. E-Estimated. NA-Not Available. NM-Not Meaningful. NR-Not Ranked. UR-Under Review.

Office: One AMD Place, Sunnyvale, CA 94088-3453.
Telephone: 408-749-4000.
Email: investor.relations@amd.com
Website: http://www.amd.com

Chrmn & CEO: H.d. Ruiz
Pres & COO: D.R. Meyer
EVP & CFO: R.J. Rivet
EVP & Chief Admin: T.M. McCoy

SVP & General Counsel: H. Wolin
Board of Directors: W. M. Barnes, B. Claflin, H. P. Eberhart, R. B. Palmer, H. d. Ruiz, L. M. Silverman, M. L. Topfer

Founded: 1969
Domicile: Delaware
Employees: 9,860

AES Corporation (The)

STANDARD &POOR'S

S&P Recommendation HOLD ★★★★★

Price $21.73 (as of Oct 27, 2006)

12-Mo. Target Price $22.00

Investment Style Large-Cap Growth

GICS Sector Utilities
Sub-Industry Independent Power Producers & Energy Traders

Comment The world's largest independent power producer, AES produces and distributes electricity in international and domestic markets.

Key Stock Statistics (Source S&P, Vickers, company reports)

52-Wk Range	$22.11–14.64	S&P Oper. EPS 2006E	1.05	P/E on S&P Oper. EPS 2006E	20.7	Dividend Rate/Share	Nil
Trailing 12-Month EPS	$1.39	S&P Oper. EPS 2007E	1.20	Common Shares Outstg. (M)	661.4	Yield (%)	Nil
Trailing 12-Month P/E	15.6	S&P Core EPS 2006E	NA	Market Capitalization(B)	$14.373	Beta	2.87
$10K Invested 5 Yrs Ago	$14,843	S&P Core EPS 2007E	NA	Institutional Ownership (%)	79	S&P Credit Rating	BB-

Price Performance

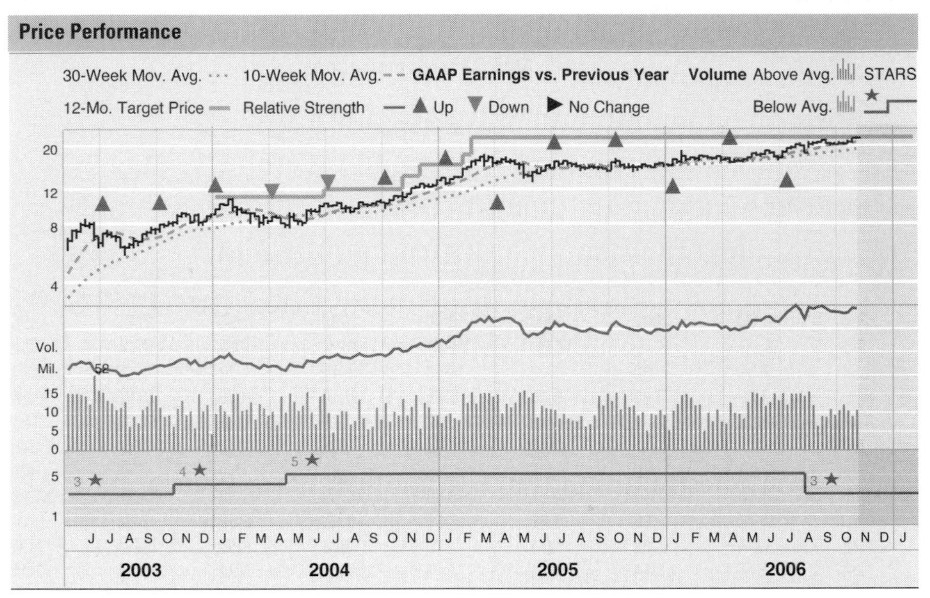

Options: ASE, CBOE, P, Ph

Analysis prepared by **Kenneth M. Leon, CPA** on August 11, 2006, when the stock traded at **$ 20.25**.

Highlights

- In 2006, we see earnings growth driven by 10% revenue gains. We project better results from international operations, particularly in South American utility operations, on improving economic conditions in emerging markets along with reduced power losses and performance improvements.
- Gross margins should expand in North American and South American generation as revenue gains on higher power prices and sales volumes offset increased purchased power and fuel costs. Rising demand in Pakistan and East Europe should also drive growth in operating income. We expect results to be boosted by significantly higher sales of excess emission allowances in the U.S.
- With lower interest expense and a level share count, we see 2006 EPS of $1.05. We think AES's projected five-year compound annual EPS growth within a range of 15% to 20%, driven by expected debt reduction, cost cuts, and new investment opportunities, is achievable given strong international growth opportunities.

Investment Rationale/Risk

- We think AES should see above-average earnings growth and an improving balance sheet over the next couple of years, in part due to stronger economic growth in emerging markets. Results will also likely be driven by cost control initiatives and potential EPS benefits from favorable foreign exchange currency translation and lower effective tax rates than historically.
- Risks to our recommendation and target price include sharp declines in certain foreign exchange currency rates, political and regulatory uncertainty regarding utility rates and U.S. power margins, counterparty default risk, and potential terrorist attacks on the infrastructure.
- We believe AES's shares are near our view of fair valuation which is our 12-month target price of $22, and is based on 18.3X our 2007 EPS estimate, near its peer average. Despite our recent recommendation downgrade to hold, from strong buy, due to valuation metrics, we believe AES is a superior independent power producer, and the shares are worth holding.

Qualitative Risk Assessment

LOW | **MEDIUM** | HIGH

Our risk assessment reflects the company's relatively large capitalization and mix of lower risk regulated utility businesses in North America, offset by higher risk merchant power operations and utility operations in emerging markets in South America, the Caribbean, East Europe and Asia.

Quantitative Evaluations

S&P Quality Ranking B-

D | C | **B-** | B | B+ | A- | A | A+

Relative Strength Rank MODERATE

70

LOWEST = 1 HIGHEST = 99

Revenue/Earnings Data

Revenue (Million $)

	1Q	2Q	3Q	4Q	Year
2006	3,013	3,038	--	--	--
2005	2,663	2,668	2,782	2,973	11,086
2004	2,257	2,263	2,423	2,543	9,486
2003	1,911	1,992	2,231	2,281	8,415
2002	2,228	2,080	2,110	2,214	8,632
2001	2,495	2,184	2,261	2,387	9,327

Earnings Per Share ($)

2006	0.52	0.31	E0.12	E0.10	E1.05
2005	0.19	0.13	0.37	0.27	0.95
2004	0.12	0.10	0.20	0.14	0.57
2003	0.23	0.24	0.10	0.01	0.56
2002	0.33	-0.19	-0.40	-4.50	-4.81
2001	0.22	0.27	0.02	0.35	0.87

Fiscal year ended Dec. 31. Next earnings report expected: NA. EPS Estimates based on S&P Operating Earnings; historical GAAP earnings are as reported.

Dividend Data

No cash dividends have been paid.

AES Corporation (The)

Business Summary August 11, 2006

CORPORATE OVERVIEW. AES Corporation (AES) owns and operates a portfolio of electricity generation and distribution business in 25 countries through its subsidiaries and affiliates. The company has two principal businesses: the generation business and the regulated utilities business.

The generation business provides power for sale to utilities and other wholesale customers while the regulated utilities business distributes power to retail, commercial, industrial, and governmental customers. The generation business has two segments: contract generation and competitive supply. In 2005, the contract generation unit contributed 37% of total revenues. It primarily sells electricity to utilities or other wholesale customers under power purchase agreements that are generally for five years or longer. We are positive on AES usually retaining 75% or more of a given customer's total capacity needs.

The competitive supply business contributed 11% of total revenues in 2005. It sells electricity to wholesale customers through competitive markets. The remaining 52% of total revenues in 2005 comes from the regulated utilities business. It markets electricity to residential, business, and government customers through integrated transmission and distribution systems.

CORPORATE STRATEGY. AES pursues both a global and a local growth strategy to increase its business. The global strategy focuses on large-scale projects and pursues strategic initiatives. It concentrates on mergers and acquisitions, exploring opportunities in the climate change business such as the production of greenhouse gas reduction activities and related industries that involve environmental issues.

AES has stated its interest in pursuing the renewable energy and alternative energy markets. The Wind Energy Ltd. acquisition is part of the company's alternative energy business. On the local growth level, AES focuses on expansion plans to fuel its organic growth. The company intends to identify opportunities to expand value through strategic platform expansions such as its 120 megawatts (MW) expansion project in Chile.

Company Financials

Per Share Data ($) Year Ended Dec. 31	2005	2004	2003	2002	2001	2000	1999	1998	1997	1996
Tangible Book Value	NM	NM	NM	NM	2.87	5.21	3.88	4.79	4.17	2.16
Earnings	0.95	0.57	0.56	-4.81	0.87	1.42	0.63	0.84	0.56	0.41
S&P Core Earnings	1.04	0.68	0.94	-3.66	0.74	NA	NA	NA	NA	NA
Dividends	Nil	Nil	Nil	Nil	Nil	Nil	Nil	Nil	Nil	Nil
Payout Ratio	Nil	Nil	Nil	Nil	Nil	Nil	Nil	Nil	Nil	Nil
Prices:High	18.13	13.71	9.50	17.92	60.15	72.81	38.19	29.00	24.81	12.53
Prices:Low	12.53	7.56	2.63	0.92	11.60	34.25	16.41	11.50	11.19	5.25
P/E Ratio:High	19	24	17	NM	69	51	61	35	45	31
P/E Ratio:Low	13	13	5	NM	13	24	26	14	20	13

Income Statement Analysis (Million $)	2005	2004	2003	2002	2001	2000	1999	1998	1997	1996
Revenue	11,086	9,486	8,415	8,632	9,327	6,691	3,253	2,398	1,411	835
Depreciation	889	841	781	837	859	582	278	196	114	65.0
Maintenance	NA	NA	NA	NA	NA	NA	NA	NA	NA	NA
Fixed Charges Coverage	1.73	1.30	1.38	0.34	1.42	1.80	NA	NA	NA	NA
Construction Credits	NA	NA	NA	NA	NA	NA	NA	NA	NA	NA
Effective Tax Rate	31.9%	28.2%	30.3%	NM	28.7%	24.7%	26.4%	26.6%	21.3%	31.1%
Net Income	632	366	336	-2,590	467	648	245	307	188	125
S&P Core Earnings	693	441	564	-1,970	394	NA	NA	NA	NA	NA

Balance Sheet & Other Financial Data (Million $)	2005	2004	2003	2002	2001	2000	1999	1998	1997	1996
Gross Property	24,741	24,141	23,098	23,050	26,748	19,150	NA	NA	NA	NA
Capital Expenditures	1,143	892	1,228	2,116	3,173	2,150	NA	NA	NA	NA
Net Property	18,654	18,788	18,505	18,846	23,434	17,846	NA	NA	NA	NA
Capitalization:Long Term Debt	36,674	16,823	16,792	17,684	20,564	16,927	NA	NA	NA	NA
Capitalization:% Long Term Debt	95.7	91.1	96.3	102.0	78.8	77.9	NA	NA	NA	NA
Capitalization:Preferred	Nil	Nil	Nil	Nil	Nil	NA	NA	NA	NA	NA
Capitalization:% Preferred	Nil	Nil	Nil	Nil	Nil	NA	NA	NA	NA	NA
Capitalization:Common	1,649	1,645	645	-341	5,539	4,811	NA	NA	NA	NA
Capitalization:% Common	4.30	8.91	3.70	-1.97	21.2	22.1	NA	NA	NA	NA
Total Capital	40,655	20,758	19,293	19,142	29,537	24,752	17,708	8,585	7,414	3,185
% Operating Ratio	85.5	84.2	84.5	88.5	89.7	88.3	NA	NA	NA	NA
% Earned on Net Property	20.9	18.5	17.0	14.3	13.6	14.0	NA	NA	NA	NA
% Return on Revenue	5.7	3.9	4.0	NM	5.0	9.7	NA	NA	NA	NA
% Return on Invested Capital	7.0	13.6	13.6	21.6	7.3	9.8	NA	NA	NA	NA
% Return on Common Equity	48.5	33.4	221.1	NM	8.4	17.4	NA	NA	NA	NA

Data as orig reptd.; bef. results of disc opers/spec. items. Per share data adj. for stk. divs.; EPS diluted. E-Estimated. NA-Not Available. NM-Not Meaningful. NR-Not Ranked. UR-Under Review.

Office: 4300 Wilson Blvd., Arlington, VA 22203-4167.
Telephone: 703-522-1315.
Email: invest@aes.com
Website: http://www.aes.com

Chrmn: R. Darman
Pres & CEO: P.T. Hanrahan
EVP & CFO: V. Harker
EVP, Secy & General Counsel: B. Miller

Investor Contact: S. Cunningham (703-682-6336)
Board of Directors: R. Darman, P. T. Hanrahan, K. Johnson, J. A. Koskinen, P. Lader, J. H. McArthur, S. O. Moose, P. A. Odeen, C. O. Rossotti, S. Sandstrom

Founded: 1981
Domicile: Delaware
Employees: 30,000

STANDARD &POOR'S

Aetna Inc.

S&P Recommendation BUY ★★★★★	Price $41.58 (as of Oct 27, 2006)	12-Mo. Target Price $49.00	Investment Style Large-Cap Value

GICS Sector Health Care
Sub-Industry Managed Health Care

Comment This company is a leading U.S. provider of health care, dental, pharmacy, group life, disability and long-term care benefits.

Key Stock Statistics (Source S&P, Vickers, company reports)

52-Wk Range	$52.48–30.94	S&P Oper. EPS 2006E	2.80	P/E on S&P Oper. EPS 2006E	14.9	Dividend Rate/Share	$0.04
Trailing 12-Month EPS	$2.98	S&P Oper. EPS 2007E	3.20	Common Shares Outstg. (M)	522.0	Yield (%)	0.10
Trailing 12-Month P/E	14.0	S&P Core EPS 2006E	2.78	Market Capitalization(B)	$21.705	Beta	0.54
$10K Invested 5 Yrs Ago	$59,020	S&P Core EPS 2007E	3.17	Institutional Ownership (%)	85	S&P Credit Rating	A-

Price Performance

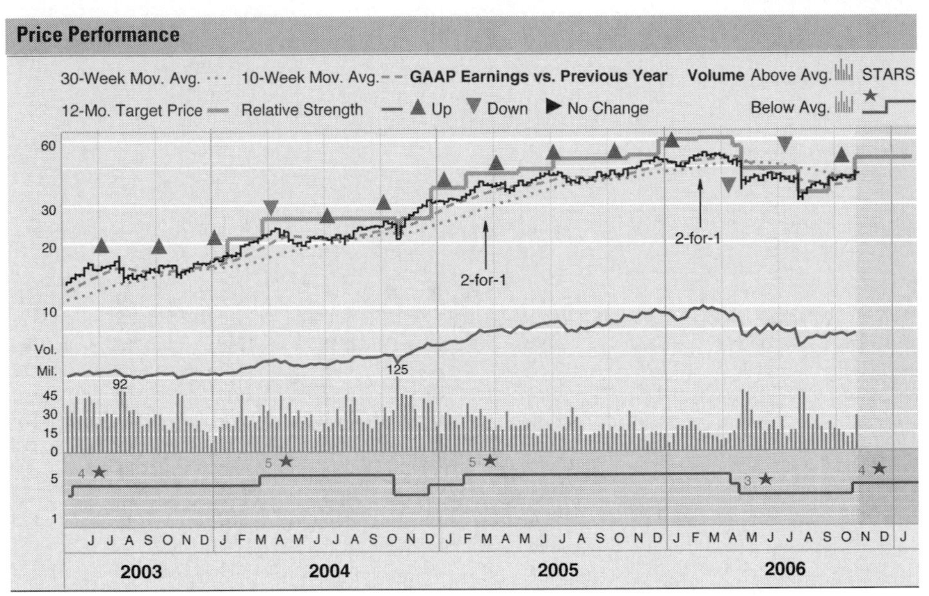

Options: ASE, CBOE, P, Ph

Highlights

➤ The STARS recommendation for AET has recently been changed to 4 (buy) from 3 (hold) and the 12-month target price has recently been changed to $49.00 from $40.00. The Highlights section of this Stock Report will be updated accordingly.

Investment Rationale/Risk

➤ The Investment Rationale/Risk section of this Stock Report will be updated shortly. For the latest News story on AET from MarketScope, see below.

➤ 10/26/06 12:05 pm EDT... S&P UPGRADES OPINION ON AETNA SHARES TO BUY FROM HOLD (AET 41.22****): Q3 operating EPS of $0.78 vs. $0.59, before reserve development, is $0.06 above our estimate. We are encouraged by lower medical costs than expected, but disappointed by second cut in enrollment guidance for '06 and attrition in national accounts that yielded net member adds of only 250K for 1/1/07. We do see new products/geographies opening growth opportunities, but also expect more competition. By raising P/E-to-growth to a still below-peer 1.0X from 0.95X, and using our '07 EPS estimate of $3.26, raised today from $3.20, we are boosting our 12-month target price $9 to $49. /P.Seligman

Qualitative Risk Assessment

LOW | **MEDIUM** | HIGH

Our risk assessment reflects AET's leadership in the highly fragmented managed care market. While its recent history of improving financial performance appears to have come to a halt, we think this halt is temporary, and believe AET's expanding product, market and geographic diversity will permit stable operational performance over the long term.

Quantitative Evaluations

S&P Quality Ranking NR

D | C | B- | B | B+ | A- | A | A+

Relative Strength Rank STRONG

75

LOWEST = 1 HIGHEST = 99

Revenue/Earnings Data

Revenue (Million $)

	1Q	2Q	3Q	4Q	Year
2006	6,235	6,252	6,300	--	--
2005	5,427	5,497	5,701	5,867	22,492
2004	4,821	4,875	5,040	5,168	19,904
2003	4,467	4,466	4,469	4,575	17,976
2002	5,265	5,064	4,832	4,718	19,879
2001	6,429	6,536	6,183	6,043	25,191

Earnings Per Share ($)

	1Q	2Q	3Q	4Q	Year
2006	0.65	0.67	0.85	**E**0.79	**E**2.80
2005	0.70	0.68	0.63	0.71	2.70
2004	0.51	0.45	0.48	0.49	1.94
2003	0.53	0.22	0.34	0.39	1.48
2002	0.15	0.18	0.16	0.16	0.65
2001	-0.09	0.02	-0.10	-0.35	-0.51

Fiscal year ended Dec. 31. Next earnings report expected: Early February. EPS Estimates based on S&P Operating Earnings; historical GAAP earnings are as reported.

Dividend Data (Dates: mm/dd Payment Date: mm/dd/yy)

Amount ($)	Date Decl.	Ex-Div. Date	Stk. of Record	Payment Date
0.040	09/30	11/14	11/16	11/30/05
2-for-1 Stk.	01/27	02/21	02/07	02/17/06
0.040	09/29	11/13	11/15	11/30/06

Dividends have been paid since 2001. Source: Company reports.

Aetna Inc.

Business Summary September 14, 2006

CORPORATE OVERVIEW. In December 2000, Aetna sold its financial services and international operations for $5 billion ($35.33 a share, not adjusted) and the assumption of $2.7 billion in debt. AET shareholders received $35.33 a share in cash, plus one share of a new health care company named Aetna. Revenue contributions (excluding net investment and other income) from the company's business operations in 2005 were: Health Care 90%; Group Insurance 9%; and Large Case Pensions 1%.

The Health Care segment offers health maintenance organization (HMO), point-of-service (POS), preferred provider organization (PPO) and indemnity benefit products. The company had total health care enrollment of 15,407,000 lives at June 30, 2006, up from 14,755,000 at December 31, 2005. Commercial risk enrollment was 5,103,000 lives, versus 5,115,000, while commercial administrative services (for self-funded accounts) was 10,054,000 lives, versus 9,406,000. Medicare enrollment was 137,000 lives, versus 120,000, while Medicaid risk enrollment was 113,000 lives, versus 114,000. The company also provides dental benefits to 13,374,000 members, versus 13,098,000.

Group Insurance provides group life, disability and long-term care products; membership was 15,265,000 at June 30, 2006, up from 13, 618,000 at December 31, 2005.

Large Case Pensions manages various retirement products, including pension and annuity products, for defined benefit and defined contribution plans. Aetna has not marketed its Large Case Pension products since 1993, but continues to manage the run-off of existing business. At December 31, 2005, assets under management totaled $21.0 billion, up from $19.7 billion at December 31, 2004.

Company Financials

Per Share Data ($) Year Ended Dec. 31	**2005**	**2004**	**2003**	**2002**	**2001**	**2000**	**1999**	**1998**	**1997**	**1996**
Tangible Book Value	8.57	8.42	6.15	4.69	4.51	4.25	NA	NA	NA	NA
Cash Flow	3.04	2.22	1.79	1.14	0.54	0.82	NA	NA	NA	NA
Earnings	2.70	1.94	1.48	0.64	-0.51	-0.23	0.84	NA	NA	NA
S&P Core Earnings	2.55	1.71	1.51	0.19	-1.12	NA	NA	NA	NA	NA
Dividends	0.02	0.01	0.01	0.01	0.01	Nil	NA	NA	NA	NA
Payout Ratio	NM	NM	1%	2%	NM	Nil	NA	NA	NA	NA
Prices:High	49.68	31.89	17.56	12.98	10.67	10.59	NA	NA	NA	NA
Prices:Low	29.93	16.41	9.98	7.48	5.75	8.23	NA	NA	NA	NA
P/E Ratio:High	18	16	12	20	NM	NM	NA	NA	NA	NA
P/E Ratio:Low	11	8	7	12	NM	NM	NA	NA	NA	NA

Income Statement Analysis (Million $)	2005	2004	2003	2002	2001	2000	1999	1998	1997	1996
Revenue	22,492	19,904	17,976	19,879	25,191	26,819	NA	NA	NA	NA
Operating Income	2,807	2,184	1,596	1,119	460	1,104	NA	NA	NA	NA
Depreciation	204	182	200	302	598	588	NA	NA	NA	NA
Interest Expense	123	105	103	120	143	248	NA	NA	NA	NA
Pretax Income	2,547	1,899	1,442	545	-379	-39.0	NA	NA	NA	NA
Effective Tax Rate	35.8%	36.0%	35.2%	27.8%	NM	NM	NA	NA	NA	NA
Net Income	1,635	1,215	934	393	-292	-127	NA	NA	NA	NA
S&P Core Earnings	1,542	1,072	957	140	-639	NA	NA	NA	NA	NA

Balance Sheet & Other Financial Data (Million $)	2005	2004	2003	2002	2001	2000	1999	1998	1997	1996
Cash	1,378	1,595	1,655	2,017	1,631	2,204	NA	NA	NA	NA
Current Assets	18,235	19,516	19,557	19,349	18,751	19,768	NA	NA	NA	NA
Total Assets	44,365	42,134	40,950	40,048	43,255	47,446	NA	NA	NA	NA
Current Liabilities	7,617	7,011	7,368	7,719	8,139	10,003	NA	NA	NA	NA
Long Term Debt	1,156	1,610	1,614	1,633	1,591	Nil	NA	NA	NA	NA
Common Equity	12,167	9,081	7,924	6,980	9,890	10,127	NA	NA	NA	NA
Total Capital	13,338	10,691	9,538	8,613	11,481	10,127	NA	NA	NA	NA
Capital Expenditures	272	190	211	156	143	36.9	NA	NA	NA	NA
Cash Flow	1,839	1,397	1,133	695	306	461	NA	NA	NA	NA
Current Ratio	2.4	2.8	2.7	2.5	2.3	2.0	NA	NA	NA	NA
% Long Term Debt of Capitalization	8.7	15.1	16.9	19.0	13.9	Nil	NA	NA	NA	NA
% Net Income of Revenue	7.6	6.4	5.2	2.0	NM	NM	NA	NA	NA	NA
% Return on Assets	3.8	2.9	2.3	0.9	NM	NM	NA	NA	NA	NA
% Return on Equity	14.0	14.3	12.5	4.7	NM	NM	NA	NA	NA	NA

Data as orig reptd.; bef. results of disc opers/spec. items. Per share data adj. for stk. divs.; EPS diluted. E-Estimated. NA-Not Available. NM-Not Meaningful. NR-Not Ranked. UR-Under Review.

Office: 151 Farmington Avenue, Hartford, CT 06156.
Telephone: 860-273-0123.
Email: investorrelations@aetna.com
Website: http://www.aetna.com

Chrmn, Pres & CEO: R.A. Williams
SVP & CFO: A.M. Bennett
SVP & General Counsel: W.J. Casazza
Investor Contact: D.W. Entrekin (860-273-7830)

Board of Directors: F. M. Clark, B. Z. Cohen, M. J. Coye, B. H. Franklin, J. E. Garten, E. G. Graves, G. Greenwald, E. M. Hancock, M. H. Jordan, E. J. Ludwig, J. P. Newhouse, R. A. Williams

Founded: 1982
Domicile: Pennsylvania
Employees: 28,200

STANDARD
&POOR'S

Affiliated Computer Services Inc.

S&P Recommendation HOLD ★★★★★	Price	12-Mo. Target Price	Investment Style
	$53.57 (as of Oct 27, 2006)	$55.00	Mid-Cap Growth

GICS Sector Information Technology
Sub-Industry Data Processing & Outsourced Services

Comment This company provides a full range of information technology services, including technology outsourcing, business process outsourcing, and professional services.

Key Stock Statistics (Source S&P, Vickers, company reports)

52-Wk Range	$63.66–46.50	S&P Oper. EPS 2007E	3.33	P/E on S&P Oper. EPS 2007E	16.1	Dividend Rate/Share	Nil
Trailing 12-Month EPS	$2.90	S&P Oper. EPS 2008E	3.77	Common Shares Outstg. (M)	118.6	Yield (%)	Nil
Trailing 12-Month P/E	18.5	S&P Core EPS 2007E	3.33	Market Capitalization(B)	$5.998	Beta	0.77
$10K Invested 5 Yrs Ago	$11,558	S&P Core EPS 2008E	3.77	Institutional Ownership (%)	84	S&P Credit Rating	B+

Price Performance

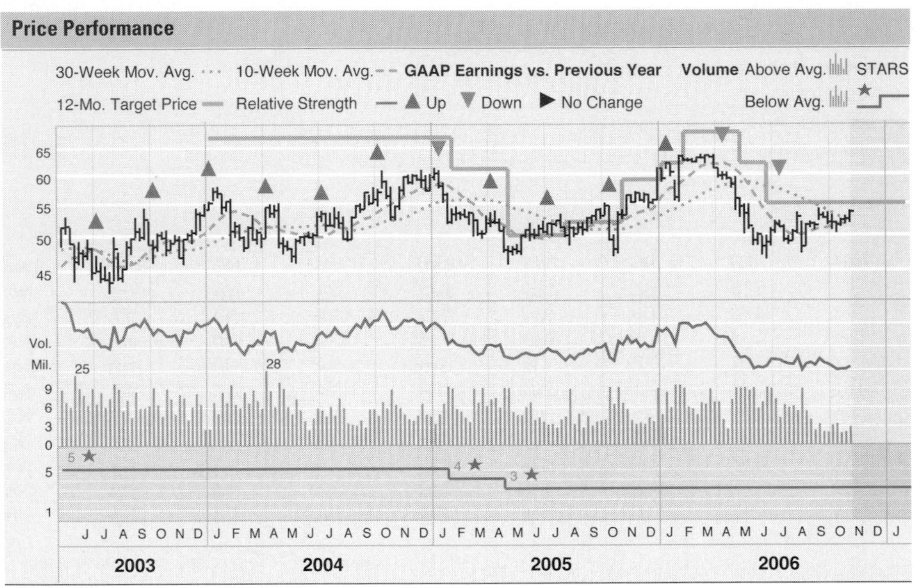

Options: ASE, CBOE, P, Ph

Analysis prepared by **Dylan Cathers** on August 24, 2006, when the stock traded at **$ 51.62**.

Highlights

- We expect revenues to grow 8% in FY 07 (Jun.) and 6% in FY 08, reflecting recent contract renewals and accelerating growth of business process outsourcing (BPO) related tasks. We are concerned, however, about weakness in ACS's government business segment, due to the loss of non-recurring contracts as well as increased competition, and its potential impact on future revenue growth.

- We see operating margins widening modestly in FY 07, to 12% from 11.5% in FY 06, due to ongoing restructurings, acquisition-related integration costs, elevated start-up costs from recently signed BPO contracts, and increased investment in sales personnel, offset by higher revenues.

- Our FY 07 EPS estimate is $3.33, including projected stock option expense. We expect the company to continue to take restructurings charges during FY 07. For FY 08, we look for EPS of $3.77. Our estimates assume a repurchase of seven million shares, which is part of ACS's ongoing $2 billion repurchase plan announced early in 2006.

Investment Rationale/Risk

- Our hold recommendation reflects our concerns that continued weakness and competition in the government segment could distract management's focus from its commercial business. While we continue to see ACS as a key beneficiary of the strong demand for outsourcing, we also have some concern about delays in recent contract signings as well as a slower ramp-up cycle for new contracts.

- Risks to our recommendation and target price include competition in the IT services marketplace, particularly the BPO arena, which could cause pricing pressures and adversely affect ACS's profit margins. We also have corporate governance concerns, including a non-shareholder approved "poison pill" and an ongoing investigation of ACS's historical stock option pricing practices.

- Our 12-month target price is $55, based on our discounted cash flow analysis. Our assumptions include a weighted average cost of capital of 10.5%, an average growth rate of 4% over the next five years, and a terminal growth rate of 3%.

Qualitative Risk Assessment

LOW	MEDIUM	**HIGH**

Our risk assessment reflects what we see as the highly competitive nature of the IT outsourcing and business process outsourcing markets, the company's recently increased debt load, and the ongoing investigation surrounding the timing of ACS's stock options.

Quantitative Evaluations

S&P Quality Ranking B+

D	C	B-	B	**B+**	A-	A	A+

Relative Strength Rank MODERATE

54

LOWEST = 1 HIGHEST = 99

Revenue/Earnings Data

Revenue (Million $)

	1Q	2Q	3Q	4Q	Year
2006	1,311	1,348	1,314	1,381	5,354
2005	1,046	1,027	1,063	1,214	4,351
2004	1,037	997.9	1,009	1,062	4,106
2003	822.6	908.8	981.6	1,014	3,787
2002	655.0	750.4	800.7	856.8	3,063
2001	478.6	500.9	533.6	550.5	2,064

Earnings Per Share ($)

	1Q	2Q	3Q	4Q	Year
2006	0.74	0.81	0.62	0.73	2.90
2005	0.72	0.73	0.88	0.87	3.19
2004	0.62	1.80	0.72	0.68	3.83
2003	0.50	0.53	0.57	0.60	2.20
2002	0.39	0.46	0.46	0.49	1.76
2001	0.29	0.29	0.32	0.33	1.23

Fiscal year ended Jun. 30. Next earnings report expected: NA. EPS Estimates based on S&P Operating Earnings; historical GAAP earnings are as reported.

Dividend Data

No cash dividends have been paid.

Affiliated Computer Services Inc.

Business Summary August 24, 2006

CORPORATE OVERVIEW. ACS provides business process and information technology outsourcing solutions to commercial and government clients. In the commercial sector, the company provides business outsourcing, systems integration services and technology outsourcing to a variety of clients. The business process outsourcing division provides services such as claims processing, finance and accounting, and loan processing. The technology outsourcing division offers the delivery of information processing services on a remote basis from host data centers that provide processing capacity, network management and desktop support. The systems integration services unit offers application development and implementation, applications outsourcing, technical support and training, network design and installation.

In the federal government sector, ACS offers business process outsourcing and systems integration services. The business process outsourcing unit consists primarily of loan servicing and human resource services for federal agencies. Within the state and local governments sector, ACS designs, implements and operates large scale health and human services programs and the supporting information technology solutions. ACS also provides child support and payment processing with high volume remittance processing and service center operations.

CORPORATE STRATEGY. Key elements of the company's business strategy include developing long-term relationships with new clients, expanding existing customer relationships, building recurring revenue streams, investing in technology, and completing strategic and tactical acquisitions. ACS provides a full range of information technology services to clients with time critical, transaction intensive business and information processing needs. Its services are designed to enable businesses and government agencies to focus on core operations, respond to rapidly changing technologies, and reduce expenses.

Company Financials

Per Share Data ($) Year Ended Jun. 30	**2006**	**2005**	**2004**	**2003**	**2002**	**2001**	**2000**	**1999**	**1998**	**1997**
Tangible Book Value	NA	0.30	2.64	1.94	0.11	0.90	0.44	NM	0.86	0.80
Cash Flow	NA	4.98	5.11	3.20	2.47	1.96	1.74	1.37	1.01	0.95
Earnings	2.90	3.19	3.83	2.20	1.76	1.23	1.04	0.83	0.56	0.52
S&P Core Earnings	NA	3.03	2.48	2.11	1.73	1.11	NA	NA	NA	NA
Dividends	Nil	Nil	Nil	Nil	Nil	Nil	Nil	Nil	Nil	Nil
Payout Ratio	Nil	Nil	Nil	Nil	Nil	Nil	Nil	Nil	Nil	Nil
Prices:High	63.66	61.16	61.23	56.56	57.05	53.63	31.31	26.50	22.50	15.13
Prices:Low	46.50	45.81	46.01	40.01	32.70	26.81	15.50	15.88	11.19	9.75
P/E Ratio:High	22	19	16	26	32	44	30	32	41	29
P/E Ratio:Low	16	14	12	18	19	22	15	19	20	19

Income Statement Analysis (Million $)										
Revenue	NA	4,351	4,106	3,787	3,063	2,064	1,963	1,642	1,189	625
Operating Income	NA	887	742	671	511	317	265	225	159	103
Depreciation	NA	233	184	152	110	93.6	84.8	66.7	47.5	31.3
Interest Expense	NA	18.6	17.0	25.2	30.6	23.7	24.0	17.6	12.1	6.41
Pretax Income	NA	641	829	491	360	221	195	146	94.1	65.0
Effective Tax Rate	NA	35.1%	36.1%	37.5%	36.3%	39.3%	44.0%	40.8%	42.2%	40.7%
Net Income	NA	416	530	307	230	134	109	86.2	54.4	38.5
S&P Core Earnings	NA	393	339	291	225	119	NA	NA	NA	NA

Balance Sheet & Other Financial Data (Million $)										
Cash	NA	62.7	76.9	51.2	33.8	242	44.5	32.8	84.0	21.3
Current Assets	NA	1,244	1,044	979	874	810	772	416	365	168
Total Assets	NA	4,851	3,907	3,699	3,404	1,892	1,656	1,224	950	577
Current Liabilities	NA	838	638	557	486	281	358	222	167	102
Long Term Debt	NA	750	372	498	708	649	526	382	235	89.5
Common Equity	NA	2,838	2,590	2,429	2,095	886	711	607	504	349
Total Capital	NA	3,829	3,197	3,104	2,899	1,590	1,272	989	763	449
Capital Expenditures	NA	253	225	206	144	99.1	71.5	61.1	43.8	38.2
Cash Flow	NA	649	714	459	340	228	194	153	102	69.8
Current Ratio	NA	1.5	1.6	1.8	1.8	2.9	2.2	1.9	2.2	1.6
% Long Term Debt of Capitalization	NA	19.6	11.6	16.1	24.4	40.8	41.3	38.6	30.8	19.9
% Net Income of Revenue	NA	9.6	12.9	8.1	7.5	6.5	5.6	5.3	4.6	6.2
% Return on Assets	NA	9.5	13.9	8.6	8.7	7.6	7.6	7.9	7.1	6.9
% Return on Equity	NA	15.3	21.1	13.6	15.4	16.8	16.6	15.5	12.8	11.8

Data as orig reptd.; bef. results of disc opers/spec. items. Per share data adj. for stk. divs.; EPS diluted. E-Estimated. NA-Not Available. NM-Not Meaningful. NR-Not Ranked. UR-Under Review.

Office: 2828 North Haskell Avenue, Dallas, TX 75204-2988.
Telephone: 214-841-6111.
Email: info@acs-inc.com
Website: http://www.acs-inc.com

Chrmn: D. Deason
Pres & CEO: M.A. King
COO & EVP: L. Blodgett
EVP & CFO: W.D. Edwards

EVP, Secy & General Counsel: W.L. Deckelman, Jr.
Investor Contact: K. Kyser (214-841-8281)
Board of Directors: L. R. Blodgett, D. Deason, M. A. King, J. L. Kosberg, D. McCuistion, J. P. O'Neill, F. A. Rossi

Founded: 1971
Domicile: Pennsylvania
Employees: 52,000

STANDARD &POOR'S

AFLAC Inc

S&P Recommendation BUY ★★★★★	Price	12-Mo. Target Price	Investment Style
	$45.41 (as of Oct 30, 2006)	$53.00	Large-Cap Growth

GICS Sector Financials
Sub-Industry Life & Health Insurance

Comment This company provides supplemental health and life insurance in the U.S. and Japan.

Key Stock Statistics (Source S&P, Vickers, company reports)

52-Wk Range	$49.65–41.63	S&P Oper. EPS 2006E	2.91	P/E on S&P Oper. EPS 2006E	15.6	Dividend Rate/Share	$0.74
Trailing 12-Month EPS	$3.01	S&P Oper. EPS 2007E	3.30	Common Shares Outstg. (M)	496.3	Yield (%)	1.63
Trailing 12-Month P/E	15.1	S&P Core EPS 2006E	2.91	Market Capitalization(B)	$22.537	Beta	0.30
$10K Invested 5 Yrs Ago	$18,649	S&P Core EPS 2007E	3.30	Institutional Ownership (%)	59	S&P Credit Rating	A

Price Performance

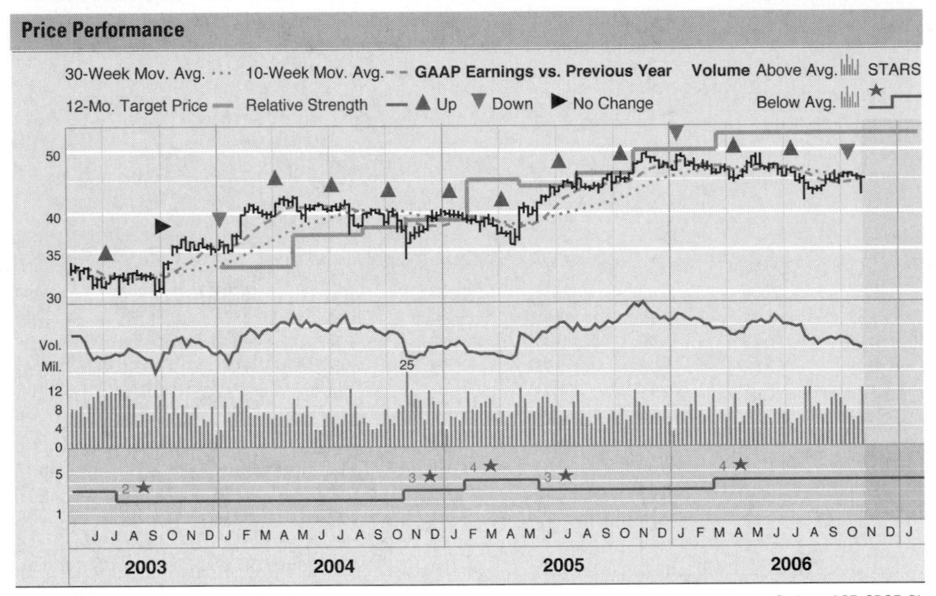

Options: ASE, CBOE, Ph

Analysis prepared by **Frank Braden** on October 30, 2006, when the stock traded at **$ 45.17**.

Highlights

- We forecast declining total new annualized premium sales in 2006 and the first half of 2007, on slowing corporate channel sales and an increasingly crowded market. We believe AFL's focus on training and distribution in Japan should improve sales results beginning around mid-year 2007. We anticipate sales of cancer life and the new WAYS life insurance product to remain strong. We believe increased ad spending and a solid distribution network should help AFL remain competitive, particularly in Japan. We see management's goal of an 8%-12% increase in 2006 sales at Aflac U.S. as obtainable.
- We expect the benefit ratio in Japan to improve another 60 to 80 basis points, as new sales of products such as EVER have a lower average benefit ratio. We see the combined ratio remaining relatively flat for Aflac U.S., with increased ad spending limiting further improvements in the ratio.
- We forecast operating EPS growth of 14% in 2006, to $2.91, including projected stock option expense. Our forecast for 2007 operating EPS is $3.30, a 13% increase from our 2006 estimate.

Investment Rationale/Risk

- We believe Aflac will be able to turn around its Japanese sales by the second half of 2007, as it focuses on strengthening its regional sales force and builds on its market leading position. We also think that slowly rising interest rates in Japan along with its rebounding economy should help boost both net investment income and new premium sales. We are encouraged by AFL's strong financial position and management's commitment to share repurchases and dividend increases.
- Risks to our opinion and target price include unfavorable movements in the yen/dollar exchange rate, less organic premium growth than we expect, particularly on new product sales and changes in distribution in Japan, less than anticipated investment income in a low interest rate environment in Japan, higher than projected underwriting and marketing expenses, and lower than forecast share repurchases.
- Our 12-month target price of $53 is based on a P/E multiple of 16X applied to our 2007 operating EPS estimate of $3.30. This multiple is a premium to AFL's peer group.

Qualitative Risk Assessment

LOW	**MEDIUM**	HIGH

Our risk assessment for Aflac reflects its strong market share position and high risk-based capital ratio, and management's consistent track record for share repurchases and dividend increases. This is offset by AFL's large exposure to earnings variability, which arises from currency exposure to the Japanese yen, from which 75% of AFL's earnings are derived.

Quantitative Evaluations

S&P Quality Ranking A

D	C	B-	B	B+	A-	**A**	A+

Relative Strength Rank MODERATE

38

LOWEST = 1 HIGHEST = 99

Revenue/Earnings Data

Revenue (Million $)

	1Q	2Q	3Q	4Q	Year
2006	3,559	3,697	3,672	--	--
2005	3,559	3,567	3,669	3,567	14,363
2004	3,280	3,233	3,321	3,448	13,281
2003	2,807	2,861	2,931	2,847	11,447
2002	2,371	2,513	2,707	2,666	10,257
2001	2,401	2,348	2,446	2,404	9,598

Earnings Per Share ($)

	1Q	2Q	3Q	4Q	Year
2006	0.74	0.81	0.71	E0.72	E2.91
2005	0.64	0.66	0.90	0.72	2.92
2004	0.61	0.51	0.58	0.81	2.52
2003	0.45	0.48	0.45	0.14	1.52
2002	0.34	0.40	0.45	0.35	1.55
2001	0.33	0.28	0.36	0.31	1.28

Fiscal year ended Dec. 31. Next earnings report expected: Late January. EPS Estimates based on S&P Operating Earnings; historical GAAP earnings are as reported.

Dividend Data (Dates: mm/dd Payment Date: mm/dd/yy)

Amount ($)	Date Decl.	Ex-Div. Date	Stk. of Record	Payment Date
0.130	04/25	05/17	05/19	06/01/06
0.130	07/25	08/16	08/18	09/01/06
0.160	10/24	11/15	11/17	12/01/06
0.185	10/24	02/14	02/16	03/01/07

Dividends have been paid since 1973. Source: Company reports.

Business Summary October 30, 2006

CORPORATE OVERVIEW. Aflac provides supplemental health and life insurance in the U.S. and Japan. Most of Aflac's policies are individually underwritten and marketed at work sites through independent agents, with premiums paid by the employee. As of March 2006, Aflac believed it was the world's leading underwriter of individually issued policies marketed at work sites.

In 2005, Aflac Japan accounted for 74% of total revenues, compared to 75% in 2004. At December 31, 2005, Aflac Japan accounted for 83% of total company assets, compared to 80% a year earlier. As of year-end 2005, Aflac Japan ranked first in terms of individual insurance policies in force, surpassing Nippon Life in March 2003.

Aflac Japan's insurance products are designed to help pay for costs that are not reimbursed under Japan's national health insurance system. Products include cancer life plans (26% of total sales in 2005; 23% in 2004); Rider MAX (11%; 20%), a rider for cancer life policies that provides accident and medical/sickness benefits; and EVER (37%; 31%), a stand-alone whole life medical plan. Aflac Japan also offers ordinary life products (18%; 19%) and other products such as living benefit life plans and care products.

Under a marketing alliance established in 2001, Dai-ichi Mutual Life Insurance Co. sold roughly 277,700 AFL cancer life policies in 2005, up from about 244,000 policies in 2004, and contributed 8% and 7%, respectively, of total new annualized premium sales in Japan. During 2005, the number of licensed sales associates rose 14.6% to approximately 81,700, compared with 71,400 at December 31, 2004. The growth in licensed sales associates resulted primarily from individual agency recruitment.

Aflac U.S. sells cancer plans (19% of total sales in 2005; 20% in 2004) and various types of health insurance, including accident and disability (51%; 52%), fixed-benefit dental (8%; 7%), and hospital indemnity (11%; 11%). Other products include long-term care, short-term disability, and ordinary life policies.

Company Financials

Per Share Data ($) Year Ended Dec. 31	**2005**	**2004**	**2003**	**2002**	**2001**	**2000**	**1999**	**1998**	**1997**	**1996**
Tangible Book Value	15.89	15.03	13.03	12.41	10.39	8.87	7.28	7.10	6.44	3.74
Operating Earnings	NA	NA	NA	1.56	1.34	1.21	1.00	0.78	0.67	0.60
Earnings	2.92	2.52	1.52	1.55	1.28	1.26	1.04	0.88	1.04	0.68
S&P Core Earnings	2.60	2.47	1.85	1.49	1.25	NA	NA	NA	NA	NA
Dividends	0.44	0.38	0.30	0.23	0.19	0.17	0.15	0.13	0.11	0.10
Payout Ratio	15%	15%	20%	15%	15%	13%	14%	14%	11%	14%
Prices:High	49.65	42.60	36.91	33.45	36.09	37.47	28.38	22.66	14.47	11.00
Prices:Low	35.50	33.85	28.00	23.10	23.00	16.78	19.50	11.34	9.38	7.06
P/E Ratio:High	17	17	24	22	28	30	27	26	14	16
P/E Ratio:Low	12	13	18	15	18	13	19	13	9	10
Income Statement Analysis (Million $)										
Life Insurance in Force	80,610	80,496	69,582	56,680	46,610	51,496	44,993	28,182	19,310	15,913
Premium Income:Life	1,139	1,031	876	761	697	716	625	508	474	206
Premium Income:A & H	10,851	10,271	9,052	7,839	7,366	7,523	6,639	5,435	5,400	5,704
Net Investment Income	2,071	1,957	1,787	1,614	1,550	1,550	1,369	1,138	1,078	1,022
Total Revenue	14,363	13,281	11,447	10,257	9,598	9,720	8,640	7,104	6,983	7,100
Pretax Income	2,226	1,807	1,225	1,259	1,081	1,012	778	551	865	650
Net Operating Income	NA	NA	NA	825	720	657	550	429	374	347
Net Income	1,483	1,299	795	821	687	687	571	487	585	394
S&P Core Earnings	1,321	1,274	962	791	670	NA	NA	NA	NA	NA
Balance Sheet & Other Financial Data (Million $)										
Cash & Equivalent	1,781	4,308	1,508	1,793	1,233	989	985	690	265	254
Premiums Due	479	417	547	435	347	301	270	229	216	227
Investment Assets:Bonds	47,551	48,024	42,893	37,483	31,677	31,305	31,175	26,424	22,584	20,589
Investment Assets:Stocks	84.0	77.0	73.0	258	245	236	215	177	146	136
Investment Assets:Loans	Nil	Nil	Nil	Nil	Nil	Nil	Nil	9.00	Nil	17.8
Investment Assets:Total	47,692	48,142	42,999	37,768	31,941	31,558	31,408	26,620	22,644	20,747
Deferred Policy Costs	5,590	5,595	5,044	4,277	3,645	3,685	3,692	3,067	2,582	2,583
Total Assets	56,361	59,326	50,964	45,058	37,860	37,232	37,041	31,183	29,454	25,023
Debt	1,050	1,141	1,409	1,312	1,000	956	931	596	523	354
Common Equity	7,927	7,573	6,646	6,394	5,425	4,694	3,868	3,770	3,430	2,126
% Return on Revenue	10.4	9.8	6.9	8.0	7.2	7.1	6.6	6.9	8.4	5.6
% Return on Assets	2.6	2.4	1.7	2.0	1.8	1.8	1.7	1.6	2.1	1.6
% Return on Equity	19.1	18.3	12.2	13.9	13.6	16.0	15.0	13.5	21.1	18.5
% Investment Yield	4.3	4.3	4.4	4.6	4.9	4.9	4.7	4.6	4.9	5.0

Data as orig reptd.; bef. results of disc opers/spec. items. Per share data adj. for stk. divs.; EPS diluted. E-Estimated. NA-Not Available. NM-Not Meaningful. NR-Not Ranked. UR-Under Review.

Office: 1932 Wynnton Road, Columbus, GA 31999.
Telephone: 706-323-3431.
Email: ir@aflac.com
Website: http://www.aflac.com

Chrmn & CEO: D.P. Amos
Pres, CFO & Treas: K. Cloninger, III
EVP, Secy & General Counsel: J.M. Loudermilk
SVP & Chief Admin: R.C. Davis

SVP & Chief Acctg Officer: R.A. Rogers, Jr.
Investor Contact: K.S. Janke, Jr. (706-596-3264)
Board of Directors: D. P. Amos, J. S. Amos, II, M. H. Armacost, K. Cloninger, III, J. F. Harris, E. J. Hudson, K. S. Janke, Sr., D. W. Johnson, R. B. Johnson, C. B. Knapp, H. Matsui, E. S. Purdom, B. K. Rimer, M. R. Schuster, D. G. Thompson, T. Tonoike, R. L. Wright

Founded: 1973
Domicile: Georgia
Employees: 6,970

STANDARD &POOR'S

Agilent Technologies Inc.

S&P Recommendation	Price	12-Mo. Target Price	Investment Style
HOLD ★★★★★	$34.88 (as of Oct 27, 2006)	$39.00	Large-Cap Value

GICS Sector Information Technology
Sub-Industry Electronic Equipment Manufacturers

Comment This Hewlett-Packard (HPQ) spinoff is a diversified global manufacturer of test and measurement instruments, and life sciences and chemical analysis instruments.

Key Stock Statistics (Source S&P, Vickers, company reports)

52-Wk Range	$39.54–26.96	S&P Oper. EPS 2006E	1.55	P/E on S&P Oper. EPS 2006E	22.5	Dividend Rate/Share	Nil
Trailing 12-Month EPS	$7.07	S&P Oper. EPS 2007E	1.74	Common Shares Outstg. (M)	408.7	Yield (%)	Nil
Trailing 12-Month P/E	4.9	S&P Core EPS 2006E	1.55	Market Capitalization(B)	$14.255	Beta	2.27
$10K Invested 5 Yrs Ago	$14,330	S&P Core EPS 2007E	1.74	Institutional Ownership (%)	72	S&P Credit Rating	BB+

Price Performance

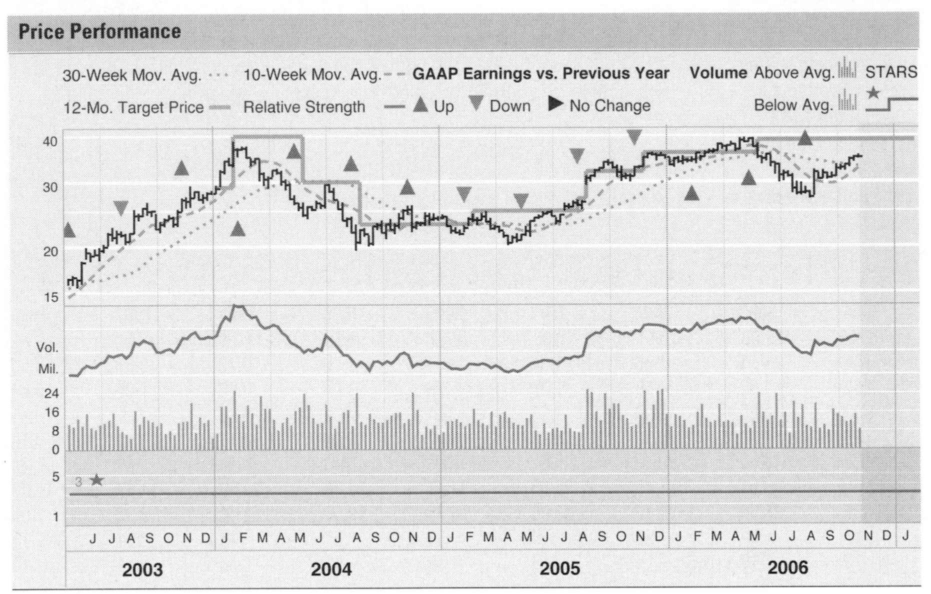

Options: ASE, CBOE, P, Ph

Analysis prepared by **David A Kaplan** on August 25, 2006, when the stock traded at **$ 30.57**.

Highlights

- We project a 13% increase in revenues in FY 06 (Oct.) and 11% for FY 07. Agilent spun off Verigy Ltd. (VRGY), its semiconductor back-end test equipment operation, in FY 06. Demand for A's semiconductor test equipment and semiconductor products had been highly cyclical, and we believe the divestitures of these units allow Agilent to better focus on its measurement business, which is expected to grow about 8% over the next year.
- We see gross margins widening to about 54.4% for FY 06, from 51.4% in FY 05 (49.1% adjusted to exclude the semiconductor business), driven by programs to improve efficiencies in the company's business.
- We see FY 06 operating EPS of $1.55, and FY 07 EPS of $1.74, including projected stock option expense. For FY 05, Agilent reported operating EPS of $0.99, excluding costs of $0.33 related to the sale of its semiconductor products business and the FY 06 spinoff of its semiconductor test solutions business.

Investment Rationale/Risk

- In an effort to reduce the volatility of its quarterly results and improve the company's focus and predictability of results, Agilent in August 2005 announced several divestitures, including the sale of its semiconductor products business to Avago Technologies Ltd. for $2.66 billion. In addition, the company sold its stake in Lumileds to Royal Philips Electronics for $948.5 million plus repayment of $51 million of debt, and in FY 06, spun off its SOC and memory test business (VRGY).
- Risks to our opinion and target price include an unsuccessful transition to a new business model following the divestiture of the company's semiconductor unit.
- Our 12-month target price of $39 is based on our price to book value and price to sales ratio analyses. We believe the shares should trade around 2.6X sales, higher than their historical levels, to reflect the reduced volatility of results we expect going forward; applying this multiple to our FY 07 revenue per share estimate, we arrive at a value of $39.

Qualitative Risk Assessment

LOW | **MEDIUM** | HIGH

Our risk assessment reflects the variability of Agilent's results in the past, balanced by recent efforts to streamline its businesses and divest parts of its portfolio that contributed to this variability.

Quantitative Evaluations

S&P Quality Ranking NR

D | C | B- | B | B+ | A- | A | A+

Relative Strength Rank STRONG

75

LOWEST = 1 HIGHEST = 99

Revenue/Earnings Data

Revenue (Million $)

	1Q	2Q	3Q	4Q	Year
2006	1,336	1,431	1,453	--	--
2005	1,212	1,688	1,242	1,407	5,139
2004	1,643	1,831	1,885	1,822	7,181
2003	1,412	1,467	1,502	1,675	6,056
2002	1,426	1,457	1,391	1,736	6,010
2001	2,565	2,406	1,819	1,606	8,396

Earnings Per Share ($)

2006	2.03	0.30	0.55	E0.43	E1.55
2005	0.10	0.11	0.10	-0.03	0.28
2004	0.14	0.21	0.20	0.15	0.71
2003	-0.24	-0.31	-3.25	0.03	-3.78
2002	-0.68	-0.54	-0.48	-0.51	-2.20
2001	0.37	0.19	-0.48	-0.98	-0.89

Fiscal year ended Oct. 31. Next earnings report expected: NA. EPS Estimates based on S&P Operating Earnings; historical GAAP earnings are as reported.

Dividend Data (Dates: mm/dd Payment Date: mm/dd/yy)

Amount ($)	Date Decl.	Ex-Div. Date	Stk. of Record	Payment Date
Stk.	09/21	11/01	10/16	10/31/06

Source: Company reports.

Please read the Required Disclosures and Analyst Certification on the last page of this report.

Agilent Technologies Inc.

Business Summary August 25, 2006

Agilent Technologies, which was spun off from Hewlett Packard (HPQ) in 1999, provides investors with exposure to the communications, electronics, life sciences, and chemical analysis industries. The company had consisted of HPQ's heralded test and measurement business, its automated test equipment business, its semiconductor products, and its life sciences and chemical analysis businesses, however, in August 2005, Agilent announced the sale of its semiconductor products business (to Avago Technologies Ltd. for $2.66 billion), and that it would spin off its SOC and memory test business in 2006. Based on Agilent's new reporting segments, following this restructuring effort, segment contributions in FY 05 (Oct.) were: Bio-Analytical Measurement, 28% of sales; Electronic Measurement, 63%; and Semiconductor Test Solutions, 9%.

A's test and measurement business was HPQ's founding technology, dating back to the late 1930s. The company is a global leader in electronic measurement. Its products are used by communications network equipment manufacturers and service providers, as well by its general purpose test customers. A also sells electronic test equipment products which are used for electronics manufacturing testing, parametric testing, and flat panel display (FPD) markets.

Agilent's bio-analytical measurement business products include microarrays, microfluidics, gas chromatography, liquid chromatography, mass spectrometry, software and informatics, and related consumables and services used in pharmaceutical analysis, the proteomics and gene expression markets, as well as the petrochemical and environmental markets, among others. Applications include measuring octane levels in gasoline, and analyzing pesticide levels in drinking water. Customers span the hydrocarbon-processing, environmental, pharmaceutical and bioscience markets. In the pharmaceutical and biopharmaceutical markets, A's instruments help lower the cost of discovering and developing new drugs.

Company Financials

Per Share Data ($) Year Ended Oct. 31	**2005**	**2004**	**2003**	**2002**	**2001**	**2000**	**1999**	**1998**	**1997**	**1996**
Tangible Book Value	7.39	6.42	5.09	8.44	9.95	10.37	8.90	NM	NA	NA
Cash Flow	0.65	1.31	-3.02	-0.62	0.72	2.75	2.60	1.93	NA	NA
Earnings	0.28	0.71	-3.78	-2.20	-0.89	1.66	1.35	0.56	NA	NA
S&P Core Earnings	-0.11	0.27	-5.70	-3.10	-2.63	NA	NA	NA	NA	NA
Dividends	Nil	Nil	Nil	Nil	Nil	Nil	Nil	NA	NA	NA
Payout Ratio	Nil	Nil	Nil	Nil	Nil	Nil	Nil	NA	NA	NA
Prices:High	36.10	38.80	29.42	38.00	68.00	162.00	80.00	NA	NA	NA
Prices:Low	20.11	19.51	18.35	10.50	18.00	38.06	30.00	NA	NA	NA
P/E Ratio:High	NM	55	NM	NM	NM	98	59	NA	NA	NA
P/E Ratio:Low	NM	27	NM	NM	NM	23	22	NA	NA	NA
Income Statement Analysis (Million $)										
Revenue	5,139	7,181	6,056	6,010	8,396	10,773	8,331	7,952	NA	NA
Operating Income	367	678	-363	-872	-44.0	1,548	1,216	919	NA	NA
Depreciation	186	292	362	735	734	495	475	477	NA	NA
Interest Expense	27.0	36.0	Nil	Nil	Nil	Nil	Nil	Nil	NA	NA
Pretax Income	306	440	-690	-1,547	-477	1,164	787	396	NA	NA
Effective Tax Rate	50.7%	20.7%	NM	NM	NM	35.0%	34.9%	35.1%	NA	NA
Net Income	141	349	-1,790	-1,022	-406	757	512	257	NA	NA
S&P Core Earnings	-55.1	137	-2,695	-1,438	-1,202	NA	NA	NA	NA	NA
Balance Sheet & Other Financial Data (Million $)										
Cash	2,251	2,315	1,607	1,844	1,170	996	Nil	Nil	NA	NA
Current Assets	4,447	4,577	3,889	4,880	4,799	5,655	3,538	3,075	NA	NA
Total Assets	6,751	7,056	6,297	8,203	7,986	8,425	5,444	4,987	NA	NA
Current Liabilities	1,936	1,871	1,906	2,181	2,002	2,758	1,681	1,599	NA	NA
Long Term Debt	Nil	1,150	1,150	1,150	Nil	Nil	Nil	Nil	NA	NA
Common Equity	4,081	3,569	2,824	4,627	5,659	5,265	3,382	3,022	NA	NA
Total Capital	4,081	4,719	3,974	5,777	5,659	5,265	3,382	3,022	NA	NA
Capital Expenditures	139	118	205	301	881	824	434	410	NA	NA
Cash Flow	327	641	-1,428	-287	328	1,252	987	734	NA	NA
Current Ratio	2.3	2.4	2.0	2.2	2.4	2.1	2.1	1.9	NA	NA
% Long Term Debt of Capitalization	Nil	24.4	28.9	19.9	Nil	Nil	Nil	Nil	NA	NA
% Net Income of Revenue	2.7	4.9	NM	NM	NM	7.0	6.1	3.2	NA	NA
% Return on Assets	2.0	5.2	NM	NM	NM	10.9	9.8	5.1	NA	NA
% Return on Equity	3.7	10.9	NM	NM	NM	17.5	16.0	8.4	NA	NA

Data as orig reptd.; bef. results of disc opers/spec. items. Per share data adj. for stk. divs.; EPS diluted. E-Estimated. NA-Not Available. NM-Not Meaningful. NR-Not Ranked. UR-Under Review.

Office: 395 Page Mill Road, Palo Alto, CA 94306.
Telephone: 650-752-5000.
Email: investor_relations@agilent.com
Website: http://www.agilent.com

Chrmn: J.G. Cullen
Pres & CEO: W.P. Sullivan
EVP & CFO: A.T. Dillon
SVP, Secy & General Counsel: D.C. Nordlund

Investor Contact: H. Terry
Board of Directors: P. N. Clark, J. G. Cullen, R. J. Herbold, W. B. Hewlett, K. B. Hwee, R. L. Joss, H. Kunz, D. M. Lawrence, A. B. Rand, W. P. Sullivan

Founded: 1999
Domicile: Delaware
Employees: 21,000

STANDARD &POOR'S

Air Products and Chemicals Inc.

S&P Recommendation SELL ★★★★★

Price $68.67 (as of Oct 27, 2006)

12-Mo. Target Price $60.00

Investment Style Large-Cap Value

GICS Sector Materials
Sub-Industry Industrial Gases

Comment This major producer of industrial gases and specialty and intermediate chemicals also has interests in environmental and energy-related businesses.

Key Stock Statistics (Source S&P, Vickers, company reports)

52-Wk Range	$69.80–56.18	S&P Oper. EPS 2007E	3.80	P/E on S&P Oper. EPS 2007E	18.1	Dividend Rate/Share	$1.36
Trailing 12-Month EPS	$3.29	S&P Oper. EPS 2008E	NA	Common Shares Outstg. (M)	220.3	Yield (%)	1.98
Trailing 12-Month P/E	20.9	S&P Core EPS 2007E	3.95	Market Capitalization(B)	$15.131	Beta	0.88
$10K Invested 5 Yrs Ago	$18,500	S&P Core EPS 2008E	NA	Institutional Ownership (%)	86	S&P Credit Rating	A

Price Performance

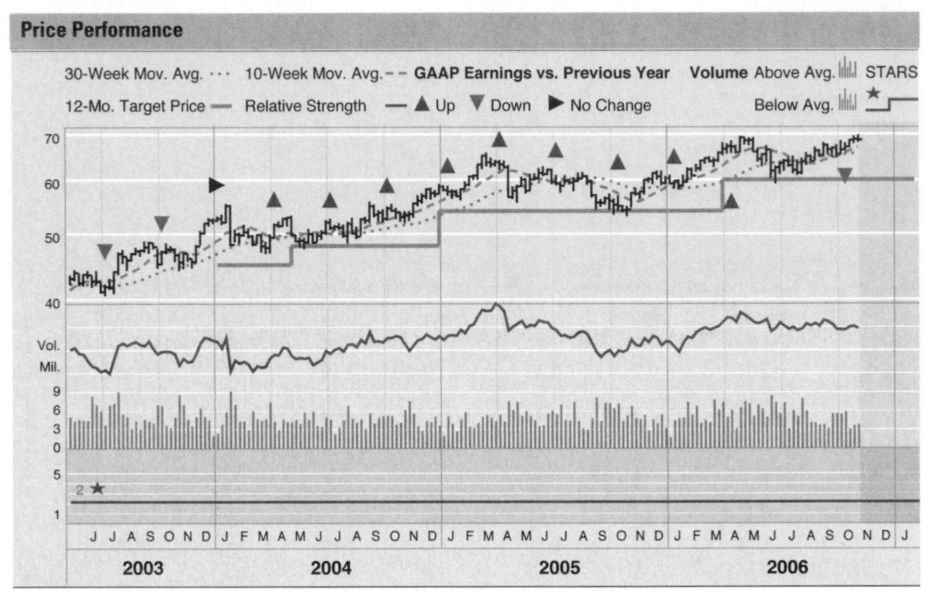

Options: P, Ph

Analysis prepared by **Richard O'Reilly, CFA** on September 28, 2006, when the stock traded at **$ 67.61**.

Highlights

- We see EPS rising to $3.80 in FY 07 (Sep.), up from the $3.50 expected for FY 06, including projected stock option expense of about $0.13. We believe sales comparisons for industrial gases will remain favorable, on continued good volume growth for many key products. We see on-site gases volumes continuing to rise, driven by six new domestic hydrogen facilities that started-up during FY 06.

- U.S. merchant gases volumes should show low-single digit percentage growth, while achieving continued good price hikes. European and Asian volumes should also continue to increase at good rates. We see continuing good volume growth for electronics products. We expect that the chemicals segment will have lower sales as a result of the planned sale of businesses accounting for about two-thirds of segment sales. We believe that volumes declined in FY 06, largely due to the loss of two major customers for polyurethane intermediates; volumes in core products rose modestly.

- We think equipment segment profits in FY 07 should remain at FY 06's projected $90 million, due to strong sales activity resulting from a record backlog for LNG heat exchangers.

Investment Rationale/Risk

- Our sell recommendation is based on our view of a premium valuation. The shares are trading at a P/E multiple of 19.5X, based on our calendar 2006 EPS estimate, above the level of the S&P 500 (15.2X). We think overall fundamentals remain sound, as APD holds strong positions in several growth products and markets for industrial gases and chemicals. However, we expect energy and raw material costs to remain high, limiting the potential for rapid margin recovery in the chemicals business.

- Risks to our recommendation and target price include stronger than expected growth in U.S. industrial activity and in the global electronics materials industry, and lower than forecast raw material and energy prices.

- The dividend was raised in 2006 for the 24th consecutive year, a record that we expect to be extended. The company plans a $1.5 billion stock repurchase program through 2008. Based on a P/E multiple of about 16X, closer to that of APD's chemical industry peer group, applied to our FY 07 earnings estimate, our 12-month target price is $60.

Qualitative Risk Assessment

LOW	**MEDIUM**	HIGH

Our risk assessment reflects the stable growth of the industrial gases industry versus commodity chemicals and what we see as the company's relatively strong balance sheet, partially offset by volatile raw material cost exposure in the chemical segment.

Quantitative Evaluations

S&P Quality Ranking B+

D	C	B-	B	**B+**	A-	A	A+

Relative Strength Rank MODERATE

53

LOWEST = 1 HIGHEST = 99

Revenue/Earnings Data

Revenue (Million $)

	1Q	2Q	3Q	4Q	Year
2006	2,099	2,317	2,320	2,359	8,850
2005	1,991	2,003	2,078	2,071	8,144
2004	1,685	1,857	1,893	1,978	7,411
2003	1,447	1,578	1,630	1,642	6,297
2002	1,317	1,313	1,374	1,398	5,401
2001	1,441	1,498	1,424	1,362	5,717

Earnings Per Share ($)

	1Q	2Q	3Q	4Q	Year
2006	0.80	0.89	E0.88	0.73	3.38
2005	0.72	0.75	0.82	0.79	3.08
2004	0.58	0.62	0.71	0.73	2.64
2003	0.58	0.51	0.12	0.58	1.79
2002	0.52	0.57	0.63	0.65	2.36
2001	0.62	0.43	0.60	0.47	2.12

Fiscal year ended Sep. 30. Next earnings report expected: Late January. EPS Estimates based on S&P Operating Earnings; historical GAAP earnings are as reported.

Dividend Data (Dates: mm/dd Payment Date: mm/dd/yy)

Amount ($)	Date Decl.	Ex-Div. Date	Stk. of Record	Payment Date
0.320	11/17	12/29	01/03	02/13/06
0.340	03/22	03/30	04/03	05/08/06
0.340	05/18	06/29	07/03	08/14/06
0.340	09/21	09/28	10/02	11/13/06

Dividends have been paid since 1954. Source: Company reports.

Air Products and Chemicals Inc.

Business Summary September 28, 2006

CORPORATE OVERVIEW. Air Products & Chemicals is one of the largest global producers of industrial gases, and has a large specialty chemicals business. APD is focusing on several areas for growth in industrial gases, including electronics, hydrogen for petroleum refining, health care and Asia. International operations accounted for 43% of FY 05 (Sep.) sales.

The industrial gases segment (71% of sales and 81% of profits in FY 05) includes nitrogen, oxygen, argon, hydrogen, helium, carbon monoxide, synthesis gas, and fluorine compounds for both merchant and tonnage (on-site) customers. Sales of atmospheric gases (oxygen, nitrogen and argon) accounted for 23% of the total in FY 05. APD is the world's leading supplier of hydrogen and carbon monoxide products (HYCO) and helium, and also supplies bulk and high purity gases, equipment, and chemicals to the electronics industry (about 23% of segment sales).

APD had total health care sales of $750 million (13% of segment total) in FY 05, with home care accounting for about 75% of revenues. In October 2002, the company entered the U.S. home health care market by purchasing American Homecare Supply (AHS) for $166 million. AHS had annual revenues of $110 million, and was one of the 10 largest home care providers of respiratory therapy and medical equipment. APD has since made a series of small U.S. home care acquisitions, including four in FY 05. The segment also includes 50%-owned ventures in power cogeneration and flue gas desulfurization facilities.

Chemicals (24%, 15%) include performance materials (epoxy and polyurethane additives, specialty amines, and surfactants); water-based polymers (emulsions, pressure-sensitive adhesives); and intermediates (polyurethanes and amines) used for adhesives, textiles, coatings, paper, pesticide, furniture, building products, and automotive markets. Commodity chemicals (ammonia and acetic acid) are also produced as raw materials or co-products.

Equipment and services (5%, 4%) includes cryogenic and process equipment for air separation, gas processing, natural gas liquefaction (LNG), and hydrogen purification. The segment also includes membranes technology for recovering gas.

Company Financials

Per Share Data ($) Year Ended Sep. 30	**2006**	**2005**	**2004**	**2003**	**2002**	**2001**	**2000**	**1999**	**1998**	**1997**
Tangible Book Value	NA	16.03	15.45	12.99	13.33	10.79	10.78	11.39	10.17	10.02
Cash Flow	NA	6.22	5.76	4.65	4.97	4.95	3.24	4.53	4.78	4.04
Earnings	3.38	3.08	2.64	1.79	2.36	2.12	0.57	2.09	2.48	1.91
S&P Core Earnings	NA	3.03	2.63	1.66	1.67	1.70	NA	NA	NA	NA
Dividends	1.34	1.25	1.04	0.88	0.82	0.78	0.74	0.70	0.64	0.58
Payout Ratio	40%	41%	30%	40%	35%	37%	130%	33%	26%	30%
Prices:High	69.80	65.81	59.18	53.07	53.52	49.00	42.25	49.25	45.34	44.81
Prices:Low	58.01	53.00	46.71	36.97	40.00	32.25	23.00	25.69	29.00	33.19
P/E Ratio:High	21	21	22	30	23	23	74	24	18	23
P/E Ratio:Low	17	17	18	21	17	15	40	12	12	17
Income Statement Analysis (Million $)										
Revenue	NA	8,144	7,411	6,297	5,401	5,717	5,496	5,020	4,919	4,638
Operating Income	NA	1,700	1,567	1,218	1,319	1,313	1,407	725	1,320	1,160
Depreciation	NA	720	715	640	581	573	576	527	506	474
Interest Expense	NA	110	121	124	122	191	197	159	163	161
Pretax Income	NA	998	851	565	784	737	118	669	824	630
Effective Tax Rate	NA	26.4%	26.6%	26.0%	30.7%	29.7%	NM	30.4%	33.6%	31.9%
Net Income	NA	712	604	400	525	513	124	451	547	429
S&P Core Earnings	NA	701	601	369	369	370	NA	NA	NA	NA
Balance Sheet & Other Financial Data (Million $)										
Cash	NA	55.8	146	76.2	254	66.2	94.1	61.6	61.5	52.5
Current Assets	NA	2,415	2,417	2,068	1,909	1,685	1,805	1,782	1,642	1,624
Total Assets	NA	10,409	10,040	9,432	8,495	8,084	8,271	8,236	7,490	7,244
Current Liabilities	NA	1,943	1,706	1,581	1,256	1,352	1,375	1,858	1,266	1,125
Long Term Debt	NA	2,053	Nil	2,169	2,041	2,028	2,616	1,962	2,279	2,292
Common Equity	NA	4,576	4,444	3,783	3,460	3,106	2,821	2,962	2,667	2,648
Total Capital	NA	7,644	5,401	6,845	6,411	6,030	6,334	5,782	5,649	5,670
Capital Expenditures	NA	930	706	613	628	708	768	889	771	870
Cash Flow	NA	1,440	1,319	1,040	1,106	1,086	700	978	1,053	903
Current Ratio	NA	1.2	1.4	1.3	1.5	1.2	1.3	1.0	1.3	1.4
% Long Term Debt of Capitalization	NA	26.9	Nil	31.7	31.8	33.6	41.3	33.9	40.3	40.4
% Net Income of Revenue	NA	8.7	8.2	6.4	9.7	9.0	2.3	9.0	11.1	9.3
% Return on Assets	NA	7.0	6.2	4.5	6.3	6.3	1.5	5.7	7.4	6.2
% Return on Equity	NA	15.8	14.7	11.1	16.0	17.3	4.3	16.0	20.6	16.4

Data as orig reptd.; bef. results of disc opers/spec. items. Per share data adj. for stk. divs.; EPS diluted. E-Estimated. NA-Not Available. NM-Not Meaningful. NR-Not Ranked. UR-Under Review.

Office: 7201 Hamilton Boulevard, Allentown, PA 18195-1501.
Telephone: 610-481-4911.
Website: http://www.airproducts.com
Chrmn & CEO: J.P. Jones, III

Pres & COO: J.F. McGlade
VP & CFO: P.E. Huck
VP, Secy & General Counsel: W.D. Brown
Investor Contact: N. Squires

Board of Directors: M. Baeza, W. Davis, III, M. J. Donahue, U. F. Fairbairn, W. D. Ford, E. E. Hagenlocker, E. Henkes, J. P. Jones, III, M. G. McGlynn, T. Murray, C. Noski, L. S. Smith

Founded: 1940
Domicile: Delaware
Employees: 20,200

STANDARD &POOR'S

Alberto-Culver Co

S&P Recommendation HOLD ★★★★★

Price $50.37 (as of Oct 27, 2006)

12-Mo. Target Price $51.00

Investment Style Mid-Cap Growth

GICS Sector Consumer Staples
Sub-Industry Personal Products

Comment This company produces well known hair care products and other health and beauty aids, and operates Sally Beauty, the world's largest chain of professional beauty supply stores.

Key Stock Statistics (Source S&P, Vickers, company reports)

52-Wk Range	$51.96–41.99	S&P Oper. EPS 2007E	2.79	P/E on S&P Oper. EPS 2007E	18.1	Dividend Rate/Share	$0.52
Trailing 12-Month EPS	$2.20	S&P Oper. EPS 2008E	NA	Common Shares Outstg. (M)	92.9	Yield (%)	1.03
Trailing 12-Month P/E	22.9	S&P Core EPS 2007E	2.79	Market Capitalization(B)	$4.680	Beta	0.35
$10K Invested 5 Yrs Ago	$18,592	S&P Core EPS 2008E	NA	Institutional Ownership (%)	71	S&P Credit Rating	BBB+

Price Performance

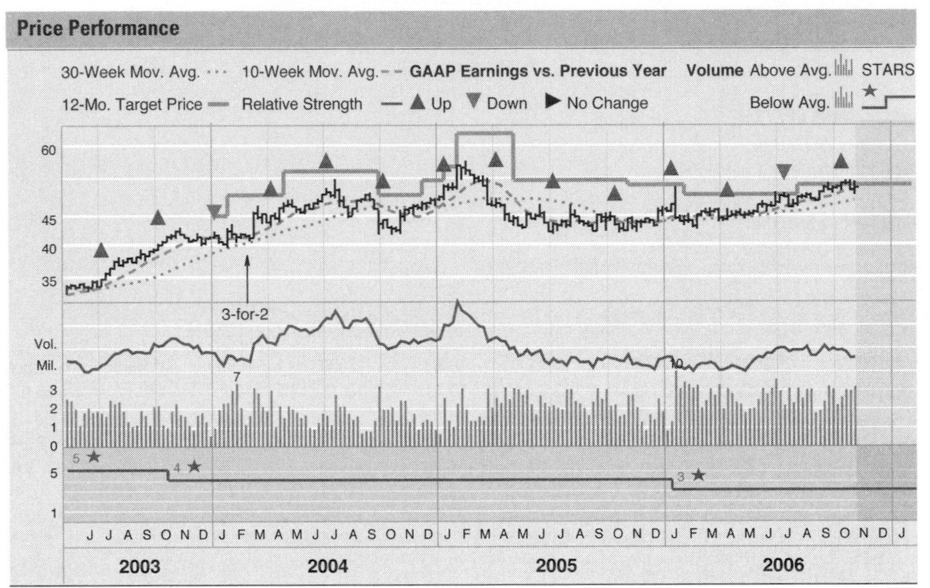

Options: ASE, CBOE, Ph

Analysis prepared by **Howard Choe** on August 02, 2006, when the stock traded at **$ 48.77**.

Highlights

- In June, ACV agreed to sell a 47.5% interest in the Sally Beauty Company, its beauty supply division, to Clayton, Dubilier & Rice, for $575 million. Under the proposed deal, expected to be completed in the fourth quarter of 2006, subject to neccessary approvals, ACV shareholders will receive a special $25 cash dividend and one share of the Sally Beauty Company.
- We expect ACV sales to increase about 6% in FY 06 (Sep.), compared to 8% growth in FY 05. We project about 4% growth for the specialty distribution division and nearly 9% growth for the consumer products division.
- We look for operating margins in FY 06 to be about even with FY 05, at 9.9%, largely due to the expensing of nearly $16 million of stock options. On a comparable basis, we believe margins will expand modestly. We see FY 06 operating EPS advancing 7% (10% on a comparable basis), to $2.54, from $2.37 in FY 05. Given that projected options are included in our FY 06 EPS estimate, our FY 06 Standard & Poor's Core EPS estimate is also $2.54.

Investment Rationale/Risk

- Our hold opinion reflects our positive view of ACV's consumer products business, partly offset by concerns over increased competition and some uncertainty related to inventory reductions at Wal-Mart, a key customer. In the long run, we believe ACV will remain competitive in its respective categories.
- Risks to our recommendation and target price include increased competition in the hair and skin care categories and in hair care retail operations, as well as integration risk associated with acquired stores.
- We view the shares as fairly valued, recently trading at nearly 19X our calendar 2006 EPS estimate of $2.58, which is modestly above our personal care group. We believe the current price amply reflects ACV's prospects over the next 12 months. Our 12-month target price of $51 assumes a P/E of about 18X our calendar 2007 EPS estimate, in line with peers.

Qualitative Risk Assessment

LOW	MEDIUM	HIGH

Demand for household and personal care products is generally static and generally not impacted by changes in the economy or geopolitical factors. However, these industries are mature and consequently competitive in nature.

Quantitative Evaluations

S&P Quality Ranking A+

D	C	B-	B	B+	A-	A	A+

Relative Strength Rank MODERATE

42

LOWEST = 1 HIGHEST = 99

Revenue/Earnings Data

Revenue (Million $)

	1Q	2Q	3Q	4Q	Year
2006	898.3	946.8	952.7	974.3	3,772
2005	847.5	884.1	898.9	900.7	3,531
2004	764.8	819.3	823.2	850.7	3,258
2003	696.8	707.0	736.1	751.6	2,891
2002	614.3	657.8	681.1	698.0	2,651
2001	593.6	622.6	634.4	643.7	2,494

Earnings Per Share ($)

	1Q	2Q	3Q	4Q	Year
2006	0.56	0.61	0.33	0.70	2.20
2005	0.53	0.53	0.57	0.63	2.27
2004	0.02	0.44	0.56	0.52	1.54
2003	0.40	0.42	0.47	0.51	1.80
2002	0.33	0.37	0.41	0.44	1.55
2001	0.27	0.30	0.33	0.37	1.27

Fiscal year ended Sep. 30. Next earnings report expected: Late January. EPS Estimates based on S&P Operating Earnings; historical GAAP earnings are as reported.

Dividend Data (Dates: mm/dd Payment Date: mm/dd/yy)

Amount ($)	Date Decl.	Ex-Div. Date	Stk. of Record	Payment Date
0.115	10/27	11/03	11/07	11/18/05
0.115	01/26	02/02	02/06	02/17/06
0.130	04/27	05/04	05/08	05/19/06
0.130	08/01	08/03	08/07	08/18/06

Dividends have been paid since 1967. Source: Company reports.

Alberto-Culver Co

Business Summary August 02, 2006

Alberto-Culver is best known for its very first product, Alberto VO5 conditioning hairdressing. The company's Global Consumer Products division (formerly Alberto-Culver Consumer Products Worldwide and Cederroth International) develops, manufactures, distributes and markets branded consumer products worldwide, including health and beauty care products (33% of FY 05 (Sep.) sales) and food and household products (4%). Its specialty distribution business (Sally Beauty Company and Sally Beauty Systems Group), which accounted for 63% of FY 05 sales, distributes professional beauty supplies.

ACV's prominent health and beauty care products marketed in the U.S. include Alberto VO5, the TRESemme, Nexxus, and Consort lines of hair care products, the St. Ives Swiss Formula line of hair and skin care products, FDS feminine deodorant sprays, and the TCB line of hair care products targeted toward ethnic markets. Well known food and household products sold in the U.S. include Mrs. Dash salt-free seasonings, Molly McButter dairy sprinkles, Sugartwin sugar substitute, and Static Guard antistatic spray. Alberto-Culver N.A. also includes the company's custom label manufacturing business.

Outside the U.S., the company sells health and beauty products in Europe and Latin America, as well as in Australia, Asia and Africa. In addition to Alberto VO5 and St. Ives Swiss Formula, products sold internationally include Salve adhesive bandages, Samarin antacids, Seltin salt substitute, Suketter artificial sweetener, Topz cotton buds, Savette wet wipes, Bliw liquid soaps, Date antiperspirants and cologne, Alberto Family Fresh shampoo and shower products, HTH and L300 skin care products, Grumme Tvattsapa detergents, and Pharbio natural pharmaceuticals.

Company Financials

Per Share Data ($) Year Ended Sep. 30	**2006**	**2005**	**2004**	**2003**	**2002**	**2001**	**2000**	**1999**	**1998**	**1997**
Tangible Book Value	NA	13.62	8.24	7.03	5.03	4.60	3.68	3.87	3.83	3.71
Cash Flow	NA	2.92	2.10	2.39	2.08	1.86	1.81	1.50	1.29	1.37
Earnings	2.20	2.27	1.54	1.80	1.55	1.27	1.22	1.01	0.91	0.94
S&P Core Earnings	NA	2.27	1.48	1.71	1.47	1.21	NA	NA	NA	NA
Dividends	0.49	0.45	0.37	0.27	0.24	0.22	0.19	0.17	0.15	0.13
Payout Ratio	22%	20%	24%	15%	15%	17%	16%	17%	17%	14%
Prices:High	51.96	56.31	52.30	42.93	38.61	30.84	29.00	18.58	21.62	21.67
Prices:Low	42.51	41.70	39.51	31.39	27.70	24.58	12.92	14.37	13.17	15.71
P/E Ratio:High	24	25	34	24	25	24	24	18	24	23
P/E Ratio:Low	19	18	26	17	18	19	11	14	14	17

Income Statement Analysis (Million $)										
Revenue	NA	3,531	3,258	2,891	2,651	2,494	2,247	1,976	1,835	1,775
Operating Income	NA	407	373	323	202	240	223	189	179	168
Depreciation	NA	60.5	51.1	48.8	47.2	51.4	49.6	42.2	38.1	38.9
Interest Expense	NA	10.6	25.7	22.4	26.0	16.4	23.7	14.8	12.2	11.8
Pretax Income	NA	324	213	251	212	167	154	134	132	136
Effective Tax Rate	NA	35.0%	33.3%	35.5%	35.0%	34.0%	33.1%	35.5%	37.3%	37.2%
Net Income	NA	211	142	162	138	110	103	86.3	83.1	85.4
S&P Core Earnings	NA	211	136	153	131	105	NA	NA	NA	NA

Balance Sheet & Other Financial Data (Million $)										
Cash	NA	104	202	370	217	202	115	55.9	72.4	76.0
Current Assets	NA	1,190	1,118	1,165	984	877	741	646	592	580
Total Assets	NA	2,302	2,059	1,946	1,729	1,517	1,390	1,185	1,068	1,000
Current Liabilities	NA	536	532	466	460	390	341	336	314	311
Long Term Debt	NA	124	121	321	320	321	341	225	172	149
Common Equity	NA	1,532	1,314	1,062	862	736	636	569	534	497
Total Capital	NA	1,689	1,459	1,422	1,221	1,096	1,016	828	734	672
Capital Expenditures	NA	91.0	74.7	61.4	55.5	36.8	37.5	47.8	55.9	58.2
Cash Flow	NA	271	193	211	185	162	153	128	121	124
Current Ratio	NA	2.2	2.1	2.5	2.1	2.2	2.2	1.9	1.9	1.9
% Long Term Debt of Capitalization	NA	7.3	8.3	22.5	26.2	29.3	33.6	27.2	23.4	22.2
% Net Income of Revenue	NA	6.0	4.4	5.6	5.2	4.4	4.6	4.4	4.5	4.8
% Return on Assets	NA	9.7	7.1	8.8	8.5	7.6	8.0	7.7	8.0	8.9
% Return on Equity	NA	14.8	11.9	16.9	17.2	16.1	17.1	15.6	16.1	18.5

Data as orig reptd.; bef. results of disc opers/spec. items. Per share data adj. for stk. divs.; EPS diluted. E-Estimated. NA-Not Available. NM-Not Meaningful. NR-Not Ranked. UR-Under Review.

Office: 2525 Armitage Avenue, Melrose Park, IL 60160-1163.
Telephone: 708-450-3000.
Email: crelations@alberto.com
Website: http://www.alberto.com

Chrmn: C.L. Bernick
Pres & CEO: H.B. Bernick
SVP & CFO: W.J. Cernugel
SVP, Secy & General Counsel: G.P. Schmidt

Investor Contact: W.C. Davidson (708 450 3145)
Board of Directors: A. G. Atwater, Jr., C. Bernick, H. B. Bernick, J. G. Brocksmith, Jr., J. Edgar, K. Harris, L. H. Lavin, J. A. Miller, R. H. Rock, S. J. Susser, W. W. Wirtz

Founded: 1961
Domicile: Delaware
Employees: 19,000

Alcoa Inc.

STANDARD &POOR'S

S&P Recommendation BUY ★★★★★

Price $28.30 (as of Oct 27, 2006)

12-Mo. Target Price $35.00

Investment Style Large-Cap Value

GICS Sector Materials
Sub-Industry Aluminum

Comment This company is the world's largest producer of aluminum and alumina, and a major participant in all segments of the industry.

Key Stock Statistics (Source S&P, Vickers, company reports)

52-Wk Range	$36.96–24.00	S&P Oper. EPS 2006E	2.82	P/E on S&P Oper. EPS 2006E	10.0	Dividend Rate/Share	$0.60
Trailing 12-Month EPS	$2.41	S&P Oper. EPS 2007E	3.00	Common Shares Outstg. (M)	867.1	Yield (%)	2.12
Trailing 12-Month P/E	11.7	S&P Core EPS 2006E	2.76	Market Capitalization(B)	$24.539	Beta	1.95
$10K Invested 5 Yrs Ago	$9,004	S&P Core EPS 2007E	2.93	Institutional Ownership (%)	81	S&P Credit Rating	A-

Price Performance

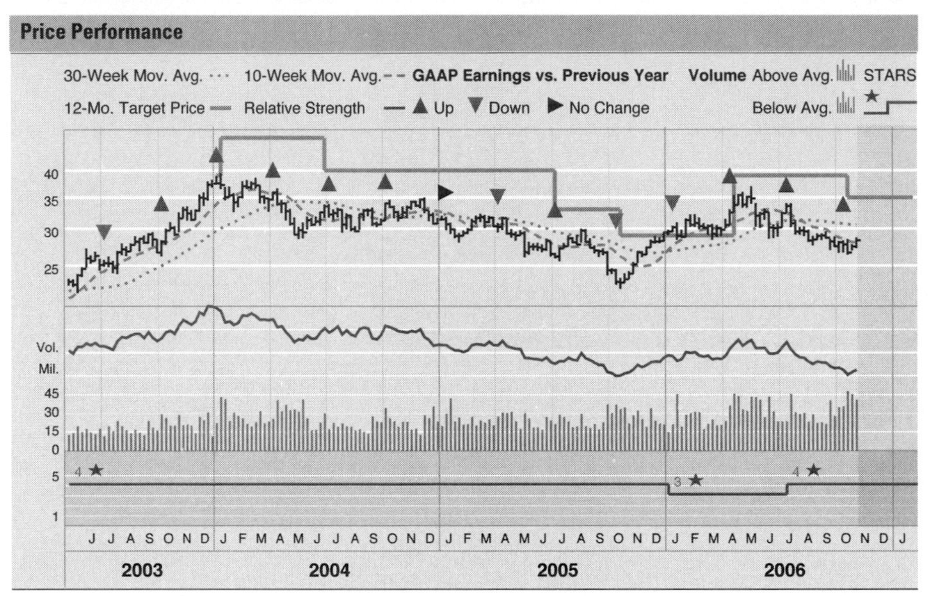

Options: ASE, CBOE, P, Ph

Analysis prepared by **Leo J. Larkin** on October 12, 2006, when the stock traded at **$ 26.95**.

Highlights

- Assuming 2.2% U.S. GDP growth in 2007, versus 2006's projected growth of 3.4% and a reduced rate of growth in the global economy, we look for a 9% sales increase in 2007, compared with 2006's estimated gain of 16%. We expect continued gains in demand from the aerospace and power generation industries and stabilization in demand from motor vehicles. Demand from residential construction is likely to be down, given the S&P forecast for a 14.6% drop in housing starts in 2007 versus 2006's projected decline of 10.1%. We estimate an average aluminum price of about $1.18 a pound in 2007, versus $1.14 projected for 2006. Our expectation for a higher price assumes that global inventories will remain tight in 2007, offsetting the impact of less robust demand.
- Aided by less rapidly rising raw material costs, lower plant start-up costs and the likely absence of unplanned plant outages, we project an increase in EPS in 2007 to $3.00 from $2.82 estimated for 2006.
- Long term, we think EPS will benefit from aluminum industry consolidation and a shift to lower cost aluminum plants.

Investment Rationale/Risk

- We believe that AA will benefit from ongoing consolidation of the aluminum industry and a slightly higher aluminum price in 2007. In our view, consolidation will result in a more disciplined pricing environment and less volatility in sales and EPS over the course of the business cycle. We believe aluminum prices hit a cyclical bottom in 2002, and will move higher through 2007. In our view, a higher aluminum price will result from rising global consumption combined with continued tight inventories. Also, production increases in China may moderate due to higher power costs. Recently trading with a current dividend yield of 2.2% and about 9X our 2007 estimate, we believe the shares are attractive.
- Risks to our recommendation and target price include a drop, rather than an increase, in aluminum prices in 2007.
- Our 12-month target price of $35 is based on our view that Alcoa's P/E on 2007's projected EPS will be at the low end of its historical range given our assumption that 2007 may represent EPS at the peak of a cycle.

Qualitative Risk Assessment

LOW | MEDIUM | **HIGH**

Our risk assessment reflects our view that AA's sales and EPS are exposed to cyclical markets such as autos and construction. While we do not believe the company's balance sheet is overly leveraged, its unfunded liabilities for pension and health care totaled $5.5 billion at the end of 2005.

Quantitative Evaluations

S&P Quality Ranking B+

D | C | B- | B | **B+** | A- | A | A+

Relative Strength Rank MODERATE

33

LOWEST = 1 HIGHEST = 99

Revenue/Earnings Data

Revenue (Million $)

	1Q	2Q	3Q	4Q	Year
2006	7,244	7,959	7,631	--	--
2005	6,226	6,698	6,566	6,669	26,159
2004	5,588	5,971	5,878	6,041	23,478
2003	5,140	5,497	5,335	5,532	21,504
2002	4,900	5,158	5,144	5,061	20,263
2001	6,176	5,991	5,511	5,181	22,859

Earnings Per Share ($)

2006	0.70	0.86	0.62	E0.65	E2.82
2005	0.30	0.53	0.33	0.24	1.40
2004	0.41	0.46	0.34	0.39	1.60
2003	0.23	0.26	0.33	0.39	1.20
2002	0.22	0.28	0.24	-0.15	0.58
2001	0.46	0.35	0.39	-0.17	1.05

Fiscal year ended Dec. 31. Next earnings report expected: Early January. EPS Estimates based on S&P Operating Earnings; historical GAAP earnings are as reported.

Dividend Data (Dates: mm/dd Payment Date: mm/dd/yy)

Amount ($)	Date Decl.	Ex-Div. Date	Stk. of Record	Payment Date
0.150	01/13	02/01	02/03	02/25/06
0.150	04/21	05/03	05/05	05/25/06
0.150	07/14	08/02	08/04	08/25/06
0.150	09/15	11/01	11/03	11/25/06

Dividends have been paid since 1939. Source: Company reports.

Alcoa Inc.

Business Summary October 12, 2006

CORPORATE OVERVIEW. Alcoa is the world's largest producer of primary aluminum and is also the world's largest supplier of alumina, an intermediate raw material used to make aluminum. In 2005, primary aluminum production totaled 3.6 million metric tons.

MARKET PROFILE. The primary factor affecting demand for aluminum products is economic growth, in general, and growth in demand for durable goods, in particular. The three largest end markets for aluminum in North America are transportation, containers/packaging, and construction. In 2004, these markets accounted for 69% of demand in North America. Other markets include consumer durables, machinery and equipment, and other. In 2005, containers/packaging accounted for 24% of Alcoa's revenues by end market; aluminum and alumina 26%; industrial products 13%; automotive, 10%; building and construction, 10%; aerospace 10%; and commercial transportation, 7%. In terms of primary production, the size of the world market was 23.4 million metric tons in 2005. Alcoa's market share was 14.6%. From 1996 through 2005, global consumption rose at a compound annual growth rate (CAGR) of 4.8%.

Company Financials

Per Share Data ($) Year Ended Dec. 31	**2005**	**2004**	**2003**	**2002**	**2001**	**2000**	**1999**	**1998**	**1997**	**1996**
Tangible Book Value	7.02	7.70	6.30	3.27	4.96	6.19	6.62	6.08	5.59	5.56
Cash Flow	2.85	2.98	2.61	3.20	2.49	3.29	2.61	2.42	2.24	1.84
Earnings	1.40	1.60	1.20	0.58	1.05	1.81	1.41	1.21	1.16	0.74
S&P Core Earnings	1.05	1.52	0.92	-0.17	0.17	NA	NA	NA	NA	NA
Dividends	0.60	0.60	0.60	0.60	0.60	0.50	0.40	0.38	0.24	0.33
Payout Ratio	43%	38%	50%	103%	57%	28%	29%	31%	21%	45%
Prices:High	32.29	39.44	38.92	39.75	45.71	43.63	41.69	20.31	22.41	16.56
Prices:Low	22.28	28.51	18.45	17.62	27.36	23.13	17.97	14.50	16.06	12.28
P/E Ratio:High	23	25	32	69	44	24	30	17	19	23
P/E Ratio:Low	16	18	15	30	26	13	13	12	14	17
Income Statement Analysis (Million $)										
Revenue	26,159	23,478	21,504	20,263	22,859	22,936	16,323	15,340	13,482	13,061
Operating Income	3,398	3,397	2,885	2,663	3,523	4,304	2,821	2,509	2,238	2,111
Depreciation	1,267	1,212	1,202	2,224	1,253	1,219	901	856	754	764
Interest Expense	339	270	314	350	393	427	195	198	141	139
Pretax Income	1,933	2,204	1,669	925	1,641	2,812	1,849	1,605	1,602	1,082
Effective Tax Rate	22.8%	25.3%	24.2%	31.6%	32.0%	33.5%	29.9%	32.0%	33.0%	33.3%
Net Income	1,233	1,402	1,034	498	908	1,489	1,054	853	805	515
S&P Core Earnings	924	1,334	777	-143	146	NA	NA	NA	NA	NA
Balance Sheet & Other Financial Data (Million $)										
Cash	762	457	576	344	512	315	237	342	801	617
Current Assets	8,790	7,493	6,740	6,313	6,792	7,578	4,800	5,025	4,417	4,281
Total Assets	33,696	32,609	31,711	29,810	28,355	31,691	17,066	17,463	13,071	13,450
Current Liabilities	7,368	6,298	5,084	4,461	5,003	7,954	3,003	3,268	2,453	2,373
Long Term Debt	5,279	5,346	6,692	8,365	6,388	4,987	2,657	2,877	1,457	1,690
Common Equity	13,318	13,245	12,020	9,872	10,614	11,366	6,262	6,000	4,363	4,407
Total Capital	20,892	20,852	20,911	20,087	18,927	18,892	10,870	10,767	6,140	8,080
Capital Expenditures	2,124	1,142	863	1,263	1,177	1,121	920	932	912	996
Cash Flow	2,498	2,612	2,234	2,720	2,159	2,706	1,953	1,707	1,557	1,279
Current Ratio	1.2	1.2	1.3	1.4	1.4	1.0	1.6	1.5	1.8	1.8
% Long Term Debt of Capitalization	25.3	25.6	32.0	41.6	33.8	26.4	24.4	26.7	23.7	20.9
% Net Income of Revenue	4.7	6.0	4.8	2.5	4.0	6.5	6.5	5.6	6.0	3.9
% Return on Assets	3.7	4.4	3.4	1.7	3.0	6.1	6.1	5.6	6.1	3.8
% Return on Equity	9.3	11.1	9.4	4.9	8.2	16.9	17.2	16.4	18.3	11.7

Data as orig reptd.; bef. results of disc opers/spec. items. Per share data adj. for stk. divs.; EPS diluted. E-Estimated. NA-Not Available. NM-Not Meaningful. NR-Not Ranked. UR-Under Review.

Office: 390 Park Ave, New York, NY 10022-4608.
Telephone: 212-836-2674.
Email: investor.relations@alcoa.com
Website: http://www.alcoa.com

Chrmn & CEO: A.J. Belda
EVP & CFO: J.C. Muscari
EVP & General Counsel: L.R. Purtell
VP & Cntlr: C.D. McLane , Jr.

Investor Contact: T. Thene (212-836-2674)
Board of Directors: A. J. Belda, K. S. Fuller, C. Ghosn, J. T. Gorman, J. M. Gueron, K. Kleinfeld, J. Owens, H. B. Schacht, F. A. Thomas, E. Zedillo

Founded: 1888
Domicile: Pennsylvania
Employees: 129,000

STANDARD &POOR'S

Allegheny Energy Inc.

S&P Recommendation HOLD ★★★★★ | **Price** $41.99 (as of Oct 27, 2006) | **12-Mo. Target Price** $48.00 | **Investment Style** Mid-Cap Value

GICS Sector Utilities
Sub-Industry Electric Utilities

Comment This diversified energy company engages in electric generation and electric and natural gas delivery, and invests in and develops telecommunications and energy-related projects.

Key Stock Statistics (Source S&P, Vickers, company reports)

52-Wk Range	**$43.15–26.40**	S&P Oper. EPS 2006**E**	**1.81**	P/E on S&P Oper. EPS 2006**E**	**23.2**	Dividend Rate/Share	**Nil**
Trailing 12-Month EPS	**$1.56**	S&P Oper. EPS 2007**E**	**2.28**	Common Shares Outstg. (M)	**164.6**	Yield (%)	**Nil**
Trailing 12-Month P/E	**26.9**	S&P Core EPS 2006**E**	**1.80**	Market Capitalization(B)	**$6.911**	Beta	**1.28**
$10K Invested 5 Yrs Ago	**$12,403**	S&P Core EPS 2007**E**	**2.27**	Institutional Ownership (%)	**77**	S&P Credit Rating	**BB+**

Price Performance

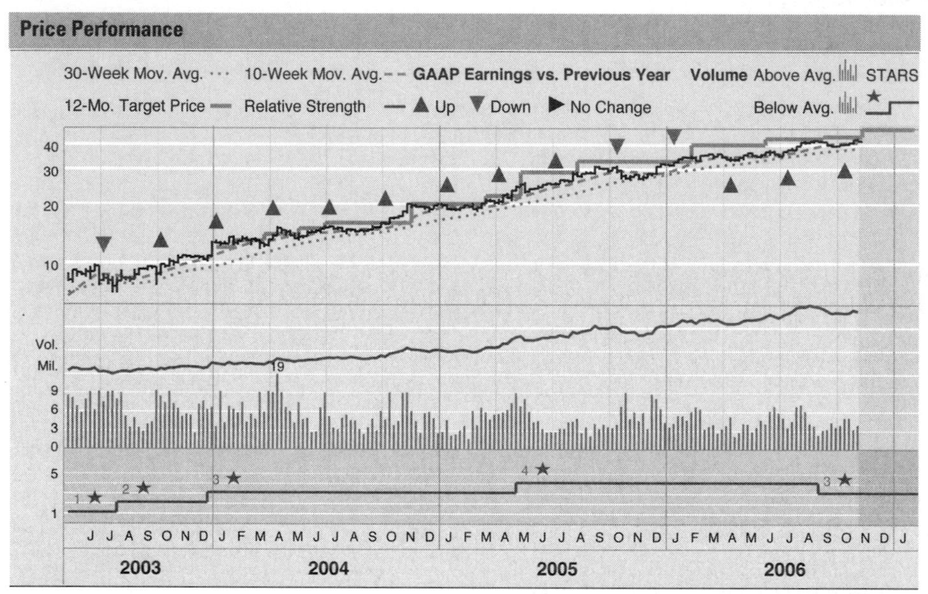

Options: ASE, CBOE, P

Highlights

➤ The 12-month target price for AYE has recently been changed to $48.00 from $44.00. The Highlights section of this Stock Report will be updated accordingly.

Investment Rationale/Risk

➤ The Investment Rationale/Risk section of this Stock Report will be updated shortly. For the latest News story on AYE from MarketScope, see below.

➤ 10/27/06 12:02 pm EDT... S&P MAINTAINS HOLD OPINION ON SHARES OF ALLEGHENY ENERGY (AYE 42.37***): AYE reports Q3 EPS from continuing operations of $0.56 vs. $0.45, a penny above our estimate. Higher Pennsylvania generation rates, the expiration of a below-market contract and lower costs were partly offset by lower market prices and costs related to an equipment failure. We expect higher power prices and slightly lower depreciation and interest costs to drive above-peer growth in '07. We are raising our '06 and '07 EPS estimates by $0.03 each to $1.81 and $2.28, respectively. Our 12-month target price rises by $4 to $48 due to a change in our medium-term growth assumptions. /CMuir

Qualitative Risk Assessment

LOW | **MEDIUM** | HIGH

Our risk assessment reflects the company's mid-level capitalization and balanced sources of earnings which include both low risk regulated electric utility and higher risk unregulated power generation operations.

Quantitative Evaluations

S&P Quality Ranking **B-**

D | C | **B-** | B | B+ | A- | A | A+

Relative Strength Rank **MODERATE**

57

LOWEST = 1 HIGHEST = 99

Revenue/Earnings Data

Revenue (Million $)

	1Q	2Q	3Q	4Q	Year
2006	845.7	722.2	816.7	--	--
2005	754.0	714.7	845.1	724.1	3,038
2004	735.4	608.9	723.3	688.5	2,756
2003	715.7	359.2	637.6	760.0	2,472
2002	1,005	784.6	537.1	661.7	2,988
2001	1,693	2,940	3,690	2,055	10,379

Earnings Per Share ($)

	1Q	2Q	3Q	4Q	Year
2006	0.68	0.19	0.65	**E**0.38	**E**1.81
2005	0.24	-0.04	0.26	0.02	0.47
2004	0.23	-0.26	0.37	0.53	0.99
2003	-0.30	-1.82	-0.40	-0.11	-2.64
2002	0.61	-0.27	-2.09	-2.23	-4.00
2001	0.93	0.97	1.33	0.50	3.73

Fiscal year ended Dec. 31. Next earnings report expected: Early February. EPS Estimates based on S&P Operating Earnings; historical GAAP earnings are as reported.

Dividend Data

Dividend payments were suspended in December 2002.

Please read the Required Disclosures and Analyst Certification on the last page of this report.

Allegheny Energy Inc.

Business Summary August 29, 2006

CORPORATE OVERVIEW. AYE is an integrated electric distribution and generation company operating in the Mid-Atlantic region. Its three distribution businesses operate under the trade name Allegheny Power. West Penn operates an electric transmission and distribution (T&D) system in southwestern, northern and south central Pennsylvania, serving approximately 702,800 customers. Potomac Edison operates an electric T&D system in portions of West Virginia, Maryland and Virginia. Potomac Edison serves approximately 454,400 electric customers. Monongahela conducts an electric T&D business that serves roughly 371,400 electric customers in northern West Virginia. In December 2005, AYE sold its Ohio service territory to American Electric Power for net cash proceeds of approximately $52 million. In September 2005, Monongahela sold its Mountaineer natural gas operations in West Virginia for $161 million with the assumption of $87 million of debt by the purchaser.

Allegheny Energy Supply, AYE's primary unregulated generating division, ended 2005 with 8,245 megawatts (MW) of capacity. The division's capacity grew from 1999 to 2001 through the transfer of regulated power plants in Pennsylvania, Maryland, Virginia and Ohio from AYE utilities, acquisition of existing plants, and construction activities. In July 2005, Allegheny Energy Supply was awarded contracts to meet Allegheny Power's 2009 and 2010 generation supply needs in Pennsylvania. In August 2005, Allegheny Energy Supply completed the sale of its Indiana-based Wheatland generating facility for approximately $100 million. The division has also placed its 526 MW natural gas-fired Gleason, TN, power plant for sale.

Monongahela owns or controls about 2,130 MW of generating capacity, most of which is delivered to AYE's electric utilities. Additionally, AYE owns a 40% interest (about 1,010 MW) in the Bath County pumped-storage hydroelectric power station.

As of December 31, 2005, about 75.5% of AYE's 10,375 MW of owned and controlled capacity was coal-fired, 13.4% was gas-fired, 10.3% was hydroelectric and 0.8% oil-fired.

Company Financials

Per Share Data ($) Year Ended Dec. 31	**2005**	**2004**	**2003**	**2002**	**2001**	**2000**	**1999**	**1998**	**1997**	**1996**
Tangible Book Value	7.98	6.94	9.05	12.05	16.48	13.80	14.97	16.49	18.31	17.68
Earnings	0.47	0.99	-2.64	-4.00	3.73	2.84	2.45	2.15	2.30	1.73
S&P Core Earnings	0.45	0.56	-2.60	-4.22	3.24	NA	NA	NA	NA	NA
Dividends	Nil	Nil	Nil	1.29	1.72	1.72	1.72	1.72	1.72	1.69
Payout Ratio	Nil	Nil	Nil	NM	46%	61%	77%	74%	75%	98%
Prices:High	32.32	20.20	13.09	43.86	55.09	48.75	35.19	34.94	32.59	31.13
Prices:Low	18.25	11.75	4.70	2.95	32.99	23.63	26.19	26.63	25.50	28.00
P/E Ratio:High	69	20	NM	NM	15	17	14	15	14	18
P/E Ratio:Low	39	12	NM	NM	9	8	11	11	11	16
Income Statement Analysis (Million $)										
Revenue	3,038	2,756	2,472	2,988	10,379	4,012	2,808	2,576	2,369	2,328
Depreciation	308	299	327	309	302	248	257	270	266	263
Maintenance	NA	NA	NA	NA	288	230	224	218	231	255
Fixed Charges Coverage	1.39	1.28	-0.35	-1.21	3.38	3.11	3.25	3.25	3.24	3.28
Construction Credits	NA	NA	NA	13.0	11.5	7.28	6.91	5.02	NA	5.89
Effective Tax Rate	46.1%	NM	NM	NM	35.2%	37.1%	36.6%	39.0%	37.4%	37.9%
Net Income	75.1	130	-334	-502	449	314	285	263	281	210
S&P Core Earnings	72.0	61.8	-329	-530	391	NA	NA	NA	NA	NA
Balance Sheet & Other Financial Data (Million $)										
Gross Property	10,786	10,644	11,831	11,357	11,087	9,507	8,840	8,630	8,451	8,207
Capital Expenditures	306	266	254	403	463	402	467	234	280	289
Net Property	6,277	6,303	7,453	6,883	6,853	5,539	5,207	5,234	5,296	5,296
Capitalization:Long Term Debt	3,665	4,639	5,234	229	3,274	2,634	2,328	2,349	2,193	2,397
Capitalization:% Long Term Debt	58.8	77.4	77.5	10.6	54.7	60.2	57.9	53.6	47.5	50.7
Capitalization:Preferred	Nil	Nil	Nil	Nil	Nil	Nil	Nil	Nil	170	170
Capitalization:% Preferred	Nil	Nil	Nil	Nil	Nil	Nil	Nil	Nil	3.70	3.60
Capitalization:Common	1,695	1,354	1,516	1,932	2,710	1,741	1,695	2,034	2,257	2,169
Capitalization:% Common	98.6	22.6	22.5	89.4	45.3	39.8	42.1	46.4	48.8	45.8
Total Capital	6,228	6,733	7,713	3,358	7,090	5,372	5,062	5,351	5,784	5,878
% Operating Ratio	83.5	82.1	99.3	101.9	93.1	86.6	83.1	82.9	80.9	83.2
% Earned on Net Property	8.5	11.5	NM	NM	11.5	10.0	9.3	8.3	8.5	7.6
% Return on Revenue	2.5	4.7	NM	NM	4.3	7.8	10.2	10.2	11.9	9.1
% Return on Invested Capital	23.3	7.4	2.6	4.2	11.9	10.5	9.2	11.9	8.1	10.9
% Return on Common Equity	4.9	9.0	NM	NM	20.2	18.3	15.3	12.3	12.7	9.8

Data as orig reptd.; bef. results of disc opers/spec. items. Per share data adj. for stk. divs.; EPS diluted. E-Estimated. NA-Not Available. NM-Not Meaningful. NR-Not Ranked. UR-Under Review.

Office: 800 Cabin Hill Dr, Greensburg, PA 15601-1650.
Telephone: 724-837-3000.
Email: investorinfo@alleghenypower.com
Website: http://www.alleghenyenergy.com

Chrmn, Pres & CEO: P.J. Evanson
SVP & CFO: P.L. Goulding
VP, Chief Acctg Officer, Cntlr & CIO: T.R. Gardner
VP & General Counsel: D.M. Feinberg

Investor Contact: M. Kuniansky (724-838-6895)
Board of Directors: H. F. Baldwin, E. Baum, P. J. Evanson, C. F. Freidheim, Jr., J. L. Johnson, T. J. Kleisner, S. H. Rice, G. E. Sarsten, M. H. Sutton

Founded: 1925
Domicile: Maryland
Employees: 4,460

Allegheny Technologies Inc

STANDARD &POOR'S

S&P Recommendation BUY ★★★★☆

Price $80.09 (as of Oct 27, 2006)

12-Mo. Target Price $95.00

Investment Style Mid-Cap Value

GICS Sector Materials
Sub-Industry Steel

Comment This company is a leading producer of specialty metals for a wide variety of end markets.

Key Stock Statistics (Source S&P, Vickers, company reports)

52-Wk Range	**$87.50–27.40**	S&P Oper. EPS 2006E	**5.40**	P/E on S&P Oper. EPS 2006E	**14.8**	Dividend Rate/Share	**$0.40**
Trailing 12-Month EPS	**$5.15**	S&P Oper. EPS 2007E	**6.40**	Common Shares Outstg. (M)	**100.6**	Yield (%)	**0.50**
Trailing 12-Month P/E	**15.6**	S&P Core EPS 2006E	**5.39**	Market Capitalization(B)	**$8.057**	Beta	**3.10**
$10K Invested 5 Yrs Ago	**$58,399**	S&P Core EPS 2007E	**5.41**	Institutional Ownership (%)	**74**	S&P Credit Rating	**BB**

Price Performance

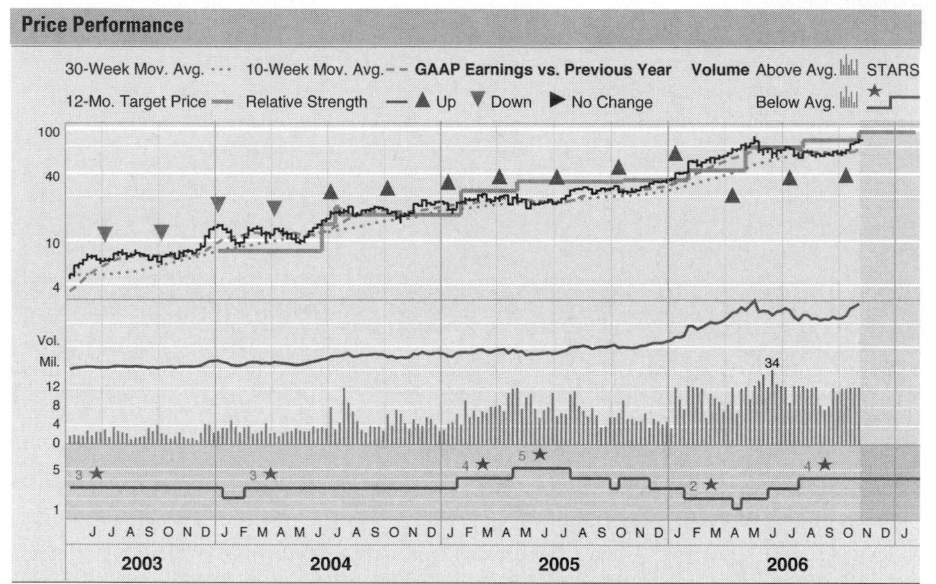

Options: ASE, CBOE, P, Ph

Highlights

➤ The 12-month target price for ATI has recently been changed to $95.00 from $80.00. The Highlights section of this Stock Report will be updated accordingly.

Investment Rationale/Risk

➤ The Investment Rationale/Risk section of this Stock Report will be updated shortly. For the latest News story on ATI from MarketScope, see below.

➤ 10/26/06 02:34 pm EDT... S&P REITERATES BUY OPINION ON SHARES OF ALLEGHENY TECHNOLOGIES (ATI 81.76****): ATI posts Q3 EPS of $1.58 versus $0.87 on a 50% sales gain, exceeding our estimate of $1.41. Higher sales and EPS reflect strong demand from aerospace, energy and chemical processing industries. We are increasing our '06 EPS estimate to $5.40 from $5.25, and our '07 estimate to $6.40 from $5.50, to reflect our expectation for increased demand from ATI's main markets. On our revised '07 estimate, we are raising our P/E-based 12-month target price to $95 from $80. On our new '07 estimate, the projected P/E is toward the midpoint of ATI's historical range. /L.Larkin

Qualitative Risk Assessment

LOW | MEDIUM | **HIGH**

Our risk assessment reflects the exposure of ATI's sales and earnings to cyclical markets and its highly leveraged balance sheet. Additionally, the company's unfunded liabilities for pension and health care benefits were 94% of shareholders' equity at the end of 2005.

Quantitative Evaluations

S&P Quality Ranking B-

D | C | **B-** | B | B+ | A- | A | A+

Relative Strength Rank STRONG

95

LOWEST = 1 HIGHEST = 99

Revenue/Earnings Data

Revenue (Million $)

	1Q	2Q	3Q	4Q	Year
2006	1,041	1,211	1,288	--	--
2005	879.6	904.2	861.7	894.4	3,540
2004	577.8	646.5	730.6	778.1	2,733
2003	480.5	489.9	482.6	484.4	1,937
2002	493.1	491.2	469.3	454.2	1,908
2001	542.5	554.7	537.7	493.1	2,128

Earnings Per Share ($)

	1Q	2Q	3Q	4Q	Year
2006	1.00	1.37	1.58	**E**1.45	**E**5.40
2005	0.61	0.91	0.87	1.19	3.59
2004	-0.63	0.31	0.09	0.35	0.22
2003	-0.32	-0.32	-0.36	-2.89	-3.87
2002	-0.14	-0.09	-0.09	-0.49	-0.82
2001	0.08	0.08	0.10	-0.57	-0.31

Fiscal year ended Dec. 31. Next earnings report expected: Late January. EPS Estimates based on S&P Operating Earnings; historical GAAP earnings are as reported.

Dividend Data (Dates: mm/dd Payment Date: mm/dd/yy)

Amount ($)	Date Decl.	Ex-Div. Date	Stk. of Record	Payment Date
0.100	12/09	12/15	12/19	12/27/05
0.100	02/24	03/16	03/20	03/28/06
0.100	05/04	05/25	05/30	06/13/06
0.100	09/14	09/20	09/22	09/29/06

Dividends have been paid since 1996. Source: Company reports.

Allegheny Technologies Inc

Business Summary July 31, 2006

In November 1999, Allegheny Technologies spun off all of the common stock of Teledyne Technologies Inc. (NYSE: TDY) and Water Pik Technologies, Inc. to ATI stockholders, and changed its name from Allegheny Teledyne Inc.

Following the spin-offs, ATI operates in three segments: Flat-Rolled Products, High Performance Metals, and Engineered Products. Markets for the three units include aerospace, oil and gas, transportation, food, chemical processing, consumer products, medical, and power generation.

The Flat-Rolled Products segment (35% of 2005 sales; 28% of operating profits) consists of Allegheny Ludlum Corp., Rodney Metals, the Allegheny Rodney Strip division of Allegheny Ludlum, and the company's interest in a Chinese joint venture, Shanghai STAL Precision Stainless Steel Ltd. The companies in this segment produce, convert and distribute stainless steel sheet, strip and plate, precision rolled strip products, flat-rolled nickel-based alloys and titanium, silicon electrical steels and tool steels. Shipments totaled 574,369 tons in 2005, versus 587,753 tons in 2004. The average realized price per ton was $2,169 in 2005, versus $2,796 in 2004. Operating profits totaled $149.9 million in 2005, versus $61.5 million in 2004.

Company Financials

Per Share Data ($) Year Ended Dec. 31	**2005**	**2004**	**2003**	**2002**	**2001**	**2000**	**1999**	**1998**	**1997**	**1996**
Tangible Book Value	6.11	2.30	NM	3.15	9.42	10.51	11.02	11.12	9.52	7.96
Cash Flow	4.47	1.00	-2.96	0.30	0.91	2.80	2.15	3.53	4.44	3.80
Earnings	3.59	0.22	-3.87	-0.82	-0.31	1.60	1.16	2.44	3.34	2.56
S&P Core Earnings	3.76	0.26	-3.19	-2.17	-2.09	NA	NA	NA	NA	NA
Dividends	0.28	0.24	0.24	0.66	0.80	0.80	1.28	1.28	1.28	0.32
Payout Ratio	8%	109%	NM	NM	NM	50%	110%	52%	38%	12%
Prices:High	36.66	23.48	14.00	19.10	21.07	26.81	48.37	59.12	65.75	47.50
Prices:Low	17.30	8.64	2.10	5.21	12.50	12.50	20.25	28.00	42.00	39.75
P/E Ratio:High	10	NM	NM	NM	NM	17	42	24	20	19
P/E Ratio:Low	5	NM	NM	NM	NM	8	17	11	13	16
Income Statement Analysis (Million $)										
Revenue	3,540	2,733	1,937	1,908	2,128	2,460	2,296	3,923	3,745	3,816
Operating Income	452	87.7	-110	65.0	166	358	284	579	531	504
Depreciation	77.0	70.1	74.0	90.0	98.0	99.7	95.3	109	98.5	105
Interest Expense	38.6	35.5	27.7	34.3	29.3	34.4	25.9	19.3	19.6	48.5
Pretax Income	307	19.8	-280	-104	-36.4	209	174	391	475	385
Effective Tax Rate	NM	NM	NM	NM	NM	36.5%	36.3%	38.3%	37.4%	41.2%
Net Income	362	19.8	-313	-65.8	-25.2	133	111	241	298	227
S&P Core Earnings	378	23.3	-258	-176	-168	NA	NA	NA	NA	NA
Balance Sheet & Other Financial Data (Million $)										
Cash	363	251	79.6	59.4	33.7	26.2	50.7	74.8	50.3	62.5
Current Assets	1,484	1,160	743	812	926	1,023	1,034	1,365	1,229	1,200
Total Assets	2,732	2,316	1,885	2,093	2,643	2,776	2,751	3,176	2,605	2,606
Current Liabilities	561	493	395	342	333	414	540	622	562	586
Long Term Debt	547	553	504	509	573	491	200	447	326	443
Common Equity	800	426	175	449	945	1,039	1,200	1,340	1,000	872
Total Capital	1,347	979	679	958	1,671	1,689	1,401	1,787	1,326	1,315
Capital Expenditures	90.1	49.9	74.4	48.7	104	60.2	74.1	173	96.3	88.6
Cash Flow	439	95.9	-239	24.2	73.4	232	206	350	396	330
Current Ratio	2.6	2.4	1.9	2.4	2.8	2.5	1.9	2.2	2.2	2.1
% Long Term Debt of Capitalization	40.6	56.5	74.3	53.2	34.3	29.1	14.3	25.0	24.6	33.7
% Net Income of Revenue	10.2	0.7	NM	NM	NM	5.4	4.8	6.1	7.9	6.0
% Return on Assets	14.3	0.9	NM	NM	NM	4.8	3.9	8.3	11.4	8.7
% Return on Equity	59.0	6.6	NM	NM	NM	11.8	8.7	20.6	31.8	27.1

Data as orig reptd.; bef. results of disc opers/spec. items. Per share data adj. for stk. divs.; EPS diluted. E-Estimated. NA-Not Available. NM-Not Meaningful. NR-Not Ranked. UR-Under Review.

Office: 1000 PPG Place, Pittsburgh, PA 15222-5479.
Telephone: 412-394-2800.
Website: http://www.alleghenytechnologies.com
Chrmn, Pres & CEO: L.P. Hassey

EVP & CFO: R.J. Harshman
EVP, Secy & General Counsel: J.D. Walton
VP, Chief Acctg Officer, Treas & Cntlr: D.G. Reid
Investor Contact: D.L. Greenfield (412-394-3004)

Board of Directors: H. K. Bowen, R. P. Bozzone, D. C. Creel, J. C. Diggs, L. P. Hassey, M. J. Joyce, W. C. McClelland, J. E. Rohr, L. J. Thomas, J. D. Turner

Founded: 1960
Domicile: Delaware
Employees: 9,300

Allergan Inc.

STANDARD &POOR'S

S&P Recommendation BUY ★★★★★

Price $115.25 (as of Oct 27, 2006)

12-Mo. Target Price $127.00

Investment Style Large-Cap Growth

GICS Sector Health Care
Sub-Industry Pharmaceuticals

Comment This technology-driven global health care company develops and commercializes products in the eye care, neuromodulator, skin care and other specialty markets.

Key Stock Statistics (Source S&P, Vickers, company reports)

52-Wk Range	$117.99–88.61	S&P Oper. EPS 2006E	3.65	P/E on S&P Oper. EPS 2006E	31.6	Dividend Rate/Share	$0.40
Trailing 12-Month EPS	$-0.45	S&P Oper. EPS 2007E	4.30	Common Shares Outstg. (M)	150.8	Yield (%)	0.35
Trailing 12-Month P/E	NM	S&P Core EPS 2006E	2.07	Market Capitalization(B)	$17.379	Beta	0.68
$10K Invested 5 Yrs Ago	$16,416	S&P Core EPS 2007E	4.01	Institutional Ownership (%)	97	S&P Credit Rating	A

Price Performance

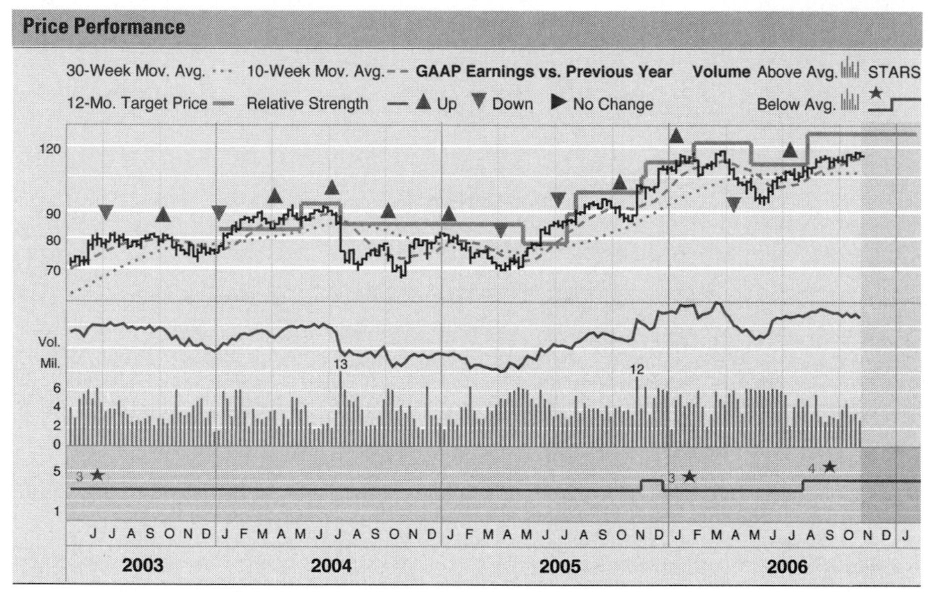

Options: ASE, CBOE, Ph

Analysis prepared by **Phillip M. Seligman** on August 16, 2006, when the stock traded at **$ 113.38**.

Highlights

- We look for 2006 revenue growth of over 28%, to $2.975 billion, driven mainly by the March 23 acquisition of Inamed Corp., which we expect to contribute $375 million in the nine months to year end. Other drivers include new drugs and new indications for existing drugs. We adjusted for the shift of Botox injectable muscle relaxant sales in Japan to GlaxoSmithKline (GSK: buy, $56) and its partial replacement by royalty and promotional/development revenue.
- We see a gross margin of about 82.0%, below 2005's 82.8%, partly on product mix, an R&D expense ratio of 16%, below 2005's 16.7%, on revenue leverage, and an SG&A cost ratio of 41.5%, above 2005's 39.8%, on sales and marketing investments. We see all three ratios also affected by stock option expense.
- We see 2006 operating EPS of $3.65, including $0.20 of projected stock option expense but excluding $0.30 of goodwill amortization, up from 2005's adjusted $3.29, excluding $0.25 of stock option expense. For 2007, we foresee EPS of $4.30. Our 2006 and 2007 S&P Core EPS estimates, including one-time charges in 2006 only and projected pension adjustments in both years, are $2.07 and $4.01, respectively.

Investment Rationale/Risk

- We are encouraged by the 16% rise in AGN's pharmaceutical sales in the second quarter, and see momentum continuing, partly on the pending EU launch of Ganfort for intra-ocular pressure in patients with open-angle glaucoma or ocular hypertension, and Lumigan's new indication as a first-line treatment for intra-ocular pressure. While we think future Botox growth rates will slow, we believe the deceleration will be modest with direct-to-consumer advertising for Botox Cosmetic. We also continue to think AGN will benefit from the pending launch of Juvederm dermal filler and from its acquisition of Inamed. We see the combined entity as a powerful force in medical aesthetics, given Inamed's dermal fillers, breast aesthetics portfolio, and LAP-BAND obesity treatment system. We see the deal boosting AGN's free cash flow and operating EPS over time.
- Risks to our recommendation and target price include FDA rejection or postponement of a new drug, and problems integrating Inamed.
- Our 12-month target price of $127 reflects a target peer-level 1.8X P/E to growth (with growth projected at 17% annually over the next three years) ratio, and our 2007 EPS estimate.

Qualitative Risk Assessment

LOW | **MEDIUM** | HIGH

Our risk assessment reflects AGN's increased diversification of aesthetic products and markets via the acquisition of Inamed, our view of its strong focus on R&D, leading market position in several ophthalmic drugs, and continued strong demand for Botox. However, we view the eyecare and aesthetics markets as competitive, and think that certain pipeline products may not be successful.

Quantitative Evaluations

S&P Quality Ranking **B**

D | C | B- | **B** | B+ | A- | A | A+

Relative Strength Rank **MODERATE**

48

LOWEST = 1 HIGHEST = 99

Revenue/Earnings Data

Revenue (Million $)

	1Q	2Q	3Q	4Q	Year
2006	615.2	801.7	--	--	--
2005	527.2	591.0	606.1	594.9	2,319
2004	472.4	506.2	510.8	556.2	2,046
2003	391.2	447.7	443.3	479.4	1,771
2002	327.7	346.7	360.0	390.9	1,425
2001	423.0	431.8	427.0	463.7	1,746

Earnings Per Share ($)

	1Q	2Q	3Q	4Q	Year
2006	-3.29	0.49	**E**0.93	**E**1.04	**E**3.65
2005	0.60	0.25	1.12	1.03	3.01
2004	0.61	0.69	0.70	0.85	2.82
2003	0.53	-0.83	0.57	-0.70	-0.40
2002	0.30	-0.02	-0.28	0.49	0.49
2001	0.40	0.16	0.50	0.63	1.69

Fiscal year ended Dec. 31. Next earnings report expected: Early November. EPS Estimates based on S&P Operating Earnings; historical GAAP earnings are as reported.

Dividend Data (Dates: mm/dd Payment Date: mm/dd/yy)

Amount ($)	Date Decl.	Ex-Div. Date	Stk. of Record	Payment Date
0.100	11/01	11/14	11/16	12/12/05
0.100	02/06	02/15	02/17	03/14/06
0.100	05/03	05/17	05/19	06/13/06
0.100	08/02	08/16	08/18	09/12/06

Dividends have been paid since 1989. Source: Company reports.

Allergan Inc.

Business Summary August 16, 2006

CORPORATE OVERVIEW. Allergan is a leading producer of ophthalmic, neuromuscular and skin care pharmaceuticals. Eye care drugs accounted for 57% of 2005 sales from continuing operations, Botox/neuromodulator 36%, skin care treatments 5%, and other, 2%. About 33% of 2005 sales were derived from foreign markets.

Eye care drugs include prescription and nonprescription products to treat eye diseases and disorders, including glaucoma, inflammation, infection, allergy, and dry eye. Important products are Alphagan, Alphagan P, and Combigan (sales of $277 million in 2005, versus $269 million in 2004) and Lumigan ($268 million versus $233 million) treatments, which are used to lower eye pressure in patients with open-angle glaucoma or ocular hypertension. Other eye care products include Restasis, for dry eye disease; Acular, Alocril, and Elestat, for seasonal allergic conjunctivitis; and Zymar and Ocuflox, for bacterial conjunctivitis.

Originally used for ophthalmic movement disorders, AGN believes that Botox (botulinum toxin type A) is the widely accepted treatment for neuromuscular disorders and related pain. More recently, Botox garnered a rapidly growing market as a facial cosmetic agent. In April 2002, the FDA approved the injectable drug for removing brow furrows and other facial wrinkles. About 57% of Botox sales in 2005 (58% in 2004) were for therapeutic indications, with cosmetic uses comprising the balance. Botox is being studied for treating excessive sweating, post-stroke spasticity, back spasms, and migraines.

Skin care products include Zorac/Tazorac receptor-selective retinoids for acne and psoriasis; Prevage for fine lines and wrinkles; and Avage for facial fine wrinkling and blotchy skin discoloration.

PRIMARY BUSINESS DYNAMICS. We believe that AGN has a strong R&D focus. Its R&D expenses, excluding one-time items, totaled $387 million in 2005 (16.7% of sales), versus $346 million (16.9%) in 2004. The R&D pipeline includes new treatments for glaucoma, dry eye, chronic pain, macular degeneration, infections, acid reflux, and other conditions.

Company Financials

Per Share Data ($) Year Ended Dec. 31	**2005**	**2004**	**2003**	**2002**	**2001**	**2000**	**1999**	**1998**	**1997**	**1996**
Tangible Book Value	10.67	7.98	4.95	6.04	6.48	5.63	3.73	3.99	4.81	3.90
Cash Flow	3.63	3.39	0.05	0.84	2.38	2.19	1.94	-0.10	1.50	1.14
Earnings	3.01	2.82	-0.40	0.49	1.69	1.61	1.39	-0.69	0.98	0.58
S&P Core Earnings	2.71	2.52	-0.66	0.90	1.39	NA	NA	NA	NA	NA
Dividends	0.40	0.36	0.36	0.36	0.36	0.32	0.28	0.26	0.26	0.25
Payout Ratio	13%	13%	NM	73%	21%	20%	20%	NM	27%	42%
Prices:High	110.50	92.61	81.80	75.10	99.38	101.13	57.81	33.25	18.59	21.00
Prices:Low	69.01	66.78	71.65	49.05	59.00	44.50	31.69	15.88	12.94	15.00
P/E Ratio:High	37	33	NM	NM	59	63	42	NM	19	36
P/E Ratio:Low	23	24	NM	NM	35	28	23	NM	13	26

Income Statement Analysis (Million $)										
Revenue	2,319	2,046	1,771	1,425	1,746	1,626	1,452	1,296	1,138	1,147
Operating Income	694	603	39.1	349	404	372	326	294	207	253
Depreciation	78.9	68.3	59.6	45.0	85.5	77.7	73.8	76.5	68.8	72.9
Interest Expense	12.4	18.1	15.6	17.4	21.4	19.8	15.1	16.4	8.90	12.5
Pretax Income	599	532	-29.5	89.8	336	304	269	-57.7	157	108
Effective Tax Rate	32.1%	28.9%	NM	28.0%	32.4%	29.0%	30.0%	NM	18.5%	29.0%
Net Income	404	377	-52.5	64.0	227	215	188	-90.2	128	77.1
S&P Core Earnings	363	339	-87.3	118	187	NA	NA	NA	NA	NA

Balance Sheet & Other Financial Data (Million $)										
Cash	1,296	895	508	774	782	774	163	182	181	112
Current Assets	1,826	1,376	928	1,200	1,325	1,326	698	661	636	600
Total Assets	2,851	2,257	1,755	1,807	2,046	1,971	1,339	1,334	1,390	1,350
Current Liabilities	1,044	460	383	404	490	433	420	369	363	375
Long Term Debt	57.5	570	573	526	521	585	209	201	143	170
Common Equity	1,567	1,116	719	808	977	874	634	696	841	750
Total Capital	1,626	1,689	1,294	1,337	1,499	1,459	843	897	984	921
Capital Expenditures	78.5	96.4	110	78.8	89.9	66.9	63.3	50.6	64.4	59.7
Cash Flow	483	445	7.10	109	312	293	262	-13.7	197	150
Current Ratio	1.7	3.0	2.4	3.0	2.7	3.1	1.7	1.8	1.8	1.6
% Long Term Debt of Capitalization	3.5	33.8	44.3	39.4	34.7	40.1	24.8	22.4	14.5	18.5
% Net Income of Revenue	17.4	18.4	NM	4.5	13.0	13.2	13.0	NM	11.3	6.8
% Return on Assets	15.8	18.8	NM	3.3	11.3	13.0	14.1	NM	9.4	5.8
% Return on Equity	30.1	41.1	NM	7.2	24.5	28.5	28.3	NM	16.1	10.9

Data as orig reptd.; bef. results of disc opers/spec. items. Per share data adj. for stk. divs.; EPS diluted. E-Estimated. NA-Not Available. NM-Not Meaningful. NR-Not Ranked. UR-Under Review.

Office: 2525 Dupont Drive, Irvine, CA 92612.
Telephone: 714-246-4500.
Email: corpinfo@allergan.com
Website: http://www.alergan.com

Chrmn, Pres & CEO: D.E. Pyott
Pres: F.M. Ball
Vice Chrmn: H.W. Boyer
EVP & CFO: J.L. Edwards

EVP, Secy & General Counsel: D.S. Ingram
Investor Contact: J. Hindman (714-246-4636)
Board of Directors: H. W. Boyer, H. E. Evans, M. R. Gallagher, G. S. Herbert, R. A. Ingram, T. M. Jones, L. J. Lavigne, Jr., D. E. Pyott, R. T. Ray, S. J. Ryan, L. D. Shaeffer

Founded: 1948
Domicile: Delaware
Employees: 5,055

Allied Waste Industries Inc.

STANDARD &POOR'S

S&P Recommendation HOLD ★★★★★

Price $12.50 (as of Oct 27, 2006)

12-Mo. Target Price $12.00

Investment Style Mid-Cap Value

GICS Sector Industrials
Sub-Industry Environmental & Facilities Services

Comment This leading waste services company provides collection, recycling and disposal services to residential, commercial and industrial customers in the U.S.

Key Stock Statistics (Source S&P, Vickers, company reports)

52-Wk Range	$14.38–7.91	S&P Oper. EPS 2006**E**	0.49	P/E on S&P Oper. EPS 2006**E**	25.5	Dividend Rate/Share	Nil
Trailing 12-Month EPS	$0.45	S&P Oper. EPS 2007**E**	0.54	Common Shares Outstg. (M)	367.6	Yield (%)	Nil
Trailing 12-Month P/E	27.8	S&P Core EPS 2006**E**	0.49	Market Capitalization(B)	$4.595	Beta	2.11
$10K Invested 5 Yrs Ago	$9,032	S&P Core EPS 2007**E**	0.54	Institutional Ownership (%)	95	S&P Credit Rating	BB

Price Performance

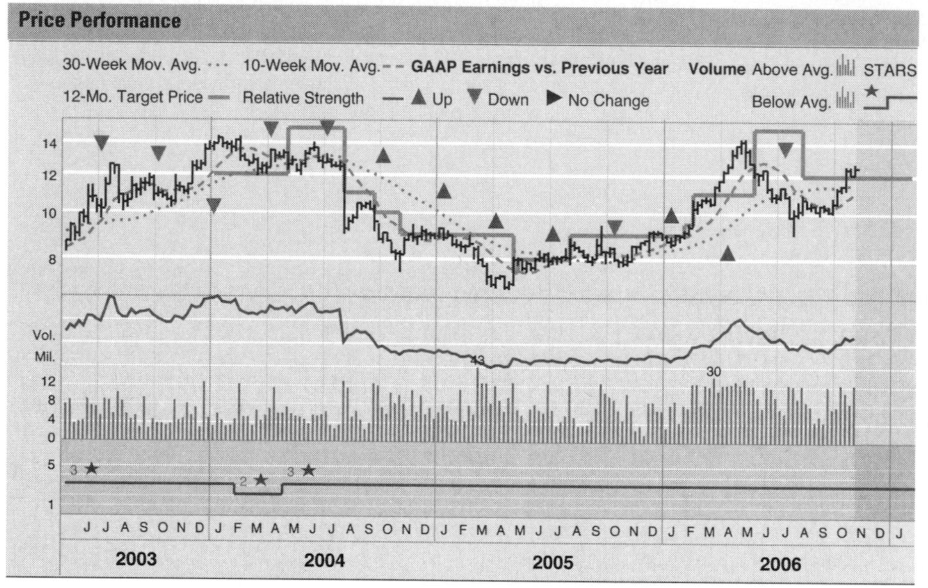

Options: ASE, CBOE, P, Ph

Analysis prepared by **Stewart Scharf** on August 21, 2006, when the stock traded at **$ 10.40**.

Highlights

- We project organic revenue growth of about 7% for 2006, driven by price initiatives and, to a lesser extent, volume growth from new national commercial accounts; price includes a 2% fuel recovery fee, while we expect recycling commodity and special waste prices to remain soft. Core volume growth will likely remain weak, as AW sacrifices market share for higher returns.
- We think 2006 EBITDA margins will widen modestly from 25.6% in 2005, as price hikes and better operating efficiencies outweigh a change in the business mix due to subcontracting costs related to the rollout of a new national account, and higher fuel costs. We see further margin expansion into 2007, on lower maintenance and labor costs, improved productivity, and new employee safety programs. SG&A expense should remain under 10% of revenues.
- We project an effective tax rate of 51% for 2006 as gas credits are phased out, and see EPS of $0.49 (before $0.07 refinancing and other charges, after $0.01 of estimated stock option expense), rising 10%, to $0.54, in 2007.

Investment Rationale/Risk

- We maintain our hold opinion, based primarily on our valuation models, as well as AW's still high leverage ratio.
- Risks to our recommendation and target price include weaker than expected economic growth, an inability to implement sustainable price hikes across the board, a significant market share loss resulting from pricing initiatives, higher than projected repair, fuel and insurance costs, increased debt levels and a decline in free cash flow generation. We have some corporate governance concerns, as the position of chairman and CEO is held by the same person.
- The stock traded recently at about 21X our 2006 EPS estimate, in line with the projected P/E multiple of AW's peers, but well above our forward P/E for the S&P 500. However, our DCF model suggests that the shares are at a 20% discount to their intrinsic value of $13, assuming a terminal growth rate of 3.5% and a weighted average cost of capital (WACC) of 8%. Blending these measures, our 12-month target price is $12.

Qualitative Risk Assessment

LOW	**MEDIUM**	HIGH

Our risk assessment reflects the cyclical nature of the business, volatile energy costs, landfill overcapacity, a high leverage ratio, and concerns related to corporate governance practices, which are offset by what we view as AW's positive cash generation and improving working capital.

Quantitative Evaluations

S&P Quality Ranking B-

D	C	**B-**	B	B+	A-	A	A+

Relative Strength Rank STRONG

87

LOWEST = 1 HIGHEST = 99

Revenue/Earnings Data

Revenue (Million $)

	1Q	2Q	3Q	4Q	Year
2006	1,439	1,541	--	--	--
2005	1,341	1,449	1,477	1,468	5,735
2004	1,275	1,362	1,378	1,347	5,362
2003	1,231	1,343	1,362	1,313	5,248
2002	1,316	1,402	1,429	1,371	5,517
2001	1,354	1,413	1,413	1,385	5,565

Earnings Per Share ($)

2006	0.08	0.08	**E**0.18	**E**0.09	**E**0.49
2005	0.05	0.12	0.10	0.15	0.43
2004	Nil	-0.05	0.13	0.04	0.11
2003	0.07	Nil	0.12	-2.29	-2.36
2002	0.17	0.18	0.23	0.19	0.76
2001	-0.14	0.18	Nil	-0.03	0.01

Fiscal year ended Dec. 31. Next earnings report expected: NA. EPS Estimates based on S&P Operating Earnings; historical GAAP earnings are as reported.

Dividend Data

No cash dividend has been paid.

Allied Waste Industries Inc.

Business Summary August 21, 2006

CORPORATE OVERVIEW. Allied Waste Industries provides non-hazardous waste collection, transfer, recycling and disposal services to 10 million residential, municipal and commercial customers in 37 states. As of July 2006, it had 304 collection companies, 162 transfer stations, 57 recycling facilities, and 169 active landfills in 37 states and Puerto Rico. In 2005, revenues were derived from collection (71%), disposal (22%, including 7.6% from transfer), recycling (commodity; 3.9%), and other (3.2%). Collection operations involve collecting and transporting nonhazardous waste from the point of generation to the transfer station or the site of disposal. A transfer station receives solid waste from third-party and company-owned collection vehicles and then compacts and transfers the waste to specially constructed trailers for transportation to disposal facilities. At June 30, 2006, the customer defection (turnover) rate was near an historical low of less than 8%. The churn (negative spread between price of new work and price of business lost) rate on the commercial business declined to less than 5% from 14% a year earlier.

At June 30, 2006, AW's leverage ratio (debt to EBITDA) was 4.8X, above peer levels, while its interest coverage (EBITDA to interest expense) was 2.4X. We expect free cash flow (FCF) to improve significantly, to about $175 million in 2006, with $100 million slated for debt paydowns and $50 million for preferred dividend payments.

We believe the company will continue to make progress with its strategic turnaround plan, divesting non-core assets and completing asset swaps with its closest competitors Waste Management and Republic Services. In the 2006 first quarter, AW divested seven underperforming operations for $12 million in proceeds, while identifying several other assets for which it is negotiating both divestiture and buy/sell agreements. The company is also implementing changes, including the temporary closing of certain landfills and the divestiture of low density collection routes.

Company Financials

Per Share Data ($) Year Ended Dec. 31	**2005**	**2004**	**2003**	**2002**	**2001**	**2000**	**1999**	**1998**	**1997**	**1996**
Tangible Book Value	NM	NM	NM	NM	NM	NM	NM	NM	NM	NM
Cash Flow	2.11	1.86	2.76	3.33	3.57	3.89	0.13	0.45	1.78	-0.61
Earnings	0.43	0.11	-2.36	0.76	0.01	0.36	-1.33	-0.54	0.57	-1.15
S&P Core Earnings	0.37	0.07	-2.43	0.53	0.13	NA	NA	NA	NA	NA
Dividends	Nil	Nil	Nil	Nil	Nil	Nil	Nil	Nil	Nil	Nil
Payout Ratio	Nil	Nil	Nil	Nil	Nil	Nil	Nil	Nil	Nil	Nil
Prices:High	9.46	14.44	14.05	14.55	19.90	14.75	24.06	31.63	24.38	10.38
Prices:Low	6.90	7.50	7.51	5.54	8.90	5.31	6.50	16.13	7.25	6.44
P/E Ratio:High	22	NM	NM	19	NM	41	NM	NM	43	NM
P/E Ratio:Low	16	NM	NM	7	NM	15	NM	NM	13	NM
Income Statement Analysis (Million $)										
Revenue	5,735	5,362	5,248	5,517	5,565	5,707	3,341	1,576	875	247
Operating Income	1,470	1,446	1,581	1,743	1,931	2,010	1,161	528	300	69.6
Depreciation	554	559	546	496	693	674	273	180	113	31.5
Interest Expense	588	588	707	774	854	882	443	88.4	94.0	9.26
Pretax Income	328	128	202	411	270	381	-227	-54.5	90.7	-66.4
Effective Tax Rate	40.9%	56.6%	44.0%	44.7%	70.7%	62.3%	NM	NM	40.9%	NA
Net Income	194	58.0	111	225	75.5	138	-221	-98.3	53.6	-66.0
S&P Core Earnings	120	26.9	-494	105	28.2	NA	NA	NA	NA	NA
Balance Sheet & Other Financial Data (Million $)										
Cash	56.1	68.0	445	180	159	122	121	39.7	11.9	50.1
Current Assets	920	923	1,286	1,072	1,198	1,272	2,248	500	187	710
Total Assets	13,626	13,440	13,861	13,929	14,347	14,514	14,963	3,753	2,449	2,318
Current Liabilities	1,576	1,757	1,568	1,450	1,434	1,600	2,629	455	233	683
Long Term Debt	6,853	7,429	7,985	8,719	9,238	9,635	9,240	2,119	1,356	1,149
Common Equity	2,526	2,272	2,185	689	586	698	638	930	596	276
Total Capital	10,598	10,242	10,631	11,165	11,411	11,761	11,085	3,049	1,967	1,478
Capital Expenditures	696	583	492	542	501	390	339	302	120	33.0
Cash Flow	696	596	562	644	695	743	24.3	81.7	167	-35.7
Current Ratio	0.6	0.5	0.8	0.7	0.8	0.8	0.9	1.1	0.8	1.0
% Long Term Debt of Capitalization	64.7	72.5	75.1	78.1	81.0	81.9	83.4	69.5	68.9	77.7
% Net Income of Revenue	3.4	1.1	2.1	4.1	1.4	2.4	NM	NM	6.1	NM
% Return on Assets	1.4	0.4	0.8	1.6	0.5	0.9	NM	NM	2.2	NM
% Return on Equity	5.9	1.6	1.1	23.1	0.4	10.4	NM	NM	12.2	NM

Data as orig reptd.; bef. results of disc opers/spec. items. Per share data adj. for stk. divs.; EPS diluted. E-Estimated. NA-Not Available. NM-Not Meaningful. NR-Not Ranked. UR-Under Review.

Office: 15880 North Greenway-Hayden Loop, Scottsdale, AZ 85260-1649.
Telephone: 480-627-2700.
Email: info@awin.com
Website: http://www.alliedwaste.com

Chrmn & CEO: J.J. Zillmer
Pres & COO: D.W. Slager
EVP & CFO: P.S. Hathaway
EVP, Secy & General Counsel: S.M. Helm

Investor Contact: M. Burnett (480-627-2785)
Board of Directors: R. M. Agate, C. H. Cotros, J. W. Crownover, S. Drescher, D. I. Foley, J. J. Harris, D. R. Hendrix, N. Lehmann, S. Martinez, J. A. Quella, J. J. Zillmer

Founded: 1987
Domicile: Delaware
Employees: 26,000

Allstate Corp (The)

STANDARD &POOR'S

S&P Recommendation STRONG BUY ★★★★★

Price $61.74 (as of Oct 27, 2006)

12-Mo. Target Price $75.00

Investment Style Large-Cap Value

GICS Sector Financials
Sub-Industry Property & Casualty Insurance

Comment Allstate, the second largest U.S. personal lines property-casualty insurer, has expanded into the life insurance and retirement savings arena.

Key Stock Statistics (Source S&P, Vickers, company reports)

52-Wk Range	**$64.50–50.22**	S&P Oper. EPS 2006**E**	**7.35**	P/E on S&P Oper. EPS 2006**E**	**8.4**	Dividend Rate/Share	**$1.40**
Trailing 12-Month EPS	**$7.47**	S&P Oper. EPS 2007**E**	**7.60**	Common Shares Outstg. (M)	**629.5**	Yield (%)	**2.27**
Trailing 12-Month P/E	**8.3**	S&P Core EPS 2006**E**	**7.12**	Market Capitalization(B)	**$38.866**	Beta	**0.65**
$10K Invested 5 Yrs Ago	**$21,397**	S&P Core EPS 2007**E**	**7.37**	Institutional Ownership (%)	**67**	S&P Credit Rating	**A+**

Price Performance

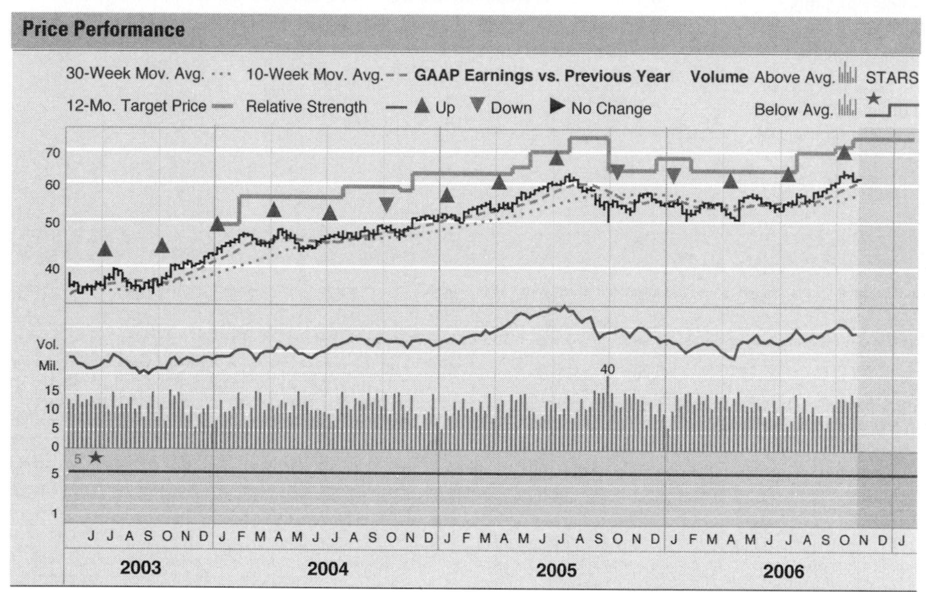

Options: ASE, CBOE, P, Ph

Analysis prepared by **Cathy A. Seifert** on October 25, 2006, when the stock traded at **$ 61.71**.

Highlights

- We expect operating revenue growth of 5% in 2006, reflecting an estimated increase of less than 5% in property-casualty earned premiums, flat to very little growth of financial services revenues, and a mid- to high-single digit increase in net investment income. Premium growth in 2007 is projected to benefit from a modest firming of insurance rates that we believe will begin to emerge in 2006, partly offset by the impact of reinsurance as ALL seeks to reduce its catastrophe risk.
- The rebound in underwriting results and profitability that we anticipate for 2006 is skewed by nearly $5.7 billion of catastrophe losses ALL incurred in 2005.
- We estimate 2006 operating EPS of $7.35, and 2007 operating EPS of $7.60, versus the $2.37 of operating EPS that ALL reported for 2005. Our operating EPS estimates assume a "normal" level of catastrophe losses and modestly firmer premium rates in the wake of record catastrophe claims in 2004 and 2005.

Investment Rationale/Risk

- We have a strong buy recommendation on the shares of this leading property-casualty insurer, which outperformed the broader market averages in 2005 and year-to-date through late October 2006, despite ALL's significant exposure to Hurricane Katrina, et al. ALL's results, excluding catastrophes, are being aided by what we view as a continued underlying improvement in core personal lines underwriting results.
- Risks to our opinion and target price include a sharp rise in loss costs and greatly increased premium price competition.
- Our favorable outlook is tempered by the near-term uncertainty surrounding the degree to which ALL will be able to leverage its exposure to hurricane losses into a stronger rate of premium increases. However, we believe ALL's underlying fundamentals are improving. In our opinion, the shares deserve an expansion of their current discounted forward P/E. Our 12-month target price of $75 assumes the shares trade at 9.9X our 2007 EPS estimate of $7.60, still a discount to many of ALL's peers.

Qualitative Risk Assessment

LOW | **MEDIUM** | HIGH

Our risk assessment reflects our view of ALL as a solid underwriter with sound risk management and capital management practices and a diversified base of business, offset by our concern over the company's exposure to catastrophe losses.

Quantitative Evaluations

S&P Quality Ranking **B**

D | C | B- | **B** | B+ | A- | A | A+

Relative Strength Rank **MODERATE**

51

LOWEST = 1 HIGHEST = 99

Revenue/Earnings Data

Revenue (Million $)

	1Q	2Q	3Q	4Q	Year
2006	9,081	8,875	8,738	--	--
2005	8,705	8,791	8,942	8,945	35,383
2004	8,311	8,304	8,442	8,879	33,936
2003	7,861	7,899	8,127	8,262	32,149
2002	7,298	7,455	7,239	7,587	29,579
2001	7,131	7,203	7,173	7,358	28,865

Earnings Per Share ($)

2006	2.19	1.89	1.83	**E**1.46	**E**7.35
2005	1.64	1.71	-2.36	1.59	2.64
2004	1.59	1.47	0.09	1.64	4.79
2003	0.94	0.84	0.98	1.09	3.85
2002	0.60	0.48	0.35	0.63	1.13
2001	0.69	0.23	0.32	0.37	1.61

Fiscal year ended Dec. 31. Next earnings report expected: Early February. EPS Estimates based on S&P Operating Earnings; historical GAAP earnings are as reported.

Dividend Data (Dates: mm/dd Payment Date: mm/dd/yy)

Amount ($)	Date Decl.	Ex-Div. Date	Stk. of Record	Payment Date
0.320	11/08	11/28	11/30	01/03/06
0.350	02/21	03/08	03/10	04/03/06
0.350	05/16	05/26	05/31	07/03/06
0.350	07/18	08/29	08/31	10/02/06

Dividends have been paid since 1993. Source: Company reports.

Allstate Corp (The)

Business Summary October 25, 2006

Established in 1931 by Sears, Roebuck & Co., Allstate is the second largest U.S. personal lines property-casualty insurer (based on earned premiums), and the 13th largest life insurer (based on life insurance in force). It writes business mainly through 12,500 exclusive agencies. ALL has also implemented a multi-access distribution model designed to allow customers to purchase company products through agents, over the Internet, via telephone, and through The Good Hands Network. ALL became an independent company in June 1995, when Sears, Roebuck & Co. spun off its 80% interest in the company.

The company's primary business is the sale of private passenger automobile and homeowners insurance, and it maintains national market shares of about 11% to 12% in each of these lines. ALL is licensed to write policies in all 50 states, the District of Columbia, Puerto Rico, and Canada. In 2005, property-liability net written premiums equaled $27.4 billion, up from the $26.5 billion in net written premiums recorded in 2004. Of the 2005 total, standard automobile policies accounted for 60%, non-standard automobile policies 6%, homeowners' coverage 24%, and other lines 10%. Property-liability premiums earned increased 3.9% in 2005, to $27.0 billion. Underwriting results in 2005 and 2004 were affected by catastrophe losses. As a result, the combined loss and expense ratio deteriorated to 102.4% in 2005, from 93.0% in 2004.

Allstate Financial (formerly Allstate Life) offers an array of life insurance, annuity, savings and investment and pension products through Allstate agents, financial institutions, independent agents and brokers, and direct marketing. Total premiums and contract charges declined 1.1% in 2005, to $2.05 billion from $2.07 billion. Of the 2005 total, traditional life insurance accounted for 14%, immediate annuities 10%, accident/health 21%, interest-sensitive life 38%, fixed annuities 3% and variable annuities 14%.

Company Financials

Per Share Data ($) Year Ended Dec. 31	**2005**	**2004**	**2003**	**2002**	**2001**	**2000**	**1999**	**1998**	**1997**	**1996**
Tangible Book Value	29.97	30.74	27.89	23.52	22.35	22.26	21.09	21.08	18.37	15.24
Operating Earnings	NA	NA	3.77	2.94	2.06	2.68	2.59	3.08	2.78	1.79
Earnings	2.64	4.79	3.85	1.13	1.61	2.95	3.38	3.94	3.56	2.32
S&P Core Earnings	2.21	4.33	3.82	2.64	1.66	NA	NA	NA	NA	NA
Dividends	1.28	1.12	0.92	0.84	0.76	0.68	0.58	0.52	0.48	0.43
Relative Payout	48%	23%	24%	74%	47%	23%	17%	13%	14%	18%
Prices:High	63.22	51.99	43.27	41.95	45.90	44.75	41.00	52.38	47.19	30.44
Prices:Low	49.66	42.55	30.05	31.03	30.00	17.19	22.88	36.06	28.13	18.69
P/E Ratio:High	24	11	11	37	29	15	12	13	13	13
P/E Ratio:Low	19	9	8	27	19	6	7	9	8	8
Income Statement Analysis (Million $)										
Life Insurance in Force	NA	NA	409,068	396,943	387,039	367,914	334,895	276,032	247,192	NA
Premium Income:Life A & H	27,039	25,989	24,677	23,361	2,230	2,205	1,623	1,519	1,502	1,336
Premium Income:Casualty/Property.	2,049	2,072	2,304	2,293	22,197	21,871	20,112	19,307	18,604	18,366
Net Investment Income	5,746	5,284	4,972	4,854	4,796	4,633	4,112	3,890	3,861	3,813
Total Revenue	35,383	33,936	32,149	29,579	28,865	29,134	26,959	25,879	24,949	24,299
Pretax Income	2,088	4,586	3,566	868	1,240	3,006	3,868	4,716	4,429	2,694
Net Operating Income	NA	NA	2,662	2,075	1,492	2,004	2,082	2,573	2,429	1,600
Net Income	1,765	3,356	2,720	803	1,167	2,211	2,720	3,294	3,105	2,075
S&P Core Earnings	1,487	3,028	2,692	1,879	1,201	NA	NA	NA	NA	NA
Balance Sheet & Other Financial Data (Million $)										
Cash & Equivalent	1,387	1,428	1,434	1,408	1,146	1,164	1,066	1,009	220	831
Premiums Due	4,739	4,721	4,386	6,958	6,674	3,802	3,927	3,082	NA	2,691
Investment Assets:Bonds	98,065	95,715	87,741	77,152	65,720	60,758	55,286	53,560	50,860	47,095
Investment Assets:Stocks	6,164	5,895	5,288	3,683	5,245	6,086	6,738	6,421	6,765	5,561
Investment Assets:Loans	8,748	7,856	6,539	6,092	5,710	4,599	4,068	3,458	3,002	3,146
Investment Assets:Total	118,297	115,530	103,081	90,650	79,876	74,483	69,645	66,525	8,000	58,329
Deferred Policy Costs	5,802	4,968	4,842	4,385	4,421	4,309	4,119	3,096	2,826	2,614
Total Assets	156,072	149,725	134,142	117,426	109,175	104,808	98,119	87,691	80,918	74,508
Debt	4,887	5,291	5,073	4,161	3,894	3,862	3,150	2,103	2,446	1,386
Common Equity	20,186	21,823	20,565	34,128	17,196	17,451	16,601	17,240	15,610	13,452
Combined Loss-Expense Ratio	102.4	93.0	94.6	98.9	102.9	99.2	97.4	93.2	94.0	100.5
% Return on Revenue	5.0	9.9	8.5	2.7	4.0	7.6	10.1	12.7	12.4	8.6
% Return on Equity	8.4	15.8	14.3	2.4	6.7	13.0	16.1	20.1	21.4	12.3
% Investment Yield	4.9	4.8	5.1	5.7	6.2	6.4	6.0	10.4	6.4	6.7

Data as orig reptd.; bef. results of disc opers/spec. items. Per share data adj. for stk. divs.; EPS diluted. E-Estimated. NA-Not Available. NM-Not Meaningful. NR-Not Ranked. UR-Under Review.

Office: 2775 Sanders Road, Northbrook, IL 60062-6127.
Telephone: 800-574-3553.
Website: http://www.allstate.com
Chrmn & CEO: E.M. Liddy

Pres & COO: T. Wilson
SVP & CIO: C. Brune
Investor Contact: D.L. Hale (800 416 8803)
VP & CFO: D.L. Hale

Board of Directors: D. Ackerman, J. G. Andress, R. D. Beyer, E. A. Brennan, W. J. Farrell, J. M. Greenberg, R. T. LeMay, E. M. Liddy, J. C. Reyes, H. J. Riley, Jr., J. I. Smith, J. A. Sprieser, M. A. Taylor, T. J. Wilson

Founded: 1953
Domicile: Delaware
Employees: 39,500

ALLTEL Corp

STANDARD &POOR'S

S&P Recommendation HOLD ★★★☆☆

Price $53.99 (as of Oct 27, 2006)

12-Mo. Target Price $56.00

Investment Style Large-Cap Value

GICS Sector Telecommunication Services
Sub-Industry Wireless Telecommunication Services

Comment This rural wireless company, based in Arkansas, acquired Western Wireless in August 2005 and spun off its wireline assets in July 2006 in a stock dividend.

Key Stock Statistics (Source S&P, Vickers, company reports)

52-Wk Range	$68.19–52.34	S&P Oper. EPS 2006E	3.05	P/E on S&P Oper. EPS 2006E	17.7	Dividend Rate/Share	$0.50
Trailing 12-Month EPS	$3.52	S&P Oper. EPS 2007E	3.00	Common Shares Outstg. (M)	388.1	Yield (%)	0.93
Trailing 12-Month P/E	15.3	S&P Core EPS 2006E	2.95	Market Capitalization(B)	$20.956	Beta	1.19
$10K Invested 5 Yrs Ago	$12,559	S&P Core EPS 2007E	2.95	Institutional Ownership (%)	71	S&P Credit Rating	A-

Price Performance

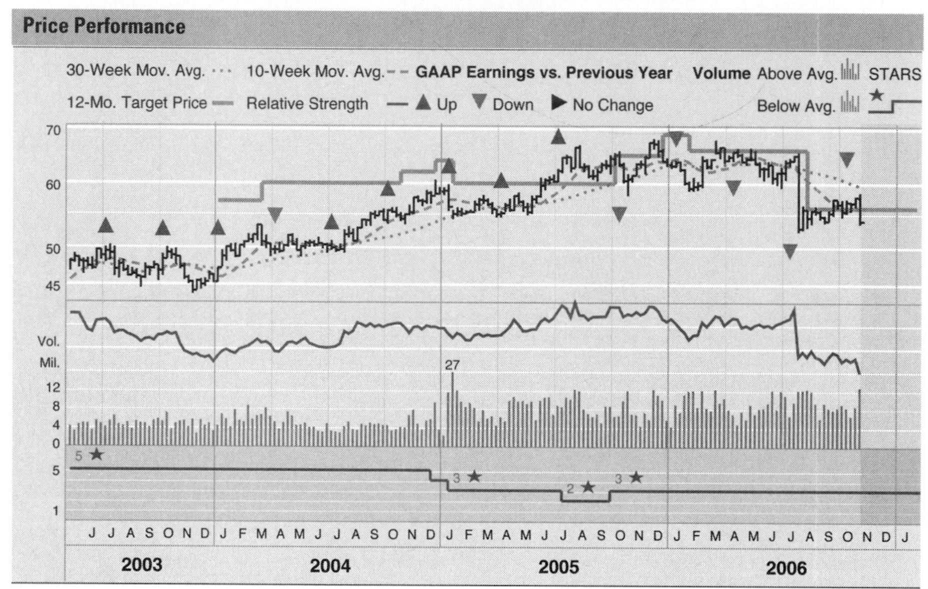

Options: ASE, CBOE, P, Ph

Analysis prepared by **Todd Rosenbluth** on August 07, 2006, when the stock traded at **$ 54.49**.

Highlights

- Including $1.4 billion in wireline revenues that were a part of AT in the first half of 2006, we forecast 2006 revenues of $9.3 billion. We see growth from the remaining wireless business being aided by previously made acquisitions, organic customer growth from new service offerings, and roaming revenues. We forecast revenues of $8.8 billion in 2007.
- We look for consolidated 2006 EBITDA margins of 36%, which we see helped by the wider margin wireline assets. In the second half of 2006 and on average in 2007, we expect wireless margins of 33% due to AT's increased dependence on prepaid services and our expectation of higher advertising and handset subsidies.
- We expect AT to help offset the loss of high margin wireline assets through its share repurchase program. We project operating EPS of $3.05 in 2006 and $3.00 in 2007. Our S&P Core EPS estimates reflect pension adjustments. First half 2006 EPS includes a net benefit of $0.12 for the sale of rural phone bank assets counterbalanced by one-time wireless amortization costs.

Investment Rationale/Risk

- Following the spin-off of its wireline assets, completed in July, we believe AT is better positioned to benefit from the growth in wireless usage. We believe its roaming partnerships will help to offset some of the challenges we believe the company faces being a mid-size carrier, in an industry dominated by four larger players that have greater scale. We also see a reduced debt load helping support its network buildout.
- Risks to our recommendation and target price include pricing pressure from competitors, weaker than expected customer growth, and a shift in strategy toward becoming more aggressive in its marketing efforts that would reduce EBITDA.
- We view positively AT's previous success in its integration of acquisitions and its strong dividend history. Our 12-month target price of $56 is derived from a P/E of 18.5X, slightly higher than peer averages, given what we see as less integration challenges than peers. AT's dividend yield provides additional downside support to its share price, in our view.

Qualitative Risk Assessment

LOW | **MEDIUM** | HIGH

Our risk assessment reflects the competitive nature of the wireless markets the company serves, offset by AT's history of dividend payments, and our view of its average debt load.

Quantitative Evaluations

S&P Quality Ranking B+

D | C | B- | B | **B+** | A- | A | A+

Relative Strength Rank WEAK

15

LOWEST = 1 HIGHEST = 99

Revenue/Earnings Data

Revenue (Million $)

	1Q	2Q	3Q	4Q	Year
2006	2,540	2,674	2,007	--	--
2005	2,126	2,260	2,519	2,582	9,487
2004	1,961	2,042	2,103	2,140	8,246
2003	1,906	2,010	2,050	2,014	7,980
2002	1,833	1,924	2,082	2,144	7,983
2001	1,853	1,920	1,899	1,927	7,599

Earnings Per Share ($)

	1Q	2Q	3Q	4Q	Year
2006	0.72	1.12	0.43	E0.62	E3.05
2005	1.03	1.27	0.91	0.67	3.80
2004	0.61	0.85	0.99	0.89	3.33
2003	0.73	0.72	0.78	0.83	3.05
2002	0.68	0.69	0.76	0.82	2.96
2001	1.19	0.70	0.71	0.74	3.34

Fiscal year ended Dec. 31. Next earnings report expected: Mid January. EPS Estimates based on S&P Operating Earnings; historical GAAP earnings are as reported.

Dividend Data (Dates: mm/dd Payment Date: mm/dd/yy)

Amount ($)	Date Decl.	Ex-Div. Date	Stk. of Record	Payment Date
Stk.	06/30	07/18	07/12	07/17/06
.048 Ext.	07/20	09/06	09/08	10/03/06
0.125	07/20	09/06	09/08	10/03/06
0.125	10/19	12/06	12/08	01/03/07

Dividends have been paid since 1961. Source: Company reports.

Please read the Required Disclosures and Analyst Certification on the last page of this report.

ALLTEL Corp

Business Summary August 07, 2006

CORPORATE OVERVIEW. ALLTEL Corp.'s wireless telephone services, which accounted for 67% of operating profits in the first half of 2006, are the fifth largest in the U.S. At the end of June 2006, AT provided wireless communications service to 11.1 million customers, had monthly customer churn of 1.9%, and generated monthly revenue per user of $53. In July 2006, AT spun off its wireline operations, the second largest independent local telephone service provider in the U.S., and merged them with VALOR Communications to form Windstream Corp. (WIN: $13). ALLTEL shareholders received 1.03 shares of VALOR stock for each share of ALLTEL they owned.

CORPORATE STRATEGY. In the second half of 2005, ALLTEL acquired wireless assets, including the August acquisition of Western Wireless Corp. (WWCA) for $6 billion and the September wireless asset swap with U.S. Cellular; the November 2006 planned acquisition of Midwest Wireless Holdings LLC for $1 billion was still waiting for necessary approvals as of August 2006. Operating in some of the smaller U.S. markets, AT has aimed to be the roaming partner of choice for the four national wireless carriers, reaching 95% of the population, in addition to looking to grow its own customer base. We believe these acquisitions paved the way for AT's decision to spin off its wireline assets. As a pure wireless company, we believe AT can better benefit from the industry-wide trend that has some customers eliminating their local phone line and using wireless plans to make their calls.

MARKET PROFILE. The four national carriers that AT competes with in its U.S. metropolitan markets have greater marketing and capital spending budgets that we believe allows them to be more aggressive than AT in discounting service plans and offering handset subsidies to add customers. Intense wireless rivalry has raised the level of competition with new service plans, messaging and data services, and game and ring-tone features. More than 65% of the population has subscribed to the services, and we believe that affordable prepaid service plans and network reliability may drive a higher penetration of wireline substitution.

Company Financials

Per Share Data ($) Year Ended Dec. 31	**2005**	**2004**	**2003**	**2002**	**2001**	**2000**	**1999**	**1998**	**1997**	**1996**
Tangible Book Value	5.63	3.13	2.65	NM	6.87	5.92	7.03	5.95	8.67	8.88
Cash Flow	7.28	2.22	7.04	6.73	7.07	9.39	5.19	4.44	5.10	3.77
Earnings	3.80	3.33	3.05	2.96	3.34	6.20	2.59	1.89	2.70	1.53
S&P Core Earnings	3.31	3.26	2.97	2.75	2.46	NA	NA	NA	NA	NA
Dividends	1.53	1.49	1.42	1.37	1.33	1.29	1.22	1.16	1.12	1.05
Payout Ratio	40%	45%	47%	46%	40%	21%	47%	61%	41%	69%
Prices:High	68.19	60.62	56.22	63.25	68.69	82.94	91.81	61.38	41.63	35.63
Prices:Low	54.20	46.65	40.68	35.33	49.43	47.75	56.31	38.25	29.75	26.63
P/E Ratio:High	18	18	18	21	21	13	35	32	15	23
P/E Ratio:Low	14	14	13	12	15	8	22	20	11	17

Income Statement Analysis (Million $)										
Revenue	9,487	8,246	7,980	7,983	7,599	7,067	6,302	5,194	3,264	3,192
Depreciation	1,483	1,300	1,248	1,179	1,168	988	862	707	451	424
Maintenance	NA	NA	NA	NA	NA	NA	NA	NA	NA	147
Construction Credits	NA	NA	NA	NA	NA	NA	NA	NA	NA	NA
Effective Tax Rate	36.8%	33.8%	36.0%	35.2%	38.6%	40.2%	37.8%	41.6%	36.9%	36.8%
Net Income	1,309	1,027	954	924	1,048	1,965	784	525	508	292
S&P Core Earnings	1,143	1,005	929	859	772	NA	NA	NA	NA	NA

Balance Sheet & Other Financial Data (Million $)										
Gross Property	17,498	15,836	14,910	14,768	13,082	12,113	10,291	8,233	5,531	5,114
Net Property	8,064	7,548	7,621	7,709	6,781	6,549	5,735	4,828	3,190	3,042
Capital Expenditures	1,302	1,125	161	1,194	1,232	1,165	1,006	869	546	464
Total Capital	20,659	14,196	14,021	13,302	10,165	9,924	9,015	7,701	4,754	4,535
Fixed Charges Coverage	6.7	5.5	5.3	5.3	6.9	12.1	5.8	4.6	5.4	5.3
Capitalization:Long Term Debt	5,783	5,352	5,581	6,146	3,862	4,612	3,750	3,492	1,874	1,756
Capitalization:Preferred	0.30	0.30	0.40	0.40	0.40	0.50	2.05	14.0	14.8	15.7
Capitalization:Common	13,015	7,128	7,022	5,998	5,565	5,095	4,205	3,262	2,199	2,088
% Return on Revenue	13.8	12.5	11.9	11.6	13.8	27.8	12.4	10.1	15.6	9.1
% Return on Invested Capital	10.1	10.7	10.3	12.4	14.9	25.3	14.3	23.7	16.6	16.2
% Return on Common Equity	13.0	14.5	14.6	16.0	19.7	42.3	20.0	19.2	23.6	14.5
% Earned on Net Property	46.5	43.1	41.7	42.9	43.9	43.7	45.1	47.5	24.5	23.4
% Long Term Debt of Capitalization	30.8	42.9	44.3	50.6	41.0	47.5	47.1	51.6	45.8	45.4
Capital % Preferred	0.0	0.0	0.0	0.0	0.0	0.0	0.0	0.2	0.4	0.6
Capitalization:% Common	69.2	57.1	55.7	49.4	59.0	52.5	52.8	48.2	53.8	54.0

Data as orig reptd.; bef. results of disc opers/spec. items. Per share data adj. for stk. divs.; EPS diluted. E-Estimated. NA-Not Available. NM-Not Meaningful. NR-Not Ranked. UR-Under Review.

Office: One Allied Drive, Little Rock, AR 72202.
Telephone: 501-905-8000.
Website: http://www.alltel.com
Chrmn: J.T. Ford

Pres & CEO: S.T. Ford
EVP & CFO: S.S. Gasaway
EVP, Secy & General Counsel: R.N. Massey
Investor Contact: J.A. Ebner

Board of Directors: J. R. Belk, P. A. Bridgman, W. H. Crown, J. T. Ford, S. T. Ford, L. L. Gellerstedt III, E. A. Mahony, Jr., J. P. McConnell, J. C. Natori, G. W. Penske, J. W. Stanton, W. A. Stephens, R. Townsend

Founded: 1954
Domicile: Delaware
Employees: 21,373

Altera Corp

STANDARD &POOR'S

S&P Recommendation HOLD ★★★★★

Price $17.94 (as of Oct 27, 2006)

12-Mo. Target Price $25.00

Investment Style Mid-Cap Growth

GICS Sector Information Technology
Sub-Industry Semiconductors

Comment ALTR is one of the largest makers of high-performance, high-density programmable logic devices (PLDs) and associated computer-aided engineering logic development tools.

Key Stock Statistics (Source S&P, Vickers, company reports)

52-Wk Range	$22.29–15.54	S&P Oper. EPS 2006E	0.82	P/E on S&P Oper. EPS 2006E	21.9	Dividend Rate/Share	Nil
Trailing 12-Month EPS	$0.76	S&P Oper. EPS 2007E	1.10	Common Shares Outstg. (M)	361.8	Yield (%)	Nil
Trailing 12-Month P/E	23.6	S&P Core EPS 2006E	0.82	Market Capitalization(B)	$6.490	Beta	2.55
$10K Invested 5 Yrs Ago	$8,211	S&P Core EPS 2007E	1.10	Institutional Ownership (%)	90	S&P Credit Rating	NA

Price Performance

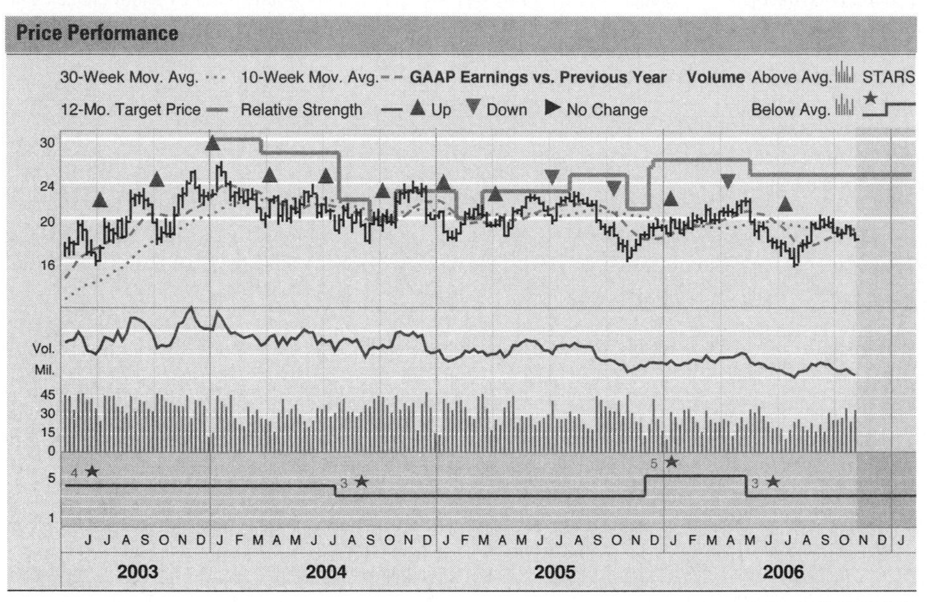

Options: ASE, CBOE, P, Ph

Analysis prepared by **Thomas W. Smith, CFA** on August 10, 2006, when the stock traded at **$ 17.92**.

Highlights

- We forecast sales growth of 18% for 2006 and 16% for 2007. We believe programmable chip makers such as ALTR should be able to outgrow the overall semiconductor industry sales pace of 10% that we foresee for 2006 and for 2007. Supply chain constraints that developed in the first quarter are fading away, in our view.
- We believe the company's new products should continue to drive growth in consumer, industrial and automotive markets, some of which represent new markets for Altera. In particular, we think that the Stratix and Cyclone products are attracting business from new customers.
- We see gross margins narrowing about 1%, to 66%, in 2006 and 2007, as new product rollouts and the inclusion of stock-based compensation that is in line with a new accounting rule add to costs. We also expect R&D and SG&A costs to increase as a percentage of sales in 2006. We project 2006 operating EPS of $0.82, including projected stock option expense, and $1.10 for 2007.

Investment Rationale/Risk

- We have a hold opinion on the shares following a May 8 announcement that management is self-initiating a review of stock option pricing practices for the period 1996-2000. The review made ALTR unable to file its Form 10-Q report for the first quarter. The preliminary results for the second quarter reported sales but, but did not have EPS. We think it is unlikely that the review will result in material changes to past earnings. However, we believe the review is dampening investor sentiment.
- Risks to our opinion and target price include possible sudden downturns in demand for semiconductors, a reliance on chip foundry partners overseas for production, and stock option expense levels that we view as above those of most companies.
- Our 12-month target price of $25 for these volatile shares is based mainly on our historical price-to-sales (P/S) analysis. In arriving at our target price, we applied a target P/S ratio of 7X, below the norm over the past three years, to our 2006 sales per share estimate of $3.59.

Qualitative Risk Assessment

LOW | **MEDIUM** | HIGH

Our risk assessment reflects our view that Altera is subject to the sales swings of the semiconductor industry and competition from a larger rival. It pays no dividend and the shares have above-average price volatility, as indicated by a high beta. This is offset by a lack of debt and participation in a high-growth niche market.

Quantitative Evaluations

S&P Quality Ranking **B**

D | C | B- | **B** | B+ | A- | A | A+

Relative Strength Rank **WEAK**

18

LOWEST = 1 HIGHEST = 99

Revenue/Earnings Data

Revenue (Million $)

	1Q	2Q	3Q	4Q	Year
2006	292.8	334.1	--	--	--
2005	264.8	285.5	291.5	281.9	1,124
2004	242.9	269.0	264.6	239.9	1,016
2003	195.1	205.3	209.5	217.4	827.2
2002	172.0	178.9	180.1	180.7	711.7
2001	287.4	215.3	174.2	162.5	839.4

Earnings Per Share ($)

2006	0.16	0.21	**E**0.21	**E**0.24	**E**0.82
2005	0.17	0.18	0.21	0.19	0.74
2004	0.15	0.20	0.22	0.15	0.72
2003	0.08	0.09	0.11	0.12	0.40
2002	0.05	0.06	0.06	0.07	0.23
2001	0.16	-0.23	0.05	-0.09	-0.10

Fiscal year ended Dec. 31. Next earnings report expected: Late January. EPS Estimates based on S&P Operating Earnings; historical GAAP earnings are as reported.

Dividend Data

No cash dividends have been paid.

Altera Corp

Business Summary August 10, 2006

Altera Corp. is a worldwide supplier of programmable logic devices (PLDs), HardCopy brand structured application-specific integrated circuits (ASICs), pre-defined design building blocks known as intellectual property cores, and associated software for logic development. PLDs are a high-growth category of semiconductors that address many applications in the communications, computer peripheral, consumer and industrial markets. PLDs offer high speed, high density, and low power characteristics. We believe competitive advantages offered to electronic system manufacturers by its products include enhanced design flexibility, shorter design cycles, lower up-front development costs, and the ability to get end-products to market faster, which can lead to significant cost savings for the customer. Drawbacks to PLDs compared to traditional application specific integrated circuits (ASICs) include larger die size and higher cost per chip.

The company's PLDs are standard products, shipped blank for user programming. They are programmed at the customer's PC or workstation, using ALTR's proprietary software. Since the company's chips are programmed at a desktop and not at a foundry, product time to market is dramatically shortened. In addition, because ALTR's integrated circuits are standard products, inventory risks are minimized for both the company and customers. The HardCopy product line assists customers who use PLDs for prototyping ASIC chips in converting the design for low cost production of non-programmable ASIC products.

In 2005, sales were as follows: 42% (40% in 2004) communications end-markets, 32% (35%) industrial, 16% (14%) consumer, and 10% (11%) computer and storage. Sales from the new product category rose 73% in 2005 and comprised 43% of total sales in the year (27% in 2004).

Company Financials

Per Share Data ($) Year Ended Dec. 31	**2005**	**2004**	**2003**	**2002**	**2001**	**2000**	**1999**	**1998**	**1997**	**1996**
Tangible Book Value	3.52	3.42	2.93	2.95	2.89	3.21	2.82	2.26	1.49	1.03
Cash Flow	0.82	0.80	0.51	0.36	0.04	1.29	0.61	0.45	0.44	0.36
Earnings	0.74	0.72	0.40	0.23	-0.10	1.19	0.54	0.39	0.39	0.30
S&P Core Earnings	0.55	0.48	0.19	-0.02	-0.28	NA	NA	NA	NA	NA
Dividends	Nil	Nil	Nil	Nil	Nil	Nil	Nil	Nil	Nil	Nil
Payout Ratio	Nil	Nil	Nil	Nil	Nil	Nil	Nil	Nil	Nil	Nil
Prices:High	22.99	26.82	25.64	26.18	34.69	67.13	34.28	15.47	16.44	9.98
Prices:Low	15.96	17.50	10.30	8.32	14.66	19.63	11.97	7.06	7.59	3.28
P/E Ratio:High	31	37	64	NM	NM	56	63	40	42	34
P/E Ratio:Low	22	24	26	NM	NM	16	22	18	20	11

Income Statement Analysis (Million $)	2005	2004	2003	2002	2001	2000	1999	1998	1997	1996
Revenue	1,124	1,016	827	712	839	1,377	837	654	631	497
Operating Income	352	345	243	146	48.8	598	335	262	254	189
Depreciation	29.4	30.5	45.3	48.5	54.3	40.1	29.4	30.0	27.1	20.9
Interest Expense	Nil	Nil	Nil	Nil	Nil	Nil	Nil	6.36	11.7	12.3
Pretax Income	357	331	213	123	-13.0	744	335	234	230	169
Effective Tax Rate	21.9%	16.8%	27.0%	26.0%	NM	33.2%	33.2%	34.0%	34.0%	35.5%
Net Income	279	275	155	91.3	-39.8	497	224	154	152	109
S&P Core Earnings	205	182	70.7	-8.66	-106	NA	NA	NA	NA	NA

Balance Sheet & Other Financial Data (Million $)	2005	2004	2003	2002	2001	2000	1999	1998	1997	1996
Cash	788	580	259	255	145	496	164	131	22.8	281
Current Assets	1,495	1,537	1,270	1,176	1,129	1,769	1,107	800	616	473
Total Assets	1,823	1,747	1,488	1,372	1,361	2,004	1,440	1,093	953	778
Current Liabilities	555	468	385	241	247	756	322	212	186	178
Long Term Debt	3.87	Nil	Nil	Nil	Nil	Nil	Nil	Nil	230	230
Common Equity	1,326	1,279	1,102	1,131	1,115	1,248	1,118	882	537	370
Total Capital	1,330	1,279	1,102	1,131	1,115	1,248	1,118	882	767	600
Capital Expenditures	25.9	24.7	13.9	9.87	65.8	87.5	29.8	24.0	80.9	45.2
Cash Flow	308	306	200	140	14.5	537	253	184	179	130
Current Ratio	2.7	3.3	3.3	4.9	4.6	2.3	3.4	3.8	3.3	2.7
% Long Term Debt of Capitalization	0.3	Nil	Nil	Nil	Nil	Nil	Nil	Nil	30.0	38.3
% Net Income of Revenue	24.8	27.1	18.8	12.8	NM	36.1	26.8	23.6	24.0	21.9
% Return on Assets	15.5	17.1	10.9	6.7	NM	28.9	17.7	15.1	17.5	14.6
% Return on Equity	21.0	23.1	13.9	8.1	NM	42.0	22.4	21.8	33.4	34.9

Data as orig reptd.; bef. results of disc opers/spec. items. Per share data adj. for stk. divs.; EPS diluted. E-Estimated. NA-Not Available. NM-Not Meaningful. NR-Not Ranked. UR-Under Review.

Office: 101 Innovation Drive, San Jose, CA 95134.
Telephone: 408-544-7000.
Email: inv_rel@altera.com
Website: http://www.altera.com

Chrmn, Pres & CEO: J.P. Daane
Vice Chrmn: R.W. Reed
COO & EVP: D.M. Berlan
VP, CFO, Chief Acctg Officer & Cntlr: J.W. Callas

VP, Secy & General Counsel: K.E. Schuelke
Investor Contact: S. Wylie (408-544-6996)
Board of Directors: J. P. Daane, R. J. Finocchio, Jr., K. McGarity, P. Newhagen, R. W. Reed, W. E. Terry, S. Wang

Founded: 1983
Domicile: Delaware
Employees: 2,361

Altria Group Inc.

STANDARD &POOR'S

S&P Recommendation STRONG BUY ★★★★★

Price $81.85 (as of Oct 27, 2006)

12-Mo. Target Price $97.00

Investment Style Large-Cap Growth

GICS Sector Consumer Staples
Sub-Industry Tobacco

Comment Altria Group (formerly Philip Morris Companies) is the world's largest cigarette producer and the largest U.S. food processor (Kraft Foods).

Key Stock Statistics (Source S&P, Vickers, company reports)

52-Wk Range	$85.00–68.36	S&P Oper. EPS 2006E	5.50	P/E on S&P Oper. EPS 2006E	14.9	Dividend Rate/Share	$3.44
Trailing 12-Month EPS	$5.40	S&P Oper. EPS 2007E	5.70	Common Shares Outstg. (M)	2,093.5	Yield (%)	4.20
Trailing 12-Month P/E	15.2	S&P Core EPS 2006E	5.25	Market Capitalization(B)	$171.349	Beta	0.76
$10K Invested 5 Yrs Ago	$21,194	S&P Core EPS 2007E	5.70	Institutional Ownership (%)	73	S&P Credit Rating	BBB+

Price Performance

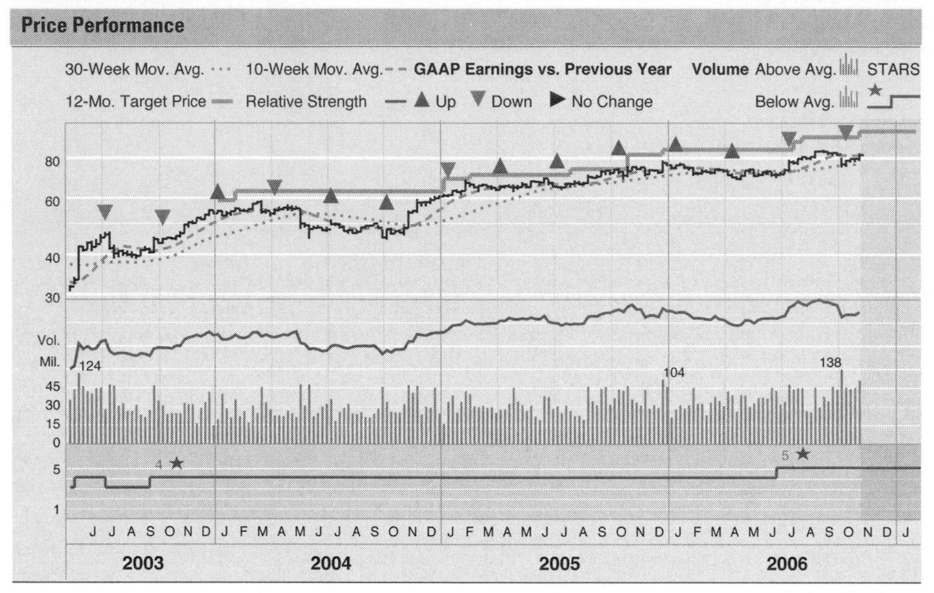

Options: ASE, CBOE, P, Ph

Highlights

- The 12-month target price for MO has recently been changed to $97.00 from $93.00. The Highlights section of this Stock Report will be updated accordingly.

Investment Rationale/Risk

- The Investment Rationale/Risk section of this Stock Report will be updated shortly. For the latest News story on MO from MarketScope, see below.
- 10/26/06 04:59 pm EDT... UPDATE - S&P REITERATES STRONG BUY OPINION ON SHARES OF ALTRIA GROUP (MO 82.0*****): MO's board of directors announces that it will move ahead with the breakup of the company. It intends to provide details, including a precise timetable, for the distribution of shares of 89% owned Kraft Foods (KFT 34.49***), to existing MO shareholders following the January 31 board meeting. We believe such a move should unlock shareholder value, providing a catalyst to move MO shares higher over the next 12 months. Giving heavier weight to our sum-of-the-parts analysis, we are raising our 12-month target price by $4, to $97. /R.Mathis

Qualitative Risk Assessment

LOW | **MEDIUM** | HIGH

MO is a large-cap company in an industry that is operationally very stable. However, the tobacco industry is beset by litigation. The company is subject to several ongoing legal actions, which could have a material impact on future cash flows.

Quantitative Evaluations

S&P Quality Ranking A+

D | C | B- | B | B+ | A- | A | **A+**

Relative Strength Rank MODERATE

54

LOWEST = 1 HIGHEST = 99

Revenue/Earnings Data

Revenue (Million $)

	1Q	2Q	3Q	4Q	Year
2006	24,355	25,769	25,885	--	--
2005	23,618	24,784	24,962	24,490	97,854
2004	21,721	22,894	22,615	22,380	89,610
2003	19,371	20,831	20,939	20,691	81,832
2002	20,535	21,103	19,996	18,774	80,408
2001	22,359	23,188	22,404	21,973	89,924

Earnings Per Share ($)

2006	1.65	1.29	1.36	**E**1.26	**E**5.50
2005	1.24	1.40	1.38	1.09	5.10
2004	1.06	1.26	1.28	0.96	4.57
2003	1.07	1.20	1.22	1.02	4.52
2002	1.09	1.21	2.06	0.85	5.21
2001	0.80	1.03	1.06	0.99	3.88

Fiscal year ended Dec. 31. Next earnings report expected: Late January. EPS Estimates based on S&P Operating Earnings; historical GAAP earnings are as reported.

Dividend Data (Dates: mm/dd Payment Date: mm/dd/yy)

Amount ($)	Date Decl.	Ex-Div. Date	Stk. of Record	Payment Date
0.800	12/14	12/23	12/28	01/10/06
0.800	02/21	03/13	03/15	04/10/06
0.800	06/02	06/13	06/15	07/10/06
0.860	08/30	09/13	09/15	10/10/06

Dividends have been paid since 1928. Source: Company reports.

Altria Group Inc.

Business Summary September 28, 2006

CORPORATE OVERVIEW. Altria Group (formerly Philip Morris Cos., Inc.) is a holding company for wholly owned and majority owned subsidiaries that make and market various consumer products, including cigarettes and packaged foods, around the world. Altria Group's reportable segments are domestic tobacco, international tobacco, North American food, international food and financial services. International operations accounted for 57.4% of sales and 54.0% of operating profits in 2005.

Philip Morris U.S.A. (PM USA) is the largest U.S. tobacco company, with total U.S. cigarette shipments amounting to 185.5 billion units in 2005 (down 0.8% from the 2004 level), accounting for 50% of total U.S. cigarette market shipments, (up from 49.8% market share in 2004). PM USA contributed 18.5% of total company sales and 27.6% of operating profits in 2005. Focus brands include Marlboro (the largest selling brand in the U.S.), Virginia Slims and Parliament in the premium category, and Basic in the discount category. Philip Morris International's (PMI) total cigarette shipments rose 5.7% in 2005, to 804.5 billion units. PMI contributed 46.3% of total company sales and 47.2% of operating profits in 2005.

Majority-owned (87.2%) Kraft Foods (KFNA) is the largest packaged food company in North America, accounting for 23.8% of total company sales and 23.1% of operating profits in 2005. Kraft Foods International (11.1% of 2005 sales, 6.8% of profits), in addition to KFNA, produces a wide variety of snacks, beverages, cheese, grocery and convenient meals in the U.S, Europe, the Middle East, Africa, and Asia/Pacific.

CORPORATE STRATEGY. MO is looking at a number of restructuring alternatives, including the possibility of separating Altria Group, Inc. into two, or potentially three, independent entities. Continuing improvements in the litigation environment are a prerequisite to such action. In January 2004, Kraft announced a three-year restructuring program to leverage its global scale, realign and lower its cost structure, and optimize its capacity utilization. The program was expected to cost about $1.2 billion, and Mo projected cost savings of about $400 million by 2000.

Company Financials

Per Share Data ($) Year Ended Dec. 31	**2005**	**2004**	**2003**	**2002**	**2001**	**2000**	**1999**	**1998**	**1997**	**1996**
Tangible Book Value	NM	NM	NM	NM	NM	NM	NM	NM	NM	NM
Cash Flow	5.92	5.35	5.22	6.10	4.93	4.50	3.90	2.89	3.28	3.25
Earnings	5.10	4.57	4.52	5.21	3.88	3.75	3.19	2.20	2.58	2.56
S&P Core Earnings	5.14	4.54	4.49	4.03	3.62	NA	NA	NA	NA	NA
Dividends	3.06	2.82	2.64	2.44	2.22	2.02	1.80	1.64	1.60	1.47
Payout Ratio	60%	62%	58%	47%	57%	54%	56%	75%	62%	57%
Prices:High	78.68	61.88	55.03	57.79	53.88	45.94	55.56	59.50	48.13	39.67
Prices:Low	60.40	44.50	27.70	35.40	38.75	18.69	21.25	34.75	36.00	28.54
P/E Ratio:High	15	14	12	11	14	12	17	27	19	15
P/E Ratio:Low	12	10	6	7	10	5	7	16	14	11
Income Statement Analysis (Million $)										
Revenue	97,854	89,610	81,832	80,408	89,924	80,356	78,596	74,391	72,055	69,204
Operating Income	19,004	17,929	17,663	18,476	18,039	16,396	15,192	15,048	14,820	13,460
Depreciation	1,675	1,607	1,440	1,331	2,337	1,717	1,702	1,690	1,700	1,691
Interest Expense	1,556	1,417	1,367	1,327	1,659	1,078	1,100	1,144	1,185	1,183
Pretax Income	15,435	14,004	14,760	18,098	14,284	13,960	12,695	9,087	10,611	10,683
Effective Tax Rate	29.9%	32.4%	34.9%	35.5%	37.9%	39.0%	39.5%	40.9%	40.5%	41.0%
Net Income	10,668	9,420	9,204	11,102	8,566	8,510	7,675	5,372	6,310	6,303
S&P Core Earnings	10,766	9,348	9,145	8,593	7,959	NA	NA	NA	NA	NA
Balance Sheet & Other Financial Data (Million $)										
Cash	6,258	5,744	3,777	565	453	937	5,100	4,081	2,282	240
Current Assets	25,781	25,901	21,382	17,441	17,275	17,238	20,895	20,230	17,440	15,190
Total Assets	107,949	101,648	96,175	87,540	84,968	79,067	61,381	59,920	55,947	54,871
Current Liabilities	26,158	23,574	21,393	19,082	20,141	25,949	18,017	16,379	15,071	14,867
Long Term Debt	17,868	18,683	21,163	21,355	18,651	19,154	12,226	12,615	12,430	12,961
Common Equity	35,707	30,714	25,077	19,478	19,620	15,005	15,305	16,197	14,920	14,218
Total Capital	71,945	67,714	64,110	56,832	52,768	40,824	33,211	33,892	32,116	31,546
Capital Expenditures	2,206	1,913	1,974	2,009	1,922	1,682	1,749	1,804	1,874	1,782
Cash Flow	12,343	11,027	10,644	12,433	10,903	10,227	9,377	7,062	8,010	7,994
Current Ratio	1.0	1.1	1.0	0.9	0.9	0.7	1.2	1.2	1.2	1.0
% Long Term Debt of Capitalization	24.8	27.6	33.0	37.6	35.3	46.9	36.8	37.2	38.7	41.0
% Net Income of Revenue	10.9	10.5	11.2	13.8	9.5	10.6	9.8	7.2	8.7	9.1
% Return on Assets	10.2	9.5	10.0	12.9	10.4	12.1	12.7	9.3	11.4	11.6
% Return on Equity	32.1	33.8	41.3	56.8	49.5	56.2	48.7	34.5	43.3	44.7

Data as orig reptd.; bef. results of disc opers/spec. items. Per share data adj. for stk. divs.; EPS diluted. E-Estimated. NA-Not Available. NM-Not Meaningful. NR-Not Ranked. UR-Under Review.

Office: 120 Park Avenue, New York, NY 10017-5592.
Telephone: 917-663-4000.
Website: http://www.altria.com
Chrmn & CEO: L.C. Camilleri

Investor Contact: D.S. Devitre (917-663-2200)
SVP & CFO: D.S. Devitre
SVP & General Counsel: C.R. Wall
SVP & CCO: D.I. Greenberg

Board of Directors: E. E. Bailey, H. Brown, M. Cabiallavetta, L. C. Camilleri, J. D. Fishburn, R. E. Huntley, T. W. Jones, G. Munoz, L. A. Noto, J. S. Reed, C. Slim Helu, S. M. Wolf

Founded: 1919
Domicile: Virginia
Employees: 199,000

Amazon.com Inc

S&P Recommendation HOLD ★★★★★

Price $38.15 (as of Oct 30, 2006)

12-Mo. Target Price $40.00

Investment Style Large-Cap Growth

GICS Sector Consumer Discretionary
Sub-Industry Internet Retail

Comment This leading online retailer sells a broad range of items from books to consumer electronics to home and garden products.

Key Stock Statistics (Source S&P, Vickers, company reports)

52-Wk Range	**$50.00–25.76**	S&P Oper. EPS 2006E	**0.44**	P/E on S&P Oper. EPS 2006E	**86.7**	Dividend Rate/Share	**Nil**
Trailing 12-Month EPS	**$0.68**	S&P Oper. EPS 2007E	**0.72**	Common Shares Outstg. (M)	**411.9**	Yield (%)	**Nil**
Trailing 12-Month P/E	**56.1**	S&P Core EPS 2006E	**0.44**	Market Capitalization(B)	**$15.715**	Beta	**2.07**
$10K Invested 5 Yrs Ago	**$50,582**	S&P Core EPS 2007E	**0.72**	Institutional Ownership (%)	**76**	S&P Credit Rating	**BB-**

Price Performance

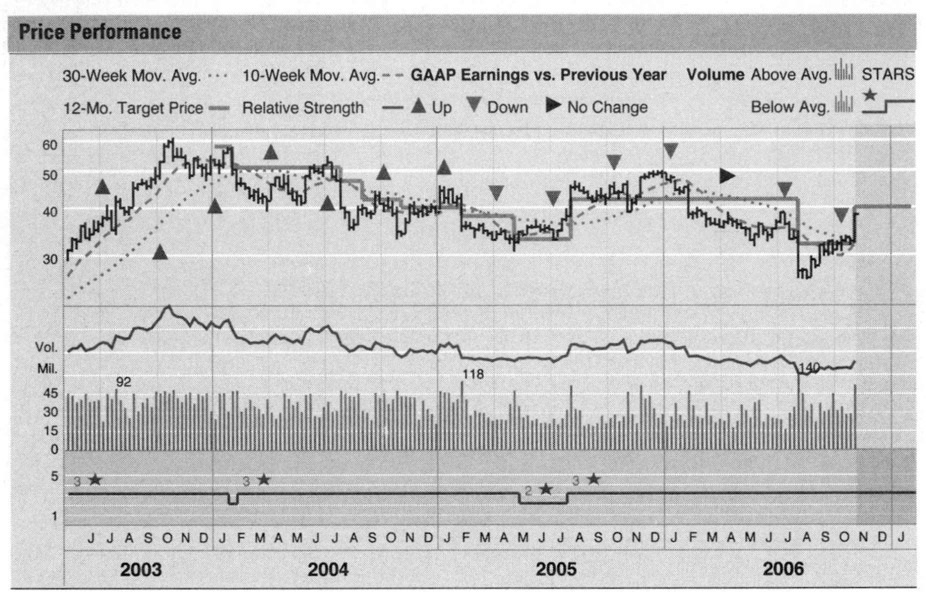

Options: ASE, CBOE, P, Ph

Analysis prepared by **Jason N. Asaeda** on October 26, 2006, when the stock traded at **$ 38.30**.

Highlights

- AMZN has become what we consider to be the first viable online marketplace in the U.S. From a projected $10.6 billion in 2006, we see net sales climbing 20% in 2007, to $12.7 billion, driven by new products, low pricing and international expansion. Shipping promotions, including the Amazon Prime membership program, which offers customers unlimited, express two-day shipping for an annual fee of $79, could also increase website traffic and conversion rates, in our view.

- Gross margins are likely to remain pressured in 2007 by the impact of free shipping offers, continued price reductions, and other promotions. Technology and content investments and increased marketing spending have contributed to lower operating margins in 2006. As the company plans to slow its pace of investments in 2007, we look for operating margins to widen by 10 basis points, to 3.7%, from a projected 3.6% in 2006.

- Factoring anticipated share buybacks under AMZN's $500 million authorization, we see operating and Standard & Poor's Core EPS of $0.44 in 2006 and $0.72 in 2007.

Investment Rationale/Risk

- While AMZN's continued investments in long-term growth opportunities, such as Amazon Prime, seller platforms, web services, and search technology, should provide the company with new sources of revenue over the next few years, we think that related margin pressure due to investment spending will limit significant upside to the shares. Longer term, we expect AMZN's initiatives to result in margin expansion, as it leverages its leading brand name and position as a leading Internet retailer.

- Risks to our recommendation and target price include the potential for lower-than-projected revenues due to heightened competition, lower-than-projected payoffs from AMZN's investments in growth initiatives, a decline in consumer discretionary spending, and/or a loss of the company's commercial agreements and strategic alliances with merchant partners.

- Our 12-month target price of $40 is based on our discounted cash flow analysis, which assumes a weighted average cost of capital of 9.9% and a terminal growth rate of 3%. We caution investors that these shares are highly volatile.

Qualitative Risk Assessment

LOW | **MEDIUM** | HIGH

Our risk assessment reflects our positive view of AMZN's large market capitalization and leading position in the e-commerce industry, offset by increasing competition and the stock's high beta.

Quantitative Evaluations

S&P Quality Ranking B-

D | C | **B-** | B | B+ | A- | A | A+

Relative Strength Rank STRONG

94

LOWEST = 1 HIGHEST = 99

Revenue/Earnings Data

Revenue (Million $)

	1Q	2Q	3Q	4Q	Year
2006	2,279	2,139	2,307	--	--
2005	1,902	1,753	1,858	2,977	8,490
2004	1,530	1,387	1,462	2,541	6,921
2003	1,084	1,100	1,134	1,946	5,264
2002	847.4	805.6	851.3	1,429	3,933
2001	700.4	667.6	639.3	1,115	3,122

Earnings Per Share ($)

2006	0.12	0.05	0.05	**E**0.22	**E**0.44
2005	0.12	0.12	0.07	0.47	0.78
2004	0.26	0.18	0.13	0.82	1.39
2003	-0.03	-0.11	0.04	0.17	0.08
2002	-0.06	-0.25	-0.09	0.01	-0.40
2001	-0.63	-0.47	-0.46	0.01	-1.53

Fiscal year ended Dec. 31. Next earnings report expected: Early February. EPS Estimates based on S&P Operating Earnings; historical GAAP earnings are as reported.

Dividend Data

No cash dividends have been paid.

Amazon.com Inc

Business Summary October 26, 2006

Since opening for business as "Earth's Biggest Bookstore" in July 1995, Amazon.com has expanded into a number of other product areas, such as apparel, shoes and accessories, electronics, computers, kitchen and housewares, books, music, DVDs, videos, cameras and photo items, office products, toys, baby items and baby registry, software, computer and video games, cell phones and service, tools and hardware, travel services, outdoor living items, and, most recently, jewelry.

AMZN has virtually unlimited online shelf space, and can offer customers a vast selection of products through an efficient search and retrieval interface. The company personalizes shopping by recommending items that, based on previous purchases, are likely to interest a particular customer. Key website features also include editorial and customer reviews, manufacturer product information, secure payment systems, wedding and baby registries, customer wish lists, and the ability to view selected interior pages and search the entire contents of many books (Look Inside the Book and Search Inside the Book).

The company currently operates six internationally focused retail websites: www.amazon.com (U.S.), www.amazon.co.uk (U.K.), www.amazon.de (Germany), www.amazon.fr (France), www.amazon.co.jp (Japan), and www.amazon.ca (Canada). All websites share a common Amazon.com experience, but are localized in terms of language, products, customer service, and fulfillment. AMZN also operates www.a9.com and www.alexa.com, which enable search and navigation, and www.imdb.com, a comprehensive movie database.

As well as being the seller of record for a broad range of new products, AMZN allows other businesses and individuals to sell new, used and collectible products on its websites through its Merchant and Amazon Marketplace programs. The company earns fixed fees, sales commissions, and/or per-unit activity fees under these programs.

The company also sells its products on the websites of other businesses through its Syndicated Stores program. Under this arrangement, AMZN generally owns the inventory, sets prices, and is responsible for fulfillment and customer service. The other businesses earn sales commission on product sales.

Company Financials

Per Share Data ($) Year Ended Dec. 31	**2005**	**2004**	**2003**	**2002**	**2001**	**2000**	**1999**	**1998**	**1997**	**1996**
Tangible Book Value	0.15	NM	NM	NM	NM	NM	NM	NM	0.10	0.02
Cash Flow	1.07	1.56	0.27	-0.16	-0.80	-2.86	-3.26	-0.23	-0.09	-0.02
Earnings	0.78	1.39	0.08	-0.40	-1.53	-4.02	-2.20	-0.42	-0.11	-0.02
S&P Core Earnings	0.83	1.27	0.02	-0.64	-2.49	NA	NA	NA	NA	NA
Dividends	Nil	Nil	Nil	Nil	Nil	Nil	Nil	Nil	Nil	NA
Payout Ratio	Nil	Nil	Nil	Nil	Nil	Nil	Nil	Nil	Nil	NA
Prices:High	50.00	57.82	61.15	25.00	22.38	91.50	113.00	60.31	5.50	NA
Prices:Low	30.60	33.00	18.55	9.03	5.51	14.88	41.00	4.15	1.31	NA
P/E Ratio:High	64	42	NM	NM	NM	NM	NM	NM	NM	NA
P/E Ratio:Low	39	24	NM	NM	NM	NM	NM	NM	NM	NA
Income Statement Analysis (Million $)										
Revenue	8,490	6,921	5,264	3,933	3,122	2,762	1,640	610	148	15.7
Operating Income	553	508	349	193	35.1	-257	-346	-55.2	-25.8	-5.69
Depreciation	121	75.7	78.3	87.8	266	406	253	56.0	3.39	0.29
Interest Expense	92.0	107	130	143	139	131	84.6	26.6	0.28	Nil
Pretax Income	428	356	35.3	-150	-557	-1,411	-720	-125	-27.6	-5.78
Effective Tax Rate	22.2%	NM	NM	NM	NM	NM	NM	NM	NM	NM
Net Income	333	588	35.3	-150	-557	-1,411	-720	-125	-27.6	-5.78
S&P Core Earnings	354	539	10.3	-242	-910	NA	NA	NA	NA	NA
Balance Sheet & Other Financial Data (Million $)										
Cash	2,000	1,779	1,395	1,301	997	1,101	706	373	110	56.5
Current Assets	2,929	2,539	1,821	1,616	1,208	1,361	1,012	424	137	NA
Total Assets	3,696	3,249	2,162	1,990	1,638	2,135	2,472	648	149	61.1
Current Liabilities	1,929	1,620	1,253	1,066	921	975	739	162	43.8	NA
Long Term Debt	1,521	1,855	1,945	2,277	2,156	2,127	1,466	348	76.7	Nil
Common Equity	246	-227	-1,036	-1,353	-1,440	-967	266	139	28.5	52.1
Total Capital	1,767	1,628	909	924	716	1,160	1,733	487	105	52.1
Capital Expenditures	204	89.1	46.0	39.2	50.3	135	287	28.3	7.20	1.21
Cash Flow	454	664	114	-62.2	-291	-1,005	-1,015	-67.7	-24.2	-5.49
Current Ratio	1.5	1.6	1.5	1.5	1.3	1.4	1.4	2.6	3.1	NA
% Long Term Debt of Capitalization	86.1	113.9	213.9	246.3	301.1	183.4	84.6	71.5	72.9	Nil
% Net Income of Revenue	3.9	8.5	0.7	NM	NM	NM	NM	NM	NM	NM
% Return on Assets	9.6	21.8	1.7	NM	NM	NM	NM	NM	NM	NM
% Return on Equity	NM	NM	NM	NM	NM	NM	NM	NM	NM	NM

Data as orig reptd.; bef. results of disc opers/spec. items. Per share data adj. for stk. divs.; EPS diluted. E-Estimated. NA-Not Available. NM-Not Meaningful. NR-Not Ranked. UR-Under Review.

Office: 1200 12th Avenue South, Seattle, WA 98144-2734.
Telephone: 206-266-1000.
Email: ir@amazon.com
Website: http://www.amazon.com

Chrmn, Pres & CEO: J.P. Bezos
SVP & CFO: T.J. Szkutak
SVP, Secy & General Counsel: L.M. Wilson
SVP & CIO: R.L. Dalzell

VP & Chief Acctg Officer: M.S. Peek
Board of Directors: T. A. Alberg, J. P. Bezos, J. S. Brown, L. J. Doerr, W. B. Gordon, M. S. Potter, T. O. Ryder, P. Q. Stonesifer

Founded: 1994
Domicile: Delaware
Employees: 12,000

STANDARD & POOR'S

Ambac Financial Group Inc.

S&P Recommendation HOLD ★★★★★ | **Price** $83.97 (as of Oct 27, 2006) | **12-Mo. Target Price** $93.00 | **Investment Style** Mid-Cap Growth

GICS Sector Financials
Sub-Industry Property & Casualty Insurance

Comment ABK, the second largest municipal bond insurer, has leveraged that strength and expanded into other types of financial guarantees.

Key Stock Statistics (Source S&P, Vickers, company reports)

52-Wk Range	$87.50–69.69	S&P Oper. EPS 2006E	7.45	P/E on S&P Oper. EPS 2006E	11.3	Dividend Rate/Share	$0.72
Trailing 12-Month EPS	$8.16	S&P Oper. EPS 2007E	7.85	Common Shares Outstg. (M)	105.9	Yield (%)	0.86
Trailing 12-Month P/E	10.3	S&P Core EPS 2006E	7.45	Market Capitalization(B)	$8.894	Beta	1.05
$10K Invested 5 Yrs Ago	$17,427	S&P Core EPS 2007E	7.85	Institutional Ownership (%)	NA	S&P Credit Rating	AA

Price Performance

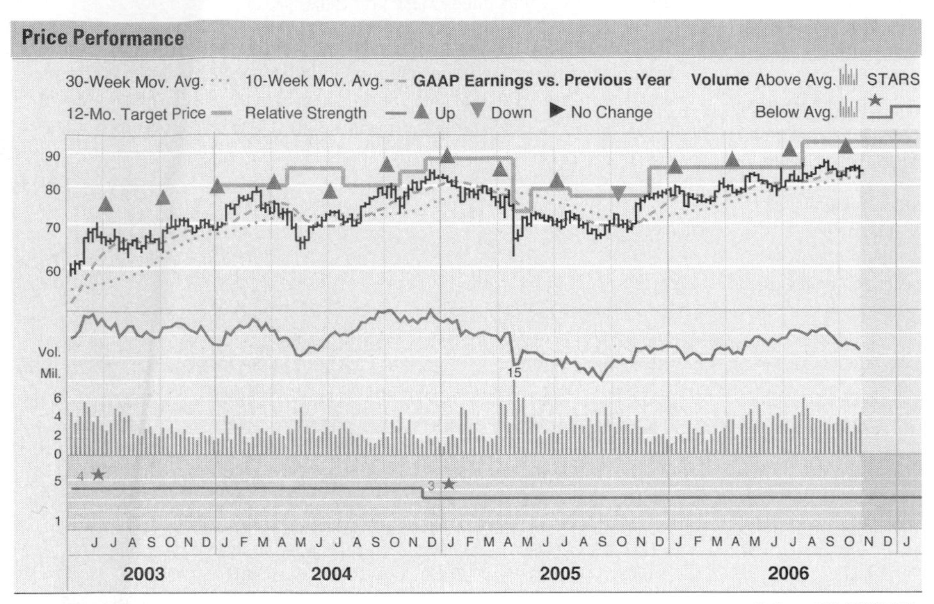

Options: ASE, CBOE, P, Ph

Analysis prepared by **Cathy A. Seifert** on August 31, 2006, when the stock traded at **$ 86.81**.

Highlights

- Earned premium growth in 2006 is expected to be modest, but will likely accelerate in 2007, in our view. Credit enhancement production (CEP), which is defined as direct and assumed up-front premiums plus the present value of installment premiums on policies and structured credit derivatives, advanced 28%, year to year, during the first six months of 2006. CEP, or "deal flow", declined 17% in public finance, but advanced 39% in structured finance and surged 131% in international units. (We do not see this rate of international growth as a run rate.)
- We believe fundamentals remain positive for the longer term. We also view ABK as one of the better underwriters in this industry, and believe it has done a superior job (versus some of its peers) in assessing and pricing risk.
- Our 2006 operating EPS estimate of $7.35 (versus $6.47 of operating EPS reported for 2005) assumes that share buybacks partly offset the impact of contracting margins. We see operating EPS of $7.85 in 2007.

Investment Rationale/Risk

- We view ABK as a well managed, financially sound franchise, and believe its shares are worth holding. Our near-term outlook is tempered by what we see as a competitive operating environment. However, we are encouraged by the first half 2006 year-to-date deal pipeline. Moreover, we believe an erosion in macro credit trends could actually aid ABK's results, since it may increase demand for the company's credit enhancement products. At recent levels, the shares were trading in line with their historical average P/E multiple. We do not advise adding to positions.
- Risks to our opinion and target price include a sharper than anticipated rise in interest rates, and a significant deterioration in credit quality.
- Our 12-month target price of $93 assumes that the stock trades at a forward P/E of about 12X our 2007 operating EPS estimate. This represents a modest premium to ABK's peers. Our target price also assumes that the shares trade at about 1.5X estimated 2007 tangible book value. This is in line with most of ABK's financial guaranty peers and at about the midpoint of ABK's historical range.

Qualitative Risk Assessment

LOW | **MEDIUM** | HIGH

Our risk assessment reflects our view of ABK as a sound underwriter with acceptable risk and capital management practices in place. This is offset by the impact that alternative credit enhancements have had on the company's production.

Quantitative Evaluations

S&P Quality Ranking A+

D | C | B- | B | B+ | A- | A | **A+**

Relative Strength Rank MODERATE

33

LOWEST = 1 HIGHEST = 99

Revenue/Earnings Data

Revenue (Million $)

	1Q	2Q	3Q	4Q	Year
2006	453.9	500.9	460.3	--	--
2005	390.8	406.4	438.3	429.8	1,662
2004	337.4	352.0	352.1	363.2	1,411
2003	290.7	321.6	321.7	338.1	1,272
2002	196.9	202.0	220.4	121.2	971.8
2001	167.6	179.5	181.3	197.1	725.0

Earnings Per Share ($)

2006	2.06	2.22	1.98	E1.63	E7.45
2005	1.66	1.69	1.61	1.90	6.87
2004	1.55	1.63	1.65	1.69	6.54
2003	1.27	1.48	1.45	1.52	5.74
2002	1.07	1.09	1.21	0.59	3.97
2001	0.90	0.99	1.02	1.07	3.97

Fiscal year ended Dec. 31. Next earnings report expected: Late January. EPS Estimates based on S&P Operating Earnings; historical GAAP earnings are as reported.

Dividend Data (Dates: mm/dd Payment Date: mm/dd/yy)

Amount ($)	Date Decl.	Ex-Div. Date	Stk. of Record	Payment Date
0.150	01/27	02/08	02/10	03/01/06
0.150	05/02	05/11	05/15	06/07/06
0.180	07/27	08/08	08/10	09/06/06
0.180	10/25	11/08	11/10	12/06/06

Dividends have been paid since 1991. Source: Company reports.

Please read the Required Disclosures and Analyst Certification on the last page of this report.

The McGraw·Hill Companies

Ambac Financial Group Inc.

Business Summary August 31, 2006

Ambac Financial Group is the second largest municipal bond insurer, and has leveraged that strength and market dominance into a diversification effort centered on other types of financial guarantees and investment management services. At December 31, 2005, the composition of the $479.2 billion of outstanding guaranteed debt was as follows: public finance 55% ($264.1 billion); structured finance 30% ($144.4 billion); and international 15% ($70.7 billion).

The company guarantees payment when due of principal and interest on the bond insured. Ambac primarily insures newly issued bonds, and the issuer normally pays a single premium to the company when the policy becomes effective. Premium rates are based on a percentage of the spread between a bond's intrinsic credit quality and an AAA-rated bond. At year-end 2005, 45% of the insured portfolio had an internal credit rating of A, 26% was rated AA, 20% was rated BBB, 8% was rated AAA, and 1% was rated below investment grade.

At December 31, 2005, the $264.1 billion public finance insured portfolio was comprised of lease and tax backed bonds (31%); general obligation bonds (22%); utility revenue bonds (14%); health care revenue bonds (10%); transportation revenue bonds (9%); and other (14%).

The Specialized Finance division is a significant participant, in our opinion, in the structured, asset-backed and mortgage-backed finance markets in the U.S. and abroad. At the end of 2005, the $144.4 billion U.S. structured finance portfolio was comprised of mortgage-backed and home equity obligations (34%); asset-backed and conduits (23%); pooled debt obligations (16%); investor owned utilities (11%); student loan obligations (11%); and other (5%). At December 31, 2005, ABK's $70.7 billion international portfolio was comprised of pooled debt obligations (33%); asset-backed and conduits (22%); mortgage-backed and home equity loans (21%); investor owned and public utilities (11%); and other international credits (13%).

Company Financials

Per Share Data ($) Year Ended Dec. 31	**2005**	**2004**	**2003**	**2002**	**2001**	**2000**	**1999**	**1998**	**1997**	**1996**
Tangible Book Value	50.85	46.13	39.71	34.20	28.26	24.60	19.23	19.98	17.85	15.34
Operating Earnings	NA	NA	NA	4.68	4.00	3.46	2.93	2.40	1.98	1.79
Earnings	6.87	6.54	5.74	3.97	3.97	3.41	2.87	2.37	2.09	2.63
S&P Core Earnings	6.82	6.27	5.41	4.39	3.87	NA	NA	NA	NA	NA
Dividends	0.55	0.47	0.42	0.38	0.34	0.31	0.28	0.25	0.23	0.21
Payout Ratio	8%	7%	7%	10%	9%	Nil	10%	11%	11%	8%
Prices:High	82.92	84.73	72.21	71.25	64.00	58.31	42.00	43.96	31.71	23.17
Prices:Low	62.20	63.80	43.79	49.86	42.20	25.92	29.79	27.25	20.67	15.17
P/E Ratio:High	12	13	13	18	16	17	15	19	15	9
P/E Ratio:Low	9	10	8	13	11	8	10	11	10	6
Income Statement Analysis (Million $)										
Premium Income	816	717	620	472	379	311	383	311	154	137
Net Investment Income	429	363	321	297	268	241	209	186	160	145
Other Revenue	404	331	652	500	78.3	380	324	-40.0	25.8	-15.3
Total Revenue	1,662	1,411	1,272	972	725	621	533	457	339	266
Pretax Income	1,023	977	850	564	569	482	405	329	286	376
Net Operating Income	NA	NA	NA	510	436	372	313	263	212	188
Net Income	751	726	628	433	433	366	308	254	223	276
S&P Core Earnings	745	695	592	479	422	NA	NA	NA	NA	NA
Balance Sheet & Other Financial Data (Million $)										
Cash & Equivalent	207	182	184	25.8	10.3	20.5	142	134	9.26	73.7
Premiums Due	3.70	16.8	3.03	4.84	2.26	1.09	15.4	16.2	106	18.5
Investment Assets:Bonds	15,495	14,243	13,521	12,141	9,871	8,065	8,738	8,622	6,774	5,088
Investment Assets:Stocks	Nil	Nil	Nil	Nil	Nil	Nil	Nil	Nil	Nil	Nil
Investment Assets:Loans	Nil	Nil	Nil	Nil	Nil	Nil	685	Nil	Nil	Nil
Investment Assets:Total	16,400	15,121	13,830	12,539	10,288	8,324	8,963	9,698	7,281	5,201
Deferred Policy Costs	202	185	175	174	163	153	135	121	106	94.2
Total Assets	19,725	18,585	16,747	15,356	12,268	10,120	11,345	11,212	8,250	5,876
Debt	2,234	1,866	792	617	1,044	424	424	424	224	224
Common Equity	5,372	5,024	4,444	3,797	3,136	2,729	2,018	2,096	1,872	1,615
Property & Casualty:Loss Ratio	NA	NA	NA	NA	NA	NA	NA	NA	NA	NA
Property & Casualty:Expense Ratio	NA	NA	NA	NA	NA	NA	NA	NA	NA	NA
Property & Casualty Combined Ratio	NA	NA	NA	NA	NA	NA	NA	NA	NA	NA
% Return on Revenue	45.5	51.4	49.4	44.5	59.7	58.9	57.7	62.2	65.8	103.8
% Return on Equity	14.4	15.6	15.2	12.5	14.8	15.0	15.0	12.8	12.8	18.3

Data as orig reptd.; bef. results of disc opers/spec. items. Per share data adj. for stk. divs.; EPS diluted. E-Estimated. NA-Not Available. NM-Not Meaningful. NR-Not Ranked. UR-Under Review.

Office: 1 State Street Plz, New York, NY 10004-1505.
Telephone: 212-668-0340.
Website: http://www.ambac.com
Chrmn, Pres & CEO: R.J. Genader

SVP & CFO: S.T. Leonard
Treas: D. Trick
General Counsel: K.J. Doyle
Investor Contact: P. Poillon (212-208-3333)

Board of Directors: M. A. Callen, J. M. Considine, R. J. Genader, W. G. Gregory, P. B. Lassiter, T. C. Theobald, L. S. Unger, H. D. Wallace

Founded: 1971
Domicile: Delaware
Employees: 354

STANDARD &POOR'S

Ameren Corp

S&P Recommendation HOLD ★★★★★

Price $54.77 (as of Oct 27, 2006)

12-Mo. Target Price $53.00

Investment Style Large-Cap Value

GICS Sector Utilities
Sub-Industry Multi-Utilities

Comment Ameren is the holding company for the largest electric utility in the state of Missouri, and several utilities in Illinois.

Key Stock Statistics (Source S&P, Vickers, company reports)

52-Wk Range	$55.24–47.96	S&P Oper. EPS 2006E	2.85	P/E on S&P Oper. EPS 2006E	19.2	Dividend Rate/Share	$2.54
Trailing 12-Month EPS	$2.52	S&P Oper. EPS 2007E	3.85	Common Shares Outstg. (M)	205.9	Yield (%)	4.64
Trailing 12-Month P/E	21.7	S&P Core EPS 2006E	2.93	Market Capitalization(B)	$11.275	Beta	0.41
$10K Invested 5 Yrs Ago	$18,159	S&P Core EPS 2007E	3.92	Institutional Ownership (%)	56	S&P Credit Rating	BBB

Price Performance

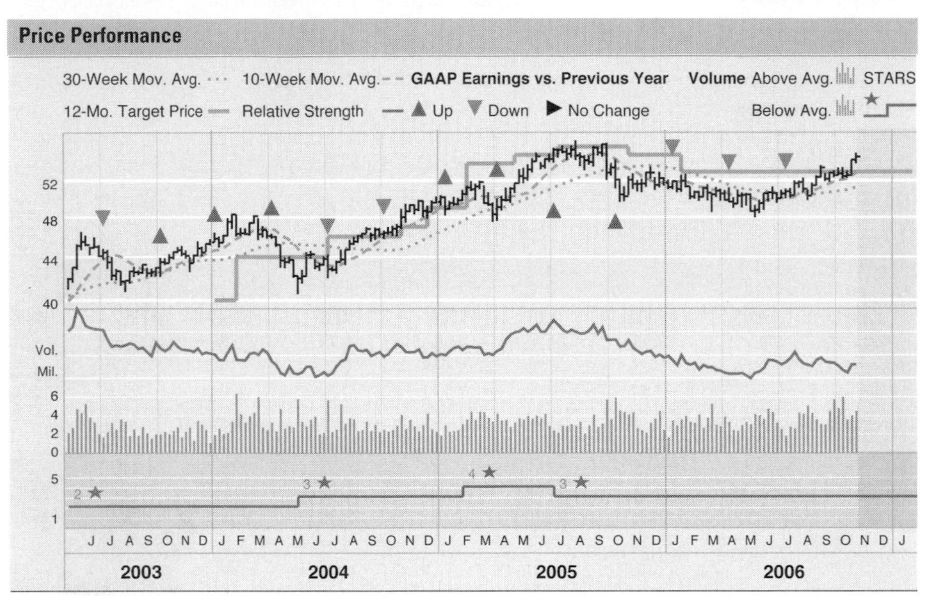

Options: P, Ph

Analysis prepared by **Justin McCann** on September 21, 2006, when the stock traded at **$ 52.56**.

Highlights

- After a projected EPS decline of nearly 10% in 2006 (from 2005's operating EPS of $3.13), we expect EPS in 2007 to advance around 30% from anticipated 2006 results. We see results in 2006 being negatively affected by an unplanned nuclear outage, increased coal and related transportation costs, milder weather, the absence of power from the Taum Sauk hydroelectric plant, and the impact of two very severe summer storms.
- We believe EPS in 2007 will benefit from expected rate increases, as well as an absence of the negative factors affecting 2006. In addition, we see earnings benefiting from the expiration of below-market power supply agreements for AEE's unregulated generation units in Illinois.
- Ameren is under investigation by the state's attorney general for the December 14, 2005 collapse of a wall at the Taum Sauk hydroelectric reservoir, which resulted in the surrounding area being flooded by 1 billion gallons of water. In May, the utility estimated the damages and liabilities to be in the range of $53 million to $73 million, and said it believes all of the costs will be covered by insurance.

Investment Rationale/Risk

- We believe the shares will by restricted by the uncertainties related to both AEE's proposed auction process for future power purchases (which has been opposed by the Governor of Illinois) once rate caps expire at the end of 2006, and the Taum Sauk litigation. However, we expect the shares to be supported by a dividend yield (recently 4.8%) that is well above the industry average. With the current 15% federal tax rate on dividends (which Congress extended two years through the end of 2010), this would indicate an after-tax yield of about 4.1%.
- Risks to our recommendation and target price include not being able to recover rising power supply costs, unfavorable rulings related to the Taum Sauk litigation, and a sharp drop in the average P/E of AEE's peer group as a whole.
- While we do not expect AEE's dividend to be increased (it has not been raised since 1997), we view it as stable, despite the above-average payout ratio of 89% of our EPS estimate for 2006. Our 12-month target price is $53, projecting an approximate peer P/E of 14.1X our EPS estimate for 2007.

Qualitative Risk Assessment

LOW | MEDIUM | HIGH

Our risk assessment reflects our expectation of steady cash flow from the company's regulated utilities, which have the benefit of fuel costs that are well below the industry average. We believe this should more than offset the increased level of purchased power needed due to the absence of power from the Taum Sauk hydroelectric plant, as well as the uncertainties related to the proposed reverse auction process for the procurement of power beginning in January 2007.

Quantitative Evaluations

S&P Quality Ranking A-

D | C | B- | B | B+ | A- | A | A+

Relative Strength Rank MODERATE

60

LOWEST = 1 HIGHEST = 99

Revenue/Earnings Data

Revenue (Million $)

	1Q	2Q	3Q	4Q	Year
2006	1,800	1,550	--	--	--
2005	1,626	1,590	1,868	1,701	6,780
2004	1,216	1,152	1,317	1,475	5,160
2003	1,108	1,088	1,350	1,047	4,593
2002	1,115	1,111	1,232	823.0	3,841
2001	1,025	1,057	1,432	992.7	4,506

Earnings Per Share ($)

2006	0.34	0.60	E1.32	E0.59	E2.85
2005	0.62	0.93	1.37	0.21	3.13
2004	0.55	0.65	1.20	0.42	2.84
2003	0.52	0.68	1.70	0.24	3.14
2002	0.42	0.80	1.63	-0.20	2.60
2001	0.48	0.69	1.94	0.34	3.45

Fiscal year ended Dec. 31. Next earnings report expected: Early November. EPS Estimates based on S&P Operating Earnings; historical GAAP earnings are as reported.

Dividend Data (Dates: mm/dd Payment Date: mm/dd/yy)

Amount ($)	Date Decl.	Ex-Div. Date	Stk. of Record	Payment Date
0.635	02/10	03/06	03/08	03/31/06
0.635	05/02	06/05	06/07	06/30/06
0.635	08/25	09/05	09/07	09/29/06
0.635	10/13	12/04	12/06	12/29/06

Dividends have been paid since 1906. Source: Company reports.

Ameren Corp

Business Summary September 21, 2006

CORPORATE OVERVIEW. Ameren Corporation (AEE) is a holding company that operates regulated electric and natural gas utilities and non-regulated operations, including energy marketing, trading and consulting services, in Missouri and Illinois. AEE's Utility Operations segment is comprised of its electric generation and electric and gas transmission and distribution operations. The company's subsidiaries include Union Electric Company (UE), Central Illinois Public Service Company (CIPS), Ameren Energy Generating Company (Genco), CILCORP Inc., and Illinois Power Company (IP). In 2005, electric services contributed to 80.1% of total revenues while gas services contributed to the rest.

CORPORATE STRATEGY. AEE has undertaken a cost control initiative related to its strategic sourcing of purchases and the streamlining of all aspects of its business. In 2005, the company faced lower coal inventory due to disruptions in coal deliveries. In case of future disruptions, AEE would pursue a strategy that could include reducing sales of power during low-margin periods or utilizing higher cost fuels to generate required electricity and purchasing power. To meet projected demand growth, the company has decided to expand its generating capacity through asset purchases. It has also entered into long-term supply agreements for ensuring its future gas supply. AEE is focused on realizing the integration synergies associated with the CILCORP and IP acquisitions, which include utilizing more economical fuels at CILCORP and reducing administrative and operating expenses at IP.

Company Financials

Per Share Data ($) Year Ended Dec. 31	**2005**	**2004**	**2003**	**2002**	**2001**	**2000**	**1999**	**1998**	**1997**	**1996**
Tangible Book Value	25.08	24.92	23.19	24.95	24.20	23.34	22.55	22.27	21.92	22.86
Earnings	3.13	2.84	3.14	2.60	3.45	3.33	2.81	2.82	2.82	2.86
S&P Core Earnings	3.32	3.12	3.28	2.36	2.81	NA	NA	NA	NA	NA
Dividends	2.54	2.54	2.54	2.54	2.54	2.54	2.54	2.54	2.54	2.51
Payout Ratio	81%	89%	81%	98%	74%	76%	90%	90%	90%	88%
Prices:High	56.77	50.36	46.50	45.25	46.00	46.94	42.94	44.31	43.75	44.13
Prices:Low	47.51	40.55	42.55	34.72	36.53	27.56	32.00	35.56	34.50	36.00
P/E Ratio:High	18	18	15	17	13	14	15	16	16	15
P/E Ratio:Low	15	14	14	13	11	8	11	13	12	13
Income Statement Analysis (Million $)										
Revenue	6,780	5,160	4,593	3,841	4,506	3,856	3,524	3,318	3,327	2,260
Depreciation	632	557	519	431	406	382	351	348	346	241
Maintenance	NA	NA	NA	NA	382	368	371	312	310	224
Fixed Charges Coverage	4.32	3.81	3.61	4.04	4.65	4.86	4.48	NA	4.08	4.25
Construction Credits	NA	NA	4.00	11.0	20.8	14.0	14.0	12.0	12.7	13.5
Effective Tax Rate	35.6%	34.7%	37.3%	38.3%	38.7%	39.7%	40.2%	40.9%	38.0%	39.3%
Net Income	628	530	506	382	475	457	385	386	387	305
S&P Core Earnings	666	582	530	347	387	NA	NA	NA	NA	NA
Balance Sheet & Other Financial Data (Million $)										
Gross Property	20,800	20,291	17,511	15,745	14,962	13,910	13,056	12,531	12,273	9,040
Capital Expenditures	947	806	682	787	1,103	929	571	325	381	376
Net Property	13,572	13,297	10,917	8,914	8,427	7,706	7,165	6,928	6,987	5,383
Capitalization:Long Term Debt	5,568	5,236	4,273	3,626	3,071	2,980	2,683	2,525	2,506	1,799
Capitalization:% Long Term Debt	46.7	47.4	49.5	48.6	47.8	48.3	46.5	45.2	43.5	41.0
Capitalization:Preferred	Nil	Nil	Nil	Nil	Nil	Nil	Nil	NA	235	219
Capitalization:% Preferred	Nil	Nil	Nil	Nil	Nil	Nil	Nil	NA	4.10	5.00
Capitalization:Common	6,364	5,800	4,354	3,842	3,349	3,196	3,089	3,056	3,019	2,355
Capitalization:% Common	53.3	52.6	50.5	51.4	52.2	51.7	53.5	54.8	52.4	54.0
Total Capital	14,047	13,075	10,653	9,339	8,144	7,884	7,441	7,285	7,507	5,851
% Operating Ratio	86.3	84.6	83.9	81.0	85.2	83.4	84.1	82.8	82.5	81.1
% Earned on Net Property	9.6	8.9	10.7	7.2	8.2	8.6	8.0	8.2	8.4	8.0
% Return on Revenue	9.3	10.3	11.0	9.9	10.6	11.9	10.9	11.6	11.6	13.5
% Return on Invested Capital	7.0	6.9	7.4	8.1	8.6	8.5	7.7	11.3	7.7	7.4
% Return on Common Equity	10.3	10.4	12.3	10.6	14.5	14.5	12.5	12.7	12.8	12.5

Data as orig reptd.; bef. results of disc opers/spec. items. Per share data adj. for stk. divs.; EPS diluted. E-Estimated. NA-Not Available. NM-Not Meaningful. NR-Not Ranked. UR-Under Review.

Office: 1901 Chouteau Avenue, St. Louis, MO 63103.
Telephone: 314-621-3222.
Email: invest@ameren.com
Website: http://www.ameren.com

Chrmn, Pres & CEO: G.L. Rainwater
COO & EVP: T.R. Voss
EVP & CFO: W.L. Baxter
SVP, Secy & General Counsel: S.R. Sullivan

VP & Treas: J.E. Birdsong
Investor Contact: B. Steinke (314-554-2574)
Board of Directors: S. F. Brauer, S. S. Elliott, G. P. Jackson, J. C. Johnson, R. A. Liddy, G. R. Lohman, R. A. Lumpkin, C. W. Mueller, D. R. Oberhelman, G. L. Rainwater, H. Saligman, P. T. Stokes, J. D. Woodard

Founded: 1881
Domicile: Missouri
Employees: 9,136

STANDARD &POOR'S

American Electric Power

S&P Recommendation BUY ★★★★★

Price $41.43 (as of Oct 31, 2006)

12-Mo. Target Price $47.00

Investment Style Large-Cap Value

GICS Sector Utilities
Sub-Industry Electric Utilities

Comment This Ohio-based electric utility holding company has subsidiaries operating in 11 states in the U.S.

Key Stock Statistics (Source S&P, Vickers, company reports)

52-Wk Range	**$41.85–32.27**	S&P Oper. EPS 2006**E**	**2.72**	P/E on S&P Oper. EPS 2006**E**	**15.2**	Dividend Rate/Share	**$1.56**
Trailing 12-Month EPS	**$2.30**	S&P Oper. EPS 2007**E**	**2.95**	Common Shares Outstg. (M)	**394.0**	Yield (%)	**3.77**
Trailing 12-Month P/E	**18.0**	S&P Core EPS 2006**E**	**2.58**	Market Capitalization(B)	**$16.322**	Beta	**0.84**
$10K Invested 5 Yrs Ago	**$12,414**	S&P Core EPS 2007**E**	**2.79**	Institutional Ownership (%)	**66**	S&P Credit Rating	**BBB**

Price Performance

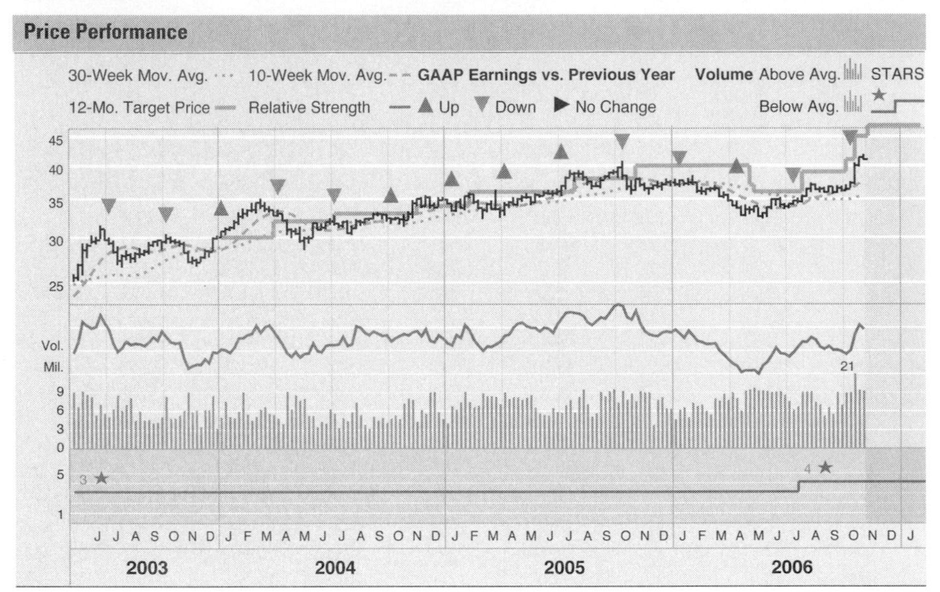

Options: ASE, CBOE, P, Ph

Highlights

➤ The 12-month target price for AEP has recently been changed to $47.00 from $45.00. The Highlights section of this Stock Report will be updated accordingly.

Investment Rationale/Risk

➤ The Investment Rationale/Risk section of this Stock Report will be updated shortly. For the latest News story on AEP from MarketScope, see below.

➤ 10/31/06 02:18 pm EST... S&P REITERATES BUY OPINION ON SHARES OF AMERICAN ELECTRIC POWER (AEP 41.25****): Q3 operating EPS of $0.99 vs. $0.95 is in line with our estimate. Results benefited from rate increases in Ohio and Kentucky, higher river barge earnings, and a sharp increase in off-system sales, which more than offset higher interest and amortization expenses. We are keeping our EPS estimates of $2.72 for '06 and $2.95 for '07. We continue to see longer-term EPS growth of 5% to 7%, driven by rate base investments in AEP's generation and transmission operations. We are raising our target price by $2 to $47, reflecting premium-to-peers P/E of 15.9X our '07 estimate. / J.McCann

Qualitative Risk Assessment

LOW | MEDIUM | HIGH

Our risk assessment reflects our view of the steady cash flow expected from the regulated utilities, with their low-cost fuel sources and generally supportive regulatory environments. The proceeds from the divestiture of most of its high-risk unregulated energy businesses were used to enhance its balance sheet and financial strength.

Quantitative Evaluations

S&P Quality Ranking **B**

D | C | B- | **B** | B+ | A- | A | A+

Relative Strength Rank **STRONG**

82

LOWEST = 1 HIGHEST = 99

Revenue/Earnings Data

Revenue (Million $)

	1Q	2Q	3Q	4Q	Year
2006	3,108	2,936	3,600	--	--
2005	3,065	2,819	3,328	2,899	12,111
2004	3,364	3,408	3,780	3,505	14,057
2003	3,834	3,451	3,940	3,320	14,545
2002	3,169	3,575	3,870	3,941	14,555
2001	14,165	14,528	18,385	14,179	61,257

Earnings Per Share ($)

2006	0.95	0.43	0.67	**E**0.36	**E**2.72
2005	0.90	0.57	0.94	0.23	2.63
2004	0.73	0.38	1.04	0.69	2.85
2003	0.83	0.47	0.75	-0.65	1.35
2002	0.49	0.49	1.14	-2.01	0.06
2001	0.83	0.87	1.25	0.17	3.11

Fiscal year ended Dec. 31. Next earnings report expected: Early February. EPS Estimates based on S&P Operating Earnings; historical GAAP earnings are as reported.

Dividend Data (Dates: mm/dd Payment Date: mm/dd/yy)

Amount ($)	Date Decl.	Ex-Div. Date	Stk. of Record	Payment Date
0.370	01/25	02/08	02/10	03/10/06
0.370	04/25	05/08	05/10	06/09/06
0.370	07/26	08/08	08/10	09/08/06
0.390	10/24	11/08	11/10	12/08/06

Dividends have been paid since 1909. Source: Company reports.

American Electric Power

Business Summary October 13, 2006

CORPORATE OVERVIEW. AEP is a holding company that primarily operates electric utility services through its regulated subsidiaries. The utility services include the generation, transmission and distribution of electricity for sale to retail and wholesale customers in the U.S. AEP's non-regulated operations include the Memco Barge Line subsidiary, which is engaged in the transportation of coal and dry bulk commodities, mainly on the Ohio, Illinois and lower Mississippi rivers. In 2005, the utility segment contributed to 92% of total revenues.

CORPORATE STRATEGY. AEP's strategy is to focus on its core utility operations and to deliver low-cost electric power to the communities served. The company plans to improve its efficiency and to maximize the power that is delivered from its generation facilities. In order to provide safe and reliable power, AEP is making investments to upgrade its transmission and distribution infrastructure, as well as to be in compliance with the appropriate environmental standards. The company intends to form a joint venture that will fund and own new electric transmission assets in Texas. AEP invested more than $1.1 billion in its energy delivery system in 2005, $370 million more than the prior year, and has projected a $1.3 billion investment in 2006. We believe AEP will be able to recover most of the costs related to these investments through rate increases.

Company Financials

Per Share Data ($) Year Ended Dec. 31	**2005**	**2004**	**2003**	**2002**	**2001**	**2000**	**1999**	**1998**	**1997**	**1996**
Tangible Book Value	22.87	21.31	19.74	19.67	20.92	20.72	25.80	25.21	24.62	23.96
Earnings	2.63	2.85	1.35	0.06	3.11	0.94	2.69	2.81	3.20	3.14
S&P Core Earnings	2.26	2.58	1.47	0.07	2.17	NA	NA	NA	NA	NA
Dividends	1.42	1.40	1.65	2.40	2.40	2.40	2.40	2.40	2.40	2.40
Payout Ratio	54%	49%	NM	NM	77%	255%	89%	85%	73%	76%
Prices:High	40.80	35.53	31.51	48.80	51.20	48.94	48.19	53.31	52.00	44.75
Prices:Low	32.25	28.50	19.01	15.10	39.25	25.94	30.56	42.06	39.13	38.63
P/E Ratio:High	16	12	23	NM	16	52	18	19	16	14
P/E Ratio:Low	12	10	14	NM	13	28	11	15	12	12
Income Statement Analysis (Million $)										
Revenue	12,111	14,057	14,545	14,555	61,257	13,694	6,916	6,346	6,161	5,849
Depreciation	1,318	1,300	1,299	1,377	1,383	1,062	600	580	591	601
Maintenance	NA	NA	NA	NA	NA	NA	NA	543	483	503
Fixed Charges Coverage	2.80	2.60	2.97	2.84	2.64	1.95	2.44	2.98	3.27	3.20
Construction Credits	21.0	NA	NA	NA	NA	NA	NA	NA	NA	NA
Effective Tax Rate	29.4%	33.7%	39.8%	79.3%	35.9%	66.4%	33.3%	37.1%	35.5%	36.8%
Net Income	1,029	1,127	522	21.0	1,003	302	520	536	620	587
S&P Core Earnings	883	1,021	573	21.1	698	NA	NA	NA	NA	NA
Balance Sheet & Other Financial Data (Million $)										
Gross Property	39,121	37,286	36,033	37,857	40,709	38,088	22,205	20,146	19,596	18,970
Capital Expenditures	2,404	1,693	1,358	1,722	1,832	1,773	867	792	760	578
Net Property	24,284	22,801	22,029	21,684	24,543	22,393	13,055	11,730	11,633	11,420
Capitalization:Long Term Debt	11,073	11,069	12,459	9,329	10,230	10,097	6,500	6,974	5,304	5,397
Capitalization:% Long Term Debt	54.9	56.5	61.3	56.9	55.4	55.6	56.5	59.0	53.1	54.3
Capitalization:Preferred	Nil	Nil	Nil	Nil	Nil	Nil	Nil	Nil	Nil	Nil
Capitalization:% Preferred	Nil	Nil	Nil	Nil	Nil	Nil	Nil	Nil	Nil	Nil
Capitalization:Common	9,088	8,515	7,874	7,064	8,229	8,054	5,006	4,841	4,677	4,545
Capitalization:% Common	45.1	43.5	38.7	43.1	44.6	44.4	43.5	41.0	46.9	45.7
Total Capital	25,032	24,403	24,290	21,523	24,523	23,554	14,577	14,767	12,918	12,990
% Operating Ratio	84.1	85.8	88.8	91.3	96.1	85.2	81.1	84.9	84.0	82.8
% Earned on Net Property	8.2	8.9	7.7	5.8	10.2	9.2	10.1	8.2	8.5	8.8
% Return on Revenue	8.5	8.0	3.6	0.1	1.6	2.2	7.5	8.4	10.1	10.0
% Return on Invested Capital	6.2	6.1	9.4	8.8	8.4	6.8	7.2	7.0	8.1	7.8
% Return on Common Equity	11.7	13.8	7.0	0.3	12.3	3.6	10.6	11.3	13.4	13.2

Data as orig reptd.; bef. results of disc opers/spec. items. Per share data adj. for stk. divs.; EPS diluted. E-Estimated. NA-Not Available. NM-Not Meaningful. NR-Not Ranked. UR-Under Review.

Office: 1 Riverside Plz, Columbus , OH 43215-2373.
Telephone: 614-716-1000.
Email: corpcomm@aep.com
Website: http://www.aep.com

Chrmn, Pres & CEO: M.G. Morris
EVP & CFO: H. Koeppel
SVP, Secy & General Counsel: J.B. Keane
Investor Contact: J. Sloat (614-716-2885)

Board of Directors: E. R. Brooks, D. M. Carlton, R. D. Crosby, Jr., J. P. DesBarres, R. W. Fri, L. A. Goodspeed, W. R. Howell, L. A. Hudson, Jr., M. G. Morris, L. L. Nowell, III, R. L. Sandor, D. G. Smith, K. D. Sullivan

Founded: 1906
Domicile: New York
Employees: 19,630

STANDARD &POOR'S

American Express Co

S&P Recommendation HOLD ★★★★★

Price $57.27 (as of Oct 27, 2006)

12-Mo. Target Price $60.00

Investment Style Large-Cap Growth

GICS Sector Financials
Sub-Industry Consumer Finance

Comment American Express is a leading global payments, network and travel company.

Key Stock Statistics (Source S&P, Vickers, company reports)

52-Wk Range	$58.43–48.21	S&P Oper. EPS 2006E	3.08	P/E on S&P Oper. EPS 2006E	18.6	Dividend Rate/Share	$0.60
Trailing 12-Month EPS	$2.83	S&P Oper. EPS 2007E	3.47	Common Shares Outstg. (M)	1,214.9	Yield (%)	1.05
Trailing 12-Month P/E	20.2	S&P Core EPS 2006E	3.04	Market Capitalization(B)	$69.575	Beta	1.29
$10K Invested 5 Yrs Ago	$22,225	S&P Core EPS 2007E	3.45	Institutional Ownership (%)	82	S&P Credit Rating	A+

Price Performance

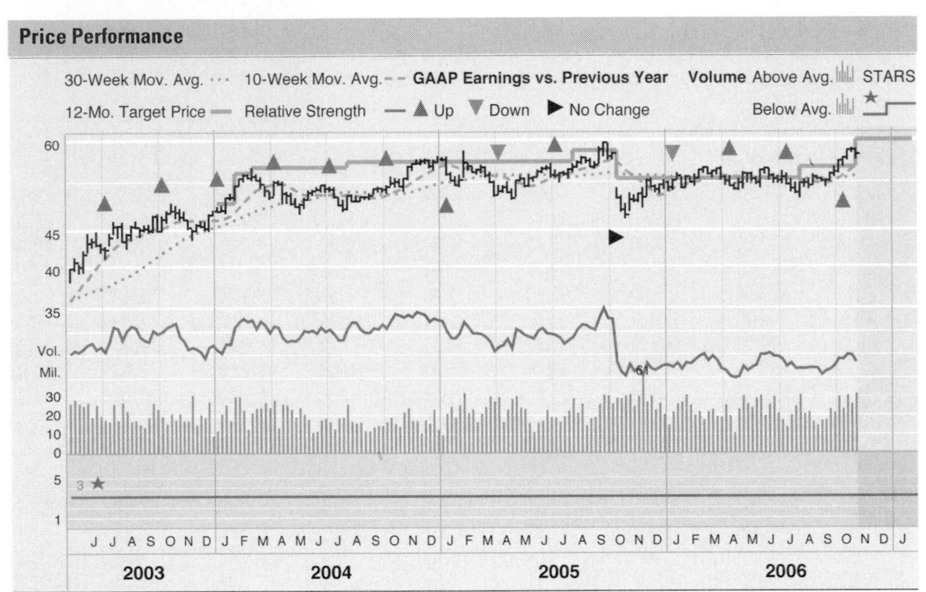

Options: ASE, CBOE, P, Ph

Analysis prepared by **Mark Hebeka, CFA** on October 25, 2006, when the stock traded at **$ 56.70**.

Highlights

- We see AXP exceeding its long-term annual revenue growth target of 8% for 2006 and 2007, mainly due to strong cardmember average spending, growth in cards in force, and acquisition benefits. We believe expense control, combined with solid credit quality, will generate positive operating leverage for the year and further boost the bottom line.
- We look for continued, albeit, sequentially slower, growth in corporate and consumer spending, while increases in marketing expenses and moderating trends in credit quality should hold back net income growth. We believe the issuance of American Express cards through partnerships with various large banking players should have a slightly negative impact on proprietary cardmember growth but a long-term positive impact on total billed business for AXP's merchant network.
- We see EPS of $3.08 in 2006 and $3.47 in 2007, up from $2.56 in 2005, with the spin-off of AXP's financial advisory business excluded from our estimates.

Investment Rationale/Risk

- We believe the current valuation, a significant premium versus diversified peers, fairly reflects our view of AXP's strong brand name and growth prospects. The stock recently traded above its average 12-month forward P/E multiple during the past three years, which we view as justified due to the recent Ameriprise spin-off. We view AXP as having exceptionally strong credit and solid growth prospects. While we see competition continuing to increase, we view AXP as the market leader and look for it to continue to innovate.
- Risks to our recommendation and target price include a possible deterioration in consumer confidence that would have an impact on domestic consumer spending, and a rise in unemployment that would pressure credit quality.
- Our 12-month target price of $60 values the stock at 17.3X our 2007 EPS estimate, a premium to its historical P/E. We think this is an appropriate valuation multiple based on our view of the company's new, less capital intensive structure, and improved growth prospects.

Qualitative Risk Assessment

LOW | MEDIUM | HIGH

Our risk assessment reflects what we see as solid business fundamentals and a strong customer base. We view AXP as able to withstand a major global or U.S. economic downturn and consider its credit quality solid.

Quantitative Evaluations

S&P Quality Ranking A-

D | C | B- | B | B+ | A- | A | A+

Relative Strength Rank MODERATE

60

LOWEST = 1 HIGHEST = 99

Revenue/Earnings Data

Revenue (Million $)

	1Q	2Q	3Q	4Q	Year
2006	6,332	6,878	6,759	--	--
2005	5,672	6,090	6,068	6,437	24,267
2004	6,910	7,232	7,202	7,771	29,115
2003	6,023	6,356	6,419	7,068	25,866
2002	5,759	5,945	5,907	6,196	23,807
2001	5,719	5,268	5,724	5,871	22,582

Earnings Per Share ($)

	1Q	2Q	3Q	4Q	Year
2006	0.70	0.78	0.78	E0.81	E3.08
2005	0.59	0.69	0.69	0.60	2.56
2004	0.66	0.68	0.69	0.71	2.74
2003	0.53	0.59	0.59	0.60	2.31
2002	0.46	0.51	0.52	0.52	2.01
2001	0.40	0.13	0.22	0.22	0.98

Fiscal year ended Dec. 31. Next earnings report expected: Late January. EPS Estimates based on S&P Operating Earnings; historical GAAP earnings are as reported.

Dividend Data (Dates: mm/dd Payment Date: mm/dd/yy)

Amount ($)	Date Decl.	Ex-Div. Date	Stk. of Record	Payment Date
0.120	11/21	01/04	01/06	02/10/06
0.120	03/27	04/05	04/07	05/10/06
0.150	05/22	07/05	07/07	08/10/06
0.150	09/27	10/04	10/06	11/10/06

Dividends have been paid since 1870. Source: Company reports.

American Express Co

Business Summary October 25, 2006

CORPORATE PROFILE. AXP is a leading global payments, network and travel company that is principally engaged in businesses comprising three operating segments: U.S. Card Services; International Card & Global Commercial Services; and Global Network & Merchant Services.

U.S. Card Services includes the U.S. proprietary consumer card business, OPEN from American Express, the global Travelers Cheques and Prepaid Services business, and the American Express U.S. Consumer Travel Network.

International Card & Global Commercial Services provides proprietary consumer cards and small business cards outside the United States. This division also offers global corporate products and services, including the corporate card, issued to individuals through a corporate account established by their employer; business travel, which helps businesses manage their travel expenses through a variety of travel-related products and services; and corporate purchasing solutions, addressing a business need to pay for everyday expenses such as office and computer supplies. International Card & Global Commercial Services also includes international banking operations that provide financial products and services to retail customers and wealthy individuals outside the United States and financial institutions around the world.

Global Network & Merchant Services consists of the merchant services businesses and global network services. Global network services develops and manages relationships with third parties that issue American Express branded cards. The global merchant services businesses develop and manage relationships with merchants that accept American Express branded cards; authorize and record transactions; pay merchants; and provide a variety of value-added point of sale and back office services. In addition, in particular emerging markets, issuance of certain proprietary cards is managed within the global network services business.

Company Financials

Per Share Data ($) Year Ended Dec. 31	**2005**	**2004**	**2003**	**2002**	**2001**	**2000**	**1999**	**1998**	**1997**	**1996**
Tangible Book Value	8.50	12.83	11.93	10.62	9.04	8.81	7.53	7.18	6.84	6.01
Earnings	2.56	2.74	2.31	2.01	0.98	2.07	1.81	1.54	1.38	1.30
S&P Core Earnings	2.49	2.53	2.09	1.68	0.73	NA	NA	NA	NA	NA
Dividends	0.48	0.32	0.38	0.32	0.32	0.32	0.30	0.30	0.30	0.38
Payout Ratio	19%	12%	16%	16%	33%	15%	17%	19%	22%	29%
Prices:High	59.50	57.05	49.11	44.91	57.06	63.00	56.29	39.54	30.50	20.13
Prices:Low	46.59	47.32	30.90	26.55	24.20	39.83	31.63	22.33	17.88	12.88
P/E Ratio:High	23	21	21	22	58	30	31	26	22	15
P/E Ratio:Low	18	17	13	13	25	19	18	14	13	10

Income Statement Analysis (Million $)	2005	2004	2003	2002	2001	2000	1999	1998	1997	1996
Cards in Force	71.0	65.4	60.5	57.3	55.2	51.7	46.0	42.7	42.7	41.5
Card Charge Volume	484,400	416,100	352,200	311,400	298,000	296,700	254,100	227,500	209,200	184,000
Premium Income	Nil	1,525	1,366	802	674	575	517	469	424	395
Commissions	4,236	4,079	3,484	3,521	3,969	4,165	3,626	3,304	4,386	2,540
Interest & Dividends	3,635	3,118	3,063	2,991	3,049	4,277	4,679	4,631	2,750	4,357
Total Revenue	24,267	29,115	25,866	23,807	22,582	23,675	16,599	14,501	17,760	16,237
Net Before Taxes	4,248	4,951	4,247	3,727	1,596	3,908	3,438	2,925	2,750	2,664
Net Income	3,221	3,516	3,000	2,671	1,311	2,810	2,475	2,141	1,991	1,901
S&P Core Earnings	3,144	3,244	2,723	2,245	986	NA	NA	NA	NA	NA

Balance Sheet & Other Financial Data (Million $)	2005	2004	2003	2002	2001	2000	1999	1998	1997	1996
Total Assets	113,960	192,638	175,001	157,253	151,100	154,423	148,517	126,933	120,003	108,512
Cash Items	7,126	9,907	5,726	10,288	7,222	8,487	7,471	4,092	4,179	2,677
Investment Assets:Bonds	Nil	Nil	Nil	Nil	Nil	Nil	Nil	Nil	Nil	Nil
Investment Assets:Stocks	Nil	Nil	Nil	Nil	Nil	Nil	Nil	Nil	Nil	Nil
Investment Assets:Loans	40,801	35,942	33,421	29,003	27,401	26,884	24,332	21,861	20,816	18,518
Investment Assets:Total	62,135	60,809	57,067	53,638	46,488	43,747	43,052	41,299	59,757	56,857
Accounts Receivable	35,497	34,650	31,269	29,087	29,498	30,543	26,467	22,224	21,774	20,491
Customer Deposits	24,579	21,091	21,250	18,317	14,557	13,870	12,197	10,398	9,444	9,555
Travel Cheques Outstanding	7,175	7,287	6,819	6,623	6,190	6,127	6,213	5,823	5,634	5,838
Debt	30,781	33,061	30,809	16,819	8,288	5,211	6,495	7,519	7,873	6,552
Common Equity	10,549	16,020	15,323	13,861	12,037	11,684	10,095	9,698	9,574	8,528
% Return on Assets	2.1	1.9	1.8	1.7	0.9	1.9	1.8	1.7	1.7	1.8
% Return on Equity	24.2	22.4	20.6	20.6	11.1	25.8	25.0	22.2	22.0	22.9

Data as orig reptd.; bef. results of disc opers/spec. items. Per share data adj. for stk. divs.; EPS diluted. E-Estimated. NA-Not Available. NM-Not Meaningful. NR-Not Ranked. UR-Under Review.

Office: 200 Vesey Street, New York, NY 10285-4814.
Telephone: 212-640-2000.
Website: http://www.americanexpress.com
Chrmn & CEO: K.I. Chenault

EVP & CFO: G. Crittenden
EVP & General Counsel: L.M. Parent
EVP & CIO: S. Squeri
SVP & Treas: D. Yowan

Investor Contact: R. Stovall (212-640-5574)
Board of Directors: D. F. Akerson, C. Barshefsky, W. G. Bowen, U. M. Burns, K. I. Chenault, P. Chernin, P. R. Dolan, V. E. Jordan, Jr., J. Leschly, R. A. McGinn, E. D. Miller, F. P. Popoff, R. D. Walter

Founded: 1868
Domicile: New York
Employees: 65,800

American International Group Inc

STANDARD &POOR'S

S&P Recommendation BUY ★★★★★

Price $67.39 (as of Oct 27, 2006)

12-Mo. Target Price $76.00

Investment Style Large-Cap Growth

GICS Sector Financials
Sub-Industry Multi-line Insurance

Comment One of the world's leading insurance organizations, AIG provides property, casualty and life insurance, as well as other financial services, in 130 countries and territories.

Key Stock Statistics (Source S&P, Vickers, company reports)

52-Wk Range	$71.09–57.52	S&P Oper. EPS 2006E	5.55	P/E on S&P Oper. EPS 2006E	12.1	Dividend Rate/Share	$0.66
Trailing 12-Month EPS	$3.25	S&P Oper. EPS 2007E	6.15	Common Shares Outstg. (M)	2,598.8	Yield (%)	0.98
Trailing 12-Month P/E	20.7	S&P Core EPS 2006E	5.44	Market Capitalization(B)	$175.131	Beta	1.04
$10K Invested 5 Yrs Ago	$8,265	S&P Core EPS 2007E	6.03	Institutional Ownership (%)	64	S&P Credit Rating	AA

Price Performance

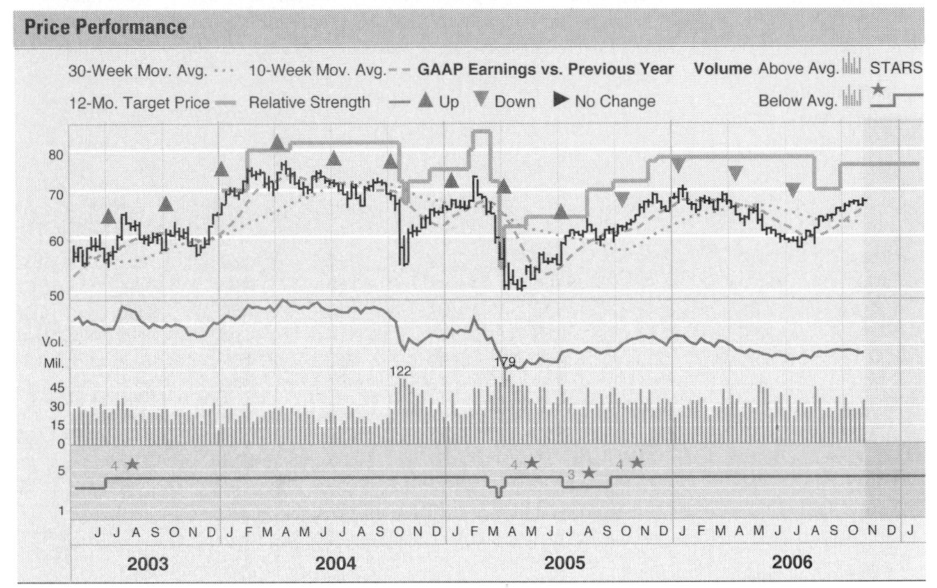

Options: ASE, CBOE, P, Ph

Analysis prepared by **Cathy A. Seifert** on October 03, 2006, when the stock traded at **$ 66.70**.

Highlights

- We forecast earned premium growth of 6% in 2006, reflecting what we view as a more competitive pricing environment and the possibility that investigations and management changes may have impaired AIG's ability to write business. Net written premiums advanced 3.1% during 2005, versus growth of 16% in 2004 (as restated). We see 2006 written premium growth of 7% to 10%, which should translate into an above average (versus the overall industry) rate of earned premium growth in 2007.
- We believe AIG's significant overseas life insurance franchise will continue to be a core contributor to operating profits. AIG is well positioned, in our view, to exploit growth opportunities that exist in a number of Asian and developing economies.
- We forecast operating EPS of $5.55 for 2006, versus operating EPS of $3.92 in 2005. The rebound in operating EPS that we forecast for 2006 is skewed by the impact of higher catastrophe losses and charges totaling $1.15 billion to settle regulatory issues, and $1.19 billion to boost loss reserves.

Investment Rationale/Risk

- Given its industry leading position, our recommendation is buy. However, our favorable outlook is tempered by concerns that AIG could have additional internal control issues that may need to be addressed. We also believe there is some uncertainty over whether AIG will be able to regain the superior (versus peers) rate of property-casualty premium growth it once enjoyed. However, we believe that AIG has a number of competitive advantages, including its low property-casualty expense ratio and its global franchise (particularly in Asia), which is unmatched, in our view.
- Risks to our recommendation and target price include a significant deterioration in loss reserve levels, and the possibility of additional significant disclosures related to internal control and/or regulatory issues.
- Our 12-month target price of $76 assumes the shares will trade at about 2X estimated 2007 tangible book value, a premium to some peers. We do not believe the shares will regain all of the premium multiple they were once awarded, owing to the downgrade of AIG's financial strength rating.

Qualitative Risk Assessment

LOW | **MEDIUM** | HIGH

Our risk assessment reflects our view of the company as a leading underwriter with an unmatched global franchise. This is partially offset by our concern that AIG may have to incur additional one-time charges as its new senior management team continues its transition and tightens internal controls.

Quantitative Evaluations

S&P Quality Ranking A+

D | C | B- | B | B+ | A- | A | **A+**

Relative Strength Rank MODERATE

57

LOWEST = 1 HIGHEST = 99

Revenue/Earnings Data

Revenue (Million $)

	1Q	2Q	3Q	4Q	Year
2006	27,259	26,743	--	--	--
2005	27,202	27,903	26,408	27,392	108,905
2004	23,637	23,809	25,411	25,760	97,987
2003	18,927	19,891	20,306	22,179	81,303
2002	16,137	16,662	17,150	17,533	67,482
2001	--	--	--	--	52,852

Earnings Per Share ($)

	1Q	2Q	3Q	4Q	Year
2006	1.21	1.21	--	--	E5.55
2005	1.45	1.71	0.66	0.17	3.99
2004	1.08	1.09	0.95	1.15	3.75
2003	0.74	0.87	0.89	1.03	3.53
2002	0.75	0.68	0.70	-0.03	2.10
2001	0.65	0.69	0.15	0.70	2.07

Fiscal year ended Dec. 31. Next earnings report expected: Mid November. EPS Estimates based on S&P Operating Earnings; historical GAAP earnings are as reported.

Dividend Data (Dates: mm/dd Payment Date: mm/dd/yy)

Amount ($)	Date Decl.	Ex-Div. Date	Stk. of Record	Payment Date
0.150	11/16	03/01	03/03	03/17/06
0.150	03/15	05/31	06/02	06/16/06
0.165	05/17	08/30	09/01	09/15/06
0.165	09/20	11/29	12/01	12/15/06

Dividends have been paid since 1969. Source: Company reports.

Please read the Required Disclosures and Analyst Certification on the last page of this report.

American International Group Inc

Business Summary October 03, 2006

Investigations by the New York Attorney General and the SEC into AIG's use of non-traditional insurance products and certain assumed reinsurance transactions (sometimes referred to as finite reinsurance) culminated in a number of events, including a management shake-up that led to: the resignation of AIG's long-time CEO, Maurice Greenberg; a write-down to earnings from 2000-2004 totaling nearly $4 billion; and a write-down of shareholders' equity of $2.26 billion. During 2005, AIG also incurred after-tax charges totaling $1.15 billion to settle its numerous regulatory issues and $1.19 billion to boost loss reserves. Revenues totaled $108.9 billion in 2005, with general insurance accounting for 42%, life insurance 43%, financial services, asset management and other 15%. The Far East provided 29% of 2005 revenues, domestic operations 55%, and other foreign 16%.

General Insurance net written premiums totaled $41.9 billion in 2005, of which the Domestic Brokerage Group accounted for 55%, Foreign General 24%, Domestic Personal Lines 11%, Reinsurance 8%, and Mortgage Guaranty 2%. The Domestic Brokerage Group underwrites an array of standard and specialty lines of commercial coverage. AIG maintains a majority ownership in Transatlantic Holdings (TRH), through which it underwrites reinsurance. The Foreign General division conducts AIG's international property-casualty operations.

Life insurance and retirement services premiums totaled $29.4 billion in 2005 and were divided as such: foreign life insurance 77%, domestic life insurance 18%, domestic retirement services 3%, and foreign retirement services 2%. Within the domestic life insurance segment, life insurance accounted for 39% of premiums in 2005, payout annuities 27%, group products 19%, and home service life insurance 15%. Life insurance accounted for 69% of foreign life insurance premiums, personal health and accident policies 22%, and group products 9%.

Company Financials

Per Share Data ($) Year Ended Dec. 31	**2005**	**2004**	**2003**	**2002**	**2001**	**2000**	**1999**	**1998**	**1997**	**1996**
Tangible Book Value	30.13	27.73	24.39	20.32	19.94	16.98	14.33	13.78	12.20	11.13
Operating Earnings	NA	NA	NA	NA	NA	2.45	2.13	1.87	1.64	1.43
Earnings	3.99	3.75	3.53	2.10	2.07	2.41	2.15	1.91	1.68	1.46
S&P Core Earnings	4.35	3.77	3.89	2.63	2.06	NA	NA	NA	NA	NA
Dividends	0.55	0.28	0.22	0.18	0.16	0.14	0.13	0.11	0.10	0.09
Relative Payout	14%	7%	6%	8%	8%	6%	6%	6%	6%	6%
Prices:High	73.46	77.36	66.35	80.00	98.31	103.75	75.25	54.73	40.02	27.59
Prices:Low	49.91	54.28	42.92	47.61	66.00	52.38	51.00	34.60	25.24	20.89
P/E Ratio:High	18	21	19	38	47	43	35	29	24	19
P/E Ratio:Low	13	14	12	23	32	22	24	18	15	14
Income Statement Analysis (Million $)										
Life Insurance in Force	1,852,833	1,858,094	1,596,626	1,324,451	1,228,501	583,059	584,959	499,167	436,573	421,983
Premium Income:Life A & H	29,400	28,082	22,879	20,320	19,243	13,610	11,942	10,247	9,926	8,978
Premium Income:Casualty/Property.	41,872	40,607	31,734	24,269	19,365	17,407	15,544	14,098	12,421	11,855
Net Investment Income	22,165	18,434	16,662	15,034	14,628	9,824	8,723	5,424	4,750	4,365
Total Revenue	108,905	97,987	81,303	67,482	52,852	40,717	36,356	29,939	27,246	25,298
Pretax Income	15,213	14,950	13,908	8,142	8,139	8,349	7,512	5,529	4,731	4,013
Net Operating Income	105	NA	NA	NA	NA	5,737	4,999	3,689	49,662	45,965
Net Income	10,477	9,875	9,265	5,519	5,499	5,636	5,055	3,766	3,332	2,897
S&P Core Earnings	11,396	9,928	10,208	6,931	5,476	NA	NA	NA	NA	NA
Balance Sheet & Other Financial Data (Million $)										
Cash & Equivalent	7,624	7,597	5,881	1,165	698	256	132	1,874	87.0	3,265
Premiums Due	15,333	15,137	14,166	13,088	11,647	11,832	12,737	11,679	10,283	9,617
Investment Assets:Bonds	385,680	365,677	309,254	243,366	200,616	102,010	90,144	61,906	51,566	48,625
Investment Assets:Stocks	23,588	17,851	9,584	7,066	7,937	7,181	6,714	5,893	5,209	6,006
Investment Assets:Loans	24,909	22,463	21,249	19,928	18,092	12,243	12,134	8,247	7,920	7,877
Investment Assets:Total	614,759	494,592	449,657	339,320	357,602	140,910	185,882	141,923	116,221	103,982
Deferred Policy Costs	33,248	29,736	26,398	22,256	17,443	10,189	9,624	7,647	6,593	6,471
Total Assets	853,370	798,660	678,346	561,229	492,982	306,577	268,238	194,398	163,971	148,431
Debt	78,625	66,850	57,877	50,076	34,503	5,801	23,795	31,093	25,260	23,521
Common Equity	86,317	80,607	71,253	59,103	52,150	39,619	33,306	27,131	24,002	22,044
Combined Loss-Expense Ratio	104.7	100.1	92.4	106.0	100.7	96.7	96.4	96.4	96.2	96.9
% Return on Revenue	9.6	10.1	11.4	8.2	10.5	13.8	13.9	12.6	14.8	11.2
% Return on Equity	12.6	13.1	14.2	9.9	11.0	15.5	15.9	14.7	14.5	13.8
% Investment Yield	3.7	3.9	4.1	4.8	4.5	7.4	4.9	4.9	4.3	4.5

Data as orig reptd.; bef. results of disc opers/spec. items. Per share data adj. for stk. divs.; EPS diluted. E-Estimated. NA-Not Available. NM-Not Meaningful. NR-Not Ranked. UR-Under Review.

Office: 70 Pine St , New York, NY 10270-0094.
Telephone: 212-770-7000.
Website: http://www.aigcorporate.com
Chrmn: F.G. Zarb

Pres & CEO: M.J. Sullivan
Vice Chrmn: E.S. Tse
Vice Chrmn: F.G. Wisner
Vice Chrmn: J.A. Frenkel

Investor Contact: C.M. Hamrah
Board of Directors: P. Chia, M. A. Cohen, M. S. Feldstein, E. V. Futter, S. L. Hammerman, R. C. Holbrooke, F. H. Langhammer, G. L. Miles, Jr., M. W. Offit, J. F. Orr, III, V. M. Rometty, M. J. Sullivan, M. H. Sutton, E. S. Tse, R. B. Willumstad, F. G. Zarb

Founded: 1967
Domicile: Delaware
Employees: 97,000

STANDARD &POOR'S

American Power Conversion Corp

S&P Recommendation HOLD ★★★★★

Price $30.23 (as of Oct 31, 2006)

12-Mo. Target Price $31.00

Investment Style Mid-Cap Growth

GICS Sector Industrials
Sub-Industry Electrical Components & Equipment

Comment APCC manufactures uninterruptible power supply (UPS) products that protect data in PCs and other electronic devices from disruptions or surges in electric power.

Key Stock Statistics (Source S&P, Vickers, company reports)

52-Wk Range	$30.30–16.28	S&P Oper. EPS 2006E	0.67	P/E on S&P Oper. EPS 2006E	45.1	Dividend Rate/Share	$0.40
Trailing 12-Month EPS	$0.53	S&P Oper. EPS 2007E	1.05	Common Shares Outstg. (M)	190.5	Yield (%)	1.32
Trailing 12-Month P/E	57.0	S&P Core EPS 2006E	0.61	Market Capitalization(B)	$5.758	Beta	2.15
$10K Invested 5 Yrs Ago	$18,469	S&P Core EPS 2007E	0.98	Institutional Ownership (%)	81	S&P Credit Rating	NA

Price Performance

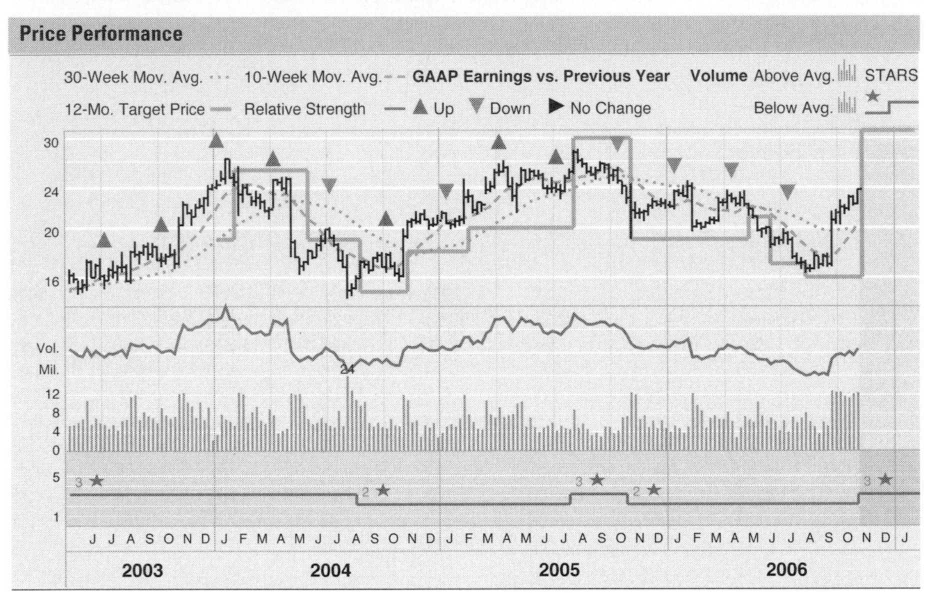

Options: ASE, CBOE, P, Ph

Highlights

➤ The STARS recommendation for APCC has recently been changed to 3 (hold) from 2 (sell) and the 12-month target price has recently been changed to $31.00 from $16.00. The Highlights section of this Stock Report will be updated accordingly.

Investment Rationale/Risk

➤ The Investment Rationale/Risk section of this Stock Report will be updated shortly. For the latest News story on APCC from MarketScope, see below.

➤ 10/30/06 09:40 am EST... S&P UPGRADES OPINION ON SHARES OF AMERICAN POWER CONVERSION TO HOLD FROM SELL (APCC 29.89***): France-based Schneider Electric SA has agreed to purchase all outstanding shares of APCC at $31 per share in cash, an aggregate of about $6.1B. The proposed deal values APCC shares at about 2.8X sales, above the company's 10-year average of 2.7X sales. Given what we view as a substantial premium on the shares amid declining profit margins, we expect shareholder approval, but note that the deal is also subject to other conditions. The transaction is projected to close during the first quarter of 2007. We are raising our target price to $31 from $16. /R.Tortoriello

Qualitative Risk Assessment

LOW | MEDIUM | **HIGH**

Our risk assessment reflects APCC's relatively inconsistent record of earnings growth, high stock volatility as reflected in its beta, and a downward trend over the past three years in profit margins.

Quantitative Evaluations

S&P Quality Ranking B

D | C | B- | **B** | B+ | A- | A | A+

Relative Strength Rank STRONG

99

LOWEST = 1 HIGHEST = 99

Revenue/Earnings Data

Revenue (Million $)

	1Q	2Q	3Q	4Q	Year
2006	478.8	560.0	--	--	--
2005	408.0	480.6	512.3	578.6	1,980
2004	351.8	395.7	441.7	510.8	1,700
2003	309.0	331.5	393.7	430.6	1,465
2002	296.7	308.2	337.1	358.0	1,300
2001	359.7	364.5	360.9	348.1	1,433

Earnings Per Share ($)

2006	0.07	0.13	**E**0.21	**E**0.27	**E**0.67
2005	0.18	0.21	0.24	0.09	0.72
2004	0.17	0.13	0.34	0.27	0.90
2003	0.15	0.17	0.28	0.28	0.88
2002	0.08	0.15	0.21	0.14	0.59
2001	0.14	0.18	0.11	0.15	0.58

Fiscal year ended Dec. 31. Next earnings report expected: NA. EPS Estimates based on S&P Operating Earnings; historical GAAP earnings are as reported.

Dividend Data (Dates: mm/dd Payment Date: mm/dd/yy)

Amount ($)	Date Decl.	Ex-Div. Date	Stk. of Record	Payment Date
0.100	11/02	11/17	11/21	12/14/05
0.100	02/01	02/15	02/20	03/15/06
0.100	05/12	05/24	05/26	06/14/06
0.100	08/15	08/24	08/28	09/13/06

Dividends have been paid since 2003. Source: Company reports.

American Power Conversion Corp

Business Summary August 04, 2006

CORPORATE OVERVIEW. Founded in 1981, American Power Conversion manufactures power protection and management solutions for computer, communications, and electronics applications worldwide. Products include uninterruptible power supply products (UPSs), electrical surge protection devices, power conditioning products, DC-power systems, management and monitoring tools, racks and enclosures, cooling solutions, and other products. These products are used primarily with sensitive electronic devices that rely on electric utility power.

APCC operates within three segments: The Small Systems segment develops power devices and accessories for servers and networking equipment commonly used in local area and wide area networks and for personal computers. Major products include Back-UPS, Smart-UPS, and the Symmetra Power Array single-phase family of UPSs.

The Large Systems segment provides systems, products, and services that primarily provide back-up power, power distribution and cooling for data centers, facilities, and communications equipment. Products include InfraStruXure systems, Silicon UPSs, NetworkAIR precision cooling equipment, DC and broadband power systems, and APC Global Services. The Other segment consists mainly of mobile accessories and replacement batteries.

Sales outside the U.S. accounted for 55% and 56% of net sales in 2005 and 2004, respectively. The Small Systems segment accounted for 74% of sales in 2005, large systems for 22%, and other for 4%.

APCC markets its products to businesses, small offices/home offices, and home users around the world through distribution channels that include: information technology and electrical equipment distributors and dealers, value added resellers, mass merchandisers, catalog merchandisers, e-commerce vendors, direct-to-customers, and strategic partnerships. Two computer distributor customers, Tech Data Product Management and Ingram Micro, accounted for 16.5% and 8.8%, respectively, of net sales in 2005 (12.7% and 8.9% in 2004).

Company Financials

Per Share Data ($) Year Ended Dec. 31	**2005**	**2004**	**2003**	**2002**	**2001**	**2000**	**1999**	**1998**	**1997**	**1996**
Tangible Book Value	8.11	7.58	7.28	6.34	5.67	5.00	4.42	3.32	2.74	2.08
Cash Flow	0.91	1.14	1.11	0.79	0.86	1.03	1.21	0.88	0.73	0.56
Earnings	0.72	0.90	0.88	0.59	0.58	0.83	1.05	0.76	0.64	0.49
S&P Core Earnings	0.69	0.85	0.77	0.46	0.33	NA	NA	NA	NA	NA
Dividends	0.40	0.36	0.16	Nil	Nil	Nil	Nil	Nil	Nil	Nil
Payout Ratio	56%	40%	18%	Nil	Nil	Nil	Nil	Nil	Nil	Nil
Prices:High	28.56	27.42	24.69	16.60	19.39	48.84	29.38	24.78	17.19	14.06
Prices:Low	19.00	14.55	13.72	9.06	10.25	9.50	13.09	11.75	7.63	3.94
P/E Ratio:High	40	30	28	28	33	59	28	33	27	29
P/E Ratio:Low	26	16	16	15	18	11	12	15	12	8
Income Statement Analysis (Million $)										
Revenue	1,980	1,700	1,465	1,300	1,433	1,484	1,337	1,126	873	707
Operating Income	225	253	277	191	201	298	310	235	189	147
Depreciation	38.3	48.5	47.5	39.7	55.9	40.9	30.6	23.0	17.7	13.5
Interest Expense	Nil	Nil	Nil	Nil	Nil	Nil	Nil	Nil	Nil	Nil
Pretax Income	209	214	239	162	159	233	293	216	178	139
Effective Tax Rate	31.0%	15.3%	26.0%	28.0%	28.5%	29.0%	29.5%	31.6%	31.5%	33.5%
Net Income	144	181	177	117	113	166	206	148	122	92.4
S&P Core Earnings	137	171	157	91.6	64.8	NA	NA	NA	NA	NA
Balance Sheet & Other Financial Data (Million $)										
Cash	774	716	252	209	288	283	456	220	270	153
Current Assets	1,809	1,605	1,498	1,277	1,067	961	900	675	540	424
Total Assets	2,075	1,844	1,806	1,605	1,421	1,317	1,107	872	641	504
Current Liabilities	421	326	281	277	183	206	194	181	114	106
Long Term Debt	Nil	Nil	Nil	Nil	Nil	Nil	Nil	Nil	Nil	Nil
Common Equity	1,640	1,502	1,511	1,312	1,221	1,097	902	681	522	392
Total Capital	1,655	1,518	1,525	1,327	1,238	1,111	913	691	528	398
Capital Expenditures	49.2	29.3	21.6	19.6	47.9	73.7	36.0	55.7	37.2	25.0
Cash Flow	182	230	224	156	169	207	237	171	140	106
Current Ratio	4.3	4.9	5.3	4.6	5.8	4.7	4.6	3.7	4.8	4.0
% Long Term Debt of Capitalization	Nil	Nil	Nil	Nil	Nil	Nil	Nil	Nil	Nil	Nil
% Net Income of Revenue	7.3	10.7	12.1	9.0	7.9	11.2	15.4	13.1	13.9	13.1
% Return on Assets	7.4	9.9	10.4	7.7	8.3	13.7	20.8	19.5	21.3	21.7
% Return on Equity	9.2	12.0	12.5	9.2	9.8	16.6	26.0	24.5	26.7	27.1

Data as orig reptd.; bef. results of disc opers/spec. items. Per share data adj. for stk. divs.; EPS diluted. E-Estimated. NA-Not Available. NM-Not Meaningful. NR-Not Ranked. UR-Under Review.

Office: 132 Fairgrounds Road, West Kingston, RI 02892-1517.
Telephone: 401-789-5735.
Email: investorrelations@apcc.com
Website: http://www.apc.com

Chrmn, Pres & CEO: R.B. Dowdell, Jr.
COO & SVP: E.W. Machala
SVP & CFO: R.J. Thompson
SVP & CTO: N.E. Rasmussen

Investor Contact: D. Hancock (800-788-2208)
Board of Directors: R. B. Dowdell, Jr., J. D. Gerson, J. G. Kassakian, E. F. Lyon, N. E. Rasmussen, E. B. Richstone

Founded: 1981
Domicile: Massachusetts
Employees: 7,580

American Standard Cos Inc

STANDARD &POOR'S

S&P Recommendation BUY ★★★★★

Price $43.66 (as of Oct 27, 2006)

12-Mo. Target Price $51.00

Investment Style Mid-Cap Growth

GICS Sector Industrials
Sub-Industry Building Products

Comment ASD is a leading worldwide maker of air conditioning systems and bathroom and kitchen fixtures and a major European producer of commercial vehicle braking systems.

Key Stock Statistics (Source S&P, Vickers, company reports)

52-Wk Range	$47.14–35.01	S&P Oper. EPS 2006E	2.75	P/E on S&P Oper. EPS 2006E	15.9	Dividend Rate/Share	$0.72
Trailing 12-Month EPS	$2.36	S&P Oper. EPS 2007E	3.10	Common Shares Outstg. (M)	199.4	Yield (%)	1.65
Trailing 12-Month P/E	18.5	S&P Core EPS 2006E	2.78	Market Capitalization(B)	$8.705	Beta	1.02
$10K Invested 5 Yrs Ago	$22,494	S&P Core EPS 2007E	3.13	Institutional Ownership (%)	86	S&P Credit Rating	BBB

Price Performance

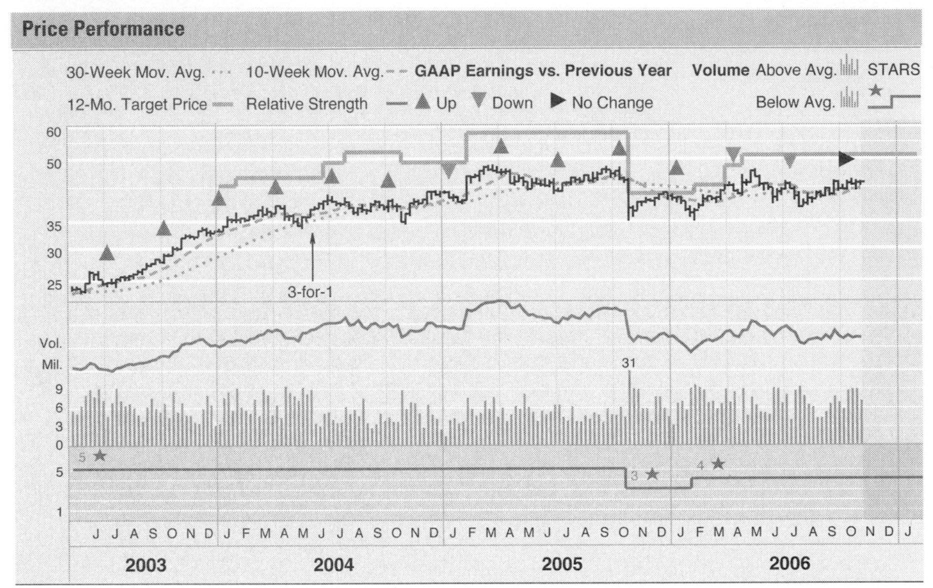

Options: ASE, CBOE, P, Ph

Analysis prepared by **Michael W. Jaffe** on August 21, 2006, when the stock traded at **$ 40.35**.

Highlights

- We see an 8% sales increase in 2006, followed by a 6% gain in 2007. We expect commercial air conditioning sales to be lifted by a relatively healthy U.S. economy. We also see flattish residential air conditioner sales in 2006 and a mid-single-digit drop in 2007. In that area, we see reduced sales volume, as macroeconomic factors have been slowing housing markets, and renovations, to a lesser extent. Yet, given a mandated shift to more energy efficient residential central air conditioners, we expect higher average prices in both years. Also, with ASD's brands still struggling, we expect flat bath and kitchen sales in both years.
- Net margins, excluding the impact of stock option expense, should widen slightly in both 2006 and 2007. We see profits aided by the better demand that we forecast in commercial air conditioning and projected benefits of streamlining actions. We expect these factors to be offset by some likely ongoing but lessening inefficiencies in bath and kitchen, and by our outlook for still high material costs.
- Our 2006 and 2007 EPS forecasts include $0.10 of projected stock option expense; $0.08 of stock option expense was excluded in 2005.

Investment Rationale/Risk

- We see ASD's primary commercial air conditioning segment continuing its revival through at least 2007. In addition, although we think ASD has operated inefficiently in its bath and kitchen segment in recent years, we see the company's ongoing initiatives allowing that business to bottom over the coming year. Based on these factors and valuation considerations, we believe the shares are undervalued.
- Risks to our recommendation and target price include a major slowdown in U.S. commercial construction markets, a greater than expected reduction in home buying and remodeling activity, and an inability to revive the struggling bath and kitchen segment.
- The shares recently traded at 13X our 2007 EPS forecast, a slight discount to the S&P 500. We believe this discount is warranted, in light of the cyclicality of ASD's businesses and its struggles in bath and kitchen. We thus determine a value of $40 for the shares on a forward P/E basis. Using DCF, and assuming 7% free cash flow growth for the next 15 years, 3% growth in perpetuity, and a 9.6% WACC, we calculate an intrinsic value of $61. Using a blend, our 12-month target price is $51.

Qualitative Risk Assessment

LOW | MEDIUM | HIGH

Our risk assessment reflects that while ASD's businesses are inherently cyclical in nature, we believe its risk profile is greatly reduced by what we view as a very strong business model, which has brought consistently strong levels of free cash flow over the past decade.

Quantitative Evaluations

S&P Quality Ranking B

D | C | B- | B | B+ | A- | A | A+

Relative Strength Rank MODERATE

55

LOWEST = 1 HIGHEST = 99

Revenue/Earnings Data

Revenue (Million $)

	1Q	2Q	3Q	4Q	Year
2006	2,552	2,991	2,965	--	--
2005	2,340	2,755	2,624	2,545	10,264
2004	2,185	2,575	2,396	2,352	9,509
2003	1,951	2,265	2,234	2,118	8,568
2002	1,762	2,087	2,070	1,877	7,795
2001	1,791	2,039	1,885	1,750	7,465

Earnings Per Share ($)

2006	0.40	0.93	0.74	E0.57	E2.75
2005	0.57	0.95	0.74	0.30	2.56
2004	0.38	0.73	0.71	-0.41	1.42
2003	0.29	0.61	0.55	0.38	1.83
2002	0.26	0.57	0.52	0.34	1.68
2001	0.30	0.54	0.41	0.09	1.35

Fiscal year ended Dec. 31. Next earnings report expected: Late January. EPS Estimates based on S&P Operating Earnings; historical GAAP earnings are as reported.

Dividend Data (Dates: mm/dd Payment Date: mm/dd/yy)

Amount ($)	Date Decl.	Ex-Div. Date	Stk. of Record	Payment Date
0.180	02/02	02/27	03/01	03/20/06
0.180	05/03	05/30	06/01	06/20/06
0.180	07/07	08/30	09/01	09/20/06
0.180	10/05	11/29	12/01	12/20/06

Dividends have been paid since 2005. Source: Company reports.

American Standard Cos Inc

Business Summary August 21, 2006

American Standard Companies is a major global maker of air conditioning systems, bathroom and kitchen fixtures and fittings, and commercial vehicle control systems.

ASD derived 59% of sales and 65% of operating profits in 2005 from its air conditioning business; 23% and 10% from bath and kitchen products; and 18% and 25% from vehicle control systems.

Brands include Trane and American Standard for air conditioning; American Standard, Ideal Standard, Porcher, Jado, Armitage Shanks and Ceramica Dolomite for bath and kitchen products; and Wabco for vehicle control systems.

Operations in Europe accounted for 30% of sales and 22% of operating profits in 2005. Other foreign operations contributed 17% and 14% to sales and profits, respectively.

The company is a leading maker of heating, ventilating and air conditioning systems, with factories in the U.S. and in foreign markets. American Standard derived 26% of the division's sales outside the U.S. in 2005. ASD makes unitary systems, which are factory-assembled central air conditioning systems; and applied systems, which are custom-engineered for commercial use. Some 70% of segment sales came from commercial markets in 2005. About 60% of air conditioning sales for the year came from replacement, renovation and repair markets, with the remainder from new construction.

ASD is a leading maker in Europe, the U.S. and several other nations of bathroom and kitchen fixtures and fittings. It supplies these products to residential and commercial markets through retail and wholesale sales channels. In 2005, 80% of the division's sales in North America, 78% in Europe and 69% in Asia, were to residential markets. Its products are used for replacement and remodeling, and new construction. About 67% of bath and kitchen segment sales in 2005 were from non-U.S. operations.

The company is a leading producer in Europe, Brazil, North America and Asia of braking and control systems for the worldwide commercial, luxury and utility vehicle sectors. The division generated 75% of its sales in Europe in 2005.

Company Financials

Per Share Data ($) Year Ended Dec. 31	**2005**	**2004**	**2003**	**2002**	**2001**	**2000**	**1999**	**1998**	**1997**	**1996**
Tangible Book Value	NM	NM	NM	NM	NM	NM	NM	NM	NM	NM
Cash Flow	3.98	2.61	2.95	2.36	2.40	2.44	2.14	1.01	1.24	0.42
Earnings	2.56	1.42	1.83	1.68	1.35	1.45	1.21	0.15	0.52	-0.20
S&P Core Earnings	2.60	2.37	1.82	1.44	1.07	NA	NA	NA	NA	NA
Dividends	0.60	Nil	Nil	Nil	Nil	Nil	Nil	Nil	Nil	Nil
Payout Ratio	23%	Nil	Nil	Nil	Nil	Nil	Nil	Nil	Nil	Nil
Prices:High	48.39	41.82	34.00	26.33	23.63	16.58	16.48	16.42	17.21	13.25
Prices:Low	35.01	33.10	21.28	19.40	15.58	11.44	10.38	7.21	11.54	8.50
P/E Ratio:High	19	29	19	16	18	11	14	NM	33	NM
P/E Ratio:Low	14	23	12	12	12	8	9	NM	22	NM

Income Statement Analysis (Million $)										
Revenue	10,264	9,509	8,568	7,795	7,465	7,598	7,190	6,654	6,008	5,805
Operating Income	1,112	1,060	924	842	886	916	839	748	711	665
Depreciation	268	262	247	150	232	213	202	190	164	146
Interest Expense	118	115	117	129	169	199	188	188	192	202
Pretax Income	726	363	549	556	476	509	452	167	247	57.6
Effective Tax Rate	23.4%	13.6%	26.2%	33.3%	38.1%	38.1%	41.5%	79.0%	47.4%	NM
Net Income	556	313	405	371	295	315	264	33.6	120	-46.7
S&P Core Earnings	562	524	403	319	234	NA	NA	NA	NA	NA

Balance Sheet & Other Financial Data (Million $)										
Cash	391	229	112	96.6	82.1	85.4	61.2	64.8	28.8	59.7
Current Assets	3,066	2,890	2,491	2,014	1,896	1,878	1,726	1,591	1,394	1,386
Total Assets	6,868	6,842	5,879	5,144	4,831	4,745	4,686	4,156	3,669	3,520
Current Liabilities	2,229	2,347	2,034	1,666	1,688	1,807	2,287	2,351	1,841	1,237
Long Term Debt	1,676	1,429	1,627	1,918	2,142	2,376	1,887	1,528	1,551	1,742
Common Equity	922	930	714	230	-90.1	-393	-497	-701	-610	-380
Total Capital	2,730	2,454	2,559	2,257	2,137	2,028	1,445	875	941	1,430
Capital Expenditures	294	216	171	165	167	219	274	255	245	212
Cash Flow	824	575	652	521	527	529	466	224	284	98.8
Current Ratio	1.4	1.2	1.2	1.2	1.1	1.0	0.8	0.7	0.8	1.1
% Long Term Debt of Capitalization	61.4	58.2	63.6	85.0	100.2	117.1	130.5	174.6	165.0	121.0
% Net Income of Revenue	5.4	3.3	4.7	4.8	4.0	4.1	3.7	0.5	2.0	NM
% Return on Assets	8.1	4.9	7.4	7.4	6.2	6.7	6.0	0.9	3.3	NM
% Return on Equity	60.0	38.1	85.9	531.1	NM	NM	NM	NM	NM	NM

Data as orig reptd.; bef. results of disc opers/spec. items. Per share data adj. for stk. divs.; EPS diluted. E-Estimated. NA-Not Available. NM-Not Meaningful. NR-Not Ranked. UR-Under Review.

Office: 1 Centennial Ave, Piscataway, NJ 08855-6820.
Telephone: 732-980-6000.
Website: http://www.americanstandard.com
Chrmn & CEO: F.M. Poses

SVP & CFO: G. D'Aloia
SVP, Secy & General Counsel: M.E. Gustafsson
VP & Treas: D.S. Kuhl
Investor Contact: B. Fisher (732-980-6000)

Board of Directors: S. E. Anderson, J. L. Cohon, P. J. Curlander, S. F. Goldstone, K. S. Hachigian, E. E. Hagenlocker, J. F. Hardymon, R. Marshall, D. F. Morrison, F. M. Poses

Founded: 1899
Domicile: Delaware
Employees: 61,200

STANDARD & POOR'S

Ameriprise Financial Inc

S&P Recommendation	Price	12-Mo. Target Price	Investment Style
BUY ★★★★★	$51.00 (as of Oct 27, 2006)	$57.00	Large-Cap Growth

GICS Sector Financials
Sub-Industry Asset Management & Custody Banks

Comment This Minneapolis-based diversified financial services company, spun off from American Express in September 2005, provides insurance, brokerage and asset management services.

Key Stock Statistics (Source S&P, Vickers, company reports)

52-Wk Range	$51.29–36.18	S&P Oper. EPS 2006E	3.43	P/E on S&P Oper. EPS 2006E	14.9	Dividend Rate/Share	$0.44
Trailing 12-Month EPS	$2.29	S&P Oper. EPS 2007E	3.79	Common Shares Outstg. (M)	243.8	Yield (%)	0.86
Trailing 12-Month P/E	22.3	S&P Core EPS 2006E	3.43	Market Capitalization(B)	$12.432	Beta	1.00
$10K Invested 5 Yrs Ago	NA	S&P Core EPS 2007E	3.79	Institutional Ownership (%)	83	S&P Credit Rating	NA

Price Performance

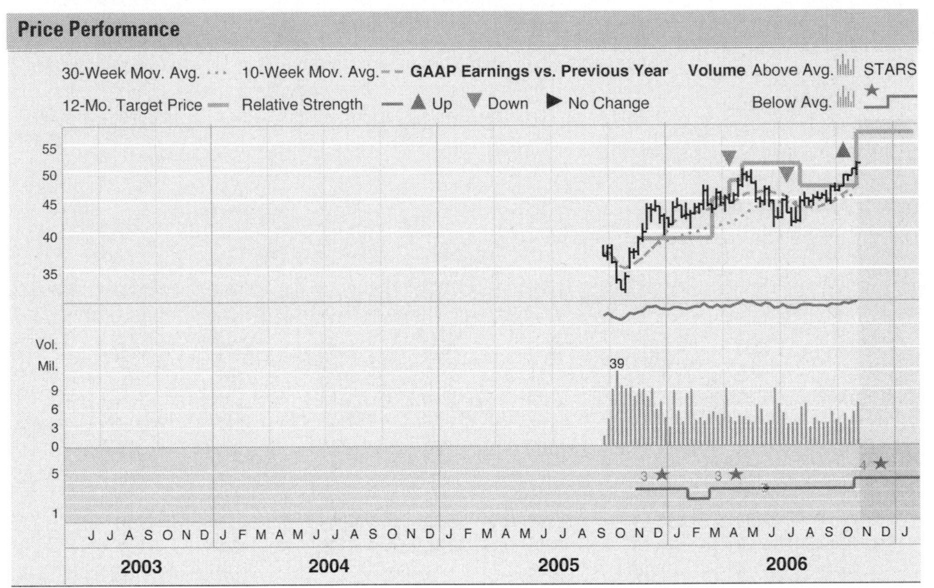

Options: ASE, CBOE, P, Ph

Highlights

➤ The STARS recommendation for AMP has recently been changed to 4 (buy) from 3 (hold) and the 12-month target price has recently been changed to $57.00 from $47.00. The Highlights section of this Stock Report will be updated accordingly.

Investment Rationale/Risk

➤ The Investment Rationale/Risk section of this Stock Report will be updated shortly. For the latest News story on AMP from MarketScope, see below.

➤ 10/25/06 07:10 am EDT... S&P UPGRADES OPINION ON SHARES OF AMERIPRISE FINANCIAL TO BUY FROM HOLD (AMP 49.6****): AMP's Q3 adjusted EPS of $0.94 vs. $0.73 beat our $0.86 estimate. Revenues rose 6%, led by 12% growth at the Protection segment, supported by auto and home insurance sales. Fee-based assets grew, helped by 31% growth in wrap accounts and 24% growth in variable annuities. Outflows continue at RiverSource funds, but we expect improved performance will reverse that trend. We are raising our '06 adjusted EPS estimate $0.28 to $3.43, and increasing our 12-month target price $10 to $57, or 15X our 2007 estimate of $3.79, raised from $3.61, in line with AMP's historical multiple. /M.Albrecht

Qualitative Risk Assessment

LOW | **MEDIUM** | HIGH

Our risk assessment reflects our view of the company's significant franchise value, offset by our concerns that the loss of the highly recognized American Express name could negatively affect AMP's ability to raise and retain client assets.

Quantitative Evaluations

S&P Quality Ranking NR

D | C | B- | B | B+ | A- | A | A+

Relative Strength Rank STRONG

81

LOWEST = 1 HIGHEST = 99

Revenue/Earnings Data

Revenue (Million $)

	1Q	2Q	3Q	4Q	Year
2006	1,959	2,053	1,977	--	--
2005	1,847	1,895	1,873	1,869	7,484
2004	--	--	--	--	6,770
2003	--	--	--	--	--
2002	--	--	--	--	--
2001	--	--	--	--	--

Earnings Per Share ($)

2006	0.57	0.57	0.71	E0.96	E3.43
2005	0.71	0.61	0.50	0.44	2.26
2004	--	--	--	--	2.80
2003	--	--	--	--	--
2002	--	--	--	--	--
2001	--	--	--	--	--

Fiscal year ended Dec. 31. Next earnings report expected: Late January. EPS Estimates based on S&P Operating Earnings; historical GAAP earnings are as reported.

Dividend Data (Dates: mm/dd Payment Date: mm/dd/yy)

Amount ($)	Date Decl.	Ex-Div. Date	Stk. of Record	Payment Date
0.110	01/26	01/31	02/02	02/17/06
0.110	04/25	05/08	05/10	05/19/06
0.110	07/25	08/04	08/08	08/18/06
0.110	10/24	11/03	11/07	11/17/06

Dividends have been paid since 2005. Source: Company reports.

Ameriprise Financial Inc

Business Summary July 28, 2006

CORPORATE OVERVIEW. Ameriprise Financial completed its spin-off from American Express on September 30, 2005, and began trading on the New York Stock Exchange on October 3 under the symbol AMP. As of December 31, 2005, Ameriprise owned, managed and administered over $428 billion of client assets, had about 2.8 million clients, and operated a network of over 12,000 financial advisers, which ranks as the fourth largest sales force among Securities Industry Association members. Ameriprise offers a broad assortment of products, including mutual funds, annuities and life insurance products. Ameriprise was originally named Investors Diversified Services before it was acquired by American Express in 1984. We think AMP will need to prove that it can grow and prosper without the benefits of its previous owner, American Express, which spun off the company in 2005. We believe the spin-off and new marketing campaign have raised AMP's visibility among prospective clients and may also help attract and retain financial advisers. In terms of corporate governance, we view favorably the high proportion of independent directors on the board, but would prefer that the company split the roles of chairman and CEO.

Ameriprise has two operating segments. Asset Accumulation and Income accounted for 67% of 2005 earnings, and Protection accounted for 33%. The Asset Accumulation and Income segment offers mutual funds and annuities to retail clients through its adviser network. This operating segment also serves institutional clients in the separately managed account, sub-advisory and 401(k) markets. We estimate that nearly 50% of the earnings within the Asset Accumulation and Income segment are derived from fixed and variable annuities, which typically combine insurance and investment features. Through its Protection segment, AMP offers various life insurance, disability income and long-term care insurance products through its adviser network. AMP also offers personal auto and home insurance products on a direct basis to retail clients principally through strategic marketing alliances, which include Costco Wholesale, Delta Air Lines, Marriott Vacation Club International, and eWomen Network.

Company Financials

Per Share Data ($) Year Ended Dec. 31	**2005**	**2004**	**2003**	**2002**	**2001**	**2000**	**1999**	**1998**	**1997**	**1996**
Tangible Book Value	30.75	6.45	NA	NA	NA	NA	NA	NA	NA	NA
Cash Flow	2.26	NA	NA	NA	NA	NA	NA	NA	NA	NA
Earnings	2.26	2.80	NA	NA	NA	NA	NA	NA	NA	NA
S&P Core Earnings	2.37	3.02	2.46	NA	NA	NA	NA	NA	NA	NA
Dividends	0.11	NA	NA	NA	NA	NA	NA	NA	NA	NA
Payout Ratio	5%	NA	NA	NA	NA	NA	NA	NA	NA	NA
Prices:High	44.78	NA	NA	NA	NA	NA	NA	NA	NA	NA
Prices:Low	32.00	NA	NA	NA	NA	NA	NA	NA	NA	NA
P/E Ratio:High	20	NA	NA	NA	NA	NA	NA	NA	NA	NA
P/E Ratio:Low	14	NA	NA	NA	NA	NA	NA	NA	NA	NA
Income Statement Analysis (Million $)										
Income Interest	2,241	2,125	NA	NA	NA	NA	NA	NA	NA	NA
Income Other	5,243	4,645	NA	NA	NA	NA	NA	NA	NA	NA
Total Income	7,484	6,770	NA	NA	NA	NA	NA	NA	NA	NA
General Expenses	6,739	5,756	NA	NA	NA	NA	NA	NA	NA	NA
Interest Expense	73.0	78.0	NA	NA	NA	NA	NA	NA	NA	NA
Depreciation	NA	NA	NA	NA	NA	NA	NA	NA	NA	NA
Net Income	556	708	NA	NA	NA	NA	NA	NA	NA	NA
S&P Core Earnings	588	762	622	NA	NA	NA	NA	NA	NA	NA
Balance Sheet & Other Financial Data (Million $)										
Cash	2,474	3,319	NA	NA	NA	NA	NA	NA	NA	NA
Receivables	2,172	2,526	NA	NA	NA	NA	NA	NA	NA	NA
Cost of Investments	39,100	40,157	NA	NA	NA	NA	NA	NA	NA	NA
Total Assets	93,121	90,934	NA	NA	NA	NA	NA	NA	NA	NA
Loss Reserve	Nil	Nil	NA	NA	NA	NA	NA	NA	NA	NA
Short Term Debt	Nil	Nil	NA	NA	NA	NA	NA	NA	NA	NA
Capitalization:Debt	1,833	1,878	NA	NA	NA	NA	NA	NA	NA	NA
Capitalization:Equity	7,687	8,058	NA	NA	NA	NA	NA	NA	NA	NA
Capitalization:Total	9,520	9,936	NA	NA	NA	NA	NA	NA	NA	NA
Price Times Book Value:High	1.5	NA	NA	NA	NA	NA	NA	NA	NA	NA
Price Times Book Value:Low	1.0	NA	NA	NA	NA	NA	NA	NA	NA	NA
Cash Flow	556	NA	NA	NA	NA	NA	NA	NA	NA	NA
% Expense/Operating Revenue	90.0	86.2	NA	NA	NA	NA	NA	NA	NA	NA
% Earnings & Depreciation/Assets	0.1	NA	NA	NA	NA	NA	NA	NA	NA	NA

Data as orig reptd.; bef. results of disc opers/spec. items. Per share data adj. for stk. divs.; EPS diluted. E-Estimated. NA-Not Available. NM-Not Meaningful. NR-Not Ranked. UR-Under Review.

Office: 55 Ameriprise Financial Ctr, Minneapolis, MN 55474-9900.
Telephone: 612-671-3131.
Website: http://www.ameriprise.com
Chrmn & CEO: J.M. Cracchiolo

Investor Contact: W.S. Berman (612-671-3131)
EVP & CFO: W.S. Berman
EVP & General Counsel: J. Junek
VP & Cntlr: D.K. Stewart

Board of Directors: J. M. Cracchiolo, I. D. Hall, W. D. Knowlton, W. W. Lewis, S. S. Marshall, J. Noddle, R. F. Powers, III, H. J. Sarles, R. F. Sharpe, Jr., W. H. Turner

Founded: 1983
Domicile: Delaware
Employees: 11,900

STANDARD &POOR'S

AmerisourceBergen Corp

S&P Recommendation HOLD ★★★★★ | **Price** $46.73 (as of Oct 27, 2006) | **12-Mo. Target Price** $48.00 | **Investment Style** Large-Cap Growth

GICS Sector Health Care
Sub-Industry Health Care Distributors

Comment This distributor of pharmaceutical products and related health care services was formed via the August 2001 merger of Amerisource Health Corp. and Bergen Brunswig Corp.

Key Stock Statistics (Source S&P, Vickers, company reports)

52-Wk Range	$48.96–37.49	S&P Oper. EPS 2006E	2.11	P/E on S&P Oper. EPS 2006E	22.1	Dividend Rate/Share	$0.10
Trailing 12-Month EPS	$1.75	S&P Oper. EPS 2007E	2.35	Common Shares Outstg. (M)	201.6	Yield (%)	0.21
Trailing 12-Month P/E	26.7	S&P Core EPS 2006E	2.13	Market Capitalization(B)	$9.419	Beta	0.02
$10K Invested 5 Yrs Ago	$14,147	S&P Core EPS 2007E	2.37	Institutional Ownership (%)	92	S&P Credit Rating	BBB-

Price Performance

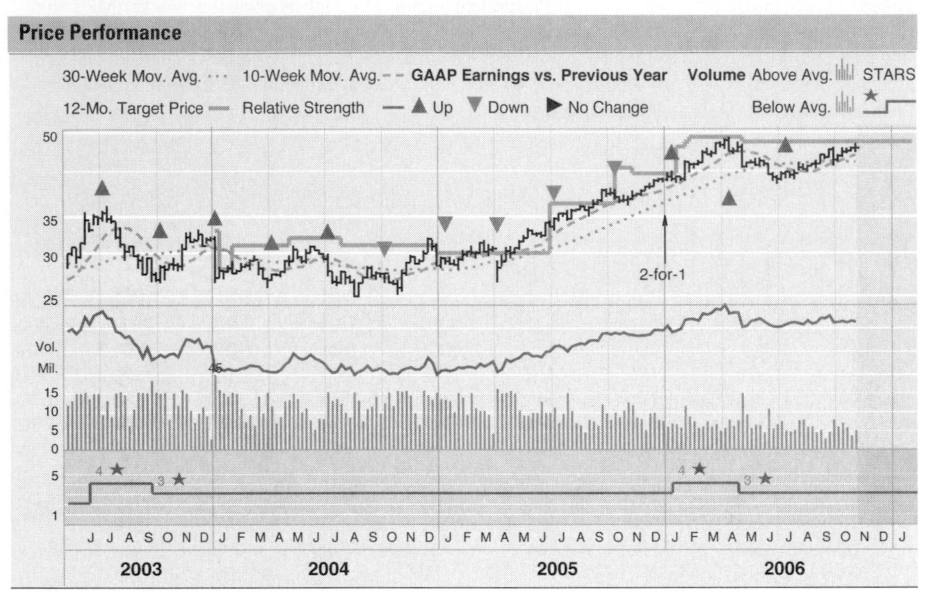

Options: ASE, CBOE, P

Analysis prepared by **Phillip M. Seligman** on September 15, 2006, when the stock traded at **$ 46.46**.

Highlights

- We look for FY 07 (Sep.) operating revenue, which excludes bulk deliveries to customers' warehouses, to rise by 7%, to about $60.7 billion, following a 9% growth we see in FY 06 to $56.7 billion. Growth drivers include an expanding and aging population and the Medicare drug program, but we see growth decelerating on the lapping of FY 06 acquisitions, the loss of two customers, and top-line pressures from increasing volumes of low-priced generic drugs.
- We look for FY 07 drug distribution operating margins to be 5 to 10 basis points above FY 06 levels, as operating efficiency improvements and generic drugs' volume discounts are partly offset by a less favorable sales mix. We see similar expansion in FY 06, but view that year's growth as mainly due to 2005's charges related to a generic drugmaker's bankruptcy and a technology inventory writedown.
- We estimate FY 06 and FY 07 operating EPS, aided by share buybacks, of $2.11 and $2.35, respectively, after $0.05 and $0.10 of projected stock option expense, compared to FY 05 operating EPS of $1.69. Our FY 06 and FY 07 Standard & Poor's Core EPS estimates, including pension plan adjustments, are $2.13 and $2.37.

Investment Rationale/Risk

- We are encouraged by ABC's healthy cash position and strong operating cash flow. We are also encouraged by the Pharmerica unit's 8% rise in revenue and wider operating margin in the June quarter, both of which were better than we expected. But firmwide operating margin improvement appears likely to be modest, in our opinion. We see savings from the distribution center rationalization and increased high-margin generic and specialty drug volumes mostly offset by the impact of higher sales to large accounts, which command steep discounts. Moreover, despite strong growth in its specialty group, a significant portion of that growth is in the group's distribution business, which has a lower EBIT margin than its service businesses.
- Risks to our opinion and target price include intensified price competition, which could outweigh cost control savings.
- We see EPS up strongly in FY 06, aided by beneficial nonoperating effects, including a lower tax rate. Our 12-month target price is $48, based on our calendar 2007 EPS estimate of $2.42 and a peer-level P/E target multiple of 20X.

Qualitative Risk Assessment

LOW | **MEDIUM** | HIGH

Our risk assessment reflects what we view as ABC's improving financial performance, ability to attract new accounts to more than compensate for account losses, and healthy operating cash flow. However, the drug distribution arena is highly competitive and ABC is less diversified than many of its large healthcare distribution peers.

Quantitative Evaluations

S&P Quality Ranking A-

D | C | B- | B | B+ | **A-** | A | A+

Relative Strength Rank MODERATE

56

LOWEST = 1 HIGHEST = 99

Revenue/Earnings Data

Revenue (Million $)

	1Q	2Q	3Q	4Q	Year
2006	14,653	15,221	15,686	--	--
2005	13,639	13,192	13,832	13,918	54,577
2004	13,355	13,364	13,072	13,389	53,179
2003	12,435	12,163	12,421	12,640	49,657
2002	11,069	10,944	11,621	11,601	45,235
2001	3,307	3,481	3,519	5,884	16,191

Earnings Per Share ($)

	1Q	2Q	3Q	4Q	Year
2006	0.46	0.61	0.58	E0.56	E2.11
2005	0.33	0.46	0.48	0.10	1.37
2004	0.47	0.62	0.55	0.41	2.03
2003	0.42	0.52	0.50	0.52	1.95
2002	0.32	0.42	0.41	0.43	1.58
2001	0.25	0.29	0.29	0.24	1.05

Fiscal year ended Sep. 30. Next earnings report expected: Early November. EPS Estimates based on S&P Operating Earnings; historical GAAP earnings are as reported.

Dividend Data (Dates: mm/dd Payment Date: mm/dd/yy)

Amount ($)	Date Decl.	Ex-Div. Date	Stk. of Record	Payment Date
2-for-1	11/15	12/29	12/13	12/28/05
0.025	02/09	02/15	02/20	03/06/06
0.025	05/11	05/18	05/22	06/05/06
0.025	08/10	08/17	08/21	09/05/06

Dividends have been paid since 2001. Source: Company reports.

Please read the Required Disclosures and Analyst Certification on the last page of this report.

AmerisourceBergen Corp

Business Summary September 15, 2006

CORPORATE OVERVIEW. AmerisourceBergen Corp., one of the largest U.S. pharmaceutical distributors, began operation in August 2001, following the merger of Amerisource Health Corp. and Bergen Brunswig Corp. ABC accounted for the merger as an acquisition by Amerisource of Bergen. National and retail drugstore chains, independent community drugstores, and pharmacy departments of supermarkets and mass merchandisers account for its retail market segment (43% of FY 05 (Sep.) operating revenues), while the hospital/acute care, mail order and specialty pharmaceuticals markets together comprise its institutional market segment (57%). The company's specialty health care distribution business (more than $7.4 billion in operating revenue) supplies goods and services to physicians in the nephrology, oncology, plasma, primary care and vaccine health care segments.

Its top 10 customers represented approximately 31% of FY 05 operating revenue. Its largest non-bulk customer represented 7.5% of operating revenue in FY 05. Revenues generated from sales to pharmacy benefit manager Medco Health Solutions accounted for 93% of bulk deliveries to customer warehouses and 6% of operating revenue in FY 05. No other individual customer accounted for more than 5% of FY 05 operating revenue. In addition, about 13% of FY 05 operating revenue was derived from three large group purchasing organizations (GPOs), each of which functions as a purchasing agent on behalf of its members, which are healthcare providers. In December 2005, United Drugs, a GPO for independent retail pharmacies, terminated its contract with ABC.

The PharMerica division, with a network of 96 pharmacies at the end of FY 05, provides institutional pharmacy care, pharmacy management services, and direct pharmaceutical services to workers' compensation and catastrophic care patients. The American Health Packaging division repackages drugs from bulk to unit dose, unit of use, blister pack, and standard bottle sizes.

Company Financials

Per Share Data ($) Year Ended Sep. 30	**2005**	**2004**	**2003**	**2002**	**2001**	**2000**	**1999**	**1998**	**1997**	**1996**
Tangible Book Value	7.38	8.62	7.21	5.22	1.80	2.41	1.44	0.75	0.14	NM
Cash Flow	1.73	2.36	2.21	1.81	1.16	1.11	0.86	0.67	0.59	0.56
Earnings	1.37	2.03	1.95	1.58	1.05	0.95	0.69	0.52	0.49	0.46
S&P Core Earnings	1.24	1.55	1.86	1.53	0.85	NA	NA	NA	NA	NA
Dividends	0.05	0.05	0.05	0.05	Nil	Nil	Nil	Nil	Nil	Nil
Payout Ratio	4%	2%	3%	3%	Nil	Nil	Nil	Nil	Nil	Nil
Prices:High	42.18	32.01	36.72	41.43	36.00	26.84	20.69	20.19	16.59	11.44
Prices:Low	26.48	24.87	22.83	25.10	20.06	6.00	5.50	11.12	10.31	6.97
P/E Ratio:High	31	16	19	26	34	28	30	39	34	25
P/E Ratio:Low	19	12	12	16	19	6	8	21	21	15
Income Statement Analysis (Million $)										
Revenue	54,577	53,179	49,657	45,235	16,191	11,645	9,760	8,575	7,816	5,552
Operating Income	723	978	963	804	302	217	191	166	132	107
Depreciation	81.2	87.1	71.0	61.2	21.6	16.1	17.4	14.8	12.4	9.20
Interest Expense	57.2	113	145	141	45.7	41.9	39.0	42.1	41.6	36.0
Pretax Income	469	760	726	572	202	160	119	82.8	78.0	61.9
Effective Tax Rate	37.7%	38.4%	39.2%	39.7%	38.6%	38.0%	40.6%	39.0%	39.2%	31.1%
Net Income	292	468	441	345	124	99.0	70.9	50.5	47.4	42.7
S&P Core Earnings	264	356	421	333	99.8	NA	NA	NA	NA	NA
Balance Sheet & Other Financial Data (Million $)										
Cash	1,316	871	800	663	298	121	59.5	85.5	68.9	71.2
Current Assets	7,988	8,295	8,859	8,350	7,513	2,321	1,920	1,418	1,625	1,115
Total Assets	11,381	11,654	12,040	11,213	10,291	2,459	2,061	1,552	1,745	1,188
Current Liabilities	6,052	6,104	6,256	6,100	5,532	1,751	1,327	1,015	1,130	786
Long Term Debt	951	1,157	1,723	1,756	1,872	413	559	454	590	434
Common Equity	4,280	4,339	4,005	3,316	5,677	565	166	75.3	14.3	-36.8
Total Capital	5,232	5,496	5,728	5,073	7,549	978	725	529	604	397
Capital Expenditures	203	189	90.6	64.2	23.4	16.6	15.8	10.4	15.9	15.7
Cash Flow	373	555	512	406	145	115	88.3	65.3	59.9	51.8
Current Ratio	1.3	1.4	1.4	1.4	1.4	1.3	1.4	1.4	1.4	1.4
% Long Term Debt of Capitalization	18.2	21.1	30.1	34.6	24.8	42.3	77.1	85.8	97.7	109.3
% Net Income of Revenue	0.5	0.9	0.9	0.8	0.8	0.9	0.7	0.6	0.6	0.8
% Return on Assets	2.5	4.0	3.8	3.2	1.9	4.4	3.9	3.1	3.2	4.2
% Return on Equity	6.8	11.2	12.1	11.2	4.0	22.1	58.8	112.7	NM	NM

Data as orig reptd.; bef. results of disc opers/spec. items. Per share data adj. for stk. divs.; EPS diluted. E-Estimated. NA-Not Available. NM-Not Meaningful. NR-Not Ranked. UR-Under Review.

Office: 1300 Morris Drive, Chesterbrook, PA 19087-5594.
Telephone: 610-727-7000.
Email: investorrelations@amerisourcebergen.com
Website: http://www.amerisourcebergen.com

Chrmn: R.C. Gozon
Pres & COO: K.J. Hilzinger
CEO: R.D. Yost
EVP & CFO: M.D. DiCandilo

VP & Secy: J.G. Chou
Investor Contact: M.N. Kilpatrick (610-727-7118)
Board of Directors: R. H. Brady, C. H. Cotros, R. C. Gozon, E. E. Hagenlocker, J. E. Henney, K. Hilzinger, M. J. Long, H. E. McGee, J. L. Wilson, R. D. Yost

Founded: 1985
Domicile: Delaware
Employees: 13,400

Amgen Inc

STANDARD & POOR'S

S&P Recommendation BUY ★★★★★

Price $75.52 (as of Oct 27, 2006)

12-Mo. Target Price $84.00

Investment Style Large-Cap Growth

GICS Sector Health Care
Sub-Industry Biotechnology

Comment Amgen, the world's leading biotech company, has major treatments for anemia, neutropenia, rheumatoid arthritis, psoriatic arthritis, and psoriasis.

Key Stock Statistics (Source S&P, Vickers, company reports)

52-Wk Range	$84.50–63.52	S&P Oper. EPS 2006E	3.72	P/E on S&P Oper. EPS 2006E	20.3	Dividend Rate/Share	Nil
Trailing 12-Month EPS	$2.44	S&P Oper. EPS 2007E	4.25	Common Shares Outstg. (M)	1,170.6	Yield (%)	Nil
Trailing 12-Month P/E	31.0	S&P Core EPS 2006E	3.72	Market Capitalization(B)	$88.402	Beta	0.84
$10K Invested 5 Yrs Ago	$12,703	S&P Core EPS 2007E	4.25	Institutional Ownership (%)	72	S&P Credit Rating	A+

Price Performance

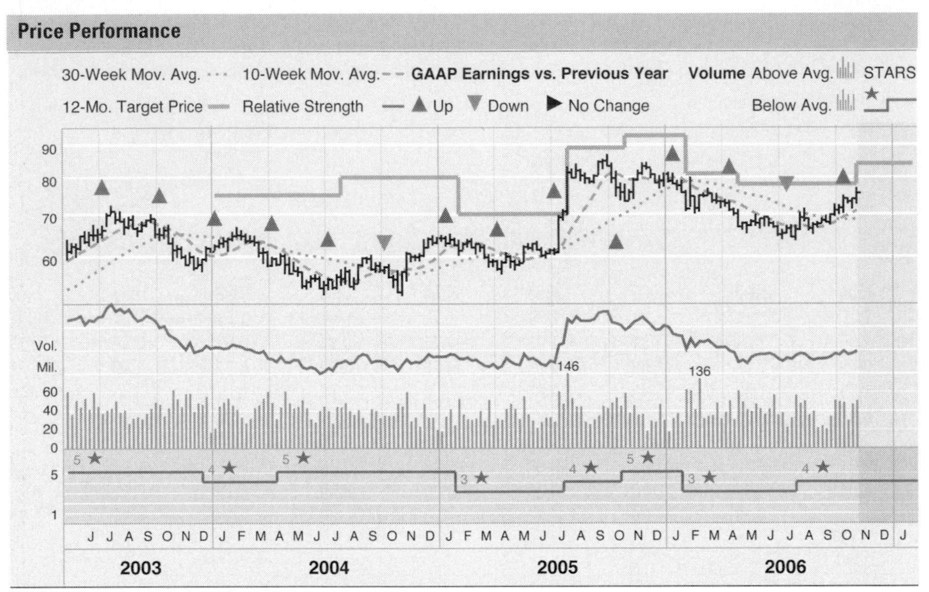

Options: ASE, CBOE, P, Ph

Analysis prepared by **Paul Starsia** on October 25, 2006, when the stock traded at **$ 75.09**.

Highlights

- Amgen reported third quarter EPS of $1.01, versus $0.82 last year, well above our $0.92 estimate (all including stock option expense). Top-line growth was mostly in line with expectations, with Aranesp and Epogen sales somewhat stronger than forecast, offset by weaker-than-projected sales of Enbrel, the company's rheumatoid arthritis treatment. A wider gross margin, a lower tax rate, and fewer-than-forecast shares outstanding led to the earnings upside.

- The gross margin increased to 86.2% in the third quarter, compared with 83.4% in the second quarter, primarily due to lower royalty expense, a more favorable product mix, and product efficiencies. The company bought back 7.3 million shares and has about $1.8 billion remaining under its stock repurchase plan.

- We project product sales of $13.7 billion in 2006, up about 14% over 2005, and about $15.9 billion in 2007. Based on the third quarter earnings upside, management's increase in its 2006 EPS guidance, and our forecast for strong 2007 operating results, we raised our 2006 and 2007 EPS estimates to $3.72 and $4.25, respectively, from $3.66 and $4.15.

Investment Rationale/Risk

- We expect sales growth to remain strong in 2007, despite the fact that Roche's CERA will likely be launched following its February 20, 2007 Prescription Drug User Fee Act date. A trial date for AMGN's patent infringement suit against Roche is expected to be set in September 2007. Important upcoming events include presentation of Phase II data on denosumab for bone erosions in early November and interim Phase II data for AMG 706 for gastrointestinal stromal tumors possibly before the end of 2006.

- Risks to our recommendation and target price include increasing competition for Aranesp/Epogen (about 50% of product sales), possible changes to Medicare reimbursement policies, and challenges to AMGN's patent portfolio.

- Our EPS growth forecast for AMGN is 14% through 2010. The current P/E-to-growth (PEG) ratio range for large-cap biotech shares is 1.4X to 1.7X, by our calculation. Given its size, product diversity and relatively mature nature of its principal products, we believe a PEG ratio at the midpoint of the current range, or 1.5X, is appropriate for AMGN shares. Assuming the stock trades to a PEG of 1.5X our 2007 EPS estimate, we derive a 12-month target price of $84.

Qualitative Risk Assessment

LOW | **MEDIUM** | HIGH

The company's products are sold in highly competitive markets and are subject to government regulation. Changes to government reimbursement policies could significantly affect AMGN's revenues and profitability. We believe that generics for Epogen could be a threat in Europe and that Roche's CERA, a competitor to Aranesp, could be launched in the U.S. in 2007.

Quantitative Evaluations

S&P Quality Ranking B+

D | C | B- | B | **B+** | A- | A | A+

Relative Strength Rank STRONG

73

LOWEST = 1 HIGHEST = 99

Revenue/Earnings Data

Revenue (Million $)

	1Q	2Q	3Q	4Q	Year
2006	3,217	3,604	3,612	--	--
2005	2,833	3,172	3,154	3,271	12,430
2004	2,343	2,585	2,713	2,909	10,550
2003	1,761	2,041	2,207	2,346	8,356
2002	1,009	1,249	1,499	1,766	5,523
2001	901.6	986.7	1,003	1,124	4,016

Earnings Per Share ($)

2006	0.82	0.01	0.94	E0.91	E3.72
2005	0.67	0.82	0.77	0.66	2.93
2004	0.52	0.57	0.18	0.53	1.81
2003	0.37	0.45	0.46	0.41	1.69
2002	0.32	0.38	-2.10	0.34	-1.21
2001	0.28	0.30	0.30	0.15	1.03

Fiscal year ended Dec. 31. Next earnings report expected: Late January. EPS Estimates based on S&P Operating Earnings; historical GAAP earnings are as reported.

Dividend Data

No cash dividends have been paid.

Please read the Required Disclosures and Analyst Certification on the last page of this report.

Amgen Inc

Business Summary October 25, 2006

CORPORATE OVERVIEW. Amgen, the world's largest biotech company, makes and markets five of the world's best-selling biotech drugs.

Epogen is a genetically engineered version of human erythropoietin (EPO), a hormone that stimulates red blood cell production in bone marrow. Its primary market is dialysis patients suffering from chronic anemia. Epogen sales were $2.46 billion in 2005 ($2.60 billion in 2004). In September 2001, Aranesp, a recombinant protein that stimulates the production of red blood cells in pre-dialysis and dialysis patients, was approved by the FDA to treat anemia associated with chronic renal failure. In July 2002, Aranesp was approved by the FDA to treat cancer patients with anemia due to chemotherapy use. Aranesp sales were $3.27 billion in 2005 ($2.47 billion). AMGN is also developing AMG 114, a third-generation EPO product.

Neupogen is a recombinant version of human granulocyte colony stimulating factor, a protein that stimulates the production of neutrophils (white blood cells that defend the body against bacterial infection). Its principal use is to build neutrophil levels in cancer patients whose natural neutrophils were destroyed by chemotherapy. Neupogen sales were $1.22 billion in 2005 ($1.18 billion). In early 2002, the FDA approved Neulasta, a long-acting white blood cell stimulant used to protect chemotherapy patients from infection. Neulasta was approved in the European Union in August 2002. Neulasta posted 2005 sales of $2.29 billion ($1.74 billion).

Enbrel, acquired through AMGN's July 2002 purchase of Immunex, had 2005 sales of $2.57 billion ($1.90 billion). It is approved to treat rheumatoid arthritis (RA), juvenile RA, and psoriatic arthritis. In addition, in July 2003, the FDA approved Enbrel to treat the spinal condition ankylosing spondylitis. In May 2004, the FDA approved Enbrel to treat adults with moderate to severe chronic plaque psoriasis.

Company Financials

Per Share Data ($) Year Ended Dec. 31	**2005**	**2004**	**2003**	**2002**	**2001**	**2000**	**1999**	**1998**	**1997**	**1996**
Tangible Book Value	5.08	4.08	4.06	2.80	4.99	4.16	2.97	2.52	2.07	1.80
Cash Flow	3.59	2.35	2.19	-0.82	1.28	1.24	1.18	0.95	0.69	0.70
Earnings	2.93	1.81	1.69	-1.21	1.03	1.05	1.02	0.82	0.59	0.61
S&P Core Earnings	2.77	1.58	1.50	-1.46	0.87	NA	NA	NA	NA	NA
Dividends	Nil	Nil	Nil	Nil	Nil	Nil	Nil	Nil	0.00	Nil
Payout Ratio	Nil	Nil	Nil	Nil	Nil	Nil	Nil	Nil	NM	Nil
Prices:High	86.92	66.88	72.37	62.94	75.06	80.44	66.44	27.25	17.34	16.63
Prices:Low	56.19	52.00	48.09	30.57	45.44	50.00	25.69	11.66	11.22	12.84
P/E Ratio:High	30	37	43	NM	73	77	65	33	30	27
P/E Ratio:Low	19	29	28	NM	44	48	25	14	19	21

Income Statement Analysis (Million $)										
Revenue	12,430	10,550	8,356	5,523	4,016	3,629	3,340	2,718	2,401	2,240
Operating Income	5,689	4,636	3,758	2,501	2,003	1,761	1,638	1,338	1,103	1,058
Depreciation	841	734	686	447	266	212	177	144	117	100
Interest Expense	99.0	38.0	31.5	44.2	13.6	15.9	15.2	10.0	3.70	6.20
Pretax Income	4,868	3,395	3,173	-684	1,686	1,674	1,566	1,224	861	962
Effective Tax Rate	24.5%	30.4%	28.8%	NM	33.6%	32.0%	30.0%	29.5%	25.2%	29.4%
Net Income	3,674	2,363	2,260	-1,392	1,120	1,139	1,096	863	644	680
S&P Core Earnings	3,470	2,074	2,006	-1,683	936	NA	NA	NA	NA	NA

Balance Sheet & Other Financial Data (Million $)										
Cash	5,255	5,808	5,123	4,664	2,662	2,028	1,333	1,276	1,027	1,077
Current Assets	9,235	9,170	7,402	6,404	3,859	2,937	2,065	1,863	1,544	1,503
Total Assets	29,297	29,221	26,177	24,456	6,443	5,400	4,078	3,672	3,110	2,766
Current Liabilities	3,595	4,157	2,246	1,529	1,003	862	831	887	742	643
Long Term Debt	3,957	3,937	3,080	3,048	223	223	223	223	229	59.0
Common Equity	20,451	19,705	19,389	18,286	5,217	4,315	3,024	2,562	2,139	1,906
Total Capital	25,571	24,936	23,930	22,927	5,440	4,538	3,247	2,785	2,368	2,122
Capital Expenditures	867	1,336	1,357	658	442	438	304	408	388	267
Cash Flow	4,515	3,097	2,946	-945	1,386	1,350	1,273	1,007	761	780
Current Ratio	2.6	2.2	3.3	4.2	3.8	3.4	2.5	2.1	2.1	2.3
% Long Term Debt of Capitalization	15.5	15.8	12.9	13.3	4.1	4.9	6.9	8.0	9.7	2.8
% Net Income of Revenue	29.6	22.4	27.0	NM	27.9	31.4	32.8	31.8	26.8	30.4
% Return on Assets	12.6	8.5	8.9	NM	18.9	24.0	28.3	25.5	21.9	26.2
% Return on Equity	18.3	12.1	12.0	NM	23.5	31.0	39.3	36.7	30.7	38.0

Data as orig reptd.; bef. results of disc opers/spec. items. Per share data adj. for stk. divs.; EPS diluted. E-Estimated. NA-Not Available. NM-Not Meaningful. NR-Not Ranked. UR-Under Review.

Office: One Amgen Center Drive, Thousand Oaks, CA 91320-1799.
Telephone: 805-447-1000.
Email: investor.relations@amgen.com
Website: http://www.amgen.com

Chrmn, Pres & CEO: K.W. Sharer
EVP & CFO: R.D. Nanula
SVP, Secy & General Counsel: D.J. Scott
SVP & CIO: T. Flanagan

VP & Chief Acctg Officer: M. Kelly
Investor Contact: A. Sood (805-447-1060)
Board of Directors: D. Baltimore, F. J. Biondi, Jr., J. D. Choate, F. W. Gluck, F. C. Herringer, G. S. Omenn, J. C. Pelham, J. P. Reason, D. B. Rice, L. D. Schaeffer, K. W. Sharer

Founded: 1980
Domicile: Delaware
Employees: 16,500

STANDARD &POOR'S

AmSouth Bancorporation

S&P Recommendation BUY ★★★★★

Price $29.84 (as of Oct 27, 2006)

12-Mo. Target Price $33.00

Investment Style Large-Cap Value

GICS Sector Financials
Sub-Industry Regional Banks

Comment This regional bank holding company, with $53 billion in assets, operates in six southeastern states.

Key Stock Statistics (Source S&P, Vickers, company reports)

52-Wk Range	**$30.89–24.90**	S&P Oper. EPS 2006**E**	**2.16**	P/E on S&P Oper. EPS 2006**E**	**13.8**	Dividend Rate/Share	**$1.04**
Trailing 12-Month EPS	**$2.10**	S&P Oper. EPS 2007**E**	**2.36**	Common Shares Outstg. (M)	**342.4**	Yield (%)	**3.49**
Trailing 12-Month P/E	**14.2**	S&P Core EPS 2006**E**	**2.17**	Market Capitalization(B)	**$10.219**	Beta	**0.37**
$10K Invested 5 Yrs Ago	**$20,226**	S&P Core EPS 2007**E**	**2.37**	Institutional Ownership (%)	**40**	S&P Credit Rating	**A**

Price Performance

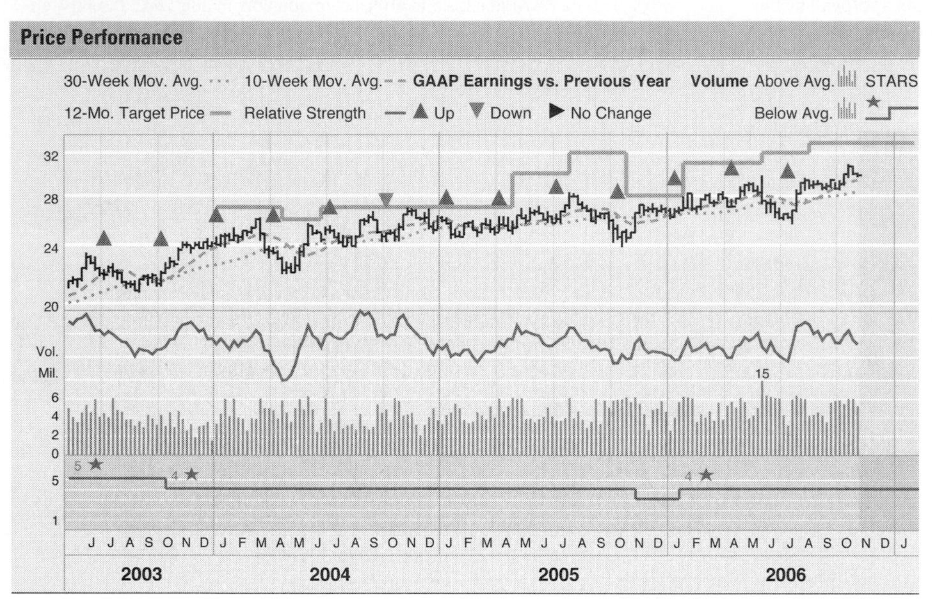

Options: ASE, CBOE, Ph

Analysis prepared by **Christopher B. Muir** on August 16, 2006, when the stock traded at **$ 29.22**.

Highlights

- We anticipate revenue growth of 3.1% in 2006 to be driven by loan and non-interest income growth and a slight increase in the net interest margin, partly offset by an anticipated reduction in the securities portfolio. Our 2006 estimates assume a net interest margin of 3.38% (down slightly from 3.39% in 2005, due to our view of continued pressure from a relatively flat yield curve), growth in earning assets of 5.3%, and non-interest income growth of 4.8%.
- We look for continued efforts to boost efficiency to be more than offset by the expensing of stock options, which began in 2006. Our 2006 non-interest expense to total revenue forecast of 53.2% is higher than the 52.9% in 2005, as a result of the expensing of stock options in 2006. Credit quality remains good and we think the company has adequate loan loss reserves. We expect loan loss provisions of $86 million in 2006, down from $94 million in 2005.
- Assuming an effective tax rate of 31.1%, we see 2006 operating EPS of $2.16, up 5.9% from the $2.04 earned in 2005. Our 2007 EPS estimate is $2.36, a further increase of 9.3%.

Investment Rationale/Risk

- We view positively ASO's diversified loan portfolio, over 65% of which is composed of variable-rate loans, as well as its high base of low-cost deposits, which have all contributed to relatively stable net interest margins. We are also encouraged by the bank's continued expansion plans in Florida. We also like the potential benefits from the recently announced merger agreement, subject to necessary approvals, with Regions Financial (RF: buy, $36). The merger is expected to close in the fourth quarter.
- Risks to our recommendation and target price include detrimental changes in the slope of the yield curve and operational performance that fails to meet our expectations.
- Our 12-month target price of $33 is based on the terms of the company's merger agreement withy RF and our 12-month target price for RF of $41. Under the terms of the agreement, each ASO share is entitled to 0.7974 shares of RF. We do not see much risk to our target price if the deal is not consummated, as our dividend discount model, which assumes a discount rate of 8.5% and a terminal growth rate of 4%, indicates an intrinsic value of $32.

Qualitative Risk Assessment

LOW | MEDIUM | HIGH

Our risk assessment reflects our view of the company's mid-cap valuation, strong credit quality of its loan portfolio, and history of profitability. While ASO operates in a highly competitive and fragmented industry, the industry tends to produce relatively stable financial results.

Quantitative Evaluations

S&P Quality Ranking A-

D | C | B- | B | B+ | A- | A | A+

Relative Strength Rank MODERATE

47

LOWEST = 1 HIGHEST = 99

Revenue/Earnings Data

Revenue (Million $)

	1Q	2Q	3Q	4Q	Year
2006	920.1	973.0	--	--	--
2005	796.6	825.7	886.2	887.9	3,396
2004	745.1	742.9	763.4	946.4	3,198
2003	730.5	733.2	734.0	744.6	2,942
2002	754.8	760.1	758.3	720.3	2,993
2001	882.1	866.2	840.7	793.7	3,383

Earnings Per Share ($)

	1Q	2Q	3Q	4Q	Year
2006	0.52	0.53	--	E0.56	E2.16
2005	0.50	0.52	0.51	0.52	2.04
2004	0.45	0.47	0.33	0.49	1.74
2003	0.44	0.44	0.45	0.45	1.77
2002	0.40	0.42	0.43	0.44	1.68
2001	0.34	0.36	0.37	0.38	1.45

Fiscal year ended Dec. 31. Next earnings report expected: Mid January. EPS Estimates based on S&P Operating Earnings; historical GAAP earnings are as reported.

Dividend Data (Dates: mm/dd Payment Date: mm/dd/yy)

Amount ($)	Date Decl.	Ex-Div. Date	Stk. of Record	Payment Date
0.260	10/20	12/16	12/20	01/02/06
0.260	01/19	03/15	03/17	04/03/06
0.260	04/20	06/14	06/16	07/03/06
0.260	07/20	09/18	09/20	10/02/06

Dividends have been paid since 1943. Source: Company reports.

Please read the Required Disclosures and Analyst Certification on the last page of this report.

AmSouth Bancorporation

Business Summary August 16, 2006

CORPORATE OVERVIEW. AmSouth Bancorporation is a regional bank holding company headquartered in Birmingham, Alabama, with approximately $53 billion in assets. It has three principal business segments: Consumer Banking, which delivers loans, deposits and other services to individuals and small businesses; Commercial Banking, which provides credit, treasury management, international, capital markets and several specialty services to corporate and middle market customers; and Wealth Management, which offers traditional trust and investment management services.

MARKET PROFILE. At December 31, 2005, ASO operated more than 675 banking offices in Tennessee (where it is ranked second, based on a deposit market share of approximately 10.7%), Florida (fifth, 2.8%), Alabama (second, 13.9%), Mississippi (third, 9.0%), Louisiana (sixth, 3.1%) and Georgia (79th, 0.2%). Based on current income levels as well as projected changes in population and household income, we believe the prospects for the bank's overall markets, with the exception of Florida and Georgia, are below average.

FINANCIAL TRENDS. Due to its above-average profit margins, ASO's performance metrics are relatively high. During 2005, its return on average assets was 1.43%, versus a median of 1.18% for its peer group of Southeastern banks. Its return on average equity during the same period was 20.44%, compared to 12.33% for peers, due partially to ASO's higher leverage levels, in our opinion.

We believe ASO's loan portfolio is fairly diversified, with a balanced mix of commercial and commercial real estate loans (approximately 51.1% of average total loans during the fourth quarter of 2005), residential mortgages (16.9%), home equity loans and lines of credit (21.8%), dealer indirect auto loans (8.8%) and other consumer loans (1.3%). We also think the bank's funding sources are well-positioned in the current environment of a flat yield curve, with roughly 53% comprised of low-cost core deposits, such as checking, savings and non-interest-bearing deposits, compared to 45% for peers. However, we note that ASO's proportion of higher-cost borrowings, which made up about 22% of total funding liabilities, is higher than the peer median of 13%. On the credit side, we believe ASO's asset quality metrics are average.

Company Financials

Per Share Data ($) Year Ended Dec. 31	**2005**	**2004**	**2003**	**2002**	**2001**	**2000**	**1999**	**1998**	**1997**	**1996**
Tangible Book Value	10.44	10.02	9.18	8.82	8.14	7.52	7.56	8.05	7.65	7.38
Earnings	2.04	1.74	1.77	1.68	1.45	0.86	0.86	1.45	1.21	0.96
S&P Core Earnings	1.85	1.50	1.66	1.51	1.27	NA	NA	NA	NA	NA
Dividends	1.01	0.97	0.93	0.89	0.85	0.81	0.67	0.53	0.51	0.48
Payout Ratio	50%	56%	53%	53%	59%	94%	78%	37%	42%	50%
Prices:High	28.29	27.00	24.62	23.06	20.24	20.06	34.58	30.42	25.36	15.07
Prices:Low	23.85	21.91	19.05	17.75	15.00	11.69	18.75	20.46	14.00	10.19
P/E Ratio:High	14	16	14	14	14	23	40	21	21	16
P/E Ratio:Low	12	13	11	11	10	14	22	14	12	11
Income Statement Analysis (Million $)										
Net Interest Income	1,525	1,476	1,415	1,473	1,395	1,379	1,508	699	676	652
Tax Equivalent Adjustment	NA	NA	44.4	51.0	63.7	62.7	4.84	5.64	7.04	9.38
Non Interest Income	915	1,032	856	739	748	669	848	347	266	235
Loan Loss Provision	94.0	128	174	214	187	228	166	58.1	67.4	65.2
% Expense/Operating Revenue	52.9%	58.1%	52.1%	49.8%	53.7%	64.7%	69.8%	55.4%	55.8%	59.5%
Pretax Income	1,055	923	891	872	771	455	541	405	349	288
Effective Tax Rate	31.2%	32.5%	29.7%	30.1%	30.4%	27.6%	37.1%	35.2%	35.1%	36.6%
Net Income	726	623	626	609	536	329	340	263	226	183
% Net Interest Margin	3.38	3.47	3.78	4.37	4.20	3.75	4.02	3.92	4.09	3.93
S&P Core Earnings	660	531	588	547	472	NA	NA	NA	NA	NA
Balance Sheet & Other Financial Data (Million $)										
Money Market Assets	98.4	38.0	42.9	138	453	2,226	205	39.0	20.4	18.9
Investment Securities	11,669	12,511	12,054	9,170	8,832	8,559	13,015	5,176	4,780	4,935
Commercial Loans	11,245	16,041	13,940	13,050	13,075	13,918	14,715	3,693	3,854	3,668
Other Loans	25,375	16,761	16,149	15,012	12,777	11,170	11,551	9,177	8,384	8,412
Total Assets	52,607	49,548	45,616	40,571	38,600	38,936	43,407	19,902	18,622	18,407
Demand Deposits	15,533	23,109	12,458	5,495	5,281	4,934	4,739	2,216	2,063	1,952
Time Deposits	20,816	11,123	17,983	21,821	20,886	21,689	23,173	11,068	10,882	10,516
Long Term Debt	5,533	7,272	7,650	6,009	6,117	5,883	5,603	3,240	1,633	1,436
Common Equity	3,635	3,569	3,230	3,116	2,955	2,813	2,959	1,428	1,385	1,396
% Return on Assets	1.4	1.3	1.5	1.5	1.4	0.8	0.8	1.4	1.2	1.0
% Return on Equity	20.1	18.3	19.7	20.1	18.6	11.4	11.0	18.7	16.3	13.1
% Loan Loss Reserve	1.0	1.1	1.3	1.4	1.4	1.5	1.4	1.4	1.5	1.5
% Loans/Deposits	99.9	96.1	96.7	100.2	97.1	92.8	94.7	96.9	95.7	96.9
% Equity to Assets	7.1	7.1	7.4	7.7	7.4	7.0	7.3	7.3	7.5	7.7

Data as orig reptd.; bef. results of disc opers/spec. items. Per share data adj. for stk. divs.; EPS diluted. E-Estimated. NA-Not Available. NM-Not Meaningful. NR-Not Ranked. UR-Under Review.

Office: 1900 5th Ave N, Birmingham, AL, USA 35203.
Telephone: 205-320-7151.
Website: http://www.amsouth.com
Chrmn, Pres & CEO: C.D. Ritter

Sr EVP: C.W. Bagby
Sr EVP: D.B. Edmonds
Sr EVP: J.M. Gaffney
Sr EVP: S. Martinez

Board of Directors: D. J. Cooper, Sr., D. DeFosset, E. W. Deavenport, Jr., M. R. Ingram, R. L. Kuehn, Jr., J. R. Malone, C. D. McCrary, C. B. Nielsen, C. D. Ritter

Founded: 1970
Domicile: Delaware
Employees: 11,600

Anadarko Petroleum Corp

S&P Recommendation HOLD ★★★★★

Price $46.52 (as of Oct 27, 2006)

12-Mo. Target Price $49.00

Investment Style Large-Cap Growth

GICS Sector Energy
Sub-Industry Oil & Gas Exploration & Production

Comment This international oil and natural gas exploration and production company has associated businesses in marketing and trading and minerals.

Key Stock Statistics (Source S&P, Vickers, company reports)

52-Wk Range	$56.98–39.51	S&P Oper. EPS 2006E	5.80	P/E on S&P Oper. EPS 2006E	8.0	Dividend Rate/Share	$0.36
Trailing 12-Month EPS	$6.29	S&P Oper. EPS 2007E	6.75	Common Shares Outstg. (M)	459.5	Yield (%)	0.77
Trailing 12-Month P/E	7.4	S&P Core EPS 2006E	5.72	Market Capitalization(B)	$21.374	Beta	0.58
$10K Invested 5 Yrs Ago	$16,161	S&P Core EPS 2007E	6.77	Institutional Ownership (%)	84	S&P Credit Rating	BBB-

Price Performance

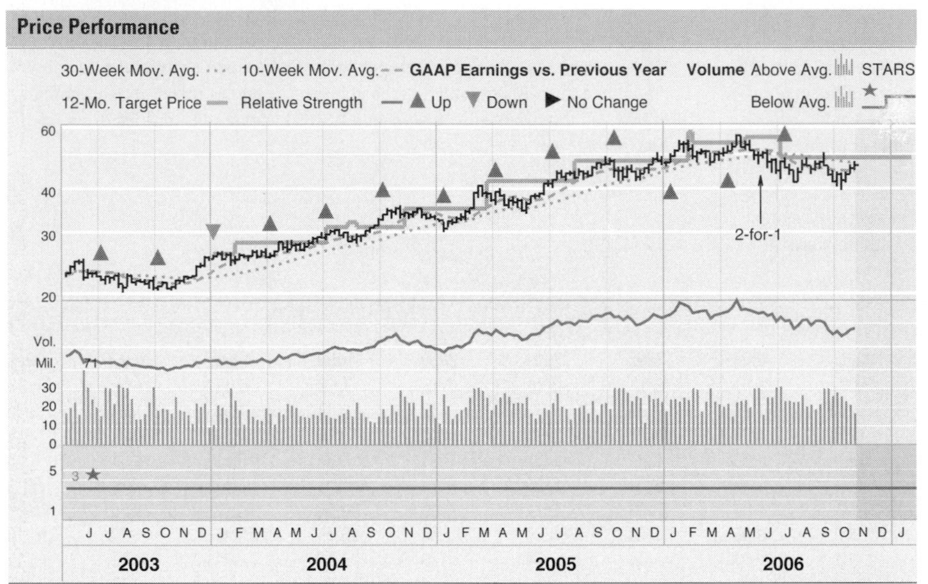

Options: ASE, CBOE, P, Ph

Analysis prepared by **Charles LaPorta, CFA** on September 13, 2006, when the stock traded at **$ 45.23**.

Highlights

- Second quarter 2006 operating EPS amounted to $1.43, versus $1.06 in 2005, and above our estimate of $1.35. The outperformance was driven by the ramp up of production in the prolific K2 Complex, which continues to expect 8 wells on line by year end.
- Per unit operating expenses increased about 3% sequentially, due to an increase in workovers, but partially offset by lower field fuel costs; we believe lifting costs will decline through year end as repair activity dissipates and deepwater volumes pick up. We believe higher per-unit depletion, depreciation and amortization charges are a result of the ramp-up in the prodigious Gulf of Mexico fields; these higher expense levels are in keeping with management guidance toward finding and development costs in the $11 per BOE area versus prior guidance of $9.
- Our EBITDA before exploration expense (EBITDAX) estimate for 2006 is $5.5 billion, on increased production and operating cost increases below industry trends. We expect interest expense to increase by $50 million in 2006 from the financing of the Kerr-McGee and Western Gas acquisitions.

Investment Rationale/Risk

- We believe APC acted on its perception that unconventional North American natural gas resources were being undervalued in the marketplace, and boldly utilized its newly strengthened balance sheet (e.g. total debt to book capitalization was 26% as of March 31, 2006) to close on the all-cash purchase of both Kerr-McGee and Western Gas Resources. These transactions have been initially financed with a 364-day bridge loan.
- Risks to our recommendation and target price include events that would cause substantial and sustained declines in oil and gas prices; a persistent inability by APC to replace its reserves; and its ability to service its pending significant debt requirements.
- APC has set formidable management execution requirements magnified by a large pending debt load (e.g. 66% pro forma debt to total capitalization) to make the pending purchases add value to shareholders. Our 12-month target price of $49 is based on a P/E of 7.3X our 2007 EPS estimate, and an enterprise value of 3.7X estimated 2006 EBITDAX, in-line with large capitalization peers.

Qualitative Risk Assessment

LOW | **MEDIUM** | HIGH

As a global exploration and production company, APC is susceptible, in our opinion, to dry hole risks in capital intensive deepwater projects. Its checkered drilling history is balanced by a large undeveloped land base and significant long-lived production assets.

Quantitative Evaluations

S&P Quality Ranking B+

D | C | B- | B | **B+** | A- | A | A+

Relative Strength Rank MODERATE

55

LOWEST = 1 HIGHEST = 99

Revenue/Earnings Data

Revenue (Million $)

	1Q	2Q	3Q	4Q	Year
2006	1,954	1,809	--	--	--
2005	1,526	1,592	1,737	2,245	7,100
2004	1,460	1,443	1,562	1,602	6,067
2003	1,255	1,249	1,340	1,278	5,122
2002	790.0	1,002	951.0	1,117	3,860
2001	3,009	2,238	1,743	1,379	8,369

Earnings Per Share ($)

2006	1.42	1.43	E1.40	E1.55	E5.80
2005	1.03	1.06	1.26	1.87	5.20
2004	0.78	0.80	0.79	0.82	3.18
2003	0.73	0.60	0.55	0.58	2.46
2002	0.17	0.47	0.37	0.61	1.61
2001	1.26	0.75	-2.71	0.21	-0.37

Fiscal year ended Dec. 31. Next earnings report expected: Late October. EPS Estimates based on S&P Operating Earnings; historical GAAP earnings are as reported.

Dividend Data (Dates: mm/dd Payment Date: mm/dd/yy)

Amount ($)	Date Decl.	Ex-Div. Date	Stk. of Record	Payment Date
0.180	02/02	03/06	03/08	03/22/06
2-for-1 Stk	02/02	05/30	05/12	05/26/06
0.090	05/11	06/12	06/14	06/28/06
0.090	08/08	09/11	09/13	09/27/06

Dividends have been paid since 1986. Source: Company reports.

Please read the Required Disclosures and Analyst Certification on the last page of this report.

Anadarko Petroleum Corp

Business Summary September 13, 2006

CORPORATE OVERVIEW. Anadarko Petroleum is an oil and gas exploration and production company whose major area of operations include Texas, Louisiana, the mid-continent region, the Rockies, the deepwater Gulf of Mexico, and Algeria. It also has production in Venezuela and Qatar, and has exploration programs in several other countries. The company's reserves have grown 5% over the past three years primarily due to successful exploration and development drilling in North America, partially offset by the implementation of a refocused strategy announced in June 2004, which resulted in APC divesting what it deemed non-core properties in a series of unrelated transactions for over $3 billion in pretax proceeds, representing about 11% of 2003 reserves and about 20% of 2004 oil and gas production. As of December 2005, APC had proved reserves of 5.6 Tcf of natural gas and 594 million barrels of oil, condensate, and NGLs. Proved developed reserves represent 62% of total reserves, and the U.S. contains 74% of APC's total reserves.

MARKET PROFILE. For a large exploration and production company that produced 158 million barrels of oil equivalent (BOE) in 2005, APC has a particularly narrow regional focus given the dominance of its North American assets on its portfolio. This market is very competitive and highly fragmented, with major competitors including XTO Energy (XTO: buy, $41) and Occidental Petroleum (OXY: buy, $46). We believe North America is a relatively mature supply source for hydrocarbons, with natural gas production changing little over the past five years. We believe the asset realignment that APC implemented in 2004 allowed the company to monetize non-core properties at attractive prices and to redeploy its energies into higher margin projects, while using the sale proceeds to strengthen its balance sheet. The company was able to simultaneously continue the development of its emerging deepwater Gulf of Mexico projects, which are currently ramping up.

The combination of substantial long-lived onshore natural gas properties, with prolific deepwater properties is unique among large capitalization independent oil and gas exploration and production companies. The capital intensity and high risk nature of deepwater developments and the accelerating pace of service cost inflation require superior execution for companies engaged in these projects. We believe APC needs a longer history of demonstrable success to attract more investors.

Company Financials

Per Share Data ($) Year Ended Dec. 31	2005	2004	2003	2002	2001	2000	1999	1998	1997	1996
Tangible Book Value	21.06	16.45	13.97	11.01	9.59	10.50	5.15	4.32	12.55	4.19
Cash Flow	8.04	6.05	5.01	3.74	2.09	3.64	1.00	0.65	1.28	1.13
Earnings	5.20	3.18	2.46	1.61	-0.37	2.13	0.13	-0.21	0.45	0.43
S&P Core Earnings	5.22	3.27	2.47	1.53	-0.49	NA	NA	NA	NA	NA
Dividends	0.36	0.28	0.22	0.16	0.11	0.10	0.10	0.09	0.08	0.08
Payout Ratio	7%	9%	9%	10%	NM	5%	80%	NM	17%	18%
Prices:High	50.71	35.78	25.86	29.28	36.99	37.97	21.38	22.44	19.19	17.22
Prices:Low	30.01	24.00	20.14	18.39	21.50	13.78	13.13	12.38	12.69	11.69
P/E Ratio:High	10	11	11	18	NM	18	NM	NM	43	41
P/E Ratio:Low	6	8	8	11	NM	6	NM	NM	29	27

Income Statement Analysis (Million $)	2005	2004	2003	2002	2001	2000	1999	1998	1997	1996
Revenue	7,100	6,067	5,122	3,860	8,369	5,686	701	560	673	569
Operating Income	5,436	4,400	3,648	2,585	3,702	2,190	421	267	402	349
Depreciation, Depletion and Amortization	1,343	1,447	1,297	1,121	1,227	593	218	204	199	167
Interest Expense	201	352	253	203	92.0	Nil	74.1	57.7	41.0	56.0
Pretax Income	3,895	2,477	1,974	1,207	-390	1,426	105	65.1	164	158
Effective Tax Rate	36.6%	35.2%	36.9%	31.2%	NM	42.2%	59.4%	NM	34.7%	36.2%
Net Income	2,471	1,606	1,245	831	-176	824	42.6	-42.2	107	101
S&P Core Earnings	2,478	1,646	1,248	785	-243	NA	NA	NA	NA	NA

Balance Sheet & Other Financial Data (Million $)	2005	2004	2003	2002	2001	2000	1999	1998	1997	1996
Cash	739	874	62.0	34.0	37.0	199	44.8	17.0	8.91	15.0
Current Assets	2,916	2,502	1,324	1,280	1,201	1,894	356	230	219	270
Total Assets	22,588	20,192	20,546	18,248	16,771	16,590	4,098	3,633	2,992	2,584
Current Liabilities	2,403	1,993	1,715	1,861	1,801	1,676	387	289	252	285
Long Term Debt	3,555	3,671	5,058	5,171	4,638	3,984	1,443	1,425	956	731
Common Equity	10,967	9,219	8,510	6,673	6,262	6,586	1,335	1,059	1,117	1,014
Total Capital	19,330	17,393	17,909	15,578	14,454	10,770	3,555	3,208	2,620	2,244
Capital Expenditures	3,408	3,064	2,772	2,388	3,316	1,708	680	917	686	427
Cash Flow	3,809	3,048	2,537	1,946	1,044	1,406	250	155	306	268
Current Ratio	1.2	1.3	0.8	0.7	0.7	1.1	0.9	0.8	0.9	0.9
% Long Term Debt of Capitalization	18.4	21.1	28.2	33.2	32.1	37.0	40.6	44.4	36.5	32.6
% Return on Assets	11.5	7.9	6.4	4.7	NM	8.0	1.1	NM	3.8	4.2
% Return on Equity	24.4	17.9	16.1	12.8	NM	20.5	2.6	NM	10.1	10.5

Data as orig reptd.; bef. results of disc opers/spec. items. Per share data adj. for stk. divs.; EPS diluted. E-Estimated. NA-Not Available. NM-Not Meaningful. NR-Not Ranked. UR-Under Review.

Office: 1201 Lake Robbins Drive, The Woodlands, TX 77380-1124.
Telephone: 832-636-1000.
Website: http://www.anadarko.com
Chrmn, Pres & CEO: J.T. Hackett

SVP & CFO: R.A. Walker
VP & Chief Acctg Officer: B.W. Busmire
VP, Chief Acctg Officer & Cntlr: D.L. Dickey
VP & Treas: R.G. Gwin

Investor Contact: S. Lawrence (832-636-3326)
Board of Directors: R. J. Allison, Jr., L. Barcus, J. L. Bryan, J. R. Butler, Jr., H. P. Eberhart, J. R. Gordon, J. T. Hackett, J. W. Poduska, Sr.

Founded: 1985
Domicile: Delaware
Employees: 3,300

STANDARD &POOR'S

Analog Devices Inc.

S&P Recommendation	Price	12-Mo. Target Price	Investment Style
HOLD ★★★★★	$31.13 (as of Oct 27, 2006)	$36.00	Large-Cap Growth

GICS Sector Information Technology
Sub-Industry Semiconductors

Comment This Massachusetts company manufactures high-performance integrated circuits (ICs) used in analog and digital signal processing applications.

Key Stock Statistics (Source S&P, Vickers, company reports)

52-Wk Range	$41.48–26.07	S&P Oper. EPS 2006E	1.45	P/E on S&P Oper. EPS 2006E	21.5	Dividend Rate/Share	$0.64
Trailing 12-Month EPS	$1.27	S&P Oper. EPS 2007E	1.62	Common Shares Outstg. (M)	352.9	Yield (%)	2.06
Trailing 12-Month P/E	24.5	S&P Core EPS 2006E	1.45	Market Capitalization(B)	$10.984	Beta	2.51
$10K Invested 5 Yrs Ago	$7,548	S&P Core EPS 2007E	1.62	Institutional Ownership (%)	82	S&P Credit Rating	BBB+

Price Performance

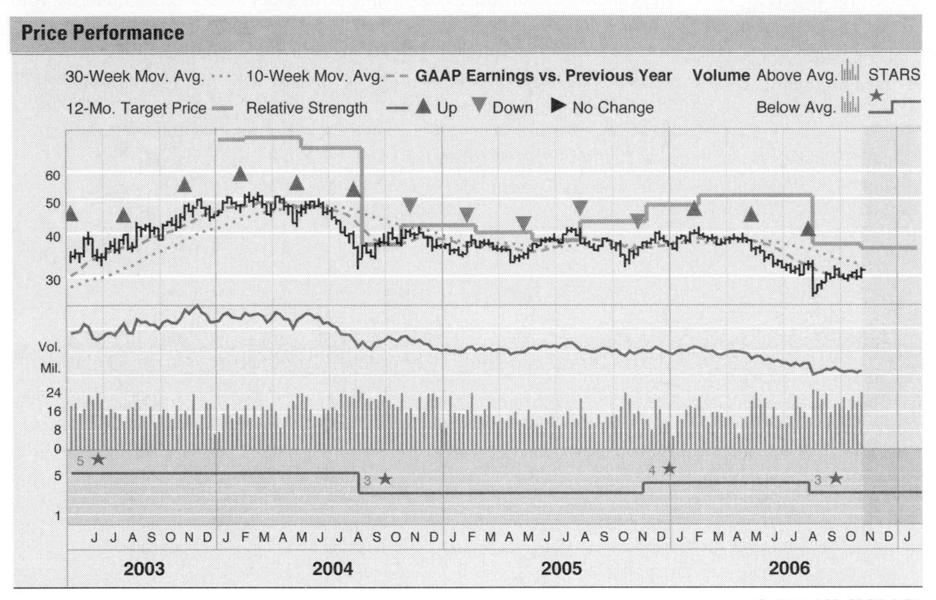

Options: ASE, CBOE, P, Ph

Analysis prepared by **Thomas W. Smith, CFA** on October 26, 2006, when the stock traded at **$ 31.54**.

Highlights

- We project that revenues will rise 8% in FY 06 (Oct.) and 8% in FY 07, following an October 24 lowering of ADI's fourth quarter revenue guidance based on weak sales to wireless handset markets. In the second quarter, the company earned $13 million on the sale of its FUSIV network processor and ADSL ASIC chip product line to Ikanos Communications; the product line represented about 2% of ADI's annual sales. We think the divestment should improve ADI's focus on higher margin products.
- We expect gross margins to be steady, near 59% in FY 06 and FY 07. Cost savings from the planned consolidation of manufacturing and product development operations should help. On October 19, 2005, ADI announced plans to close its California wafer fab and transfer production to its Massachusetts and Ireland sites, which have more advanced process technology.
- Our FY 06 operating EPS estimate of $1.45 includes projected stock option expense of $0.17, and our operating EPS estimate of $1.62 for FY 07 includes estimated stock option expense of $0.24.

Investment Rationale/Risk

- Although we believe the shares appear attractively valued on a price-to-sales basis, we also think that the near-term pace of sales growth has become less certain. Spots of inventory congestion appeared in the FY 06 third quarter at customers in the wireless handset and PC areas, and continued into the fourth quarter per ADI's October 24 sales warning. We expect the inventory overhang to clear in the first quarter of FY 07.
- Risks to our opinion and target price include possible downward fluctuations in demand for semiconductors, above-average share price volatility, and stock option expense that we view as above the norm for S&P 500 companies.
- Our 12-month target price of $36 is based on a blend of our price to sales and P/E analyses. Applying a target price to sales ratio of 4.4X, at the low end of ADI's historical range, to our FY 07 sales per share estimate of $7.77, we project a value of $34. We see a value of $37 by applying a historical trough level P/E of 23X to our FY 07 EPS estimate of $1.62.

Qualitative Risk Assessment

LOW | **MEDIUM** | HIGH

Our risk assessment reflects that ADI is subject to the sales cycles of the semiconductor industry, offset by our view of relatively stable chip pricing owing to high proprietary design content, broad end markets, a leading market share in key converter and amplifier product categories, a lack of debt, and a long corporate history.

Quantitative Evaluations

S&P Quality Ranking **B**

D | C | B- | **B** | B+ | A- | A | A+

Relative Strength Rank **MODERATE**

47

LOWEST = 1 HIGHEST = 99

Revenue/Earnings Data

Revenue (Million $)

	1Q	2Q	3Q	4Q	Year
2006	621.3	643.9	663.7	--	--
2005	580.5	603.7	582.4	622.1	2,389
2004	605.4	678.5	717.8	632.1	2,634
2003	467.4	501.9	520.5	557.5	2,047
2002	393.0	413.4	445.5	455.7	1,708
2001	772.3	601.4	479.9	423.3	2,277

Earnings Per Share ($)

	1Q	2Q	3Q	4Q	Year
2006	0.32	0.39	0.39	**E**0.36	**E**1.45
2005	0.28	0.31	0.32	0.18	1.08
2004	0.30	0.39	0.43	0.34	1.45
2003	0.16	0.19	0.21	0.38	0.78
2002	0.06	0.04	0.08	0.09	0.28
2001	0.50	0.27	0.10	0.06	0.93

Fiscal year ended Oct. 31. Next earnings report expected: Mid November. EPS Estimates based on S&P Operating Earnings; historical GAAP earnings are as reported.

Dividend Data (Dates: mm/dd Payment Date: mm/dd/yy)

Amount ($)	Date Decl.	Ex-Div. Date	Stk. of Record	Payment Date
0.120	11/15	11/22	11/25	12/14/05
0.120	02/09	02/22	02/24	03/15/06
0.160	03/14	05/24	05/26	06/14/06
0.160	08/14	08/23	08/25	09/13/06

Dividends have been paid since 2003. Source: Company reports.

Analog Devices Inc.

Business Summary October 26, 2006

Analog Devices designs, manufactures, and markets a broad line of high-performance analog, mixed-signal and digital signal processing (DSP) integrated circuits (ICs) that address a wide range of real-world signal processing applications. Real-world phenomena that these applications are designed for include temperature, pressure, sound, images, speed, acceleration, position and rotation. These phenomena are specifically analog in nature, consisting of continuously varying information.

The company's analog products are typically general purpose in nature and are used in a wide variety of equipment and systems. Accordingly, they tend to have long life cycles. ADI markets several thousand products; its 10 largest products by revenue accounted for 12% of FY 05 (Oct.) total revenue, down from 17% of FY 04 sales. A majority of the company's products are proprietary. These factors, together with greater product price stability and less intense Asian competition, have allowed the company, in our view, to post more stable operating results than those of most semiconductor makers. The semiconductor industry has displayed sharp cyclicality over the company's history.

ADI's products are sold both to OEMs and to customers building their own equipment. Key markets are industrial, which accounted for approximately 39% of sales in FY 05 (36% of FY 04 sales), communications 31% (37%), computers 15% (14%), and high-performance consumer electronics 15% (13%). The customer base is fairly broad: the 20 largest customers, excluding distributors, accounted for about 29% of sales in FY 05 (29% of sales in FY 04), and the largest customer, excluding distributors, accounted for approximately 4% (3%).

The expansion of broadband and wireless communications applications helps drive demand for analog and DSP chips. ADI's products are built into data and digital subscriber lines (DSL) modems, wireless telephones, base station equipment, and remote access servers.

The company's chips are increasingly sold to PC and digital entertainment markets, as consumer equipment to handle voice, video and images becomes increasingly complex and sells to a wider audience. ADI's chips are used in end-products that include digital televisions, DVD recorders/players, and digital camcorders and cameras.

Company Financials

Per Share Data ($) Year Ended Oct. 31	**2005**	**2004**	**2003**	**2002**	**2001**	**2000**	**1999**	**1998**	**1997**	**1996**
Tangible Book Value	9.61	9.66	8.42	7.50	7.20	5.90	4.54	3.47	3.50	2.67
Cash Flow	1.49	1.84	1.22	0.90	1.48	2.00	0.94	0.69	0.79	0.75
Earnings	1.08	1.45	0.78	0.28	0.93	1.59	0.55	0.36	0.52	0.52
S&P Core Earnings	0.29	0.91	0.20	-0.32	0.44	NA	NA	NA	NA	NA
Dividends	0.32	0.20	Nil	Nil	Nil	Nil	Nil	Nil	Nil	Nil
Payout Ratio	30%	14%	Nil	Nil	Nil	Nil	Nil	Nil	Nil	Nil
Prices:High	41.40	52.37	50.35	48.84	64.00	103.00	47.25	19.81	18.34	13.31
Prices:Low	31.71	31.36	22.58	17.88	29.00	41.31	12.19	6.00	10.31	6.38
P/E Ratio:High	38	36	65	NM	69	65	86	56	35	26
P/E Ratio:Low	29	22	29	NM	31	26	22	17	20	12

Income Statement Analysis (Million $)										
Revenue	2,389	2,634	2,047	1,708	2,277	2,578	1,450	1,231	1,243	1,194
Operating Income	703	852	552	405	675	924	391	289	337	311
Depreciation	156	153	168	238	210	157	143	128	104	83.8
Interest Expense	0.03	0.22	32.2	44.5	62.5	5.84	8.07	11.2	12.5	11.3
Pretax Income	588	733	382	140	507	866	258	150	236	231
Effective Tax Rate	29.4%	22.1%	21.9%	25.0%	29.7%	29.9%	23.6%	20.6%	24.4%	25.5%
Net Income	415	571	298	105	356	607	197	119	178	172
S&P Core Earnings	113	364	74.2	-118	170	NA	NA	NA	NA	NA

Balance Sheet & Other Financial Data (Million $)										
Cash	628	519	518	1,614	1,365	1,736	356	263	290	300
Current Assets	3,732	3,529	2,886	3,624	3,435	3,168	1,379	904	895	820
Total Assets	4,583	4,720	4,093	4,980	4,885	4,411	2,218	1,862	1,764	1,516
Current Liabilities	819	567	463	484	528	650	479	321	274	270
Long Term Debt	Nil	Nil	Nil	1,274	1,206	1,213	16.2	341	349	354
Common Equity	3,692	3,800	3,288	2,900	2,843	2,304	1,616	1,128	1,147	863
Total Capital	3,692	3,810	3,305	4,197	4,100	3,568	1,672	1,501	1,517	1,233
Capital Expenditures	85.5	146	67.7	57.4	297	275	77.5	167	179	234
Cash Flow	570	723	467	343	567	764	339	247	282	256
Current Ratio	4.6	6.2	6.2	7.5	6.5	4.9	2.9	2.8	3.3	3.0
% Long Term Debt of Capitalization	Nil	Nil	Nil	30.4	29.4	34.0	1.0	22.7	23.0	28.7
% Net Income of Revenue	17.4	21.7	14.6	6.2	15.7	23.6	13.6	9.7	14.3	14.4
% Return on Assets	8.9	13.0	6.6	2.1	7.7	18.3	9.6	6.6	10.9	13.7
% Return on Equity	11.1	16.1	9.6	3.7	13.8	31.0	14.3	10.5	17.7	22.6

Data as orig reptd.; bef. results of disc opers/spec. items. Per share data adj. for stk. divs.; EPS diluted. E-Estimated. NA-Not Available. NM-Not Meaningful. NR-Not Ranked. UR-Under Review.

Office: One Technology Way, Norwood, MA 02062-9106.
Telephone: 800-262-5643.
Email: investor.relations@analog.com
Website: http://www.analog.com

Chrmn: R. Stata
Pres & CEO: J.G. Fishman
VP & CFO: J.E. McDonough
VP, Secy & General Counsel: M.K. Seif

Treas: W.A. Martin
Investor Contact: M. Tagliaferro (781-461-3282)
Board of Directors: J. Champy, J. L. Doyle, J. G. Fishman, J. C. Hodgson, C. King, F. G. Saviers, P. J. Severino, K. Sicchitano, R. Stata, L. C. Thurow

Founded: 1965
Domicile: Massachusetts
Employees: 8,800

STANDARD &POOR'S

Anheuser-Busch Companies Inc.

S&P Recommendation HOLD ★★★★★

Price $47.70 (as of Oct 27, 2006)

12-Mo. Target Price $51.00

Investment Style Large-Cap Growth

GICS Sector Consumer Staples
Sub-Industry Brewers

Comment BUD, the parent company of the world's largest brewer, also has interests in entertainment operations.

Key Stock Statistics (Source S&P, Vickers, company reports)

52-Wk Range	$50.00–40.17	S&P Oper. EPS 2006E	2.59	P/E on S&P Oper. EPS 2006E	18.4	Dividend Rate/Share	$1.18
Trailing 12-Month EPS	$2.59	S&P Oper. EPS 2007E	2.60	Common Shares Outstg. (M)	768.7	Yield (%)	2.47
Trailing 12-Month P/E	18.4	S&P Core EPS 2006E	2.57	Market Capitalization(B)	$36.668	Beta	0.27
$10K Invested 5 Yrs Ago	$12,401	S&P Core EPS 2007E	2.65	Institutional Ownership (%)	60	S&P Credit Rating	A+

Price Performance

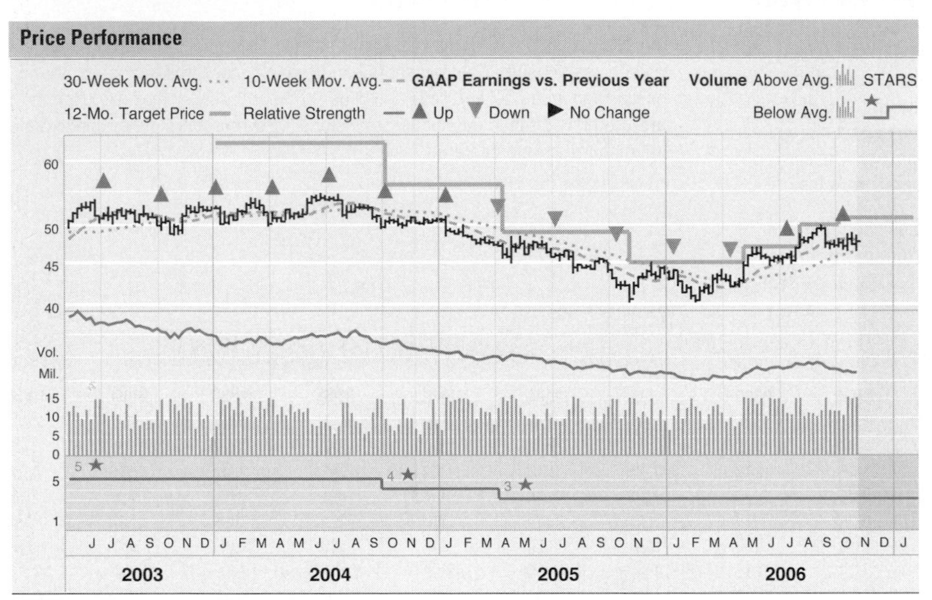

Options: ASE, CBOE, P, Ph

Analysis prepared by **Raymond Mathis** on September 26, 2006, when the stock traded at **$ 47.70**.

Highlights

- We see net sales (after excise taxes) rising 3.5% in 2006, as we expect improving domestic volume trends and strength in international sales. As competitive responses to BUD's price hikes have waned and pressure in the sub-premium segment continues to escalate, we are encouraged by the halt in price increases. We expect net revenue per barrel to rise about 1.0% to 1.5% in 2006. We see worldwide shipment volumes rising in the mid-single digits, reflecting acquisitions and strength in China and Canada.

- We see operating margins narrowing in 2006, as higher packaging and energy costs, increased marketing efforts, higher low-margin international business, and option expensing outweigh limited price increases, volume gains, and possible reductions in promotional activity. In our view, growth in equity income from BUD's Grupo Modelo interest will bolster earnings over the near term.

- We see flat interest expense, but possibly a higher effective tax rate in 2006. Aided by probable share repurchases, we see a rise in 2006 operating EPS to $2.61 from $2.35 in 2005.

Investment Rationale/Risk

- We believe recent increases in marketing activity might not be effectively fending off what we view as the main threat-- wines and spirits, as indicated by continued weakness in industry shipment volumes. We expect the pricing environment to be unfavorable going forward. However, we anticipate a turnaround in market share losses as price gaps narrow within segments and as on-premise marketing heats up. In addition, we see rising equity income from BUD's 50% stake in Modelo.

- Risks to our recommendation and target price include potential market share declines due to aggressive marketing by competitors, particularly in the wine and spirits categories, for first-time drinkers. Also, greater than expected increases in energy and commodity costs could hurt margins.

- Our 12-month target price of $51 blends our DCF and P/E analyses, giving more weight to the latter. Our DCF model calculates a $48 intrinsic value assuming a 9.0% cost of capital and a 2.4% five-year growth rate. Applying an historical average P/E ratio of 20X to our 2006 EPS estimate of $2.61, we get a $52 value.

Qualitative Risk Assessment

LOW	MEDIUM	HIGH

BUD is a large cap company, and has the largest market share in an industry that has historically demonstrated stable revenue streams.

Quantitative Evaluations

S&P Quality Ranking A+

D	C	B-	B	B+	A-	A	A+

Relative Strength Rank MODERATE

35

LOWEST = 1 HIGHEST = 99

Revenue/Earnings Data

Revenue (Million $)

	1Q	2Q	3Q	4Q	Year
2006	3,756	4,256	4,281	--	--
2005	3,564	4,018	4,089	3,365	15,036
2004	3,477	4,010	4,080	3,367	14,934
2003	3,281	3,770	3,881	3,215	14,147
2002	3,137	3,626	3,706	3,098	13,566
2001	3,044	3,452	3,522	2,893	12,911

Earnings Per Share ($)

2006	0.64	0.82	0.82	**E**0.31	**E**2.59
2005	0.65	0.78	0.66	0.26	2.35
2004	0.67	0.83	0.85	0.42	2.77
2003	0.57	0.75	0.80	0.36	2.48
2002	0.51	0.66	0.71	0.32	2.20
2001	0.43	0.58	0.62	0.26	1.89

Fiscal year ended Dec. 31. Next earnings report expected: Early February. EPS Estimates based on S&P Operating Earnings; historical GAAP earnings are as reported.

Dividend Data (Dates: mm/dd Payment Date: mm/dd/yy)

Amount ($)	Date Decl.	Ex-Div. Date	Stk. of Record	Payment Date
0.270	01/11	02/07	02/09	03/09/06
0.270	04/26	05/05	05/09	06/09/06
0.295	07/26	08/07	08/09	09/11/06
0.295	10/25	11/07	11/09	12/11/06

Dividends have been paid since 1932. Source: Company reports.

Anheuser-Busch Companies Inc.

Business Summary September 26, 2006

CORPORATE OVERVIEW. Anheuser-Busch Cos. is the holding company parent of the largest U.S. brewer, Anheuser-Busch, Inc. (ABI), which dates back to 1875, Anheuser-Busch International, Inc. (ABII), and other subsidiaries that conduct various other business operations.

Major beer brands include Budweiser, Bud Light, Bud Dry, Bud Ice (Light), Michelob, Michelob Light, Michelob Ultra, Michelob Golden Draft, Michelob Golden Draft (Light), Michelob Black & Tan Lager, Michelob Amber Bock, Michelob Honey Lager, Michelob Marzen, Busch, Busch Light, Busch Ice, Natural Light, Natural Ice, King Cobra, ZiegenBock Amber, ZiegenBock light, Hurricane Malt Liquor, Hurricane Ice, Anheuser World Select, Bare Knuckle Stout, Bacardi Silver, Bacardi Silver O3, Bacardi Silver Raz, Bacardi Limon, Bacardi Black Cherry, Bacardi Green Apple, BE, Budweiser Select and Tequiza. Non-alcoholic malt beverages include O'Doul's, O'Doul's Amber, and Busch NA.

BUD operates 12 breweries, strategically located across the U.S., to serve its distribution system economically. Worldwide sales of the company's beer brands in 2005 totaled 121.9 million barrels (up from 116.8 million barrels in 2004). U.S. sales totaled 103.0 million barrels in 2005 (up fractionally), or about 50% of U.S. industry sales. BUD's beer products are sold in more than 80 countries and U.S. territories. International beer volume was 20.8 million barrels in 2005, compared to 13.8 million barrels in 2004. In 2005, domestic beer contributed 75.8% of net sales, and 68.4% of net income, and international beer 6.4% and 22.7%.

Through various subsidiaries, the company is involved in a number of beer-related operations that help to insulate it from occasional rises in packaging and ingredient costs. These operations include can manufacturing, metalized paper printing, and barley malting. Packaging operations accounted for 10.4% of total net sales in 2005, and 3.6% of net profit.

Through Busch Entertainment Corp., the company operates nine theme parks, including Busch Gardens in Florida and Virginia; Sea World parks in Florida, Texas and California; water parks in Florida and Virginia; and an educational play park in Pennsylvania. Busch Entertainment contributed 7.4% of total net sales in 2005, 5.3% of profit.

Company Financials

Per Share Data ($) Year Ended Dec. 31	2005	2004	2003	2002	2001	2000	1999	1998	1997	1996
Tangible Book Value	2.71	1.88	2.74	3.61	4.15	4.11	3.80	3.96	3.69	3.61
Cash Flow	3.60	4.04	3.53	3.16	2.82	2.56	1.47	2.02	1.86	1.73
Earnings	2.35	2.77	2.48	2.20	1.89	1.69	1.47	1.27	1.18	1.14
S&P Core Earnings	2.38	2.61	2.33	1.96	1.67	NA	NA	NA	NA	NA
Dividends	1.03	0.93	0.83	0.75	0.69	0.63	0.58	0.54	0.50	0.46
Payout Ratio	44%	34%	33%	34%	37%	37%	39%	43%	42%	40%
Prices:High	51.32	54.74	53.84	55.00	46.95	49.88	42.00	34.13	24.13	22.50
Prices:Low	40.15	49.42	45.30	43.65	36.75	27.31	32.22	21.47	19.25	16.19
P/E Ratio:High	22	20	22	25	25	30	29	27	20	20
P/E Ratio:Low	17	18	18	20	19	16	22	17	16	14
Income Statement Analysis (Million $)										
Revenue	15,036	14,934	14,147	13,566	12,911	12,262	11,704	11,245	11,066	10,884
Operating Income	3,705	4,294	4,077	3,827	3,540	3,299	3,080	2,862	2,737	2,623
Depreciation	979	933	877	847	834	804	777	738	684	594
Interest Expense	435	405	377	351	334	315	290	265	219	233
Pretax Income	2,690	2,999	3,169	2,975	2,618	2,380	2,165	1,937	1,883	1,893
Effective Tax Rate	31.6%	38.7%	34.5%	35.0%	34.9%	34.8%	35.2%	36.3%	37.4%	38.9%
Net Income	1,839	2,240	2,076	1,934	1,705	1,552	1,402	1,233	1,179	1,156
S&P Core Earnings	1,860	2,111	1,952	1,722	1,507	NA	NA	NA	NA	NA
Balance Sheet & Other Financial Data (Million $)										
Cash	226	228	191	189	163	160	152	225	147	94.0
Current Assets	1,759	1,818	1,630	1,505	1,550	1,548	1,601	1,640	1,584	1,466
Total Assets	16,555	16,173	14,690	14,120	13,862	13,085	12,640	12,484	11,727	10,464
Current Liabilities	1,983	1,969	1,857	1,788	1,732	1,676	1,987	1,730	1,501	1,431
Long Term Debt	1,682	8,279	7,285	6,603	5,984	5,375	4,881	4,719	4,366	3,271
Common Equity	3,343	2,668	2,712	3,052	4,062	4,128	3,921	4,216	4,042	4,029
Total Capital	6,708	12,674	11,459	11,962	11,334	10,876	10,147	10,238	9,701	8,508
Capital Expenditures	1,137	1,090	993	835	1,022	1,075	856	818	1,199	1,085
Cash Flow	2,818	3,173	2,953	2,781	2,539	2,356	1,402	1,971	1,863	1,750
Current Ratio	0.9	0.9	0.9	0.8	0.9	0.9	0.8	0.9	1.1	1.0
% Long Term Debt of Capitalization	25.1	65.3	63.6	55.2	52.8	49.4	48.1	46.1	45.0	21.4
% Net Income of Revenue	12.2	15.0	14.7	14.3	13.2	12.7	12.0	11.0	10.7	10.6
% Return on Assets	11.2	14.5	14.4	13.8	12.7	12.1	11.2	10.2	10.6	11.0
% Return on Equity	61.2	83.3	72.0	45.3	41.6	38.6	34.5	29.9	29.2	27.3

Data as orig reptd.; bef. results of disc opers/spec. items. Per share data adj. for stk. divs.; EPS diluted. E-Estimated. NA-Not Available. NM-Not Meaningful. NR-Not Ranked. UR-Under Review.

Office: One Busch Place, St. Louis, MO 63118.
Telephone: 314-577-2000.
Website: http://www.anheuser-busch.com
Chrmn: A.A. Busch, III

Pres & CEO: P.T. Stokes
VP & CFO: W.R. Baker
VP & Cntlr: J. Kelly

Board of Directors: A. A. Busch IV, A. A. Busch, III, C. G. Fernandez, J. J. Forese, J. E. Jacob, J. R. Jones, C. F. Knight, V. R. Loucks, Jr., V. S. Martinez, W. P. Payne, J. M. Roche, H. H. Shelton, P. T. Stokes, A. C. Taylor, D. A. Warner, III, E. E. Whitacre, Jr.

Founded: 1852
Domicile: Delaware
Employees: 31,485

Aon Corp.

S&P Recommendation HOLD ★★★★★	**Price**	**12-Mo. Target Price**	**Investment Style**
	$34.86 (as of Oct 27, 2006)	$40.00	Large-Cap Value

GICS Sector Financials
Sub-Industry Insurance Brokers

Comment This Chicago-based holding company is comprised of a family of insurance brokerage, consulting and insurance underwriting subsidiaries.

Key Stock Statistics (Source S&P, Vickers, company reports)

52-Wk Range	**$42.76–31.01**	S&P Oper. EPS 2006**E**	**2.33**	P/E on S&P Oper. EPS 2006**E**	**15.0**	Dividend Rate/Share	**$0.60**
Trailing 12-Month EPS	**$2.14**	S&P Oper. EPS 2007**E**	**2.80**	Common Shares Outstg. (M)	**314.5**	Yield (%)	**1.72**
Trailing 12-Month P/E	**16.3**	S&P Core EPS 2006**E**	**2.33**	Market Capitalization(B)	**$10.962**	Beta	**0.39**
$10K Invested 5 Yrs Ago	**$9,644**	S&P Core EPS 2007**E**	**2.80**	Institutional Ownership (%)	**86**	S&P Credit Rating	**BBB+**

Price Performance

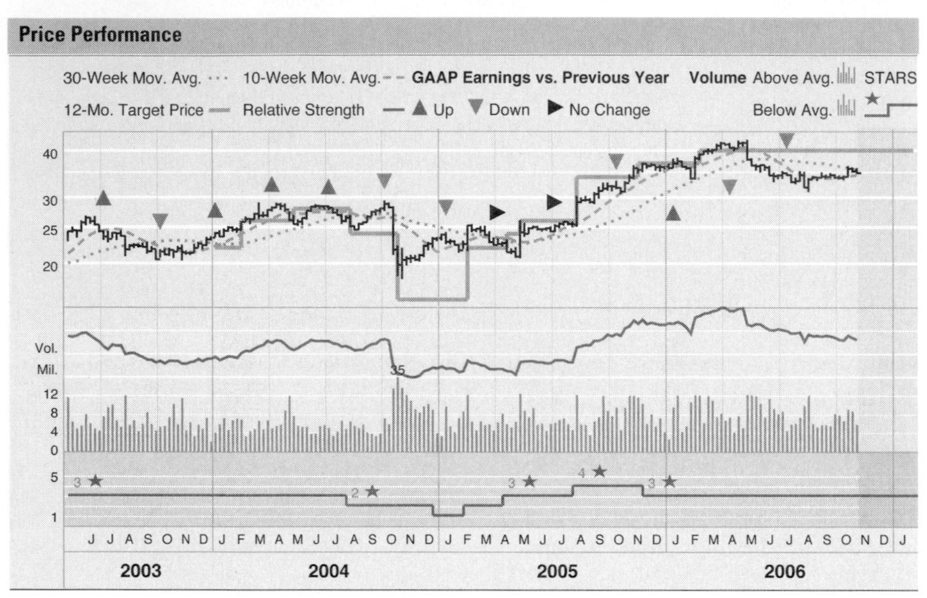

Options: ASE, CBOE, P, Ph

Analysis prepared by **Frank Braden** on August 15, 2006, when the stock traded at **$ 33.85**.

Highlights

- We see total revenues falling modestly in 2006 before rising 4% in 2007. The expected decline in 2006 revenue should be partially due to the proposed sale of Aon's warranty business. We look for restructuring costs of $95 million in 2006 to be offset by cost savings of $100 million. We forecast expenses from AOC's restructuring plan to total $300 million through the end of 2007 and expect about 60% of the expenses to come from workforce reduction. Annualized cost savings should reach $195 million by 2008. We see flat revenue growth in the risk and brokerage services and pretax margins improving to 17.3%.
- We look for modest growth for consulting revenues and expect pretax income in the segment to improve. Insurance underwriting revenues should decline in 2006 on the proposed sale of the warranty business, but results should be supported by an improving expense ratio. We expect AOC to use excess cash to fund its pension plan or repurchase shares as part of its $1 billion repurchase authorization.
- Our forecast of 2006 EPS from continuing operations is $2.33, including about $0.05 of projected stock option expense.

Investment Rationale/Risk

- We believe AOC has done a good job so far in right-sizing its operations to deal with the loss of high-margin contingent commissions. In addition, we see further opportunities for AOC to reduce operating costs and expand overall operating margins in 2006. However, results in the consulting segment have remained below our expectations, and the pricing environment remains challenging, in our view.
- Risks to our recommendation and target price include continuing pressure on operating results from the elimination of contingent commissions and from a soft property and casualty market; possible client defections following legal/regulatory settlements; currency risks; and potential additional contingent commission probes by international authorities.
- Our 12-month target price of $40 is based on a P/E multiple of 17X applied to our 2006 EPS estimate of $2.33 from continuing operations, a premium to AOC's three-year multiple of 15X, reflecting our view of rising premium rates and higher operating margins.

Qualitative Risk Assessment

LOW	**MEDIUM**	HIGH

Our risk assessment reflects our view of the well diversified operations of the company and solid balance sheet with low debt, offset by the impact of the loss of contingent commissions and business restructuring.

Quantitative Evaluations

S&P Quality Ranking **B+**

D	C	B-	B	**B+**	A-	A	A+

Relative Strength Rank **MODERATE**

38

LOWEST = 1 HIGHEST = 99

Revenue/Earnings Data

Revenue (Million $)

	1Q	2Q	3Q	4Q	Year
2006	2,523	2,265	--	--	--
2005	2,464	2,456	2,387	2,530	9,837
2004	2,564	2,544	2,402	2,662	10,172
2003	2,384	2,434	2,391	2,601	9,810
2002	2,088	2,122	2,246	2,366	8,822
2001	1,811	1,917	1,912	2,036	7,676

Earnings Per Share ($)

2006	0.57	0.53	**E**0.54	**E**0.69	**E**2.33
2005	0.58	0.54	0.35	0.42	1.89
2004	0.58	0.54	0.36	0.25	1.72
2003	0.49	0.48	0.44	0.67	2.08
2002	0.57	Nil	0.46	0.59	1.64
2001	0.07	0.11	0.26	0.30	0.73

Fiscal year ended Dec. 31. Next earnings report expected: Early November. EPS Estimates based on S&P Operating Earnings; historical GAAP earnings are as reported.

Dividend Data (Dates: mm/dd Payment Date: mm/dd/yy)

Amount ($)	Date Decl.	Ex-Div. Date	Stk. of Record	Payment Date
0.150	04/14	04/28	05/02	05/15/06
0.150	04/14	04/28	05/02	05/15/06
0.150	07/21	07/28	08/01	08/14/06
0.150	10/06	10/30	11/01	11/14/06

Dividends have been paid since 1950. Source: Company reports.

Business Summary August 15, 2006

CORPORATE OVERVIEW. Aon Corp. is a global provider of insurance brokerage services, insurance products, and risk and insurance advice, as well as other consulting services, conducting business in more than 120 countries and sovereignties. As of December 31, 2005, the company was the world's second largest insurance broker based on revenues, the largest reinsurance broker, and the leading manager of captive insurance companies worldwide, based on surveys by Business Insurance.

U.S. operations accounted for 50% of consolidated revenue in 2005, the U.K. 16%, continental Europe 18%, and the rest of the world 16%.

AOC classifies its businesses into three operating segments: risk and insurance brokerage, consulting, and insurance underwriting. The risk and insurance brokerage segment accounted for 55% of total operating segment revenues in 2005, the consulting segment 13%, and the insurance underwriting segment 32%.

LEGAL/REGULATORY ISSUES. In March 2005, AOC reached a settlement with the New York, Illinois and Connecticut attorneys general and other regulators resolving all issues related to investigations conducted by these agencies. Under the settlement, AOC agreed to institute certain business reforms and pay $190 million into a fund to be distributed to eligible U.S. clients where AOC received certain related contingent commissions, with no portion of the payments considered a fine or penalty.

Company Financials

Per Share Data ($) Year Ended Dec. 31	**2005**	**2004**	**2003**	**2002**	**2001**	**2000**	**1999**	**1998**	**1997**	**1996**
Tangible Book Value	2.48	0.76	NM	NM	NM	NM	NM	NM	NM	4.93
Operating Earnings	NA	NA	NA	NA	NA	NA	NA	NA	1.53	1.09
Earnings	1.89	1.72	2.08	1.64	0.73	1.82	1.33	2.07	1.12	1.10
S&P Core Earnings	2.10	2.29	2.05	1.00	-0.06	NA	NA	NA	NA	NA
Dividends	0.60	0.60	0.60	0.83	0.90	0.87	0.81	0.73	0.68	0.63
Relative Payout	32%	35%	29%	50%	123%	48%	61%	35%	61%	57%
Prices:High	37.14	29.44	26.79	39.63	44.80	42.75	46.67	50.37	39.25	28.78
Prices:Low	20.64	18.15	17.41	13.30	29.75	20.69	26.06	32.17	26.78	21.11
P/E Ratio:High	20	17	13	24	61	23	35	24	35	26
P/E Ratio:Low	11	11	8	8	41	11	20	16	24	19
Income Statement Analysis (Million $)										
Life Insurance in Force	17,182	20,529	26,784	28,136	31,454	28,170	22,011	16,163	19,262	21,301
Premium Income:Life A & H	NA	1,620	1,680	1,628	1,350	1,233	1,137	1,084	1,081	1,105
Premium Income:Casualty/Property.	NA	1,168	869	732	672	673	671	589	528	421
Net Investment Income	343	324	317	252	213	508	577	590	494	384
Total Revenue	9,837	10,172	9,810	8,822	7,676	7,375	7,070	6,493	5,751	3,888
Pretax Income	965	880	1,110	793	399	854	635	931	542	446
Net Operating Income	NA	NA	NA	NA	NA	NA	NA	NA	402	283
Net Income	642	577	663	466	203	481	352	541	299	292
S&P Core Earnings	709	765	652	281	-19.4	NA	NA	NA	NA	NA
Balance Sheet & Other Financial Data (Million $)										
Cash & Equivalent	476	570	540	506	439	1,118	837	786	1,085	479
Premiums Due	9,697	1,645	1,504	1,213	953	1,278	1,116	1,120	863	989
Investment Assets:Bonds	4,218	3,482	2,751	2,089	2,149	2,337	2,497	3,103	4,841	4,092
Investment Assets:Stocks	40.0	40.0	42.0	62.0	382	492	574	768	806	879
Investment Assets:Loans	Nil	Nil	Nil	Nil	Nil	Nil	NA	Nil	Nil	87.2
Investment Assets:Total	9,064	13,720	7,324	6,587	6,146	6,019	6,184	6,452	5,922	5,213
Deferred Policy Costs	1,186	1,137	1,021	882	704	656	636	573	549	599
Total Assets	27,818	28,329	27,027	25,334	22,386	22,251	21,132	19,688	18,691	13,723
Debt	2,105	2,117	2,095	1,721	2,494	1,848	1,811	1,380	2,201	475
Common Equity	5,303	5,103	4,498	3,895	3,521	3,388	3,051	3,017	2,822	2,827
Combined Loss-Expense Ratio	NA	NA	NA	NA	NA	NA	NA	NA	NA	NA
% Return on Revenue	6.5	5.7	6.8	5.3	2.6	6.5	5.0	8.3	5.2	7.6
% Return on Equity	12.3	12.0	15.7	12.6	5.8	14.8	11.5	18.4	10.1	11.5
% Investment Yield	4.6	4.4	4.6	4.0	3.5	8.3	9.1	9.5	8.9	4.9

Data as orig reptd.; bef. results of disc opers/spec. items. Per share data adj. for stk. divs.; EPS diluted. E-Estimated. NA-Not Available. NM-Not Meaningful. NR-Not Ranked. UR-Under Review.

Office: 200 East Randoph Street, Chicago, IL 60601-6436.
Telephone: 312-381-1000.
Website: http://www.aon.com
Exec Chrmn: P.G. Ryan

Pres & CEO: G.C. Case
Sr EVP: M.D. O'Halleran
EVP, CFO & Chief Admin: D.P. Bulger
EVP & General Counsel: D.C. Findlay

Investor Contact: S. Malchow (312-381-3983)
Board of Directors: G. C. Case, E. D. Jannotta, P. J. Kalff, L. B. Knight, J. M. Losh, R. E. Martin, A. J. McKenna, R. S. Morrison, R. B. Myers, R. B. Myers, R. C. Notebaert, J. W. Rogers, Jr., P. G. Ryan, G. Santona, C. Y. Woo

Founded: 1919
Domicile: Delaware
Employees: 46,600

STANDARD &POOR'S

Apache Corp

S&P Recommendation BUY ★★★★★ | **Price** $65.32 (as of Oct 30, 2006) | **12-Mo. Target Price** $82.00 | **Investment Style** Large-Cap Growth

GICS Sector Energy
Sub-Industry Oil & Gas Exploration & Production

Comment This international independent exploration and production company explores for, develops and produces natural gas, crude oil and natural gas liquids.

Key Stock Statistics (Source S&P, Vickers, company reports)

52-Wk Range	**$76.25–56.50**	S&P Oper. EPS 2006**E**	**8.00**	P/E on S&P Oper. EPS 2006**E**	**8.2**	Dividend Rate/Share	**$0.60**
Trailing 12-Month EPS	**$8.43**	S&P Oper. EPS 2007**E**	**10.40**	Common Shares Outstg. (M)	**329.2**	Yield (%)	**0.92**
Trailing 12-Month P/E	**7.8**	S&P Core EPS 2006**E**	**8.00**	Market Capitalization(B)	**$21.506**	Beta	**-0.04**
$10K Invested 5 Yrs Ago	**$30,082**	S&P Core EPS 2007**E**	**10.40**	Institutional Ownership (%)	**79**	S&P Credit Rating	**A-**

Price Performance

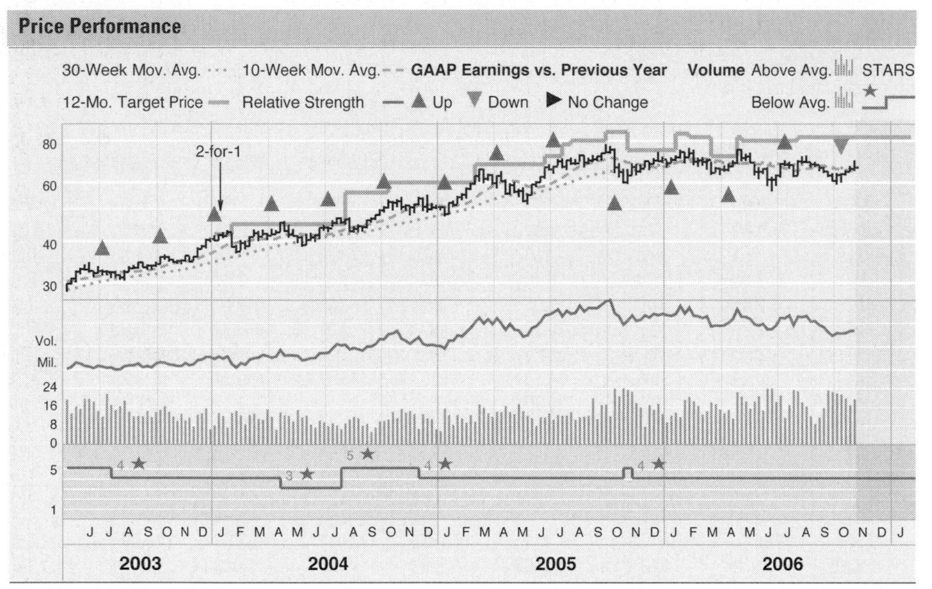

Options: ASE, CBOE, P, Ph

Analysis prepared by **Charles LaPorta, CFA** on October 26, 2006, when the stock traded at **$ 68.21**.

Highlights

- Third quarter EPS was $1.94, below the $2.08 reported last year and our estimate of $2.00, on lower than expected production volumes. We expect production growth of about 10% in 2006, driven by the recently completed purchase of Argentina properties and the recently closed acquisition of BP's (BP: buy, $70) Gulf of Mexico (GOM) assets.
- Lifting costs increased sequentially to $7.67 per BOE, due to workover expenses and lower volumes. We expect these costs to trend lower to around $6.75 by mid-2007, as production returns from under-producing basins. We expect a 300 basis point decline in EBITDA margins in 2006, resulting in EBITDA of $6.1 billion, driven by lower hydrocarbon prices and higher operating costs.
- We expect per unit depletion, depreciation and amortization charges to increase about 15% in 2006, reflecting the higher costs associated with recently announced acquisitions. The purchase of GOM assets is primarily being financed through the issuance of commercial paper, which we expect will increase interest expense by about $35 million in 2006.

Investment Rationale/Risk

- We consider APA among the most active and geographically diversified companies in the sector. Including the recent GOM transaction, APA's GOM production represents only 21% of its total production and domestic production of 39%. As of September 30, 2006, and including commercial paper issuance and outstanding volumetric production payments, debt was about 24% of capitalization. Given APA's disclosed drilling activity level and our expectation of heightened activity following the close of recent transactions, we expect over $3.5 billion in capital expenditures in 2006.
- Risks to our recommendation and target price include events that would cause substantial and sustained declines in oil and gas prices; a persistent inability by APA to replace its reserves; and acts of force majeure on production facilities. Our corporate governance concerns include a "poison pill" and a prescribed inability for shareholders to amend bylaws.
- Our 12-month target price is $82, which reflects a P/E multiple of 7.9X our 2007 EPS estimate and an enterprise value of 4.3X estimated 2007 EBITDA, both slight premiums to large-cap global E&P peers.

Qualitative Risk Assessment

LOW | **MEDIUM** | HIGH

As a global exploration and production company, we believe APA is susceptible to substantial and sustained declines in oil and gas prices and a force majeure event that could damage its production facilities. However, APA's operations are geographically diversified, and its production is about evenly split between oil and gas.

Quantitative Evaluations

S&P Quality Ranking **B+**

D | C | B- | B | **B+** | A- | A | A+

Relative Strength Rank **MODERATE**

33

LOWEST = 1 HIGHEST = 99

Revenue/Earnings Data

Revenue (Million $)

	1Q	2Q	3Q	4Q	Year
2006	1,999	2,062	2,261	--	--
2005	1,662	1,759	2,061	2,102	7,584
2004	1,150	1,241	1,407	1,535	5,333
2003	966.6	1,054	1,105	1,065	4,190
2002	528.0	656.3	645.2	730.4	2,560
2001	795.1	800.4	652.4	543.1	2,777

Earnings Per Share ($)

2006	1.97	2.17	1.94	**E**1.90	**E**8.00
2005	1.67	1.76	2.05	2.35	7.84
2004	1.05	1.16	1.30	1.53	5.04
2003	0.97	0.75	0.85	0.80	3.35
2002	0.26	0.48	0.48	0.59	1.80
2001	0.93	0.67	0.52	0.25	2.37

Fiscal year ended Dec. 31. Next earnings report expected: Early February. EPS Estimates based on S&P Operating Earnings; historical GAAP earnings are as reported.

Dividend Data (Dates: mm/dd Payment Date: mm/dd/yy)

Amount ($)	Date Decl.	Ex-Div. Date	Stk. of Record	Payment Date
0.100	02/16	04/19	04/21	05/22/06
0.100	05/22	07/19	07/21	08/22/06
0.150	09/13	10/19	10/23	11/22/06
0.150	09/13	10/19	10/23	11/22/06

Dividends have been paid since 1965. Source: Company reports.

Business Summary October 26, 2006

CORPORATE OVERVIEW. As an independent exploration and production (E&P) company, Apache explores for, develops and produces natural gas, crude oil, and natural gas liquids (NGLs). In North America, its exploration and production interests focus on the Gulf of Mexico (GOM), the Gulf Coast, the Permian Basin, the Anadarko Basin, and the Western Sedimentary Basin of Canada. Internationally, APA has exploration and production interests in offshore Western Australia, offshore U.K. in the North Sea, onshore Egypt, offshore China, and onshore Argentina.

MARKET PROFILE. APA represents a large independent E&P company that produced 166 million barrels of oil equivalent (BOE) worldwide in 2005. The company operates in seven countries, with no single basin representing more than 25% of production or reserves. We believe the value of this geographic diversity was highlighted during 2005 when hurricanes of historic severity hit the GOM, which represented 14% of production and 18.3% of reserves in 2005. Despite an 8% decline in U.S. production resulting from storm disruptions, APA's company-wide production increased 2% for the year. The company employs a deliberate portfolio approach to acquiring and producing hydrocarbons. It was one of the first to successfully implement an "acquire and exploit" strategy via an aggressive implementation of repeatable development drilling techniques. The company has since modified this strategy to include different geologic formations and geographic locations. However, the core of establishing a repeatable drilling program in each basin remains.

We believe the global energy industry is highly competitive and fragmented among a diverse number of companies of differing sizes and characteristics. These include government-owned national oil companies like Saudi Aramco and large publicly traded energy companies like Exxon Mobil (XOM:strong buy, $60). Over the past 10 years, as demand for hydrocarbons has continued to increase, an increasing proportion of the world's hydrocarbon reserves are located in developing countries whose reserves are effectively owned and managed by the government. APA estimates that only 13% of worldwide reserves are available for publicly traded energy companies to develop and produce. Many large private companies like XOM are able to utilize formidable financial resources and decades-long corporate relationships to win lucrative development deals in these areas. We believe APA has demonstrated uncommon success in this area via its successful and growing relationship with Egypt.

Company Financials

Per Share Data ($) Year Ended Dec. 31	**2005**	**2004**	**2003**	**2002**	**2001**	**2000**	**1999**	**1998**	**1997**	**1996**
Tangible Book Value	31.06	24.18	19.25	15.33	14.69	12.07	8.97	7.54	8.02	7.30
Cash Flow	12.22	8.81	6.67	4.55	5.30	4.46	2.51	2.20	2.37	2.20
Earnings	7.84	5.04	3.35	1.80	2.37	2.48	0.74	-0.58	0.72	0.61
S&P Core Earnings	7.60	5.19	3.29	1.73	2.28	NA	NA	NA	NA	NA
Dividends	0.34	0.32	0.21	0.19	0.12	0.09	0.12	0.12	0.12	0.12
Payout Ratio	4%	6%	6%	11%	5%	4%	16%	NM	17%	20%
Prices:High	78.15	55.16	41.68	28.88	31.55	32.12	21.62	16.77	19.51	16.40
Prices:Low	47.45	36.79	26.26	21.12	16.56	13.91	7.63	9.12	13.04	10.55
P/E Ratio:High	10	11	12	16	13	13	29	NM	27	27
P/E Ratio:Low	6	7	8	12	7	6	10	NM	18	17

Income Statement Analysis (Million $)	**2005**	**2004**	**2003**	**2002**	**2001**	**2000**	**1999**	**1998**	**1997**	**1996**
Revenue	7,584	5,333	4,190	2,560	2,777	2,284	1,300	876	1,176	977
Operating Income	5,792	4,119	3,241	1,048	2,146	1,310	870	509	712	577
Depreciation, Depletion and Amortization	1,416	1,222	1,073	844	821	584	443	630	388	315
Interest Expense	122	120	127	133	132	109	84.6	70.4	68.7	89.8
Pretax Income	4,206	2,663	1,922	899	1,199	1,204	345	-188	259	200
Effective Tax Rate	37.6%	37.3%	43.0%	38.3%	39.7%	40.1%	41.7%	NM	40.1%	39.4%
Net Income	2,624	1,670	1,095	554	723	721	201	-129	155	121
S&P Core Earnings	2,539	1,713	1,069	524	681	NA	NA	NA	NA	NA

Balance Sheet & Other Financial Data (Million $)	**2005**	**2004**	**2003**	**2002**	**2001**	**2000**	**1999**	**1998**	**1997**	**1996**
Cash	229	111	33.5	51.9	35.6	37.2	13.2	14.5	9.69	13.2
Current Assets	2,162	1,349	899	767	698	630	343	227	348	268
Total Assets	19,272	15,502	12,416	9,460	8,934	7,482	5,503	3,996	4,139	3,432
Current Liabilities	2,187	1,283	820	532	522	553	337	306	344	310
Long Term Debt	2,192	2,588	2,327	2,159	2,244	2,193	1,880	1,343	150	1,236
Common Equity	10,443	8,106	6,434	4,826	4,112	3,448	2,361	1,703	1,729	1,519
Total Capital	12,733	10,793	8,860	7,083	7,655	5,948	4,549	3,416	3,586	3,010
Capital Expenditures	3,716	2,456	1,595	1,037	1,525	1,011	591	700	732	124
Cash Flow	4,034	2,887	2,163	1,387	1,525	1,284	629	499	543	436
Current Ratio	1.0	1.1	1.1	1.4	1.3	1.1	1.0	0.7	1.0	0.9
% Long Term Debt of Capitalization	17.2	24.0	26.3	30.5	29.3	36.9	41.3	39.3	41.9	41.1
% Return on Assets	15.1	12.0	10.0	6.0	8.8	11.1	4.2	NM	4.1	3.9
% Return on Equity	28.2	22.9	19.4	12.2	18.6	24.1	9.2	NM	9.5	9.3

Data as orig reptd.; bef. results of disc opers/spec. items. Per share data adj. for stk. divs.; EPS diluted. E-Estimated. NA-Not Available. NM-Not Meaningful. NR-Not Ranked. UR-Under Review.

Office: 2000 Post Oak Blvd Ste 100, Houston, TX 77056-4400.
Telephone: 713-296-6000.
Website: http://www.apachecorp.com
Chrmn: R. Plank

Pres, CEO & COO: G.S. Farris
EVP & CFO: R.B. Plank
SVP & General Counsel: A. Lannie
VP & Treas: M.W. Dundrea

Investor Contact: R.J. Dye (713-296-6662)
Board of Directors: F. M. Bohen, G. S. Farris, R. M. Ferlic, E. C. Fiedorek, A. D. Frazier, Jr., P. A. Graham, J. A. Kocur, G. D. Lawrence, F. H. Merelli, R. D. Patton, C. J. Pitman, R. Plank, J. A. Precourt

Founded: 1954
Domicile: Delaware
Employees: 2,806

STANDARD &POOR'S

Apartment Investment and Management Co

S&P Recommendation SELL ★★★★★

Price $57.08 (as of Oct 27, 2006)

12-Mo. Target Price $42.00

Investment Style Mid-Cap Value

GICS Sector Financials
Sub-Industry Residential REITS

Comment This real estate investment trust is the largest U.S. owner and manager of multifamily apartment properties.

Key Stock Statistics (Source S&P, Vickers, company reports)

52-Wk Range	$59.17–36.71	S&P Oper. EPS 2006E	-0.85	P/E on S&P Oper. EPS 2006E	NM	Dividend Rate/Share	$2.40
Trailing 12-Month EPS	$0.78	S&P Oper. EPS 2007E	-0.78	Common Shares Outstg. (M)	97.4	Yield (%)	4.20
Trailing 12-Month P/E	73.2	S&P Core EPS 2006E	-0.96	Market Capitalization(B)	$5.558	Beta	0.46
$10K Invested 5 Yrs Ago	$19,075	S&P Core EPS 2007E	-0.78	Institutional Ownership (%)	94	S&P Credit Rating	BB+

Price Performance

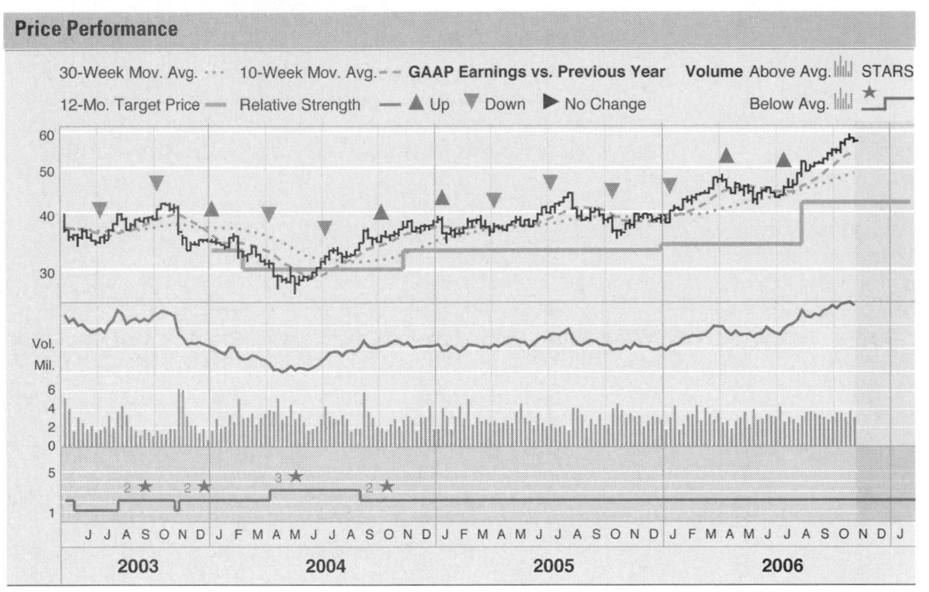

Options: CBOE, P, Ph

Analysis prepared by **Royal F. Shepard, CFA** on August 15, 2006, when the stock traded at **$ 50.50**.

Highlights

- AIV is focused on upgrading the quality of its large multi-family portfolio. During the first half, the trust sold $600 million of assets in non-core markets, well on its way toward its target of $850 million - $1,050 million for the full year. Redeveloping existing properties should also eventually contribute to better same-store performance. As of June 30, 2006, the trust had 44 active projects, and expects to spend a total of $384 million when complete.
- Portfolio rebalancing is likely to dilute EPS in 2006, in our view. On a GAAP basis, we estimate a loss of $0.85 a share after significant interest expense and large real estate depreciation expenses.
- AIV is gaining pricing flexibility, in our view, as occupancy rates exceed the 94% level. We expect revenue growth to improve as leases turn over in coming quarters. Our estimate for 2006 FFO is $2.98, up from $2.68 in 2005. Nonetheless, we project that cash flow, after taking into account recurring capital expenditures, will continue to lag the $2.40 annual dividend. As a result, we view a dividend increase over the next 12 months as unlikely.

Investment Rationale/Risk

- AIV is one of the largest residential REITs, with a diversified portfolio of conventional and affordable housing properties. Improving industry fundamentals should assist the trust in its ongoing effort to increase average unit rent. We remain concerned, however, with the trust's relatively weak financial position. As of June 30, 2006, total debt was 55% of total capitalization, higher than that of most peers. Fixed charges were covered at about 1.8X, we estimate, toward the low end of our coverage universe.
- Risks to our recommendation and target price include the possibility of stronger than expected employment growth stimulating new household formation, or faster than expected interest rate increases, which could slow home sales.
- Our 12-month target price of $42 is based on a multiple of 14X estimated 2006 FFO, a discount to peers based on AIV's below average financial position. Our dividend discount model uses a 9.4% discount rate and assumes the current payout is maintained until gradual growth resumes in 2008.

Qualitative Risk Assessment

LOW | **MEDIUM** | HIGH

Our risk assessment of AIV reflects its large, diversified operations and low stock volatility, offset by our view of a recent weak operating performance and insufficient coverage of the current common dividend.

Quantitative Evaluations

S&P Quality Ranking B-

D | C | **B-** | B | B+ | A- | A | A+

Relative Strength Rank STRONG

74

LOWEST = 1 HIGHEST = 99

Revenue/Earnings Data

Revenue (Million $)

	1Q	2Q	3Q	4Q	Year
2006	430.1	435.0	--	--	--
2005	361.6	372.3	386.8	400.9	1,522
2004	376.4	380.2	334.1	384.4	1,469
2003	397.5	378.4	377.4	381.9	1,516
2002	340.9	373.4	380.4	411.5	1,506
2001	322.2	323.8	323.8	328.0	1,464

Earnings Per Share ($)

2006	-0.19	-0.23	**E**-0.25	**E**-0.18	**E**-0.85
2005	-0.27	-0.24	-0.31	-0.41	-1.23
2004	-0.15	-0.20	-0.02	-0.01	-0.36
2003	0.01	Nil	-0.13	-0.12	-0.25
2002	0.45	0.47	0.24	-0.17	0.94
2001	-0.07	0.11	0.02	0.16	0.23

Fiscal year ended Dec. 31. Next earnings report expected: Early November. EPS Estimates based on S&P Operating Earnings; historical GAAP earnings are as reported.

Dividend Data (Dates: mm/dd Payment Date: mm/dd/yy)

Amount ($)	Date Decl.	Ex-Div. Date	Stk. of Record	Payment Date
0.600	10/27	11/16	11/18	11/30/05
0.600	12/28	12/28	12/31	01/31/06
0.600	05/02	05/17	05/19	05/31/06
0.600	08/01	08/16	08/18	08/31/06

Dividends have been paid since 1994. Source: Company reports.

Apartment Investment and Management Co

Business Summary August 15, 2006

CORPORATE OVERVIEW. Apartment Investment and Management Co. is one of the largest U.S. multifamily residential REITs in terms of units. At June 30, 2006, it owned, held an equity interest in, or managed a geographically diversified portfolio of 1,320 properties, including about 230,438 apartment units, located in 47 states, the District of Columbia and Puerto Rico.

The trust conducts substantially all its business, and owns all its assets, through AIMCO Properties, L.P., of which AIV owns approximately a 90% interest. AIV operates in two segments: the ownership, operation and management of apartment properties; and the management of apartment properties for third parties and affiliates.

MARKET PROFILE. The U.S. housing market is highly fragmented, and is characterized broadly by two types of housing units -- multi-family and single-family. At the end of 2005, the U.S. Census Bureau estimated that there were 123.93 million housing units in the country, an increase of 1.4% from 2004. Partially due to the high fragmentation, and the fact that residents have the option of either being owners or tenants (renters), the housing market can be highly competitive. Main demand drivers for apartments are household formation and employment growth. We expect 1.4 million new households to be formed in 2006, up from an estimated 1.3 million in 2005. Supply is created by new housing unit construction, which could consist of single-family homes or multi-family apartment buildings or condominiums. We forecast 1.9 million housing unit starts in 2006, down from 2.1 million in 2005, but still at what we view as a high level.

With apartment tenants on relatively short leases compared to those of commercial and industrial properties, apartment REITs are generally more sensitive to changes in market conditions than REITs in other property categories. Results could be hurt by new construction that adds new space in excess of actual demand. Trends in home price affordability also affect both rent levels and the level of new construction, since the relative price attractiveness of owning versus renting is an important factor in consumer decision making.

Company Financials

Per Share Data ($) Year Ended Dec. 31	**2005**	**2004**	**2003**	**2002**	**2001**	**2000**	**1999**	**1998**	**1997**	**1996**
Tangible Book Value	17.82	20.73	20.57	22.88	18.90	23.33	24.27	20.26	19.02	14.56
Earnings	-1.23	-0.36	-0.25	0.94	0.23	0.52	0.38	0.80	1.08	1.04
S&P Core Earnings	-1.25	-0.39	-0.32	0.89	0.19	NA	NA	NA	NA	NA
Dividends	3.00	2.40	3.06	3.28	3.12	2.80	2.50	2.25	1.85	1.70
Payout Ratio	NM	NM	NM	NM	NM	NM	NM	NM	171%	163%
Prices:High	44.14	39.25	42.05	51.46	50.13	50.06	44.13	41.00	38.00	28.38
Prices:Low	34.17	26.45	33.00	33.90	39.25	36.31	34.06	30.00	25.50	18.38
P/E Ratio:High	NM	NM	NM	55	NM	96	NM	51	35	27
P/E Ratio:Low	NM	NM	NM	36	NM	70	NM	37	24	18
Income Statement Analysis (Million $)										
Rental Income	1,460	1,402	1,446	1,292	1,298	1,051	534	377	193	101
Mortgage Income	Nil	Nil	Nil	Nil	Nil	Nil	43.5	Nil	Nil	Nil
Total Income	1,522	1,469	1,516	1,506	1,464	1,101	577	377	193	101
General Expenses	816	768	729	664	652	485	406	190	88.2	42.6
Interest Expense	368	367	373	340	316	270	140	89.4	51.4	24.8
Provision for Losses	Nil	Nil	Nil	Nil	Nil	Nil	Nil	Nil	Nil	Nil
Depreciation	412	369	328	289	364	330	151	93.4	37.7	20.0
Net Income	-27.9	55.7	70.7	175	107	99.2	83.7	64.5	28.9	12.9
S&P Core Earnings	-117	-35.5	-29.2	77.1	13.8	NA	NA	NA	NA	NA
Balance Sheet & Other Financial Data (Million $)										
Cash	330	293	98.0	97.0	820	1,068	1,123	127	37.1	13.1
Total Assets	10,017	10,072	10,113	10,317	8,323	7,700	5,685	4,268	2,101	835
Real Estate Investment	10,990	10,800	10,601	10,227	8,416	7,012	4,509	2,803	1,657	865
Loss Reserve	Nil	Nil	Nil	Nil	Nil	Nil	Nil	Nil	Nil	Nil
Net Investment	8,752	8,785	8,753	8,616	6,796	6,099	4,092	2,574	1,504	745
Short Term Debt	Nil	Nil	Nil	Nil	214	329	630	460	53.0	205
Capitalization:Debt	6,284	5,734	6,198	5,529	4,670	4,031	2,525	1,350	755	318
Capitalization:Equity	1,706	1,967	2,005	2,218	1,592	1,664	1,622	1,110	910	223
Capitalization:Total	9,436	9,246	9,580	9,180	7,904	7,037	5,181	2,795	1,948	610
% Earnings & Depreciation/Assets	3.8	4.2	3.9	5.0	5.9	1.5	4.7	4.7	4.6	4.9
Price Times Book Value:High	2.5	1.9	2.0	2.3	2.7	2.1	1.8	2.0	2.0	2.0
Price Times Book Value:Low	1.9	1.3	1.6	1.5	2.1	1.6	1.4	1.5	1.3	1.3

Data as orig reptd.; bef. results of disc opers/spec. items. Per share data adj. for stk. divs.; EPS diluted. E-Estimated. NA-Not Available. NM-Not Meaningful. NR-Not Ranked. UR-Under Review.

Office: 4582 S Ulster St Ste 1100, Denver, CO 80237-2662.
Telephone: 303-757-8101.
Email: investor@aimco.com
Website: http://www.aimco.com

Chrmn, Pres & CEO: T. Considine
EVP & CFO: T.M. Herzog
EVP & Treas: P.K. Fielding
EVP, Secy & General Counsel: M. Cortez

SVP & Chief Acctg Officer: S.W. Fordham
Investor Contact: J. Martin (303-691-4440)
Trustees: J. N. Bailey, T. Considine, R. S. Ellwood, J. L. Martin, T. L. Rhodes, M. A. Stein

Founded: 1994
Domicile: Maryland
Employees: 6,400

Apollo Group Inc

STANDARD &POOR'S

S&P Recommendation	Price	12-Mo. Target Price	Investment Style
SELL ★★★★★	$35.76 (as of Oct 27, 2006)	$35.00	Mid-Cap Growth

GICS Sector Consumer Discretionary
Sub-Industry Education Services

Comment This leading provider of higher education programs for working adults offers educational programs and services at 97 campuses and 159 learning centers.

Key Stock Statistics (Source S&P, Vickers, company reports)

52-Wk Range	**$73.01–35.39**	S&P Oper. EPS 2007**E**	**2.30**	P/E on S&P Oper. EPS 2007**E**	**15.5**	Dividend Rate/Share	**Nil**
Trailing 12-Month EPS	**$2.49**	S&P Oper. EPS 2008**E**	**2.35**	Common Shares Outstg. (M)	**172.8**	Yield (%)	**Nil**
Trailing 12-Month P/E	**14.4**	S&P Core EPS 2007**E**	**2.30**	Market Capitalization(B)	**$6.161**	Beta	**-0.03**
$10K Invested 5 Yrs Ago	**$13,083**	S&P Core EPS 2008**E**	**2.35**	Institutional Ownership (%)	**88**	S&P Credit Rating	**NA**

Price Performance

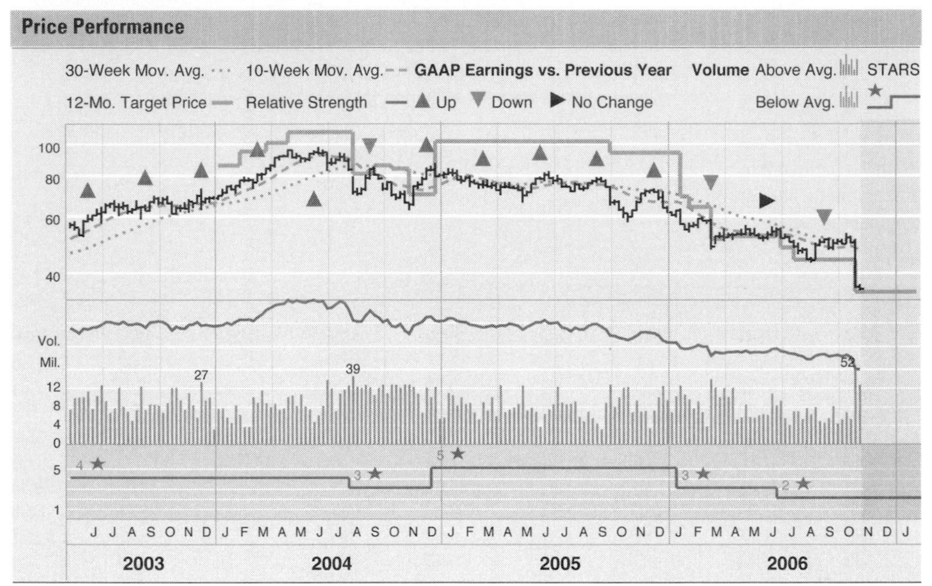

Options: ASE, CBOE, P, Ph

Highlights

- The 12-month target price for APOL has recently been changed to $35.00 from $44.00. The Highlights section of this Stock Report will be updated accordingly.

Investment Rationale/Risk

- The Investment Rationale/Risk section of this Stock Report will be updated shortly. For the latest News story on APOL from MarketScope, see below.

- 10/18/06 10:38 am EDT... S&P REITERATES SELL OPINION ON SHARES OF APOLLO GROUP (APOL 40.01**): Shares are off 18% this morning after APOL posts Aug-Q EPS of $0.54 vs. $0.65 before charges, $0.15 below our est. Enrollments rose 5%, 8th straight Q of lower growth, and margins narrowed. We attribute these trends to changing demographics, more competition and what we view as certain operating missteps. We see enrollment gains leveling off in coming year but think oper. performance will be lackluster for some time. We are lowering our FY 07 (Aug.) EPS est. by $0.60 to $2.30; we see $2.35 in FY 08. We are lowering our target price by $9 to $35, based on relative P/E and DCF. /M.Jaffe

Qualitative Risk Assessment

LOW | **MEDIUM** | HIGH

Our risk assessment reflects what we view as APOL's consistently solid levels of cash flow and a healthy balance sheet. We see these factors being offset by the company's current transformation of its business model. We also see APOL's risk levels heightened by its recent executive changeover and studies of its stock option granting practices by two separate regulatory bodies. In the corporate governance area, we have a negative view of the near 100% voting control held by insiders through separate voting shares.

Quantitative Evaluations

S&P Quality Ranking **B+**

D | C | B- | B | **B+** | A- | A | A+

Relative Strength Rank **WEAK**

3

LOWEST = 1 HIGHEST = 99

Revenue/Earnings Data

Revenue (Million $)

	1Q	2Q	3Q	4Q	Year
2006	628.9	569.6	653.6	624.2	2,476
2005	534.9	505.7	619.0	591.8	2,251
2004	411.8	396.9	497.0	492.8	1,798
2003	308.9	295.2	364.2	371.3	1,340
2002	228.2	222.6	276.4	282.3	1,009
2001	177.1	163.0	214.3	215.1	769.5

Earnings Per Share ($)

	1Q	2Q	3Q	4Q	Year
2006	0.73	0.46	0.77	0.54	2.49
2005	0.58	0.47	0.77	0.58	2.39
2004	0.44	0.35	0.56	-0.59	0.77
2003	0.30	0.24	0.39	0.37	1.30
2002	0.18	0.15	0.27	0.26	0.87
2001	0.14	0.09	0.19	0.17	0.60

Fiscal year ended Aug. 31. Next earnings report expected: Mid December. EPS Estimates based on S&P Operating Earnings; historical GAAP earnings are as reported.

Dividend Data

No cash dividends have been paid.

Apollo Group Inc

Business Summary September 26, 2006

CORPORATE OVERVIEW. Historically, Apollo Group has derived most of its revenues through the provision of higher education programs for working adults. It has several school units, but the large majority of its students have taken education programs at its University of Phoenix (UOP) unit. UOP offers its education programs at campuses, as well as through online programs. They consist mostly of bachelors and masters degree programs in business, education, information technology, criminal justice and nursing. As of June 2006, APOL offered programs and services at 97 campuses and 159 learning centers in 39 states, Puerto Rico, Canada, the Netherlands and Mexico. Combined enrollment at all divisions totaled 323,100 at May 31, 2006, up from 307,400 at FY 05 (Aug.) year end, and 255,600 at FY 04 year end. The company recently stopped giving breakdowns of students at campuses versus those in online programs. However, online started to account for a slight majority of APOL's student base in FY 05's third quarter, and has since accounted for most of its enrollment growth.

CORPORATE STRATEGY. The level of Apollo's overall enrollment growth has declined sequentially for seven straight quarters, from 27.7% in FY 04's fourth quarter, to 9.3% in FY 06's third quarter. We attribute this to changing demographic trends, greater competition and the law of big numbers. Until very recently, APOL focused almost entirely on students who were older than the traditional 18-to-22 year-old college student, particularly baby boomers. However, with the youngest baby boomers now over the age of 40, APOL has started to seek students in other demographic categories. As a result, it began to place much more focus on its Axia College program, which offers associates degrees and targets younger students. In late 2005, APOL also announced that it was consolidating Axia into UOP, from its much smaller and lesser known Western International University unit. We agree with APOL's actions, as it has become more challenging to maintain its growth. We also think Axia will attract more students by being part of the much more familiar UOP name, and it will raise the probability that these students remain in the Apollo fold, as it should be an easier transition to bachelor's degree programs at UOP, which many of these students have expressed an interest in obtaining. However, Todd Nelson's January 2006 resignation from his chairman, president and CEO posts brought some uncertainties about APOL's upper management team and its ability to successfully shift its business model.

Company Financials

Per Share Data ($) Year Ended Aug. 31	2006	2005	2004	2003	2002	2001	2000	1999	1998	1997
Tangible Book Value	NA	3.73	4.89	5.23	3.60	2.47	1.39	1.10	0.91	0.71
Cash Flow	NA	2.68	1.79	1.62	1.12	0.81	0.57	0.45	0.33	0.23
Earnings	2.49	2.39	0.77	1.30	0.87	0.60	0.41	0.33	0.26	0.19
S&P Core Earnings	NA	2.30	0.72	1.22	0.79	0.52	NA	NA	NA	NA
Dividends	Nil	Nil	Nil	Nil	Nil	Nil	Nil	Nil	Nil	Nil
Payout Ratio	Nil	Nil	Nil	Nil	Nil	Nil	Nil	Nil	Nil	Nil
Prices:High	63.26	84.20	98.01	73.09	46.15	33.31	22.64	15.22	19.22	14.56
Prices:Low	35.39	57.40	62.55	40.72	28.13	19.33	8.17	7.81	9.11	6.81
P/E Ratio:High	25	35	NM	56	53	56	55	46	73	77
P/E Ratio:Low	14	24	NM	31	32	32	20	23	35	36
Income Statement Analysis (Million $)										
Revenue	NA	2,251	1,798	1,340	1,009	769	610	499	385	279
Operating Income	NA	767	481	428	293	194	141	113	82.9	57.2
Depreciation	NA	54.5	43.2	40.3	35.2	32.7	27.4	20.6	12.8	6.55
Interest Expense	NA	Nil	Nil	Nil	Nil	Nil	Nil	Nil	Nil	Nil
Pretax Income	NA	730	456	402	266	175	120	98.0	76.3	55.0
Effective Tax Rate	NA	39.1%	39.1%	38.5%	39.4%	38.4%	40.8%	39.8%	39.3%	39.3%
Net Income	NA	445	278	247	161	108	71.2	59.0	46.3	33.4
S&P Core Earnings	NA	427	131	218	140	90.1	NA	NA	NA	NA
Balance Sheet & Other Financial Data (Million $)										
Cash	NA	595	677	800	610	375	154	108	103	106
Current Assets	NA	835	855	950	730	487	247	198	174	144
Total Assets	NA	1,303	1,452	1,378	980	680	405	348	305	195
Current Liabilities	NA	518	465	335	264	182	131	109	95.6	67.4
Long Term Debt	NA	Nil	Nil	Nil	15.5	14.8	9.97	4.22	3.80	2.48
Common Equity	NA	707	957	1,027	699	482	261	231	200	124
Total Capital	NA	707	957	1,027	715	497	272	237	205	127
Capital Expenditures	NA	104	80.3	55.8	36.7	44.4	34.8	44.7	30.9	12.8
Cash Flow	NA	499	321	287	196	141	98.6	79.6	59.1	40.0
Current Ratio	NA	1.6	1.8	2.8	2.8	2.7	1.9	1.8	1.8	2.1
% Long Term Debt of Capitalization	NA	Nil	Nil	Nil	2.2	3.0	3.7	1.8	1.9	2.0
% Net Income of Revenue	NA	19.8	15.4	18.4	16.0	14.0	11.7	11.8	12.0	12.0
% Return on Assets	NA	31.8	19.6	20.9	19.4	19.9	18.9	18.1	18.5	20.1
% Return on Equity	NA	53.5	28.0	28.6	29.3	29.0	28.9	27.4	28.6	32.6

Data as orig reptd.; bef. results of disc opers/spec. items. Per share data adj. for stk. divs.; EPS diluted. E-Estimated. NA-Not Available. NM-Not Meaningful. NR-Not Ranked. UR-Under Review.

Office: 4615 East Elwood Street, Phoenix, AZ 85040-1958.
Telephone: 480-966-5394.
Website: http://www.apollogrp.edu
Exec Chrmn: J.G. Sperling

Pres: B. Mueller
CFO, Treas & Secy: K.B. Gonzales
Chief Acctg Officer: D.E. Bachus
Investor Contact: J. Pasinski (800-990-2765)

Board of Directors: J. Blair, D. J. DeConcini, D. Diethelm, H. F. Govenar, B. Mueller, J. R. Norton III, J. G. Sperling, P. V. Sperling, G. Zimmer

Founded: 1981
Domicile: Arizona
Employees: 32,666

STANDARD &POOR'S

Apple Computer Inc

S&P Recommendation BUY ★★★★★

Price $80.41 (as of Oct 27, 2006)

12-Mo. Target Price $91.00

Investment Style Large-Cap Growth

GICS Sector Information Technology
Sub-Industry Computer Hardware

Comment This leading vendor of personal computers has broadened its reach in the digital music business with the success of its iPod MP3 player.

Key Stock Statistics (Source S&P, Vickers, company reports)

52-Wk Range	**$86.40–50.16**	S&P Oper. EPS 2007**E**	**2.72**	P/E on S&P Oper. EPS 2007**E**	**29.6**	Dividend Rate/Share	**Nil**
Trailing 12-Month EPS	**$2.27**	S&P Oper. EPS 2008**E**	**3.13**	Common Shares Outstg. (M)	**850.5**	Yield (%)	**Nil**
Trailing 12-Month P/E	**35.4**	S&P Core EPS 2007**E**	**2.72**	Market Capitalization(B)	**$68.389**	Beta	**1.58**
$10K Invested 5 Yrs Ago	**$86,138**	S&P Core EPS 2008**E**	**3.13**	Institutional Ownership (%)	**71**	S&P Credit Rating	**NR**

Price Performance

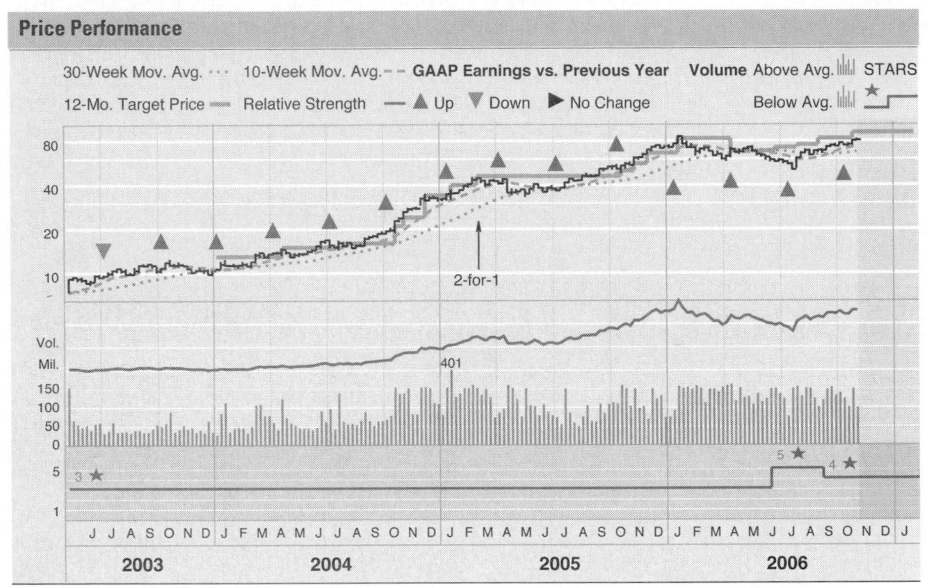

Options: ASE, CBOE, P, Ph

Analysis prepared by **Richard N. Stice, CFA** on October 19, 2006, when the stock traded at **$ 78.99**.

Highlights

- We project revenue growth of 22% for FY 07 (Sep.), following an increase of 39% in FY 06. We think revenues will continue to benefit from growth in AAPL's refreshed iPod line, but that rates should moderate from previously high levels, which we had believed were not sustainable. In addition, we see the core Mac line registering solid growth in FY 07, aided by the completion of AAPL's transition to Intel chips, and market share gains.
- We believe that FY 07 gross margins will narrow to 28.5%, from FY 06's 29.0%, as we suspect that the sales mix shift favoring some of AAPL's lower-end iPod products, as well as recent price reductions, could outweigh the benefits of higher volumes. This, however, should be somewhat offset by the growing demand for Macs, particularly in the notebook space. We also expect results to be aided by the company's net cash and short-term investments balance, which totaled over $10 billion at the end of FY 06.
- We forecast FY 07 EPS of $2.72, up 20% from FY 06's $2.27. We note that both totals include projected stock-based compensation expense.

Investment Rationale/Risk

- We expect revenue growth to remain above peers over the next 12 months, reflecting new product launches and a further improvement in Mac-related sales. Results should also benefit from AAPL's expanding retail presence, which we believe is significantly broadening the company's user base. These factors should outweigh our expectation of slowing iPod growth rates in the year ahead.
- Risks to our opinion and target price include challengers to AAPL's successful iPod line, market share losses, and additional executive departures and further negative publicity related to its internal stock option probe.
- Our 12-month target price of $91 is based on a blend of our price-to-sales and DCF analyses. Specifically, we believe AAPL shares can trade at 3.0X our FY 07 revenue per share estimate, which is a premium of 11% to its three-year historical average. Combined with $11.50 a share in net cash and short-term investments, this results in a value of $92. In addition, our DCF model assumes a weighted average cost of capital of 11.5% and an expected terminal growth rate of 4%, leading to our intrinsic value estimate of $89.

Qualitative Risk Assessment

LOW | MEDIUM | **HIGH**

Our risk assessment reflects the volatility of the shares as well as our view of the company's high degree of success in the MP3 player market, which we believe will likely present tougher future year-over-year sales comparisons.

Quantitative Evaluations

S&P Quality Ranking **B**

D | C | B- | **B** | B+ | A- | A | A+

Relative Strength Rank **STRONG**

87

LOWEST = 1 HIGHEST = 99

Revenue/Earnings Data

Revenue (Million $)

	1Q	2Q	3Q	4Q	Year
2006	5,749	4,359	4,370	4,837	19,315
2005	3,490	3,243	3,520	3,678	13,931
2004	2,006	1,909	2,014	2,350	8,279
2003	1,472	1,475	1,545	1,715	6,207
2002	1,375	1,495	1,429	1,443	5,742
2001	1,007	1,431	1,475	1,450	5,363

Earnings Per Share ($)

	1Q	2Q	3Q	4Q	Year
2006	0.65	0.47	0.54	0.62	2.27
2005	0.35	0.34	0.37	0.50	1.56
2004	0.09	0.06	0.08	0.13	0.36
2003	-0.01	0.02	0.03	0.06	0.10
2002	0.06	0.06	0.05	-0.07	0.09
2001	-0.31	0.06	0.09	0.10	-0.06

Fiscal year ended Sep. 30. Next earnings report expected: Mid January. EPS Estimates based on S&P Operating Earnings; historical GAAP earnings are as reported.

Dividend Data

No cash dividends have been paid since 1996.

Apple Computer Inc

Business Summary October 19, 2006

CORPORATE OVERVIEW. Apple Computer may have a relatively small share of the more than $200 billion market for PCs (estimated for 2005 by market research firm IDC), but in the rapidly growing MP3 player market, Apple has dominated with the success of its iPod. The worldwide portable compressed audio market was about $21 billion in 2005 and is projected by IDC to grow 29% in 2006. In the portable jukebox category of the market, IDC estimated Apple's global market share to be 72% in 2005.

Apple hopes that the success of the iPod will translate into higher demand for its computers. Over the past several years, AAPL's PC share has been maintained at roughly 3% on a global unit basis.

In August 2006, as a result of an internal stock option investigation, the company announced that it would likely need to restate its historical financial statements to record non-cash charges. While we view the news as disappointing, we believe it does not change AAPL's fundamental operating model.

COMPETITIVE LANDSCAPE. Apple, in our opinion, derives its competitive advantage from its focus on innovation. We believe the iPod is a clear example of this strategy's success. AAPL entered the consumer device market with the iPod in 2001, and by the fourth quarter of FY 05 (Sep.), iPod sales were 33% of total revenues.

Another key differentiator for the company is that its computers are based on its own operating system, enabling a further area for Apple to innovate, in our view. AAPL's computers are based on the Mac OS (versus the prevalent Windows operating system). Apple's Mac OS operating system focuses on simplicity and is viewed as graphically sophisticated, in our opinion. The Mac line also differed from peers due to its use of the PowerPC RISC-based chip, developed by IBM and Motorola (now Freescale), but transitioned to the more common Intel chip, effective January 2006. Apple differentiated its iPod from other MP3 players by launching its iTunes digital music download service (launched in 2003, with certain video content added as of October 2005 and movies in September 2006). As of October 2006, the company estimated that iTunes had an 85% share of the legal download music market.

Company Financials

Per Share Data ($) Year Ended Sep. 30	**2006**	**2005**	**2004**	**2003**	**2002**	**2001**	**2000**	**1999**	**1998**	**1997**
Tangible Book Value	NA	8.83	6.36	5.61	5.54	5.59	6.00	4.59	2.76	2.05
Cash Flow	NA	1.77	0.55	0.50	0.25	0.09	1.21	0.99	0.63	-1.84
Earnings	2.27	1.56	0.36	0.10	0.09	-0.06	1.09	0.90	0.52	-2.07
S&P Core Earnings	NA	1.47	0.22	-0.17	-0.19	-0.72	NA	NA	NA	NA
Dividends	Nil	Nil	Nil	Nil	Nil	Nil	Nil	Nil	Nil	Nil
Payout Ratio	Nil	Nil	Nil	Nil	Nil	Nil	Nil	Nil	Nil	Nil
Prices:High	86.40	75.46	34.79	12.51	13.09	13.56	37.59	29.50	10.94	7.44
Prices:Low	50.16	31.30	10.59	6.36	6.68	7.22	6.81	8.00	3.38	3.19
P/E Ratio:High	38	48	98	NM	NM	NM	34	33	21	NM
P/E Ratio:Low	22	20	30	NM	NM	NM	6	9	6	NM

Income Statement Analysis (Million $)										
Revenue	NA	13,931	8,279	6,207	5,742	5,363	7,983	6,134	5,941	7,081
Operating Income	NA	1,829	499	138	164	-231	704	471	379	-285
Depreciation	NA	179	150	113	118	102	84.0	85.0	111	118
Interest Expense	NA	Nil	3.00	8.00	11.0	16.0	21.0	47.0	62.0	71.0
Pretax Income	NA	1,815	383	92.0	87.0	-52.0	1,092	676	329	-1,045
Effective Tax Rate	NA	26.4%	27.9%	26.1%	25.3%	NM	28.0%	11.1%	6.10%	NM
Net Income	NA	1,335	276	68.0	65.0	-37.0	786	601	309	-1,045
S&P Core Earnings	NA	1,259	164	-119	-137	-465	NA	NA	NA	NA

Balance Sheet & Other Financial Data (Million $)										
Cash	NA	3,491	2,969	3,396	2,252	2,310	1,191	1,326	1,481	1,230
Current Assets	NA	10,300	7,055	5,887	5,388	5,143	5,427	4,285	3,698	3,424
Total Assets	NA	11,551	8,050	6,815	6,298	6,021	6,803	5,161	4,289	4,233
Current Liabilities	NA	3,484	2,680	2,357	1,658	1,518	1,933	1,549	1,520	1,818
Long Term Debt	NA	Nil	Nil	Nil	316	317	300	300	954	951
Common Equity	NA	7,466	5,076	4,223	4,095	3,920	4,031	2,954	1,492	1,050
Total Capital	NA	7,466	5,076	4,223	4,640	4,503	4,870	3,612	2,769	2,415
Capital Expenditures	NA	260	176	164	174	232	107	47.0	46.0	53.0
Cash Flow	NA	1,514	426	181	183	65.0	870	686	420	-927
Current Ratio	NA	3.0	2.6	2.5	3.2	3.4	2.8	2.8	2.4	1.9
% Long Term Debt of Capitalization	NA	Nil	Nil	Nil	6.8	7.0	6.2	8.3	34.5	39.4
% Net Income of Revenue	NA	9.6	3.3	1.1	1.1	NM	9.8	9.8	5.2	NM
% Return on Assets	NA	13.6	3.7	1.0	1.1	NM	13.1	12.7	7.3	NM
% Return on Equity	NA	21.3	5.9	1.6	1.6	NM	22.5	27.0	24.3	NM

Data as orig reptd.; bef. results of disc opers/spec. items. Per share data adj. for stk. divs.; EPS diluted. E-Estimated. NA-Not Available. NM-Not Meaningful. NR-Not Ranked. UR-Under Review.

Office: 1 Infinite Loop, Cupertino, CA 95014.
Telephone: 408-996-1010.
Email: investor_relations@apple.com
Website: http://www.apple.com

CEO: S.P. Jobs
COO: T.D. Cook
Investor Contact: P. Oppenheimer (408-974-3123)
SVP & CFO: P. Oppenheimer

SVP & General Counsel: N.R. Heinen
Board of Directors: F. D. Anderson, W. V. Campbell, M. S. Drexler, A. Gore, Jr., S. P. Jobs, A. D. Levinson, E. Schmidt, J. B. York

Founded: 1977
Domicile: California
Employees: 16,820

STANDARD &POOR'S

Applera Corp Applied Biosystems Group

S&P Recommendation HOLD ★★★	Price	12-Mo. Target Price	Investment Style
	$37.30 (as of Oct 31, 2006)	$40.00	Mid-Cap Growth

GICS Sector Health Care
Sub-Industry Life Sciences Tools & Services

Comment This company (formerly PE Corp. - PE Biosystems Group) supplies instrument systems, reagents, software and related services for life science research applications.

Key Stock Statistics (Source S&P, Vickers, company reports)

52-Wk Range	$39.49–24.86	S&P Oper. EPS 2007E	1.38	P/E on S&P Oper. EPS 2007E	27.0	Dividend Rate/Share	$0.17
Trailing 12-Month EPS	$0.90	S&P Oper. EPS 2008E	1.52	Common Shares Outstg. (M)	182.2	Yield (%)	0.46
Trailing 12-Month P/E	41.4	S&P Core EPS 2007E	1.38	Market Capitalization(B)	$6.798	Beta	1.27
$10K Invested 5 Yrs Ago	$12,902	S&P Core EPS 2008E	1.52	Institutional Ownership (%)	91	S&P Credit Rating	NA

Price Performance

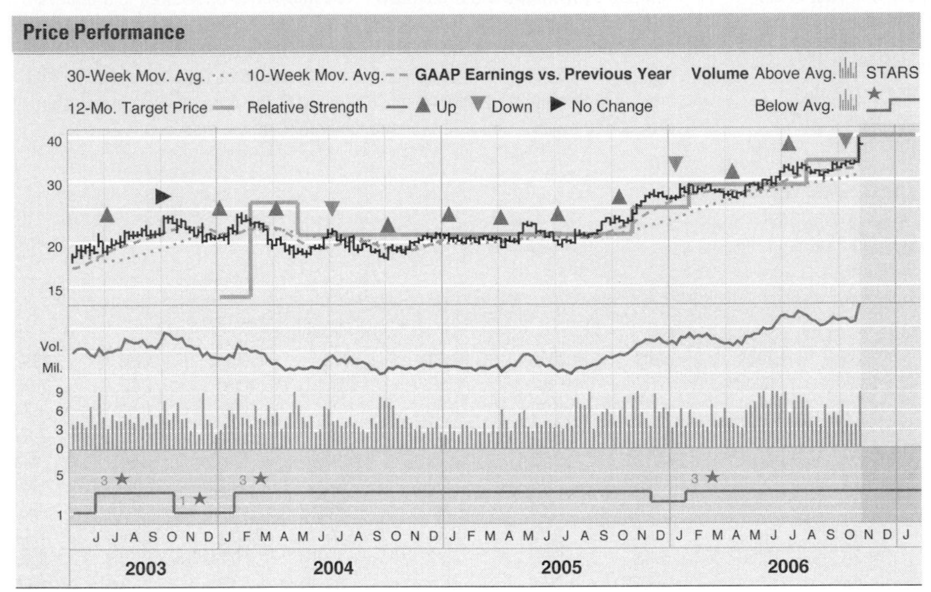

Options: ASE, CBOE, P

Analysis prepared by **Jeffrey Loo, CFA** on October 31, 2006, when the stock traded at **$ 37.23**.

Highlights

- We see sales increasing 9% in FY 07 (Jun.), to $2.07 billion, on mixed performances in ABI's five business units and contributions from recent acquisitions. We see mid-teens growth in Real-time PCR/Other Applied Genomics, aided by licensing agreements, and low double digit growth in Mass Spectrometry, partly offset by declines in Core DNA & PCR, in DNA Sequencing, and in Other product lines. We also expect ABI to seek additional acquisitions.

- We see flat gross margins, but expect operating margins to improve by 30 basis points, on operating leverage, partially offset by the inclusion of stock option expense for the full year and higher SG&A expenses. We expect flat R&D expenses, as cost savings from the integration of the MALDI TOF product line into the MDS Sciex joint venture should be offset by the integration of the Agencourt acquisition.

- Our FY 07 EPS estimate is $1.38 after $0.05 of projected stock option costs. ABI completed its share buyback program in June 2006, but we think another buyback program will be initiated. ABI's estimated stock option expense is lower than in the past, due to its decision to accelerate stock option vesting.

Investment Rationale/Risk

- We are encouraged by the improvement in sales and margins and believe ABI is now well positioned to benefit from its years-long restructuring and product portfolio rebalancing. We also view recent acquisitions positively. Although we are encouraged by ABI's sales growth we believe the shares trading at 27.5X our 2007 EPS, above peers, are fairly valued. We remain cautious due to ABI's heavy dependence on academic clients that rely on government funding as we continue to see pressure on government funding in the U.S. and Europe. We believe the academic and government-funded customer base accounts for about 40% of sales. However, ABI is focusing more on commercial clients, reflecting acquisitions.

- Risks to our recommendation and target price include lower than expected sales growth, inability to increase the commercial end-user client base, and limited market acceptance of new products.

- Our 12-month target price of $40 is based on a blend of our DCF analysis, which assumes a WACC of 9.7% and terminal growth of 3%, and our P/E analysis, using a slightly above peer multiple, due to ABI's growth rate.

Qualitative Risk Assessment

LOW | **MEDIUM** | HIGH

Our risk assessment reflects ABI's diverse product portfolio and broad geographic client base, offset by its heavy dependence on academic clients that rely on government funding and the highly competitive industry in which it competes.

Quantitative Evaluations

S&P Quality Ranking **B+**

D | C | B- | B | **B+** | A- | A | A+

Relative Strength Rank **STRONG**

90

LOWEST = 1 HIGHEST = 99

Revenue/Earnings Data

Revenue (Million $)

	1Q	2Q	3Q	4Q	Year
2007	476.3	--	--	--	--
2006	415.5	481.9	490.7	523.1	1,905
2005	390.3	463.4	454.8	478.6	1,787
2004	382.7	458.4	439.6	460.4	1,741
2003	395.9	444.7	409.4	432.9	1,683
2002	366.6	411.1	409.0	417.3	1,604

Earnings Per Share ($)

2007	-0.32	**E**0.36	**E**0.35	**E**0.38	**E**1.38
2006	0.21	0.17	0.65	0.41	1.43
2005	0.18	0.37	0.28	0.35	1.19
2004	0.16	0.25	0.22	0.20	0.83
2003	0.16	0.14	0.19	0.46	0.95
2002	0.15	0.23	0.23	0.18	0.78

Fiscal year ended Jun. 30. Next earnings report expected: Late January. EPS Estimates based on S&P Operating Earnings; historical GAAP earnings are as reported.

Dividend Data (Dates: mm/dd Payment Date: mm/dd/yy)

Amount ($)	Date Decl.	Ex-Div. Date	Stk. of Record	Payment Date
0.043	11/17	11/29	12/01	01/03/06
0.043	01/19	02/27	03/01	04/03/06
0.043	04/24	05/30	06/01	07/03/06
0.043	08/17	08/30	09/01	10/02/06

Dividends have been paid since 1971. Source: Company reports.

Please read the Required Disclosures and Analyst Certification on the last page of this report.

Applera Corp Applied Biosystems Group

Business Summary October 31, 2006

Applera Corp. - Applied Biosystems Group was formed in 1999 via a reorganization of Applera Corp. that created Applied Biosystems Group (ABI) and Celera Genomics Group (CRA). ABI serves the life science and research industry by developing and manufacturing instrument-based systems, consumables and reagents, software, and related services. Its instruments and tools are used in genomics to analyze nucleic acids (DNA and RNA), small molecule analysis and development, and proteomics to make scientific discoveries and develop new pharmaceuticals, and to conduct standardized testing.

ABI has developed technologies and products to support applications in genomics research such as sequencing, genotyping, and gene expression studies. Customers in the genomics market use ABI's instrument-based systems for the analysis of nucleic acids for basic research, pharmaceutical and diagnostic discovery and development, biosecurity, food and environmental testing, analysis of infectious diseases, and human identification and forensic analysis.

In the field of proteomics, the company has developed products for the identification, characterization, and measurement of expression of proteins and peptides. Gene codes for proteins in biological organisms and proteins are the key biological molecules that function in all aspects of living things such as growth, development and reproduction. The proteomics research market uses the company's products for the analysis of proteins and peptides for the discovery of drug targets, protein therapeutics and diagnostics.

Products such as mass spectrometers are used by researchers to analyze small molecules (generally smaller than peptides), including metabolites, other small biological molecules found naturally in the body such as hormones, and trace contaminants in food, beverages, or environmental applications.

ABI also develops and manufactures informatics software and services used to integrate and automate life sciences research, development, and manufacturing laboratories with the goal of increasing efficiency and effectiveness. Users are typically involved in gene mapping, drug discovery, drug development, and drug manufacturing. The company also offers software products for laboratory information management systems, to facilitate sample tracking, data collection, data analysis, and data mining to assist researchers in transforming data into useful information.

Company Financials

Per Share Data ($) Year Ended Jun. 30	2006	2005	2004	2003	2002	2001	2000	1999	1998	1997
Tangible Book Value	6.40	7.68	6.36	6.63	5.38	NM	NM	NM	2.86	2.49
Cash Flow	1.84	1.61	1.29	1.45	1.16	1.27	1.11	0.93	0.55	0.85
Earnings	1.43	1.19	0.83	0.95	0.78	0.96	0.86	0.72	0.28	0.65
S&P Core Earnings	1.46	0.36	0.30	0.31	0.34	0.32	NA	NA	NA	NA
Dividends	0.17	0.17	0.17	0.17	0.17	0.17	0.17	0.17	0.17	0.17
Payout Ratio	12%	14%	20%	18%	22%	18%	20%	24%	61%	26%
Prices:High	39.49	28.17	24.44	24.00	39.28	94.25	160.00	62.94	25.17	21.53
Prices:Low	26.13	19.20	17.76	14.90	13.00	18.49	42.81	21.97	13.63	14.47
P/E Ratio:High	28	24	29	25	50	98	NM	87	90	33
P/E Ratio:Low	18	16	21	16	17	19	NM	31	49	22
Income Statement Analysis (Million $)										
Revenue	1,905	1,787	1,741	1,683	1,604	1,619	1,388	1,222	1,531	1,277
Operating Income	388	357	330	324	318	347	270	234	220	189
Depreciation	77.2	82.9	96.8	106	81.2	66.8	54.5	44.3	53.1	36.0
Interest Expense	Nil	Nil	Nil	Nil	0.89	1.30	8.13	4.50	4.91	2.33
Pretax Income	317	297	240	239	238	304	276	192	101	157
Effective Tax Rate	13.3%	20.3%	28.2%	19.6%	29.1%	30.2%	32.5%	15.9%	38.4%	26.8%
Net Income	275	237	172	200	168	212	186	148	56.4	115
S&P Core Earnings	282	72.7	63.8	63.3	72.9	71.7	NA	NA	NA	NA
Balance Sheet & Other Financial Data (Million $)										
Cash	374	756	505	602	441	392	395	237	82.9	196
Current Assets	1,013	1,391	1,110	1,232	1,072	1,014	998	918	796	794
Total Assets	2,246	2,290	1,948	2,127	1,819	1,678	1,698	1,348	1,334	1,105
Current Liabilities	573	547	518	541	522	508	603	644	508	455
Long Term Debt	Nil	Nil	Nil	Nil	Nil	Nil	36.1	31.5	33.7	33.6
Common Equity	1,478	1,523	1,244	1,388	1,125	1,041	934	534	564	437
Total Capital	1,478	1,523	1,244	1,388	1,125	1,041	970	566	642	471
Capital Expenditures	41.5	84.6	60.4	132	88.3	144	94.4	82.5	101	59.9
Cash Flow	352	320	269	306	250	279	241	193	110	151
Current Ratio	1.8	2.5	2.1	2.3	2.1	2.0	1.7	1.4	1.6	1.8
% Long Term Debt of Capitalization	Nil	Nil	Nil	Nil	Nil	Nil	3.7	5.6	Nil	7.1
% Net Income of Revenue	14.4	13.3	9.9	11.9	10.5	13.1	13.4	12.1	3.7	9.0
% Return on Assets	12.2	11.2	8.5	10.1	9.6	12.6	12.2	12.0	4.6	11.3
% Return on Equity	18.5	17.1	13.1	15.9	15.5	21.5	25.4	27.0	11.3	30.3

Data as orig reptd.; bef. results of disc opers/spec. items. Per share data adj. for stk. divs.; EPS diluted. E-Estimated. NA-Not Available. NM-Not Meaningful. NR-Not Ranked. UR-Under Review.

Office: 301 Merritt 7, Norwalk, CT 06856-5435.
Telephone: 203-840-2000.
Website: http://www.appliedbiosystems.com
Chrmn, Pres & CEO: T.L. White

VP & CSO: D. Gilbert
Investor Contact: P. Dworkin (650-554-2479)

Board of Directors: R. H. Ayers, J. Belingard, R. H. Hayes, A. J. Levine, W. H. Longfield, T. E. Martin, C. W. Slayman, O. R. Smith, J. R. Tobin, T. L. White

Founded: 1937
Domicile: Delaware
Employees: 4,570

Applied Materials Inc

STANDARD &POOR'S

S&P Recommendation BUY ★★★★★	Price $17.26 (as of Oct 27, 2006)	12-Mo. Target Price $21.00	Investment Style Large-Cap Growth

GICS Sector Information Technology
Sub-Industry Semiconductor Equipment

Comment This company is the world's largest manufacturer of wafer fabrication equipment for the semiconductor industry.

Key Stock Statistics (Source S&P, Vickers, company reports)

52-Wk Range	$21.06–14.39	S&P Oper. EPS 2006E	0.98	P/E on S&P Oper. EPS 2006E	17.6	Dividend Rate/Share	$0.20
Trailing 12-Month EPS	$0.82	S&P Oper. EPS 2007E	1.41	Common Shares Outstg. (M)	1,388.9	Yield (%)	1.16
Trailing 12-Month P/E	21.1	S&P Core EPS 2006E	0.98	Market Capitalization(B)	$23.973	Beta	2.52
$10K Invested 5 Yrs Ago	$9,482	S&P Core EPS 2007E	1.41	Institutional Ownership (%)	82	S&P Credit Rating	A-

Price Performance

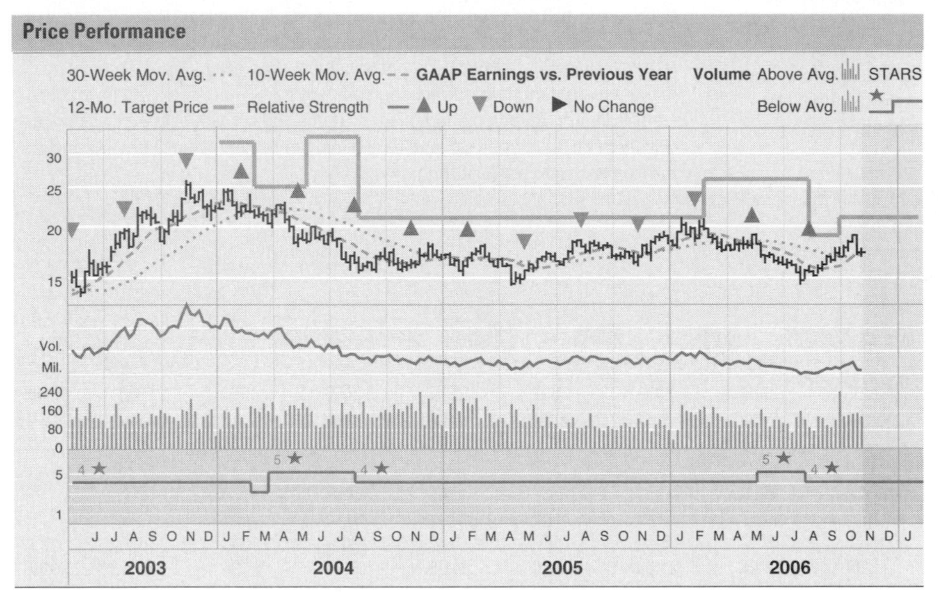

Options: ASE, CBOE, P, Ph

Analysis prepared by **David A Kaplan** on September 20, 2006, when the stock traded at **$ 17.55**.

Highlights

- AMAT reported July quarter EPS of $0.33, versus $0.23 a year earlier and surpassing our $0.30 EPS estimate, driven by strength in memory markets, which account for over half of AMAT's revenues. Revenues rose 13% sequentially and 56% year to year. We see little change in revenues for the next few quarters, as elevated levels of inventory at chipmakers and economic headwinds reduce growth. We see growth picking up in the second half of calendar 2007.
- Gross margins widened 160 basis points (bps), to 48.1%, in the July quarter, and we expect margins to remain steady in the coming quarters. The semiconductor equipment industry's three-month average book-to-bill ratio, as measured by SEMI, fell to 1.06 in July, from 1.14 in June. AMAT announced in September that it had bought back $2.5 billion, or 10%, of its shares to date in the October quarter, and it authorized further buybacks of $5 billion over the next three years.
- We see EPS of $0.98 in FY 06 (Oct.) and $1.41 for FY 07, both including estimated stock option expense, compared with FY 05 EPS of $0.73.

Investment Rationale/Risk

- We believe the semiconductor equipment industry will see a downturn in the second half of 2006 and into 2007, but we see this downturn as less severe than in the past. We view AMAT as less volatile than peers, and with the shares near a two-year low and at a discount to peers on a P/E basis, we see the stock as undervalued.
- Risks to our recommendation and target price include a greater than expected slowdown in the global economy, which could weaken demand for chips and increase pricing pressure.
- The shares recently traded at 2.9X our FY 06 sales per share estimate, a 10% premium to peers. On a P/E basis, the shares recently traded at about 17.7X our FY 06 EPS estimate, at a discount to peers. Applying a peer-based target P/E of around 15X our FY 07 EPS estimate, we arrive at our 12-month target price of $21.

Qualitative Risk Assessment

LOW | **MEDIUM** | HIGH

Our risk assessment reflects the historical cyclicality of the semiconductor equipment industry, the lack of visibility in the intermediate term, the dynamic nature of the change in semiconductor technology, and intense competition. This is offset by AMAT's market leadership, size and solid balance sheet.

Quantitative Evaluations

S&P Quality Ranking B-

D | C | **B-** | B | B+ | A- | A | A+

Relative Strength Rank MODERATE

33

LOWEST = 1 HIGHEST = 99

Revenue/Earnings Data

Revenue (Million $)

	1Q	2Q	3Q	4Q	Year
2006	1,858	2,248	2,543	--	--
2005	1,781	1,861	1,632	1,718	6,992
2004	1,555	2,018	2,236	2,203	8,013
2003	1,054	1,107	1,095	1,221	4,477
2002	1,000	1,156	1,460	1,446	5,062
2001	2,363	2,139	1,576	1,265	7,343

Earnings Per Share ($)

	1Q	2Q	3Q	4Q	Year
2006	0.09	0.26	0.33	**E**0.31	**E**0.98
2005	0.17	0.18	0.23	0.15	0.73
2004	0.05	0.22	0.26	0.27	0.78
2003	-0.04	-0.04	-0.02	0.01	-0.09
2002	-0.03	0.03	0.07	0.09	0.16
2001	0.25	0.19	0.07	-0.05	0.46

Fiscal year ended Oct. 31. Next earnings report expected: Mid November. EPS Estimates based on S&P Operating Earnings; historical GAAP earnings are as reported.

Dividend Data (Dates: mm/dd Payment Date: mm/dd/yy)

Amount ($)	Date Decl.	Ex-Div. Date	Stk. of Record	Payment Date
0.030	12/15	02/14	02/16	03/09/06
0.050	03/22	05/16	05/18	06/08/06
0.050	06/14	08/15	08/17	09/07/06
0.050	09/13	11/14	11/16	12/07/06

Dividends have been paid since 2005. Source: Company reports.

Applied Materials Inc

Business Summary September 20, 2006

CORPORATE OVERVIEW. Applied Materials leads the semiconductor capital equipment market, with FY 05 (Oct.) sales nearly twice those of its nearest competitor, Tokyo Electron. AMAT sells equipment to the front end of the semiconductor fabrication process, which consists of those steps necessary to build the transistors and wiring needed to form integrated circuits (IC). AMAT has also developed equipment used in the flat panel display manufacturing process.

AMAT products address the following chip production processes: AMAT's deposition products are used to plant thin films of conductive or insulating material to form an IC. AMAT's etch products selectively remove thin films of three different types of materials: metal, silicon, and dielectric thin films. AMAT's ion implant products are used to change the conductive properties of silicon, and thereby create active electronic components by bombarding them with beams of ions. Chemical-mechanical polishing products are used to polish the surface of a wafer following deposition in order to facilitate subsequent processing steps. Metrology and inspection tools are used to measure critical process parameters (such as the thickness of deposited films) and find and classify defects.

Sales by geographic region in FY 05 were as follows: North America 21%, Japan 20%, Europe 13%, Taiwan 23%, Asia-Pacific 9%, and Korea 14%. In total, 80% of sales were derived from Asia, representing considerable exposure (and risk) to the region, in our opinion. During FY 05, Samsung America accounted for 10% of revenue. No single customer accounted for over 10% of FY 04 revenue.

Company Financials

Per Share Data ($) Year Ended Oct. 31	**2005**	**2004**	**2003**	**2002**	**2001**	**2000**	**1999**	**1998**	**1997**	**1996**
Tangible Book Value	5.30	5.33	4.62	4.67	4.51	4.20	2.59	2.05	1.87	1.64
Cash Flow	0.91	0.99	0.14	0.39	0.69	1.41	0.63	0.38	0.48	0.51
Earnings	0.73	0.78	-0.09	0.16	0.46	1.20	0.46	0.19	0.33	0.41
S&P Core Earnings	0.54	0.59	-0.33	-0.04	0.33	NA	NA	NA	NA	NA
Dividends	0.06	Nil	Nil	Nil	Nil	Nil	Nil	Nil	Nil	Nil
Payout Ratio	8%	Nil	Nil	Nil	Nil	Nil	Nil	Nil	Nil	Nil
Prices:High	19.47	24.75	25.94	27.95	29.55	57.50	32.25	11.75	13.55	5.59
Prices:Low	14.33	15.36	11.25	10.26	13.30	17.06	10.72	5.39	4.34	2.72
P/E Ratio:High	27	32	NM	NM	65	48	70	77	41	14
P/E Ratio:Low	20	20	NM	NM	29	14	23	35	13	7
Income Statement Analysis (Million $)										
Revenue	6,992	8,013	4,477	5,062	7,343	9,564	4,859	4,042	4,074	4,145
Operating Income	1,748	2,313	440	083	1,538	3,149	1,257	910	970	1,078
Depreciation	300	356	382	388	387	362	275	285	219	149
Interest Expense	37.8	52.9	46.9	49.4	47.6	51.4	47.1	45.3	20.7	20.7
Pretax Income	1,582	1,829	-212	341	1,104	2,948	1,056	438	799	922
Effective Tax Rate	23.5%	26.1%	NM	21.0%	29.8%	30.0%	31.3%	34.0%	37.6%	35.0%
Net Income	1,210	1,351	-149	269	775	2,064	726	289	498	600
S&P Core Earnings	905	1,017	-562	-65.2	558	NA	NA	NA	NA	NA
Balance Sheet & Other Financial Data (Million $)										
Cash	990	2,282	1,365	1,285	1,356	1,648	823	575	448	404
Current Assets	9,449	10,282	8,371	8,073	7,782	8,839	5,060	3,519	3,770	2,693
Total Assets	11,269	12,093	10,312	10,225	9,829	10,546	6,707	4,930	5,071	3,638
Current Liabilities	1,765	2,288	1,641	1,501	1,533	2,760	1,669	1,118	1,402	935
Long Term Debt	407	410	456	574	565	573	584	617	623	275
Common Equity	8,929	9,262	8,068	8,020	7,607	7,104	4,337	3,121	2,942	2,370
Total Capital	9,336	9,672	8,524	8,594	8,172	7,677	4,954	3,749	3,613	2,658
Capital Expenditures	200	191	265	417	711	383	204	449	339	453
Cash Flow	1,510	1,707	233	657	1,162	2,426	1,001	573	718	748
Current Ratio	5.4	4.5	5.1	5.4	5.1	3.2	3.0	3.1	2.7	2.9
% Long Term Debt of Capitalization	4.4	4.2	5.4	6.7	6.9	7.5	11.8	16.4	17.3	10.3
% Net Income of Revenue	17.3	16.9	NM	5.3	10.5	21.6	14.9	7.1	12.2	14.4
% Return on Assets	10.4	12.1	NM	2.7	7.6	23.5	12.5	5.8	11.4	18.1
% Return on Equity	13.3	15.6	NM	3.4	10.5	35.3	19.5	9.5	18.8	28.9

Data as orig reptd.; bef. results of disc opers/spec. items. Per share data adj. for stk. divs.; EPS diluted. E-Estimated. NA-Not Available. NM-Not Meaningful. NR-Not Ranked. UR-Under Review.

Office: 3050 Bowers Avenue, Santa Clara, CA, United States 95054-3298.
Telephone: 408-727-5555.
Email: investor_relations@appliedmaterials.com
Website: http://www.appliedmaterials.com

Chrmn: J.C. Morgan
Pres & CEO: M. Splinter
SVP & CFO: N.H. Handel
SVP, Secy & General Counsel: J.J. Sweeney

VP & Cntlr: Y. Weatherford
Board of Directors: M. H. Armacost, R. H. Brust, D. A. Coleman, P. V. Gerdine, T. Iannotti, C. Y. Liu, J. C. Morgan, G. Parker, W. P. Roelandts, M. R. Splinter

Founded: 1967
Domicile: Delaware
Employees: 12,924

Archer-Daniels-Midland Co

STANDARD &POOR'S

S&P Recommendation BUY ★★★★★

Price $38.50 (as of Oct 31, 2006)

12-Mo. Target Price $45.00

Investment Style Large-Cap Value

GICS Sector Consumer Staples
Sub-Industry Agricultural Products

Comment This company is a major processor and merchandiser of agricultural commodities, including oilseeds, corn and wheat.

Key Stock Statistics (Source S&P, Vickers, company reports)

52-Wk Range	**$46.71–23.37**	S&P Oper. EPS 2007**E**	**2.50**	P/E on S&P Oper. EPS 2007**E**	**15.4**	Dividend Rate/Share	**$0.40**
Trailing 12-Month EPS	**$2.32**	S&P Oper. EPS 2008**E**	**2.75**	Common Shares Outstg. (M)	**655.7**	Yield (%)	**1.04**
Trailing 12-Month P/E	**16.6**	S&P Core EPS 2007**E**	**2.50**	Market Capitalization(B)	**$25.245**	Beta	**0.92**
$10K Invested 5 Yrs Ago	**$31,994**	S&P Core EPS 2008**E**	**2.75**	Institutional Ownership (%)	**66**	S&P Credit Rating	**A**

Price Performance

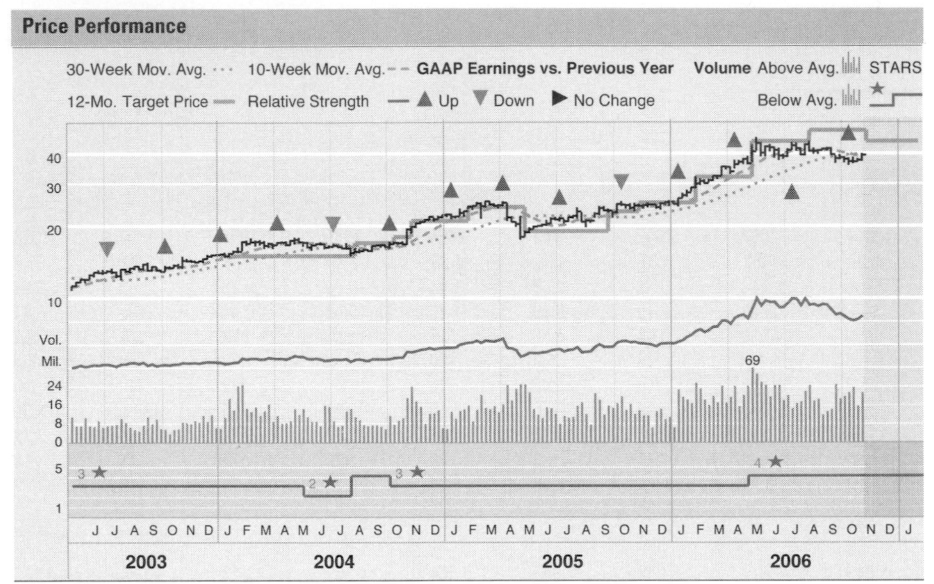

Options: ASE, CBOE, P, Ph

Highlights

- The 12-month target price for ADM has recently been changed to $45.00 from $46.00. The Highlights section of this Stock Report will be updated accordingly.

Investment Rationale/Risk

- The Investment Rationale/Risk section of this Stock Report will be updated shortly. For the latest News story on ADM from MarketScope, see below.

- 10/31/06 11:40 am EST... S&P REITERATES BUY OPINION ON SHARES OF ARCHER DANIELS MIDLAND (ADM 38.37****): ADM posts Sep-Q EPS of $0.61 vs. $0.29, $0.02 ahead of our expectations. Increases in bioproduct demand continued to be the main growth driver, although all major segments improved versus the prior year. We see benefits in FY 07 (Jun.) from improved sweetener pricing, the growing U.S. biofuel industry, and strong demand for agricultural services. On recent weakness in ethanol pricing, we see FY 08 EPS of $2.75, with growth decelerating to 10% from our forecast of 25% for FY 07. As a result, our 12-month target price falls $5 to $45, based on our updated P/E analysis. / J.Agnese

Qualitative Risk Assessment

LOW | MEDIUM | **HIGH**

Our risk assessment reflects the company's cyclical operations, which are significantly affected by exposure to crop and meat commodity markets, as well as high political risks.

Quantitative Evaluations

S&P Quality Ranking A

D | C | B- | B | B+ | A- | **A** | A+

Relative Strength Rank WEAK

28

LOWEST = 1 HIGHEST = 99

Revenue/Earnings Data

Revenue (Million $)

	1Q	2Q	3Q	4Q	Year
2007	9.45	--	--	--	--
2006	8,627	9,299	9,123	9,547	36,596
2005	8,972	9,064	8,484	9,424	35,944
2004	7,968	9,189	9,309	9,686	36,151
2003	6,944	7,807	7,909	8,048	30,708
2002	5,504	5,554	5,326	7,069	23,454

Earnings Per Share ($)

2007	0.61	**E**0.64	**E**0.63	**E**0.62	**E**2.50
2006	0.29	0.56	0.53	0.62	2.00
2005	0.41	0.48	0.41	0.30	1.59
2004	0.23	0.34	0.35	-0.16	0.76
2003	0.17	0.20	0.18	0.15	0.70
2002	0.20	0.23	0.18	0.17	0.78

Fiscal year ended Jun. 30. Next earnings report expected: Late January. EPS Estimates based on S&P Operating Earnings; historical GAAP earnings are as reported.

Dividend Data (Dates: mm/dd Payment Date: mm/dd/yy)

Amount ($)	Date Decl.	Ex-Div. Date	Stk. of Record	Payment Date
0.085	11/03	11/16	11/19	12/10/05
0.100	02/03	02/15	02/17	03/10/06
0.100	05/05	05/17	05/19	06/09/06
0.100	08/03	08/16	08/18	09/08/06

Dividends have been paid since 1927. Source: Company reports.

Archer-Daniels-Midland Co

Business Summary August 04, 2006

Archer-Daniels-Midland (ADM) calls itself "supermarket to the world." Within a network of more than 250 domestic and internationally based plants, cereal grains and oilseeds are processed into a multitude of products used in food, beverage, nutraceutical, industrial and animal feed markets worldwide.

Most of the company's business involves converting raw soybeans, corn and wheat into further-processed ingredients for the food manufacturing industry in the U.S. and abroad. In FY 06 (Jun.), oilseeds processing contributed 29% of segment operating profits (22% in FY 05); corn processing 43% (34%); agricultural services 13% (17%); and other 15% (27%).

ADM is one of the world's largest processors of oilseeds (soybeans, cottonseed, sunflower seeds, canola, peanuts, flaxseed and corn germ), which are processed to provide vegetable oils and meals principally for the food and feed industries. Crude vegetable oil is sold to others or refined and hydrogenated to produce oils for margarine, shortening, salad oils and other food products. Oilseed meals supply more than one-half of the high protein ingredients used in the manufacture of commercial livestock and poultry feeds.

The company is the world's largest corn processor. The corn processing segment is involved in corn wet and dry milling operations. Wet milling products include syrup, starch, glucose, dextrose, crystalline dextrose, high-fructose sweeteners, crystalline fructose, corn gluten feed and ethyl alcohol. Dry milled products include ethanol, distilled grains, meal and grits. In gasoline, ethanol increases octane and is used as an extender and oxygenate.

ADM is vertically integrated, with its agricultural services segment utilizing grain elevators and transportation networks to buy, store, clean and transport agricultural commodities such as oilseeds, corn, wheat milo, oats and barley. In addition to supplying its processing operations, these commodities are resold primarily as food or feed ingredients. Over the past five years, ADM spent $3.4 billion to construct new plants, expand existing plants and acquire plants and transportation equipment. ADM owns 80% of A.C. Toepfer International, one of the world's largest trading companies specializing in agricultural commodities and processed products.

ADM's other operations include the processing of wheat, corn and milo into flour, which is used in both food and industrial products. The company also produces a wide range of edible soy protein products and consumer and institutional health foods based on its soy products.

Company Financials

Per Share Data ($) Year Ended Jun. 30	**2006**	**2005**	**2004**	**2003**	**2002**	**2001**	**2000**	**1999**	**1998**	**1997**
Tangible Book Value	14.47	12.47	11.31	10.43	10.39	9.56	9.21	9.23	9.48	9.26
Cash Flow	3.00	2.60	1.82	1.69	1.64	1.44	1.35	1.26	1.36	1.19
Earnings	2.00	1.59	0.76	0.70	0.78	0.58	0.46	0.41	0.60	0.55
S&P Core Earnings	2.02	1.53	1.14	0.61	0.55	0.58	NA	NA	NA	NA
Dividends	0.37	0.32	0.27	0.24	0.20	0.19	0.14	0.13	0.17	0.16
Payout Ratio	19%	20%	36%	34%	25%	32%	30%	32%	29%	28%
Prices:High	46.71	25.55	22.55	15.24	14.85	15.80	14.46	14.74	19.44	20.26
Prices:Low	24.05	17.50	14.90	10.50	10.00	10.24	7.80	10.37	12.80	13.32
P/E Ratio:High	23	16	30	22	19	27	32	35	33	37
P/E Ratio:Low	12	11	20	15	13	18	17	25	21	24

Income Statement Analysis (Million $)	2006	2005	2004	2003	2002	2001	2000	1999	1998	1997
Revenue	36,596	35,944	36,151	30,708	23,454	20,051	12,877	14,283	16,146	13,853
Operating Income	2,430	2,015	1,432	1,423	1,424	1,272	1,094	1,116	1,247	1,071
Depreciation	657	665	686	644	567	572	604	585	527	446
Interest Expense	365	Nil	Nil	Nil	356	397	377	326	293	238
Pretax Income	1,855	1,516	718	631	719	522	353	420	610	644
Effective Tax Rate	29.3%	31.1%	31.1%	28.5%	28.9%	26.6%	14.7%	33.1%	33.8%	41.4%
Net Income	1,312	1,044	495	451	511	383	301	281	404	377
S&P Core Earnings	1,322	1,001	739	397	363	382	NA	NA	NA	NA

Balance Sheet & Other Financial Data (Million $)	2006	2005	2004	2003	2002	2001	2000	1999	1998	1997
Cash	2,334	1,430	1,412	765	844	676	477	1,461	346	728
Current Assets	11,826	9,711	10,339	8,422	7,363	6,150	6,162	5,790	5,452	4,284
Total Assets	21,269	18,598	19,369	17,183	15,416	14,340	14,423	14,030	13,834	11,354
Current Liabilities	6,165	5,367	6,750	5,147	4,719	3,867	4,333	3,840	3,717	2,249
Long Term Debt	4,050	3,530	3,740	3,872	3,111	3,351	3,277	3,192	2,847	2,345
Common Equity	9,807	8,433	7,698	7,069	6,755	6,332	6,110	6,241	6,505	6,050
Total Capital	14,614	12,743	12,092	11,485	10,498	10,327	9,948	10,053	9,985	8,993
Capital Expenditures	762	624	509	420	350	273	429	671	703	780
Cash Flow	1,969	1,709	1,180	1,095	1,078	955	905	866	931	823
Current Ratio	1.9	1.8	1.5	1.6	1.6	1.6	1.4	1.5	1.5	1.9
% Long Term Debt of Capitalization	27.7	27.7	30.9	33.7	29.6	32.4	32.9	31.8	28.5	26.1
% Net Income of Revenue	3.6	2.9	1.4	1.5	2.2	1.9	2.3	2.0	2.5	2.7
% Return on Assets	6.6	5.5	2.7	2.8	3.4	2.7	2.1	2.0	3.2	3.5
% Return on Equity	14.4	12.9	6.7	6.5	7.8	6.2	4.9	4.4	6.4	6.2

Data as orig reptd.; bef. results of disc opers/spec. items. Per share data adj. for stk. divs.; EPS diluted. E-Estimated. NA-Not Available. NM-Not Meaningful. NR-Not Ranked. UR-Under Review.

Office: 4666 Faries Parkway, Decatur, IL 62525.
Telephone: 217-424-5200.
Website: http://www.admworld.com
Chrmn: G.A. Andreas

Pres & CEO: P.A. Woertz
EVP, Secy & General Counsel: D.J. Smith
SVP & CFO: D.J. Schmalz
VP & Treas: V. Luthar

Investor Contact: C. Renshaw (217-424-4647)
Board of Directors: G. A. Andreas, A. L. Boeckmann, M. H. Carter, R. S. Joslin, A. Maciel Neto, P. J. Moore, M. B. Mulroney, T. F. O'Neill, O. G. Webb, K. R. Westbrook, P. A. Woertz

Founded: 1898
Domicile: Delaware
Employees: 26,800

STANDARD &POOR'S

Archstone-Smith Trust

S&P Recommendation HOLD ★★★★★	Price	12-Mo. Target Price	Investment Style
	$60.00 (as of Oct 30, 2006)	$59.00	Large-Cap Value

GICS Sector Financials
Sub-Industry Residential REITS

Comment This REIT (formerly Archstone Communities Trust) is a leading owner and operator of high-rise and garden-style apartments in protected locations.

Key Stock Statistics (Source S&P, Vickers, company reports)

52-Wk Range	$60.08–39.42	S&P Oper. EPS 2006E	1.07	P/E on S&P Oper. EPS 2006E	56.1	Dividend Rate/Share	$1.74
Trailing 12-Month EPS	$3.76	S&P Oper. EPS 2007E	1.25	Common Shares Outstg. (M)	214.2	Yield (%)	2.90
Trailing 12-Month P/E	16.0	S&P Core EPS 2006E	1.07	Market Capitalization(B)	$12.855	Beta	0.53
$10K Invested 5 Yrs Ago	$33,088	S&P Core EPS 2007E	1.25	Institutional Ownership (%)	93	S&P Credit Rating	BBB+

Price Performance

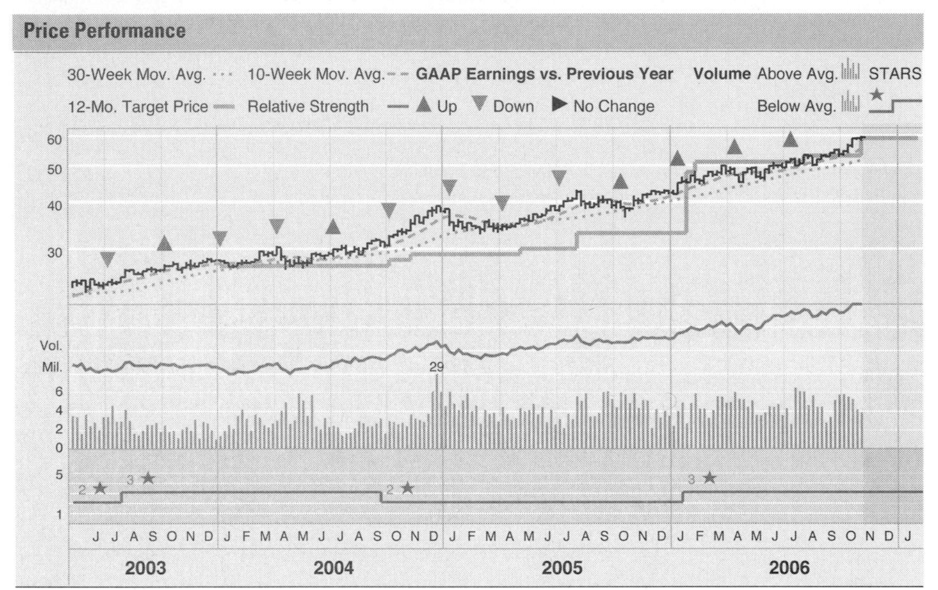

Options: CBOE, P

Analysis prepared by **Royal F. Shepard, CFA** on October 26, 2006, when the stock traded at **$ 59.49**.

Highlights

- A focus on space-constrained markets, such as Washington, DC, Southern California and New York City, is driving ASN's revenue and property-level income. As recent rental rate increases work their way through the portfolio, we expect 2007 operating income to increase 8%-10%, following a projected 8% gain in 2006. Although we think rental markets may begin to cool somewhat by the second half of 2007, ASN's large project development pipeline, totaling almost 6,000 units, should begin to contribute meaningfully in late 2007 and 2008.
- We expect Ameriton, ASN's subsidiary focused on short-term investment opportunities, to contribute about $0.23 to 2006 FFO, in line with 2005. Our total per share FFO estimate is $2.28, versus $1.99 in 2005. Our outlook for 2007 is $2.50.
- In early 2006, ASN increased its cash dividend by a modest 0.6%. Based on current funds available for distribution, we think a more significant increase of 3% - 5% is possible in January 2007.

Investment Rationale/Risk

- ASN derives about 97% of property income from core markets, setting the stage, in our view, for continued earnings growth. We expect significantly higher move-in rents to work through ASN's portfolio over the next 12 months. We also like its growing development pipeline and its opportunities to capitalize on short-term shifts in the real estate market through Ameriton. A rise in interest rates or a slowing economy, though, could limit Ameriton's available investment returns.
- Risks to our recommendation and target price include a less than expected rise in interest rates, keeping mortgage rates and the affordability of home ownership at low levels. Also, new systems might not provide expected efficiencies and a sufficient return on investment.
- Applying a multiple of 23.5X estimated 2007 FFO, a modest premium to peers, we arrive at our 12-month target price of $59. Based on recent market prices implying a one-year cash yield of 4.5%, we estimate ASN's net asset value at about $63 a share.

Qualitative Risk Assessment

LOW	MEDIUM	HIGH

Our risk assessment reflects our view of ASN's large and diversified portfolio and its lower debt to capitalization ratio than peers in our coverage universe, offset by significant upcoming debt maturities and significant acquisition and disposition activity.

Quantitative Evaluations

S&P Quality Ranking NR

D	C	B-	B	B+	A-	A	A+

Relative Strength Rank STRONG

82

LOWEST = 1 HIGHEST = 99

Revenue/Earnings Data

Revenue (Million $)

	1Q	2Q	3Q	4Q	Year
2006	266.8	293.7	--	--	--
2005	202.5	209.9	260.2	274.4	946.9
2004	204.9	215.0	222.5	231.0	873.3
2003	246.6	228.5	228.1	225.4	900.4
2002	250.6	260.2	271.5	300.1	1,082
2001	175.1	160.8	163.7	229.4	728.9

Earnings Per Share ($)

2006	0.26	0.77	E0.27	E0.28	E1.07
2005	0.19	0.18	0.25	0.18	0.78
2004	0.21	0.23	0.18	0.12	0.73
2003	0.22	0.05	0.79	0.13	0.41
2002	0.28	0.43	0.31	0.42	1.34
2001	0.52	0.58	0.36	0.37	1.81

Fiscal year ended Dec. 31. Next earnings report expected: NA. EPS Estimates based on S&P Operating Earnings; historical GAAP earnings are as reported.

Dividend Data (Dates: mm/dd Payment Date: mm/dd/yy)

Amount ($)	Date Decl.	Ex-Div. Date	Stk. of Record	Payment Date
0.435	01/04	02/13	02/15	02/28/06
0.435	04/25	05/12	05/16	05/31/06
0.435	07/25	08/14	08/16	08/31/06
0.435	10/25	11/13	11/15	11/30/06

Dividends have been paid since 1970. Source: Company reports.

Archstone-Smith Trust

Business Summary October 26, 2006

CORPORATE OVERVIEW. Archstone-Smith Trust is an equity REIT that focuses on the operation, development, redevelopment, acquisition and long-term ownership of apartment communities in protected markets throughout the U.S. At September 30, 2006, it owned or had an interest in 354 communities representing 90,093 units, including properties under construction.

With over 90% of the trust's investments concentrated in Washington, DC, Southern California, the San Francisco Bay Area, Chicago, New York, Boston, southeast Florida, and Seattle, we believe ASN has completed a transformation from a southeastern regional REIT to a nationwide REIT concentrated in protected, supply-constrained markets. We like this strategy, and believe it could help ASN operationally outperform peers. At September 30, 2006, property level income from the trust's largest markets were as follows: the greater Washington, DC, metropolitan area 35.3%; Southern California 25.7%; New York 11.6%; the San Francisco Bay Area 9.4%; Boston 4.3%; Seattle 4.3%; southeast Florida 3.1%; and Chicago 3.0%.

Ameriton, a wholly owned subsidiary, utilizes ASN's expertise to capitalize on short-term real estate investment opportunities. In 2005, Ameriton focused primarily on the sale of newly developed communities in suburban Washington, DC and Houston. On a GAAP basis, it recognized gains of $62.5 million on the sale of 11 communities, contributing $56.7 million to funds from operations and producing an average unleveraged pretax internal rate of return (IRR) of 24%.

MARKET PROFILE. The housing market is highly fragmented and is characterized broadly by two types of housing units -- multi-family and single-family. At the end of 2005, the U.S. Census Bureau estimated that there were 123.93 million housing units in the country. Partly due to the high fragmentation and because residents have the option of either being owners or tenants (renters), the housing market can be highly competitive. Main demand drivers for apartments are household formation and employment growth. S&P expects 1.4 million new households to be formed in 2006, up from an estimated number 1.3 million in 2005. Supply is created by new housing unit construction, which could consist of single-family homes, or multi-family apartment buildings or condominiums. S&P forecasts 1.8 million housing unit starts in 2006, down from 2.1 million in 2005, but still at what we consider to be a high level.

Company Financials

Per Share Data ($) Year Ended Dec. 31	**2005**	**2004**	**2003**	**2002**	**2001**	**2000**	**1999**	**1998**	**1997**	**1996**
Tangible Book Value	23.22	18.21	20.52	21.27	20.78	16.00	18.47	16.44	14.04	13.24
Earnings	0.78	0.73	0.41	1.34	1.81	1.78	1.47	1.50	0.65	1.47
S&P Core Earnings	0.55	0.72	0.40	1.17	1.91	NA	NA	NA	NA	NA
Dividends	1.73	2.72	1.71	1.70	1.64	1.54	1.48	1.39	1.30	1.55
Payout Ratio	222%	NM	NM	127%	91%	87%	101%	93%	NM	105%
Prices:High	43.10	39.05	28.35	29.19	27.85	26.56	23.50	24.50	25.13	23.63
Prices:Low	32.76	26.35	20.94	21.31	23.00	19.25	18.94	17.88	21.00	19.00
P/E Ratio:High	55	53	69	22	15	15	16	16	39	16
P/E Ratio:Low	42	36	51	16	13	11	13	12	32	13

Income Statement Analysis (Million $)										
Rental Income	891	854	881	998	702	688	638	485	335	322
Mortgage Income	Nil	Nil	Nil	Nil	Nil	34.7	29.1	29.0	20.6	4.20
Total Income	947	873	900	1,082	729	723	667	514	356	326
General Expenses	324	281	285	597	205	194	187	190	118	197
Interest Expense	188	175	187	195	142	145	121	113	61.2	35.3
Provision for Losses	Nil	Nil	Nil	Nil	Nil	Nil	Nil	Nil	Nil	Nil
Depreciation	216	203	188	206	132	144	132	96.3	52.9	44.9
Net Income	163	178	98.4	272	260	262	229	200	72.9	132
S&P Core Earnings	114	143	75.7	202	251	NA	NA	NA	NA	NA

Balance Sheet & Other Financial Data (Million $)										
Cash	10,802	435	186	12.8	127	12.4	78.8	101	4.90	5.64
Total Assets	11,467	9,066	8,922	8,855	8,550	5,020	5,302	5,060	2,806	2,282
Real Estate Investment	11,625	9,221	8,999	9,186	8,713	5,288	5,428	5,082	2,890	2,343
Loss Reserve	Nil	Nil	Nil	Nil	Nil	Nil	Nil	Nil	Nil	Nil
Net Investment	10,788	8,457	8,350	8,615	8,307	4,912	5,127	4,876	2,760	2,246
Short Term Debt	Nil	Nil	217	241	136	125	82.4	41.1	37.0	Nil
Capitalization:Debt	4,846	3,817	3,686	3,862	3,717	2,346	2,383	2,131	1,127	907
Capitalization:Equity	4,932	3,634	3,996	3,550	3,427	1,965	2,270	2,355	1,300	1,000
Capitalization:Total	10,615	8,408	8,423	8,253	8,113	4,691	5,005	4,780	2,631	2,175
% Earnings & Depreciation/Assets	3.6	4.2	3.4	5.5	5.8	7.8	7.0	7.5	4.9	8.6
Price Times Book Value:High	1.9	2.1	1.5	1.4	1.3	1.7	1.3	1.5	1.8	1.8
Price Times Book Value:Low	1.4	1.4	1.1	1.0	1.1	1.2	1.0	1.1	1.5	1.4

Data as orig reptd.; bef. results of disc opers/spec. items. Per share data adj. for stk. divs.; EPS diluted. E-Estimated. NA-Not Available. NM-Not Meaningful. NR-Not Ranked. UR-Under Review.

Office: 9200 E. Panorama Circle, Englewood, CO 80112.
Telephone: 303-708-5959.
Email: investors@archstonemail.com
Website: http://www.archstonesmith.com

Chrmn & CEO: R.S. Sellers
COO: J.L. Freeman
EVP, Secy & General Counsel: C. Brower
CFO: C.E. Mueller, Jr.

Chief Acctg Officer: M.A. Schumacher
Auditor: KPMG, Denver
Trustees: J. A. Cardwell, S. R. Demeritt, E. A. Gerardi, Jr., R. Gillis, N. S. Holmes, R. P. Kogod, J. H. Polk, III, J. M. Richman, J. C. Schweitzer, R. S. Sellers, R. H. Smith

Founded: 1963
Domicile: Maryland
Employees: 2,703

STANDARD &POOR'S

Ashland Inc

S&P Recommendation	Price	12-Mo. Target Price	Investment Style
HOLD ★★★★★	$59.10 (as of Oct 31, 2006)	$64.00	Mid-Cap Value

GICS Sector Materials
Sub-Industry Diversified Chemicals

Comment This supplier of highway construction products/services and specialty chemicals sold its 38% interest in Marathon Ashland Petroleum LLC to Marathon Oil Corp. in June 2005.

Key Stock Statistics (Source S&P, Vickers, company reports)

52-Wk Range	$75.17–53.07	S&P Oper. EPS 2007E	3.65	P/E on S&P Oper. EPS 2007E	16.2	Dividend Rate/Share	$1.10
Trailing 12-Month EPS	$5.64	S&P Oper. EPS 2008E	NA	Common Shares Outstg. (M)	71.1	Yield (%)	1.86
Trailing 12-Month P/E	10.5	S&P Core EPS 2007E	3.74	Market Capitalization(B)	$4.202	Beta	0.70
$10K Invested 5 Yrs Ago	$22,499	S&P Core EPS 2008E	NA	Institutional Ownership (%)	82	S&P Credit Rating	BBB

Price Performance

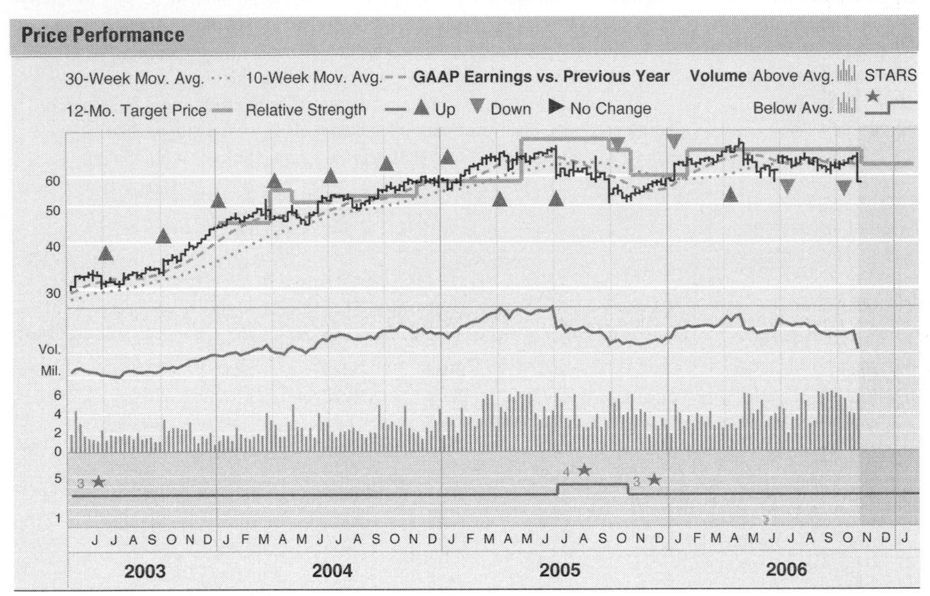

Options: ASE, CBOE, P, Ph

Highlights

- The 12-month target price for ASH has recently been changed to $64.00 from $70.00. The Highlights section of this Stock Report will be updated accordingly.

Investment Rationale/Risk

- The Investment Rationale/Risk section of this Stock Report will be updated shortly. For the latest News story on ASH from MarketScope, see below.
- 10/31/06 09:57 am EST... S&P MAINTAINS HOLD OPINION ON SHARES OF ASHLAND (ASH 58.62***): ASH posts Sep-Q EPS of $0.79 vs. $1.08, before one-time items in both periods. The company continues to exit certain businesses, and Sep-Q EPS excludes $2.03 from discontinued operations. We expect FY 07 (Sep.) results to benefit from continued global economic growth, previously implemented cost reduction efforts, and a return to profitability in its Valvoline business. All told, we forecast FY 07 operating EPS of $3.65. But our 12-month target price falls to $64 from $70, based on our revised DCF and enterprise value-to-EBITDA analyses. /A. Fiore-CFA

Qualitative Risk Assessment

LOW | **MEDIUM** | HIGH

Our risk assessment reflects the highly cyclical nature of the company's end markets, offset by what we view as a strong balance sheet with a relatively low amount of debt. As of March 2006, the company had net cash and short-term investments of about $1.0 billion.

Quantitative Evaluations

S&P Quality Ranking **B**

D | C | B- | **B** | B+ | A- | A | A+

Relative Strength Rank **WEAK**

12

LOWEST = 1 HIGHEST = 99

Revenue/Earnings Data

Revenue (Million $)

	1Q	2Q	3Q	4Q	Year
2006	2,429	2,299	2,708	1,908	7,233
2005	2,177	2,062	2,492	2,538	9,270
2004	1,974	1,812	2,425	2,334	8,301
2003	1,846	1,736	2,125	2,130	7,865
2002	1,812	1,598	2,047	2,086	7,543
2001	1,878	1,659	1,567	2,129	7,719

Earnings Per Share ($)

	1Q	2Q	3Q	4Q	Year
2006	0.91	0.67	1.29	0.79	2.53
2005	1.28	0.44	23.65	1.49	26.86
2004	0.56	-0.16	2.35	2.81	5.59
2003	0.04	-0.50	1.03	0.89	1.37
2002	0.55	-0.31	0.93	0.68	1.83
2001	0.84	0.37	0.53	1.77	5.77

Fiscal year ended Sep. 30. Next earnings report expected: Mid December. EPS Estimates based on S&P Operating Earnings; historical GAAP earnings are as reported.

Dividend Data (Dates: mm/dd Payment Date: mm/dd/yy)

Amount ($)	Date Decl.	Ex-Div. Date	Stk. of Record	Payment Date
0.275	01/25	02/15	02/20	03/15/06
0.275	05/17	05/25	05/30	06/15/06
0.275	07/20	08/17	08/21	09/15/06
10.2 Spl.	09/14	10/26	10/10	10/25/06

Dividends have been paid since 1936. Source: Company reports.

Ashland Inc

Business Summary July 31, 2006

Founded in 1936, Ashland (ASH) operates in two business sectors: chemicals and transportation construction. Its chemicals sector is operated through three business segments: Ashland Distribution (38% of FY 04 (Sep.) revenues; 10% of FY 04 operating income), Ashland Specialty Chemical (17%; 11%), and Valvoline (15%; 14%). Its transportation business is conducted through its APAC group of companies (30%; 17%).

The APAC group of companies is the largest U.S. asphalt and concrete paving company. It performs contract construction work and services, including highway paving, resurfacing and repair, as well as excavation, grading and bridge construction. The segment conducts business through 24 units that operate in 14 southern and midwestern states. About 78% of APAC's FY 04 revenues were from construction, and 22% from materials. About 82% of APAC's FY 04 construction revenues were derived from highway and public sector sources, with 18% from industrial and commercial customers. Construction backlog at June 30, 2006 was $2.0 billion, 7% below the prior year.

Through Ashland Distribution, the company distributes chemicals, plastics, reinforcements and resins, and fine ingredients in North America, and plastics in Europe. Ashland Distribution specializes in providing mixed truckloads and less-than-truckload quantities to customers in a wide range of industries. Deliveries are performed through a network of owned or leased facilities, including about 126 locations in North America. Distribution of thermoplastic resins in Europe is conducted through 17 third-party warehouses in 13 foreign countries.

Ashland Specialty Chemical focuses on two primary chemistries: thermoset and water. Ashland Specialty Chemical makes specialty chemicals for the automotive, building and construction, foundry, marine, paint, paper, ink and flexible packaging industries. The division owns and operates 38 manufacturing facilities, and participates in 12 manufacturing joint ventures in 19 countries.

Company Financials

Per Share Data ($) Year Ended Sep. 30	**2006**	**2005**	**2004**	**2003**	**2002**	**2001**	**2000**	**1999**	**1998**	**1997**
Tangible Book Value	NA	42.32	30.46	25.44	24.29	24.01	20.10	27.50	25.40	[illegible]
Cash Flow	NA	30.11	8.32	4.32	4.99	9.37	7.45	6.91	4.99	10.63
Earnings	2.53	26.86	5.59	1.37	1.83	5.77	4.10	3.89	2.63	2.51
S&P Core Earnings	NA	15.98	5.69	1.73	1.45	5.25	NA	NA	NA	NA
Dividends	1.10	1.10	1.10	1.10	1.10	1.10	1.10	1.10	1.10	1.10
Payout Ratio	43%	4%	20%	80%	60%	19%	27%	28%	42%	44%
Prices:High	75.17	72.20	60.17	44.55	46.98	46.54	37.19	50.63	57.94	54.88
Prices:Low	57.25	50.45	43.73	25.91	23.60	34.39	28.63	30.31	42.25	39.25
P/E Ratio:High	30	3	11	33	26	8	9	13	22	22
P/E Ratio:Low	23	2	8	19	13	6	7	8	16	16

Income Statement Analysis (Million $)										
Revenue	NA	9,270	8,301	7,865	7,543	7,719	7,961	6,801	6,534	14,200
Operating Income	NA	349	375	123	309	273	433	400	229	943
Depreciation, Depletion and Amortization	NA	193	193	204	220	250	237	228	181	572
Interest Expense	NA	82.0	114	128	138	170	188	140	130	170
Pretax Income	NA	1,803	548	138	58.0	681	483	482	317	335
Effective Tax Rate	NA	NM	27.4%	31.9%	NM	40.4%	39.5%	39.8%	36.0%	35.5%
Net Income	NA	2,005	398	94.0	129	406	292	290	203	192
S&P Core Earnings	NA	1,189	405	120	103	371	NA	NA	NA	NA

Balance Sheet & Other Financial Data (Million $)										
Cash	NA	985	243	223	90.0	236	67.0	110	34.0	268
Current Assets	NA	3,757	2,302	2,085	1,925	2,213	2,131	2,059	1,828	2,995
Total Assets	NA	6,815	7,502	7,006	6,725	6,945	6,771	6,424	6,082	7,777
Current Liabilities	NA	1,545	1,815	1,484	1,511	1,497	1,699	1,396	1,361	2,261
Long Term Debt	NA	82.0	1,109	1,512	1,606	1,786	1,899	1,927	1,507	1,639
Common Equity	NA	3,739	2,706	2,253	2,339	2,399	1,965	2,200	2,137	2,024
Total Capital	NA	3,821	4,182	4,056	4,201	4,625	4,152	4,353	3,644	3,936
Capital Expenditures	NA	380	210	110	185	205	232	248	274	431
Cash Flow	NA	2,198	591	298	349	656	529	518	384	755
Current Ratio	NA	2.4	1.3	1.4	1.3	1.5	1.3	1.5	1.3	1.3
% Long Term Debt of Capitalization	NA	2.1	26.5	37.3	38.2	38.6	45.7	44.3	41.4	41.6
% Return on Assets	NA	28.0	5.5	1.4	1.9	5.9	4.4	4.6	2.9	2.6
% Return on Equity	NA	62.2	16.1	4.2	5.4	17.9	14.0	13.4	9.8	10.3

Data as orig reptd.; bef. results of disc opers/spec. items. Per share data adj. for stk. divs.; EPS diluted. E-Estimated. NA-Not Available. NM-Not Meaningful. NR-Not Ranked. UR-Under Review.

Office: 50 E Rivercenter Blvd, Covington, KY 41011-1683.
Telephone: 859-815-3333.
Email: investor_relations@ashland.com
Website: http://www.ashland.com

Chrmn & CEO: J.J. O'Brien
SVP & CFO: J.M. Quin
SVP, Secy & General Counsel: D.L. Hausrath
Investor Contact: D.L. Porter (859-815-3825)

VP & Treas: D.L. Porter
Board of Directors: E. H. Drew, R. W. Hale, B. P. Healy, M. L. Jackson, K. Ligocki, P. F. Noonan, J. J. O'Brien, G. A. Schaefer, Jr., T. M. Solso, M. J. Ward

Founded: 1918
Domicile: Kentucky
Employees: 20,900

AT&T Inc

STANDARD &POOR'S

S&P Recommendation	Price	12-Mo. Target Price	Investment Style
HOLD ★★★★★	$34.22 (as of Oct 27, 2006)	$36.00	Large-Cap Value

GICS Sector Telecommunication Services
Sub-Industry Integrated Telecommunication Services

Comment AT&T Inc. (formerly SBC Communications) provides local and long distance service and holds a 60%-stake in Cingular Wireless. AT&T Corp. was acquired in late 2005.

Key Stock Statistics (Source S&P, Vickers, company reports)

52-Wk Range	$35.00–23.35	S&P Oper. EPS 2006E	2.32	P/E on S&P Oper. EPS 2006E	14.8	Dividend Rate/Share	$1.33
Trailing 12-Month EPS	$1.86	S&P Oper. EPS 2007E	2.45	Common Shares Outstg. (M)	3,884.2	Yield (%)	3.89
Trailing 12-Month P/E	18.4	S&P Core EPS 2006E	2.15	Market Capitalization(B)	$132.916	Beta	1.40
$10K Invested 5 Yrs Ago	$11,116	S&P Core EPS 2007E	2.25	Institutional Ownership (%)	65	S&P Credit Rating	A

Price Performance

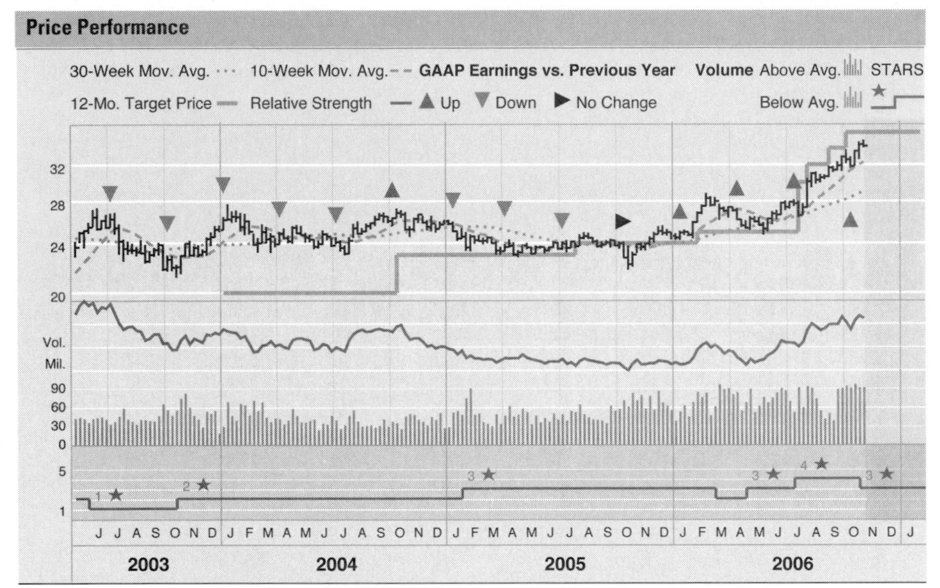

Options: ASE, CBOE, P, Ph

Analysis prepared by **Todd Rosenbluth** on October 27, 2006, when the stock traded at **$ 34.31**.

Highlights

- We expect 2006 normalized revenues, including wireless and acquired AT&T Corp. operations, to be $85.6 billion, and see modest growth in 2007. In addition to the large enterprise revenues acquired from AT&T Corp., we expect gains in small and medium business revenues. However, we project that voice revenues will decline amid increased competition. Our estimates exclude BellSouth (BLS: hold, $46), which T agreed to acquire in March 2006, subject to necessary approvals that are expected in the fourth quarter.
- We believe that wireline operating margins will be helped by workforce reductions and network integrations and will widen throughout 2007, averaging 18.5%. On the wireless side, margin improvement should stem from improved customer retention that we think will keep acquisition costs down. Our estimates exclude adjustments for integration expenses.
- For 2006 and 2007, we estimate operating EPS of $2.32 and $2.45, respectively, up from pro forma EPS of $1.72 in 2005, and see S&P Core EPS affected by pension adjustments. First nine month 2006 results include $0.34 of one-time items.

Investment Rationale/Risk

- We believe that through wireline cost reductions and growth stemming from Cingular, broadband offerings and an improving business landscape, T should generate strong free cash flow and EPS gains in 2006 and 2007. While we think T would be paying a premium for BLS in order to gain full control of Cingular and faces competitive challenges, we expect the shares will be supported by stock repurchases and believe that the regulatory arena, long negative for T, is turning positive for the company. However, with the shares up 25% since mid July, our hold opinion is based on valuation.
- Risks to our recommendation and target price include a change in federal regulations for the telecom segment, increased competition from cable carriers, weaker than projected wireless services execution, the proposed integration of BLS, and the rollout of its fiber based video services.
- Our 12-month target price of $36 is based on our relative P/E analysis, which assumes a peer average of 15X our 2007 EPS estimate and an enterprise value/EBITDA multiple of 6.2X. T's total return potential is aided by its current 4% dividend yield.

Qualitative Risk Assessment

LOW | **MEDIUM** | HIGH

Our risk assessment reflects our view of the company's strong balance sheet and T's power over its suppliers, offset by the competitive nature of the telecom landscape and the integration challenges of its numerous acquisitions.

Quantitative Evaluations

S&P Quality Ranking B+

D | C | B- | B | **B+** | A- | A | A+

Relative Strength Rank STRONG

78

LOWEST = 1 HIGHEST = 99

Revenue/Earnings Data

Revenue (Million $)

	1Q	2Q	3Q	4Q	Year
2006	15,835	15,810	15,638	--	--
2005	10,248	10,328	10,320	12,966	43,862
2004	10,128	10,314	10,292	10,287	40,787
2003	10,333	10,204	10,239	10,067	40,843
2002	10,522	10,843	10,556	11,217	43,138
2001	11,190	11,477	11,338	11,903	45,908

Earnings Per Share ($)

	1Q	2Q	3Q	4Q	Year
2006	0.37	0.46	0.56	E0.58	E2.32
2005	0.27	0.30	0.38	0.46	1.42
2004	0.59	0.35	0.38	0.21	1.50
2003	0.74	0.42	0.37	0.28	1.80
2002	0.48	0.53	0.51	0.71	2.23
2001	0.54	0.61	0.61	0.37	2.14

Fiscal year ended Dec. 31. Next earnings report expected: Late January. EPS Estimates based on S&P Operating Earnings; historical GAAP earnings are as reported.

Dividend Data (Dates: mm/dd Payment Date: mm/dd/yy)

Amount ($)	Date Decl.	Ex-Div. Date	Stk. of Record	Payment Date
0.333	12/09	01/06	01/10	02/01/06
0.333	03/31	04/06	04/10	05/01/06
0.333	06/30	07/06	07/10	08/01/06
0.333	09/29	10/05	10/10	11/01/06

Dividends have been paid since 1984. Source: Company reports.

Please read the Required Disclosures and Analyst Certification on the last page of this report.

AT&T Inc

Business Summary October 27, 2006

CORPORATE OVERVIEW. AT&T Inc. combined SBC Communications with the acquired assets of AT&T Corp. following the stock and cash acquisition completed in November 2005. AT&T Inc. was the largest U.S. local telephone service provider, with 47 million in-region local phone lines as of September 2006 (down from 50 million in June 2005), and T had a DSL penetration rate of 31% of its consumer's lines. The company also owns a 60% interest in Cingular Wireless, the nation's largest wireless provider with more than 58 million subscribers. The inclusion of AT&T Corp. added voice, data, IP, hosting and outsourcing services for small, mid-sized and large U.S. and multinational customers as well as a national network that we believe was superior to what SBC had in place. In March 2006, T agreed to acquire BellSouth (19 million access lines) for 1.325 T shares for each common share of BellSouth, subject to necessary approvals, a deal that was initially valued at $67 billion. We expect the deal to close in the fourth quarter of 2006.

CORPORATE STRATEGY. The company has grown through mergers with fellow Bell companies Pacific Telesis (a $16.5 billion acquisition in 1997) and Ameritech ($62 billion, 1999) and the more recent AT&T Corp. deal. Cingular Wireless began operations in October 2000, through the merger of the wireless operations of SBC Communications and BellSouth. In October 2004, Cingular purchased AT&T Wireless (AWE), one of its competitors, for $41 billion in cash. We believe the wireline deals will improve T's cost structure.

MARKET PROFILE. The wireline telecommunications business has been undergoing deregulation and change since the 1990s, including the introduction of competition from cable providers and the entry of the local telecom providers into new markets. A spate of merger activity has reordered the telecom sector. In about a decade, the U.S. wireline industry has shrunk to just two dominant players, AT&T Inc. (assuming its planned merger with BellSouth) and Verizon Communications, from 10 major entities. Household spending on communications services (wireless, wireline, Internet and video services) was $175 as of March 2006.

Company Financials

Per Share Data ($) Year Ended Dec. 31	**2005**	**2004**	**2003**	**2002**	**2001**	**2000**	**1999**	**1998**	**1997**	**1996**
Tangible Book Value	8.29	11.77	11.09	9.51	8.62	7.38	5.87	4.95	3.60	3.59
Cash Flow	3.68	3.80	4.16	4.79	2.25	5.16	4.37	4.66	3.47	3.58
Earnings	1.42	1.50	1.80	2.23	2.14	2.32	1.90	2.05	0.80	1.73
S&P Core Earnings	1.24	1.22	1.50	1.21	1.39	NA	NA	NA	NA	NA
Dividends	1.29	1.25	1.37	1.07	1.02	1.01	0.97	0.93	0.89	0.85
Payout Ratio	91%	83%	76%	48%	48%	43%	51%	45%	111%	49%
Prices:High	25.98	27.73	31.65	40.99	53.06	59.00	59.94	54.88	38.06	30.13
Prices:Low	21.75	22.98	18.85	19.57	36.50	34.81	44.06	35.00	24.63	23.00
P/E Ratio:High	18	18	18	18	25	25	32	27	48	17
P/E Ratio:Low	15	15	10	9	17	15	23	17	31	13
Income Statement Analysis (Million $)										
Revenue	43,862	40,787	40,843	43,138	45,908	51,476	49,489	28,777	24,856	13,898
Depreciation	7,643	7,564	7,870	8,578	9,077	9,748	8,553	5,177	4,922	2,240
Maintenance	NA	NA	NA	NA	NA	NA	NA	NA	NA	NA
Construction Credits	36.0	31.0	37.0	58.0	119	81.0	81.0	59.0	120	21.0
Effective Tax Rate	16.3%	30.5%	32.9%	28.5%	36.1%	38.2%	39.4%	36.2%	36.9%	35.7%
Net Income	4,786	4,979	5,971	7,473	7,260	7,967	6,573	4,068	1,474	2,101
S&P Core Earnings	4,189	4,031	5,000	4,048	4,717	NA	NA	NA	NA	NA
Balance Sheet & Other Financial Data (Million $)										
Gross Property	149,238	136,177	133,923	131,755	127,524	119,753	116,332	73,466	65,286	32,754
Net Property	58,727	50,046	52,128	48,490	49,827	47,195	46,571	29,920	27,339	14,007
Capital Expenditures	5,576	5,099	5,219	6,808	11,189	13,124	10,304	5,927	5,766	3,027
Total Capital	96,727	77,544	69,607	62,705	58,476	54,079	50,411	27,741	24,967	13,339
Fixed Charges Coverage	4.4	6.9	7.0	6.9	6.6	8.0	7.5	6.8	2.1	7.1
Capitalization:Long Term Debt	26,115	21,231	16,060	18,536	17,133	16,492	18,415	12,612	13,019	5,505
Capitalization:Preferred	Nil	Nil	Nil	Nil	Nil	Nil	Nil	Nil	Nil	Nil
Capitalization:Common	54,690	40,504	38,248	33,199	32,491	30,463	26,726	12,780	9,892	6,835
% Return on Revenue	10.9	12.2	14.6	17.3	15.8	15.5	13.3	14.1	5.9	15.2
% Return on Invested Capital	6.5	7.0	9.0	11.4	12.9	16.6	15.0	17.7	12.0	17.7
% Return on Common Equity	10.1	12.6	16.7	22.6	23.1	27.9	26.6	34.9	15.1	32.1
% Earned on Net Property	11.3	11.6	12.9	17.5	22.4	22.9	25.6	23.3	11.9	26.3
% Long Term Debt of Capitalization	32.3	34.4	29.6	35.8	34.5	35.1	40.9	49.7	56.8	44.7
Capital % Preferred	Nil	Nil	Nil	Nil	Nil	Nil	Nil	Nil	Nil	Nil
Capitalization:% Common	67.7	65.6	70.4	64.2	65.5	64.9	59.1	50.3	43.2	55.4

Data as orig reptd.; bef. results of disc opers/spec. items. Per share data adj. for stk. divs.; EPS diluted. E-Estimated. NA-Not Available. NM-Not Meaningful. NR-Not Ranked. UR-Under Review.

Office: 175 East Houston, San Antonio, TX 78205-2255.
Telephone: 210-821-4105.
Website: http://www.sbc.com
Chrmn & CEO: E.E. Whitacre, Jr.

COO: R.L. Stephenson
Sr EVP: K. Jennings
Sr EVP: J.W. Callaway
Sr EVP: J. Kahan

Investor Contact: R. Dietz (210-351-2100)
Board of Directors: W. F. Aldinger, III, G. F. Amelio, A. A. Busch, III, M. K. Eby, Jr., J. A. Henderson, C. F. Knight, J. C. Madonna, L. M. Martin, J. B. McCoy, M. S. Metz, T. Rembe, S. D. Ritchey, J. M. Roche, R. L. Stephenson, L. D. Tyson, P. P. Upton, E. E. Whitacre, Jr.

Founded: 1983
Domicile: Delaware
Employees: 189,950

STANDARD &POOR'S

Autodesk Inc

S&P Recommendation HOLD ★★★★★

Price $36.21 (as of Oct 27, 2006)

12-Mo. Target Price $44.00

Investment Style Mid-Cap Growth

GICS Sector Information Technology
Sub-Industry Application Software

Comment Autodesk develops, markets and supports computer-aided design and drafting (CAD) software, including its flagship AutoCAD program, for use on desktop computers and workstations.

Key Stock Statistics (Source S&P, Vickers, company reports)

52-Wk Range	**$48.27–29.56**	S&P Oper. EPS 2007**E**	**1.27**	P/E on S&P Oper. EPS 2007**E**	**28.5**	Dividend Rate/Share	**Nil**
Trailing 12-Month EPS	**$1.22**	S&P Oper. EPS 2008**E**	**1.48**	Common Shares Outstg. (M)	**231.7**	Yield (%)	**Nil**
Trailing 12-Month P/E	**29.7**	S&P Core EPS 2007**E**	**1.27**	Market Capitalization(B)	**$8.390**	Beta	**1.24**
$10K Invested 5 Yrs Ago	**$40,818**	S&P Core EPS 2008**E**	**1.48**	Institutional Ownership (%)	**88**	S&P Credit Rating	**NA**

Price Performance

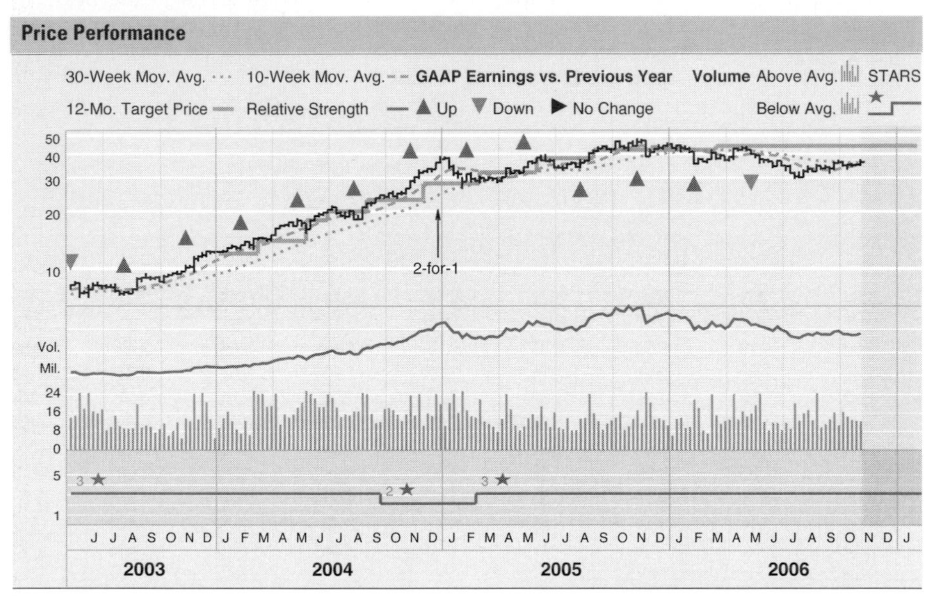

Options: ASE, CBOE, P, Ph

Analysis prepared by **Clyde Montevirgen** on August 29, 2006, when the stock traded at **$ 33.85**.

Highlights

- Following a 23% increase in FY 06 (Jan.), we expect revenues to increase 21% in FY 07 and 15% in FY 08; recent acquisitions should generate approximately 6% of ADSK's revenues in FY 07. New seat growth and new products have recently accounted for about two-thirds of ADSK's revenue, indicating an underlying strength for its products that we expect to persist for several years. We expect upgrade revenue to continue to decline as customers increasingly opt for subscriptions over upgrades.
- Operating margins rose in FY 06 for the third consecutive year, increasing to 24.8% from 21.2% in FY 05 and 6.2% in FY 04. We believe ADSK's FY 07 operating margins will narrow modestly, partly due to the impact of stock-based compensation expense and increasing research and development costs to support new products. However, we see additional operating leverage in sales and marketing costs in FY 08 and we look for wider margins.
- We expect operating EPS of $1.27 in FY 07, including $0.29 of projected stock option expense. In FY 08, we estimate operating EPS of $1.48.

Investment Rationale/Risk

- Although we see a slight deceleration in R&D spending for certain CAD products over the next year, we think ADSK's top-line will benefit from its focus on converting users from 2D to 3D design products, and from its presence in emerging markets with its infrastructure design offerings. We view ADSK's sales execution and operations as favorable, but are cautious of the pace of growth in a few of its end markets. We think ADSK's above-peer comparisons are justified because of its growth potential; however, considering our view of slowing global economics, we have a hold opinion as we see medium-term economic uncertainty posing greater risks to ADSK's growth.
- Risks to our opinion and target price include a negative impact from its internal option probe, weaker than expected company execution, market share loss, and a slowdown in global information technology (IT) spending.
- Our 12-month target price of $44 is based on our DCF model--which assumes a 9.7% WACC and 3.5% terminal growth rate, producing an intrinsic value of $42--and a P/E to growth ratio of 2.1X, valuing the shares at nearly $47.

Qualitative Risk Assessment

LOW | MEDIUM | **HIGH**

Our risk assessment reflects ADSK's exposure to cyclical business spending and intense competition, offset somewhat by our view of the company's strong market position and size.

Quantitative Evaluations

S&P Quality Ranking **B**

D | C | B- | **B** | B+ | A- | A | A+

Relative Strength Rank **MODERATE**

59

LOWEST = 1 HIGHEST = 99

Revenue/Earnings Data

Revenue (Million $)

	1Q	2Q	3Q	4Q	Year
2007	436.0	--	--	--	--
2006	355.1	373.0	378.3	416.8	1,523
2005	297.9	279.6	300.2	356.2	1,234
2004	210.8	211.7	233.9	295.3	951.6
2003	229.3	211.4	188.7	195.5	825.0
2002	245.7	231.4	216.4	254.0	947.5

Earnings Per Share ($)

2007	0.20	**E**0.29	**E**0.32	**E**0.40	**E**1.27
2006	0.31	0.30	0.38	0.33	1.33
2005	0.18	0.16	0.30	0.26	0.90
2004	0.04	0.15	0.10	0.24	0.52
2003	0.08	0.05	-0.02	0.03	0.14
2002	0.13	0.09	0.10	0.10	0.40

Fiscal year ended Jan. 31. Next earnings report expected: NA. EPS Estimates based on S&P Operating Earnings; historical GAAP earnings are as reported.

Dividend Data

Quarterly cash dividends were discontinued after April 2005.

Autodesk Inc

Business Summary August 29, 2006

Autodesk makes software products that are used across industries and in the home for architectural design and land development, manufacturing, utilities, telecommunications, and media and entertainment. ADSK is organized into two segments: the Design Solutions segment and the Discreet segment. The Design Solutions segment includes the following business divisions: Manufacturing Solutions, Building Solutions, Infrastructure Solutions, and Platform Technology and Other.

The Design Solutions segment sells design software for professionals, occasional users, and consumers who design, draft and diagram; and mapping and geographic information systems technology for public and private users. End users of design software products include architects, engineers, construction firms, designers and drafters.

The Manufacturing Solutions division accounted for 18% of Design Solutions segment revenues in FY 05 (Jan.). The Autodesk Inventor Series delivers Autodesk Mechanical Desktop, a 3D mechanical design program, and Autodesk Inventor software, a 3D mechanical design creation tool, in one solution. AutoCAD Mechanical software, a 2D mechanical design and engineering tool, is also included in this division.

The Building Solutions division accounted for 12% of Design Solutions segment revenues in FY 05. The division's main product lines are Autodesk Architectural Desktop and Autodesk Revit.

The Platform Technology division and Other accounted for 57% of Design Solutions segment revenues in FY 05. The division includes the company's flagship product, AutoCAD, a leading computer aided design (CAD) tool. It is a general-purpose CAD tool for design, modeling, drafting, mapping, rendering and facility management tasks. The most current version, AutoCAD 2006, was introduced in March 2005. Other products in the division include AutoCAD LT, a low cost CAD package with 2D and basic 3D drafting capabilities, and Autodesk Buzzsaw, an online collaboration service that allows users to store, manage, and share project documents from any Internet connection.

Company Financials

Per Share Data ($) Year Ended Jan. 31	**2006**	**2005**	**2004**	**2003**	**2002**	**2001**	**2000**	**1999**	**1998**	**1997**
Tangible Book Value	2.06	2.07	2.07	1.84	2.20	1.85	2.22	2.06	1.57	1.35
Cash Flow	1.51	1.11	0.74	0.35	0.68	0.69	0.36	0.79	0.30	0.41
Earnings	1.33	0.90	0.52	0.14	0.40	0.40	0.04	0.46	0.08	0.22
S&P Core Earnings	1.05	0.67	0.33	-0.07	0.09	0.17	NA	NA	NA	NA
Dividends	0.06	0.06	0.06	0.06	0.06	0.06	0.06	0.06	0.06	0.06
Payout Ratio	5%	7%	12%	43%	15%	15%	150%	13%	77%	27%
Calendar Year	2005	2004	2003	2002	2001	2000	1999	1998	1997	1996
Prices:High	48.27	38.98	12.45	11.84	10.55	14.02	12.36	12.52	12.78	11.06
Prices:Low	26.20	12.10	6.41	5.09	6.05	4.86	4.25	5.41	7.00	4.63
P/E Ratio:High	36	43	24	85	26	35	NM	27	NM	50
P/E Ratio:Low	20	13	12	36	15	12	NM	12	NM	21

Income Statement Analysis (Million $)	2006	2005	2004	2003	2002	2001	2000	1999	1998	1997
Revenue	1,523	1,234	952	825	947	936	820	740	632	510
Operating Income	414	314	0.16	99.7	195	208	115	200	147	99.4
Depreciation	43.7	51.9	50.3	40.8	62.9	68.8	79.7	63.2	43.9	34.8
Interest Expense	Nil	Nil	Nil	Nil	Nil	Nil	Nil	Nil	Nil	Nil
Pretax Income	383	246	117	38.5	55.1	41.7	23.9	147	55.0	66.5
Effective Tax Rate	14.1%	10.1%	NM	17.1%	NM	NM	59.0%	38.2%	72.1%	37.5%
Net Income	329	222	120	31.9	90.3	93.2	9.81	90.6	15.4	41.6
S&P Core Earnings	258	161	74.4	-16.2	19.5	38.5	NA	NA	NA	NA

Balance Sheet & Other Financial Data (Million $)	2006	2005	2004	2003	2002	2001	2000	1999	1998	1997
Cash	369	533	364	247	505	423	359	378	96.1	183
Current Assets	739	782	597	450	564	491	545	450	308	311
Total Assets	1,361	1,142	1,017	884	902	808	907	694	534	492
Current Liabilities	507	477	385	310	371	334	299	232	199	150
Long Term Debt	Nil	Nil	Nil	Nil	Nil	Nil	Nil	Nil	Nil	Nil
Common Equity	791	648	622	569	529	460	602	460	303	244
Total Capital	791	648	629	571	529	473	607	461	304	247
Capital Expenditures	20.5	40.8	25.9	36.1	45.1	32.4	14.9	30.4	15.0	17.4
Cash Flow	373	273	171	80.7	153	162	89.6	154	59.2	76.4
Current Ratio	1.5	1.6	1.6	1.5	1.5	1.5	1.8	1.9	1.5	2.1
% Long Term Debt of Capitalization	Nil	Nil	Nil	Nil	Nil	Nil	Nil	Nil	Nil	Nil
% Net Income of Revenue	21.6	18.0	12.6	3.9	9.5	10.0	1.2	12.2	2.4	8.2
% Return on Assets	26.3	20.5	12.7	3.6	10.6	10.9	1.1	14.8	3.0	8.3
% Return on Equity	45.7	34.9	20.2	5.8	18.3	17.6	1.7	23.7	5.6	14.2

Data as orig reptd.; bef. results of disc opers/spec. items. Per share data adj. for stk. divs.; EPS diluted. E-Estimated. NA-Not Available. NM-Not Meaningful. NR-Not Ranked. UR-Under Review.

Office: 111 McInnis Parkway, San Rafael, CA 94903-2700.
Telephone: 415-507-5000.
Email: investor.relations@autodesk.com
Website: http://www.autodesk.com

Exec Chrmn: C.A. Bartz
Pres & CEO: C. Bass
SVP & CFO: A.J. Castino
SVP, Secy & General Counsel: M.K. Sterling

Investor Contact: S. Pirri (415-507-6467)
Board of Directors: C. A. Bartz, C. Bass, M. A. Bertelsen, C. W. Beveridge, J. H. Dawson, M. Fister, P. Halvorsen, S. L. Scheid, M. A. Taylor, L. W. Wangberg

Founded: 1982
Domicile: Delaware
Employees: 4,813

STANDARD &POOR'S

Automatic Data Processing Inc.

S&P Recommendation STRONG BUY ★★★★★

Price $49.44 (as of Oct 31, 2006)

12-Mo. Target Price $56.00

Investment Style Large-Cap Growth

GICS Sector Information Technology
Sub-Industry Data Processing & Outsourced Services

Comment ADP, one of the world's largest independent computing services companies, provides a broad range of data processing services.

Key Stock Statistics (Source S&P, Vickers, company reports)

52-Wk Range	$49.94–42.50	S&P Oper. EPS 2007E	2.20	P/E on S&P Oper. EPS 2007E	22.5	Dividend Rate/Share	$0.74
Trailing 12-Month EPS	$2.76	S&P Oper. EPS 2008E	NA	Common Shares Outstg. (M)	555.6	Yield (%)	1.50
Trailing 12-Month P/E	17.9	S&P Core EPS 2007E	2.20	Market Capitalization(B)	$27.467	Beta	1.30
$10K Invested 5 Yrs Ago	$9,950	S&P Core EPS 2008E	NA	Institutional Ownership (%)	74	S&P Credit Rating	AAA

Price Performance

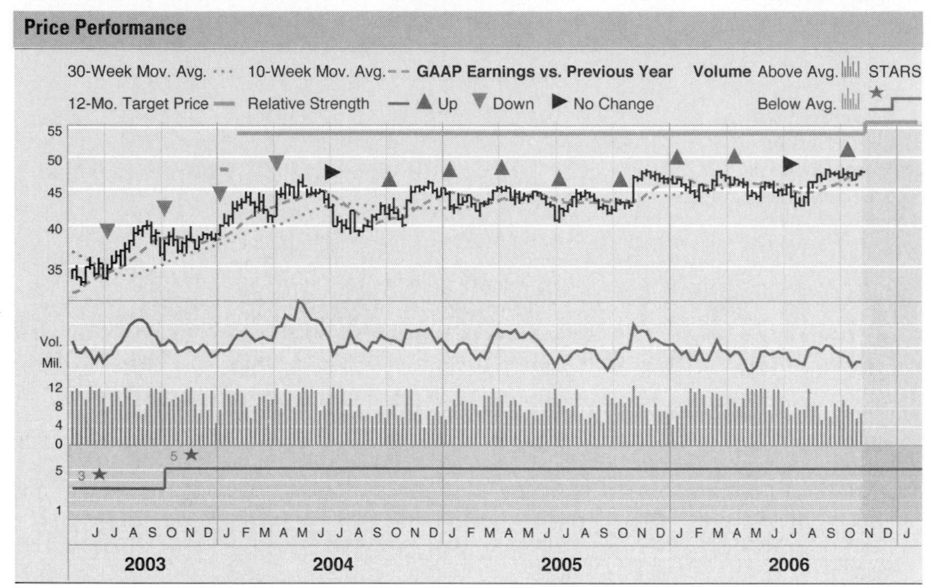

Options: ASE, CBOE, P, Ph

Highlights

➤ The 12-month target price for ADP has recently been changed to $56.00 from $54.00. The Highlights section of this Stock Report will be updated accordingly.

Investment Rationale/Risk

➤ The Investment Rationale/Risk section of this Stock Report will be updated shortly. For the latest News story on ADP from MarketScope, see below.

➤ 10/31/06 10:30 am EST... S&P REITERATES STRONG BUY RECOMMENDATION ON SHARES OF AUTOMATIC DATA PROCESSING (ADP 49.7*****): Sep-Q operating EPS of $0.43 vs. $0.36 is in line with our estimate. We expect the company to sustain current level of strong revenue growth in the core employer services segment, although we look for margin pressure in the segment due to increased levels of investment and costs from recent acquisitions. We think the dealer services unit will improve margins as FY 07 (June) progresses. Our FY 07 EPS estimate of $2.20 is unchanged. We are raising our target price by $2 to $56, on a peer-based P/E of 23X our calendar '07 EPS estimate of $2.43. /D.Cathers

Qualitative Risk Assessment

LOW | **MEDIUM** | HIGH

Our risk assessment reflects what we see as the company's strong balance sheet, steady cash inflow and recurring revenue stream, offset by intense competition in payroll processing and the threat of new entrants into the marketplace.

Quantitative Evaluations

S&P Quality Ranking A+

D | C | B- | B | B+ | A- | A | **A+**

Relative Strength Rank MODERATE

68

LOWEST = 1 HIGHEST = 99

Revenue/Earnings Data

Revenue (Million $)

	1Q	2Q	3Q	4Q	Year
2007	2,218	--	--	--	--
2006	1,922	2,047	2,439	2,474	8,882
2005	1,855	1,994	2,349	2,302	8,499
2004	1,720	1,927	2,121	2,086	7,755
2003	1,648	1,683	1,906	1,912	7,147
2002	1,608	1,681	1,870	1,845	7,004

Earnings Per Share ($)

2007	0.46	**E**0.48	**E**0.62	**E**0.67	**E**2.20
2006	0.36	0.44	0.61	0.44	1.85
2005	0.35	0.42	0.57	0.44	1.79
2004	0.32	0.38	0.50	0.36	1.56
2003	0.34	0.43	0.54	0.36	1.68
2002	0.31	0.42	0.56	0.46	1.75

Fiscal year ended Jun. 30. Next earnings report expected: Late January. EPS Estimates based on S&P Operating Earnings; historical GAAP earnings are as reported.

Dividend Data (Dates: mm/dd Payment Date: mm/dd/yy)

Amount ($)	Date Decl.	Ex-Div. Date	Stk. of Record	Payment Date
0.185	01/27	03/08	03/10	04/01/06
0.185	04/27	06/07	06/09	07/01/06
0.185	08/10	09/13	09/15	10/01/06
0.185	10/17	01/13	01/18	01/19/07

Dividends have been paid since 1974. Source: Company reports.

Automatic Data Processing Inc.

Business Summary August 07, 2006

CORPORATE OVERVIEW. ADP is the largest global provider of payroll outsourcing services based on revenue. The company also offers human resources outsourcing, tax filing, and benefits administration, with a broad range of data processing services in three business segments: employer, brokerage, and dealer.

Employer services provides payroll, human resource, benefits administration, time and attendance, and tax filing and reporting services to more than 518,000 clients in North America, Europe, Australia, Asia and Brazil. Brokerage services includes securities processing, desktop productivity applications, and investor communications services to the financial services industry. The company is the largest provider of securities processing services in North America, offering its clients solutions geared toward both retail and institutional transactions. Dealer services provides transaction systems, data products and professional services to automobile and truck dealers and manufacturers worldwide.

MARKET PROFILE. The market for payroll services, which is the largest segment of ADP's employer services division, totaled about $10.1 billion in calendar 2004, according to market researcher IDC. Between 2006 and 2009, IDC expects this area to grow at an annual compound average growth rate of 6.9%, assuming a 9% growth rate in 2005. Using IDC's data, ADP captured 29.2% of the payroll services market in 2004, while the second-largest provider Paychex (PAYX: hold, $35) had a 9.8% market share.

Company Financials

Per Share Data ($) Year Ended Jun. 30	2006	2005	2004	2003	2002	2001	2000	1999	1998	1997
Tangible Book Value	5.21	4.55	4.23	4.57	5.25	4.97	4.71	3.97	2.90	2.30
Cash Flow	5.35	2.30	2.07	2.13	2.19	1.93	1.74	1.52	1.37	1.27
Earnings	1.85	1.79	1.56	1.68	1.75	1.44	1.31	1.10	0.99	0.88
S&P Core Earnings	1.85	1.60	1.38	1.42	1.49	1.31	NA	NA	NA	NA
Dividends	0.71	0.61	0.54	0.48	0.45	0.40	0.34	0.30	0.26	0.22
Payout Ratio	38%	34%	35%	28%	26%	27%	26%	21%	26%	25%
Prices:High	49.94	48.11	47.31	40.81	59.53	63.56	69.31	54.81	42.16	31.29
Prices:Low	42.50	40.37	38.60	27.24	31.15	41.00	40.00	36.25	28.78	19.75
P/E Ratio:High	27	27	30	24	34	44	53	50	43	36
P/E Ratio:Low	23	23	25	16	18	28	31	33	29	22

Income Statement Analysis (Million $)	2006	2005	2004	2003	2002	2001	2000	1999	1998	1997
Revenue	8,882	8,499	7,755	7,147	7,004	7,018	6,288	5,540	4,798	4,112
Operating Income	1,967	1,948	1,745	1,793	1,952	1,938	1,904	1,376	1,153	1,005
Depreciation	289	304	307	275	279	321	284	273	245	223
Interest Expense	72.8	32.3	Nil	Nil	21.2	14.3	13.1	19.1	24.0	27.8
Pretax Income	3,486	1,678	1,495	1,645	1,787	1,525	1,290	1,085	884	724
Effective Tax Rate	19.2%	37.1%	37.4%	38.1%	38.4%	39.4%	34.8%	35.7%	31.5%	29.1%
Net Income	2,815	1,055	936	1,018	1,101	925	841	697	605	514
S&P Core Earnings	1,077	940	824	857	940	842	NA	NA	NA	NA

Balance Sheet & Other Financial Data (Million $)	2006	2005	2004	2003	2002	2001	2000	1999	1998	1997
Cash	2,269	1,671	1,129	2,344	2,750	1,791	1,824	1,092	752	1,025
Current Assets	4,760	4,441	2,762	3,676	2,817	3,083	3,064	2,194	1,829	1,805
Total Assets	27,490	27,615	21,121	19,834	18,277	17,889	16,851	5,825	5,175	4,383
Current Liabilities	2,593	2,801	1,768	1,999	1,411	1,336	1,297	1,286	1,221	1,020
Long Term Debt	74.3	75.8	76.2	84.7	90.6	110	132	146	192	401
Common Equity	6,012	5,784	5,418	5,371	5,114	4,701	4,583	4,062	3,406	2,661
Total Capital	6,210	6,150	5,778	5,777	5,442	5,019	4,866	4,346	3,745	3,165
Capital Expenditures	292	196	196	134	146	185	166	178	199	175
Cash Flow	3,104	1,360	1,242	1,293	1,380	1,246	1,125	970	850	737
Current Ratio	1.8	1.6	1.6	1.8	2.0	2.3	2.4	1.7	1.5	1.8
% Long Term Debt of Capitalization	1.2	1.2	1.3	1.5	1.7	2.2	2.7	3.4	5.1	12.7
% Net Income of Revenue	31.7	12.4	12.1	14.2	15.7	13.2	13.4	12.6	12.6	12.5
% Return on Assets	10.2	4.3	4.6	5.3	6.1	5.3	5.7	12.6	12.7	12.5
% Return on Equity	47.7	18.8	17.3	19.4	22.4	19.9	19.6	17.9	20.0	20.6

Data as orig reptd.; bef. results of disc opers/spec. items. Per share data adj. for stk. divs.; EPS diluted. E-Estimated. NA-Not Available. NM-Not Meaningful. NR-Not Ranked. UR-Under Review.

Office: 1 Adp Blvd, Roseland, NJ 07068-1728.
Telephone: 973-974-5000.
Website: http://www.adp.com
Chrmn: A.F. Weinbach

Pres & CEO: G.C. Bulter
COO: S.M. Martone
VP, Chief Acctg Officer & Cntlr: D. Sheldon
VP & Treas: R.L. Colotti

Board of Directors: G. D. Brenneman, L. Brun, G. C. Butler, L. G. Cooperman, G. Hubbard, J. P. Jones, A. D. Jordan, F. V. Malek, H. Taub, A. F. Weinbach

Founded: 1949
Domicile: Delaware
Employees: 46,000

AutoNation Inc

STANDARD &POOR'S

S&P Recommendation HOLD ★★★★★

Price $19.98 (as of Oct 27, 2006)

12-Mo. Target Price $22.00

Investment Style Mid-Cap Value

GICS Sector Consumer Discretionary
Sub-Industry Automotive Retail

Comment AutoNation, the largest U.S. retail auto dealer, owns and operates about 340 new vehicle franchises in 16 states.

Key Stock Statistics (Source S&P, Vickers, company reports)

52-Wk Range	$22.94–18.95	S&P Oper. EPS 2006E	1.52	P/E on S&P Oper. EPS 2006E	13.1	Dividend Rate/Share	Nil
Trailing 12-Month EPS	$1.31	S&P Oper. EPS 2007E	1.80	Common Shares Outstg. (M)	213.0	Yield (%)	Nil
Trailing 12-Month P/E	15.3	S&P Core EPS 2006E	1.52	Market Capitalization(B)	$4.256	Beta	0.95
$10K Invested 5 Yrs Ago	$19,980	S&P Core EPS 2007E	1.80	Institutional Ownership (%)	89	S&P Credit Rating	BBB-

Price Performance

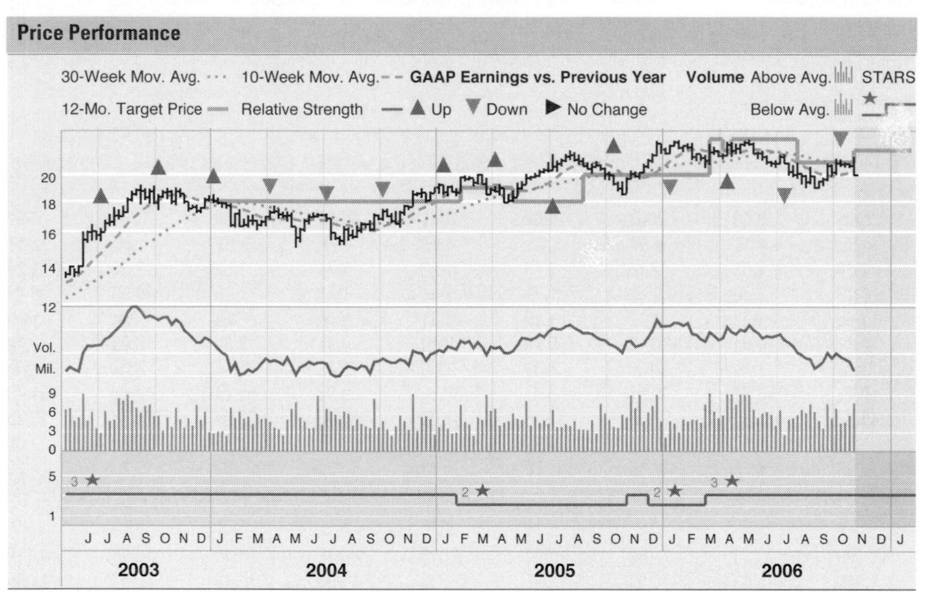

Options: ASE, CBOE, P, Ph

Qualitative Risk Assessment

LOW | **MEDIUM** | HIGH

Our risk assessment reflects the cyclical nature of the automotive retailing industry, which is affected by interest rates, consumer confidence, and personal discretionary spending; and the company's highly variable cost structure.

Quantitative Evaluations

S&P Quality Ranking B

D | C | B- | **B** | B+ | A- | A | A+

Relative Strength Rank WEAK

21

LOWEST = 1 HIGHEST = 99

Highlights

- The 12-month target price for AN has recently been changed to $22.00 from $21.00. The Highlights section of this Stock Report will be updated accordingly.

Investment Rationale/Risk

- The Investment Rationale/Risk section of this Stock Report will be updated shortly. For the latest News story on AN from MarketScope, see below.
- 10/26/06 04:18 pm EDT... S&P REITERATES HOLD OPINION ON SHARES OF AUTONATION (AN 20.88***): AN posts Q3 EPS from continuing operations of $0.40 vs. $0.45, below our $0.47 estimate. Sales and operating margins were below our forecast. We expect free cash of more than $300 million in '07, with a large portion to be used for share repurchases and acquisitions. We are lowering our '06 EPS estimate by $0.07 to $1.52, but increasing 07's by two cents to $1.80, based on an increase in the EPS benefits we see from share buybacks. We are raising our 12-month target price by $1, to $22, based on a combination of P/E and DCF analyses. /E.Levy-CFA

Revenue/Earnings Data

Revenue (Million $)

	1Q	2Q	3Q	4Q	Year
2006	4,674	5,011	4,962	--	--
2005	4,561	5,019	5,188	4,485	19,253
2004	4,630	4,916	5,041	4,838	19,425
2003	4,459	5,069	5,257	4,596	19,381
2002	4,751	5,016	5,194	4,519	19,479
2001	4,888	4,945	5,011	5,146	19,989

Earnings Per Share ($)

2006	0.37	0.32	0.40	**E**0.34	**E**1.52
2005	0.33	0.40	0.45	0.30	1.48
2004	0.32	0.35	0.35	0.43	1.45
2003	0.72	0.37	0.38	0.28	1.76
2002	0.28	0.32	0.33	0.26	1.19
2001	0.17	0.26	0.24	0.06	0.73

Fiscal year ended Dec. 31. Next earnings report expected: Early February. EPS Estimates based on S&P Operating Earnings; historical GAAP earnings are as reported.

Dividend Data

No cash dividends have been paid.

AutoNation Inc

Business Summary August 11, 2006

CORPORATE OVERVIEW. AutoNation's vehicle retailing unit segment operates in saturated markets, in our view; about 75% of total U.S. vehicle sales are to replace existing autos.

AN's new auto retailing operations (60% of 2005 revenues) consist of about 345 dealerships. Although the company is the largest U.S. auto retailer, it controls only about 2% of the nearly $1 trillion U.S. new and used car market.

The sale of used vehicles accounted for 23% of revenues in 2005. Fixed operations provided 13% of sales, while finance and insurance and other accounted for the balance.

MARKET PROFILE. The automotive retailing industry is the largest retail trade sector in the United States. It generates approximately $1.0 trillion in annual sales. The industry is highly fragmented, with the 100 largest automotive retailers generating approximately 17% of industry revenues in 2004 (latest available).

Car retailing is a very competitive business. With razor-thin profit margins and highly leveraged inventories that depreciate rapidly, dealers must generate high volume and fast turnover. However, auto demand itself is driven by volatile factors such as strength of the economy, interest rate levels, and consumer confidence. In addition, dealerships operate with high overhead costs, resulting in a high sales breakeven point.

Consolidation is an important trend, as the number of franchised stores in the U.S. has declined in the past 20 years, from approximately 24,725 in 1983 to 22,089 in 2005. The large capital requirements necessary to operate and be competitive in today's retailing environment make it likely that consolidation will continue.

U.S. new vehicle sales totaled nearly 17 million units in 2005; we expect a drop to 16.8 million in 2006.

Company Financials

Per Share Data ($) Year Ended Dec. 31	**2005**	**2004**	**2003**	**2002**	**2001**	**2000**	**1999**	**1998**	**1997**	**1996**
Tangible Book Value	0.53	4.53	3.91	3.14	3.00	2.61	1.72	11.04	4.04	4.00
Cash Flow	1.78	1.78	2.01	1.40	1.18	1.28	0.07	2.94	2.72	2.15
Earnings	1.48	1.45	1.76	1.19	0.73	0.91	-0.07	0.71	0.46	-0.12
S&P Core Earnings	1.44	1.41	1.69	1.12	0.57	NA	NA	NA	NA	NA
Dividends	Nil	Nil	Nil	Nil	Nil	Nil	Nil	Nil	Nil	Nil
Payout Ratio	Nil	Nil	Nil	Nil	Nil	Nil	Nil	Nil	Nil	Nil
Prices:High	22.84	19.33	19.19	18.73	13.07	10.75	18.38	30.00	44.38	34.63
Prices:Low	17.91	15.01	11.61	9.05	4.94	4.63	7.50	10.00	19.00	13.19
P/E Ratio:High	15	13	11	16	18	12	NM	42	96	NM
P/E Ratio:Low	12	10	7	8	7	5	NM	14	41	NM
Income Statement Analysis (Million $)										
Revenue	19,253	19,425	19,381	19,479	19,989	20,610	20,112	16,118	10,306	2,365
Operating Income	888	861	805	786	667	855	461	1,588	1,350	576
Depreciation	80.7	89.7	71.0	69.7	152	134	60.0	1,052	971	540
Interest Expense	191	159	143	125	43.7	248	35.0	22.0	17.0	33.4
Pretax Income	623	607	591	618	401	525	-27.0	523	315	-10.2
Effective Tax Rate	36.5%	34.7%	14.4%	38.3%	38.9%	37.5%	NM	35.9%	36.5%	NM
Net Income	396	396	506	382	245	328	-31.0	335	200	-27.9
S&P Core Earnings	385	385	486	359	192	NA	NA	NA	NA	NA
Balance Sheet & Other Financial Data (Million $)										
Cash	244	107	171	176	128	82.2	369	217	148	63.6
Current Assets	3,880	3,678	3,990	3,629	3,153	4,176	4,301	8,406	6,826	2,584
Total Assets	8,825	8,699	8,823	8,585	8,065	8,830	9,613	13,926	10,527	3,776
Current Liabilities	3,412	3,411	3,810	2,981	2,578	3,141	3,165	5,540	4,263	2,228
Long Term Debt	484	798	808	643	647	850	836	2,316	2,334	170
Common Equity	4,670	4,263	3,950	3,910	3,828	3,843	4,601	5,425	3,484	1,276
Total Capital	5,340	5,218	4,935	5,500	5,329	5,570	6,241	9,968	5,818	1,447
Capital Expenditures	132	133	133	183	164	148	242	438	460	203
Cash Flow	476	486	577	451	397	462	29.0	1,387	1,171	513
Current Ratio	1.1	1.1	1.0	1.2	1.2	1.3	1.4	1.5	1.6	1.2
% Long Term Debt of Capitalization	9.1	15.3	16.4	11.7	12.1	15.3	13.4	29.1	40.1	11.7
% Net Income of Revenue	2.1	2.0	2.6	2.0	1.2	1.6	NM	2.1	1.9	NM
% Return on Assets	4.5	4.5	5.8	4.6	2.9	3.6	NM	2.8	2.8	NM
% Return on Equity	8.9	9.7	12.9	9.9	6.4	7.8	NM	7.5	8.4	NM

Data as orig reptd.; bef. results of disc opers/spec. items. Per share data adj. for stk. divs.; EPS diluted. E-Estimated. NA-Not Available. NM-Not Meaningful. NR-Not Ranked. UR-Under Review.

Office: 110 SE 6th St, Ft. Lauderdale, FL 33301-5012.
Telephone: 954-769-6000.
Website: http://www.autonation.com
Chrmn & CEO: M.J. Jackson

Pres & COO: M.E. Maroone
Investor Contact: C.T. Monaghan (954-769-6000)
EVP & CFO: C.T. Monaghan
SVP, Secy & General Counsel: J.P. Ferrando

Board of Directors: R. J. Brown, R. L. Burdick, W. C. Crowley, R. R. Grusky, M. A. Jackson, E. S. Lampert, M. E. Maroone, C. A. Migoya, I. B. Rosenfield

Founded: 1991
Domicile: Delaware
Employees: 27,000

STANDARD &POOR'S

AutoZone Inc

S&P Recommendation HOLD ★★★★★

Price $110.90 (as of Oct 27, 2006)

12-Mo. Target Price $115.00

Investment Style Mid-Cap Growth

GICS Sector Consumer Discretionary
Sub-Industry Automotive Retail

Comment This retailer of automotive parts and accessories operates over 3,800 AutoZone stores throughout most of the U.S. and in Mexico.

Key Stock Statistics (Source S&P, Vickers, company reports)

52-Wk Range	**$114.56–79.94**	S&P Oper. EPS 2007**E**	**8.42**	P/E on S&P Oper. EPS 2007**E**	**13.2**	Dividend Rate/Share	**Nil**
Trailing 12-Month EPS	**$7.50**	S&P Oper. EPS 2008**E**	**9.25**	Common Shares Outstg. (M)	**71.3**	Yield (%)	**Nil**
Trailing 12-Month P/E	**14.8**	S&P Core EPS 2007**E**	**8.42**	Market Capitalization(B)	**$7.908**	Beta	**0.57**
$10K Invested 5 Yrs Ago	**$19,364**	S&P Core EPS 2008**E**	**9.25**	Institutional Ownership (%)	**90**	S&P Credit Rating	**BBB+**

Price Performance

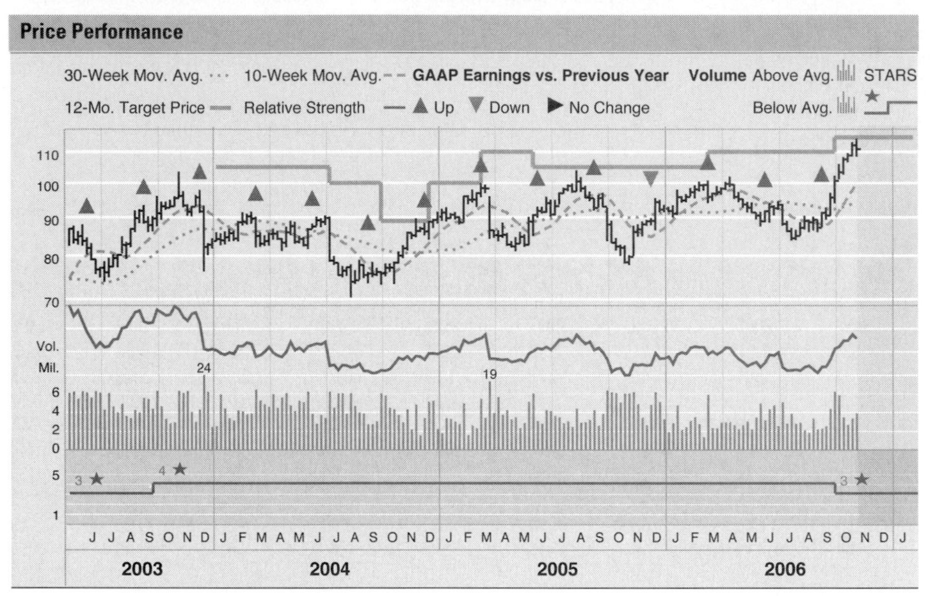

Options: ASE, CBOE, P, Ph

Analysis prepared by **Michael Souers** on October 02, 2006, when the stock traded at **$ 104.15**.

Highlights

- We see sales growth of 4%-5% in FY 07 (Aug.), reflecting the addition of approximately 200 new stores. We project a low single digit rise in same-store sales, driven primarily by gains in commercial sales. We expect do-it-yourself (DIY) sales to improve slightly, on increased average ticket.
- We look for operating margins to widen slightly, as leverage from sales growth, well controlled store and payroll costs, and a greater share of wider margin private label products in the retail segment outweigh an anticipated increased proportion of lower margin commercial sales in the mix and expected higher advertising and marketing spending.
- After our projections of slightly higher interest expense, taxes of 37.0%, and a slightly lower share count reflecting stock repurchases, we forecast that FY 07 operating EPS will grow 12%, to $8.42, from the $7.50 earned in FY 06. We project FY 08 EPS of $9.25. Our FY 07 EPS estimate includes $0.13 of projected stock option expense.

Investment Rationale/Risk

- At about 12X our FY 07 EPS estimate, the shares recently traded at modest discounts to both the S&P 500 and to peers. While the company maintains an industry leading sales to square foot ratio, as well as, sporting higher gross, operating and net margins than any of its peers, its recent sales trends have been rather anemic. Despite what we view as a rational pricing environment, margins will continue to be pressured if same-store-sales trends fail to improve from those in recent years. Longer term, we expect AZO to benefit from what we see as favorable vehicle demographic trends.
- Risks to our recommendation and target price include a slowdown in the U.S. economy; further increases in oil prices; dampening auto usage; technological changes that might reduce the need for auto parts; and execution risk for AZO as it tries to drive top line growth.
- Our 12-month target price of $115, based on our DCF analysis, is equal to about 13.7X our FY 07 EPS estimate. Our DCF model assumes a weighted average cost of capital of 8.8% and a terminal growth rate of 3.0%.

Qualitative Risk Assessment

LOW | **MEDIUM** | HIGH

Our risk assessment for AutoZone reflects the cyclical and seasonal nature of the auto parts retailing industry, which is sensitive to various economic data points, offset by what we view as the company's strong financial metrics and margins.

Quantitative Evaluations

S&P Quality Ranking **B+**

D | C | B- | B | **B+** | A- | A | A+

Relative Strength Rank **STRONG**

85

LOWEST = 1 HIGHEST = 99

Revenue/Earnings Data

Revenue (Million $)

	1Q	2Q	3Q	4Q	Year
2006	1,338	1,254	1,417	1,939	5,948
2005	1,286	1,204	1,338	1,882	5,711
2004	1,282	1,159	1,360	1,836	5,637
2003	1,219	1,121	1,288	1,830	5,457
2002	1,176	1,081	1,225	1,843	5,326
2001	1,064	974.0	1,140	1,641	4,818

Earnings Per Share ($)

	1Q	2Q	3Q	4Q	Year
2006	1.48	1.25	1.89	2.92	7.50
2005	1.52	1.16	1.86	2.66	7.18
2004	1.35	1.04	1.68	2.53	6.56
2003	1.04	0.79	1.30	2.27	5.34
2002	0.76	0.58	0.96	1.73	4.00
2001	0.46	0.28	0.56	0.24	1.54

Fiscal year ended Aug. 31. Next earnings report expected: Early December. EPS Estimates based on S&P Operating Earnings; historical GAAP earnings are as reported.

Dividend Data

No cash dividends have been paid.

AutoZone Inc

Business Summary October 02, 2006

AutoZone is a leading specialty retailer of automotive parts, chemicals and accessories, focusing primarily on do-it-yourself (DIY) consumers. As of August 27, 2005, the company operated 3,592 U.S. AutoZone stores, in 49 states and the District of Columbia, and 81 stores in Mexico. AZO also sells automotive diagnostic equipment and repair software through ALLDATA, diagnostic and repair information through alldatadiy.com, and parts and accessories online at autozone.com.

The company's 3,592 U.S. stores represented 22.8 million sq. ft., up from 3,420 stores and 21.7 million sq. ft. a year earlier.

Each store's product line includes new and remanufactured automotive hard parts, such as alternators, starters, water pumps, brake shoes and pads, carburetors, clutches and engines; maintenance items, such as oil, antifreeze, transmission, brake and power steering fluids, engine additives, protectants and waxes; and accessories, such as car stereos and floor mats. Parts are carried for domestic and foreign cars, sport utility vehicles, vans and light trucks.

Stores, generally in high-visibility locations, range in size from about 4,000 sq. ft. to 8,100 sq. ft., with new stores increasingly using a larger format. As of August 27, 2005, Autozone stores were principally in the following locations: 432 stores in Texas, 413 in California, 197 in Ohio, 172 in Illinois, 162 in Florida, 133 in Georgia, 131 in Michigan, 129 in Tennessee, 128 in North Carolina, 116 in Indiana, and 109 in New York, with the rest in other states.

AZO offers everyday low prices, and attempts to be the price leader in hard parts. Stores generally carry between 21,000 and 23,000 stock-keeping units. In addition to targeting the DIY customer, the company also has a commercial sales program in the U.S. (AZ Commercial), which provides commercial credit and delivery of parts and other products to local, regional and national repair garages, dealers and service stations. As of August 27, 2005, 2,104 stores had commercial sales programs. The hub stores provide fast replenishment of key merchandise to support the DIY and commercial sales businesses. AZO does not perform repairs or installations.

Company Financials

Per Share Data ($) Year Ended Aug. 31	2006	2005	2004	2003	2002	2001	2000	1999	1998	1997
Tangible Book Value	2.35	1.15	NM	0.90	3.87	5.13	5.49	6.83	7.37	7.00
Cash Flow	9.34	8.92	7.79	6.47	5.10	2.70	2.88	2.44	2.10	1.78
Earnings	7.50	7.18	6.56	5.34	4.00	1.54	2.00	1.63	1.48	1.28
S&P Core Earnings	NA	7.03	6.40	5.09	3.87	1.45	NA	NA	NA	NA
Dividends	Nil	Nil	Nil	Nil	Nil	Nil	Nil	Nil	Nil	Nil
Payout Ratio	Nil	Nil	Nil	Nil	Nil	Nil	Nil	Nil	Nil	Nil
Prices:High	114.56	103.94	92.35	103.63	89.34	80.00	32.50	37.01	[illegible]	[illegible]
Prices:Low	83.81	77.76	70.35	58.21	59.20	24.37	21.00	22.56	20.50	19.50
P/E Ratio:High	15	14	14	19	22	52	16	23	26	26
P/E Ratio:Low	11	11	11	11	15	16	10	14	14	15

Income Statement Analysis (Million $)	2006	2005	2004	2003	2002	2001	2000	1999	1998	1997
Revenue	5,948	5,711	5,637	5,457	5,326	4,818	4,483	4,116	3,243	2,691
Operating Income	1,239	1,114	1,106	1,028	889	646	630	555	478	399
Depreciation	139	138	107	110	118	131	118	122	95.5	77.2
Interest Expense	110	104	93.0	84.8	79.9	101	76.8	45.3	18.2	8.84
Pretax Income	902	873	906	833	691	287	435	388	364	313
Effective Tax Rate	36.9%	34.6%	37.5%	37.9%	38.1%	38.8%	38.5%	36.9%	37.4%	37.6%
Net Income	569	571	566	518	428	176	268	245	228	195
S&P Core Earnings	NA	560	553	492	415	165	NA	NA	NA	NA

Balance Sheet & Other Financial Data (Million $)	2006	2005	2004	2003	2002	2001	2000	1999	1998	1997
Cash	91.6	74.8	76.9	6.74	6.50	7.29	6.97	5.92	6.63	4.67
Current Assets	2,119	1,929	1,756	1,585	1,450	1,329	1,187	1,225	1,117	779
Total Assets	4,526	4,245	3,913	3,680	3,478	3,433	3,333	3,285	2,748	1,884
Current Liabilities	2,055	1,811	1,818	1,676	1,534	1,267	1,035	1,001	860	592
Long Term Debt	1,857	1,862	1,869	1,547	1,195	1,225	1,250	888	545	198
Common Equity	470	391	171	374	1,378	866	997	1,324	1,302	1,075
Total Capital	2,327	2,253	2,046	1,921	2,573	2,092	2,247	2,212	1,302	1,274
Capital Expenditures	264	283	185	182	117	169	250	428	337	297
Cash Flow	709	709	673	627	546	307	386	367	323	272
Current Ratio	1.0	1.1	1.0	0.9	0.9	1.0	1.1	1.2	1.3	1.3
% Long Term Debt of Capitalization	79.8	82.6	91.3	80.5	46.4	58.6	55.6	40.2	29.5	15.5
% Net Income of Revenue	9.6	10.0	10.0	9.5	8.0	3.6	6.0	5.9	7.0	7.2
% Return on Assets	13.0	14.0	14.7	14.5	12.4	5.2	8.1	8.1	9.8	11.5
% Return on Equity	132.3	203.1	207.7	97.4	27.5	18.9	23.1	18.6	19.2	20.1

Data as orig reptd.; bef. results of disc opers/spec. items. Per share data adj. for stk. divs.; EPS diluted. E-Estimated. NA-Not Available. NM-Not Meaningful. NR-Not Ranked. UR-Under Review.

Office: 123 South Front Street, Memphis, TN 38103-3607.
Telephone: 901-495-6500.
Email: investor.relations@autozone.com
Website: http://www.autozone.com

Chrmn: J.R. Hyde, III
Pres & CEO: W.C. Rhodes
EVP & CFO: W. Giles
SVP, Secy & General Counsel: H.L. Goldsmith

VP & Cntlr: C. Pleas, III
Investor Contact: B. Campbell (901-495-7005)
Board of Directors: C. M. Elson, S. E. Gove, E. G. Graves, N. G. House, J. R. Hyde, III, E. S. Lampert, W. A. McKenna, G. MrKonic, Jr., W. C. Rhodes

Founded: 1986
Domicile: Nevada
Employees: 53,000

Avaya Inc

STANDARD &POOR'S

S&P Recommendation HOLD ★★★★★	**Price** $12.82 (as of Oct 27, 2006)	**12-Mo. Target Price** $14.00	**Investment Style** Mid-Cap Value

GICS Sector Information Technology
Sub-Industry Communications Equipment

Comment Avaya, a former division of Lucent Technologies (spun off in 2000), provides communications systems and software for enterprises worldwide.

Key Stock Statistics (Source S&P, Vickers, company reports)

52-Wk Range	$13.23–8.85	S&P Oper. EPS 2007E	0.68	P/E on S&P Oper. EPS 2007E	18.9	Dividend Rate/Share	Nil
Trailing 12-Month EPS	$0.43	S&P Oper. EPS 2008E	0.75	Common Shares Outstg. (M)	457.0	Yield (%)	Nil
Trailing 12-Month P/E	29.8	S&P Core EPS 2007E	0.68	Market Capitalization(B)	$5.858	Beta	4.82
$10K Invested 5 Yrs Ago	$13,935	S&P Core EPS 2008E	0.75	Institutional Ownership (%)	78	S&P Credit Rating	BB

Price Performance

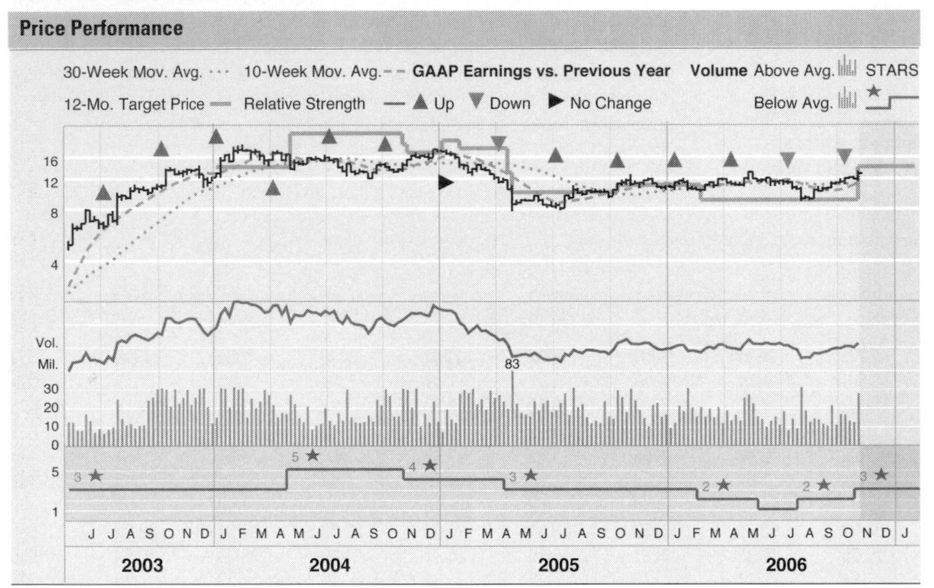

Options: ASE, CBOE, P, Ph

Analysis prepared by **Ari Bensinger** on October 26, 2006, when the stock traded at **$ 12.98**.

Highlights

- Following a 5% sales increase in FY 06 (Sep.), we see sales advancing 7% in FY 07, as higher spending for Internet Protocol (IP) convergence products, as well as disciplined product pricing outweigh a continued decline for legacy time division multiplexing (TDM) products. In the enterprise market, we believe the need to upgrade and replace relatively old network equipment should create a gradual multi-year spending cycle.
- We expect the FY 07 gross margin to widen moderately, to the 48% level, reflecting a favorable product mix shift toward more software-based product sales. We see FY 07 operating expense declining as a percentage of sales, due to aggressive cost management.
- After anticipated lower interest expense resulting from continued repurchasing of debt, but taxes at a likely higher effective rate, reflecting the reversal of tax allowance deferrals, we forecast FY 07 operating EPS of $0.68, including $0.05 of projected stock option expense, versus the $0.43 posted in FY 06. We look for a further increase to $0.75 in FY 08.

Investment Rationale/Risk

- We see competition in the IP telephony arena intensifying, especially from networking vendor Cisco Systems (CSCO: buy, $24). Nevertheless, we believe AV will be able to materially participate in what we forecast to be a prolonged and sizable industry transition to IP telephony, due to its extensive installed base in the legacy private branch exchange arena and its large services support business.
- Risks to our recommendation and target price include a slowdown in Internet telephony deployments and market share losses in the VoIP equipment arena.
- Our 12-month target price of $14 is based on 21X our FY 07 EPS estimate, in line with peers. In our opinion, the stock's P/E multiple was well below the peer average over the past two years due to the company's reliance on the slow growth private branch exchange (PBX) business. However, we believe an improving revenue growth profile, as evidenced by our view of strong September quarter revenue growth, will drive the stock's valuation multiple to expand toward industry peers.

Qualitative Risk Assessment

LOW	MEDIUM	**HIGH**

Our risk assessment reflects the highly competitive nature of the industry, the uncertain adoption rate of Internet telephony, and our view of a material decline in demand for the company's legacy voice equipment.

Quantitative Evaluations

S&P Quality Ranking NR

D	C	B-	B	B+	A-	A	A+

Relative Strength Rank STRONG

90

LOWEST = 1 HIGHEST = 99

Revenue/Earnings Data

Revenue (Million $)

	1Q	2Q	3Q	4Q	Year
2006	1,249	1,238	1,297	1,364	5,148
2005	1,148	1,222	1,236	1,296	4,902
2004	971.0	1,006	1,016	1,076	4,069
2003	1,067	1,081	1,072	1,118	4,338
2002	1,306	1,279	1,219	1,152	4,956
2001	1,785	1,852	1,714	1,442	6,793

Earnings Per Share ($)

	1Q	2Q	3Q	4Q	Year
2006	0.15	0.08	0.10	0.10	0.43
2005	0.07	0.07	0.40	0.36	1.89
2004	0.07	0.22	0.12	0.21	0.63
2003	-0.33	-0.11	0.02	0.15	-0.23
2002	-0.09	-0.63	-0.11	-1.50	-2.44
2001	0.03	-0.25	0.06	-1.17	-1.33

Fiscal year ended Sep. 30. Next earnings report expected: Late January. EPS Estimates based on S&P Operating Earnings; historical GAAP earnings are as reported.

Dividend Data

No cash dividends have been paid.

Please read the Required Disclosures and Analyst Certification on the last page of this report.

Avaya Inc

Business Summary October 26, 2006

CORPORATE OVERVIEW. Avaya (formerly the Network Enterprise Group of Lucent Technologies Inc.) provides communications systems and software for enterprises, including businesses, government agencies and other organizations. The company offers converged voice and data networks, traditional voice communications systems, customer relationship management, and unified communications. Results are reported under two segments: Global Communications Solutions (GCS) and Avaya Global Services (AGS).

The GCS segment (52% of revenue in FY 05 (Sep.)) sells communications systems, including Internet Protocol (IP) telephony solutions, multi-media contact center infrastructure and converged applications, unified communications applications, devices such as IP telephone sets, and traditional voice communications systems. The segment also includes the portion of the Tenovis rental and managed services revenue attributable to the equipment used in connection with customer contracts. The AGS segment (48%) sells end-to-end global service offerings that enable customers to plan and manage their converged communications networks worldwide. We believe AV is one of the few large equipment suppliers to offer a large in-house global service organization.

PRIMARY BUSINESS DYNAMICS. Private branch exchanges (PBX), private telephone switchboards used within an enterprise, account for the majority of the enterprise communications hardware market. These devices provide switching within the company or within specific company locations. For sizable enterprises, a PBX provides a cheaper switching alternative than providing an external connection line to every telephone in the organization. In addition, intra-office connections are easier, usually with an abbreviated three or four-digit number. A critical part of the AV's strategy focuses on the migration from circuit-switched voice communications systems to converged packet-based networks that provide for the integration of voice, data, video and other application traffic on a single unified network.

Company Financials

Per Share Data ($) Year Ended Sep. 30	2006	2005	2004	2003	2002	2001	2000	1999	1998	1997
Tangible Book Value	NA	1.51	1.18	0.13	NM	0.79	1.99	4.63	NA	NA
Cash Flow	NA	2.54	0.92	0.27	-1.74	-0.28	-0.58	NA	NA	NA
Earnings	0.43	1.89	0.63	-0.23	-2.44	-1.33	-1.39	0.70	NA	NA
S&P Core Earnings	NA	1.80	0.56	-0.32	-3.02	-0.90	NA	NA	NA	NA
Dividends	Nil	Nil	Nil	Nil	Nil	Nil	Nil	NA	NA	NA
Payout Ratio	Nil	Nil	Nil	Nil	Nil	Nil	Nil	NA	NA	NA
Prices:High	13.23	17.74	19.00	14.35	12.73	19.24	26.00	NA	NA	NA
Prices:Low	8.85	7.76	11.95	1.93	1.12	8.50	10.00	NA	NA	NA
P/E Ratio:High	31	9	30	NM	NM	NM	NM	NA	NA	NA
P/E Ratio:Low	21	4	19	NM	NM	NM	NM	NA	NA	NA
Income Statement Analysis (Million $)										
Revenue	NA	4,902	4,069	4,338	4,956	6,793	7,680	8,268	NA	NA
Operating Income	NA	592	1,469	310	620	6,218	461	NA	NA	NA
Depreciation	NA	272	147	201	229	273	220	NA	NA	NA
Interest Expense	NA	19.0	66.0	78.0	51.0	Nil	76.0	90.0	NA	NA
Pretax Income	NA	247	242	5.00	-401	-570	-448	307	NA	NA
Effective Tax Rate	NA	NM	NM	NM	NM	NM	NM	39.4%	NA	NA
Net Income	NA	923	291	-88.0	-666	-352	-375	186	NA	NA
S&P Core Earnings	NA	876	252	-125	-997	-257	NA	NA	NA	NA
Balance Sheet & Other Financial Data (Million $)										
Cash	NA	750	1,617	1,192	597	250	271	217	NA	NA
Current Assets	NA	2,171	2,724	2,569	2,303	2,769	3,362	2,763	NA	NA
Total Assets	NA	5,219	4,159	4,057	3,897	4,648	5,037	4,609	NA	NA
Current Liabilities	NA	1,319	1,423	1,168	1,324	2,018	2,589	2,233	NA	NA
Long Term Debt	NA	25.0	294	953	933	1,127	713	Nil	NA	NA
Common Equity	NA	1,961	794	266	170	660	764	1,288	NA	NA
Total Capital	NA	2,082	1,088	1,219	1,103	2,182	1,477	1,288	NA	NA
Capital Expenditures	NA	147	81.0	60.0	111	341	499	NA	NA	NA
Cash Flow	NA	1,195	438	113	-574	-79.0	-155	NA	NA	NA
Current Ratio	NA	1.6	1.9	2.2	1.7	1.4	1.3	1.2	NA	NA
% Long Term Debt of Capitalization	NA	1.2	27.0	78.2	84.6	51.6	48.3	Nil	NA	NA
% Net Income of Revenue	NA	18.8	7.2	NM	NM	NM	NM	2.2	NA	NA
% Return on Assets	NA	19.7	7.1	NM	NM	NM	NM	NA	NA	NA
% Return on Equity	NA	67.0	58.6	NM	NM	NM	NM	NA	NA	NA

Data as orig reptd.; bef. results of disc opers/spec. items. Per share data adj. for stk. divs.; EPS diluted. E-Estimated. NA-Not Available. NM-Not Meaningful. NR-Not Ranked. UR-Under Review.

Office: 211 Mount Airy Rd, Basking Ridge, NJ 07920.
Telephone: 908-953-6000.
Email: avirsvcs@avaya.com
Website: http://www.avaya.com

Chrmn: P.A. Odeen
Pres & CEO: L.J. D'Ambrosio
COO: M. Thurk
SVP & CFO: G.K. McGuire

SVP, Secy & General Counsel: P.F. Craven
Investor Contact: M. Booher (908-953-7500)
Board of Directors: B. Bond, F. J. Fanzilli, J. P. Landy, M. Leslie, P. A. Odeen, D. K. Peterson, H. S. Runtagh, D. C. Stanzione, P. Stern, A. Terracciano, R. F. Wallman, R. Zarrella

Founded: 2000
Domicile: Delaware
Employees: 19,100

Avery Dennison Corp

STANDARD &POOR'S

S&P Recommendation HOLD ★★★★★

Price $62.87 (as of Oct 27, 2006)

12-Mo. Target Price $62.00

Investment Style Mid-Cap Value

GICS Sector Industrials
Sub-Industry Office Services & Supplies

Comment AVY is a leading worldwide manufacturer of pressure-sensitive adhesives and materials, office products, labels, retail systems and specialty chemicals.

Key Stock Statistics (Source S&P, Vickers, company reports)

52-Wk Range	**$63.94–54.95**	S&P Oper. EPS 2006**E**	**3.72**	P/E on S&P Oper. EPS 2006**E**	**16.9**	Dividend Rate/Share	**$1.60**
Trailing 12-Month EPS	**$2.58**	S&P Oper. EPS 2007**E**	**4.00**	Common Shares Outstg. (M)	**109.8**	Yield (%)	**2.54**
Trailing 12-Month P/E	**24.4**	S&P Core EPS 2006**E**	**3.60**	Market Capitalization(B)	**$6.901**	Beta	**0.62**
$10K Invested 5 Yrs Ago	**$14,730**	S&P Core EPS 2007**E**	**3.95**	Institutional Ownership (%)	**76**	S&P Credit Rating	**A-**

Price Performance

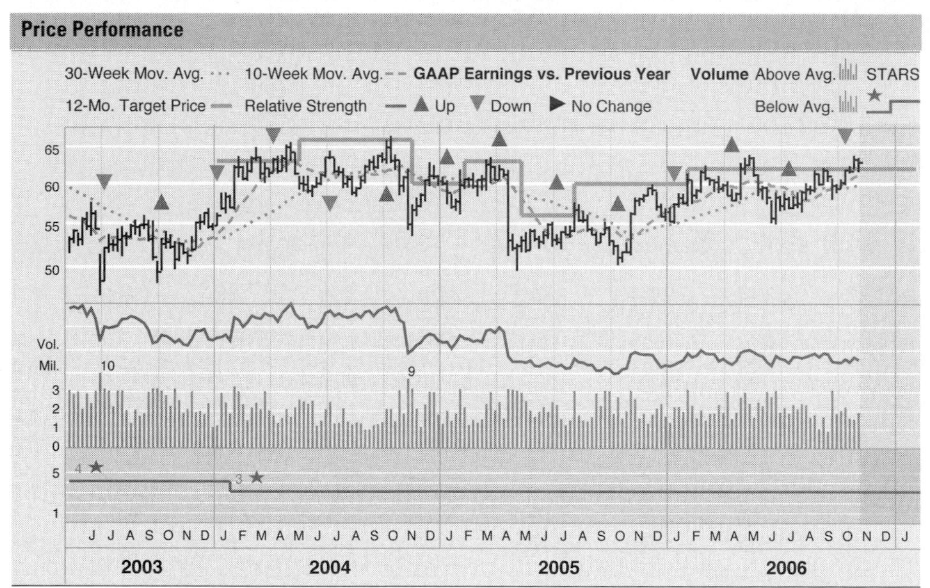

Options: ASE, CBOE, P, Ph

Analysis prepared by **Richard O'Reilly, CFA** on August 18, 2006, when the stock traded at **$ 61.09**.

Highlights

- We expect sales in 2006 to rise 2%-4%, with virtually all of the gain coming in the second half. We expect overall volumes to grow 4% in 2006, after a 1% decline in 2005, assuming a continuing rebound in volumes in the U.S. roll material and label businesses and continued good gains in Europe, Asia and Latin America. We see office products sales improving in 2006, after a 3% decline in 2005.
- The price/mix should remain slightly positive, versus the typical 2% negative rate, as AVY implements price increases to offset 2% higher raw material costs. AVY sold two product lines with total annual sales of about $70 million.
- We foresee margins widening in 2006 on the volume growth and planned overhead cost reductions of up to $50 million, partly offset by higher marketing spending. We project that radio frequency identification (RFID) development spending will modestly decline in 2006 after nearly doubling in 2005 to about $32 million. We estimate that the effective tax rate for 2006 will be about 22%, up from 2005's 19%. Our 2006 EPS estimate of $3.65 includes $0.12 of projected stock option expense, but excludes possible restructuring charges of up to $0.17.

Investment Rationale/Risk

- While recent growth had been slower than we had expected, we believe fundamentals remain sound, with growth driven by the increasing use of non-impact printing systems for computers and for product tracking and information needs. We also see a proliferation of high-quality graphics on packaging and consumer products spurring sales of pressure-sensitive labels.
- Risks to our recommendation and target price include the potentially adverse impact of antitrust investigations involving AVY, and an inability to introduce new products or raise selling prices in response to higher raw material costs.
- Our concerns regarding antitrust investigations largely offset stronger growth in organic sales that we project. Our 12-month target price is $62. We value AVY shares using a P/E of 17X our 2006 estimate, near their historical premium to the S&P 500 of almost 20% on a P/E basis. We think AVY's record of earnings and dividend growth (Standard & Poor's Earnings/Dividend Ranking of A; 30 consecutive years of dividend growth) should provide support for the shares.

Qualitative Risk Assessment

LOW | **MEDIUM** | HIGH

Our risk assessment reflects the company's leading market shares in pressure sensitive adhesives and office products, and our view of above average growth rates in key end markets and a relatively strong balance sheet, offset by possible adverse legal issues.

Quantitative Evaluations

S&P Quality Ranking **A**

D | C | B- | B | B+ | A- | **A** | A+

Relative Strength Rank **MODERATE**

56

LOWEST = 1 HIGHEST = 99

Revenue/Earnings Data

Revenue (Million $)

	1Q	2Q	3Q	4Q	Year
2006	1,337	1,410	1,418	--	--
2005	1,346	1,419	1,363	1,364	5,474
2004	1,247	1,324	1,336	1,434	5,341
2003	1,135	1,192	1,204	1,231	4,763
2002	930.8	1,056	1,115	1,105	4,207
2001	963.2	960.8	966.7	912.6	3,803

Earnings Per Share ($)

2006	0.69	0.96	0.85	**E**1.00	**E**3.72
2005	0.58	0.89	0.86	0.57	2.90
2004	0.52	0.68	0.75	0.83	2.78
2003	0.71	0.70	0.65	0.40	2.43
2002	0.66	0.74	0.64	0.56	2.59
2001	0.65	0.61	0.63	0.59	2.47

Fiscal year ended Dec. 31. Next earnings report expected: Late January. EPS Estimates based on S&P Operating Earnings; historical GAAP earnings are as reported.

Dividend Data (Dates: mm/dd Payment Date: mm/dd/yy)

Amount ($)	Date Decl.	Ex-Div. Date	Stk. of Record	Payment Date
0.390	01/26	02/27	03/01	03/15/06
0.390	04/27	06/05	06/07	06/21/06
0.390	07/26	09/01	09/06	09/20/06
0.400	10/27	12/04	12/06	12/20/06

Dividends have been paid since 1964. Source: Company reports.

Please read the Required Disclosures and Analyst Certification on the last page of this report.

Avery Dennison Corp

Business Summary August 18, 2006

CORPORATE OVERVIEW. Avery Dennison is the leading global manufacturer of pressure-sensitive technology and self-adhesive solutions for consumer products and label systems, including office products, product identification and control systems, and specialty tapes and chemicals.

Foreign operations accounted for 56% of sales in 2005.

The pressure-sensitive adhesives and materials group (57% of sales and 54% of operating profits in 2005) includes Fasson- and JAC-brand pressure sensitive, self-adhesive coated papers; plastic films and metal foils in roll and sheet form; graphic and decoration films and labels; and adhesives, protective coatings and electroconductive resins for industrial, automotive, aerospace, appliance, electronic, medical and consumer markets. The acquisition of Jackstadt in May 2002 was AVY's largest purchase in more than a decade and, we believe, strengthened its business in many developing markets worldwide.

The office and consumer products group (21% and 35%) consists of consumer and office products such as pressure-sensitive labels; copier, laser and ink-jet print labels and template software; notebooks; presentation and organizing products (binders, sheet protectors, dividers); writing instruments; marking devices; security badge systems; and many other products sold under the Avery, National and Hi-Liter brands for office, home and school uses.

Retail information services (12% and 9%) sell a variety of price marking and brand identification products for retailers, apparel manufacturers, distributors and industrial customers. Products include woven and printed labels; heat transfers; graphic and barcode tags; patches; integrated tags; price tickets; customer hard and soft good packagings; barcode printers; software; plastics fastening; and applications devices for use in identification, tracking and control applications.

Other businesses (10% and 2%) consists of industrial and automotive decoration films and graphics sold primarily to original equipment manufacturers; self-adhesive postal stamps and on-battery testing labels; and specialty fastening and bonding tapes sold in roll form. The radio frequency identification (RFID) business (inlays and labels) was reported in this segment in 2005. The RFID business had a net loss of about $32 million in 2005, but we expect the loss to decline modestly in 2006.

Company Financials

Per Share Data ($) Year Ended Dec. 31	**2005**	**2004**	**2003**	**2002**	**2001**	**2000**	**1999**	**1998**	**1997**	**1996**
Tangible Book Value	6.74	5.85	4.08	2.53	4.70	3.94	3.66	5.98	5.91	5.73
Cash Flow	4.95	4.66	4.22	4.12	4.05	4.41	3.61	3.37	3.03	2.76
Earnings	2.90	2.78	2.43	2.59	2.47	2.84	2.13	2.15	1.93	1.68
S&P Core Earnings	2.66	2.51	2.05	2.02	1.81	NA	NA	NA	NA	NA
Dividends	1.53	1.49	1.45	1.35	1.23	1.11	0.99	0.87	0.72	0.62
Payout Ratio	53%	54%	60%	52%	50%	39%	46%	40%	37%	37%
Prices:High	63.58	66.60	63.75	69.70	60.50	78.50	73.00	62.06	45.75	36.50
Prices:Low	49.60	53.50	46.25	52.06	43.25	41.13	39.38	39.44	33.38	23.75
P/E Ratio:High	22	24	26	27	24	28	34	29	24	22
P/E Ratio:Low	17	19	19	20	18	14	18	18	17	14

Income Statement Analysis (Million $)										
Revenue	5,474	5,341	4,763	4,207	3,803	3,894	3,768	3,460	3,346	3,223
Operating Income	690	655	602	593	566	638	589	499	460	419
Depreciation	202	188	179	153	156	157	150	127	117	113
Interest Expense	57.9	58.5	57.7	43.7	50.2	54.6	43.4	34.6	31.7	40.9
Pretax Income	367	373	335	365	360	426	330	337	311	271
Effective Tax Rate	20.4%	25.1%	27.5%	29.5%	32.4%	33.5%	34.8%	33.7%	34.2%	35.0%
Net Income	292	280	243	257	243	284	215	223	205	176
S&P Core Earnings	269	251	205	201	179	NA	NA	NA	NA	NA

Balance Sheet & Other Financial Data (Million $)										
Cash	98.5	84.8	29.5	22.8	19.1	11.4	6.90	18.5	3.30	3.80
Current Assets	1,558	1,542	1,441	1,216	982	982	956	802	794	805
Total Assets	4,204	4,399	4,105	3,652	2,819	2,699	2,593	2,143	2,047	2,037
Current Liabilities	1,526	1,387	1,496	1,296	951	801	850	664	630	694
Long Term Debt	723	1,007	888	837	627	773	701	466	404	371
Common Equity	1,512	1,549	1,319	1,056	929	828	810	833	838	832
Total Capital	2,235	2,647	2,274	1,968	1,647	1,695	1,610	1,363	1,292	1,247
Capital Expenditures	163	179	201	152	135	198	178	160	177	188
Cash Flow	493	468	422	410	399	440	366	351	322	289
Current Ratio	1.0	1.1	1.0	0.9	1.0	1.2	1.1	1.2	1.3	1.2
% Long Term Debt of Capitalization	32.4	38.1	39.0	42.5	38.0	45.6	43.5	34.2	31.3	29.8
% Net Income of Revenue	5.3	5.2	5.1	6.1	6.4	7.3	5.7	6.5	6.1	5.5
% Return on Assets	6.8	6.6	6.3	7.8	8.8	10.7	9.1	10.7	10.0	8.8
% Return on Equity	19.1	19.5	20.4	25.9	27.7	34.6	26.2	26.7	24.5	21.4

Data as orig reptd.; bef. results of disc opers/spec. items. Per share data adj. for stk. divs.; EPS diluted. E-Estimated. NA-Not Available. NM-Not Meaningful. NR-Not Ranked. UR-Under Review.

Office: 150 North Orange Grove Boulevard, Pasadena, CA 91103.
Telephone: 626-304-2000.
Email: investorcom@averydennison.com
Website: http://www.averydennison.com

Chrmn: K. Kresa
Pres & CEO: D.A. Scarborough
EVP & CFO: D.R. O'Bryant
EVP, Secy & General Counsel: R.G. van Schoonenberg

Investor Contact: K.E. Rodriguez (626-304-2000)
Board of Directors: P. K. Barker, R. Borjesson, J. T. Cardis, R. M. Ferry, K. Kresa, P. W. Mullin, D. E. Pyott, D. A. Scarborough, P. Siewert, J. A. Stewart

Founded: 1935
Domicile: Delaware
Employees: 22,600

STANDARD & POOR'S

Avon Products Inc.

S&P Recommendation HOLD ★★★★★

Price $29.20 (as of Oct 27, 2006)

12-Mo. Target Price $32.00

Investment Style Large-Cap Growth

GICS Sector Consumer Staples
Sub-Industry Personal Products

Comment This company is the world's leading direct marketer of cosmetics, toiletries, fashion jewelry and fragrances, with more than 3 million sales representatives worldwide.

Key Stock Statistics (Source S&P, Vickers, company reports)

52-Wk Range	$33.26–24.33	S&P Oper. EPS 2006E	1.39	P/E on S&P Oper. EPS 2006E	21.0	Dividend Rate/Share	$0.70
Trailing 12-Month EPS	$1.06	S&P Oper. EPS 2007E	1.66	Common Shares Outstg. (M)	447.7	Yield (%)	2.40
Trailing 12-Month P/E	27.6	S&P Core EPS 2006E	1.45	Market Capitalization(B)	$13.072	Beta	0.27
$10K Invested 5 Yrs Ago	$13,224	S&P Core EPS 2007E	1.72	Institutional Ownership (%)	85	S&P Credit Rating	A

Price Performance

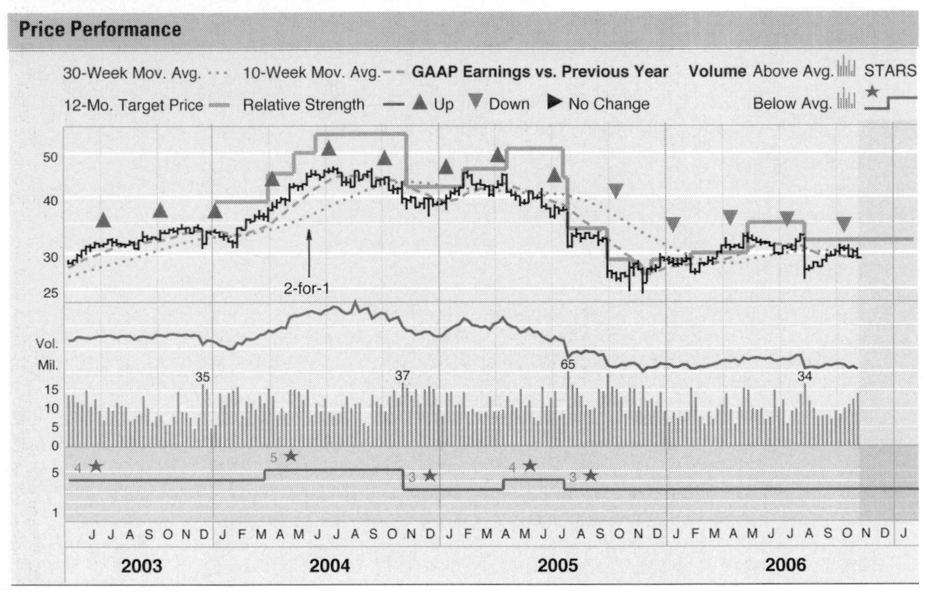

Options: ASE, CBOE, P, Ph

Analysis prepared by **Howard Choe** on August 11, 2006, when the stock traded at **$ 27.74**.

Highlights

- On February 27, 2006, the company was approved by the Chinese government to resume direct selling in China. On November 15, 2005, AVP announced a multi-year restructuring plan in an effort to drive revenue and profit growth. The plan entails reorganizing and downsizing the organization, implementing global manufacturing and increasing supply chain efficiencies. Pretax costs for the plan are estimated to be $300 million-$500 million. AVP plans to reinvest the savings from this plan in marketing, R&D and incentivizing its sales force.
- We see 2006 sales rising 4.5%, reflecting strong sales in Latin America and weakness in Asia. Sales growth in the U.S. should be modest, in our view, driven by new products but hampered by a declining sales force. Given the inclusion of stock option expense, which we see at $45 million, we expect the operating margin to decline 350 basis points to 11.3%.
- Excluding unusual items, we project that 2006 EPS will decline 23%, to $1.39, from $1.81 in 2005. We estimate S&P Core EPS of $1.45 for 2006, reflecting adjustments related to post-retirement obligations.

Investment Rationale/Risk

- We have a hold opinion on the shares, reflecting our concerns over AVP's weak performance in Asia amid a declining sales representative base and continued weakness in North America. We believe sales growth in North America will remain challenged due to the declining number of sales representatives, increased competition, and macro concerns.
- Risks to our recommendation and target price include further deterioration in the U.S. market, political and economic instability in international markets, competition from various sales channels, and unfavorable consumer reception of new products.
- Given our near-term concerns over slowing growth, we believe AVP should trade near the level of its peers. We expect volatility in the shares to be somewhat higher given near term issues. We therefore see the shares as fairly valued at a recent level of 20.2X our 2006 EPS estimate, modestly above the peer group average. Our 12-month target price is $32, which assumes a forward P/E of 18.0X applied to our 2007 EPS estimate.

Qualitative Risk Assessment

LOW | **MEDIUM** | HIGH

Demand for personal care products are generally static. Demand is generally not impacted by changes in the economy or geopolitical factors. However, certain product categories such as fragrances are more susceptible to the aforementioned factors.

Quantitative Evaluations

S&P Quality Ranking A

D | C | B- | B | B+ | A- | **A** | A+

Relative Strength Rank WEAK

22

LOWEST = 1 HIGHEST = 99

Revenue/Earnings Data

Revenue (Million $)

	1Q	2Q	3Q	4Q	Year
2006	2,003	2,080	2,059	--	--
2005	1,881	1,984	1,886	2,398	8,150
2004	1,765	1,866	1,806	2,311	7,748
2003	1,481	1,656	1,629	2,109	6,876
2002	1,384	1,527	1,463	1,854	6,228
2001	1,358	1,463	1,423	1,752	5,995

Earnings Per Share ($)

	1Q	2Q	3Q	4Q	Year
2006	0.12	0.33	0.19	**E**0.43	**E**1.39
2005	0.36	0.69	0.35	0.40	1.81
2004	0.31	0.49	0.37	0.61	1.77
2003	0.21	0.36	0.28	0.55	1.39
2002	0.20	0.32	0.19	0.40	1.11
2001	0.17	0.29	0.21	0.23	0.90

Fiscal year ended Dec. 31. Next earnings report expected: Early February. EPS Estimates based on S&P Operating Earnings; historical GAAP earnings are as reported.

Dividend Data (Dates: mm/dd Payment Date: mm/dd/yy)

Amount ($)	Date Decl.	Ex-Div. Date	Stk. of Record	Payment Date
0.165	11/03	11/15	11/17	12/01/05
0.175	01/26	02/10	02/14	03/01/06
0.175	05/04	05/12	05/16	06/01/06
0.175	08/03	08/15	08/17	09/01/06

Dividends have been paid since 1919. Source: Company reports.

Avon Products Inc.

STANDARD &POOR'S

Business Summary August 11, 2006

CORPORATE OVERVIEW. Avon Products, which began operations in 1886, is a global manufacturer and marketer of beauty and related products. The company has three product categories: Beauty, Beauty Plus and Beyond Beauty. Beauty consists of cosmetics, fragrance and toiletries and accounted for 69% of sales in 2005. Beauty Plus (18%) consists of jewelry, watches and apparel and accessories. Beyond Beauty (13%) consists of home products, gift and decorative and candles. The company has operations in 62 countries, including the U.S., and its products are distributed in 51 additional countries, for coverage in 113 markets. Geographically, 31% of 2005 sales were derived from North America, while Latin America, Asia Pacific and Europe accounted for 28%, 13% and 28% of sales, respectively. Foreign operations accounted for 76% of operating profits in 2005. Sales are made to the ultimate customer mainly through a combination of direct selling and marketing by about 5.1 million independent Avon representatives, about 468,000 of whom are in the U.S.

CORPORATE STRATEGY. In response to slowing sales and profit growth for the nine months ending in September 2005, AVP embarked on a multi-year restructuring plan in November 2005, in an effort to drive revenue and profit growth. The plan entails reorganizing and downsizing the organization, implementing global manufacturing and increasing supply chain efficiencies. AVP expects restructuring benefits will help fund an increase in consumer research, marketing and product development to ultimately enhance sales beginning in 2007. Also in 2005, Avon started implementation of a global supply chain strategy, which includes the development of a new common systems platform, known as enterprise resource planning (ERP).

MARKET PROFILE. Generating approximately $8 billion in revenue, AVP is the largest player in the global direct selling industry (estimated to be approximately $95 billion in 2004 by the Direct Selling Association). While direct selling has increased at a rapid rate (24% between 2001 and 2004), we estimate that the global cosmetics and toiletries market (we estimate to be $230 billion in revenue) has grown at a slower rate, in the mid-single digits. AVP faces competition not just from other direct sellers but also makers of personal care items that sell through the retail and Internet channels. However, as a key industry player, we expect AVP to benefit from continued growth, especially in developing markets.

Company Financials

Per Share Data ($) Year Ended Dec. 31	**2005**	**2004**	**2003**	**2002**	**2001**	**2000**	**1999**	**1998**	**1997**	**1996**
Tangible Book Value	1.68	2.02	0.79	NM	NM	NM	NM	0.55	0.54	0.46
Cash Flow	2.10	2.05	1.63	1.34	1.10	1.20	0.74	0.64	0.77	0.72
Earnings	1.81	1.77	1.39	1.11	0.90	1.01	0.58	0.51	0.64	0.60
S&P Core Earnings	1.80	1.80	1.37	0.95	0.77	NA	NA	NA	NA	NA
Dividends	0.66	0.70	0.42	0.40	0.38	0.37	0.36	0.34	0.32	0.29
Payout Ratio	36%	40%	30%	36%	42%	37%	62%	67%	50%	49%
Prices:High	45.66	46.65	34.88	28.55	25.06	24.88	29.56	23.13	19.50	14.88
Prices:Low	24.33	30.81	24.47	21.75	17.78	12.63	11.66	12.50	12.66	9.08
P/E Ratio:High	25	26	25	26	28	25	51	45	31	25
P/E Ratio:Low	13	17	18	20	20	12	20	25	20	15

Income Statement Analysis (Million $)										
Revenue	8,150	7,748	6,876	6,228	5,995	5,715	5,289	5,213	5,079	4,814
Operating Income	1,289	1,361	1,162	1,029	951	886	762	706	616	609
Depreciation	140	135	124	125	109	97.1	83.0	72.0	72.1	64.5
Interest Expense	54.1	33.8	33.3	52.0	71.1	84.7	43.2	41.0	41.8	40.0
Pretax Income	1,124	1,188	994	836	666	691	507	456	535	510
Effective Tax Rate	24.0%	27.8%	32.1%	35.0%	34.7%	29.2%	40.3%	41.9%	37.0%	37.5%
Net Income	848	846	665	535	430	485	302	270	339	318
S&P Core Earnings	845	859	652	455	367	NA	NA	NA	NA	NA

Balance Sheet & Other Financial Data (Million $)										
Cash	1,059	770	694	607	509	123	117	106	142	185
Current Assets	2,921	2,506	2,226	2,048	1,889	1,546	1,338	1,341	1,344	1,350
Total Assets	4,763	4,148	3,562	3,328	3,193	2,826	2,529	2,434	2,273	2,222
Current Liabilities	2,502	1,526	1,588	1,976	1,461	1,359	1,713	1,330	1,356	1,391
Long Term Debt	766	866	878	767	1,236	1,108	701	201	102	105
Common Equity	794	950	371	-128	-74.6	-216	-406	285	285	242
Total Capital	1,595	1,829	1,300	712	1,192	954	365	559	456	422
Capital Expenditures	207	250	163	127	155	194	203	190	169	104
Cash Flow	987	981	788	659	539	582	385	342	411	382
Current Ratio	1.2	1.6	1.4	1.0	1.3	1.1	0.8	1.0	1.0	1.0
% Long Term Debt of Capitalization	48.1	47.4	67.5	107.8	103.7	116.1	192.3	36.0	22.3	24.9
% Net Income of Revenue	10.4	10.9	9.7	8.6	7.2	8.5	5.7	5.2	6.7	6.6
% Return on Assets	19.0	21.9	19.3	16.4	14.3	18.1	12.2	11.5	15.1	14.9
% Return on Equity	97.2	128.0	545.8	NM	NM	NM	NM	94.7	128.7	146.0

Data as orig reptd.; bef. results of disc opers/spec. items. Per share data adj. for stk. divs.; EPS diluted. E-Estimated. NA-Not Available. NM-Not Meaningful. NR-Not Ranked. UR-Under Review.

Office: 1345 Avenue of the Americas, New York, NY 10105-0196.
Telephone: 212-282-5000.
Email: individual.investor@avon.com
Website: http://www.avoninvestor.com

Chrmn & CEO: A. Jung
Pres & COO: S.J. Kropf
EVP & CFO: C. Cramb
SVP, Secy & General Counsel: G.L. Klemann, II

VP & Chief Acctg Officer: K. Byrne
Investor Contact: R. Johansen (212-282-5320)
Board of Directors: W. D. Cornwell, E. T. Fogarty, S. C. Gault, F. Hassan, A. Jung, M. E. Lagomasino, A. S. Moore, P. S. Pressler, P. Stern, L. A. Weinbach

Founded: 1886
Domicile: New York
Employees: 49,000

Baker Hughes Inc

STANDARD &POOR'S

S&P Recommendation BUY ★★★★★

Price $70.59 (as of Oct 27, 2006)

12-Mo. Target Price $92.00

Investment Style Large-Cap Growth

GICS Sector Energy
Sub-Industry Oil & Gas Equipment & Services

Comment This company is one of the world's largest oilfield services companies, providing products and services to the energy industry.

Key Stock Statistics (Source S&P, Vickers, company reports)

52-Wk Range	**$89.30–51.81**	S&P Oper. EPS 2006**E**	**4.23**	P/E on S&P Oper. EPS 2006**E**	**16.7**	Dividend Rate/Share	**$0.52**
Trailing 12-Month EPS	**$6.97**	S&P Oper. EPS 2007**E**	**5.24**	Common Shares Outstg. (M)	**329.0**	Yield (%)	**0.74**
Trailing 12-Month P/E	**10.1**	S&P Core EPS 2006**E**	**4.18**	Market Capitalization(B)	**$23.221**	Beta	**0.72**
$10K Invested 5 Yrs Ago	**$20,385**	S&P Core EPS 2007**E**	**5.19**	Institutional Ownership (%)	**91**	S&P Credit Rating	**A**

Price Performance

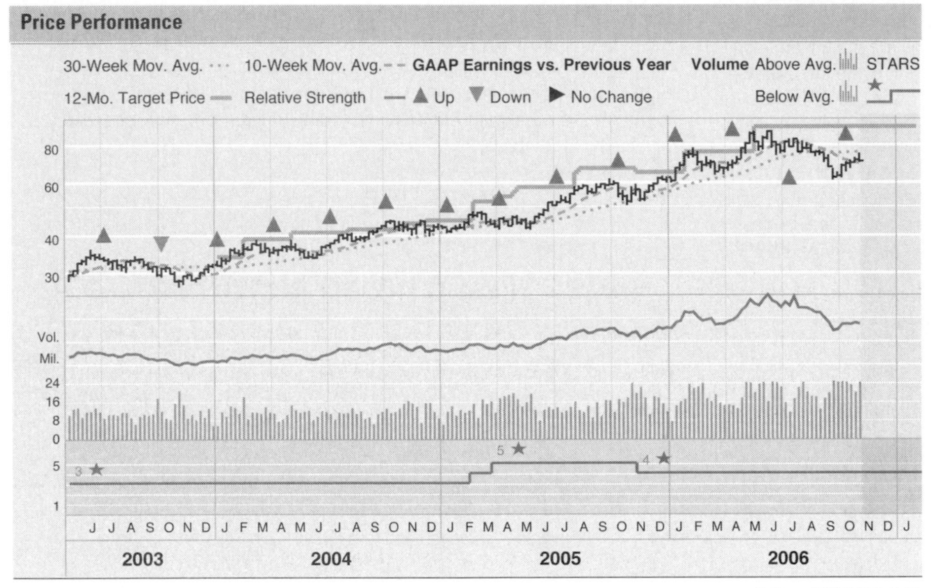

Options: ASE, CBOE, P, Ph

Analysis prepared by **Stewart Glickman, CFA** on September 29, 2006, when the stock traded at **$ 68.20**.

Highlights

- We expect total revenues to grow about 30% in 2006, with greater gains in international markets than in North America. We estimate that operating margins of the core oilfield segment will widen in 2006, to about 25%, versus 20% generated in 2005. For 2007, we see revenue growth of about 22%, with further margin gains.
- In the second quarter, BHI sold its 30% stake in Western Geco, a provider of reservoir imaging to the oil and gas industry, to Schlumberger (SLB: strong buy, $61) for $2.4 billion in cash. We like the deal for BHI, as we view it as strong value for a minority stake, and it should enable the company to focus on its core oilfield services operations. At June 30, 2006, long-term debt stood at $1.08 billion. We expect BHI to use available cash for debt reduction and share buybacks.
- We estimate 2006 EPS from continuing operations of $4.23 (which excludes the $3.07 per share gain on the sale of Western Geco), rising to $5.24 in 2007. On an S&P Core Earnings basis, we expect EPS of $4.18 and $5.19 in the respective years, with the divergence from operating EPS reflecting pension adjustments.

Investment Rationale/Risk

- We expect improving fundamentals for the company's broad line of oilfield products and services, and anticipate that BHI will generate improved pricing traction in 2006, leading, in our view, to wider operating margins, as increasing E&P activity raises demand for the company's services. Although cost inflation (both for labor and for equipment components) is a concern, we believe that higher prices should more than offset any such cost pressures.
- Risks to our recommendation and target price include lower prices for oil and natural gas; reduced drilling activity in international markets; and higher than expected cost inflation.
- Our discounted cash flow model, which assumes free cash flow growth of about 9% to 10% for 10 years, with 3% growth thereafter, discounted at a weighted average cost of capital of 9.7%, shows an intrinsic value of about $97 per share. Applying multiples of 13.5X to projected 2006 EBITDA and 18X to estimated 2006 cash flow and blending with our DCF model, our 12-month target price is $92.

Qualitative Risk Assessment

LOW | **MEDIUM** | HIGH

Our risk assessment reflects BHI's exposure to volatile crude oil and natural gas prices, capital spending decisions by its exploration and production customers, and political risk associated with operating in frontier regions. Offsetting these risks is BHI's strong position in drilling and completion products.

Quantitative Evaluations

S&P Quality Ranking **B**

D | C | B- | **B** | B+ | A- | A | A+

Relative Strength Rank **WEAK**

28

LOWEST = 1 HIGHEST = 99

Revenue/Earnings Data

Revenue (Million $)

	1Q	2Q	3Q	4Q	Year
2006	2,062	2,203	2,309	--	--
2005	1,643	1,768	1,785	1,989	7,186
2004	1,388	1,499	1,538	1,679	6,104
2003	1,200	1,315	1,338	1,440	5,293
2002	1,203	1,245	1,280	1,292	5,020
2001	1,229	1,342	1,436	1,376	5,382

Earnings Per Share ($)

	1Q	2Q	3Q	4Q	Year
2006	0.93	4.14	1.09	**E**1.19	**E**4.23
2005	0.53	0.64	0.64	0.76	2.56
2004	0.28	0.35	0.41	0.53	1.57
2003	0.15	0.24	-0.29	0.30	0.40
2002	0.21	0.21	0.19	-0.01	0.66
2001	0.21	0.31	0.41	0.37	1.31

Fiscal year ended Dec. 31. Next earnings report expected: Mid February. EPS Estimates based on S&P Operating Earnings; historical GAAP earnings are as reported.

Dividend Data (Dates: mm/dd Payment Date: mm/dd/yy)

Amount ($)	Date Decl.	Ex-Div. Date	Stk. of Record	Payment Date
0.130	01/26	02/02	02/06	02/17/06
0.130	04/27	05/04	05/08	05/19/06
0.130	07/27	08/03	08/07	08/18/06
0.130	10/26	11/02	11/06	11/17/06

Dividends have been paid since 1987. Source: Company reports.

Baker Hughes Inc

Business Summary September 29, 2006

CORPORATE OVERVIEW. Baker Hughes was formed through the 1987 merger of Baker International Corp. and Hughes Tool Co. In 1998, it acquired seismic and wireline logging company Western Atlas, creating the third largest oilfield services company. BHI has operations in over 90 countries. The U.S. accounted for 36% of 2005 revenues, followed by Canada with 6.6%, the U.K. with 5.6%, and Norway 5.2%. In 2005, the company reorganized its seven product-line focused divisions into three operating segments: Drilling & Evaluation; Completion & Production; and Western Geco (which provides reservoir imaging, monitoring and development services).

The Drilling & Evaluation segment (51% of 2005 total oilfield revenues and 50% of total oilfield segment income) consists of four operating divisions: Baker Hughes Drilling Fluids, Hughes Christensen, INTEQ, and Baker Atlas. The products and services in this segment are typically used in the drilling of crude oil and natural gas wells.

Baker Hughes Drilling Fluids provides drilling and completion fluids, and fluid environmental services. Fluids are used in order to control downhole pressure, clean the bottom of the well, and to cool and lubricate the drill bit and drill string. Hughes Christensen manufactures drill bit products, primarily Tri-cone roller cone drill bits and polycrystalline diamond compact (PDC) fixed cutter bits. INTEQ supplies directional and horizontal drilling services, coring services, subsurface surveying, logging-while-drilling, and measurement-while-drilling services.

Baker Atlas provides formation evaluation and perforating services for oil and natural gas wells. Formation evaluation involves measuring and analyzing specific physical properties of the rock in the vicinity of the wellbore to determine a reservoir's boundaries, hydrocarbon volume, and ability to produce fluids to the surface. Perforating services involve puncturing a well's steel casing and cement sheath with explosive charges; this creates a fracture in the formation, and provides a path for the hydrocarbons in the formation to enter the wellbore.

Company Financials

Per Share Data ($) Year Ended Dec. 31	2005	2004	2003	2002	2001	2000	1999	1998	1997	1996
Tangible Book Value	9.42	7.35	5.87	6.05	5.69	4.64	4.17	3.98	9.16	6.45
Cash Flow	3.68	2.69	1.59	1.56	2.32	2.14	2.52	1.43	1.93	2.32
Earnings	2.56	1.57	0.40	0.66	1.31	0.31	0.16	-0.92	0.71	1.23
S&P Core Earnings	2.47	1.50	0.62	0.55	1.17	NA	NA	NA	NA	NA
Dividends	0.48	0.46	0.46	0.46	0.46	0.46	0.46	0.46	0.46	0.43
Payout Ratio	19%	29%	115%	70%	35%	148%	NM	NM	65%	35%
Prices:High	63.13	45.30	36.15	39.95	45.29	43.38	36.25	44.13	49.63	38.88
Prices:Low	40.73	31.56	26.90	22.60	25.76	19.63	15.00	15.00	32.63	22.75
P/E Ratio:High	25	29	90	61	35	NM	NM	NM	70	32
P/E Ratio:Low	16	20	67	34	20	NM	NM	NM	46	18
Income Statement Analysis (Million $)										
Revenue	7,186	6,104	5,293	5,020	5,382	5,234	4,547	6,312	3,685	3,028
Operating Income	1,616	1,195	957	856	1,077	1,076	992	1,058	616	502
Depreciation, Depletion and Amortization	382	374	349	302	345	612	778	758	186	156
Interest Expense	72.3	83.6	103	111	126	173	159	149	48.6	55.5
Pretax Income	1,279	780	328	380	662	236	85.0	-201	213	299
Effective Tax Rate	31.6%	32.3%	45.1%	41.2%	33.7%	56.7%	37.6%	NM	48.8%	41.0%
Net Income	874	528	180	224	439	102	53.0	-297	109	176
S&P Core Earnings	842	506	209	186	393	NA	NA	NA	NA	NA
Balance Sheet & Other Financial Data (Million $)										
Cash	697	319	98.4	144	45.4	34.6	18.0	16.6	8.60	7.71
Current Assets	3,840	2,967	2,524	2,556	2,697	2,487	2,330	2,725	2,221	1,717
Total Assets	7,807	6,821	6,302	6,401	6,676	6,453	7,040	7,811	4,756	3,298
Current Liabilities	1,361	1,236	1,302	1,080	1,212	988	1,000	1,310	936	635
Long Term Debt	1,078	1,086	1,133	1,424	1,682	2,050	2,706	2,726	772	674
Common Equity	4,698	3,895	3,350	3,397	3,328	3,047	3,072	3,199	2,605	1,689
Total Capital	6,004	5,214	4,611	4,988	5,221	5,255	5,813	6,082	3,652	2,513
Capital Expenditures	478	348	405	317	319	599	634	1,318	343	182
Cash Flow	1,257	902	529	525	783	714	831	461	295	332
Current Ratio	2.8	2.4	1.9	2.4	2.2	2.5	2.3	2.1	2.4	2.7
% Long Term Debt of Capitalization	18.0	20.8	24.6	28.6	32.2	39.0	46.6	44.8	21.1	26.8
% Return on Assets	12.0	8.0	2.8	3.4	6.7	1.5	0.7	NM	2.7	5.4
% Return on Equity	20.4	14.6	5.3	6.7	13.8	3.3	1.7	NM	5.1	11.0

Data as orig reptd.; bef. results of disc opers/spec. items. Per share data adj. for stk. divs.; EPS diluted. E-Estimated. NA-Not Available. NM-Not Meaningful. NR-Not Ranked. UR-Under Review.

Office: 3900 Essex Lane, Houston, TX 77027-5177.
Telephone: 713-439-8600.
Website: http://www.bakerhughes.com
Chrmn & CEO: C.C. Deaton

Pres & COO: J.R. Clark
SVP & CFO: P.A. Ragauss
VP & General Counsel: A.R. Crain
VP & CCO: J. Martin

Founded: 1972
Domicile: Delaware
Employees: 29,100

STANDARD &POOR'S

Ball Corp

S&P Recommendation BUY ★★★★★

Price $41.26 (as of Oct 27, 2006)

12-Mo. Target Price $48.00

Investment Style Mid-Cap Growth

GICS Sector Materials
Sub-Industry Metal & Glass Containers

Comment Ball, one of the largest producers of metal beverage cans in the world, derives about 10% of its revenues from sales of hi-tech equipment to the aerospace industry.

Key Stock Statistics (Source S&P, Vickers, company reports)

52-Wk Range	$45.00–34.16	S&P Oper. EPS 2006E	2.85	P/E on S&P Oper. EPS 2006E	14.5	Dividend Rate/Share	$0.40
Trailing 12-Month EPS	$3.08	S&P Oper. EPS 2007E	3.30	Common Shares Outstg. (M)	104.2	Yield (%)	0.97
Trailing 12-Month P/E	13.4	S&P Core EPS 2006E	2.69	Market Capitalization(B)	$4.299	Beta	0.05
$10K Invested 5 Yrs Ago	$26,488	S&P Core EPS 2007E	3.41	Institutional Ownership (%)	73	S&P Credit Rating	BB+

Price Performance

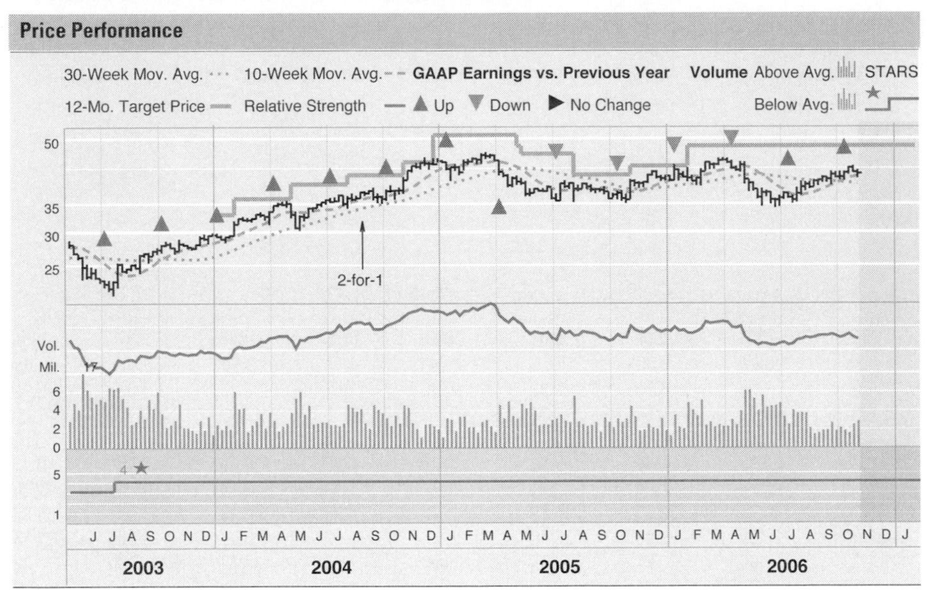

Options: ASE, CBOE, P, Ph

Analysis prepared by **Stewart Scharf** on August 15, 2006, when the stock traded at **$ 38.88**.

Highlights

- We project internal sales growth of 5% to 6% for 2006, mainly reflecting increased volume for beverage cans in the Americas, as well as in Europe and Asia, despite tight supplies due to a fire in April at a German plant. We expect beverage can volume in Germany to recover due to a new deposit redemption system, while sales of plastic containers rebound; we see the aerospace and technologies segment remaining weak. Total sales should benefit from contributions from two recent acquisitions.
- We see 2006 gross margins (before D&A) expanding modestly from 2005's 16.2% of sales, with better results in the second half, as pricing initiatives should offset high freight, energy and materials costs. We expect EBITDA margins to widen from 12.1% in 2005, on cost controls, synergies from acquisitions, global production efficiencies and a better product mix.
- We estimate EPS of $2.85 in 2006 (before a $0.43 insurance gain and a $0.01 charge, but after $0.03 of projected stock option expense), and $3.30 for 2007.

Investment Rationale/Risk

- We maintain our buy recommendation, based on valuation and our belief that trends for BLL's global markets are favorable.
- Risks to our recommendation and target price include weak exchange rates, softening domestic beer sales in favor of wine and spirits, cost pressures in Europe and China, supply disruptions, integration problems, and an inability to pass along higher raw material costs to customers. We have some concerns related to BLL's corporate governance practices, including the former CEO serving on the board.
- The shares recently traded at 13.4X our 2006 EPS estimate, a 10% discount to S&P's Metal & Glass Containers group. However, based on our DCF model, which assumes a 3.5% perpetual growth rate and a weighted average cost of capital of 8.3%, the shares recently traded at more than a 20% discount to our intrinsic value estimate of $50. We blend our metrics and apply a P/E of near 17X our 2006 EPS estimate, above BLL's average historical P/E, and we arrive at our 12-month target price of $48.

Qualitative Risk Assessment

LOW | **MEDIUM** | HIGH

Our risk assessment reflects the seasonality inherent in the beverage can business, our view of BLL's high debt levels, our corporate governance concerns related to board and audit issues, and volatile raw material prices, which are offset by our expectations of lower interest expense due to debt refinancing and redemptions.

Quantitative Evaluations

S&P Quality Ranking B+

D | C | B- | B | **B+** | A- | A | A+

Relative Strength Rank MODERATE

47

LOWEST = 1 HIGHEST = 99

Revenue/Earnings Data

Revenue (Million $)

	1Q	2Q	3Q	4Q	Year
2006	1,365	1,843	1,822	--	--
2005	1,324	1,552	1,584	1,291	5,751
2004	1,232	1,467	1,479	1,263	5,440
2003	1,071	1,353	1,359	1,194	4,977
2002	875.9	1,034	1,039	910.2	3,859
2001	850.0	992.6	1,001	843.0	3,686

Earnings Per Share ($)

2006	0.43	1.26	0.97	E0.49	E2.85
2005	0.51	0.71	0.73	0.42	2.38
2004	0.41	0.80	0.90	0.50	2.60
2003	0.28	0.65	0.61	0.49	2.01
2002	0.24	0.44	0.44	0.28	1.38
2001	0.16	-1.48	0.31	0.07	-0.93

Fiscal year ended Dec. 31. Next earnings report expected: Late January. EPS Estimates based on S&P Operating Earnings; historical GAAP earnings are as reported.

Dividend Data (Dates: mm/dd Payment Date: mm/dd/yy)

Amount ($)	Date Decl.	Ex-Div. Date	Stk. of Record	Payment Date
0.100	01/25	02/27	03/01	03/15/06
0.100	04/26	05/30	06/01	06/15/06
0.100	07/26	08/30	09/01	09/15/06
0.100	10/25	11/29	12/01	12/15/06

Dividends have been paid since 1958. Source: Company reports.

Ball Corp

Business Summary August 15, 2006

CORPORATE OVERVIEW. Ball Corp. primarily manufactures rigid packaging products for beverages and foods. Two beverage companies account for a substantial part of its packaging sales: SABMiller plc and PepsiCo. BLL is comprised of five segments: Metal Beverage Packaging (Americas); Metal Beverage Packaging (Europe/Asia); Metal Food & Household Packaging (Americas); Plastic Packaging (Americas); and Aerospace and Technologies. In 2005, BLL's segments consisted of North American Packaging, International Packaging; and Aerospace and Technologies. The A&T segment provides products and services to the defense and commercial markets. U.S. government agencies accounted for more than 80% of segment sales in 2005.

The company's packaging products include aluminum and steel two-piece beverage cans, and two- and three-piece steel food cans. Metal Beverage Packaging (Americas) segment net sales represented 42% of the total through the first half of 2006 ($122 million of pretax earnings); Metal beverage packaging (Europe/Asia) accounted for 23% ($97 million); Metal Food and Household packaging (Americas) was 16% ($16 million); Plastic Packaging (Americas) accounted for 9.4% ($9.2 million); and Aerospace and Technologies, 10% ($335 million). BLL entered the plastics business in 1995, when it began to make polyethylene terephthalate (PET) bottles. Sales volumes of metal food containers in North America tend to be highest from June through October due to seasonal vegetable and salmon packs. BLL believes this accounts for more than 30% of all North American metal beverage can shipments.

In March 2006, the company acquired U.S. Can's Argentinean and U.S. operations for 444,677 BLL common shares and the assumption of $598 million of debt. Sales for the two divisions totaled about $600 million in 2005, with EBITDA near $80 million. The transaction makes BLL the largest supplier in the U.S. of aerosol cans, primarily for food and household products. Separately, the company completed the acquisition of certain North American plastic container assets of Alcan Packaging for $185 million. The operations had annual sales of $150 million.

Company Financials

Per Share Data ($) Year Ended Dec. 31	**2005**	**2004**	**2003**	**2002**	**2001**	**2000**	**1999**	**1998**	**1997**	**1996**
Tangible Book Value	NM	NM	NM	NM	1.27	1.81	1.27	0.32	3.45	4.27
Cash Flow	0.00	4.49	3.81	2.68	0.44	1.81	2.03	1.41	1.34	0.86
Earnings	2.38	2.60	2.01	1.38	-0.93	0.54	0.79	0.23	0.44	0.09
S&P Core Earnings	2.54	2.67	2.12	1.10	-0.88	NA	NA	NA	NA	NA
Dividends	0.40	0.35	0.24	0.18	0.15	0.15	0.15	0.15	0.15	0.15
Payout Ratio	17%	13%	12%	13%	NM	28%	19%	66%	34%	176%
Prices:High	46.45	45.20	29.88	27.25	18.03	11.98	14.78	12.23	9.75	8.06
Prices:Low	35.06	28.26	21.15	16.30	9.52	6.50	8.84	7.16	5.94	5.78
P/E Ratio:High	20	17	15	20	NM	22	19	54	22	95
P/E Ratio:Low	15	11	11	12	NM	12	11	31	14	68
Income Statement Analysis (Million $)										
Revenue	5,751	5,440	4,977	3,859	3,686	3,665	3,584	2,896	2,389	2,184
Operating Income	697	739	663	458	127	445	442	334	248	177
Depreciation	214	215	206	149	153	159	163	155	118	93.5
Interest Expense	116	104	126	75.6	88.3	95.2	108	78.6	53.5	39.9
Pretax Income	362	436	331	245	-110	110	171	32.9	85.2	20.1
Effective Tax Rate	27.5%	31.9%	30.2%	34.3%	NM	38.9%	38.0%	26.7%	37.6%	35.8%
Net Income	262	296	230	159	-99.2	68.2	104	32.0	58.3	13.1
S&P Core Earnings	280	304	242	127	-96.0	NA	NA	NA	NA	NA
Balance Sheet & Other Financial Data (Million $)										
Cash	61.0	199	36.5	259	83.1	25.6	35.8	34.0	25.5	169
Current Assets	1,226	1,246	924	1,225	794	969	896	886	798	767
Total Assets	4,343	4,478	4,070	4,132	2,314	2,650	2,732	2,855	2,090	1,701
Current Liabilities	1,176	996	861	1,069	575	659	670	688	838	511
Long Term Debt	1,473	1,538	1,579	1,854	949	1,012	1,093	1,230	366	408
Common Equity	835	1,087	808	493	504	640	635	565	574	587
Total Capital	2,314	2,631	2,393	2,353	1,463	1,709	1,803	1,877	1,113	1,047
Capital Expenditures	292	196	137	158	68.5	98.7	107	84.2	97.7	196
Cash Flow	475	511	435	309	51.3	225	264	184	173	104
Current Ratio	1.0	1.3	1.1	1.1	1.4	1.5	1.3	1.3	1.0	1.5
% Long Term Debt of Capitalization	63.7	58.5	66.0	78.8	64.9	59.2	60.6	65.5	32.9	39.0
% Net Income of Revenue	4.5	5.4	4.6	4.1	NM	1.9	2.9	1.1	2.4	0.6
% Return on Assets	5.9	6.9	5.6	4.9	NM	2.5	3.7	1.3	3.1	0.8
% Return on Equity	27.2	31.2	35.4	32.0	NM	10.1	16.9	5.1	9.9	1.8

Data as orig reptd.; bef. results of disc opers/spec. items. Per share data adj. for stk. divs.; EPS diluted. E-Estimated. NA-Not Available. NM-Not Meaningful. NR-Not Ranked. UR-Under Review.

Office: 10 Longs Peak Dr, Broomfield, CO 80021-2510.
Telephone: 303-469-3131.
Website: http://www.ball.com
Chrmn, Pres & CEO: R.D. Hoover

COO & SVP: J.R. Friedery
SVP & CFO: R.J. Seabrook
SVP & Secy: D.A. Westerlund
VP & Treas: S. Morrison

Investor Contact: A.T. Scott (303-460-3537)
Board of Directors: H. M. Dean, H. C. Fiedler, R. D. Hoover, J. F. Lehman, G. R. Nelson, J. Nicholson, G. A. Sissel, G. M. Smart, T. M. Solso, S. A. Taylor, II, E. H. van der Kaay

Founded: 1880
Domicile: Indiana
Employees: 13,100

STANDARD &POOR'S

Bank of America Corp

S&P Recommendation STRONG BUY ★★★★★

Price $53.70 (as of Oct 27, 2006)

12-Mo. Target Price $63.00

Investment Style Large-Cap Value

GICS Sector Financials
Sub-Industry Other Diversified Financial Services

Comment This banking company has offices in 31 states and in Washington, D.C., and provides international corporate financial services.

Key Stock Statistics (Source S&P, Vickers, company reports)

52-Wk Range	$54.87–42.75	S&P Oper. EPS 2006E	4.60	P/E on S&P Oper. EPS 2006E	11.7	Dividend Rate/Share	$2.24
Trailing 12-Month EPS	$4.32	S&P Oper. EPS 2007E	4.88	Common Shares Outstg. (M)	4,525.9	Yield (%)	4.17
Trailing 12-Month P/E	12.4	S&P Core EPS 2006E	4.54	Market Capitalization(B)	$243.040	Beta	0.57
$10K Invested 5 Yrs Ago	$21,551	S&P Core EPS 2007E	4.83	Institutional Ownership (%)	60	S&P Credit Rating	AA-

Price Performance

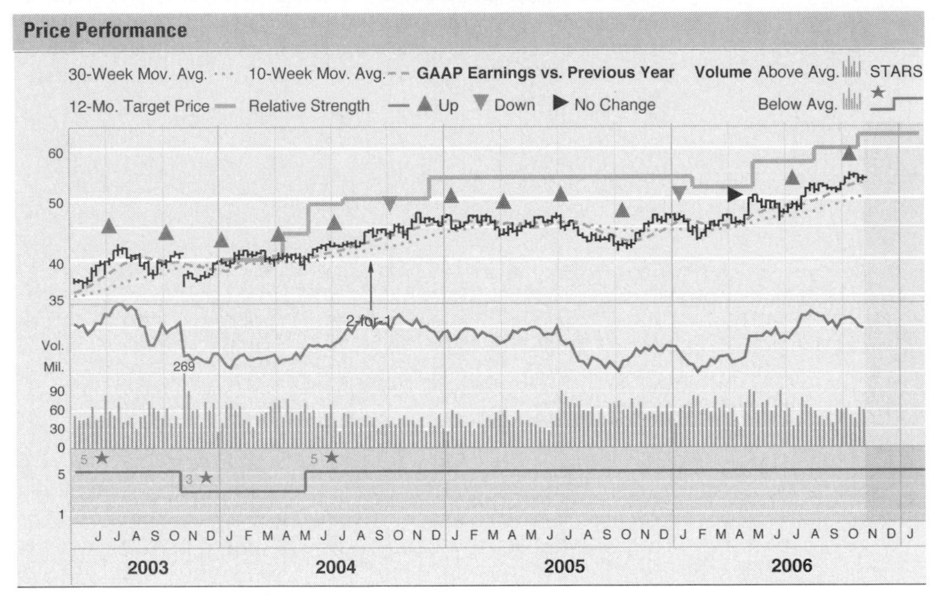

Options: ASE, CBOE, P, Ph

Analysis prepared by **Mark Hebeka, CFA** on October 24, 2006, when the stock traded at **$ 53.40**.

Highlights

- We continue to anticipate that non-mortgage consumer, commercial lending and market-sensitive fee-based businesses will drive revenue growth in a healthy economy in 2006 and 2007. We believe that continued solid credit quality and efficiency improvements are likely to make a positive contribution to the company's earnings growth. We view the acquisition of MBNA as an opportunity for BAC to add higher returning loans to its portfolio and help mitigate the effects of a challenging interest rate environment.
- We look for the net interest margin to remain relatively stable or widen slightly through 2007 if the Treasury yield curve steepens modestly from current levels. We think expenses will remain under tight control, and we see the company's efficiency ratio improving steadily in the quarters ahead.
- Excluding merger-related expense, we estimate operating EPS of $4.60 in 2006, up from operating EPS of $4.21 in 2005. Our 2007 EPS estimate is $4.88.

Investment Rationale/Risk

- We believe BAC shares offer an attractive risk/reward ratio at current valuation levels, and an above-peer dividend yield. We view BAC's acquisition of MBNA for about $35 billion in early 2006 as having a minor negative effect on credit quality but believe this will be outweighed by increased revenue from the addition of credit card loans.
- Risks to our recommendation and target price include a failure to derive projected cost savings, litigation costs potentially exceeding our expectations, significant credit quality deterioration, a severe economic downturn, or a serious event that could affect domestic equity markets.
- Our 12-month target price of $63 equates to 12.9X our 2007 operating EPS estimate, compared to about 11.5X, on average, for peers. Our valuation is based on our expectation of strong economic conditions, BAC's extensive geographic footprint, and our view of its balanced business model.

Qualitative Risk Assessment

LOW | MEDIUM | HIGH

Our risk assessment reflects what we see as strong business fundamentals and a robust customer base. We view BAC as having a diverse product line and geographic presence, which should enable it to withstand a major economic downturn.

Quantitative Evaluations

S&P Quality Ranking A-

D | C | B- | B | B+ | A- | A | A+

Relative Strength Rank MODERATE

48

LOWEST = 1 HIGHEST = 99

Revenue/Earnings Data

Revenue (Million $)

	1Q	2Q	3Q	4Q	Year
2006	27,026	28,895	--	--	--
2005	19,168	21,222	21,621	22,280	83,980
2004	12,289	16,448	16,413	--	63,324
2003	11,410	12,250	12,294	12,111	48,065
2002	11,311	11,465	11,405	--	45,732
2001	14,021	13,666	12,751	--	52,641

Earnings Per Share ($)

2006	1.07	1.19	1.18	**E**1.14	**E**4.60
2005	1.07	1.17	0.95	0.88	4.04
2004	0.92	0.93	0.91	0.94	3.69
2003	0.80	0.90	0.96	0.92	3.57
2002	0.69	0.70	0.73	0.85	2.96
2001	0.58	0.62	0.26	0.64	2.09

Fiscal year ended Dec. 31. Next earnings report expected: Late January. EPS Estimates based on S&P Operating Earnings; historical GAAP earnings are as reported.

Dividend Data (Dates: mm/dd Payment Date: mm/dd/yy)

Amount ($)	Date Decl.	Ex-Div. Date	Stk. of Record	Payment Date
0.500	01/25	03/01	03/03	03/24/06
0.500	04/26	05/31	06/02	06/23/06
0.560	07/26	08/30	09/01	09/22/06
0.560	10/25	11/29	12/01	12/22/06

Dividends have been paid since 1903. Source: Company reports.

Bank of America Corp

Business Summary October 24, 2006

CORPORATE OVERVIEW. Bank of America has operations in 31 countries, with about 6,000 banking centers and approximately 17,000 ATMs in the U.S. at the end of 2005. BAC reports the results of its operations through four business segments: Global Consumer and Small Business Banking, Global Business and Financial Services, Global Capital Markets and Investment Banking, and Global Wealth and Investment Management.

Global Consumer and Small Business Banking provides a diversified range of products and services to individuals and small businesses through multiple delivery channels. Global Business and Financial Services serves domestic and international business clients providing financial services, specialized industry expertise and local delivery through a global team of client managers and a variety of businesses. Global Capital Markets and Investment Banking provides capital-raising solutions, advisory services, derivatives capabilities, equity and debt sales and trading for BAC's clients, as well as traditional bank deposit and loan products, and treasury management and payment services for large corporations and institutional clients. Global Wealth and Investment Management offers investment services, estate management, financial planning services, fiduciary management, credit and banking expertise, and diversified asset management products to institutional clients as well as high-net-worth individuals.

IMPACT OF MAJOR DEVELOPMENTS. After the January 1, 2006, acquisition of MBNA Corp., Bank of America Card Services had more than 40 million active accounts and nearly $140 billion in managed balances, making it the largest credit card issuer in the U.S., measured by balances.

Company Financials

Per Share Data ($) Year Ended Dec. 31	**2005**	**2004**	**2003**	**2002**	**2001**	**2000**	**1999**	**1998**	**1997**	**1996**
Tangible Book Value	13.18	12.41	12.34	12.59	11.65	10.66	9.06	9.01	8.33	9.21
Earnings	4.04	3.69	3.57	2.96	2.09	2.26	2.24	1.45	2.09	2.00
S&P Core Earnings	4.06	3.75	3.54	2.70	1.96	NA	NA	NA	NA	NA
Dividends	1.90	1.70	1.44	1.22	1.14	1.03	0.93	0.80	0.69	0.60
Payout Ratio	47%	46%	40%	41%	55%	46%	41%	55%	33%	30%
Prices:High	47.44	47.47	42.45	38.54	32.77	30.50	38.19	44.22	35.84	26.31
Prices:Low	41.13	38.51	32.13	26.98	22.50	18.16	23.81	22.00	24.00	16.09
P/E Ratio:High	12	13	12	13	16	13	17	30	17	13
P/E Ratio:Low	10	10	9	9	11	8	11	15	12	8
Income Statement Analysis (Million $)										
Net Interest Income	30,737	28,797	21,464	20,923	20,290	18,442	18,237	18,298	7,898	6,329
Tax Equivalent Adjustment	832	716	643	588	343	322	215	128	116	94.0
Non Interest Income	26,438	20,097	16,422	13,571	14,348	14,489	14,069	12,189	6,351	3,646
Loan Loss Provision	4,014	2,769	2,839	3,697	4,287	2,535	182	2,920	800	605
% Expense/Operating Revenue	50.4%	54.5%	52.2%	63.1%	59.8%	63.7%	56.9%	67.4%	52.3%	57.4%
Pretax Income	24,480	21,221	15,861	12,991	10,117	11,788	12,215	8,048	4,796	3,634
Effective Tax Rate	32.7%	33.4%	31.8%	28.8%	32.9%	36.2%	35.5%	35.8%	35.8%	34.6%
Net Income	16,465	14,143	10,810	9,249	6,792	7,517	7,882	5,165	3,077	2,452
% Net Interest Margin	2.84	3.26	3.36	3.75	3.68	3.22	3.47	3.69	3.79	3.62
S&P Core Earnings	16,499	14,308	10,708	8,452	6,384	NA	NA	NA	NA	NA
Balance Sheet & Other Financial Data (Million $)										
Money Market Assets	294,292	197,308	153,090	115,687	81,384	76,544	81,226	73,498	36,095	27,491
Investment Securities	221,603	195,073	68,240	69,148	85,499	65,838	83,069	80,587	47,203	14,387
Commercial Loans	218,334	193,930	131,304	145,170	163,898	203,542	195,779	196,130	71,442	58,796
Other Loans	355,457	327,907	240,159	197,585	165,255	188,651	174,883	161,198	69,568	61,519
Total Assets	1,291,803	1,110,457	736,445	660,458	621,764	642,191	632,574	617,679	264,562	185,794
Demand Deposits	186,736	169,899	121,530	124,359	113,934	100,645	95,469	94,336	34,674	25,738
Time Deposits	447,934	448,671	292,583	262,099	259,561	263,599	251,804	262,974	103,520	80,760
Long Term Debt	100,848	98,078	75,343	67,176	68,026	72,502	60,441	50,842	27,204	22,985
Common Equity	101,262	99,374	47,926	50,261	48,455	47,556	44,355	45,855	21,243	13,538
% Return on Assets	1.4	1.5	1.5	1.4	1.1	1.2	1.3	0.9	1.4	13.0
% Return on Equity	16.3	19.2	22.0	18.7	14.1	16.3	17.5	11.5	17.6	18.0
% Loan Loss Reserve	1.4	1.7	1.7	2.0	2.1	1.7	1.8	2.0	1.9	1.9
% Loans/Deposits	87.4	84.4	89.7	88.4	97.8	107.7	106.7	99.4	104.1	113.0
% Equity to Assets	8.4	8.0	7.0	7.7	7.6	7.2	7.2	7.6	7.7	7.0

Data as orig reptd.; bef. results of disc opers/spec. items. Per share data adj. for stk. divs.; EPS diluted. E-Estimated. NA-Not Available. NM-Not Meaningful. NR-Not Ranked. UR-Under Review.

Office: 100 N Tryon St, Charlotte, NC 28255.
Telephone: 704-386-8486.
Website: http://www.bankofamerica.com
Chrmn, Pres & CEO: K.D. Lewis

CFO: A.G. de Molina
Investor Contact: K. Stitt (704-386-5667)

Board of Directors: W. Barnet, III, F. P. Bramble, Sr., J. T. Collins, G. L. Countryman, T. R. Franks, P. Fulton, C. K. Gifford, W. S. Jones, K. D. Lewis, M. C. Lozano, W. E. Massey, T. J. May, P. E. Mitchell, T. M. Ryan, O. T. Sloan, Jr., M. R. Spangler, R. L. Tillman, J. M. Ward

Founded: 1874
Domicile: Delaware
Employees: 176,638

STANDARD &POOR'S

Bank of New York Co Inc. (The)

S&P Recommendation	Price	12-Mo. Target Price	Investment Style
HOLD ★★★★★	$34.42 (as of Oct 30, 2006)	$39.00	Large-Cap Value

GICS Sector Financials
Sub-Industry Asset Management & Custody Banks

Comment BK is a leader in securities processing, and also provides a complete range of banking and other financial services.

Key Stock Statistics (Source S&P, Vickers, company reports)

52-Wk Range	$38.00–30.81	S&P Oper. EPS 2006E	2.23	P/E on S&P Oper. EPS 2006E	15.4	Dividend Rate/Share	$0.88
Trailing 12-Month EPS	$2.11	S&P Oper. EPS 2007E	2.43	Common Shares Outstg. (M)	763.0	Yield (%)	2.56
Trailing 12-Month P/E	16.3	S&P Core EPS 2006E	2.20	Market Capitalization(B)	$26.262	Beta	1.52
$10K Invested 5 Yrs Ago	$10,888	S&P Core EPS 2007E	2.42	Institutional Ownership (%)	71	S&P Credit Rating	A+

Price Performance

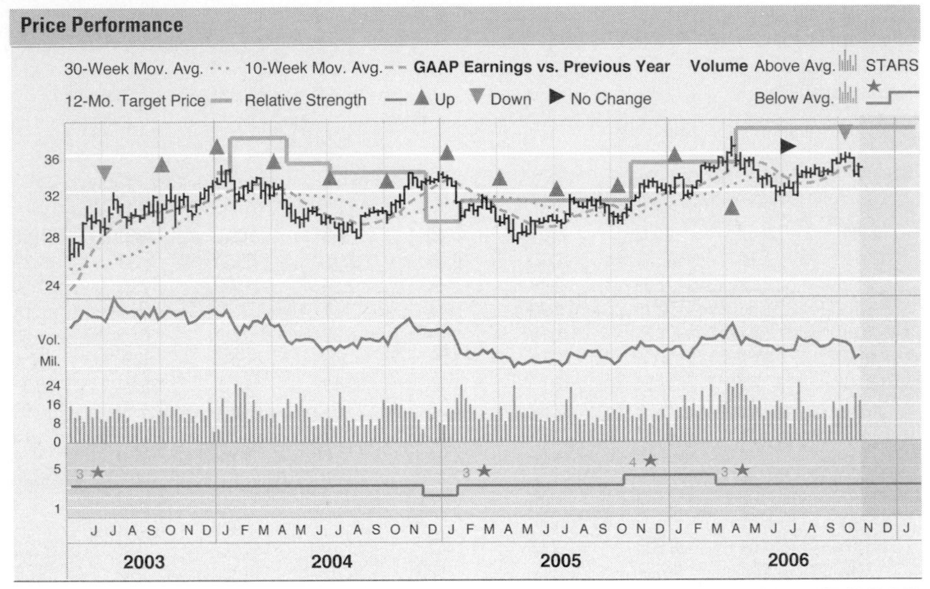

Options: ASE, CBOE, P, Ph

Analysis prepared by **Mark Hebeka, CFA** on October 30, 2006, when the stock traded at **$ 34.50**.

Highlights

- We expect 2006 and 2007 revenue growth based on our projections of healthy capital markets activity and strong economic conditions. Key areas that we believe offer growth through 2007 are execution and clearing services, foreign exchange, and trading. In the longer term, we think a trend on the part of investment advisors and brokers toward outsourcing middle and back-office processing will be a driver for revenue growth.
- We look for foreign partnerships to help diversify the business mix and we believe they will be an area of healthy growth in the future. We are encouraged by BK's business strategy and see continued expense discipline and expansion through acquisitions and international alliances going forward.
- We project 2006 operating EPS of $2.23, up from 2005's $2.03, implying EPS growth slightly below our long-term EPS growth projection of 10% a year. Our 2007 operating EPS estimate is $2.43.

Investment Rationale/Risk

- On October 1, BK swapped its retail banking and regional middle-market business for the corporate trust business of JP Morgan Chase (JPM: hold, $48) plus $150 million in cash. We have a positive view on the long-term growth prospects of this deal for BK, but it is not expected to be accretive to the company's operating earnings until 2009.
- Risks to our recommendation and target price include a significant decline in capital markets activity, credit losses and/or loan loss reserve provisions that are greater than our expectations, and adverse resolutions of ongoing regulatory investigations and other legal proceedings.
- Our 12-month target price of $39 is based on our dividend discount model, assuming 10% annual EPS growth over the next five years and a discount rate of 8.5%. This equates to a P/E of approximately 16X our 2007 EPS estimate, slightly below peers.

Qualitative Risk Assessment

LOW	MEDIUM	HIGH

Our risk assessment for Bank of New York reflects what we view as solid fundamentals and diverse business lines. BK has provided stable earnings over the long term and we believe it would be able to sustain a prolonged economic downturn.

Quantitative Evaluations

S&P Quality Ranking A-

D	C	B-	B	B+	A-	A	A+

Relative Strength Rank MODERATE

32

LOWEST = 1 HIGHEST = 99

Revenue/Earnings Data

Revenue (Million $)

	1Q	2Q	3Q	4Q	Year
2006	2,330	2,276	2,219	--	--
2005	1,917	2,077	2,126	2,230	8,312
2004	1,671	1,767	1,739	1,968	7,144
2003	1,420	1,591	1,638	1,686	6,336
2002	1,480	1,530	1,285	1,461	5,756
2001	1,891	1,781	1,745	1,777	7,160

Earnings Per Share ($)

	1Q	2Q	3Q	4Q	Year
2006	0.55	0.52	0.39	E0.54	E2.23
2005	0.49	0.52	0.51	0.53	2.03
2004	0.47	0.48	0.46	0.45	1.85
2003	0.41	0.39	0.34	0.40	1.52
2002	0.50	0.50	0.11	0.14	1.24
2001	0.52	0.52	0.33	0.45	1.81

Fiscal year ended Dec. 31. Next earnings report expected: Mid January. EPS Estimates based on S&P Operating Earnings; historical GAAP earnings are as reported.

Dividend Data (Dates: mm/dd Payment Date: mm/dd/yy)

Amount ($)	Date Decl.	Ex-Div. Date	Stk. of Record	Payment Date
0.210	01/10	01/23	01/25	02/02/06
0.210	04/11	04/24	04/26	05/05/06
0.220	07/11	07/24	07/26	08/04/06
0.220	10/10	10/23	10/25	11/03/06

Dividends have been paid since 1785. Source: Company reports.

Please read the Required Disclosures and Analyst Certification on the last page of this report.

Bank of New York Co Inc. (The)

Business Summary October 30, 2006

CORPORATE OVERVIEW. Bank of New York provides a comprehensive array of services that enable institutions and individuals to move and manage their financial assets in more than 100 markets worldwide. The company has several core competencies: institutional services, private banking, and asset management. Its global client base includes a broad range of leading financial institutions, corporations, government entities, endowments, and foundations.

Key products include advisory and asset management services to support the investment decision, trade execution, clearance and settlement capabilities, custody, securities lending, accounting, and administrative services for investment portfolios, sophisticated risk and performance measurement tools for analyzing portfolios, and services for issuers of both equity and debt securities.

CORPORATE STRATEGY. BK's strategy over the past decade has been to focus on scalable, fee-based securities servicing and fiduciary businesses, and it has achieved top three market share in most of its major product lines. The company attempts to distinguish itself competitively by offering products and services around the investment lifecycle.

By providing integrated solutions for clients' needs, BK strives to be the preferred partner in helping its clients succeed in the world's rapidly evolving financial markets. The company's key objectives include achieving positive operating leverage on an annual basis and sustaining top-line growth by expanding client relationships and winning new ones.

To achieve its top objectives, BK has grown both through internal reinvestments as well as the execution of strategic acquisitions to expand product offerings and increase market share in its scale businesses. Internal reinvestment occurs mainly through increased technology spending, staffing levels, marketing/branding initiatives, quality programs, and product development. The company invests in technology to improve the breadth and quality of its product offerings, and to increase economies of scale. BK has acquired over 90 businesses over the past 10 years, almost exclusively in its securities servicing and asset management areas.

Company Financials

Per Share Data ($) Year Ended Dec. 31	2005	2004	2003	2002	2001	2000	1999	1998	1997	1996
Tangible Book Value	7.06	6.45	5.59	5.66	5.79	8.30	6.95	7.05	6.67	6.50
Earnings	2.03	1.85	1.52	1.24	1.81	1.92	2.27	1.53	1.36	1.24
S&P Core Earnings	1.99	1.73	1.46	1.01	1.56	NA	NA	NA	NA	NA
Dividends	0.82	0.79	0.76	0.76	0.72	0.66	0.58	0.54	0.49	0.42
Payout Ratio	40%	43%	50%	61%	40%	34%	26%	35%	36%	34%
Prices:High	33.69	34.85	33.49	46.50	58.13	59.38	45.19	40.56	29.28	18.06
Prices:Low	26.93	27.25	19.25	20.85	29.75	29.75	31.81	24.00	16.38	10.88
P/E Ratio:High	17	19	22	37	32	31	20	27	22	15
P/E Ratio:Low	13	15	13	17	16	15	14	16	12	9

Income Statement Analysis (Million $)	2005	2004	2003	2002	2001	2000	1999	1998	1997	1996
Net Interest Income	1,909	1,645	1,609	1,665	1,681	1,870	1,701	1,651	1,855	1,961
Tax Equivalent Adjustment	29.0	30.0	35.0	49.0	60.0	54.0	44.0	58.0	35.0	38.0
Non Interest Income	4,888	4,613	3,971	3,261	3,386	2,959	3,294	2,108	2,001	2,033
Loan Loss Provision	15.0	15.0	155	685	375	105	135	20.0	280	600
% Expense/Operating Revenue	65.7%	65.6%	65.9%	55.3%	54.4%	51.4%	44.0%	50.5%	48.6%	45.6%
Pretax Income	2,367	2,199	1,762	1,372	2,058	2,251	2,840	1,891	1,773	1,656
Effective Tax Rate	33.6%	34.5%	34.3%	34.3%	34.7%	36.5%	38.8%	37.0%	37.7%	38.3%
Net Income	1,571	1,440	1,157	902	1,343	1,429	1,739	1,192	1,104	1,020
% Net Interest Margin	2.36	2.07	2.22	2.62	2.57	2.96	3.11	3.24	3.89	4.35
S&P Core Earnings	1,536	1,350	1,097	728	1,159	NA	NA	NA	NA	NA

Balance Sheet & Other Financial Data (Million $)	2005	2004	2003	2002	2001	2000	1999	1998	1997	1996
Money Market Assets	16,999	18,527	18,521	13,798	19,684	23,178	20,948	9,422	7,562	3,249
Investment Securities	27,326	23,802	22,903	18,300	12,862	7,401	6,899	6,415	6,628	5,053
Commercial Loans	13,252	12,624	13,646	20,335	19,034	21,327	17,851	16,407	14,429	12,844
Other Loans	27,474	23,157	21,637	11,004	16,713	14,934	21,251	21,979	20,698	24,162
Total Assets	102,074	94,529	92,397	77,564	81,025	77,114	74,756	63,503	59,961	55,765
Demand Deposits	18,236	17,442	14,789	13,301	12,635	13,255	12,162	11,480	12,561	11,812
Time Deposits	46,188	41,279	41,617	42,086	43,076	43,121	43,589	33,152	28,796	27,531
Long Term Debt	Nil	Nil	Nil	Nil	Nil	4,536	4,311	3,386	1,809	1,816
Common Equity	9,876	9,290	8,428	6,684	6,317	6,151	5,142	5,447	5,001	5,015
% Return on Assets	1.6	1.5	1.4	1.1	1.7	1.9	2.5	1.9	1.9	1.9
% Return on Equity	16.4	16.3	15.3	13.9	21.5	25.3	32.8	22.8	21.9	20.0
% Loan Loss Reserve	1.0	1.7	1.9	2.7	1.7	1.7	1.6	1.7	1.8	2.4
% Loans/Deposits	63.2	60.9	62.6	56.6	64.2	64.3	67.3	86.0	84.9	94.1
% Equity to Assets	9.7	9.5	8.9	8.2	7.9	7.4	7.7	8.5	8.7	9.3

Data as orig reptd.; bef. results of disc opers/spec. items. Per share data adj. for stk. divs.; EPS diluted. E-Estimated. NA-Not Available. NM-Not Meaningful. NR-Not Ranked. UR-Under Review.

Office: One Wall Street, New York, NY 10286.
Telephone: 212-495-1784.
Email: shareowner-svcs@bankofny.com
Website: http://www.bankofny.com

Chrmn & CEO: T.A. Renyi
Pres: G.L. Hassell
Vice Chrmn: B.W. Van Saun
Vice Chrmn & Chief Admin: D.R. Monks

Vice Chrmn, Secy & General Counsel: J.M. Liftin
Investor Contact: J.F. Murphy (212- 635-7740)
Board of Directors: F. J. Biondi, Jr., N. M. Donofrio, G. L. Hassell, R. J. Kogan, M. J. Kowalski, J. A. Luke, Jr., J. C. Malone, P. Myners, C. A. Rein, T. A. Renyi, W. C. Richardson, B. L. Roberts, S. C. Scott, III, R. C. Vaughan

Founded: 1784
Domicile: New York
Employees: 23,451

STANDARD &POOR'S

Bard (C.R.) Inc

S&P Recommendation HOLD ★★★★★

Price $81.81 (as of Oct 27, 2006)

12-Mo. Target Price $85.00

Investment Style Mid-Cap Growth

GICS Sector Health Care
Sub-Industry Health Care Equipment

Comment This diversified maker of therapeutic and diagnostic medical devices has exposure to the vascular, urology, oncology and specialty surgical markets.

Key Stock Statistics (Source S&P, Vickers, company reports)

52-Wk Range	$84.96–59.89	S&P Oper. EPS 2006E	3.31	P/E on S&P Oper. EPS 2006E	24.7	Dividend Rate/Share	$0.56
Trailing 12-Month EPS	$3.09	S&P Oper. EPS 2007E	3.78	Common Shares Outstg. (M)	103.5	Yield (%)	0.68
Trailing 12-Month P/E	26.5	S&P Core EPS 2006E	3.31	Market Capitalization(B)	$8.468	Beta	0.49
$10K Invested 5 Yrs Ago	$30,569	S&P Core EPS 2007E	3.78	Institutional Ownership (%)	86	S&P Credit Rating	A

Price Performance

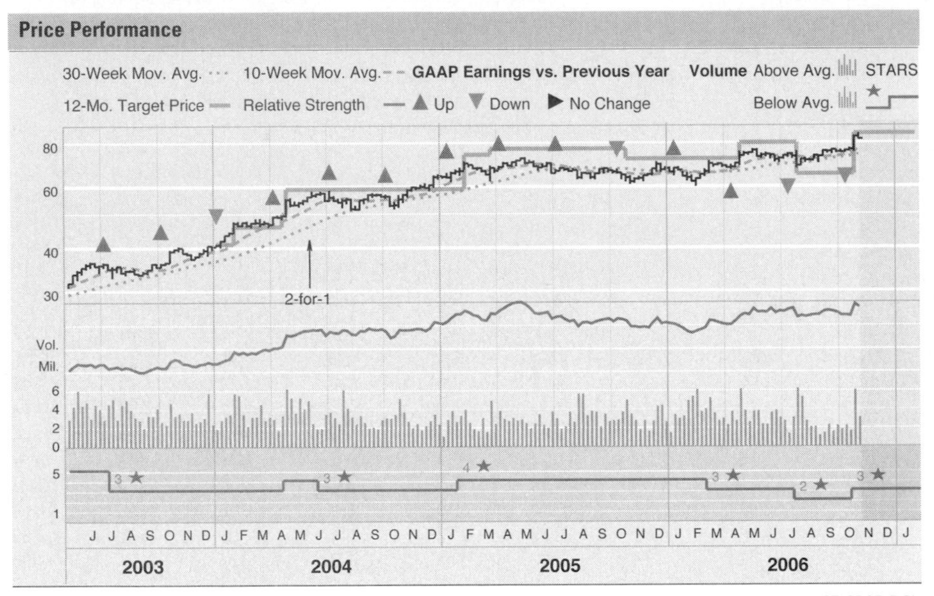

Options: ASE, CBOE, P, Ph

Analysis prepared by **Robert M. Gold** on October 20, 2006, when the stock traded at **$ 83.06**.

Highlights

- We believe net sales in 2007 will approximate $2.20 billion, up from a projected $1.98 billion in 2006, as balanced growth across the vascular, urology and oncology business segments joins with modest expectations in the specialty surgical area. We believe new product launches will continue to provide incremental sales growth in 2007, and note that expected launches in 2007 will include a new PTA balloon, ablation catheter, hernia fixation system and vena cava filter.
- We think significant gross margin expansion opportunities will be available in 2007, driven by new product introductions and the favorable impact of increased product manufacturing at a facility in Puerto Rico. We expect that SG&A costs will remain at about 30% of sales, with R&D costs absorbing 6% to 7% of sales. We see an effective tax rate of 27.0% to 27.5% through 2008.
- We estimate 2006 operating EPS of $3.31, with an approximate 14% rise to $3.78 in 2007. Both years include $0.20 of projected stock-based compensation costs.

Investment Rationale/Risk

- We believe new products in the oncology, hernia repair and urology segments, plus momentum in existing categories, will help drive low double digit constant currency sales growth over the coming three years. In our view, the adverse gross margin impact from the Venetec International acquisition will abate in 2007, and we think this deal can potentially boost sales to acute care hospitals. We do have some concerns about the sustainable growth rate in the hernia repair franchise.
- Risks to our opinion and target price include unfavorable patent litigation outcomes, adverse reimbursement changes and failure to commercialize new products in a timely fashion.
- BCR's projected growth rate is slightly below peers, with organic sales growth of about 10% annually expected in coming years. However, we think the revenue stream is less volatile than peers, and think the prospect of rising gross and operating margins justifies a slight valuation premium. By applying a forward P/E to growth (PEG) ratio of 1.6X to our 2007 EPS estimate of $3.78, and assuming three-year EPS growth of 14%, our 12-month target price is $85.

Qualitative Risk Assessment

LOW | **MEDIUM** | HIGH

Our risk assessment reflects that BCR operates in a highly competitive environment. In addition, hospital customers generate a large portion of revenues from Medicare, and are therefore subject to reimbursement risks that could reduce prices paid to suppliers. However, we believe BCR's product line is largely focused on areas that have not been subject to intense pricing pressure, and we think management has a solid track record in terms of identifying and integrating acquisitions.

Quantitative Evaluations

S&P Quality Ranking A-

D | C | B- | B | B+ | **A-** | A | A+

Relative Strength Rank STRONG

78

LOWEST = 1 HIGHEST = 99

Revenue/Earnings Data

Revenue (Million $)

	1Q	2Q	3Q	4Q	Year
2006	467.5	498.2	498.9	--	--
2005	428.6	447.4	443.3	452.0	1,771
2004	393.8	416.3	421.9	424.1	1,656
2003	335.9	354.2	361.8	381.2	1,433
2002	301.9	317.5	322.7	331.7	1,274
2001	284.8	295.9	297.8	302.8	1,181

Earnings Per Share ($)

	1Q	2Q	3Q	4Q	Year
2006	0.76	0.76	0.82	E0.86	E3.31
2005	0.75	0.79	0.83	0.75	3.12
2004	0.68	0.55	0.95	0.65	2.82
2003	0.45	0.47	0.49	0.20	1.60
2002	0.33	0.42	0.29	0.45	1.47
2001	0.33	0.34	0.34	0.37	1.38

Fiscal year ended Dec. 31. Next earnings report expected: Late January. EPS Estimates based on S&P Operating Earnings; historical GAAP earnings are as reported.

Dividend Data (Dates: mm/dd Payment Date: mm/dd/yy)

Amount ($)	Date Decl.	Ex-Div. Date	Stk. of Record	Payment Date
0.130	12/14	01/19	01/23	02/03/06
0.130	04/19	04/27	05/01	05/12/06
0.140	06/14	07/20	07/24	08/04/06
0.140	10/11	10/19	10/23	11/03/06

Dividends have been paid since 1960. Source: Company reports.

Bard (C.R.) Inc

Business Summary October 20, 2006

CORPORATE OVERVIEW. This company offers a range of medical, surgical, diagnostic and patient care devices. Sales in 2005 came from urology (30%), vascular (24%), oncology (23%), surgery (19%), and other (4%) products.

Bard's vascular products include percutaneous transluminal angioplasty catheters, guide wires, introducers and accessories, peripheral stents, vena cava filters and biopsy devices; electrophysiology products such as lab systems, and diagnostic therapeutic and temporary pacing electrode catheters; and fabrics, meshes and implantable vascular grafts.

Urological diagnosis and intervention products include Foley catheters, procedure kits and trays, and related urine monitoring and collection systems; urethral stents; and specialty devices for incontinence, endoscopic procedures, and stone removal. Newer products include the Infection Control Foley catheter that reduces the rate of urinary tract infections; a collagen implant and sling materials used to treat urinary incontinence; and brachytherapy services, devices, and radioactive seeds to treat prostate cancer.

Oncology products include specialty access catheters and ports; gastroenterological products (endoscopic accessories, percutaneous feeding devices and stents); biopsy devices; and a suturing system for gastroesophageal reflux disease.

Surgical specialties products include meshes for hernia and other soft tissue repairs; irrigation devices for orthopedic, laparoscopic and gynecological procedures; and topical hemostatic devices. In January 2003, Bard introduced the VentralexT hernia patch, a simplified intra-abdominal hernia repair technology characterized by minimal suturing, small incisions, and potentially shorter recovery times. To further expand its markets around the hernia repair call point, in June 2004, Bard acquired the Salute Fixation system and related technology from Onux Inc. The device is used to attach mesh to host tissue for laparoscopic hernia repair procedures.

Company Financials

Per Share Data ($) Year Ended Dec. 31	**2005**	**2004**	**2003**	**2002**	**2001**	**2000**	**1999**	**1998**	**1997**	**1996**
Tangible Book Value	10.39	7.26	5.35	4.84	3.97	2.53	2.34	2.03	1.31	1.36
Cash Flow	3.71	3.33	2.03	1.87	1.89	1.53	1.61	2.78	1.13	1.32
Earnings	3.12	2.82	1.60	1.47	1.38	1.04	1.14	2.26	0.63	0.81
S&P Core Earnings	2.86	2.29	1.73	1.27	1.21	NA	NA	NA	NA	NA
Dividends	0.50	0.47	0.45	0.43	0.42	0.41	0.39	0.37	0.35	0.33
Payout Ratio	16%	17%	28%	29%	31%	39%	34%	16%	56%	41%
Prices:High	72.79	65.13	40.80	31.97	32.47	27.47	29.94	25.13	19.50	18.69
Prices:Low	60.82	40.09	27.02	22.05	20.43	17.50	20.84	14.25	13.19	12.94
P/E Ratio:High	23	23	25	22	24	26	26	11	31	23
P/E Ratio:Low	19	14	17	15	15	17	18	6	21	16
Income Statement Analysis (Million $)										
Revenue	1,771	1,656	1,433	1,274	1,181	1,099	1,037	1,165	1,214	1,194
Operating Income	503	418	333	295	266	244	239	217	222	227
Depreciation	63.8	54.7	44.7	42.3	53.2	49.6	49.1	58.7	57.3	57.4
Interest Expense	12.2	12.7	12.5	12.6	14.2	19.3	19.3	26.4	32.9	26.4
Pretax Income	450	414	223	211	205	154	173	464	105	103
Effective Tax Rate	25.0%	26.9%	24.5%	26.5%	30.1%	30.6%	31.9%	45.7%	31.1%	10.0%
Net Income	337	303	169	155	143	107	118	252	72.3	92.5
S&P Core Earnings	309	244	182	134	126	NA	NA	NA	NA	NA
Balance Sheet & Other Financial Data (Million $)										
Cash	754	541	417	23.1	30.8	21.3	17.3	25.6	8.00	78.0
Current Assets	1,264	1,054	875	758	647	527	529	489	564	577
Total Assets	2,266	2,009	1,692	1,417	1,231	1,089	1,126	1,080	1,279	1,333
Current Liabilities	641	390	422	317	235	225	353	303	311	336
Long Term Debt	0.80	151	152	152	156	204	158	160	341	343
Common Equity	1,536	1,360	1,046	880	789	614	574	568	573	602
Total Capital	1,544	1,534	1,197	1,033	945	818	733	728	914	945
Capital Expenditures	97.2	74.0	72.1	41.0	27.4	19.4	26.1	43.8	32.8	41.6
Cash Flow	401	358	213	197	196	157	167	311	130	150
Current Ratio	2.0	2.7	2.1	2.4	2.8	2.3	1.5	1.6	1.8	1.7
% Long Term Debt of Capitalization	0.1	9.9	12.7	14.7	16.5	25.0	21.6	22.0	37.3	36.3
% Net Income of Revenue	19.0	18.3	11.8	12.2	12.1	9.7	11.4	21.7	6.0	7.8
% Return on Assets	15.8	16.4	10.8	11.5	12.3	9.6	10.7	21.4	5.5	7.7
% Return on Equity	23.3	25.2	17.5	18.6	20.4	18.0	20.7	44.2	12.3	15.9

Data as orig reptd.; bef. results of disc opers/spec. items. Per share data adj. for stk. divs.; EPS diluted. E-Estimated. NA-Not Available. NM-Not Meaningful. NR-Not Ranked. UR-Under Review.

Office: 730 Central Avenue, Murray Hill, NJ 07974.
Telephone: 908-277-8000.
Website: http://www.crbard.com
Chrmn & CEO: T.M. Ring

Pres & COO: J.H. Weiland
SVP & CFO: T.C. Schermerhorn
VP & Treas: S.T. Lowry
VP, Secy & General Counsel: J.A. Reinsdorf

Investor Contact: E.J. Shick
Board of Directors: M. C. Breslawsky, T. K. Dunnigan, H. L. Henkel, T. E. Martin, G. K. Naughton, T. M. Ring, T. G. Thompson, J. H. Weiland, A. Welters, T. L. White

Founded: 1907
Domicile: New Jersey
Employees: 8,900

STANDARD &POOR'S

Barr Pharmaceuticals Inc

S&P Recommendation BUY ★★★★★

Price $50.70 (as of Oct 27, 2006)

12-Mo. Target Price $67.00

Investment Style Mid-Cap Growth

GICS Sector Health Care
Sub-Industry Pharmaceuticals

Comment This company (formerly Barr Laboratories) produces a wide range of generic pharmaceuticals in varying strengths. BRL also offers its own line of proprietary drug products. In June 2006, BRL agreed to acquire Croatia-based Pliva for about $2.3 billion in cash.

Key Stock Statistics (Source S&P, Vickers, company reports)

52-Wk Range	$70.25–44.60	S&P Oper. EPS 2007E	3.50	P/E on S&P Oper. EPS 2007E	14.5	Dividend Rate/Share	Nil
Trailing 12-Month EPS	$3.12	S&P Oper. EPS 2008E	4.00	Common Shares Outstg. (M)	106.2	Yield (%)	Nil
Trailing 12-Month P/E	16.3	S&P Core EPS 2007E	3.50	Market Capitalization(B)	$5.385	Beta	0.39
$10K Invested 5 Yrs Ago	$15,010	S&P Core EPS 2008E	4.00	Institutional Ownership (%)	85	S&P Credit Rating	NA

Price Performance

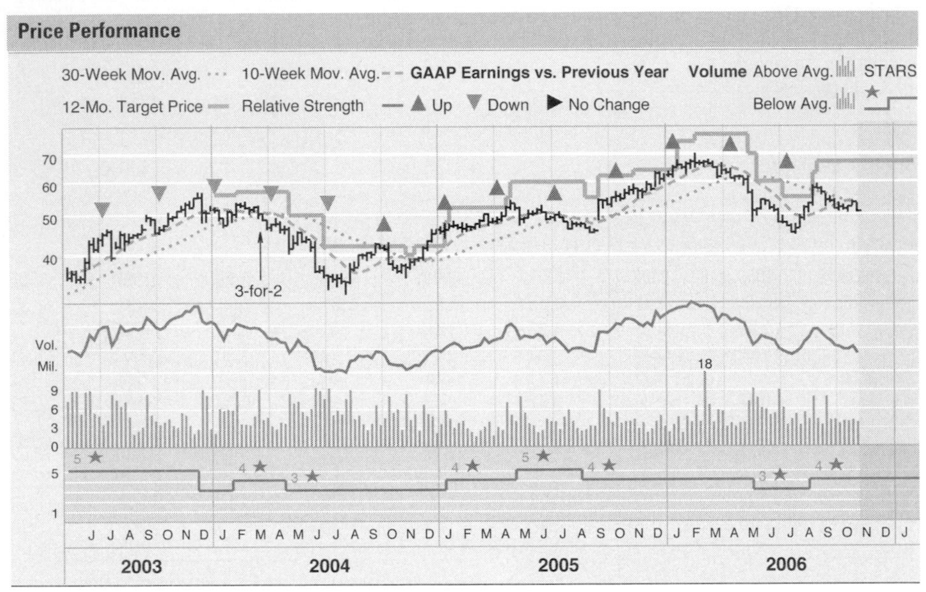

Options: ASE, CBOE, P, Ph

Analysis prepared by **Herman B. Saftlas** on August 29, 2006, when the stock traded at **$ 57.00**.

Highlights

- Barr is changing its fiscal year end from June to December. Based on Barr being an independent entity (excluding the planned acquisition of Pliva), we expect revenues for calendar 2007 to reach $1.6 billion, up from an indicated $1.5 billion for calendar 2006. We see volume augmented by generic versions of Allegra-D, Actiq, Adderall XR and Ortho-Cylen oral contraceptive. On the branded side, sales should be boosted by new products such as Seasonique and Kariva oral contraceptives, ParaGard IUD and Plan B emergency oral contraceptive.
- We foresee an improvement in gross margins on increased product sales, helped by a more profitable sales mix and manufacturing efficiencies. Results should also benefit from tight control over operating costs.
- We project calendar 2007 operating EPS of $3.70 (after estimated stock option expense), up from an estimated $3.25 for calendar 2006. Adjusted EPS (before special items) for FY 06 (Jun.) was $3.23.

Investment Rationale/Risk

- We are encouraged by positive developments at BRL, the most recent being FDA approval of the OTC sale of Plan B emergency oral contraceptive. BRL also recently settled patent litigation with Shire Pharmaceuticals, which will enable Barr to launch a generic version of Shire's Adderall XR drug for ADHD in 2009 and receive payments from Shire in exchange for certain assets. We think the planned acquisition of Croatian drugmaker Pliva, subject to necessary approvals, could provide significant long-term benefits. However, consummation of this deal depends on the outcome of a bidding contest with Iceland-based Actavis.
- Risks to our recommendation and target price include stronger than expected competition in key generic and branded drug lines, and failure to complete the proposed Pliva acquisition.
- Our 12-month target price of $67 applies a modest premium-to-peers P/E of 18.1X to our calendar 2007 EPS estimate of $3.70. Our DCF model, which assumes a WACC of 8.2%, and terminal growth of 2%, also supports intrinsic value of about $67.

Qualitative Risk Assessment

LOW | **MEDIUM** | HIGH

Our risk assessment reflects risks inherent in the generic pharmaceutical business, which include the ability to develop generic products and legally challenge branded patents. However, we believe Barr's proven expertise in developing novel generic and proprietary drugs, and successfully litigating patent challenges, together with our view of a strong balance sheet, provide a measure of stability to the company.

Quantitative Evaluations

S&P Quality Ranking **B**

D | C | B- | **B** | B+ | A- | A | A+

Relative Strength Rank **WEAK**

19

LOWEST = 1 HIGHEST = 99

Revenue/Earnings Data

Revenue (Million $)

	1Q	2Q	3Q	4Q	Year
2006	310.4	325.5	326.8	351.7	1,314
2005	244.5	257.4	265.0	280.5	1,047
2004	310.7	374.1	321.1	303.2	1,309
2003	220.4	209.0	171.9	301.5	902.9
2002	352.1	366.1	261.4	209.4	1,189
2001	111.8	135.2	137.3	140.9	509.7

Earnings Per Share ($)

	1Q	2Q	3Q	4Q	Year
2006	0.78	0.88	0.70	0.76	3.12
2005	0.49	0.56	0.58	0.40	2.03
2004	0.37	0.33	0.33	0.13	1.15
2003	0.41	0.42	0.44	0.35	1.62
2002	0.72	0.40	0.52	0.44	2.08
2001	0.15	0.19	0.20	0.22	0.74

Fiscal year ended Jun. 30. Next earnings report expected: Early November. EPS Estimates based on S&P Operating Earnings; historical GAAP earnings are as reported.

Dividend Data

No cash dividends have been paid.

Barr Pharmaceuticals Inc

Business Summary August 29, 2006

CORPORATE OVERVIEW. Founded in 1970, Barr Pharmaceuticals (formerly Barr Laboratories) is a leading developer, producer and marketer of generic pharmaceuticals, with a product focus on the therapeutic areas of psychotherapeutics, oncology, female health care (including hormone replacement and oral contraceptives), heart disease, and infection. BRL also sells a number of proprietary products. Acquisitions in recent years included Duramed Pharmaceuticals, a maker of women's health and hormone replacement products, and Enhance Pharmaceuticals, a research and development concern that is developing a vaginal ring drug delivery system.

Sales of generic oral contraceptives accounted for about 30% of total revenues in FY 06 (Jun.); other generic drugs 34%; proprietary products 28%; and alliance, development and other revenues 11%.

The company's generic division manufactures and distributes some 70 generic pharmaceuticals comprising more than 100 different dosage forms and strengths. Generic oral contraceptive sales totaled $399 million in FY 06, up from $397 million in FY 05. The company's oral contraceptives are sold under the Tri-Sprintec, Sprintec, Apri, Aviane, Kariva, Lessina, Nortrel, Sprintec and Errin names. Barr's portfolio of generic oral contraceptives comprises some 22 products. In December 2004, the FDA approved Barr's Enjuvia hormone replacement product.

The company also sells generic versions of antidepressants Prozac and Remeron, Tamoxifen for breast cancer, anticoagulant Coumadin, and Adderall, a treatment for attention deficit hyperactivity disorder (ADHD).

In its proprietary business, Barr manufactures and distributes some 13 branded pharmaceutical products, largely concentrated in the female healthcare arena. These products include Seasonale, an extended-cycle oral contraceptive product; Seasonique, a next-generation version of Seasonale; Cenestin, a synthetic conjugated estrogen; Plan B, an emergency contraceptive; Trexall, a methotrexate drug used to treat cancer, psoriasis and rheumatoid arthritis; and Viaspan, an organ transplant preservation solution. During FY 03, the company acquired U.S. rights from Wyeth to four branded drugs, including treatments for hypertension and glaucoma.

Company Financials

Per Share Data ($) Year Ended Jun. 30	**2006**	**2005**	**2004**	**2003**	**2002**	**2001**	**2000**	**1999**	**1998**	**1997**
Tangible Book Value	11.54	10.81	9.18	8.07	6.80	4.59	3.60	2.78	2.07	1.42
Cash Flow	3.70	2.41	1.45	1.84	2.21	0.86	0.66	0.74	0.50	0.32
Earnings	3.12	2.03	1.15	1.62	2.08	0.74	0.53	0.62	0.43	0.26
S&P Core Earnings	3.20	2.20	1.49	2.03	2.43	0.97	NA	NA	NA	NA
Dividends	Nil	Nil	Nil	Nil	Nil	Nil	Nil	Nil	Nil	Nil
Payout Ratio	Nil	Nil	Nil	Nil	Nil	Nil	Nil	Nil	Nil	Nil
Prices:High	70.25	63.60	53.99	56.91	35.56	40.27	35.61	14.39	14.74	14.78
Prices:Low	44.60	43.71	32.01	28.93	21.96	19.78	8.89	8.39	7.30	4.86
P/E Ratio:High	23	31	47	35	17	55	67	23	34	57
P/E Ratio:Low	14	22	28	18	11	27	17	14	17	19
Income Statement Analysis (Million $)										
Revenue	1,314	1,047	1,309	903	1,189	510	482	444	377	284
Operating Income	549	357	225	249	341	72.4	75.2	88.9	58.9	35.4
Depreciation	62.0	40.8	32.1	22.7	15.3	10.8	10.4	9.31	5.52	4.99
Interest Expense	0.49	1.46	2.64	1.47	3.53	1.86	2.41	2.70	0.86	0.94
Pretax Income	523	330	194	263	338	101	67.8	80.1	54.7	32.1
Effective Tax Rate	35.7%	34.8%	36.7%	36.2%	37.1%	38.2%	37.5%	38.5%	38.7%	39.3%
Net Income	336	215	123	168	212	62.5	42.3	49.3	33.5	19.4
S&P Core Earnings	345	233	159	141	166	55.3	NA	NA	NA	NA
Balance Sheet & Other Financial Data (Million $)										
Cash	602	643	452	412	331	222	156	103	73.0	31.9
Current Assets	1,109	993	878	848	638	437	315	248	217	127
Total Assets	1,921	1,483	1,333	1,181	889	543	424	348	311	204
Current Liabilities	187	213	208	275	177	152	113	101	122	85.3
Long Term Debt	7.43	15.5	32.4	34.0	42.6	24.9	28.1	30.0	32.2	14.9
Common Equity	1,691	1,234	1,042	868	667	366	282	214	156	102
Total Capital	1,698	1,249	1,074	902	709	391	311	246	189	118
Capital Expenditures	61.0	55.2	46.9	80.6	47.2	17.7	12.1	12.3	20.4	35.1
Cash Flow	398	256	155	190	226	73.3	52.8	58.6	39.0	24.4
Current Ratio	5.9	4.7	4.2	3.1	3.6	2.9	2.8	2.5	1.8	1.5
% Long Term Debt of Capitalization	0.4	1.2	3.0	3.8	6.0	6.4	9.0	12.2	17.0	12.6
% Net Income of Revenue	25.6	20.5	9.4	18.6	17.9	12.3	8.8	11.1	8.9	6.8
% Return on Assets	19.7	15.3	9.8	16.2	27.3	12.9	11.0	15.0	13.0	10.4
% Return on Equity	23.0	18.9	12.9	21.8	38.8	19.3	17.1	26.6	26.0	21.3

Data as orig reptd.; bef. results of disc opers/spec. items. Per share data adj. for stk. divs.; EPS diluted. E-Estimated. NA-Not Available. NM-Not Meaningful. NR-Not Ranked. UR-Under Review.

Office: 400 Chestnut Ridge Rd, Woodcliff Lake, NJ 07677-7604.
Telephone: 201-930-3300.
Email: ir@barrlabs.com
Website: http://www.barrlabs.com

Chrmn & CEO: B.L. Downey
VP, CFO, Treas & Secy: W.T. McKee
VP & General Counsel: F.J. Killion
Investor Contact: C.A. Cox (845-348-6808)

Board of Directors: P. M. Bisaro, H. N. Chefitz, B. L. Downey, R. R. Frankovic, J. S. Gilmore, III, P. R. Seaver, G. P. Stephan

Founded: 1970
Domicile: Delaware
Employees: 2,040

STANDARD &POOR'S

Bausch & Lomb Inc

S&P Recommendation HOLD ★★★★★ | **Price** $53.45 (as of Oct 27, 2006) | **12-Mo. Target Price** $47.00 | **Investment Style** Mid-Cap Value

GICS Sector Health Care
Sub-Industry Health Care Supplies

Comment The world's leading maker of contact lenses and related solutions, this company also produces ophthalmic drugs and consumer items.

Key Stock Statistics (Source S&P, Vickers, company reports)

52-Wk Range	**$84.30–40.75**	S&P Oper. EPS 2005**E**	**3.65**	P/E on S&P Oper. EPS 2005**E**	**14.6**	Dividend Rate/Share	**$0.52**
Trailing 12-Month EPS	**$2.68**	S&P Oper. EPS 2006**E**	**0.90**	Common Shares Outstg. (M)	**53.8**	Yield (%)	**0.97**
Trailing 12-Month P/E	**19.9**	S&P Core EPS 2005**E**	**3.15**	Market Capitalization(B)	**$2.866**	Beta	**0.74**
$10K Invested 5 Yrs Ago	**$16,497**	S&P Core EPS 2006**E**	**0.90**	Institutional Ownership (%)	**90**	S&P Credit Rating	**BBB**

Price Performance

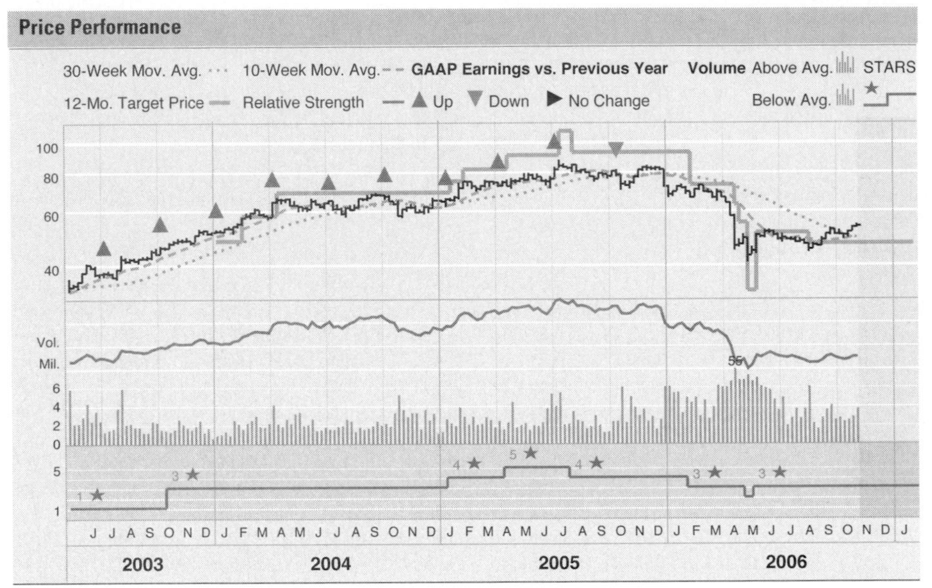

Options: ASE, CBOE, P, Ph

Analysis prepared by **Robert M. Gold** on August 14, 2006, when the stock traded at **$ 45.04**.

Highlights

- As of early August, BOL had not yet issued financial statements for the first half of 2006. Our 2006 revenue forecast is $2.3 billion, including an estimated $150 million of lost contact lens solution sales as a result of consumer concerns over possible fungus contamination. We believe concerns over the MoistureLoc product will result in lost sales of other BOL lens care products for the balance of 2006. We think 2007 sales can reach $2.5 billion.
- In our view, BOL's margins are at risk from the ReNu MoistureLoc contact lens solution issues, due to idle plant capacity, higher SG&A spending and litigation-related costs. Reflecting ongoing efforts to broaden the product pipeline and gain FDA approval to market new drugs, we expect R&D costs to consume 7.5% to 8.0% of sales through 2007.
- We believe the company's effective tax rate in 2006 and 2007 will be higher than originally anticipated, due to a revision on the amount of deferred tax assets on the balance sheet. We think 2006 operating EPS will approximate $0.90, including stock option expense of $0.28, and see 2007 EPS rising to $2.50.

Investment Rationale/Risk

- We think the company continues to face significant operational and financial challenges stemming from the removal of ReNu with MoistureLoc from the market, along with an internal investigation of accounting irregularities. In our opinion, Bausch & Lomb will need to significantly boost SG&A spending in order to rebuild consumer confidence in the Bausch & Lomb brand name. It will also need to issue audited financial statements for 2005 and through the first half of 2006 in a timely manner to restore investor confidence and avoid an outright default on its debt covenants.
- Risks to our recommendation and target price include an unfavorable resolution of internal accounting investigations and a slower than expected recovery in the lens solution segment.
- Our 12-month target price of $47, or nearly 19X our 2007 EPS estimate, is a premium to the P/E of the S&P 500 but below the company's medical device peers. In our opinion, a discount to peers is justified by the continued lack of visibility on forward sales and earnings growth, along with the lack of financial statement filings with the SEC for the past three quarters.

Qualitative Risk Assessment

LOW | MEDIUM | **HIGH**

Bausch & Lomb operates in a competitive and relatively low-margined segment of the health care sector. In addition, we think the company faces an extended period of litigation tied to possible eye fungal infections associated with the use of its ReNu with MoistureLoc product. We are also concerned about the company's failure to file audited financial statements with the SEC for several quarters (including for 2005), which put it in technical default of some debt covenants.

Quantitative Evaluations

S&P Quality Ranking **B**

D | C | B- | **B** | B+ | A- | A | A+

Relative Strength Rank **STRONG**

71

LOWEST = 1 HIGHEST = 99

Revenue/Earnings Data

Revenue (Million $)

	1Q	2Q	3Q	4Q	Year
2005	554.3	608.3	588.7	--	--
2004	510.3	566.5	548.9	606.6	2,232
2003	448.0	512.5	508.9	550.1	2,020
2002	414.2	458.4	466.7	477.4	1,817
2001	412.2	414.0	433.7	452.0	1,712
2000	408.9	455.2	443.2	465.1	1,772

Earnings Per Share ($)

	1Q	2Q	3Q	4Q	Year
2005	0.63	0.81	0.32	**E**1.20	**E**3.65
2004	0.43	0.78	0.79	0.94	2.93
2003	0.31	0.53	0.60	0.92	2.36
2002	0.16	0.40	0.17	0.60	1.34
2001	-0.02	0.13	0.43	0.24	0.78
2000	0.68	0.64	0.27	-0.09	1.49

Fiscal year ended Dec. 31. Next earnings report expected: NA. EPS Estimates based on S&P Operating Earnings; historical GAAP earnings are as reported.

Dividend Data (Dates: mm/dd Payment Date: mm/dd/yy)

Amount ($)	Date Decl.	Ex-Div. Date	Stk. of Record	Payment Date
0.130	10/25	11/29	12/01	01/03/06
0.130	02/28	03/02	03/06	04/03/06
0.130	05/02	05/30	06/01	07/05/06
0.130	07/25	08/30	09/01	10/02/06

Dividends have been paid since 1952. Source: Company reports.

Please read the Required Disclosures and Analyst Certification on the last page of this report.

Bausch & Lomb Inc

STANDARD &POOR'S

Business Summary August 14, 2006

CORPORATE OVERVIEW. Bausch & Lomb, which makes well-known contact lenses and contact lens solution brands, also produces ophthalmic pharmaceuticals and equipment used for eye surgery. Sales in Europe and Asia accounted for 57% of the total in 2004 (latest available).

Contact lenses (30% of 2004 sales) include traditional planned replacement disposable, daily disposable, multifocal, continuous wear and toric soft contact lenses and rigid gas permeable (RGP) materials. These products are sold under the Bausch & Lomb, Boston, Medalist, PureVision and SofLens trademarks. The SofLens66 Toric lens, a cast-molded multifocal lens for people with presbyopia, is the number one prescribed mutifocal lens in the U.S. and Europe. The PureVision spherical (or non-toric) lens, a breakthrough silicone hydrogel lens for up to 30 days of wear, was launched in the U.S. in 2005.

In July 2004, BOL and CIBA Vision Corp. resolved patent disputes concerning contact lens manufacturing. The parties also agreed to cross-license rights to their silicone hydrogel contact lens technologies. BOL will pay CIBA a royalty on net U.S. sales of PureVision brand contact lenses until 2014 and on net sales outside the U.S. until 2016.

Lens care products (23%) include multi-purpose solutions, enzyme cleaners and saline solutions sold under the Bausch & Lomb, Boston, ReNu and Sensitive Eyes brands. During 2004, BOL launched ReNu with MoistureLoc, a new multi-purpose solution, in the U.S. and Europe, and expanded the availability of ReNu with MoistureLoc into Asian markets in 2005.

Company Financials

Per Share Data ($) Year Ended Dec. 31	**2004**	**2003**	**2002**	**2001**	**2000**	**1999**	**1998**	**1997**	**1996**	**1995**
Tangible Book Value	9.14	5.20	2.87	2.48	4.18	1.10	1.52	7.41	8.86	9.62
Cash Flow	5.23	4.70	3.75	3.65	4.20	4.42	3.35	2.90	3.47	3.62
Earnings	2.93	2.36	1.34	0.78	1.49	1.75	0.45	0.89	1.47	1.94
S&P Core Earnings	2.80	2.26	0.49	-0.07	NA	NA	NA	NA	NA	NA
Dividends	0.52	0.52	0.65	1.04	1.04	1.04	1.04	1.04	1.04	1.01
Payout Ratio	18%	22%	49%	133%	70%	59%	NM	117%	71%	52%
Prices:High	69.00	52.66	44.80	54.93	80.88	84.75	60.00	47.88	44.50	44.50
Prices:Low	50.70	36.05	27.16	27.20	33.56	51.38	37.75	32.50	32.50	30.88
P/E Ratio:High	24	22	33	70	54	48	NM	54	30	23
P/E Ratio:Low	17	15	20	35	22	29	NM	37	22	16
Income Statement Analysis (Million $)										
Revenue	2,232	2,020	1,817	1,712	1,772	1,756	2,363	1,916	1,927	1,933
Operating Income	405	354	329	263	371	424	425	332	319	343
Depreciation	125	125	130	155	148	156	164	112	113	105
Interest Expense	48.4	54.2	53.9	58.3	68.5	88.4	101	56.0	51.7	45.8
Pretax Income	247	197	137	85.0	161	185	130	118	169	212
Effective Tax Rate	33.5%	34.0%	34.5%	33.8%	40.8%	36.0%	60.9%	38.6%	37.7%	36.9%
Net Income	160	126	72.5	42.0	82.0	103	25.2	49.4	83.1	112
S&P Core Earnings	152	121	27.0	-3.36	NA	NA	NA	NA	NA	NA
Balance Sheet & Other Financial Data (Million $)										
Cash	502	563	465	534	660	827	429	184	168	194
Current Assets	1,381	1,421	1,285	1,397	1,646	1,810	1,587	1,090	948	930
Total Assets	3,022	3,006	2,908	2,994	3,086	3,274	3,492	2,773	2,603	2,550
Current Liabilities	832	876	829	704	809	620	812	887	929	859
Long Term Debt	543	652	656	703	763	977	1,281	511	236	191
Common Equity	1,427	1,203	1,018	975	1,039	1,234	845	818	882	929
Total Capital	2,059	1,982	1,950	2,190	2,179	2,554	2,573	1,129	1,550	1,551
Capital Expenditures	119	91.5	91.9	96.4	95.0	156	202	126	130	95.0
Cash Flow	285	251	203	197	230	259	189	161	196	217
Current Ratio	1.7	1.6	1.5	2.0	2.0	2.9	2.0	1.2	1.0	1.1
% Long Term Debt of Capitalization	26.4	32.9	33.6	32.1	35.0	38.2	49.8	45.3	15.2	12.4
% Net Income of Revenue	7.1	6.3	4.0	2.5	4.6	5.8	1.1	2.6	4.3	5.8
% Return on Assets	5.3	4.4	2.5	1.3	2.6	3.0	0.8	1.8	3.2	4.5
% Return on Equity	12.1	11.4	7.3	4.2	7.2	9.9	3.0	5.8	9.2	12.2

Data as orig reptd.; bef. results of disc opers/spec. items. Per share data adj. for stk. divs.; EPS diluted. E-Estimated. NA-Not Available. NM-Not Meaningful. NR-Not Ranked. UR-Under Review.

Office: One Bausch & Lomb Pl, Rochester, NY 14604-2701.
Telephone: 585-338-6000.
Website: http://www.bausch.com
Chrmn & CEO: R.L. Zarrella

SVP & CFO: S.C. McCluski
SVP & CSO: P. Tyle
SVP & General Counsel: R.B. Stiles
VP & Treas: E. Rivera

Investor Contact: B.M. Kelley
Board of Directors: A. M. Bennett, D. De Solo, P. A. Friedman, J. S. Linen, R. R. McMullin, L. J. Rice, W. H. Waltrip, B. W. Wilson, K. L. Wolfe, R. L. Zarrella

Founded: 1853
Domicile: New York
Employees: 12,400

STANDARD &POOR'S

Baxter International Inc

S&P Recommendation HOLD ★★★★★

Price $46.34 (as of Oct 27, 2006)

12-Mo. Target Price $46.00

Investment Style Large-Cap Growth

GICS Sector Health Care
Sub-Industry Health Care Equipment

Comment This global medical products and services company provides critical therapies for people with life-threatening conditions.

Key Stock Statistics (Source S&P, Vickers, company reports)

52-Wk Range	$47.49–35.12	S&P Oper. EPS 2006E	2.15	P/E on S&P Oper. EPS 2006E	21.6	Dividend Rate/Share	$0.58
Trailing 12-Month EPS	$1.93	S&P Oper. EPS 2007E	2.48	Common Shares Outstg. (M)	652.4	Yield (%)	1.26
Trailing 12-Month P/E	24.0	S&P Core EPS 2006E	2.15	Market Capitalization(B)	$30.232	Beta	0.97
$10K Invested 5 Yrs Ago	$10,081	S&P Core EPS 2007E	2.48	Institutional Ownership (%)	83	S&P Credit Rating	A-

Price Performance

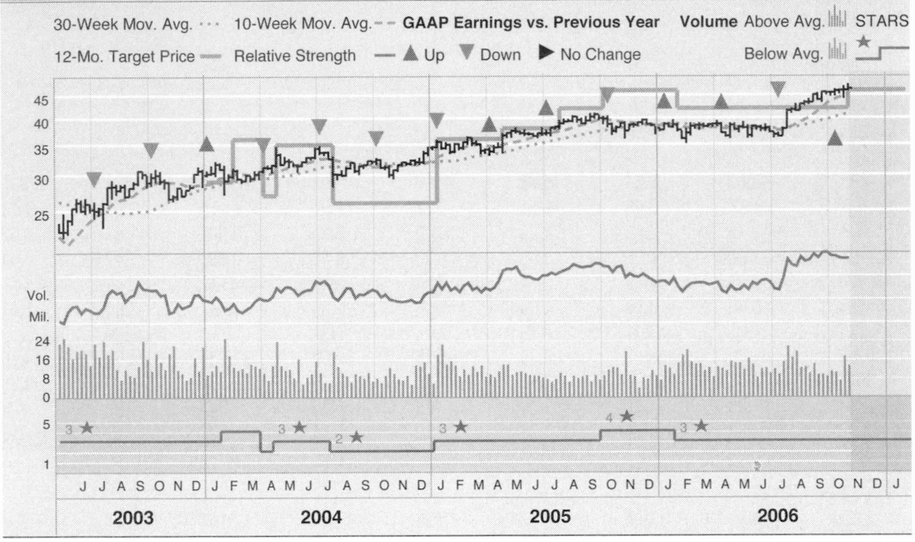

30-Week Mov. Avg. ··· 10-Week Mov. Avg. - - GAAP Earnings vs. Previous Year Volume Above Avg. STARS
12-Mo. Target Price — Relative Strength — ▲ Up ▼ Down ▶ No Change Below Avg.

45 40 35 30 25

Vol. Mil.

24 16 8 0

5 3★ 3★ 2★ 3★ 4★ 3★ 1

J J A S O N D J F M A M J J A S O N D J F M A M J J A S O N D J F M A M J J A S O N D J

2003 2004 2005 2006

Options: ASE, CBOE, P, Ph

Highlights

➤ The 12-month target price for BAX has recently been changed to $46.00 from $42.00. The Highlights section of this Stock Report will be updated accordingly.

Investment Rationale/Risk

➤ The Investment Rationale/Risk section of this Stock Report will be updated shortly. For the latest News story on BAX from MarketScope, see below.

➤ 10/20/06 02:42 pm EDT... S&P REITERATES HOLD OPINION ON SHARES OF BAXTER INTERNATIONAL (BAX 46.05***): BAX posts 21% rise in Q3 operating EPS, to $0.57, topping our estimate by $0.03. The increase largely reflects gross margin expansion, to 47.5% from 43.2%, with strong growth in sales of higher-margin plasma proteins. However, medical delivery sales remained weak, hurt by generic competition in the anesthesia market. Now available overseas, we expect BAX's Colleague infusion pump to return to the U.S. market, subject to FDA clearance. We are raising our target price by $4 to $46, which applies peer-level P/E of 18.5X to our $2.48 EPS estimate for '07. /H. Saftlas

Qualitative Risk Assessment

LOW **MEDIUM** HIGH

Our risk assessment reflects that BAX operates in a highly competitive business characterized by rapid technological change and new market entrants. In addition, the business entails regulatory and reimbursement risks, as well as liability risks from malfunctioning products. This is offset by our belief that health care products are immune to economic cycles, and that long-term demand should benefit from demographic growth in the elderly and a greater penetration of developing global markets.

Quantitative Evaluations

S&P Quality Ranking **B+**

D C B- B **B+** A- A A+

Relative Strength Rank **MODERATE**

64

LOWEST = 1 HIGHEST = 99

Revenue/Earnings Data

Revenue (Million $)

	1Q	2Q	3Q	4Q	Year
2006	2,409	2,649	2,557	--	--
2005	2,383	2,577	2,398	2,491	9,849
2004	2,209	2,379	2,320	2,601	9,509
2003	1,997	2,163	2,219	2,537	8,916
2002	1,875	1,945	2,029	2,261	8,110
2001	1,757	1,870	1,900	2,136	7,663

Earnings Per Share ($)

2006	0.43	0.47	0.57	**E**0.61	**E**2.15
2005	0.36	0.51	0.18	0.46	1.52
2004	0.30	-0.28	0.42	0.17	0.62
2003	0.36	0.08	0.47	0.62	1.52
2002	0.41	0.32	0.51	0.42	1.67
2001	0.36	0.42	0.45	-0.13	1.09

Fiscal year ended Dec. 31. Next earnings report expected: Late January. EPS Estimates based on S&P Operating Earnings; historical GAAP earnings are as reported.

Dividend Data (Dates: mm/dd Payment Date: mm/dd/yy)

Amount ($)	Date Decl.	Ex-Div. Date	Stk. of Record	Payment Date
0.582	11/15	12/07	12/09	01/05/06

Dividends have been paid since 1934. Source: Company reports.

Baxter International Inc

Business Summary July 28, 2006

CORPORATE OVERVIEW. Founded in 1931 as the first producer of commercially prepared intravenous (IV) solutions, Baxter International produces and distributes medical products and equipment, with a focus on the blood and circulatory system. In 2005, international sales accounted for 55% of the total.

The Medication Delivery unit (41% of 2005 net sales) makes IV solutions and various specialty products such as critical-care generic injectable drugs, anesthetic agents, and nutrition and oncology products. The products work with devices such as drug-reconstitution systems, IV infusion pumps, nutritional compounding equipment, and medication management systems to provide fluid replenishment, general anesthesia, parenteral nutrition, pain management, antibiotic therapy and chemotherapy.

The BioSciences unit (39%) produces plasma-based and recombinant clotting factors for hemophilia, as well as biopharmaceuticals for immune deficiencies, cancer and other disorders. It also offers biosurgery products for hemostasis, tissue sealing and tissue regeneration, vaccines, and blood processing and storage systems used by hospitals, blood banks and others. BAX also sells a meningitis C vaccine, and is developing cell culture-derived vaccines for influenza, smallpox, Severe Acute Respiratory Syndrome and other diseases. In 2003, the company received FDA approval to sell Advate, a recombinant blood clotting agent produced without adding human or animal proteins in the cell culture, purification or final formulation process. During 2003, BAX acquired Alpha Therapeutic Corp.'s Aralast alpha-1 proteinase inhibitor (A1PI) treatment for hereditary emphysema, and 42 FDA-licensed plasma collection centers in the U.S.

Renal Care products (20%) comprise dialysis equipment and other products and services provided for kidney failure patients. BAX sells products for peritoneal dialysis (PD), including solutions, container systems and automated machines that cleanse patients' blood overnight while they sleep. The company also makes dialyzers and instrumentation for hemodialysis (HD). During 2003, BAX launched its Extraneal (icodextrin) solution in the U.S. and Japan, which offers the potential for increased fluid removal from the bloodstream during dialysis.

Company Financials

Per Share Data ($) Year Ended Dec. 31	**2005**	**2004**	**2003**	**2002**	**2001**	**2000**	**1999**	**1998**	**1997**	**1996**
Tangible Book Value	3.61	2.45	1.74	1.53	3.44	2.43	4.19	1.79	1.78	2.05
Cash Flow	2.45	1.59	2.42	2.38	1.81	1.91	1.95	1.28	1.24	1.70
Earnings	1.52	0.62	1.52	1.67	1.09	1.24	1.32	0.55	0.53	1.05
S&P Core Earnings	1.38	0.52	1.25	1.30	0.53	NA	NA	NA	NA	NA
Dividends	0.58	0.58	0.58	0.58	0.58	0.15	0.58	0.58	0.57	0.58
Payout Ratio	38%	94%	38%	35%	53%	12%	44%	107%	107%	55%
Prices:High	41.07	34.84	31.32	59.90	55.90	45.13	38.00	33.00	30.13	24.06
Prices:Low	33.08	27.10	18.18	24.07	40.06	25.88	28.41	24.25	19.94	19.88
P/E Ratio:High	27	56	21	36	51	37	29	61	57	23
P/E Ratio:Low	22	44	12	14	37	21	22	44	38	19
Income Statement Analysis (Million $)										
Revenue	9,849	9,509	8,916	8,110	7,663	6,896	6,380	6,599	6,138	5,438
Operating Income	2,110	2,039	2,161	2,168	1,934	1,673	1,522	1,545	1,403	1,259
Depreciation	580	601	545	439	441	405	372	426	398	348
Interest Expense	166	99.0	118	71.0	108	124	152	193	198	103
Pretax Income	1,444	430	1,150	1,397	964	946	1,052	549	523	793
Effective Tax Rate	33.7%	10.9%	19.8%	26.1%	31.1%	22.0%	26.0%	42.6%	42.6%	27.5%
Net Income	958	383	922	1,033	664	738	779	315	300	575
S&P Core Earnings	864	323	756	794	313	NA	NA	NA	NA	NA
Balance Sheet & Other Financial Data (Million $)										
Cash	841	1,109	927	1,169	582	579	606	709	465	761
Current Assets	5,116	6,019	5,437	5,160	3,977	3,651	3,819	4,651	3,870	3,480
Total Assets	12,727	14,147	13,779	12,478	10,343	8,733	9,644	10,085	8,707	7,596
Current Liabilities	4,165	4,286	3,819	3,851	3,294	3,372	2,700	2,988	2,557	2,445
Long Term Debt	2,414	3,933	4,421	4,398	2,486	1,726	2,601	3,096	2,635	1,695
Common Equity	4,299	3,705	3,323	2,939	3,757	2,659	3,348	2,839	2,619	2,504
Total Capital	6,713	7,638	7,744	7,366	6,461	4,545	6,260	6,440	5,570	4,454
Capital Expenditures	444	558	789	734	669	101	529	492	403	318
Cash Flow	1,538	984	1,467	1,472	1,105	1,143	1,151	741	698	923
Current Ratio	1.2	1.4	1.4	1.3	1.2	1.1	1.4	1.6	1.5	1.4
% Long Term Debt of Capitalization	36.0	51.5	57.1	59.7	38.5	38.0	41.5	48.1	47.3	38.1
% Net Income of Revenue	9.7	4.0	10.3	12.7	8.7	10.7	12.2	4.8	4.9	10.6
% Return on Assets	7.1	2.8	7.0	9.1	7.0	8.0	8.0	3.4	3.7	6.8
% Return on Equity	23.9	10.8	29.4	30.9	20.7	24.6	25.2	11.5	11.7	18.5

Data as orig reptd.; bef. results of disc opers/spec. items. Per share data adj. for stk. divs.; EPS diluted. E-Estimated. NA-Not Available. NM-Not Meaningful. NR-Not Ranked. UR-Under Review.

Office: One Baxter Parkway, Deerfield, IL 60015.
Telephone: 847-948-2000.
Website: http://www.baxter.com
Chrmn & CEO: R.L. Parkinson, Jr.

VP, CFO & Treas: R.M. Davis
VP & CSO: N.J. Riedel
VP & Secy: D.P. Scharf
VP & Cntlr: M.J. Baughman

Investor Contact: M. Ladone (847-948-3371)
Board of Directors: W. E. Boomer, B. E. Devitt, J. D. Forsyth, G. D. Fosler, J. R. Gavin, III, P. S. Hellman, J. B. Martin, R. L. Parkinson, Jr., C. U. Shapazian, T. T. Stallkamp, K. J. Storm, A. P. Stroucken

Founded: 1931
Domicile: Delaware
Employees: 47,000

STANDARD &POOR'S

BB&T Corp

S&P Recommendation BUY ★★★★★

Price $43.03 (as of Oct 27, 2006)

12-Mo. Target Price $49.00

Investment Style Large-Cap Value

GICS Sector Financials
Sub-Industry Regional Banks

Comment This North Carolina bank holding company, through subsidiaries, operates banking offices in 11 states and Washington, DC.

Key Stock Statistics (Source S&P, Vickers, company reports)

52-Wk Range	$44.54–38.24	S&P Oper. EPS 2006E	3.25	P/E on S&P Oper. EPS 2006E	13.2	Dividend Rate/Share	$1.68
Trailing 12-Month EPS	$3.13	S&P Oper. EPS 2007E	3.50	Common Shares Outstg. (M)	537.0	Yield (%)	3.90
Trailing 12-Month P/E	13.8	S&P Core EPS 2006E	3.33	Market Capitalization(B)	$23.109	Beta	0.47
$10K Invested 5 Yrs Ago	$15,350	S&P Core EPS 2007E	3.72	Institutional Ownership (%)	29	S&P Credit Rating	A+

Price Performance

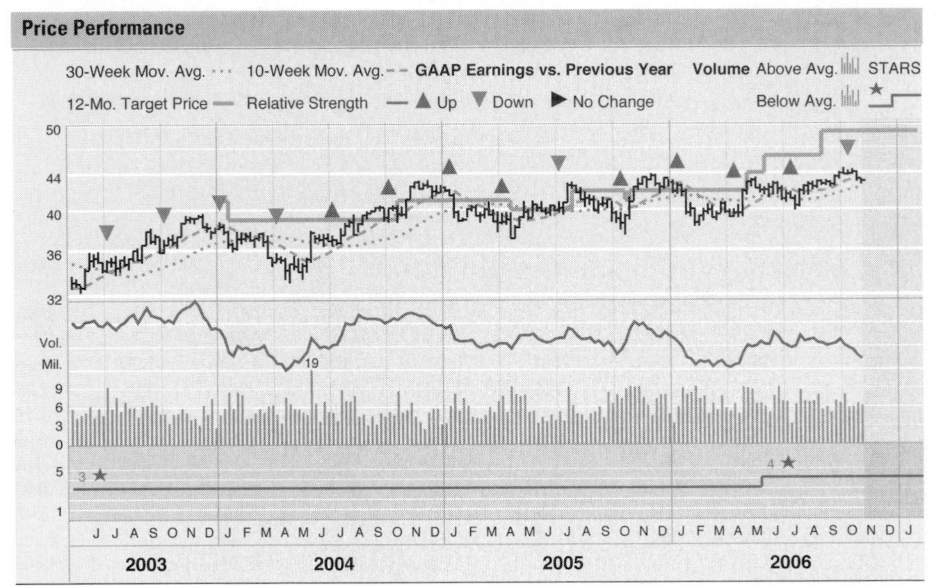

Options: ASE, CBOE, P, Ph

Analysis prepared by **Christopher B. Muir** on August 24, 2006, when the stock traded at **$ 42.70**.

Highlights

- We expect earning asset growth of 12% in 2006, as a result of continued loan growth. We see net interest income increasing 7.2% as a result of projected earning asset growth, partly offset by a lower net interest margin of 3.72% (3.89% in 2005). In our view, non-interest income growth will be strong, at about 11%, as a result of growth in several areas. As a result, we forecast a 8.7% increase in total revenues.
- We expect that stock option expense in 2006 will more than offset improvements related to merger savings in 2006 that would have led to an improved efficiency ratio. We expect the efficiency ratio to begin showing an improvement in 2007. As a result, our 2006 non-interest expense to total revenues forecast of 54.0% is slightly worse than 2005's 53.6%. We expect to see continued strong credit quality in 2006, with loan loss provisions rising slightly, to $222 million from $217 million in 2005.
- We see 2006 EPS rising to $3.35, a 12% increase from the $3.00 earned in 2005. Our 2007 EPS forecast is $3.74, a further 12% increase.

Investment Rationale/Risk

- Although we believe that BBT has a solid track record of merger integrations, we think that management is under pressure to show success from recent acquisitions, including First Virginia Banks. Merger savings should help to keep the company's expense growth in check for the next few years. BBT's shares recently traded at 11.4X our 2007 EPS estimate, or at a 12% discount to its large-cap regional banking peers, a level that leaves room for multiple expansion, in our view.
- Risks to our opinion and target price include detrimental changes in the slope of the yield curve, and operational performance that fails to meet our expectations.
- Our 12-month target price of $49 is based on our dividend discount and relative valuation analyses. Our target price is equal to 13X our 2007 EPS estimate, or even with the average for large-cap regional banking peers, which we think is appropriate, given our view of BBT's growth prospects. Our dividend discount model assumes a terminal growth rate of 4% and a discount rate of 8.5%.

Qualitative Risk Assessment

LOW | MEDIUM | HIGH

Our risk assessment reflects the company's large-cap valuation, our view of the strong credit quality of its loan portfolio, and its history of profitability. While the company operates in a highly competitive and fragmented industry, the industry tends to produce relatively stable financial results.

Quantitative Evaluations

S&P Quality Ranking A-

D | C | B- | B | B+ | A- | A | A+

Relative Strength Rank MODERATE

30

LOWEST = 1 HIGHEST = 99

Revenue/Earnings Data

Revenue (Million $)

	1Q	2Q	3Q	4Q	Year
2006	2,165	2,319	2,462	--	--
2005	1,760	1,918	2,036	2,118	7,831
2004	1,559	1,693	1,698	1,736	6,666
2003	1,500	1,507	1,611	1,627	6,244
2002	1,456	1,526	1,549	1,629	6,127
2001	1,476	1,487	1,550	1,500	6,228

Earnings Per Share ($)

	1Q	2Q	3Q	4Q	Year
2006	0.79	0.79	0.77	E0.86	E3.25
2005	0.71	0.70	0.80	0.78	3.00
2004	0.60	0.72	0.74	0.75	2.80
2003	0.69	0.67	0.21	0.55	2.07
2002	0.64	0.68	0.68	0.70	2.70
2001	0.53	0.60	0.48	0.61	2.12

Fiscal year ended Dec. 31. Next earnings report expected: Mid January. EPS Estimates based on S&P Operating Earnings; historical GAAP earnings are as reported.

Dividend Data (Dates: mm/dd Payment Date: mm/dd/yy)

Amount ($)	Date Decl.	Ex-Div. Date	Stk. of Record	Payment Date
0.380	12/13	01/11	01/13	02/01/06
0.380	02/21	04/11	04/14	05/01/06
0.420	06/27	07/12	07/14	08/01/06
0.420	08/22	10/11	10/13	11/01/06

Dividends have been paid since 1934. Source: Company reports.

BB&T Corp

Business Summary August 24, 2006

CORPORATE OVERVIEW. BBT has bank operations providing loan, deposit and financial products primarily in the Southeast. BBT has seven reportable business segments: Banking Network, Mortgage Banking, Trust Services, Insurance Services, Investment Banking and Brokerage, Specialized Lending, and Treasury.

The Banking Network generated 65% of total revenues and 76% of segment net income in 2005. In addition to providing banking services, BBT's bank subsidiaries also offer brokerage, insurance and other financial services. The Mortgage Banking segment generated 28% of revenues and 8% of segment net income, Insurance services 13% and 3%, Specialized Lending 7% and 3%, Investment Banking 6% and 1%, Trust 3% and 0%, and others 8% and 9%.

MARKET PROFILE. BBT's southeastern footprint includes 400 branches in Virginia, 329 in North Carolina, 136 in Georgia, 123 in Maryland, 96 in South Carolina, 95 in Kentucky, 88 in Florida, 72 in West Virginia, 63 in Tennessee, nine in Washington, DC, two in Alabama, and one in Indiana, according to Highline Data. Based on data from the U.S. Census Bureau, the projection for average population growth from 2005 to 2010 in the states where the company has more than a trivial presence is as follows: 5.9% in Virginia, 7.6% in North Carolina, 5.7% in Georgia, 5.4% in Maryland, 4.5% in South Carolina, 2.2% in Kentucky, 8.2% in Florida, 0.7% in West Virginia, 4.5% in Tennessee, and -3.8% in Washington, DC. The projected population weighted average growth rate for these states is 6.0%. The estimated national growth rate is 4.2%.

COMPETITIVE LANDSCAPE. Competition for low cost deposits is fierce in the banking industry. Demand deposit accounts are typically the least expensive, followed by interest bearing demand accounts and interest bearing time deposit accounts. Banks try to attract demand deposit accounts by offering additional services tied to the accounts. In addition, primary lending products are commodity type products and there are few ways to differentiate them.

Company Financials

Per Share Data ($) Year Ended Dec. 31	**2005**	**2004**	**2003**	**2002**	**2001**	**2000**	**1999**	**1998**	**1997**	**1996**
Tangible Book Value	11.76	12.26	11.66	12.04	13.50	11.91	9.66	9.95	8.23	7.91
Earnings	3.00	2.80	2.07	2.70	2.12	1.55	1.83	1.71	1.30	1.28
S&P Core Earnings	2.90	2.75	1.97	2.59	2.02	NA	NA	NA	NA	NA
Dividends	1.46	1.34	1.22	1.10	0.98	0.86	0.75	0.66	0.58	0.50
Payout Ratio	49%	48%	59%	41%	46%	55%	41%	39%	45%	39%
Prices:High	43.92	43.25	39.69	39.47	38.84	38.25	40.63	40.75	32.50	18.50
Prices:Low	37.04	33.02	30.66	31.03	30.24	21.69	27.19	26.25	17.50	12.88
P/E Ratio:High	15	15	19	15	18	25	22	24	25	14
P/E Ratio:Low	12	12	15	11	14	14	15	15	13	10
Income Statement Analysis (Million $)										
Net Interest Income	3,525	3,348	3,082	2,747	2,434	2,018	1,582	1,247	1,100	775
Tax Equivalent Adjustment	82.7	NA	21.2	151	19.1	130	86.7	64.0	52.9	34.2
Non Interest Income	2,326	2,113	1,782	1,522	1,256	996	639	520	473	294
Loan Loss Provision	217	249	248	264	224	127	92.1	80.3	89.9	53.7
% Expense/Operating Revenue	53.4%	57.6%	63.6%	54.0%	60.1%	56.0%	58.4%	52.5%	59.6%	74.4%
Pretax Income	2,467	2,322	1,617	1,791	1,360	906	904	734	547	418
Effective Tax Rate	33.0%	32.9%	34.1%	27.8%	28.4%	30.8%	32.2%	31.6%	34.2%	32.2%
Net Income	1,654	1,558	1,065	1,293	974	626	613	502	360	284
% Net Interest Margin	3.89	4.04	4.06	4.25	4.17	3.56	4.27	3.75	4.55	4.45
S&P Core Earnings	1,608	1,529	1,012	1,241	927	NA	NA	NA	NA	NA
Balance Sheet & Other Financial Data (Million $)										
Money Market Assets	697	1,244	604	591	458	379	390	168	178	21.0
Investment Securities	20,489	19,173	16,317	17,655	16,662	13,851	10,579	8,099	6,629	5,262
Commercial Loans	37,655	34,321	12,429	7,061	6,551	5,894	4,593	3,444	3,018	2,375
Other Loans	36,739	33,228	49,151	44,079	38,985	33,561	24,320	19,932	16,499	12,150
Total Assets	109,170	100,509	90,467	80,217	70,870	59,340	43,481	34,427	29,178	21,247
Demand Deposits	13,477	12,246	11,098	7,864	6,940	5,064	3,908	3,247	2,829	1,990
Time Deposits	60,805	55,453	48,252	43,416	37,794	32,951	23,343	19,800	17,381	12,963
Long Term Debt	13,119	11,420	10,808	13,588	11,721	8,355	5,492	4,737	3,283	2,052
Common Equity	11,129	10,874	9,935	7,388	6,150	4,786	3,199	2,759	2,238	1,729
% Return on Assets	1.6	1.6	1.2	1.7	1.4	1.1	1.5	1.6	1.4	1.4
% Return on Equity	15.0	15.0	12.3	19.1	16.8	14.2	19.2	20.1	18.1	16.5
% Loan Loss Reserve	1.1	1.2	1.3	1.4	1.4	1.3	1.3	1.4	1.3	1.3
% Loans/Deposits	99.0	100.7	105.0	104.4	106.1	106.0	107.1	98.3	97.9	97.2
% Equity to Assets	10.5	10.9	10.1	9.0	8.4	7.9	7.7	7.9	7.9	8.1

Data as orig reptd.; bef. results of disc opers/spec. items. Per share data adj. for stk. divs.; EPS diluted. E-Estimated. NA-Not Available. NM-Not Meaningful. NR-Not Ranked. UR-Under Review.

Office: 200 West Second Street, Winston-Salem, NC 27101.
Telephone: 336-733-2000.
Website: http://www.bbandt.com
Chrmn & CEO: J.A. Allison, IV

COO: K.S. King
Sr EVP: C.L. Wilson, III
Sr EVP: W.K. Chalk
Sr EVP: R.E. Greene

Investor Contact: T. Gjesdal
Board of Directors: J. A. Allison, IV, J. S. Banner, A. R. Cablik, N. R. Chilton, R. E. Deal, T. D. Efird, B. J. Fitzpatrick, L. V. Hackley, J. P. Helm, J. P. Howe, III, J. H. Maynard, A. O. McCauley, J. H. Morrison, N. R. Qubein, E. R. Sasser

Founded: 1968
Domicile: North Carolina
Employees: 27,700

STANDARD &POOR'S

Bear Stearns Companies Inc (The)

S&P Recommendation HOLD ★★★★★	**Price**	**12-Mo. Target Price**	**Investment Style**
	$149.21 (as of Oct 27, 2006)	$150.00	Large-Cap Value

GICS Sector Financials
Sub-Industry Investment Banking & Brokerage

Comment This company's Bear, Stearns & Co. unit is a leading investment bank and broker, and is ranked as one of the largest NYSE member firms.

Key Stock Statistics (Source S&P, Vickers, company reports)

52-Wk Range	$155.02–104.20	S&P Oper. EPS 2006E	13.48	P/E on S&P Oper. EPS 2006E	11.1	Dividend Rate/Share	$1.12
Trailing 12-Month EPS	$13.17	S&P Oper. EPS 2007E	13.77	Common Shares Outstg. (M)	117.3	Yield (%)	0.75
Trailing 12-Month P/E	11.3	S&P Core EPS 2006E	13.48	Market Capitalization(B)	$17.504	Beta	0.83
$10K Invested 5 Yrs Ago	$27,033	S&P Core EPS 2007E	13.77	Institutional Ownership (%)	69	S&P Credit Rating	A+

Price Performance

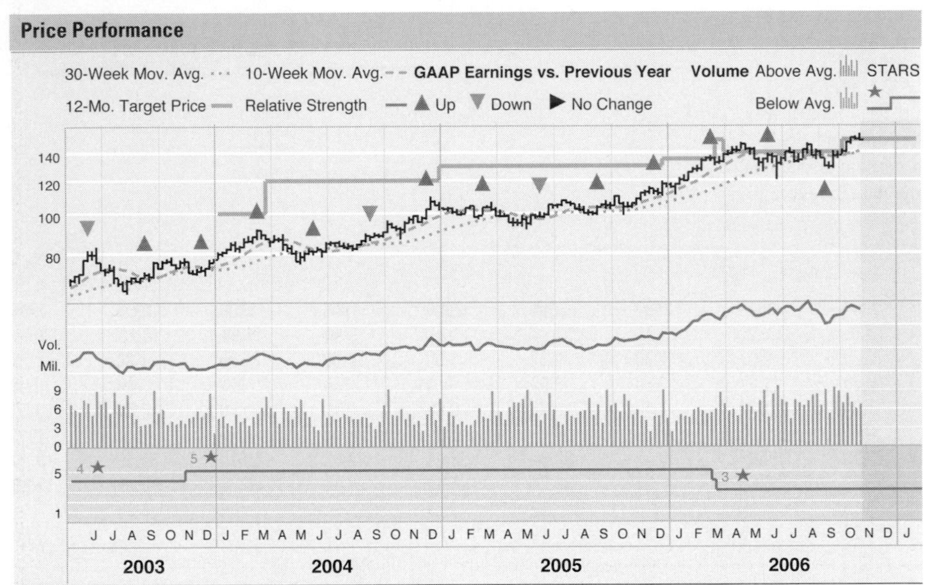

Options: ASE, CBOE, P, Ph

Analysis prepared by **Christopher B. Muir** on October 02, 2006, when the stock traded at **$ 141.73**.

Highlights

- We think BSC has a strong competitive position, due to the breadth of its fixed income franchise, the stability and consistency of its trading revenues, and the growth of its prime brokerage business. We are pleased with the diversification within BSC's fixed income business, but think the company remains heavily dependent on mortgage and high yield related businesses.
- Despite what we view as a strong August quarter, we think the higher interest rate environment could hurt the company's mortgage franchise in FY 07 (Nov.). However, we expect strong revenue growth in institutional equities, global clearing services, and wealth management to offset a modest decline that we see for fixed income.
- We forecast EPS of $13.48 in FY 06 and $13.77 in FY 07, aided by higher merchant banking gains, improving equity trading volumes, and continued prudent expense management. We think that BSC's ratio of compensation expense to net revenue will rise slightly from FY 05, but remain within its guidance of 48%-52%, including projected stock option expense.

Investment Rationale/Risk

- We think BSC shares merit a lower valuation than larger peers given that we view the company as generally less diversified by business and by region. Furthermore, we think BSC has been slow to focus on faster growing areas. We view the current valuation as appropriate given our concerns about a slowing in the company's capital markets segment due to rising interest rates.
- Risks to our recommendation and target price include sharply higher interest rates, wider credit spreads, potential trading losses, and regulatory issues.
- The shares recently traded at a P/E of about 10X our FY 07 EPS estimate and a ratio of 1.7X book value per share, discounts to the company's peer group in our coverage universe. Our 12-month target price of $150 is equal to nearly 10.9X our FY 07 EPS estimate, which is modestly above BSC's historical average. We see limited potential for the multiple to expand given that we expect a less favorable fixed income environment.

Qualitative Risk Assessment

LOW | **MEDIUM** | HIGH

Our risk assessment is based on our view that the company has a strong competitive position. However, we believe BSC is less diversified by business and by region relative to certain larger peers; we also note significant industry cyclicality.

Quantitative Evaluations

S&P Quality Ranking A

D | C | B- | B | B+ | A- | **A** | A+

Relative Strength Rank MODERATE

64

LOWEST = 1 HIGHEST = 99

Revenue/Earnings Data

Revenue (Million $)

	1Q	2Q	3Q	4Q	Year
2006	3,638	4,304	4,136	--	--
2005	2,622	2,824	2,925	3,181	11,552
2004	2,081	2,064	1,894	2,382	8,422
2003	1,838	1,850	1,842	1,865	7,395
2002	1,718	2,070	1,581	1,521	6,891
2001	2,136	2,449	2,302	1,814	8,701

Earnings Per Share ($)

2006	3.54	3.72	3.02	E3.19	E13.48
2005	2.64	2.09	2.69	2.90	10.31
2004	2.57	2.49	2.09	2.61	9.76
2003	2.00	2.05	2.30	2.19	8.52
2002	2.00	2.59	1.23	1.36	6.47
2001	1.10	1.18	0.95	1.08	4.31

Fiscal year ended Nov. 30. Next earnings report expected: Mid December. EPS Estimates based on S&P Operating Earnings; historical GAAP earnings are as reported.

Dividend Data (Dates: mm/dd Payment Date: mm/dd/yy)

Amount ($)	Date Decl.	Ex-Div. Date	Stk. of Record	Payment Date
0.280	12/15	01/12	01/17	01/27/06
0.280	03/16	04/13	04/18	04/28/06
0.280	06/21	07/14	07/18	07/28/06
0.280	09/20	10/13	10/17	10/27/06

Dividends have been paid since 1986. Source: Company reports.

Bear Stearns Companies Inc (The)

Business Summary October 02, 2006

The Bear Stearns Companies is the fifth largest company in the highly cyclical and increasingly concentrated investment banking and brokerage industry, serving corporate, government, institutional and individual clients. Although it operates in three segments (Capital Markets, Global Clearing Services and Wealth Management), the company is best known for its significant fixed income trading prowess, particularly in mortgage and high-yield securities. International revenue rose to 13% of total revenue in FY 05 (Nov.), up from 8% in FY 03, and we estimate is largely generated in BSC's Capital Markets segment in London. We see strong growth in international revenue, but view BSC as largely a domestic player.

From a corporate governance perspective, we believe the interests of BSC's management are closely aligned with those of its shareholders given that all directors, nominees and executive officers owned 9.1% of the outstanding common stock as of January 31, 2006. However, we view executive compensation as very generous, and would prefer that the company split the positions of chairman and chief executive officer. We believe that BSC would make an attractive acquisition candidate, but think significant insider ownership of about 41% of the shares (fully diluted) outstanding significantly reduces the probability of its acquisition.

Company Financials

Per Share Data ($) Year Ended Nov. 30	**2005**	**2004**	**2003**	**2002**	**2001**	**2000**	**1999**	**1998**	**1997**	**1996**
Tangible Book Value	91.50	82.31	67.58	57.91	45.25	45.49	33.90	27.84	22.69	17.57
Cash Flow	9.75	9.06	7.76	5.75	3.85	4.89	4.64	4.47	4.16	3.27
Earnings	10.31	9.76	8.52	6.47	4.31	5.35	4.27	4.17	3.81	2.96
S&P Core Earnings	10.76	9.44	8.16	6.15	4.09	NA	NA	NA	NA	NA
Dividends	1.00	0.85	0.74	0.62	0.60	0.55	0.55	0.54	0.53	0.52
Payout Ratio	10%	9%	9%	10%	14%	10%	13%	13%	14%	17%
Prices:High	119.40	109.85	83.12	67.55	64.45	72.50	50.48	58.05	43.99	24.51
Prices:Low	91.27	75.44	57.58	50.50	40.65	36.50	31.90	23.58	23.22	15.73
P/E Ratio:High	12	11	10	10	15	14	12	14	12	8
P/E Ratio:Low	9	8	7	8	9	7	7	6	6	5

Income Statement Analysis (Million $)	2005	2004	2003	2002	2001	2000	1999	1998	1997	1996
Commissions	1,200	1,178	1,078	1,111	1,117	1,207	1,014	903	732	687
Interest Income	5,107	2,317	1,955	2,232	4,339	5,642	4,009	4,286	3,058	2,393
Total Revenue	11,552	8,422	7,395	6,891	8,701	10,277	7,882	7,980	6,077	4,964
Interest Expense	4,142	1,609	1,401	1,763	3,794	4,801	3,380	3,639	2,551	1,981
Pretax Income	2,207	2,022	1,772	1,311	934	1,172	1,064	1,063	1,014	835
Effective Tax Rate	33.8%	33.5%	34.8%	33.0%	33.1%	34.0%	36.8%	37.9%	39.5%	41.2%
Net Income	1,462	1,345	1,156	878	625	773	673	660	613	491
S&P Core Earnings	1,555	1,341	1,154	883	622	NA	NA	NA	NA	NA

Balance Sheet & Other Financial Data (Million $)	2005	2004	2003	2002	2001	2000	1999	1998	1997	1996
Total Assets	292,635	255,950	212,168	184,854	185,530	171,166	153,894	154,496	121,434	92,085
Cash Items	11,129	8,596	12,495	12,620	16,620	6,093	5,020	3,357	2,698	1,830
Receivables	37,233	35,364	23,645	19,762	23,702	19,305	18,065	90,537	79,258	63,221
Securities Owned	93,364	81,203	59,233	53,116	51,911	61,760	41,943	44,620	38,437	26,222
Securities Borrowed	10,104	10,719	6,648	58,879	63,794	69,036	64,819	59,960	53,848	43,222
Due Brokers & Customers	75,888	84,535	71,343	62,365	61,470	51,236	43,019	47,175	32,730	23,753
Other Liabilities	3,665	5,180	2,688	2,378	2,660	23,863	25,954	29,423	23,109	16,171
Capitalization:Debt	43,490	36,843	29,993	24,244	24,192	17,243	15,147	13,296	8,120	6,044
Capitalization:Equity	10,562	8,538	6,932	5,689	4,829	4,958	4,156	3,499	2,941	2,307
Capitalization:Total	54,424	45,829	37,463	30,626	29,820	22,898	20,103	17,938	11,746	8,789
% Return on Revenue	14.1	18.6	18.3	15.2	8.2	8.5	9.8	8.3	10.1	9.9
% Return on Assets	0.5	0.6	0.6	0.5	0.4	0.5	0.4	0.5	0.6	0.6
% Return on Equity	14.9	17.0	17.8	16.0	12.1	16.2	16.6	19.5	22.1	25.6

Data as orig reptd.; bef. results of disc opers/spec. items. Per share data adj. for stk. divs.; EPS diluted. E-Estimated. NA-Not Available. NM-Not Meaningful. NR-Not Ranked. UR-Under Review.

Office: 383 Madison Avenue, New York, NY 10179.
Telephone: 212-272-2000.
Email: ir@bear.com
Website: http://www.bearstearns.com

Chrmn & CEO: J.E. Cayne
COO & Co-Pres: A.D. Schwartz
COO & Co-Pres: W.J. Spector
EVP & CFO: S.L. Molinaro, Jr.

Treas: M. Minikes
Investor Contact: E. Ventura (212-272-9251)
Board of Directors: H. S. Bienen, J. E. Cayne, C. D. Glickman, A. C. Greenberg, D. J. Harrington, F. T. Nickell, P. A. Novelly, F. V. Salerno, A. D. Schwartz, W. J. Spector, V. Tese, W. S. Williams, Jr.

Founded: 1923
Domicile: Delaware
Employees: 11,843

STANDARD &POOR'S

Becton, Dickinson and Co

S&P Recommendation BUY ★★★★★	Price	12-Mo. Target Price	Investment Style
	$70.69 (as of Oct 27, 2006)	$75.00	Large-Cap Growth

GICS Sector Health Care
Sub-Industry Health Care Equipment

Comment BDX provides a wide range of medical devices and diagnostic products used in hospitals, doctors' offices, research labs, and other settings.

Key Stock Statistics (Source S&P, Vickers, company reports)

52-Wk Range	**$74.25–50.48**	S&P Oper. EPS 2006**E**	**3.26**	P/E on S&P Oper. EPS 2006**E**	**21.7**	Dividend Rate/Share	**$0.86**
Trailing 12-Month EPS	**$2.83**	S&P Oper. EPS 2007**E**	**3.65**	Common Shares Outstg. (M)	**244.7**	Yield (%)	**1.22**
Trailing 12-Month P/E	**25.0**	S&P Core EPS 2006**E**	**3.26**	Market Capitalization(B)	**$17.297**	Beta	**0.58**
$10K Invested 5 Yrs Ago	**$20,498**	S&P Core EPS 2007**E**	**3.65**	Institutional Ownership (%)	**84**	S&P Credit Rating	**A+**

Price Performance

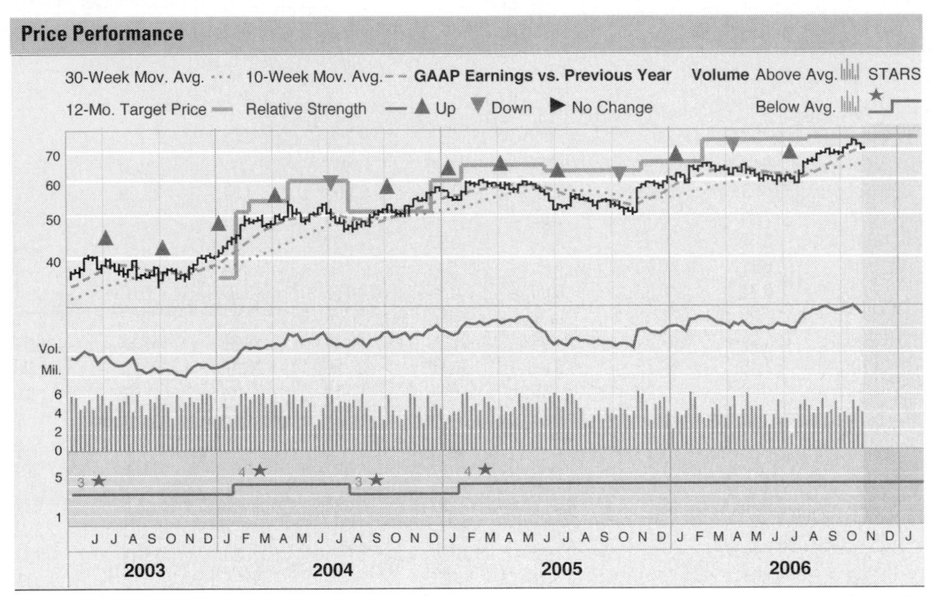

Options: CBOE, P, Ph

Analysis prepared by **Robert M. Gold** on August 07, 2006, when the stock traded at **$ 65.68**.

Highlights

- We look for FY 06 (Sep.) revenues of $5.8 billion, excluding foreign exchange fluctuations, which BDX believes could lower reported sales growth by about 1%. Broken down by segment, we see FY 06 medical systems sales growth of about 8%, with biosciences advancing 9% and diagnostics gaining 6%. We expect strength will be seen in sales of safety-engineered products, blood glucose monitoring and diabetes care products, immunization products, infectious disease diagnostics, and immunocytometry instrument platforms. We think sales in FY 07 will reach $6.3 billion.
- In our view, modest gross margin expansion is possible during FY 06, due to a more favorable sales mix and manufacturing efficiencies. R&D outlays could range from 5.0% to 5.5% of sales, while SG&A may account for 26% of sales. We look for FY 06 free cash flow of about $900 million. BDX's tax rate in FY 06 is seen at 26%.
- Excluding a non-recurring insurance settlement gain and acquired in-process R&D charges, we estimate FY 06 operating EPS of $3.26. Our forecast removes $0.25 of projected stock option expense. Looking into FY 07, our EPS estimate is $3.65, including $0.30 of stock option costs.

Investment Rationale/Risk

- We think BDX should continue to benefit from recovering end user demand in the life sciences industry and momentum in the diagnostics and diabetes management areas. With a recent dividend yield of 1.3%, BDX provides the largest yield in our medical equipment coverage universe, and the stock offers one of the highest S&P Quality Rankings in the health care sector. Given our expectation that high quality, defensive names will lead the market over the next 12-months, and our opinion that Becton shares are underpriced relative to both the S&P 500 and its medical device peers, we continue to recommend purchase.
- Risks to our recommendation and target price include a slower-than-expected recovery in key life science markets, adverse patent litigation and unfavorable foreign currency fluctuations.
- Recently priced at 17.9X our FY 07 EPS forecast, BDX was at a steep discount to our medical device coverage universe, a discount we feel is unwarranted given the company's sales momentum and well-managed cost structure. Our 12-month target price of $75 assumes a P/E of about 20.5X our FY 07 EPS estimate and a forward PEG ratio of 1.5X, in line with peers.

Qualitative Risk Assessment

LOW | **MEDIUM** | HIGH

BDX's markets are competitive, and new product introductions by current and future competitors have the potential to significantly impact market dynamics. In addition, changes in domestic and foreign healthcare industry practices and regulations may result in increased pricing pressures and lower reimbursements for some of its products. On the other hand, we believe Becton's product line has more favorable demand and pricing characteristics than for those of the medical equipment industry in general.

Quantitative Evaluations

S&P Quality Ranking A

D | C | B- | B | B+ | A- | **A** | A+

Relative Strength Rank MODERATE

48

LOWEST = 1 HIGHEST = 99

Revenue/Earnings Data

Revenue (Million $)

	1Q	2Q	3Q	4Q	Year
2006	1,414	1,449	1,484	--	--
2005	1,288	1,366	1,381	1,379	5,415
2004	1,185	1,254	1,243	1,253	4,935
2003	1,052	1,134	1,165	1,177	4,528
2002	945.0	1,013	998.5	1,077	4,033
2001	843.3	961.2	954.2	987.5	3,754

Earnings Per Share ($)

2006	0.85	0.61	0.81	**E**0.84	**E**3.26
2005	0.74	0.71	0.73	0.47	2.66
2004	0.48	0.62	0.41	0.70	2.21
2003	0.43	0.54	0.49	0.61	2.07
2002	0.37	0.48	0.44	0.50	1.79
2001	0.23	0.44	0.46	0.49	1.63

Fiscal year ended Sep. 30. Next earnings report expected: Early November. EPS Estimates based on S&P Operating Earnings; historical GAAP earnings are as reported.

Dividend Data (Dates: mm/dd Payment Date: mm/dd/yy)

Amount ($)	Date Decl.	Ex-Div. Date	Stk. of Record	Payment Date
0.215	11/22	12/09	12/13	01/03/06
0.215	01/31	03/08	03/10	03/31/06
0.215	05/23	06/07	06/09	06/30/06
0.215	07/25	09/06	09/08	09/29/06

Dividends have been paid since 1926. Source: Company reports.

Becton, Dickinson and Co

Business Summary August 07, 2006

Becton, Dickinson traces its roots to a concern started by Maxwell Becton and Fairleigh Dickinson in 1897. One of the first companies to sell U.S.-made glass syringes, BDX was also a pioneer in the production of hypodermic needles. The company now manufactures and sells medical supplies, devices, lab equipment and diagnostic products used by health care institutions, life science researchers, clinical laboratories, industry and the general public. In FY 05 (Sep.), about 52% of sales were generated from foreign markets.

Major products in the core medical systems division (55% of FY 05 revenue from continuing operations) include hypodermic syringes and needles for injection, insulin syringes and pen needles and blood glucose monitoring systems for diabetes care, infusion therapy devices, prefillable drug delivery systems and surgical blades and scalpels. The segment also markets specialty blades and cannulas for ophthalmic surgery procedures, anesthesia needles, critical care systems, elastic support products and thermometers.

The diagnostics segment (30%) sells clinical and industrial microbiology products, sample collection products, specimen management systems, hematology instruments and other diagnostic systems, including immunodiagnostic test kits. The segment also includes consulting services and customized, automated bar-code systems for patient identification and point-of-care data capture.

The biosciences unit (15%) provides research tools and reagents to clinicians and medical researchers studying genes, proteins and cells in order to better understand disease, improve diagnosis and disease management and facilitate the discovery and development of novel therapeutics. Products include instrument systems for cell sorting and analysis, monoclonal antibody reagents and kits for diagnostic and research use, tools to aid in drug discovery and vaccine development, molecular biology products, fluid handling, cell growth and screening products.

Research and development spending in FY 05 was $272 million, or 5.0% of revenues, compared with $236 million (4.8%) in FY 04. In FY 06, BDX expects R&D spending to rise approximately 12%.

Company Financials

Per Share Data ($) Year Ended Sep. 30	2005	2004	2003	2002	2001	2000	1999	1998	1997	1996
Tangible Book Value	10.28	9.28	8.82	6.06	5.35	3.80	2.74	3.30	4.11	4.44
Cash Flow	4.36	3.57	3.54	2.92	2.76	2.58	2.01	1.77	1.97	1.81
Earnings	2.66	2.21	2.07	1.79	1.63	1.49	1.04	0.90	1.15	1.05
S&P Core Earnings	2.74	2.39	2.01	1.57	1.38	NA	NA	NA	NA	NA
Dividends	0.72	0.60	0.40	0.39	0.38	0.37	0.34	0.29	0.26	0.23
Payout Ratio	27%	27%	19%	22%	23%	25%	33%	32%	23%	22%
Prices:High	61.17	58.18	41.82	38.60	39.25	35.31	44.19	49.63	27.81	22.75
Prices:Low	49.71	40.90	28.82	24.70	29.96	23.75	22.38	24.38	20.94	17.69
P/E Ratio:High	23	26	20	22	24	24	42	55	24	22
P/E Ratio:Low	19	19	14	14	18	16	21	27	18	17

Income Statement Analysis (Million $)	2005	2004	2003	2002	2001	2000	1999	1998	1997	1996
Revenue	5,415	4,935	4,528	4,033	3,754	3,618	3,418	3,117	2,811	2,770
Operating Income	1,419	1,244	1,094	1,002	952	861	780	714	661	632
Depreciation	387	357	344	305	306	288	259	229	210	200
Interest Expense	55.7	29.6	73.1	33.3	47.1	78.3	72.1	64.2	48.6	64.4
Pretax Income	1,005	753	710	629	577	520	373	341	423	394
Effective Tax Rate	31.1%	22.6%	22.9%	23.6%	24.0%	24.4%	26.0%	30.6%	29.0%	28.0%
Net Income	692	583	547	480	438	393	276	237	300	283
S&P Core Earnings	712	628	523	417	364	NA	NA	NA	NA	NA

Balance Sheet & Other Financial Data (Million $)	2005	2004	2003	2002	2001	2000	1999	1998	1997	1996
Cash	1,043	719	520	243	82.1	49.2	59.9	83.3	113	165
Current Assets	2,975	2,641	2,339	1,929	1,763	1,661	1,684	1,543	1,313	1,277
Total Assets	6,072	5,753	5,572	5,040	4,802	4,505	4,437	3,846	3,080	2,890
Current Liabilities	1,299	1,050	1,043	1,252	1,265	1,354	1,329	1,092	678	766
Long Term Debt	1,061	1,172	1,184	803	1,902	780	954	765	665	468
Common Equity	3,284	3,037	2,863	2,450	2,288	1,912	1,722	1,565	1,334	1,272
Total Capital	4,345	4,328	4,200	3,396	4,321	2,823	2,764	2,428	2,095	1,829
Capital Expenditures	318	266	261	260	371	376	312	181	170	146
Cash Flow	1,080	940	889	783	742	679	532	463	507	481
Current Ratio	2.3	2.5	2.2	1.5	1.4	1.2	1.3	1.4	1.9	1.7
% Long Term Debt of Capitalization	24.4	27.1	28.2	23.6	44.0	27.6	34.5	31.5	31.7	25.6
% Net Income of Revenue	12.8	11.8	12.1	11.9	11.7	10.9	8.1	7.6	10.7	10.2
% Return on Assets	11.7	10.3	10.3	9.8	9.4	8.8	6.7	6.8	10.1	9.6
% Return on Equity	21.9	19.7	20.5	20.2	20.8	21.5	16.6	16.1	22.8	21.5

Data as orig reptd.; bef. results of disc opers/spec. items. Per share data adj. for stk. divs.; EPS diluted. E-Estimated. NA-Not Available. NM-Not Meaningful. NR-Not Ranked. UR-Under Review.

Office: One Becton Drive, Franklin Lakes, NJ 07417-1880.
Telephone: 201-847-6800.
Email: investor_relations@bdhq.bd.com
Website: http://www.bd.com

Chrmn, Pres & CEO: E.J. Ludwig
EVP & CFO: J. Considine
VP & Secy: D. Paranicas
VP & General Counsel: J.S. Sherman

VP & Cntlr: W. Tozzi
Investor Contact: P.A. Spinella (201-847-5453)
Board of Directors: B. L. Anderson, H. P. Becton, Jr., E. F. DeGraan, C. M. Fraser-Liggett, E. J. Ludwig, A. A. Mahmoud, G. A. Mecklenburg, J. F. Orr, W. J. Overlock, Jr., J. E. Perrella, B. L. Scott, A. Sommer, M. af Ugglas

Founded: 1897
Domicile: New Jersey
Employees: 24,800

STANDARD &POOR'S

Bed Bath & Beyond Inc

S&P Recommendation STRONG BUY ★★★★★

Price $39.70 (as of Oct 27, 2006)

12-Mo. Target Price $47.00

Investment Style Large-Cap Growth

GICS Sector Consumer Discretionary
Sub-Industry Homefurnishing Retail

Comment BBBY operates a nationwide chain of more than 700 superstores selling better-quality domestics merchandise and home furnishings at prices below those offered by department stores.

Key Stock Statistics (Source S&P, Vickers, company reports)

52-Wk Range	$44.10–30.92	S&P Oper. EPS 2007E	2.19	P/E on S&P Oper. EPS 2007E	18.1	Dividend Rate/Share	Nil
Trailing 12-Month EPS	$1.98	S&P Oper. EPS 2008E	2.50	Common Shares Outstg. (M)	282.7	Yield (%)	Nil
Trailing 12-Month P/E	20.1	S&P Core EPS 2007E	2.19	Market Capitalization(B)	$11.222	Beta	0.93
$10K Invested 5 Yrs Ago	$14,775	S&P Core EPS 2008E	2.50	Institutional Ownership (%)	86	S&P Credit Rating	BBB

Price Performance

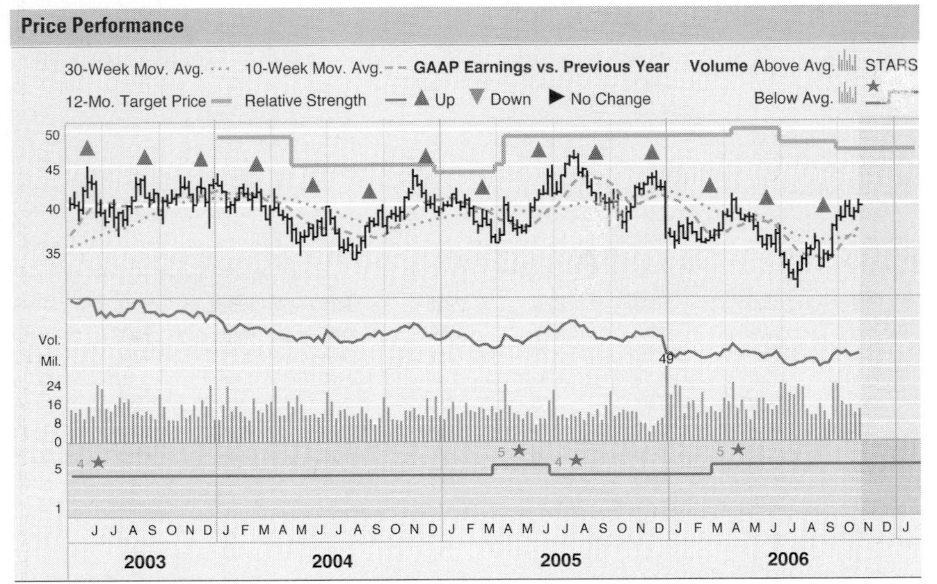

Options: ASE, CBOE, Ph

Analysis prepared by **Michael Souers** on October 10, 2006, when the stock traded at **$ 40.05**.

Highlights

- We expect sales to increase 12% to 13% in FY 07 (Feb.), reflecting the projected addition of about 70 to 75 new Bed Bath & Beyond stores, representing nearly 2.5 million square feet of store space, and same-store sales increases of 3% to 5%. We also anticipate the opening of a handful of new Christmas Tree Shops and Harmon Stores. We see same-store sales growth likely being driven by an increase in the average ticket.
- We project that gross margins will widen slightly, on a more favorable product mix. We expect a modest narrowing in operating margins, as the inclusion of stock option expense for the first half of FY 07, increased occupancy costs, and slightly higher store opening costs are partly offset by the leveraging of SG&A expenses.
- After higher interest income, an anticipated level tax rate of 36.6% versus 37.4%, and approximately 5% fewer shares, we see FY 07 EPS of $2.19, a 14% increase from the $1.92 the company earned in FY 06. We estimate EPS of $2.50 in FY 08. Our FY 07 EPS estimate includes $0.12 of projected stock option expense.

Investment Rationale/Risk

- BBBY recently traded at a P/E to earnings growth (PEG) ratio of under 1.0X, a discount to both peers and the S&P 500 (1.3X). In addition, BBBY's forward P/E of about 15X is low on a historical basis, as the company's average forward P/E has been approximately 30X over the past four years. The company has approved 1,100 domestic sites, and we believe that annual sales will rise at a compound annual growth rate (CAGR) of 10%-11% over the next five years. We expect that BBBY will continue to gain market share in home furnishings, with better merchandising and store level execution than peers.
- Risks to our recommendation and target price include a potential slowdown in the U.S. economy, an unanticipated shift in consumer spending away from home-centered products, and possible miscues in BBBY's store expansion strategy.
- Our 12-month target price of $47, or about 19X our FY 08 EPS estimate, is based on our discounted cash flow analysis, which assumes a weighted average cost of capital of 10.8% and a terminal growth rate of 4.0%.

Qualitative Risk Assessment

LOW | **MEDIUM** | HIGH

Our risk assessment reflects the cyclical nature of the home furnishing retail industry, which relies heavily on consumer spending, and, to a lesser extent, housing turnover; the untapped growth areas in major domestic metro markets and Canada; and an S&P Quality Ranking of A-, which reflects consistent historical earnings growth, in our opinion.

Quantitative Evaluations

S&P Quality Ranking A-

D | C | B- | B | B+ | **A-** | A | A+

Relative Strength Rank STRONG

72

LOWEST = 1 HIGHEST = 99

Revenue/Earnings Data

Revenue (Million $)

	1Q	2Q	3Q	4Q	Year
2007	1,396	1,607	--	--	--
2006	1,244	1,431	1,449	1,685	5,810
2005	1,101	1,274	1,305	1,468	5,148
2004	893.9	1,111	1,175	1,298	4,478
2003	776.8	903.0	936.0	1,049	3,665
2002	575.8	713.6	759.4	879.1	2,928

Earnings Per Share ($)

2007	0.35	0.51	E0.53	E0.80	E2.19
2006	0.33	0.47	0.45	0.67	1.92
2005	0.27	0.39	0.40	0.59	1.65
2004	0.19	0.32	0.33	0.47	1.31
2003	0.15	0.25	0.25	0.35	1.00
2002	0.10	0.18	0.18	0.28	0.74

Fiscal year ended Feb. 28. Next earnings report expected: Late December. EPS Estimates based on S&P Operating Earnings; historical GAAP earnings are as reported.

Dividend Data

No cash dividends have been paid.

Bed Bath & Beyond Inc

Business Summary October 10, 2006

CORPORATE OVERVIEW. Bed Bath & Beyond operates one of the largest U.S. chains of superstores selling domestics merchandise and home furnishings. BBBY stores range in size from 20,000 sq. ft. to 50,000 sq. ft., with some exceeding 80,000 sq. ft. The company has grown rapidly, from 38 stores at the end of FY 93 (Feb.) to 742 stores in 46 states and Puerto Rico at year-end FY 06. BBBY opened 83 stores in FY 06, after opening 85 stores in FY 05; it expects to open 70 to 75 new stores in FY 07. During FY 06, total square footage of Bed Bath & Beyond stores grew 11%, to 25.5 million sq. ft., from 22.9 million sq. ft. Company stores are principally located in suburban areas of medium and large sized cities. These stores are situated in strip and power strip shopping centers, as well as in major off-price and conventional malls, and freestanding buildings.

In March 2002, the company acquired Harmon Stores, Inc., a health and beauty care retailer. The Harmon chain had 38 stores in three states at February 28, 2006, ranging in size from approximately 5,000 to 9,000 sq. ft. In June 2003, BBBY acquired Christmas Tree Shops, a retailer of home decor, giftware, housewares, food, paper goods and seasonal products, for approximately $194.4 million, net of cash acquired. The company operated 29 Christmas Tree Shops in eight states at year-end FY 06, ranging in size between 30,000 and 50,000 sq. ft.

BBBY believes that the breadth and depth of selection that it offers in most product categories exceeds what is generally available in department stores or other specialty retail stores and that this enables it to offer customers the convenience of one-stop shopping for most household items. The company sells domestics merchandise such as bed linens, sheets, comforters, bedspreads, draperies, pillows and blankets. Bath accessories include towels, shower curtains, waste baskets, hampers and rugs. Kitchen textiles include tablecloths, placemats, napkins, and dish towels. BBBY stores also sell home furnishings such as kitchen and tabletop items, including cookware, cutlery, flatware and glassware; basic housewares, consisting of storage items and closet items; small electric appliances such as blenders, coffee makers, vacuum cleaners, toaster ovens and hair dryers; and miscellaneous gift items, consisting of picture frames, luggage, small toys and seasonal merchandise.

Company Financials

Per Share Data ($) Year Ended Feb. 28	**2006**	**2005**	**2004**	**2003**	**2002**	**2001**	**2000**	**1999**	**1998**	**1997**
Tangible Book Value	8.05	6.99	6.14	4.93	3.75	2.84	1.99	1.48	1.07	0.78
Cash Flow	2.29	1.96	1.59	1.25	0.94	0.75	0.57	0.42	0.32	0.24
Earnings	1.92	1.65	1.31	1.00	0.74	0.59	0.46	0.34	0.26	0.20
S&P Core Earnings	1.87	1.55	1.23	0.92	0.67	0.53	NA	NA	NA	NA
Dividends	Nil	Nil	Nil	Nil	Nil	Nil	Nil	Nil	Nil	Nil
Payout Ratio	Nil	Nil	Nil	Nil	Nil	Nil	Nil	Nil	Nil	Nil
Calendar Year	2005	2004	2003	2002	2001	2000	1999	1998	1997	1996
Prices:High	46.99	44.43	45.00	37.90	35.70	27.31	19.69	17.59	9.81	7.88
Prices:Low	35.50	33.88	30.18	26.70	18.70	11.00	12.75	8.56	5.72	4.09
P/E Ratio:High	24	27	34	38	48	46	43	52	38	40
P/E Ratio:Low	18	21	23	27	25	19	28	25	22	21
Income Statement Analysis (Million $)										
Revenue	5,810	5,148	4,478	3,665	2,928	2,397	1,878	1,397	1,067	823
Operating Income	990	890	724	555	409	319	241	181	137	104
Depreciation	111	97.5	84.6	74.8	62.5	46.7	31.6	23.2	18.2	13.4
Interest Expense	Nil	Nil	Nil	Nil	Nil	Nil	Nil	Nil	Nil	Nil
Pretax Income	915	811	650	491	357	282	215	162	121	91.3
Effective Tax Rate	37.4%	37.8%	38.5%	38.5%	38.5%	39.0%	39.0%	39.7%	39.8%	39.8%
Net Income	573	505	399	302	220	172	131	97.3	73.1	55.0
S&P Core Earnings	557	470	370	277	200	155	NA	NA	NA	NA
Balance Sheet & Other Financial Data (Million $)										
Cash	652	851	867	617	429	239	144	90.4	53.3	38.8
Current Assets	2,072	2,097	1,969	1,594	1,227	886	647	455	326	228
Total Assets	3,382	3,200	2,865	2,189	1,648	1,196	866	633	458	330
Current Liabilities	990	874	770	680	511	353	287	206	150	106
Long Term Debt	Nil	Nil	Nil	Nil	Nil	Nil	Nil	Nil	Nil	Nil
Common Equity	2,262	2,204	1,991	1,452	1,094	817	559	411	295	214
Total Capital	2,262	2,204	1,991	1,452	1,094	817	559	411	295	214
Capital Expenditures	220	191	113	135	121	140	90.1	62.3	41.2	35.1
Cash Flow	684	602	484	377	282	219	163	121	91.4	68.5
Current Ratio	2.1	2.4	2.6	2.3	2.4	2.5	2.3	2.2	2.2	2.2
% Long Term Debt of Capitalization	Nil	Nil	Nil	Nil	Nil	Nil	Nil	Nil	Nil	Nil
% Net Income of Revenue	9.9	9.8	8.9	8.2	7.5	7.2	7.0	7.0	6.9	6.7
% Return on Assets	17.4	16.7	15.8	15.8	15.4	16.7	17.5	17.8	18.6	19.5
% Return on Equity	25.7	24.1	23.2	23.7	23.0	25.0	27.1	27.6	28.7	30.1

Data as orig reptd.; bef. results of disc opers/spec. items. Per share data adj. for stk. divs.; EPS diluted. E-Estimated. NA-Not Available. NM-Not Meaningful. NR-Not Ranked. UR-Under Review.

Office: 650 Liberty Ave, Union, NJ 07083-8135.
Telephone: 908-688-0888.
Website: http://www.bedbathandbeyond.com
Co-Chrmn: W. Eisenberg

Co-Chrmn: L. Feinstein
Pres: A. Stark
CEO: S.H. Temares
Investor Contact: R. Curwin (908-688-0888)

Board of Directors: D. S. Adler, S. F. Barshay, W. Eisenberg, K. Eppler, L. Feinstein, J. Heller, R. S. Kaplan, V. A. Morrison, F. Stoller, S. H. Temares

Founded: 1971
Domicile: New York
Employees: 33,000

STANDARD &POOR'S

BellSouth Corp

S&P Recommendation HOLD ★★★★★

Price $45.04 (as of Oct 27, 2006)

12-Mo. Target Price $46.00

Investment Style Large-Cap Value

GICS Sector Telecommunication Services
Sub-Industry Integrated Telecommunication Services

Comment BellSouth, which provides wireline service in the southeastern U.S. and co-owns Cingular Wireless, has agreed to be sold to AT&T Inc., subject to necessary approvals.

Key Stock Statistics (Source S&P, Vickers, company reports)

52-Wk Range	$45.99–25.22	S&P Oper. EPS 2006E	2.36	P/E on S&P Oper. EPS 2006E	19.1	Dividend Rate/Share	$1.16
Trailing 12-Month EPS	$1.85	S&P Oper. EPS 2007E	2.49	Common Shares Outstg. (M)	1,815.8	Yield (%)	2.58
Trailing 12-Month P/E	24.4	S&P Core EPS 2006E	2.20	Market Capitalization(B)	$81.783	Beta	1.67
$10K Invested 5 Yrs Ago	$14,289	S&P Core EPS 2007E	2.30	Institutional Ownership (%)	60	S&P Credit Rating	A

Price Performance

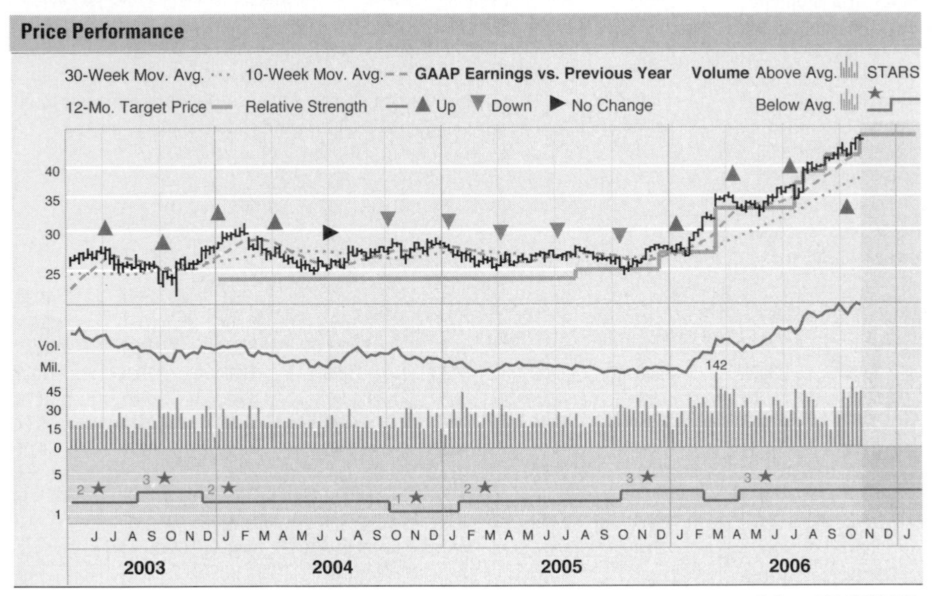

Options: ASE, CBOE, P, Ph

Analysis prepared by **Todd Rosenbluth** on October 25, 2006, when the stock traded at **$ 45.08**.

Highlights

- In March 2006, BLS agreed to be acquired by AT&T (T: hold, $35) in an all stock deal, subject to necessary approvals, which are expected by the end of 2006. We expect BLS's normalized revenues (including the Cingular wireless joint venture) to be up 4% in 2006 and 2.5% in 2007. Revenues should be driven primarily by customer growth at Cingular. On the wireline side, we project a continued decline in total access lines.
- With wireline work force and other operational cuts combined with improving customer retention at Cingular helping to keep marketing costs under control, we see EBITDA margins widening to approximately 38% in 2006. We believe these cost savings will also be helped by the impact of work force reductions on the wireline side.
- We expect operating EPS of $2.36 in 2006 and $2.49 in 2007. Our S&P Core EPS estimates reflect pension adjustments. Our 2006 operating estimate excludes integration expense from the AT&T Wireless deal in 2004 and other one-time charges that totaled $0.29 a share in the first nine months.

Investment Rationale/Risk

- BLS shareholders are expected to receive 1.325 T shares for each BLS share, but there is no downside price protection. As a stand-alone company, we believe BLS will continue to benefit from growth at Cingular as customer loyalty and data service growth improves. On the wireline side, while we have concerns about continued residential line losses from increased competition, operating margins should remain strong. We see T benefiting from BLS's more efficient wireline operations.
- Risks to our recommendation and target price include the failure of T to close on its planned purchase of BLS, increased competition from wireless, wireline and cable carriers, and weaker than expected fundamentals at AT&T.
- Our 12-month target price of $46 for BLS reflects a slight discount to the proposed deal terms and reflects our 12-month target price of $36 for AT&T. While we believe a premium to peers P/E of 18X and an enterprise value to EBITDA multiple of 7X is excessive for a company facing BLS's operational challenges, we expect the planned deal, subject to necessary approvals, to be approved by the end of the year.

Qualitative Risk Assessment

LOW | **MEDIUM** | HIGH

Our risk assessment reflects our view of the company's strong balance sheet and its buying power over suppliers, offset by the proposed merger with AT&T and the competitive nature of serving telecom customers in its region of the country.

Quantitative Evaluations

S&P Quality Ranking B+

D | C | B- | B | **B+** | A- | A | A+

Relative Strength Rank STRONG

79

LOWEST = 1 HIGHEST = 99

Revenue/Earnings Data

Revenue (Million $)

	1Q	2Q	3Q	4Q	Year
2006	5,171	5,206	5,218	--	--
2005	5,091	5,142	5,072	5,242	20,547
2004	4,976	5,083	5,095	5,146	20,300
2003	5,523	5,642	5,728	5,742	22,635
2002	5,534	5,780	5,434	5,692	22,440
2001	5,919	5,985	6,013	6,213	24,130

Earnings Per Share ($)

	1Q	2Q	3Q	4Q	Year
2006	0.43	0.49	0.58	**E**0.62	**E**2.36
2005	0.37	0.43	0.44	0.34	1.59
2004	0.63	0.51	0.46	0.25	1.85
2003	0.49	0.51	0.51	0.43	1.94
2002	0.61	0.16	0.35	0.32	1.44
2001	0.47	0.47	Nil	0.42	1.36

Fiscal year ended Dec. 31. Next earnings report expected: Late January. EPS Estimates based on S&P Operating Earnings; historical GAAP earnings are as reported.

Dividend Data (Dates: mm/dd Payment Date: mm/dd/yy)

Amount ($)	Date Decl.	Ex-Div. Date	Stk. of Record	Payment Date
0.290	11/28	01/10	01/12	02/01/06
0.290	02/27	04/11	04/13	05/01/06
0.290	06/26	07/11	07/13	08/01/06
0.290	09/25	10/05	10/10	11/01/06

Dividends have been paid since 1984. Source: Company reports.

BellSouth Corp

Business Summary October 25, 2006

CORPORATE OVERVIEW. BellSouth Corp. is the third largest Regional Bell Operating Company (behind Verizon, and AT&T Inc.--formerly SBC Communications), with approximately 19 million local phone lines, a long-distance penetration rate of about 60% of its mass market customers, and approximately 3.5 million DSL customers as of September 2006. In 2005, BLS lost 100,000 access lines due to the hurricanes in the Gulf Coast region. The company owns a 40% interest in Cingular Wireless, the largest U.S. wireless provider with 58.7 million subscribers, which generated 42% of BLS's normalized operating revenues in the first nine months of 2006.

COMPETITIVE LANDSCAPE. In 2006, BLS's wireline operations have faced technology substitution effects, primarily from wireless, as customers have eliminated their access line. We believe this trend is continuing and expect the more urban consumer markets to be similarly challenged by cable telephony competition from Time Warner, Comcast, and others. As of June 2006, BLS faced cable telephony competition in markets where 50% of its access lines reside. In an effort to combat substitution from cable carriers and national wireless carriers with large buckets of minutes, BLS has partnered with DirectTV to provide video services and offered DSL services with different speeds.

In our opinion, one of the challenges for wireless carriers such as Cingular, currently co-owned by BLS and AT&T, is keeping customers loyal, as there are three other national carriers and other regional carriers in most markets. We believe Cingular has begun to differentiate itself by using initially exclusive wireless handsets offered by suppliers Motorola and Samsung. In the third quarter of 2006, it added 1.4 million net subscribers. We expect Cingular's additions to improve as the integration of the previously acquired AT&T Wireless business continues.

Company Financials

Per Share Data ($) Year Ended Dec. 31	**2005**	**2004**	**2003**	**2002**	**2001**	**2000**	**1999**	**1998**	**1997**	**1996**
Tangible Book Value	12.24	11.73	9.33	8.05	7.51	6.81	5.86	6.79	6.67	5.98
Cash Flow	3.59	3.83	4.19	3.92	3.90	4.84	4.24	3.97	3.64	3.31
Earnings	1.59	1.85	1.94	1.44	1.36	2.23	1.80	1.78	1.65	1.44
S&P Core Earnings	1.38	1.68	1.95	0.56	1.21	NA	NA	NA	NA	NA
Dividends	1.12	1.04	0.87	0.78	0.76	0.76	0.76	0.72	0.72	0.72
Payout Ratio	70%	56%	45%	54%	56%	34%	42%	40%	44%	50%
Prices:High	28.12	31.00	30.00	40.90	45.88	53.50	51.31	50.00	29.06	22.94
Prices:Low	24.32	24.46	19.79	18.32	36.26	34.94	39.75	27.06	19.06	17.63
P/E Ratio:High	18	17	15	28	34	24	29	28	18	16
P/E Ratio:Low	15	13	10	13	27	16	22	15	12	12

Income Statement Analysis (Million $)										
Revenue	20,547	20,300	22,635	22,440	24,130	26,151	24,224	23,123	20,561	19,040
Depreciation	3,661	3,636	4,179	4,643	4,782	4,935	4,671	4,357	3,964	3,719
Maintenance	NA	NA	NA	NA	NA	NA	NA	NA	NA	NA
Construction Credits	NA	NA	NA	NA	NA	NA	NA	NA	NA	NA
Effective Tax Rate	32.3%	34.6%	35.9%	40.8%	36.0%	36.0%	37.2%	38.7%	39.4%	37.9%
Net Income	2,913	3,394	3,589	2,708	2,570	4,220	3,448	3,527	3,270	2,863
S&P Core Earnings	2,523	3,062	3,594	1,045	2,269	NA	NA	NA	NA	NA

Balance Sheet & Other Financial Data (Million $)										
Gross Property	64,574	63,601	65,715	64,435	64,332	24,157	61,009	57,974	53,828	50,059
Net Property	21,723	22,039	23,807	23,445	24,943	24,157	24,631	23,940	22,861	21,825
Capital Expenditures	3,457	3,193	3,200	3,785	5,997	6,995	6,200	5,212	4,858	4,455
Total Capital	43,220	44,666	36,550	34,641	36,817	32,955	26,759	17,862	25,324	21,365
Fixed Charges Coverage	4.6	6.1	6.3	4.6	3.9	5.9	6.6	7.5	7.1	6.8
Capitalization:Long Term Debt	13,079	15,108	11,489	12,283	15,014	12,463	9,113	8,715	7,348	8,116
Capitalization:Preferred	Nil	Nil	Nil	Nil	Nil	Nil	Nil	Nil	Nil	Nil
Capitalization:Common	23,534	23,066	19,712	17,686	18,597	16,912	14,815	17,862	15,740	13,249
% Return on Revenue	14.2	16.7	15.9	12.1	10.7	16.1	14.2	15.3	15.9	15.0
% Return on Invested Capital	9.8	10.7	13.6	13.7	12.2	20.7	17.7	26.0	14.0	12.2
% Return on Common Equity	12.5	15.9	19.1	14.9	14.5	26.6	22.3	21.0	22.2	22.8
% Earned on Net Property	39.3	39.1	43.6	43.6	46.8	50.9	47.1	43.8	41.8	39.6
% Long Term Debt of Capitalization	35.7	39.6	36.8	41.0	44.7	42.4	38.1	29.8	31.8	37.9
Capital % Preferred	Nil	Nil	Nil	Nil	Nil	Nil	Nil	Nil	Nil	Nil
Capitalization:% Common	64.3	60.4	63.2	59.0	55.3	57.6	61.9	70.2	68.2	66.7

Data as orig reptd.; bef. results of disc opers/spec. items. Per share data adj. for stk. divs.; EPS diluted. E-Estimated. NA-Not Available. NM-Not Meaningful. NR-Not Ranked. UR Under Review.

Office: 1155 Peachtree St NE Rm 15G03, Atlanta, GA 30309-7629.
Telephone: 404-249-2000.
Email: investor@bellsouth.com
Website: http://www.bellsouth.com

Chrmn & CEO: F.D. Ackerman
Pres & COO: M. Feidler
Vice Chrmn: D. Anderson
VP & General Counsel: M. Gary

Investor Contact: P. Shannon (800-241-3419)
Board of Directors: F. D. Ackerman, R. V. Anderson, J. H. Blanchard, J. H. Brown, A. M. Codina, M. Feidler, K. F. Feldstein, J. P. Kelly, L. F. Mullin, R. B. Smith, W. S. Stavropoulos

Founded: 1983
Domicile: Georgia
Employees: 63,066

STANDARD &POOR'S

Bemis Co Inc

S&P Recommendation BUY ★★★★★

Price $33.60 (as of Oct 27, 2006)

12-Mo. Target Price $40.00

Investment Style Mid-Cap Value

GICS Sector Materials
Sub-Industry Paper Packaging

Comment This Minneapolis-based company is a leading maker of a broad range of flexible packaging and pressure-sensitive materials.

Key Stock Statistics (Source S&P, Vickers, company reports)

52-Wk Range	$34.76–25.75	S&P Oper. EPS 2006E	1.85	P/E on S&P Oper. EPS 2006E	18.2	Dividend Rate/Share	$0.76
Trailing 12-Month EPS	$1.68	S&P Oper. EPS 2007E	2.05	Common Shares Outstg. (M)	104.8	Yield (%)	2.26
Trailing 12-Month P/E	20.0	S&P Core EPS 2006E	1.87	Market Capitalization(B)	$3.522	Beta	0.76
$10K Invested 5 Yrs Ago	$16,829	S&P Core EPS 2007E	2.08	Institutional Ownership (%)	67	S&P Credit Rating	A

Price Performance

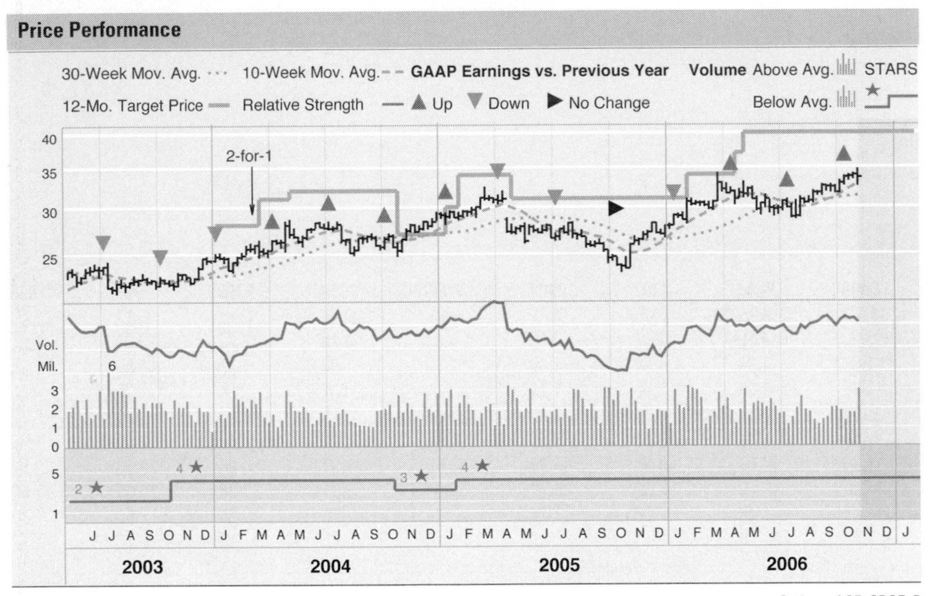

Options: ASE, CBOE, P

Analysis prepared by **Stewart Scharf** on August 16, 2006, when the stock traded at **$ 31.54**.

Highlights

- We project high single digit sales growth for 2006, mainly driven by demand for innovative flexible packaging products. We see a sequential pickup in orders for new flexible and pressure-sensitive products in Europe and Brazil, while BMS focuses on growing its higher-margin graphics and technical product lines. We expect 5% sales growth in 2007.
- In our view, gross margins will widen somewhat in 2006 from 19.5% in 2005, reflecting pricing initiatives, more balanced order patterns and a change in the product mix to include more higher value added products, especially in Europe. Although rising material costs are likely to restrict second half margins, we believe operating margins will expand from 2005's 10.8%, based on a capacity build and better production efficiencies, along with SG&A expenses below 9.5% of sales. We see further margin expansion during 2007.
- We estimate 2006 EPS of $1.85 (before $0.18 of projected restructuring and related charges), advancing to $2.05 in 2007 (before an estimated $0.03 restructuring charge).

Investment Rationale/Risk

- Based on our valuation metrics, which we believe indicate attractive potential on a total return basis, and favorable market drivers, we maintain our buy recommendation.
- Risks to our recommendation and target price include a significant rise in petrochemical prices that the company is unable to pass on to customers, a further change in customer order patterns due to rising resin costs, and negative foreign exchange rates. We have concern regarding corporate governance practices, mainly due to board and audit issues, including the CEO being a party to one or more related-party transactions.
- At less than 17X our 2006 EPS estimate, the shares were recently trading at a modest premium to S&P's paper packaging group. However, based on our DCF analysis, the stock is nearly 30% below its intrinsic value of $43, based on our assumption of 3.5% terminal growth rate and 8.3% cost of capital. Blending our metrics, we think the stock deserves a forward P/E of 21.5X our 2006 estimate, which leads to our 12-month target price of $40.

Qualitative Risk Assessment

LOW | **MEDIUM** | HIGH

Our risk assessment reflects the possibility of softer global economic conditions, weaker foreign exchange rates, rising raw material prices and interest rates, and difficulty in integrating acquisitions. However, it also considers the S&P Quality Ranking of A, which indicates historically stable earnings and dividend growth.

Quantitative Evaluations

S&P Quality Ranking A

D | C | B- | B | B+ | A- | **A** | A+

Relative Strength Rank MODERATE

55

LOWEST = 1 HIGHEST = 99

Revenue/Earnings Data

Revenue (Million $)

	1Q	2Q	3Q	4Q	Year
2006	901.7	933.8	903.3	--	--
2005	831.9	879.9	870.1	892.1	3,474
2004	684.0	712.9	711.9	725.6	2,834
2003	638.6	670.2	662.0	664.3	2,635
2002	552.7	584.8	601.0	630.6	2,369
2001	577.4	581.6	575.6	558.6	2,293

Earnings Per Share ($)

2006	0.35	0.46	0.45	E0.44	E1.85
2005	0.30	0.38	0.41	0.42	1.51
2004	0.40	0.42	0.41	0.44	1.67
2003	0.33	0.36	0.32	0.35	1.37
2002	0.33	0.41	0.41	0.40	1.54
2001	0.28	0.34	0.34	0.37	1.32

Fiscal year ended Dec. 31. Next earnings report expected: Late January. EPS Estimates based on S&P Operating Earnings; historical GAAP earnings are as reported.

Dividend Data (Dates: mm/dd Payment Date: mm/dd/yy)

Amount ($)	Date Decl.	Ex-Div. Date	Stk. of Record	Payment Date
0.190	02/02	02/13	02/15	03/01/06
0.190	05/04	05/17	05/19	06/01/06
0.190	08/03	08/16	08/18	09/01/06
0.190	10/26	11/15	11/17	12/01/06

Dividends have been paid since 1922. Source: Company reports.

Please read the Required Disclosures and Analyst Certification on the last page of this report.

Bemis Co Inc

Business Summary August 16, 2006

CORPORATE OVERVIEW. Bemis Co., a leading North American producer of flexible packaging products, as well as pressure-sensitive materials, focuses on the food industry (65% of sales). Markets also include the chemicals, agribusiness, pharmaceutical, personal care products, electronics, automotive and graphic industries. BMS has 61 manufacturing plants in 11 countries.

Although BMS focuses on marketing its products in the U.S. (66% of 2005 net sales), Europe (17%) and Canada (2.2%), it has broadened its reach to Southeast Asia, South America and Mexico (15% of sales combined), due to strong demand for barrier films to extend the shelf life of perishable foods.

In January 2005, the company acquired majority ownership of Brazil-based Dixie Toga, a leading South American packaging company, for $250 million in cash (less than 6X Dixie's 2004 EBITDA). Dixie had annual sales of over $450 million in 2005. BMS, which controls 85% of Dixie's preferred shares, is building a plant in Brazil. In our view, this acquisition will greatly contribute to the company's exposure overseas.

The Flexible Packaging Products segment (82% of net sales in 2005; $333 million of operating profits) produces a wide range of consumer and industrial packaging products, including high barrier, polyethylene and paper products. High barrier products, which comprise more than 50% of net sales, include flexible polymer film structures and barrier laminates for food, medical and personal care products.

The Pressure Sensitive Materials segment (18% of net sales in 2005; $41 million in operating profits) produces printing products, decorative and sheet products, and technical products.

Flexible packaging competitors include Alcan Packaging, Sealed Air, Sonoco Products, Smurfit-Stone Container and Intertape Polymer Group. Pressure-sensitive materials competitors include Avery Dennison, Minnesota Mining and Manufacturing (3M), Ricoh and Spinnaker Industries.

Company Financials

Per Share Data ($) Year Ended Dec. 31	2005	2004	2003	2002	2001	2000	1999	1998	1997	1996
Tangible Book Value	6.29	7.48	5.81	4.11	4.39	4.76	5.52	4.88	4.62	4.38
Cash Flow	2.98	2.88	2.56	2.65	2.49	2.24	2.02	1.88	1.73	1.57
Earnings	1.51	1.67	1.37	1.54	1.32	1.22	1.09	1.04	1.00	0.95
S&P Core Earnings	1.48	1.65	1.32	1.28	1.02	NA	NA	NA	NA	NA
Dividends	0.72	0.64	0.56	0.52	0.50	0.48	0.46	0.44	0.40	0.36
Payout Ratio	48%	38%	41%	34%	38%	39%	42%	42%	40%	38%
Prices:High	32.50	29.49	25.58	29.12	26.24	19.66	20.19	23.47	23.97	18.81
Prices:Low	23.20	23.24	19.67	19.70	14.34	11.47	15.09	16.75	16.81	12.81
P/E Ratio:High	22	18	19	19	20	16	19	22	24	20
P/E Ratio:Low	15	14	14	13	11	9	14	16	17	13

Income Statement Analysis (Million $)	2005	2004	2003	2002	2001	2000	1999	1998	1997	1996
Revenue	3,474	2,834	2,635	2,369	2,293	2,165	1,918	1,848	1,877	1,655
Operating Income	472	420	384	401	384	363	316	297	274	242
Depreciation	151	131	128	119	124	108	97.7	88.9	78.9	66.2
Interest Expense	38.7	15.5	12.6	15.4	30.3	31.6	21.2	21.9	18.9	13.4
Pretax Income	282	294	240	268	228	212	190	186	180	163
Effective Tax Rate	40.3%	38.7%	38.4%	37.9%	38.2%	38.2%	37.4%	37.8%	37.4%	27.9%
Net Income	163	180	147	166	140	131	115	111	108	101
S&P Core Earnings	160	179	142	137	108	NA	NA	NA	NA	NA

Balance Sheet & Other Financial Data (Million $)	2005	2004	2003	2002	2001	2000	1999	1998	1997	1996
Cash	91.1	93.9	76.5	56.4	35.1	28.9	18.2	23.7	13.8	10.2
Current Assets	988	874	752	722	587	640	584	518	516	467
Total Assets	2,965	2,487	2,293	2,257	1,923	1,889	1,532	1,453	1,363	1,169
Current Liabilities	474	375	316	326	238	495	253	243	251	214
Long Term Debt	790	534	583	718	595	438	372	371	317	241
Common Equity	1,349	1,308	1,139	959	886	799	726	671	640	567
Total Capital	2,336	2,019	1,878	1,788	1,606	1,342	1,227	1,156	1,055	865
Capital Expenditures	187	135	106	91.0	117	100	137	140	168	112
Cash Flow	313	311	275	285	264	239	212	200	186	167
Current Ratio	2.1	2.3	2.4	2.2	2.5	1.3	2.3	2.1	2.1	2.2
% Long Term Debt of Capitalization	33.8	26.4	31.1	40.2	37.1	32.6	30.3	32.1	30.0	27.9
% Net Income of Revenue	4.7	6.3	5.6	7.0	6.1	6.0	6.0	6.0	5.7	6.1
% Return on Assets	6.0	7.5	6.5	7.9	7.4	7.6	7.6	7.9	8.5	9.2
% Return on Equity	12.2	14.7	14.0	17.9	16.7	17.1	16.2	17.0	17.8	18.8

Data as orig reptd.; bef. results of disc opers/spec. items. Per share data adj. for stk. divs.; EPS diluted. E-Estimated. NA-Not Available. NM-Not Meaningful. NR-Not Ranked. UR-Under Review.

Office: 222 South 9th Street, Minneapolis, MN 55402-4099.
Telephone: 612-376-3000.
Website: http://www.bemis.com
Pres & CEO: J.H. Curler

COO & EVP: H.J. Theisen
VP, CFO & Treas: G.C. Wulf
VP, Secy & General Counsel: J.J. Seifert
Investor Contact: M.E. Miller (612-376-3030)

Board of Directors: W. J. Bolton, J. H. Curler, D. S. Haffner, B. L. Johnson, T. M. Manganello, N. P. McDonald, R. D. O'Shaughnessy, P. S. Peercy, E. N. Perry, W. J. Scholle, H. J. Theisen, P. Weaver, G. C. Wulf

Founded: 1858
Domicile: Missouri
Employees: 15,903

STANDARD & POOR'S

Best Buy Co. Inc.

S&P Recommendation	Price	12-Mo. Target Price	Investment Style
BUY ★★★★★	$54.14 (as of Oct 27, 2006)	$64.00	Large-Cap Growth

GICS Sector Consumer Discretionary
Sub-Industry Computer & Electronics Retail

Comment This leading retailer of consumer electronics and entertainment software operates more than 1,100 stores in the U.S., Canada and China.

Key Stock Statistics (Source S&P, Vickers, company reports)

52-Wk Range	$59.50–42.75	S&P Oper. EPS 2007E	2.79	P/E on S&P Oper. EPS 2007E	19.4	Dividend Rate/Share	$0.40
Trailing 12-Month EPS	$2.50	S&P Oper. EPS 2008E	3.20	Common Shares Outstg. (M)	480.3	Yield (%)	0.74
Trailing 12-Month P/E	21.7	S&P Core EPS 2007E	2.79	Market Capitalization(B)	$26.001	Beta	1.64
$10K Invested 5 Yrs Ago	$22,674	S&P Core EPS 2008E	3.20	Institutional Ownership (%)	73	S&P Credit Rating	BBB

Price Performance

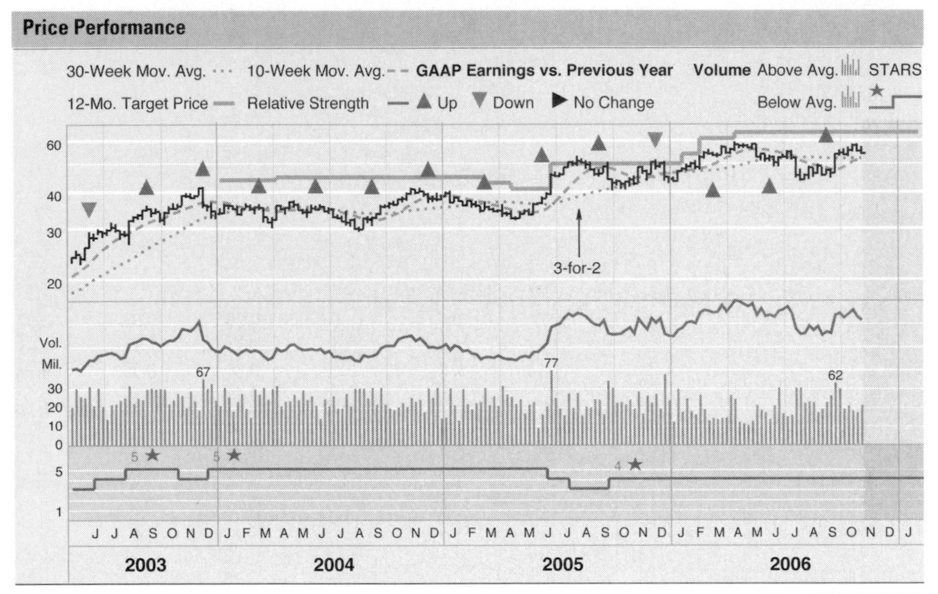

Options: ASE, CBOE, P, Ph

Analysis prepared by **Marie Driscoll, CFA** on September 26, 2006, when the stock traded at **$ 55.87**.

Highlights

- We view BBY as the best-of-class U.S. consumer electronics retailer, based on its digital product focus, knowledgeable sales staff, and effective advertising and marketing campaigns. BBY's focus on advanced TVs, laptops and digital imaging products should support double digit revenue growth. Declining average selling prices of digital TVs should ignite mass adoption and be a key driver of BBY's growth, in our opinion.

- We see a 13% rise in revenues for FY 07 (Feb.), to $34.7 billion, followed by a 10% increase in FY 08, driven by new store contributions and a projected low- to mid-single digit comparable-store sales gain. We look for flat gross margins in FY 07 and a modest 10 basis point expansion in FY 08, aided by an expanded service suite and efficiency initiatives. Despite continued growth initiatives, we expect SG&A leverage on higher sales, and we look for operating margins to widen 70 basis points in FY 07, to 6.0%, and another 20 basis points in FY 08.

- We estimate FY 07 EPS of $2.79, up 23% from $2.27 in FY 06, and we see $3.20 in FY 08.

Investment Rationale/Risk

- We continue to have confidence in Best Buy's ability to execute on its growth strategy. In addition to capitalizing on the strength of the current consumer electronics product cycle, we believe BBY is positioned to grow its market share through initiatives such as Best Buy for Business, Geek Squad and Magnolia store-within-a-store offerings. Combined with BBY's customer focus, we think these initiatives will enable BBY to continue to differentiate itself in a competitive marketplace.

- Risks to our opinion and target price include an adverse shift in the economic climate and consumer confidence, and the risk that BBY will be unable to successfully execute its strategic objectives and meet market expectations for sales growth and profitability.

- Our 12-month target price of $64 is based on our historical P/E model, and assumes a target P/E of 23X applied to our FY 07 EPS estimate. Based on our view of strong growth opportunities over the next five years, we think this target multiple, in line with BBY's three-year historical average, is warranted.

Qualitative Risk Assessment

LOW | **MEDIUM** | HIGH

Our risk assessment reflects what we view as BBY's strong balance sheet, sizable market share, numerous suppliers and buyers, and a history of profitability, offset by a highly competitive environment for consumer electronics retailing, with numerous rivals and strong price competition.

Quantitative Evaluations

S&P Quality Ranking B+

D | C | B- | B | **B+** | A- | A | A+

Relative Strength Rank MODERATE

51

LOWEST = 1 HIGHEST = 99

Revenue/Earnings Data

Revenue (Million $)

	1Q	2Q	3Q	4Q	Year
2007	6,959	7,603	--	--	--
2006	6,118	6,702	7,335	10,693	30,848
2005	5,479	6,080	6,647	9,227	27,433
2004	4,668	5,396	6,034	8,449	24,547
2003	4,202	4,624	5,131	6,989	20,946
2002	3,697	4,164	4,756	6,980	19,597

Earnings Per Share ($)

	1Q	2Q	3Q	4Q	Year
2007	0.47	0.47	**E**0.36	**E**1.51	**E**2.79
2006	0.34	0.37	0.28	1.29	2.27
2005	0.23	0.30	0.29	1.03	1.86
2004	0.14	0.28	0.25	0.95	1.63
2003	0.16	0.16	0.18	0.77	1.27
2002	0.11	0.17	0.17	0.72	1.18

Fiscal year ended Feb. 28. Next earnings report expected: Mid December. EPS Estimates based on S&P Operating Earnings; historical GAAP earnings are as reported.

Dividend Data (Dates: mm/dd Payment Date: mm/dd/yy)

Amount ($)	Date Decl.	Ex-Div. Date	Stk. of Record	Payment Date
0.080	12/14	12/29	01/03	01/24/06
0.080	03/31	04/18	04/20	05/11/06
0.080	06/15	06/29	07/03	07/25/06
0.100	06/21	09/29	10/03	10/24/06

Dividends have been paid since 2003. Source: Company reports.

Best Buy Co. Inc.

Business Summary September 26, 2006

CORPORATE OVERVIEW. This leading consumer electronics retailer operated, as of the end of the FY 07 (Feb.) second quarter, 815 Best Buy stores (771 in the U.S. and 44 in Canada), 20 Magnolia Audio Video stores, 14 Pacific Sales showrooms and 12 Geek Squad stores in the U.S., 119 Future Shop stores in Canada, and 131 Five Star stores in China. For the five years ended FY 06, BBY posted a five-year sales compound annual growth rate (CAGR) of 15.2%, surpassing the Computer and Electronics Retail sub-industry average CAGR of 9.2%. BBY's growth has been a function of new stores opening at higher levels of productivity, with total square footage increasing at a CAGR of 4% during the five-year period. Average annual same-store sales gains of 4.3% also contributed to the top-line advance.

CORPORATE STRATEGY. BBY's business strategy centers on meeting individual consumer electronics needs with end-to-end solutions, which involves greater employee involvement and increased services. Some 40% of U.S. Best Buy stores have been converted or opened with the customer-centric operating model, and BBY is committed to scaling BBY customer-centricity across the organization in FY 07. This year, BBY plans to open nearly 90 new stores in North America, add 200 Magnolia Home Theaters to U.S. Best Buy stores, and build its small business capabilities at 200 stores accompanied by 900 Microsoft-certified professionals.

BBY sees an opportunity to expand to at least 1,200 superstores in North America. Based on our expectations for approximately 75 net new store openings per year, we believe BBY has about five years of organic growth potential from its core business. However, we expect the majority of new store openings to be in smaller 20,000 square foot locations, compared to BBY's average store square footage of 38,000. We expect new concepts, such as stand-alone Geek Squad stores, to provide incremental growth opportunities. In total, we project a five-year square footage CAGR in the mid- to high single digits.

Company Financials

Per Share Data ($) Year Ended Feb. 28	**2006**	**2005**	**2004**	**2003**	**2002**	**2001**	**2000**	**1999**	**1998**	**1997**
Tangible Book Value	9.60	7.91	5.97	4.70	3.65	3.07	2.44	2.32	1.39	1.13
Cash Flow	3.16	2.76	2.41	1.91	1.91	1.18	0.95	0.64	0.36	0.17
Earnings	2.27	1.86	1.63	1.27	1.18	0.83	0.72	0.48	0.23	0.00
S&P Core Earnings	2.27	1.77	1.45	1.11	1.08	0.76	NA	NA	NA	NA
Dividends	0.31	0.50	0.27	Nil	Nil	Nil	Nil	Nil	Nil	Nil
Payout Ratio	14%	38%	17%	Nil	Nil	Nil	Nil	Nil	Nil	Nil
Calendar Year	2005	2004	2003	2002	2001	2000	1999	1998	1997	1996
Prices:High	18.03	41.47	41.80	35.83	33.42	39.50	35.78	13.83	4.56	2.92
Prices:Low	14.84	29.25	15.77	11.33	12.36	9.33	13.72	4.00	0.88	1.08
P/E Ratio:High	14	22	26	28	28	48	49	29	20	NM
P/E Ratio:Low	11	16	10	9	10	11	19	8	4	NM

Income Statement Analysis (Million $)										
Revenue	30,848	27,433	24,547	20,946	19,597	15,327	12,494	10,078	8,358	7,771
Operating Income	2,100	1,901	1,699	1,320	1,246	772	649	443	255	120
Depreciation	456	459	385	310	309	167	110	78.4	68.3	66.8
Interest Expense	30.0	44.0	31.0	25.0	2.00	6.90	5.10	23.8	37.7	50.9
Pretax Income	1,721	1,443	1,296	1,014	936	642	563	365	154	2.87
Effective Tax Rate	33.8%	35.3%	38.3%	38.7%	39.1%	38.3%	38.3%	38.5%	38.6%	39.0%
Net Income	1,140	934	800	622	570	396	347	224	94.5	1.75
S&P Core Earnings	1,140	873	704	538	512	361	NA	NA	NA	NA

Balance Sheet & Other Financial Data (Million $)										
Cash	681	470	2,600	1,914	1,855	747	751	786	520	89.8
Current Assets	7,985	6,903	5,724	4,867	4,611	2,929	2,238	2,063	1,710	1,385
Total Assets	11,864	10,294	8,652	7,663	7,375	4,840	2,995	2,512	2,056	1,734
Current Liabilities	6,056	4,959	4,501	3,793	3,730	2,715	1,785	1,387	1,034	818
Long Term Debt	178	528	482	828	813	181	14.9	30.5	490	447
Common Equity	5,257	4,449	3,422	2,730	2,521	1,822	1,096	1,064	558	438
Total Capital	5,435	4,977	3,904	3,558	3,334	2,003	1,111	1,095	1,005	889
Capital Expenditures	648	502	545	725	627	658	361	166	72.0	87.5
Cash Flow	1,596	1,393	1,185	932	925	563	457	303	163	68.5
Current Ratio	1.3	1.4	1.3	1.3	1.2	1.1	1.3	1.5	1.7	1.7
% Long Term Debt of Capitalization	3.3	10.6	12.3	23.3	24.4	9.0	1.4	2.8	48.8	50.3
% Net Income of Revenue	3.7	3.4	3.3	3.0	2.9	2.6	2.8	2.2	1.1	Nil
% Return on Assets	10.3	9.9	9.8	8.3	9.3	10.1	12.6	9.8	5.0	Nil
% Return on Equity	23.5	23.7	26.0	23.8	26.2	27.1	32.6	27.7	19.0	Nil

Data as orig reptd.; bef. results of disc opers/spec. items. Per share data adj. for stk. divs.; EPS diluted. E-Estimated. NA-Not Available. NM-Not Meaningful. NR-Not Ranked. UR-Under Review.

Office: 7075 Flying Cloud Drive, Eden Prairie, MN 55344-3538.
Telephone: 952-947-2000.
Email: moneytalk@bestbuy.com
Website: http://www.bestbuy.com

Chrmn: R.M. Schulze
Pres & COO: B.J. Dunn
Vice Chrmn: A.U. Lenzmeier
Vice Chrmn & CEO: B.H. Anderson

EVP & CFO: D.R. Jackson
Investor Contact: J. Driscoll (612-291-6110)
Auditor: Ernst & Young
Board of Directors: B. H. Anderson, R. T. Blanchard, A. Bousbib, K. J. Higgins Victor, R. James, E. S. Kaplan, A. U. Lenzmeier, M. H. Paull, R. M. Rebolledo, R. M. Schulze, M. A. Tolan, F. D. Trestman, H. A. Tyabji, J. C. Wetherbe

Founded: 1966
Domicile: Minnesota
Employees: 128,000

STANDARD & POOR'S

Big Lots Inc

S&P Recommendation HOLD ★★★★★

Price $20.17 (as of Oct 27, 2006)

12-Mo. Target Price $20.00

Investment Style Mid-Cap Value

GICS Sector Consumer Discretionary
Sub-Industry General Merchandise Stores

Comment This leading broadline closeout retailer, based in Ohio, has about 1,400 Big Lots stores in 47 states.

Key Stock Statistics (Source S&P, Vickers, company reports)

52-Wk Range	$21.18–11.16	S&P Oper. EPS 2007E	0.66	P/E on S&P Oper. EPS 2007E	30.6	Dividend Rate/Share	Nil
Trailing 12-Month EPS	$0.12	S&P Oper. EPS 2008E	0.75	Common Shares Outstg. (M)	108.9	Yield (%)	Nil
Trailing 12-Month P/E	NM	S&P Core EPS 2007E	0.66	Market Capitalization(B)	$2.196	Beta	0.78
$10K Invested 5 Yrs Ago	$26,263	S&P Core EPS 2008E	0.76	Institutional Ownership (%)	NA	S&P Credit Rating	NA

Price Performance

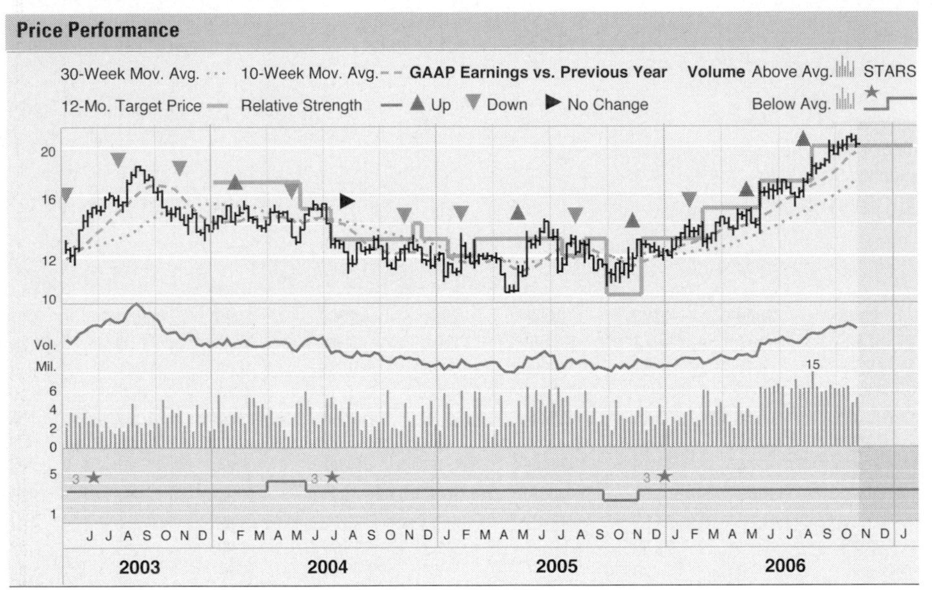

Options: P, Ph

Analysis prepared by **Jason N. Asaeda** on September 14, 2006, when the stock traded at **$ 19.96**.

Highlights

- We look for FY 07 (Jan.) net sales of $4.6 billion. Excluding the selling square footage of 130 stores reported as discontinued operations, and based on BIG's plans to open only 15 new stores and to close 40 underperforming locations in FY 07 as part of its What's Important Now (WIN) strategy, we see a modest decline in retail selling square footage. However, we look for an increased focus on brand-name closeouts and "treasure hunt" items, and improved product quality and in-stock levels to support a 3% to 4% rise in same-store sales.
- Operating margins are likely to widen on better inventory turnover due to a more productive sales mix; the elimination of losses from underperforming stores; distribution center efficiencies; and well controlled payrolls. This should be partly offset by rising utility and inbound freight costs, and stock option expense.
- Factoring in likely share buybacks under BIG's new $150 million authorization, we see FY 07 operating and S&P Core EPS of $0.66.

Investment Rationale/Risk

- As part of its WIN strategy, BIG has reduced its home office work force and is closely managing store payroll, as it sees a near-term opportunity to lower its general office, store, and, to a lesser extent, distribution center expenses annually by $30 million to $35 million. BIG is also taking markdowns more consistently in an effort to drive both same-store sales growth and higher inventory turns. In addition, the company is attempting to raise sales productivity by better aligning products with customer preferences, and by accelerating the closure of underperforming stores. We view these actions favorably and look for company fundamentals to begin to improve this fiscal year.
- Risks to our recommendation and target price include sales shortfalls due to reduced consumer discretionary spending, and/or poor customer response to new merchandise assortments.
- We arrive at our 12-month target price of $20 by applying a peer-median forward price/sales multiple of 0.5X to our FY 07 net sales estimate.

Qualitative Risk Assessment

LOW | **MEDIUM** | HIGH

Our risk assessment reflects our expectation of improving company fundamentals, supported by BIG's new merchandising and cost reduction initiatives, offset by what we see as a challenging retail environment that adds to execution risk of a turnaround.

Quantitative Evaluations

S&P Quality Ranking B-

D | C | **B-** | B | B+ | A- | A | A+

Relative Strength Rank MODERATE

66

LOWEST = 1 HIGHEST = 99

Revenue/Earnings Data

Revenue (Million $)

	1Q	2Q	3Q	4Q	Year
2007	1,092	1,057	--	--	--
2006	1,099	1,051	1,041	1,395	4,430
2005	1,019	995.0	980.0	1,381	4,375
2004	948.4	949.3	948.1	1,329	4,174
2003	904.1	879.3	868.2	1,217	3,869
2002	773.6	748.4	773.1	1,138	3,433

Earnings Per Share ($)

2007	0.13	0.04	**E**-0.08	**E**0.57	**E**0.66
2006	0.07	-0.12	-0.17	0.33	0.14
2005	0.05	-0.07	-0.23	0.51	0.27
2004	0.08	-0.07	-0.05	0.80	0.77
2003	0.11	0.03	-0.04	0.57	0.65
2002	Nil	-0.09	-0.14	-0.02	-0.25

Fiscal year ended Jan. 31. Next earnings report expected: Mid November. EPS Estimates based on S&P Operating Earnings; historical GAAP earnings are as reported.

Dividend Data

Proceeds from the sale of rights amounting to $0.01 a share were distributed in 2001.

Big Lots Inc

Business Summary September 14, 2006

CORPORATE OVERVIEW. BIG's strategy is to position itself as a preferred shopping destination for consumers seeking savings on brand-name closeouts and other value-priced merchandise. The company's product offerings range from everyday essentials such as food and other consumables, to more discretionary-purchase items, including furniture, holiday assortments, electronics, apparel, and small appliances. In our view, FY 07 (Jan.) will be a transitional year for BIG, as the company plans to slow chain expansion in order to better focus on implementing operational changes to reverse a two-year trend of declining operating profits.

CORPORATE STRATEGY. BIG's primary growth driver is expansion. The company seeks to build on its leadership position in broadline closeout retailing by expanding its market presence in both existing and new markets. From FY 00 through FY 05, the company increased its selling square footage at a compound annual growth rate (CAGR) of about 6% as it expanded its store count from 1,230 to 1,502. In FY 06, BIG continued to expand its store base, adding 73 new stores. However, the company also accelerated the closure of underperforming locations as part of its What's Important Now (WIN) turnaround strategy, which was announced in November 2005. As a result, BIG ended FY 06 with 1,401 stores in 47 states, reflecting a 3.5% decline in selling square footage.

WIN is aimed at improving financial performance via changes in the company's merchandising, cost structure and real estate. As its first steps, BIG is attempting to raise productivity of its chain by closing low-volume stores located mainly in small, rural, or weaker performing markets, and by moving from an opportunistic real estate strategy to one focused on its most successful trade areas. These areas include California, Arizona, Washington, New York and New Jersey. The company closed 174 stores in FY 06 and plans to scale back new store openings to 15 and to close 40 more underperforming stores in FY 07.

Company Financials

Per Share Data ($) Year Ended Jan. 31	2006	2005	2004	2003	2002	2001	2000	1999	1998	1997
Tangible Book Value	9.47	9.54	9.51	8.83	8.11	8.28	11.71	10.79	9.60	8.15
Cash Flow	1.15	1.17	1.56	1.38	0.37	1.44	1.74	1.71	1.47	1.93
Earnings	0.14	0.27	0.77	0.65	-0.25	0.87	0.85	0.97	0.77	1.44
S&P Core Earnings	0.05	0.25	0.78	0.60	-0.32	0.83	NA	NA	NA	NA
Dividends	Nil	Nil	Nil	Nil	Nil	Nil	Nil	Nil	Nil	Nil
Payout Ratio	Nil	Nil	Nil	Nil	Nil	Nil	Nil	Nil	Nil	Nil
Calendar Year	2005	2004	2003	2002	2001	2000	1999	1998	1997	1996
Prices:High	14.29	15.62	18.39	19.90	15.75	16.38	38.13	46.13	50.00	28.32
Prices:Low	10.06	11.05	9.92	9.75	7.15	8.25	13.69	15.50	24.50	12.40
P/E Ratio:High	NM	58	24	31	NM	19	45	48	65	21
P/E Ratio:Low	NM	41	13	15	NM	9	16	16	32	9
Income Statement Analysis (Million $)										
Revenue	4,430	4,375	4,174	3,869	3,433	3,277	4,700	4,194	4,055	2,648
Operating Income	141	172	222	231	43.4	249	271	288	268	245
Depreciation	115	104	93.7	85.7	72.0	64.5	100	84.0	79.2	48.4
Interest Expense	6.27	24.8	16.4	21.0	20.5	23.6	25.3	24.3	25.7	16.8
Pretax Income	20.9	43.3	113	125	-48.7	161	145	179	162	180
Effective Tax Rate	24.8%	29.8%	20.6%	39.5%	NM	39.5%	39.5%	39.0%	47.0%	37.0%
Net Income	15.7	30.4	89.9	75.7	-29.5	97.6	96.1	109	85.9	113
S&P Core Earnings	4.93	27.8	91.6	70.7	-36.7	92.6	NA	NA	NA	NA
Balance Sheet & Other Financial Data (Million $)										
Cash	1.71	2.52	174	160	NA	NA	96.3	75.9	41.7	30.0
Current Assets	994	1,035	1,134	NA	NA	NA	1,420	1,335	1,107	926
Total Assets	1,625	1,734	1,801	1,656	1,470	1,528	2,187	2,043	1,746	1,331
Current Liabilities	437	413	416	NA	NA	NA	711	460	525	457
Long Term Debt	5.50	159	204	204	204	268	60.5	296	115	151
Common Equity	1,167	1,075	1,109	1,020	923	924	1,300	1,182	1,035	682
Total Capital	1,173	1,235	1,313	1,224	1,127	1,192	1,468	1,583	1,106	870
Capital Expenditures	68.5	135	170	110	NA	NA	147	167	146	93.6
Cash Flow	130	135	184	161	42.5	162	197	193	165	162
Current Ratio	2.3	2.5	2.7	NA	NA	NA	2.0	2.9	2.1	2.0
% Long Term Debt of Capitalization	0.5	12.9	15.5	16.7	18.1	22.5	4.1	18.7	11.1	17.4
% Net Income of Revenue	0.4	0.7	2.2	2.0	NM	3.0	2.0	2.6	2.1	4.2
% Return on Assets	0.9	1.7	5.2	4.8	NM	5.3	4.5	5.8	5.6	11.5
% Return on Equity	1.4	2.8	8.4	7.8	NM	8.8	7.7	9.9	10.0	21.2

Data as orig reptd.; bef. results of disc opers/spec. items. Per share data adj. for stk. divs.; EPS diluted. E-Estimated. NA-Not Available. NM-Not Meaningful. NR-Not Ranked. UR-Under Review.

Office: 300 Phillipi Road, Columbus, OH 43228-1310.
Telephone: 614-278-6800.
Website: http://www.biglots.com
Chrmn, Pres & CEO: S.S. Fishman

SVP & CFO: J.R. Cooper
SVP, Secy & General Counsel: C.W. Haubiel, II
Investor Contact: T.A. Johnson (614-278-6622)
VP & Cntlr: P.A. Schroeder

Board of Directors: J. P. Berger, S. M. Berman, S. S. Fishman, D. T. Kollat, B. J. Lauderback, P. E. Mallott, R. Solt, J. R. Tener, D. B. Tishkoff

Founded: 1983
Domicile: Ohio
Employees: 43,985

Biogen Idec Inc

STANDARD &POOR'S

S&P Recommendation HOLD ★★★★★

Price $47.60 (as of Oct 31, 2006)

12-Mo. Target Price $51.00

Investment Style Large-Cap Growth

GICS Sector Health Care
Sub-Industry Biotechnology

Comment This major biopharmaceutical concern develops and markets targeted therapies for the treatment of multiple sclerosis, non-Hodgkin's lymphoma, and rheumatoid arthritis.

Key Stock Statistics (Source S&P, Vickers, company reports)

52-Wk Range	$50.72–39.95	S&P Oper. EPS 2006**E**	2.00	P/E on S&P Oper. EPS 2006**E**	23.8	Dividend Rate/Share	Nil
Trailing 12-Month EPS	$0.46	S&P Oper. EPS 2007**E**	2.36	Common Shares Outstg. (M)	343.6	Yield (%)	Nil
Trailing 12-Month P/E	NM	S&P Core EPS 2006**E**	2.00	Market Capitalization(B)	$16.355	Beta	0.53
$10K Invested 5 Yrs Ago	$7,270	S&P Core EPS 2007**E**	2.36	Institutional Ownership (%)	85	S&P Credit Rating	BB

Price Performance

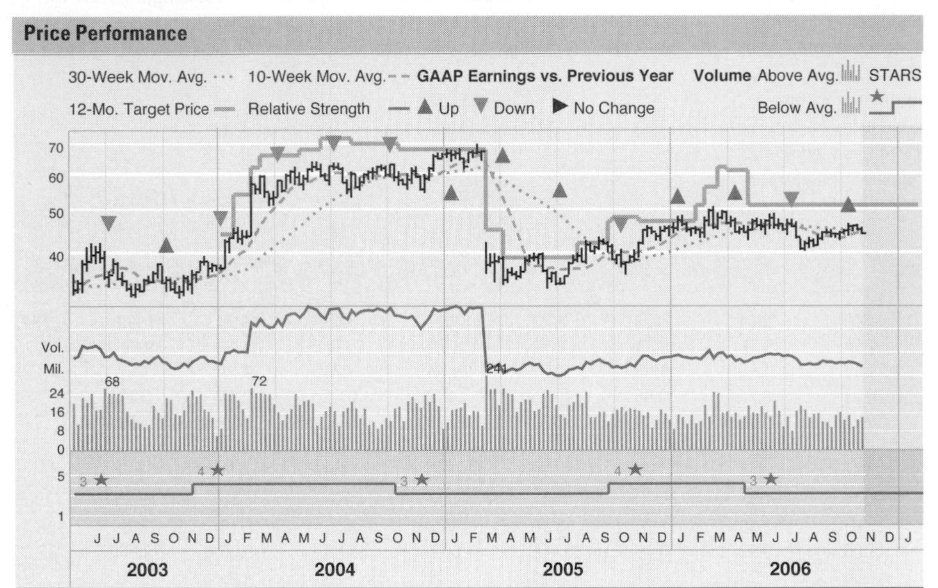

Options: ASE, CBOE, P, Ph

Analysis prepared by **Paul Starsia** on September 29, 2006, when the stock traded at **$ 44.54**.

Highlights

- In June 2006, the FDA and European Commission approved the reintroduction of Tysabri as a monotherapy treatment for relapsing forms of multiple sclerosis (MS). However, revised labeling is required, and patients and caregivers will be required to enroll in the TOUCH prescribing program, which is designed to provide information on the drug's risks and benefits and to minimize the potential risk of progressive multifocal leukoencephalopathy (PML). We believe Tysabri will likely be given to patients not responding to other approved MS therapies.
- In the second quarter 2006, BIIB completed two acquisitions, Conforma and Fumapharm. Conforma is a development stage company focused on the treatment of cancer, and Fumapharm currently has a commercialized product in Germany for the treatment of psoriasis and a compound, BG-12, in Phase II for the treatment of MS, which BIIB has been jointly developing.
- We project 2006 U.S. Rituxan sales of $2 billion. We look for global Avonex sales of $1.65 billion. We forecast 2006 Tysabri sales of $31 million. Including projected stock option expense of $0.10, we estimate 2006 EPS of $2.00.

Investment Rationale/Risk

- Following FDA and European approval for the reintroduction of Tysabri, we continue to look for a slow ramp-up in Tysabri sales due to our view of a strict distribution program. Aside from Tysabri, we think growth in royalties and Avonex sales will continue to moderate. We continue to like Rituxan's long-term prospects, with its recent approval to treat rheumatoid arthritis and ongoing trials in other indications, including lupus and MS. Also, we think recent acquisitions have bolstered its pipeline.
- Risks to our recommendation and target price include lower than expected sales of Rituxan and Avonex, new cases of PML in Tysabri patients, and the failure of compounds in development to show efficacy or to have adverse safety events.
- We project an annualized EPS growth rate of about 15.3% for BIIB through 2010. Our growth rate forecast for BIIB's peers is 23%. We consider a forward P/E to growth (PEG) ratio of 1.4X to 1.6X to be appropriate for most biotech stocks. Assuming BIIB trades at a PEG ratio of 1.4X our 2007 EPS estimate, our 12-month target price is $51.

Qualitative Risk Assessment

LOW | MEDIUM | **HIGH**

Biogen Idec sells products in competitive markets and must contend with the potential for generic threats, additional regulatory oversight, and changes in drug reimbursement. Also, the company is engaged in the development of new drugs, which is a highly risky endeavor.

Quantitative Evaluations

S&P Quality Ranking B-

D | C | **B-** | B | B+ | A- | A | A+

Relative Strength Rank STRONG

75

LOWEST = 1 HIGHEST = 99

Revenue/Earnings Data

Revenue (Million $)

	1Q	2Q	3Q	4Q	Year
2006	611.2	660.0	703.5	--	--
2005	587.8	605.6	596.2	632.9	2,423
2004	541.7	538.8	543.3	587.8	2,212
2003	117.3	123.6	138.5	299.9	679.2
2002	79.74	97.13	103.7	123.7	404.2
2001	56.54	64.85	69.62	81.68	272.7

Earnings Per Share ($)

	1Q	2Q	3Q	4Q	Year
2006	0.35	-0.50	0.45	**E**0.46	**E**2.00
2005	0.12	0.10	0.08	0.16	0.47
2004	-0.12	Nil	0.10	0.08	0.07
2003	0.24	0.17	0.26	-4.03	-4.92
2002	0.17	0.20	0.22	0.26	0.85
2001	0.12	0.15	0.16	0.16	0.59

Fiscal year ended Dec. 31. Next earnings report expected: Mid February. EPS Estimates based on S&P Operating Earnings; historical GAAP earnings are as reported.

Dividend Data

No cash dividends have been paid.

Biogen Idec Inc

Business Summary September 29, 2006

CORPORATE OVERVIEW. Biogen Idec researches, develops and markets therapeutics to treat cancer and autoimmune diseases. The company was formed through the November 2003 merger of IDEC Pharmaceuticals and Biogen.

The company's largest selling drug is Rituxan, a treatment for relapsed or refractory low grade or follicular B-cell non-Hodgkin's lymphomas (NHL). There are over 300,000 U.S. patients with various forms of this disease. Rituxan is being marketed and sold in the U.S. under a co-promotion agreement with Genentech; BIIB receives joint business revenues on a percentage of sales. F. Hoffman-La Roche has marketing rights (under the name MabThera) outside the U.S., with BIIB receiving royalties on sales. U.S. Rituxan sales were $1.83 billion in 2005, up from $1.57 billion in 2004.

Avonex was approved by the FDA to treat relapsing forms of MS in 1996. European approval was granted in 1997. Avonex sales were $1.54 billion in 2005 ($1.42 billion in 2004). The company estimates that more than 120,000 patients use Avonex worldwide.

BIIB co-developed Tysabri with Elan Corp. The FDA approved Tysabri for the treatment of relapsing MS in November 2004. However, three adverse events related to progressive multifocal leukoencephalopathy (PML), a rare fatal nervous system disorder, were reported in 2005, causing the drug to be removed from the market. Following safety evaluations and analysis of additional clinical data, a supplemental application for approval was filed with the FDA in September 2005. On June 5, 2006, the FDA approved Tysabri for a relaunch into the U.S. market, contingent upon a restricted distribution program designed to limit risks associated with Tysabri, most notably PML.

Company Financials

Per Share Data ($) Year Ended Dec. 31	2005	2004	2003	2002	2001	2000	1999	1998	1997	1996
Tangible Book Value	8.38	7.08	6.85	7.25	6.22	4.63	1.11	0.88	0.53	0.61
Cash Flow	1.63	1.35	-4.57	0.88	0.62	0.39	0.31	0.18	-0.10	-0.02
Earnings	0.47	0.07	-4.92	0.85	0.59	0.36	0.29	0.15	-0.14	-0.06
S&P Core Earnings	0.16	-0.06	-5.13	0.54	0.34	NA	NA	NA	NA	NA
Dividends	Nil	Nil	Nil	Nil	Nil	Nil	Nil	Nil	Nil	Nil
Payout Ratio	Nil	Nil	Nil	Nil	Nil	Nil	Nil	Nil	Nil	Nil
Prices:High	70.00	68.13	42.15	71.40	75.00	77.65	35.00	8.03	7.71	5.44
Prices:Low	33.18	36.60	27.80	20.76	32.63	18.54	6.60	2.88	2.63	2.31
P/E Ratio:High	NM	NM	NM	84	NM	NM	NM	52	NM	NM
P/E Ratio:Low	NM	NM	NM	24	NM	NM	NM	19	NM	NM

Income Statement Analysis (Million $)	2005	2004	2003	2002	2001	2000	1999	1998	1997	1996
Revenue	2,423	2,212	679	404	273	155	118	87.0	44.6	30.0
Operating Income	756	483	14.6	285	137	60.6	45.8	23.2	-14.0	-2.79
Depreciation	402	439	61.3	10.2	6.31	4.74	4.37	4.28	4.01	2.64
Interest Expense	Nil	18.9	15.2	16.1	7.30	7.05	6.06	0.63	0.92	2.70
Pretax Income	256	64.1	-881	232	162	69.3	45.6	21.9	-15.5	-4.96
Effective Tax Rate	37.3%	60.9%	NM	36.0%	37.1%	17.2%	5.37%	1.93%	NM	NM
Net Income	161	25.1	-875	148	102	57.4	43.2	21.5	-15.5	-4.96
S&P Core Earnings	56.6	-21.6	-914	93.4	61.4	NA	NA	NA	NA	NA

Balance Sheet & Other Financial Data (Million $)	2005	2004	2003	2002	2001	2000	1999	1998	1997	1996
Cash	851	1,058	836	373	426	401	61.4	73.5	34.8	25.3
Current Assets	1,618	1,931	1,839	978	700	631	279	101	79.2	91.6
Total Assets	8,367	9,166	9,504	2,060	1,141	856	307	125	106	114
Current Liabilities	583	1,261	405	56.2	35.3	23.0	15.6	14.5	19.4	13.7
Long Term Debt	43.4	102	887	866	136	129	123	2.10	2.02	5.00
Common Equity	6,906	6,826	7,053	1,110	956	695	160	106	80.7	66.0
Total Capital	7,712	7,850	9,049	1,976	1,092	824	283	109	84.4	71.0
Capital Expenditures	318	361	301	166	0.07	31.4	4.29	1.72	5.88	6.30
Cash Flow	563	465	-814	158	108	62.1	47.5	25.8	-11.5	-2.31
Current Ratio	2.8	1.5	4.5	17.4	19.8	27.4	17.8	7.0	4.1	6.7
% Long Term Debt of Capitalization	0.6	1.3	9.8	43.8	12.4	15.7	43.4	1.9	2.4	7.0
% Net Income of Revenue	6.6	1.1	NM	36.6	37.3	37.1	36.6	24.7	NM	NM
% Return on Assets	1.8	0.3	NM	9.3	10.2	9.9	20.0	18.6	NM	NM
% Return on Equity	2.3	0.4	NM	14.3	12.3	13.4	32.4	23.0	NM	NM

Data as orig reptd.; bef. results of disc opers/spec. items. Per share data adj. for stk. divs.; EPS diluted. E-Estimated. NA-Not Available. NM-Not Meaningful. NR-Not Ranked. UR-Under Review.

Office: 14 Cambridge Center, Cambridge, MA 02142.
Telephone: 617-679-2000.
Website: http://www.biogenidec.com
Chrmn: B.R. Ross

Pres & CEO: J.C. Mullen
EVP & CFO: P.N. Kellogg
EVP, Secy & General Counsel: S.H. Alexander
Investor Contact: E. Woo (617-679-2812)

Board of Directors: A. Belzer, L. C. Best, A. B. Glassberg, M. L. Good, T. F. Keller, J. C. Mullen, R. W. Pangia, B. R. Ross, L. Schenk, P. A. Sharp, W. D. Young

Founded: 1985
Domicile: Delaware
Employees: 3,400

STANDARD &POOR'S

Biomet Inc

S&P Recommendation HOLD ★★★★★

Price
$36.22 (as of Oct 27, 2006)

12-Mo. Target Price
$35.00

Investment Style
Mid-Cap Growth

GICS Sector Health Care
Sub-Industry Health Care Equipment

Comment Biomet makes surgical implants for the replacement of hip and knee joints, orthopedic support items, fracture fixation devices, and other related medical devices.

Key Stock Statistics (Source S&P, Vickers, company reports)

52-Wk Range	**$39.45–30.22**	S&P Oper. EPS 2007E	**1.85**	P/E on S&P Oper. EPS 2007E	**19.6**	Dividend Rate/Share	**$0.30**
Trailing 12-Month EPS	**$1.65**	S&P Oper. EPS 2008E	**2.12**	Common Shares Outstg. (M)	**244.9**	Yield (%)	**0.83**
Trailing 12-Month P/E	**22.0**	S&P Core EPS 2007E	**1.85**	Market Capitalization(B)	**$8.871**	Beta	**0.02**
$10K Invested 5 Yrs Ago	**$11,602**	S&P Core EPS 2008E	**2.12**	Institutional Ownership (%)	**67**	S&P Credit Rating	**NA**

Price Performance

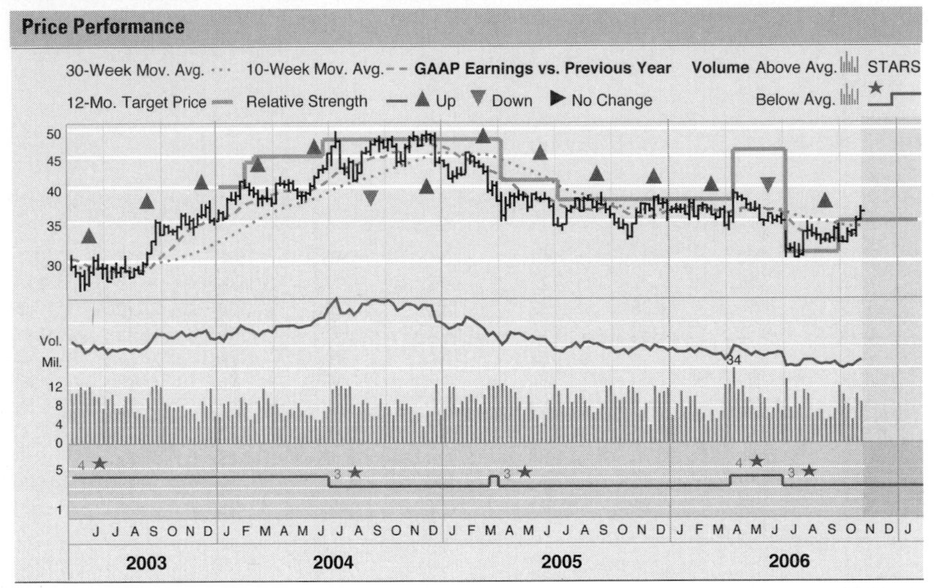

Options: ASE, CBOE, P, Ph

Analysis prepared by **Robert M. Gold** on September 21, 2006, when the stock traded at **$ 32.87**.

Highlights

- We see FY 07 (May) revenues approximating $2.1 billion, as an approximate 9% advance in the reconstructive implant segment joins with more modest growth in the spine and fracture fixation areas. In our view, the overall reconstruction market has slowed in recent quarters, and we believe global unit pricing across the industry will remain under pressure.
- We believe gross margin expansion will be challenging in FY 07 absent new product introductions and increased global pricing pressures. In addition, we think SG&A spending will continue to accelerate as the company seeks to capture market share through a more aggressive direct-to-consumer advertising campaign. Research and development spending is expected to remain at about 4.0% to 4.3% of sales, but we think the company has some opportunities to boost net margins by managing the income tax rate.
- Our FY 07 operating EPS estimate is $1.85, which includes $0.05 of projected stock option expense. Looking into FY 08, we see EPS of $2.12, also after $0.05 of estimated stock option expense.

Investment Rationale/Risk

- We are concerned about the potential impact on orthopedic implant pricing from a Department of Justice (DOJ) investigation focused on Biomet and its peers, which could, in our view, alter the longstanding relationships between implant makers and orthopedic surgeons. However, we think unit sales trends will remain positive, and believe the stock will gain support from takeover speculation. In April 2006, BMET retained Morgan Stanley to assist in exploring strategic alternatives.
- Risks to our opinion and target price include a less favorable acquisition environment, adverse changes to Medicare reimbursement rates, loss of market share in key device markets, and an adverse outcome in government investigations of BMET and the industry.
- We see BMET generating three-year EPS growth of 13%, versus 15% for peers, and we think the DOJ investigation will remove the valuation premium the orthopedic device stocks have enjoyed relative to our broader medical device coverage universe. Based on a forward P/E-to-growth (PEG) valuation and price/sales ratio in line with the group, our 12-month target price is $35.

Qualitative Risk Assessment

LOW | **MEDIUM** | HIGH

Our risk assessment reflects that Biomet operates in an industry characterized by product innovation and market share volatility. In addition, hospital customers receive a significant amount of reimbursement from Medicare, and ongoing federal budgetary pressures could result in lower Medicare prices for orthopedic and other devices.

Quantitative Evaluations

S&P Quality Ranking **A**

D | C | B- | B | B+ | A- | **A** | A+

Relative Strength Rank **STRONG**

78

LOWEST = 1 HIGHEST = 99

Revenue/Earnings Data

Revenue (Million $)

	1Q	2Q	3Q	4Q	Year
2007	508.2	--	--	--	--
2006	484.9	494.7	506.3	539.9	2,026
2005	438.2	456.7	482.0	503.1	1,880
2004	370.3	387.6	410.2	447.2	1,615
2003	317.6	341.5	354.0	377.2	1,390
2002	272.0	289.4	304.6	325.9	1,192

Earnings Per Share ($)

2007	0.42	**E**0.43	**E**0.48	**E**0.52	**E**1.85
2006	0.40	0.41	0.43	0.40	1.63
2005	0.24	0.36	0.38	0.41	1.38
2004	0.30	0.32	0.34	0.31	1.27
2003	0.25	0.27	0.28	0.30	1.10
2002	0.21	0.23	0.23	0.23	0.88

Fiscal year ended May 31. Next earnings report expected: Late December. EPS Estimates based on S&P Operating Earnings; historical GAAP earnings are as reported.

Dividend Data (Dates: mm/dd Payment Date: mm/dd/yy)

Amount ($)	Date Decl.	Ex-Div. Date	Stk. of Record	Payment Date
0.300	06/28	07/12	07/14	07/21/06

Dividends have been paid since 1996. Source: Company reports.

Business Summary September 21, 2006

CORPORATE OVERVIEW. Biomet sells reconstructive orthopedic implants, electrical bone stimulators and related products that are used primarily by orthopedic medical specialists in the surgical replacement of hip and knee joints and in fracture fixation procedures to aid healing.

Reconstructive devices (68% of FY 06 (May) sales) are used to replace joints that have deteriorated due to disease or injury, including implants for replacement of hips, knees, shoulders, ankles and elbows. For minimally invasive knee arthroplasty procedures, BMET sells devices that include the Repicci II Unicondylar Knee System, the Oxford Phase 3 Unicompartmental Knee, and the Vanguard Complete Knee Replacement System. The company also offers over 20 hip systems in various sizes and configurations, mostly using titanium or cobalt chromium alloy femoral components and proprietary ARCom polyethylene-lined or metal-on-metal acetabular components. BMET makes orthopedic surgical instruments, and sells dental reconstruction implants and related instrumentation, regenerative products and materials.

Fixation products (12%) include electrical stimulation devices to treat recalcitrant bone fractures that have not healed with conventional surgical and/or non-surgical methods; external fixation devices for complicated trauma, limb-lengthening and deformity correction uses, and for fracture repair; craniomaxillofacial fixation systems and neurosurgical titanium implants; internal fixation devices such as nails, plates, screws, pins and wires; and bone substitutes.

Spinal products (11%) include implantable, direct current electrical stimulation devices that provide an adjunct to surgical intervention in the treatment of nonunions and spinal fusions; spinal fixation systems that address the inherent drawbacks of traditional rod and plate systems; and spinal surgery products including implants, orthobiologics and minimally-invasive surgery products.

Company Financials

Per Share Data ($) Year Ended May 31	2006	2005	2004	2003	2002	2001	2000	1999	1998	1997
Tangible Book Value	4.88	4.16	4.44	4.46	3.96	3.73	3.28	2.84	2.40	2.11
Cash Flow	1.97	1.66	1.50	1.27	1.06	0.89	0.80	0.57	0.58	0.49
Earnings	1.63	1.38	1.27	1.10	0.88	0.73	0.65	0.46	0.49	0.42
S&P Core Earnings	1.59	1.35	1.23	1.08	0.88	0.72	NA	NA	NA	NA
Dividends	0.20	0.15	0.10	NA	0.07	0.06	0.06	0.05	0.05	0.04
Payout Ratio	12%	11%	8%	NA	8%	9%	10%	12%	10%	11%
Calendar Year	2005	2004	2003	2002	2001	2000	1999	1998	1997	1996
Prices:High	45.71	49.64	38.02	33.26	34.36	27.83	20.33	18.31	12.00	9.17
Prices:Low	32.50	35.07	26.74	21.75	20.46	12.06	10.94	10.50	6.33	5.56
P/E Ratio:High	28	36	30	38	39	38	31	40	24	22
P/E Ratio:Low	20	25	21	25	23	17	17	23	13	13
Income Statement Analysis (Million $)										
Revenue	2,026	1,880	1,615	1,390	1,192	1,031	921	757	651	580
Operating Income	691	643	553	472	419	360	315	256	204	178
Depreciation	82.2	69.6	59.5	45.7	47.8	42.8	39.8	29.5	23.5	18.5
Interest Expense	Nil	8.86	3.54	4.40	3.38	4.11	3.19	Nil	0.34	0.70
Pretax Income	611	550	509	452	376	311	281	186	204	169
Effective Tax Rate	33.5%	36.0%	34.6%	34.7%	33.9%	34.1%	35.5%	33.6%	38.8%	37.1%
Net Income	406	352	326	287	240	198	174	116	125	106
S&P Core Earnings	394	343	317	281	240	193	NA	NA	NA	NA
Balance Sheet & Other Financial Data (Million $)										
Cash	161	105	159	226	154	235	214	129	117	123
Current Assets	1,315	1,174	1,116	1,112	953	968	790	682	571	464
Total Assets	2,264	2,097	1,788	1,672	1,522	1,489	1,218	1,068	849	628
Current Liabilities	520	501	313	267	238	242	181	201	98.1	72.9
Long Term Debt	Nil	Nil	Nil	Nil	Nil	Nil	Nil	Nil	Nil	Nil
Common Equity	1,716	1,564	1,448	1,286	1,176	1,146	943	776	667	553
Total Capital	1,743	1,595	1,474	1,405	1,284	1,247	1,037	866	750	555
Capital Expenditures	109	97.4	61.3	59.8	62.3	35.3	43.1	51.1	44.1	21.4
Cash Flow	488	421	385	332	288	240	214	146	148	125
Current Ratio	2.5	2.3	3.6	4.2	4.0	4.0	4.4	3.4	5.8	6.4
% Long Term Debt of Capitalization	Nil	Nil	Nil	Nil	Nil	Nil	Nil	Nil	Nil	Nil
% Net Income of Revenue	20.0	18.7	20.2	20.6	20.1	19.2	18.9	15.4	19.1	18.3
% Return on Assets	18.6	18.1	18.8	18.0	15.9	14.6	14.9	12.1	16.9	17.4
% Return on Equity	24.8	23.3	23.8	23.3	20.6	18.9	20.0	16.1	20.4	19.6

Data as orig reptd.; bef. results of disc opers/spec. items. Per share data adj. for stk. divs.; EPS diluted. E-Estimated. NA-Not Available. NM-Not Meaningful. NR-Not Ranked. UR-Under Review.

Office: 56 East Bell Drive, Warsaw, IN 46582.
Telephone: 574-267-6639.
Email: investors@biomet.com
Website: http://www.biomet.com

Chrmn: N.L. Noblitt
Pres & CEO: D.P. Hann
Vice Chrmn: J.L. Ferguson
SVP, CFO & Treas: G.D. Hartman

VP, Secy & General Counsel: B.J. Tandy
Investor Contact: B. Goslee (574-267-6639)
Board of Directors: J. L. Ferguson, D. P. Hann, C. S. Harrison, M. R. Harroff, T. F. Kearns, Jr., S. A. Lamb, J. L. Miller, K. V. Miller, C. E. Niemier, N. L. Noblitt, M. T. Quayle, L. G. Tanner

Founded: 1977
Domicile: Indiana
Employees: 6,357

BJ Services Co

STANDARD & POOR'S

S&P Recommendation BUY ★★★★★

Price $30.16 (as of Oct 31, 2006)

12-Mo. Target Price $38.00

Investment Style Mid-Cap Growth

GICS Sector Energy
Sub-Industry Oil & Gas Equipment & Services

Comment This company provides pressure pumping and other oilfield services to the petroleum industry worldwide.

Key Stock Statistics (Source S&P, Vickers, company reports)

52-Wk Range	$42.85–27.43	S&P Oper. EPS 2007E	3.20	P/E on S&P Oper. EPS 2007E	9.4	Dividend Rate/Share	$0.20
Trailing 12-Month EPS	$2.52	S&P Oper. EPS 2008E	NA	Common Shares Outstg. (M)	299.2	Yield (%)	0.66
Trailing 12-Month P/E	12.0	S&P Core EPS 2007E	3.18	Market Capitalization(B)	$9.022	Beta	1.01
$10K Invested 5 Yrs Ago	$23,359	S&P Core EPS 2008E	NA	Institutional Ownership (%)	91	S&P Credit Rating	BBB+

Price Performance

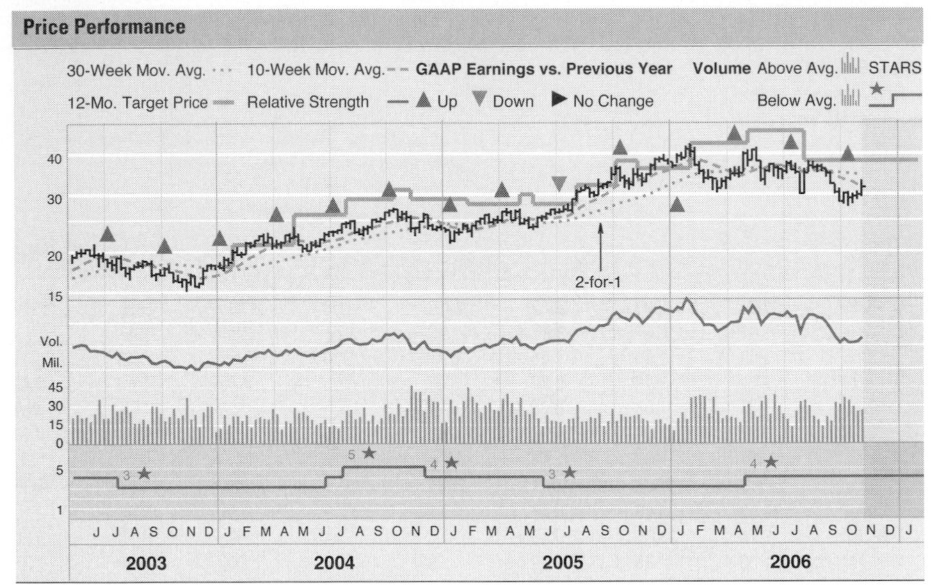

Options: ASE, CBOE, P, Ph

Analysis prepared by **Stewart Glickman, CFA** on July 28, 2006, when the stock traded at **$ 34.80**.

Highlights

- We expect total revenues to increase about 33% in FY 06 (Sep.) and 15% in FY 07, based on our view that pricing traction for BJS should be sustained in the near term as rig activity continues to rise. We estimate that operating margins will be in the high-20% to low-30% range in both FY 06 and FY 07.
- We believe the main growth driver continues to be the U.S. market, where we expect the rig count to rise about 8% in FY 07. In July, natural gas prices were at about the $6.40/MMBtu level, versus an average of more than $11/MMBtu in January 2006, yielding some concern that rig demand (and thus ancillary demand for pressure pumping) could be deferred. Although we view this scenario as unlikely, we do believe that the prospect of material adverse changes in demand does elevate the company's risk profile.
- We project FY 06 EPS from continuing operations of $2.50, rising to $3.03 in FY 07. On an S&P Core Earnings basis, we expect EPS of $2.47 and $3.01 in the respective years, with the divergence from operating EPS reflecting adjustments for pension gains.

Investment Rationale/Risk

- We now see an elevated risk profile for BJS, given concerns over potential for deferral of oilfield activity in North America. As a result, despite BJS' strong historical financial performance, with return on equity exceeding 10% in six of the last seven years, we think a modest discount to peers is warranted.
- Risks to our recommendation and target price include reduced demand for pressure pumping services; higher than expected cost inflation; lower than projected natural gas and oil prices; and lower than anticipated returns from International operations.
- Our discounted cash flow model, which assumes free cash flow growth of about 10% for 10 years and 3% thereafter, discounted at a weighted average cost of capital of 11.4%, indicates that the shares have an intrinsic value of about $38. Applying a 9X multiple to our calendar 2006 EBITDA projection and 14X estimated 2006 cash flow (both discounts to peers), blended with our DCF analysis, we arrive at our 12-month target price of $38.

Qualitative Risk Assessment

LOW | MEDIUM | **HIGH**

Our risk assessment for BJS reflects its exposure to volatile hydrocarbon prices, particularly natural gas, the company's leverage to the North American market, and concerns over capacity additions for pressure pumping. Partly offsetting these risks is the company's strong position in pressure pumping services.

Quantitative Evaluations

S&P Quality Ranking **B**

D | C | B- | **B** | B+ | A- | A | A+

Relative Strength Rank **WEAK**

16

LOWEST = 1 HIGHEST = 99

Revenue/Earnings Data

Revenue (Million $)

	1Q	2Q	3Q	4Q	Year
2006	956.2	1,079	1,117	1,216	4,368
2005	737.8	795.9	817.3	892.3	3,243
2004	600.8	647.1	658.7	694.5	2,601
2003	473.1	534.6	546.6	588.6	2,143
2002	510.1	442.4	439.7	473.7	1,866
2001	489.7	549.7	579.8	614.3	2,234

Earnings Per Share ($)

	1Q	2Q	3Q	4Q	Year
2006	0.48	0.62	0.67	0.76	2.52
2005	0.29	0.33	0.35	0.41	1.38
2004	0.19	0.23	0.40	0.29	1.11
2003	0.11	0.14	0.16	0.19	0.59
2002	0.21	0.12	0.09	0.11	0.52
2001	0.19	0.23	0.32	0.31	1.04

Fiscal year ended Sep. 30. Next earnings report expected: Late January. EPS Estimates based on S&P Operating Earnings; historical GAAP earnings are as reported.

Dividend Data (Dates: mm/dd Payment Date: mm/dd/yy)

Amount ($)	Date Decl.	Ex-Div. Date	Stk. of Record	Payment Date
0.050	12/08	12/16	12/20	01/13/06
0.050	01/31	03/13	03/15	04/13/06
0.050	05/25	06/13	06/15	07/14/06
0.050	07/27	09/13	09/15	10/13/06

Dividends have been paid since 2004. Source: Company reports.

BJ Services Co

Business Summary July 28, 2006

CORPORATE OVERVIEW. BJ Services is a leading provider of pressure pumping and other oilfield services to the petroleum industry worldwide. Demand for its services depends on the number of oil and natural gas wells being drilled, the depth and drilling conditions of the wells, the number of well completions, and the level of workover activity worldwide. BJS's principal customers consist of major and independent oil and natural gas producing companies. The company operates in 49 countries in the major international oil and natural gas producing areas of Canada, Latin America, Europe, Africa, Russia, Asia, the Middle East, Russia and China. In FY 05 (Sep.), 52% of revenues were generated by U.S./Mexico pressure pumping; 32% from International pressure pumping; and 16% other oilfield services. Other than Canada, the international market tends to be less volatile than the U.S. due to the size and complexity of investment, and projects tend to be managed with a longer-term perspective with regard to commodity prices. In addition, the international market is dominated by major oil and national oil companies, which tend to have different objectives and more operating stability than typical independent U.S. producers.

Pressure pumping services (84% of FY 05 revenues and 91% of segment operating profits) are used in the completion of oil and gas wells, both onshore and offshore. Customers are mainly served in the U.S. Stimulation services are designed to improve the flow of oil and natural gas from producing formations using fracturing, acidizing, sand control, nitrogen, coiled tubing and downhole tool services. Cementing is done between the casing pipe and the wellbore during the drilling and completion phase of a well. This is done to isolate fluids that could damage productivity, seal the casing from corrosive fluids and provide structural support for the casing string. Cementing services are also used when recompleting wells from one producing zone to another, and when plugging and abandoning wells.

Company Financials

Per Share Data ($) Year Ended Sep. 30	**2006**	**2005**	**2004**	**2003**	**2002**	**2001**	**2000**	**1999**	**1998**	**1997**
Tangible Book Value	NA	4.94	3.73	2.44	1.74	2.79	2.40	1.36	1.54	2.90
Cash Flow	NA	1.79	1.49	0.96	0.84	1.36	0.65	0.25	0.64	1.20
Earnings	2.52	1.38	1.11	0.59	0.52	1.04	0.35	-0.11	0.36	0.33
S&P Core Earnings	NA	1.35	0.90	0.54	0.45	0.97	NA	NA	NA	NA
Dividends	0.20	0.12	0.04	Nil	Nil	Nil	Nil	Nil	Nil	Nil
Payout Ratio	8%	9%	4%	Nil	Nil	Nil	Nil	Nil	Nil	Nil
Prices:High	42.85	39.78	27.33	21.20	19.75	21.55	19.19	10.86	10.95	11.34
Prices:Low	27.43	21.13	17.42	14.63	11.50	7.28	9.53	3.36	2.97	4.78
P/E Ratio:High	17	29	25	36	38	21	53	NM	30	35
P/E Ratio:Low	11	15	16	25	22	7	26	NM	8	15
Income Statement Analysis (Million $)										
Revenue	NA	3,243	2,601	2,143	1,866	2,234	1,555	1,131	1,527	1,467
Operating Income	NA	788	567	414	368	641	297	125	316	273
Depreciation, Depletion and Amortization	NA	137	126	120	105	105	102	99.8	91.0	90.4
Interest Expense	NA	11.0	16.4	31.9	8.98	13.3	20.0	31.4	26.0	30.7
Pretax Income	NA	653	521	276	253	529	175	-44.9	175	154
Effective Tax Rate	NA	30.7%	30.7%	31.7%	34.1%	34.0%	32.7%	NM	31.1%	30.1%
Net Income	NA	453	361	188	166	349	118	-29.7	117	108
S&P Core Earnings	NA	447	295	174	142	324	NA	NA	NA	NA
Balance Sheet & Other Financial Data (Million $)										
Cash	NA	357	425	278	84.7	84.1	6.47	3.92	2.00	3.90
Current Assets	NA	1,334	1,424	942	649	733	506	439	452	475
Total Assets	NA	3,396	3,331	2,786	2,442	1,985	1,785	1,825	1,743	1,727
Current Liabilities	NA	684	910	471	356	390	337	445	513	385
Long Term Debt	NA	Nil	78.9	494	489	79.4	142	423	242	299
Common Equity	NA	2,484	2,094	1,651	1,419	1,370	1,170	877	900	960
Total Capital	NA	2,548	2,262	2,152	1,917	1,460	1,320	1,306	1,151	1,314
Capital Expenditures	NA	324	201	167	179	183	80.5	111	168	102
Cash Flow	NA	590	487	308	271	454	220	70.1	208	198
Current Ratio	NA	2.0	1.6	2.0	1.8	1.9	1.5	1.0	0.9	1.2
% Long Term Debt of Capitalization	NA	Nil	3.5	22.9	25.5	5.4	10.8	32.4	21.0	22.7
% Return on Assets	NA	13.5	11.8	7.2	7.5	18.5	6.5	NM	6.7	6.3
% Return on Equity	NA	19.8	19.3	12.3	11.9	27.5	11.5	NM	12.6	12.0

Data as orig reptd.; bef. results of disc opers/spec. items. Per share data adj. for stk. divs.; EPS diluted. E-Estimated. NA-Not Available. NM-Not Meaningful. NR-Not Ranked. UR-Under Review.

Office: 5500 NorthWest Central Drive, Houston, TX 77092.
Telephone: 713-462-4239.
Website: http://www.bjservices.com
Chrmn, Pres & CEO: J.W. Stewart

VP & CFO: J.E. Smith
VP, Secy & General Counsel: M.B. Shannon
Treas: B. Wells
Cntlr: B. McCole

Board of Directors: L. W. Heiligbrodt, J. R. Huff, D. D. Jordan, M. E. Patrick, J. L. Payne, J. W. Stewart, W. H. White

Founded: 1872
Domicile: Delaware
Employees: 13,600

STANDARD &POOR'S

Black & Decker Corp (The)

S&P Recommendation HOLD ★★★★★

Price
$84.74 (as of Oct 27, 2006)

12-Mo. Target Price
$86.00

Investment Style
Mid-Cap Growth

GICS Sector Consumer Discretionary
Sub-Industry Household Appliances

Comment BDK is a leading global producer of power tools, hardware and home improvement products and fastening systems.

Key Stock Statistics (Source S&P, Vickers, company reports)

52-Wk Range	**$94.90–66.04**	S&P Oper. EPS 2006**E**	**7.04**	P/E on S&P Oper. EPS 2006**E**	**12.0**	Dividend Rate/Share	**$1.52**
Trailing 12-Month EPS	**$8.39**	S&P Oper. EPS 2007**E**	**7.80**	Common Shares Outstg. (M)	**74.0**	Yield (%)	**1.79**
Trailing 12-Month P/E	**10.1**	S&P Core EPS 2006**E**	**7.04**	Market Capitalization(B)	**$6.275**	Beta	**0.88**
$10K Invested 5 Yrs Ago	**$25,950**	S&P Core EPS 2007**E**	**7.80**	Institutional Ownership (%)	**87**	S&P Credit Rating	**BBB**

Price Performance

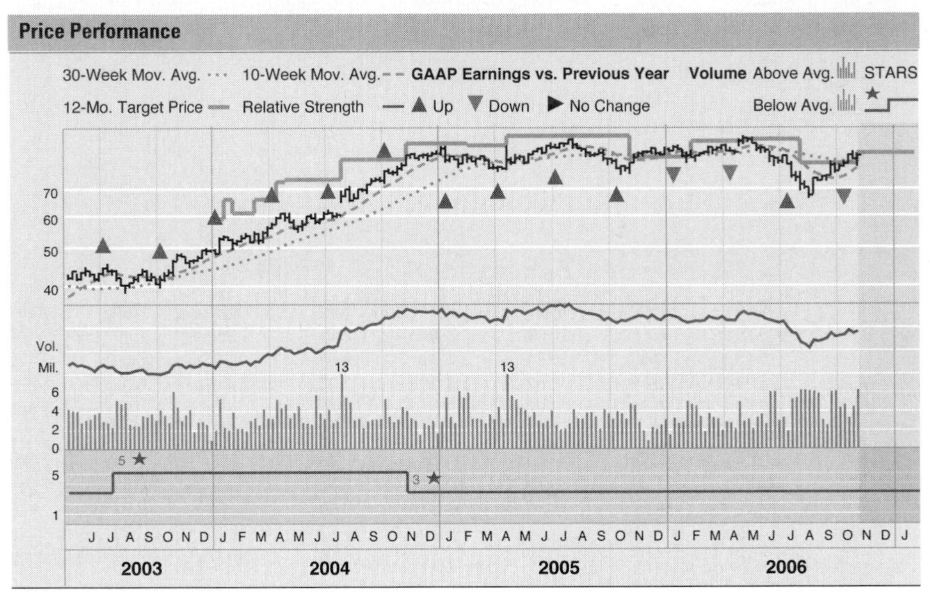

Options: ASE, CBOE, P, Ph

Highlights

➤ The 12-month target price for BDK has recently been changed to $86.00 from $81.00. The Highlights section of this Stock Report will be updated accordingly.

Investment Rationale/Risk

➤ The Investment Rationale/Risk section of this Stock Report will be updated shortly. For the latest News story on BDK from MarketScope, see below.

➤ 10/26/06 12:26 pm EDT... S&P REITERATES HOLD OPINION ON SHARES OF BLACK & DECKER (BDK 83.9***): Q3 EPS of $1.74 vs. $1.69 is $0.01 below our forecast. Greater-than-expected share buybacks largely offset weaker sales and margins. Despite the lower share count, we are reducing our '06 EPS estimate by $0.14 to $7.04, and '07's by $0.09 to $7.80 to reflect a slower sales outlook combined with margin pressure. We think there could be additional share repurchases from what we view as healthy cash flow. Based on historical P/E and improved peer valuations, we are raising our target price by $5 to $86, or 11X our '07 EPS estimate. /ELevy-CFA

Qualitative Risk Assessment

LOW | **MEDIUM** | HIGH

Our risk assessment reflects our positive view of BDK's strong brand name and cash flow, offset by our negative view of industry cyclicality.

Quantitative Evaluations

S&P Quality Ranking **B+**

D | C | B- | B | **B+** | A- | A | A+

Relative Strength Rank **STRONG**

71

LOWEST = 1 HIGHEST = 99

Revenue/Earnings Data

Revenue (Million $)

	1Q	2Q	3Q	4Q	Year
2006	1,529	1,697	1,576	--	--
2005	1,519	1,699	1,576	1,730	6,524
2004	1,093	1,298	1,283	1,725	5,398
2003	939.2	1,090	1,116	1,338	4,483
2002	951.7	1,125	1,085	1,232	4,394
2001	979.0	1,070	1,063	1,221	4,333

Earnings Per Share ($)

2006	1.45	1.98	1.69	**E**1.88	**E**7.04
2005	1.79	1.88	1.73	1.28	6.69
2004	0.93	1.50	1.35	1.60	5.40
2003	0.55	0.94	0.95	1.23	3.68
2002	0.41	0.81	0.68	0.94	2.84
2001	0.40	0.51	0.57	-0.16	1.33

Fiscal year ended Dec. 31. Next earnings report expected: Late January. EPS Estimates based on S&P Operating Earnings; historical GAAP earnings are as reported.

Dividend Data (Dates: mm/dd Payment Date: mm/dd/yy)

Amount ($)	Date Decl.	Ex-Div. Date	Stk. of Record	Payment Date
0.380	02/09	03/15	03/17	03/31/06
0.380	04/27	06/14	06/16	06/30/06
0.380	07/20	09/13	09/15	09/29/06
0.380	10/26	12/13	12/15	12/29/06

Dividends have been paid since 1937. Source: Company reports.

Black & Decker Corp (The)

Business Summary August 01, 2006

Black & Decker, incorporated in 1910, is a global manufacturer and marketer of power tools and accessories, hardware and home improvement products, and technology-based fastening systems. Its products are sold under a number of well known brand names in more than 100 countries. The company has 44 manufacturing facilities, including 24 located outside the U.S. in 10 foreign countries.

Operations consist of three segments: Power Tools and Accessories (74% of 2005 sales and 71% in 2004), Hardware and Home Improvement (16% and 18%), and Fastening and Assembly Systems (10% and 11%). The U.S. accounted for 66% of sales in 2005, Europe 21%, and other countries 13%.

BDK is one of the world's leading producers of portable electric power tools and electric lawn and garden tools, as well as one of the largest suppliers of power tool accessories and specialized, engineered fastening and assembly systems in the markets it serves. Its plumbing products business is one of the largest North American faucet makers.

The Power Tools and Accessories segment manufactures and sells consumer and professional power tools (such as drills, screwdrivers and saws) and accessories, outdoor products (electric lawn and garden tools), cleaning and lighting products and product services. Products are sold mainly to retailers, wholesalers, jobbers, and distributors, although some discontinued or reconditioned products are sold through company-operated service centers and factory outlets directly to end users. Principal materials used to manufacture products in this segment include plastics, aluminum, copper, steel, certain electronic components, and batteries.

The Hardware and Home Improvement segment (formerly building products) makes and sells security hardware (locksets and deadbolts) and plumbing products (faucets, shower heads and bath accessories). Products are sold primarily to retailers, wholesalers, distributors, and jobbers. Certain security hardware products are sold to commercial, institutional, and industrial customers. The principal materials used in the manufacture of products in this segment are plastics, aluminum, steel, brass, zamak, and ceramics.

Company Financials

Per Share Data ($) Year Ended Dec. 31	**2005**	**2004**	**2003**	**2002**	**2001**	**2000**	**1999**	**1998**	**1997**	**1996**
Tangible Book Value	5.27	4.57	0.96	NM	NM	NM	0.66	NM	NM	NM
Cash Flow	8.97	7.12	5.40	4.49	3.30	5.28	5.21	-6.52	4.55	4.11
Earnings	6.69	5.40	3.68	2.84	1.33	3.34	3.40	-8.22	2.35	1.64
S&P Core Earnings	6.22	4.93	3.23	1.56	0.11	NA	NA	NA	NA	NA
Dividends	1.12	0.84	0.57	0.48	0.48	0.48	0.48	0.48	0.48	0.48
Payout Ratio	17%	16%	15%	17%	36%	14%	14%	NM	20%	29%
Prices:High	93.71	89.64	49.90	50.50	46.95	52.38	64.63	65.50	43.44	44.25
Prices:Low	75.70	48.07	33.20	35.00	28.26	27.56	41.00	37.94	29.63	29.00
P/E Ratio:High	14	17	14	18	35	16	19	NM	18	27
P/E Ratio:Low	11	9	9	12	21	8	12	NM	13	18
Income Statement Analysis (Million $)										
Revenue	6,524	5,398	4,483	4,394	4,333	4,561	4,521	4,560	4,940	4,914
Operating Income	964	772	594	549	407	686	696	639	703	572
Depreciation	151	143	133	128	159	163	160	155	214	215
Interest Expense	81.9	57.9	60.7	84.3	84.3	104	126	145	133	140
Pretax Income	819	604	391	307	155	405	441	-589	349	203
Effective Tax Rate	33.6%	27.0%	26.5%	25.3%	30.5%	30.3%	32.0%	NM	35.0%	21.6%
Net Income	544	441	287	230	108	282	300	-755	227	159
S&P Core Earnings	506	401	251	126	9.48	NA	NA	NA	NA	NA
Balance Sheet & Other Financial Data (Million $)										
Cash	968	514	308	517	245	135	147	88.0	247	142
Current Assets	3,347	2,927	2,203	2,194	1,892	1,962	1,911	1,752	2,079	1,804
Total Assets	5,817	5,531	4,223	4,131	4,014	4,090	4,013	3,853	5,361	5,154
Current Liabilities	2,264	1,793	1,312	1,453	1,071	1,632	1,573	1,375	1,373	507
Long Term Debt	1,030	1,201	916	928	1,191	798	847	1,149	1,624	1,416
Common Equity	1,524	1,559	846	600	751	692	801	573	1,791	1,632
Total Capital	2,742	2,930	1,942	1,739	2,204	1,712	1,892	2,002	3,473	3,116
Capital Expenditures	111	118	103	96.6	135	200	171	146	203	196
Cash Flow	695	584	421	358	267	445	460	-600	441	374
Current Ratio	1.5	1.6	1.7	1.5	1.8	1.2	1.2	1.3	1.5	1.2
% Long Term Debt of Capitalization	37.6	41.0	47.1	53.4	54.1	46.6	44.8	57.4	46.8	45.4
% Net Income of Revenue	8.3	8.2	6.4	5.2	2.5	6.2	6.6	NM	4.6	3.2
% Return on Assets	9.6	9.0	6.9	5.6	2.7	7.0	7.6	NM	4.3	3.0
% Return on Equity	35.3	36.7	39.7	34.0	15.0	37.8	43.7	NM	13.3	10.[illegible]

Data as orig reptd.; bef. results of disc opers/spec. items. Per share data adj. for stk. divs.; EPS diluted. E-Estimated. NA-Not Available. NM-Not Meaningful. NR-Not Ranked. UR-Under Review.

Office: 701 East Joppa Road, Towson, MD 21286.
Telephone: 410-716-3900.
Email: investor.relations@bdk.com
Website: http://www.bdk.com

Chrmn, Pres & CEO: N.D. Archibald
SVP & CFO: M.D. Mangan
SVP & Secy: B.B. Lucas
SVP & General Counsel: C.E. Fenton

Investor Contact: M.M. Rothleitner (410-716-3979)
Board of Directors: N. D. Archibald, N. R. Augustine, B. L. Bowles, G. W. Buckley, M. A. Burns, K. B. Clark, M. A. Fernandez, B. H. Griswold, IV, A. Luiso, R. L. Ryan, M. Willes

Founded: 1910
Domicile: Maryland
Employees: 27,200

STANDARD &POOR'S

BMC Software Inc.

S&P Recommendation HOLD ★★★★★

Price $29.59 (as of Oct 27, 2006)

12-Mo. Target Price $30.00

Investment Style Mid-Cap Value

GICS Sector Information Technology
Sub-Industry Systems Software

Comment This Houston-based company provides systems management software that improves the availability, performance and recovery of applications and data.

Key Stock Statistics (Source S&P, Vickers, company reports)

52-Wk Range	$30.58–18.50	S&P Oper. EPS 2007**E**	1.20	P/E on S&P Oper. EPS 2007**E**	24.7	Dividend Rate/Share	Nil
Trailing 12-Month EPS	$0.81	S&P Oper. EPS 2008**E**	1.39	Common Shares Outstg. (M)	205.0	Yield (%)	Nil
Trailing 12-Month P/E	36.5	S&P Core EPS 2007**E**	1.20	Market Capitalization(B)	$6.065	Beta	1.66
$10K Invested 5 Yrs Ago	$17,426	S&P Core EPS 2008**E**	1.39	Institutional Ownership (%)	92	S&P Credit Rating	NA

Price Performance

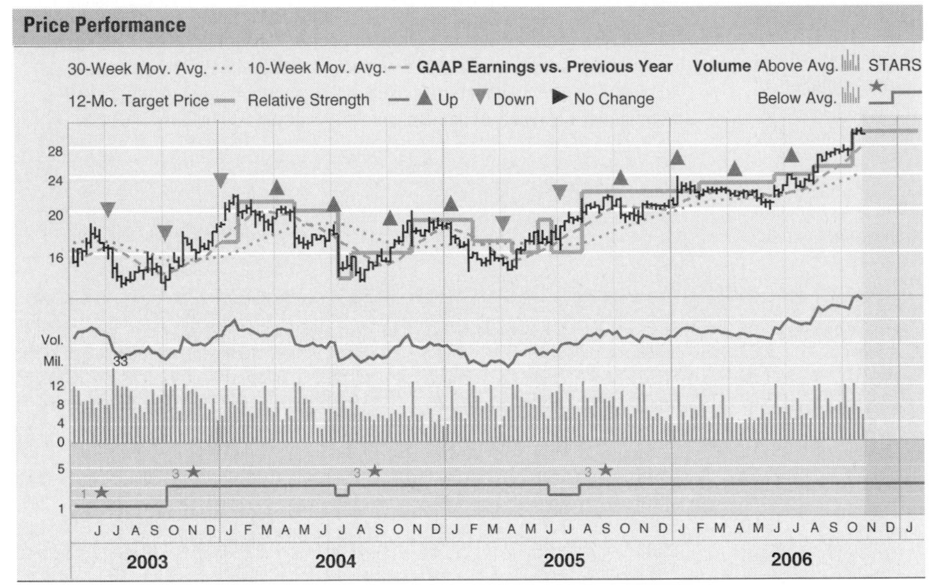

Options: ASE, CBOE, P, Ph

Analysis prepared by **Zaineb Bokhari** on October 16, 2006, when the stock traded at **$ 29.94**.

Highlights

- We expect revenues to increase about 5% in FY 07 (Mar.) and 4% in FY 08, as strong projected double-digit growth in service management solutions is partly offset by modest declines in solutions for mainframe and distributed systems. We note that in FY 06 the percentage of transactions for which revenue was recognized ratably (versus upfront) rose to 40% on average, from 35% in FY 05. This trend has contributed to our modest growth outlook for revenues.

- Operating margins should widen to about 20% in FY 07 and 21% in FY 08, from about 16% in FY 06, due to recent cost-cutting efforts, which include head count reductions and property sales.

- We estimate operating EPS of $1.20 for FY 07, up from $1.06 (using a 28% effective tax rate in both years). Our FY 08 EPS estimate is $1.39. We expect EPS to benefit from interest income earned on the $1.2 billion in cash and investments on BMC's balance sheet. Our EPS estimates for FY 07 and FY 08 include $0.20 of projected stock option expense for each year. We look for continued aggressive share repurchases in future periods, following a recent authorization to repurchase $1 billion of stock.

Investment Rationale/Risk

- We have a favorable view of BMC's recent workforce reduction as well as its decision to focus resources on its growth businesses. BMC's balance sheet showed no debt and about $1.2 billion in cash and short-term marketable securities at June 30, 2006. Recent tax legislation has allowed BMC to repatriate up to $717 million in overseas earnings at favorable tax rates. We expect BMC to employ this liquidity to repurchase shares and to seek growth via acquisitions that it believes will be complementary to its newer service management business.

- Risks to our recommendation and target price include increased competition from large platform vendors, a significant decline in corporate spending on information technology, and greater pricing pressures.

- We arrive at our 12-month target price of $30 by applying a 1.7X P/E-to-growth ratio to our calendar 2007 EPS estimate of $1.35, within the historical range for the shares of 1.3X-2.0X.

Qualitative Risk Assessment

LOW	**MEDIUM**	HIGH

Our risk assessment for BMC Software reflects our concern that the company's legacy mainframe business remains vulnerable to competition from hardware vendors, notably IBM. We see this competitive pressure, and an ongoing business transition within BMC, impacting growth. Despite this, we look for strong earnings gains supported by cost-cutting measures.

Quantitative Evaluations

S&P Quality Ranking C

D	**C**	B-	B	B+	A-	A	A+

Relative Strength Rank STRONG

82

LOWEST = 1 HIGHEST = 99

Revenue/Earnings Data

Revenue (Million $)

	1Q	2Q	3Q	4Q	Year
2007	361.4	--	--	--	--
2006	348.3	361.8	380.3	407.9	1,498
2005	326.0	355.1	386.8	395.1	1,463
2004	309.9	333.8	374.8	400.2	1,419
2003	305.2	291.2	349.6	380.7	1,327
2002	341.0	295.1	321.0	311.8	1,289

Earnings Per Share ($)

2007	0.15	**E**0.29	**E**0.30	**E**0.35	**E**1.20
2006	-0.19	0.19	0.22	0.31	0.47
2005	0.05	0.06	0.16	0.07	0.34
2004	-0.03	-0.06	-0.20	0.16	-0.12
2003	0.02	0.04	0.05	0.09	0.20
2002	-0.14	-0.22	-0.39	-0.01	-0.75

Fiscal year ended Mar. 31. Next earnings report expected: Early November. EPS Estimates based on S&P Operating Earnings; historical GAAP earnings are as reported.

Dividend Data

No cash dividends have been paid.

BMC Software Inc.

Business Summary October 16, 2006

CORPORATE OVERVIEW. BMC Software is a leading independent software vendor. The company's information technology (IT) infrastructure management solutions span enterprise systems, applications, databases, and service management. In FY 06 (Mar.), the company's product solutions fell into four broad categories: Mainframe Management, Distributed Systems Management, Services Management, and Identity Management.

The Mainframe Management segment includes automated tools that enhance the performance and availability of database management systems on mainframe platforms. This segment includes BMC's mainframe performance monitoring and management product line, MAINVIEW. It also includes SmartDBA, for the management and recovery of IBM's DB2 and IMS databases. The segment contributed 34% of license revenues in FY 06, down from 35% in FY 05 and 39% in FY 04.

The Distributed Systems Management segment includes solutions and software tools for businesses to manage their distributed IT infrastructure. Solutions include the PATROL product line for distributed computing environments and SmartDBA for Oracle, IBM DB2 UDB, Microsoft SQL Server, and Sybase databases. Other products in this category include enterprise job scheduling and output management and application management solutions. The segment contributed 30% of license revenues in FY 06, down from 33% in FY 05 and 37% in FY 04.

The Service Management segment includes software that allows organizations to automate and manage internal and external service and support processes. This segment includes service, change and asset management, IT discovery and software configuration management solutions gained through the acquisitions of Remedy, Magic and Marimba. The segment contributed 34% of license revenue in FY 06, up from 30% in FY 05 and 22% in FY 04.

The Identity Management segment includes products for the management of user identities and access to the IT systems of an organization. The main product in this category is the BMC Software Identity Management Suite, an integrated suite of products that allows for user administration and provisioning, password administration, enterprise directory management, Web access control and audit and compliance management. The segment contributed 2% of license revenues in FY 06, FY 05 and FY 04.

Company Financials

Per Share Data ($) Year Ended Mar. 31	2006	2005	2004	2003	2002	2001	2000	1999	1998	1997
Tangible Book Value	2.31	2.60	3.11	3.70	5.49	5.67	5.67	5.64	3.68	2.73
Cash Flow	1.40	1.33	1.03	1.25	0.78	1.42	1.89	1.77	1.03	0.92
Earnings	0.47	0.34	-0.12	0.20	-0.75	0.17	0.96	1.47	0.76	0.77
S&P Core Earnings	0.29	-0.03	-0.56	-0.01	-0.94	-0.19	NA	NA	NA	NA
Dividends	Nil	Nil	Nil	Nil	Nil	Nil	Nil	Nil	Nil	Nil
Payout Ratio	Nil	Nil	Nil	Nil	Nil	Nil	Nil	Nil	Nil	Nil
Calendar Year	2005	2004	2003	2002	2001	2000	1999	1998	1997	1996
Prices:High	21.68	21.87	19.84	23.00	33.00	86.63	84.06	60.25	35.63	23.38
Prices:Low	14.44	13.70	13.18	10.85	11.50	13.00	30.00	29.25	19.81	9.31
P/E Ratio:High	41	64	NM	NM	NM	NM	88	41	47	31
P/E Ratio:Low	27	40	NM	NM	NM	NM	31	20	26	12
Income Statement Analysis (Million $)										
Revenue	1,498	1,463	1,419	1,327	1,289	1,504	1,719	1,304	731	563
Operating Income	334	264	162	349	400	336	656	548	357	261
Depreciation	205	222	259	248	376	315	236	76.8	58.0	32.5
Interest Expense	1.70	2.00	1.10	Nil	0.40	11.3	23.4	Nil	Nil	Nil
Pretax Income	204	98.2	-29.4	69.3	-231	60.4	311	478	257	237
Effective Tax Rate	50.0%	23.3%	NM	30.7%	NM	29.8%	22.1%	23.8%	35.4%	30.9%
Net Income	102	75.3	-26.8	48.0	-184	42.4	243	364	166	164
S&P Core Earnings	63.9	-5.94	-128	-3.42	-232	-46.6	NA	NA	NA	NA
Balance Sheet & Other Financial Data (Million $)										
Cash	1,063	929	909	1,015	546	146	152	1,205	72.1	139
Current Assets	1,506	1,440	1,425	1,098	997	903	896	873	374	248
Total Assets	3,211	3,298	3,045	2,846	2,676	3,034	2,962	2,283	1,248	844
Current Liabilities	1,202	1,085	987	839	681	829	884	651	336	205
Long Term Debt	Nil	Nil	Nil	Nil	Nil	Nil	Nil	Nil	Nil	Nil
Common Equity	1,099	1,262	1,215	1,383	1,507	1,815	1,781	1,334	759	546
Total Capital	1,099	1,262	1,215	1,383	1,507	1,815	1,781	1,334	803	546
Capital Expenditures	24.1	57.7	50.4	23.6	64.3	183	148	116	67.0	26.8
Cash Flow	307	297	233	296	192	357	478	441	224	196
Current Ratio	1.3	1.3	1.4	1.3	1.5	1.1	1.0	1.3	1.1	1.2
% Long Term Debt of Capitalization	Nil	Nil	Nil	Nil	Nil	Nil	Nil	Nil	Nil	Nil
% Net Income of Revenue	6.8	5.1	NM	3.6	NM	2.8	14.1	27.9	22.7	29.1
% Return on Assets	3.1	2.4	NM	1.7	NM	1.4	9.2	20.6	15.9	22.6
% Return on Equity	8.6	6.1	NM	3.3	NM	2.4	15.6	34.8	25.4	35.2

Data as orig reptd.; bef. results of disc opers/spec. items. Per share data adj. for stk. divs.; EPS diluted. E-Estimated. NA-Not Available. NM-Not Meaningful. NR-Not Ranked. UR-Under Review.

Office: 2101 Citywest Boulevard, Houston, TX 77042-2827.
Telephone: 713-918-8800.
Email: investor@bmc.com
Website: http://www.bmc.com

Chrmn: B.G. Cupp
Pres & CEO: R.E. Beauchamp
SVP, CFO & Treas: S.B. Solcher
SVP, Secy & General Counsel: D.M. Clolery

VP, Chief Acctg Officer & Cntlr: L.E. Travis
Board of Directors: J. E. Barfield, J. W. Barter, R. E. Beauchamp, B. G. Cupp, M. K. Gafner, L. W. Gray, P. T. Jenkins, L. J. Lavigne, Jr., K. A. O'Neill, G. F. Raymond, T. C. Tinsley

Founded: 1980
Domicile: Delaware
Employees: 6,200

STANDARD &POOR'S

Boeing Co (The)

S&P Recommendation BUY ★★★★★

Price $79.74 (as of Oct 27, 2006)

12-Mo. Target Price $106.00

Investment Style Large-Cap Value

GICS Sector Industrials
Sub-Industry Aerospace & Defense

Comment This company is the world's second-largest commercial jet and military weapons manufacturer.

Key Stock Statistics (Source S&P, Vickers, company reports)

52-Wk Range	**$89.58–64.20**	S&P Oper. EPS 2006**E**	**2.50**	P/E on S&P Oper. EPS 2006**E**	**31.9**	Dividend Rate/Share	**$1.20**
Trailing 12-Month EPS	**$2.12**	S&P Oper. EPS 2007**E**	**4.50**	Common Shares Outstg. (M)	**790.7**	Yield (%)	**1.50**
Trailing 12-Month P/E	**37.6**	S&P Core EPS 2006**E**	**3.15**	Market Capitalization(B)	**$63.054**	Beta	**1.01**
$10K Invested 5 Yrs Ago	**$23,106**	S&P Core EPS 2007**E**	**4.58**	Institutional Ownership (%)	**67**	S&P Credit Rating	**A**

Price Performance

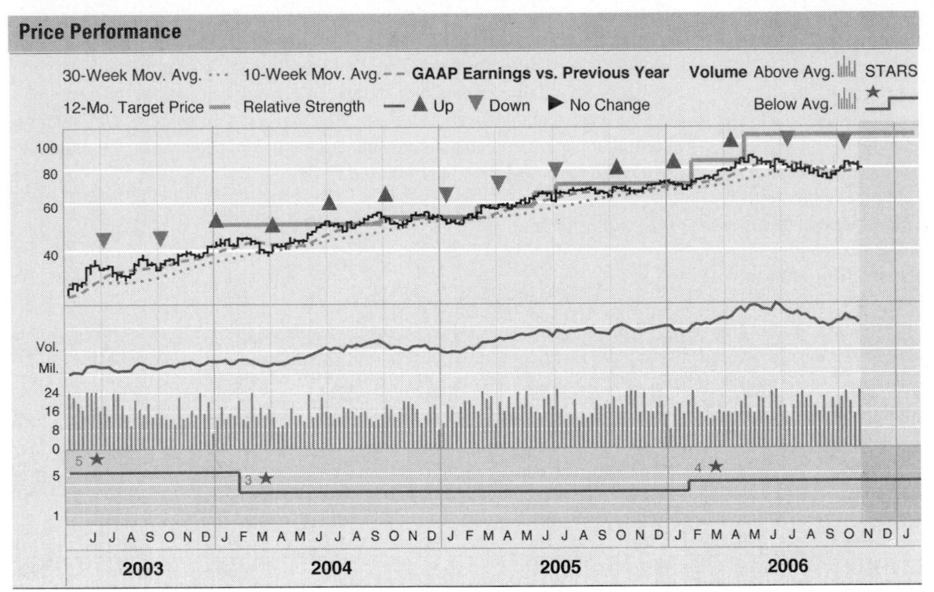

Options: ASE, CBOE, P, Ph

Analysis prepared by **Richard Tortoriello** on August 21, 2006, when the stock traded at **$ 76.65**.

Highlights

- We estimate that the Commercial Airlines segment will rise to 46% of sales in 2006, from 40% in 2005, driving overall sales growth of 12%. We expect Integrated Defense System segment sales to rise by about 1%, and see sales increasing strongly at the much smaller Boeing Capital segment. For 2007, we project an overall sales increase of 8%.
- We believe a recent spike in commercial aircraft orders will help support operating margins, despite our forecast of declines in defense-related margins, on lower volumes and contract mix. Overall, we project operating margins in 2006 of 4.7%, down from 5.2% in 2005. In 2007, we project an increase in overall operating margins to 6.9%.
- We project earnings per share for 2006, including $1.15 of special charges related to the settlement of government litigation and a customer contract, of $2.56, and project growth to $4.45 in 2007. We expect free cash flow (cash from operating activities less capital expenditures) of greater than $5 per share in each year.

Investment Rationale/Risk

- Our analysis of past cycles indicates that peaks in delivery of aircraft follow peaks in orders by three years. We believe that 2005 was the peak in BA's order cycle, with over 1,000 commercial aircraft ordered, but we expect that 2006 orders will not be far below 2005. As a result, we see the peak of the current delivery cycle stretching out into late 2008 or early 2009. We also note that BA now has over $10 of cash per share, which we expect to be spent on continued share repurchases and debt reductions.
- Risks to our recommendation and target price include loss of significant defense contracts leading to lower defense sales, and manufacturing difficulties encountered by Boeing or its suppliers as commercial aircraft production shifts into high gear.
- Our 12-month target price of $106 is based on a P/E ratio of 24X our 2007 EPS estimate, above BA's 10-year historical average forward P/E of 17.3X, but in line with historical high P/E ratios in the 24X to 26X range. We believe that given the current strong aerospace cycle, BA deserves to trade at the high end of its historical range.

Qualitative Risk Assessment

LOW | **MEDIUM** | HIGH

Our risk assessment reflects that BA participates in highly cyclical, very competitive and capital intensive businesses. This is offset by what we see as a strong cash position and likely strong generation of free cash flow, along with a healthy and rising backlog of business.

Quantitative Evaluations

S&P Quality Ranking A-

D | C | B- | B | B+ | **A-** | A | A+

Relative Strength Rank **MODERATE**

33

LOWEST = 1 HIGHEST = 99

Revenue/Earnings Data

Revenue (Million $)

	1Q	2Q	3Q	4Q	Year
2006	14,264	14,986	14,739	--	--
2005	12,987	15,025	12,629	14,204	54,845
2004	12,903	13,088	13,152	13,314	52,457
2003	12,258	12,772	12,241	13,214	50,485
2002	13,821	13,857	12,690	13,701	54,069
2001	13,293	15,516	13,687	15,702	58,198

Earnings Per Share ($)

2006	0.88	-0.21	0.89	**E**0.95	**E**2.50
2005	0.64	0.70	1.26	0.59	3.19
2004	0.76	0.72	0.54	0.23	2.24
2003	-0.60	-0.24	0.32	1.40	0.89
2002	0.72	0.96	0.46	0.73	2.87
2001	1.45	0.99	0.80	0.12	3.41

Fiscal year ended Dec. 31. Next earnings report expected: Early February. EPS Estimates based on S&P Operating Earnings; historical GAAP earnings are as reported.

Dividend Data (Dates: mm/dd Payment Date: mm/dd/yy)

Amount ($)	Date Decl.	Ex-Div. Date	Stk. of Record	Payment Date
0.250	10/31	11/08	11/11	12/02/05
0.300	12/12	02/08	02/10	03/03/06
0.300	05/02	05/10	05/12	06/02/06
0.300	06/26	08/09	08/11	09/01/06

Dividends have been paid since 1942. Source: Company reports.

Boeing Co (The)

Business Summary August 21, 2006

CORPORATE OVERVIEW. This global aerospace giant conducts business through four segments: Boeing Commercial Aircraft (BCA; 41% of revenues, 27% of operating profits in 2005) and EADS's 80%-owned Airbus division are the world's only makers of 100-plus seat passenger jets. Integrated Defense Systems (IDS; 56%, 75%), the world's second-largest military contractor, makes a wide range of military aircraft and missiles, as well as computer-based information networking systems used in everything from missile defense systems to combat vehicles. BA's BCC segment (2%, 4%) primarily finances commercial aircraft for airlines. Boeing's Other segment (1%, -6%) primarily consists of the fledgling Connexion by Boeing unit, which provides in-flight Internet services.

MARKET PROFILE. Based on total dollar sales of 100-plus seat jetliners in 2004 (latest available), BCA and Airbus control about 45% and 55%, respectively, of the global commercial jetliner market. Demand for jetliners is driven primarily by growth in the global 100-plus seat commercial aircraft fleet. Based on the latest statistics provided by independent research firm Avitas, Inc., from 1993 through 2003, the global airliner fleet grew at a 3.0% average annual rate, to 13,265 jets.

Examining BA's military weapons market profile, demand for IDS's equipment and systems is primarily driven by growth in the procurement and R&D sectors of the U.S. defense budget, which accounts for about 40% of global military weapons spending. The market for military weapons systems is mature. Based on U.S. Department of Defense statistics, from FY 94 (Oct.) through FY 04 (latest available), the procurement and R&D sectors of the total U.S. defense budget grew at 5.3% and 5.1% average annual rates, respectively.

Company Financials

Per Share Data ($) Year Ended Dec. 31	**2005**	**2004**	**2003**	**2002**	**2001**	**2000**	**1999**	**1998**	**1997**	**1996**
Tangible Book Value	10.33	10.08	6.17	4.53	5.23	6.63	10.14	10.25	10.56	11.75
Cash Flow	5.08	4.00	2.68	2.46	5.52	4.14	4.27	2.84	1.32	3.03
Earnings	3.19	2.24	0.89	2.87	3.41	2.44	2.49	1.15	-0.18	1.60
S&P Core Earnings	3.05	1.99	1.33	0.26	-0.06	NA	NA	NA	NA	NA
Dividends	1.00	0.77	0.68	0.68	0.68	0.56	0.56	0.56	0.56	0.55
Payout Ratio	31%	34%	76%	24%	20%	23%	22%	49%	NM	34%
Prices:High	72.40	55.48	43.37	51.07	69.85	70.94	48.50	56.25	60.50	53.75
Prices:Low	49.52	38.04	24.73	28.53	27.60	32.00	32.56	29.00	43.00	37.06
P/E Ratio:High	23	25	49	18	20	29	19	49	NM	34
P/E Ratio:Low	16	17	28	10	8	13	13	25	NM	23

Income Statement Analysis (Million $)										
Revenue	54,845	52,457	50,485	54,069	58,198	51,321	57,993	56,154	45,800	22,681
Operating Income	3,707	3,405	3,198	5,447	6,467	4,996	4,724	3,189	2,503	2,212
Depreciation	1,503	1,509	1,450	1,497	1,750	1,479	1,645	1,622	1,458	991
Interest Expense	653	685	800	730	650	445	431	453	513	203
Pretax Income	2,819	1,960	550	1,353	3,565	2,999	3,324	1,397	-341	1,363
Effective Tax Rate	9.12%	7.14%	NM	63.6%	20.7%	29.0%	30.5%	19.8%	NM	19.7%
Net Income	2,562	1,820	718	492	2,827	2,128	2,309	1,120	-178	1,095
S&P Core Earnings	2,450	1,616	1,074	203	284	NA	NA	NA	NA	NA

Balance Sheet & Other Financial Data (Million $)										
Cash	5,412	3,204	4,633	2,333	633	1,010	3,354	2,462	4,420	5,258
Current Assets	21,968	15,100	17,258	16,855	16,206	15,864	15,712	16,375	19,263	15,080
Total Assets	60,058	53,963	53,035	52,342	48,343	42,028	36,147	36,672	38,024	27,254
Current Liabilities	28,188	20,835	18,448	19,810	20,486	18,289	13,656	13,422	14,152	8,642
Long Term Debt	9,538	10,879	13,299	12,589	10,866	7,567	5,980	6,103	6,123	3,980
Common Equity	11,059	11,286	8,139	7,696	10,825	11,020	11,462	12,316	12,953	10,941
Total Capital	22,664	23,255	21,438	20,285	21,868	18,587	17,614	18,419	19,076	14,921
Capital Expenditures	1,547	978	741	1,001	1,068	932	1,236	1,584	1,391	726
Cash Flow	4,065	3,329	2,168	1,989	4,577	3,607	3,954	2,742	1,280	2,086
Current Ratio	0.8	0.7	0.9	0.9	0.8	0.9	1.2	1.2	1.4	1.8
% Long Term Debt of Capitalization	42.1	46.8	62.0	62.1	49.7	40.7	34.0	33.1	47.2	26.7
% Net Income of Revenue	4.7	3.5	1.4	0.9	4.9	4.1	4.0	2.0	NM	4.8
% Return on Assets	4.4	3.4	1.4	1.0	6.2	5.4	6.3	3.0	NM	4.4
% Return on Equity	22.9	18.7	9.1	5.3	25.9	18.9	19.4	8.9	NM	10.5

Data as orig reptd.; bef. results of disc opers/spec. items. Per share data adj. for stk. divs.; EPS diluted. E-Estimated. NA-Not Available. NM-Not Meaningful. NR-Not Ranked. UR-Under Review.

Office: 100 N. Riverside, Chicago, IL 60606.
Telephone: 312-544-2000.
Website: http://www.boeing.com
Chrmn, Pres & CEO: W.J. McNerney, Jr.

EVP & CFO: J.A. Bell
SVP & General Counsel: D.G. Bain
Investor Contact: P. Kinscherff (312-544-2140)

Board of Directors: J. H. Biggs, J. E. Bryson, L. Z. Cook, W. M. Daley, K. M. Duberstein, J. F. McDonnell, W. J. McNerney, Jr., R. D. Nanula, R. L. Ridgway, M. S. Zafirovski

Founded: 1934
Domicile: Delaware
Employees: 153,000

STANDARD &POOR'S

Boston Properties Inc

S&P Recommendation SELL ★★★★★

Price $104.36 (as of Oct 27, 2006)

12-Mo. Target Price $91.00

Investment Style Large-Cap Value

GICS Sector Financials
Sub-Industry Office REITS

Comment This REIT primarily owns office buildings in the Boston, Washington, DC, New York City, San Francisco, and Princeton, NJ markets.

Key Stock Statistics (Source S&P, Vickers, company reports)

52-Wk Range	$106.62–66.17	S&P Oper. EPS 2006E	2.40	P/E on S&P Oper. EPS 2006E	43.5	Dividend Rate/Share	$2.72
Trailing 12-Month EPS	$8.13	S&P Oper. EPS 2007E	2.50	Common Shares Outstg. (M)	114.3	Yield (%)	2.61
Trailing 12-Month P/E	12.8	S&P Core EPS 2006E	2.40	Market Capitalization(B)	$11.928	Beta	0.47
$10K Invested 5 Yrs Ago	$39,388	S&P Core EPS 2007E	2.50	Institutional Ownership (%)	96	S&P Credit Rating	NA

Price Performance

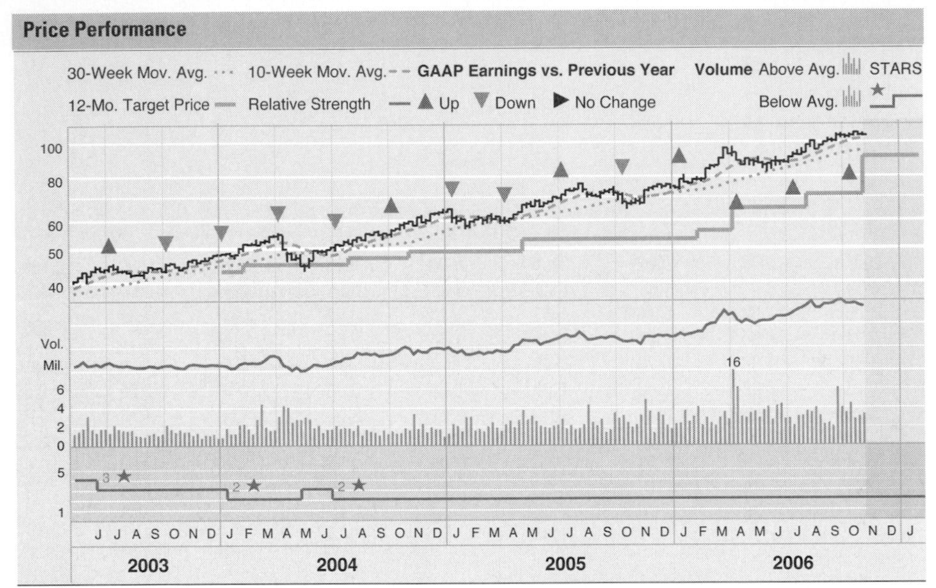

Options: ASE, P

Highlights

- The 12-month target price for BXP has recently been changed to $91.00 from $71.00. The Highlights section of this Stock Report will be updated accordingly.

Investment Rationale/Risk

- The Investment Rationale/Risk section of this Stock Report will be updated shortly. For the latest News story on BXP from MarketScope, see below.

- 10/25/06 12:10 pm EDT... S&P MAINTAINS SELL OPINION ON SHARES OF BOSTON PROPERTIES (BXP 104.81**): Q3 EPS of $0.91, vs. $0.50, exceeds our $0.59 est., boosted by property sales. Per-share funds from operations of $1.16, compared with Street's $1.10 estimate, includes higher lease termination fees. In '07, we see limited chances to roll up leases, leading to EPS of $2.50, versus our '06 estimate of $2.49, raised by $0.05 today. We see '07 FFO of $4.55 vs. $4.45 we expect in '06. We think BXP is realizing value from asset sales, new projects. We are raising our target price by $20 to $91, 20X our '07 FFO est., excl. expected $5.25 special dividend, which is a premium to peers. /R.Shepard

Qualitative Risk Assessment

LOW | MEDIUM | HIGH

Our risk assessment reflects what we see as BXP's large and diverse asset portfolio, relatively unleveraged balance sheet, consistent cash distribution, and low stock volatility as measured by its beta.

Quantitative Evaluations

S&P Quality Ranking A-

D | C | B- | B | B+ | A- | A | A+

Relative Strength Rank MODERATE

53

LOWEST = 1 HIGHEST = 99

Revenue/Earnings Data

Revenue (Million $)

	1Q	2Q	3Q	4Q	Year
2006	356.1	370.4	372.5	--	--
2005	356.2	360.6	361.8	366.3	1,438
2004	333.3	344.9	359.7	362.6	1,400
2003	319.7	323.4	331.2	336.2	1,310
2002	279.6	295.6	313.7	346.0	1,235
2001	233.5	256.3	277.2	266.1	1,033

Earnings Per Share ($)

2006	0.59	5.24	0.91	E0.63	E2.40
2005	0.55	1.36	0.50	1.00	3.46
2004	0.61	0.61	0.58	0.55	2.35
2003	1.13	0.64	0.57	0.61	2.94
2002	0.53	0.59	0.74	2.64	4.40
2001	0.57	0.53	0.45	0.60	2.26

Fiscal year ended Dec. 31. Next earnings report expected: Late January. EPS Estimates based on S&P Operating Earnings; historical GAAP earnings are as reported.

Dividend Data (Dates: mm/dd Payment Date: mm/dd/yy)

Amount ($)	Date Decl.	Ex-Div. Date	Stk. of Record	Payment Date
0.680	12/19	12/28	12/30	01/30/06
0.680	03/17	03/29	03/31	04/28/06
0.680	06/19	06/28	06/30	07/31/06
0.680	09/18	09/27	09/29	10/31/06

Dividends have been paid since 1997. Source: Company reports.

Boston Properties Inc

Business Summary August 03, 2006

CORPORATE OVERVIEW. Boston Properties, founded in 1970, is a REIT that develops, acquires, manages, and operates, and is one of the largest U.S. owners of Class A office properties. BXP conducts substantially all of its business through its limited partnership, of which it is the sole general partner, and holds an 80.9% economic interest.

At June 30, 2006, the property portfolio consisted of 124 properties, totaling 42.1 million new rentable sq. ft. and parking facilities for 31,837 vehicles. The properties included 120 office buildings, including four development properties, two retail properties, and two hotels.

MARKET PROFILE The market for office leases is inherently cyclical. Local economic conditions, particularly the employment level, play an important role in determining competitive dynamics. Standard & Poor's estimates that non-farm payrolls will increase 170,000 per month, on average, in 2006, comparable to growth in 2005.

The U.S. office market tends to track the overall economy on a lagged basis. At the end of the second quarter of 2006, we believe the national vacancy rate was approximately 14%, reflecting an improvement since cyclical lows in 2002-2003. In our opinion, BXP's Washington DC and midtown Manhattan markets are among the nation's strongest. The metropolitan Boston, San Francisco, and Princeton, New Jersey markets are trailing the current recovery. Boston and San Francisco, which account for 74% of BXP's 2006 lease expirations, are expected to roll down rents between 7% and 10%. Overall, as of June 30, 2006, BXP had an office vacancy rate of 5.6%, well ahead of the national averages.

Competition for leasing real estate is high. In addition, we believe that competition for the acquisition of new properties is intensifying from other REITs, private real estate funds, financial institutions, insurance companies and others. As a result, we think BXP could have difficulty finding new assets at attractive prices.

Company Financials

Per Share Data ($) Year Ended Dec. 31	**2005**	**2004**	**2003**	**2002**	**2001**	**2000**	**1999**	**1998**	**1997**	**1996**
Tangible Book Value	25.92	26.61	22.51	20.79	19.34	19.02	15.57	14.93	4.52	2.71
Earnings	3.46	2.35	2.94	4.40	2.26	2.01	1.71	1.61	0.70	1.19
S&P Core Earnings	3.46	2.34	2.88	4.37	2.20	NA	NA	NA	NA	NA
Dividends	5.19	2.58	2.50	2.41	2.27	1.96	1.73	1.64	0.85	NA
Payout Ratio	150%	110%	85%	55%	100%	96%	101%	101%	121%	NA
Prices:High	76.67	64.90	48.47	41.55	43.88	44.88	37.50	36.06	35.25	NA
Prices:Low	56.66	42.99	34.80	32.95	34.00	29.00	27.25	23.44	25.00	NA
P/E Ratio:High	22	28	16	9	19	22	22	22	NM	NA
P/E Ratio:Low	16	18	12	7	15	14	16	14	NM	NA
Income Statement Analysis (Million $)										
Rental Income	1,339	1,293	1,219	1,174	1,008	859	765	488	140	218
Mortgage Income	Nil	Nil	Nil	Nil	Nil	Nil	Nil	Nil	Nil	Nil
Total Income	1,438	1,400	1,310	1,235	1,033	879	787	514	146	226
General Expenses	545	528	498	464	351	300	279	173	46.8	110
Interest Expense	308	306	299	272	223	217	205	125	38.3	56.0
Provision for Losses	Nil	Nil	Nil	Nil	Nil	Nil	Nil	Nil	Nil	NA
Depreciation	267	252	210	186	150	133	120	75.4	21.7	36.9
Net Income	393	255	290	420	215	153	120	98.6	27.2	40.6
S&P Core Earnings	393	254	284	413	203	NA	NA	NA	NA	NA
Balance Sheet & Other Financial Data (Million $)										
Cash	377	345	133	199	201	378	88.7	78.0	34.9	6.00
Total Assets	8,902	9,063	8,551	8,427	7,254	6,226	5,435	5,235	1,673	919
Real Estate Investment	9,151	9,291	8,983	8,671	7,458	6,113	5,612	4,917	1,797	1,080
Loss Reserve	Nil	Nil	Nil	Nil	Nil	Nil	Nil	Nil	Nil	NA
Net Investment	7,886	8,148	7,981	7,848	6,738	5,526	5,142	4,560	1,502	808
Short Term Debt	Nil	Nil	Nil	Nil	282	194	680	26.9	9.00	NA
Capitalization:Debt	4,679	4,733	5,005	3,336	4,033	3,415	2,642	3,062	1,332	739
Capitalization:Equity	2,917	2,936	2,400	2,160	1,754	1,648	1,058	948	175	103
Capitalization:Total	8,335	8,455	8,235	6,340	6,732	6,040	4,582	5,089	1,498	890
% Earnings & Depreciation/Assets	7.3	5.8	5.9	7.7	5.4	4.9	4.5	5.0	NM	NA
Price Times Book Value:High	3.0	2.4	2.1	2.0	2.3	2.4	2.4	2.4	7.8	NA
Price Times Book Value:Low	2.2	1.6	1.5	1.6	1.8	1.5	1.8	1.6	5.5	NA

Data as orig reptd.; bef. results of disc opers/spec. items. Per share data adj. for stk. divs.; EPS diluted. E-Estimated. NA-Not Available. NM-Not Meaningful. NR-Not Ranked. UR-Under Review.

Office: 111 Hungtington Avenue , Boston, MA 02199-7627.
Telephone: 617-236-3300.
Email: investor_relations@bostonproperties.com
Website: http://www.bostonproperties.com

Chrmn: M.B. Zuckerman
Pres & CEO: E.H. Linde
SVP & CFO: D.T. Linde
SVP, Secy & General Counsel: F.D. Burt

Trustees: L. S. Bacow, Z. Baird, W. M. Daley, C. Einiger, E. H. Linde, A. J. Patricof, R. E. Salomon, M. Turchin, D. A. Twardock, M. B. Zuckerman

Founded: 1970
Domicile: Delaware
Employees: 673

STANDARD &POOR'S

Boston Scientific Corp

S&P Recommendation STRONG SELL ★★★★★

Price $16.05 (as of Oct 27, 2006)

12-Mo. Target Price $13.00

Investment Style Large-Cap Growth

GICS Sector Health Care
Sub-Industry Health Care Equipment

Comment This manufacturer of minimally invasive medical devices acquired device rival Guidant Corp. in April 2006 for $27 billion in cash and stock.

Key Stock Statistics (Source S&P, Vickers, company reports)

52-Wk Range	$27.82–14.43	S&P Oper. EPS 2006E	0.85	P/E on S&P Oper. EPS 2006E	18.9	Dividend Rate/Share	Nil
Trailing 12-Month EPS	$-2.79	S&P Oper. EPS 2007E	0.90	Common Shares Outstg. (M)	1,472.4	Yield (%)	Nil
Trailing 12-Month P/E	NM	S&P Core EPS 2006E	0.85	Market Capitalization(B)	$23.633	Beta	0.56
$10K Invested 5 Yrs Ago	$13,741	S&P Core EPS 2007E	0.90	Institutional Ownership (%)	65	S&P Credit Rating	BBB+

Price Performance

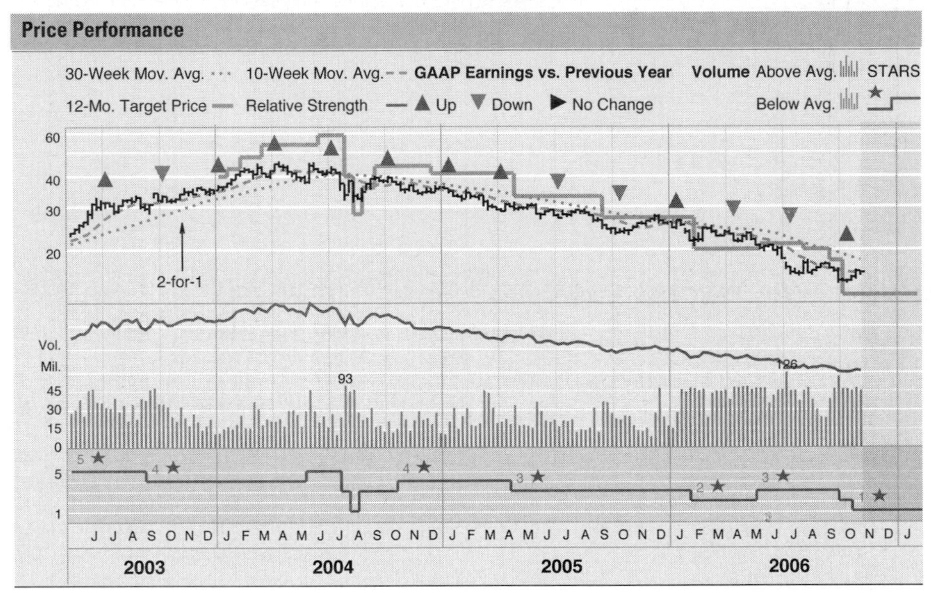

Options: ASE, CBOE, P, Ph

Analysis prepared by **Robert M. Gold** on October 20, 2006, when the stock traded at **$ 16.14**.

Highlights

- We look for 2006 revenues of $7.9 billion, including $1.4 billion from the cardiac rhythm management businesses acquired from Guidant. We believe the drug-coated stent market will slow in 2006 as pricing erodes, penetration rates approach 90%, and competition intensifies. We are also concerned about recent evidence of a decline in the global implantable cardioverter defibrillator (ICD) markets into the single digit area. We see 2007 sales of $9.0 billion, with approximately 7% sales growth envisioned in both 2008 and 2009.
- We believe the Guidant merger will prove to be significantly dilutive to EPS through at least 2009. We are also apprehensive about new product launches following the recent warning from the FDA regarding device complaint notification procedures.
- For 2006, our operating EPS estimate for the combined BSX/GDT, excluding non-cash charges, integration-related costs, and litigation expenses, is $0.85, below our former EPS estimate of $1.70 for a stand-alone Boston Scientific. We estimate 2007 EPS of $0.90.

Investment Rationale/Risk

- In our opinion, the acquisition of Guidant's cardiac rhythm management businesses is capable of fueling a higher long-term revenue growth rate for BSX. However, we are concerned about the substantial dilution to BSX shareholders stemming from the merger, particularly amid the recent slowdown in the global ICD and interventional cardiology device markets.
- Risks to our recommendation and target price include unfavorable litigation outcomes, intensified competition in key markets, and a failure to successfully commercialize key products in the pipeline.
- Our 12-month target price is $13, or 14.4X our 2007 EPS estimate and 2.1X projected 2007 sales, below peers but in line with the S&P 500. We believe a discount to peers is warranted by the financial risks associated with the GDT purchase. We are also apprehensive about Medicare price cuts for both defibrillators and cardiac stents, categories that we view as critical to the company's long-term growth potential. In addition, we believe that safety concerns about BSX's drug-coated coronary stents could result in further market share losses into 2007.

Qualitative Risk Assessment

LOW | MEDIUM | **HIGH**

The company operates within intensely competitive areas of the health care industry, and its ability to sustain growth largely depends on its ability to develop and commercialize new products. In addition, a large percentage of customers are reimbursed by the federal Medicare program, and we believe the government is likely to reduce the pace of expenditure growth by lowering reimbursement rates for expensive medical devices such as defibrillators and cardiac stents.

Quantitative Evaluations

S&P Quality Ranking B

D | C | B- | **B** | B+ | A- | A | A+

Relative Strength Rank WEAK

29

LOWEST = 1 HIGHEST = 99

Revenue/Earnings Data

Revenue (Million $)

	1Q	2Q	3Q	4Q	Year
2006	1,620	2,110	2,206	--	--
2005	1,615	1,617	1,511	1,540	6,283
2004	1,082	1,460	1,482	1,600	5,624
2003	807.0	854.0	876.0	939.0	3,476
2002	675.0	708.0	722.0	814.0	2,919
2001	654.0	672.0	670.0	677.0	2,673

Earnings Per Share ($)

	1Q	2Q	3Q	4Q	Year
2006	0.40	-3.21	0.05	**E**0.12	**E**0.85
2005	0.42	0.24	-0.33	0.40	0.75
2004	0.23	0.36	0.30	0.35	1.24
2003	0.12	0.14	0.15	0.16	0.56
2002	0.10	0.03	0.20	0.13	0.45
2001	-0.01	-0.22	0.07	0.08	-0.07

Fiscal year ended Dec. 31. Next earnings report expected: Early February. EPS Estimates based on S&P Operating Earnings; historical GAAP earnings are as reported.

Dividend Data

No cash dividends have been paid.

Boston Scientific Corp

Business Summary October 20, 2006

Boston Scientific develops and markets minimally invasive medical devices that are used in a broad range of interventional medical specialties, including interventional cardiology, peripheral intervention, electrophysiology, gastroenterology, gynecology, oncology, and urology. Following the April 2006 acquisition of Guidant Corp., Boston Scientific also sells cardiac rhythm management products.

Within the cardiovascular market, the company sells products used to treat the coronary vessel disease known as arteriosclerosis. The majority of BSX's cardiovascular products are used in percutaneous transluminal coronary angioplasty (PTCA) and percutaneous transluminal coronary rotational atherectomy. These products include PTCA balloon catheters, rotational atherectomy systems, guide wires, guide catheters, diagnostic catheters, and, more recently, a cutting balloon catheter. Other products include thrombectomy catheters, peripheral vascular stents, embolic protection filters, blood clot filter systems, and electrophysiology products such as catheters and systems for use in less-invasive procedures to diagnose abnormally fast heart rhythms.

In addition, BSX markets balloon-expandable and self-expanding coronary stent systems. Stents are tiny mesh tubes that are used in the treatment of coronary artery disease. They are implanted in patients to prop open arteries and facilitate blood flow to the heart. In 2002, the company launched its Express 2 coronary stent system, featuring both the Express stent and the Maverick balloon dilatation catheter. In early 2004, BSX launched Taxus, essentially an Express stent coated with a polymer embedded with the anticancer compound paclitaxel. Clinical studies showed that this stent significantly reduced the rate of instent restenosis, or vessel reclosure, which occurs in about one-third of patients who undergo angioplasty and stenting. In January 2005, BSX launched its next generation Taxus Liberte paclitaxel-eluting coronary stent in 18 Inter-Continental countries and in Europe.

Company Financials

Per Share Data ($) Year Ended Dec. 31	**2005**	**2004**	**2003**	**2002**	**2001**	**2000**	**1999**	**1998**	**1997**	**1996**
Tangible Book Value	0.67	0.82	0.49	0.12	NM	0.33	NM	NM	0.87	0.85
Cash Flow	1.12	1.60	0.79	0.64	0.22	0.68	0.67	-0.18	0.31	0.32
Earnings	0.75	1.24	0.56	0.45	-0.07	0.46	0.45	-0.34	0.20	0.23
S&P Core Earnings	1.39	1.27	0.50	0.33	-0.10	NA	NA	NA	NA	NA
Dividends	Nil	Nil	Nil	Nil	Nil	Nil	Nil	Nil	Nil	Nil
Payout Ratio	Nil	Nil	Nil	Nil	Nil	Nil	Nil	Nil	Nil	Nil
Prices:High	35.50	46.10	36.85	22.15	13.95	14.59	23.53	20.42	19.59	15.38
Prices:Low	22.80	31.25	19.10	10.24	6.63	6.09	8.78	10.06	10.25	9.44
P/E Ratio:High	47	37	66	49	NM	32	52	NM	112	67
P/E Ratio:Low	30	25	34	23	NM	13	20	NM	59	41

Income Statement Analysis (Million $)	2005	2004	2003	2002	2001	2000	1999	1998	1997	1996
Revenue	6,283	5,624	3,476	2,919	2,673	2,664	2,842	2,234	1,872	1,462
Operating Income	2,338	1,989	945	757	614	819	857	-93.8	502	403
Depreciation	314	275	196	161	232	181	178	129	86.7	61.4
Interest Expense	90.0	64.0	46.0	43.0	59.0	70.0	118	67.6	14.3	11.2
Pretax Income	891	1,494	643	549	44.0	527	562	-274	259	297
Effective Tax Rate	29.5%	28.9%	26.6%	32.1%	NM	29.2%	34.0%	NM	38.0%	43.7%
Net Income	628	1,062	472	373	-54.0	373	371	-263	160	167
S&P Core Earnings	1,162	1,082	423	269	-77.0	NA	NA	NA	NA	NA

Balance Sheet & Other Financial Data (Million $)	2005	2004	2003	2002	2001	2000	1999	1998	1997	1996
Cash	848	1,640	671	277	180	54.0	64.0	70.3	58.0	75.5
Current Assets	2,631	3,289	1,880	1,208	1,106	992	1,055	1,267	1,064	749
Total Assets	8,196	8,170	5,699	4,450	3,974	3,427	3,572	3,893	1,968	1,512
Current Liabilities	1,479	2,605	1,393	923	831	819	1,055	1,620	808	464
Long Term Debt	1,864	1,139	1,172	847	973	562	678	1,364	46.3	Nil
Common Equity	4,282	4,025	2,862	2,467	2,015	1,935	1,724	821	986	916
Total Capital	6,408	5,423	4,185	3,414	2,988	2,497	2,402	2,185	1,091	976
Capital Expenditures	341	274	188	112	121	76.0	80.0	174	220	135
Cash Flow	942	1,337	668	534	178	554	549	-135	247	229
Current Ratio	1.8	1.3	1.3	1.3	1.3	1.2	1.0	0.8	1.3	1.6
% Long Term Debt of Capitalization	29.1	21.0	28.0	24.8	32.6	22.5	28.2	62.4	4.2	Nil
% Net Income of Revenue	10.0	18.9	13.6	12.8	NM	14.0	13.1	9.6	8.6	11.4
% Return on Assets	7.7	15.3	9.3	8.9	NM	10.7	9.9	NM	9.2	12.7
% Return on Equity	15.1	30.8	17.7	16.6	NM	20.4	29.2	NM	16.9	19.8

Data as orig reptd.; bef. results of disc opers/spec. items. Per share data adj. for stk. divs.; EPS diluted. E-Estimated. NA-Not Available. NM-Not Meaningful. NR-Not Ranked. UR-Under Review.

Office: One Boston Scientific Place, Natick, MA 01760-1537.
Telephone: 508-650-8000.
Email: investor_relations@bsci.com
Website: http://www.bostonscientific.com

Chrmn: P.M. Nicholas
Pres & CEO: J.R. Tobin
COO: P.A. LaViolette
EVP & CFO: L.C. Best

EVP & CTO: F.A. Colen
Investor Contact: M. Kofol (508-650-8569)
Board of Directors: J. E. Abele, U. M. Burns, N. DeParle, J. L. Fleishman, M. A. Fox, R. J. Groves, K. M. Johnson, E. Mario, P. M. Nicholas, N. J. Nicholas, Jr., J. E. Pepper, U. E. Reinhardt, W. B. Rudman, J. R. Tobin

Founded: 1979
Domicile: Delaware
Employees: 19,800

STANDARD &POOR'S

Bristol-Myers Squibb Co

S&P Recommendation HOLD ★★★★★ | **Price** $24.69 (as of Oct 27, 2006) | **12-Mo. Target Price** $25.00 | **Investment Style** Large-Cap Value

GICS Sector Health Care
Sub-Industry Pharmaceuticals

Comment This leading global drugmaker is strong in both prescription and nonprescription products.

Key Stock Statistics (Source S&P, Vickers, company reports)

52-Wk Range	$26.14–20.08	S&P Oper. EPS 2006E	0.95	P/E on S&P Oper. EPS 2006E	26.0	Dividend Rate/Share	$1.12
Trailing 12-Month EPS	$1.13	S&P Oper. EPS 2007E	1.15	Common Shares Outstg. (M)	1,966.5	Yield (%)	4.54
Trailing 12-Month P/E	21.9	S&P Core EPS 2006E	0.95	Market Capitalization(B)	$48.554	Beta	1.11
$10K Invested 5 Yrs Ago	$5,484	S&P Core EPS 2007E	1.15	Institutional Ownership (%)	77	S&P Credit Rating	A+

Price Performance

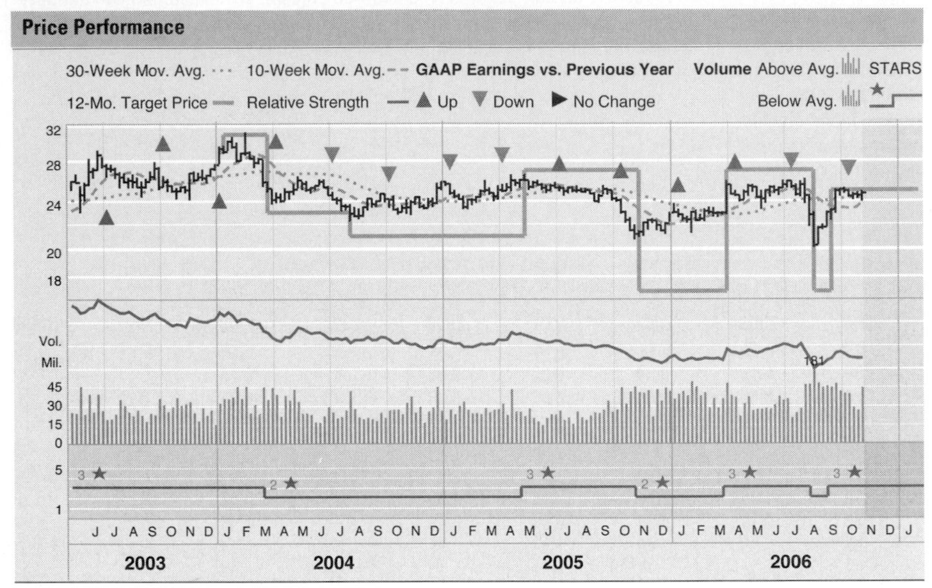

Options: ASE, CBOE, P, Ph

Analysis prepared by **Herman B. Saftlas** on September 19, 2006, when the stock traded at **$ 24.68**.

Highlights

- We expect revenues to decline about 7% in 2006, largely reflecting lower sales of patent expired drugs such as Pravachol anticholesterol and Taxol anticancer drugs. Sales of Plavix, an anticlotting agent (BMY's largest selling drug), are also expected to drop about 8%, given the large amount of generic Plavix from Apotex now in wholesaler inventory channels. As an offset, we see growing momentum in newer products such as Abilify antipsychotic, Reyataz HIV/AIDS therapy, Erbitux anticancer, and Orencia for rheumatoid arthritis.
- We expect gross margins to narrow, due to projected declines in sales of older, higher-margin products. Operating results are also likely to remain under pressure from new product launch costs. We anticipate a higher effective tax rate in 2006. Equity income, however, will probably increase.
- We project operating EPS of $0.95 for 2006, after projected stock option expense. Assuming BMY prevails in upcoming Plavix patent litigation, we believe EPS will improve to $1.15 in 2007.

Investment Rationale/Risk

- In early September, a federal judge issued an injunction blocking Canadian drugmaker Apotex from selling its generic version of Plavix, pending the resolution of patent litigation. But the issuing judge stopped short of ordering a recall of generic Plavix already shipped. Based on wholesaler stockpiles of generic Plavix, BMY reduced 2006 EPS guidance to no less than $0.95, from $1.15-$1.25. However, we now believe BMY has a better chance to prevail in upcoming Plavix patent litigation (to begin in January 2007). We also think BMY has done an admirable job building its new drug portfolio, and that the stock has takeover appeal at current levels.
- Risks to our opinion and target price include the possibility of BMY losing the Plavix litigation, and possible pipeline setbacks.
- Our 12-month target price of $25 applies a peer-level P/E of 17.8X to our 2008 EPS estimate of $1.40. Our DCF model, which assumes a weighted average cost of capital of 8.4% and terminal growth of 1%, also supports intrinsic value of $25.

Qualitative Risk Assessment

LOW | MEDIUM | **HIGH**

In common with other large capitalization drugmakers, BMY is subject to the threat of generic challenges to its branded drugs, as well as risks associated with new drug development and regulatory approval. We believe BMY is more heavily reliant on the success of its R&D pipeline than many of its peers, given the large number of patent expirations of BMY drugs in recent years.

Quantitative Evaluations

S&P Quality Ranking A-

D | C | B- | B | B+ | **A-** | A | A+

Relative Strength Rank MODERATE

48

LOWEST = 1 HIGHEST = 99

Revenue/Earnings Data

Revenue (Million $)

	1Q	2Q	3Q	4Q	Year
2006	4,676	4,871	4,154	--	--
2005	4,532	4,889	4,767	5,019	19,207
2004	4,626	4,819	4,778	5,157	19,380
2003	4,728	5,129	5,372	5,665	20,894
2002	4,661	4,127	4,537	4,794	18,119
2001	4,689	4,709	4,743	5,282	19,423

Earnings Per Share ($)

2006	0.36	0.34	0.17	E0.11	E0.95
2005	0.27	0.50	0.49	0.26	1.52
2004	0.49	0.27	0.38	0.07	1.21
2003	0.41	0.46	0.47	0.26	1.59
2002	0.43	0.25	0.17	0.19	1.05
2001	0.63	0.56	0.63	-0.54	1.29

Fiscal year ended Dec. 31. Next earnings report expected: Late January. EPS Estimates based on S&P Operating Earnings; historical GAAP earnings are as reported.

Dividend Data (Dates: mm/dd Payment Date: mm/dd/yy)

Amount ($)	Date Decl.	Ex-Div. Date	Stk. of Record	Payment Date
0.280	12/06	01/04	01/06	02/01/06
0.280	03/07	04/05	04/07	05/01/06
0.280	06/14	07/05	07/07	08/01/06
0.280	09/12	10/04	10/06	11/01/06

Dividends have been paid since 1900. Source: Company reports.

Bristol-Myers Squibb Co

Business Summary September 19, 2006

CORPORATE PROFILE. Bristol-Myers Squibb ranks among the world's largest pharmaceutical concerns, offering a wide range of prescription drugs. In recent years, BMY divested its Clairol beauty care and Zimmer orthopedic device subsidiaries, in an effort to focus on wider margin prescription drugs. In 2005, BMY sold its anticancer drug distribution division, as well as its U.S. and Canadian consumer medications businesses.

Prescription drugs accounted for 80% of sales in 2005, nutritionals 11%, medical devices 8%, and consumer health care 1%. Foreign sales accounted for 46% of total sales in 2005. A relatively large portion of BMY's pharmaceutical portfolio is now off patent and subject to generic erosion. These products include: Taxol and Paraplatin, anticancer drugs; Glucophage and Glucovance, diabetes drugs; and Monopril, a cardiovascular drug.

Cardiovasculars include Pravachol, a cholesterol-reducing agent (sales of $2.3 billion in 2005); Monopril, an antihypertensive agent ($208 million); and Coumadin, an anticoagulant ($212 million). Through a joint venture with Sanofi-Aventis SA, BMY produces Plavix ($3.8 billion), a platelet aggregation inhibitor for the prevention of stroke, heart attack, and vascular disease; and Avapro/Avalide ($982 million), an angiotensin II receptor blocker for hypertension. Principal anticancer drugs are Taxol ($747 million), Erbitux ($413 million) and Paraplatin ($157 million).

The company's principal anti-infective drugs are HIV/AIDS treatments such as Reyataz ($696 million) Sustiva ($680 million), Zerit ($216 million), and Videx ($174 million). BMY also offers Cefzil, Tequin, Maxipime, and other antibiotics; and central nervous system agents, including Abilify, an antipsychotic agent ($912 million), Sinemet for Parkinson's disease, and various other drugs. Diabetes products ($172 million) comprise off-patent Glucophage products. Orencia, a new treatment for rheumatoid arthritis, was approved in December 2005.

The Mead Johnson division offers nutritionals, consisting of infant formulas such as Enfamil and ProSobee, as well as vitamins and nutritional supplements. The Convatec unit offers ostomy and wound care products.

Company Financials

Per Share Data ($) Year Ended Dec. 31	**2005**	**2004**	**2003**	**2002**	**2001**	**2000**	**1999**	**1998**	**1997**	**1996**
Tangible Book Value	2.28	1.76	1.62	0.88	1.70	3.96	3.61	3.01	2.82	2.53
Cash Flow	1.98	1.66	1.99	1.43	1.68	2.42	2.39	1.85	1.86	1.68
Earnings	1.52	1.21	1.59	1.05	1.29	2.36	2.06	1.55	1.57	1.42
S&P Core Earnings	1.43	1.24	1.57	1.07	0.67	NA	NA	NA	NA	NA
Dividends	1.12	1.12	1.12	1.12	1.10	0.98	0.86	0.78	0.77	0.75
Payout Ratio	74%	93%	70%	107%	85%	42%	42%	50%	49%	53%
Prices:High	26.60	31.30	29.21	51.95	73.50	74.88	79.25	67.63	49.09	29.09
Prices:Low	20.70	22.22	21.00	19.49	48.50	42.44	57.25	44.16	26.63	19.50
P/E Ratio:High	17	26	18	49	57	32	38	44	31	20
P/E Ratio:Low	14	18	13	19	38	18	28	29	17	14

Income Statement Analysis (Million $)										
Revenue	19,207	19,380	20,894	18,119	19,423	18,216	20,222	18,284	16,701	15,065
Operating Income	4,880	5,373	5,726	4,851	7,034	6,732	6,531	5,746	5,029	4,472
Depreciation	929	909	779	735	781	746	678	625	591	519
Interest Expense	349	310	277	410	182	108	130	154	118	93.0
Pretax Income	4,516	4,418	4,694	2,647	2,986	5,478	5,767	4,268	4,482	4,013
Effective Tax Rate	20.6%	34.4%	25.9%	16.4%	15.4%	25.2%	27.7%	26.4%	28.5%	29.0%
Net Income	2,992	2,378	3,106	2,034	2,527	4,096	4,167	3,141	3,205	2,850
S&P Core Earnings	2,808	2,448	3,043	2,076	1,321	NA	NA	NA	NA	NA

Balance Sheet & Other Financial Data (Million $)										
Cash	5,799	7,474	5,457	3,989	5,654	3,385	2,957	2,529	1,794	2,185
Current Assets	12,283	14,801	11,918	9,975	12,349	9,824	9,267	8,782	7,736	7,528
Total Assets	28,138	30,435	27,471	24,874	27,057	17,578	17,114	16,272	14,977	14,685
Current Liabilities	6,890	9,843	7,530	8,220	8,826	5,632	5,537	5,791	5,032	5,050
Long Term Debt	8,364	8,463	8,522	6,261	6,237	1,336	1,342	1,364	1,279	966
Common Equity	11,208	10,202	19,572	8,967	10,736	9,180	8,645	7,576	7,219	6,570
Total Capital	19,572	18,665	28,094	15,228	16,973	10,516	9,987	8,940	8,498	7,536
Capital Expenditures	738	676	937	997	1,023	589	709	788	767	601
Cash Flow	3,921	3,287	3,885	2,769	3,308	4,842	4,845	3,766	3,796	3,369
Current Ratio	1.8	1.5	1.6	1.2	1.4	1.7	1.7	1.5	1.5	1.5
% Long Term Debt of Capitalization	42.7	45.3	30.3	41.1	36.7	12.7	13.4	15.3	15.1	12.8
% Net Income of Revenue	15.6	12.3	14.9	11.2	13.0	22.5	20.6	17.2	19.2	18.9
% Return on Assets	10.2	8.2	11.8	7.7	11.3	23.6	25.0	20.1	21.6	19.9
% Return on Equity	27.9	23.8	16.8	22.5	25.4	46.0	51.4	42.5	46.5	46.0

Data as orig reptd.; bef. results of disc opers/spec. items. Per share data adj. for stk. divs.; EPS diluted. E-Estimated. NA-Not Available. NM-Not Meaningful. NR-Not Ranked. UR-Under Review.

Office: 345 Park Ave, New York, NY 10154-0004.
Telephone: 212-546-4000.
Website: http://www.bms.com
Chrmn: J.D. Robinson, III

CEO: J.M. Cornelius
SVP & CFO: A.R. Bonfield
VP & Treas: E.M. Dwyer
VP & Secy: S. Leung

Investor Contact: J. Elicker (212-546-3775)
Board of Directors: R. E. Allen, L. B. Campbell, V. D. Coffman, J. M. Cornelius, P. R. Dolan, L. J. Freeh, L. V. Gerstner, Jr., L. H. Glimcher, L. Johansson, J. D. Robinson, III, V. L. Sato, L. W. Sullivan, R. S. Williams

Founded: 1887
Domicile: Delaware
Employees: 43,000

Broadcom Corp

STANDARD &POOR'S

S&P Recommendation SELL ★★★★★

Price
$29.19 (as of Oct 27, 2006)

12-Mo. Target Price
$24.00

Investment Style
Large-Cap Growth

GICS Sector Information Technology
Sub-Industry Semiconductors

Comment This company provides semiconductors for broadband communications markets, including cable set-top boxes, cable modems, office networks and home networking.

Key Stock Statistics (Source S&P, Vickers, company reports)

52-Wk Range	$50.00–21.98	S&P Oper. EPS 2006E	0.75	P/E on S&P Oper. EPS 2006E	38.9	Dividend Rate/Share	Nil
Trailing 12-Month EPS	$0.82	S&P Oper. EPS 2007E	0.85	Common Shares Outstg. (M)	545.3	Yield (%)	Nil
Trailing 12-Month P/E	35.6	S&P Core EPS 2006E	0.75	Market Capitalization(B)	$13.684	Beta	3.65
$10K Invested 5 Yrs Ago	$11,818	S&P Core EPS 2007E	0.85	Institutional Ownership (%)	83	S&P Credit Rating	NA

Price Performance

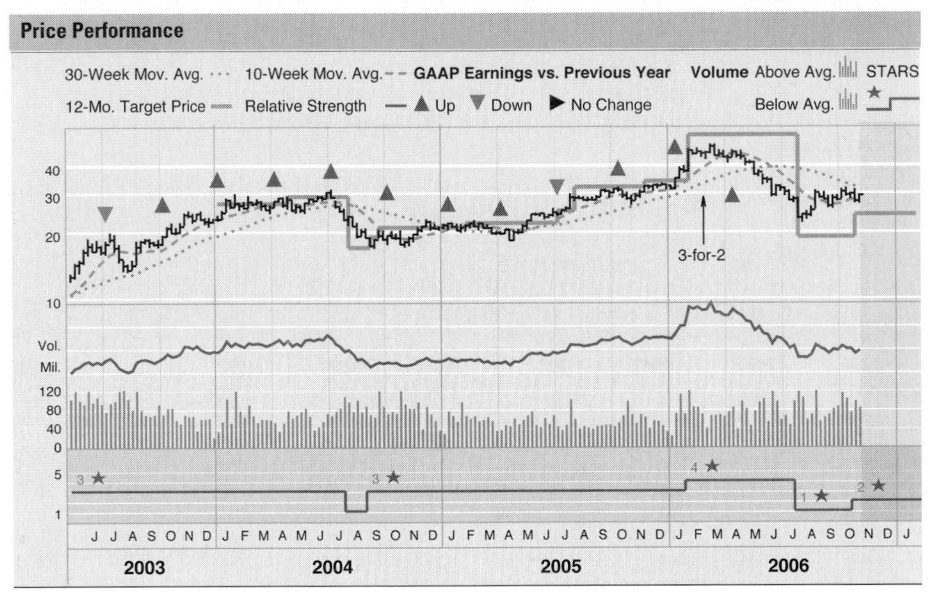

Options: ASE, CBOE, P, Ph

Qualitative Risk Assessment

LOW | MEDIUM | **HIGH**

Our risk assessment reflects that Broadcom is exposed to the sales cycles of the semiconductor industry, has a limited number of key customers, is dependent on foundry partners for production, and relies on stock-based compensation more than most companies. This is partially offset by a lack of debt and a broadening base of end users.

Quantitative Evaluations

S&P Quality Ranking B-

D | C | **B-** | B | B+ | A- | A | A+

Relative Strength Rank MODERATE

40

LOWEST = 1 HIGHEST = 99

Highlights

➤ The STARS recommendation for BRCM has recently been changed to 2 (sell) from 1 (strong sell) and the 12-month target price has recently been changed to $24.00 from $19.00. The Highlights section of this Stock Report will be updated accordingly.

Investment Rationale/Risk

➤ The Investment Rationale/Risk section of this Stock Report will be updated shortly. For the latest News story on BRCM from MarketScope, see below.

➤ 10/20/06 07:21 am EDT... S&P UPGRADES RECOMMENDATION ON BROADCOM SHARES TO SELL FROM STRONG SELL (BRCM 28.97**): BRCM posts Q3 sales increase of 30% Y/Y and decrease of 4% Q/Q, in line with our view. However, BRCM guided for Q4 growth of 1% Q/Q, below our 6% growth forecast. EPS was not reported because of its stock options review. Inventory congestion in DSL and other markets lingers, but we foresee resolution by '07 and thus some improvement in investor sentiment. Still, we are lowering our '06 EPS estimate to $0.75 from $0.80 and '07's to $0.85 from $0.95, including option costs. Our target price rises to $24 from $19, based on a higher target P/S in the lower half of historical range. /T.Smith-CFA

Revenue/Earnings Data

Revenue (Million $)

	1Q	2Q	3Q	4Q	Year
2006	900.7	--	--	--	--
2005	550.3	604.9	695.0	820.6	2,671
2004	573.4	641.3	646.5	539.4	2,401
2003	327.5	377.9	425.6	479.1	1,610
2002	238.8	258.2	290.0	296.0	1,083
2001	310.5	210.9	213.6	226.8	961.8

Earnings Per Share ($)

2006	0.22	**E**0.22	**E**0.16	**E**0.16	**E**0.75
2005	0.13	0.03	0.23	0.33	0.73
2004	0.08	0.12	0.09	0.13	0.42
2003	-0.17	-2.05	-0.01	0.01	-2.19
2002	-0.42	-0.33	-0.45	-4.27	-5.57
2001	-0.95	-1.15	-4.24	-0.85	-7.19

Fiscal year ended Dec. 31. Next earnings report expected: NA. EPS Estimates based on S&P Operating Earnings; historical GAAP earnings are as reported.

Dividend Data (Dates: mm/dd Payment Date: mm/dd/yy)

Amount ($)	Date Decl.	Ex-Div. Date	Stk. of Record	Payment Date
3-for-2 Stk.	01/26	02/22	02/06	02/21/06

Source: Company reports.

Broadcom Corp

Business Summary August 03, 2006

Founded in 1991, Broadcom designs, develops and supplies semiconductor products that address business and consumer demand for high-speed access to multimedia information and entertainment content consisting of voice, video and data. The company sees its mission as "connecting everything."

The company's integrated circuits (ICs) address all major broadband communications markets, including digital cable, direct broadcast satellite and Internet Protocol set-top boxes and media servers; cable and DSL modems; high definition television; high-speed transmission and switching for local, metropolitan, wide area and storage networking; wireless and personal area networking; wireless communications; Voice over Internet Protocol (VoIP) gateway and telephony systems; broadband network processors; and system I/O server solutions.

Broadband products mainly consist of high-performance digital signal processing ICs working with analog and mixed-signal ICs and often with radio-frequency ICs that are increasingly offered as system-on-a-chip solutions with related software. According to the company, BRCM aims to make highly integrated, comprehensive systems solutions on single chips or chipsets, reducing board space, simplifying the customer's manufacturing process, lowering the customer's system costs, and boosting performance.

In 2005, net revenue by major target market was 40% (47% in 2004) enterprise networking; 34% (32%) broadband communications; and 26% (21%) mobile and wireless.

Customers include leading communications equipment and computer companies such as Alcatel, Apple, 3Com, Cisco Systems, Echostar, Nortel Networks, IBM, Samsung, and Scientific-Atlanta. BRCM does most of its business with a small number of customers. Motorola accounted for 15.5% of 2005 sales. In 2005, the five leading customers accounted for approximately 52% of total revenue, up from 51% of total revenue in 2004 and 45% in 2003.

Company Financials

Per Share Data ($) Year Ended Dec. 31	**2005**	**2004**	**2003**	**2002**	**2001**	**2000**	**1999**	**1998**	**1997**	**1996**
Tangible Book Value	3.79	2.59	1.43	0.94	2.19	3.31	1.59	0.78	0.81	NA
Cash Flow	0.85	0.59	-1.98	-5.20	-4.87	-1.59	0.28	0.16	0.02	NA
Earnings	0.73	0.42	-2.19	-5.57	-7.19	-2.09	0.24	0.13	-0.01	NA
S&P Core Earnings	0.16	-0.70	-2.31	-5.07	-6.87	NA	NA	NA	NA	NA
Dividends	Nil	Nil	Nil	Nil	Nil	Nil	Nil	Nil	NA	NA
Payout Ratio	Nil	Nil	Nil	Nil	Nil	Nil	Nil	Nil	NA	NA
Prices:High	33.28	31.37	25.10	35.57	93.00	183.17	96.33	22.50	NA	NA
Prices:Low	18.25	16.83	7.91	6.35	12.27	49.83	15.42	4.00	NA	NA
P/E Ratio:High	46	75	NM	NM	NM	NM	NM	NM	NA	NA
P/E Ratio:Low	25	40	NM	NM	NM	NM	NM	NM	NA	NA
Income Statement Analysis (Million $)										
Revenue	2,671	2,401	1,610	1,083	962	1,096	518	203	37.0	NA
Operating Income	557	450	-30.4	-442	-573	-169	157	59.7	0.81	NA
Depreciation	68.5	91.7	90.9	147	889	165	14.0	7.50	3.04	NA
Interest Expense	Nil	Nil	Nil	3.60	5.00	0.33	0.55	0.47	0.26	NA
Pretax Income	392	294	-935	-1,939	-2,799	-692	119	56.0	-1.95	NA
Effective Tax Rate	NM	25.7%	NM	NM	NM	NM	30.2%	35.0%	NM	NA
Net Income	412	219	-960	-2,237	-2,742	-688	83.3	36.4	-1.17	NA
S&P Core Earnings	88.6	-330	-1,011	-2,039	-2,617	NA	NA	NA	NA	NA
Balance Sheet & Other Financial Data (Million $)										
Cash	1,733	1,183	606	503	540	524	174	62.6	91.2	NA
Current Assets	2,336	1,584	996	722	674	876	391	157	NA	NA
Total Assets	3,752	2,886	2,018	2,216	3,623	4,678	585	237	114	NA
Current Liabilities	595	497	504	534	412	203	86.1	27.1	NA	NA
Long Term Debt	Nil	Nil	Nil	1.21	4.01	Nil	0.55	Nil	0.10	NA
Common Equity	3,145	2,366	1,490	1,645	3,207	4,475	499	210	105	NA
Total Capital	3,145	2,366	1,490	1,646	3,211	4,475	499	210	NA	NA
Capital Expenditures	41.8	49.9	47.9	75.2	71.4	80.7	29.2	27.3	NA	NA
Cash Flow	480	310	-869	-2,090	-1,853	-523	97.3	43.9	1.87	NA
Current Ratio	3.9	3.2	2.0	1.4	1.6	4.3	4.5	5.8	NA	NA
% Long Term Debt of Capitalization	Nil	Nil	Nil	0.1	0.1	Nil	0.1	Nil	NA	NA
% Net Income of Revenue	15.4	9.1	NM	NM	NM	NM	16.1	17.9	NM	NA
% Return on Assets	12.4	8.9	NM	NM	NM	NM	19.7	25.8	NM	NA
% Return on Equity	14.9	11.3	NM	NM	NM	NM	23.3	33.8	NM	NA

Data as orig reptd.; bef. results of disc opers/spec. items. Per share data adj. for stk. divs.; EPS diluted. E-Estimated. NA-Not Available. NM-Not Meaningful. NR-Not Ranked. UR-Under Review.

Office: 16215 Alton Parkway, Irvine, CA 92618-3616.
Telephone: 949-450-8700.
Email: investorinfo@broadcom.com
Website: http://www.broadcom.com

Chrmn: H. Samueli
Pres & CEO: S.A. McGregor
SVP & CFO: W.J. Ruehle
SVP, Secy & General Counsel: D.A. Dull

VP & Cntlr: B.E. Kiddoo
Investor Contact: P. Andrew (949-926-5663)
Board of Directors: G. L. Farinsky, M. E. Grzelakowski, N. H. Handel, J. E. Major, S. A. McGregor, A. E. Ross, H. Samueli, R. E. Switz, W. F. Wolfen

Founded: 1991
Domicile: California
Employees: 4,287

STANDARD & POOR'S

Brown-Forman Corp

S&P Recommendation HOLD ★★★★★

Price $72.36 (as of Oct 27, 2006)

12-Mo. Target Price $78.00

Investment Style Mid-Cap Growth

GICS Sector Consumer Staples
Sub-Industry Distillers & Vintners

Comment This leading distiller and importer of alcoholic beverages, based in Kentucky, markets such brands as Jack Daniel's, Southern Comfort, Finlandia, Korbel and Bolla.

Key Stock Statistics (Source S&P, Vickers, company reports)

52-Wk Range	$82.55–62.41	S&P Oper. EPS 2007E	3.20	P/E on S&P Oper. EPS 2007E	22.6	Dividend Rate/Share	$1.12
Trailing 12-Month EPS	$3.26	S&P Oper. EPS 2008E	NA	Common Shares Outstg. (M)	123.0	Yield (%)	1.55
Trailing 12-Month P/E	22.2	S&P Core EPS 2007E	3.23	Market Capitalization(B)	$4.785	Beta	0.35
$10K Invested 5 Yrs Ago	$25,700	S&P Core EPS 2008E	NA	Institutional Ownership (%)	56	S&P Credit Rating	A

Price Performance

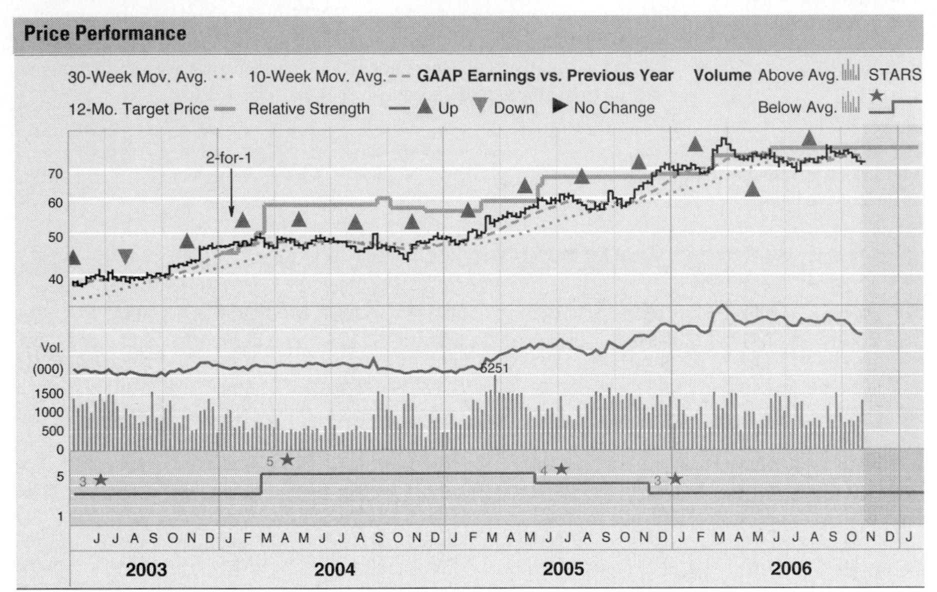

Analysis prepared by **Raymond Mathis** on June 13, 2006, when the stock traded at **$ 70.77**.

Highlights

- We look for 7.5% wine and spirits sales growth, down from the low double digits, limited by anticipated trade inventory reductions. In addition to price increases, our FY 07 (Apr.) growth projection reflects continued momentum in top spirits brands Jack Daniel's, Southern Comfort and Finlandia. We anticipate that new wine introductions and increased marketing will boost growth in the wine segment. All told, we see beverage volumes benefiting further from strong advertising and marketing.
- We look for gross margin expansion to be tempered by rising grape costs and increased promotions, partly offsetting a likely improvement in the product mix. Operating margins should benefit from improvements in global distribution arrangements, in our view, partly offset by increased marketing support and higher SG&A costs related to the recent Chambord liqueur acquisition.
- We expect lower net interest expense as the company pays down debt, but a higher effective tax rate. Excluding unusual items, we estimate FY 07 EPS of $3.20, on a higher share count. We project FY 07 S&P Core EPS of $3.23, reflecting estimated pension cost adjustments.

Investment Rationale/Risk

- Long term, we look for continued strength in the global market, and think that spirits will continue to make successful inroads in the 21- to 27-year-old demographic. BF.B should continue to capitalize on what we see as positive industry trends with its strong portfolio of spirits and international reach, particularly with its Jack Daniel's brand. In addition, we believe BF.B's commitment to improving distribution and brand building will support outperformance.
- Risks to our recommendation and target price include an unexpected slowdown in the growth of top-performing brands. Also, we believe BF.B's dual-class structure and the majority representation of insiders on its board of directors pose corporate governance concerns.
- Based on our discounted cash flow model, assuming an 8.5% cost of capital, we estimate intrinsic value of $78. We apply a P/E of 26X, above the stock's historical average, to our calendar 2006 EPS estimate of $3.10, which leads to a value of $79. Our 12-month target price of $78 reflects a blend of our DCF and P/E analyses. With a 1.6% dividend yield, we recommend holding the shares for their total return potential.

Qualitative Risk Assessment

LOW | **MEDIUM** | HIGH

Brown-Forman is a large-cap competitor in an industry that has historically demonstrated relative stability. However, we believe the company's dual-class structure and the majority representation of insiders on its board of directors pose corporate governance concerns.

Quantitative Evaluations

S&P Quality Ranking A

D | C | B- | B | B+ | A- | **A** | A+

Relative Strength Rank WEAK

22

LOWEST = 1 HIGHEST = 99

Revenue/Earnings Data

Revenue (Million $)

	1Q	2Q	3Q	4Q	Year
2007	639.7	--	--	--	--
2006	547.0	666.0	637.0	594.0	2,444
2005	578.0	780.0	758.0	613.0	2,729
2004	532.6	725.2	697.0	625.0	2,577
2003	479.0	692.0	636.0	571.0	2,378
2002	469.7	644.1	570.5	523.9	1,958

Earnings Per Share ($)

2007	0.76	**E**0.96	**E**0.80	**E**0.79	**E**3.20
2006	0.71	0.91	0.98	0.61	3.20
2005	0.42	0.83	0.78	0.49	2.52
2004	0.26	0.73	0.66	0.47	2.11
2003	0.26	0.59	0.51	0.45	1.82
2002	0.29	0.58	0.42	0.38	1.66

Fiscal year ended Apr. 30. Next earnings report expected: Early December. EPS Estimates based on S&P Operating Earnings; historical GAAP earnings are as reported.

Dividend Data (Dates: mm/dd Payment Date: mm/dd/yy)

Amount ($)	Date Decl.	Ex-Div. Date	Stk. of Record	Payment Date
0.280	01/26	03/06	03/08	04/01/06
0.280	05/25	06/05	06/07	07/01/06
0.280	07/27	09/05	09/07	10/01/06

Dividends have been paid since 1960. Source: Company reports.

Brown-Forman Corp

Business Summary June 13, 2006

Brown-Forman Corp.'s origins date back to 1870. It is the world's fourth largest producer of distilled spirits. With a portfolio of well known brands, the company is best known for its popular Jack Daniel's Tennessee Whiskey, which continues to be its largest sales and profit producer. BF.B also manufactures and sells consumer durables, primarily under the Hartmann luggage brand. The wines and spirits segment contributed 98% to operating profits in FY 05 (Apr.), and consumer durables the remaining 2%.

Although many alcoholic beverage companies have moved in recent years to reduce their dependence on the highly mature brown spirits market, BF.B has remained whiskey-oriented. Its product line is stocked with well known whiskies, bourbons, vodkas, tequilas, rums, and liqueurs. Brands include Jack Daniel's, Canadian Mist, Southern Comfort and Early Times. Jack Daniel's volume growth in FY 05 was 9%, with the U.S. market accounting for 55% of its sales. Statistics based on case sales rank Jack Daniel's as the largest selling Tennessee whiskey in the U.S., Canadian Mist as the second largest selling Canadian whiskey in the U.S., and Southern Comfort as the largest selling domestic proprietary liqueur in the U.S. The company's other major alcoholic beverage lines include wine brands such as Fetzer and Bolla wines, and Korbel Champagnes.

BF.B's strategy is to expand the beverage division through international expansion and the continual introduction of successful new products. Since 2004, BF.B has launched a variety of new products, including One.6 Chardonnay and One.9 Merlot targeted to diet-conscious individuals. In FY 05, the company purchased the remaining 20% equity interest in Finlandia vodka; the initial investment was made in FY 97 along with Michel Picard French wines.

International sales, consisting principally of exports of wines and spirits, increased 20% in FY 05, to about $907 million, accounting for 33% of total net revenues. Beverage growth in recent years has come primarily from international markets for the company's spirits brands. The key export markets for brands include the U.K., Australia, South Africa, Japan and China.

Company Financials

Per Share Data ($) Year Ended Apr. 30	**2006**	**2005**	**2004**	**2003**	**2002**	**2001**	**2000**	**1999**	**1998**	**1997**
Tangible Book Value	8.49	5.69	4.29	2.41	7.72	6.75	5.68	4.77	4.04	3.37
Cash Flow	3.60	2.98	2.29	2.21	2.05	2.15	2.03	1.87	1.70	1.58
Earnings	3.20	2.52	2.11	1.82	1.66	1.70	1.59	1.47	1.34	1.23
S&P Core Earnings	3.17	2.38	2.07	1.55	1.39	1.52	NA	NA	NA	NA
Dividends	0.92	0.80	0.73	0.73	0.68	0.64	0.61	0.58	0.55	0.53
Payout Ratio	29%	32%	34%	40%	41%	38%	38%	39%	41%	43%
Calendar Year	2005	2004	2003	2002	2001	2000	1999	1998	1997	1996
Prices:High	72.40	50.09	47.56	40.27	36.00	34.63	38.63	38.44	27.69	23.75
Prices:Low	46.62	42.80	30.13	29.35	28.83	20.94	27.47	25.88	21.00	17.63
P/E Ratio:High	23	20	23	22	22	20	24	20	21	19
P/E Ratio:Low	15	17	14	16	17	12	17	18	16	14

Income Statement Analysis (Million $)										
Revenue	2,444	2,729	2,577	2,378	1,958	1,924	1,877	1,776	1,669	1,584
Operating Income	560	513	473	429	408	438	410	377	358	337
Depreciation	44.0	58.0	56.0	55.0	55.0	64.0	62.0	55.0	51.0	50.0
Interest Expense	18.0	21.0	21.0	8.00	8.00	16.0	15.0	10.0	14.0	17.0
Pretax Income	559	476	388	373	348	366	343	318	296	273
Effective Tax Rate	29.3%	35.3%	33.5%	34.3%	34.5%	36.3%	36.4%	36.5%	37.5%	38.0%
Net Income	395	308	258	245	228	233	218	202	185	169
S&P Core Earnings	391	289	252	209	190	208	NA	NA	NA	NA

Balance Sheet & Other Financial Data (Million $)										
Cash	475	295	68.0	72.0	116	86.0	180	171	78.0	58.0
Current Assets	1,610	1,317	1,083	1,068	1,029	994	1,020	999	869	802
Total Assets	2,728	2,624	2,376	2,264	2,016	1,939	1,802	1,735	1,494	1,428
Current Liabilities	569	638	369	548	495	538	522	517	382	399
Long Term Debt	351	352	630	629	40.0	40.0	41.0	53.0	50.0	63.0
Common Equity	1,563	1,310	1,085	840	1,311	1,187	1,048	917	805	718
Total Capital	2,047	1,794	1,837	1,547	1,409	1,289	1,184	1,107	1,005	975
Capital Expenditures	52.0	49.0	56.0	119	71.0	96.0	78.0	46.0	44.0	55.0
Cash Flow	439	366	314	300	283	297	280	257	235	218
Current Ratio	2.8	2.1	2.9	1.9	2.1	1.8	2.0	1.9	2.3	2.0
% Long Term Debt of Capitalization	17.1	19.6	34.3	40.7	2.8	3.1	3.5	4.8	4.9	6.4
% Net Income of Revenue	16.2	11.3	10.0	10.3	11.6	12.1	11.6	11.4	11.1	10.6
% Return on Assets	14.7	12.3	11.1	11.4	11.5	12.5	12.3	12.3	12.7	12.0
% Return on Equity	27.5	25.6	26.8	22.8	18.3	20.9	22.2	23.5	24.3	25.2

Data as orig reptd.; bef. results of disc opers/spec. items. Per share data adj. for stk. divs.; EPS diluted. E-Estimated. NA-Not Available. NM-Not Meaningful. NR-Not Ranked. UR-Under Review.

Office: 850 Dixie Highway, Louisville, KY 40210-1091.
Telephone: 502-585-1100.
Website: http://www.brown-forman.com
Chrmn: O. Brown, II

Pres & CEO: P.C. Varga
Vice Chrmn: J.S. Welch, Jr.
Vice Chrmn, Secy & General Counsel: M.B. Crutcher
EVP & CFO: P.A. Wood

Investor Contact: T. Graven (502-774-7442)
Board of Directors: P. Bousquet-Chavanne, B. D. Bramley, I. Brown Bond, G. G. Brown III, O. Brown, II, D. G. Calder, S. A. Frazier, R. P. Mayer, S. E. O'Neil, M. R. Simmons, W. M. Street, D. B. Stubbs, P. C. Varga

Founded: 1870
Domicile: Delaware
Employees: 3,750

STANDARD &POOR'S

Brunswick Corp

S&P Recommendation HOLD ★★★★★	**Price** $32.46 (as of Oct 27, 2006)	**12-Mo. Target Price** $34.00	**Investment Style** Mid-Cap Value

GICS Sector Consumer Discretionary
Sub-Industry Leisure Products

Comment This leading manufacturer of marine engines and boats also has other recreational businesses.

Key Stock Statistics (Source S&P, Vickers, company reports)

52-Wk Range	$43.39–27.08	S&P Oper. EPS 2006E	2.44	P/E on S&P Oper. EPS 2006E	13.3	Dividend Rate/Share	$0.60
Trailing 12-Month EPS	$2.86	S&P Oper. EPS 2007E	3.02	Common Shares Outstg. (M)	92.7	Yield (%)	1.85
Trailing 12-Month P/E	11.4	S&P Core EPS 2006E	2.44	Market Capitalization(B)	$3.010	Beta	1.11
$10K Invested 5 Yrs Ago	$18,180	S&P Core EPS 2007E	3.02	Institutional Ownership (%)	89	S&P Credit Rating	BBB+

Price Performance

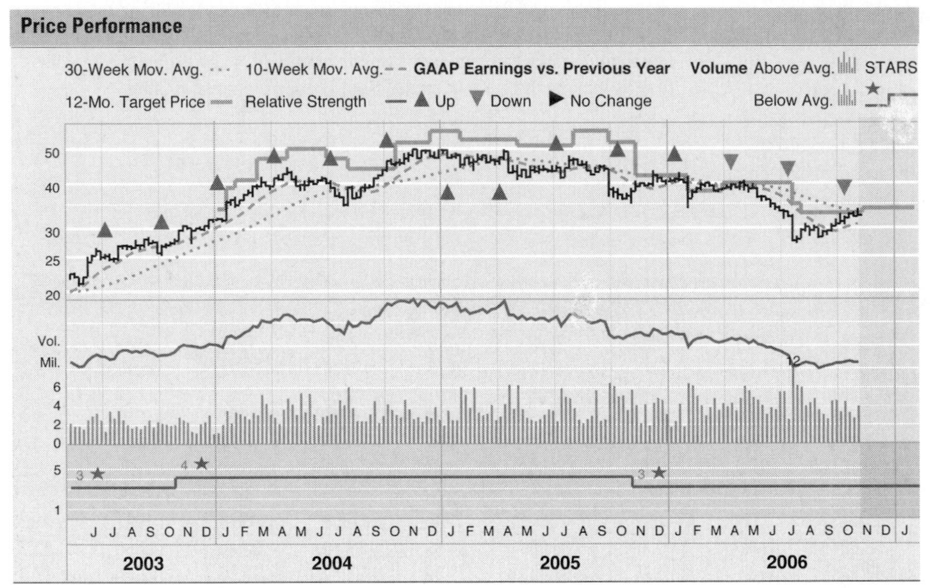

Options: ASE, CBOE, P, Ph

Highlights

- The 12-month target price for BC has recently been changed to $34.00 from $33.00. The Highlights section of this Stock Report will be updated accordingly.

Investment Rationale/Risk

- The Investment Rationale/Risk section of this Stock Report will be updated shortly. For the latest News story on BC from MarketScope, see below.

- 10/27/06 01:28 pm EDT... S&P MAINTAINS HOLD RECOMMENDATION ON SHARES OF BRUNSWICK CORP. (BC 32.92***): Adjusted for tax credits in both periods, BC posts Q3 EPS of $0.48 vs. $0.69, $0.04 below our estimate. The shortfall reflects higher-than-expected SG&A and R&D expenses. Sales fell 1%, with the marine segment off 2%. We are reducing our '06 EPS estimate by $0.04 to $2.44. Reflecting our more cautious outlook for the marine segment, we are cutting our '07 EPS estimate by $0.36 to $3.02. However, we are raising our 12-month target price by $1 to $34, to reflect the shift in the base for our valuation model from our '06 EPS estimate to an average of our '06 and '07 estimates. /L.Braverman-CFA

Qualitative Risk Assessment

LOW	MEDIUM	HIGH

Our risk assessment for Brunswick Corp. reflects the highly discretionary nature of its products, its significant unit prices, and the integration risks of BC's many acquisitions. This is partially offset by the company's corporate governance practices, which we view as more favorable than its peers.

Quantitative Evaluations

S&P Quality Ranking **B**

D	C	B-	B	B+	A-	A	A+

Relative Strength Rank **MODERATE**

53

LOWEST = 1 HIGHEST = 99

Revenue/Earnings Data

Revenue (Million $)

	1Q	2Q	3Q	4Q	Year
2006	1,458	1,543	1,338	--	--
2005	1,401	1,599	1,435	1,490	5,924
2004	1,200	1,423	1,273	1,334	5,229
2003	934.5	1,071	1,036	1,087	4,129
2002	866.7	1,017	900.0	928.0	3,712
2001	913.2	928.8	811.0	717.8	3,371

Earnings Per Share ($)

	1Q	2Q	3Q	4Q	Year
2006	0.70	0.99	0.54	E0.46	E2.44
2005	0.96	1.15	0.89	0.90	3.90
2004	0.50	0.93	0.75	0.59	2.77
2003	0.04	0.59	0.41	0.43	1.47
2002	0.15	0.51	0.26	0.22	1.14
2001	0.45	0.47	0.07	-0.03	0.96

Fiscal year ended Dec. 31. Next earnings report expected: Late January. EPS Estimates based on S&P Operating Earnings; historical GAAP earnings are as reported.

Dividend Data (Dates: mm/dd Payment Date: mm/dd/yy)

Amount ($)	Date Decl.	Ex-Div. Date	Stk. of Record	Payment Date
0.600	10/26	11/18	11/22	12/15/05
0.600	10/25	11/22	11/27	12/15/06

Dividends have been paid since 1969. Source: Company reports.

Brunswick Corp

Business Summary August 01, 2006

CORPORATE OVERVIEW. Brunswick Corp. is a major marine products company that also sells fitness equipment as well as products related to bowling and billiards. In addition, the company operates Brunswick bowling centers in the U.S. and internationally and retail billiards stores in the U.S.

In 2005, the company's marine-related businesses accounted for 83% of net sales, or $4.9 billion (after eliminations); $2.6 billion was from the Marine Engine area and $2.8 billion was from the Boat segment. Operating profits totaled $261 million for the Marine Engine segment and $193 million for the Boat segment. The Marine Engine group consists of the Mercury Marine Group and Brunswick New Technologies (BNT). Mercury Marine manufactures and markets a full range of outboard, inboard and sterndrive engines; water-jet propulsion systems; and related parts and accessories. BNT manufactures and markets engine electronics and controls and other marine technologies, including navigation systems, chart plotters, telematics, and GPS equipment. The Boat segment designs, manufactures and markets fiberglass pleasure boats, high-performance boats, offshore fishing boats, and aluminum fishing, deck and pontoon boats.

The Fitness segment includes cardiovascular fitness equipment (including treadmills, total body cross trainers, stair climbers, and stationary exercise bicycles) and strength-training equipment under the Life Fitness, Hammer Strength, and ParaBody brands. In 2005, the company reported Fitness segment sales of $551 million (9% of total net sales), and operating earnings of $56 million. Fitness segment sales are derived from commercial as well as high-end consumer markets.

In 2005, BC's Bowling and Billiards segment had net sales of $465 million (8%) and operating earnings of $37.2 million. The segment includes the production of bowling balls and bowling capital equipment; the operation of more than 100 bowling centers; and the marketing of billiards tables, cues and accessories.

In addition, BC owns 49% of Brunswick Acceptance Co. (BAC), a joint venture with GE Commercial Finance. BAC provides secured wholesale floor-plan financing to BC's boat and engine dealers and purchases and services a portion of Mercury Marine's domestic accounts receivables related to its boatbuilder and dealer customers. In 2005, BAC purchased $913.3 million of receivables from BC.

Company Financials

Per Share Data ($) Year Ended Dec. 31	**2005**	**2004**	**2003**	**2002**	**2001**	**2000**	**1999**	**1998**	**1997**	**1996**
Tangible Book Value	9.99	7.85	6.77	5.90	5.78	6.41	6.98	5.34	4.75	7.02
Cash Flow	5.54	4.39	3.11	2.78	2.78	3.96	2.20	3.42	3.07	3.19
Earnings	3.90	2.77	1.47	1.14	0.96	2.28	0.41	1.80	1.51	1.88
S&P Core Earnings	3.58	2.78	1.77	0.69	0.42	NA	NA	NA	NA	NA
Dividends	0.60	0.60	0.50	0.50	0.50	0.50	0.50	0.50	0.50	0.50
Payout Ratio	15%	22%	34%	44%	52%	22%	122%	28%	33%	27%
Prices:High	49.77	49.85	32.08	30.01	25.01	22.13	30.00	35.69	37.00	25.88
Prices:Low	35.00	31.25	16.35	18.30	14.03	14.75	18.06	12.00	23.13	17.25
P/E Ratio:High	13	18	22	26	26	10	73	20	25	14
P/E Ratio:Low	9	11	11	16	15	6	44	7	15	9

Income Statement Analysis (Million $)										
Revenue	5,924	5,229	4,129	3,712	3,371	3,812	4,284	3,945	3,657	3,160
Operating Income	641	558	397	345	352	601	544	560	526	435
Depreciation	162	158	151	148	160	149	166	160	157	130
Interest Expense	53.2	45.2	41.0	43.3	52.9	67.6	61.0	62.7	51.3	33.4
Pretax Income	496	379	201	162	132	323	55.0	284	236	290
Effective Tax Rate	22.3%	28.7%	32.8%	36.0%	35.9%	37.5%	31.1%	37.1%	36.0%	36.0%
Net Income	385	270	135	104	84.7	202	37.9	179	151	186
S&P Core Earnings	354	271	163	63.7	37.1	NA	NA	NA	NA	NA

Balance Sheet & Other Financial Data (Million $)										
Cash	488	500	346	351	109	125	101	126	85.6	242
Current Assets	2,235	2,099	1,715	1,660	1,401	1,832	1,578	1,454	1,366	1,242
Total Assets	4,622	4,346	3,603	3,407	3,158	3,397	3,355	3,352	3,241	2,802
Current Liabilities	1,305	1,254	1,102	1,006	903	1,248	1,088	1,036	948	831
Long Term Debt	724	728	584	590	600	602	Nil	635	646	455
Common Equity	1,979	1,658	1,323	1,102	1,111	1,067	1,300	1,311	1,366	1,198
Total Capital	2,850	2,567	1,907	1,691	1,896	1,884	1,432	2,112	2,105	1,809
Capital Expenditures	234	171	160	113	111	156	198	198	191	170
Cash Flow	548	427	286	252	245	351	204	338	308	316
Current Ratio	1.7	1.7	1.6	1.7	1.6	1.5	1.5	1.4	1.4	1.5
% Long Term Debt of Capitalization	25.4	28.4	30.6	34.9	31.7	31.9	Nil	30.1	30.7	25.2
% Net Income of Revenue	6.5	5.2	3.3	2.8	2.5	5.3	0.9	4.5	4.1	5.9
% Return on Assets	8.6	6.8	3.9	3.2	2.7	6.1	1.1	5.4	5.0	7.2
% Return on Equity	20.9	18.6	11.2	9.4	7.8	17.1	2.9	13.3	11.7	16.6

Data as orig reptd.; bef. results of disc opers/spec. items. Per share data adj. for stk. divs.; EPS diluted. E-Estimated. NA-Not Available. NM-Not Meaningful. NR-Not Ranked. UR-Under Review.

Office: 1 North Field Court, Lake Forest, IL 60045-4811.
Telephone: 847-735-4700.
Website: http://www.brunswick.com
Chrmn & CEO: D.E. McCoy

Vice Chrmn: P.B. Hamilton
SVP & CFO: P.G. Leemputte
VP & Treas: W.L. Metzger
VP, Secy & General Counsel: M.I. Smith

Investor Contact: K.J. Chieger (847-735-4700)
Board of Directors: N. D. Archibald, J. L. Bleustein, M. J. Callahan, C. W. Dunaway, M. A. Fernandez, P. B. Hamilton, P. Harf, D. E. McCoy, G. H. Phillips, R. W. Schipke, R. Stayer, L. A. Zimmerman

Founded: 1844
Domicile: Delaware
Employees: 27,500

STANDARD & POOR'S

Burlington Northern Santa Fe Corp

S&P Recommendation HOLD ★★★★★

Price $77.99 (as of Oct 27, 2006)

12-Mo. Target Price $80.00

Investment Style Large-Cap Value

GICS Sector Industrials
Sub-Industry Railroads

Comment Through BNSF Railway Co. (formerly The Burlington Northern and Santa Fe Railway Co.), BNI owns one of the largest railroad networks in the U.S.

Key Stock Statistics (Source S&P, Vickers, company reports)

52-Wk Range	$87.99–60.50	S&P Oper. EPS 2006E	4.99	P/E on S&P Oper. EPS 2006E	15.6	Dividend Rate/Share	$1.00
Trailing 12-Month EPS	$4.81	S&P Oper. EPS 2007E	5.60	Common Shares Outstg. (M)	359.2	Yield (%)	1.28
Trailing 12-Month P/E	16.2	S&P Core EPS 2006E	4.93	Market Capitalization(B)	$28.015	Beta	0.85
$10K Invested 5 Yrs Ago	$31,298	S&P Core EPS 2007E	5.58	Institutional Ownership (%)	78	S&P Credit Rating	BBB+

Price Performance

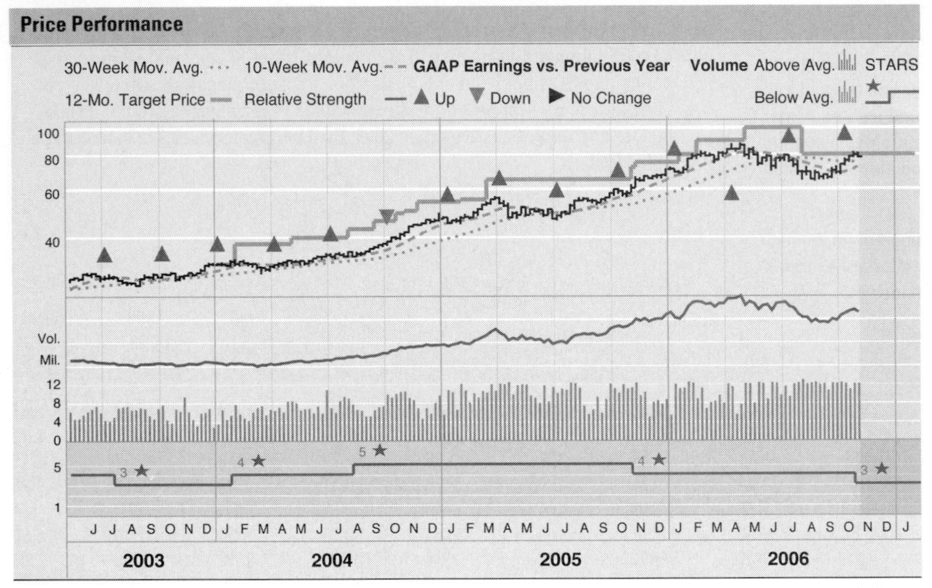

Options: ASE, CBOE, P

Highlights

➤ The STARS recommendation for BNI has recently been changed to 3 (hold) from 4 (buy). The Highlights section of this Stock Report will be updated accordingly.

Investment Rationale/Risk

➤ The Investment Rationale/Risk section of this Stock Report will be updated shortly. For the latest News story on BNI from MarketScope, see below.

➤ 10/24/06 11:56 am EDT... S&P DOWNGRADES SHARES OF BURLINGTON NORTHERN SANTA FE TO HOLD FROM BUY (BNI 78.13***): Q3 EPS of $1.33 vs. $1.09 is $0.04 ahead of our estimate, with revenue 19% higher on equal parts volume, pricing, and fuel surcharge. We expect revenue momentum to slow in '07, as we believe the majority of contracts have been repriced and about 90% of clients are now under some type of fuel recovery clause. BNI's asset utilization rates are at 10-year highs. We are increasing our '06 EPS estimate to $4.99 from $4.95, while '07's remains $5.60. However, with shares bit below our target price of $80 and valuations above 10-year average, we think BNI is fairly valued. /KKirkeby-CFA

Qualitative Risk Assessment

LOW | MEDIUM | HIGH (rating: LOW)

Our risk assessment reflects what we believe is BNI's strong profitability, cash flow generation, and balance sheet, and a diverse customer base, offset somewhat by its exposure to economic cycles, freight demand, and regulations.

Quantitative Evaluations

S&P Quality Ranking A-

D | C | B- | B | B+ | A- | A | A+

Relative Strength Rank MODERATE

70

LOWEST = 1 HIGHEST = 99

Revenue/Earnings Data

Revenue (Million $)

	1Q	2Q	3Q	4Q	Year
2006	3,463	3,701	3,939	--	--
2005	2,982	3,138	3,317	3,550	12,987
2004	2,490	2,685	2,793	2,978	10,946
2003	2,232	2,294	2,395	2,492	9,413
2002	2,163	2,207	2,308	2,301	8,979
2001	2,293	2,271	2,343	2,301	9,208

Earnings Per Share ($)

	1Q	2Q	3Q	4Q	Year
2006	1.09	1.27	1.33	E1.34	E4.99
2005	0.83	0.96	1.09	1.13	4.01
2004	0.52	0.67	0.01	0.91	2.10
2003	0.40	0.54	0.55	0.61	2.09
2002	0.45	0.51	0.51	0.54	2.00
2001	0.36	0.50	0.58	0.46	1.89

Fiscal year ended Dec. 31. Next earnings report expected: Late January. EPS Estimates based on S&P Operating Earnings; historical GAAP earnings are as reported.

Dividend Data (Dates: mm/dd Payment Date: mm/dd/yy)

Amount ($)	Date Decl.	Ex-Div. Date	Stk. of Record	Payment Date
0.200	02/14	03/09	03/13	04/03/06
0.200	04/24	06/08	06/12	07/03/06
0.250	07/20	09/07	09/11	10/02/06
0.250	10/19	12/08	12/12	01/02/07

Dividends have been paid since 1940. Source: Company reports.

Burlington Northern Santa Fe Corp

Business Summary July 26, 2006

CORPORATE OVERVIEW. Burlington Northern Santa Fe Corp., through its BNSF Railway Co. subsidiary, operates the second largest U.S. rail system, delivering about 45% of rail traffic in the West, and about 23% of U.S. rail traffic. BNSF operates a rail system of about 32,000 miles (24,000 owned, 8,000 trackage rights) that spans 28 western and midwestern states and two Canadian provinces.

MARKET PROFILE. We believe BNI's consumer/intermodal business, sensitive to U.S. import and consumption trends, is the industry volume leader, and at the heart of its competitive strategy. Consumer freight provided 41% of freight revenues in 2005 and consisted primarily of intermodal service: international container traffic, services to United Parcel Service, less-than-truckload and truckload carriers, and automotive and perishables traffic. Industrial products, sensitive to U.S. GDP trends, provided 23% of freight revenues in 2005, and was comprised of construction and building products, chemicals, and petroleum. Coal, which we believe is BNI's most profitable segment, accounted for 19% of 2005 freight revenues. A major transporter of low-sulfur coal, 90% of BNI's coal traffic originates in the Powder River Basin of Wyoming and Montana, primarily delivered to power utilities. Agricultural products, sensitive to annual crop volumes, accounted for 17% of 2005 freight revenues, including deliveries of grains, ethanol and fertilizer.

COMPETITIVE LANDSCAPE. The U.S. rail industry has an oligopoly-like structure, with over 80% of revenues generated by the four largest railroads: BNI and Union Pacific Corp. operating on the West Coast, and CSX Corp. and Norfolk Southern Corp. operating on the East Coast. Railroads simultaneously compete for customers while cooperating by sharing assets, interfacing systems, and cooperatively fulfilling customer transports. Key suppliers include locomotive and rail equipment manufacturers, fuel suppliers, and labor. BNI's employees, about 85% of whom are unionized, enjoy above national average compensation due to their significant bargaining power.

Company Financials

Per Share Data ($) Year Ended Dec. 31	**2005**	**2004**	**2003**	**2002**	**2001**	**2000**	**1999**	**1998**	**1997**	**1996**
Tangible Book Value	25.57	24.71	22.84	21.10	20.33	19.08	17.96	16.53	14.53	12.95
Cash Flow	6.83	4.79	4.53	4.44	4.21	4.52	4.36	4.17	3.52	3.52
Earnings	4.01	2.10	2.09	2.00	1.89	2.36	2.45	2.43	1.88	1.90
S&P Core Earnings	4.10	2.03	2.01	1.75	1.73	NA	NA	NA	NA	NA
Dividends	0.74	0.64	0.54	0.48	0.49	0.48	0.48	0.42	0.40	0.40
Payout Ratio	18%	30%	26%	24%	26%	20%	20%	17%	21%	21%
Prices:High	72.00	49.25	32.50	31.75	34.00	29.56	37.94	35.71	33.65	30.04
Prices:Low	44.58	29.52	23.29	23.18	22.40	19.06	22.88	26.88	23.42	24.50
P/E Ratio:High	18	23	16	16	18	13	15	15	18	16
P/E Ratio:Low	11	14	11	12	12	8	9	11	12	13
Income Statement Analysis (Million $)										
Revenue	12,987	10,946	9,413	8,979	9,208	9,205	9,100	8,941	8,413	8,187
Operating Income	3,997	2,698	2,575	2,587	2,664	3,003	3,096	2,990	2,630	2,508
Depreciation	1,075	1,012	910	931	909	895	897	832	773	760
Interest Expense	437	409	420	428	463	453	387	354	344	301
Pretax Income	2,448	1,273	1,231	1,216	1,182	1,585	1,819	1,849	1,404	1,440
Effective Tax Rate	37.5%	37.9%	36.9%	37.5%	37.6%	38.2%	37.5%	37.5%	37.0%	38.3%
Net Income	1,531	791	777	760	737	980	1,137	1,155	885	889
S&P Core Earnings	1,563	767	743	667	676	NA	NA	NA	NA	NA
Balance Sheet & Other Financial Data (Million $)										
Cash	75.0	322	18.0	28.0	26.0	11.0	22.0	25.0	31.0	47.0
Current Assets	1,880	1,615	862	791	723	976	1,066	1,206	1,234	1,331
Total Assets	30,304	28,925	26,939	25,767	24,721	24,375	23,700	22,690	21,336	19,846
Current Liabilities	3,229	2,716	2,346	2,091	2,161	2,186	2,075	2,197	2,060	2,311
Long Term Debt	6,698	6,051	6,440	6,641	6,363	6,614	5,655	5,188	5,181	4,546
Common Equity	9,925	9,311	8,495	7,932	7,849	7,480	8,172	7,770	6,812	5,981
Total Capital	24,539	23,182	22,416	21,548	20,943	20,516	19,924	18,620	17,168	15,256
Capital Expenditures	1,750	1,527	1,726	1,358	1,459	1,399	1,788	2,147	2,182	2,234
Cash Flow	2,606	1,803	1,687	1,691	1,646	1,875	2,034	1,987	1,658	1,649
Current Ratio	0.6	0.6	0.4	0.4	0.3	0.4	0.5	0.5	0.6	0.6
% Long Term Debt of Capitalization	27.3	26.1	28.7	30.8	30.4	32.2	28.4	27.9	30.2	29.8
% Net Income of Revenue	11.8	7.2	8.3	8.5	8.0	10.6	12.5	12.9	10.5	10.9
% Return on Assets	5.2	2.8	2.9	3.0	3.0	4.1	4.9	5.2	4.3	4.7
% Return on Equity	15.6	8.9	9.5	9.6	9.6	12.5	14.3	15.8	13.8	16.1

Data as orig reptd.; bef. results of disc opers/spec. items. Per share data adj. for stk. divs.; EPS diluted. E-Estimated. NA-Not Available. NM-Not Meaningful. NR-Not Ranked. UR-Under Review.

Office: 2650 Lou Menk Dr, Fort Worth, TX 76131-2830.
Telephone: 800-795-2673.
Email: investor.relations@bnsf.com
Website: http://www.bnsf.com

Chrmn, Pres & CEO: M.K. Rose
EVP & CFO: T.N. Hund
EVP & Secy: J.R. Moreland
Investor Contact: J. Ayers (817-352-4813)

Board of Directors: A. L. Boeckman, D. G. Cook, V. S. Martinez, M. F. Racicot, R. S. Roberts, M. K. Rose, M. J. Shapiro, J. C. Watts, Jr., R. H. West, J. S. Whisler, E. E. Whitacre, Jr.

Founded: 1994
Domicile: Delaware
Employees: 40,000

Campbell Soup Co

STANDARD &POOR'S

S&P Recommendation HOLD ★★★★★

Price $36.49 (as of Oct 27, 2006)

12-Mo. Target Price $38.00

Investment Style Large-Cap Growth

GICS Sector Consumer Staples
Sub-Industry Packaged Foods & Meats

Comment Campbell Soup is a major producer of branded soups and other grocery food products.

Key Stock Statistics (Source S&P, Vickers, company reports)

52-Wk Range	$38.49–28.30	S&P Oper. EPS 2007E	1.85	P/E on S&P Oper. EPS 2007E	19.7	Dividend Rate/Share	$0.80
Trailing 12-Month EPS	$1.85	S&P Oper. EPS 2008E	1.98	Common Shares Outstg. (M)	403.4	Yield (%)	2.19
Trailing 12-Month P/E	19.7	S&P Core EPS 2007E	1.83	Market Capitalization(B)	$14.721	Beta	0.56
$10K Invested 5 Yrs Ago	$14,502	S&P Core EPS 2008E	1.96	Institutional Ownership (%)	43	S&P Credit Rating	A

Price Performance

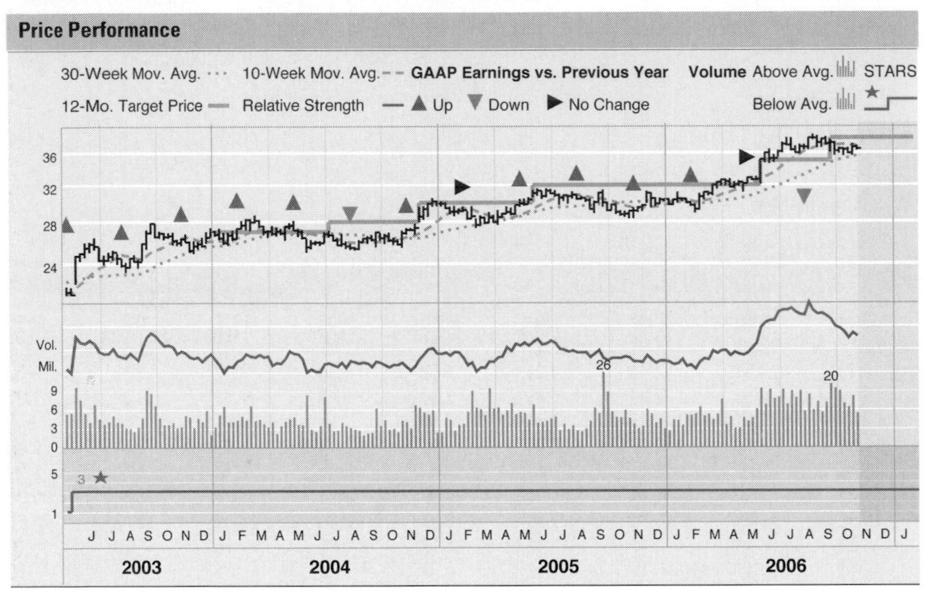

Options: ASE, CBOE, P, Ph

Analysis prepared by **Rick Joy** on September 22, 2006, when the stock traded at **$ 35.95**.

Highlights

- We expect net sales from continuing operations to advance 3% to 4% in FY 07 (Jul.), reflecting our expectations of growth in the low single digits for the U.S. soups, sauces and beverages business, a mid-single digit gain for the baking and snacking segment, no growth for the international soup business, and high single digit growth for the Godiva and Away from Home business. Foreign currency translations are expected to be a modest positive. Volumes should benefit from new products and packaging, and from higher levels of marketing spending, in our opinion.
- We think margins are likely to remain unchanged, as we expect rising soup prices and savings from cost reduction initiatives to be offset by increased energy and commodity costs, technology investments and increased marketing spending.
- After an expected modest reduction in interest expense and shares outstanding, we project that FY 07 operating EPS will increase to $1.85, from EPS of $1.81 in FY 06. For the longer term, we project 5% to 7% annual operating EPS growth.

Investment Rationale/Risk

- We have a hold opinion on the shares, based on total return. While CPB managed to achieve growth across several business segments during FY 06 (Jul.), competitive activity in its core ready-to-serve soup business remains intense, and we believe that the company's turnaround plan needs more time to gain traction. We think CPB's long-term annual EPS growth target of 5% to 7% is achievable, but we note that this EPS range falls below that of many of CPB's large capitalization food peers.
- Risks to our recommendation and target price include competitive pressures in CPB's businesses, consumer acceptance of new products, and the company's ability to achieve sales and earnings growth forecasts.
- Our DCF model, which assumes a 9% cost of capital and a terminal growth rate for cash flow of 3%, calculates intrinsic value of $39. Our relative valuation model, based on our analyses of comparable peer P/E and enterprise value (EV)-to-EBITDA multiples, arrives at a value of $37. Blending our valuations, our 12-month target price is $38.

Qualitative Risk Assessment

LOW | MEDIUM | HIGH

Our risk assessment for Campbell Soup reflects the relatively stable nature of the company's end markets, our view of its strong balance sheet and cash flow, and corporate governance practices that we see as favorable relative to peers.

Quantitative Evaluations

S&P Quality Ranking B+

D | C | B- | B | **B+** | A- | A | A+

Relative Strength Rank MODERATE

32

LOWEST = 1 HIGHEST = 99

Revenue/Earnings Data

Revenue (Million $)

	1Q	2Q	3Q	4Q	Year
2006	2,002	2,159	1,728	1,454	7,343
2005	2,091	2,223	1,736	1,498	7,548
2004	1,909	2,100	1,667	1,433	7,109
2003	1,705	1,918	1,600	1,455	6,678
2002	1,729	1,810	1,371	1,223	6,133
2001	1,778	1,958	1,439	1,330	6,664

Earnings Per Share ($)

	1Q	2Q	3Q	4Q	Year
2006	0.69	0.58	0.35	0.20	1.82
2005	0.56	0.57	0.35	0.23	1.71
2004	0.51	0.57	0.34	0.14	1.57
2003	0.47	0.56	0.31	0.18	1.52
2002	0.42	0.49	0.23	0.13	1.28
2001	0.47	0.65	0.30	0.13	1.55

Fiscal year ended Jul. 31. Next earnings report expected: Late November. EPS Estimates based on S&P Operating Earnings; historical GAAP earnings are as reported.

Dividend Data (Dates: mm/dd Payment Date: mm/dd/yy)

Amount ($)	Date Decl.	Ex-Div. Date	Stk. of Record	Payment Date
0.180	11/17	12/28	01/02	01/30/06
0.180	03/23	04/06	04/10	05/01/06
0.180	06/22	07/06	07/10	07/31/06
0.200	09/28	10/04	10/09	10/30/06

Dividends have been paid since 1902. Source: Company reports.

Please read the Required Disclosures and Analyst Certification on the last page of this report.

Campbell Soup Co

Business Summary September 22, 2006

Probably known best for its ubiquitous red and white soup cans (elevated to icon status by Andy Warhol), Campbell Soup Co. is a major force in the U.S. packaged foods industry. The company, which traces its origins in the food business back to 1869, manufactures and markets a wide array of branded, prepared convenience food products worldwide.

Operations outside the U.S. accounted for 36% of net sales and 27% of pretax earnings in FY 05 (Jul.), mostly in Europe (15% and 11%) and Australia/Asia Pacific (14% and 9%). As of the first quarter of FY 05, the company changed its organizational structure and now reports results based on the following segments: U.S. Soup, Sauces and Beverages (41% of FY 05 sales, 58% of FY 05 operating profits), Baking and Snacking (23%, 16%), International Soup and Sauces (23%, 17%), and Other (13%, 9%).

Campbell's U.S. Soup, Sauces and Beverages segment includes major U.S. products such as both condensed and ready-to-serve soups (Campbell's, Home Cookin', Chunky, Healthy Request); broth (Swanson); chili (Campbell's Chunky); meal kits (Campbell's Supper Bakes); juices (Campbell's Tomato, V8, V8 Splash); canned pasta, gravies and beans (Campbell's); spaghetti sauce (Prego); and Mexican sauces (Pace).

The company's Baking and Snacking division includes Pepperidge Farm cookies, crackers, breads and frozen products in the U.S.; Arnotts biscuits in Australia and Asia Pacific; and Arnotts salty snacks in Australia. The International Soup and Sauces segment includes the soup, sauces and beverage businesses outside of the United States, including Europe, Mexico, Latin America, the Asia Pacific region, and the retail business in Canada.

The balance of the portfolio reported in Other includes Godiva Chocolatier (worldwide) and the company's Away From Home operations, which represent the distribution of products such as soup, specialty entrees, beverage products, other prepared foods and Pepperidge Farm products through various foodservice channels in the U.S. and Canada.

Company Financials

Per Share Data ($) Year Ended Jul. 31	**2006**	**2005**	**2004**	**2003**	**2002**	**2001**	**2000**	**1999**	**1998**	**1997**
Tangible Book Value	NM	NM	NM	NM	NM	NM	NM	NM	NM	NM
Cash Flow	2.52	2.39	2.20	2.11	2.05	2.19	2.23	2.20	2.07	2.21
Earnings	1.82	1.71	1.57	1.52	1.28	1.55	1.65	1.63	1.50	1.51
S&P Core Earnings	1.81	1.63	1.47	1.46	1.00	1.28	NA	NA	NA	NA
Dividends	0.72	0.68	0.63	0.63	0.63	0.90	0.68	0.89	0.82	0.75
Payout Ratio	40%	40%	40%	41%	49%	58%	41%	55%	55%	50%
Prices:High	38.49	31.60	30.52	27.90	30.00	35.44	39.63	55.75	62.88	59.38
Prices:Low	28.88	27.35	25.03	19.95	19.65	25.52	23.75	37.44	46.69	39.38
P/E Ratio:High	21	18	19	18	23	23	24	34	42	39
P/E Ratio:Low	16	16	16	13	15	16	14	23	31	26

Income Statement Analysis (Million $)	2006	2005	2004	2003	2002	2001	2000	1999	1998	1997
Revenue	7,343	7,548	7,109	6,678	6,133	6,664	6,267	6,424	6,696	7,964
Operating Income	1,445	1,483	1,394	1,376	1,442	1,470	1,516	1,625	1,782	1,950
Depreciation	289	279	260	243	319	266	251	255	261	382
Interest Expense	165	184	174	186	190	216	192	184	189	167
Pretax Income	1,001	1,030	947	924	798	987	1,077	1,097	1,079	1,114
Effective Tax Rate	24.6%	31.4%	31.7%	32.3%	34.2%	34.2%	33.7%	34.0%	35.6%	35.4%
Net Income	755	707	647	626	525	649	714	724	689	713
S&P Core Earnings	751	675	603	604	413	536	NA	NA	NA	NA

Balance Sheet & Other Financial Data (Million $)	2006	2005	2004	2003	2002	2001	2000	1999	1998	1997
Cash	657	40.0	32.0	32.0	21.0	24.0	27.0	6.00	16.0	26.0
Current Assets	2,112	1,512	1,481	1,290	1,199	1,221	1,168	1,294	1,440	1,583
Total Assets	7,870	6,776	6,675	6,205	5,721	5,927	5,196	5,522	5,633	6,459
Current Liabilities	2,962	2,002	2,339	2,783	2,678	3,120	3,032	3,146	2,803	2,981
Long Term Debt	2,116	2,542	2,543	2,249	2,449	2,243	1,218	1,330	1,169	1,153
Common Equity	1,768	1,270	874	387	-114	-247	137	275	874	1,420
Total Capital	3,884	3,812	3,417	2,636	2,335	1,996	1,355	1,564	2,293	2,656
Capital Expenditures	309	332	288	283	269	200	200	297	256	331
Cash Flow	1,044	986	907	869	844	915	965	979	950	1,095
Current Ratio	0.7	0.8	0.6	0.5	0.4	0.4	0.4	0.4	0.5	0.5
% Long Term Debt of Capitalization	54.5	66.7	74.4	85.3	104.9	112.4	89.9	85.0	51.0	43.4
% Net Income of Revenue	10.3	9.4	9.1	9.4	8.6	9.7	11.4	11.3	10.3	9.0
% Return on Assets	10.3	10.5	10.0	10.5	9.0	11.7	13.3	13.0	11.4	10.9
% Return on Equity	49.7	66.0	102.6	458.6	NA	NA	383.9	130.6	60.1	34.3

Data as orig reptd.; bef. results of disc opers/spec. items. Per share data adj. for stk. divs.; EPS diluted. E-Estimated. NA-Not Available. NM-Not Meaningful. NR-Not Ranked. UR-Under Review.

Office: 1 Campbell Pl, Camden, NJ 08103-1799.
Telephone: 856-342-4800.
Website: http://www.campbellsoup.com
Chrmn: H. Golub

Pres & CEO: D.R. Conant
Investor Contact: R.A. Schiffner (856-342-4800)
SVP & CFO: R.A. Schiffner
SVP & CIO: D.A. Wright

Founded: 1869
Domicile: New Jersey
Employees: 24,000

STANDARD &POOR'S

CA Inc

S&P Recommendation HOLD ★★★★★

Price $24.51 (as of Oct 27, 2006)

12-Mo. Target Price $24.00

Investment Style Large-Cap Value

GICS Sector Information Technology
Sub-Industry Systems Software

Comment This Long Island-based company (formerly Computer Associates International) develops systems software, database management systems, and applications software.

Key Stock Statistics (Source S&P, Vickers, company reports)

52-Wk Range	**$29.71–18.97**	S&P Oper. EPS 2007**E**	**0.95**	P/E on S&P Oper. EPS 2007**E**	**25.8**	Dividend Rate/Share	**$0.16**
Trailing 12-Month EPS	**$0.17**	S&P Oper. EPS 2008**E**	**NA**	Common Shares Outstg. (M)	**526.5**	Yield (%)	**0.65**
Trailing 12-Month P/E	**NM**	S&P Core EPS 2007**E**	**0.95**	Market Capitalization(B)	**$12.904**	Beta	**2.60**
$10K Invested 5 Yrs Ago	**$7,460**	S&P Core EPS 2008**E**	**NA**	Institutional Ownership (%)	**80**	S&P Credit Rating	**BBB-**

Price Performance

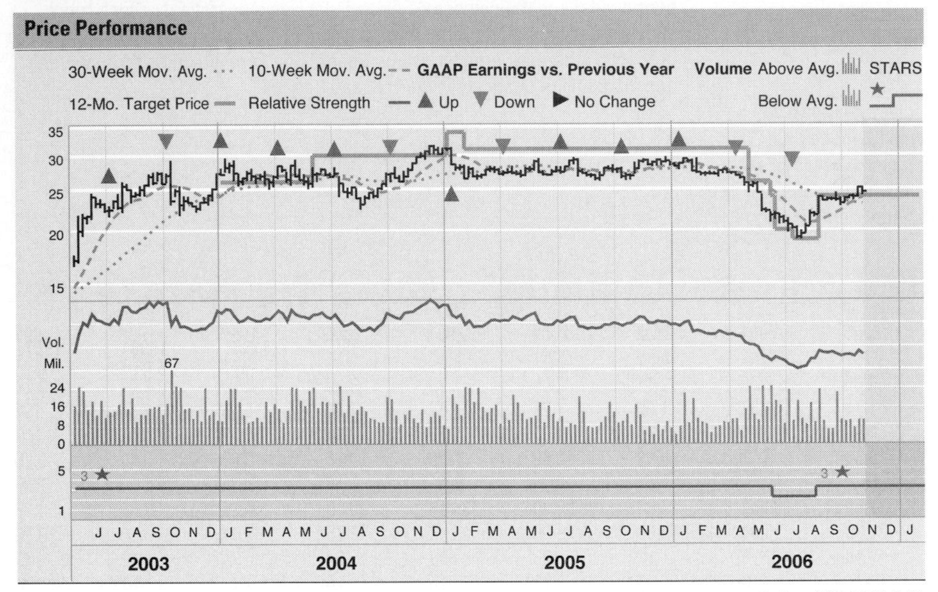

Options: ASE, CBOE, P, Ph

Analysis prepared by **Zaineb Bokhari** on August 16, 2006, when the stock traded at **$ 23.54**.

Highlights

- In view of recent management turnover and our expectation that added disruptions from a recent sales force realignment are likely, we see FY 07 (Mar.) sales rising about 3% to $3.9 billion, slowing from FY 06's 5%. We expect bookings to rise modestly in FY 07 despite a 19% drop in FY 06, impacted by a decline in the early customer license renewals. In addition, contribution from recent acquisitions of Niku Corp. (August 2005) and Wily Technology (March 2006) has been muted by a sooner-than-expected transition to CA's ratable revenue recognition model.
- We anticipate that the company will benefit from recently announced plans to reduce its work force by 1,700 (about 11%), with potential annual cost savings of up to $200 million when completed. As a result, we forecast wider operating margins in FY 07.
- We project FY 07 operating EPS of $0.95, up 13% from $0.84 (revised) in FY 06. We expect EPS to be aided by the company's plans to repurchase $2 billion in shares during FY 07, partly financed by bank debt. Despite higher expected interest expense, we expect the planned buybacks to be accretive to EPS.

Investment Rationale/Risk

- We believe that CA's legacy mainframe software business will continue to be the major source of organic revenue, large deals and cash flow. CA has made several smaller acquisitions in recent quarters, that we believe have added to its technology portfolio and raised its profile in higher growth areas. Despite this, trends in trailing billings and bookings (organic and overall) have been weak, in our view. We view favorably the company's efforts to clear accounting issues that have been mainly historical in nature. Recent management turnover lowers our confidence in the company's ability to break from its uneven past record in the near term. We expect limited acquisition activity in view of planned share repurchases that we expect will restrict sales growth.
- Risks to our opinion and target price include significant declines in corporate spending on enterprise software from current levels, and a deterioration in the pricing environment.
- We derive our 12-month target price of $24 by applying a 25X P/E multiple to our FY 07 EPS estimate, which is near the low end of the three-year average trading range of 34.2X-22.2X.

Qualitative Risk Assessment

LOW | MEDIUM | **HIGH**

Our risk assessment for the company reflects our concerns regarding the number of recent departures of senior executives, and what we consider to be poor execution, weak financial results and modest underlying growth. We think it will be some time before the company can show a meaningful improvement.

Quantitative Evaluations

S&P Quality Ranking **B-**

D | C | **B-** | B | B+ | A- | A | A+

Relative Strength Rank **MODERATE**

62

LOWEST = 1 HIGHEST = 99

Revenue/Earnings Data

Revenue (Million $)

	1Q	2Q	3Q	4Q	Year
2007	956.0	--	--	--	--
2006	927.0	950.0	971.0	948.0	3,796
2005	850.0	858.0	910.0	912.0	3,530
2004	813.0	833.0	844.0	850.0	3,276
2003	765.0	772.0	778.0	801.0	3,116
2002	712.0	733.0	747.0	772.0	2,964

Earnings Per Share ($)

2007	0.06	**E**0.21	**E**0.27	**E**0.30	**E**0.95
2006	0.16	0.08	0.09	-0.07	0.26
2005	0.08	-0.16	0.06	0.04	0.02
2004	0.02	-0.15	0.04	0.05	-0.06
2003	-0.11	-0.09	-0.08	-0.18	-0.46
2002	-0.59	-0.50	-0.40	-0.41	-1.91

Fiscal year ended Mar. 31. Next earnings report expected: NA. EPS Estimates based on S&P Operating Earnings; historical GAAP earnings are as reported.

Dividend Data (Dates: mm/dd Payment Date: mm/dd/yy)

Amount ($)	Date Decl.	Ex-Div. Date	Stk. of Record	Payment Date
0.040	11/11	12/13	12/15	12/30/05
0.040	03/07	03/15	03/17	03/31/06
0.040	06/07	06/15	06/19	06/30/06
0.040	09/18	09/20	09/22	09/29/06

Dividends have been paid since 1990. Source: Company reports.

CA Inc

Business Summary August 16, 2006

CORPORATE OVERVIEW. CA, Inc. (formerly Computer Associates International) is a leading provider of enterprise software. In FY 06 (Mar.), the company had five business units: Enterprise Systems Management (32% of total FY 06 billings), Security Management (10%), Storage Management (10%), Business Service Optimization (12%), and the CA Products Group (which includes application development tools and database, approximately 26%). The balance of FY 06 billings came from professional services and other products. CA's products are comprised of both mainframe and distributed solutions, each of which made up about half of FY 06 revenue.

In FY 05, the company sold its product primarily though a direct sales force of more than 2,200 quoted sales people. While a comparable number was not given for FY 06, we note that the number of sales and support personnel fell to 4,900 in FY 06 from 5,100 in FY 05. In FY 05, the company moved to a named account structure under which its sales organization focused on what CA considered its largest and most important accounts and relied on resellers to sell into other accounts. The company also sells its products to large enterprises through partnerships with original equipment manufacturers (OEMs) and system integrators. CA has also pursued channel partnerships to more cost effectively sell into the small- and mid-sized business segment.

CORPORATE STRATEGY. In recent quarters, the company has made several small- and mid-sized acquisitions of technologies that it considers strategic and complementary to its systems and security management offerings. In August 2004, CA acquired Pest Patrol, a private provider of antispyware and security solutions, for about $40 million in cash. In November 2004, CA acquired Netegrity, a provider of access and identity management software, for about $455 million, including $439 million in cash paid for Netegrity's common stock. In June 2005, CA acquired Concord Communications, a provider of network service management software for $337 million in cash plus the assumption of $20 million in net debt. In August 2005, CA acquired Niku Corp., a provider of information technology management and governance solutions, for $350 million in cash. In March 2006, CA acquired Wily Technology, a private provider of application management software, for $375 million in cash.

Company Financials

Per Share Data ($) Year Ended Mar. 31	2006	2005	2004	2003	2002	2001	2000	1999	1998	1997
Tangible Book Value	NM	0.50	8.09	NM	NM	0.66	1.71	2.06	2.53	0.95
Cash Flow	1.22	0.24	0.17	0.60	-0.01	0.89	2.32	1.69	2.68	2.08
Earnings	0.26	0.02	-0.06	-0.46	-1.91	-1.02	1.25	1.11	2.06	0.65
S&P Core Earnings	0.26	0.22	0.02	-0.53	-2.05	-1.18	NA	NA	NA	NA
Dividends	0.08	0.08	0.08	0.08	0.08	0.08	0.08	0.08	0.07	0.06
Payout Ratio	31%	NM	NM	NM	NM	NM	6%	7%	3%	10%
Calendar Year	2005	2004	2003	2002	2001	2000	1999	1998	1997	1996
Prices:High	31.35	31.71	29.29	38.74	39.03	79.44	70.63	61.94	57.50	45.25
Prices:Low	26.04	22.37	12.39	7.47	18.31	18.13	32.13	26.00	24.83	22.56
P/E Ratio:High	NM	NM	NM	NM	NM	NM	56	56	28	70
P/E Ratio:Low	NM	NM	NM	NM	NM	NM	26	23	12	35

Income Statement Analysis (Million $)										
Revenue	3,796	3,530	3,276	3,116	2,964	4,198	6,766	5,253	4,719	4,040
Operating Income	836	504	417	421	-62.0	604	3,318	2,529	2,366	2,056
Depreciation	583	130	134	612	1,096	1,110	594	325	349	424
Interest Expense	41.0	106	Nil	172	227	344	339	154	147	104
Pretax Income	121	11.0	-54.0	-363	-1,385	-666	1,590	1,010	1,874	932
Effective Tax Rate	NM	NM	NM	NM	NM	NM	56.2%	38.0%	37.6%	60.7%
Net Income	156	13.0	-36.0	-267	-1,102	-591	696	626	1,169	366
S&P Core Earnings	155	136	7.10	-301	-1,185	-688	NA	NA	NA	NA

Balance Sheet & Other Financial Data (Million $)										
Cash	1,865	3,125	1,902	1,512	1,180	850	1,387	536	251	143
Current Assets	2,648	3,954	3,358	3,565	3,061	2,643	3,992	2,631	2,255	1,780
Total Assets	10,438	11,082	10,679	11,054	12,226	14,143	17,493	8,070	6,706	6,084
Current Liabilities	3,377	3,664	2,455	2,974	2,321	2,286	3,004	1,863	1,876	1,727
Long Term Debt	1,810	1,810	2,298	2,298	3,334	3,639	4,527	2,032	1,027	1,663
Common Equity	4,680	4,840	4,718	4,363	4,617	5,780	7,037	2,729	2,481	1,503
Total Capital	6,536	6,822	7,634	7,525	9,218	11,319	13,929	5,795	4,460	4,019
Capital Expenditures	143	69.0	30.0	30.0	25.0	89.0	198	222	84.0	41.4
Cash Flow	739	143	98.0	345	-6.00	519	1,290	951	1,518	790
Current Ratio	0.8	1.1	1.4	1.2	1.3	1.2	1.3	1.4	1.2	1.0
% Long Term Debt of Capitalization	27.7	26.5	30.1	30.5	36.2	32.1	32.5	35.1	23.0	43.0
% Net Income of Revenue	4.1	0.4	NM	NM	NM	NM	10.2	11.9	24.8	9.1
% Return on Assets	1.4	0.1	NM	NM	NM	NM	5.4	8.5	18.3	6.6
% Return on Equity	3.2	0.3	NM	NM	NM	NM	14.3	24.0	58.7	24.5

Data as orig reptd.; bef. results of disc opers/spec. items. Per share data adj. for stk. divs.; EPS diluted. E-Estimated. NA-Not Available. NM-Not Meaningful. NR-Not Ranked. UR-Under Review.

Office: 1 Computer Associates Plz, Islandia, NY 11749-7000.
Telephone: 631-342-6000.
Email: cainvestor@ca.com
Website: http://www.ca.com

Chrmn: L.S. Ranieri
Pres & CEO: J.A. Swainson
COO & EVP: M.J. Christenson
EVP & CFO: N.E. Cooper

EVP & Chief Admin: J.E. Bryant
Board of Directors: K. D. Cron, A. M. D'Amato, G. J. Fernandes, R. E. La Blanc, C. B. Lofgren, J. W. Lorsch, W. E. McCracken, L. S. Ranieri, W. P. Schuetze, J. A. Swainson, L. S. Unger, R. Zambonini

Founded: 1974
Domicile: Delaware
Employees: 16,000

Capital One Financial Corp.

STANDARD &POOR'S

S&P Recommendation BUY ★★★★★

Price $81.66 (as of Oct 27, 2006)

12-Mo. Target Price $92.00

Investment Style Large-Cap Growth

GICS Sector Financials
Sub-Industry Consumer Finance

Comment This company is one of the largest issuers of Visa and MasterCard credit cards in the world.

Key Stock Statistics (Source S&P, Vickers, company reports)

52-Wk Range	$90.04–69.30	S&P Oper. EPS 2006E	8.12	P/E on S&P Oper. EPS 2006E	10.1	Dividend Rate/Share	$0.11
Trailing 12-Month EPS	$7.44	S&P Oper. EPS 2007E	8.15	Common Shares Outstg. (M)	306.1	Yield (%)	0.13
Trailing 12-Month P/E	11.0	S&P Core EPS 2006E	8.07	Market Capitalization(B)	$24.998	Beta	1.73
$10K Invested 5 Yrs Ago	$17,881	S&P Core EPS 2007E	8.11	Institutional Ownership (%)	85	S&P Credit Rating	BBB

Price Performance

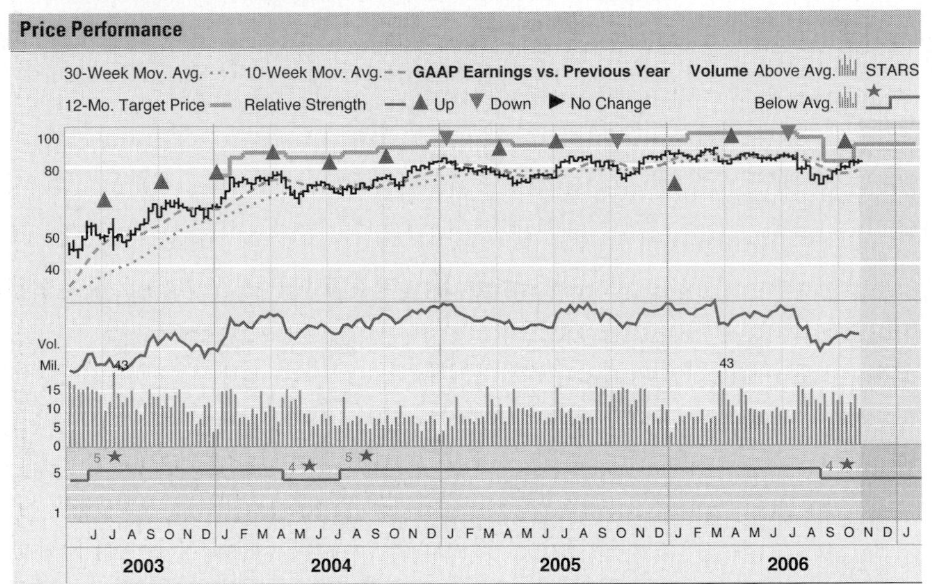

Options: ASE, CBOE, P, Ph

Analysis prepared by **Mark Hebeka, CFA** on October 25, 2006, when the stock traded at **$ 82.26**.

Highlights

- In March, COF announced a definitive agreement to purchase North Fork Bancorp (NFB: hold, $29) for about $14.6 billion, subject to necessary approvals. The proposed transaction is expected to close in the fourth quarter of 2006. We see increased integration risk associated with this proposed acquisition, but believe it is consistent with COF's goal of national scale lending combined with local scale banking. We see a potential for continued pressure on margins in the quarters ahead due to increased loan repayments, a challenging interest rate environment, and strong competition.
- In 2006 and 2007, we expect further stable loan growth due to continued strong consumer spending and our positive outlook for demand for the company's consumer lending products. We see results benefiting from COF's strategic shift toward higher credit quality and higher average balance (but lower margin) products.
- We see operating EPS of $8.12 in 2006 (excluding the planned NFB acquisition) and $8.15 in 2007, versus $6.73 in 2005.

Investment Rationale/Risk

- Our buy recommendation is based on what we see as the company's progress in implementing its dual operating strategy of diversification and emphasis on lower loss rate products. We have concerns about intense competition and credit exposure in U.K. operations, but remain optimistic about long-term prospects. We believe our expectations are not appropriately reflected in the stock's valuation.
- Risks to our recommendation and target price include increased competition from larger credit card issuers; a decline in consumer confidence that could restrict consumer spending; integration risk; and a rise in unemployment that could negatively affect credit quality.
- Our 12-month target price of $92 is equal to about 11.3X our 2007 EPS estimate. We believe this is an appropriate valuation multiple based on a discount to historical averages, justified, we believe, by increased integration and credit risk and the current stage of the economic expansion.

Qualitative Risk Assessment

LOW | MEDIUM | HIGH

Our risk assessment reflects what we see as solid business fundamentals, diverse product offerings and a strong customer base. We view COF as well diversified and able to withstand a major economic downturn.

Quantitative Evaluations

S&P Quality Ranking A+

D | C | B- | B | B+ | A- | A | A+

Relative Strength Rank MODERATE

58

LOWEST = 1 HIGHEST = 99

Revenue/Earnings Data

Revenue (Million $)

	1Q	2Q	3Q	4Q	Year
2006	3,737	3,607	3,826	--	--
2005	2,852	2,934	2,999	3,300	12,085
2004	2,608	2,548	2,768	2,771	10,695
2003	2,411	2,381	2,466	2,525	9,784
2002	2,133	2,369	2,628	2,434	9,648
2001	1,675	1,731	1,867	1,982	7,254

Earnings Per Share ($)

2006	2.86	1.78	1.89	**E**1.72	**E**8.12
2005	1.99	2.03	1.81	0.97	6.73
2004	1.84	1.65	1.97	0.77	6.21
2003	1.35	1.23	1.23	1.11	4.92
2002	0.83	0.92	1.13	1.05	3.93
2001	0.66	0.70	0.75	0.80	2.91

Fiscal year ended Dec. 31. Next earnings report expected: Mid January. EPS Estimates based on S&P Operating Earnings; historical GAAP earnings are as reported.

Dividend Data (Dates: mm/dd Payment Date: mm/dd/yy)

Amount ($)	Date Decl.	Ex-Div. Date	Stk. of Record	Payment Date
0.027	01/26	02/08	02/10	02/21/06
0.027	04/27	05/08	05/10	05/22/06
0.027	07/27	08/08	08/10	08/21/06
0.027	10/26	11/08	11/10	11/20/06

Dividends have been paid since 1995. Source: Company reports.

Capital One Financial Corp.

Business Summary October 25, 2006

CORPORATE OVERVIEW. COF is one of the world's largest financial services franchises. It is a diversified financial services corporation focused primarily on consumer lending and deposits. Its principal business segments are domestic credit card lending, automobile and other motor vehicle financing, global financial services and banking.

U.S. Card Segment. COF offers a wide variety of credit card products throughout the US. It customizes products to appeal to different consumer preferences and needs by combining different product features, including annual percentage rates, fees and credit limits, rewards programs and other special features. COF's pricing strategies are risk based; lower risk customers may likely be offered products with more favorable pricing and we expect these products to yield lower delinquencies and credit losses. On products offered to higher risk customers, however, COF is likely to experience higher delinquencies and losses, and it prices these products accordingly.

Auto Finance Segment. Through Capital One Auto Finance, Inc., the company purchases retail installment contracts, secured by automobiles or other motor vehicles, through dealer networks throughout the U.S. In addition, COF utilizes direct marketing to offer automobile financing directly to consumers. Its direct marketed products include financing for the purchase of new and used vehicles, as well as refinancing of existing motor vehicle loans. As of December 31, 2005, COF was the second largest non-captive auto lender in the U.S. In January 2005, it acquired Onyx Acceptance Corporation, an auto finance company that provides financing to franchised and select independent dealerships throughout the U.S. The corporation also completed the acquisition of Key Bank's non-prime auto loan portfolio in 2005. Similar to its credit card strategy, COF customizes product features, such as interest rate, loan amount and loan terms, enabling it to lend to customers with a wide range of credit profiles.

Company Financials

Per Share Data ($) Year Ended Dec. 31	**2005**	**2004**	**2003**	**2002**	**2001**	**2000**	**1999**	**1998**	**1997**	**1996**
Tangible Book Value	33.99	33.98	25.75	20.44	15.33	9.94	7.69	6.45	4.55	3.72
Earnings	6.73	6.21	4.92	3.93	2.91	2.24	1.72	1.32	0.93	0.77
S&P Core Earnings	6.61	5.72	4.41	3.37	2.55	NA	NA	NA	NA	NA
Dividends	0.11	0.11	0.11	0.11	0.11	0.11	0.11	0.11	0.11	0.11
Payout Ratio	2%	2%	2%	3%	4%	5%	6%	8%	11%	14%
Prices:High	88.56	84.45	64.25	66.50	72.58	73.25	60.25	43.31	18.10	12.29
Prices:Low	69.09	60.04	24.91	24.05	36.40	32.06	35.81	16.85	10.17	7.25
P/E Ratio:High	13	14	13	17	25	33	35	33	19	16
P/E Ratio:Low	10	10	5	6	13	14	21	13	11	9
Income Statement Analysis (Million $)										
Net Interest Income	3,680	3,003	2,785	2,719	1,663	1,589	1,053	695	383	365
Non Interest Income	6,358	5,900	5,416	5,467	4,420	3,034	2,372	1,488	1,069	763
Loan Loss Provision	1,491	1,221	1,517	2,149	990	718	383	267	263	167
Non Interest Expenses	5,718	5,322	4,857	4,586	4,058	3,148	2,465	1,472	884	713
% Expense/Operating Revenue	57.0%	59.8%	59.2%	56.0%	66.7%	68.1%	72.0%	67.4%	60.9%	63.2%
Pretax Income	2,829	2,360	1,827	1,451	1,035	757	577	444	305	248
Effective Tax Rate	36.1%	34.6%	37.0%	38.0%	38.0%	38.0%	37.1%	38.0%	38.0%	37.5%
Net Income	1,809	1,543	1,151	900	642	470	363	275	189	155
% Net Interest Margin	6.63	6.44	7.45	8.73	8.03	12.0	10.8	9.95	8.86	8.16
S&P Core Earnings	1,792	1,431	1,012	742	545	NA	NA	NA	NA	NA
Balance Sheet & Other Financial Data (Million $)										
Money Market Assets	2,049	1,084	1,598	641	352	162	112	284	174	450
Investment Securities	14,350	9,300	5,867	4,424	3,116	1,697	1,856	1,797	1,243	895
Earning Assets:Total Loans	59,848	38,216	32,850	27,854	20,921	14,059	9,914	6,157	4,862	4,225
Total Assets	88,701	53,747	46,284	37,382	28,184	18,889	13,336	9,419	7,078	6,467
Demand Deposits	NA	NA	Nil	Nil	Nil	Nil	Nil	Nil	Nil	Nil
Time Deposits	43,092	NA	22,416	17,326	12,839	8,379	3,784	2,000	1,314	943
Long Term Debt	14,863	Nil	14,813	8,124	Nil	4,051	4,181	3,038	3,633	3,994
Common Equity	14,129	8,388	6,052	4,623	3,324	1,963	1,518	1,270	893	740
% Return on Assets	2.5	3.1	2.8	2.7	2.7	2.9	3.2	3.3	2.8	2.8
% Return on Equity	16.1	21.4	21.6	22.6	24.3	27.0	26.0	25.4	23.2	22.9
% Loan Loss Reserve	3.0	3.9	4.9	6.2	4.0	3.7	3.5	3.8	3.8	2.7
% Loans/Deposits	124.8	149.1	146.5	160.8	162.9	167.8	262.0	307.9	370.1	NM
% Loans/Assets	68.8	71.0	71.9	74.4	74.3	72.3	70.6	66.8	68.0	77.4
% Equity to Assets	15.8	14.4	12.8	12.1	11.2	10.8	12.3	13.1	12.1	15.7

Data as orig reptd.; bef. results of disc opers/spec. items. Per share data adj. for stk. divs.; EPS diluted. E-Estimated. NA-Not Available. NM-Not Meaningful. NR-Not Ranked. UR-Under Review.

Office: 1680 Capital One Drive, McLean, VA 22102-3406.
Telephone: 703-720-1000.
Email: investor.relations@capitalone.com
Website: http://www.capitalone.com

Chrmn, Pres & CEO: R.D. Fairbank
EVP, CFO & Chief Acctg Officer: G.L. Perlin
EVP, Secy & General Counsel: J.G. Finneran, Jr.
EVP & CIO: G.S. Bailar

Investor Contact: M. Rowen (703-720-2455)
Board of Directors: E. R. Campbell, W. R. Dietz, R. D. Fairbank, P. W. Gross, A. F. Hackett, L. Hay, III, P. E. Leroy, M. A. Shattuck, III, S. Westreich

Founded: 1993
Domicile: Delaware
Employees: 21,000

STANDARD &POOR'S

Cardinal Health Inc

S&P Recommendation HOLD ★★★★★	**Price** $64.47 (as of Oct 27, 2006)	**12-Mo. Target Price** $74.00	**Investment Style** Large-Cap Growth

GICS Sector Health Care
Sub-Industry Health Care Distributors

Comment This company is one of the leading wholesale distributors of pharmaceuticals, medical/surgical supplies and related products to a broad range of health care customers.

Key Stock Statistics (Source S&P, Vickers, company reports)

52-Wk Range	$75.74–60.15	S&P Oper. EPS 2007E	3.65	P/E on S&P Oper. EPS 2007E	17.7	Dividend Rate/Share	$0.36
Trailing 12-Month EPS	$2.46	S&P Oper. EPS 2008E	4.20	Common Shares Outstg. (M)	405.5	Yield (%)	0.56
Trailing 12-Month P/E	26.2	S&P Core EPS 2007E	3.64	Market Capitalization(B)	$26.144	Beta	0.66
$10K Invested 5 Yrs Ago	$9,083	S&P Core EPS 2008E	4.19	Institutional Ownership (%)	85	S&P Credit Rating	BBB

Price Performance

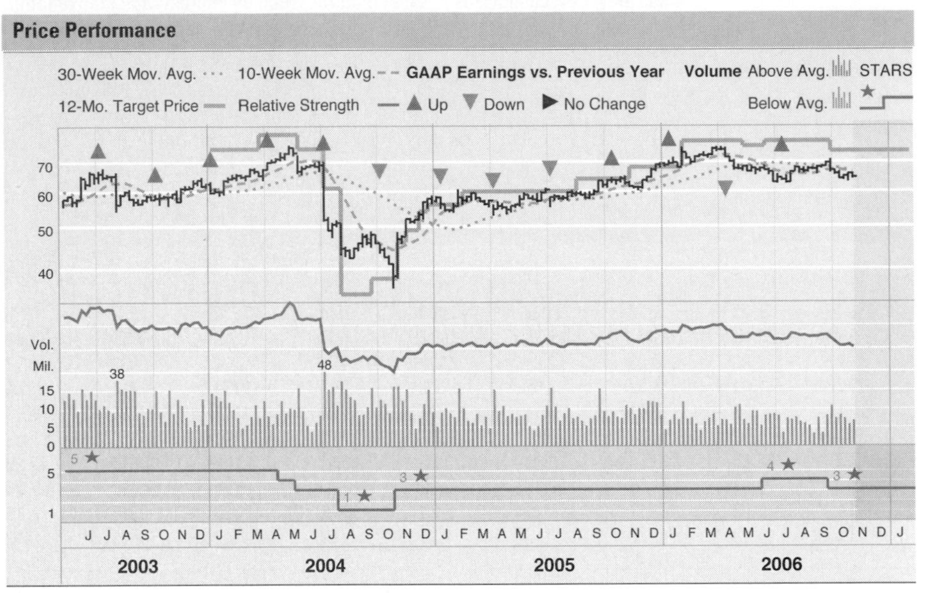

Options: ASE, CBOE, P, Ph

Analysis prepared by **Phillip M. Seligman** on September 26, 2006, when the stock traded at **$ 66.52**.

Highlights

- We see total revenue growing about 10%, to $90.5 billion, in FY 07 (Jun.), above FY 06's 8.6% advance, driven by expected strong direct store delivery and bulk-customer sales growth by Supply Chain Services - Pharmaceutical (SCSP; formerly known as Pharmaceutical Distribution and Provider Services), new products from Medical Product Manufacturing (MPM) and Clinical Technologies and Services (CTS), and demand for drug manufacturing at Pharmaceutical Technologies and Services (PTS), partly offset by the divestiture of noncore businesses.
- We see some relief from pressure on SCSP operating margins from the recent and expected launches of new generic drugs, but note competitive sell-side margin pressures. We look for an improving product mix and international expansion to aid MPM's and CTS's respective earnings growth, while PTS exhibits operating improvement following its recent restructuring.
- Including stock option expense, we look for FY 07 operating EPS of $3.65, compared to FY 06's $3.12, and $4.20 in FY 08. Our FY 07 and FY 08 S&P Core EPS estimates of $3.64 and $4.19, respectively, reflect modest pension and post-retirement plan adjustments.

Investment Rationale/Risk

- We see uncertainty surrounding a potential rise in sell-side pricing pressure on CAH's generic drug business from Wal-Mart's (WMT: strong buy, $48) decision to slash generic drug prescription prices. While WMT is piloting the program in Tampa, Fla., and limiting it to 291 older, already deeply discounted generics, we would not be surprised to see the program expanded nationwide and eventually matched by CVS (CVS: strong buy, $33) and Walgreen's (WAG: buy, $47), CAH's largest retail customers. Elsewhere, however, we are encouraged by CAH's turnaround efforts, reorganized business structure, and the new CEO's willingness to divest underperforming units.
- Risks to our recommendation and target price include the loss of major accounts and unfavorable changes in contracts with drugmakers. Another risk is the SEC's formal investigation of CAH's accounting, which we view as a significant overhang, possibly leading to further financial restatements and/or a financial penalty.
- Our 12-month target price of $74 reflects a peer-level P/E of 19.5X applied to our calendar 2007 operating EPS estimate of $3.80.

Qualitative Risk Assessment

LOW	**MEDIUM**	HIGH

Our risk assessment reflects CAH's diversified products and services and what we believe are good growth prospects for its contract drugmaking and its drug dispensing systems. However, we also see intense competition in the drug distribution market and believe that future drugmaker-distributor contract negotiations might be less favorable for distributors.

Quantitative Evaluations

S&P Quality Ranking **A+**

D	C	B-	B	B+	A-	A	**A+**

Relative Strength Rank **WEAK**

21

LOWEST = 1 HIGHEST = 99

Revenue/Earnings Data

Revenue (Million $)

	1Q	2Q	3Q	4Q	Year
2006	21,357	19,781	20,638	21,708	81,364
2005	17,796	18,555	19,103	19,457	74,911
2004	15,388	16,351	16,392	16,923	65,054
2003	11,417	12,706	12,837	13,506	50,467
2002	9,865	11,222	11,541	11,766	44,394
2001	8,735	9,638	12,580	12,401	47,947

Earnings Per Share ($)

	1Q	2Q	3Q	4Q	Year
2006	0.73	0.72	0.83	0.80	2.90
2005	0.50	0.47	0.84	0.59	2.40
2004	0.72	0.85	0.99	0.91	3.47
2003	0.64	0.82	0.74	0.82	3.12
2002	0.53	0.62	0.66	0.64	2.45
2001	0.41	0.49	0.42	0.55	1.88

Fiscal year ended Jun. 30. Next earnings report expected: Late January. EPS Estimates based on S&P Operating Earnings; historical GAAP earnings are as reported.

Dividend Data (Dates: mm/dd Payment Date: mm/dd/yy)

Amount ($)	Date Decl.	Ex-Div. Date	Stk. of Record	Payment Date
0.060	11/09	12/28	01/01	01/15/06
0.060	02/23	03/29	04/01	04/15/06
0.090	05/10	06/28	07/01	07/15/06
0.090	08/02	09/27	10/01	10/15/06

Dividends have been paid since 1983. Source: Company reports.

Cardinal Health Inc

Business Summary September 26, 2006

CORPORATE OVERVIEW. As of FY 07 (Jun.), Cardinal Health's reportable segments have been realigned into two main businesses comprised of five reportable segments: Supply Chain Services, which is comprised of Supply Chain Services - Pharmaceutical (SCSP) and Supply Chain Services - Medical (SCSM), and Pharmaceutical & Medical Products, which is comprised of Medical Products Manufacturing (MPM), Pharmaceutical Technologies and Services, and Clinical Technologies and Services. The description below is based on the historical segment structure.

Pharmaceutical Distribution and Provider Services (PDS; 82% of FY 06 operating revenue) distributes pharmaceutical and related health care products to independent and chain drug stores, hospitals, alternate care centers, and supermarket and mass merchandiser pharmacies. PDS operates a pharmaceutical repackaging and distribution program for retail and mail order customers. It is also a franchiser of retail pharmacies (Medicine Shoppe International, Inc. and Medicap Pharmacies Inc.).

Medical-Surgical Products and Services (MPS; 12%), operating through Allegiance Corp., provides non-pharmaceutical health care products for hospitals and other health care providers. It also manufactures sterile and non-sterile procedure kits, single-use surgical drapes, gowns and apparel, exam and surgical gloves, fluid suction and collection systems, respiratory therapy products, surgical instruments, special procedure products and other products.

Pharmaceutical Technologies and Services (PTS; 3%) provides contract manufacturing and packaging services to drugmakers. It provides proprietary drug delivery technologies, as well as manufacturing for nearly all traditional oral dosage and sterile dose forms. The group also provides drug discovery, development and analytical science services, and medical education, marketing and contract sales services. Its Nuclear Pharmacy Services unit prepares and deliver radiopharmaceuticals for use in nuclear imaging and other procedures in hospitals and clinics.

Clinical Technologies and Services (CTS; 3%) provides automation and information products and services. One unit, Pyxis Corp., develops, manufactures and markets point-of-use pharmacy systems that automate the distribution and management of medications and supplies in hospitals and other health care facilities.

Company Financials

Per Share Data ($) Year Ended Jun. 30	**2006**	**2005**	**2004**	**2003**	**2002**	**2001**	**2000**	**1999**	**1998**	**1997**
Tangible Book Value	8.52	8.20	7.05	12.10	11.50	9.50	7.28	6.13	9.04	4.94
Cash Flow	3.82	3.34	4.15	3.70	2.98	2.50	2.17	1.65	1.86	0.95
Earnings	2.90	2.40	3.47	3.12	2.45	1.88	1.59	1.09	0.97	0.74
S&P Core Earnings	2.88	2.16	3.14	2.78	2.26	1.69	NA	NA	NA	NA
Dividends	0.27	0.15	0.12	0.11	0.10	0.09	0.05	0.05	0.05	0.04
Payout Ratio	9%	6%	3%	4%	4%	5%	3%	5%	5%	6%
Prices:High	75.74	69.64	76.54	67.96	73.70	77.32	69.96	55.50	50.92	35.00
Prices:Low	62.35	52.85	36.08	50.00	46.60	56.67	24.67	24.67	30.97	22.89
P/E Ratio:High	26	29	22	22	30	41	44	51	53	47
P/E Ratio:Low	21	22	10	16	19	30	15	23	32	31
Income Statement Analysis (Million $)										
Revenue	81,364	74,911	65,054	50,467	44,394	47,948	29,871	25,034	15,918	10,968
Operating Income	2,474	2,555	2,694	3,723	2,216	1,893	1,377	1,257	538	443
Depreciation	393	410	299	266	244	281	246	234	64.3	51.3
Interest Expense	132	134	98.9	115	133	155	117	99.4	23.0	28.0
Pretax Income	1,835	1,629	2,238	2,127	1,701	1,332	1,078	759	403	312
Effective Tax Rate	32.2%	35.8%	31.9%	33.6%	33.8%	35.6%	36.9%	39.9%	38.6%	42.0%
Net Income	1,245	1,047	1,525	1,412	1,126	857	680	456	247	181
S&P Core Earnings	1,236	936	1,369	1,266	1,045	771	NA	NA	NA	NA
Balance Sheet & Other Financial Data (Million $)										
Cash	1,321	1,412	1,096	1,724	1,382	934	505	165	305	243
Current Assets	14,777	13,443	13,058	13,250	11,907	10,716	6,871	5,147	3,229	2,504
Total Assets	23,374	22,059	21,369	18,521	16,438	14,642	10,265	8,289	3,961	3,109
Current Liabilities	11,373	10,105	9,369	7,314	6,810	6,575	4,262	2,959	1,844	1,409
Long Term Debt	2,600	2,320	2,835	2,472	2,207	1,871	1,486	1,224	273	278
Common Equity	8,491	8,593	7,976	7,758	6,393	5,437	3,981	3,463	1,625	1,332
Total Capital	11,090	10,913	12,000	11,207	8,600	7,308	5,467	5,208	1,898	1,610
Capital Expenditures	443	572	410	423	285	341	308	320	111	75.2
Cash Flow	1,637	1,456	1,824	1,678	1,370	1,138	926	690	311	232
Current Ratio	1.3	1.3	1.4	1.8	1.7	1.6	1.6	1.7	1.8	1.8
% Long Term Debt of Capitalization	23.4	21.3	23.6	22.1	25.7	25.6	27.2	23.5	14.4	17.3
% Net Income of Revenue	1.5	1.4	2.3	2.8	2.5	1.8	2.3	1.8	1.6	1.7
% Return on Assets	5.5	4.8	7.7	8.1	7.2	6.4	7.3	5.8	7.0	6.1
% Return on Equity	14.6	12.6	19.5	20.0	19.0	17.4	18.0	14.2	16.7	15.3

Data as orig reptd.; bef. results of disc opers/spec. items. Per share data adj. for stk. divs.; EPS diluted. E-Estimated. NA-Not Available. NM-Not Meaningful. NR-Not Ranked. UR-Under Review.

Office: 7000 Cardinal Place, Dublin, OH 43017.
Telephone: 614-757-5000.
Website: http://www.cardinal.com
Chrmn: R.D. Walter

Pres & CEO: R.K. Clark
EVP & CFO: J.W. Henderson
EVP, Secy & Chief Lgl Officer: I. Fong
EVP & CCO: D. Walsh

Board of Directors: R. K. Clark, G. H. Conrades, C. Darden, J. F. Finn, R. L. Gerbig, J. M. Losh, J. B. McCoy, R. C. Notebaert, M. D. O'Halleran, D. Raisbeck, J. G. Spaulding, M. D. Walter, R. D. Walter

Founded: 1979
Domicile: Ohio
Employees: 55,000

STANDARD &POOR'S

Caremark Rx Inc

S&P Recommendation BUY ★★★★★

Price $49.66 (as of Oct 27, 2006)

12-Mo. Target Price $60.00

Investment Style Large-Cap Growth

GICS Sector Health Care
Sub-Industry Health Care Services

Comment This pharmacy benefits manager provides drug benefit services to more than 2,000 health plan sponsors.

Key Stock Statistics (Source S&P, Vickers, company reports)

52-Wk Range	$59.89–42.40	S&P Oper. EPS 2006E	2.35	P/E on S&P Oper. EPS 2006E	21.1	Dividend Rate/Share	$0.40
Trailing 12-Month EPS	$2.24	S&P Oper. EPS 2007E	2.77	Common Shares Outstg. (M)	426.9	Yield (%)	0.81
Trailing 12-Month P/E	22.2	S&P Core EPS 2006E	2.35	Market Capitalization(B)	$21.200	Beta	0.58
$10K Invested 5 Yrs Ago	$34,500	S&P Core EPS 2007E	2.77	Institutional Ownership (%)	88	S&P Credit Rating	NA

Price Performance

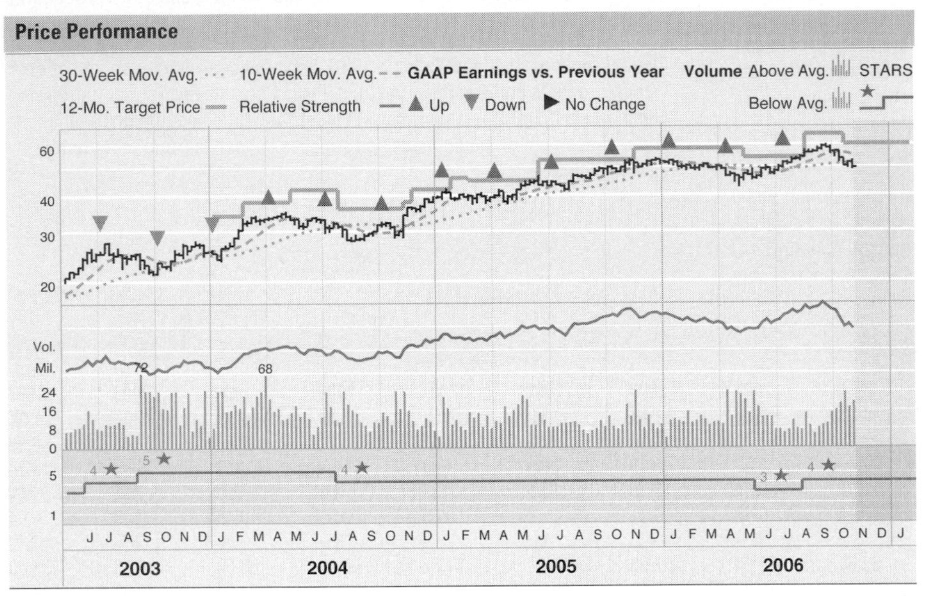

Options: ASE, CBOE, Ph

Analysis prepared by **Phillip M. Seligman** on October 13, 2006, when the stock traded at **$ 50.71**.

Highlights

- We see 2006 revenues rising about 10.5%, to $36.5 billion, slower than 2005's 28% growth, on the lapping of the March 2005 AdvancePCS acquisition, and First DataBank's decision in early October 2006 to cut its published average wholesale prices (AWPs) of branded drugs, used as a reimbursement benchmark, by 5%. We believe revenue drivers will be new accounts, drug price inflation, increased service usage by existing accounts, and the Medicare prescription drug program (PDP), which started in 2006. We also think the launches of low-priced, yet highly profitable generic equivalents of blockbuster drugs will pressure the top line.
- We expect EBITDA per adjusted claim to rise, on a better customer mix, continued growth in mail-order, specialty and generic drug penetration, and the lapping of Medicare drug program start-up costs. We see these positives partly offset by the decline in AWPs.
- We look for 2006 operating EPS of $2.35, including estimated stock option expense of $0.08, compared to 2005's $1.97, which excluded stock option expense of $0.02. We project 2007 EPS of $2.77. We see EPS growth aided by CMX's $3 billion share repurchase program.

Investment Rationale/Risk

- We are encouraged by the 12% rise in EBITDA per adjusted claim in the second quarter, partly on increased generic drug and specialty drug penetration, and we see it continuing to expand going forward, mainly aided by the large stream of generic drug launches that are slated to continue past the end of the decade. However, we think expansion will slow, at least temporarily, in the fourth quarter and in most of 2007, assuming a one-time decline in AWPs without a concurrent decline in the cost of goods. We view CMX's cash flow as strong, which provides financial flexibility. We believe investors are looking beyond the U.S. Attorney's subpoena issue and the SEC letter of informal inquiry on stock option grant timing.
- Risks to our recommendation and target price include pressure on margins from clients seeking greater discounts and/or enhanced services, increased government oversight and adverse regulatory changes, loss of key accounts, and risks due to investigations.
- Our 12-month target price of $60 reflects a P/E to earnings growth ratio of 1.2X, on an expected 3-year growth rate of 18%, matching historical peer levels, and our 2007 EPS estimate.

Qualitative Risk Assessment

LOW | **MEDIUM** | HIGH

Our risk assessment reflects rising drug demand and our view of an improving financial performance and low debt leverage. However, we believe that intense competition and increased government regulation of pharmacy benefit managers, which we view as likely, could slow long-term progress in profits.

Quantitative Evaluations

S&P Quality Ranking B-

D | C | **B-** | B | B+ | A- | A | A+

Relative Strength Rank WEAK

12

LOWEST = 1 HIGHEST = 99

Revenue/Earnings Data

Revenue (Million $)

	1Q	2Q	3Q	4Q	Year
2006	8,907	9,438	--	--	--
2005	8,352	8,199	8,072	8,368	32,991
2004	3,026	7,304	7,458	8,013	25,801
2003	2,164	2,204	2,257	2,443	9,067
2002	1,614	1,626	1,713	1,851	6,805
2001	1,374	1,373	1,380	1,486	5,614

Earnings Per Share ($)

	1Q	2Q	3Q	4Q	Year
2006	0.51	0.58	E0.63	E0.63	E2.35
2005	0.43	0.47	0.51	0.64	2.05
2004	0.29	0.30	0.37	0.45	1.43
2003	0.24	0.26	0.29	0.31	1.10
2002	0.24	0.27	0.31	2.34	3.15
2001	0.15	0.16	0.19	0.23	0.73

Fiscal year ended Dec. 31. Next earnings report expected: Early November. EPS Estimates based on S&P Operating Earnings; historical GAAP earnings are as reported.

Dividend Data (Dates: mm/dd Payment Date: mm/dd/yy)

Amount ($)	Date Decl.	Ex-Div. Date	Stk. of Record	Payment Date
0.100	04/05	06/28	06/30	07/17/06
0.100	08/17	09/27	09/29	10/16/06

Dividends have been paid since 2006. Source: Company reports.

Caremark Rx Inc

Business Summary October 13, 2006

CORPORATE OVERVIEW. CMX provides pharmacy benefit management (PBM) services and therapeutic pharmaceutical services that assist employers, insurance companies, unions, government employee group, HMOs and other sponsors of health benefit plans and individuals throughout the U.S. in delivering prescription drugs in a cost-effective manner. In 2005, the company managed 536.3 million prescriptions for individuals from more than 2,000 organizations. The Federal Employees Health Benefit Plan accounted for approximately 16% of its net revenue.

Pharmacy benefits management involves the design and administration of programs aimed at reducing costs and improving the safety, effectiveness and convenience of prescription drug use. Prescription drugs are dispensed to patients through more than 60,000 third party retail pharmacies and CMX's seven mail service pharmacies and 21 specialty pharmacies. In 2005, it processed 478.0 million retail prescriptions (down from 544.9 million in 2004), and filled 58.3 million (47.0 million) mail order prescriptions.

Caremark Specialty Pharmacy Services, through the specialty pharmacies, delivers advanced medications, including injectable and other specialized infusion drugs, to individuals with chronic or genetic diseases and disorders.

CORPORATE STRATEGY. From the discontinuance of its physician practice management in 1998 until 2003, CMX primarily grew organically. In March 2004, it acquired AdvancePCS, a PBM that focused on a different customer market (mainly health plans) than CMX (mainly employers). The combination, in our view, yielded increased scale, a diversified customer base, and opportunities for increased cost efficiencies. We look for additional, primarily "tuck-in" acquisitions going forward, to improve existing services and add new ones.

Company Financials

Per Share Data ($) Year Ended Dec. 31	2005	2004	2003	2002	2001	2000	1999	1998	1997	1996
Tangible Book Value	0.70	NM	2.18	0.75	NM	NM	NM	NM	NA	0.49
Cash Flow	2.37	1.72	1.27	3.22	0.78	0.55	-0.62	0.29	-3.09	0.05
Earnings	2.05	1.43	1.10	3.15	0.73	0.43	-0.74	0.16	-4.25	-0.58
S&P Core Earnings	1.97	1.40	1.07	3.10	0.66	NA	NA	NA	NA	NA
Dividends	Nil	Nil	Nil	Nil	Nil	Nil	Nil	Nil	Nil	Nil
Payout Ratio	Nil	Nil	Nil	Nil	Nil	Nil	Nil	Nil	Nil	Nil
Prices:High	53.90	39.95	27.92	21.95	18.50	13.94	9.00	22.38	32.00	36.00
Prices:Low	37.00	23.50	16.20	12.24	10.75	3.75	2.88	1.63	17.88	16.38
P/E Ratio:High	26	28	25	7	25	32	NM	NM	NM	NM
P/E Ratio:Low	18	16	15	4	15	9	NM	NM	NM	NM
Income Statement Analysis (Million $)										
Revenue	32,991	25,801	9,067	6,805	5,614	4,430	3,308	2,634	6,331	4,813
Operating Income	1,628	1,178	576	411	297	236	201	163	110	318
Depreciation	147	124	45.1	29.9	26.9	25.4	22.1	24.7	120	81.9
Interest Expense	Nil	31.0	42.5	46.8	77.3	110	120	78.8	55.7	23.9
Pretax Income	1,498	998	485	334	193	99.9	-138	49.6	-772	-95.1
Effective Tax Rate	37.8%	39.8%	40.0%	NM	8.01%	8.49%	NM	38.0%	NM	NM
Net Income	932	600	291	829	177	91.4	-143	30.8	-694	-89.8
S&P Core Earnings	896	589	285	807	159	NA	NA	NA	NA	NA
Balance Sheet & Other Financial Data (Million $)										
Cash	1,269	1,079	815	307	159	2.35	6.80	23.1	216	124
Current Assets	4,645	4,220	1,947	1,226	647	453	535	1,186	1,313	947
Total Assets	12,851	12,310	2,474	1,913	874	686	771	1,862	2,891	2,266
Current Liabilities	3,712	3,764	1,064	877	679	635	563	1,100	1,237	777
Long Term Debt	387	450	693	696	896	933	1,430	1,735	1,471	716
Common Equity	8,181	7,540	641	258	-772	-969	-1,281	-1,144	90.9	739
Total Capital	8,813	7,990	1,334	953	123	-35.7	149	591	1,562	1,455
Capital Expenditures	138	80.5	63.2	48.4	39.9	23.2	20.4	28.7	123	122
Cash Flow	1,080	724	336	849	204	117	-121	55.5	-573	-7.90
Current Ratio	1.3	1.1	1.8	1.4	1.0	0.7	0.9	1.1	1.1	1.2
% Long Term Debt of Capitalization	4.4	5.6	52.0	73.0	727.2	NM	962.7	293.6	94.1	49.2
% Net Income of Revenue	2.8	2.3	3.2	12.2	3.2	2.1	NM	1.2	NM	NM
% Return on Assets	7.4	8.1	13.3	59.5	22.7	12.6	NM	1.3	NM	NM
% Return on Equity	11.9	14.7	64.8	NM	NM	NM	NM	NA	NM	NM

Data as orig reptd.; bef. results of disc opers/spec. items. Per share data adj. for stk. divs.; EPS diluted. E-Estimated. NA-Not Available. NM-Not Meaningful. NR-Not Ranked. UR-Under Review

Office: 211 Commerce Street, Nashville, TN 37201-1817.
Telephone: 615-743-6600.
Website: http://www.caremarkrx.com
Chrmn, Pres & CEO: E.M. Crawford

Vice Chrmn: C.L. Piccolo
COO & Sr EVP: H.A. McLure
EVP & CFO: P.J. Clemens, IV
EVP & General Counsel: E.L. Hardin, Jr.

Board of Directors: E. M. Banks, C. D. Brown, II, C. Conway-Welch, E. M. Crawford, H. Diamond, K. E. Gibney Williams, E. L. Hardin, Jr., R. L. Headrick, J. Millon, C. L. Piccolo, M. D. Ware

Founded: 1993
Domicile: Delaware
Employees: 13,628

STANDARD &POOR'S

Carnival Corp

S&P Recommendation SELL ★★★★★	Price	12-Mo. Target Price	Investment Style
	$48.81 (as of Oct 27, 2006)	$46.00	Large-Cap Growth

GICS Sector Consumer Discretionary
Sub-Industry Hotels, Resorts & Cruise Lines

Comment Carnival Corp. and Carnival plc own businesses that operate more than 75 cruise ships.

Key Stock Statistics (Source S&P, Vickers, company reports)

52-Wk Range	$56.14–36.40	S&P Oper. EPS 2006**E**	2.71	P/E on S&P Oper. EPS 2006**E**	18.0	Dividend Rate/Share	$1.10
Trailing 12-Month EPS	$2.58	S&P Oper. EPS 2007**E**	3.00	Common Shares Outstg. (M)	626.7	Yield (%)	2.25
Trailing 12-Month P/E	18.9	S&P Core EPS 2006**E**	2.71	Market Capitalization(B)	$30.591	Beta	1.38
$10K Invested 5 Yrs Ago	$24,975	S&P Core EPS 2007**E**	3.00	Institutional Ownership (%)	72	S&P Credit Rating	A-

Price Performance

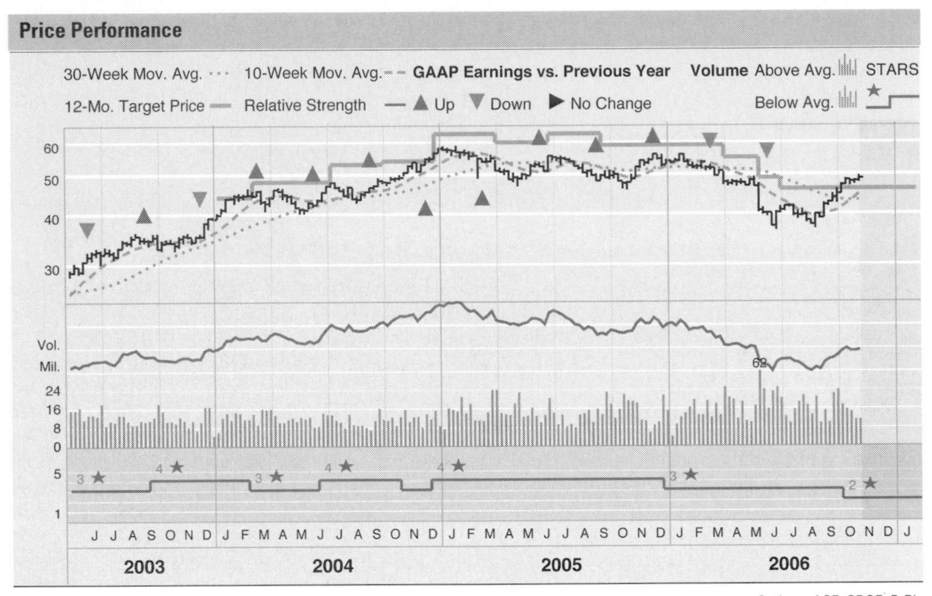

Options: ASE, CBOE, P, Ph

Analysis prepared by **Tom Graves, CFA** on October 05, 2006, when the stock traded at **$ 48.23**.

Highlights

- In 2003, this leading cruise ship company merged with P&O Princess Cruises plc, which was renamed Carnival plc. With a dual listing format, CCL shares continue to trade on the NYSE, while Carnival plc shares trade on the London Stock Exchange, and are represented by American Depositary Shares (CUK: sell, $49) in the U.S.
- In FY 07 (Nov.), including additional capacity from new ships, we estimate the combined Carnival businesses revenue of $12.8 billion, up from the $11.8 billion that we project for FY 06. We estimate FY 07 net income of $2.4 billion, compared to the $2.2 billion that we project for FY 06. We estimate FY 07 EPS of $3.00, up from the $2.71 that we project for FY 06. Our FY 06 estimate includes about $0.02 of special charges in the first quarter, an estimated $0.04 negative impact related to a March 2006 ship fire, $0.06 of option expensing, and an $0.08 negative impact from a change in accounting for dry-dock costs.
- In September 2006, Carnival said that there was a little less than $800 million remaining under a recent authorization to repurchase $1 billion of Carnival stock.

Investment Rationale/Risk

- In our view, the stock is amply priced. We expect that a new U.S. travel document requirement for cruiseship passengers will be delayed, with implementation possibly in 2008 or 2009, rather than in January 2007. Such a delay should be beneficial to Carnival. However, we are wary about growth prospects for overall U.S. consumer spending in 2007, and we remain concerned about potential profit pressure on Carnival from fuel costs and prospective higher taxes related to Alaska.
- Risks to our recommendation and target price include the possibility that demand for cruise travel will be stronger than we anticipate, and that fuel costs will be more favorable than we expect.
- Based on our calendar 2007 EPS estimates, CCL shares were recently at about a 16% P/E premium to the S&P 500, which we believe more than amply reflects what we see as favorable demographics for the cruiseship industry and Carnival's leadership position. Our 12-month target price of $46 is about 15X our FY 07 EPS estimate, which would be about a 13% P/E premium to what we are targeting for shares of an industry competitor.

Qualitative Risk Assessment

LOW | **MEDIUM** | HIGH

We believe that Carnival has competitive advantages related to its industry leading position, and we view the company's financial condition as being relatively strong. However, in our view, Carnival's operations are subject to external factors, including economic conditions and hurricane activity.

Quantitative Evaluations

S&P Quality Ranking **A+**

D | C | B- | B | B+ | A- | A | **A+**

Relative Strength Rank **STRONG**

82

LOWEST = 1 HIGHEST = 99

Revenue/Earnings Data

Revenue (Million $)

	1Q	2Q	3Q	4Q	Year
2006	2,461	2,662	--	--	--
2005	2,396	2,519	3,605	2,567	11,087
2004	1,980	2,256	3,245	2,243	9,727
2003	1,031	1,335	2,524	1,817	6,718
2002	905.8	989.2	1,438	1,036	4,368
2001	1,008	1,079	1,490	959.1	4,536

Earnings Per Share ($)

2006	0.34	0.46	**E**1.46	**E**0.46	**E**2.71
2005	0.42	0.49	1.36	0.43	2.70
2004	0.25	0.41	1.23	0.36	2.24
2003	0.22	0.19	0.90	0.26	1.66
2002	0.22	0.33	0.85	0.33	1.73
2001	0.22	0.32	0.84	0.20	1.58

Fiscal year ended Nov. 30. Next earnings report expected: NA. EPS Estimates based on S&P Operating Earnings; historical GAAP earnings are as reported.

Dividend Data (Dates: mm/dd Payment Date: mm/dd/yy)

Amount ($)	Date Decl.	Ex-Div. Date	Stk. of Record	Payment Date
0.250	01/25	02/15	02/17	03/10/06
0.250	04/21	05/17	05/19	06/09/06
0.250	07/07	08/16	08/18	09/08/06
0.275	10/18	11/15	11/17	12/08/06

Dividends have been paid since 1988. Source: Company reports.

Carnival Corp

Business Summary October 05, 2006

CORPORATE OVERVIEW. Carnival Corp. is the world's largest cruiseship company and has grown significantly through both acquisitions and the addition of new ships. In 2003, Carnival merged with P&O Princess Cruises plc, which was renamed Carnival plc. As of September 2006, the combined Carnival had 81 cruise ships with capacity for more than 140,000 passengers (based on two passengers per cabin, although some cabins can accommodate three or more passengers). Also, Carnival has tour operations in Alaska and the Canadian Yukon.

With Carnival's dual listing company (DLC) format, there are separate stocks trading under the Carnival Corp. and Carnival plc names. Each company has retained its separate legal identity, but the two share a single senior executive management team, have identical boards of directors, and are run as if they were a single economic enterprise. In valuing CCL shares, we look at the combined financial results and equity base of the Carnival entities.

PRIMARY BUSINESS DYNAMICS. In FY 06 (Nov.), we look for fuel costs to increase again, but for most of the incremental pressure occurring in the year's first half. Also, we look for some softness in demand for CCL Caribbean cruises, which could be related to hurricane activity in 2005.

MARKET PROFILE. We believe that the cruise industry carried more than 12 million passengers in 2005, with more than half of them coming from the North American market. In FY 05, CCL carried 6.8 million passengers. Looking ahead, we expect demand for cruiseship vacations to grow. In the U.S., we believe that most people have never taken a multi-night cruiseship vacation, and we expect that an aging of the U.S. population will lead to more interest in cruises. Also, we believe that a continued industry emphasis on providing ships with more features and the addition of more local ports will encourage passenger demand.

COMPETITIVE LANDSCAPE. We see Carnival enhancing its competitive position through the addition of new ships, which should encourage both returning and new customers. As of September 2006, there were 15 new Carnival ships scheduled to enter service between March 2007 and spring 2010. However, it is possible that some older ships may be sold or retired during the next few years. Carnival is much larger than its biggest competitor -- Royal Caribbean Cruises Ltd. (RCL) -- which operates 29 ships with about 63,000 berths.

Company Financials

Per Share Data ($) Year Ended Nov. 30	2005	2004	2003	2002	2001	2000	1999	1998	1997	1996
Tangible Book Value	15.47	13.96	11.83	11.48	10.13	8.84	8.86	6.46	4.82	4.77
Cash Flow	3.91	3.13	2.46	2.38	2.21	2.08	2.06	1.73	1.40	1.23
Earnings	2.70	2.24	1.66	1.73	1.58	1.60	1.66	1.40	1.12	0.98
Dividends	0.80	0.52	0.44	0.42	0.42	0.42	0.38	0.32	0.24	0.19
Payout Ratio	30%	23%	27%	24%	27%	26%	23%	22%	22%	19%
Prices:High	58.98	58.75	39.84	34.64	34.94	51.25	53.50	48.50	27.94	16.56
Prices:Low	45.78	39.75	20.34	22.07	16.95	18.31	38.13	19.00	15.69	11.63
P/E Ratio:High	22	26	24	20	22	32	32	35	25	17
P/E Ratio:Low	17	18	12	13	11	11	23	14	14	12
Income Statement Analysis (Million $)										
Revenue	11,087	9,727	6,718	4,368	4,536	3,779	3,497	3,009	2,447	2,213
Operating Income	3,541	2,985	1,968	1,444	1,448	1,233	1,188	1,020	828	697
Depreciation	902	812	585	382	372	288	244	201	167	145
Interest Expense	330	284	195	111	121	41.4	47.0	57.8	55.9	90.0
Pretax Income	2,184	1,901	1,223	959	948	967	1,044	851	672	575
Effective Tax Rate	NM	2.47%	2.37%	NM	2.34%	0.11%	0.27%	0.45%	0.93%	1.56%
Net Income	2,257	1,854	1,194	1,016	926	965	1,027	836	666	566
Balance Sheet & Other Financial Data (Million $)										
Cash	1,178	643	1,070	667	1,421	189	522	137	140	124
Current Assets	2,215	1,728	2,132	1,132	1,959	549	792	370	336	291
Total Assets	28,432	27,636	24,491	12,335	11,564	9,831	8,286	7,179	5,427	5,102
Current Liabilities	5,192	5,034	3,315	1,620	1,480	1,715	1,405	1,135	786	663
Long Term Debt	5,727	6,291	6,918	3,012	2,955	2,099	868	1,563	1,015	1,317
Common Equity	16,972	15,760	13,793	7,418	6,591	5,871	5,931	4,285	3,605	3,031
Total Capital	22,699	22,051	20,711	10,430	9,546	7,970	6,799	5,981	4,620	4,348
Capital Expenditures	1,977	3,586	2,516	1,986	827	1,003	873	1,150	498	902
Cash Flow	3,159	2,666	1,779	1,398	1,298	1,253	1,271	1,037	833	711
Current Ratio	0.4	0.3	0.6	0.7	1.3	0.3	0.6	0.3	0.4	0.4
% Long Term Debt of Capitalization	25.2	28.5	33.4	28.9	31.0	26.3	12.8	26.1	22.0	30.3
% Net Income of Revenue	20.4	19.1	17.8	23.3	20.4	25.6	29.4	27.8	27.2	25.5
% Return on Assets	8.1	7.1	6.5	8.5	8.7	10.7	13.3	13.3	12.7	13.2
% Return on Equity	13.8	12.5	11.3	14.5	14.9	16.4	20.1	21.2	20.1	21.1

Data as orig reptd.; bef. results of disc opers/spec. items. Per share data adj. for stk. divs.; EPS diluted. E-Estimated. NA-Not Available. NM-Not Meaningful. NR-Not Ranked. UR-Under Review.

Office: 3655 NW 87th Avenue, Doral, FL 33178-2428.
Telephone: 305-599-2600.
Website: http://www.carnivalcorp.com
Chrmn & CEO: M. Arison

Vice Chrmn & COO: H.S. Frank
EVP, CFO & Chief Acctg Officer: G.R. Cahill
SVP, Secy & General Counsel: A. Perez
Investor Contact: B. Roberts (305-599-2600)

Board of Directors: M. Arison, R. G. Capen, Jr., R. H. Dickinson, A. W. Donald, P. L. Foschi, H. S. Frank, R. J. Glasier, B. Hogg, A. K. Lanterman, M. A. Maidique, J. Parker, P. Ratcliffe, S. S. Subotnick, U. Zucker

Founded: 1974
Domicile: Panama
Employees: 71,200

Caterpillar Inc

STANDARD &POOR'S

S&P Recommendation HOLD ★★★★★

Price
$61.27 (as of Oct 27, 2006)

12-Mo. Target Price
$65.00

Investment Style
Large-Cap Value

GICS Sector Industrials
Sub-Industry Construction & Farm Machinery & Heavy Trucks

Comment CAT, the world's largest producer of earthmoving equipment, is also a big maker of truck engines and power generators.

Key Stock Statistics (Source S&P, Vickers, company reports)

52-Wk Range	$82.03–51.68	S&P Oper. EPS 2006**E**	5.18	P/E on S&P Oper. EPS 2006**E**	11.8	Dividend Rate/Share	$1.20
Trailing 12-Month EPS	$5.06	S&P Oper. EPS 2007**E**	5.50	Common Shares Outstg. (M)	655.7	Yield (%)	1.96
Trailing 12-Month P/E	12.1	S&P Core EPS 2006**E**	5.19	Market Capitalization(B)	$40.178	Beta	1.33
$10K Invested 5 Yrs Ago	$28,873	S&P Core EPS 2007**E**	5.51	Institutional Ownership (%)	69	S&P Credit Rating	A

Price Performance

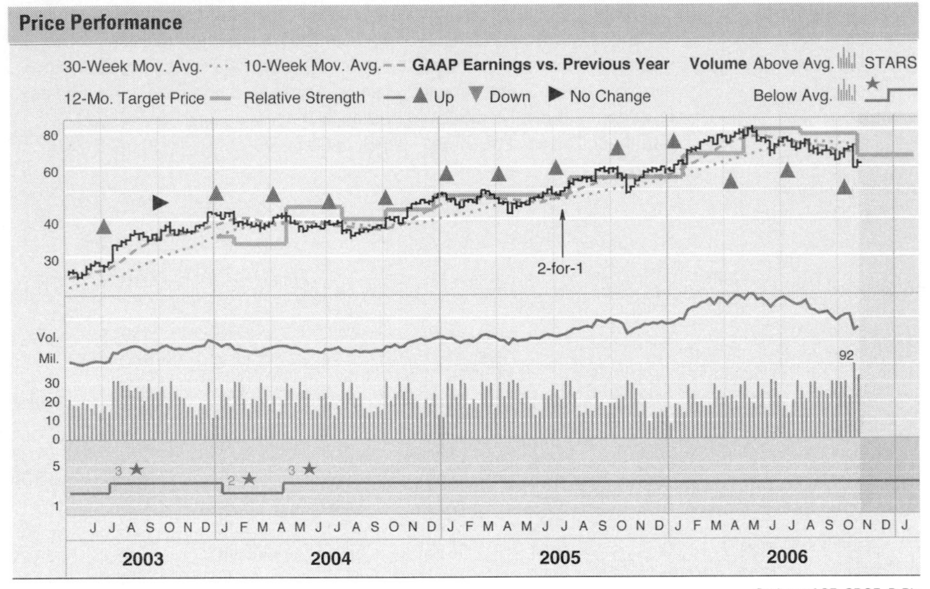

Options: ASE, CBOE, P, Ph

Analysis prepared by **Anthony M. Fiore, CFA** on October 24, 2006, when the stock traded at **$ 61.02**.

Highlights

- We expect net sales of machinery and engines to rise about 4% in 2007, following a projected advance of 13% in 2006. We expect sales to modestly underperform end-market demand in 2007 on an anticipated reduction in dealer inventories. We see a continued build-out of infrastructure in developing countries, combined with expected strength in mining, and oil exploration and production more than offsetting a projected downturn in heavy-truck engine production and U.S. residential construction activity. We also believe sales should benefit from previously announced price increases of CAT products.

- We expect operating margins to remain about flat in 2007, as we expect a combination of improved price realization and benefits from cost control efforts to be mostly offset by higher raw material costs and certain supply chain constraints.

- We regard the quality of earnings as high versus peers, with only a minimal difference between our 2007 Standard & Poor's Core EPS estimate and our operating EPS forecast. Our 2006 and 2007 operating EPS estimates each include $0.20 of projected stock option expense.

Investment Rationale/Risk

- While we expect favorable end market conditions to continue over the next 12 months, we believe that our outlook is largely reflected in the price of the stock. As in prior industry cycles, we expect the stock to trade at lower multiples during peak or near-peak EPS years.

- Risks to our opinion and target price include slower than expected economic growth and/or industrial production; a downturn in the nonresidential construction, trucking, power and/or mining end markets; delays in legislation needed to fund public construction; continued escalation of raw material costs; and further supply constraints.

- Our discounted cash flow model, which assumes a 7.5% average annual free cash flow (operating cash flow less net capital expenditures) growth rate over the next 10 years, 3.5% growth in perpetuity, and a 9% weighted average cost of capital, indicates intrinsic value of about $64. In terms of relative valuation, applying a target P/E multiple of 12X, in line with historical norms, to our 2007 EPS estimate of $5.50 suggests a value of $66. Our 12-month target price of $65 is based on a weighted blend of these two methodologies.

Qualitative Risk Assessment

LOW | **MEDIUM** | HIGH

Our risk assessment for Caterpillar reflects its leading position in many of the end markets it serves and our positive outlook for improving nonresidential construction activity, offset by the highly cyclical nature of the construction equipment and engine businesses.

Quantitative Evaluations

S&P Quality Ranking B+

D | C | B- | B | **B+** | A- | A | A+

Relative Strength Rank WEAK

11

LOWEST = 1 HIGHEST = 99

Revenue/Earnings Data

Revenue (Million $)

	1Q	2Q	3Q	4Q	Year
2006	9,392	10,605	10,517	--	--
2005	8,339	9,360	8,977	9,663	36,339
2004	6,467	7,564	7,649	8,571	30,251
2003	4,821	5,932	5,545	6,465	22,763
2002	4,409	5,291	5,075	5,377	20,152
2001	4,810	5,488	5,056	5,096	20,450

Earnings Per Share ($)

2006	1.20	1.52	1.14	**E**1.32	**E**5.18
2005	0.81	1.08	0.94	1.20	4.04
2004	0.60	0.80	0.71	0.78	2.88
2003	0.19	0.58	0.31	0.49	1.57
2002	0.12	0.29	0.31	0.44	1.15
2001	0.24	0.39	0.29	0.24	1.16

Fiscal year ended Dec. 31. Next earnings report expected: NA. EPS Estimates based on S&P Operating Earnings; historical GAAP earnings are as reported.

Dividend Data (Dates: mm/dd Payment Date: mm/dd/yy)

Amount ($)	Date Decl.	Ex-Div. Date	Stk. of Record	Payment Date
0.250	12/14	01/18	01/20	02/18/06
0.250	04/12	04/20	04/24	05/20/06
0.300	06/14	07/18	07/20	08/19/06
0.300	10/11	10/19	10/23	11/20/06

Dividends have been paid since 1914. Source: Company reports.

Caterpillar Inc

Business Summary October 24, 2006

CORPORATE OVERVIEW. Caterpillar's distinctive yellow machines are in service in nearly every country in the world; roughly half of the company's revenues are derived from outside of North America. About 70% of CAT's 220 independent dealers are located outside the U.S.

CAT's largest operating segment, the Machinery unit (63% of revenues in 2005 and 11% operating margin), makes the company's well known earthmoving equipment. Machinery's end-markets include heavy construction, general construction, and mining quarry and aggregate, industrial, waste, forestry and agriculture. End markets are very cyclical and competitive; demand for CAT's earthmoving equipment is driven by many volatile factors, including the health of global economies, commodity prices, and interest rates, in our view. Principal competitors include Japan's Komatsu Ltd.; CNH Global NV (Case and NewHolland brands); Deere & Co.; and Sweden's Volvo.

For decades, the Engine segment (30% and 10%) made diesel engines solely for CAT's own earthmoving equipment. Currently, however, Engine derives about 90% of sales from third-party customers, such as Paccar, Inc., the maker of well known Kenworth and Peterbilt brand tractor/trailer trucks. Engine's major end markets are electric power generation, on-highway truck, oil and gas, industrial/OEM and marine. In recent years, sales of on-highway engines have benefited from a replacement cycle that has historically averaged about three to five years. We expect industry sales of on-highway engines to peak in 2006 before falling sharply in 2007. CAT, Cummins Inc., and DaimlerChrysler's Detroit Diesel division each account for about 30% of the world diesel engine market.

The Financial Products segment (7% and 23%) primarily provides equipment financing to CAT dealers and customers. Financing plans include operating and finance leases, installment sales contracts, working capital loans and wholesale financing plans. At December 31, 2005, total long-term finance related receivables and long-term finance related debt stood at $10.3 billion and $13.0 billion, respectively.

Company Financials

Per Share Data ($) Year Ended Dec. 31	**2005**	**2004**	**2003**	**2002**	**2001**	**2000**	**1999**	**1998**	**1997**	**1996**
Tangible Book Value	9.77	8.34	6.48	5.51	5.75	5.97	5.56	5.45	6.05	5.10
Cash Flow	6.14	4.85	3.48	2.91	2.85	2.97	2.63	3.23	3.16	2.64
Earnings	4.04	2.88	1.57	1.15	1.16	1.51	1.32	2.06	2.19	1.77
S&P Core Earnings	4.05	2.76	1.50	0.20	0.16	NA	NA	NA	NA	NA
Dividends	0.91	0.78	0.71	0.70	0.69	0.67	0.63	0.55	0.45	0.38
Payout Ratio	23%	27%	45%	61%	59%	44%	48%	27%	21%	21%
Prices:High	59.88	49.36	42.48	30.00	28.42	27.56	33.22	30.38	30.81	20.25
Prices:Low	41.31	34.25	20.62	16.88	19.88	14.78	21.00	19.53	18.13	13.50
P/E Ratio:High	15	17	27	26	24	18	25	15	14	11
P/E Ratio:Low	10	12	13	15	17	10	16	10	8	8
Income Statement Analysis (Million $)										
Revenue	36,339	30,251	22,763	20,152	20,450	20,175	19,702	20,977	18,925	16,522
Operating Income	6,029	4,650	3,505	3,060	3,137	3,447	2,999	3,607	3,529	2,983
Depreciation	1,477	1,397	1,347	1,220	1,169	1,022	945	865	738	696
Interest Expense	1,028	750	716	800	942	980	829	753	580	510
Pretax Income	3,974	2,766	1,497	1,110	1,172	1,500	1,401	2,178	2,461	1,974
Effective Tax Rate	28.2%	26.4%	26.6%	28.1%	31.3%	29.8%	32.5%	30.5%	32.3%	31.5%
Net Income	2,854	2,035	1,099	798	805	1,053	946	1,513	1,665	1,361
S&P Core Earnings	2,860	1,951	1,052	133	98.7	NA	NA	NA	NA	NA
Balance Sheet & Other Financial Data (Million $)										
Cash	1,108	445	342	309	400	334	548	360	292	487
Current Assets	22,790	20,856	16,791	14,628	13,400	12,521	11,734	11,459	9,814	8,783
Total Assets	47,069	43,091	36,465	32,851	30,657	28,464	26,635	25,128	20,756	18,728
Current Liabilities	19,092	16,210	12,621	11,344	10,276	8,568	8,178	7,945	6,379	7,013
Long Term Debt	15,677	15,837	14,078	11,596	11,291	11,334	9,928	9,404	6,942	4,532
Common Equity	8,432	7,467	6,078	5,472	5,611	5,600	5,465	5,131	4,679	4,116
Total Capital	24,109	23,304	20,156	17,068	16,902	16,934	15,393	14,535	11,621	8,648
Capital Expenditures	2,415	2,114	1,765	1,773	1,968	1,388	1,280	1,269	1,106	771
Cash Flow	4,331	3,432	2,446	2,018	1,974	2,075	1,891	2,378	2,403	2,057
Current Ratio	1.2	1.3	1.3	1.3	1.3	1.5	1.4	1.4	1.5	1.3
% Long Term Debt of Capitalization	65.0	68.0	69.8	67.9	66.8	66.9	64.5	64.7	59.7	52.4
% Net Income of Revenue	7.9	6.7	4.8	4.0	3.9	5.2	4.8	7.2	8.8	8.2
% Return on Assets	6.3	5.1	3.2	2.5	2.7	3.8	3.7	6.6	8.4	7.7
% Return on Equity	35.9	30.0	19.0	14.4	14.4	19.0	17.9	30.8	37.9	36.3

Data as orig reptd.; bef. results of disc opers/spec. items. Per share data adj. for stk. divs.; EPS diluted. E-Estimated. NA-Not Available. NM-Not Meaningful. NR-Not Ranked. UR-Under Review.

Office: 100 N.E. Adams Street, Peoria, IL 61629.
Telephone: 309-675-1000.
Email: catir@cat.com
Website: http://www.cat.com

Chrmn & CEO: J.W. Owens
VP & CFO: D.B. Burritt
VP, Secy & General Counsel: J.B. Buda
Treas: K.E. Colgan

Investor Contact: M. DeWalt (309-675-4549)
Board of Directors: W. F. Blount, J. R. Brazil, J. T. Dillon, E. V. Fife, G. D. Fosler, J. Gallardo, D. R. Goode, P. A. Magowan, W. A. Osborn, J. W. Owens, C. D. Powell, E. B. Rust, Jr., J. I. Smith

Auditor: PricewaterhouseCoopers
Founded: 1925
Domicile: Delaware
Employees: 85,116

STANDARD &POOR'S

CBS Corp

S&P Recommendation HOLD ★★★★★

Price $28.97 (as of Oct 27, 2006)

12-Mo. Target Price $30.00

Investment Style Large-Cap Value

GICS Sector Consumer Discretionary
Sub-Industry Broadcasting & Cable TV

Comment This major operator of TV, radio and outdoor advertising properties is one of the two companies recently created after the separation of the "old" Viacom into two public entities.

Key Stock Statistics (Source S&P, Vickers, company reports)

52-Wk Range	**$70.40–23.85**	S&P Oper. EPS 2006**E**	**1.64**	P/E on S&P Oper. EPS 2006**E**	**17.7**	Dividend Rate/Share	**$0.80**
Trailing 12-Month EPS	**$-4.83**	S&P Oper. EPS 2007**E**	**1.72**	Common Shares Outstg. (M)	**780.6**	Yield (%)	**2.76**
Trailing 12-Month P/E	**NM**	S&P Core EPS 2006E	**1.64**	Market Capitalization(B)	**$20.792**	Beta	**0.93**
$10K Invested 5 Yrs Ago	**NA**	S&P Core EPS 2007E	**1.72**	Institutional Ownership (%)	**77**	S&P Credit Rating	**BBB**

Price Performance

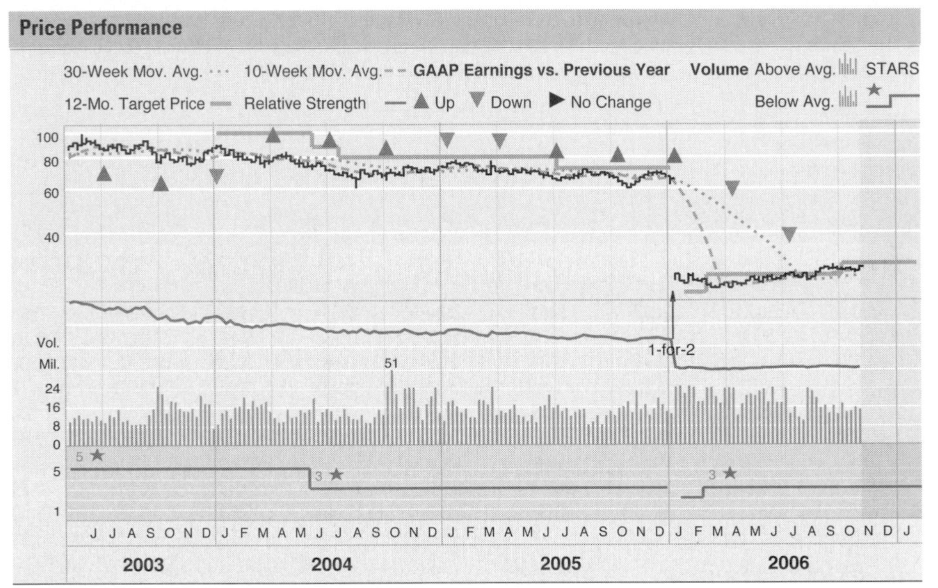

Options: ASE, CBOE, P

Analysis prepared by **Tuna N. Amobi, CFA, CPA** on September 29, 2006, when the stock traded at **$ 28.15**.

Highlights

- For the company as presently constituted (excluding parks), we estimate that total revenues will rise 2.5% in 2006, reflecting strength in the outdoor division (constant dollars) and modest growth in the TV segment (with incremental political advertising), partly offset by a sharp decline in the radio business. In 2007, we see 4.7% total revenue growth, with radio up modestly and relatively stronger TV gains (with the Super Bowl on CBS) and continued relatively strong growth for the outdoor unit.
- We expect 2006 results to reflect a significant margin contraction in the radio division, as well as various new media investments that should continue into 2007. However, we see radio margins improving in 2007, and results should further benefit from the expiration of certain unprofitable outdoor contracts.
- We estimate total EBITDA of about $3.06 billion in 2006, and $3.2 billion in 2007. With higher interest costs, and relatively high effective taxes, we forecast EPS of $1.64 and $1.72 in the respective years (including about $0.07 of option expense).

Investment Rationale/Risk

- Our hold opinion reflects a soft radio and TV ad environment, which was reflected in 2006 second quarter results. We also see radio adversely affected by the loss of Howard Stern in several top markets and, despite strong CBS ratings, we note relatively soft 2006-07 upfront and current scatter advertising markets. We are cautious on the new CW network joint venture, but encouraged by improved operating leverage at the outdoor unit, and by certain restructuring steps completed by the radio division in the third quarter. We also see solid cash reserves leading to a possible dividend increase.
- Risks to our recommendation and target price include relatively high advertising exposure (about 70% of total revenues), continued challenges for the radio division, and uncertainties regarding a dividend increase or other use of growing free cash flow.
- We expect CBS to generate about $1.5 billion of free cash flow in 2006 and 2007. Our 12-month target price of $30 reflects what we view as an ample 2X forward P/E-to-growth ratio (or 15.5X 2006 free cash flow) relative to the peer group's average of 1.6X.

Qualitative Risk Assessment

LOW	**MEDIUM**	HIGH

Our risk assessment reflects CBS's leading TV and outdoor properties, the company's strong balance sheet and free cash flow generation, offset by continued challenges in the radio business and a soft advertising market.

Quantitative Evaluations

S&P Quality Ranking B-

D	C	**B-**	B	B+	A-	A	A+

Relative Strength Rank MODERATE

54

LOWEST = 1 HIGHEST = 99

Revenue/Earnings Data

Revenue (Million $)

	1Q	2Q	3Q	4Q	Year
2006	3,582	3,483	--	--	--
2005	5,577	5,876	5,943	3,828	14,536
2004	6,772	6,842	5,485	6,296	22,526
2003	6,051	6,418	6,600	7,516	26,585
2002	5,672	5,850	6,307	6,778	24,606
2001	5,752	5,717	5,714	6,040	23,223

Earnings Per Share ($)

2006	0.30	0.64	**E**0.41	**E**0.44	**E**1.64
2005	0.72	0.94	0.94	-6.07	-5.27
2004	0.82	0.86	0.84	-20.42	-17.56
2003	0.52	0.74	0.80	-0.44	1.62
2002	0.42	0.62	0.72	0.72	2.48
2001	Nil	0.02	-0.22	-0.04	-0.26

Fiscal year ended Dec. 31. Next earnings report expected: Early November. EPS Estimates based on S&P Operating Earnings; historical GAAP earnings are as reported.

Dividend Data (Dates: mm/dd Payment Date: mm/dd/yy)

Amount ($)	Date Decl.	Ex-Div. Date	Stk. of Record	Payment Date
0.160	01/30	02/24	02/28	04/01/06
0.180	05/25	06/01	06/05	07/01/06
0.200	08/14	08/29	08/31	10/01/06
0.200	10/19	11/28	11/30	01/01/07

Dividends have been paid since 2003. Source: Company reports.

Please read the Required Disclosures and Analyst Certification on the last page of this report.

CBS Corp

Business Summary September 29, 2006

CORPORATE OVERVIEW. In its current form, the company is one of the two independent public entities created after the early 2006 separation of the "old" Viacom (which was renamed CBS Corp., while the other entity adopted the "Viacom" name). Pursuant to the separation, each Class A and B shareholder of the "old" Viacom received 0.5 of a share of corresponding A or B stock of each of the new entities. We believe that CBS Corp. was the lower-growth entity resulting from the separation, and that it was targeted to value-oriented investors. Nearly 70% of its revenues are generated from advertising-related businesses.

The television segment includes the CBS and UPN broadcast networks, CW network (a new joint venture with Time Warner's WB), 39 owned and operated (O&O) TV stations, Showtime cable networks and Paramount/King World TV production and syndication. The radio division, CBS Radio, operates 178 radio stations in 40 U.S. markets (and owns interests of 18% in Westwood One and 10% in Spanish Broadcasting). The outdoor unit, Viacom Outdoor, operates billboards and out-of-home displays in the U.S. and abroad. The Publishing segment mainly includes book publishers Simon & Schuster. In 2006, the company sold its Paramount Parks for $1.24 billion in cash.

CORPORATE STRATEGY. Increasingly, the company plans to leverage its TV (entertainment and news) franchises across both traditional and emerging platforms. Recent announcements include several deals with Internet, technology and cable companies to offer CBS's prime-time shows for on-demand and mobile users. The company recently launched CBSNews.com, broadband channels (Inner Tube and Showbiz), and for the first time in March 2006, streamed its NCAA sports event on the CBS site. CEO Moonves recently estimated potential revenue upside for the various new media initiatives in the tens of millions of dollars over the next few years.

Company Financials

Per Share Data ($) Year Ended Dec. 31	**2005**	**2004**	**2003**	**2002**	**2001**	**2000**	**1999**	**1998**	**1997**	**1996**
Tangible Book Value	NM	NM	NM	NM	NM	NM	NM	NM	NM	NM
Cash Flow	-9.91	-16.62	2.77	3.55	3.31	3.04	3.43	1.90	3.55	2.53
Earnings	-5.27	-17.56	1.62	2.48	-0.26	-0.60	1.02	-0.20	0.89	0.30
S&P Core Earnings	1.10	2.92	2.40	2.08	-0.76	NA	NA	NA	NA	NA
Dividends	0.56	0.50	0.24	Nil	Nil	Nil	Nil	Nil	Nil	Nil
Payout Ratio	NM	NM	15%	Nil	Nil	Nil	Nil	Nil	Nil	Nil
Prices:High	77.98	90.10	99.50	103.78	119.00	151.75	120.87	74.25	42.25	47.63
Prices:Low	59.86	60.18	66.22	59.50	56.50	88.63	70.75	40.50	25.25	29.75
P/E Ratio:High	NM	NM	61	42	NM	NM	NM	NM	47	NM
P/E Ratio:Low	NM	NM	41	24	NM	NM	NM	NM	28	NM

Income Statement Analysis (Million $)										
Revenue	14,536	22,526	26,585	24,606	23,223	20,044	12,859	12,096	13,206	12,084
Operating Income	3,165	5,838	5,957	5,542	4,667	4,243	2,102	1,529	1,696	2,181
Depreciation	499	810	1,000	946	3,087	2,224	845	777	943	818
Interest Expense	720	719	776	848	963	822	449	622	782	832
Pretax Income	-7,513	-13,676	2,861	3,695	656	436	783	96.0	1,060	468
Effective Tax Rate	NM	NM	55.9%	39.2%	NM	NM	52.5%	145.0%	65.1%	63.2%
Net Income	-8,322	-15,060	1,435	2,207	-220	-364	372	-44.0	375	171
S&P Core Earnings	871	2,497	2,087	1,845	-656	NA	NA	NA	NA	NA

Balance Sheet & Other Financial Data (Million $)										
Cash	1,655	928	851	631	727	934	681	267	292	209
Current Assets	6,796	7,494	7,736	7,167	7,206	7,832	5,198	5,065	5,714	5,718
Total Assets	43,030	68,002	89,849	89,754	90,810	82,646	24,486	23,613	28,289	28,834
Current Liabilities	5,379	6,880	7,585	7,341	7,562	7,758	4,400	5,633	5,053	4,269
Long Term Debt	7,153	9,649	9,683	10,205	10,824	12,474	Nil	3,813	7,423	9,856
Common Equity	21,737	59,862	63,205	62,488	62,717	47,967	11,132	11,450	12,184	11,394
Total Capital	31,007	70,879	73,812	74,337	75,884	67,481	12,379	15,863	19,607	22,450
Capital Expenditures	376	415	534	537	515	659	706	604	530	599
Cash Flow	-7,823	-14,250	2,435	3,152	2,867	1,860	1,216	676	1,318	929
Current Ratio	1.3	1.1	1.0	1.0	1.0	1.0	1.2	0.9	1.1	1.3
% Long Term Debt of Capitalization	23.1	13.6	13.1	13.7	14.3	18.5	Nil	24.0	37.8	43.9
% Net Income of Revenue	NM	NM	5.4	9.0	NM	NM	2.9	NM	2.8	1.4
% Return on Assets	NM	NM	1.6	2.4	NM	NM	1.5	NM	1.3	0.6
% Return on Equity	NM	NM	2.3	3.5	NM	NM	3.3	NM	2.7	0.9

Data as orig reptd.; bef. results of disc opers/spec. items. Per share data adj. for stk. divs.; EPS diluted. Data as orig reptd., for "old" Viacom through third qtr 2005. E-Estimated. NA-Not Available. NM-Not Meaningful. NR-Not Ranked. UR-Under Review.

Office: 51 W 52nd St, New York, NY 10019-6188.
Telephone: 212-975-4321.
Website: http://www.cbscorporation.com
Chrmn: S.M. Redstone

Pres & CEO: L. Moonves
EVP & CFO: F.G. Reynolds
EVP & General Counsel: L.J. Briskman
Investor Contact: M.M. Shea

Founded: 1986
Domicile: Delaware
Employees: 32,160

STANDARD &POOR'S

CenterPoint Energy Inc.

S&P Recommendation HOLD ★★★★★

Price $15.41 (as of Oct 27, 2006)

12-Mo. Target Price $14.00

Investment Style Mid-Cap Value

GICS Sector Utilities
Sub-Industry Multi-Utilities

Comment This Houston-based energy company (formerly Reliant Energy) is one of the largest electric and natural gas delivery companies in the U.S.

Key Stock Statistics (Source S&P, Vickers, company reports)

52-Wk Range	$15.70–11.62	S&P Oper. EPS 2006E	1.00	P/E on S&P Oper. EPS 2006E	15.4	Dividend Rate/Share	$0.60
Trailing 12-Month EPS	$1.28	S&P Oper. EPS 2007E	1.00	Common Shares Outstg. (M)	311.8	Yield (%)	3.89
Trailing 12-Month P/E	12.0	S&P Core EPS 2006E	0.98	Market Capitalization(B)	$4.804	Beta	1.08
$10K Invested 5 Yrs Ago	$8,453	S&P Core EPS 2007E	0.98	Institutional Ownership (%)	70	S&P Credit Rating	BBB

Price Performance

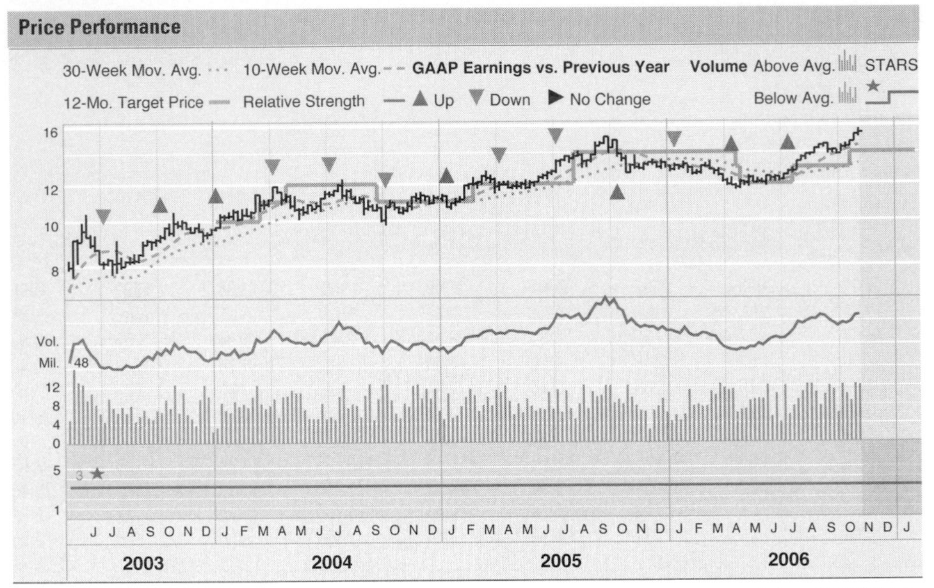

Options: ASE, CBOE, P, Ph

Analysis prepared by **Justin McCann** on October 09, 2006, when the stock traded at **$ 14.40**.

Highlights

- Aided by a sharp reduction in interest and other finance charges, we expect operating EPS in 2006 to advance to $1.00, up from 2005's EPS from continuing operations of $0.67. The company reported operating EPS of $0.58 in the first half of 2006, which excludes net EPS of $0.31 from one-time items. For 2007, we expect CNP's operating EPS to remain essentially flat with anticipated results in 2006.
- Minnesota Gas filed a request for an annual rate increase of $41 million with the state's utilities commission last November. A decision is expected in the fourth quarter of 2006, but the utility was authorized, effective January 1, 2006, to charge an interim rate increase equivalent to an annual increase of $35 million. Any excess between the interim rate and the final rate would be refunded to customers.
- On June 1, 2006, the gas transmission units of CNP and Duke Energy signed a memorandum of understanding to jointly develop a proposed pipeline that could stretch from Texas to Pennsylvania. Should the companies commit themselves to the project, they believe it would be ready for service by the fourth quarter of 2008.

Investment Rationale/Risk

- We would hold the shares on a total return basis. While the stock had traded at a significant premium to its peers' P/E multiple on its 2005 earnings, it has recently been trading at a discount to its peers' P/E on our EPS estimates for 2006 and 2007. We think investors had been looking past the modest earnings advance in 2005 to what we view as a marked improvement in CNP's financial strength and EPS outlook for 2006; however, essentially flat results are expected for 2007.
- Risks to our investment recommendation and target price include the impact that would likely result from a potential decline in its credit ratings, including the difficulty in accessing capital markets on reasonable terms; as well as a sharp drop in the average P/E multiple of the stock's industry peers.
- We expect CNP to use the bulk of the proceeds received from its "true-up" recovery to reduce its debt, which, at the end of 2005 was $8.57 billion. With our view that CNP will emerge from this transitional period financially stronger, we see the stock trading at a modest discount to its peers' P/E of about 14X our EPS estimate for 2007. Our 12-month target price is $14.

Qualitative Risk Assessment

LOW | MEDIUM | HIGH

Our risk assessment reflects the strong and steady cash flow that we expect from the Houston electric operations, which have a growing service territory; a low commodity risk profile; a generally supportive regulatory environment; and the gas purchase adjustment clauses that reduce the commodity risks related to the company's more diversified gas distribution operations.

Quantitative Evaluations

S&P Quality Ranking B

D | C | B- | **B** | B+ | A- | A | A+

Relative Strength Rank STRONG

79

LOWEST = 1 HIGHEST = 99

Revenue/Earnings Data

Revenue (Million $)

	1Q	2Q	3Q	4Q	Year
2006	3,077	1,843	--	--	--
2005	2,762	1,932	2,073	3,212	9,722
2004	2,959	2,241	1,667	2,618	8,510
2003	2,900	2,090	2,250	2,519	9,760
2002	2,078	1,804	1,923	2,117	7,923
2001	13,284	11,991	12,511	8,440	46,226

Earnings Per Share ($)

	1Q	2Q	3Q	4Q	Year
2006	0.28	0.61	E0.20	E0.22	E1.00
2005	0.20	0.09	0.15	0.25	0.67
2004	0.24	0.19	0.05	0.46	0.61
2003	0.27	0.27	0.60	0.23	1.37
2002	0.49	0.29	0.54	-0.03	1.29
2001	0.69	1.08	1.21	0.16	3.14

Fiscal year ended Dec. 31. Next earnings report expected: Early November. EPS Estimates based on S&P Operating Earnings; historical GAAP earnings are as reported.

Dividend Data (Dates: mm/dd Payment Date: mm/dd/yy)

Amount ($)	Date Decl.	Ex-Div. Date	Stk. of Record	Payment Date
0.150	01/26	02/14	02/16	03/10/06
0.150	04/28	05/12	05/16	06/09/06
0.150	07/27	08/14	08/16	09/08/06
0.150	10/26	11/14	11/16	12/08/06

Dividends have been paid since 1922. Source: Company reports.

CenterPoint Energy Inc.

Business Summary October 09, 2006

CORPORATE OVERVIEW. CenterPoint Energy (formerly Reliant Energy) is a Houston-based energy delivery company with operations that include electric transmission and distribution, natural gas distribution, and interstate natural gas pipelines and a gas gathering company.

MARKET PROFILE. The CenterPoint Energy Houston Electric (CEHE) utility serves approximately 1.9 million customers in a 5,000 square mile territory that includes the cities of Houston and Galveston, TX, and (with the exception of Texas City), nearly all of the Houston/Galveston metropolitan area. Following the deregulation of the industry in Texas, wholesale and retail suppliers pay the company to deliver the electricity over its transmission lines. The natural gas subsidiary, CenterPoint Energy Resources Corp. (CERC), serves about 3.1 million customers in six states, through two unincorporated divisions: Minnesota Gas and Southern Gas Operations. Minnesota Gas serves about 780,000 customers in Minneapolis and other communities in Minnesota, with residential customers accounting for 44% of total volume in 2005, and commercial and industrial customers 56%; Southern Gas Operations distributes natural gas to approximately 2.3 million customers in Arkansas, Louisiana, Mississippi, Oklahoma and Texas (with Houston being the largest metropolitan area), with residential customers accounting for 42% of total volume in 2005, and commercial and industrial customers 58%.

CNP operates two interstate natural gas pipelines: CenterPoint Energy-Mississippi River Transmission Corp. and CenterPoint Energy Gas Transmission Co. With over 8,200 miles of pipe, they combine into one of the largest interstate pipelines in the mid-continent U.S. CNP's gas gathering company, CenterPoint Energy Field Services, operates 4,300 miles of gathering pipelines, and about 200 natural gas gathering systems in Arkansas, Oklahoma, Louisiana, and Texas.

Company Financials

Per Share Data ($) Year Ended Dec. 31	**2005**	**2004**	**2003**	**2002**	**2001**	**2000**	**1999**	**1998**	**1997**	**1996**
Tangible Book Value	NM	NM	NM	NM	13.05	8.11	7.69	6.77	9.01	14.88
Earnings	0.67	0.61	1.37	1.29	3.14	2.68	5.82	-0.50	1.66	1.66
S&P Core Earnings	0.75	0.65	1.28	2.17	3.00	NA	NA	NA	NA	NA
Dividends	0.40	0.40	0.40	1.07	1.50	1.50	1.50	1.50	1.50	1.50
Payout Ratio	60%	66%	29%	83%	48%	56%	26%	NM	90%	90%
Prices:High	15.14	12.32	10.49	27.10	50.45	49.00	32.50	33.38	27.25	25.63
Prices:Low	10.55	9.66	4.35	4.24	23.27	19.75	22.75	25.00	18.88	20.50
P/E Ratio:High	23	20	8	21	16	18	6	NM	16	15
P/E Ratio:Low	16	16	3	3	7	7	4	NM	11	12

Income Statement Analysis (Million $)										
Revenue	16,231	8,510	9,760	7,923	46,226	29,339	15,303	11,488	6,873	4,095
Depreciation	541	490	625	616	911	906	911	857	652	550
Maintenance	NA	NA	NA	NA	NA	NA	NA	NA	NA	NA
Fixed Charges Coverage	1.35	1.15	1.37	1.80	3.33	2.60	2.32	1.64	2.56	3.31
Construction Credits	NA	NA	NA	NA	NA	NA	Nil	4.00	3.00	6.72
Effective Tax Rate	40.5%	NM	35.6%	35.0%	33.3%	32.9%	35.0%	NM	32.9%	33.1%
Net Income	225	206	420	386	919	771	1,666	-141	421	405
S&P Core Earnings	254	224	390	642	868	NA	NA	NA	NA	NA

Balance Sheet & Other Financial Data (Million $)										
Gross Property	11,558	10,963	11,812	11,409	24,214	15,260	20,133	17,030	16,039	13,015
Capital Expenditures	693	530	648	854	2,053	1,842	1,179	743	329	318
Net Property	8,492	8,186	11,812	11,409	15,857	15,260	13,267	11,531	11,269	8,756
Capitalization:Long Term Debt	8,568	7,193	10,783	9,194	6,448	5,701	5,666	7,153	5,218	3,026
Capitalization:% Long Term Debt	86.9	86.7	86.0	71.0	48.4	51.0	51.6	62.4	49.8	43.3
Capitalization:Preferred	Nil	Nil	Nil	Nil	Nil	10.0	10.0	10.0	10.0	135
Capitalization:% Preferred	Nil	Nil	Nil	Nil	Nil	0.09	0.09	0.01	0.10	1.40
Capitalization:Common	1,296	1,106	1,761	3,756	6,881	5,472	5,296	4,312	4,887	3,828
Capitalization:% Common	13.1	13.3	14.0	29.0	51.6	48.9	48.3	37.6	46.7	39.8
Total Capital	12,769	10,767	12,934	13,180	16,970	13,998	13,694	14,158	13,619	9,628
% Operating Ratio	15.0	88.2	85.8	85.8	96.6	94.9	97.8	86.9	87.5	80.7
% Earned on Net Property	11.3	10.6	21.8	17.2	12.8	13.2	10.0	13.0	10.6	4.6
% Return on Revenue	1.4	2.4	4.3	4.9	2.0	2.6	10.9	NM	6.1	9.9
% Return on Invested Capital	7.9	7.6	11.1	14.7	11.2	10.3	20.5	16.6	7.9	10.3
% Return on Common Equity	18.7	14.4	26.4	10.3	14.8	14.3	34.7	NM	9.7	10.2

Data as orig reptd.; bef. results of disc opers/spec. items. Per share data adj. for stk. divs.; EPS diluted. E-Estimated. NA-Not Available. NM-Not Meaningful. NR-Not Ranked. UR-Under Review.

Office: 1111 Louisiana Street, Houston, TX 77002-5230.
Telephone: 713-207-1111.
Email: info@reliantenergy.nl
Website: http://www.centerpointenergy.com

Chrmn: M. Carroll
Pres & CEO: D.M. McClanahan
EVP & CFO: G.L. Whitlock
EVP, Secy & General Counsel: S.E. Rozzell

SVP & Chief Acctg Officer: J.S. Brian
Investor Contact: M. Paulsen (713-207-6500)
Board of Directors: D. R. Campbell, M. Carroll, J. T. Cater, D. Cody, O. H. Crosswell, J. M. Longoria, T. F. Madison, D. M. McClanahan, R. T. O'Connell, M. E. Shannon, P. S. Wareing

Founded: 1882
Domicile: Texas
Employees: 9,001

STANDARD &POOR'S

Centex Corp.

S&P Recommendation BUY ★★★★☆

Price $52.51 (as of Oct 27, 2006)

12-Mo. Target Price $59.00

Investment Style Mid-Cap Growth

GICS Sector Consumer Discretionary
Sub-Industry Homebuilding

Comment This major U.S. homebuilder sells homes in 25 states, and also engages in mortgage banking and general construction contracting.

Key Stock Statistics (Source S&P, Vickers, company reports)

52-Wk Range	$79.40–42.90	S&P Oper. EPS 2007E	4.20	P/E on S&P Oper. EPS 2007E	12.5	Dividend Rate/Share	$0.16
Trailing 12-Month EPS	$7.87	S&P Oper. EPS 2008E	3.20	Common Shares Outstg. (M)	118.5	Yield (%)	0.30
Trailing 12-Month P/E	6.7	S&P Core EPS 2007E	4.20	Market Capitalization(B)	$6.224	Beta	1.35
$10K Invested 5 Yrs Ago	$30,341	S&P Core EPS 2008E	3.20	Institutional Ownership (%)	98	S&P Credit Rating	BBB

Price Performance

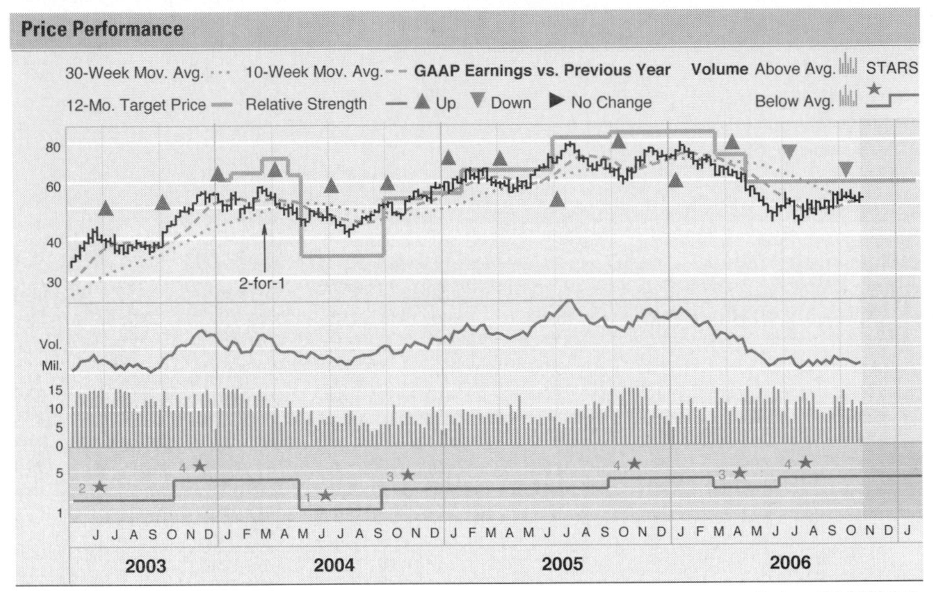

Options: ASE, CBOE, P, Ph

Analysis prepared by **William R. Mack, CFA** on October 16, 2006, when the stock traded at **$ 52.78**.

Highlights

- CTX is aggressively reducing its share count, cautiously managing its land holdings and closely managing its balance sheet. The recent divestiture of Centex Home Equity (CHEQ) should generate about $540 million, which we see mostly being used for further buybacks and debt reduction.
- We think every geographic region is suffering from slower new home demand and, in those markets that had become most frothy, like Phoenix, southwest Florida, and Orange County (CA), we believe demand still remains well short of existing home supply. Further, we see slower sales translating into home price decreases through calendar year end 2006, and additional gross margin diminution in FY 08 (Mar.).
- Management is allowing an increasing number of option contracts for the purchase of land to lapse. Through the first six months of FY 07, we estimate the company has taken close to $200 million in write-downs, option abandonments and other measures aimed at reducing the estimated value of its land. Indeed, we expect more of the same into FY 08.

Investment Rationale/Risk

- Relative to other builders, the company is highly diverse--both in terms of its geographic markets and its business lines. Following the divestiture of Fairclough in FY 06 (Mar.) and CHEQ recently, we expect traditional homebuilding revenues to account for about 85% of the total, less than any builder we cover.
- Risks to our opinion and target price include a significant jump in mortgage rates and weakening job growth. These factors are key demand inputs for the highly cyclical homebuilding industry.
- We arrive at our 12-month target price of $59 by applying a 1.5X multiple to the company's current $41 book value. Given the current lack of predictability in earnings arising from the cycle's recent turn, we think P/E has less validity than price-to-book, which we believe more closely represents intrinsic value. Our $59 target implies a P/E multiple of about 12.7X our FY 07 EPS estimate. Each of these valuations is above peer levels, reflecting our view that the company's balance sheet is the industry's best for large builders.

Qualitative Risk Assessment

LOW	MEDIUM	HIGH

Centex has a relatively low leverage ratio of less than 50% (before proceeds from its Centex Home Equity divestiture), and its debt to total capital has consistently been around this level for the past several years. At less than 6%, its cost of debt is relatively low and, in our view, reflects the company's investment grade balance sheet.

Quantitative Evaluations

S&P Quality Ranking **A+**

D	C	B-	B	B+	A-	A	A+

Relative Strength Rank **MODERATE**

44

LOWEST = 1 HIGHEST = 99

Revenue/Earnings Data

Revenue (Million $)

	1Q	2Q	3Q	4Q	Year
2007	3,273	3,323	--	--	--
2006	3,222	3,630	3,738	4,550	14,400
2005	2,766	2,985	3,119	3,990	12,860
2004	2,173	2,428	2,570	3,193	10,363
2003	1,844	2,084	2,305	2,885	9,117
2002	1,709	1,884	1,894	2,261	7,748

Earnings Per Share ($)

	1Q	2Q	3Q	4Q	Year
2007	1.39	0.70	**E**0.95	**E**1.16	**E**4.20
2006	1.74	2.49	2.52	2.92	9.20
2005	1.35	1.61	1.91	2.75	7.64
2004	1.04	1.56	1.43	2.05	6.01
2003	0.69	0.92	1.25	1.56	4.41
2002	0.61	0.75	0.77	0.93	3.06

Fiscal year ended Mar. 31. Next earnings report expected: Late January. EPS Estimates based on S&P Operating Earnings; historical GAAP earnings are as reported.

Dividend Data (Dates: mm/dd Payment Date: mm/dd/yy)

Amount ($)	Date Decl.	Ex-Div. Date	Stk. of Record	Payment Date
0.040	02/14	02/27	03/01	03/22/06
0.040	05/11	05/25	05/30	06/20/06
0.040	07/13	07/31	08/02	08/23/06
0.040	10/13	10/30	11/01	11/22/06

Dividends have been paid since 1973. Source: Company reports.

Centex Corp.

Business Summary October 16, 2006

CORPORATE OVERVIEW. Centex Corp. constructs site-built homes in 86 markets throughout the U.S. CTX sells homes to first-time and move-up buyers, as well as active adult and second home buyers. It also has operations in various construction and real estate-related businesses.

To reduce exposure to local market volatility, the company built homes in an average of 626 neighborhoods in FY 06 (Mar.), versus 559 in FY 05. CTX delivered 39,232 homes in FY 06, up 17% from the FY 05 level. Sales prices vary widely, with an average of about $304,000 in FY 06 (up 13%). In this past year, 80% of the homes closed were single-family detached homes, which includes homes from resort and second homes, as well as on-your-lot operations.

IMPACT OF MAJOR DEVELOPMENTS. Relative to peers, Centex has historically relied less on acquisitions for its expansion. Its most recent acquisition occurred in January 2003, with the purchase of The Jones Company. Since that time, as the homebuilding up-cycle entered its later stages, the company has become even more cautious about businesses it considers non-core. As a result, Centex has been on the selling end of most strategic activity in the past few years.

In June 2003, CTX spun off its Cavco Industries manufactured home business to shareholders. Likewise, in January 2004, CTX spun off its 65% stake in Centex Construction Products, which was renamed Eagle Materials (EXP).

In September 2005, CTX sold Fairclough Homes, which operates in the United Kingdom, generating cash proceeds of almost $320 million. (In February 2004, CTX acquired the partnership through merger transactions. Prior to the merger, it accounted for its investment in the partnership using the equity method of accounting.) In July 2006, the company sold its sub-prime lending operations for about $540 million, or a slight premium to the unit's book value.

Company Financials

Per Share Data ($) Year Ended Mar. 31	**2006**	**2005**	**2004**	**2003**	**2002**	**2001**	**2000**	**1999**	**1998**	**1997**
Tangible Book Value	44.51	32.97	23.89	19.05	14.49	11.59	10.32	8.77	7.20	6.31
Cash Flow	9.67	8.08	6.79	5.31	3.75	2.65	2.51	2.17	1.39	1.02
Earnings	9.20	7.64	6.01	4.41	3.06	2.33	2.11	1.88	1.18	0.91
S&P Core Earnings	9.20	7.64	5.90	4.25	2.86	2.17	NA	NA	NA	NA
Dividends	0.16	0.14	0.08	0.08	0.08	0.08	0.08	0.08	0.07	0.05
Payout Ratio	2%	2%	1%	2%	3%	3%	4%	4%	6%	6%
Calendar Year	2005	2004	2003	2002	2001	2000	1999	1998	1997	1996
Prices:High	79.66	59.98	56.54	31.55	29.40	20.00	22.88	22.88	16.50	9.44
Prices:Low	54.60	39.94	24.15	19.16	14.02	8.75	11.19	13.19	8.38	6.31
P/E Ratio:High	9	8	9	7	10	9	11	12	14	10
P/E Ratio:Low	6	5	4	4	5	4	5	7	7	7
Income Statement Analysis (Million $)										
Revenue	14,400	12,860	10,363	9,117	7,748	6,711	5,956	5,155	3,975	3,785
Operating Income	1,884	1,583	1,221	1,058	846	608	597	505	334	243
Depreciation	63.1	58.3	102	113	91.0	41.0	49.0	36.2	25.6	13.5
Interest Expense	12.1	22.2	39.9	120	116	99.0	67.0	41.6	33.3	34.1
Pretax Income	1,895	1,574	1,149	825	640	468	481	427	232	164
Effective Tax Rate	35.6%	35.7%	32.4%	29.0%	37.0%	32.9%	33.1%	33.1%	37.5%	34.9%
Net Income	1,221	1,011	777	556	382	282	257	232	145	107
S&P Core Earnings	1,221	1,011	765	536	358	264	NA	NA	NA	NA
Balance Sheet & Other Financial Data (Million $)										
Cash	47.2	503	193	644	326	115	140	111	98.3	31.3
Current Assets	NA	NA	NA	NA	NA	NA	NA	NA	NA	NA
Total Assets	21,365	20,011	16,069	11,611	8,985	6,649	4,039	4,335	3,416	2,679
Current Liabilities	NA	NA	NA	NA	NA	NA	NA	NA	NA	NA
Long Term Debt	6,059	12,968	8,616	6,237	4,944	3,041	751	284	238	237
Common Equity	5,012	4,281	3,050	2,459	2,116	1,714	1,420	1,198	991	836
Total Capital	11,604	17,706	12,002	8,866	7,214	4,899	2,300	1,623	1,464	1,314
Capital Expenditures	92.2	43.3	53.8	63.0	60.0	52.0	88.0	52.5	36.9	16.1
Cash Flow	1,284	1,070	879	669	473	323	306	268	170	120
Current Ratio	NA	NA	NA	NA	NA	NA	NA	NA	NA	NA
% Long Term Debt of Capitalization	52.2	73.2	71.8	70.3	68.5	62.1	32.7	17.5	16.2	18.0
% Net Income of Revenue	8.5	7.9	7.5	6.1	4.9	4.2	4.3	4.5	3.6	2.8
% Return on Assets	5.9	5.6	5.6	5.4	4.9	5.3	6.1	6.0	4.8	4.2
% Return on Equity	26.3	27.6	27.2	24.3	19.9	18.0	19.6	21.2	15.9	13.7

Data as orig reptd.; bef. results of disc opers/spec. items. Per share data adj. for stk. divs.; EPS diluted. E-Estimated. NA-Not Available. NM-Not Meaningful. NR-Not Ranked. UR-Under Review.

Office: 2728 N Harwood St., Dallas, TX, USA 75201-1516.
Telephone: 214-981-5000.
Email: ir@centex.com
Website: http://www.centex.com

Chrmn, Pres & CEO: T.R. Eller
EVP & CFO: C.R. Smith
SVP & General Counsel: B.J. Woram
SVP & Cntlr: M.D. Kemp

Investor Contact: M.G. Moyer (214-981-5000)
Board of Directors: B. T. Alexander, D. W. Cook, III, J. L. Elek, T. R. Eller, U. Fairbairn, T. J. Falk, C. W. Murchison, III, F. M. Poses, J. J. Postl, D. W. Quinn, M. K. Rose, T. M. Schoewe

Founded: 1950
Domicile: Nevada
Employees: 18,544

STANDARD &POOR'S

CenturyTel Inc.

S&P Recommendation BUY ★★★★★

Price $41.34 (as of Oct 30, 2006)

12-Mo. Target Price $45.00

Investment Style Mid-Cap Value

GICS Sector Telecommunication Services
Sub-Industry Integrated Telecommunication Services

Comment This holding company provides a range of telephone services in 22 states, with operations concentrated in Wisconsin, Louisiana, Michigan and Ohio.

Key Stock Statistics (Source S&P, Vickers, company reports)

52-Wk Range	$41.51–31.76	S&P Oper. EPS 2006E	2.46	P/E on S&P Oper. EPS 2006E	16.8	Dividend Rate/Share	$0.25
Trailing 12-Month EPS	$3.06	S&P Oper. EPS 2007E	2.55	Common Shares Outstg. (M)	116.4	Yield (%)	0.60
Trailing 12-Month P/E	13.5	S&P Core EPS 2006E	2.40	Market Capitalization(B)	$4.812	Beta	1.22
$10K Invested 5 Yrs Ago	$13,381	S&P Core EPS 2007E	2.50	Institutional Ownership (%)	88	S&P Credit Rating	BBB

Price Performance

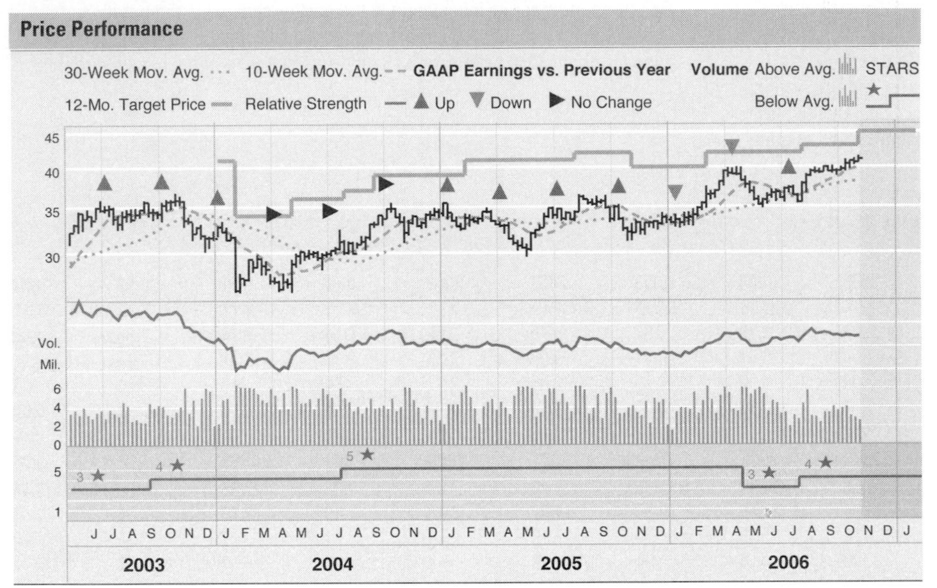

Options: Cycle P, Ph

Analysis prepared by **Todd Rosenbluth** on October 30, 2006, when the stock traded at **$ 41.37**.

Highlights

- We see revenues up fractionally in 2006 and 2007, with increased penetration of DSL, long-distance and enhanced services offsetting an anticipated 4.5% fewer access lines and lower universal funding. We believe CTL's recent access line count reduction is primarily the result of younger customers staying with competitors' wireless service, and note that in the 12 months ended June 2006, CTL has more DSL additions than line losses. We expect wireless and video services to make modest contributions for CTL in 2006.
- Despite strong cost cutting efforts, we look for EBITDA margins, among the industry's best, to narrow in 2006, to about 49%, as benefits from system integrations are counterbalanced by increased selling and marketing costs related to the rollout of new services and the inclusion of stock option expense.
- We project operating EPS of $2.46 in 2006, aided by the repurchase of 10% of the company's shares, and we see $2.55 for 2007. We expect CTL to exceed its third quarter EPS guidance. Our Standard & Poor's Core EPS estimates reflect pension adjustments.

Investment Rationale/Risk

- We believe this rural carrier faces less competitive pressures from wireless and cable carriers than its peers. We view positively CTL's share repurchases, and believe the company remains cautious in its guidance, following strong first half results. We expect CTL to continue to seek to acquire access lines but, in the continued absence of acquisition candidates, will look to further buy back some of its shares.
- Risks to our recommendation and target price include adjustments to the universal service fund or access charges, from which CTL receives revenues, a dilutive acquisition, or an increase in customer migration.
- Even with a smaller dividend payout than rural carrier peers, we believe CTL trades at an unwarranted discount using our enterprise value/EBITDA analysis, given our view of its its stable margins and a balance sheet that is less leveraged than peers. Based on the aforementioned analyses, our 12-month target price is $45, or an enterprise value of 6.5X our 2007 EBITDA projection. CTL has raised its dividend 33 years in a row, but recently yielded only 0.6%.

Qualitative Risk Assessment

LOW	MEDIUM	HIGH

Our risk assessment reflects what we see as CTL's strong balance sheet, the rural nature of most of the company's operations, and the less competitive nature of its markets relative to peers.

Quantitative Evaluations

S&P Quality Ranking A

D	C	B-	B	B+	A-	A	A+

Relative Strength Rank MODERATE

61

LOWEST = 1 HIGHEST = 99

Revenue/Earnings Data

Revenue (Million $)

	1Q	2Q	3Q	4Q	Year
2006	611.7	609.1	--	--	--
2005	595.3	606.4	657.1	620.5	2,479
2004	593.7	603.6	603.9	606.2	2,407
2003	580.5	590.2	603.8	606.3	2,381
2002	422.9	438.7	524.5	585.9	1,972
2001	516.0	367.9	539.4	543.2	2,117

Earnings Per Share ($)

	1Q	2Q	3Q	4Q	Year
2006	0.55	1.26	**E**0.64	**E**0.64	**E**2.46
2005	0.59	0.64	0.68	0.59	2.49
2004	0.58	0.60	0.63	0.62	2.41
2003	0.58	0.60	0.63	0.57	2.38
2002	0.30	0.28	0.45	0.30	1.33
2001	0.33	1.09	0.65	0.35	2.41

Fiscal year ended Dec. 31. Next earnings report expected: NA. EPS Estimates based on S&P Operating Earnings; historical GAAP earnings are as reported.

Dividend Data (Dates: mm/dd Payment Date: mm/dd/yy)

Amount ($)	Date Decl.	Ex-Div. Date	Stk. of Record	Payment Date
0.060	11/17	11/30	12/02	12/16/05
0.063	02/21	03/02	03/06	03/17/06
0.063	05/23	06/01	06/05	06/16/06
0.063	08/22	08/31	09/05	09/15/06

Dividends have been paid since 1974. Source: Company reports.

Please read the Required Disclosures and Analyst Certification on the last page of this report.

CenturyTel Inc.

Business Summary October 30, 2006

CORPORATE OVERVIEW. At June 2006, CTL operated 2.2 million telephone access lines, primarily in rural and suburban areas in 22 states. The company also generated revenues by offering long distance service to more than 1 million customers, as well as by offering DSL broadband to 313,000 customers, plus caller ID and call waiting. In October 2004, CTL completed the installation of a new billing and customer care system. In addition, the company partnered with Echostar Communications to offer wholesale satellite services in CTL's product bundles in late 2005. The company has also begun to offer wholesale wireless services in select markets. Combined, wireless and video services comprised less than 1% of CTL's second quarter revenues, and we believe these services are being currently being offered as a customer retention approach.

COMPETITIVE LANDSCAPE. We believe CTL faces fewer challenges from technology substitution to cable telephony as the penetration of the necessary broadband connection is smaller in the Tier II and Tier III markets in which CTL operates. Furthermore, as of mid-2006, more than 52% of its customers had the choice for cable broadband and 19% had the choice for cable Voice over Internet Protocol (VoIP) telephone service. CTL's local access lines declined 4.6% in the 12 months ended June 2006, partly due to, we think, the displacement of traditional wireline telephone services by other competitive service providers and partly due to fewer customers signing up for new local phone services.

Telecom providers such as BellSouth and Verizon Communications, which serve more metropolitan markets, lost 7% of lines or more in the same period mentioned above. To better compete with broadband cable providers, CTL is testing ADSL2+ technology to offer higher speed data and video services to its customers in addition to its partnership with Echostar Communications.

CORPORATE GOVERNANCE. We have some corporate governance concerns related to CTL's "poison pill" antitakeover provision, which expires in November 2006. However, the board is controlled by a majority of outside directors and many directors own shares of CTL, which we view favorably.

Company Financials

Per Share Data ($) Year Ended Dec. 31	**2005**	**2004**	**2003**	**2002**	**2001**	**2000**	**1999**	**1998**	**1997**	**1996**
Tangible Book Value	1.41	NM	0.37	NM	NM	NM	1.39	NM	NM	3.60
Cash Flow	6.37	5.90	5.63	4.21	5.73	4.36	4.16	2.65	3.02	1.94
Earnings	2.49	2.41	2.38	1.33	2.41	1.63	1.70	1.63	1.87	0.96
S&P Core Earnings	2.30	2.36	2.35	1.08	1.21	NA	NA	NA	NA	NA
Dividends	0.24	0.23	0.22	0.21	0.20	0.19	0.09	0.17	0.16	0.16
Payout Ratio	10%	10%	9%	16%	8%	12%	5%	11%	9%	17%
Prices:High	36.50	35.54	36.76	35.50	39.88	47.31	49.00	45.17	22.42	15.78
Prices:Low	20.66	26.20	25.25	21.10	25.45	24.44	35.19	21.50	12.67	12.67
P/E Ratio:High	15	15	15	27	17	29	29	28	12	17
P/E Ratio:Low	12	11	11	16	11	15	21	13	7	13

Income Statement Analysis (Million $)										
Revenue	2,479	2,407	2,381	1,972	2,117	1,846	1,677	1,577	902	750
Depreciation	532	501	471	412	473	388	349	329	159	132
Maintenance	NA	NA	NA	NA	NA	NA	NA	NA	NA	NA
Construction Credits	NA	NA	NA	NA	NA	NA	NA	NA	NA	NA
Effective Tax Rate	37.0%	38.4%	35.2%	35.3%	37.2%	39.0%	41.5%	39.7%	36.8%	36.6%
Net Income	334	337	345	190	343	231	240	229	256	129
S&P Core Earnings	307	330	339	153	171	NA	NA	NA	NA	NA

Balance Sheet & Other Financial Data (Million $)										
Gross Property	7,801	7,431	3,455	6,668	5,839	5,915	4,194	4,290	3,845	1,686
Net Property	3,304	3,341	3,455	3,532	3,000	2,959	2,256	2,351	2,259	1,149
Capital Expenditures	415	385	378	386	507	450	390	311	181	223
Total Capital	5,993	6,172	6,588	6,666	4,425	5,082	3,926	4,471	4,237	1,802
Fixed Charges Coverage	3.6	3.6	3.4	2.3	3.4	3.2	3.4	2.9	5.3	5.6
Capitalization:Long Term Debt	2,376	2,762	3,109	3,578	2,088	3,050	2,078	2,558	2,610	626
Capitalization:Preferred	Nil	Nil	7.98	7.98	7.98	7.98	7.98	8.11	8.11	10.0
Capitalization:Common	3,617	3,410	3,471	3,080	2,329	2,024	1,840	1,523	1,292	1,018
% Return on Revenue	13.5	14.0	14.5	9.6	16.2	12.5	14.3	14.5	28.4	17.2
% Return on Invested Capital	8.8	8.6	8.6	7.4	12.2	9.4	10.4	14.1	15.8	10.5
% Return on Common Equity	9.5	9.8	10.5	7.0	15.7	12.0	14.2	16.2	22.1	13.5
% Earned on Net Property	38.2	36.9	35.0	31.5	34.6	35.0	37.2	35.1	25.1	13.5
% Long Term Debt of Capitalization	39.6	44.8	47.2	53.7	47.2	60.0	52.9	62.6	61.7	37.8
Capital % Preferred	Nil	Nil	0.1	0.1	0.2	0.2	0.2	0.2	1.9	0.6
Capitalization:% Common	60.4	55.2	52.7	46.2	52.6	39.8	46.9	37.3	30.5	61.6

Data as orig reptd.; bef. results of disc opers/spec. items. Per share data adj. for stk. divs.; EPS diluted. E-Estimated. NA-Not Available. NM-Not Meaningful. NR-Not Ranked. UR-Under Review.

Office: 100 CenturyTel Drive, Monroe, LA 71203.
Telephone: 318-388-9000.
Website: http://www.centurytel.com
Chrmn & CEO: G.F. Post, III

Pres & COO: K.A. Puckett
EVP & CFO: R.S. Ewing, Jr.
SVP, Secy & General Counsel: S.W. Goff
SVP & CIO: M. Maslowski

Investor Contact: T. Davis (318-388-9525)
Auditor: KPMG
Board of Directors: W. R. Boles, Jr., V. Boulet, C. Czeschin, J. B. Gardner, W. B. Hanks, G. J. McCray, C. G. Melville, Jr., F. Nichols, H. P. Perry, G. F. Post, III, J. D. Reppond, J. Zimmel

Founded: 1968
Domicile: Louisiana
Employees: 6,900

STANDARD &POOR'S

Chesapeake Energy Corp

S&P Recommendation STRONG BUY ★★★★★

Price $31.98 (as of Oct 30, 2006)

12-Mo. Target Price $43.00

Investment Style Large-Cap Growth

GICS Sector Energy
Sub-Industry Oil & Gas Exploration & Production

Comment The third largest independent producer of natural gas in the U.S., CHK has operations in the Mid-Continent, Permian Basin, South Texas, Texas Gulf Coast, Barnett Shale, Ark-La-Tex, and Appalachian Basin regions.

Key Stock Statistics (Source S&P, Vickers, company reports)

52-Wk Range	$35.57–26.59	S&P Oper. EPS 2006E	3.61	P/E on S&P Oper. EPS 2006E	8.9	Dividend Rate/Share	$0.24
Trailing 12-Month EPS	$4.59	S&P Oper. EPS 2007E	3.80	Common Shares Outstg. (M)	425.2	Yield (%)	0.75
Trailing 12-Month P/E	7.0	S&P Core EPS 2006E	3.61	Market Capitalization(B)	$13.596	Beta	0.48
$10K Invested 5 Yrs Ago	$45,653	S&P Core EPS 2007E	3.80	Institutional Ownership (%)	59	S&P Credit Rating	BB

Price Performance

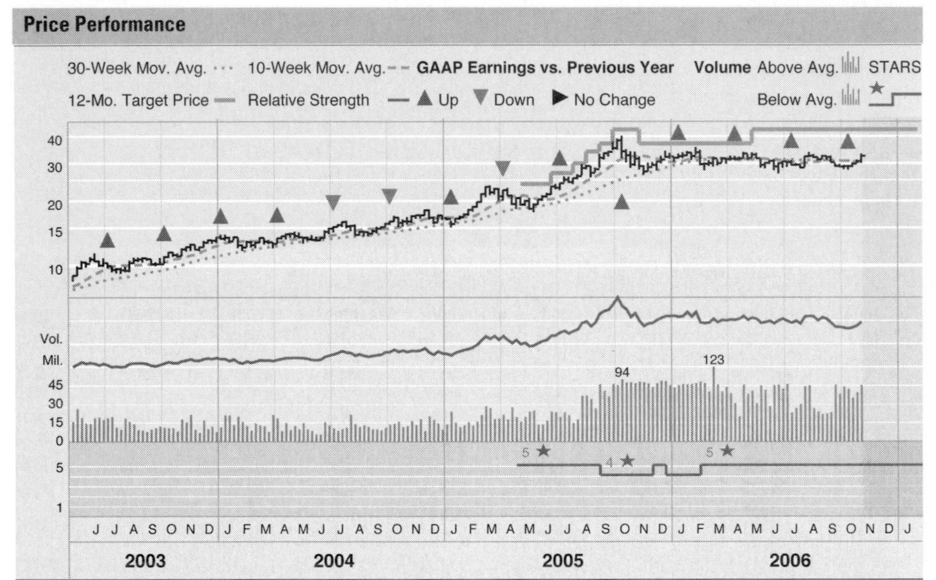

Options: ASE, CBOE, P, Ph

Analysis prepared by **Charles LaPorta, CFA** on September 14, 2006, when the stock traded at **$ 29.17**.

Highlights

- Second quarter operating EPS was $0.82, versus $0.50 last year, above our $0.80 estimate. We expect production volumes to increase about 25% in 2006, reflecting an aggressive drilling program. CHK currently operates 101 rigs and expects to be running 135 rigs by year end.
- We believe cash operating costs will increase over 20% in 2006, due to industrywide service cost inflation. However, CHK has an effective hedge against higher service costs through its ownership of 57 rigs (expected to rise to 79 by the 2007 first quarter), and should be able to benefit from higher rig rates by billing out these services on jointly operated wells.
- Our EBITDAX (EBITDA before exploration expense) estimate for 2006 is $4.7 billion, about an 80% increase over last year. We project that per unit depreciation, depletion and amortization (DD&A) charges will increase about 20%, due to substantial acquisitions last year. We expect CHK's aggressive use of debt to drive interest expense about $90 million higher before the impact of hedging transactions.

Investment Rationale/Risk

- We believe CHK has opportunistically minimized the effect of recent natural gas price declines, as over 90% of its 2006 production and over 72% of its 2007 production has been hedged at $9.17 per Mmbtu and $9.88 per Mmbtu, respectively. CHK currently has a reserve life of about 14 years, and a nine-year drilling inventory.
- Risks to our recommendation and target price include CHK's desire for acquisitions, which could lead to an aggressively priced and financed deal; events that would cause substantial and sustained declines in gas prices; and a persistent inability to replace reserves.
- CHK has demonstrated a consistent ability to economically find and produce primarily natural gas hydrocarbons both organically and via acquisitions. We believe the stock should trade at a premium to other onshore large capitalization producers, given CHK's very attractive production hedges amidst a steep decline in natural gas prices. Our 12-month target price of $43 is based on a P/E of 11.3X our 2007 EPS estimate, and an enterprise value of 4.7X our EBITDAX estimate, both premiums to peers.

Qualitative Risk Assessment

LOW | MEDIUM | **HIGH**

CHK operates in a very capital intensive industry that is cyclical and derives value from producing a commodity whose price is very volatile. Magnifying the inherent risk in this industry, CHK has utilized an aggressive growth through acquisition strategy, and maintains relatively high financial leverage.

Quantitative Evaluations

S&P Quality Ranking B-

D | C | **B-** | B | B+ | A- | A | A+

Relative Strength Rank MODERATE

69

LOWEST = 1 HIGHEST = 99

Revenue/Earnings Data

Revenue (Million $)

	1Q	2Q	3Q	4Q	Year
2006	1,945	1,584	1,929	--	--
2005	783.5	1,048	1,083	1,751	4,665
2004	563.1	574.3	629.8	942.1	2,709
2003	374.4	429.6	454.6	456.7	1,717
2002	89.84	194.3	198.2	255.4	737.8
2001	277.4	275.7	238.9	177.1	969.1

Earnings Per Share ($)

2006	1.44	0.82	1.13	E0.89	E3.61
2005	0.36	0.52	0.43	1.11	2.51
2004	0.38	0.30	0.29	0.52	1.53
2003	0.31	0.31	0.33	0.25	1.20
2002	-0.18	0.13	0.08	0.13	0.17
2001	0.41	0.50	0.38	0.23	1.51

Fiscal year ended Dec. 31. Next earnings report expected: Late February. EPS Estimates based on S&P Operating Earnings; historical GAAP earnings are as reported.

Dividend Data (Dates: mm/dd Payment Date: mm/dd/yy)

Amount ($)	Date Decl.	Ex-Div. Date	Stk. of Record	Payment Date
0.050	12/21	12/28	01/02	01/16/06
0.050	03/06	03/30	04/03	04/17/06
0.060	06/14	06/29	07/03	07/17/06
0.060	09/25	09/28	10/02	10/16/06

Dividends have been paid since 2002. Source: Company reports.

Chesapeake Energy Corp

Business Summary September 14, 2006

CORPORATE OVERVIEW. Chesapeake Energy Corp., the third largest independent producer of natural gas in the U.S., is engaged in exploratory and developmental drilling and producing property acquisitions. The company is focusing on building and developing one of the largest onshore natural gas resource bases in the U.S. Its primary operating area is the Mid-Continent region of the U.S., which includes Oklahoma, Arkansas, Kansas, and the Texas Panhandle. In addition, CHK is building secondary operating areas in South Texas and the Texas Gulf Coast region, the Permian Basin of western Texas and eastern New Mexico, the Barnett Shale area of north-central TX, the Ark-La-Tex Basin of eastern Texas and northern Louisiana, and most recently, the emerging Fayetteville Shale play located in Arkansas. As a result of its recent acquisition of Columbia Natural Resources, CHK has a significant presence in the Appalachian Basin, in West Virginia, eastern Kentucky, eastern Ohio and southern New York.

As of December 31, 2005, CHK had 7.5 Tcfe of proved reserves (92% natural gas, 100% onshore). Total reserve additions in 2005 were internally estimated at 3.088 Tcfe, for a reserve replacement rate of 659% of production. Reserve replacement through the drill bit was 1.047 Tcfe, or 223% of production (including a positive 17 Bcfe for performance revisions and a positive 24 Bcfe from oil and natural gas price increases), and reserve replacement through acquisitions was 2.041 Tcfe, or 436% of production. During 2005 CHK led the nation in drilling activity with an average utilization of 73 operated rigs and 66 non-operated rigs. Through this drilling activity, it drilled 902 (686 net) wells and participated in another 1,066 (130 net) wells operated by other companies. As of December 31, 2005, proved developed reserves were 65% of total proved reserves.

MARKET PROFILE. CHK's addressable market is the North American continent. As a large onshore natural gas producer, CHK competes in a fragmented market that is beginning to rationalize with several large onshore players such as Devon Energy (DVN: strong buy, $66) and XTO Energy (XTO: buy, $41). We believe North America is a relatively mature supply source for hydrocarbons, and natural gas production has been relatively flat over the past seven years. From January 1, 1998 to December 31, 2005, CHK has been one of the most active consolidators of onshore U.S. natural gas assets, having purchased about 5.9 Tcfe of proved reserves, at a total cost of about $10.3 billion for a per proved Bcfe acquisition cost of $1.37.

Company Financials

Per Share Data ($) Year Ended Dec. 31	**2005**	**2004**	**2003**	**2002**	**2001**	**2000**	**1999**	**1998**	**1997**	**1996**
Tangible Book Value	12.42	8.57	5.45	3.99	3.75	2.05	NM	NM	3.77	4.08
Cash Flow	5.05	3.56	2.61	1.54	2.52	3.67	1.30	-8.18	0.43	-1.08
Earnings	2.51	1.53	1.20	0.17	1.51	3.01	0.16	-9.83	-0.45	-3.52
S&P Core Earnings	2.48	1.50	1.19	0.17	1.36	NA	NA	NA	NA	NA
Dividends	0.20	0.17	0.14	0.06	Nil	Nil	Nil	0.06	0.04	0.06
Payout Ratio	8%	11%	11%	35%	Nil	Nil	Nil	NM	NM	NM
Prices:High	40.20	18.31	14.00	8.55	11.06	10.50	4.13	7.75	31.75	31.75
Prices:Low	15.06	11.70	7.27	4.50	4.50	1.94	0.63	0.75	6.31	6.31
P/E Ratio:High	16	12	12	50	7	3	26	NM	NM	NM
P/E Ratio:Low	6	8	6	26	3	1	4	NM	NM	NM
Income Statement Analysis (Million $)										
Revenue	4,665	2,709	1,717	738	969	628	355	378	233	280
Operating Income	1,773	992	675	191	597	384	207	177	158	180
Depreciation, Depletion and Amortization	945	611	386	235	178	105	99.5	152	62.0	106
Interest Expense	220	167	154	111	98.3	86.3	81.1	68.2	29.8	17.5
Pretax Income	1,493	805	501	67.1	438	196	35.0	-921	-31.6	-180
Effective Tax Rate	36.5%	36.0%	38.0%	40.0%	39.9%	NM	5.04%	NM	Nil	NM
Net Income	948	515	311	40.3	263	456	33.3	-921	-31.6	-177
S&P Core Earnings	871	431	283	29.9	235	NA	NA	NA	NA	NA
Balance Sheet & Other Financial Data (Million $)										
Cash	60.0	6.90	40.6	248	125	3.50	38.9	35.3	124	124
Current Assets	1,183	568	342	435	361	167	97.5	118	218	298
Total Assets	16,118	8,245	4,572	2,876	2,287	1,440	851	813	953	949
Current Liabilities	1,964	964	513	266	173	163	88.2	131	153	146
Long Term Debt	5,490	3,075	2,058	1,651	1,329	945	964	919	509	509
Common Equity	4,598	2,672	1,180	758	617	282	-447	-479	280	287
Total Capital	13,469	7,172	3,982	2,559	2,097	1,270	753	671	789	796
Capital Expenditures	484	127	71.5	33.6	24.9	78.9	49.9	271	217	468
Cash Flow	1,851	1,087	674	265	439	556	133	-776	30.5	-71.2
Current Ratio	0.6	0.6	0.7	1.6	2.1	1.0	1.1	0.9	1.4	2.0
% Long Term Debt of Capitalization	40.8	42.9	51.7	64.5	63.4	74.4	128.0	137.1	NM	63.9
% Return on Assets	7.8	8.0	8.3	1.6	14.1	39.8	4.0	NM	NM	NM
% Return on Equity	24.9	24.7	29.7	4.4	58.1	NM	NM	NM	NM	NM

Data as orig reptd.; bef. results of disc opers/spec. items. Per share data adj. for stk. divs.; EPS diluted. E-Estimated. NA-Not Available. NM-Not Meaningful. NR-Not Ranked. UR-Under Review.

Office: 6100 North Western Avenue, Oklahoma City, OK 73118.
Telephone: 405-848-8000.
Website: http://www.chkenergy.com
Chrmn & CEO: A.K. McClendon

COO & EVP: S.C. Dixon
EVP & CFO: M.C. Rowland
SVP & Chief Acctg Officer: M.A. Johnson
SVP & Treas: M.A. Burger

Investor Contact: J.L. Mobley
Board of Directors: R. K. Davidson, F. Keating, B. M. Kerr, C. T. Maxwell, A. K. McClendon, D. Nickles, F. B. Whittemore

Founded: 1991
Domicile: Oklahoma
Employees: 2,885

STANDARD &POOR'S

Chevron Corp

S&P Recommendation STRONG BUY ★★★★★

Price $67.20 (as of Oct 31, 2006)

12-Mo. Target Price $84.00

Investment Style Large-Cap Growth

GICS Sector Energy
Sub-Industry Integrated Oil & Gas

Comment This global integrated oil company (formerly ChevronTexaco) has interests in exploration, production, refining and marketing, and petrochemicals.

Key Stock Statistics (Source S&P, Vickers, company reports)

52-Wk Range	**$68.50–53.76**	S&P Oper. EPS 2006**E**	**8.07**	P/E on S&P Oper. EPS 2006**E**	**8.3**	Dividend Rate/Share	**$2.08**
Trailing 12-Month EPS	**$7.92**	S&P Oper. EPS 2007**E**	**8.34**	Common Shares Outstg. (M)	**2,198.0**	Yield (%)	**3.10**
Trailing 12-Month P/E	**8.5**	S&P Core EPS 2006**E**	**8.02**	Market Capitalization(B)	**$147.705**	Beta	**0.65**
$10K Invested 5 Yrs Ago	**$18,095**	S&P Core EPS 2007**E**	**8.41**	Institutional Ownership (%)	**62**	S&P Credit Rating	**AA**

Price Performance

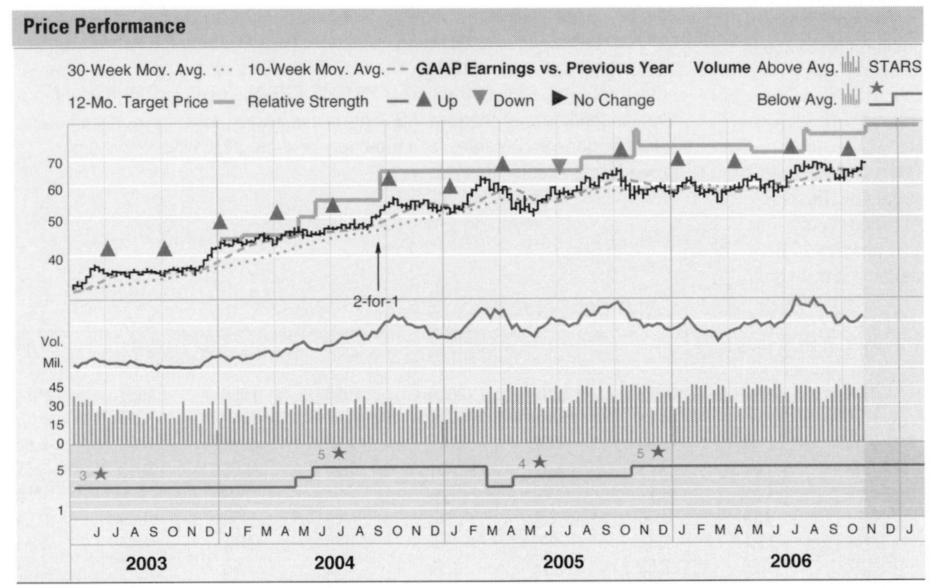

Options: ASE, CBOE, P, Ph

Highlights

- The 12-month target price for CVX has recently been changed to $84.00 from $80.00. The Highlights section of this Stock Report will be updated accordingly.

Investment Rationale/Risk

- The Investment Rationale/Risk section of this Stock Report will be updated shortly. For the latest News story on CVX from MarketScope, see below.

- 10/30/06 07:37 am EST... S&P REITERATES STRONG BUY RECOMMENDATION ON SHARES OF CHEVRON (CVX 67.68*****): CVX posted Q3 operating EPS of $2.29 vs. $1.64, beating our estimate by $0.26 on better-than-expected marketing and chemical margins. Contributions from Unocal helped to boost oil & gas production by 6%, in line with our expectations; we forecast 6% growth in '06, and 4% in '07. We are raising our '06 operating EPS estimate by $0.05 to $8.07, but trimming '07s by $0.10 to $8.34. A blend of our DCF and relative valuations leads us to incease our 12-month target price by $4 to $84, representing an expected enterprise value of 4.9X our '07 EBITDA estimate; a discount to peers. /T.Vital

Qualitative Risk Assessment

LOW | MEDIUM | HIGH

Our risk assessment reflects Chevron's diversified and strong business profile in volatile, cyclical and capital intensive segments of the energy industry. With improved returns since the Texaco merger in 2001, we view its corporate governance practices as generally sound and its earnings stability as favorable.

Quantitative Evaluations

S&P Quality Ranking **B+**

D | C | B- | B | B+ | A- | A | A+

Relative Strength Rank **MODERATE**

61

LOWEST = 1 HIGHEST = 99

Revenue/Earnings Data

Revenue (Million $)

	1Q	2Q	3Q	4Q	Year
2006	54,624	53,536	54.21	--	--
2005	41,607	48,343	54,456	53,794	198,200
2004	33,063	36,579	39,611	41,612	155,300
2003	30,965	29,361	30,970	30,465	121,761
2002	21,155	25,333	25,503	27,058	99,049
2001	12,298	13,006	11,563	19,606	106,245

Earnings Per Share ($)

2006	1.80	1.97	2.29	**E**1.89	**E**8.07
2005	1.28	1.76	1.64	1.86	6.54
2004	1.20	1.93	1.38	1.63	6.14
2003	1.00	0.75	1.01	0.82	3.57
2002	0.34	0.20	-0.43	0.43	0.54
2001	1.25	1.03	0.91	-1.11	1.85

Fiscal year ended Dec. 31. Next earnings report expected: Late January. EPS Estimates based on S&P Operating Earnings; historical GAAP earnings are as reported.

Dividend Data (Dates: mm/dd Payment Date: mm/dd/yy)

Amount ($)	Date Decl.	Ex-Div. Date	Stk. of Record	Payment Date
0.450	01/25	02/14	02/16	03/10/06
0.520	04/26	05/17	05/19	06/12/06
0.520	07/26	08/16	08/18	09/11/06
0.520	10/25	11/15	11/17	12/11/06

Dividends have been paid since 1912. Source: Company reports.

Chevron Corp

Business Summary September 29, 2006

CORPORATE OVERVIEW. In October 2001, Chevron Corp. (CHV) and Texaco Inc. (TX) merged, creating the second largest U.S.-based oil company, ChevronTexaco Corp. (CVX). In May 2005, the company changed its name to Chevron Corp.

CVX separately manages its exploration and production (22% of 2005 revenues; 79% of 2005 segment income); refining, marketing and transportation (76%; 19%); chemicals (less than 1%; 2%); and other businesses, including its 24% common equity interest in Dynegy, mining operations of coal and other minerals, power generation, and other businesses.

We estimate CVX's three year (2003-2005) organic reserve replacement rate (including affiliated companies) at a subpar 58%. Net production of crude oil and natural gas liquids (excluding affiliates) declined 3.2%, to 1.493 million barrels per day (b/d) in 2005. Net production of natural gas rose 7.0%, to 4.01 billion cubic feet (Bcf) per day in 2005. Proved liquids reserves (excluding affiliates) rose 2.1%, to 5.626 billion barrels, as of year-end 2005, and proved natural gas reserves (excluding affiliates) increased by 27%, to 20.466 trillion cubic feet (Tcf). The average sales price for liquids was $47.56 per barrel in 2005, and $5.18 per thousand cubic feet (Mcf) for natural gas. Three-year (2003-2005) average production costs were $5.58 per barrel of oil equivalent (boe).

As of December 31, 2005, CVX owned 19 fuel refineries and an asphalt plant, for a total refining capacity of 2.195 million b/d (45% U.S., 10% Europe, 3% Canada, and 42% Asia Pacific and Africa). As of year-end 2005, it had a network of 20,354 retail sites in nearly 90 countries (46% U.S.). In April 2006, CVX agreed to buy a 5% stake (for $300 million) in Reliance Petroleum Limited, a company formed to own and operate a new export refinery in Jamnagar, India.

Company Financials

Per Share Data ($) Year Ended Dec. 31	**2005**	**2004**	**2003**	**2002**	**2001**	**2000**	**1999**	**1998**	**1997**	**1996**
Tangible Book Value	25.99	21.47	16.98	14.80	15.92	15.54	13.53	13.05	13.32	11.97
Cash Flow	8.96	8.53	5.99	2.98	5.17	6.17	3.74	2.78	4.22	3.70
Earnings	6.54	6.14	3.57	0.54	1.85	3.99	1.57	1.02	2.47	2.00
S&P Core Earnings	6.62	5.88	3.50	1.22	1.66	NA	NA	NA	NA	NA
Dividends	1.75	1.53	1.43	1.40	1.33	1.30	1.24	1.22	1.14	1.04
Payout Ratio	27%	25%	40%	NM	72%	33%	79%	120%	46%	52%
Prices:High	65.98	56.07	43.50	45.80	49.25	47.44	52.47	45.09	44.59	34.19
Prices:Low	49.81	42.00	30.66	32.71	39.22	34.97	36.56	33.88	30.88	25.50
P/E Ratio:High	10	9	12	86	27	12	33	44	18	17
P/E Ratio:Low	8	7	9	61	21	9	23	33	12	13

Income Statement Analysis (Million $)										
Revenue	193,641	150,865	120,032	98,691	104,409	50,592	35,448	29,943	40,583	42,782
Operating Income	27,129	21,542	49,336	28,848	16,031	15,834	5,848	3,945	6,747	6,209
Depreciation, Depletion and Amortization	5,913	4,935	5,384	5,231	7,059	2,848	2,866	2,320	2,300	2,216
Interest Expense	482	406	474	565	833	460	463	405	312	472
Pretax Income	25,293	20,636	12,850	4,213	8,412	9,270	3,648	1,834	5,502	4,740
Effective Tax Rate	43.9%	36.4%	41.6%	71.8%	51.8%	44.1%	43.3%	27.0%	40.8%	45.0%
Net Income	14,099	13,034	7,426	1,132	3,931	5,185	2,070	1,339	3,256	2,607
S&P Core Earnings	14,277	12,471	7,454	2,590	3,518	NA	NA	NA	NA	NA

Balance Sheet & Other Financial Data (Million $)										
Cash	11,144	10,742	5,267	3,781	3,150	2,630	2,032	1,413	1,015	1,637
Current Assets	34,336	28,503	19,426	17,776	18,327	8,213	8,297	6,297	7,006	7,942
Total Assets	125,833	93,208	81,470	77,359	77,572	41,264	40,668	36,540	35,473	34,854
Current Liabilities	25,011	18,795	16,111	19,876	20,654	7,674	8,889	7,166	6,946	8,907
Long Term Debt	12,131	10,456	10,894	10,911	8,989	5,153	5,485	4,393	4,431	3,988
Common Equity	66,722	48,575	40,022	36,176	37,120	21,761	17,749	17,034	17,472	15,623
Total Capital	90,315	66,471	57,601	53,009	52,524	31,822	28,244	25,072	25,118	22,462
Capital Expenditures	8,701	6,310	5,625	7,597	9,713	3,657	4,366	3,880	3,899	3,424
Cash Flow	20,012	17,969	12,810	6,363	10,990	8,033	4,936	3,659	5,556	4,823
Current Ratio	1.4	1.5	1.2	0.9	0.9	1.1	0.9	0.9	1.0	0.9
% Long Term Debt of Capitalization	13.4	15.7	18.9	20.6	17.1	16.2	19.4	17.5	17.6	17.8
% Return on Assets	12.9	14.9	9.4	1.5	5.1	12.7	5.4	3.7	9.3	7.6
% Return on Equity	24.5	29.4	19.5	3.1	10.7	25.1	11.9	7.8	19.7	17.4

Data as orig reptd.; bef. results of disc opers/spec. items. Per share data adj. for stk. divs.; EPS diluted. Quarterly revs. incl. other inc. E-Estimated. NA-Not Available. NM-Not Meaningful. NR-Not Ranked. UR-Under Review.

Office: 6001 Bollinger Canyon Road, San Ramon, CA 94583-2324.
Telephone: 925-842-1000.
Email: invest@chevrontexaco.com
Website: http://www.chevrontexaco.com

Chrmn & CEO: D.J. O'Reilly
Vice Chrmn: P.J. Robertson
VP & CFO: S.J. Crowe
VP & Chief Acctg Officer: M.A. Humphrey

Investor Contact: R. Richards (925-842-5690)
Board of Directors: S. H. Armacost, L. F. Deily, R. E. Denham, R. J. Eaton, S. Ginn, C. A. Hills, F. G. Jenifer, S. Nunn, D. J. O'Reilly, D. B. Rice, P. J. Robertson, C. R. Shoemate, R. D. Sugar, C. Ware

Founded: 1901
Domicile: Delaware
Employees: 59,000

STANDARD &POOR'S

Chicago Mercantile Exchange Holdings Inc.

S&P Recommendation HOLD ★★★★★

Price $505.30 (as of Oct 27, 2006)

12-Mo. Target Price $500.00

Investment Style Large-Cap Growth

GICS Sector Financials
Sub-Industry Specialized Finance

Comment This company operates the largest futures exchange in the U.S.

Key Stock Statistics (Source S&P, Vickers, company reports)

52-Wk Range	$535.01–344.00	S&P Oper. EPS 2006E	11.60	P/E on S&P Oper. EPS 2006E	43.6	Dividend Rate/Share	$2.52
Trailing 12-Month EPS	$10.86	S&P Oper. EPS 2007E	14.84	Common Shares Outstg. (M)	35.6	Yield (%)	0.50
Trailing 12-Month P/E	46.5	S&P Core EPS 2006E	11.60	Market Capitalization(B)	$17.563	Beta	1.20
$10K Invested 5 Yrs Ago	NA	S&P Core EPS 2007E	14.84	Institutional Ownership (%)	80	S&P Credit Rating	NA

Price Performance

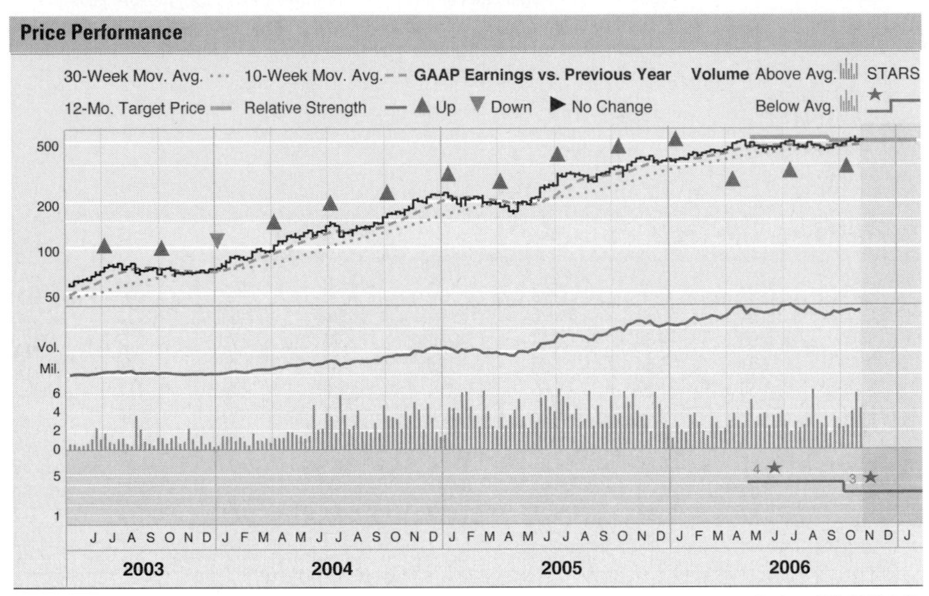

Options: ASE, CBOE, P, Ph

Analysis prepared by **Jason Willey** on October 26, 2006, when the stock traded at **$ 499.45**.

Highlights

- We believe CME's trading volumes are benefiting from increased investor sophistication, more active investment strategies, and growing demand for alternative investment products. We view CME's market leading position in key interest rate and equity index futures as highly defensible, and see ongoing volatility in interest rates, energy costs, and equity markets benefiting derivatives trading, and CME, specifically.
- Third quarter results were aided by a 28% rise in average daily volume (ADV), as demand remained strong across all of CME's products. Driving upside to our estimates was a better-than-expected contribution from CME's relationship with the New York Mercantile Exchange. We believe ongoing volume growth, a shift in trading from CME's floor to its electronic platform, and the company's low variable cost model, will enable CME's operating margin to expand by 340 basis points in 2006, to 57.1%.
- Driven by growth in the ADV, which we see rising 28% in 2006, and the expansion of newer initiatives in foreign exchange and energy, we forecast EPS of $11.60 in 2006 and $14.84 in 2007. We expect free cash flow per share to closely mirror EPS.

Investment Rationale/Risk

- We believe CME holds a dominant position in the futures markets for interest rates, equities and commodities, and is expanding its presence in foreign exchange and energy. With broad product exposure, highly defensible positioning, and a low variable cost model, we see CME delivering sustained revenue and margin growth. We believe the company's proposed merger with the Chicago Board of Trade (BOT: hold, 149), subject to necessary approvals, will help CME further diversify its revenue base and more easily expand its over-the-counter offerings. Despite our positive operational outlook, we believe CME's valuation fully incorporates our positive outlook.
- Risks to our recommendation and target price include a decrease in trading volumes, a faster than expected mix shift to lower margin member trading, and enhanced regulatory scrutiny.
- Our 12-month target price of $500 is based on a P/E of 33.5X our 2007 EPS estimate, a small premium to the current 32.5X peer group multiple. We believe this premium is justified given CME's leading market share and strong margin leverage.

Qualitative Risk Assessment

LOW | MEDIUM | **HIGH**

Our risk assessment reflects the potential volatility in results due to changes in futures trading volumes, recent acquisition activity in the sector, and a changing regulatory environment.

Quantitative Evaluations

S&P Quality Ranking **NR**

D | C | B- | B | B+ | A- | A | A+

Relative Strength Rank **MODERATE**

70

LOWEST = 1 HIGHEST = 99

Revenue/Earnings Data

Revenue (Million $)

	1Q	2Q	3Q	4Q	Year
2006	290.5	318.1	274.7	--	--
2005	223.9	252.2	249.6	251.6	977.3
2004	169.6	190.5	192.4	196.0	752.8
2003	128.6	142.4	135.0	134.6	544.8
2002	453.2	107.5	125.2	119.4	469.1
2001	--	--	--	--	396.6

Earnings Per Share ($)

	1Q	2Q	3Q	4Q	Year
2006	2.61	3.12	2.95	**E**2.92	**E**11.60
2005	2.04	2.36	2.22	2.18	8.81
2004	1.35	1.66	1.72	1.64	6.38
2003	0.77	1.03	0.93	0.87	3.60
2002	0.63	0.71	0.77	1.02	3.13
2001	0.62	0.64	0.60	0.46	2.33

Fiscal year ended Dec. 31. Next earnings report expected: Late January. EPS Estimates based on S&P Operating Earnings; historical GAAP earnings are as reported.

Dividend Data (Dates: mm/dd Payment Date: mm/dd/yy)

Amount ($)	Date Decl.	Ex-Div. Date	Stk. of Record	Payment Date
0.460	10/25	12/07	12/09	12/27/05
0.630	02/02	03/08	03/10	03/27/06
0.630	04/27	06/07	06/09	06/26/06
0.630	08/02	09/06	09/08	09/25/06

Dividends have been paid since 2003. Source: Company reports.

Please read the Required Disclosures and Analyst Certification on the last page of this report.

Chicago Mercantile Exchange Holdings Inc.

Business Summary October 26, 2006

CORPORATE OVERVIEW. The Chicago Mercantile Exchange is the largest futures exchange in the United States. CME serves the risk management needs of clients worldwide through a diverse range of futures and options-on-futures products on its CME Globex electronic trading platform and on its trading floors. CME offers futures and options on futures primarily in four product areas: interest rates, stock indexes, foreign exchange, and commodities. CME is the leading exchange for trading Eurodollar futures, the world's most actively traded futures contract and a benchmark for measuring the relative value of U.S. dollar denominated short-term fixed income securities.

CME operates its own clearing house, which clears, settles and guarantees every contract traded through its exchange. In addition, CME has a multi-year agreement with the Chicago Board of Trade (CBOT) to provide clearing services for all future and options on futures contracts traded through the CBOT. We view CME's internal clearing capabilities as a key competitive advantage as CME is able to capture the revenue associated with both the trading and clearing of its products. We expect CME to expand its clearing business by partnering with other exchanges and clearing over-the-counter (OTC) transactions.

In 2005, CME derived 71% of its net revenues from fees associated with trading and clearing its products. These fees include per contract charges for trade execution, clearing and CME Globex fees. Fees are charged at various rates based on the product traded, the method of trade and the exchange trading privileges of the customer making the trade. Generally, members are charged lower fees than non-members. Certain customers benefit from volume discounts and limits on fees as part of an effort to encourage increased liquidity.

Company Financials

Per Share Data ($) Year Ended Dec. 31	2005	2004	2003	2002	2001	2000	1999	1998	1997	1996
Tangible Book Value	32.38	23.83	17.10	13.71	12.39	NA	NA	NA	NA	NA
Cash Flow	10.71	7.93	5.16	4.76	3.61	NA	NA	NA	NA	NA
Earnings	8.81	6.38	3.60	3.13	2.33	NA	NA	NA	NA	NA
S&P Core Earnings	8.80	6.37	3.61	3.23	NA	NA	NA	NA	NA	NA
Dividends	1.84	1.04	0.63	Nil	NA	NA	NA	NA	NA	NA
Payout Ratio	21%	16%	18%	Nil	NA	NA	NA	NA	NA	NA
Prices:High	396.90	229.80	79.30	45.50	NA	NA	NA	NA	NA	NA
Prices:Low	163.80	72.50	41.35	35.00	NA	NA	NA	NA	NA	NA
P/E Ratio:High	45	36	22	15	NA	NA	NA	NA	NA	NA
P/E Ratio:Low	19	11	11	11	NA	NA	NA	NA	NA	NA
Income Statement Analysis (Million $)										
Revenue	977	753	545	469	397	NA	NA	NA	NA	NA
Operating Income	631	464	290	NA	NA	NA	NA	NA	NA	NA
Depreciation	66.0	53.0	53.0	48.5	37.0	NA	NA	NA	NA	NA
Interest Expense	57.0	19.0	8.74	15.9	9.48	NA	NA	NA	NA	NA
Pretax Income	508	368	206	154	114	NA	NA	NA	NA	NA
Effective Tax Rate	39.6%	40.2%	40.7%	39.0%	40.3%	NA	NA	NA	NA	NA
Net Income	307	220	122	94.1	68.3	NA	NA	NA	NA	NA
S&P Core Earnings	307	219	123	97.2	NA	NA	NA	NA	NA	NA
Balance Sheet & Other Financial Data (Million $)										
Cash	904	660	442	339	292	NA	NA	NA	NA	NA
Current Assets	3,783	2,695	4,723	3,215	2,818	NA	NA	NA	NA	NA
Total Assets	3,969	2,857	4,873	3,355	2,958	NA	NA	NA	NA	NA
Current Liabilities	2,830	2,026	4,288	2,889	2,544	NA	NA	NA	NA	NA
Long Term Debt	Nil	Nil	Nil	2.33	8.22	NA	NA	NA	NA	NA
Common Equity	1,119	813	563	446	394	NA	NA	NA	NA	NA
Total Capital	1,119	813	563	448	402	NA	NA	NA	NA	NA
Capital Expenditures	85.6	67.0	63.0	56.3	NA	NA	NA	NA	NA	NA
Cash Flow	373	273	175	143	106	NA	NA	NA	NA	NA
Current Ratio	1.3	1.3	1.1	1.1	1.1	NA	NA	NA	NA	NA
% Long Term Debt of Capitalization	Nil	Nil	Nil	0.5	2.0	NA	NA	NA	NA	NA
% Net Income of Revenue	31.4	29.2	22.5	20.1	17.2	NA	NA	NA	NA	NA
% Return on Assets	8.9	5.6	3.0	3.5	NA	NA	NA	NA	NA	NA
% Return on Equity	31.7	31.9	24.2	27.1	NA	NA	NA	NA	NA	NA

Data as orig reptd.; bef. results of disc opers/spec. items. Per share data adj. for stk. divs.; EPS diluted. E-Estimated. NA-Not Available. NM-Not Meaningful. NR-Not Ranked. UR-Under Review.

Office: 20 S Wacker Dr, Chicago, IL 60606-7408.
Telephone: 312-930-1000.
Email: info@cme.com
Website: http://www.cme.com

Chrmn: T.A. Duffy
Pres & COO: P. Gill
Vice Chrmn: J.E. Oliff
Vice Chrmn: W.R. Shepard

CEO: C.S. Donohue
Investor Contact: J. Perschier (312-930-8491)
Board of Directors: D. H. Chookaszian, C. S. Donohue, T. A. Duffy, M. J. Gepsman, D. R. Glickman, E. Harrington, B. F. Johnson, G. M. Katler, P. B. Lynch, L. Melamed, W. P. Miller, II, J. E. Oliff, A. J. Pollock, W. G. Salatich, Jr., J. F. Sandner, T. L. Savage, M. S. Scholes, W. R. Shepard, H. J. Siegel, D. J. Wescott

Founded: 2001
Domicile: Delaware
Employees: 1,321

STANDARD &POOR'S

Chubb Corp (The)

S&P Recommendation STRONG BUY ★★★★★

Price $52.44 (as of Oct 27, 2006)

12-Mo. Target Price $67.00

Investment Style Large-Cap Value

GICS Sector Financials
Sub-Industry Property & Casualty Insurance

Comment As one of the largest U.S. property-casualty insurers, Chubb has carved out a number of niches, including high-end personal lines and specialty liability lines coverage.

Key Stock Statistics (Source S&P, Vickers, company reports)

52-Wk Range	**$54.73–45.98**	S&P Oper. EPS 2006E	**5.40**	P/E on S&P Oper. EPS 2006E	**9.7**	Dividend Rate/Share	**$1.00**
Trailing 12-Month EPS	**$5.05**	S&P Oper. EPS 2007E	**5.60**	Common Shares Outstg. (M)	**410.8**	Yield (%)	**1.91**
Trailing 12-Month P/E	**10.4**	S&P Core EPS 2006E	**5.24**	Market Capitalization(B)	**$21.543**	Beta	**0.88**
$10K Invested 5 Yrs Ago	**$15,473**	S&P Core EPS 2007E	**5.43**	Institutional Ownership (%)	**86**	S&P Credit Rating	**A**

Price Performance

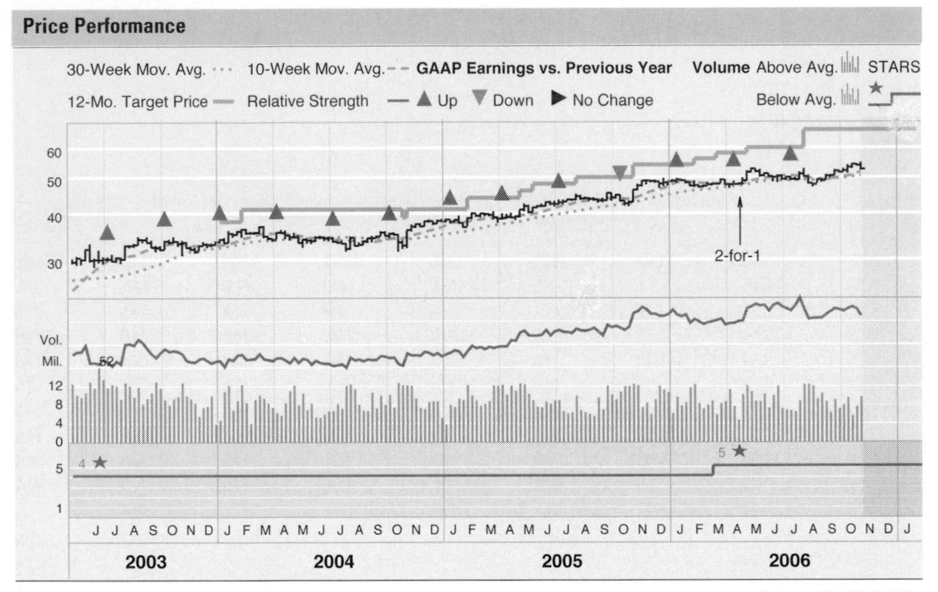

Options: ASE, CBOE, P, Ph

Analysis prepared by **Cathy A. Seifert** on August 31, 2006, when the stock traded at **$ 49.65**.

Highlights

- We anticipate earned premium growth in 2006 of 5% to 7%, faster that our projection for the property-casualty industry as a whole. We expect pricing in a number of catastrophe-exposed lines of business to firm considerably. This will likely boost earned premium growth in 2007. We anticipate that underwriting margins will be buoyed by continued favorable claim trends in a number of core lines. Barring a surge in catastrophe claims, we expect CB to earn an underwriting profit in 2006.
- We see investment income growth climbing 9% to 11% in 2006, as still relatively low investment yields are being offset by continued favorable cash flow trends. Assuming these trends continue into 2007, investment income growth should advance by double digits.
- Our operating EPS estimates of $4.90 for 2006 and $5.35 for 2007 assume that the company does not incur any large one-time reserve boosts, such as those for asbestos, and that its exposure to catastrophe losses remains stable.

Investment Rationale/Risk

- We view the shares of this property-casualty insurer as undervalued on both a relative and an historical basis. We believe the stock deserves a premium-to-peers P/E and price/tangible book multiple, based on what we see as CB's superior personal lines franchise and its wider-margin mix of business. Our outlook is tempered a bit by our concerns over the adequacy of loss reserves in certain lines of business.
- Risks to our opinion and target price include a deterioration in claim trends and loss reserves, a continuation of record catastrophe losses, or a significant terrorist attack or catastrophe in the U.S.
- Our 12-month target price of $67 assumes that the stock's forward P/E multiple will increase to approximately 12.5X our $5.35 operating EPS estimate for 2007 and 1.9X estimated 2007 tangible book value. These represent slight premiums to the peer group average multiples, which we believe are warranted.

Qualitative Risk Assessment

LOW | **MEDIUM** | HIGH

Our risk assessment reflects our view that CB is a superior underwriter with sound capital and risk management practices and an attractive mix of business. This is partly offset by concerns over the adequacy of loss reserves in certain lines of business and by CB's exposure to catastrophe claims.

Quantitative Evaluations

S&P Quality Ranking **B+**

D | C | B- | B | **B+** | A- | A | A+

Relative Strength Rank **MODERATE**

41

LOWEST = 1 HIGHEST = 99

Revenue/Earnings Data

Revenue (Million $)

	1Q	2Q	3Q	4Q	Year
2006	3,506	3,445	--	--	--
2005	3,449	3,451	3,479	3,703	14,082
2004	3,178	3,206	3,345	3,448	13,177
2003	2,616	2,839	2,947	2,992	11,394
2002	2,105	2,224	2,364	2,447	9,140
2001	1,892	1,915	1,956	1,992	7,754

Earnings Per Share ($)

2006	1.58	1.41	**E**0.95	**E**1.26	**E**5.40
2005	1.18	1.23	0.60	1.46	4.47
2004	0.94	0.93	0.94	1.20	4.01
2003	0.66	0.73	0.69	0.19	2.23
2002	0.58	0.60	-0.71	0.17	0.65
2001	0.49	0.42	-0.70	0.08	0.32

Fiscal year ended Dec. 31. Next earnings report expected: NA. EPS Estimates based on S&P Operating Earnings; historical GAAP earnings are as reported.

Dividend Data (Dates: mm/dd Payment Date: mm/dd/yy)

Amount ($)	Date Decl.	Ex-Div. Date	Stk. of Record	Payment Date
0.500	03/03	03/15	03/17	04/04/06
2-for-1 Stk.	03/03	04/19	03/31	04/18/06
0.250	06/09	06/21	06/23	07/11/06
0.250	09/08	09/20	09/22	10/10/06

Dividends have been paid since 1902. Source: Company reports.

Please read the Required Disclosures and Analyst Certification on the last page of this report.

Business Summary August 31, 2006

CORPORATE OVERVIEW. CB's property-casualty operations are divided into three strategic business units: Personal Lines (29% of net written premiums in 2005); Commercial Insurance (44%); and Specialty Insurance (27%). Net written premiums approached $12.3 billion in 2005, up 1.7% from net written premiums of $12.1 billion recorded in 2004.

The Personal Insurance division offers primarily automobile and homeowners' insurance coverage. The company's products are typically targeted to individuals with upscale homes and automobiles, requiring more coverage choices and higher policy limits than are offered under standard insurance policies. Net written premiums totaled $3.3 billion in 2005 (up 6.5% from $3.1 billion in 2004), and were divided as follows: homeowners' 58%, automobile 22%, and other (mainly personal article coverage) 20%. Chubb Commercial Insurance underwrites an array of commercial insurance policies, including those for multiple peril, casualty, workers' compensation, and property and marine coverage. Net written premiums totaled $4.6 billion in 2004 (up 12% from $4.1 billion in 2003) and were divided as follows: commercial casualty 34%, commercial multi-peril 26%, property and marine 24%, and workers' compensation 16%.

Chubb Specialty Insurance offers a variety of specialized executive protection and professional liability products for privately and publicly owned companies, financial institutions, professional firms, and health care organizations. Net written premiums totaled $4.7 billion in 2004 (up 6.8% from $4.4 billion in 2003), and were divided as follows: executive protection 47%, financial institutions 19%, and other 34%.

Company Financials

Per Share Data ($) Year Ended Dec. 31	**2005**	**2004**	**2003**	**2002**	**2001**	**2000**	**1999**	**1998**	**1997**	**1996**
Tangible Book Value	28.56	25.06	21.50	18.67	17.81	18.58	16.42	17.42	16.74	15.62
Operating Earnings	NA	NA	NA	0.58	0.31	1.91	1.67	1.83	2.00	1.79
Earnings	4.47	4.01	2.23	0.65	0.32	2.01	1.83	2.10	2.20	1.38
S&P Core Earnings	3.87	3.63	2.08	0.42	0.19	NA	NA	NA	NA	NA
Dividends	1.08	0.78	0.72	0.70	0.68	0.66	0.64	0.61	0.58	0.54
Payout Ratio	24%	19%	32%	109%	NM	33%	35%	29%	26%	39%
Prices:High	49.73	38.73	34.65	39.32	43.31	45.13	38.19	44.41	39.25	28.13
Prices:Low	36.51	31.50	20.89	25.96	27.77	21.63	22.00	27.69	25.56	20.44
P/E Ratio:High	11	10	16	61	NM	23	21	21	18	20
P/E Ratio:Low	8	8	9	40	NM	11	12	13	12	15

Income Statement Analysis (Million $)										
Premium Income	12,176	11,636	10,183	8,035	6,656	6,146	5,652	5,304	5,157	4,569
Net Investment Income	1,408	1,256	1,118	997	983	957	893	822	785	712
Other Revenue	12,675	286	93.2	57.7	115	6,294	184	224	721	400
Total Revenue	14,082	13,177	11,394	9,140	7,754	7,252	6,730	6,350	6,664	5,681
Pretax Income	2,447	2,068	934	168	-66.0	851	710	850	973	547
Net Operating Income	NA	NA	NA	201	111	681	565	615	701	434
Net Income	1,826	1,548	809	223	112	715	621	707	770	486
S&P Core Earnings	1,578	1,402	754	146	65.2	NA	NA	NA	NA	NA

Balance Sheet & Other Financial Data (Million $)										
Cash & Equivalent	427	392	1,044	1,644	691	720	735	229	12.0	200
Premiums Due	2,319	2,336	2,188	6,112	6,198	3,263	1,235	1,199	1,144	985
Investment Assets:Bonds	30,523	28,009	22,412	18,263	16,117	15,564	14,519	13,319	12,454	11,158
Investment Assets:Stocks	2,212	1,841	1,514	795	710	831	769	1,092	871	646
Investment Assets:Loans	Nil	Nil	Nil	Nil	Nil	Nil	Nil	Nil	Nil	Nil
Investment Assets:Total	34,893	31,504	26,934	21,279	17,784	17,001	16,019	14,755	14,049	1,281
Deferred Policy Costs	1,445	1,435	1,343	1,150	929	842	780	729	677	601
Total Assets	48,061	44,260	38,361	34,114	29,449	25,027	23,537	20,746	19,616	19,939
Debt	2,467	2,814	2,814	1,959	2,901	754	759	608	399	1,071
Common Equity	12,407	10,126	8,522	6,859	6,525	6,982	6,272	5,644	5,657	5,463
Property & Casualty:Loss Ratio	64.3	63.1	67.6	75.4	80.8	67.5	70.3	66.3	64.5	66.2
Property & Casualty:Expense Ratio	28.0	29.2	30.4	31.3	32.6	32.9	32.5	33.5	32.4	32.1
Property & Casualty Combined Ratio	92.3	92.3	98.0	106.7	113.4	100.4	102.8	99.8	96.9	98.3
% Return on Revenue	13.0	11.8	7.1	2.4	1.4	9.9	9.2	11.1	11.6	8.6
% Return on Equity	16.2	16.6	10.5	3.3	1.7	10.8	10.4	12.5	13.8	9.1

Data as orig reptd.; bef. results of disc opers/spec. items. Per share data adj. for stk. divs.; EPS diluted. E-Estimated. NA-Not Available. NM-Not Meaningful. NR-Not Ranked. UR-Under Review.

Office: 15 Mountain View Road, Warren, NJ 07061-1615.
Telephone: 908-903-2000.
Email: info@chubb.com
Website: http://www.chubb.com

Chrmn, Pres & CEO: J.D. Finnegan
Vice Chrmn & COO: T.F. Motamed
Vice Chrmn & CFO: M. O'Reilly
Vice Chrmn & Chief Admin: J.J. Degnan

SVP & Chief Acctg Officer: H.B. Schram
Investor Contact: G.A. Montgomery (908-903-2365)
Board of Directors: Z. Baird, S. P. Burke, J. I. Cash, Jr., J. J. Cohen, J. M. Cornelius, J. Finnegan, K. J. Mangold, D. G. Scholey, R. G. Seitz, L. M. Small, D. E. Somers, K. H. Williams, A. W. Zollar

Founded: 1967
Domicile: New Jersey
Employees: 10,800

STANDARD & POOR'S

CIENA Corp

S&P Recommendation HOLD ★★★★★	Price	12-Mo. Target Price	Investment Style
	$23.59 (as of Oct 27, 2006)	$32.00	Mid-Cap Value

GICS Sector Information Technology
Sub-Industry Communications Equipment

Comment This company manufactures telecommunications equipment used to increase the capacity of fiber optic networks.

Key Stock Statistics (Source S&P, Vickers, company reports)

52-Wk Range	$39.36–16.32	S&P Oper. EPS 2006E	0.15	P/E on S&P Oper. EPS 2006E	NM	Dividend Rate/Share	Nil
Trailing 12-Month EPS	$-3.22	S&P Oper. EPS 2007E	0.53	Common Shares Outstg. (M)	84.4	Yield (%)	Nil
Trailing 12-Month P/E	NM	S&P Core EPS 2006E	0.15	Market Capitalization(B)	$1.992	Beta	3.19
$10K Invested 5 Yrs Ago	$1,701	S&P Core EPS 2007E	0.53	Institutional Ownership (%)	77	S&P Credit Rating	B

Price Performance

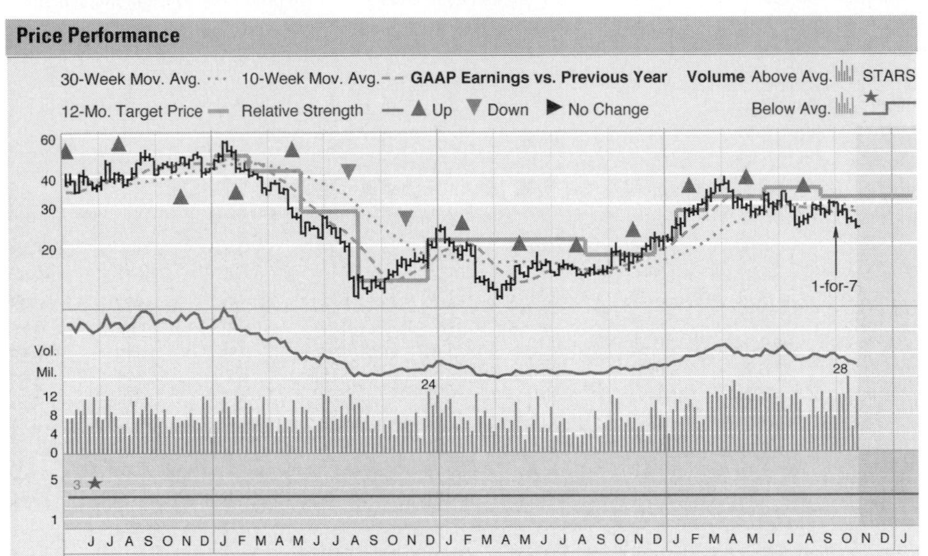

Options: ASE, CBOE, P, Ph

Analysis prepared by **Ari Bensinger** on September 28, 2006, when the stock traded at **$ 27.16**.

Highlights

- After an estimated 32% increase in FY 06 (Oct.), we project sales advancing 25% in FY 07, reflecting higher demand for optical transport and switching products. We expect sales to benefit from higher telecom capital expenditures on network infrastructure to support a material increase in bandwidth demand.
- Despite the higher sales volume, we forecast FY 07 gross margin remaining relatively flat with the prior period at the 46% level, owing to an unfavorable product mix. With major restructuring complete, we see FY 07 operating expense as a percentage of sales decreasing from the prior period. Interest income should increase moderately on a higher cash balance.
- After an expected 35% effective tax rate, and factoring in a 1-for-7 reverse stock split that was effective in September 2006, we forecast EPS of $0.53 in FY 07, versus the $0.15 EPS that we estimate for FY 06. Our FY 06 and FY 07 estimates include projected stock option expense of $0.09 in each fiscal year.

Investment Rationale/Risk

- We believe a fundamental turnaround is developing for the company, and we see operating profits in the second half of FY 06. In our opinion, the company has expanded its product areas and addressable markets, which now require a broader direct and indirect sales organization. We believe CIEN is beginning to get sales traction with its broader portfolio of networking solutions, which should ease pressure on operating margins.
- Risks to our opinion and target price include lower than expected sales growth for the company's core optical products and poor execution in realizing higher sales from several acquisitions in the networking market.
- We view the stock, recently trading at 4X book value, slightly above the peer average, as worth holding for an expected turnaround of the company. To arrive at our 12-month target price of $32, we apply an assumed price to sales ratio of 4.5X to our FY 07 estimate and an enterprise value of 4.4X to our FY 07 sales estimate, both in line with other next generation equipment peers.

Qualitative Risk Assessment

LOW	MEDIUM	HIGH

Our risk assessment is tied to the company's intense competitive landscape and the increased buying power of customers. Competing against larger equipment companies, which have broader product offerings and larger service teams to meet customer needs, we believe CIEN is at risk of pressure on its profitability.

Quantitative Evaluations

S&P Quality Ranking C

D	C	B-	B	B+	A-	A	A+

Relative Strength Rank WEAK

8

LOWEST = 1 HIGHEST = 99

Revenue/Earnings Data

Revenue (Million $)

	1Q	2Q	3Q	4Q	Year
2006	120.4	131.2	152.5	--	--
2005	94.75	103.9	110.5	118.2	427.3
2004	66.41	74.70	75.59	82.01	298.7
2003	70.47	73.54	68.48	70.64	283.1
2002	162.2	87.05	50.03	61.92	361.2
2001	352.0	425.4	458.1	367.8	1,603

Earnings Per Share ($)

	1Q	2Q	3Q	4Q	Year
2006	-0.07	Nil	-0.07	**E**0.09	**E**0.15
2005	-0.70	-0.91	-0.63	-3.08	-5.32
2004	-1.12	-1.12	-1.75	-6.09	-10.57
2003	-1.75	-1.19	-1.40	-1.68	-6.09
2002	-1.54	-13.03	-2.94	-12.25	-30.60
2001	1.26	-1.19	0.14	-38.59	-40.27

Fiscal year ended Oct. 31. Next earnings report expected: Early December. EPS Estimates based on S&P Operating Earnings; historical GAAP earnings are as reported.

Dividend Data (Dates: mm/dd Payment Date: mm/dd/yy)

Amount ($)	Date Decl.	Ex-Div. Date	Stk. of Record	Payment Date
1-for-7 REV.	--	09/25	--	09/25/06

Source: Company reports.

Please read the Required Disclosures and Analyst Certification on the last page of this report.

CIENA Corp

Business Summary September 28, 2006

CORPORATE OVERVIEW. Ciena Corp. supplies application-focused communications networking equipment, software and services to communications service providers, cable operators, governments and enterprises. CIEN has sought to diversify its customer base and broaden its networking solutions portfolio from its historical expertise in core optical systems. Largely untested in the networking business, the company may face many challenges in gaining market penetration, in our view. In FY 06 (Oct.), CIEN also expects to take additional steps to reduce operating expenses, which may be disruptive to its business.

PRIMARY BUSINESS DYNAMICS. Product sales provided 89% of total revenues, and service revenues 11%, in the second quarter of FY 06. Revenue from optical transport and switching products were 64% of total sales in the second quarter of FY 06, followed by 17% for broadband access products, 11% for global networking services, and 8% for data networking solutions. We believe CIEN continues to focus on cost reductions across all product lines. It relies on electronic manufacturing service (EMS) providers to perform the majority of the manufacturing operations for its products and components, and is increasingly utilizing overseas suppliers in Asia.

MARKET PROFILE. The market for communications networking equipment, software and services is characterized, in our view, by rapid technological change, frequent introductions of new products, and recurring changes in customer requirements. We believe CIEN's future success will depend on its ability to maintain and expand its sales to existing and new communications service provider customers, particularly overseas. In April 2005, CIEN was selected as a preferred supplier for BT Group's 21st Century Network, which is deploying CIEN's optical switching and transport systems and its Ethernet transport products.

Company Financials

Per Share Data ($) Year Ended Oct. 31	**2005**	**2004**	**2003**	**2002**	**2001**	**2000**	**1999**	**1998**	**1997**	**1996**
Tangible Book Value	4.62	6.58	13.10	20.24	40.62	19.54	26.19	15.55	12.82	5.71
Cash Flow	-4.41	-9.17	-4.59	-28.08	-33.96	3.39	2.44	2.81	4.13	0.56
Earnings	-5.32	-10.57	-6.09	-30.60	-40.27	1.89	-0.11	1.72	3.82	0.53
S&P Core Earnings	-4.48	-7.70	-6.09	-23.52	-22.47	NA	NA	NA	NA	NA
Dividends	Nil	Nil	Nil	Nil	Nil	Nil	Nil	Nil	Nil	NA
Payout Ratio	Nil	Nil	Nil	Nil	Nil	Nil	Nil	Nil	Nil	NA
Prices:High	24.02	57.00	54.20	121.15	756.30	1057	261.07	323.44	222.78	NA
Prices:Low	11.51	11.69	29.35	16.88	64.43	158.88	47.71	28.45	77.91	NA
P/E Ratio:High	NM	NM	NM	NM	NM	NM	NM	NM	58	NA
P/E Ratio:Low	NM	NM	NM	NM	NM	NM	NM	NM	20	NA
Income Statement Analysis (Million $)										
Revenue	427	299	283	361	1,603	859	482	508	374	54.8
Operating Income	-115	-185	-209	-569	324	163	43.5	157	187	17.4
Depreciation	76.0	107	93.7	131	283	63.6	50.4	33.3	10.2	1.01
Interest Expense	25.4	26.8	36.3	45.3	30.6	0.34	0.50	0.26	0.34	0.30
Pretax Income	-434	-788	-385	-1,487	-1,707	121	-5.99	93.4	184	17.0
Effective Tax Rate	NM	NM	NM	NM	NM	32.5%	NM	43.1%	38.6%	13.3%
Net Income	-436	-789	-387	-1,597	-1,794	81.4	-3.92	53.2	113	14.7
S&P Core Earnings	-367	-573	-386	-1,225	-1,001	NA	NA	NA	NA	NA
Balance Sheet & Other Financial Data (Million $)										
Cash	373	203	310	377	398	238	262	243	263	129
Current Assets	1,102	1,079	1,229	1,638	2,191	813	533	428	379	NA
Total Assets	1,675	2,137	2,378	2,751	3,317	1,027	678	572	447	174
Current Liabilities	178	159	186	224	254	173	106	61.9	53.6	NA
Long Term Debt	650	692	794	919	870	Nil	Nil	1.41	1.88	2.67
Common Equity	735	1,154	1,331	1,527	2,129	810	530	475	364	152
Total Capital	1,385	1,846	2,125	2,246	3,063	849	567	510	394	155
Capital Expenditures	11.3	33.0	29.5	66.3	239	124	46.8	86.4	66.6	NA
Cash Flow	-360	-682	-293	-1,466	-1,511	145	46.5	86.5	123	15.7
Current Ratio	6.2	6.8	6.6	7.3	8.6	4.7	5.1	6.9	7.1	NA
% Long Term Debt of Capitalization	46.9	37.5	37.4	37.6	28.4	Nil	Nil	2.8	0.5	1.7
% Net Income of Revenue	NM	NM	NM	NM	NM	9.5	NM	10.5	30.2	26.8
% Return on Assets	NM	NM	NM	NM	NM	9.5	NM	10.4	43.9	NA
% Return on Equity	NM	NM	NM	NM	NM	12.1	NM	12.7	61.3	NA

Data as orig reptd.; bef. results of disc opers/spec. items. Per share data adj. for stk. divs.; EPS diluted. E-Estimated. NA-Not Available. NM-Not Meaningful. NR-Not Ranked. UR-Under Review.

Office: 1201 Winterson Road, Linthicum, MD 21090-2205.
Telephone: 410-865-8500.
Website: http://www.ciena.com
Exec Chrmn: P.H. Nettles

Pres & CEO: G. Smith
COO & SVP: A. Smith
Investor Contact: J.R. Chinnici (888-243-6223)
SVP & CFO: J.R. Chinnici

Board of Directors: S. P. Bradley, H. B. Cash, B. L. Claflin, D. H. Davis, Jr., L. W. Fitt, P. H. Nettles, J. M. O'Brien, M. J. Rowny, G. B. Smith, G. H. Taylor

Founded: 1992
Domicile: Delaware
Employees: 1,497

STANDARD &POOR'S

CIGNA Corp.

S&P Recommendation BUY ★★★★★

Price $118.20 (as of Oct 27, 2006)

12-Mo. Target Price $129.00

Investment Style Large-Cap Growth

GICS Sector Health Care
Sub-Industry Managed Health Care

Comment CIGNA is one of the largest investor-owned employee benefits organizations in the U.S. Its subsidiaries are major providers of employee benefits offered through the workplace.

Key Stock Statistics (Source S&P, Vickers, company reports)

52-Wk Range	$133.77–88.05	S&P Oper. EPS 2006**E**	8.85	P/E on S&P Oper. EPS 2006**E**	13.4	Dividend Rate/Share	$0.10
Trailing 12-Month EPS	$8.98	S&P Oper. EPS 2007**E**	10.00	Common Shares Outstg. (M)	110.9	Yield (%)	0.08
Trailing 12-Month P/E	13.2	S&P Core EPS 2006**E**	9.18	Market Capitalization(B)	$13.108	Beta	0.91
$10K Invested 5 Yrs Ago	$16,252	S&P Core EPS 2007**E**	10.68	Institutional Ownership (%)	83	S&P Credit Rating	BBB

Price Performance

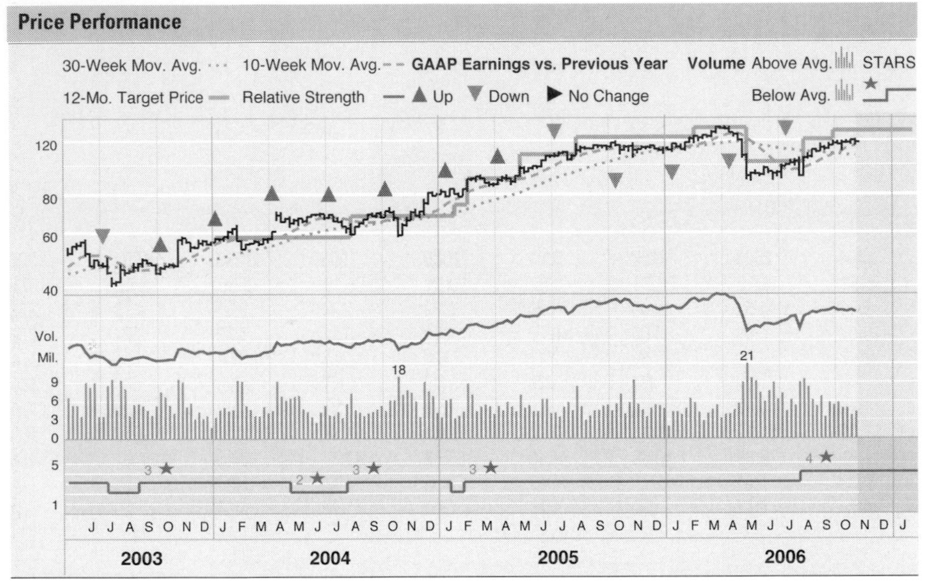

Options: ASE, CBOE, P, Ph

Analysis prepared by **Phillip M. Seligman** on September 18, 2006, when the stock traded at **$ 116.34**.

Highlights

- We expect 2006 Health Care segment revenue to decline about 2%, as lower premium revenue outweighs higher ASO fee revenue. We see 6.0% to 6.5% higher premium yields (rates minus buydowns) in the guaranteed cost book of business, and 1% to 2% higher organic medical enrollment for the year, with 2% to 3% growth in the second half, primarily in regional and national commercial account markets.
- CI's view of 7.0% to 7.5% medical cost trends suggests to us that 2006's medical cost ratio will be 120 to 170 basis points above 2005's 85.3%, excluding reserve development. Much of the gains that we expect for Health Care should come from lower SG&A spending via cost control, partly offset by spending on new initiatives.
- We forecast operating EPS of $8.85 in 2006, compared to 2005's $7.17, before favorable reserve development, and we look for $10.00 in 2007. We see share buybacks aiding EPS growth. Our 2006 and 2007 S&P Core EPS estimates of $9.18 and $10.68, respectively, exclude realized investment gains in 2006 but include pension and post-retirement adjustments in both years.

Investment Rationale/Risk

- We view positively the health care unit's improved enrollment retention, its recent promising alliances that should provide market expansion opportunities, and its progress in the national accounts market where the company sees a larger pipeline for the 2007 selling season. Moreover, we are less concerned that CI will face adverse selection (i.e., more profitable accounts going to peers). We also view favorably CI's product development, pricing discipline, and improved medical and SG&A cost control.
- Risks to our recommendation and target price include enrollment deterioration, a decline in the proportion of CI's more profitable accounts, and unfavorable medical cost trends. Our corporate governance concerns include that the positions of chairman and CEO are combined, and hurdles faced by shareholders seeking to change company policies.
- Our 12-month target price of $129 is based on an above-peer P/E to growth ratio of 1.15X, using a three-year growth rate of 12.7%, and our 2006 EPS estimate.

Qualitative Risk Assessment

LOW | **MEDIUM** | HIGH

Our risk assessment reflects our view of CI's improving cost structure, account retention, significant provider network, and wide range of attractive product and service offerings. However, the managed care market is intensely competitive, and we believe CI's national peers have strengthened competitively while CI had to focus on turning itself around.

Quantitative Evaluations

S&P Quality Ranking B

D | C | B- | **B** | B+ | A- | A | A+

Relative Strength Rank MODERATE

60

LOWEST = 1 HIGHEST = 99

Revenue/Earnings Data

Revenue (Million $)

	1Q	2Q	3Q	4Q	Year
2006	4,107	4,098	--	--	--
2005	4,345	4,107	4,022	4,210	16,684
2004	4,722	4,633	4,479	4,342	18,176
2003	4,900	4,634	4,773	4,501	18,808
2002	4,690	4,877	5,083	4,748	19,348
2001	4,732	4,663	4,778	4,942	19,115

Earnings Per Share ($)

2006	2.87	2.33	**E**2.19	**E**2.25	**E**8.85
2005	3.28	2.82	2.00	1.78	9.83
2004	1.47	3.59	2.26	4.16	11.44
2003	1.34	-0.38	1.39	2.06	4.41
2002	1.52	1.50	-6.27	0.33	-2.83
2001	1.78	1.66	1.81	1.32	6.59

Fiscal year ended Dec. 31. Next earnings report expected: Early November. EPS Estimates based on S&P Operating Earnings; historical GAAP earnings are as reported.

Dividend Data (Dates: mm/dd Payment Date: mm/dd/yy)

Amount ($)	Date Decl.	Ex-Div. Date	Stk. of Record	Payment Date
0.025	02/22	03/09	03/13	04/10/06
0.025	04/26	06/08	06/12	07/10/06
0.025	07/26	09/07	09/11	10/10/06
0.025	10/25	12/07	12/11	01/08/07

Dividends have been paid since 1867. Source: Company reports.

Please read the Required Disclosures and Analyst Certification on the last page of this report.

CIGNA Corp.

Business Summary September 18, 2006

CORPORATE OVERVIEW. CIGNA Corp., one of the largest U.S. employee benefits organizations, provides health care products and services and group life, accident and disability insurance.

Health Care offers group medical, dental, behavioral health and pharmacy services products. Medical products include consumer directed health plans (CDHPs), HMOs, network only, point-of-service (POS) plans, preferred provider organizations (PPOs), and traditional indemnity coverage. The health care products and services are offered through guaranteed cost, retrospectively experience-rated, administrative services only (ASO) and minimum premium funding arrangements. Under ASO, the employer or other plan sponsor self-funds all of its claims and assumes the risk for claim costs incurred. CI's CDHPs offer a modular product portfolio that offers a choice of benefits network and various funding, medical management, consumerism and health advocacy options for employers and consumers.

Medical covered lives at June 30, 2006, totaled 9.0 million (versus 9.1 million as of December 31, 2005): 1,116,000 (1,059,000) guaranteed cost (commercial HMO, Medicare, and Medicaid); 906,000 (1,129,000) experience-related indemnity; and 6,997,000 (6,902,000) ASO.

Disability and Life, which provides employer-paid and voluntary life, accident and disability products, held group life insurance policies covering 5.8 million lives at year-end 2005, versus 5.6 million at year-end 2004. International operates in selected markets outside the U.S., providing individual and group life, accident and health, health care and pension products. CI's assets under management at year-end 2005 totaled $21.4 billion, versus $21.9 billion at year-end 2004.

Company Financials

Per Share Data ($) Year Ended Dec. 31	**2005**	**2004**	**2003**	**2002**	**2001**	**2000**	**1999**	**1998**	**1997**	**1996**
Tangible Book Value	30.89	27.14	20.56	8.23	22.87	23.26	24.67	28.07	24.95	27.66
Operating Earnings	NA	NA	NA	NA	7.34	6.05	3.52	4.63	4.72	4.38
Earnings	9.83	11.44	4.41	-2.83	6.59	6.08	3.54	6.05	4.88	4.62
S&P Core Earnings	8.41	7.85	3.63	-0.71	5.31	NA	NA	NA	NA	NA
Dividends	0.10	0.41	1.32	1.32	1.28	1.24	1.19	1.14	1.11	1.07
Relative Payout	1%	4%	30%	NM	19%	20%	34%	19%	23%	23%
Prices:High	119.82	83.27	58.58	111.00	134.95	136.75	98.63	82.38	66.92	47.79
Prices:Low	78.11	52.90	39.10	34.15	69.86	60.75	63.44	56.00	44.71	33.58
P/E Ratio:High	12	7	13	NM	20	22	28	14	14	10
P/E Ratio:Low	8	5	9	NM	11	10	18	9	9	7

Income Statement Analysis (Million $)										
Life Insurance in Force	NA	NA	459,995	516,661	609,970	647,464	662,693	670,667	695,272	NA
Premium Income:Life A & H	13,695	14,236	15,441	15,737	15,367	16,328	15,079	13,913	12,251	9,518
Premium Income:Casualty/Property.	Nil	Nil	Nil	Nil	Nil	Nil	Nil	2,500	2,684	4,398
Net Investment Income	1,359	1,643	2,594	2,716	2,843	2,942	2,959	3,705	4,245	4,333
Total Revenue	16,684	18,176	18,808	19,348	19,115	19,994	18,781	21,437	20,038	18,950
Pretax Income	1,793	2,375	903	-569	1,497	1,497	1,219	2,010	1,650	1,601
Net Operating Income	NA	NA	NA	NA	1,101	983	695	1,190	971	1,000
Net Income	1,276	1,577	620	397	989	987	699	1,292	1,086	1,056
S&P Core Earnings	1,090	1,082	509	-99.2	794	NA	NA	NA	NA	NA

Balance Sheet & Other Financial Data (Million $)										
Cash & Equivalent	1,991	2,804	1,860	2,079	2,455	2,739	2,732	3,797	2,625	2,177
Premiums Due	8,616	16,223	9,421	9,981	2,832	2,814	2,475	4,469	4,265	4,229
Investment Assets:Bonds	14,947	16,136	17,121	27,803	23,401	24,776	22,944	32,634	36,358	36,253
Investment Assets:Stocks	135	33.0	11,300	295	404	569	585	1,043	854	701
Investment Assets:Loans	5,271	5,123	10,227	11,134	12,694	12,755	12,816	15,784	18,112	18,223
Investment Assets:Total	21,376	21,919	39,658	40,362	38,261	41,516	38,295	50,707	37,697	56,534
Deferred Policy Costs	618	544	580	494	448	1,052	927	1,069	1,542	1,230
Total Assets	44,863	81,059	90,953	88,950	91,589	95,088	95,333	114,612	108,199	98,932
Debt	1,338	1,438	1,500	1,500	1,627	1,163	1,359	1,431	2,155	1,021
Common Equity	5,360	5,203	4,465	3,665	5,055	5,634	6,149	8,277	7,932	7,208
Combined Loss-Expense Ratio	NA	NA	NA	NA	NA	NA	NA	107.1	NA	132.0
% Return on Revenue	7.6	8.7	3.3	NM	5.2	4.9	3.7	6.0	5.4	5.6
% Return on Equity	24.2	32.2	15.3	NM	18.9	16.5	9.1	15.9	14.3	14.7
% Investment Yield	6.3	5.3	6.5	6.9	7.3	7.1	7.4	8.4	7.5	7.6

Data as orig reptd.; bef. results of disc opers/spec. items. Per share data adj. for stk. divs.; EPS diluted. E-Estimated. NA-Not Available. NM-Not Meaningful. NR-Not Ranked. UR-Under Review.

Office: Two Liberty Place, Philadelphia, PA 19192-0004.
Telephone: 215-761-1000.
Website: http://www.cigna.com
Chrmn, Pres & CEO: H.E. Hanway

EVP & CFO: M.W. Bell
EVP & General Counsel: C.A. Petren
Investor Contact: T. Detrick (215-761-1414)

Board of Directors: R. H. Campbell, H. E. Hanway, I. Harris, Jr., J. E. Henney, P. N. Larson, R. Martinez IV, L. W. Sullivan, H. A. Wagner, C. C. Wait, D. F. Zarcone, W. D. Zollars

Founded: 1792
Domicile: Delaware
Employees: 28,000

STANDARD &POOR'S

Cincinnati Financial Corp

S&P Recommendation HOLD ★★★★★

Price $46.06 (as of Oct 27, 2006)

12-Mo. Target Price $50.00

Investment Style Mid-Cap Value

GICS Sector Financials
Sub-Industry Property & Casualty Insurance

Comment This insurance holding company markets primarily property and casualty coverage; it also conducts life insurance and asset management operations.

Key Stock Statistics (Source S&P, Vickers, company reports)

52-Wk Range	**$49.19–41.21**	S&P Oper. EPS 2006**E**	**2.95**	P/E on S&P Oper. EPS 2006**E**	**15.6**	Dividend Rate/Share	**$1.34**
Trailing 12-Month EPS	**$5.60**	S&P Oper. EPS 2007**E**	**3.10**	Common Shares Outstg. (M)	**173.2**	Yield (%)	**2.91**
Trailing 12-Month P/E	**8.2**	S&P Core EPS 2006**E**	**2.86**	Market Capitalization(B)	**$7.979**	Beta	**0.59**
$10K Invested 5 Yrs Ago	**$14,870**	S&P Core EPS 2007**E**	**3.04**	Institutional Ownership (%)	**52**	S&P Credit Rating	**A**

Price Performance

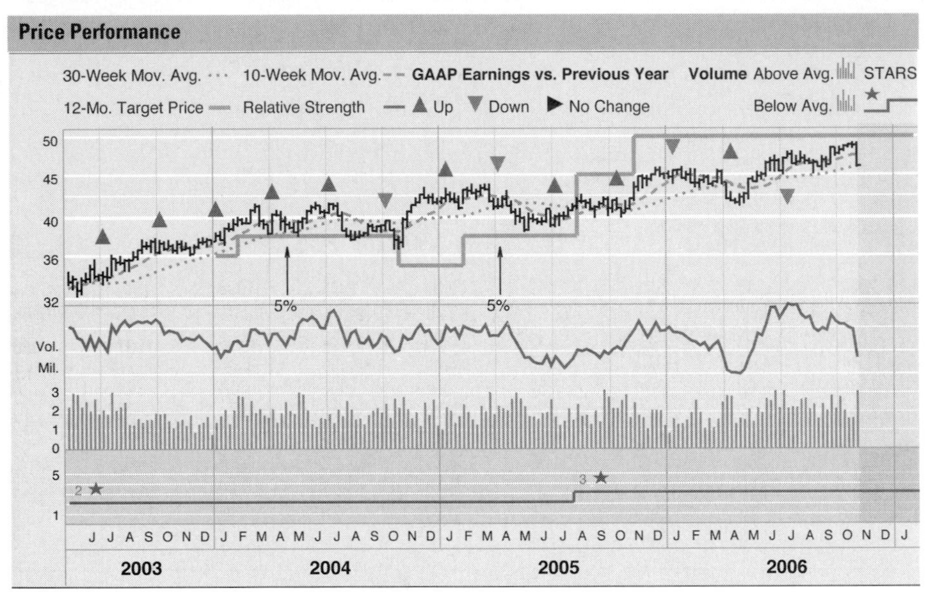

Options: ASE

Analysis prepared by **Cathy A. Seifert** on October 04, 2006, when the stock traded at **$ 48.50**.

Highlights

- We project property casualty earned premium growth of 3% to 5% in 2006, versus the 4.8% recorded for 2005. We see the effects of CINF's expansion being offset by continued price competition. Though we expect pricing for many lines of insurance to firm in the aftermath of 2005's record catastrophe losses, we believe that competition in many non-coastal regions (like those in which CINF operates) will increase.
- We estimate net investment income growth of approximately 4% to 6% in 2006. This rate of growth is below that of a number of CINF's peers and is partly due to a different asset mix. At December 31, 2005, nearly 56% of CINF's invested assets were in equity securities, versus an industry average that we estimate is less than 15%.
- We expect tepid premium growth, narrower underwriting margins, and a more modest rate of investment income growth to lead to a decline in operating earnings in 2006. We see operating EPS of $2.95 in 2006, and $3.10 in 2007, versus $3.17 reported in 2005.

Investment Rationale/Risk

- We believe that CINF has done an admirable job of improving its underwriting results and profitability. We also note that CINF's lack of meaningful exposure to hurricane losses has resulted in superior results relative to many of its peers. But, we anticipate CINF will face price competition in its core markets. Moreover, we regard the current valuation as fair. The stock's P/E multiple and P/E-to-growth (PEG) ratios were recently at premiums to peers. CINF also has among the lowest rates of return on equity in its peer group.
- Risks to our opinion and target price include a lower than expected premium growth rate and a sharp deterioration in underwriting results and profitability.
- Our 12-month target price of $50 assumes a modest expansion in the shares' forward P/E, to about 17X our 2006 EPS estimate, more than a 25% premium to peers. Our target price also assumes a forward price/book multiple of about 1.4X, a discount to peers.

Qualitative Risk Assessment

LOW | **MEDIUM** | HIGH

Our risk assessment reflects our view of the company as a fairly conservative underwriter with sound risk and capital management policies. However, CINF's investment allocation is more heavily weighted toward equity holdings than the company's peers.

Quantitative Evaluations

S&P Quality Ranking A-

D | C | B- | B | B+ | **A-** | A | A+

Relative Strength Rank WEAK

20

LOWEST = 1 HIGHEST = 99

Revenue/Earnings Data

Revenue (Million $)

	1Q	2Q	3Q	4Q	Year
2006	1,607	981.0	--	--	--
2005	916.0	940.0	944.0	967.0	3,767
2004	870.0	923.0	879.0	942.0	3,614
2003	707.0	798.0	836.0	840.0	3,181
2002	687.0	703.0	731.0	722.0	2,843
2001	618.0	645.0	644.0	654.0	2,561

Earnings Per Share ($)

	1Q	2Q	3Q	4Q	Year
2006	3.13	0.76	**E**0.67	**E**0.85	**E**2.95
2005	0.81	0.89	0.66	1.03	3.40
2004	0.82	0.87	0.50	1.09	3.28
2003	0.31	0.48	0.58	0.72	2.10
2002	0.42	0.19	0.40	0.31	1.32
2001	0.41	0.27	0.20	0.20	1.08

Fiscal year ended Dec. 31. Next earnings report expected: Early November. EPS Estimates based on S&P Operating Earnings; historical GAAP earnings are as reported.

Dividend Data (Dates: mm/dd Payment Date: mm/dd/yy)

Amount ($)	Date Decl.	Ex-Div. Date	Stk. of Record	Payment Date
0.305	11/21	12/21	12/23	01/17/06
0.335	02/03	03/22	03/24	04/14/06
0.335	05/26	06/21	06/23	07/14/06
0.335	08/14	09/20	09/22	10/16/06

Dividends have been paid since 1954. Source: Company reports.

Cincinnati Financial Corp

Business Summary October 04, 2006

Cincinnati Financial Corp. underwrites and sells property-casualty insurance primarily in the Midwest and Southeast, through a network of independent agents. Operations as of 2005 year-end were conducted in 32 states, through a network of 1,024 independent insurance agents, many of whom own stock in the company. The company is licensed in all 50 states, the District of Columbia, and Puerto Rico. An ongoing geographical expansion plan is being implemented.

Property-casualty net earned premiums totaled $3.1 billion in 2005, with commercial lines accounting for 74% and personal lines for 26%. Four lines of business (commercial multi-peril, workers compensation, commercial auto and other liability) accounted for 90% of commercial lines earned premiums in 2005. Personal auto and homeowners coverage accounted for over 89% of personal lines earned premiums in 2005.

Underwriting results improved slightly in 2005, due in part to a lower level of catastrophe losses The loss ratio in 2005 equaled 59.2% (including 4.1 points of catastrophe losses), versus 60.1% (including 5.1 points of catastrophe losses). The expense ratio inched upward, to 29.8%, from 229.4%. The policyholder dividend ratio declined to 0.2% in 2005 from 0.3% in 2004. Taken together, the GAAP combined ratio equaled 89.2% in 2005, a modest improvement from 2004's combined ratio of 89.8%.

Life, accident and health insurance is marketed through property-casualty agents and independent life insurance agents. This unit has been expanding its worksite marketing activities, introducing a new product line and exploring expansion opportunities. Term life insurance represents this unit's largest product line.

Total invested assets of more than $12.6 billion at December 31, 2005, were divided as follows: fixed maturities 43%, equity securities 55%, and preferred equities and other investments 2%. CinFin Capital Management offers asset management services to institutions and high net worth individuals.

Company Financials

Per Share Data ($) Year Ended Dec. 31	2005	2004	2003	2002	2001	2000	1999	1998	1997	1996
Tangible Book Value	34.98	35.60	35.10	31.42	33.62	33.80	30.35	30.58	25.71	17.19
Operating Earnings	3.02	2.93	NA	1.67	1.17	0.82	1.38	1.08	1.39	1.02
Earnings	3.40	3.28	2.10	1.32	1.08	0.66	1.38	1.28	1.61	1.19
S&P Core Earnings	3.10	2.87	2.09	1.55	1.06	NA	NA	NA	NA	NA
Dividends	1.21	1.04	0.91	0.81	0.76	0.69	0.60	0.54	0.50	0.45
Relative Payout	35%	32%	43%	61%	71%	104%	44%	42%	31%	38%
Prices:High	45.95	43.52	38.01	42.90	38.94	39.29	38.55	42.55	42.78	19.80
Prices:Low	38.38	36.57	30.00	29.42	30.84	23.75	27.32	27.66	18.75	16.10
P/E Ratio:High	14	13	18	32	36	59	28	33	27	17
P/E Ratio:Low	11	11	14	22	29	36	20	22	12	14
Income Statement Analysis (Million $)										
Life Insurance in Force	51,493	44,921	48,492	32,486	27,534	23,525	17,890	13,048	10,845	9,776
Premium Income:Life A & H	106	101	95.0	87.0	81.0	79.3	75.0	70.1	62.9	56.0
Premium Income:Casualty/Property.	3,058	2,919	2,653	2,391	2,071	1,828	1,657	1,543	1,454	1,367
Net Investment Income	526	492	465	445	421	415	387	368	349	327
Total Revenue	3,767	3,614	3,181	2,843	2,561	2,331	2,120	2,054	1,942	1,809
Pretax Income	823	800	480	279	221	109	322	307	395	282
Net Operating Income	562	524	286	300	210	120	255	199	254	193
Net Income	602	584	374	238	193	118	255	242	299	224
S&P Core Earnings	549	512	372	279	189	NA	NA	NA	NA	NA
Balance Sheet & Other Financial Data (Million $)										
Cash & Equivalent	119	306	91.0	112	93.0	60.3	420	135	80.2	130
Premiums Due	1,797	1,799	1,677	1,483	732	652	192	164	159	162
Investment Assets:Bonds	5,476	5,141	3,925	3,305	3,010	2,721	2,617	2,812	2,751	2,562
Investment Assets:Stocks	7,106	7,498	8,524	7,884	8,495	8,526	7,511	7,455	5,999	3,740
Investment Assets:Loans	Nil	Nil	Nil	Nil	Nil	Nil	Nil	Nil	Nil	Nil
Investment Assets:Total	75.0	12,677	12,527	11,257	11,571	11,316	10,194	10,325	8,797	6,344
Deferred Policy Costs	429	400	372	343	286	259	154	143	135	128
Total Assets	16,003	16,107	15,509	14,059	13,959	13,287	11,380	11,087	9,493	7,046
Debt	791	791	603	420	609	449	457	472	339	342
Common Equity	4,145	6,249	6,204	5,998	5,998	5,995	5,420	5,621	4,717	3,163
Combined Loss-Expense Ratio	89.2	89.8	94.7	98.4	104.9	112.5	100.0	103.6	97.7	103.0
% Return on Revenue	16.0	16.2	11.8	8.4	7.5	5.1	12.0	11.8	15.4	12.4
% Return on Equity	15.4	8.0	5.4	3.6	3.2	1.0	4.6	4.7	7.6	7.7
% Investment Yield	720.5	3.9	3.9	3.9	3.7	3.9	3.8	3.8	4.6	5.5

Data as orig reptd.; bef. results of disc opers/spec. items. Per share data adj. for stk. divs.; EPS diluted. E-Estimated. NA-Not Available. NM-Not Meaningful. NR-Not Ranked. UR-Under Review.

Office: 6200 South Gilmore Road, Fairfield, OH 45014-5141.
Telephone: 513-870-2000.
Email: investor_inquiries@cinfin.com
Website: http://www.cinfin.com

Chrmn & CEO: J.J. Schiff, Jr.
Pres, Vice Chrmn & COO: J.E. Benoski
EVP, CFO, Treas & Secy: K.W. Stecher
Investor Contact: H.J. Wietzel (513-870-2768)

Board of Directors: W. F. Bahl, J. E. Benoski, M. Brown, D. J. Debbink, K. C. Lichtendahl, W. R. McMullen, G. W. Price, T. R. Schiff, J. J. Schiff, Jr., J. M. Shepherd, D. S. Skidmore, J. Steele, Jr., L. R. Webb, E. A. Woods

Founded: 1968
Domicile: Ohio
Employees: 3,983

STANDARD &POOR'S

Cintas Corp

S&P Recommendation BUY ★★★★★

Price $41.15 (as of Oct 27, 2006)

12-Mo. Target Price $45.00

Investment Style Mid-Cap Growth

GICS Sector Industrials
Sub-Industry Diversified Commercial & Professional Services

Comment A leader in the corporate identity uniform business, Cintas also provides entrance mats, sanitation supplies, and first aid and safety products.

Key Stock Statistics (Source S&P, Vickers, company reports)

52-Wk Range	$45.40–34.57	S&P Oper. EPS 2007E	2.20	P/E on S&P Oper. EPS 2007E	18.7	Dividend Rate/Share	$0.35
Trailing 12-Month EPS	$2.01	S&P Oper. EPS 2008E	2.33	Common Shares Outstg. (M)	160.6	Yield (%)	0.85
Trailing 12-Month P/E	20.5	S&P Core EPS 2007E	2.20	Market Capitalization(B)	$6.607	Beta	1.25
$10K Invested 5 Yrs Ago	$9,827	S&P Core EPS 2008E	2.33	Institutional Ownership (%)	66	S&P Credit Rating	A

Price Performance

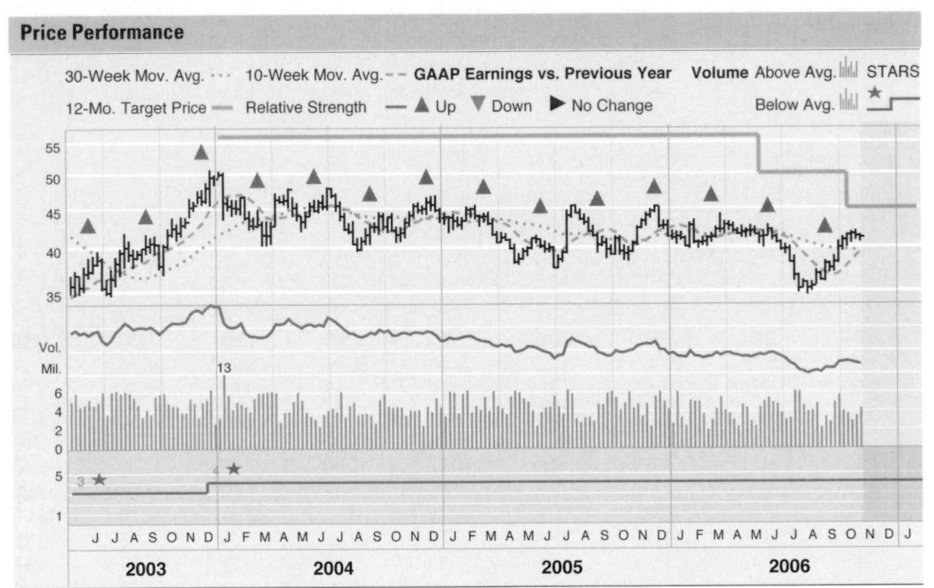

Options: ASE, CBOE, P, Ph

Analysis prepared by **Kevin Kirkeby** on October 04, 2006, when the stock traded at **$ 41.23**.

Highlights

- We forecast revenues will increase about 10% in FY 07 (May), with new client wins contributing to a likely 8% rise in rental and facility services (75% of total revenues). Including acquisitions, the other services segment should show a 15% gain, down from nearly 19% in FY 06, as the businesses become larger. We see contract renewals remaining above 90%, but believe CTAS has little ability to increase prices.

- CTAS recently introduced a new sales structure that emphasizes the cross selling of services and has added additional salespeople in an effort to counteract slowing organic growth. These efforts and investments in labor and equipment for its new businesses are expected to largely offset margin improvements from plant rationalizations and lower cost sourcing initiatives in FY 07.

- We estimate EPS to rise 13% in FY 07 to $2.20, including three cents per share in stock option expenses. The comparison against FY 06 benefits from a repurchase program that reduced shares outstanding by more than 6 million shares, or 4% of the total outstanding. Cash flow is projected to be $328 million in FY 07.

Investment Rationale/Risk

- CTAS has historically traded at a premium valuation to the S&P 500 and peers, in our view, due to its consistent growth. We think it can achieve a 38th consecutive year of sales and profit growth in FY 07. However, as employment growth nationwide has slowed and a greater percentage of earnings gains have come from acquisitions and share buybacks, valuations have compressed to near historical lows. As the newer service businesses achieve sufficient scale and demonstrate margin expansion, we expect valuations to expand modestly.

- Risks to our recommendation and target price include slower than expected growth in employment levels and uniform rentals, and potentially rising labor costs.

- The shares have traded in a range of 16X to 55X forward EPS over the last 10 years. Using an 18X multiple, near the low end of its historical range, applied to our FY 07 EPS estimate, we calculate a value of $40. Our DCF model yields an intrinsic value of $50, based on a 10.4% WACC, 8% annual free cash flow growth over the next 10 years, and 3.5% growth in perpetuity. Blending our valuation models results in a 12-month target price of $45.

Qualitative Risk Assessment

LOW | MEDIUM | HIGH

Our risk assessment reflects the company's leading position in its core business, other related services that we believe are showing good growth, and what we view as a relatively strong balance sheet and cash flow.

Quantitative Evaluations

S&P Quality Ranking A+

D | C | B- | B | B+ | A- | A | A+

Relative Strength Rank MODERATE

58

LOWEST = 1 HIGHEST = 99

Revenue/Earnings Data

Revenue (Million $)

	1Q	2Q	3Q	4Q	Year
2007	914.2	--	--	--	--
2006	823.5	835.8	836.4	907.9	3,404
2005	746.0	756.8	755.2	809.3	3,067
2004	677.7	701.3	696.9	738.2	2,814
2003	665.7	681.0	663.8	676.1	2,687
2002	564.6	557.2	545.5	603.8	2,271

Earnings Per Share ($)

	1Q	2Q	3Q	4Q	Year
2007	0.53	E0.53	E0.53	E0.61	E2.20
2006	0.47	0.46	0.46	0.55	1.94
2005	0.42	0.43	0.41	0.48	1.74
2004	0.37	0.40	0.39	0.42	1.58
2003	0.36	0.37	0.34	0.38	1.45
2002	0.33	0.34	0.32	0.37	1.36

Fiscal year ended May 31. Next earnings report expected: Late December. EPS Estimates based on S&P Operating Earnings; historical GAAP earnings are as reported.

Dividend Data (Dates: mm/dd Payment Date: mm/dd/yy)

Amount ($)	Date Decl.	Ex-Div. Date	Stk. of Record	Payment Date
0.350	01/24	02/03	02/07	03/14/06

Dividends have been paid since 1984. Source: Company reports.

Cintas Corp

Business Summary October 04, 2006

CORPORATE OVERVIEW. Cintas Corp. is North America's leading supplier of corporate uniforms, as well as a significant provider of related services. FY 06 (May) marked Cintas Corp.'s 37th consecutive year of sales and profit growth.

The Rental operating segment (75% of total revenues in FY 06 (May) and 79% of gross profits, with a 45.2% margin) designs and manufactures corporate uniforms that it rents (about 43% of total company sales)--together with other items--to its customers. Services provided to the rental markets by the company also include the cleaning of uniforms, as well as the provision of ongoing replacements as required by each customer. CTAS rents uniforms to a variety of industries, including hospitality, auto aftermarket, and food service. The company also offers ancillary products, including the rental or sale of entrance and special purpose mats, towels, mops, and linen products.

The Other Services segment (25%, 21%, and 35.1% margin) includes the design, manufacture and direct sale of uniforms to CTAS's national account customers. In addition, the segment sells ancillary products, including sanitation supplies and services and cleanroom supplies.

The company offers first aid, safety, and emergency care supplies and training. These services are available through local distributors in 42 major U.S. cities. The company has broadened its product line to include fire protection services, including the inspection, repair and recharging of portable fire extinguishers, fire suppression systems, and emergency and exit lights. In a short period of time, the company believes it has become the second largest fire protection services company in the U.S., with capabilities in 23 of the top 50 cities. The company estimates the market size for first aid and fire protection services at a combined $4.5 billion a year.

The company also provides on-site and off-site shredding of confidential documents. In FY 06, CTAS made several small acquisitions in the document storage business. Document management services are now available in 70 of the 100 largest markets in the U.S. and Canada. The company estimates the potential annual market is $8 billion.

Company Financials

Per Share Data ($) Year Ended May 31	2006	2005	2004	2003	2002	2001	2000	1999	1998	1997
Tangible Book Value	4.73	6.15	6.32	5.42	4.39	6.42	5.42	4.54	3.71	3.14
Cash Flow	2.78	2.43	2.26	2.12	1.95	1.82	1.60	1.23	1.09	0.89
Earnings	1.94	1.74	1.58	1.45	1.36	1.30	1.14	0.82	0.79	0.64
S&P Core Earnings	1.92	1.69	1.54	1.43	1.33	1.27	NA	NA	NA	NA
Dividends	0.32	0.32	0.29	0.27	0.25	0.22	0.19	0.15	0.12	0.10
Payout Ratio	16%	18%	18%	19%	18%	17%	17%	18%	15%	16%
Calendar Year	2005	2004	2003	2002	2001	2000	1999	1998	1997	1996
Prices:High	45.50	50.35	50.68	56.62	53.25	54.00	52.25	47.50	28.33	21.17
Prices:Low	37.51	39.51	30.60	39.15	33.75	23.17	26.00	26.00	17.00	13.92
P/E Ratio:High	23	29	32	42	39	42	46	50	30	33
P/E Ratio:Low	19	23	19	29	25	18	23	32	21	22
Income Statement Analysis (Million $)										
Revenue	3,404	3,067	2,814	2,687	2,271	2,161	1,902	1,752	1,198	840
Operating Income	674	614	602	539	478	459	423	338	258	198
Depreciation	127	120	117	115	101	90.2	78.5	68.8	45.8	35.8
Interest Expense	31.8	24.4	25.1	30.9	11.0	15.1	15.9	16.4	9.08	7.97
Pretax Income	522	477	432	396	372	356	312	224	179	147
Effective Tax Rate	37.3%	37.0%	37.0%	37.0%	37.0%	37.6%	38.0%	38.0%	31.5%	38.0%
Net Income	327	301	272	249	234	222	193	139	123	90.8
S&P Core Earnings	324	293	265	245	229	219	NA	NA	NA	NA
Balance Sheet & Other Financial Data (Million $)										
Cash	241	309	254	57.7	85.1	110	110	88.1	12.7	103
Current Assets	1,178	1,167	1,034	878	853	820	721	634	509	365
Total Assets	3,425	3,060	2,810	2,583	2,519	1,752	1,581	1,408	1,018	762
Current Liabilities	412	356	326	305	313	251	235	212	159	116
Long Term Debt	794	465	474	535	703	221	254	284	180	111
Common Equity	2,088	2,104	1,888	1,646	1,424	1,231	1,043	871	654	512
Total Capital	3,013	2,703	2,485	2,278	2,207	1,501	1,346	1,196	858	646
Capital Expenditures	157	141	113	115	170	147	161	171	97.0	67.8
Cash Flow	454	420	389	365	335	313	272	208	169	127
Current Ratio	2.9	3.3	3.2	2.9	2.7	3.3	3.1	3.0	3.2	3.1
% Long Term Debt of Capitalization	26.4	17.2	19.1	23.5	31.9	14.7	18.9	23.7	21.0	17.3
% Net Income of Revenue	9.6	9.8	44.4	9.3	10.3	10.3	10.3	7.9	10.3	10.8
% Return on Assets	10.1	10.2	10.1	9.8	11.0	13.3	12.9	10.2	13.8	12.7
% Return on Equity	15.6	15.1	15.4	16.2	17.6	19.6	20.2	17.1	21.1	19.3

Data as orig reptd.; bef. results of disc opers/spec. items. Per share data adj. for stk. divs.; EPS diluted. E-Estimated. NA-Not Available. NM-Not Meaningful. NR-Not Ranked. UR-Under Review.

Office: 6800 Cintas Boulevard, Cincinnati, OH 45262-5737.
Telephone: 513-459-1200.
Website: http://www.cintas.com
Chrmn: R.T. Farmer

Pres & CEO: S.D. Farmer
Vice Chrmn: R.J. Kohlhepp
Investor Contact: W.C. Gale (513-459-1200)
SVP & CFO: W.C. Gale

Board of Directors: G. S. Adolph, P. R. Carter, G. V. Dirvin, R. T. Farmer, S. D. Farmer, J. Hergenhan, R. L. Howe, R. J. Kohlhepp, D. C. Phillips

Founded: 1968
Domicile: Washington
Employees: 32,000

STANDARD &POOR'S

Circuit City Stores Inc

S&P Recommendation HOLD ★★★★★	Price	12-Mo. Target Price	Investment Style
	$27.00 (as of Oct 27, 2006)	$30.00	Mid-Cap Value

GICS Sector Consumer Discretionary
Sub-Industry Computer & Electronics Retail

Comment Circuit City is a large retailer of brand-name consumer electronics, personal computers, and entertainment software.

Key Stock Statistics (Source S&P, Vickers, company reports)

52-Wk Range	$31.54–17.39	S&P Oper. EPS 2007E	1.08	P/E on S&P Oper. EPS 2007E	25.0	Dividend Rate/Share	$0.16
Trailing 12-Month EPS	$0.93	S&P Oper. EPS 2008E	1.25	Common Shares Outstg. (M)	175.2	Yield (%)	0.59
Trailing 12-Month P/E	29.0	S&P Core EPS 2007E	1.08	Market Capitalization(B)	$4.729	Beta	0.70
$10K Invested 5 Yrs Ago	$43,967	S&P Core EPS 2008E	1.25	Institutional Ownership (%)	97	S&P Credit Rating	NA

Price Performance

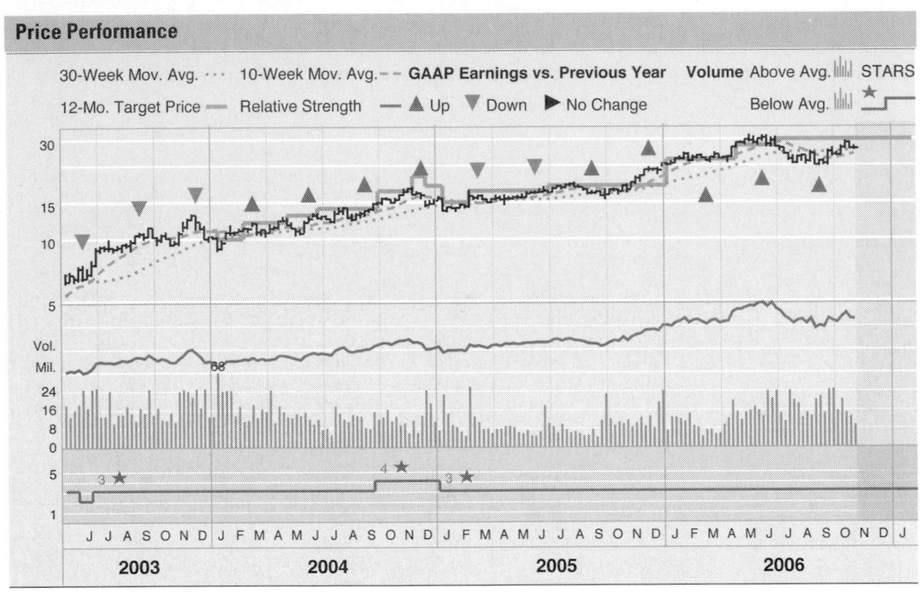

Options: ASE, CBOE, P

Analysis prepared by **Marie Driscoll, CFA** on September 22, 2006, when the stock traded at **$ 25.25**.

Highlights

- We see an 11% sales gain in FY 07 (Feb.) and an 8% gain in FY 08, supported by mid- to high-single digit comparable-store sales gains and new store expansion. We think that CC, as well as peer companies, will continue to benefit from strong consumer demand for advanced TVs, as declines in average selling prices of about 25% should make the TVs more affordable to a larger customer base. We also expect notebook computers, digital imaging products, MP3 players, and services to be strong.
- We see a FY 07 operating margin of 2.3% (versus 1.9% in FY 06), at the high end of CC's guidance of 2.0% to 2.4%, and up another 40 basis points in FY 08. We expect leverage on higher sales volumes, continued operational improvements, and growing sales of higher margin service offerings to be partly offset by investments in infrastructure that should help to enhance CC's competitive positioning over the long term. We expect these incremental investments to affect FY 07's operating margin by approximately 100 basis points.
- We see FY 07 EPS of $1.08, up 32%, and look for EPS of $1.25 in FY 08.

Investment Rationale/Risk

- At about 0.38X our estimate of FY 07 sales per share, CC trades just below its five-year historical average price to sales ratio. By this metric, CC trades at a significant--and we think warranted--discount to Best Buy (BBY: buy, $55). However, we believe that CC is making significant progress in improving its operations, as evidenced by strong results posted in the past four consecutive quarters. We view investments in business upgrades, marketing and store revitalizations, which we expect will cap margin improvement in FY 07, as necessary to position CC for sustainable, consistent and profitable growth over the long term. However, we think the current valuation largely reflects CC's improved growth prospects.
- Risks to our recommendation and target price include an adverse shift in the economic climate and consumer confidence, and the possibility that CC will fail to achieve its strategic objectives and will be unable to meet sales growth and profitability expectations.
- Our 12-month target price of $30 reflects a price to sales ratio of 0.41X our estimate of FY 07 sales per share, in line with CC's five-year historical average.

Qualitative Risk Assessment

LOW | **MEDIUM** | HIGH

Our risk assessment reflects our view of CC's strong balance sheet, with little debt, and improving financial trends, offset by intense rivalry in the consumer electronics industry.

Quantitative Evaluations

S&P Quality Ranking B-

D | C | **B-** | B | B+ | A- | A | A+

Relative Strength Rank MODERATE

56

LOWEST = 1 HIGHEST = 99

Revenue/Earnings Data

Revenue (Million $)

	1Q	2Q	3Q	4Q	Year
2007	2,617	2,839	--	--	--
2006	2,228	2,562	2,906	3,911	11,598
2005	2,067	2,345	2,493	3,469	10,472
2004	1,933	2,156	2,407	3,249	9,745
2003	2,118	2,221	2,422	3,192	9,954
2002	2,678	2,888	3,054	4,171	12,791

Earnings Per Share ($)

2007	0.03	0.07	**E**0.11	**E**0.88	**E**1.08
2006	-0.07	0.01	0.06	0.84	0.83
2005	-0.03	-0.06	-0.03	0.43	0.31
2004	-0.14	-0.19	-0.14	0.46	Nil
2003	-0.01	-0.05	-0.10	0.36	0.20
2002	0.05	0.03	0.10	0.73	0.92

Fiscal year ended Feb. 28. Next earnings report expected: Mid December. EPS Estimates based on S&P Operating Earnings; historical GAAP earnings are as reported.

Dividend Data (Dates: mm/dd Payment Date: mm/dd/yy)

Amount ($)	Date Decl.	Ex-Div. Date	Stk. of Record	Payment Date
0.018	12/15	12/28	12/31	01/16/06
0.018	03/15	03/29	03/31	04/17/06
0.018	06/15	06/28	06/30	07/17/06
0.040	06/29	09/27	09/30	10/16/06

Dividends have been paid since 1979. Source: Company reports.

Please read the Required Disclosures and Analyst Certification on the last page of this report.

Circuit City Stores Inc

Business Summary September 22, 2006

CORPORATE OVERVIEW. This large specialty retailer of consumer electronics goods has two reportable segments: domestic (95% of FY 06 (Feb.) revenues) and international (5%). Domestically, CC sells brand-name products through Circuit City Superstores (626 as of year-end FY 06), mall-based stores (5) and its Web site. The international segment sells private-label and brand-name consumer electronics through 540 company-owned stores, 300 dealer outlets, 93 Rogers Plus stores and 21 Battery Plus stores.

Major merchandise categories are: video (44% of FY 06 sales); information technology (28%); audio (16%); and entertainment software (12%). CC also provides services, including narrowband, broadband, wireless telephone, digital video services, extended warranty programs, car audio installation and in-home video installation. With our view of increasing price deflation and the commoditization of consumer electronic goods, we expect retailers such as CC to increasingly focus on growing service revenues. In addition to generating a higher margin, we think services can help companies differentiate themselves in the marketplace, as well as build brand loyalty.

In May 2004, CC acquired Ontario-based consumer electronics retailer InterTAN for $14 a share in cash. Also in May, CC sold its private-label credit card operation to Bank One Corp. In November 2003, the company completed the sale of its bank card operation to FleetBoston Financial. In October 2002, the CarMax vehicle retail business was separated from CC, becoming part of a separately traded public company, CarMax, Inc. (KMX). CarMax Group common stock had been about 64%-owned by CC.

Company Financials

Per Share Data ($) Year Ended Feb. 28	2006	2005	2004	2003	2002	2001	2000	1999	1998	1997
Tangible Book Value	9.73	9.78	10.91	11.15	11.13	10.13	9.33	7.69	7.12	6.73
Cash Flow	1.74	1.09	0.96	0.95	1.78	1.53	2.33	1.41	1.11	1.18
Earnings	0.83	0.31	Nil	0.20	0.92	0.73	1.60	0.74	0.57	0.69
S&P Core Earnings	0.81	0.32	0.01	0.08	0.80	0.63	NA	NA	NA	NA
Dividends	0.07	0.07	0.07	0.07	0.07	0.07	0.07	0.07	0.07	0.07
Payout Ratio	9%	23%	NM	35%	8%	10%	4%	9%	8%	9%
Calendar Year	2005	2004	2003	2002	2001	2000	1999	1998	1997	1996
Prices:High	23.12	17.87	13.21	31.40	26.65	65.19	53.88	27.25	22.75	19.38
Prices:Low	13.40	8.69	3.91	6.95	9.55	8.69	23.69	14.41	14.31	12.50
P/E Ratio:High	28	60	NM	NM	29	89	34	37	33	28
P/E Ratio:Low	16	29	NM	NM	10	12	15	19	21	18

Income Statement Analysis (Million $)										
Revenue	11,598	10,472	9,745	9,954	12,791	12,959	12,614	10,804	8,871	7,664
Operating Income	384	247	166	163	519	462	701	399	311	-8.00
Depreciation	164	155	198	157	151	153	148	140	110	99.0
Interest Expense	3.14	2.07	1.80	1.09	5.84	19.4	24.2	28.3	36.5	6.28
Pretax Income	239	95.8	-1.24	67.0	353	259	529	231	168	15.9
Effective Tax Rate	36.8%	37.5%	NM	38.0%	38.0%	38.0%	38.0%	38.0%	38.0%	41.5%
Net Income	151	59.9	-0.79	41.6	219	161	328	143	104	136
S&P Core Earnings	144	61.9	0.83	16.3	166	129	NA	NA	NA	NA

Balance Sheet & Other Financial Data (Million $)										
Cash	316	880	783	885	1,252	446	644	266	117	203
Current Assets	2,833	2,686	2,919	3,103	3,653	2,847	2,943	2,395	2,146	2,163
Total Assets	4,069	3,789	3,633	3,799	4,539	3,871	3,955	3,445	3,232	3,081
Current Liabilities	1,622	12,164	1,177	1,280	1,641	1,292	1,406	964	906	837
Long Term Debt	52.0	11.5	22.7	11.3	14.1	116	249	427	424	430
Common Equity	1,955	2,087	2,224	2,342	2,734	2,356	2,142	1,905	1,730	1,615
Total Capital	2,007	2,099	2,247	2,353	2,749	2,488	2,419	2,369	2,181	2,078
Capital Expenditures	255	269	176	151	214	286	222	367	588	542
Cash Flow	315	215	197	199	370	314	476	283	221	235
Current Ratio	1.7	0.2	2.5	2.4	2.2	2.2	2.1	2.5	2.4	2.6
% Long Term Debt of Capitalization	2.6	0.5	1.0	0.5	0.5	4.7	10.3	18.0	24.5	20.7
% Net Income of Revenue	1.3	0.6	NM	0.4	1.7	1.2	2.6	1.3	1.2	1.8
% Return on Assets	3.8	1.6	NM	1.0	5.2	4.1	8.9	4.3	3.3	4.9
% Return on Equity	7.5	2.8	NM	1.6	8.6	7.1	16.2	7.9	6.2	10.2

Data as orig reptd.; bef. results of disc opers/spec. items. Per share data adj. for stk. divs.; EPS diluted. E-Estimated. NA-Not Available. NM-Not Meaningful. NR-Not Ranked. UR-Under Review.

Office: 9950 Mayland Drive, Richmond, VA 23233-1464.
Telephone: 804-527-4000.
Website: http://www.circuitcity.com
Chrmn, Pres & CEO: P.J. Schoonover

EVP & CFO: M.E. Foss
SVP, Treas & Cntlr: P.J. Dunn
SVP, Secy & General Counsel: R.D. Hedgebeth
SVP & CIO: W.E. McCorey, Jr.

Board of Directors: R. M. Brill, C. H. Byrd, U. O. Fairbairn, B. S. Feigin, M. E. Foss, J. F. Hardymon, A. Kane, A. B. King, M. Salovaara, P. J. Schoonover, J. P. Spainhour, C. Y. Woo

Founded: 1949
Domicile: Virginia
Employees: 42,359

STANDARD &POOR'S

Cisco Systems Inc

S&P Recommendation BUY ★★★★★

Price $23.72 (as of Oct 27, 2006)

12-Mo. Target Price $26.00

Investment Style Large-Cap Growth

GICS Sector Information Technology
Sub-Industry Communications Equipment

Comment CSCO offers a complete line of routers and switching products that connect and manage communications among local and wide area computer networks employing a variety of protocols.

Key Stock Statistics (Source S&P, Vickers, company reports)

52-Wk Range	**$24.78–16.87**	S&P Oper. EPS 2007**E**	**1.18**	P/E on S&P Oper. EPS 2007**E**	**20.1**	Dividend Rate/Share	**Nil**
Trailing 12-Month EPS	**$0.89**	S&P Oper. EPS 2008**E**	**1.35**	Common Shares Outstg. (M)	**6,070.1**	Yield (%)	**Nil**
Trailing 12-Month P/E	**26.7**	S&P Core EPS 2007E	**1.35**	Market Capitalization(B)	**$143.984**	Beta	**2.08**
$10K Invested 5 Yrs Ago	**$13,719**	S&P Core EPS 2008E	**NA**	Institutional Ownership (%)	**66**	S&P Credit Rating	**A+**

Price Performance

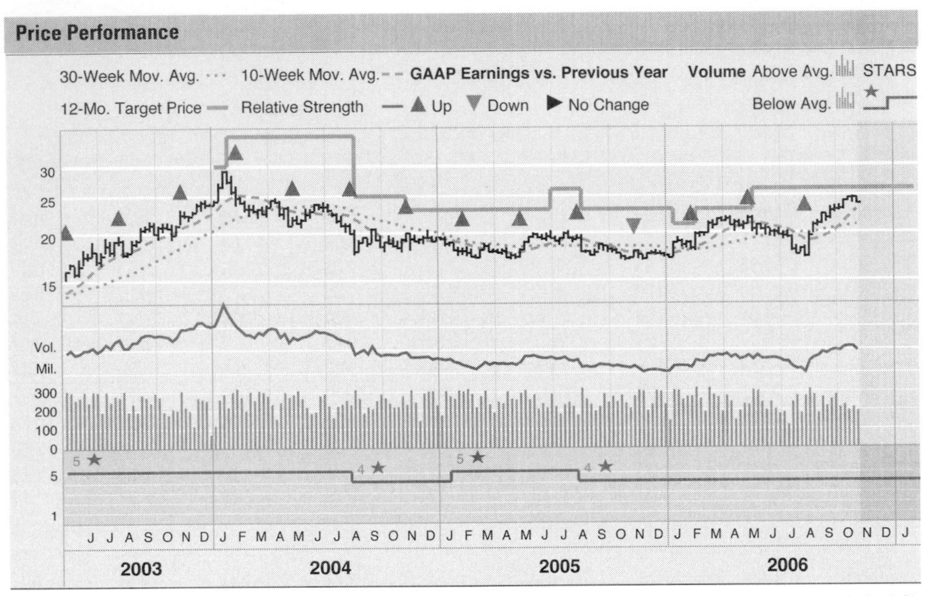

Options: ASE, CBOE, P, Ph

Analysis prepared by **Ari Bensinger** on August 14, 2006, when the stock traded at **$ 20.12**.

Highlights

- Following a 15% rise in FY 06 (Jul.), we project that revenues will advance 17% in FY 07, including a full fiscal year contribution from Scientific-Atlanta, which was acquired in February 2006. We expect the maturing switching and routing divisions to post high single digit growth. We believe the advanced technologies division could increase more than 40%, fueled by the new video systems segment.
- We look for the gross margin to narrow modestly, to about 65%, in FY 07, primarily attributable to a less favorable sales mix reflecting strong advanced technology growth, as well as the addition of Scientific Atlanta products. Other factors affecting profitability include component costs, channel mix, and competitive pricing pressures.
- Reflecting anticipated higher sales volume, we forecast operating expenses declining as a percentage of sales. We forecast FY 07 operating EPS of $1.18, including $0.11 of projected stock option expense in accordance with the new FASB 123R mandate, versus the $0.95 posted in FY 06.

Investment Rationale/Risk

- In our view, CSCO is maintaining its dominant market position in the large network routing and switching markets, while successfully positioning itself in attractive subsegments. We see the early 2006 acquisition of Scientific-Atlanta as adding cable video integration solutions to CSCO's IP transport expertise, enabling an end-to-end video distribution offering.
- Risks to our opinion and target price include potential market share losses as peers increasingly target CSCO's dominant share, and narrowing margins due to intensifying pricing pressures.
- Our 12-month target price of $26 is based on a P/E of about 22X our FY 07 operating EPS estimate, slightly below the peer mean. Using our five-year earnings growth rate projection of 13%, our target price reflects a forward P/E to growth (PEG) ratio of 1.7X, in line with the industry average. Our discounted cash flow model, assuming a weighted average cost of capital of 11.9% and terminal growth of free cash flow of 3%, indicates an intrinsic value of $26.

Qualitative Risk Assessment

LOW | **MEDIUM** | HIGH

Our risk assessment reflects the highly competitive nature of the industry balanced by our view of CSCO's strong financials, including roughly $18 billion in cash, and its dominant market position.

Quantitative Evaluations

S&P Quality Ranking B+

D | C | B- | B | **B+** | A- | A | A+

Relative Strength Rank MODERATE

66

LOWEST = 1 HIGHEST = 99

Revenue/Earnings Data

Revenue (Million $)

	1Q	2Q	3Q	4Q	Year
2006	6,550	6,628	7,322	7,984	28,484
2005	5,971	6,062	6,187	6,581	24,801
2004	5,101	5,398	5,620	5,926	22,045
2003	4,845	4,713	4,618	4,702	18,878
2002	4,448	4,816	4,822	4,829	18,915
2001	6,519	6,748	4,728	4,298	22,293

Earnings Per Share ($)

	1Q	2Q	3Q	4Q	Year
2006	0.20	0.22	0.22	0.25	0.89
2005	0.21	0.21	0.21	0.24	0.87
2004	0.15	0.18	0.17	0.20	0.70
2003	0.08	0.14	0.14	0.14	0.50
2002	-0.04	0.09	0.10	0.10	0.25
2001	0.11	0.12	-0.37	Nil	-0.14

Fiscal year ended Jul. 31. Next earnings report expected: Early November. EPS Estimates based on S&P Operating Earnings; historical GAAP earnings are as reported.

Dividend Data

No cash dividends have been paid.

Please read the Required Disclosures and Analyst Certification on the last page of this report.

Cisco Systems Inc

Business Summary August 14, 2006

CORPORATE OVERVIEW. Cisco Systems, which supplies the majority of networking gear used for the Internet, is the world's largest supplier of high-performance computer internetworking systems. The company's sales strategy is primarily based on distribution channel partners (approximately 90% of sales), with about 40,000 reseller partner sales representatives around the world.

Product families are categorized into four segments: switches (50% of total product sales), routers (25%), advanced technologies (20%), and other. There are currently six such advanced technologies: home networking, IP telephony, optical networking, security, storage area networking, and wireless technology. We estimate that the home networking, IP telephony and security sub-segments are all above or near the billion dollar level on an annual basis. Other products are comprised of primarily access and network management software. The company also offers a broad range of service offerings, including technical support services and advanced services.

MARKET PROFILE. With a dominant market share of approximately 70% of the overall Ethernet switching market, we believe CSCO has become the de facto choice for Ethernet switches. We view the company's large installed base as a significant competitive advantage over peers, especially in cases of modular switching solutions, where it is very difficult for competitors to displace the large modular chassis equipment. Because of its reputation and related large market share, in our opinion, Cisco products typically enjoy a price premium over the competition.

CSCO leads the overall routing market, with a more than 50% share. For core routers, which have speeds of more than 2.5 gigabits per second, CSCO and Juniper Networks dominate the market, with a combined market share of over 95%. In May 2004, Cisco introduced its new high-end core router, the Carrier Routing System-1 (CRS-1), with capacity for 1.2 terabits per second.

IMPACT OF MAJOR DEVELOPMENTS. In February 2006, CSCO acquired cable set top maker Scientific-Atlanta for about $6.9 billion. We think the transaction will help pull through additional network transport demand, especially in the attractive IP television (IPTV) and video-on-demand markets. In addition, Scientific-Atlanta's set-top portfolio should augment CSCO's home networking Linksys gear.

Company Financials

Per Share Data ($) Year Ended Jul. 31	**2006**	**2005**	**2004**	**2003**	**2002**	**2001**	**2000**	**1999**	**1998**	**1997**
Tangible Book Value	2.07	2.74	3.16	3.35	3.33	3.07	3.14	3.57	1.14	1.07
Cash Flow	1.10	1.02	0.91	0.72	0.52	0.17	0.47	0.76	0.26	0.30
Earnings	0.89	0.87	0.70	0.50	0.25	-0.14	0.36	0.31	0.21	0.17
S&P Core Earnings	0.88	0.70	0.52	0.28	0.12	-0.37	NA	NA	NA	NA
Dividends	Nil	Nil	Nil	Nil	Nil	Nil	Nil	Nil	Nil	Nil
Payout Ratio	Nil	Nil	Nil	Nil	Nil	Nil	Nil	Nil	Nil	Nil
Prices:High	24.78	20.25	29.39	24.60	21.84	44.50	82.00	53.59	24.44	10.10
Prices:Low	17.10	16.83	17.53	12.33	12.24	11.04	35.16	22.47	8.58	5.03
P/E Ratio:High	28	23	42	49	87	NM	NM	NM	NM	60
P/E Ratio:Low	19	19	25	25	49	NM	98	72	41	30

Income Statement Analysis (Million $)										
Revenue	28,484	24,801	22,045	18,878	18,915	22,293	18,928	12,154	8,459	6,440
Operating Income	8,380	8,451	7,738	6,477	4,941	2,257	4,098	3,470	2,432	1,839
Depreciation	1,293	1,009	1,443	1,591	1,957	2,236	863	486	327	212
Interest Expense	Nil	Nil	Nil	Nil	Nil	Nil	Nil	Nil	Nil	Nil
Pretax Income	7,633	8,036	6,992	5,013	2,710	-874	4,343	3,316	2,302	1,889
Effective Tax Rate	26.9%	28.6%	28.9%	28.6%	30.1%	NM	38.6%	36.8%	41.4%	44.5%
Net Income	5,580	5,741	4,968	3,578	1,893	-1,014	2,668	2,096	1,350	1,049
S&P Core Earnings	5,499	4,645	3,652	2,051	931	-2,641	NA	NA	NA	NA

Balance Sheet & Other Financial Data (Million $)										
Cash	3,297	4,742	3,722	3,925	9,484	4,873	4,234	829	535	270
Current Assets	25,676	13,031	14,343	13,415	17,433	12,835	11,110	4,615	3,762	3,101
Total Assets	43,315	33,883	35,594	37,107	37,795	35,238	32,870	14,725	8,917	5,452
Current Liabilities	11,313	9,511	8,703	8,294	8,375	8,096	5,196	3,003	1,767	1,120
Long Term Debt	6,332	Nil	Nil	Nil	Nil	Nil	Nil	Nil	Nil	Nil
Common Equity	23,912	23,174	25,826	28,029	28,656	27,120	26,497	11,678	7,107	4,290
Total Capital	30,250	23,184	25,916	28,039	28,671	27,142	27,674	11,722	7,150	4,332
Capital Expenditures	772	692	613	717	2,641	2,271	1,086	584	415	330
Cash Flow	6,873	6,750	6,411	5,169	3,850	1,222	3,531	2,582	1,677	1,261
Current Ratio	2.3	1.4	1.6	1.6	2.1	1.6	2.1	1.5	2.1	2.8
% Long Term Debt of Capitalization	20.9	Nil	Nil	Nil	Nil	Nil	Nil	Nil	Nil	Nil
% Net Income of Revenue	19.6	23.1	22.5	19.0	10.0	NM	14.1	17.2	16.0	16.3
% Return on Assets	14.5	16.5	13.7	9.6	5.2	NM	11.2	17.7	18.8	23.1
% Return on Equity	23.7	23.4	18.4	12.6	6.8	NM	13.9	22.3	23.7	29.5

Data as orig reptd.; bef. results of disc opers/spec. items. Per share data adj. for stk. divs.; EPS diluted. E-Estimated. NA-Not Available. NM-Not Meaningful. NR-Not Ranked. UR-Under Review.

Office: 170 West Tasman Drive, San Jose, CA 95134-1706.
Telephone: 408-526-4000.
Email: investor-relations@cisco.com
Website: http://www.cisco.com

Chrmn: J. Morgridge
Pres & CEO: J. Chambers
SVP & CTO: C.H. Giancarlo
SVP & CIO: R. Jacoby

VP, CFO & Cntlr: J. Chadwick
Board of Directors: C. A. Bartz, M. M. Burns, M. Capellas, L. R. Carter, J. T. Chambers, J. L. Hennessy, R. M. Kovacevich, R. McGeary, S. M. West, J. Yang

Founded: 1984
Domicile: California
Employees: 49,926

STANDARD &POOR'S

Citigroup Inc.

S&P Recommendation STRONG BUY ★★★★★

Price $50.36 (as of Oct 27, 2006)

12-Mo. Target Price $60.00

Investment Style Large-Cap Value

GICS Sector Financials
Sub-Industry Other Diversified Financial Services

Comment This diversified financial services company provides a wide range of financial services to consumers and corporate customers in more than 100 countries and territories.

Key Stock Statistics (Source S&P, Vickers, company reports)

52-Wk Range	$51.33–44.81	S&P Oper. EPS 2006**E**	4.33	P/E on S&P Oper. EPS 2006**E**	11.6	Dividend Rate/Share	$1.96
Trailing 12-Month EPS	$4.64	S&P Oper. EPS 2007**E**	4.61	Common Shares Outstg. (M)	4,943.9	Yield (%)	3.89
Trailing 12-Month P/E	10.9	S&P Core EPS 2006**E**	4.32	Market Capitalization(B)	$248.977	Beta	1.29
$10K Invested 5 Yrs Ago	$12,896	S&P Core EPS 2007**E**	4.60	Institutional Ownership (%)	64	S&P Credit Rating	AA-

Price Performance

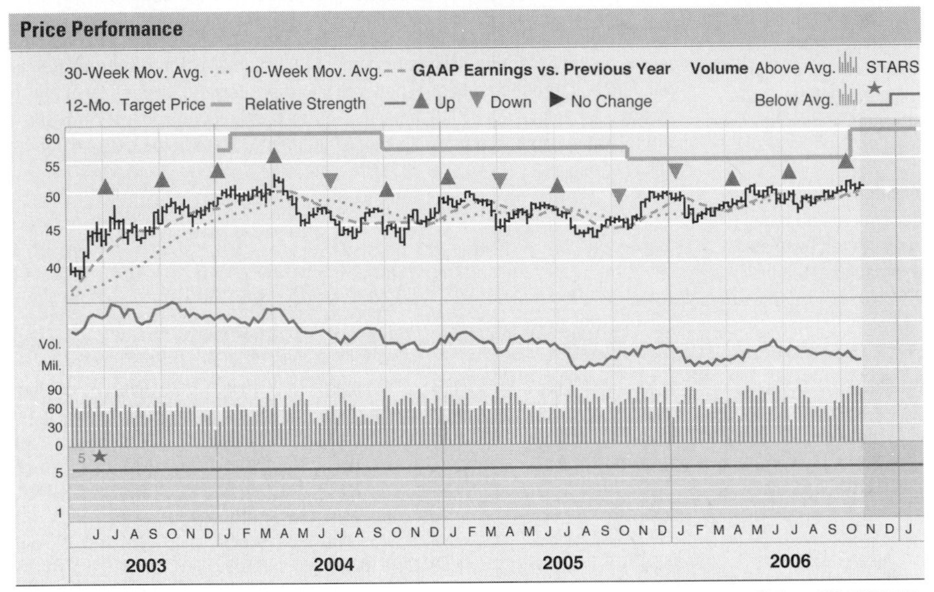

Options: ASE, CBOE, P, Ph

Analysis prepared by **Mark Hebeka, CFA** on October 25, 2006, when the stock traded at **$ 50.48**.

Highlights

- We believe that the company's business mix of high growth consumer businesses, combined with a strong corporate lending and investment banking market, should benefit from healthy global economies. We look for revenues to increase at a modest pace in 2006 and 2007, with challenging banking and credit card conditions in the U.S. being offset by strong growth in emerging markets.
- We expect C's corporate and investment banking businesses to make an increasing contribution to earnings in the quarters ahead. We believe earnings from consumer businesses, such as credit cards, consumer finance, and retail banking, will continue to be driven by a mixture of market growth and acquisitions. We look for C to focus on the U.S. consumer business to help it continue to gain traction and improve upon on what we view as its recent weak performance.
- We forecast 2006 operating EPS of $4.33, up from $3.82 in 2005. Our 2007 EPS estimate is $4.61, under our primary assumption of continuing healthy global economic conditions.

Investment Rationale/Risk

- Our strong buy recommendation is based on the company's geographic and product diversity and improving earnings quality that we expect in 2006 and 2007. It is also based on what we view as the potential for long-term above peer average revenue growth and profitability prospects that we believe are not reflected in the stock's current valuation.
- Risks to our recommendation and target price include a severe downturn in global economic conditions, a significant rise in credit losses, the failure to implement announced cost reduction initiatives, and a serious geopolitical event that could affect global capital markets.
- We expect the stock's valuation to trend toward its historical average as global economic activity likely remains healthy. Our 12-month target price of $60 is based on our sum-of-the-parts analysis and is equal to 13X our 2007 EPS estimate, reflecting our view of solid earnings quality and improved growth prospects.

Qualitative Risk Assessment

LOW | MEDIUM | HIGH

Our risk assessment reflects our view of C's strong fundamentals, solid credit quality, large customer base, and a healthy economy. We also believe C's diversity in its geographic presence and product offerings provide significant protection from a local or regional downturn.

Quantitative Evaluations

S&P Quality Ranking A+

D | C | B- | B | B+ | A- | A | A+

Relative Strength Rank MODERATE

43

LOWEST = 1 HIGHEST = 99

Revenue/Earnings Data

Revenue (Million $)

	1Q	2Q	3Q	4Q	Year
2006	34,290	35,899	36,323	--	--
2005	28,620	28,837	31,147	31,714	120,318
2004	25,976	27,287	26,408	28,605	108,276
2003	23,199	23,840	23,334	24,340	94,713
2002	22,654	23,601	23,505	22,796	92,556
2001	29,804	27,854	27,714	26,650	112,022

Earnings Per Share ($)

2006	1.11	1.05	1.06	**E**1.09	**E**4.33
2005	0.98	0.91	0.97	0.98	3.82
2004	1.01	0.22	1.02	1.02	3.26
2003	0.79	0.83	0.90	0.91	3.42
2002	0.66	0.73	0.72	0.47	2.59
2001	0.70	0.71	0.61	0.74	2.75

Fiscal year ended Dec. 31. Next earnings report expected: Late January. EPS Estimates based on S&P Operating Earnings; historical GAAP earnings are as reported.

Dividend Data (Dates: mm/dd Payment Date: mm/dd/yy)

Amount ($)	Date Decl.	Ex-Div. Date	Stk. of Record	Payment Date
0.490	01/20	02/02	02/06	02/24/06
0.490	04/18	04/27	05/01	05/26/06
0.490	07/17	08/03	08/07	08/25/06
0.490	10/19	11/02	11/06	11/22/06

Dividends have been paid since 1986. Source: Company reports.

Citigroup Inc.

Business Summary October 25, 2006

CORPORATE OVERVIEW. Citigroup is organized into three major business groups: Global Consumer; Corporate and Investment Banking (CIB); and Global Wealth Management. The Citigroup Global Consumer business includes banking services, credit cards, loans and insurance. The CIB business is in about 100 countries and advises companies, governments, and institutional investors on the best way to realize their strategic objectives. The Global Wealth Management division at Citigroup is comprised of The Citigroup Private Bank, Smith Barney (private wealth management), and Citigroup Investment Research, and serves both private and institutional clients.

CORPORATE STRATEGY. Citigroup has five strategic initiatives: expand international distribution; increase U.S. distribution; transfer expertise; invest in technology and people; and allocate capital.

C plans to expand internationally through the addition of 150-200 branches, 400-500 consumer finance centers, and about 150 automated loan machines. In our view, these large increases show the growing importance that C is putting on organic growth. C also plans to build 70-100 new retail bank and 125-200 consumer finance branches in the U.S. during 2006. C expects to use what we believe is an innovative new strategy for branch building (other than demographics) by placing locations in areas with large existing customer bases with the hope of building deeper relationships with those customers.

UPCOMING CATALYSTS. We see various catalysts coming into play in 2006 and beyond. They include interest rates, housing, competition, and mergers and acquisitions. We believe the narrowing spread between short-term and long-term rates will continue to put pressure on core banking operations. Standard & Poor's is forecasting an average 3-month Treasury-Bill rate of 4.7% and a 10-year Treasury-Bill average of 5.0% in 2006, leaving the spread at a relatively narrow 30 basis points.

Company Financials

Per Share Data ($) Year Ended Dec. 31	2005	2004	2003	2002	2001	2000	1999	1998	1997	1996
Tangible Book Value	12.76	11.72	10.75	9.70	15.49	12.84	10.64	8.95	6.99	4.97
Earnings	3.82	3.26	3.42	2.59	2.75	2.62	2.12	1.22	1.27	1.17
S&P Core Earnings	3.69	4.02	3.35	2.33	2.51	NA	NA	NA	NA	NA
Dividends	1.76	1.60	1.10	0.70	0.60	0.52	0.41	0.28	0.20	0.15
Payout Ratio	46%	49%	32%	27%	22%	20%	19%	23%	16%	13%
Prices:High	49.99	52.88	49.15	52.20	57.38	59.13	43.69	36.75	28.69	15.83
Prices:Low	42.91	42.10	30.25	24.48	34.51	35.34	24.50	14.25	14.58	9.42
P/E Ratio:High	13	16	14	20	21	23	21	30	23	14
P/E Ratio:Low	11	13	9	9	13	13	12	12	11	8
Income Statement Analysis (Million $)										
Premium Income	3,132	3,993	3,749	3,410	13,460	12,429	10,441	9,850	8,995	7,633
Investment Income	28,833	22,728	18,937	21,036	26,949	27,562	21,728	23,696	16,214	5,549
Other Revenue	88,353	81,555	72,027	68,110	71,613	71,835	49,836	42,885	12,400	8,163
Total Revenue	120,318	108,276	94,713	92,556	112,022	111,826	82,005	76,431	37,609	21,345
Interest Expense	36,676	22,086	17,271	21,248	31,965	36,638	24,768	27,495	11,443	2,259
% Expense/Operating Revenue	75.5%	77.6%	72.2%	77.8%	80.5%	81.1%	80.6%	87.9%	86.7%	85.9%
Pretax Income	29,433	24,182	26,333	20,537	21,897	21,143	15,948	9,269	5,012	3,398
Effective Tax Rate	30.8%	28.6%	31.1%	34.1%	34.4%	35.6%	35.8%	34.9%	33.8%	30.9%
Net Income	19,806	17,046	17,853	13,448	14,284	13,519	9,994	5,807	3,104	2,300
S&P Core Earnings	19,114	20,934	17,424	12,000	12,943	NA	NA	NA	NA	NA
Balance Sheet & Other Financial Data (Million $)										
Receivables	42,823	44,056	31,053	29,714	47,528	36,237	32,677	30,905	30,939	22,408
Cash & Investment	208,970	236,799	204,041	186,839	179,352	134,743	127,284	117,509	65,867	58,613
Loans	583,503	548,829	478,006	447,805	391,933	367,022	244,206	221,958	10,816	7,885
Total Assets	1,494,037	1,484,101	1,264,032	1,097,190	1,051,450	902,210	716,937	668,641	386,555	151,067
Capitalization:Debt	217,499	207,910	168,759	133,079	128,756	116,698	52,012	52,991	30,597	13,227
Capitalization:Equity	111,412	108,166	96,889	85,318	79,722	64,461	47,761	40,395	19,443	12,410
Capitalization:Total	330,036	317,201	284,251	219,797	210,003	182,904	101,698	95,839	51,905	26,441
Price Times Book Value:High	3.9	4.5	4.6	5.4	3.7	4.6	4.1	4.1	4.1	3.2
Price Times Book Value:Low	3.4	3.5	2.8	2.5	2.2	2.7	2.3	1.6	2.1	1.9
% Return on Revenue	16.5	15.7	18.8	14.5	12.8	12.9	12.2	7.6	8.3	10.8
% Return on Assets	1.3	1.2	1.5	1.3	1.5	1.6	1.4	1.1	1.2	1.7
% Return on Equity	18.0	16.6	19.5	11.6	19.7	22.2	22.3	14.2	18.6	18.9
Loans/Equity	5.2	5.1	5.1	3.6	5.3	5.6	5.3	516.9	51.7	50.0

Data as orig reptd.; bef. results of disc opers/spec. items. Per share data adj. for stk. divs.; EPS diluted. E-Estimated. NA-Not Available. NM-Not Meaningful. NR-Not Ranked. UR-Under Review.

Office: 399 Park Avenue, New York, NY, USA 10043.
Telephone: 212-559-1000.
Website: http://www.citigroup.com
Chrmn & CEO: C.O. Prince

Vice Chrmn: S.R. Volk
Vice Chrmn & Chief Admin: L.B. Kaden
CFO: S. Krawcheck
Chief Acctg Officer & Cntlr: J.C. Gerspach

Board of Directors: C. M. Armstrong, A. J. Belda, G. David, K. T. Derr, J. M. Deutch, A. Dibble Jordan, R. Hernandez, K. Kleinfeld, A. N. Liveris, D. C. Mecum, A. Mulcahy, R. D. Parsons, J. Rodin, R. E. Rubin, F. A. Thomas, S. I. Weill

Founded: 1901
Domicile: Delaware
Employees: 307,000

STANDARD &POOR'S

Citizens Communications Co

S&P Recommendation BUY ★★★★★

Price $14.78 (as of Oct 27, 2006)

12-Mo. Target Price $15.00

Investment Style Mid-Cap Value

GICS Sector Telecommunication Services
Sub-Industry Integrated Telecommunication Services

Comment CZN provides wireline communications services in rural areas and small and medium sized towns and cities. In September 2006, CZN agreed to acquire Commonwealth Telephone Enterprises, subject to necessary approvals.

Key Stock Statistics (Source S&P, Vickers, company reports)

52-Wk Range	$14.87–11.97	S&P Oper. EPS 2006E	0.65	P/E on S&P Oper. EPS 2006E	22.7	Dividend Rate/Share	$1.00
Trailing 12-Month EPS	$0.81	S&P Oper. EPS 2007E	0.68	Common Shares Outstg. (M)	320.8	Yield (%)	6.77
Trailing 12-Month P/E	18.3	S&P Core EPS 2006E	0.60	Market Capitalization(B)	$4.742	Beta	1.57
$10K Invested 5 Yrs Ago	$23,926	S&P Core EPS 2007E	0.63	Institutional Ownership (%)	75	S&P Credit Rating	BB+

Price Performance

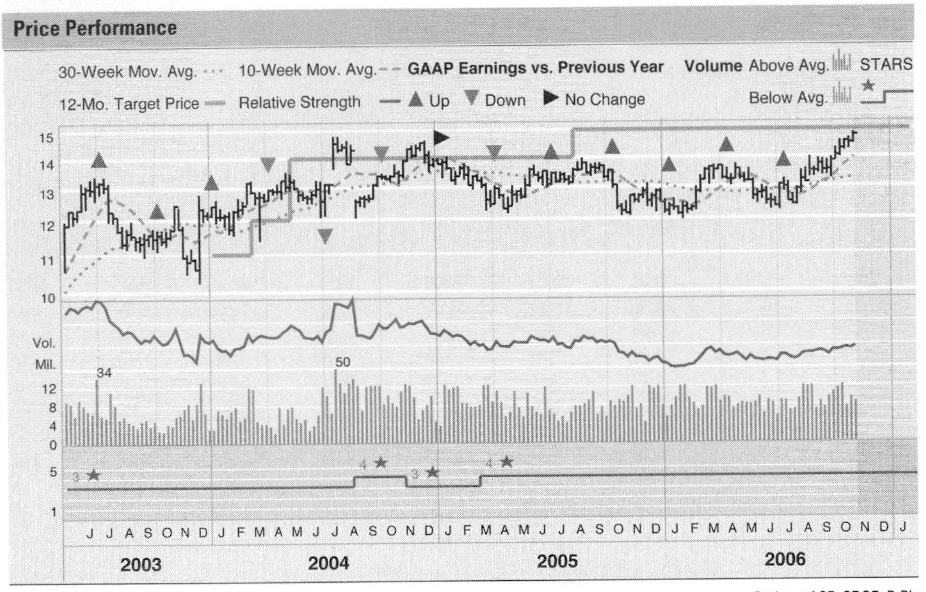

Options: ASE, CBOE, P, Ph

Analysis prepared by **Todd Rosenbluth** on September 19, 2006, when the stock traded at **$ 13.51**.

Highlights

- We expect revenues to be up 1.5% in 2006 and 1% in 2007, as additional long-distance and DSL penetration will likely be offset by lower access charges, due to a decline in universal service support and total access line weakness. We also see selective price increases beginning to help in the second half of 2006. The sale of Electric Lightwave (7% of 2005 revenues) was completed in the third quarter of 2006. Our estimates do not include Commonwealth Telephone (CTCO: $41, buy) operations.
- We believe EBITDA margins will widen to 56% in 2006 and stay near this level in 2007, remaining among the industry's best--following the sale of lower-margin CLEC operations--as we see the company benefiting from work force cuts, its billing and call center conversion, and continued deployment of higher-margin calling services. We look for depreciation charges to decrease modestly.
- Aided by share buybacks, we see operating EPS of $0.65 (including $0.02 for projected stock option expense) in 2006 and $0.68 in 2007. S&P Core EPS estimates reflect projected pension adjustments.

Investment Rationale/Risk

- What we consider as CZN's relatively strong margins reflect its limited vulnerability to pricing pressures compared to national telecom peers and the strong cost-cutting measures taken in the past 12 months, in our opinion. We contend that the terms of the planned CTCO deal, subject to necessary approvals, are fair, and believe that CZN can gain synergies from increasing enhanced services penetration and lowering operating expenses.
- Risks to our opinion and target price include a balance sheet that appears more leveraged than those of most telecom peers; a failure to close on its proposed acquisition; and changes to the universal service fund, from which CZN receives revenues.
- Our 12-month target price of $15 is based on an enterprise value/EBITDA multiple of 7.5X, in line with rural peers. The recent 7.3% dividend yield adds to total return potential. CZN began paying quarterly dividends in the second half of 2004. In the first half of 2006, 52% of free cash flow was paid out in dividends, lower than most small telecom peers. We believe the dividend is secure regardless of any merger outcome.

Qualitative Risk Assessment

LOW | MEDIUM | HIGH

Our risk assessment for Citizens Communications reflects the rural, less competitive nature of its operations, and what we see as the strong and stable cash flow that supports its dividend policy.

Quantitative Evaluations

S&P Quality Ranking B-

D | C | **B-** | B | B+ | A- | A | A+

Relative Strength Rank STRONG

72

LOWEST = 1 HIGHEST = 99

Revenue/Earnings Data

Revenue (Million $)

	1Q	2Q	3Q	4Q	Year
2006	506.9	506.9	--	--	--
2005	537.2	531.8	537.4	556.1	2,162
2004	558.5	544.1	545.4	545.0	2,193
2003	651.9	644.0	595.0	554.1	2,445
2002	679.3	662.4	668.8	658.7	2,669
2001	624.3	505.7	661.1	665.9	2,457

Earnings Per Share ($)

2006	0.13	0.29	**E**0.16	**E**0.16	**E**0.65
2005	0.11	0.13	0.11	0.23	0.59
2004	0.15	0.08	-0.04	0.05	0.23
2003	0.22	0.12	0.04	0.05	0.42
2002	-0.16	-0.15	-2.49	-0.13	-2.93
2001	0.07	-0.06	-0.11	-0.41	-0.28

Fiscal year ended Dec. 31. Next earnings report expected: Early November. EPS Estimates based on S&P Operating Earnings; historical GAAP earnings are as reported.

Dividend Data (Dates: mm/dd Payment Date: mm/dd/yy)

Amount ($)	Date Decl.	Ex-Div. Date	Stk. of Record	Payment Date
0.250	02/24	03/07	03/09	03/31/06
0.250	05/25	06/07	06/09	06/30/06
0.250	07/28	09/06	09/09	09/29/06
0.250	10/26	12/06	12/09	12/29/06

Dividends have been paid since 2004. Source: Company reports.

Citizens Communications Co

Business Summary September 19, 2006

CORPORATE PROFILE. Citizens Communications provides wireline services to rural areas and small and medium sized towns and cities in 24 states, including Arizona, California, and New York, as an incumbent local exchange carrier (ILEC) for 2.2 million access lines as of June 2006. The company also had 350,000 DSL subscribers, up 31% from a year earlier. CZN grew its revenues in the first half of 2006 due to, in our opinion, increased penetration of its bundle of services, including enhanced features such as caller ID, voicemail, and DSL. Electric Lightwave, which CZN ran to provide competitive local access services to business customers, was sold at the end of July for $247 million.

CORPORATE STRATEGY. Over the past four years, CZN has transitioned from a utility with gas, water and electric businesses into a telecom company with the purchase of Frontier Communications and the sale of its non-telecom businesses for more than $1.7 billion. CZN has focused on growing by providing rural local residential phone customers with enhanced services as well as long-distance and DSL. The penetration rates for enhanced services in many of CZN's territories are below the national average, creating what we believe is an opportunity for CZN.

In September 2006, CZN agreed to acquire Commonwealth Telephone Enterprises (CTCO) in a proposed deal, subject to necessary approvals, initially valued at $1.2 billion; CZN would pay $31.31 in cash and 0.768 of its shares. Assuming the planned deal is completed as we expect in the middle of 2007, the combined company would have 2.6 million access lines and 388,000 broadband connections. CZN anticipates taking on additional debt to complete the proposed transaction. CTCO is rural wireline provider in Pennsylvania with penetration levels for long distance, broadband, and overall service bundles lower than CZN.

In July 2004, the company announced a $2 special dividend and initiated a $0.25 quarterly dividend. We expect CZN's dividend payout to exceed its EPS in 2006 and be supported by asset sales and cash flow generation. In April 2006, CZN received $65 million following the liquidation of the rural Telephone Bank.

Company Financials

Per Share Data ($) Year Ended Dec. 31	**2005**	**2004**	**2003**	**2002**	**2001**	**2000**	**1999**	**1998**	**1997**	**1996**
Tangible Book Value	NM	NM	NM	NM	NM	4.09	7.36	7.27	6.93	6.90
Cash Flow	2.26	2.09	2.37	-0.24	2.08	1.30	1.45	1.22	NA	NA
Earnings	0.59	0.23	0.42	-2.93	-0.28	-0.15	0.45	0.23	0.04	0.72
S&P Core Earnings	0.59	0.19	0.68	-2.89	-0.58	NA	NA	NA	NA	NA
Dividends	1.00	0.50	Nil	Nil	Nil	Nil	Nil	Nil	Nil	Nil
Payout Ratio	169%	NM	Nil	Nil	Nil	Nil	Nil	Nil	Nil	Nil
Prices:High	14.05	14.80	13.40	11.52	15.88	19.00	14.31	11.18	11.71	11.23
Prices:Low	12.08	11.37	8.81	2.51	8.20	12.50	7.25	6.89	7.61	9.45
P/E Ratio:High	24	62	32	NM	NM	NM	32	51	NM	16
P/E Ratio:Low	20	47	21	NM	NM	NM	16	31	NM	13
Income Statement Analysis (Million $)										
Revenue	2,162	2,193	2,445	2,669	2,457	1,802	1,087	1,542	1,394	1,307
Operating Income	1,149	1,148	1,173	1,179	927	549	8.07	178	15.8	296
Depreciation	542	573	595	756	632	388	262	258	236	194
Interest Expense	339	379	423	478	386	194	93.2	112	114	96.1
Pretax Income	285	85.5	189	-1,238	-78.7	-44.0	158	73.9	23.5	269
Effective Tax Rate	29.6%	15.6%	35.5%	NM	NM	NM	40.8%	25.4%	41.5%	31.5%
Net Income	200	72.2	122	-823	-63.9	-40.1	117	59.6	16.3	185
S&P Core Earnings	201	57.7	198	-811	-164	NA	NA	NA	NA	NA
Balance Sheet & Other Financial Data (Million $)										
Cash	266	167	584	393	57.7	31.2	37.1	31.9	35.1	24.2
Current Assets	542	450	896	1,201	2,533	2,263	309	414	377	370
Total Assets	6,412	6,668	7,689	8,147	10,554	6,955	5,772	5,293	4,873	4,523
Current Liabilities	617	418	536	771	1,567	992	467	508	418	409
Long Term Debt	3,999	4,267	4,397	5,159	5,736	3,264	2,309	1,900	1,707	1,510
Common Equity	1,042	1,362	1,415	1,172	1,946	1,720	1,920	1,793	1,679	1,678
Total Capital	5,366	5,629	6,259	6,468	8,112	5,474	4,700	4,669	4,305	3,536
Capital Expenditures	268	276	278	469	531	537	485	483	531	348
Cash Flow	742	645	717	-67.5	568	348	380	318	252	379
Current Ratio	0.9	1.1	1.7	1.6	1.6	2.3	0.7	0.8	0.9	0.9
% Long Term Debt of Capitalization	74.5	75.8	70.2	79.8	70.7	59.6	49.1	52.0	50.0	47.0
% Net Income of Revenue	9.3	3.3	5.0	NM	NM	NM	10.8	3.9	1.2	14.1
% Return on Assets	3.1	1.0	1.5	NM	NM	NM	2.1	1.2	0.3	4.4
% Return on Equity	16.7	5.2	9.4	NM	NM	NM	6.5	3.4	3.4	11.1

Data as orig reptd.; bef. results of disc opers/spec. items. Per share data adj. for stk. divs.; EPS diluted. E-Estimated. NA-Not Available. NM-Not Meaningful. NR-Not Ranked. UR-Under Review.

Office: 3 High Ridge Park, Stamford, CT 06905-1337.
Telephone: 203-614-5600.
Email: citizens@cnz.com
Website: http://www.czn.net

Chrmn & CEO: M. Wilderrotter
Pres: J. Elliott
COO & EVP: D.J. McCarthy
SVP & Chief Acctg Officer: R.J. Larson

SVP, Secy & General Counsel: L.R. Mitten
Investor Contact: M. Bromley (203-614-5218)
Board of Directors: K. Q. Abernathy, L. T. Barnes, Jr., J. Elliott, J. B. Finard, L. Fitt, S. Harfenist, W. Kraus, H. L. Schrott, L. D. Segil, B. E. Singer, E. Tornberg, D. H. Ward, M. A. Wick, III, M. Wilderotter

Founded: 1927
Domicile: Delaware
Employees: 6,103

STANDARD &POOR'S

CIT Group Inc.

S&P Recommendation HOLD ★★★★★ | **Price** $51.25 (as of Oct 27, 2006) | **12-Mo. Target Price** $54.00 | **Investment Style** Large-Cap Value

GICS Sector Financials
Sub-Industry Specialized Finance

Comment This diversified finance company engages in vendor, equipment, commercial, consumer and structured financing as well as leasing activities.

Key Stock Statistics (Source S&P, Vickers, company reports)

52-Wk Range	$56.48–41.91	S&P Oper. EPS 2006E	4.60	P/E on S&P Oper. EPS 2006E	11.1	Dividend Rate/Share	$0.80
Trailing 12-Month EPS	$4.50	S&P Oper. EPS 2007E	5.40	Common Shares Outstg. (M)	198.8	Yield (%)	1.56
Trailing 12-Month P/E	11.4	S&P Core EPS 2006E	4.80	Market Capitalization(B)	$10.190	Beta	2.03
$10K Invested 5 Yrs Ago	NA	S&P Core EPS 2007E	5.40	Institutional Ownership (%)	92	S&P Credit Rating	A

Price Performance

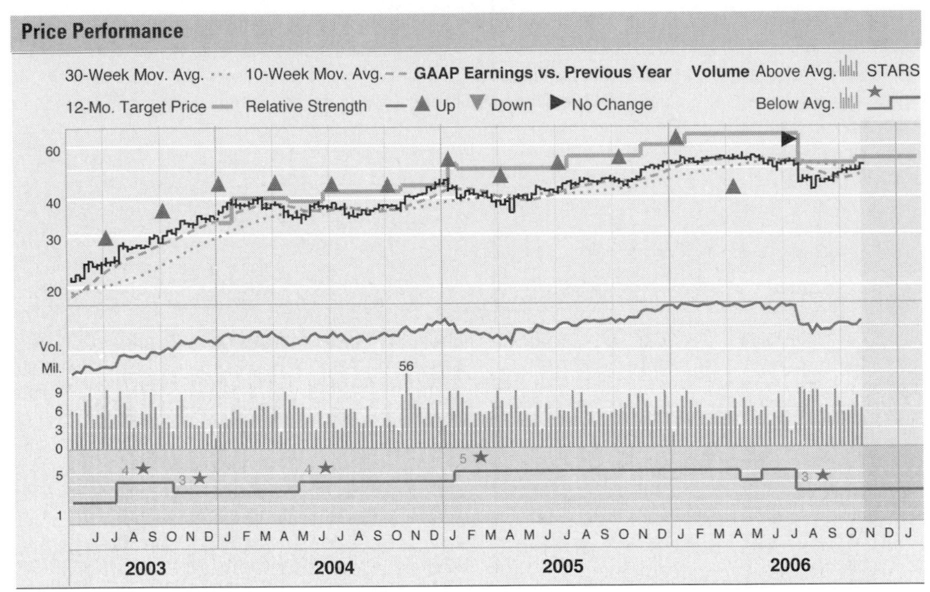

Options: ASE, CBOE, P, Ph

Analysis prepared by **Matthew Albrecht** on October 23, 2006, when the stock traded at **$ 49.21**.

Highlights

- Over the past several years, CIT Group has benefited from an improvement in utilization, lease rates and credit quality, due to strengthening in the economy. Although credit quality remains strong, we believe that changes in the macro economy raise the risk of a negative shift in credit trends, specifically related to home lending, but we think CIT's well diversified asset base should help limit the potential risk.

- The company has benefited from 17% year-to-year growth in managed assets in recent periods, but net finance revenue as a percentage of average earning assets was down to 3.17% in the first nine months of 2006, compared to 3.41% in the comparable 2005 period, due to a narrower credit spread. Net charge-offs remained at low levels, but growth in non-performing loans and delinquencies gives us concern about the potential for a worsening of credit quality in the future.

- We forecast EPS of $4.60 in 2006 and $5.40 in 2007, aided by growth in managed assets, productivity gains, and higher nonspread revenues, partially offset by a contraction in net finance margins and higher expenses.

Investment Rationale/Risk

- We view CIT as well managed, with an established brand and disciplined risk management policies. Despite recent positive trends in loan demand, we are increasingly concerned that growing competition will limit future asset growth and net financing margins. We view favorably the company's efforts to exit underperforming businesses and redeploy capital in higher return businesses.

- Risks to our recommendation and target price include sharply higher interest rates and declining demand for commercial or consumer financing services. We think that a deterioration in credit quality in the company's target markets, notably commercial aerospace, represents an additional risk. Regarding corporate governance, we would prefer that CIT split the roles of chairman and CEO.

- The shares recently traded at a P/E of 10.7X our 2006 EPS estimate and 1.4X book value, in line with recently reduced peer multiples. Our 12-month target price of $54 is 10X our 2007 EPS estimate, a slight discount to the historical average, which reflects what we view as CIT's strong financial position but an increasingly risky operating environment.

Qualitative Risk Assessment

LOW | MEDIUM | HIGH

Our risk assessment reflects our view of the company's disciplined risk management policies and sound competitive position, only partially offset by potentially narrower net interest margins.

Quantitative Evaluations

S&P Quality Ranking **NR**

D | C | B- | B | B+ | A- | A | A+

Relative Strength Rank **STRONG**

71

LOWEST = 1 HIGHEST = 99

Revenue/Earnings Data

Revenue (Million $)

	1Q	2Q	3Q	4Q	Year
2006	1,555	1,379	--	--	--
2005	1,261	1,387	1,408	1,522	5,653
2004	1,134	1,149	1,180	1,219	4,676
2003	1,175	1,161	1,142	1,172	4,678
2002	1,199	1,107	1,022	--	5,275
2001	--	--	--	--	4,548

Earnings Per Share ($)

	1Q	2Q	3Q	4Q	Year
2006	1.12	1.16	**E**1.25	**E**1.07	**E**4.60
2005	1.06	1.16	1.02	1.21	4.44
2004	0.88	0.82	0.86	0.95	3.50
2003	0.60	0.65	0.69	0.72	2.66
2002	0.87	-21.84	-11.33	0.64	-31.66
2001	--	--	--	--	--

Fiscal year ended Dec. 31. Next earnings report expected: NA. EPS Estimates based on S&P Operating Earnings; historical GAAP earnings are as reported.

Dividend Data (Dates: mm/dd Payment Date: mm/dd/yy)

Amount ($)	Date Decl.	Ex-Div. Date	Stk. of Record	Payment Date
0.200	01/17	02/13	02/15	02/28/06
0.200	04/17	05/11	05/15	05/30/06
0.200	07/18	08/11	08/15	08/30/06
0.200	10/17	11/13	11/15	11/30/06

Dividends have been paid since 2002. Source: Company reports.

CIT Group Inc.

Business Summary October 23, 2006

CIT Group is a leading global commercial and consumer finance company that has provided financing and leasing capital since 1908. In 2001, the company was acquired by Tyco International and renamed Tyco Capital Corp.; it was subsequently spun off in July 2002. CIT had total managed assets of $62.9 billion at December 31, 2005. The company intends to maintain its competitive position by expanding its existing markets, industries and products, improving overall efficiency and flexibility, and restoring debt credit ratings to higher levels. We think CIT's target markets will remain competitive in 2006 as customers increasingly access the bank and high yield markets.

Transactions are generated through direct calling efforts with borrowers, lessees, equipment end-users, vendors, manufacturers and distributors and through referral sources and other intermediaries. In addition, the company's business units jointly structure certain transactions and refer transactions to other CIT units to meet overall customer financing needs. The company also buys and sells participations in, and syndications of, finance receivables and/or lines of credit. The company operates in five business segments.

In September 2003, CIT purchased $446 million of factoring receivables from GE Commercial Services, and in December 2003, acquired $1 billion in U.S. factoring assets from HSBC. In February 2005, CIT acquired Education Lending Group, which offers student loans, primarily guaranteed by the U.S. government. We project that the acquisition will be accretive to EPS in 2006.

Company Financials

Per Share Data ($) Year Ended Dec. 31	2005	2004	2003	2002	2001	2000	1999	1998	1997	1996
Tangible Book Value	27.38	25.94	23.14	20.67	NA	NA	NA	NA	NA	NA
Cash Flow	9.10	7.95	7.61	-25.75	NA	NA	NA	NA	NA	NA
Earnings	4.44	3.50	2.66	-31.66	NA	NA	NA	NA	NA	NA
S&P Core Earnings	3.80	3.42	2.58	-1.03	NA	NA	NA	NA	NA	NA
Dividends	0.61	0.52	0.48	Nil	NA	NA	NA	NA	NA	NA
Payout Ratio	14%	15%	18%	Nil	NA	NA	NA	NA	NA	NA
Prices:High	52.94	46.23	36.20	24.05	NA	NA	NA	NA	NA	NA
Prices:Low	35.41	32.65	16.08	13.80	NA	NA	NA	NA	NA	NA
P/E Ratio:High	12	13	14	NM	NA	NA	NA	NA	NA	NA
P/E Ratio:Low	8	9	6	NM	NA	NA	NA	NA	NA	NA

Income Statement Analysis (Million $)	2005	2004	2003	2002	2001	2000	1999	1998	1997	1996
Revenue	5,653	4,676	4,678	5,275	4,548	NA	NA	NA	NA	NA
Operating Income	3,410	3,481	3,270	2,299	2,394	NA	NA	NA	NA	NA
Depreciation	1,001	956	1,053	1,241	1,037	NA	NA	NA	NA	NA
Interest Expense	1,912	1,260	1,319	2,102	1,620	NA	NA	NA	NA	NA
Pretax Income	1,417	1,237	937	-6,314	622	NA	NA	NA	NA	NA
Effective Tax Rate	32.8%	39.1%	38.9%	NM	45.0%	NA	NA	NA	NA	NA
Net Income	949	754	567	-6,699	334	NA	NA	NA	NA	NA
S&P Core Earnings	802	735	549	-200	379	NA	NA	NA	NA	NA

Balance Sheet & Other Financial Data (Million $)	2005	2004	2003	2002	2001	2000	1999	1998	1997	1996
Cash	4,811	3,438	1,974	2,274	808	NA	NA	NA	NA	NA
Accounts Receivable	45,293	36,072	31,575	27,681	31,387	NA	NA	NA	NA	NA
Accounts Payable	4,188	3,847	3,895	2,514	2,393	NA	NA	NA	NA	NA
Total Assets	63,387	51,111	46,343	42,710	51,090	NA	NA	NA	NA	NA
Long Term Debt	33,468	25,569	20,758	17,327	18,907	NA	NA	NA	NA	NA
Lease Obligations	NA	NA	NA	NA	NA	NA	NA	NA	NA	NA
Common Equity	6,463	6,055	5,394	4,758	10,598	NA	NA	NA	NA	NA
Total Capital	40,480	31,665	26,191	22,085	29,505	NA	NA	NA	NA	NA
Capital Expenditures	2,359	1,489	2,096	1,877	1,451	NA	NA	NA	NA	NA
Cash Flow	1,950	1,710	1,620	-5,458	1,371	NA	NA	NA	NA	NA
% Long Term Debt of Capitalization	82.6	80.7	79.3	78.5	64.1	NA	NA	NA	NA	NA
% Net Income of Revenue	16.7	16.1	12.1	NM	7.3	NA	NA	NA	NA	NA
% Return on Assets	1.6	1.6	1.3	NM	NM	NA	NA	NA	NA	NA
% Return on Equity	15.1	13.1	11.2	NM	NM	NA	NA	NA	NA	NA

Data as orig reptd.; bef. results of disc opers/spec. items. Per share data adj. for stk. divs.; EPS diluted. E-Estimated. NA-Not Available. NM-Not Meaningful. NR-Not Ranked. UR-Under Review.

Office: 1 CIT Drive, Livingston, NJ 07039.
Telephone: 973-740-5000.
Email: investor.relations@cit.com
Website: http://www.citgroup.com

Chrmn & CEO: J.M. Peek
Vice Chrmn: F. Wolfert
Vice Chrmn: L. Marsiello
Vice Chrmn: T. Hallman

Vice Chrmn, EVP & CFO: J.M. Leone
Investor Contact: S. Klimas (866-542-4847)
Board of Directors: G. C. Butler, W. M. Freeman, T. H. Kean, S. Lyne, M. M. Parrs, J. M. Peek, T. Ring, J. R. Ryan, S. Sternberg, P. J. Tobin, L. M. Van Deusen

Auditor: Pricewaterhousecoopers
Founded: 1908
Domicile: Delaware
Employees: 5,860

STANDARD &POOR'S

Citrix Systems Inc

S&P Recommendation BUY ★★★★★

Price $29.25 (as of Oct 27, 2006)

12-Mo. Target Price $36.00

Investment Style Mid-Cap Growth

GICS Sector Information Technology
Sub-Industry Application Software

Comment This company is a leading developer and supplier of access infrastructure software and services.

Key Stock Statistics (Source S&P, Vickers, company reports)

52-Wk Range	**$45.50–26.48**	S&P Oper. EPS 2006**E**	**1.16**	P/E on S&P Oper. EPS 2006**E**	**25.2**	Dividend Rate/Share	**Nil**
Trailing 12-Month EPS	**$1.05**	S&P Oper. EPS 2007**E**	**1.29**	Common Shares Outstg. (M)	**183.8**	Yield (%)	**Nil**
Trailing 12-Month P/E	**27.9**	S&P Core EPS 2006**E**	**1.16**	Market Capitalization(B)	**$5.376**	Beta	**2.64**
$10K Invested 5 Yrs Ago	**$11,386**	S&P Core EPS 2007**E**	**1.29**	Institutional Ownership (%)	**83**	S&P Credit Rating	**NR**

Price Performance

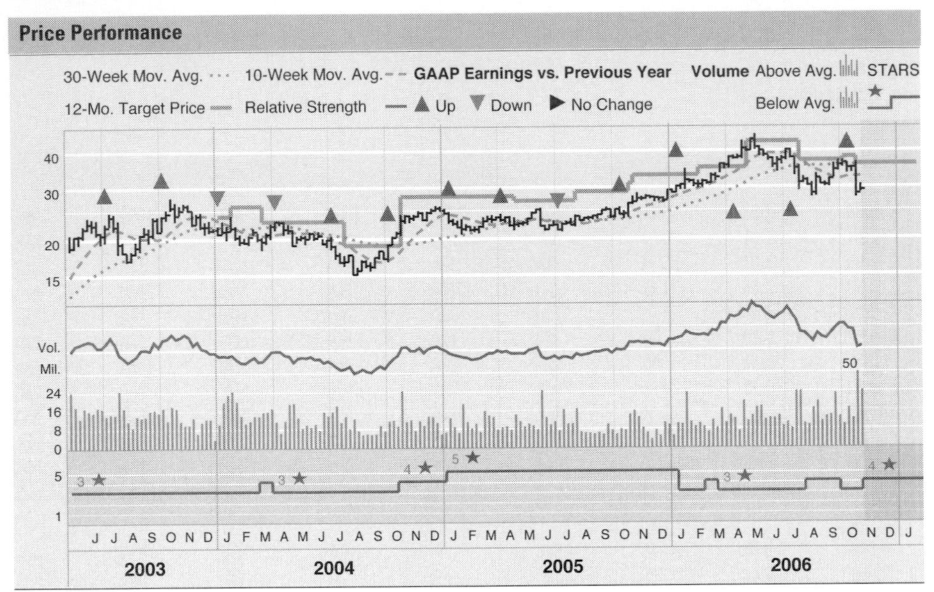

Options: ASE, CBOE, P, Ph

Highlights

➤ The STARS recommendation for CTXS has recently been changed to 4 (buy) from 3 (hold). The Highlights section of this Stock Report will be updated accordingly.

Investment Rationale/Risk

➤ The Investment Rationale/Risk section of this Stock Report will be updated shortly. For the latest News story on CTXS from MarketScope, see below.

➤ 10/27/06 12:18 pm EDT... S&P UPGRADES SHARES OF CITRIX SYSTEMS TO BUY FROM HOLD, BASED ON VALUATION (CTXS 29.64****): The price of CTXS shares has declined 16% since the company reporting Q3 results that showed weakness in its presentation server product. Although we expect the weakness to continue into the first half of '07, we believe it is being offset by faster growth in other products. CTXS is trading at 23X our '07 operating EPS estimate of $1.29 (after $0.23 of stock option expense), a slight premium to the 20X industry average even though CTXS has historically grown much faster. Our 12-month target price is $36, reflecting a blend of our DCF and P/E analysis. /J.Yin

Qualitative Risk Assessment

LOW | **MEDIUM** | HIGH

Our risk assessment reflects the rapid pace of technological change in the company's areas of focus, offset by notable acquisition activity that we believe has enabled CTXS to build leading positions in certain segments, and our view of strong cash flow generation and balance sheet attributes.

Quantitative Evaluations

S&P Quality Ranking **B+**

D | C | B- | B | **B+** | A- | A | A+

Relative Strength Rank **WEAK**

8

LOWEST = 1 HIGHEST = 99

Revenue/Earnings Data

Revenue (Million $)

	1Q	2Q	3Q	4Q	Year
2006	260.0	275.5	277.9	--	--
2005	201.9	211.2	227.0	268.7	908.7
2004	161.3	178.3	187.6	214.0	741.2
2003	143.5	143.1	144.3	157.7	588.6
2002	142.3	117.5	118.9	148.8	527.5
2001	132.8	147.3	153.5	158.1	591.6

Earnings Per Share ($)

2006	0.24	0.24	0.25	**E**0.31	**E**1.16
2005	0.22	0.16	0.23	0.32	0.93
2004	0.05	0.18	0.22	0.30	0.75
2003	0.18	0.17	0.18	0.21	0.74
2002	0.14	0.06	0.10	0.23	0.52
2001	0.15	0.12	0.14	0.13	0.54

Fiscal year ended Dec. 31. Next earnings report expected: Mid January. EPS Estimates based on S&P Operating Earnings; historical GAAP earnings are as reported.

Dividend Data

No cash dividends have been paid.

Citrix Systems Inc

Business Summary October 23, 2006

CORPORATE OVERVIEW. Citrix Systems designs, develops and markets technology solutions that enable on-demand access to information and applications. More and more people conduct business in remote and mobile contexts--moving from location to location, using multiple devices, and connecting with a wide range of heterogeneous applications over wired, wireless, and Internet networks. IDC identified CTXS as the tenth largest software vendor in the world in 2004 (based on indirect sales), with a notable presence in the networking software and system software segments.

The company's offerings are designed for three primary markets: individual consumers and professionals, small businesses, and enterprises. Citrix GoToMyPC (remote access to PCs via the Internet) and Citrix GoToMeeting (for online collaborative gatherings) are the company's primary solutions for individuals. Small business offerings consist of Citrix Access Essentials, Citrix Access Gateway, and Citrix GoToMeeting Corporate. Enterprise products include Citrix Access Suite, Citrix Presentation Server (virtualization solution), Citrix Access Gateway, Citrix Password Manager, Citrix NetScaler Application offerings, Citrix GoToAssist (for technical support), and Citrix GoToMeeting Corporate. Presentation Server offerings accounted for 85% of product license revenues for 2005, and 93% of them for 2004, indicating the importance of this area to the company. However, we expect this percentage to continue to decline to reflect growth in the company's NetScaler, Access Suite, and Access Gateway solutions.

Company Financials

Per Share Data ($) Year Ended Dec. 31	**2005**	**2004**	**2003**	**2002**	**2001**	**2000**	**1999**	**1998**	**1997**	**1996**
Tangible Book Value	2.68	2.80	3.24	2.57	2.48	2.94	2.59	2.92	1.19	0.89
Cash Flow	1.06	0.95	0.94	0.75	0.95	0.72	0.75	0.84	0.25	0.12
Earnings	0.93	0.75	0.74	0.52	0.54	0.47	0.61	0.34	0.24	0.11
S&P Core Earnings	0.74	0.48	0.23	-0.34	-0.19	NA	NA	NA	NA	NA
Dividends	Nil	Nil	Nil	Nil	Nil	Nil	Nil	Nil	Nil	Nil
Payout Ratio	Nil	Nil	Nil	Nil	Nil	Nil	Nil	Nil	Nil	Nil
Prices:High	29.46	26.00	27.86	24.70	37.19	122.31	65.00	24.44	14.08	9.46
Prices:Low	20.70	15.02	10.48	4.70	16.88	14.25	13.25	9.09	1.63	1.96
P/E Ratio:High	32	35	38	47	69	NM	NM	73	59	83
P/E Ratio:Low	22	20	14	9	31	NM	NM	27	7	17
Income Statement Analysis (Million $)										
Revenue	909	741	589	527	592	471	403	249	124	44.5
Operating Income	233	212	189	145	216	172	201	119	60.4	18.1
Depreciation	22.0	33.6	34.3	41.4	79.6	50.2	27.6	15.2	1.71	0.38
Interest Expense	2.23	4.37	18.3	18.2	20.6	17.0	12.6	Nil	NA	Nil
Pretax Income	226	164	161	113	153	135	183	95.5	64.6	22.3
Effective Tax Rate	26.2%	20.0%	21.0%	17.0%	31.0%	30.0%	36.0%	36.0%	36.0%	16.0%
Net Income	166	132	127	93.9	105	94.5	117	61.1	41.4	18.7
S&P Core Earnings	131	83.5	39.3	-60.5	-36.2	NA	NA	NA	NA	NA
Balance Sheet & Other Financial Data (Million $)										
Cash	484	73.5	359	143	140	375	216	128	140	99.1
Current Assets	726	427	809	375	346	587	570	244	258	147
Total Assets	1,682	1,286	1,345	1,162	1,208	1,113	1,038	431	283	150
Current Liabilities	426	342	626	189	193	159	137	85.1	35.4	7.72
Long Term Debt	31.0	Nil	Nil	334	346	330	314	Nil	Nil	Nil
Common Equity	1,203	925	707	622	647	593	533	297	197	142
Total Capital	1,234	925	707	955	994	923	847	297	197	142
Capital Expenditures	26.4	24.4	11.1	19.1	60.6	43.5	26.3	11.4	6.10	2.16
Cash Flow	188	165	161	135	185	145	145	76.3	43.1	19.1
Current Ratio	1.7	1.2	1.3	2.0	1.8	3.7	4.2	2.9	7.3	19.1
% Long Term Debt of Capitalization	2.5	Nil	Nil	34.9	34.8	35.8	37.1	Nil	Nil	NA
% Net Income of Revenue	18.3	17.7	21.6	17.8	17.8	10.0	29.0	24.6	33.4	42.0
% Return on Assets	11.2	10.0	10.1	7.9	9.1	8.8	15.9	17.1	19.1	19.1
% Return on Equity	15.6	16.1	19.1	14.6	17.0	16.8	28.2	24.7	24.4	20.2

Data as orig reptd.; bef. results of disc opers/spec. items. Per share data adj. for stk. divs.; EPS diluted. E-Estimated. NA-Not Available. NM-Not Meaningful. NR-Not Ranked. UR-Under Review.

Office: 851 West Cypress Creek Road, Fort Lauderdale, FL 33309.
Telephone: 954-267-3000.
Email: investor@citrix.com
Website: http://www.citrix.com

Chrmn: T.F. Bogan
Pres & CEO: M.B. Templeton
VP & CFO: D.J. Henshall
VP, Secy & General Counsel: D.R. Friedman

Investor Contact: J. Lilly (954-267-2886)
Board of Directors: T. Bogan, M. J. Demo, S. M. Dow, A. Hirji, G. Morin, G. R. Sullivan, M. B. Templeton

Founded: 1989
Domicile: Delaware
Employees: 3,171

STANDARD &POOR'S

Clear Channel Communications Inc.

S&P Recommendation	Price	12-Mo. Target Price	Investment Style
HOLD ★★★★★	$34.85 (as of Oct 31, 2006)	$37.00	Large-Cap Growth

GICS Sector Consumer Discretionary
Sub-Industry Broadcasting & Cable TV

Comment The nation's largest radio operator, with nearly 1,200 stations, this company also owns 90% of publicly traded Clear Channel Outdoor, a leading global operator of outdoor advertising displays.

Key Stock Statistics (Source S&P, Vickers, company reports)

52-Wk Range	$35.55–27.17	S&P Oper. EPS 2006E	1.36	P/E on S&P Oper. EPS 2006E	25.6	Dividend Rate/Share	$0.75
Trailing 12-Month EPS	$1.80	S&P Oper. EPS 2007E	1.51	Common Shares Outstg. (M)	496.3	Yield (%)	2.15
Trailing 12-Month P/E	19.4	S&P Core EPS 2006E	1.36	Market Capitalization(B)	$17.296	Beta	1.51
$10K Invested 5 Yrs Ago	$9,134	S&P Core EPS 2007E	1.51	Institutional Ownership (%)	87	S&P Credit Rating	BBB-

Price Performance

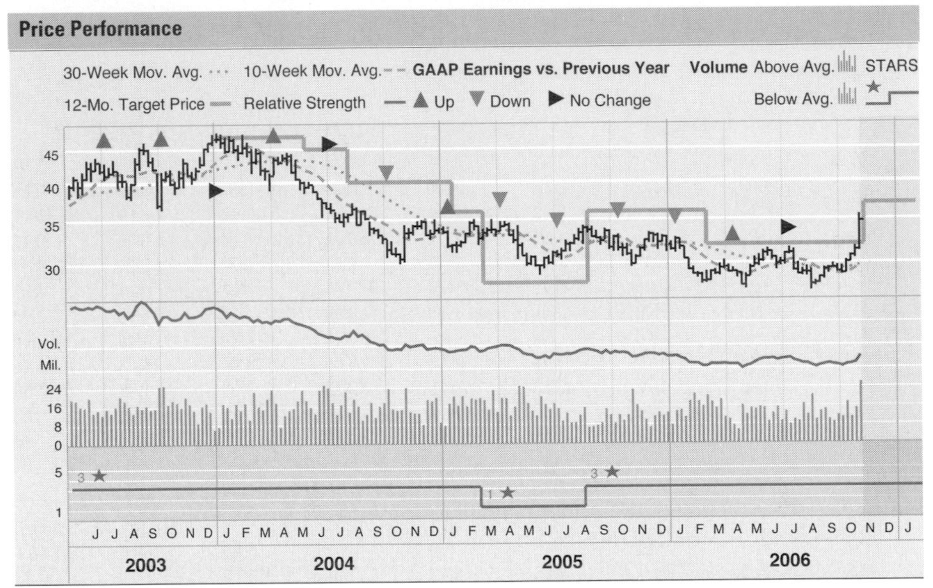

Options: ASE, CBOE, P, Ph

Highlights

- The 12-month target price for CCU has recently been changed to $37.00 from $32.00. The Highlights section of this Stock Report will be updated accordingly.

Investment Rationale/Risk

- The Investment Rationale/Risk section of this Stock Report will be updated shortly. For the latest News story on CCU from MarketScope, see below.

- 10/30/06 11:19 am EST... S&P MAINTAINS HOLD OPINION ON SHARES OF CLEAR CHANNEL COMMUNICATIONS (CCU 35.05***): Before $0.01 one-time gain, Q3 EPS of $0.37 vs. $0.35 is $0.02 above our estimate. Radio revenues grew 5%, above peers, bit shy of Less Is More target. We see healthy operating leverage at U.S. Outdoor. CCU says Q4 radio pacings are up 8.8%, which we view as solid. We see strong 2nd half '06 TV political ads. CCU did not comment on last week's decision to mull strategic options. But we see strong interest from several private consortia, and initial bids could arrive in coming weeks. We are raising our target price by $5 to $37, on attractiveness as acquisition candidate. /T. Amobi-CPA, CFA

Qualitative Risk Assessment

LOW | **MEDIUM** | HIGH

Our risk assessment reflects the company's leading radio market share, a rebounding outdoor business, and our view of ample financial flexibility, offset by high exposure to cyclical advertising, uncertainties with the Less Is More initiative, and increased competition from satellite radio and other newer digital platforms.

Quantitative Evaluations

S&P Quality Ranking B-

D | C | **B-** | B | B+ | A- | A | A+

Relative Strength Rank STRONG

92

LOWEST = 1 HIGHEST = 99

Revenue/Earnings Data

Revenue (Million $)

	1Q	2Q	3Q	4Q	Year
2006	1,504	1,851	--	--	--
2005	1,448	1,723	1,683	1,757	6,610
2004	1,970	2,485	2,649	2,315	9,419
2003	1,779	2,317	2,544	2,290	8,931
2002	1,698	2,173	2,340	2,210	8,421
2001	1,628	2,179	2,300	1,862	7,970

Earnings Per Share ($)

2006	0.19	0.39	**E**0.35	**E**0.41	**E**1.36
2005	0.12	0.39	0.32	0.34	1.16
2004	0.19	0.41	0.44	0.37	1.41
2003	0.12	0.41	1.03	0.30	1.85
2002	0.15	0.39	0.34	0.30	1.18
2001	-0.53	-0.40	-0.39	-0.61	-1.93

Fiscal year ended Dec. 31. Next earnings report expected: Mid November. EPS Estimates based on S&P Operating Earnings; historical GAAP earnings are as reported.

Dividend Data (Dates: mm/dd Payment Date: mm/dd/yy)

Amount ($)	Date Decl.	Ex-Div. Date	Stk. of Record	Payment Date
0.188	02/14	03/29	03/31	04/15/06
0.188	04/26	06/28	06/30	07/15/06
0.188	07/25	09/27	09/30	10/15/06
0.188	10/25	12/27	12/31	01/15/07

Dividends have been paid since 2003. Source: Company reports.

Clear Channel Communications Inc.

Business Summary September 29, 2006

CORPORATE OVERVIEW. Clear Channel Communications is the nation's leading radio operator, with nearly 1,200 radio stations (many in the top markets) and a national radio network. The company also owns 90% of Clear Channel Outdoor (CCO: hold, $21), a leading global outdoor advertising company with nearly 900,000 displays worldwide. Its other interests include 41 TV stations and Katz Media, a media representation firm. In November 2005, CCU completed an IPO of 10% of its outdoor business, and in December 2005, spun off its live entertainment assets to create Live Nation (LYV: $21).

CORPORATE STRATEGY. In December 2004, in a move to stimulate demand and improve inventory pricing, CCU's radio division launched a major companywide initiative dubbed Less Is More (LIM). The program entailed a lower ceiling on commercial minutes played per hour, and another ceiling on the length and number of units in any given commercial break (with some variations by station, format and time of day). LIM has resulted in a 20% reduction in commercial and promotional minutes, as local managers sell fewer of the traditional 60-second spot lengths, and more of the newly created 30s, 15s, and premium spots. CCU recently said that about 35% of its inventory had been migrated to the shorter spot lengths. Despite likely further potential hurdles ahead, we are encouraged by recent management updates showing gains in ratings, time spent listening (TSL) and yield per minute (YPM).

Company Financials

Per Share Data ($) Year Ended Dec. 31	**2005**	**2004**	**2003**	**2002**	**2001**	**2000**	**1999**	**1998**	**1997**	**1996**
Tangible Book Value	NM	NM	NM	NM	NM	NM	NM	0.35	NM	NM
Cash Flow	2.35	2.57	2.93	2.19	2.40	2.82	2.49	1.44	0.97	0.56
Earnings	1.16	1.41	1.85	1.18	-1.93	0.57	0.26	0.22	0.34	0.25
S&P Core Earnings	1.06	1.21	1.06	1.04	-2.00	NA	NA	NA	NA	NA
Dividends	0.69	0.45	0.20	Nil	Nil	Nil	Nil	Nil	Nil	Nil
Payout Ratio	59%	32%	11%	Nil	Nil	Nil	Nil	Nil	Nil	Nil
Prices:High	35.07	47.76	47.48	54.90	68.08	95.50	91.50	62.31	39.94	22.63
Prices:Low	28.75	29.96	31.00	20.00	35.20	43.87	52.00	31.00	16.81	10.19
P/E Ratio:High	30	34	26	47	NM	NM	NM	NM	NM	90
P/E Ratio:Low	25	21	17	17	NM	NM	NM	NM	NM	41

Income Statement Analysis (Million $)										
Revenue	6,610	9,419	8,931	8,421	7,970	5,345	2,678	1,351	697	352
Operating Income	2,053	2,368	2,263	2,186	1,899	1,722	976	546	282	145
Depreciation	630	694	671	621	2,562	1,401	722	305	114	45.8
Interest Expense	443	368	388	433	560	383	192	136	75.1	30.1
Pretax Income	1,079	1,364	1,925	1,218	-1,249	714	236	126	111	76.4
Effective Tax Rate	39.5%	38.0%	40.5%	40.5%	NM	65.1%	63.8%	57.2%	42.6%	37.2%
Net Income	635	846	1,146	725	-1,144	249	85.7	54.0	63.6	37.7
S&P Core Earnings	581	724	653	635	-1,181	NA	NA	NA	NA	NA

Balance Sheet & Other Financial Data (Million $)										
Cash	82.8	210	123	170	159	825	81.1	36.5	24.7	16.7
Current Assets	2,248	2,270	2,186	2,123	1,941	2,343	925	410	199	113
Total Assets	18,703	19,928	28,353	27,672	47,603	50,056	16,822	7,540	3,456	1,325
Current Liabilities	2,107	2,185	1,893	3,011	2,960	2,129	686	258	86.9	43.5
Long Term Debt	6,275	6,963	7,075	7,382	7,968	1,597	4,584	2,324	1,540	725
Common Equity	8,826	9,488	15,554	14,210	29,736	30,347	10,084	4,483	1,747	513
Total Capital	15,920	16,756	25,736	24,109	44,269	38,777	15,987	7,206	3,318	1,256
Capital Expenditures	328	357	378	549	598	496	239	142	31.0	19.7
Cash Flow	1,266	1,540	1,817	1,346	1,418	1,650	808	359	178	83.5
Current Ratio	1.1	1.0	1.2	0.7	0.7	1.1	1.3	1.6	2.3	2.6
% Long Term Debt of Capitalization	39.4	41.6	27.5	30.6	18.0	4.1	28.7	32.2	46.4	57.7
% Net Income of Revenue	9.6	9.0	12.8	8.6	NM	4.7	3.2	4.0	9.1	10.7
% Return on Assets	3.3	3.5	4.1	1.9	NM	0.7	0.7	1.0	2.7	4.0
% Return on Equity	6.9	6.8	7.7	3.3	NM	1.2	1.2	1.7	5.6	11.1

Data as orig reptd.; bef. results of disc opers/spec. items. Per share data adj. for stk. divs.; EPS diluted. E-Estimated. NA-Not Available. NM-Not Meaningful. NR-Not Ranked. UR-Under Review.

Office: 200 East Basse Road, San Antonio, TX 78209-8328.
Telephone: 210-822-2828.
Website: http://www.clearchannel.com
Chrmn: L.L. Mays

Pres & CFO: R.T. Mays
CEO & COO: M.P. Mays
EVP & General Counsel: A. Levin
SVP & Chief Acctg Officer: H.W. Hill, Jr.

Investor Contact: R. Hollinger (212-622-3516)
Board of Directors: A. D. Feld, P. J. Lewis, L. L. Mays, M. P. Mays, R. T. Mays, B. J. McCombs, P. B. Riggins, T. H. Strauss, J. Watts, J. H. Williams, J. B. Zachry

Founded: 1974
Domicile: Texas
Employees: 31,800

STANDARD &POOR'S

Clorox Co (The)

S&P Recommendation HOLD ★★★☆☆

Price $64.28 (as of Oct 27, 2006)

12-Mo. Target Price $64.00

Investment Style Large-Cap Growth

GICS Sector Consumer Staples
Sub-Industry Household Products

Comment This company is a diversified producer of household cleaning, grocery and specialty food products.

Key Stock Statistics (Source S&P, Vickers, company reports)

52-Wk Range	$66.00–53.42	S&P Oper. EPS 2007E	3.20	P/E on S&P Oper. EPS 2007E	20.1	Dividend Rate/Share	$1.16
Trailing 12-Month EPS	$2.90	S&P Oper. EPS 2008E	NA	Common Shares Outstg. (M)	151.2	Yield (%)	1.80
Trailing 12-Month P/E	22.2	S&P Core EPS 2007E	3.08	Market Capitalization(B)	$9.716	Beta	0.45
$10K Invested 5 Yrs Ago	$19,422	S&P Core EPS 2008E	NA	Institutional Ownership (%)	77	S&P Credit Rating	A-

Price Performance

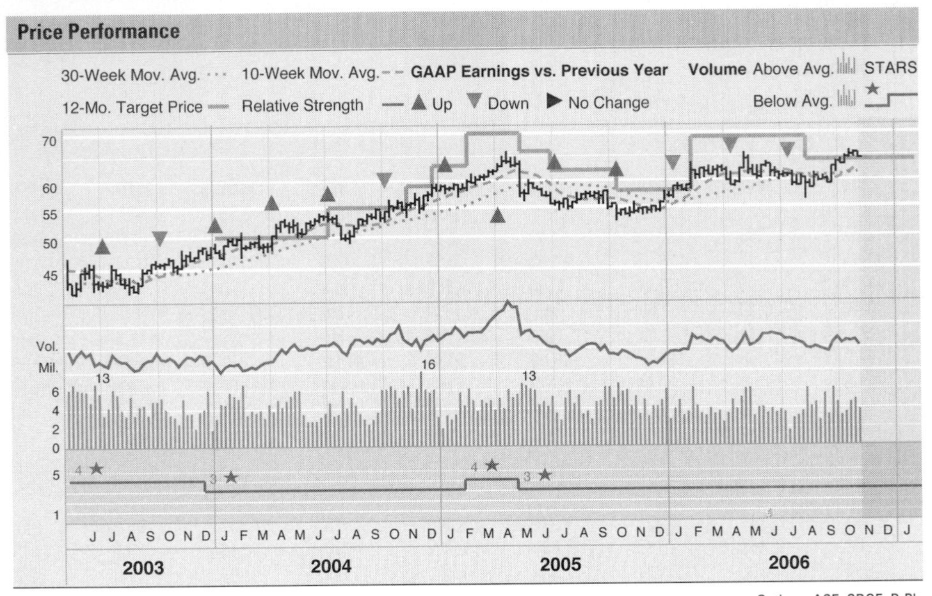

Options: ASE, CBOE, P, Ph

Analysis prepared by **Howard Choe** on August 18, 2006, when the stock traded at **$ 60.57**.

Highlights

- We expect sales to increase approximately 4% in FY 07 (Jun.) versus 6% in the prior year, reflecting modest volume growth driven by new product introductions across most business segments. We expect the international segment to again lead volume growth. We think the household products group, CLX's largest segment, will experience mid-single digit sales growth.
- We believe operating margins will widen to 18.2% in FY 07 from 17.5% in FY 06, as easier raw material cost comparisons, cost savings derived from more efficient manufacturing, promotional spending, sourcing and distribution more than offset higher general and administrative expenses.
- We see FY 07 EPS from continuing operations increasing 7% to $3.20, from FY 06's $3.00. Our FY 07 operating EPS estimate includes a projected $0.17 for stock option expense versus $0.14 in FY 06. We estimate S&P Core EPS of $3.08 in FY 07, reflecting costs related to post retirement obligations.

Investment Rationale/Risk

- In recent years, CLX's performance has been positive but erratic, in our view, due to the seasonal nature of some businesses and the diverse categories in which they operate. We also believe the timing of new product introductions adds to the volatility. However, the level of CLX's product innovation is respectable, in our view, and bolsters the company's pricing power as well its competitive stance.
- Risks to our recommendation and target price include increased competition and promotional activity that would affect profitability, low consumer acceptance of new products, unfavorable foreign exchange, and potential challenges in the implementation of new enterprise resource planning system software.
- With the shares recently trading at a slight premium to peers, at 20X our calendar 2006 EPS estimate, we view them as fairly valued given that we think CLX peers have a stronger sales outlook and steadier earnings growth. Our 12-month target price of $64 is based on our assumption that the shares will trade more in line with peers, at 19.1X our calendar 2007 EPS estimate of $3.35.

Qualitative Risk Assessment

LOW	MEDIUM	HIGH

Our risk assessment reflects our view of stable demand for household and personal care products, generally not affected by changes in the economy or geopolitical factors.

Quantitative Evaluations

S&P Quality Ranking A

D	C	B-	B	B+	A-	A	A+

Relative Strength Rank MODERATE

50

LOWEST = 1 HIGHEST = 99

Revenue/Earnings Data

Revenue (Million $)

	1Q	2Q	3Q	4Q	Year
2006	1,104	1,064	1,157	1,319	4,644
2005	1,048	1,000	1,086	1,254	4,388
2004	1,048	947.0	1,086	1,243	4,324
2003	1,047	926.0	1,019	1,152	4,144
2002	991.0	901.0	1,033	1,136	4,061
2001	985.0	899.0	989.0	1,102	3,903

Earnings Per Share ($)

2006	0.70	0.55	0.72	0.92	2.89
2005	0.50	0.72	0.75	1.00	2.88
2004	0.60	0.52	0.59	0.83	2.55
2003	0.71	0.39	0.51	0.72	2.33
2002	0.33	0.22	0.20	0.63	1.37
2001	0.42	0.27	0.33	0.34	1.36

Fiscal year ended Jun. 30. Next earnings report expected: Early November. EPS Estimates based on S&P Operating Earnings; historical GAAP earnings are as reported.

Dividend Data (Dates: mm/dd Payment Date: mm/dd/yy)

Amount ($)	Date Decl.	Ex-Div. Date	Stk. of Record	Payment Date
0.290	11/16	01/25	01/28	02/15/06
0.290	03/14	04/26	04/28	05/12/06
0.290	05/17	07/27	07/31	08/15/06
0.290	09/20	10/27	10/31	11/15/06

Dividends have been paid since 1968. Source: Company reports.

Clorox Co (The)

Business Summary August 18, 2006

Following its divestiture from The Procter & Gamble Company in 1969 through its January 1999 acquisition of First Brands, Clorox has grown into a company with approximately $4.5 billion in annual sales. Over that time, the name Clorox became nearly synonymous with household bleach.

CLX's strategy is to continue to expand strategic capabilities that drive value into the categories in which it competes. In order to succeed over the long term, the company plans to continue to develop its strategic capabilities in six key areas: consumers, customers, cost, people, process and partnerships.

Sales contributions in FY 05 were as follows: Household Group - North America 46%; Specialty Products 41%, and International 13%. In FY 05, Wal-Mart Stores and its affiliated companies accounted for 27% of consolidated net sales.

The company's Household Group - North America segment includes household cleaning, bleach and other home care products, water filtration products, and food storage and trash disposal categories marketed in the U.S. and Canada. Its International segment includes operations outside the U.S. and Canada, primarily focusing on the laundry, household cleaning, automotive care, insecticides (Brazil and Korea), and food storage and trash disposal categories. The Specialty Products segment includes charcoal, U.S. and European automotive care, cat litter, insecticides, dressings and sauces, and professional products categories.

Most non-durable household consumer products are nationally advertised and sold in the U.S. to grocery stores through a network of brokers and sold to mass merchandisers, warehouse clubs, and military and other retail stores primarily through a direct sales force. Within the U.S., Clorox also sells institutional versions of specialty food and non-food products. Outside the U.S., the company sells consumer products through subsidiaries, licensees, distributors and joint-venture arrangements with local partners.

CLX owns and operates 21 manufacturing facilities in the U.S. The company also owns and operates 21 manufacturing facilities internationally. CLX leases nine distribution centers located in the U.S., Canada, and Chile.

Company Financials

Per Share Data ($) Year Ended Jun. 30	2006	2005	2004	2003	2002	2001	2000	1999	1998	1997
Tangible Book Value	NM	NM	0.77	NM	0.24	1.38	1.10	0.31	NM	NM
Cash Flow	4.12	3.95	3.47	3.19	2.18	2.30	2.48	1.87	2.27	1.82
Earnings	2.89	2.88	2.55	2.33	1.37	1.36	1.64	1.03	1.41	1.21
S&P Core Earnings	2.94	2.73	2.43	2.26	1.63	1.11	NA	NA	NA	NA
Dividends	1.14	1.10	1.08	0.88	0.84	0.84	0.61	0.76	0.64	0.58
Payout Ratio	39%	38%	42%	38%	61%	62%	37%	74%	45%	48%
Prices:High	66.00	66.04	59.45	49.16	47.95	40.85	56.38	66.47	58.75	40.19
Prices:Low	56.17	52.50	46.50	37.40	31.92	29.95	28.38	37.50	37.19	24.31
P/E Ratio:High	23	23	23	21	35	30	34	65	42	33
P/E Ratio:Low	19	18	18	16	23	22	17	36	26	20

Income Statement Analysis (Million $)										
Revenue	4,644	4,388	4,324	4,144	4,061	3,903	4,083	4,003	2,741	2,533
Operating Income	967	1,011	1,069	1,046	942	895	981	933	676	593
Depreciation	188	190	197	191	190	225	201	202	137	126
Interest Expense	127	79.0	30.0	28.0	39.0	88.0	98.0	97.0	69.7	55.6
Pretax Income	653	731	840	802	498	487	622	430	472	416
Effective Tax Rate	32.2%	29.3%	35.0%	35.9%	35.3%	33.3%	36.7%	42.8%	36.9%	40.0%
Net Income	443	517	546	514	322	325	394	246	298	249
S&P Core Earnings	450	489	521	496	383	266	NA	NA	NA	NA

Balance Sheet & Other Financial Data (Million $)										
Cash	192	293	232	172	177	251	245	132	89.7	101
Current Assets	1,007	1,090	1,043	951	1,002	1,103	1,454	1,116	799	673
Total Assets	3,616	3,617	3,834	3,652	3,630	3,995	4,353	4,132	3,030	2,778
Current Liabilities	1,130	1,348	1,268	1,451	1,225	1,069	1,541	1,368	1,225	893
Long Term Debt	1,966	2,122	475	495	678	685	590	702	316	566
Common Equity	-156	-553	1,540	1,215	1,354	1,900	1,794	1,178	1,085	1,036
Total Capital	1,939	1,651	2,189	1,825	2,174	2,732	2,608	2,117	1,401	1,773
Capital Expenditures	180	151	172	205	177	192	158	176	99.0	95.2
Cash Flow	631	707	743	705	512	550	595	448	480	376
Current Ratio	0.9	0.8	0.8	0.7	0.8	1.0	0.9	0.8	0.7	0.8
% Long Term Debt of Capitalization	101.4	128.5	21.7	27.1	31.2	25.1	22.6	33.2	22.6	31.9
% Net Income of Revenue	9.5	11.8	12.6	12.4	7.9	8.3	9.6	6.1	10.9	9.8
% Return on Assets	12.2	13.9	14.6	14.3	8.4	7.8	9.3	6.0	10.3	10.1
% Return on Equity	NA	104.8	39.6	39.8	19.8	17.6	23.4	19.6	28.1	25.1

Data as orig reptd.; bef. results of disc opers/spec. items. Per share data adj. for stk. divs.; EPS diluted. E-Estimated. NA-Not Available. NM-Not Meaningful. NR-Not Ranked. UR-Under Review.

Office: 1221 Broadway, Oakland, CA, USA 94612.
Telephone: 510-271-7000.
Email: investor_relations@clorox.com
Website: http://www.thecloroxcompany.com

Chrmn & CEO: D.R. Knauss
SVP & CFO: D.J. Heinrich
SVP & General Counsel: L. Stein
Investor Contact: S. Austenfeld (510-271-2270)

Board of Directors: D. Boggan, Jr., T. M. Friedman, G. Harad, D. K. Knauss, R. W. Matschullat, G. G. Michael, J. L. Murley, M. E. Shannon, P. Thomas-Graham, C. M. Ticknor

Founded: 1913
Domicile: Delaware
Employees: 7,600

STANDARD &POOR'S

CMS Energy Corp

S&P Recommendation HOLD ★★★★★

Price $15.12 (as of Oct 27, 2006)

12-Mo. Target Price $15.00

Investment Style Mid-Cap Value

GICS Sector Utilities
Sub-Industry Multi-Utilities

Comment This energy holding company's principal subsidiary is Consumers Energy, the largest utility in Michigan and the sixth largest gas and 13th largest electric utility in the U.S.

Key Stock Statistics (Source S&P, Vickers, company reports)

52-Wk Range	$15.37–12.09	S&P Oper. EPS 2006E	1.02	P/E on S&P Oper. EPS 2006E	14.8	Dividend Rate/Share	Nil
Trailing 12-Month EPS	$-1.06	S&P Oper. EPS 2007E	1.15	Common Shares Outstg. (M)	221.6	Yield (%)	Nil
Trailing 12-Month P/E	NM	S&P Core EPS 2006E	1.11	Market Capitalization(B)	$3.350	Beta	2.38
$10K Invested 5 Yrs Ago	$8,054	S&P Core EPS 2007E	1.24	Institutional Ownership (%)	92	S&P Credit Rating	BB

Price Performance

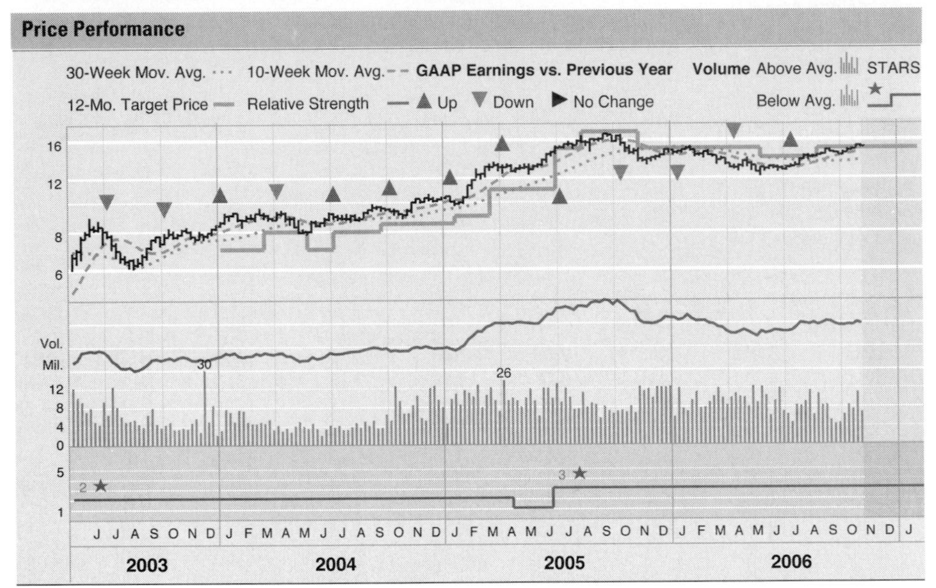

Options: ASE, CBOE, P, Ph

Analysis prepared by **Justin McCann** on August 21, 2006, when the stock traded at **$ 14.25**.

Highlights

- We expect operating EPS in 2006 to increase about 6% from 2005's $0.96, which excludes net one-time charges of $1.40. Results in the first half of 2006 benefited from the December 2005 electric rate increase as well as the tax benefit from a settlement with the IRS, which more than offset the impact of nuclear refueling costs and the adverse effect of milder weather in the second quarter.
- For 2006, we expect EPS to benefit from rate increases and a further reduction in interest expense. On December 22, 2005, the Michigan Public Service Commission (MPSC) authorized a total electric rate increase of $177.4 million for the Consumers Energy subsidiary, based on an allowed return on equity of 11.15%.
- On July 12, 2006, CMS agreed to sell its 798-megawatt Palisades nuclear power plant to Entergy (ETR). The proposed transaction, valued at $380 million, includes a 15-year power purchase agreement for 100% of the plant's production of nuclear power for Consumers Energy's customers. We expect the transaction to be completed, subject to required approvals, in the first quarter of 2007.

Investment Rationale/Risk

- While the stock has underperformed the company's electric and gas utility peers year to date, we expect it to perform more in line over the next 12 months. CMS remains burdened with a high level of debt, a below investment grade credit rating, and higher than average financing costs. However, we expect the shares to be supported by the company's improved liquidity profile and the recent rate increases. We also see a possibility that the dividend (which was suspended in January 2003) may be restored.
- Risks to our recommendation and target price include CMS making slower than anticipated progress in the strengthening of its balance sheet and the restoration of its dividend, as well as a sharp decrease in the average P/E of the group as a whole.
- While we believe the shares could benefit from a potential restoration of the dividend, this could be partially offset by the possibility that the company's financial flexibility could be lowered. We expect the stock to trade at a discount-to-peers P/E of about 13X our 2007 EPS estimate. Our 12-month target price is $15.

Qualitative Risk Assessment

LOW | **MEDIUM** | HIGH

Our risk assessment reflects a balance between the steady cash flow from the regulated electric and gas utility businesses, which operate within a generally supportive regulatory environment, and an improved but still weak financial risk profile, reflecting a high level of debt, and a well above average cost of capital due to the company's below investment grade credit rating.

Quantitative Evaluations

S&P Quality Ranking C

D | **C** | B- | B | B+ | A- | A | A+

Relative Strength Rank MODERATE

62

LOWEST = 1 HIGHEST = 99

Revenue/Earnings Data

Revenue (Million $)

	1Q	2Q	3Q	4Q	Year
2006	2,032	1,396	--	--	--
2005	1,845	1,230	1,307	1,906	6,288
2004	1,754	1,093	1,063	1,562	5,472
2003	1,968	1,126	1,047	1,372	5,513
2002	2,263	2,137	2,579	1,708	8,687
2001	2,859	2,237	2,150	2,351	9,597

Earnings Per Share ($)

2006	-0.12	0.30	**E**0.26	**E**0.27	**E**1.02
2005	0.74	0.12	-1.21	-0.09	-0.51
2004	-0.06	0.10	0.29	0.29	0.67
2003	0.47	-0.08	-0.47	-0.22	-0.30
2002	0.70	0.27	0.07	-3.78	-2.99
2001	0.85	0.40	-2.89	-1.03	-2.53

Fiscal year ended Dec. 31. Next earnings report expected: Early November. EPS Estimates based on S&P Operating Earnings; historical GAAP earnings are as reported.

Dividend Data

Dividend payments were suspended in January 2003.

CMS Energy Corp

Business Summary August 21, 2006

CORPORATE OVERVIEW. CMS Energy (CMS) is the energy holding company for Consumers Energy (formerly Consumers Power Co.), a regulated electric and gas utility serving Michigan's Lower Peninsula, and CMS Enterprises, which is engaged in U.S. and international energy-related businesses. CMS operates in three business segments: electric utility, gas utility, and enterprises. CMS's electric utility operations include generation, purchase, distribution, and sale of electricity. CMS's gas utility purchases, transports, stores, distributes, and sells natural gas. The enterprises segment, through its various subsidiaries and equity investments, is engaged in diversified energy businesses, including independent power production, electric distribution, and natural gas transmission, storage and processing.

CORPORATE STRATEGY. CMS's business strategy is to focus on its core areas of utility operations and services. We believe this should result in capital redeployment and a stronger balance sheet. The non-utility segment will strive to improve earnings and cash flow. In this segment, CMS seeks to optimize cash flow and further reduce business risk and leverage by selling non-strategic assets. In 2005, CMS repatriated $377 million from the enterprises segment to capitalize on the tax break under the American Jobs Creation Act. The company has deployed the earnings in the utility business.

Company Financials

Per Share Data ($) Year Ended Dec. 31	**2005**	**2004**	**2003**	**2002**	**2001**	**2000**	**1999**	**1998**	**1997**	**1996**
Tangible Book Value	10.53	10.51	9.69	7.47	8.11	12.15	13.23	20.30	19.49	17.86
Earnings	-0.51	0.67	-0.30	-2.99	-2.53	0.36	2.17	2.22	2.61	2.45
S&P Core Earnings	-0.44	0.38	0.25	-3.75	-3.29	NA	NA	NA	NA	NA
Dividends	Nil	Nil	Nil	1.09	1.46	1.46	1.39	1.26	1.14	1.02
Payout Ratio	Nil	Nil	Nil	NM	NM	NM	64%	57%	44%	42%
Prices:High	16.80	10.65	10.74	24.80	31.80	32.25	48.44	50.13	44.06	33.75
Prices:Low	9.70	7.81	3.41	5.45	19.49	16.06	30.31	38.75	31.13	27.81
P/E Ratio:High	NM	16	NM	NM	NM	NM	22	23	17	14
P/E Ratio:Low	NM	12	NM	NM	NM	NM	14	17	12	11

Income Statement Analysis (Million $)										
Revenue	6,288	5,472	5,513	8,687	9,597	8,998	6,103	5,141	4,787	4,333
Depreciation	525	431	428	403	530	637	595	484	477	441
Maintenance	249	256	226	211	263	298	216	176	174	178
Fixed Charges Coverage	-0.56	1.01	1.23	0.12	1.26	1.63	1.73	1.75	2.28	2.32
Construction Credits	NA	NA	NA	NA	NA	NA	Nil	Nil	16.0	8.00
Effective Tax Rate	NM	NM	NM	NM	NM	57.7%	18.8%	29.2%	30.4%	36.7%
Net Income	-98.0	127	-43.0	-416	-331	41.0	277	242	268	240
S&P Core Earnings	-93.1	63.4	40.6	-522	-431	NA	NA	NA	NA	NA

Balance Sheet & Other Financial Data (Million $)										
Gross Property	12,448	14,751	11,790	11,344	15,195	14,087	14,278	11,253	10,705	10,147
Capital Expenditures	593	525	535	747	1,262	1,032	1,124	1,295	711	659
Net Property	7,325	8,636	6,944	5,234	8,362	7,835	8,121	6,040	5,435	5,280
Capitalization:Long Term Debt	7,286	7,307	8,652	6,399	6,983	7,913	7,075	5,486	3,347	2,945
Capitalization:% Long Term Debt	73.8	75.8	84.5	85.0	78.7	77.0	74.2	71.2	60.1	58.9
Capitalization:Preferred	261	261	Nil	Nil	Nil	Nil	Nil	Nil	238	356
Capitalization:% Preferred	2.64	2.71	Nil	Nil	Nil	Nil	Nil	Nil	4.28	7.10
Capitalization:Common	2,322	2,072	1,585	1,133	1,890	2,361	2,456	2,216	1,977	1,702
Capitalization:% Common	23.5	21.5	15.5	15.0	21.3	23.0	25.8	28.8	35.5	34.0
Total Capital	10,566	11,123	11,010	8,058	9,834	11,221	10,359	8,486	6,456	5,962
% Operating Ratio	84.8	88.2	91.5	92.1	89.6	88.9	84.7	86.9	86.9	87.6
% Earned on Net Property	NM	7.6	8.1	1.8	3.7	9.1	12.9	13.5	13.9	13.1
% Return on Revenue	NM	2.3	NM	NM	NM	0.5	4.5	4.7	5.6	5.5
% Return on Invested Capital	11.0	9.5	6.7	7.9	9.4	9.5	10.0	12.0	9.9	11.5
% Return on Common Equity	NM	6.3	NM	NM	NM	1.7	11.9	11.5	14.6	15.1

Data as orig reptd.; bef. results of disc opers/spec. items. Per share data adj. for stk. divs.; EPS diluted. E-Estimated. NA-Not Available. NM-Not Meaningful. NR-Not Ranked. UR-Under Review.

Office: 1 Energy Plaza Dr, Jackson, MI 49201-2357.
Telephone: 517-788-0550.
Email: invest@cmsenergy.com
Website: http://www.cmsenergy.com

Chrmn & CEO: K. Whipple
Pres & CEO: D.W. Joos
Vice Chrmn & Chief Lgl Officer: S.K. Smith, Jr.
EVP & CFO: T.J. Webb

SVP & General Counsel: J.E. Brunner
Investor Contact: L.L. Mountcastle (517-788-2590)
Board of Directors: M. S. Ayres, J. E. Barfield, R. M. Gabrys, D. W. Joos, P. R. Lochner, Jr., M. T. Monahan, J. F. Paquette, Jr., P. A. Pierre, K. L. Way, K. Whipple, J. B. Yasinsky

Founded: 1987
Domicile: Michigan
Employees: 8,713

STANDARD &POOR'S

Coach Inc.

S&P Recommendation STRONG BUY ★★★★★

Price $39.01 (as of Oct 27, 2006)

12-Mo. Target Price $48.00

Investment Style Large-Cap Growth

GICS Sector Consumer Discretionary
Sub-Industry Apparel, Accessories & Luxury Goods

Comment COH designs, makes and markets fine accessories for women and men, including handbags, weekend and travel accessories, outerwear, footwear and business cases.

Key Stock Statistics (Source S&P, Vickers, company reports)

52-Wk Range	$40.15–25.18	S&P Oper. EPS 2007**E**	1.65	P/E on S&P Oper. EPS 2007**E**	23.6	Dividend Rate/Share	Nil
Trailing 12-Month EPS	$1.37	S&P Oper. EPS 2008**E**	1.90	Common Shares Outstg. (M)	365.9	Yield (%)	Nil
Trailing 12-Month P/E	28.5	S&P Core EPS 2007**E**	1.65	Market Capitalization(B)	$14.272	Beta	1.27
$10K Invested 5 Yrs Ago	$103,406	S&P Core EPS 2008**E**	1.90	Institutional Ownership (%)	85	S&P Credit Rating	NA

Price Performance

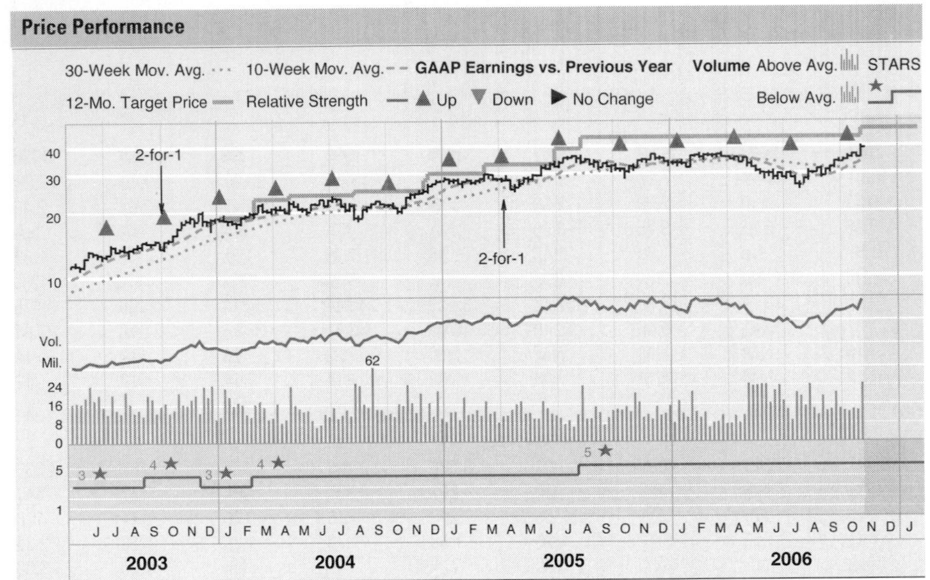

Options: ASE, CBOE, P, Ph

Highlights

- The 12-month target price for COH has recently been changed to $48.00 from $44.00. The Highlights section of this Stock Report will be updated accordingly.

Investment Rationale/Risk

- The Investment Rationale/Risk section of this Stock Report will be updated shortly. For the latest News story on COH from MarketScope, see below.
- 10/24/06 11:34 am EDT... S&P REITERATES STRONG BUY RECOMMENDATION ON SHARES OF COACH INC. (COH 38.67*****): Beats our $0.30 Sep-Q EPS estimate, posting $0.34 vs. $0.24. U.S. same-store sales growth accelerated to 21.4% from June-Q's 18.5%, driven by full-price retail, where comps rose 510 bps to 16%. COH's operating margin widened 340 bps on SG&A leverage. The company estimates 35% of Sep-Q sales were generated by consumers new to its franchise and lifted its estimate of its market size to $7.5B, from $5B. We are raising our FY 07 (June) and FY 08 EPS est both by $0.10, to $1.65 and $1.90, and our target price by $4 to $48, 25X our FY 08 estimate, in line with expected growth rate. /M. Driscoll-CFA

Qualitative Risk Assessment

LOW | **MEDIUM** | HIGH

Our risk assessment reflects our view of COH's strong brand equity and growing cash flow, offset by a highly competitive market amid retail consolidation.

Quantitative Evaluations

S&P Quality Ranking NR

D | C | B- | B | B+ | A- | A | A+

Relative Strength Rank STRONG

93

LOWEST = 1 HIGHEST = 99

Revenue/Earnings Data

Revenue (Million $)

	1Q	2Q	3Q	4Q	Year
2007	553.9	--	--	--	--
2006	449.0	650.3	497.9	514.4	2,112
2005	344.1	531.8	415.9	418.7	1,710
2004	258.4	411.5	313.1	338.2	1,321
2003	192.8	308.5	220.4	231.5	953.2
2002	150.7	235.8	161.6	171.4	719.4

Earnings Per Share ($)

2007	0.34	**E**0.56	**E**0.35	**E**0.40	**E**1.65
2006	0.24	0.45	0.28	0.31	1.27
2005	0.17	0.34	0.23	0.25	1.00
2004	0.11	0.25	0.15	0.17	0.68
2003	0.06	0.17	0.09	0.08	0.40
2002	0.04	0.12	0.03	0.05	0.24

Fiscal year ended Jun. 30. Next earnings report expected: Late January. EPS Estimates based on S&P Operating Earnings; historical GAAP earnings are as reported.

Dividend Data

No cash dividends have been paid.

The McGraw-Hill Companies

Coach Inc.

STANDARD &POOR'S

Business Summary September 06, 2006

CORPORATE OVERVIEW. Coach is a leading U.S. designer and marketer of high quality accessories. Founded in 1941, over the past several years, COH has transformed the Coach brand, building on its popular core categories by introducing new products in a broader array of materials, styles and categories. The company has also implemented a flexible sourcing and manufacturing model, which, it believes, enables it to bring a broader range of products to market more rapidly and efficiently.

MARKET PROFILE. Coach is the number one luxury accessories brand in the U.S., with an estimated 23% share of this $4.8 billion market ($100 handbags). This sub-segment of the handbag/accessories market grew at an estimated 17% pace in 2005, following a 30% year-over-year gain in 2004, and 23% in 2003. COH was able to outpace industry growth and add an estimated five market share points in the 2002-2005 period, as it executed its five pronged multi-channel growth strategy. The Japanese consumer makes up about 40% of the global luxury handbag market. COH estimates that it currently has 8% of the domestic Japanese market and aims to increase its share to 15% over the next five years by opening new stores.

Company Financials

Per Share Data ($) Year Ended Jun. 30	**2006**	**2005**	**2004**	**2003**	**2002**	**2001**	**2000**	**1999**	**1998**	**1997**
Tangible Book Value	2.57	2.07	2.00	1.11	0.67	0.43	0.15	NA	NA	NA
Cash Flow	1.44	1.14	0.79	0.48	0.31	0.24	0.17	NA	NA	NA
Earnings	1.27	1.00	0.68	0.40	0.24	0.19	0.10	NA	NA	NA
S&P Core Earnings	1.27	0.91	0.61	0.35	0.21	0.17	NA	NA	NA	NA
Dividends	Nil	Nil	Nil	Nil	Nil	Nil	NA	NA	NA	NA
Payout Ratio	Nil	Nil	Nil	Nil	Nil	Nil	NA	NA	NA	NA
Prices:High	40.15	36.84	28.85	20.42	8.93	5.34	3.67	NA	NA	NA
Prices:Low	25.18	24.51	16.88	7.26	4.30	2.50	2.00	NA	NA	NA
P/E Ratio:High	32	37	42	52	38	28	NM	NA	NA	NA
P/E Ratio:Low	20	25	25	18	18	13	NM	NA	NA	NA
Income Statement Analysis (Million $)										
Revenue	2,112	1,710	1,321	953	719	616	549	NA	NA	NA
Operating Income	830	679	487	274	163	130	78.5	NA	NA	NA
Depreciation	65.1	57.0	42.9	30.2	25.5	24.1	22.6	NA	NA	NA
Interest Expense	Nil	1.22	0.81	0.70	1.12	2.26	6.60	NA	NA	NA
Pretax Income	797	638	448	245	133	99.4	51.1	NA	NA	NA
Effective Tax Rate	38.0%	36.9%	37.5%	37.0%	35.5%	35.6%	30.6%	NA	NA	NA
Net Income	494	389	262	147	85.8	64.0	35.4	NA	NA	NA
S&P Core Earnings	494	356	236	129	74.9	58.3	NA	NA	NA	NA
Balance Sheet & Other Financial Data (Million $)										
Cash	143	155	263	229	94.0	3.69	NA	NA	NA	NA
Current Assets	974	709	706	449	288	152	134	NA	NA	NA
Total Assets	1,627	1,347	1,029	618	441	259	233	NA	NA	NA
Current Liabilities	342	266	182	161	159	104	79.6	NA	NA	NA
Long Term Debt	3.10	3.27	3.42	3.54	3.62	3.69	87.8	NA	NA	NA
Common Equity	1,189	1,033	782	427	260	148	65.0	NA	NA	NA
Total Capital	1,223	1,041	842	453	279	152	153	NA	NA	NA
Capital Expenditures	134	94.6	67.7	57.1	42.8	31.9	NA	NA	NA	NA
Cash Flow	559	446	305	177	111	88.2	58.0	NA	NA	NA
Current Ratio	2.9	2.7	3.9	2.8	1.8	1.5	1.7	NA	NA	NA
% Long Term Debt of Capitalization	0.3	0.3	0.4	0.8	1.3	2.4	57.4	NA	NA	NA
% Net Income of Revenue	23.4	22.7	19.8	15.4	11.9	10.4	6.4	NA	NA	NA
% Return on Assets	33.0	32.5	31.8	27.7	24.5	23.1	NA	NA	NA	NA
% Return on Equity	44.0	42.8	43.3	42.7	42.0	35.5	NA	NA	NA	NA

Data as orig reptd.; bef. results of disc opers/spec. items. Per share data adj. for stk. divs.; EPS diluted. E-Estimated. NA-Not Available. NM-Not Meaningful. NR-Not Ranked. UR-Under Review.

Office: 516 W 34th St, New York, NY 10001-1394.
Telephone: 212-594-1850.
Email: info@coach.com
Website: http://www.coach.com

Chrmn & CEO: L. Frankfort
Pres & COO: K. Monda
SVP, CFO & Chief Acctg Officer: M. Devine
SVP, Secy & General Counsel: C. Sadler

Investor Contact: A. Shaw Resnick (212-629-2618)
Board of Directors: L. Frankfort, S. J. Kropf, G. Loveman, I. Menezes, I. Miller, K. Monda, M. Murphy, J. Zeitlin

Founded: 1941
Domicile: Maryland
Employees: 7,500

STANDARD &POOR'S

Coca-Cola Co (The)

S&P Recommendation BUY ★★★★★

Price $46.76 (as of Oct 30, 2006)

12-Mo. Target Price $50.00

Investment Style Large-Cap Growth

GICS Sector Consumer Staples
Sub-Industry Soft Drinks

Comment Coca-Cola is the world's largest soft drink company and has a sizable fruit juice business. Its bottling interests include a 36% stake in NYSE-listed Coca-Cola Enterprises.

Key Stock Statistics (Source S&P, Vickers, company reports)

52-Wk Range	**$47.50–39.36**	S&P Oper. EPS 2006**E**	**2.36**	P/E on S&P Oper. EPS 2006**E**	**19.8**	Dividend Rate/Share	**$1.24**
Trailing 12-Month EPS	**$2.24**	S&P Oper. EPS 2007**E**	**2.55**	Common Shares Outstg. (M)	**2,343.8**	Yield (%)	**2.65**
Trailing 12-Month P/E	**20.9**	S&P Core EPS 2006E	**2.36**	Market Capitalization(B)	**$109.596**	Beta	**0.43**
$10K Invested 5 Yrs Ago	**$10,642**	S&P Core EPS 2007E	**2.55**	Institutional Ownership (%)	**63**	S&P Credit Rating	**A+**

Price Performance

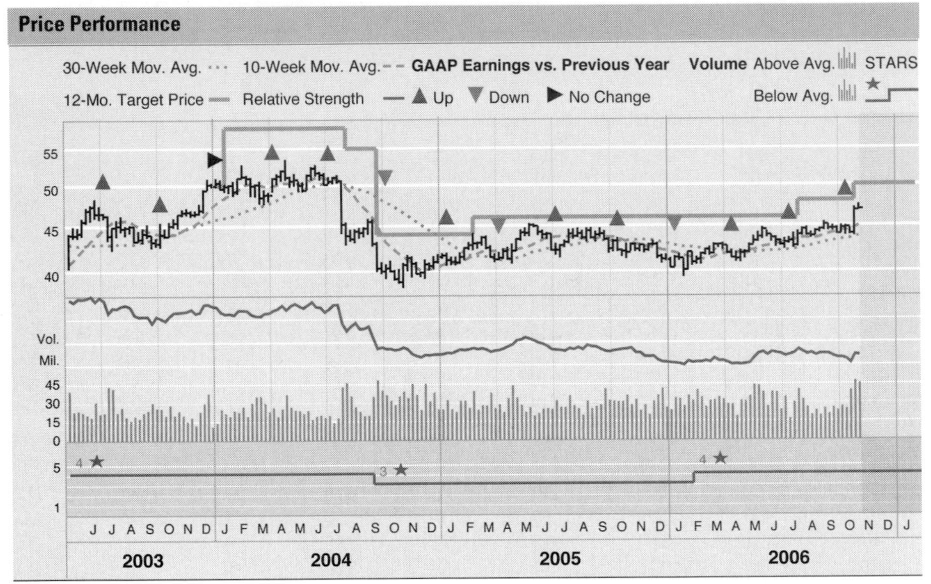

Options: ASE, CBOE, P, Ph

Analysis prepared by **Rick Joy** on October 26, 2006, when the stock traded at **$ 47.11**.

Highlights

- While 2005 was largely a transition year for the company, we expect an improved operating performance in 2006 and 2007. KO's longer-term financial objectives include 3% to 4% annual volume growth, 6% to 8% operating income growth, and EPS growth in the high single digits.
- We see net sales rising about 5% in 2007, reflecting 3% to 4% higher worldwide volumes and higher net prices. Volume growth should benefit from new products and increased marketing spending, but will likely be tempered by challenges in Northern Europe. We expect operating profits to advance at a mid-single digit rate, as a more favorable product mix and improved leverage are partially offset by higher commodity costs and increased marketing spending. We believe equity income will rise moderately, reflecting operating improvements at Coca-Cola Enterprises and other bottlers.
- Based on our expectation for a 1% to 2% reduction in KO's shares outstanding, we expect EPS of $2.55 in 2007, up 8% from estimated operating EPS of $2.36 in 2006. Longer term, we expect annual EPS growth of 8%-9%.

Investment Rationale/Risk

- Our buy recommendation reflects what we see as improving volume trends for the company's businesses and our expectation that the company can generate sustainable volume and earnings growth longer term. We view KO's long-term growth targets as reasonable, and expect the company to perform in line with those targets in 2007. We see the shares as attractive, given our view of KO's strong free cash flow generation and long-term growth potential.
- Risks to our recommendation and target price include a rise in competitive pressures for KO's beverage businesses, an inability to meet growth targets, and unfavorable weather conditions in the company's markets. With regard to corporate governance, we would prefer the separation of the chairman and CEO roles.
- Our DCF model, which assumes a 9% cost of capital and 4% terminal growth, calculates intrinsic value at $48. Our relative valuation model is derived from an analysis of comparable peer P/E and EV/EBITDA multiples and targets a value of $51. Blending our valuations, our 12-month target price is $50.

Qualitative Risk Assessment

LOW	MEDIUM	HIGH

Our risk assessment for the Coca-Cola Company reflects the relatively stable nature of the company's end markets, dominant market share positions around the world and our view of a strong balance sheet and cash flow.

Quantitative Evaluations

S&P Quality Ranking B+

D	C	B-	B	**B+**	A-	A	A+

Relative Strength Rank MODERATE

63

LOWEST = 1 HIGHEST = 99

Revenue/Earnings Data

Revenue (Million $)

	1Q	2Q	3Q	4Q	Year
2006	5,226	6,476	6,454	--	--
2005	5,206	6,310	6,037	5,551	23,104
2004	5,078	5,965	5,662	5,257	21,962
2003	4,502	5,695	5,671	5,176	21,044
2002	4,079	5,368	5,322	4,795	19,564
2001	4,479	5,293	5,397	4,923	20,092

Earnings Per Share ($)

	1Q	2Q	3Q	4Q	Year
2006	0.47	0.78	0.62	**E**0.51	**E**2.36
2005	0.42	0.72	0.54	0.36	2.04
2004	0.46	0.65	0.39	0.50	2.00
2003	0.34	0.55	0.50	0.38	1.77
2002	0.29	0.49	0.44	0.38	1.60
2001	0.35	0.45	0.43	0.37	1.60

Fiscal year ended Dec. 31. Next earnings report expected: Early February. EPS Estimates based on S&P Operating Earnings; historical GAAP earnings are as reported.

Dividend Data (Dates: mm/dd Payment Date: mm/dd/yy)

Amount ($)	Date Decl.	Ex-Div. Date	Stk. of Record	Payment Date
0.310	02/16	03/13	03/15	04/01/06
0.310	04/20	06/13	06/15	07/01/06
0.310	07/20	09/13	09/15	10/01/06
0.310	10/19	11/29	12/01	12/15/06

Dividends have been paid since 1893. Source: Company reports.

Coca-Cola Co (The)

Business Summary October 26, 2006

The Coca-Cola Company is the world's largest producer of soft drink concentrates and syrups, as well as the world's largest producer of juice and juice-related products. Finished soft drink products bearing the company's trademarks have been sold in the U.S. since 1886, and are now sold in more than 200 countries. Sales and operating profits (before accounting for intercompany sales and corporate overhead) in 2005 by geographic region were distributed as follows: North America (29% of revenues, 21% of segment operating profits); European Union (29.5%, 31%); North Asia, Eurasia and Middle East (19.5%, 23%); Latin America (11%, 16%); East, South Asia and Pacific Rim (5.5%, 3%); and Africa (5.5%, 6%).

The company's business, which is extremely focused, in our view, encompasses the production and sale of soft drink and non-carbonated beverage concentrates and syrups. These products are sold to the company's authorized independent and company-owned bottling/canning operations, and fountain wholesalers. These customers then either combine the syrup with carbonated water, or combine the concentrate with sweetener, water and carbonated water to produce finished soft drinks. The finished soft drinks are packaged in authorized containers bearing the company's well-known trademarks, which include Coca-Cola (best-selling soft drink in the world, including Coca-Cola classic), caffeine free Coca-Cola (classic), diet Coke (sold as Coke light in many markets outside the U.S.), Cherry Coke, diet Cherry Coke, diet Coke with lemon, Vanilla Coke, diet Vanilla Coke, Fanta, Full Throttle, Sprite, diet Sprite, Barq's, Surge, Mr. PiBB, Mello Yello, TAB, Fresca, PowerAde, Minute Maid, Hi-C, Fruitopia, and other products developed for specific markets, including Georgia ready-to-drink coffees. The company also markets the Schweppes and Canada Dry mixer (such as tonic water, club soda and ginger ale), Crush and Dr. Pepper brands in more than 160 countries outside of the U.S. In 2005, concentrates and syrups for beverages bearing the trademark "Coca-Cola" or including the trademark "Coke" accounted for approximately 55% of the company's total gallon sales.

Company Financials

Per Share Data ($) Year Ended Dec. 31	**2005**	**2004**	**2003**	**2002**	**2001**	**2000**	**1999**	**1998**	**1997**	**1996**
Tangible Book Value	5.29	5.02	4.14	3.34	3.53	2.98	3.06	3.19	2.67	2.18
Cash Flow	2.43	2.36	2.11	1.93	1.92	1.19	1.30	1.67	1.89	1.59
Earnings	2.04	2.00	1.77	1.60	1.60	0.88	0.98	1.42	1.64	1.40
S&P Core Earnings	2.03	2.08	1.77	1.62	1.46	NA	NA	NA	NA	NA
Dividends	1.12	1.00	0.88	0.80	0.72	0.68	0.64	0.60	0.56	0.50
Payout Ratio	55%	50%	50%	50%	45%	77%	65%	42%	34%	36%
Prices:High	45.26	53.50	50.90	57.91	62.19	66.88	70.88	88.94	72.63	54.25
Prices:Low	40.31	38.30	37.01	42.90	42.37	42.88	47.31	53.63	51.13	36.06
P/E Ratio:High	22	27	29	36	39	76	72	63	44	39
P/E Ratio:Low	20	19	21	27	26	49	48	38	31	26

Income Statement Analysis (Million $)	2005	2004	2003	2002	2001	2000	1999	1998	1997	1996
Revenue	23,104	21,962	21,044	19,564	20,092	20,458	19,805	18,813	18,868	18,546
Operating Income	7,017	6,591	6,071	6,264	6,155	4,464	4,774	5,612	5,627	4,394
Depreciation	932	893	850	806	803	773	792	645	626	479
Interest Expense	240	196	178	199	289	447	337	277	258	286
Pretax Income	6,690	6,222	5,495	5,499	5,670	3,399	3,819	5,198	6,055	4,596
Effective Tax Rate	27.2%	22.1%	20.9%	27.7%	29.8%	36.0%	36.3%	32.0%	31.8%	24.0%
Net Income	4,872	4,847	4,347	3,976	3,979	2,177	2,431	3,533	4,129	3,492
S&P Core Earnings	4,854	5,063	4,350	4,021	3,654	NA	NA	NA	NA	NA

Balance Sheet & Other Financial Data (Million $)	2005	2004	2003	2002	2001	2000	1999	1998	1997	1996
Cash	4,767	6,768	3,482	2,345	1,934	1,892	1,812	1,807	1,737	1,658
Current Assets	10,250	12,094	8,396	7,352	7,171	6,620	6,480	6,380	5,969	5,910
Total Assets	29,427	31,327	27,342	24,501	22,417	20,834	21,623	19,145	16,940	16,161
Current Liabilities	9,836	10,971	7,886	7,341	8,429	9,321	9,856	8,640	7,379	7,416
Long Term Debt	1,154	1,157	2,517	2,701	1,219	835	854	687	801	1,116
Common Equity	16,355	15,935	14,090	11,800	11,366	9,316	9,513	8,403	7,311	6,156
Total Capital	17,861	17,542	16,944	14,900	13,027	10,509	10,865	9,514	8,560	7,573
Capital Expenditures	899	755	812	851	769	733	1,069	863	1,093	990
Cash Flow	5,804	5,740	5,197	4,782	4,782	2,950	3,223	4,178	4,755	3,971
Current Ratio	1.0	1.1	1.1	1.0	0.9	0.7	0.7	0.7	0.8	0.8
% Long Term Debt of Capitalization	6.5	6.6	14.9	18.1	9.4	7.9	7.9	7.2	9.4	14.7
% Net Income of Revenue	21.1	22.1	20.7	20.3	19.8	10.6	12.3	18.8	21.9	18.8
% Return on Assets	16.0	16.5	16.8	16.9	18.4	10.3	11.9	19.6	24.9	22.4
% Return on Equity	30.2	32.3	33.6	34.3	38.5	23.1	27.1	45.0	61.3	60.5

Data as orig reptd.; bef. results of disc opers/spec. items. Per share data adj. for stk. divs.; EPS diluted. E-Estimated. NA-Not Available. NM-Not Meaningful. NR-Not Ranked. UR-Under Review.

Office: 1 Coca Cola Plz NW, Atlanta, GA 30313-2499.
Telephone: 404-676-2121.
Website: http://www.coca-cola.com
Chrmn & CEO: E.N. Isdell

Investor Contact: G.P. Fayard (404-676-2121)
EVP & CFO: G.P. Fayard
Chief Acctg Officer & Cntlr: C. McDaniel
Secy: C. Hayes

Board of Directors: H. A. Allen, R. W. Allen, C. P. Black, W. Buffett, B. Diller, E. N. Isdell, D. R. Keough, M. E. Lagomasino, D. F. McHenry, S. Nunn, J. P. Reinhard, J. D. Robinson, III, P. V. Ueberroth, J. B. Williams

Founded: 1886
Domicile: Delaware
Employees: 55,000

STANDARD &POOR'S

Coca-Cola Enterprises Inc.

S&P Recommendation HOLD ★★★★★

Price $20.10 (as of Oct 30, 2006)

12-Mo. Target Price $23.00

Investment Style Large-Cap Value

GICS Sector Consumer Staples
Sub-Industry Soft Drinks

Comment This company is the world's largest bottler of Coca-Cola beverage products, distributing to about 78% of the North American market. Coca-Cola Co. holds 36% of CCE's common stock.

Key Stock Statistics (Source S&P, Vickers, company reports)

52-Wk Range	**$22.49–18.52**	S&P Oper. EPS 2006**E**	**1.26**	P/E on S&P Oper. EPS 2006**E**	**16.0**	Dividend Rate/Share	**$0.24**
Trailing 12-Month EPS	**$1.06**	S&P Oper. EPS 2007**E**	**1.35**	Common Shares Outstg. (M)	**477.8**	Yield (%)	**1.19**
Trailing 12-Month P/E	**19.0**	S&P Core EPS 2006**E**	**1.31**	Market Capitalization(B)	**$9.605**	Beta	**0.37**
$10K Invested 5 Yrs Ago	**$11,267**	S&P Core EPS 2007**E**	**1.41**	Institutional Ownership (%)	**41**	S&P Credit Rating	**A**

Price Performance

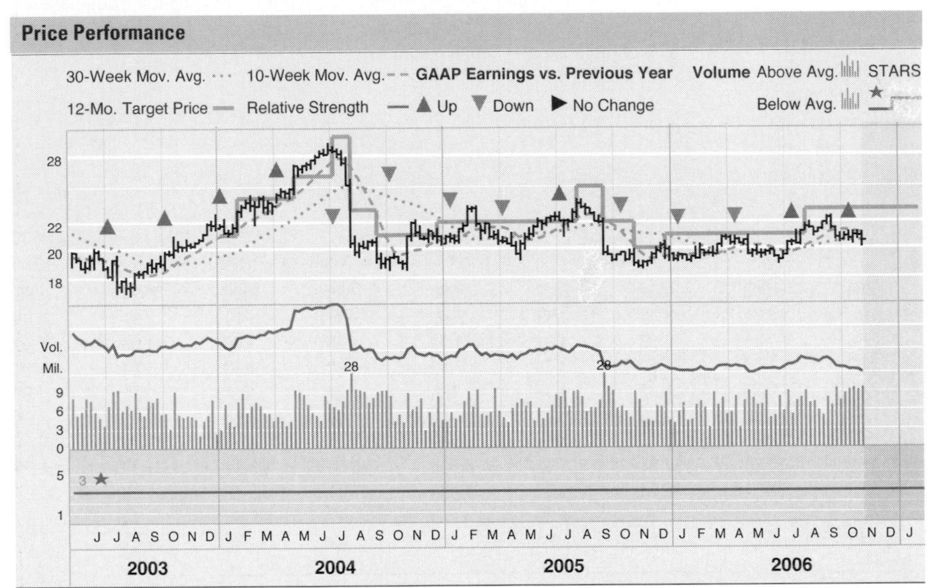

Options: ASE, CBOE, P, Ph

Analysis prepared by **Rick Joy** on October 27, 2006, when the stock traded at **$ 20.76**.

Highlights

- We expect net revenues in 2007 to advance 3% to 4%, reflecting consolidated bottle and can unit case volume growth of 1% to 2%, a 2% increase in net revenues per case, and a modest positive impact from foreign currency translations. We project that North American volumes will rise 1% to 2%, while European volumes will likely be up less than 1%.
- We see gross margins remaining unchanged, as benefits from a product mix shift toward cold channel sales and higher pricing are offset by higher sweetener, energy and packaging costs. We think SG&A expenses will decrease modestly as a percentage of sales, as productivity savings outweigh higher pension and fuel costs.
- Following a reduction in interest expense and a modest decrease in shares outstanding, we estimate that 2007 EPS will increase 7% to $1.35, from operating EPS of $1.26 in 2006. We see 2007 EPS of $1.35. For the longer term, we expect annual EPS growth of 7% to 9%.

Investment Rationale/Risk

- Our hold recommendation reflects our expectation for a challenging operating environment for the company over the next 12 months. We see results benefiting from pricing gains, but we expect commodity cost inflation, high energy prices and sluggish soft drink trends to be offsets. In light of our expectations of sluggish volume trends for CCE's European business in the near term, we believe appreciation potential is limited, as we wait for signs of an improvement in volume and earnings growth trends.
- Risks to our recommendation and target price include rising commodity costs, consumer acceptance of new product introductions, and CCE's ability to achieve sales and earnings growth forecasts. In terms of corporate governance, the board is controlled by a majority of insiders and affiliated insiders, which we view unfavorably.
- Our 12-month target price of $23 is based on our analysis of peer P/E and enterprise value to EBITDA multiples, and our DCF model, which assumes a weighted average cost of capital of 9% and a terminal growth rate of 3%.

Qualitative Risk Assessment

LOW | MEDIUM | HIGH

Our risk assessment for Coca-Cola Enterprises reflects our view of the relatively stable nature of the company's end markets, strong cash flows and its relationship with corporate partner Coca-Cola Company.

Quantitative Evaluations

S&P Quality Ranking **B**

D | C | B- | **B** | B+ | A- | A | A+

Relative Strength Rank **WEAK**

18

LOWEST = 1 HIGHEST = 99

Revenue/Earnings Data

Revenue (Million $)

	1Q	2Q	3Q	4Q	Year
2006	4,333	5,467	5,206	--	--
2005	4,196	5,128	4,895	4,487	18,706
2004	4,240	4,844	4,670	4,404	18,158
2003	3,667	4,617	4,734	4,312	17,330
2002	3,642	4,448	4,549	4,249	16,889
2001	3,352	4,105	4,276	3,967	15,700

Earnings Per Share ($)

	1Q	2Q	3Q	4Q	Year
2006	0.03	0.71	0.44	**E**0.15	**E**1.26
2005	0.10	0.70	0.40	-0.12	1.08
2004	0.22	0.43	0.44	0.17	1.26
2003	0.06	0.56	0.56	0.28	1.48
2002	0.02	0.47	0.42	0.17	1.07
2001	-0.24	0.24	0.02	-0.08	-0.05

Fiscal year ended Dec. 31. Next earnings report expected: Early February. EPS Estimates based on S&P Operating Earnings; historical GAAP earnings are as reported.

Dividend Data (Dates: mm/dd Payment Date: mm/dd/yy)

Amount ($)	Date Decl.	Ex-Div. Date	Stk. of Record	Payment Date
0.060	02/17	03/15	03/17	03/30/06
0.060	04/25	06/14	06/16	06/29/06
0.060	07/25	09/13	09/15	09/28/06
0.060	10/25	11/29	12/01	12/14/06

Dividends have been paid since 1986. Source: Company reports.

Coca-Cola Enterprises Inc.

Business Summary October 27, 2006

Coca-Cola Enterprises is the world's largest bottler of Coca-Cola beverage products, distributing about 79% of all bottle/can volume of carbonated soft-drink products of The Coca-Cola Co. (KO) in North America. KO owns about 36% of the company's common stock. CCE's product line also includes other nonalcoholic beverages, such as still and sparkling waters, juices, isotonics and teas. In 2005, the company sold approximately 42 billion bottles and cans throughout its territories, representing about 20% of The Coca-Cola Company's worldwide volume. About 93% of this volume consisted of beverages produced and sold under licenses from The Coca-Cola Company. CCE also distributes Dr Pepper and several other beverage brands.

Based on net operating revenues in 2005, North America accounted for 72% of total revenues, and Europe for 28%. CCE operates in parts of 46 states in the U.S., the District of Columbia, the U.S. Virgin Islands, all 10 Canadian provinces, and portions of Europe that include Belgium, France, the U.K., Luxembourg, Monaco, and the Netherlands. At December 31, 2005, CCE's bottling territories encompassed an aggregate population of 407 million people. The company's five leading brands in North America in 2005 were Coca-Cola classic, Diet Coke, Dasani, Sprite and caffeine free diet Coke, while the five leading brands in Europe were Coca-Cola, diet Coke/Coke light, Fanta, Schweppes and Sprite.

The company conducts its business primarily under bottle contracts with KO. CCE has the exclusive right to produce and market Coca-Cola soft drinks in authorized containers in specified territories; KO has the ability, at its sole discretion, to set prices for concentrates and syrups. At the end of 2005, CCE operated 428 production and distribution facilities, approximately 54,000 vehicles, and about 2.4 million coolers, beverage dispensers and vending machines used to market, distribute and produce the company's products.

Company Financials

Per Share Data ($) Year Ended Dec. 31	**2005**	**2004**	**2003**	**2002**	**2001**	**2000**	**1999**	**1998**	**1997**	**1996**
Tangible Book Value	NM	NM	NM	NM	6.25	6.67	6.83	6.08	4.61	3.75
Cash Flow	3.27	3.52	3.88	3.35	3.08	3.48	3.22	3.11	2.82	1.98
Earnings	1.08	1.26	1.48	1.07	-0.05	0.54	0.13	0.35	0.43	0.28
S&P Core Earnings	1.01	1.19	1.22	0.78	-0.34	NA	NA	NA	NA	NA
Dividends	0.16	0.16	0.16	0.16	0.12	0.16	0.16	0.15	0.08	0.03
Payout Ratio	15%	13%	11%	15%	NM	30%	123%	41%	19%	12%
Prices:High	23.92	29.34	23.30	24.50	23.90	30.25	37.50	41.56	36.00	16.38
Prices:Low	18.52	18.45	16.85	15.94	13.46	14.00	16.81	22.88	15.71	8.00
P/E Ratio:High	22	23	16	23	NM	56	NM	NM	84	58
P/E Ratio:Low	17	15	11	15	NM	26	NM	NM	37	28
Income Statement Analysis (Million $)										
Revenue	18,706	18,158	17,330	16,889	15,700	14,750	14,406	13,414	11,278	7,921
Operating Income	2,475	2,504	2,674	2,409	1,954	2,387	2,187	1,989	1,666	1,172
Depreciation	1,044	1,068	1,097	1,045	1,353	1,261	1,348	1,120	946	627
Interest Expense	633	619	607	662	753	791	751	703	538	353
Pretax Income	790	818	972	705	-150	333	88.0	169	178	194
Effective Tax Rate	34.9%	27.1%	30.5%	29.9%	NM	29.1%	33.0%	16.0%	3.90%	41.2%
Net Income	514	596	676	494	-19.0	236	59.0	142	171	114
S&P Core Earnings	478	563	563	356	-147	NA	NA	NA	NA	NA
Balance Sheet & Other Financial Data (Million $)										
Cash	107	155	80.0	68.0	284	294	141	68.0	45.0	47.0
Current Assets	3,395	3,264	3,000	2,844	2,876	2,631	2,581	2,285	1,813	1,319
Total Assets	25,357	26,354	25,700	24,375	23,719	22,162	22,730	21,132	17,487	11,234
Current Liabilities	3,846	3,431	3,941	3,455	4,522	3,094	3,614	3,397	3,032	1,690
Long Term Debt	9,165	10,523	10,552	11,236	10,365	10,348	10,153	9,605	7,760	4,814
Common Equity	5,643	5,378	4,365	3,310	2,783	2,790	2,877	2,389	1,782	1,416
Total Capital	19,914	21,139	19,882	19,122	17,521	17,956	18,028	16,758	13,538	6,230
Capital Expenditures	914	946	1,099	1,029	972	1,181	1,480	1,551	967	622
Cash Flow	1,558	1,664	1,771	1,536	1,331	1,494	1,404	1,262	1,115	741
Current Ratio	0.9	1.0	0.8	0.8	0.6	0.9	0.7	0.7	0.6	0.8
% Long Term Debt of Capitalization	46.0	49.8	53.1	58.8	59.2	57.6	56.3	57.3	57.3	77.2
% Net Income of Revenue	2.7	3.3	3.9	2.9	NM	1.6	0.4	1.1	1.5	1.4
% Return on Assets	2.0	2.3	2.7	2.1	NM	1.1	0.3	0.7	1.2	1.1
% Return on Equity	9.3	12.2	17.6	16.1	NM	8.2	2.1	6.8	10.6	8.1

Data as orig reptd.; bef. results of disc opers/spec. items. Per share data adj. for stk. divs.; EPS diluted. E-Estimated. NA-Not Available. NM-Not Meaningful. NR Not Ranked. UR-Under Review.

Office: 2500 Windy Ridge Parkway , Atlanta, GA 30339.
Telephone: 770-989-3000.
Website: http://www.cokecce.com
Chrmn: L.F. Kline

Pres & CEO: J.F. Brock
COO & EVP: G.D. Van Houten, Jr.
EVP & General Counsel: J.J. Culhane
SVP & CFO: W.W. Douglas, III

Board of Directors: F. Aguirre, J. Brock, J. E. Copeland, Jr., C. Darden, J. A. Douglas, Jr., J. T. Eyton, G. P. Fayard, I. Finan, M. J. Herb, L. P. Humann, D. A. James, S. K. Johnston, III, L. F. Kline, P. R. Reynolds

Founded: 1944
Domicile: Delaware
Employees: 73,000

STANDARD &POOR'S

Colgate-Palmolive Co

S&P Recommendation STRONG BUY ★★★★★

Price $63.80 (as of Oct 30, 2006)

12-Mo. Target Price $71.00

Investment Style Large-Cap Growth

GICS Sector Consumer Staples
Sub-Industry Household Products

Comment This major consumer products company markets oral, personal and household care and pet nutrition products in more than 200 countries and territories.

Key Stock Statistics (Source S&P, Vickers, company reports)

52-Wk Range	$63.88–51.19	S&P Oper. EPS 2006E	2.89	P/E on S&P Oper. EPS 2006E	22.1	Dividend Rate/Share	$1.28
Trailing 12-Month EPS	$2.38	S&P Oper. EPS 2007E	3.22	Common Shares Outstg. (M)	514.3	Yield (%)	2.01
Trailing 12-Month P/E	26.8	S&P Core EPS 2006E	2.94	Market Capitalization(B)	$32.814	Beta	0.27
$10K Invested 5 Yrs Ago	$11,852	S&P Core EPS 2007E	3.26	Institutional Ownership (%)	69	S&P Credit Rating	AA-

Price Performance

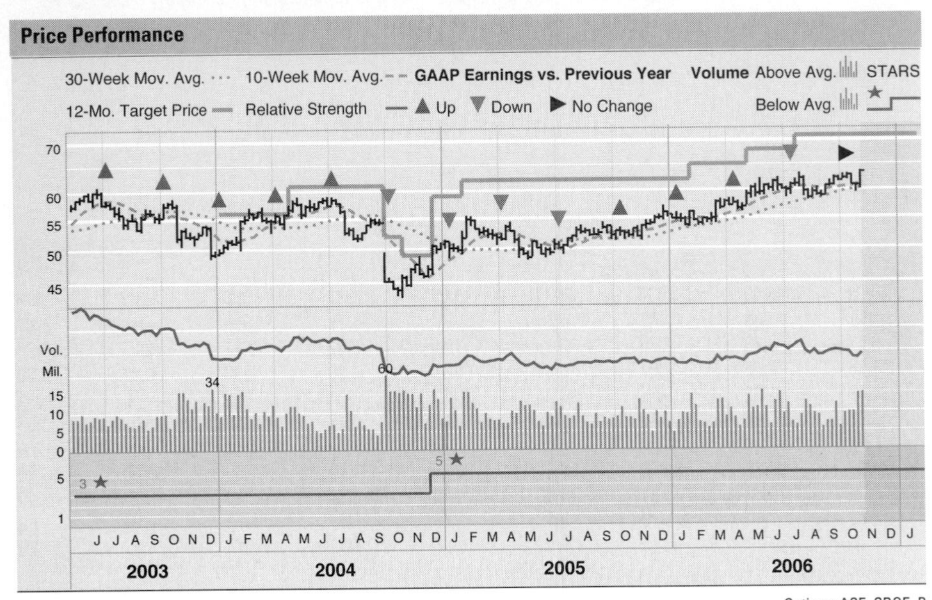

Options: ASE, CBOE, P

Analysis prepared by **Loran Braverman, CFA** on October 30, 2006, when the stock traded at **$ 63.39**.

Highlights

- In December 2004, CL embarked on a four-year restructuring program that involves: a 12% workforce reduction, the closing of a third of CL's factories, an increased focus on faster growing markets, new product innovation, and more efficient spending on marketing.
- For 2006, we expect sales to increase 6%, primarily reflecting solid volume growth and price increases. We project a gross margin expansion of approximately 100 basis points. We expect the selling, general and administrative expense ratio to be flat, excluding our estimate of $77 million for stock option expense. Overall, we look for the operating margin to rise by 80 basis points (bps) in 2006 and another 40 bps in 2007. All of the expense ratios exclude one-time and restructuring charges. Our 2007 sales growth forecast is 5.5%.
- With our assumption of a 32% effective tax rate and 1% fewer shares as a result of share repurchases, we expect 2006 EPS to increase to $2.89. This includes $0.10 of stock-option related expense but excludes $0.40 of restructuring charges. We project 2006 S&P Core EPS of $2.94, reflecting post-retirement adjustments.

Investment Rationale/Risk

- We have a strong buy opinion on the shares, reflecting our belief that CL's restructuring initiatives are likely to drive improved profitability. We think that savings derived from the restructuring program will be reinvested in R&D and marketing. The program is also expected to allocate more resources to faster growing markets. We believe these efforts will culminate in greater gross margin expansion and EPS growth in the low double digits from 2006 onward.
- Risks to our recommendation and target price include intensified competition in the global oral care market, unfavorable currency translations, and low consumer acceptance of new products.
- Given the stable and improving outlook that we see for CL, we believe the shares should trade at a premium to peers. The shares were recently trading at a modest premium to peers on a P/E basis. However, on a forward P/E basis, the shares were trading at a 25% discount to their 10-year average of 27X. Our 12-month target price of $71 applies a P/E of 22X to our 2007 EPS estimate of $3.22.

Qualitative Risk Assessment

LOW	MEDIUM	HIGH

Our risk assessment reflects that demand for household and personal care products is generally static, and not affected by changes in the economy or geopolitical factors. This is partially offset by our view that these industries are mature and competitive in nature.

Quantitative Evaluations

S&P Quality Ranking A+

D	C	B-	B	B+	A-	A	A+

Relative Strength Rank MODERATE

62

LOWEST = 1 HIGHEST = 99

Revenue/Earnings Data

Revenue (Million $)

	1Q	2Q	3Q	4Q	Year
2006	2,871	3,014	3,144	--	--
2005	2,743	2,838	2,912	2,905	11,397
2004	2,514	2,572	2,696	2,803	10,584
2003	2,348	2,459	2,524	2,573	9,903
2002	2,195	2,297	2,382	2,420	9,294
2001	2,293	2,330	2,391	2,414	9,428

Earnings Per Share ($)

	1Q	2Q	3Q	4Q	Year
2006	0.59	0.51	0.63	E0.76	E2.89
2005	0.53	0.62	0.63	0.65	2.43
2004	0.59	0.66	0.58	0.50	2.33
2003	0.56	0.62	0.63	0.65	2.46
2002	0.49	0.55	0.57	0.59	2.19
2001	0.44	0.47	0.49	0.49	1.89

Fiscal year ended Dec. 31. Next earnings report expected: Late January. EPS Estimates based on S&P Operating Earnings; historical GAAP earnings are as reported.

Dividend Data (Dates: mm/dd Payment Date: mm/dd/yy)

Amount ($)	Date Decl.	Ex-Div. Date	Stk. of Record	Payment Date
0.290	01/12	01/24	01/26	02/15/06
0.320	03/09	04/20	04/24	05/15/06
0.320	07/13	07/24	07/26	08/15/06
0.320	10/05	10/20	10/24	11/15/06

Dividends have been paid since 1895. Source: Company reports.

Colgate-Palmolive Co

Business Summary October 30, 2006

CORPORATE OVERVIEW. Colgate-Palmolive Co. is a leading global consumer products company that operates in the oral, personal, and household care, and pet food markets. Its products are marketed in more than 200 countries and territories worldwide. Sales of oral, personal, and home care products accounted for 87% of total worldwide sales in 2005. The balance of revenues was derived from the sale of pet foods. The company's oral care products include toothbrushes, toothpaste and pharmaceutical products for oral health professionals. CL's personal care products include bar and liquid soaps, shampoos, conditioners, deodorants antiperspirants, and shave products. The home care division produces major brands such as Palmolive and Ajax soaps. Oral, personal and home care sales outside of North America accounted for 64% of total sales in 2005. Sales in Latin America, Europe and Asia/Africa accounted for 23%, 24% and 18% of total oral, personal and home care sales segment sales, respectively.

MARKET PROFILE. CL is a dominant player in its categories. According to Information Resources Inc., CL held about a 36% volume share of toothpaste in the U.S. as of November 2005, about in line with its main competitor, Procter & Gamble (PG: $62, strong buy). According to company sources, CL holds a nearly 34% market share in Europe. The company is the U.S. market leader in liquid hand soap, with about a 44% market share. While volume growth for CL's categories in developed countries has been modest, in our view, growth in the developing and emerging markets is projected to rise at a rate two to three times that of developed markets in the near term. Colgate has the advantage of having operated in these markets for an extended period of time (several decades) and this is evident in the leading market shares that the company enjoys. In countries such as Venezuela and Mexico, Colgate has a toothpaste market share above 80%, more than 75 percentage points over its nearest competitor. In Eastern Europe, Colgate has more than a 35% share, India 50%, China 32%, and Russia 17%. With plans to increase consumer awareness and product innovation, coupled with growing economies, we believe Colgate is well situated to benefit from this market growth.

Company Financials

Per Share Data ($) Year Ended Dec. 31	**2005**	**2004**	**2003**	**2002**	**2001**	**2000**	**1999**	**1998**	**1997**	**1996**
Tangible Book Value	NM	NM	NM	NM	NM	NM	NM	NM	NM	NM
Cash Flow	2.97	2.86	3.15	2.65	2.40	2.32	1.96	1.69	1.60	1.58
Earnings	2.43	2.33	2.46	2.19	1.89	1.70	1.47	1.31	1.14	1.05
S&P Core Earnings	2.21	2.26	2.31	2.00	1.71	NA	NA	NA	NA	NA
Dividends	1.11	0.96	0.90	0.72	0.68	0.63	0.59	0.55	0.53	0.47
Payout Ratio	46%	41%	37%	33%	36%	37%	40%	42%	47%	45%
Prices:High	57.15	59.04	60.99	58.86	64.75	66.75	65.00	49.44	39.34	24.13
Prices:Low	48.25	42.89	48.56	44.05	48.50	40.50	36.56	32.53	22.50	17.22
P/E Ratio:High	24	25	25	27	34	39	44	38	35	23
P/E Ratio:Low	20	18	20	20	26	24	25	25	20	16
Income Statement Analysis (Million $)										
Revenue	11,397	10,584	9,903	9,294	9,428	9,358	9,118	8,972	9,057	8,749
Operating Income	2,613	2,540	2,467	2,333	2,198	2,132	1,904	1,733	1,591	1,470
Depreciation	329	328	316	297	336	410	340	330	320	316
Interest Expense	143	124	124	151	192	200	212	205	232	244
Pretax Income	2,134	2,050	2,042	1,870	1,709	1,600	1,425	1,278	1,131	955
Effective Tax Rate	34.1%	32.9%	30.4%	31.1%	30.6%	31.4%	32.1%	31.4%	32.0%	33.5%
Net Income	1,351	1,327	1,421	1,288	1,147	1,064	937	849	740	635
S&P Core Earnings	1,207	1,262	1,309	1,152	1,011	NA	NA	NA	NA	NA
Balance Sheet & Other Financial Data (Million $)										
Cash	341	320	265	168	173	213	235	182	183	308
Current Assets	2,757	2,740	2,497	2,228	2,203	2,347	2,355	2,245	2,196	2,372
Total Assets	8,507	8,673	7,479	7,087	6,985	7,252	7,423	7,685	7,539	7,902
Current Liabilities	2,743	2,731	2,445	2,149	2,124	2,244	2,274	2,114	1,959	1,904
Long Term Debt	2,918	3,090	2,685	3,211	2,812	2,537	2,243	2,301	2,341	2,787
Common Equity	1,380	971	594	27.3	505	1,115	1,467	1,709	1,793	1,641
Total Capital	5,106	4,845	4,028	4,050	4,139	4,453	4,701	4,834	4,805	5,055
Capital Expenditures	389	348	302	344	340	367	373	390	479	459
Cash Flow	1,653	1,629	1,736	1,563	1,461	1,453	1,255	1,158	1,039	930
Current Ratio	1.0	1.0	1.0	1.0	1.0	1.0	1.0	1.1	1.1	1.3
% Long Term Debt of Capitalization	57.1	63.8	66.7	79.3	67.9	57.0	47.7	47.6	48.7	55.2
% Net Income of Revenue	11.9	12.5	14.4	13.9	12.2	11.4	10.3	9.5	8.2	7.3
% Return on Assets	15.7	16.4	19.5	18.3	16.1	14.5	12.4	11.2	9.6	7.9
% Return on Equity	99.5	166.2	457.2	475.7	139.0	80.8	57.6	47.3	41.9	42.1

Data as orig reptd.; bef. results of disc opers/spec. items. Per share data adj. for stk. divs.; EPS diluted. E-Estimated. NA-Not Available. NM-Not Meaningful. NR-Not Ranked. UR-Under Review.

Office: 300 Park Avenue, New York, NY 10022.
Telephone: 212-310-2000.
Email: investor_relations@colpal.com
Website: http://www.colgate.com

Chrmn & CEO: R. Mark
Pres & COO: I. Cook
Vice Chrmn: J.G. Teruel
SVP, Secy & General Counsel: A.D. Hendry

VP & Treas: E.J. Filusch
Investor Contact: D.H. Thompson
Board of Directors: J. T. Cahill, J. K. Conway, E. M. Hancock, D. W. Johnson, R. J. Kogan, D. E. Lewis, R. Mark, J. P. Reinhard, H. B. Wentz, Jr.

Founded: 1806
Domicile: Delaware
Employees: 35,800

STANDARD &POOR'S

Comcast Corp

S&P Recommendation BUY ★★★★★

Price
$40.67 (as of Oct 31, 2006)

12-Mo. Target Price
$45.00

Investment Style
Large-Cap Value

GICS Sector Consumer Discretionary
Sub-Industry Broadcasting & Cable TV

Comment This company is the largest U.S. cable multiple system operator (MSO), with over 24 million basic customers.

Key Stock Statistics (Source S&P, Vickers, company reports)

52-Wk Range	**$40.75–25.35**	S&P Oper. EPS 2006**E**	**0.79**	P/E on S&P Oper. EPS 2006**E**	**51.5**	Dividend Rate/Share	**Nil**
Trailing 12-Month EPS	**$1.07**	S&P Oper. EPS 2007**E**	**1.09**	Common Shares Outstg. (M)	**2,092.8**	Yield (%)	**Nil**
Trailing 12-Month P/E	**38.0**	S&P Core EPS 2006**E**	**0.79**	Market Capitalization(B)	**$55.555**	Beta	**0.86**
$10K Invested 5 Yrs Ago	**$10,881**	S&P Core EPS 2007**E**	**1.09**	Institutional Ownership (%)	**75**	S&P Credit Rating	**BBB**

Price Performance

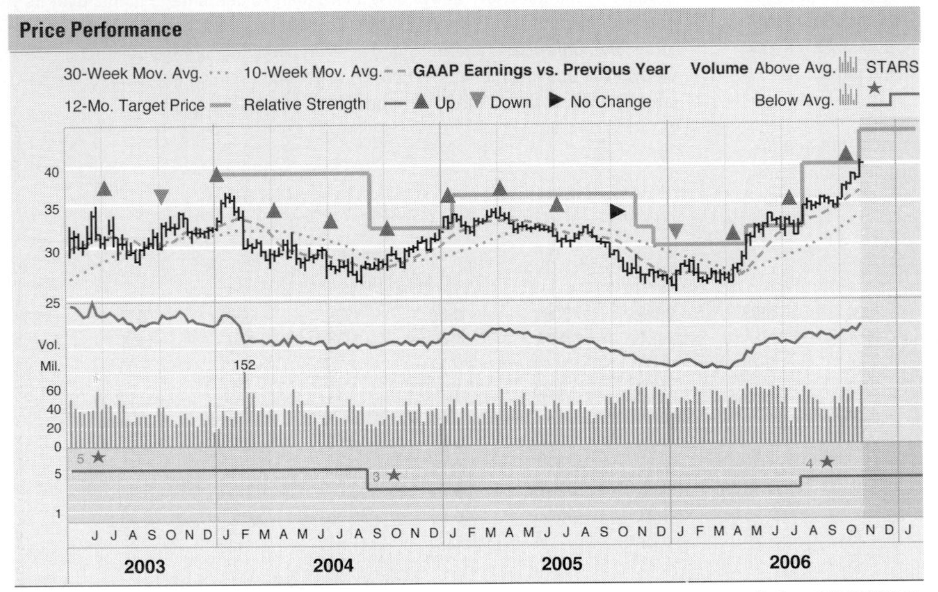

Options: ASE, CBOE, P, Ph

Analysis prepared by **Tuna N. Amobi, CFA, CPA** on October 30, 2006, when the stock traded at **$ 40.28**.

Highlights

- We see total revenue growth of about 11% in 2006 and 10% in 2007 (pro forma for the transaction with Adelphia/Time Warner that closed July 31, 2006), with over 4.4 million revenue-generating units (RGUs) net adds in 2006, including over 1.4 million for digital phone service, which could double in 2007, outweighing likely further contraction in the circuit-switched phone business. Newer video offerings could aid overall pricing. We see improved local cable ad sales, as well as continued strong low double-digit growth in the content segment.
- We see margin expansion each year driven by the triple-play offer, and aided by the integration of newly acquired Adelphia systems, partly offset by further investments in content, technology and wireless initiatives. We estimate consolidated EBITDA growth of approximately 13% in each of 2006 and 2007, to about $9.6 billion and $10.8 billion, respectively.
- With higher interest expense and a relatively high effective tax rate over 40%, we estimate EPS of $0.79 in 2006 (including $0.08 of employee stock option expense) and $1.09 in 2007 ($0.06), with further share buybacks under a current $5 billion program.

Investment Rationale/Risk

- Our opinion reflects what we expect to be significantly improving cable fundamentals, after what we saw as strong 2006 third quarter results, continuing the momentum for much of the year. With an accelerating deployment and marketing of digital phone service driving overall penetration of triple-play services, management reiterated its 2006 RGU guidance, recently raised in July. The bundling strategy could also benefit from a wireless product to be launched in the 2006 second half. We see potentially sizable scale economies from new acquisitions.
- Risks to our recommendation and target price include increased competition from satellite and telco rivals; and regulatory issues related to national franchising, "net neutrality", digital multi-casting and a la carte pricing.
- With over $7 billion of total projected free cash flow in 2006 and 2007, we see ample flexibility, likely further enhanced by an imminent unwinding of cable joint ventures with Time Warner. With projected double-digit growth, our 12-month target price is $45, with a premium to peers implied by a projected 10.5X cable-only enterprise value to 2007 EBITDA, or nearly $3,800 per subscriber.

Qualitative Risk Assessment

LOW | **MEDIUM** | HIGH

Our risk assessment reflects our view of the company's sound financial condition, and likely further significant increases in economies of scale through integration of recent acquisitions, against a backdrop of increased competition from satellite operators and the telephone companies.

Quantitative Evaluations

S&P Quality Ranking B-

D | C | **B-** | B | B+ | A- | A | A+

Relative Strength Rank STRONG

89

LOWEST = 1 HIGHEST = 99

Revenue/Earnings Data

Revenue (Million $)

	1Q	2Q	3Q	4Q	Year
2006	5,901	6,228	6,432	--	--
2005	5,363	5,598	5,578	5,716	22,255
2004	4,908	5,066	5,098	5,235	20,307
2003	4,466	4,594	4,546	4,742	18,348
2002	2,672	2,709	2,705	4,374	12,460
2001	--	--	--	--	19,697

Earnings Per Share ($)

	1Q	2Q	3Q	4Q	Year
2006	0.22	0.22	0.46	**E**0.20	**E**0.79
2005	0.06	0.19	0.10	0.06	0.42
2004	0.03	0.12	0.10	0.19	0.43
2003	-0.16	-0.01	-0.07	0.17	-0.10
2002	-0.09	-0.22	0.08	-0.03	-0.25
2001	--	--	--	--	-1.34

Fiscal year ended Dec. 31. Next earnings report expected: Early February. EPS Estimates based on S&P Operating Earnings; historical GAAP earnings are as reported.

Dividend Data

No cash dividends have been paid since 1999.

Comcast Corp

Business Summary October 30, 2006

CORPORATE OVERVIEW. Comcast Corp. became the largest U.S. cable multiple system operator (MSO) after its acquisition of the former AT&T Broadband (ATTB) in November 2002. As of September 30, 2006, the company counted about 24.1 million subscribers to its basic service, about 12.1 million for digital video, 11.0 million for high-speed Internet service; and nearly 2.1 million for telephone (1.4 million digital phone and 740,000 for circuit-switched phone). The company's content assets include cable networks E! Entertainment Television, The Golf Channel, Outdoor Life Network and G4, among other programming investments.

COMPETITIVE LANDSCAPE. In a typical market, Comcast faces competition from direct broadcast satellite (DBS) providers DirecTV Group and EchoStar Communications, and from incumbent phone companies such as Verizon Communications and AT&T (formerly SBC Communications). In the past two years, the satellite companies and the telcos have also aligned to offer integrated bundles of video, voice and data services through co-branding partnerships.

We expect this competition to intensify in the years ahead, as both DBS companies launch new satellites to drive advanced video offerings, while the telcos accelerate their own deployment of fiber-based video and broadband offerings. A possible national franchising bill could also help the new entrants attain a much quicker time-to-market in head-to-head competition with cable operators. With DSL discounts already aggressive in several markets, we believe the pending AT&T acquisition of BellSouth could create a stronger competitor that could further drive increased promotional activity.

However, we think Comcast has thus far successfully resisted price competition, focusing instead on product differentiation through newer offerings such as VOD, and enhanced features such as higher data speeds and a broadband portal. We expect cable operators to increasingly experiment with package discounts, as the rapidly changing competitive landscape continues to evolve.

Company Financials

Per Share Data ($) Year Ended Dec. 31	**2005**	**2004**	**2003**	**2002**	**2001**	**2000**	**1999**	**1998**	**1997**	**1996**
Tangible Book Value	NM	NM	NM	NM	NM	NM	NM	NM	NM	NM
Cash Flow	2.68	2.53	0.36	1.58	1.48	4.90	2.40	2.38	1.05	1.30
Earnings	0.42	0.43	-0.10	-0.25	-1.34	2.16	0.95	1.25	-0.33	-0.11
S&P Core Earnings	0.49	0.21	-0.45	0.71	-1.54	NA	NA	NA	NA	NA
Dividends	Nil	Nil	Nil	Nil	Nil	Nil	0.01	0.05	0.05	0.05
Payout Ratio	Nil	Nil	Nil	Nil	Nil	Nil	1%	4%	NM	NM
Prices:High	34.50	36.50	34.85	37.55	45.81	52.37	54.63	29.50	16.56	10.56
Prices:Low	25.80	26.25	23.42	17.05	31.85	27.93	28.06	14.75	7.19	6.88
P/E Ratio:High	82	85	NM	NM	NM	24	57	24	NM	NM
P/E Ratio:Low	61	61	NM	NM	NM	13	30	12	NM	NM
Income Statement Analysis (Million $)										
Revenue	22,255	20,307	18,348	12,460	19,697	8,219	6,209	5,145	4,913	4,038
Operating Income	8,493	7,531	6,392	3,691	1,576	2,470	1,880	1,497	1,469	1,207
Depreciation	4,803	4,623	4,438	2,032	6,345	2,631	1,216	940	936	698
Interest Expense	1,796	1,876	2,018	884	2,341	691	538	467	565	541
Pretax Income	1,880	1,810	-137	70.0	-5,927	3,602	1,500	1,557	-229	-16.1
Effective Tax Rate	49.6%	45.6%	NM	NM	NM	40.0%	48.2%	38.1%	NM	NM
Net Income	928	970	-218	276	-3,021	2,045	781	1,008	-209	-52.5
S&P Core Earnings	1,090	465	-979	792	-1,482	NA	NA	NA	NA	NA
Balance Sheet & Other Financial Data (Million $)										
Cash	693	452	1,550	781	558	652	922	871	414	331
Current Assets	2,594	3,535	5,403	7,076	4,944	5,144	9,759	5,624	1,560	1,406
Total Assets	103,146	104,694	109,159	113,105	109,319	35,745	28,686	14,817	12,804	12,089
Current Liabilities	6,269	8,635	9,654	15,383	12,489	4,042	5,527	3,093	1,418	1,365
Long Term Debt	21,682	20,093	23,835	27,957	27,528	10,517	8,707	5,464	6,559	7,103
Common Equity	40,219	41,422	41,662	38,329	38,451	28,113	9,772	3,243	1,101	520
Total Capital	89,928	88,798	91,689	92,070	94,758	45,734	23,159	10,780	10,317	9,796
Capital Expenditures	3,621	3,660	4,161	1,975	NA	1,637	894	899	926	670
Cash Flow	5,731	5,593	4,220	1,756	3,324	4,653	1,967	1,918	713	646
Current Ratio	0.4	0.4	0.6	0.5	0.4	1.3	1.8	1.8	1.1	1.0
% Long Term Debt of Capitalization	24.1	22.6	26.0	30.4	29.1	23.0	37.6	50.7	63.6	72.5
% Net Income of Revenue	4.2	4.8	NM	NM	NM	24.9	12.6	19.6	NM	NM
% Return on Assets	0.9	0.9	NM	NM	NM	6.3	3.6	7.3	NM	NM
% Return on Equity	2.3	2.3	NM	NM	NM	8.4	11.5	45.1	NM	NM

Data as orig reptd.; bef. results of disc opers/spec. items. Per share data adj. for stk. divs.; EPS diluted. E-Estimated. NA-Not Available. NM-Not Meaningful. NR-Not Ranked. UR-Under Review.

Office: 1500 Market St , Philadelphia, PA 19102-2148.
Telephone: 215-665-1700.
Website: http://www.comcast.com
Chrmn, Pres & CEO: B.L. Roberts

COO & EVP: S. Burke
EVP & CFO: L.S. Smith
EVP, CFO & Treas: J.R. Alchin
SVP, Chief Acctg Officer & Cntlr: L.J. Salva

Investor Contact: M. Dooner (215-981-7392)
Board of Directors: S. D. Anstrom, K. J. Bacon, S. M. Bonovitz, E. D. Breen, J. A. Brodsky, J. J. Collins, J. M. Cook, J. A. Honickman, B. L. Roberts, R. J. Roberts, J. Rodin, M. I. Sovern

Founded: 1969
Domicile: Pennsylvania
Employees: 80,000

STANDARD &POOR'S

Comerica Inc

S&P Recommendation HOLD ★★★★★	Price $58.58 (as of Oct 27, 2006)	12-Mo. Target Price $62.00	Investment Style Large-Cap Value

GICS Sector Financials
Sub-Industry Diversified Banks

Comment This Detroit-based bank holding company operates banking affiliates in Michigan, Texas, California and Florida.

Key Stock Statistics (Source S&P, Vickers, company reports)

52-Wk Range	$60.25–50.12	S&P Oper. EPS 2006E	4.80	P/E on S&P Oper. EPS 2006E	12.2	Dividend Rate/Share	$2.36
Trailing 12-Month EPS	$4.90	S&P Oper. EPS 2007E	5.01	Common Shares Outstg. (M)	162.2	Yield (%)	4.03
Trailing 12-Month P/E	12.0	S&P Core EPS 2006E	4.79	Market Capitalization(B)	$9.502	Beta	0.82
$10K Invested 5 Yrs Ago	$14,781	S&P Core EPS 2007E	4.99	Institutional Ownership (%)	61	S&P Credit Rating	A

Price Performance

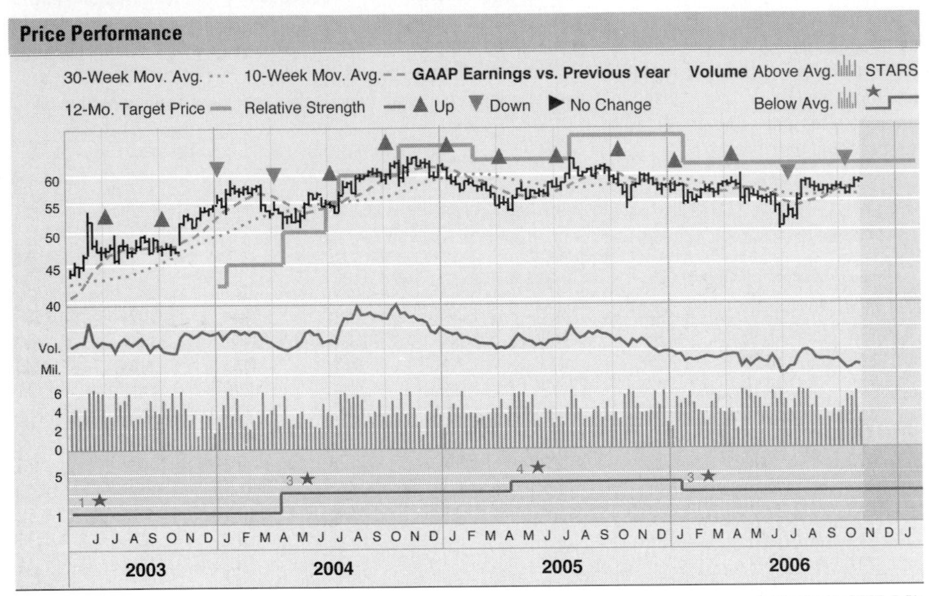

Options: ASE, CBOE, P, Ph

Analysis prepared by **Mark Hebeka, CFA** on August 16, 2006, when the stock traded at **$ 58.10**.

Highlights

- We expect the net interest margin to continue to be flat or experience a slight narrowing in 2006 as funding costs begin to catch up with higher yielding investment securities. We believe a challenging interest rate environment and intense competition in the Midwest will continue to challenge earnings growth over the next several quarters. We remain favorable on CMA's de novo branch building strategy and look for the addition of 24 new branches in higher-growth markets during 2006.
- In the past several quarters, CMA has continued to see improvements in asset quality, and we believe net chargeoffs are likely to remain flat in the quarters ahead as we think credit quality may have peaked. We believe prudent expense management will be of critical importance in 2006, given the company's expectation of margin pressure and new branch expenses.
- We estimate 2006 operating EPS of $4.80, down from $5.11 in 2005, followed by $5.01 in 2007, in a stable regional and national economy that we expect.

Investment Rationale/Risk

- While we believe CMA has strong fundamentals, diverse product offerings, a well-established customer base, and a presence in some higher growth markets such as Florida, Texas and California, we remain cautious as we see the interest rate environment and competition remaining fierce for the long term in CMA's primary market of the Midwest. We continue to view credit quality as solid, and believe CMA's exposure to the auto industry and challenged markets as limited.
- Risks to our recommendation and target price include a severe economic downturn in combination with higher short-term interest rates that could result in an inverted yield curve, legal and regulatory risks, and a decline in business spending.
- Our 12-month target price of $62 equates to approximately 12.4X our 2007 operating EPS estimate, a slight premium to peers and in line with the stock's average historical valuation multiple.

Qualitative Risk Assessment

LOW	MEDIUM	HIGH

Our risk assessment reflects what we see as solid business fundamentals and a strong customer base. We view CMA as well diversified and able to withstand a major regional or U.S. economic downturn.

Quantitative Evaluations

S&P Quality Ranking A

D	C	B-	B	B+	A-	**A**	A+

Relative Strength Rank MODERATE

51

LOWEST = 1 HIGHEST = 99

Revenue/Earnings Data

Revenue (Million $)

	1Q	2Q	3Q	4Q	Year
2006	987.0	1,072	1,089	--	--
2005	817.0	874.0	951.0	1,026	3,668
2004	763.0	773.0	764.0	794.0	3,094
2003	866.0	853.0	800.0	780.0	3,299
2002	920.0	927.0	910.0	940.0	3,697
2001	1,110	1,078	1,039	970.3	4,197

Earnings Per Share ($)

	1Q	2Q	3Q	4Q	Year
2006	1.23	1.22	1.20	**E**1.21	**E**4.80
2005	1.16	1.28	1.41	1.25	5.11
2004	0.92	1.10	1.13	1.21	4.36
2003	1.00	0.97	0.89	0.89	3.75
2002	1.20	0.88	0.14	1.18	3.40
2001	0.50	1.13	1.14	1.11	3.88

Fiscal year ended Dec. 31. Next earnings report expected: Mid January. EPS Estimates based on S&P Operating Earnings; historical GAAP earnings are as reported.

Dividend Data (Dates: mm/dd Payment Date: mm/dd/yy)

Amount ($)	Date Decl.	Ex-Div. Date	Stk. of Record	Payment Date
0.550	11/15	12/13	12/15	01/01/06
0.590	01/24	03/13	03/15	04/01/06
0.590	05/16	06/13	06/15	07/01/06
0.590	07/25	09/13	09/15	10/01/06

Dividends have been paid since 1936. Source: Company reports.

Comerica Inc

Business Summary August 16, 2006

CORPORATE OVERVIEW. The owner of one of Michigan's oldest banks, Comerica is a Detroit-based bank holding company that operates banking units in Michigan, California, Texas and Florida. It also has banking subsidiaries in Canada and Mexico.

Operations are divided into three major lines of business: the Business Bank, the Retail Bank (formerly known as Small Business and Personal Financial Services), and Wealth and Institutional Management. The Business Bank is primarily comprised of middle market, commercial real estate, national dealer services, global finance, large corporate, leasing, financial services, and technology and life sciences. This business segment offers various products and services, including commercial loans and lines of credit, deposits, cash management, capital market products, international trade finance, letters of credit, foreign exchange management services and loan syndication services.

The Retail Bank includes small business banking (entities with annual sales under $10 million) and personal financial services, consisting of consumer lending, consumer deposit gathering and mortgage loan origination. In addition to a full range of financial services provided to small businesses and their owners, this business segment offers a variety of consumer products, including deposit accounts, installment loans, credit and debit cards, student loans, home equity loans and lines of credit, and residential mortgage loans.

Wealth & Institutional Management offers products and services consisting of personal trust, which is designed to meet the personal financial needs of affluent, private banking, institutional trust, retirement services, investment management and advisory services, investment banking, and discount securities brokerage services. This business segment also offers the sale of mutual funds and annuity products, as well as life, disability and long-term care insurance products.

Company Financials

Per Share Data ($) Year Ended Dec. 31	2005	2004	2003	2002	2001	2000	1999	1998	1997	1996
Tangible Book Value	31.09	29.85	29.20	28.31	27.15	23.94	20.60	17.94	16.02	14.70
Earnings	5.11	4.36	3.75	3.40	3.88	4.63	4.14	3.72	3.19	2.37
S&P Core Earnings	4.90	4.27	3.72	3.30	3.27	NA	NA	NA	NA	NA
Dividends	2.20	2.08	2.00	1.92	1.76	1.60	1.40	1.25	1.15	1.01
Payout Ratio	43%	48%	53%	56%	45%	35%	34%	34%	36%	43%
Prices:High	63.38	63.80	56.34	66.09	65.15	61.13	70.00	73.00	61.87	39.58
Prices:Low	53.17	50.45	37.10	35.20	44.02	32.94	44.00	46.50	34.17	24.17
P/E Ratio:High	12	15	15	19	17	13	17	20	19	17
P/E Ratio:Low	10	12	10	10	11	7	11	12	11	10

Income Statement Analysis (Million $)	2005	2004	2003	2002	2001	2000	1999	1998	1997	1996
Net Interest Income	1,956	1,810	1,926	2,132	2,102	1,659	1,547	1,461	1,443	1,412
Tax Equivalent Adjustment	4.00	3.00	3.00	4.00	4.00	4.00	5.00	7.00	9.00	15.0
Non Interest Income	942	857	837	819	784	827	711	597	522	493
Loan Loss Provision	-47.0	64.0	377	635	236	145	114	113	146	114
% Expense/Operating Revenue	57.4%	55.9%	53.6%	51.3%	53.9%	53.6%	49.3%	49.4%	51.3%	55.7%
Pretax Income	1,279	1,110	953	882	1,111	1,151	1,033	931	817	646
Effective Tax Rate	32.7%	31.8%	30.6%	31.9%	36.1%	34.9%	34.9%	34.8%	35.0%	35.4%
Net Income	861	757	661	601	710	749	673	607	530	417
% Net Interest Margin	4.06	3.86	3.95	4.55	4.61	4.54	4.55	4.57	4.53	4.54
S&P Core Earnings	826	744	657	584	587	NA	NA	NA	NA	NA

Balance Sheet & Other Financial Data (Million $)	2005	2004	2003	2002	2001	2000	1999	1998	1997	1996
Money Market Assets	1,159	3,230	4,013	2,446	1,079	165	613	110	203	65.5
Investment Securities	5,399	7,173	8,502	5,499	5,370	2,843	2,739	2,822	4,006	4,800
Commercial Loans	33,707	31,540	32,153	33,732	32,660	28,001	25,429	23,266	16,323	13,926
Other Loans	9,540	9,303	7,274	8,549	8,536	8,060	7,265	7,339	12,572	12,281
Total Assets	53,013	51,766	52,592	53,301	50,732	41,985	38,653	36,601	36,292	34,206
Demand Deposits	15,666	15,164	14,104	16,335	12,596	6,815	6,136	6,999	6,761	6,713
Time Deposits	26,765	25,772	27,359	25,440	24,974	20,353	17,155	17,314	15,825	15,654
Long Term Debt	47,945	4,286	4,801	5,216	5,503	8,089	8,580	5,282	7,286	4,242
Common Equity	5,068	5,105	5,110	4,947	4,807	3,757	3,225	2,797	2,512	2,366
% Return on Assets	1.6	1.5	1.2	1.2	1.4	1.9	1.8	1.7	1.5	1.2
% Return on Equity	16.9	14.8	13.1	12.3	15.4	21.0	21.8	22.2	21.1	16.4
% Loan Loss Reserve	1.2	-1.6	2.0	1.9	-1.6	1.5	1.5	1.5	1.5	1.4
% Loans/Deposits	101.9	99.8	99.3	101.2	109.7	132.7	140.4	125.9	127.9	117.2
% Equity to Assets	9.7	9.8	9.5	9.4	9.0	8.7	8.0	7.3	6.9	7.1

Data as orig reptd.; bef. results of disc opers/spec. items. Per share data adj. for stk. divs.; EPS diluted. E-Estimated. NA-Not Available. NM-Not Meaningful. NR-Not Ranked. UR-Under Review.

Office: 500 Woodward Ave MC3391, Detroit, MI 48226.
Telephone: 248-371-5000.
Website: http://www.comerica.com
Chrmn, Pres & CEO: R.W. Babb, Jr.

Vice Chrmn: J.J. Buttigieg, III
EVP & CFO: E.S. Acton
SVP & Treas: P.E. Burdiss
Investor Contact: J.S. Love (313-222-2840)

Board of Directors: R. W. Babb, Jr., L. Bauder, J. J. Buttigieg, III, J. F. Cordes, P. D. Cummings, A. F. Earley, Jr., R. Fridholm, T. W. Herrick, A. A. Piergallini, R. S. Taubman, R. M. Turner, Jr., W. P. Vititoe, P. M. Wallington, G. L. Warden, K. L. Way

Founded: 1849
Domicile: Delaware
Employees: 11,343

STANDARD &POOR'S

Commerce Bancorp Inc.

S&P Recommendation HOLD ★★★★★

Price $34.96 (as of Oct 27, 2006)

12-Mo. Target Price $38.00

Investment Style Mid-Cap Growth

GICS Sector Financials
Sub-Industry Regional Banks

Comment This multibank holding company operates a network of branch offices serving New Jersey, Pennsylvania, Connecticut, Delaware, New York, Washington, DC, Virginia, and Florida.

Key Stock Statistics (Source S&P, Vickers, company reports)

52-Wk Range	$41.20–29.76	S&P Oper. EPS 2006**E**	1.69	P/E on S&P Oper. EPS 2006**E**	20.7	Dividend Rate/Share	$0.48
Trailing 12-Month EPS	$1.48	S&P Oper. EPS 2007**E**	2.09	Common Shares Outstg. (M)	186.5	Yield (%)	1.37
Trailing 12-Month P/E	23.6	S&P Core EPS 2006**E**	1.69	Market Capitalization(B)	$6.520	Beta	0.64
$10K Invested 5 Yrs Ago	$20,373	S&P Core EPS 2007**E**	2.09	Institutional Ownership (%)	95	S&P Credit Rating	NA

Price Performance

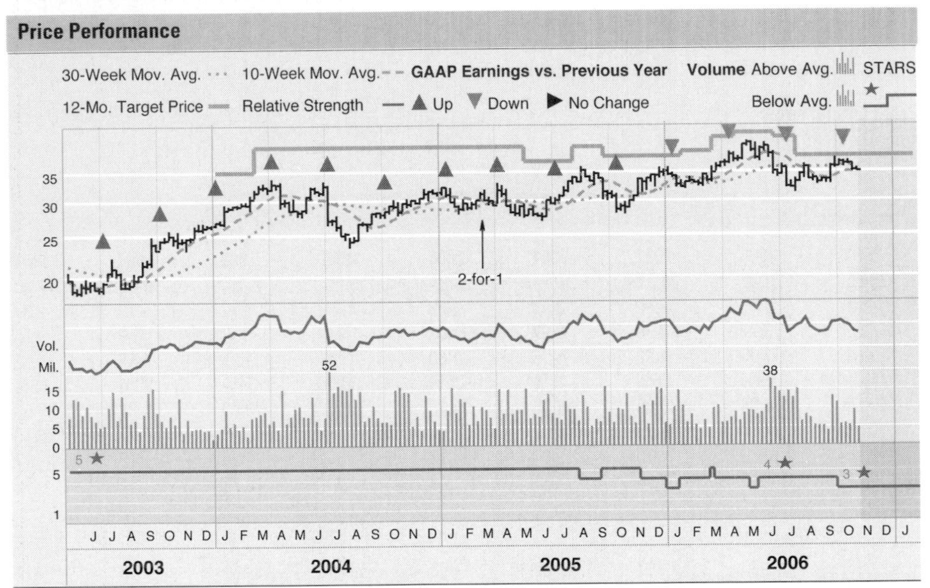

Options: ASE, CBOE, P, Ph

Analysis prepared by **Christopher B. Muir** on September 29, 2006, when the stock traded at **$ 36.87**.

Highlights

- We expect that well above average core deposit and earning asset growth coupled with strong fee income growth will result in total revenue growth of 18% in 2006. Our 2006 estimates include a net interest margin of 3.36% (down from 3.77% in 2005 due to continued pressure from a relatively flat yield curve), average earning asset growth of 28%, and noninterest income growth of 26%.
- We expect the company's noninterest expenses to remain relatively high as a result of the company's push to open new branches in several regions. Our 2006 noninterest expense to total revenue forecast of 71.9% is slightly worse than 2005's 71.8%, due to the inclusion of stock option expense in 2006. Credit quality remains strong, in our view, but we expect loan loss provisions to increase to about $31 million in 2006, from $19 million in 2005.
- Assuming an effective tax rate of 34.0%, we see operating EPS rising to $1.69 in 2006, a 5.0% increase from 2005's $1.61. Our 2007 EPS estimate is $2.09, a further 24% increase.

Investment Rationale/Risk

- We believe CBH's retail banking model offers a competitive advantage in an industry marked by commodity pricing and intense competition. We like the company's customer focused business approach as well as its branch expansion strategy. The stock recently traded at 17.6X our 2007 EPS estimate, or a 33% P/E premium to its mid-cap regional banking peers.
- Risks to our opinion and target price include detrimental changes in the slope of the yield curve and operational performance that fails to meet our expectations. We are also concerned about corporate governance issues related to compensation and the CEO's involvement in related-party transactions.
- Our 12-month target price of $38 is based on our dividend discount model and relative valuation analysis. Our target price is 18.2X our 2007 EPS estimate, or a 37% premium to its peers, which we believe is justified by our EPS growth projections. Our dividend discount model assumes a terminal growth rate of 4%, a weighted average cost of capital of 8.7%, and yields an intrinsic value of $37.

Qualitative Risk Assessment

LOW | MEDIUM | HIGH

Our risk assessment reflects our view of the company's mid-cap valuation, the strong credit quality of its loan portfolio, and CBH's history of profitability. While the company operates in a highly competitive and fragmented industry, the industry tends to produce relatively stable financial results.

Quantitative Evaluations

S&P Quality Ranking A+

D | C | B- | B | B+ | A- | A | A+

Relative Strength Rank WEAK

28

LOWEST = 1 HIGHEST = 99

Revenue/Earnings Data

Revenue (Million $)

	1Q	2Q	3Q	4Q	Year
2006	641.5	705.1	748.0	--	--
2005	474.2	513.3	548.6	571.9	2,108
2004	358.3	384.3	420.9	449.9	1,613
2003	282.9	302.1	319.1	344.0	1,248
2002	224.1	250.1	220.2	272.2	1,013
2001	187.2	194.5	204.8	214.7	801.2

Earnings Per Share ($)

2006	0.41	0.41	0.41	**E**0.45	**E**1.69
2005	0.45	0.46	0.45	0.26	1.61
2004	0.38	0.40	0.42	0.44	1.63
2003	0.30	0.32	0.34	0.36	1.31
2002	0.23	0.25	0.26	0.29	1.02
2001	0.18	0.19	0.19	0.21	0.76

Fiscal year ended Dec. 31. Next earnings report expected: Mid January. EPS Estimates based on S&P Operating Earnings; historical GAAP earnings are as reported.

Dividend Data (Dates: mm/dd Payment Date: mm/dd/yy)

Amount ($)	Date Decl.	Ex-Div. Date	Stk. of Record	Payment Date
0.120	12/20	01/04	01/06	01/20/06
0.120	03/21	04/03	04/05	04/20/06
0.120	06/20	06/30	07/05	07/18/06
0.120	09/19	10/02	10/04	10/20/06

Dividends have been paid since 1984. Source: Company reports.

Commerce Bancorp Inc.

Business Summary September 29, 2006

CORPORATE OVERVIEW. Commerce Bancorp, Inc. owns three nationally chartered bank subsidiaries and one New Jersey chartered bank subsidiary. At the end of 2005, the company had assets of $38.5 billion and a market capitalization of $6.1 billion. It has a stated goal of having 700 offices and $104 billion in assets by the end of 2009. The company operates two reportable segments: Community Banks and Parent/Other.

The Community Banks segment accounts for 92.5% of total revenues. The segment offers a relatively standard group of banking services, which include: free minimum balance checking accounts, savings programs, money market accounts, negotiable orders of withdrawal (NOW) accounts, certificates of deposit (CDs), safe deposit facilities, free coin counting, consumer installment loan programs (such as home improvement or automobile loans), home equity and revolving lines of credit, overdraft checking, construction loans, and home mortgages. The segment also provides corporate trust services.

The Parent/Other Segment includes Commerce Insurance, Commerce Capital Markets (CCMI), and the holding company. Commerce Insurance operates an insurance brokerage agency concentrating on commercial property, casualty and surety, as well as personal lines of insurance and employee benefits for clients, primarily in Delaware, New Jersey, New York and Pennsylvania. CCMI engages in various securities, investment banking and brokerage activities.

MARKET PROFILE. CBH's footprint includes 373 branches in New Jersey, 82 branches in New York, 75 branches in Pennsylvania, 8 branches in Delaware, seven branches in Florida, four branches in Virginia, three branches in Connecticut, and one branch in Washington, D.C. The projection for deposit weighted average population growth in the company's service territory is 3.2% from 2005 to 2010, according to SNL Financial. The projected national growth rate is 6.3% and the population weighted average growth rate of the states in the company's service territory is 3.5%.

Company Financials

Per Share Data ($) Year Ended Dec. 31	**2005**	**2004**	**2003**	**2002**	**2001**	**2000**	**1999**	**1998**	**1997**	**1996**
Tangible Book Value	12.33	10.42	8.35	6.77	4.84	3.89	2.99	2.98	2.69	2.35
Earnings	1.61	1.63	1.31	1.02	0.76	0.63	0.54	0.47	0.41	0.36
S&P Core Earnings	1.30	1.56	1.24	0.97	0.70	NA	NA	NA	NA	NA
Dividends	0.44	0.38	0.33	0.30	0.28	0.24	0.21	0.22	0.15	0.11
Payout Ratio	27%	23%	25%	29%	36%	39%	38%	46%	34%	32%
Prices:High	35.98	33.83	26.74	25.25	19.80	17.70	11.90	12.02	8.97	5.47
Prices:Low	26.87	23.35	18.12	18.05	13.00	7.72	9.23	7.53	4.51	3.31
P/E Ratio:High	22	21	20	25	26	28	22	25	21	15
P/E Ratio:Low	17	14	14	18	17	12	17	16	11	9
Income Statement Analysis (Million $)										
Net Interest Income	1,154	1,018	756	573	401	297	244	174	147	109
Tax Equivalent Adjustment	19.7	18.4	15.6	13.1	11.4	9.22	5.19	2.37	1.36	0.88
Non Interest Income	457	372	329	257	196	148	112	86.0	55.1	30.0
Loan Loss Provision	19.2	39.2	31.9	33.2	26.4	13.9	9.18	5.87	4.67	3.00
% Expense/Operating Revenue	70.3%	66.6%	69.4%	68.7%	69.0%	69.5%	69.8%	69.4%	68.2%	69.7%
Pretax Income	431	415	293	218	152	118	97.3	74.8	61.9	41.5
Effective Tax Rate	34.3%	34.1%	33.7%	33.5%	32.1%	32.4%	32.2%	34.1%	34.9%	35.7%
Net Income	283	273	194	145	103	80.0	66.0	49.3	40.3	26.6
% Net Interest Margin	3.77	4.28	4.36	4.69	4.76	4.62	4.65	4.38	4.55	4.63
S&P Core Earnings	227	262	184	136	94.9	NA	NA	NA	NA	NA
Balance Sheet & Other Financial Data (Million $)										
Money Market Assets	156	169	170	326	283	161	123	85.4	168	173
Investment Securities	22,524	18,508	13,141	8,570	5,285	3,535	2,866	2,411	2,197	1,449
Commercial Loans	5,591	4,115	3,298	3,859	3,034	2,440	1,766	367	254	661
Other Loans	7,068	5,340	4,143	1,963	1,549	1,247	1,195	1,564	1,157	435
Total Assets	38,466	30,502	22,712	16,404	11,364	8,297	6,636	4,894	3,939	2,862
Demand Deposits	30,793	18,011	13,149	3,243	6,012	1,789	1,421	1,037	763	1,303
Time Deposits	3,933	9,648	7,552	11,306	4,173	5,598	4,188	3,398	2,607	1,271
Long Term Debt	Nil	200	200	200	80.5	80.5	80.5	80.5	23.0	26.3
Common Equity	2,309	1,666	1,277	918	640	492	358	302	248	181
% Return on Assets	0.8	1.0	1.0	1.0	1.0	1.1	1.1	1.1	1.2	1.0
% Return on Equity	14.2	18.6	17.7	18.6	18.1	18.9	19.3	17.9	18.6	15.5
% Loan Loss Reserve	1.1	1.4	1.5	1.5	1.4	1.3	1.3	1.4	1.5	1.4
% Loans/Deposits	36.5	34.3	36.1	40.7	45.7	50.5	52.9	43.5	39.9	42.1
% Equity to Assets	5.8	5.5	5.6	5.6	5.8	5.7	5.7	6.2	6.3	6.5

Data as orig reptd.; bef. results of disc opers/spec. items. Per share data adj. for stk. divs.; EPS diluted. E-Estimated. NA-Not Available. NM-Not Meaningful. NR-Not Ranked. UR-Under Review.

Office: 1701 Route 70 E, Cherry Hill, NJ 08003-2335.
Telephone: 856-751-9000.
Website: http://www.commerceonline.com
Chrmn, Pres, CEO & Secy: V.W. Hill, II

EVP & Treas: P.M. Musumeci, Jr.
Investor Contact: C.E. Jordan, Jr. (888-751-9000)
SVP, CFO & Chief Acctg Officer: D.J. Pauls

Board of Directors: J. R. Bershad, J. E. Buckelew, D. T. DiFrancesco, V. W. Hill, II, M. N. Kerr, S. M. Lewis, J. K. Lloyd, G. E. Norcross, III, III, D. J. Ragone, W. A. Schwartz, Jr., J. T. Tarquini, Jr., J. S. Vassalluzzo

Founded: 1982
Domicile: New Jersey
Employees: 10,800

STANDARD &POOR'S

Compass Bancshares Inc

S&P Recommendation HOLD ★★★★★

Price $55.80 (as of Oct 27, 2006)

12-Mo. Target Price $55.00

Investment Style Mid-Cap Value

GICS Sector Financials
Sub-Industry Regional Banks

Comment This bank holding company, based in Birmingham, AL, has subsidiaries with banking offices in Alabama, Texas, Florida, Arizona, Colorado and New Mexico.

Key Stock Statistics (Source S&P, Vickers, company reports)

52-Wk Range	$59.95–47.56	S&P Oper. EPS 2006E	3.55	P/E on S&P Oper. EPS 2006E	15.7	Dividend Rate/Share	$1.56
Trailing 12-Month EPS	$3.44	S&P Oper. EPS 2007E	3.91	Common Shares Outstg. (M)	129.4	Yield (%)	2.80
Trailing 12-Month P/E	16.2	S&P Core EPS 2006E	3.61	Market Capitalization(B)	$7.220	Beta	0.56
$10K Invested 5 Yrs Ago	$25,389	S&P Core EPS 2007E	4.05	Institutional Ownership (%)	43	S&P Credit Rating	A-

Price Performance

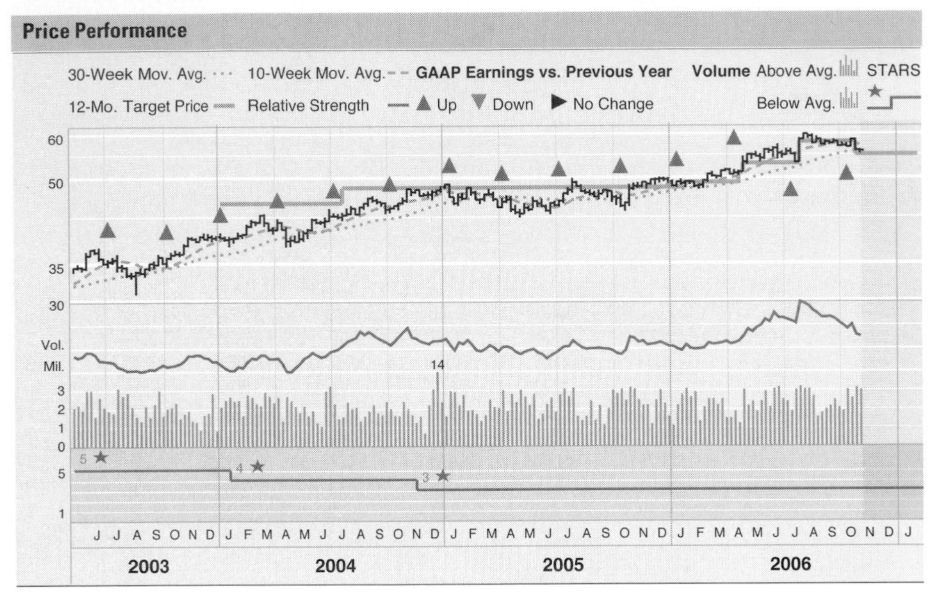

Options: P, Ph

Highlights

➤ The 12-month target price for CBSS has recently been changed to $55.00 from $58.00. The Highlights section of this Stock Report will be updated accordingly.

Investment Rationale/Risk

➤ The Investment Rationale/Risk section of this Stock Report will be updated shortly. For the latest News story on CBSS from MarketScope, see below.

➤ 10/18/06 04:11 pm EDT... UPDATE - S&P MAINTAINS HOLD RECOMMENDATION ON SHARES OF COMPASS BANCSHARES (CBSS 56.01***): On its Q3 conference call, CBSS notes 21% total deposit growth, year over year, despite competition and a difficult interest rate environment, but cautions that pricing pressures are not abating. Earning asset growth is in line with our forecast. Credit quality remains strong, in our view, with just 0.28% of assets classified as non-performing, despite some exposure to regional and national homebuilders. Even so, we are reducing our '06 EPS estimate to $3.55 from $3.61, '07's to $3.91 from $4.05. We are lowering our 12-month target price by $3 to $55, 14X our '07 EPS estimate. /E. Oja

Qualitative Risk Assessment

LOW	MEDIUM	HIGH

Our risk assessment for CBSS reflects our view of the company's mid-cap valuation, strong credit quality of its loan portfolio, and history of profitability. While the company operates in a highly competitive and fragmented industry, the industry tends to produce relatively stable financial results.

Quantitative Evaluations

S&P Quality Ranking A+

D	C	B-	B	B+	A-	A	A+

Relative Strength Rank WEAK

23

LOWEST = 1 HIGHEST = 99

Revenue/Earnings Data

Revenue (Million $)

	1Q	2Q	3Q	4Q	Year
2006	615.5	692.8	--	--	--
2005	497.9	545.6	565.8	594.5	2,204
2004	452.6	463.0	488.7	486.8	1,891
2003	449.4	449.7	450.9	453.6	1,803
2002	447.2	458.1	464.4	458.4	1,828
2001	481.6	476.8	472.3	463.4	1,894

Earnings Per Share ($)

	1Q	2Q	3Q	4Q	Year
2006	0.85	0.88	0.90	E0.91	E3.55
2005	0.74	0.83	0.80	0.81	3.18
2004	0.69	0.73	0.75	0.78	2.95
2003	0.64	0.68	0.68	0.69	2.69
2002	0.59	0.60	0.61	0.62	2.42
2001	0.50	0.52	0.53	0.56	2.11

Fiscal year ended Dec. 31. Next earnings report expected: Mid January. EPS Estimates based on S&P Operating Earnings; historical GAAP earnings are as reported.

Dividend Data (Dates: mm/dd Payment Date: mm/dd/yy)

Amount ($)	Date Decl.	Ex-Div. Date	Stk. of Record	Payment Date
0.350	11/14	12/13	12/15	01/02/06
0.390	02/21	03/13	03/15	04/03/06
0.390	05/23	06/13	06/15	07/03/06
0.390	08/28	09/13	09/15	10/02/06

Dividends have been paid since 1939. Source: Company reports.

Compass Bancshares Inc

Business Summary July 26, 2006

CORPORATE OVERVIEW. CBSS is a bank holding company that owns Compass Bank, the company's main banking subsidiary, and Central Bank of the South, which has limited activities. The company's four segments are Corporate Banking, Retail Banking, Wealth Management, and Treasury. The company operates in Texas, Alabama, Arizona, Florida, and Colorado.

The company's two banking segments make up 88% of the company's 2005 total revenues. Banking operations consist of lending and deposit gathering as well as other banking-related products and services, including investment and trust services. Corporate Banking's (33% of revenues) target market includes business, commercial and institutional clients in each of the company's major metropolitan markets. Retail Banking's (55% of revenues) target market includes consumer and small business clients.

Wealth Management (6% of revenues) provides specialized investment portfolio management, credit products, trust and estate services, financial counseling and services to private clients and foundations, as well as investment management and retirement services to companies and their employees. Treasury (3% of revenues) manages the company's investment securities portfolio, public entity deposits, balance sheet interest rate sensitivity, and liquidity and funding positions. Corporate activities make up the remaining 3% of revenues.

CBSS uses derivative instruments to manage the risk of earnings fluctuations caused by interest rate volatility. Additionally, the company manages its credit risk of default by its corporate customers through credit limit approval and monitoring procedures.

MARKET PROFILE. CBSS's footprint includes 167 branches in Texas, 90 in Alabama, 73 in Arizona, 42 in Florida, 32 in Colorado, and 11 in New Mexico. Based on data from the US Census Bureau, the projection for average population growth from 2005 to 2010 in the states that the company operates in are as follows: 7.8% in Texas, 0.9% in Alabama, 29.4% in Arizona, 20.5% in Florida, 12.3% in Colorado, and 8.9% in New Mexico. The projected population weighted average growth rate for these states is 8.3%. The projected national growth rate is 4.5%.

Company Financials

Per Share Data ($) Year Ended Dec. 31	**2005**	**2004**	**2003**	**2002**	**2001**	**2000**	**1999**	**1998**	**1997**	**1996**
Tangible Book Value	15.54	14.14	12.93	13.06	13.53	9.77	10.52	10.55	9.70	13.21
Earnings	3.18	2.95	2.69	2.42	2.11	2.00	1.88	1.57	1.56	1.42
S&P Core Earnings	3.06	2.79	2.58	2.27	1.99	NA	NA	NA	NA	NA
Dividends	1.40	1.25	1.12	1.00	0.92	0.88	0.78	0.68	0.71	0.57
Payout Ratio	44%	42%	42%	41%	44%	44%	41%	43%	46%	0%
Prices:High	50.06	48.82	39.84	36.12	29.46	24.44	30.75	36.00	31.67	17.83
Prices:Low	42.34	37.50	29.60	26.00	18.75	15.50	20.50	18.75	17.22	13.67
P/E Ratio:High	16	17	15	15	14	12	16	23	20	12
P/E Ratio:Low	13	13	11	11	9	8	11	12	11	9
Income Statement Analysis (Million $)										
Net Interest Income	969	912	910	925	826	681	639	579	475	402
Tax Equivalent Adjustment	4.09	3.58	3.70	4.40	5.05	4.73	4.71	4.10	3.80	4.00
Non Interest Income	659	590	526	437	369	299	239	218	174	145
Loan Loss Provision	118	106	120	136	106	53.5	31.1	38.4	22.4	17.6
% Expense/Operating Revenue	55.4%	57.7%	55.4%	55.1%	57.2%	57.9%	58.7%	61.6%	61.0%	61.6%
Pretax Income	608	555	518	477	410	357	331	272	238	202
Effective Tax Rate	33.9%	33.4%	34.0%	34.1%	34.1%	32.5%	34.5%	33.6%	34.8%	36.2%
Net Income	402	370	342	314	270	241	217	181	156	129
% Net Interest Margin	2.99	3.60	3.98	4.37	4.15	3.88	3.97	4.13	4.11	4.00
S&P Core Earnings	386	350	329	294	257	NA	NA	NA	NA	NA
Balance Sheet & Other Financial Data (Million $)										
Money Market Assets	123	107	137	24.8	40.5	142	134	155	182	147
Investment Securities	6,950	7,165	7,312	5,282	7,271	6,467	5,694	5,542	3,311	3,155
Commercial Loans	7,976	10,720	8,907	8,660	7,802	3,963	3,436	3,088	2,209	1,729
Other Loans	13,396	8,136	8,459	7,821	5,905	7,531	7,353	7,015	6,468	5,731
Total Assets	30,798	28,185	26,963	23,885	23,015	19,992	18,151	17,289	13,460	11,814
Demand Deposits	6,098	5,476	4,627	3,964	3,576	3,105	2,656	2,552	2,010	1,749
Time Deposits	14,286	11,563	11,061	11,171	10,159	10,928	10,153	9,461	7,623	7,472
Long Term Debt	4,111	3,841	4,828	4,251	3,424	2,529	2,564	1,373	1,387	701
Common Equity	2,236	2,045	1,872	1,932	1,716	1,480	1,196	1,167	960	803
% Return on Assets	1.4	1.3	1.3	1.3	1.2	1.3	1.2	1.2	1.2	1.2
% Return on Equity	18.7	18.9	18.0	17.2	16.8	17.8	18.1	16.7	17.6	17.1
% Loan Loss Reserve	0.8	1.4	-1.4	1.4	1.4	1.3	1.3	1.4	1.4	1.6
% Loans/Deposits	170.6	110.7	110.7	108.9	99.8	81.9	84.2	84.1	85.2	80.9
% Equity to Assets	7.3	7.1	7.5	7.8	7.3	7.0	6.7	6.9	7.0	6.8

Data as orig reptd.; bef. results of disc opers/spec. items. Per share data adj. for stk. divs.; EPS diluted. E-Estimated. NA-Not Available. NM-Not Meaningful. NR-Not Ranked. UR-Under Review.

Office: 15 South 20th Street, Birmingham, AL 35233-2000.
Telephone: 205-297-3000.
Website: http://www.compassbank.com
Chrmn & CEO: D.P. Jones, Jr.

Sr EVP: G.R. Stone
Sr EVP: G.M. Boltwood
CFO: G.R. Hegel
Chief Acctg Officer: K.P. Pressley

Investor Contact: E. Bilek (205-297-3331)
Board of Directors: J. H. Click, Jr., C. W. Daniel, W. E. Davenport, T. Fitzpatrick, C. J. Gessler, Jr., D. P. Jones, Jr., C. E. McMahen, J. S. Stein, J. T. Strange

Founded: 1970
Domicile: Delaware
Employees: 8,000

STANDARD &POOR'S

Computer Sciences Corp

S&P Recommendation HOLD ★★★★★	**Price** $52.77 (as of Oct 27, 2006)	**12-Mo. Target Price** $52.00	**Investment Style** Mid-Cap Value

GICS Sector Information Technology
Sub-Industry Data Processing & Outsourced Services

Comment This leading computer services company provides consulting, systems integration, and outsourcing services.

Key Stock Statistics (Source S&P, Vickers, company reports)

52-Wk Range	**$60.39–46.23**	S&P Oper. EPS 2007**E**	**3.71**	P/E on S&P Oper. EPS 2007**E**	**14.2**	Dividend Rate/Share	**Nil**
Trailing 12-Month EPS	**$2.41**	S&P Oper. EPS 2008**E**	**4.21**	Common Shares Outstg. (M)	**171.7**	Yield (%)	**Nil**
Trailing 12-Month P/E	**21.9**	S&P Core EPS 2007**E**	**2.82**	Market Capitalization(B)	**$9.062**	Beta	**1.65**
$10K Invested 5 Yrs Ago	**$14,379**	S&P Core EPS 2008**E**	**4.21**	Institutional Ownership (%)	**93**	S&P Credit Rating	**A-**

Price Performance

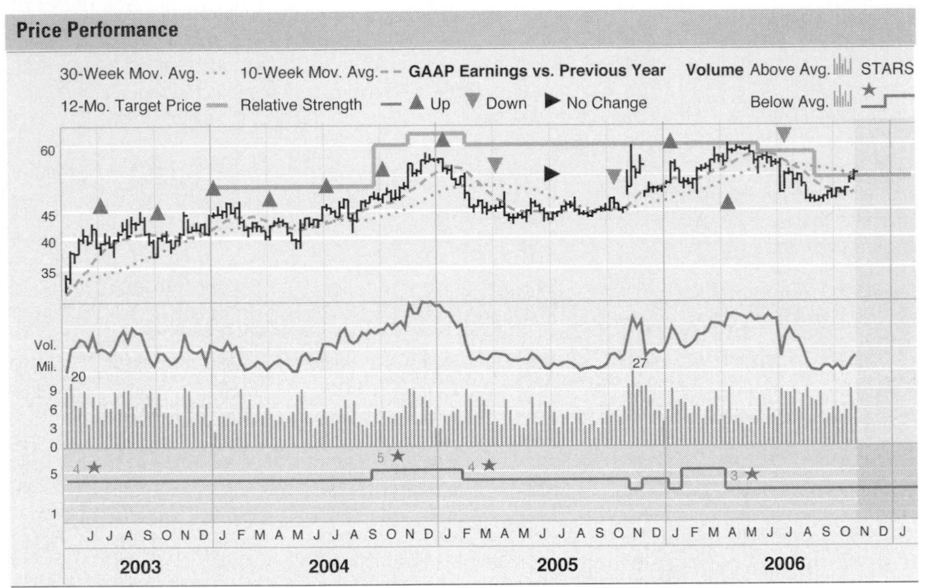

Options: ASE, CBOE, P, Ph

Analysis prepared by **Dylan Cathers** on August 23, 2006, when the stock traded at **$ 47.43**.

Highlights

- We see revenues from operations increasing 2.5% in FY 07 (Mar.) and 3.5% in FY 08. We anticipate continued strong demand in the U.S. federal government segment. Recent awards in this area include the U.S. Army of the Information Technology Enterprise Solutions II services contract, which the company values at about $2 billion over nine years. CSC sees its addressable federal market pipeline of opportunities consisting of $36 billion in awards that are expected to be allocated over the next 20 months. In FY 06, CSC's major business awards in the federal market totaled about $7.2 billion.
- We expect CSC's commercial operations to remain weak, with particular softness in Europe, partially offset by strength in Asia and Australia.
- We think that CSC's margins will be flat in FY 07, but improve as the year progresses due to restructuring activities. We estimate FY 07 EPS of $3.71, including projected stock option expense, versus operating EPS of $3.33 in FY 06. Our FY 08 EPS estimate is $4.21.

Investment Rationale/Risk

- Our hold recommendation is based on valuation. The shares have been under pressure recently, despite management's July announcement that it intends to repurchase up to $2 billion (about 19%) of CSC shares. We think increased levels of U.S. federal government outsourcing, cost-cutting initiatives from the current restructuring program, as well as a continued upward momentum in outsourcing in general in calendars 2006 and 2007 are likely sources of future revenue and profit gains.
- Risks to our recommendation and target price stem from increased competition for large and long-term contracts in the IT infrastructure and outsourcing arena, and shareholder litigation and investigations by the SEC and U.S. Attorney regarding stock option pricing practices. We also have concerns regarding corporate governance, including a combination of the chairman and CEO roles and a poison pill in place.
- Our 12-month target price of $52 is based on a peer-level P/E ratio of 15X and a P/E-to-growth ratio of 1.05X, using our calendar 2006 EPS estimate of $3.47.

Qualitative Risk Assessment

LOW | **MEDIUM** | HIGH

Our risk assessment reflects what we see as the highly competitive nature of the IT consulting and outsourcing market, offset by our view of CSC's strong balance sheet and the stability afforded the company by the numerous long-term contracts that it has signed with customers.

Quantitative Evaluations

S&P Quality Ranking **B+**

D | C | B- | B | **B+** | A- | A | A+

Relative Strength Rank **STRONG**

71

LOWEST = 1 HIGHEST = 99

Revenue/Earnings Data

Revenue (Million $)

	1Q	2Q	3Q	4Q	Year
2007	3,556	--	--	--	--
2006	3,583	3,573	3,577	3,884	14,616
2005	3,736	3,935	3,517	3,879	14,059
2004	3,555	3,591	3,621	4,000	14,768
2003	2,754	2,720	2,794	3,079	11,347
2002	2,714	2,765	2,901	3,046	11,426

Earnings Per Share ($)

2007	-0.29	**E**0.69	**E**1.02	**E**1.40	**E**3.71
2006	0.58	0.53	0.88	1.08	3.07
2005	0.58	0.68	0.69	0.86	2.59
2004	0.49	0.57	0.68	1.01	2.75
2003	0.46	0.54	0.61	0.93	2.54
2002	0.28	0.40	0.51	0.82	2.01

Fiscal year ended Mar. 31. Next earnings report expected: Early November. EPS Estimates based on S&P Operating Earnings; historical GAAP earnings are as reported.

Dividend Data

No cash dividends have been paid since 1998.

Computer Sciences Corp

Business Summary August 23, 2006

CORPORATE OVERVIEW. Computer Sciences offers a broad array of services to clients in the global commercial and government markets. The company specializes in the application of complex information technology (IT) to achieve the strategic objectives of its customers. Offerings include IT and business process outsourcing, and IT and professional services.

Outsourcing involves operating all or a portion of a customer's technology infrastructure, including systems analysis, applications development, network operations, desktop computing, and data center management. CSC also provides business process outsourcing, which involves managing key functions for clients such as claims processing, credit checking, logistics, and customer call centers.

IT and professional services includes systems integration, consulting, and professional services. Systems integration encompasses designing, developing, implementing, and integrating complete information systems. Consulting and professional services includes advising clients on the strategic acquisition and utilization of IT, and on business strategy, security, modeling, engineering, and business process re-engineering. CSC also licenses sophisticated software systems for healthcare and financial services markets, and provides a broad array of end-to-end e-business solutions to meet the needs of large commercial and government clients.

Company Financials

Per Share Data ($) Year Ended Mar. 31	**2006**	**2005**	**2004**	**2003**	**2002**	**2001**	**2000**	**1999**	**1998**	**1997**
Tangible Book Value	23.85	21.71	15.44	11.78	11.58	9.26	12.78	10.98	9.32	7.23
Cash Flow	9.42	8.56	8.29	6.95	7.02	5.17	5.59	4.85	4.08	3.36
Earnings	3.07	2.59	2.75	2.54	2.01	1.37	2.37	2.11	1.64	1.23
S&P Core Earnings	3.00	2.59	2.68	1.84	1.48	0.80	NA	NA	NA	NA
Dividends	Nil	Nil	Nil	Nil	Nil	Nil	Nil	Nil	Nil	Nil
Payout Ratio	Nil	Nil	Nil	Nil	Nil	Nil	Nil	Nil	Nil	Nil
Calendar Year	2005	2004	2003	2002	2001	2000	1999	1998	1997	1996
Prices:High	59.90	58.00	44.99	53.47	66.71	99.88	94.63	74.88	43.88	43.25
Prices:Low	42.31	38.07	26.52	24.30	28.99	58.25	52.38	39.97	28.94	32.06
P/E Ratio:High	20	22	16	21	33	73	40	35	27	35
P/E Ratio:Low	14	15	10	10	14	43	22	19	18	26

Income Statement Analysis (Million $)										
Revenue	14,616	14,059	14,768	11,347	11,426	10,524	9,371	7,660	6,601	5,616
Operating Income	2,149	1,845	1,868	1,609	1,497	1,302	1,239	990	849	718
Depreciation	1,188	1,146	1,038	858	858	649	546	445	387	333
Interest Expense	104	157	170	143	155	106	58.1	48.5	51.0	40.3
Pretax Income	821	715	747	612	497	330	611	511	191	303
Effective Tax Rate	29.7%	30.6%	30.5%	28.0%	30.7%	29.4%	34.1%	33.3%	NM	36.7%
Net Income	577	496	519	440	344	233	403	341	260	192
S&P Core Earnings	565	495	507	319	254	137	NA	NA	NA	NA

Balance Sheet & Other Financial Data (Million $)										
Cash	1,291	1,010	610	300	149	185	260	603	275	110
Current Assets	6,306	5,690	4,867	4,088	3,304	3,204	2,766	2,669	1,983	1,612
Total Assets	12,943	12,634	11,804	10,433	8,611	8,175	5,874	5,008	4,047	3,581
Current Liabilities	4,141	3,878	3,253	2,987	2,708	3,589	1,984	2,081	1,215	1,087
Long Term Debt	1,377	1,303	2,306	2,205	1,873	1,029	652	398	736	631
Common Equity	6,772	6,495	5,504	4,606	3,624	3,215	3,044	2,400	2,001	1,670
Total Capital	8,149	7,798	7,810	6,811	5,497	4,245	3,780	2,798	2,737	2,416
Capital Expenditures	827	855	725	638	672	897	586	426	349	322
Cash Flow	1,765	1,642	1,558	1,298	1,202	882	949	786	647	526
Current Ratio	1.5	1.5	1.5	1.4	1.2	0.9	1.4	1.3	1.6	1.5
% Long Term Debt of Capitalization	16.9	16.7	29.5	32.4	34.1	24.3	17.3	14.2	26.9	26.1
% Net Income of Revenue	3.9	3.5	3.5	3.9	3.0	2.2	4.3	4.5	3.9	3.4
% Return on Assets	4.5	4.1	4.7	4.6	4.1	3.3	7.2	7.5	6.8	5.9
% Return on Equity	8.7	8.3	10.3	10.7	10.1	7.5	14.3	15.5	14.2	12.5

Data as orig reptd.; bef. results of disc opers/spec. items. Per share data adj. for stk. divs.; EPS diluted. E-Estimated. NA-Not Available. NM-Not Meaningful. NR-Not Ranked. UR-Under Review.

Office: 2100 East Grand Avenue, El Segundo, CA 90245.
Telephone: 310-615-0311.
Email: investorrelations@csc.com
Website: http://www.csc.com

Chrmn & CEO: V.B. Honeycutt
Pres & COO: M.W. Laphen
VP & CFO: M.E. Keane
VP & Treas: T.R. Irvin

VP, Secy & General Counsel: H.D. Fisk
Investor Contact: L. Runge (310-615-1680)
Board of Directors: I. W. Bailey, II, D. J. Barram, S. L. Baum, R. F. Chase, V. B. Honeycutt, F. W. McFarlan, T. H. Patrick

Founded: 1959
Domicile: Nevada
Employees: 79,000

STANDARD &POOR'S

Compuware Corp

S&P Recommendation HOLD ★★★★★	**Price** $7.61 (as of Oct 27, 2006)	**12-Mo. Target Price** $9.00	**Investment Style** Mid-Cap Value

GICS Sector Information Technology
Sub-Industry Application Software

Comment This company provides software products and professional services designed to increase the productivity of information systems departments.

Key Stock Statistics (Source S&P, Vickers, company reports)

52-Wk Range	**$9.99–6.02**	S&P Oper. EPS 2007**E**	**0.41**	P/E on S&P Oper. EPS 2007**E**	**18.6**	Dividend Rate/Share	**Nil**
Trailing 12-Month EPS	**$0.39**	S&P Oper. EPS 2008**E**	**0.47**	Common Shares Outstg. (M)	**372.5**	Yield (%)	**Nil**
Trailing 12-Month P/E	**19.5**	S&P Core EPS 2007**E**	**0.41**	Market Capitalization(B)	**$2.835**	Beta	**3.31**
$10K Invested 5 Yrs Ago	**$6,937**	S&P Core EPS 2008**E**	**0.47**	Institutional Ownership (%)	**74**	S&P Credit Rating	**NR**

Price Performance

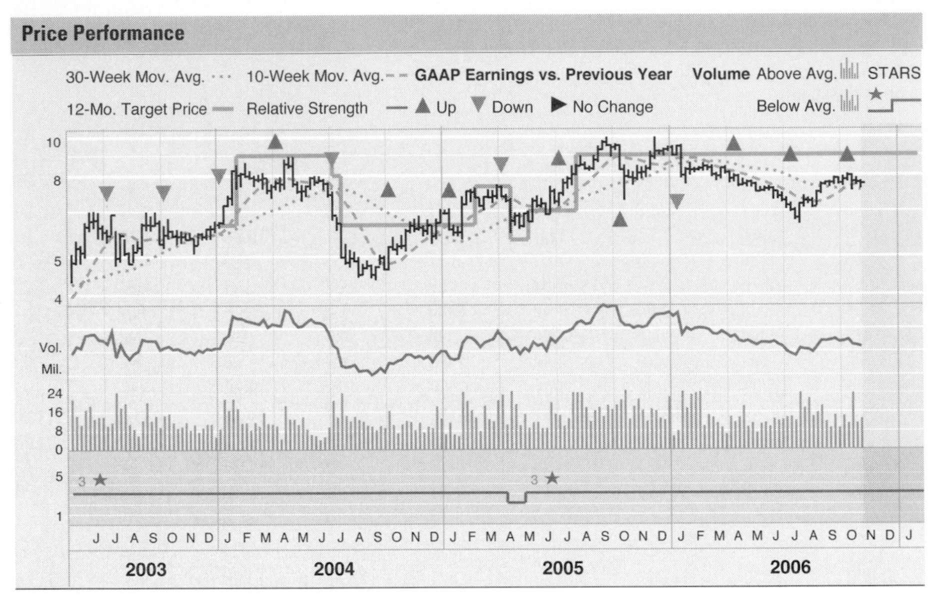

Options: ASE, CBOE, P

Analysis prepared by **Zaineb Bokhari** on October 13, 2006, when the stock traded at **$ 7.70**.

Highlights

- We expect revenues to rise about 3% in FY 07 (Mar.) and 4% in FY 08, based on our outlook for modest growth in licenses and single digit growth for maintenance revenues, and professional services fees. We expect much of this revenue growth to occur in the second half of the fiscal years, in keeping with seasonal patterns.
- With tight cost controls, we anticipate that operating margins will widen in FY 07 and in FY 08. Including acquisitions, CPWR lowered its headcount by about 20% from FY 03 to FY 06; CPWR's professional services organization saw headcount fall by 31% over this period. In view of the modest revenue growth we forecast for CPWR, we expect future declines to be more modest.
- After effective taxes projected at 33%, we expect FY 07 EPS of $0.41, up from $0.37 in FY 06. Our FY 08 EPS estimate is $0.47. We expect EPS in both years to be aided by ongoing share repurchases. Our EPS estimates include approximately $0.10 of interest income in FY 07 and about $0.08 in FY 08. Our EPS estimate also include $0.02-$0.03 of projected stock option expense in each year.

Investment Rationale/Risk

- Despite what we view as CPWR's operational struggles, we have a hold opinion on these volatile shares, primarily based on valuation. The shares recently traded at an enterprise value to projected calendar 2006 sales multiple of about 1.9X, a discount to the 2.3X average for software peers. We view the balance sheet as strong, with about $896 million in cash and short-term investments at June 30, 2006 (about $2.37 a share), and no debt.
- Risks to our opinion and target price include weaker than expected corporate IT spending. We are also concerned that software vendors such as Compuware are vulnerable to competition from hardware vendors, most notably IBM, particularly in mainframes. In addition, we are concerned about CPWR's corporate governance related to its stock compensation practices.
- Our 12-month target price of $9 is derived from our valuation of discounted free cash flow, assuming a weighted average cost of capital (WACC) of 13.5% and a terminal growth rate of 3%.

Qualitative Risk Assessment

LOW	MEDIUM	**HIGH**

Our risk assessment reflects our concern over CPWR's ability to generate future revenue growth, as newer initiatives have been slow to bear fruit, in our opinion. Absent a meaningful pickup in revenue growth, we expect ongoing cost reduction and interest income to drive future earnings growth.

Quantitative Evaluations

S&P Quality Ranking **NR**

D	C	B-	B	B+	A-	A	A+

Relative Strength Rank **MODERATE**

38

LOWEST = 1 HIGHEST = 99

Revenue/Earnings Data

Revenue (Million $)

	1Q	2Q	3Q	4Q	Year
2007	296.3	288.5	--	--	--
2006	297.3	292.7	305.9	309.5	1,205
2005	287.1	295.5	330.5	318.8	1,232
2004	306.0	302.8	318.2	337.7	1,265
2003	346.6	358.0	333.1	337.6	1,375
2002	446.8	424.0	450.6	407.2	1,729

Earnings Per Share ($)

2007	0.08	0.07	**E**0.13	**E**0.13	**E**0.41
2006	0.06	0.06	0.10	0.15	0.37
2005	Nil	0.02	0.11	0.07	0.20
2004	0.01	-0.02	0.06	0.09	0.13
2003	0.06	0.09	0.07	0.06	0.27
2002	0.09	0.07	0.08	-0.90	-0.66

Fiscal year ended Mar. 31. Next earnings report expected: Late January. EPS Estimates based on S&P Operating Earnings; historical GAAP earnings are as reported.

Dividend Data

No cash dividends have been paid.

Compuware Corp

Business Summary October 13, 2006

CORPORATE OVERVIEW. Originally founded as a professional services company, Compuware provides software, maintenance and professional services intended to increase the productivity of the information technology (IT) departments of businesses. CPWR offers mainframe software for testing, debugging and system maintenance of IBM and IBM-compatible mainframes. The company's distributed products support requirements management (Changepoint), application development (Uniface, Optimal, and DevPartner), testing (QA Center and File-AID/CS), and application performance analysis (Vantage).

LEGAL/REGULATORY ISSUES. On March 21, 2005, Compuware settled all pending litigation with IBM (originally filed in March 2002). Pursuant to the terms of the settlement agreement, IBM also entered into a four-year license and maintenance arrangement with Compuware, worth $140 million, and offered to purchase $260 million of the company's services over a four-year period extending from March 2005 through March 2009. In late 2005, this settlement agreement was amended to extend the period over which IBM could purchase $140 million of Compuware's software and maintenance to five years (ending March 31, 2010). In addition, according to this amendment, IBM will offer Compuware the opportunity to bid on a minimum of $260 million of IBM-sourced services over a four-and-a-half year period. We do not see the resolution of CPWR's lawsuit against IBM having a meaningful impact on the competitive environment.

FINANCIAL TRENDS. Like those of many of its enterprise software peers, and, in particular, those with sizable mainframe-related revenues, CPWR's revenues peaked in FY 00, driven by Y2K-related spending. Revenues declined annually from FY 00 (Mar.) to FY 06, despite a number of acquisitions. Operating income has followed a similar pattern, although it seems to us to have bottomed in FY 04 due to ongoing expense reductions.

Company Financials

Per Share Data ($) Year Ended Mar. 31	**2006**	**2005**	**2004**	**2003**	**2002**	**2001**	**2000**	**1999**	**1998**	**1997**
Tangible Book Value	3.33	3.15	3.11	2.93	2.60	2.02	1.51	2.70	1.81	4.54
Cash Flow	0.51	0.34	0.27	0.41	-0.40	0.60	1.10	0.97	0.59	0.63
Earnings	0.37	0.20	0.13	0.27	-0.66	0.32	0.91	0.87	0.50	0.27
S&P Core Earnings	0.33	0.12	0.03	0.14	-0.15	0.17	NA	NA	NA	NA
Dividends	Nil	Nil	Nil	Nil	Nil	Nil	Nil	Nil	Nil	Nil
Payout Ratio	Nil	Nil	Nil	Nil	Nil	Nil	Nil	Nil	Nil	Nil
Calendar Year	2005	2004	2003	2002	2001	2000	1999	1998	1997	1996
Prices:High	9.99	8.95	6.52	14.00	14.50	37.81	40.00	39.91	19.75	7.78
Prices:Low	5.51	4.35	3.22	2.35	6.25	5.63	16.38	15.56	6.03	1.94
P/E Ratio:High	27	45	50	52	NM	NM	44	46	39	29
P/E Ratio:Low	15	22	25	9	NM	NM	18	18	12	7
Income Statement Analysis (Million $)										
Revenue	1,205	1,232	1,265	1,375	1,729	2,010	2,231	1,638	1,139	813
Operating Income	198	143	90.5	188	264	296	641	547	317	181
Depreciation	50.2	56.4	55.2	53.8	98.2	104	71.5	41.5	36.5	15.5
Interest Expense	Nil	Nil	Nil	6.10	7.43	31.3	24.5	Nil	Nil	Nil
Pretax Income	191	106	56.0	156	-245	192	562	530	291	149
Effective Tax Rate	25.3%	28.0%	11.0%	34.0%	NM	38.0%	37.3%	34.0%	33.3%	34.8%
Net Income	143	76.5	49.8	103	-245	119	352	350	194	97.4
S&P Core Earnings	126	46.1	9.72	51.2	-55.3	62.2	NA	NA	NA	NA
Balance Sheet & Other Financial Data (Million $)										
Cash	612	498	455	319	233	53.3	30.5	193	206	107
Current Assets	1,445	1,358	1,143	1,050	1,063	1,004	988	1,072	676	452
Total Assets	2,511	2,478	2,234	2,123	1,994	2,279	2,416	1,677	1,073	755
Current Liabilities	545	578	493	469	556	569	596	522	314	272
Long Term Debt	Nil	Nil	Nil	Nil	Nil	140	450	Nil	6.96	6.07
Common Equity	1,579	1,516	1,414	1,332	1,170	1,377	1,204	1,080	708	446
Total Capital	1,605	1,516	1,418	1,332	1,170	1,538	1,667	1,080	715	452
Capital Expenditures	14.5	134	74.6	225	90.4	39.8	34.9	26.4	28.0	23.4
Cash Flow	193	133	105	157	-147	223	423	391	230	113
Current Ratio	2.6	2.3	2.3	2.2	1.9	1.8	1.7	2.1	2.2	1.7
% Long Term Debt of Capitalization	Nil	Nil	Nil	Nil	Nil	9.1	27.0	Nil	1.0	1.3
% Net Income of Revenue	11.9	6.2	3.9	7.5	NM	5.9	15.8	21.4	17.0	12.0
% Return on Assets	5.7	3.2	2.3	5.0	NM	5.1	17.2	25.5	21.2	14.9
% Return on Equity	9.2	5.2	3.6	8.2	NM	9.2	30.8	39.1	33.6	25.5

Data as orig reptd.; bef. results of disc opers/spec. items. Per share data adj. for stk. divs.; EPS diluted. E-Estimated. NA-Not Available. NM-Not Meaningful. NR-Not Ranked. UR-Under Review.

Office: 1 Campus Martius, Detroit, MI 48226-5099.
Telephone: 313-227-7300.
Email: investor.relations@compuware.com
Website: http://www.compuware.com

Chrmn, Pres & CEO: P. Karmanos, Jr.
SVP, CFO & Treas: L.L. Fournier
SVP, Secy & General Counsel: T. Costello, Jr.
Investor Contact: L. Elkin (248-737-7345)

Board of Directors: D. W. Archer, G. S. Bedi, W. O. Grabe, W. R. Halling, P. Karmanos, Jr., F. A. Nelson, G. D. Price, W. J. Prowse, G. S. Romney

Founded: 1973
Domicile: Michigan
Employees: 7,510

STANDARD & POOR'S

Comverse Technology Inc

S&P Recommendation HOLD ★★★★★

Price $21.74 (as of Oct 27, 2006)

12-Mo. Target Price $22.00

Investment Style Mid-Cap Value

GICS Sector Information Technology
Sub-Industry Communications Equipment

Comment This company manufactures computer and telecommunications systems and software for communications and information processing applications.

Key Stock Statistics (Source S&P, Vickers, company reports)

52-Wk Range	**$29.64–17.04**	S&P Oper. EPS 2006**E**	**0.61**	P/E on S&P Oper. EPS 2006**E**	**35.6**	Dividend Rate/Share	**Nil**
Trailing 12-Month EPS	**$0.55**	S&P Oper. EPS 2007**E**	**0.66**	Common Shares Outstg. (M)	**202.0**	Yield (%)	**Nil**
Trailing 12-Month P/E	**39.5**	S&P Core EPS 2006**E**	**0.38**	Market Capitalization(B)	**$4.392**	Beta	**2.12**
$10K Invested 5 Yrs Ago	**$11,919**	S&P Core EPS 2007**E**	**0.66**	Institutional Ownership (%)	**NA**	S&P Credit Rating	**BB-**

Price Performance

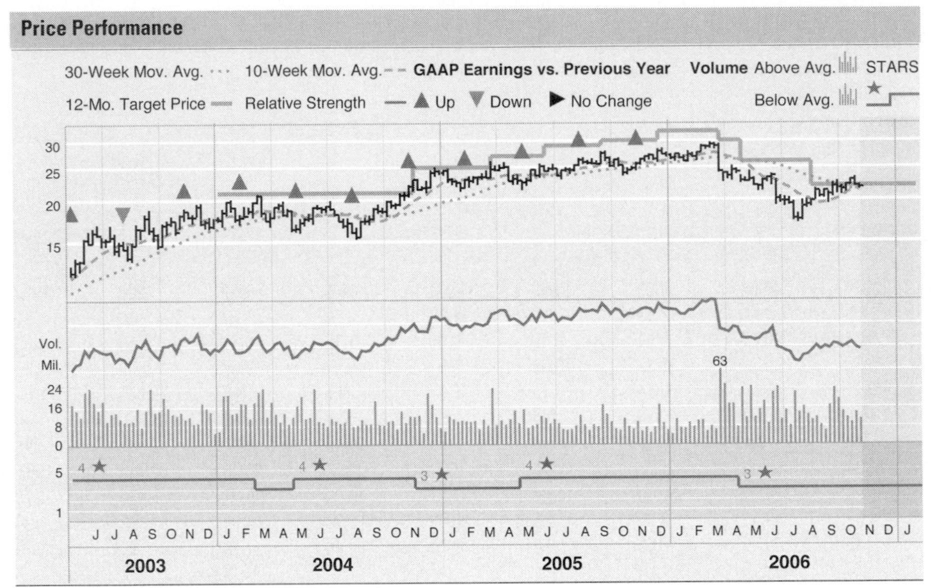

Options: ASE, CBOE, P, Ph

Analysis prepared by **Todd Rosenbluth** on August 07, 2006, when the stock traded at **$ 19.62**.

Highlights

- In March, CMVT delayed the reporting of its fourth quarter FY 06 earnings results due to a review of its stock option grant procedures, and the company was still reviewing its full accounting as of early August. However, CMVT reported revenues in the fourth quarter of FY 06 and in the first quarter of FY 07 that were higher than we projected. We see 28% sales growth for FY 07, reflecting our view of an increasing mix of wireless software in wireless carriers' spending programs and the addition of the GSS division that was acquired in December 2005.
- We expect a gross margin of 59% in FY 07, and we believe the lower margin billing segment integration will be offset by cost saving efforts and volume increases that should outweigh any pricing pressures. The company enjoys a low tax rate, which provides significant tax incentives.
- We project operating EPS of $0.61 in FY 06 before projected stock option expense. We see EPS of $0.66 in FY 07 and $0.77 in FY 08, including projected stock option expense of $0.21 in each year, to which we believe CMVT has modestly more exposure than its peers.

Investment Rationale/Risk

- We believe CMVT will take advantage of strong demand for enhanced wireless service applications around the globe, as we see CMVT's product portfolio in strong demand as carriers expand their networks, increase enhanced service applications, and provide billing. However, we have corporate governance concerns related to its still ongoing accounting restatement and the departure of senior executives.
- Risks to our recommendation and target price include risks in Israel, where a substantial number of CMVT's facilities are located; and potential long delays in realizing sales from the order backlog.
- We are pleased with what we view as CMVT's steady operational execution, and we believe its balance sheet will remain strong, with about $8 per share in net cash (after debt). Using our relative P/E to growth analysis based on expected 15% growth and factoring in our increased corporate governance concerns, we arrive at our 12-month target price of $22.

Qualitative Risk Assessment

LOW | **MEDIUM** | HIGH

Our risk assessment reflects the company's planned accounting restatement, and the competitive telecom landscape, offset by its long-term relationships with its telecom customers.

Quantitative Evaluations

S&P Quality Ranking B-

D | C | **B-** | B | B+ | A- | A | A+

Relative Strength Rank MODERATE

42

LOWEST = 1 HIGHEST = 99

Revenue/Earnings Data

Revenue (Million $)

	1Q	2Q	3Q	4Q	Year
2006	272.8	285.8	299.0	--	--
2005	221.4	233.4	245.5	259.1	959.4
2004	180.6	188.5	193.8	203.0	765.9
2003	211.2	181.2	167.5	176.0	735.9
2002	365.0	345.1	295.0	265.1	1,270
2001	261.3	292.1	318.0	346.6	1,225

Earnings Per Share ($)

2006	0.11	0.16	0.18	**E**0.18	**E**0.61
2005	0.03	0.06	0.08	0.10	0.28
2004	-0.03	-0.01	-0.02	0.02	-0.03
2003	-0.13	0.02	-0.43	-0.16	-0.69
2002	0.43	0.15	0.01	-0.29	0.29
2001	0.33	0.30	0.35	0.41	1.39

Fiscal year ended Jan. 31. Next earnings report expected: NA. EPS Estimates based on S&P Operating Earnings; historical GAAP earnings are as reported.

Dividend Data

No cash dividends have been paid.

Comverse Technology Inc

Business Summary August 07, 2006

CORPORATE SUMMARY. Comverse Technology's multimedia communications and information processing technology and products cover four primary categories: call completion and call management solutions; advanced messaging solutions; management and delivery of data and content-based services; and real-time billing and account management. In October 2005, CMVT agreed to acquire the GSS division of CSG Systems for $251 million in cash. The deal closed in December 2005 and is expected to be slightly accretive to FY 06 pro forma net income. GSS handles converged billing services for telecom and cable companies such as Vodafone, France Telecom, Telecom Italia, British Sky Broadcasting and China Telecom.

PRIMARY BUSINESS DYNAMICS. Comverse Network Systems Products (68% of FY 05 (Jan.) sales) include enhanced service platforms (ESP) for telecommunications carriers. These platforms enable the provision of revenue generating value added services, including call answering, unified messaging, short text messaging, one-touch call return and other personal communications services. Customers benefit from receiving service subscription fees and from traffic revenue generated by the increase in completed calls. In addition, the services help reduce overall network traffic due to repeated busy or no-answer calls. In June 2005, CMVT announced the availability of MIMail, an integrated Mobile IM and e-mail solution that migrates the two popular messaging services to the mobile environment.

More than 400 wireless and wireline network operators use CMVT's ESP systems, in more than 110 countries. Users include a majority of the world's largest telephone companies. Major customers include: AT&T (U.S.), Deutsche Telekom (Germany), KDDI (Japan), MCI Worldcom (U.S.), O2 (Germany and the U.K.), NTT (Japan), Orange (several countries), SFR (France), Sprint Nextel (U.S.), Telecom Italia (Italy), Telmex (Mexico), Telstra (Australia), Verizon (USA), and Vodafone (multiple countries).

Company Financials

Per Share Data ($) Year Ended Jan. 31	**2005**	**2004**	**2003**	**2002**	**2001**	**2000**	**1999**	**1998**	**1997**	**1996**
Tangible Book Value	9.02	8.60	8.25	8.63	7.24	4.62	2.71	3.46	2.84	1.86
Cash Flow	0.62	0.35	-0.33	0.64	1.59	1.15	0.92	0.65	0.44	0.34
Earnings	0.28	-0.03	-0.69	0.29	1.39	1.07	0.78	0.54	0.39	0.25
S&P Core Earnings	-0.25	-0.68	-1.35	-0.54	0.92	NA	NA	NA	NA	NA
Dividends	Nil	Nil	Nil	Nil	Nil	Nil	Nil	Nil	Nil	Nil
Payout Ratio	Nil	Nil	Nil	Nil	Nil	Nil	Nil	Nil	Nil	Nil
Calendar Year	2004	2003	2002	2001	2000	1999	1998	1997	1996	1995
Prices:High	25.07	19.65	28.28	124.75	123.88	72.50	23.83	18.29	13.96	8.67
Prices:Low	15.25	8.50	6.65	15.03	61.81	21.67	9.79	10.46	5.38	3.67
P/E Ratio:High	90	NM	NM	NM	89	68	31	34	36	35
P/E Ratio:Low	54	NM	NM	NM	44	20	13	19	14	15

Income Statement Analysis (Million $)										
Revenue	959	766	736	1,270	1,225	872	696	280	207	137
Operating Income	118	39.3	-48.7	192	304	205	136	51.5	34.8	20.5
Depreciation	66.7	71.8	67.4	63.8	53.2	33.5	20.9	9.70	7.13	5.87
Interest Expense	Nil	6.98	Nil	Nil	18.0	19.3	15.2	9.77	7.10	4.40
Pretax Income	83.2	8.58	-126	59.1	268	186	123	48.3	31.3	19.1
Effective Tax Rate	15.9%	NM	NM	7.51%	7.03%	8.38%	9.56%	9.96%	10.7%	10.8%
Net Income	57.3	-5.39	-129	54.6	249	170	112	43.5	28.0	17.1
S&P Core Earnings	-48.9	-129	-252	-94.8	162	NA	NA	NA	NA	NA

Balance Sheet & Other Financial Data (Million $)										
Cash	721	1,531	1,403	1,362	1,275	339	584	174	236	123
Current Assets	2,627	2,462	2,127	2,397	2,276	1,176	933	405	351	190
Total Assets	2,925	2,728	2,404	2,704	2,625	1,352	1,031	458	391	221
Current Liabilities	487	321	360	367	415	327	225	75.2	58.7	35.2
Long Term Debt	420	Nil	391	600	900	300	415	115	115	60.0
Common Equity	1,794	1,673	1,550	1,616	1,236	711	382	261	212	122
Total Capital	2,410	1,834	2,024	2,278	2,190	1,011	797	377	327	182
Capital Expenditures	46.2	35.4	34.1	54.6	97.3	84.8	24.7	12.6	9.75	5.56
Cash Flow	124	66.4	-62.1	118	302	204	132	53.2	35.1	22.9
Current Ratio	5.4	7.7	5.9	6.5	5.5	3.6	4.1	5.4	6.0	5.4
% Long Term Debt of Capitalization	17.4	Nil	19.3	26.3	41.1	29.7	52.1	30.5	35.1	33.0
% Net Income of Revenue	6.0	NM	NM	4.3	20.3	19.5	16.0	15.5	25.9	12.4
% Return on Assets	2.0	NM	NM	2.0	12.5	14.3	15.0	15.0	9.2	8.2
% Return on Equity	3.3	NM	NM	3.8	25.4	31.2	34.8	34.7	16.8	15.3

Data as orig reptd.; bef. results of disc opers/spec. items. Per share data adj. for stk. divs.; EPS diluted. E-Estimated. NA-Not Available. NM-Not Meaningful. NR-Not Ranked. UR-Under Review.

Office: 909 3rd Ave, New York, NY 10022-4731.
Telephone: 212-652-6801.
Email: info@comverse.com
Website: http://www.cmvt.com

Chrmn: R. Hiram
CEO: R. Alon
EVP, Chief Admin, Secy & General Counsel: P.L. Robinson
VP, CFO & Treas: A.T. Aronovitz

Investor Contact: P.D. Baker (516-677-7226)
Board of Directors: K. Alexander, R. Alon, I. Danziger, J. H. Friedman, R. Hiram, S. Oolie, W. F. Sorin, M. C. Terrell

Founded: 1984
Domicile: New York
Employees: 5,050

STANDARD &POOR'S

ConAgra Foods Inc.

S&P Recommendation HOLD ★★★★★

Price $26.02 (as of Oct 30, 2006)

12-Mo. Target Price $25.00

Investment Style Large-Cap Value

GICS Sector Consumer Staples
Sub-Industry Packaged Foods & Meats

Comment This company is one of the largest U.S. packaged food processors.

Key Stock Statistics (Source S&P, Vickers, company reports)

52-Wk Range	**$26.10–18.85**	S&P Oper. EPS 2007**E**	**1.19**	P/E on S&P Oper. EPS 2007**E**	**21.9**	Dividend Rate/Share	**$0.72**
Trailing 12-Month EPS	**$0.69**	S&P Oper. EPS 2008**E**	**1.27**	Common Shares Outstg. (M)	**509.5**	Yield (%)	**2.77**
Trailing 12-Month P/E	**37.7**	S&P Core EPS 2007**E**	**1.20**	Market Capitalization(B)	**$13.258**	Beta	**0.36**
$10K Invested 5 Yrs Ago	**$13,853**	S&P Core EPS 2008**E**	**1.28**	Institutional Ownership (%)	**68**	S&P Credit Rating	**BBB+**

Price Performance

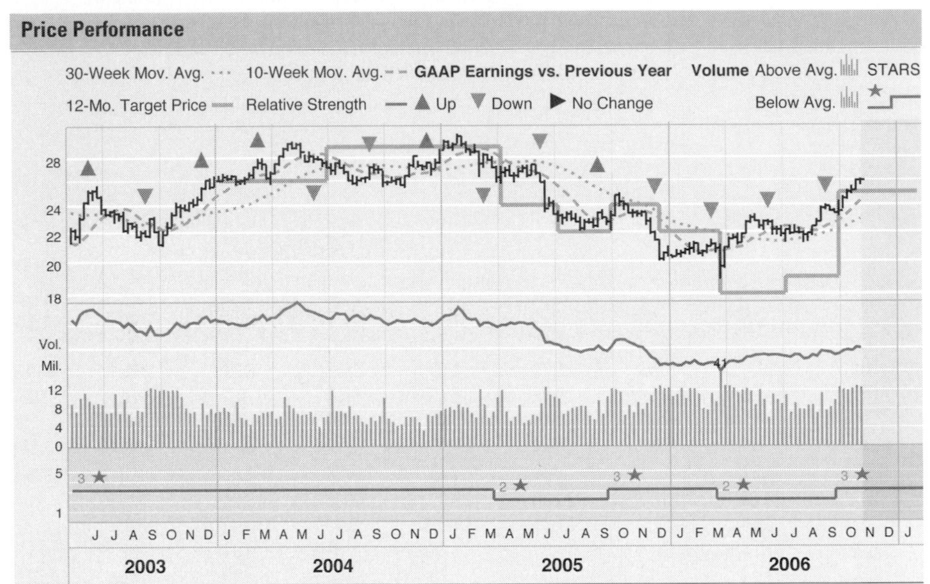

Options: ASE, CBOE, P

Analysis prepared by **Rick Joy** on October 27, 2006, when the stock traded at **$ 25.87**.

Highlights

- The company recently announced a new restructuring program, which includes further portfolio streamlining, a rationalization of manufacturing assets and an increase in marketing spending and focus on strategic brands. ConAgra expects the impact of the divestitures and restructuring costs to depress operating earnings until FY 09 (May).

- We expect net sales to decline in FY 07, primarily reflecting divestitures and SKU (stock keeping unit) reductions. The company is pursuing plans to divest its seafood, refrigerated meats and cheese businesses, with annual sales of approximately $2.8 billion. We see a substantial decline in operating profits due to divestitures, increased advertising and marketing spending, and higher commodity, energy and packaging costs.

- Following a reduction in net interest expense, we estimate FY 07 operating EPS of $1.19, down from FY 06 operating EPS of $1.38. For FY 08, we see earnings growing 7% to $1.27. For the longer-term, we expect annual operating earnings growth of 7% to 8%.

Investment Rationale/Risk

- Our hold recommendation primarily reflects our view of mixed operating results in recent quarters and the near-term operational risk we see as the company implements a major restructuring program. While encouraged by results for the first quarter of FY 07 that were above our forecasts and the longer-term potential of planned restructuring actions, we believe it will be several quarters before we see improved earnings visibility and consistency.

- Risks to our recommendation and target price include competitive pressures in CAG's businesses, the potential for increased commodity cost inflation, and the company's ability to achieve cost savings and efficiency targets.

- Our 12-month target price of $25 is based on our analysis of peer P/E multiples and enterprise value to EBITDA ratios, and our discounted cash flow analysis, which assumes a weighted average cost of capital of 9% and a terminal growth rate for free cash flows of 3%.

Qualitative Risk Assessment

LOW | MEDIUM | HIGH

Our risk assessment reflects the relatively stable nature of the company's end markets, strong cash flows, and corporate governance practices that we view as favorable relative to peers.

Quantitative Evaluations

S&P Quality Ranking A-

D | C | B- | B | B+ | A- | A | A+

Relative Strength Rank STRONG

77

LOWEST = 1 HIGHEST = 99

Revenue/Earnings Data

Revenue (Million $)

	1Q	2Q	3Q	4Q	Year
2007	2,689	--	--	--	--
2006	2,700	3,026	2,879	2,975	11,579
2005	3,496	4,116	3,570	3,706	14,567
2004	4,394	3,873	3,598	3,962	14,522
2003	6,529	5,438	3,963	3,910	19,839
2002	7,608	7,364	6,245	6,414	27,630

Earnings Per Share ($)

2007	0.21	**E**0.33	**E**0.31	**E**0.26	**E**1.19
2006	0.63	0.24	0.18	0.10	1.15
2005	0.26	0.47	0.32	0.20	1.27
2004	0.38	0.45	0.36	0.37	1.50
2003	0.42	0.44	0.30	0.42	1.58
2002	0.36	0.44	0.31	0.36	1.47

Fiscal year ended May 31. Next earnings report expected: Late December. EPS Estimates based on S&P Operating Earnings; historical GAAP earnings are as reported.

Dividend Data (Dates: mm/dd Payment Date: mm/dd/yy)

Amount ($)	Date Decl.	Ex-Div. Date	Stk. of Record	Payment Date
0.273	12/01	01/26	01/30	03/01/06
0.180	03/16	04/27	05/01	06/01/06
0.180	07/14	07/27	07/31	09/01/06
0.180	09/28	10/26	10/30	12/01/06

Dividends have been paid since 1976. Source: Company reports.

ConAgra Foods Inc.

Business Summary October 27, 2006

ConAgra Foods (formerly ConAgra, Inc.) is one of the largest food companies in North America. In recent years, CAG has been pursuing an acquisition and divestiture strategy to shift its focus toward its core branded and value-added food products, while exiting commodity-related businesses. The company's businesses are divided into four reporting segments: consumer foods, which provided 57% of total sales in FY 06 (May); foods and ingredients (28%); trading and merchandising (10%); and international foods (5%).

The consumer foods segment consists of branded shelf-stable, frozen and refrigerated food products that are sold in various retail channels. The company's shelf-stable products include tomato products, cooking oils, popcorn, soup, puddings, meat snacks, canned beans, canned pasta, canned chili, cocoa mixes and peanut butter. Major shelf-stable brands include Hunt's, Healthy Choice, Chef Boyardee, Wesson, Orville Redenbacher, PAM, Slim Jim, ACT II, Peter Pan, Van Kamp's, Gulden's, Beanee Weenee, Manwich, Hunt's Snack Pack, Swiss Miss, Knott's Berry Farm, La Choy, Gebhardt, DAVID, Wolf Brand, Pemmican, Penrose and Andy Capp's. Major frozen grocery brands include Healthy Choice, Banquet, Marie Callender's, Kid Cuisine, Morton, Chun King, La Choy and Wolfgang Puck. Refrigerated products include brands such as Armour, Butterball, Cook's, Brown 'N Serve, Healthy Choice, Louis Kemp, Hebrew National, Parkay, Blue Bonnet, Fleischmann's, Egg Beaters, and Reddi-wip.

The foods and ingredients segment includes branded and customized food products, including meals, entrees, prepared potatoes, meats, seafood, sauces, and a variety of custom-manufactured culinary products for sale to restaurants and other foodservice establishments. Food ingredients includes certain branded and commodity food ingredients, including milled grain ingredients, seasonings, blends and flavorings, which are sold to food processors, as well as certain commodity sourcing and merchandising operations.

The trading and merchandising segment includes the sourcing, merchandising, trading, marketing and distribution of agricultural and energy commodities. International foods includes branded food products which are sold principally in retail channels in North America, Europe and Asia.

Company Financials

Per Share Data ($) Year Ended May 31	2006	2005	2004	2003	2002	2001	2000	1999	1998	1997
Tangible Book Value	0.79	0.47	0.41	NM	NM	NM	1.22	1.02	0.81	0.08
Cash Flow	1.74	1.95	2.16	2.30	2.39	2.30	1.98	1.80	2.33	2.23
Earnings	1.15	1.27	1.50	1.58	1.47	1.33	0.86	0.75	1.36	1.34
S&P Core Earnings	0.91	1.14	1.39	1.42	1.27	1.20	NA	NA	NA	NA
Dividends	1.08	1.03	0.98	NA	0.88	0.79	0.74	0.65	0.60	0.53
Payout Ratio	94%	81%	65%	NA	60%	59%	86%	86%	44%	39%
Calendar Year	2005	2004	2003	2002	2001	2000	1999	1998	1997	1996
Prices:High	30.24	29.65	26.41	27.65	26.00	26.19	34.38	33.63	38.75	27.38
Prices:Low	19.99	25.38	17.75	20.90	17.50	15.06	20.63	22.56	24.50	18.81
P/E Ratio:High	26	23	18	18	18	20	40	45	28	20
P/E Ratio:Low	17	20	12	14	12	11	24	30	18	14

Income Statement Analysis (Million $)	2006	2005	2004	2003	2002	2001	2000	1999	1998	1997
Revenue	11,579	14,567	14,522	19,839	27,630	27,194	25,386	24,594	23,841	24,022
Operating Income	1,184	1,618	1,735	1,123	2,144	2,026	1,028	1,940	1,767	1,709
Depreciation	311	351	352	392	474	499	537	500	446	414
Interest Expense	307	341	275	276	402	423	303	354	338	332
Pretax Income	906	1,133	1,151	1,276	1,268	1,104	666	682	1,021	1,081
Effective Tax Rate	34.2%	41.5%	30.9%	34.2%	38.1%	38.2%	38.0%	47.5%	38.5%	39.6%
Net Income	596	663	796	840	785	682	413	358	628	615
S&P Core Earnings	470	589	740	750	668	612	NA	NA	NA	NA

Balance Sheet & Other Financial Data (Million $)	2006	2005	2004	2003	2002	2001	2000	1999	1998	1997
Cash	332	208	589	629	158	198	158	62.8	95.0	106
Current Assets	4,790	4,524	5,145	6,060	6,434	7,363	5,967	5,656	5,487	5,205
Total Assets	11,970	12,792	14,230	15,071	15,496	16,481	12,296	12,146	11,703	11,277
Current Liabilities	2,965	2,389	3,002	3,803	4,313	6,936	5,489	5,386	5,070	4,990
Long Term Debt	3,155	4,349	5,281	5,570	5,919	4,635	3,092	3,068	3,028	2,356
Common Equity	4,650	4,859	4,840	4,622	4,308	3,983	2,964	2,909	2,780	2,472
Total Capital	7,805	9,209	10,120	10,192	10,227	8,618	6,056	5,977	5,808	5,352
Capital Expenditures	263	453	352	390	531	560	539	662	569	670
Cash Flow	907	1,014	1,148	1,232	1,259	1,181	950	858	1,074	1,029
Current Ratio	1.6	1.9	1.7	1.6	1.5	1.1	1.1	1.1	1.1	1.0
% Long Term Debt of Capitalization	40.4	47.2	52.2	54.7	57.9	53.8	51.1	51.3	52.1	44.0
% Net Income of Revenue	5.1	4.6	5.5	4.2	2.8	2.5	1.6	1.5	2.6	2.6
% Return on Assets	4.8	4.9	5.4	5.5	4.9	4.8	3.4	3.0	5.5	5.5
% Return on Equity	12.5	13.7	16.8	18.8	18.9	19.9	14.1	12.5	23.9	26.0

Data as orig reptd.; bef. results of disc opers/spec. items. Per share data adj. for stk. divs.; EPS diluted. E-Estimated. NA-Not Available. NM-Not Meaningful. NR-Not Ranked. UR-Under Review.

Office: 1 Conagra Dr, Omaha, NE 68102-5001.
Telephone: 402-595-4000.
Website: http://www.conagra.com
Chrmn: S.F. Goldstone

Pres & CEO: G.M. Rodkin
EVP & CFO: A.J. Hawaux
EVP & Chief Admin: O.C. Johnson
EVP & Secy: R.F. Sharpe Jr.

Investor Contact: C.W. Klinefelter (402-595-4154)
Board of Directors: D. H. Batchelder, M. C. Bay, S. G. Butler, J. T. Chain, Jr., S. F. Goldstone, A. B. Hayes, W. G. Jurgensen, M. H. Rauenhorst, C. E. Reichardt, G. M. Rodkin, R. W. Roskens, K. E. Stinson

Founded: 1919
Domicile: Delaware
Employees: 33,000

STANDARD
&POOR'S

ConocoPhillips

S&P Recommendation BUY ★★★★★

Price
$60.24 (as of Oct 31, 2006)

12-Mo. Target Price
$77.00

Investment Style
Large-Cap Value

GICS Sector Energy
Sub-Industry Integrated Oil & Gas

Comment This integrated oil and gas company (formerly Phillips Petroleum), the second largest U.S. refiner, acquired Tosco Corp. in 2001, and merged with Conoco Inc. in 2002.

Key Stock Statistics (Source S&P, Vickers, company reports)

52-Wk Range	**$72.50–54.90**	S&P Oper. EPS 2006**E**	**10.47**	P/E on S&P Oper. EPS 2006**E**	**5.8**	Dividend Rate/Share	**$1.44**
Trailing 12-Month EPS	**$10.45**	S&P Oper. EPS 2007**E**	**10.47**	Common Shares Outstg. (M)	**1,647.8**	Yield (%)	**2.39**
Trailing 12-Month P/E	**5.8**	S&P Core EPS 2006**E**	**10.16**	Market Capitalization(B)	**$99.264**	Beta	**0.61**
$10K Invested 5 Yrs Ago	**$24,142**	S&P Core EPS 2007**E**	**10.51**	Institutional Ownership (%)	**76**	S&P Credit Rating	**A-**

Price Performance

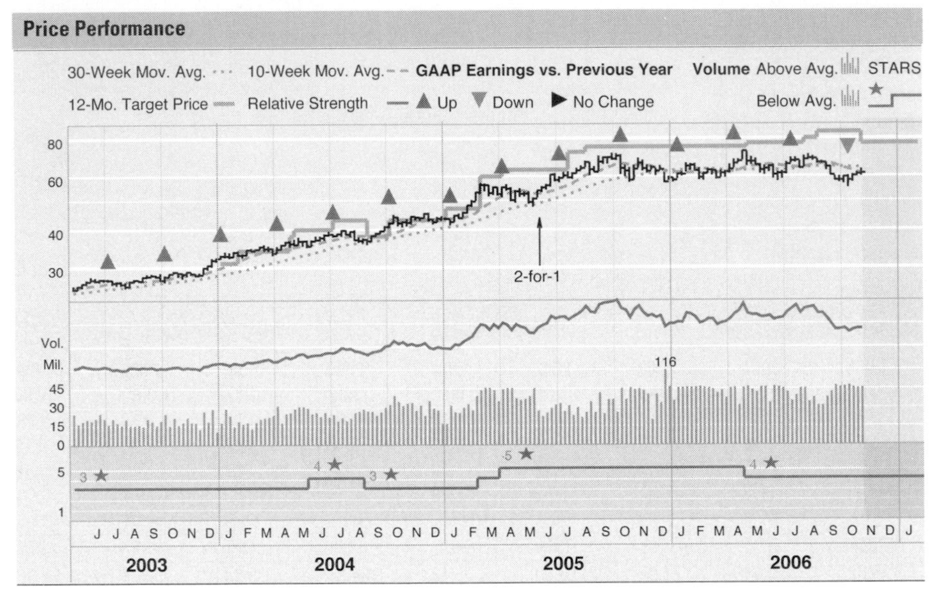

Options: ASE, CBOE, P, Ph

Analysis prepared by **Tina J. Vital** on October 31, 2006, when the stock traded at **$ 60.15**.

Highlights

- Third quarter operating earnings rose 18%, to $4.498 billion, or $2.68 per share. Results excluded net special charges of $0.37 per share, and surpassed our estimate by $0.26, reflecting better than expected domestic price realizations and marketing results.

- Reflecting contributions from Burlington Resources, we expect oil and gas production growth of 32% in 2006. On August 6, 2006, BP (BP: buy, $69) began a partial shut-down of its Prudhoe Bay oilfield (COP stake 36.1%) due to unexpected corrosion in its Eastern Operating Area pipelines. By the end of October, production had ramped back up to near normal levels. With international development projects under way, and increased investment in Russia, we look for hydrocarbon production growth of over 3% per annum during 2007-2010. Spending reached $11.62 billion in 2005, and COP has budgeted $18 billion for 2006 and $15 billion per annum in 2007-2010.

- COP's after-tax operating earnings rose 63% in 2005, and we project an increase of 28% in 2006 and 4% in 2007.

Investment Rationale/Risk

- COP has been reshaping its upstream portfolio to focus on higher growth assets. On March 31, 2006, COP acquired Burlington Resources. While we believe the purchase was pricey, we like it and see its premium justified by Burlington Resources' relatively low cost and its strong organic growth focused on North American natural gas. As of the 2006 third quarter, COP bought 19% of Lukoil shares, which should boost reserves and production by over 10%, and we estimate its re-entry into Libya should raise its oil production at an attractive cost.

- Risks to our opinion and target price include geopolitical risk associated with COP's international operations, an inability to achieve upstream production targets, and operational risk from large development projects.

- A blend of our DCF (assuming a WACC of 8.41% and a terminal growth rate of 3%) and relative valuations leads to our 12-month target price of $77. This represents an expected enterprise value of about 4.2X our 2006 EBITDA estimate, a discount to peers.

Qualitative Risk Assessment

LOW | MEDIUM | HIGH

Our risk assessment reflects the company's diversified and strong business profile in volatile, cyclical and capital intensive segments of the energy industry. While COP has a history of aggressive acquisition activity, we believe that its earnings stability is good and that its corporate governance practices are sound.

Quantitative Evaluations

S&P Quality Ranking **B+**

D | C | B- | B | B+ | A- | A | A+

Relative Strength Rank **WEAK**

25

LOWEST = 1 HIGHEST = 99

Revenue/Earnings Data

Revenue (Million $)

	1Q	2Q	3Q	4Q	Year
2006	47,927	48,476	48,400	--	--
2005	38,918	42,614	49,659	51,258	183,364
2004	29,800	31,886	34,741	40,100	136,916
2003	27,077	25,347	26,493	25,830	105,097
2002	8,431	10,414	14,557	23,346	57,224
2001	4,904	5,000	6,159	9,964	26,868

Earnings Per Share ($)

	1Q	2Q	3Q	4Q	Year
2006	2.34	3.09	2.31	**E**2.36	**E**10.47
2005	2.06	2.21	2.68	2.69	9.63
2004	1.16	1.44	1.44	1.76	5.79
2003	0.93	0.79	0.91	0.74	3.53
2002	-0.14	0.48	-0.06	0.43	0.74
2001	0.96	1.20	0.67	0.21	2.79

Fiscal year ended Dec. 31. Next earnings report expected: Late January. EPS Estimates based on S&P Operating Earnings; historical GAAP earnings are as reported.

Dividend Data (Dates: mm/dd Payment Date: mm/dd/yy)

Amount ($)	Date Decl.	Ex-Div. Date	Stk. of Record	Payment Date
0.360	02/10	02/16	02/21	03/01/06
0.360	05/10	05/18	05/22	06/01/06
0.360	07/12	07/27	07/31	09/01/06
0.360	10/04	10/27	10/31	12/01/06

Dividends have been paid since 1934. Source: Company reports.

ConocoPhillips

Business Summary October 31, 2006

CORPORATE OVERVIEW. On August 30, 2002, Phillips Petroleum and Conoco merged, creating ConocoPhillips (COP), the third largest oil company in the U.S. COP operates in six operating segments: exploration and production (E&P; 27% of 2005 sales, 62% of 2005 net income); refining and marketing (R&M; 71%, 31%); midstream (2%, 5%); Lukoil Investment; chemicals; and emerging businesses.

We estimate COP's three-year (2003-2005) organic reserve replacement rate (including equity affiliates) at 104%. Proved crude oil reserves (excluding equity affiliates) rose 5.3%, to 3.336 billion barrels (75% developed) in 2005. Proved natural gas reserves (excluding equity affiliates) declined 1.9%, to 16.513 trillion cubic feet (Tcf; 86% developed) in 2005. Crude oil production rose to 907,000 barrels per day (b/d) in 2005, from 905,000 b/d in 2004. Natural gas liquids (NGL) production increased to 91,000 b/d in 2005, from 84,000 b/d in 2004. Natural gas production declined to 3.270 billion cubic feet (Bcf) per day in 2005, from 3.317 Bcf per day in 2004. The average worldwide sales price for crude oil was $49.87 per barrel in 2005, and $6.30 per thousand cubic feet (Mcf) for natural gas. Three-year (2003-2005) production costs averaged $4.07 per barrel oil equivalent (boe).

As of December 31, 2005, COP owned or had interests in 12 U.S. refineries, five European refineries, and one refinery in Malaysia, with a capacity of 2.61 million b/d. In April 2005, COP unveiled a five year $3 billion program to expand its ability to refine heavy-sour crude oils. At year-end 2005, gasoline and distillates were sold through approximately 13,600 branded outlets in the U.S. (under Phillips 66, Conoco and 76 brands), Europe and Asia Pacific (under the JET and ProJET brands).

Company Financials

Per Share Data ($) Year Ended Dec. 31	**2005**	**2004**	**2003**	**2002**	**2001**	**2000**	**1999**	**1998**	**1997**	**1996**
Tangible Book Value	25.49	18.53	12.85	9.91	14.07	10.77	8.06	7.51	8.25	7.28
Cash Flow	12.63	8.49	5.90	5.31	5.14	5.94	2.97	2.96	3.44	4.27
Earnings	9.63	5.79	3.53	0.74	2.79	3.63	1.20	0.46	1.81	2.48
S&P Core Earnings	9.72	5.88	3.43	0.64	2.60	NA	NA	NA	NA	NA
Dividends	1.18	0.90	0.82	0.74	0.70	0.68	0.68	0.68	0.67	0.63
Payout Ratio	12%	15%	23%	101%	25%	19%	57%	149%	37%	25%
Prices:High	71.48	45.61	33.02	32.05	34.00	35.00	28.63	26.63	26.13	22.94
Prices:Low	41.40	32.15	26.80	22.02	25.00	17.97	18.84	20.09	18.69	15.56
P/E Ratio:High	7	8	9	44	12	10	24	59	14	9
P/E Ratio:Low	4	6	8	30	9	5	16	44	10	6

Income Statement Analysis (Million $)	2005	2004	2003	2002	2001	2000	1999	1998	1997	1996
Revenue	183,364	135,076	104,196	56,748	26,868	21,113	13,751	11,545	15,210	15,731
Operating Income	24,077	17,033	11,866	4,571	8,393	5,528	2,452	1,630	2,748	2,730
Depreciation, Depletion and Amortization	4,253	3,798	3,485	4,446	1,391	1,179	902	1,302	863	941
Interest Expense	497	546	864	614	391	422	332	253	280	250
Pretax Income	23,580	14,401	8,337	2,164	3,302	3,769	1,185	421	1,900	2,172
Effective Tax Rate	42.0%	43.5%	44.9%	67.0%	50.2%	50.6%	48.6%	43.7%	49.5%	40.0%
Net Income	13,640	8,107	4,593	714	1,643	1,862	609	237	959	1,303
S&P Core Earnings	13,753	8,241	4,697	618	1,533	NA	NA	NA	NA	NA

Balance Sheet & Other Financial Data (Million $)	2005	2004	2003	2002	2001	2000	1999	1998	1997	1996
Cash	2,214	1,387	490	307	142	149	138	97.0	163	615
Current Assets	19,612	15,021	11,192	10,903	4,363	2,606	2,773	2,349	2,648	3,306
Total Assets	106,999	92,861	82,455	76,836	35,217	20,509	15,201	14,216	13,860	13,548
Current Liabilities	21,359	15,586	14,011	12,816	4,542	3,492	2,520	2,132	2,445	3,137
Long Term Debt	10,758	14,370	16,340	19,267	9,295	7,272	4,921	4,756	2,775	2,555
Common Equity	52,731	42,723	34,366	29,517	14,340	6,093	4,549	4,219	4,814	4,251
Total Capital	76,137	68,583	60,113	57,796	27,650	15,259	10,950	10,292	9,497	9,286
Capital Expenditures	11,620	9,496	6,169	4,388	3,085	2,022	1,690	2,052	2,043	1,544
Cash Flow	17,893	11,905	8,078	5,160	3,034	3,041	1,511	1,539	1,822	2,244
Current Ratio	0.9	1.0	0.8	0.9	1.0	0.7	1.1	1.1	1.1	1.1
% Long Term Debt of Capitalization	14.1	21.0	27.2	33.3	33.6	47.7	44.9	46.2	29.2	27.5
% Return on Assets	13.6	9.2	5.8	1.3	5.9	10.4	4.1	1.7	7.0	10.2
% Return on Equity	28.6	21.0	14.4	3.3	16.1	35.0	13.9	5.2	21.2	35.0

Data as orig reptd.; bef. results of disc opers/spec. items. Per share data adj. for stk. divs.; EPS diluted. E-Estimated. NA-Not Available. NM-Not Meaningful. NR-Not Ranked. UR-Under Review.

Office: 600 N Dairy Ashford St, Houston, TX 77079-1175.
Telephone: 281-293-1000.
Website: http://www.conocophillips.com
Chrmn, Pres & CEO: J.J. Mulva

EVP & CFO: J.A. Carrig
SVP & General Counsel: S.F. Gates
VP & Cntlr: R.C. Berney
Investor Contact: G. Russell (212-207-1996)

Board of Directors: R. L. Armitage, N. H. Auchinleck, N. R. Augustine, J. Copeland, K. M. Duberstein, R. R. Harkin, L. D. Horner, C. C. Krulak, H. McGraw, III, J. J. Mulva, H. Norvik, W. K. Reilly, W. R. Rhodes, J. S. Roy, B. S. Shackouls, V. J. Tschinkel, K. C. Turner, W. E. Wade Jr.

Founded: 1917
Domicile: Delaware
Employees: 38,000

STANDARD & POOR'S

Consolidated Edison Inc.

S&P Recommendation HOLD ★★★★★	Price	12-Mo. Target Price	Investment Style
	$48.23 (as of Oct 27, 2006)	$45.00	Large-Cap Value

GICS Sector Utilities
Sub-Industry Multi-Utilities

Comment This electric and gas utility holding company serves parts of New York, New Jersey and Pennsylvania.

Key Stock Statistics (Source S&P, Vickers, company reports)

52-Wk Range	$48.70–41.17	S&P Oper. EPS 2006E	2.90	P/E on S&P Oper. EPS 2006E	16.6	Dividend Rate/Share	$2.30
Trailing 12-Month EPS	$2.96	S&P Oper. EPS 2007E	3.13	Common Shares Outstg. (M)	246.5	Yield (%)	4.77
Trailing 12-Month P/E	16.3	S&P Core EPS 2006E	2.63	Market Capitalization(B)	$11.887	Beta	0.10
$10K Invested 5 Yrs Ago	$15,703	S&P Core EPS 2007E	2.76	Institutional Ownership (%)	48	S&P Credit Rating	A

Price Performance

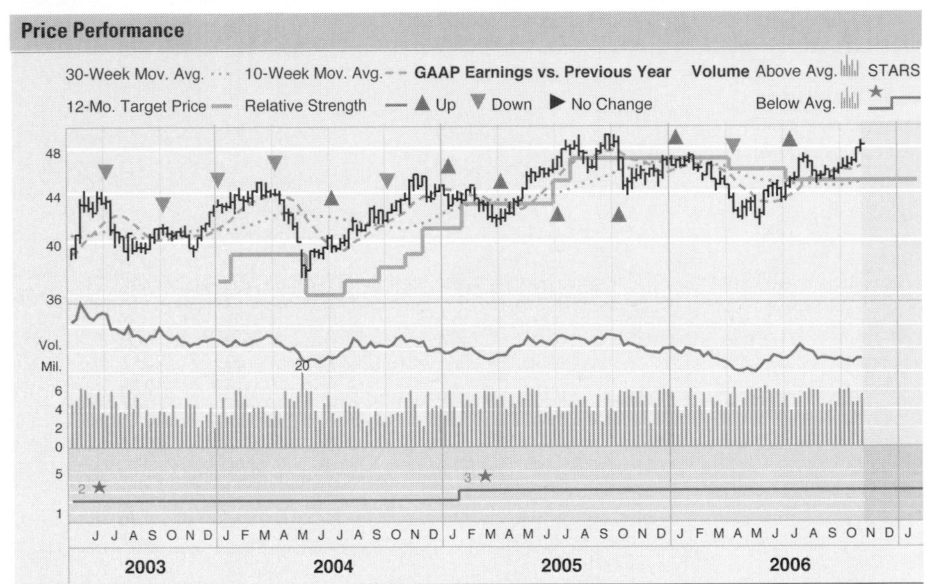

Options: ASE, CBOE, P, Ph

Analysis prepared by **Justin McCann** on September 27, 2006, when the stock traded at **$ 46.65**.

Highlights

- After an anticipated 3% decline in 2006, we expect EPS to increase about 8% in 2007. While results in 2006 should benefit from a full year of the April 2005 gas, steam and electric rate increases, we believe this will be more than offset by a return to normal weather (in contrast to the much warmer than normal weather in 2005), and from the costs related to the extended power outages during the July heatwave. We expect ED to spend more than $1.8 billion on its electric infrastructure in 2006.
- We see 2007 EPS being aided by the continuing strength in the local New York economy and the rate increases that will take effect next April. We also expect EPS in the final quarter of 2006 and in 2007 to be restricted by more shares outstanding. While ED issued a small amount of new equity in 2005, it issued nearly 9.72 million shares in late September 2006, for proceeds of approximately $450 million.
- In March 2005, the New York Public Service Commission approved a three-year electric rate plan for Con Edison of New York's, under which rates were increased $104.6 million, effective April 1, 2005, and would be increased $220.4 million effective April 1, 2007.

Investment Rationale/Risk

- The stock has underperformed ED's electric and gas utility peers year to date reflecting, in our view, the reduced EPS outlook for 2006, as well as a recent revision to the outlook for its A credit rating from stable to negative from Standard & Poor's Rating Services (an entity that operates separately from S&P Equity Research). We expect the company to increase the dividend at an annual rate of around 1%.
- Risks to our recommendation and target price include a significant weakening of the economy in the utility's service territory, the emergence of an unfavorable regulatory environment, and a sharp decline in the average P/E multiple of the peer group as a whole.
- Given a dividend yield (recently at 4.9%) that is well above the industry average (recently at 3.9%), we believe the shares should be valued at a premium to peers. However, in light of a higher interest rate environment, we expect a contraction in the peer P/E multiple over the next 12 months, and expect the shares to trade at a modest premium-to-peers P/E multiple of 14.4X our EPS estimate for 2007. Our 12-month target price is $45.

Qualitative Risk Assessment

LOW	MEDIUM	HIGH

Our risk assessment reflects our view of the company's strong and steady cash flows from regulated electric and gas utility operations, strong balance sheet and A credit rating, a healthy economy in its service territory, and a historically supportive regulatory environment.

Quantitative Evaluations

S&P Quality Ranking B+

D	C	B-	B	B+	A-	A	A+

Relative Strength Rank MODERATE

61

LOWEST = 1 HIGHEST = 99

Revenue/Earnings Data

Revenue (Million $)

	1Q	2Q	3Q	4Q	Year
2006	3,317	2,555	--	--	--
2005	2,801	2,406	3,375	3,108	11,690
2004	2,679	2,164	2,734	2,182	9,758
2003	2,570	2,175	2,801	2,279	9,827
2002	2,099	1,900	2,539	2,057	8,482
2001	2,886	2,112	2,693	1,943	9,634

Earnings Per Share ($)

	1Q	2Q	3Q	4Q	Year
2006	0.74	0.51	E1.10	E0.55	E2.90
2005	0.75	0.48	1.17	0.59	2.99
2004	0.69	0.38	1.03	0.22	2.32
2003	0.72	0.29	1.16	0.19	2.36
2002	0.78	0.46	1.33	0.56	3.13
2001	0.84	0.48	1.30	0.59	3.21

Fiscal year ended Dec. 31. Next earnings report expected: NA. EPS Estimates based on S&P Operating Earnings; historical GAAP earnings are as reported.

Dividend Data (Dates: mm/dd Payment Date: mm/dd/yy)

Amount ($)	Date Decl.	Ex-Div. Date	Stk. of Record	Payment Date
0.575	01/26	02/13	02/15	03/15/06
0.575	04/20	05/11	05/15	06/15/06
0.575	07/20	08/14	08/16	09/15/06
0.575	10/19	11/13	11/15	12/15/06

Dividends have been paid since 1885. Source: Company reports.

Consolidated Edison Inc.

Business Summary September 27, 2006

CORPORATE OVERVIEW. Consolidated Edison is a holding company with electric and gas utilities serving a territory that includes New York City (except part of Queens), most of Westchester County, southeastern New York state, northern New Jersey, and northeastern Pennsylvania. Although the company also has some competitive subsidiaries that participate in energy-related businesses, we expect the two regulated utilities to provide substantially all of ED's earnings over the next few years.

MARKET PROFILE. The company's principal business operations are Con Edison of New York's regulated electric, gas and steam utility operations, and Orange and Rockland Utilities' regulated electric and gas utility operations. In 2005, electric revenues accounted for 64.9% of consolidated sales (68.2% in 2004); gas revenues 15.9% (15.4%); non-utility revenues 13.6% (10.8%); and steam revenues 5.5% (5.6%). At December 31, 2005, the distribution system of Consolidated Edison Company of New York had about 36,047 miles of overhead distribution lines and around 93,612 miles of underground distribution lines. The distribution system of O&R had about 3,632 miles of overhead distribution lines, and 1,485 miles of underground distribution lines.

The company's Con Edison of New York (CENY) unit provides electric service (75% of CENY's operating revenues in 2005) to about 3.2 million customers and gas service (18%) to around 1.1 million customers in New York City and Westchester County. It also provides steam service (7%) in parts of Manhattan to around 2,000 customers (mostly large office buildings, apartment houses and hospitals). Most of the electricity sold by CENY in 2005 was purchased under firm power contracts (primarily with non-utility generators) or through the wholesale electricity market administered by the New York Independent System Operator (NYISO). We expect this to continue for the foreseeable future.

The company's O&R unit provides electric and gas service in southeastern New York and adjacent areas of eastern Pennsylvania, and electric service in areas of New Jersey adjacent to its New York service territory. In 2005, electric sales accounted for 72% of its operating revenues and gas sales, 28%.

Company Financials

Per Share Data ($) Year Ended Dec. 31	**2005**	**2004**	**2003**	**2002**	**2001**	**2000**	**1999**	**1998**	**1997**	**1996**
Tangible Book Value	30.69	29.86	29.09	25.40	24.23	23.50	22.41	25.19	24.52	23.69
Earnings	2.99	2.32	2.36	3.13	3.21	2.74	3.13	3.04	2.95	2.93
S&P Core Earnings	2.54	1.78	1.66	0.50	0.66	NA	NA	NA	NA	NA
Dividends	2.28	2.26	2.24	2.22	2.20	2.18	2.14	2.12	2.10	2.08
Payout Ratio	76%	97%	95%	71%	69%	80%	68%	70%	71%	71%
Prices:High	49.29	45.59	46.02	45.40	43.37	39.50	53.44	56.13	41.50	34.75
Prices:Low	41.10	37.23	36.55	32.65	31.44	26.19	33.56	39.06	27.00	25.88
P/E Ratio:High	16	20	20	15	14	14	17	18	14	12
P/E Ratio:Low	14	16	15	10	10	10	11	13	9	9

Income Statement Analysis (Million $)	2005	2004	2003	2002	2001	2000	1999	1998	1997	1996
Revenue	11,090	9,758	9,827	8,482	9,634	9,431	7,491	7,093	7,121	6,960
Depreciation	584	551	529	495	526	586	526	519	503	496
Maintenance	NA	NA	353	387	430	458	438	477	475	459
Fixed Charges Coverage	3.19	2.64	3.13	3.25	3.46	3.06	4.03	4.24	4.05	4.25
Construction Credits	16.0	43.0	27.0	14.0	9.00	8.00	6.00	4.00	7.00	5.00
Effective Tax Rate	34.6%	33.1%	37.5%	35.6%	38.9%	34.0%	34.3%	35.7%	34.8%	36.4%
Net Income	732	549	525	680	696	596	715	730	713	694
S&P Core Earnings	621	421	370	106	141	NA	NA	NA	NA	NA

Balance Sheet & Other Financial Data (Million $)	2005	2004	2003	2002	2001	2000	1999	1998	1997	1996
Gross Property	21,467	20,394	19,294	18,000	16,630	17,021	16,088	16,132	15,659	15,352
Capital Expenditures	1,617	1,359	1,292	1,216	1,104	986	695	626	669	724
Net Property	17,112	16,106	15,225	13,330	12,136	11,786	11,354	11,406	11,267	11,067
Capitalization:Long Term Debt	7,641	6,807	6,769	6,206	5,542	5,447	4,560	4,087	4,229	4,281
Capitalization:% Long Term Debt	50.5	48.5	51.3	50.3	48.3	48.8	44.5	39.4	40.4	41.4
Capitalization:Preferred	Nil	Nil	Nil	Nil	250	250	250	250	233	323
Capitalization:% Preferred	Nil	Nil	Nil	Nil	2.18	2.24	2.44	2.41	3.00	3.10
Capitalization:Common	7,477	7,234	6,423	5,921	5,690	5,471	5,448	6,026	5,930	5,728
Capitalization:% Common	49.5	51.5	48.7	48.0	49.6	49.0	53.1	58.1	56.6	55.4
Total Capital	18,804	17,806	16,406	15,037	13,835	13,602	12,666	12,911	12,949	12,793
% Operating Ratio	90.3	90.3	88.8	74.1	88.1	117.8	86.0	85.1	85.3	85.4
% Earned on Net Property	7.0	5.9	6.4	8.3	9.4	8.8	9.0	9.3	9.4	9.3
% Return on Revenue	6.3	5.6	5.3	8.0	7.2	6.3	9.5	10.3	10.0	10.0
% Return on Invested Capital	6.7	5.9	7.3	7.8	8.3	7.7	8.2	11.1	8.1	8.0
% Return on Common Equity	10.0	7.9	8.5	11.5	12.2	10.7	12.2	11.9	11.9	12.2

Data as orig reptd.; bef. results of disc opers/spec. items. Per share data adj. for stk. divs.; EPS diluted. E-Estimated. NA-Not Available. NM-Not Meaningful. NR-Not Ranked. UR-Under Review.

Office: 4 Irving Place, New York, NY 10003.
Telephone: 212-460-4600.
Email: corpcom@coned.com
Website: http://www.coned.com

Chrmn: E.R. McGrath
Pres & CEO: K. Burke
EVP & CFO: J.S. Freilich
VP & Treas: J.P. Oates

General Counsel: C.E. McTiernan
Board of Directors: K. Burke, V. A. Calarco, G. Campbell, Jr., G. J. Davis, M. J. Del Giudice, E. V. Futter, S. Hernandez-Pinero, P. W. Likins, E. R. McGrath, F. V. Salerno, S. R. Volk

Founded: 1884
Domicile: New York
Employees: 14,537

STANDARD &POOR'S

CONSOL Energy Inc.

S&P Recommendation BUY ★★★★★ | **Price** $37.58 (as of Oct 27, 2006) | **12-Mo. Target Price** $45.00 | **Investment Style** Mid-Cap Value

GICS Sector Energy
Sub-Industry Coal & Consumable Fuels

Comment This Pittsburgh-based company is a major producer of high-bituminous coal and coalbed methane gas.

Key Stock Statistics (Source S&P, Vickers, company reports)

52-Wk Range	$49.09–26.80	S&P Oper. EPS 2006E	2.14	P/E on S&P Oper. EPS 2006E	17.6	Dividend Rate/Share	$0.28
Trailing 12-Month EPS	$1.97	S&P Oper. EPS 2007E	3.05	Common Shares Outstg. (M)	183.4	Yield (%)	0.75
Trailing 12-Month P/E	19.1	S&P Core EPS 2006E	2.11	Market Capitalization(B)	$6.890	Beta	1.42
$10K Invested 5 Yrs Ago	$31,247	S&P Core EPS 2007E	3.05	Institutional Ownership (%)	93	S&P Credit Rating	BB

Price Performance

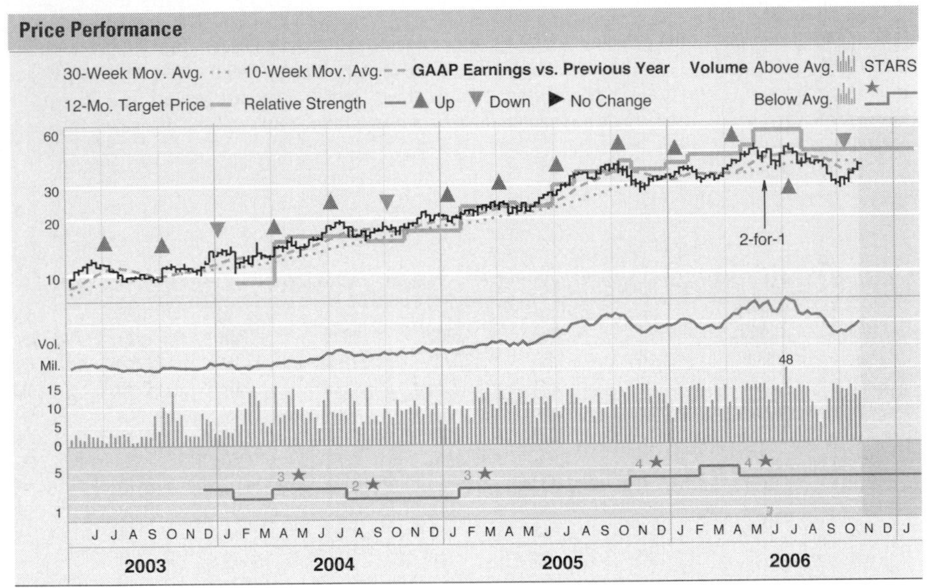

Options: ASE, CBOE, P, Ph

Analysis prepared by **John F. Hingher, CFA** on July 31, 2006, when the stock traded at **$ 39.79**.

Highlights

- We see revenues growing nearly 14% in 2006, as we expect higher prices for steam and metallurgical coal, as well as improved volumes due to the recent permitting of mines, and a reduction in production-related difficulties in northern Appalachia. Longer term, while we foresee difficulties in significantly increasing coal volumes due to deteriorating geological conditions, we expect solid demand and price growth for northern Appalachian coal as more scrubber capacity comes on line.
- In light of the high fixed costs and resulting earnings leverage of the coal mining industry, we see coal segment margins widening in 2006, primarily as a result of the volume and price increases.
- We estimate 2006 income before extraordinary items of $444.7 million, or $2.40 per share, including projected stock option expense. Our 2006 Standard & Poor's Core EPS projection is $2.36, with the difference from our operating estimate primarily reflecting pension and post-retirement adjustments.

Investment Rationale/Risk

- We think CNX will benefit from a steady pricing environment in the near term and from rising market share for northern Appalachian coal over the longer term. Demand for steam coal from utilities should increase, as more coal-powered generation comes online and supply has been somewhat hampered by rail disruptions. While we think CNX faces a challenge in improving coal segment profits given that difficult geological conditions could reduce volumes and offset the expected higher pricing, we believe this is overly discounted in the stock price.
- Risks to our opinion and target price include lower than anticipated increases in coal and/or gas prices, transportation problems, and lower production volumes from existing mines.
- CNX recently traded in line with its peer group average based on our forward 12-month EPS estimate of $2.51 and at an enterprise value of 7.4X our estimate of 2006 EBITDA, versus a peer multiple of 8.4X. Our 12-month target price is $45, implying an 8.4X EV/2006 EBITDA estimate multiple, in line with the peer group average.

Qualitative Risk Assessment

LOW | **MEDIUM** | HIGH

Our risk assessment reflects the cyclical nature of the coal market, corporate governance practices regarding takeover defense, and the heavily regulated nature of the industry and its utilities end market; offset by expected benefits from the pricing cycle and rising market share.

Quantitative Evaluations

S&P Quality Ranking NR

D | C | B- | B | B+ | A- | A | A+

Relative Strength Rank STRONG

78

LOWEST = 1 HIGHEST = 99

Revenue/Earnings Data

Revenue (Million $)

	1Q	2Q	3Q	4Q	Year
2006	985.9	932.3	843.4	--	--
2005	817.0	817.2	879.9	969.1	3,483
2004	650.9	674.6	659.9	791.4	2,777
2003	559.8	556.5	552.2	554.0	2,222
2002	552.0	536.3	546.4	554.6	2,184
2001	--	--	--	--	2,368

Earnings Per Share ($)

2006	0.67	0.57	0.27	E0.64	E2.14
2005	0.41	0.22	2.02	0.47	3.13
2004	0.18	0.15	-0.07	0.37	0.64
2003	0.02	0.07	-0.04	-0.14	-0.05
2002	0.04	0.06	-0.05	0.03	0.08
2001	0.03	0.19	0.64	0.31	1.17

Fiscal year ended Dec. 31. Next earnings report expected: Late January. EPS Estimates based on S&P Operating Earnings; historical GAAP earnings are as reported.

Dividend Data (Dates: mm/dd Payment Date: mm/dd/yy)

Amount ($)	Date Decl.	Ex-Div. Date	Stk. of Record	Payment Date
0.140	04/28	05/05	05/09	05/30/06
2-for-1 Stk.	05/04	06/01	05/15	05/31/06
0.070	07/28	08/08	08/10	08/28/06
0.070	10/27	11/06	11/08	11/24/06

Dividends have been paid since 1999. Source: Company reports.

Please read the Required Disclosures and Analyst Certification on the last page of this report.

CONSOL Energy Inc.

Business Summary July 31, 2006

CORPORATE OVERVIEW. Through expansion and acquisitions, CONSOL Energy has grown from a single-fuel mining company formed in 1860 into a multi-energy producer of coal and gas. CNX produces high Btu coal and gas, two fuels that collectively generate two thirds of all U.S. electric power, from reserves located mainly east of the Mississippi River.

The coal segment (CNX Coal) has 17 mining complexes in the U.S., and sells steam coal to power generators and metallurgical coal to metal and coke producers. The company had an estimated 4.5 billion tons of proven and probable coal reserves at the end of 2005, nearly all of which was located in underground mines. About 60% of CNX's reserves are found in northern Appalachia, with 17% in the Midwest, 10% in central Appalachia, 10% in the western U.S., and 3% in western Canada. The company is a major fuel supplier to the electric power industry in the Northeast quadrant of the U.S. Coal produced at CNX's mines is transported to customers via railroad cars, barges, trucks and conveyor belts, or by a combination of such methods. In 2005, the company sold 68.9 million produced tons of coal, up from 67.3 million tons in 2004. Approximately 91% of coal produced in 2005 was sold under contracts with terms of one year or more. The average sales price per produced ton sold in 2005 was $35.54, versus $29.84 in 2004. In 2005, one customer, Allegheny Energy, accounted for 10% of total company revenue.

CONSOL Energy owns 81.5% of CNX Gas Corporation, which is one of the largest U.S. producers of coalbed methane (CBM), with daily gas production of 173 MMcf. CBM is pipeline quality gas that is found in coal seams, usually in formations at depths of less than 2,500 feet versus conventional natural gas fields with depths of up to 15,000 feet. At the end of 2005, CNX Gas had 1.1 Tcf of proved CBM reserves, of which approximately 49% was developed, and more than 2,000 active wells connected to over 1,000 miles of gathering lines. In 2005, the company sold 54.4 Bcf of gas at an average price of $6.00, versus 54.6 Bcf at $5.04 in 2004.

Company Financials

Per Share Data ($) Year Ended Dec. 31	2005	2004	2003	2002	2001	2000	1999	1998	1997	1996
Tangible Book Value	5.54	2.59	NM	1.03	2.23	1.62	1.59	NA	NA	NA
Cash Flow	4.54	2.17	1.40	1.74	2.71	2.24	1.24	NA	NA	NA
Earnings	3.13	0.64	-0.05	0.08	1.17	0.68	0.31	NA	NA	NA
S&P Core Earnings	2.05	0.69	0.04	0.03	0.98	NA	NA	NA	NA	NA
Dividends	0.28	0.28	0.28	0.42	0.56	0.56	Nil	NA	NA	NA
Payout Ratio	9%	44%	NM	NM	48%	83%	Nil	NA	NA	NA
Prices:High	39.91	21.95	13.40	14.16	21.24	14.00	8.00	NA	NA	NA
Prices:Low	18.58	10.12	7.28	4.90	9.15	4.97	4.81	NA	NA	NA
P/E Ratio:High	13	35	NM	NM	18	21	NM	NA	NA	NA
P/E Ratio:Low	6	16	NM	NM	8	7	NM	NA	NA	NA

Income Statement Analysis (Million $)	2005	2004	2003	2002	2001	2000	1999	1998	1997	1996
Revenue	3,483	2,777	2,222	2,184	2,368	2,159	1,110	NA	NA	NA
Operating Income	617	308	246	268	418	599	409	NA	NA	NA
Depreciation	262	280	242	263	243	250	121	NA	NA	NA
Interest Expense	27.3	31.4	34.5	46.2	57.6	55.0	30.5	NA	NA	NA
Pretax Income	655	82.6	-33.5	-40.4	240	107	40.2	NA	NA	NA
Effective Tax Rate	9.83%	NM	NM	NM	23.6%	NM	0.30%	NA	NA	NA
Net Income	581	115	-12.6	11.7	184	107	40.0	NA	NA	NA
S&P Core Earnings	381	125	6.95	3.70	154	NA	NA	NA	NA	NA

Balance Sheet & Other Financial Data (Million $)	2005	2004	2003	2002	2001	2000	1999	1998	1997	1996
Cash	341	6.42	6.51	11.5	16.6	8.20	23.6	NA	NA	NA
Current Assets	998	470	471	623	566	578	623	NA	NA	NA
Total Assets	5,088	4,196	4,319	4,293	3,895	3,866	3,875	NA	NA	NA
Current Liabilities	804	705	825	814	934	953	884	NA	NA	NA
Long Term Debt	438	426	442	488	231	301	313	NA	NA	NA
Common Equity	1,025	469	291	162	352	254	255	NA	NA	NA
Total Capital	1,557	895	733	650	583	555	567	NA	NA	NA
Capital Expenditures	523	411	291	295	214	143	105	NA	NA	NA
Cash Flow	843	396	230	275	427	357	161	NA	NA	NA
Current Ratio	1.2	0.7	0.6	0.8	0.6	0.6	0.7	NA	NA	NA
% Long Term Debt of Capitalization	28.2	47.6	60.3	75.1	39.6	54.1	55.1	NA	NA	NA
% Net Income of Revenue	17.2	4.1	NM	NM	7.8	4.9	3.6	NA	NA	NA
% Return on Assets	12.5	2.7	NM	NM	4.7	2.7	NM	NA	NA	NA
% Return on Equity	77.7	30.3	NM	NM	60.6	42.0	NM	NA	NA	NA

Data as orig reptd.; bef. results of disc opers/spec. items. Per share data adj. for stk. divs.; EPS diluted. E-Estimated. NA-Not Available. NM-Not Meaningful. NR-Not Ranked. UR-Under Review.

Office: 1800 Washington Road, Pittsburgh, PA 15241.
Telephone: 412-831-4000.
Website: http://www.consolenergy.com
Chrmn: J.L. Whitmire

Pres & CEO: J.B. Harvey
COO: P.B. Lilly
Investor Contact: W.J. Lyons (412-831-4000)
EVP & CFO: W.J. Lyons

Board of Directors: J. Altmeyer, Sr., W. E. Davis, R. K. Gupta, P. A. Hammick, D. C. Hardesty, Jr., J. B. Harvey, W. P. Powell, J. L. Whitmire, J. T. Williams

Founded: 1991
Domicile: Delaware
Employees: 7,257

STANDARD &POOR'S

Constellation Brands Inc.

S&P Recommendation HOLD ★★★★★ | **Price** $27.60 (as of Oct 27, 2006) | **12-Mo. Target Price** $31.00 | **Investment Style** Mid-Cap Value

GICS Sector Consumer Staples
Sub-Industry Distillers & Vintners

Comment This leading international producer and marketer of alcoholic beverages has a broad portfolio of wine, imported beer and distilled spirits brands.

Key Stock Statistics (Source S&P, Vickers, company reports)

52-Wk Range	**$29.09–22.56**	S&P Oper. EPS 2007**E**	**1.74**	P/E on S&P Oper. EPS 2007**E**	**15.9**	Dividend Rate/Share	**Nil**
Trailing 12-Month EPS	**$1.34**	S&P Oper. EPS 2008**E**	**NA**	Common Shares Outstg. (M)	**233.4**	Yield (%)	**Nil**
Trailing 12-Month P/E	**20.6**	S&P Core EPS 2007**E**	**1.74**	Market Capitalization(B)	**$5.784**	Beta	**0.35**
$10K Invested 5 Yrs Ago	**$24,989**	S&P Core EPS 2008**E**	**NA**	Institutional Ownership (%)	**77**	S&P Credit Rating	**BB**

Price Performance

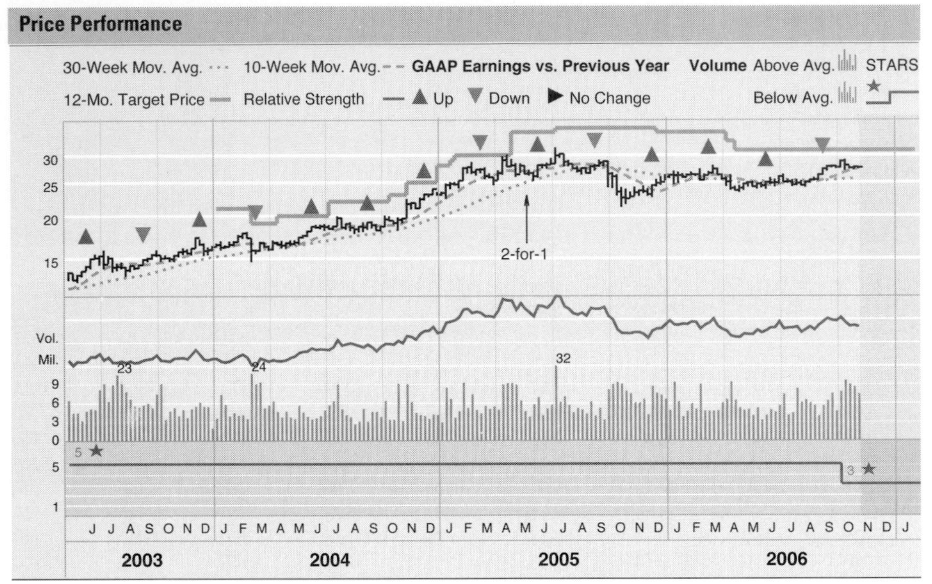

Options: ASE, CBOE, P, Ph

Analysis prepared by **Raymond Mathis** on October 17, 2006, when the stock traded at **$ 27.53**.

Highlights

- We expect FY 07 (Feb.) net revenue to advance 15%, benefiting from growth in global wine sales, Australian and U.S. wine exports, and a stronger fine wines portfolio following the purchase of Mondavi, and the acquisition of Vincor. We see heavy competition in the U.K. market limiting growth in the branded and wholesale businesses, and competitive pressures continuing in the Australian market. We look for spirits sales to strengthen as STZ invests in new products and seeks acquisitions, and we see high single digit growth in beer volumes.
- We look for operating margin expansion in late FY 07 on well controlled SG&A expenses and likely distribution and sourcing synergies. We expect some pressure on margins from the expansion of the U.K. wholesale business and continued brand investments behind Corona and Mondavi's lead brands. We see higher interest expense due to acquisition financing.
- With an expected effective tax rate of 39%, reflecting the sale of a subsidiary, and a higher anticipated share count, we project a rise in FY 07 operating EPS, to $1.74, excluding restructuring charges and potential integration costs for Vincor. Including charges, we see EPS of $1.38.

Investment Rationale/Risk

- We believe the MOND and VN acquisitions will support strong growth in the long term, as STZ's distribution provides significant reach for the major acquired brands. We see healthy global demand for premium wines continuing, and U.S. wine exports benefiting from a relatively weak U.S. dollar. We expect the proposed joint venture to distribute Modelo brands nationwide, to further boost Corona, but we expect these results to be deconsolidated. We look for a turnaround in grape supply issues in 2007, and believe U.S. and U.K. competitive pressures will ease over the longer term.
- Risks to our recommendation and target price include continued pricing pressures in the U.S. wine market, and resistance to further beer price increases. We are concerned about potential integration risk with regard to MOND and VN.
- Our discounted cash flow analysis, which assumes a 9% discount rate and 11% annual sales growth for five years, calculates intrinsic value of $33. Combining our DCF model with an above-historical-average P/E multiple of 17X applied to our FY 07 EPS estimate of $1.74, our 12-month target price is $31.

Qualitative Risk Assessment

LOW | MEDIUM | HIGH

STZ is a large-cap company in an industry that has demonstrated stable revenue streams. This is only partially offset by our corporate governance concerns relating to STZ's dual class stock structure with unequal voting rights.

Quantitative Evaluations

S&P Quality Ranking **B+**

D | C | B- | B | **B+** | A- | A | A+

Relative Strength Rank **MODERATE**

45

LOWEST = 1 HIGHEST = 99

Revenue/Earnings Data

Revenue (Million $)

	1Q	2Q	3Q	4Q	Year
2007	1,156	1,715	--	--	--
2006	1,097	1,192	1,267	1,048	4,603
2005	927.3	1,037	1,086	1,038	4,088
2004	772.8	911.1	987.3	881.3	3,552
2003	650.4	689.8	738.4	653.0	2,732
2002	642.1	740.8	764.1	673.5	2,821

Earnings Per Share ($)

	1Q	2Q	3Q	4Q	Year
2007	0.36	0.28	**E**0.50	**E**0.45	**E**1.74
2006	0.32	0.34	0.46	0.24	1.36
2005	0.23	0.35	0.42	0.20	1.19
2004	0.21	0.17	0.37	0.28	1.03
2003	0.20	0.26	0.35	0.28	1.10
2002	0.14	0.21	0.28	0.16	0.79

Fiscal year ended Feb. 28. Next earnings report expected: Early January. EPS Estimates based on S&P Operating Earnings; historical GAAP earnings are as reported.

Dividend Data

No cash dividends have been paid.

The McGraw-Hill Companies

Constellation Brands Inc.

Business Summary October 17, 2006

CORPORATE OVERVIEW. Through an aggressive acquisition program over the past few years, Constellation Brands (formerly Canandaigua Brands) has become a leading international producer and marketer of alcoholic beverages in North America, Europe and Australia. With the April 2003 acquisition of BRL Hardy Ltd., Australia's largest producer of wine, STZ became the world's largest wine business. In addition, the Hardy acquisition led STZ to restructure its operating segments into Constellation Wines, and Constellation Beers and Spirits.

Constellation Wines produces and markets table wines, dessert wines and sparkling wines. It is the second largest producer and marketer in the U.S., the largest producer in Canada and Australia, and the largest marketer in the U.K. The company sells wines in the popular, premium, super-premium and ultra-premium categories. The higher category wines are supported by vineyard holdings in California, Canada, Australia, New Zealand and Chile. At the end of FY 06 (Feb.), the company operated 19 wineries in the U.S., 10 in Australia, three in New Zealand, and one in Chile.

STZ has developed a premium wine portfolio through acquisitions since 1999. Leading wine brands include Almaden, Arbor Mist, Vendange, Woodbridge by Robert Mondavi, Hardys, Nobilo, Alice White, Ruffino, Robert Mondavi Private Selection, Blackstone, Ravenswood, Estancia, Franciscan Oakville Estate, Simi and Robert Mondavi Winery brands.

The Constellation Beers and Spirits segment imports and markets a diversified line of beer, and produces, bottles, imports and markets a diversified line of distilled spirits. The company is the largest marketer of imported beer in 25 mostly western states. It distributes six of the top 20 imported beer brands in the U.S.: Corona Extra, the best selling imported beer, Modelo Especial, Corona Light, Pacifico, St. Pauli Girl, and Negra Modelo. It also imports the top-selling Chinese beer, Tsingtao.

Distilled spirits brands are marketed primarily in the value and mid-premium priced category. Principal brands include Balck Velvet, Barton, Skol, Fleischmann's Canadian LTD, Montezuma, Ten High, Chi-Chi's, Mr. Boston, Inver House, and Monte Alban. STZ also sells bulk spirits and other related products and services. The company operates seven facilities for the production of spirits.

Company Financials

Per Share Data ($) Year Ended Feb. 28	**2006**	**2005**	**2004**	**2003**	**2002**	**2001**	**2000**	**1999**	**1998**	**1997**
Tangible Book Value	NM	NM	NM	0.39	NM	NM	NM	NM	1.16	2.42
Cash Flow	1.86	1.59	1.39	1.42	1.08	0.95	0.80	0.67	0.55	0.38
Earnings	1.36	1.19	1.03	1.10	0.79	0.65	0.52	0.41	0.33	0.18
S&P Core Earnings	1.24	1.02	0.96	0.97	0.66	0.54	NA	NA	NA	NA
Dividends	Nil	Nil	Nil	Nil	Nil	Nil	Nil	Nil	Nil	Nil
Payout Ratio	Nil	Nil	Nil	Nil	Nil	Nil	Nil	Nil	Nil	Nil
Calendar Year	2005	2004	2003	2002	2001	2000	1999	1998	1997	1996
Prices:High	31.60	23.91	17.33	16.00	11.63	7.38	7.69	7.47	7.20	4.94
Prices:Low	21.15	14.65	10.95	10.53	6.63	5.05	5.36	4.41	2.73	1.97
P/E Ratio:High	23	20	17	15	15	11	15	18	22	28
P/E Ratio:Low	16	12	11	10	8	8	10	11	8	11

Income Statement Analysis (Million $)										
Revenue	4,603	4,088	3,552	2,732	2,821	2,397	2,340	1,497	1,213	1,135
Operating Income	840	689	601	470	394	315	281	187	150	113
Depreciation	128	104	82.0	60.1	51.9	44.6	40.9	38.6	33.2	31.9
Interest Expense	190	138	145	105	114	109	106	41.5	32.2	34.1
Pretax Income	477	432	344	335	230	162	129	104	84.9	47.8
Effective Tax Rate	31.8%	36.0%	36.0%	39.3%	40.0%	40.0%	40.0%	59.3%	41.0%	42.1%
Net Income	325	276	220	203	138	97.3	77.4	61.9	50.1	27.8
S&P Core Earnings	288	230	199	181	115	80.7	NA	NA	NA	NA

Balance Sheet & Other Financial Data (Million $)										
Cash	10.9	17.6	37.1	13.8	8.96	146	34.3	27.6	1.20	10.0
Current Assets	2,701	2,734	2,071	1,330	1,231	1,191	996	856	564	501
Total Assets	7,401	7,804	5,559	3,196	3,069	2,512	2,349	1,794	1,073	1,020
Current Liabilities	1,298	1,138	1,030	585	595	427	438	832	283	247
Long Term Debt	2,516	3,205	1,779	1,192	1,293	1,307	1,237	415	309	339
Common Equity	2,975	2,780	2,378	1,207	956	616	521	435	415	365
Total Capital	5,862	6,375	4,344	2,544	2,412	2,056	1,874	1,355	783	765
Capital Expenditures	132	120	105	71.6	71.1	68.2	57.7	49.9	31.2	31.6
Cash Flow	444	370	297	263	190	142	118	101	83.2	59.7
Current Ratio	2.1	2.4	2.0	2.3	2.1	2.8	2.3	1.0	2.0	2.0
% Long Term Debt of Capitalization	42.9	50.3	41.0	46.8	53.6	63.6	66.0	30.6	39.5	44.3
% Net Income of Revenue	7.1	6.8	6.2	7.4	4.9	4.1	3.3	4.1	4.1	2.4
% Return on Assets	4.3	4.1	5.0	6.5	4.9	4.0	3.7	4.3	4.8	2.7
% Return on Equity	11.0	10.3	12.1	18.5	17.5	17.1	16.2	14.6	12.8	7.7

Data as orig reptd.; bef. results of disc opers/spec. items. Per share data adj. for stk. divs.; EPS diluted. E-Estimated. NA-Not Available. NM-Not Meaningful. NR-Not Ranked. UR-Under Review.

Office: 370 Woodcliff Dr., Suite 300, Fairport, NY 14450-4238.
Telephone: 585-218-3600.
Website: http://www.cbrands.com
Chrmn & CEO: R. Sands

Pres & COO: R. Sands
EVP & CFO: T.S. Summer
EVP & General Counsel: T.J. Mullin
Secy: D.S. Sorce

Investor Contact: L.M. Schnorr (585-218-3677)
Board of Directors: B. A. Fromberg, J. K. Hauswald, J. A. Locke, III, T. C. McDermott, R. Sands, R. Sands, P. L. Smith

Founded: 1972
Domicile: Delaware
Employees: 7,900

Constellation Energy Group Inc.

STANDARD &POOR'S

S&P Recommendation HOLD ★★★★★

Price $62.40 (as of Oct 31, 2006)

12-Mo. Target Price $67.00

Investment Style Large-Cap Value

GICS Sector Utilities
Sub-Industry Independent Power Producers & Energy Traders

Comment The largest wholesale power supplier in the U.S. and the parent of Baltimore Gas and Electric, CEG agreed to the termination of its planned merger with FPL Group.

Key Stock Statistics (Source S&P, Vickers, company reports)

52-Wk Range	$63.00–50.40	S&P Oper. EPS 2006E	3.45	P/E on S&P Oper. EPS 2006E	18.1	Dividend Rate/Share	$1.51
Trailing 12-Month EPS	$4.07	S&P Oper. EPS 2007E	4.56	Common Shares Outstg. (M)	179.7	Yield (%)	2.42
Trailing 12-Month P/E	15.3	S&P Core EPS 2006E	3.47	Market Capitalization(B)	$11.211	Beta	0.52
$10K Invested 5 Yrs Ago	$30,435	S&P Core EPS 2007E	4.57	Institutional Ownership (%)	64	S&P Credit Rating	BBB+

Price Performance

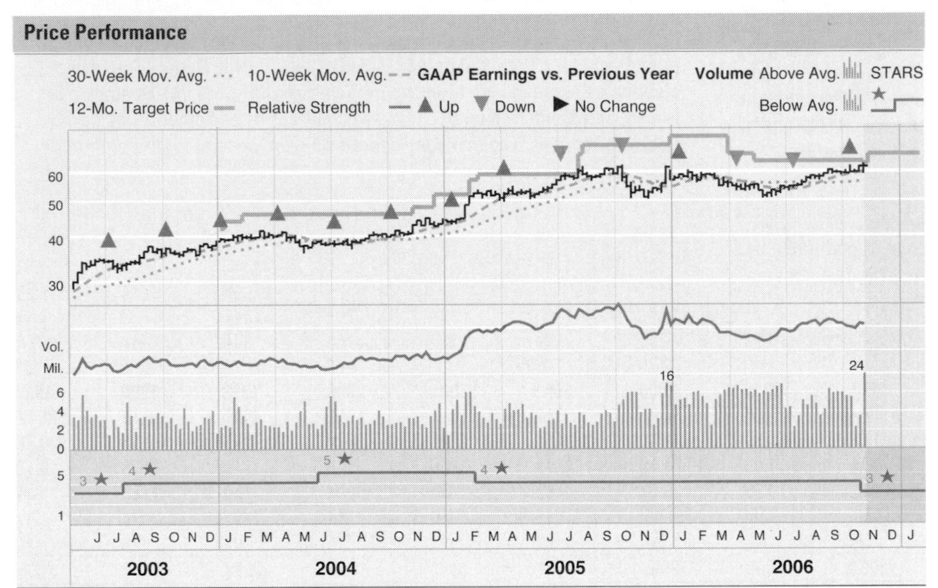

Options: ASE, CBOE, P, Ph

Analysis prepared by **Justin McCann** on October 31, 2006, when the stock traded at **$ 62.40**.

Highlights

- Given the regulatory and judicial uncertainties that marred the Maryland approval process for the company's planned merger with FPL Group (FPL: buy, $50), we believe the termination of the merger was in the best interest of CEG and its shareholders. Driven by its merchant energy operations, we expect CEG's earnings growth to remain strong for the next several years.
- Following the recent agreed-to $1.6 billion sale of six generating plants, we believe EPS from continuing operations in 2006 will decline by 4.7% from 2005 operating EPS of $3.62. (Our 2006 EPS estimate including the plants would have been $3.75). We see double-digit earnings growth from the energy merchant segment, but given the abnormally warm weather in 2005, we see a drop in earnings from BG&E.
- We expect the loss of competitive transition charges and synfuel tax credits to restrict EPS growth. We expect 2007 EPS to grow more than 32% from our 2006 estimate, driven by rising power margins. The Maryland senate bill (SB1) limited the initial stage of the July 1, 2006 phased-in rate increase to 15%, but authorized BGE to securitize $604 million for the deferred recovery of its unrecovered power costs.

Investment Rationale/Risk

- The stock has risen more than 5% since the beginning of October, and is up more than 8% year-to-date. Given this rise, we expect a reduced level of total return from the current level and have lowered our recommendation to hold, from buy. While we thought the proposed merger with FPL would have created a significant national presence for the combined company and a strong platform for the growth of its unregulated operations, CEG maintains its position as the nation's largest wholesale seller and its largest competitive electricity supplier to large commercial and industrial customers.
- Risks to our recommendation and target price include trading-related risks for contracted electric load obligations, and increased competition in wholesale power and competitive commercial and industrial markets.
- The dividend, which was raised 12.6% with the April 2006 payment, was recently yielding about 2.5%. This approximates the yield of other utility holding companies where earnings are driven by their high-growth non-regulated operations. Our 12-month target price of $67 is based on a modest premium-to-peers P/E of 14.7X our EPS estimate for 2007.

Qualitative Risk Assessment

LOW | **MEDIUM** | HIGH

Our risk assessment reflects a balance between stable and steady earnings provided by CEG's regulated electric and gas utility operations and cyclical and volatile earnings from the unregulated merchant energy business, including power generation, energy and energy-related marketing and trading.

Quantitative Evaluations

S&P Quality Ranking B

D | C | B- | **B** | B+ | A- | A | A+

Relative Strength Rank MODERATE

65

LOWEST = 1 HIGHEST = 99

Revenue/Earnings Data

Revenue (Million $)

	1Q	2Q	3Q	4Q	Year
2006	4,898	4,422	5,434	--	--
2005	3,630	3,549	4,922	5,159	17,132
2004	3,037	2,793	3,435	3,286	12,550
2003	2,330	2,271	2,604	2,498	9,703
2002	1,046	1,021	1,270	1,372	4,703
2001	1,147	843.2	1,036	901.9	3,928

Earnings Per Share ($)

	1Q	2Q	3Q	4Q	Year
2006	0.63	0.52	1.79	E1.18	E3.45
2005	0.67	0.66	1.02	1.04	3.38
2004	0.66	0.77	1.19	0.76	3.40
2003	0.40	0.58	1.15	0.71	2.85
2002	1.40	0.50	0.92	0.39	3.20
2001	0.68	0.46	1.00	-1.59	0.52

Fiscal year ended Dec. 31. Next earnings report expected: Late January. EPS Estimates based on S&P Operating Earnings; historical GAAP earnings are as reported.

Dividend Data (Dates: mm/dd Payment Date: mm/dd/yy)

Amount ($)	Date Decl.	Ex-Div. Date	Stk. of Record	Payment Date
0.378	01/30	03/08	03/10	04/03/06
0.378	05/19	06/08	06/12	07/03/06
0.378	07/21	09/07	09/11	10/02/06
0.378	10/20	12/07	12/11	01/02/07

Dividends have been paid since 1910. Source: Company reports.

Constellation Energy Group Inc.

Business Summary October 31, 2006

CORPORATE OVERVIEW. Constellation Energy is the nation's largest wholesale power seller and largest competitive supplier of electricity to large commercial and industrial customers. It is also the holding company for Baltimore Gas & Electric Company, a regulated utility.

MARKET PROFILE. CEG's Merchant Energy operations (which accounted for 71% of net income in 2005) include wholesale power generation, energy marketing and risk management services for wholesale customers, competitive retail supply services for commercial and industrial customers, and consulting services. Merchant Energy also houses energy marketing and risk management operations, which are conducted by NewEnergy, serving the commercial and industrial (C&I) market, and Constellation Commodities Group, serving the wholesale market. The company's regulated electric (25%) and gas (4%) utility operations are performed by Baltimore Gas and Electric (BGE), which serves around 1.2 million electric customers and approximately 620,000 gas customers in a service territory that covers the city of Baltimore and all or part of 10 counties in central Maryland.

IMPACT OF MAJOR DEVELOPMENTS. On October 25, 2006, CEG and FPL Group (FPL), announced the termination of the merger agreement that had been announced on December 19, 2005. If the merger had been completed, the shareholders of FPL, the holding company for Florida Power & Light Company and FPL Energy (an independent power supplier), would have had an approximate 60% interest in the new company, and CEG shareholders a 40% interest. The combined entity would have been one of the largest electric companies in the U.S. Although we were disappointed that the merger was terminated, we believe the regulatory and judicial uncertainties surrounding the approval process in Maryland justified the decision.

Company Financials

Per Share Data ($) Year Ended Dec. 31	2005	2004	2003	2002	2001	2000	1999	1998	1997	1996
Tangible Book Value	26.76	25.99	23.81	22.71	23.44	20.88	19.95	19.98	19.44	19.25
Earnings	3.38	3.40	2.85	3.20	0.52	2.30	2.18	2.06	1.72	1.85
S&P Core Earnings	3.31	3.33	2.66	1.75	0.34	NA	NA	NA	NA	NA
Dividends	1.34	1.14	1.04	0.96	0.48	1.68	1.68	1.66	1.63	1.59
Payout Ratio	40%	34%	36%	30%	92%	73%	77%	81%	95%	86%
Prices:High	62.60	44.90	39.61	32.38	50.14	52.06	31.50	35.25	34.31	29.50
Prices:Low	43.01	35.89	25.17	19.30	20.90	27.06	24.69	29.25	24.75	25.00
P/E Ratio:High	19	13	14	10	96	23	14	17	20	16
P/E Ratio:Low	13	11	9	6	40	12	11	14	14	14
Income Statement Analysis (Million $)										
Revenue	17,132	12,550	9,703	4,703	3,928	3,879	3,787	3,358	3,308	3,153
Depreciation	542	526	479	481	419	470	450	377	343	330
Maintenance	NA	NA	NA	NA	NA	NA	186	178	179	174
Fixed Charges Coverage	3.50	3.40	3.12	2.90	3.01	3.12	2.98	2.81	2.92	2.59
Construction Credits	NA	NA	NA	NA	NA	NA	NA	9.70	5.30	10.0
Effective Tax Rate	25.2%	22.6%	36.2%	37.1%	31.5%	40.0%	36.3%	35.2%	35.8%	34.9%
Net Income	607	589	476	526	82.4	345	326	328	283	311
S&P Core Earnings	594	578	444	290	54.9	NA	NA	NA	NA	NA
Balance Sheet & Other Financial Data (Million $)										
Gross Property	14,403	14,315	13,580	12,354	11,862	10,442	8,989	8,744	8,495	8,196
Capital Expenditures	760	704	658	850	1,318	1,079	436	339	373	361
Net Property	10,067	10,087	9,602	7,957	7,700	6,644	5,523	5,657	5,652	5,582
Capitalization:Long Term Debt	4,559	5,003	5,229	4,804	2,903	3,349	2,765	3,128	2,989	2,759
Capitalization:% Long Term Debt	48.1	51.4	55.8	55.4	43.0	51.5	48.0	51.3	48.5	46.3
Capitalization:Preferred	Nil	Nil	Nil	Nil	Nil	Nil	Nil	-7.00	23.0	345
Capitalization:% Preferred	Nil	Nil	Nil	Nil	Nil	Nil	Nil	NM	4.87	5.80
Capitalization:Common	4,916	4,727	4,141	3,862	3,844	3,153	2,993	2,982	2,870	2,857
Capitalization:% Common	51.9	48.6	44.2	44.6	57.0	48.5	52.0	48.9	46.6	48.0
Total Capital	10,720	11,105	10,833	10,083	8,271	7,943	7,157	7,727	7,432	7,261
% Operating Ratio	94.5	92.2	91.6	87.2	78.3	84.3	84.8	82.5	75.4	84.1
% Earned on Net Property	10.5	17.0	17.1	17.8	5.0	13.3	13.6	13.1	11.9	12.1
% Return on Revenue	3.5	4.7	4.9	11.2	2.1	8.9	8.6	9.8	8.6	9.9
% Return on Invested Capital	9.2	9.0	8.2	9.8	10.5	8.2	7.8	11.0	8.6	9.2
% Return on Common Equity	12.6	13.3	11.9	13.6	2.3	11.2	10.9	10.5	8.9	9.6

Data as orig reptd.; bef. results of disc opers/spec. items. Per share data adj. for stk. divs.; EPS diluted. E-Estimated. NA-Not Available. NM-Not Meaningful. NR-Not Ranked. UR-Under Review.

Office: 750 E Pratt St, Baltimore, MD 21202-3142.
Telephone: 410-783-2800.
Website: http://www.constellationenergy.com
Chrmn, Pres & CEO: M.A. Shattuck, III

Vice Chrmn & EVP: T.V. Brooks
EVP, CFO & Chief Admin: E.F. Smith
EVP & General Counsel: I.B. Yoskowitz
SVP & CIO: B.S. Perlman

Investor Contact: K. Hadlock (410-864-6440)
Board of Directors: D. L. Becker, J. T. Brady, F. P. Bramble, Sr., E. A. Crooke, J. R. Curtiss, F. A. Hrabowski, III, N. Lampton, R. J. Lawless, L. M. Martin, M. A. Shattuck, III, M. D. Sullivan, Y. C. de Balmann

Founded: 1906
Domicile: Maryland
Employees: 9,850

STANDARD &POOR'S

Convergys Corp

S&P Recommendation SELL ★★★★★ | **Price** $21.11 (as of Oct 27, 2006) | **12-Mo. Target Price** $19.00 | **Investment Style** Mid-Cap Value

GICS Sector Information Technology
Sub-Industry Data Processing & Outsourced Services

Comment This company is a provider of outsourced billing and customer management solutions for communications companies and state governments.

Key Stock Statistics (Source S&P, Vickers, company reports)

52-Wk Range	**$21.72–15.32**	S&P Oper. EPS 2006**E**	**1.15**	P/E on S&P Oper. EPS 2006**E**	**18.4**	Dividend Rate/Share	**Nil**
Trailing 12-Month EPS	**$1.03**	S&P Oper. EPS 2007**E**	**1.25**	Common Shares Outstg. (M)	**138.8**	Yield (%)	**Nil**
Trailing 12-Month P/E	**20.5**	S&P Core EPS 2006E	**1.15**	Market Capitalization(B)	**$2.931**	Beta	**1.70**
$10K Invested 5 Yrs Ago	**$7,249**	S&P Core EPS 2007E	**1.25**	Institutional Ownership (%)	**77**	S&P Credit Rating	**BBB**

Price Performance

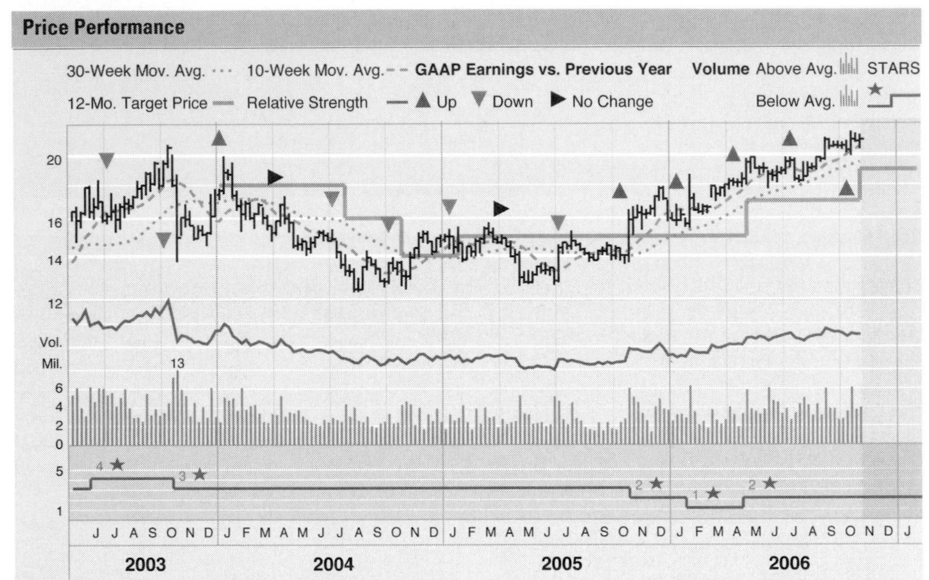

Options: CBOE, P, Ph

Analysis prepared by **Todd Rosenbluth** on October 26, 2006, when the stock traded at **$ 21.37**.

Highlights

- We expect revenues to rise 7% in 2006 and 4% in 2007, as gains at the larger Customer Care Group (CCG) are likely to be somewhat offset by declines at the Information Management Group (IMG). Employee Care should also exhibit growth, in our view, though we were surprised with the segment's relatively light third quarter 2006 revenue. We see IMG being hurt as key telecommunications customers Cingular and Sprint Nextel migrate off of CVG's billing systems.
- We see operating margins remaining around 9.5% in 2006 and 2007, as we project that high fixed costs and growth in lower-margin operations will be offset by a reduction in employees and increased volumes. Given that growth is expected to stem from the customer care segment, we view restructuring efforts, totaling $21 million, skeptically.
- We estimate EPS of $1.15 in 2006 and $1.25 in 2007 (including projected stock compensation expense). We believe that in 2006 CVG's cellular partnership will contribute $0.05 of after-tax non-operating income.

Investment Rationale/Risk

- We believe recent restructuring efforts and the buildout of the small employee care segment are beginning to offset the longer-term challenges we see related to customer migration. However, we believe CVG will have difficulty growing earnings in 2007. Given our expectation of modest revenue growth while peers are seeing stronger gains, we have a sell recommendation on the shares.
- Risks to our recommendation and target price include contract extensions with large customers, above average growth from non-communications companies, new government contracts, and currency gains from international operations.
- On a forward P/E-to-growth basis, CVG shares trade in line with our peer group of companies that provide enhanced services to communications companies. However, we believe a discount is warranted given what we view as sizable customer migration risk, narrower margins, and sluggish top-line growth. Our 12-month target price is $19, based on a P/E to growth rate of 1.5X, or a multiple of 15X applied to our 2007 EPS estimate.

Qualitative Risk Assessment

LOW | **MEDIUM** | HIGH

Our risk assessment for Convergys reflects the competitive nature of serving the communications industry, and the concentration of its customer base, with 33% of 2005 revenues stemming from three companies. These considerations are partially offset by the use of long-term contracts.

Quantitative Evaluations

S&P Quality Ranking **NR**

D | C | B- | B | B+ | A- | A | A+

Relative Strength Rank **MODERATE**

57

LOWEST = 1 HIGHEST = 99

Revenue/Earnings Data

Revenue (Million $)

	1Q	2Q	3Q	4Q	Year
2006	675.3	691.8	702.7	--	--
2005	637.3	630.4	644.8	669.6	2,582
2004	573.9	601.7	639.9	672.2	2,488
2003	560.4	563.2	570.7	594.5	2,289
2002	587.5	572.7	561.2	564.8	2,286
2001	577.8	571.2	567.2	590.7	2,321

Earnings Per Share ($)

	1Q	2Q	3Q	4Q	Year
2006	0.26	0.28	0.32	**E**0.32	**E**1.15
2005	0.22	0.18	0.30	0.16	0.86
2004	0.22	0.20	0.21	0.14	0.77
2003	0.22	0.29	0.31	0.33	1.15
2002	0.35	0.35	0.34	-0.18	0.88
2001	0.34	0.16	0.02	0.33	0.80

Fiscal year ended Dec. 31. Next earnings report expected: Late January. EPS Estimates based on S&P Operating Earnings; historical GAAP earnings are as reported.

Dividend Data

No cash dividends have been paid.

Please read the Required Disclosures and Analyst Certification on the last page of this report.

Convergys Corp

Business Summary October 26, 2006

CORPORATE OVERVIEW. Convergys Corp. is a leading provider of outsourced, integrated billing, and employee and customer care software and services. CVG focuses on developing long-term strategic relationships with clients in employee- and customer-intensive industries, including telecommunications, cable, broadband, direct satellite broadcasting, financial services, and government.

The information management group, known as IMG (28% of first half 2006 revenues), serves clients principally by providing and managing complex billing and information software that addresses all segments of the communications industry. The customer care group, known as CCG (64%), provides outsourced customer management services for clients, utilizing its advanced information systems capabilities and industry experience through call centers and web-based assistance programs. Communications customers contributed 51% of CCG revenues in the first half of 2006. Non communications clients include technology companies and a number of financial institutions. The employee care segment (7.5%) helps clients with the administration of benefits, human resources, recruiting, and payroll services using a single point of contact system. The company has a 45% limited partnership interest in the Cellular Partnership, which operates a cellular telecommunications business in central and southwestern Ohio and northern Kentucky.

MARKET PROFILE. Intense rivalry between wireless, wireline, and cable companies has raised the level of competition in the U.S., in our opinion. Companies in these industries have launched new offerings such as broadband, and looked to improve their customer service to improve loyalty. By March 2006, consumers were spending approximately $175 a month on wireline, wireless, Internet, and television services. Telecom companies are offering three or more of these services in a bundle and focusing on improving customer loyalty through strong customer care services and billing integration. Meanwhile, we expect the trend of oursourcing of human resources functions by large corporations to continue as they look for efficiencies following major acquisitions.

Company Financials

Per Share Data ($) Year Ended Dec. 31	**2005**	**2004**	**2003**	**2002**	**2001**	**2000**	**1999**	**1998**	**1997**	**1996**
Tangible Book Value	3.13	2.62	2.60	2.54	3.08	2.41	1.13	0.29	NM	NA
Cash Flow	1.89	1.74	1.99	1.70	1.81	2.25	1.73	1.28	1.07	NA
Earnings	0.86	0.77	1.15	0.88	0.80	1.23	0.89	0.57	0.54	NA
S&P Core Earnings	0.81	0.60	0.91	0.54	0.51	NA	NA	NA	NA	NA
Dividends	Nil	Nil	Nil	Nil	Nil	Nil	Nil	Nil	NA	NA
Payout Ratio	Nil	Nil	Nil	Nil	Nil	Nil	Nil	Nil	NA	NA
Prices:High	17.90	19.96	20.80	37.98	50.25	55.44	31.75	23.75	NA	NA
Prices:Low	12.57	12.30	11.30	12.50	24.46	26.63	14.50	9.63	NA	NA
P/E Ratio:High	21	26	18	43	63	45	36	42	NA	NA
P/E Ratio:Low	15	16	10	14	31	22	16	17	NA	NA

Income Statement Analysis (Million $)	2005	2004	2003	2002	2001	2000	1999	1998	1997	1996
Revenue	2,582	2,488	2,289	2,286	2,321	2,163	1,763	1,447	988	NA
Operating Income	392	327	415	498	543	489	388	313	220	NA
Depreciation	147	141	124	137	176	161	130	101	61.0	NA
Interest Expense	21.2	10.3	6.90	11.0	20.0	32.9	32.5	33.9	5.40	NA
Pretax Income	213	173	272	244	255	317	223	131	131	NA
Effective Tax Rate	42.5%	35.7%	36.8%	40.3%	45.5%	38.6%	38.4%	38.0%	33.7%	NA
Net Income	123	112	172	146	139	195	137	81.0	86.6	NA
S&P Core Earnings	117	87.6	133	88.9	91.3	NA	NA	NA	NA	NA

Balance Sheet & Other Financial Data (Million $)	2005	2004	2003	2002	2001	2000	1999	1998	1997	1996
Cash	196	58.4	37.2	12.2	41.1	28.2	30.8	3.80	2.10	NA
Current Assets	849	593	420	418	523	481	298	361	266	NA
Total Assets	2,411	2,208	1,810	1,620	1,743	1,780	1,580	1,451	654	NA
Current Liabilities	618	577	543	462	492	359	387	698	217	NA
Long Term Debt	298	302	58.8	4.60	3.60	291	250	Nil	430	NA
Common Equity	1,355	1,285	1,144	1,126	1,227	1,113	927	732	431	NA
Total Capital	1,697	1,588	1,202	1,131	1,230	1,403	1,178	732	NA	NA
Capital Expenditures	131	156	174	90.8	114	175	155	93.5	NA	NA
Cash Flow	270	253	296	283	315	356	267	182	148	NA
Current Ratio	1.4	1.0	0.8	0.9	1.1	1.3	0.8	0.5	1.2	NA
% Long Term Debt of Capitalization	17.5	19.0	4.9	0.4	0.3	20.7	21.3	Nil	NA	NA
% Net Income of Revenue	4.7	4.5	7.5	6.4	6.0	9.0	7.8	5.6	8.8	NA
% Return on Assets	5.3	5.5	10.0	8.7	7.8	11.6	9.0	7.7	NA	NA
% Return on Equity	9.3	9.2	15.1	12.4	11.8	19.1	16.5	13.9	NA	NA

Data as orig reptd.; bef. results of disc opers/spec. items. Per share data adj. for stk. divs.; EPS diluted. E-Estimated. NA-Not Available. NM-Not Meaningful. NR-Not Ranked. UR-Under Review.

Office: 201 East Fourth Street, Cincinnati, OH 45202.
Telephone: 513-723-7000.
Email: investor@convergys.com
Website: http://www.convergys.com

Chrmn & CEO: J.F. Orr
Pres & COO: D.F. Dougherty
SVP, Secy & General Counsel: W.H. Hawkins II
Investor Contact: E. Shanks (800-344-3000)

Board of Directors: Z. Baird, J. F. Barrett, D. B. Dillon, D. F. Dougherty, E. C. Fast, J. E. Gibbs, R. L. Howe, S. C. Mason, P. A. Odeen, J. F. Orr, S. A. Ribeau, D. R. Whitwam

Founded: 1998
Domicile: Ohio
Employees: 65,700

STANDARD &POOR'S

Cooper Industries Ltd.

S&P Recommendation HOLD ★★★★★

Price $90.00 (as of Oct 27, 2006)

12-Mo. Target Price $98.00

Investment Style Mid-Cap Value

GICS Sector Industrials
Sub-Industry Electrical Components & Equipment

Comment Cooper Industries is a diversified worldwide manufacturer of electrical products, tools, and hardware.

Key Stock Statistics (Source S&P, Vickers, company reports)

52-Wk Range	$96.12–69.88	S&P Oper. EPS 2006E	5.12	P/E on S&P Oper. EPS 2006E	17.6	Dividend Rate/Share	$1.48
Trailing 12-Month EPS	$2.23	S&P Oper. EPS 2007E	5.80	Common Shares Outstg. (M)	91.5	Yield (%)	1.64
Trailing 12-Month P/E	40.4	S&P Core EPS 2006E	5.14	Market Capitalization(B)	$8.238	Beta	1.07
$10K Invested 5 Yrs Ago	$26,579	S&P Core EPS 2007E	5.82	Institutional Ownership (%)	80	S&P Credit Rating	NA

Price Performance

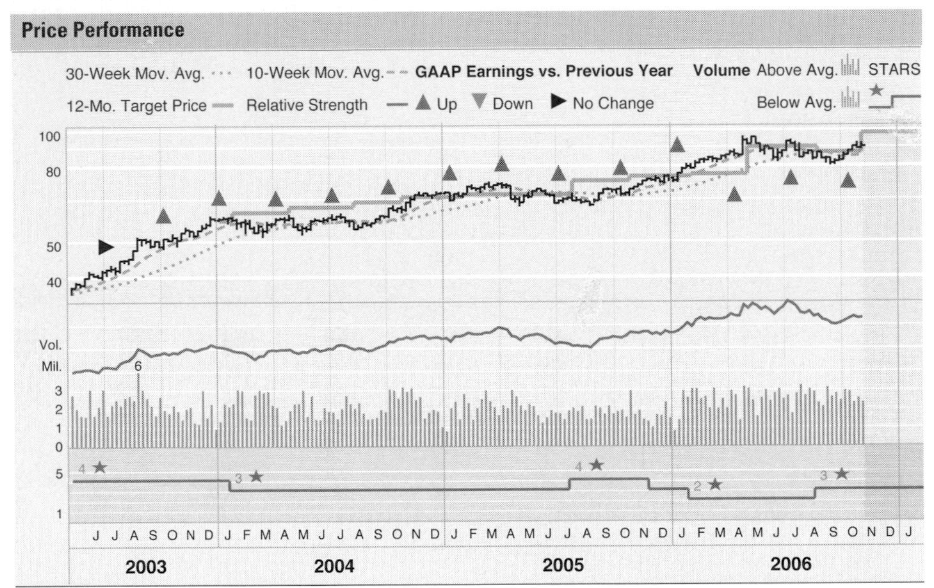

Options: ASE, CBOE, P, Ph

Analysis prepared by **Efraim Levy, CFA** on October 27, 2006, when the stock traded at **$ 90.00**.

Highlights

- Based on our expectation of continued improving economic conditions, we look for sales growth of 7% to 9% in 2006 and 7% to 8% in 2007, with margin improvement from restructuring. Our EPS estimates for CBE reflect the relatively low tax rates the company enjoys as a Bermuda corporation; rates should rise modestly in 2006 after increasing slightly in 2005.
- Our 2006 operating EPS estimate of $5.12, which we raised from $5.03, is up from 2005's $4.12. We expect EPS of $5.80 in 2007. We see the company exceeding the high end of its 2006 EPS guidance of $5.04 to $5.10.
- We forecast that free cash flow (net income before depreciation but after capital expenditures) will exceed net income in 2006 and 2007. We think that a focus on cash generation should help boost cash flow and allow for share repurchases and acquisitions. Long-term debt amounted to 41% of total capitalization at the end of 2005, and we expect a reduction by year-end 2006.

Investment Rationale/Risk

- Cooper's P/E is toward the lower end of the peer range, while its projected P/E to growth ratio, price to free cash ratio, and net margin of 9.8% in 2006 are within its peer group ranges. The shares recently yielded 1.6%. Possible exposure to asbestos liabilities stemming from the 2001 Federal-Mogul (FMO) bankruptcy filing remains a concern to us. FMO has said it may not fulfill an agreement to indemnify CBE for asbestos claims stemming from Pneumo-Abex product lines that it bought from CBE. However, an agreement to limit CBE obligations could be reached in 2006.
- Risks to our opinion and target price include weaker than expected industrial and other economic demand.
- Our use of a P/E multiple of 17.2X applied to our 2007 EPS estimate reflects peer and historical P/E multiple comparisons and implies a $100 value. Our discounted cash flow model, which assumes a weighted average cost of capital of 10.4%, a compound annual growth rate of 6.6% over the next 15 years, and a terminal growth rate of 3.5%, calculates intrinsic value of about $96. Based on a combination of our P/E and DCF analyses, our 12-month target price is $98.

Qualitative Risk Assessment

LOW | **MEDIUM** | HIGH

Our risk assessment reflects what we see as favorable growth prospects in the markets CBE serves, and what we consider good corporate governance and a healthy balance sheet, offset by the company's vulnerability to a possible economic slowdown.

Quantitative Evaluations

S&P Quality Ranking B+

D | C | B- | B | **B+** | A- | A | A+

Relative Strength Rank MODERATE

57

LOWEST = 1 HIGHEST = 99

Revenue/Earnings Data

Revenue (Million $)

	1Q	2Q	3Q	4Q	Year
2006	1,241	1,288	1,315	--	--
2005	1,145	1,189	1,210	1,186	4,730
2004	1,065	1,109	1,140	1,149	4,463
2003	957.8	1,011	1,049	1,044	4,061
2002	975.0	1,001	999.3	985.0	3,961
2001	1,095	1,073	1,052	999.6	4,210

Earnings Per Share ($)

2006	1.14	1.27	1.38	**E**1.33	**E**5.12
2005	0.92	1.02	1.08	1.10	4.12
2004	0.81	0.89	0.95	0.94	3.58
2003	0.61	0.78	0.75	0.78	2.92
2002	0.52	0.78	0.68	0.30	2.28
2001	0.60	0.72	0.78	0.66	2.75

Fiscal year ended Dec. 31. Next earnings report expected: Late January. EPS Estimates based on S&P Operating Earnings; historical GAAP earnings are as reported.

Dividend Data (Dates: mm/dd Payment Date: mm/dd/yy)

Amount ($)	Date Decl.	Ex-Div. Date	Stk. of Record	Payment Date
0.370	11/01	11/29	12/01	01/03/06
0.370	02/13	02/27	03/01	04/03/06
0.370	04/25	06/01	06/05	07/03/06
0.370	08/01	08/29	08/31	10/02/06

Dividends have been paid since 1947. Source: Company reports.

Cooper Industries Ltd.

Business Summary October 27, 2006

CORPORATE OVERVIEW. Cooper Industries, a diversified, worldwide manufacturer of electrical products, tools and hardware, focuses on leveraging its strong brand name recognition by broadening its product line; strengthening its manufacturing and distribution systems to lower costs and improve customer service; expanding globally via acquisitions and joint ventures to participate in growing economies; and improving working capital efficiency and increasing cash flow to fuel future growth.

Electrical products contributed nearly 85% of revenues in 2005, and tools and hardware provided more than 15%.

About 27% of sales in 2005 were outside the U.S. and Canada.

The countries that generate the most international revenues for CBE are Canada, Germany, Mexico and the U.K. The company has several small joint ventures with operations in China.

Cash flow from operations in 2005 was $574 million, up from 2004's $474 million and 2003's $440 million.

CORPORATE STRATEGY. In the four years through 2000, CBE completed 33 acquisitions: 23 in the electrical products group and 10 in the tools and hardware segment. Six acquisitions in 2000 cost about $578 million. The company did not make any acquisitions in 2001 through 2003, but concluded two acquisitions at an aggregate cost of nearly $49 million in 2004. The company did not complete any acquisitions in 2005.

Reflecting slowing demand, the company reduced 2001 capital spending to $115 million, from 2000's $175 million. A further reduction was seen in 2002, to $74 million. Capital spending in 2003 totaled $80 million, but such expenditures increased to $103 million in 2004, as CBE invested in new products, new business systems, and cost reduction programs. However, capital expenditures dropped again in 2005, to $97 million. For 2006, we expect capital spending to rise to approximately $100 million.

Company Financials

Per Share Data ($) Year Ended Dec. 31	**2005**	**2004**	**2003**	**2002**	**2001**	**2000**	**1999**	**1998**	**1997**	**1996**
Tangible Book Value	1.32	1.54	0.66	0.07	1.25	NM	0.04	0.91	1.60	NM
Cash Flow	5.48	4.80	4.22	3.58	4.72	5.69	5.05	4.19	5.26	5.08
Earnings	4.12	3.58	2.92	2.28	2.75	3.80	3.50	2.93	3.26	2.93
Dividends	1.48	1.40	1.40	1.40	1.40	1.40	1.32	1.32	1.32	1.32
Payout Ratio	36%	39%	48%	61%	51%	37%	38%	45%	40%	45%
Prices:High	75.75	68.44	58.85	47.01	60.45	47.00	56.75	70.38	58.63	44.63
Prices:Low	62.08	51.34	33.86	27.14	31.61	29.38	39.63	36.88	40.00	34.13
P/E Ratio:High	18	19	20	21	22	12	16	24	18	15
P/E Ratio:Low	15	14	12	12	11	8	11	13	12	12
Income Statement Analysis (Million $)										
Revenue	4,730	4,483	4,061	3,961	4,210	4,460	3,869	3,651	5,289	5,284
Operating Income	671	614	516	516	662	825	725	683	939	869
Depreciation	111	118	121	122	186	174	148	138	220	234
Interest Expense	64.8	68.1	74.1	74.5	84.7	100	55.2	102	90.0	142
Pretax Income	495	429	347	280	316	550	519	524	627	558
Effective Tax Rate	21.0%	20.7%	20.8%	23.7%	17.4%	35.0%	36.0%	35.9%	37.0%	43.5%
Net Income	391	340	274	214	261	357	332	336	395	315
Balance Sheet & Other Financial Data (Million $)										
Cash	453	653	464	302	11.5	26.4	26.9	21.0	30.0	16.0
Current Assets	2,131	2,219	1,961	1,689	1,651	1,735	1,467	1,417	2,137	2,098
Total Assets	5,215	5,341	4,965	4,688	4,611	4,789	4,143	3,779	6,053	6,053
Current Liabilities	1,161	1,828	1,022	960	1,106	1,174	1,086	971	1,385	1,381
Long Term Debt	1,003	699	1,337	1,281	1,107	1,301	894	775	1,272	1,738
Common Equity	2,205	2,287	2,118	2,002	2,023	1,904	1,743	1,563	2,577	1,890
Total Capital	3,208	2,985	3,455	3,283	3,130	3,205	2,638	2,338	3,849	3,628
Capital Expenditures	96.7	103	79.9	73.8	115	175	166	142	196	202
Cash Flow	502	457	396	335	448	532	480	474	615	549
Current Ratio	1.8	1.2	1.9	1.8	1.5	1.5	1.4	1.5	1.5	1.5
% Long Term Debt of Capitalization	31.3	23.4	38.7	39.0	35.4	40.6	33.9	33.1	33.0	47.9
% Net Income of Revenue	8.3	7.6	6.8	5.4	6.2	8.0	8.6	9.2	7.5	6.0
% Return on Assets	7.4	6.6	5.7	4.6	5.6	8.0	8.4	6.8	6.6	5.2
% Return on Equity	17.4	15.4	13.3	10.6	13.3	19.6	20.1	16.2	17.7	17.5

Data as orig reptd.; bef. results of disc opers/spec. items. Per share data adj. for stk. divs.; EPS diluted. E-Estimated. NA-Not Available. NM-Not Meaningful. NR-Not Ranked. UR-Under Review.

Office: 600 Travis, Houston, TX 77002-1001.
Telephone: 713-209-8400.
Email: info@cooperindustries.com
Website: http://www.cooperindustries.com

Chrmn, Pres & CEO: K.S. Hachigian
SVP & CFO: T.A. Klebe
SVP & General Counsel: K.M. McDonald
VP & Chief Acctg Officer: J.B. Levos

VP & Treas: A.J. Hill
Investor Contact: R.J. Bajenski (713-209-8610)
Board of Directors: S. G. Butler, K. S. Hachigian, L. A. Hill, J. J. Postl, D. F. Smith, G. B. Smith

Founded: 1833
Domicile: Bermuda
Employees: 28,903

STANDARD &POOR'S

Corning Inc

S&P Recommendation HOLD ★★★★★

Price $20.59 (as of Oct 27, 2006)

12-Mo. Target Price $25.00

Investment Style Large-Cap Value

GICS Sector Information Technology
Sub-Industry Communications Equipment

Comment GLW, once an old-line housewares company, is now a leading maker of fiber optics and semiconductor components for the telecommunications and electronics industries.

Key Stock Statistics (Source S&P, Vickers, company reports)

52-Wk Range	$29.61–17.50	S&P Oper. EPS 2006E	1.10	P/E on S&P Oper. EPS 2006E	18.7	Dividend Rate/Share	Nil
Trailing 12-Month EPS	$0.73	S&P Oper. EPS 2007E	1.25	Common Shares Outstg. (M)	1,559.8	Yield (%)	Nil
Trailing 12-Month P/E	28.2	S&P Core EPS 2006E	1.09	Market Capitalization(B)	$32.116	Beta	3.26
$10K Invested 5 Yrs Ago	$23,859	S&P Core EPS 2007E	1.25	Institutional Ownership (%)	74	S&P Credit Rating	BBB

Price Performance

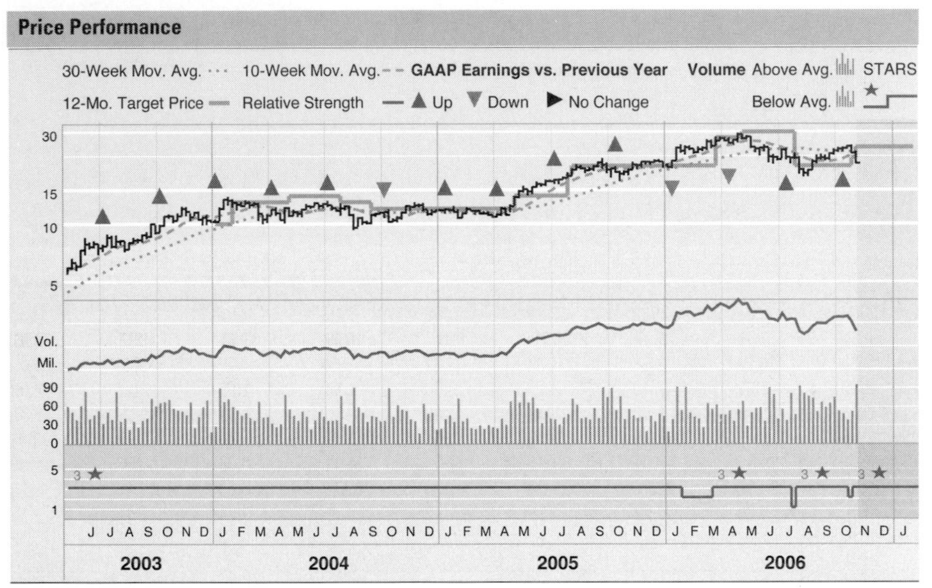

Options: ASE, CBOE, P, Ph

Analysis prepared by **Kenneth M. Leon, CPA** on October 25, 2006, when the stock traded at **$ 21.91**.

Highlights

- Following what we expect to be a 45% sales increase in 2006, we see sales advancing 15% to 17% in 2007, due to higher demand for liquid crystal display (LCD) glass substrates, where GLW is the market leader. Our sales forecast reflects the LCD market as volatile in terms of end user demand for notebooks, PC monitors and flat panel televisions. In 2007, we expect 5% to 10% sales growth from GLW's telecom unit as carriers expand their fiber-to-the-premise (FTTP) spending.
- We believe cost-cutting efforts may offset some of the decline in product pricing. We see GLW's 2006 gross margins stable near 45% in both 2006 and 2007. With less visibility on product demand from GLW's addressable markets, we expect 2007 operating expenses to be held to the levels of 2006.
- With a lower effective tax rate, and factoring in increased equity earnings expected from Dow Corning and Samsung Corning, we project operating EPS of $1.10 in 2006 and $1.25 in 2007, including $0.07 of projected stock option expense in both years.

Investment Rationale/Risk

- We believe GLW's markets for LCD glass panels remain strong while telecom fiber optic systems sales are less predictable and trending less favorable with increased pricing pressure. Leading LCD peers such as AU Optronics, LG Philips LCD and Hoya remain competitive, but GLW's strong relationship with Samsung and Sony, market leaders in flat panel televisions, benefits GLW's 2007 sales outlook, in our opinion.
- Risks to our recommendation and target price include weak demand for flat panel LCD televisions and telecom spending, unstable pricing on display technologies products, and narrower margins in the telecom unit. Capital investments by flat panel display competitors may decline.
- Our 12-month target price of $25 is largely based on a P/E of 20X our 2007 EPS estimate, slightly above the peer average. Our target price reflects a price to sales ratio of 6.7X, above the peer average. With mid-teens sales growth forecast for 2007, we have a hold recommendation on GLW shares, which are trading somewhat below our view of fair value.

Qualitative Risk Assessment

LOW | **MEDIUM** | HIGH

Our risk assessment reflects Corning's exposure to intense competition in its major businesses, offset by its market leadership, positive cash flow, and what we consider a strong balance sheet.

Quantitative Evaluations

S&P Quality Ranking C

D | **C** | B- | B | B+ | A- | A | A+

Relative Strength Rank WEAK

9

LOWEST = 1 HIGHEST = 99

Revenue/Earnings Data

Revenue (Million $)

	1Q	2Q	3Q	4Q	Year
2006	1,262	1,261	1,282	--	--
2005	1,050	1,141	1,188	1,200	4,579
2004	844.0	971.0	1,006	1,033	3,854
2003	746.0	752.0	772.0	820.0	3,090
2002	839.0	827.0	762.0	736.0	3,164
2001	1,921	1,868	1,509	974.0	6,272

Earnings Per Share ($)

2006	0.16	0.32	0.27	**E**0.29	**E**1.10
2005	0.17	0.11	0.13	-0.02	0.38
2004	0.04	0.07	-1.79	0.11	-1.57
2003	-0.17	-0.02	0.02	-0.02	-0.18
2002	-0.10	-0.41	-0.27	-0.96	-1.85
2001	0.14	-5.13	-0.24	-0.69	-5.89

Fiscal year ended Dec. 31. Next earnings report expected: Late January. EPS Estimates based on S&P Operating Earnings; historical GAAP earnings are as reported.

Dividend Data

Dividends were omitted in July 2001.

Please read the Required Disclosures and Analyst Certification on the last page of this report.

Corning Inc

Business Summary October 25, 2006

CORPORATE OVERVIEW. Corning (GLW) has completed a transformation from an old-line, slow-growing housewares company into a leading maker of high technology fiber optics and high performance glass components for the global telecommunications and personal computer industries. Results are reported in four primary business segments: display technologies (40% of 2006 third quarter sales), telecommunications (35%), environmental technologies (12%), life sciences (5%) and other (8%). GLW's 10 largest customers account for about 50% of its sales, but no individual customer accounted for more than 10% of consolidated sales in its 2005 results.

PRIMARY BUSINESS DYNAMICS. The display technologies segment manufactures glass substrates for active matrix liquid crystal displays (LCDs), which are used primarily in notebook computers, flat panel desktop monitors, and LCD televisions.

The telecommunications segment produces optical fiber and cable, and hardware and equipment products for the worldwide telecommunications industry. A significant portion of GLW's optical fiber is sold to its own subsidiaries. GLW's hardware and equipment products include cable assemblies, fiber optic hardware, fiber optic connectors, optical components and couplers, and other equipment. We believe fiber-to-the-premise (FTTP) products may be exposed to selling price declines and uneven order patterns from large carriers in their fiber deployment spending.

The environmental technologies segment includes ceramic technologies and solutions for emissions and pollution control in mobile and stationary applications, including gasoline and diesel substrate and filter products. Although sales are to the emission control systems manufacturers, the use of substrates and filters is also required by the automotive and diesel engine manufacturers. We look to new diesel products as a larger contributor to revenues in late 2007 and future years.

GLW's conventional glass television business includes a 50% interest in Samsung Corning Company, Ltd., a producer of components for cathode ray tubes in televisions and computer monitors.

Company Financials

Per Share Data ($) Year Ended Dec. 31	**2005**	**2004**	**2003**	**2002**	**2001**	**2000**	**1999**	**1998**	**1997**	**1996**
Tangible Book Value	3.43	2.38	2.65	2.14	3.39	3.56	2.60	1.72	1.28	0.92
Cash Flow	0.71	-1.20	0.23	-1.04	-4.74	1.34	1.15	0.85	1.03	0.88
Earnings	0.38	-1.57	-0.18	-1.85	-5.89	0.46	0.65	0.46	0.62	0.49
S&P Core Earnings	0.48	-1.01	-0.16	-2.14	-3.11	NA	NA	NA	NA	NA
Dividends	Nil	Nil	Nil	Nil	0.12	0.24	0.24	0.24	0.24	0.24
Payout Ratio	Nil	Nil	Nil	Nil	NM	52%	37%	52%	39%	49%
Prices:High	21.95	13.89	12.34	11.15	72.19	113.29	43.02	15.23	21.71	15.42
Prices:Low	10.61	9.29	3.34	1.10	6.92	34.33	14.92	7.63	11.25	9.29
P/E Ratio:High	58	NM	NM	NM	NM	NM	66	33	35	31
P/E Ratio:Low	28	NM	NM	NM	NM	NM	23	16	18	19
Income Statement Analysis (Million $)										
Revenue	4,579	3,854	3,090	3,164	6,272	7,127	4,297	3,484	4,090	3,652
Operating Income	1,284	892	386	21.0	805	1,929	1,053	847	1,083	850
Depreciation	512	523	517	661	1,080	765	381	298	322	288
Interest Expense	116	141	154	179	153	107	79.9	56.7	85.0	69.1
Pretax Income	1,170	-1,137	-550	-2,604	-5,963	840	735	535	757	572
Effective Tax Rate	49.4%	NM	NM	NM	NM	48.4%	25.7%	24.8%	30.0%	28.5%
Net Income	585	-2,185	-223	-1,780	-5,498	410	477	328	440	343
S&P Core Earnings	738	-1,420	-200	-2,207	-2,908	NA	NA	NA	NA	NA
Balance Sheet & Other Financial Data (Million $)										
Cash	1,342	1,009	833	1,471	1,037	138	116	12.2	65.3	51.9
Current Assets	3,860	3,281	2,694	3,825	4,107	4,634	1,783	1,310	1,424	1,419
Total Assets	11,175	9,710	10,752	11,548	12,793	17,526	6,012	4,982	4,811	4,321
Current Liabilities	2,216	2,336	1,553	1,680	1,994	1,949	1,488	1,075	1,017	808
Long Term Debt	1,789	2,214	2,668	3,963	4,461	3,966	1,289	1,364	1,499	1,574
Common Equity	5,609	3,752	5,379	4,536	5,414	10,633	2,227	1,506	1,246	961
Total Capital	7,441	6,059	8,168	8,713	10,001	14,808	3,814	3,233	3,116	2,868
Capital Expenditures	1,553	857	366	357	1,800	1,525	733	714	775	598
Cash Flow	1,097	-1,662	294	-1,247	-4,418	1,175	858	626	761	631
Current Ratio	1.7	1.4	1.7	2.3	2.1	2.4	1.2	1.2	1.4	1.8
% Long Term Debt of Capitalization	24.0	36.5	32.7	45.5	44.6	26.8	33.8	42.2	32.6	54.9
% Net Income of Revenue	12.8	NM	NM	NM	NM	5.7	11.1	9.4	10.8	9.4
% Return on Assets	5.6	NM	NM	NM	NM	3.4	8.7	6.7	9.6	7.0
% Return on Equity	12.5	NM	NM	NM	NM	6.2	25.5	23.7	39.7	22.3

Data as orig reptd.; bef. results of disc opers/spec. items. Per share data adj. for stk. divs.; EPS diluted. E-Estimated. NA-Not Available. NM-Not Meaningful. NR-Not Ranked. UR-Under Review.

Office: One Riverfront Plaza, Corning, NY 14831-0001.
Telephone: 607-974-9000.
Email: info@corning.com
Website: http://www.corning.com

Chrmn: J.R. Houghton
Pres & CEO: W.P. Weeks
Vice Chrmn & CFO: J.B. Flaws
COO: P.F. Volanakis

EVP & Chief Admin: K.P. Gregg
Investor Contact: M.S. Rogus (888-267-6464)
Board of Directors: J. S. Brown, R. F. Cummings, Jr., J. B. Flaws, G. Gund, J. M. Hennessy, J. R. Houghton, J. Knowles, J. J. O'Connor, D. D. Rieman, H. O. Ruding, W. D. Smithburg, H. E. Tookes II, P. F. Volanakis, P. Warrior, W. P. Weeks

Founded: 1851
Domicile: New York
Employees: 26,000

STANDARD &POOR'S

Costco Wholesale Corp

S&P Recommendation BUY ★★★★★

Price $53.01 (as of Oct 27, 2006)

12-Mo. Target Price $58.00

Investment Style Large-Cap Value

GICS Sector Consumer Staples
Sub-Industry Hypermarkets & Super Centers

Comment This company operates about 470 membership warehouses in the U.S., Puerto Rico, Canada, the U.K., Taiwan, Japan, Korea and Mexico.

Key Stock Statistics (Source S&P, Vickers, company reports)

52-Wk Range	**$57.94–46.00**	S&P Oper. EPS 2007**E**	**2.65**	P/E on S&P Oper. EPS 2007**E**	**20.0**	Dividend Rate/Share	**$0.52**
Trailing 12-Month EPS	**$2.30**	S&P Oper. EPS 2008**E**	**NA**	Common Shares Outstg. (M)	**468.0**	Yield (%)	**0.98**
Trailing 12-Month P/E	**23.1**	S&P Core EPS 2007**E**	**2.65**	Market Capitalization(B)	**$24.807**	Beta	**0.77**
$10K Invested 5 Yrs Ago	**$13,402**	S&P Core EPS 2008**E**	**NA**	Institutional Ownership (%)	**80**	S&P Credit Rating	**A**

Price Performance

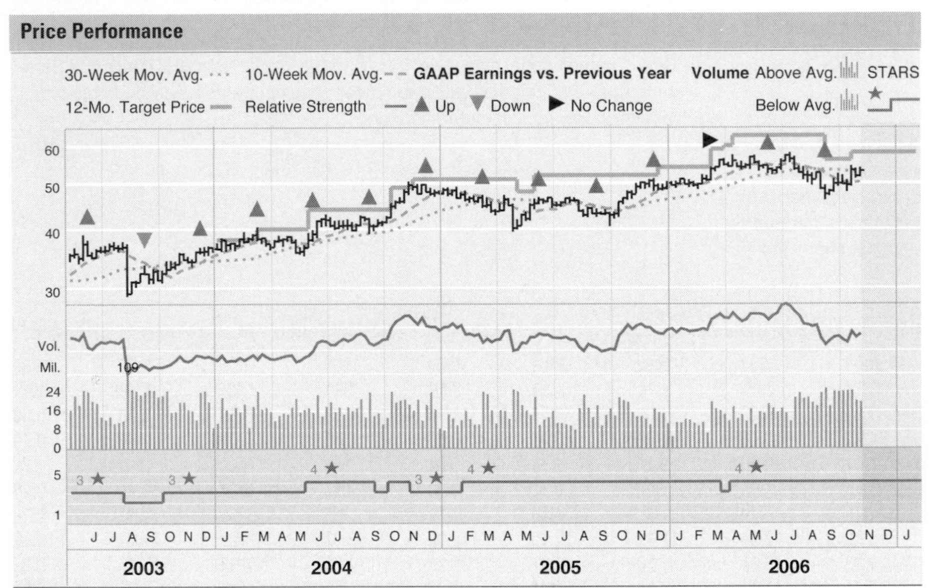

Options: ASE, CBOE, P, Ph

Analysis prepared by **Joseph Agnese** on October 16, 2006, when the stock traded at **$ 52.98**.

Highlights

- We see net sales advancing about 12% in FY 07 (Aug.), reflecting a same-store sales increase of 8% and about 7% square footage growth. We look for membership fees to equal around 2.1% of sales, benefiting from rising membership retention and rates and growing conversions to executive memberships.
- We project that gross margins will be flat, as the benefits of wider margins on food and sundries, soft and hard lines and fresh foods are likely to be offset by narrower ancillary business margins and the impact of a 2% reward on executive memberships. We look for operating margins to expand on benefits from increased sales leverage, health care cost reductions, and lower workers' compensation costs.
- After a projected modest reduction in the share count, as we believe the company will become more active at repurchasing shares, we estimate that FY 07 EPS will increase 15%, to $2.65, from operating income of $2.30 for FY 06.

Investment Rationale/Risk

- We expect COST to maintain or capture market share, reflecting what we view as a strong value proposition and a relatively upscale product mix that appeals to a more affluent customer base. We believe that declining gasoline prices may benefit gross margins in the near term, and with labor cost controls in place and store expansion accelerating, we think the company is well positioned to generate future earnings growth.
- Risks to our recommendation and target price include a slowdown in sales due to weakness in the economy and increased pricing competition in an intensely competitive environment.
- Our 12-month target price of $58 is derived from a blend of our relative P/E and discounted cash flow (DCF) analyses. We assume that the stock will trade at a P/E of 21X our FY 07 EPS estimate of $2.65, in line with its three year historical average, and we calculate a value of about $56. Our DCF assumptions include a weighted average cost of capital of 9% and an expected terminal growth rate of 3.5%, resulting in an intrinsic value of $58 to $60.

Qualitative Risk Assessment

LOW | MEDIUM | HIGH

Our risk assessment for Costco Wholesale incorporates our view of a strong balance sheet, its market leadership position, and our expectations for consistent earnings and dividend growth to continue.

Quantitative Evaluations

S&P Quality Ranking A-

D | C | B- | B | B+ | A- | A | A+

Relative Strength Rank MODERATE

55

LOWEST = 1 HIGHEST = 99

Revenue/Earnings Data

Revenue (Million $)

	1Q	2Q	3Q	4Q	Year
2006	12,927	14,055	13,273	19.88	60.15
2005	11,578	12,658	11,997	16,702	52,935
2004	10,521	11,549	10,897	15,139	48,107
2003	9,199	10,114	9,543	13,690	42,546
2002	8,467	9,383	8,617	12,296	38,763
2001	7,637	8,306	7,719	11,135	34,797

Earnings Per Share ($)

	1Q	2Q	3Q	4Q	Year
2006	0.45	0.62	0.49	0.75	2.30
2005	0.40	0.62	0.43	0.73	2.18
2004	0.34	0.48	0.42	0.62	1.85
2003	0.31	0.39	0.33	0.51	1.53
2002	0.28	0.41	0.28	0.52	1.48
2001	0.28	0.38	0.23	0.41	1.29

Fiscal year ended Aug. 31. Next earnings report expected: Early December. EPS Estimates based on S&P Operating Earnings; historical GAAP earnings are as reported.

Dividend Data (Dates: mm/dd Payment Date: mm/dd/yy)

Amount ($)	Date Decl.	Ex-Div. Date	Stk. of Record	Payment Date
0.115	11/07	11/16	11/18	12/02/05
0.115	01/26	02/07	02/09	02/24/06
0.130	04/25	05/08	05/10	05/26/06
0.130	07/18	07/28	08/01	08/25/06

Dividends have been paid since 2004. Source: Company reports.

Costco Wholesale Corp

Business Summary October 16, 2006

Costco Wholesale (formerly Costco Companies, Inc., and prior to that, Price/Costco, Inc.) began the pioneering "I can get it for you wholesale" membership warehouse concept in 1976, in San Diego, CA. The company operated 471 warehouses worldwide as of March 2, 2006, mainly in the U.S. and Canada (including 28 stores operated through a joint venture in Mexico). COST also operates an e-commerce Web site, costco.com.

The company believes that low prices on a limited selection of national brand merchandise and selected private-label products in a wide range of merchandise categories produce high sales volume and rapid inventory turnover. According to COST, high levels of turnover, combined with operating efficiencies achieved by volume purchasing in a no-frills, self-service warehouse facility enable the company to operate profitably at significantly narrower gross margins than traditional retailers and even discounters and supermarkets. COST buys virtually all of its merchandise directly from manufacturers, for shipment either directly to warehouse clubs or to a consolidation point (depot), at which shipments are combined in order to minimize freight and handling costs. The company generally receives cash from the sale of a substantial portion of its inventory at mature warehouse operations before it is required to pay vendors, even though COST often pays early to obtain payment discounts.

COST has two primary types of memberships: Gold Star (individual) and Business members. Individual memberships are available to employees of federal, state and local governments; financial institutions; corporations; utility and transportation companies; public and private educational institutions; and other organizations. Gold Star membership is $45 annually. There were 16.2 million Gold Star memberships as of August 28, 2005.

Businesses, including individuals with retail sales or business licenses, may become Business members by paying an annual $45 fee, with add-on membership cards available for an annual fee of $35. As of August 28, 2005, there were 5.0 million Business memberships. Executive memberships, available for a $100 annual fee, offer business and individual members savings on services such as merchant credit card processing and small business loans, as well as a 2% reward, up to a maximum of $500 annually, on qualified purchases. Approximately 4.2 million members have upgraded to the Executive membership program.

Company Financials

Per Share Data ($) Year Ended Aug. 31	**2006**	**2005**	**2004**	**2003**	**2002**	**2001**	**2000**	**1999**	**1998**	**1997**
Tangible Book Value	NA	18.80	16.48	14.33	12.51	10.71	9.37	7.98	6.71	5.66
Cash Flow	NA	3.13	2.74	2.32	2.17	1.90	1.86	1.57	1.41	1.16
Earnings	2.30	2.18	1.85	1.53	1.48	1.29	1.35	1.12	1.02	0.73
S&P Core Earnings	NA	2.12	1.76	1.40	1.32	1.12	NA	NA	NA	NA
Dividends	0.49	0.43	0.20	Nil	Nil	Nil	Nil	Nil	Nil	Nil
Payout Ratio	21%	20%	11%	Nil	Nil	Nil	Nil	Nil	Nil	Nil
Prices:High	57.94	51.21	50.46	39.02	46.90	46.38	60.50	49.38	38.06	22.56
Prices:Low	46.00	39.48	35.05	27.00	27.09	29.83	25.94	32.69	20.63	11.88
P/E Ratio:High	25	23	27	26	32	36	45	44	38	31
P/E Ratio:Low	20	18	19	18	18	23	19	29	20	16
Income Statement Analysis (Million $)										
Revenue	NA	52,935	48,107	42,546	38,763	34,797	32,164	27,456	24,270	21,874
Operating Income	NA	1,969	1,827	1,567	1,494	1,312	1,299	1,141	989	838
Depreciation	NA	478	441	391	342	301	254	225	196	182
Interest Expense	NA	34.4	36.7	36.9	29.1	32.0	39.3	45.5	48.0	76.0
Pretax Income	NA	1,549	1,401	1,158	1,138	1,003	1,052	859	766	520
Effective Tax Rate	NA	31.4%	37.0%	37.8%	38.5%	40.0%	40.0%	40.0%	39.9%	40.0%
Net Income	NA	1,063	882	721	700	602	631	515	460	312
S&P Core Earnings	NA	1,044	837	660	624	525	NA	NA	NA	NA
Balance Sheet & Other Financial Data (Million $)										
Cash	NA	2,063	2,823	1,545	806	603	525	441	362	176
Current Assets	NA	8,086	7,269	5,712	4,631	3,882	3,470	3,316	2,628	2,110
Total Assets	NA	16,514	15,093	13,192	11,620	10,090	8,634	7,505	6,260	5,476
Current Liabilities	NA	6,609	6,171	5,011	4,450	4,112	3,404	2,866	2,197	1,964
Long Term Debt	NA	711	994	1,290	1,211	859	790	919	930	917
Common Equity	NA	8,881	7,625	6,555	5,694	4,883	4,240	3,532	2,966	2,468
Total Capital	NA	9,650	8,922	8,181	7,025	5,858	5,139	4,572	3,896	3,507
Capital Expenditures	NA	995	706	811	1,039	1,448	1,228	788	572	553
Cash Flow	NA	1,541	1,323	1,112	1,042	903	886	740	656	494
Current Ratio	NA	1.2	1.2	1.1	1.0	0.9	1.0	1.2	1.2	1.1
% Long Term Debt of Capitalization	NA	7.4	11.1	15.8	17.2	14.7	15.4	20.1	23.9	26.1
% Net Income of Revenue	NA	2.0	1.8	1.7	1.8	1.7	2.0	1.9	1.9	1.4
% Return on Assets	NA	6.7	6.2	5.8	6.4	6.4	7.8	7.5	7.8	6.0
% Return on Equity	NA	12.9	12.4	11.8	13.2	13.2	16.2	15.9	16.9	14.7

Data as orig reptd.; bef. results of disc opers/spec. items. Per share data adj. for stk. divs.; EPS diluted. E-Estimated. NA-Not Available. NM-Not Meaningful. NR-Not Ranked. UR-Under Review.

Office: 999 Lake Dr, Issaquah, WA 98027.
Telephone: 425-313-8100.
Email: investor@costco.com
Website: http://www.costco.com

Chrmn: J.H. Brotman
Pres & CEO: J.D. Sinegal
COO & Sr EVP: R.D. DiCerchio
Investor Contact: R.A. Galanti (425-313-8203)

EVP & CFO: R.A. Galanti
Board of Directors: J. H. Brotman, B. S. Carson, Sr., S. Decker, R. D. DiCerchio, D. J. Evans, R. A. Galanti, W. H. Gates, II, H. E. James, R. M. Libenson, J. W. Meisenbach, C. T. Munger, J. S. Ruckelshaus, J. D. Sinegal

Founded: 1976
Domicile: Washington
Employees: 110,000

Countrywide Financial Corp

STANDARD &POOR'S

S&P Recommendation HOLD ★★★★★

Price $38.12 (as of Oct 31, 2006)

12-Mo. Target Price $40.00

Investment Style Large-Cap Growth

GICS Sector Financials
Sub-Industry Thrifts & Mortgage Finance

Comment This financial services company originates, purchases, securitizes, sells and services mortgages and offers loan closing, banking and insurance services.

Key Stock Statistics (Source S&P, Vickers, company reports)

52-Wk Range	**$43.67–30.60**	S&P Oper. EPS 2006**E**	**4.42**	P/E on S&P Oper. EPS 2006**E**	**8.6**	Dividend Rate/Share	**$0.60**
Trailing 12-Month EPS	**$4.33**	S&P Oper. EPS 2007**E**	**4.96**	Common Shares Outstg. (M)	**612.0**	Yield (%)	**1.57**
Trailing 12-Month P/E	**8.8**	S&P Core EPS 2006**E**	**4.41**	Market Capitalization(B)	**$23.330**	Beta	**0.55**
$10K Invested 5 Yrs Ago	**$39,746**	S&P Core EPS 2007**E**	**4.95**	Institutional Ownership (%)	**93**	S&P Credit Rating	**A**

Price Performance

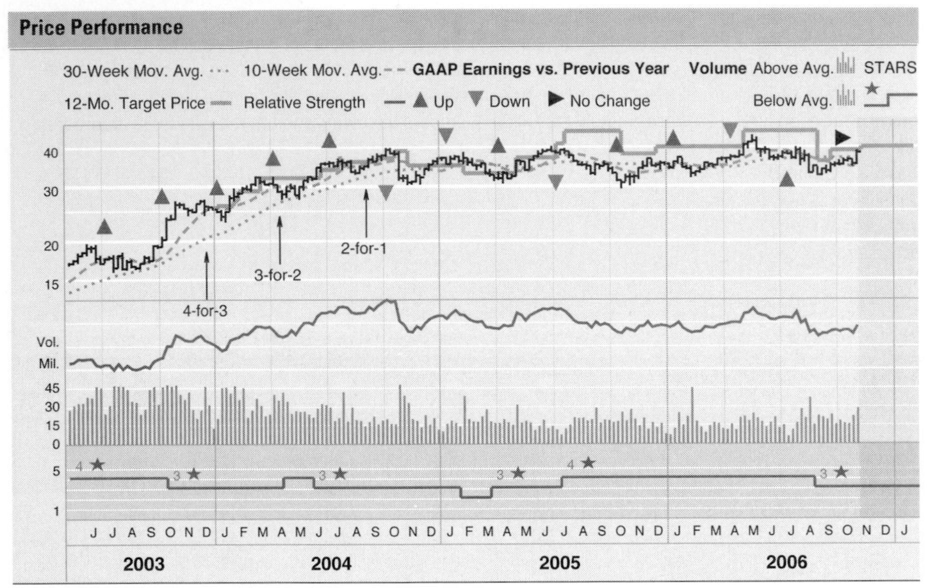

Options: ASE, CBOE, P

Analysis prepared by **Stuart Plesser** on October 31, 2006, when the stock traded at **$ 38.09**.

Highlights

- We expect mortgage originations to decline in 2006 and 2007, reflecting a decrease in refinancing transactions and a weakening of the housing market. Our projections call for CFC's loan production volume to experience low single digit growth in 2007, with less gains on sales of loans due to narrower margins stemming from competitive pricing pressures. We see double digit growth in net interest income, fueled by robust growth in earning assets.
- Based on our expectation for continued growth in CFC's servicing portfolio, a recovery in mortgage servicing rights due to higher long-term rates, and our view of its successful hedging strategy, we forecast double digit growth in net loan servicing fees in 2007. Combined with our projections for stronger insurance premiums, we estimate that total revenues will increase by about 12%. Given CFC's expense and head-count initiatives, we see operating margins improving in 2007.
- We forecast operating EPS of $4.42 in 2006 and assuming a 2% decline in diluted shares, $4.96 in 2007, which would represent growth of about 12%.

Investment Rationale/Risk

- A combination of margin pressure and a pickup in competition in the mortgage banking business will likely limit CFC's plans to expand loan origination market share for most of 2007. However, a likely slowdown in loan production growth should be largely offset by an increase in earnings from mortgage servicing rights. Continued growth in Banking segment earning assets should result in higher net interest income, thus helping to boost CFC's bottom line. Nevertheless, we have become concerned about credit issues, as pay option ARMs--among the riskier types of home loans--currently comprise over 40% of CFC's earning assets. In addition, reserves for loans held for investment are below peer levels.
- Risks to our recommendation and target price include sharply higher mortgage rates and a sudden deterioration in credit quality.
- Our 12-month target price of $40 implies a P/E of 8.4X applied to our 12-month forward EPS estimate of $4.77. This represents a discount to peers, warranted, in our view, due to CFC's high exposure to option ARM loans.

Qualitative Risk Assessment

LOW | **MEDIUM** | HIGH

As a leader in mortgage originations and servicing, we believe CFC is exposed to the mortgage cycle. However, we see this offset by its strong market position and diversification of earnings that stem from its banking and insurance businesses.

Quantitative Evaluations

S&P Quality Ranking A-

D | C | B- | B | B+ | **A-** | A | A+

Relative Strength Rank STRONG

71

LOWEST = 1 HIGHEST = 99

Revenue/Earnings Data

Revenue (Million $)

	1Q	2Q	3Q	4Q	Year
2006	1,361	--	2,823	--	--
2005	2,405	2,308	2,712	2,592	10,017
2004	1,965	2,475	2,110	2,017	8,567
2003	1,451	1,636	2,934	2,006	8,027
2002	913.8	998.3	1,211	1,397	4,519
2001	--	--	--	--	2,636

Earnings Per Share ($)

	1Q	2Q	3Q	4Q	Year
2006	1.10	1.15	1.03	**E**1.13	**E**4.42
2005	1.13	0.92	1.03	1.03	4.11
2004	0.90	1.29	0.81	0.61	3.63
2003	0.61	0.68	1.93	0.91	4.15
2002	0.33	0.37	0.44	0.49	1.62
2001	--	--	--	--	0.97

Fiscal year ended Dec. 31. Next earnings report expected: Late January. EPS Estimates based on S&P Operating Earnings; historical GAAP earnings are as reported.

Dividend Data (Dates: mm/dd Payment Date: mm/dd/yy)

Amount ($)	Date Decl.	Ex-Div. Date	Stk. of Record	Payment Date
0.150	02/01	02/09	02/13	03/02/06
0.150	04/27	05/10	05/12	05/31/06
0.150	07/26	08/11	08/15	08/31/06
0.150	10/25	11/09	11/13	11/30/06

Dividends have been paid since 1979. Source: Company reports.

Countrywide Financial Corp

Business Summary October 31, 2006

CORPORATE OVERVIEW. Countrywide Financial Corporation is a financial holding company primarily engaged in residential mortgage banking and related businesses. It has five operating segments: Mortgage Banking, 59% of pretax earnings in 2005 (65% of pretax earnings in 2004), Banking, 25% (16%), Capital Markets, 11% (13%), Insurance, 4% (5%) and Global Operations, 1% (1%). Recently, the company has been focusing on diversification in an attempt to leverage its core Mortgage Banking business and provide earnings that are less cyclical.

The Mortgage Banking segment produces loans through four divisions of Countrywide Home Loans: its primary subsidiary, Consumer Markets, which originates loans directly with consumers as well as through real estate agents, builders, relocation companies and other entities; Wholesale Lending, which originates mortgages through mortgage brokers and other financial intermediaries; Correspondent Lending, which purchases loans from other lenders; and Full Spectrum Lending, which originates non-prime loans. Nearly all mortgage loans produced in this segment are sold in the secondary market in the form of mortgage backed securities but CFC generally retains mortgage servicing rights (MSRs), or the rights to service these loans, as well as other residual interests related to these loans. As the value of MSRs and other retained interests typically decline when mortgage rates decline, CFC maintains a portfolio of financial instruments called the Servicing Hedge, which tend to increase in value when interest rates decline.

The Banking segment consists of: Treasury Bank, which originates and invests in mortgage loans and home equity lines of credit while funding its operations with retail and commercial deposits, borrowings and repurchase agreements; and Countrywide Warehouse Lending, which provides lines of credit to mortgage bankers to finance their mortgage loan inventories, or warehouse. Properties securing mortgage loans held in CFC's portfolio are mainly concentrated in California (47%).

The Capital Markets segment consists of: Countrywide Securities, a broker-dealer specializing in underwriting and trading mortgage securities; Countrywide Asset Management, which acquires and disposes of loans from third parties as well as CFC's Mortgage Banking segment; and Countrywide Commercial Real Estate Finance, which originates and holds commercial mortgages for sale or securitization.

Company Financials

Per Share Data ($) Year Ended Dec. 31	2005	2004	2003	2002	2001	2000	1999	1998	1997	1996
Tangible Book Value	22.03	17.73	14.61	10.20	8.33	7.56	6.36	5.59	4.78	3.80
Cash Flow	4.35	3.63	4.15	1.62	3.42	2.08	0.88	0.93	0.88	0.71
Earnings	4.11	3.63	4.15	1.62	0.97	0.79	0.88	0.82	0.77	0.61
S&P Core Earnings	3.94	3.58	4.12	1.59	0.93	NA	NA	NA	NA	NA
Dividends	0.59	0.37	0.15	0.11	0.10	0.10	0.10	0.08	0.08	0.08
Payout Ratio	14%	10%	4%	7%	10%	13%	11%	10%	10%	13%
Prices:High	40.31	39.93	27.27	13.75	13.00	12.63	12.86	14.06	10.81	7.56
Prices:Low	29.34	23.01	12.62	9.40	9.35	5.58	6.16	7.16	6.00	4.94
P/E Ratio:High	10	11	7	8	13	16	15	17	14	12
P/E Ratio:Low	7	6	3	6	10	7	7	9	8	8

Income Statement Analysis (Million $)	2005	2004	2003	2002	2001	2000	1999	1998	1997	1996
Loan Fees	NA	NA	2,804	2,029	2,048	1,600	1,599	1,647	1,209	967
Interest Income	7,970	4,630	3,342	2,253	1,822	1,341	999	999	440	350
Total Revenue	13,675	9,421	10,430	10,663	5,331	4,022	3,394	3,676	2,495	1,656
Interest Expense	5,616	2,608	1,940	1,461	1,475	1,348	930	984	424	317
% Expense/Operating Revenue	108.3%	110.2%	78.5%	58.5%	70.1%	82.6%	131.6%	205.3%	119.4%	164.0%
Pretax Income	4,148	3,596	3,846	1,343	789	586	631	632	566	422
Effective Tax Rate	39.0%	38.9%	38.3%	37.3%	38.4%	36.2%	35.0%	39.0%	39.0%	39.0%
Net Income	2,528	2,198	2,373	842	486	374	410	385	345	257
S&P Core Earnings	2,430	2,166	2,351	826	462	NA	NA	NA	NA	NA

Balance Sheet & Other Financial Data (Million $)	2005	2004	2003	2002	2001	2000	1999	1998	1997	1996
Net Property	1,280	985	755	577	447	397	411	312	226	274
Cash & Securities	73,291	73,229	58,962	41,388	9,876	8,337	2,044	1,519	5,303	18.3
Loans	70,260	37,350	24,104	15,026	10,369	1,964	2,653	6,231	5,292	2,580
Total Assets	175,085	128,496	97,950	58,031	37,217	22,956	15,822	15,648	12,219	8,089
Capitalization:Debt	40,553	66,614	20,104	14,117	11,309	8,144	7,753	6,453	7,975	2,368
Capitalization:Equity	12,816	10,310	8,085	5,161	4,088	3,559	2,888	2,519	2,088	1,612
Capitalization:Total	53,369	76,924	28,188	19,278	17,212	13,273	10,641	8,972	6,284	3,980
Price Times Book Value:High	1.8	2.3	1.9	1.3	1.6	1.7	2.0	2.5	2.3	2.1
Price Times Book Value:Low	1.3	1.3	0.9	0.9	1.1	0.7	1.0	1.3	1.3	1.6
Cash Flow	2,528	2,198	2,373	842	1,706	991	476	435	390	298
% Return on Revenue	19.9	25.4	22.8	8.3	9.1	9.3	12.1	10.5	13.8	15.6
% Return on Assets	1.7	1.9	3.0	1.8	1.6	1.9	2.6	2.9	3.4	3.1
% Return on Equity	21.9	23.9	35.8	18.2	12.7	11.6	14.2	16.7	18.7	17.6

Data as orig reptd.; bef. results of disc opers/spec. items. Per share data adj. for stk. divs.; EPS diluted. E-Estimated. NA-Not Available. NM-Not Meaningful. NR-Not Ranked. UR-Under Review.

Office: 4500 Park Granada, Calabasas, CA 91302-7137.
Telephone: 818-225-3000.
Email: ir@countrywide.com
Website: http://www.countrywide.com

Chrmn & CEO: A.R. Mozilo
Pres & COO: D. Sambol
CFO: E.P. Sieracki
Chief Admin: M.M. Gates

Chief Acctg Officer: L. Milleman
Investor Contact: D. Bigelow (818-225-3550)
Board of Directors: K. Brown, H. G. Cisneros, J. M. Cunningham, R. J. Donato, M. E. Dougherty, S. S. Kurland, M. R. Melone, A. R. Mozilo, R. T. Parry, O. P. Robertson, K. P. Russell, H. W. Snyder

Founded: 1969
Domicile: Delaware
Employees: 54,456

STANDARD & POOR'S

Coventry Health Care Inc.

S&P Recommendation STRONG BUY ★★★★★	**Price** $49.80 (as of Oct 27, 2006)	**12-Mo. Target Price** $62.00	**Investment Style** Mid-Cap Growth

GICS Sector Health Care
Sub-Industry Managed Health Care

Comment This national managed health care company operates health plans, insurance companies, network rental/managed care services companies, and workers' compensation services companies.

Key Stock Statistics (Source S&P, Vickers, company reports)

52-Wk Range	**$61.88–45.37**	S&P Oper. EPS 2006**E**	**3.52**	P/E on S&P Oper. EPS 2006**E**	**14.1**	Dividend Rate/Share	**Nil**
Trailing 12-Month EPS	**$3.27**	S&P Oper. EPS 2007**E**	**4.00**	Common Shares Outstg. (M)	**158.9**	Yield (%)	**Nil**
Trailing 12-Month P/E	**15.2**	S&P Core EPS 2006**E**	**3.52**	Market Capitalization(B)	**$7.913**	Beta	**0.14**
$10K Invested 5 Yrs Ago	**$50,247**	S&P Core EPS 2007**E**	**4.00**	Institutional Ownership (%)	**90**	S&P Credit Rating	**BBB-**

Price Performance

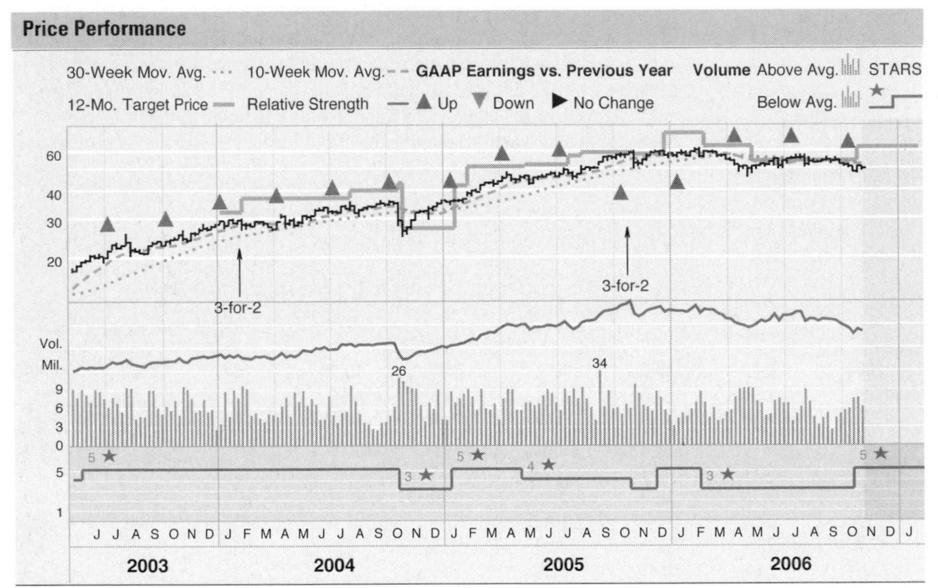

Options: ASE, CBOE, P, Ph

Analysis prepared by **Phillip M. Seligman** on October 19, 2006, when the stock traded at **$ 50.15**.

Highlights

- For 2006, we look for revenues to grow 18%, to $7.8 billion, on $600 million from the Medicare prescription drug program (PDP), 6% commercial premium yield (rates minus buydowns), and 1% higher health plan enrollment. We see the latter driven by 7% more Medicare Advantage members and 2% to 3% gains, which we see in the second half, in commercial enrollment, offset by fewer Medicaid members (due to the impact of Hurricane Katrina and Missouri eligibility recertification).
- We see the companywide medical loss ratio (MLR) up by 70 bps, as lower commercial MLR is outweighed by an increase in Medicare Advantage enrollment, the start of the PDP, and the rise of the Medicaid MLR, as Medicaid premiums are determined by the states. We look for a 110 bps decline in the SG&A cost ratio, despite PDP start-up costs and stock option expense. We expect PDP claim costs to decline as the year progresses.
- We see operating EPS of $3.52 in 2006, after $0.12 of stock option expense, versus $3.15 in 2005, before $0.08 of stock option expense, and $4.00 in 2007.

Investment Rationale/Risk

- We are encouraged by what we believe is good management execution and CVH's overarching focus on cost control, which continues to yield the highest EBITDA margin among peers. We see this as a competitive advantage, permitting CVH to compete effectively against larger rivals. Even so, we now look for overall commercial health plan enrollment to rise at slightly below industry-level rates in 2006, given competition. But we see good growth prospects for CVH's Medicare unit, since its Medicare PDP is one of only a few covering branded drugs in the "donut hole," and because of its move into Medicare private-fee-for-service. We also see CVH expanding into new markets and returning to the M&A front, but believe that most acquisition prospects have become more expensive.
- Risks to our recommendation and target price include a potential government probe of the managed care industry, higher than expected medical costs, and a weakened job market.
- Our 12-month target price of $62 is derived by applying an above-peer 1.1X PEG ratio to our 14% three-year EPS growth projection and our 2007 EPS estimate.

Qualitative Risk Assessment

LOW | **MEDIUM** | HIGH

Our risk assessment reflects CVH's industry leading operating margins and its January 2005 acquisition of First Health, which we think provides good growth prospects. Even so, CVH faces intense competition, which has limited enrollment growth, and we do not see an opportunity for membership to grow more strongly until CVH can successfully reduce more of First Health's costs.

Quantitative Evaluations

S&P Quality Ranking **B**

D | C | B- | **B** | B+ | A- | A | A+

Relative Strength Rank **WEAK**

18

LOWEST = 1 HIGHEST = 99

Revenue/Earnings Data

Revenue (Million $)

	1Q	2Q	3Q	4Q	Year
2006	1,939	1,945	1,909	--	--
2005	1,565	1,653	1,674	1,719	6,611
2004	1,288	1,310	1,330	1,384	5,312
2003	1,065	1,096	1,150	1,223	4,535
2002	848.6	890.1	892.0	946.3	3,577
2001	751.4	786.7	794.7	814.5	3,147

Earnings Per Share ($)

	1Q	2Q	3Q	4Q	Year
2006	0.74	0.84	0.92	**E**1.01	**E**3.52
2005	0.73	0.79	0.81	0.77	3.10
2004	0.55	0.62	0.64	0.67	2.48
2003	0.37	0.47	0.49	0.51	1.83
2002	0.20	0.27	0.29	0.30	1.06
2001	0.12	0.13	0.14	0.15	0.55

Fiscal year ended Dec. 31. Next earnings report expected: Early February. EPS Estimates based on S&P Operating Earnings; historical GAAP earnings are as reported.

Dividend Data

No Dividend Data Available

Please read the Required Disclosures and Analyst Certification on the last page of this report.

Coventry Health Care Inc.

Business Summary October 19, 2006

CORPORATE OVERVIEW. Coventry Health Care is a diversified national managed care company. It offers a full range of managed care products, including HMO, PPO, POS, Medicare Risk and Medicaid plans. As of June 30, 2006, it had 2,543,000 members in 17 health plans in 20 states (versus 2,546,000 as of December 31, 2005).

CVH offers individual and employer groups a full range of commercial risk products, including health maintenance organization (HMO), preferred provider organization (PPO) and point-of service (POS) products. As of June 30, 2006, it had 1,473,000 (1,474,000 at December 31, 2005) commercial risk members. Commercial risk accounted for 65% of total 2005 revenue.

CVH offers management services and access to its provider networks to employers that self-insure their employee health benefits. As of June 30, 2006, CVH had 611,000 (592,000) non-risk health plan members. These services accounted for about 2% of 2005 revenue.

As of June 30, 2006, the company's Medicare Advantage enrollment was 80,000 (75,000) members. Enrollment in its stand-alone Medicare Prescription Drug Program, which started in 2006, was 663,000 as of June 30, 2006. The MA line accounted for 10% of total 2005 revenue.

CVH offers health care coverage to Medicaid beneficiaries in eight states which, as of June 30, 2006, covered 379,000 (393,000) members. Medicaid accounted for over 11% of total 2005 revenue.

In January 2005, CVH acquired First Health Group, gaining a nationwide provider network and high-margin, fee-based service businesses, such as network rental, clinical programs, workers' compensation administration, Medicaid health care management services, and pharmacy benefit management. CVH also gained additional PPO members, including the Federal Employee Health Benefit program, the largest employer-sponsored group health program in the U.S., and an administrative services only (ASO, or non-risk) product for large employers with locations in several states that self-insure. We believe FH offers CVH many growth opportunities, such as the ability to develop local health plans in more states.

Company Financials

Per Share Data ($) Year Ended Dec. 31	**2005**	**2004**	**2003**	**2002**	**2001**	**2000**	**1999**	**1998**	**1997**	**1996**
Tangible Book Value	3.21	6.60	4.57	2.85	2.89	2.31	1.60	1.06	0.12	NM
Cash Flow	3.63	2.61	1.97	1.24	0.72	0.60	0.50	0.12	0.32	-0.25
Earnings	3.10	2.48	1.83	1.06	0.55	0.41	0.31	-0.10	0.16	-0.83
S&P Core Earnings	3.01	2.41	1.80	1.03	0.52	NA	NA	NA	NA	NA
Dividends	Nil	Nil	Nil	Nil	Nil	Nil	Nil	Nil	Nil	Nil
Payout Ratio	Nil	Nil	Nil	Nil	Nil	Nil	Nil	Nil	Nil	Nil
Prices:High	60.31	36.20	29.46	16.89	12.22	13.31	6.81	8.56	8.94	9.50
Prices:Low	34.21	24.66	10.80	8.67	5.78	3.06	2.22	1.72	2.94	3.94
P/E Ratio:High	19	15	16	16	22	32	22	NM	56	NM
P/E Ratio:Low	11	10	6	8	11	7	7	NM	18	NM
Income Statement Analysis (Million $)										
Revenue	6,611	5,312	4,535	3,577	3,147	2,605	2,162	2,110	1,228	1,057
Operating Income	878	514	384	220	117	81.1	71.8	51.1	18.5	-38.7
Depreciation	86.2	17.6	18.2	18.9	25.9	27.0	28.2	25.8	12.7	42.9
Interest Expense	58.4	14.3	15.1	13.4	Nil	Nil	Nil	8.57	10.3	6.26
Pretax Income	799	527	393	226	135	102	76.0	-17.5	20.3	-84.2
Effective Tax Rate	37.3%	36.0%	36.4%	35.5%	38.0%	39.9%	42.8%	NM	41.4%	NM
Net Income	502	337	250	146	83.5	61.3	43.4	-11.7	11.9	-61.3
S&P Core Earnings	485	328	245	143	78.5	NA	NA	NA	NA	NA
Balance Sheet & Other Financial Data (Million $)										
Cash	392	418	253	187	312	256	240	409	154	98.0
Current Assets	1,326	973	534	424	579	507	483	591	237	208
Total Assets	4,895	2,341	1,982	1,643	1,451	1,239	1,082	1,091	469	449
Current Liabilities	1,270	932	855	801	752	632	523	566	261	282
Long Term Debt	760	171	171	175	Nil	Nil	Nil	46.4	85.7	57.3
Common Equity	2,555	1,212	929	646	689	662	480	437	118	100
Total Capital	3,315	1,383	1,099	821	689	662	527	483	204	158
Capital Expenditures	71.4	15.0	13.4	13.0	11.9	16.0	14.7	3.24	7.20	12.7
Cash Flow	588	355	268	164	109	88.4	71.6	14.1	24.6	-18.4
Current Ratio	1.0	1.0	0.6	0.5	0.8	0.8	0.9	1.0	0.9	0.7
% Long Term Debt of Capitalization	22.9	12.3	15.5	21.3	Nil	Nil	Nil	9.6	42.1	36.3
% Net Income of Revenue	7.6	6.3	5.5	4.1	2.7	2.4	2.0	NM	1.0	NM
% Return on Assets	13.9	15.6	13.8	9.4	6.2	5.3	4.0	NM	2.6	NM
% Return on Equity	26.6	31.5	31.8	21.8	13.0	10.7	9.5	NM	10.9	NM

Data as orig reptd.; bef. results of disc opers/spec. items. Per share data adj. for stk. divs.; EPS diluted. E-Estimated. NA-Not Available. NM-Not Meaningful. NR-Not Ranked. UR-Under Review.

Office: 6705 Rockledge Drive, Bethesda, MD 20817.
Telephone: 301-581-0600.
Email: investor-relations@cvty.com
Website: http://www.coventryhealth.com

Chrmn: A.F. Wise
Pres: T.P. McDonough
CEO: D.B. Wolf
EVP, CFO & Treas: S.M. Guertin

EVP & CIO: H.C. DeMovick, Jr.
Investor Contact: D. Asher (301-581-5717)
Board of Directors: J. Ackerman, J. H. Austin, L. D. Crandall, E. D. Farley, Jr., L. N. Kugelman, D. N. Mendelson, R. W. Moorhead, III, R. W. Morey, E. E. Tallett, T. T. Weglicki, A. F. Wise, D. B. Wolf

Founded: 1986
Domicile: Delaware
Employees: 9,830

STANDARD &POOR'S

CSX Corp

S&P Recommendation HOLD ★★★★★

Price $36.44 (as of Oct 27, 2006)

12-Mo. Target Price $39.00

Investment Style Large-Cap Value

GICS Sector Industrials
Sub-Industry Railroads

Comment This company operates a major U.S. rail network, and provides intermodal and U.S. container shipping services.

Key Stock Statistics (Source S&P, Vickers, company reports)

52-Wk Range	$38.30–22.26	S&P Oper. EPS 2006E	2.19	P/E on S&P Oper. EPS 2006E	16.6	Dividend Rate/Share	$0.40
Trailing 12-Month EPS	$2.59	S&P Oper. EPS 2007E	2.54	Common Shares Outstg. (M)	435.2	Yield (%)	1.10
Trailing 12-Month P/E	14.1	S&P Core EPS 2006E	2.13	Market Capitalization(B)	$15.858	Beta	1.02
$10K Invested 5 Yrs Ago	$22,631	S&P Core EPS 2007E	2.50	Institutional Ownership (%)	76	S&P Credit Rating	BBB

Price Performance

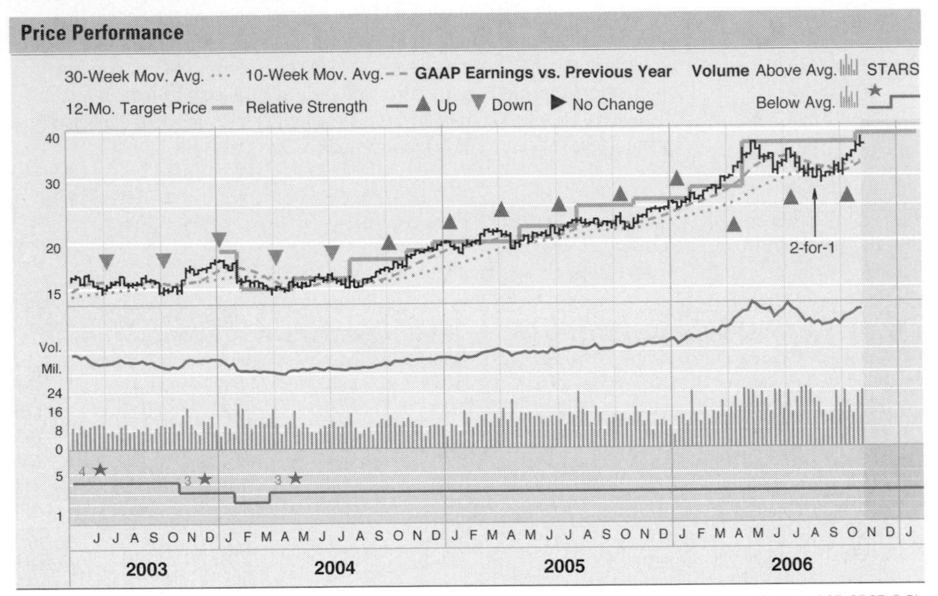

Options: ASE, CBOE, P, Ph

Analysis prepared by **Kevin Kirkeby** on October 19, 2006, when the stock traded at **$ 35.29**.

Highlights

- We expect revenue to increase 11% in 2006 and another 8% in 2007, with underlying volume gains of 1% anticipated for both years, and freight rates rising 5% and 3% in the respective years. Demand for coal and intermodal will likely be the primary contributors to the pricing gains, as we anticipate fuel surcharges stabilizing in 2007. We see a challenging environment for fertilizers and phosphates, as well as auto parts and forest products, and forecast volume declines in those segments.
- We expect operating margins in 2007 to widen modestly from the 20% level we anticipate for 2006, as several customer contracts come up for renewal and the roughly 20 capacity expansion projects scheduled for completion in late 2006 improve network dwell time and velocity. Partially offsetting these gains is the likely increase in CSX's cost of fuel, as the last of its fuel hedges rolled off in the third quarter of 2006.
- Results in 2007 are expected to benefit from reduced interest expense on lower debt levels. Excluding $0.29 of one-time gains, we see 2007 EPS of $2.54, up 16% from the $2.19, before special items, projected for 2006.

Investment Rationale/Risk

- We believe that the recent improvements to operations and profitability will start to slow in 2007 following several quarters of above-average price gains and margin expansion. Revenue per unit in CSX's merchandise segment, for example, was up 17% in the 2006 third quarter. While volume trends are expected to remain favorable in key markets such as coal and intermodal, we see fewer opportunities to raise freight rates or to drop lower-profit customers.
- Risks to our opinion and target price include an economic slowdown that affects freight volumes, declining railroad system fluidity, unusually severe weather, and rapid changes in diesel prices.
- Our DCF model derives an intrinsic value of $41, based on a weighted average cost of capital of 9% and a 3.5% terminal growth rate. Applying a 7.3X forward enterprise value to EBITDA multiple, which we calculate as the historical five-year average and consider appropriate for the current stage of sector expansion, to our 2007 EBITDA estimate, we derive a value of $37. Blending these models, we arrive at our 12-month target price of $39.

Qualitative Risk Assessment

LOW | **MEDIUM** | HIGH

Our risk assessment reflects what we believe is CSX's exposure to economic cycles, freight demand and pricing and fuel prices, offset by its consistently positive cash flow generation, moderate debt levels and diverse customer base.

Quantitative Evaluations

S&P Quality Ranking B

D | C | B- | **B** | B+ | A- | A | A+

Relative Strength Rank STRONG

86

LOWEST = 1 HIGHEST = 99

Revenue/Earnings Data

Revenue (Million $)

	1Q	2Q	3Q	4Q	Year
2006	2,331	2,421	2,418	--	--
2005	2,108	2,166	2,125	2,219	8,618
2004	1,915	1,995	1,938	2,172	8,020
2003	2,016	1,942	1,882	1,953	7,793
2002	1,964	2,073	2,055	2,060	8,152
2001	2,025	2,057	2,019	2,009	8,110

Earnings Per Share ($)

	1Q	2Q	3Q	4Q	Year
2006	0.53	0.83	0.71	**E**0.54	**E**2.19
2005	0.34	0.37	0.36	0.52	1.59
2004	0.06	0.26	0.26	0.36	0.94
2003	0.10	0.29	-0.24	0.29	0.44
2002	0.16	0.32	0.30	0.32	1.10
2001	0.05	0.26	0.24	0.16	0.69

Fiscal year ended Dec. 31. Next earnings report expected: Late January. EPS Estimates based on S&P Operating Earnings; historical GAAP earnings are as reported.

Dividend Data (Dates: mm/dd Payment Date: mm/dd/yy)

Amount ($)	Date Decl.	Ex-Div. Date	Stk. of Record	Payment Date
0.130	05/03	05/23	05/25	06/15/06
2-for-1 Stk.	07/18	08/16	08/03	08/15/06
0.200	07/18	08/23	08/25	09/15/06
0.100	09/13	11/21	11/24	12/15/06

Dividends have been paid since 1922. Source: Company reports.

CSX Corp

Business Summary October 19, 2006

CORPORATE OVERVIEW. CSX operates the largest rail network in the eastern U.S., with a 22,000-mile rail network linking commercial markets in 23 states and two Canadian provinces, and owns companies providing intermodal and rail-to-truck transload services. In 1997, the company purchased a 42% stake in Conrail, bringing CSX's system into New York City, Boston, Philadelphia and Buffalo; in 2004, CSX gained direct ownership and control of Conrail's New York Central Lines. With these routes, the company was able to offer shippers broader geographic coverage, access more ports, and expand its share of north-south traffic. In 2003, CSX saw a decline in certain performance measures, including personal injury frequency, train accident frequency, train velocity, train recrews, and on-time originations and arrivals. CSX experienced continuing operational difficulties in 2004, with train velocity and on-time performance worsening. In the third quarter of 2004, CSX initiated a major initiative to improve network performance called the "One Plan," which we believe is leading to improving safety, efficiency and service quality.

MARKET PROFILE. We believe CSX's intermodal business, representing 16% of 2005 revenue, will be its fastest growing segment longer term, driven by rising international trade and its cost savings over trucks for long-distance container movements, though we see CSX's service quality as inferior to its primary competitor. Coal, which we believe is CSX's most profitable segment, accounted for 23% of 2005 revenues. Most of this traffic originates from the Appalachian coal fields, and is primarily delivered to power utilities. CSX's merchandise freight provided 49% of freight revenues in 2005, and includes chemical, forest products, metals, and agricultural products. We believe this business is sensitive to U.S. GDP trends, and faces average long-term volume growth prospects. We believe automotive freight, at 10% of revenues in 2005, has a weak volume growth outlook, due to slowing domestic manufacturing trends.

COMPETITIVE LANDSCAPE. The US rail industry has an oligopoly-like structure, with over 80% of revenues generated by the four largest railroads: CSX and Norfolk Southern Corp. operating on the East Coast, and Union Pacific Corp. and Burlington Northern Santa Fe Corp. operating on the West Coast. Railroads simultaneously compete for customers while cooperating by sharing assets, interfacing systems, and completing customer movements.

Company Financials

Per Share Data ($) Year Ended Dec. 31	2005	2004	2003	2002	2001	2000	1999	1998	1997	1996
Tangible Book Value	18.25	15.77	15.01	14.52	14.32	14.13	13.20	13.55	13.23	11.51
Cash Flow	3.41	2.55	1.94	2.62	2.16	2.76	1.46	2.73	3.36	3.45
Earnings	1.59	0.94	0.44	1.10	0.69	0.44	0.12	1.26	1.81	2.00
S&P Core Earnings	1.60	0.90	0.66	0.85	0.59	NA	NA	NA	NA	NA
Dividends	0.22	0.20	0.20	0.20	0.40	0.60	0.60	0.60	0.54	0.52
Payout Ratio	14%	21%	45%	18%	58%	136%	NM	48%	30%	26%
Prices:High	25.80	20.23	18.15	20.70	20.65	16.72	26.97	30.38	31.22	26.56
Prices:Low	18.45	14.40	12.75	12.55	12.41	9.75	14.41	18.25	20.63	21.06
P/E Ratio:High	16	22	41	19	30	38	NM	24	17	13
P/E Ratio:Low	12	15	29	11	18	22	NM	15	11	11

Income Statement Analysis (Million $)	2005	2004	2003	2002	2001	2000	1999	1998	1997	1996
Revenue	8,618	8,020	7,793	8,152	8,110	8,191	10,811	9,898	10,621	10,536
Operating Income	2,345	1,730	1,269	1,776	1,579	1,405	1,685	1,790	2,271	2,142
Depreciation	833	730	643	649	622	600	621	630	688	620
Interest Expense	423	435	418	445	518	543	521	506	451	249
Pretax Income	1,036	637	265	723	448	656	130	808	1,224	1,316
Effective Tax Rate	30.5%	34.4%	28.7%	35.4%	34.6%	13.9%	67.7%	29.2%	31.4%	35.0%
Net Income	720	418	189	467	293	565	51.0	537	799	855
S&P Core Earnings	729	405	280	363	249	NA	NA	NA	NA	NA

Balance Sheet & Other Financial Data (Million $)	2005	2004	2003	2002	2001	2000	1999	1998	1997	1996
Cash	309	859	368	264	618	684	974	533	690	682
Current Assets	2,372	2,987	1,903	1,789	2,074	2,046	2,563	1,984	2,175	2,072
Total Assets	24,232	24,581	21,760	20,951	20,801	20,491	20,720	20,427	19,957	19,957
Current Liabilities	2,979	3,317	2,210	2,454	3,303	3,280	3,473	2,600	2,707	2,757
Long Term Debt	5,093	6,234	6,886	6,519	5,839	5,810	6,196	6,432	6,416	4,331
Common Equity	8,918	7,858	7,569	7,091	7,060	6,017	5,756	5,880	5,766	4,995
Total Capital	20,093	20,071	18,207	17,177	16,520	15,211	15,179	15,485	15,121	12,046
Capital Expenditures	1,136	1,030	1,059	1,080	930	913	1,517	1,479	1,125	1,223
Cash Flow	1,553	1,148	832	1,116	915	1,165	623	1,167	1,487	1,475
Current Ratio	0.8	0.9	0.9	0.7	0.6	0.6	0.7	0.8	0.8	0.8
% Long Term Debt of Capitalization	25.3	31.1	37.8	38.0	35.3	38.2	40.8	41.5	42.4	36.0
% Net Income of Revenue	8.4	5.2	2.4	5.7	3.6	6.9	0.5	5.4	7.5	8.1
% Return on Assets	2.9	1.8	0.9	2.2	1.4	2.7	0.2	2.7	4.3	5.5
% Return on Equity	8.6	5.4	2.6	6.6	4.2	9.6	0.9	9.2	14.8	18.5

Data as orig reptd.; bef. results of disc opers/spec. items. Per share data adj. for stk. divs.; EPS diluted. E-Estimated. NA-Not Available. NM-Not Meaningful. NR-Not Ranked. UR-Under Review.

Office: 500 Water Street , Jacksonville , FL 32202.
Telephone: 904-359-3200.
Website: http://www.csx.com
Chrmn, Pres & CEO: M.J. Ward

EVP & CFO: O. Munoz
VP & Cntlr: C.T. Sizemore
Investor Contact: D. Baggs (904-359-4812)

Board of Directors: D. M. Alvarado, E. E. Bailey, J. B. Breaux, S. T. Halverson, E. J. Kelly, R. D. Kunisch, S. J. Morcott, D. M. Ratcliffe, C. E. Rice, W. C. Richardson, F. S. Royal, D. J. Shepard, M. J. Ward

Founded: 1978
Domicile: Virginia
Employees: 35,109

STANDARD & POOR'S

Cummins Inc.

S&P Recommendation HOLD ★★★★★

Price $126.98 (as of Oct 31, 2006)

12-Mo. Target Price $128.00

Investment Style Mid-Cap Value

GICS Sector Industrials
Sub-Industry Construction & Farm Machinery & Heavy Trucks

Comment This Indiana-based company, a leading manufacturer of truck engines, also makes stand-by power equipment and industrial filters.

Key Stock Statistics (Source S&P, Vickers, company reports)

52-Wk Range	**$139.20–85.47**	S&P Oper. EPS 2006**E**	**14.00**	P/E on S&P Oper. EPS 2006**E**	**9.1**	Dividend Rate/Share	**$1.44**
Trailing 12-Month EPS	**$13.77**	S&P Oper. EPS 2007**E**	**9.00**	Common Shares Outstg. (M)	**50.7**	Yield (%)	**1.13**
Trailing 12-Month P/E	**9.2**	S&P Core EPS 2006**E**	**14.00**	Market Capitalization(B)	**$6.438**	Beta	**1.56**
$10K Invested 5 Yrs Ago	**$45,092**	S&P Core EPS 2007**E**	**9.00**	Institutional Ownership (%)	**NA**	S&P Credit Rating	**BBB-**

Price Performance

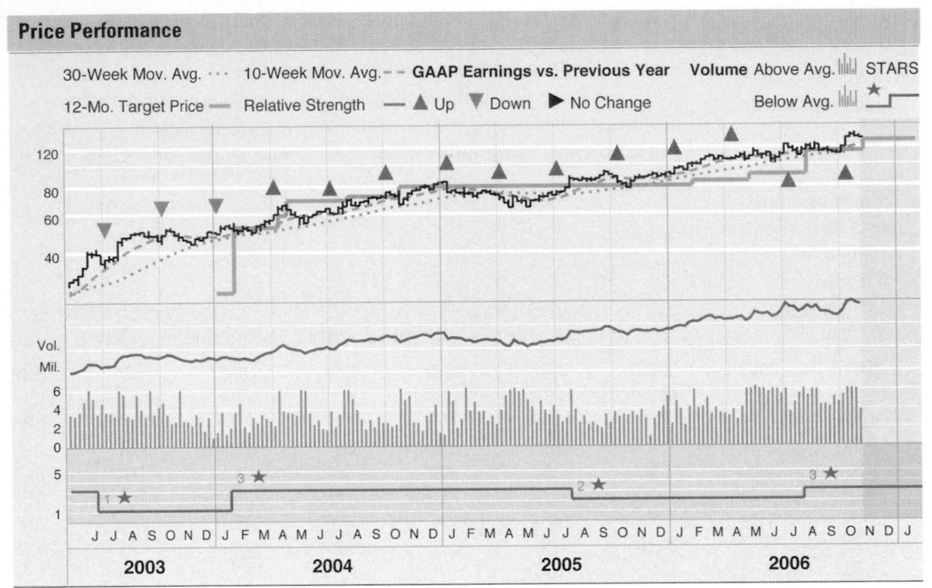

Options: ASE, CBOE, P, Ph

Highlights

- The 12-month target price for CMI has recently been changed to $128.00 from $115.00. The Highlights section of this Stock Report will be updated accordingly.

Investment Rationale/Risk

- The Investment Rationale/Risk section of this Stock Report will be updated shortly. For the latest News story on CMI from MarketScope, see below.

- 10/31/06 02:50 pm EST... S&P MAINTAINS HOLD OPINION ON SHARES OF CUMMINS (CMI 126.18***): Q3 operating EPS of $3.37 vs. $2.90 is below our $3.55 estimate. Sales increased 14%, slightly above our forecast, led by a 24% rise in the power generation business. Despite higher overall sales than we expected, profitability was limited, in our view, by higher costs than we anticipated in the components segment, reflecting certain manufacturing inefficiencies. We are keeping our '06 and '07 operating EPS estimates of $14.00 and $9.00, respectively. But our 12-month target price rises to $128 from $115, based on revised DCF analysis and higher peer group P/Es. /A. Fiore-CFA

Qualitative Risk Assessment

LOW | **MEDIUM** | HIGH

Our risk assessment reflects the highly cyclical nature of the North America medium (class 5-7) and heavy-duty (class 8) truck markets and significant pension and post-retirement benefit obligations, offset by a geographically diverse mix of business.

Quantitative Evaluations

S&P Quality Ranking **B**

D | C | B- | **B** | B+ | A- | A | A+

Relative Strength Rank **MODERATE**

52

LOWEST = 1 HIGHEST = 99

Revenue/Earnings Data

Revenue (Million $)

	1Q	2Q	3Q	4Q	Year
2006	2,678	2,842	2,809	--	--
2005	2,208	2,490	2,467	2,753	9,918
2004	1,771	2,124	2,194	2,349	8,438
2003	1,387	1,539	1,634	1,736	6,296
2002	1,333	1,458	1,648	1,414	5,853
2001	1,349	1,461	1,408	1,463	5,681

Earnings Per Share ($)

2006	2.70	4.38	3.37	**E**3.70	**E**14.00
2005	1.96	2.83	2.90	3.31	11.01
2004	0.76	1.76	2.40	2.41	7.39
2003	-0.79	0.34	0.60	1.07	1.36
2002	-0.69	0.40	1.06	1.10	2.06
2001	-0.68	-2.14	0.08	0.08	-2.66

Fiscal year ended Dec. 31. Next earnings report expected: Late January. EPS Estimates based on S&P Operating Earnings; historical GAAP earnings are as reported.

Dividend Data (Dates: mm/dd Payment Date: mm/dd/yy)

Amount ($)	Date Decl.	Ex-Div. Date	Stk. of Record	Payment Date
0.300	02/13	02/17	02/22	03/01/06
0.300	05/09	05/16	05/18	06/01/06
0.360	07/11	08/16	08/18	09/01/06
0.360	10/10	11/14	11/16	12/01/06

Dividends have been paid since 1948. Source: Company reports.

Cummins Inc.

Business Summary August 01, 2006

Truck engine makers such as Cummins continue to contend with price wars, highly cyclical markets, and an overabundance of global engine-making capacity. In addition, engine makers are constantly plowing back profits into engine development and plant and machinery, just to maintain market share. Over the past 10 years, research and development expenses and capital spending averaged 4.1% and 3.8% of revenues, respectively.

Strong, consistent earnings growth and return on equity (ROE) have been hard to achieve in the truck engine-making business. Over the past 10 years, earnings have been very erratic. During this period, CMI reported EPS as high as $7.39, and losses per share of as much as $2.66. ROE over the past 10 years averaged only 12%, versus an estimated 14% for the S&P 500.

In an effort to reduce earnings cyclicality and enter markets with better long-term growth potential, the company has been expanding into the power generation equipment and industrial filter arenas. As a result, these segments have been accounting for an increasing proportion of CMI's total sales and profits.

CMI's diesel engine making segment (57% and 63% of sales and operating profits in 2004; 6.2% operating margin) consists of heavy, medium and small truck/bus engines (67% of the engine segments sales), and machinery engines (23%). Major competitors include Caterpillar's truck engine operations and DaimlerChrysler's Detroit Diesel subsidiary.

The power generation segment (19% and 13%; 3.7%) primarily makes backup power generators for homes, offices and hospitals. Increasing unreliability of power utility authorities, improving technology, and the need to prevent computer and Internet systems from power outages are driving consumer and institutional demand for the company's stand-by power generators. Primary competitors include Caterpillar, Emerson Electric, Ingersoll Rand, and Honeywell International.

Company Financials

Per Share Data ($) Year Ended Dec. 31	**2005**	**2004**	**2003**	**2002**	**2001**	**2000**	**1999**	**1998**	**1997**	**1996**
Tangible Book Value	30.24	20.71	11.15	9.66	16.24	20.20	25.66	13.26	29.57	28.12
Cash Flow	18.17	13.52	7.01	7.16	3.39	6.49	10.08	4.56	9.49	7.92
Earnings	11.01	7.39	1.36	2.06	-2.66	-0.20	4.13	-0.55	5.48	4.01
S&P Core Earnings	11.40	8.01	1.59	-1.56	-5.75	NA	NA	NA	NA	NA
Dividends	1.20	1.20	1.20	1.20	1.20	1.20	1.13	1.10	1.08	1.00
Payout Ratio	11%	16%	88%	58%	NM	NM	27%	NM	20%	25%
Prices:High	93.88	84.67	52.31	50.29	45.50	50.00	65.69	62.75	83.00	47.75
Prices:Low	63.59	48.12	21.72	19.60	28.00	27.06	34.56	28.31	44.25	34.50
P/E Ratio:High	9	11	38	24	NM	NM	16	NM	15	12
P/E Ratio:Low	6	7	16	10	NM	NM	8	NM	8	9
Income Statement Analysis (Million $)										
Revenue	9,918	8,438	6,296	5,853	5,681	6,597	6,639	6,266	5,625	5,257
Operating Income	1,058	696	316	327	304	479	625	498	434	357
Depreciation	295	272	223	219	231	240	233	199	158	149
Interest Expense	109	113	101	82.0	87.0	86.0	75.0	71.0	26.0	18.0
Pretax Income	798	432	80.0	57.0	-129	3.00	221	-6.00	286	214
Effective Tax Rate	27.1%	13.0%	15.0%	NM	NM	NM	24.9%	NM	25.9%	25.2%
Net Income	550	350	54.0	79.0	-102	8.00	160	-21.0	212	160
S&P Core Earnings	570	380	62.8	-61.4	-221	NA	NA	NA	NA	NA
Balance Sheet & Other Financial Data (Million $)										
Cash	840	690	195	298	92.0	62.0	74.0	38.0	49.0	108
Current Assets	3,916	3,273	2,130	1,982	1,635	1,830	2,180	1,876	1,710	1,553
Total Assets	6,885	6,527	5,126	4,837	4,335	4,500	4,697	4,542	3,765	3,369
Current Liabilities	2,218	2,197	1,391	1,329	970	1,223	1,314	1,071	1,055	1,021
Long Term Debt	1,213	1,299	1,380	1,290	1,206	1,032	1,092	1,137	522	283
Common Equity	1,864	2,802	949	841	1,025	1,336	1,429	1,272	1,422	1,312
Total Capital	3,302	4,309	2,452	2,223	2,314	2,440	2,595	2,471	1,997	1,595
Capital Expenditures	186	151	111	90.0	206	228	215	271	405	304
Cash Flow	845	622	277	298	129	248	393	178	370	309
Current Ratio	1.8	1.5	1.5	1.5	1.7	1.5	1.7	1.8	1.6	1.5
% Long Term Debt of Capitalization	36.7	30.1	56.3	58.0	52.1	42.3	42.1	46.0	26.1	17.7
% Net Income of Revenue	5.5	4.1	0.9	1.3	NM	0.1	2.4	NM	3.8	3.0
% Return on Assets	8.2	6.0	1.1	1.7	NM	0.2	3.5	NM	5.9	5.0
% Return on Equity	33.7	14.9	6.0	8.7	NM	0.6	11.8	NM	15.5	12.8

Data as orig reptd.; bef. results of disc opers/spec. items. Per share data adj. for stk. divs.; EPS diluted. E-Estimated. NA-Not Available. NM-Not Meaningful. NR-Not Ranked. UR-Under Review.

Office: 500 Jackson Street, Columbus, IN 47202-3005.
Telephone: 812-377-5000.
Email: investor_relations@cummins.com
Website: http://www.cummins.com

Chrmn & CEO: T.M. Solso
Pres & COO: F.J. Loughrey
EVP & CFO: J.S. Blackwell
VP & Treas: R. Harris

VP, Secy & General Counsel: M.M. Rose
Investor Contact: D.A. Cantrell (812-377-3121)
Board of Directors: R. J. Darnall, J. M. Deutch, A. M. Herman, F. J. Loughrey, W. I. Miller, G. Nelson, T. M. Solso, C. Ware, J. L. Wilson

Founded: 1919
Domicile: Indiana
Employees: 33,500

STANDARD & POOR'S

CVS Corp

S&P Recommendation	Price	12-Mo. Target Price	Investment Style
STRONG BUY ★★★★★	$31.20 (as of Oct 27, 2006)	$40.00	Large-Cap Value

GICS Sector Consumer Staples
Sub-Industry Drug Retail

Comment This company is one of the largest U.S. drug store operators with about 6,200 stores and $37 billion in sales.

Key Stock Statistics (Source S&P, Vickers, company reports)

52-Wk Range	$36.14–23.89	S&P Oper. EPS 2006**E**	1.55	P/E on S&P Oper. EPS 2006**E**	20.1	Dividend Rate/Share	$0.16
Trailing 12-Month EPS	$1.56	S&P Oper. EPS 2007**E**	1.95	Common Shares Outstg. (M)	821.4	Yield (%)	0.50
Trailing 12-Month P/E	20.0	S&P Core EPS 2006**E**	1.55	Market Capitalization(B)	$25.628	Beta	1.03
$10K Invested 5 Yrs Ago	$20,172	S&P Core EPS 2007**E**	1.95	Institutional Ownership (%)	81	S&P Credit Rating	BBB+

Price Performance

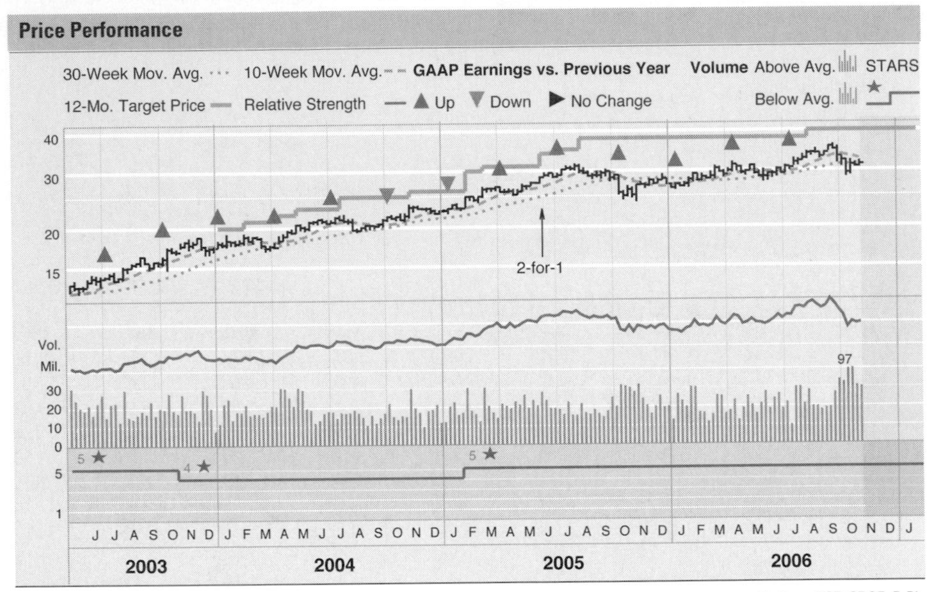

Options: ASE, CBOE, P, Ph

Analysis prepared by **Joseph Agnese** on October 12, 2006, when the stock traded at **$ 31.47**.

Highlights

- We expect total sales to increase about 18% in 2006, reflecting acquisitions, 3.5% organic square footage growth and same-store sales growth of about 8%. We look for pharmacy sales growth to be restricted by increased sales of lower priced generic drugs, but non-prescription sales should benefit from improved merchandising and increased customer traffic within acquired drug stores.
- We see margins narrowing slightly in 2006, as integration expenses from recent acquisitions, a rise in the mix of lower margin pharmacy sales, and higher employee benefit costs offset synergies from prior acquisitions that include increased sales leverage and improved purchasing power. Margin benefits we foresee also include an increased proportion of sales of wider margin generic drugs and improved cost management, due to inventory and pharmacy efficiency programs.
- We estimate 2006 operating EPS of $1.55 (including $0.05 of projected stock option expense), up 12% from $1.38 in 2005.

Investment Rationale/Risk

- We anticipate significant earnings benefits from the acquisition of 700 drugstores from Albertson's in June 2006 and from the integration of 1,100 former Eckerd drug stores that were acquired in July 2004. We believe the integration of both Albertson's and Eckerd stores provides an opportunity to accelerate earnings growth over the next few years from improved shrink control and increased customer counts due to more efficient service levels and improved merchandising.
- Risks to our recommendation and target price include potential problems that may arise in implementing and managing the acquisition of Albertson's drug stores.
- Assuming that the shares trade at 1.5X our projected long-term growth rate of 15%, and applying that ratio to our 2007 EPS estimate of $1.95, results in a value of $44. Our analysis of discounted cash flow, assuming a weighted average cost of capital of 9.0% and a terminal growth rate of 3.5%, suggests an intrinsic value of about $36. Blending our valuation metrics, our 12-month target price is $40.

Qualitative Risk Assessment

LOW	**MEDIUM**	HIGH

Our risk assessment reflects our view of the company's leadership position, and strong market share position, in a relatively stable U.S. retail drug industry, offset by the potential for acquisition integration risk and growth in non-traditional competitors.

Quantitative Evaluations

S&P Quality Ranking B+

D	C	B-	B	**B+**	A-	A	A+

Relative Strength Rank WEAK

21

LOWEST = 1 HIGHEST = 99

Revenue/Earnings Data

Revenue (Million $)

	1Q	2Q	3Q	4Q	Year
2006	9,979	10,561	--	--	--
2005	9,182	9,122	8,970	9,732	37,006
2004	6,819	6,943	7,909	8,923	30,594
2003	6,313	6,445	6,378	7,452	26,588
2002	5,971	5,990	5,876	6,345	24,182
2001	5,386	5,494	5,411	5,951	22,241

Earnings Per Share ($)

2006	0.39	0.40	**E**0.32	**E**0.44	**E**1.55
2005	0.35	0.33	0.30	0.48	1.45
2004	0.29	0.28	0.22	0.31	1.10
2003	0.24	0.25	0.23	0.32	1.03
2002	0.22	0.22	0.20	0.25	0.88
2001	0.27	0.24	0.15	-0.17	0.50

Fiscal year ended Dec. 31. Next earnings report expected: Early November. EPS Estimates based on S&P Operating Earnings; historical GAAP earnings are as reported.

Dividend Data (Dates: mm/dd Payment Date: mm/dd/yy)

Amount ($)	Date Decl.	Ex-Div. Date	Stk. of Record	Payment Date
0.039	01/12	01/19	01/23	02/03/06
0.039	03/01	04/20	04/24	05/03/06
0.039	07/06	07/19	07/21	08/01/06
0.039	09/20	10/18	10/21	11/01/06

Dividends have been paid since 1916. Source: Company reports.

Business Summary October 12, 2006

CORPORATE OVERVIEW. CVS Corp. operates one of the largest drug store chains in the U.S., based on revenues, net income and store count. The company offers prescription drugs and a wide assortment of general merchandise, including OTC drugs, beauty products and cosmetics, film and photo finishing services, seasonal merchandise, greeting cards and convenience foods. As of December 2005, net selling space in retail and specialty drugstores was 45 million sq. ft., with about half of its store base opened or significantly remodeled within the past five years. A typical store ranges in size from 8,000 sq. ft. to 13,000 sq. ft. Most new stores being built range in size between 10,000 sq. ft. and 13,000 sq. ft. and typically include a drive-thru pharmacy.

MARKET PROFILE. CVS is the largest U.S. drug store chain, based on store count, with about 6,150 stores as of August 2006, in 37 states and the District of Columbia. The company has stores in 71 of the top 100 U.S. drug store markets, holding the number one or number two market share in 50 of these markets, and 70% of all markets in which it operates. It filled more than 433 million prescriptions in 2005, accounting for about 14% of the U.S. retail pharmacy market. Pharmacy operations are critical to CVS's success, in our view, accounting for 70% of sales in 2005. Payments by third party managed care providers under prescription drug plans accounted for 94% of total pharmacy sales in 2005. Sales to Medicaid plans were approximately 9% of total sales and 13% of pharmacy sales in 2005. CVS's pharmacy benefit management (PBM) business operates under the PharmaCare Management Services name. This business generated $3.0 billion in sales in 2005 and covered approximately 30 million lives as of January 2005, ranking as the fourth largest full service PBM in the U.S., based on lives covered.

Company Financials

Per Share Data ($) Year Ended Dec. 31	**2005**	**2004**	**2003**	**2002**	**2001**	**2000**	**1999**	**1998**	**1997**	**1996**
Tangible Book Value	6.77	4.98	5.98	5.05	4.45	4.11	3.44	2.70	1.99	1.97
Cash Flow	2.14	1.69	1.46	1.25	0.88	1.26	1.10	0.78	0.36	0.71
Earnings	1.45	1.10	1.03	0.88	0.50	0.92	0.78	0.49	0.04	0.53
S&P Core Earnings	1.41	1.06	0.98	0.80	0.41	NA	NA	NA	NA	NA
Dividends	0.15	0.13	0.12	0.12	0.12	0.12	0.12	0.14	0.11	0.11
Payout Ratio	10%	12%	11%	13%	23%	13%	15%	29%	NM	21%
Prices:High	31.60	23.67	18.78	17.85	31.88	30.22	29.19	28.00	17.50	11.50
Prices:Low	22.02	16.87	10.92	11.52	11.45	13.88	15.00	15.22	9.75	6.81
P/E Ratio:High	22	22	18	20	64	33	38	57	NM	22
P/E Ratio:Low	15	15	11	13	23	15	19	31	NM	13

Income Statement Analysis (Million $)										
Revenue	37,006	30,594	26,588	24,182	22,241	20,088	18,098	15,274	12,738	5,528
Operating Income	2,609	1,952	1,765	1,517	1,091	1,619	1,413	1,181	664	370
Depreciation	589	497	342	310	321	297	278	250	222	76.0
Interest Expense	111	58.3	48.0	50.4	61.0	79.3	59.1	61.0	45.0	31.0
Pretax Income	1,909	1,396	1,376	1,156	710	1,243	1,076	711	155	403
Effective Tax Rate	35.8%	34.2%	38.4%	38.0%	41.8%	40.0%	41.0%	44.3%	76.1%	40.6%
Net Income	1,225	919	847	717	413	746	635	396	37.0	239
S&P Core Earnings	1,171	869	785	635	323	NA	NA	NA	NA	NA

Balance Sheet & Other Financial Data (Million $)										
Cash	513	392	843	700	236	337	230	181	169	424
Current Assets	8,393	7,920	6,497	5,982	5,454	4,937	4,608	4,349	3,685	1,973
Total Assets	15,283	14,547	10,543	9,645	8,628	7,950	7,275	6,736	5,637	2,832
Current Liabilities	4,584	4,859	3,489	3,106	3,066	2,964	2,890	3,183	2,855	1,182
Long Term Debt	1,594	1,926	753	1,076	810	537	558	276	273	304
Common Equity	8,109	6,759	6,022	4,991	4,306	4,037	3,404	2,830	2,077	946
Total Capital	9,925	8,913	6,817	6,318	12,706	4,869	4,265	3,386	2,634	1,569
Capital Expenditures	1,495	1,348	1,122	1,109	714	695	494	502	312	224
Cash Flow	1,800	1,401	1,189	1,012	719	1,028	898	632	245	301
Current Ratio	1.8	1.6	1.9	1.9	1.8	1.7	1.6	1.4	1.3	1.7
% Long Term Debt of Capitalization	16.1	21.6	11.0	17.0	63.8	11.0	13.1	8.2	10.4	19.4
% Net Income of Revenue	3.3	3.0	3.2	3.0	1.9	3.7	3.5	2.6	0.3	4.3
% Return on Assets	8.2	7.3	8.4	7.8	5.0	9.8	9.1	6.4	0.9	7.1
% Return on Equity	16.3	14.4	15.4	15.1	9.6	19.7	19.9	15.6	1.5	20.8

Data as orig reptd.; bef. results of disc opers/spec. items. Per share data adj. for stk. divs.; EPS diluted. E-Estimated. NA-Not Available. NM-Not Meaningful. NR-Not Ranked. UR-Under Review.

Office: One CVS Drive, Woonsocket, RI 02895-6184.
Telephone: 401-765-1500.
Email: investorinfo@cvs.com
Website: http://www.cvs.com

Chrmn, Pres & CEO: T.M. Ryan
EVP, CFO & Chief Admin: D.B. Rickard
SVP, Chief Acctg Officer & Cntlr: P.A. Price
VP & Treas: C. DeNale

Investor Contact: N.R. Christal (914-722-4704)
Board of Directors: W. D. Cornwell, D. W. Dorman, T. B. Gerrity, S. P. Goldstein, M. Heard, W. H. Joyce, T. Murray, S. Z. Rosenberg, T. M. Ryan, A. J. Verrecchia

Founded: 1892
Domicile: Delaware
Employees: 148,000

Danaher Corp

S&P Recommendation HOLD ★★★★★

Price $70.28 (as of Oct 27, 2006)

12-Mo. Target Price $75.00

Investment Style Large-Cap Growth

GICS Sector Industrials
Sub-Industry Industrial Machinery

Comment This company is a leading maker of tools, including Sears Craftsman hand tools, and of process/environmental controls and telecommunications equipment.

Key Stock Statistics (Source S&P, Vickers, company reports)

52-Wk Range	$72.16–51.11	S&P Oper. EPS 2006**E**	3.24	P/E on S&P Oper. EPS 2006**E**	21.7	Dividend Rate/Share	$0.08
Trailing 12-Month EPS	$3.26	S&P Oper. EPS 2007**E**	3.77	Common Shares Outstg. (M)	307.8	Yield (%)	0.11
Trailing 12-Month P/E	21.6	S&P Core EPS 2006**E**	3.22	Market Capitalization(B)	$21.632	Beta	0.80
$10K Invested 5 Yrs Ago	$23,796	S&P Core EPS 2007**E**	3.79	Institutional Ownership (%)	72	S&P Credit Rating	A+

Price Performance

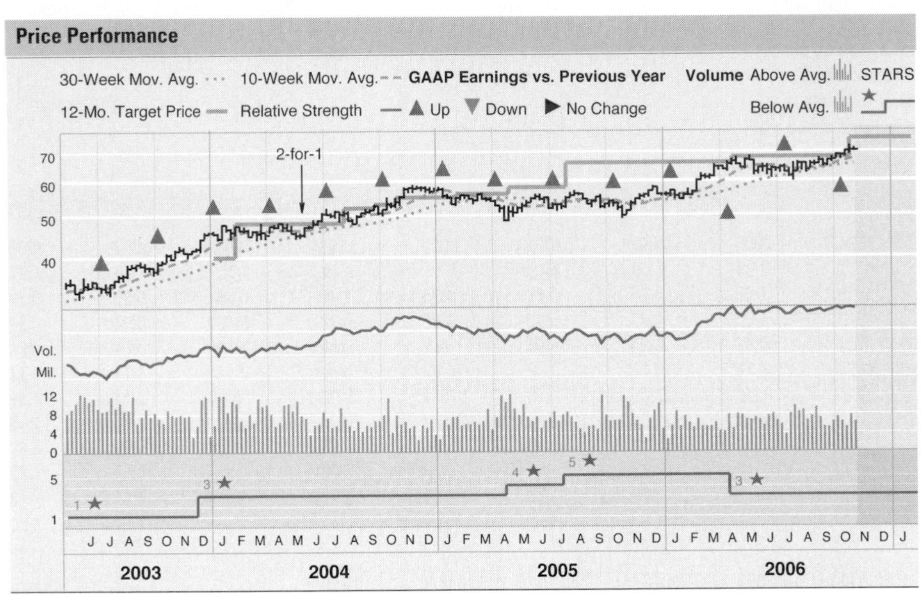

Options: ASE, CBOE, P, Ph

Analysis prepared by **Efraim Levy, CFA** on October 19, 2006, when the stock traded at **$ 70.33**.

Highlights

- We expect revenue growth of 14% in 2007 and 20% in 2006, driven by a combination of U.S. and foreign economic growth, and acquisitions. We project organic sales growth from all three operating segments.
- We see margins benefiting from employment reductions and other streamlining activities, partly offset by narrower margins at some acquired businesses. In October, the company said it expected EPS for 2006 of between $3.19 and $3.24, after $0.11 of projected stock option expense. Our $3.24 EPS estimate for 2006 includes estimated stock option expense, as we expect Danaher to match the high end of company forecasts.
- For the long term, we look for sales increases to be driven by internal growth, supplemented by acquisitions. We anticipate that a steady flow of new and enhanced products, as well as greater sales of traditional tool lines, will aid comparisons. We expect margins to widen over time, as DHR consolidates acquisitions and likely benefits from higher capacity utilization, productivity gains, and cost-cutting efforts. DHR has authorized a 10 million share buyback program that we view positively.

Investment Rationale/Risk

- The balance sheet appears healthy to us. Based on several valuation measures, the stock is at a premium to that of some peers. We believe this reflects DHR's wider net margins and faster growth. Its quality of earnings appears high to us, as we expect free cash flow in 2007 and 2006 to exceed net income, and we think that S&P Core EPS adjustments will be less than 1% in both 2007 and 2006.
- Risks to our recommendation and target price include slowing demand for DHR's products, and unfavorable changes in foreign exchange rates. Also, we are concerned about some of Danaher's corporate governance practices, particularly its classified board of directors with its staggered terms, which may allow certain policies to be entrenched longer despite shareholders' possible desire to change them.
- Given what we see as a sound balance sheet and in view of the strong cash flow growth that we expect in coming years, we think the company could raise its $0.08 annual cash dividend. Our 12-month target price of $75 is derived by applying a P/E of 20X to our 2007 EPS estimate of $3.77, reflecting peer and historical P/E multiples.

Qualitative Risk Assessment

LOW | **MEDIUM** | HIGH

Our risk assessment reflects our view of favorable growth prospects in most of the markets, good corporate leadership, and a healthy balance sheet, offset by corporate governance issues.

Quantitative Evaluations

S&P Quality Ranking A+

D | C | B- | B | B+ | A- | A | **A+**

Relative Strength Rank MODERATE

61

LOWEST = 1 HIGHEST = 99

Revenue/Earnings Data

Revenue (Million $)

	1Q	2Q	3Q	4Q	Year
2006	2,144	2,350	2,443	--	--
2005	1,826	1,929	1,966	2,264	7,985
2004	1,543	1,621	1,745	1,980	6,889
2003	1,196	1,299	1,309	1,489	5,294
2002	1,004	1,146	1,152	1,275	4,577
2001	1,005	956.6	901.6	918.9	3,782

Earnings Per Share ($)

	1Q	2Q	3Q	4Q	Year
2006	0.67	0.98	0.83	**E**0.94	**E**3.24
2005	0.58	0.70	0.70	0.78	2.76
2004	0.45	0.56	0.62	0.67	2.30
2003	0.33	0.40	0.44	0.53	1.69
2002	0.28	0.33	0.37	0.52	1.49
2001	0.28	0.32	0.29	0.12	1.01

Fiscal year ended Dec. 31. Next earnings report expected: Late January. EPS Estimates based on S&P Operating Earnings; historical GAAP earnings are as reported.

Dividend Data (Dates: mm/dd Payment Date: mm/dd/yy)

Amount ($)	Date Decl.	Ex-Div. Date	Stk. of Record	Payment Date
0.020	12/06	12/28	12/31	01/27/06
0.020	02/28	03/29	03/31	04/28/06
0.020	05/04	06/28	06/30	07/28/06
0.020	09/14	09/27	09/29	10/27/06

Dividends have been paid since 1993. Source: Company reports.

Danaher Corp

Business Summary October 19, 2006

CORPORATE OVERVIEW. Danaher Corp. is a leading maker of hand tools and process and environmental controls. The company has three reporting segments: professional instrumentation (more than 47% of 2005 sales), industrial technologies (37%), and tools and components (16%).

The professional instrumentation segment offers professional and technical customers various products and services that are used in connection with the performance of their work.

The industrial technologies segment manufactures products and sub-systems that are typically incorporated by original equipment manufacturers (OEMs) into various end-products and systems, as well as by customers and systems integrators into production and packaging lines.

The tools and components segment encompasses one strategic line of business, mechanics' hand tools, and four focused niche businesses--Delta Consolidated Industries, Hennessy Industries, Jacobs Chuck Manufacturing Company, and Jacobs Vehicle Systems.

Sales in 2005 by geographic destination were U.S. 53%, Europe 29%, Asia 12%, and other regions 6%.

CORPORATE STRATEGY. The company's strategy is to expand revenues through a combination of internal growth and acquisitions. We expect the company to continue its tradition of successful acquisition integrations.

In May 2006, as part of its acquisition strategy, the company acquired Sybron Dental Specialties Inc. for $47 per share. The total transaction, including the assumption of debt, is valued at about $2 billion. Sybron manufactures a broad range of equipment for the dental industry and had about $650 million in revenues in its fiscal year ended September 30, 2005.

Company Financials

Per Share Data ($) Year Ended Dec. 31	**2005**	**2004**	**2003**	**2002**	**2001**	**2000**	**1999**	**1998**	**1997**	**1996**
Tangible Book Value	NM	NM	0.99	0.01	NM	0.28	1.46	0.25	0.27	0.03
Cash Flow	3.28	2.75	2.07	1.87	1.57	1.63	1.33	1.05	0.96	0.82
Earnings	2.76	2.30	1.69	1.49	1.01	1.12	0.90	0.66	0.64	0.53
S&P Core Earnings	2.70	2.20	1.55	1.20	0.85	NA	NA	NA	NA	NA
Dividends	0.06	0.06	0.06	0.05	0.04	0.04	0.03	0.03	0.03	0.02
Payout Ratio	2%	2%	4%	3%	4%	3%	3%	4%	4%	4%
Prices:High	58.40	58.90	46.18	37.73	34.34	34.91	34.50	27.63	16.00	11.66
Prices:Low	48.32	43.83	29.78	26.30	21.95	18.22	21.38	14.00	9.75	7.31
P/E Ratio:High	21	26	27	25	34	31	39	42	25	22
P/E Ratio:Low	18	19	18	18	22	16	24	21	15	14
Income Statement Analysis (Million $)										
Revenue	7,985	6,889	5,294	4,577	3,782	3,770	3,197	2,910	2,051	1,812
Operating Income	1,446	1,253	957	824	750	702	584	475	343	295
Depreciation	177	156	133	130	178	150	126	109	76.1	68.6
Interest Expense	44.9	55.0	59.0	43.7	25.7	29.2	16.7	24.9	13.1	16.4
Pretax Income	1,234	1,058	797	657	476	523	430	301	254	210
Effective Tax Rate	27.3%	29.5%	32.6%	29.4%	37.5%	38.0%	39.1%	39.2%	39.0%	39.0%
Net Income	898	746	537	464	298	324	262	183	155	128
S&P Core Earnings	876	715	491	373	249	NA	NA	NA	NA	NA
Balance Sheet & Other Financial Data (Million $)										
Cash	316	609	1,230	810	707	177	260	41.9	33.3	26.4
Current Assets	2,945	2,919	2,942	2,387	1,875	1,474	1,202	887	618	547
Total Assets	9,163	8,494	6,890	6,029	4,820	4,032	3,047	2,739	1,880	1,765
Current Liabilities	2,269	2,202	1,380	1,265	1,017	1,019	709	689	524	475
Long Term Debt	858	926	1,284	1,197	1,119	714	341	413	163	220
Common Equity	5,080	4,620	3,647	3,010	2,229	1,942	1,709	1,352	917	800
Total Capital	5,938	5,545	4,931	4,207	3,348	2,656	2,050	1,765	1,080	1,020
Capital Expenditures	121	116	80.3	65.4	80.6	88.5	88.9	90.3	62.8	51.3
Cash Flow	1,075	902	670	594	476	474	388	292	231	197
Current Ratio	1.3	1.3	2.1	1.9	1.8	1.4	1.7	1.3	1.2	1.2
% Long Term Debt of Capitalization	14.4	16.7	26.0	28.5	33.4	26.9	16.6	23.4	15.1	21.5
% Net Income of Revenue	11.2	10.8	10.1	10.1	7.9	8.6	8.2	6.3	7.5	7.1
% Return on Assets	10.2	9.7	8.3	8.6	6.7	9.2	8.9	7.4	8.5	7.9
% Return on Equity	18.5	18.0	16.1	17.7	14.3	17.8	16.8	14.7	18.0	18.5

Data as orig reptd.; bef. results of disc opers/spec. items. Per share data adj. for stk. divs.; EPS diluted. E-Estimated. NA-Not Available. NM-Not Meaningful. NR-Not Ranked. UR-Under Review.

Office: 2099 Pennsylvania Ave NW Fl 12, Washington, DC 20006-6807.
Telephone: 202-828-0850.
Email: ir@danaher.com
Website: http://www.danaher.com

Chrmn: S.M. Rales
Pres & CEO: H.L. Culp, Jr.
EVP & Secy: P.W. Allender
SVP & General Counsel: J.P. Graham

Investor Contact: A. Wilson (202-828-0850)
Board of Directors: M. M. Caplin, H. L. Culp, Jr., D. J. Ehrlich, L. P. Hefner, W. G. Lohr, Jr., M. P. Rales, S. M. Rales, J. T. Schwieters, A. G. Spoon, A. E. Stephenson, Jr.

Founded: 1969
Domicile: Delaware
Employees: 40,000

STANDARD & POOR'S

Darden Restaurants Inc.

S&P Recommendation HOLD ★★★★★	Price $41.00 (as of Oct 27, 2006)	12-Mo. Target Price $42.00	Investment Style Mid-Cap Growth

GICS Sector Consumer Discretionary
Sub-Industry Restaurants

Comment This restaurant company operates the Red Lobster, Olive Garden, Smokey Bones and Bahama Breeze chains.

Key Stock Statistics (Source S&P, Vickers, company reports)

52-Wk Range	$44.43–32.00	S&P Oper. EPS 2007E	2.32	P/E on S&P Oper. EPS 2007E	17.7	Dividend Rate/Share	$0.46
Trailing 12-Month EPS	$2.22	S&P Oper. EPS 2008E	NA	Common Shares Outstg. (M)	146.8	Yield (%)	1.12
Trailing 12-Month P/E	18.5	S&P Core EPS 2007E	2.22	Market Capitalization(B)	$6.020	Beta	0.41
$10K Invested 5 Yrs Ago	$20,292	S&P Core EPS 2008E	NA	Institutional Ownership (%)	86	S&P Credit Rating	BBB+

Price Performance

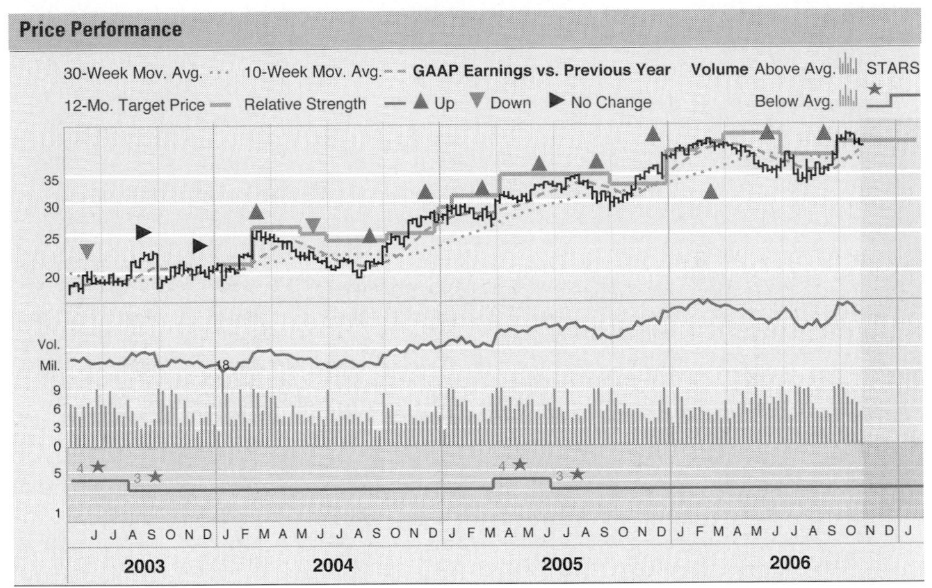

Options: ASE, CBOE, P, Ph

Highlights

- The 12-month target price for DRI has recently been changed to $42.00 from $39.00. The Highlights section of this Stock Report will be updated accordingly.

Investment Rationale/Risk

- The Investment Rationale/Risk section of this Stock Report will be updated shortly. For the latest News story on DRI from MarketScope, see below.

- 09/20/06 10:34 am EDT... S&P REITERATES HOLD RECOMMENDATION ON SHARES OF DARDEN RESTAURANTS (DRI 41.24***): The company posts Aug-Q EPS of $0.61, before one-time items, vs. $0.53, $0.09 above our estimate. Results benefited from same-store sales growth at Olive Garden units, lower food costs, well-controlled corporate expenses, and share repurchases. We are raising our FY 07 (May) EPS estimate by $0.10, to $2.32, and our 12-month target price by $2, to $42, to reflect improved operating margin projections. At 17.7X our FY 07 estimate, DRI is trading in line with peers. We believe this valuation adequately reflects the company's growth prospects / D.Milton

Qualitative Risk Assessment

LOW | **MEDIUM** | HIGH

DRI competes in the stable, and growing casual dining industry, and we believe that its Red Lobster and Olive Garden concepts have among the strongest brand name recognition in the industry. The company's balance sheet is somewhat more leveraged than most of its peers.

Quantitative Evaluations

S&P Quality Ranking A

D | C | B- | B | B+ | A- | **A** | A+

Relative Strength Rank MODERATE

49

LOWEST = 1 HIGHEST = 99

Revenue/Earnings Data

Revenue (Million $)

	1Q	2Q	3Q	4Q	Year
2007	1,456	--	--	--	--
2006	1,409	1,325	1,474	1,512	5,721
2005	1,279	1,229	1,376	1,394	5,278
2004	1,260	1,143	1,242	1,359	5,003
2003	1,175	1,143	1,181	1,227	4,655
2002	1,074	1,007	1,125	1,162	4,369

Earnings Per Share ($)

	1Q	2Q	3Q	4Q	Year
2007	0.59	E0.36	E0.71	E0.64	E2.32
2006	0.53	0.35	0.67	0.60	2.16
2005	0.44	0.26	0.56	0.52	1.78
2004	0.40	0.18	0.46	0.32	1.36
2003	0.40	0.18	0.35	0.35	1.31
2002	0.34	0.20	0.36	0.40	1.30

Fiscal year ended May 31. Next earnings report expected: Mid December. EPS Estimates based on S&P Operating Earnings; historical GAAP earnings are as reported.

Dividend Data (Dates: mm/dd Payment Date: mm/dd/yy)

Amount ($)	Date Decl.	Ex-Div. Date	Stk. of Record	Payment Date
0.200	09/22	10/05	10/10	11/01/05
0.200	03/21	04/06	04/10	05/01/06
0.230	09/19	10/05	10/10	11/01/06

Dividends have been paid since 1995. Source: Company reports.

Darden Restaurants Inc.

Business Summary June 22, 2006

With annual sales of more than $5.7 billion, Darden Restaurants is the world's largest publicly held casual dining restaurant company. At May 28, 2006, it operated 1,427 restaurants in the U.S. and Canada, including 682 Red Lobster units, 582 Olive Garden units, 126 Smokey Bones BBQ Sports Bar units, 32 Bahama Breeze restaurants, and five Seasons 52 locations.

Olive Garden is the U.S. market share leader among casual dining Italian food restaurants. FY 06 (May) systemwide sales grew 9.0%, to $2.6 billion. Same-restaurant sales were up 5.5%, after rising 7.2% in FY 05 and 4.6% in FY 04, and average restaurant sales were $4.6 million. The average check per person was $14 to $15 in FY 05 (latest available).

Red Lobster, founded by William Darden in 1968, is the largest U.S. casual dining, seafood-specialty restaurant operator. System sales totaled $2.6 billion in FY 06, up 5.9% from FY 05. Average restaurant sales were $3.8 million in FY 06, up from $3.6 in FY 05. Same-store sales rose 4.9% in FY 06, following a 0.9% increase in FY 05 and a 3.5% decline in FY 04. The average check per person in FY 05 (latest available) was $17.00 to $18.00.

The company's other concepts, Bahama Breeze and Smokey Bones, are relatively new, and have not yet gained enough scale to contribute meaningfully to profits. Bahama Breeze, first opened in 1996, is a Caribbean-themed restaurant that offers a distinctive island dining experience. Smokey Bones, first opened in 1999, combines barbecue with a relaxed sports bar atmosphere. The company expects the concepts to contribute only slightly to profits in FY 07, due to high operating costs and expansion-related expenses. It is currently experimenting with a new prototype for the Bahama Breeze chain in an attempt to closely match its cost structure with expected revenues. The company believes that Smokey Bones can contribute significantly to revenue and profit growth in the near future, but has recently slowed expansion plans to study unit costs.

Company Financials

Per Share Data ($) Year Ended May 31	**2006**	**2005**	**2004**	**2003**	**2002**	**2001**	**2000**	**1999**	**1998**	**1997**
Tangible Book Value	8.20	8.25	7.86	7.03	6.56	5.66	5.00	4.01	4.04	4.81
Cash Flow	3.57	3.08	2.60	2.43	2.20	1.85	1.55	1.34	1.00	0.20
Earnings	2.16	1.78	1.36	1.31	1.30	1.06	0.89	0.66	0.45	0.23
S&P Core Earnings	2.10	1.68	1.27	1.18	1.16	0.97	NA	NA	NA	NA
Dividends	0.08	0.08	0.08	0.05	0.05	0.05	0.05	0.05	0.05	0.05
Payout Ratio	4%	4%	6%	4%	4%	5%	6%	8%	12%	23%
Calendar Year	2005	2004	2003	2002	2001	2000	1999	1998	1997	1996
Prices:High	39.53	28.54	23.01	29.76	24.98	18.00	15.58	12.62	8.33	9.33
Prices:Low	25.78	18.48	16.50	18.00	12.67	8.29	10.42	7.83	4.50	5.00
P/E Ratio:High	18	16	17	23	19	17	17	19	19	40
P/E Ratio:Low	12	10	12	14	10	8	12	12	10	21

Income Statement Analysis (Million $)	2006	2005	2004	2003	2002	2001	2000	1999	1998	1997
Revenue	5,721	5,278	5,003	4,655	4,369	4,021	3,701	3,458	3,287	3,172
Operating Income	757	685	636	588	563	479	421	352	300	235
Depreciation	221	213	210	198	166	147	130	125	126	137
Interest Expense	43.1	43.1	43.7	44.1	37.8	31.5	23.1	40.6	20.5	23.3
Pretax Income	483	424	340	348	363	301	274	216	154	27.6
Effective Tax Rate	29.9%	31.4%	31.9%	33.2%	34.5%	34.6%	35.5%	34.9%	33.8%	NM
Net Income	338	291	231	232	238	197	177	141	102	-91.0
S&P Core Earnings	330	274	214	208	212	181	NA	NA	NA	NA

Balance Sheet & Other Financial Data (Million $)	2006	2005	2004	2003	2002	2001	2000	1999	1998	1997
Cash	42.3	42.8	36.7	48.6	153	61.8	26.1	41.0	33.5	25.5
Current Assets	378	407	346	326	450	328	290	328	398	337
Total Assets	3,010	2,938	2,780	2,665	2,530	2,218	1,971	1,906	1,985	1,964
Current Liabilities	1,026	1,045	683	640	601	554	607	534	559	481
Long Term Debt	495	350	653	658	663	518	304	314	311	313
Common Equity	1,230	1,273	1,246	1,196	1,129	1,035	960	964	1,020	1,081
Total Capital	1,815	1,738	2,075	2,005	1,909	1,644	1,344	1,350	1,408	1,464
Capital Expenditures	338	329	354	423	318	355	269	124	112	160
Cash Flow	560	504	441	430	404	344	307	266	228	45.8
Current Ratio	0.4	0.4	0.5	0.5	0.7	0.6	0.5	0.6	0.7	0.7
% Long Term Debt of Capitalization	27.3	20.2	31.5	32.8	34.7	31.5	22.6	23.3	22.0	21.4
% Net Income of Revenue	5.9	5.5	4.6	5.0	5.4	4.9	4.8	4.1	3.1	NM
% Return on Assets	11.4	10.2	8.5	8.9	10.0	9.4	9.2	7.2	5.2	NM
% Return on Equity	27.0	23.7	19.0	20.0	22.0	19.7	18.4	14.2	9.7	NM

Data as orig reptd.; bef. results of disc opers/spec. items. Per share data adj. for stk. divs.; EPS diluted. E-Estimated. NA-Not Available. NM-Not Meaningful. NR-Not Ranked. UR-Under Review.

Office: 5900 Lake Ellenor Drive, Orlando, FL 32809-4634.
Telephone: 407-245-4000.
Email: irinfo@darden.com
Website: http://www.darden.com

Chrmn & CEO: C. Otis, Jr.
Pres & COO: A.H. Madsen
SVP & CFO: L.J. Dimopoulos
SVP, Secy & General Counsel: P.J. Shives

SVP & Cntlr: C.B. Richmond
Board of Directors: L. L. Berry, O. C. Donald, D. H. Hughes, C. A. Ledsinger, Jr., W. M. Lewis, Jr., C. Mack, III, A. H. Madsen, C. McGillicuddy, III, C. Otis, Jr., M. D. Rose, M. A. Sastre, J. A. Smith, B. Sweatt, III, R. P. Wilson

Founded: 1968
Domicile: Florida
Employees: 157,300

STANDARD &POOR'S

Dean Foods Co

S&P Recommendation BUY ★★★★★

Price $42.10 (as of Oct 27, 2006)

12-Mo. Target Price $46.00

Investment Style Mid-Cap Growth

GICS Sector Consumer Staples
Sub-Industry Packaged Foods & Meats

Comment This leading U.S. dairy processor and distributor was formed in December 2001 when Suiza Foods acquired Dean Foods.

Key Stock Statistics (Source S&P, Vickers, company reports)

52-Wk Range	$43.27–34.66	S&P Oper. EPS 2006E	2.13	P/E on S&P Oper. EPS 2006E	19.8	Dividend Rate/Share	Nil
Trailing 12-Month EPS	$1.82	S&P Oper. EPS 2007E	2.45	Common Shares Outstg. (M)	133.5	Yield (%)	Nil
Trailing 12-Month P/E	23.1	S&P Core EPS 2006E	2.15	Market Capitalization(B)	$5.619	Beta	0.07
$10K Invested 5 Yrs Ago	$25,107	S&P Core EPS 2007E	2.48	Institutional Ownership (%)	82	S&P Credit Rating	NA

Price Performance

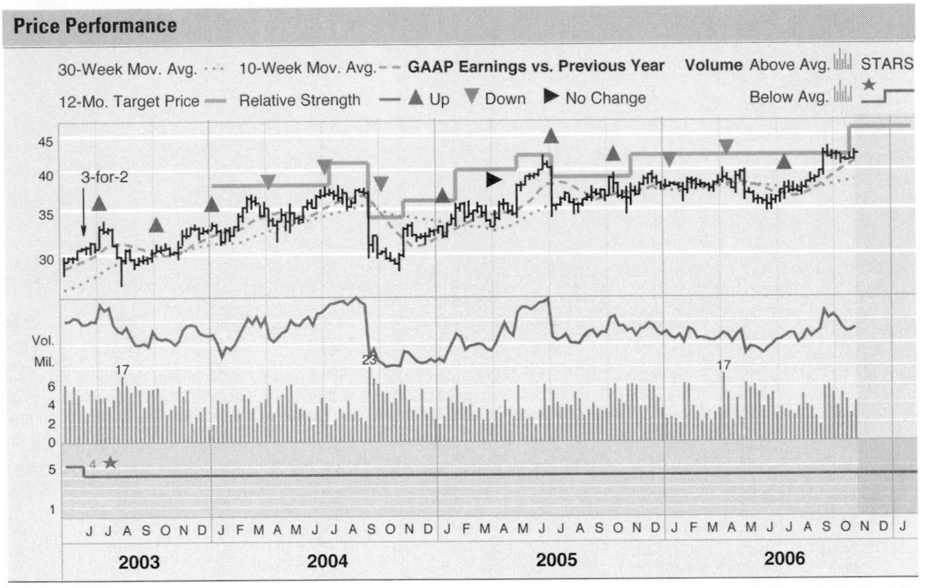

Options: ASE, CBOE, P, Ph

Analysis prepared by **Rick Joy** on October 24, 2006, when the stock traded at **$ 42.03**.

Highlights

- We expect net sales to advance less than 1% at DF in 2006, as increased demand for milk and strong branded products growth outweigh lower milk prices. We see continued strong growth for soy milk and organic products.
- We believe operating margins in 2006 will be aided by a moderation in dairy cost volatility, improving economies of scale in the dairy business, and better input cost trends. Margin gains are likely to be tempered somewhat as the company maintains high levels of branded product advertising and marketing spending. We expect spending to be focused particularly on the company's Silk, Sun Soy and International Delight brands. We look for operating income to advance at a high single digit rate in 2006.
- Following higher interest expense and a 7% to 8% reduction in shares outstanding, we estimate EPS of $2.13 (includes projected stock option expense of $0.10) in 2006, up 8% from 2005 EPS of $1.97. For the long term, we see annual EPS growth of 8% to 10%. Our 2006 Standard & Poor's Core EPS estimate is $2.15.

Investment Rationale/Risk

- Our buy recommendation on the shares reflects our expectation for modest dairy commodity cost volatility in 2007, and strong long-term earnings growth and margin expansion as the company continues its transition to a more value-added product line, and as it realizes the benefits of plant rationalizations and scale efficiencies. At a recent price of approximately 17X our 2007 EPS estimate of $2.40, a premium to the P/E multiple for the S&P 400 but in line with food industry peers, we consider the shares attractive.
- Risks to our recommendation and target price include commodity cost volatility in the dairy markets, a possible lack of consumer acceptance of new product introductions, and the company's ability to achieve sales and earnings growth forecasts.
- Our DCF model, which assumes an 8.5% cost of capital and 3.5% terminal growth, calculates an intrinsic value of $48. Our relative valuation model, which is based on peer P/E and enterprise value (EV)/EBITDA multiples, targets a value of $44 to $45. Blending these valuations, our 12-month target price is $46.

Qualitative Risk Assessment

LOW | MEDIUM | HIGH

Our risk assessment for Dean Foods reflects the relatively stable nature of the company's end markets, our view of its strong cash flow, and corporate governance practices that we consider favorable relative to peers.

Quantitative Evaluations

S&P Quality Ranking B+

D | C | B- | B | B+ | A- | A | A+

Relative Strength Rank MODERATE

60

LOWEST = 1 HIGHEST = 99

Revenue/Earnings Data

Revenue (Million $)

	1Q	2Q	3Q	4Q	Year
2006	2,592	2,478	--	--	--
2005	2,562	2,603	2,647	2,695	10,506
2004	2,452	2,807	2,773	2,791	10,822
2003	2,145	2,223	2,307	2,510	9,185
2002	2,226	2,295	2,230	2,240	8,991
2001	1,474	1,527	1,556	1,673	6,230

Earnings Per Share ($)

	1Q	2Q	3Q	4Q	Year
2006	0.37	0.53	**E**0.55	**E**0.63	**E**2.13
2005	0.43	0.52	0.43	0.49	1.78
2004	0.43	0.47	0.25	0.64	1.78
2003	0.43	0.54	0.76	0.54	2.27
2002	0.37	0.48	0.45	0.47	1.77
2001	0.27	0.37	0.32	0.29	1.23

Fiscal year ended Dec. 31. Next earnings report expected: Early November. EPS Estimates based on S&P Operating Earnings; historical GAAP earnings are as reported.

Dividend Data

No cash dividends have been paid.

Please read the Required Disclosures and Analyst Certification on the last page of this report.

The McGraw-Hill Companies

Dean Foods Co

Business Summary October 24, 2006

Dean Foods Co. is the leading U.S. processor and distributor of milk and other dairy products. In December 2001, Suiza Foods Corp., the largest U.S. dairy, acquired Dean Foods Co. Suiza subsequently changed its name to Dean Foods Co. DF currently has three operating divisions: Dairy Group, White Wave Foods Company, and International. The company has grown primarily through an aggressive acquisition strategy and by realizing regional economies of scale and operating efficiencies by consolidating manufacturing and distribution operations in each of its core businesses.

Through the Dairy Group ($8.96 billion of sales in 2005), the company sells primarily fresh dairy products with a product mix weighted heavily toward fluid milk. Products sold include fluid milk, ice cream, half-and-half, condensed milk, cottage cheese, sour cream, yogurt, dips, coffee creamers, juice and juice drinks, and water. The decentralized group is organized by geographic regions, with products manufactured in 97 plants throughout 34 states. Products are delivered directly from plants or distribution warehouses to customers in trucks in a form of delivery called direct store delivery (DSD). With one of the most extensive refrigerated DSD systems in the U.S., DF has more than 6,000 routes, covering nearly the entire country. Products are sold to a variety of retail and food service customers, including grocery stores, club stores, convenience stores, mass merchandisers, schools, restaurants, hotels and distributors. Wal-Mart accounted for 15.6% of the Dairy Group's sales in 2005.

The White Wave Foods Company ($1.14 billion) develops, manufactures and markets a variety of nationally branded soy, dairy and dairy-related products, such as Silk soymilk and cultured soy products; Horizon Organic dairy products; juices and other products; International Delight coffee creamers; LAND O'LAKES creamers and cultured products; Sun Soy soymilk; Hershey's milks and milkshakes; Marie's dips and dressings; and Naturally Yours sour cream. The company licenses the LAND O'LAKES and Hershey's names from third parties.

Company Financials

Per Share Data ($) Year Ended Dec. 31	2005	2004	2003	2002	2001	2000	1999	1998	1997	1996
Tangible Book Value	NM	NM	NM	NM	NM	NM	NM	NM	NM	NM
Cash Flow	3.22	1.58	3.41	2.71	2.44	2.35	2.05	1.55	0.95	1.27
Earnings	1.78	1.78	2.27	1.77	1.23	1.27	1.04	0.97	0.42	0.94
S&P Core Earnings	1.66	1.58	1.85	1.57	0.91	NA	NA	NA	NA	NA
Dividends	Nil	Nil	Nil	Nil	Nil	Nil	Nil	Nil	Nil	Nil
Payout Ratio	Nil	Nil	Nil	Nil	Nil	Nil	Nil	Nil	Nil	Nil
Prices:High	42.10	38.00	33.75	27.03	24.16	17.48	16.75	22.33	20.83	6.92
Prices:Low	31.60	28.25	24.60	18.05	14.00	12.00	9.88	8.56	6.42	4.67
P/E Ratio:High	24	21	15	15	20	14	16	23	49	7
P/E Ratio:Low	18	16	11	10	11	9	10	9	15	5
Income Statement Analysis (Million $)										
Revenue	10,506	10,822	9,185	8,991	6,230	5,756	4,482	3,321	1,795	521
Operating Income	867	919	889	856	542	524	406	334	177	45.1
Depreciation	221	224	192	174	155	145	155	91.8	44.6	9.93
Interest Expense	169	205	195	231	135	147	87.8	82.3	36.7	17.5
Pretax Income	439	462	574	421	231	234	193	164	82.7	21.1
Effective Tax Rate	37.9%	38.3%	38.0%	36.4%	36.3%	38.4%	39.1%	36.4%	52.4%	NM
Net Income	272	285	356	268	116	114	109	103	39.3	27.9
S&P Core Earnings	254	253	288	236	79.2	NA	NA	NA	NA	NA
Balance Sheet & Other Financial Data (Million $)										
Cash	25.1	27.6	47.1	45.9	78.3	31.0	25.2	54.9	24.4	8.95
Current Assets	1,477	1,596	1,401	1,311	1,482	818	639	814	396	87.5
Total Assets	7,051	7,756	6,993	6,582	6,732	3,780	2,659	3,014	1,403	384
Current Liabilities	1,137	1,106	1,170	1,268	1,175	700	479	559	233	60.6
Long Term Debt	3,329	3,116	2,611	3,140	3,556	1,809	1,373	1,576	778	227
Common Equity	1,872	2,661	2,543	1,643	1,476	599	584	656	356	93.5
Total Capital	5,688	6,308	5,542	5,077	5,313	3,047	2,145	2,390	1,157	324
Capital Expenditures	307	356	292	242	137	137	188	177	62.1	14.0
Cash Flow	494	509	548	442	270	259	264	195	83.9	37.9
Current Ratio	1.3	1.4	1.2	1.0	1.3	1.2	1.3	1.5	1.7	1.4
% Long Term Debt of Capitalization	58.5	49.4	47.1	61.8	66.9	59.3	64.0	65.9	67.2	70.1
% Net Income of Revenue	2.6	2.6	3.9	3.0	1.9	1.9	2.4	3.1	2.2	5.4
% Return on Assets	3.7	3.9	5.2	4.0	2.2	3.5	3.8	4.7	4.4	9.1
% Return on Equity	12.0	11.0	17.0	17.2	11.1	19.2	17.6	20.3	17.5	54.2

Data as orig reptd.; bef. results of disc opers/spec. items. Per share data adj. for stk. divs.; EPS diluted. E-Estimated. NA-Not Available. NM-Not Meaningful. NR-Not Ranked. UR-Under Review.

Office: 2515 McKinney Avenue, Dallas, TX 75201.
Telephone: 214-303-3400.
Website: http://www.deanfoods.com
Chrmn & CEO: G.L. Engles

EVP & CFO: J.F. Callahan, Jr.
EVP, Secy & General Counsel: M.P. Goolsby
SVP & Chief Acctg Officer: R.L. McCrummen
VP & Treas: T.A. Smith

Board of Directors: A. J. Bernon, L. M. Collens, T. Davis, G. L. Engles, S. L. Green, J. S. Hardin, Jr., J. Hill, R. Kirk, J. Llewellyn, Jr., J. R. Muse, H. M. Nevares, P. E. Pender, P. Schenkel, J. L. Turner

Founded: 1925
Domicile: Delaware
Employees: 27,030

STANDARD &POOR'S

Deere & Co

S&P Recommendation HOLD ★★★★★

Price $87.00 (as of Oct 27, 2006)

12-Mo. Target Price $78.00

Investment Style Large-Cap Value

GICS Sector Industrials
Sub-Industry Construction & Farm Machinery & Heavy Trucks

Comment DE, the world's largest producer of farm equipment, is also a large maker of construction machinery and lawn and garden equipment.

Key Stock Statistics (Source S&P, Vickers, company reports)

52-Wk Range	$91.98–59.70	S&P Oper. EPS 2006E	6.16	P/E on S&P Oper. EPS 2006E	14.1	Dividend Rate/Share	$1.56
Trailing 12-Month EPS	$6.94	S&P Oper. EPS 2007E	7.00	Common Shares Outstg. (M)	231.2	Yield (%)	1.79
Trailing 12-Month P/E	12.5	S&P Core EPS 2006E	6.35	Market Capitalization(B)	$20.114	Beta	1.10
$10K Invested 5 Yrs Ago	$24,191	S&P Core EPS 2007E	7.19	Institutional Ownership (%)	83	S&P Credit Rating	A-

Price Performance

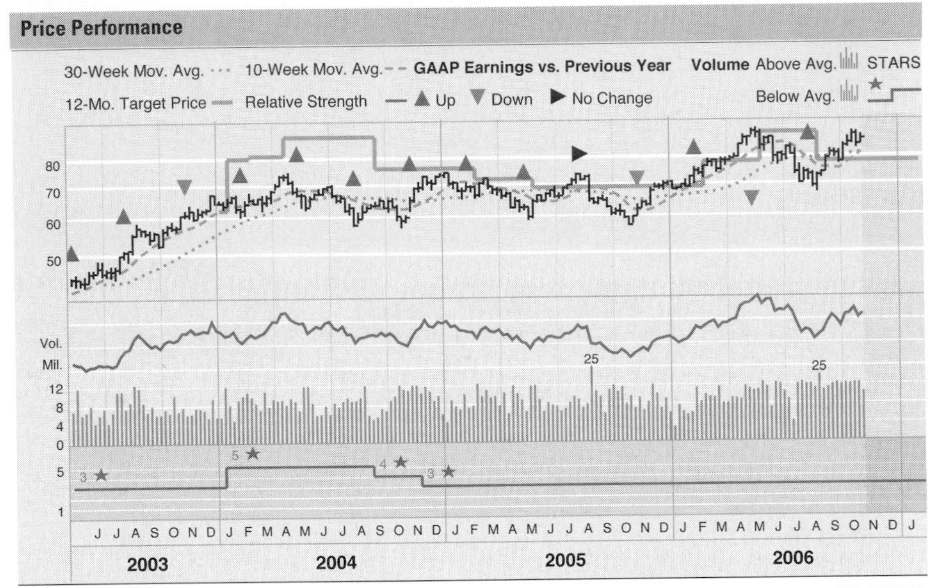

Options: ASE, CBOE, Ph

Analysis prepared by **Anthony M. Fiore, CFA** on August 18, 2006, when the stock traded at **$ 72.43**.

Highlights

- We expect revenue growth of about 5% in FY 07 (Oct.), following a projected advance of 3% in FY 06, based on our outlook for continued strength in U.S. farm cash receipts, combined with expected sales of new products and improved pricing. We anticipate that payments to farmers as a result of the current farm bill will continue to provide support for farm equipment sales in FY 07.
- In terms of profitability, we anticipate operating margins to widen only fractionally in FY 07, as we see improving price realization and lower expected pension and other post-retirement benefit expense, partially offset by a continuation of high raw material costs that we anticipate. For the longer term, we expect growth in the production of ethanol from corn over the next five years will increase demand for corn, which in turn should boost prices of corn and, ultimately, cash receipts for farmers.
- Our 2006 operating EPS estimate includes $0.20 of projected stock option expense. Our 2007 S&P Core EPS estimate is $0.19 a share above our operating EPS forecast, with the difference reflecting pension and post-retirement related adjustments.

Investment Rationale/Risk

- Our enthusiasm for the stock is tempered by our belief that near-term profitability will be limited by a projected decline in unit sales volumes of agricultural equipment and also due to what we see as difficult earnings comparisons. As in prior industry cycles, we expect DE shares to trade at lower multiples during peak or near-peak EPS years.
- Risks to our recommendation and target price include the potential for lower crop prices to negatively affect spending on farm equipment; weaker than expected European demand as a result of Common Agricultural Policy reform; continued raw material cost escalation; and an unexpected slowdown in end markets.
- Our 12-month target price of $78 combines two valuation metrics. Our discounted cash flow model, which assumes a 5% average annual free cash flow growth rate over the next 10 years, 3.5% growth in perpetuity, and a 9% discount rate, indicates intrinsic value of about $79. In terms of relative valuation, applying a target P/E multiple of about 11X, in line with historical norms, to our FY 07 EPS estimate leads to a value of $78. By blending these two methodologies, we arrive at our target price.

Qualitative Risk Assessment

LOW	**MEDIUM**	HIGH

Our risk assessment for Deere & Co. reflects the highly cyclical nature of the company's business, its leading position in many of the markets it serves, and our view of a strong equipment operations balance sheet with large cash balances offset by its significant post retirement benefit obligations.

Quantitative Evaluations

S&P Quality Ranking B

D	C	B-	**B**	B+	A-	A	A+

Relative Strength Rank MODERATE

70

LOWEST = 1 HIGHEST = 99

Revenue/Earnings Data

Revenue (Million $)

	1Q	2Q	3Q	4Q	Year
2006	4,202	6,562	6,267	--	--
2005	4,127	6,621	6,005	5,177	21,931
2004	2,912	5,877	5,418	5,207	19,986
2003	2,794	4,400	4,402	3,939	15,535
2002	2,522	3,987	3,969	3,469	13,947
2001	2,680	3,776	3,584	3,161	13,293

Earnings Per Share ($)

2006	0.94	2.17	1.85	E0.96	E6.16
2005	0.89	2.43	1.58	0.96	5.87
2004	0.68	1.88	1.58	1.41	5.56
2003	0.28	1.07	1.02	0.27	2.64
2002	-0.16	0.59	0.61	0.28	1.33
2001	0.24	0.54	0.30	-1.36	-0.27

Fiscal year ended Oct. 31. Next earnings report expected: Late November. EPS Estimates based on S&P Operating Earnings; historical GAAP earnings are as reported.

Dividend Data (Dates: mm/dd Payment Date: mm/dd/yy)

Amount ($)	Date Decl.	Ex-Div. Date	Stk. of Record	Payment Date
0.390	11/30	12/28	12/31	02/01/06
0.390	02/22	03/29	03/31	05/01/06
0.390	05/31	06/28	06/30	08/01/06
0.390	08/30	09/27	09/30	11/01/06

Dividends have been paid since 1937. Source: Company reports.

Please read the Required Disclosures and Analyst Certification on the last page of this report.

Deere & Co

Business Summary August 18, 2006

CORPORATE OVERVIEW. Deere & Co. is the world's largest maker of farm tractors and combines, and a leading maker of construction equipment. Its largest competitors include construction equipment behemoth Caterpillar Inc.; Netherlands-based CNH Global N.V., a worldwide maker of both farm and construction equipment; and AGCO Corp., the world's third largest global farm equipment maker.

The farm equipment segment (54% of FY 05 (Oct.) revenues; 9.2% operating margin) primarily makes tractors; combine, cotton and sugar cane harvesters; tillage, seeding and soil preparation machinery; hay and forage equipment; material handling equipment; and integrated agricultural management systems technology for the global farming industry. Over the past five years, segment margins averaged about 7.4%.

The commercial and consumer equipment segment (C&CE; 19%; 5.1%) manufactures and distributes equipment and service parts for commercial uses. Products include small tractors for lawn, garden, commercial and utility purposes; riding and walk-behind mowers; golf course equipment; utility vehicles; landscape and irrigation equipment; and other outdoor products. In addition, this division also includes John Deere Landscapes, Inc., a distributor of irrigation equipment, nursery products and landscape products. Over the past five years, segment margins averaged 4.1%.

The construction and forestry segment (27%; 13%) manufactures and distributes a broad range of machines and service parts used in construction, earthmoving, material handling and timber harvesting. Products include backhoe loaders; crawler dozers and loaders; four-wheel-drive loaders; excavators; motor graders; articulated dump trucks; landscape loaders; skid-steer loaders; and log skidders, feller bunchers, harvesters and related attachments. Over the past five years, margins for this segment averaged 6.1%.

The credit segment finances sales and leases by John Deere dealers of new and used agricultural, commercial and consumer, and construction and forestry equipment. In addition, this division provides wholesale financing to dealers, provides operating loans and finances retail revolving charge accounts. Credit operations had receivables under management of $12.9 billion at October 31, 2005. Over the past five years, margins for the segment averaged about 27%.

Company Financials

Per Share Data ($) Year Ended Oct. 31	2005	2004	2003	2002	2001	2000	1999	1998	1997	1996
Tangible Book Value	24.25	21.86	11.82	9.49	13.14	15.56	16.24	16.65	15.96	12.72
Cash Flow	8.46	8.01	5.24	4.34	2.78	4.80	3.21	5.85	5.30	4.39
Earnings	5.87	5.56	2.64	1.33	-0.27	2.06	1.02	4.16	3.78	3.14
S&P Core Earnings	6.04	5.67	3.07	-0.38	-1.63	NA	NA	NA	NA	NA
Dividends	1.21	1.06	0.88	0.88	0.88	0.88	0.88	0.88	0.80	0.80
Payout Ratio	21%	19%	33%	66%	NM	43%	86%	21%	21%	25%
Prices:High	74.41	74.93	67.41	51.60	46.13	49.63	45.94	64.13	60.50	47.13
Prices:Low	56.99	56.72	37.56	37.50	33.50	30.31	31.56	28.38	39.88	33.00
P/E Ratio:High	13	13	26	39	NM	24	45	15	16	15
P/E Ratio:Low	10	10	14	28	NM	15	31	7	11	11

Income Statement Analysis (Million $)	2005	2004	2003	2002	2001	2000	1999	1998	1997	1996
Revenue	21,931	19,986	15,535	13,947	13,293	13,137	11,751	13,749	12,791	11,229
Operating Income	3,553	2,976	2,231	1,696	1,274	2,102	1,435	2,197	2,295	1,999
Depreciation	636	621	631	725	718	648	513	418	366	311
Interest Expense	761	592	1,257	637	766	676	557	519	422	402
Pretax Income	2,162	2,115	980	578	-46.3	779	374	1,575	1,511	1,298
Effective Tax Rate	33.1%	33.5%	34.4%	44.7%	NM	37.7%	36.1%	35.2%	36.5%	37.0%
Net Income	1,447	1,406	643	319	-64.0	486	239	1,021	960	817
S&P Core Earnings	1,483	1,430	743	-94.8	-385	NA	NA	NA	NA	NA

Balance Sheet & Other Financial Data (Million $)	2005	2004	2003	2002	2001	2000	1999	1998	1997	1996
Cash	4,708	3,428	4,616	3,004	1,206	419	612	1,177	330	1,161
Current Assets	NA	NA	NA	NA	NA	NA	NA	NA	NA	NA
Total Assets	33,637	28,754	26,258	23,768	22,663	20,469	17,578	18,002	16,320	14,653
Current Liabilities	NA	NA	NA	NA	NA	NA	NA	NA	NA	NA
Long Term Debt	11,739	11,090	10,404	8,950	6,561	4,764	3,806	2,792	2,623	2,425
Common Equity	6,825	6,350	2,834	1,797	3,992	4,302	4,094	4,080	4,148	3,557
Total Capital	18,564	17,441	13,238	10,772	10,566	9,141	7,963	6,892	6,792	5,991
Capital Expenditures	513	364	310	359	491	427	316	435	485	687
Cash Flow	2,083	2,027	1,275	1,045	654	1,133	752	1,439	1,326	1,128
Current Ratio	NA	NA	NA	NA	NA	NA	NA	NA	NA	NA
% Long Term Debt of Capitalization	63.2	63.6	78.6	83.1	62.1	52.1	47.8	40.5	38.6	40.5
% Net Income of Revenue	6.6	7.0	4.2	2.4	NM	3.8	2.0	7.4	7.5	7.3
% Return on Assets	4.6	5.1	2.6	1.4	NM	2.6	1.3	5.9	6.2	5.7
% Return on Equity	22.0	30.6	27.8	11.8	NM	11.6	5.8	24.8	24.9	24.6

Data as orig reptd.; bef. results of disc opers/spec. items. Per share data adj. for stk. divs.; EPS diluted. E-Estimated. NA-Not Available. NM-Not Meaningful. NR-Not Ranked. UR-Under Review.

Office: One John Deere Place, Moline, IL 61265.
Telephone: 309-765-8000.
Email: stockholder@deere.com
Website: http://www.deere.com

Chrmn, Pres & CEO: R.W. Lane
SVP & CFO: M.J. Mack, Jr.
SVP & General Counsel: J.R. Jenkins
Investor Contact: M. Ziegler (309-765-4491)

Secy: M.H. Howze
Board of Directors: J. R. Block, C. C. Bowles, V. D. Coffman, T. K. Dunnigan, L. A. Hadley, D. C. Jain, A. L. Kelly, R. W. Lane, A. Madero, J. Milberg, R. B. Myers, T. H. Patrick, A. L. Peters, J. R. Walter

Founded: 1837
Domicile: Delaware
Employees: 47,400

STANDARD & POOR'S

Dell Inc

S&P Recommendation HOLD ★★★★★

Price $23.11 (as of Oct 27, 2006)

12-Mo. Target Price $23.00

Investment Style Large-Cap Growth

GICS Sector Information Technology
Sub-Industry Computer Hardware

Comment Dell (formerly Dell Computer Corp.) is the leading direct marketer and one of the world's 10 leading manufacturers of PCs compatible with industry standards established by IBM.

Key Stock Statistics (Source S&P, Vickers, company reports)

52-Wk Range	$33.22–18.95	S&P Oper. EPS 2007**E**	1.15	P/E on S&P Oper. EPS 2007**E**	20.1	Dividend Rate/Share	Nil
Trailing 12-Month EPS	$1.23	S&P Oper. EPS 2008**E**	1.45	Common Shares Outstg. (M)	2,271.6	Yield (%)	Nil
Trailing 12-Month P/E	18.8	S&P Core EPS 2007**E**	1.15	Market Capitalization(B)	$52.497	Beta	1.15
$10K Invested 5 Yrs Ago	$9,063	S&P Core EPS 2008**E**	1.45	Institutional Ownership (%)	66	S&P Credit Rating	A-

Price Performance

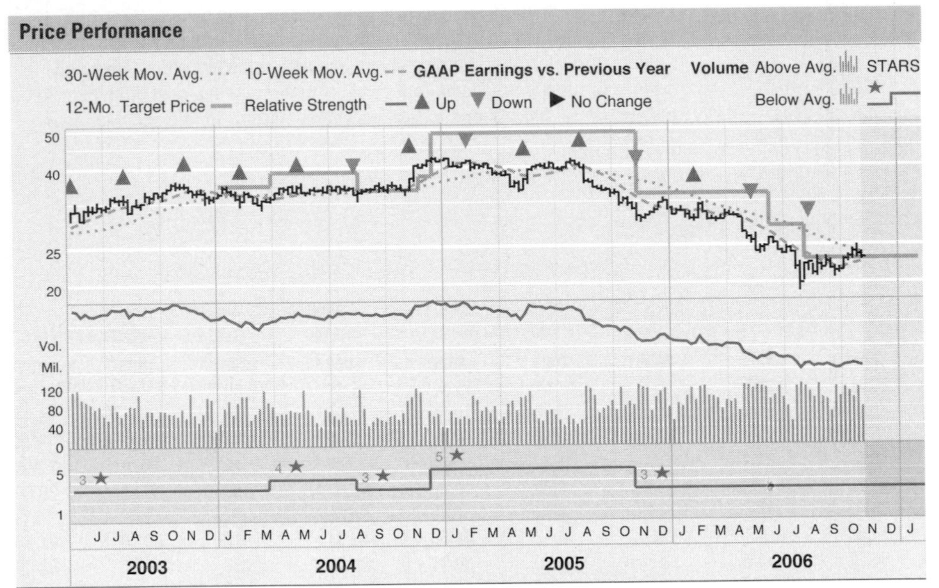

Options: ASE, CBOE, P, Ph

Analysis prepared by **Richard N. Stice, CFA** on August 22, 2006, when the stock traded at **$ 21.62**.

Highlights

- We forecast revenue growth of 7% in FY 08 (Jan.), compared with our estimated rise of 3% in FY 07. We believe demand will be stimulated in part by the expected release of Microsoft Corp.'s (MSFT: strong buy, $25) new operating system. In addition, we expect more robust growth in international markets, particularly in the Asian region, where DELL is now the second largest PC provider. We also anticipate further improvement in the company's data storage business.
- We see gross margins widening in FY 08 to 17%, from FY 07's projected 16.4%. We expect this expansion to be driven by higher volumes, a decline in component costs and manufacturing efficiencies. We estimate SG&A declining as a percentage of revenue, as new investments related to customer service are likely to be completed. We also believe that additional share repurchases are likely.
- We estimate FY 08 earnings per share of $1.45, a 26% increase from FY 07's projected $1.15. Both estimates include charges related to stock-based compensation expense.

Investment Rationale/Risk

- Dell's results have recently been challenged by a shift in the industry toward lower end PC products, in our view. While Dell has been able to take advantage of a lower cost structure versus peers, reflecting the cost advantages of its direct sales model, we believe the company is witnessing new and more aggressive competition. However, with what we see as Dell's solid focus on asset management enabling it to generate strong cash flow from operations, we believe the shares are worth holding.
- Risks to our opinion and target price include market share losses as Dell's peers improve their cost position in PCs, a slowdown in technology spending, and costs associated with a recently disclosed informal SEC inquiry.
- Our 12-month target price of $23 is based on our discounted cash flow (DCF) and price to sales analyses. Our DCF model assumes a WACC of 13.2% and leads to a value of $27. On a price to sales basis, we allocate the shares a rate of 0.75X, below their recent historical trading range, due to what we view as a tough competitive environment. This metric indicates a value of $19.

Qualitative Risk Assessment

LOW | **MEDIUM** | HIGH

Our risk assessment reflects our view of Dell's solid balance sheet and strong execution in asset management, offset by what we see as heightened competitive pressures from peers over the past year.

Quantitative Evaluations

S&P Quality Ranking **B+**

D | C | B- | B | **B+** | A- | A | A+

Relative Strength Rank **MODERATE**

37

LOWEST = 1 HIGHEST = 99

Revenue/Earnings Data

Revenue (Million $)

	1Q	2Q	3Q	4Q	Year
2007	14,216	14,094	--	--	--
2006	13,386	13,428	13,911	15,183	55,908
2005	11,540	11,706	12,502	13,457	49,205
2004	9,532	9,778	10,622	11,512	41,444
2003	8,066	8,459	9,144	9,735	35,404
2002	8,028	7,611	7,468	8,061	31,168

Earnings Per Share ($)

2007	0.33	0.22	**E**0.27	**E**0.33	**E**1.15
2006	0.37	0.41	0.25	0.43	1.46
2005	0.28	0.31	0.33	0.26	1.18
2004	0.23	0.34	0.26	0.29	1.01
2003	0.17	0.19	0.21	0.23	0.80
2002	0.17	-0.04	0.16	0.17	0.46

Fiscal year ended Jan. 31. Next earnings report expected: Early November. EPS Estimates based on S&P Operating Earnings; historical GAAP earnings are as reported.

Dividend Data

No cash dividends have been paid.

Business Summary August 22, 2006

CORPORATE OVERVIEW. Dell is a key player in the global market for information technology (IT), which totaled more than $1 trillion in 2005, according to data from IDC, a market researcher based in Framingham, MA. Total IT spending growth is slowing to a five-year compound annual growth rate of about 6%, from double digit rates last decade, partly reflecting the law of large numbers, but also due to intense pricing pressure in many key categories, especially computer hardware.

Computer hardware comprises about 40% of total IT spending, according to IDC, with PCs accounting for approximately 70% of that category. While leading computer hardware manufacturers have been grappling with plunging PC prices over the past decade, Dell has been leading this charge, in our opinion, and we think it has emerged as a key force with whom all computer hardware vendors have had to reckon.

Dell's share of the global PC market, currently at 19%, is up dramatically from 10.5% in FY 00 (Jan.). Dell has been the leader in this market for the past two years. In servers, Dell commands the number three spot (based on global system revenues). The majority of Dell's sales are from PCs (61%), but other categories are increasingly important to sales, such as servers (9%), services (10%), storage (4%) and software and peripherals (16%).

IMPACT OF MAJOR DEVELOPMENTS. In August 2006, the company announced a recall of up to 4.1 million battery packs manufactured by Sony Corp. (SNE: hold, $46). While it is difficult to calculate the total amount, we believe that SNE is likely to be responsible for the majority of the relevant expenses. Also in August 2006, DELL disclosed that it was being informally investigated by the SEC. The primary focus of the probe involves DELL's revenue recognition practices, but the company does not believe any material adjustment will be necessary. We think this issue adds another element of uncertainty to DELL's business. Moreover, with the investigation originating in August of 2005, we are disappointed in the company's delay in disclosing the information.

Company Financials

Per Share Data ($) Year Ended Jan. 31	2006	2005	2004	2003	2002	2001	2000	1999	1998	1997
Tangible Book Value	1.77	2.61	2.46	1.89	1.80	2.16	2.06	0.91	0.50	0.29
Cash Flow	1.62	1.32	1.11	0.88	0.54	0.90	0.67	0.56	0.34	0.19
Earnings	1.46	1.18	1.01	0.80	0.46	0.81	0.61	0.53	0.32	0.17
S&P Core Earnings	1.03	0.88	0.68	0.49	0.28	0.58	NA	NA	NA	NA
Dividends	Nil	Nil	Nil	Nil	Nil	Nil	Nil	Nil	Nil	Nil
Payout Ratio	Nil	Nil	Nil	Nil	Nil	Nil	Nil	Nil	Nil	Nil
Calendar Year	2005	2004	2003	2002	2001	2000	1999	1998	1997	1996
Prices:High	42.30	42.57	37.18	31.06	31.32	59.69	55.00	37.91	12.98	4.02
Prices:Low	28.62	31.14	22.59	21.90	16.01	16.25	31.37	9.92	3.12	0.72
P/E Ratio:High	29	36	37	39	68	74	90	73	41	23
P/E Ratio:Low	20	26	22	27	35	20	51	19	10	4

Income Statement Analysis (Million $)										
Revenue	55,908	49,205	41,444	35,404	31,168	31,888	25,265	18,243	12,327	7,759
Operating Income	4,740	4,588	3,807	3,055	2,510	3,008	2,613	2,149	1,383	761
Depreciation	393	334	263	211	239	240	156	103	67.0	47.0
Interest Expense	28.0	16.0	14.0	17.0	29.0	47.0	34.0	Nil	3.00	7.00
Pretax Income	4,574	4,445	3,724	3,027	1,731	3,194	2,451	2,084	1,368	747
Effective Tax Rate	21.9%	31.5%	29.0%	29.9%	28.0%	30.0%	32.0%	29.9%	31.0%	28.9%
Net Income	3,572	3,043	2,645	2,122	1,246	2,236	1,666	1,460	944	531
S&P Core Earnings	2,494	2,227	1,806	1,356	781	1,602	NA	NA	NA	NA

Balance Sheet & Other Financial Data (Million $)										
Cash	7,042	4,747	4,317	4,232	3,641	4,910	3,809	3,181	1,844	1,352
Current Assets	17,706	16,897	10,633	8,924	7,877	9,491	7,681	6,339	3,912	2,747
Total Assets	23,109	23,215	19,311	15,470	13,535	13,435	11,471	6,877	4,268	2,993
Current Liabilities	15,927	14,136	10,896	8,933	7,519	6,543	5,192	3,695	2,697	1,658
Long Term Debt	504	505	505	506	520	509	508	512	17.0	18.0
Common Equity	4,129	6,485	6,280	4,873	4,694	5,622	5,308	2,321	1,293	806
Total Capital	4,633	6,990	6,785	5,379	5,214	6,131	5,816	2,833	1,310	824
Capital Expenditures	728	525	329	305	303	482	397	296	187	114
Cash Flow	3,965	3,377	2,908	2,333	1,485	2,476	1,822	1,563	1,011	578
Current Ratio	1.1	1.2	1.0	1.0	1.0	1.5	1.5	1.7	1.5	1.7
% Long Term Debt of Capitalization	10.9	7.2	7.4	9.4	10.0	8.3	8.7	18.1	1.3	2.2
% Net Income of Revenue	6.4	6.2	6.4	6.0	4.0	7.0	6.6	8.0	7.7	6.8
% Return on Assets	15.4	14.3	15.2	14.6	9.2	18.0	18.2	26.2	26.0	20.7
% Return on Equity	67.3	47.7	47.4	44.4	24.2	40.9	43.7	80.8	89.9	59.9

Data as orig reptd.; bef. results of disc opers/spec. items. Per share data adj. for stk. divs.; EPS diluted. E-Estimated. NA-Not Available. NM-Not Meaningful. NR-Not Ranked. UR-Under Review.

Office: 1 Dell Way, Round Rock, TX 78682.
Telephone: 512-338-4400.
Email: investor_relations_fulfillment@dell.com
Website: http://www.dell.com

Chrmn: M.S. Dell
Pres & CEO: K.B. Rollins
SVP & CFO: J.M. Schneider
SVP & General Counsel: L. Tu

VP & Chief Acctg Officer: J.S. Hooper
Investor Contact: L.A. Tyson (512-723-1130)
Auditor: PricewaterhouseCoopers
Board of Directors: D. J. Carty, M. S. Dell, W. H. Gray, III, S. L. Krawcheck, A. Lafley, J. C. Lewent, T. Luce, K. S. Luft, A. J. Mandl, M. A. Miles, S. S. Nunn, Jr., K. B. Rollins

Founded: 1984
Domicile: Delaware
Employees: 66,100

STANDARD &POOR'S

Devon Energy Corp

S&P Recommendation STRONG BUY ★★★★★

Price $67.18 (as of Oct 27, 2006)

12-Mo. Target Price $88.00

Investment Style Large-Cap Growth

GICS Sector Energy
Sub-Industry Oil & Gas Exploration & Production

Comment This independent oil and gas exploration and production company has grown through its acquisitions of Ocean Energy, Mitchell Energy, and Anderson Exploration.

Key Stock Statistics (Source S&P, Vickers, company reports)

52-Wk Range	$74.75–48.94	S&P Oper. EPS 2006E	7.15	P/E on S&P Oper. EPS 2006E	9.4	Dividend Rate/Share	$0.45
Trailing 12-Month EPS	$7.20	S&P Oper. EPS 2007E	11.00	Common Shares Outstg. (M)	441.1	Yield (%)	0.67
Trailing 12-Month P/E	9.3	S&P Core EPS 2006E	7.05	Market Capitalization(B)	$29.630	Beta	0.59
$10K Invested 5 Yrs Ago	$34,604	S&P Core EPS 2007E	8.25	Institutional Ownership (%)	80	S&P Credit Rating	BBB

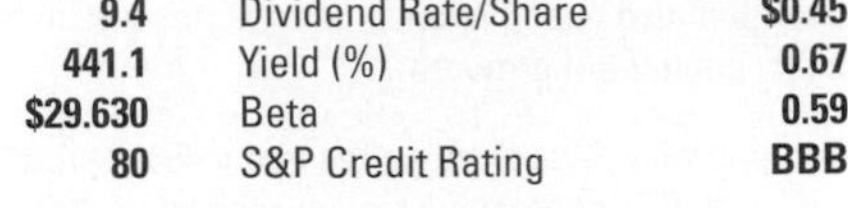

Price Performance

Options: ASE, CBOE, P

Analysis prepared by **Charles LaPorta, CFA** on September 14, 2006, when the stock traded at **$ 64.73**.

Highlights

- Second quarter operating EPS was $1.53, versus $1.38 the year before, and below our estimate of $1.55. Given 2005 asset divestitures and hurricane-related curtailments, and that DVN hit break points in production sharing contracts in international properties, we estimate about a 5% decline in 2006 production.
- Operating costs per BOE were flat sequentially, as lower field fuel costs were offset by maintenance, and service cost increases. We expect that lease operating expenses will remain flat in 2006, as service cost inflation is offset by more profitable projects coming on line. A combination of lower production volumes and a stronger Canadian dollar resulted in higher depreciation, depletion and amortization (DD&A) per BOE. We believe DD&A per BOE will trend lower through 2006.
- Our EBITDA projection for 2006 is about $8.0 billion, which suggests 69% EBITDA margins, flat with last year. Partial commercial paper financing of the June 2006 Chief acquisition should lead to $38 million in added interest expense in the second half of 2006; DVN's share repurchase program has been suspended until further notice.

Investment Rationale/Risk

- We believe DVN has transformed the company from a value-enhancing restructuring story to a production growth story as several long-term projects come online simultaneously in 2007. We think the announced lower tertiary Gulf of Mexico discovery has secured the DVN production growth story for the long-term (meaning 2009 to 2015), while its recent Barnett Shale acquisition will immediately help secure DVN's dominance in a core area.
- Risks to our recommendation and target price include events that would cause substantial and sustained declines in oil and gas prices, and a persistent inability of the company to replace its reserves. We are somewhat concerned about corporate governance policies, including a "poison pill" and no shareholder approval of board size.
- We believe DVN's announcement of the largest domestic hydrocarbon find in a generation should allow the shares to trade at a premium to its large capitalization pees. Our 12-month target price of $88 is based on a P/E of about 8.0X our 2007 EPS estimate, and an enterprise value of 4.2X our 2007 EBITDAX estimate, both premiums to peers.

Qualitative Risk Assessment

LOW | **MEDIUM** | HIGH

Our risk assessment reflects our view that DVN is susceptible to substantial and sustained declines in oil and gas prices, and a force majeure event that could damage its production facilities. This is offset by DVN's sizable operations, which are primarily located in North America, minimizing political risk, and its production, which is about evenly split between oil and gas.

Quantitative Evaluations

S&P Quality Ranking **B+**

D | C | B- | B | **B+** | A- | A | A+

Relative Strength Rank **MODERATE**

67

LOWEST = 1 HIGHEST = 99

Revenue/Earnings Data

Revenue (Million $)

	1Q	2Q	3Q	4Q	Year
2006	2,717	2,617	--	--	--
2005	2,351	2,468	2,704	3,218	10,741
2004	2,238	2,219	2,267	2,465	9,189
2003	1,671	1,813	1,948	1,921	7,352
2002	903.0	1,149	1,031	1,233	4,316
2001	1,024	725.2	586.7	740.0	3,075

Earnings Per Share ($)

2006	1.56	1.92	**E**1.60	**E**2.46	**E**7.15
2005	1.14	1.38	1.63	2.14	6.26
2004	1.00	1.01	1.04	1.35	4.38
2003	1.29	0.81	0.86	1.13	4.00
2002	0.20	-0.65	0.35	0.25	0.16
2001	1.30	0.51	0.32	-2.07	0.17

Fiscal year ended Dec. 31. Next earnings report expected: Early November. EPS Estimates based on S&P Operating Earnings; historical GAAP earnings are as reported.

Dividend Data (Dates: mm/dd Payment Date: mm/dd/yy)

Amount ($)	Date Decl.	Ex-Div. Date	Stk. of Record	Payment Date
0.075	12/01	12/13	12/15	12/31/05
0.113	03/01	03/13	03/15	03/31/06
0.113	06/01	06/13	06/15	06/30/06
0.113	09/01	09/13	09/15	09/29/06

Dividends have been paid since 1993. Source: Company reports.

Please read the Required Disclosures and Analyst Certification on the last page of this report.

Devon Energy Corp

Business Summary September 14, 2006

CORPORATE OVERVIEW. DVN is an independent energy company, engaged primarily in oil and natural gas exploration, development, and production; the acquisition of producing properties; the transportation of oil, natural gas, and natural gas liquids (NGLs); and the processing of natural gas. The company operates oil and gas properties in the U.S., Canada, and internationally. U.S. operations focus on the Permian Basin, the Mid-Continent, the Rocky Mountains, and onshore and offshore the Gulf of Mexico. Canadian operations focus on the Western Canadian Sedimentary Basin in Alberta and British Columbia. Operations outside North America currently include Azerbaijan, Brazil, China, Egypt, and West Africa (including Equatorial Guinea). At year-end 2005, DVN had proved reserves of about 2.11 billion barrels of oil equivalent (BOE) (58% natural gas, 42% liquids; 88% North America), with 24% of reserves proved undeveloped.

MARKET PROFILE. DVN was one of the first independent oil and gas exploration and production companies to successfully implement an "acquire and exploit" strategy via an aggressive implementation of repeatable development drilling techniques. The company has since modified this strategy to include different geologic formations and geographic locations. However, the core of establishing a repeatable drilling program in each basin remains.

We believe the global energy industry is highly competitive and fragmented among a diverse number of companies of differing sizes and characteristics. These include government-owned national oil companies like Saudi Aramco and large publicly traded energy companies like Exxon Mobil (XOM: $65; strong buy). Over the past 10 years, as demand for hydrocarbons has continued to rise, an increasing proportion of the world's hydrocarbon reserves are located in developing countries with reserves that are effectively owned and managed by the government. Many large private companies like XOM have benefited from, in our view, their formidable financial resources and decades-long corporate relationships with these governments. DVN's strategy has been focused on North American properties, given the extensive history of private property rights and the strong enforceability of contracts.

Company Financials

Per Share Data ($) Year Ended Dec. 31	**2005**	**2004**	**2003**	**2002**	**2001**	**2000**	**1999**	**1998**	**1997**	**1996**
Tangible Book Value	20.31	16.30	11.50	3.20	4.32	11.03	16.03	5.40	8.41	7.35
Cash Flow	10.87	8.95	8.10	4.04	3.54	5.37	2.65	0.66	2.49	1.77
Earnings	6.26	4.38	4.00	0.16	0.17	2.75	0.73	-0.63	1.09	0.79
S&P Core Earnings	6.01	4.30	3.99	0.47	0.09	NA	NA	NA	NA	NA
Dividends	0.30	0.20	0.10	0.10	0.10	0.10	0.10	0.10	0.10	0.07
Payout Ratio	5%	5%	3%	63%	59%	4%	14%	NM	9%	9%
Prices:High	70.35	41.64	29.40	26.55	33.38	32.37	22.47	20.56	24.56	18.50
Prices:Low	36.48	25.90	21.23	16.94	15.28	15.69	10.06	13.06	13.69	9.94
P/E Ratio:High	11	10	7	NM	NM	12	31	NM	23	24
P/E Ratio:Low	6	6	5	NM	NM	6	14	NM	13	13
Income Statement Analysis (Million $)										
Revenue	10,741	9,189	7,352	4,316	3,075	2,784	734	388	306	163
Operating Income	7,290	6,038	4,589	2,403	2,350	2,094	491	237	209	111
Depreciation, Depletion and Amortization	2,191	2,290	1,793	1,211	876	693	254	124	85.3	43.4
Interest Expense	533	475	504	533	220	154	66.9	22.6	0.27	5.28
Pretax Income	4,552	3,293	2,245	-134	84.0	1,142	160	-75.8	121	59.3
Effective Tax Rate	35.6%	33.6%	22.9%	NM	35.7%	36.0%	40.8%	NM	38.0%	41.4%
Net Income	2,930	2,186	1,731	59.0	54.0	730	94.6	-60.3	75.3	34.8
S&P Core Earnings	2,801	2,136	1,715	147	22.9	NA	NA	NA	NA	NA
Balance Sheet & Other Financial Data (Million $)										
Cash	1,606	2,119	1,273	292	193	228	167	19.2	42.1	9.40
Current Assets	4,206	3,583	2,364	1,064	1,081	934	417	111	93.2	43.4
Total Assets	30,273	29,736	27,162	16,225	13,184	6,860	4,623	1,226	846	746
Current Liabilities	2,934	3,100	2,071	1,042	919	629	227	80.7	30.8	23.6
Long Term Debt	5,957	7,031	8,635	7,562	6,589	2,049	1,787	555	Nil	8.00
Common Equity	14,999	13,673	11,055	4,652	3,258	3,276	2,024	523	544	472
Total Capital	26,362	25,505	24,061	14,842	11,990	5,953	4,204	1,111	795	711
Capital Expenditures	4,090	3,103	2,587	3,426	5,326	1,280	315	376	130	98.9
Cash Flow	5,111	4,466	3,514	1,260	920	1,414	345	63.6	161	78.2
Current Ratio	1.4	1.2	1.1	1.0	1.2	1.5	1.8	1.4	3.0	1.8
% Long Term Debt of Capitalization	22.6	27.6	35.9	51.0	55.0	34.4	42.5	49.9	Nil	1.2
% Return on Assets	9.7	7.7	8.0	NM	0.5	11.3	3.2	NM	9.5	6.0
% Return on Equity	20.3	17.6	21.9	NM	1.3	24.9	7.1	NM	14.8	10.1

Data as orig reptd.; bef. results of disc opers/spec. items. Per share data adj. for stk. divs.; EPS diluted. E-Estimated. NA-Not Available. NM-Not Meaningful. NR-Not Ranked. UR-Under Review.

Office: 20 North Broadway, Oklahoma City, OK 73102-8260.
Telephone: 405-235-3611.
Website: http://www.devonenergy.com
Chrmn & CEO: J.L. Nichols

Pres: J. Richels
SVP & CFO: B.J. Jennings
SVP & General Counsel: D.R. Ligon
VP & Cntlr: R.A. Marcum

Investor Contact: V. White (405-552-4526)
Board of Directors: T. F. Ferguson, P. J. Fluor, D. M. Gavrin, J. A. Hill, R. L. Howard, W. J. Johnson, M. M. Kanovsky, J. T. Mitchell, R. A. Mosbacher, Jr., J. L. Nichols

Founded: 1988
Domicile: Delaware
Employees: 4,075

STANDARD &POOR'S

Dillard's Inc.

S&P Recommendation HOLD ★★★★★ | **Price** $30.46 (as of Oct 27, 2006) | **12-Mo. Target Price** $34.00 | **Investment Style** Mid-Cap Value

GICS Sector Consumer Discretionary
Sub-Industry Department Stores

Comment Dillard's operates about 325 department stores, located primarily in the South and the Midwest.

Key Stock Statistics (Source S&P, Vickers, company reports)

52-Wk Range	$33.87–19.87	S&P Oper. EPS 2007E	2.18	P/E on S&P Oper. EPS 2007E	14.0	Dividend Rate/Share	$0.16
Trailing 12-Month EPS	$2.15	S&P Oper. EPS 2008E	2.64	Common Shares Outstg. (M)	79.6	Yield (%)	0.53
Trailing 12-Month P/E	14.2	S&P Core EPS 2007E	2.20	Market Capitalization(B)	$2.301	Beta	1.28
$10K Invested 5 Yrs Ago	$23,164	S&P Core EPS 2008E	2.66	Institutional Ownership (%)	97	S&P Credit Rating	BB

Price Performance

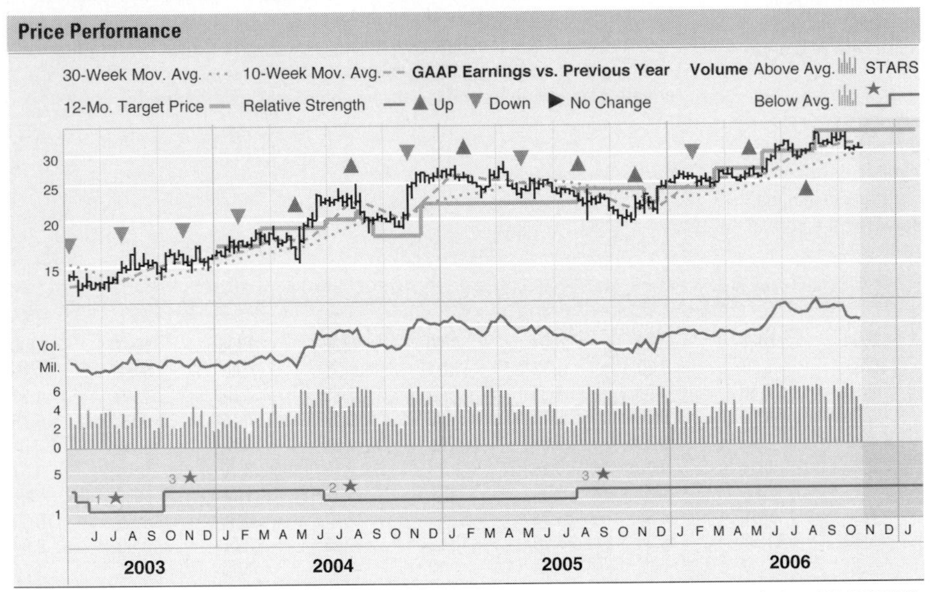

Options: ASE, CBOE, P, Ph

Analysis prepared by **Jason N. Asaeda** on August 18, 2006, when the stock traded at **$ 33.52**.

Highlights

- In FY 07 (Jan.), we expect net sales to reach $7.62 billion. DDS plans to open nine new stores. Balancing our view of a challenging retail environment against the company's efforts to increase differentiation in its assortments by offering more upscale and contemporary choices, we look for same-store sales to be flat to up 1%.
- Gross margins should widen on an anticipated shift in the sales mix to higher margin merchandise and better customer response to new assortments, which should help reduce markdown exposure. We expect expense ratios to improve, reflecting the sale of DDS's credit card business, and lower interest and debt expense due to the redemption of notes in FY 05. The company also anticipates that income from its credit marketing and servicing alliance with GE Consumer Finance could approximate earnings previously derived from Dillard National Bank.
- We see FY 07 operating EPS of $2.18 and S&P Core EPS of $2.20, with the difference reflecting projected pension income.

Investment Rationale/Risk

- As a result of a strong performance in the first half of FY 07, we have confidence that DDS has the merchandising skills to remain competitive in a market soon to be dominated by Federated Department Stores' (FD: buy, $38) Macy's division. Despite soft projected top line growth, we see improved inventory management enabling DDS to achieve margin gains over the balance of the year.
- Risks to our recommendation and target price include a long record of inconsistent sales and earnings under the Dillard family's management, which raises concerns about turnaround execution. With regard to DDS's corporate governance practices, we are concerned about a non-shareholder approved poison pill and a dual class capital structure with unequal voting rights. In addition, no governance committee has been established by directors.
- Our 12-month target price of $34 is based on our discounted cash flow analysis, which assumes a weighted average cost of capital of 8.4% and a terminal growth rate of 2.5%.

Qualitative Risk Assessment

LOW | **MEDIUM** | HIGH

Our risk assessment reflects our view of DDS's improving sales and profit margins, driven by successful turnaround initiatives, offset by its history of inconsistent results under the Dillard family's management.

Quantitative Evaluations

S&P Quality Ranking B+

D | C | B- | B | **B+** | A- | A | A+

Relative Strength Rank WEAK

23

LOWEST = 1 HIGHEST = 99

Revenue/Earnings Data

Revenue (Million $)

	1Q	2Q	3Q	4Q	Year
2007	1,837	1,688	--	--	--
2006	1,803	1,692	1,727	2,338	7,560
2005	1,854	1,671	1,699	2,304	7,529
2004	1,814	1,721	1,764	2,299	7,599
2003	1,911	1,818	1,794	2,388	7,911
2002	1,920	1,828	1,872	2,534	8,155

Earnings Per Share ($)

2007	0.77	0.20	**E**0.07	**E**1.28	**E**2.18
2006	0.46	-0.15	-0.03	1.24	1.49
2005	0.64	-0.31	-0.23	1.30	1.41
2004	0.29	-0.60	-0.19	0.61	0.11
2003	0.68	0.15	-0.07	0.85	1.60
2002	0.30	-0.24	-0.48	1.20	0.35

Fiscal year ended Jan. 31. Next earnings report expected: Early December. EPS Estimates based on S&P Operating Earnings; historical GAAP earnings are as reported.

Dividend Data (Dates: mm/dd Payment Date: mm/dd/yy)

Amount ($)	Date Decl.	Ex-Div. Date	Stk. of Record	Payment Date
0.040	12/01	12/28	12/30	02/01/06
0.040	03/10	03/29	03/31	05/01/06
0.040	06/01	06/28	06/30	08/01/06
0.040	08/30	09/27	09/29	11/01/06

Dividends have been paid since 1969. Source: Company reports.

Dillard's Inc.

Business Summary August 18, 2006

Dillard's is an outgrowth of a department store originally founded in 1938 by William Dillard. At July 29, 2006, the company operated 325 traditional department stores (net of four locations closed at the time due to hurricane damage) offering fashion apparel and home furnishings in 29 states. The heaviest concentrations of stores were in the Southwest, the Southeast and the Midwest.

Given a highly competitive retail environment, DDS has adopted a number of strategies intended to improve its profitability. In FY 06 (Jan.), the company increased its emphasis on nationally known contemporary and better lines, and expanded its better exclusive brand lines such as Antonio Melani, Gianni Bini, and Daniel Cremieux.

DDS continues to focus on improving its merchandise mix, eliminating and replacing underperforming products from both national and exclusive sources with more promising brands, and tailoring its assortments to local demographics. Exclusive brand merchandise accounted for 24.0% of sales in FY 06, up from 23.1% in FY 05.

Company Financials

Per Share Data ($) Year Ended Jan. 31	**2006**	**2005**	**2004**	**2003**	**2002**	**2001**	**2000**	**1999**	**1998**	**1997**
Tangible Book Value	29.08	27.51	26.35	26.25	25.02	25.06	22.68	20.39	25.76	23.83
Cash Flow	5.37	5.01	3.67	5.21	4.49	4.40	4.31	3.47	4.09	3.80
Earnings	1.49	1.41	0.11	1.60	0.35	1.06	1.55	1.26	2.31	2.09
S&P Core Earnings	1.23	0.72	-0.03	1.01	0.71	0.92	NA	NA	NA	NA
Dividends	0.16	0.16	0.16	0.16	0.16	0.16	0.16	0.16	0.16	0.14
Payout Ratio	11%	11%	145%	10%	46%	15%	10%	13%	7%	7%
Calendar Year	2005	2004	2003	2002	2001	2000	1999	1998	1997	1996
Prices:High	28.60	27.50	17.80	31.20	22.50	20.01	37.44	44.50	44.75	41.75
Prices:Low	18.91	15.21	12.32	12.94	11.44	9.43	17.75	26.50	28.00	27.13
P/E Ratio:High	19	20	NM	20	64	20	24	35	19	20
P/E Ratio:Low	13	11	NM	8	33	9	11	21	12	13
Income Statement Analysis (Million $)										
Revenue	7,560	7,529	7,599	7,911	8,155	8,567	8,921	7,797	6,632	6,228
Operating Income	604	645	538	429	386	469	640	441	554	511
Depreciation	304	302	297	306	314	303	293	240	200	194
Interest Expense	106	139	181	183	190	224	237	197	129	121
Pretax Income	136	185	16.0	211	112	141	284	219	410	380
Effective Tax Rate	10.5%	36.2%	41.6%	35.4%	41.0%	31.2%	42.3%	38.4%	37.1%	37.1%
Net Income	121	118	9.34	136	65.8	97.0	164	135	258	239
S&P Core Earnings	100	60.6	-2.90	85.8	60.1	83.8	NA	NA	NA	NA
Balance Sheet & Other Financial Data (Million $)										
Cash	300	498	161	142	153	194	199	72.0	42.0	64.0
Current Assets	2,150	2,293	3,024	3,130	2,815	2,843	3,424	3,438	2,998	2,761
Total Assets	5,517	5,692	6,411	6,676	7,075	7,199	7,918	8,178	5,592	5,060
Current Liabilities	1,147	1,045	1,336	886	928	877	811	1,094	1,099	895
Long Term Debt	1,291	1,543	2,073	2,743	2,677	2,906	3,452	3,562	1,378	1,187
Common Equity	2,341	2,325	2,237	2,264	2,668	2,630	2,832	2,840	2,807	2,716
Total Capital	4,110	4,377	4,927	5,007	5,989	6,175	6,986	7,084	4,493	4,165
Capital Expenditures	456	285	227	233	271	226	247	248	509	350
Cash Flow	426	420	307	442	379	400	457	375	458	433
Current Ratio	1.9	2.2	2.3	3.5	3.0	3.2	4.2	3.1	2.7	3.1
% Long Term Debt of Capitalization	31.4	35.3	42.1	54.8	44.7	47.1	49.4	50.3	30.6	28.5
% Net Income of Revenue	1.6	1.6	0.1	1.7	0.8	1.1	1.9	1.7	3.9	3.8
% Return on Assets	2.2	1.9	0.1	2.0	0.9	1.3	2.0	2.0	4.8	4.9
% Return on Equity	5.2	5.2	0.4	5.5	2.5	3.6	5.8	4.8	9.3	9.2

Data as orig reptd.; bef. results of disc opers/spec. items. Per share data adj. for stk. divs.; EPS diluted. E-Estimated. NA-Not Available. NM-Not Meaningful. NR-Not Ranked. UR-Under Review.

Office: 1600 Cantrell Rd, Little Rock, AR 72201-1145.
Telephone: 501-376-5200.
Website: http://www.dillards.com
Chrmn & CEO: W. Dillard, II

Pres: A. Dillard
Investor Contact: J.I. Freeman
SVP & CFO: J.I. Freeman
VP, Secy & General Counsel: P.J. Schroeder, Jr.

Board of Directors: R. C. Connor, D. Corbusier, W. D. Davis, A. Dillard, M. J. Dillard, W. Dillard, II, J. I. Freeman, J. P. Hammerschmidt, P. R. Johnson, W. A. Stephens, W. H. Sutton, J. C. Watts, Jr.

Founded: 1938
Domicile: Delaware
Employees: 52,056

STANDARD &POOR'S

Walt Disney Co (The)

S&P Recommendation BUY ★★★★★

Price $31.73 (as of Oct 27, 2006)

12-Mo. Target Price $35.00

Investment Style Large-Cap Value

GICS Sector Consumer Discretionary
Sub-Industry Movies & Entertainment

Comment This media and entertainment conglomerate has diversified global operations in theme parks, motion pictures, and television and radio broadcasting.

Key Stock Statistics (Source S&P, Vickers, company reports)

52-Wk Range	$31.99–23.77	S&P Oper. EPS 2006E	1.62	P/E on S&P Oper. EPS 2006E	19.6	Dividend Rate/Share	$0.27
Trailing 12-Month EPS	$1.49	S&P Oper. EPS 2007E	1.79	Common Shares Outstg. (M)	2,090.1	Yield (%)	0.85
Trailing 12-Month P/E	21.3	S&P Core EPS 2006E	1.62	Market Capitalization(B)	$66.320	Beta	1.27
$10K Invested 5 Yrs Ago	$17,844	S&P Core EPS 2007E	1.79	Institutional Ownership (%)	69	S&P Credit Rating	A-

Price Performance

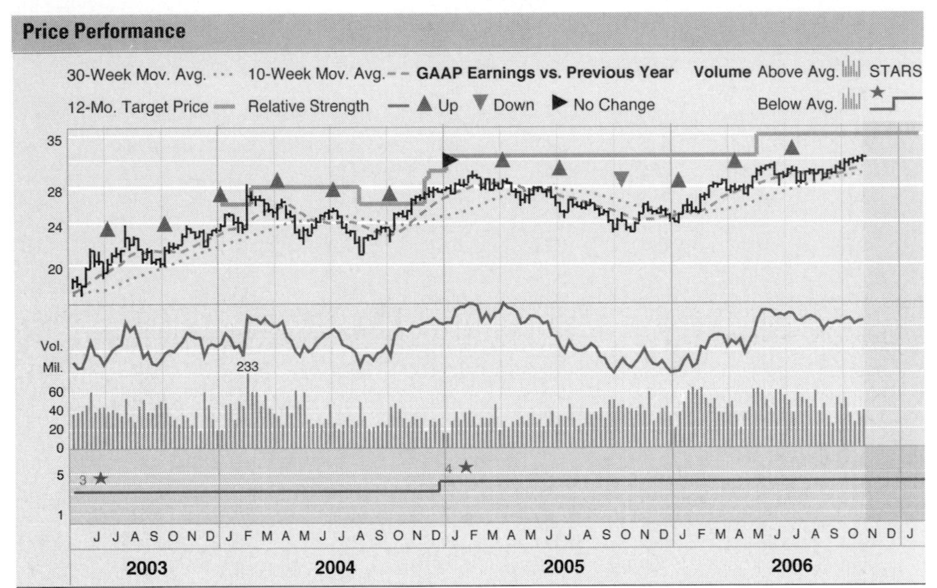

Options: ASE, CBOE, P, Ph

Analysis prepared by **Tuna N. Amobi, CFA, CPA** on September 28, 2006, when the stock traded at **$ 31.12**.

Highlights

- We estimate that total revenues will rise about 7% each in FY 06 (Sep.) and FY 07, helped by higher advertising and affiliate revenues at the media networks businesses (excluding a discontinued ABC radio unit). Despite potentially difficult comparisons, we see a continued rebound at the U.S theme parks, and a strong slate of film/DVD releases through the FY 07 first half, which should drive healthy gains in consumer licensing. In FY 06, we project nearly $500 million of Internet revenues, increasing by an estimated 25% in FY 07.
- We expect margin expansion through FY 07, on reduced cost pressures at the parks, improved ABC profits, and studio restructuring savings, partly offset by higher NFL rights fees at ESPN, and new media investments. We estimate consolidated EBITDA of $6.75 billion in FY 06, and $7.42 billion in FY 07.
- With ongoing stock buybacks, we forecast EPS of $1.62 in FY 06, and $1.79 in FY 07 (including about $0.10 of projected option expense). DIS sees about $0.10 in FY 06 EPS dilution on the Pixar deal, and recently reiterated its double digit earnings growth target through at least FY 08.

Investment Rationale/Risk

- DIS's fiscal third quarter results reflected a continued strong rebound in theme park attendance, and a solid film performance on Cars, Chronicles of Narnia, and Pirates 2 which, combined with the upcoming release of Pirates 3, should significantly aid FY 07 results. The parks could further benefit from a new marketing campaign with the end of the 50th anniversary celebrations, and the studios from the Pixar integration and a recent major restructuring. After the 2006-07 upfront market, we see a strong programming lineup at ABC, and potentially sustainable double-digit ESPN operating income growth in the next few years. We also see ample flexibility for stock buybacks.
- Risks to our recommendation and target price include exposure to cyclical advertising and theme park attendance; an ABC ratings slide; lower-than-projected ESPN growth; and volatility of film results.
- Our 12-month target price of $35 is based on sum-of-the parts valuation using relative enterprise value targets for each of the four business segments, including corporate overheads. DIS offers a modest 0.9% dividend yield.

Qualitative Risk Assessment

LOW | **MEDIUM** | HIGH

Our risk assessment reflects the strength of the company's content oriented media and entertainment brands, counterbalanced by a relatively high exposure to cyclical advertising-related and theme parks businesses.

Quantitative Evaluations

S&P Quality Ranking B

D | C | B- | **B** | B+ | A- | A | A+

Relative Strength Rank MODERATE

60

LOWEST = 1 HIGHEST = 99

Revenue/Earnings Data

Revenue (Million $)

	1Q	2Q	3Q	4Q	Year
2006	8,854	8,027	8,620	--	--
2005	8,666	7,829	7,715	7,734	31,944
2004	8,549	7,189	7,471	7,543	30,752
2003	7,170	6,500	6,377	7,014	27,061
2002	7,016	5,856	5,795	6,662	25,329
2001	7,433	6,049	5,975	5,812	25,269

Earnings Per Share ($)

2006	0.37	0.37	0.53	**E**0.36	**E**1.62
2005	0.33	0.31	0.39	0.20	1.24
2004	0.33	0.26	0.29	0.25	1.12
2003	0.06	0.15	0.24	0.20	0.65
2002	0.21	0.13	0.18	0.09	0.60
2001	0.16	-0.26	0.19	0.03	0.11

Fiscal year ended Sep. 30. Next earnings report expected: Mid November. EPS Estimates based on S&P Operating Earnings; historical GAAP earnings are as reported.

Dividend Data (Dates: mm/dd Payment Date: mm/dd/yy)

Amount ($)	Date Decl.	Ex-Div. Date	Stk. of Record	Payment Date
0.270	12/02	12/08	12/12	01/06/06

Dividends have been paid since 1957. Source: Company reports.

Please read the Required Disclosures and Analyst Certification on the last page of this report.

Walt Disney Co (The)

Business Summary September 28, 2006

CORPORATE OVERVIEW. The Walt Disney Co. is a leading media conglomerate with key operations in theme parks, television, filmed entertainment and merchandise licensing. Theme Parks and Resorts (28% of FY 05 (Sep.) revenues) includes the company's best known assets -- Disney World and Disneyland parks in Orlando, FL, and Anaheim, CA, respectively; Disney Cruise Line; Euro Disney, Paris (39%-owned); and Hong Kong Disneyland (43%-owned).

Media Networks (41% of revenues) includes the ABC broadcast network; 10 television stations; and cable networks ESPN (80%-owned), The Disney Channel, ABC Family, Lifetime (50%) and E! (39.6%). Studio entertainment (24% of revenues) includes the film, television and home video businesses under the Walt Disney, Touchstone and Miramax brands. Consumer products (7% of revenues) includes merchandise licensing, children's book publishing, video game development, and 104 retail stores mainly in Europe (the 315-store U.S. chain is operated by specialty retailer Children's Place under a licensing deal).

CORPORATE STRATEGY. As a content-oriented company, DIS's top strategic priorities include creativity and innovation, international expansion, and leveraging new technology applications. Under CEO Robert Iger, we see senior management aggressively exploring new avenues to offer its branded content, characters and entertainment franchises across emerging digital platforms such as broadband and wireless, while making further investments in other areas such as video games. Recent initiatives include: a deal to provide content from its ABC networks and the film studios on Apple's video iPod, the launches of ESPN Mobile and Disney Mobile cellular phone services, and an ad-supported streaming of ABC's shows. Internet revenues will likely top $500 million in FY 06.

Meanwhile, in July 2006, DIS unveiled a key restructuring of its studio division, with more focus on Disney-branded films, and a sharp reduction in its annual slate (to 10 live-action/animation films plus two to three Touchstone titles), resulting in a headcount reduction of about 650. The company has aggressively expanded its Disney Channel in the past few years, and in September 2005, opened Hong Kong Disneyland.

Company Financials

Per Share Data ($) Year Ended Sep. 30	2005	2004	2003	2002	2001	2000	1999	1998	1997	1996
Tangible Book Value	3.24	3.15	2.01	1.78	3.99	2.24	2.59	1.75	0.63	NM
Cash Flow	1.93	1.69	1.17	1.11	0.89	1.48	2.22	2.70	3.36	2.78
Earnings	1.24	1.12	0.65	0.60	0.11	0.57	0.62	0.89	0.95	0.65
S&P Core Earnings	1.27	1.04	0.49	0.29	0.21	NA	NA	NA	NA	NA
Dividends	0.24	0.21	0.21	0.21	0.21	0.21	0.21	0.19	0.16	0.13
Payout Ratio	19%	19%	32%	35%	191%	37%	34%	21%	17%	20%
Prices:High	29.99	28.41	23.80	25.17	34.80	43.88	38.69	42.79	33.42	25.75
Prices:Low	22.89	20.88	14.84	13.48	15.50	26.00	23.38	22.50	22.13	17.75
P/E Ratio:High	24	25	37	42	NM	77	62	48	35	39
P/E Ratio:Low	18	19	23	22	NM	46	38	25	23	27

Income Statement Analysis (Million $)	2005	2004	2003	2002	2001	2000	1999	1998	1997	1996
Revenue	31,944	30,752	27,061	25,329	25,269	25,402	23,402	22,976	22,473	18,739
Operating Income	5,446	5,258	3,790	3,426	4,586	5,043	7,010	7,533	8,903	6,968
Depreciation	1,339	1,210	1,077	1,042	1,754	2,195	3,323	3,754	4,958	3,944
Interest Expense	605	629	666	453	417	558	717	685	741	545
Pretax Income	3,987	3,739	2,254	2,190	1,283	2,633	2,314	3,157	3,387	2,061
Effective Tax Rate	31.1%	32.0%	35.0%	38.9%	82.5%	61.0%	43.8%	41.4%	42.0%	41.1%
Net Income	2,569	2,345	1,338	1,236	120	920	1,300	1,850	1,966	1,214
S&P Core Earnings	2,635	2,201	1,006	606	458	NA	NA	NA	NA	NA

Balance Sheet & Other Financial Data (Million $)	2005	2004	2003	2002	2001	2000	1999	1998	1997	1996
Cash	1,723	2,042	1,583	1,239	618	842	414	127	317	732
Current Assets	8,845	9,369	8,314	7,849	7,029	10,007	10,200	9,375	NA	NA
Total Assets	53,158	53,902	49,988	50,045	43,699	45,027	43,679	41,378	37,776	37,777
Current Liabilities	9,168	11,059	8,669	7,819	6,219	8,402	7,707	7,525	NA	NA
Long Term Debt	10,157	9,395	10,643	12,467	8,940	6,959	9,278	9,562	11,068	12,342
Common Equity	26,210	26,081	23,791	23,445	22,672	24,100	20,975	19,388	17,285	16,086
Total Capital	40,045	39,224	37,574	38,943	34,724	34,248	32,913	31,438	30,032	29,172
Capital Expenditures	1,823	1,427	1,049	1,086	1,795	2,013	2,134	2,314	1,922	1,745
Cash Flow	3,908	3,555	2,415	2,278	1,874	3,115	4,623	5,604	6,924	5,158
Current Ratio	1.0	0.8	1.0	1.0	1.1	1.2	1.3	1.2	NA	NA
% Long Term Debt of Capitalization	25.4	24.0	28.3	32.0	25.7	20.3	28.2	30.4	36.9	42.3
% Net Income of Revenue	8.0	7.6	4.9	4.9	0.5	3.6	5.6	8.1	8.7	6.5
% Return on Assets	4.8	4.5	2.7	2.6	0.3	2.1	3.1	4.7	5.2	4.7
% Return on Equity	9.8	9.4	5.7	5.4	0.5	4.1	6.4	10.1	11.8	10.7

Data as orig reptd.; bef. results of disc opers/spec. items. Per share data adj. for stk. divs.; EPS diluted. E-Estimated. NA-Not Available. NM-Not Meaningful. NR-Not Ranked. UR-Under Review.

Office: 500 South Buena Vista Street, Burbank, CA 91521.
Telephone: 818-560-1000.
Website: http://www.disney.com
Chrmn: G.J. Mitchell

Pres & CEO: R.A. Iger
Sr EVP: J.M. Renfro
Investor Contact: T.O. Staggs (818-560-1000)
Sr EVP & CFO: T.O. Staggs

Board of Directors: J. E. Bryson, J. Chen, J. L. Estrin, R. A. Iger, F. H. Langhammer, A. Lewis, M. C. Lozano, R. W. Matschullat, G. J. Mitchell, L. J. O'Donovan, J. E. Pepper, Jr., O. C. Smith, G. L. Wilson

Auditor: PricewaterhouseCoopers
Founded: 1936
Domicile: Delaware
Employees: 133,000

STANDARD &POOR'S

Dollar General Corp

S&P Recommendation HOLD ★★★★★

Price $13.82 (as of Oct 27, 2006)

12-Mo. Target Price $15.00

Investment Style Mid-Cap Growth

GICS Sector Consumer Discretionary
Sub-Industry General Merchandise Stores

Comment This discount retailer sells inexpensive soft and hard goods to low-, middle- and fixed-income families through over 8,100 stores in 32 states.

Key Stock Statistics (Source S&P, Vickers, company reports)

52-Wk Range	$19.84–12.10	S&P Oper. EPS 2007E	0.88	P/E on S&P Oper. EPS 2007E	15.7	Dividend Rate/Share	$0.20
Trailing 12-Month EPS	$0.95	S&P Oper. EPS 2008E	1.05	Common Shares Outstg. (M)	312.0	Yield (%)	1.45
Trailing 12-Month P/E	14.6	S&P Core EPS 2007E	0.88	Market Capitalization(B)	$4.311	Beta	0.92
$10K Invested 5 Yrs Ago	$10,165	S&P Core EPS 2008E	1.05	Institutional Ownership (%)	75	S&P Credit Rating	BBB-

Price Performance

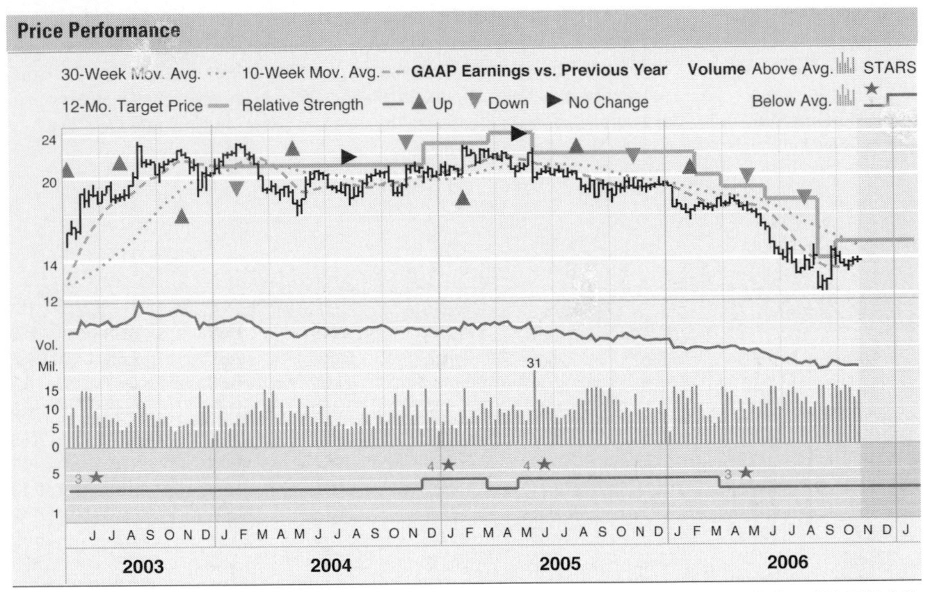

Options: ASE, CBOE, P, Ph

Analysis prepared by **Jason N. Asaeda** on September 26, 2006, when the stock traded at **$ 14.00**.

Highlights

- In FY 07 (Jan.), we look for sales to rise 10%, to $9.5 billion, driven by the opening of over 800 stores. We see a potential sales lift from new product offerings, store layout changes, broader tender options, and increased customer awareness of Dollar General stores as a result of heightened promotional activity.
- Gross margins are likely to remain under pressure from the shift in sales mix to lower-margin consumables, promotional markdowns, high inventory shrinkage, and rising transportation expense, partly offset by DG's efforts to improve merchandise markups with direct sourcing. As was the case in FY 06, we look for the company's EZstore project to curtail costs from store labor, damaged merchandise and workers' compensation. However, with likely expense deleveraging on a projected 3% same-store sales increase, infrastructure investments, and stock option expensing, we anticipate further operating margin erosion.
- Factoring in projected share buybacks, we expect FY 07 operating and S&P Core EPS of $0.88.

Investment Rationale/Risk

- We look favorably on store productivity gains and cost reductions that have been achieved as part of DG's EZstore project. However, we think management's decision to plan for an aggressive expansion in FY 07 without having fully resolved store issues--which we believe include high carryover inventory of seasonal merchandise and weak sales of higher-margin categories such as home products and apparel--reduces the likelihood of the company achieving a turnaround in FY 07, particularly in light of external challenges.
- Risks to our recommendation and target price include sales shortfalls due to a weakening in consumer spending, and merchandising missteps. Our corporate governance concerns include a non-shareholder approved poison pill plan and the non-disclosure of specific hurdle rates for performance-based equity incentive awards.
- Our 12-month target price of $15 is based on our discounted cash flow analysis, which assumes a weighted average cost of capital of 9.3% and a terminal growth rate of 3.0%.

Qualitative Risk Assessment

LOW | **MEDIUM** | HIGH

Our risk assessment reflects DG's earnings erosion in recent years, partly reflecting difficult economic conditions for customers, offset by promising new merchandising and productivity initiatives that we expect to boost sales and profit margins going forward.

Quantitative Evaluations

S&P Quality Ranking A+

D | C | B- | B | B+ | A- | A | **A+**

Relative Strength Rank MODERATE

37

LOWEST = 1 HIGHEST = 99

Revenue/Earnings Data

Revenue (Million $)

	1Q	2Q	3Q	4Q	Year
2007	2,151	2,251	--	--	--
2006	1,978	2,066	2,058	2,481	8,582
2005	1,748	1,836	1,879	2,198	7,661
2004	1,569	1,836	1,685	1,966	6,872
2003	1,389	1,454	1,498	1,760	6,100
2002	1,203	1,225	1,309	1,586	5,323

Earnings Per Share ($)

2007	0.15	0.15	E0.14	E0.44	E0.88
2006	0.20	0.23	0.20	0.46	1.08
2005	0.20	0.22	0.22	0.41	1.04
2004	0.18	0.22	0.23	0.30	0.89
2003	0.14	0.13	0.20	0.32	0.79
2002	0.11	0.08	0.14	0.29	0.62

Fiscal year ended Jan. 31. Next earnings report expected: Late November. EPS Estimates based on S&P Operating Earnings; historical GAAP earnings are as reported.

Dividend Data (Dates: mm/dd Payment Date: mm/dd/yy)

Amount ($)	Date Decl.	Ex-Div. Date	Stk. of Record	Payment Date
0.045	11/21	12/27	12/29	01/12/06
0.050	03/17	04/04	04/06	04/20/06
0.050	05/31	07/03	07/06	07/20/06
0.050	08/29	10/03	10/05	10/19/06

Dividends have been paid since 1975. Source: Company reports.

Dollar General Corp

Business Summary September 26, 2006

CORPORATE OVERVIEW. DG focuses on customers that most other retailers ignore: the low-, middle- and fixed-income brackets. About 48% of customers live in households with incomes under $30,000, and about 26% earn under $20,000. DG's assortment of private label and national brand products includes consumables (i.e., food, health and beauty aids, cleaning supplies, stationery, and pet supplies), housewares/domestics, seasonal goods and basic apparel. The majority of items are priced at $10 or less, with approximately 30% at $1 or less.

As of August 4, 2006, DG operated 8,178 stores, including 50 Dollar General Market stores, mainly in the southern, southwestern, midwestern and eastern U.S. The average Dollar General store has about 6,800 sq. ft. of selling space, 4,250 items, and serves customers living within a five mile radius. The company believes its customers prefer the convenience of small, neighborhood stores. Over 50% of the stores are located in communities with populations below 20,000. Dollar General Market stores have an average of 17,400 sq. ft. of selling space and carry an expanded assortment of grocery products and perishable items.

PRIMARY BUSINESS DYNAMICS. DG's primary growth drivers are same-store sales (sales results for stores open more than 13 months) and new store openings. Same-store sales advanced 2.0% in FY 06 (Jan.), mainly attributable to an increase in the average customer purchase, versus a 3.2% rise in FY 05. The company believes that FY 06 sales were hurt by the adverse effect of rising fuel prices, interest rates and consumer debt levels, as well as increased promotional efforts of competitors on customers' spending.

DG thinks that its focus on towns that many retailers find too small to support their business models has enabled it to expand its chain faster than most retailers. From FY 01 through FY 06, the company increased its store count from 5,000 to 7,929 at a compound annual growth rate (CAGR) of nearly 10%. In FY 07, DG plans to open at least 800 new Dollar General stores and up to 25 new Dollar General Market stores.

Company Financials

Per Share Data ($) Year Ended Jan. 31	**2006**	**2005**	**2004**	**2003**	**2002**	**2001**	**2000**	**1999**	**1998**	**1997**
Tangible Book Value	5.45	5.13	4.69	3.86	3.13	2.60	3.50	2.61	2.65	1.78
Cash Flow	1.66	1.53	1.34	1.19	0.99	0.55	1.05	0.69	0.67	0.53
Earnings	1.08	1.04	0.89	0.79	0.62	0.21	0.55	0.45	0.43	0.34
S&P Core Earnings	0.98	1.00	0.89	0.69	0.59	0.45	NA	NA	NA	NA
Dividends	0.16	0.14	0.13	0.13	0.13	0.12	0.10	0.08	0.07	0.06
Payout Ratio	15%	13%	14%	16%	21%	57%	18%	17%	15%	18%
Calendar Year	2005	2004	2003	2002	2001	2000	1999	1998	1997	1996
Prices:High	22.80	23.19	23.40	19.95	24.05	23.19	26.10	24.19	16.38	9.14
Prices:Low	17.75	16.91	9.50	11.70	10.50	13.44	15.08	12.80	7.80	4.04
P/E Ratio:High	21	22	26	25	39	NM	47	54	38	27
P/E Ratio:Low	16	16	11	15	17	NM	27	28	18	12
Income Statement Analysis (Million $)										
Revenue	8,582	7,661	6,872	6,100	5,323	4,551	3,888	3,221	2,627	2,134
Operating Income	749	721	674	563	497	427	413	342	274	221
Depreciation	187	164	152	135	123	111	63.9	53.1	38.7	31.0
Interest Expense	26.2	28.8	31.5	42.6	45.8	45.4	5.16	8.35	3.76	4.70
Pretax Income	545	535	480	415	328	109	344	281	232	185
Effective Tax Rate	35.7%	35.6%	37.3%	36.1%	36.7%	35.0%	36.2%	35.2%	37.6%	37.8%
Net Income	350	344	301	265	208	70.6	219	182	145	115
S&P Core Earnings	318	333	300	231	196	150	NA	NA	NA	NA
Balance Sheet & Other Financial Data (Million $)										
Cash	201	233	398	121	262	262	58.8	22.3	7.13	6.60
Current Assets	1,763	1,731	1,652	1,324	1,556	1,125	1,096	879	667	505
Total Assets	2,992	2,841	2,653	2,333	2,552	2,282	1,451	1,212	915	718
Current Liabilities	934	826	744	665	1,134	538	472	455	308	224
Long Term Debt	270	258	265	330	339	721	1.20	0.79	1.30	2.60
Common Equity	1,721	1,684	1,577	557	1,042	862	926	725	583	485
Total Capital	2,058	2,015	1,909	938	1,419	1,583	979	757	607	494
Capital Expenditures	284	292	149	134	125	217	153	140	108	84.4
Cash Flow	537	509	453	400	330	182	282	232	180	144
Current Ratio	1.9	2.1	2.2	2.0	1.4	2.1	2.3	1.9	2.2	2.2
% Long Term Debt of Capitalization	13.1	12.8	13.9	35.2	23.9	45.5	0.1	0.1	0.2	0.5
% Net Income of Revenue	4.1	4.5	4.4	4.3	3.9	1.6	5.6	5.7	5.5	5.4
% Return on Assets	12.0	12.6	12.1	10.8	8.6	3.4	16.5	17.1	17.7	16.5
% Return on Equity	20.6	21.3	21.0	33.1	21.8	8.3	26.4	27.3	26.5	24.9

Data as orig reptd.; bef. results of disc opers/spec. items. Per share data adj. for stk. divs.; EPS diluted. E-Estimated. NA-Not Available. NM-Not Meaningful. NR-Not Ranked. UR-Under Review.

Office: 100 Mission Ridge, Goodlettsville, TN 37072.
Telephone: 615-855-4000.
Website: http://www.dollargeneral.com
Chrmn & CEO: D.A. Perdue

Investor Contact: D.M. Tehle (615-855-4000)
EVP & CFO: D.M. Tehle
EVP, Secy & General Counsel: S.S. Lanigan
SVP & Cntlr: A.C. Elliott

Board of Directors: D. L. Bere, D. C. Bottorff, B. L. Bowles, J. L. Clayton, R. D. Dickson, E. G. Gee, B. M. Knuckles, D. A. Perdue, J. N. Purcell, J. D. Robbins, R. E. Thornburgh, D. M. Wilds

Founded: 1939
Domicile: Tennessee
Employees: 64,500

STANDARD &POOR'S

Dominion Resources Inc.

S&P Recommendation HOLD ★★★★★

Price $80.64 (as of Oct 27, 2006)

12-Mo. Target Price $79.00

Investment Style Large-Cap Value

GICS Sector Utilities
Sub-Industry Multi-Utilities

Comment This energy holding company's principal subsidiaries are Virginia Electric & Power Co. and Consolidated Natural Gas.

Key Stock Statistics (Source S&P, Vickers, company reports)

52-Wk Range	$81.91–68.72	S&P Oper. EPS 2006E	5.17	P/E on S&P Oper. EPS 2006E	15.6	Dividend Rate/Share	$2.76
Trailing 12-Month EPS	$2.78	S&P Oper. EPS 2007E	6.18	Common Shares Outstg. (M)	352.8	Yield (%)	3.42
Trailing 12-Month P/E	29.0	S&P Core EPS 2006E	4.99	Market Capitalization(B)	$28.454	Beta	0.47
$10K Invested 5 Yrs Ago	$16,145	S&P Core EPS 2007E	6.07	Institutional Ownership (%)	62	S&P Credit Rating	BBB

Price Performance

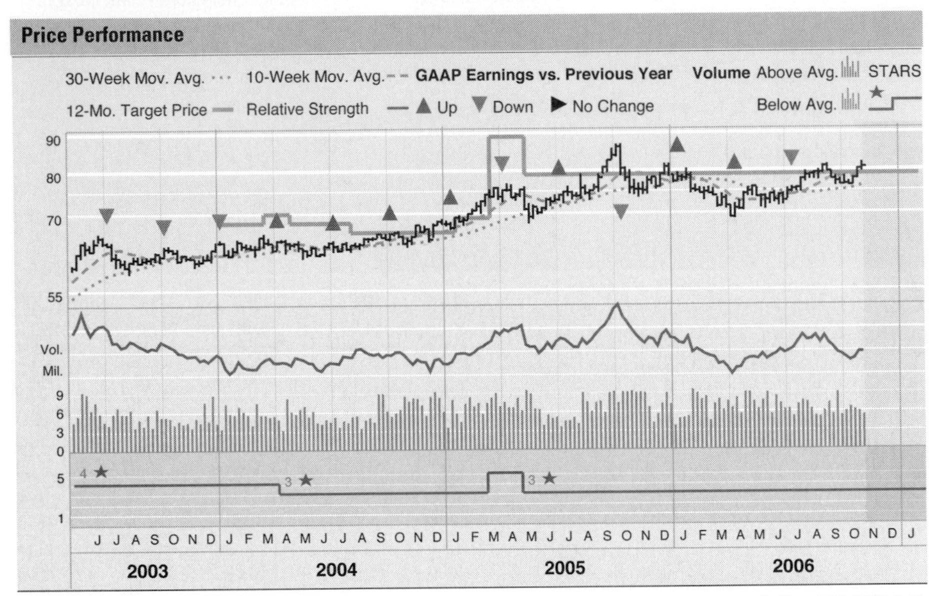

Options: ASE, CBOE, P, Ph

Analysis prepared by **Todd Rosenbluth** on September 27, 2006, when the stock traded at **$ 77.45**.

Highlights

- We expect E&P operations to see mid-single digit growth in 2006, aided by high teens production growth and higher hedged prices. We look for offshore deepwater projects to get back on track following damage from 2005 hurricanes. We think E&P profits will be restricted by rising labor and production costs, offset by higher business insurance recoveries.
- At regulated utilities, we look for slightly higher earnings as a return to normal weather offsets customer growth and purchased power savings. The generation segment should benefit, in our view, from improved power pricing and contributions from acquisitions, partly offset by an under-recovery in fuel expenses in Virginia. We see overall revenues down fractionally in 2006, but expect that EBITDA growth will stem from operating expense savings.
- We project 2006 operating EPS of $5.17 and 2007 operating EPS of $6.18. Our S&P Core Earnings estimate reflects pension adjustments.

Investment Rationale/Risk

- We think D's strategy of acquiring power plants that serve its utilities should reduce purchased power costs, and provide greater operational flexibility. We believe that strong natural gas fundamentals will drive growth in E&P operations, but we remain concerned about potential hurricane-related damage to offshore operations. The scheduled reset of rates in Virginia in 2007 should help D recover from the impact of high fuel costs.
- Risks to our recommendation and target price include potential delays or cost overruns related to development projects; a sharp decline in natural gas prices; higher than expected interest rates; and a weaker economy.
- The shares recently traded near the average 2007 P/E for peer multi-utilities. Our 12-month target price of $79 is roughly equal to 13X our 2007 EPS estimate, on par with target peer valuations, as we think that what we view as D's stronger long-term growth outlook is balanced by our near-term regulatory and execution concerns.

Qualitative Risk Assessment

LOW | **MEDIUM** | HIGH

Our risk assessment reflects our view of Dominion's relatively large capitalization and balanced sources of earnings, which include low-risk regulated electric and gas distribution and pipeline operations, offset by higher risk exploration and production and energy marketing businesses.

Quantitative Evaluations

S&P Quality Ranking B+

D | C | B- | B | **B+** | A- | A | A+

Relative Strength Rank MODERATE

56

LOWEST = 1 HIGHEST = 99

Revenue/Earnings Data

Revenue (Million $)

	1Q	2Q	3Q	4Q	Year
2006	4,957	3,556	--	--	--
2005	4,736	3,646	4,564	5,095	18,041
2004	3,879	3,040	3,292	3,761	13,972
2003	3,579	2,630	2,853	3,016	12,078
2002	2,634	2,332	2,545	2,707	10,218
2001	3,198	2,309	2,544	2,507	10,558

Earnings Per Share ($)

	1Q	2Q	3Q	4Q	Year
2006	1.53	0.46	**E**1.39	**E**1.40	**E**5.17
2005	1.25	0.97	0.03	0.76	3.00
2004	1.36	0.79	1.02	0.67	3.82
2003	1.32	0.78	1.01	-0.10	2.98
2002	1.20	0.97	1.54	1.12	4.82
2001	1.20	0.62	1.37	-0.45	2.15

Fiscal year ended Dec. 31. Next earnings report expected: Early November. EPS Estimates based on S&P Operating Earnings; historical GAAP earnings are as reported.

Dividend Data (Dates: mm/dd Payment Date: mm/dd/yy)

Amount ($)	Date Decl.	Ex-Div. Date	Stk. of Record	Payment Date
0.670	10/28	11/23	11/28	12/20/05
0.690	01/26	02/22	02/24	03/20/06
0.690	04/28	11/29	12/01	12/20/06

Dividends have been paid since 1925. Source: Company reports.

Dominion Resources Inc.

Business Summary September 27, 2006

CORPORATE OVERVIEW. Dominion Resources is a fully integrated gas and electric holding company. The company operates in four primary segments: Delivery, Energy, Generation, and Exploration and Production. The Delivery segment (22.6% of operating revenue before adjustments and eliminations in 2005) operates regulated electric and gas distribution businesses as well as non-regulated retail energy marketing. The Energy segment (16.0%) operates in tariff-based electric transmission, natural gas transmission and storage businesses, and the Cove Point LNG facility. The Generation segment (43.1%) is involved in generation for the electric utility and merchant power along with energy marketing and risk management activities. Exploration and Production segment (15.1%) explores and produces gas and oil in the U.S., the Gulf of Mexico, and western Canada.

CORPORATE STRATEGY. D focuses its efforts mainly on the energy-intensive Northeast, Mid-Atlantic and Midwest regions of the US. As part of a strategy to concentrate on growing its core businesses in the above-mentioned markets, the company is committed to divesting all of its energy-related operations outside the U.S., primarily equity investments in Australia and Argentina. The company believes that the integrated energy model and diverse generation source will enable it to balance the volatility in commodity prices. It has a proactive risk management strategy and has entered into commodity derivative agreements to hedge against the commodity price risk.

MARKET PROFILE. As of December 31, 2005, D had a total power generation capacity of 28,053 MW. The Delivery segment served a total of 3.9 million electric and gas utility customers in five states, and has 1.2 million competitive retail marketing customers in eight states. Due to a Virginia regulatory electric rate freeze through 2007, the company is allowed to retain cost savings in this jurisdiction.

Company Financials

Per Share Data ($) Year Ended Dec. 31	**2005**	**2004**	**2003**	**2002**	**2001**	**2000**	**1999**	**1998**	**1997**	**1996**
Tangible Book Value	17.58	32.73	19.19	18.18	15.69	14.20	24.80	26.56	16.55	27.21
Earnings	3.00	3.82	2.98	4.82	2.15	1.76	2.81	2.75	2.15	2.65
S&P Core Earnings	2.94	3.79	3.15	3.84	1.31	NA	NA	NA	NA	NA
Dividends	2.68	2.60	2.58	2.58	2.58	2.58	2.58	2.58	2.58	2.58
Payout Ratio	89%	68%	87%	54%	120%	147%	92%	94%	120%	97%
Prices:High	86.97	68.85	65.95	67.06	69.99	67.94	49.38	48.94	42.88	44.38
Prices:Low	66.51	60.78	51.74	35.40	55.13	34.81	36.56	37.81	33.25	36.88
P/E Ratio:High	29	18	22	14	33	39	18	18	20	17
P/E Ratio:Low	22	16	17	7	26	20	13	14	15	14
Income Statement Analysis (Million $)										
Revenue	18,041	13,972	12,078	10,218	10,558	9,260	5,520	6,086	7,678	4,042
Depreciation	1,412	1,305	1,216	1,258	1,245	1,176	716	734	819	615
Maintenance	NA	NA	NA	NA	NA	NA	NA	NA	NA	251
Fixed Charges Coverage	2.63	3.09	2.63	3.15	2.02	1.99	2.44	1.83	2.38	3.12
Construction Credits	Nil	Nil	Nil	Nil	Nil	Nil	Nil	Nil	Nil	Nil
Effective Tax Rate	36.0%	35.6%	38.6%	33.3%	40.5%	30.5%	31.3%	35.2%	34.3%	31.1%
Net Income	1,034	1,264	949	1,362	544	415	551	536	399	472
S&P Core Earnings	1,010	1,254	1,004	1,088	331	NA	NA	NA	NA	NA
Balance Sheet & Other Financial Data (Million $)										
Gross Property	42,063	38,663	37,107	32,631	33,105	31,011	18,646	18,106	19,520	16,816
Capital Expenditures	1,683	1,451	2,138	2,828	1,224	1,385	737	755	649	484
Net Property	28,940	26,716	25,850	20,257	18,681	14,849	10,764	10,637	12,533	10,509
Capitalization:Long Term Debt	14,910	15,764	16,033	13,714	12,119	10,486	7,321	5,071	7,196	4,728
Capitalization:% Long Term Debt	58.9	58.0	60.3	57.3	58.1	58.3	58.2	44.2	49.1	45.2
Capitalization:Preferred	Nil	Nil	Nil	Nil	Nil	509	509	1,074	1,074	824
Capitalization:% Preferred	Nil	Nil	Nil	Nil	Nil	2.83	4.05	9.40	7.30	7.90
Capitalization:Common	10,397	11,426	10,538	10,213	8,368	6,992	4,752	5,315	5,040	4,924
Capitalization:% Common	41.1	42.0	39.7	42.7	40.1	38.9	37.8	46.4	34.4	47.0
Total Capital	30,291	32,689	31,134	28,136	24,811	20,955	14,427	13,475	14,658	12,474
% Operating Ratio	89.7	85.6	83.7	78.5	85.6	80.5	80.9	64.4	83.6	81.6
% Earned on Net Property	8.8	10.3	10.6	21.4	10.6	11.9	9.7	9.4	13.0	11.5
% Return on Revenue	5.7	9.0	7.9	13.3	5.2	4.5	10.0	8.8	5.2	9.8
% Return on Invested Capital	6.4	6.5	6.5	8.5	7.2	10.7	7.9	8.4	7.6	9.8
% Return on Common Equity	9.5	11.5	9.1	14.7	7.1	7.1	10.9	10.4	8.0	9.8

Data as orig reptd.; bef. results of disc opers/spec. items. Per share data adj. for stk. divs.; EPS diluted. E-Estimated. NA-Not Available. NM-Not Meaningful. NR-Not Ranked. UR-Under Review.

Office: 120 Tredegar Street, Richmond, VA 23219.
Telephone: 804-819-2000.
Email: investor_relations@domres.com
Website: http://www.dom.com

Chrmn: T.E. Capps
Pres & CEO: T.F. Farrell II
EVP & CFO: T.N. Chewning
SVP & Chief Admin: M.C. Doswell

SVP & Treas: G.S. Hetzer
Investor Contact: J. O'Hare (804-819-2156)
Board of Directors: P. W. Brown, R. J. Calise, T. E. Capps, G. A. Davidson, Jr., T. F. Farrell II, J. W. Harris, R. S. Jepson, Jr., M. J. Kington, B. J. Lambert, III, R. L. Leatherwood, M. A. McKenna, F. S. Royal, S. D. Simmons, D. A. Wollard

Founded: 1909
Domicile: Virginia
Employees: 17,400

STANDARD &POOR'S

R.R. Donnelley & Sons Co

S&P Recommendation BUY ★★★★★

Price $34.07 (as of Oct 27, 2006)

12-Mo. Target Price $39.00

Investment Style Mid-Cap Value

GICS Sector Industrials
Sub-Industry Commercial Printing

Comment R.R. Donnelley, the largest U.S. commercial printer, specializes in the production of catalogs, inserts, magazines, books, directories, and financial and computer documentation.

Key Stock Statistics (Source S&P, Vickers, company reports)

52-Wk Range	$36.43–28.50	S&P Oper. EPS 2006E	2.51	P/E on S&P Oper. EPS 2006E	13.6	Dividend Rate/Share	$1.04
Trailing 12-Month EPS	$0.80	S&P Oper. EPS 2007E	2.66	Common Shares Outstg. (M)	216.3	Yield (%)	3.05
Trailing 12-Month P/E	42.6	S&P Core EPS 2006E	2.19	Market Capitalization(B)	$7.369	Beta	0.80
$10K Invested 5 Yrs Ago	$15,534	S&P Core EPS 2007E	2.33	Institutional Ownership (%)	82	S&P Credit Rating	A-

Price Performance

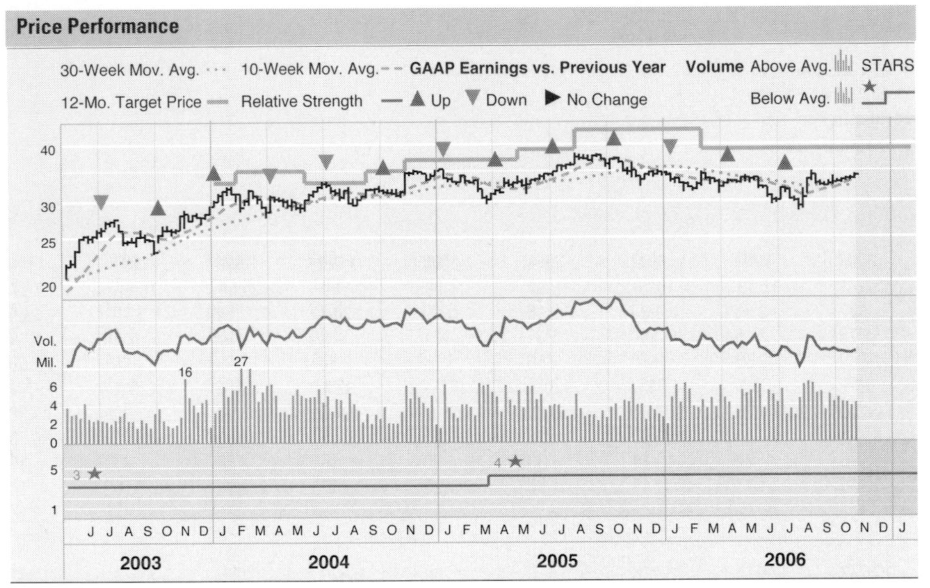

Options: ASE, CBOE, P, Ph

Analysis prepared by **James Peters, CFA** on August 31, 2006, when the stock traded at **$ 32.42**.

Highlights

- For 2006, we forecast revenue growth of 12%, including the full year effect of acquiring the Astron Group, Asia Printers and Poligrafia in 2005. We see organic revenue growth of 6.4%, driven by new business wins and a greater wallet share from existing customers as the company leverages its expanding product and platform capabilities. We also foresee more favorable foreign exchange comparisons boosting growth as the year progresses.
- We expect incremental stock option expense of $4.0 million, pricing pressure, and higher energy and paper costs to be offset by operating leverage from revenue growth as well as continued productivity advances. We forecast a slight operating margin expansion, to 10.5% in 2006, from 10.4% in 2005, before restructuring, impairment and acquisition integration charges.
- After higher expected interest payments, we see 2006 EPS rising to $2.51. Our 2006 S&P Core EPS estimate of $2.19 reflects $0.32 of projected pension expense. EPS in 2005 excluded an impairment charge of $1.66 in the Forms and Labels segment.

Investment Rationale/Risk

- We expect RRD to continue to gain market share by leveraging its geographic and product breadth, and through its low cost structure. We look for the company to deploy free cash flow in 2006 by refreshing its platform with above long-term trend capital expenditures of about $380 million, down from $471 million in 2005 and paying down about $225 million of debt maturing in November. We believe the company will continue to pursue selective acquisitions as RRD aims to expand its global reach and further increase its operating leverage.
- Risks to our opinion and target price include acquisition integration, substantially higher input costs, and greater than expected growth of information disseminated electronically.
- We derive our 12-month target price of $39 based on a blend of relative valuation analyses. We arrive at a $37 valuation by applying a peer average 6.9X enterprise value/EBITDA multiple to our 2007 EBITDA estimate of $1.53 billion. We derive a $42 valuation by applying a peer average P/E of 15.9X to our 2007 EPS estimate of $2.66.

Qualitative Risk Assessment

LOW | **MEDIUM** | HIGH

Our risk assessment reflects economies of scale that the company realizes as the largest U.S. commercial printer in a fragmented print industry and the company's low weighted average cost of capital, offset by industry pricing pressure and the increasingly electronic nature of communication.

Quantitative Evaluations

S&P Quality Ranking B

D | C | B- | **B** | B+ | A- | A | A+

Relative Strength Rank MODERATE

56

LOWEST = 1 HIGHEST = 99

Revenue/Earnings Data

Revenue (Million $)

	1Q	2Q	3Q	4Q	Year
2006	2,267	2,274	--	--	--
2005	1,927	1,932	2,184	2,388	8,430
2004	1,289	1,843	1,913	2,112	7,156
2003	1,074	1,142	1,194	1,377	4,787
2002	1,094	1,149	1,177	1,335	4,755
2001	1,303	1,292	1,288	1,415	5,298

Earnings Per Share ($)

	1Q	2Q	3Q	4Q	Year
2006	0.52	0.57	**E**0.67	**E**0.66	**E**2.51
2005	0.50	0.44	0.59	-1.09	0.44
2004	-0.35	-0.06	0.52	0.61	0.88
2003	0.05	0.17	0.47	0.85	1.54
2002	0.20	0.22	0.42	0.42	1.24
2001	0.12	0.05	0.36	-0.33	0.21

Fiscal year ended Dec. 31. Next earnings report expected: Early November. EPS Estimates based on S&P Operating Earnings; historical GAAP earnings are as reported.

Dividend Data (Dates: mm/dd Payment Date: mm/dd/yy)

Amount ($)	Date Decl.	Ex-Div. Date	Stk. of Record	Payment Date
0.260	01/05	02/08	02/10	03/01/06
0.260	04/26	05/08	05/10	06/01/06
0.260	07/26	08/08	08/10	09/01/06
0.260	10/26	11/08	11/10	12/01/06

Dividends have been paid since 1911. Source: Company reports.

Please read the Required Disclosures and Analyst Certification on the last page of this report.

R.R. Donnelley & Sons Co

Business Summary August 31, 2006

RRD is the largest printing company in North America, serving customers in the publishing, health care, advertising, retail, telecommunications, technology, financial services and other industries. The company provides solutions in long- and short-run commercial printing, direct mail, financial printing, print fulfillment, forms and labels, logistics, digital printing, call centers, transactional print-and-mail, print management, online services, digital photography, color services, and content and database management. Geographically, the company derives the majority of its revenues from the U.S. (86% of 2005 revenues), with Europe accounting for 6% and the rest of the world 8%. In 2005, no customer accounted for 10% or more of the company's sales.

The company was reorganized in 2004 into three reportable segments, including Publishing and Retail Services, Integrated Print Communications, and Forms and Labels. The Publishing and Retail Services segment (50% of revenues in 2005) consists of the following businesses: magazine, catalog and retail, which includes print services to consumer magazine and catalog publishers as well as retailers; directories, which serves the global printing needs of yellow and white pages directory publishers; logistics, which delivers company and third party printed products as well as performs the distribution of time-sensitive and secure material, warehousing and fulfillment services; and premedia, which offers conventional and digital photography, creative, color matching, page production and content management services. The segment also includes results from Asia and Europe, except for results from the Astron Group. The company states that historically, demand in several of the end markets serviced by this segment is higher in the second half of the year, driven by increased advertising pages within magazines, and holiday catalog, retail and book volumes.

Company Financials

Per Share Data ($) Year Ended Dec. 31	2005	2004	2003	2002	2001	2000	1999	1998	1997	1996
Tangible Book Value	NM	3.81	5.14	4.51	3.92	5.89	6.01	6.85	8.31	7.22
Cash Flow	2.40	5.07	4.43	4.32	3.41	5.34	5.29	4.66	3.91	1.53
Earnings	0.44	0.88	1.54	1.24	0.21	2.17	2.40	2.08	1.40	-1.04
S&P Core Earnings	1.27	1.20	1.18	0.18	-0.65	NA	NA	NA	NA	NA
Dividends	1.04	1.04	1.02	0.98	0.94	0.90	0.86	0.82	0.78	0.74
Payout Ratio	NM	118%	66%	79%	NM	41%	36%	39%	56%	NM
Prices:High	38.27	35.37	30.15	32.10	31.90	27.50	44.75	48.00	41.75	39.88
Prices:Low	29.54	27.62	16.94	18.50	24.30	19.00	21.50	33.75	29.50	29.38
P/E Ratio:High	87	40	20	26	NM	13	19	23	30	NM
P/E Ratio:Low	67	31	11	15	NM	9	9	16	21	NM

Income Statement Analysis (Million $)										
Revenue	8,430	7,156	4,787	4,755	5,298	5,764	5,183	5,018	4,850	6,599
Operating Income	1,295	952	617	686	722	891	905	856	811	813
Depreciation	425	771	329	352	379	390	374	367	371	389
Interest Expense	111	85.9	50.4	62.8	71.2	89.6	88.2	78.0	91.0	95.0
Pretax Income	332	357	208	176	74.9	434	507	510	304	-110
Effective Tax Rate	71.5%	26.0%	15.3%	19.1%	66.6%	38.5%	38.5%	42.2%	31.9%	NM
Net Income	95.6	265	177	142	25.0	267	312	295	207	-158
S&P Core Earnings	275	243	136	21.3	-78.3	NA	NA	NA	NA	NA

Balance Sheet & Other Financial Data (Million $)										
Cash	367	642	60.8	60.5	48.6	60.9	41.9	66.0	48.0	31.1
Current Assets	2,622	2,601	1,000	866	940	1,206	1,230	1,145	1,147	1,753
Total Assets	9,374	8,554	3,189	3,152	3,400	3,914	3,853	3,788	4,134	4,849
Current Liabilities	1,814	1,487	884	955	984	1,191	1,203	898	813	1,148
Long Term Debt	2,365	1,581	752	753	881	739	748	999	1,153	1,431
Common Equity	3,724	3,987	983	915	888	1,233	1,138	1,301	1,592	1,631
Total Capital	6,686	6,144	1,970	1,882	1,982	2,205	2,140	2,585	2,974	3,316
Capital Expenditures	471	265	203	242	273	237	276	225	360	403
Cash Flow	521	1,036	506	495	404	657	686	662	578	232
Current Ratio	1.4	1.7	1.1	0.9	1.0	1.0	1.0	1.3	1.4	1.5
% Long Term Debt of Capitalization	35.4	25.7	38.2	40.0	44.5	33.5	35.0	38.6	38.8	43.1
% Net Income of Revenue	1.1	3.7	3.7	3.0	0.5	4.6	6.0	5.9	4.3	NM
% Return on Assets	1.1	4.5	5.5	4.4	0.7	6.9	8.1	7.4	4.6	NM
% Return on Equity	2.5	10.7	18.6	15.8	2.4	22.5	25.5	20.4	12.8	NM

Data as orig reptd.; bef. results of disc opers/spec. items. Per share data adj. for stk. divs.; EPS diluted. E-Estimated. NA-Not Available. NM-Not Meaningful. NR-Not Ranked. UR-Under Review.

Office: 111 W Wacker Dr, Chicago, IL 60606.
Telephone: 312-326-8000.
Email: investor.info@rrd.com
Website: http://www.rrdonnelley.com

Chrmn, Pres & CEO: M.A. Angelson
EVP & CFO: T.J. Quinlan, III
SVP & General Counsel: S.S. Bettman
SVP & Cntlr: M.W. McHugh

Investor Contact: D.N. Leib (312-326-8000)
Board of Directors: M. A. Angelson, R. F. Cummings, Jr., J. H. Hamilton, T. S. Johnson, J. C. Pope, M. T. Riordan, L. H. Schipper, O. R. Sockwell, B. L. Thomas, N. Wesley, S. M. Wolf

Founded: 1864
Domicile: Delaware
Employees: 50,000

STANDARD &POOR'S

Dover Corp

S&P Recommendation HOLD ★★★★★ | **Price** $47.50 (as of Oct 31, 2006) | **12-Mo. Target Price** $52.00 | **Investment Style** Large-Cap Value

GICS Sector Industrials
Sub-Industry Industrial Machinery

Comment This company manufactures a broad range of specialized industrial products and sophisticated manufacturing equipment.

Key Stock Statistics (Source S&P, Vickers, company reports)

52-Wk Range	$51.92–38.44	S&P Oper. EPS 2006E	2.93	P/E on S&P Oper. EPS 2006E	16.2	Dividend Rate/Share	$0.74
Trailing 12-Month EPS	$2.73	S&P Oper. EPS 2007E	3.35	Common Shares Outstg. (M)	204.2	Yield (%)	1.56
Trailing 12-Month P/E	17.4	S&P Core EPS 2006E	2.86	Market Capitalization(B)	$9.698	Beta	1.47
$10K Invested 5 Yrs Ago	$14,588	S&P Core EPS 2007E	3.25	Institutional Ownership (%)	82	S&P Credit Rating	A

Price Performance

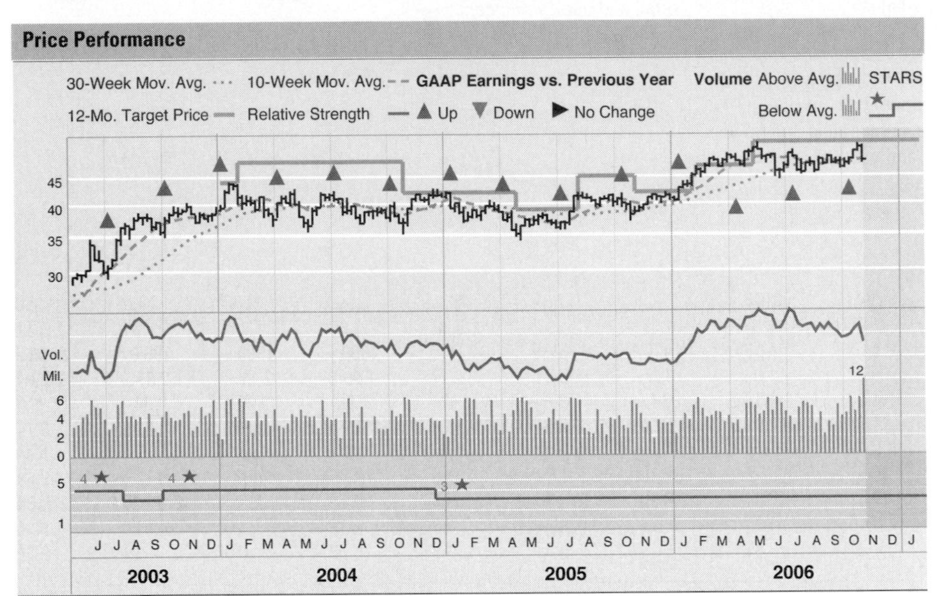

Options: ASE, P, Ph

Analysis prepared by **Stewart Scharf** on October 31, 2006, when the stock traded at **$ 47.55**.

Highlights

- We expect total revenues to advance over 20%, with low-double digit organic growth, driven by strength in the oil and gas, electronic components and process equipment markets, which should offset softness in the light construction, automotive and food equipment sectors, as well as the semiconductor market. We believe industrial-related equipment spending will continue to rise into 2007. However, we project more moderate growth of about 10% for 2007.

- We expect gross margins to widen to near 36% in 2006, from about 35% in 2005, with further expansion likely in 2007, based on pricing initiatives, and stabilizing raw material costs. Operating margins should also widen on price hikes and productivity improvements, as SG&A declines to about 22% of revenues in 2006, and near 21% in 2007. We expect further cost controls, while cash generation remains strong.

- We project 2006 operating EPS of $2.93, rising 14% in 2007 to $3.35. We see S&P Core EPS of $2.86 and $3.25, respectively, due mainly to pension costs.

Investment Rationale/Risk

- We view positively DOV's ability to generate strong free cash flow ($455 million through the first nine months of 2006), operating leverage and consistent dividend payments that have grown at a 10-year CAGR of about 8%, as evidenced by S&P's above average A-minus Quality Ranking. However, we think these factors are appropriately reflected in the current price.

- Risks to our opinion and target price include reduced industrial capital spending should interest rates rise; a longer-than-expected downturn in the semiconductor market, impacting demand for technology products; and another significant rise in raw material costs.

- Our DCF model, which assumes a 4% terminal growth rate and a cost of capital of 11.4%, derives intrinsic value of $51. The shares traded recently at about 14X our 2007 EPS projection, in line with peers, but at a small discount to the stock's four-year historical average, which we apply to our estimate to arrive at a value of $53. Blending these methodologies leads to our 12-month target price of $52.

Qualitative Risk Assessment

LOW | MEDIUM | **HIGH**

Our risk assessment reflects the company's acquisition strategy, its model of operating numerous different businesses as stand-alone entities, and its exposure to several cyclical end markets.

Quantitative Evaluations

S&P Quality Ranking A-

D | C | B- | B | B+ | **A-** | A | A+

Relative Strength Rank WEAK

25

LOWEST = 1 HIGHEST = 99

Revenue/Earnings Data

Revenue (Million $)

	1Q	2Q	3Q	4Q	Year
2006	1,668	1,655	1,652	--	--
2005	1,383	1,525	1,556	1,614	6,078
2004	1,242	1,380	1,444	1,421	5,488
2003	1,028	1,124	1,154	1,198	4,413
2002	994.6	1,082	1,062	1,045	4,184
2001	1,210	1,115	1,085	1,050	4,460

Earnings Per Share ($)

2006	0.65	0.77	0.77	E0.74	E2.93
2005	0.47	0.59	0.65	0.61	2.32
2004	0.41	0.53	0.58	0.48	2.00
2003	0.29	0.36	0.37	0.39	1.40
2002	0.22	0.31	0.29	0.19	1.04
2001	0.38	0.24	0.02	0.18	0.82

Fiscal year ended Dec. 31. Next earnings report expected: NA. EPS Estimates based on S&P Operating Earnings; historical GAAP earnings are as reported.

Dividend Data (Dates: mm/dd Payment Date: mm/dd/yy)

Amount ($)	Date Decl.	Ex-Div. Date	Stk. of Record	Payment Date
0.170	11/03	11/28	11/30	12/15/05
0.170	02/02	02/24	02/28	03/15/06
0.170	05/04	05/26	05/31	06/15/06
0.185	08/03	08/29	08/31	09/15/06

Dividends have been paid since 1947. Source: Company reports.

Dover Corp

Business Summary October 31, 2006

CORPORATE OVERVIEW. Dover Corporation is a diversified manufacturer of a broad range of specialized industrial products and manufacturing equipment. The company has been formed largely through acquisitions, completing 68 acquisitions for approximately $2.9 billion between January 2000 and December 2005. The company is comprised of six operating segments: Diversified, Electronics, Industries, Resources, Systems, and Technologies.

Dover Diversified manufactures equipment and components for use in the defense, aerospace and automotive aftermarket industries, heat transfer equipment, specialized bearings, construction and agricultural cabs, and color measurement and control systems for printing presses. Dover Electronics manufactures an array of specialized electronic, electromechanical, and plastic components for OEMs in multiple end markets including hearing aids, telecom, defense and aerospace electronics, and life sciences. Electronics also supplies ATM hardware and software for retail applications and financial institutions, and chemical proportioning and dispensing systems for janitorial/sanitation applications.

Dover Industries manufactures a diverse mix of equipment and components for use in the waste handling, bulk transport, and automotive service industries. Major units include PDQ Manufacturing, Heil Environmental, Rotary Lift, Heil Trailer International, Chief Automotive, and Marathon Equipment. Dover Resources manufactures products primarily for the oil and gas, automotive fueling, fluid handling, engineered components, material handling and chemical equipment industries. Dover Systems manufactures food equipment (refrigeration systems, display cases, walk-in coolers, etc.) and packaging machinery. The food equipment businesses (Hill Phoenix and Unified Brands) sell to the institutional and commercial foodservice markets. The packaging machinery businesses sell to the beverage and food processing industries. Dover Technologies manufactures products in two broad groupings: Circuit Board Assembly and Test equipment (CBAT), and Product Identification and Printing systems.

Company Financials

Per Share Data ($) Year Ended Dec. 31	2005	2004	2003	2002	2001	2000	1999	1998	1997	1996
Tangible Book Value	NM	2.16	2.71	2.66	1.97	1.79	1.08	2.11	2.81	2.29
Cash Flow	3.18	2.78	2.14	1.83	1.89	3.60	2.79	2.20	2.54	2.28
Earnings	2.32	2.00	1.40	1.04	0.82	2.61	1.92	1.45	1.79	1.73
S&P Core Earnings	2.25	1.92	1.31	0.90	0.68	NA	NA	NA	NA	NA
Dividends	0.66	0.62	0.57	0.54	0.52	0.48	0.44	0.40	0.36	0.32
Payout Ratio	28%	31%	41%	52%	63%	18%	23%	28%	20%	19%
Prices:High	42.11	44.13	40.45	43.55	43.55	54.38	47.94	39.94	36.69	27.56
Prices:Low	34.11	35.12	22.85	23.54	26.40	34.13	29.31	25.50	24.13	18.31
P/E Ratio:High	18	22	29	42	53	21	25	28	20	16
P/E Ratio:Low	15	18	16	23	32	13	15	18	13	11

Income Statement Analysis (Million $)	2005	2004	2003	2002	2001	2000	1999	1998	1997	1996
Revenue	6,078	5,488	4,413	4,184	4,460	5,401	4,446	3,978	4,548	4,076
Operating Income	876	773	595	503	518	1,047	819	700	783	664
Depreciation	176	161	151	161	219	203	183	168	171	125
Interest Expense	72.2	61.3	62.2	70.0	91.2	97.5	53.4	60.7	46.9	42.0
Pretax Income	644	552	372	270	238	772	615	489	617	589
Effective Tax Rate	26.3%	25.9%	23.3%	21.7%	30.0%	31.0%	34.1%	33.2%	34.3%	33.7%
Net Income	474	409	285	211	167	533	405	326	405	390
S&P Core Earnings	460	392	267	182	138	NA	NA	NA	NA	NA

Balance Sheet & Other Financial Data (Million $)	2005	2004	2003	2002	2001	2000	1999	1998	1997	1996
Cash	191	358	370	295	177	187	138	96.8	125	218
Current Assets	1,976	2,150	1,850	1,658	1,655	1,975	1,612	1,305	1,591	1,490
Total Assets	6,573	5,792	5,134	4,437	4,602	4,892	4,132	3,627	3,278	2,993
Current Liabilities	1,207	1,356	911	697	819	1,605	1,345	990	1,197	1,139
Long Term Debt	1,344	753	1,004	1,030	1,033	632	608	610	263	253
Common Equity	3,330	3,119	2,743	2,395	2,520	2,442	2,039	1,911	1,778	1,490
Total Capital	5,046	4,168	3,980	3,561	3,656	3,141	2,689	2,571	2,007	1,797
Capital Expenditures	152	107	96.4	102	167	198	130	126	146	126
Cash Flow	650	570	437	372	386	737	588	494	576	515
Current Ratio	1.6	1.6	2.0	2.4	2.0	1.2	1.2	1.3	1.3	1.3
% Long Term Debt of Capitalization	26.6	18.1	25.2	28.9	28.3	20.1	22.6	23.7	13.1	14.1
% Net Income of Revenue	7.8	7.5	6.5	5.0	3.7	9.9	9.1	8.2	8.9	9.6
% Return on Assets	7.7	7.5	6.0	4.7	3.5	11.8	10.4	9.5	12.9	13.8
% Return on Equity	14.7	14.0	11.1	8.6	6.7	23.8	20.5	17.7	24.4	28.7

Data as orig reptd.; bef. results of disc opers/spec. items. Per share data adj. for stk. divs.; EPS diluted. E-Estimated. NA-Not Available. NM-Not Meaningful. NR-Not Ranked. UR-Under Review.

Office: 280 Park Avenue, New York, NY 10017-1215.
Telephone: 212-922-1640.
Website: http://www.dovercorporation.com
Chrmn: T.L. Reece

Pres, CEO & COO: R.L. Hoffman
VP & CFO: R.G. Kuhbach
VP, Secy & General Counsel: J.W. Schmidt
VP & Cntlr: R.T. McKay, Jr.

Investor Contact: P.E. Goldberg (212-922-1640)
Board of Directors: D. H. Benson, R. W. Cremin, J. M. Ergas, K. C. Graham, R. L. Hoffman, J. L. Koley, R. K. Lochridge, T. L. Reece, B. G. Rethore, M. B. Stubbs, M. A. Winston

Founded: 1947
Domicile: Delaware
Employees: 31,650

Dow Chemical Co (The)

S&P Recommendation HOLD ★★★★★

Price $40.96 (as of Oct 27, 2006)

12-Mo. Target Price $40.00

Investment Style Large-Cap Value

GICS Sector Materials
Sub-Industry Diversified Chemicals

Comment The largest U.S. chemical company, DOW provides chemical, plastic and agricultural products and services to many consumer markets.

Key Stock Statistics (Source S&P, Vickers, company reports)

52-Wk Range	$47.21–33.00	S&P Oper. EPS 2006**E**	4.50	P/E on S&P Oper. EPS 2006**E**	9.1	Dividend Rate/Share	$1.50
Trailing 12-Month EPS	$3.95	S&P Oper. EPS 2007**E**	5.00	Common Shares Outstg. (M)	959.3	Yield (%)	3.66
Trailing 12-Month P/E	10.4	S&P Core EPS 2006**E**	5.17	Market Capitalization(B)	$39.295	Beta	1.14
$10K Invested 5 Yrs Ago	$14,042	S&P Core EPS 2007**E**	5.91	Institutional Ownership (%)	63	S&P Credit Rating	A-

Price Performance

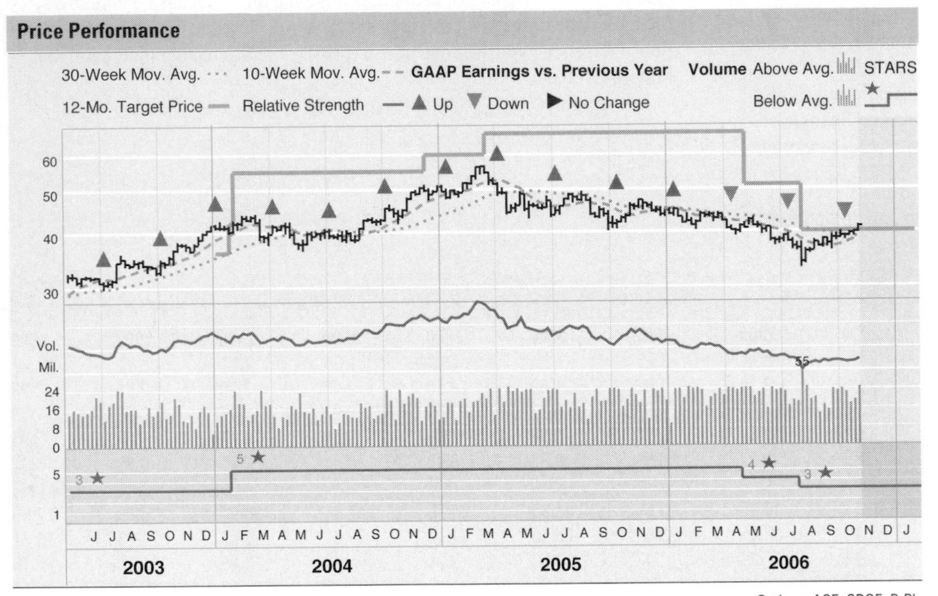

Options: ASE, CBOE, P, Ph

Analysis prepared by **Richard O'Reilly, CFA** on August 10, 2006, when the stock traded at **$ 36.08**.

Highlights

- We expect the company to post modestly lower EPS in 2006, as rising feedstock costs outweigh higher average selling prices. We anticipate favorable industry fundamentals continuing in 2007 on further good global economic growth combined with limited industry capacity additions.
- We expect sales to increase in 2006 as volume growth resumes after a 2% decline in 2005. Dow's Gulf Coast operations were disrupted by both of 2005's major hurricanes, with one major complex taking weeks to resume normal operations. We expect prices for many of the company's basic plastics and chemicals to increase in the second half following the second quarter's softness. We see the joint ventures in low-cost feedstock locations such as Kuwait performing better in the second half in the absence of first-half planned outages.
- We project that agricultural segment profits will be somewhat below 2005's reduced level as a result of lower U.S. sales. Interest expense should be lower due to a further reduction of debt in 2006. We expect the effective tax rate to be about 26%.

Investment Rationale/Risk

- We recently downgraded our opinion to hold, from buy, after disappointing second quarter earnings. We believe the commodity chemical industry's supply/demand fundamentals will show cyclical strength over the next two years, but historically high and volatile feedstock costs should limit margin improvements. DOW plans to control overhead costs and continue to focus on capital discipline, as capital spending in 2006 should again remain below depreciation. The net cash to capital ratio was recently down to about 30%, and we expect the company to continue to repurchase its common stock.
- Risks to our recommendation and target price include an unexpected softening of the U.S. economy, higher than expected energy costs, and unplanned production outages and interruptions. We remain somewhat concerned about possible additional asbestos liabilities for DOW, largely related to its Union Carbide unit.
- Our 12-month target price of $40 is based on a historical peak-of-cycle P/E multiple of 8X and an annualized earnings rate of about $5.00 a share that we believe DOW should achieve in 2007.

Qualitative Risk Assessment

LOW | **MEDIUM** | HIGH

Our risk assessment reflects the diverse business and geographic sales mix and manufacturing integration of this company, partly offset by the cyclical nature of the commodity chemical industry and volatility of raw material costs.

Quantitative Evaluations

S&P Quality Ranking B

D | C | B- | **B** | B+ | A- | A | A+

Relative Strength Rank MODERATE

70

LOWEST = 1 HIGHEST = 99

Revenue/Earnings Data

Revenue (Million $)

	1Q	2Q	3Q	4Q	Year
2006	12,020	12,509	12,359	--	--
2005	11,679	11,450	11,261	11,917	46,307
2004	9,309	9,844	10,072	10,936	40,161
2003	8,081	8,242	7,977	8,332	32,632
2002	6,305	7,259	7,084	6,961	27,609
2001	7,386	7,344	6,729	6,346	27,805

Earnings Per Share ($)

2006	1.24	1.05	0.53	**E**1.21	**E**4.50
2005	1.39	1.30	0.82	1.14	4.64
2004	0.50	0.72	0.65	1.06	2.93
2003	0.09	0.43	0.36	0.99	1.88
2002	0.04	0.26	0.14	-0.89	-0.44
2001	-0.80	0.31	0.06	-0.04	-0.46

Fiscal year ended Dec. 31. Next earnings report expected: Late January. EPS Estimates based on S&P Operating Earnings; historical GAAP earnings are as reported.

Dividend Data (Dates: mm/dd Payment Date: mm/dd/yy)

Amount ($)	Date Decl.	Ex-Div. Date	Stk. of Record	Payment Date
0.335	12/08	12/28	12/30	01/30/06
0.375	02/09	03/29	03/31	04/28/06
0.375	05/11	06/28	06/30	07/28/06
0.375	09/14	09/27	09/29	10/30/06

Dividends have been paid since 1911. Source: Company reports.

Dow Chemical Co (The)

Business Summary August 10, 2006

CORPORATE OVERVIEW. The 2001 purchase of Union Carbide Corp., a leading producer of polyethylene, ethylene glycol, solvents and specialty chemicals, made DOW the largest U.S. chemical company. Foreign operations accounted for 62% of 2005 sales.

Chemicals (12% of sales and 14% of profits in 2005) include inorganics (chlorine, caustic soda, chlorinated solvents, calcium chlorides, ethylene dichloride and vinyl chloride), ethylene oxide/glycol and vinyl acetate monomer, used primarily as raw materials in the manufacture of customer products. Performance chemicals (17%, 16%) consist of latex coatings and binders, water-based emulsions (acrylic latexes), water soluble polymers, cellulose ethers and resins, biocides, custom manufacturing, fine chemicals, superabsorbent polymers, ion exchange resins, membranes, glycine, glycols, amines, surfactants, heat transfer and deicing fluids, lubricants and solvents.

Dow AgroSciences (7%, 7%) is a leading global maker of herbicides (Clincher, Starane), insecticides (Dursban, Lorsban, Sentricon termite colony elimination system, Tracer) and fungicides for crop protection and industrial/commercial pest control. It is also building a plant genetics and biotechnology business in crop seeds (Mycogen), traits (Herculex) and value-added grains.

The company, a major producer of plastics (26%, 31%), is the world's largest producer of polyethylene and polystyrene resins, which are used in a broad variety of applications. It also makes polypropylene and PET polyester plastics, and styrene-butadiene and polybutadiene rubbers. Performance plastics (25%, 32%) consist of engineering plastics (polycarbonates, ABS), adhesives and sealants, polyurethanes, polyols, isocyanates, propylene oxide/glycol, epoxy resins and intermediates (phenol and acetone), fabricated products (foams and films, STYROFOAM products), polyolefins for wire and cable insulation, and technology licensing (UNIPOL for polyethylene and polypropylene, Meteor for ethylene oxide/glycol).

The hydrocarbons and energy business (13%, nil) procures fuels and raw materials and produces ethylene, propylene, aromatics, styrene, and power and steam. Other businesses include advanced electronic materials, the company's insurance and environmental operations, and the Dow Corning joint venture.

Company Financials

Per Share Data ($) Year Ended Dec. 31	**2005**	**2004**	**2003**	**2002**	**2001**	**2000**	**1999**	**1998**	**1997**	**1996**
Tangible Book Value	12.14	9.01	5.79	4.19	7.59	10.78	9.59	8.77	8.69	9.73
Cash Flow	6.77	5.12	3.93	4.57	1.55	4.14	3.91	3.83	4.46	4.33
Earnings	4.64	2.93	1.88	-0.44	-0.46	2.22	1.98	1.91	2.57	2.57
S&P Core Earnings	4.04	2.34	1.58	-1.41	-1.43	NA	NA	NA	NA	NA
Dividends	1.34	1.34	1.34	1.34	1.30	1.16	1.16	1.16	1.12	1.00
Payout Ratio	29%	46%	71%	NM	NM	52%	59%	61%	44%	39%
Prices:High	56.75	51.34	42.00	37.00	39.67	47.17	46.00	33.81	34.21	30.83
Prices:Low	40.18	36.35	24.83	23.66	25.06	23.00	28.50	24.90	25.46	22.75
P/E Ratio:High	12	18	22	NM	NM	21	23	18	13	12
P/E Ratio:Low	9	12	13	NM	NM	10	14	13	10	9
Income Statement Analysis (Million $)										
Revenue	46,307	40,161	32,632	27,609	27,805	23,008	18,929	18,441	20,018	20,053
Operating Income	7,437	5,466	3,922	2,925	2,953	3,462	3,407	3,498	4,013	4,385
Depreciation	2,079	2,088	1,903	1,825	1,815	1,315	1,301	1,305	1,287	1,298
Interest Expense	702	747	828	774	733	460	431	493	471	529
Pretax Income	6,399	3,796	1,751	-622	-613	2,401	2,166	2,012	2,948	3,288
Effective Tax Rate	27.8%	23.1%	NM	NM	NM	34.3%	35.4%	34.0%	35.3%	36.1%
Net Income	4,535	2,797	1,739	-405	-417	1,513	1,331	1,310	1,808	1,907
S&P Core Earnings	3,956	2,236	1,462	-1,295	-1,303	NA	NA	NA	NA	NA
Balance Sheet & Other Financial Data (Million $)										
Cash	3,838	3,192	2,434	1,573	264	304	1,212	390	235	2,302
Current Assets	17,404	15,890	13,002	11,681	10,308	9,260	8,847	8,040	8,640	9,830
Total Assets	45,934	45,885	41,891	39,562	35,515	27,645	25,499	23,830	24,040	24,673
Current Liabilities	10,663	10,506	9,534	8,856	8,125	7,873	6,295	6,842	7,340	6,004
Long Term Debt	10,186	12,629	12,763	12,659	10,266	5,365	5,022	4,051	4,196	4,196
Common Equity	15,324	12,270	9,175	7,626	9,993	9,186	8,323	7,429	7,626	7,954
Total Capital	27,241	26,649	23,438	21,645	21,376	15,848	14,642	12,802	13,196	15,280
Capital Expenditures	1,597	1,333	1,100	1,623	1,587	1,349	1,412	1,546	1,198	1,344
Cash Flow	6,614	4,885	3,642	1,420	1,398	2,828	2,627	2,609	3,089	3,198
Current Ratio	1.6	1.5	1.4	1.3	1.3	1.2	1.4	1.2	1.2	1.6
% Long Term Debt of Capitalization	37.4	47.4	54.5	58.5	48.0	33.9	34.3	31.6	31.7	15.0
% Net Income of Revenue	9.8	7.0	5.3	NM	NM	6.6	7.0	7.1	9.0	9.5
% Return on Assets	9.9	6.4	4.3	NM	NM	5.7	5.4	5.5	7.4	7.9
% Return on Equity	32.9	26.1	20.7	NM	NM	17.3	16.8	17.3	23.1	24.8

Data as orig reptd.; bef. results of disc opers/spec. items. Per share data adj. for stk. divs.; EPS diluted. E-Estimated. NA-Not Available. NM-Not Meaningful. NR-Not Ranked. UR-Under Review.

Office: 2030 Dow Center, Midland, MI 48674-0001.
Telephone: 989-636-1000.
Website: http://www.dow.com
Chrmn, Pres & CEO: A.N. Liveris

EVP & CFO: G.E. Merszei
SVP & CIO: D.E. Kepler II
VP & CTO: W.F. Banholzer
VP & Treas: F. Ruiz

Investor Contact: T. McNeill (989-636-0626)
Board of Directors: A. A. Allemang, J. K. Barton, J. A. Bell, J. M. Fettig, B. H. Franklin, J. B. Hess, A. N. Liveris, G. E. Merszei, J. P. Reinhard, J. M. Ringler, R. G. Shaw, P. G. Stern

Founded: 1897
Domicile: Delaware
Employees: 42,413

STANDARD &POOR'S

Dow Jones and Co Inc.

S&P Recommendation HOLD ★★★★★ | **Price** $35.57 (as of Oct 27, 2006) | **12-Mo. Target Price** $39.00 | **Investment Style** Mid-Cap Growth

GICS Sector Consumer Discretionary
Sub-Industry Publishing

Comment Dow Jones publishes The Wall Street Journal and Barron's, provides newswire, news retrieval and financial information services, and publishes general circulation newspapers.

Key Stock Statistics (Source S&P, Vickers, company reports)

52-Wk Range	$41.39–32.16	S&P Oper. EPS 2006E	1.08	P/E on S&P Oper. EPS 2006E	32.9	Dividend Rate/Share	$1.00
Trailing 12-Month EPS	$1.78	S&P Oper. EPS 2007E	1.65	Common Shares Outstg. (M)	83.3	Yield (%)	2.81
Trailing 12-Month P/E	20.0	S&P Core EPS 2006E	1.06	Market Capitalization(B)	$2.247	Beta	1.15
$10K Invested 5 Yrs Ago	$8,623	S&P Core EPS 2007E	1.63	Institutional Ownership (%)	NA	S&P Credit Rating	BBB+

Price Performance

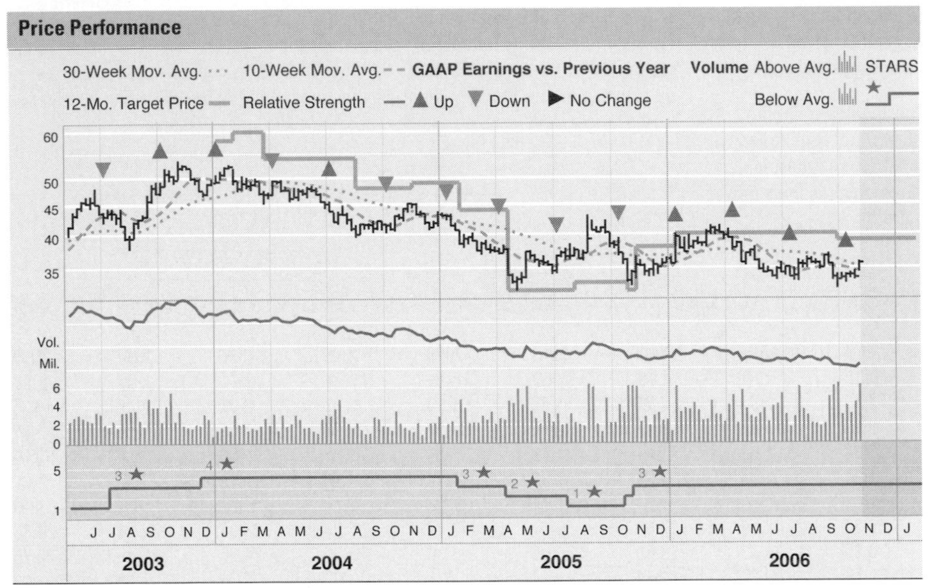

Options: ASE, CBOE, P, Ph

Analysis prepared by **James Peters, CFA** on September 20, 2006, when the stock traded at **$ 32.88**.

Highlights

- For 2006, we see revenues rising about 7.0%, led by advances in electronic publishing, advertising sales from the September 2005 launch of Weekend Journal, and slightly higher anticipated advertising rates.
- We forecast an expansion in the operating margin of about 90 basis points, to 8.4% in 2006. We expect DJ to incur an estimated $46 million in expenses related to a project to retrofit 19 company presses, which, when completed, will enable the presses to print on a smaller page size and result in estimated annual savings of about $18 million beginning in 2007. We see $6 million in annual savings from changes to the company's prescription drug plans, and another $14 million primarily from reduced employee expense as a result of DJ's recent operational realignment.
- DJ assumed additional debt to pay for its legal dispute settlement with Cantor Fitzgerald for $202 million; it also realized a one-time gain of $63 million, since $265 million was reserved for the potential loss. After higher projected interest expense, we see 2006 EPS, excluding one-time items, of $1.08, versus $0.98 in 2005.

Investment Rationale/Risk

- We think DJ has become much more competitive since mid-2005 as a result of management changes and various cost cutting and revenue growth initiatives, including the recent announcement to sell advertising on the front page of the Wall Street Journal. However, we also believe these efforts indicate that DJ is unlikely to seek a buyer in the near term. We would not add to positions, as the shares were recently trading at a premium to the S&P 500, at about 20X our 2007 EPS estimate.
- Risks to our opinion and target price include a rapid decline in business-to-business (B2B) advertising, the possibility that revenues for MarketWatch and Weekend Journal will grow more slowly than we anticipate, and the possibility that the company will not achieve planned savings from cost-cutting actions.
- We expect free cash flow growth to be limited in 2006 by above-trend, planned capital expenditures of $100 million and by substantial costs associated with various initiatives. Our 12-month target price of $39 is derived from our DCF analysis, which assumes an 8.3% WACC and a 3.5% terminal growth rate.

Qualitative Risk Assessment

LOW | **MEDIUM** | HIGH

Our risk assessment reflects the cyclical nature of technology and financial advertising, and significant competition from various media for advertising, offset by what we view as the company's superior-to-peer ability to monetize its reputation via sales of Web-based content and other products.

Quantitative Evaluations

S&P Quality Ranking B

D | C | B- | **B** | B+ | A- | A | A+

Relative Strength Rank MODERATE

55

LOWEST = 1 HIGHEST = 99

Revenue/Earnings Data

Revenue (Million $)

	1Q	2Q	3Q	4Q	Year
2006	452.2	481.2	412.4	--	--
2005	412.1	454.2	421.2	482.2	1,770
2004	401.6	437.8	394.9	437.2	1,671
2003	358.2	393.6	376.0	420.7	1,548
2002	392.9	417.0	352.4	396.9	1,559
2001	459.9	484.1	397.6	431.5	1,773

Earnings Per Share ($)

2006	0.74	0.34	0.15	E0.44	E1.08
2005	0.10	0.01	0.12	0.49	0.73
2004	0.22	0.41	0.15	0.43	1.21
2003	0.82	0.38	0.35	0.54	2.08
2002	1.53	0.64	0.03	0.18	2.40
2001	0.07	0.50	0.19	0.38	1.14

Fiscal year ended Dec. 31. Next earnings report expected: Late January. EPS Estimates based on S&P Operating Earnings; historical GAAP earnings are as reported.

Dividend Data (Dates: mm/dd Payment Date: mm/dd/yy)

Amount ($)	Date Decl.	Ex-Div. Date	Stk. of Record	Payment Date
0.250	01/18	01/30	02/01	03/01/06
0.250	04/19	04/27	05/01	06/01/06
0.250	06/21	07/28	08/01	09/01/06
0.250	09/20	10/30	11/01	12/01/06

Dividends have been paid since 1906. Source: Company reports.

Dow Jones and Co Inc.

Business Summary September 20, 2006

CORPORATE OVERVIEW. Dow Jones & Co., a global provider of and financial news and information, is the parent of The Wall Street Journal and Barron's. In February 2006, DJ was realigned into the consumer, enterprise and community media segments in order to reflect its markets and customers, rather than its media distribution methods.

The Consumer Media Group (about 61% of total revenues for the quarter ended March 2006, the first quarter since revenues were re-classified) includes the Wall Street Journal Franchise (including domestic and international print, online, television and radio), the Barron's Franchise (print, online and conferences), and the MarketWatch Franchise (online, newsletters, television and radio). The Enterprise Media Group (21%) includes Dow Jones Newswires, Dow Jones Licensing Services, Dow Jones Indexes, Dow Jones Financial Information Services, and Dow Jones Reprints and Permissions. The Community Media Group (18%) includes the Ottaway Community newspaper properties.

COMPETITIVE LANDSCAPE. The Wall Street Journal (WSJ) is one of only three national newspapers, along with the New York Times and Gannett's USA Today. Because of wide national distribution of the paper, WSJ's advertiser base is skewed more toward national advertisers than most newspaper publishers. In turn, this makes WSJ's advertising levels more volatile than most newspaper publishers since there is a greater level of competition for national advertiser spending, in our view. DJ's advertiser base is also more skewed toward B2B advertising than that of most newspaper publishers, with a reliance on technology and financial advertising that has hurt revenue results in recent years, as those advertising categories have struggled. In September 2005, DJ launched the Weekend Edition of the WSJ on Saturdays in attempt to diversify its advertising base by incorporating more consumer based advertising.

Company Financials

Per Share Data ($) Year Ended Dec. 31	2005	2004	2003	2002	2001	2000	1999	1998	1997	1996
Tangible Book Value	NM	NM	NM	NM	NM	0.98	5.24	4.60	4.07	3.89
Cash Flow	2.03	2.48	3.38	3.71	2.36	-0.13	4.13	1.56	-5.74	4.22
Earnings	0.73	1.21	2.08	2.40	1.14	-1.35	2.99	0.09	-8.36	1.96
S&P Core Earnings	0.89	0.88	0.91	0.16	1.09	NA	NA	NA	NA	NA
Dividends	1.00	1.00	1.00	1.00	1.00	1.00	0.96	0.96	0.96	0.96
Payout Ratio	137%	83%	48%	42%	88%	NM	32%	NM	NM	49%
Prices:High	43.35	52.74	53.62	60.20	64.30	77.31	71.38	59.00	55.88	41.88
Prices:Low	31.94	39.50	33.25	29.50	43.05	51.38	43.63	41.56	33.38	31.88
P/E Ratio:High	59	44	26	25	56	NM	24	NM	NM	21
P/E Ratio:Low	44	33	16	12	38	NM	15	NM	NM	16
Income Statement Analysis (Million $)										
Revenue	1,770	1,671	1,548	1,559	1,773	2,203	2,002	2,158	2,573	2,482
Operating Income	241	271	231	209	289	606	496	437	510	555
Depreciation	108	105	106	110	106	108	104	142	251	218
Interest Expense	19.3	3.74	2.83	3.08	0.50	2.04	5.27	7.19	19.4	18.8
Pretax Income	104	156	221	258	99.7	76.4	418	71.7	-764	331
Effective Tax Rate	41.7%	37.5%	23.4%	24.8%	98.5%	NM	34.8%	88.0%	NM	44.6%
Net Income	60.4	99.5	171	202	98.2	-119	272	8.36	-802	190
S&P Core Earnings	74.5	72.0	74.9	12.3	93.2	NA	NA	NA	NA	NA
Balance Sheet & Other Financial Data (Million $)										
Cash	10.6	17.2	23.5	39.3	21.0	49.3	86.4	143	23.8	6.77
Current Assets	284	254	246	251	246	368	456	442	507	404
Total Assets	1,782	1,380	1,304	1,208	1,298	1,362	1,531	1,491	1,920	2,760
Current Liabilities	1,018	717	614	622	602	587	579	600	672	601
Long Term Debt	225	136	153	92.9	174	151	150	150	229	332
Common Equity	1,905	151	130	40.6	41.8	159	553	509	781	1,644
Total Capital	2,130	290	289	134	220	318	703	659	1,010	1,976
Capital Expenditures	65.3	76.0	55.9	77.7	129	187	191	226	348	232
Cash Flow	169	204	277	311	204	-11.1	376	151	-551	408
Current Ratio	0.3	0.4	0.4	0.4	0.4	0.6	0.8	0.7	0.8	0.7
% Long Term Debt of Capitalization	10.6	46.7	52.9	69.3	79.2	47.4	21.3	22.7	22.7	16.8
% Net Income of Revenue	3.4	6.0	11.0	12.9	5.5	NM	13.6	0.4	NM	7.7
% Return on Assets	3.8	7.4	13.6	16.1	7.4	NM	18.1	0.5	NM	7.1
% Return on Equity	3.1	5.0	7.7	489.5	98.0	NM	51.3	1.3	NM	11.7

Data as orig reptd.; bef. results of disc opers/spec. items. Per share data adj. for stk. divs.; EPS diluted. E-Estimated. NA-Not Available. NM-Not Meaningful. NR-Not Ranked. UR-Under Review.

Office: 200 Liberty Street, New York, NY 10281.
Telephone: 212-416-2000.
Email: investorrelations@dowjones.com
Website: http://www.dowjones.com

Chrmn: P.R. Kann
CEO: R.F. Zannino
VP & CFO: C.W. Vieth
VP, Secy & General Counsel: J.A. Stern

Investor Contact: M. Donohue (609-520-5660)
Board of Directors: C. Bancroft, J. E. Barfield, L. B. Campbell, E. Castro-Wright, M. B. Elefante, J. M. Engler, H. Golub, L. Hill, I. O. Hockaday, Jr., V. E. Jordan, Jr., P. R. Kann, D. K. Li, M. P. McPherson, F. N. Newman, J. H. Ottaway, Jr., E. Steele, W. C. Steere, Jr., R. F. Zannino, D. von Holtzbrinck

Founded: 1882
Domicile: Delaware
Employees: 7,501

STANDARD &POOR'S

D.R. Horton Inc.

S&P Recommendation HOLD ★★★★★

Price $23.75 (as of Oct 27, 2006)

12-Mo. Target Price $24.00

Investment Style Mid-Cap Growth

GICS Sector Consumer Discretionary
Sub-Industry Homebuilding

Comment DHI is the largest homebuilder in the U.S., based on the number of homes sold.

Key Stock Statistics (Source S&P, Vickers, company reports)

52-Wk Range	**$41.66–19.52**	S&P Oper. EPS 2006**E**	**4.10**	P/E on S&P Oper. EPS 2006**E**	**5.8**	Dividend Rate/Share	**$0.60**
Trailing 12-Month EPS	**$4.79**	S&P Oper. EPS 2007**E**	**3.55**	Common Shares Outstg. (M)	**313.1**	Yield (%)	**2.53**
Trailing 12-Month P/E	**5.0**	S&P Core EPS 2006**E**	**4.10**	Market Capitalization(B)	**$7.437**	Beta	**1.39**
$10K Invested 5 Yrs Ago	**$33,175**	S&P Core EPS 2007**E**	**3.55**	Institutional Ownership (%)	**75**	S&P Credit Rating	**BBB-**

Price Performance

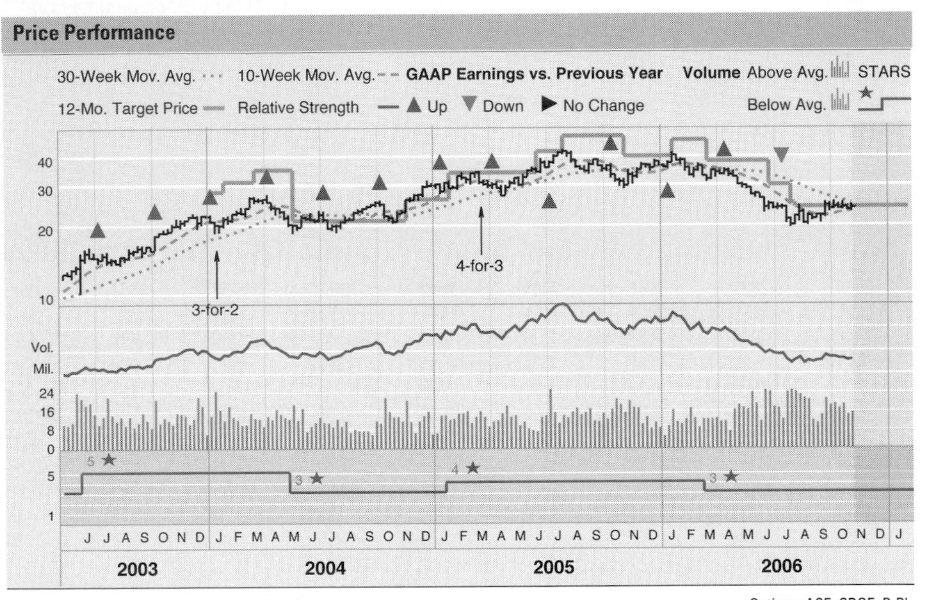

Options: ASE, CBOE, P, Ph

Analysis prepared by **William R. Mack, CFA** on July 24, 2006, when the stock traded at **$ 20.15**.

Highlights

- In FY 06 (Sep.) and FY 07, we believe DHI will remain the largest builder in the U.S. However, in our view, the company will likely have to materially compromise its profit margins in order to keep unit sales volumes above 50,000 homes.

- Our forecast assumes the current quarter's pretax margin will decline nearly six percentage points, to about 12.0%, or slightly below the same period in 2003. Once the current industry-wide oversupply of homes is worked through, which we think could happen by this time next year, we believe the company's pretax margin will stabilize at around 10%, a level it held at the start of this decade, when mortgage rates were near current levels (about 7%).

- Like most of its peers, DHI remains a net accumulator of land even as its sales have slowed. We like the company's relatively strong dividend yield, and we think investors would be even better served if DHI were to use most of its operating cash flow for purposes other than land investment, namely, share repurchases and debt reduction.

Investment Rationale/Risk

- We expect DHI's valuation to improve modestly, since we think markedly lower procurement costs will enable it to increase operating profits even in markets where home prices soften. As the housing cycle matures, we would look for land and other operating costs to gain increasing importance. In our view, this factor, along with what we believe is the best track record of increasing profits in the industry, argues for a multiple that is above the group average.

- Risks to our recommendation and target price include the possibility of sharply higher mortgage rates and a land surplus, which might be compounded if home prices nationally should fall. Moreover, DHI's inventories have risen nearly 40% in a year. If new unit orders fail to turn positive by this coming spring, a critical selling season, we think the company could suffer from a dangerous overhang of land.

- We think DHI deserves a slight premium to its current book value of $20. Our 12-month target price of $24 is 20% above this level.

Qualitative Risk Assessment

LOW | **MEDIUM** | HIGH

Our risk assessment reflects our view that DHI's operations are highly diversified geographically. In combination with its leading market capitalization and outstanding track record, in our opinion, the company has better access to capital than most of its peers. Offsetting this is DHI's vast land holdings that could hamper its ability to adjust to a geographically broad slowdown in demand.

Quantitative Evaluations

S&P Quality Ranking **A+**

D | C | B- | B | B+ | A- | A | **A+**

Relative Strength Rank **MODERATE**

40

LOWEST = 1 HIGHEST = 99

Revenue/Earnings Data

Revenue (Million $)

	1Q	2Q	3Q	4Q	Year
2006	2,903	3,527	3,594	--	--
2005	2,520	2,877	3,370	5,097	13,864
2004	2,205	2,335	2,790	3,511	10,841
2003	1,745	1,909	2,212	2,862	8,728
2002	1,160	1,600	1,808	2,170	6,739
2001	887.7	906.8	1,121	1,540	4,456

Earnings Per Share ($)

2006	0.98	1.11	0.93	**E**1.08	**E**4.10
2005	0.76	0.92	1.17	1.77	4.62
2004	0.58	0.60	0.80	1.10	3.08
2003	0.38	0.43	0.50	0.73	2.05
2002	0.31	0.32	0.34	0.46	1.44
2001	0.21	0.22	0.30	0.37	1.11

Fiscal year ended Sep. 30. Next earnings report expected: Mid November. EPS Estimates based on S&P Operating Earnings; historical GAAP earnings are as reported.

Dividend Data (Dates: mm/dd Payment Date: mm/dd/yy)

Amount ($)	Date Decl.	Ex-Div. Date	Stk. of Record	Payment Date
0.100	01/12	01/25	01/27	02/10/06
0.100	04/24	05/03	05/05	05/19/06
0.150	08/09	08/17	08/21	09/01/06
0.150	10/12	10/19	10/23	11/01/06

Dividends have been paid since 1997. Source: Company reports.

Please read the Required Disclosures and Analyst Certification on the last page of this report.

D.R. Horton Inc.

Business Summary July 24, 2006

CORPORATE OVERVIEW. D.R. Horton was founded in 1978 by Donald Horton, now chairman. In 1992, it went public in order to gain broader access to capital markets, which has helped fuel its subsequent growth beyond its base in the Dallas/Fort Worth area. With operating divisions in 25 states and 74 markets, D.R. Horton is the largest domestic homebuilder (by unit volume as well as by market capitalization) and the most geographically diversified.

The company was the first U.S. builder to sell 50,000 homes in a single year (FY 05-Sep.) and it aims to be the first to eclipse the 100,000 unit mark (by FY 10). By emphasizing entry-level and first-time move-up buyers, it targets the broadest segments of the population. With an average selling price slightly above $260,000 in FY 05, DHI's homes are among the most affordable of all public builders; and with a pretax margin in the upper quartile of its peers, it ranks among the most efficient.

CORPORATE STRATEGY. Most of D.R. Horton's growth in the past 15 to 20 years has been the result of organic initiatives. Generally, the company has established satellite operations in new markets located in relatively close proximity to existing markets. The company has been successful at quickly ramping up volumes in these satellite operations--often at the expense of smaller competitors--aided by materials purchasing agreements struck at the regional level and relatively favorable access to capital markets.

Complementing this organic growth has been an aggressive takeover program, with close to 20 acquisitions since DHI went public. Most of these deals have occurred in new markets in an effort to either create a platform for future growth in a locale or to expand an existing satellite operation there. The majority of these acquisitions have been focused on a single market and have been asset-based transactions, rather than purchases of companies. However, in 2002, DHI bought Schuler Homes for about $1.8 billion, in a deal that increased its revenue base about 25%.

Company Financials

Per Share Data ($) Year Ended Sep. 30	**2005**	**2004**	**2003**	**2002**	**2001**	**2000**	**1999**	**1998**	**1997**	**1996**
Tangible Book Value	15.28	10.87	7.93	5.77	4.83	3.81	3.01	2.43	1.73	1.48
Cash Flow	4.87	3.24	2.16	1.54	1.24	0.94	0.78	0.46	0.31	0.26
Earnings	4.62	3.08	2.05	1.44	1.10	0.84	0.69	0.43	0.28	0.24
S&P Core Earnings	4.61	3.07	2.04	1.44	1.16	NA	NA	NA	NA	NA
Dividends	0.31	0.22	0.14	0.10	0.06	0.05	0.03	0.02	0.02	Nil
Payout Ratio	7%	7%	7%	7%	5%	5%	5%	6%	6%	Nil
Prices:High	42.82	31.41	22.69	14.58	11.17	7.81	6.34	6.87	5.79	3.28
Prices:Low	26.83	18.47	8.48	8.02	5.83	3.00	2.76	2.93	2.48	2.07
P/E Ratio:High	9	10	11	10	10	9	9	16	21	14
P/E Ratio:Low	6	6	4	6	5	4	4	7	9	9
Income Statement Analysis (Million $)										
Revenue	13,864	10,841	8,728	6,739	4,456	3,654	3,156	2,177	837	547
Operating Income	2,402	1,430	1,049	693	480	339	273	189	66.9	47.0
Depreciation	52.8	49.6	41.8	32.8	31.2	22.0	20.8	9.83	4.41	2.58
Interest Expense	21.2	9.30	12.6	11.5	14.1	15.8	16.5	16.2	5.15	14.8
Pretax Income	2,379	1,583	1,008	648	408	309	264	159	59.9	44.4
Effective Tax Rate	38.2%	38.4%	37.9%	37.5%	37.5%	38.0%	39.4%	41.3%	39.6%	38.4%
Net Income	1,471	975	626	405	255	192	160	93.4	36.2	36.2
S&P Core Earnings	1,463	969	622	406	267	NA	NA	NA	NA	NA
Balance Sheet & Other Financial Data (Million $)										
Cash	1,150	518	583	104	239	72.5	129	76.8	44.0	32.5
Current Assets	NA	NA	NA	NA	NA	NA	NA	NA	NA	NA
Total Assets	12,515	8,985	7,279	6,018	3,652	2,695	2,362	1,668	720	403
Current Liabilities	NA	NA	NA	NA	NA	NA	NA	NA	NA	NA
Long Term Debt	3,660	3,032	2,665	2,636	1,884	1,344	1,191	855	355	159
Common Equity	5,360	3,961	3,031	2,270	1,250	970	798	549	263	159
Total Capital	9,224	7,159	5,832	4,927	3,143	2,319	1,993	1,407	618	336
Capital Expenditures	68.2	55.2	48.7	39.8	33.4	19.6	17.3	11.6	5.30	2.67
Cash Flow	1,523	1,025	668	437	286	214	181	103	40.6	30.0
Current Ratio	NA	NA	NA	NA	NA	NA	NA	NA	NA	NA
% Long Term Debt of Capitalization	39.7	42.4	45.7	53.5	59.9	58.0	59.7	60.8	57.5	47.2
% Net Income of Revenue	10.6	8.9	7.2	6.0	5.7	5.2	5.1	4.3	4.3	5.0
% Return on Assets	13.7	12.0	9.4	8.4	8.0	7.6	7.9	7.8	6.4	7.6
% Return on Equity	31.5	27.9	23.6	23.0	23.0	21.7	23.7	23.0	16.4	19.0

Data as orig reptd.; bef. results of disc opers/spec. items. Per share data adj. for stk. divs.; EPS diluted. E-Estimated. NA-Not Available. NM-Not Meaningful. NR-Not Ranked. UR-Under Review.

Office: 301 Commerce St Ste 500, Fort Worth, TX 76102-4140.
Telephone: 817-390-8200.
Website: http://www.drhorton.com
Chrmn: D.R. Horton

Pres, Vice Chrmn & CEO: D.J. Tomnitz
COO & EVP: G.D. Jones
COO & EVP: T.F. Noon
COO & EVP: G.W. Seagraves

Investor Contact: S.H. Dwyer (817-390-8200)
Board of Directors: B. S. Anderson, M. R. Buchanan, R. I. Galland, M. W. Hewatt, D. R. Horton, D. J. Tomnitz, B. Wheat

Founded: 1991
Domicile: Delaware
Employees: 8,900

STANDARD &POOR'S

DTE Energy Co

S&P Recommendation SELL ★★☆☆☆

Price $45.17 (as of Oct 27, 2006)

12-Mo. Target Price $41.00

Investment Style Mid-Cap Value

GICS Sector Utilities
Sub-Industry Multi-Utilities

Comment This Detroit-based diversified energy company is involved in the development and management of energy-related businesses and services nationwide.

Key Stock Statistics (Source S&P, Vickers, company reports)

52-Wk Range	$45.97–38.77	S&P Oper. EPS 2006E	2.55	P/E on S&P Oper. EPS 2006E	17.7	Dividend Rate/Share	$2.06
Trailing 12-Month EPS	$2.77	S&P Oper. EPS 2007E	2.75	Common Shares Outstg. (M)	177.8	Yield (%)	4.56
Trailing 12-Month P/E	16.3	S&P Core EPS 2006E	2.67	Market Capitalization(B)	$8.029	Beta	0.45
$10K Invested 5 Yrs Ago	$13,810	S&P Core EPS 2007E	2.87	Institutional Ownership (%)	60	S&P Credit Rating	BBB

Price Performance

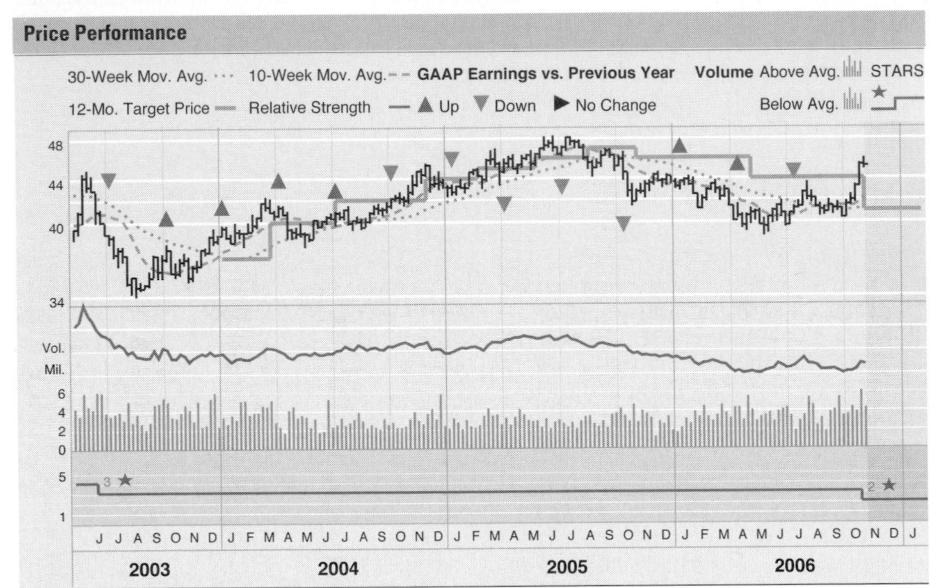

Options: ASE, Ph

Analysis prepared by **Justin McCann** on October 25, 2006, when the stock traded at **$ 45.78**.

Highlights

- Excluding synfuel-related tax credits, we expect DTE to earn $2.55 in 2006. Due to the sharp rise in oil prices, DTE halted its synfuel production on May 12; but, after prices declined, it resumed production at some of its plants on September 18. Excluding synfuel-related credits, DTE earned $1.72 in 2005. However, we expect hedges on its synfuel production to contribute about $1 billion in cash between 2006 and 2009.
- We expect EPS in 2006 to be aided by a residential electric rate hike and a significant increase in cost reductions. While earnings in 2006 could be significantly restricted by a reduction or elimination of synfuel-related tax credits as a result of the rise in oil prices, oil hedges and tax credit carryforwards should protect about 60% of related cash flow.
- On August 31, 2006, the Michigan Public Service Commission ordered Detroit Edison to reduce electric rates by $78.8 million, with $52.5 million reduced as of September 5, 2006, and the remaining $26.3 million as of January 1, 2007. The reductions will continue through the later of March 31, 2008, or 12 months from the filing of the utility's general rate case, which must be filed prior to July 1, 2007.

Investment Rationale/Risk

- Given the recent sharp rise in the shares, we have lowered our opinion to sell, from hold. We believe the stock is overvalued at 16.5X our operating EPS estimate for 2007, an approximate 10% premium to peers. While we believe the stock has benefited from the resumption of some of its synfuel production, it is uncertain what DTE will receive in tax credits (which are scheduled to expire at the end of 2007). We believe, however, that the projected decline in synfuel-related tax credits and earnings will be partially offset by the $1 billion in cash produced from synfuel-related hedges.
- Risks to our opinion and target price include a sharp rise in the average P/E multiple of the peer group, as well as successful reform of the electric choice program, which has resulted in a loss of industrial and commercial customers.
- The shares recently yielded about 4.5% on what we consider a secure dividend, well above the recent industry average of 3.7%. Given the above-peer yield, and despite the reduced level of synfuel-related tax credits, we expect the shares to trade at a more modest premium-to-peers P/E of about 14.9X our EPS estimate for 2007. Our 12-month target price is $41.

Qualitative Risk Assessment

LOW | **MEDIUM** | HIGH

Our risk assessment reflects a balance between the steady cash flow that we expect from both the regulated utilities, which operate within a generally supportive regulatory environment, and most of the unregulated operations, which are expected to contribute approximately one-third of DTE's consolidated cash flow, with the higher risk and far less predictable contribution from the synthetic fuel operations.

Quantitative Evaluations

S&P Quality Ranking B+

D | C | B- | B | **B+** | A- | A | A+

Relative Strength Rank STRONG

74

LOWEST = 1 HIGHEST = 99

Revenue/Earnings Data

Revenue (Million $)

	1Q	2Q	3Q	4Q	Year
2006	2,635	1,895	--	--	--
2005	2,309	1,941	2,060	2,712	9,022
2004	2,093	1,501	1,594	1,926	7,114
2003	2,095	1,600	1,654	1,692	7,041
2002	1,896	1,478	1,636	1,739	6,749
2001	1,842	1,790	2,081	2,136	7,849

Earnings Per Share ($)

	1Q	2Q	3Q	4Q	Year
2006	0.76	-0.18	**E**0.44	**E**1.06	**E**2.55
2005	0.72	0.19	0.17	2.18	3.27
2004	1.15	0.20	0.54	0.68	2.55
2003	0.64	-0.22	1.06	1.36	2.85
2002	1.24	0.42	0.96	1.21	3.83
2001	0.95	-0.60	0.38	1.34	2.14

Fiscal year ended Dec. 31. Next earnings report expected: Early November. EPS Estimates based on S&P Operating Earnings; historical GAAP earnings are as reported.

Dividend Data (Dates: mm/dd Payment Date: mm/dd/yy)

Amount ($)	Date Decl.	Ex-Div. Date	Stk. of Record	Payment Date
0.515	12/01	12/15	12/19	01/15/06
0.515	03/06	03/16	03/20	04/15/06
0.515	06/01	06/15	06/19	07/15/06
0.515	09/01	09/14	09/18	10/15/06

Dividends have been paid since 1909. Source: Company reports.

Please read the Required Disclosures and Analyst Certification on the last page of this report.

DTE Energy Co

Business Summary October 25, 2006

CORPORATE OVERVIEW. DTE Energy, formed on January 1, 1996, is the holding company for The Detroit Edison Company and Michigan Consolidated Gas (MichCon), regulated electric and gas utilities serving customers within the state of Michigan, and three non-utility operations engaged in a variety of energy-related businesses in various portions of the United States. In 2005, the regulated utility operations accounted for 73.2% of consolidated revenues and 54.5% of income from continuing operations, and the non-utility operations 26.8% and 45.5%.

MARKET PROFILE. Detroit Edison is a regulated electric utility serving approximately 2.2 million customers in southeastern Michigan. In 2005, residential customers accounted for 37.2% of the utility's revenues; commercial customers 32.6%; industrial customers 17.1%; other 11.4%; and wholesale 1.8%. With its high percentage of commercial and industrial customers, the utility has been hurt by the state's Customer Choice program, losing about 12% of retail sales in 2005, 18% in 2004, and 12% in 2003. However, the loss of customers also had the effect of reducing the need for purchased power, and allowed it to sell excess power into the wholesale market when conditions were favorable. The utility's generating capability is heavily dependent on the availability of coal, which accounts for more than 70% of its fuel requirements. The majority of the utility's coal needs are obtained through long-term contracts, with the remainder purchased through short-term agreements or purchases in the spot market.

MichCon is a regulated natural gas utility serving about 1.3 million residential, commercial and industrial customers in the state of Michigan. It also has subsidiaries involved in the gathering and transmission of natural gas in northern Michigan, and operates one of the largest natural gas distribution and transmission systems in the U.S, with connections to interstate pipelines providing access to most of the major natural gas producing regions in the Gulf Coast, Mid-Continent and Canadian regions. The company purchases its natural gas supplies on the open market through a diversified portfolio of supply contracts, and given its storage capacity, should be able to meet its supply requirements.

Company Financials

Per Share Data ($) Year Ended Dec. 31	**2005**	**2004**	**2003**	**2002**	**2001**	**2000**	**1999**	**1998**	**1997**	**1996**
Tangible Book Value	20.88	20.01	19.05	14.61	16.06	28.15	26.96	25.49	24.55	23.41
Earnings	3.27	2.55	2.85	3.83	2.14	3.27	3.33	3.05	2.88	2.13
S&P Core Earnings	2.13	1.97	3.22	2.80	2.09	NA	NA	NA	NA	NA
Dividends	2.06	2.06	2.06	2.06	2.06	2.06	2.06	2.06	2.06	2.06
Payout Ratio	63%	81%	72%	54%	96%	63%	62%	68%	72%	97%
Prices:High	48.31	45.49	49.50	47.70	47.13	41.31	44.69	49.25	34.75	37.25
Prices:Low	41.39	37.88	34.00	33.05	33.13	28.44	31.06	33.44	26.13	27.63
P/E Ratio:High	15	18	17	12	22	13	13	16	12	17
P/E Ratio:Low	13	15	12	9	15	9	9	11	9	13
Income Statement Analysis (Million $)										
Revenue	9,022	7,114	7,041	6,749	7,849	5,597	4,728	4,221	3,764	3,645
Depreciation	869	744	687	759	795	758	735	661	660	527
Maintenance	NA	NA	NA	NA	NA	NA	NA	NA	NA	278
Fixed Charges Coverage	1.21	1.35	1.49	2.00	2.04	2.42	2.60	2.84	3.21	3.19
Construction Credits	NA	NA	NA	NA	NA	NA	NA	Nil	Nil	5.36
Effective Tax Rate	NM	NM	24.0%	NM	NM	1.89%	11.0%	25.8%	38.1%	41.9%
Net Income	576	443	480	632	329	468	483	443	417	309
S&P Core Earnings	374	344	542	463	322	NA	NA	NA	NA	NA
Balance Sheet & Other Financial Data (Million $)										
Gross Property	18,660	18,011	17,679	17,862	17,067	13,162	12,746	12,178	14,495	13,777
Capital Expenditures	1,065	904	751	984	1,096	749	739	555	456	531
Net Property	10,830	10,491	10,324	9,813	9,543	7,387	7,148	6,943	8,934	8,501
Capitalization:Long Term Debt	7,080	7,606	7,669	7,785	7,928	4,062	4,052	4,323	3,914	3,895
Capitalization:% Long Term Debt	55.1	57.8	59.2	63.0	63.0	50.3	50.9	53.9	51.3	52.1
Capitalization:Preferred	Nil	Nil	Nil	Nil	Nil	Nil	Nil	Nil	144	144
Capitalization:% Preferred	Nil	Nil	Nil	Nil	Nil	Nil	Nil	Nil	1.80	1.90
Capitalization:Common	5,769	5,548	5,287	4,565	4,657	4,015	3,909	3,698	3,562	3,444
Capitalization:% Common	44.9	42.2	40.8	37.0	37.0	49.7	49.1	46.1	46.7	46.0
Total Capital	14,468	13,429	14,256	13,434	14,063	9,878	9,886	9,909	9,904	9,822
% Operating Ratio	96.1	93.4	91.1	82.8	86.3	85.3	82.2	81.4	80.2	79.1
% Earned on Net Property	8.9	8.1	7.2	11.4	8.2	11.4	12.8	11.8	8.4	7.2
% Return on Revenue	6.4	6.2	6.8	9.4	4.2	8.4	10.2	10.5	11.1	8.5
% Return on Invested Capital	6.0	6.1	7.5	9.1	8.9	8.1	8.3	6.2	9.9	6.2
% Return on Common Equity	10.2	8.2	9.7	13.8	7.6	11.8	12.7	12.2	11.9	8.9

Data as orig reptd.; bef. results of disc opers/spec. items. Per share data adj. for stk. divs.; EPS diluted. E-Estimated. NA-Not Available. NM-Not Meaningful. NR-Not Ranked. UR-Under Review.

Office: 2000 2nd Ave, Detroit, MI 48226-1279.
Telephone: 313-235-4000.
Email: shareholdersvcs@dteenergy.com
Website: http://www.dteenergy.com

Chrmn & CEO: A.F. Earley, Jr.
Pres & COO: G.M. Anderson
Vice Chrmn: S. Ewing
EVP & CFO: D.E. Meador

SVP & General Counsel: B.D. Peterson
Investor Contact: D. McClung (313-235-8030)
Board of Directors: L. Bauder, A. F. Earley, Jr., A. D. Gilmour, A. R. Glancy, III, F. M. Hennessey, J. W. Laymon, J. E. Lobbia, G. J. McGovern, E. A. Miller, C. W. Pryor, Jr., J. Robles, Jr., H. F. Sims, J. H. Vandenberghe

Founded: 1995
Domicile: Michigan
Employees: 11,410

Duke Energy Corp

STANDARD &POOR'S

S&P Recommendation HOLD ★★★★★	Price	12-Mo. Target Price	Investment Style
	$31.78 (as of Oct 27, 2006)	$33.00	Large-Cap Value

GICS Sector Utilities
Sub-Industry Multi-Utilities

Comment DUK provides electric service to about 2 million customers in North and South Carolina, and is one of the largest U.S. transporters and marketers of natural gas.

Key Stock Statistics (Source S&P, Vickers, company reports)

52-Wk Range	$32.12–25.58	S&P Oper. EPS 2006E	1.80	P/E on S&P Oper. EPS 2006E	17.7	Dividend Rate/Share	$1.28
Trailing 12-Month EPS	$1.32	S&P Oper. EPS 2007E	2.00	Common Shares Outstg. (M)	1,253.0	Yield (%)	4.03
Trailing 12-Month P/E	24.1	S&P Core EPS 2006E	1.77	Market Capitalization(B)	$39.821	Beta	1.05
$10K Invested 5 Yrs Ago	$10,378	S&P Core EPS 2007E	1.97	Institutional Ownership (%)	60	S&P Credit Rating	BBB

Price Performance

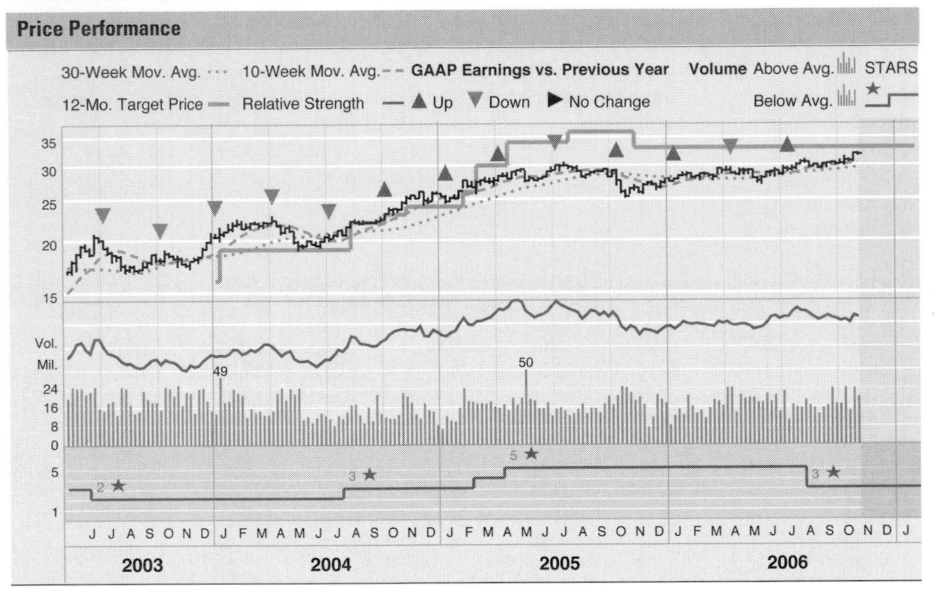

Options: ASE, CBOE, P, Ph

Analysis prepared by **Kenneth M. Leon, CPA** on August 04, 2006, when the stock traded at **$ 30.68**.

Highlights

- We think DUK's merger with Cinergy, which was completed at the end of the first quarter, will be accretive to earnings by late 2006. We see DUK's underutilized Midwest gas-fired plants benefiting from additional sales to Cinergy's electric utilities. We think the combined entity has an improved profile, with 80% or more of operating income expected to be derived from regulated electric and gas operations.
- The electric utility segment should see high single digit earnings gains in 2006, mainly on contributions from the acquisition, customer growth and higher power sales. In natural gas distribution, we see level income as customer growth is offset by lower usage per customer and higher operating expenses. We expect Crescent to see a drop in earnings on a slowdown in the real estate market.
- We think higher single digit natural gas prices will drive upper single digit income growth in DUK's midstream businesses. With level interest expense, but a significantly higher share count, we see 2006 EPS at $1.80.

Investment Rationale/Risk

- We believe DUK's exit from derivative contracts related to its merchant power business removes a major impediment to DUK's ongoing efforts to sell its Northeast and West-based merchant power assets. The divestiture of power assets would eliminate a potential drag on earnings growth, in our view. We expect DUK to realize cost synergies over time in excess of $150 million from its merger with Cinergy starting in 2007.
- Risks to our recommendation and target price include lower electric margins, a sharper than expected rise in interest rates, unfavorable commodity price trends, and integration issues stemming from the merger with Cinergy.
- Our 12-month target price of $33 is based on a combination of our DCF (weighted average cost of capital: 7.5%, terminal growth rate: 3%) and relative valuation analyses. Our target price assigns DUK's stock a P/E of 17.3X our 2006 estimate, a 10% premium to peers, reflecting earnings growth above peers. While we view DUK's strategy favorably, we believe the shares are fairly valued at current levels.

Qualitative Risk Assessment

LOW | **MEDIUM** | HIGH

Our risk assessment reflects DUK's large market capitalization and a balanced portfolio of businesses that include regulated electric utility and pipelines, offset by unregulated merchant power generation, exploration and production, and energy marketing operations.

Quantitative Evaluations

S&P Quality Ranking B+

D | C | B- | B | **B+** | A- | A | A+

Relative Strength Rank MODERATE

62

LOWEST = 1 HIGHEST = 99

Revenue/Earnings Data

Revenue (Million $)

	1Q	2Q	3Q	4Q	Year
2006	3,201	3,973	--	--	--
2005	5,328	5,274	3,028	3,116	16,746
2004	5,635	5,318	5,504	6,046	22,503
2003	6,228	5,235	5,609	5,457	22,529
2002	3,227	3,698	3,982	4,756	15,663
2001	16,491	15,580	16,718	10,714	59,503

Earnings Per Share ($)

	1Q	2Q	3Q	4Q	Year
2006	0.50	0.34	E0.60	E0.41	E1.80
2005	0.88	0.32	0.96	0.43	2.61
2004	0.07	0.43	0.42	0.36	1.27
2003	0.43	0.46	0.05	-1.99	-1.13
2002	0.48	0.56	0.27	-0.06	1.22
2001	0.73	0.53	1.01	0.28	2.56

Fiscal year ended Dec. 31. Next earnings report expected: Early November. EPS Estimates based on S&P Operating Earnings; historical GAAP earnings are as reported.

Dividend Data (Dates: mm/dd Payment Date: mm/dd/yy)

Amount ($)	Date Decl.	Ex-Div. Date	Stk. of Record	Payment Date
0.310	10/25	11/09	11/14	12/16/05
0.310	01/05	02/15	02/17	03/16/06
0.320	06/28	08/09	08/11	09/18/06
0.320	10/24	11/15	11/17	12/18/06

Dividends have been paid since 1926. Source: Company reports.

Duke Energy Corp

Business Summary August 04, 2006

At the end of 2005, Duke Energy Corp. was the sixth largest U.S. owner of interstate natural gas pipelines (by route miles) and the largest producer of natural gas liquids. The company also provides electric and gas utility services, and sells wholesale power.

Operating segments include Franchised Electric (27% of 2005 segment EBIT), Natural Gas Transmission (25%), Duke Energy Field Services (DEFS; 36%), Duke Energy International (DEI; 5.8%), and Crescent Real Estate (5.8%). Franchised Electric served about 2.3 million electric utility customers in North Carolina and South Carolina and owned 18,387 MW of power (net) as of December 2005.

Transmission operations consist of 17,500 miles of gas pipelines and 250 Bcf of gas storage capacity and significant natural gas gathering and processing facilities in the U.S. and Canada. It also includes Union Gas, a natural gas utility serving almost 1.3 million residential, commercial and industrial customers in Ontario.

DEFS is a 50-50 joint venture between DUK and ConocoPhillips. It gathers natural gas, processes it (separating out natural gas liquids, or NGLs), transports gas and NGLs, and fractionates NGLs (dividing them into component parts). DEI primarily consists of power generation (4,139 net MW) in Central and South America. In April 2004, the company sold its Australian pipeline assets for $1.24 billion (including $900 million of assumed debt). Crescent develops and manages commercial, residential and multi-family real estate projects in the Southeast and Southwest, and manages legacy land holdings in North and South Carolina.

In September 2005, Duke began disposing of DENA's (DUK's wholesale power generation and marketing unit, with 9,860 net MW of generation capacity at 2004 year end) assets and contracts outside the Midwest. DUK intends to retain DENA's Midwestern generation assets, consisting of approximately 3,600 MW of power generation, and certain contracts related to those facilities.

Company Financials

Per Share Data ($) Year Ended Dec. 31	2005	2004	2003	2002	2001	2000	1999	1998	1997	1996
Tangible Book Value	13.65	12.54	10.74	12.51	14.11	11.21	10.69	10.09	9.36	11.57
Earnings	2.61	1.27	-1.13	1.22	2.56	2.38	1.13	1.71	1.25	1.69
S&P Core Earnings	1.29	1.24	-1.10	1.01	2.29	NA	NA	NA	NA	NA
Dividends	1.17	1.10	1.10	1.10	1.10	1.10	1.10	1.10	1.08	1.04
Payout Ratio	45%	87%	NM	90%	43%	46%	98%	64%	86%	62%
Prices:High	30.55	26.16	21.57	40.00	47.74	45.22	32.66	35.50	28.28	26.50
Prices:Low	24.37	18.85	12.21	16.42	32.22	22.88	23.38	26.56	20.94	21.69
P/E Ratio:High	12	21	NM	33	19	19	29	21	23	16
P/E Ratio:Low	9	15	NM	13	13	10	21	16	17	13
Income Statement Analysis (Million $)										
Revenue	16,746	22,503	22,529	15,663	59,503	49,318	21,742	17,610	16,309	4,758
Depreciation	1,728	1,851	1,803	1,571	1,336	1,167	968	909	841	492
Maintenance	NA	NA	NA	NA	NA	NA	NA	NA	NA	NA
Fixed Charges Coverage	2.91	2.40	1.96	2.46	5.33	4.25	3.16	4.78	3.67	4.20
Construction Credits	NA	NA	NA	NA	53.0	63.0	82.0	88.0	109	112
Effective Tax Rate	29.5%	27.5%	NM	35.1%	33.1%	32.9%	31.4%	36.4%	39.1%	40.0%
Net Income	2,533	1,232	-1,005	1,034	1,994	1,776	847	1,260	974	730
S&P Core Earnings	1,249	1,199	-994	908	1,777	NA	NA	NA	NA	NA
Balance Sheet & Other Financial Data (Million $)										
Gross Property	40,574	46,806	47,157	48,677	39,464	34,615	30,436	27,128	25,448	14,946
Capital Expenditures	2,309	2,055	2,470	4,924	5,930	5,634	NA	2,159	1,323	646
Net Property	29,200	33,506	34,986	36,219	28,415	24,469	20,995	16,875	15,736	9,386
Capitalization:Long Term Debt	14,547	16,932	20,622	21,629	13,728	12,425	10,087	7,191	6,530	3,538
Capitalization:% Long Term Debt	46.9	50.5	59.8	58.9	51.5	54.7	52.0	45.9	44.8	39.0
Capitalization:Preferred	Nil	134	134	157	234	247	313	313	489	684
Capitalization:% Preferred	Nil	0.40	0.39	0.43	0.88	1.09	1.61	2.00	3.40	7.50
Capitalization:Common	16,439	16,441	13,748	14,944	12,689	10,056	8,998	8,150	7,540	4,889
Capitalization:% Common	53.1	49.1	39.8	40.7	47.6	44.2	46.4	52.1	51.8	54.3
Total Capital	36,988	40,375	40,490	43,644	33,393	29,225	24,225	19,882	18,673	11,737
% Operating Ratio	89.6	88.6	85.4	87.1	95.0	94.3	93.8	90.6	91.8	81.4
% Earned on Net Property	11.5	8.9	NM	7.6	15.5	16.8	9.5	14.9	15.4	14.5
% Return on Revenue	15.1	5.5	NM	6.6	3.4	3.6	3.9	7.2	6.0	15.3
% Return on Invested Capital	11.1	7.0	8.7	6.3	10.5	11.2	7.6	13.2	11.2	16.9
% Return on Common Equity	15.3	8.1	NM	7.4	17.4	18.4	9.6	15.5	14.1	14.2

Data as orig reptd.; bef. results of disc opers/spec. items. Per share data adj. for stk. divs.; EPS diluted. E-Estimated. NA-Not Available. NM-Not Meaningful. NR-Not Ranked. UR-Under Review.

Office: 526 South Church Street, Charlotte, NC 28202-1904.
Telephone: 704-594-6200.
Website: http://www.duke-energy.com
Chrmn & CEO: P. Anderson

Pres & COO: F. Fowler
VP & CFO: D. Hauser
VP, Secy & General Counsel: B.K. Trent

Board of Directors: R. Agnelli, P. M. Anderson, W. Barnet III, G. A. Bernhardt, Sr., W. T. Esrey, A. M. Gray, J. Hance, D. Hendrix, A. M. Lennon, J. G. Martin, M. Phelps, J. T. Rhodes

Founded: 1916
Domicile: North Carolina
Employees: 20,400

STANDARD &POOR'S

E. I. du Pont de Nemours and Co

S&P Recommendation HOLD ★★★★★	Price $45.55 (as of Oct 27, 2006)	12-Mo. Target Price $50.00	Investment Style Large-Cap Value

GICS Sector Materials
Sub-Industry Diversified Chemicals

Comment This broadly diversified company is the second largest U.S. chemicals manufacturer.

Key Stock Statistics (Source S&P, Vickers, company reports)

52-Wk Range	$46.90–38.52	S&P Oper. EPS 2006E	2.85	P/E on S&P Oper. EPS 2006E	16.0	Dividend Rate/Share	$1.48
Trailing 12-Month EPS	$2.62	S&P Oper. EPS 2007E	3.10	Common Shares Outstg. (M)	921.8	Yield (%)	3.25
Trailing 12-Month P/E	17.4	S&P Core EPS 2006E	2.72	Market Capitalization(B)	$41.988	Beta	1.02
$10K Invested 5 Yrs Ago	$13,020	S&P Core EPS 2007E	3.04	Institutional Ownership (%)	64	S&P Credit Rating	A

Price Performance

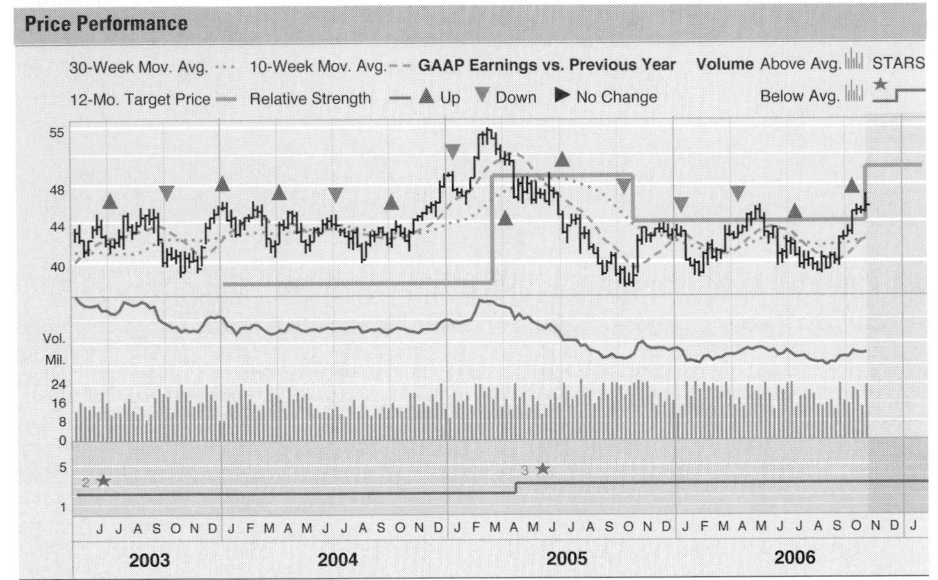

Options: ASE, CBOE, P, Ph

Highlights

➤ The 12-month target price for DD has recently been changed to $50.00 from $44.00. The Highlights section of this Stock Report will be updated accordingly.

Investment Rationale/Risk

➤ The Investment Rationale/Risk section of this Stock Report will be updated shortly. For the latest News story on DD from MarketScope, see below.

➤ 10/24/06 11:04 am EDT... S&P MAINTAINS HOLD OPINION ON SHARES OF DUPONT (DD 46.05***): Q3 EPS of $0.49 vs. $0.33 before special items topped our $0.43 estimate, helped by $0.03 from a lower-than-expected tax rate. Sales rose 7.5%, as volumes and prices each rose 3%. But domestic volume growth remained sluggish at 1%, partly reflecting exposure to Big 3 makers. In our opinion, improving prices should again offset higher material costs in Q4 and we see a possible favorable cost trend going into '07. Our '06 EPS outlook remains $2.85. On higher relative P/E multiples, we are raising our target price to $50 from $44, 16X our $3.10 '07 EPS estimate. /R. O'Reilly-CFA

Qualitative Risk Assessment

LOW | **MEDIUM** | HIGH

Our risk assessment reflects the company's diverse business and geographic sales mix and its leadership positions in key products, partly offset by the cyclical nature of the chemical industry and the volatility of raw material costs.

Quantitative Evaluations

S&P Quality Ranking B

D | C | B- | **B** | B+ | A- | A | A+

Relative Strength Rank STRONG

73

LOWEST = 1 HIGHEST = 99

Revenue/Earnings Data

Revenue (Million $)

	1Q	2Q	3Q	4Q	Year
2006	7,394	7,442	6,645	--	--
2005	7,431	7,511	5,870	5,827	26,639
2004	8,073	7,527	5,740	6,000	27,340
2003	7,008	7,369	6,142	6,477	26,996
2002	6,142	6,700	5,482	5,682	24,006
2001	6,859	6,997	5,641	5,229	24,726

Earnings Per Share ($)

2006	0.88	1.04	0.52	**E**0.42	**E**2.85
2005	0.96	1.01	-0.09	0.16	2.07
2004	0.66	0.50	0.33	0.28	1.77
2003	0.56	0.67	-0.88	0.63	0.99
2002	0.48	0.54	0.47	0.35	1.84
2001	0.46	-0.21	0.13	3.82	4.15

Fiscal year ended Dec. 31. Next earnings report expected: Late January. EPS Estimates based on S&P Operating Earnings; historical GAAP earnings are as reported.

Dividend Data (Dates: mm/dd Payment Date: mm/dd/yy)

Amount ($)	Date Decl.	Ex-Div. Date	Stk. of Record	Payment Date
0.370	01/25	02/13	02/15	03/14/06
0.370	04/26	05/11	05/15	06/12/06
0.370	07/26	08/11	08/15	09/12/06
0.370	10/25	11/13	11/15	12/14/06

Dividends have been paid since 1904. Source: Company reports.

E. I. du Pont de Nemours and Co

Business Summary September 18, 2006

E.I. du Pont de Nemours and Company, the second largest domestic chemicals producer, has made several major changes in recent years, including divesting its Conoco energy business in 1999, and expanding its life sciences businesses (now crop pesticides and nutrition). In April 2004, it sold the Textile and Interiors unit (consisting of nylon, polyester and Lycra fibers, with total annual sales of $6.3 billion) for $4.2 billion; proceeds were largely used to repay debt. The sale of the fiber businesses reduced DD's exposure to raw material cost changes by about 55%.

Foreign sales accounted for 58% of the total in 2005.

The Agricultural and Nutrition segment (24% of sales in 2005, and 21% of pretax operating income) consists of Pioneer Hi-Bred (43% of segment sales in 2005), the world's largest seed company, including corn (72% of sales) and soybeans; DuPont is also a major global supplier of crop protection chemicals (35%). In mid-2006, Pioneer estimated that its U.S. corn market share declined in 2006--partly due to a limited supply of certain biotech traits--but that its share in soybean increased. The segment also includes nutrition and health (including the Solae soy business and food packaging products) and microbial diagnostic testing products.

The Coatings and Color Technologies unit (23%, 14%) is one of the largest global auto paint suppliers (including OEM and refinish markets) and the largest maker of titanium pigments (33% of segment sales). Pigment volumes declined in the second half of 2005 as one large plant suffered extensive hurricane damage. The segment also includes industrial and powder coatings, and inks for digital printing. The Electronic and Communication Technologies segment (12%, 13%) includes electronic materials and display products (photoresins, films), and flexographic printing and proofing systems. DD is the world's largest maker of fluorochemicals (refrigerants, blowing agents, aerosols) and fluoropolymers (Teflon resins and coatings). Performance Materials (22%, 13%) includes engineering polymers for auto, electrical, consumer and industrial uses; packaging and industrial polymers; polyester films; and elastomers. Safety & Protection (19%, 23%) consists of Kevlar and Nomex aramid fibers and Tyvek and Sontara nonwovens for industrial, packaging and textile uses; specialty and intermediate chemicals; solid surfaces (Corian products); and safety consulting services.

Company Financials

Per Share Data ($) Year Ended Dec. 31	2005	2004	2003	2002	2001	2000	1999	1998	1997	1996
Tangible Book Value	4.24	6.25	4.63	4.54	7.30	4.50	3.72	9.78	8.66	8.85
Cash Flow	3.45	3.11	2.58	3.35	5.83	3.96	1.73	2.70	4.16	5.47
Earnings	2.07	1.77	0.99	1.84	4.15	2.19	0.19	1.43	2.08	3.24
S&P Core Earnings	1.98	2.00	1.14	0.40	-1.04	NA	NA	NA	NA	NA
Dividends	1.46	1.40	1.40	1.40	1.40	1.40	1.40	1.37	1.23	1.12
Payout Ratio	71%	79%	141%	76%	34%	64%	NM	96%	59%	34%
Prices:High	54.90	49.39	46.00	49.80	49.88	74.00	75.19	84.44	69.75	49.69
Prices:Low	37.60	39.88	38.60	35.02	32.64	38.19	50.06	51.69	46.38	34.81
P/E Ratio:High	27	28	46	27	12	34	NM	59	34	15
P/E Ratio:Low	18	23	39	19	8	17	NM	36	22	11

Income Statement Analysis (Million $)	2005	2004	2003	2002	2001	2000	1999	1998	1997	1996
Revenue	26,639	27,340	26,996	24,006	24,726	28,268	26,918	24,767	45,079	43,810
Operating Income	3,507	3,574	3,176	4,263	4,130	5,244	5,469	5,680	8,118	7,975
Depreciation	1,358	1,347	1,584	1,515	1,754	1,860	1,690	1,452	2,385	2,621
Interest Expense	518	362	347	359	590	810	535	640	642	714
Pretax Income	3,558	1,442	143	2,124	6,844	3,447	1,690	2,613	4,680	5,981
Effective Tax Rate	41.3%	NM	NM	8.71%	36.0%	31.1%	83.4%	36.0%	48.6%	39.2%
Net Income	2,053	1,780	1,002	1,841	4,328	2,314	219	1,648	2,405	3,636
S&P Core Earnings	1,965	2,008	1,132	398	-1,087	NA	NA	NA	NA	NA

Balance Sheet & Other Financial Data (Million $)	2005	2004	2003	2002	2001	2000	1999	1998	1997	1996
Cash	1,851	3,536	3,298	4,143	5,848	1,617	1,582	1,069	1,146	1,319
Current Assets	12,422	15,211	18,462	13,459	14,801	11,656	12,653	9,236	11,874	11,103
Total Assets	33,250	35,632	37,039	34,621	40,319	39,426	40,777	38,536	42,942	37,987
Current Liabilities	7,463	7,939	13,043	7,096	8,067	9,255	11,228	11,610	14,070	10,987
Long Term Debt	6,783	5,548	4,301	5,647	5,350	6,658	6,625	4,495	5,929	5,087
Common Equity	8,670	11,140	9,544	8,826	14,215	13,062	12,638	13,717	11,033	10,472
Total Capital	17,346	19,001	15,087	18,755	24,916	22,442	21,677	19,286	19,953	18,549
Capital Expenditures	1,340	1,232	1,713	1,280	1,494	1,925	2,055	2,240	4,768	3,303
Cash Flow	3,411	3,117	2,576	3,346	6,072	4,164	1,899	3,090	4,780	6,247
Current Ratio	1.7	1.9	1.4	1.9	1.8	1.3	1.1	0.8	0.8	1.0
% Long Term Debt of Capitalization	39.1	29.2	28.5	30.1	21.5	29.7	30.6	23.3	29.7	27.4
% Net Income of Revenue	7.7	6.5	3.7	7.7	17.5	8.2	0.8	6.7	5.3	8.3
% Return on Assets	6.0	4.9	2.8	4.9	10.9	5.8	0.6	4.4	5.9	9.7
% Return on Equity	20.6	17.1	10.8	15.9	31.7	17.9	1.6	13.3	22.3	38.8

Data as orig reptd.; bef. results of disc opers/spec. items. Per share data adj. for stk. divs.; EPS diluted. E-Estimated. NA-Not Available. NM-Not Meaningful. NR-Not Ranked. UR-Under Review.

Office: 1007 Market Street, Wilmington, DE 19898.
Telephone: 302-774-1000.
Email: info@dupont.com
Website: http://www.dupont.com

Chrmn & CEO: C.O. Holliday, Jr.
COO & EVP: R.R. Goodmanson
EVP & CFO: J.L. Keefer
SVP, Chief Admin & General Counsel: S.J. Mobley

SVP & CTO: U. Chowdhry
Investor Contact: C.J. Lukach (800-441-7515)
Board of Directors: A. J. Belda, R. H. Brown, C. J. Crawford, J. T. Dillon, L. C. Duemling, C. O. Holliday, Jr., L. D. Juliber, M. Naitoh, S. O'Keefe, W. K. Reilly, H. R. Sharp, III, C. M. Vest, T. du Pont

Founded: 1802
Domicile: Delaware
Employees: 60,000

STANDARD & POOR'S

Dynegy Inc.

S&P Recommendation HOLD ★★★★★

Price $6.16 (as of Oct 27, 2006)

12-Mo. Target Price $6.50

Investment Style Mid-Cap Value

GICS Sector Utilities
Sub-Industry Independent Power Producers & Energy Traders

Comment This company generates and sells wholesale power from plants located primarily in the U.S. Midwest, Northeast and South.

Key Stock Statistics (Source S&P, Vickers, company reports)

52-Wk Range	$6.38–4.06	S&P Oper. EPS 2006E	-0.25	P/E on S&P Oper. EPS 2006E	NM	Dividend Rate/Share	Nil
Trailing 12-Month EPS	$0.36	S&P Oper. EPS 2007E	-0.15	Common Shares Outstg. (M)	497.7	Yield (%)	Nil
Trailing 12-Month P/E	17.1	S&P Core EPS 2006E	-0.31	Market Capitalization(B)	$2.469	Beta	2.75
$10K Invested 5 Yrs Ago	$1,624	S&P Core EPS 2007E	-0.15	Institutional Ownership (%)	63	S&P Credit Rating	NA

Price Performance

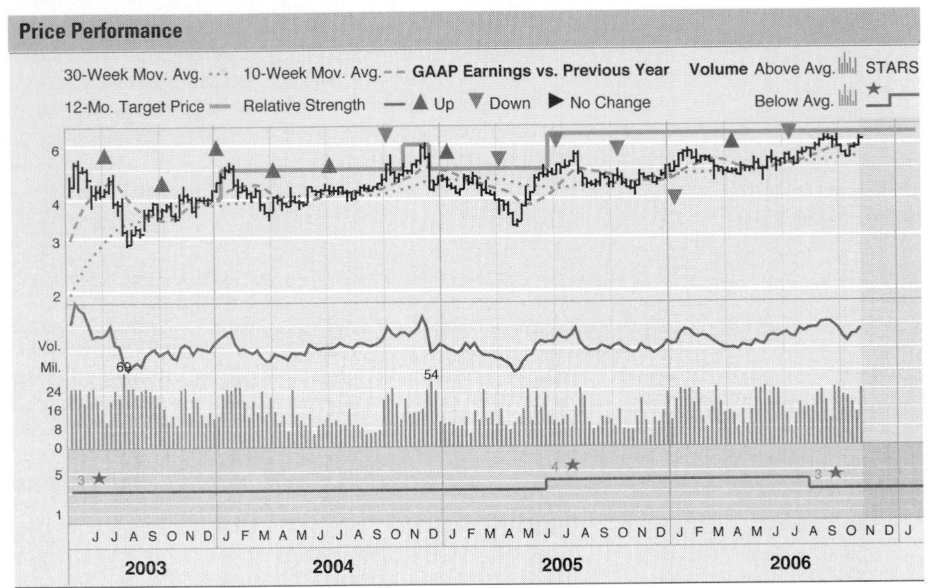

Options: ASE, CBOE, P, Ph

Analysis prepared by **Kenneth M. Leon, CPA** on August 14, 2006, when the stock traded at **$ 5.64**.

Highlights

- In 2006, we see fluctuating power prices on lower regional reserve margins and demand dependent on economic growth. The Midwest should see mid-single digit volume declines, despite contributions from its acquisition of the remaining 50% of the Rocky Road power plant. We also expect higher transportation costs for coal to narrow margins.
- The Northeast and South regions are experiencing lower shipment volumes in the absence of 2005's warmer than normal summer weather. We expect increased operating and maintenance costs to have a negative impact on operating earnings. Results for 2006 will also be negatively impacted by the absence of equity income following DYN's sale of its 50% stake in West Coast Power.
- We forecast lower earnings from the power generation unit, modest cost control savings, and flat projected interest costs on total debt outstanding. These drivers lead to our net loss estimate of $0.25 in 2006 and a $0.15 loss in 2007, compared to a $0.30 operating loss in 2005, excluding one-time items.

Investment Rationale/Risk

- We believe potential declines in DYN's outlook for shipment volumes and commodity pricing may delay its effort to improve the balance sheet with the proceeds from asset sales. We are less confident that DYN's plans to use about $2.3 billion from the sale of its natural gas liquids business will be used fully to lower debt with lower average commodity prices negatively impacting its revenue and EBITDA from regional operations.
- Risks to our recommendation and target price include higher coal transportation costs and lower electricity demand. The variability of sales volumes, fuel and commodity prices, and operational activities leads to less earnings visibility and volatility, in our opinion.
- Based on a blend of our DCF and enterprise value/EBITDA models, our 12-month target price is $6.50. Our DCF model incorporates a weighted average cost of capital of 8.5% and a terminal growth rate of 3%. Our target price implies a valuation of 1.3X book value (versus 0.8X recently, and 1.9X for regulated utilities).

Qualitative Risk Assessment

LOW | MEDIUM | **HIGH**

Our risk assessment is based on Dynegy's significant exposure to cyclical power markets and volatile commodity markets for fuels that it uses to generate power.

Quantitative Evaluations

S&P Quality Ranking C

D | **C** | B- | B | B+ | A- | A | A+

Relative Strength Rank STRONG

76

LOWEST = 1 HIGHEST = 99

Revenue/Earnings Data

Revenue (Million $)

	1Q	2Q	3Q	4Q	Year
2006	600.0	439.0	--	--	--
2005	462.0	459.0	770.0	622.0	2,313
2004	1,657	1,440	1,650	1,406	6,153
2003	1,879	1,067	1,385	1,456	5,787
2002	1,444	1,380	1,407	1,322	5,553
2001	14,168	10,812	8,519	8,743	42,242

Earnings Per Share ($)

2006	-0.01	-0.48	**E**-0.09	**E**-0.07	**E**-0.25
2005	-0.71	-0.30	-0.05	-0.98	-2.13
2004	0.14	Nil	0.16	-0.47	-0.09
2003	-0.03	-0.99	2.65	-0.54	1.30
2002	-0.26	-1.76	-4.71	-0.98	-6.24
2001	0.42	0.43	0.85	0.21	1.89

Fiscal year ended Dec. 31. Next earnings report expected: Early November. EPS Estimates based on S&P Operating Earnings; historical GAAP earnings are as reported.

Dividend Data

No cash dividends have been paid since 2002.

The McGraw-Hill Companies

Dynegy Inc.

Business Summary August 14, 2006

CORPORATE OVERVIEW. At the end of 2005, DYN owned or leased 12,638 net Megawatts (MW) of generating capacity. In January 2005, DYN completed the acquisition of Sithe Energies for $135 million in cash and the assumption of $919 million of project debt. The acquisition included the 1,021 MW Independence power generation facility located near Scriba, NY, four natural gas-fired merchant facilities in New York and four hydroelectric generation facilities in Pennsylvania. In addition, Dynegy acquired a 750 MW firm capacity sales agreement with Con Edison, which runs through 2014, and provides annual cash receipts of $100 million.

On December 27, 2005, DYN entered into an agreement to sell its 50% equity interest in West Coast Power, a joint venture with 1,800 MW of generation capacity in Southern California, to NRG Energy. At the same time, DYN purchased NRG' 50% stake in a 364 MW gas-fired peaking facility in Illinois. The transactions, which resulted in net cash proceeds of $160 million to DYN, closed in the second quarter of 2006. In addition, the company in December 2005 entered into an agreement to sell its 50% interest in a generating facility in Panama.

The power generation business consists of three segments -- Midwest (7,369 MW), Northeast (2,803 MW) and South (2,466 MW). About 24% of DYN's generation capacity is coal-fired, 30% can use either coal, gas or oil, while the remainder is primarily gas-fired. In terms of dispatch type, about 34% is base-load generation, 18% intermediate, and the rest peaking.

By 2006, DYN had completed fuel conversion of all its Midwest coal generation facilities to exclusively burn Powder River Basin (PRB) coal. PRB coal is a cleaner-burning coal with lower sulfur content, making it more economic to burn while emitting lower amounts of sulfur dioxide. DYN believes the conversions to PRB coal and attendant upgrades to new equipment and technologies will allow its units to improve operating margins and reliability.

Company Financials

Per Share Data ($) Year Ended Dec. 31	2005	2004	2003	2002	2001	2000	1999	1998	1997	1996
Tangible Book Value	5.58	4.87	5.04	4.57	8.85	6.49	4.03	3.15	4.52	2.67
Cash Flow	-1.06	0.64	-0.05	-4.00	3.23	2.71	1.22	0.93	1.41	0.55
Earnings	-2.13	-0.09	1.30	-6.24	1.89	1.48	0.65	0.48	-0.42	0.60
S&P Core Earnings	-0.71	0.06	1.76	-1.96	0.73	NA	NA	NA	NA	NA
Dividends	Nil	Nil	Nil	0.15	0.30	0.32	0.04	0.04	0.04	0.05
Payout Ratio	Nil	Nil	Nil	NM	16%	22%	5%	8%	NM	6%
Prices:High	5.70	6.09	5.43	32.19	59.00	59.88	17.93	12.68	17.48	17.93
Prices:Low	3.21	3.40	1.13	0.49	20.00	17.12	7.34	6.79	10.67	6.25
P/E Ratio:High	NM	NM	4	NM	31	40	27	27	NM	30
P/E Ratio:Low	NM	NM	1	NM	11	12	11	14	NM	10

Income Statement Analysis (Million $)	2005	2004	2003	2002	2001	2000	1999	1998	1997	1996
Revenue	2,313	6,153	5,787	5,553	42,242	29,445	15,430	14,258	13,378	7,280
Operating Income	507	620	367	327	1,424	1,130	343	225	490	Nil
Depreciation	284	356	454	613	454	389	129	103	379	0.50
Interest Expense	389	480	509	374	259	251	78.2	75.0	63.5	28.1
Pretax Income	-1,199	-74.0	-675	-2,546	977	791	243	175	140	170
Effective Tax Rate	NM	NM	NM	NM	27.5%	33.0%	30.7%	28.7%	NM	33.2%
Net Income	-804	-10.0	-474	-1,955	646	501	152	108	-87.7	113
S&P Core Earnings	274	27.6	734	-711	246	NA	NA	NA	NA	NA

Balance Sheet & Other Financial Data (Million $)	2005	2004	2003	2002	2001	2000	1999	1998	1997	1996
Cash	1,549	628	496	774	218	86.0	45.2	28.4	23.0	NM
Current Assets	3,706	2,752	3,030	7,586	9,507	10,150	2,805	2,117	2,019	456
Total Assets	10,126	9,852	13,293	20,030	24,874	21,406	6,525	5,264	4,517	1,278
Current Liabilities	2,116	1,802	2,576	6,748	8,555	9,405	2,539	2,026	1,753	393
Long Term Debt	4,228	4,332	5,893	5,666	3,854	3,174	1,499	1,247	1,202	333
Common Equity	2,153	1,867	2,045	2,087	4,719	3,613	1,234	1,053	944	552
Total Capital	7,326	7,302	9,221	10,062	12,694	8,214	3,144	2,692	2,475	885
Capital Expenditures	195	311	333	947	1,845	769	365	299	220	Nil
Cash Flow	-542	324	-20.0	-1,672	1,097	855	281	211	291	114
Current Ratio	1.8	1.5	1.2	1.1	1.1	1.1	1.1	1.0	1.2	1.2
% Long Term Debt of Capitalization	57.7	59.3	63.9	56.3	30.4	38.6	47.7	46.3	40.5	37.6
% Net Income of Revenue	NM	NM	NM	NM	1.5	1.7	1.0	0.8	NM	1.6
% Return on Assets	NM	NM	NM	NM	2.8	3.6	2.6	2.2	NM	7.3
% Return on Equity	NM	NM	NM	NM	15.5	19.2	13.2	10.8	NM	13.6

Data as orig reptd.; bef. results of disc opers/spec. items. Per share data adj. for stk. divs.; EPS diluted. E-Estimated. NA-Not Available. NM-Not Meaningful. NR-Not Ranked. UR-Under Review.

Office: 1000 Louisiana Street, Houston, TX 77002-5050.
Telephone: 713-507-6400.
Email: ir@dynegy.com
Website: http://www.dynegy.com

Chrmn & CEO: B.A. Williamson
Pres & COO: S.A. Furbacher
EVP & CFO: H.C. Nichols
EVP & General Counsel: J.K. Blodgett

SVP & Cntlr: C.J. Stone
Investor Contact: J. Sousa
Board of Directors: C. E. Bayless, D. W. Biegler, L. W. Bynoe, T. D. Clark, Jr., B. J. Galt, P. A. Hammick, G. L. Mazanec, R. C. Oelkers, R. Roberts, H. B. Sheppard, J. J. Stewart, W. L. Trubeck, B. A. Williamson

Founded: 1985
Domicile: Illinois
Employees: 1,371

STANDARD &POOR'S

Eastman Chemical Co

S&P Recommendation	Price	12-Mo. Target Price	Investment Style
BUY ★★★★★	$60.92 (as of Oct 31, 2006)	$70.00	Mid-Cap Value

GICS Sector Materials
Sub-Industry Diversified Chemicals

Comment This global company manufactures and markets more than 1,200 chemicals, fibers and plastics products.

Key Stock Statistics (Source S&P, Vickers, company reports)

52-Wk Range	$61.29–47.30	S&P Oper. EPS 2006E	4.90	P/E on S&P Oper. EPS 2006E	12.4	Dividend Rate/Share	$1.76
Trailing 12-Month EPS	$4.59	S&P Oper. EPS 2007E	5.00	Common Shares Outstg. (M)	82.3	Yield (%)	2.89
Trailing 12-Month P/E	13.3	S&P Core EPS 2006E	4.75	Market Capitalization(B)	$5.011	Beta	0.90
$10K Invested 5 Yrs Ago	$21,251	S&P Core EPS 2007E	5.10	Institutional Ownership (%)	86	S&P Credit Rating	BBB

Price Performance

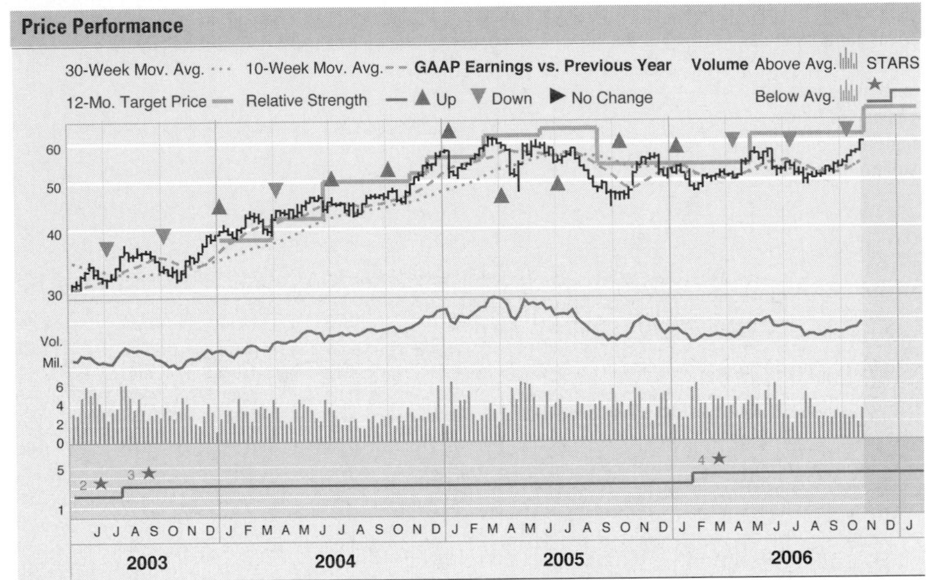

Options: ASE, CBOE, P, Ph

Highlights

- The 12-month target price for EMN has recently been changed to $70.00 from $62.00. The Highlights section of this Stock Report will be updated accordingly.

Investment Rationale/Risk

- The Investment Rationale/Risk section of this Stock Report will be updated shortly. For the latest News story on EMN from MarketScope, see below.

- 10/30/06 01:16 pm EST... S&P MAINTAINS BUY OPINION ON SHARES OF EASTMAN CHEMICAL (EMN 60.88****): Q3 EPS of $1.24 vs. $1.53 tops our $1.10 estimate. Sales rose 8%, driven by higher prices. Profits were hurt by higher raw material costs, planned maintenance outages, and polyester resins profit that fell to near breakeven. We expect the specialty and fibers units to continue to perform well while a new plant technology and restructuring in Europe helps polyester. We expect EMN to soon set a stock buyback. We now see '06 EPS at $4.90, raised from $4.65, but are keeping our above-consensus $5.00 for '07. Our 12-month target price rises $8 to $70 on higher relative multiples. /R.O'Reilly-CFA

Qualitative Risk Assessment

LOW | **MEDIUM** | HIGH

Our risk assessment reflects the diverse business and geographic sales mix of the company, partly offset by the cyclical nature of the chemicals industry and volatility of raw material costs.

Quantitative Evaluations

S&P Quality Ranking B-

D | C | **B-** | B | B+ | A- | A | A+

Relative Strength Rank STRONG

88

LOWEST = 1 HIGHEST = 99

Revenue/Earnings Data

Revenue (Million $)

	1Q	2Q	3Q	4Q	Year
2006	1,803	1,929	1,966	--	--
2005	1,762	1,752	1,816	1,729	7,059
2004	1,597	1,676	1,649	1,658	6,580
2003	1,441	1,481	1,444	1,434	5,800
2002	1,236	1,395	1,374	1,315	5,320
2001	1,344	1,402	1,367	1,271	5,384

Earnings Per Share ($)

2006	1.27	1.37	1.15	E0.90	E4.90
2005	2.00	2.51	1.50	0.81	6.81
2004	-0.07	1.07	0.49	0.68	2.18
2003	0.23	0.46	-4.35	0.13	-3.54
2002	0.30	0.58	0.31	-0.16	1.02
2001	0.48	-1.92	0.31	-1.20	-2.33

Fiscal year ended Dec. 31. Next earnings report expected: Late January. EPS Estimates based on S&P Operating Earnings; historical GAAP earnings are as reported.

Dividend Data (Dates: mm/dd Payment Date: mm/dd/yy)

Amount ($)	Date Decl.	Ex-Div. Date	Stk. of Record	Payment Date
0.440	12/01	12/13	12/15	01/02/06
0.440	03/02	03/13	03/15	04/03/06
0.440	05/04	06/13	06/15	07/03/06
0.440	08/03	09/13	09/15	10/02/06

Dividends have been paid since 1994. Source: Company reports.

Eastman Chemical Co

Business Summary August 21, 2006

CORPORATE OVERVIEW. Eastman Chemical Co. is a large global maker of a broad range of chemicals, plastics and fibers. International operations accounted for 45% of sales in 2005.

In early 2006 the company realigned its organization structure. The Chemicals and Fibers group consists of three segments. The coatings, adhesive, specialty polymers, and inks segment (19% of 2005 sales, operating profits of $229 million) is a leading supplier of alcohols and solvents used in coatings (59% of segment sales) and resins, dispersions and specialty polymers used in adhesives. In August 2004, EMN sold certain product lines acquired in the late 1990s with annual sales of about $600 million, for $215 million. Performance chemicals and intermediates (23%, $161 million) includes oxo chemicals, acetyls, plasticizers, and glycols used for polymers, photographic and home care products, agricultural chemicals, and pharmaceutical intermediates; additives for food and beverage ingredients; and custom manufacturing. In the fibers business (12%, $207 million), EMN is one of the world's two largest suppliers of acetate cigarette filter tow and with the exit of a major competitor in 2005, is now the leader in acetate yarn. The company projects global growth in demand for filter tow of 3% annually through 2010, with Asia and Eastern Europe having the fastest growth rates.

The Polyester group consists of polymers (36%, $159 million) and specialty plastics (10%, $64 million). EMN is the world's largest producer of polyester plastics, including polyethylene terephthalate (PET), used for packaging applications and beverage containers such as soft-drink bottles; it also makes polyethylene resins used for packaging, films and containers. The company has annual PET capacity of 3.3 billion lbs. In March 2005, EMN began construction of a new plant with annual capacity of 770 million lbs. using new IntegRex technology, with the start-up expected in late 2006 and full production in 2007. EMN plans to then close higher cost domestic capacity. EMN believes that it could expand the new plant by up to 30% within two years. The company is also evaluating a second facility using refinements to the new technology. The polyethylene business is a U.S.-based business, and had a relatively small market share, accounting for about 20% of annual polymers segment sales. Specialty plastics includes modified copolyesters and cellulosic plastics for consumer, medical, packaging, and specialty applications; the segment also sells films and sheet products. EMN's products compete with alternative polymers, primarily acrylic and polycarbonate.

Company Financials

Per Share Data ($) Year Ended Dec. 31	2005	2004	2003	2002	2001	2000	1999	1998	1997	1996
Tangible Book Value	15.85	10.70	9.00	9.06	9.92	15.64	16.81	24.45	22.40	21.28
Cash Flow	10.50	6.23	1.22	6.18	3.33	9.36	5.46	7.59	7.86	9.01
Earnings	6.81	2.18	-3.54	1.02	-2.33	3.94	0.61	3.13	3.63	4.80
S&P Core Earnings	5.63	2.23	-3.45	0.26	-3.06	NA	NA	NA	NA	NA
Dividends	1.76	1.76	1.76	1.76	1.76	1.76	1.76	1.76	1.76	1.72
Payout Ratio	26%	81%	NM	173%	NM	45%	NM	56%	48%	36%
Prices:High	61.80	58.17	39.57	49.55	55.65	54.75	60.31	72.94	65.38	76.25
Prices:Low	44.10	38.00	27.56	34.53	29.03	33.63	36.00	43.50	50.75	50.75
P/E Ratio:High	9	27	NM	49	NM	14	99	23	18	16
P/E Ratio:Low	6	17	NM	34	NM	9	59	14	14	11
Income Statement Analysis (Million $)										
Revenue	7,059	6,580	5,800	5,320	5,384	5,292	4,590	4,481	4,678	4,782
Operating Income	1,092	696	590	610	755	989	663	785	895	977
Depreciation	304	322	367	397	435	418	383	351	327	314
Interest Expense	100	115	124	128	140	135	126	96.0	87.0	67.0
Pretax Income	783	64.0	-381	84.0	-297	452	72.0	360	446	607
Effective Tax Rate	28.9%	NM	NM	5.95%	NM	33.0%	33.3%	30.8%	35.9%	37.3%
Net Income	557	170	-273	79.0	-179	303	48.0	249	286	380
S&P Core Earnings	459	173	-266	20.4	-236	NA	NA	NA	NA	NA
Balance Sheet & Other Financial Data (Million $)										
Cash	524	325	558	77.0	66.0	101	186	29.0	29.0	24.0
Current Assets	1,924	1,768	2,010	1,529	1,458	1,523	1,489	1,415	1,490	1,345
Total Assets	5,773	5,872	6,230	6,273	6,086	6,550	6,303	5,876	5,778	5,266
Current Liabilities	1,051	1,099	1,477	1,224	958	1,258	1,608	985	954	787
Long Term Debt	1,621	2,061	2,089	2,054	2,143	1,914	1,506	1,649	1,714	1,523
Common Equity	1,612	1,184	1,913	1,271	1,378	1,812	2,521	1,934	1,753	1,639
Total Capital	3,550	3,455	4,318	3,809	3,973	4,333	4,512	3,998	3,864	3,510
Capital Expenditures	343	248	230	427	234	226	292	500	749	789
Cash Flow	861	492	94.0	476	256	721	431	600	613	694
Current Ratio	1.8	1.6	1.4	1.2	1.5	1.2	0.9	1.4	1.6	1.7
% Long Term Debt of Capitalization	45.7	59.7	48.4	53.9	53.9	44.2	33.4	41.2	44.4	43.3
% Net Income of Revenue	7.9	2.6	NM	1.5	NM	5.7	1.0	5.6	6.1	7.9
% Return on Assets	9.6	2.8	NM	1.3	NM	4.7	0.8	4.3	5.6	7.5
% Return on Equity	39.8	15.3	NM	6.0	NM	17.0	1.9	13.5	16.9	24.0

Data as orig reptd.; bef. results of disc opers/spec. items. Per share data adj. for stk. divs.; EPS diluted. E-Estimated. NA-Not Available. NM-Not Meaningful. NR-Not Ranked. UR-Under Review.

Office: 200 S Wilcox Dr, Kingsport, TN, USA 37660-5147.
Telephone: 423-229-2000.
Website: http://www.eastman.com
Chrmn & CEO: J.B. Ferguson

SVP & CFO: R.A. Lorraine
SVP & CTO: R.C. Lindsay
SVP, Secy & General Counsel: T.K. Lee
VP & Cntlr: C.E. Espeland

Investor Contact: G. Riddle (423-229-8692)
Board of Directors: M. P. Connors, S. R. Demeritt, J. B. Ferguson, D. W. Griffin, R. M. Hernandez, R. J. Hornbaker, L. M. Kling, H. L. Lance, T. H. McLain, D. W. Raisbeck, P. M. Wood

Founded: 1993
Domicile: Delaware
Employees: 12,000

Eastman Kodak Co

S&P Recommendation HOLD ★★★★★	**Price** $24.40 (as of Oct 31, 2006)	**12-Mo. Target Price** $24.00	**Investment Style** Mid-Cap Value

GICS Sector Consumer Discretionary
Sub-Industry Photographic Products

Comment This multinational company has a large presence in consumer, professional and health imaging.

Key Stock Statistics (Source S&P, Vickers, company reports)

52-Wk Range	**$30.91–18.93**	S&P Oper. EPS 2006**E**	**0.80**	P/E on S&P Oper. EPS 2006**E**	**30.5**	Dividend Rate/Share	**$0.50**
Trailing 12-Month EPS	**$-2.46**	S&P Oper. EPS 2007**E**	**0.98**	Common Shares Outstg. (M)	**287.3**	Yield (%)	**2.05**
Trailing 12-Month P/E	**NM**	S&P Core EPS 2006**E**	**-2.70**	Market Capitalization(B)	**$7.009**	Beta	**1.21**
$10K Invested 5 Yrs Ago	**$9,103**	S&P Core EPS 2007**E**	**0.75**	Institutional Ownership (%)	**NA**	S&P Credit Rating	**B+**

Price Performance

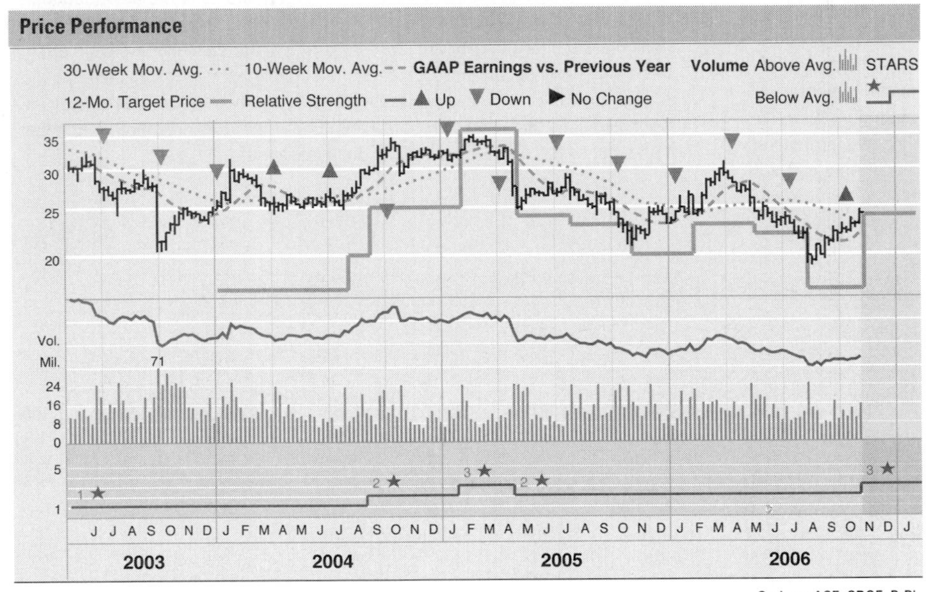

Options: ASE, CBOE, P, Ph

Highlights

➤ The STARS recommendation for EK has recently been changed to 3 (hold) from 2 (sell) and the 12-month target price has recently been changed to $24.00 from $17.00. The Highlights section of this Stock Report will be updated accordingly.

Investment Rationale/Risk

➤ The Investment Rationale/Risk section of this Stock Report will be updated shortly. For the latest News story on EK from MarketScope, see below.

➤ 10/31/06 04:49 pm EST... S&P UPGRADES SHARES OF EASTMAN KODAK TO HOLD, FROM SELL (EK 24.4***): Before special items, a Q3 operating profit rise of 38% is much better than we expected, primarily reflecting only a 20% profit decline from the film and photofinishing segment. Assuming a 35% tax rate, and with $0.10 from Q3 asset sale gains, we are increasing our '06 EPS estimate to $0.80 from $0.43, and our '07's to $0.98 from $0.72. This assumes retention of health care business, though it could be divested. We are raising our 12-month target price to $24, from $17, which still reflects 24X P/E, but with an upwardly revised '07 EPS estimate. EK has 2.0% indicated dividend. / T.Graves-CFA

Qualitative Risk Assessment

LOW	MEDIUM	**HIGH**

Our risk assessment is based on the company's ongoing shift toward digital photography. While we think EK has made progress in this endeavor, we are concerned about competitive threats and margin declines in this space. We also note that EK has posted losses for seven consecutive quarters.

Quantitative Evaluations

S&P Quality Ranking B-

D	C	**B-**	B	B+	A-	A	A+

Relative Strength Rank STRONG

81

LOWEST = 1 HIGHEST = 99

Revenue/Earnings Data

Revenue (Million $)

	1Q	2Q	3Q	4Q	Year
2006	2,889	3,360	3,204	--	--
2005	2,832	3,686	3,553	4,197	14,268
2004	2,919	3,469	3,364	3,765	13,517
2003	2,740	3,352	3,447	3,778	13,317
2002	2,707	3,339	3,354	3,441	12,835
2001	2,975	3,592	3,308	3,441	13,234

Earnings Per Share ($)

	1Q	2Q	3Q	4Q	Year
2006	-1.04	-0.98	-0.13	**E**0.47	**E**0.80
2005	-0.49	-0.49	-3.62	-0.47	-5.05
2004	0.06	0.50	0.16	-0.06	0.28
2003	-0.01	0.39	0.42	0.03	0.83
2002	0.13	0.97	1.15	0.39	2.72
2001	0.52	0.12	0.33	0.39	0.26

Fiscal year ended Dec. 31. Next earnings report expected: Late January. EPS Estimates based on S&P Operating Earnings; historical GAAP earnings are as reported.

Dividend Data (Dates: mm/dd Payment Date: mm/dd/yy)

Amount ($)	Date Decl.	Ex-Div. Date	Stk. of Record	Payment Date
0.250	10/18	10/28	11/01	12/14/05
0.250	05/10	05/30	06/01	07/18/06
0.250	10/17	10/30	11/01	12/14/06

Dividends have been paid since 1902. Source: Company reports.

Eastman Kodak Co

Business Summary August 07, 2006

CORPORATE OVERVIEW. Eastman Kodak offers products in the photographic, graphic communications and health care markets. For 2005, based on a new reporting structure, the Film & Photofinishing System Group accounted for 37% of revenue, while the Consumer Digital area represented 22%, the Graphic Communications Group 20%, the Health Group 18%, and other activities 1%.

The company has continued to increase its presence in the digital photography market. During 2005, sales attributable to this technology accounted for 54% of the overall total, marking the first time in EK's history that the majority of its revenue base was not derived via traditional film products. According to market research firm IDC, EK shipped more than seven million digital cameras in 2005, and possessed a market share of 25% within this category, an increase from 21% in 2004.

CORPORATE STRATEGY. As consumers continue to migrate away from film (U.S. consumer film volumes declined by 25% in 2005), EK has implemented a number of restructuring initiatives. In January 2004, the company introduced a cost reduction program that was expected to result in charges of $1.3 billion to $1.7 billion and 12,000 to 15,000 layoffs by the end of 2006. However, in July 2005, EK extended its original forecast to accelerate its shift toward digital businesses and to respond to a faster than expected decline in consumer film sales. In August 2006, EK estimated that the total restructuring program would result in an employee headcount reduction of 25,000 to 27,000 positions and a total cost of $3.0 billion to $3.4 billion, with the program to be essentially completed in 2007. Through June 20, 2006, EK had recorded charges of $2.4 billion, including $1.1 billion for severance, $697 million for accelerated depreciation, $308 million for long-lived asset impairments, $222 million for exit costs, and $62 million for inventory. We look for the restructuring activity to lead to annual cost savings of more than $1 billion.

Company Financials

Per Share Data ($) Year Ended Dec. 31	**2005**	**2004**	**2003**	**2002**	**2001**	**2000**	**1999**	**1998**	**1997**	**1996**
Tangible Book Value	NM	6.57	5.53	6.27	6.71	8.56	9.45	8.54	8.09	12.51
Cash Flow	-0.18	3.88	3.72	5.52	3.42	7.48	7.19	6.84	2.51	5.68
Earnings	-5.05	0.28	0.83	2.72	0.26	4.59	4.33	4.24	0.01	3.00
S&P Core Earnings	-4.93	-0.42	0.53	0.44	-1.86	NA	NA	NA	NA	NA
Dividends	0.50	0.50	1.15	1.80	1.77	1.76	1.76	1.76	1.76	1.60
Payout Ratio	NM	179%	139%	68%	NM	38%	41%	42%	NM	53%
Prices:High	35.19	34.74	41.08	38.48	49.95	67.50	80.38	88.94	94.75	85.00
Prices:Low	20.77	24.25	20.39	25.58	24.40	35.31	56.63	57.94	53.31	65.13
P/E Ratio:High	NM	NM	49	15	19	15	19	21	NM	28
P/E Ratio:Low	NM	NM	25	10	9	8	13	14	NM	22

Income Statement Analysis (Million $)										
Revenue	14,268	13,517	13,317	12,835	13,234	13,994	14,089	13,406	14,538	15,967
Operating Income	1,483	1,638	1,605	2,898	1,923	3,103	2,908	2,783	2,431	3,107
Depreciation	1,402	1,030	830	818	919	889	918	853	828	903
Interest Expense	211	168	148	173	219	178	142	110	98.0	83.0
Pretax Income	-762	-92.0	196	946	97.0	2,132	2,109	2,106	53.0	1,556
Effective Tax Rate	NM	NM	NM	16.1%	33.0%	34.0%	34.0%	34.0%	90.6%	35.1%
Net Income	-1,455	81.0	238	793	76.0	1,407	1,392	1,390	5.00	1,011
S&P Core Earnings	-1,419	-119	149	127	-541	NA	NA	NA	NA	NA

Balance Sheet & Other Financial Data (Million $)										
Cash	1,665	1,255	1,250	569	448	251	393	500	728	1,796
Current Assets	5,781	5,648	5,455	4,534	4,683	5,491	5,444	5,599	5,475	6,965
Total Assets	14,921	14,737	14,818	13,369	13,362	14,212	14,370	14,733	13,145	14,438
Current Liabilities	5,489	4,990	5,307	5,377	5,354	6,215	5,769	6,178	5,177	5,417
Long Term Debt	2,764	1,852	2,302	1,164	1,666	1,166	Nil	504	585	559
Common Equity	1,967	3,811	3,264	2,777	2,894	3,428	3,912	3,988	3,161	4,734
Total Capital	4,731	5,663	5,566	3,941	4,560	4,655	3,971	1,108	3,746	5,395
Capital Expenditures	472	460	506	577	743	945	1,127	4,561	1,485	1,341
Cash Flow	-53.0	1,111	1,068	1,611	995	2,296	2,310	2,243	833	1,914
Current Ratio	1.1	1.1	1.0	0.8	0.9	0.9	0.9	0.9	1.1	1.3
% Long Term Debt of Capitalization	58.4	32.7	41.4	29.5	36.5	25.0	Nil	11.1	15.6	10.4
% Net Income of Revenue	NM	NM	1.8	6.2	0.6	10.1	9.9	10.4	0.0	6.4
% Return on Assets	NM	NM	1.7	5.9	0.6	9.8	9.6	10.0	0.0	7.0
% Return on Equity	NM	NM	7.9	27.9	2.4	38.3	35.2	38.9	0.1	20.6

Data as orig reptd.; bef. results of disc opers/spec. items. Per share data adj. for stk. divs.; EPS diluted. E-Estimated. NA-Not Available. NM-Not Meaningful. NR-Not Ranked. UR-Under Review.

Office: 343 State Street, Rochester, NY 14650.
Telephone: 585-724-4000.
Website: http://www.kodak.com
Chrmn, Pres & CEO: A.M. Perez

SVP & Chief Admin: C.S. Brown, Jr.
SVP & General Counsel: J.P. Haag
VP & CIO: K. VanGelder
CFO: F. Sklarsky

Investor Contact: D. Flick (585-724-4352)
Board of Directors: R. S. Braddock, M. L. Collins, T. M. Donahue, M. Hawley, W. H. Hernandez, D. L. Lee, D. E. Lewis, A. M. Perez, H. D. Ruiz, L. D. Tyson

Founded: 1880
Domicile: New Jersey
Employees: 51,100

STANDARD &POOR'S

Eaton Corp

S&P Recommendation HOLD ★★★★★

Price $72.99 (as of Oct 27, 2006)

12-Mo. Target Price $80.00

Investment Style Large-Cap Value

GICS Sector Industrials
Sub-Industry Industrial Machinery

Comment This diversified industrial manufacturer's products include electrical systems and components for power management; truck transmissions; and fluid power systems and services for industrial, mobile and aircraft equipment.

Key Stock Statistics (Source S&P, Vickers, company reports)

52-Wk Range	$79.98–57.83	S&P Oper. EPS 2006E	6.25	P/E on S&P Oper. EPS 2006E	11.7	Dividend Rate/Share	$1.56
Trailing 12-Month EPS	$6.00	S&P Oper. EPS 2007E	6.50	Common Shares Outstg. (M)	150.0	Yield (%)	2.14
Trailing 12-Month P/E	12.2	S&P Core EPS 2006E	6.55	Market Capitalization(B)	$10.949	Beta	1.17
$10K Invested 5 Yrs Ago	$24,050	S&P Core EPS 2007E	6.80	Institutional Ownership (%)	79	S&P Credit Rating	A

Price Performance

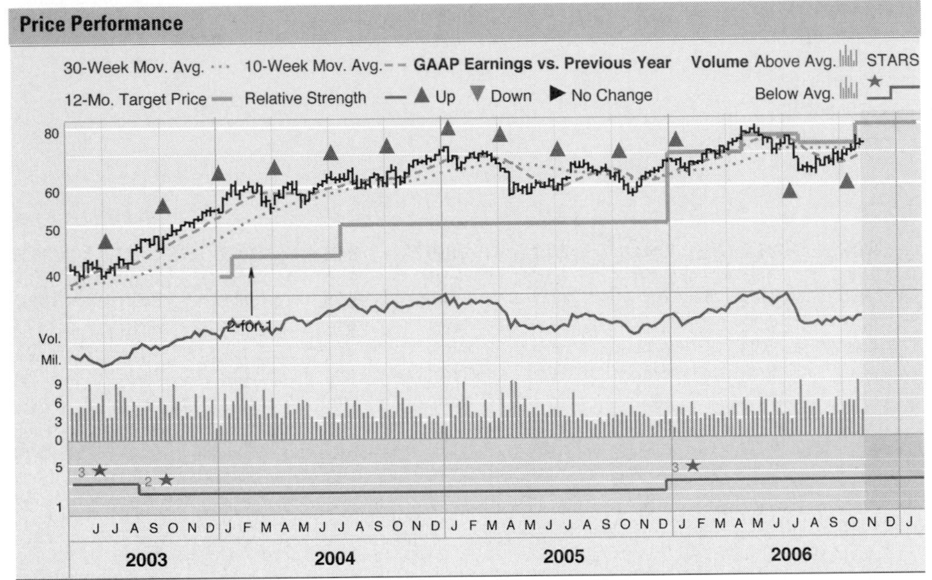

Options: ASE, CBOE, P, Ph

Analysis prepared by **Anthony M. Fiore, CFA** on October 17, 2006, when the stock traded at **$ 73.27**.

Highlights

- We expect sales to increase about 13% in 2006, following a similar advance in 2005. We see sales in 2006 being bolstered by continued strong demand in ETN's truck, electrical and fluid power businesses, combined with contributions from recent acquisitions. We see growth moderating in 2007, to around 5%, largely reflecting an anticipated decline in the medium and heavy duty truck markets.
- In terms of profitability, we see a fractionally wider operating margin in 2006 based on our outlook for improving profitability in the electrical and fluid power businesses, partially offset by our expectation of reduced profitability in the automotive segment. With regard to the electrical segment, we think margin expansion will largely be driven by improving nonresidential construction activity in North America.
- We forecast that operating earnings will increase to $6.25 in 2006, versus $5.38 in 2005, before one-time items, and then grow in 2007, to $6.50. Our operating EPS estimates for 2006 and 2007 each include $0.14 of projected stock option expense.

Investment Rationale/Risk

- While we expect favorable conditions in many of ETN's end markets to continue in 2007, we think that our outlook is largely reflected in the price of the stock. With the shares recently trading near our target price, we do not recommend adding to positions.
- Risks to our opinion and target price include a downturn in the North American and/or European truck markets; the potential for supply disruptions; a continued escalation in raw material costs; and any significant deterioration in the structural growth prospects of ETN's main end markets, market positions, cost structure, and/or competitive positions.
- Our 12-month target price of $80 combines two valuation metrics. Our discounted cash flow model, which assumes an 8%-10% average annual free cash flow growth rate over the next 10 years, 3.5% in perpetuity, and a 9% discount rate, indicates intrinsic value of about $74 a share. In terms of relative valuation, applying a target P/E multiple of 13X, in line with historical norms, to our 2007 EPS estimate of $6.50 suggests a value of $85. By blending these two methodologies, we arrive at our target price.

Qualitative Risk Assessment

LOW | **MEDIUM** | HIGH

Our risk assessment for Eaton Corp. reflects our view that it has good geographic and product diversification, offset by the highly cyclical nature of the company's various end markets, and significant pension and other postretirement benefit obligations.

Quantitative Evaluations

S&P Quality Ranking B+

D | C | B- | B | **B+** | A- | A | A+

Relative Strength Rank MODERATE

61

LOWEST = 1 HIGHEST = 99

Revenue/Earnings Data

Revenue (Million $)

	1Q	2Q	3Q	4Q	Year
2006	3,013	3,186	3,115	--	--
2005	2,654	2,834	2,789	2,838	11,115
2004	2,238	2,403	2,543	2,633	9,817
2003	1,925	2,027	2,026	2,083	8,061
2002	1,723	1,881	1,830	1,775	7,209
2001	1,983	1,871	1,750	1,695	7,299

Earnings Per Share ($)

2006	E1.40	1.64	1.39	E1.62	E6.25
2005	1.19	1.37	1.30	1.38	5.23
2004	0.85	1.03	1.09	1.16	4.13
2003	0.50	0.64	0.70	0.72	2.56
2002	0.24	0.61	0.65	0.47	1.96
2001	0.36	0.35	0.29	0.21	1.20

Fiscal year ended Dec. 31. Next earnings report expected: Late January. EPS Estimates based on S&P Operating Earnings; historical GAAP earnings are as reported.

Dividend Data (Dates: mm/dd Payment Date: mm/dd/yy)

Amount ($)	Date Decl.	Ex-Div. Date	Stk. of Record	Payment Date
0.350	01/24	02/02	02/06	02/24/06
0.350	04/26	05/04	05/08	05/26/06
0.390	07/17	08/03	08/07	08/25/06
0.390	10/25	11/02	11/06	11/24/06

Dividends have been paid since 1923. Source: Company reports.

Eaton Corp

Business Summary October 17, 2006

Eaton Corp., a $10 billion in revenues industrial equipment and parts manufacturer, conducts business through four business segments.

The Fluid Power (FP) segment (29% of revenues and 11% operating margin in 2005) makes hydraulics for everything from jet planes to farm tractors. FP sells its hydraulics equipment to three market channels: mobile (primarily earth-movers and farm tractors; about 40% of FP sales); stationary (primarily machine tools; 35%); and aerospace (mainly commercial and military aircraft; 25%).

Parker Hannifin, the world's largest hydraulics equipment maker, Eaton (the second largest), Germany-based Sauer Danfoss (the third), and Germany-based Mannesmann (fourth) account for about 40% of the $50 billion in revenue global hydraulics equipment industry. The 60% balance is comprised of hundreds of small hydraulics equipment makers.

ETN's growing Electrical segment (34% and 11%) makes a wide range of electrical distribution equipment, such as switchboards, circuit boards and circuit breakers. The segment also makes electronic sensors that control industrial machinery, as well as electricity quality-monitoring systems. The unit's primary competitors include GE, Germany-based Siemens and Schneider Electric. Demand for ETN's electrical equipment and components is primarily driven by the health of the residential and commercial construction industry.

ETN's Automotive Components segment (16% and 13%) is the world's largest maker of engine valves, which are used to control the air flow of internal combustion engines of cars and small trucks. TRW Automotive and Germany-based INA are the world's second and third largest engine valve makers. The segment also makes safety and environmental related automotive components and actuators that move certain auto components (such as side-view mirrors). Demand for ETN's automotive components is primarily driven by the health of the auto and light-truck market.

Company Financials

Per Share Data ($) Year Ended Dec. 31	**2005**	**2004**	**2003**	**2002**	**2001**	**2000**	**1999**	**1998**	**1997**	**1996**
Tangible Book Value	0.09	3.46	3.14	NM	0.29	NM	0.64	7.17	7.37	7.16
Cash Flow	8.08	6.67	5.18	4.49	3.78	5.05	7.25	4.66	5.17	4.34
Earnings	5.23	4.13	2.56	1.96	1.20	2.50	4.18	2.40	2.97	2.25
S&P Core Earnings	5.40	4.15	2.43	0.99	-0.18	NA	NA	NA	NA	NA
Dividends	1.24	1.08	0.92	0.88	0.88	0.88	0.88	0.88	0.86	0.80
Payout Ratio	24%	26%	36%	45%	74%	35%	21%	37%	29%	36%
Prices:High	72.69	72.64	54.70	44.34	40.72	43.28	51.75	49.81	51.69	35.44
Prices:Low	56.65	52.74	33.01	29.55	27.56	28.75	31.00	28.75	33.63	25.19
P/E Ratio:High	14	18	21	23	34	17	12	21	17	16
P/E Ratio:Low	11	13	13	15	23	11	7	12	11	11

Income Statement Analysis (Million $)	2005	2004	2003	2002	2001	2000	1999	1998	1997	1996
Revenue	11,115	9,817	8,061	7,209	7,299	8,309	8,402	6,625	7,563	6,961
Operating Income	1,468	1,287	984	870	703	1,013	1,170	813	1,042	854
Depreciation	409	400	394	353	355	364	441	331	342	320
Interest Expense	90.0	78.0	87.0	104	142	177	152	88.0	86.0	93.0
Pretax Income	996	781	508	399	278	552	963	485	668	485
Effective Tax Rate	19.2%	17.0%	24.0%	29.6%	39.2%	34.2%	35.9%	28.0%	30.5%	28.1%
Net Income	805	648	386	281	169	363	617	349	464	349
S&P Core Earnings	832	651	367	141	-25.0	NA	NA	NA	NA	NA

Balance Sheet & Other Financial Data (Million $)	2005	2004	2003	2002	2001	2000	1999	1998	1997	1996
Cash	110	85.0	61.0	75.0	112	82.0	81.0	80.0	53.0	60.0
Current Assets	3,578	3,182	3,093	2,457	2,387	2,571	2,782	1,982	2,055	2,017
Total Assets	10,218	9,075	8,223	7,138	7,646	8,180	8,437	5,665	5,465	5,307
Current Liabilities	2,968	2,262	2,126	1,734	1,669	2,107	2,649	1,516	1,357	1,230
Long Term Debt	1,830	Nil	1,651	1,887	2,252	2,447	1,915	1,191	1,272	1,062
Common Equity	3,778	3,606	3,117	2,302	2,475	2,410	2,624	2,057	2,071	2,160
Total Capital	5,608	3,606	4,768	4,752	5,307	4,857	4,539	3,248	3,343	3,222
Capital Expenditures	363	330	2,733	228	295	386	496	483	438	347
Cash Flow	1,214	1,048	780	634	524	727	1,058	680	806	669
Current Ratio	1.2	1.4	1.5	1.4	1.4	1.2	1.1	1.3	1.5	1.6
% Long Term Debt of Capitalization	32.6	Nil	34.6	39.7	42.4	50.4	42.2	36.7	38.0	33.0
% Net Income of Revenue	7.2	6.6	4.8	3.9	2.3	4.4	7.3	5.3	6.1	5.1
% Return on Assets	8.3	7.5	5.0	3.8	2.1	4.4	8.8	6.3	8.6	6.8
% Return on Equity	21.8	19.3	14.2	11.8	6.9	14.4	26.4	16.9	21.9	16.9

Data as orig reptd.; bef. results of disc opers/spec. items. Per share data adj. for stk. divs.; EPS diluted. E-Estimated. NA-Not Available. NM-Not Meaningful. NR-Not Ranked. UR-Under Review.

Office: Eaton Center, Cleveland, OH 44114-2535.
Telephone: 216-523-5000.
Website: http://www.eaton.com
Chrmn, Pres & CEO: A.M. Cutler

EVP & CFO: R.H. Fearon
VP & CTO: Y. Tsavalas
VP & Treas: R.E. Parmenter
VP & Secy: E.R. Franklin

Investor Contact: B. Hartman (216-523-4501)
Board of Directors: C. M. Connor, M. J. Critelli, A. M. Cutler, E. Green, N. C. Lautenbach, D. L. McCoy, J. R. Miller, G. R. Page, V. A. Pelson, G. L. Tooker

Founded: 1916
Domicile: Ohio
Employees: 59,000

STANDARD &POOR'S

eBay Inc

S&P Recommendation STRONG BUY ★★★★★	**Price** $32.07 (as of Oct 27, 2006)	**12-Mo. Target Price** $35.00	**Investment Style** Large-Cap Growth

GICS Sector Information Technology
Sub-Industry Internet Software & Services

Comment EBAY owns one of the world's most popular e-commerce destinations, which bears its name, as well as PayPal, an online payments company, and Skype, an Internet telephony business.

Key Stock Statistics (Source S&P, Vickers, company reports)

52-Wk Range	**$47.86–22.83**	S&P Oper. EPS 2006**E**	**0.83**	P/E on S&P Oper. EPS 2006**E**	**38.6**	Dividend Rate/Share	**Nil**
Trailing 12-Month EPS	**$0.74**	S&P Oper. EPS 2007**E**	**1.04**	Common Shares Outstg. (M)	**1,415.4**	Yield (%)	**Nil**
Trailing 12-Month P/E	**43.3**	S&P Core EPS 2006**E**	**0.83**	Market Capitalization(B)	**$45.392**	Beta	**1.71**
$10K Invested 5 Yrs Ago	**$22,505**	S&P Core EPS 2007**E**	**1.04**	Institutional Ownership (%)	**66**	S&P Credit Rating	**NA**

Price Performance

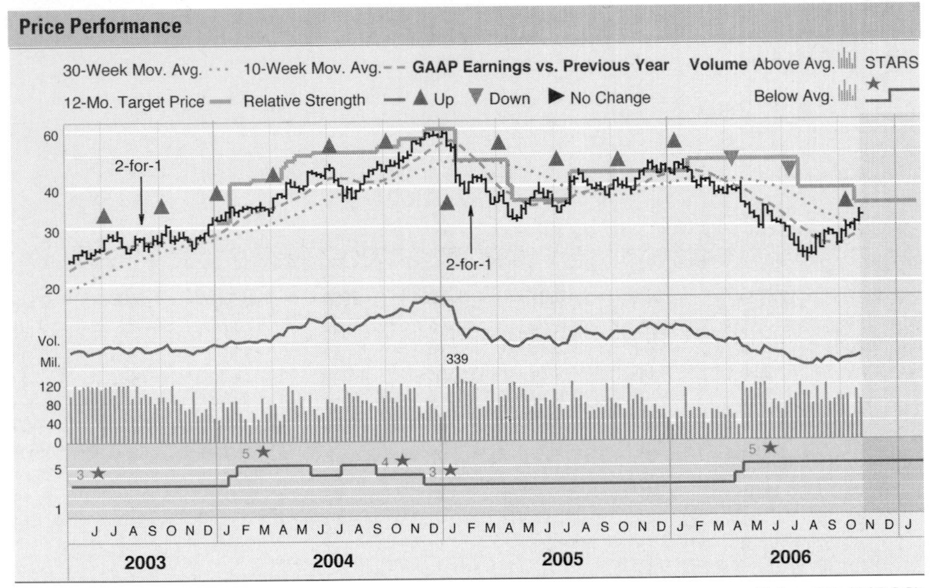

Options: ASE, CBOE, P, Ph

Analysis prepared by **Scott H. Kessler** on October 24, 2006, when the stock traded at **$ 31.74**.

Highlights

- We expect revenues to rise 29% in 2006 and 19% in 2007. We look for international operations (47% of 2006 third quarter revenues) to continue to contribute significant additional listing and transaction fees, and to account for an increasing percentage of revenues.
- We project that EBAY's annual margins will be flat to lower in 2006 versus last year. Following major acquisitions in 2005, we expect that EBAY will invest significantly to build and integrate these businesses. We believe EBAY will continue to focus on international opportunities, especially in China, where we think it faces notable competition. Margins should improve in 2007.
- In October 2005, EBAY acquired Skype Technologies, a provider of Internet communications offerings, in a transaction valued at up to $3.9 billion in cash and stock. In August 2005, EBAY acquired Shopping.com, a comparison shopping service, for $634 million. In July 2006, EBAY announced a $2 billion share buyback. Our EPS estimates include projected stock option expense.

Investment Rationale/Risk

- We see EBAY as the clear leader in online auctions, a mainstream Internet retail destination, a major facilitator of large transactions involving cars and real estate, a growing international presence, and the owner of the world's leading purely online payment platform. We are optimistic about its international and payment segments.
- Risks to our recommendation and target price include a material weakening of consumer sentiment and/or spending, potentially greater regulation and taxation associated with EBAY's businesses, and significant and increasing international competition. We also believe the Skype purchase was not very strategic and was excessively priced.
- EBAY's recent P/E of 37X our 2006 EPS estimate was well above that of the S&P 500, but its recent 2006 P/E to growth (PEG) ratio was comparable. Based on our DCF model, with assumptions that include a weighted average cost of capital of 12.8% and projected average annual free cash flow growth of 23% over the next five years, our 12-month target price is $35.

Qualitative Risk Assessment

LOW	MEDIUM	**HIGH**

In our view, EBAY is a well established leader in the Internet segment, possesses a business model that we see as compelling, and sports a strong balance sheet. However, the company operates in fast-changing areas and faces notable competition. The stock also is generally much more volatile than the S&P 500.

Quantitative Evaluations

S&P Quality Ranking **NR**

D	C	B-	B	B+	A-	A	A+

Relative Strength Rank **STRONG**

89

LOWEST = 1 HIGHEST = 99

Revenue/Earnings Data

Revenue (Million $)

	1Q	2Q	3Q	4Q	Year
2006	1,390	1,411	1,449	--	--
2005	1,032	1,086	1,106	1,329	4,552
2004	756.2	773.4	805.9	935.8	3,271
2003	476.5	509.3	530.9	648.4	2,165
2002	245.1	266.3	288.8	413.9	1,214
2001	154.1	180.9	194.4	219.4	748.8

Earnings Per Share ($)

2006	0.17	0.17	0.20	**E**0.23	**E**0.83
2005	0.19	0.21	0.18	0.20	0.78
2004	0.15	0.14	0.13	0.15	0.57
2003	0.08	0.07	0.08	0.11	0.34
2002	0.04	0.05	0.05	0.07	0.21
2001	0.02	0.02	0.02	0.02	0.08

Fiscal year ended Dec. 31. Next earnings report expected: Mid January. EPS Estimates based on S&P Operating Earnings; historical GAAP earnings are as reported.

Dividend Data

No cash dividends have been paid.

The McGraw-Hill Companies

eBay Inc

Business Summary October 24, 2006

CORPORATE OVERVIEW. eBay operates the world's largest online trading community. As of September 2006, eBay had 211.9 million confirmed registered users (up from 168.1 million a year earlier) and 79.8 million active users (68.0 million), which accounted for 488.3 million non-store listings (407.0 million) and 95.4 million store listings (51.6 million). Following acquisitions in recent years, the company also owns Half.com (fixed price retail sales), PayPal (online payments), Rent.com (apartment and home rentals), Shopping.com (comparison shopping) and Skype (Internet calling).

The company and its affiliates have Web sites directed toward the following geographies: Argentina, Australia, Austria, Belgium, Brazil, Canada, China, France, Germany, Hong Kong, India, Ireland, Italy, Malaysia, Mexico, the Netherlands, New Zealand, the Philippines, Poland, Singapore, South Korea, Spain, Sweden, Switzerland, Taiwan, and the U.K. It discontinued its Web site in Japan in early 2002. Much of this expansion was achieved through acquisitions from 2001 to 2004.

CORPORATE STRATEGY. The company's stated goal is to become the world's most efficient and abundant marketplace, by expanding its community of users, delivering value to buyers and sellers, creating a global marketplace, and providing a faster, easier and safer trading experience. EBAY has increasingly employed acquisitions to fulfill the aforementioned goal, with a focus on international expansion and offering more choices and services to its buyers and sellers. In our view, PayPal was an extremely successful acquisition because it dramatically enhanced the user experience. Moreover, the combination accelerated the benefits the companies already derived from the Network Effect, in our opinion. However, we are skeptical as to whether the November 2005 purchase of Skype will yield comparable results. Nonetheless, we are growing increasingly optimistic on Skype's potential as a stand-alone business, and also see synergies with PayPal.

Company Financials

Per Share Data ($) Year Ended Dec. 31	**2005**	**2004**	**2003**	**2002**	**2001**	**2000**	**1999**	**1998**	**1997**	**1996**
Tangible Book Value	2.21	2.73	2.23	1.46	1.11	0.93	0.81	0.09	0.07	NA
Cash Flow	1.05	0.75	0.46	0.28	0.16	0.08	0.03	0.01	NA	NA
Earnings	0.78	0.57	0.34	0.21	0.08	0.04	0.01	Nil	Nil	NA
S&P Core Earnings	0.61	0.43	0.21	0.04	-0.00	NA	NA	NA	NA	NA
Dividends	Nil	Nil	Nil	Nil	Nil	Nil	Nil	Nil	NA	NA
Payout Ratio	Nil	Nil	Nil	Nil	Nil	NM	Nil	Nil	NA	NA
Prices:High	58.89	59.21	32.40	17.71	18.19	31.88	29.25	12.97	NA	NA
Prices:Low	30.78	31.30	16.88	12.21	7.11	6.69	6.92	0.75	NA	NA
P/E Ratio:High	75	NM	95	83	NM	NM	NM	NM	NA	NA
P/E Ratio:Low	39	NM	50	57	NM	NM	NM	NM	NA	NA
Income Statement Analysis (Million $)										
Revenue	4,552	3,271	2,165	1,214	749	431	225	47.4	5.76	NA
Operating Income	1,820	1,313	828	431	227	74.6	23.8	8.88	NA	NA
Depreciation	378	254	159	76.6	86.6	38.1	20.7	2.79	NA	NA
Interest Expense	3.48	8.88	4.31	1.49	2.85	3.37	1.94	0.04	Nil	NA
Pretax Income	1,549	1,128	662	398	163	78.0	20.5	7.03	-1.98	NA
Effective Tax Rate	30.2%	30.5%	31.3%	36.7%	49.1%	42.0%	45.8%	65.9%	NM	NA
Net Income	1,082	778	447	250	90.4	48.3	10.8	2.40	-1.91	NA
S&P Core Earnings	853	589	270	52.2	-4.04	NA	NA	NA	NA	NA
Balance Sheet & Other Financial Data (Million $)										
Cash	1,314	1,330	1,382	1,109	524	202	220	31.8	67.7	NA
Current Assets	3,183	2,911	2,146	1,468	884	675	460	83.4	NA	NA
Total Assets	11,789	7,991	5,820	4,124	1,679	1,182	964	92.5	76.8	NA
Current Liabilities	1,485	1,085	647	386	180	137	88.8	8.04	NA	NA
Long Term Debt	Nil	0.08	124	13.8	12.0	11.4	15.0	Nil	0.01	NA
Common Equity	10,048	6,728	4,896	3,556	1,429	1,014	852	84.4	71.1	NA
Total Capital	10,264	6,868	5,139	3,715	1,479	1,038	867	84.4	71.1	NA
Capital Expenditures	338	293	365	139	57.4	49.8	141	8.86	NA	NA
Cash Flow	1,460	1,032	606	326	177	86.3	31.5	5.19	NA	NA
Current Ratio	2.1	2.7	3.3	3.8	4.9	4.9	5.2	10.4	NA	NA
% Long Term Debt of Capitalization	Nil	NM	2.4	0.4	0.8	1.1	1.7	Nil	6.9	NA
% Net Income of Revenue	23.8	23.8	20.7	20.6	12.1	11.2	4.8	5.1	NM	NA
% Return on Assets	10.9	11.3	9.1	8.6	6.3	4.5	1.9	4.9	NM	NA
% Return on Equity	12.9	13.4	10.6	10.0	7.4	5.2	2.3	5.6	NM	NA

Data as orig reptd.; bef. results of disc opers/spec. items. Per share data adj. for stk. divs.; EPS diluted. E-Estimated. NA-Not Available. NM-Not Meaningful. NR-Not Ranked. UR-Under Review.

Office: 2145 Hamilton Ave, San Jose, CA 95125-5905.
Telephone: 408-376-7400.
Email: investor_relations@ebay.com
Website: http://www.ebay.com

Chrmn: P.M. Omidyar
Pres & CEO: M.C. Whitman
SVP & CFO: R.H. Swan
SVP, Secy & General Counsel: M.R. Jacobson

Board of Directors: F. D. Anderson, E. Barnholt, P. Bourguignon, S. D. Cook, W. C. Ford, Jr., R. C. Kagle, D. G. Lepore, P. M. Omidyar, R. T. Schlosberg, III, T. J. Tierney, M. C. Whitman

Founded: 1995
Domicile: Delaware
Employees: 12,600

STANDARD &POOR'S

Ecolab Inc.

S&P Recommendation HOLD ★★★★★

Price $45.29 (as of Oct 27, 2006)

12-Mo. Target Price $46.00

Investment Style Large-Cap Growth

GICS Sector Materials
Sub-Industry Specialty Chemicals

Comment This company is the leading worldwide marketer of cleaning, sanitizing and maintenance products and services for the hospitality, institutional and industrial markets.

Key Stock Statistics (Source S&P, Vickers, company reports)

52-Wk Range	$45.48–32.42	S&P Oper. EPS 2006E	1.42	P/E on S&P Oper. EPS 2006E	31.9	Dividend Rate/Share	$0.40
Trailing 12-Month EPS	$1.36	S&P Oper. EPS 2007E	1.62	Common Shares Outstg. (M)	251.6	Yield (%)	0.88
Trailing 12-Month P/E	33.3	S&P Core EPS 2006E	1.40	Market Capitalization(B)	$11.396	Beta	0.49
$10K Invested 5 Yrs Ago	$26,429	S&P Core EPS 2007E	1.60	Institutional Ownership (%)	54	S&P Credit Rating	A

Price Performance

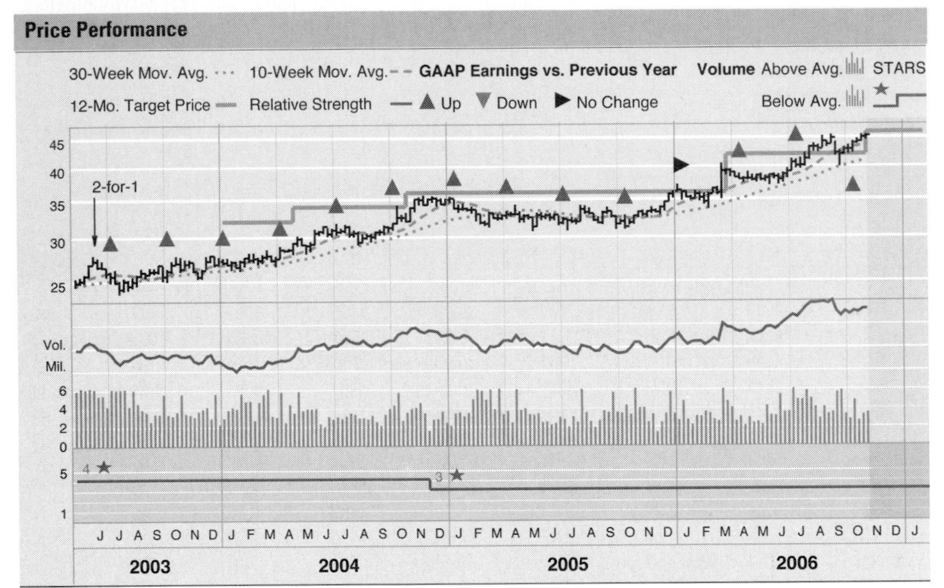

Options: ASE, P, Ph

Analysis prepared by **Richard O'Reilly, CFA** on October 27, 2006, when the stock traded at **$ 45.29**.

Highlights

- We expect sales to grow in 2007 at a similar rate as the 7% increase expected for 2006, which includes the adverse impact of slightly unfavorable currency rates. We see organic sales growth from existing businesses growing about the same rate as the 8% for 2006, aided by expected healthy conditions in key domestic markets, continued benefits from new products and customers, a projected price increase of 2%, and a 5% annual expansion in the salesforce for each of the past two years.
- We look for the domestic institutional, Kay, food & beverage, health care and pest elimination units to continue to grow. We also see growth for newer businesses such as vehicle care. We believe international sales will increase in most parts of the world, although Europe may continue to lag. Margins will likely remain unchanged for the rest of 2006 as selling price increases offset higher raw material costs. We expect the loss from the GCS kitchen repair unit to decline in the second half of 2007 following completion of investments to build the business.
- We assume an effective tax rate of about 35%. Our operating EPS estimate of $1.42 for 2006 includes projected stock option expense of $0.10.

Investment Rationale/Risk

- We expect ECL to post ongoing solid sales and EPS gains in coming periods, based on our belief that conditions will remain healthy in the global industries that it serves. However, we think that our overall positive views are already reflected in the shares.
- Risks to our recommendation and target price include unexpected slowdowns in the hospitality, travel and foodservice industries, an inability to continue to successfully introduce new products and services, and higher than expected raw material costs.
- The shares recently traded at about 31X our 2006 EPS forecast, a large premium to the S&P 500 and at the upper end of ECL's annual P/E multiple for the past decade. Although we believe that a steady grower such as ECL will be sought by investors as the economic recovery matures, we think it is near an appropriate valuation. Our 12-month target price is $46, which is 28X our 2007 EPS forecast and a P/E-to growth multiple of 1.9X the 15% EPS gains we see for the next few years.

Qualitative Risk Assessment

LOW | MEDIUM | HIGH

Our risk assessment reflects the company's leading share positions in its core businesses, the stable nature of end markets and customers, and our view of its strong balance sheet and cash generation. The stock's S&P Quality Ranking is A, the second highest possible, indicating a solid 10-year historical record of earnings and dividend growth.

Quantitative Evaluations

S&P Quality Ranking A

D | C | B- | B | B+ | A- | A | A+

Relative Strength Rank MODERATE

65

LOWEST = 1 HIGHEST = 99

Revenue/Earnings Data

Revenue (Million $)

	1Q	2Q	3Q	4Q	Year
2006	1,120	1,226	1,279	--	--
2005	1,070	1,159	1,165	1,142	4,535
2004	979.4	1,043	1,090	1,073	4,185
2003	875.9	946.7	982.8	956.5	3,762
2002	786.1	839.2	894.9	883.4	3,404
2001	580.9	595.8	616.2	561.8	2,355

Earnings Per Share ($)

	1Q	2Q	3Q	4Q	Year
2006	0.30	0.36	0.43	E0.33	E1.42
2005	0.27	0.31	0.38	0.27	1.23
2004	0.25	0.30	0.36	0.27	1.19
2003	0.21	0.25	0.33	0.26	1.06
2002	0.14	0.20	0.28	0.20	0.81
2001	0.17	0.19	0.23	0.15	0.73

Fiscal year ended Dec. 31. Next earnings report expected: Early February. EPS Estimates based on S&P Operating Earnings; historical GAAP earnings are as reported.

Dividend Data (Dates: mm/dd Payment Date: mm/dd/yy)

Amount ($)	Date Decl.	Ex-Div. Date	Stk. of Record	Payment Date
0.100	12/08	12/16	12/20	01/17/06
0.100	02/24	03/10	03/14	04/17/06
0.100	05/12	06/16	06/20	07/17/06
0.100	08/04	09/15	09/19	10/16/06

Dividends have been paid since 1936. Source: Company reports.

Please read the Required Disclosures and Analyst Certification on the last page of this report.

Ecolab Inc.

Business Summary October 27, 2006

CORPORATE OVERVIEW. Ecolab is a global supplier of cleaning, sanitizing, and maintenance products and services for hospitality, institutional, and industrial markets. In the U.S. cleaning and sanitizing business (43% of 2005 sales, 51% of profits), the institutional division (25% of 2005 total sales) is the leading provider of cleaners and sanitizers for warewashing, on-premise laundry, kitchen cleaning and general housekeeping, product dispensing equipment and dishwashing racks and related kitchen sundries to the foodservice, lodging and health care industries. It also provides pool and spa treatment products.

The Kay division (5%) is the largest supplier of cleaning and sanitizing products (surface cleaners, degreasers, sanitizers and hand care products) for the quick-service restaurant, convenience store and food retail markets. The Food and Beverage division (8%) offers cleaning and sanitizing products and services to farms, dairy plants, food and beverage processors, and pharmaceutical plants.

ECL also sells professional janitorial products (detergents, floor care, disinfectants, odor control; 1%) under the Airkem brand name; health care products (skin care, disinfectants and sterilants; 1%) under the Huntington name; textile care products (1%) for large institutional and commercial laundries; vehicle care products (soaps, polishes, wheel treatments) for rental, fleet and retail car washes (1%); and water treatment products (1%) to institutional, laundry and food and beverage, and processing markets for boilers, cooling and waste treatment systems.

Other U.S. services (8%, 7%) include institutional and commercial pest elimination and prevention services (5%) and GCS Services, a provider of commercial kitchen equipment repair and maintenance services (3%). ECL bought GCS Service in 1998, and has added to this business through small acquisitions; this business has had operating losses for the three years through 2005.

The International business (49%, 42%) provides services similar to those offered in the U.S. to Canada (3%) and about 70 countries in Europe (35%), Latin America (3%), the Asia/Pacific region (7%), and other (1%). The institutional and food & beverage businesses constitute a larger protion of the international business compared to the U.S.

Company Financials

Per Share Data ($) Year Ended Dec. 31	**2005**	**2004**	**2003**	**2002**	**2001**	**2000**	**1999**	**1998**	**1997**	**1996**
Tangible Book Value	2.00	1.33	1.14	0.83	0.41	1.77	1.98	1.76	1.30	1.63
Cash Flow	2.22	2.13	1.93	1.67	1.35	1.35	1.15	1.03	0.88	0.79
Earnings	1.23	1.19	1.06	0.81	0.73	0.79	0.66	0.58	0.50	0.44
S&P Core Earnings	1.24	1.10	0.98	0.64	0.61	NA	NA	NA	NA	NA
Dividends	0.36	0.33	0.30	0.28	0.26	0.25	0.21	0.19	0.17	0.15
Payout Ratio	29%	28%	28%	34%	36%	31%	32%	33%	34%	33%
Prices:High	37.15	35.59	27.92	25.20	22.09	22.84	22.22	19.00	14.00	9.88
Prices:Low	30.68	26.12	23.08	18.27	14.25	14.00	15.84	13.06	9.00	7.28
P/E Ratio:High	30	30	26	31	30	29	34	33	28	23
P/E Ratio:Low	25	22	22	23	20	18	24	23	18	17
Income Statement Analysis (Million $)										
Revenue	4,535	4,185	3,762	3,404	2,355	2,264	2,080	1,888	1,640	1,490
Operating Income	799	786	713	656	482	471	714	384	319	275
Depreciation	257	247	230	223	163	148	135	122	101	89.5
Interest Expense	49.8	45.3	45.3	43.9	28.4	24.6	22.7	25.0	12.6	14.4
Pretax Income	498	489	448	354	306	338	286	256	219	184
Effective Tax Rate	35.9%	36.5%	38.1%	39.6%	38.4%	38.3%	38.4%	39.7%	38.9%	38.5%
Net Income	319	310	277	214	188	209	176	155	134	113
S&P Core Earnings	322	283	260	167	157	NA	NA	NA	NA	NA
Balance Sheet & Other Financial Data (Million $)										
Cash	104	71.2	85.6	49.2	41.8	44.0	47.7	28.4	61.2	69.3
Current Assets	1,422	1,279	1,150	1,016	930	601	577	504	510	436
Total Assets	3,797	3,716	3,229	2,878	2,525	1,714	1,586	1,471	1,416	1,208
Current Liabilities	1,119	940	851	866	828	532	471	400	404	328
Long Term Debt	519	Nil	604	540	512	234	169	227	259	149
Common Equity	1,649	1,563	1,295	1,100	880	757	929	691	552	520
Total Capital	2,169	1,563	1,900	1,639	1,393	991	1,098	918	811	669
Capital Expenditures	269	276	212	213	158	150	146	148	122	112
Cash Flow	576	558	507	437	351	357	310	276	235	203
Current Ratio	1.3	1.4	1.4	1.2	1.1	1.1	1.2	1.3	1.3	1.3
% Long Term Debt of Capitalization	23.9	Nil	31.8	32.9	36.8	23.6	15.4	24.7	31.9	22.2
% Net Income of Revenue	7.0	7.4	7.4	6.3	8.0	9.2	8.5	8.2	8.2	7.6
% Return on Assets	8.5	8.9	9.1	7.9	8.9	12.6	11.5	10.7	10.2	10.0
% Return on Equity	19.7	21.7	23.2	21.6	23.0	27.5	18.9	24.9	25.0	23.2

Data as orig reptd.; bef. results of disc opers/spec. items. Per share data adj. for stk. divs.; EPS diluted. E-Estimated. NA-Not Available. NM-Not Meaningful. NR-Not Ranked. UR-Under Review.

Office: 370 North Wabasha Street, Saint Paul, MN 55102-1390.
Telephone: 651-293-2233.
Email: investor.info@ecolab.com
Website: http://www.ecolab.com

Chrmn, Pres & CEO: D.M. Baker
EVP & CFO: S.L. Fritze
SVP, Secy & General Counsel: L.T. Bell
SVP & Cntlr: D.J. Schmechel

VP & CIO: R.P. Tabb
Investor Contact: M.J. Monahan (651-293-2809)
Board of Directors: D. M. Baker, Jr., L. S. Biller, R. U. De Schutter, J. A. Grundhofer, S. Hamelmann, J. W. Johnson, U. Lehner, J. W. Levin, R. L. Lumpkins, B. M. Pritchard, K. Rorsted, J. J. Zillmer

Founded: 1924
Domicile: Delaware
Employees: 21,338

Edison International

STANDARD &POOR'S

S&P Recommendation BUY ★★★★★

Price $44.12 (as of Oct 27, 2006)

12-Mo. Target Price $49.00

Investment Style Large-Cap Growth

GICS Sector Utilities
Sub-Industry Electric Utilities

Comment EIX is the holding company for Southern California Edison. Other businesses include electric power generation, financial investments, and real estate development.

Key Stock Statistics (Source S&P, Vickers, company reports)

52-Wk Range	$47.30–37.90	S&P Oper. EPS 2006E	3.00	P/E on S&P Oper. EPS 2006E	14.7	Dividend Rate/Share	$1.08
Trailing 12-Month EPS	$3.53	S&P Oper. EPS 2007E	3.35	Common Shares Outstg. (M)	325.8	Yield (%)	2.45
Trailing 12-Month P/E	12.5	S&P Core EPS 2006E	2.92	Market Capitalization(B)	$14.375	Beta	0.81
$10K Invested 5 Yrs Ago	$32,004	S&P Core EPS 2007E	3.28	Institutional Ownership (%)	71	S&P Credit Rating	BBB-

Price Performance

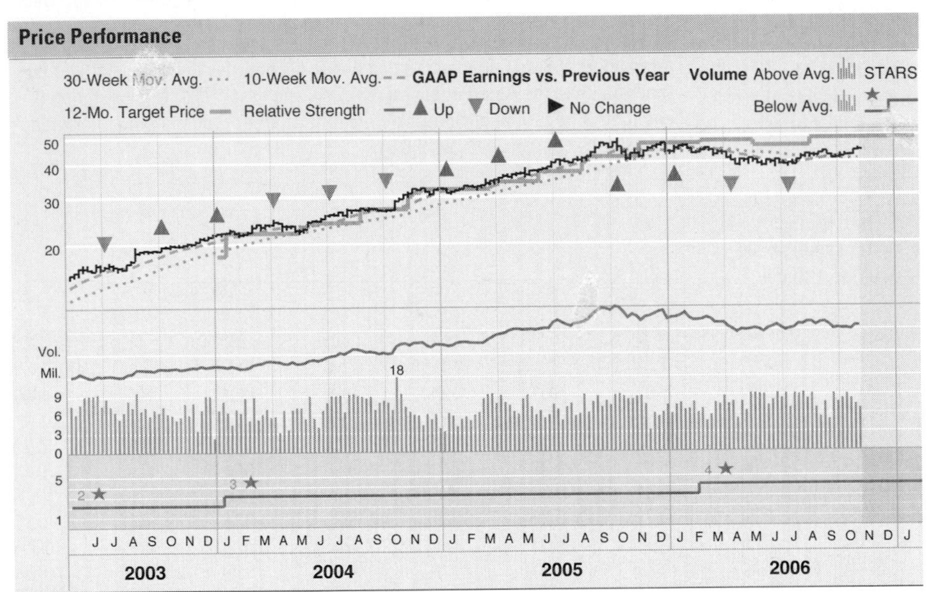

Options: ASE, CBOE, P

Analysis prepared by **Justin McCann** on August 11, 2006, when the stock traded at **$ 42.23**.

Highlights

- We expect operating EPS in 2006 to decline about 4% from 2005's operating EPS of $3.13. Operating EPS of $1.10 in the first half of 2006 was down $0.09 from the year-earlier level, as higher operating expenses and income tax outweighed the benefit of rate increases for Southern California Edison (SCE) and higher wholesale margins, net interest income, and energy trading income at Edison Mission Energy.

- We do not expect EIX's earnings in 2006 to reflect the level of transmission-related congestion and energy price volatility that significantly benefited its energy marketing and trading operations in 2005. While we expect EIX to continue to benefit from the spread between high wholesale energy prices and its low-cost 7,500 megawatt coal-fired production, we do not expect energy prices to have the exceptionally high level of volatility seen in 2005.

- On January 26, 2006, the California Public Utilities Commission (CPUC) granted SCE a 5.5% annual rate increase due to the sharp rise in natural gas prices. The increase, which became effective on February 4, brought to 15.2% the rate hikes the CPUC granted SCE for 2006.

Investment Rationale/Risk

- After significantly outperforming the S&P Index of Electric Utilities in 2005 (up 36%), the stock has retreated about 2% year to date through early August. Given the decline, we believe the stock has become increasingly attractive for its total return potential. With earnings expected to benefit from the rate increases granted to Southern California Edison and higher wholesale power margins, we believe the shares are undervalued at their recent discount-to-peers P/E of 14.2X our EPS estimate for 2006.

- Risks to our opinion and target price include the potential for unfavorable regulatory or legislative acts that could strain the company's recovered financial and credit strength, and a significant market-related change in the P/E of the electric utility group as a whole.

- Given our favorable outlook for Southern California Edison and Edison Mission Energy, we expect the stock to trade near a peer P/E of about 14.6X our EPS estimate for 2007. After the recent increase in peer valuations, we believe the stock, despite its below-peer dividend yield (recently 2.5%), has above-peer total return potential over the next 12 months. Our 12-month target price is $49.

Qualitative Risk Assessment

LOW	MEDIUM	HIGH

Our risk assessment reflects our view of the strong and steady earnings and cash flows expected from the regulated Southern California Edison utility, with its large and rapidly growing service territory and a generally supportive regulatory environment.

Quantitative Evaluations

S&P Quality Ranking B

D	C	B-	B	B+	A-	A	A+

Relative Strength Rank MODERATE

62

LOWEST = 1 HIGHEST = 99

Revenue/Earnings Data

Revenue (Million $)

	1Q	2Q	3Q	4Q	Year
2006	2,751	3,001	--	--	--
2005	2,446	2,649	3,783	2,975	11,852
2004	2,116	2,565	3,188	2,327	10,199
2003	2,523	3,125	3,833	2,654	12,135
2002	2,488	2,824	3,707	2,469	11,488
2001	2,196	2,446	3,882	2,912	11,436

Earnings Per Share ($)

	1Q	2Q	3Q	4Q	Year
2006	0.56	0.53	E1.29	E0.61	E3.00
2005	0.59	0.55	1.31	0.90	3.34
2004	0.16	-1.21	0.95	0.78	0.68
2003	0.19	0.07	1.52	0.59	2.37
2002	0.24	1.99	1.05	0.17	3.46
2001	-1.93	0.18	6.66	6.66	7.36

Fiscal year ended Dec. 31. Next earnings report expected: Early November. EPS Estimates based on S&P Operating Earnings; historical GAAP earnings are as reported.

Dividend Data (Dates: mm/dd Payment Date: mm/dd/yy)

Amount ($)	Date Decl.	Ex-Div. Date	Stk. of Record	Payment Date
0.270	12/15	12/28	12/30	01/31/06
0.270	03/01	03/29	03/31	04/30/06
0.270	04/27	06/28	06/30	07/31/06
0.270	09/07	09/27	09/29	10/31/06

Dividends have been paid since 2004. Source: Company reports.

Edison International

Business Summary August 11, 2006

CORPORATE OVERVIEW. Edison International (EIX) is the holding company of the regulated Southern California Edison (SCE) utility and several non-regulated subsidiaries. The principal non-utility companies are Edison Mission Energy (EME), an independent power producer that also conducts price risk management and energy trading activities, and Edison Capital, which holds equity investments in energy and infrastructure projects. In 2005, SCE accounted for 80% of EIX's consolidated revenues, the non-utility power generation business accounted for 19%, and investments and other operations 1%. The utility's retail operations are regulated by the purview of the California Public Utilities Commission (CPUC), while its wholesale operations fall under the oversight of the Federal Energy Regulatory Commission (FERC).

CORPORATE STRATEGY. In 2005, EIX's strategic plan established a balanced approach for growth, dividends and balance sheet strength. To implement this strategy, the company initiated efforts to reduce administration expenses in the non-utility companies and a multi-year productivity effort at the utility. EIX has taken steps to rebalance its capital structure so as to further reduce debt, and has worked to enhance liquidity through strong cash flow generation. SCE is working on new projects that will expand its transmission and distribution systems and intends to implement a comprehensive software system to support the majority of its critical business processes. We also expect to see EIX further strengthen the independent power business, expand investment in renewable energy, and evaluate prospects for growth in the non-utility sector.

Company Financials

Per Share Data ($) Year Ended Dec. 31	**2005**	**2004**	**2003**	**2002**	**2001**	**2000**	**1999**	**1998**	**1997**	**1996**
Tangible Book Value	20.30	18.56	13.86	11.59	8.10	7.43	14.03	13.55	13.75	14.25
Earnings	3.34	0.68	2.37	3.46	7.36	-5.84	1.79	1.84	1.73	1.64
S&P Core Earnings	3.35	0.60	2.45	2.81	6.78	NA	NA	NA	NA	NA
Dividends	1.02	1.05	Nil	Nil	Nil	1.11	1.07	1.04	1.00	1.25
Payout Ratio	31%	154%	Nil	Nil	Nil	NM	60%	56%	58%	76%
Prices:High	49.16	32.52	22.07	19.60	16.12	30.00	29.63	31.00	27.81	20.38
Prices:Low	30.43	21.24	10.57	7.80	6.25	14.13	21.63	25.13	19.38	15.00
P/E Ratio:High	15	48	9	6	2	NM	17	17	16	12
P/E Ratio:Low	9	31	4	2	1	NM	12	14	11	9

Income Statement Analysis (Million $)										
Revenue	11,852	10,199	12,135	11,488	11,436	11,717	9,670	10,208	9,235	8,545
Depreciation	1,061	1,022	1,184	1,030	973	1,933	1,794	1,662	1,362	1,173
Maintenance	NA	NA	NA	NA	NA	NA	NA	411	406	331
Fixed Charges Coverage	3.28	2.20	1.73	1.81	3.38	-0.90	1.90	1.71	2.27	3.20
Construction Credits	NA	NA	NA	NA	NA	NA	Nil	12.0	17.0	26.0
Effective Tax Rate	26.4%	NM	21.5%	25.6%	40.7%	NM	32.0%	40.4%	40.3%	44.0%
Net Income	1,108	226	779	1,135	2,402	-1,943	623	668	700	717
S&P Core Earnings	1,111	199	808	921	2,211	NA	NA	NA	NA	NA

Balance Sheet & Other Financial Data (Million $)										
Gross Property	24,775	23,214	24,674	23,264	22,396	25,737	27,203	17,223	24,661	21,134
Capital Expenditures	1,868	1,733	1,288	1,590	933	1,488	1,231	963	783	744
Net Property	18,588	17,397	20,288	15,170	14,427	17,903	19,683	10,326	14,117	11,703
Capitalization:Long Term Debt	9,552	9,807	12,221	12,915	14,007	13,660	15,050	8,543	8,871	7,475
Capitalization:% Long Term Debt	59.1	61.3	69.4	74.4	81.1	85.0	74.3	62.6	59.1	51.3
Capitalization:Preferred	Nil	Nil	9.00	Nil	Nil	Nil	Nil	Nil	609	709
Capitalization:% Preferred	Nil	Nil	0.05	Nil	Nil	Nil	Nil	Nil	4.05	4.80
Capitalization:Common	6,615	6,049	5,383	4,437	3,272	2,420	5,211	5,099	5,527	6,397
Capitalization:% Common	40.9	37.8	30.6	25.6	18.9	15.0	25.7	37.4	36.8	43.9
Total Capital	21,854	21,688	24,246	23,786	24,163	21,609	26,252	18,520	19,452	19,943
% Operating Ratio	80.7	80.6	75.2	82.8	93.2	86.4	92.9	96.9	87.8	82.7
% Earned on Net Property	6.9	6.6	9.1	16.0	36.9	NM	11.6	6.4	10.2	12.4
% Return on Revenue	9.3	2.2	6.4	9.9	21.0	NM	6.4	6.5	7.6	8.4
% Return on Invested Capital	12.2	10.4	14.9	10.9	4.8	7.8	3.6	7.9	10.5	7.1
% Return on Common Equity	17.1	3.8	15.9	29.4	84.4	NM	12.1	12.6	11.7	11.2

Data as orig reptd.; bef. results of disc opers/spec. items. Per share data adj. for stk. divs.; EPS diluted. E-Estimated. NA-Not Available. NM-Not Meaningful. NR-Not Ranked. UR-Under Review.

Office: 2244 Walnut Grove Avenue, Rosemead, CA 91770-3714.
Telephone: 877-379-9515.
Website: http://www.edison.com
Chrmn, Pres & CEO: J.E. Bryson

Investor Contact: T.R. McDaniel (877-379-9515)
EVP, CFO & Treas: T.R. McDaniel
EVP & General Counsel: J.A. Bouknight, Jr.
VP & Cntlr: L.G. Sullivan

Board of Directors: J. E. Bryson, F. A. Cordova, C. B. Curtis, B. M. Freeman, B. Karatz, L. G. Nogales, R. L. Olson, J. M. Rosser, R. T. Schlosberg, III, R. H. Smith, T. C. Sutton

Founded: 1886
Domicile: California
Employees: 15,838

STANDARD & POOR'S

Electronic Arts Inc

S&P Recommendation HOLD ★★★★★

Price $54.51 (as of Oct 27, 2006)

12-Mo. Target Price $54.00

Investment Style Large-Cap Growth

GICS Sector Information Technology
Sub-Industry Home Entertainment Software

Comment This California-based company produces entertainment software for PCs, home video game consoles, and mobile gaming devices.

Key Stock Statistics (Source S&P, Vickers, company reports)

52-Wk Range	$61.97–39.99	S&P Oper. EPS 2007E	0.13	P/E on S&P Oper. EPS 2007E	NM	Dividend Rate/Share	Nil
Trailing 12-Month EPS	$0.68	S&P Oper. EPS 2008E	1.13	Common Shares Outstg. (M)	306.7	Yield (%)	Nil
Trailing 12-Month P/E	80.2	S&P Core EPS 2007E	0.11	Market Capitalization(B)	$16.716	Beta	1.18
$10K Invested 5 Yrs Ago	$19,978	S&P Core EPS 2008E	1.10	Institutional Ownership (%)	96	S&P Credit Rating	NA

Price Performance

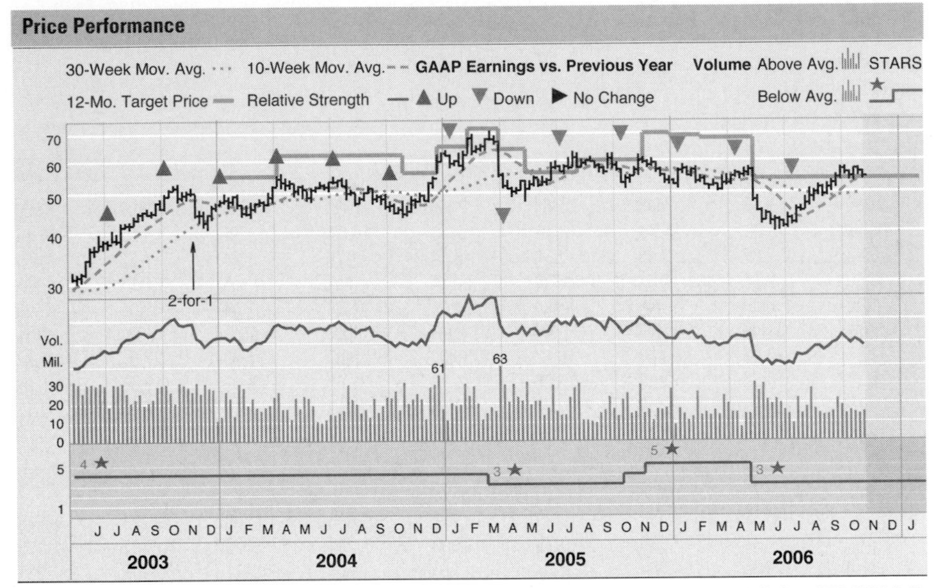

Options: ASE, CBOE, P, Ph

Analysis prepared by **Clyde Montevirgen** on August 23, 2006, when the stock traded at **$ 49.76**.

Highlights

- We see a moderate revenue increase of 2.1% in FY 07 (Mar.), following a 7.0% decline in FY 06. We believe sales are likely to be negatively impacted by our view of a limited installed base for Microsoft's X-Box 360 and with consumers postponing purchases until the release of other next-generation consoles. However, as the transition to next generation consoles proceeds, we expect game sales to accelerate, providing a 10% revenue increase in FY 08.
- We see a negative operating margin in FY 07, compared to an 11% margin in FY 06, as ERTS expenses stock options and increases product development spending in preparation for the next generation of hardware consoles; this expense hits ERTS more quickly than its peers as it expenses, rather than capitalizes, the majority of its development costs. However, we see operating margins of nearly 15% in FY 08 as increased sales levels should provide leverage.
- We are projecting operating EPS of $0.13 and $1.13 in FY 07 and FY 08, including $0.31 of projected stock option expense in each year, respectively.

Investment Rationale/Risk

- We have a hold opinion based on increased uncertainty and our less optimistic outlook for video game sales associated with the growth rate for next-generation consoles. We think the combination of a possible economic slowdown and the relatively high price for PlayStation 3 will hinder total installed base growth, causing possible delays in game releases and slowing revenue growth. However, we believe the company's industry position remains attractive with its library of hit titles. Moreover, ERTS has a strong balance sheet, in our view, with nearly $2.4 billion in cash and short-term investments ($7.83 per share), and no debt.
- Risks to our recommendation and target price include a sharper-than-expected slowdown in the video game industry as the next generation hardware cycle begins to ramp up, pricing pressure for certain titles, and a potential slowdown in consumer spending.
- Our discounted cash flow analysis assumes a WACC of 11.6% and terminal growth of 3%, and shows intrinsic value of $65. Blending with a P/E to growth ratio of 3.1X our FY 07 operating estimate, our 12-month target price is $54.

Qualitative Risk Assessment

LOW | **MEDIUM** | HIGH

Our risk assessment takes into account the volatile nature of the home entertainment software industry and the company's focus on the consumer market. Offsetting these characteristics, in our view, is ERTS's leading market share position and advantageous financial structure.

Quantitative Evaluations

S&P Quality Ranking **B+**

D | C | B- | B | **B+** | A- | A | A+

Relative Strength Rank **MODERATE**

53

LOWEST = 1 HIGHEST = 99

Revenue/Earnings Data

Revenue (Million $)

	1Q	2Q	3Q	4Q	Year
2007	413.0	--	--	--	--
2006	365.0	675.0	1,270	641.0	2,951
2005	431.6	715.7	1,428	553.0	3,129
2004	353.4	530.0	1,475	598.4	2,957
2003	331.9	453.5	1,234	463.1	2,482
2002	182.0	240.2	832.9	469.7	1,725

Earnings Per Share ($)

2007	-0.26	E-0.10	E0.38	E0.05	E0.13
2006	-0.19	0.16	0.83	-0.05	0.75
2005	0.08	0.31	1.18	0.02	1.59
2004	0.06	0.25	1.26	0.29	1.87
2003	0.03	0.17	0.85	0.03	1.09
2002	-0.17	-0.12	0.46	0.17	0.36

Fiscal year ended Mar. 31. Next earnings report expected: Early November. EPS Estimates based on S&P Operating Earnings; historical GAAP earnings are as reported.

Dividend Data

No cash dividends have been paid.

The McGraw-Hill Companies

Electronic Arts Inc

Business Summary August 23, 2006

CORPORATE OVERVIEW. Electronic Arts is of the primary third-party video game publishers, earning close to $3.0 billion in revenue in FY 06 (Mar.). ERTS owns many of today's most popular video game franchises, including Madden NFL, The Sims, and Need for Speed, and publishes games under three primary brands: EA Sports, EA, EA Sports BIG and Pogo, which publishes online and downloadable casual games. The company also co-publishes with outside developers under its EA Partners unit and distributes games for other developers; these activities generated 7% of FY 06 revenues.

CORPORATE STRATEGY. We believe that one of ERTS's main advantages is its ability to publish titles across all major platforms, including consoles (61% of FY 06 revenues), PCs (14%), and handheld gaming devices (14%). Within the console segment, ERTS's revenues are spread among the PlayStation 2 (38%), X-Box (13%), X-Box 360 (5%) and GameCube (5%), which we believe reduces the risk ERTS faces that sales of any particular console will languish. We believe ERTS further diversified its revenue base with the February 2006 acquisition of cellular phone game developer JAMDAT Mobile. We believe that ERTS attempts to maintain diversity among genres and individual titles. During FY 06, ERTS published 31 titles, representing 131 SKUs, compared to 35 titles and 109 SKUs in FY 05; 27 titles sold over one million units in FY 06 compared to 31 in FY 05. During FY 06, the company had one title, Need For Speed Most Wanted, which accounted for 10% of total revenue. ERTS has also secured several exclusive licenses, including those for the NFL, ESPN, NCAA football, NASCAR, Tiger Woods, and the PGA, which we believe will enable it to attain higher market shares in certain genres, offsetting the increased cost for exclusivity.

Company Financials

Per Share Data ($) Year Ended Mar. 31	**2006**	**2005**	**2004**	**2003**	**2002**	**2001**	**2000**	**1999**	**1998**	**1997**
Tangible Book Value	8.29	10.66	8.52	11.62	3.92	3.33	2.86	2.38	2.34	1.80
Cash Flow	1.05	1.82	2.12	2.79	0.74	0.22	0.62	0.47	0.41	0.34
Earnings	0.75	1.59	1.87	1.09	0.36	-0.04	0.44	0.29	0.30	0.24
S&P Core Earnings	0.49	1.35	1.59	0.82	0.10	-0.25	NA	NA	NA	NA
Dividends	Nil	Nil	Nil	Nil	Nil	Nil	Nil	Nil	Nil	Nil
Payout Ratio	Nil	Nil	Nil	Nil	Nil	Nil	Nil	Nil	Nil	Nil
Calendar Year	2005	2004	2003	2002	2001	2000	1999	1998	1997	1996
Prices:High	71.16	63.71	52.89	36.22	33.46	28.97	31.11	14.28	10.06	9.97
Prices:Low	47.45	43.38	23.76	24.74	17.25	12.25	9.50	8.31	4.81	5.28
P/E Ratio:High	95	40	28	33	94	NM	71	50	34	42
P/E Ratio:Low	63	27	13	23	49	NM	22	29	16	22
Income Statement Analysis (Million $)										
Revenue	2,951	3,129	2,957	2,482	1,725	1,322	1,420	1,222	909	625
Operating Income	454	759	863	629	267	42.1	207	190	123	88.8
Depreciation	95.0	75.0	77.5	91.6	111	69.7	46.7	40.4	26.9	21.5
Interest Expense	Nil	Nil	Nil	Nil	Nil	Nil	Nil	Nil	Nil	0.01
Pretax Income	389	725	797	461	148	-13.4	170	118	108	79.0
Effective Tax Rate	37.8%	30.5%	27.5%	30.9%	31.0%	NM	30.9%	38.3%	33.0%	34.5%
Net Income	236	504	577	317	102	-11.1	117	72.9	72.6	53.0
S&P Core Earnings	153	425	482	239	28.0	-68.2	NA	NA	NA	NA
Balance Sheet & Other Financial Data (Million $)										
Cash	1,402	1,410	2,151	951	804	477	340	318	378	236
Current Assets	3,012	3,706	2,911	1,911	1,153	819	705	569	590	369
Total Assets	4,386	4,370	3,401	2,360	1,699	1,379	1,192	902	746	517
Current Liabilities	869	828	722	571	453	340	265	236	182	127
Long Term Debt	Nil	Nil	Nil	Nil	Nil	Nil	Nil	Nil	Nil	Nil
Common Equity	3,408	3,498	2,678	1,785	1,243	1,034	923	663	564	389
Total Capital	3,449	3,509	2,678	1,789	1,246	1,039	927	666	564	389
Capital Expenditures	123	126	89.6	59.1	51.5	120	135	116	45.2	36.2
Cash Flow	331	579	655	409	212	58.6	163	119	99.5	74.5
Current Ratio	3.5	4.5	4.0	3.3	2.5	2.4	2.7	2.4	3.2	2.9
% Long Term Debt of Capitalization	Nil	Nil	Nil	Nil	Nil	Nil	Nil	Nil	Nil	Nil
% Net Income of Revenue	8.0	16.1	19.5	12.8	5.9	NM	8.2	6.0	8.0	8.5
% Return on Assets	5.4	12.9	20.0	15.6	6.6	NM	11.2	8.8	11.5	11.3
% Return on Equity	6.8	16.3	25.9	20.9	8.9	NM	14.7	11.9	15.2	14.9

Data as orig reptd.; bef. results of disc opers/spec. items. Per share data adj. for stk. divs.; EPS diluted. E-Estimated. NA-Not Available. NM-Not Meaningful. NR-Not Ranked. UR-Under Review.

Office: 209 Redwood Shores Parkway, Redwood City, CA 94065-1175.
Telephone: 650-628-1500.
Email: investorrelations@ea.com
Website: http://www.ea.com

Chrmn & CEO: L.F. Probst III
Pres: V.P. Lee
EVP, CFO & Chief Admin: W.C. Jenson
SVP & Chief Acctg Officer: K.A. Barker

SVP, Secy & General Counsel: S.G. Bene
Investor Contact: T. Gugler (650-628-7327)
Board of Directors: M. R. Asher, L. S. Coleman, G. M. Kusin, G. B. Maffei, T. Mott, V. Paul, L. F. Probst III, R. A. Simonson, L. J. Srere

Founded: 1982
Domicile: Delaware
Employees: 7,200

STANDARD &POOR'S

Electronic Data Systems Corp

S&P Recommendation BUY ★★★★★

Price $24.83 (as of Oct 27, 2006)

12-Mo. Target Price $28.00

Investment Style Large-Cap Value

GICS Sector Information Technology
Sub-Industry Data Processing & Outsourced Services

Comment This Texas-based company, which was split off from GM in 1996, is a leading provider of a full range of information technology (IT) services.

Key Stock Statistics (Source S&P, Vickers, company reports)

52-Wk Range	**$28.09–22.42**	S&P Oper. EPS 2006**E**	**0.83**	P/E on S&P Oper. EPS 2006**E**	**29.9**	Dividend Rate/Share	**$0.20**
Trailing 12-Month EPS	**$0.46**	S&P Oper. EPS 2007**E**	**1.37**	Common Shares Outstg. (M)	**517.6**	Yield (%)	**0.81**
Trailing 12-Month P/E	**54.0**	S&P Core EPS 2006**E**	**0.83**	Market Capitalization(B)	**$12.852**	Beta	**1.96**
$10K Invested 5 Yrs Ago	**$4,224**	S&P Core EPS 2007**E**	**1.37**	Institutional Ownership (%)	**90**	S&P Credit Rating	**BBB-**

Price Performance

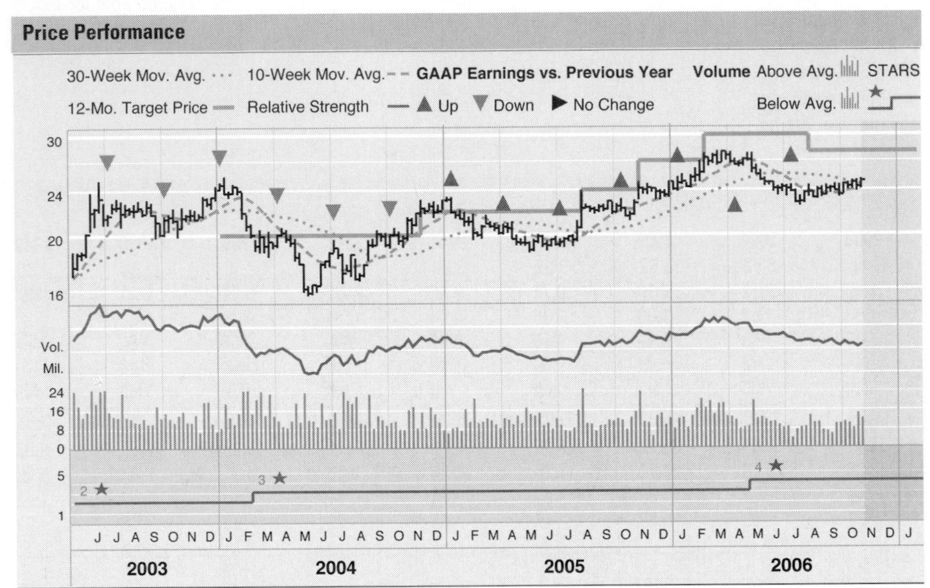

Options: ASE, CBOE, P, Ph

Analysis prepared by **Dylan Cathers** on August 08, 2006, when the stock traded at **$ 23.60.**

Highlights

- We expect revenues to rise 5% in 2006, in contrast with a 2% decline in 2005. We believe that the company's backlog of opportunities is strong, bolstered by the recent GM contract award. In our opinion, the GM contract, along with further expected Medicaid wins, growth of the U.K. Ministry of Defense contract, the extension of the Navy deal, and increased traction in the business process outsourcing segment should help revenues increase by nearly 3% in 2007.

- We see operating margins widening to the mid-single digits by the end of 2006, due to benefits resulting from restructuring efforts and a slowdown in investment spending, despite the inclusion of stock option expense. We expect the company to continue to invest heavily in automation and standardization in the IT Outsourcing segment and in business process outsourcing. Also aiding margins will likely be improvements in the profitability of EDS's Navy contract.

- We forecast 2006 and 2007 EPS of $0.83 and $1.37, respectively. Our estimates reflect the expensing of stock options.

Investment Rationale/Risk

- We see efforts by the company to refocus its business strategy, increase liquidity, and focus on productivity as finally being successful. Nonetheless, we still think EDS faces challenges in the coming months as it seeks to deal with poorly performing contracts, addresses intensifying competition, and increases investment spending.

- Risks to our recommendation and target price include accelerating competition in the outsourcing market, which could cause pricing pressures and negatively affect profit margins. Other risks include increased expenses related to early-stage contract start-up costs, higher commission expenses from a larger sales force, and risks associated with the ramp-up of EDS's global delivery platform.

- Our 12-month target price of $28 is based on a P/E-to-growth (PEG) ratio of 0.9X our 2006 EPS estimate. Our discounted cash flow analysis, which assumes a weighted average cost of capital of 11%, an average annual compound growth rate of 13% over the next five years, and an expected terminal growth rate of 3%, yields an intrinsic value of $28.

Qualitative Risk Assessment

LOW | MEDIUM | **HIGH**

Our risk assessment reflects our view of the difficulties surrounding some of EDS's megadeals and in implementing a global sourcing model, and the intense competition in the IT services and outsourcing industry.

Quantitative Evaluations

S&P Quality Ranking **B**

D | C | B- | **B** | B+ | A- | A | A+

Relative Strength Rank **MODERATE**

52

LOWEST = 1 HIGHEST = 99

Revenue/Earnings Data

Revenue (Million $)

	1Q	2Q	3Q	4Q	Year
2006	5,078	5,194	--	--	--
2005	4,737	5,000	4,874	5,146	19,757
2004	5,196	5,235	4,943	5,295	20,669
2003	5,221	5,273	5,220	5,762	21,476
2002	5,266	5,395	5,334	5,507	21,502
2001	4,987	5,091	5,559	5,906	21,543

Earnings Per Share ($)

2006	0.06	0.21	**E**0.21	**E**0.37	**E**0.83
2005	0.03	0.06	0.22	0.24	0.54
2004	-0.07	-0.27	-0.33	0.08	-0.59
2003	0.01	0.19	Nil	-0.73	-0.53
2002	0.70	0.63	0.21	0.52	2.06
2001	0.98	0.62	0.44	0.82	2.86

Fiscal year ended Dec. 31. Next earnings report expected: Early November. EPS Estimates based on S&P Operating Earnings; historical GAAP earnings are as reported.

Dividend Data (Dates: mm/dd Payment Date: mm/dd/yy)

Amount ($)	Date Decl.	Ex-Div. Date	Stk. of Record	Payment Date
0.050	02/07	02/15	02/20	03/10/06
0.050	04/18	05/11	05/15	06/09/06
0.050	07/18	08/11	08/15	09/11/06
0.050	10/18	11/13	11/15	12/11/06

Dividends have been paid since 1984. Source: Company reports.

Electronic Data Systems Corp

Business Summary August 08, 2006

CORPORATE OVERVIEW. Electronic Data Systems is a leading provider of professional information technology (IT) services. The company was purchased by General Motors in 1984, and was a wholly owned subsidiary of the auto manufacturer until 1996, when GM spun it off.

EDS has three main segments. Infrastructure Services is the company's largest division, accounting for over half of EDS's revenues. It delivers hosting, workplace, store security and privacy and communications services to customers in an attempt to decrease costs and increase productivity. Applications Services assists its clients in planning, developing, and integrating and managing custom applications, packaged software and industry-specific solutions. The Business Process Outsourcing segment allows companies to outsource entire non-core segments of their business, such as human resources, finance and accounting, and supply-chain management

PRIMARY BUSINESS DYNAMICS. One of the prominent features of EDS's business model is its dependence on large contracts, in our opinion. For example, in October 2000, EDS was awarded a contract by the U.S. Navy and Marine Corps to provide end-to-end IT infrastructure on a seat management basis. The contract had a base period of five years, extended in October 2002 to seven years, with a minimum aggregate order obligation of $6 billion. Since its inception, the contract has been problematic for EDS, in our view, as it took charges against long-term assets and recorded losses. In 2005, the company recorded revenues of $817 million, but booked an operating loss of $75 million. The deal, which was recently extended to 2010, has shown some signs of improvement for EDS, in our opinion, as it was cash flow positive last year. The company expects free cash flow to be about $2.4 billion between 2005 and 2010.

Another large contract of EDS's is with General Motors, its former parent company, which accounted for about 9% of total revenues in 2005. In February 2006, GM announced about half of its $15 billion worth of five-year contracts with IT outsourcers. EDS accounted for the majority of the awards, but with slightly less than under its previous contracts.

Company Financials

Per Share Data ($) Year Ended Dec. 31	**2005**	**2004**	**2003**	**2002**	**2001**	**2000**	**1999**	**1998**	**1997**	**1996**
Tangible Book Value	5.62	5.58	NM	3.22	3.05	4.53	6.04	11.06	8.15	7.54
Cash Flow	3.33	3.25	4.73	5.01	5.93	5.40	3.73	4.31	3.95	3.32
Earnings	0.54	-0.59	-0.53	2.06	2.86	2.40	0.85	1.50	1.48	0.89
S&P Core Earnings	0.52	-0.93	-0.97	1.16	1.64	NA	NA	NA	NA	NA
Dividends	0.20	0.40	0.60	0.60	0.60	0.60	0.60	0.60	0.60	0.60
Payout Ratio	37%	NM	NM	29%	21%	25%	71%	40%	41%	67%
Prices:High	24.82	25.44	25.03	68.55	72.45	76.69	70.00	51.31	49.63	63.38
Prices:Low	18.60	16.62	10.05	10.09	50.90	38.38	44.13	30.44	25.50	40.75
P/E Ratio:High	46	NM	NM	33	25	32	82	34	34	71
P/E Ratio:Low	34	NM	NM	5	18	16	52	20	17	46
Income Statement Analysis (Million $)										
Revenue	19,757	20,669	21,476	21,502	21,543	19,227	18,534	16,891	15,236	14,441
Operating Income	1,972	2,040	2,601	3,312	3,707	3,252	1,909	2,509	2,753	2,767
Depreciation	1,456	1,974	2,529	1,443	1,482	1,431	1,436	1,394	1,210	1,181
Interest Expense	241	321	266	258	247	210	150	131	176	153
Pretax Income	439	-388	-389	1,525	2,199	1,800	658	1,133	1,142	674
Effective Tax Rate	34.9%	NM	NM	34.0%	36.9%	36.5%	36.0%	34.4%	36.0%	36.0%
Net Income	286	-295	-252	1,007	1,387	1,143	421	743	731	432
S&P Core Earnings	275	-464	-461	560	795	NA	NA	NA	NA	NA
Balance Sheet & Other Financial Data (Million $)										
Cash	3,220	3,592	2,313	1,890	839	693	729	1,312	677	963
Current Assets	8,502	8,479	6,823	9,385	7,374	6,167	5,878	5,633	5,169	5,008
Total Assets	17,087	17,744	18,280	18,880	16,353	12,700	12,522	11,526	11,174	11,174
Current Liabilities	5,048	5,256	7,473	6,129	4,367	4,318	4,996	3,657	3,258	3,163
Long Term Debt	2,939	3,168	3,488	4,148	4,692	2,586	2,391	1,184	1,791	2,324
Common Equity	7,512	7,440	5,714	7,022	6,446	5,139	4,535	5,917	5,310	4,783
Total Capital	10,866	10,608	9,686	11,221	11,986	8,382	7,194	7,869	7,575	8,030
Capital Expenditures	718	666	703	973	1,285	768	685	870	769	1,158
Cash Flow	1,742	1,679	2,277	2,450	2,869	2,575	1,857	2,137	1,941	1,613
Current Ratio	1.7	1.6	0.9	1.5	1.7	1.4	1.2	1.5	1.6	1.6
% Long Term Debt of Capitalization	27.0	29.9	36.0	37.0	39.1	30.8	33.2	15.0	23.6	28.9
% Net Income of Revenue	1.4	NM	NM	4.7	6.4	5.9	2.3	4.4	4.8	3.0
% Return on Assets	1.6	NM	NM	5.7	9.6	9.1	3.5	6.5	6.5	3.9
% Return on Equity	3.8	NM	NM	15.0	23.9	23.6	8.1	13.2	14.5	8.9

Data as orig reptd.; bef. results of disc opers/spec. items. Per share data adj. for stk. divs.; EPS diluted. E-Estimated. NA-Not Available. NM-Not Meaningful. NR-Not Ranked. UR-Under Review.

Office: 5400 Legacy Drive, Plano, TX 75024-3199.
Telephone: 972-605-6000.
Email: invest@eds.com
Website: http://www.eds.com

Chrmn & CEO: M.H. Jordan
Pres: J.M. Heller
COO: R. Rittenmeyer
EVP & CFO: R. Vargo

EVP & General Counsel: S. Gordon
Investor Contact: A. Hamood (972-605-6661)
Board of Directors: W. R. Dunbar, R. A. Enrico, M. C. Faga, S. M. Gillis, R. J. Groves, E. M. Hancock, J. M. Heller, R. L. Hunt, M. H. Jordan, E. A. Kangas, J. K. Sims, R. D. Yost

Founded: 1962
Domicile: Delaware
Employees: 117,000

STANDARD & POOR'S

El Paso Corp

S&P Recommendation HOLD ★★★★★

Price $13.82 (as of Oct 27, 2006)

12-Mo. Target Price $15.00

Investment Style Large-Cap Value

GICS Sector Energy
Sub-Industry Oil & Gas Storage & Transportation

Comment This provider of natural gas and related energy products owns North America's largest natural gas pipeline system and is one of its biggest independent natural gas producers.

Key Stock Statistics (Source S&P, Vickers, company reports)

52-Wk Range	$16.39–10.76	S&P Oper. EPS 2006E	0.93	P/E on S&P Oper. EPS 2006E	14.9	Dividend Rate/Share	$0.16
Trailing 12-Month EPS	$-0.46	S&P Oper. EPS 2007E	1.25	Common Shares Outstg. (M)	695.9	Yield (%)	1.16
Trailing 12-Month P/E	NM	S&P Core EPS 2006E	0.93	Market Capitalization(B)	$9.618	Beta	2.11
$10K Invested 5 Yrs Ago	$3,146	S&P Core EPS 2007E	1.25	Institutional Ownership (%)	75	S&P Credit Rating	B+

Price Performance

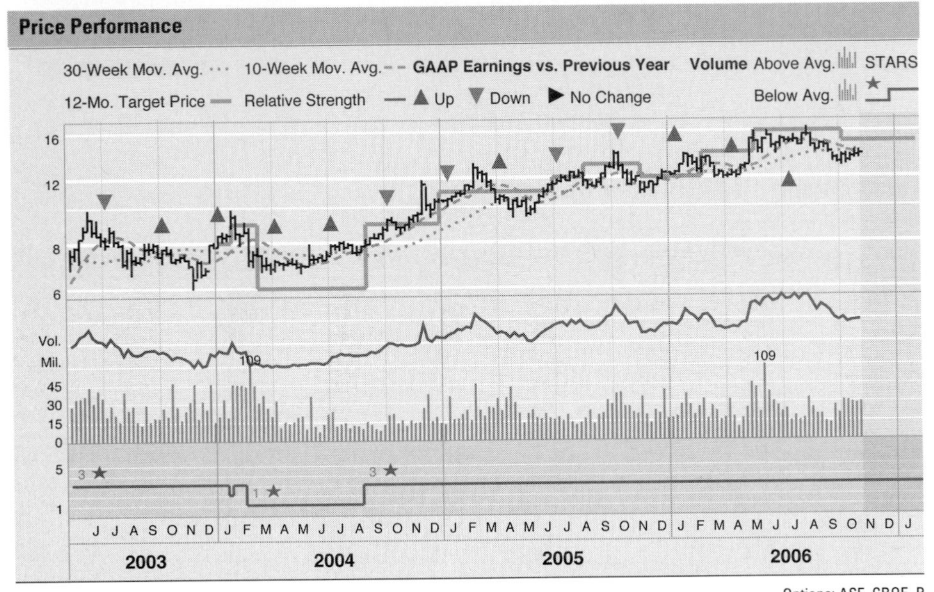

Options: ASE, CBOE, P

Analysis prepared by **Michael Kay** on September 27, 2006, when the stock traded at **$ 13.32**.

Highlights

- The expiration of discounted rates to certain El Paso Natural Gas (EPNG) customers boosted the Pipeline segment in the first half of 2006. While we believe project inventory in 2006 should provide for modest production growth in the exploration and production (E&P) segment, we think high operating costs will make it difficult for EP to grow this segment. In our view, 2006 results will provide a much clearer operating picture of the restructured EP, largely clear of extraordinary items.
- In 2006, the Pipelines segment has placed several projects into service, completing the Elba Island LNG terminal, the expansion of Wyoming Interstate Company's 143-mile Piceance pipeline, and the Cheyenne Plains pipeline expansion. Oil and gas production is up from last year, but remains challenged by the slow pace of recovery in production knocked off by last summer's hurricanes.
- The Pipeline segment should rebound, in our view, from the impact of hurricanes and record solid growth. While we are still skeptical of the E&P business, we view as positive EP's lower risk onshore emphasis.

Investment Rationale/Risk

- Apart from the final outcome of the Continental Connector pipeline project, we see few near-term catalysts for the shares. We find the Pipeline segment to be well run and a cash flow contributor. However, we continue to believe the company has a disadvantage in its E&P segment, as we view EP's assets as mature, high-cost properties, adding to future downside risk in earnings. We would prefer reserve additions through the drillbit rather than acquisitions, but EP has not demonstrated a successful drilling history, in our opinion.
- Risks to our recommendation and target price include a prolonged decline in natural gas prices, an inability to wind down remaining energy trading positions, a slowing economy, and warmer than normal winter weather.
- Although we remain attracted to EP's premier gas pipeline franchise and its strong and diverse organic growth potential, the company's E&P segment remains a concern. Our 12-month target price of $15 is based on an enterprise value to EBITDA ratio of 6.8X.

Qualitative Risk Assessment

LOW	MEDIUM	HIGH

Our risk assessment is based on our view of EP's struggling exploration and production segment, which has proven to be very volatile. EP's balance sheet is highly leveraged, in our opinion, making it difficult to turn around the E&P segment. Partly offsetting these risks is EP's involvement in several different business lines, including regulated pipelines.

Quantitative Evaluations

S&P Quality Ranking B-

D	C	B-	B	B+	A-	A	A+

Relative Strength Rank MODERATE

30

LOWEST = 1 HIGHEST = 99

Revenue/Earnings Data

Revenue (Million $)

	1Q	2Q	3Q	4Q	Year
2006	1,531	1,214	--	--	--
2005	1,108	1,184	768.0	957.0	4,017
2004	1,557	1,524	1,429	1,364	5,874
2003	1,844	1,574	1,724	1,569	6,711
2002	3,755	2,987	2,656	2,796	12,194
2001	17,754	13,363	13,845	12,115	57,475

Earnings Per Share ($)

	1Q	2Q	3Q	4Q	Year
2006	0.52	0.21	**E**0.16	**E**0.20	**E**0.93
2005	0.18	-0.34	-0.51	-0.45	-1.13
2004	-0.15	0.07	-0.31	-0.86	-1.25
2003	-0.33	-0.53	0.12	-0.28	-1.03
2002	0.43	0.02	-0.06	-2.54	-2.30
2001	-0.78	-0.26	0.42	0.72	0.13

Fiscal year ended Dec. 31. Next earnings report expected: Early November. EPS Estimates based on S&P Operating Earnings; historical GAAP earnings are as reported.

Dividend Data (Dates: mm/dd Payment Date: mm/dd/yy)

Amount ($)	Date Decl.	Ex-Div. Date	Stk. of Record	Payment Date
0.040	02/14	03/01	03/03	04/03/06
0.040	04/13	05/31	06/02	07/03/06
0.040	07/20	08/30	09/01	10/02/06
0.040	10/26	11/29	12/01	01/02/07

Dividends have been paid since 1992. Source: Company reports.

El Paso Corp

Business Summary September 27, 2006

CORPORATE OVERVIEW. Founded in 1928, El Paso originally served as a regional natural gas pipeline company that ultimately expanded geographically and into complimentary business lines. By 2001, its total assets exceeded $44 billion and included natural gas production, power generation, trading operations and its traditional natural gas pipeline businesses. In late 2001 through 2003, various industry and company-specific events led to a substantial decline in EP's fundamentals. In late 2003, EP announced a long-term business strategy principally focused on core pipeline and production businesses. During the past several years, EP has sold nearly $12 billion of assets to reduce debt and improve liquidity. These divestitures have resulted in significant financial losses through asset impairments, realized losses on asset sales and a reduction of income from the businesses sold.

PRIMARY BUSINESS DYNAMICS. The Pipeline segment is the largest U.S. owner of interstate natural gas pipelines and owns or has interests in 56,000 miles of pipeline. The division also has 420 billion cubic feet (Bcf) of natural gas storage capacity, and a liquefied natural gas terminal at Elba Island, GA with 806 million cubic feet (Mmcf) of daily base load sendout capacity. Each pipeline system and storage facility operates under Federal Energy Regulatory Commission (FERC) approved tariffs that establish rates, cost recovery mechanisms, and service terms and conditions. The established rates are a function of EP's costs of providing services, including a "reasonable" return on invested capital.

EP's strategy to create value in this segment is to: (1) Expand systems into new markets (e.g., the Continental Connector project in the Rockies, LNG in the Gulf of Mexico and the Atlantic Coast), while leveraging existing assets; (2) recontract or contract available or expiring capacity and resolve open rate cases; (3) leverage its coast-to-coast scale economies; and (4) invest in maintenance and pipeline integrity projects to maintain the value and ensure the safety of its pipeline systems and assets.

Company Financials

Per Share Data ($) Year Ended Dec. 31	**2005**	**2004**	**2003**	**2002**	**2001**	**2000**	**1999**	**1998**	**1997**	**1996**
Tangible Book Value	3.38	4.68	5.36	11.70	17.65	15.25	10.47	13.06	15.39	13.77
Cash Flow	0.61	0.45	0.99	0.21	2.76	4.82	1.61	3.92	3.60	1.93
Earnings	-1.13	-1.25	-1.03	-2.30	0.13	2.44	-1.06	1.85	1.59	0.53
S&P Core Earnings	-1.07	-0.84	-0.68	-1.95	-0.37	NA	NA	NA	NA	NA
Dividends	0.16	0.16	0.16	0.87	0.85	0.82	0.79	0.76	0.73	0.70
Payout Ratio	NM	NM	NM	NM	NM	34%	NM	41%	46%	131%
Prices:High	14.16	11.85	10.30	46.89	75.30	74.25	43.44	38.94	33.75	26.63
Prices:Low	9.30	6.57	3.33	4.39	36.00	30.31	30.69	24.69	24.44	14.31
P/E Ratio:High	NM	NM	NM	NM	NM	30	NM	21	21	50
P/E Ratio:Low	NM	NM	NM	NM	NM	12	NM	13	15	27
Income Statement Analysis (Million $)										
Revenue	4,017	5,874	6,711	12,194	57,475	21,950	10,581	5,782	5,638	3,010
Operating Income	934	2,386	2,907	2,872	4,391	2,155	1,482	775	757	370
Depreciation	1,121	1,088	1,207	1,405	1,359	589	609	269	236	101
Interest Expense	1,389	1,632	1,839	1,400	1,155	538	453	267	238	110
Pretax Income	-991	-777	-1,200	-1,567	466	1,012	-287	377	340	65.0
Effective Tax Rate	NM	NM	NM	NM	39.1%	28.3%	NM	33.7%	37.9%	38.5%
Net Income	-702	-802	-616	-1,289	67.0	582	-242	225	186	38.0
S&P Core Earnings	-696	-531	-401	-1,096	-194	NA	NA	NA	NA	NA
Balance Sheet & Other Financial Data (Million $)										
Cash	2,132	2,117	1,429	1,591	1,139	688	545	90.0	116	200
Current Assets	6,185	5,632	8,922	11,924	12,659	10,076	2,911	1,209	1,629	1,965
Total Assets	31,838	31,383	37,084	46,224	48,171	27,445	16,657	10,069	9,532	9,532
Current Liabilities	5,712	4,572	7,074	10,350	13,565	10,467	3,702	2,162	2,464	2,712
Long Term Debt	17,054	18,608	20,722	19,727	14,109	6,574	5,548	3,177	2,119	2,215
Common Equity	2,639	3,439	4,474	8,377	9,356	3,569	2,947	2,108	1,959	1,638
Total Capital	21,850	23,358	25,196	31,680	31,012	14,623	11,601	6,914	5,993	5,280
Capital Expenditures	1,718	1,782	2,452	3,716	4,079	1,336	1,086	406	293	119
Cash Flow	392	286	591	116	1,426	1,171	367	494	422	139
Current Ratio	1.1	1.2	1.3	1.2	0.9	1.0	0.8	0.6	0.7	0.7
% Long Term Debt of Capitalization	78.1	79.7	82.2	62.3	45.5	45.0	47.8	46.0	35.4	42.0
% Net Income of Revenue	NM	NM	NM	NM	0.1	2.7	NM	3.9	3.3	1.3
% Return on Assets	NM	NM	NM	NM	0.1	2.6	NM	2.3	2.0	0.7
% Return on Equity	NM	NM	NM	NM	0.8	17.9	NM	11.1	10.3	3.2

Data as orig reptd.; bef. results of disc opers/spec. items. Per share data adj. for stk. divs.; EPS diluted. E-Estimated. NA-Not Available. NM-Not Meaningful. NR-Not Ranked. UR-Under Review.

Office: El Paso Energy Building, Houston, TX 77002-5089.
Telephone: 713-420-2600.
Email: investorrelations@epenergy.com
Website: http://www.elpaso.com

Chrmn: R.L. Keuhn, Jr.
Pres & CEO: D.L. Foshee
EVP & CFO: D.M. Leland
EVP & General Counsel: R.W. Baker

SVP, Chief Acctg Officer & Cntlr: J. Sult
Investor Contact: B. Connery (713-420-5855)
Board of Directors: J. C. Braniff, J. Dunlap, D. L. Foshee, R. W. Goldman, A. W. Hall, Jr., T. R. Hix, W. H. Joyce, R. L. Kuehn, Jr., F. P. McClean, M. Talbert, R. F. Vagt, J. L. Whitmire, J. B. Wyatt

Founded: 1928
Domicile: Delaware
Employees: 5,700

STANDARD &POOR'S

Embarq Corp

S&P Recommendation HOLD ★★★★★

Price $48.73 (as of Oct 30, 2006)

12-Mo. Target Price $52.00

Investment Style Mid-Cap Value

GICS Sector Telecommunication Services
Sub-Industry Integrated Telecommunication Services

Comment Embarq, which provides wireline services to 7 million access lines, is the fifth largest wireline provider in the U.S. EQ was spun off from Sprint Nextel in May 2006.

Key Stock Statistics (Source S&P, Vickers, company reports)

52-Wk Range	$52.49–38.81	S&P Oper. EPS 2006E	4.68	P/E on S&P Oper. EPS 2006E	10.4	Dividend Rate/Share	$2.00
Trailing 12-Month EPS	$0.00	S&P Oper. EPS 2007E	4.60	Common Shares Outstg. (M)	149.1	Yield (%)	4.10
Trailing 12-Month P/E	NM	S&P Core EPS 2006E	4.45	Market Capitalization(B)	$7.267	Beta	1.00
$10K Invested 5 Yrs Ago	NA	S&P Core EPS 2007E	4.40	Institutional Ownership (%)	84	S&P Credit Rating	NA

Price Performance

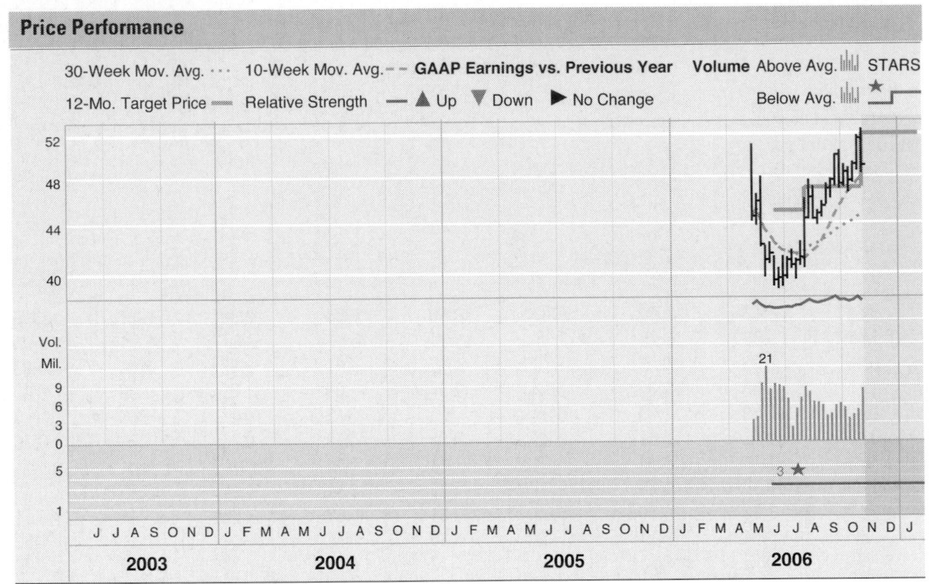

Analysis prepared by **Todd Rosenbluth** on October 30, 2006, when the stock traded at **$ 48.73**.

Highlights

- We see revenues declining 3% in 2006 and holding flat in 2007, as this newly formed telecom carrier faces increased competition from cable and wireless carriers in its urban markets. We expect access line losses to rise to approximately 6% by the end of 2006, up from 4% in 2005, as customers move to the newly launched cable telephony bundle. We believe EQ will offset some of the customer losses with the expansion of its DSL services through its own service bundle.
- We look for EBITDA margins to narrow to 40.4% in 2006 and to 40% in 2007, from 43.5% in 2005, as revenues decline and operating costs rise. We believe EQ will have higher sales and marketing costs than it did as a Sprint segment, and expect a rebranding campaign to increase costs.
- We see lower interest costs in 2006, and assume an effective 39% tax rate. Our EPS estimate of $4.68 in 2006, down from a pro forma $5.49 in 2005, reflects weaker results expected in the second half. We see EPS of $4.60 in 2007.

Investment Rationale/Risk

- Despite a short operating history following its spin-off from Sprint Nextel (S: buy, $19) in mid-May, we believe EQ has the flexibility to repurchase shares or look for acquisitions. We think the company's wireline operations have greater exposure to cable telephony competition, which will cause a larger percentage of access line losses. We believe the key driver for EQ will be bundling of broadband services in an effort to keep customers loyal.
- Risks to our recommendation and target price include a new management team operating independently, greater than expected cable competition, a dividend cut, increased shareholder turnover, and higher customer migration from wireless substitution.
- EQ trades at an enterprise value/EBITDA multiple below that of rural peers. We believe a discount to rural peers is warranted given the company's short history and its less stable customer base. Our 12-month target price of $52 values EQ at an enterprise value/EBITDA multiple of 5.5X, in line with larger Bell carriers.

Qualitative Risk Assessment

LOW | **MEDIUM** | HIGH

Our risk assessment reflects the competitive nature of the telecom industry and the company's short operating history, offset by our view of its steady operating cash flow that supports its dividend.

Quantitative Evaluations

S&P Quality Ranking NR

D | C | B- | B | B+ | A- | A | A+

Relative Strength Rank MODERATE

50

LOWEST = 1 HIGHEST = 99

Revenue/Earnings Data

Revenue (Million $)

	1Q	2Q	3Q	4Q	Year
2006	1,561	1.58	1,606	--	--
2005	--	--	--	--	6,701
2004	--	--	--	--	--
2003	--	--	--	--	--
2002	--	--	--	--	--
2001	--	--	--	--	--

Earnings Per Share ($)

	1Q	2Q	3Q	4Q	Year
2006	1.42	1.44	1.06	E0.98	E4.68
2005	--	--	--	--	4.96
2004	--	--	--	--	--
2003	--	--	--	--	--
2002	--	--	--	--	--
2001	--	--	--	--	--

Fiscal year ended Dec. 31. Next earnings report expected: NA. EPS Estimates based on S&P Operating Earnings; historical GAAP earnings are as reported.

Dividend Data (Dates: mm/dd Payment Date: mm/dd/yy)

Amount ($)	Date Decl.	Ex-Div. Date	Stk. of Record	Payment Date
0.500	07/20	09/06	09/08	09/30/06
0.500	10/09	12/06	12/08	12/31/06

Dividends have been paid since 2006. Source: Company reports.

Please read the Required Disclosures and Analyst Certification on the last page of this report.

Embarq Corp

Business Summary October 30, 2006

CORPORATE OVERVIEW. In mid-May 2006, Sprint Nextel spun off its local telephone business as a separate entity now known as Embarq Corp. (EQ). The corporate action was a tax-free distribution to S's shareholders, who received one share of EQ for every 20 shares of S. As of September 2006, EQ provided local service to 7 million access lines in 18 states, down from 7.4 million a year earlier. The majority of EQ's access lines are located in Florida, North Carolina, Nevada and Ohio. The company serves customers in Fort Myers, Las Vegas, Orlando and Raleigh-Durham, in addition to numerous smaller markets. The company's offerings include local and long distance voice and data services, including high-speed DSL Internet services, both for residential and corporate customers.

CORPORATE STRATEGY. EQ's business strategy is to bundle services to sell the commoditized wireline services with high growth services such as broadband. It has launched an MVNO wireless service under the Embarq brand name to cash in on the growing wireless segment. The company also has an agency arrangement with EchoStar Communications for providing video services. As of September 2006, the company had 933,000 DSL customers, up 58% from a year earlier, and 146,000 video customers.

COMPETITIVE LANDSCAPE. We believe that to date, wireless substitution has been the greatest threat to EQ's access lines, which fell 6% in the 12 months ended September 2006. Wireless coverage has improved over the past couple of years, and we believe that many of these customers have dropped their landlines and switched to Sprint Nextel, the former parent of EQ. However, with approximately 55% of EQ's access lines being covered by cable competition as of September 2006 and our expectation that this figure will grow to more than 70% by the end of 2006, EQ should face higher cable telephony competition. Among the largest of the competitors in EQ's territory include Time Warner, Comcast, Charter and Cox.

Company Financials

Per Share Data ($) Year Ended Dec. 31	2005	2004	2003	2002	2001	2000	1999	1998	1997	1996
Tangible Book Value	NM	NA	NA	NA	NA	NA	NA	NA	NA	NA
Cash Flow	12.09	NA	NA	NA	NA	NA	NA	NA	NA	NA
Earnings	4.96	NA	NA	NA	NA	NA	NA	NA	NA	NA
S&P Core Earnings	5.91	6.04	NA	NA	NA	NA	NA	NA	NA	NA
Dividends	NA	NA	NA	NA	NA	NA	NA	NA	NA	NA
Payout Ratio	NA	NA	NA	NA	NA	NA	NA	NA	NA	NA
Prices:High	NA	NA	NA	NA	NA	NA	NA	NA	NA	NA
Prices:Low	NA	NA	NA	NA	NA	NA	NA	NA	NA	NA
P/E Ratio:High	NA	NA	NA	NA	NA	NA	NA	NA	NA	NA
P/E Ratio:Low	NA	NA	NA	NA	NA	NA	NA	NA	NA	NA
Income Statement Analysis (Million $)										
Revenue	6,701	NA	NA	NA	NA	NA	NA	NA	NA	NA
Operating Income	2,911	NA	NA	NA	NA	NA	NA	NA	NA	NA
Depreciation	1,070	NA	NA	NA	NA	NA	NA	NA	NA	NA
Interest Expense	520	NA	NA	NA	NA	NA	NA	NA	NA	NA
Pretax Income	1,245	NA	NA	NA	NA	NA	NA	NA	NA	NA
Effective Tax Rate	40.2%	NA	NA	NA	NA	NA	NA	NA	NA	NA
Net Income	744	NA	NA	NA	NA	NA	NA	NA	NA	NA
S&P Core Earnings	887	907	NA	NA	NA	NA	NA	NA	NA	NA
Balance Sheet & Other Financial Data (Million $)										
Cash	200	NA	NA	NA	NA	NA	NA	NA	NA	NA
Current Assets	1,194	NA	NA	NA	NA	NA	NA	NA	NA	NA
Total Assets	9,473	NA	NA	NA	NA	NA	NA	NA	NA	NA
Current Liabilities	1,157	NA	NA	NA	NA	NA	NA	NA	NA	NA
Long Term Debt	7,248	NA	NA	NA	NA	NA	NA	NA	NA	NA
Common Equity	-1,071	NA	NA	NA	NA	NA	NA	NA	NA	NA
Total Capital	7,268	NA	NA	NA	NA	NA	NA	NA	NA	NA
Capital Expenditures	NA	NA	NA	NA	NA	NA	NA	NA	NA	NA
Cash Flow	1,814	NA	NA	NA	NA	NA	NA	NA	NA	NA
Current Ratio	1.0	NA	NA	NA	NA	NA	NA	NA	NA	NA
% Long Term Debt of Capitalization	99.7	NA	NA	NA	NA	NA	NA	NA	NA	NA
% Net Income of Revenue	11.1	NA	NA	NA	NA	NA	NA	NA	NA	NA
% Return on Assets	NA	NA	NA	NA	NA	NA	NA	NA	NA	NA
% Return on Equity	NA	NA	NA	NA	NA	NA	NA	NA	NA	NA

Data as orig reptd.; bef. results of disc opers/spec. items. Per share data adj. for stk. divs.; EPS diluted. E-Estimated. NA-Not Available. NM-Not Meaningful. NR-Not Ranked. UR-Under Review.

Office: 5454 W. 110th Street, Overland Park, KS 66211.
Telephone: 913-323-4637.
Website: http://www.embarq.com
Chrmn, Pres & CEO: D.R. Hesse

COO: M.B. Fuller
CFO: G.M. Betts
Treas: L.H. Meredith
General Counsel: T.A. Gerke

Board of Directors: P. C. Brown, S. A. Davis, D. R. Hesse, J. P. Mullen, W. A. Owens, D. C. Paliwal, S. M. Shern, L. A. Siegel

Auditor: KPMG, Kansas City
Founded: 2005
Domicile: Delaware
Employees: 20,000

STANDARD &POOR'S

EMC Corp

S&P Recommendation BUY ★★★★★

Price $12.42 (as of Oct 27, 2006)

12-Mo. Target Price $15.00

Investment Style Large-Cap Growth

GICS Sector Information Technology
Sub-Industry Computer Storage & Peripherals

Comment This company is the leading supplier of enterprise data storage systems and software.

Key Stock Statistics (Source S&P, Vickers, company reports)

52-Wk Range	$14.75–9.44	S&P Oper. EPS 2006E	0.53	P/E on S&P Oper. EPS 2006E	23.4	Dividend Rate/Share	Nil
Trailing 12-Month EPS	$0.43	S&P Oper. EPS 2007E	0.69	Common Shares Outstg. (M)	2,298.5	Yield (%)	Nil
Trailing 12-Month P/E	28.9	S&P Core EPS 2006E	0.53	Market Capitalization(B)	$28.547	Beta	2.28
$10K Invested 5 Yrs Ago	$9,262	S&P Core EPS 2007E	0.69	Institutional Ownership (%)	68	S&P Credit Rating	BBB+

Price Performance

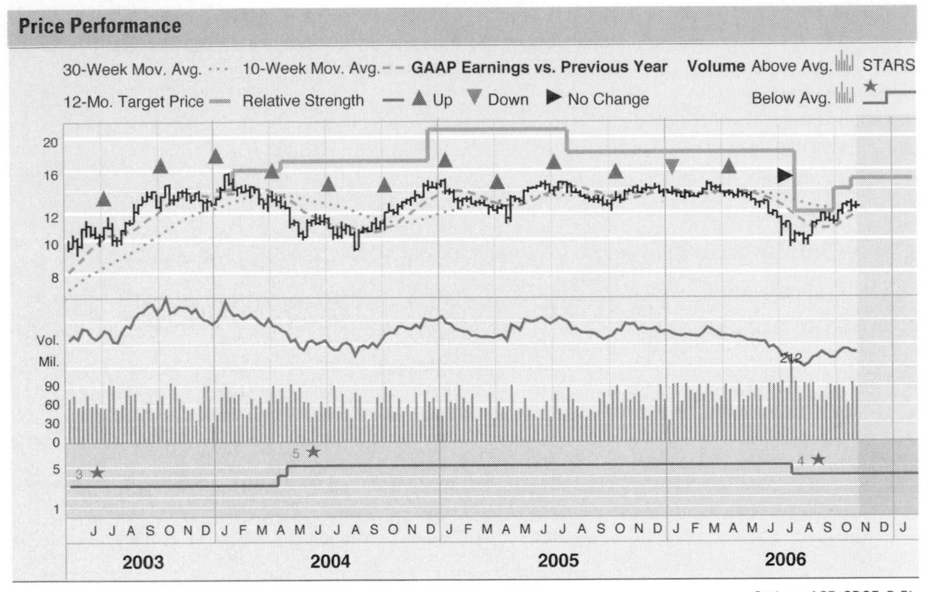

Options: ASE, CBOE, P, Ph

Analysis prepared by **Richard N. Stice, CFA** on October 19, 2006, when the stock traded at **$ 12.18**.

Highlights

- We see 2007 revenues increasing about 13%, following an anticipated gain of 15% in 2006. We expect sales to be aided by a consistent level of IT spending, the continued expansion of digital content, acquisition benefits, the completion of major product transitions, market share gains and international expansion. We believe companies continue to view data storage as a high level priority and think that they are likely to devote an increasing amount of resources toward this industry.
- We expect gross margins to widen, as projected volume increases outweigh the likelihood of a less favorable business mix. Our 2007 gross margin target is 53.7%, versus an estimated 52.8% for 2006. We see operating expenses declining as a percentage of revenues due to efficiency improvements. Results should also benefit from ongoing share repurchases, albeit at a slower pace than what we expect for 2006.
- We forecast 2007 EPS of $0.69, which includes the impact of projected stock option expense and intangible asset amortization, a 30% increase from 2006's projected total of $0.53.

Investment Rationale/Risk

- We believe EMC will continue to benefit from what we view as a steady IT spending environment, given its leading position in the data storage sector. Moreover, we think the expansion of its product portfolio, resulting from recent acquisition activity and R&D efforts, will have a positive impact. Finally, we view EMC's capital structure favorably, with close to $2.50 per share in cash and investments and no long-term debt.
- Risks to our recommendation and target price include further component shortages, an elongated sales cycle, and greater than anticipated pricing declines. Regarding corporate governance practices, we are somewhat concerned that the roles of chairman and CEO are held by the same individual.
- Our 12-month target price of $15 combines two valuation techniques. The first is a relative P/E measure that equates EMC with the S&P Information Technology sector and results in a value of $13. The second is based on our discounted cash flow analysis, which leads to an intrinsic value calculation of $16. Our assumptions include a WACC of 12.7% and an expected terminal growth rate of 3%.

Qualitative Risk Assessment

LOW | **MEDIUM** | HIGH

Our risk assessment reflects our view that EMC boasts an industry leading market share position, consistent free cash flow generation, and a strong balance sheet with no long-term debt. However, we see the data storage industry as cyclical, highly competitive, and prone to precipitous declines in average selling prices.

Quantitative Evaluations

S&P Quality Ranking **B**

D | C | B- | **B** | B+ | A- | A | A+

Relative Strength Rank **MODERATE**

66

LOWEST = 1 HIGHEST = 99

Revenue/Earnings Data

Revenue (Million $)

	1Q	2Q	3Q	4Q	Year
2006	2,551	2,575	2,815	--	--
2005	2,243	2,345	2,366	2,710	9,664
2004	1,872	1,971	2,029	2,358	8,229
2003	1,384	1,479	1,511	1,863	6,237
2002	1,302	1,388	1,259	1,489	5,438
2001	2,345	2,021	1,212	1,513	7,091

Earnings Per Share ($)

	1Q	2Q	3Q	4Q	Year
2006	0.12	0.12	--	E0.17	E0.53
2005	0.11	0.12	0.17	0.06	0.47
2004	0.06	0.08	0.09	0.13	0.36
2003	0.02	0.04	0.07	0.09	0.22
2002	-0.03	Nil	0.01	-0.03	-0.05
2001	0.18	0.05	-0.43	-0.03	-0.23

Fiscal year ended Dec. 31. Next earnings report expected: Late January. EPS Estimates based on S&P Operating Earnings; historical GAAP earnings are as reported.

Dividend Data

No cash dividends have been paid.

EMC Corp

Business Summary October 19, 2006

CORPORATE OVERVIEW. EMC offers a wide range of information storage systems, software and services designed to meet the specific needs of its customers in terms of performance, functionality, scalability, data availability and cost. Customers are located worldwide and represent a cross section of industries and government agencies. The company's products and services are used in conjunction with a variety of computing platforms that support key business processes, including transaction processing, data warehousing, electronic commerce, and content management. In 2005, revenues reached a record level of $9.7 billion. This eclipsed the previous high of $8.9 billion that was achieved in 2000.

Revenues outside of the United States accounted for 43% of EMC's total in 2005, down from 44% in 2004. Moreover, all of EMC's markets expanded at a double digit rate during the year, with Latin America, at 26%, generating the fastest level of growth.

CORPORATE STRATEGY. EMC's strategy focuses on the concept of information lifecycle management (ILM). This idea centers on the management of information across its entire life, from creation and use to archive and disposal Through its utilization, ILM simultaneously lowers the cost and reduces the risk of managing data, in our view, regardless of what format it is in (documents, images or e-mail). ILM also provides for cost effective business continuity and more efficient compliance with government and industry regulations.

As part of this plan, EMC has engaged in a number of acquisitions over the past two years. One of its more successful deals, in our view, was the purchase of VMware, Inc., a virtual infrastructure software company, which is operated as an independent subsidiary. VMware's software provides a layer of abstraction between the computing, storage, and networking hardware and the software that runs on it. This is designed to enable customers to achieve much higher utilization of the server, storage, and network resources deployed within their operations, while dramatically simplifying how the workloads that are run on those systems are operated and managed. In 2005, VMware's revenues rose 78%.

Company Financials

Per Share Data ($) Year Ended Dec. 31	**2005**	**2004**	**2003**	**2002**	**2001**	**2000**	**1999**	**1998**	**1997**	**1996**
Tangible Book Value	3.20	3.22	3.19	3.05	3.31	3.72	2.38	1.60	1.19	0.83
Cash Flow	0.73	0.61	0.45	0.24	0.07	1.02	0.66	0.46	0.32	0.24
Earnings	0.47	0.36	0.22	-0.05	-0.23	0.79	0.46	0.37	0.26	0.20
S&P Core Earnings	0.35	0.21	0.04	-0.23	-0.33	NA	NA	NA	NA	NA
Dividends	Nil	Nil	Nil	Nil	Nil	Nil	Nil	Nil	Nil	Nil
Payout Ratio	Nil	Nil	Nil	Nil	Nil	Nil	Nil	Nil	Nil	Nil
Prices:High	15.09	15.80	14.66	17.97	82.00	104.94	55.50	21.66	8.14	4.55
Prices:Low	11.10	9.24	5.98	3.67	10.01	47.50	21.00	6.00	3.97	1.89
P/E Ratio:High	32	44	67	NM	NM	NM	NM	58	31	23
P/E Ratio:Low	24	26	27	NM	NM	NM	NM	16	15	10

Income Statement Analysis (Million $)	2005	2004	2003	2002	2001	2000	1999	1998	1997	1996
Revenue	9,664	8,229	6,237	5,438	7,091	8,873	6,716	3,974	2,938	2,274
Operating Income	2,222	1,716	988	310	355	2,774	1,897	1,185	798	583
Depreciation	640	616	521	654	655	517	447	203	136	86.9
Interest Expense	7.99	7.52	3.03	11.4	11.3	14.6	33.5	20.2	15.5	12.0
Pretax Income	1,652	1,185	571	-296	-577	2,441	1,357	1,058	718	519
Effective Tax Rate	31.4%	26.5%	13.1%	NM	NM	27.0%	25.5%	25.0%	25.0%	25.6%
Net Income	1,133	871	496	-119	-508	1,782	1,011	793	539	386
S&P Core Earnings	839	504	84.2	-477	-720	NA	NA	NA	NA	NA

Balance Sheet & Other Financial Data (Million $)	2005	2004	2003	2002	2001	2000	1999	1998	1997	1996
Cash	2,322	1,477	1,869	1,687	2,129	1,983	1,109	705	955	496
Current Assets	6,574	4,831	4,687	4,217	4,923	6,100	4,320	3,105	2,627	1,754
Total Assets	16,790	15,423	14,093	9,590	9,890	10,628	7,173	4,569	3,490	2,294
Current Liabilities	3,674	2,949	2,547	2,042	2,179	2,114	1,398	653	506	418
Long Term Debt	127	128	130	Nil	Nil	14.5	687	539	559	191
Common Equity	12,065	11,523	10,885	7,226	7,601	8,177	4,952	3,324	2,376	1,637
Total Capital	12,368	11,793	11,015	7,226	7,601	8,494	5,764	3,914	2,980	1,874
Capital Expenditures	601	371	369	391	889	858	524	373	211	126
Cash Flow	1,773	1,488	1,017	535	147	2,299	1,458	997	675	473
Current Ratio	1.8	1.6	1.8	2.1	2.3	2.9	3.1	4.8	5.2	4.2
% Long Term Debt of Capitalization	1.0	1.1	1.2	Nil	Nil	0.2	11.9	13.8	18.8	10.2
% Net Income of Revenue	11.7	10.6	8.0	NM	NM	20.1	15.0	20.0	18.3	17.0
% Return on Assets	7.0	5.9	4.2	NM	NM	20.0	15.8	19.7	18.6	19.1
% Return on Equity	9.6	7.8	5.5	NM	NM	27.1	34.4	27.8	26.8	27.8

Data as orig reptd.; bef. results of disc opers/spec. items. Per share data adj. for stk. divs.; EPS diluted. E-Estimated. NA-Not Available. NM-Not Meaningful. NR-Not Ranked. UR-Under Review.

Office: 176 South Street, Hopkinton, MA 01748-2230.
Telephone: 508-435-1000.
Email: emc_ir@emc.com
Website: http://www.emc.com

Chrmn, Pres & CEO: J.M. Tucci
Vice Chrmn & CFO: W.J. Teuber, Jr.
SVP & General Counsel: P.T. Dacier

Board of Directors: M. W. Brown, M. J. Cronin, G. Deegan, J. R. Egan, W. P. Fitzgerald, O. Kallasvuo, W. B. Priem, D. N. Strohm, J. M. Tucci, A. M. Zeien

Founded: 1979
Domicile: Massachusetts
Employees: 26,500

STANDARD &POOR'S

Emerson Electric Co.

S&P Recommendation HOLD ★★★★★ | **Price** $84.16 (as of Oct 27, 2006) | **12-Mo. Target Price** $90.00 | **Investment Style** Large-Cap Value

GICS Sector Industrials
Sub-Industry Electrical Components & Equipment

Comment This company primarily makes backup power equipment for telecom and Internet providers and users; climate control components; and electric motors.

Key Stock Statistics (Source S&P, Vickers, company reports)

52-Wk Range	$90.42–68.83	S&P Oper. EPS 2006E	4.38	P/E on S&P Oper. EPS 2006E	19.2	Dividend Rate/Share	$1.78
Trailing 12-Month EPS	$4.20	S&P Oper. EPS 2007E	5.00	Common Shares Outstg. (M)	407.7	Yield (%)	2.12
Trailing 12-Month P/E	20.0	S&P Core EPS 2006E	4.37	Market Capitalization(B)	$34.312	Beta	1.12
$10K Invested 5 Yrs Ago	$18,459	S&P Core EPS 2007E	4.99	Institutional Ownership (%)	73	S&P Credit Rating	A

Price Performance

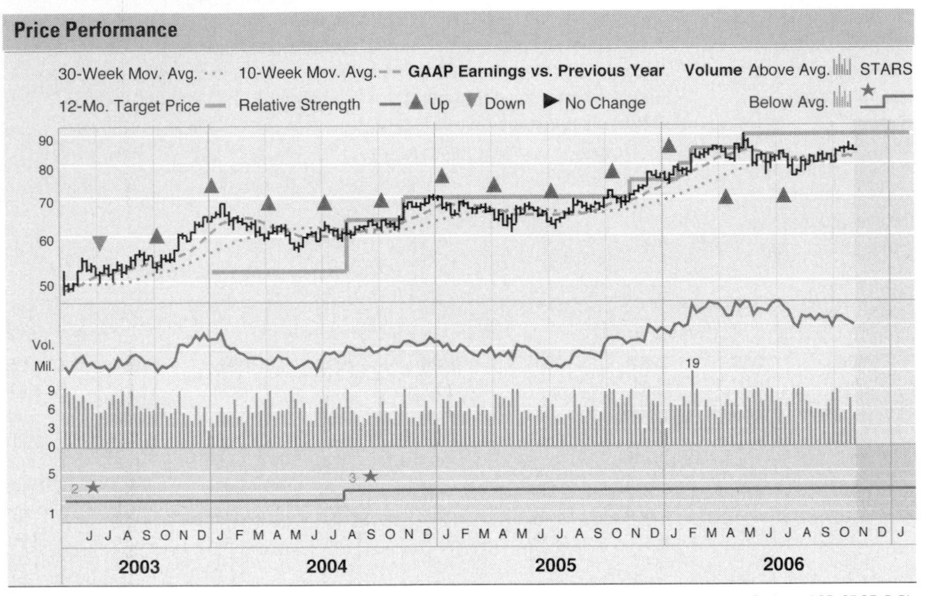

Options: ASE, CBOE, P, Ph

Analysis prepared by **John F. Hingher, CFA** on August 03, 2006, when the stock traded at **$ 80.74**.

Highlights

- We see pent-up replacement demand for capital equipment in a number of end-market segments, new capacity additions in some end-markets, and anticipated price increases driving revenue growth of 14% in FY 06 (Sep.). We believe management will aim for price increases and productivity improvements to offset rising raw material costs. In FY 07, we forecast 6% sales growth.
- We forecast an increase in margins in FY 06 and FY 07, aided by the anticipated greater volumes, a shift to low-cost manufacturing, improved productivity, lower restructuring costs, and increased operating leverage resulting from management's continued focus on cost control.
- We see operating EPS growing about 23% in FY 06, to $4.38, and 14% in FY 07, to $5.00. We estimate S&P Core EPS for FY 06 of $4.37. For the longer term, we have confidence in management's ability to continue to control costs and maintain a strong balance sheet. We see our view supported by the company's 10-year historical average ROE of about 20%.

Investment Rationale/Risk

- We project an uptick in some of EMR's important end-markets, and believe that strong growth in emerging markets, particularly in Asia and Latin America, will continue. We are optimistic regarding the short-term outlook and what we view as EMR's solid cash flow generating ability, but based on the shares' valuation, we would not add to positions.
- Risks to our opinion and target price include slowing customer capital spending; less growth in Asia; and rising prices for key inputs. We also have concerns regarding EMR's corporate governance policies related to takeover defenses and the election of directors.
- Our DCF model, which assumes annual FCF growth of 9% for the next 10 years, 3.5% thereafter, and a WACC of 11.3%, suggests intrinsic value of $87. EMR recently traded at 16X our forward 12-month EPS estimate of $4.83, below its historical average, but above peers' 14X average. Blending methodologies leads to our 12-month target price of $90, or 19X our forward EPS estimate, a premium we think is warranted given EMR's superior ROE.

Qualitative Risk Assessment

LOW | **MEDIUM** | HIGH

Our risk assessment reflects the cyclical nature of several of the company's major end markets, its acquisition strategy, and corporate governance practices that we view as unfavorable versus peers. This is offset by our view of its strong competitive position in its major product categories and a S&P Quality Ranking of A, which indicates above-average stability in earnings and dividends growth.

Quantitative Evaluations

S&P Quality Ranking A

D | C | B- | B | B+ | A- | **A** | A+

Relative Strength Rank MODERATE

43

LOWEST = 1 HIGHEST = 99

Revenue/Earnings Data

Revenue (Million $)

	1Q	2Q	3Q	4Q	Year
2006	4,548	4,852	5,217	--	--
2005	3,970	4,227	4,465	4,643	17,305
2004	3,600	3,859	4,036	4,120	15,615
2003	3,226	3,465	3,573	3,694	13,958
2002	3,295	3,421	3,571	3,538	13,824
2001	3,920	4,103	3,905	3,552	15,480

Earnings Per Share ($)

	1Q	2Q	3Q	4Q	Year
2006	0.96	1.05	1.18	**E**1.19	**E**4.38
2005	0.70	0.83	0.86	1.01	3.40
2004	0.58	0.75	0.81	0.84	2.98
2003	0.52	0.56	0.66	0.66	2.41
2002	0.61	0.65	0.67	0.59	2.52
2001	0.83	0.83	0.77	-0.03	2.40

Fiscal year ended Sep. 30. Next earnings report expected: Early November. EPS Estimates based on S&P Operating Earnings; historical GAAP earnings are as reported.

Dividend Data (Dates: mm/dd Payment Date: mm/dd/yy)

Amount ($)	Date Decl.	Ex-Div. Date	Stk. of Record	Payment Date
0.445	11/01	11/08	11/11	12/09/05
0.445	02/07	02/15	02/17	03/10/06
0.445	05/02	05/10	05/12	06/09/06
0.445	08/01	08/09	08/11	09/11/06

Dividends have been paid since 1947. Source: Company reports.

Emerson Electric Co.

Business Summary August 03, 2006

CORPORATE OVERVIEW. Emerson is an industrial conglomerate operating more than 60 diverse businesses in five primary business segments: Process Management, Industrial Automation, Network Power, Climate Technologies, and Appliance and Tools.

The company's Process Management segment, which accounted for 24% of FY 05 (Sep.) total revenues and 27% of profits, and had 16% margins, produces process management software and systems, analytical instrumentation, valves, control systems for measurement and control of fluid flow, and integrated solutions for process and industrial applications. The Industrial Automation segment (18%, 19%, 14%) primarily makes industrial motors and drives, transmissions, alternators, controls and equipment for automated equipment. The Network Power segment (19%, 15%, 11%) mainly makes power systems and precision cooling products used in computer, telecommunications and Internet infrastructure. The Climate Technologies segment (17%, 18%, 15%) mostly makes home and building thermostats and compressors. Compressors are cooling components used in air conditioning units and refrigerators. The Appliance and Tools segment (22%, 21%, 13%) mainly makes various household appliances, electric motors and controls for appliances, hand-held tools, and storage solutions. In terms of geography, total sales in FY 05 broke down as follows: United States 53%, Europe 22%, Asia 14%, and other regions 11%.

Company Financials

Per Share Data ($) Year Ended Sep. 30	**2005**	**2004**	**2003**	**2002**	**2001**	**2000**	**1999**	**1998**	**1997**	**1996**
Tangible Book Value	4.67	4.72	3.61	1.98	2.22	2.53	4.43	4.70	5.20	5.77
Cash Flow	4.83	8.75	3.67	3.80	4.15	4.87	4.45	4.04	3.67	3.32
Earnings	3.40	2.98	2.41	2.52	2.40	3.30	3.00	2.77	2.52	2.28
S&P Core Earnings	3.40	2.97	2.26	1.87	1.76	NA	NA	NA	NA	NA
Dividends	1.66	1.60	1.57	1.55	1.53	1.45	1.33	1.18	1.08	0.98
Payout Ratio	49%	54%	65%	62%	64%	44%	44%	43%	43%	43%
Prices:High	77.84	70.88	65.00	66.09	79.25	79.75	71.44	67.44	60.38	51.75
Prices:Low	60.69	56.22	43.78	41.74	44.04	40.50	51.44	54.50	45.00	38.75
P/E Ratio:High	23	24	27	26	33	24	24	24	24	23
P/E Ratio:Low	18	19	18	17	18	12	17	20	18	17

Income Statement Analysis (Million $)	2005	2004	2003	2002	2001	2000	1999	1998	1997	1996
Revenue	17,305	15,615	13,958	13,824	15,480	15,545	14,270	13,447	12,298	11,150
Operating Income	3,150	2,842	2,497	2,443	2,988	3,219	2,943	2,738	2,494	2,259
Depreciation	562	557	534	541	708	678	638	563	512	465
Interest Expense	243	234	246	260	304	288	190	152	121	127
Pretax Income	2,149	3,704	1,414	1,565	1,589	2,178	2,021	1,924	1,784	1,609
Effective Tax Rate	33.8%	16.1%	28.4%	32.3%	35.0%	34.7%	35.0%	36.1%	37.1%	36.7%
Net Income	1,422	3,109	1,013	1,060	1,032	1,422	1,314	1,229	1,122	1,019
S&P Core Earnings	1,424	1,250	951	784	753	NA	NA	NA	NA	NA

Balance Sheet & Other Financial Data (Million $)	2005	2004	2003	2002	2001	2000	1999	1998	1997	1996
Cash	1,233	1,346	696	381	356	281	266	210	221	149
Current Assets	6,837	6,416	5,500	4,961	5,320	5,483	5,124	5,001	4,717	4,187
Total Assets	17,227	16,361	15,194	14,545	15,046	15,164	13,624	12,660	11,463	10,481
Current Liabilities	4,931	4,339	3,417	4,400	5,379	5,219	4,590	4,022	3,842	3,021
Long Term Debt	3,128	3,136	3,733	2,990	2,256	2,248	1,317	1,057	571	773
Common Equity	7,400	12,266	6,460	5,741	6,114	10,248	6,181	5,803	5,420	5,353
Total Capital	10,528	15,402	10,193	8,731	8,370	12,496	7,498	6,860	5,992	6,126
Capital Expenditures	518	400	337	384	554	692	592	603	575	514
Cash Flow	1,984	3,666	1,547	1,601	1,740	2,101	1,951	1,792	1,634	1,484
Current Ratio	1.4	1.5	1.6	1.1	1.0	1.1	1.1	1.2	1.2	1.4
% Long Term Debt of Capitalization	29.7	20.4	36.6	34.2	26.9	18.0	17.6	15.4	9.6	12.6
% Net Income of Revenue	8.2	19.9	7.3	7.7	6.7	9.2	9.2	9.1	9.1	9.1
% Return on Assets	8.5	19.7	6.8	7.2	6.8	9.9	10.0	10.2	10.2	10.3
% Return on Equity	19.4	26.1	16.6	17.9	16.5	14.5	21.9	21.9	20.8	19.9

Data as orig reptd.; bef. results of disc opers/spec. items. Per share data adj. for stk. divs.; EPS diluted. E-Estimated. NA-Not Available. NM-Not Meaningful. NR-Not Ranked. UR-Under Review.

Office: 8000 W Florissant Ave, Saint Louis, MO 63136.
Telephone: 314-553-2000.
Website: http://www.gotoemerson.com
Chrmn, Pres & CEO: D.N. Farr

COO: E.L. Monser
Sr EVP: C.A. Peters
Sr EVP & CFO: W.J. Galvin
EVP, Secy & General Counsel: W.W. Withers

Investor Contact: R.T. Sharp (314-553-2197)
Board of Directors: A. A. Busch, III, D. N. Farr, D. C. Farrell, C. G. Fernandez, W. J. Galvin, A. F. Golden, R. B. Horton, G. A. Lodge, V. R. Loucks, Jr., J. B. Menzer, C. A. Peters, J. W. Prueher, R. L. Ridgway, R. L. Stephenson

Founded: 1890
Domicile: Missouri
Employees: 114,200

STANDARD &POOR'S

Entergy Corp.

S&P Recommendation HOLD ★★★★★ | **Price** $85.83 (as of Oct 31, 2006) | **12-Mo. Target Price** $87.00 | **Investment Style** Large-Cap Value

GICS Sector Utilities
Sub-Industry Electric Utilities

Comment This electric utility holding company serves 2.7 million customers in Arkansas, Louisiana, Mississippi and Texas.

Key Stock Statistics (Source S&P, Vickers, company reports)

52-Wk Range	**$86.94–66.78**	S&P Oper. EPS 2006**E**	**4.70**	P/E on S&P Oper. EPS 2006**E**	**18.3**	Dividend Rate/Share	**$2.16**
Trailing 12-Month EPS	**$4.52**	S&P Oper. EPS 2007**E**	**5.55**	Common Shares Outstg. (M)	**208.4**	Yield (%)	**2.52**
Trailing 12-Month P/E	**19.0**	S&P Core EPS 2006**E**	**4.75**	Market Capitalization(B)	**$17.883**	Beta	**0.24**
$10K Invested 5 Yrs Ago	**$26,485**	S&P Core EPS 2007**E**	**5.59**	Institutional Ownership (%)	**79**	S&P Credit Rating	**NA**

Price Performance

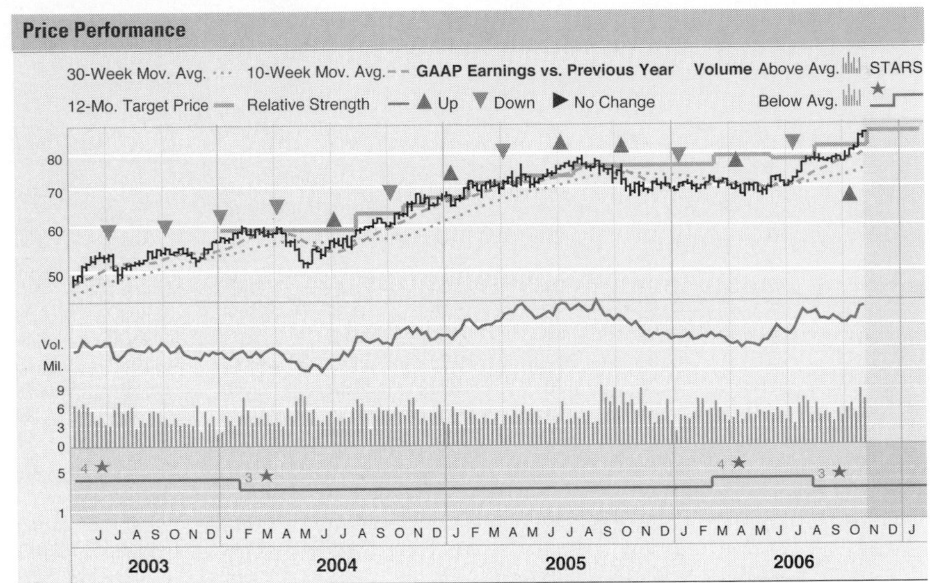

Options: ASE, CBOE, P, Ph

Highlights

- The 12-month target price for ETR has recently been changed to $87.00 from $82.00. The Highlights section of this Stock Report will be updated accordingly.

Investment Rationale/Risk

- The Investment Rationale/Risk section of this Stock Report will be updated shortly. For the latest News story on ETR from MarketScope, see below.

- 10/31/06 03:02 pm EST... S&P REITERATES HOLD OPINION ON SHARES OF ENTERGY CORP. (ETR 85.92***): ETR posts Q3 operating EPS of $1.80 vs. $1.68, $0.03 below our estimate. Results benefited from sharply higher nuclear earnings, which more than offset impact of higher operational expenses at ETR's utilities, and higher interest expense. Although we are lowering our '06 EPS estimate by $0.05 to $4.70, we are raising our '07 estimate by $0.05 to $5.55. We see '07 primarily driven by higher price contracts and a new acqusition in its nuclear operation. We are raising our 12-month target price $5 to $87, reflecting a premium-to-peers P/E of 15.7X our '07 estimate. /J.McCann

Qualitative Risk Assessment

LOW | **MEDIUM** | HIGH

Our risk assessment reflects the steady cash flow we expect from most of the regulated utilities and the nuclear operations, balanced by the uncertainties related to the recovery of the utility operations in New Orleans.

Quantitative Evaluations

S&P Quality Ranking B+

D | C | B- | B | **B+** | A- | A | A+

Relative Strength Rank STRONG

76

LOWEST = 1 HIGHEST = 99

Revenue/Earnings Data

Revenue (Million $)

	1Q	2Q	3Q	4Q	Year
2006	2,568	2,629	3,255	--	--
2005	2,323	2,710	3,130	2,652	10,106
2004	2,252	2,485	2,964	2,424	10,124
2003	2,038	2,354	2,700	2,103	9,195
2002	1,861	2,097	2,469	1,879	8,305
2001	2,653	2,495	2,576	1,885	9,621

Earnings Per Share ($)

2006	0.93	1.27	1.83	**E**0.70	**E**4.70
2005	0.79	1.33	1.65	0.59	4.40
2004	0.88	1.14	1.22	0.68	3.93
2003	1.10	0.89	1.57	-0.14	3.42
2002	-0.36	1.06	1.59	0.35	2.64
2001	0.69	1.06	1.39	-0.01	3.13

Fiscal year ended Dec. 31. Next earnings report expected: Late January. EPS Estimates based on S&P Operating Earnings; historical GAAP earnings are as reported.

Dividend Data (Dates: mm/dd Payment Date: mm/dd/yy)

Amount ($)	Date Decl.	Ex-Div. Date	Stk. of Record	Payment Date
0.540	01/27	02/08	02/10	03/01/06
0.540	04/11	05/09	05/11	06/01/06
0.540	08/04	08/11	08/15	09/01/06
0.540	10/27	11/08	11/10	12/01/06

Dividends have been paid since 1988. Source: Company reports.

Business Summary September 29, 2006

CORPORATE OVERVIEW. Entergy is an integrated energy company primarily engaged in electric power production and retail electric distribution operations. It owns and operates power plants with about 30,000 megawatts (MW) of electric generating capacity, and is the second largest nuclear power generator in the U.S. As the holding company for Entergy Arkansas, Entergy Gulf States, Entergy Louisiana, Entergy Mississippi, and Entergy New Orleans, Entergy Corp. provides electricity to 2.6 million U.S. retail customers. ETR also owns System Energy Resources, which has a 90% interest in the Grand Gulf 1 nuclear plant. The non-utility nuclear business owns and operates five nuclear plants in the northeastern U.S., selling mainly to wholesale customers.

IMPACT OF MAJOR DEVELOPMENTS. Hurricanes Katrina and Rita caused catastrophic damage to large portions of ETR's service territories in Louisiana, Mississippi, and Texas, including the effect of extensive flooding in and around greater New Orleans. Entergy estimated its total restoration costs at around $1.5 billion. It also estimated that the impact will result in lost non-fuel revenues in 2006 of $123 million for Entergy New Orleans and $39 million for Entergy Louisiana.

In September 2005, Entergy New Orleans filed for Chapter 11 reorganization. Entergy continues to work with authorities to resolve the bankruptcy in a satisfactory manner, but we think some of the key factors will remain the amount and timing of both insurance proceeds and federal and state assistance funding, as well as the number and timing of customers that return to New Orleans, and the overall economic recovery of the city.

Company Financials

Per Share Data ($) Year Ended Dec. 31	**2005**	**2004**	**2003**	**2002**	**2001**	**2000**	**1999**	**1998**	**1997**	**1996**
Tangible Book Value	35.49	36.43	36.38	33.61	33.74	31.83	29.71	28.82	19.72	25.77
Earnings	4.40	3.93	3.42	2.64	3.13	2.97	2.25	3.00	1.03	1.83
S&P Core Earnings	4.49	3.99	3.70	2.14	2.21	NA	NA	NA	NA	NA
Dividends	2.16	1.89	1.60	1.34	1.28	1.22	1.20	1.50	1.80	1.80
Payout Ratio	49%	48%	47%	51%	41%	41%	53%	50%	175%	98%
Prices:High	79.22	68.67	57.24	46.85	44.67	43.88	33.50	32.44	30.25	30.38
Prices:Low	64.48	50.64	42.26	32.12	32.56	15.94	23.69	23.25	22.38	24.88
P/E Ratio:High	18	17	17	18	14	15	15	11	29	17
P/E Ratio:Low	15	13	12	12	10	5	11	8	22	14

Income Statement Analysis (Million $)										
Revenue	10,106	10,124	9,195	8,305	9,621	10,016	8,773	11,495	9,562	7,164
Depreciation	856	896	851	839	721	785	745	985	980	791
Maintenance	NA	NA	NA	NA	NA	NA	NA	NA	NA	NA
Fixed Charges Coverage	3.69	3.54	2.66	2.23	2.25	2.83	2.34	1.91	1.87	2.51
Construction Credits	75.1	65.3	75.9	57.0	48.0	56.0	52.0	23.0	18.0	18.3
Effective Tax Rate	36.6%	28.2%	37.6%	32.1%	38.5%	40.3%	37.5%	24.4%	59.4%	50.1%
Net Income	969	933	813	623	727	711	595	786	301	420
S&P Core Earnings	961	922	856	487	495	NA	NA	NA	NA	NA

Balance Sheet & Other Financial Data (Million $)										
Gross Property	32,437	32,055	31,181	32,964	32,403	29,865	28,178	26,892	29,102	25,109
Capital Expenditures	1,458	1,411	1,569	1,580	1,380	1,494	1,196	1,144	847	572
Net Property	19,426	18,915	18,561	20,657	20,597	18,501	17,279	16,816	19,517	16,223
Capitalization:Long Term Debt	8,838	7,034	7,498	7,458	7,536	8,014	7,253	7,349	9,304	7,838
Capitalization:% Long Term Debt	53.2	44.5	45.2	47.6	49.1	52.2	49.3	49.7	54.7	50.9
Capitalization:Preferred	Nil	365	334	359	361	335	338	338	1,003	928
Capitalization:% Preferred	Nil	2.31	2.01	2.29	2.35	2.18	2.30	2.28	5.80	6.00
Capitalization:Common	7,761	8,400	8,773	7,839	7,456	7,003	7,118	7,107	6,693	6,641
Capitalization:% Common	46.8	53.2	52.8	50.1	48.6	45.6	48.4	48.0	39.3	43.1
Total Capital	22,399	21,266	21,805	20,355	19,399	19,095	18,539	18,942	22,156	19,876
% Operating Ratio	63.3	87.6	89.4	85.8	88.6	89.0	88.3	86.8	81.3	82.4
% Earned on Net Property	9.3	8.8	8.1	5.8	8.1	8.6	7.3	8.3	10.1	7.9
% Return on Revenue	9.6	9.2	8.8	7.5	7.6	7.1	6.8	6.8	3.1	5.9
% Return on Invested Capital	6.6	6.5	2.4	7.7	7.6	7.1	7.0	14.8	7.7	6.2
% Return on Common Equity	11.7	10.6	9.5	7.8	9.7	9.6	7.8	10.7	3.7	6.3

Data as orig reptd.; bef. results of disc opers/spec. items. Per share data adj. for stk. divs.; EPS diluted. E-Estimated. NA-Not Available. NM-Not Meaningful. NR-Not Ranked. UR-Under Review.

Office: 500 Clinton Center Dr, Clinton, MS 39056-5630.
Telephone: 504-576-4000.
Website: http://www.entergy.com
Chrmn & CEO: J.W. Leonard

Pres: R.J. Smith
EVP & CFO: L. Denault
EVP & General Counsel: R.D. Sloan
SVP & Chief Acctg Officer: N.E. Langston

Investor Contact: N. Morovich (504-576-5506)
Board of Directors: M. S. Bateman, W. F. Blount, C. P. Deming, G. Edwards, A. M. Herman, D. C. Hintz, J. W. Leonard, S. L. Levenick, R. V. Luft, K. A. Murphy, J. R. Nichols, W. A. Percy, II, W. J. Tauzin, S. V. Wilkinson, S. D. deBree

Founded: 1989
Domicile: Delaware
Employees: 14,136

STANDARD &POOR'S

EOG Resources Inc.

S&P Recommendation STRONG BUY ★★★★★

Price $66.53 (as of Oct 31, 2006)

12-Mo. Target Price $88.00

Investment Style Large-Cap Growth

GICS Sector Energy
Sub-Industry Oil & Gas Exploration & Production

Comment This company explores for, develops, produces and markets natural gas and crude oil in the U.S., Trinidad and Canada.

Key Stock Statistics (Source S&P, Vickers, company reports)

52-Wk Range	$86.91–56.31	S&P Oper. EPS 2006E	5.52	P/E on S&P Oper. EPS 2006E	12.1	Dividend Rate/Share	$0.24
Trailing 12-Month EPS	$6.16	S&P Oper. EPS 2007E	7.20	Common Shares Outstg. (M)	242.6	Yield (%)	0.36
Trailing 12-Month P/E	10.8	S&P Core EPS 2006E	5.52	Market Capitalization(B)	$16.141	Beta	0.50
$10K Invested 5 Yrs Ago	$36,784	S&P Core EPS 2007E	7.20	Institutional Ownership (%)	91	S&P Credit Rating	BBB+

Price Performance

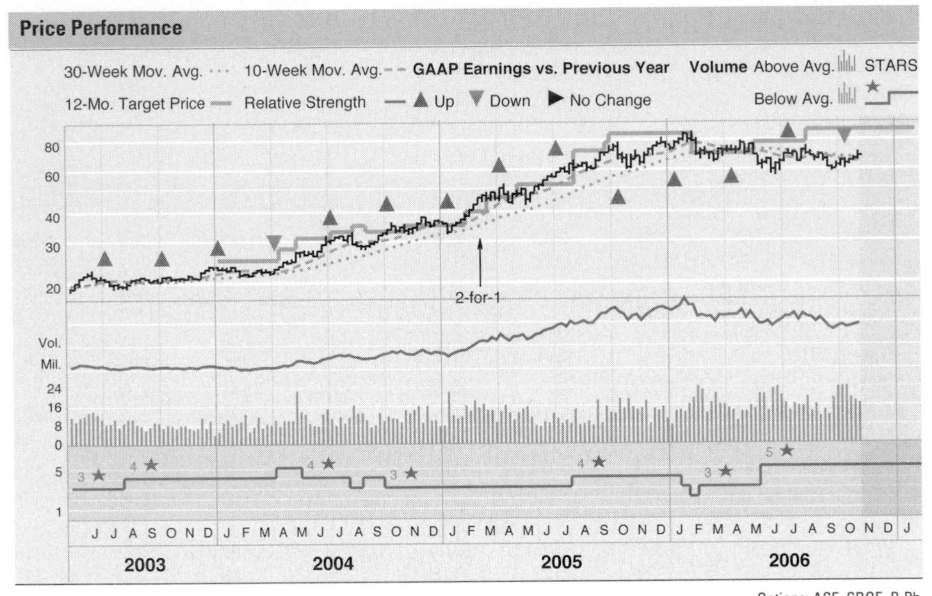

Options: ASE, CBOE, P, Ph

Analysis prepared by **Charles LaPorta, CFA** on August 28, 2006, when the stock traded at **$ 67.83**.

Highlights

- Second quarter operating EPS of $1.16, versus $1.02 last year, exceeded our estimate of $1.00. The company has acquired leases and continues to test six "conceptual" shale plays in hopes of replicating its Barnett Shale success. We believe North American operations will drive 2006 production growth of 10%, as the North Sea suffers from a lack of available equipment, and Trinidad suffers from available takeaway capacity.
- Surprisingly prolific wells in its Johnson County, TX acreage helped drive lifting costs per mcfe down 6% versus last year. We are looking for flat per unit cash operating costs in 2006 due to strong overhead control and lower field fuel costs. We also expect finding and development costs to remain in line with the three-year average, which should help restrain the growth of depreciation, depletion and amortization (DD&A) per unit to about $1.40 per mcfe for 2006.
- Our 2006 EBITDAX estimate is $3.0 billion. With EOG's debt to capitalization ratio at 13% as of June 30, 2006, we expect interest expense to decline about $15 million in 2006. We estimate the effective tax rate for 2006 at 34%.

Investment Rationale/Risk

- We expect double-digit organic production growth through the next two years, and the hedging of a portion of the company's 2006 production at what we believe are attractive prices. EOG's cost structure is among the lowest of its peers in our coverage universe, and, as a result, its five-year return on capital employed (ROCE) of 17.1% is among the highest. We estimate 2006 capital spending of $2.6 billion, given the increase in activity in the Barnett Shale and in East Texas.
- Risks to our recommendation and target price include events that would cause substantial and sustained declines in oil and gas prices; a persistent inability to replace reserves; and acts of terrorism against EOG's production facilities.
- We find it exceptional that a company of EOG's size is able to grow as fast as it has organically, and to fund such growth internally. Our 12-month target price is $88, based on a P/E of 12.2X applied to our 2007 EPS estimate and an enterprise value of 5.0X our 2007 EBITDAX projection, a premium to peers, which we believe is warranted.

Qualitative Risk Assessment

LOW | **MEDIUM** | HIGH

Our risk assessment reflects that EOG operates in a capital intensive industry that is cyclical and derives value from producing a commodity whose price is very volatile. This is balanced by EOG's history of relatively low operating costs and our view of its essentially debt-free balance sheet after netting out cash balances.

Quantitative Evaluations

S&P Quality Ranking B

D | C | B- | **B** | B+ | A- | A | A+

Relative Strength Rank MODERATE

43

LOWEST = 1 HIGHEST = 99

Revenue/Earnings Data

Revenue (Million $)

	1Q	2Q	3Q	4Q	Year
2006	1,085	919.1	968.3	--	--
2005	688.2	783.9	934.5	1,214	3,620
2004	464.3	519.0	594.2	693.7	2,271
2003	464.7	424.8	458.7	396.5	1,745
2002	186.5	290.5	279.9	338.2	1,095
2001	597.3	466.1	354.2	237.4	1,655

Earnings Per Share ($)

2006	1.73	1.34	1.21	**E**1.51	**E**5.52
2005	0.83	1.02	1.40	1.88	5.13
2004	0.42	0.60	0.71	0.85	2.58
2003	0.58	0.46	0.50	0.31	1.83
2002	-0.12	0.15	0.11	0.18	0.33
2001	0.90	0.57	0.29	-0.12	1.65

Fiscal year ended Dec. 31. Next earnings report expected: Early February. EPS Estimates based on S&P Operating Earnings; historical GAAP earnings are as reported.

Dividend Data (Dates: mm/dd Payment Date: mm/dd/yy)

Amount ($)	Date Decl.	Ex-Div. Date	Stk. of Record	Payment Date
0.040	10/28	01/12	01/17	01/31/06
0.060	02/01	04/11	04/13	04/28/06
0.060	05/02	07/13	07/17	07/31/06
0.060	09/07	10/13	10/17	10/31/06

Dividends have been paid since 1990. Source: Company reports.

EOG Resources Inc.

Business Summary August 28, 2006

CORPORATE OVERVIEW. EOG Resources, Inc. (EOG), a Delaware corporation organized in 1985, together with its subsidiaries, explores for, develops, produces and markets natural gas and crude oil primarily in major producing basins in the U.S., Canada, offshore Trinidad, and the U.K. North Sea. At December 31, 2005, EOG's total estimated net proved reserves were 6.19 trillion cubic feet equivalent (Tcfe), of which 5.56 Tcf were natural gas reserves and 106 million barrels (MMBbl), or 637 Bcfe, were crude oil and hydrocarbon liquids reserves. About 56% of EOG's reserves were in the U.S., 21% Trinidad, 22% Canada and 1% the North Sea.

MARKET PROFILE. EOG's addressable markets include North American operations, where about 75% of its reserve base is located, with the remainder in Trinidad. As a large onshore primarily natural gas producer, EOG competes in a fragmented market that is beginning to rationalize with several large onshore players such as Devon Energy (DVN: buy, $63) and XTO Energy (XTO: buy, $48). We believe North America is a relatively mature supply source for hydrocarbons, and natural gas production has been little changed in North America over the past five years. We think EOG has overcome this situation by astutely purchasing land in attractive regions such as the Barnett Shale, East Texas, and the Rocky Mountains, and employing unconventional drilling and production techniques to successfully boost production volumes. Such unconventional resource plays include basin-centered tight gas formations, coal-bed methane formations, and fractured shale formations, which are characterized by a low proportion of exploration capital expenditures, resulting in relatively low risk resource acquisition capability. In our view, the main driver of value in these resource plays is the development of drilling techniques--in a basin--that are repeatable, increasing productivity organically and moving reserves characterized as probable and possible to the proven category.

The company also has producing operations in offshore Trinidad (116 MMcf, 2.2 MBbl per day). EOG sells natural gas to Trinidad under five separate take-or-pay contracts, with terminations ranging from 2015 to 2025.

Company Financials

Per Share Data ($) Year Ended Dec. 31	**2005**	**2004**	**2003**	**2002**	**2001**	**2000**	**1999**	**1998**	**1997**	**1996**
Tangible Book Value	17.21	11.97	8.95	6.64	6.47	5.27	4.11	4.17	4.13	3.96
Cash Flow	7.81	4.69	3.73	2.02	3.32	3.17	3.61	1.20	1.27	1.23
Earnings	5.13	2.58	1.83	0.33	1.65	1.12	2.00	0.18	0.39	0.44
S&P Core Earnings	5.08	2.54	1.77	0.26	1.60	NA	NA	NA	NA	NA
Dividends	0.15	0.12	0.09	0.08	0.08	0.07	0.06	0.06	0.06	0.06
Payout Ratio	3%	5%	5%	25%	5%	6%	3%	33%	15%	14%
Prices:High	82.00	38.25	23.76	22.08	27.75	28.34	12.69	12.25	13.50	15.31
Prices:Low	32.05	21.23	17.85	15.01	12.90	6.84	7.19	5.88	8.75	11.19
P/E Ratio:High	16	15	13	68	17	25	6	68	35	35
P/E Ratio:Low	6	8	10	46	8	6	4	33	22	25

Income Statement Analysis (Million $)										
Revenue	3,620	2,271	1,745	1,095	1,655	1,490	801	769	774	731
Operating Income	1,992	979	697	648	1,181	697	18.2	114	193	209
Depreciation, Depletion and Amortization	654	504	442	398	392	370	460	315	278	251
Interest Expense	62.5	63.1	58.7	59.7	45.1	61.0	61.8	48.6	27.7	22.0
Pretax Income	1,965	926	654	120	631	634	568	60.3	163	191
Effective Tax Rate	35.9%	32.5%	33.1%	27.2%	36.9%	37.3%	NM	6.82%	25.4%	26.7%
Net Income	1,260	625	437	87.2	399	397	569	56.2	122	140
S&P Core Earnings	1,238	605	412	62.4	376	NA	NA	NA	NA	NA

Balance Sheet & Other Financial Data (Million $)										
Cash	644	21.0	4.44	9.85	2.51	20.2	24.8	6.30	9.33	7.64
Current Assets	1,563	587	396	395	272	394	201	246	282	326
Total Assets	7,753	5,799	4,749	3,814	3,414	3,001	2,611	3,018	2,723	2,458
Current Liabilities	1,172	632	477	276	311	370	219	263	291	317
Long Term Debt	859	1,078	1,109	1,145	856	859	990	1,143	741	466
Common Equity	4,217	2,847	2,098	1,524	1,495	1,234	982	1,280	1,281	1,265
Total Capital	6,298	4,925	4,125	3,478	3,050	2,580	2,346	2,683	2,310	2,040
Capital Expenditures	1,725	1,417	1,204	714	974	603	403	690	626	539
Cash Flow	1,906	1,118	868	474	780	756	1,028	371	400	391
Current Ratio	1.3	0.9	0.8	1.4	0.9	1.1	0.9	0.9	1.0	1.0
% Long Term Debt of Capitalization	13.6	21.9	26.9	32.9	28.1	33.3	42.2	42.6	32.1	22.8
% Return on Assets	18.6	11.8	10.2	2.4	12.4	14.1	20.2	2.0	4.7	6.1
% Return on Equity	35.5	24.9	23.4	5.0	28.4	34.8	50.3	4.4	9.6	11.5

Data as orig reptd.; bef. results of disc opers/spec. items. Per share data adj. for stk. divs.; EPS diluted. E-Estimated. NA-Not Available. NM-Not Meaningful. NR-Not Ranked. UR-Under Review.

Office: 333 Clay Street, Houston, TX 77002-4006.
Telephone: 877-363-3647.
Email: ir@eogresources.com
Website: http://www.eogresources.com

Chrmn & CEO: M.G. Papa
Pres: E.P. Segner, III
SVP & General Counsel: B. Hunsaker, Jr.
VP & Chief Acctg Officer: T.K. Driggers

VP & Secy: P.L. Edwards
Investor Contact: M.A. Baldwin (713-651-6364)
Board of Directors: G. A. Alcorn, C. R. Crisp, M. G. Papa, E. P. Segner, III, W. Stevens, H. L. Steward, D. F. Textor, F. G. Wisner

Founded: 1985
Domicile: Delaware
Employees: 1,400

E TRADE Financial Corporation

STANDARD &POOR'S

S&P Recommendation STRONG BUY ★★★★★

Price $23.83 (as of Oct 27, 2006)

12-Mo. Target Price $30.00

Investment Style Large-Cap Growth

GICS Sector Financials
Sub-Industry Investment Banking & Brokerage

Comment E*TRADE provides online discount brokerage, mortgage and banking services, primarily to retail customers.

Key Stock Statistics (Source S&P, Vickers, company reports)

52-Wk Range	$27.76–18.15	S&P Oper. EPS 2006E	1.41	P/E on S&P Oper. EPS 2006E	16.9	Dividend Rate/Share	Nil
Trailing 12-Month EPS	$1.36	S&P Oper. EPS 2007E	1.84	Common Shares Outstg. (M)	427.2	Yield (%)	Nil
Trailing 12-Month P/E	17.5	S&P Core EPS 2006E	1.41	Market Capitalization(B)	$10.180	Beta	2.22
$10K Invested 5 Yrs Ago	$32,030	S&P Core EPS 2007E	1.84	Institutional Ownership (%)	80	S&P Credit Rating	BB-

Price Performance

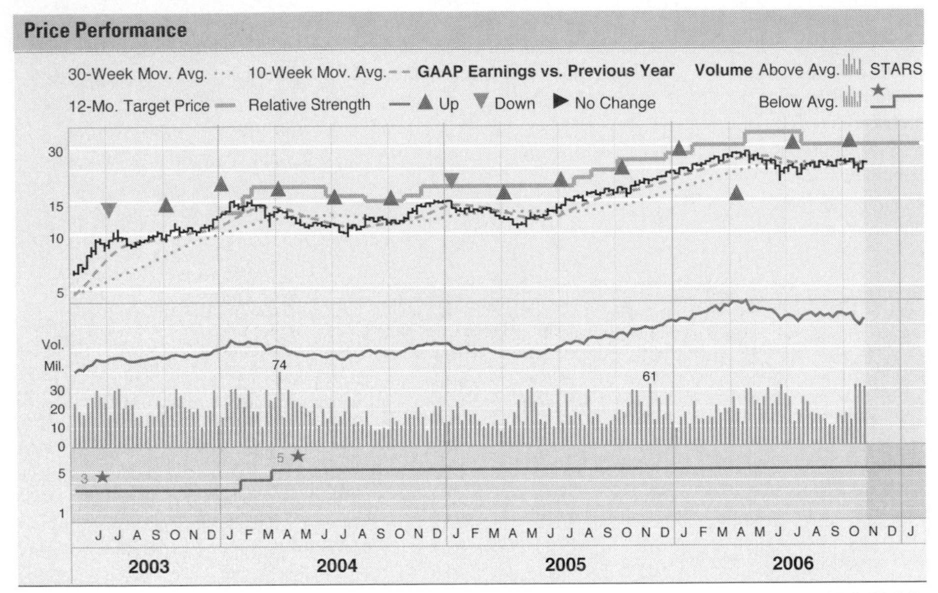

Options: ASE, CBOE, P, Ph

Analysis prepared by **Matthew Albrecht** on October 24, 2006, when the stock traded at **$ 22.71**.

Highlights

- We think ET is gaining market share, aided by its attractive commission rates, expanding branch network, and recent acquisitions. We like ET's diversification between its retail brokerage and banking businesses, which provide synergies and have resulted in more stable operating earnings, in our view. We expect ET to increasingly segment its customer base and target international clients, active investors, and option trading opportunities.
- Results through the first nine months of 2006 were aided by growth in client accounts, specifically banking accounts, wider net interest spreads, and higher trading volume. We view positively the fact that ET has largely completed the integration of two major acquisitions ahead of schedule and without excessive account attrition. We see some pressure on retail trading volume from recent market volatility, but expect banking profits to increase, aided by growth in assets and lower funding costs.
- We forecast EPS of $1.41 in 2006 and $1.84 in 2007, reflecting our expectations for higher trading activity, organic growth in customer cash balances, stable net interest margins, and merger synergies.

Investment Rationale/Risk

- We think recently completed acquisitions put ET back into a four-horse race with rivals and strengthen the company's competitive position. The integration of BrownCo and Harrisdirect are largely complete, which should add to economies of scale through 2007. Although we see pressure on commission rates, we think market share gains, earnings growth and industry consolidation will help the shares move higher.
- Risks to our recommendation and target price include interest rate volatility, increased price competition, various regulatory issues, and potential equity market depreciation, notably in the Nasdaq. Also, we have corporate governance concerns including generous executive compensation and anti-takeover provisions.
- The shares recently traded at about 12.3X our 2007 EPS estimate, a discount to peers. Our 12-month target price of $30 is arrived at by applying a multiple of about 16X to our 2007 EPS estimate, also a discount to online broker peers, warranted, in our view, by ET's heavier reliance on banking.

Qualitative Risk Assessment

LOW | MEDIUM | **HIGH**

Our risk assessment reflects our concern with significant industry volatility and formidable competition, only partially offset by ET's strong client relationships and successful acquisition strategy.

Quantitative Evaluations

S&P Quality Ranking B-

D | C | **B-** | B | B+ | A- | A | A+

Relative Strength Rank MODERATE

48

LOWEST = 1 HIGHEST = 99

Revenue/Earnings Data

Revenue (Million $)

	1Q	2Q	3Q	4Q	Year
2006	598.4	937.4	581.8	--	--
2005	417.4	387.7	419.8	478.9	1,704
2004	400.5	380.9	337.1	409.5	1,947
2003	322.2	381.1	397.7	382.8	1,719
2002	554.6	531.2	468.6	484.7	2,302
2001	550.1	516.0	481.4	514.6	2,062

Earnings Per Share ($)

	1Q	2Q	3Q	4Q	Year
2006	0.33	0.36	0.34	--	E1.41
2005	0.27	0.29	0.29	0.31	1.16
2004	0.23	0.24	0.21	0.24	0.92
2003	0.06	0.03	0.17	0.27	0.55
2002	0.05	0.09	0.06	0.08	0.30
2001	-0.02	-0.04	-0.77	0.02	-0.81

Fiscal year ended Dec. 31. Next earnings report expected: Late January. EPS Estimates based on S&P Operating Earnings; historical GAAP earnings are as reported.

Dividend Data

No cash dividends have been paid.

The McGraw-Hill Companies

E TRADE Financial Corporation

Business Summary October 24, 2006

E*TRADE Financial (ET) is one of the industry's leading online financial services concerns. The company provides online discount brokerage and banking services, primarily to retail customers. Although most of the company's business is done over the Internet, ET also serves customers through branches, automated and live telephone service, and Internet-enabled wireless devices. Retail customers can move money electronically between brokerage, banking and lending accounts. As of June 30 2006, ET had about 3.6 million brokerage accounts and about 749,000 banking accounts. We expect the company to open about 20 branches over the next two years, bringing its total to about 36, and to continue to shed non-core businesses.

Through its Brokerage segment, ET's customers can buy and sell stocks, bonds, options, futures, and over 6,000 non-proprietary mutual funds. Customers can also obtain streaming quotes and charts, access real-time market commentary and research reports, and perform personalized portfolio tracking. Brokerage customers can obtain margin loans collateralized by their securities. The company uses sophisticated proprietary transaction-enabling technology to automate traditionally labor-intensive transactions. The brokerage business continues to be the primary point of introduction for the majority of ET's customers, who are typically self-directed investors.

Through its Banking segment, the company offers residential mortgage products, home equity loans and home equity lines of credit (HELOC). The segment also offers credit card, automobile, recreational vehicle (RV), marine and other consumer loans. In late 2003, the Banking segment began sweeping Brokerage customer money market balances into an FDIC-insured Sweep Deposit Account (SDA) product, which lowered its cost of funds. At the end of 2005, ET had $7.7 billion in the SDA product, up from $4.3 billion at the end of 2003. We look for the transfer of nearly $5 billion in additional cash balances into ET's Sweep Deposit Account program, which was introduced in 2003. We estimate that nearly half of the bank's customers are also brokerage customers. ET's loan portfolio consists of first mortgages, the majority of which are adjustable-rate, home equity lines of credit (HELOC) and second mortgage loan products, and consumer loans for recreational vehicle (RV), marine, automobile, and credit card loans. We think credit quality looks good, given ET's total allowance for loan losses as a percentage of total nonperforming loans increased to 183% at the end of 2005, up from 96% at the end of 2001.

Company Financials

Per Share Data ($) Year Ended Dec. 31	**2005**	**2004**	**2003**	**2002**	**2001**	**2000**	**1999**	**1998**	**1997**	**1996**
Tangible Book Value	2.07	4.58	3.73	2.68	2.54	4.43	3.81	3.14	1.82	0.59
Cash Flow	1.36	1.07	0.55	1.20	-0.28	0.37	-0.09	0.07	0.13	0.00
Earnings	1.16	0.92	0.55	0.30	-0.81	-0.06	-0.23	-0.01	0.10	-0.01
S&P Core Earnings	0.88	0.66	0.27	0.27	-0.86	NA	NA	NA	NA	NA
Dividends	Nil	Nil	Nil	Nil	Nil	Nil	Nil	Nil	Nil	Nil
Payout Ratio	Nil	Nil	Nil	Nil	Nil	Nil	Nil	Nil	Nil	Nil
Prices:High	21.71	15.40	12.91	12.64	15.38	34.25	72.25	16.25	11.97	3.47
Prices:Low	10.53	9.51	3.65	2.81	4.07	6.66	12.74	2.50	2.75	2.06
P/E Ratio:High	19	17	23	42	NM	NM	NM	NM	119	NM
P/E Ratio:Low	9	10	7	9	NM	NM	NM	NM	27	NM
Income Statement Analysis (Million $)										
Commissions	459	350	337	302	407	739	356	162	110	44.2
Interest Income	1,650	1,146	6.54	12.7	22.2	17.2	196	95.7	40.2	7.00
Total Revenue	1,704	1,947	1,719	2,302	2,062	1,973	695	285	158	58.6
Interest Expense	853	558	532	609	832	630	73.4	39.7	14.9	2.22
Pretax Income	676	514	310	194	-310	104	-91.5	-1.67	23.3	-1.38
Effective Tax Rate	34.0%	31.6%	36.2%	43.9%	NM	81.8%	NM	NM	40.4%	NM
Net Income	446	351	203	107	-271	19.2	-54.4	-0.71	13.9	-0.83
S&P Core Earnings	339	247	101	96.1	-291	NA	NA	NA	NA	NA
Balance Sheet & Other Financial Data (Million $)										
Total Assets	44,568	31,033	26,049	21,534	18,172	17,317	3,927	1,969	990	990
Cash Items	844	940	921	2,223	1,601	301	189	26.8	36.8	50.1
Receivables	7,174	3,035	2,298	1,500	2,139	6,543	2,913	1,310	728	193
Securities Owned	12,565	12,589	9,876	8,702	4,726	985	189	503	191	35.0
Securities Borrowed	Nil	Nil	Nil	Nil	Nil	NA	NA	NA	NA	NA
Due Brokers & Customers	7,316	3,619	3,696	2,792	2,700	6,056	2,824	1,185	681	0.22
Other Liabilities	38.1	52.2	79.3	775	818	471	189	73.8	18.1	6.10
Capitalization:Debt	6,189	586	695	907	605	3,336	Nil	Nil	9.40	0.02
Capitalization:Equity	3,400	2,228	1,918	1,506	1,571	1,857	914	710	281	69.3
Capitalization:Total	9,589	2,814	2,614	2,412	2,175	5,192	914	710	291	69.3
% Return on Revenue	68.4	18.0	11.8	5.4	NM	1.6	NM	NM	8.8	NM
% Return on Assets	1.2	1.2	0.9	0.5	NM	0.2	NM	NM	2.2	NM
% Return on Equity	15.9	16.9	11.9	7.0	NM	1.2	NM	NM	7.9	NM

Data as orig reptd.; bef. results of disc opers/spec. items. Per share data adj. for stk. divs.; EPS diluted. E-Estimated. NA-Not Available. NM-Not Meaningful. NR-Not Ranked. UR-Under Review.

Office: 135 E 57th St, New York, NY 10022-2050.
Telephone: 646-521-4300.
Email: ir@etrade.com
Website: http://www.etrade.com

Chrmn: G. Hayter
Pres & COO: R.J. Lilien
CEO: M. Caplan
CFO: R.J. Simmons

Chief Admin: A.W. Gelbard
Investor Contact: C. Dotson (650-331-6000)
Board of Directors: D. Brewster, M. H. Caplan, R. D. Fisher, G. Hayter, M. K. Parks, C. C. Raffaeli, L. E. Randall, D. L. Weaver, S. H. Willard

Founded: 1982
Domicile: Delaware
Employees: 3,400

STANDARD & POOR'S

Equifax Inc.

S&P Recommendation HOLD ★★★★★

Price $37.40 (as of Oct 27, 2006)

12-Mo. Target Price $39.00

Investment Style Mid-Cap Growth

GICS Sector Industrials
Sub-Industry Diversified Commercial & Professional Services

Comment This company is a leading worldwide source of consumer and commercial credit information.

Key Stock Statistics (Source S&P, Vickers, company reports)

52-Wk Range	$39.42–30.15	S&P Oper. EPS 2006E	2.05	P/E on S&P Oper. EPS 2006E	18.2	Dividend Rate/Share	$0.16
Trailing 12-Month EPS	$2.09	S&P Oper. EPS 2007E	2.25	Common Shares Outstg. (M)	126.6	Yield (%)	0.43
Trailing 12-Month P/E	17.9	S&P Core EPS 2006E	2.05	Market Capitalization(B)	$4.736	Beta	1.18
$10K Invested 5 Yrs Ago	$16,476	S&P Core EPS 2007E	2.25	Institutional Ownership (%)	79	S&P Credit Rating	A-

Price Performance

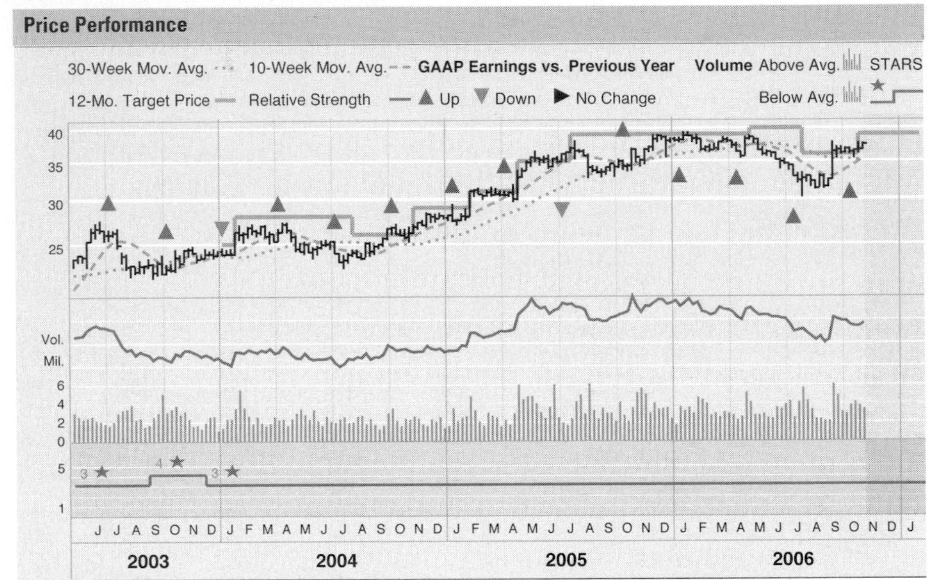

Options: ASE, P, Ph

Analysis prepared by **Zaineb Bokhari** on October 20, 2006, when the stock traded at **$ 36.37**.

Highlights

- After rising about 13% in 2005, we expect revenues to increase by 7% in 2006, to about $1.5 billion, aided by EFX's ongoing participation under the Fair and Accurate Credit Transaction (FACT) Act and, to some extent, by recent acquisitions. We look for revenue growth of about 5% in 2007.
- While we believe EFX's participation under the FACT Act had a positive impact on revenue (of about $38 million) and EPS in 2005, we think it had a negative impact on operating margins. We expect operating margins of about 34% in 2006, versus 35% in 2005, to be affected by EFX's continued participation under the act. We also expect 2006 operating margins to be affected somewhat as EFX continues to broaden its service offerings in international markets, particularly Latin America. We see modestly wider operating margins in 2007.
- We estimate operating EPS of $2.05 in 2006 (excluding gains and one-time items), up from $1.79 in 2005 (excluding a contribution of about $0.07 from the company's FACT Act participation). We see EPS rising 10%, to $2.25, in 2007.

Investment Rationale/Risk

- While we believe that heightened consumer awareness of identity theft and the importance of protecting credit information will benefit the company, we believe this will be offset, to some extent, by the increased attention this issue is receiving from federal regulators, such as the FACT Act, which allows consumers to receive a free credit report annually from the credit bureaus. International markets should offer avenues for growth for EFX, in our view, particularly in the United Kingdom and Latin America. However, slower-growing North America remains the largest contributor to total revenues (81% in 2005).
- Risks to our opinion and target price include increasing competition from the other major credit bureaus, Experian and TransUnion. We are also concerned about the possibility of a slowdown in the company's North American mortgage services business if domestic interest rates trend higher.
- Our 12-month target price of $39 is derived by applying a 17.5X P/E to our 2007 EPS estimate, within the shares' average historical range of 12.9X to 18.7X, and at a modest discount to the average for peers of 19.3X.

Qualitative Risk Assessment

LOW | **MEDIUM** | HIGH

Our risk assessment reflects our view that the majority of the company's domestic operations are relatively mature, offset by our positive outlook for its European and Latin American operations, which we see growing faster than domestic operations.

Quantitative Evaluations

S&P Quality Ranking B+

D | C | B- | B | **B+** | A- | A | A+

Relative Strength Rank MODERATE

70

LOWEST = 1 HIGHEST = 99

Revenue/Earnings Data

Revenue (Million $)

	1Q	2Q	3Q	4Q	Year
2006	374.0	387.7	394.6	--	--
2005	343.4	363.4	375.3	361.3	1,443
2004	309.9	315.4	319.9	327.6	1,273
2003	301.6	317.0	309.8	297.0	1,225
2002	259.0	268.0	289.7	292.6	1,109
2001	285.2	289.6	282.4	281.9	1,139

Earnings Per Share ($)

	1Q	2Q	3Q	4Q	Year
2006	0.48	0.53	0.61	**E**0.56	**E**2.05
2005	0.44	0.47	0.47	0.48	1.86
2004	0.38	0.58	0.40	0.42	1.78
2003	0.33	0.36	0.39	0.23	1.31
2002	0.30	0.34	0.36	0.38	1.39
2001	0.24	0.28	0.26	0.07	0.84

Fiscal year ended Dec. 31. Next earnings report expected: Early February. EPS Estimates based on S&P Operating Earnings; historical GAAP earnings are as reported.

Dividend Data (Dates: mm/dd Payment Date: mm/dd/yy)

Amount ($)	Date Decl.	Ex-Div. Date	Stk. of Record	Payment Date
0.040	11/03	11/21	11/24	12/15/05
0.040	02/24	02/27	03/01	03/15/06
0.040	05/17	05/23	05/25	06/15/06
0.040	08/16	08/23	08/25	09/15/06

Dividends have been paid since 1914. Source: Company reports.

Equifax Inc.

Business Summary October 20, 2006

CORPORATE OVERVIEW. Equifax is one of three main providers of consumer and commercial credit information in the U.S. Equifax collects, organizes and manages credit, financial, demographic and marketing information regarding individuals and businesses, which the company collects from various sources. These sources include financial or credit granting institutions (which provide accounts receivable information), government organizations and consumers. The company maintains information in proprietary databases regarding approximately 400 million consumers and businesses worldwide. EFX amasses and processes this data using proprietary systems, and makes the data available to customers in various formats.

Products and services include consumer credit information, information database management, marketing information, business credit information, decisioning and analytical tools, and identity verification services that enable businesses to make informed decisions about extending credit or providing services, managing portfolio risk, and developing marketing strategies. According to the company, EFX allows consumers to manage and protect their financial affairs through products that the company sells directly to individuals using the Internet.

Equifax derived 81% of operating revenue from North America in 2005, down from 82% in 2004. The company's largest operating segment, North American Information Services (56% of revenues in both 2005 and 2004), includes Consumer Services (credit information regarding individuals), Small Business Services (credit information regarding small businesses), Mortgage Services (credit loan origination information) and Canadian operations (commercial credit reporting). Other North American operating segments include Personal Solutions (credit information sales to consumers) and Marketing Services (credit and direct marketing services), which collectively accounted for 26% of revenues in each of 2005 and 2004.

Company Financials

Per Share Data ($) Year Ended Dec. 31	**2005**	**2004**	**2003**	**2002**	**2001**	**2000**	**1999**	**1998**	**1997**	**1996**
Tangible Book Value	NM	NM	NM	NM	NM	NM	NM	NM	NM	NM
Cash Flow	2.49	2.39	2.00	1.96	1.61	2.77	2.44	2.06	1.78	1.81
Earnings	1.86	1.78	1.31	1.39	0.84	1.68	1.55	1.34	1.25	1.03
S&P Core Earnings	1.88	1.59	1.18	1.04	0.52	NA	NA	NA	NA	NA
Dividends	0.15	0.11	0.08	0.08	0.25	0.37	0.36	0.35	0.35	0.33
Payout Ratio	8%	6%	6%	6%	29%	22%	23%	26%	28%	32%
Prices:High	39.00	28.46	27.59	31.30	38.76	36.50	39.88	45.00	37.19	34.50
Prices:Low	26.97	22.60	17.84	18.95	18.60	19.88	20.13	29.75	26.50	17.75
P/E Ratio:High	21	16	21	23	46	22	26	34	30	33
P/E Ratio:Low	14	13	14	14	22	12	13	22	21	17

Income Statement Analysis (Million $)	2005	2004	2003	2002	2001	2000	1999	1998	1997	1996
Revenue	1,443	1,273	1,225	1,109	1,139	1,966	1,773	1,621	1,366	1,811
Operating Income	504	459	438	432	420	604	540	469	401	401
Depreciation	82.2	81.1	95.3	80.5	106	149	125	104	77.1	85.9
Interest Expense	35.6	34.9	39.6	41.2	47.8	76.0	61.0	42.7	20.8	23.0
Pretax Income	396	388	286	317	205	385	366	327	323	304
Effective Tax Rate	36.5%	38.1%	36.5%	39.0%	41.7%	40.8%	41.0%	40.9%	42.6%	41.5%
Net Income	247	237	179	191	117	228	216	193	186	178
S&P Core Earnings	248	211	162	146	73.6	NA	NA	NA	NA	NA

Balance Sheet & Other Financial Data (Million $)	2005	2004	2003	2002	2001	2000	1999	1998	1997	1996
Cash	37.5	52.1	39.3	30.5	33.2	89.4	137	90.6	52.3	49.9
Current Assets	280	300	286	286	358	605	609	520	401	437
Total Assets	1,832	1,557	1,553	1,507	1,423	2,070	1,840	1,829	1,177	1,303
Current Liabilities	295	457	355	428	276	426	505	419	328	375
Long Term Debt	464	399	663	691	694	994	934	869	339	306
Common Equity	820	524	372	221	244	384	393	366	349	425
Total Capital	1,410	961	1,079	938	1,026	1,467	1,400	1,286	688	731
Capital Expenditures	17.2	16.5	14.6	12.8	13.0	37.1	39.0	44.9	34.5	56.0
Cash Flow	329	318	274	272	224	377	341	297	263	264
Current Ratio	1.0	0.7	0.8	0.7	1.3	1.4	1.2	1.2	1.2	1.2
% Long Term Debt of Capitalization	32.9	41.5	61.5	73.7	67.6	67.7	66.7	67.6	49.2	41.9
% Net Income of Revenue	17.1	18.6	14.6	17.2	10.3	11.6	12.2	11.9	13.6	9.8
% Return on Assets	14.5	15.3	11.7	13.1	7.1	11.7	11.8	12.9	15.0	15.1
% Return on Equity	36.7	53.0	60.3	82.4	37.4	76.1	49.7	54.0	47.9	45.6

Data as orig reptd.; bef. results of disc opers/spec. items. Per share data adj. for stk. divs.; EPS diluted. E-Estimated. NA-Not Available. NM-Not Meaningful. NR-Not Ranked. UR-Under Review.

Office: 1550 Peachtree St NW, Atlanta, GA 30309.
Telephone: 404-885-8000.
Email: investor@equifax.com
Website: http://www.equifax.com

Chrmn & CEO: R.F. Smith
VP & Chief Acctg Officer: N.M. King
VP, Secy & General Counsel: K.E. Mast
CFO: L. Andrean

Chief Admin: C.M. Rushing
Investor Contact: J. Dodge
Board of Directors: C. G. Betty, J. L. Clendenin, J. E. Copeland Jr., A. W. Dahlberg, R. D. Daleo, L. P. Humann, L. A. Kennedy, S. S. Marshall, L. L. Prince, D. R. Riddle, R. F. Smith, J. M. Ward

Founded: 1913
Domicile: Georgia
Employees: 4,600

STANDARD & POOR'S

Equity Office Properties Trust

S&P Recommendation SELL ★★★★★

Price $42.50 (as of Oct 31, 2006)

12-Mo. Target Price $37.00

Investment Style Large-Cap Value

GICS Sector Financials
Sub-Industry Office REITS

Comment This REIT is the largest publicly held owner and manager of office properties in the U.S.

Key Stock Statistics (Source S&P, Vickers, company reports)

52-Wk Range	$42.57–28.20	S&P Oper. EPS 2006E	0.09	P/E on S&P Oper. EPS 2006E	NM	Dividend Rate/Share	$1.32
Trailing 12-Month EPS	$0.03	S&P Oper. EPS 2007E	0.25	Common Shares Outstg. (M)	350.1	Yield (%)	3.11
Trailing 12-Month P/E	NM	S&P Core EPS 2006E	0.09	Market Capitalization(B)	$14.880	Beta	0.57
$10K Invested 5 Yrs Ago	$21,333	S&P Core EPS 2007E	0.25	Institutional Ownership (%)	96	S&P Credit Rating	BBB

Price Performance

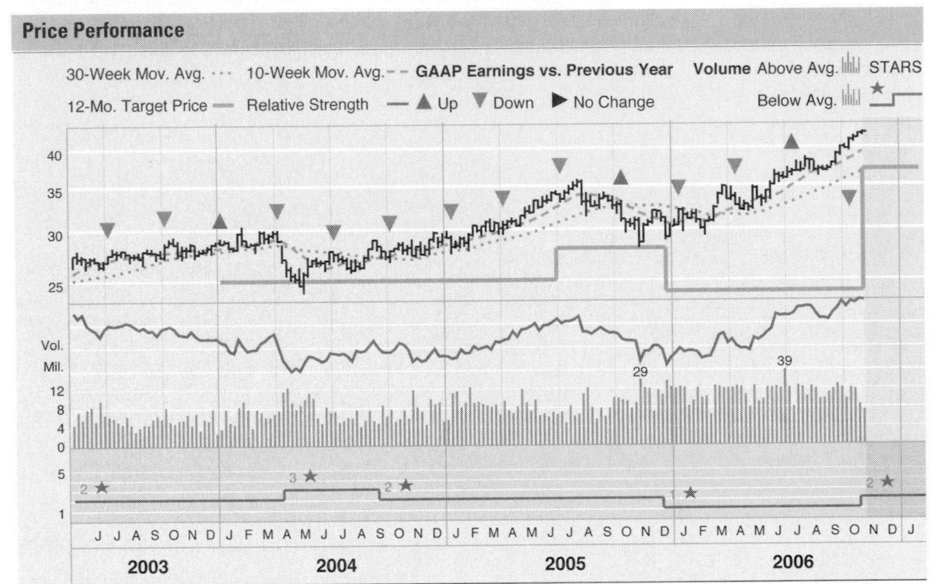

Options: ASE, CBOE, P, Ph

Analysis prepared by **Royal F. Shepard, CFA** on October 24, 2006, when the stock traded at **$ 41.98**.

Highlights

- We think EOP will remain aggressive in recycling its office portfolio. Since early 2005, the trust has sold more than $3 billion in assets. In addition, EOP is exploring the sale of $3.0 billion-$3.5 billion in additional assets through year-end 2007. Proceeds are likely, in our view, to go toward new investments and share buy backs. We see pressure in 2006 from the roll-down of rents by an average of 5%-10% as leases expire. We think better market conditions may begin easing that pressure in 2007.

- We expect occupancy levels to increase about 100 basis points in 2006, from an average of 90.4% in 2005. Asset sales, however, could dilute reported earnings. Also, EOP is spending more on tenant improvements due to higher construction and labor costs. We estimate 2006 EPS of $0.20, versus $0.38 from continuing operations in 2005. Per share FFO for 2006 is projected at $2.15, down from $2.26.

- During the first half of 2006, EOP repurchased 35.6 million shares for $1.2 billion. Based on our cash flow projections, however, EOP may need to use some cash proceeds from planned dispositions to cover its already reduced dividend payout.

Investment Rationale/Risk

- In our view, EOP faces several challenges, including in-place rents that are above the current market, customer concessions in the form of capital improvements, and dilution from asset turnover. We expect a decline in property operating income in 2006 without a significant rebound until 2008. Ongoing asset sales will, in our opinion, eventually provide some value to investors.

- Risks to our recommendation and target price include the possibility that national employment growth will exceed our expectations or that a major geographic market will experience an economic surge.

- We think EOP deserves to sell at a discount to peers based on our view of its weak financial profile, including minimal (1.1X) coverage of fixed charges. Our 12-month target price of $37 is a blend of our relative price to FFO estimate (16.5X our 2007 FFO estimate of $2.40) and our net asset value estimate, based on the stock's recent price.

Qualitative Risk Assessment

LOW	MEDIUM	HIGH

Our risk assessment of EOP reflects our view of its large and diversified portfolio, offset by what we see as its above-average financial leverage and low fixed charge coverage, and a recent dividend cut.

Quantitative Evaluations

S&P Quality Ranking **B**

D	C	B-	B	B+	A-	A	A+

Relative Strength Rank **STRONG**

76

LOWEST = 1 HIGHEST = 99

Revenue/Earnings Data

Revenue (Million $)

	1Q	2Q	3Q	4Q	Year
2006	853.7	840.4	860.4	--	--
2005	758.1	723.8	732.1	786.6	3,001
2004	789.4	793.0	793.9	819.5	3,196
2003	829.3	811.0	806.2	828.8	3,196
2002	873.4	872.9	875.2	884.5	3,506
2001	666.2	668.9	893.7	901.4	3,130

Earnings Per Share ($)

	1Q	2Q	3Q	4Q	Year
2006	0.04	0.03	-0.20	E0.06	E0.09
2005	0.22	-0.25	0.16	-0.03	0.38
2004	0.23	0.24	-0.33	0.16	0.28
2003	0.33	0.30	0.28	0.45	1.26
2002	0.51	0.41	0.41	0.42	1.75
2001	0.39	0.40	0.49	0.30	1.58

Fiscal year ended Dec. 31. Next earnings report expected: Early February. EPS Estimates based on S&P Operating Earnings; historical GAAP earnings are as reported.

Dividend Data (Dates: mm/dd Payment Date: mm/dd/yy)

Amount ($)	Date Decl.	Ex-Div. Date	Stk. of Record	Payment Date
0.500	12/01	12/13	12/15	12/30/05
0.330	03/10	03/29	03/31	04/17/06
0.330	06/15	06/28	06/30	07/17/06
0.330	09/15	09/27	09/29	10/16/06

Dividends have been paid since 1997. Source: Company reports.

Please read the Required Disclosures and Analyst Certification on the last page of this report.

Equity Office Properties Trust

Business Summary October 24, 2006

CORPORATE OVERVIEW. Equity Office Properties Trust is the largest publicly held owner and operator of U.S. office buildings, in terms of both market capitalization and square footage. The trust's strategy is to achieve sustainable long-term growth in cash flow and portfolio value. EOP is the sole general partner of--and owns approximately 89.7% of--the partnership units of EOP Operating Limited Partnership, through which it owns substantially all its assets and conducts substantially all its operations.

At June 30, 2006, EOP owned or had interests in 595 office properties, with 109.2 million rentable sq. ft. of space. The trust has sold all of its 77 industrial properties over the past three years. The office properties, by rentable square foot, were about 39.4% in central business districts and 60.6% in suburban markets. Occupancy levels at EOP's office properties have trended down in recent years, from 95% at year-end 1998 to 86.6% by year-end 2003. However, they bounced back to 87.7% at year-end 2004 and 90.7% by June 30, 2006. In part, we believe this reflects the disposition of lower occupancy properties.

The trust owns a geographically diversified portfolio, with properties in 27 metropolitan areas, including 17 core markets. At year-end 2005, EOP's largest markets for its office properties were Boston (11.4% of rentable sq. ft., 14.0% of property net operating income), San Francisco (9.3%, 10.9%), San Jose (6.4%, 8.8%), New York (5.3%, 8.9%), Los Angeles (7.2%, 9.5%), Seattle (8.6%, 7.6%), Chicago (10.3%, 6.9%), and Washington, DC (6.0%, 7.6%).

MARKET PROFILE. The market for office leases is inherently cyclical. Local economic conditions, particularly the employment level, play an important role in determining competitive dynamics. Standard & Poor's estimates that non-farm payrolls will increase 170,000 per month, on average, in 2006, comparable to growth in 2005.

Company Financials

Per Share Data ($) Year Ended Dec. 31	**2005**	**2004**	**2003**	**2002**	**2001**	**2000**	**1999**	**1998**	**1997**	**1996**
Tangible Book Value	18.27	22.28	24.96	24.67	27.09	24.01	26.91	24.56	24.80	14.28
Earnings	0.38	0.28	1.26	1.75	1.58	1.53	1.52	1.24	1.11	0.91
S&P Core Earnings	0.38	0.26	1.24	1.59	1.77	NA	NA	NA	NA	NA
Dividends	2.00	2.00	2.00	2.00	1.90	1.71	1.58	1.38	0.56	NA
Payout Ratio	NM	NM	159%	114%	120%	112%	61%	111%	50%	NA
Prices:High	35.79	30.40	29.30	31.36	33.19	33.50	29.38	32.00	34.68	NA
Prices:Low	27.45	23.90	23.31	22.78	26.20	22.88	20.81	20.19	21.00	NA
P/E Ratio:High	94	NM	23	18	21	22	11	26	31	NA
P/E Ratio:Low	72	NM	18	13	17	15	8	16	19	NA
Income Statement Analysis (Million $)										
Rental Income	2,763	2,554	2,537	2,715	2,426	1,733	1,493	1,538	1,127	503
Mortgage Income	Nil	Nil	Nil	Nil	Nil	2,264	14.2	11.7	23.1	9.85
Total Income	3,001	3,196	3,190	3,508	3,130	2,264	1,942	1,680	1,451	670
General Expenses	931	895	858	137	767	865	751	664	838	422
Interest Expense	832	851	820	815	734	526	414	339	275	111
Provision for Losses	Nil	Nil	Nil	Nil	Nil	Nil	Nil	Nil	Nil	Nil
Depreciation	750	784	716	684	575	427	359	306	253	135
Net Income	204	156	549	732	630	473	442	357	282	134
S&P Core Earnings	169	109	490	660	654	NA	NA	NA	NA	NA
Balance Sheet & Other Financial Data (Million $)										
Cash	21,458	107	69.4	58.5	61.1	53.3	2.30	67.0	229	31.5
Total Assets	22,974	24,672	24,189	25,247	25,808	18,794	14,046	14,261	11,752	5,009
Real Estate Investment	24,717	26,422	25,439	25,164	24,816	17,619	13,203	13,684	11,041	NA
Loss Reserve	Nil	Nil	Nil	Nil	Nil	Nil	Nil	Nil	Nil	NA
Net Investment	21,380	23,257	22,861	23,086	23,322	16,641	13,438	13,332	10,976	4,843
Short Term Debt	1,631	548	334	1,008	130	159	187	1,332	2,041	240
Capitalization:Debt	11,088	12,809	11,479	11,743	11,859	8,644	5,665	4,693	2,243	1,358
Capitalization:Equity	7,536	9,059	9,733	10,209	10,445	7,453	6,211	7,052	6,205	3,059
Capitalization:Total	20,172	23,628	23,214	24,261	24,772	17,930	13,375	13,077	9,403	4,662
% Earnings & Depreciation/Assets	4.0	3.8	5.1	5.5	5.4	5.4	5.7	5.1	6.4	NA
Price Times Book Value:High	2.0	1.4	1.2	1.3	1.2	1.4	1.1	1.3	1.4	NA
Price Times Book Value:Low	1.5	1.1	0.9	0.9	1.0	0.9	0.8	0.8	0.9	NA

Data as orig reptd.; bef. results of disc opers/spec. items. Per share data adj. for stk. divs.; EPS diluted. E-Estimated. NA-Not Available. NM-Not Meaningful. NR-Not Ranked. UR-Under Review.

Office: Two North Riverside Plaza, Chicago, IL 60606-2621.
Telephone: 312-466-3300.
Website: http://www.equityoffice.com
Chrmn: S. Zell

Pres & CEO: R. Kincaid
COO & EVP: P. Owen, Jr.
EVP & CFO: M.C. Williams
EVP, Secy & General Counsel: S.M. Stevens

Investor Contact: C. Shipstead (312-466-4336)
Trustees: M. Alexander, T. E. Dobrowski, W. M. Goodyear, J. D. Harper, Jr., R. D. Kincaid, S. Z. Rosenberg, S. I. Sadove, S. Susman, S. Zell, J. H. van der Vlist

Founded: 1996
Domicile: Maryland
Employees: 2,300

STANDARD &POOR'S

Equity Residential

S&P Recommendation SELL ★★★★★

Price $54.45 (as of Oct 27, 2006)

12-Mo. Target Price $33.00

Investment Style Large-Cap Value

GICS Sector Financials
Sub-Industry Residential REITS

Comment This equity REIT (formerly Equity Residential Properties Trust) owns and operates a nationally diversified portfolio of apartment properties.

Key Stock Statistics (Source S&P, Vickers, company reports)

52-Wk Range	$54.91–37.31	S&P Oper. EPS 2006E	0.40	P/E on S&P Oper. EPS 2006E	NM	Dividend Rate/Share	$1.77
Trailing 12-Month EPS	$3.39	S&P Oper. EPS 2007E	0.55	Common Shares Outstg. (M)	291.0	Yield (%)	3.25
Trailing 12-Month P/E	16.1	S&P Core EPS 2006E	0.40	Market Capitalization(B)	$15.843	Beta	0.85
$10K Invested 5 Yrs Ago	$27,906	S&P Core EPS 2007E	0.55	Institutional Ownership (%)	92	S&P Credit Rating	A-

Price Performance

Options: ASE, P, Ph

Analysis prepared by **Royal F. Shepard, CFA** on August 21, 2006, when the stock traded at **$ 47.58**.

Highlights

- We expect EQR to make ongoing progress in improving revenues across its established properties in 2006. During the first half, same-store units increased revenues 6% on higher occupancy and rental rates. In our estimation, the full year will show a similar comparison. An accelerated disposition program, however, could dilute reported earnings, in our view. The trust has agreed to sell its Lexford Housing Division, consisting of 27,390 low rent properties, subject to necessary approvals. In total, we expect about $2 billion in dispositions for the year.
- The sale of Lexford, if completed, will dilute earnings by about $0.05 a share in the second half, about offsetting better operating fundamentals. We also think higher mortgage rates could cool demand for EQR's for-sale condominium projects as 2006 progresses. In our view, earnings and cash flow contributed from the sale of units in EQR's developments will likely fall below the approximately $0.29 a share added to FFO in 2005.
- For 2006, we see EPS from continuing operations of $0.40, increasing to $0.55 in 2007. Per share FFO is estimated at $2.40, compared to recurring FFO of about $2.33 in 2005.

Investment Rationale/Risk

- We believe EQR shares should trade at a discount to peers, based on the trust's continued exposure to what we view as less attractive markets, such as Boston, Atlanta, and Texas. In our view, the recent agreement to sell the Lexford division represents significant progress toward moving the trust out of slower growth mid-continent markets. Near term, we expect dilution from dispositions until proceeds are reinvested. At the same time, we think rising operating expenses and a slowing market for condominium conversions will limit upside in earnings and cash flow.
- Risks to our recommendation and target price include the potential for a sharp rise in interest rates, which might curtail single-family home sales. Higher than expected levels of household formation could also boost demand for apartments.
- Our 12-month target price of $33 is based on our calculation of net asset value, reflecting recent sales transactions. Our dividend discount model assumes a 9.4% discount rate and a gradual return to historical growth levels, leading to an intrinsic value of $32.

Qualitative Risk Assessment

LOW | MEDIUM | HIGH

Our risk assessment of EQR reflects our view that it is one of the largest, most diversified residential REITs and has below average financial leverage and moderate stock price volatility.

Quantitative Evaluations

S&P Quality Ranking B+

D | C | B- | B | B+ | A- | A | A+

Relative Strength Rank STRONG

79

LOWEST = 1 HIGHEST = 99

Revenue/Earnings Data

Revenue (Million $)

	1Q	2Q	3Q	4Q	Year
2006	521.0	491.9	--	--	--
2005	461.6	478.9	495.5	518.9	1,955
2004	443.9	474.7	483.5	487.4	1,890
2003	448.5	455.9	459.4	459.5	1,823
2002	498.8	502.7	499.6	492.9	1,994
2001	537.9	544.4	552.4	536.5	2,171

Earnings Per Share ($)

2006	0.06	0.08	E0.13	E0.14	E0.40
2005	0.27	0.10	0.04	0.11	0.51
2004	0.12	0.13	0.07	0.10	0.37
2003	0.13	0.17	0.15	0.02	0.43
2002	0.28	0.32	0.23	0.43	0.78
2001	0.40	0.28	0.26	0.43	1.36

Fiscal year ended Dec. 31. Next earnings report expected: Early November. EPS Estimates based on S&P Operating Earnings; historical GAAP earnings are as reported.

Dividend Data (Dates: mm/dd Payment Date: mm/dd/yy)

Amount ($)	Date Decl.	Ex-Div. Date	Stk. of Record	Payment Date
0.443	12/09	12/15	12/19	01/13/06
0.443	02/21	03/16	03/20	04/13/06
0.443	05/19	06/15	06/19	07/14/06
0.443	08/21	09/14	09/18	10/13/06

Dividends have been paid since 1993. Source: Company reports.

Equity Residential

Business Summary August 21, 2006

CORPORATE OVERVIEW. Equity Residential is one of the largest publicly-held owners of multifamily properties. Structured as a REIT, it owns, manages and operates properties through its 93.4% interest in its operating limited partnership. At June 30, 2006, EQR owned or had interests in 898 multifamily properties with 191,582 units in 31 states. The trust adopted its current name in May 2002.

EQR's properties fall into three categories: garden, mid-rise/high-rise, and ranch. Garden-style properties have two or three floors, while mid-rise/high-rise properties have more than three floors. At the end of 2005, the trust's 568 garden-style properties each had an average of 265 units, and an average occupancy rate of 93.9%. The 57 mid-rise/high-rise properties had an average of 279 units, and an average occupancy rate of 94.5%. The 300 ranch properties had an average of 92 units, and an occupancy rate of 91.8%. The trust also owned a single military housing property with 3,603 units and an occupancy rate of 95.3%.

MARKET PROFILE. The housing market is highly fragmented, and is characterized broadly by two types of housing units--multi-family and single-family. At the end 2005, the U.S. Census Bureau estimated that there were 123.93 million housing units in the country. Partly due to the high fragmentation, and the fact that residents have the option of either being owners, or tenants (renters), the housing market can be highly competitive, in our view. Main demand drivers for apartments are household formation and employment growth. S&P expects 1.4 million new households to be formed in 2006, up from an estimated 1.3 million in 2005. Supply is created by new housing unit construction, which could consist of single-family homes, or multi family apartment buildings or condominiums. Standard & Poor's forecasts 1.9 million housing unit starts in 2006, down from 2.1 million in 2005, but still at what we consider a high level.

Company Financials

Per Share Data ($) Year Ended Dec. 31	**2005**	**2004**	**2003**	**2002**	**2001**	**2000**	**1999**	**1998**	**1997**	**1996**
Tangible Book Value	16.65	15.28	15.43	15.57	16.20	20.82	16.33	16.46	14.74	10.28
Earnings	0.51	0.37	0.43	0.78	1.36	1.67	1.15	0.82	0.88	0.85
S&P Core Earnings	0.51	0.34	0.41	0.72	1.38	NA	NA	NA	NA	NA
Dividends	1.74	1.73	1.73	1.73	1.68	1.58	1.47	1.36	1.27	1.20
Payout Ratio	NM	NM	NM	222%	124%	94%	128%	167%	145%	169%
Prices:High	42.17	36.75	30.30	30.96	30.45	28.63	24.19	26.28	27.50	21.75
Prices:Low	30.70	26.65	23.12	21.55	24.80	19.34	19.06	17.34	19.88	14.13
P/E Ratio:High	83	99	70	40	22	17	21	32	31	26
P/E Ratio:Low	60	72	54	28	18	12	17	21	23	17
Income Statement Analysis (Million $)										
Rental Income	1,944	1,878	1,809	1,970	2,075	1,960	1,712	1,296	708	454
Mortgage Income	Nil	Nil	Nil	Nil	8.79	11.2	12.6	18.6	20.4	12.8
Total Income	1,955	1,090	1,823	1,994	2,171	2,030	1,753	1,337	747	478
General Expenses	925	870	802	841	924	812	673	833	291	288
Interest Expense	391	349	333	343	361	388	341	249	124	85.6
Provision for Losses	Nil	Nil	Nil	Nil	Nil	Nil	Nil	Nil	Nil	Nil
Depreciation	508	484	444	462	457	450	409	302	157	93.3
Net Income	152	135	212	302	474	555	394	258	177	102
S&P Core Earnings	97.1	74.5	86.4	194	374	NA	NA	NA	NA	NA
Balance Sheet & Other Financial Data (Million $)										
Cash	13,798	83.5	49.6	540	449	417	114	4.00	209	147
Total Assets	14,099	12,645	11,467	11,811	12,236	12,264	11,716	10,700	7,095	2,986
Real Estate Investment	16,597	14,864	12,874	13,046	13,016	12,591	12,239	10,942	7,121	2,984
Loss Reserve	Nil	Nil	Nil	Nil	Nil	Nil	Nil	Nil	Nil	Nil
Net Investment	13,709	12,264	10,578	10,934	11,297	11,239	11,168	10,224	6,677	2,682
Short Term Debt	Nil	Nil	Nil	334	699	Nil	250	151	61.1	28.2
Capitalization:Debt	7,032	5,642	4,836	5,050	5,044	5,706	5,224	4,530	2,887	1,226
Capitalization:Equity	4,891	4,436	4,345	4,251	4,447	4,436	4,195	5,330	3,690	1,459
Capitalization:Total	12,850	10,714	10,452	10,858	11,094	11,938	11,186	9,860	6,851	2,685
% Earnings & Depreciation/Assets	4.9	5.1	5.6	6.4	7.6	8.3	7.2	6.3	6.6	7.6
Price Times Book Value:High	2.5	2.4	2.0	2.0	1.9	1.4	1.5	1.6	1.9	2.1
Price Times Book Value:Low	1.8	1.7	1.5	1.4	1.5	0.9	1.2	1.1	1.3	1.4

Data as orig reptd.; bef. results of disc opers/spec. items. Per share data adj. for stk. divs.; EPS diluted. E-Estimated. NA-Not Available. NM-Not Meaningful. NR-Not Ranked. UR-Under Review.

Office: Two North Riverside Plaza, Chicago, IL 60606.
Telephone: 312-474-1300.
Email: investorrelations@eqrworld.com
Website: http://www.equityresidential.com

Chrmn: S. Zell
Pres & CEO: D.J. Neithercut
COO & EVP: G.A. Spector
EVP & CFO: D. Brandin

EVP, Secy & General Counsel: B.C. Strohm
Investor Contact: M. McKenna (888-879-6356)
Trustees: J. W. Alexander, C. L. Atwood, S. O. Evans, J. D. Harper, Jr., B. A. Knox, J. E. Neal, D. J. Neithercut, D. G. Rogers, S. Z. Rosenberg, G. A. Spector, B. J. White, S. Zell

Founded: 1993
Domicile: Maryland
Employees: 6,000

STANDARD &POOR'S

Exelon Corp

S&P Recommendation BUY ★★★★★

Price $62.40 (as of Oct 27, 2006)

12-Mo. Target Price $70.00

Investment Style Large-Cap Growth

GICS Sector Utilities
Sub-Industry Electric Utilities

Comment This holding company for Philadelphia-based PECO Energy and Chicago-based Unicom terminated its merger with New Jersey-based Public Service Enterprise Group.

Key Stock Statistics (Source S&P, Vickers, company reports)

52-Wk Range	$63.62–49.76	S&P Oper. EPS 2006**E**	3.33	P/E on S&P Oper. EPS 2006**E**	18.7	Dividend Rate/Share	$1.60
Trailing 12-Month EPS	$1.44	S&P Oper. EPS 2007**E**	4.55	Common Shares Outstg. (M)	669.5	Yield (%)	2.56
Trailing 12-Month P/E	43.3	S&P Core EPS 2006**E**	3.29	Market Capitalization(B)	$41.776	Beta	0.47
$10K Invested 5 Yrs Ago	$35,956	S&P Core EPS 2007**E**	4.50	Institutional Ownership (%)	66	S&P Credit Rating	BBB+

Price Performance

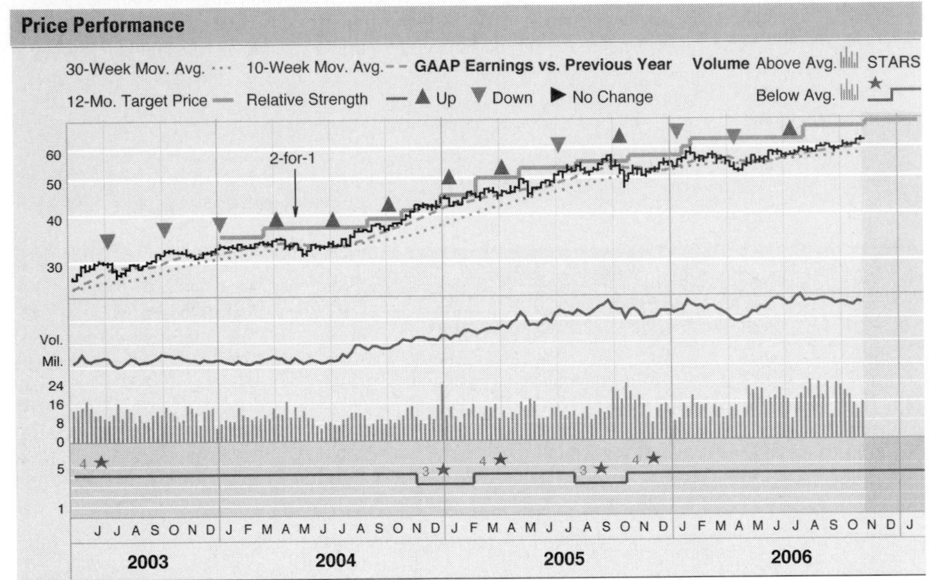

Options: ASE, CBOE, P, Ph

Highlights

- The 12-month target price for EXC has recently been changed to $70.00 from $68.00. The Highlights section of this Stock Report will be updated accordingly.

Investment Rationale/Risk

- The Investment Rationale/Risk section of this Stock Report will be updated shortly. For the latest News story on EXC from MarketScope, see below.

- 10/27/06 04:00 pm EDT... S&P REITERATES BUY OPINION ON SHARES OF EXELON CORP (EXC 62.41****): Q3 operating EPS of $1.02 vs. $0.95 is $0.04 below our estimate. EPS excludes $1.15 charge for goodwill impairment of ComEd unit, related to rate case ruling that allowed an $8 million increase, well below the $317 million requested. Should Illinois general assembly extend current rate freeze through 2010, ComEd expects to file for bankruptcy. However, as a separate legal entity, EXC does not expect to be impacted. We still see EPS of $3.33 for '06 and $4.55 for '07. We are raising our 12-month target price $2 to $70, reflecting a premium-to-peers P/E of 15.4X our '07 estimate. / J.McCann

Qualitative Risk Assessment

LOW	MEDIUM	HIGH

Our risk assessment reflects Exelon's strong and steady cash flows from the regulated PECO Energy and ComEd utilities, as well as the strong earnings and cash flows from very profitable but higher risk power generating and energy marketing operations.

Quantitative Evaluations

S&P Quality Ranking B+

D	C	B-	B	B+	A-	A	A+

Relative Strength Rank MODERATE

58

LOWEST = 1 HIGHEST = 99

Revenue/Earnings Data

Revenue (Million $)

	1Q	2Q	3Q	4Q	Year
2006	3,861	3,697	--	--	--
2005	3,561	3,484	4,473	3,838	15,357
2004	3,722	3,550	3,865	3,378	14,515
2003	4,074	3,721	4,441	3,577	15,812
2002	3,357	3,519	4,370	3,709	14,955
2001	3,823	3,651	4,285	3,381	15,140

Earnings Per Share ($)

	1Q	2Q	3Q	4Q	Year
2006	0.59	0.95	**E**1.06	**E**0.80	**E**3.33
2005	0.77	0.76	1.07	-1.19	1.40
2004	0.57	0.78	0.86	0.54	2.75
2003	0.39	0.57	-0.16	0.42	1.20
2002	0.37	0.75	0.85	0.61	2.58
2001	0.60	0.49	0.58	0.52	2.20

Fiscal year ended Dec. 31. Next earnings report expected: NA. EPS Estimates based on S&P Operating Earnings; historical GAAP earnings are as reported.

Dividend Data (Dates: mm/dd Payment Date: mm/dd/yy)

Amount ($)	Date Decl.	Ex-Div. Date	Stk. of Record	Payment Date
0.400	01/25	05/11	05/15	06/10/06
0.400	01/25	05/11	05/15	06/10/06
0.400	06/28	08/11	08/15	09/11/06
0.400	07/25	11/13	11/15	12/11/06

Dividends have been paid since 1902. Source: Company reports.

Exelon Corp

Business Summary September 22, 2006

CORPORATE OVERVIEW. Exelon Corp. was formed in October 2000, through the acquisition by Philadelphia-based PECO Energy of Chicago-based Unicom Corp. The company, along with its subsidiaries, is engaged in the energy delivery, generation and other businesses. Exelon operates in three business segments: ComEd, PECO and Generation. Segment contributions to 2005 net income were: ComEd, after a goodwill impairment charge of $1,207 million, a loss of $676 million (income of $676 million in 2004); PECO, $520 million ($455 million); Generation, $1,109 million ($657 million); and other, a loss of $2 million (income of $82 million). We see ComEd's contribution to total operating income declining from about 25% in 2005 and 2006 to about 15% in 2007, and the contribution from the generation business increasing to about 65% from 50%.

IMPACT OF MAJOR DEVELOPMENTS. On September 14, 2006, the company and Public Service Enterprise Group (PEG) announced the termination of the merger agreement that had been announced on December 20, 2004. If the merger had been completed, the combined company would have been the largest electric utility, the seventh largest gas utility, and one of the largest power generators in the U.S. While the company's nuclear services contract with PEG expires in January 2007, PEG has options to renew it for up to three years. Although we were disappointed that a settlement could not be reached with the New Jersey Board of Public Utilities, we believe the rate concessions and additional power plant divestitures demanded by the BPU would have significantly diluted many of the benefits of the proposed transaction.

Company Financials

Per Share Data ($) Year Ended Dec. 31	**2005**	**2004**	**2003**	**2002**	**2001**	**2000**	**1999**	**1998**	**1997**	**1996**
Tangible Book Value	8.48	7.10	5.77	4.26	4.51	3.18	4.57	6.81	6.13	10.44
Earnings	1.40	2.75	1.20	2.58	2.20	1.44	1.58	1.16	0.72	1.12
S&P Core Earnings	3.01	2.79	1.74	1.64	1.49	NA	NA	NA	NA	NA
Dividends	1.60	1.53	0.96	0.88	0.91	0.46	0.50	0.50	0.90	0.88
Payout Ratio	114%	56%	80%	34%	41%	32%	32%	43%	125%	78%
Prices:High	57.46	44.90	33.31	28.50	35.13	35.50	25.25	21.09	13.19	16.25
Prices:Low	41.77	30.92	23.04	18.92	19.38	16.50	15.38	9.44	9.38	11.50
P/E Ratio:High	41	16	28	11	16	25	16	18	18	15
P/E Ratio:Low	30	11	19	7	9	11	10	8	13	10

Income Statement Analysis (Million $)										
Revenue	15,357	14,515	15,812	14,955	15,140	7,499	5,437	5,210	4,618	4,284
Depreciation	1,334	1,305	1,126	1,340	1,449	458	237	643	581	489
Maintenance	NA	NA	NA	NA	NA	NA	NA	NA	NA	325
Fixed Charges Coverage	4.88	3.94	2.19	3.56	2.98	2.94	3.24	3.52	2.41	3.05
Construction Credits	NA	NA	NA	NA	NA	Nil	4.00	3.52	21.8	19.9
Effective Tax Rate	49.8%	27.5%	29.4%	37.4%	39.7%	27.3%	36.6%	37.5%	46.5%	39.7%
Net Income	951	1,841	793	1,670	1,416	907	619	532	337	517
S&P Core Earnings	2,035	1,865	1,142	1,062	962	NA	NA	NA	NA	NA

Balance Sheet & Other Financial Data (Million $)										
Gross Property	29,853	28,711	27,578	25,904	21,526	19,886	9,412	7,228	6,574	14,945
Capital Expenditures	2,165	1,921	1,954	2,150	2,041	752	491	415	490	549
Net Property	21,981	21,482	20,630	17,134	13,742	12,936	5,045	4,337	3,884	9,898
Capitalization:Long Term Debt	11,760	12,235	13,576	14,580	13,492	14,398	6,098	3,269	4,325	4,371
Capitalization:% Long Term Debt	56.3	56.5	61.5	65.3	62.1	66.6	75.6	49.9	59.4	47.0
Capitalization:Preferred	Nil	Nil	Nil	Nil	Nil	Nil	193	230	230	292
Capitalization:% Preferred	Nil	Nil	Nil	Nil	Nil	Nil	2.39	3.51	3.20	3.10
Capitalization:Common	9,125	9,423	8,503	7,742	8,230	7,215	1,773	3,057	3,079	4,646
Capitalization:% Common	43.7	43.5	38.5	34.7	37.9	33.4	22.0	46.6	37.4	49.9
Total Capital	25,964	26,463	26,724	26,325	26,341	26,352	10,760	9,233	9,897	13,390
% Operating Ratio	80.5	81.1	82.2	73.1	83.9	80.5	80.7	81.5	84.6	78.9
% Earned on Net Property	12.5	16.3	11.4	21.3	25.2	17.0	28.6	31.2	14.4	9.1
% Return on Revenue	6.2	12.7	5.0	11.2	9.4	12.1	11.4	10.2	7.3	12.1
% Return on Invested Capital	11.4	10.3	10.2	10.2	9.8	9.8	10.3	14.3	6.3	6.8
% Return on Common Equity	10.2	20.5	9.8	21.1	18.3	20.2	25.1	16.9	8.0	10.9

Data as orig reptd.; bef. results of disc opers/spec. items. Per share data adj. for stk. divs.; EPS diluted. E-Estimated. NA-Not Available. NM-Not Meaningful. NR-Not Ranked. UR-Under Review.

Office: 10 S Dearborn St 37th Fl, Chicago, IL 60603-2300.
Telephone: 312-394-7398.
Website: http://www.exeloncorp.com
Chrmn, Pres & CEO: J.W. Rowe

EVP & CFO: J.F. Young
EVP, Chief Admin & Chief Lgl Officer: R.E. Mehrberg
SVP & Cntlr: M.F. Hilzinger
Investor Contact: J. Carson (312-394-7398)

Board of Directors: E. A. Brennan, M. W. D'Alessio, N. DeBenedictis, B. DeMars, N. A. Diaz, S. L. Gin, R. B. Greco, E. D. Jannotta, J. M. Palms, W. Richardson, T. Ridge, J. W. Rogers, Jr., R. Rubin, R. L. Thomas

Founded: 1887
Domicile: Pennsylvania
Employees: 17,200

Express Scripts Inc

STANDARD &POOR'S

S&P Recommendation HOLD ★★★★★

Price $64.97 (as of Oct 27, 2006)

12-Mo. Target Price $73.00

Investment Style Mid-Cap Growth

GICS Sector Health Care
Sub-Industry Health Care Services

Comment This company offers prescription benefits and disease state management services.

Key Stock Statistics (Source S&P, Vickers, company reports)

52-Wk Range	$95.00–63.83	S&P Oper. EPS 2006E	3.25	P/E on S&P Oper. EPS 2006E	20.0	Dividend Rate/Share	Nil
Trailing 12-Month EPS	$3.03	S&P Oper. EPS 2007E	3.75	Common Shares Outstg. (M)	135.4	Yield (%)	Nil
Trailing 12-Month P/E	21.4	S&P Core EPS 2006E	3.25	Market Capitalization(B)	$8.799	Beta	-0.06
$10K Invested 5 Yrs Ago	$30,459	S&P Core EPS 2007E	3.75	Institutional Ownership (%)	88	S&P Credit Rating	BBB

Price Performance

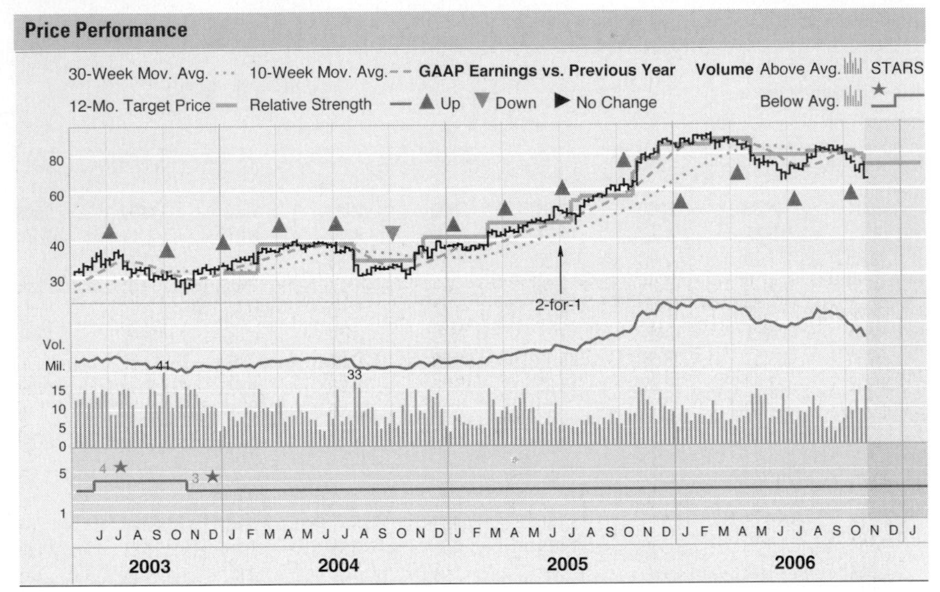

Options: ASE, CBOE, P

Highlights

- The 12-month target price for ESRX has recently been changed to $73.00 from $79.00. The Highlights section of this Stock Report will be updated accordingly.

Investment Rationale/Risk

- The Investment Rationale/Risk section of this Stock Report will be updated shortly. For the latest News story on ESRX from MarketScope, see below.

- 10/25/06 12:09 pm EDT... S&P MAINTAINS HOLD RECOMMENDATION ON SHARES OF EXPRESS SCRIPTS (ESRX 65.73***): ESRX's Q3 operating EPS of $0.83 vs. $0.67 is $0.01 below our estimate. We view positively a 39% rise in EBITDA per adjusted claim. However, we are concerned by account losses in the pharmacy benefit management unit and specialty drug unit's difficulties. We also see risk of negative impact on EPS from a proposed decline in published average wholesale prices of branded drugs, used as a reimbursement benchmark by pharmacy benefit managers. We cut P/E-to-growth to 1.15X from 1.2X, below historic peer levels, and our target price drops $6 to $73. We would not add to positions. /P.Seligman

Qualitative Risk Assessment

LOW | **MEDIUM** | HIGH

Our risk assessment partly reflects rising drug demand, improving financial performance, and healthy operating cash flow. However, we believe that intense competition and increased government regulation of pharmacy benefit managers, which we view as likely, could result in changes in industry conditions.

Quantitative Evaluations

S&P Quality Ranking **B+**

D | C | B- | B | **B+** | A- | A | A+

Relative Strength Rank **WEAK**

7

LOWEST = 1 HIGHEST = 99

Revenue/Earnings Data

Revenue (Million $)

	1Q	2Q	3Q	4Q	Year
2006	4,445	4,452	4,330	--	--
2005	3,839	3,944	3,848	4,635	16,266
2004	3,628	3,780	3,768	3,940	15,115
2003	3,224	3,334	3,249	3,488	13,295
2002	2,540	3,178	3,177	3,366	12,261
2001	2,091	2,247	2,381	2,610	9,329

Earnings Per Share ($)

2006	0.70	0.75	0.83	**E**0.96	**E**3.25
2005	0.57	0.68	0.68	0.75	2.68
2004	0.45	0.42	0.40	0.54	1.80
2003	0.38	0.37	0.41	0.43	1.59
2002	0.28	0.31	0.34	0.36	1.28
2001	0.17	0.19	0.20	0.22	0.78

Fiscal year ended Dec. 31. Next earnings report expected: Late February. EPS Estimates based on S&P Operating Earnings; historical GAAP earnings are as reported.

Dividend Data

No cash dividends have been paid.

Business Summary October 13, 2006

CORPORATE OVERVIEW. Express Scripts is one of the largest U.S. pharmacy benefits managers (PBMs). Its PBM services (88.2% of 2005 revenue, versus 94.3% in 2004) include retail network pharmacy management, mail pharmacy services, benefit design consultation, drug utilization review, formulary management, disease management, and compliance and therapy management for thousands of client groups that include health insurers, third-party administrators, employers, union-sponsored benefit plans and government health programs.

Specialty services (10.0%, versus 4.1%) include patient care and delivery of injectable and infusion drugs, including biopharmaceutical drugs, to patient homes, physician offices, hospitals, clinics and infusion centers, third-party logistics services, fertility services, and bio-pharma services including reimbursement and customized logistics solutions.

Pharma Business Solutions (PBS; 1.9%, versus 1.6%) services include distribution of pharmaceuticals to low-income patients through pharmaceutical manufacturer- and company-sponsored generic patient assistance programs, distribution of pharmaceuticals requiring special handling or packaging, and distribution of sample units to physicians and verification of practitioner.

Revenues are generated primarily from the delivery of prescription drugs through 58,000 contracted retail pharmacies, four home delivery fulfillment pharmacies and 33 specialty drug pharmacies, as of December 31, 2005. Revenues from the delivery of prescription drugs to members represented 98.2% of revenues in 2005, versus 98.6% in 2004 and 2003. Revenues from services, such as the administration of some clients' retail pharmacy networks, and certain services provided by PBS comprised the remainder.

The five largest clients accounted for 23.6% of revenues in 2005, compared to 22.8% in 2004. In 2005, the company processed 437 million network pharmacy claims, 40 million mail pharmacy claims and 5 million PBS and specialty claims, compared to 399 million, 38 million and 3.5 million, respectively, in 2004.

Company Financials

Per Share Data ($) Year Ended Dec. 31	**2005**	**2004**	**2003**	**2002**	**2001**	**2000**	**1999**	**1998**	**1997**	**1996**
Tangible Book Value	NM	NM	NM	NM	NM	NM	NM	NM	1.54	1.26
Cash Flow	3.25	2.25	1.93	1.79	1.29	0.46	1.56	0.52	0.33	0.25
Earnings	2.68	1.80	1.59	1.28	0.78	-0.06	1.06	0.32	0.25	0.20
S&P Core Earnings	2.60	1.73	1.51	1.20	0.72	NA	NA	NA	NA	NA
Dividends	Nil	Nil	Nil	Nil	Nil	Nil	Nil	Nil	Nil	Nil
Payout Ratio	Nil	Nil	Nil	Nil	Nil	Nil	Nil	Nil	Nil	Nil
Prices:High	90.80	40.60	37.72	32.95	30.73	26.75	26.38	17.25	8.09	7.25
Prices:Low	36.54	29.15	23.17	19.33	17.42	7.13	11.09	6.75	3.91	3.31
P/E Ratio:High	34	23	24	26	39	NM	25	54	32	36
P/E Ratio:Low	14	16	15	15	22	NM	10	21	15	17
Income Statement Analysis (Million $)										
Revenue	16,266	15,115	13,295	12,261	9,329	6,787	4,288	2,825	1,231	774
Operating Income	727	563	503	454	317	279	241	116	59.3	46.3
Depreciation	84.0	70.0	54.0	82.0	80.1	78.6	74.0	27.0	10.5	6.71
Interest Expense	37.0	41.7	41.4	42.2	34.2	47.9	60.0	20.2	0.23	0.06
Pretax Income	615	451	405	330	208	-4.47	265	76.2	54.7	43.1
Effective Tax Rate	35.0%	38.3%	38.2%	38.2%	39.9%	NM	40.7%	44.0%	38.9%	39.3%
Net Income	400	278	251	204	125	-8.02	157	42.7	33.4	26.2
S&P Core Earnings	389	270	239	192	115	NA	NA	NA	NA	NA
Balance Sheet & Other Financial Data (Million $)										
Cash	478	166	396	191	178	53.2	283	123	64.2	79.6
Current Assets	2,257	1,443	1,560	1,394	1,213	998	1,066	657	364	263
Total Assets	5,493	3,600	3,409	3,207	2,500	2,277	2,487	1,095	403	300
Current Liabilities	2,394	1,813	1,626	1,544	1,246	1,116	1,100	539	198	135
Long Term Debt	1,401	412	455	563	346	396	636	306	Nil	Nil
Common Equity	1,465	1,196	1,194	1,003	832	705	699	250	204	164
Total Capital	2,866	1,608	1,649	1,565	1,178	1,102	1,335	556	204	166
Capital Expenditures	60.0	51.5	53.1	61.3	57.3	80.2	37.0	23.9	13.0	9.48
Cash Flow	484	348	305	286	205	70.6	231	69.7	43.9	32.9
Current Ratio	0.9	0.8	1.0	0.9	1.0	0.9	1.0	1.2	1.8	2.0
% Long Term Debt of Capitalization	48.9	25.6	27.6	35.9	29.4	36.0	47.6	55.1	Nil	Nil
% Net Income of Revenue	2.5	1.8	1.9	1.7	1.3	NM	3.7	1.5	2.7	3.4
% Return on Assets	8.8	7.9	7.6	7.1	5.2	NM	8.8	5.7	9.5	11.3
% Return on Equity	30.1	23.3	22.8	22.2	16.3	NM	33.2	18.8	18.2	21.7

Data as orig reptd.; bef. results of disc opers/spec. items. Per share data adj. for stk. divs.; EPS diluted. E-Estimated. NA-Not Available. NM-Not Meaningful. NR-Not Ranked. UR-Under Review.

Office: 13900 Riverport Drive, Maryland Heights, MO 63043-4804.
Telephone: 314-770-1666.
Email: investor.relations@express-scripts.com
Website: http://www.express-scripts.com

Chrmn: B.A. Toan
Pres & CEO: G. Paz
COO: D.A. Lowenberg
SVP & CFO: E. Stiften

SVP, Secy & General Counsel: T.M. Boudreau
Investor Contact: D. Myers (314-702-7173)
Board of Directors: G. G. Benanav, F. J. Borelli, M. C. Breen, N. J. LaHowchic, T. P. Mac Mahon, J. O. Parker, Jr., G. Paz, S. Skinner, S. Sternberg, B. A. Toan, H. L. Waltman

Founded: 1986
Domicile: Delaware
Employees: 14,020

STANDARD &POOR'S

Exxon Mobil Corp

S&P Recommendation STRONG BUY ★★★★★

Price $71.42 (as of Oct 31, 2006)

12-Mo. Target Price $87.00

Investment Style Large-Cap Growth

GICS Sector Energy
Sub-Industry Integrated Oil & Gas

Comment XOM, formed through the merger of Exxon and Mobil in late 1999, is the world's largest publicly owned integrated oil company.

Key Stock Statistics (Source S&P, Vickers, company reports)

52-Wk Range	$72.33–55.60	S&P Oper. EPS 2006E	6.45	P/E on S&P Oper. EPS 2006E	11.1	Dividend Rate/Share	$1.28
Trailing 12-Month EPS	$6.57	S&P Oper. EPS 2007E	6.66	Common Shares Outstg. (M)	5,945.0	Yield (%)	1.79
Trailing 12-Month P/E	10.9	S&P Core EPS 2006E	6.43	Market Capitalization(B)	$424.589	Beta	0.62
$10K Invested 5 Yrs Ago	$19,561	S&P Core EPS 2007E	6.72	Institutional Ownership (%)	52	S&P Credit Rating	AAA

Price Performance

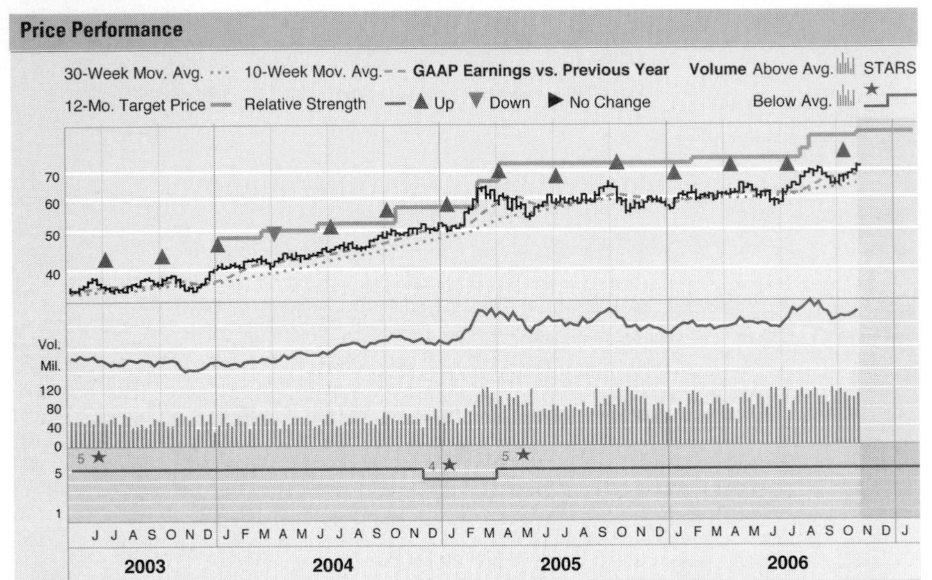

Options: ASE, CBOE, P, Ph

Analysis prepared by **Tina J. Vital** on October 31, 2006, when the stock traded at **$ 71.03**.

Highlights

- Third quarter operating earnings rose 26% to $10.49 billion, or $1.77 per share. Results beat our estimate by $0.17 per share, reflecting better than expected marketing and chemical margins.
- Hydrocarbon production rose 7.2% in the third quarter, slightly below our estimate due to field declines, entitlement effects and divestment impacts, and we expect 5% growth for 2006. With international development projects progressing on schedule, we expect upstream production will increase 3% per annum during 2007-2010. We believe the company will benefit from "big-pocket" upstream growth opportunities in deepwater, in liquefied natural gas (LNG), and in ventures with state-owned oil companies.
- XOM's after-tax operating earnings rose by 31% in 2005, and we expect an increase of 14% in 2006 and 2% in 2007. Gross share repurchases totaled $21.2 billion in the first nine months of 2006, which reduced shares by 4.9%.

Investment Rationale/Risk

- We expect XOM's upstream to benefit from high oil prices, and its complex refineries to benefit from significant cost discounts due to its ability to refine lower quality crude feedstocks. We estimate that its refineries hold upgrading capacity of over 2.6 million barrels per day (b/d), among the largest in the world. We view XOM's three-year (2003-05) upstream unit costs as below its peer average, its upstream production growth prospects as in line, and its three-year organic reserve replacement rate as above average.
- Risks to our recommendation and target price include geopolitical risk, lack of success at replacing reserves through the drillbit, and changes in economic, industry and operating conditions.
- A blend of our discounted cash flow (assuming a WACC of 9.1% and terminal growth of 3%) and peer multiples leads to our 12-month target price of $87, at an enterprise value of 7.3X our 2007 EBITDA estimate, a premium to peers, warranted, in our view, by XOM's high earnings quality and substantial refining conversion capacity.

Qualitative Risk Assessment

LOW | MEDIUM | HIGH (LOW)

Our risk assessment reflects our view of the company's diversified and strong business profile in volatile, cyclical and capital intensive segments of the energy industry. We view ExxonMobil's earnings stability and corporate governance practices as above average.

Quantitative Evaluations

S&P Quality Ranking A-

D | C | B- | B | B+ | A- | A | A+

Relative Strength Rank MODERATE

70

LOWEST = 1 HIGHEST = 99

Revenue/Earnings Data

Revenue (Million $)

	1Q	2Q	3Q	4Q	Year
2006	88,980	99,034	99,593	--	--
2005	82,051	88,568	100,717	99,662	370,680
2004	67,602	70,693	76,375	83,357	298,035
2003	63,780	57,165	59,841	65,952	246,738
2002	43,531	50,909	54,182	56,211	204,506
2001	57,278	56,184	52,113	47,300	213,488

Earnings Per Share ($)

	1Q	2Q	3Q	4Q	Year
2006	1.37	1.72	1.77	E1.52	E6.45
2005	1.22	1.20	1.58	1.71	5.71
2004	0.83	0.88	0.88	1.30	3.89
2003	0.97	0.62	0.55	1.01	3.15
2002	0.30	0.38	0.39	0.54	1.61
2001	0.70	0.63	0.46	0.39	2.18

Fiscal year ended Dec. 31. Next earnings report expected: Late January. EPS Estimates based on S&P Operating Earnings; historical GAAP earnings are as reported.

Dividend Data (Dates: mm/dd Payment Date: mm/dd/yy)

Amount ($)	Date Decl.	Ex-Div. Date	Stk. of Record	Payment Date
0.320	01/25	02/08	02/10	03/10/06
0.320	04/26	05/10	05/12	06/09/06
0.320	07/26	08/10	08/14	09/11/06
0.320	10/25	11/09	11/13	12/11/06

Dividends have been paid since 1882. Source: Company reports.

Exxon Mobil Corp

Business Summary October 31, 2006

CORPORATE OVERVIEW. In late 1999, the FTC allowed Exxon and Mobil to reunite, creating Exxon Mobil Corp. (XOM). ExxonMobil's businesses include oil and natural gas exploration and production (8% of 2005 sales; 67% of 2005 segment earnings); refining and marketing (83%; 22%); chemicals (9%; 11%); and other operations, such as electric power generation, coal and minerals.

Historically, XOM reported proved reserve data excluding year-end price/cost revisions; using this information, we estimate its three-year (2003-2005) organic reserve replacement at 116%. Based on regulatory guidance, in 2004, XOM began reporting proved reserve data on the basis of December 31 prices and costs (year-end prices). Including year-end price/cost revisions, we estimate XOM's three-year (2003-2005) organic reserve replacement at 108%. Using year-end pricing, proved liquids (including tar sands and nonconsolidated) reserves declined to 11.229 billion barrels (63% developed) at year-end 2005, from 11.651 billion barrels in 2004. Proved natural gas reserves (including nonconsolidated reserves) rose to 66.907 trillion cubic feet (Tcf; 65% developed) in 2005, from 60.362 Tcf in 2004. Liquids production declined 1.9%, to 2.523 million b/d in 2005, and natural gas production available for sale dropped 6.2%, to 9.251 billion cubic feet per day (Bcf)/d in 2005.

As of year-end 2005, the company had an ownership interest in 43 refineries in 25 countries, with 6.35 million b/d of atmospheric distillation capacity (U.S. 31%, Europe 28%, Asia Pacific 15%, Japan 12%, Canada 8%, and Latin America/other 6%).

MANAGEMENT. We believe XOM is one of the best managed companies in the energy sector. In January 2006, Lee R. Raymond retired and Rex W. Tillerson became chairman and CEO. We expect Tillerson to benefit from plans made by Raymond over the past 12 years, and see Tillerson's diplomatic skills as playing an important role in enhancing those plans.

Company Financials

Per Share Data ($) Year Ended Dec. 31	**2005**	**2004**	**2003**	**2002**	**2001**	**2000**	**1999**	**1998**	**1997**	**1996**
Tangible Book Value	18.13	15.90	13.69	11.13	10.74	10.21	9.13	8.83	8.69	8.32
Cash Flow	7.34	5.38	4.50	2.84	3.32	3.43	2.30	2.38	2.81	2.58
Earnings	5.71	3.89	3.15	1.61	2.18	2.27	1.13	1.31	1.69	1.51
S&P Core Earnings	5.72	4.01	3.03	1.52	2.03	NA	NA	NA	NA	NA
Dividends	1.14	1.06	0.98	0.92	0.91	0.88	0.84	0.82	0.81	0.78
Payout Ratio	20%	27%	31%	57%	42%	39%	74%	63%	48%	52%
Prices:High	65.96	52.05	41.13	44.58	45.84	47.72	43.63	38.66	33.63	25.31
Prices:Low	49.25	39.91	31.58	29.75	35.01	34.94	32.16	28.31	24.13	19.41
P/E Ratio:High	12	13	13	28	21	21	39	30	20	17
P/E Ratio:Low	9	10	10	18	16	15	29	22	14	13

Income Statement Analysis (Million $)	**2005**	**2004**	**2003**	**2002**	**2001**	**2000**	**1999**	**1998**	**1997**	**1996**
Revenue	370,680	298,035	246,738	204,506	213,488	232,748	185,527	117,772	137,242	134,249
Operating Income	59,255	45,639	32,230	23,280	29,602	33,309	17,921	12,326	16,993	15,387
Depreciation, Depletion and Amortization	10,253	9,767	9,047	8,310	7,944	8,130	8,304	5,340	5,474	5,329
Interest Expense	496	638	207	398	293	589	695	100	415	984
Pretax Income	60,231	42,017	32,660	17,719	24,688	27,493	11,295	9,241	13,204	12,300
Effective Tax Rate	38.7%	37.9%	33.7%	36.7%	36.5%	40.3%	28.7%	28.3%	32.9%	35.8%
Net Income	36,130	25,330	20,960	11,011	15,105	15,990	7,910	6,440	8,460	7,510
S&P Core Earnings	36,164	26,089	20,214	10,418	14,042	NA	NA	NA	NA	NA

Balance Sheet & Other Financial Data (Million $)	**2005**	**2004**	**2003**	**2002**	**2001**	**2000**	**1999**	**1998**	**1997**	**1996**
Cash	28,671	18,531	10,626	7,229	6,547	7,081	1,761	1,461	4,062	2,969
Current Assets	73,342	60,377	45,960	38,291	35,681	40,399	31,141	17,593	21,192	19,910
Total Assets	208,335	195,256	174,278	152,644	143,174	149,000	144,521	92,630	96,064	95,527
Current Liabilities	46,307	42,981	38,386	33,175	30,114	38,191	38,733	19,412	19,654	19,505
Long Term Debt	6,220	5,013	4,756	6,655	7,099	7,280	8,402	4,530	7,050	7,236
Common Equity	111,186	101,756	89,915	74,597	73,161	70,757	63,466	43,645	43,470	43,239
Total Capital	138,284	131,813	118,171	100,504	99,444	97,709	91,807	63,229	66,533	66,167
Capital Expenditures	13,839	11,986	12,859	11,437	9,989	8,446	10,849	8,359	7,393	7,209
Cash Flow	46,383	35,097	30,007	19,321	23,049	24,120	16,178	11,770	13,915	12,812
Current Ratio	1.6	1.4	1.2	1.2	1.2	1.1	0.8	0.9	1.1	2.1
% Long Term Debt of Capitalization	4.4	3.8	4.0	6.6	7.1	7.5	9.2	7.2	10.6	10.9
% Return on Assets	17.9	13.7	12.8	7.4	10.3	10.9	5.6	6.8	8.8	8.0
% Return on Equity	33.9	26.4	25.5	14.9	21.0	23.8	12.6	14.8	19.5	18.0

Data as orig reptd.; bef. results of disc opers/spec. items. Per share data adj. for stk. divs.; EPS diluted. E-Estimated. NA-Not Available. NM-Not Meaningful. NR-Not Ranked. UR-Under Review.

Office: 5959 Las Colinas Blvd, Irving, TX 75039-2298.
Telephone: 972-444-1000.
Website: http://www.exxonmobil.com
Chrmn, Pres & CEO: R.W. Tillerson

SVP & Treas: D.D. Humphreys
Investor Contact: P.T. Mulva (800-252-1800)
VP & Secy: P.T. Mulva
VP & General Counsel: C.W. Matthews

Board of Directors: M. J. Boskin, W. W. George, J. R. Houghton, W. R. Howell, R. C. King, P. E. Lippincott, H. A. McKinnell, Jr., M. C. Nelson, S. J. Palmisano, W. V. Shipley, J. S. Simon, R. W. Tillerson

Founded: 1870
Domicile: New Jersey
Employees: 83,700

STANDARD & POOR'S

Family Dollar Stores Inc.

S&P Recommendation HOLD ★★★★★

Price $29.81 (as of Oct 27, 2006)

12-Mo. Target Price $29.00

Investment Style Mid-Cap Growth

GICS Sector Consumer Discretionary
Sub-Industry General Merchandise Stores

Comment This company operates a chain of over 6,170 retail discount stores in 44 states across the U.S.

Key Stock Statistics (Source S&P, Vickers, company reports)

52-Wk Range	**$30.91–21.57**	S&P Oper. EPS 2007**E**	**1.68**	P/E on S&P Oper. EPS 2007**E**	**17.7**	Dividend Rate/Share	**$0.42**
Trailing 12-Month EPS	**$1.30**	S&P Oper. EPS 2008**E**	**1.90**	Common Shares Outstg. (M)	**151.6**	Yield (%)	**1.41**
Trailing 12-Month P/E	**22.9**	S&P Core EPS 2007**E**	**1.68**	Market Capitalization(B)	**$4.520**	Beta	**0.70**
$10K Invested 5 Yrs Ago	**$10,734**	S&P Core EPS 2008**E**	**1.90**	Institutional Ownership (%)	**96**	S&P Credit Rating	**NA**

Price Performance

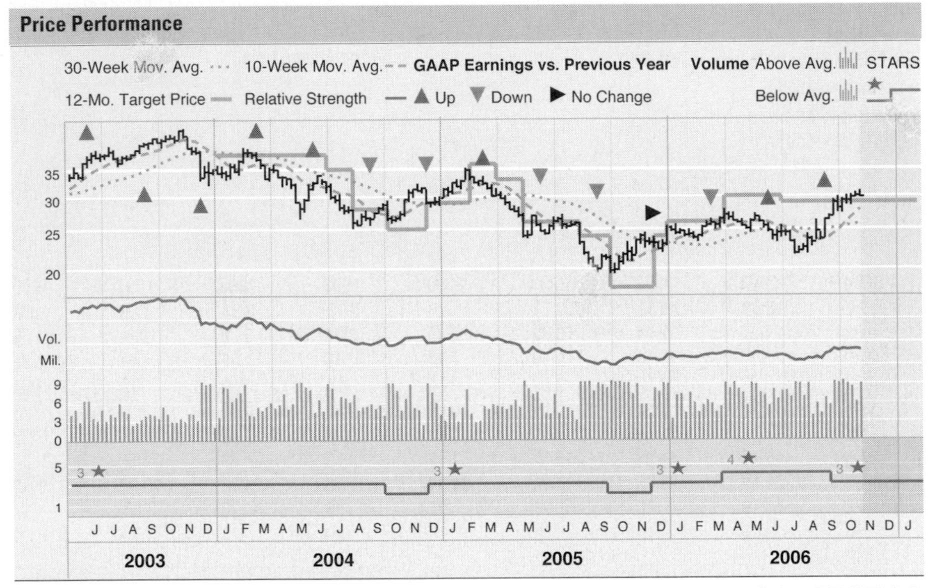

Options: ASE, CBOE, P, Ph

Analysis prepared by **Jason N. Asaeda** on September 29, 2006, when the stock traded at **$ 29.13**.

Highlights

- We look for sales to rise 9.5%, to $7.0 billion in FY 07 (Aug.), mainly driven by the planned opening of approximately 400 new stores. We think FDO will control its pace of expansion in an effort to open stores more cost effectively and on schedule. We look for productivity gains at about 1,300 "Urban Initiative" stores, as well as a sales mix that addresses the basic needs of customers to drive 3% to 4% same-store sales growth. The company plans to expand its cooler program to an additional 1,000 stores, and to increase its food assortment in about 1,300 stores in FY 07.
- FDO's expanding network of distribution centers should help mitigate rising freight costs. The gross margin should also benefit from higher purchase markups and shrink reduction, partly offset by growth in sales of lower-margin hardline consumables and the taking of more timely markdowns to keep inventories clean. We expect the company to leverage SG&A expenses on the improving performance of Urban Initiative stores.
- Factoring in likely share buybacks, we see FY 07 operating and S&P Core EPS of $1.68.

Investment Rationale/Risk

- With FDO's growing focus on food assortments and treasure-hunt items supporting a positive same-store sales trend, we see an opportunity for the company to increase its share of the customer wallet in FY 07. We are also encouraged by FDO's report of ongoing productivity gains at its Urban Initiative stores. We think these positive factors, coupled with a faster pace of new store growth relative to FY 06, and expense controls, should drive an appreciable lift in sales and earnings over the next 12 months despite difficult macro conditions for customers. However, we do not see a near-term catalyst for the shares.
- Risks to our recommendation and target price include sales shortfalls due to a slower-than-anticipated increase in consumer discretionary spending, delays in new store openings/product receipts, and increased competition.
- Our 12-month target price of $29 is based on our discounted cash flow model, which assumes a weighted average cost of capital of 11% and a terminal growth rate of 3%.

Qualitative Risk Assessment

LOW | **MEDIUM** | HIGH

Our risk assessment reflects our view of FDO's earnings erosion in recent years, partly reflecting difficult economic conditions for core lower-income customers, offset by promising new merchandising and productivity initiatives that could, in our opinion, boost sales and profit margins going forward.

Quantitative Evaluations

S&P Quality Ranking **A+**

D | C | B- | B | B+ | A- | A | **A+**

Relative Strength Rank **STRONG**

77

LOWEST = 1 HIGHEST = 99

Revenue/Earnings Data

Revenue (Million $)

	1Q	2Q	3Q	4Q	Year
2006	1,511	1,736	1,570	1,578	6,395
2005	1,380	1,587	1,428	1,430	5,825
2004	1,245	1,403	1,310	1,324	5,282
2003	1,109	1,256	1,177	1,208	4,750
2002	977.1	1,105	1,022	1,058	4,163
2001	820.2	1,037	887.0	920.8	3,665

Earnings Per Share ($)

	1Q	2Q	3Q	4Q	Year
2006	0.32	0.35	0.37	0.26	1.30
2005	0.32	0.48	0.32	0.18	1.30
2004	0.37	0.47	0.43	0.26	1.53
2003	0.33	0.42	0.40	0.28	1.43
2002	0.29	0.37	0.35	0.24	1.25
2001	0.24	0.35	0.31	0.20	1.10

Fiscal year ended Aug. 31. Next earnings report expected: Late December. EPS Estimates based on S&P Operating Earnings; historical GAAP earnings are as reported.

Dividend Data (Dates: mm/dd Payment Date: mm/dd/yy)

Amount ($)	Date Decl.	Ex-Div. Date	Stk. of Record	Payment Date
0.095	11/03	12/13	12/15	01/16/06
0.105	01/19	03/13	03/15	04/15/06
0.105	05/15	06/13	06/15	07/14/06
0.105	08/18	09/13	09/15	10/13/06

Dividends have been paid since 1976. Source: Company reports.

Family Dollar Stores Inc.

Business Summary September 29, 2006

CORPORATE OVERVIEW. FDO operates a chain of over 6,170 retail discount stores in 44 states. The company provides primarily low to lower-middle income consumers with an assortment of hardlines and softlines priced from under $1 to $10. Hardlines include consumables such as food, household chemicals and paper products, as well as pet, hardware and automotive supplies, electronics, housewares and seasonal merchandise. Softlines include apparel, shoes and domestic items. Family Dollar stores are operated on a self-service basis, which contributes to its low overhead, with limited advertising support and promotional activity. The once cash-only stores now accept PIN-based debit card payments in most locations. Food stamp acceptance is also being piloted. In our view, broader tender options offer the company an opportunity to improve its share of customer wallet as shopping is more convenient and available cash does not limit basket size.

PRIMARY BUSINESS DYNAMICS. FDO's primary growth drivers are same-store sales (sales results for stores open more than 13 months) and new store openings. The company believes difficult macro conditions, including inflation, lack of real wage growth and rising energy costs, have prompted its customers to increasingly cut back on discretionary spending in recent years. As a result, annual same-store sales growth weakened from an average of 5% from FY 00 (Aug.) through FY 02, to 3.8% in FY 03, and 1.9% in FY 04. Same-store sales recovered modestly in FY 05, rising 2.3%, driven by FDO's efforts to improve performance at about 1,300 high-volume urban market stores, as well as favorable customer response to the company's expanded assortments of frequently purchased hardline consumables such as food, household chemicals and paper products, as well as opportunistically purchased "treasure-hunt" items that added interest to the sales mix. These factors contributed to a 3.7% same-store sales increase in FY 06.

Company Financials

Per Share Data ($) Year Ended Aug. 31	**2006**	**2005**	**2004**	**2003**	**2002**	**2001**	**2000**	**1999**	**1998**	**1997**
Tangible Book Value	NA	8.64	8.13	7.61	6.66	5.57	4.66	4.00	3.36	2.92
Cash Flow	NA	1.99	2.10	1.94	1.69	1.49	1.31	1.06	0.80	0.61
Earnings	1.30	1.30	1.53	1.43	1.25	1.10	1.00	0.81	0.60	0.44
S&P Core Earnings	NA	1.21	1.45	1.39	1.22	1.08	NA	NA	NA	NA
Dividends	0.40	0.36	0.32	0.28	0.25	0.23	0.22	0.20	0.17	0.15
Payout Ratio	31%	28%	21%	20%	20%	21%	21%	24%	28%	35%
Prices:High	30.91	35.25	39.66	44.13	37.25	31.35	24.50	26.75	22.44	15.06
Prices:Low	21.57	19.40	25.09	25.46	23.75	18.38	14.25	14.00	11.50	6.25
P/E Ratio:High	24	27	26	31	30	29	25	33	37	35
P/E Ratio:Low	17	15	16	18	19	17	14	17	19	14
Income Statement Analysis (Million $)										
Revenue	NA	5,825	5,282	4,750	4,163	3,665	3,133	2,751	2,362	1,995
Operating Income	NA	458	512	478	419	366	325	266	201	151
Depreciation	NA	115	97.9	88.3	77.0	67.7	54.5	43.8	34.8	29.1
Interest Expense	NA	Nil	Nil	Nil	Nil	Nil	Nil	Nil	0.01	0.31
Pretax Income	NA	343	414	390	342	298	271	223	166	121
Effective Tax Rate	NA	36.5%	36.6%	36.5%	36.5%	36.5%	36.5%	37.1%	37.8%	38.5%
Net Income	NA	218	263	247	217	190	172	140	103	74.7
S&P Core Earnings	NA	202	250	241	213	186	NA	NA	NA	NA
Balance Sheet & Other Financial Data (Million $)										
Cash	NA	105	150	207	220	21.8	43.6	95.3	134	42.5
Current Assets	NA	1,355	1,225	1,156	1,056	807	751	720	647	545
Total Assets	NA	2,410	2,167	1,986	1,755	1,400	1,244	1,095	942	780
Current Liabilities	NA	895	714	595	531	390	412	379	343	261
Long Term Debt	NA	Nil	Nil	Nil	Nil	Nil	Nil	Nil	Nil	Nil
Common Equity	NA	2,187	1,360	1,533	1,245	959	798	691	578	500
Total Capital	NA	2,274	1,454	1,612	1,314	1,009	832	717	599	519
Capital Expenditures	NA	229	218	220	187	163	172	125	96.4	77.1
Cash Flow	NA	332	361	336	294	257	227	184	138	104
Current Ratio	NA	1.5	1.7	1.9	2.0	2.1	1.8	1.9	1.9	2.1
% Long Term Debt of Capitalization	NA	Nil	Nil	Nil	Nil	Nil	Nil	Nil	Nil	Nil
% Net Income of Revenue	NA	3.7	5.0	5.2	5.2	5.2	5.5	5.1	4.4	3.7
% Return on Assets	NA	9.4	12.7	13.2	13.8	14.3	14.7	13.7	12.0	10.1
% Return on Equity	NA	10.6	19.7	17.8	18.9	21.6	23.1	22.1	19.2	15.8

Data as orig reptd.; bef. results of disc opers/spec. items. Per share data adj. for stk. divs.; EPS diluted. E-Estimated. NA-Not Available. NM-Not Meaningful. NR-Not Ranked. UR-Under Review.

Office: 10401 Monroe Rd, Matthews, NC 28105-5349.
Telephone: 704-847-6961.
Website: http://www.familydollar.com
Chrmn & CEO: H.R. Levine

Pres, COO & CFO: R.J. Kelly
SVP, Secy & General Counsel: J.G. Kelley
Investor Contact: K.F. Rawlins (704-847-6961)

Board of Directors: M. R. Bernstein, S. A. Decker, E. C. Dolby, G. A. Eisenberg, H. R. Levine, G. R. Mahoney, Jr., J. G. Martin, D. C. Pond

Founded: 1959
Domicile: Delaware
Employees: 42,000

STANDARD &POOR'S

Federal Home Loan Mortgage Corp.

S&P Recommendation HOLD ★★★★★ | **Price** $69.10 (as of Oct 27, 2006) | **12-Mo. Target Price** $70.00 | **Investment Style** Large-Cap Growth

GICS Sector Financials
Sub-Industry Thrifts & Mortgage Finance

Comment Federal Home Loan Mortgage (Freddie Mac), a U.S. government-sponsored enterprise (GSE), buys mortgages from lenders to increase the supply of funds for housing.

Key Stock Statistics (Source S&P, Vickers, company reports)

52-Wk Range	$70.37–55.64	S&P Oper. EPS 2006E	6.52	P/E on S&P Oper. EPS 2006E	10.6	Dividend Rate/Share	$1.88
Trailing 12-Month EPS	$2.83	S&P Oper. EPS 2007E	6.75	Common Shares Outstg. (M)	693.0	Yield (%)	2.72
Trailing 12-Month P/E	24.4	S&P Core EPS 2006E	6.53	Market Capitalization(B)	$47.886	Beta	0.52
$10K Invested 5 Yrs Ago	$11,358	S&P Core EPS 2007E	6.76	Institutional Ownership (%)	92	S&P Credit Rating	AAA

Price Performance

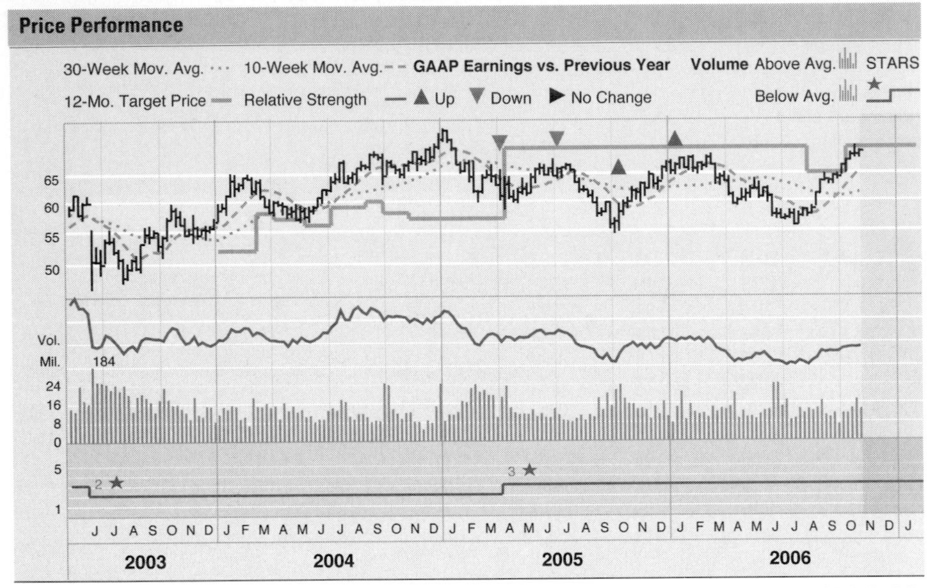

Options: ASE, CBOE, P, Ph

Analysis prepared by **Stuart Plesser** on October 09, 2006, when the stock traded at **$ 67.65**.

Highlights

- Based on our expectations for a modest easing of margin compression on FRE's retained portfolio and a single-digit increase in assets, somewhat offset by lower nominal margins on floating-rate mortgage-related security purchases, we see net interest income increasing in 2006.
- We project higher management and guarantee income in 2006 due to continued growth in outstanding Participation Certificates (PCs) and structured securities. Combined with our expectations for lower fair value losses on derivative instruments not in qualifying hedge relationships, we see significantly higher non-interest income in 2006. Due to FRE's low exposure to interest only and option adjustable-rate mortgages (ARMs) and low loan-to-value ratios, we do not foresee a material increase in credit losses in the near term. With FRE's cost control measures, we see non-interest expenses growing at a slower rate than total revenues, resulting in modest improvements in operating margins.
- Taking into account moderate share repurchase activity, we forecast EPS of $6.52 for 2006.

Investment Rationale/Risk

- We see continued growth in the fair value of FRE's net assets, due to income from its retained portfolio and fee-based income, offset by a widening of FRE's mortgage-to-debt option adjusted spreads (OAS). We are encouraged by FRE's low interest rate and credit risk metrics and high capital surplus levels, as well as its use of callable debt to mitigate interest rate risk. Although we remain concerned about a potential negative impact from pending GSE legislation--specifically, restrictions on portfolio size--we believe restrictions will be less severe than our previous expectations.
- Risks to our recommendation and target price include more stringent government regulation, greater than expected competition from other financial institutions and higher than expected credit losses. We believe regulatory and political risks will continue to overshadow the shares until final legislation is passed.
- Our 12-month target price of $70 implies a price to book ratio of 1.8 applied to our 12-month forward book value estimate of $42.30, in line with FRE's price/book trading multiple over the last three years.

Qualitative Risk Assessment

LOW | **MEDIUM** | HIGH

Our risk assessment takes into account FRE's unique position as a government-sponsored enterprise (GSE), offset by our view of a potential negative impact from pending government GSE legislation, including portfolio limits.

Quantitative Evaluations

S&P Quality Ranking A

D | C | B- | B | B+ | A- | **A** | A+

Relative Strength Rank STRONG

74

LOWEST = 1 HIGHEST = 99

Revenue/Earnings Data

Revenue (Million $)

	1Q	2Q	3Q	4Q	Year
2005	--	--	--	--	36,653
2004	--	--	--	--	32,564
2003	--	--	--	--	36,839
2002	9,799	9,268	9,650	10,704	46,258
2001	8,528	8,876	9,108	9,661	36,173
2000	6,930	7,323	7,652	8,064	29,969

Earnings Per Share ($)

2005	0.33	0.41	1.19	0.90	2.83
2004	1.82	3.91	-2.26	0.47	3.94
2003	--	--	--	--	6.68
2002	2.07	1.50	1.90	2.38	14.18
2001	1.12	1.29	1.49	2.06	5.96
2000	0.81	0.83	0.86	0.89	3.39

Fiscal year ended Dec. 31. Next earnings report expected: NA. EPS Estimates based on S&P Operating Earnings; historical GAAP earnings are as reported.

Dividend Data (Dates: mm/dd Payment Date: mm/dd/yy)

Amount ($)	Date Decl.	Ex-Div. Date	Stk. of Record	Payment Date
0.470	12/01	12/08	12/12	12/30/05
0.470	03/03	03/08	03/10	03/31/06
0.470	06/01	06/08	06/12	06/30/06
0.470	09/08	09/14	09/18	09/29/06

Dividends have been paid since 1989. Source: Company reports.

Federal Home Loan Mortgage Corp.

Business Summary October 09, 2006

CORPORATE OVERVIEW. The Federal Home Loan Mortgage Corp., better known as Freddie Mac, is one of two public government-sponsored enterprises (the other is rival Fannie Mae) formed to promote home ownership by increasing the availability of mortgage financing. The company was originally part of the Federal Home Loan Bank Board, which was dismantled under the S&L bailout law of 1989.

PRIMARY BUSINESS DYNAMICS. The company generates income primarily from two business activities: portfolio investment activities and credit guarantee activities. In regard to investment activities, FRE purchases mortgage loans and mortgage-related securities and holds them in its retained portfolio. This business is quite profitable for Freddie Mac, because its cost of funds is, in a sense, subsidized by its quasi-agency status. While FRE functions in a manner similar to a savings and loan that originates home mortgage loans to hold for its own account, the major difference is that FRE uses capital market borrowings to finance its mortgage purchases, whereas thrifts use retail savings. Also, Freddie Mac purchases mortgages from various lenders, while thrifts actually issue mortgages to homebuyers. The retained portfolio business generates the majority of the company's profits.

The company also derives income from guaranteeing the payment of principal and interest on mortgage-related securities in exchange for a fee, which is referred to as a guarantee fee. The types of mortgage fee guarantees include: mortgage Participation Certificates (PCs), in which customers sell FRE mortgages in exchange for PCs; single-class and multi-class Structured Securities, which represent beneficial interests in pools of PCs; and securities related to tax-exempt multifamily housing revenue bonds.

The company's mortgage-backed securities (MBS) operation is best illustrated by an example. Typically, a bank or thrift decides that it prefers to hold MBSs, as opposed to originated loans. The institution then turns over the loan, or more often a pool of loans, to Freddie Mac, which gives the lender MBSs in return. The transaction helps both parties, in our opinion. Freddie Mac receives a fee of about one-fifth of 1% to guarantee the principal and interest on the MBSs. Meanwhile, the lender has a nearly risk-free instrument on which it receives principal and interest payments. Freddie Mac makes money in this business because its loss rate is very low: people will default on all sorts of bills, but the basic need for shelter provides a powerful incentive to keep mortgages more or less current.

Company Financials

Per Share Data ($) Year Ended Dec. 31	**2005**	**2004**	**2003**	**2002**	**2001**	**2000**	**1999**	**1998**	**1997**	**1996**
Tangible Book Value	32.59	38.79	39.01	45.58	15.51	16.80	11.99	11.55	8.74	9.63
Earnings	2.83	3.94	6.68	14.18	5.96	3.39	2.95	2.31	1.88	1.67
S&P Core Earnings	2.84	3.95	6.70	14.22	5.91	NA	NA	NA	NA	NA
Dividends	1.52	1.20	1.04	0.88	0.80	0.68	0.60	0.48	0.40	0.35
Payout Ratio	54%	32%	16%	6%	13%	20%	20%	21%	21%	21%
Prices:High	73.91	74.20	64.78	69.50	71.25	70.13	65.25	66.38	44.56	29.25
Prices:Low	54.50	56.45	46.48	52.60	58.75	36.88	45.38	38.69	26.69	19.06
P/E Ratio:High	26	19	10	5	12	21	22	29	24	18
P/E Ratio:Low	19	14	7	4	10	11	15	17	14	11

Income Statement Analysis (Million $)										
Interest on:Mortgages	33,721	32,467	33,302	34,239	30,180	23,989	19,714	14,269	11,030	9,038
Interest on:Investment	2,606	3,136	3,796	4,147	4,180	4,361	3,039	2,369	1,971	1,745
Interest Expense	29,899	26,566	28,150	26,564	28,808	25,512	20,213	14,711	11,119	8,241
Guaranty Fees	NA	NA	NA	NA	1,639	1,489	1,405	1,307	1,298	1,249
Loan Loss Provision	251	143	10.0	128	45.0	40.0	60.0	190	310	320
Administration Expenses	2,666	2,242	2,064	1,553	1,020	883	655	578	495	440
Pretax Income	2,652	3,856	7,175	14,987	6,300	3,534	3,161	2,356	2,215	1,797
Effective Tax Rate	13.8%	20.5%	30.7%	31.4%	30.6%	28.2%	29.8%	27.8%	25.7%	30.0%
Net Income	2,189	2,937	4,816	10,090	4,373	2,539	2,218	1,700	1,395	1,243
S&P Core Earnings	1,974	2,737	4,605	9,881	4,121	NA	NA	NA	NA	NA

Balance Sheet & Other Financial Data (Million $)										
Mortgages	709,503	664,582	660,531	589,722	494,585	385,117	322,569	255,348	164,250	137,520
Investment	57,324	62,027	83,936	124,245	75,894	40,718	31,747	44,753	13,402	16,331
Cash & Equivalent	10,468	35,253	23,142	10,792	1,508	366	5,144	2,565	438	9,141
Total Assets	806,222	795,284	803,449	752,249	617,340	459,297	386,684	321,421	194,597	173,866
Short Term Debt	288,532	282,303	295,262	244,429	250,338	183,576	175,525	193,871	85,128	80,105
Long Term Debt	460,260	449,394	444,351	421,267	311,608	243,178	185,056	Nil	83,446	76,386
Equity	22,582	26,807	26,878	24,381	10,777	11,642	8,330	8,028	5,934	6,685
% Return on Assets	0.3	0.4	0.6	1.4	0.8	0.6	0.6	0.7	0.8	0.8
% Return on Equity	8.0	10.2	17.2	49.3	37.1	23.6	25.2	22.6	20.6	18.5
Equity/Assets Ratio	32.4	29.8	29.0	34.9	2.1	2.4	2.3	2.7	3.1	4.0
Price Times Book Value:High	2.3	1.9	1.7	1.5	4.6	4.2	5.4	5.7	5.1	3.0
Price Times Book Value:Low	1.7	1.5	1.2	1.2	3.8	2.2	3.8	3.3	4.1	2.0

Data as orig reptd.; bef. results of disc opers/spec. items. Per share data adj. for stk. divs.; EPS diluted. E-Estimated. NA-Not Available. NM-Not Meaningful. NR-Not Ranked. UR-Under Review.

Office: 8200 Jones Branch Drive, McLean, VA 22102.
Telephone: 703-903-2000.
Website: http://www.freddiemac.com
Chrmn & CEO: R.F. Syron

Pres & COO: E.M. McQuade
EVP & CFO: A.S. Piszel
EVP & General Counsel: R. Bostrom
SVP & Chief Admin: M.A. Colon

Board of Directors: B. T. Alexander, G. T. Boisi, M. Engler, R. K. Goeltz, T. S. Johnson, W. M. Lewis, Jr., E. M. McQuade, S. F. O'Malley, J. M. Peek, R. F. Poe, S. A. Ross, R. F. Syron, W. Turner

Auditor: PricewaterhouseCoopers
Founded: 1970
Domicile: United States
Employees: 5,217

STANDARD & POOR'S

Federal National Mortgage Association

S&P Recommendation HOLD ★★★★★ | **Price** $59.42 (as of Oct 27, 2006) | **12-Mo. Target Price** $55.00 | **Investment Style** Large-Cap Growth

GICS Sector Financials
Sub-Industry Thrifts & Mortgage Finance

Comment This government-sponsored enterprise (GSE) buys mortgage assets from other lenders and holds them in its portfolio or securitizes them for sale to investors.

Key Stock Statistics (Source S&P, Vickers, company reports)

52-Wk Range	$60.17–45.21	S&P Oper. EPS 2004E	7.42	P/E on S&P Oper. EPS 2004E	8.0	Dividend Rate/Share	$1.04
Trailing 12-Month EPS	$0.00	S&P Oper. EPS 2005E	6.42	Common Shares Outstg. (M)	967.9	Yield (%)	1.75
Trailing 12-Month P/E	NM	S&P Core EPS 2004E	7.37	Market Capitalization(B)	$57.513	Beta	0.64
$10K Invested 5 Yrs Ago	$8,222	S&P Core EPS 2005E	6.38	Institutional Ownership (%)	100	S&P Credit Rating	AA-

Price Performance

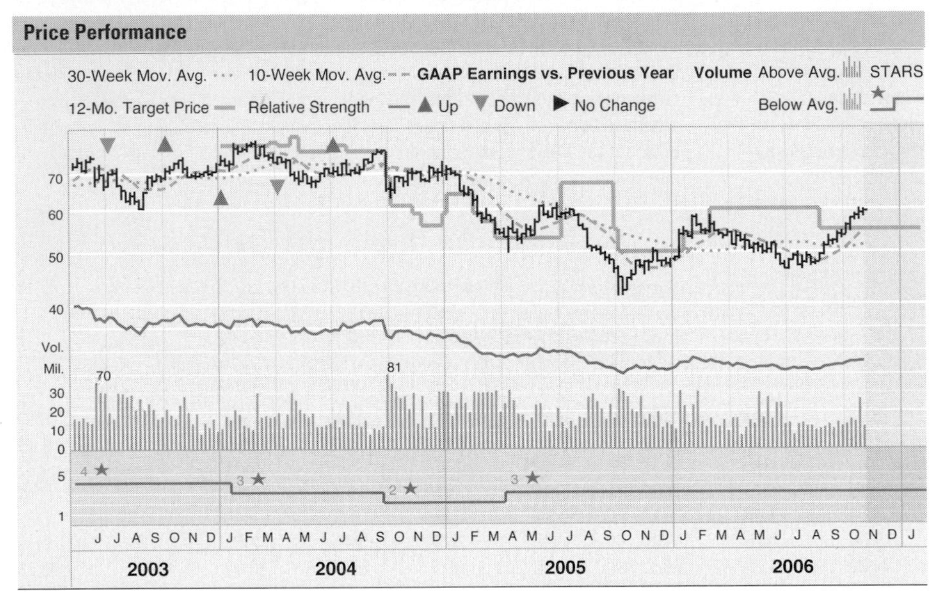

Options: ASE, CBOE, P, Ph

Analysis prepared by **Stuart Plesser** on August 31, 2006, when the stock traded at **$ 52.75**.

Highlights

- Under regulatory mandate, FNM is restating results for 2004, and still hasn't provided results for 2005 and 2006. Given that FNM has uncovered various accounting errors, including an $8.4 billion after-tax loss related to hedge accounting and an after-tax loss related to mortgage commitments that will likely total up to $2.4 billion, we believe the company lacks earnings visibility. Reflecting FNM's need to maintain a 30% surplus over the minimum capital requirement, we see average investment balances decreasing, which, despite rising investment yields, will likely result in double-digit declines in net interest income in 2006.
- Based on our projections for continued growth in outstanding mortgage-backed securities albeit at a slower rate than in previous years due to investor demand for higher yields, we see guarantee fee income increasing in the low teens in 2006. Due to higher administrative expenses associated with FNM's ongoing restatement process, we see little improvement in pretax margins.
- Taking into account moderate anticipated share repurchase activity, we forecast operating EPS of $5.40 in 2006.

Investment Rationale/Risk

- Although we believe FNM's primary growth driver, residential mortgage debt outstanding, will generate stable increases in the mid- to high-single digit range in the long run, we are concerned about the lack of earnings visibility. The settlement with the OFHEO and the SEC resulted in a $400 million penalty, but we believe FNM management now has proper guidance on correcting its internal controls and corporate culture. We see near-term growth limited by restrictions on FNM's mortgage asset portfolio. We see the potential for increased competition, both for the purchase of mortgage assets from other financial institutions and the issuance of MBSs from the private label securitization market.
- Risks to our recommendation and target price include the discovery of additional accounting errors, more stringent regulation and greater than expected competition.
- Our 12-month target price of $55 implies a P/E of approximately 10.2X applied to our 2006 EPS estimate, a discount to FNM's 5-year average to reflect the possibility of additional regulatory issues and the uncovering of further accounting troubles.

Qualitative Risk Assessment

LOW | **MEDIUM** | HIGH

Our risk assessment takes into account FNM's delay in filing its restated financial statements, which could lead to the discovery of additional accounting-related issues, as well as our view of a potential negative impact from pending government-sponsored enterprise legislation, including portfolio limits. These issues are tempered by its unique position as a government-sponsored enterprise.

Quantitative Evaluations

S&P Quality Ranking NR

D | C | B- | B | B+ | A- | A | A+

Relative Strength Rank STRONG

82

LOWEST = 1 HIGHEST = 99

Revenue/Earnings Data

Revenue (Million $)

	1Q	2Q	3Q	4Q	Year
2004	13,083	12,542	--	--	--
2003	13,557	13,456	13,275	13,480	53,768
2002	12,988	13,211	13,319	13,383	52,901
2001	12,366	12,560	12,880	12,958	50,803
2000	10,305	10,658	11,204	11,921	44,088
1999	8,658	8,938	9,433	9,939	36,968

Earnings Per Share ($)

2004	1.90	1.10	E2.19	E2.23	E7.42
2003	1.93	1.09	2.50	2.21	7.72
2002	1.17	1.44	0.98	0.94	4.53
2001	1.14	1.45	1.32	1.98	5.89
2000	1.02	1.02	1.09	1.13	4.26
1999	0.88	0.92	0.94	0.99	3.73

Fiscal year ended Dec. 31. Next earnings report expected: NA. EPS Estimates based on S&P Operating Earnings; historical GAAP earnings are as reported.

Dividend Data (Dates: mm/dd Payment Date: mm/dd/yy)

Amount ($)	Date Decl.	Ex-Div. Date	Stk. of Record	Payment Date
0.260	01/24	01/27	01/31	02/25/06
0.260	04/25	04/26	04/28	05/25/06
0.260	07/18	07/27	07/31	08/25/06
0.260	10/17	10/27	10/31	11/27/06

Dividends have been paid since 1956. Source: Company reports.

Federal National Mortgage Association

Business Summary August 31, 2006

The Federal National Mortgage Association (known as Fannie Mae) is a government-sponsored enterprise, chartered by Congress to increase the availability of mortgage credit for homebuyers. Its mission is essentially to increase the rate of home ownership, making American society more stable. The company's predecessor was formed during the Great Depression, in an effort to make home ownership possible at a time when it was nearly impossible for people in certain parts of the U.S. to obtain a mortgage. FNM basically operates in two business segments.

In its retained mortgage portfolio business, which accounts for most of its profits, the company buys mortgages from lenders such as thrifts, banks and mortgage bankers, and holds them on account. It funds mortgage purchases with debt of various maturities, earning a spread on the difference between the yield on the mortgages and the cost of the debt. FNM purchased $573 billion of mortgages in 2003, versus $371 billion in 2002 and $271 billion in 2001.

In securitization operations, which account for much of FNM's remaining profits, the company swaps mortgage-backed securities (MBSs) for mortgages with various lending institutions, and in the process, earns a fee of about 0.20%. One reason that lenders swap loans for MBSs is that the latter add to liquidity. FNM functions as a mortgage insurer in that it accepts the risk of default on the mortgage in exchange for a fee or a premium. In 2003, it issued $850 billion in MBSs for other investors, versus $478 billion in 2002 and $345 billion in 2001.

Congress is constantly concerned about the government's risk exposure on over $1 trillion of mortgages and mortgage-backed securities outstanding, since the U.S. government might have to ultimately make good on large-scale defaults. Congress has therefore established capital standards, which the company is required to meet.

Company Financials

Per Share Data ($) Year Ended Dec. 31	2003	2002	2001	2000	1999	1998	1997	1996	1995	1994
Tangible Book Value	18.73	13.76	15.86	18.58	16.03	13.95	12.34	11.10	10.04	8.74
Earnings	7.72	4.53	5.89	4.26	3.73	3.26	2.84	2.50	1.94	1.95
S&P Core Earnings	7.66	4.45	5.65	NA	NA	NA	NA	NA	NA	NA
Dividends	1.68	1.32	1.20	1.12	1.08	0.96	0.84	0.76	0.68	0.60
Payout Ratio	22%	29%	20%	26%	29%	29%	30%	30%	35%	31%
Prices:High	75.95	84.10	87.94	89.38	75.88	76.19	57.31	41.63	31.50	22.59
Prices:Low	58.40	58.85	72.08	47.88	58.56	49.56	36.13	27.50	17.19	17.03
P/E Ratio:High	10	19	15	21	20	23	20	17	16	12
P/E Ratio:Low	8	13	12	11	16	15	13	11	9	9
Income Statement Analysis (Million $)										
Interest on:Mortgages	49,754	49,265	46,478	39,403	32,672	25,878	22,716	20,560	18,154	15,851
Interest on:Investment	1,166	1,588	2,692	3,378	2,823	4,319	3,662	3,212	2,917	1,496
Interest Expense	37,351	40,287	41,080	37,107	30,001	25,885	22,429	20,180	18,024	14,524
Guaranty Fees	2,411	1,816	1,482	1,351	1,282	1,229	1,274	1,196	1,086	1,083
Loan Loss Provision	100	128	Nil	Nil	-120	50.0	100	195	140	155
Administration Expenses	1,463	1,219	1,017	905	800	708	636	560	546	525
Pretax Income	10,413	6,048	8,291	5,982	5,440	4,645	4,337	3,905	2,995	3,146
Effective Tax Rate	25.9%	23.6%	26.8%	26.2%	27.9%	25.9%	29.3%	29.5%	28.0%	31.9%
Net Income	7,720	4,619	6,067	4,416	3,921	3,444	3,068	2,754	2,155	2,141
S&P Core Earnings	7,518	4,440	5,688	NA	NA	NA	NA	NA	NA	NA
Balance Sheet & Other Financial Data (Million $)										
Mortgages	901,795	797,693	705,167	607,399	522,780	415,223	313,316	286,259	252,588	220,525
Investment	59,493	59,844	74,554	54,968	39,751	58,213	64,596	56,606	57,273	46,335
Cash & Equivalent	1,415	1,710	1,518	617	2,099	743	2,205	850	318	231
Total Assets	1,009,569	887,515	799,791	675,072	575,167	485,014	391,673	351,041	316,550	272,508
Short Term Debt	483,193	382,412	343,492	280,322	226,582	205,413	175,400	159,900	146,153	112,602
Long Term Debt	478,539	468,570	419,975	362,360	321,037	254,878	194,374	171,370	153,021	144,628
Equity	18,265	13,610	15,815	18,560	16,329	14,303	12,793	12,773	10,959	9,541
% Return on Assets	0.8	1.0	0.8	0.7	0.7	0.8	0.8	0.8	0.7	0.9
% Return on Equity	47.5	30.7	34.5	24.6	25.1	25.4	24.4	23.9	21.0	24.3
Equity/Assets Ratio	1.7	1.7	2.3	3.6	2.9	3.1	3.6	3.4	3.5	3.6
Price Times Book Value:High	4.1	6.1	5.5	4.8	4.7	5.5	4.6	3.8	3.1	2.6
Price Times Book Value:Low	3.1	4.3	4.5	2.6	3.7	3.6	2.9	2.5	1.7	1.9

Data as orig reptd.; bef. results of disc opers/spec. items. Per share data adj. for stk. divs.; EPS diluted. E-Estimated. NA-Not Available. NM-Not Meaningful. NR-Not Ranked. UR-Under Review.

Office: 3900 Wisconsin Avenue NW, Washington, DC 20016-2892.
Telephone: 202-752-7000.
Email: investor_relations1@fanniemae.com
Website: http://www.fanniemae.com

Chrmn: S.B. Ashley
Pres & CEO: D.H. Mudd
COO: M.J. Williams
EVP & Secy: T.E. Donilon

EVP & General Counsel: B. Wilkinson
Investor Contact: M. Christy
Board of Directors: S. B. Ashley, D. R. Beresford, K. M. Duberstein, B. Gaines, K. Horn, A. M. Korologos, B. Macaskill, D. B. Marron, D. H. Mudd, J. K. Pickett, L. Rahl, H. P. Swygert, J. K. Wulff

Founded: 1938
Domicile: United States
Employees: 5,055

STANDARD &POOR'S

Federated Department Stores Inc.

S&P Recommendation BUY ★★★★★

Price $43.88 (as of Oct 27, 2006)

12-Mo. Target Price $46.00

Investment Style Large-Cap Value

GICS Sector Consumer Discretionary
Sub-Industry Department Stores

Comment Following its merger with May Department Stores in August 2005, FD operates over 850 department stores under the Macy's and Bloomingdale's names.

Key Stock Statistics (Source S&P, Vickers, company reports)

52-Wk Range	$45.01–29.90	S&P Oper. EPS 2007E	2.15	P/E on S&P Oper. EPS 2007E	20.4	Dividend Rate/Share	$0.51
Trailing 12-Month EPS	$2.92	S&P Oper. EPS 2008E	3.12	Common Shares Outstg. (M)	543.5	Yield (%)	1.16
Trailing 12-Month P/E	15.0	S&P Core EPS 2007E	2.19	Market Capitalization(B)	$23.851	Beta	1.31
$10K Invested 5 Yrs Ago	$27,986	S&P Core EPS 2008E	3.16	Institutional Ownership (%)	91	S&P Credit Rating	BBB

Price Performance

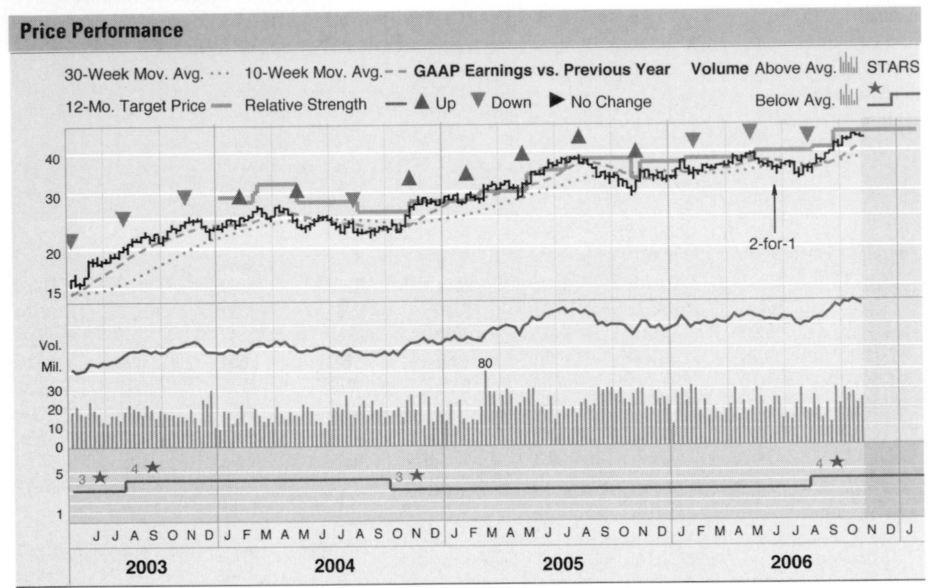

Options: ASE, CBOE, P, Ph

Analysis prepared by **Jason N. Asaeda** on September 13, 2006, when the stock traded at **$ 41.58**.

Highlights

- Factoring in the impact of FD's merger with May Department Stores, the sale of its credit card business in FY 06 (Jan.), and planned divestitures, we project net sales of $27 billion in FY 07. At Federated stores, we see improved customer perceptions of fair value in less discounted prices, and fashion-right private label offerings supporting a 3% rise in same-store sales. FD converted about 400 former May stores, which are excluded from the same-store sales base, to the Macy's format on September 9. We foresee limited near-term sales upside at these store locations due to ongoing inventory change-outs.
- Balancing sales growth in higher-margin private brands and initial merger cost savings against carrying costs of former May divisions, higher depreciation and amortization charges, loss of profit contributions from credit assets, and option expensing, we see operating margins narrowing.
- Factoring in likely share buybacks, we estimate FY 07 operating EPS of $2.15 and S&P Core EPS of $2.19, with the difference reflecting projected pension plan income and post-retirement costs.

Investment Rationale/Risk

- In our view, FD will need good execution of regional merchandising and higher customer service to retain loyal customers of former May stores at recently Macy's-rebranded locations. Based on improving sales and margin trends at legacy Macy's stores, which we attribute to higher quality, trend-right assortments that are now being flowed into new Macy's doors, we think FD will succeed.
- Risks to our recommendation and target price include sales shortfalls due to fashion merchandising mistakes; negative response by former May store customers to assortments and likely lower promotional levels at Macy's; and cutbacks in consumer spending. Our corporate governance concerns include the non-disclosure of specific hurdle rates for performance-based equity awards and of stock ownership for executives.
- We believe FD shares are undervalued, recently trading at 13.2X our FY 08 EPS estimate of $3.12 vs. a peer-median forward P/E multiple of 15.0X. Our 12-month target price of $46 is based on our discounted cash flow model, which assumes a weighted average cost of capital of 9.8% and a terminal growth rate of 2.5%.

Qualitative Risk Assessment

LOW | **MEDIUM** | HIGH

Our risk assessment reflects our view of FD's very strong brand and geographical presence in a consolidating industry, offset by potential merger-related integration challenges and uncertainty over consumer discretionary spending in light of rising interest rates and debt levels.

Quantitative Evaluations

S&P Quality Ranking B

D | C | B- | **B** | B+ | A- | A | A+

Relative Strength Rank STRONG

73

LOWEST = 1 HIGHEST = 99

Revenue/Earnings Data

Revenue (Million $)

	1Q	2Q	3Q	4Q	Year
2007	5,930	5,995	--	--	--
2006	3,641	3,623	5,785	9,571	22,390
2005	3,517	3,548	3,491	5,074	15,630
2004	3,291	3,434	3,486	5,053	15,264
2003	3,453	3,486	3,479	5,017	15,435
2002	3,556	3,488	3,475	5,132	15,651

Earnings Per Share ($)

2007	-0.13	0.51	E0.20	E1.45	E2.15
2006	0.36	0.84	0.89	1.23	3.16
2005	0.26	0.22	0.21	1.28	1.93
2004	0.12	0.32	0.18	1.25	1.86
2003	0.22	0.33	0.19	0.89	1.61
2002	0.15	0.31	0.07	0.78	1.30

Fiscal year ended Jan. 31. Next earnings report expected: Early November. EPS Estimates based on S&P Operating Earnings; historical GAAP earnings are as reported.

Dividend Data (Dates: mm/dd Payment Date: mm/dd/yy)

Amount ($)	Date Decl.	Ex-Div. Date	Stk. of Record	Payment Date
2-for-1 Stk.	03/28	06/12	05/26	06/09/06
0.128	03/28	06/14	06/16	07/03/06
0.128	08/25	09/13	09/15	10/02/06
0.128	10/26	12/13	12/15	01/02/07

Dividends have been paid since 2003. Source: Company reports.

Please read the Required Disclosures and Analyst Certification on the last page of this report.

Federated Department Stores Inc.

Business Summary September 13, 2006

CORPORATE OVERVIEW. In February 2005, FD and The May Department Stores Co. announced merger plans. At that time, May was in need of new leadership to revive its business, and FD was in the midst of a successful turnaround and on the lookout for acquisitions that would expand its presence in underserved markets. Both companies viewed the merger as a win-win proposition, as FD would roll out its profit-driving merchandising, pricing, and service initiatives to May's stores, and May would add 15 new states to FD's existing 34-state operating base.

As a result of the $17 billion May merger, which closed in August 2005, FD is now the fourth largest U.S. mass merchandiser in annual revenues, with over 850 department stores in 45 states under the Macy's and Bloomingdale's names.

CORPORATE STRATEGY. In 2005, FD focused on three key priorities to better position its business for long term growth: growing "better" and "affordable luxury" assortments, with an emphasis on private label merchandise; improving customer perceptions of fair value in less discounted prices; and enriching the overall shopping experience. With its merger with May, the company also expanded its core Macy's brand nationwide. Going forward, FD sees an opportunity to accelerate the sales performance in about 400 former May locations that were rebranded Macy's on September 9, 2006.

Effective February 1, 2006, FD began to operate Macy's through seven geographic divisions, each responsible for store management and operations, soft goods merchandise buying and planning, human resources, finance marketing, visual merchandising, and other functions. The Macy's Home Store division has responsibility for home-related merchandising and marketing in all Macy's stores.

Company Financials

Per Share Data ($) Year Ended Jan. 31	**2006**	**2005**	**2004**	**2003**	**2002**	**2001**	**2000**	**1999**	**1998**	**1997**
Tangible Book Value	5.34	16.55	NM	13.47	12.16	12.47	11.26	12.15	10.87	9.50
Cash Flow	4.29	4.09	3.92	3.31	2.94	1.32	3.49	2.91	2.61	1.96
Earnings	3.16	1.93	1.86	1.61	1.30	-0.45	1.81	1.53	1.29	0.62
S&P Core Earnings	2.21	1.83	1.69	1.24	0.91	0.25	NA	NA	NA	NA
Dividends	0.26	0.19	Nil	Nil	Nil	Nil	Nil	Nil	Nil	Nil
Payout Ratio	8%	10%	Nil	Nil	Nil	Nil	Nil	Nil	Nil	Nil
Calendar Year	2005	2004	2003	2002	2001	2000	1999	1998	1997	1996
Prices:High	39.03	29.08	25.30	22.13	24.95	26.94	28.53	28.09	24.44	18.50
Prices:Low	27.10	21.40	11.76	11.80	13.03	10.50	18.22	16.41	15.00	12.50
P/E Ratio:High	12	15	14	14	19	NM	16	18	19	29
P/E Ratio:Low	9	11	6	7	10	NM	10	11	12	20

Income Statement Analysis (Million $)										
Revenue	22,390	15,630	15,264	15,435	15,651	18,407	17,716	15,833	15,668	15,229
Operating Income	3,087	2,143	2,047	2,019	1,923	2,239	2,443	2,085	1,951	1,760
Depreciation	974	743	706	676	657	727	742	630	610	558
Interest Expense	422	299	266	311	331	444	368	304	418	499
Pretax Income	2,044	1,116	1,084	1,048	780	113	1,346	1,163	958	441
Effective Tax Rate	32.8%	38.3%	36.1%	39.1%	33.6%	NM	40.9%	41.1%	40.0%	39.9%
Net Income	1,373	689	693	638	518	-184	795	685	575	266
S&P Core Earnings	967	655	628	490	364	102	NA	NA	NA	NA

Balance Sheet & Other Financial Data (Million $)										
Cash	248	868	925	716	636	322	218	307	142	149
Current Assets	10,145	7,510	7,452	7,154	7,280	8,700	8,522	5,972	6,194	6,429
Total Assets	33,168	14,885	14,550	14,441	15,044	17,012	17,692	13,464	13,738	14,264
Current Liabilities	7,590	4,301	3,883	3,601	3,714	4,869	4,552	3,068	3,060	3,596
Long Term Debt	8,860	2,637	3,151	3,408	3,859	4,374	4,589	3,057	3,919	4,606
Common Equity	13,519	6,167	5,940	5,762	5,564	5,822	6,552	5,709	5,256	4,669
Total Capital	24,083	10,003	10,089	10,168	10,768	11,589	12,585	9,826	10,114	10,106
Capital Expenditures	568	467	508	568	615	742	770	695	696	846
Cash Flow	2,347	1,432	1,399	1,314	1,175	543	1,537	1,315	1,185	824
Current Ratio	1.3	1.7	1.9	2.0	2.0	1.8	1.9	1.9	2.0	1.8
% Long Term Debt of Capitalization	36.8	26.4	31.2	33.5	35.8	37.7	36.5	31.1	38.7	45.6
% Net Income of Revenue	6.1	4.4	4.5	4.1	3.3	NM	4.5	4.3	3.7	1.8
% Return on Assets	5.7	4.7	4.8	4.2	3.4	NM	5.1	5.0	4.1	1.9
% Return on Equity	13.9	11.4	11.8	11.3	9.1	NM	13.0	12.5	11.6	6.0

Data as orig reptd.; bef. results of disc opers/spec. items. Per share data adj. for stk. divs.; EPS diluted. E-Estimated. NA-Not Available. NM-Not Meaningful. NR-Not Ranked. UR-Under Review.

Office: 7 W Seventh St, Cincinnati, OH 45202.
Telephone: 513-579-7000.
Website: http://www.fds.com
Chrmn, Pres & CEO: T.J. Lundgren

Vice Chrmn: R.W. Tysoe
Vice Chrmn: T.L. Cole
Vice Chrmn: T.G. Cody
Vice Chrmn: J.E. Grove

Board of Directors: M. Feldberg, S. Levinson, T. J. Lundgren, J. Neubauer, J. A. Pichler, J. M. Roche, W. P. Stiritz, C. E. Weatherup, M. C. Whittington, K. M. von der Heyden

Founded: 1858
Domicile: Delaware
Employees: 232,000

STANDARD & POOR'S

Federated Investors Inc.

S&P Recommendation BUY ★★★★★

Price $34.44 (as of Oct 27, 2006)

12-Mo. Target Price $40.00

Investment Style Mid-Cap Growth

GICS Sector Financials
Sub-Industry Asset Management & Custody Banks

Comment This leading U.S. investment management company has a strong market share in money market products.

Key Stock Statistics (Source S&P, Vickers, company reports)

52-Wk Range	$40.17–29.56	S&P Oper. EPS 2006E	1.81	P/E on S&P Oper. EPS 2006E	19.0	Dividend Rate/Share	$0.72
Trailing 12-Month EPS	$1.83	S&P Oper. EPS 2007E	2.03	Common Shares Outstg. (M)	105.3	Yield (%)	2.09
Trailing 12-Month P/E	18.8	S&P Core EPS 2006E	1.81	Market Capitalization(B)	$3.628	Beta	0.66
$10K Invested 5 Yrs Ago	$13,519	S&P Core EPS 2007E	2.03	Institutional Ownership (%)	63	S&P Credit Rating	NA

Price Performance

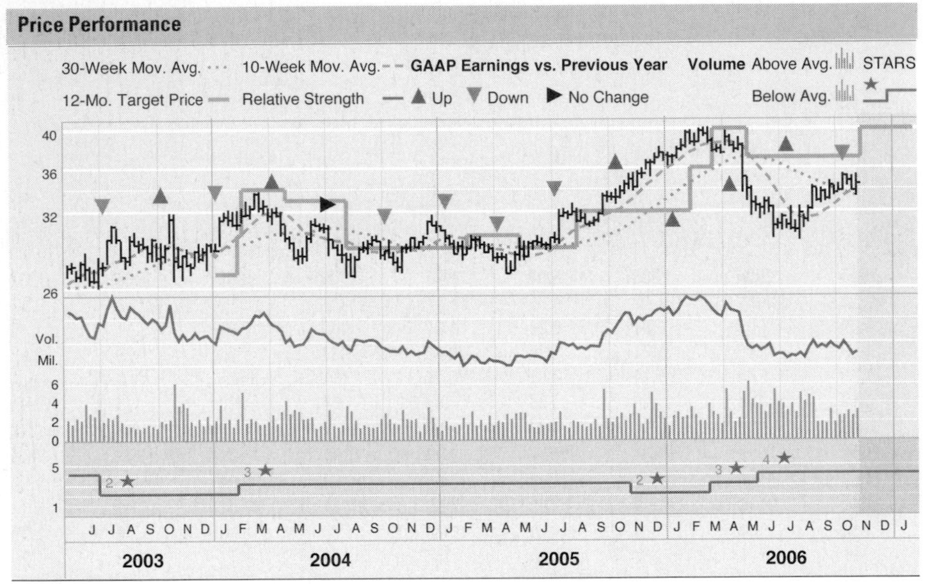

Options: ASE, P

Highlights

- The 12-month target price for FII has recently been changed to $40.00 from $37.00. The Highlights section of this Stock Report will be updated accordingly.

Investment Rationale/Risk

- The Investment Rationale/Risk section of this Stock Report will be updated shortly. For the latest News story on FII from MarketScope, see below.

- 10/27/06 10:08 am EDT... S&P REITERATES BUY RECOMMENDATION ON SHARES OF FEDERATED INVESTORS (FII 34.8****): FII posts Q3 EPS of $0.43 vs. $0.61, $0.05 lower than our estimate. A settlement payment reduced EPS by a penny. Assets under management were up 6% sequentially, aided by the early-period acquisition of equity manager MDTA, which added $6.7 billion of assets. We have a favorable view of that acquisition, which brought higher-margined equity assets. We are cutting our '06 EPS estimate by $0.04 to $1.81, but are raising '07's by $0.08 to $2.03. Our 12-month target price of $40, raised $3 today, is 19.7X our '07 estimate, in line with FII's 5-year average P/E. /M.Albrecht

Qualitative Risk Assessment

LOW | MEDIUM | **HIGH**

Our risk assessment reflects the company's relatively narrow product offering and significant competition from larger, more diversified fund management companies.

Quantitative Evaluations

S&P Quality Ranking B+

D | C | B- | B | **B+** | A- | A | A+

Relative Strength Rank MODERATE

49

LOWEST = 1 HIGHEST = 99

Revenue/Earnings Data

Revenue (Million $)

	1Q	2Q	3Q	4Q	Year
2006	238.8	236.4	243.9	--	--
2005	205.4	220.7	241.4	241.8	909.2
2004	220.7	213.1	205.2	208.1	847.0
2003	194.1	202.5	210.0	216.8	823.3
2002	181.6	182.4	173.2	173.8	711.1
2001	171.4	180.9	181.2	182.3	715.8

Earnings Per Share ($)

	1Q	2Q	3Q	4Q	Year
2006	0.43	0.44	0.43	E0.50	E1.81
2005	0.07	0.35	0.61	0.48	1.51
2004	0.46	0.44	0.43	0.29	1.62
2003	0.43	0.44	0.46	0.38	1.71
2002	0.44	0.45	0.43	0.42	1.74
2001	0.35	0.36	0.36	0.38	1.44

Fiscal year ended Dec. 31. Next earnings report expected: Late January. EPS Estimates based on S&P Operating Earnings; historical GAAP earnings are as reported.

Dividend Data (Dates: mm/dd Payment Date: mm/dd/yy)

Amount ($)	Date Decl.	Ex-Div. Date	Stk. of Record	Payment Date
0.150	01/26	02/06	02/08	02/15/06
0.180	04/27	05/04	05/08	05/15/06
0.180	07/31	08/04	08/08	08/15/06
0.180	10/26	11/06	11/08	11/15/06

Dividends have been paid since 1998. Source: Company reports.

Federated Investors Inc.

Business Summary August 04, 2006

CORPORATE OVERVIEW. A leading provider of investment management products and related financial services, Federated Investors (FII) has been in the mutual fund business for more than 40 years. The company is one of the largest mutual fund managers in the United States, based on assets under management. Assets under management at the end of 2005 totaled $213 billion, up from $179 billion at the end of 2004.

Federated manages assets across a wide range of asset categories, including substantial participation in fast growing areas such as equity and international investments. It is among the industry leaders in money market and fixed income funds, based on assets under management, and offers one of the industry's most comprehensive product lines. Assets under management by class at the end of 2005 included money market (75% of total), equity (14%), and fixed income (11%). By product type, mutual funds represented about 89% of total assets under management, with the balance held in separately managed accounts.

Company Financials

Per Share Data ($) Year Ended Dec. 31	**2005**	**2004**	**2003**	**2002**	**2001**	**2000**	**1999**	**1998**	**1997**	**1996**
Tangible Book Value	1.50	1.30	2.05	1.48	0.79	0.86	0.62	0.28	NM	NM
Cash Flow	1.75	1.79	1.95	1.90	1.65	1.40	1.10	0.88	0.70	0.77
Earnings	1.51	1.62	1.71	1.74	1.44	1.27	0.96	0.71	0.61	0.13
S&P Core Earnings	1.67	1.70	1.67	1.69	1.46	NA	NA	NA	NA	NA
Dividends	0.50	0.41	0.30	0.22	0.22	0.14	0.11	0.05	0.07	0.13
Payout Ratio	38%	26%	17%	12%	15%	11%	11%	7%	Nil	34%
Prices:High	38.11	33.79	31.90	36.18	32.80	31.69	14.12	13.46	NA	NA
Prices:Low	26.99	26.72	23.85	23.43	23.31	12.46	10.04	7.33	NA	NA
P/E Ratio:High	25	21	19	21	23	25	15	19	NA	NA
P/E Ratio:Low	18	16	14	13	16	10	10	10	NA	NA
Income Statement Analysis (Million $)										
Income Interest	8.73	3.39	2.15	2.40	9.74	19.0	13.9	8.88	3.03	2.16
Income Other	0.05	-0.11	0.00	2.27	706	662	587	513	401	320
Total Income	909	847	823	711	716	681	601	522	401	322
General Expenses	634	530	531	399	388	394	364	340	294	272
Interest Expense	17.9	21.0	4.71	4.79	29.7	34.2	31.8	27.6	20.1	18.6
Depreciation	24.0	19.0	20.6	19.2	26.0	15.8	18.1	22.9	22.4	18.3
Net Income	163	179	191	204	173	155	124	92.4	51.0	13.6
S&P Core Earnings	181	188	187	199	175	NA	NA	NA	NA	NA
Balance Sheet & Other Financial Data (Million $)										
Cash	246	258	234	151	73.5	150	171	186	NA	NA
Receivables	45.8	33.8	38.3	31.2	32.6	36.9	35.2	31.0	NA	NA
Cost of Investments	38.4	2.10	1.53	1.00	4.60	85.3	66.4	13.4	NA	NA
Total Assets	897	955	879	530	432	705	673	580	NA	NA
Loss Reserve	Nil	Nil	Nil	Nil	0.32	0.09	0.18	1.27	NA	NA
Short Term Debt	Nil	Nil	Nil	Nil	Nil	14.3	14.3	0.24	0.28	NA
Capitalization:Debt	160	285	328	59.2	55.0	394	394	372	284	NA
Capitalization:Equity	540	458	396	341	237	148	119	88.7	-41.1	NA
Capitalization:Total	723	767	744	416	299	583	551	491	244	NA
Price Times Book Value:High	24.0	24.8	15.6	24.8	41.5	36.7	22.0	49.0	NA	NA
Price Times Book Value:Low	17.0	19.6	11.6	16.0	29.5	14.5	16.0	27.0	NA	NA
Cash Flow	187	198	212	223	199	171	142	115	73.4	25.9
% Expense/Operating Revenue	71.7	65.1	65.1	56.7	58.4	62.9	65.9	70.4	78.3	84.0
% Earnings & Depreciation/Assets	20.2	19.5	25.3	46.4	35.0	24.8	22.7	NA	NA	NA

Data as orig reptd.; bef. results of disc opers/spec. items. Per share data adj. for stk. divs.; EPS diluted. E-Estimated. NA-Not Available. NM-Not Meaningful. NR-Not Ranked. UR-Under Review.

Office: 1001 Liberty Avenue, Pittsburgh, PA 15222-3779.
Telephone: 412-288-1900.
Email: investors@federatedinv.com
Website: http://www.FederatedInvestors.com

Chrmn: J.F. Donahue
Pres & CEO: J.C. Donahue
Vice Chrmn, EVP, Secy & Chief Lgl Officer: J.W. McGonigle
VP, CFO & Treas: T.R. Donahue

VP & Chief Acctg Officer: D. McAuley, III
Investor Contact: R. Hanley (412-288-1934)
Board of Directors: J. C. Donahue, J. F. Donahue, M. J. Farrell, D. M. Kelly, J. W. McGonigle, J. L. Murdy, E. G. O'Connor

Founded: 1955
Domicile: Pennsylvania
Employees: 1,289

STANDARD
&POOR'S

FedEx Corp.

S&P Recommendation STRONG BUY ★★★★★

Price $114.03 (as of Oct 27, 2006)

12-Mo. Target Price $143.00

Investment Style Large-Cap Growth

GICS Sector Industrials
Sub-Industry Air Freight & Logistics

Comment This company provides guaranteed domestic and international air express, residential and business ground package delivery, heavy freight and logistics services.

Key Stock Statistics (Source S&P, Vickers, company reports)

52-Wk Range	**$120.01–90.68**	S&P Oper. EPS 2007**E**	**6.65**	P/E on S&P Oper. EPS 2007**E**	**17.1**	Dividend Rate/Share	**$0.36**
Trailing 12-Month EPS	**$6.26**	S&P Oper. EPS 2008**E**	**7.60**	Common Shares Outstg. (M)	**306.6**	Yield (%)	**0.32**
Trailing 12-Month P/E	**18.2**	S&P Core EPS 2007**E**	**6.00**	Market Capitalization(B)	**$34.965**	Beta	**0.60**
$10K Invested 5 Yrs Ago	**$29,332**	S&P Core EPS 2008**E**	**7.00**	Institutional Ownership (%)	**75**	S&P Credit Rating	**BBB**

Price Performance

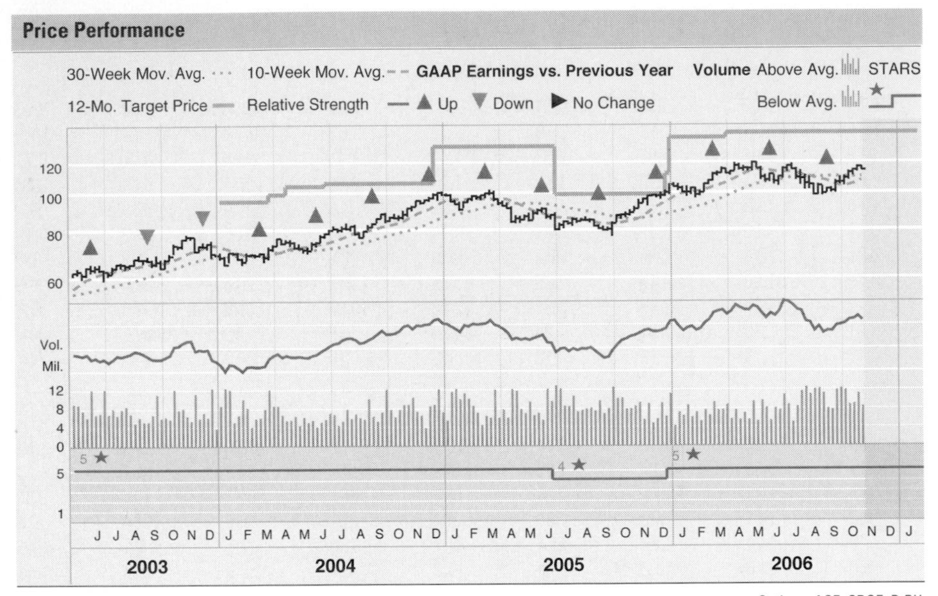

Options: ASE, CBOE, P, PH

Analysis prepared by **Jim Corridore** on September 26, 2006, when the stock traded at **$ 107.02**.

Highlights

- We see FY 07 (May) revenues rising 9%-10%, after growing 10% in FY 06. We expect about 5% volume growth at Ground, with revenues increasing about 10%, which should be aided by market share gains and price hikes. We see 6% revenue growth and 4% volume growth at Express. We estimate that international revenues will continue to grow in the double digits, driven by export activity out of China.
- We think operating margins are likely to widen, aided by lower salaries and benefits, purchased transportation, maintenance and depreciation as a percentage of revenues. We think efforts to focus on a better mix of products should help margins. The company is also attempting to push lower margin shipments into ground and freight channels, which we also see aiding margins in FY 07.
- We estimate FY 07 operating EPS of $6.65 (which includes $0.10 of projected stock option expense), up 14% from FY 06 EPS of $5.83. We forecast S&P Core EPS of $6.00 in FY 07, based on projected pension costs.

Investment Rationale/Risk

- We think FDX is likely to improve operating margins, which should help drive strong net income and free cash flow growth. We also believe the U.S. and global economy is likely to remain healthy into 2007, which argues for a higher valuation for this cyclical stock, in our opinion. FDX was recently trading at a P/E below the S&P 500, while we believe FDX is likely to grow EPS faster than the overall market. We think FDX will achieve its goals of improving operating margins, cash flow, and return on invested capital.
- Risks to our recommendation and target price include a possible price war or a major economic slowdown. In addition, we are concerned about some of FDX's corporate governance practices, such as the presence of affiliated outsiders on the board of directors and the audit committee.
- Our 12-month target price of $143 is based on a P/E of 21.5X applied to our FY 07 EPS estimate of $6.65, still toward the lower end of the company's five-year historical P/E range of 16.3X-36.6X EPS, and below UPS (UPS: buy, $81).

Qualitative Risk Assessment

LOW | MEDIUM | HIGH

Our risk assessment reflects our view of the company's strong and stable balance sheet, healthy cash flow generation and strong earnings growth potential amid the inherent cyclicality of its business segment. This is only partly offset by the potential that FDX could suffer from any material economic slowdown.

Quantitative Evaluations

S&P Quality Ranking B+

D | C | B- | B | B+ | A- | A | A+

Relative Strength Rank MODERATE

62

LOWEST = 1 HIGHEST = 99

Revenue/Earnings Data

Revenue (Million $)

	1Q	2Q	3Q	4Q	Year
2007	8,545	--	--	--	--
2006	7,707	8,090	8,003	8,494	32,294
2005	6,975	7,334	7,339	7,715	29,363
2004	5,687	5,920	6,062	7,041	24,710
2003	5,445	5,667	5,545	5,830	22,487
2002	5,037	5,135	5,019	5,416	20,607

Earnings Per Share ($)

2007	1.53	**E**1.60	**E**1.52	**E**2.00	**E**6.65
2006	1.10	1.53	1.38	1.82	5.83
2005	1.08	1.15	1.03	1.46	4.72
2004	0.42	0.30	0.68	1.36	2.76
2003	0.52	0.81	0.49	0.92	2.74
2002	0.41	0.81	0.39	0.78	2.39

Fiscal year ended May 31. Next earnings report expected: Late December. EPS Estimates based on S&P Operating Earnings; historical GAAP earnings are as reported.

Dividend Data (Dates: mm/dd Payment Date: mm/dd/yy)

Amount ($)	Date Decl.	Ex-Div. Date	Stk. of Record	Payment Date
0.080	11/18	12/09	12/13	01/03/06
0.080	02/17	03/09	03/13	04/03/06
0.090	05/26	06/08	06/12	07/03/06
0.090	08/18	09/07	09/11	10/02/06

Dividends have been paid since 2002. Source: Company reports.

FedEx Corp.

STANDARD &POOR'S

Business Summary September 26, 2006

CORPORATE OVERVIEW. FedEx Corp. provides global time-definite air express services for packages, documents and freight in 220 countries, and ground-based delivery of small packages in North America. In addition, the company offers expedited critical shipment delivery, customs brokerage solutions, less-than-truckload (LTL) freight transportation, and customized logistics. In February 2004, FDX paid $2.4 billion in cash for Kinko's, which operates about 1,200 copy centers that also provide business services. Kinko's has annual revenues of about $2 billion. Kinko's joined three other FedEx companies: Express, Ground, and Freight.

CORPORATE STRATEGY: The company intends to leverage and extend the FedEx brand and to provide customers with seamless access to its entire portfolio of integrated transportation services. Sales and marketing activities are coordinated among operating companies. Advanced information technology makes it convenient for customers to use the full range of FedEx services and provides a single point of contact for customers to access shipment tracking, customer service and invoicing information. The company intends to continue to operate independent express, ground and freight networks, but has increased its emphasis on having the individual business units work together to compete more effectively.

Company Financials

Per Share Data ($) Year Ended May 31	**2006**	**2005**	**2004**	**2003**	**2002**	**2001**	**2000**	**1999**	**1998**	**1997**
Tangible Book Value	28.39	22.36	17.45	21.03	18.38	16.20	14.33	14.50	12.26	11.29
Cash Flow	10.83	9.48	7.28	7.20	6.89	6.35	6.23	5.55	4.91	4.91
Earnings	5.83	4.72	2.76	2.74	2.39	1.99	2.32	2.10	1.68	1.56
S&P Core Earnings	5.60	4.48	2.61	1.38	0.95	0.44	NA	NA	NA	NA
Dividends	0.33	0.29	0.22	0.20	Nil	Nil	Nil	Nil	Nil	Nil
Payout Ratio	6%	6%	8%	7%	Nil	Nil	Nil	Nil	Nil	Nil
Calendar Year	2005	2004	2003	2002	2001	2000	1999	1998	1997	1996
Prices:High	105.82	100.92	78.05	61.35	53.48	49.85	61.88	46.56	42.25	22.50
Prices:Low	76.81	64.84	47.70	42.75	33.15	30.56	34.88	21.81	21.00	16.72
P/E Ratio:High	18	21	28	22	22	25	27	22	25	14
P/E Ratio:Low	13	14	17	16	14	15	15	10	12	11

Income Statement Analysis (Million $)										
Revenue	32,294	29,363	24,710	22,487	20,607	19,629	18,257	16,773	15,873	11,520
Operating Income	4,564	3,933	3,250	2,822	2,804	2,347	2,376	2,198	2,047	1,477
Depreciation	1,550	1,462	1,375	1,351	1,364	1,276	1,155	1,035	964	778
Interest Expense	142	160	136	118	139	144	100	98.0	124	91.0
Pretax Income	2,899	2,313	1,319	1,338	1,160	928	1,138	1,061	899	628
Effective Tax Rate	37.7%	37.4%	36.5%	38.0%	37.5%	37.0%	39.5%	40.5%	44.6%	42.5%
Net Income	1,806	1,449	838	830	725	584	688	631	498	361
S&P Core Earnings	1,733	1,376	790	415	286	130	NA	NA	NA	NA

Balance Sheet & Other Financial Data (Million $)										
Cash	1,937	1,039	1,046	538	331	121	68.0	325	230	122
Current Assets	6,464	5,269	4,970	3,941	3,665	3,449	3,285	3,141	2,880	2,133
Total Assets	22,690	20,404	19,134	15,385	13,812	13,340	11,527	10,648	9,686	7,625
Current Liabilities	5,473	4,734	4,732	3,335	2,942	3,250	2,891	2,785	2,804	1,963
Long Term Debt	1,592	2,427	2,837	1,709	1,800	1,900	1,776	1,360	1,385	1,398
Common Equity	11,511	9,588	8,036	7,288	6,545	5,900	4,785	4,664	3,961	2,962
Total Capital	14,470	13,221	12,054	9,879	8,944	8,256	6,906	6,317	5,620	4,520
Capital Expenditures	2,518	2,236	1,271	1,511	1,615	1,893	1,627	1,550	1,880	1,471
Cash Flow	3,356	2,911	2,213	2,181	2,089	1,860	1,843	1,665	1,462	1,139
Current Ratio	1.2	1.1	1.1	1.2	1.2	1.1	1.1	1.1	1.0	1.1
% Long Term Debt of Capitalization	11.0	18.3	23.5	17.2	20.1	23.0	25.7	21.5	24.6	31.0
% Net Income of Revenue	5.6	4.9	3.4	3.7	3.5	3.0	3.8	3.8	3.1	3.1
% Return on Assets	8.4	7.3	4.9	5.7	5.3	4.7	6.2	6.2	5.8	5.0
% Return on Equity	17.1	16.4	10.9	11.8	11.7	10.9	14.6	14.6	14.4	13.0

Data as orig reptd.; bef. results of disc opers/spec. items. Per share data adj. for stk. divs.; EPS diluted. E-Estimated. NA-Not Available. NM-Not Meaningful. NR-Not Ranked. UR-Under Review.

Office: 942 South Shady Grove Road, Memphis, TN 38120-4117.
Telephone: 901-818-7500.
Website: http://www.fedex.com
Chrmn, Pres & CEO: F.W. Smith

EVP & CFO: A.B. Graf, Jr.
EVP, Secy & General Counsel: C.P. Richards
EVP & CIO: R.B. Carter
Investor Contact: J. Clippard Jr. (901-818-7200)

Board of Directors: J. L. Barksdale, A. A. Busch, IV, J. A. Edwardson, J. L. Estrin, J. K. Glass, P. Greer, J. R. Hyde, III, S. A. Jackson, S. R. Loranger, C. T. Manatt, F. W. Smith, J. I. Smith, P. S. Walsh, P. S. Willmott

Founded: 1971
Domicile: Delaware
Employees: 243,650

STANDARD &POOR'S

Fifth Third Bancorp

S&P Recommendation HOLD ★★★★★ | **Price** $39.53 (as of Oct 27, 2006) | **12-Mo. Target Price** $41.00 | **Investment Style** Large-Cap Growth

GICS Sector Financials
Sub-Industry Regional Banks

Comment This regional bank holding company operates banking centers in Ohio, Kentucky, Indiana, Michigan, Illinois, Florida, West Virginia, Pennsylvania, and Tennessee.

Key Stock Statistics (Source S&P, Vickers, company reports)

52-Wk Range	**$42.50–35.86**	S&P Oper. EPS 2006**E**	**2.68**	P/E on S&P Oper. EPS 2006**E**	**14.7**	Dividend Rate/Share	**$1.60**
Trailing 12-Month EPS	**$2.60**	S&P Oper. EPS 2007**E**	**2.87**	Common Shares Outstg. (M)	**557.9**	Yield (%)	**4.05**
Trailing 12-Month P/E	**15.2**	S&P Core EPS 2006**E**	**2.66**	Market Capitalization(B)	**$22.054**	Beta	**0.32**
$10K Invested 5 Yrs Ago	**$7,808**	S&P Core EPS 2007**E**	**2.85**	Institutional Ownership (%)	**67**	S&P Credit Rating	**A+**

Price Performance

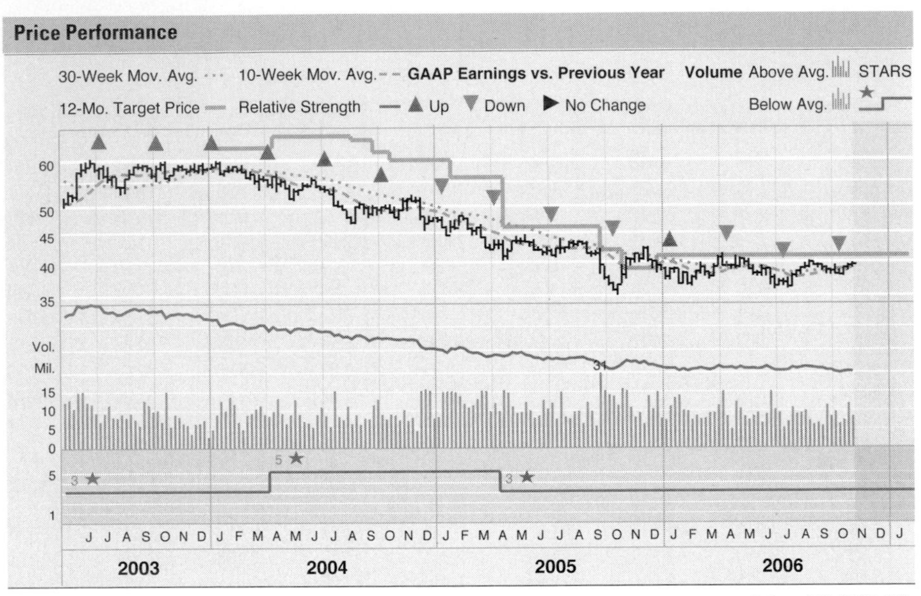

Options: ASE, CBOE, P, Ph

Analysis prepared by **Mark Hebeka, CFA** on September 18, 2006, when the stock traded at **$ 38.30**.

Highlights

- We believe that challenging operating conditions on the deposit and loan pricing fronts will make the company's projected return to its historical profitability levels a longer process than we had originally anticipated. With continued higher interest rates, coupled with a flattened yield curve, we think that FITB will not have a meaningful expansion in its net interest margin, or an acceleration in net interest income and revenue, until at least 2007.
- We believe quarterly credit losses during 2006 are likely to increase slightly based on our expectation for strong economic conditions and relatively low levels of non-performers. We look for the company to grow loans at a healthy rate while deposit growth should lag until aggressive deposit pricing takes hold. We expect expense growth to continue at a healthy pace in 2006, based on FITB's large investments in revenue producing personnel and branch network expansion during the past year.
- Our 2006 operating EPS estimate is $2.68, versus $2.77 in 2005. We project 2007 EPS of $2.87.

Investment Rationale/Risk

- We continue to believe that FITB can generate above peer average loan growth and can eventually return to its historical levels of profitability. However, we think that this process is going to take longer than we had originally expected, and, in the mean time, we do not believe the shares are likely to regain their historical above average valuation. We look for de novo expansion to pick up in the coming quarters as fewer branches than anticipated were recently opened. We believe this will be one of FITB's main drivers to achieve growth.
- Risks to our recommendation and target price include a severe economic downturn combined with a sharper than expected rise in short-term interest rates that could result in an inverted yield curve, and a further deterioration in consumer confidence that could affect consumer spending levels.
- We continue to view FITB as one of the bank industry's better operators, with above average fundamentals. We therefore believe that the stock's current P/E multiple should remain stable. Our 12-month target price of $41 is equal to about 14X our 2007 EPS estimate.

Qualitative Risk Assessment

LOW | MEDIUM | HIGH

Our risk assessment reflects what we see as solid business fundamentals and a strong customer base. We view FITB as well diversified and able to withstand a major regional or U.S. economic downturn.

Quantitative Evaluations

S&P Quality Ranking **A+**

D | C | B- | B | B+ | A- | A | A+

Relative Strength Rank **MODERATE**

46

LOWEST = 1 HIGHEST = 99

Revenue/Earnings Data

Revenue (Million $)

	1Q	2Q	3Q	4Q	Year
2006	2,015	2,132	1,381	--	--
2005	1,752	1,850	1,905	1,988	7,495
2004	1,617	1,749	1,654	1,560	6,579
2003	1,588	1,641	1,666	1,587	6,474
2002	1,514	1,554	1,644	1,611	6,324
2001	1,110	1,653	1,621	1,560	6,506

Earnings Per Share ($)

	1Q	2Q	3Q	4Q	Year
2006	0.65	0.69	0.68	**E**0.68	**E**2.68
2005	0.72	0.75	0.71	0.60	2.77
2004	0.75	0.79	0.83	0.31	2.68
2003	0.72	0.75	0.78	0.73	2.97
2002	0.66	0.68	0.70	0.72	2.76
2001	0.51	0.22	0.47	0.65	1.86

Fiscal year ended Dec. 31. Next earnings report expected: Mid January. EPS Estimates based on S&P Operating Earnings; historical GAAP earnings are as reported.

Dividend Data (Dates: mm/dd Payment Date: mm/dd/yy)

Amount ($)	Date Decl.	Ex-Div. Date	Stk. of Record	Payment Date
0.380	12/21	12/29	12/30	01/17/06
0.380	03/28	03/30	03/31	04/18/06
0.400	06/20	06/28	06/30	07/20/06
0.400	09/19	09/27	09/29	10/19/06

Dividends have been paid since 1952. Source: Company reports.

Fifth Third Bancorp

Business Summary September 18, 2006

CORPORATE OVERVIEW. FITB is divided into five segments: commercial banking, branch banking, consumer lending, investment advisors and processing solutions. Commercial banking provides a comprehensive range of financial services and products to large and middle-market businesses, governments and professional customers. In addition to the traditional lending and depository offerings, commercial banking products and services include cash management, foreign exchange and international trade finance, derivatives and capital markets services, asset-based lending, real estate finance, public finance, commercial leasing and syndicated finance.

Branch banking provides a full range of deposit and loan and lease products to individuals and small businesses through over 1,100 banking centers. Branch banking offers depository and loan products, such as checking and savings accounts, home equity lines of credit, credit cards and loans for automobile and other personal financing needs, as well as products designed to meet the specific needs of small businesses, including cash management services.

Consumer lending includes mortgage and home equity lending activities and other indirect lending activities. Mortgage and home equity lending activities include the origination, retention and servicing of mortgage and home equity loans or lines of credit, sales and securitizations of those loans or pools of loans or lines of credit and all associated hedging activities. Other indirect lending activities include loans to consumers through dealers and federal and private student education loans.

Investment advisors provides a full range of investment alternatives for individuals, companies and not-for-profit organizations. Primary services include trust, asset management, retirement plans and custody. Fifth Third Securities, Inc., an indirect wholly-owned subsidiary, offers full service retail brokerage services to individual clients and broker dealer services to the institutional marketplace. Fifth Third Asset Management, Inc., an indirect wholly-owned subsidiary, provides asset management services and also advises a proprietary family of mutual funds, Fifth Third Funds. Fifth Third Processing Solutions provides electronic funds transfer, debit, credit and merchant transaction processing, operates the Jeanie ATM network, and provides other data processing services to affiliated and unaffiliated customers.

Company Financials

Per Share Data ($) Year Ended Dec. 31	2005	2004	2003	2002	2001	2000	1999	1998	1997	1996
Tangible Book Value	12.72	13.33	13.46	13.12	13.09	10.50	8.79	7.04	8.47	5.19
Earnings	2.77	2.68	2.97	2.76	1.86	1.83	1.43	1.17	1.13	0.95
S&P Core Earnings	2.78	2.69	2.84	2.56	1.63	NA	NA	NA	NA	NA
Dividends	1.46	1.31	1.13	0.98	0.83	0.70	0.56	0.44	0.38	0.33
Payout Ratio	53%	49%	38%	36%	45%	38%	39%	37%	33%	34%
Prices:High	48.12	60.00	62.15	69.70	64.77	60.88	50.29	49.42	37.11	22.00
Prices:Low	35.04	45.32	47.05	55.26	45.69	29.33	38.58	31.67	18.00	12.89
P/E Ratio:High	17	22	21	25	35	33	35	42	33	23
P/E Ratio:Low	13	17	16	20	25	16	27	27	16	14
Income Statement Analysis (Million $)										
Net Interest Income	2,965	3,012	2,905	2,700	2,433	1,470	1,405	1,003	745	689
Tax Equivalent Adjustment	31.0	36.0	39.0	39.5	45.5	93.0	73.0	49.2	43.0	39.0
Non Interest Income	2,461	2,502	2,399	2,047	1,626	1,013	876	626	439	364
Loan Loss Provision	330	268	399	247	236	89.0	134	109	80.3	64.0
% Expense/Operating Revenue	53.6%	53.5%	46.0%	51.9%	57.7%	45.1%	47.7%	47.9%	42.7%	45.0%
Pretax Income	2,208	2,237	2,547	2,432	1,653	1,275	1,026	726	604	500
Effective Tax Rate	29.8%	31.8%	31.6%	31.2%	33.3%	32.3%	34.9%	34.4%	33.6%	33.0%
Net Income	1,549	1,525	1,722	1,635	1,101	863	668	476	401	335
% Net Interest Margin	3.23	3.48	3.62	3.96	3.82	3.77	3.99	3.94	4.11	3.99
S&P Core Earnings	1,555	1,529	1,650	1,513	965	NA	NA	NA	NA	NA
Balance Sheet & Other Financial Data (Million $)										
Money Market Assets	117	77.0	55.0	312	225	198	355	119	29.4	44.6
Investment Securities	22,471	25,474	29,402	25,828	20,748	15,827	12,817	8,539	6,469	6,401
Commercial Loans	33,214	30,601	28,242	22,614	10,839	12,382	11,141	9,093	5,684	5,903
Other Loans	38,024	29,207	25,493	23,314	30,709	13,570	14,746	9,375	7,555	7,060
Total Assets	105,225	94,456	91,143	80,894	71,026	45,857	41,589	28,922	21,375	20,549
Demand Deposits	53,778	37,288	31,899	11,139	10,595	5,604	8,011	6,355	2,426	2,496
Time Deposits	13,656	20,938	25,196	41,069	35,259	25,344	18,072	12,425	12,488	11,879
Long Term Debt	15,227	13,983	9,063	8,179	7,030	4,034	1,977	2,288	458	278
Common Equity	9,437	8,915	8,516	8,466	7,630	4,891	4,306	3,179	2,277	2,144
% Return on Assets	1.6	1.6	2.0	2.2	1.6	2.0	1.7	1.9	1.9	1.8
% Return on Equity	16.9	17.3	20.3	20.3	15.4	19.2	16.6	17.5	18.1	17.3
% Loan Loss Reserve	1.0	1.2	1.4	1.4	1.4	1.4	4.9	1.5	1.5	1.5
% Loans/Deposits	105.6	103.7	94.9	94.4	95.4	85.6	100.4	94.7	90.1	87.1
% Equity to Assets	9.2	9.5	9.9	10.6	10.2	10.3	10.3	10.8	10.5	10.3

Data as orig reptd.; bef. results of disc opers/spec. items. Per share data adj. for stk. divs.; EPS diluted. E-Estimated. NA-Not Available. NM-Not Meaningful. NR-Not Ranked. UR-Under Review.

Office: 38 Fountain Square Plaza, Cincinnati, OH 45263.
Telephone: 513-534-5300.
Website: http://www.53.com
Chrmn & CEO: G.A. Schaefer, Jr.

Pres: K.T. Kabat
COO & EVP: G.D. Carmichael
EVP & CFO: C.G. Marshall
EVP, Secy & General Counsel: P.L. Reynolds

Investor Contact: J. Richardson
Board of Directors: D. F. Allen, J. F. Barrett, J. P. Hackett, J. R. Herschede, A. M. Hill, R. L. Koch, II, M. D. Livingston, K. W. Lowe, H. G. Meijer, J. E. Rogers, G. A. Schaefer, Jr., J. J. Schiff, Jr., D. S. Taft, T. W. Traylor

Founded: 1862
Domicile: Ohio
Employees: 21,681

STANDARD &POOR'S

FirstEnergy Corp.

S&P Recommendation HOLD ★★★★★	Price	12-Mo. Target Price	Investment Style
	$59.53 (as of Oct 27, 2006)	$62.00	Large-Cap Value

GICS Sector Utilities
Sub-Industry Electric Utilities

Comment This electric utility holding company serves about 4.5 million customers in portions of Ohio, Pennsylvania and New Jersey.

Key Stock Statistics (Source S&P, Vickers, company reports)

52-Wk Range	$60.41–45.78	S&P Oper. EPS 2006E	3.85	P/E on S&P Oper. EPS 2006E	15.5	Dividend Rate/Share	$1.80
Trailing 12-Month EPS	$3.64	S&P Oper. EPS 2007E	4.15	Common Shares Outstg. (M)	329.8	Yield (%)	3.02
Trailing 12-Month P/E	16.4	S&P Core EPS 2006E	3.71	Market Capitalization(B)	$19.635	Beta	0.29
$10K Invested 5 Yrs Ago	$20,989	S&P Core EPS 2007E	4.00	Institutional Ownership (%)	70	S&P Credit Rating	BBB

Price Performance

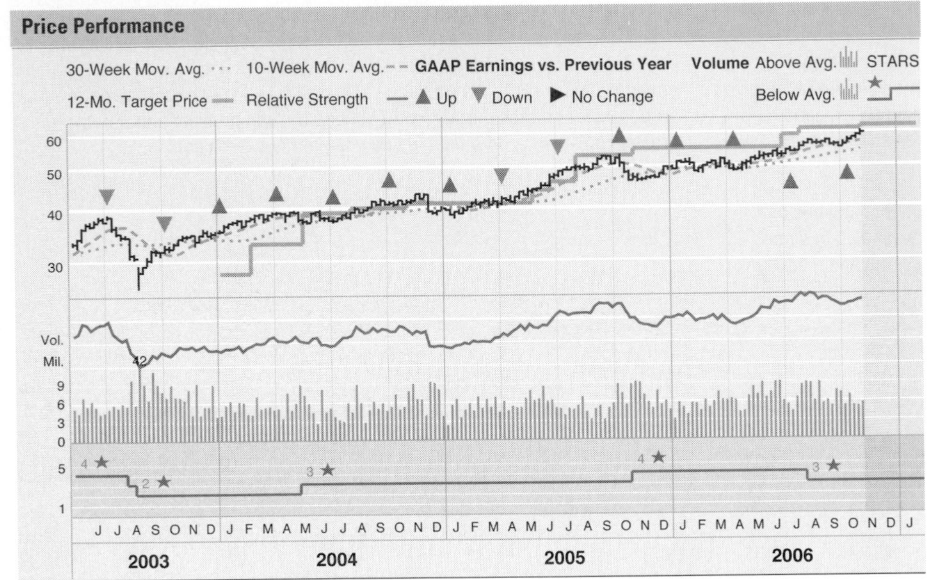

Options: ASE, CBOE, P, Ph

Analysis prepared by **Justin McCann** on October 26, 2006, when the stock traded at **$ 59.33**.

Highlights

- After a more than 25% anticipated advance in 2006 (from 2005's operating EPS of $3.00), we expect operating EPS to increase by nearly 8% in 2007. Results in the third quarter of 2006 benefited by $0.24 from the reduction in the amortization of transition costs; $0.07 from the deferral of costs related to the upgrading of the company's electric distribution infrastructure; and $0.08 from the deferral of certain fuel and distribution costs.
- We expect operating EPS in 2006 to be driven by the net reduction in transition cost amortization in Ohio, higher generation margins, and growth in the wires business. We also look for FE to generate more than $2 billion in net cash from operations in 2006, and approximately $450 million in free cash flow.
- In June 2006, the company's generation subsidiary entered into a new coal supply agreement with CONSOL Energy (CNX), under which CNX would supply a total of more than 128 million tons of high-BTU coal for the 20 year period 2009 through 2028. The agreement replaced an existing agreement that ran through 2020, and should result in the shipment of an additional two million tons per year.

Investment Rationale/Risk

- With the shares up more than 20% year to date, and having outperformed its electric utility peers for the past two years, we expect a reduced level of total return from the stock's current value. After having completed its four-year debt reduction program of nearly $4 billion, FE's enhanced financial strength allowed the company's board to authorize a stock repurchase program of up to 12 million common shares. This was largely implemented on August 10, 2006, when FE repurchased 10.6 million shares, or about 3.2% of its outstanding shares.
- Risks to our recommendation and target price include the possibility of higher than anticipated or inadequately hedged replacement power costs, as well as a reduction in the average P/E of FE's electric utility peers.
- FE has adopted a new dividend policy that has targeted future annual increases of about 4% to 5% and a dividend payout ratio of 50% to 60%. The targeted growth rate is above both the expected dividend growth rate of the industry and FE's own expected longer-term EPS growth rate of 3% to 4%. Our 12-month target price of $62 represents a discount to peers P/E multiple of 14.9X our EPS estimate for 2007.

Qualitative Risk Assessment

LOW	MEDIUM	HIGH

Our risk assessment reflects the strong and steady cash flow we expect from the company's regulated electric utility subsidiaries; its low-cost baseload power generation in Ohio and Pennsylvania; its low-risk transmission distribution operations in New Jersey and Pennsylvania; and its rate certainty in Ohio. This is partially offset by the company's below average nuclear operations and our view of its high level of debt and environmental spending.

Quantitative Evaluations

S&P Quality Ranking **B+**

D	C	B-	B	**B+**	A-	A	A+

Relative Strength Rank **MODERATE**

66

LOWEST = 1 HIGHEST = 99

Revenue/Earnings Data

Revenue (Million $)

	1Q	2Q	3Q	4Q	Year
2006	2,845	2,790	3,401	--	--
2005	2,813	2,900	3,588	2,892	11,989
2004	3,183	3,150	3,536	2,950	12,453
2003	3,221	2,853	3,434	2,799	12,307
2002	2,762	2,899	3,451	3,040	12,152
2001	2,000	1,804	1,952	2,300	7,999

Earnings Per Share ($)

	1Q	2Q	3Q	4Q	Year
2006	0.67	0.91	1.40	E0.81	E3.85
2005	0.42	0.54	1.01	0.67	2.65
2004	0.53	0.62	0.91	0.61	2.66
2003	0.39	0.03	0.51	0.44	1.39
2002	0.29	0.79	1.05	0.20	2.33
2001	0.49	0.67	1.06	0.64	2.84

Fiscal year ended Dec. 31. Next earnings report expected: Mid February. EPS Estimates based on S&P Operating Earnings; historical GAAP earnings are as reported.

Dividend Data (Dates: mm/dd Payment Date: mm/dd/yy)

Amount ($)	Date Decl.	Ex-Div. Date	Stk. of Record	Payment Date
0.450	11/15	02/03	02/07	03/01/06
0.450	03/21	05/03	05/05	06/01/06
0.450	06/20	08/03	08/07	09/01/06
0.450	09/19	11/03	11/07	12/01/06

Dividends have been paid since 1930. Source: Company reports.

FirstEnergy Corp.

Business Summary October 26, 2006

CORPORATE OVERVIEW. FirstEnergy (FE) is a diversified energy company involved in the generation, transmission and distribution of electricity as well as energy management and related services. The company operates primarily through two core business segments: Regulated Services, which provides transmission and distribution services, and Power Supply Management Services (PSM). The Regulated Services segment, which is comprised of seven electric utility operating companies, contributed to 98.7% of the net income in 2005. The PSM Services segment, which owns and operates the generation assets and wholesale purchase of electricity, energy management and other energy-related services, contributed to 1.3% of 2005 net income.

CORPORATE STRATEGY. FE intends to be a leading regional supplier of energy services in the northeast quadrant of the U.S. On the generation front, the company is working to optimize its generation portfolio and to effectively manage its commodity supplies and risks. FE is committed to reinvesting in the operations of its utilities for a continuous improvement in their customer service quality and reliability. To this end, FE is upgrading its transmission and distribution system, implementing new technologies and incorporating industry-best practices. The company has made safety and environmental compliance one of its top priorities, both within the nuclear fleet and across the organization.

Company Financials

Per Share Data ($) Year Ended Dec. 31	**2005**	**2004**	**2003**	**2002**	**2001**	**2000**	**1999**	**1998**	**1997**	**1996**
Tangible Book Value	9.63	7.70	6.55	4.11	6.04	11.42	10.47	9.62	8.91	16.41
Earnings	2.65	2.66	1.39	2.33	2.84	2.69	2.50	1.95	1.94	2.10
S&P Core Earnings	2.56	2.77	1.61	1.69	2.36	NA	NA	NA	NA	NA
Dividends	1.67	1.50	1.50	1.50	1.13	1.50	1.50	1.50	1.50	1.50
Payout Ratio	63%	56%	108%	64%	40%	56%	60%	77%	77%	71%
Prices:High	53.36	43.41	38.90	39.12	36.98	32.13	33.19	34.06	29.00	24.88
Prices:Low	37.70	35.24	25.82	24.85	26.10	10.00	22.13	27.06	19.25	19.25
P/E Ratio:High	20	16	28	17	13	12	13	17	15	12
P/E Ratio:Low	14	13	19	11	9	7	9	14	10	9
Income Statement Analysis (Million $)										
Revenue	11,989	12,453	12,307	12,152	7,999	7,029	6,320	5,861	2,821	2,470
Depreciation	1,870	1,756	1,282	1,106	890	934	938	741	475	356
Maintenance	NA	NA	NA	NA	NA	NA	NA	NA	NA	NA
Fixed Charges Coverage	3.39	3.25	1.88	2.25	2.85	2.71	2.62	2.21	2.64	2.87
Construction Credits	NA	NA	NA	24.5	35.5	27.1	13.4	7.64	3.50	3.10
Effective Tax Rate	46.3%	43.4%	49.0%	44.5%	42.0%	38.6%	41.0%	42.2%	40.5%	39.0%
Net Income	873	874	422	686	655	599	568	441	306	315
S&P Core Earnings	841	911	482	406	540	NA	NA	NA	NA	NA
Balance Sheet & Other Financial Data (Million $)										
Gross Property	23,790	22,892	22,374	21,231	20,589	12,839	15,013	15,255	17,516	8,733
Capital Expenditures	1,208	846	856	998	852	588	625	653	204	140
Net Property	13,998	13,478	13,269	12,680	12,428	7,575	9,093	9,243	11,880	5,418
Capitalization:Long Term Debt	8,339	10,348	9,789	11,636	12,508	6,552	6,906	7,307	6,970	2,713
Capitalization:% Long Term Debt	47.1	53.7	53.1	62.0	62.8	58.5	60.2	62.2	57.5	48.6
Capitalization:Preferred	184	335	352	Nil	Nil	Nil	Nil	Nil	995	367
Capitalization:% Preferred	1.04	1.74	1.91	Nil	Nil	Nil	Nil	Nil	8.20	6.60
Capitalization:Common	9,188	8,589	8,289	7,120	7,399	4,653	4,564	4,449	4,160	2,503
Capitalization:% Common	51.9	44.6	45.0	38.0	37.2	41.5	39.8	37.8	34.3	44.8
Total Capital	20,437	21,597	20,608	21,360	22,852	13,540	13,970	14,325	14,754	7,560
% Operating Ratio	89.0	87.3	90.4	86.6	50.8	37.8	82.0	82.2	81.2	78.5
% Earned on Net Property	15.0	16.5	11.2	17.4	16.8	18.1	16.7	NA	6.0	9.5
% Return on Revenue	7.3	7.0	3.4	5.6	8.2	8.5	9.0	7.5	10.8	12.8
% Return on Invested Capital	7.3	7.4	6.5	7.4	21.8	32.0	7.8	NA	5.5	7.5
% Return on Common Equity	9.8	10.4	5.5	9.5	10.9	13.0	12.6	NA	9.2	12.3

Data as orig reptd.; bef. results of disc opers/spec. items. Per share data adj. for stk. divs.; EPS diluted. E-Estimated. NA-Not Available. NM-Not Meaningful. NR-Not Ranked. UR-Under Review.

Office: 76 South Main Street, Akron, OH 44308-1890.
Telephone: 800-736-3402.
Website: http://www.firstenergycorp.com
Chrmn: G.M. Smart

Pres & CEO: A.J. Alexander
COO & EVP: R.R. Grigg
SVP & CFO: R.H. Marsh
SVP & General Counsel: L.L. Vespoli

Investor Contact: R.E. Seeholzer
Board of Directors: P. T. Addison, A. J. Alexander, C. A. Cartwright, W. T. Cottle, R. B. Heisler Jr., R. W. Maier, E. J. Novak, Jr., R. N. Pokelwaldt, P. J. Powers, C. A. Rein, R. C. Savage, G. M. Smart, W. M. Taylor, J. T. Williams, Sr., P. K. Woolf

Founded: 1996
Domicile: Ohio
Employees: 14,586

STANDARD &POOR'S

First Data Corp.

S&P Recommendation HOLD ★★★★★

Price $24.30 (as of Oct 30, 2006)

12-Mo. Target Price $24.00

Investment Style Large-Cap Growth

GICS Sector Information Technology
Sub-Industry Data Processing & Outsourced Services

Comment FDC provides card and check processing services. In October 2006, FDC completed the spin-off of Western Union.

Key Stock Statistics (Source S&P, Vickers, company reports)

52-Wk Range	$48.88–21.93	S&P Oper. EPS 2006**E**	1.13	P/E on S&P Oper. EPS 2006**E**	21.5	Dividend Rate/Share	$0.24
Trailing 12-Month EPS	$1.96	S&P Oper. EPS 2007**E**	1.21	Common Shares Outstg. (M)	765.2	Yield (%)	0.99
Trailing 12-Month P/E	12.4	S&P Core EPS 2006**E**	1.13	Market Capitalization(B)	$18.593	Beta	0.98
$10K Invested 5 Yrs Ago	$12,761	S&P Core EPS 2007**E**	1.21	Institutional Ownership (%)	87	S&P Credit Rating	A

Price Performance

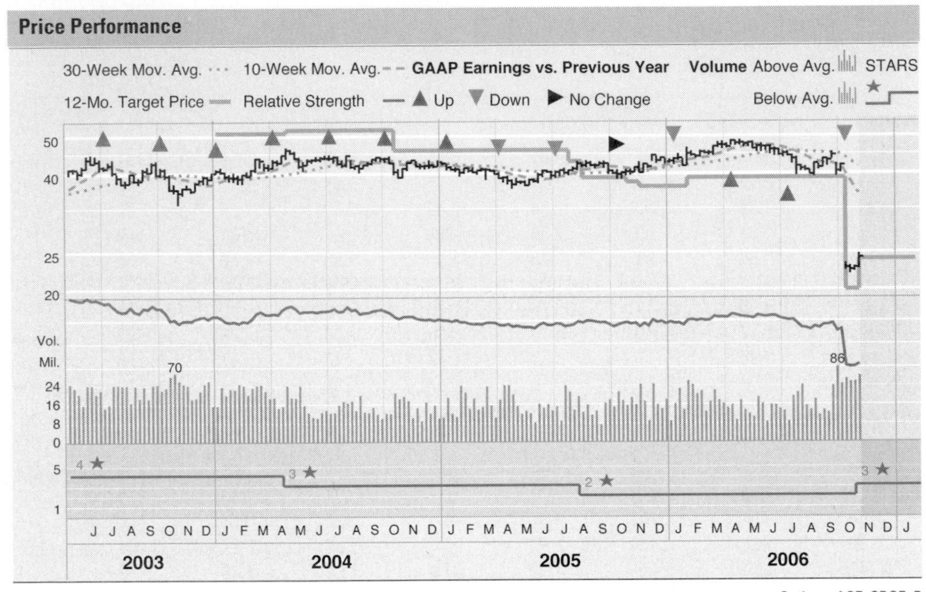

Options: ASE, CBOE, P

Analysis prepared by **Zaineb Bokhari** on October 30, 2006, when the stock traded at **$ 24.36**.

Highlights

- In October 2006, FDC completed the spin-off of Western Union (WU: $22) which accounted for 37% of segment revenues in 2005. Post-divestiture, we forecast revenue growth of approximately 8% in 2006 and 7% in 2007. We expect the company's core commercial services and international segments to remain the primary drivers of growth in 2006 and 2007.
- We expect FDC's operating margins in 2006 and 2007 to remain consistent with levels seen in 2005. We think the company's card processing services face significant challenges given recent developments regarding changes in control of notable credit card portfolios. We also expect ongoing pricing pressure within FDC's card processing operations to limit margin expansion.
- EPS has been aided by share repurchases that led to sequential reductions in shares outstanding from 2002 to 2005. We expect future repurchases as indicated by a recent announcement of the company's plans to repurchase $700 million in shares by 2007. We project FDC's post-divestiture annual EPS from continuing operations of $1.13 in 2006 and $1.21 in 2007.

Investment Rationale/Risk

- Although we think FDC intended to deliver shareholder value with the spin-off of WU, we see this action as paramount to selling its most attractive and important business. In addition, on a recurring quarterly basis, FDC has described multiple one-time items related to acquired businesses and other developments. We think the WU divestiture will detract from earnings quality. Despite this, we expect renewed corporate focus on continuing operations to improve following the spin-off. We think this will lead to incrementally better execution for FDC's continuing businesses.
- Risks to our recommendation and target price include increasing competition (particularly on price) from other payment processors, and the potential for business disruptions or loss due to ongoing consolidation within the financial services industry, which FDC serves.
- As earnings normalize following the WU spin-off, we expect FDC shares to trade in line with the data processing and outsourced services peers at approximately 20.0X our 2007 estimate; as a result, we set our 12-month target price at $24.

Qualitative Risk Assessment

LOW | **MEDIUM** | HIGH

Our risk assessment reflects our view of FDC's market leadership in multiple businesses, notable revenue diversification, and a solid and flexible balance sheet, offset by our belief that operations are mostly mature, inconsistent financial execution, and somewhat lacking earnings quality.

Quantitative Evaluations

S&P Quality Ranking A

D | C | B- | B | B+ | A- | **A** | A+

Relative Strength Rank WEAK

2

LOWEST = 1 HIGHEST = 99

Revenue/Earnings Data

Revenue (Million $)

	1Q	2Q	3Q	4Q	Year
2006	2,696	2,861	1,796	--	--
2005	2,466	2,595	2,662	2,767	10,490
2004	2,258	2,529	2,536	2,690	10,013
2003	2,009	2,114	2,140	2,244	8,400
2002	1,740	1,890	1,948	2,059	7,636
2001	1,509	1,608	1,652	1,682	6,451

Earnings Per Share ($)

2006	0.56	0.60	0.17	**E**0.35	**E**1.13
2005	0.47	0.50	0.54	0.53	2.04
2004	0.61	0.53	0.54	0.56	2.22
2003	0.39	0.47	0.49	0.55	1.86
2002	0.32	0.39	0.45	0.46	1.61
2001	0.24	0.31	0.19	0.37	1.10

Fiscal year ended Dec. 31. Next earnings report expected: Late January. EPS Estimates based on S&P Operating Earnings; historical GAAP earnings are as reported.

Dividend Data (Dates: mm/dd Payment Date: mm/dd/yy)

Amount ($)	Date Decl.	Ex-Div. Date	Stk. of Record	Payment Date
0.060	02/22	03/30	04/03	04/13/06
0.060	05/10	06/29	07/03	07/13/06
Stk	09/08	10/02	09/22	09/29/06
0.060	09/08	10/03	10/02	10/12/06

Dividends have been paid since 1992. Source: Company reports.

First Data Corp.

Business Summary October 30, 2006

CORPORATE OVERVIEW. In 2005, First Data had more than 460 million card accounts on file, processed 23.4 billion North American merchant transactions, and operated 271,000 Western Union agent locations. FDC transformed itself from a small credit card processing operation (part of American Express) into one of the world's largest independent data services companies. In January 2006, the company announced that it would be realigning into new operating segments. In October 2006, FDC completed the spin-off of Western Union. Every FDC share was provided with a WU share.

The Merchant Services segment (which accounted for 37% of total revenues in 2005 and 2004) facilitated the acceptance of consumer transactions at the point of sale, whether that is a physical merchant location, the Internet, or an ATM. Offerings include merchant acquiring (facilitation of credit and debit card acceptance by merchants, through authorization, transaction capture, settlement, chargeback handling, and Internet-based transaction processing), check verification and guarantee services, and network acquiring and processing (ATM processing, access to the STAR network, and debit-card transaction processing services).

Card Issuing Services (22%, 23%) provided U.S. and international card processing for card issuers. Offerings include (credit, debit, and private label) card processing services for financial institutions and other issuers of cards, including account maintenance, transaction authorization and posting, statement generation and printing, card embossing, fraud and risk management services, debit network issuing and processing (STAR network access, and ATM/debit and signature debit processing) and card processing software (VisionPLUS card processing software to financial institutions, retailers, and third-party processors primarily in international markets).

The Payment Services segment (40%, 38%) included WU, and provided money transfer services to consumers and businesses from one location to another, or through the issuance of an official check or money order from a bank or other institution.

Company Financials

Per Share Data ($) Year Ended Dec. 31	**2005**	**2004**	**2003**	**2002**	**2001**	**2000**	**1999**	**1998**	**1997**	**1996**
Tangible Book Value	NM	NM	NM	NM	NM	0.20	0.51	NM	NM	NM
Cash Flow	3.03	3.10	2.62	2.30	1.90	1.83	2.09	1.18	0.95	1.12
Earnings	2.04	2.22	1.86	1.61	1.10	1.13	1.38	0.52	0.40	0.69
S&P Core Earnings	1.77	1.90	1.71	1.42	1.12	NA	NA	NA	NA	NA
Dividends	0.24	0.08	0.08	0.07	0.04	0.04	0.04	0.04	0.04	0.04
Payout Ratio	12%	4%	4%	4%	4%	4%	3%	8%	10%	5%
Prices:High	44.75	46.80	44.90	45.08	40.10	28.84	25.75	18.03	23.06	22.00
Prices:Low	36.50	37.67	30.90	23.75	24.88	18.50	15.66	9.84	12.50	15.19
P/E Ratio:High	22	21	24	28	36	26	19	35	58	32
P/E Ratio:Low	18	17	17	15	23	16	11	19	32	22
Income Statement Analysis (Million $)										
Revenue	10,490	10,013	8,400	7,636	6,451	5,705	5,540	5,118	5,235	4,934
Operating Income	3,713	3,193	2,519	2,374	2,154	1,925	1,831	1,726	1,726	1,548
Depreciation	777	738	569	538	638	589	618	591	534	424
Interest Expense	228	137	107	117	120	99.2	104	104	117	110
Pretax Income	2,269	2,657	1,978	1,773	1,211	1,308	1,825	712	706	1,032
Effective Tax Rate	23.9%	25.4%	23.5%	24.4%	27.8%	28.9%	34.3%	34.6%	49.5%	38.3%
Net Income	1,597	1,868	1,394	1,238	875	930	1,200	466	357	637
S&P Core Earnings	1,387	1,599	1,285	1,103	887	NA	NA	NA	NA	NA
Balance Sheet & Other Financial Data (Million $)										
Cash	1,181	895	840	819	918	853	3,324	460	411	272
Current Assets	NA	NA	NA	NA	NA	NA	NA	NA	NA	NA
Total Assets	34,249	32,719	25,586	26,591	21,912	17,295	17,005	16,587	15,315	14,340
Current Liabilities	NA	NA	NA	NA	NA	NA	NA	NA	NA	NA
Long Term Debt	3,962	3,703	2,916	2,562	2,685	975	1,072	1,129	1,134	1,709
Common Equity	18,019	18,403	4,047	6,691	3,520	6,025	3,908	3,756	3,657	3,710
Total Capital	21,981	22,106	6,963	9,253	6,205	7,000	4,980	4,885	5,408	5,417
Capital Expenditures	225	177	162	212	187	149	244	326	297	393
Cash Flow	2,375	2,606	1,963	1,776	1,513	1,518	1,818	1,057	891	106
Current Ratio	NA	NA	NA	NA	NA	NA	NA	NA	NA	NA
% Long Term Debt of Capitalization	18.0	16.8	41.9	27.7	43.3	13.9	21.5	23.1	32.4	31.5
% Net Income of Revenue	15.2	18.7	16.6	16.2	13.6	16.3	21.7	9.1	6.8	12.9
% Return on Assets	4.8	6.4	5.3	5.1	4.5	5.4	7.1	2.9	2.4	4.8
% Return on Equity	8.8	14.9	34.0	19.6	24.1	15.3	20.0	12.6	9.7	18.6

Data as orig reptd.; bef. results of disc opers/spec. items. Per share data adj. for stk. divs.; EPS diluted. E-Estimated. NA-Not Available. NM-Not Meaningful. NR-Not Ranked. UR-Under Review.

Office: 6200 South Quebec Street, Greenwood Village, CO 80111-4729.
Telephone: 303-967-8000.
Email: fdc.ir@firstdatacorp.com
Website: http://www.firstdata.com

Chrmn & CEO: H.C. Duques
EVP & CFO: K.S. Patmore
EVP & CTO: D. Dibble
EVP, Secy & General Counsel: M.T. Whealy

Board of Directors: D. P. Burnham, D. A. Coulter, A. Davis, H. C. Duques, P. B. Ellwood, C. T. Fote, J. M. Greenberg, C. F. Jones, R. P. Kiphart, J. D. Robinson, III, C. T. Russell, J. E. Spero, A. F. Weinbach

Founded: 1989
Domicile: Delaware
Employees: 33,000

STANDARD &POOR'S

First Horizon National Corp

S&P Recommendation HOLD ★★★★★

Price $39.30 (as of Oct 27, 2006)

12-Mo. Target Price $36.00

Investment Style Mid-Cap Value

GICS Sector Financials
Sub-Industry Regional Banks

Comment FHN (formerly First Tennessee National) owns First Tennessee Bank and First Horizon Home Loan Corporation.

Key Stock Statistics (Source S&P, Vickers, company reports)

52-Wk Range	**$43.07–37.10**	S&P Oper. EPS 2006**E**	**2.10**	P/E on S&P Oper. EPS 2006**E**	**18.7**	Dividend Rate/Share	**$1.80**
Trailing 12-Month EPS	**$3.96**	S&P Oper. EPS 2007**E**	**2.95**	Common Shares Outstg. (M)	**123.9**	Yield (%)	**4.58**
Trailing 12-Month P/E	**9.9**	S&P Core EPS 2006**E**	**2.06**	Market Capitalization(B)	**$4.871**	Beta	**0.40**
$10K Invested 5 Yrs Ago	**$12,649**	S&P Core EPS 2007**E**	**2.90**	Institutional Ownership (%)	**46**	S&P Credit Rating	**A-**

Price Performance

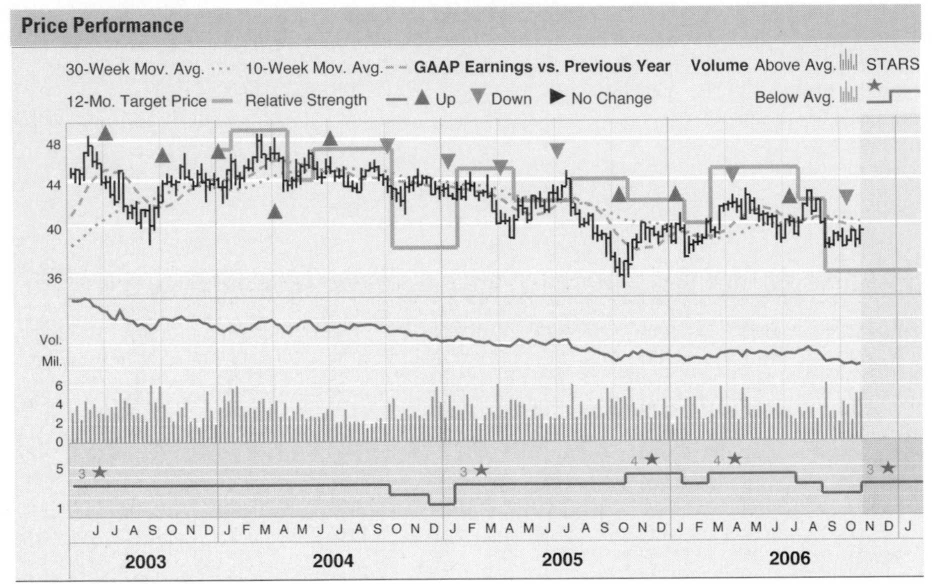

Options: P, Ph

Highlights

- The STARS recommendation for FHN has recently been changed to 3 (hold) from 2 (sell). The Highlights section of this Stock Report will be updated accordingly.

Investment Rationale/Risk

- The Investment Rationale/Risk section of this Stock Report will be updated shortly. For the latest News story on FHN from MarketScope, see below.

- 10/27/06 10:35 am EDT... S&P UPGRADES SHARES OF FIRST HORIZON TO HOLD FROM SELL, BASED ON VALUATION (FHN 39.45***): The shares are down about 8% over the last two months, compared with about a 2.5% gain for the S&P 500 Regional Banks Index. Although FHN's mortgage banking division will likely pressure results, we see this offset by continued growth in earning assets and fee income. The possibility of FHN being acquired should lend support to its shares. We continue to look for '06 and '07 EPS of $2.16 and $2.90, but are raising our 12-month target price by $3 to $39. At 14X our 12-month forward EPS estimate of $2.80, this is in line with FHN's 5-year historical P/E average. /S. Plesser

Qualitative Risk Assessment

LOW | MEDIUM | HIGH

Our risk assessment for FHN reflects our view of its long-term trend of stability and moderate growth in earnings and its long-term trend of increasing dividends. While the company operates in a highly competitive and fragmented industry, the industry tends to produce relatively stable financial results, in our view.

Quantitative Evaluations

S&P Quality Ranking **A+**

D | C | B- | B | B+ | A- | A | **A+**

Relative Strength Rank **MODERATE**

34

LOWEST = 1 HIGHEST = 99

Revenue/Earnings Data

Revenue (Million $)

	1Q	2Q	3Q	4Q	Year
2006	739.1	910.6	994.0	--	--
2005	728.3	781.8	867.0	862.9	3,240
2004	624.1	630.1	627.8	647.9	2,530
2003	685.6	698.3	669.7	639.8	2,693
2002	582.9	585.3	652.5	759.4	2,580
2001	643.3	693.1	664.5	633.2	2,515

Earnings Per Share ($)

2006	0.03	0.82	0.53	**E**0.67	**E**2.10
2005	0.85	0.80	0.90	0.87	3.42
2004	0.92	0.92	0.89	0.81	3.54
2003	0.91	0.90	0.91	0.90	3.62
2002	0.67	0.69	0.73	0.80	2.89
2001	0.47	0.68	0.68	0.68	2.51

Fiscal year ended Dec. 31. Next earnings report expected: Mid January. EPS Estimates based on S&P Operating Earnings; historical GAAP earnings are as reported.

Dividend Data (Dates: mm/dd Payment Date: mm/dd/yy)

Amount ($)	Date Decl.	Ex-Div. Date	Stk. of Record	Payment Date
0.450	01/18	03/15	03/17	04/01/06
0.450	04/21	06/14	06/16	07/01/06
0.450	07/20	09/13	09/15	10/01/06
0.450	10/18	12/13	12/15	01/01/07

Dividends have been paid since 1895. Source: Company reports.

First Horizon National Corp

Business Summary September 01, 2006

CORPORATE OVERVIEW. First Horizon National (formerly First Tennessee National) is a Memphis, TN-based regional bank holding company with $36.6 billion in assets at December 31, 2005. Through its three major brands--First Horizon, First Tennessee National, and FTN Financial--the bank provides retail commercial banking services, mortgage banking, and capital markets operations. During 2005, 57% of revenues came from fee income and 43% from net interest income. This contrasts with the average regional bank, which derives about 32% of its revenues from fee income sources.

Retail/commercial banking contributed 58% of revenues in 2005, mortgage banking 28%, and capital markets 14%.

Income from mortgage banking operations was the largest contributor to fee income. As of December 2005, First Horizon Home Loan had 413 offices in 44 states, and ranked among the 20 U.S. leaders in mortgage loan originations and mortgage loan servicing, as reported by Inside Mortgage Finance.

CORPORATE STRATEGY. Unlike many of its competitors, the company has generally not grown through an aggressive acquisition strategy, but has focused on expanding its nationally ranked specialty lines of business. FHN's strategy is to expand into 15 major markets that it has identified as targets, establish a large number of customers in those markets through its mortgage operations, and then cross-sell them other financial products. As of 2005, the bank was expanding in Georgia, northern Virginia, and Texas.

In January 2005, FTN Financial, FHN's capital markets division, acquired the fixed income business of Spear, Leeds & Kellogg, a division of Goldman Sachs, Inc. Following the acquisition, FTN Financial had about 1,000 employees in 15 states, with over 5,000 customers. In March 2006, FHN sold its merchant processing business--First Horizon Merchant Services--to NOVA Information Systems, a subsidiary of U.S. Bancorp. Partial proceeds from the sale were used to fund a 4 million common share accelerated repurchase program, which was estimated to cost $158 million, excluding transaction costs.

Company Financials

Per Share Data ($) Year Ended Dec. 31	**2005**	**2004**	**2003**	**2002**	**2001**	**2000**	**1999**	**1998**	**1997**	**1996**
Tangible Book Value	15.19	14.73	13.43	11.92	10.27	9.81	8.53	2.34	3.38	4.26
Earnings	3.42	3.54	3.62	2.89	2.51	1.77	1.91	1.72	1.50	1.34
S&P Core Earnings	3.26	3.41	3.32	2.59	1.88	NA	NA	NA	NA	NA
Dividends	1.74	1.63	1.30	1.05	0.91	0.88	0.76	0.66	0.62	0.55
Payout Ratio	51%	46%	36%	36%	36%	50%	40%	38%	41%	41%
Prices:High	44.80	48.65	48.50	41.00	37.49	29.31	45.38	38.38	34.81	19.44
Prices:Low	34.78	40.79	35.58	29.76	27.13	15.94	27.38	23.38	18.38	14.25
P/E Ratio:High	13	14	13	14	15	17	24	22	23	15
P/E Ratio:Low	10	12	10	10	11	9	14	14	12	11
Income Statement Analysis (Million $)										
Net Interest Income	984	856	806	753	686	598	590	541	483	451
Tax Equivalent Adjustment	1.10	1.10	1.26	1.50	2.10	2.60	3.00	NA	NA	5.40
Non Interest Income	1,400	1,342	1,638	1,550	1,321	1,068	1,121	982	669	574
Loan Loss Provision	67.7	48.3	86.7	92.2	93.5	67.4	57.9	51.4	51.1	35.7
% Expense/Operating Revenue	70.1%	68.4%	67.1%	71.3%	67.7%	75.5%	74.4%	73.7%	68.1%	68.7%
Pretax Income	645	667	719	558	494	337	379	353	315	282
Effective Tax Rate	31.6%	31.9%	34.2%	32.5%	33.2%	31.0%	34.8%	36.0%	37.3%	36.2%
Net Income	441	454	473	376	330	233	248	226	197	180
% Net Interest Margin	3.08	3.62	3.78	4.33	4.27	3.73	3.80	3.80	4.23	4.13
S&P Core Earnings	423	438	434	337	248	NA	NA	NA	NA	NA
Balance Sheet & Other Financial Data (Million $)										
Money Market Assets	3,629	1,676	1,182	1,157	877	380	430	484	482	291
Investment Securities	2,912	2,681	2,470	2,700	2,526	2,839	3,101	2,426	2,186	2,240
Commercial Loans	9,899	7,730	6,904	5,723	5,598	5,327	4,431	4,117	3,769	3,522
Other Loans	10,702	8,698	7,087	5,622	4,685	4,912	4,933	4,440	4,416	4,088
Total Assets	36,579	29,772	24,507	23,823	20,617	18,555	18,373	18,734	14,388	13,059
Demand Deposits	10,027	4,995	4,540	5,149	4,010	2,847	2,798	3,058	2,536	2,123
Time Deposits	13,411	14,788	11,140	10,564	9,596	9,342	8,560	8,665	7,136	6,910
Long Term Debt	3,733	2,617	1,117	1,074	3,066	3,119	459	514	169	175
Common Equity	2,312	2,041	1,850	1,691	1,478	1,384	1,241	1,100	954	955
% Return on Assets	1.3	1.7	2.0	1.7	1.7	1.3	1.3	1.4	1.4	1.4
% Return on Equity	20.3	23.1	26.7	23.8	23.0	17.7	21.1	23.0	20.7	20.1
% Loan Loss Reserve	0.8	0.7	0.9	0.9	1.1	1.2	1.2	1.6	1.5	1.5
% Loans/Deposits	106.8	109.2	108.2	102.7	100.6	98.2	100.5	78.3	85.9	84.3
% Equity to Assets	6.6	7.2	7.3	7.1	7.3	7.1	6.3	6.2	7.0	7.1

Data as orig reptd.; bef. results of disc opers/spec. items. Per share data adj. for stk. divs.; EPS diluted. E-Estimated. NA-Not Available. NM-Not Meaningful. NR-Not Ranked. UR-Under Review.

Office: 165 Madison Avenue, Memphis, TN 38103.
Telephone: 901-523-4444.
Website: http://www.firsttennessee.com
Chrmn, Pres & CEO: J.K. Glass

COO: G.L. Baker
EVP & CFO: M.L. Mosby, III
EVP, Chief Acctg Officer & Cntlr: J.F. Keen
EVP & General Counsel: H.A. Johnson, III

Investor Contact: M. Yates (901-523-4068)
Board of Directors: R. C. Blattberg, S. F. Cooper, J. K. Glass, J. A. Haslam, III, R. B. Martin, V. R. Palmer, M. D. Rose, M. F. Sammons, W. B. Sansom, J. P. Ward, L. Yancy, III

Founded: 1968
Domicile: Tennessee
Employees: 13,175

STANDARD &POOR'S

Fiserv Inc

S&P Recommendation BUY ★★★★★

Price $48.44 (as of Oct 27, 2006)

12-Mo. Target Price $57.00

Investment Style Mid-Cap Growth

GICS Sector Information Technology
Sub-Industry Data Processing & Outsourced Services

Comment This company is a full-service provider of computerized account processing and integrated information management systems for financial institutions.

Key Stock Statistics (Source S&P, Vickers, company reports)

52-Wk Range	**$49.96–40.29**	S&P Oper. EPS 2006**E**	**2.56**	P/E on S&P Oper. EPS 2006**E**	**18.9**	Dividend Rate/Share	**Nil**
Trailing 12-Month EPS	**$2.73**	S&P Oper. EPS 2007**E**	**2.85**	Common Shares Outstg. (M)	**174.2**	Yield (%)	**Nil**
Trailing 12-Month P/E	**17.7**	S&P Core EPS 2006**E**	**2.56**	Market Capitalization(B)	**$8.440**	Beta	**1.09**
$10K Invested 5 Yrs Ago	**$12,737**	S&P Core EPS 2007**E**	**2.85**	Institutional Ownership (%)	**81**	S&P Credit Rating	**NA**

Price Performance

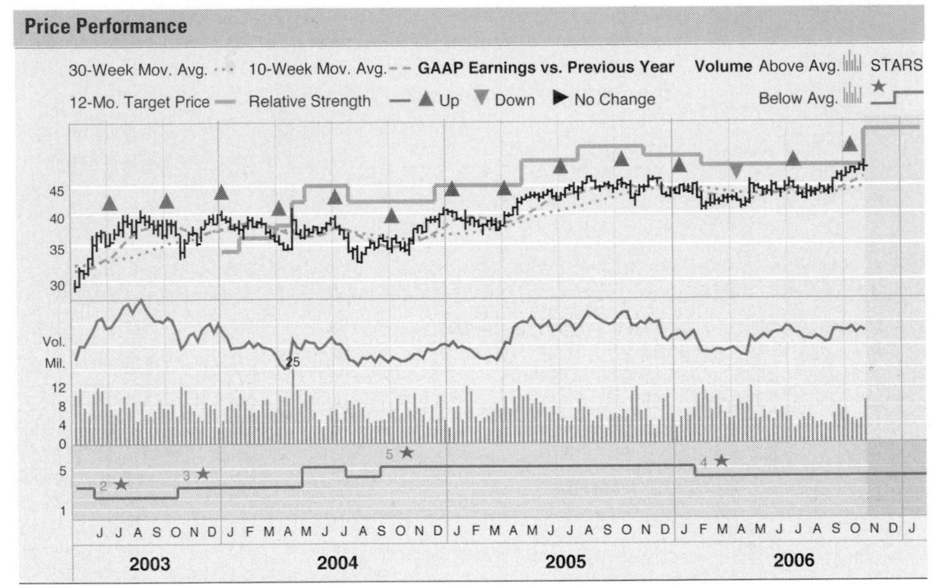

Options: ASE, CBOE, Ph

Highlights

➤ The 12-month target price for FISV has recently been changed to $57.00 from $49.00. The Highlights section of this Stock Report will be updated accordingly.

Investment Rationale/Risk

➤ The Investment Rationale/Risk section of this Stock Report will be updated shortly. For the latest News story on FISV from MarketScope, see below.

➤ 10/25/06 10:03 am EDT... S&P REITERATES BUY OPINION ON SHARES OF FISERV (FISV 47.3****): FISV posts Q3 EPS of $0.63 vs. $0.56, in line with our forecast. Revenues rose 14% and adjusted internal growth was 5%, reflecting solid results in the financial segment. We are trimming our '06 EPS estimate to $2.56 from $2.59, due to our slightly more conservative outlook for Q4. However, based on revised peer and DCF analyses, we are raising our target price to $57 from $49. We think FISV should benefit from focus on revenue synergies and cost-cutting, and a more measured approach to acquisitions. We believe today's share price decline is an enhanced purchasing opportunity. /S.Kessler

Qualitative Risk Assessment

LOW | **MEDIUM** | HIGH

Our risk assessment reflects our view of FISV's notable size, market position, and flexible balance sheet, offset by its relatively modest internal growth rate and active acquisition strategy.

Quantitative Evaluations

S&P Quality Ranking **B+**

D | C | B- | B | **B+** | A- | A | A+

Relative Strength Rank **MODERATE**

61

LOWEST = 1 HIGHEST = 99

Revenue/Earnings Data

Revenue (Million $)

	1Q	2Q	3Q	4Q	Year
2006	1,097	1,093	1,157	--	--
2005	973.1	996.4	1,012	1,078	4,059
2004	937.5	946.0	958.1	966.4	3,730
2003	707.5	738.6	796.1	837.3	3,034
2002	631.9	632.4	635.7	668.9	2,569
2001	453.9	472.7	467.2	496.7	1,890

Earnings Per Share ($)

	1Q	2Q	3Q	4Q	Year
2006	0.64	0.62	1.89	**E**0.67	**E**2.56
2005	0.71	0.59	0.58	0.80	2.68
2004	0.49	0.49	0.53	0.50	2.00
2003	0.38	0.40	0.41	0.42	1.61
2002	0.33	0.34	0.34	0.35	1.37
2001	0.27	0.27	0.27	0.27	1.09

Fiscal year ended Dec. 31. Next earnings report expected: Late January. EPS Estimates based on S&P Operating Earnings; historical GAAP earnings are as reported.

Dividend Data

No cash dividends have been paid.

Please read the Required Disclosures and Analyst Certification on the last page of this report.

Fiserv Inc

Business Summary July 31, 2006

CORPORATE OVERVIEW. Fiserv's Financial Institution Outsourcing, Systems and Services segment, which accounted for (treating the securities clearing business as discontinued) 69% of 2005 operating revenues (70% in 2004), provides solutions to thousands of financial institutions, including banks, credit unions, leasing companies, mortgage lenders, savings institutions, and insurance companies. "Core" products integrate account services and management information functions, and include systems to process accounts, general ledgers, central information files, and report generation. Complementary offerings allow financial institutions to provide additional services to their clients, such as home banking and ATM access; asset-liability modeling and cash management are also offered. IDC projects that U.S. IT outsourcing spending by banking and insurance firms will rise from $6.3 billion in 2004, to $7.8 billion in 2009.

The Health Plan Management Services segment (27%, 24%) provides solutions for the administration of health plans to customers nationwide, including claim adjudication and payment, customer service, reporting, and other related offerings. These offerings are provided to employers that self-fund their health plans, and to insurance companies and HMOs. Additional services include utilization and case management, health and prevention programs, prescription benefit management and pharmacy mail-order services, data management, and claim repricing. IDC estimates that U.S. health care companies will increase their spending on IT outsourcing from $1.3 billion in 2004, to $1.7 billion in 2009.

Company Financials

Per Share Data ($) Year Ended Dec. 31	**2005**	**2004**	**2003**	**2002**	**2001**	**2000**	**1999**	**1998**	**1997**	**1996**
Tangible Book Value	NM	0.96	NM	2.60	2.60	2.18	1.57	1.57	1.50	1.08
Cash Flow	3.62	2.94	2.48	2.09	1.86	1.33	1.18	1.00	0.64	0.67
Earnings	2.68	2.00	1.61	1.37	1.09	0.93	0.73	0.60	0.50	0.40
S&P Core Earnings	2.28	1.91	1.47	1.26	1.00	NA	NA	NA	NA	NA
Dividends	Nil	Nil	Nil	Nil	Nil	Nil	Nil	Nil	Nil	Nil
Payout Ratio	Nil	Nil	Nil	Nil	Nil	Nil	Nil	Nil	Nil	Nil
Prices:High	46.89	41.01	40.77	47.24	44.61	42.75	27.17	23.83	15.26	11.96
Prices:Low	36.33	32.20	27.23	22.50	29.08	16.21	16.08	13.33	9.63	7.41
P/E Ratio:High	17	21	25	34	41	46	37	40	30	30
P/E Ratio:Low	14	16	17	16	27	17	22	22	19	19
Income Statement Analysis (Million $)										
Revenue	4,059	3,730	3,034	2,569	1,890	1,654	1,408	1,234	974	798
Operating Income	925	845	704	734	501	429	347	282	229	191
Depreciation	179	185	172	141	148	70.1	86.3	76.5	63.2	42.2
Interest Expense	27.8	24.9	22.9	17.8	12.1	22.1	19.4	16.0	11.9	19.1
Pretax Income	818	641	516	436	347	300	234	194	154	105
Effective Tax Rate	37.5%	38.4%	39.0%	39.0%	40.0%	41.0%	41.0%	41.0%	41.0%	41.0%
Net Income	511	395	315	266	208	177	138	114	90.8	61.7
S&P Core Earnings	435	377	288	246	191	NA	NA	NA	NA	NA
Balance Sheet & Other Financial Data (Million $)										
Cash	184	516	203	227	136	98.9	80.6	71.6	89.4	80.8
Current Assets	NA	NA	NA	NA	NA	NA	NA	NA	NA	NA
Total Assets	6,040	8,383	7,214	6,439	5,322	5,586	5,308	3,958	3,636	1,909
Current Liabilities	NA	NA	NA	NA	NA	NA	NA	NA	NA	NA
Long Term Debt	595	505	699	483	343	335	326	390	252	273
Common Equity	2,466	2,564	2,200	1,828	1,605	1,252	1,091	886	769	507
Total Capital	3,227	3,204	2,990	2,357	1,948	1,622	1,477	1,276	1,021	780
Capital Expenditures	165	161	143	142	68.0	73.0	69.7	77.5	39.8	36.2
Cash Flow	691	580	487	407	356	247	224	191	154	104
Current Ratio	NA	NA	NA	NA	NA	NA	NA	NA	NA	NA
% Long Term Debt of Capitalization	18.4	15.8	23.4	20.5	17.6	20.7	22.1	30.6	24.7	35.0
% Net Income of Revenue	12.6	10.6	10.4	10.4	11.0	10.7	9.8	9.3	9.3	7.7
% Return on Assets	7.1	5.1	4.6	4.5	3.8	3.2	3.0	3.0	3.3	3.3
% Return on Equity	20.3	16.6	15.6	15.5	14.6	15.1	13.9	13.8	14.2	13.1

Data as orig reptd.; bef. results of disc opers/spec. items. Per share data adj. for stk. divs.; EPS diluted. E-Estimated. NA-Not Available. NM-Not Meaningful. NR-Not Ranked. UR-Under Review.

Office: 255 Fiserv Drive, Brookfield, WI 53045.
Telephone: 262-879-5000.
Email: general_info@fiserv.com
Website: http://www.fiserv.com

Chrmn: D.F. Dillon
Pres & CEO: J.W. Yabuki
COO & Sr EVP: N.J. Balthasar
EVP & CFO: T. Hirsch

EVP, Chief Admin, Secy & General Counsel: C.W. Sprague
Board of Directors: D. F. Dillon, K. R. Jensen, D. P. Kearney, G. J. Levy, L. M. Muma, G. M. Renwick, K. M. Robak, L. W. Seidman, T. C. Wertheimer, J. W. Yabuki

Founded: 1984
Domicile: Wisconsin
Employees: 22,000

STANDARD &POOR'S

Fisher Scientific International Inc.

S&P Recommendation STRONG BUY ★★★★★

Price $86.29 (as of Oct 27, 2006)

12-Mo. Target Price $104.00

Investment Style Large-Cap Growth

GICS Sector Health Care
Sub-Industry Life Sciences Tools & Services

Comment This company serves as a one-stop source of products, services and global solutions for the scientific research, clinical laboratory and industrial safety markets.

Key Stock Statistics (Source S&P, Vickers, company reports)

52-Wk Range	**$88.78–54.70**	S&P Oper. EPS 2006**E**	**4.06**	P/E on S&P Oper. EPS 2006**E**	**21.3**	Dividend Rate/Share	**Nil**
Trailing 12-Month EPS	**$3.77**	S&P Oper. EPS 2007**E**	**4.65**	Common Shares Outstg. (M)	**125.0**	Yield (%)	**Nil**
Trailing 12-Month P/E	**22.9**	S&P Core EPS 2006**E**	**4.06**	Market Capitalization(B)	**$10.789**	Beta	**0.21**
$10K Invested 5 Yrs Ago	**$29,251**	S&P Core EPS 2007**E**	**4.65**	Institutional Ownership (%)	**99**	S&P Credit Rating	**BBB-**

Price Performance

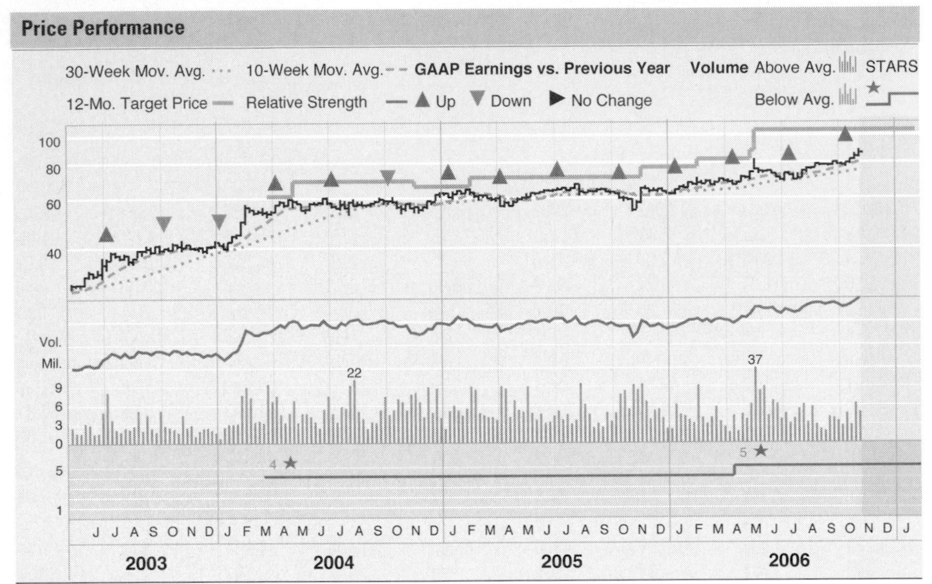

Options: ASE, CBOE, P, Ph

Analysis prepared by **Jeffrey Loo, CFA** on August 10, 2006, when the stock traded at **$ 76.39**.

Highlights

- In May 2006, Thermo Electron (TMO: strong buy, $38) agreed to acquire FSH in a stock-for-stock reverse merger for about $10.6 billion based on TMO's closing price on May 5, 2006, subject to necessary approvals. FSH shareholders will receive 2 TMO shares for each FSH share and will own 61% of the combined company that will be named Thermo Fisher Scientific, with projected sales exceeding $9 billion. The proposed deal is expected to close in the fourth quarter of 2006.
- On a stand-alone basis, we see 2006 sales of $5.9 billion, reflecting 9% growth in scientific products and 6% growth in health care products and excluding the lab workstation unit, which we expect FSH to divest in 2006. We see gross margins improving 130 basis points on a product mix shift to higher margin proprietary products. Despite the inclusion of projected stock option expense, we see a 70 basis point improvement in the operating margin, to 13.9%, on cost saving synergies from the Apogent acquisition and from operating leverage.
- After $0.28 of projected stock option expense, our 2006 EPS estimate is $3.96.

Investment Rationale/Risk

- We think the proposed deal for TMO to acquire FSH makes sense. We expect FSH to grow sales faster than its peers, and we think the planned integration of TMO's products will result in the most comprehensive life science product offering, potentially accelerating sales growth. The global sales and distribution network of each company should result in revenue and cost synergies. We think these potential synergies will add to FSH's operating margin expansion. Further, we see FSH's cash flow improving as a result of the proposed merger, allowing the pay down of a portion of FSH's debt.
- Risks to our recommendation and target price include a slowdown in research spending, adverse regulatory actions preventing the proposed transaction, and potential sales channel disruption due to the planned deal.
- We expect FSH's share price to track the movement of TMO's share price. Based on our 12-month target price of $52 for TMO and terms of 2 TMO shares for each FSH share, our 12-month target price is $104.

Qualitative Risk Assessment

LOW | **MEDIUM** | HIGH

Our risk assessment reflects what we view as FSH's broad product offering and diverse client base, which helps reduce risk. However, the company has a proactive acquisition strategy that we believe increases its risk profile.

Quantitative Evaluations

S&P Quality Ranking B-

D | C | **B-** | B | B+ | A- | A | A+

Relative Strength Rank STRONG

82

LOWEST = 1 HIGHEST = 99

Revenue/Earnings Data

Revenue (Million $)

	1Q	2Q	3Q	4Q	Year
2006	1,412	1,466	1,508	--	--
2005	1,351	1,391	1,413	1,424	5,579
2004	1,011	1,058	1,263	1,331	4,663
2003	833.4	864.5	890.0	976.5	3,564
2002	775.5	809.9	830.9	822.1	3,238
2001	687.0	708.8	729.5	754.7	2,880

Earnings Per Share ($)

2006	0.81	0.92	1.12	**E**1.10	**E**4.06
2005	0.60	0.67	0.73	0.91	2.92
2004	0.51	0.64	0.34	0.41	1.80
2003	-0.02	0.57	0.47	0.28	1.29
2002	0.34	0.35	0.52	0.46	1.67
2001	-0.59	0.23	0.30	0.19	0.31

Fiscal year ended Dec. 31. Next earnings report expected: Early February. EPS Estimates based on S&P Operating Earnings; historical GAAP earnings are as reported.

Dividend Data

No cash dividends have been paid since 1996.

Please read the Required Disclosures and Analyst Certification on the last page of this report.

Fisher Scientific International Inc.

Business Summary August 10, 2006

CORPORATE OVERVIEW. Fisher Scientific is a leading global manufacturer and provider of scientific research, health care and safety-related products and services. It provides a broad range of product offerings, including more than 600,000 products and services to more than 350,000 customers located in over 150 countries. Customers include pharmaceutical and biotechnology companies; colleges and universities; medical research institutions; hospitals and reference labs; and research and development laboratories. Approximately 80% of FSH's revenues are from the sale of consumable products. The company currently operates through three segments: scientific products and services, which accounted for 73% of sales in 2005 (73% in 2004); health care products and services, 23% (23%); and laboratory workstations, 4% (4%). However, FSH announced in early 2006 that it intends to divest laboratory workstations. The scientific products segment provides products and services to entities conducting scientific research, including quality control and basic research and development, and drug discovery and development. This segment manufactures and distributes a broad range of biochemicals and bioreagents, custom peptide, organic and inorganic chemicals, sera, cell culture media, safety products, and other consumable products. This segment also provides services to pharmaceutical and biotechnology companies engaged in clinical trials, including specialized packaging, over-encapsulation, and labeling and distribution for Phase III and Phase IV clinical trials. The health care segment manufactures and distributes diagnostic kits and reagents, consumable supplies, instruments and medical devices to hospitals, clinical labs, reference labs and physician's offices in the U.S. The laboratory workstations segment manufactures and sells workstations and fume hoods for laboratories. Products include steel, wood and plastic laminate casework systems, adaptable furniture systems, airflow products and other laboratory fixtures and accessories.

Company Financials

Per Share Data ($) Year Ended Dec. 31	**2005**	**2004**	**2003**	**2002**	**2001**	**2000**	**1999**	**1998**	**1997**	**1996**
Tangible Book Value	NM	NM	NM	NM	NM	NM	NM	NM	0.71	0.69
Cash Flow	4.48	3.36	2.66	2.96	1.86	1.94	2.00	0.09	0.16	0.87
Earnings	2.92	1.80	1.29	1.67	0.31	0.51	0.55	-1.24	-0.30	0.39
S&P Core Earnings	2.63	1.71	0.93	1.23	-0.04	NA	NA	NA	NA	NA
Dividends	Nil	Nil	Nil	Nil	Nil	Nil	Nil	Nil	0.01	0.02
Payout Ratio	Nil	Nil	Nil	Nil	Nil	Nil	Nil	Nil	NM	4%
Prices:High	67.50	63.10	42.80	33.43	40.00	51.00	44.00	22.50	10.25	9.55
Prices:Low	53.50	39.27	24.55	22.85	21.00	19.88	16.13	9.52	7.03	6.65
P/E Ratio:High	23	35	33	20	NM	NM	80	NM	NM	24
P/E Ratio:Low	18	22	19	14	NM	NM	29	NM	NM	17
Income Statement Analysis (Million $)										
Revenue	5,579	4,663	3,564	3,238	2,880	2,622	2,470	2,252	2,175	2,144
Operating Income	880	503	341	318	213	218	219	186	120	139
Depreciation	200	143	82.8	74.9	82.0	63.6	62.4	53.0	47.0	44.6
Interest Expense	109	105	84.8	91.3	99.5	99.1	104	90.3	23.0	27.1
Pretax Income	488	192	96.1	142	30.3	37.8	57.8	-60.3	-5.10	67.6
Effective Tax Rate	23.8%	13.5%	18.4%	31.7%	45.9%	39.9%	59.5%	NM	NM	45.6%
Net Income	372	166	78.4	96.7	16.4	22.7	23.4	-49.5	-30.5	36.8
S&P Core Earnings	335	158	56.4	70.4	-2.39	NA	NA	NA	NA	NA
Balance Sheet & Other Financial Data (Million $)										
Cash	407	163	83.8	38.8	75.1	66.0	50.3	65.6	18.2	24.7
Current Assets	1,991	1,691	1,011	769	758	651	635	561	592	653
Total Assets	8,430	8,090	2,859	1,871	1,839	1,386	1,403	1,358	1,177	1,263
Current Liabilities	1,015	968	648	583	638	508	520	453	355	877
Long Term Debt	2,136	2,309	1,386	922	956	991	1,011	1,022	268	282
Common Equity	4,304	3,870	575	134	23.3	-312	-331	-325	347	386
Total Capital	6,440	6,179	1,962	1,055	979	679	680	697	615	668
Capital Expenditures	128	93.4	80.2	43.9	40.1	23.1	41.1	67.2	59.2	40.7
Cash Flow	572	310	161	172	98.4	86.3	85.8	3.50	16.5	81.4
Current Ratio	2.0	1.7	1.6	1.3	1.2	1.3	1.2	1.2	1.7	0.7
% Long Term Debt of Capitalization	33.2	37.4	70.7	87.3	97.6	145.9	148.6	146.6	43.5	42.2
% Net Income of Revenue	6.7	3.6	2.2	3.0	0.6	0.9	0.9	NM	NM	1.7
% Return on Assets	4.5	3.0	3.3	5.2	1.0	1.6	1.7	NM	NM	2.9
% Return on Equity	9.1	7.5	22.1	123.3	NM	NM	NM	NM	NM	12.0

Data as orig reptd.; bef. results of disc opers/spec. items. Per share data adj. for stk. divs.; EPS diluted. E-Estimated. NA-Not Available. NM-Not Meaningful. NR-Not Ranked. UR-Under Review.

Office: One Liberty Lane, Hampton, NH 03842.
Telephone: 603-926-5911.
Website: http://www.fishersci.com
Chrmn & CEO: P.M. Montrone

Pres & COO: D.T. Della Penta
Vice Chrmn: P.M. Meister
VP & CFO: K.P. Clark
Investor Contact: C. Miller (603-929-2381)

Board of Directors: R. F. Coppola, M. D. Dingman, B. L. Koepfgen, P. M. Meister, P. M. Montrone, S. B. Rich, C. A. Sanders, S. M. Sperling, W. C. Stephens, R. W. Vieser

Founded: 1991
Domicile: Delaware
Employees: 19,500

STANDARD &POOR'S

Fluor Corp.

S&P Recommendation HOLD ★★★★★

Price $78.67 (as of Oct 27, 2006)

12-Mo. Target Price $88.00

Investment Style Mid-Cap Value

GICS Sector Industrials
Sub-Industry Construction & Engineering

Comment FLR is one of the world's largest engineering, procurement and construction companies.

Key Stock Statistics (Source S&P, Vickers, company reports)

52-Wk Range	$103.85–62.54	S&P Oper. EPS 2006E	2.45	P/E on S&P Oper. EPS 2006E	32.1	Dividend Rate/Share	$0.80
Trailing 12-Month EPS	$4.00	S&P Oper. EPS 2007E	3.75	Common Shares Outstg. (M)	87.6	Yield (%)	1.02
Trailing 12-Month P/E	19.7	S&P Core EPS 2006E	2.47	Market Capitalization(B)	$6.890	Beta	0.92
$10K Invested 5 Yrs Ago	$18,574	S&P Core EPS 2007E	3.78	Institutional Ownership (%)	91	S&P Credit Rating	A

Price Performance

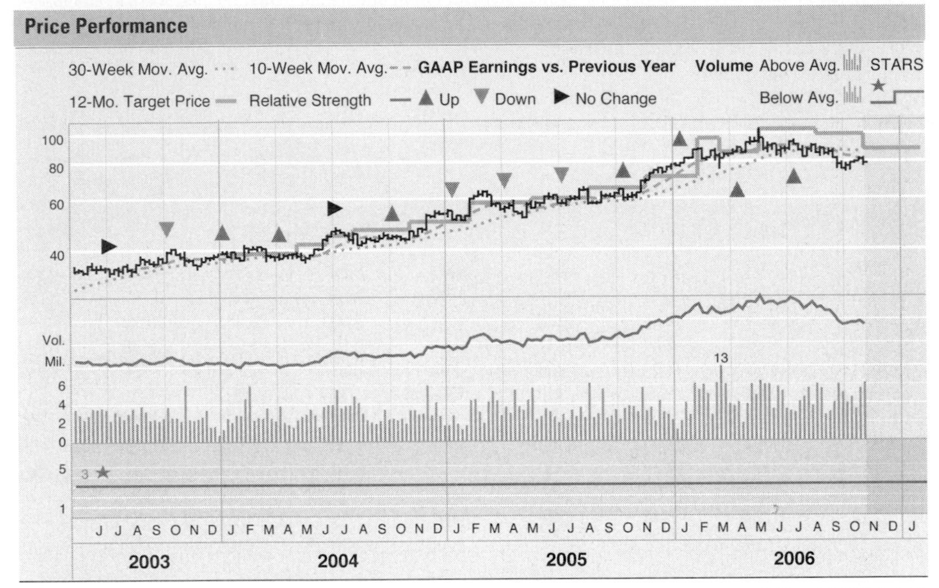

Options: ASE, CBOE, P, Ph

Analysis prepared by **Stewart Scharf** on October 27, 2006, when the stock traded at **$ 78.49**.

Highlights

- We forecast low- to mid-teens revenue growth for 2006, although second half contributions from government work should decline as programs for FEMA disaster relief, the rebuilding of Iraq and the DOE near completion. We see strength in 2007 driven by new awards in the oil and gas, power, petrochemical and infrastructure markets.
- In our view, gross margins should widen during 2006 to near 4.5%, from 2005's 3.3%, driven by higher-margin new awards and a return to normal earnings in the industrial and infrastructure group. However, $168 million in pretax cost overruns in the third quarter, mainly due to various problems at fixed-price U.S. embassy projects, will impact earnings. We see oil & gas operating margins in the 5% range in the second half and into 2007, based on more front-end work, which carries higher margins. As FLR books larger projects, we expect the absolute profit value to rise significantly while margins narrow.
- We project EPS of $2.45 (after charges for cost overruns), advancing to $3.75 for 2007.

Investment Rationale/Risk

- We maintain our hold opinion on the stock, based on our valuation models and growth prospects.
- Risks to our recommendation and target price include margin pressures due to a shift in oil and gas projects, geopolitical unrest, project delays or cancellations, unproductive or unavailable labor, further problems with an embassy project in Haiti, and timing issues for new awards. We also are concerned about corporate governance practices, as three or more related party transactions involved directors or officers other than the CEO.
- The stock recently traded at about 33X our 2006 EPS estimate, a premium to our projected P/E for the S&P 500 and FLR's peers. However, our DCF model suggests the stock is 20% below its intrinsic value of $100, assuming a 3.5% terminal growth rate and an 8.3% weighted average cost of capital. We project return on equity (ROE) at or above 2005's 16%. We blend our DCF metric with relative P/E multiples, and apply a near-peer P/E of 23.5X to our 2007 EPS estimate to arrive at our 12-month target price of $88.

Qualitative Risk Assessment

LOW | **MEDIUM** | HIGH

Our risk assessment reflects the cyclical nature of the company's markets, and geopolitical issues, as more projects are in unstable regions of the world, volatile energy prices, a tight engineering labor market, and our view of lumpiness in new bookings and corporate governance issues, which are offset by FLR's balance sheet, which we believe remains strong as debt levels are well controlled.

Quantitative Evaluations

S&P Quality Ranking B+

D | C | B- | B | **B+** | A- | A | A+

Relative Strength Rank WEAK

19

LOWEST = 1 HIGHEST = 99

Revenue/Earnings Data

Revenue (Million $)

	1Q	2Q	3Q	4Q	Year
2006	3,625	3,456	--	--	--
2005	2,860	2,920	3,419	3,963	13,161
2004	2,063	2,214	2,363	2,740	9,380
2003	2,077	2,243	2,121	2,365	8,806
2002	2,507	2,536	2,451	2,465	9,959
2001	1,911	2,227	2,199	2,635	8,972

Earnings Per Share ($)

2006	1.00	0.74	E0.05	E0.65	E2.45
2005	0.56	-0.19	1.51	0.74	2.62
2004	0.57	0.54	0.57	0.57	2.25
2003	0.51	0.54	0.55	0.63	2.23
2002	0.45	0.54	0.58	0.56	2.13
2001	0.21	0.44	0.56	0.39	1.61

Fiscal year ended Dec. 31. Next earnings report expected: Early November. EPS Estimates based on S&P Operating Earnings; historical GAAP earnings are as reported.

Dividend Data (Dates: mm/dd Payment Date: mm/dd/yy)

Amount ($)	Date Decl.	Ex-Div. Date	Stk. of Record	Payment Date
0.160	10/26	12/05	12/07	01/02/06
0.200	02/10	03/07	03/09	04/03/06
0.200	05/23	09/05	09/07	10/02/06

Dividends have been paid since 1974. Source: Company reports.

Business Summary October 27, 2006

CORPORATE OVERVIEW. Fluor Corp. is one of the world's largest engineering, procurement, construction and maintenance companies. It has five principal operating segments.

The Oil & Gas segment provides design and engineering, procurement and construction (EPC) services to oil, gas, refining, chemical, polymer and petrochemical customers. A new front-end oil & gas award typically takes 6 to 12 months to transition to a full EPS award. Industrial & Infrastructure provides EPC services to businesses, including industrial, commercial, telecommunications, mining and technology. Global Services provides operations and maintenance support, equipment and outsourcing, and asset management solutions through TRS Staffing Solutions. Government Services provides support services to the federal government and other government parties. In early 2005, the company realigned its chemicals business from the industrial and infrastructure segment to oil and gas in anticipation of a large increase in petrochemical projects over the next few years. Prior periods were restated.

Contributions to revenues and operating profits in 2005 were as follows: Oil and Gas, 40% of revenues and 53% of operating profits ($242 million); Industrial & Infrastructure, 24% ($17 million operating loss); Power, 2.9% and 2.9% ($13 million); Global Services, 12% and 25% ($114 million); and Government Services, 21% and 19% ($84 million).

Total backlog of $14.9 billion at year-end 2005, up 1% from a year earlier, was divided by segment as follows: Oil & Gas $6.0 billion, up 12%; Industrial & Infrastructure $3.9 billion, down 23%; Power $1.1 billion versus $552 million; Global Services $2.5 billion, up 8.8%; and Government Services $1.4 billion, down 1.9%. Backlog by geographic region at the end of 2005 was: U.S. 35%; the Americas 17%; Europe, Africa and the Middle East 39%; and Asia Pacific (including Australia) 8.2%.

FLR expects new awards of $4.8 billion in the third quarter of 2006, bringing backlog to over $19 billion. New awards in 2005 amounted to $12.5 billion. New awards by segment were: Oil & Gas, 36% of total awards; Industrial & Infrastructure, 19%; Government, 10%; Global Services, 17%; and Power, 8%. By segment, Oil & Gas more than doubled, to $1.6 billion; Industrial & Infrastructure dropped 33%, to $720 million; Government rose 48%, to $601 million; Global Services plunged 73%, to $165 million; and Power was down 20%, to $300 million.

Company Financials

Per Share Data ($) Year Ended Dec. 31	**2005**	**2004**	**2003**	**2002**	**2001**	**2000**	**1999**	**1998**	**1997**	**1996**
Tangible Book Value	17.84	14.89	12.51	10.76	9.57	19.96	19.27	18.35	18.84	18.86
Cash Flow	3.82	3.36	3.22	3.11	2.52	5.39	5.56	6.63	4.64	5.46
Earnings	2.62	2.25	2.23	2.13	1.61	1.31	1.37	2.97	1.73	3.17
S&P Core Earnings	2.61	2.07	2.33	1.79	1.13	NA	NA	NA	NA	NA
Dividends	0.64	0.64	0.64	0.64	0.64	1.00	0.80	0.80	0.76	0.68
Payout Ratio	24%	28%	29%	30%	40%	76%	58%	27%	44%	21%
Prices:High	79.10	55.19	40.82	44.95	63.20	48.50	46.60	52.50	75.88	71.00
Prices:Low	50.11	36.10	26.65	20.06	31.20	23.94	26.19	34.13	33.50	57.75
P/E Ratio:High	30	25	18	21	39	37	34	18	44	23
P/E Ratio:Low	19	16	12	9	19	18	19	11	19	18

Income Statement Analysis (Million $)	2005	2004	2003	2002	2001	2000	1999	1998	1997	1996
Revenue	13,161	9,380	8,806	9,959	8,972	9,970	12,417	13,505	14,299	11,015
Operating Income	396	370	344	332	258	451	654	676	511	596
Depreciation	104	91.9	79.7	78.0	71.9	312	318	289	248	194
Interest Expense	16.3	15.4	10.1	8.93	25.0	26.3	50.9	45.0	31.0	16.0
Pretax Income	300	281	268	261	185	142	186	362	255	413
Effective Tax Rate	24.1%	33.6%	33.0%	34.8%	31.1%	29.8%	44.0%	35.1%	42.7%	35.1%
Net Income	227	187	180	170	128	99.8	104	235	146	268
S&P Core Earnings	226	171	188	143	90.2	NA	NA	NA	NA	NA

Balance Sheet & Other Financial Data (Million $)	2005	2004	2003	2002	2001	2000	1999	1998	1997	1996
Cash	789	605	497	753	573	69.4	210	341	309	316
Current Assets	3,108	2,723	2,214	1,941	1,851	1,448	1,910	2,277	2,226	1,797
Total Assets	4,574	3,970	3,449	3,142	3,091	3,653	4,886	5,019	4,698	3,952
Current Liabilities	2,339	1,764	1,829	1,756	1,811	1,620	2,204	2,496	1,991	1,646
Long Term Debt	92.0	348	44.7	17.6	17.6	17.6	318	300	301	3.00
Common Equity	1,631	1,336	1,082	884	789	1,609	1,581	1,526	1,741	1,670
Total Capital	1,723	1,683	1,126	901	807	1,627	2,061	1,932	2,108	1,716
Capital Expenditures	213	104	79.2	63.0	148	284	504	601	466	392
Cash Flow	331	279	259	248	200	412	422	524	394	462
Current Ratio	1.3	1.5	1.2	1.1	1.0	0.9	0.9	0.9	1.1	1.1
% Long Term Debt of Capitalization	5.3	20.7	4.0	2.0	2.2	1.1	15.4	15.5	14.3	0.1
% Net Income of Revenue	1.7	2.0	2.0	1.7	1.4	1.0	0.8	1.7	1.0	2.4
% Return on Assets	5.3	5.0	5.4	5.4	4.4	2.3	2.1	4.8	3.4	7.5
% Return on Equity	15.3	15.4	18.3	20.3	18.0	6.3	6.7	14.4	8.6	17.3

Data as orig reptd.; bef. results of disc opers/spec. items. Per share data adj. for stk. divs.; EPS diluted. E-Estimated. NA-Not Available. NM-Not Meaningful. NR-Not Ranked. UR-Under Review.

Office: One Enterprise Dr, Aliso Viejo, CA 92656-2606.
Telephone: 949-349-2000.
Email: investor@fluor.com
Website: http://www.fluor.com

Chrmn & CEO: A.L. Boeckmann
SVP & CFO: D.M. Steuert
VP & Cntlr: V.L. Prechtl
Secy & Chief Lgl Officer: L.N. Fisher

Investor Contact: K. Lockwood (949-349-3815)
Board of Directors: A. L. Boeckmann, P. J. Fluor, J. T. Hackett, K. Kresa, V. S. Martinez, D. R. O'Hare, J. W. Prueher, R. Renwick, P. S. Watson, S. H. Woolsey

Founded: 1924
Domicile: Delaware
Employees: 34,836

STANDARD &POOR'S

Ford Motor Co

S&P Recommendation HOLD ★★★★★ | **Price** $8.29 (as of Oct 27, 2006) | **12-Mo. Target Price** $10.00 | **Investment Style** Large-Cap Value

GICS Sector Consumer Discretionary
Sub-Industry Automobile Manufacturers

Comment Ford, the world's second largest producer of cars and trucks, also has automotive financing and insurance operations.

Key Stock Statistics (Source S&P, Vickers, company reports)

52-Wk Range	$9.48–6.06	S&P Oper. EPS 2006**E**	-1.50	P/E on S&P Oper. EPS 2006**E**	NM	Dividend Rate/Share	Nil
Trailing 12-Month EPS	$-0.67	S&P Oper. EPS 2007**E**	-1.24	Common Shares Outstg. (M)	1,881.0	Yield (%)	Nil
Trailing 12-Month P/E	NM	S&P Core EPS 2006E	-1.42	Market Capitalization(B)	$15.006	Beta	1.85
$10K Invested 5 Yrs Ago	$5,952	S&P Core EPS 2007E	-1.21	Institutional Ownership (%)	69	S&P Credit Rating	B

Price Performance

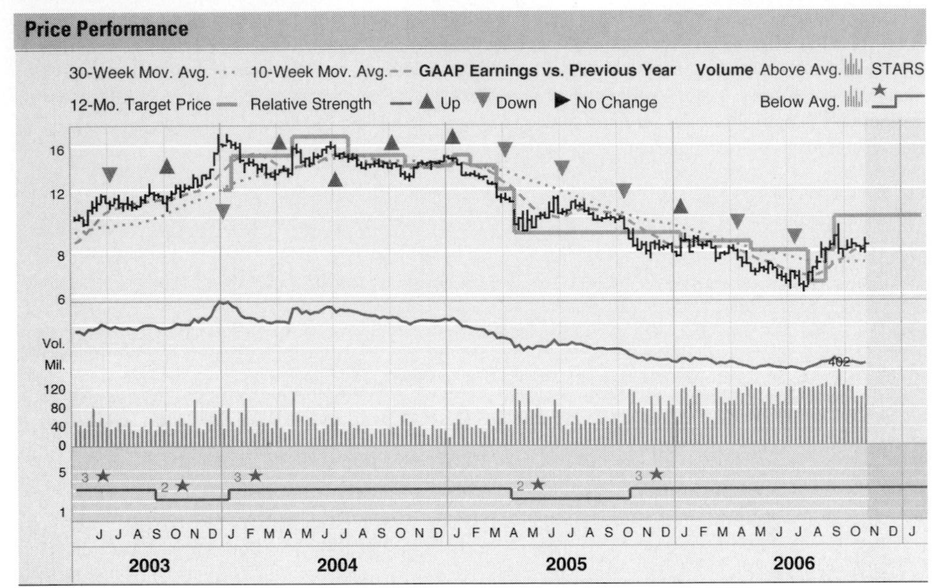

Options: ASE, CBOE, P, Ph

Analysis prepared by **Efraim Levy, CFA** on October 24, 2006, when the stock traded at **$ 8.14**.

Highlights

- We see Ford's automotive revenue falling 5% in 2007, following an expected decrease in 2006, despite about $7 billion of 2006 sales from former Visteon (VC: sell, $8) facilities. We expect financial services revenues to drop 24% and 8% in 2006 and 2007, respectively. Ford faces challenges, in our view, from intense competition, lower market share, excess capacity, high gas prices, and rising legacy pension and health care costs. The financial services segment has been an important contributor to recent sales and earnings, in our opinion, but we expect its income to decline. We think that the addition of facilities from Visteon will hurt margins until operations can be significantly improved, shut or sold.
- Pension and other retiree benefit expenses should increase, but F does not anticipate required pension fund payments before 2009. We believe that the most recent contract with the UAW will enhance productivity by allowing Ford to close several production plants.
- We expect losses per share of $1.50 in 2006 and $1.24 in 2007. The difference between our operating EPS projections and our S&P Core EPS estimates reflects pension adjustments.

Investment Rationale/Risk

- We think the addition of a new president and CEO, who is an automotive industry outsider with experience in turning around an international manufacturer, is a potential plus regarding the company's improvement efforts. However, it is not a panacea, in our view. In 2006 and 2007, we expect F to lose market share. While we believe that Ford needs to stabilize volumes, we would hold the shares in anticipation of our view that net income will benefit from restructuring activities.
- Risks to our opinion and target price include increased competitive challenges; a decline in expected demand and production; and weaker than projected financial services income. We are also concerned about Ford's corporate governance that gives Ford family members greater voting rights than other shareholders.
- With our forecasts for losses for both 2006 and 2007, a P/E multiple is not a meaningful valuation method for Ford. The stock traded recently at a price to sales (P/S) multiple in line with GM. Based on peer comparative P/S multiples, our 12-month target price is $10, equal to 0.15X projected 2007 sales per share.

Qualitative Risk Assessment

LOW | MEDIUM | **HIGH**

Our risk assessment reflects the highly cyclical nature of Ford's markets as well as our view of the current and long-term challenges that it faces, with intensifying competition and high fixed and legacy costs.

Quantitative Evaluations

S&P Quality Ranking B-

D | C | **B-** | B | B+ | A- | A | A+

Relative Strength Rank MODERATE

61

LOWEST = 1 HIGHEST = 99

Revenue/Earnings Data

Revenue (Million $)

	1Q	2Q	3Q	4Q	Year
2006	41,055	41,965	--	--	--
2005	45,136	44,548	40,856	46,549	177,089
2004	44,691	42,802	38,996	44,930	171,652
2003	40,815	40,582	36,791	46,008	164,196
2002	39,541	42,127	39,338	41,580	163,420
2001	42,446	42,314	36,502	41,150	162,412

Earnings Per Share ($)

2006	-0.64	-0.14	**E**-0.46	**E**-1.09	**E**-1.50
2005	0.58	0.47	-0.16	0.21	1.14
2004	0.95	0.57	0.25	0.03	1.80
2003	0.45	0.22	0.13	-0.35	0.50
2002	-0.05	0.31	-0.14	0.01	0.15
2001	0.56	-0.42	-0.39	-2.81	-3.02

Fiscal year ended Dec. 31. Next earnings report expected: NA. EPS Estimates based on S&P Operating Earnings; historical GAAP earnings are as reported.

Dividend Data (Dates: mm/dd Payment Date: mm/dd/yy)

Amount ($)	Date Decl.	Ex-Div. Date	Stk. of Record	Payment Date
0.100	12/08	01/26	01/30	03/01/06
0.100	03/09	04/28	05/02	06/01/06
0.050	07/13	07/31	08/02	09/01/06

Dividends have been paid since 1983. Source: Company reports.

Business Summary October 24, 2006

CORPORATE OVERVIEW. Ford is the world's second largest motor vehicle manufacturer. It produces cars and trucks, and many of the vehicles' plastic, glass and electronic components, and replacement parts. It also owns a 33% stake in Mazda Motor Corp. Financial services include Ford Motor Credit (automotive financing and insurance) and American Road Insurance Co.

Despite historically high new light vehicle industry volume, Ford's margins have been pressured by an increase in competition--primarily from Asian companies--and a shift away from the more profitable large SUV segment to smaller, less profitable crossover utility vehicles (CUVs), in our opinion. We think this is likely to hurt Ford's market share, at least until the company can introduce more of its own CUVs.

In recent years, the company's business and product portfolio has changed several times as Ford sought to optimize its financial health and performance. In December 2005, Ford sold its Hertz Corp. unit for about $15 billion, including around $5.6 billion in cash proceeds. We believe the sale will dilute EPS in 2006, as Hertz had contributed $0.16 per share to EPS in 2004 and $0.19 in the first nine months of 2005, according to company estimates. In 1999, the company acquired the car operations of AB Volvo for $6.45 billion. In 2000, Ford acquired Land Rover from BMW Group for $1.9 billion.

CORPORATE STRATEGY. Challenged by a shrinking U.S. market share, the company has announced restructuring plans in recent years in an attempt to lower its costs. However, even as Ford works to reduce its costs, the company now faces expenses stemming from assistance F is giving its former in-house parts manufacturing unit, Visteon Corp. In October 2005, Ford acquired 23 money-losing plants and facilities from Visteon. It also provided financial assistance to Visteon. In exchange, it received warrants to purchase Visteon common shares.

In March 2005, the company agreed to: relieve Visteon of a portion (about $25 million per month) of its obligation to reimburse Ford for the costs of Ford's employees assigned to Visteon; reduce by about one-fourth the number of days within which Ford will make payment to Visteon for materials and components it purchases from Visteon; and acquire up to about $150 million of new machinery and equipment for use by Visteon necessary for its production of components for Ford. In exchange, Visteon agreed to continue to supply Ford with certain components without cost surcharges. In December 2003, Ford assumed about $1.05 billion in post-retirement health care and insurance obligations from Visteon.

In January 2002, the company said that, including earlier initiatives since January 2001, it planned to eliminate up to 35,000 employees worldwide as part of a restructuring. It recorded a related charge of $4.1 billion ($2.27 a share) in 2001 for asset impairment, restructuring and other costs.

Company Financials

Per Share Data ($) Year Ended Dec. 31	2005	2004	2003	2002	2001	2000	1999	1998	1997	1996
Tangible Book Value	3.68	4.60	2.30	NM	NM	6.10	16.60	16.80	21.01	17.52
Cash Flow	7.62	9.12	8.31	8.45	5.78	13.46	13.36	24.70	11.86	9.60
Earnings	1.14	1.80	0.50	0.15	-3.02	3.59	5.86	17.76	5.62	3.72
S&P Core Earnings	0.94	1.80	1.03	-1.16	-4.56	NA	NA	NA	NA	NA
Dividends	0.40	0.40	0.40	0.40	1.05	2.30	1.88	2.18	1.65	1.47
Payout Ratio	35%	22%	80%	NM	NM	64%	32%	12%	29%	40%
Prices:High	14.75	17.34	17.33	18.23	31.42	57.25	67.88	65.94	50.25	37.25
Prices:Low	7.57	12.61	6.58	6.90	14.70	21.69	46.25	37.50	30.00	27.25
P/E Ratio:High	13	10	35	NM	NM	16	12	4	9	10
P/E Ratio:Low	7	7	13	NM	NM	6	8	2	5	7

Income Statement Analysis (Million $)	2005	2004	2003	2002	2001	2000	1999	1998	1997	1996
Revenue	177,089	171,652	164,196	163,420	162,412	170,064	162,558	144,416	153,731	146,991
Operating Income	21,052	24,945	24,770	25,034	22,941	34,530	29,311	27,400	31,017	25,267
Depreciation	14,042	13,052	14,297	15,177	15,922	14,849	9,254	8,589	7,645	6,875
Interest Expense	7,643	7,071	7,690	8,824	10,848	10,902	9,076	8,865	10,500	10,399
Pretax Income	1,996	4,853	1,370	953	-7,584	8,234	11,026	25,396	10,939	6,793
Effective Tax Rate	NM	19.3%	9.85%	31.7%	NM	32.9%	33.3%	12.5%	34.2%	31.9%
Net Income	2,228	3,634	921	284	-5,453	5,410	7,237	22,071	6,920	4,446
S&P Core Earnings	1,794	3,637	1,905	-2,202	-8,266	NA	NA	NA	NA	NA

Balance Sheet & Other Financial Data (Million $)	2005	2004	2003	2002	2001	2000	1999	1998	1997	1996
Cash	39,082	33,018	33,642	30,521	15,028	16,490	23,585	23,805	20,835	15,414
Total Assets	269,476	292,654	304,594	289,357	276,543	284,421	276,229	237,545	279,097	262,867
Long Term Debt	94,428	106,540	119,751	125,806	121,430	99,560	78,734	64,898	80,245	77,136
Total Debt	154,332	172,973	179,804	167,892	168,009	166,229	152,738	132,835	168,925	150,239
Common Equity	12,957	16,045	11,651	5,590	7,786	18,610	27,537	23,409	30,734	26,068
Capital Expenditures	7,517	6,745	7,749	7,278	7,008	8,348	8,535	8,617	8,717	8,651
Cash Flow	16,270	16,686	15,218	15,446	10,454	20,244	16,476	30,553	14,511	11,321
% Return on Assets	0.8	1.2	0.3	0.1	NM	2.0	2.8	8.5	2.6	1.8
% Return on Equity	15.4	26.2	10.7	4.0	NM	23.3	28.4	81.1	23.9	17.7
% Long Term Debt of Capitalization	82.9	82.2	87.5	87.8	87.2	78.3	68.6	73.5	68.5	71.3

Data as orig reptd.; bef. results of disc opers/spec. items. Per share data adj. for stk. divs.; EPS diluted. E-Estimated. NA-Not Available. NM-Not Meaningful. NR-Not Ranked. UR-Under Review.

Office: One American Rd, Dearborn, MI 48126-2798.
Telephone: 313-322-3000.
Website: http://www.ford.com
Exec Chrmn: W.C. Ford, Jr.

Pres & CEO: A. Mulally
Investor Contact: D.R. Leclair (800-555-5259)
EVP & CFO: D.R. Leclair
SVP & General Counsel: D. Leitch

Board of Directors: J. R. Bond, S. G. Butler, K. A. Casiano, E. B. Ford, II, W. C. Ford, Jr., I. O. Hockaday, Jr., R. A. Manoogian, E. R. Marram, A. Mulally, H. A. Neal, J. Ollila, J. L. Thornton

Founded: 1903
Domicile: Delaware
Employees: 300,000

Forest Laboratories Inc.

STANDARD &POOR'S

S&P Recommendation HOLD ★★★★★

Price $47.88 (as of Oct 27, 2006)

12-Mo. Target Price $53.00

Investment Style Large-Cap Growth

GICS Sector Health Care
Sub-Industry Pharmaceuticals

Comment This company develops and makes branded and generic ethical drug products, sold primarily in the U.S., Puerto Rico, and Western and Eastern Europe.

Key Stock Statistics (Source S&P, Vickers, company reports)

52-Wk Range	$54.70–36.18	S&P Oper. EPS 2007E	2.65	P/E on S&P Oper. EPS 2007E	18.1	Dividend Rate/Share	Nil
Trailing 12-Month EPS	$2.23	S&P Oper. EPS 2008E	2.90	Common Shares Outstg. (M)	318.0	Yield (%)	Nil
Trailing 12-Month P/E	21.5	S&P Core EPS 2007E	2.65	Market Capitalization(B)	$15.224	Beta	0.39
$10K Invested 5 Yrs Ago	$12,613	S&P Core EPS 2008E	2.90	Institutional Ownership (%)	91	S&P Credit Rating	NA

Price Performance

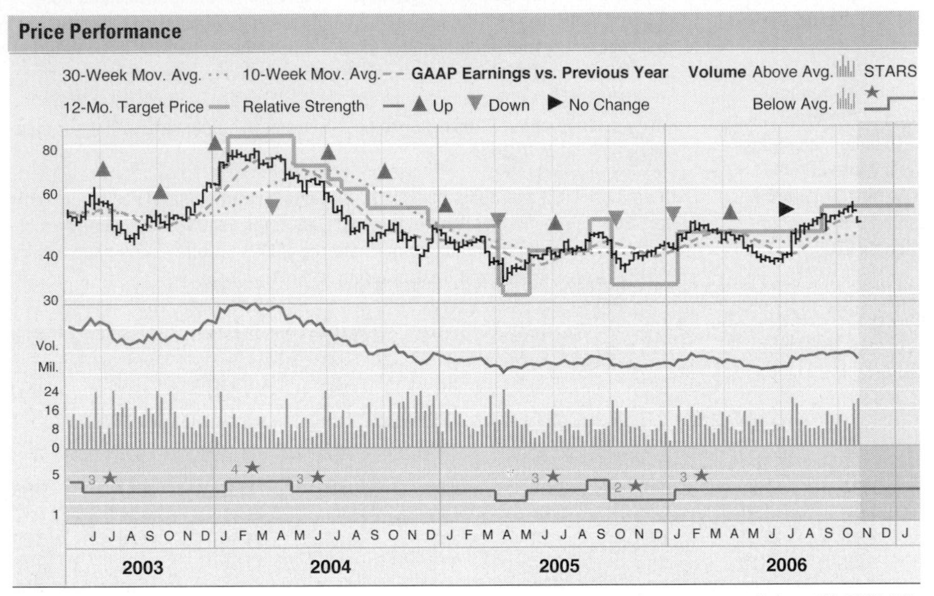

Options: ASE, CBOE, P, Ph

Analysis prepared by **Herman B. Saftlas** on October 20, 2006, when the stock traded at **$ 51.47**.

Highlights

- We expect revenues in FY 07 (Mar.) to advance about 12%, to over $3.3 billion. Despite heightened competitive pressures in the antidepressant market, we project a 10% rise in Lexapro sales, reflecting our view of that drug's efficacy and side effect advantages, an expanded salesforce and higher prices. Sales of Namenda should increase over 20%, lifted by greater acceptance of this Alzheimer's drug by the medical community.
- We think gross margins will remain fairly steady, in the 76%-77% range. While R&D expenses will likely increase, they should be much lower than previously expected, reflecting a decision to shift some $43 million in product milestone payments to FY 08. SG&A spending as a percentage of total revenues should be lower. Other income should be higher, boosted by greater contributions from Benicar, a heart drug sold through a joint venture with Sankyo.
- Our FY 07 operating EPS forecast is $2.65, after product licensing and milestone payments and projected stock option expense. We see further EPS progress, to $2.90, in FY 08.

Investment Rationale/Risk

- We believe that Forest has become one of the world's leading specialty drug companies, with particular expertise in central nervous system drugs such as Lexapro, an antidepressant, and Namenda, a treatment for Alzheimer's disease. While sales of Lexapro and Namenda should remain strong over the foreseeable future, we think greater investor focus will be on as yet unproven pipeline drugs needed to drive long-term growth. Lexapro and Namenda patents expire in 2012. In our opinion, key R&D opportunities include nebivolol for heart disease, milnacipran for fibromyalgia, and Orapem novel antibiotic.
- Risks to our opinion and target price include greater than expected competition in principal markets, as well as possible setbacks in the R&D pipeline.
- Our 12-month target price of $53 applies a peer-level P/E of about 18.3X to our FY 08 EPS estimate of $2.90. This valuation is also supported by our DCF model, which assumes decelerated cash flow growth over the next 15 years, a weighted average cost of capital of 8%, and terminal growth of 1%.

Qualitative Risk Assessment

LOW | **MEDIUM** | HIGH

We view positively the company's recent legal victory against generic challengers to its important Lexapro patent. We also think its R&D pipeline shows promise. However, Forest's relatively small size among big pharma competitors and our view of its somewhat limited product line represent negative risk factors.

Quantitative Evaluations

S&P Quality Ranking B+

D | C | B- | B | **B+** | A- | A | A+

Relative Strength Rank WEAK

24

LOWEST = 1 HIGHEST = 99

Revenue/Earnings Data

Revenue (Million $)

	1Q	2Q	3Q	4Q	Year
2007	816.3	847.0	--	--	--
2006	711.8	736.5	757.8	756.3	2,962
2005	--	--	--	640.6	3,114
2004	614.4	625.5	707.2	733.1	2,680
2003	467.2	531.6	586.8	621.1	2,207
2002	350.5	376.3	403.1	436.8	1,602

Earnings Per Share ($)

	1Q	2Q	3Q	4Q	Year
2007	0.62	--	E0.64	E0.64	E2.65
2006	0.62	0.59	0.57	0.28	2.08
2005	0.60	0.79	0.70	0.15	2.25
2004	0.48	0.49	0.60	0.38	1.95
2003	0.34	0.39	0.47	0.48	1.66
2002	0.20	0.22	0.24	0.26	0.91

Fiscal year ended Mar. 31. Next earnings report expected: Mid January. EPS Estimates based on S&P Operating Earnings; historical GAAP earnings are as reported.

Dividend Data

No cash dividends have been paid.

Please read the Required Disclosures and Analyst Certification on the last page of this report.

Business Summary October 20, 2006

CORPORATE OVERVIEW. Forest Laboratories is a leading producer of niche-oriented branded and generic prescription pharmaceuticals. Most of Forest's products were developed in collaboration with licensing partners. FRX's most important products are antidepressants, which accounted for about 68% of net sales in FY 06 (Mar.).

Lexapro antidepressant is now the company's single most important product. A single enanitomer version of Celexa (an older, off-patent FRX antidepressant), Lexapro is an advanced selective serotonin reuptake inhibitor (SSRI) indicated for the treatment of both depression and generalized anxiety disorder. Lexapro had sales of $1.9 billion in FY 06, up from $1.6 billion in FY 05. FRX licensed both Celexa and Lexapro from H. Lundbeck A/S, a Danish pharmaceutical company. As of September 2006, Lexapro had a 13.3% share of the relatively crowded U.S. prescription antidepressant drug market, based on data from IMS Health.

FRX's second most important product is Namenda (licensed from Merz Pharmaceuticals of Germany), a treatment for moderate to severe Alzheimer's disease. Sales of Namenda totaled $508 million in FY 06, up from $333 million in FY 05. In July 2005, the FDA issued a non-approvable letter regarding the company's supplemental filing for clearance to market Namenda also for mild-to-moderate Alzheimer's disease. As of September 2006, Namenda had about 32% of the Alzheimer's prescription drug market, according to IMS Health.

Other products include Tiazac, a once daily diltiazem calcium channel blocker for hypertension; Aerobid, a metered-dose inhaled steroid to treat asthma; Campral for alcohol addiction; Combunox for the short-term management of severe pain; Aero-chamber, a device used to improve the delivery of aerosol products; Levothroid, a thyroid product; and Cervidil, used to aid in cervical dilation.

COMPETITIVE LANDSCAPE. The U.S. selective serotonin reuptake inhibitor (SSRI) antidepressant drug market totaled about $6.8 billion in 2005, down 18% from 2004, based on data from IMS Health. We think the decline reflected the impact of inexpensive generic versions of several patent-expired branded antidepressants, negative publicity about SSRIs, and competition from new non-SSRI antidepressants. We expect further attrition in the SSRI market in 2006, reflecting anticipated generic erosion in Pfizer's Zoloft line.

Company Financials

Per Share Data ($) Year Ended Mar. 31	2006	2005	2004	2003	2002	2001	2000	1999	1998	1997
Tangible Book Value	7.69	8.21	8.03	5.66	3.75	2.60	1.79	1.60	1.25	1.22
Cash Flow	2.20	2.32	2.01	1.80	1.06	0.71	0.44	0.29	0.17	-0.01
Earnings	2.08	2.25	1.95	1.66	0.91	0.59	0.32	0.23	0.11	-0.07
S&P Core Earnings	1.97	2.15	1.85	1.58	0.74	0.47	NA	NA	NA	NA
Dividends	Nil	Nil	Nil	Nil	Nil	Nil	Nil	Nil	Nil	Nil
Payout Ratio	Nil	Nil	Nil	Nil	Nil	Nil	Nil	Nil	Nil	Nil
Calendar Year	2005	2004	2003	2002	2001	2000	1999	1998	1997	1996
Prices:High	45.21	78.81	63.23	54.99	41.60	35.33	15.44	13.31	6.16	6.97
Prices:Low	32.46	36.10	41.85	32.12	23.25	14.34	10.31	6.08	3.95	3.53
P/E Ratio:High	22	35	32	33	46	60	48	59	56	NM
P/E Ratio:Low	16	16	21	19	26	24	32	27	36	NM
Income Statement Analysis (Million $)										
Revenue	2,962	3,114	2,650	2,207	1,567	1,181	882	546	427	281
Operating Income	701	1,164	929	833	490	318	181	54.3	27.2	-48.1
Depreciation	40.7	25.4	22.2	51.6	54.6	43.3	40.6	21.3	20.1	19.2
Interest Expense	Nil	Nil	Nil	Nil	Nil	Nil	Nil	Nil	Nil	Nil
Pretax Income	870	1,185	937	821	470	299	157	111	54.8	-39.0
Effective Tax Rate	18.5%	29.2%	21.5%	24.2%	28.1%	28.0%	28.4%	30.4%	33.0%	NM
Net Income	709	839	736	622	338	215	113	77.2	36.7	-23.5
S&P Core Earnings	673	800	697	589	272	170	NA	NA	NA	NA
Balance Sheet & Other Financial Data (Million $)										
Cash	1,323	1,619	2,131	1,556	893	506	355	279	150	172
Current Assets	2,207	2,708	2,916	2,255	1,195	884	645	502	372	360
Total Assets	3,120	3,705	3,863	2,918	1,952	1,447	1,098	875	744	700
Current Liabilities	421	564	605	564	325	224	211	130	130	73.5
Long Term Debt	Nil	Nil	Nil	Nil	Nil	Nil	Nil	Nil	Nil	Nil
Common Equity	2,698	3,132	3,256	2,352	1,625	1,222	885	744	614	626
Total Capital	2,699	3,141	3,258	2,354	1,627	1,223	887	745	614	626
Capital Expenditures	55.0	89.0	102	79.6	36.4	30.9	35.3	17.2	6.89	9.66
Cash Flow	749	864	758	674	393	258	153	98.4	56.8	-4.36
Current Ratio	5.2	4.8	4.8	4.0	3.7	4.0	3.1	3.9	2.9	4.9
% Long Term Debt of Capitalization	Nil	Nil	Nil	Nil	Nil	Nil	Nil	Nil	Nil	Nil
% Net Income of Revenue	24.3	26.9	27.8	28.2	21.6	18.2	12.8	14.1	8.6	NM
% Return on Assets	20.8	22.2	21.7	25.5	19.9	16.7	11.4	9.5	5.1	NM
% Return on Equity	24.3	26.3	26.2	31.3	23.7	20.4	13.8	11.4	5.9	NM

Data as orig reptd.; bef. results of disc opers/spec. items. Per share data adj. for stk. divs.; EPS diluted. E-Estimated. NA-Not Available. NM-Not Meaningful. NR-Not Ranked. UR-Under Review.

Office: 909 3rd Ave, New York, NY 10022-4748.
Telephone: 212-421-7850.
Email: investor.relations@frx.com
Website: http://www.frx.com

Chrmn & CEO: H. Solomon
Pres & COO: L.S. Olanoff
Investor Contact: F.I. Perier, Jr. (212-421-7850)
SVP & CFO: F.I. Perier, Jr.

Secy: W.J. Candee, III
Board of Directors: N. Basgoz, W. J. Candee, III, G. S. Cohan, D. L. Goldwasser, K. E. Goodman, L. S. Olanoff, L. B. Salans, H. Solomon

Founded: 1956
Domicile: Delaware
Employees: 5,050

STANDARD &POOR'S

Fortune Brands Inc.

S&P Recommendation HOLD ★★★★★

Price $76.95 (as of Oct 27, 2006)

12-Mo. Target Price $85.00

Investment Style Large-Cap Growth

GICS Sector Consumer Discretionary
Sub-Industry Housewares & Specialties

Comment This diversified holding company has interests in consumer businesses that include home improvement, spirits and wine, office products, and golf-related products.

Key Stock Statistics (Source S&P, Vickers, company reports)

52-Wk Range	**$82.87–68.45**	S&P Oper. EPS 2006**E**	**5.30**	P/E on S&P Oper. EPS 2006**E**	**14.5**	Dividend Rate/Share	**$1.56**
Trailing 12-Month EPS	**$4.93**	S&P Oper. EPS 2007**E**	**5.65**	Common Shares Outstg. (M)	**150.8**	Yield (%)	**2.03**
Trailing 12-Month P/E	**15.6**	S&P Core EPS 2006**E**	**5.34**	Market Capitalization(B)	**$11.606**	Beta	**0.75**
$10K Invested 5 Yrs Ago	**$23,579**	S&P Core EPS 2007**E**	**5.69**	Institutional Ownership (%)	**63**	S&P Credit Rating	**BBB**

Price Performance

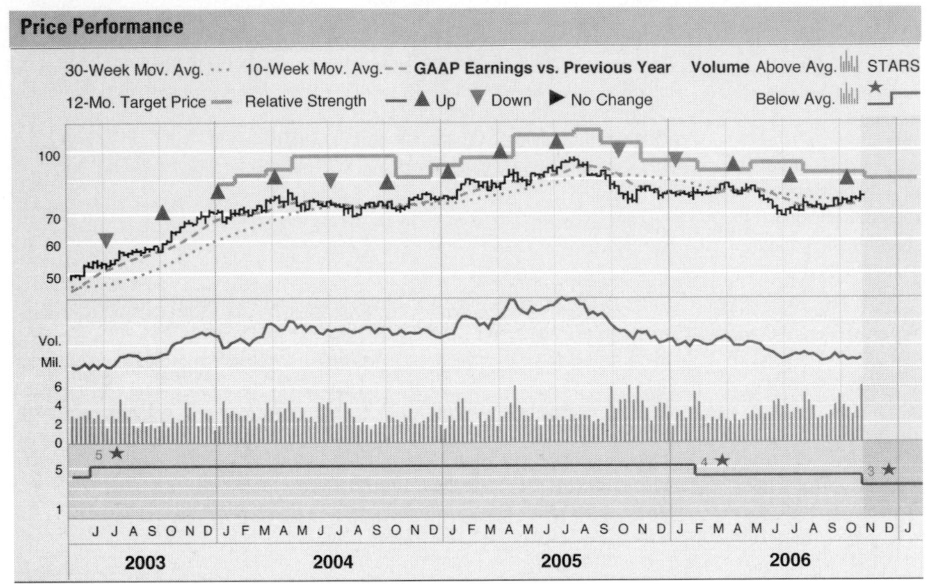

Options: ASE, CBOE, P, Ph

Highlights

- The STARS recommendation for FO has recently been changed to 3 (hold) from 4 (buy) and the 12-month target price has recently been changed to $85.00 from $88.00. The Highlights section of this Stock Report will be updated accordingly.

Investment Rationale/Risk

- The Investment Rationale/Risk section of this Stock Report will be updated shortly. For the latest News story on FO from MarketScope, see below.

- 10/27/06 11:59 am EDT... S&P DOWNGRADES RECOMMENDATION ON SHARES OF FORTUNE BRANDS TO HOLD FROM BUY (FO 77.58***): Excluding one-time items, FO posted Q3 EPS from continuing operations of $1.30 vs. $1.12, in line with our estimate. The strength was primarily due to the Spirits & Wine division. We are maintaining our EPS estimate of $5.30 for '06, but reducing our '07 estimate by $0.20 to $5.65 to reflect our more cautious outlook for FO's housing-related business. We are also reducing our P/E-based 12-month target price by $3 to $85. With the recent strong stock appreciation and our reduced target price, we believe the FO shares are fairly valued. / L.Braverman-CFA

Qualitative Risk Assessment

LOW | MEDIUM | HIGH

Our risk assessment reflects our view that FO has a long track record of consistent sales and earnings growth. While the company has exposure to the home building market, more of its products are geared for remodeling. Its spirits/wine and golf businesses are generally stable, in our opinion.

Quantitative Evaluations

S&P Quality Ranking **B**

D | C | B- | B | B+ | A- | A | A+

Relative Strength Rank **MODERATE**

57

LOWEST = 1 HIGHEST = 99

Revenue/Earnings Data

Revenue (Million $)

	1Q	2Q	3Q	4Q	Year
2006	2,017	2,257	2,219	--	--
2005	1,518	1,783	1,802	1,959	7,061
2004	1,708	1,890	1,812	1,912	7,321
2003	1,392	1,582	1,584	1,657	6,215
2002	1,271	1,513	1,463	1,432	5,678
2001	1,301	1,433	1,472	1,472	5,679

Earnings Per Share ($)

	1Q	2Q	3Q	4Q	Year
2006	1.15	1.63	0.98	**E**1.40	**E**5.30
2005	0.95	1.22	0.52	1.17	3.87
2004	0.92	1.11	1.52	1.68	5.23
2003	0.66	1.18	0.98	1.04	3.86
2002	0.55	1.27	0.73	0.86	3.41
2001	0.39	0.66	0.60	0.84	2.49

Fiscal year ended Dec. 31. Next earnings report expected: Early February. EPS Estimates based on S&P Operating Earnings; historical GAAP earnings are as reported.

Dividend Data (Dates: mm/dd Payment Date: mm/dd/yy)

Amount ($)	Date Decl.	Ex-Div. Date	Stk. of Record	Payment Date
0.360	01/24	02/06	02/08	03/01/06
0.360	04/25	05/08	05/10	06/01/06
0.390	07/25	08/07	08/09	09/01/06
0.390	09/26	11/06	11/08	12/01/06

Dividends have been paid since 1905. Source: Company reports.

Fortune Brands Inc.

Business Summary August 07, 2006

Fortune Brands is a holding company with subsidiaries that produce home and hardware products, spirits and wine, and golf products.

Major units of FO's home and hardware products segment include MasterBrand Cabinets, Moen, Master Lock, Waterloo and Therma-Tru. Moen is a leading producer of faucets, sinks, and plumbing accessories in the U.S. and Asia. Master Lock makes key-controlled and combination locks, and door locksets and related hardware. MasterBrand Cabinets manufactures stock and semi-custom kitchen cabinets and vanities and ready-to-assemble kitchen cabinets and bathroom vanities under the Aristokraft, Schrock, Omega, Kemper, Decora and Diamond names. Waterloo makes tool storage products for Sears Craftsman and other private labels. Therma-Tru (acquired in November 2003) is the leading U.S. manufacturer of residential entry doors. In 2005, hardware and home improvement products accounted for 59% of total sales and 56% of operating company contributions (before corporate expenses).

Golf products (18%, 15%) operations are conducted through Acushnet, a leading producer of golf balls (Titleist, Pinnacle), golf shoes (FootJoy), golf clubs (Cobra, Titleist), and golf gloves. Other products include bags, carts, dress and athletic shoes, socks and accessories.

Spirits and wine (23%, 34%) are sold through the Beam Global Spirits & Wine subsidiary. Leading brands include Jim Beam Bourbon whiskey, DeKuyper cordials, Gilbey's gin, Kamchatka vodka, and Geyser Peak wine. Principal markets are the U.S., the U.K., and Australia. About 25% of the division's sales come from international markets. In July 2005, the company acquired various spirits and wine brands from Pernod Ricard, which in turn were acquired by Pernod from Allied Domecq PLC. This transaction more than doubled the sales of FO's spirits and wine segment. Some of the key brands that were acquired are Sauza tequila, Courvoisier cognac, Canadian Club whiskey, and Maker's Mark bourbon brand, which remains subject to regulatory clearance in the U.S.

In August 2005, FO spun off the office products division, which has merged with General Binding Corp.

Company Financials

Per Share Data ($) Year Ended Dec. 31	**2005**	**2004**	**2003**	**2002**	**2001**	**2000**	**1999**	**1998**	**1997**	**1996**
Tangible Book Value	NM	NM	NM	NM	2.06	0.89	0.83	1.91	1.93	NM
Cash Flow	5.35	6.70	5.14	4.57	3.89	0.63	-3.96	3.09	1.64	4.46
Earnings	3.87	5.23	3.86	3.41	2.49	-0.88	-5.35	1.67	0.23	2.86
S&P Core Earnings	3.73	4.58	3.79	3.14	2.38	NA	NA	NA	NA	NA
Dividends	1.38	1.26	1.14	1.02	0.97	0.93	0.89	0.85	1.41	2.00
Payout Ratio	36%	24%	30%	30%	39%	NM	NM	51%	NM	70%
Prices:High	96.18	80.50	71.80	57.86	40.54	33.25	45.88	42.25	56.00	50.13
Prices:Low	73.50	66.10	40.60	36.85	28.38	19.19	29.38	25.25	30.25	39.88
P/E Ratio:High	25	15	19	17	16	NM	NM	25	NM	18
P/E Ratio:Low	19	13	11	11	11	NM	NM	15	NM	14

Income Statement Analysis (Million $)	2005	2004	2003	2002	2001	2000	1999	1998	1997	1996
Revenue	7,061	7,321	6,215	5,678	5,679	5,845	5,525	5,241	4,845	5,776
Operating Income	1,748	1,374	1,142	1,011	870	938	853	871	723	1,363
Depreciation	224	221	193	179	219	237	231	251	243	275
Interest Expense	159	87.9	73.8	74.1	96.8	134	107	103	117	179
Pretax Income	926	1,086	884	756	492	38.9	-721	512	140	824
Effective Tax Rate	35.0%	26.1%	32.7%	28.3%	19.2%	NM	NM	42.6%	70.0%	39.8%
Net Income	582	784	579	526	386	-138	-891	294	42.0	497
S&P Core Earnings	559	684	567	484	367	NA	NA	NA	NA	NA

Balance Sheet & Other Financial Data (Million $)	2005	2004	2003	2002	2001	2000	1999	1998	1997	1996
Cash	93.6	165	105	15.4	48.7	20.9	72.0	40.0	54.0	120
Current Assets	3,193	2,642	2,282	1,903	1,970	2,265	2,313	2,265	2,096	3,873
Total Assets	13,202	7,884	7,445	5,822	5,301	5,764	6,417	7,360	6,943	9,504
Current Liabilities	2,818	2,036	2,134	1,515	1,258	2,040	2,003	1,845	1,769	3,695
Long Term Debt	4,890	1,240	1,243	200	950	1,152	1,205	982	739	1,598
Common Equity	3,639	3,203	2,712	2,305	2,094	2,127	2,728	4,087	4,006	3,671
Total Capital	9,788	5,207	4,664	2,983	3,444	3,343	3,991	5,080	4,795	5,402
Capital Expenditures	222	242	194	194	207	227	241	252	197	240
Cash Flow	805	1,005	772	704	605	99.0	-661	544	284	771
Current Ratio	1.1	1.3	1.1	1.3	1.6	1.1	1.2	1.2	1.2	1.1
% Long Term Debt of Capitalization	50.0	23.8	26.6	6.7	27.6	34.5	30.2	19.3	15.4	29.6
% Net Income of Revenue	8.2	10.7	9.3	9.3	6.8	NM	NM	5.6	0.9	8.6
% Return on Assets	5.5	10.2	8.7	9.5	7.0	NM	NM	4.1	0.5	5.7
% Return on Equity	17.2	26.5	23.1	23.9	18.3	NM	NM	7.2	1.1	13.2

Data as orig reptd.; bef. results of disc opers/spec. items. Per share data adj. for stk. divs.; EPS diluted. E-Estimated. NA-Not Available. NM-Not Meaningful. NR-Not Ranked. UR-Under Review.

Office: 520 Lake Cook Rd, Deerfield, IL 60015-5611.
Telephone: 847-484-4400.
Email: investorrelations@fortunebrands.com
Website: http://www.fortunebrands.com

Chrmn & CEO: N.H. Wesley
SVP & CFO: C.P. Omtvedt
SVP & Treas: M. Hausberg
SVP, Secy & General Counsel: M.A. Roche

Investor Contact: T. Diaz (847-484-4410)
Board of Directors: P. O. Ewers, R. A. Goldstein, T. C. Hays, P. E. Leroy, G. R. Lohman, A. D. Mackay, E. A. Renna, J. C. Reyes, A. M. Tatlock, D. M. Thomas, N. H. Wesley, P. M. Wilson

Founded: 1904
Domicile: Delaware
Employees: 27,476

STANDARD &POOR'S

FPL Group Inc.

S&P Recommendation BUY ★★★★★ | **Price** $50.77 (as of Oct 30, 2006) | **12-Mo. Target Price** $57.00 | **Investment Style** Large-Cap Value

GICS Sector Utilities
Sub-Industry Electric Utilities

Comment The holding company for Florida Power & Light and FPL Energy, FPL Group has agreed to the termination of its planned merger with Constellation Energy.

Key Stock Statistics (Source S&P, Vickers, company reports)

52-Wk Range	$51.00–37.81	S&P Oper. EPS 2006E	2.91	P/E on S&P Oper. EPS 2006E	17.4	Dividend Rate/Share	$1.50
Trailing 12-Month EPS	$3.07	S&P Oper. EPS 2007E	3.40	Common Shares Outstg. (M)	404.4	Yield (%)	2.95
Trailing 12-Month P/E	16.5	S&P Core EPS 2006E	2.63	Market Capitalization(B)	$20.532	Beta	0.45
$10K Invested 5 Yrs Ago	$22,814	S&P Core EPS 2007E	3.10	Institutional Ownership (%)	69	S&P Credit Rating	A

Price Performance

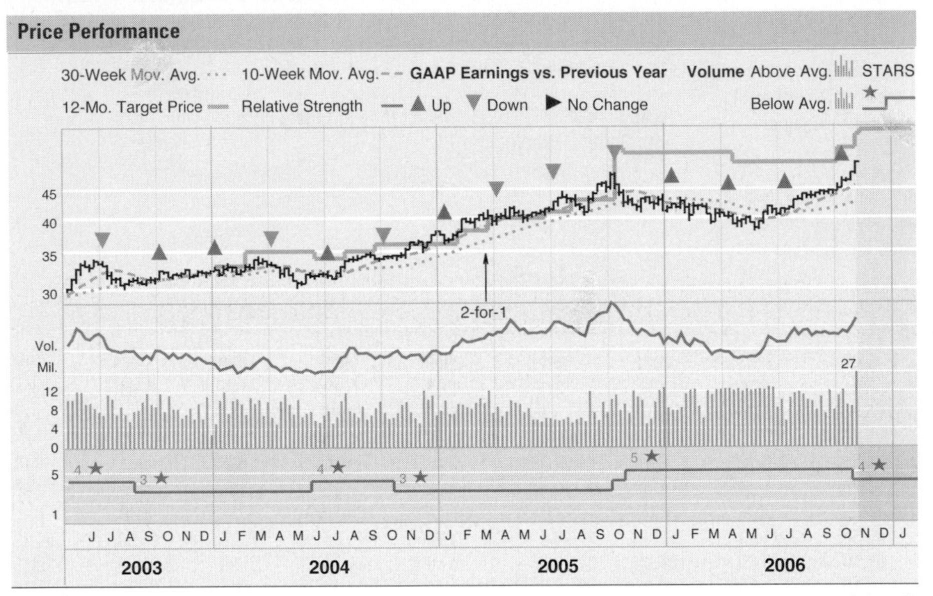

Options: Ph

Analysis prepared by **Justin McCann** on October 30, 2006, when the stock traded at **$ 50.75**.

Highlights

- Given the regulatory and judicial uncertainties that marred the Maryland approval process for the company's planned merger with Constellation Energy (CEG: hold, $62), we believe the termination of the merger was in the best interests of FPL and its shareholders. While we thought the merger would have created a significant national presence for the combined company and a stronger platform for the growth of its unregulated operations, we believe that given the strengths of its regulated and unregulated operations, FPL will remain one of the premier electric companies in the U.S.

- After an anticipated increase of nearly 13% in 2006 (from 2005 operating EPS of $2.58), we expect operating EPS to advance nearly 17% in 2007. In 2006, we look for Florida Power & Light to contribute operating EPS of about $2.09; FPL Energy about $0.99; and for the corporate and other operations to record a loss of about $0.17.

- We believe the EPS growth we project for both 2006 and 2007 will be driven by a sharp increase in earnings from FPL Energy, as it benefits from contracts with higher power prices.

Investment Rationale/Risk

- Given the recent rise in the shares, we have lowered our investment recommendation to buy, from strong buy. The shares rose more than 3% on the day the termination of planned merger with Constellation Energy was announced, and have advanced around 20% year-to-date. We still see strong growth on a stand-alone basis, and continue to project nearly 17% EPS growth for 2007, and close to 10% growth in 2008 and 2009. While we believe the well-above-peer earnings growth we project for FPL will more than offset a below-peer dividend yield, we expect a less robust level of total return from the stock's current level.

- Risks to our recommendation and target price include lower than expected results from the unregulated FPL Energy business, and a reduction in the average P/E of the group as a whole.

- Given the rise in the shares, the yield from the dividend has declined to about 3%. We still expect to see annual dividend increases at about a 3% rate. Our 12-month target price of $57 reflects a premium-to-peers P/E of 16.8X our EPS estimate for 2007, justified, we think, by above-average earnings growth.

Qualitative Risk Assessment

LOW | MEDIUM | HIGH

Our risk assessment reflects FPL's strong and steady cash flows from its Florida Power & Light utility, which enjoys well above average customer growth, and a generally supportive regulatory environment. We believe this largely offsets the fast growing but higher-risk cash flows from its independent power subsidiary.

Quantitative Evaluations

S&P Quality Ranking A-

D | C | B- | B | B+ | A- | A | A+

Relative Strength Rank STRONG

89

LOWEST = 1 HIGHEST = 99

Revenue/Earnings Data

Revenue (Million $)

	1Q	2Q	3Q	4Q	Year
2006	3,584	3,809	4,694	--	--
2005	2,437	2,741	3,504	3,164	11,846
2004	2,331	2,619	2,983	2,589	10,522
2003	2,082	2,339	2,775	2,435	9,630
2002	1,843	2,248	2,353	2,029	8,311
2001	1,941	2,166	2,529	1,839	8,475

Earnings Per Share ($)

	1Q	2Q	3Q	4Q	Year
2006	0.63	0.60	1.32	**E**0.53	**E**2.91
2005	0.36	0.52	0.87	0.53	2.29
2004	0.39	0.72	0.88	0.47	2.46
2003	0.50	0.67	0.94	0.41	2.51
2002	0.49	0.73	0.43	0.37	2.00
2001	0.33	0.65	0.99	0.35	2.31

Fiscal year ended Dec. 31. Next earnings report expected: Late January. EPS Estimates based on S&P Operating Earnings; historical GAAP earnings are as reported.

Dividend Data (Dates: mm/dd Payment Date: mm/dd/yy)

Amount ($)	Date Decl.	Ex-Div. Date	Stk. of Record	Payment Date
0.375	02/17	03/03	03/07	03/15/06
0.375	05/26	06/07	06/09	06/15/06
0.375	08/04	08/23	08/25	09/15/06
0.375	10/13	11/21	11/24	12/15/06

Dividends have been paid since 1944. Source: Company reports.

FPL Group Inc.

Business Summary October 30, 2006

CORPORATE OVERVIEW. FPL Group, one of the largest providers of electricity-related services in the U.S., is the holding company for Florida Power & Light Co., a regulated and vertically integrated utility, and FPL Energy, a wholesale generator of electricity with operations in 24 states.

MARKET PROFILE. Florida Power & Light provides electricity to about 4.2 million customers in an area covering nearly all of Florida's eastern seaboard, as well as the southern part of the state. As is true of most states in the Southeast, Florida has shown little interest in restructuring its electric utility industry. Although there have been efforts to introduce a competitive wholesale generation market within the state, there has not been any legislation that would allow it to take place, and we don't expect to see any within the next several years.

Electric revenues by customer class in 2005 were: residential 55%; commercial 37%; industrial 3%; and other 5%. Given its unusually low level of exposure to industrial customers, we consider the company to be much less vulnerable to economic downturns. This, along with an above average customer growth rate (2.4% in 2005), and a recent regulatory ruling that has provided rate certainty through 2009 and set up a storm cost recovery mechanism, helps to establish, we think, a more favorable foundation for the utility's long-term annual EPS growth, which we project at 3% to 4%.

IMPACT OF MAJOR DEVELOPMENTS. On October 25, 2006, the company and Baltimore-based Constellation Energy Group (CEG) announced the termination of the merger agreement that had been announced on December 19, 2005. If the merger had been completed, FPL shareholders would have had an approximate 60% interest in the new company, and CEG shareholders a 40% interest. Since CEG is not only the holding company for Baltimore Gas & Electric Company, but the nation's largest wholesale power seller and its largest competitive supplier of electricity to large commercial and industrial customers, the merger would have made the combined entity one of the largest electric companies in the U.S. Although we were disappointed that the merger was terminated, we believe the regulatory and judicial uncertainties surrounding the approval process in Maryland justified the decision.

Company Financials

Per Share Data ($) Year Ended Dec. 31	2005	2004	2003	2002	2001	2000	1999	1998	1997	1996
Tangible Book Value	21.52	20.24	18.93	17.46	17.09	15.89	15.00	14.16	13.31	12.31
Earnings	2.29	2.46	2.51	2.01	2.31	2.07	2.04	1.93	1.79	1.67
S&P Core Earnings	2.06	2.17	2.21	1.52	1.83	NA	NA	NA	NA	NA
Dividends	1.42	1.30	1.20	1.16	1.12	1.08	1.04	1.00	0.96	0.92
Payout Ratio	62%	53%	48%	58%	48%	52%	51%	52%	54%	55%
Prices:High	48.11	38.05	34.04	32.66	35.81	36.50	30.97	36.28	30.00	24.06
Prices:Low	35.90	30.10	26.78	22.50	25.61	18.19	20.56	28.03	21.31	20.75
P/E Ratio:High	21	15	14	16	16	18	15	19	17	14
P/E Ratio:Low	16	12	11	11	11	9	10	15	12	12

Income Statement Analysis (Million $)	2005	2004	2003	2002	2001	2000	1999	1998	1997	1996
Revenue	11,846	10,522	9,630	8,311	8,475	7,082	6,438	6,661	6,369	6,037
Depreciation	1,285	1,198	1,105	952	983	1,032	1,040	1,284	1,061	960
Maintenance	NA	NA	NA	NA	NA	NA	NA	NA	NA	NA
Fixed Charges Coverage	2.87	3.26	3.95	4.52	4.51	4.55	4.96	NA	3.97	4.01
Construction Credits	28.0	37.0	NA	NA	NA	Nil	Nil	Nil	Nil	2.00
Effective Tax Rate	23.5%	23.1%	29.2%	26.0%	32.7%	32.3%	31.7%	29.6%	33.0%	33.6%
Net Income	885	887	893	695	781	704	697	664	618	579
S&P Core Earnings	797	782	786	527	616	NA	NA	NA	NA	NA

Balance Sheet & Other Financial Data (Million $)	2005	2004	2003	2002	2001	2000	1999	1998	1997	1996
Gross Property	33,351	31,720	30,272	26,505	23,388	21,022	19,554	17,952	17,820	17,034
Capital Expenditures	1,616	1,394	1,383	1,277	1,544	1,299	861	617	551	488
Net Property	22,463	21,226	20,297	14,304	11,662	9,934	9,264	8,555	9,354	9,384
Capitalization:Long Term Debt	8,039	8,027	8,728	6,016	5,084	4,202	3,704	2,347	2,949	3,144
Capitalization:% Long Term Debt	48.6	51.6	55.6	47.4	45.8	42.9	40.8	30.5	36.8	39.0
Capitalization:Preferred	Nil	Nil	Nil	Nil	Nil	Nil	Nil	226	226	332
Capitalization:% Preferred	Nil	Nil	Nil	Nil	Nil	Nil	Nil	2.90	2.80	4.10
Capitalization:Common	8,499	7,537	6,967	6,688	6,015	5,593	5,370	5,126	4,845	4,592
Capitalization:% Common	51.4	48.4	44.4	52.6	54.2	57.1	59.2	66.6	60.4	56.9
Total Capital	19,615	15,645	17,850	14,444	12,629	11,442	10,337	9,159	9,493	10,201
% Operating Ratio	88.6	87.8	87.9	85.7	87.6	86.3	88.0	85.4	85.5	85.5
% Earned on Net Property	6.7	7.1	8.1	9.5	10.3	12.9	18.2	14.0	13.1	9.1
% Return on Revenue	7.5	8.4	9.3	8.4	9.2	9.9	10.8	10.0	9.7	9.6
% Return on Invested Capital	8.6	9.2	8.1	9.0	9.6	9.7	11.4	10.7	9.4	8.5
% Return on Common Equity	11.0	12.0	13.4	10.7	13.5	12.8	13.3	13.3	13.1	12.9

Data as orig reptd.; bef. results of disc opers/spec. items. Per share data adj. for stk. divs.; EPS diluted. E-Estimated. NA-Not Available. NM-Not Meaningful. NR-Not Ranked. UR-Under Review.

Office: 700 Universe Boulevard, Juno Beach, FL 33408-0420.
Telephone: 561-694-4000.
Website: http://www.fplgroup.com
Chrmn, Pres & CEO: L. Hay, III

VP & CFO: M.P. Dewhurst
VP & General Counsel: E.F. Tancer
Chief Acctg Officer: K.M. Davis
Investor Contact: P. Cutler (800-222-4511)

Board of Directors: H. J. Arnelle, S. S. Barrat, R. M. Beall, II, J. H. Brown, J. L. Camaren, J. B. Ferguson, L. Hay, III, R. E. Schupp, M. Thaman, H. E. Tookes, II, P. R. Tregurtha, F. G. Zarb

Founded: 1984
Domicile: Florida
Employees: 12,400

STANDARD & POOR'S

Franklin Resources Inc.

S&P Recommendation STRONG BUY ★★★★★	**Price** $110.90 (as of Oct 27, 2006)	**12-Mo. Target Price** $136.00	**Investment Style** Large-Cap Growth

GICS Sector Financials
Sub-Industry Asset Management & Custody Banks

Comment This company is one of the world's largest asset managers, serving retail, institutional and high-net-worth clients.

Key Stock Statistics (Source S&P, Vickers, company reports)

52-Wk Range	$112.19–80.16	S&P Oper. EPS 2007E	6.05	P/E on S&P Oper. EPS 2007E	18.3	Dividend Rate/Share	$0.48
Trailing 12-Month EPS	$4.86	S&P Oper. EPS 2008E	NA	Common Shares Outstg. (M)	252.6	Yield (%)	0.43
Trailing 12-Month P/E	22.8	S&P Core EPS 2007E	6.05	Market Capitalization(B)	$28.011	Beta	1.08
$10K Invested 5 Yrs Ago	$35,596	S&P Core EPS 2008E	NA	Institutional Ownership (%)	46	S&P Credit Rating	A+

Price Performance

Options: P

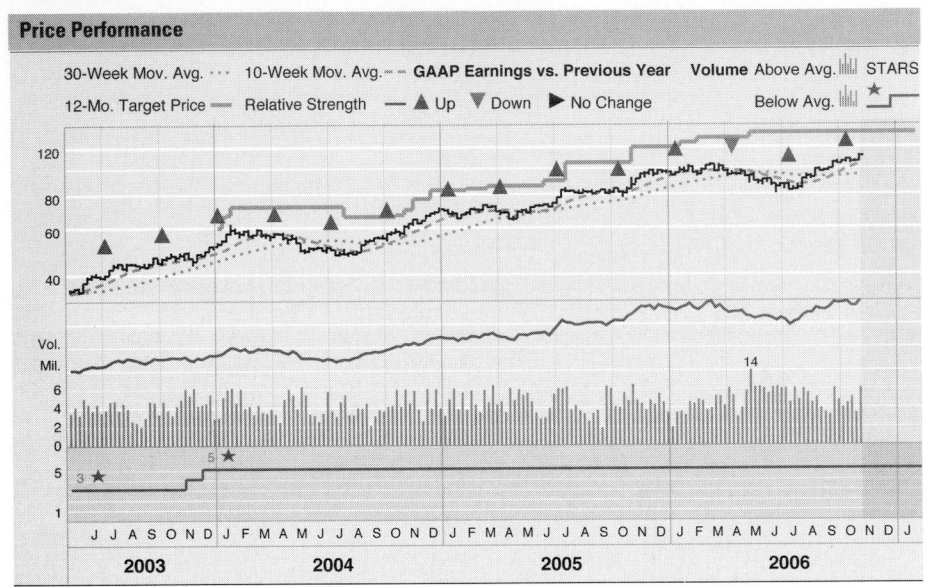

Analysis prepared by **Robert McMillan** on August 03, 2006, when the stock traded at **$ 92.05**.

Highlights

- We believe that BEN's broad product offerings, dominated by value and global investment strategies, have contributed to strong relative investment performance. We think that this, coupled with a continued focus on customer service, has generated a loyal following among its clients and the financial advisers who recommend and distribute its funds. We also see a significant rise in operating margins, aided by prudent expense growth and the continued shift by investors toward higher fee equity and global funds.
- In the third quarter of FY 06 (Sep.), average assets under management rose 19%, to $495 billion, aided by client inflows and market appreciation. We see strong demand for BEN's global investment strategies in FY 07, a competitive strength, in our view. We also expect continued strong inflows into hybrid products, aided by robust demand for BEN's Income Fund.
- We see EPS of $5.37 in FY 06 and $6.05 in FY 07, driven by higher client assets, prudent expense growth, and an expected mix shift toward higher-margin equity and global funds. We expect the company to reallocate about $2 billion in repatriated earnings in FY 06.

Investment Rationale/Risk

- We believe the shares deserve to trade at a higher multiple, based on our view of BEN's consistent net client inflows, strong relative investment performance, and low ratio of debt to total capitalization. We view favorably the company's strong operating free cash flow, but would prefer that the company raise its dividend or repurchase additional shares given increasing cash balances.
- Risks to our recommendation and target price include potential depreciation in global equity, bond and currency markets that can materially affect assets under management and net investor flows. We think the shift by investors toward discount brokerage firms could hurt net inflows, given that BEN's funds typically have front-end sales charges.
- Having declined about 2.6% thus far in 2006, the shares recently traded at about 15X our FY 07 EPS estimate, a significant discount to the company's peer group average. Our 12-month target price of $136 is equal to nearly 23X our FY 07 EPS estimate and is comparable to peers. We have a strong buy recommendation on the shares, as we see BEN gaining market share.

Qualitative Risk Assessment

LOW | MEDIUM | HIGH

Our risk assessment reflects our view of the company's strong relative investment performance, consistent net client inflows, and low ratio of debt to total capitalization.

Quantitative Evaluations

S&P Quality Ranking A-

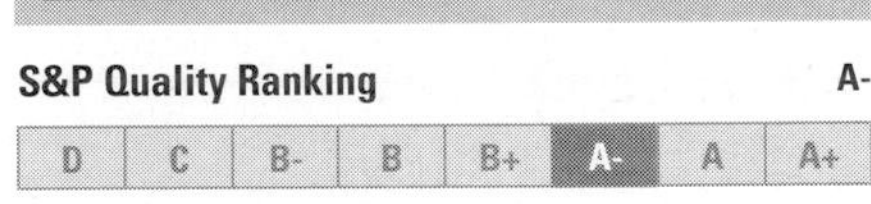

Relative Strength Rank STRONG

82

LOWEST = 1 HIGHEST = 99

Revenue/Earnings Data

Revenue (Million $)

	1Q	2Q	3Q	4Q	Year
2006	1,181	1,255	1,317	1,297	5,051
2005	986.0	1,051	1,110	1,163	4,310
2004	809.7	879.0	867.8	881.7	3,438
2003	605.5	613.1	683.9	722.0	2,624
2002	618.2	626.0	666.1	608.3	2,519
2001	564.1	577.4	609.5	603.9	2,355

Earnings Per Share ($)

2006	1.21	0.74	1.41	1.49	4.86
2005	0.92	0.85	1.00	1.28	4.06
2004	0.67	0.68	0.69	0.74	2.78
2003	0.43	0.43	0.52	0.61	1.97
2002	0.45	0.46	0.48	0.26	1.65
2001	0.61	0.54	0.46	0.32	1.91

Fiscal year ended Sep. 30. Next earnings report expected: Late January. EPS Estimates based on S&P Operating Earnings; historical GAAP earnings are as reported.

Dividend Data (Dates: mm/dd Payment Date: mm/dd/yy)

Amount ($)	Date Decl.	Ex-Div. Date	Stk. of Record	Payment Date
0.120	12/16	12/28	12/30	01/13/06
0.120	03/14	03/29	03/31	04/13/06
0.120	06/20	06/30	07/05	07/14/06
0.120	09/20	10/02	10/04	10/13/06

Dividends have been paid since 1981. Source: Company reports.

Franklin Resources Inc.

Business Summary August 03, 2006

CORPORATE OVERVIEW. Franklin Resources is one of the largest U.S. money managers, with $453.1 billion in assets under management at the end of FY 05 (Sep.), up from $361.9 billion at the end of FY 04. At the end of FY 05, equity-based investments accounted for 58% of assets under management, fixed income investments 23%, hybrid funds 17%, and money funds 1%. Global equity and fixed income accounted for 45% of assets under management. We think that a potential decline in the dollar relative to other major currencies would aid BEN, as we estimate that roughly 47% of client assets are invested in global products. We estimate that about 25% of assets under management are from non-U.S. shareholders.

The company's sponsored investment products are distributed under five distinct names: Franklin, Templeton, Mutual Series, Bisset and Fiduciary. We are impressed with BEN's broad range of investment products, but think the company lacks a compelling roster of growth equity products. BEN has targeted key market segments including retail (76% of assets at the end of FY 05), institutional (22%), and high net-worth (2%).

CORPORATE STRATEGY. Despite its acquisitive history, we think BEN's management favors organic growth. We believe that the interests of BEN's management are closely aligned with those of shareholders given that directors, director nominees and executive officers as a group owned about 35% of the common shares outstanding as of November 30, 2005. We expect that BEN would be opportunistic should it pursue any acquisitions, given significant insider ownership at the company.

Through several acquisitions, BEN has shifted its asset mix from predominantly fixed-income securities toward equity-based investments. In April 2001, BEN acquired Fiduciary Trust Co. International, an investment management company catering to high net worth and institutional clients, for about $776 million. In 1996, BEN acquired certain assets and liabilities of Heine Securities Corp., which managed the value-oriented Mutual Series funds. The Templeton funds were acquired in 1992, with the purchase of Templeton, Galbraith & Hansberger.

Company Financials

Per Share Data ($) Year Ended Sep. 30	**2006**	**2005**	**2004**	**2003**	**2002**	**2001**	**2000**	**1999**	**1998**	**1997**
Tangible Book Value	NA	14.39	12.23	9.31	8.69	7.23	7.37	5.79	4.08	5.00
Cash Flow	NA	5.02	3.51	2.67	2.35	2.79	3.13	2.48	2.74	4.40
Earnings	4.86	4.06	2.78	1.97	1.65	1.91	2.28	1.69	1.98	1.72
S&P Core Earnings	NA	3.97	2.47	1.70	1.56	1.61	NA	NA	NA	NA
Dividends	0.36	0.40	0.33	0.29	0.28	0.26	0.24	0.22	0.20	0.17
Payout Ratio	7%	10%	12%	15%	17%	14%	11%	13%	10%	10%
Prices:High	112.19	98.86	71.45	52.25	44.48	48.30	45.63	45.00	57.88	51.91
Prices:Low	80.16	63.56	46.85	29.99	27.90	30.85	24.63	27.00	25.75	22.08
P/E Ratio:High	23	24	26	27	27	25	20	27	29	30
P/E Ratio:Low	16	16	17	15	17	16	11	16	13	13

Income Statement Analysis (Million $)										
Income Interest	NA	NA	NA	NA	NA	NA	NA	NA	NA	NA
Income Other	NA	NA	NA	NA	NA	NA	NA	NA	NA	NA
Total Income	NA	4,310	3,438	2,624	2,519	2,355	2,340	2,262	2,577	2,163
General Expenses	NA	3,004	NA	NA	NA	NA	NA	NA	NA	NA
Interest Expense	NA	34.0	30.7	19.9	12.3	10.6	14.0	21.0	22.5	25.3
Depreciation	NA	17.5	NA	NA	NA	NA	200	200	191	124
Net Income	NA	1,058	702	503	433	485	562	427	500	434
S&P Core Earnings	NA	1,033	622	432	410	407	NA	NA	NA	NA

Balance Sheet & Other Financial Data (Million $)										
Cash	NA	3,152	2,917	1,054	981	569	746	819	537	435
Receivables	NA	549	444	441	393	603	693	552	318	438
Cost of Investments	NA	1,566	NA	NA	NA	NA	NA	NA	NA	NA
Total Assets	NA	8,894	8,228	6,971	6,423	6,266	4,042	3,667	3,480	3,095
Loss Reserve	NA	Nil	NA	NA	NA	NA	NA	NA	NA	NA
Short Term Debt	NA	169	NA	0.29	7.80	NA	NA	NA	NA	NA
Capitalization:Debt	NA	1,208	1,196	1,109	595	566	294	294	612	493
Capitalization:Equity	NA	5,684	5,107	4,310	4,267	3,978	2,965	2,657	2,281	1,854
Capitalization:Total	NA	7,204	6,615	5,622	5,037	4,544	3,260	2,951	2,775	2,347
Price Times Book Value:High	NA	6.9	NA	5.5	5.1	NA	NA	NA	NA	NA
Price Times Book Value:Low	NA	4.4	NA	3.2	3.2	NA	NA	NA	NA	NA
Cash Flow	NA	1,075	NA	NA	NA	NA	762	627	691	558
% Expense/Operating Revenue	NA	70.1	NA	NA	NA	NA	NA	NA	NA	NA
% Earnings & Depreciation/Assets	NA	12.6	NA	NA	NA	NA	NA	NA	NA	NA

Data as orig reptd.; bef. results of disc opers/spec. items. Per share data adj. for stk. divs.; EPS diluted. E-Estimated. NA-Not Available. NM-Not Meaningful. NR-Not Ranked. UR-Under Review.

Office: One Franklin Parkway, San Mateo, CA 94403.
Telephone: 650-312-2000.
Website: http://www.franklintempleton.com
Chrmn: C.B. Johnson

Pres & CEO: G.E. Johnson
Vice Chrmn: H.E. Burns
Vice Chrmn: R.H. Johnson, Jr.
Vice Chrmn: A.M. Tatlock

Board of Directors: S. H. Armacost, H. E. Burns, C. Crocker, J. R. Hardiman, R. Joffe, C. B. Johnson, R. H. Johnson, Jr., T. Kean, C. Ratnathicam, P. M. Sacerdote, L. Stein, A. M. Tatlock, L. E. Woodworth

Founded: 1947
Domicile: Delaware
Employees: 7,156

STANDARD &POOR'S

Freeport-McMoran Copper & Gold Inc.

S&P Recommendation BUY ★★★★★

Price $59.05 (as of Oct 27, 2006)

12-Mo. Target Price $70.00

Investment Style Large-Cap Growth

GICS Sector Materials
Sub-Industry Diversified Metals & Mining

Comment This company explores for, mines and mills copper, gold and silver in Indonesia, and has a copper smelting and refining operation in Spain.

Key Stock Statistics (Source S&P, Vickers, company reports)

52-Wk Range	$72.20–43.10	S&P Oper. EPS 2006E	6.43	P/E on S&P Oper. EPS 2006E	9.2	Dividend Rate/Share	$1.25
Trailing 12-Month EPS	$6.83	S&P Oper. EPS 2007E	5.45	Common Shares Outstg. (M)	196.5	Yield (%)	2.12
Trailing 12-Month P/E	8.7	S&P Core EPS 2006E	6.19	Market Capitalization(B)	$11.601	Beta	1.34
$10K Invested 5 Yrs Ago	$65,509	S&P Core EPS 2007E	5.03	Institutional Ownership (%)	88	S&P Credit Rating	BB-

Price Performance

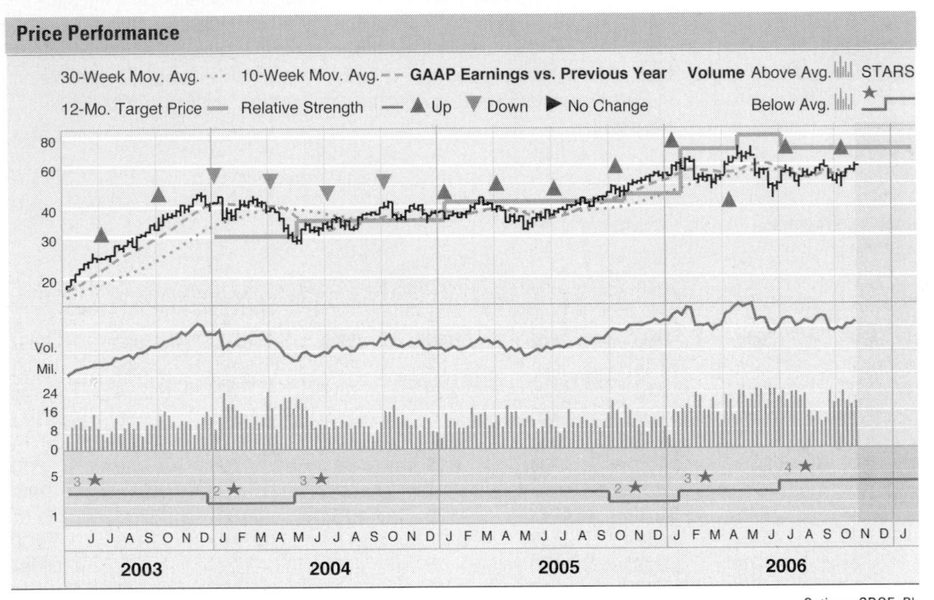

Options: CBOE, Ph

Analysis prepared by **Leo J. Larkin** on October 10, 2006, when the stock traded at **$ 54.21**.

Highlights

- Following a sales gain of 76% in 2005, we anticipate a 45% increase in sales in 2006 as a higher price for copper offsets a lower volume of production in 2006 compared with 2005. In 2005, copper production totaled 1.46 billion lbs. and gold output totaled 2.8 million oz. For 2006, copper production is projected to total 1.2 billion lbs. and gold output is expected to decline to 1.7 million oz. However, given our expectation for a higher average price for copper, sales should increase despite a forecast for a decline in output.

- Despite lower volume, reduced by-product credits and costs for deferred stripping, margins will likely expand as a result of higher revenue per pound. Benefiting further from lower interest expense and a lower tax rate, we project an increase in operating EPS to $6.20 in 2006. Assuming a lower copper price in 2007 and a small decline in production, we estimate a decline in EPS in 2007 to $5.05.

- We expect long-term EPS to benefit from a secular rise in copper demand, share repurchases, and a decline in interest expense resulting from a projected decrease in total debt.

Investment Rationale/Risk

- Aided by a steady increase in sales and EPS from 2000 through the second quarter of 2006, FCX reinstated its dividend and reduced debt substantially. In 2004, 2005 and 2006, FCX paid supplemental dividends and repurchased shares. Based on our expectation for generally higher EPS and free cash flow in the years ahead, we believe FCX should be able to increase shareholder value by increasing its dividend, reducing debt or repurchasing shares. In our view, EPS and cash flow will trend higher as growth in demand for copper is likely to exceed the rate of gain in supply. We see this occurring due to the absence of new large mines coming on stream and lower production from existing mines due to depletion.

- Risks to our opinion and target price include a drop in the price of copper in 2007 in excess of what we currently project and the risk posed by having all of FCX's mining assets in Indonesia.

- Our 12-month target price of $70 assumes that FCX will sell at 13.9X our 2007 EPS estimate, which is high for a copper stock but low for a gold company. Our target P/E is at the low end of the historical range of the past 10 years.

Qualitative Risk Assessment

LOW | MEDIUM | **HIGH**

Our risk assessment reflects the concentration of FCX's mining assets in Indonesia, the exposure of its earnings per share to copper and gold, both cyclical commodities, and its stagnant reserve profile. Partially offsetting this is the large debt reduction seen in recent years and solid free cash flow generation.

Quantitative Evaluations

S&P Quality Ranking B

D | C | B- | **B** | B+ | A- | A | A+

Relative Strength Rank STRONG

75

LOWEST = 1 HIGHEST = 99

Revenue/Earnings Data

Revenue (Million $)

	1Q	2Q	3Q	4Q	Year
2006	1,086	1,426	1,636	--	--
2005	803.1	902.9	1,490	--	4,179
2004	360.2	486.3	600.6	924.8	2,372
2003	524.6	609.5	632.0	446.1	2,212
2002	392.7	408.0	538.7	571.0	1,910
2001	447.1	538.3	441.2	412.3	1,839

Earnings Per Share ($)

2006	1.23	1.74	1.67	**E**1.81	**E**6.43
2005	0.70	0.91	0.86	2.19	4.67
2004	-0.10	-0.30	0.10	1.08	0.85
2003	0.28	0.37	0.41	Nil	1.07
2002	-0.01	0.04	0.39	0.41	0.89
2001	0.26	0.25	0.03	-0.01	0.53

Fiscal year ended Dec. 31. Next earnings report expected: Mid January. EPS Estimates based on S&P Operating Earnings; historical GAAP earnings are as reported.

Dividend Data (Dates: mm/dd Payment Date: mm/dd/yy)

Amount ($)	Date Decl.	Ex-Div. Date	Stk. of Record	Payment Date
.75 Spl.	05/02	06/13	06/15	06/30/06
0.313	07/05	07/13	07/17	08/01/06
.75 Spl.	08/01	09/12	09/14	09/29/06
0.313	10/04	10/12	10/16	11/01/06

Dividends have been paid since 2003. Source: Company reports.

Freeport-McMoran Copper & Gold Inc.

Business Summary October 10, 2006

Freeport-McMoRan Copper & Gold is one of the world's largest and lowest cost copper and gold producers. The company conducts mining operations in Indonesia through majority-owned subsidiaries PT Freeport Indonesia Co. (PT-FI) and PT IRJA Eastern Minerals Corp. FCX is also engaged in copper smelting and refining through Atlantic Copper Holding, S.A., and PT Smelting.

Mill throughput was 216,200 metric tons in 2005, versus 185,100 metric tons in 2004. Copper cash production costs were $0.07 a lb. in 2005, versus $0.40 a lb. in 2004.

Copper sales amounted to 1,456,500,000 lbs. in 2005 at an average price of $1.85 a lb., versus 991,600,000 lbs. in 2004 at an average price of $1.37 a lb.

Gold sales totaled 2,790,200 oz. in 2005 at an average price of $456.27 an oz., versus 1,443,000 oz. in 2004 at an average price of $412.32 an oz.

Company Financials

Per Share Data ($) Year Ended Dec. 31	**2005**	**2004**	**2003**	**2002**	**2001**	**2000**	**1999**	**1998**	**1997**	**1996**
Tangible Book Value	3.98	0.36	4.23	NM	NM	NM	NM	NM	NM	1.61
Cash Flow	5.38	1.96	2.52	2.67	2.49	2.09	2.39	2.25	2.32	2.03
Earnings	4.67	0.85	1.07	0.89	0.53	0.26	0.61	0.67	1.06	0.89
S&P Core Earnings	4.63	0.48	1.03	0.84	0.49	NA	NA	NA	NA	NA
Dividends	1.25	0.85	0.27	Nil	Nil	Nil	Nil	0.20	0.90	0.90
Payout Ratio	27%	100%	25%	Nil	Nil	Nil	Nil	30%	85%	101%
Prices:High	56.35	44.90	46.74	20.83	17.15	21.44	21.38	21.44	34.88	36.13
Prices:Low	31.52	27.76	16.01	9.95	8.31	6.75	9.13	9.81	14.94	27.38
P/E Ratio:High	12	53	44	23	32	82	35	32	33	41
P/E Ratio:Low	7	33	15	11	16	26	15	15	14	31

Income Statement Analysis (Million $)	**2005**	**2004**	**2003**	**2002**	**2001**	**2000**	**1999**	**1998**	**1997**	**1996**
Revenue	4,179	2,372	2,212	1,910	1,839	1,869	1,887	1,757	2,001	1,905
Operating Income	2,429	823	1,054	901	827	778	876	852	878	812
Depreciation	252	206	231	260	284	284	293	277	214	174
Interest Expense	132	148	197	171	174	205	194	225	175	140
Pretax Income	2,037	574	584	450	359	273	381	361	517	522
Effective Tax Rate	44.9%	57.6%	57.9%	54.6%	56.6%	58.4%	51.4%	47.2%	44.8%	47.3%
Net Income	995	202	197	168	113	77.0	136	154	245	226
S&P Core Earnings	919	77.7	167	123	70.8	NA	NA	NA	NA	NA

Balance Sheet & Other Financial Data (Million $)	**2005**	**2004**	**2003**	**2002**	**2001**	**2000**	**1999**	**1998**	**1997**	**1996**
Cash	764	551	464	7.84	7.59	7.97	6.70	5.90	9.00	37.1
Current Assets	2,022	1,460	1,100	638	548	569	564	46.0	463	661
Total Assets	5,550	5,087	4,718	4,192	4,212	3,951	4,083	4,193	4,152	3,866
Current Liabilities	1,369	698	632	538	628	634	515	518	476	598
Long Term Debt	1,003	1,874	2,076	1,961	2,133	1,988	2,033	2,329	2,308	1,426
Common Equity	743	63.6	776	-83.2	-246	-312	-153	-247	-71.1	325
Total Capital	3,971	4,189	3,925	3,514	3,464	3,204	3,453	3,599	3,551	3,066
Capital Expenditures	143	141	139	188	167	292	161	292	595	490
Cash Flow	1,186	363	401	391	360	323	394	395	459	400
Current Ratio	1.5	2.1	1.7	1.2	0.9	0.9	1.1	1.1	1.0	1.1
% Long Term Debt of Capitalization	25.2	44.7	52.9	55.8	61.6	62.0	58.9	64.7	65.0	46.5
% Net Income of Revenue	23.8	8.5	8.9	8.8	6.1	4.1	7.2	8.8	12.2	11.9
% Return on Assets	18.7	4.1	4.4	4.0	2.8	1.9	3.3	3.7	6.1	7.1
% Return on Equity	231.7	37.3	49.0	NM	NM	NA	NM	NM	NM	56.7

Data as orig reptd.; bef. results of disc opers/spec. items. Per share data adj. for stk. divs.; EPS diluted. E-Estimated. NA-Not Available. NM-Not Meaningful. NR-Not Ranked. UR-Under Review.

Office: 1615 Poydras Street, New Orleans, LA 70112-1254.
Telephone: 504-582-4000.
Email: ir@fmi.com
Website: http://www.fcx.com

Chrmn: J.R. Moffett
Pres & CEO: R.C. Adkerson
Vice Chrmn: B.M. Rankin, Jr.
COO & SVP: M.J. Johnson

SVP, CFO & Treas: K.L. Quirk
Board of Directors: R. J. Allison, Jr., R. A. Day, G. J. Ford, H. D. Graham, Jr., J. B. Johnston, B. L. Lackey, G. K. McDonald, J. R. Moffett, B. M. Rankin, J. S. Roy, S. H. Siegele, J. T. Wharton

Founded: 1987
Domicile: Delaware
Employees: 8,738

STANDARD &POOR'S

Freescale Semiconductor Inc

S&P Recommendation HOLD ★★★★★

Price $39.32 (as of Oct 27, 2006)

12-Mo. Target Price $40.00

Investment Style Large-Cap Value

GICS Sector Information Technology
Sub-Industry Semiconductors

Comment This global semiconductor company provides embedded processing and connectivity products to the automotive, networking, and wireless communications industries.

Key Stock Statistics (Source S&P, Vickers, company reports)

52-Wk Range	$39.54–23.22	S&P Oper. EPS 2006E	2.30	P/E on S&P Oper. EPS 2006E	17.1	Dividend Rate/Share	Nil
Trailing 12-Month EPS	$2.15	S&P Oper. EPS 2007E	2.40	Common Shares Outstg. (M)	405.8	Yield (%)	Nil
Trailing 12-Month P/E	18.3	S&P Core EPS 2006E	2.30	Market Capitalization(B)	$10.616	Beta	1.00
$10K Invested 5 Yrs Ago	NA	S&P Core EPS 2007E	2.40	Institutional Ownership (%)	82	S&P Credit Rating	BB+

Price Performance

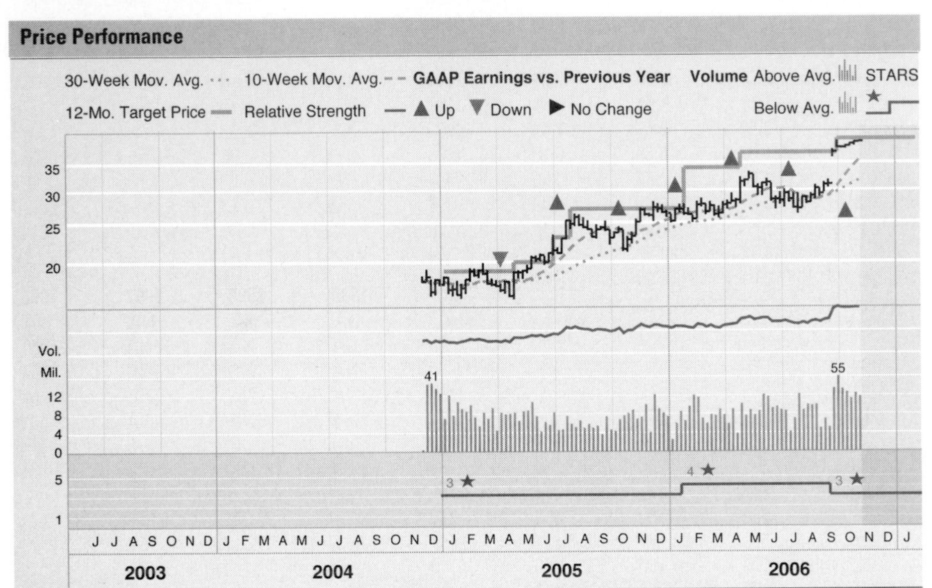

Analysis prepared by **Thomas W. Smith, CFA** on September 18, 2006, when the stock traded at **$ 39.23**.

Highlights

- We see revenues advancing 10% in 2006 and 9% in 2007. Orders rose 14%, year to year, in the second quarter, indicating likely growth ahead. We expect the Wireless and Mobile Solutions Group to lead other segments in sales performance in the near term.
- Gross margins have widened in recent quarters as plant utilization increased. We project a further improvement in gross margins as the company sharpens its product focus and depreciation charges are reduced. We see gross margins widening to 46% in 2006 and 47% in 2007, from 42% in 2005. We project operating margins of 15% in 2006, versus 11% in 2005. Debt reduction in recent quarters should help reduce interest expense. We model an effective tax rate of 8% for 2006 and 20% for 2007, which is lower than many peers; the effective tax rate reflects international profits taxed at lower than U.S. rates.
- We estimate EPS of $2.22 for 2006 and $2.30 for 2007, both including projected stock-based compensation expense.

Investment Rationale/Risk

- We recently lowered our recommendation to hold, from buy, following Freescale's September 11 announcement that it was in discussions related to a possible business transaction, and a one-day increase of about 20% in the share price. On September 15, the company announced its agreement to be acquired by a private equity consortium led by The Blackstone Group in a $17.6 billion planned deal. The consortium would pay $40 a share in cash for all Freescale class A and class B shares under the proposed merger plan, which is subject to necessary approvals, including a vote by Freescale shareholders.
- Risks to our opinion and target price include the possibility that the proposed merger might not occur. An ongoing risk is Freescale's reliance on a single large customer--Motorola--which accounted for 27% of sales in 2005.
- Our 12-month target price of $40 is in line with the acquisition price that was agreed to by the Blackstone-led consortium.

Qualitative Risk Assessment

LOW | MEDIUM | **HIGH**

Freescale is subject to the sales cycles of the semiconductor industry, demand trends in wireless communications, and buying patterns of several big customers. While the company had a long corporate history as part of Motorola, we believe it faces new marketing challenges and opportunities as a stand-alone chipmaker.

Quantitative Evaluations

S&P Quality Ranking NR

D | C | B- | B | B+ | A- | A | A+

Relative Strength Rank STRONG

87

LOWEST = 1 HIGHEST = 99

Revenue/Earnings Data

Revenue (Million $)

	1Q	2Q	3Q	4Q	Year
2006	1,526	1,599	1,619	--	--
2005	1,442	1,472	1,450	1,479	5,843
2004	1,396	1,461	1,430	1,428	5,715
2003	1,151	1,115	1,225	1,373	4,864
2002	--	--	--	--	--
2001	--	--	--	--	--

Earnings Per Share ($)

	1Q	2Q	3Q	4Q	Year
2006	0.48	0.61	0.61	E0.60	E2.30
2005	0.20	0.29	0.38	0.45	1.33
2004	0.28	0.15	0.15	0.01	0.62
2003	--	--	--	--	-0.78
2002	--	--	--	--	--
2001	--	--	--	--	--

Fiscal year ended Dec. 31. Next earnings report expected: Mid January. EPS Estimates based on S&P Operating Earnings; historical GAAP earnings are as reported.

Dividend Data

No cash dividends have been paid.

Freescale Semiconductor Inc

Business Summary September 18, 2006

Freescale is a global semiconductor company focused on providing embedded processing and connectivity products to large, high-growth markets. Based in Austin, Texas, and operating in 30 countries, the company is currently focused on providing products to the automotive, consumer, industrial, networking, and wireless communications industries.

In their simplest forms, embedded processors provide the basic intelligence for electronic devices and can be programmed to address specific applications or functions. Examples of Freescale's embedded processors include microprocessors, digital signal processors, and communications processors. In addition to its embedded processors, the company also offers a portfolio of complementary devices that facilitate connectivity between products, across networks, and to real-world signals, such as sound, vibration and pressure. These complementary devices include sensors, radio frequency semiconductors, power management and other analog and mixed-signal integrated circuits. Through complex combinations of its embedded processors and complementary products, Freescale offers its customers platform-level products.

Freescale has three primary segments: the Transportation and Standard Products Group (TSPG), the Networking and Computing Systems Group (NCSG), and the Wireless and Mobile Solutions Group (WMSG). TSPG (44% of total 2005 sales) provides products for the automotive electronics, industrial and other markets. Over 70% of TSPG's sales were made to the automotive market in 2005. NCSG (25%) supplies products to the wired and wireless infrastructure and embedded computing markets. WMSG (30%) provides products for wireless mobile devices. Over 90% of WMSG revenue in 2005 came from cellular handsets and Motorola was the largest customer with 69% of WMSG sales. In addition, the company has an Other business segment (1%) that includes all of its other operations, including sales of wafers to other chipmakers.

Company Financials

Per Share Data ($) Year Ended Dec. 31	**2005**	**2004**	**2003**	**2002**	**2001**	**2000**	**1999**	**1998**	**1997**	**1996**
Tangible Book Value	10.30	9.11	8.43	NA	NA	NA	NA	NA	NA	NA
Cash Flow	2.96	4.76	1.41	NA	NA	NA	NA	NA	NA	NA
Earnings	1.33	0.62	-0.78	NA	NA	NA	NA	NA	NA	NA
S&P Core Earnings	1.10	0.62	-1.91	NA	NA	NA	NA	NA	NA	NA
Dividends	Nil	Nil	NA	NA	NA	NA	NA	NA	NA	NA
Payout Ratio	Nil	Nil	NA	NA	NA	NA	NA	NA	NA	NA
Prices:High	28.11	19.20	NA	NA	NA	NA	NA	NA	NA	NA
Prices:Low	16.20	16.49	NA	NA	NA	NA	NA	NA	NA	NA
P/E Ratio:High	21	31	NA	NA	NA	NA	NA	NA	NA	NA
P/E Ratio:Low	12	27	NA	NA	NA	NA	NA	NA	NA	NA
Income Statement Analysis (Million $)										
Revenue	5,843	5,715	4,864	NA	NA	NA	NA	NA	NA	NA
Operating Income	1,310	1,116	617	NA	NA	NA	NA	NA	NA	NA
Depreciation	691	740	858	NA	NA	NA	NA	NA	NA	NA
Interest Expense	85.0	31.0	NA	NA	NA	NA	NA	NA	NA	NA
Pretax Income	613	263	-265	NA	NA	NA	NA	NA	NA	NA
Effective Tax Rate	8.16%	19.8%	NM	NA	NA	NA	NA	NA	NA	NA
Net Income	563	211	-312	NA	NA	NA	NA	NA	NA	NA
S&P Core Earnings	465	125	-531	-1,852	NA	NA	NA	NA	NA	NA
Balance Sheet & Other Financial Data (Million $)										
Cash	1,421	2,374	1,755	NA	NA	NA	NA	NA	NA	NA
Current Assets	2,970	4,001	3,168	NA	NA	NA	NA	NA	NA	NA
Total Assets	7,170	6,622	5,794	NA	NA	NA	NA	NA	NA	NA
Current Liabilities	1,139	1,161	614	NA	NA	NA	NA	NA	NA	NA
Long Term Debt	1,230	1,250	1,250	NA	NA	NA	NA	NA	NA	NA
Common Equity	4,447	3,936	3,651	NA	NA	NA	NA	NA	NA	NA
Total Capital	5,677	5,212	4,936	NA	NA	NA	NA	NA	NA	NA
Capital Expenditures	491	522	NA	NA	NA	NA	NA	NA	NA	NA
Cash Flow	1,254	951	546	NA	NA	NA	NA	NA	NA	NA
Current Ratio	2.6	3.4	5.2	NA	NA	NA	NA	NA	NA	NA
% Long Term Debt of Capitalization	21.7	24.0	25.3	NA	NA	NA	NA	NA	NA	NA
% Net Income of Revenue	9.6	3.7	NM	NA	NA	NA	NA	NA	NA	NA
% Return on Assets	8.1	3.8	NA	NA	NA	NA	NA	NA	NA	NA
% Return on Equity	13.4	5.6	NA	NA	NA	NA	NA	NA	NA	NA

Data as orig reptd.; bef. results of disc opers/spec. items. Per share data adj. for stk. divs.; EPS diluted. E-Estimated. NA-Not Available. NM-Not Meaningful. NR-Not Ranked. UR-Under Review.

Office: 6501 William Cannon Drive West, Austin, TX 78735.
Telephone: 512-895-2000.
Website: http://www.freescale.com
Chrmn & CEO: M. Mayer

SVP & CFO: A. Campbell
SVP & CTO: C. Simson
SVP, Secy & General Counsel: J.D. Torres
VP & Treas: G. Heinlein

Investor Contact: M. Haws (512-895-2454)
Board of Directors: H. R. Bingham, S. P. Kaufman, K. Kennedy, M. Mayer, A. M. Perez, K. A. Prabhu, B. K. West

Founded: 1953
Domicile: Delaware
Employees: 22,700

STANDARD & POOR'S

Gannett Co Inc.

S&P Recommendation HOLD ★★★★★

Price $60.29 (as of Oct 27, 2006)

12-Mo. Target Price $58.00

Investment Style Large-Cap Growth

GICS Sector Consumer Discretionary
Sub-Industry Publishing

Comment Gannett publishes about 100 daily U.S. newspapers, more than 750 non-daily publications in the U.S. and Guam, and some 300 U.K. titles, and operates 21 TV stations in the U.S.

Key Stock Statistics (Source S&P, Vickers, company reports)

52-Wk Range	$66.16–51.65	S&P Oper. EPS 2006**E**	4.92	P/E on S&P Oper. EPS 2006**E**	12.3	Dividend Rate/Share	$1.24
Trailing 12-Month EPS	$4.83	S&P Oper. EPS 2007**E**	4.96	Common Shares Outstg. (M)	236.4	Yield (%)	2.06
Trailing 12-Month P/E	12.5	S&P Core EPS 2006**E**	4.83	Market Capitalization(B)	$14.251	Beta	0.42
$10K Invested 5 Yrs Ago	$9,980	S&P Core EPS 2007**E**	4.87	Institutional Ownership (%)	83	S&P Credit Rating	A

Price Performance

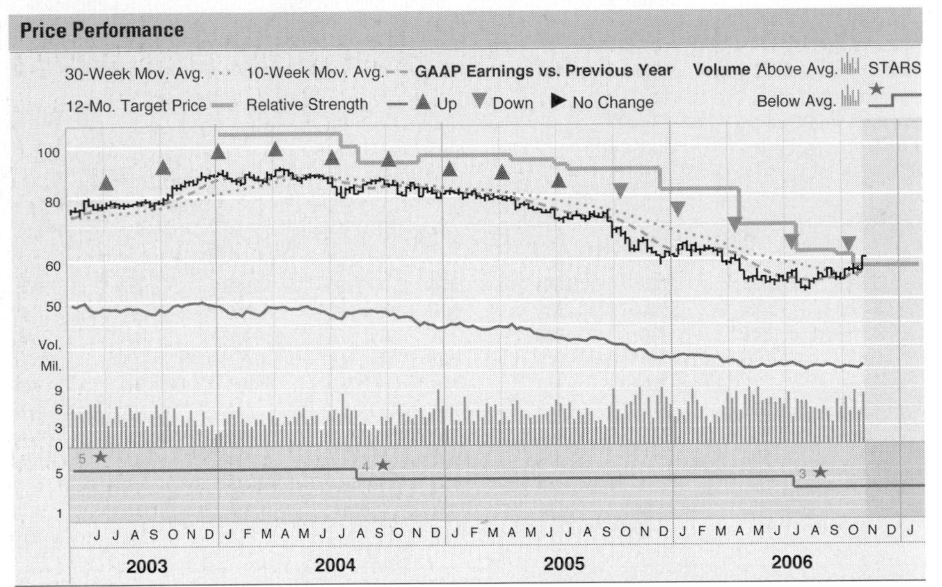

Options: P

Analysis prepared by **James Peters, CFA** on October 13, 2006, when the stock traded at **$ 57.07**.

Highlights

- For 2006, we forecast revenue growth of approximately 3.1%, led by anticipated advertising gains from mid-term political elections in the fourth quarter. Looking to 2007, we see modest revenue growth of about 1.4%, buoyed by strong gains in online revenues. We expect publishing revenues to remain soft due to our weak outlook for US classified advertising. We also believe the company's Newsquest operations will struggle due to the continued economic sluggishness we foresee in the UK. We see organic broadcast revenues falling slightly on tough political revenue comparisons.
- We see a slight operating margin expansion in 2007 to 25.6%, up from the 25.2% we foresee for 2006. We see gains coming from modest improvement at the company's Detroit operations and from lower energy costs. We also expect paper price increases to moderate.
- After higher anticipated interest expense, we estimate 2006 EPS of $4.92. Our 2006 S&P Core EPS estimate of $4.83 reflects $0.09 of pension adjustments. We expect GCI to continue to use free cash flow for Internet acquisitions and for media properties that create duopolies.

Investment Rationale/Risk

- We think GCI will ultimately be successful in transitioning to a more internet based media company, and think the company will generate strong revenue growth in 2007 from its online initiatives. We also believe ratings improvements at NBC will provide a boost for the broadcasting division in the upcoming year. However, with continued near term investments we foresee to support its Internet transition and with our outlook for continued economic weakness in the Detroit region and in the UK, we see no near term catalyst for the stock.
- Risks to our recommendation and target price include worse than anticipated weakness in Great Britain; drops in audience ratings at network-affiliated TV stations; and a weakening of the British pound versus the U.S. dollar.
- Our 12-month target price is $58, derived by applying a peer average EBITDA multiple of 8.1X to our 2007 EBITDA estimate of $2.35 billion. The multiple represents a significant discount to GCI's historical 10.7X EBITDA multiple, which we think is warranted by slower near-term EPS growth prospects we foresee.

Qualitative Risk Assessment

LOW | **MEDIUM** | HIGH

Our risk assessment reflects our view of a highly competitive advertising environment, offset by the company's consistently strong free cash flow and profitability, and its relatively low weighted average cost of capital.

Quantitative Evaluations

S&P Quality Ranking A

D | C | B- | B | B+ | A- | **A** | A+

Relative Strength Rank STRONG

77

LOWEST = 1 HIGHEST = 99

Revenue/Earnings Data

Revenue (Million $)

	1Q	2Q	3Q	4Q	Year
2006	882.5	2,028	1,915	--	--
2005	1,768	1,911	1,865	2,055	7,599
2004	1,730	1,873	1,816	1,962	7,381
2003	1,552	1,705	1,631	1,822	6,711
2002	1,513	1,613	1,570	1,726	6,422
2001	1,575	1,627	1,518	1,624	6,344

Earnings Per Share ($)

	1Q	2Q	3Q	4Q	Year
2006	0.99	1.31	1.11	**E**1.52	**E**4.92
2005	1.03	1.34	1.13	1.44	4.92
2004	1.00	1.30	1.18	1.47	4.92
2003	0.93	1.20	1.03	1.31	4.46
2002	0.91	1.13	0.99	1.29	4.31
2001	0.66	0.88	0.66	0.93	3.12

Fiscal year ended Dec. 31. Next earnings report expected: Late January. EPS Estimates based on S&P Operating Earnings; historical GAAP earnings are as reported.

Dividend Data (Dates: mm/dd Payment Date: mm/dd/yy)

Amount ($)	Date Decl.	Ex-Div. Date	Stk. of Record	Payment Date
0.290	02/21	03/08	03/10	04/03/06
0.290	04/18	06/07	06/09	07/03/06
0.310	07/25	09/13	09/15	10/02/06
0.310	10/24	12/13	12/15	01/02/07

Dividends have been paid since 1929. Source: Company reports.

Gannett Co Inc.

Business Summary October 13, 2006

Gannett is a diversified news and information company that publishes newspapers, operates broadcasting stations, operates Web sites in connection with its newspaper and broadcast operations, and is engaged in marketing, commercial printing, a newswire service, data services, and news programming. Approximately 85% of 2005 revenues were from domestic operations in 41 states, the District of Columbia and Guam, and approximately 15% of revenues were from foreign operations, primarily in the U.K.

The newspaper publishing segment (90% of 2005 revenues) consists of the operations of 108 daily newspapers, nearly 1,000 non-daily publications in the U.S. and Guam, and approximately 300 titles in the U.K. The company's 91 U.S. daily newspapers have a combined circulation of approximately 7.3 million, making it the largest newspaper group in terms of circulation in the U.S. The segment includes the publication of USA TODAY, the nation's largest selling daily newspaper, with a circulation of about 2.3 million. The company's strategy for non-daily publications is to target these products at communities of interest, defined by geography, demographics or life style. In the U.K., the company is the second largest regional publisher via its wholly owned subsidiary Newsquest plc. Newsquest operations generated approximately 17% and 11% of segment advertising and circulation revenues, respectively.

The broadcast segment (10% of 2005 revenues) consists of 21 network-affiliated TV stations, including 12 NBC, six CBS, and three ABC affiliates, and Captivate Network, a national news and entertainment network that delivers programming and full-motion video advertising through video screens located in office tower elevators across North America. The principal sources of GCI's television revenues are: local advertising focusing on the immediate geographic area of the stations; national advertising, compensation paid by the networks for carrying commercial network programs; advertising on the stations' Web sites; and payments by advertisers to television stations for other services, such as the production of advertising material. Captivate derives its revenue principally from national advertising.

Company Financials

Per Share Data ($) Year Ended Dec. 31	**2005**	**2004**	**2003**	**2002**	**2001**	**2000**	**1999**	**1998**	**1997**	**1996**
Tangible Book Value	NM	NM	NM	NM	NM	NM	NM	0.66	NM	NM
Cash Flow	6.24	6.14	5.30	5.13	4.78	4.99	3.87	4.59	3.55	4.36
Earnings	4.92	4.92	4.46	4.31	3.12	3.63	3.26	3.50	2.50	2.21
S&P Core Earnings	4.43	4.45	4.23	3.70	2.39	NA	NA	NA	NA	NA
Dividends	1.12	1.04	0.98	0.94	0.90	0.86	0.81	0.78	0.74	0.71
Payout Ratio	23%	21%	22%	22%	29%	24%	25%	22%	30%	32%
Prices:High	82.41	91.38	89.63	79.90	71.14	81.56	83.63	75.13	61.81	39.38
Prices:Low	58.37	78.84	66.70	62.76	53.00	48.38	60.63	47.63	35.69	29.50
P/E Ratio:High	17	19	20	19	23	22	26	21	25	18
P/E Ratio:Low	12	16	15	15	17	13	19	14	14	13
Income Statement Analysis (Million $)										
Revenue	7,599	7,381	6,711	6,422	6,344	6,222	5,260	5,121	4,729	4,421
Operating Income	2,322	2,392	2,213	2,149	2,034	2,190	1,843	1,754	1,617	1,354
Depreciation	274	244	232	215	444	376	169	310	301	193
Interest Expense	211	141	139	146	222	219	94.6	79.4	98.2	136
Pretax Income	1,818	1,995	1,840	1,765	1,371	1,609	1,527	1,669	1,209	1,087
Effective Tax Rate	33.4%	34.0%	34.2%	34.3%	39.4%	39.6%	39.8%	40.1%	41.1%	42.6%
Net Income	1,211	1,317	1,211	1,160	831	972	919	1,000	713	624
S&P Core Earnings	1,092	1,191	1,150	998	638	NA	NA	NA	NA	NA
Balance Sheet & Other Financial Data (Million $)										
Cash	163	136	67.2	90.4	141	193	46.2	66.2	52.8	27.0
Current Assets	1,462	1,371	1,223	1,133	1,178	1,302	1,075	906	885	767
Total Assets	15,743	15,399	14,706	13,733	13,096	12,980	9,006	6,979	6,890	6,350
Current Liabilities	1,096	1,005	962	959	1,128	1,174	884	728	768	719
Long Term Debt	5,438	4,608	3,835	4,547	5,080	5,748	2,463	1,307	1,741	1,880
Common Equity	7,571	8,164	8,423	6,912	5,736	5,103	4,630	3,980	3,480	2,931
Total Capital	13,897	13,685	13,094	12,138	11,319	11,126	7,572	5,709	5,623	4,811
Capital Expenditures	263	280	281	275	325	351	258	244	221	260
Cash Flow	1,486	1,561	1,443	1,375	1,275	1,348	1,089	1,310	1,014	1,230
Current Ratio	1.3	1.4	1.3	1.2	1.0	1.1	1.2	1.2	1.2	1.1
% Long Term Debt of Capitalization	39.1	33.7	29.3	37.5	44.9	51.7	32.5	22.8	30.9	39.0
% Net Income of Revenue	15.9	17.8	18.0	18.1	13.1	15.6	17.5	19.5	15.1	14.1
% Return on Assets	7.8	8.8	8.5	8.6	6.4	8.8	11.5	14.4	10.8	9.7
% Return on Equity	15.4	15.9	15.8	18.3	15.3	20.0	21.4	26.8	22.2	24.6

Data as orig reptd.; bef. results of disc opers/spec. items. Per share data adj. for stk. divs.; EPS diluted. E-Estimated. NA-Not Available. NM-Not Meaningful. NR-Not Ranked. UR-Under Review.

Office: 7950 Jones Branch Dr, McLean, VA 22107-0910.
Telephone: 703-854-6000.
Email: gcishare@gannett.com
Website: http://www.gannett.com

Chrmn, Pres & CEO: C.A. Dubow
EVP & CFO: G.C. Martore
SVP & General Counsel: K. Wimmer
VP & Treas: M.A. Hart

VP & Secy: T.A. Mayman
Investor Contact: J. Heinz (703-854-6917)
Board of Directors: L. D. Boccardi, C. A. Dubow, J. J. Louis, M. Magner, D. M. McFarland, S. P. Munn, D. Shalala, K. H. Williams

Founded: 1923
Domicile: Delaware
Employees: 52,600

STANDARD &POOR'S

Gap Inc. (The)

S&P Recommendation SELL ★★★★★

Price $20.72 (as of Oct 27, 2006)

12-Mo. Target Price $15.00

Investment Style Large-Cap Growth

GICS Sector Consumer Discretionary
Sub-Industry Apparel Retail

Comment This specialty apparel retailer operates Gap, Banana Republic and Old Navy stores, offering casual clothing to moderate, upper and value-oriented market segments.

Key Stock Statistics (Source S&P, Vickers, company reports)

52-Wk Range	$20.84–15.91	S&P Oper. EPS 2007**E**	1.04	P/E on S&P Oper. EPS 2007**E**	19.9	Dividend Rate/Share	$0.32
Trailing 12-Month EPS	$1.06	S&P Oper. EPS 2008**E**	1.25	Common Shares Outstg. (M)	828.5	Yield (%)	1.54
Trailing 12-Month P/E	19.6	S&P Core EPS 2007**E**	1.04	Market Capitalization(B)	$17.167	Beta	1.35
$10K Invested 5 Yrs Ago	$15,528	S&P Core EPS 2008**E**	1.25	Institutional Ownership (%)	59	S&P Credit Rating	BBB-

Price Performance

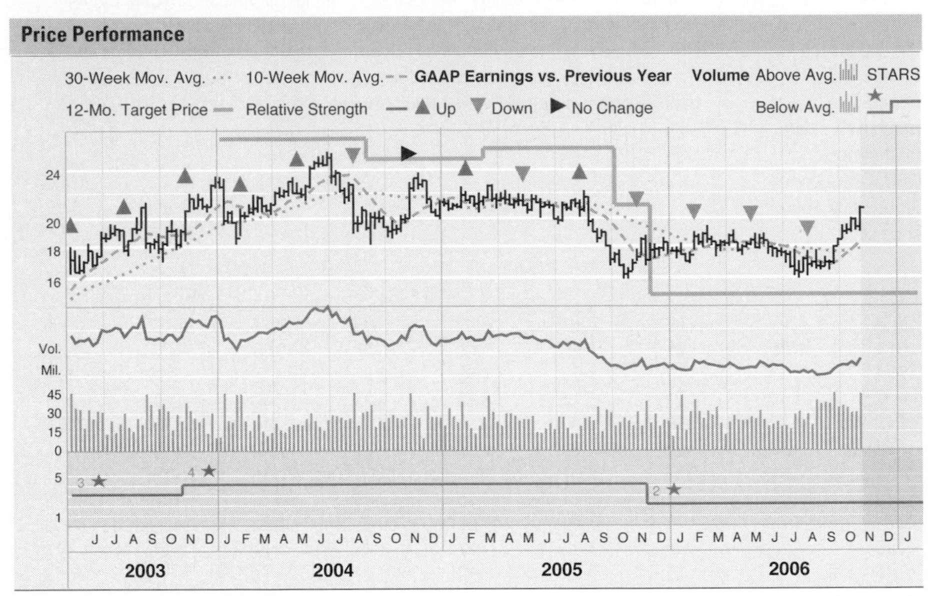

Options: ASE, CBOE, P, Ph

Analysis prepared by **Marie Driscoll, CFA** on September 29, 2006, when the stock traded at **$ 19.16**.

Highlights

- Mature and overdistributed brands stymied GPS's FY 06 (Jan.) sales growth, leading to a 2% sales drop and a 5% same-store sales decline. For FY 07, we see a low single digit sales gain, as an estimated 1% to 2% increase in selling square footage is likely to offset a low single digit comp store sales decline. For the second half of FY 07, same-store sales trends are expected to remain difficult despite easy comparisons. Second quarter comps declined 5% (lapping the 3% second quarter comp decline a year ago), with all concepts participating in the lackluster results.
- We believe GPS's focus on expenses, labor scheduling, inventory flows, and the supply chain is producing an inferior store experience and apparel silhouettes that are too basic. Given GPS's long lead times, we do not expect merchandise changes to affect sales until the second half of FY 07. We project about a 260 basis point contraction in the operating margin--to 8.3% of sales--driven equally by the cost of goods and SG&A expense.
- Our FY 07 EPS estimate of $1.04 includes about $0.03 of projected stock option expense and around 5% fewer shares outstanding.

Investment Rationale/Risk

- Until same-store sales trends revive and are in a sustainable positive trajectory, we believe the shares lack a catalyst. While we think the present management team restored credibility to GPS's business model, we regard the brands as mature and anticipate further difficulties as the iconic Gap and Old Navy brands attempt to incorporate fashion into product assortments. As difficult as this will be to execute, in our opinion, we wonder when and if the consumer will respond--at full price. We would like to see GPS accelerate its Forth & Towne test (currently five stores targeted at the 35-year-old woman) and repurpose some GAP real estate as Forth & Towne.
- Risks to our recommendation and target price include a recovery in same-store sales trends in the next few quarters that would lead to better than expected sales and earnings.
- Our 12-month target price of $15 assumes that GPS will trade at about a 20% discount to its peer group, due to weak same-store sales trends, and thus incorporates a P/E multiple of 12X applied to our FY 08 EPS estimate. Historically, the stock has traded at a modest premium to peers.

Qualitative Risk Assessment

LOW | **MEDIUM** | HIGH

Our risk assessment reflects our view of GPS's strong cash flow and balance sheet, offset by weakness in its two largest brands and increased competition.

Quantitative Evaluations

S&P Quality Ranking A

D | C | B- | B | B+ | A- | **A** | A+

Relative Strength Rank STRONG

89

LOWEST = 1 HIGHEST = 99

Revenue/Earnings Data

Revenue (Million $)

	1Q	2Q	3Q	4Q	Year
2007	3,441	3,716	--	--	--
2006	3,626	3,716	3,860	4,821	16,023
2005	3,668	3,721	3,980	4,898	16,267
2004	3,353	3,685	3,929	4,886	15,854
2003	2,891	3,268	3,645	4,651	14,455
2002	3,180	3,245	3,333	4,089	13,848

Earnings Per Share ($)

2007	0.28	0.15	**E**0.26	**E**0.36	**E**1.04
2006	0.31	0.30	0.24	0.39	1.24
2005	0.33	0.21	0.28	0.40	1.21
2004	0.22	0.22	0.28	0.37	1.09
2003	0.04	0.06	0.15	0.27	0.54
2002	0.13	0.10	-0.21	-0.04	-0.01

Fiscal year ended Jan. 31. Next earnings report expected: Mid November. EPS Estimates based on S&P Operating Earnings; historical GAAP earnings are as reported.

Dividend Data (Dates: mm/dd Payment Date: mm/dd/yy)

Amount ($)	Date Decl.	Ex-Div. Date	Stk. of Record	Payment Date
0.045	11/30	12/30	01/04	01/25/06
0.080	03/21	03/31	04/04	04/25/06
0.080	05/09	06/30	07/05	07/25/06
0.080	09/26	10/05	10/10	10/24/06

Dividends have been paid since 1976. Source: Company reports.

Gap Inc. (The)

Business Summary September 29, 2006

CORPORATE OVERVIEW. Gap is a specialty retailer that operates stores selling casual apparel, accessories, and personal care products for men, women and children. As of July 29, 2006, it operated 3,085 stores: 1,327 Gap North America; 503 Banana Republic North America; 982 Old Navy North America; five Forth & Towne and 268 international locations with 38.2 million sq. ft. of total retail space. In FY 06 (Jan.), North America accounted for 91% of sales.

MARKET PROFILE. GPS participates in the men's, women's and children's apparel market, which generated approximately $181 billion at U.S. retail in 2005, according to NPD Fashionworld consumer estimated data. The apparel market is fragmented, with national brands marketed by 20 companies accounting for about 30% of total apparel sales, and the remaining 70% comprised of smaller and/or private label "store" brands. The market is mature, in our view, with demand largely mirroring population growth, and fashion trends accounting for a modicum of incremental volume. Deflationary pricing pressure is a function of channel competition and production steadily moving offshore to low-cost producers in India, Asia and China. S&P forecasts 2006 apparel sales increasing in the low single digits, generally in line with GDP growth.

COMPETITIVE LANDSCAPE. By channel, specialty stores account for the largest share of apparel sales, at 30% in 2005, according to NPD. Mass merchants (e.g. Wal-Mart and Target) came in second, at 18%, up 100 basis points, and department stores came in third, at 17%, down from their year-ago number two spot and losing 200 basis points of market share. National chains (e.g. Sears and JC Penney) captured 15% of 2005 fourth quarter apparel sales, and off-price retailers (e.g. TJX and Ross Stores) were at 8%. The remaining 12% was divided among factory outlets and direct and e-mail pure plays. GPS is the largest U.S. specialty retailer, with an estimated 25% of the channel's volume.

Company Financials

Per Share Data ($) Year Ended Jan. 31	**2006**	**2005**	**2004**	**2003**	**2002**	**2001**	**2000**	**1999**	**1998**	**1997**
Tangible Book Value	6.33	5.73	5.33	4.12	3.48	3.43	2.63	1.83	1.79	1.79
Cash Flow	1.93	1.79	1.71	1.43	0.93	1.67	1.75	1.25	0.87	0.70
Earnings	1.24	1.21	1.09	0.54	-0.01	1.00	1.26	0.91	0.58	0.47
S&P Core Earnings	1.15	1.13	1.03	0.50	-0.10	0.86	NA	NA	NA	NA
Dividends	0.09	0.09	0.09	0.09	0.09	0.09	0.09	0.09	0.09	0.09
Payout Ratio	7%	7%	8%	17%	NM	9%	7%	9%	15%	19%
Calendar Year	2005	2004	2003	2002	2001	2000	1999	1998	1997	1996
Prices:High	22.70	25.72	23.47	17.14	34.98	53.75	52.69	40.92	17.15	10.81
Prices:Low	15.90	18.12	12.01	8.35	11.12	18.50	30.81	15.31	8.26	6.22
P/E Ratio:High	18	21	22	32	NM	54	42	45	30	23
P/E Ratio:Low	13	15	11	15	NM	18	24	17	14	13
Income Statement Analysis (Million $)										
Revenue	16,023	16,267	15,854	14,455	13,848	13,674	11,635	9,054	6,508	5,284
Operating Income	2,370	2,705	2,543	1,794	1,148	2,035	2,253	1,659	1,121	944
Depreciation	625	620	664	781	810	590	436	326	270	215
Interest Expense	45.0	167	234	249	109	74.9	31.8	13.6	Nil	NA
Pretax Income	1,793	1,872	1,683	801	242	1,382	1,785	1,319	854	749
Effective Tax Rate	37.9%	38.6%	38.8%	40.4%	NM	36.5%	36.9%	37.5%	37.5%	39.4%
Net Income	1,113	1,150	1,030	477	-7.76	877	1,127	825	534	453
S&P Core Earnings	1,033	1,073	978	439	-89.1	760	NA	NA	NA	NA
Balance Sheet & Other Financial Data (Million $)										
Cash	2,987	7,139	2,261	3,389	1,036	409	450	565	913	622
Current Assets	5,239	6,304	6,689	5,740	3,045	2,648	2,198	1,872	1,831	1,329
Total Assets	8,821	10,048	10,343	9,902	7,591	7,013	5,189	3,964	3,338	2,627
Current Liabilities	1,942	2,242	2,492	2,727	2,056	2,799	1,753	1,553	992	775
Long Term Debt	513	1,886	2,487	2,896	1,961	780	785	496	496	Nil
Common Equity	5,425	4,936	4,783	3,658	3,010	2,928	2,233	1,574	1,584	1,654
Total Capital	5,938	6,822	7,270	6,554	4,971	3,708	3,018	2,070	2,080	1,654
Capital Expenditures	600	442	272	303	940	1,859	1,239	798	466	372
Cash Flow	1,738	1,770	1,694	1,258	803	1,468	1,563	1,151	804	668
Current Ratio	2.7	2.8	2.7	2.1	1.5	0.9	1.3	1.2	1.8	1.7
% Long Term Debt of Capitalization	8.6	27.6	34.2	44.2	39.5	21.0	26.0	24.0	23.8	Nil
% Net Income of Revenue	6.9	7.1	6.5	3.3	NM	6.4	9.7	9.1	8.2	8.6
% Return on Assets	11.8	11.1	10.2	5.4	NM	14.4	24.6	22.6	17.9	18.2
% Return on Equity	21.5	24.0	24.4	14.3	NM	34.0	59.2	52.2	33.0	27.5

Data as orig reptd.; bef. results of disc opers/spec. items. Per share data adj. for stk. divs.; EPS diluted. E-Estimated. NA-Not Available. NM-Not Meaningful. NR-Not Ranked. UR-Under Review.

Office: 2 Folsom St, San Francisco, CA 94105-1205.
Telephone: 650-952-4400 .
Email: investor_relations@gap.com
Website: http://www.gapinc.com

Chrmn: R.J. Fisher
Pres & CEO: P. Pressler
EVP & CFO: B.H. Pollitt
EVP, Secy, General Counsel & CCO: L. Shanahan

Investor Contact: M. Webb (415-427-2161)
Board of Directors: H. Behar, A. D. Bellamy, D. De Sole, D. G. Fisher, D. F. Fisher, R. J. Fisher, P. L. Hughes, B. Martin, J. P. Montoya, P. Pressler, J. M. Schneider, M. A. Shattuck, III

Founded: 1969
Domicile: Delaware
Employees: 153,000

STANDARD &POOR'S

General Dynamics Corp

S&P Recommendation HOLD ★★★★★

Price $70.91 (as of Oct 27, 2006)

12-Mo. Target Price $80.00

Investment Style Large-Cap Growth

GICS Sector Industrials
Sub-Industry Aerospace & Defense

Comment This major military contractor is also one of the world's largest makers of corporate jets.

Key Stock Statistics (Source S&P, Vickers, company reports)

52-Wk Range	$77.98–55.09	S&P Oper. EPS 2006**E**	4.18	P/E on S&P Oper. EPS 2006**E**	17.0	Dividend Rate/Share	$0.92
Trailing 12-Month EPS	$4.55	S&P Oper. EPS 2007**E**	4.62	Common Shares Outstg. (M)	403.4	Yield (%)	1.30
Trailing 12-Month P/E	15.6	S&P Core EPS 2006**E**	3.70	Market Capitalization(B)	$28.606	Beta	0.63
$10K Invested 5 Yrs Ago	$17,760	S&P Core EPS 2007**E**	4.10	Institutional Ownership (%)	79	S&P Credit Rating	A

Price Performance

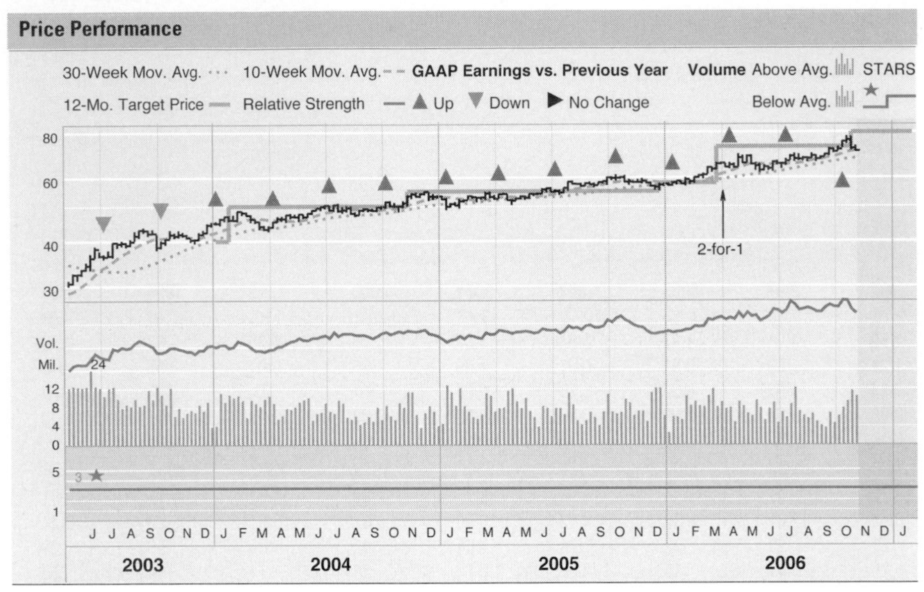

Options: ASE, CBOE, Ph

Highlights

- The 12-month target price for GD has recently been changed to $80.00 from $73.00. The Highlights section of this Stock Report will be updated accordingly.

Investment Rationale/Risk

- The Investment Rationale/Risk section of this Stock Report will be updated shortly. For the latest News story on GD from MarketScope, see below.
- 10/18/06 01:14 pm EDT... S&P REITERATES HOLD RECOMMENDATION ON SHARES OF GENERAL DYNAMICS (GD 74.96***): Q3 EPS of $1.08 vs. $0.90 is $0.03 above our estimate on a 14.5% sales rise. Operating margin rose 30 bps to 11.2%, aided by improvement in marine systems. Funded backlog rose 3.8% from Q2, with strong gains in all segments. We view fundamental outlook for GD's business segments including ships, land systems, Gulfstream, and info systems as bright. We are raising our '06 EPS estimate $0.02 to $4.20, and '07 $0.13 to $4.75. We are also raising our target price $7 to $80, which, at 16.8X our '07 estimate, is above GD's 10-year historical average P/E of 15.2X. / R.Tortoriello

Qualitative Risk Assessment

LOW | MEDIUM | HIGH

Our risk assessment reflects GD's long-term record of consistency and growth in earnings and dividends, as reflected in its S&P Quality Ranking of A. Our assessment also reflects GD's relatively low volatility, as reflected in a recent beta below 0.5.

Quantitative Evaluations

S&P Quality Ranking A

D | C | B- | B | B+ | A- | A | A+

Relative Strength Rank WEAK

29

LOWEST = 1 HIGHEST = 99

Revenue/Earnings Data

Revenue (Million $)

	1Q	2Q	3Q	4Q	Year
2006	5,570	5,934	6,069	--	--
2005	4,819	5,214	5,380	5,831	21,244
2004	4,661	4,666	4,661	5,190	19,178
2003	3,421	3,935	4,427	4,834	16,617
2002	3,102	3,506	3,284	3,937	13,829
2001	2,673	2,962	3,020	3,508	12,163

Earnings Per Share ($)

2006	0.94	1.03	1.08	**E**1.16	**E**4.18
2005	0.85	0.85	0.92	1.00	3.63
2004	0.66	0.73	0.79	0.82	2.99
2003	0.56	0.61	0.64	0.70	2.50
2002	0.57	0.67	0.69	0.67	2.59
2001	0.60	0.56	0.57	0.61	2.33

Fiscal year ended Dec. 31. Next earnings report expected: Late January. EPS Estimates based on S&P Operating Earnings; historical GAAP earnings are as reported.

Dividend Data (Dates: mm/dd Payment Date: mm/dd/yy)

Amount ($)	Date Decl.	Ex-Div. Date	Stk. of Record	Payment Date
0.400	12/07	01/18	01/20	02/10/06
2-for-1 Stk.	03/01	03/27	03/13	03/24/06
0.230	06/07	07/05	07/07	08/11/06
0.230	08/02	10/04	10/06	11/10/06

Dividends have been paid since 1979. Source: Company reports.

Business Summary September 05, 2006

CORPORATE OVERVIEW. General Dynamics is a defense contractor and corporate jet maker that conducts business through five operating segments.

Information Systems & Technology (IS&T) segment (37% of sales, 39% of operating profits in 2005) primarily makes sophisticated electronics for land-, sea- and air-based weapons systems. IS&T also provides computer hardware and software for the U.S. military and federal government. We believe the $60 billion U.S. government IT market is fragmented; IS&T's main competitors are the IT divisions of Northrop Grumman, Lockheed Martin and Boeing.

Marine Systems (22%; 11%) is the Pentagon's second largest military shipbuilder (Northrop Grumman is the largest). Although the U.S. military shipbuilding industry operates as a duopoly, profit margins are low due to excess production capacity.

Combat Systems (21%; 26%) makes wheeled armored vehicles and munitions. GD is also the only U.S. tank maker. Reflecting the U.S. Army's desire to transform itself into a highly agile fighting force, demand is expected to slow for tanks, but to accelerate for its various wheeled combat vehicles. CS's main competitor is United Defense Industries.

Demand for GD's military weapons systems is driven mainly by growth in the procurement and R&D sectors of the U.S. military budget (40% of world military spending, according to independent aerospace and defense researcher Teal Group). Based on Pentagon statistics, from FY 94 (Oct.) through FY 04, procurement and R&D spending grew at 5.3% and 5.1% average annual growth rates, respectively.

Aerospace (16%; 23%) makes the well-known Gulfstream business jet. Based on revenues, Gulfstream is the world's second-largest corporate jet maker. Canada-based Bombardier, Textron's Cessna division, France's Dassault and Raytheon's aircraft-making unit are the world's first-, third-, fourth- and fifth-largest corporate aircraft makers, respectively. The $9 billion global corporate jet market is oligopolistic; based on statistics provided by independent aviation research firm Teal Group, the five largest corporate jet makers account for 99% of global corporate jet sales.

Company Financials

Per Share Data ($) Year Ended Dec. 31	**2005**	**2004**	**2003**	**2002**	**2001**	**2000**	**1999**	**1998**	**1997**	**1996**
Tangible Book Value	1.40	NM	NM	2.81	1.92	3.22	1.64	2.74	2.83	6.79
Cash Flow	4.48	3.57	3.20	3.14	2.99	2.80	2.66	1.93	0.80	1.33
Earnings	3.63	2.99	2.50	2.59	2.33	2.24	2.18	1.43	1.25	1.07
S&P Core Earnings	3.34	2.81	2.34	1.62	1.57	NA	NA	NA	NA	NA
Dividends	0.78	0.70	0.63	0.59	0.55	0.51	0.47	0.43	0.41	0.40
Payout Ratio	22%	23%	25%	23%	24%	23%	22%	30%	33%	38%
Prices:High	61.14	54.99	45.40	55.59	48.00	39.50	37.72	31.00	22.88	18.88
Prices:Low	48.80	42.48	25.00	36.63	30.25	18.13	23.09	20.13	15.78	14.25
P/E Ratio:High	17	18	18	21	21	18	17	22	18	18
P/E Ratio:Low	13	14	10	14	13	8	11	14	13	13
Income Statement Analysis (Million $)										
Revenue	21,244	19,178	16,617	13,829	12,163	10,356	8,959	4,970	4,062	3,581
Operating Income	2,539	2,173	1,744	1,795	1,756	1,555	1,396	668	549	434
Depreciation	342	232	277	213	271	226	193	126	91.0	67.0
Interest Expense	154	157	98.0	45.0	56.0	60.0	34.0	12.0	12.0	14.0
Pretax Income	2,100	1,785	1,372	1,584	1,424	1,262	1,126	549	479	409
Effective Tax Rate	30.1%	32.6%	27.3%	33.6%	33.8%	28.6%	21.8%	33.7%	34.0%	34.0%
Net Income	1,468	1,203	997	1,051	943	901	880	364	316	270
S&P Core Earnings	1,354	1,130	931	658	636	NA	NA	NA	NA	NA
Balance Sheet & Other Financial Data (Million $)										
Cash	2,331	976	860	328	442	177	270	220	336	894
Current Assets	9,173	7,287	6,394	5,098	4,893	3,551	3,491	1,873	1,689	1,858
Total Assets	19,591	17,544	16,183	11,731	11,069	7,987	7,774	4,572	4,091	3,299
Current Liabilities	6,907	5,374	5,616	4,582	4,579	2,901	3,453	1,461	1,291	833
Long Term Debt	2,781	3,291	3,296	718	724	162	169	249	257	156
Common Equity	8,145	7,189	5,921	5,199	4,528	3,820	3,171	2,219	1,915	1,714
Total Capital	10,926	10,480	9,217	5,917	5,252	3,982	3,340	2,468	2,172	1,870
Capital Expenditures	279	266	224	264	356	288	197	158	83.0	75.0
Cash Flow	1,810	1,435	1,274	1,264	1,214	1,127	1,073	490	407	337
Current Ratio	1.3	1.4	1.1	1.1	1.1	1.2	1.0	1.3	1.3	2.2
% Long Term Debt of Capitalization	25.5	31.4	35.8	12.1	13.8	4.1	5.1	10.1	11.8	8.3
% Net Income of Revenue	6.9	6.3	6.0	7.6	7.8	8.7	9.8	7.3	7.8	7.5
% Return on Assets	7.9	7.1	7.1	9.2	9.9	11.4	12.6	8.4	8.6	8.3
% Return on Equity	19.1	18.4	17.9	21.6	22.6	25.8	31.5	17.6	17.4	16.5

Data as orig reptd.; bef. results of disc opers/spec. items. Per share data adj. for stk. divs.; EPS diluted. E-Estimated. NA-Not Available. NM-Not Meaningful. NR-Not Ranked. UR-Under Review.

Office: 2941 Fairview Park Dr Ste 100, Falls Church, VA 22042-4513.
Telephone: 703-876-3000.
Website: http://www.generaldynamics.com
Chrmn & CEO: N.D. Chabraja

SVP & CFO: L.H. Redd
SVP, Secy & General Counsel: D.A. Savner
Investor Contact: R. Lewis (703-876-3195)
VP & Cntlr: J.M. Schwartz

Board of Directors: N. D. Chabraja, J. S. Crown, W. P. Fricks, C. H. Goodman, J. L. Johnson, G. A. Joulwan, P. G. Kaminski, J. M. Keane, D. Lucas, L. L. Lyles, C. E. Mundy, Jr., R. Walmsley

Founded: 1899
Domicile: Delaware
Employees: 72,700

STANDARD &POOR'S

General Electric Co

S&P Recommendation BUY ★★★★★

Price $35.21 (as of Oct 27, 2006)

12-Mo. Target Price $40.00

Investment Style Large-Cap Growth

GICS Sector Industrials
Sub-Industry Industrial Conglomerates

Comment This industrial conglomerate sells products ranging from jet engines and gas turbines to consumer appliances, railroad locomotives and medical equipment. It also owns NBC Universal, and is one of the world's largest providers of financing.

Key Stock Statistics (Source S&P, Vickers, company reports)

52-Wk Range	$36.48–32.06	S&P Oper. EPS 2006E	1.98	P/E on S&P Oper. EPS 2006E	17.8	Dividend Rate/Share	$1.00
Trailing 12-Month EPS	$1.66	S&P Oper. EPS 2007E	2.25	Common Shares Outstg. (M)	10,323.4	Yield (%)	2.84
Trailing 12-Month P/E	21.2	S&P Core EPS 2006E	1.82	Market Capitalization(B)	$363.485	Beta	0.82
$10K Invested 5 Yrs Ago	$10,304	S&P Core EPS 2007E	2.07	Institutional Ownership (%)	56	S&P Credit Rating	AAA

Price Performance

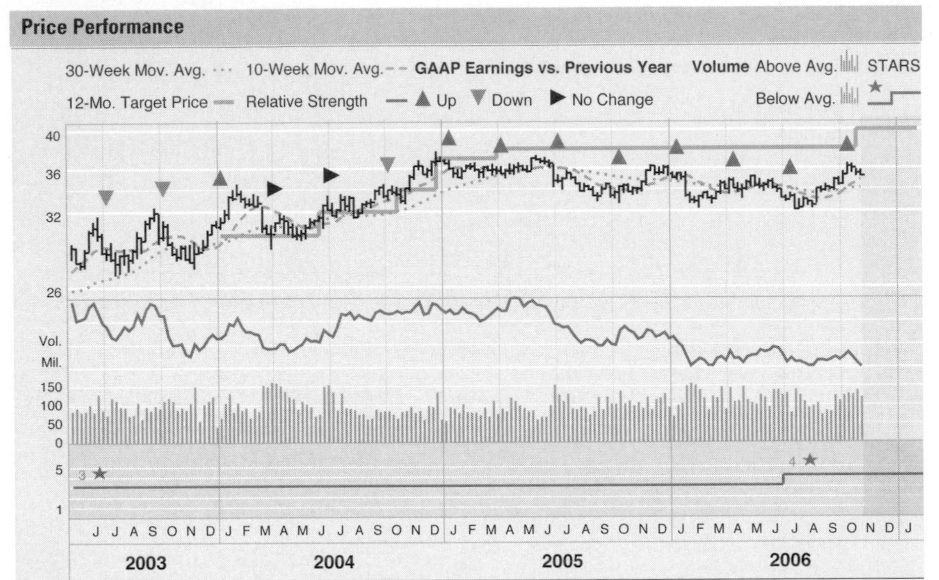

Options: ASE, CBOE, P, Ph

Analysis prepared by **Richard Tortoriello** on October 18, 2006, when the stock traded at **$ 35.56**.

Highlights

- We estimate 8.6% revenue growth in 2006, above S&P's estimate of U.S. real GDP growth of 3.4%. For 2007, we project further sales growth of about 7%, versus S&P's projected real GDP growth of 2.3%. The U.S. accounts for about 48% of GE's sales. Global Insight, an economic forecasting firm, projects 2.1% real GDP growth in 2006 and 1.7% in 2007 for the 12 Eurozone countries (27% of GE's sales occur in Europe), and 5.4% growth in 2006 and 4.8% in 2007 for the Asia-Pacific region (13%).
- We see operating margins widening slightly, to 15.4% in 2006, from 15.0% in 2005, and project further operating margin improvement in 2007. In particular, we look for continued margin improvement in the infrastructure, health care and commercial finance segments, driven by strong volume gains and improved productivity.
- We project EPS of $1.98 in 2006, with growth to $2.25 in 2007. The company's quality of earnings is high, in our opinion, with GE's S&P Core EPS at 96% of reported earnings in 2005 and free cash flow at 127% of reported earnings.

Investment Rationale/Risk

- Given what we see as an environment of increased investment risk, we view GE's S&P Quality Ranking of A+ as providing a measure of safety for shareholders. We also like the repositioning of GE's portfolio of businesses that has taken place over the past few years, and we see reasons --including a strong aerospace market, increasing demand for energy infrastructure, increased global consumer wealth, etc. -- why GE's businesses should continue to grow for the foreseeable future.
- Risks to our recommendation and target price include slower than expected global economic growth, and unanticipated manufacturing, competitive or other difficulties with GE's main product lines.
- Our 12-month target price of $40 is based on a ratio of 18X our 2007 EPS estimate. This compares to a 20-year average two-year forward P/E ratio for GE of 17.9X, with lows (following the 1987 market crash) near 10X and highs (during 2000) near 40X. GE's recent earnings yield (the inverse of its P/E ratio) on 2007 EPS was 6.4%, which we believe compares favorably with the recent 10-year Treasury bond yield of 4.8%.

Qualitative Risk Assessment

LOW | MEDIUM | HIGH

Our risk assessment reflects our view of GE's long-term record of steady growth in earnings, cash flow and dividends, which we attribute to good management of a diversified portfolio of growing and profitable businesses, as well as GE's relatively low stock volatility, as reflected in its recent beta of 0.84.

Quantitative Evaluations

S&P Quality Ranking **A+**

D | C | B- | B | B+ | A- | A | **A+**

Relative Strength Rank **MODERATE**

41

LOWEST = 1 HIGHEST = 99

Revenue/Earnings Data

Revenue (Million $)

	1Q	2Q	3Q	4Q	Year
2006	37,821	39,900	40,856	--	--
2005	--	--	--	40,705	149,702
2004	33,350	37,035	38,272	43,706	152,363
2003	30,456	33,373	33,394	36,964	134,187
2002	30,521	33,214	32,585	35,378	131,698
2001	30,493	31,977	29,468	33,975	125,913

Earnings Per Share ($)

2006	0.39	0.47	0.49	E0.64	E1.98
2005	0.33	0.41	0.43	0.55	1.72
2004	0.32	0.38	0.38	0.51	1.59
2003	0.32	0.38	0.40	0.45	1.55
2002	0.35	0.44	0.41	0.31	1.51
2001	0.30	0.39	0.33	0.39	1.41

Fiscal year ended Dec. 31. Next earnings report expected: Mid January. EPS Estimates based on S&P Operating Earnings; historical GAAP earnings are as reported.

Dividend Data (Dates: mm/dd Payment Date: mm/dd/yy)

Amount ($)	Date Decl.	Ex-Div. Date	Stk. of Record	Payment Date
0.250	11/18	12/22	12/27	01/25/06
0.250	02/10	02/23	02/27	04/25/06
0.250	06/09	06/22	06/26	07/25/06
0.250	09/08	09/21	09/25	10/25/06

Dividends have been paid since 1899. Source: Company reports.

General Electric Co

Business Summary October 18, 2006

CORPORATE OVERVIEW. This multi-industry, media and financing giant does business through six segments: Infrastructure, Industrial, Healthcare, NBC Universal, Commercial Finance, and Consumer Finance.

The Infrastructure segment (29% of 2005 revenues, 33.2% of operating profits) produces, sells, finances and services equipment for the air transportation and energy generation industries (products range from jet engines and maintenance operations to power generation equipment). It also produces, sells and services equipment for the rail transportation, oil & gas, and water treatment industries. The Aviation and Energy sub-segments, excluding financial services, together made up 70% of 2005 segment revenues and 69% of operating profits.

The Industrial segment (22.6%, 10.9%) produces and sells products, including consumer appliances, industrial equipment and plastics, and related services. GE makes, sells and services major home appliances; it also makes a variety of electrical equipment and motors. Plastics are used for a number of applications, including automobile and appliance parts, computer enclosures, compact disks, etc. In addition, it finances business equipment for a wide variety of customer applications. Consumer and industrial products accounted for 43% of 2005 segment revenues and 34% of operating profits.

The Healthcare segment (10.5%, 11.4%) manufactures, sells and services a wide range of medical equipment, including equipment for magnetic resonance (MR), computed tomography (CT), positron emission tomography (PET) imaging, x-ray, patient monitoring, diagnostic cardiology, nuclear imaging, ultrasound, bone densitometry, anesthesiology and oxygen therapy, neonatal and critical care, and therapy.

NBC Universal (10.2%, 13.2%) is principally engaged in the broadcast of network television services to affiliated television stations within the U.S.; the production of live and recorded TV programs; the production and distribution of motion pictures; the operation of TV broadcasting stations; the ownership of several cable/satellite networks around the world; the operation of theme parks; and investment and programming activities in multimedia and the Internet.

Company Financials

Per Share Data ($) Year Ended Dec. 31	**2005**	**2004**	**2003**	**2002**	**2001**	**2000**	**1999**	**1998**	**1997**	**1996**
Tangible Book Value	2.64	2.55	2.40	1.76	2.34	2.32	1.68	1.55	1.56	1.36
Cash Flow	2.53	2.39	2.24	2.11	2.11	2.04	1.74	1.52	1.25	1.12
Earnings	1.72	1.59	1.55	1.51	1.41	1.27	1.07	0.93	0.82	0.73
S&P Core Earnings	1.68	1.54	1.41	1.10	0.98	NA	NA	NA	NA	NA
Dividends	0.91	0.82	0.77	0.73	0.66	0.57	0.49	0.42	0.36	0.32
Payout Ratio	53%	52%	50%	48%	47%	45%	46%	45%	44%	43%
Prices:High	37.34	37.75	32.42	41.84	53.55	60.50	53.17	34.65	25.52	17.69
Prices:Low	32.67	28.88	21.30	21.40	28.50	41.65	31.35	23.00	15.98	11.58
P/E Ratio:High	22	24	21	28	38	48	50	37	31	24
P/E Ratio:Low	19	18	14	14	20	33	29	25	19	16

Income Statement Analysis (Million $)	2005	2004	2003	2002	2001	2000	1999	1998	1997	1996
Revenue	149,702	152,363	134,187	131,698	125,913	129,853	111,630	100,469	90,840	79,179
Operating Income	46,840	40,262	36,792	35,431	38,200	38,329	32,646	29,355	23,885	22,764
Depreciation	8,538	8,385	6,956	5,998	7,089	7,736	6,691	5,860	4,082	3,785
Interest Expense	15,187	11,907	10,432	10,216	11,062	11,720	10,013	9,753	8,384	7,904
Pretax Income	23,115	21,034	20,194	19,217	20,049	18,873	15,577	13,742	11,419	11,075
Effective Tax Rate	16.7%	16.7%	21.4%	19.6%	27.8%	30.3%	31.1%	30.4%	26.1%	32.6%
Net Income	18,275	16,593	15,589	15,133	14,128	12,735	10,717	9,296	8,203	7,280
S&P Core Earnings	17,848	16,138	14,195	11,038	9,889	NA	NA	NA	NA	NA

Balance Sheet & Other Financial Data (Million $)	2005	2004	2003	2002	2001	2000	1999	1998	1997	1996
Cash	9,011	150,864	133,388	125,772	110,099	99,534	90,312	83,034	76,482	64,080
Current Assets	NA	NA	NA	NA	NA	NA	NA	NA	NA	NA
Total Assets	673,342	750,330	647,483	575,244	495,023	437,006	405,200	355,935	304,012	272,402
Current Liabilities	NA	NA	NA	NA	NA	NA	NA	NA	NA	NA
Long Term Debt	212,281	213,161	170,004	140,632	79,806	82,132	71,427	59,663	46,603	49,246
Common Equity	109,354	110,284	79,180	63,706	54,824	50,492	42,557	38,880	34,438	31,125
Total Capital	346,019	354,242	267,611	222,328	148,975	146,250	128,436	112,158	93,374	91,651
Capital Expenditures	14,441	13,118	9,767	13,351	15,520	13,967	15,502	8,982	8,388	7,760
Cash Flow	26,813	24,978	22,545	21,131	21,217	20,471	17,408	15,156	12,285	11,065
Current Ratio	NA	NA	NA	NA	NA	NA	NA	NA	NA	NA
% Long Term Debt of Capitalization	61.3	60.2	63.5	63.3	53.6	56.2	55.6	53.2	50.0	53.7
% Net Income of Revenue	12.2	10.8	11.6	11.5	11.2	9.8	9.6	9.3	9.0	9.2
% Return on Assets	2.6	2.4	2.5	2.8	3.0	3.0	2.8	2.8	2.8	2.9
% Return on Equity	16.6	17.5	21.8	25.5	26.8	27.4	26.3	25.4	25.0	24.0

Data as orig reptd.; bef. results of disc opers/spec. items. Per share data adj. for stk. divs.; EPS diluted. E-Estimated. NA-Not Available. NM-Not Meaningful. NR-Not Ranked. UR-Under Review.

Office: 3135 Easton Tpke, Fairfield, CT 06828-0001.
Telephone: 203-373-2211.
Website: http://www.ge.com
Chrmn & CEO: J.R. Immelt

Vice Chrmn: R.C. Wright
Vice Chrmn: W.M. Castell
Vice Chrmn: D.D. Dammerman
Vice Chrmn: D.L. Calhoun

Investor Contact: D. Janki
Board of Directors: J. I. Cash, Jr., W. M. Castell, A. M. Fudge, C. X. Gonzalez, J. R. Immelt, A. Jung, A. G. Lafley, R. W. Lane, R. S. Larsen, R. B. Lazarus, S. Nunn, R. S. Penske, R. J. Swieringa, D. A. Warner, III, R. C. Wright

Founded: 1892
Domicile: New York
Employees: 316,000

STANDARD & POOR'S

General Mills Inc.

S&P Recommendation BUY ★★★★★

Price $56.40 (as of Oct 30, 2006)

12-Mo. Target Price $61.00

Investment Style Large-Cap Growth

GICS Sector Consumer Staples
Sub-Industry Packaged Foods & Meats

Comment This company is a major producer of packaged consumer food products, including Big G cereals and Betty Crocker desserts/baking mixes.

Key Stock Statistics (Source S&P, Vickers, company reports)

52-Wk Range	$57.00–47.05	S&P Oper. EPS 2007E	3.10	P/E on S&P Oper. EPS 2007E	18.2	Dividend Rate/Share	$1.40
Trailing 12-Month EPS	$3.00	S&P Oper. EPS 2008E	3.40	Common Shares Outstg. (M)	343.1	Yield (%)	2.48
Trailing 12-Month P/E	18.8	S&P Core EPS 2007E	2.90	Market Capitalization(B)	$19.349	Beta	0.21
$10K Invested 5 Yrs Ago	$14,330	S&P Core EPS 2008E	3.19	Institutional Ownership (%)	78	S&P Credit Rating	BBB+

Price Performance

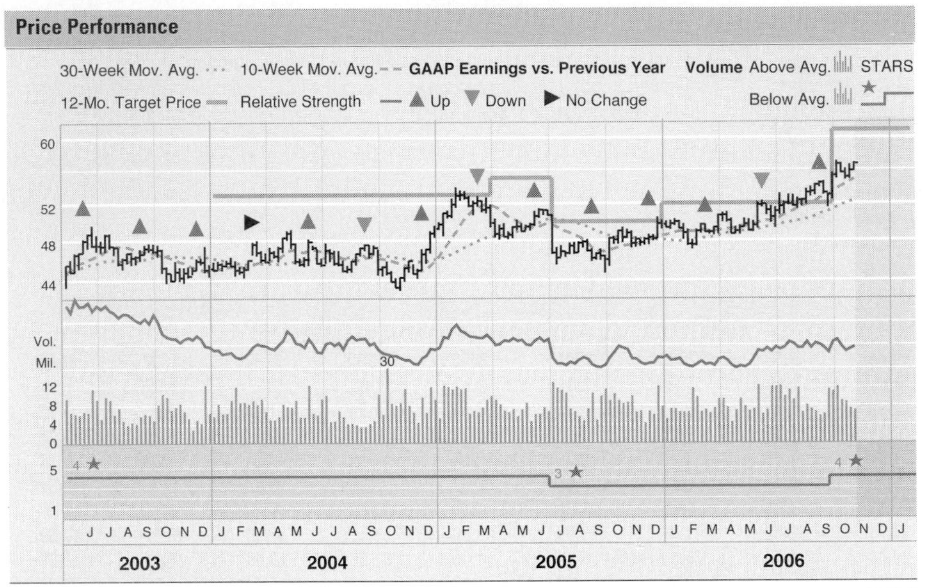

Options: CBOE, P

Analysis prepared by **Rick Joy** on October 26, 2006, when the stock traded at **$ 56.42**.

Highlights

- General Mills renewed its share repurchase program last year, and during the first quarter of FY 07 (May), the company repurchased 14.1 million shares of common stock. Long-term annual growth targets include low single digit growth in net sales, mid-single digit operating profit growth, and high single digit growth in EPS.
- We see net sales advancing 4% to 5% in FY 07, led by 2% to 3% unit volume growth and higher prices. We expect operating margins to see some benefit from a combination of productivity gains and volume-based efficiencies, improved price realization, and higher profits from international joint venture operations. However, we look for higher marketing and promotional spending in support of new products, commodity cost inflation and high energy costs to temper any margin gains.
- Following a reduction in shares outstanding and the inclusion of an estimated $0.12 per share in stock option expense, we see FY 07 operating EPS increasing to $3.10, from $3.00 in FY 06. For the longer term, we see annual EPS growth of 7% to 9%.

Investment Rationale/Risk

- Our buy recommendation reflects our belief that accelerating brand momentum and operating leverage will lead to improved EPS visibility and consistency. Several key brands showed strong growth during the first quarter of FY 07, and we believe results will continue to benefit from new product introductions and productivity gains. We view the shares as attractive given what we consider strong cash flows, improving brand momentum, good cost management, and healthy long-term growth potential.
- Risks to our recommendation and target price relate to competitive pressures in General Mills' businesses, a lack of consumer acceptance of new product introductions, the potential for commodity cost inflation and an inability to achieve sales and earnings growth forecasts.
- Our 12-month target price of $61 is based on an analysis of peer P/E and EV/EBITDA multiples, and our discounted free cash flow model, which assumes a weighted average cost of capital of 9% and a terminal growth rate for free cash flows of 3%.

Qualitative Risk Assessment

LOW | MEDIUM | HIGH

Our risk assessment reflects the relatively stable nature of the company's end markets, strong cash flows, corporate governance practices that we view as favorable versus peers, and an S&P Quality Ranking of A- that reflects historical stability of earnings and dividends.

Quantitative Evaluations

S&P Quality Ranking A-

D | C | B- | B | B+ | A- | A | A+

Relative Strength Rank MODERATE

56

LOWEST = 1 HIGHEST = 99

Revenue/Earnings Data

Revenue (Million $)

	1Q	2Q	3Q	4Q	Year
2007	2,860	--	--	--	--
2006	2,662	3,273	2,860	2,845	11,640
2005	2,585	3,168	2,772	2,719	11,244
2004	2,518	3,060	2,703	2,789	11,070
2003	2,362	2,953	2,645	2,546	10,506
2002	1,404	1,842	2,379	2,324	7,949

Earnings Per Share ($)

	1Q	2Q	3Q	4Q	Year
2007	0.74	E1.02	E0.70	E0.64	E3.10
2006	0.64	0.97	0.68	0.61	2.90
2005	0.45	0.92	0.58	1.14	3.08
2004	0.59	0.81	0.63	0.72	2.75
2003	0.47	0.73	0.63	0.59	2.43
2002	0.65	0.41	0.22	0.15	1.35

Fiscal year ended May 31. Next earnings report expected: Late December. EPS Estimates based on S&P Operating Earnings; historical GAAP earnings are as reported.

Dividend Data (Dates: mm/dd Payment Date: mm/dd/yy)

Amount ($)	Date Decl.	Ex-Div. Date	Stk. of Record	Payment Date
0.340	12/12	01/06	01/10	02/01/06
0.340	03/13	04/06	04/10	05/01/06
0.350	06/26	07/06	07/10	08/01/06
0.350	09/25	10/05	10/10	11/01/06

Dividends have been paid since 1898. Source: Company reports.

General Mills Inc.

Business Summary October 26, 2006

General Mills (GIS) is the second largest U.S. producer of ready-to-eat breakfast cereals, and a leading producer of other well known packaged consumer foods. Following the company's October 2001 acquisition of The Pillsbury Company, GIS organized its businesses into three reportable segments: U.S. Retail (69% of FY 06 (May) sales, 84% of operating income); Bakeries and Foodservice (15%, 7%); and International (16%, 9%). The U.S. Retail segment consists of cereals, meals, refrigerated and frozen dough products, baking products, snacks, yogurt and organic foods. The Bakeries and Foodservice segment consists of products marketed to retail and wholesale bakeries and offered to commercial and noncommercial foodservice sectors throughout the United States and Canada, such as restaurants and businesses and school cafeterias. The International segment is made up of retail business outside the United States and foodservice business outside of the U.S. and Canada.

Major cereal brands, most of which bear the Big G label, include Cheerios, Wheaties, Lucky Charms, Total and Chex cereals. Other consumer packaged food products include baking mixes (Betty Crocker, Bisquick); meals (Betty Crocker dry packaged dinner mixes), Progresso soups, Green Giant canned and frozen vegetables; snacks (Pop Secret microwave popcorn, Bugles snacks, grain and fruit snack products); Pillsbury refrigerated and frozen dough products, frozen breakfast products and frozen pizza and snack products; and organic foods and other products, including Yoplait and Colombo yogurt. The company also engages in grain merchandising, produces its own ingredient flour requirements, and sells flour to bakeries. Products are also made and sold in Canada and Europe, Japan, Korea and Latin America.

Company Financials

Per Share Data ($) Year Ended May 31	**2006**	**2005**	**2004**	**2003**	**2002**	**2001**	**2000**	**1999**	**1998**	**1997**
Tangible Book Value	NM	NM	NM	NM	NM	NM	NM	NM	NM	NM
Cash Flow	3.99	4.11	3.79	3.39	2.21	3.04	2.68	4.63	1.90	1.99
Earnings	2.90	3.08	2.75	2.43	1.35	2.28	2.00	1.70	1.30	1.41
S&P Core Earnings	2.72	2.17	2.43	1.74	0.55	1.79	NA	NA	NA	NA
Dividends	1.34	1.24	1.10	1.10	1.10	1.10	1.10	1.08	1.06	1.02
Payout Ratio	46%	40%	40%	45%	81%	48%	55%	64%	82%	72%
Calendar Year	2005	2004	2003	2002	2001	2000	1999	1998	1997	1996
Prices:High	53.89	49.96	49.66	51.73	52.86	45.31	43.94	39.84	39.13	33.75
Prices:Low	44.67	43.01	41.43	37.38	37.26	29.38	32.50	29.59	28.88	26.00
P/E Ratio:High	19	16	18	21	39	20	22	23	30	24
P/E Ratio:Low	15	14	15	15	28	13	16	17	22	18
Income Statement Analysis (Million $)										
Revenue	11,640	11,244	11,070	10,506	7,949	7,078	6,700	6,246	6,033	5,609
Operating Income	2,420	2,435	2,442	2,290	1,569	1,392	1,308	1,212	1,145	1,042
Depreciation	424	443	399	365	296	223	209	194	195	183
Interest Expense	427	488	537	589	445	223	168	134	130	116
Pretax Income	1,631	1,904	1,583	1,377	700	1,015	950	838	664	703
Effective Tax Rate	33.2%	34.9%	33.4%	33.4%	34.1%	34.5%	35.3%	36.3%	36.4%	36.7%
Net Income	1,090	1,240	1,055	917	461	665	614	535	422	445
S&P Core Earnings	1,024	863	931	652	189	512	NA	NA	NA	NA
Balance Sheet & Other Financial Data (Million $)										
Cash	647	573	751	703	975	64.1	25.6	3.90	6.00	13.0
Current Assets	3,176	3,055	3,215	3,179	3,437	1,408	1,190	1,103	1,035	1,011
Total Assets	18,207	18,066	18,448	18,227	16,540	5,091	4,574	4,141	3,861	3,902
Current Liabilities	6,138	4,184	2,757	3,444	5,747	2,209	2,529	1,700	1,444	1,293
Long Term Debt	2,415	4,255	7,410	7,516	5,591	2,221	1,760	1,702	1,640	1,530
Common Equity	5,772	5,676	5,248	4,175	3,576	52.2	-289	164	190	495
Total Capital	11,145	12,915	14,730	13,652	9,727	2,696	1,859	2,156	2,244	2,441
Capital Expenditures	360	414	628	711	506	308	268	281	184	163
Cash Flow	1,514	1,683	1,454	1,282	757	888	823	729	617	628
Current Ratio	0.5	0.7	1.2	0.9	0.6	0.6	0.5	0.6	0.7	0.8
% Long Term Debt of Capitalization	21.7	32.9	50.3	55.1	57.5	82.4	94.7	79.0	73.1	62.7
% Net Income of Revenue	9.4	11.0	9.5	8.7	5.8	9.4	9.2	8.6	7.0	8.0
% Return on Assets	6.0	6.8	5.8	5.3	4.3	13.8	14.1	13.4	10.9	12.4
% Return on Equity	18.7	22.7	22.4	23.7	25.4	NM	NM	301.6	123.2	110.7

Data as orig reptd.; bef. results of disc opers/spec. items. Per share data adj. for stk. divs.; EPS diluted. E-Estimated. NA-Not Available. NM-Not Meaningful. NR-Not Ranked. UR-Under Review.

Office: 1 General Mills Blvd, Minneapolis, MN 55426-1348.
Telephone: 763-764-7600.
Website: http://www.generalmills.com
Chrmn & CEO: S.W. Sanger

Pres & COO: K.J. Powell
Vice Chrmn & CFO: J.A. Lawrence
SVP, Secy, General Counsel & CCO: S.S. Marshall
Investor Contact: K. Wenker (800-245-5703)

Board of Directors: P. Danos, W. T. Esrey, R. V. Gilmartin, J. R. Hope, H. G. Miller, H. Ochoa-Brillembourg, S. Odland, K. J. Powell, M. D. Rose, R. L. Ryan, S. W. Sanger, A. M. Spence, D. A. Terrell

Founded: 1928
Domicile: Delaware
Employees: 28,100

STANDARD &POOR'S

General Motors Corp.

S&P Recommendation HOLD ★★★★★ | **Price** $33.93 (as of Oct 27, 2006) | **12-Mo. Target Price** $37.00 | **Investment Style** Large-Cap Value

GICS Sector Consumer Discretionary
Sub-Industry Automobile Manufacturers

Comment GM is the world's largest producer of cars and trucks, and has significant finance, aerospace, defense and electronics operations.

Key Stock Statistics (Source S&P, Vickers, company reports)

52-Wk Range	**$36.56–18.33**	S&P Oper. EPS 2006**E**	**4.73**	P/E on S&P Oper. EPS 2006**E**	**7.2**	Dividend Rate/Share	**$1.00**
Trailing 12-Month EPS	**$-16.99**	S&P Oper. EPS 2007**E**	**5.20**	Common Shares Outstg. (M)	**565.6**	Yield (%)	**2.95**
Trailing 12-Month P/E	**NM**	S&P Core EPS 2006**E**	**5.46**	Market Capitalization(B)	**$19.191**	Beta	**1.31**
$10K Invested 5 Yrs Ago	**$9,549**	S&P Core EPS 2007**E**	**5.63**	Institutional Ownership (%)	**87**	S&P Credit Rating	**B**

Price Performance

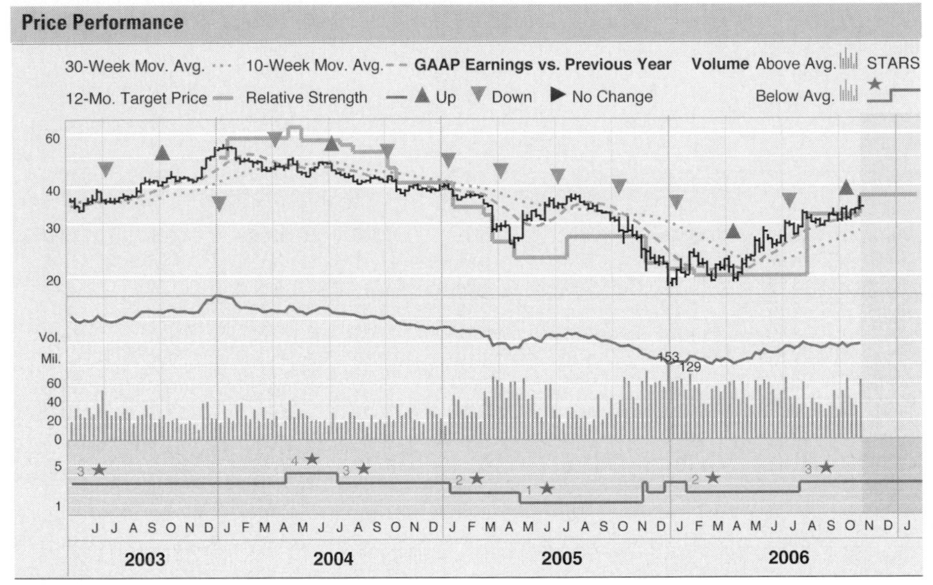

Options: ASE, CBOE, P, Ph

Highlights

➤ The 12-month target price for GM has recently been changed to $37.00 from $32.00. The Highlights section of this Stock Report will be updated accordingly.

Investment Rationale/Risk

➤ The Investment Rationale/Risk section of this Stock Report will be updated shortly. For the latest News story on GM from MarketScope, see below.

➤ 10/25/06 01:00 pm EDT... S&P REITERATES HOLD OPINION ON SHARES OF GENERAL MOTORS (GM 34.65***): GM posts adjusted Q3 EPS of $0.93 versus an adjusted loss of $1.97 per share. On largely favorable tax items, EPS exceeds our $0.08 EPS projection. A $4.5B reduction of expected costs in connection with a potential Delphi settlement suggests to us that negotiations with the former unit and the UAW are making progress. Still, GM faces lower earnings contributions from GMAC following its planned sale in Q4. We are raising our '06 EPS forecast $0.92 to $4.73, and we see $4.50 for '07. We are also raising our 12-month target price $5 to $37, within GM's historical P/E range. / E.Levy-CFA

Qualitative Risk Assessment

LOW | MEDIUM | **HIGH**

Our risk assessment for General Motors reflects the highly cyclical nature of its markets as well as our view of the current and long-term challenges that GM faces, with its highly leveraged balance sheet, intensifying competition, high fixed and legacy costs and the risk of a strike at a bankrupt major parts supplier.

Quantitative Evaluations

S&P Quality Ranking **B-**

D | C | **B-** | B | B+ | A- | A | A+

Relative Strength Rank **STRONG**

77

LOWEST = 1 HIGHEST = 99

Revenue/Earnings Data

Revenue (Million $)

	1Q	2Q	3Q	4Q	Year
2006	52,245	54,395	48,821	--	--
2005	45,773	48,469	47,182	51,180	192,604
2004	47,862	49,293	44,934	51,428	193,517
2003	47,146	45,944	43,351	49,084	185,524
2002	46,264	48,265	43,578	48,656	186,763
2001	42,615	46,220	42,475	45,950	177,260

Earnings Per Share ($)

2006	0.78	-5.97	-0.20	**E**0.97	**E**4.73
2005	-2.22	-1.75	-2.94	-11.59	-18.50
2004	2.12	2.42	0.56	-0.17	4.95
2003	2.74	1.57	0.80	Nil	5.03
2002	0.57	2.43	-1.42	1.71	3.35
2001	0.53	1.03	-0.41	0.60	1.77

Fiscal year ended Dec. 31. Next earnings report expected: Late January. EPS Estimates based on S&P Operating Earnings; historical GAAP earnings are as reported.

Dividend Data (Dates: mm/dd Payment Date: mm/dd/yy)

Amount ($)	Date Decl.	Ex-Div. Date	Stk. of Record	Payment Date
0.500	10/31	11/08	11/10	12/10/05
0.250	02/07	02/14	02/16	03/10/06
0.250	05/02	05/10	05/12	06/10/06
0.250	08/01	08/09	08/11	09/09/06

Dividends have been paid since 1915. Source: Company reports.

General Motors Corp.

Business Summary August 01, 2006

CORPORATE OVERVIEW. General Motors is the world's largest manufacturer of cars and trucks. The majority of its business is derived from the automotive industry, but it also has financing and insurance and financial services operations through its General Motors Acceptance Corp. (GMAC) unit, and produces products and provides services in other industries. Competition has been increasing for this once dominant market leader. With Toyota Motor (TM: hold, $105), already the world's most profitable automaker, steadily and rapidly expanding its global vehicle sales and production, the Japanese company is likely to overtake GM as the world volume leader in vehicle sales and production in either 2006 or 2007, in our opinion.

IMPACT OF MAJOR DEVELOPMENTS. GM has reached an agreement to sell 51% of GMAC to an investor group that the company believes would enhance GMAC's credit rating and thereby reduce the unit's borrowing costs, as well as raise funds for the parent company. The downside of a potential transaction, in our view, would be a partial loss of GMAC income contributions. The transaction is subject to customary and other conditions and is expected to close in the second half of 2006.

In October 2005, Delphi Corp. (formerly Delphi Automotive Systems) filed for Chapter 11 bankruptcy protection. Delphi is GM's largest parts supplier. We have assumed that the direct costs of the Delphi bankruptcy filing, including a possible but unlikely strike by Delphi workers, could hurt the 2006 bottom line by $300 million, although visibility for these costs is very low. Workers at GM's largest parts supplier have threatened to strike if a wage and benefits agreement cannot be worked out with Delphi. A work stoppage at General Motors itself in mid-1998 cost GM about $2 billion in lost profits; a strike against Delphi that could halt GM production could be even more costly for the struggling automaker, in our view.

In October 2002, GM invested $251 million for a 42.1% controlling stake in a new company that owns selected assets of South Korea's Daewoo Motor Co. GM partners own 24.9%, and Daewoo creditors own the remaining 33%. GM's strategy is to use these vehicles to compete in low-priced vehicle segments around the world. We see profit contributions and market gains via these operations.

In May 2005, Kirk Kerkorian's Tracinda Corp. announced its intent to make a cash tender offer for up to 28 million GM common shares for $31 cash per share, subject to certain conditions. Following the completion of the offer and after subsequent transactions, Tracinda owns 56 million GM shares, or about 9.9% of the shares outstanding. Representing Tracinda, in February, Jerome York, with his automotive industry and company turnaround experience, joined GM's board of directors.

General Motors, Nissan Motor (NSANY: hold, $22) and Renault SA are reviewing the possibility of forming a three-way alliance.

Company Financials

Per Share Data ($) Year Ended Dec. 31	**2005**	**2004**	**2003**	**2002**	**2001**	**2000**	**1999**	**1998**	**1997**	**1996**
Tangible Book Value	18.12	40.35	36.49	NM	1.93	13.60	16.03	6.25	5.80	7.30
Cash Flow	9.38	29.91	29.60	26.03	24.12	30.04	27.20	22.39	31.93	22.11
Earnings	-18.50	4.95	5.03	3.35	1.77	6.68	8.53	4.18	8.62	6.07
S&P Core Earnings	-11.92	7.11	7.91	-1.49	-5.77	NA	NA	NA	NA	NA
Dividends	2.00	2.00	2.00	2.00	2.00	2.00	2.00	2.00	2.00	1.60
Payout Ratio	NM	40%	40%	60%	113%	30%	23%	48%	23%	26%
Prices:High	40.80	55.55	54.39	68.17	67.80	94.63	94.88	76.69	72.44	59.38
Prices:Low	18.33	36.90	29.75	30.80	39.17	48.44	59.75	47.06	52.25	45.75
P/E Ratio:High	NM	11	11	20	38	14	11	18	8	10
P/E Ratio:Low	NM	7	6	9	22	7	7	11	6	8
Income Statement Analysis (Million $)										
Revenue	192,604	193,517	185,524	186,763	177,260	184,632	176,558	161,315	178,174	164,069
Operating Income	14,606	27,324	26,423	22,733	23,016	30,127	29,115	23,706	30,443	23,484
Depreciation	15,769	14,152	13,978	12,938	12,908	13,411	12,318	12,201	16,616	11,840
Interest Expense	15,768	11,980	9,464	7,715	8,590	9,552	7,750	6,893	6,113	5,695
Pretax Income	-16,336	1,894	3,593	2,080	1,518	7,164	8,722	4,428	7,714	6,676
Effective Tax Rate	NM	NM	20.3%	25.6%	50.6%	33.4%	35.7%	33.0%	13.9%	25.8%
Net Income	-10,458	2,805	2,862	1,736	601	4,452	5,576	2,956	6,698	4,953
S&P Core Earnings	-6,741	4,040	4,510	-838	-3,209	NA	NA	NA	NA	NA
Balance Sheet & Other Financial Data (Million $)										
Cash	50,452	57,730	54,769	38,274	30,014	21,040	21,250	20,024	22,984	22,262
Total Assets	476,078	479,603	448,507	370,782	323,969	303,100	274,730	257,389	228,888	222,142
Long Term Debt	202,177	207,174	191,133	134,272	104,638	65,843	62,963	52,794	42,194	38,074
Total Debt	285,750	300,279	271,756	201,940	166,314	144,655	131,906	114,372	93,249	85,300
Common Equity	14,597	27,726	25,268	6,814	19,707	30,175	20,644	14,983	17,505	23,417
Capital Expenditures	8,179	7,753	7,330	7,443	8,631	9,722	7,384	9,618	10,320	9,949
Cash Flow	5,311	16,957	16,840	14,627	13,410	17,753	17,814	15,094	23,216	16,712
% Return on Assets	NM	0.6	0.7	0.5	0.2	1.5	2.1	1.2	3.0	2.3
% Return on Equity	NM	10.6	17.8	12.7	2.0	17.1	30.8	17.8	32.4	21.1
% Long Term Debt of Capitalization	91.0	85.5	85.2	89.0	79.4	63.8	69.3	71.0	66.6	58.8

Data as orig reptd.; bef. results of disc opers/spec. items. Per share data adj. for stk. divs.; EPS diluted. E-Estimated. NA-Not Available. NM-Not Meaningful. NR-Not Ranked. UR-Under Review.

Office: 300 Renaissance Center, Detroit, MI 48265-3000.
Telephone: 313-556-5000.
Website: http://www.gm.com
Chrmn & CEO: G.R. Wagoner, Jr.

Vice Chrmn: J.M. Devine
Vice Chrmn: R.A. Lutz
Vice Chrmn & CFO: F. Henderson
EVP & General Counsel: T.A. Gottschalk

Board of Directors: P. N. Barnevik, E. Bowles, J. H. Bryan, A. M. Codina, G. M. Fisher, K. Katen, K. Kresa, E. J. Kullman, P. A. Laskawy, E. Pfeiffer, G. R. Wagoner, Jr.

Founded: 1908
Domicile: Delaware
Employees: 335,000

Genuine Parts Co

STANDARD &POOR'S

S&P Recommendation HOLD ★★★★★

Price $45.60 (as of Oct 27, 2006)

12-Mo. Target Price $46.00

Investment Style Mid-Cap Value

GICS Sector Consumer Discretionary
Sub-Industry Distributors

Comment This company is a leading wholesale distributor of automotive replacement parts, industrial parts and supplies, and office products.

Key Stock Statistics (Source S&P, Vickers, company reports)

52-Wk Range	$46.16–40.00	S&P Oper. EPS 2006E	2.76	P/E on S&P Oper. EPS 2006E	16.5	Dividend Rate/Share	$1.35
Trailing 12-Month EPS	$2.69	S&P Oper. EPS 2007E	3.04	Common Shares Outstg. (M)	171.3	Yield (%)	2.96
Trailing 12-Month P/E	17.0	S&P Core EPS 2006E	2.73	Market Capitalization(B)	$7.812	Beta	0.66
$10K Invested 5 Yrs Ago	$15,625	S&P Core EPS 2007E	3.01	Institutional Ownership (%)	73	S&P Credit Rating	NA

Price Performance

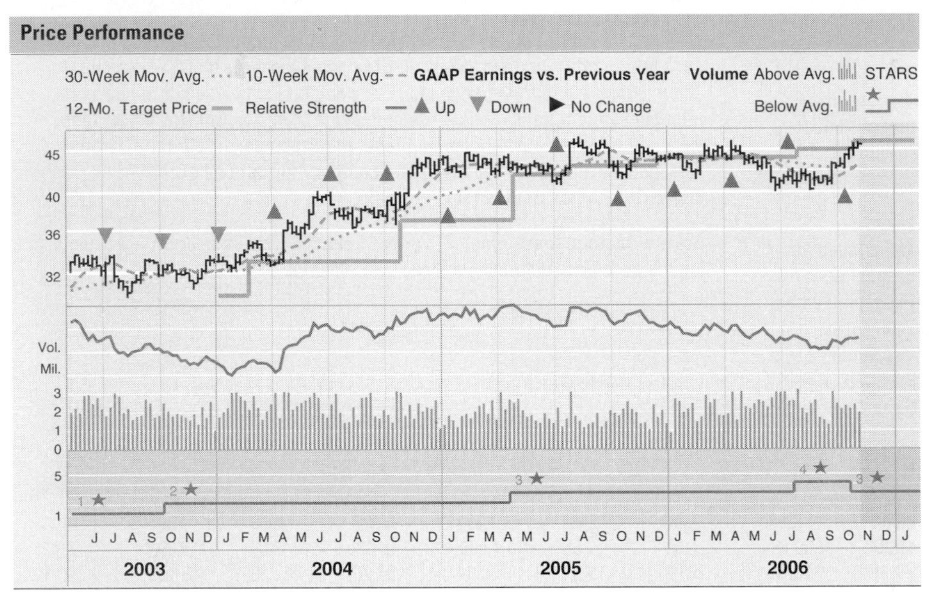

Options: P

Analysis prepared by **Efraim Levy, CFA** on October 19, 2006, when the stock traded at **$ 44.67**.

Highlights

- We expect revenues to grow 7.3% in both 2006 and 2007. We see sales gains in all four segments. We think pricing will remain competitive, and foresee gross margins rising modestly as GPC divests some low-margin businesses and cuts costs. Margin improvement, however, should be limited, as we expect other lower margin businesses to grow more rapidly than higher margin segments.
- We expect longer-term prospects for GPC's auto parts segment to be enhanced by the rising number and increasing complexity of vehicles. The average vehicle in the U.S. is currently more than eight years old. We believe GPC will benefit from an expanding market share, as long-term industry consolidation continues to drive out smaller participants. We also see GPC as likely to use its distribution strength to leverage sales of acquired parts companies.
- What we view as GPC's solid balance sheet, low debt, and strong cash flow are resources that could potentially be used to accelerate earnings growth in the longer term. We see GPC using cash flow to repurchase shares, invest in growing the business, make modest-sized acquisitions, and increase its dividend.

Investment Rationale/Risk

- Based on our 2007 EPS estimate, the stock's recent P/E multiple of about 15X is above the average for peers, reflecting, in our view, above average projected net margins. Earnings quality appears high to us, and we look for only minor adjustments to reported EPS using Standard & Poor's Core Earnings methodology. An above-average dividend yield adds to GPC's total return potential.
- Risks to our recommendation and target price include weaker than expected demand for the company's products, and a weaker than anticipated improvement in operating margins.
- We assume a P/E multiple of about 15X applied to our 2007 EPS estimate of $3.04 in our target price calculation, reflecting historical P/E multiple comparisons and leading to a value of nearly $46. Our DCF model, which assumes a weighted average cost of capital of 9.8%, a compound annual growth rate of 7% over the next 15 years, and a terminal growth rate of 3%, calculates an intrinsic value above $47. Based on a combination of our P/E and DCF analyses, our 12-month target price is $46.

Qualitative Risk Assessment

LOW | MEDIUM | HIGH

Our risk assessment reflects GPC's long-term record of rising sales and earnings and what we view as good, albeit conservative, corporate leadership and a healthy balance sheet.

Quantitative Evaluations

S&P Quality Ranking **A**

D | C | B- | B | B+ | A- | A | A+

Relative Strength Rank **MODERATE**

67

LOWEST = 1 HIGHEST = 99

Revenue/Earnings Data

Revenue (Million $)

	1Q	2Q	3Q	4Q	Year
2006	2,554	2,662	2,700	--	--
2005	2,342	2,476	2,556	2,410	9,783
2004	2,197	2,298	2,349	2,253	9,097
2003	2,022	2,153	2,189	2,085	8,449
2002	1,978	2,131	2,157	1,994	8,259
2001	2,055	2,119	2,099	1,948	8,221

Earnings Per Share ($)

2006	0.66	0.70	0.71	E0.70	E2.76
2005	0.61	0.63	0.63	0.63	2.50
2004	0.57	0.58	0.56	0.55	2.25
2003	0.51	0.52	0.51	0.50	2.03
2002	0.50	0.55	0.54	0.52	2.10
2001	0.52	0.55	0.51	0.14	1.71

Fiscal year ended Dec. 31. Next earnings report expected: Late February. EPS Estimates based on S&P Operating Earnings; historical GAAP earnings are as reported.

Dividend Data (Dates: mm/dd Payment Date: mm/dd/yy)

Amount ($)	Date Decl.	Ex-Div. Date	Stk. of Record	Payment Date
0.313	11/21	12/07	12/09	01/02/06
0.338	02/20	03/08	03/10	04/03/06
0.338	04/18	06/07	06/09	07/03/06
0.338	08/21	09/06	09/08	10/02/06

Dividends have been paid since 1948. Source: Company reports.

Genuine Parts Co

Business Summary October 19, 2006

CORPORATE OVERVIEW. Genuine Parts is the leading independent U.S. distributor of automotive replacement parts. As of December 2005, it operated 58 NAPA warehouse distribution centers in the U.S., about 1,000 company-owned jobbing stores, six Rayloc auto parts rebuilding plants, four Balkamp distribution centers, and four Johnson Industries facilities. The company has been expanding via a combination of internal growth and acquisitions.

The automotive parts segment (51% of 2005 revenues, 51% of profits) serves about 5,800 NAPA Auto Parts stores, including about 1,000 company-owned stores, selling to garages, service stations, car and truck dealers, fleet operators, leasing companies, bus and truck lines, etc.

The industrial parts segment (29%, 27%) distributes about three million industrial replacement parts and related supply items, including bearings, power transmission equipment replacement parts, including hydraulic and pneumatic products, material handling components, agricultural and irrigation equipment, and related items from locations in the U.S. and Canada.

Through S. P. Richards Co., the office products group (17%, 20%) distributes more than 30,000 office product items, including information processing supplies and office furniture, machines and supplies to office suppliers, from facilities in the U.S. and Canada.

The EIS electrical/electronics materials group (3%, 2%) was formed via the 1998 acquisition of EIS, Inc., for $200 million. EIS is a wholesale distributor of material and supplies to the electrical and electronic industries.

Company Financials

Per Share Data ($) Year Ended Dec. 31	**2005**	**2004**	**2003**	**2002**	**2001**	**2000**	**1999**	**1998**	**1997**	**1996**
Tangible Book Value	15.21	14.21	12.95	11.88	10.97	10.50	9.80	9.52	10.39	6.41
Cash Flow	2.87	2.61	2.42	2.50	2.21	2.72	2.61	2.36	2.23	2.09
Earnings	2.50	2.25	2.03	2.10	1.71	2.20	2.11	1.98	1.90	1.82
S&P Core Earnings	2.40	2.22	1.95	1.80	1.53	NA	NA	NA	NA	NA
Dividends	1.25	1.20	1.18	1.16	1.14	1.10	1.03	0.99	0.96	0.89
Payout Ratio	50%	53%	58%	55%	67%	50%	49%	50%	51%	49%
Prices:High	46.64	44.32	33.75	38.80	37.94	26.69	35.75	38.25	35.88	31.67
Prices:Low	40.75	32.03	27.20	27.10	23.91	18.25	22.25	28.25	28.67	26.67
P/E Ratio:High	19	20	17	18	22	12	17	19	19	17
P/E Ratio:Low	16	14	13	13	14	8	11	14	15	15
Income Statement Analysis (Million $)										
Revenue	9,783	9,097	8,449	8,259	8,221	8,370	7,982	6,614	6,005	5,720
Operating Income	804	698	641	676	656	739	718	658	624	596
Depreciation	65.5	62.2	69.0	70.2	85.8	92.3	90.0	69.3	58.9	50.4
Interest Expense	29.6	Nil	Nil	Nil	Nil	Nil	Nil	Nil	Nil	NM
Pretax Income	709	636	572	606	496	647	628	589	566	545
Effective Tax Rate	38.3%	37.8%	38.1%	39.3%	40.1%	40.4%	39.9%	39.6%	39.5%	39.5%
Net Income	437	396	354	368	297	385	378	356	342	330
S&P Core Earnings	420	388	339	316	265	NA	NA	NA	NA	NA
Balance Sheet & Other Financial Data (Million $)										
Cash	189	135	15.4	20.0	85.8	27.7	45.7	85.0	72.8	67.4
Current Assets	3,807	3,633	3,418	3,336	3,146	3,019	2,895	2,683	2,094	1,938
Total Assets	4,772	4,455	4,116	4,020	4,207	4,142	3,930	3,600	2,754	2,522
Current Liabilities	1,249	1,133	1,017	1,070	919	988	916	818	557	568
Long Term Debt	500	500	625	675	836	771	702	589	210	110
Common Equity	2,694	2,544	2,312	2,130	2,345	2,261	2,178	2,053	1,859	1,732
Total Capital	3,408	3,212	3,100	2,950	3,287	3,154	3,014	2,782	2,198	1,953
Capital Expenditures	85.7	72.1	73.9	64.8	41.9	71.1	88.3	88.2	90.4	95.2
Cash Flow	503	458	423	438	383	478	468	425	401	380
Current Ratio	3.0	3.2	3.4	3.1	3.4	3.1	3.2	3.3	3.8	3.4
% Long Term Debt of Capitalization	14.7	15.6	20.2	22.9	25.4	24.4	23.3	21.1	9.5	5.6
% Net Income of Revenue	4.5	4.3	4.2	4.4	3.6	4.6	4.7	5.4	5.7	5.8
% Return on Assets	9.5	9.2	8.6	8.9	7.1	9.5	10.0	11.2	13.0	13.8
% Return on Equity	16.7	16.3	15.9	16.4	12.9	17.4	17.9	18.2	19.1	19.5

Data as orig reptd.; bef. results of disc opers/spec. items. Per share data adj. for stk. divs.; EPS diluted. E-Estimated. NA-Not Available. NM-Not Meaningful. NR-Not Ranked. UR-Under Review.

Office: 2999 Circle 75 Parkway, Atlanta, GA 30339.
Telephone: 770-953-1700.
Website: http://www.genpt.com
Chrmn, Pres & CEO: T.C. Gallagher

Vice Chrmn, EVP & CFO: J.W. Nix
SVP & Secy: C.B. Yancey
Investor Contact: S.G. Jones (770-953-1700)

Board of Directors: M. B. Bullock, R. W. Courts, II, J. Douville, T. C. Gallagher, J. D. Johns, M. M. Johns, J. H. Lanier, W. B. Needham, J. W. Nix, L. L. Prince, G. W. Rollins, L. G. Steiner

Founded: 1928
Domicile: Georgia
Employees: 31,700

STANDARD &POOR'S

Genworth Financial Inc

S&P Recommendation	Price	12-Mo. Target Price	Investment Style
BUY ★★★★★	$33.69 (as of Oct 27, 2006)	$39.00	Large-Cap Value

GICS Sector Financials
Sub-Industry Multi-line Insurance

Comment This insurance holding company serves lifestyle protection, retirement income, investment and mortgage insurance needs around the world.

Key Stock Statistics (Source S&P, Vickers, company reports)

52-Wk Range	$36.47–30.90	S&P Oper. EPS 2006E	2.82	P/E on S&P Oper. EPS 2006E	11.9	Dividend Rate/Share	$0.36
Trailing 12-Month EPS	$2.65	S&P Oper. EPS 2007E	3.18	Common Shares Outstg. (M)	455.0	Yield (%)	1.07
Trailing 12-Month P/E	12.7	S&P Core EPS 2006E	2.79	Market Capitalization(B)	$15.329	Beta	0.97
$10K Invested 5 Yrs Ago	NA	S&P Core EPS 2007E	3.15	Institutional Ownership (%)	98	S&P Credit Rating	A

Price Performance

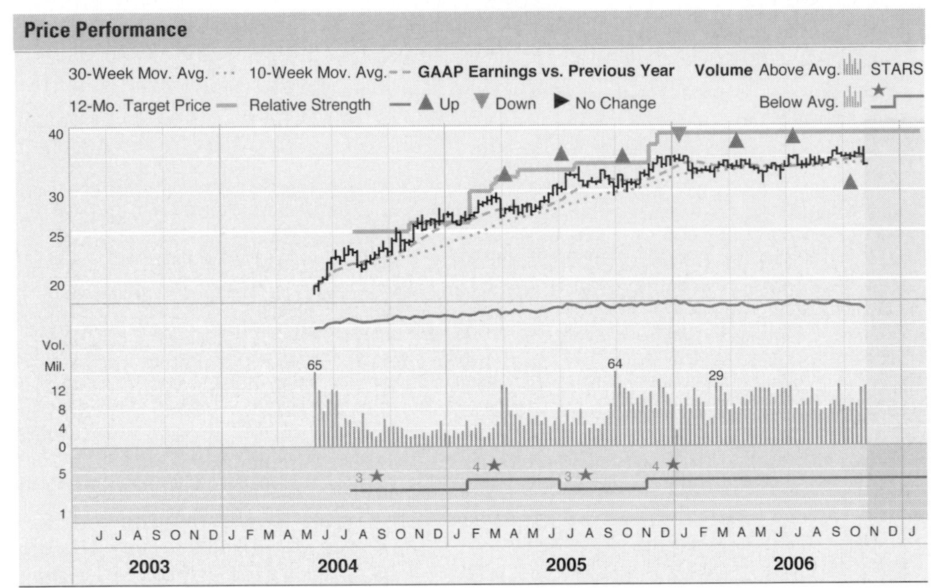

Analysis prepared by **Frank Braden** on August 02, 2006, when the stock traded at **$ 34.52**.

Highlights

- We forecast operating earnings increases for the protection segment of 8% in 2006, on double digit growth in life and single digit growth in long-term care (LTC) product earnings. We expect operating earnings for the retirement income and investments segment to benefit from the strong growth we foresee in earnings for fee-based products, partially offset by weaker sales of fixed annuity products, reflecting the difficult interest rate environment.

- We see operating earnings from the mortgage insurance segment growing near 20% in 2006. We expect premiums to climb 35% in 2006 in the international mortgage insurance businesses, based on GNW's aggressive expansion in Continental Europe. We project that premiums for the U.S. mortgage insurance businesses will see a modest rise as management focuses on the higher margin European business. We see GNW reaching 12% ROE prior to management's goal of year-end 2008.

- We estimate 15% growth in operating EPS in 2006, to $2.90, on approximately 3% fewer shares, including projected stock option expense.

Investment Rationale/Risk

- We believe GNW will benefit from growth in its higher margin businesses, including international mortgage insurance, European payment protection insurance, and traditional life. We expect $1.5 billion of capital redeployment in 2006, with $1 billion of excess capital at year end. We remain concerned with the overall health of the long-term care industry and expect low terminations of older blocks and the loss of some reinsurance coverage to remain a drag on earnings.

- Risks to our opinion and target price include low interest rates environment; higher investment portfolio risks; high concentrations of product line sales associated with certain third parties; and price, integration and execution risks associated with potential acquisitions.

- We arrive at our 12-month target price of $39 by applying a 13.4X P/E multiple to our 2006 operating EPS estimate of $2.90, a premium to the peer group average to account for our forecast of higher than average growth over the next several years.

Qualitative Risk Assessment

LOW | MEDIUM | HIGH

Our risk assessment reflects what we see as GNW's strong balance sheet and large amount of excess capital. The company should benefit from improved financial flexibility now that GE has fully divested its shares of GNW.

Quantitative Evaluations

S&P Quality Ranking **NR**

D | C | B- | B | B+ | A- | A | A+

Relative Strength Rank **WEAK**

19

LOWEST = 1 HIGHEST = 99

Revenue/Earnings Data

Revenue (Million $)

	1Q	2Q	3Q	4Q	Year
2006	2,625	2,754	2.80	--	--
2005	2,611	2,610	2,628	2,655	10,504
2004	3,024	2,921	2,470	2,642	11,057
2003	--	--	--	--	9,775
2002	--	--	--	--	--
2001	--	--	--	--	--

Earnings Per Share ($)

	1Q	2Q	3Q	4Q	Year
2006	0.69	0.68	0.65	**E**0.71	**E**2.82
2005	0.65	0.60	0.64	0.64	2.52
2004	0.53	0.55	0.55	0.70	2.34
2003	--	--	--	--	1.82
2002	--	--	--	--	--
2001	--	--	--	--	--

Fiscal year ended Dec. 31. Next earnings report expected: Late January. EPS Estimates based on S&P Operating Earnings; historical GAAP earnings are as reported.

Dividend Data (Dates: mm/dd Payment Date: mm/dd/yy)

Amount ($)	Date Decl.	Ex-Div. Date	Stk. of Record	Payment Date
0.075	12/02	01/10	01/12	01/27/06
0.075	03/22	04/10	04/12	04/27/06
0.075	05/17	07/10	07/12	07/27/06
0.090	09/20	10/10	10/12	10/27/06

Dividends have been paid since 2004. Source: Company reports.

Genworth Financial Inc

Business Summary August 02, 2006

CORPORATE OVERVIEW. Genworth Financial, Inc., carved out from General Electric (GE) in May 2004, is a U.S. insurance company with an expanding international presence. As of February 2006, GNW had operations in 24 countries, and believed it was the largest provider of private mortgage insurance outside the U.S. based on new insurance written. According to reports by VARDS, LIMRA International and Inside Mortgage Finance magazine, GNW in 2005 was the largest U.S. provider of variable income annuities and the second largest provider of fixed immediate annuities, based on total premiums and deposits, and the fifth largest provider of mortgage insurance, based on new insurance written.

U.S. operations accounted for 80% of total revenues in 2005 (81% in 2004), while international operations accounted for 20% (19%).

The company conducts its business through three major segments. The protection business (58% of 2005 total revenues) offers U.S. customers life insurance, long-term care insurance and, for companies with fewer than 1,000 employees, group life and health insurance. In 2005, GNW was the leading provider of individual long-term care insurance based on annualized first-year premiums, according to LIMRA International. In Europe, it offers payment protection insurance, which helps consumers meet their payment obligations in the event of illness, involuntary unemployment, disability or death. The retirement income and investments business (28%) offers U.S. customers fixed, variable and income annuities, variable life insurance, asset management and specialized products, including guaranteed investment contracts, funding agreements and structured settlements. The mortgage insurance business (12%) offers mortgage insurance products in the U.S., Canada, Australia, New Zealand and Europe that facilitate home ownership by enabling borrowers to buy homes with low-down-payment mortgages. These products also help financial institutions manage their capital efficiently by reducing the capital required for low-down-payment mortgages.

Company Financials

Per Share Data ($) Year Ended Dec. 31	2005	2004	2003	2002	2001	2000	1999	1998	1997	1996
Tangible Book Value	24.51	21.69	20.18	NA	NA	NA	NA	NA	NA	NA
Operating Earnings	NA	NA	NA	NA	NA	NA	NA	NA	NA	NA
Earnings	2.52	2.34	1.82	NA	NA	NA	NA	NA	NA	NA
S&P Core Earnings	2.52	2.29	1.96	NA	NA	NA	NA	NA	NA	NA
Dividends	0.27	0.07	NA	NA	NA	NA	NA	NA	NA	NA
Relative Payout	11%	3%	NA	NA	NA	NA	NA	NA	NA	NA
Prices:High	35.25	27.84	NA	NA	NA	NA	NA	NA	NA	NA
Prices:Low	25.72	18.75	NA	NA	NA	NA	NA	NA	NA	NA
P/E Ratio:High	14	12	NA	NA	NA	NA	NA	NA	NA	NA
P/E Ratio:Low	10	8	NA	NA	NA	NA	NA	NA	NA	NA
Income Statement Analysis (Million $)										
Life Insurance in Force	NA	NA	NA	NA	NA	NA	NA	NA	NA	NA
Premium Income:Life A & H	NA	NA	6,252	NA	NA	NA	NA	NA	NA	NA
Premium Income:Casualty/Property.	NA	NA	Nil	NA	NA	NA	NA	NA	NA	NA
Net Investment Income	3,536	3,648	2,928	NA	NA	NA	NA	NA	NA	NA
Total Revenue	10,504	11,057	9,775	NA	NA	NA	NA	NA	NA	NA
Pretax Income	1,798	1,638	1,263	NA	NA	NA	NA	NA	NA	NA
Net Operating Income	NA	NA	NA	NA	NA	NA	NA	NA	NA	NA
Net Income	1,221	1,145	892	NA	NA	NA	NA	NA	NA	NA
S&P Core Earnings	1,221	1,126	956	NA	NA	NA	NA	NA	NA	NA
Balance Sheet & Other Financial Data (Million $)										
Cash & Equivalent	2,608	2,125	1,630	NA	NA	NA	NA	NA	NA	NA
Premiums Due	NA	NA	NA	NA	NA	NA	NA	NA	NA	NA
Investment Assets:Bonds	53,791	52,424	50,081	NA	NA	NA	NA	NA	NA	NA
Investment Assets:Stocks	367	374	387	NA	NA	NA	NA	NA	NA	NA
Investment Assets:Loans	8,908	7,275	6,794	NA	NA	NA	NA	NA	NA	NA
Investment Assets:Total	66,573	65,747	61,749	NA	NA	NA	NA	NA	NA	NA
Deferred Policy Costs	5,586	5,020	4,421	NA	NA	NA	NA	NA	NA	NA
Total Assets	105,292	103,878	100,216	NA	NA	NA	NA	NA	NA	NA
Debt	3,336	3,042	3,016	NA	NA	NA	NA	NA	NA	NA
Common Equity	13,310	12,866	12,258	NA	NA	NA	NA	NA	NA	NA
Combined Loss-Expense Ratio	NA	NA	NA	NA	NA	NA	NA	NA	NA	NA
% Return on Revenue	11.6	10.4	9.1	NA	NA	NA	NA	NA	NA	NA
% Return on Equity	9.3	8.0	NA	NA	NA	NA	NA	NA	NA	NA
% Investment Yield	NA	NA	NA	NA	NA	NA	NA	NA	NA	NA

Data as orig reptd.; bef. results of disc opers/spec. items. Per share data adj. for stk. divs.; EPS diluted. E-Estimated. NA-Not Available. NM-Not Meaningful. NR-Not Ranked. UR-Under Review.

Office: 6620 West Broad Street, Richmond, VA 23230.
Telephone: 804-281-6000.
Email: investorinfo@genworth.com
Website: http://www.genworth.com

Chrmn, Pres & CEO: M.D. Fraizer
SVP & CFO: R.P. McKenney
SVP, Secy & General Counsel: L.E. Roday
Investor Contact: J.S. Peters (804-662-2693)

VP & Cntlr: S.R. Lindquist
Board of Directors: F. J. Borelli, M. D. Fraizer, N. J. Karch, J. R. Kerrey, S. T. Naqvi, J. A. Parke, J. S. Riepe, B. A. Toan, T. B. Wheeler

Auditor: KPMG, Richmond, VA
Founded: 2003
Domicile: Delaware
Employees: 6,900

Genzyme Corp

S&P Recommendation	Price	12-Mo. Target Price	Investment Style
BUY ★★★★★	$68.69 (as of Oct 27, 2006)	$76.00	Large-Cap Growth

GICS Sector Health Care
Sub-Industry Biotechnology

Comment This biopharmaceutical concern makes and markets human therapeutic and diagnostic products. Its largest selling product is Cerezyme, a drug to treat Gaucher disease.

Key Stock Statistics (Source S&P, Vickers, company reports)

52-Wk Range	$77.82–54.64	S&P Oper. EPS 2006E	2.32	P/E on S&P Oper. EPS 2006E	29.6	Dividend Rate/Share	Nil
Trailing 12-Month EPS	$1.32	S&P Oper. EPS 2007E	2.83	Common Shares Outstg. (M)	261.4	Yield (%)	Nil
Trailing 12-Month P/E	52.0	S&P Core EPS 2006E	2.32	Market Capitalization(B)	$17.954	Beta	1.45
$10K Invested 5 Yrs Ago	$12,645	S&P Core EPS 2007E	2.83	Institutional Ownership (%)	91	S&P Credit Rating	BBB

Price Performance

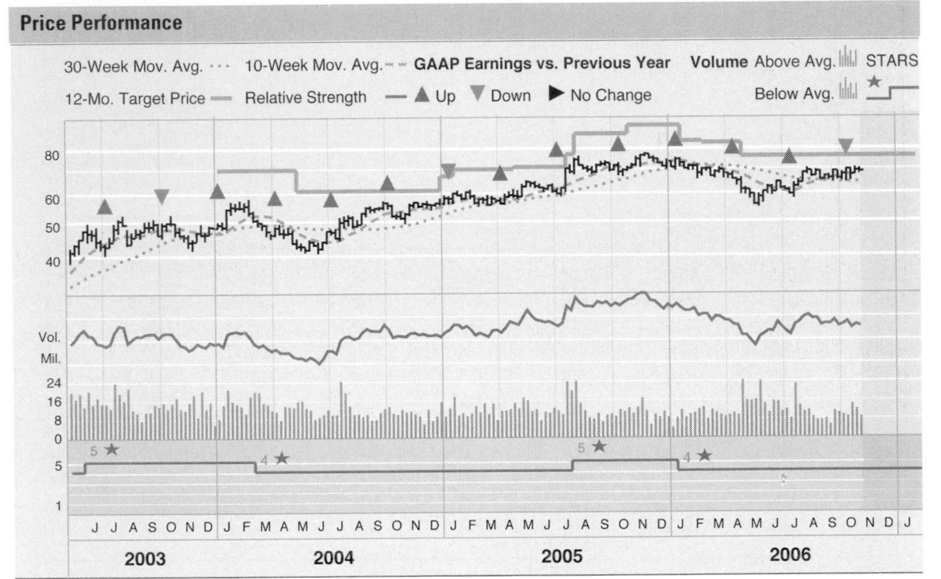

Options: ASE, CBOE

Analysis prepared by **Paul Starsia** on October 13, 2006, when the stock traded at **$ 66.74**.

Highlights

- Third quarter EPS, before charges and after stock option expense, was $0.60, compared with $0.61 in the prior year. Revenue growth was somewhat disappointing to us, due to the entrance of a new competitor for Synvisc and slower Fabrazyme patient accruals. Myozyme sales were within expectations.

- The company exceeded its third quarter earning guidance due to a higher gross margin that was the result of manufacturing efficiencies, as well as tight expense control. GENZ expects steady improvement in the gross margin as it achieves higher capacity utilization with the addition of new products.

- We see revenues of about $3.1 billion in 2006, a 17% gain from 2005, and $3.6 billion in 2007. Sales growth should be led by new products Hectoral and Myozyme, as well as solid demand for Renagel and Fabrazyme. GENZ appears on track to meet its goal of 20% EPS growth for 2006, and we are maintaining our 2006 and 2007 EPS estimates of $2.32 and $2.83, respectively, both including option expense.

Investment Rationale/Risk

- Fresenius, a large dialysis operator in the U.S., recently bought the rights to PhosLo, a direct competitor to GENZ's Renagel. Fresenius said that it would not switch patients to PhosLo if there were no clinical justification. We think the threat to Renagel is modest in the near term but will require monitoring going forward. We see the weakness in Synvisc as temporary and due to price discounting, rather than clinical superiority of competing Euflexxa. We expect the introduction of next generation, once a day, longer lasting Synvisc to overcome sales weakness in coming quarters.

- Risks to our recommendation and target price include increased competition for Cerazyme, Renagel, and Synvisc, clinical and regulatory risks for pipeline products Tolevamer, Campath, and Sevelamer Carbonate, and changes in Medicare reimbursement policies.

- Assuming that GENZ trades at a P/E to earnings growth (PEG) ratio of 1.3X (the recent PEG range for profitable biotechs was 1.0X to 1.6X), based on our 2008 EPS estimate of $3.45 and our 5-year EPS growth projections of 16%, our 12-month target price is $76.

Qualitative Risk Assessment

LOW | **MEDIUM** | HIGH

Due to the diversity of Genzyme's portfolio of therapeutic products, as well as its diagnostic business, we believe it carries less risk than most biotech issues. With regard to the firm's individual drugs of importance, we think Renagel faces the greatest competition and should continue to see a strong competitive landscape for the foreseeable future.

Quantitative Evaluations

S&P Quality Ranking **B**

D | C | B- | **B** | B+ | A- | A | A+

Relative Strength Rank **MODERATE**

49

LOWEST = 1 HIGHEST = 99

Revenue/Earnings Data

Revenue (Million $)

	1Q	2Q	3Q	4Q	Year
2006	730.8	793.4	808.6	--	--
2005	630.0	668.1	708.1	728.7	2,735
2004	491.3	549.6	569.2	591.1	2,201
2003	381.9	418.9	437.0	476.1	1,714
2002	242.2	267.2	272.8	298.1	1,080
2001	222.7	239.0	255.1	265.2	981.9

Earnings Per Share ($)

	1Q	2Q	3Q	4Q	Year
2006	0.37	0.49	0.06	E0.62	E2.32
2005	0.36	0.46	0.43	0.39	1.65
2004	0.29	0.33	0.41	-0.68	0.37
2003	0.28	0.32	-0.43	0.25	0.42
2002	0.14	0.23	0.25	0.20	0.81
2001	0.18	0.31	-0.37	0.20	0.19

Fiscal year ended Dec. 31. Next earnings report expected: Mid February. EPS Estimates based on S&P Operating Earnings; historical GAAP earnings are as reported.

Dividend Data

No cash dividends have been paid.

Please read the Required Disclosures and Analyst Certification on the last page of this report.

Genzyme Corp

Business Summary October 13, 2006

CORPORATE OVERVIEW. Genzyme develops, manufactures and markets therapeutic and diagnostic products. The company's lead therapeutic product is Cerezyme, an enzyme replacement therapy for Gaucher disease, a debilitating genetic disorder that causes fatigue, anemia, and bone erosion. Cerezyme sales totaled $933 million in 2005 ($839 million in 2004).

Renagel, a treatment to reduce elevated serum phosphorus in patients on kidney dialysis, is GENZ's second largest selling product. Sales in 2005 were $418 million ($364 million). GENZ markets Renagel in the U.S. and Europe.

Enzyme replacement therapy Fabrazyme was approved in Europe in August 2001 and in the U.S. in April 2003 for the treatment of Fabry disease, a rare genetic disorder. Fabrazyme sales were $305 million in 2005, up from $210 million in 2004. Aldurazyme, an enzyme replacement therapy for MPS-I, was approved by the FDA in April 2003. Aldurazyme is partnered with BioMarin through a 50%-owned joint venture. GENZ has developed Myozyme, another enzyme replacement therapy for the treatment of Pompe disease. This is a rare and often fatal disorder with an estimated patent population of less than 10,000 worldwide. Myozyme has been approved by the FDA. In the third quarter of 2006, Myozyme sales totaled $20.4 million. Synvisc is an injectable hyaluronan-based biomaterial to treat osteoarthritis of the knee by improving joint lubrication. In January 2005, GENZ reacquired U.S. marketing rights to Synvisc from Wyeth.

In July 2005, GENZ acquired Bone Care International Inc. for $604 million, net of Bone Care's cash. Bone Care's main product is Hectorol, a vitamin D2 product to treat secondary hyperparathyroidism in patients with chronic kidney disease. In December 2004, GENZ acquired ILEX Oncology for about $1 billion. Two approved drugs obtained through this deal are Clolar, to treat children with relapsed or refractory acute lymphoblastic leukemia, and Campath, to treat chronic lymphocytic leukemia. In September 2003, GENZ acquired SangStat Medical for $637 million cash. The primary product stemming from this purchase was Thymoglobulin, approved by the FDA to treat kidney transplant rejection

Company Financials

Per Share Data ($) Year Ended Dec. 31	**2005**	**2004**	**2003**	**2002**	**2001**	**2000**	**1999**	**1998**	**1997**	**1996**
Tangible Book Value	7.99	8.11	6.31	NM	6.10	4.05	5.54	5.56	4.75	4.22
Cash Flow	2.67	1.24	0.41	1.16	0.75	0.91	1.27	1.02	0.77	-0.01
Earnings	1.65	0.37	0.42	0.81	0.19	0.68	1.00	0.74	0.49	-0.23
S&P Core Earnings	1.23	-0.03	-0.26	0.59	0.02	NA	NA	NA	NA	NA
Dividends	Nil	Nil	Nil	Nil	Nil	Nil	Nil	0.01	Nil	Nil
Payout Ratio	Nil	Nil	Nil	Nil	Nil	Nil	Nil	1%	Nil	Nil
Prices:High	77.82	59.14	52.45	58.55	64.00	51.88	31.56	25.00	16.50	19.25
Prices:Low	55.15	40.67	28.45	15.64	34.34	19.84	15.38	11.75	10.38	9.88
P/E Ratio:High	47	NM	NM	72	NM	77	32	34	34	NM
P/E Ratio:Low	33	NM	NM	19	NM	29	15	16	21	NM

Income Statement Analysis (Million $)	2005	2004	2003	2002	2001	2000	1999	1998	1997	1996
Revenue	2,735	2,201	1,714	1,080	982	752	635	673	597	511
Operating Income	915	717	463	318	380	-185	280	185	140	128
Depreciation	285	205	160	96.0	118	41.2	50.2	45.8	43.7	29.3
Interest Expense	19.6	38.2	26.6	17.8	23.2	14.2	19.9	17.1	8.11	6.84
Pretax Income	641	222	2.82	207	56.5	-179	226	164	90.6	-27.3
Effective Tax Rate	29.2%	63.7%	NM	27.3%	93.1%	51.9%	37.3%	38.2%	37.1%	NM
Net Income	441	86.5	-67.6	151	3.88	85.9	142	101	57.0	-47.5
S&P Core Earnings	326	-6.61	-61.0	125	5.25	NA	NA	NA	NA	NA

Balance Sheet & Other Financial Data (Million $)	2005	2004	2003	2002	2001	2000	1999	1998	1997	1996
Cash	292	481	293	373	167	136	94.5	100	66.3	77.2
Current Assets	1,665	1,634	1,323	1,100	721	605	605	610	406	491
Total Assets	6,879	6,069	5,005	3,556	3,225	2,499	1,400	1,646	1,203	1,230
Current Liabilities	550	624	392	275	243	167	117	197	97.5	110
Long Term Debt	816	811	1,415	600	600	454	273	275	118	224
Common Equity	5,150	4,380	2,936	2,586	2,280	1,750	1,008	1,167	981	884
Total Capital	6,301	5,417	4,558	3,268	2,961	2,329	1,280	1,442	1,099	1,108
Capital Expenditures	19.2	187	260	220	171	72.6	52.9	55.3	28.5	42.5
Cash Flow	726	292	92.9	247	122	127	192	147	101	-18.2
Current Ratio	3.0	2.6	3.4	4.0	3.0	3.6	5.2	3.1	4.2	4.5
% Long Term Debt of Capitalization	12.9	15.0	30.1	18.4	20.3	31.1	21.3	19.1	10.7	20.2
% Net Income of Revenue	16.1	3.9	NM	14.0	0.4	11.4	22.4	15.0	9.5	NM
% Return on Assets	6.8	1.6	NM	4.4	0.2	4.0	10.1	7.1	4.7	NM
% Return on Equity	9.3	2.4	NM	6.2	0.1	5.5	14.6	9.4	6.1	NM

Data as orig reptd.; bef. results of disc opers/spec. items. Per share data adj. for stk. divs.; EPS diluted. E-Estimated. NA-Not Available. NM-Not Meaningful. NR-Not Ranked. UR-Under Review.

Office: 500 Kendall St, Cambridge, MA 02142-1108.
Telephone: 617-252-7570.
Email: information@genzyme.com
Website: http://www.genzyme.com

Chrmn, Pres & CEO: H.A. Termeer
EVP, CFO & Chief Acctg Officer: M.S. Wyzga
EVP & Secy: P. Wirth
SVP & CSO: A.E. Smith

Investor Contact: K. Galfetti (617-768-6563)
Board of Directors: D. A. Berthiaume, H. E. Blair, G. K. Boudreaux, R. J. Carpenter, C. L. Cooney, V. J. Dzau, C. Mack, III, R. F. Syron, H. A. Termeer

Founded: 1991
Domicile: Massachusetts
Employees: 8,200

STANDARD &POOR'S

Gilead Sciences Inc

S&P Recommendation HOLD ★★★★★

Price $68.18 (as of Oct 27, 2006)

12-Mo. Target Price $70.00

Investment Style Large-Cap Growth

GICS Sector Health Care
Sub-Industry Biotechnology

Comment This biopharmaceutical company is engaged in the discovery, development and commercialization of treatments to fight bacterial, fungal, and viral infections.

Key Stock Statistics (Source S&P, Vickers, company reports)

52-Wk Range	**$69.63–46.54**	S&P Oper. EPS 2006**E**	**2.40**	P/E on S&P Oper. EPS 2006**E**	**28.4**	Dividend Rate/Share	**Nil**
Trailing 12-Month EPS	**$1.58**	S&P Oper. EPS 2007**E**	**2.50**	Common Shares Outstg. (M)	**456.8**	Yield (%)	**Nil**
Trailing 12-Month P/E	**43.2**	S&P Core EPS 2006**E**	**2.40**	Market Capitalization(B)	**$31.147**	Beta	**0.92**
$10K Invested 5 Yrs Ago	**$40,296**	S&P Core EPS 2007**E**	**2.50**	Institutional Ownership (%)	**91**	S&P Credit Rating	**NA**

Price Performance

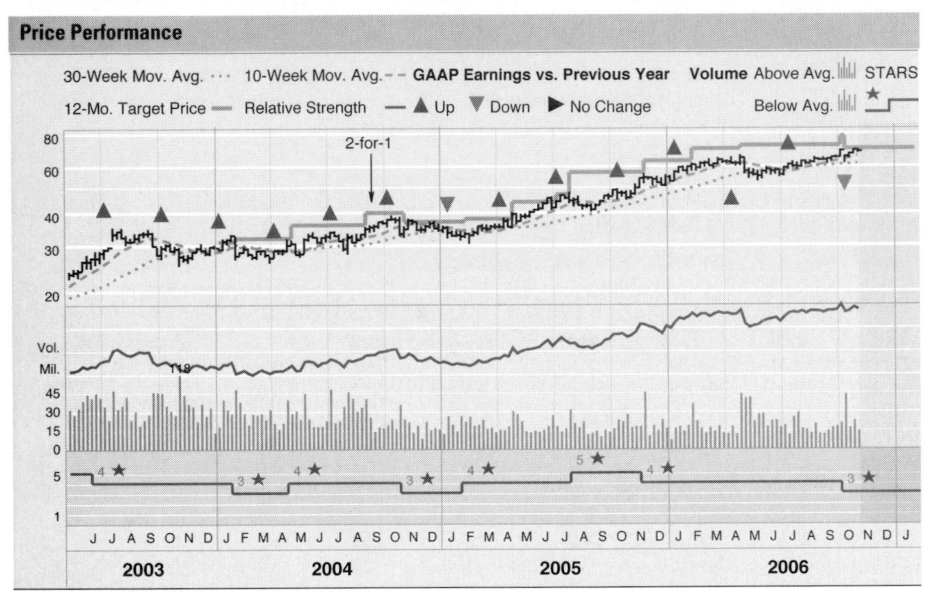

Options: CBOE, P, Ph

Analysis prepared by **Paul Starsia** on October 23, 2006, when the stock traded at **$ 69.38**.

Highlights

- Excluding a one-time charge of $356 million and including projected stock option expense of $25 million, GILD reported third quarter EPS of $0.58, well ahead of our $0.51 estimate. The earnings upside was primarily due to, in our opinion, much better than expected sales of Atripla, GILD's newly launched triple-combination HIV drug, which generated sales of $65 million versus our $35 million forecast. Truvada sequential sales growth was just 3.3%.

- On October 2, 2006, GILD announced that it plans to acquire Myogen (MYOG: $52) for $2.5 billion in cash. The proposed deal, subject to necessary approvals, gives GILD access to two late-stage product candidates: ambrisentan for pulmonary arterial hypertension, and darusentan for resistant hypertension. The proposed transaction should be dilutive to 2007 and 2008 EPS, neutral in 2009, and accretive in 2010.

- Following the strong third quarter results, we raised our 2006 EPS from $2.25 to $2.40, but lowered our 2007 forecast from $2.70 to $2.50 (all estimates include projected stock option expense), to reflect increased expenses associated with the planned MYOG deal.

Investment Rationale/Risk

- Atripla's launch exceeded expectations by a wide margin, and we anticipate that the drug will become the gold standard of care in the HIV treatment market, due to its convenient dosing regimen and favorable side-effect profile. We believe that Truvada sales may have reached a plateau, but look for Atripla market share gains to maintain HIV franchise sales momentum going forward. We believe that ambrisentan will help support the company's long-term growth rate, and that additional acquisitions are likely in the future.

- Risks to our recommendation and target price include slower than expected sales of the company's HIV drugs, pipeline setbacks, and acquisition integration issues.

- Our 12-month target price of $70 is based on our P/E analysis, which assigns a 28X multiple applied to our 2007 EPS estimate of $2.50. This is in line with the average for our universe of large-cap biotech stocks, and reflects a significant premium to the company's estimated five-year EPS growth rate of 16%.

Qualitative Risk Assessment

LOW | MEDIUM | **HIGH**

Our risk assessment reflects that Gilead is highly dependent on the growth of its antiHIV drug portfolio. Also, the company operates in a highly competitive market, and a lack of pipeline development could result in diminished growth expectations in the future.

Quantitative Evaluations

S&P Quality Ranking B-

D | C | **B-** | B | B+ | A- | A | A+

Relative Strength Rank MODERATE

67

LOWEST = 1 HIGHEST = 99

Revenue/Earnings Data

Revenue (Million $)

	1Q	2Q	3Q	4Q	Year
2006	692.9	685.3	748.7	--	--
2005	430.4	495.3	493.5	609.3	2,028
2004	309.1	319.7	326.2	369.6	1,325
2003	165.1	238.9	200.4	263.5	867.9
2002	78.42	109.4	134.0	145.0	466.8
2001	57.84	50.69	50.92	74.33	233.8

Earnings Per Share ($)

	1Q	2Q	3Q	4Q	Year
2006	0.55	0.56	-0.11	**E**0.58	**E**2.40
2005	0.34	0.41	0.38	0.59	1.72
2004	0.25	0.24	0.25	0.24	0.99
2003	-1.11	0.23	0.17	0.43	-0.18
2002	-0.01	0.05	0.05	0.09	0.17
2001	-0.06	-0.09	-0.07	0.31	0.13

Fiscal year ended Dec. 31. Next earnings report expected: Late January. EPS Estimates based on S&P Operating Earnings; historical GAAP earnings are as reported.

Dividend Data

No cash dividends have been paid.

Gilead Sciences Inc

Business Summary October 23, 2006

CORPORATE OVERVIEW. Gilead Sciences focuses on the research, development and marketing of anti-infective medications, with a primary focus on treatments for HIV.

In October 2001, the FDA approved Viread to treat HIV patients. In addition to being used on patients who have become resistant to other reverse transcriptase inhibitors, clinical data on Viread's use in treating naive patients has helped to drive sales in the frontline treatment setting. Viread sales were $779 million in 2005, compared to $783 million in 2004.

In January 2003, GILD acquired Triangle Pharmaceuticals (VIRS) for about $464 million in cash. VIRS's lead product was Emtriva, an antiHIV medication. Emtriva was approved by the FDA in July 2003, and in October 2003 in Europe. In August 2004, the FDA approved Truvada, a once-daily combination tablet formulated with Viread and Emtriva. Truvada sales were $568 million in 2005.

In September 2002, Hepsera was approved by the FDA. In March 2003, it was approved in the European Union (EU). GILD recorded $187 million in Hepsera sales in 2005, up from $113 million in 2004. The company out-licensed rights to Hepsera for Asia and Latin America to GlaxoSmithKline (GSK) in exchange for milestones and royalties.

AmBisome is a liposomal formulation of amphotericin B, an antifungal agent that can attack and kill a broad variety of life-threatening fungal infections. AmBisome is co-marketed in the U.S. with Fujisawa Healthcare, and is also approved by the FDA to treat cryptococcal meningitis in AIDS patients. Sales were $221 million in 2005, up from $212 million in 2004.

Company Financials

Per Share Data ($) Year Ended Dec. 31	**2005**	**2004**	**2003**	**2002**	**2001**	**2000**	**1999**	**1998**	**1997**	**1996**
Tangible Book Value	6.59	4.17	2.35	1.45	1.17	0.93	0.84	0.94	1.15	1.27
Cash Flow	1.79	1.02	-0.13	0.21	0.16	-0.09	-0.16	-0.22	0.13	-0.08
Earnings	1.72	0.99	-0.18	0.17	0.13	-0.12	-0.19	-0.23	-0.12	-0.10
S&P Core Earnings	1.56	0.78	-0.33	0.02	-0.27	NA	NA	NA	NA	NA
Dividends	Nil	Nil	Nil	Nil	Nil	Nil	Nil	Nil	Nil	Nil
Payout Ratio	Nil	Nil	Nil	Nil	Nil	Nil	Nil	Nil	Nil	Nil
Prices:High	56.51	39.10	35.31	20.00	18.42	14.77	11.94	5.53	5.91	5.31
Prices:Low	30.39	25.75	15.62	13.04	6.22	5.41	4.41	2.25	2.64	2.03
P/E Ratio:High	33	39	NM	NM	NM	NM	NM	NM	NM	NM
P/E Ratio:Low	18	26	NM	NM	NM	NM	NM	NM	NM	NM

Income Statement Analysis (Million $)										
Revenue	2,028	1,325	868	467	234	196	169	32.6	40.0	33.4
Operating Income	1,148	656	361	95.4	-106	-40.3	-39.2	-71.6	-42.8	-31.6
Depreciation	36.8	24.4	20.9	14.4	14.7	12.0	12.6	2.76	2.98	4.48
Interest Expense	0.44	7.35	21.9	13.9	14.0	Nil	6.52	0.19	0.49	0.71
Pretax Income	1,158	656	-168	73.4	55.3	-41.9	-65.6	-56.1	28.0	-21.7
Effective Tax Rate	30.0%	31.5%	NM	1.77%	7.48%	NM	NM	NM	NM	NM
Net Income	814	449	-72.0	72.1	51.2	-43.1	-66.5	-56.1	28.0	-21.7
S&P Core Earnings	737	354	-133	8.55	-108	NA	NA	NA	NA	NA

Balance Sheet & Other Financial Data (Million $)										
Cash	2,324	1,254	707	942	583	513	294	32.5	32.0	132
Current Assets	3,092	1,850	1,266	1,184	708	594	372	288	340	300
Total Assets	3,765	2,156	1,555	1,288	795	678	437	303	352	311
Current Liabilities	455	253	186	105	80.1	58.2	47.9	31.8	33.4	16.1
Long Term Debt	241	0.23	345	595	250	252	84.8	0.56	1.33	2.91
Common Equity	3,028	1,871	1,003	571	452	351	297	271	317	292
Total Capital	3,277	1,871	1,348	1,166	703	603	382	271	318	295
Capital Expenditures	2,226	51.4	38.6	17.6	26.3	15.6	12.5	2.50	3.86	3.72
Cash Flow	851	474	-51.1	86.5	65.9	-31.1	-53.9	-53.3	31.0	-17.3
Current Ratio	6.8	7.3	6.8	11.3	8.8	10.2	7.8	9.1	10.2	18.7
% Long Term Debt of Capitalization	7.3	NM	25.6	51.0	35.6	41.8	22.2	0.2	0.0	1.0
% Net Income of Revenue	40.1	33.9	NM	15.4	21.9	NM	NM	NM	69.9	NM
% Return on Assets	27.5	24.2	NM	6.9	6.9	NM	NM	NM	8.4	NM
% Return on Equity	33.2	31.3	NM	14.1	12.7	NM	NM	NM	9.2	NM

Data as orig reptd.; bef. results of disc opers/spec. items. Per share data adj. for stk. divs.; EPS diluted. E-Estimated. NA-Not Available. NM-Not Meaningful. NR Not Ranked. UR-Under Review.

Office: 333 Lakeside Drive, Foster City, CA 94404.
Telephone: 650-574-3000.
Email: investor_relations@gilead.com
Website: http://www.gilead.com

Chrmn: J.M. Denny
Pres & CEO: J.C. Martin
EVP & CFO: J.F. Milligan
SVP & General Counsel: G.H. Alton

Investor Contact: S. Hubbard ((650) 522-5715)
Board of Directors: P. Berg, J. F. Cogan, E. F. Davignon, J. M. Denny, J. W. Madigan, J. C. Martin, G. E. Moore, N. G. Moore, G. E. Wilson

Founded: 1987
Domicile: Delaware
Employees: 1,900

STANDARD &POOR'S

Goldman Sachs Group Inc. (The)

S&P Recommendation STRONG BUY ★★★★★

Price $188.67 (as of Oct 27, 2006)

12-Mo. Target Price $220.00

Investment Style Large-Cap Value

GICS Sector Financials
Sub-Industry Investment Banking & Brokerage

Comment Goldman Sachs is one of the world's leading investment banking and securities companies.

Key Stock Statistics (Source S&P, Vickers, company reports)

52-Wk Range	$193.60–124.23	S&P Oper. EPS 2006E	17.10	P/E on S&P Oper. EPS 2006E	11.0	Dividend Rate/Share	$1.40
Trailing 12-Month EPS	$16.44	S&P Oper. EPS 2007E	19.82	Common Shares Outstg. (M)	425.8	Yield (%)	0.74
Trailing 12-Month P/E	11.5	S&P Core EPS 2006E	17.10	Market Capitalization(B)	$80.342	Beta	1.27
$10K Invested 5 Yrs Ago	$23,706	S&P Core EPS 2007E	19.82	Institutional Ownership (%)	70	S&P Credit Rating	AA-

Price Performance

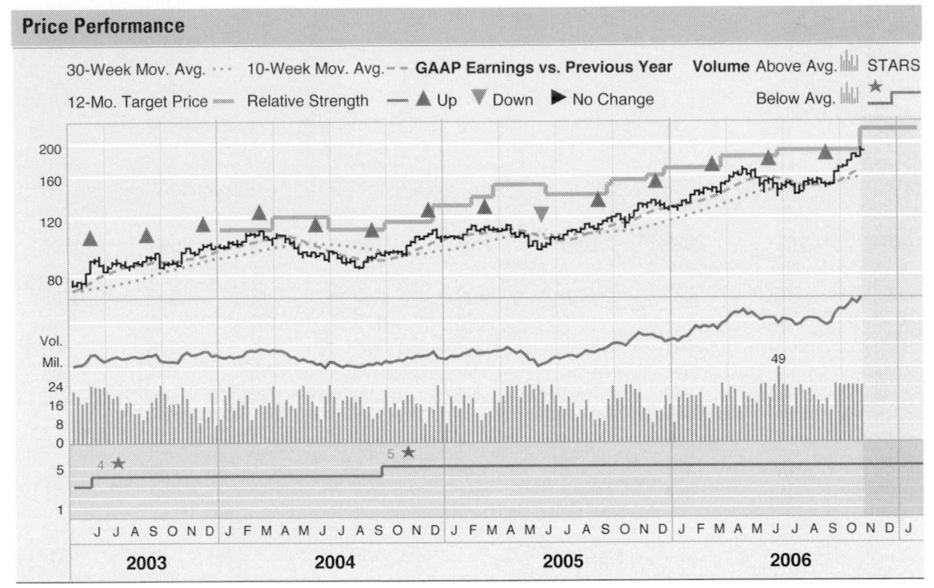

Options: ASE, CBOE, P, Ph

Analysis prepared by **Matthew Albrecht** on October 25, 2006, when the stock traded at **$ 188.09**.

Highlights

- We think Goldman Sachs maintains a strong competitive position across its segments, notably in its trading, principal investments, prime brokerage and asset management businesses. Despite quarterly volatility, GS is benefiting, in our view, from growth in its trading businesses, continued strength in merger and acquisition activity, and higher merchant banking gains.
- We expect strong growth in investment banking revenues to continue into FY 07 (Nov.). Specifically, we expect the merger and acquisition advisory business to flourish, and we expect debt underwriting volume to remain elevated as interest rates persist at favorable levels. We also believe the principal investments business will improve, based on the company's investments in economies around the globe, and particularly in Asia, where it may soon realize gains from investments in companies going public. We expect trading levels to remain elevated, led by fixed income and commodity trading.
- We forecast EPS of $17.10 for FY 06 and $19.82 for FY 07, despite a slight increase in the ratio of compensation to revenues, due to cost controls related to brokerage and clearing costs and technology expenses.

Investment Rationale/Risk

- We believe the company's original partnership structure has contributed to an ownership mentality within the company, resulting in a competitive advantage for GS. We think the shares should trade at a much higher valuation, based on our view of the company's global footprint, significant operating leverage, and strong client relationships. Prudent growth in head count and compensation should also benefit GS's valuation, in our view. We view favorably the company's stock buyback program and return on tangible equity above its 20% target.
- Risks to our recommendation and target price include stock and bond market depreciation, sharply higher interest rates, widening credit spreads, and greater regulatory scrutiny.
- The shares recently traded at about 11X our FY 06 EPS estimate, in line with brokerage peers, but at a discount to the historical multiple and that of the S&P 500. Our 12-month target price of $220 is based on a P/E multiple of about 11X applied to our FY 07 EPS estimate.

Qualitative Risk Assessment

LOW | MEDIUM | HIGH

Our risk assessment reflects our view of the company's global footprint, strong client relationships, and ownership mentality within the company.

Quantitative Evaluations

S&P Quality Ranking **NR**

D | C | B- | B | B+ | A- | A | A+

Relative Strength Rank **STRONG**

89

LOWEST = 1 HIGHEST = 99

Revenue/Earnings Data

Revenue (Million $)

	1Q	2Q	3Q	4Q	Year
2006	17,246	18,002	15,979	--	--
2005	9,964	8,949	12,333	12,145	43,391
2004	7,905	7,676	6,803	7,455	29,839
2003	6,094	5,985	5,715	5,829	23,623
2002	5,700	6,234	5,872	5,048	22,854
2001	9,502	8,158	7,360	6,118	31,138

Earnings Per Share ($)

2006	5.08	4.78	3.26	**E**3.99	**E**17.10
2005	2.94	1.71	3.25	3.35	11.21
2004	2.50	2.31	1.74	2.36	8.92
2003	1.29	1.36	1.32	1.89	5.87
2002	0.98	1.06	1.00	0.98	4.03
2001	1.40	1.06	0.87	0.93	4.26

Fiscal year ended Nov. 30. Next earnings report expected: Mid December. EPS Estimates based on S&P Operating Earnings; historical GAAP earnings are as reported.

Dividend Data (Dates: mm/dd Payment Date: mm/dd/yy)

Amount ($)	Date Decl.	Ex-Div. Date	Stk. of Record	Payment Date
0.250	12/15	01/20	01/24	02/23/06
0.350	03/14	04/21	04/25	05/25/06
0.350	06/13	07/21	07/25	08/24/06
0.350	09/13	10/19	10/23	11/20/06

Dividends have been paid since 1999. Source: Company reports.

Please read the Required Disclosures and Analyst Certification on the last page of this report.

Goldman Sachs Group Inc. (The)

Business Summary October 25, 2006

CORPORATE OVERVIEW. Goldman Sachs (GS) is a global investment banking, securities and investment management firm that provides a wide range of services to corporations, financial institutions, governments and high-net-worth individuals. GS operates through three core businesses: Investment Banking, Trading and Principal Investments, and Asset Management and Securities Services.

The Trading and Principal Investments business (66% of 2005 net revenues) facilitates customer transactions with a diverse group of corporations, financial institutions, governments and individuals and takes proprietary positions through market making in, and trading of, fixed income and equity products, currencies, commodities and derivatives. The activities of the Trading and Principal Investments business can be grouped under three segments: Fixed Income, Currency and Commodities (FICC), Equities, and Principal Investments. The FICC business makes markets in and trades interest rate and credit products, mortgage-backed securities and loans and other asset-backed securities, currencies and commodities. The Equities business makes markets in, trades, and acts as a specialist for, equities and equity-related products. It generates commissions from executing and clearing client transactions on major stock, options, and futures exchanges worldwide through its Equities customer franchise and clearing activities.

The Principal Investments business primarily represents net revenues from corporate and real estate merchant banking investments. These net revenues are from three primary sources -- returns on corporate and real estate investments, its investment in the convertible preferred stock of Sumitomo Mitsui Financial Group, Inc. (SMFG), and overrides. Overrides represent net revenues from the increased share of the income and gains derived from GS's merchant banking funds when the return on a fund's investments exceeds certain threshold returns.

Company Financials

Per Share Data ($) Year Ended Nov. 30	**2005**	**2004**	**2003**	**2002**	**2001**	**2000**	**1999**	**1998**	**1997**	**1996**
Tangible Book Value	52.15	52.14	45.73	40.18	38.30	34.15	22.65	NA	NA	NA
Cash Flow	12.22	9.90	6.97	5.20	5.39	6.94	6.27	NA	NA	NA
Earnings	11.21	8.92	5.87	4.03	4.26	6.00	5.27	2.62	NA	NA
S&P Core Earnings	11.12	8.63	5.26	3.30	3.60	NA	NA	NA	NA	NA
Dividends	1.00	1.00	0.74	0.48	0.48	0.48	0.24	NA	NA	NA
Payout Ratio	9%	11%	13%	12%	11%	8%	4%	NA	NA	NA
Prices:High	134.99	110.88	100.78	97.25	120.00	133.63	94.81	NA	NA	NA
Prices:Low	94.75	83.29	61.02	58.57	63.27	65.50	53.00	NA	NA	NA
P/E Ratio:High	12	12	17	24	28	22	17	NA	NA	NA
P/E Ratio:Low	8	9	10	15	15	11	10	NA	NA	NA

Income Statement Analysis (Million $)	2005	2004	2003	2002	2001	2000	1999	1998	1997	1996
Commissions	6,689	5,941	4,317	3,273	3,020	2,307	Nil	NA	NA	NA
Interest Income	21,250	11,914	10,751	11,269	16,620	17,396	12,722	NA	NA	NA
Total Revenue	43,391	29,839	23,623	22,854	31,138	33,000	25,363	22,478	NA	NA
Interest Expense	18,153	8,888	7,600	8,868	15,327	16,410	12,018	13,986	NA	NA
Pretax Income	8,273	6,676	4,445	3,253	3,696	5,020	1,992	2,129	NA	NA
Effective Tax Rate	32.0%	31.8%	32.4%	35.0%	37.5%	38.9%	NM	41.0%	NA	NA
Net Income	5,626	4,553	3,005	2,114	2,310	3,067	2,708	1,256	NA	NA
S&P Core Earnings	5,560	4,406	2,693	1,737	1,949	NA	NA	NA	NA	NA

Balance Sheet & Other Financial Data (Million $)	2005	2004	2003	2002	2001	2000	1999	1998	1997	1996
Total Assets	706,804	531,379	403,799	355,574	312,218	289,760	250,491	231,796	NA	NA
Cash Items	61,666	52,544	36,802	25,211	29,043	21,002	12,190	2,702	NA	NA
Receivables	75,381	52,545	36,377	28,938	33,463	159,019	150,154	NA	NA	NA
Securities Owned	238,043	183,880	160,719	129,775	108,885	95,260	81,809	NA	NA	NA
Securities Borrowed	23,331	19,394	17,528	12,238	81,579	40,211	49,352	NA	NA	NA
Due Brokers & Customers	188,318	161,221	109,028	95,590	97,297	82,148	59,534	NA	NA	NA
Other Liabilities	13,830	10,360	8,144	6,002	7,129	11,116	110,508	NA	NA	NA
Capitalization:Debt	100,007	80,696	57,482	38,711	31,016	31,395	20,952	20,776	NA	NA
Capitalization:Equity	26,252	25,079	21,632	19,003	18,231	16,530	10,145	7,627	NA	NA
Capitalization:Total	128,009	105,775	79,114	57,714	49,247	47,925	31,097	28,403	NA	NA
% Return on Revenue	13.0	15.3	12.7	9.3	7.4	9.3	10.7	5.6	NA	NA
% Return on Assets	0.9	1.0	0.8	0.6	0.8	1.1	1.2	NA	NA	NA
% Return on Equity	21.9	19.5	14.8	11.4	13.3	23.0	30.4	NA	NA	NA

Data as orig reptd.; bef. results of disc opers/spec. items. Per share data adj. for stk. divs.; EPS diluted. E-Estimated. NA-Not Available. NM-Not Meaningful. NR-Not Ranked. UR-Under Review.

Office: 85 Broad Street, New York, NY 10004.
Telephone: 212-902-1000.
Email: gs-investor-relations@gs.com
Website: http://www.gs.com

Chrmn & CEO: H.M. Paulson, Jr.
Pres & COO: L.C. Blankfein
Vice Chrmn: S.M. Nora Johnson
Vice Chrmn: R. Zoellick

EVP & CFO: D.A. Viniar
Investor Contact: S. Smith (212-902-0300)
Auditor: PricewaterhouseCoopers
Board of Directors: L. C. Blankfein, J. H. Bryan, C. Dahlback, S. Friedman, W. George, J. A. Johnson, L. D. Juliber, E. M. Liddy, B. o. Madingley, H. M. Paulson, Jr., R. J. Simmons

Founded: 1869
Domicile: Delaware
Employees: 22,425

STANDARD &POOR'S

Goodrich Corp

S&P Recommendation BUY ★★★★★	Price	12-Mo. Target Price	Investment Style
	$43.00 (as of Oct 27, 2006)	$49.00	Mid-Cap Value

GICS Sector Industrials
Sub-Industry Aerospace & Defense

Comment This company is one of the world's largest providers of commercial jet equipment, parts and services.

Key Stock Statistics (Source S&P, Vickers, company reports)

52-Wk Range	$47.45–33.60	S&P Oper. EPS 2006E	2.55	P/E on S&P Oper. EPS 2006E	16.9	Dividend Rate/Share	$0.80
Trailing 12-Month EPS	$3.59	S&P Oper. EPS 2007E	3.05	Common Shares Outstg. (M)	124.7	Yield (%)	1.86
Trailing 12-Month P/E	12.0	S&P Core EPS 2006E	2.58	Market Capitalization(B)	$5.363	Beta	1.13
$10K Invested 5 Yrs Ago	$22,908	S&P Core EPS 2007E	2.91	Institutional Ownership (%)	84	S&P Credit Rating	BBB

Price Performance

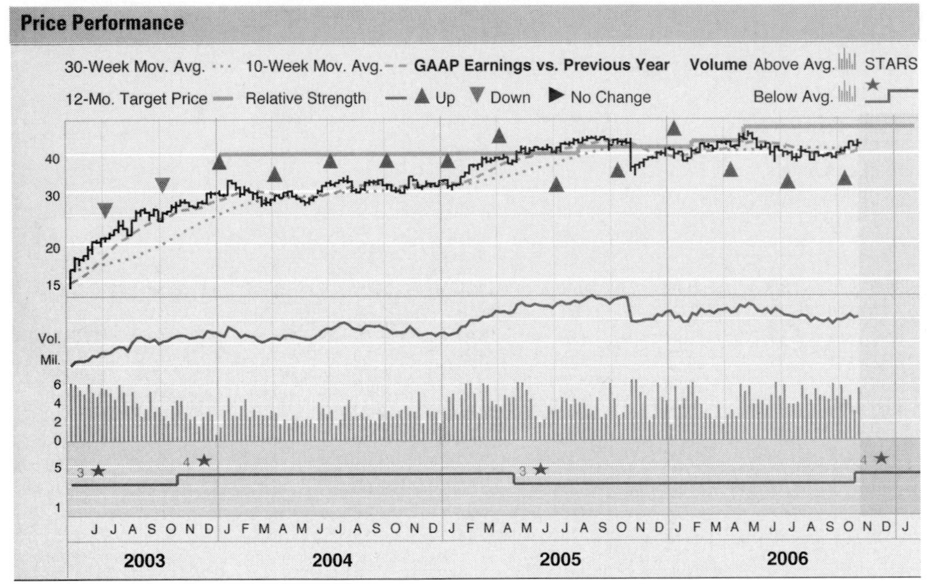

Options: CBOE, Ph

Highlights

- The STARS recommendation for GR has recently been changed to 4 (buy) from 3 (hold). The Highlights section of this Stock Report will be updated accordingly.

Investment Rationale/Risk

- The Investment Rationale/Risk section of this Stock Report will be updated shortly. For the latest News story on GR from MarketScope, see below.

- 10/26/06 01:45 pm EDT... S&P UPGRADES SHARES OF GOODRICH CORP. TO BUY FROM HOLD (GR 43.2****): Q3 EPS of $0.80 vs. $0.49 on 4.8% higher sales exceeds our $0.60 estimate. Operating margins rose 2.2 points to 13.7%, with notable improvement in airframe systems. With aviation fleets growing and demand for air travel strong, we expect good demand for GR's parts and its maintenance, repair & overhaul services to continue for at least next two years. We are raising our '06 EPS estimate, which excludes $1.15 tax gain, by $0.15 to $2.55, and '07's by $0.15 to $3.05. We are maintaining our 12-month target price of $49, 16X our '07 estimate, below historical highs of 18X-20X. / R.Tortoriello

Qualitative Risk Assessment

LOW | **MEDIUM** | HIGH

Our risk assessment reflects GR's history of cyclical earnings growth and its long record of dividend payments, offset by lack of growth in dividends, as reflected in an S&P Quality Ranking of B (below average). We also take into account GR's recent long-term debt-to-capital ratio of 50%, which is above average for peers in the aerospace & defense subindustry.

Quantitative Evaluations

S&P Quality Ranking **B**

D | C | B- | **B** | B+ | A- | A | A+

Relative Strength Rank **MODERATE**

66

LOWEST = 1 HIGHEST = 99

Revenue/Earnings Data

Revenue (Million $)

	1Q	2Q	3Q	4Q	Year
2006	1,424	1,483	1,436	--	--
2005	1,276	1,353	1,371	1,398	5,397
2004	1,162	1,134	1,167	1,262	4,725
2003	1,094	1,095	1,064	1,130	4,383
2002	921.2	925.5	882.1	1,181	3,910
2001	1,008	1,072	1,052	1,053	4,185

Earnings Per Share ($)

2006	1.59	0.64	0.80	**E**0.56	**E**2.55
2005	0.46	0.51	0.49	0.51	1.97
2004	0.26	0.32	0.41	0.30	1.30
2003	-0.28	0.12	0.29	0.19	0.33
2002	0.47	0.56	0.45	0.11	1.57
2001	0.66	0.70	0.76	-0.50	1.65

Fiscal year ended Dec. 31. Next earnings report expected: Early February. EPS Estimates based on S&P Operating Earnings; historical GAAP earnings are as reported.

Dividend Data (Dates: mm/dd Payment Date: mm/dd/yy)

Amount ($)	Date Decl.	Ex-Div. Date	Stk. of Record	Payment Date
0.200	04/25	06/01	06/05	07/03/06
0.200	07/25	08/31	09/05	10/02/06
0.200	07/25	09/21	09/25	10/02/06
0.200	10/24	11/30	12/04	01/02/07

Dividends have been paid since 1939. Source: Company reports.

Goodrich Corp

Business Summary August 09, 2006

CORPORATE PROFILE. This global aircraft components maker conducts business through three segments:

The Engine Systems segment (41% of revenues and 64% of operating income in 2005, with operating margins of 18%) makes an array of jet engine components and parts. Its largest customers include Airbus, Boeing, Rolls-Royce and global airlines. Primary competitors in this market include United Technologies, BAE Systems and Honeywell.

Airframe Systems (34%; 12%; 4.0%) primarily makes landing gear, wheels and brakes for passenger jets with at least 100 seats. AS and Messier-Dowty (a division of France-based SNECMA) each control 50% of the global landing gear market. The unit is also a major global provider of aircraft maintenance, repair and overhaul (MRO) services. AS's MRO customers mostly comprise the world's major airlines. Primary aircraft maintenance competitors include TIMCO Aviation Services, SIA Engineering Co., Singapore Technologies and Lufthansa Technik.

Electronic Systems (24%; 23%; 11%) makes mostly equipment that either controls or monitors the performance of aircraft. Primary offerings include sensor equipment for military and commercial rockets and satellites, flight and jet engine controls equipment, and electrical power equipment for civil and military aircraft. In addition, it is a major maker of inflatable evacuation slides and ice detection equipment. Primary competitors include Smiths Group, Parker Hannifin and Honeywell.

The company derives a material amount of revenues from sales to Boeing, Airbus and the U.S. government (primarily the Department of Defense). In 2005, the U.S. government, Airbus and Boeing accounted for 18%, 16% and 12% of total revenues, respectively.

The company projects capital expenditures of $240 million to $260 million for 2006.

Company Financials

Per Share Data ($) Year Ended Dec. 31	**2005**	**2004**	**2003**	**2002**	**2001**	**2000**	**1999**	**1998**	**1997**	**1996**
Tangible Book Value	NM	NM	NM	NM	4.66	3.48	1.41	9.63	11.35	8.53
Cash Flow	3.79	3.18	2.18	3.31	3.28	4.39	3.62	5.25	3.38	4.16
Earnings	1.97	1.30	0.33	1.57	1.65	2.68	1.53	3.04	1.53	1.97
S&P Core Earnings	2.10	1.57	0.42	0.42	0.41	NA	NA	NA	NA	NA
Dividends	0.80	0.80	0.80	0.88	1.10	1.10	1.10	1.10	1.10	1.10
Payout Ratio	41%	62%	242%	56%	67%	41%	72%	36%	72%	56%
Prices:High	45.82	33.90	30.30	34.45	44.50	43.13	45.69	56.00	48.25	45.88
Prices:Low	30.11	26.60	12.20	14.17	15.91	21.56	21.00	26.50	35.13	33.38
P/E Ratio:High	23	26	92	22	27	16	30	18	32	23
P/E Ratio:Low	15	20	37	9	10	8	14	9	23	17
Income Statement Analysis (Million $)										
Revenue	5,397	4,725	4,383	3,910	4,185	4,364	5,538	3,951	3,373	2,239
Operating Income	759	636	515	586	666	830	973	653	501	361
Depreciation	226	223	219	184	174	193	231	165	139	118
Interest Expense	131	143	163	117	118	129	138	79.0	73.0	40.4
Pretax Income	375	199	61.3	259	271	443	316	374	207	178
Effective Tax Rate	31.8%	21.7%	37.2%	36.0%	34.8%	35.4%	46.3%	39.1%	45.4%	34.5%
Net Income	244	156	38.5	166	177	286	170	228	113	106
S&P Core Earnings	260	189	48.6	44.9	44.7	NA	NA	NA	NA	NA
Balance Sheet & Other Financial Data (Million $)										
Cash	251	298	378	150	85.8	77.5	66.4	31.7	47.0	48.7
Current Assets	2,425	2,357	2,087	2,008	1,921	3,080	2,101	1,615	1,401	912
Total Assets	6,454	6,218	5,890	5,990	4,638	5,718	5,456	4,193	3,494	2,663
Current Liabilities	1,615	1,565	1,401	1,554	1,159	2,147	1,511	991	935	663
Long Term Debt	1,742	1,899	2,137	2,254	1,432	1,590	1,788	995	564	400
Common Equity	1,473	1,343	1,194	933	1,361	1,227	1,293	1,600	1,423	1,050
Total Capital	3,215	3,276	3,330	3,187	2,808	2,819	3,208	2,718	2,110	1,573
Capital Expenditures	216	152	125	107	191	148	246	209	160	184
Cash Flow	470	379	258	349	351	479	400	394	252	225
Current Ratio	1.5	1.5	1.5	1.3	1.7	1.4	1.4	1.6	1.5	1.4
% Long Term Debt of Capitalization	54.2	58.0	64.2	70.7	51.0	56.4	55.7	36.6	26.7	25.5
% Net Income of Revenue	4.5	3.3	0.9	4.2	4.2	6.6	3.1	5.8	3.4	4.8
% Return on Assets	3.8	2.6	0.6	3.0	3.6	5.3	3.2	5.9	3.7	4.2
% Return on Equity	17.3	12.3	3.6	14.5	13.7	22.7	13.4	15.1	9.2	11.1

Data as orig reptd.; bef. results of disc opers/spec. items. Per share data adj. for stk. divs.; EPS diluted. E-Estimated. NA-Not Available. NM-Not Meaningful. NR-Not Ranked. UR-Under Review.

Office: Four Coliseum Centre, Charlotte, NC 28217-4578.
Telephone: 704-423-7000.
Website: http://www.goodrich.com
Chrmn, Pres & CEO: M.O. Larsen

EVP & General Counsel: T.G. Linnert
SVP & CFO: S.E. Kuechle
VP & Cntlr: S. Cottrill
Investor Contact: P. Gifford (704-423-5517)

Board of Directors: D. C. Creel, G. A. Davidson, Jr., H. E. DeLoach, Jr., J. W. Griffith, W. R. Holland, J. P. Jumper, M. O. Larsen, D. E. Olesen, A. M. Rankin, Jr., J. R. Wilson, A. T. Young

Founded: 1912
Domicile: New York
Employees: 22,600

STANDARD &POOR'S

Goodyear Tire & Rubber Co

S&P Recommendation HOLD ★★★★★	Price $14.96 (as of Oct 27, 2006)	12-Mo. Target Price $14.00	Investment Style Mid-Cap Growth

GICS Sector Consumer Discretionary
Sub-Industry Tires & Rubber

Comment GT is the largest U.S. manufacturer of tires, and one of the largest worldwide. Operations also include rubber and plastic products and chemicals.

Key Stock Statistics (Source S&P, Vickers, company reports)

52-Wk Range	$19.31–9.75	S&P Oper. EPS 2006E	0.99	P/E on S&P Oper. EPS 2006E	15.1	Dividend Rate/Share	Nil
Trailing 12-Month EPS	$0.92	S&P Oper. EPS 2007E	1.35	Common Shares Outstg. (M)	177.3	Yield (%)	Nil
Trailing 12-Month P/E	16.3	S&P Core EPS 2006E	1.59	Market Capitalization(B)	$2.653	Beta	1.95
$10K Invested 5 Yrs Ago	$7,830	S&P Core EPS 2007E	1.94	Institutional Ownership (%)	86	S&P Credit Rating	B+

Price Performance

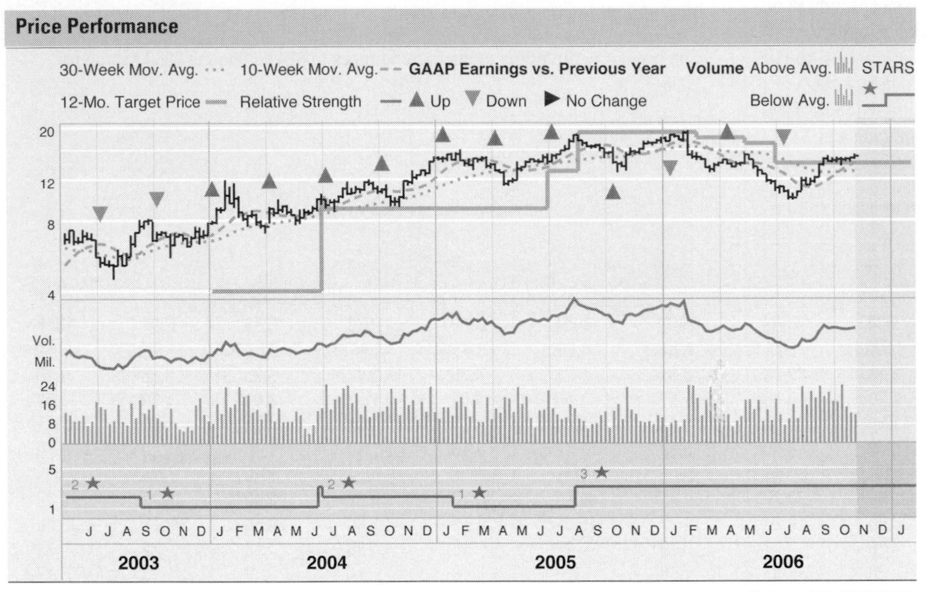

Options: ASE, CBOE, P, Ph

Analysis prepared by **Efraim Levy, CFA** on August 24, 2006, when the stock traded at **$ 11.77**.

Highlights

- We estimate that 2007 revenues will expand 2% to 3%. We see sales driven mostly by a better product mix and price increases. However, we anticipate lower heavy vehicle production reducing U.S. original equipment tire shipments. Although we expect margins to benefit from the implementation of higher selling prices and expense reduction due to past and ongoing restructuring activities, high raw material prices and increased pension expense should be partly offsetting. Interest expenses should rise on increasing interest rates. We expect all operating segments to be profitable in 2007
- We see reductions in higher cost plant capacity and a shift to Asian-based production providing savings. However, the company has significant debt obligations coming due that must be paid or refinanced during 2006 and 2007, as well as obligations due to retirees that must be paid.
- We expect the restructuring of credit facilities will give GT more time and flexibility to make operating improvements in the key North American market. The difference between our operating and S&P Core EPS estimates mainly reflects projected net pension credits.

Investment Rationale/Risk

- The potential sale of certain assets would provide cash to repay some debt, and GT has been extending its debt maturities. We see a $350 million convertible debt offering helping liquidity. While we have increased confidence in the near-term liquidity, we regard liquidity challenges from debt and employee retirement obligations as matters of concern for the longer term. We think GT will ultimately issue equity in order to strengthen the balance sheet.
- Risks to our recommendation and target price include an increase in GT's need for cash and weaker than anticipated demand for tires; less favorable selling prices; lower than expected cost savings; and faster than projected raw material price increases.
- We look for cash flow to be negative in 2006 after cash contributions to fund its pension plan. To reflect cash needs not included in net income, we are using a P/E of about 10X our 2007 EPS estimate of $1.35, at the low end of its historical range. From this method, we derive our 12-month target price of $14. Given the sizable, in our view, estimated unfunded retiree benefit obligations, we would not add to GT positions.

Qualitative Risk Assessment

LOW | MEDIUM | **HIGH**

Our risk assessment reflects the highly cyclical nature of the company's markets as well as our view of the current and long-term challenges that GT faces with its highly leveraged balance sheet, intensifying competition, high fixed costs and legacy costs.

Quantitative Evaluations

S&P Quality Ranking B-

D | C | **B-** | B | B+ | A- | A | A+

Relative Strength Rank STRONG

82

LOWEST = 1 HIGHEST = 99

Revenue/Earnings Data

Revenue (Million $)

	1Q	2Q	3Q	4Q	Year
2006	4,856	5,142	--	--	--
2005	4,767	4,992	5,030	4,934	19,723
2004	4,302	4,519	4,714	4,835	18,370
2003	3,546	3,753	3,906	3,914	15,119
2002	3,311	3,479	3,530	3,530	13,850
2001	3,414	3,583	3,678	3,473	14,147

Earnings Per Share ($)

2006	0.37	0.01	**E**0.26	**E**0.18	**E**0.99
2005	0.35	0.34	0.70	-0.23	1.21
2004	-0.44	0.17	0.20	0.62	0.63
2003	-1.12	-0.30	-0.67	-2.49	-4.58
2002	-0.39	0.18	0.20	-6.30	-6.62
2001	-0.30	0.05	0.06	-1.07	-1.27

Fiscal year ended Dec. 31. Next earnings report expected: NA. EPS Estimates based on S&P Operating Earnings; historical GAAP earnings are as reported.

Dividend Data

No cash dividends have been paid.

Please read the Required Disclosures and Analyst Certification on the last page of this report.

Goodyear Tire & Rubber Co

Business Summary August 24, 2006

CORPORATE OVERVIEW. Goodyear Tire & Rubber is the largest U.S. manufacturer of tires, and one of the largest worldwide. Operations also include rubber and plastic products and chemicals. Despite efforts to rationalize operations, divest non-core operations, and explore international growth opportunities, the company posted annual losses during 2001 through 2003. However, Goodyear made operational progress and returned to profitability in 2004. Goodyear posted further income gains in 2005, and we project an additional improvement for 2006. GT holds the leading market share in North America, Latin America, China and India.

In 2005, 92% of segment sales and 91% of profits came from tire products. Engineered products accounted for the balance of revenues and profits.

CORPORATE STRATEGY. The company sometimes uses joint ventures to facilitate growth of its business. In 1999, GT and Sumitomo Rubber Industries (SRI) completed a global alliance that again made GT the world's leading tire manufacturer. GT created a European joint venture with SRI. GT and SRI owned 75% and 25%, respectively, of both the North American and European joint ventures. In Japan, the ownership ratio is reversed.

GT and Pacific Dunlop Ltd. participate in equally owned joint ventures in South Pacific Tyres, an Australian partnership, and South Pacific Tyres N.Z. Ltd., a New Zealand company.

At December 31, 2004, the company said that it did not maintain effective control over the preparation and review of account reconciliations of certain general ledger accounts. This control deficiency resulted in misstatements that were part of the restatement of the company's consolidated financial statements for 2003, 2002 and 2001, for each of the quarters for the year ended December 31, 2003 and for the first, second and third quarters for the year ended December 31, 2004. In February 2006, GT said that the matters about weakness in internal controls had been fixed as of December 31, 2005.

In October 2003, the company determined that it was appropriate to restate previously issued financial statements. GT restated financial statements for 1998 through 2002, and for parts of 2003.

Company Financials

Per Share Data ($) Year Ended Dec. 31	**2005**	**2004**	**2003**	**2002**	**2001**	**2000**	**1999**	**1998**	**1997**	**1996**
Tangible Book Value	NM	NM	NM	NM	14.06	18.49	19.87	24.01	21.68	21.03
Cash Flow	4.16	3.87	-0.62	-3.01	2.71	4.22	5.18	7.63	6.51	3.63
Earnings	1.21	0.63	-4.58	-6.62	-1.27	0.26	1.52	4.53	3.53	0.66
S&P Core Earnings	2.61	0.84	-3.32	-8.16	-3.09	NA	NA	NA	NA	NA
Dividends	Nil	Nil	Nil	0.48	1.02	1.20	1.20	1.20	1.14	1.03
Payout Ratio	Nil	Nil	Nil	NM	NM	NM	79%	26%	32%	156%
Prices:High	18.59	15.01	8.19	28.85	32.10	31.63	66.75	76.75	71.25	53.00
Prices:Low	11.24	7.06	3.35	6.50	17.37	15.60	25.50	45.88	49.25	41.50
P/E Ratio:High	15	24	NM	NM	NM	NM	44	17	20	80
P/E Ratio:Low	9	11	NM	NM	NM	NM	17	10	14	63
Income Statement Analysis (Million $)										
Revenue	19,723	18,370	15,119	13,850	14,147	14,417	12,881	12,626	13,155	13,113
Operating Income	1,706	1,457	-549	915	916	1,173	1,094	1,560	1,689	1,657
Depreciation	630	629	693	603	637	630	582	488	469	461
Interest Expense	411	369	296	241	292	283	179	147	119	134
Pretax Income	584	381	-655	37.9	273	92.3	337	1,035	845	122
Effective Tax Rate	42.8%	54.6%	NM	NM	NM	20.0%	16.5%	27.6%	28.5%	16.8%
Net Income	239	115	-802	-1,106	-204	40.3	241	717	559	102
S&P Core Earnings	522	142	-584	-1,362	-495	NA	NA	NA	NA	NA
Balance Sheet & Other Financial Data (Million $)										
Cash	2,178	1,968	1,565	947	959	253	241	239	259	239
Current Assets	8,680	8,632	6,988	5,227	5,255	5,467	5,261	4,529	4,164	4,025
Total Assets	15,627	16,533	15,006	13,147	13,513	13,568	13,103	10,589	9,917	9,672
Current Liabilities	4,811	5,113	3,686	4,071	3,327	4,226	3,960	3,277	3,251	2,766
Long Term Debt	4,742	449	4,826	2,989	3,204	2,350	2,348	1,187	845	1,132
Common Equity	73.0	72.8	-13.1	651	2,864	3,503	3,617	3,746	3,395	3,279
Total Capital	5,910	1,774	5,639	4,380	6,855	6,698	6,856	5,192	4,240	4,652
Capital Expenditures	634	519	375	458	435	614	805	838	699	618
Cash Flow	869	744	-109	-503	433	671	823	1,205	1,028	563
Current Ratio	1.8	1.7	1.9	1.3	1.6	1.3	1.3	1.4	1.3	1.5
% Long Term Debt of Capitalization	80.2	25.3	85.6	68.2	46.7	35.1	34.2	22.9	19.9	24.3
% Net Income of Revenue	1.2	0.6	NM	NM	NM	0.3	1.9	5.7	4.2	0.8
% Return on Assets	1.5	0.7	NM	NM	NM	0.3	2.0	7.0	5.7	1.0
% Return on Equity	325.2	565.5	NM	NM	NM	1.1	6.5	20.1	16.7	3.1

Data as orig reptd.; bef. results of disc opers/spec. items. Per share data adj. for stk. divs.; EPS diluted. E-Estimated. NA-Not Available. NM-Not Meaningful. NR-Not Ranked. UR-Under Review.

Office: 1144 East Market Street, Akron, OH, USA 44316-0002.
Telephone: 330-796-2121.
Email: goodyear.investor.relations@goodyear.com
Website: http://www.goodyear.com

Chrmn, Pres & CEO: R.J. Keegan
EVP & CFO: R.J. Kramer
SVP & Treas: D.R. Wells
SVP, Secy & General Counsel: C.T. Harvie

VP & Cntlr: T.A. Connell
Investor Contact: B. Gould (330-796-8576)
Board of Directors: J. C. Boland, J. G. Breen, G. D. Forsee, W. J. Hudson, Jr., R. J. Keegan, S. A. Minter, D. M. Morrison, R. O'Neal, S. D. Peterson, G. C. Sullivan, T. H. Weidemeyer, M. R. Wessel

Founded: 1898
Domicile: Ohio
Employees: 80,000

STANDARD &POOR'S

Google Inc

S&P Recommendation HOLD ★★★★★

Price $475.20 (as of Oct 27, 2006)

12-Mo. Target Price $500.00

Investment Style Large-Cap Growth

GICS Sector Information Technology
Sub-Industry Internet Software & Services

Comment GOOG, which completed its initial public offering in August 2004, is the world's largest Internet company. It specializes in online search and advertising.

Key Stock Statistics (Source S&P, Vickers, company reports)

52-Wk Range	**$491.96–331.55**	S&P Oper. EPS 2006**E**	**8.83**	P/E on S&P Oper. EPS 2006**E**	**53.8**	Dividend Rate/Share	**Nil**
Trailing 12-Month EPS	**$7.86**	S&P Oper. EPS 2007**E**	**10.62**	Common Shares Outstg. (M)	**304.4**	Yield (%)	**Nil**
Trailing 12-Month P/E	**60.5**	S&P Core EPS 2006**E**	**8.83**	Market Capitalization(B)	**$144.632**	Beta	**1.00**
$10K Invested 5 Yrs Ago	**NA**	S&P Core EPS 2007**E**	**10.62**	Institutional Ownership (%)	**57**	S&P Credit Rating	**NA**

Price Performance

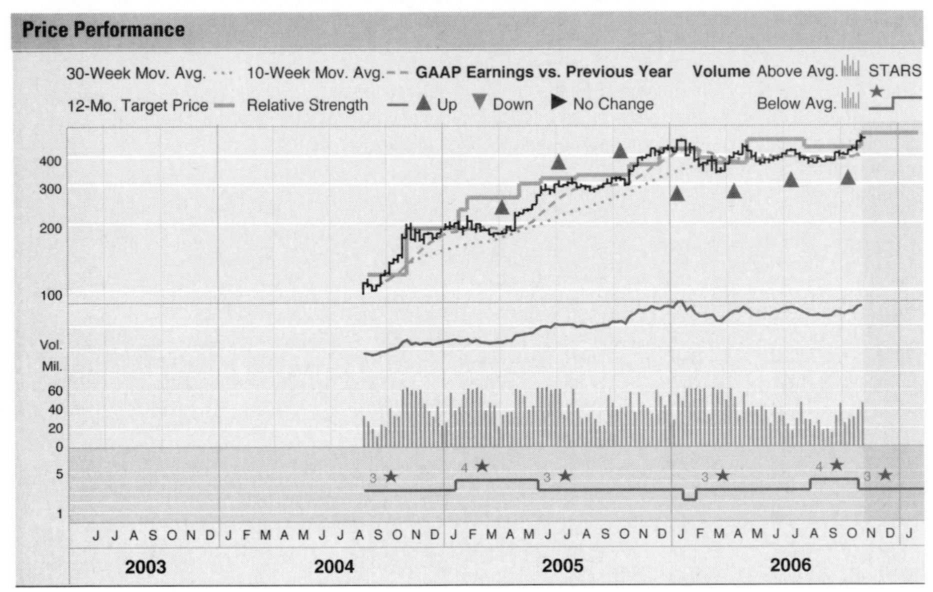

Options: ASE, CBOE, P, Ph

Analysis prepared by **Scott H. Kessler** on October 27, 2006, when the stock traded at **$ 481.59**.

Highlights

- We expect gross revenues to increase 72% in 2006 and 55% in 2007. We believe revenues will benefit from increased spending on Internet advertising, the efficiency and appeal of keyword search advertising, market share gains in certain segments, new offerings, and international expansion. Revenue increases should continue to be paced, in our view, by revenues derived from GOOG's Web sites. We anticipate that GOOG will employ some of the proceeds from the $1.7 billion raised through its IPO (August 2004) and $6.3 billion from stock offerings (September 2005 and March 2006) for investments in, and acquisitions of, businesses and companies.

- We project that operating and net margins will narrow modestly in 2006 and 2007, owing to continuing substantial investments for business expansion, partly due to anticipated heightened competition.

- We believe EPS will benefit from a lower effective corporate tax rate in 2006, which we project at about 26%. We foresee 2007 taxes at 28%. Our EPS estimates include notable projected stock option expenses.

Investment Rationale/Risk

- We believe GOOG could start to be impacted by launches of Microsoft's (MSFT: hold, $28) adCenter search advertising system, and major search improvements by Yahoo (YHOO: hold, $25). We expect keyword pricing and GOOG's market share to be adversely affected by growing competition and concerns related to "click fraud." Nonetheless, we believe GOOG will benefit from continuing growth in Internet advertising, and are particularly keen on video efforts that should be bolstered by the planned acquisition of YouTube (we expect the proposed deal to close by December 2006, subject to necessary approvals).

- Risks to our recommendation and target price include possible market share losses, new product/service introductions that do not occur or succeed as some expect, and challenges related to growing legal and regulatory issues.

- Our relative P/E and P/E to growth analyses lead to a value of around $470. Our DCF model (with assumptions including a discount rate of 13.1%, and five-year average annual growth cf 48%) yields an intrinsic value of roughly $525. Based upon a blend of these methodologies, our 12-month target price is $500.

Qualitative Risk Assessment

LOW | MEDIUM | **HIGH**

Our risk assessment reflects what we see as the Internet segment's emerging nature and relatively low barriers to entry, significant and mounting competition, the corporation's short history as an operating entity and publicly traded company, our view of somewhat lacking corporate governance practices, and notable share-price volatility.

Quantitative Evaluations

S&P Quality Ranking **NR**

D | C | B- | B | B+ | A- | A | A+

Relative Strength Rank **STRONG**

92

LOWEST = 1 HIGHEST = 99

Revenue/Earnings Data

Revenue (Million $)

	1Q	2Q	3Q	4Q	Year
2006	2,254	2,456	2,690	--	--
2005	1,257	1,385	1,578	1,919	6,139
2004	651.6	700.2	805.9	1,032	3,189
2003	248.6	311.2	393.9	512.2	1,466
2002	42.29	78.53	130.8	187.9	439.5
2001	--	--	--	--	86.40

Earnings Per Share ($)

	1Q	2Q	3Q	4Q	Year
2006	1.95	2.33	2.36	**E**2.53	**E**8.83
2005	1.29	1.19	1.32	1.22	5.02
2004	0.24	0.30	0.19	0.71	1.46
2003	--	--	--	--	0.51
2002	--	--	--	--	0.45
2001	--	--	--	--	0.04

Fiscal year ended Dec. 31. Next earnings report expected: Early February. EPS Estimates based on S&P Operating Earnings; historical GAAP earnings are as reported.

Dividend Data

No cash dividends have been paid.

Please read the Required Disclosures and Analyst Certification on the last page of this report.

Google Inc

Business Summary October 27, 2006

CORPORATE OVERVIEW. Google is a global technology company whose stated mission is to organize the world's information and make it universally accessible and useful. GOOG has amassed and maintains what we believe is the Internet's largest index of information (consisting of billions of items, including Web pages, images and videos), and makes most of it freely accessible and usable to anyone with online access. GOOG's Web sites are a leading Internet destination, and its brand is one of the most recognized in the world. International sources contributed 44% of 2006 third quarter revenues, versus 39% in the 2005 third quarter.

GOOG's advertising program, called AdWords, enables advertisers to present online ads when users are searching for related information. Advertisers employ GOOG's tools to create text-based ads, bid on keywords that trigger display of their ads, and set daily spending budgets. Ads are ranked for presentation based on the maximum cost per click set by the advertiser, click-through rates, and other factors used to determine ad relevance. This process is designed to favor the most relevant ads. GOOG's AdSense technology enables Google Network Web sites to provide targeted ads from AdWords advertisers.

Advertising accounted for 99% of revenues in the third quarters of both 2006 and 2005. Google Web sites accounted for 60% of 2006 third quarter revenues and 56% of the prior year period's revenues. Google Network Web sites contributed 39% of 2006 third quarter revenues and 43% in the 2005 quarter. Forrester Research projects that marketing spending for U.S. online search will increase from $4.3 billion in 2004 to $11.6 billion in 2010 (average annual growth of 18%).

Company Financials

Per Share Data ($) Year Ended Dec. 31	2005	2004	2003	2002	2001	2000	1999	1998	1997	1996
Tangible Book Value	31.20	10.25	7.66	NA	NA	NA	NA	NA	NA	NA
Cash Flow	5.90	1.93	0.75	NA	NA	NA	NA	NA	NA	NA
Earnings	5.02	1.46	0.51	0.45	0.04	-0.22	-0.14	NA	NA	NA
S&P Core Earnings	4.68	1.85	0.40	0.44	NA	NA	NA	NA	NA	NA
Dividends	Nil	Nil	NA	NA	NA	NA	NA	NA	NA	NA
Payout Ratio	Nil	Nil	NA	NA	NA	NA	NA	NA	NA	NA
Prices:High	446.21	201.60	NA	NA	NA	NA	NA	NA	NA	NA
Prices:Low	172.57	85.00	NA	NA	NA	NA	NA	NA	NA	NA
P/E Ratio:High	89	NM	NA	NA	NA	NA	NA	NA	NA	NA
P/E Ratio:Low	34	NM	NA	NA	NA	NA	NA	NA	NA	NA

Income Statement Analysis (Million $)	2005	2004	2003	2002	2001	2000	1999	1998	1997	1996
Revenue	6,139	3,189	1,466	440	86.4	19.1	0.22	NA	NA	NA
Operating Income	2,274	970	393	204	21.0	NA	NA	NA	NA	NA
Depreciation	257	129	50.2	18.0	10.0	NA	NA	NA	NA	NA
Interest Expense	0.78	0.86	1.93	2.57	1.76	NA	NA	NA	NA	NA
Pretax Income	2,142	650	347	185	10.1	-14.7	-6.08	NA	NA	NA
Effective Tax Rate	31.6%	38.6%	69.5%	46.1%	30.6%	Nil	Nil	NA	NA	NA
Net Income	1,465	399	106	99.7	6.99	-14.7	-6.08	NA	NA	NA
S&P Core Earnings	1,366	503	103	97.4	NA	NA	NA	NA	NA	NA

Balance Sheet & Other Financial Data (Million $)	2005	2004	2003	2002	2001	2000	1999	1998	1997	1996
Cash	8,034	2,132	1,712	146	33.6	19.1	20.0	NA	NA	NA
Current Assets	9,001	2,693	NA	232	NA	NA	NA	NA	NA	NA
Total Assets	10,272	3,313	2,492	286	84.5	46.9	25.8	NA	NA	NA
Current Liabilities	745	340	NA	89.5	NA	NA	NA	NA	NA	NA
Long Term Debt	Nil	Nil	NA	6.50	NA	NA	NA	NA	NA	NA
Common Equity	9,419	2,929	2,181	130	NA	NA	NA	NA	NA	NA
Total Capital	9,454	2,929	NA	178	50.2	27.2	20.0	NA	NA	NA
Capital Expenditures	838	319	177	37.2	13.1	NA	NA	NA	NA	NA
Cash Flow	1,722	528	156	118	17.0	NA	NA	NA	NA	NA
Current Ratio	12.1	7.9	NA	2.6	NA	NA	NA	NA	NA	NA
% Long Term Debt of Capitalization	Nil	Nil	NA	3.7	NA	NA	NA	NA	NA	NA
% Net Income of Revenue	23.9	12.5	7.2	22.7	8.1	NM	NM	NA	NA	NA
% Return on Assets	21.6	19.1	NA	NA	NA	NA	NA	NA	NA	NA
% Return on Equity	23.7	23.0	NA	NA	NA	NA	NA	NA	NA	NA

Data as orig reptd.; bef. results of disc opers/spec. items. Per share data adj. for stk. divs.; EPS diluted. E-Estimated. NA-Not Available. NM-Not Meaningful. NR-Not Ranked. UR-Under Review.

Office: 1600 Amphitheatre Parkway, Mountain View, CA 94043.
Telephone: 650-623-4000.
Email: info@google.com
Website: http://www.google.com

Exec Chrmn & CEO: E. Schmidt
Pres: S. Brin
Pres: L. Page
SVP & CFO: G. Reyes

SVP, Secy & General Counsel: D.C. Drummond
Investor Contact: M. Shim (650-253-7663)
Board of Directors: S. Brin, L. J. Doerr, J. L. Hennessy, A. D. Levinson, A. Mather, M. Moritz, P. S. Otellini, L. Page, E. Schmidt, K. R. Shriram, S. M. Tilghman

Auditor: Ernst & Young
Employees: 5,680

STANDARD &POOR'S

Grainger (W W) Inc.

S&P Recommendation STRONG BUY ★★★★★

Price $72.84 (as of Oct 27, 2006)

12-Mo. Target Price $86.00

Investment Style Mid-Cap Value

GICS Sector Industrials
Sub-Industry Trading Companies & Distributors

Comment Grainger is the largest global distributor of industrial and commercial supplies, such as hand tools, electric motors, light bulbs, and janitorial items.

Key Stock Statistics (Source S&P, Vickers, company reports)

52-Wk Range	**$79.95–60.60**	S&P Oper. EPS 2006**E**	**4.10**	P/E on S&P Oper. EPS 2006**E**	**17.8**	Dividend Rate/Share	**$1.16**
Trailing 12-Month EPS	**$4.24**	S&P Oper. EPS 2007**E**	**4.70**	Common Shares Outstg. (M)	**88.6**	Yield (%)	**1.59**
Trailing 12-Month P/E	**17.2**	S&P Core EPS 2006**E**	**4.10**	Market Capitalization(B)	**$6.452**	Beta	**0.81**
$10K Invested 5 Yrs Ago	**$18,081**	S&P Core EPS 2007**E**	**4.70**	Institutional Ownership (%)	**69**	S&P Credit Rating	**AA+**

Price Performance

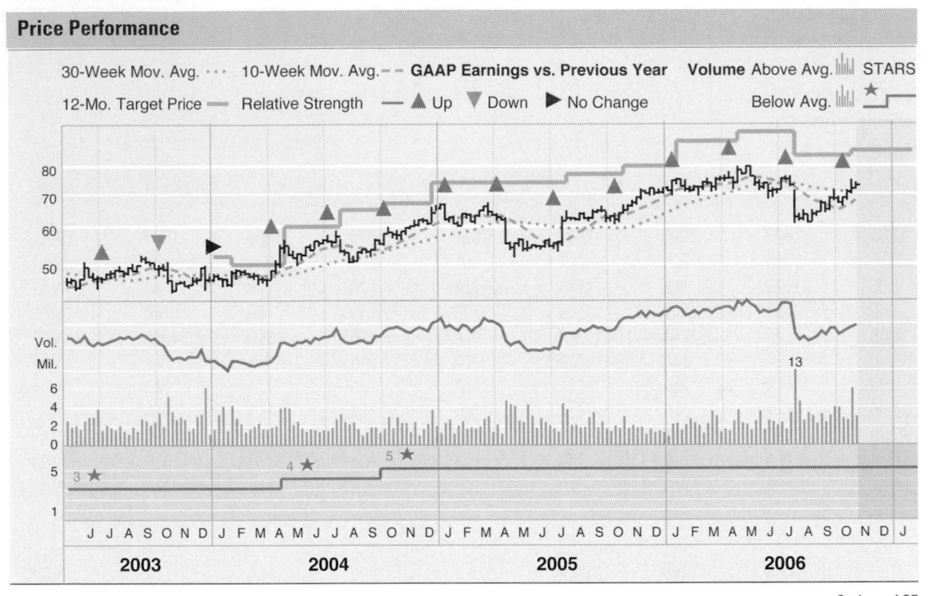

Options: ASE

Analysis prepared by **Stewart Scharf** on October 18, 2006, when the stock traded at **$ 72.99**.

Highlights

- We expect sales to advance about 7% through 2007, driven by market and product line expansion in the branch-based business, based on sales to government, manufacturing and commercial customers. We think acquisitions will continue to aid lab safety sales, while sales in Canada should benefit from strength in oil, gas and mining, and favorable exchange rates.
- In our view, gross margins should widen by 60 basis points in 2006 to 39.6%, with further expansion likely in 2007, reflecting pricing pass-throughs and a more favorable product mix, as GWW reduces sales to lower-margin integrated supply and automotive customers. We see EBITDA margins expanding this year to 11.6% from 11%, and by 50 to 100 basis points in 2007, based on supply chain cost savings and $15 million in annualized savings from other technology programs.
- We estimate 2006 operating EPS of $4.10 (before gains of $0.16, including a $0.09 tax benefit, but after $0.14 of projected stock option expense), advancing 15%, to EPS of $4.70 for 2007.

Investment Rationale/Risk

- We believe general market trends are favorable and strategic initiatives will enhance the distribution network. We also find the shares attractive based on valuation. We expect 2006 free cash flow to approximate $300 million, targeted for internal investments, share buybacks, and bolt-on lab safety acquisitions.
- Risks to our recommendation and target price include a significant downturn in industrial production; a greater than expected negative impact from entering new markets, especially China; and an inability to maintain GWW's large customer base.
- Our 12-month target price of $86 is based on a blend of our relative and DCF analyses. The stock trades at a discount to peers due to, in our opinion, signs of softening in some markets earlier this year. Applying a P/E of 20.5X our 2006 EPS estimate, near peers and modestly above GWW's five-year historical average, we value the stock at $84. Our DCF-based model, assuming a 3.5% terminal growth rate and an 8.3% weighted average cost of capital, targets intrinsic value of $88.

Qualitative Risk Assessment

LOW | **MEDIUM** | HIGH

Our risk assessment reflects uncertain economic conditions, pricing pressures, facilities disruptions or shutdowns, and corporate governance practices in which the positions of chairman and CEO are held by the same person. This is offset by S&P's Quality Ranking of A-, which indicates above average dividend and earnings growth.

Quantitative Evaluations

S&P Quality Ranking A-

D | C | B- | B | B+ | **A-** | A | A+

Relative Strength Rank STRONG

71

LOWEST = 1 HIGHEST = 99

Revenue/Earnings Data

Revenue (Million $)

	1Q	2Q	3Q	4Q	Year
2006	1,419	1,483	1,519	--	--
2005	1,335	1,373	1,428	1,391	5,527
2004	1,228	1,256	1,301	1,265	5,050
2003	1,139	1,173	1,201	1,154	4,667
2002	1,125	1,195	1,203	1,120	4,644
2001	1,219	1,225	1,199	1,111	4,754

Earnings Per Share ($)

2006	0.93	1.02	1.16	**E**1.08	**E**4.10
2005	0.79	0.89	0.97	1.13	3.78
2004	0.69	0.72	0.74	0.98	3.13
2003	0.57	0.60	0.62	0.67	2.46
2002	0.61	0.57	0.64	0.67	2.50
2001	0.45	0.15	0.59	0.65	1.84

Fiscal year ended Dec. 31. Next earnings report expected: Late January. EPS Estimates based on S&P Operating Earnings; historical GAAP earnings are as reported.

Dividend Data (Dates: mm/dd Payment Date: mm/dd/yy)

Amount ($)	Date Decl.	Ex-Div. Date	Stk. of Record	Payment Date
0.240	01/25	02/09	02/13	03/01/06
0.290	04/26	05/04	05/08	06/01/06
0.290	07/26	08/10	08/14	09/01/06
0.290	10/25	11/09	11/13	12/01/06

Dividends have been paid since 1965. Source: Company reports.

Please read the Required Disclosures and Analyst Certification on the last page of this report.

Grainger (W W) Inc.

Business Summary October 18, 2006

CORPORATE OVERVIEW. W.W. Grainger distributes facilities maintenance and other industrial and commercial supplies, including pumps, tools, motors, and electrical and safety products. It has nearly 600 branches and 17 distribution centers. Starting in 2006, the company began reporting its Canadian branch-based business as a separate segment: Acklands-Grainger Branch-based. Through the first nine months of 2006, the Grainger Branch-based segment accounted for 83% of revenues, while the operating margin was 9.7% and pretax return on invested capital (ROIC) was over 34%. The segment mainly consists of 408 U.S. brick and mortar branch stores (two in Puerto Rico) and 20 Will Call Express branches, as well as eight stores in Mexico. In the 2006 third quarter, GWW opened a branch and Will-Call Express location in China. These branches sell company-made--as well as third-party--industrial supplies, via in-store catalogs and Internet services. Acklands-Grainger, with 160 branches, accounted for nearly 10% of revenues and 5% of ROIC. Lab Safety (7% and 35%) is a direct marketer of safety and other industrial products. Approximately 25% of GWW's sales consist of private label items.

The company uses a multichannel business model to provide customers with a range of options for finding and purchasing products through a network of branches, field sales forces, direct marketing (including catalogs), and a variety of electronic and Internet channels. The company's 2006 catalog features more than 115,000 products, a 40% increase from 2005. GWW also offers 300,000 products from its Web site, while an additional 500,000 can be accessed through its sourcing service. Product line expansion is expected to contribute nearly 2% to GWW's projected sales growth for 2006. In July, GWW lowered its sales guidance for 2006 to 7% to 9%, from 8% to 11%. In our view, most markets will remain strong into 2007.

We believe that GWW's financial strength, including what we consider its low debt and strong cash flow, positions it to fund acquisitions and major initiatives, improve its effectiveness and accelerate top line growth. We see favorable trends continuing. In October 2006, GWW authorized an additional 10 million share buyback plan following the repurchase of 2.6 million shares in the third quarter (4.7 million for $319 million year to date). Since 1984, the company repurchased an adjusted 47 million shares for $1.7 billion, or 25% of the shares outstanding.

Company Financials

Per Share Data ($) Year Ended Dec. 31	2005	2004	2003	2002	2001	2000	1999	1998	1997	1996
Tangible Book Value	23.47	20.89	18.43	16.92	15.51	14.67	14.00	11.74	11.13	11.65
Cash Flow	4.85	4.06	3.28	3.30	2.73	3.01	2.85	3.20	3.05	2.74
Earnings	3.78	3.13	2.46	2.50	1.84	2.05	1.92	2.44	2.27	2.02
S&P Core Earnings	3.65	2.96	2.36	2.29	1.87	NA	NA	NA	NA	NA
Dividends	0.92	0.79	0.74	0.72	0.70	0.67	0.63	0.58	0.53	0.49
Payout Ratio	24%	25%	30%	29%	38%	33%	33%	24%	23%	24%
Prices:High	72.45	66.99	53.30	59.40	48.99	56.88	58.13	54.72	49.88	40.75
Prices:Low	51.65	45.00	41.40	39.20	29.51	24.31	36.88	36.44	35.25	31.31
P/E Ratio:High	19	21	22	24	27	28	30	22	22	20
P/E Ratio:Low	14	14	17	16	16	12	19	15	16	16
Income Statement Analysis (Million $)										
Revenue	5,527	5,050	4,667	4,644	4,754	4,977	4,534	4,341	4,137	3,537
Operating Income	617	525	463	467	461	426	406	482	473	420
Depreciation	98.1	85.6	76.1	75.9	83.7	90.6	88.4	74.2	79.7	74.3
Interest Expense	1.86	4.39	6.02	6.16	10.7	24.4	15.6	6.65	5.46	3.00
Pretax Income	533	445	381	398	297	332	304	401	390	349
Effective Tax Rate	35.0%	35.5%	40.4%	40.8%	41.3%	41.8%	40.5%	40.5%	40.5%	40.2%
Net Income	346	287	227	235	175	193	181	239	232	209
S&P Core Earnings	336	272	217	213	177	NA	NA	NA	NA	NA
Balance Sheet & Other Financial Data (Million $)										
Cash	545	429	403	209	169	63.4	62.7	43.1	46.9	127
Current Assets	1,998	1,755	1,633	1,485	1,393	1,483	1,471	1,206	1,183	1,320
Total Assets	3,108	2,810	2,625	2,437	2,331	2,460	2,565	2,104	1,998	2,119
Current Liabilities	727	662	707	586	554	747	871	664	534	616
Long Term Debt	4.90	Nil	4.90	120	118	125	125	123	131	6.15
Common Equity	2,289	2,068	1,845	1,668	1,603	1,537	1,481	1,279	1,295	1,463
Total Capital	2,301	2,072	1,850	1,787	1,723	1,663	1,654	1,402	1,429	1,471
Capital Expenditures	112	128	74.1	134	100	65.5	114	130	108	62.1
Cash Flow	444	372	303	311	258	284	269	313	311	283
Current Ratio	2.7	2.6	2.3	2.5	2.5	2.0	1.7	1.8	2.2	2.1
% Long Term Debt of Capitalization	0.2	Nil	0.3	6.7	6.9	7.5	7.6	8.8	9.2	0.4
% Net Income of Revenue	6.3	5.7	4.9	5.1	3.7	3.9	4.0	5.5	5.6	5.9
% Return on Assets	11.7	10.6	9.0	9.9	7.3	7.7	7.7	11.6	11.3	11.0
% Return on Equity	15.9	14.7	12.9	14.4	11.1	12.8	13.1	18.5	16.8	15.8

Data as orig reptd.; bef. results of disc opers/spec. items. Per share data adj. for stk. divs.; EPS diluted. E-Estimated. NA-Not Available. NM-Not Meaningful. NR-Not Ranked. UR-Under Review.

Office: 100 Grainger Pkwy, Lake Forest, IL 60045.
Telephone: 847-535-1000.
Website: http://www.grainger.com
Chrmn & CEO: R.L. Keyser

Pres: J.T. Ryan
SVP & CFO: P.O. Loux
SVP & General Counsel: J.L. Howard
VP & Cntlr: J.E. Andringa

Investor Contact: W.D. Chapman (847-535-0881)
Board of Directors: B. P. Anderson, W. H. Gantz, D. W. Grainger, V. A. Hailey, W. K. Hall, R. L. Keyser, S. L. Levenick, J. W. McCarter, Jr., N. S. Novich, M. J. Roberts, G. L. Rogers, J. D. Slavik, H. B. Smith

Founded: 1927
Domicile: Illinois
Employees: 16,732

STANDARD &POOR'S

Halliburton Co

S&P Recommendation	Price	12-Mo. Target Price	Investment Style
BUY ★★★★★	$32.15 (as of Oct 27, 2006)	$43.00	Large-Cap Value

GICS Sector Energy
Sub-Industry Oil & Gas Equipment & Services

Comment This Houston-based oilfield services and engineering and construction company provides products and services to energy, industrial and governmental customers.

Key Stock Statistics (Source S&P, Vickers, company reports)

52-Wk Range	$41.99–26.33	S&P Oper. EPS 2006E	2.14	P/E on S&P Oper. EPS 2006E	15.0	Dividend Rate/Share	$0.30
Trailing 12-Month EPS	$2.64	S&P Oper. EPS 2007E	2.87	Common Shares Outstg. (M)	1,031.2	Yield (%)	0.93
Trailing 12-Month P/E	12.2	S&P Core EPS 2006E	2.11	Market Capitalization(B)	$33.152	Beta	1.49
$10K Invested 5 Yrs Ago	$25,199	S&P Core EPS 2007E	2.83	Institutional Ownership (%)	85	S&P Credit Rating	BBB+

Price Performance

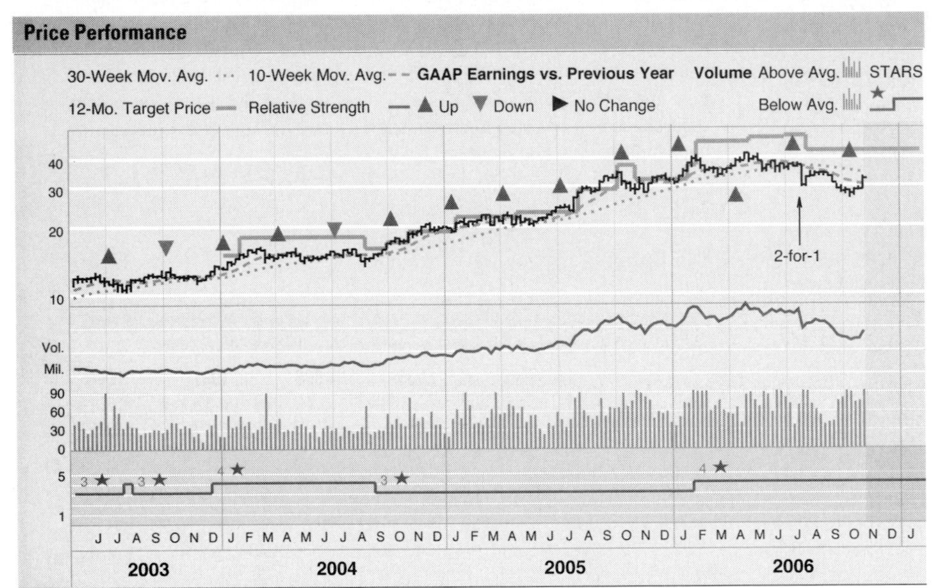

Options: ASE, CBOE, P, Ph

Analysis prepared by **Stewart Glickman, CFA** on July 25, 2006, when the stock traded at **$ 31.45**.

Highlights

- In the Energy Services Group (ESG), we look for 2006 revenue growth of about 30%, led by improvements in the Fluid Systems and Drilling & Formation Evaluation businesses, and 21% growth in 2007. In the E&C segment, we expect lower revenues in 2006 and 2007, but with operating margins of 3% to 4% -- above the historical 1% to 3% range. In July, HAL reported charges from a gas-to-liquid project in Escravos, Nigeria; given that the project is only 30% complete, we see potential for further charges beyond current expectations.

- In July 2006, HAL said it plans to effect a tax-free spinoff of KBR to HAL shareholders within nine months, predicated on IRS approval of tax-free status, with the possibility of also completing an initial public offering of up to 20% of KBR prior to the eventual spinoff.

- For 2006, we expect split-adjusted EPS of $2.06, rising to $2.83 in 2007. On an S&P Core Earnings basis, we expect EPS of $2.02 and $2.80 in the respective years, with the divergence between operating and Core earnings reflecting estimated pension adjustments.

Investment Rationale/Risk

- The shares have typically traded at a discount to those of oilfield services peers, which we attribute mainly to HAL's less-profitable KBR unit. But with HAL's plans to effect a spinoff of KBR, we believe the discount should narrow. We estimate that ESG's operating margins (excluding one-time items) should continue to exceed peers' oilfield services margins in 2006.

- Risks to our recommendation and target price include reduced oil and gas drilling activity; lower than expected oil and natural gas prices; and political risk.

- Our sum-of-the-parts model, based on projected peer average EBITDA multiples for the ESG segment and Energy & Chemicals segment of KBR, and assigning a 5X EBITDA multiple to the G&I segment of KBR, yields a value of $47 ($1 from KBR). On a relative basis, we think shares still merit a discount to peers in light of uncertainty related to the KBR spinoff, as well as HAL's relatively higher exposure to North America. Using multiples of 11X estimated 2006 EBITDA and 15X projected 2006 cash flow (both discounts to peers) produces values of $41 per share and $37, respectively. Blending with our DCF model, our 12-month target price is $43.

Qualitative Risk Assessment

LOW | MEDIUM | **HIGH**

Our risk assessment reflects HAL's exposure to volatile crude oil and natural gas prices, leverage to the North American oilfield services market, and political risk associated with operating in frontier regions such as Nigeria and Iraq. Partially offsetting these risks is HAL's leadership position in oilfield services and its growing liquefied natural gas (LNG)-related businesses.

Quantitative Evaluations

S&P Quality Ranking B

D | C | B- | **B** | B+ | A- | A | A+

Relative Strength Rank MODERATE

66

LOWEST = 1 HIGHEST = 99

Revenue/Earnings Data

Revenue (Million $)

	1Q	2Q	3Q	4Q	Year
2006	5,210	5,545	5,831	--	--
2005	4,938	5,163	5,095	5,798	20,994
2004	5,519	4,956	4,790	5,201	20,466
2003	3,060	3,599	4,148	5,464	16,271
2002	3,007	3,235	2,982	3,348	12,572
2001	3,144	3,339	3,391	3,172	13,046

Earnings Per Share ($)

	1Q	2Q	3Q	4Q	Year
2006	0.45	0.48	0.58	E0.64	E2.14
2005	0.36	0.38	0.48	1.04	2.27
2004	0.09	-0.07	0.21	0.20	0.44
2003	0.07	0.05	0.11	0.17	0.39
2002	0.06	-0.42	0.11	-0.15	-0.40
2001	0.10	0.17	0.21	0.17	0.64

Fiscal year ended Dec. 31. Next earnings report expected: Late January. EPS Estimates based on S&P Operating Earnings; historical GAAP earnings are as reported.

Dividend Data (Dates: mm/dd Payment Date: mm/dd/yy)

Amount ($)	Date Decl.	Ex-Div. Date	Stk. of Record	Payment Date
0.150	02/16	02/28	03/02	03/23/06
0.150	05/17	05/30	06/01	06/22/06
2-for-1 Stk.	02/16	07/17	06/23	07/14/06
0.075	07/19	08/30	09/01	09/22/06

Dividends have been paid since 1947. Source: Company reports.

Halliburton Co

Business Summary July 25, 2006

CORPORATE OVERVIEW. HAL is a leading global provider of oilfield services to the energy industry, and provides engineering and construction expertise to energy, industrial and governmental customers. HAL is comprised of two main business units: the Energy Services Group (ESG: 48% of 2005 revenues and 82% of operating income), and the KBR unit (KBR: 52%, 18%). ESG is further categorized by four operating segments: Production Optimization (20%, 40%), Fluid Systems (14%, 20%), Drilling & Formation Evaluation (11%, 17%), and Digital & Consulting Solutions (3%, 5%). KBR is further divided into two operating segments: the Energy & Chemicals segment (E&C: 13%, 6%) and the Government & Infrastructure segment (G&I: 39%, 12%). The former segment includes both upstream and downstream oil and gas projects, including liquefied natural gas (LNG) and gas-to-liquid (GTL) projects, while the latter segment includes reconstruction work in Iraq; Iraq generated 24% of total revenues in 2005, down from 26% in 2004.

CORPORATE STRATEGY. In April 2006, the company filed an S-1 prospectus for the partial spinoff of up to 20% of KBR in an initial public offering. We believe this is a potential first step in a plan to eventually spin off the entire KBR business unit and transform the company into a pure-play oilfield services company. While we expect HAL to defend its strong market position in North America, we believe that future capital expenditures will increasingly flow to the Eastern Hemisphere, which we see as growing faster in the long term.

MARKET PROFILE. ESG generated 2005 revenues of about $10 billion, or approximately a 26% market share for those oilfield services markets in which it competes. We believe HAL has a commanding market share in the pressure pumping market (largely North America- and natural gas-driven), and strong shares in drilling and completion fluids and completion equipment. HAL's customer base includes integrated oil companies, nationalized oil companies (such as Brazil's Petrobras or Saudi Arabia's Saudi Aramco), as well as independent exploration and production companies. The United States is the single largest oilfield services market in the world, although we believe other regions, such as the Eastern Hemisphere, are currently growing at a relatively faster pace. The Eastern Hemisphere is typically a longer-term contract market than the North American oilfield services market; as a result, pricing gains typically take longer to manifest themselves internationally.

Company Financials

Per Share Data ($) Year Ended Dec. 31	**2005**	**2004**	**2003**	**2002**	**2001**	**2000**	**1999**	**1998**	**1997**	**1996**
Tangible Book Value	5.46	3.55	2.14	3.25	4.65	3.90	3.98	3.74	4.32	3.85
Cash Flow	2.76	1.01	0.98	0.18	1.26	0.77	1.53	0.65	1.47	1.13
Earnings	2.27	0.44	0.39	-0.40	0.64	0.21	0.34	-0.02	0.88	0.60
S&P Core Earnings	2.11	0.37	0.34	-0.52	0.33	NA	NA	NA	NA	NA
Dividends	0.25	0.25	0.25	0.25	0.25	0.25	0.25	0.25	0.25	0.25
Payout Ratio	11%	57%	64%	NM	39%	119%	75%	NM	29%	42%
Prices:High	34.89	20.85	13.60	10.83	24.63	27.59	25.88	28.63	31.63	15.91
Prices:Low	18.59	12.90	8.60	4.30	5.47	16.13	14.06	12.50	14.84	11.19
P/E Ratio:High	15	48	35	NM	38	NM	77	NM	36	27
P/E Ratio:Low	8	30	22	NM	9	NM	42	NM	17	19

Income Statement Analysis (Million $)	2005	2004	2003	2002	2001	2000	1999	1998	1997	1996
Revenue	20,994	20,466	16,246	12,498	13,046	11,856	14,765	17,159	8,819	7,385
Operating Income	2,972	1,291	1,166	289	1,615	789	1,069	1,769	1,117	772
Depreciation, Depletion and Amortization	504	509	518	505	531	503	599	587	310	269
Interest Expense	207	229	139	113	147	146	144	137	43.0	24.0
Pretax Income	2,492	651	612	-228	954	335	1,012	278	766	404
Effective Tax Rate	3.17%	37.0%	38.2%	NM	40.3%	38.5%	21.1%	NM	39.2%	25.5%
Net Income	2,357	385	339	-346	551	188	755	-15.0	454	300
S&P Core Earnings	2,181	320	299	-445	287	NA	NA	NA	NA	NA

Balance Sheet & Other Financial Data (Million $)	2005	2004	2003	2002	2001	2000	1999	1998	1997	1996
Cash	2,391	2,808	1,815	1,107	290	231	466	203	221	214
Current Assets	9,327	9,962	7,919	5,560	5,573	5,568	6,022	6,083	2,972	2,398
Total Assets	15,010	15,796	15,463	12,844	10,966	10,103	10,728	11,112	5,603	4,437
Current Liabilities	4,437	7,064	6,542	3,272	2,908	3,826	3,693	4,004	1,773	1,505
Long Term Debt	2,813	3,593	3,415	1,181	1,403	1,049	1,056	1,370	539	200
Common Equity	6,372	3,932	2,547	3,558	4,752	5,618	4,287	4,061	2,585	2,159
Total Capital	9,330	7,633	6,062	4,810	6,196	6,705	5,496	5,601	3,144	2,359
Capital Expenditures	651	575	515	764	797	578	593	914	577	396
Cash Flow	2,861	894	857	159	1,082	691	1,354	572	764	568
Current Ratio	2.1	1.4	1.2	1.7	1.9	1.5	1.6	1.5	1.7	1.6
% Long Term Debt of Capitalization	30.2	47.1	56.3	24.6	22.6	15.6	19.2	24.5	17.1	8.5
% Return on Assets	15.3	2.5	2.4	NM	5.2	1.9	6.9	NM	9.0	7.3
% Return on Equity	45.7	14.4	11.1	NM	12.7	3.7	18.1	NM	19.1	14.7

Data as orig reptd.; bef. results of disc opers/spec. items. Per share data adj. for stk. divs.; EPS diluted. E-Estimated. NA-Not Available. NM-Not Meaningful. NR-Not Ranked. UR-Under Review.

Office: 1401 McKinney St Ste 2400, Houston, TX 77010-4040.
Telephone: 713-759-2600.
Email: investors@haliburton.com
Website: http://www.halliburton.com

Chrmn, Pres & CEO: D.J. Lesar
COO & EVP: A.R. Lane
EVP & CFO: C.C. Gaut
EVP & General Counsel: A.O. Cornelison, Jr.

SVP & Chief Acctg Officer: M.A. McCollum
Investor Contact: P. Koeller (713-759-2688)
Board of Directors: A. M. Bennett, J. R. Boyd, R. L. Crandall, K. T. Derr, S. M. Gillis, W. R. Howell, R. L. Hunt, D. J. Lesar, J. L. Martin, J. A. Precourt, D. L. Reed

Founded: 1919
Domicile: Delaware
Employees: 106,000

STANDARD & POOR'S

Harley-Davidson Inc.

S&P Recommendation HOLD ★★★★★

Price $67.62 (as of Oct 27, 2006)

12-Mo. Target Price $64.00

Investment Style Large-Cap Growth

GICS Sector Consumer Discretionary
Sub-Industry Motorcycle Manufacturers

Comment This leading maker of heavyweight motorcycles also produces a line of motorcycle parts and accessories.

Key Stock Statistics (Source S&P, Vickers, company reports)

52-Wk Range	**$70.14–47.86**	S&P Oper. EPS 2006**E**	**3.92**	P/E on S&P Oper. EPS 2006**E**	**17.3**	Dividend Rate/Share	**$0.84**
Trailing 12-Month EPS	**$3.80**	S&P Oper. EPS 2007**E**	**4.36**	Common Shares Outstg. (M)	**262.2**	Yield (%)	**1.24**
Trailing 12-Month P/E	**17.8**	S&P Core EPS 2006**E**	**3.92**	Market Capitalization(B)	**$17.731**	Beta	**0.98**
$10K Invested 5 Yrs Ago	**$14,815**	S&P Core EPS 2007**E**	**4.36**	Institutional Ownership (%)	**79**	S&P Credit Rating	**A+**

Price Performance

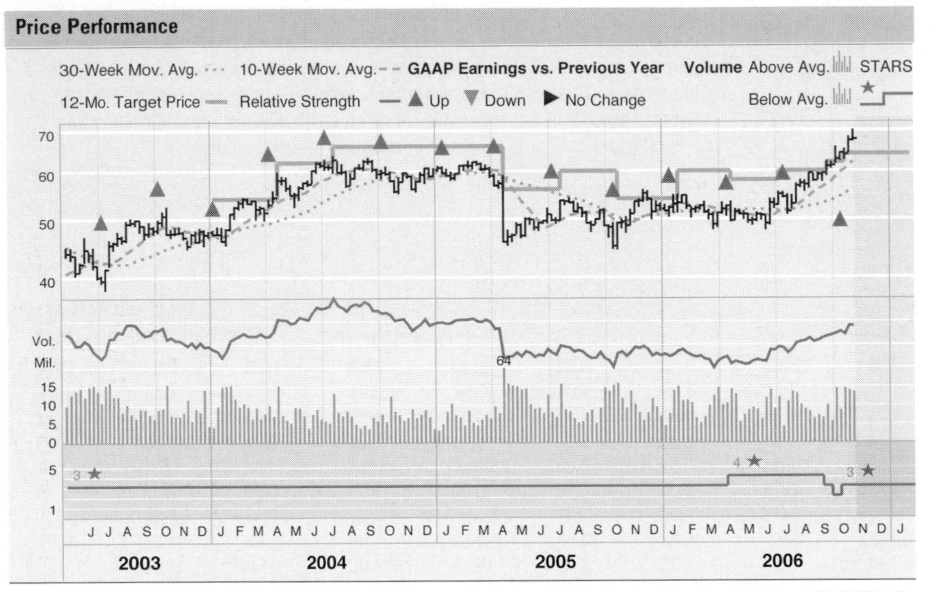

Options: ASE, CBOE, P, Ph

Analysis prepared by **Tom Graves, CFA** on October 13, 2006, when the stock traded at **$ 63.81**.

Highlights

- We look for revenues in 2007 to increase 7.0% from the $5.8 billion projected for 2006. We expect that sales of Harley-Davidson brand bikes will account for almost 80% of HOG's total revenues. In 2007, we estimate net income of $1.11 billion ($4.36 a share, with 3.7% fewer diluted shares), up 7% from the $1.04 billion ($3.92) we project for 2006. Our EPS estimates for 2007 and 2006 as well as reported EPS for 2005, include the expensing of stock options.

- In October 2006, HOG said that it expected 2006 wholesale shipments of Harley-Davidson brand motorcycles to total between 349,000 to 351,000 units, compared to 329,017 units shipped in 2005.

- As of September 24, 2006, HOG had cash equivalents and marketable securities totaling about $953 million, down from $1.018 billion at the end of 2005's third quarter. In 2006's first nine months, the company repurchased 17.2 million shares of its common stock at a cost of $911 million. In October 2006, directors authorized a new share repurchase program for up to 20 million additional shares. In August 2006, the stock's ticker symbol on the NYSE was changed to HOG, from HDI.

Investment Rationale/Risk

- We continue to like HOG's strong brand and market leadership. We also expect further stock repurchase and dividend hikes as HOG utilizes free cash flow. In 2006's second quarter, HOG increased its quarterly dividend by nearly 17%, continuing a series of payout boosts in recent years. In our view, based on expected EPS growth in 2006 and 2007, the stock was recently at what we consider to be adequate P/E premiums of 3% and 4%, respectively, to the S&P 500. Also, we have some concern that an aging U.S. population will limit longer-term domestic motorcycle sales.

- Risks to our recommendation and target price include the possibility that demand for HOG bikes will be weaker than expected.

- We have a hold recommendation on the stock. The shares were recently trading near our 12-month target price of $64, which is based on our DCF model that assumes a blended weighted average cost of capital of 10.1% and an annual perpetuity cash flow growth of 2%. The stock recently had an indicated dividend yield of 1.3%.

Qualitative Risk Assessment

LOW | **MEDIUM** | HIGH

Our risk assessment reflects our view that this company's market leadership position and strong brand should help offset the prospect that an aging U.S. population will limit future domestic demand for motorcycles. Also, we expect the company to generate free cash flow, with some of it likely to be used for dividend increases and to repurchase stock.

Quantitative Evaluations

S&P Quality Ranking **A+**

D | C | B- | B | B+ | A- | A | **A+**

Relative Strength Rank **STRONG**

84

LOWEST = 1 HIGHEST = 99

Revenue/Earnings Data

Revenue (Million $)

	1Q	2Q	3Q	4Q	Year
2006	1,285	1,377	1,636	--	--
2005	1,235	1,333	1,431	1,342	5,342
2004	1,166	1,328	1,301	1,221	5,015
2003	1,114	1,219	1,134	1,158	4,624
2002	927.9	1,001	1,136	1,027	4,091
2001	767.3	850.9	850.8	894.4	3,363

Earnings Per Share ($)

2006	0.86	0.91	1.20	**E**0.97	**E**3.92
2005	0.77	0.84	0.96	0.84	3.41
2004	0.68	0.83	0.77	0.71	3.00
2003	0.61	0.66	0.62	0.60	2.50
2002	0.39	0.47	0.54	0.49	1.90
2001	0.30	0.38	0.36	0.39	1.43

Fiscal year ended Dec. 31. Next earnings report expected: Mid January. EPS Estimates based on S&P Operating Earnings; historical GAAP earnings are as reported.

Dividend Data (Dates: mm/dd Payment Date: mm/dd/yy)

Amount ($)	Date Decl.	Ex-Div. Date	Stk. of Record	Payment Date
0.180	12/08	12/14	12/16	12/28/05
0.180	02/15	03/07	03/09	03/24/06
0.210	04/29	06/05	06/07	06/26/06
0.210	09/14	09/29	10/03	10/13/06

Dividends have been paid since 1993. Source: Company reports.

Harley-Davidson Inc.

Business Summary October 13, 2006

CORPORATE OVERVIEW. Harley-Davidson is a leading supplier of heavyweight motorcycles (engine displacement exceeding about 651 cubic centimeters). The company also sells motorcycle parts, accessories, clothing and collectibles, and has a sizeable financial services business.

HOG manufactures five families of Harley-Davidson brand motorcycles: Sportster, Dyna, Softail, Touring and VRSC. As of early 2006, the engines in these product lines ranged in size from 883 cc to 1690 cc. The company's 2006 model year line-up included 33 models of Harley-Davidson heavyweight motorcycles, with domestic manufacturer's suggested retail prices ranging from $6,595 to $20,685. Also, as of early 2006, HOG was offering some limited-edition custom motorcycles having suggested retail prices ranging from $26,495 to $31,995.

In 2005, HOG shipped 329,017 Harley-Davidson brand motorcycles, up from 317,209 in 2004. Also, HOG shipped 11,166 Buell motorcycles in 2005, up from 9,857 in 2004.

In July 2006, the company said that its 2007 line of motorcycles would include four new models, and that a new Twin Cam 96 engine is being used for all 2007 models in the Harley-Davidson Dyna, Softail and Touring product families.

CORPORATE STRATEGY. We expect the company to focus on both current owners of HOG motorcycles and on potential new customers. We believe that many purchasers of a new Harley-Davidson motorcycle previously owned a HOG bike.

We expect HOG's marketing focus to include international markets, where we expect that HOG's opportunities for growth are stronger than they are in the U.S. In 2005, HOG's international sales totaled about $1.04 billion, up from $917 million in 2005.

In addition to selling motorcycle-related products, we see HOG making a sizable profit related to financial services that it provides to independent dealers and to retail customers of those dealers. During 2005, Harley-Davidson Financial Services financed 45% of the new Harley-Davidson motorcycles retailed by independent dealers in the United States, as compared to 40% in 2004.

Company Financials

Per Share Data ($) Year Ended Dec. 31	**2005**	**2004**	**2003**	**2002**	**2001**	**2000**	**1999**	**1998**	**1997**	**1996**
Tangible Book Value	11.05	10.73	9.63	7.21	5.64	4.47	3.65	3.20	2.59	2.06
Cash Flow	4.25	3.72	3.18	2.48	1.93	1.56	1.23	0.97	0.79	0.66
Earnings	3.41	3.00	2.50	1.90	1.43	1.13	0.87	0.69	0.57	0.48
S&P Core Earnings	3.44	2.98	2.51	1.85	1.34	NA	NA	NA	NA	NA
Dividends	0.63	0.41	0.20	0.14	0.12	0.10	0.09	0.08	0.07	0.06
Payout Ratio	18%	13%	8%	7%	8%	9%	10%	11%	12%	12%
Prices:High	62.49	63.75	52.51	57.25	55.99	50.63	32.03	23.75	15.63	12.38
Prices:Low	44.40	45.20	35.01	42.60	32.00	29.53	21.38	12.47	8.34	6.59
P/E Ratio:High	18	21	21	30	39	45	37	34	28	26
P/E Ratio:Low	13	15	14	22	22	26	25	18	15	14
Income Statement Analysis (Million $)										
Revenue	5,342	5,015	4,624	4,091	3,363	2,906	2,453	2,064	1,763	1,531
Operating Income	1,676	1,576	1,346	1,059	816	648	530	421	340	284
Depreciation	206	214	197	176	153	133	114	87.4	70.2	55.2
Interest Expense	Nil	Nil	Nil	Nil	Nil	Nil	Nil	Nil	Nil	Nil
Pretax Income	1,488	1,379	1,166	886	673	549	421	336	276	228
Effective Tax Rate	35.5%	35.5%	34.7%	34.5%	35.0%	36.6%	36.5%	36.5%	37.0%	36.9%
Net Income	960	890	761	580	438	348	267	214	174	143
S&P Core Earnings	969	881	763	564	411	NA	NA	NA	NA	NA
Balance Sheet & Other Financial Data (Million $)										
Cash	1,046	1,612	1,323	796	635	420	183	165	147	142
Total Assets	5,255	5,483	4,923	3,861	3,118	2,436	2,112	1,920	1,599	1,320
Long Term Debt	1,000	800	670	380	380	355	280	280	280	258
Total Debt	1,205	1,295	794	763	597	445	461	427	371	258
Common Equity	3,084	3,218	2,958	2,233	1,756	1,406	1,161	1,080	827	663
Capital Expenditures	198	214	227	324	204	204	166	183	186	179
Cash Flow	1,165	1,104	958	756	591	481	381	301	244	199
% Return on Assets	17.9	17.1	17.3	16.6	15.8	15.3	13.3	12.2	11.9	12.3
% Return on Equity	30.5	28.8	29.3	29.1	27.7	27.1	24.4	23.0	23.4	24.6
% Long Term Debt of Capitalization	23.6	19.7	17.8	14.4	17.6	20.2	19.4	21.4	25.3	NM

Data as orig reptd.; bef. results of disc opers/spec. items. Per share data adj. for stk. divs.; EPS diluted. E-Estimated. NA-Not Available. NM-Not Meaningful. NR-Not Ranked. UR-Under Review.

Office: 3700 W Juneau Ave, Milwaukee, WI 53208.
Telephone: 414-342-4680.
Email: investor_relations@harley-davidson.com
Website: http://www.harley-davidson.com

Chrmn: J.L. Bleustein
Pres & CEO: J.L. Ziemer
VP & CFO: T.E. Bergmann
VP, Chief Acctg Officer & Treas: J.M. Brostowitz

VP, Secy, General Counsel & CCO: G.A. Lione
Board of Directors: B. K. Allen, R. I. Beattie, J. L. Bleustein, G. H. Conrades, J. C. Green, D. A. James, S. L. Levinson, G. L. Miles, Jr., J. A. Norling, J. L. Ziemer

Founded: 1903
Domicile: Wisconsin
Employees: 9,700

STANDARD &POOR'S

Harman International Industries Inc.

S&P Recommendation HOLD ★★★★★

Price $102.35 (as of Oct 31, 2006)

12-Mo. Target Price $110.00

Investment Style Mid-Cap Growth

GICS Sector Consumer Discretionary
Sub-Industry Consumer Electronics

Comment This Washington, DC-based company manufactures and markets high-fidelity audio products and electronic systems targeted primarily at OEM, consumer, and professional markets.

Key Stock Statistics (Source S&P, Vickers, company reports)

52-Wk Range	$115.85–74.65	S&P Oper. EPS 2007E	4.44	P/E on S&P Oper. EPS 2007E	23.1	Dividend Rate/Share	$0.05
Trailing 12-Month EPS	$3.81	S&P Oper. EPS 2008E	5.25	Common Shares Outstg. (M)	66.1	Yield (%)	0.05
Trailing 12-Month P/E	26.9	S&P Core EPS 2007E	4.44	Market Capitalization(B)	$6.762	Beta	1.36
$10K Invested 5 Yrs Ago	$58,982	S&P Core EPS 2008E	5.25	Institutional Ownership (%)	96	S&P Credit Rating	BBB+

Price Performance

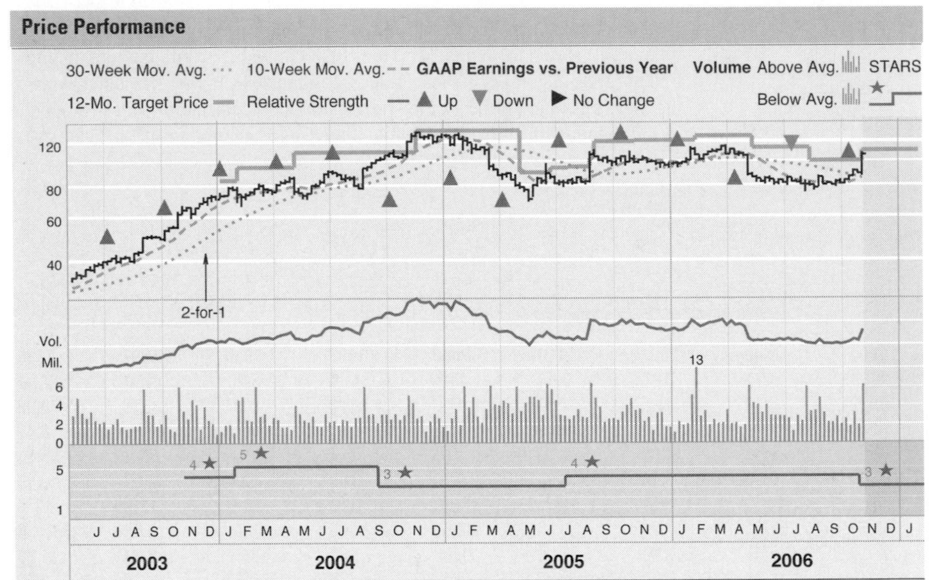

Analysis prepared by **James Peters, CFA** on October 31, 2006, when the stock traded at **$ 102.35**.

Highlights

- We believe visibility into automotive segment revenues remains high due to long lead times associated with infotainment awards programs, and we expect revenue growth in HAR's largest segment to be about 12% in FY 07 (Jun.) and at least as much in FY 08 as the pipeline of awarded contracts is fulfilled. We see overall revenue growth of about 10% in FY 07, supported by more moderate advances in the professional and consumer segments.
- We see research and development costs remaining stable in FY 07 at about 9.3%, and contributing to operating margin expansion in the latter part of FY 07 and into FY 08 as sales associated with these expenditures grow. We see operating margins widening to about 12.7% in FY 07, and believe HAR is on track to achieve its goal of 16% operating margins over the next four to five years.
- Including lower anticipated net interest expense, we see operating earnings rising to $4.44 in FY 07 from $3.89 in FY 06, on slightly fewer shares. FY 06 EPS excludes $0.14 of one-time charges.

Investment Rationale/Risk

- We see HAR as the market leader in supplying high-end infotainment systems to automobile manufacturers. We view HAR's sales to automotive OEM customers as the key driver of its record sales and earnings over the past few years, and we expect this to continue, with an acceleration from current levels expected for FY 08. We also believe that HAR has an opportunity to expand into mid-priced autos and international markets. In the Consumer group, we expect HAR to benefit from the adoption of music-enabled cell phones.
- Risks to our recommendation and target price include a deterioration in economic conditions, insufficient market acceptance of new products, the loss of business from a major customer, and unfavorable currency fluctuations.
- By applying a slight discount to historical EBITDA multiple of 13X to our FY 07 EBITDA estimate of $584 million, which we believe is appropriate given our view of a higher level of near-term uncertainty regarding consumer spending, we derive a 12-month target price of $110.

Qualitative Risk Assessment

LOW | **MEDIUM** | HIGH

Our risk assessment reflects our view of HAR's strong balance sheet, offset by its high customer concentration in the automotive segment and sensitivity to the cyclical automobile industry.

Quantitative Evaluations

S&P Quality Ranking B+

D | C | B- | B | **B+** | A- | A | A+

Relative Strength Rank STRONG

94

LOWEST = 1 HIGHEST = 99

Revenue/Earnings Data

Revenue (Million $)

	1Q	2Q	3Q	4Q	Year
2007	825.5	--	--	--	--
2006	754.7	832.7	801.5	859.1	3,248
2005	691.7	788.6	742.6	808.0	3,031
2004	597.3	691.6	690.4	732.0	2,711
2003	490.8	560.0	554.5	623.3	2,229
2002	399.0	467.4	458.3	501.4	1,826

Earnings Per Share ($)

2007	0.85	E1.28	E1.07	E1.25	E4.44
2006	0.79	1.07	0.94	0.95	3.75
2005	0.48	0.92	0.90	1.01	3.31
2004	0.29	0.60	0.63	0.76	2.27
2003	0.15	0.41	0.45	0.55	1.55
2002	0.08	0.18	0.22	0.38	0.85

Fiscal year ended Jun. 30. Next earnings report expected: Late January. EPS Estimates based on S&P Operating Earnings; historical GAAP earnings are as reported.

Dividend Data (Dates: mm/dd Payment Date: mm/dd/yy)

Amount ($)	Date Decl.	Ex-Div. Date	Stk. of Record	Payment Date
0.013	01/26	02/06	02/08	02/22/06
0.013	05/01	05/08	05/10	05/24/06
0.013	07/28	08/07	08/09	08/23/06
0.013	10/30	11/06	11/08	11/22/06

Dividends have been paid since 1994. Source: Company reports.

Harman International Industries Inc.

Business Summary October 31, 2006

CORPORATE OVERVIEW. HAR has three operating segments: Automotive (70% of FY 05 (Jun.) sales); Consumer (14%); and Professional (16%). Within Automotive, HAR designs, manufactures and markets audio, electronic and infotainment systems to be installed as original equipment by automotive manufacturers. Brand names include JBL, Infinity and Harmon/Kardon, and customers include DaimlerChrysler, BMW, Toyota, Audi, Porsche, Hyundai, Kia, and Volvo, among others. HAR has traditionally served the luxury market. However, we see opportunities to grow share through penetration into lower-priced vehicles.

In Consumer, HAR produces audio, video and electronic systems for home, computer and multimedia applications. Brands include JBL, Infinity, Harman/Kardon, Lexicon, and Mark Levinson. In Professional, HAR produces loudspeakers and electronics used by audio professionals in concert halls, stadiums, and other buildings and for recording, broadcast, cinema and music reproduction applications. Brands include JBL Professional, Soundcraft, AKG, Lexicon, BSS, and Studer.

IMPACT OF MAJOR DEVELOPMENTS. We believe the level of visibility into HAR's future revenue stream based on current and future awards programs is high. Some such awards include the FY 05 Chrysler program for an entry-level entertainment system that is expected to start in FY 08. In FY 05, HAR also received awards for substantially all of Audi's infotainment systems business beginning from FY 08 to FY 12. These two awards are expected to represent $550 million in annual sales in FY 08. In FY 06, HAR was selected by BMW Group as the supplier to enter into final contract negotiations to develop its next generation infotainment head, with an introduction planned in three to four years. Harman also received the award for the 2009 Mercedes-Benz E Class mid-level infotainment system and for its sound system. We think the pipeline looks strong and expect to see sales growth ramp up in FY 08 based on the expected timing of these awards.

Company Financials

Per Share Data ($) Year Ended Jun. 30	**2006**	**2005**	**2004**	**2003**	**2002**	**2001**	**2000**	**1999**	**1998**	**1997**
Tangible Book Value	12.82	10.74	9.43	6.66	5.04	4.33	4.69	4.61	4.70	4.84
Cash Flow	5.66	4.99	3.80	2.85	2.00	1.48	1.95	1.09	1.54	1.46
Earnings	3.75	3.31	2.27	1.55	0.85	0.48	1.03	0.16	0.72	0.74
S&P Core Earnings	3.75	3.28	2.27	1.51	0.76	0.41	NA	NA	NA	NA
Dividends	0.05	0.05	0.05	0.05	0.05	0.05	0.04	0.05	0.05	0.05
Payout Ratio	1%	2%	2%	3%	6%	10%	4%	31%	7%	7%
Prices:High	115.85	130.45	131.74	75.35	32.65	23.31	25.18	14.03	11.70	14.25
Prices:Low	74.65	68.54	66.12	26.15	19.09	11.64	13.75	8.56	7.88	8.09
P/E Ratio:High	31	39	58	49	38	49	24	86	16	19
P/E Ratio:Low	20	21	29	17	22	24	13	53	11	11
Income Statement Analysis (Million $)										
Revenue	3,248	3,031	2,711	2,229	1,826	1,717	1,678	1,500	1,513	1,474
Operating Income	527	470	360	255	181	138	186	143	163	155
Depreciation	130	119	106	88.5	78.1	67.2	64.6	66.8	62.5	53.1
Interest Expense	13.0	10.5	17.2	22.6	22.4	25.0	18.5	23.6	24.9	23.6
Pretax Income	376	335	228	142	80.2	45.1	103	14.4	75.7	77.9
Effective Tax Rate	32.4%	30.6%	30.6%	26.0%	28.2%	28.2%	29.1%	18.7%	28.9%	29.5%
Net Income	255	233	158	105	57.5	32.4	72.8	11.7	53.8	54.8
S&P Core Earnings	256	231	158	102	51.5	27.3	NA	NA	NA	NA
Balance Sheet & Other Financial Data (Million $)										
Cash	292	291	378	148	116	2.75	4.36	2.96	16.2	4.23
Current Assets	1,249	1,183	1,204	968	877	709	671	647	695	679
Total Assets	2,355	2,187	1,989	1,704	1,480	1,162	1,138	1,066	1,131	1,014
Current Liabilities	869	729	662	487	433	350	361	287	327	251
Long Term Debt	179	331	388	498	470	Nil	255	280	260	266
Common Equity	1,228	1,061	875	656	527	423	486	468	512	467
Total Capital	1,410	1,392	1,263	1,154	999	424	742	749	772	734
Capital Expenditures	131	176	135	116	114	88.1	80.4	67.8	57.5	68.4
Cash Flow	385	352	264	194	136	99.6	137	78.5	116	108
Current Ratio	1.4	1.6	1.8	2.0	2.0	2.0	1.9	2.3	2.1	2.7
% Long Term Debt of Capitalization	12.7	23.8	30.7	43.2	47.1	Nil	34.3	37.4	33.6	36.2
% Net Income of Revenue	7.9	7.7	5.8	4.7	3.1	1.9	4.3	0.8	3.6	3.7
% Return on Assets	11.2	11.2	8.6	6.6	4.4	2.8	6.6	1.1	5.0	5.5
% Return on Equity	22.3	24.1	20.6	17.8	12.1	7.1	15.3	2.4	11.0	12.1

Data as orig reptd.; bef. results of disc opers/spec. items. Per share data adj. for stk. divs.; EPS diluted. E-Estimated. NA-Not Available. NM-Not Meaningful. NR-Not Ranked. UR-Under Review.

Office: 1101 Pennsylvania Avenue, N.W., Washington, DC 20004.
Telephone: 202-393-1101.
Website: http://www.harman.com
Exec Chrmn: S. Harman

Vice Chrmn & CEO: B.A. Girod
EVP & CTO: E. Geiger
VP & CFO: K.L. Brown
Investor Contact: S.B. Robinson (202-393-1101)

Board of Directors: G. Harman, S. Harman, S. M. Hufstedler, A. McLaughlin Korologos, E. H. Meyer

Founded: 1980
Domicile: Delaware
Employees: 11,246

STANDARD &POOR'S

Harrah's Entertainment Inc

S&P Recommendation HOLD ★★★★★

Price $74.08 (as of Oct 27, 2006)

12-Mo. Target Price $81.00

Investment Style Large-Cap Growth

GICS Sector Consumer Discretionary
Sub-Industry Casinos & Gaming

Comment This geographically diverse company, based in Las Vegas, operates and/or has ownership interests in more than 30 gaming properties.

Key Stock Statistics (Source S&P, Vickers, company reports)

52-Wk Range	$83.33–58.22	S&P Oper. EPS 2006E	3.60	P/E on S&P Oper. EPS 2006E	20.6	Dividend Rate/Share	$1.60
Trailing 12-Month EPS	$1.47	S&P Oper. EPS 2007E	4.20	Common Shares Outstg. (M)	185.8	Yield (%)	2.16
Trailing 12-Month P/E	50.4	S&P Core EPS 2006E	3.41	Market Capitalization(B)	$13.765	Beta	0.50
$10K Invested 5 Yrs Ago	$26,660	S&P Core EPS 2007E	4.10	Institutional Ownership (%)	87	S&P Credit Rating	BB+

Price Performance

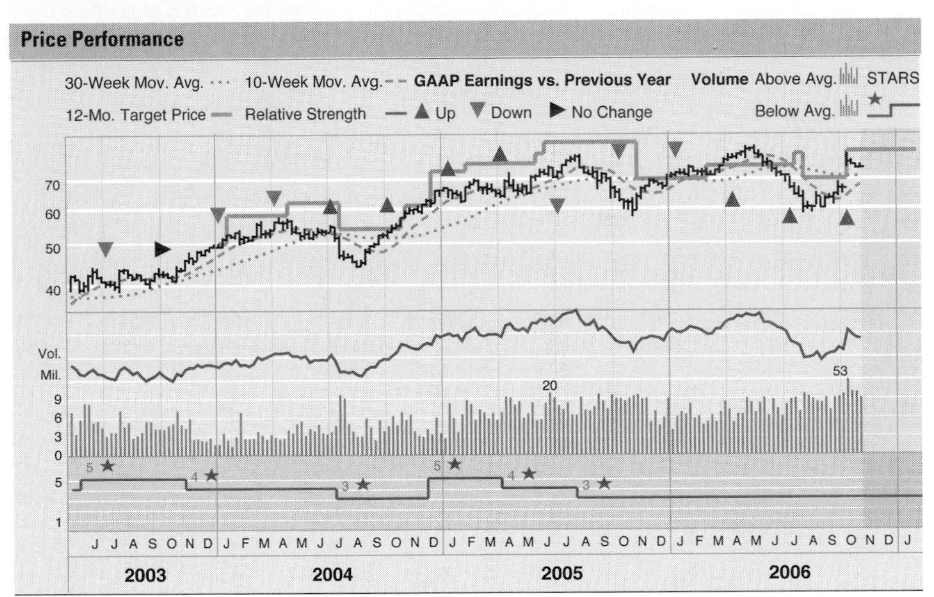

Options: ASE, CBOE

Analysis prepared by **Tom Graves, CFA** on October 09, 2006, when the stock traded at **$ 75.99**.

Highlights

- On October 2, 2006, HET said that its Board of Directors had received a proposal from Apollo Management and Texas Pacific Group to acquire all of HET's outstanding common stock for $81 per share in cash. HET's directors have established a special committee, consisting of all non-management directors, to review the proposal.
- In June 2005, HET acquired gaming company Caesars Entertainment through a stock-and-cash transaction. For 2006, we look for HET's revenue from continuing operations to increase 35%, largely due to the full-year inclusion of various properties that were part of the Caesars acquisition.
- Before some special items, we look for 2006 EPS of $3.67. This includes costs related to master planning for prospective development in Las Vegas and Atlantic City, plus $0.16 a share related to the expensing of stock options. Primarily due to the Caesars acquisition, we expect the average number of shares outstanding (fully diluted) for 2006 to be up about 25%, year to year. For 2007, excluding any future acquisitions, we estimate EPS of $4.25.

Investment Rationale/Risk

- The stock was recently trading about 6% below the $81 per share acquisition price proposed by a pair of private equity firms. We believe this reflects a variety of factors, including concern about whether HET directors will favor the proposed transaction, and the prospect of a lengthy regulatory review process. We would not be surprised if HET makes an effort to have the price sweetened to exceed the company's intra-day high of $83.33 reached in May 2006. Subject to approvals, we look for a deal to occur in the second half of 2007.
- Risks to our recommendation and target price include the possibility that expectations of HET being acquired for at least $81 a share will diminish.
- Our 12-month target price of $81 a share reflects our opinion that HET will be acquired. In our view, the prospect that the proposed acquisition price will be sweetened is offset by risk that a deal will not occur. An acquisition price of $81 a share would be 19X our 2007 EPS estimate, which is modestly above the average P/E recently received by a small group of peers.

Qualitative Risk Assessment

LOW | **MEDIUM** | HIGH

Our risk assessment reflects our view that economic or regulatory changes in local or regional markets that can have an adverse impact on operating results are likely to be diluted by the company's geographic diversification. We expect the company to generate a large amount of cash flow from operating activities, portions of which are likely to be used to help finance expansion projects.

Quantitative Evaluations

S&P Quality Ranking B

D | C | B- | **B** | B+ | A- | A | A+

Relative Strength Rank STRONG

73

LOWEST = 1 HIGHEST = 99

Revenue/Earnings Data

Revenue (Million $)

	1Q	2Q	3Q	4Q	Year
2006	2,357	2,374	2,513	--	--
2005	1,257	1,458	2,301	2,095	7,111
2004	1,012	1,037	1,310	1,189	4,548
2003	1,059	1,080	1,139	1,044	4,323
2002	974.7	1,021	1,124	1,016	4,136
2001	867.2	873.5	1,008	960.6	3,709

Earnings Per Share ($)

2006	0.95	0.69	0.96	E0.69	E3.60
2005	0.81	0.66	0.85	-0.39	1.75
2004	0.67	0.74	0.99	0.53	2.92
2003	0.73	0.70	0.89	0.32	2.64
2002	0.75	0.75	0.89	0.48	2.86
2001	0.38	0.40	0.55	0.49	1.81

Fiscal year ended Dec. 31. Next earnings report expected: Late February. EPS Estimates based on S&P Operating Earnings; historical GAAP earnings are as reported.

Dividend Data (Dates: mm/dd Payment Date: mm/dd/yy)

Amount ($)	Date Decl.	Ex-Div. Date	Stk. of Record	Payment Date
0.363	02/06	02/13	02/15	02/22/06
0.363	04/24	05/08	05/10	05/24/06
0.400	07/20	08/07	08/09	08/23/06
0.400	10/19	11/06	11/08	11/22/06

Dividends have been paid since 2003. Source: Company reports.

Please read the Required Disclosures and Analyst Certification on the last page of this report.

Harrah's Entertainment Inc

Business Summary October 09, 2006

CORPORATE OVERVIEW. Harrah's Entertainment is the most geographically diversified casino company in North America. The company has ownership interests in and/or manages more than 30 gaming properties.

CORPORATE STRATEGY. This company has grown partly through acquisitions, the largest of which was the June 2005 acquisition of Caesars Entertainment. Earlier acquisitions included Horseshoe Gaming Holding Corp. (2004), Harveys Casino Resorts (2001), Players International (2000), Rio Hotel and Casino Inc. (1999), and Showboat Inc. (1998). In August 2006, HET said that it had offered to acquire casino company London Clubs International plc. Subject to approvals, the transaction could be completed in the fourth quarter of 2006. Also, outside the U.S., we have seen the company looking to participate in gaming development through joint ventures in various places. However, a joint venture proposal for a Singapore casino project was unsuccessful. Also, we have seen the company looking to expand a number of existing U.S. properties. The company's future strategy could be affected if HET is acquired.

MARKET PROFILE. In 2005, we estimate U.S. casino winnings at $48 billion, which excludes gaming activity at racetracks. In the two largest U.S. gaming markets--Las Vegas and Atlantic City--HET operates a total of 11 casino/hotels, including six that were part of the Caesars acquisition. In December 2005, HET acquired the Imperial Palace on the Las Vegas Strip, and we look for at least a portion of the 18.5-acre site to be used for future redevelopment. In other states, expansion possibilities for HET include the introduction of slot machine casinos in Pennsylvania. In Chester, PA, if the necessary regulatory approvals are received, we look for HET to operate a 50%-owned "racino," where both slot machines and harness racing would be available. Also, in Pittsburgh, HET and a partner have presented a proposal for a large multi-use project development, which would include a slot machine casino.

PRIMARY BUSINESS DYNAMICS. HET operates casinos on boats or barges in Illinois, Indiana, Iowa, Louisiana, Mississippi and Missouri. However, three of HET's water-based gaming projects, plus a land-based casino in New Orleans, were closed following hurricane-related damage in the second half of 2005. The New Orleans casino and a Lake Charles, LA, hotel reopened in February 2006, and a Biloxi, MS, gaming project reopened in August 2006. HET has sold or has agreed to sell assets related to two of the closed gaming projects.

Company Financials

Per Share Data ($) Year Ended Dec. 31	**2005**	**2004**	**2003**	**2002**	**2001**	**2000**	**1999**	**1998**	**1997**	**1996**
Tangible Book Value	2.78	NM	4.41	2.50	2.26	5.04	6.43	2.41	6.79	6.43
Cash Flow	5.32	6.12	5.75	5.55	4.68	2.30	3.40	2.77	2.27	1.94
Earnings	1.75	2.92	2.64	2.86	1.81	-0.09	1.71	1.19	1.06	0.95
S&P Core Earnings	1.53	2.66	2.51	2.66	1.62	NA	NA	NA	NA	NA
Dividends	1.39	1.26	0.60	Nil	Nil	Nil	Nil	Nil	Nil	Nil
Payout Ratio	79%	43%	23%	Nil	Nil	Nil	Nil	Nil	Nil	Nil
Prices:High	79.69	67.25	49.94	51.35	38.29	30.06	30.75	26.38	23.06	38.88
Prices:Low	57.29	43.94	30.30	34.95	22.00	17.00	14.19	11.06	15.50	16.38
P/E Ratio:High	46	23	19	18	21	NM	18	22	22	41
P/E Ratio:Low	33	15	11	12	12	NM	8	9	15	17
Income Statement Analysis (Million $)										
Revenue	7,111	4,548	4,323	4,136	3,709	3,471	3,024	2,004	1,619	1,588
Operating Income	1,816	1,165	1,081	1,100	939	1,088	755	484	385	392
Depreciation	534	362	343	306	333	282	218	159	122	102
Interest Expense	481	272	234	240	256	227	193	117	79.1	70.9
Pretax Income	505	529	476	536	348	17.8	79.4	203	184	172
Effective Tax Rate	45.1%	36.1%	36.2%	36.8%	36.4%	NM	NM	36.7%	37.4%	39.1%
Net Income	265	330	292	325	209	-11.3	220	122	108	98.8
S&P Core Earnings	236	301	277	303	187	NA	NA	NA	NA	NA
Balance Sheet & Other Financial Data (Million $)										
Cash	724	489	410	416	361	299	234	159	116	105
Current Assets	1,629	787	685	686	618	583	487	279	212	202
Total Assets	20,518	8,586	6,579	6,350	6,129	5,166	4,767	3,286	2,006	1,974
Current Liabilities	1,598	754	583	626	569	778	372	233	211	205
Long Term Debt	11,039	5,151	3,672	3,763	3,719	2,836	2,540	1,999	924	889
Common Equity	5,665	2,035	1,738	1,471	1,374	12,853	1,486	851	736	720
Total Capital	18,583	7,632	5,791	5,538	5,386	15,794	4,274	2,941	1,696	1,654
Capital Expenditures	1,160	654	405	369	530	421	340	140	230	314
Cash Flow	799	691	635	631	542	270	438	281	230	201
Current Ratio	1.0	1.0	1.2	1.1	1.1	0.7	1.3	1.2	1.0	1.0
% Long Term Debt of Capitalization	59.4	67.5	63.4	68.0	69.1	17.9	59.4	68.0	54.5	53.7
% Net Income of Revenue	3.7	7.2	6.8	7.8	5.6	NM	7.3	6.1	6.6	6.2
% Return on Assets	1.8	4.3	4.5	5.2	3.7	NM	5.5	4.6	5.4	9.1
% Return on Equity	6.9	17.5	18.2	22.8	15.8	NM	18.8	15.3	14.8	15.1

Data as orig reptd.; bef. results of disc opers/spec. items. Per share data adj. for stk. divs.; EPS diluted. E-Estimated. NA-Not Available. NM-Not Meaningful. NR-Not Ranked. UR-Under Review.

Office: One Harrah's Court, Las Vegas, NV 89119.
Telephone: 702-407-6000.
Email: investors@harrahs.com
Website: http://www.harrahs.com

Chrmn, Pres & CEO: G.W. Loveman
Vice Chrmn: C.L. Atwood
COO: T.J. Wilmott
SVP, CFO & Treas: J.S. Halkyard

SVP, Chief Acctg Officer & Cntlr: A.D. McDuffie
Investor Contact: D. Foley (702-407-6370)
Board of Directors: B. T. Alexander, C. L. Atwood, F. J. Biondi, Jr., S. F. Bollenbach, J. M. Henson, W. B. Hilton, R. Horn, G. W. Loveman, R. B. Martin, G. G. Michael, R. G. Miller, B. A. Sells, C. J. Williams

Founded: 1989
Domicile: Delaware
Employees: 85,000

STANDARD &POOR'S

Hartford Financial Services Group Inc. (The)

S&P Recommendation STRONG BUY ★★★★★	Price	12-Mo. Target Price	Investment Style
	$87.25 (as of Oct 27, 2006)	$105.00	Large-Cap Value

GICS Sector Financials
Sub-Industry Multi-line Insurance

Comment Based in Hartford, CT, HIG is one of the largest U.S. multi-line insurance holding companies, and a leading writer of individual variable annuities in the U.S. and Japan.

Key Stock Statistics (Source S&P, Vickers, company reports)

52-Wk Range	**$94.03–78.25**	S&P Oper. EPS 2006**E**	**8.75**	P/E on S&P Oper. EPS 2006**E**	**10.0**	Dividend Rate/Share	**$2.00**
Trailing 12-Month EPS	**$7.75**	S&P Oper. EPS 2007**E**	**9.50**	Common Shares Outstg. (M)	**316.9**	Yield (%)	**2.29**
Trailing 12-Month P/E	**11.3**	S&P Core EPS 2006**E**	**8.54**	Market Capitalization(B)	**$27.653**	Beta	**1.42**
$10K Invested 5 Yrs Ago	**$17,099**	S&P Core EPS 2007**E**	**9.28**	Institutional Ownership (%)	**90**	S&P Credit Rating	**A**

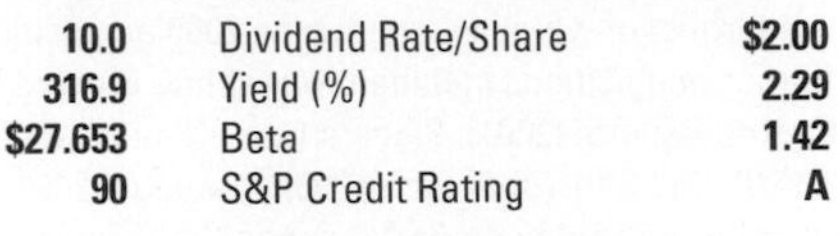

Price Performance

30-Week Mov. Avg. ··· 10-Week Mov. Avg. - - **GAAP Earnings vs. Previous Year** ▲ Up ▼ Down ▶ No Change **Volume** Above Avg. Below Avg. STARS 12-Mo. Target Price — Relative Strength —

2003 2004 2005 2006

Options: CBOE

Qualitative Risk Assessment

LOW | **MEDIUM** | HIGH

Our risk assessment reflects our view of HIG's position as a leader in both the property-casualty and life insurance/retirement savings areas, combined with what we view as the company's diversified revenue and earnings streams and sound capital position. However, exposure to catastrophe losses always exists.

Quantitative Evaluations

S&P Quality Ranking **B**

D | C | B- | **B** | B+ | A- | A | A+

Relative Strength Rank **MODERATE**

35

LOWEST = 1 HIGHEST = 99

Highlights

- The 12-month target price for HIG has recently been changed to $105.00 from $112.00. The Highlights section of this Stock Report will be updated accordingly.

Investment Rationale/Risk

- The Investment Rationale/Risk section of this Stock Report will be updated shortly. For the latest News story on HIG from MarketScope, see below.

- 10/27/06 12:27 pm EDT... S&P MAINTAINS STRONG BUY OPINION ON SHARES OF HARTFORD FINANCIAL SERVICES (HIG 88.0*****): HIG reports $2.30 vs. $1.81 Q3 operating EPS, ahead of our $1.94 forecast amid lower catastrophe losses. We are raising our '06 operating EPS estimate $0.25 to $8.75 to reflect these results, but keeping our $9.50 '07 operating EPS estimate amid cautious comments given on today's call. We continue to view HIG as one of the better managed franchises in the insurance industry, with superior risk and capital management capabilities. Our $105 12-mo. target price (cut $7) assumes shares trade at 11X our '07 estimate, and 2X est '07 tangible book, still a slight discount to peers. /C.Seifert

Revenue/Earnings Data

Revenue (Million $)

	1Q	2Q	3Q	4Q	Year
2006	6,543	4,971	7,407	--	--
2005	6,002	6,064	7,307	7,710	27,083
2004	5,732	5,444	5,416	6,101	22,693
2003	4,331	4,682	4,947	4,773	18,733
2002	3,900	3,885	3,961	4,161	15,907
2001	3,722	3,847	3,722	3,856	15,147

Earnings Per Share ($)

2006	2.34	1.52	2.39	**E**2.07	**E**8.75
2005	2.21	1.98	1.76	1.51	7.44
2004	2.01	1.46	1.66	2.08	7.20
2003	-5.33	1.88	1.20	1.59	-0.33
2002	1.17	0.74	1.06	1.01	3.97
2001	1.12	0.94	-0.43	0.58	2.27

Fiscal year ended Dec. 31. Next earnings report expected: Late January. EPS Estimates based on S&P Operating Earnings; historical GAAP earnings are as reported.

Dividend Data (Dates: mm/dd Payment Date: mm/dd/yy)

Amount ($)	Date Decl.	Ex-Div. Date	Stk. of Record	Payment Date
0.400	02/16	02/27	03/01	04/03/06
0.400	05/18	05/30	06/01	07/03/06
0.400	07/20	08/30	09/01	10/02/06
0.500	10/19	11/29	12/01	01/02/07

Dividends have been paid since 1996. Source: Company reports.

Hartford Financial Services Group Inc. (The)

Business Summary September 15, 2006

CORPORATE OVERVIEW. As a multi-line insurer, HIG underwrites life as well as property-casualty insurance. Segment revenues totaled $27.1 billion in 2005, of which life accounted for 56% and property-casualty for the remaining 44%.

HIG's property-casualty operation provides a wide range of commercial, personal, specialty and reinsurance coverages. It constitutes one of the largest U.S. property-casualty insurance organizations, and is the endorsed provider of automobile and homeowners coverages to members of the American Association of Retired Persons (AARP). Earned premiums of $10.2 billion in 2005 were divided: business insurance 47%, personal lines 36%, and specialty commercial 17%.

HIG's life insurance operations are conducted by Hartford Life, Inc. The Retail Investment Products Group (which accounted for 47% of the life divisions' more than $1.3 billion of segment operating profits in 2005) provides an array of investment and savings products to individual investors, including annuities, mutual funds, 401(k) plans and 529 college savings plans. Group Benefits (21% of segment profits in 2005) offers short- and long-term disability insurance, group life and accident insurance, and other specialty products to employers, associations and affinity groups. The Individual Life segment (13%) offers an array of life insurance, including variable universal life, universal life, whole life and term life insurance. The Institutional Financial Solutions Group (7%) provides customized wealth creation and financial protection solutions for institutions, corporations, and high net worth individuals. The Retirement Plans Group (6% of 2005 segment operating profits) provides retirement plans for corporate clients and non-profit organizations. The International unit (6%) offers fixed and variable annuities in Japan, Brazil and the U. K.

Company Financials

Per Share Data ($) Year Ended Dec. 31	**2005**	**2004**	**2003**	**2002**	**2001**	**2000**	**1999**	**1998**	**1997**	**1996**
Tangible Book Value	45.05	42.58	34.80	35.31	29.87	32.88	25.07	28.17	25.79	19.23
Operating Earnings	NA	NA	-0.93	4.96	3.00	4.29	3.68	3.45	4.70	-1.30
Earnings	7.44	7.20	-0.33	3.97	2.27	4.36	3.79	4.30	5.58	-0.42
S&P Core Earnings	7.68	6.52	-1.15	4.27	2.22	NA	NA	NA	NA	NA
Dividends	1.17	1.13	1.09	1.05	1.01	0.97	0.90	0.85	0.80	0.80
Relative Payout	16%	16%	NM	26%	44%	22%	24%	20%	14%	NM
Prices:High	89.49	69.57	59.27	70.24	71.15	80.00	66.44	60.00	47.25	34.94
Prices:Low	65.35	52.73	31.64	37.25	45.50	29.38	36.50	37.63	32.44	22.25
P/E Ratio:High	12	10	NM	18	31	18	18	14	8	NM
P/E Ratio:Low	9	7	NM	9	20	7	10	9	6	NM
Income Statement Analysis (Million $)										
Life Insurance in Force	764,293	139,889	704,369	629,028	534,489	585,582	527,285	528,608	407,860	312,176
Premium Income:Life A & H	14,359	13,566	11,891	4,884	4,903	4,565	4,069	4,371	3,323	3,185
Premium Income:Casualty/Property.	NA	NA	8,805	8,114	7,266	6,975	6,488	7,245	7,000	6,891
Net Investment Income	8,231	5,162	3,233	2,953	2,850	2,674	2,627	3,102	2,655	2,523
Total Revenue	27,083	22,693	18,733	15,907	15,147	14,703	13,528	15,022	13,305	12,473
Pretax Income	2,985	2,523	-550	1,068	354	1,418	1,235	1,475	1,703	-318
Net Operating Income	NA	NA	-253	1,250	724	962	837	816	1,117	-318
Net Income	2,274	2,138	-91.0	1,000	549	974	862	1,015	1,332	NA
S&P Core Earnings	2,356	1,936	-315	1,078	538	NA	NA	NA	NA	NA
Balance Sheet & Other Financial Data (Million $)										
Cash & Equivalent	1,273	1,148	462	377	353	227	182	123	140	112
Premiums Due	6,360	6,178	9,043	7,706	2,432	6,874	2,071	1,833	1,873	1,797
Investment Assets:Bonds	76,440	75,100	61,263	48,889	40,046	34,492	32,875	35,331	35,053	31,449
Investment Assets:Stocks	25,495	14,466	565	917	1,349	1,056	1,286	1,066	1,922	1,865
Investment Assets:Loans	3,747	2,662	2,512	2,934	3,317	3,610	4,222	6,687	3,759	3,839
Investment Assets:Total	106,935	94,408	65,847	54,530	46,689	40,669	39,141	43,696	37,363	33,800
Deferred Policy Costs	9,702	8,509	7,599	6,689	6,420	5,305	5,038	4,579	4,181	3,535
Total Assets	285,557	259,735	225,853	182,043	181,238	171,532	167,051	150,632	131,743	108,840
Debt	4,048	4,308	4,613	4,064	3,377	3,105	2,798	2,798	1,773	1,532
Common Equity	15,325	14,238	11,639	10,734	9,013	7,464	5,466	6,423	6,085	4,520
Combined Loss-Expense Ratio	93.2	95.3	98.0	99.2	112.4	102.4	103.3	102.9	102.3	105.2
% Return on Revenue	8.4	9.4	NM	6.3	3.6	6.6	6.4	6.8	10.0	NM
% Return on Equity	15.4	16.5	NM	10.1	6.7	15.1	14.5	16.2	25.1	NM
% Investment Yield	8.2	6.4	5.4	5.8	6.5	6.7	6.3	7.7	6.7	6.8

Data as orig reptd.; bef. results of disc opers/spec. items. Per share data adj. for stk. divs.; EPS diluted. E-Estimated. NA-Not Available. NM-Not Meaningful. NR-Not Ranked. UR-Under Review.

Office: Hartford Plaza, Hartford, CT 06115.
Telephone: 860-547-5000.
Website: http://www.thehartford.com
Chrmn & CEO: R. Ayer

EVP & CFO: D.M. Johnson
EVP & General Counsel: N.S. Wolin
VP & Secy: R.D. Costello

Board of Directors: R. Ayer, E. J. Kelly, III, P. G. Kirk, Jr., T. M. Marra, G. J. McGovern, M. G. Morris, R. W. Selander, C. B. Strauss, H. P. Swygert, D. K. Zwiener, R. de Oliveira

Founded: 1810
Domicile: Delaware
Employees: 30,000

STANDARD &POOR'S

Hasbro Inc.

S&P Recommendation	Price	12-Mo. Target Price	Investment Style
BUY ★★★★★	$25.10 (as of Oct 27, 2006)	$29.00	Mid-Cap Value

GICS Sector Consumer Discretionary
Sub-Industry Leisure Products

Comment This large toy company has brands that include Monopoly, Playskool and Tonka, as well as various items related to categories such as Star Wars and Pokemon.

Key Stock Statistics (Source S&P, Vickers, company reports)

52-Wk Range	$25.95–17.00	S&P Oper. EPS 2006E	1.30	P/E on S&P Oper. EPS 2006E	19.3	Dividend Rate/Share	$0.48
Trailing 12-Month EPS	$1.16	S&P Oper. EPS 2007E	1.45	Common Shares Outstg. (M)	163.6	Yield (%)	1.91
Trailing 12-Month P/E	21.6	S&P Core EPS 2006E	1.30	Market Capitalization(B)	$4.106	Beta	1.32
$10K Invested 5 Yrs Ago	$15,723	S&P Core EPS 2007E	1.45	Institutional Ownership (%)	85	S&P Credit Rating	BBB-

Price Performance

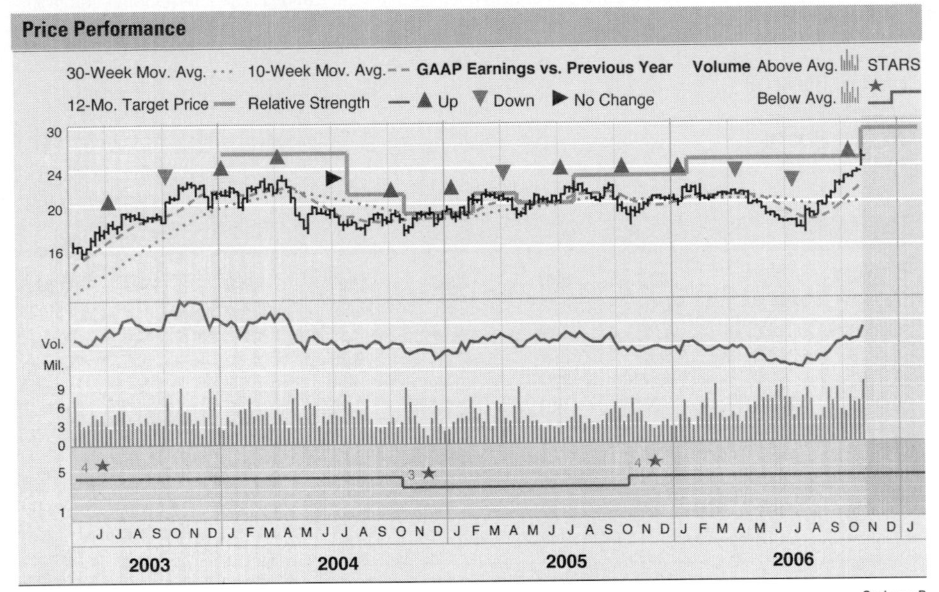

Options: P

Qualitative Risk Assessment

LOW | **MEDIUM** | HIGH

Our risk assessment takes into account our positive view of HAS's strong market share position and healthy balance sheet, offset by our negative view of intense industry rivalry and the concentrated buying power of U.S. toy retailers.

Quantitative Evaluations

S&P Quality Ranking B

D | C | B- | **B** | B+ | A- | A | A+

Relative Strength Rank STRONG

92

LOWEST = 1 HIGHEST = 99

Highlights

➤ The 12-month target price for HAS has recently been changed to $29.00 from $25.00. The Highlights section of this Stock Report will be updated accordingly.

Investment Rationale/Risk

➤ The Investment Rationale/Risk section of this Stock Report will be updated shortly. For the latest News story on HAS from MarketScope, see below.

➤ 10/23/06 02:58 pm EDT... S&P MAINTAINS BUY OPINION ON SHARES OF HASBRO (HAS 25.56****): Q3 EPS of $0.58 vs. $0.47 tops our estimate by $0.07, including higher-than-anticipated revenue and profit margins. We are raising our '06 EPS estimate to $1.30 from $1.17, and our '07 EPS projection to $1.45 from $1.32. Although Star Wars-related sales are likely to decline in Q4 (vs. a year ago), we have a generally favorable profit outlook for HAS for the '06 holiday season. We look for a Marvel license pact to become a bigger revenue driver in '07, and we expect further stock repurchases. With increased EPS estimates, our 12-month target price rises to $29 from $25. /T.Graves-CFA

Revenue/Earnings Data

Revenue (Million $)

	1Q	2Q	3Q	4Q	Year
2006	468.2	527.8	1,039	--	--
2005	454.9	572.4	988.1	1,072	3,088
2004	474.3	516.4	947.3	1,060	2,998
2003	461.8	581.5	581.5	1,124	3,139
2002	452.3	546.0	820.5	997.4	2,816
2001	463.3	511.0	893.4	988.7	2,856

Earnings Per Share ($)

	1Q	2Q	3Q	4Q	Year
2006	-0.03	0.07	0.58	E0.62	E1.30
2005	-0.02	0.13	0.47	0.48	1.09
2004	0.03	0.06	0.43	0.44	0.96
2003	0.01	0.06	0.06	0.43	0.98
2002	-0.10	-0.15	0.32	0.36	0.43
2001	-0.14	-0.11	0.29	0.30	0.35

Fiscal year ended Dec. 31. Next earnings report expected: Early February. EPS Estimates based on S&P Operating Earnings; historical GAAP earnings are as reported.

Dividend Data (Dates: mm/dd Payment Date: mm/dd/yy)

Amount ($)	Date Decl.	Ex-Div. Date	Stk. of Record	Payment Date
0.090	12/15	01/30	02/01	02/15/06
0.120	02/16	04/27	05/01	05/15/06
0.120	05/25	07/28	08/01	08/15/06
0.120	07/27	10/30	11/01	11/15/06

Dividends have been paid since 1981. Source: Company reports.

Please read the Required Disclosures and Analyst Certification on the last page of this report.

Hasbro Inc.

Business Summary July 31, 2006

CORPORATE OVERVIEW. Hasbro is a worldwide leader in children's and family leisure time and entertainment products and services, including the design, manufacture and marketing of games and toys ranging from traditional to high-tech. Some of the company's widely recognized core brands, both internationally and in the U.S., are Playskool, Tonka, Super Soaker, Milton Bradley, Parker Brothers, Tiger And Wizards of the Coast. Offerings in the games segment include traditional board games, hand-held electronic, trading card, plug and play and DVD games, as well as electronic learning aids and puzzles. Toy offerings include boys' action figures, vehicles and playsets, girls' toys, electronic toys, plush products, preschool toys and infant products, children's consumer electronics, electronic interactive products and toy related specialty products.

Part of HAS growth strategy includes licensing, which has been successful in the past for HAS. In 2005, revenues generated from the sale of Star Wars products produced under its license with Lucas Licensing and Lucasfilm represented approximately 16% of total company revenues. In January 2006, HAS completed a licensing agreement with Marvel Entertainment, Inc. to product action figures and other toys and games based on their library of intellectual property, including Spiderman and the Fantastic 4. We expect products related to this license to begin shipping late in 2006, with the bulk of the licensed products expected in 2007 and thereafter.

Company Financials

Per Share Data ($) Year Ended Dec. 31	2005	2004	2003	2002	2001	2000	1999	1998	1997	1996
Tangible Book Value	3.61	3.01	1.32	0.08	NM	NM	0.64	2.05	4.30	4.27
Cash Flow	2.20	1.75	2.37	0.95	1.66	0.69	2.31	1.48	1.20	1.51
Earnings	1.09	0.96	0.98	0.43	0.35	-0.82	0.93	1.01	0.68	1.01
S&P Core Earnings	1.02	0.90	0.93	0.44	0.19	NA	NA	NA	NA	NA
Dividends	0.33	0.21	0.12	0.12	0.12	0.24	0.23	0.21	0.23	0.25
Payout Ratio	30%	22%	12%	28%	34%	NM	25%	21%	33%	25%
Prices:High	22.35	23.33	22.63	17.30	18.44	18.94	37.00	27.29	24.33	20.78
Prices:Low	17.75	16.90	11.23	9.87	10.31	8.38	16.88	18.67	15.25	12.83
P/E Ratio:High	21	24	23	40	53	NM	40	27	36	21
P/E Ratio:Low	16	18	11	23	29	NM	18	18	22	13

Income Statement Analysis (Million $)	2005	2004	2003	2002	2001	2000	1999	1998	1997	1996
Revenue	3,088	2,998	3,139	2,816	2,856	3,787	4,232	3,304	3,189	3,002
Operating Income	491	439	509	309	435	268	669	442	473	430
Depreciation	180	146	240	89.3	226	264	277	97.0	113	98.2
Interest Expense	30.5	31.7	52.5	77.5	104	114	69.3	36.1	27.5	31.5
Pretax Income	311	260	244	104	96.2	-226	274	303	205	307
Effective Tax Rate	31.8%	24.6%	28.3%	27.9%	36.8%	NM	31.0%	32.0%	34.0%	34.9%
Net Income	212	196	175	75.1	60.8	-145	189	206	135	200
S&P Core Earnings	199	184	166	79.1	33.8	NA	NA	NA	NA	NA

Balance Sheet & Other Financial Data (Million $)	2005	2004	2003	2002	2001	2000	1999	1998	1997	1996
Cash	942	725	521	495	233	127	280	178	362	219
Current Assets	1,830	1,718	1,509	1,432	1,369	1,580	2,132	1,790	1,574	1,487
Total Assets	3,301	3,241	3,163	3,143	3,369	3,828	4,463	3,794	2,900	2,702
Current Liabilities	911	1,149	930	967	759	1,240	2,071	1,366	1,004	831
Long Term Debt	496	303	687	857	1,166	1,168	421	407	Nil	149
Common Equity	1,723	1,640	1,405	1,191	1,353	1,327	1,879	1,945	1,838	1,652
Total Capital	2,219	1,942	2,092	2,049	2,519	2,495	2,300	2,352	1,838	1,801
Capital Expenditures	70.6	79.2	63.1	58.7	50.0	125	107	142	99.3	102
Cash Flow	392	342	415	164	287	120	466	303	248	298
Current Ratio	2.0	1.5	1.6	1.5	1.8	1.3	1.0	1.3	1.6	1.8
% Long Term Debt of Capitalization	22.3	15.6	32.8	41.8	46.3	46.8	18.3	17.3	Nil	8.3
% Net Income of Revenue	6.9	6.5	5.6	2.7	2.1	NM	4.5	6.2	4.2	6.7
% Return on Assets	6.5	6.1	5.6	2.3	1.7	NM	4.6	6.2	4.8	7.5
% Return on Equity	12.6	12.9	13.5	5.9	4.5	NM	9.9	10.9	7.7	12.6

Data as orig reptd.; bef. results of disc opers/spec. items. Per share data adj. for stk. divs.; EPS diluted. E-Estimated. NA-Not Available. NM-Not Meaningful. NR-Not Ranked. UR-Under Review.

Office: 1027 Newport Ave, Pawtucket, RI, USA 02862.
Telephone: 401-431-8697.
Website: http://www.hasbro.com
Chrmn: A.G. Hassenfeld

Pres & CEO: A.J. Verrecchia
COO: B. Goldner
SVP & CFO: D.D. Hargreaves
SVP & Treas: M.R. Trueb

Investor Contact: K.A. Warren (401-727-5401)
Board of Directors: B. L. Anderson, A. R. Batkin, F. J. Biondi, Jr., J. M. Connors, Jr., M. Garrett, E. G. Gee, J. M. Greenberg, A. G. Hassenfeld, C. B. Malone, E. M. Philip, P. Stern, A. J. Verrecchia

Founded: 1926
Domicile: Rhode Island
Employees: 5,900

STANDARD & POOR'S

HCA Inc.

S&P Recommendation HOLD ★★★★★

Price $50.45 (as of Oct 27, 2006)

12-Mo. Target Price $51.00

Investment Style Large-Cap Growth

GICS Sector Health Care
Sub-Industry Health Care Facilities

Comment This company, which owns and operates the largest U.S. chain of for-profit acute care hospitals, and some outpatient surgery centers and psychiatric facilities, has agreed to a $51 a share buyout.

Key Stock Statistics (Source S&P, Vickers, company reports)

52-Wk Range	$52.74–41.80	S&P Oper. EPS 2006E	2.69	P/E on S&P Oper. EPS 2006E	18.8	Dividend Rate/Share	$0.68
Trailing 12-Month EPS	$2.96	S&P Oper. EPS 2007E	3.10	Common Shares Outstg. (M)	423.9	Yield (%)	1.35
Trailing 12-Month P/E	17.0	S&P Core EPS 2006E	2.69	Market Capitalization(B)	$20.327	Beta	-0.37
$10K Invested 5 Yrs Ago	$13,090	S&P Core EPS 2007E	3.10	Institutional Ownership (%)	79	S&P Credit Rating	B+

Price Performance

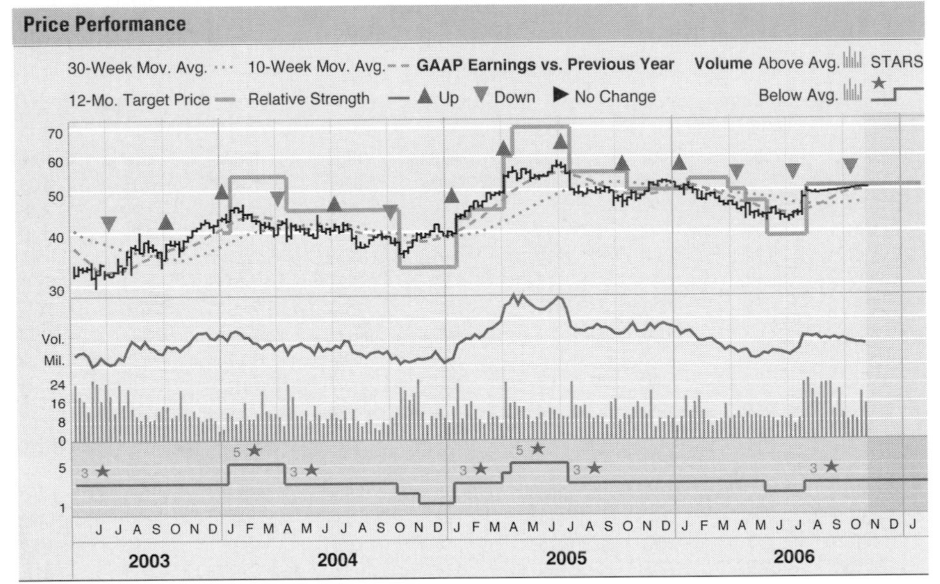

Options: ASE, CBOE, P

Analysis prepared by **Cameron Lavey** on October 23, 2006, when the stock traded at **$ 50.35**.

Highlights

- We see 2006 revenue rising 4.6%, which includes a price hike of about 4% and 1% volume growth. In addition, we expect HCA's exposure to self-pay revenue to increase in the high single digits on higher co-pays and deductibles for the insured and a rise in uninsured admissions. In 2007, we think that Medicare and managed care reimbursement increases will help drive top-line growth, but we forecast a flat to slightly negative Medicaid environment. All told, we forecast a 2% increase in revenue.
- We anticipate 2006 bad debt expense equal to 10.4% of revenue. This is above the 9.6% reported for 2005; however, the 2006 figure reflects a higher level of discounts for uninsured patients, which lowers reported bad debt expense. We expect an increase in total uncompensated care. In 2007, we anticipate slightly wider EBITDA margins on a reduction in salaries and benefits expense. We see supplies expense remaining flat, and bad debt expense trending down slightly to 10.2% of revenue.
- We see EPS of $2.69 in 2006 and $3.10 in 2007, both after $0.08 of projected stock option expense.

Investment Rationale/Risk

- The company has agreed to be acquired by a group of private equity firms for $51 per share, subject to approvals. We think the deal will be approved and expect the shares to trade in line with the proposed offer price. HCA recently reported what we view as weak third quarter operating results, including a fractional increase in same-facility admissions and a 10.1% rise in same-facility uninsured admissions.
- Risks to our recommendation and target price include a higher than anticipated rise in bad debt expense, a decrease in volumes, lower pricing from Medicare and/or managed care payors, and lower collections from uninsured patients.
- The $51 buyout price is supported by our discounted cash flow (DCF) and relative valuation analyses. Our DCF model assumes a weighted average cost of capital of 7.5%, five-year growth of 8%, and perpetual growth of 3%, resulting in a price of $50. Our target price assumes that the shares will trade at 16.5X our 2007 EPS estimate of $3.10, slightly above peers and in line with a buyout offer.

Qualitative Risk Assessment

LOW | **MEDIUM** | HIGH

We think HCA's geographic diversity provides a stable operating base. However, the company is dependent on third-party reimbursements, including Medicare and Medicaid, which can be unpredictable. HCA also has a higher level of debt than peers in our coverage universe.

Quantitative Evaluations

S&P Quality Ranking B+

D | C | B- | B | **B+** | A- | A | A+

Relative Strength Rank MODERATE

50

LOWEST = 1 HIGHEST = 99

Revenue/Earnings Data

Revenue (Million $)

	1Q	2Q	3Q	4Q	Year
2006	6,415	6,360	6,213	--	--
2005	6,182	6,070	6,025	6,178	24,455
2004	5,937	5,833	5,792	5,940	23,502
2003	5,273	5,467	5,471	5,597	21,808
2002	4,873	4,903	4,929	5,024	19,729
2001	4,501	4,476	4,438	4,538	17,953

Earnings Per Share ($)

	1Q	2Q	3Q	4Q	Year
2006	0.92	0.72	0.58	E0.64	E2.69
2005	0.95	0.90	0.62	0.74	3.19
2004	0.69	0.72	0.47	0.70	2.58
2003	0.90	0.47	0.61	0.63	2.61
2002	0.74	0.66	0.38	-0.20	1.59
2001	0.59	0.48	0.48	0.11	1.68

Fiscal year ended Dec. 31. Next earnings report expected: Early February. EPS Estimates based on S&P Operating Earnings; historical GAAP earnings are as reported.

Dividend Data (Dates: mm/dd Payment Date: mm/dd/yy)

Amount ($)	Date Decl.	Ex-Div. Date	Stk. of Record	Payment Date
0.150	09/22	10/28	11/01	12/01/05
0.150	11/23	01/30	02/01	03/01/06
0.170	02/01	04/27	05/01	06/01/06
0.170	05/25	07/28	08/01	09/01/06

Dividends have been paid since 1993. Source: Company reports.

Please read the Required Disclosures and Analyst Certification on the last page of this report.

Business Summary October 23, 2006

CORPORATE OVERVIEW. HCA operates the largest U.S. chain of acute care hospitals, as well as an extensive network of outpatient surgery centers and some psychiatric hospitals. Most of HCA's acute care hospitals provide a full range of medical and surgical services, including inpatient care, intensive care, cardiac care, diagnostic services and emergency services. They also provide outpatient services such as surgery, laboratory, radiology, respiratory therapy, cardiology and physical therapy. At September 30, 2006, HCA owned and/or operated 172 hospitals, plus another seven hospitals through joint ventures. In addition, HCA operated 94 freestanding surgery centers, including seven operated through joint ventures, as well as six psychiatric hospitals and one rehabilitation hospital. In the third quarter of 2006, on a same-facility basis (which includes facilities in operation for a full year), admissions rose 0.1%, and equivalent admissions declined 0.9%. Outpatient surgery cases fell 2.8% while inpatient surgeries increased 0.1%. Emergency room visits decreased 1.5%, to 1.27 million.

Company Financials

Per Share Data ($) Year Ended Dec. 31	2005	2004	2003	2002	2001	2000	1999	1998	1997	1996
Tangible Book Value	5.18	4.18	7.44	7.08	5.33	4.14	5.85	7.26	5.81	7.30
Cash Flow	6.27	5.16	4.98	3.51	3.63	2.20	2.96	2.75	2.14	3.92
Earnings	3.19	2.58	2.61	1.59	1.68	0.39	1.11	0.82	0.27	2.22
S&P Core Earnings	2.95	2.10	2.28	2.32	1.66	NA	NA	NA	NA	NA
Dividends	0.58	0.41	0.08	0.08	0.08	0.08	0.08	0.08	0.07	0.08
Payout Ratio	18%	16%	3%	5%	5%	21%	7%	10%	26%	4%
Prices:High	58.60	46.60	44.45	52.05	47.28	45.25	29.44	34.63	44.88	41.88
Prices:Low	38.97	34.70	34.50	36.21	33.93	18.75	17.25	17.00	25.75	31.67
P/E Ratio:High	18	18	17	33	28	NM	27	42	NM	19
P/E Ratio:Low	12	13	13	23	20	NM	16	21	NM	14

Income Statement Analysis (Million $)	2005	2004	2003	2002	2001	2000	1999	1998	1997	1996
Revenue	24,455	23,502	21,808	19,729	17,953	16,670	16,657	18,681	18,819	19,909
Operating Income	4,004	3,716	3,721	3,697	3,200	3,051	2,798	2,756	2,783	4,136
Depreciation	1,374	1,250	1,112	1,010	1,048	1,033	1,094	1,247	1,238	1,155
Interest Expense	655	563	491	446	536	559	471	561	493	498
Pretax Income	2,327	2,141	2,306	1,603	1,624	600	1,284	1,151	538	2,656
Effective Tax Rate	31.2%	34.0%	35.7%	38.8%	37.1%	49.5%	44.4%	47.7%	38.3%	38.0%
Net Income	1,424	1,246	1,332	833	903	219	657	532	182	1,505
S&P Core Earnings	1,316	1,019	1,169	1,207	894	NA	NA	NA	NA	NA

Balance Sheet & Other Financial Data (Million $)	2005	2004	2003	2002	2001	2000	1999	1998	1997	1996
Cash	336	129	115	161	85.0	314	190	297	110	113
Current Assets	5,215	4,683	4,822	4,505	4,141	4,453	3,597	3,863	4,423	4,413
Total Assets	22,225	21,465	21,063	18,741	17,730	17,568	16,885	19,429	22,022	21,272
Current Liabilities	3,895	3,174	3,168	3,739	3,184	4,141	3,332	3,559	2,773	2,946
Long Term Debt	9,889	10,044	8,042	6,497	6,953	5,631	5,284	5,685	9,276	6,781
Common Equity	4,863	4,407	6,209	5,702	4,762	4,405	5,617	7,581	7,250	8,609
Total Capital	15,580	15,260	16,581	12,810	12,278	10,608	11,664	14,031	17,362	17,490
Capital Expenditures	1,592	1,513	1,838	1,718	1,370	1,155	1,287	1,255	1,422	1,400
Cash Flow	2,798	2,496	2,444	1,843	1,951	1,252	1,751	1,779	1,420	2,660
Current Ratio	1.3	1.5	1.5	1.2	1.3	1.1	1.1	1.1	1.6	1.5
% Long Term Debt of Capitalization	63.5	65.8	48.5	50.7	56.6	53.1	45.3	40.5	53.4	38.8
% Net Income of Revenue	5.8	5.3	6.1	4.2	5.0	1.3	3.9	2.8	1.0	7.6
% Return on Assets	6.5	5.9	6.7	4.6	5.1	1.3	3.6	2.6	0.8	7.3
% Return on Equity	30.7	23.5	22.4	15.9	19.7	4.4	10.0	7.2	2.3	19.0

Data as orig reptd.; bef. results of disc opers/spec. items. Per share data adj. for stk. divs.; EPS diluted. E-Estimated. NA-Not Available. NM-Not Meaningful. NR-Not Ranked. UR-Under Review.

Office: 1 Park Plz, Nashville, TN 37203-6527.
Telephone: 615-344-9551.
Website: http://www.hcahealthcare.com
Chrmn & CEO: J.O. Bovender, Jr.

Pres & COO: R.M. Bracken
EVP & CFO: R.M. Johnson
SVP & Treas: D.G. Anderson
SVP & General Counsel: R.A. Waterman

Board of Directors: C. M. Armstrong, M. H. Averhoff, J. O. Bovender, Jr., R. M. Bracken, M. Feldstein, T. F. Frist, Jr., F. W. Gluck, G. A. Hatchett, C. O. Holliday, Jr., T. M. Long, J. H. McArthur, K. C. Nelson, F. S. Royal, H. T. Shapiro

Founded: 1990
Domicile: Delaware
Employees: 191,100

STANDARD &POOR'S

Health Management Associates Inc.

S&P Recommendation HOLD ★★★★★ | **Price** $19.99 (as of Oct 27, 2006) | **12-Mo. Target Price** $21.00 | **Investment Style** Mid-Cap Growth

GICS Sector Health Care
Sub-Industry Health Care Facilities

Comment HMA operates a network of general acute care hospitals located primarily in nonurban areas in the Southeast and Southwest.

Key Stock Statistics (Source S&P, Vickers, company reports)

52-Wk Range	$24.00–19.04	S&P Oper. EPS 2007E	1.40	P/E on S&P Oper. EPS 2007E	14.3	Dividend Rate/Share	$0.24
Trailing 12-Month EPS	$0.98	S&P Oper. EPS 2008E	NA	Common Shares Outstg. (M)	240.3	Yield (%)	1.20
Trailing 12-Month P/E	20.4	S&P Core EPS 2007E	1.40	Market Capitalization(B)	$4.803	Beta	-0.10
$10K Invested 5 Yrs Ago	$10,498	S&P Core EPS 2008E	NA	Institutional Ownership (%)	92	S&P Credit Rating	BBB+

Price Performance

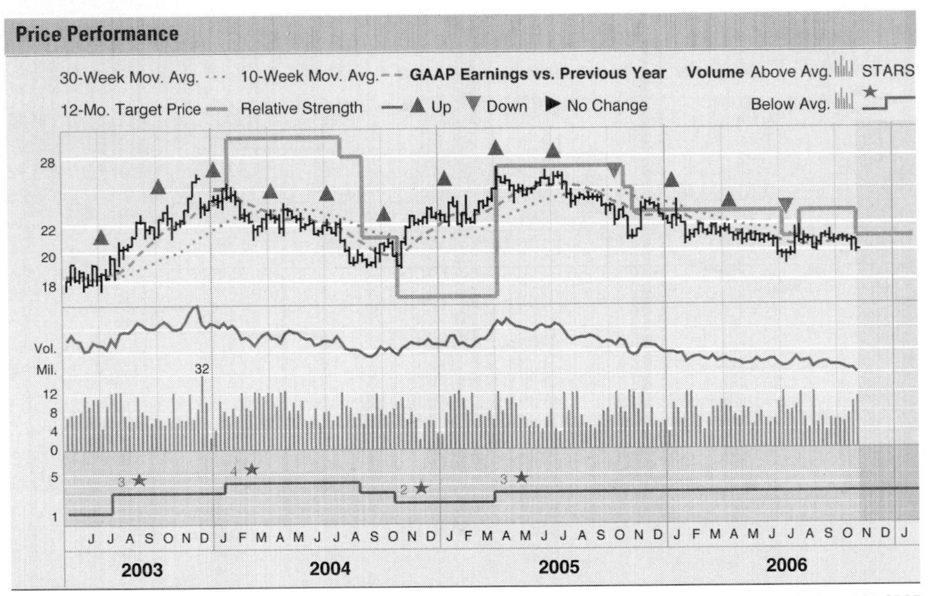

Options: ASE, CBOE

Analysis prepared by **Cameron Lavey** on October 25, 2006, when the stock traded at **$ 20.07**.

Highlights

- We expect a revenue increase of 13% in 2006, including same-facility revenue growth of 4%-5%. Our forecast assumes a same-facility admissions gain of 1% and mid-single digit price increases; we look for acquisitions to supply the rest of our forecast revenue growth. In 2007, we see a 6% rise in revenue, driven entirely by organic growth. Our 2007 forecast assumes similar trends to 2006, with low single digit volume gains and mid-single digit price increases.
- We anticipate that the company will generate 2006 EBITDA of about $735 million, implying an EBITDA margin of 18.1%. We think EBITDA margins will remain flat in 2007 as a decline in salary expense is offset by higher costs for supplies and other operating expenses. We anticipate double digit growth in charity care write-offs. HMA's practice of writing off higher levels of charity care distorts EBITDA margins relative to peers, in our view.
- We estimate 2006 EPS of $1.30, which includes projected stock option expense of $0.05, but does not include any gains from sales of facilities. In 2007, we forecast EPS of $1.40.

Investment Rationale/Risk

- While we think that some industry trends are showing signs of improvement, including labor costs and malpractice expenses, we would not add to positions due to HMA's high level of charity care and the continued pressure we see from bad debts from uninsured patients. In addition, volume growth remains challenging, in our view. HMA's charity care write-offs as a percentage of gross revenue were 4.4% in the third quarter of 2006, versus 4.5% in the prior year period. We expect this measure to remain in the mid-single digits in 2007.
- Risks to our recommendation and target price include potentially higher supply costs, decreased pricing power, and unanticipated cuts in Medicare and/or Medicaid reimbursement rates. Continued rises in uninsured admissions could further increase bad debts.
- On the basis of a P/E to growth (PEG) ratio of about 1.0X, matching the peer group average PEG, we believe the shares are fairly valued. Our 12-month target price of $21 is based on a P/E of 15X our 2007 EPS estimate, in line with peers.

Qualitative Risk Assessment

LOW | **MEDIUM** | HIGH

Our risk assessment reflects our view of stable demand for HMA's services, driven by a rising senior population in the U.S. HMA also carries the lowest amount of debt among its peers in our coverage universe. However, this is offset by the company's dependence on third-party reimbursements, including Medicare and Medicaid, for revenue. Such payments can change unexpectedly.

Quantitative Evaluations

S&P Quality Ranking B+

D | C | B- | B | **B+** | A- | A | A+

Relative Strength Rank WEAK

20

LOWEST = 1 HIGHEST = 99

Revenue/Earnings Data

Revenue (Million $)

	1Q	2Q	3Q	4Q	Year
2006	1,033	1,022	--	994.1	3,006
2005	--	--	--	905.6	3,555
2004	756.6	833.9	817.3	798.1	3,206
2003	609.4	646.5	647.1	657.6	2,561
2002	495.8	580.0	592.5	594.4	2,263
2001	434.2	481.1	473.2	491.2	1,880

Earnings Per Share ($)

	1Q	2Q	3Q	4Q	Year
2006	0.36	0.32	E0.34	0.26	0.93
2005	0.32	0.40	0.35	0.35	1.42
2004	0.29	0.37	0.36	0.30	1.32
2003	0.24	0.31	0.30	0.28	1.13
2002	0.20	0.27	0.26	0.24	0.97
2001	0.16	0.19	0.21	0.20	0.76

Fiscal year ended Dec. 31. Next earnings report expected: Late January. EPS Estimates based on S&P Operating Earnings; historical GAAP earnings are as reported.

Dividend Data (Dates: mm/dd Payment Date: mm/dd/yy)

Amount ($)	Date Decl.	Ex-Div. Date	Stk. of Record	Payment Date
0.060	09/22	11/02	11/04	11/29/05
0.060	02/03	02/13	02/15	03/09/06
0.060	05/02	05/10	05/12	06/05/06
0.060	08/01	08/09	08/11	09/05/06

Dividends have been paid since 2002. Source: Company reports.

Please read the Required Disclosures and Analyst Certification on the last page of this report.

Health Management Associates Inc.

Business Summary October 25, 2006

CORPORATE OVERVIEW. Health Management Associates operates acute care facilities in growing, non-urban communities, primarily in the southeastern and southwestern U.S. The majority of HMA's facilities are located in Florida and Mississippi. Excluding three hospitals held for sale, it operated 57 hospitals with a total of 8,331 beds as of September 30, 2006. HMA believes it can acquire acute care facilities and boost their financial performance through capital improvement projects, better physician recruiting and retention, and implementing the latest medical technologies and services. Reimbursement rates tend to be higher for non-urban providers, mainly as an incentive to offer needed care in underserved areas. Many non-urban hospitals have limited access to the capital needed to keep pace with advances in medical technology. In addition, they sometimes lack management resources needed to recruit and retain physicians. As a result, patients may migrate to, be referred by local physicians to, or be encouraged by managed care plans to travel to hospitals in larger, urban markets.

In 2005, HMA acquired five acute care facilities with a total of 795 beds for $341.9 million. In the first quarter of 2006, the company purchased two facilities with a total of 151 beds for $89.0 million. HMA also bought an 80% ownership interest in an 84-bed facility. In the second quarter of 2006, HMA acquired two additional facilities, entered into one joint venture to own and operate a cardiac catheterization program, and announced an agreement to sell three facilities by November 2006. In the third quarter of 2006, the company sold two psychiatric hospitals for an after-tax gain of $12.7 million. We do not expect any additional acquisitions in 2006, as HMA focuses on improving the operating performance of existing and recently acquired facilities. In 2007, we think the company will continue to focus on its existing portfolio of assets; our forecasts do not assume any acquisitions in 2007.

Company Financials

Per Share Data ($) Year Ended Dec. 31	**2006**	**2005**	**2004**	**2003**	**2002**	**2001**	**2000**	**1999**	**1998**	**1997**
Tangible Book Value	NA	5.89	5.05	5.16	4.24	4.08	3.44	2.98	2.82	2.29
Cash Flow	NA	2.04	1.86	1.54	1.31	1.08	0.98	0.83	0.73	0.58
Earnings	0.93	1.42	1.32	1.13	0.97	0.76	0.68	0.59	0.54	0.43
S&P Core Earnings	NA	1.23	1.28	1.08	0.93	0.72	NA	NA	NA	NA
Dividends	0.18	0.16	0.08	0.08	Nil	Nil	Nil	Nil	Nil	Nil
Payout Ratio	19%	11%	6%	7%	Nil	Nil	Nil	Nil	Nil	Nil
Prices:High	24.00	27.00	25.55	26.45	22.99	22.22	22.75	21.63	25.75	17.67
Prices:Low	19.04	20.75	18.80	15.89	16.24	13.42	9.63	7.00	14.92	9.50
P/E Ratio:High	26	19	19	23	24	29	33	37	48	41
P/E Ratio:Low	20	15	14	14	17	18	14	12	28	22
Income Statement Analysis (Million $)										
Revenue	NA	3,555	3,206	2,561	2,263	1,880	1,578	1,356	1,139	895
Operating Income	NA	702	683	593	518	432	376	316	280	219
Depreciation	NA	155	135	110	95.3	90.6	74.5	61.3	50.4	36.6
Interest Expense	NA	12.9	16.2	30.4	15.5	20.0	25.4	8.39	4.76	3.71
Pretax Income	NA	568	532	463	407	321	276	247	225	178
Effective Tax Rate	NA	37.2%	37.8%	37.9%	39.2%	39.2%	39.3%	39.2%	39.3%	39.3%
Net Income	NA	354	325	283	246	195	168	150	137	108
S&P Core Earnings	NA	308	313	273	235	185	NA	NA	NA	NA
Balance Sheet & Other Financial Data (Million $)										
Cash	NA	78.6	113	395	124	70.3	16.5	12.9	12.7	67.4
Current Assets	NA	988	942	1,093	696	565	487	425	309	236
Total Assets	NA	3,988	3,507	2,979	2,364	1,942	1,772	1,517	1,112	728
Current Liabilities	NA	1,069	320	273	274	188	170	175	121	82.9
Long Term Debt	NA	367	926	925	650	429	520	402	177	49.7
Common Equity	NA	2,289	1,978	1,637	1,347	1,254	1,030	891	757	560
Total Capital	NA	2,702	3,090	2,648	2,048	1,717	1,585	1,325	974	629
Capital Expenditures	NA	273	202	166	116	73.5	121	159	237	111
Cash Flow	NA	509	460	393	342	286	242	211	187	145
Current Ratio	NA	0.9	2.9	4.0	2.5	3.0	2.9	2.4	2.6	2.8
% Long Term Debt of Capitalization	NA	13.6	29.9	34.9	31.7	25.0	32.8	30.3	18.2	7.9
% Net Income of Revenue	NA	9.8	10.1	11.1	10.9	10.4	10.6	11.1	12.0	12.1
% Return on Assets	NA	9.5	10.0	10.6	11.4	10.5	10.2	11.4	14.9	16.4
% Return on Equity	NA	16.6	18.0	19.0	19.0	17.1	17.5	18.2	20.8	22.2

Data as orig reptd.; bef. results of disc opers/spec. items. Per share data adj. for stk. divs.; EPS diluted. Prior to 2006, fiscal year ended September 30. E-Estimated. NA-Not Available. NM-Not Meaningful. NR-Not Ranked. UR-Under Review.

Office: 5811 Pelican Bay Boulevard, Naples, FL 34108-2711.
Telephone: 239-598-3131.
Website: http://www.hma-corp.com
Chrmn: W.J. Schoen

Pres & COO: B.W. Whitman
Vice Chrmn & CEO: J.V. Vumbacco
SVP & CFO: R.E. Farnham
SVP, Secy & General Counsel: T.R. Parry

Investor Contact: J.C. Merriwether (239-598-3104)
Board of Directors: K. P. Dauten, D. E. Kiernan, R. A. Knox, W. E. Mayberry, V. A. O'Meara, W. J. Schoen, W. C. Steere, Jr., J. V. Vumbacco, R. W. Westerfield

Founded: 1977
Domicile: Delaware
Employees: 31,000

STANDARD &POOR'S

Heinz (H J) Co

S&P Recommendation HOLD ★★★★★

Price
$42.00 (as of Oct 27, 2006)

12-Mo. Target Price
$45.00

Investment Style
Large-Cap Growth

GICS Sector Consumer Staples
Sub-Industry Packaged Foods & Meats

Comment This company produces a wide variety of food products worldwide, with a major presence in the U.S. in condiments, frozen potatoes, and convenience meals.

Key Stock Statistics (Source S&P, Vickers, company reports)

52-Wk Range	**$44.15–33.42**	S&P Oper. EPS 2007**E**	**2.35**	P/E on S&P Oper. EPS 2007**E**	**17.9**	Dividend Rate/Share	**$1.40**
Trailing 12-Month EPS	**$2.02**	S&P Oper. EPS 2008**E**	**2.50**	Common Shares Outstg. (M)	**331.5**	Yield (%)	**3.33**
Trailing 12-Month P/E	**20.8**	S&P Core EPS 2007**E**	**2.41**	Market Capitalization(B)	**$13.922**	Beta	**0.42**
$10K Invested 5 Yrs Ago	**$13,012**	S&P Core EPS 2008**E**	**2.56**	Institutional Ownership (%)	**69**	S&P Credit Rating	**BBB**

Price Performance

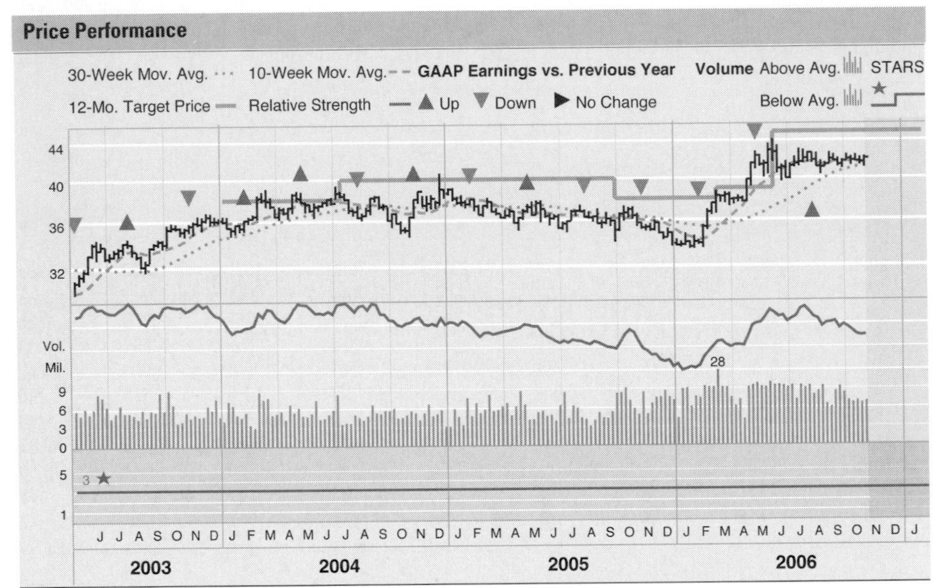

Options: ASE, CBOE, P

Analysis prepared by **Rick Joy** on September 29, 2006, when the stock traded at **$ 41.93**.

Highlights

- We expect net sales from continuing operations to rise 3% to 4% in FY 07 (Apr.) on volume growth and modest pricing gains. We see sales growth of 5% to 6% for the North American consumer products business, 3% to 4% for foodservice operations, 2% to 3% for the European business, and 5% to 6% for the Asia/Pacific business.
- We look for operating margins to benefit from an improving sales mix, SKU rationalizations, better working capital management, and cost savings from restructuring programs. However, we think that higher commodity, energy and packaging costs, and increased levels of advertising and marketing spending could partially offset some of these benefits.
- After a 3% to 4% reduction in shares outstanding, we project FY 07 operating EPS of $2.35 (including projected stock option expense of $0.05), up 7% from pro forma FY 06 EPS of $2.14. For FY 08, we see EPS rising to $2.50. For the longer term, we see annual EPS growth of 6% to 8%.

Investment Rationale/Risk

- Our hold opinion on the shares primarily reflects commodity cost inflation, mixed results in recent quarters for HNZ's various food businesses and the execution risk associated with the company's divestiture plans. We view the shares as a worthwhile holding at a recent 18.6X our calendar 2006 EPS estimate of $2.25, in line with the average P/E multiple of other leading packaged foods companies and a premium to the multiple for the S&P 500.
- Risks to our recommendation and target price include competitive product and pricing pressures in HNZ's markets, raw material cost inflation, consumer acceptance of new product introductions and the impact from foreign currency.
- Based on our discounted cash flow analysis, we see intrinsic value of $46 (key assumptions: 5% free cash flow a compound annual growth rate (CAGR) in years one to 10; 3% terminal growth; 9% discount rate). Our 12-month target price of $45 is derived from our analysis of discounted free cash flow and relative P/E and EV/EBITDA multiples.

Qualitative Risk Assessment

LOW	MEDIUM	HIGH

Our risk assessment for H. J. Heinz reflects the relatively stable nature of the company's end markets, strong cash flow and corporate governance practices that we view as favorable relative to peers.

Quantitative Evaluations

S&P Quality Ranking **B**

D	C	B-	B	B+	A-	A	A+

Relative Strength Rank **MODERATE**

39

LOWEST = 1 HIGHEST = 99

Revenue/Earnings Data

Revenue (Million $)

	1Q	2Q	3Q	4Q	Year
2007	2,060	--	--	--	--
2006	2,110	2,339	2,187	2,400	8,643
2005	2,003	2,200	2,261	2,448	8,912
2004	1,896	2,090	2,097	2,331	8,415
2003	1,839	2,099	2,105	2,193	8,237
2002	2,077	2,414	2,365	2,574	9,431

Earnings Per Share ($)

2007	0.58	**E**0.60	**E**0.57	**E**0.63	**E**2.35
2006	0.45	0.50	0.40	Nil	1.29
2005	0.55	0.56	0.50	0.58	2.08
2004	0.60	0.54	0.57	0.56	2.20
2003	0.50	0.60	0.37	0.29	1.57
2002	0.57	0.59	0.57	0.37	2.36

Fiscal year ended Apr. 30. Next earnings report expected: Late November. EPS Estimates based on S&P Operating Earnings; historical GAAP earnings are as reported.

Dividend Data (Dates: mm/dd Payment Date: mm/dd/yy)

Amount ($)	Date Decl.	Ex-Div. Date	Stk. of Record	Payment Date
0.300	11/09	12/21	12/23	01/10/06
0.300	03/08	03/22	03/24	04/10/06
0.350	06/01	06/21	06/24	07/10/06
0.350	08/16	09/20	09/22	10/10/06

Dividends have been paid since 1911. Source: Company reports.

Heinz (H J) Co

Business Summary September 29, 2006

Although largely known for its familiar ketchup, H.J. Heinz boasts many other branded food products, ranging from Ore-Ida frozen potatoes to Weight Watchers frozen dinners, which are consumed by millions of people daily. The company's current operating strategy rests on three pillars: a renewed focus on core competencies, niche acquisitions, and cost control. Sales are broadly based geographically, with contributions by major region in FY 06 (Apr.) as follows: North America (47.7% of sales), Europe (34.6%), Asia/Pacific (12.9%), and other (4.8%).

The company's revenues are generated via the manufacture and sale of products in the following categories: ketchup, condiments and sauces (40.8% of FY 06 sales), sold under names such as Heinz and Classico; meals and snacks (44.9%), which include items such as Boston Market HomeStyle Meals, Ore-Ida potatoes, and Smart Ones; infant foods (10%); and other products (4.3%). Total marketing support in FY 06 increased $108.8 million, to $2.2 billion, and is recorded either as a reduction in revenue or as a component of SG&A expenses.

In December 2002, HNZ completed the spin-off of its North American Pet Food and Pet Snacks, U.S. Tuna, U.S. Private Label Soup, College Inn Broth, and U.S. Infant Feeding businesses, merging them with Del Monte Foods Co. At the close of the transaction, HNZ shareholders owned about 74.5% and Del Monte shareholders about 25.5% of the fully diluted share capital of the new Del Monte. As a result of the merger, HNZ received $1.1 billion in cash, which was used to retire debt.

The strategic rationale behind the Del Monte transaction was to make HNZ a more focused and faster growing business, leveraging the global strategic platforms of Meal Enhancers (ketchup, condiments and sauces) and Meals & Snacks (frozen and ambient). Upon completion of the transaction, HNZ reduced its annual dividend rate to $1.08 a share beginning in April 2003, from an annual rate of $1.62 a share. As of June 1, 2006, the current annual dividend is $1.40.

Company Financials

Per Share Data ($) Year Ended Apr. 30	**2006**	**2005**	**2004**	**2003**	**2002**	**2001**	**2000**	**1999**	**1998**	**1997**
Tangible Book Value	NM	NM	NM	NM	NM	NM	NM	NM	NM	0.02
Cash Flow	2.07	2.82	2.86	2.17	3.22	2.26	3.32	2.11	2.99	1.72
Earnings	1.29	2.08	2.20	1.57	2.36	1.41	2.47	1.29	2.15	0.81
S&P Core Earnings	1.72	2.29	2.11	1.43	1.99	1.31	NA	NA	NA	NA
Dividends	1.14	1.10	1.08	1.61	1.55	1.45	1.40	1.34	1.24	1.14
Payout Ratio	88%	53%	49%	88%	65%	102%	56%	104%	57%	140%
Calendar Year	2005	2004	2003	2002	2001	2000	1999	1998	1997	1996
Prices:High	39.13	40.61	36.82	43.48	47.94	48.00	58.81	61.75	56.69	38.38
Prices:Low	33.64	34.53	28.90	29.60	36.90	30.81	39.50	48.50	35.25	29.75
P/E Ratio:High	30	20	17	24	20	34	24	48	26	47
P/E Ratio:Low	26	17	13	16	16	22	16	38	16	37

Income Statement Analysis (Million $)	2006	2005	2004	2003	2002	2001	2000	1999	1998	1997
Revenue	8,643	8,912	8,415	8,237	9,431	9,430	9,408	9,300	9,209	9,357
Operating Income	1,377	1,607	1,613	1,389	1,892	1,282	1,575	1,412	1,834	1,096
Depreciation	264	252	234	215	302	299	306	302	314	340
Interest Expense	316	232	212	224	294	333	270	259	259	274
Pretax Income	693	1,059	1,169	869	1,279	673	1,464	835	1,255	479
Effective Tax Rate	36.2%	30.5%	33.3%	36.1%	34.8%	26.5%	39.2%	43.2%	36.1%	37.0%
Net Income	443	736	779	555	834	495	891	474	802	302
S&P Core Earnings	587	809	747	500	702	458	NA	NA	NA	NA

Balance Sheet & Other Financial Data (Million $)	2006	2005	2004	2003	2002	2001	2000	1999	1998	1997
Cash	445	1,084	1,180	802	207	139	138	116	96.0	189
Current Assets	2,704	3,646	3,611	3,284	3,374	3,117	3,170	2,887	2,687	3,013
Total Assets	9,738	10,578	9,877	9,225	10,278	9,035	8,851	8,054	8,023	8,438
Current Liabilities	2,018	2,587	2,469	1,926	2,509	3,655	2,126	2,786	2,164	2,880
Long Term Debt	4,357	4,122	4,538	4,776	4,643	3,015	3,936	2,472	2,769	2,284
Common Equity	2,049	2,614	8,841	2,876	1,719	1,374	1,596	1,804	2,216	2,440
Total Capital	7,045	7,359	13,797	8,252	7,197	4,642	5,804	4,587	5,276	4,989
Capital Expenditures	231	241	232	154	213	411	452	317	374	377
Cash Flow	707	988	1,013	770	1,136	794	1,197	776	1,116	642
Current Ratio	1.3	1.4	1.5	1.7	1.3	0.9	1.5	1.0	1.2	1.1
% Long Term Debt of Capitalization	61.8	56.0	32.9	57.9	64.5	64.9	67.8	53.9	52.5	45.8
% Net Income of Revenue	5.1	8.3	9.3	6.7	8.8	5.2	9.5	5.1	8.7	3.2
% Return on Assets	4.4	7.2	8.2	5.7	8.6	5.5	10.5	5.9	9.7	3.5
% Return on Equity	19.0	26.3	8.9	17.9	53.9	33.3	52.4	23.6	34.5	11.7

Data as orig reptd.; bef. results of disc opers/spec. items. Per share data adj. for stk. divs.; EPS diluted. E-Estimated. NA-Not Available. NM-Not Meaningful. NR-Not Ranked. UR-Under Review.

Office: 600 Grant Street, Pittsburgh, PA 15219-2200.
Telephone: 412-456-5700.
Website: http://www.heinz.com
Chrmn, Pres & CEO: W.R. Johnson

EVP & CFO: A. Winkleblack
SVP & General Counsel: T. Bobby
SVP & Cntlr: E.J. McMenamin
Investor Contact: J. Runkel (412-456-6034)

Board of Directors: C. E. Bunch, M. C. Choksi, L. S. Coleman, Jr., P. H. Coors, J. G. Drosdick, E. E. Holiday, W. R. Johnson, C. Kendle, D. R. O'Hare, D. H. Reilley, L. C. Swann, T. J. Usher

Founded: 1869
Domicile: Pennsylvania
Employees: 36,000

STANDARD &POOR'S

Hercules Inc

S&P Recommendation	Price	12-Mo. Target Price	Investment Style
HOLD ★★★★★	$17.91 (as of Oct 27, 2006)	$17.00	Mid-Cap Value

GICS Sector Materials
Sub-Industry Diversified Chemicals

Comment This company manufactures and markets chemical specialties globally for use in making a variety of products for home, office and industrial markets.

Key Stock Statistics (Source S&P, Vickers, company reports)

52-Wk Range	$18.01–10.00	S&P Oper. EPS 2006**E**	1.17	P/E on S&P Oper. EPS 2006**E**	15.3	Dividend Rate/Share	Nil
Trailing 12-Month EPS	$-0.62	S&P Oper. EPS 2007**E**	1.30	Common Shares Outstg. (M)	113.3	Yield (%)	Nil
Trailing 12-Month P/E	NM	S&P Core EPS 2006**E**	1.21	Market Capitalization(B)	$2.030	Beta	1.36
$10K Invested 5 Yrs Ago	$21,071	S&P Core EPS 2007**E**	1.38	Institutional Ownership (%)	93	S&P Credit Rating	BB

Price Performance

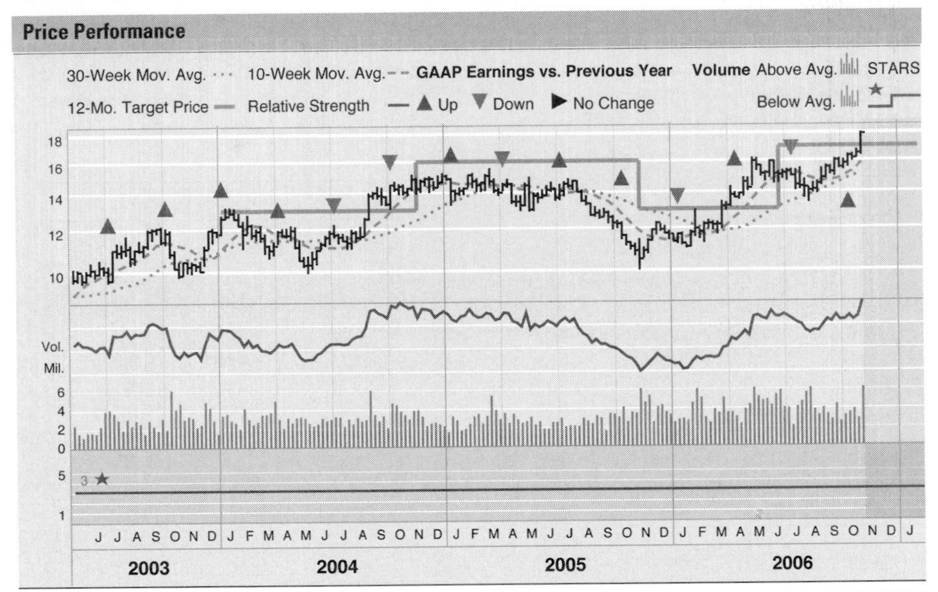

Options: ASE, CBOE, P

Analysis prepared by **Richard O'Reilly, CFA** on September 11, 2006, when the stock traded at **$ 15.18**.

Highlights

- We expect sales for 2006 to be about $2.0 billion, reflecting the absence of FiberVisions, reported on the equity basis since March 2006. We believe that sales for HPC's remaining businesses will grow at about 6%, benefiting from higher selling prices for paper chemicals and stronger overall demand. The early 2006 purchase of a guar business with annual sales of almost $50 million and the consolidation of a venture in China will both add to sales.
- We see operating profits improving modestly as HPC continues to achieve productivity gains. HPC is implementing additional restructuring actions designed to generate annual overhead cost savings of $20 million by 2008, with $10 million expected in 2006. We expect raw material and freight costs to increase in 2006, although at a slower pace than in 2005. HPC estimates that hurricane-related impacts were $0.10 a share in 2005, including $0.07 in the fourth quarter.
- We believe that interest expense in 2006 will decline to about $70 million, reflecting the elimination of $200 million of high-cost debt over the past year. Reported results for the Q2 of 2006 included a litigation charge of $0.62 a share.

Investment Rationale/Risk

- We expect positive operating EPS comparisons to resume in 2006, driven by mid-single digit sales growth and lower interest expense. We expect price boosts being implemented to offset a projected $50 million increase in raw material and freight costs. The sale in early 2006 of 51% of FiberVisions should be modestly accretive to annual EPS.
- Risks to our recommendation and target price include the company's high net debt-to-capital ratio (almost 100% at June 30, 2006), unexpected increases in raw material costs, and the possibility that any increase in asbestos-related legal exposure could dampen interest in the shares.
- We expect HPC to have free cash flow of about $100 million in 2006, up from $88 million in 2005, with funds used to retire debt. We expect 2006 capital expenditures to remain below depreciation and believe that asbestos-related spending will continue to be reimbursed. Assuming a multiple of 8.5X our projected 2006 EBITDA of $340 million, modestly below recent industry transactions, our 12-month target price is $17.

Qualitative Risk Assessment

LOW | **MEDIUM** | HIGH

Our risk assessment reflects the broad and stable nature of the company's end markets, with low exposure to petrochemicals, partly offset by a high debt ratio and potentially large environmental claims.

Quantitative Evaluations

S&P Quality Ranking B-

D | C | **B-** | B | B+ | A- | A | A+

Relative Strength Rank STRONG

91

LOWEST = 1 HIGHEST = 99

Revenue/Earnings Data

Revenue (Million $)

	1Q	2Q	3Q	4Q	Year
2006	527.3	501.0	513.1	--	--
2005	505.1	538.6	522.9	502.2	2,069
2004	475.0	510.0	501.0	511.0	1,997
2003	447.0	478.0	463.0	458.0	1,846
2002	402.0	437.0	443.0	423.0	1,705
2001	702.0	670.0	637.0	611.0	2,620

Earnings Per Share ($)

	1Q	2Q	3Q	4Q	Year
2006	0.13	-0.46	0.31	**E**0.25	**E**1.17
2005	0.04	0.08	0.22	-0.71	-0.25
2004	0.24	0.04	-0.47	0.44	0.25
2003	0.13	0.30	0.16	0.10	0.69
2002	-0.03	-0.19	-0.32	0.09	-0.45
2001	-0.09	0.21	-0.66	Nil	-0.54

Fiscal year ended Dec. 31. Next earnings report expected: Early February. EPS Estimates based on S&P Operating Earnings; historical GAAP earnings are as reported.

Dividend Data

No cash dividends have been paid since 2000.

Business Summary September 11, 2006

CORPORATE OVERVIEW. Hercules makes specialty chemicals that are used in a broad range of consumer and industrial markets. Key markets for the company's products include pulp and paper (48% of sales in 2005), food, pharmaceutical and personal care (21%), industrial (12%), paints and adhesives (10%), and construction materials (9%). International operations contributed 52% of sales in 2005, including 36% from Europe.

The paper technologies and ventures group (49% of sales and 35% of operating profits in 2005) consists of pulp and paper chemicals (39% -- sizing agents, coatings, emulsions, defoamers, deposition, corrosion and foam control, deinking, felt conditioning, fiber recovery, and water treatment for utility systems, cooling water and water clarification). Hercules is the largest global supplier in a fragmented $4.0 billion annual market for paper and pulp chemicals. Ventures (10%) consists of water management, pulp and biorefining, polyols and lubricants, adhesives, and a water treatment chemicals tolling business.

The Aqualon group (37%, 68%) is the global leader in water-soluble polymers and coatings derived from cellulose pulps and guar, and used in paints, adhesives, paper, construction materials, personal care products, drugs, foods and beverages, inks, and oil well drilling. Coatings and construction markets account for about 50% of annual sales. The group also includes the former Pinova resins unit, the world's only maker of rosin resins ($70 million of annual sales) for flavors and fragrances, adhesives and disinfectants for use in consumer and industrial products such as masking, packaging, and duct tapes, beverages, construction materials, and plastics. The global market size for the products in which Aqualon compete is about $2.5 billion. About 60% of Aqualon sales are outside the U.S.

In late March 2006, HPC sold for $109 million a 51% interest in FiberVisions (14%, -3%), one of the world's largest producers of polypropylene staple fiber used in disposable hygiene products and wipes, as well as olefin textile fibers and yarn. The buyer has an option to buy an additional 14% interest for $7.4 million in 2007. HPC reported a related pretax charge of $41.6 million in the 2005 fourth quarter. HPC's remaining 49% interest in FiberVisions is now reported using the equity earnings method.

Company Financials

Per Share Data ($) Year Ended Dec. 31	**2005**	**2004**	**2003**	**2002**	**2001**	**2000**	**1999**	**1998**	**1997**	**1996**
Tangible Book Value	NM	NM	NM	NM	NM	NM	NM	NM	7.18	8.75
Cash Flow	0.62	1.17	1.61	0.47	1.43	3.22	2.94	1.20	3.88	4.03
Earnings	-0.25	0.25	0.69	-0.45	-0.54	0.91	1.62	0.10	3.18	3.04
S&P Core Earnings	0.27	0.27	0.70	-0.58	-1.96	NA	NA	NA	NA	NA
Dividends	Nil	Nil	Nil	Nil	Nil	0.62	1.08	1.08	1.00	0.92
Payout Ratio	Nil	Nil	Nil	Nil	Nil	68%	67%	NM	31%	30%
Prices:High	15.55	15.25	12.50	13.70	20.00	28.00	40.69	51.38	54.50	66.25
Prices:Low	10.00	9.93	7.40	8.45	6.50	11.38	22.38	24.63	37.75	42.75
P/E Ratio:High	NM	61	18	NM	NM	31	25	NM	17	22
P/E Ratio:Low	NM	40	11	NM	NM	12	14	NM	12	14

Income Statement Analysis (Million $)	2005	2004	2003	2002	2001	2000	1999	1998	1997	1996
Revenue	2,069	1,997	1,846	1,705	2,620	3,152	3,248	2,145	1,866	2,060
Operating Income	289	328	355	-323	482	598	624	506	466	528
Depreciation	106	101	100	100	212	246	144	108	73.0	106
Interest Expense	89.4	109	131	154	254	260	236	103	39.0	40.0
Pretax Income	-45.8	29.0	95.0	-53.0	14.0	164	243	77.0	593	485
Effective Tax Rate	NM	6.90%	22.1%	NM	NM	40.2%	30.9%	88.3%	45.4%	32.9%
Net Income	-38.6	27.0	74.0	-49.0	-58.0	98.0	168	9.00	324	325
S&P Core Earnings	28.3	28.9	76.1	-62.8	-212	NA	NA	NA	NA	NA

Balance Sheet & Other Financial Data (Million $)	2005	2004	2003	2002	2001	2000	1999	1998	1997	1996
Cash	77.3	127	125	334	76.0	54.0	63.0	68.0	17.0	30.0
Current Assets	843	772	820	907	842	1,022	1,338	1,240	689	739
Total Assets	2,569	2,710	2,766	2,693	5,049	5,309	5,896	5,833	2,411	2,386
Current Liabilities	512	477	457	616	917	922	1,559	1,317	799	694
Long Term Debt	1,092	1,210	1,326	1,362	2,583	2,964	2,769	3,296	799	345
Common Equity	-24.7	97.0	66.0	-123	4,402	4,600	4,733	559	690	887
Total Capital	1,143	1,384	1,470	1,319	7,319	7,751	7,789	4,080	1,649	1,361
Capital Expenditures	67.5	77.0	48.0	43.0	63.0	187	196	157	119	120
Cash Flow	67.3	128	174	51.0	154	344	312	117	397	431
Current Ratio	1.6	1.6	1.8	1.5	0.9	1.1	0.9	0.9	0.9	1.1
% Long Term Debt of Capitalization	95.5	87.4	90.2	103.3	35.3	38.2	35.6	80.8	48.5	25.3
% Net Income of Revenue	NM	1.4	4.0	NM	NM	3.1	5.2	0.4	17.4	15.8
% Return on Assets	NM	1.0	2.7	NM	NM	1.7	2.9	0.2	13.5	13.3
% Return on Equity	NM	50.0	NA	NM	NM	2.1	3.7	1.4	41.1	32.9

Data as orig reptd.; bef. results of disc opers/spec. items. Per share data adj. for stk. divs.; EPS diluted. E-Estimated. NA-Not Available. NM-Not Meaningful. NR-Not Ranked. UR-Under Review.

Office: 1313 N Market St Ofc, Wilmington, DE 19894-0001.
Telephone: 302-594-5000.
Website: http://www.herc.com
Chrmn: J.K. Wulff

Pres & CEO: C.A. Rogerson
VP & CFO: A.A. Spizzo
VP & Treas: S.C. Shears
VP & Cntlr: F.G. Aanonsen

Investor Contact: S.L. Fornoff (302-594-7151)
Board of Directors: A. Cheng Catalano, T. P. Gerrity, J. C. Hunter, III, B. M. Joyce, R. D. Kennedy, J. M. Lipton, C. A. Rogerson, J. K. Wulff, J. B. Wyatt

Founded: 1912
Domicile: Delaware
Employees: 4,650

STANDARD
&POOR'S

Hershey Co (The)

S&P Recommendation BUY ★★★★★

Price
$52.41 (as of Oct 27, 2006)

12-Mo. Target Price
$56.00

Investment Style
Mid-Cap Growth

GICS Sector Consumer Staples
Sub-Industry Packaged Foods & Meats

Comment Hershey (formerly Hershey Foods Corp.) is the leading U.S. producer of chocolate and confectionery products.

Key Stock Statistics (Source S&P, Vickers, company reports)

52-Wk Range	**$59.05–48.20**	S&P Oper. EPS 2006**E**	**2.48**	P/E on S&P Oper. EPS 2006**E**	**21.1**	Dividend Rate/Share	**$1.08**
Trailing 12-Month EPS	**$2.38**	S&P Oper. EPS 2007**E**	**2.75**	Common Shares Outstg. (M)	**234.2**	Yield (%)	**2.06**
Trailing 12-Month P/E	**22.0**	S&P Core EPS 2006E	**2.48**	Market Capitalization(B)	**$9.085**	Beta	**0.14**
$10K Invested 5 Yrs Ago	**$17,686**	S&P Core EPS 2007E	**2.75**	Institutional Ownership (%)	**56**	S&P Credit Rating	**A+**

Price Performance

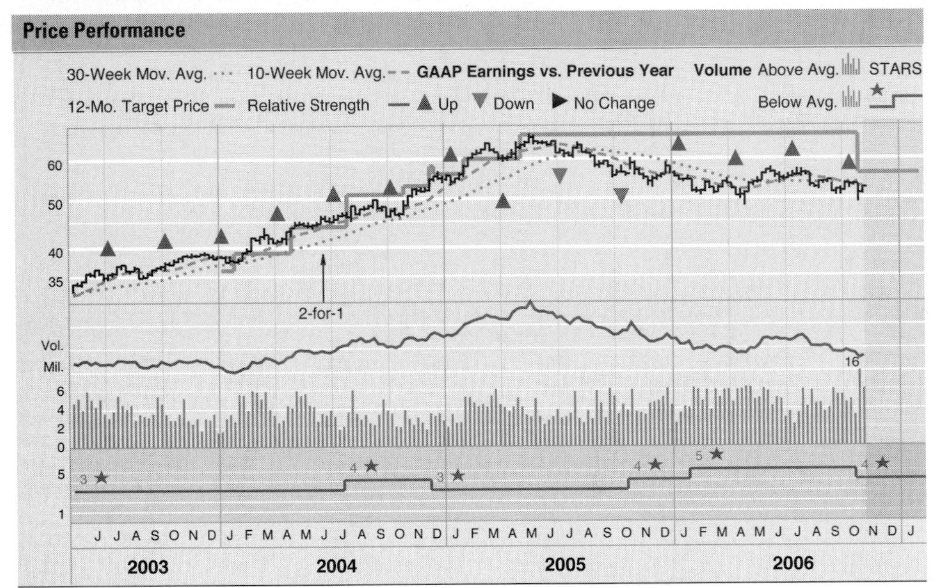

Options: ASE

Analysis prepared by **Rick Joy** on October 26, 2006, when the stock traded at **$ 51.61**.

Highlights

- Hershey is pursuing a realignment program that includes a work force reduction, a streamlining of North American operations, and the closure of a manufacturing facility. HSY expects ongoing annual cost savings of $45 million to $50 million when this program is fully implemented.
- We expect net sales to increase more than 4% in 2007, as growth in core U.S. brands, acquisition contributions, new product introductions and an improved product mix outweigh SKU (stock keeping unit) reductions. We see margins benefiting from improved logistics and supply chain costs, facility closures, a more favorable product mix, and improved price realizations. Advertising and marketing spending will likely increase and should continue to focus on core brands.
- Based on our expectations for a modest increase in interest expense and a 2% to 3% reduction in shares outstanding, we project 2007 operating EPS of $2.75, up 11% from anticipated 2006 EPS of $2.48. For the longer term, we believe 9% to 11% annual EPS growth is possible.

Investment Rationale/Risk

- Our buy recommendation reflects our expectation for strong sales growth trends and expanding margins in the coming quarters. We think core brand momentum, earnings visibility and cash flow will remain solid, supported by strong new product introductions. We think the shares are attractive in light of our view of HSY's strong balance sheet and dominant position in the U.S. confectionery market.
- Risks to our recommendation and target price include competitive pressures, a lack of consumer acceptance of new products, commodity cost inflation, and a potential inability to achieve sales and earnings growth forecasts. In terms of corporate governance, the company has a dual class capital structure with unequal voting rights, which we view unfavorably.
- Our discounted cash flow model, which assumes a 9% weighted average cost of capital and a terminal growth rate for cash flows of 3.5%, calculates intrinsic value of $58. Our relative valuation model, based on our analyses of comparable peer P/E and EV-to-EBITDA multiples, arrives at a value of $55. Blending our valuations, our 12-month target price is $56.

Qualitative Risk Assessment

LOW | MEDIUM | HIGH

Our risk assessment reflects the relatively stable nature of Hershey's end markets, dominant market share positions and our view of a strong balance sheet and cash flow.

Quantitative Evaluations

S&P Quality Ranking **B+**

D | C | B- | B | **B+** | A- | A | A+

Relative Strength Rank **WEAK**

29

LOWEST = 1 HIGHEST = 99

Revenue/Earnings Data

Revenue (Million $)

	1Q	2Q	3Q	4Q	Year
2006	1,133	1,052	1,413	--	--
2005	1,126	988.5	1,368	1,353	4,836
2004	1,013	893.7	1,255	1,268	4,429
2003	953.2	849.1	1,191	1,179	4,173
2002	988.5	823.5	1,152	1,156	4,120
2001	1,080	898.9	1,304	1,274	4,557

Earnings Per Share ($)

2006	0.50	0.41	0.77	**E**0.79	**E**2.48
2005	0.47	0.39	0.48	0.70	1.99
2004	0.41	0.56	0.66	0.68	2.30
2003	0.37	0.27	0.58	0.55	1.76
2002	0.32	0.23	0.45	0.48	1.46
2001	0.29	0.19	0.44	-0.17	0.75

Fiscal year ended Dec. 31. Next earnings report expected: Late January. EPS Estimates based on S&P Operating Earnings; historical GAAP earnings are as reported.

Dividend Data (Dates: mm/dd Payment Date: mm/dd/yy)

Amount ($)	Date Decl.	Ex-Div. Date	Stk. of Record	Payment Date
0.245	02/16	02/22	02/24	03/15/06
0.245	04/18	05/23	05/25	06/15/06
0.270	08/08	08/23	08/25	09/15/06
0.270	10/03	11/20	11/22	12/15/06

Dividends have been paid since 1930. Source: Company reports.

Hershey Co (The)

Business Summary October 26, 2006

The Hershey Company (formerly Hershey Foods Corporation), primarily through its Hershey Chocolate U.S.A., Hershey International and Hershey Canada Inc. units, produces and distributes a broad line of chocolate, confectionery and grocery products. Financial results have strengthened over the past few years, driven mainly by a rationalization of product lines that offered subpar investment returns, the integration of a number of complementary acquisitions, and a high rate of new product success.

The company makes chocolate and confectionery products in various packaged forms, and markets them under more than 50 brands. Principal chocolate and confectionery products in the U.S. are: Hershey's, Hershey's with almonds, and Cookies 'N' Mint bars; Hugs and Kisses (both also with almonds) chocolates; Kit Kat wafer bars; Mr. Goodbar chocolate bars; Reese's Pieces candies; Rolo caramels in milk chocolate; Skor toffee bars; Y&S Twizzlers licorice; and Amazin' Fruit gummy bears fruit candy. HSY significantly increased its participation in the non-chocolate side of the confectionery industry through its 1996 acquisition of Leaf North America, with major brands that included Jolly Rancher, Whoppers, Milk Duds, and Good & Plenty. Grocery products include Hershey's chocolate chips, cocoa and syrup; and Reese's peanut butter and peanut butter chips. Hershey's chocolate milk is produced and sold under license by independent dairies throughout the U.S., using a chocolate milk mix manufactured by HSY. The most significant raw material used in the production of the company's chocolate and confectionery products is cocoa beans.

In December 2004, Hershey acquired the Mauna Loa Macadamia Nut Corp. from The Shansby Group, a private equity investment firm. Mauna Loa is the leading processor and marketer of macadamia snacks, with annual sales of approximately $80 million.

Company Financials

Per Share Data ($) Year Ended Dec. 31	2005	2004	2003	2002	2001	2000	1999	1998	1997	1996
Tangible Book Value	1.63	2.03	3.29	3.55	2.65	2.57	2.34	1.79	1.05	1.95
Cash Flow	2.96	3.17	2.44	2.17	1.44	1.84	2.21	1.71	1.62	1.32
Earnings	1.99	2.30	1.76	1.46	0.75	1.21	1.63	1.17	1.12	0.89
S&P Core Earnings	1.94	2.23	1.73	1.37	0.94	NA	NA	NA	NA	NA
Dividends	0.93	0.84	0.72	0.63	0.58	0.54	0.50	0.46	0.42	0.38
Payout Ratio	47%	36%	41%	43%	78%	45%	31%	39%	38%	43%
Prices:High	67.37	56.75	39.33	39.75	35.08	33.22	32.44	38.19	31.94	25.88
Prices:Low	52.49	37.28	30.35	28.23	27.56	18.88	22.88	29.84	21.06	15.97
P/E Ratio:High	34	25	22	27	47	27	20	33	29	29
P/E Ratio:Low	26	16	17	19	37	16	14	26	19	18
Income Statement Analysis (Million $)										
Revenue	4,836	4,429	4,173	4,120	4,557	4,221	3,971	4,436	4,302	3,989
Operating Income	1,175	1,092	992	904	812	799	722	801	783	697
Depreciation	218	190	181	178	190	176	163	158	153	133
Interest Expense	89.5	66.5	63.5	60.7	71.5	81.0	77.3	88.6	79.1	53.6
Pretax Income	773	836	733	638	344	547	728	557	554	480
Effective Tax Rate	36.2%	29.3%	36.6%	36.7%	39.7%	38.8%	36.8%	38.8%	39.3%	43.1%
Net Income	493	591	465	404	207	335	460	341	336	273
S&P Core Earnings	482	573	455	377	258	NA	NA	NA	NA	NA
Balance Sheet & Other Financial Data (Million $)										
Cash	67.2	54.8	115	298	134	32.0	118	39.0	54.2	61.4
Current Assets	1,409	1,182	1,132	1,264	1,168	1,295	1,280	1,134	1,035	986
Total Assets	4,295	3,798	3,583	3,481	3,247	3,448	3,347	3,404	3,291	3,185
Current Liabilities	1,518	1,285	586	547	606	767	713	815	796	817
Long Term Debt	943	691	968	852	877	878	878	879	1,029	655
Common Equity	1,021	1,089	1,280	1,372	1,147	1,175	1,099	1,042	853	1,161
Total Capital	2,364	2,109	2,626	2,572	2,280	2,353	2,303	2,243	2,149	2,040
Capital Expenditures	181	182	219	133	160	138	115	161	173	159
Cash Flow	711	781	646	581	398	511	624	499	489	407
Current Ratio	0.9	0.9	1.9	2.3	1.9	1.7	1.8	1.4	1.3	1.2
% Long Term Debt of Capitalization	39.9	32.7	36.9	33.1	38.5	37.3	38.1	39.2	47.9	32.1
% Net Income of Revenue	10.2	13.3	11.1	9.8	4.5	7.9	11.6	7.7	7.8	6.9
% Return on Assets	12.2	16.0	13.2	12.0	6.2	9.8	13.6	10.2	10.4	9.1
% Return on Equity	45.7	46.4	35.1	32.0	17.8	29.4	43.0	36.0	33.4	24.4

Data as orig reptd.; bef. results of disc opers/spec. items. Per share data adj. for stk. divs.; EPS diluted. E-Estimated. NA-Not Available. NM-Not Meaningful. NR-Not Ranked. UR-Under Review.

Office: 100 Crystal A Dr, Hershey, PA 17033-0810.
Telephone: 717-534-4000.
Website: http://www.hersheys.com
Chrmn, Pres & CEO: R.H. Lenny

SVP & CFO: D.J. West
SVP, Secy & General Counsel: B.H. Snyder
VP & Chief Acctg Officer: D.W. Tacka
Investor Contact: J.A. Edris (800-539-0261)

Board of Directors: J. A. Boscia, R. H. Campbell, R. F. Cavanaugh, G. P. Coughlan, H. Edelman, B. G. Hill, A. F. Kelly, Jr., R. H. Lenny, M. J. McDonald, M. J. Toulantis

Founded: 1893
Domicile: Delaware
Employees: 13,750

STANDARD &POOR'S

Hess Corp

S&P Recommendation HOLD ★★★★★

Price $42.40 (as of Oct 31, 2006)

12-Mo. Target Price $47.00

Investment Style Large-Cap Growth

GICS Sector Energy
Sub-Industry Integrated Oil & Gas

Comment This integrated oil and natural gas company has exploration and production activities worldwide, but markets refined petroleum products on the U.S. East Coast.

Key Stock Statistics (Source S&P, Vickers, company reports)

52-Wk Range	$56.45–37.62	S&P Oper. EPS 2006E	6.77	P/E on S&P Oper. EPS 2006E	6.3	Dividend Rate/Share	$0.40
Trailing 12-Month EPS	$6.37	S&P Oper. EPS 2007E	5.95	Common Shares Outstg. (M)	280.5	Yield (%)	0.94
Trailing 12-Month P/E	6.7	S&P Core EPS 2006E	5.68	Market Capitalization(B)	$11.894	Beta	0.57
$10K Invested 5 Yrs Ago	$20,440	S&P Core EPS 2007E	6.00	Institutional Ownership (%)	85	S&P Credit Rating	BBB-

Price Performance

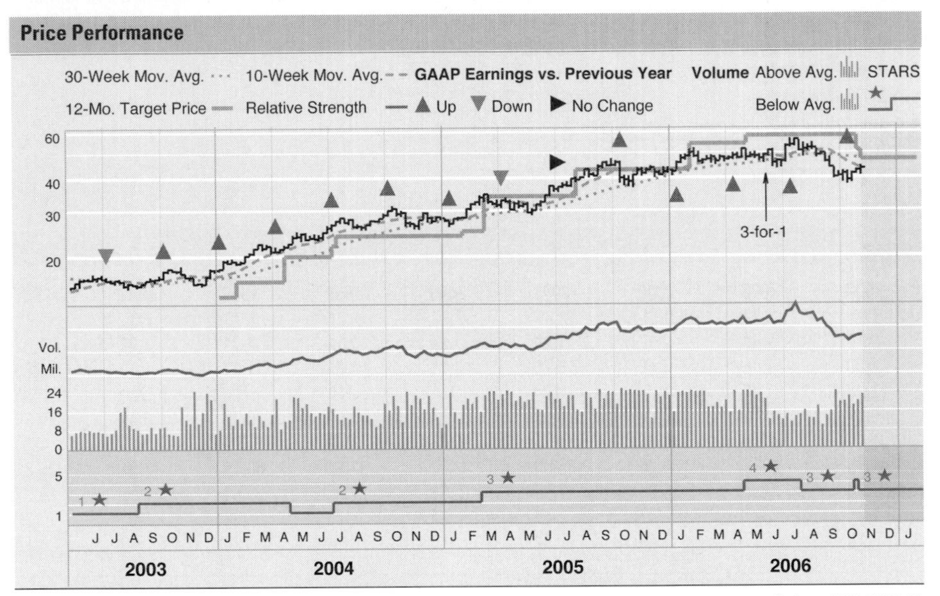

Options: ASE, CBOE, Ph

Analysis prepared by **Tina J. Vital** on October 31, 2006, when the stock traded at **$ 42.26**.

Highlights

- Third quarter operating earnings rose 42%, to $390 million, or $1.23 per share. Results excluded special charges of $0.33 per share, but missed our estimate by $0.28 per share, reflecting $0.29 per share in dry hole costs related to two deepwater Gulf of Mexico wells.
- Hydrocarbon production rose 13% in the third quarter, but missed our expectations. We expect strong 7% hydrocarbon production growth in 2006, and over 5% in both 2007 and 2008, on the start-up of key projects, such as in Equatorial Guinea, the Malaysia/Thailand joint development area (JDA), and its reentry into Libya.
- While U.S. refining margins have narrowed since July, we believe this decline is temporary and expect the switch to winter fuels, combined with scheduled maintenance, to boost refining margins in the 2006 fourth quarter. As a result, we project after-tax operating earnings will rise 78% in 2006 before declining 12% in 2007 on lower estimated pricing. HES had entered into a number of unprofitable oil hedges, but the company expects a significant portion of these hedges to roll off in 2006.

Investment Rationale/Risk

- We believe HES's 2006 re-entry into Libya will raise its oil production and proved reserves by over 10% at an attractive cost, which we estimate at near $4.31 per barrel. We estimate HES's three-year (2003-2005) organic reserve replacement rate as below average compared to peers, and its three-year finding, development and reserve replacement costs as above peers. Thus, HES, in our view, needs to spend more going forward to achieve greater exploration success; since 2004, the company has raised its capital spending by over 60% per year.
- Risks to our recommendation and target price include geopolitical risk, changes in economic, industry and operating conditions, and an inability to achieve upstream production targets.
- A blend of our discounted cash flow (weighted average cost of capital of 6.6% and terminal growth of 3%) and relative valuations leads to our 12-month target price of $47, representing an expected enterprise value of about 3X our 2006 EBITDA estimate, a discount to peers, reflecting our view of increased spending requirements to maintain and grow HES's upstream portfolio.

Qualitative Risk Assessment

LOW | **MEDIUM** | HIGH

Our risk assessment reflects HES's diversified business profile in volatile, cyclical and capital intensive segments of the energy industry. However, we see increased risk from its investments in politically challenged locales, and a relatively high cost structure in exploration and production.

Quantitative Evaluations

S&P Quality Ranking B

D | C | B- | **B** | B+ | A- | A | A+

Relative Strength Rank WEAK

20

LOWEST = 1 HIGHEST = 99

Revenue/Earnings Data

Revenue (Million $)

	1Q	2Q	3Q	4Q	Year
2006	7,159	6,718	7,130	--	--
2005	4,956	4,963	5,769	7,059	22,747
2004	4,488	3,803	3,830	4,612	16,733
2003	4,254	3,199	3,230	3,628	14,480
2002	3,021	2,796	2,818	3,297	12,093
2001	4,183	3,461	2,888	2,881	13,413

Earnings Per Share ($)

	1Q	2Q	3Q	4Q	Year
2006	2.21	1.79	0.94	**E**1.55	**E**6.77
2005	0.71	0.92	0.87	1.44	3.98
2004	0.92	0.92	0.58	0.74	3.17
2003	0.81	0.24	0.55	0.24	1.72
2002	0.53	0.55	-0.51	-1.40	-0.83
2001	1.26	1.33	0.62	0.20	3.42

Fiscal year ended Dec. 31. Next earnings report expected: Late January. EPS Estimates based on S&P Operating Earnings; historical GAAP earnings are as reported.

Dividend Data (Dates: mm/dd Payment Date: mm/dd/yy)

Amount ($)	Date Decl.	Ex-Div. Date	Stk. of Record	Payment Date
0.300	03/01	03/09	03/13	03/31/06
3-for-1 Stk.	05/03	06/01	05/17	05/31/06
0.100	06/08	06/14	06/16	06/30/06
0.100	09/06	09/14	09/18	09/29/06

Dividends have been paid since 1922. Source: Company reports.

Please read the Required Disclosures and Analyst Certification on the last page of this report.

Hess Corp

Business Summary October 31, 2006

Hess Corp. (HES; formerly Amerada Hess Corp.) has two operating segments: exploration and production (18% of 2005 revenues, and 67% of 2005 net income), and marketing and refining (82%; 33%). Business is conducted in the U.S. (86% of 2005 revenues), Europe (9%), Africa (3%), Asia and other countries (2%). As of May 2005, the Hess family and related interests owned about 14% of the common shares.

We estimate HES's three-year (2003-2005) organic reserve replacement (including equity investees)at a subpar 68%. Crude oil production declined to 244,000 barrels per day (b/d) in 2005, from 246,000 b/d in 2004. Natural gas production dropped to 544,000 thousand cubic feet (Mcf) per day in 2005, from 575,000 Mcf per day in 2004. The impact of Hurricanes Katrina and Rita reduced 2005 full year production by an average of 7,000 barrels of oil equivalent (boe) per day. HES estimates its 2006 hydrocarbon production will average about 360,000 boe/d. Average selling prices (including the effects of hedging) for liquids was $33.69 per barrel in 2005, and $5.65 per Mcf for natural gas. Hedge losses totaled $228 million for the nine months ended September 30, 2006, and HES had $1.4 billion of deferred hedging losses, after income taxes, included in accumulated other comprehensive income. As of September 30, 2006, the company's outstanding hedge positions included 30,000 b/d of crude oil in 2006, and 24,000 b/d during 2007-2012. Three year (2003-2005) average production (lifting) costs were $6.85 per boe.

Company Financials

Per Share Data ($) Year Ended Dec. 31	**2005**	**2004**	**2003**	**2002**	**2001**	**2000**	**1999**	**1998**	**1997**	**1996**
Tangible Book Value	16.61	14.34	13.62	12.17	14.70	14.59	11.17	9.99	11.72	12.12
Cash Flow	7.11	6.18	5.61	4.17	7.04	6.43	4.02	0.73	2.47	5.17
Earnings	3.98	3.17	1.72	-0.83	3.42	3.79	1.62	-1.71	0.03	2.36
S&P Core Earnings	3.78	3.06	1.75	-1.28	3.25	NA	NA	NA	NA	NA
Dividends	0.40	0.40	0.40	0.40	0.40	0.20	0.20	0.20	0.20	0.20
Payout Ratio	10%	13%	23%	NM	12%	5%	12%	NM	NM	8%
Prices:High	47.50	31.30	19.07	28.23	30.13	25.42	22.10	20.35	21.50	20.17
Prices:Low	25.94	17.75	13.71	16.47	17.92	15.94	14.58	15.33	15.79	15.83
P/E Ratio:High	12	10	11	NM	9	7	14	NM	NM	9
P/E Ratio:Low	7	6	8	NM	5	4	9	NM	NM	7
Income Statement Analysis (Million $)										
Revenue	22,747	16,733	14,480	12,093	13,413	11,993	7,039	6,590	8,234	8,272
Operating Income	2,967	2,769	2,127	2,382	2,399	2,264	1,214	475	910	1,306
Depreciation, Depletion and Amortization	1,025	970	1,053	1,320	967	714	648	657	673	783
Interest Expense	224	241	293	269	194	162	158	153	136	166
Pretax Income	2,226	1,558	781	-51.0	1,438	1,672	702	-514	127	1,014
Effective Tax Rate	44.2%	37.7%	40.2%	NM	36.4%	30.0%	37.6%	NM	93.7%	34.9%
Net Income	1,242	970	467	-218	914	1,023	438	-459	8.00	660
S&P Core Earnings	1,131	888	468	-339	870	NA	NA	NA	NA	NA
Balance Sheet & Other Financial Data (Million $)										
Cash	315	877	518	197	37.0	312	41.0	74.0	91.0	113
Current Assets	5,290	4,335	3,186	2,756	3,946	4,115	1,828	1,887	2,204	2,427
Total Assets	19,115	16,312	13,983	13,262	15,369	10,274	7,728	7,883	7,935	7,784
Current Liabilities	6,447	4,697	2,669	2,553	3,718	3,538	1,579	1,797	1,740	1,737
Long Term Debt	3,759	3,785	3,868	4,976	5,283	1,985	2,287	2,476	2,003	1,712
Common Equity	6,272	5,583	5,326	8,498	4,907	3,883	3,038	2,643	3,216	3,384
Total Capital	11,446	10,566	10,352	14,518	11,301	6,378	5,767	5,603	5,781	5,712
Capital Expenditures	2,341	1,521	1,358	1,404	2,501	938	797	1,439	1,346	861
Cash Flow	2,219	1,892	1,515	1,102	1,881	1,737	1,086	198	681	1,443
Current Ratio	0.8	0.9	1.2	1.1	1.1	1.2	1.2	1.1	1.3	1.4
% Long Term Debt of Capitalization	32.8	35.8	37.4	34.3	46.7	31.1	39.7	44.2	34.6	30.0
% Return on Assets	7.0	6.4	3.4	NM	7.1	11.4	5.6	NM	0.1	8.5
% Return on Equity	20.1	16.9	9.7	NM	20.8	29.6	15.4	NM	0.2	21.8

Data as orig reptd.; bef. results of disc opers/spec. items. Per share data adj. for stk. divs.; EPS diluted. E-Estimated. NA-Not Available. NM-Not Meaningful. NR-Not Ranked. UR-Under Review.

Office: 1185 Avenue Of The Americas, New York, NY 10036.
Telephone: 212-997-8500.
Email: investorrelations@hess.com
Website: http://www.hess.com

Chrmn & CEO: J.B. Hess
EVP & General Counsel: J.B. Collins, II
SVP & CFO: J.P. Reilly
VP & Treas: R.J. Vogel

Investor Contact: J.R. Wilson (212-536-8940)
Board of Directors: N. F. Brady, J. B. Collins, II, J. B. Hess, E. E. Holiday, T. H. Kean, R. Lavizzo-Mourey, C. G. Matthews, J. J. O'Connor, F. A. Olson, F. B. Walker, R. N. Wilson, E. H. von Metzsch

Founded: 1920
Domicile: Delaware
Employees: 11,610

STANDARD &POOR'S

Hewlett-Packard Co

S&P Recommendation HOLD ★★★★★

Price $38.46 (as of Oct 27, 2006)

12-Mo. Target Price $40.00

Investment Style Large-Cap Value

GICS Sector Information Technology
Sub-Industry Computer Hardware

Comment This leading maker of computer products, including printers, servers, and PCs, has a large service and support network. It acquired Compaq Computer in May 2002.

Key Stock Statistics (Source S&P, Vickers, company reports)

52-Wk Range	$40.10–27.68	S&P Oper. EPS 2006E	2.22	P/E on S&P Oper. EPS 2006E	17.3	Dividend Rate/Share	$0.32
Trailing 12-Month EPS	$1.71	S&P Oper. EPS 2007E	2.42	Common Shares Outstg. (M)	2,739.0	Yield (%)	0.83
Trailing 12-Month P/E	22.5	S&P Core EPS 2006E	2.22	Market Capitalization(B)	$105.340	Beta	1.92
$10K Invested 5 Yrs Ago	$23,205	S&P Core EPS 2007E	2.42	Institutional Ownership (%)	77	S&P Credit Rating	A-

Price Performance

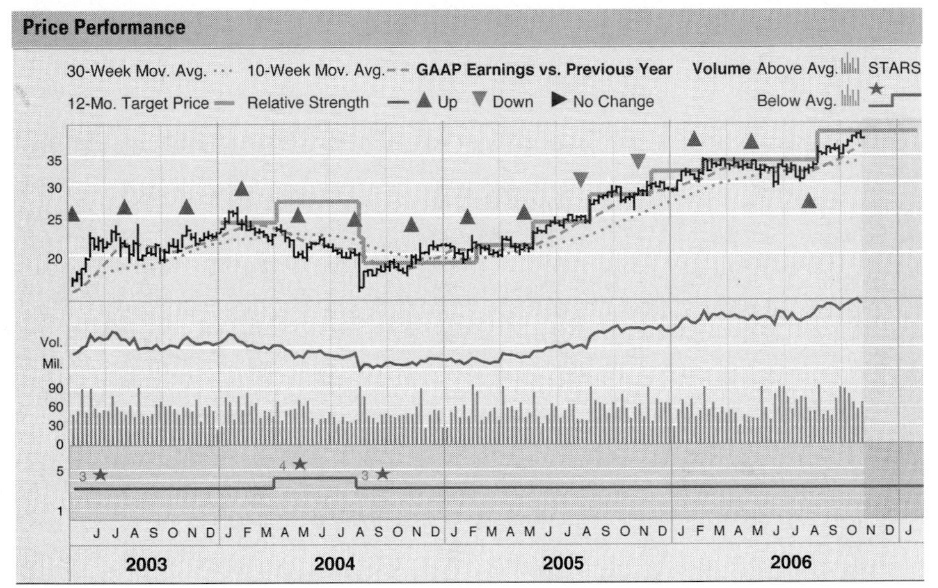

Options: ASE, CBOE, P, Ph

Analysis prepared by **Richard N. Stice, CFA** on September 18, 2006, when the stock traded at **$ 36.40**.

Highlights

- We project revenue growth of 5% in FY 07 (Oct.), a similar rate to our FY 06 forecast. We expect overall technology spending to receive a lift from the scheduled launch of Microsoft Corp.'s (MSFT: strong buy, $26) new operating system. However, we anticipate this demand being somewhat offset by sluggish growth in HPQ's services business as well as more aggressive pricing in the PC market.
- We expect gross margins to widen to 25% in FY 07, from FY 06's expected 24.4%, on higher volumes and manufacturing efficiencies. We see a further reduction in SG&A expenses, on a percentage of revenue basis, and we believe that FY 07 operating margins are likely to approach 9%, versus FY 06's forecast of 7.9%. We also think results will be aided by additional share buybacks, as the company has instituted a new $6 billion share repurchase program.
- Based on these assumptions, our FY 07 operating EPS estimate is $2.42, a 9% increase from our FY 06 EPS estimate of $2.22. Both estimates include projected costs associated with stock-based compensation expense.

Investment Rationale/Risk

- Our hold opinion is based on total return potential. We continue to believe that information technology spending will expand over the next 12 months, but at a moderate pace. In light of HPQ's broad product and customer base, we expect the company to benefit from this trend. We believe HPQ, under CEO Mark Hurd, has made substantial progress in its cost reduction efforts. However, we see further endeavors to lower expenses as unlikely to have as meaningful an impact on HPQ's operating leverage. Moreover, we think that overall top line growth remains somewhat sluggish.
- Risks to our opinion and target price include what we view as HPQ's need to augment its capabilities in software and services in order to offer a more attractive long-term competitive position.
- Our 12-month target price is $40. Our DCF model assumes a weighted average cost of capital of 11.3% and leads to an intrinsic value of $44. On a relative P/E basis, in which we allocate HPQ a 10% premium to the S&P 500, we arrive at a value of $36 on a blended basis.

Qualitative Risk Assessment

LOW | **MEDIUM** | HIGH

Our risk assessment reflects the intensely price competitive environment in the computer hardware industry, balanced by our view of the company's successful efforts in reducing its cost structure.

Quantitative Evaluations

S&P Quality Ranking B+

D | C | B- | B | **B+** | A- | A | A+

Relative Strength Rank MODERATE

68

LOWEST = 1 HIGHEST = 99

Revenue/Earnings Data

Revenue (Million $)

	1Q	2Q	3Q	4Q	Year
2006	22,659	22,554	21,890	--	--
2005	21,454	21,570	20,759	22,913	86,696
2004	19,514	20,113	18,889	21,389	79,905
2003	17,877	17,983	17,348	19,853	73,061
2002	11,383	10,621	16,536	18,048	56,588
2001	12,398	11,668	10,284	10,876	45,226

Earnings Per Share ($)

	1Q	2Q	3Q	4Q	Year
2006	0.42	0.66	0.48	E0.62	E2.22
2005	0.32	0.33	0.03	0.14	0.82
2004	0.30	0.29	0.19	0.37	1.15
2003	0.24	0.22	0.10	0.28	0.83
2002	0.25	0.12	-0.67	0.13	-0.37
2001	0.20	0.02	0.06	0.04	0.32

Fiscal year ended Oct. 31. Next earnings report expected: Mid November. EPS Estimates based on S&P Operating Earnings; historical GAAP earnings are as reported.

Dividend Data (Dates: mm/dd Payment Date: mm/dd/yy)

Amount ($)	Date Decl.	Ex-Div. Date	Stk. of Record	Payment Date
0.080	11/18	12/12	12/14	01/04/06
0.080	02/03	03/13	03/15	04/05/06
0.080	05/19	06/12	06/14	07/05/06
0.080	07/21	09/11	09/13	10/04/06

Dividends have been paid since 1965. Source: Company reports.

Hewlett-Packard Co

Business Summary September 18, 2006

CORPORATE OVERVIEW. Hewlett-Packard provides computers and related products, technologies, solutions and services to all segments of the computer industry worldwide. The ongoing elimination of 15,300 positions through retirement programs and work force restructurings has enabled the company to develop a global delivery structure that has improved margins by taking advantage of low cost technical expertise. In February 2005, Chairman and CEO Carly Fiorina stepped down following the failure of the company's board to agree on how to execute HP's strategy. Effective April 1, 2005, former NCR Corp. CEO Mark Hurd was named CEO and president. In addition, Mr. Hurd is slated to take over the chairman's role in January 2007.

In July 2006, HPQ agreed to acquire Mercury Interactive Corp. (MERQ), a provider of software and services, for $4.5 billion. HPQ anticipates that the planned transaction, which is expected to close during the fourth quarter of calendar 2006, subject to necessary approvals, will be $0.04 dilutive to FY 07 (Oct.) EPS and $0.02 accretive in FY 08. We believe the proposed deal would strengthen and improve the profitability of HPQ's business mix, but think the price being paid is a bit steep, particularly given the ongoing formal SEC investigation of MERQ.

PRIMARY BUSINESS DYNAMICS. Large corporations and small offices/home offices are the primary drivers of spending on information technology products and services. Industrywide trends, exchange rates, and distribution channels influence HPQ's financial performance. Most players sell broad product lines and have a global sourcing and distribution system. Persistent pricing pressure in a competitive industry led to increased merger and acquisition activity by top vendors, creating market share concentration of 49% (2005) among the top five players.

Company Financials

Per Share Data ($) Year Ended Oct. 31	**2005**	**2004**	**2003**	**2002**	**2001**	**2000**	**1999**	**1998**	**1997**	**1996**
Tangible Book Value	6.04	6.06	6.08	5.35	7.20	7.30	9.10	8.33	7.76	6.63
Cash Flow	1.63	1.93	1.65	0.48	1.01	2.37	2.10	2.25	2.21	1.85
Earnings	0.82	1.15	0.83	-0.37	0.32	1.73	1.49	1.39	1.48	1.23
S&P Core Earnings	0.74	0.94	0.65	-0.65	0.16	NA	NA	NA	NA	NA
Dividends	0.32	0.32	0.32	0.32	0.32	0.32	0.32	0.30	0.26	0.22
Payout Ratio	39%	28%	39%	NM	100%	18%	22%	22%	18%	18%
Prices:High	30.25	26.28	23.90	24.12	37.95	77.75	59.22	41.19	36.47	28.84
Prices:Low	18.89	16.08	14.18	10.75	12.50	29.13	31.69	23.53	24.06	18.41
P/E Ratio:High	37	23	29	NM	NM	45	40	30	25	23
P/E Ratio:Low	23	14	17	NM	NM	17	21	17	16	15
Income Statement Analysis (Million $)										
Revenue	86,696	79,905	73,061	56,588	45,226	48,782	42,370	47,061	42,895	38,420
Operating Income	7,520	7,017	6,713	4,570	3,192	5,257	5,004	5,710	5,895	5,023
Depreciation	2,344	2,395	2,527	2,119	1,369	1,368	1,316	1,869	1,556	1,297
Interest Expense	334	247	277	212	234	233	202	235	215	327
Pretax Income	3,543	4,196	2,888	-1,052	702	4,625	4,194	4,091	4,445	3,694
Effective Tax Rate	32.3%	16.7%	12.1%	NM	11.1%	23.0%	26.0%	28.0%	30.0%	30.0%
Net Income	2,398	3,497	2,539	-923	624	3,561	3,104	2,945	3,119	2,586
S&P Core Earnings	2,150	2,886	1,983	-1,635	285	NA	NA	NA	NA	NA
Balance Sheet & Other Financial Data (Million $)										
Cash	13,911	12,663	14,188	11,192	4,197	3,415	5,411	4,046	3,072	2,885
Current Assets	43,334	42,901	40,996	36,075	21,305	23,244	21,642	21,584	20,947	17,991
Total Assets	77,317	76,138	74,708	70,710	32,584	34,009	35,297	33,673	31,749	27,699
Current Liabilities	31,460	28,588	26,630	24,310	13,964	15,197	14,321	13,473	11,219	10,623
Long Term Debt	3,392	4,623	6,494	6,035	3,729	3,402	1,764	2,063	3,158	2,579
Common Equity	37,176	37,564	37,746	36,262	13,953	14,209	18,295	16,919	16,155	13,438
Total Capital	40,568	42,187	44,240	42,297	17,682	17,611	20,059	18,982	19,313	16,017
Capital Expenditures	1,995	2,126	1,995	1,710	1,527	1,737	1,134	1,997	2,338	2,201
Cash Flow	4,742	5,892	5,066	1,196	1,993	4,929	4,420	4,814	4,675	3,883
Current Ratio	1.4	1.5	1.5	1.5	1.5	1.5	1.5	1.6	1.9	1.7
% Long Term Debt of Capitalization	8.4	11.0	14.7	14.3	21.1	19.3	8.8	10.9	16.4	16.1
% Net Income of Revenue	2.8	4.4	3.5	NM	1.4	7.3	7.3	6.3	7.3	6.7
% Return on Assets	3.1	4.6	3.5	NM	1.9	10.3	9.3	9.0	10.5	9.9
% Return on Equity	6.4	9.3	6.9	NM	4.4	21.9	17.6	17.8	14.5	20.5

Data as orig reptd.; bef. results of disc opers/spec. items. Per share data adj. for stk. divs.; EPS diluted. E-Estimated. NA-Not Available. NM-Not Meaningful. NR-Not Ranked. UR-Under Review.

Office: 3000 Hanover Street, Palo Alto, CA 94304-1112.
Telephone: 650-857-1501.
Website: http://www.hp.com
Chrmn, Pres & CEO: M. Hurd

EVP & CFO: R.P. Wayman
EVP & CTO: S.V. Robison
EVP & CIO: R.D. Mott
SVP & Chief Acctg Officer: J.E. Flaxman

Investor Contact: B. Humphries (866-438-4771)
Board of Directors: L. T. Babbio, Jr., S. M. Baldauf, R. A. Hackborn, J. H. Hammergren, M. V. Hurd, T. Perkins, R. Ryan, L. S. Salhany, R. P. Wayman

Founded: 1939
Domicile: Delaware
Employees: 150,000

STANDARD &POOR'S

Hilton Hotels Corp

S&P Recommendation HOLD ★★★★★

Price $28.92 (as of Oct 31, 2006)

12-Mo. Target Price $30.00

Investment Style Large-Cap Growth

GICS Sector Consumer Discretionary
Sub-Industry Hotels, Resorts & Cruise Lines

Comment This leading hospitality company owns, manages or franchises more than 2,700 hotels, resorts and vacation ownership properties.

Key Stock Statistics (Source S&P, Vickers, company reports)

52-Wk Range	$29.79–19.07	S&P Oper. EPS 2006E	1.14	P/E on S&P Oper. EPS 2006E	25.4	Dividend Rate/Share	$0.16
Trailing 12-Month EPS	$1.09	S&P Oper. EPS 2007E	1.33	Common Shares Outstg. (M)	385.8	Yield (%)	0.55
Trailing 12-Month P/E	26.5	S&P Core EPS 2006E	1.01	Market Capitalization(B)	$11.157	Beta	1.22
$10K Invested 5 Yrs Ago	$34,509	S&P Core EPS 2007E	1.33	Institutional Ownership (%)	85	S&P Credit Rating	BB

Price Performance

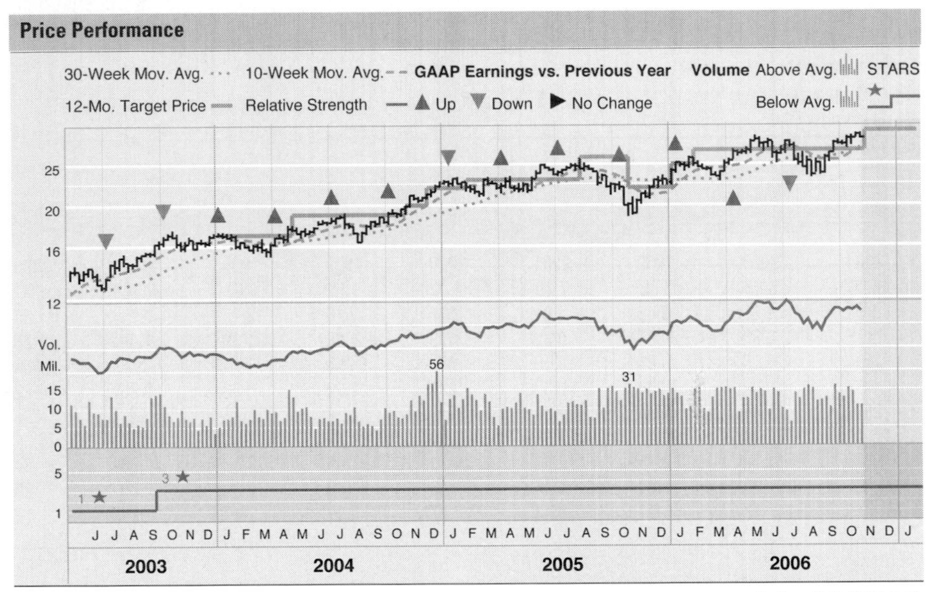

Options: ASE, CBOE, P, Ph

Highlights

- The 12-month target price for HLT has recently been changed to $30.00 from $27.00. The Highlights section of this Stock Report will be updated accordingly.

Investment Rationale/Risk

- The Investment Rationale/Risk section of this Stock Report will be updated shortly. For the latest News story on HLT from MarketScope, see below.

- 10/31/06 03:12 pm EST... S&P REITERATES HOLD RECOMMENDATION ON SHARES OF HILTON HOTELS (HLT 29.01***): Q3 EPS of $0.30, before one-time items, vs. $0.21 a year ago, was $0.02 above our estimate. EBITDA jumped 58% to $440 million, reflecting the acquisition of Hilton Plc, expansion elsewhere, and 9.8% growth in worldwide revenue per available room. We are raising our '06 EPS estimate by $0.04 to $1.14, and our 12-month target price by $3 to $30. At 25X our '06 EPS estimate, the shares are trading at a premium to the S&P 500. We believe this valuation is justified by HLT's relative strong growth prospects and low capex requirements. /D. Milton

Qualitative Risk Assessment

LOW | **MEDIUM** | HIGH

Our risk assessment reflects our view that HLT's recent acquisition of Hilton Group's lodging assets has added geographic diversity and boosted opportunities for international growth. The purchase has added a considerable amount of debt to HLT's balance sheet, though we expect that the company will be looking to reduce its debt level.

Quantitative Evaluations

S&P Quality Ranking B

D | C | B- | **B** | B+ | A- | A | A+

Relative Strength Rank MODERATE

64

LOWEST = 1 HIGHEST = 99

Revenue/Earnings Data

Revenue (Million $)

	1Q	2Q	3Q	4Q	Year
2006	1,137	2,204	--	--	--
2005	1,076	1,176	1,102	1,083	4,437
2004	994.0	1,065	1,033	1,054	4,146
2003	909.0	976.0	952.0	982.0	3,819
2002	921.0	782.0	942.0	957.0	3,847
2001	833.0	844.0	711.0	662.0	3,050

Earnings Per Share ($)

	1Q	2Q	3Q	4Q	Year
2006	0.26	0.35	**E**0.30	**E**0.32	**E**1.14
2005	0.16	0.49	0.22	0.26	1.13
2004	0.10	0.19	0.16	0.16	0.60
2003	0.02	0.14	0.09	0.17	0.43
2002	0.09	0.20	0.13	0.11	0.53
2001	0.15	0.23	0.06	0.01	0.45

Fiscal year ended Dec. 31. Next earnings report expected: NA. EPS Estimates based on S&P Operating Earnings; historical GAAP earnings are as reported.

Dividend Data (Dates: mm/dd Payment Date: mm/dd/yy)

Amount ($)	Date Decl.	Ex-Div. Date	Stk. of Record	Payment Date
0.040	11/16	11/30	12/02	12/16/05
0.040	01/19	03/01	03/03	03/17/06
0.040	05/24	06/07	06/09	06/23/06
0.040	07/21	08/30	09/02	09/15/06

Dividends have been paid since 1946. Source: Company reports.

Hilton Hotels Corp

Business Summary August 08, 2006

CORPORATE OVERVIEW. This hotel company includes about 2,900 properties, with more than 475,000 rooms, operating under various brands. Most of the hotels are franchises operated by others, but Hilton Hotels Corp. owns, leases or manages a number of lodging properties. In February 2006, HLT acquired the lodging assets of British company Hilton Group plc for about $5.7 billion. The assets acquired included 392 hotels with 102,455 rooms, of which 39 hotels were owned, 201 were leased, four were partially owned through joint ventures, 118 were managed, and 30 were franchised. Also, as a result of the acquisition, HLT acquired rights to the Hilton brand name outside of the U.S.

As of June 30, 2006, HLT had 66 owned hotels and 206 leased hotels. Owned hotels include the Waldorf-Astoria in New York City. In addition, HLT managed and/or had a joint venture interest in 389 other hotels, and was the franchisor of 2,160 lodging properties.

At June 30, 2006, HLT's business included 491 properties (170,842 rooms) with the Hilton brand, 1,365 Hampton hotels (136,161 rooms), 181 Embassy Suites hotels (43,992 rooms), 167 Doubletree hotels (43,649 rooms), 279 Hilton Garden Inn properties (38,374 rooms), 130 Scandic hotels (23,147 rooms), 174 Homewood Suites by Hilton (19,280 rooms), 16 Conrad hotels (5,302 rooms), and 18 other properties (6,995 rooms). Also, HLT had 40 timeshare properties.

CORPORATE STRATEGY. With the acquisition of the Hilton's Group's lodging business, we see HLT boosting its global presence, creating additional expansion opportunities (especially outside of the U.S.), and gaining more control over the Hilton brand. As of March 2006, following the acquisition, about 2,400 of HLT's hotels (about 382,000 rooms) were in the Americas, and about 370 hotels (about 90,000 rooms) were elsewhere.

PRIMARY BUSINESS DYNAMICS. In 2005, on a pro forma basis (assuming asset sale activity had occurred at the start of the year) HLT had adjusted EBITDA (which likely excludes some items) of $1.52 billion, of which 43% came from owned hotels, 33% from managed and franchised properties, 16% from leased hotels, and 8% from timeshare operations. Viewed another way, 71% of the adjusted EBITDA came from the Americas, while 9% was from the United Kingdom and Ireland, 9% from the Nordic area, 8% from Europe and Africa, and 3% from elsewhere. Also, HLT said that its top 10 markets contributed about 30% of adjusted EBITDA, with roughly half of this from New York and Hawaii.

Company Financials

Per Share Data ($) Year Ended Dec. 31	**2005**	**2004**	**2003**	**2002**	**2001**	**2000**	**1999**	**1998**	**1997**	**1996**
Tangible Book Value	0.83	0.06	0.08	NM	NM	NM	NM	0.72	8.25	7.63
Cash Flow	1.95	1.38	1.30	1.39	1.41	1.67	1.25	1.09	2.21	1.34
Earnings	1.13	0.60	0.43	0.53	0.45	0.73	0.58	0.71	0.94	0.79
S&P Core Earnings	0.83	0.57	0.44	0.50	0.48	NA	NA	NA	NA	NA
Dividends	0.12	0.08	0.08	0.08	0.08	0.08	0.08	0.32	0.32	0.31
Payout Ratio	11%	13%	19%	15%	18%	11%	14%	45%	34%	39%
Prices:High	25.81	22.96	17.50	17.09	13.57	12.13	17.13	35.50	35.81	31.75
Prices:Low	18.78	15.10	10.38	9.56	6.15	6.38	8.38	12.00	24.00	15.28
P/E Ratio:High	23	38	41	32	30	17	30	50	38	40
P/E Ratio:Low	17	25	24	18	14	9	14	17	26	19
Income Statement Analysis (Million $)										
Revenue	4,437	4,146	3,819	3,847	3,050	3,451	2,150	1,769	5,316	3,940
Operating Income	1,067	953	850	972	1,023	1,212	682	589	896	507
Depreciation	299	339	347	348	391	382	187	125	300	178
Interest Expense	259	300	315	347	402	462	239	141	190	106
Pretax Income	638	373	223	285	250	479	313	336	448	267
Effective Tax Rate	26.0%	34.0%	23.8%	28.4%	30.8%	41.7%	41.5%	40.5%	41.7%	39.7%
Net Income	460	238	164	198	166	272	176	188	250	156
S&P Core Earnings	335	225	165	187	179	NA	NA	NA	NA	NA
Balance Sheet & Other Financial Data (Million $)										
Cash	1,154	303	82.0	54.0	35.0	47.0	104	47.0	330	438
Current Assets	2,089	1,106	1,020	630	996	840	763	469	1,011	1,151
Total Assets	8,743	8,242	8,178	8,348	8,785	9,140	9,253	3,944	7,826	7,577
Current Liabilities	864	629	895	575	902	646	629	506	941	998
Long Term Debt	3,672	3,733	3,801	4,554	4,950	5,693	6,085	3,037	2,709	2,606
Common Equity	2,811	2,568	2,239	2,053	1,783	3,284	3,252	187	3,368	3,196
Total Capital	7,161	7,082	6,815	7,432	7,604	9,879	10,216	3,289	6,695	6,415
Capital Expenditures	423	178	202	245	370	458	254	171	531	242
Cash Flow	759	577	511	546	557	654	363	303	550	334
Current Ratio	2.4	1.8	1.1	1.1	1.1	1.3	1.2	0.9	1.1	1.2
% Long Term Debt of Capitalization	51.3	52.7	55.8	61.3	65.1	57.6	59.6	92.3	40.5	40.6
% Net Income of Revenue	10.4	5.7	4.3	5.1	5.4	7.8	8.2	10.6	4.7	3.9
% Return on Assets	5.4	2.9	2.0	2.3	1.9	2.9	2.7	3.2	3.2	2.8
% Return on Equity	17.1	9.9	7.6	10.3	9.7	17.8	9.1	10.0	7.6	7.0

Data as orig reptd.; bef. results of disc opers/spec. items. Per share data adj. for stk. divs.; EPS diluted. E-Estimated. NA-Not Available. NM-Not Meaningful. NR-Not Ranked. UR-Under Review.

Office: 9336 Civic Center Dr, Beverly Hills, CA 90210.
Telephone: 310-278-4321.
Website: http://www.hilton.com
Co-Chrmn: B. Hilton

Co-Chrmn & CEO: S.F. Bollenbach
Pres & COO: M.J. Hart
EVP & CFO: R.M. La Forgia
EVP, Secy & General Counsel: M. Kleiner

Investor Contact: M.A. Grossman (310-205-4030)
Board of Directors: S. F. Bollenbach, B. B. Coleman, A. S. Crown, C. Garvey, P. M. George, B. Hilton, B. V. Lambert, J. H. Myers, J. L. Notter, D. F. Tuttle, P. V. Ueberroth

Founded: 1946
Domicile: Delaware
Employees: 61,000

STANDARD &POOR'S

Home Depot Inc. (The)

S&P Recommendation STRONG BUY ★★★★★

Price $37.07 (as of Oct 27, 2006)

12-Mo. Target Price $51.00

Investment Style Large-Cap Growth

GICS Sector Consumer Discretionary
Sub-Industry Home Improvement Retail

Comment HD operates a chain of more than 2,000 retail warehouse-type stores, selling a wide variety of home improvement products for the do-it-yourself and home remodeling markets.

Key Stock Statistics (Source S&P, Vickers, company reports)

52-Wk Range	$43.95–32.85	S&P Oper. EPS 2007E	3.02	P/E on S&P Oper. EPS 2007E	12.3	Dividend Rate/Share	$0.60
Trailing 12-Month EPS	$2.92	S&P Oper. EPS 2008E	3.29	Common Shares Outstg. (M)	2,064.0	Yield (%)	1.62
Trailing 12-Month P/E	12.7	S&P Core EPS 2007E	3.02	Market Capitalization(B)	$76.514	Beta	1.54
$10K Invested 5 Yrs Ago	$9,639	S&P Core EPS 2008E	3.29	Institutional Ownership (%)	66	S&P Credit Rating	AA

Price Performance

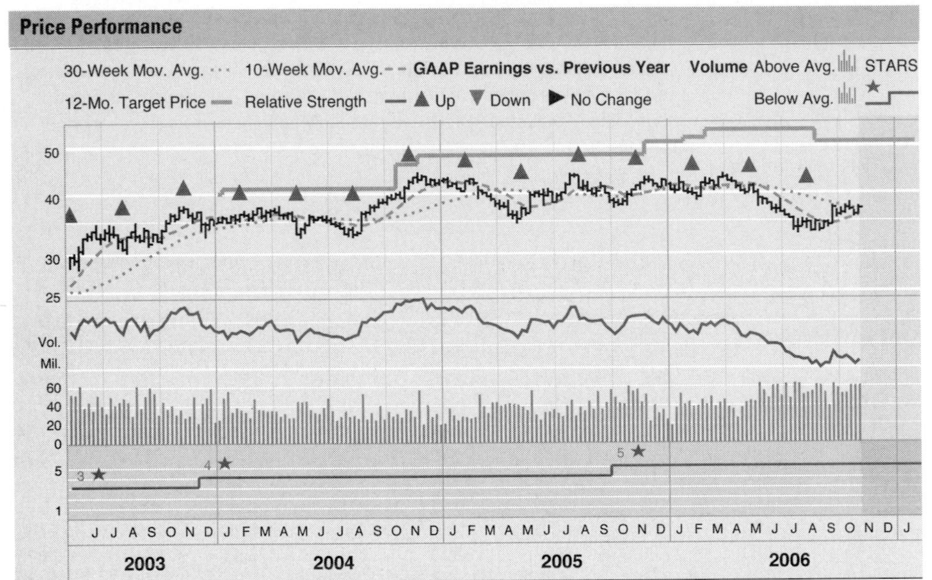

Options: ASE, CBOE, P, Ph

Analysis prepared by **Michael Souers** on September 28, 2006, when the stock traded at **$ 36.57**.

Highlights

- We expect sales to grow 14% to 15% in FY 07 (Jan.), driven by acquisitions in HD's Supply division, about 115 new retail store additions, including international store openings, and a decline in same-store sales of approximately 1%. We think declines in store traffic will outpace penetration of appliance programs and improvements in the merchandise mix.
- We see FY 07 margins narrowing 30-50 basis points, as operating margins of acquisitions in the professional market are lower than those of core retail operations. However, this negative impact will likely be nearly offset by a greater proportion of higher margin private label brands and more upscale merchandise, firmer pricing, and economies of scale.
- After higher expected interest expense stemming from increased debt levels, an effective tax rate projected at 38.0%, and a diluted share count that is about 3% lower--reflecting HD's active share repurchase program--we project FY 07 EPS of $3.02, an 11% increase from the $2.72 the company earned in FY 06. We estimate FY 08 EPS of $3.29.

Investment Rationale/Risk

- At about 11X our FY 08 EPS estimate, the shares recently traded at a modest discount to key peer Lowe's (LOW: buy, $29) and a significant discount to the S&P 500. We think HD's recent acquisitions in the $410 billion U.S. professional market--complementing its core business--have reduced HD's cyclicality and should provide HD with a steady stream of cash flow over the foreseeable future. In addition, we look for growth prospects in Canada, Mexico and China to fuel the company's international expansion plans. Lastly, the rebuilding efforts from Hurricane Katrina should bolster EPS results for the next several years, and provide a cushion against any loss of revenues from what we see as a likely slowdown in the housing market.
- Risks to our recommendation and target price include a potential slowdown in the economy; a sharp rise in interest rates; and unfavorable currency movements.
- Our 12-month target price of $51 is equal to about 15.5X our FY 08 EPS estimate, and is derived from our DCF model, which assumes a weighted average cost of capital of 10.3% and a terminal growth rate of 3.5%.

Qualitative Risk Assessment

LOW | MEDIUM | HIGH

Our risk assessment for Home Depot reflects the cyclical nature of the home improvement retail industry, which is reliant on economic growth; our view of ample opportunities for growth in the professional market domestically and the retail business overseas; and an S&P Quality Ranking of A+.

Quantitative Evaluations

S&P Quality Ranking **A+**

D | C | B- | B | B+ | A- | A | **A+**

Relative Strength Rank **MODERATE**

51

LOWEST = 1 HIGHEST = 99

Revenue/Earnings Data

Revenue (Million $)

	1Q	2Q	3Q	4Q	Year
2007	21,461	26,026	--	--	--
2006	18,973	22,305	20,744	19,489	81,511
2005	17,550	19,960	18,772	16,812	73,094
2004	15,104	17,989	16,598	15,125	64,816
2003	14,282	16,277	14,475	13,213	58,247
2002	12,200	14,576	13,289	13,488	53,553

Earnings Per Share ($)

2007	0.70	0.90	E0.77	E0.62	E3.02
2006	0.57	0.82	0.72	0.60	2.72
2005	0.49	0.70	0.60	0.47	2.26
2004	0.39	0.56	0.50	0.42	1.88
2003	0.36	0.50	0.40	0.30	1.56
2002	0.27	0.39	0.33	0.30	1.29

Fiscal year ended Jan. 31. Next earnings report expected: Mid November. EPS Estimates based on S&P Operating Earnings; historical GAAP earnings are as reported.

Dividend Data (Dates: mm/dd Payment Date: mm/dd/yy)

Amount ($)	Date Decl.	Ex-Div. Date	Stk. of Record	Payment Date
0.100	11/17	11/29	12/01	12/15/05
0.150	01/19	03/07	03/09	03/23/06
0.150	05/24	06/06	06/08	06/22/06
0.150	08/24	09/05	09/07	09/21/06

Dividends have been paid since 1987. Source: Company reports.

Home Depot Inc. (The)

Business Summary September 28, 2006

CORPORATE OVERVIEW. Home Depot is the world's largest home improvement retailer, with revenues in excess of $80 billion. The company mainly operates retail warehouse-type stores that sell a wide assortment of building materials, home improvement and lawn and garden products. At January 29, 2006, HD operated 2,042 stores, including 1,984 Home Depot stores (137 in Canada and 54 in Mexico), 34 EXPO Design Centers, three Home Depot Supply stores, 11 Home Depot Landscape Supply stores, and two Home Depot Floor stores.

Home Depot stores average approximately 105,000 sq. ft., plus 23,000 sq. ft. of garden center and storage space. It stocks 35,000 to 45,000 items, including brand name and proprietary items. Home Depot stores serve three primary customer groups: Do-It-Yourself (DIY) customers, typically homeowners who complete their own projects and installations; Do-It-For-Me (DIFM) Customers, usually homeowners who purchase materials and hire third parties to complete the project and/or installation and; Professional Customers, consisting of professional remodelers, general contractors, repairpeople and tradespeople. By product group, plumbing, electrical and kitchen (29% of FY 06 revenues) represented HD's largest source of revenue, followed by hardware and seasonal (27%), building materials, lumber and millwork (24%) and paint, flooring and wall covering (19%).

CORPORATE STRATEGY. We believe HD is in a period of transition after years of expanding rapidly as a big-box retailer. Home Depot appears to have shifted its focus for future expansion toward the $410 billion Professional market, and recently completed the acquisition of Hughes Supply, effectively doubling the size of Home Depot Supply.

At the end of 2004, Home Depot entered into an arrangement to lease commercial space in Shanghai to support a retail initiative in China. The company is pursuing its strategy for entry into the China home improvement marketplace. We anticipate that HD will make an acquisition in late 2006 in order to gain a small foothold of retail stores from which it can expand.

Company Financials

Per Share Data ($) Year Ended Jan. 31	**2006**	**2005**	**2004**	**2003**	**2002**	**2001**	**2000**	**1999**	**1998**	**1997**
Tangible Book Value	11.12	9.54	9.56	8.39	7.53	6.32	5.22	3.83	3.17	2.71
Cash Flow	3.45	2.85	2.35	1.95	1.62	1.35	1.19	0.86	0.63	0.53
Earnings	2.72	2.26	1.88	1.56	1.29	1.10	1.00	0.71	0.52	0.43
S&P Core Earnings	2.68	2.19	1.78	1.46	1.18	1.01	NA	NA	NA	NA
Dividends	0.40	0.33	0.26	0.21	0.17	0.16	0.11	0.08	0.06	0.05
Payout Ratio	15%	15%	14%	13%	13%	15%	11%	11%	12%	12%
Calendar Year	2005	2004	2003	2002	2001	2000	1999	1998	1997	1996
Prices:High	43.98	44.30	37.89	52.60	53.73	70.00	69.75	41.33	20.17	13.22
Prices:Low	34.56	32.34	20.10	23.01	30.30	34.69	34.58	18.44	10.61	9.22
P/E Ratio:High	16	20	20	41	43	64	70	58	39	31
P/E Ratio:Low	13	14	11	18	24	32	35	26	21	21

Income Statement Analysis (Million $)	2006	2005	2004	2003	2002	2001	2000	1999	1998	1997
Revenue	81,511	73,094	64,816	58,247	53,553	45,738	38,434	30,219	24,156	19,536
Operating Income	10,942	9,245	7,922	6,733	5,696	4,792	4,258	3,034	2,299	1,766
Depreciation	1,579	1,319	1,076	903	764	601	463	373	283	232
Interest Expense	143	70.0	62.0	37.0	28.0	21.0	28.0	37.0	42.0	39.0
Pretax Income	9,282	7,912	6,843	5,872	4,957	4,217	3,804	2,654	1,914	1,543
Effective Tax Rate	37.1%	36.8%	37.1%	37.6%	38.6%	38.8%	39.0%	39.2%	38.6%	38.7%
Net Income	5,838	5,001	4,304	3,664	3,044	2,581	2,320	1,614	1,160	938
S&P Core Earnings	5,751	4,843	4,067	3,414	2,780	2,364	NA	NA	NA	NA

Balance Sheet & Other Financial Data (Million $)	2006	2005	2004	2003	2002	2001	2000	1999	1998	1997
Cash	793	506	2,826	2,188	2,477	167	168	62.0	172	146
Current Assets	15,346	14,190	13,328	11,917	10,361	7,777	6,390	4,933	4,460	3,709
Total Assets	44,482	38,907	34,437	30,011	26,394	21,385	17,081	13,465	11,229	9,342
Current Liabilities	12,901	10,529	9,554	8,035	6,501	4,385	3,656	2,857	2,456	1,842
Long Term Debt	2,672	2,148	856	1,321	1,250	1,545	750	1,566	1,303	1,247
Common Equity	26,909	24,158	22,407	19,802	18,082	15,004	12,341	8,740	7,098	5,955
Total Capital	30,604	27,615	24,230	21,485	19,521	16,755	13,188	10,400	8,595	7,366
Capital Expenditures	3,881	3,948	3,508	2,749	3,393	3,558	2,581	2,059	1,525	1,194
Cash Flow	7,417	6,320	5,380	4,567	3,808	3,182	2,783	1,987	1,443	1,170
Current Ratio	1.2	1.3	1.4	1.5	1.6	1.8	1.7	1.7	1.8	2.0
% Long Term Debt of Capitalization	8.7	7.8	3.5	6.1	6.4	9.2	5.7	15.1	15.2	16.9
% Net Income of Revenue	7.2	6.8	6.6	6.3	5.7	5.6	6.0	5.3	4.8	4.8
% Return on Assets	14.0	13.6	13.4	13.0	12.7	13.4	15.2	13.1	11.3	11.2
% Return on Equity	22.9	21.5	20.4	19.3	18.4	18.9	22.0	20.4	17.8	17.1

Data as orig reptd.; bef. results of disc opers/spec. items. Per share data adj. for stk. divs.; EPS diluted. E-Estimated. NA-Not Available. NM-Not Meaningful. NR-Not Ranked. UR-Under Review.

Office: 2455 Paces Ferry Rd, N.W., Atlanta, GA 30339-1834.
Telephone: 770-433-8211.
Website: http://www.homedepot.com
Chrmn, Pres & CEO: R.L. Nardelli

Vice Chrmn: F.S. Blake
EVP & CFO: C.B. Tome
EVP, Secy & General Counsel: F.L. Fernandez
EVP & CIO: R.P. DeRodes

Investor Contact: D. Dayhoff (770-384-2666)
Board of Directors: G. D. Brenneman, J. L. Clendenin, C. X. Gonzalez, M. A. Hart, III, B. G. Hill, L. P. Jackson, Jr., L. R. Johnston, K. G. Langone, A. Mozilo, R. L. Nardelli, T. J. Ridge

Founded: 1978
Domicile: Delaware
Employees: 344,810

STANDARD &POOR'S

Honeywell International Inc.

S&P Recommendation HOLD ★★★★★	Price	12-Mo. Target Price	Investment Style
	$42.30 (as of Oct 27, 2006)	$42.00	Large-Cap Value

GICS Sector Industrials
Sub-Industry Aerospace & Defense

Comment HON, the world's largest maker of cockpit controls, small jet engines and climate control equipment, also makes industrial materials and consumer automotive products.

Key Stock Statistics (Source S&P, Vickers, company reports)

52-Wk Range	$44.48–33.75	S&P Oper. EPS 2006E	2.50	P/E on S&P Oper. EPS 2006E	16.9	Dividend Rate/Share	$0.91
Trailing 12-Month EPS	$2.46	S&P Oper. EPS 2007E	2.90	Common Shares Outstg. (M)	816.5	Yield (%)	2.15
Trailing 12-Month P/E	17.2	S&P Core EPS 2006E	2.45	Market Capitalization(B)	$34.538	Beta	1.64
$10K Invested 5 Yrs Ago	$15,873	S&P Core EPS 2007E	2.85	Institutional Ownership (%)	76	S&P Credit Rating	A

Price Performance

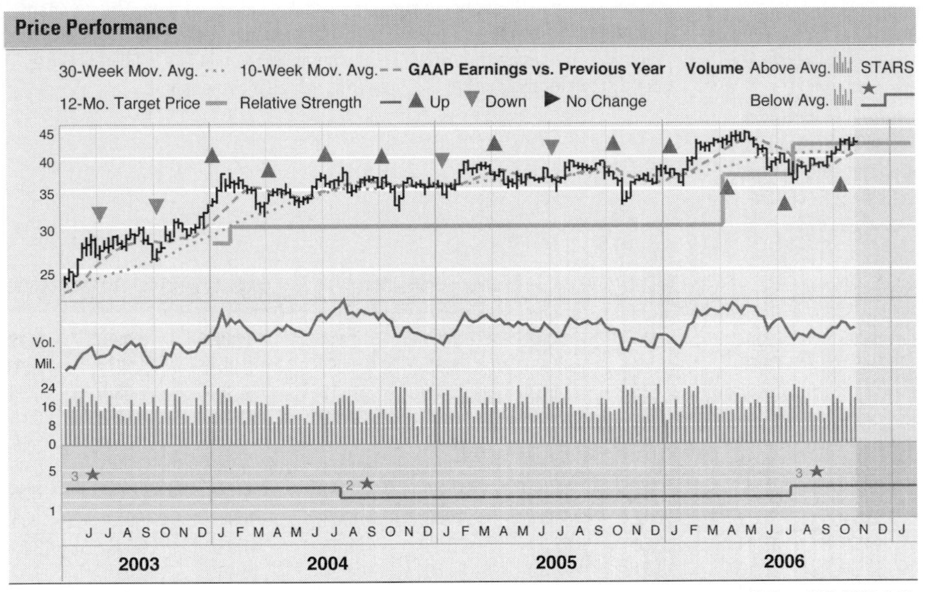

Options: ASE, CBOE, P, Ph

Analysis prepared by **Richard Tortoriello** on July 26, 2006, when the stock traded at **$ 37.97**.

Highlights

- With a strong global economy, HON's automation and control systems and specialty materials segments have been driving top-line growth in the 12% area (including acquisitions). We expect a return to growth in the aviation segment in the second half of 2006, where HON's growth has been below what we expected given the current strong aerospace cycle. We also expect sluggish, but improving, growth from HON's transportation business, where it has been gaining product wins in turbochargers. Overall, we look for 12% sales growth in 2006, and 7% in 2007 (absent acquisitions).
- Margins have been holding up well, in our view, with total segment profit margins improving to 13.1% in the second quarter of 2006, from 12.1% a year earlier. We project further margin increases, on increased sales volumes and cost-containment efforts, and estimate operating margins of 13.3% for 2006 and 13.9% in 2007.
- We expect EPS to advance to $2.50 in 2006 and $2.90 in 2007. We project free cash flow (cash flow from operating activities less capital expenditures) per share near or above reported EPS in 2006, and see HON using this cash partly for continued share repurchases.

Investment Rationale/Risk

- HON's return on invested capital has risen from near 0% in 2002 and 2003 to over 10% in 2005 and over 11% for the past four quarters. We believe that, given growth that we expect in HON's markets and assuming improved growth in aerospace, HON can continue to improve on this profitability. In the meantime, we see shareholders benefiting from HON's substantial cash generation.
- Risks to our recommendation and target price include a downturn in the global economy or in any of HON's core markets, the potential for competitive pressures in its core markets, as well as the potential for manufacturing or other operational difficulties.
- Our 12-month target price of $42 is based on a P/E multiple of 14.5X our 2007 EPS estimate. This compares to a historical 10-year average of HON's forward P/E 15.3X. We note that the current average P/E, on 2007 estimated earnings, for our coverage of 18 aerospace & defence stocks is 14.7X.

Qualitative Risk Assessment

LOW | **MEDIUM** | HIGH

Our risk assessment reflects what we believe is above average exposure to market movements, sensitivity to economic cycles, currency fluctuations, and raw material costs, and potential legal and environmental liabilities, offset by what we view as a strong balance sheet.

Quantitative Evaluations

S&P Quality Ranking **B**

D | C | B- | **B** | B+ | A- | A | A+

Relative Strength Rank **MODERATE**

59

LOWEST = 1 HIGHEST = 99

Revenue/Earnings Data

Revenue (Million $)

	1Q	2Q	3Q	4Q	Year
2006	7,241	7,898	7,952	--	--
2005	6,453	7,026	6,899	7,275	27,653
2004	6,178	6,388	6,395	6,640	25,601
2003	5,399	5,749	5,768	6,187	23,103
2002	5,199	5,651	5,569	5,855	22,274
2001	5,944	6,066	5,789	5,853	23,652

Earnings Per Share ($)

	1Q	2Q	3Q	4Q	Year
2006	0.51	0.63	0.66	**E**0.72	**E**2.50
2005	0.42	0.33	0.51	0.61	1.86
2004	0.34	0.42	0.43	0.30	1.49
2003	0.32	0.37	0.40	0.47	1.56
2002	0.46	0.56	0.50	-1.78	-0.27
2001	0.05	0.06	-0.38	0.14	-0.12

Fiscal year ended Dec. 31. Next earnings report expected: Late January. EPS Estimates based on S&P Operating Earnings; historical GAAP earnings are as reported.

Dividend Data (Dates: mm/dd Payment Date: mm/dd/yy)

Amount ($)	Date Decl.	Ex-Div. Date	Stk. of Record	Payment Date
0.227	02/16	02/23	02/27	03/10/06
0.227	04/24	05/17	05/19	06/09/06
0.227	07/28	08/16	08/18	09/08/06
0.227	10/27	11/16	11/20	12/08/06

Dividends have been paid since 1887. Source: Company reports.

Honeywell International Inc.

Business Summary July 26, 2006

CORPORATE OVERVIEW. This $25 billion-revenue, aerospace-oriented industrial conglomerate conducts business through four operating segments.

The Aerospace segment (38% of 2005 revenues and 47% of earnings before interest and taxes (EBIT), and 16% EBIT margins) primarily makes cockpit controls, power generation equipment, and wheels and brakes for commercial and military aircraft. It is also a leading maker of jet engines for regional and business jet manufacturers.

Demand for HON's aircraft equipment is driven primarily by growth in the global 100+ seat jetliner fleet. Based on the latest statistics provided by independent research firm Avitas, Inc., from 1993 through 2003, the global airliner fleet expanded at a 3.0% average annual growth rate.

The Aerospace segment is also a major player in the $35 billion global aircraft maintenance, repair and overhaul (MRO) industry. Based on statistics provided by aviation trade group Aerospace Industries Association, from 1994 through 2004, the MRO market expanded at a 2.2% average annual growth rate.

HON's Automation and Control Solutions segment (34%; 30%; 11%) is best known as a global maker of home and office climate controls equipment. It also makes home automation systems, energy-efficient lighting controls, and security and fire alarms. With more than 20,000 providers, the $110 billion security systems industry is fragmented (based on statistics provided by trade group Security Industry Association).

The Specialty Materials segment (12%; 7%; 8%) makes specialty chemicals and fibers. HON sells its industrial materials primarily to the food, pharmaceutical, and electronic packaging industries.

The Transportation Systems segment (16%; 16%; 12%) consists of a portfolio of brand name car care products, such as FRAM filters, Prestone antifreeze, Autolite spark plugs, and Simoniz car waxes. The unit is also a large truck brake maker.

Company Financials

Per Share Data ($) Year Ended Dec. 31	2005	2004	2003	2002	2001	2000	1999	1998	1997	1996
Tangible Book Value	1.95	4.70	4.46	2.52	3.45	4.71	4.95	4.12	3.47	4.89
Cash Flow	2.74	2.24	2.25	0.53	1.02	3.28	2.99	3.38	3.07	2.87
Earnings	1.86	1.49	1.56	-0.27	-0.12	2.05	1.90	2.32	2.02	1.81
S&P Core Earnings	1.83	1.42	1.57	0.15	-0.26	NA	NA	NA	NA	NA
Dividends	1.03	0.75	0.75	0.75	0.75	0.75	0.68	0.60	0.52	0.45
Payout Ratio	55%	50%	48%	NM	NM	37%	36%	26%	26%	25%
Prices:High	39.50	38.46	33.50	40.95	53.90	60.50	68.63	47.56	47.13	37.19
Prices:Low	32.68	31.23	20.20	18.77	22.15	32.13	37.81	32.63	31.63	23.56
P/E Ratio:High	21	26	21	NM	NM	30	36	21	23	21
P/E Ratio:Low	18	21	13	NM	NM	16	20	14	16	13
Income Statement Analysis (Million $)										
Revenue	27,653	25,601	23,103	22,274	23,652	25,023	23,735	15,128	14,472	13,971
Operating Income	3,178	2,350	2,513	2,573	1,085	3,794	2,905	2,571	2,019	1,456
Depreciation	697	650	595	671	926	995	881	609	609	602
Interest Expense	356	331	335	344	405	481	265	162	175	186
Pretax Income	2,323	1,600	1,647	-945	-422	2,398	2,248	1,980	1,761	1,553
Effective Tax Rate	31.9%	23.8%	18.0%	NM	NM	30.8%	31.5%	30.9%	31.0%	34.3%
Net Income	1,581	1,281	1,344	-220	NA	1,659	1,541	1,331	1,170	1,020
S&P Core Earnings	1,554	1,225	1,363	119	-207	NA	NA	NA	NA	NA
Balance Sheet & Other Financial Data (Million $)										
Cash	1,234	3,586	2,950	2,021	1,393	1,196	1,991	712	611	1,766
Current Assets	11,962	12,820	11,523	10,195	9,894	10,661	10,422	5,593	5,573	5,839
Total Assets	32,294	31,062	29,344	27,559	24,226	25,175	23,527	15,560	13,707	12,829
Current Liabilities	10,430	8,739	6,783	6,574	6,220	7,214	8,272	5,185	4,436	3,696
Long Term Debt	3,082	4,069	4,961	4,719	4,731	3,941	2,457	1,476	1,215	1,317
Common Equity	11,254	11,252	7,243	8,925	9,170	9,707	8,599	5,297	4,205	4,180
Total Capital	14,839	15,718	12,520	14,063	14,776	14,821	11,920	7,568	6,114	6,107
Capital Expenditures	684	629	655	671	876	853	986	684	717	755
Cash Flow	2,278	1,931	1,939	451	827	2,654	2,422	1,940	1,779	1,622
Current Ratio	1.1	1.5	1.7	1.6	1.6	1.5	1.3	1.1	1.3	1.6
% Long Term Debt of Capitalization	20.8	25.9	39.6	33.6	32.0	26.6	20.6	19.5	19.3	21.6
% Net Income of Revenue	5.7	5.0	5.8	NM	NM	6.6	6.5	8.8	8.1	7.3
% Return on Assets	5.0	4.2	4.7	NM	NM	6.8	6.7	9.1	8.8	8.1
% Return on Equity	14.0	11.7	21.1	NM	NM	18.1	18.5	28.0	27.9	26.2

Data as orig reptd.; bef. results of disc opers/spec. items. Per share data adj. for stk. divs.; EPS diluted. E-Estimated. NA-Not Available. NM-Not Meaningful. NR-Not Ranked. UR-Under Review.

Office: 101 Columbia Rd, Morristown, NJ 07960-4640.
Telephone: 973-455-2000.
Website: http://www.honeywell.com
Chrmn & CEO: D.M. Cote

SVP & CFO: D.J. Anderson
SVP & General Counsel: P.M. Kreindler
SVP & CIO: L.E. Kittelberger
VP & Secy: T.F. Larkins

Investor Contact: N. Noviello (973-455-2222)
Board of Directors: G. M. Bethune, D. M. Cote, D. S. Davis, L. F. Deily, C. Hollick, J. J. Howard, B. Karatz, R. E. Palmer, J. C. Pardo, I. G. Seidenberg, B. T. Sheares, E. K. Shinseki, J. R. Stafford, M. W. Wright

Founded: 1920
Domicile: Delaware
Employees: 116,000

STANDARD &POOR'S

Hospira Inc

S&P Recommendation HOLD ★★★★★

Price $36.97 (as of Oct 27, 2006)

12-Mo. Target Price $39.00

Investment Style Mid-Cap Growth

GICS Sector Health Care
Sub-Industry Health Care Equipment

Comment Spun off from Abbott Laboratories in May 2004, this Illinois-based company provides a variety of hospital products, including injectable generic drugs, pumps, and syringes.

Key Stock Statistics (Source S&P, Vickers, company reports)

52-Wk Range	$47.99–33.75	S&P Oper. EPS 2006E	1.93	P/E on S&P Oper. EPS 2006E	19.2	Dividend Rate/Share	Nil
Trailing 12-Month EPS	$1.36	S&P Oper. EPS 2007E	2.30	Common Shares Outstg. (M)	157.0	Yield (%)	Nil
Trailing 12-Month P/E	27.2	S&P Core EPS 2006E	1.93	Market Capitalization(B)	$5.804	Beta	0.42
$10K Invested 5 Yrs Ago	NA	S&P Core EPS 2007E	2.30	Institutional Ownership (%)	71	S&P Credit Rating	NA

Price Performance

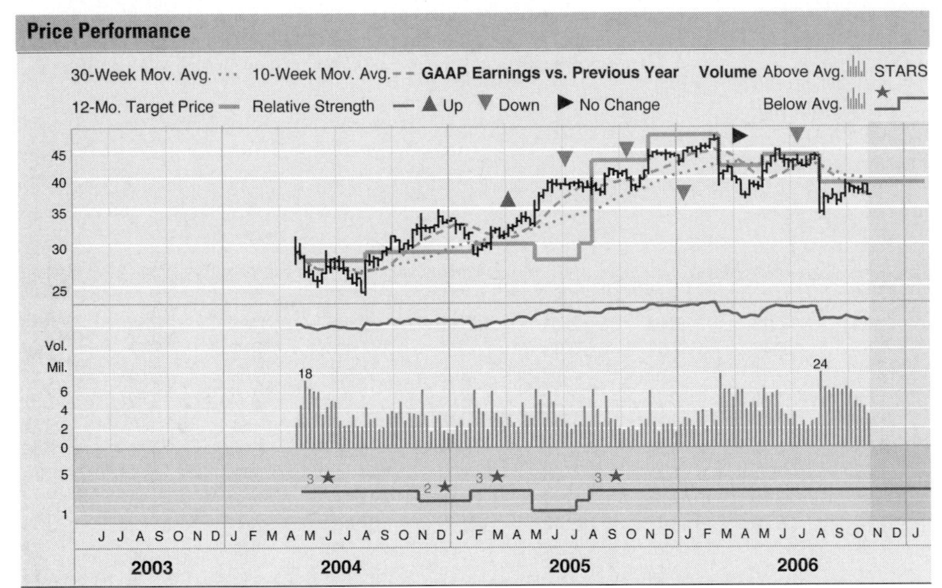

Analysis prepared by **Cameron Lavey** on October 17, 2006, when the stock traded at **$ 37.46**.

Highlights

- We expect 2006 revenues to rise about 5%, to $2.76 billion. Our forecast assumes low single digit growth of specialty injectables and low double digit growth in medication delivery systems, partially offset by less sales to Abbott Labs (ABT: buy, $47); we see growth of about 10% in the contract manufacturing division. For 2007, we project revenue growth of 7%, driven by low double digit growth in contract manufacturing.
- We expect gross margins to widen slightly in 2006 as HSP transitions to higher margin products and eliminates lower margin contracts in the contract manufacturing segment. We think increased pricing will be partially offset by a rise in SG&A expenses as HSP continues to expand its infrastructure as an independent public company. In 2007, we believe an improved product mix will lead to wider gross margins, while lower SG&A expenses (as a percentage of sales) drive EBITDA margin expansion.
- We estimate 2006 operating EPS of $1.93, followed by EPS of $2.30 in 2007. Our EPS estimates include projected stock option expense of $0.16 per year.

Investment Rationale/Risk

- Our hold recommendation is based on valuation. While we are encouraged by gross margin improvements and higher than anticipated sales of medication delivery systems, we think the shares are fairly valued at current levels. We see annualized EPS growth of 8% to 10% over the next four years, and believe that EPS gains will largely come from operational efficiencies, as we forecast mid-single digit sales growth. With the shares recently trading at a slight premium to peers on a P/E basis, we would not add to positions.
- Risks to our recommendation and target price include lower than expected sales, higher than anticipated operating costs, and a failure to gain approval for injectable drugs. In addition, the transition to a stand-alone company could take more time or be more costly than we anticipate.
- Our 12-month target price of $39 is based on our DCF analysis, which assumes a weighted average cost of capital of 9.7%, a compound annual growth rate in free cash flow of 9.8% over the next five years, and terminal growth of 3%.

Qualitative Risk Assessment

LOW | **MEDIUM** | HIGH

Our risk assessment reflects our view that HSP has a broad product portfolio, which reduces its dependence on any one product category. We see stable demand for hospital products due to our belief that demand for hospital services will remain strong. However, HSP still faces challenges in converting to a standalone company, in our opinion.

Quantitative Evaluations

S&P Quality Ranking **NR**

D | C | B- | B | B+ | A- | A | A+

Relative Strength Rank **WEAK**

20

LOWEST = 1 HIGHEST = 99

Revenue/Earnings Data

Revenue (Million $)

	1Q	2Q	3Q	4Q	Year
2006	664.3	629.9	--	--	--
2005	662.1	618.5	656.6	646.2	2,627
2004	609.0	667.4	656.1	700.3	2,645
2003	--	--	--	--	2,545
2002	--	--	--	--	--
2001	--	--	--	--	--

Earnings Per Share ($)

	1Q	2Q	3Q	4Q	Year
2006	0.49	0.34	**E**0.46	**E**0.47	**E**1.93
2005	0.49	0.44	0.37	0.16	1.46
2004	0.43	0.80	0.39	0.31	1.92
2003	--	--	--	--	1.65
2002	--	--	--	--	--
2001	--	--	--	--	--

Fiscal year ended Dec. 31. Next earnings report expected: Early November. EPS Estimates based on S&P Operating Earnings; historical GAAP earnings are as reported.

Dividend Data

No cash dividends have been paid.

Hospira Inc

Business Summary October 17, 2006

CORPORATE OVERVIEW. Hospira (HSP) was created on May 3, 2004, as a spin-off from Abbott Laboratories. Abbott shareholders received one share of Hospira for every 10 shares of Abbott. HSP provides medication delivery systems and specialty pharmaceuticals to hospitals, clinics and physicians. The legal separation to a stand-alone company was completed in the second quarter of 2006.

Hospira has an international presence, with operations in close to 70 countries. International sales accounted for 17% of total revenues in 2005. The company operates 14 manufacturing facilities domestically and internationally.

Operating segments include specialty injectable pharmaceuticals (2005 sales of $845 million, 32% of sales), medication delivery systems ($796 million, 30%), and injectable pharmaceutical contract manufacturing services ($179 million, 7%). Sales to Abbott Laboratories totaled $169 million in 2005, down from $180 million in 2004. Sales in the other category and to international third parties constitute the remainder of total sales. Major competitors include Baxter International, Becton Dickinson, Edwards Lifesciences, Fresenius AG, Patheon, and Sicor.

The specialty injectable pharmaceuticals division provides over 130 generic injectable drugs available in a wide array of dosages and formulations. Therapeutic areas of focus include cardiovascular, anesthesia, anti-infectives, analgesics, and other. Some other products include Carpuject prefilled syringes; patient-controlled analgesia syringes for use with its LifeCare PCA drug delivery pumps; and the ADD-Vantage System, which aids in the preparation of drug solutions from prepackaged powders or concentration.

Company Financials

Per Share Data ($) Year Ended Dec. 31	2005	2004	2003	2002	2001	2000	1999	1998	1997	1996
Tangible Book Value	7.57	5.74	NM	NA	NA	NA	NA	NA	NA	NA
Cash Flow	2.42	2.84	NA	NA	NA	NA	NA	NA	NA	NA
Earnings	1.46	1.92	1.65	NA	NA	NA	NA	NA	NA	NA
S&P Core Earnings	1.35	1.31	1.46	NA	NA	NA	NA	NA	NA	NA
Dividends	Nil	Nil	NA	NA	NA	NA	NA	NA	NA	NA
Payout Ratio	Nil	Nil	NA	NA	NA	NA	NA	NA	NA	NA
Prices:High	45.10	34.86	NA	NA	NA	NA	NA	NA	NA	NA
Prices:Low	28.35	24.02	NA	NA	NA	NA	NA	NA	NA	NA
P/E Ratio:High	31	18	NA	NA	NA	NA	NA	NA	NA	NA
P/E Ratio:Low	19	13	NA	NA	NA	NA	NA	NA	NA	NA

Income Statement Analysis (Million $)	2005	2004	2003	2002	2001	2000	1999	1998	1997	1996
Revenue	2,627	2,645	2,624	NA	NA	NA	NA	NA	NA	NA
Operating Income	493	509	506	NA	NA	NA	NA	NA	NA	NA
Depreciation	156	146	146	NA	NA	NA	NA	NA	NA	NA
Interest Expense	28.3	18.8	Nil	NA	NA	NA	NA	NA	NA	NA
Pretax Income	322	412	359	NA	NA	NA	NA	NA	NA	NA
Effective Tax Rate	26.8%	26.7%	27.5%	NA	NA	NA	NA	NA	NA	NA
Net Income	236	302	260	NA	NA	NA	NA	NA	NA	NA
S&P Core Earnings	217	206	231	187	NA	NA	NA	NA	NA	NA

Balance Sheet & Other Financial Data (Million $)	2005	2004	2003	2002	2001	2000	1999	1998	1997	1996
Cash	521	200	Nil	NA	NA	NA	NA	NA	NA	NA
Current Assets	1,561	1,198	1,075	NA	NA	NA	NA	NA	NA	NA
Total Assets	2,789	2,343	2,250	NA	NA	NA	NA	NA	NA	NA
Current Liabilities	596	536	360	NA	NA	NA	NA	NA	NA	NA
Long Term Debt	695	699	Nil	NA	NA	NA	NA	NA	NA	NA
Common Equity	1,328	984	1,453	NA	NA	NA	NA	NA	NA	NA
Total Capital	2,027	1,687	1,453	NA	NA	NA	NA	NA	NA	NA
Capital Expenditures	256	229	197	NA	NA	NA	NA	NA	NA	NA
Cash Flow	392	447	406	NA	NA	NA	NA	NA	NA	NA
Current Ratio	2.6	2.2	3.0	NA	NA	NA	NA	NA	NA	NA
% Long Term Debt of Capitalization	34.3	41.4	Nil	NA	NA	NA	NA	NA	NA	NA
% Net Income of Revenue	9.0	11.4	9.9	NA	NA	NA	NA	NA	NA	NA
% Return on Assets	9.2	13.1	11.8	NA	NA	NA	NA	NA	NA	NA
% Return on Equity	20.4	24.7	18.7	NA	NA	NA	NA	NA	NA	NA

Data as orig reptd.; bef. results of disc opers/spec. items. Per share data adj. for stk. divs.; EPS diluted. E-Estimated. NA-Not Available. NM-Not Meaningful. NR-Not Ranked. UR-Under Review.

Office: 275 North Field Drive, Lake Forest, IL 60045.
Telephone: 847-937-6100.
Chrmn: D.A. Jones
CEO: C.B. Begley

COO: T.C. Kearney
SVP & CFO: T.E. Werner
SVP, Secy & General Counsel: B.J. Smith
Investor Contact: L. McHugh (224-212-2363)

Board of Directors: I. W. Bailey, II, C. B. Begley, C. R. Curran, D. A. Jones, J. C. Pelham, J. J. Sokolov, J. C. Staley, W. L. Weiss

Auditor: Deloitte & Touche
Founded: 2003
Domicile: Delaware
Employees: 14,000

STANDARD & POOR'S

Block (H&R) Inc.

S&P Recommendation SELL ★★☆☆☆	Price $21.43 (as of Oct 27, 2006)	12-Mo. Target Price $19.00	Investment Style Mid-Cap Growth

GICS Sector Consumer Discretionary
Sub-Industry Specialized Consumer Services

Comment This diversified company provides a wide range of financial products and services, including income tax preparation, mortgage loans and investment services.

Key Stock Statistics (Source S&P, Vickers, company reports)

52-Wk Range	$26.96–19.80	S&P Oper. EPS 2007E	1.42	P/E on S&P Oper. EPS 2007E	15.1	Dividend Rate/Share	$0.54
Trailing 12-Month EPS	$1.14	S&P Oper. EPS 2008E	NA	Common Shares Outstg. (M)	321.7	Yield (%)	2.52
Trailing 12-Month P/E	18.8	S&P Core EPS 2007E	1.42	Market Capitalization(B)	$6.894	Beta	0.26
$10K Invested 5 Yrs Ago	$13,805	S&P Core EPS 2008E	NA	Institutional Ownership (%)	88	S&P Credit Rating	BBB+

Price Performance

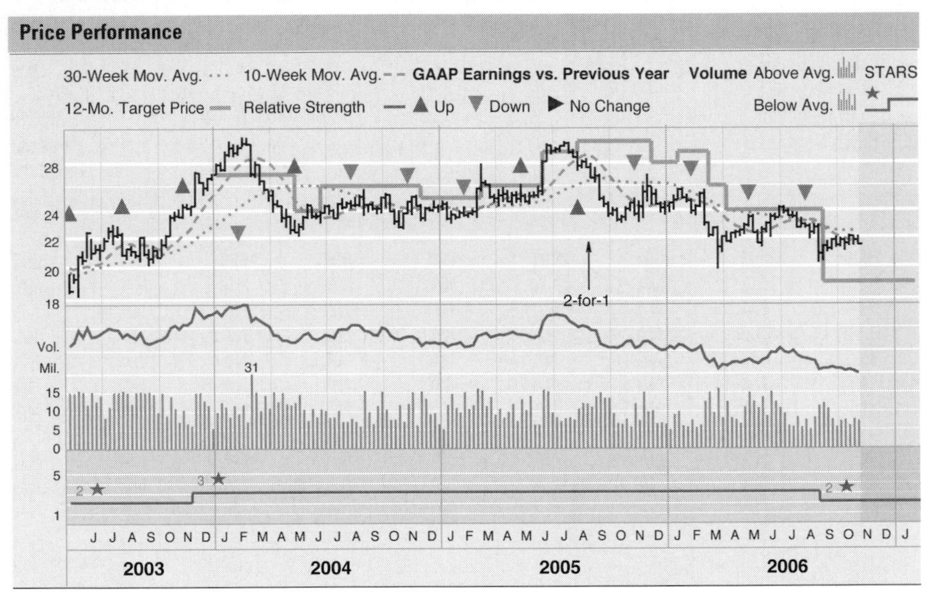

Options: ASE, P

Analysis prepared by **Loran Braverman, CFA** on September 01, 2006, when the stock traded at **$ 21.04**.

Highlights

- Revenues declined 12% in the first quarter of FY 07 (Apr.), caused by, in our opinion, a 44% decline in mortgage services revenues. The mortgage services segment, which, as of the start of FY 07, consists solely of the non-prime Option One business, was affected, we believe, by a softening in the housing market. Business services had a gain of 62%, helped by an acquisition. Tax services rose 15%, but were seasonally unimportant. In FY 07, we expect revenue growth of 4.5%. We think tax services can show growth of 6.0%, if HRB has fewer missteps than seen in FY 06.
- Due to the highly seasonal nature of the tax service business, HRB typically has losses in the first two fiscal quarters. Of the $173 million increase in the first quarter pretax loss year to year, $136 million was due to the mortgage services segment, which included a loss provision of $102 million. For full year FY 07, we look for the pretax margin to decline 130 basis points, with a drop in the mortgage services margin offsetting ongoing significant cost cutting efforts.
- For FY 07, we look for EPS of $1.42, including projected stock option expense of $0.10.

Investment Rationale/Risk

- HRB shares recently traded at 13.2X trailing 12-month EPS, slightly below the average multiple of 13.8X since mid-2002. Although we believe HRB owns the premier name in consumer tax preparation services, it faces growing competition from other multi-office providers and from increased public acceptance of software-based self-filed returns. In addition, its second largest business, mortgage services, is fully participating in a softening mortgage market.
- Risks to our opinion and target price the include a positive resolution of litigation and regulatory issues; tax law changes; and a near-term improvement in the subprime, variable rate mortgage, and refinancing businesses. In February 2006, HRB announced that it was restating results for FY 04, FY 05, and FY 06 to date, principally due to errors in determining its effective state income tax rate.
- Our 12-month target price of $19 is based on a blend of our historical and peer analyses. Our historical analysis leads us to apply a 14.4X P/E ratio to our FY 07 EPS estimate, valuing the shares at $20. Our peer model, based a on sum-of-the-parts analysis, values the stock at $17.

Qualitative Risk Assessment

LOW	MEDIUM	**HIGH**

Our risk assessment reflects HRB's leading position in its market, offset by the higher overall risk to HRB from its heightened emphasis on cross-selling financial products to its tax service clients and on its subprime variable rate mortgage and refinancing businesses, internal accounting control issues, which, in 2006, caused HRB to restate almost three years of results, and HRB being the target of a number of recent lawsuits.

Quantitative Evaluations

S&P Quality Ranking A-

D	C	B-	B	B+	**A-**	A	A+

Relative Strength Rank WEAK

23

LOWEST = 1 HIGHEST = 99

Revenue/Earnings Data

Revenue (Million $)

	1Q	2Q	3Q	4Q	Year
2007	540.8	--	--	--	--
2006	615.0	605.0	1,157	2,496	4,873
2005	482.7	539.3	1,032	2,357	4,420
2004	494.8	579.9	977.2	2,192	4,206
2003	431.4	471.4	958.4	1,919	3,780
2002	329.0	373.9	733.5	1,881	3,318

Earnings Per Share ($)

2007	-0.41	E-0.26	E0.17	E1.90	E1.42
2006	-0.08	-0.25	0.04	1.77	1.47
2005	-0.13	-0.16	0.28	1.83	1.88
2004	0.03	0.03	0.29	1.62	1.95
2003	-0.03	-0.11	0.37	1.36	1.58
2002	-0.09	-0.08	0.08	1.23	1.16

Fiscal year ended Apr. 30. Next earnings report expected: Mid November. EPS Estimates based on S&P Operating Earnings; historical GAAP earnings are as reported.

Dividend Data (Dates: mm/dd Payment Date: mm/dd/yy)

Amount ($)	Date Decl.	Ex-Div. Date	Stk. of Record	Payment Date
0.125	11/17	12/09	12/13	01/03/06
0.125	02/23	03/09	03/13	04/03/06
0.125	05/23	06/08	06/12	07/03/06
0.135	06/09	09/07	09/11	10/02/06

Dividends have been paid since 1962. Source: Company reports.

Please read the Required Disclosures and Analyst Certification on the last page of this report.

Block (H&R) Inc.

Business Summary September 01, 2006

CORPORATE OVERVIEW. HRB provides various financial products and services, which the company believes are complementary. In FY 06 (Apr.), Tax Services accounted for 50% of revenues and 71% of profits, Mortgage 26% and 39%, Business Services 18% and 7%, and Investment Services 6% and (4)%; the corporate division was (13)% of profits. The Tax Services division served about 19.5 million clients in FY 06, including 15.7 million retail clients (down 1.9%) and more than 3.7 million digital clients (up 23%). Tax Services also offers refund anticipation loans (RALs). There were 12,165 company-owned and franchised U.S. H&R Block offices at April 30, 2006. In addition, HRB offers tax preparation services at hundreds of H&R Block Premium offices for more complex returns. International operations are located primarily in Australia, Canada, and the U.K., with combined company owned and franchise offices numbering 1,383 at April 30, 2006. Tax Services also offers online tax preparation, tax preparation software, and guarantee programs.

HRB also originates, services and sells conforming and non-conforming loans in the U.S. through more than 49,000 mortgage broker locations (as of April 30, 2006); and provides brokerage services, investment planning, accounting, tax and consulting services, and tax, estate planning, and financial planning services.

MARKET PROFILE. HRB's largest segment, tax services, has competition from other tax service chains, professional CPA/accounting firms, "mom and pop" local tax service providers and do-it-yourselfers (DIYers). In addition, HRB and some other online tax service product providers participate in the Free Filing Alliance, which offers free online federal return preparation with no income limitations. We believe HRB competes successfully by offering many services at what customers believe is an acceptable price to value relationship. These services include: the convenience of the largest retail tax office network in the U.S.; a "Peace of Mind" Guarantee" (POM) whereby HRB commits to representing its clients if audited by the IRS and to assuming the cost of additional taxes resulting from errors attributable to an HRB tax professional; "Refund Anticipation Loans" and "Refund Anticipation Checks" and a service whereby DIYers using HRB's online service can have an HRB tax professional check their returns and receive the POM guarantee. By offering increased value, HRB has been able to raise rates 5%-7% annually since 2002.

Company Financials

Per Share Data ($) Year Ended Apr. 30	**2006**	**2005**	**2004**	**2003**	**2002**	**2001**	**2000**	**1999**	**1998**	**1997**
Tangible Book Value	1.90	1.64	1.41	1.69	0.73	0.67	0.32	1.68	2.46	2.21
Cash Flow	2.05	2.43	2.42	2.02	1.57	2.61	1.01	0.77	0.53	0.51
Earnings	1.47	1.88	1.95	1.58	1.16	0.76	0.64	0.59	0.41	0.34
S&P Core Earnings	1.53	1.76	1.85	1.44	1.07	0.73	NA	NA	NA	NA
Dividends	0.54	0.39	0.39	0.35	0.29	0.27	0.26	0.21	0.20	0.26
Payout Ratio	37%	21%	20%	22%	25%	35%	40%	36%	49%	NM
Calendar Year	2005	2004	2003	2002	2001	2000	1999	1998	1997	1996
Prices:High	30.00	30.50	27.89	26.75	23.19	12.38	14.88	12.27	11.44	10.53
Prices:Low	22.99	22.08	17.64	14.50	9.16	6.73	9.50	8.83	7.00	5.91
P/E Ratio:High	20	16	14	17	20	16	23	21	20	94
P/E Ratio:Low	16	12	9	9	8	9	15	15	17	52
Income Statement Analysis (Million $)										
Revenue	4,873	4,420	4,206	3,780	3,318	3,002	2,452	1,645	1,307	1,916
Operating Income	128	215	1,411	240	987	913	704	499	364	171
Depreciation	192	184	172	162	155	206	147	74.6	55.8	167
Interest Expense	49.1	62.4	84.6	92.6	116	243	154	69.3	52.3	11.7
Pretax Income	827	1,018	1,164	987	717	473	412	384	281	62.4
Effective Tax Rate	40.7%	37.5%	39.5%	41.2%	39.4%	41.5%	38.9%	38.0%	38.0%	23.5%
Net Income	490	636	704	580	434	277	252	238	174	47.8
S&P Core Earnings	509	593	665	527	400	268	NA	NA	NA	NA
Balance Sheet & Other Financial Data (Million $)										
Cash	1,088	1,617	1,617	1,337	617	326	442	250	901	680
Current Assets	2,824	3,071	2,961	2,747	2,245	2,271	3,864	1,087	2,143	1,270
Total Assets	5,989	5,539	5,380	4,604	4,231	4,122	5,699	1,910	2,904	1,906
Current Liabilities	2,893	2,209	2,472	1,897	1,880	1,988	3,520	554	1,277	713
Long Term Debt	418	923	546	822	868	871	872	250	250	Nil
Common Equity	2,148	1,976	1,897	1,664	1,369	1,174	1,219	1,062	1,342	999
Total Capital	2,565	2,899	2,443	2,486	2,238	2,045	2,091	1,312	1,591	1,025
Capital Expenditures	251	209	128	151	112	90.0	113	78.8	44.3	165
Cash Flow	682	820	876	742	590	482	399	312	230	215
Current Ratio	1.0	1.4	1.2	1.4	1.2	1.1	1.1	2.0	1.7	1.8
% Long Term Debt of Capitalization	16.3	31.8	22.3	33.1	38.8	42.6	41.7	19.0	15.7	Nil
% Net Income of Revenue	12.4	14.3	16.7	21.4	13.1	9.2	10.3	14.5	13.3	2.5
% Return on Assets	8.5	11.8	13.9	13.1	10.4	5.6	6.6	9.9	7.2	2.6
% Return on Equity	23.9	33.5	39.6	38.2	34.2	23.1	22.1	19.8	14.9	4.7

Data as orig reptd.; bef. results of disc opers/spec. items. Per share data adj. for stk. divs.; EPS diluted. E-Estimated. NA-Not Available. NM-Not Meaningful. NR-Not Ranked. UR-Under Review.

Office: 4400 Main Street, Kansas City, MO 64111-1812.
Telephone: 816-753-6900.
Email: investorrelations@hrblock.com
Website: http://www.hrblock.com

Chrmn, Pres & CEO: M.A. Ernst
EVP & CFO: W. Trubeck
SVP & General Counsel: N.J. Spaeth
SVP & Cntlr: J. Nachbor

VP & Treas: B. Shulman
Investor Contact: S. Dudley (816-932-8342)
Board of Directors: T. M. Bloch, J. D. Choate, D. R. Ecton, M. A. Ernst, H. F. Frigon, R. W. Hale, L. Lauer, D. B. Lewis, T. D. Seip, L. W. Smith, R. Wilkins, Jr

Founded: 1946
Domicile: Missouri
Employees: 134,500

STANDARD &POOR'S

Humana Inc.

S&P Recommendation HOLD ★★★★★	Price	12-Mo. Target Price	Investment Style
	$60.00 (as of Oct 31, 2006)	$71.00	Large-Cap Growth

GICS Sector Health Care
Sub-Industry Managed Health Care

Comment This company provides a broad range of managed health care services to more than 9 million individuals.

Key Stock Statistics (Source S&P, Vickers, company reports)

52-Wk Range	$68.24–41.08	S&P Oper. EPS 2006E	2.86	P/E on S&P Oper. EPS 2006E	21.0	Dividend Rate/Share	Nil
Trailing 12-Month EPS	$2.43	S&P Oper. EPS 2007E	3.90	Common Shares Outstg. (M)	165.1	Yield (%)	Nil
Trailing 12-Month P/E	24.7	S&P Core EPS 2006E	2.86	Market Capitalization(B)	$9.904	Beta	0.57
$10K Invested 5 Yrs Ago	$58,661	S&P Core EPS 2007E	3.90	Institutional Ownership (%)	86	S&P Credit Rating	BBB

Price Performance

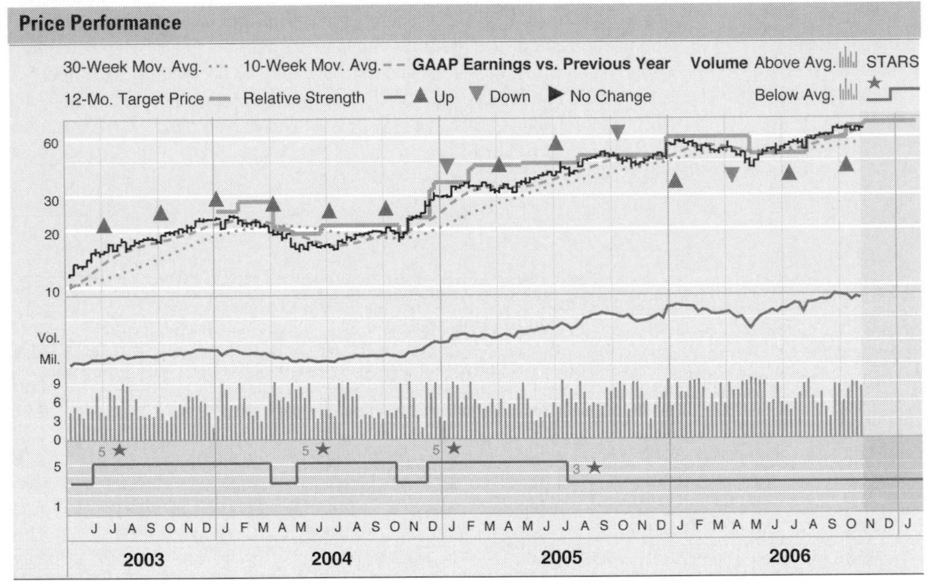

Options: ASE, CBOE, Ph

Highlights

➤ The 12-month target price for HUM has recently been changed to $71.00 from $68.00. The Highlights section of this Stock Report will be updated accordingly.

Investment Rationale/Risk

➤ The Investment Rationale/Risk section of this Stock Report will be updated shortly. For the latest News story on HUM from MarketScope, see below.

➤ 10/30/06 10:42 am EST... S&P MAINTAINS HOLD RECOMMENDATION ON SHARES OF HUMANA (HUM 63.26***): Q3 oper. EPS of $0.95 vs. $0.60 is $0.01 below our estimate. We expect strong '07 gains in its Medicare unit on higher Medicare HMO enrollment, new drug plan members offsetting attrition and drug plan price hikes. We view HUM's Medicare sales capability as a strength, but see competition rising and slower-than-expected conversion of drug plan members to HMOs. We are raising our '07 EPS estimate by $0.55 to $3.90, but cutting our ratio of P/E to growth from 1.2X to peer-level 1.1X, and our 3-year growth estimate to 16.5% from 17%. We are raising our target price by $3 to $71. /P.Seligman

Qualitative Risk Assessment

LOW | **MEDIUM** | HIGH

Our risk assessment reflects HUM's product, market and geographic diversity and its competitive strength in the Medicare market. However, despite HUM being a pioneer in consumer-directed health plans, we believe that intense competition will continue to limit commercial enrollment growth.

Quantitative Evaluations

S&P Quality Ranking B

D | C | B- | **B** | B+ | A- | A | A+

Relative Strength Rank WEAK

17

LOWEST = 1 HIGHEST = 99

Revenue/Earnings Data

Revenue (Million $)

	1Q	2Q	3Q	4Q	Year
2006	4,704	5,407	5,650	--	--
2005	3,887	3,546	3,821	3,663	14,418
2004	3,287	3,431	3,176	3,210	13,104
2003	2,932	3,030	3,112	3,153	12,226
2002	2,733	2,832	2,842	2,855	11,261
2001	2,464	2,497	2,611	2,623	10,195

Earnings Per Share ($)

2006	0.50	0.53	0.95	E0.88	E2.86
2005	0.54	0.51	0.30	0.39	1.87
2004	0.41	0.50	0.52	0.29	1.72
2003	0.19	0.43	0.38	0.41	1.41
2002	0.28	0.27	0.31	Nil	0.85
2001	0.16	0.15	0.18	0.21	0.70

Fiscal year ended Dec. 31. Next earnings report expected: Early February. EPS Estimates based on S&P Operating Earnings; historical GAAP earnings are as reported.

Dividend Data

No cash dividends have been paid since 1993.

Humana Inc.

Business Summary October 10, 2006

CORPORATE OVERVIEW. One of the largest managed care organizations, Humana's medical membership totaled 11,025,500 as of June 30, 2006 (versus 7,075,600 at December 31, 2005).

The Commercial segment consists of members enrolled in products marketed to employer groups and individuals, including fully insured medical (1,893,100 versus 1,999,800), administrative services only (ASO; 1,420,800 versus 1,170,000), and specialty (1,894,900 versus 1,902,100). Health maintenance organizations (HMOs; 17.1% of total premium and fee revenues in 2005) require members to use only doctors in its network and generally reimburse providers on a capitated basis. Preferred provider organizations (PPOs; 25.5%) allow members the option to go to doctors outside of the network, with the members paying a portion of the provider's fees. ASO products (1.4%), which include HMOs, PPOs and consumer-directed health plans, are offered to employers that self-insure their employee health plans. Specialty products (2.7%) include dental, group and individual life, and short-term disability.

The Government segment consists of Medicare Advantage (MA; HMO: 457,000 versus 427,900; PPO: 64,500 versus 8,600; private-fee-for-service, or PFFS, 438,200 versus 121,300); Medicare Prescription Drug Program (Medicare PDP, as of June 30, 2006, only; Standard: 2,066,500, Enhanced: 977,200, Complete: 415,100); Medicaid (418,500 versus 457,900), and the Department of Defense health program, TRICARE (fully insured: 1,732,600 versus 1,750,900; administrative services: 1,141,900 versus 1,138,200).

In 2005, MA revenues were $4.6 billion (32.2%). Florida contracts covered approximately 295,400 members and accounted for premium revenues of $2.8 billion (60.9% of MA premium revenues, or 19.9% of the total). As of January 1, 2006, MA plans included 12 local HMOs, 12 local PPOs, a regional PPO in 23 states, and private fee-for-service (PFFS) programs in 35 states, and HUM offered the Medicare Prescription Drug Program in 46 states. (Reflecting, we believe, Medicare's increasing importance to Humana's business, in the six months ended June 30, 2006, MA accounted for 39.1% of total premium and revenues and Medicare - standalone PDP members accounted for 13.5%.)

The Medicaid business (3.8%) has contracts in Puerto Rico, Florida and Illinois.

HUM's current TRICARE South Region contract (fully insured: 16.9%; administrative services fees: 0.4%) covers beneficiaries in 10 states.

Company Financials

Per Share Data ($) Year Ended Dec. 31	2005	2004	2003	2002	2001	2000	1999	1998	1997	1996
Tangible Book Value	7.41	7.52	6.54	5.09	4.33	3.43	2.75	2.98	1.68	4.93
Cash Flow	2.68	2.45	2.20	1.57	1.67	1.42	-1.53	1.53	1.69	0.68
Earnings	1.87	1.72	1.41	0.85	0.70	0.54	-2.28	0.77	1.05	0.07
S&P Core Earnings	1.99	1.55	1.23	0.87	0.63	NA	NA	NA	NA	NA
Dividends	Nil	Nil	Nil	Nil	Nil	Nil	Nil	Nil	Nil	Nil
Payout Ratio	Nil	Nil	Nil	Nil	Nil	Nil	Nil	Nil	Nil	Nil
Prices:High	55.70	31.02	23.39	17.45	15.63	15.81	20.75	32.13	25.31	28.88
Prices:Low	28.82	15.20	8.80	9.78	8.38	4.75	5.88	12.25	17.38	15.00
P/E Ratio:High	30	18	17	21	22	29	NM	42	24	NM
P/E Ratio:Low	15	9	6	12	12	9	NM	16	17	NM
Income Statement Analysis (Million $)										
Revenue	14,418	13,104	12,226	11,261	10,195	10,395	9,959	9,597	7,880	6,677
Operating Income	590	415	489	384	114	171	59.0	228	242	112
Depreciation	129	118	127	121	162	147	124	128	108	98.0
Interest Expense	39.3	23.2	17.4	17.0	25.0	29.0	33.0	47.0	20.0	11.0
Pretax Income	422	416	345	210	183	114	-404	203	270	18.0
Effective Tax Rate	26.9%	32.7%	33.6%	32.0%	36.1%	21.1%	NM	36.5%	35.9%	33.3%
Net Income	308	280	229	143	117	90.0	-382	129	173	12.0
S&P Core Earnings	330	252	200	145	104	NA	NA	NA	NA	NA
Balance Sheet & Other Financial Data (Million $)										
Cash	732	580	931	721	651	2,067	2,485	2,812	627	1,584
Current Assets	4,206	3,596	3,321	2,795	2,623	2,499	3,064	3,119	2,750	2,002
Total Assets	6,870	5,658	5,293	4,600	4,404	4,167	4,900	5,496	5,418	3,153
Current Liabilities	3,220	2,327	2,265	2,390	2,307	2,665	3,164	2,643	2,263	1,500
Long Term Debt	514	637	643	340	315	Nil	324	1,011	1,486	225
Common Equity	2,474	2,090	1,836	1,606	1,508	1,374	1,268	1,688	1,501	1,292
Total Capital	2,988	2,727	2,479	1,946	1,823	1,374	1,592	2,699	2,987	1,517
Capital Expenditures	166	114	101	112	115	135	89.0	104	73.0	72.0
Cash Flow	437	398	356	264	279	237	-258	257	281	110
Current Ratio	1.3	1.5	1.5	1.2	1.1	0.9	1.0	1.2	1.2	1.3
% Long Term Debt of Capitalization	17.2	23.3	25.9	17.5	17.3	Nil	20.4	37.5	49.7	14.8
% Net Income of Revenue	2.1	102.6	1.9	1.3	1.2	0.9	NM	1.3	2.2	0.2
% Return on Assets	4.9	5.1	4.5	3.2	2.7	2.0	NM	2.4	4.0	0.4
% Return on Equity	13.5	14.3	13.3	9.2	8.2	6.8	NM	8.1	12.4	1.0

Data as orig reptd.; bef. results of disc opers/spec. items. Per share data adj. for stk. divs.; EPS diluted. E-Estimated. NA-Not Available. NM-Not Meaningful. NR-Not Ranked. UR-Under Review.

Office: 500 West Main Street, Louisville, KY 40202-4268.
Telephone: 502-580-1000.
Website: http://www.humana.com
Chrmn: D.A. Jones, Jr.

Pres & CEO: M.B. McCallister
COO: J.E. Murray
SVP, CFO & Treas: J.H. Bloem
SVP & General Counsel: A.P. Hipwell

Investor Contact: T. Noland (502-580-3674)
Board of Directors: F. A. D'Amelio, W. R. Dunbar, K. J. Hilzinger, D. A. Jones, Jr., M. B. McCallister, J. J. O'Brien, W. A. Reynolds, J. O. Robbins

Founded: 1964
Domicile: Delaware
Employees: 18,700

STANDARD &POOR'S

Huntington Bancshares Inc

S&P Recommendation HOLD ★★★★★ | **Price** $24.23 (as of Oct 27, 2006) | **12-Mo. Target Price** $25.00 | **Investment Style** Mid-Cap Value

GICS Sector Financials
Sub-Industry Regional Banks

Comment This $33 billion regional bank holding company has a network of branches throughout the Midwest.

Key Stock Statistics (Source S&P, Vickers, company reports)

52-Wk Range	$24.82–22.56	S&P Oper. EPS 2006E	1.84	P/E on S&P Oper. EPS 2006E	13.2	Dividend Rate/Share	$1.00
Trailing 12-Month EPS	$2.00	S&P Oper. EPS 2007E	1.92	Common Shares Outstg. (M)	237.5	Yield (%)	4.13
Trailing 12-Month P/E	12.1	S&P Core EPS 2006E	1.83	Market Capitalization(B)	$5.755	Beta	0.43
$10K Invested 5 Yrs Ago	$17,846	S&P Core EPS 2007E	1.90	Institutional Ownership (%)	42	S&P Credit Rating	BBB+

Price Performance

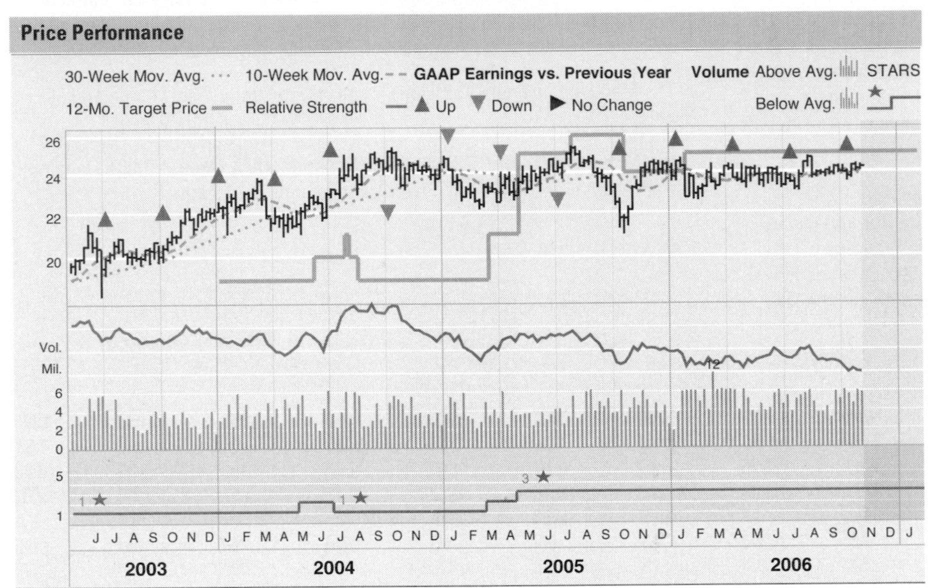

Options: CBOE, Ph

Analysis prepared by **Mark Hebeka, CFA** on August 08, 2006, when the stock traded at **$ 24.50**.

Highlights

- HBAN's net interest margin has remained relatively stable throughout the past several quarters, despite continued increases in short-term rates and a flat yield curve, due, in our opinion, to solid growth in loans (over 50% of which are variable rate) and deposits as well as decreases in its lower-yielding securities portfolio. Based on our expectations for moderate growth in average earning assets and stable to slightly improving margins, we forecast that HBAN's net interest income will increase in the mid-single digits in 2006.
- For 2006, we see strong growth in trust services, reflecting more assets under management, and moderately higher brokerage and insurance income and other service fees. As operating lease costs and regulatory-related expenses decline, we see continued operating leverage aiding earnings, leading to improvements in efficiency ratios.
- Taking into account expected share repurchase activity, we forecast operating EPS of $1.84 in 2006 and $1.92 in 2007.

Investment Rationale/Risk

- We view positively HBAN's loan portfolio, over 50% of which is comprised of variable rate commercial and consumer loans, as well as its shorter-duration securities portfolio and high base of low-cost deposits, all of which we believe have contributed to relatively stable net interest margins. We also think that once the run-off of its operating lease portfolio is complete, HBAN's efficiency ratios will improve.
- Risks to our recommendation and target price include a flatter-than-expected yield curve, integration risk related to pending acquisitions, and corporate governance issues regarding compensation and ownership. We are also concerned about potential asset quality issues, given our view of HBAN's somewhat lackluster markets in the Midwest, as well as the company's relatively high proportion of borrowings as a funding source.
- Our 12-month target price of $25 represents a P/E multiple of about 13X, in line with the peer group of Midwestern banks, applied to our 2007 EPS estimate.

Qualitative Risk Assessment

LOW | MEDIUM | HIGH

Our risk assessment reflects what we see as solid business fundamentals and a strong customer base. We view HBAN as well diversified and able to withstand a major economic downturn.

Quantitative Evaluations

S&P Quality Ranking B+

D | C | B- | B | **B+** | A- | A | A+

Relative Strength Rank MODERATE

39

LOWEST = 1 HIGHEST = 99

Revenue/Earnings Data

Revenue (Million $)

	1Q	2Q	3Q	4Q	Year
2006	624.3	684.9	--	--	--
2005	544.2	558.5	581.6	589.8	2,274
2004	553.6	542.3	527.9	542.2	2,166
2003	599.6	604.7	606.1	564.6	2,375
2002	695.0	491.8	522.7	506.9	2,216
2001	635.7	627.2	609.3	576.9	2,449

Earnings Per Share ($)

	1Q	2Q	3Q	4Q	Year
2006	0.45	0.46	0.65	**E**0.47	**E**1.84
2005	0.41	0.45	0.47	0.44	1.77
2004	0.45	0.47	0.40	0.39	1.71
2003	0.39	0.42	0.45	0.40	1.67
2002	0.39	0.33	0.41	0.36	1.49
2001	0.27	0.01	0.17	0.26	0.71

Fiscal year ended Dec. 31. Next earnings report expected: Mid January. EPS Estimates based on S&P Operating Earnings; historical GAAP earnings are as reported.

Dividend Data (Dates: mm/dd Payment Date: mm/dd/yy)

Amount ($)	Date Decl.	Ex-Div. Date	Stk. of Record	Payment Date
0.250	01/18	03/15	03/17	04/03/06
0.250	04/20	06/14	06/16	07/03/06
0.250	07/18	09/13	09/15	10/02/06
0.250	10/17	12/13	12/15	01/02/07

Dividends have been paid since 1912. Source: Company reports.

Huntington Bancshares Inc

Business Summary August 08, 2006

CORPORATE OVERVIEW. Huntington Bancshares Inc. (HBAN) is a multi-state diversified financial holding company focused on the Midwest region of the United States. It provides full-service commercial and consumer banking services, mortgage banking services, automobile financing, equipment leasing, investment management, trust services, and brokerage services. The company also offers insurance services, including reinsurance of private mortgages, credit life and disability insurance, and other products.

On March 1, 2006, Unizan Financial Corp. (UNIZ) was merged into HBAN. UNIZ shareholders were entitled to receive 1.1424 shares of HBAN common stock for each share of UNIZ held. The deal added 42 offices, 48 automated teller machines (ATMs), $2.5 billion in total assets, $1.7 billion in loans, and $1.8 billion in deposits. Furthermore, the combination added leading positions in Muskingum and Stark counties in Ohio, increased market share in the Dayton and Columbus areas, and created a new Eastern Ohio region.

The company has one banking subsidiary and several non-bank subsidiaries. As of December 2005, the Huntington Bank subsidiary had 165 banking offices in Ohio, 113 in Michigan, 26 in West Virginia, 23 in Indiana, and 12 in Kentucky. The company also had five private banking offices in Florida, and two foreign offices in the Cayman Islands and Hong Kong. Including all its other offices, HBAN has 380 locations with 998 ATMs at the end of 2005.

CORPORATE STRATEGY. Since 2001, the bank has focused on operations in the Midwest. It has sought to strengthen its leadership team and has decentralized each office's decision-making ability, adopting the "local bank with national resources" model. The bank continues to invest in its systems and front-line technology. All told, we believe Huntington has improved its portfolio mix, reducing exposure to higher risk loans and increasing the level of low-risk loans. It lowered its exposure in auto lending to 18% in 2005, from 33% in 2001, and reduced its non-performing assets and net charge-off ratios to historically low levels.

Company Financials

Per Share Data ($) Year Ended Dec. 31	2005	2004	2003	2002	2001	2000	1999	1998	1997	1996
Tangible Book Value	11.41	10.02	8.99	8.95	6.77	9.43	8.66	8.43	7.93	7.24
Earnings	1.77	1.71	1.67	1.49	0.71	1.32	1.65	1.17	1.14	1.23
S&P Core Earnings	1.73	1.66	1.56	0.67	0.60	NA	NA	NA	NA	NA
Dividends	0.85	0.75	0.67	0.64	0.72	0.74	0.68	0.62	0.57	0.52
Payout Ratio	48%	44%	40%	43%	101%	56%	41%	53%	50%	42%
Prices:High	25.41	25.38	22.55	21.77	19.28	21.82	30.89	28.55	29.21	19.72
Prices:Low	20.97	20.89	17.78	16.00	12.63	12.52	19.49	18.18	17.08	13.97
P/E Ratio:High	14	15	14	15	27	17	19	25	26	16
P/E Ratio:Low	12	12	11	11	18	9	12	16	15	11
Income Statement Analysis (Million $)										
Net Interest Income	962	911	849	984	996	942	1,042	1,021	1,027	759
Tax Equivalent Adjustment	NA	NA	9.68	5.21	6.35	8.31	9.42	10.3	11.9	5.10
Non Interest Income	640	803	1,064	680	509	494	561	408	335	255
Loan Loss Provision	81.3	55.1	164	227	309	90.5	88.4	105	108	65.0
% Expense/Operating Revenue	60.5%	65.5%	64.3%	50.6%	67.4%	61.7%	56.6%	63.9%	59.0%	55.7%
Pretax Income	544	553	524	589	173	460	615	440	459	399
Effective Tax Rate	24.2%	27.8%	26.4%	38.4%	NM	28.6%	31.3%	31.4%	36.3%	34.3%
Net Income	412	399	386	363	179	328	422	302	293	262
% Net Interest Margin	3.33	3.33	3.49	4.19	4.02	3.73	4.11	4.28	4.44	4.11
S&P Core Earnings	405	388	360	165	152	NA	NA	NA	NA	NA
Balance Sheet & Other Financial Data (Million $)										
Money Market Assets	105	960	138	86.6	118	143	28.9	243	556	12.0
Investment Securities	4,527	4,239	4,929	3,411	2,862	4,107	4,889	4,806	5,743	4,804
Commercial Loans	10,845	10,303	9,486	9,336	10,415	8,887	8,452	6,027	5,271	4,463
Other Loans	13,627	13,257	11,590	11,619	11,187	11,723	12,216	13,428	12,468	9,798
Total Assets	32,765	32,565	30,484	27,579	28,500	28,599	29,037	28,296	26,731	20,852
Demand Deposits	3,390	3,392	2,987	3,074	3,741	3,505	7,594	7,771	2,550	5,050
Time Deposits	19,020	17,376	15,500	14,425	16,446	16,272	11,613	11,951	3,768	8,336
Long Term Debt	4,597	6,227	6,808	3,304	3,039	3,338	4,269	3,247	2,886	1,556
Common Equity	2,594	2,538	2,275	2,304	2,416	2,366	2,182	2,149	2,025	1,512
% Return on Assets	1.3	1.3	1.3	1.3	0.6	1.1	1.5	1.1	1.2	1.3
% Return on Equity	16.0	16.6	17.3	15.4	7.5	14.4	19.5	14.5	16.5	17.3
% Loan Loss Reserve	-0.7	1.1	1.6	1.7	1.8	1.4	-1.4	1.5	1.5	1.4
% Loans/Deposits	171.3	114.5	115.2	122.8	110.1	105.0	NA	98.6	98.6	106.5
% Equity to Assets	7.9	7.6	7.7	8.4	8.4	7.9	7.6	7.6	7.4	7.4

Data as orig reptd.; bef. results of disc opers/spec. items. Per share data adj. for stk. divs.; EPS diluted. E-Estimated. NA-Not Available. NM-Not Meaningful. NR-Not Ranked. UR-Under Review.

Office: Huntington Center, Columbus, OH 43287.
Telephone: 614-480-8300.
Website: http://www.huntington.com
Chrmn, Pres & CEO: T.E. Hoaglin

Vice Chrmn: R. Baldwin
Investor Contact: M.J. McMennamin (614-480-5676)
Sr EVP: D. Benhase
Sr EVP: N. Stanhutz

Board of Directors: R. Biggs, D. M. Casto, III, M. J. Endres, J. B. Gerlach, Jr., T. E. Hoaglin, K. A. Holbrook, D. P. Lauer, W. J. Lhota, G. E. Little, D. L. Porteous, K. H. Ransier

Founded: 1966
Domicile: Maryland
Employees: 7,602

STANDARD &POOR'S

Illinois Tool Works Inc.

S&P Recommendation HOLD ★★★★★

Price $47.03 (as of Oct 27, 2006)

12-Mo. Target Price $50.00

Investment Style Large-Cap Growth

GICS Sector Industrials
Sub-Industry Industrial Machinery

Comment This diversified manufacturer operates a portfolio of about 700 industrial and consumer businesses located throughout the world.

Key Stock Statistics (Source S&P, Vickers, company reports)

52-Wk Range	**$53.54–41.54**	S&P Oper. EPS 2006**E**	**3.03**	P/E on S&P Oper. EPS 2006**E**	**15.5**	Dividend Rate/Share	**$0.84**
Trailing 12-Month EPS	**$2.95**	S&P Oper. EPS 2007**E**	**3.30**	Common Shares Outstg. (M)	**567.9**	Yield (%)	**1.79**
Trailing 12-Month P/E	**15.9**	S&P Core EPS 2006**E**	**3.01**	Market Capitalization(B)	**$26.708**	Beta	**0.89**
$10K Invested 5 Yrs Ago	**$16,496**	S&P Core EPS 2007**E**	**3.28**	Institutional Ownership (%)	**80**	S&P Credit Rating	**AA**

Price Performance

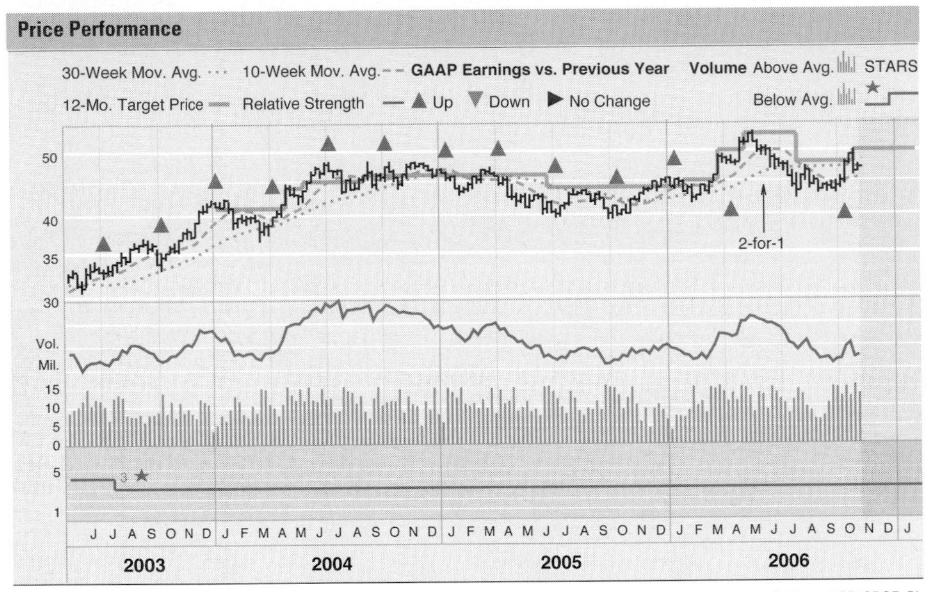

Options: ASE, CBOE, Ph

Analysis prepared by **Anthony M. Fiore, CFA** on October 19, 2006, when the stock traded at **$ 47.22**.

Highlights

- We see revenues increasing 6% to 8% in 2007, following a projected advance of about 9% in 2006, driven by contributions from acquisitions, combined with an expected improvement in North America commercial construction and industrial activity in many of the company's international end markets. We foresee these drivers outweighing what we view as deteriorating end-market conditions in the North American auto and residential housing sectors.

- We expect a modest expansion in operating margins in 2007, due to projected benefits from ongoing cost-cutting measures, combined with a modest improvement in volumes. In addition, we see EPS benefiting from a lower anticipated share count in 2007, as we believe the company will likely continue its share repurchase program.

- Our Standard & Poor's Core EPS estimates for 2006 and 2007 are each $0.02 below our respective operating EPS forecasts, with the differences reflecting projected pension and post-retirement related cost adjustments. Our 2006 and 2007 S&P Core EPS and operating EPS estimates each include $0.06 of projected stock option expense.

Investment Rationale/Risk

- While we expect contributions from acquisitions, share repurchases, and favorable conditions in many of ITW's end markets to continue over the next 12 months, we believe that our outlook is largely reflected in the price of the stock.

- Risks to our recommendation and target price include an unexpected downturn in industrial activity and/or capital spending; execution risk associated with acquisitions; continued escalation of raw material costs; and a greater than anticipated slowing of the residential housing and/or automotive markets.

- Our discounted cash flow model, which assumes an 8% average annual free cash flow growth rate over the next 10 years, 3.5% growth in perpetuity, and an 8% weighted average cost of capital, indicates intrinsic value of about $49. In terms of relative valuation, applying a target P/E multiple of about 15X, in line with historical norms, to our 2007 EPS estimate of $3.30, suggests a value of about $50 a share. We arrive at our 12-month target price of $50 using a weighted blend of these valuation metrics.

Qualitative Risk Assessment

LOW	MEDIUM	HIGH

Our risk assessment reflects an S&P Earnings & Dividend Rank of A+ for ITW, a balance sheet we see as strong with a relatively low amount of debt, and free cash flow that has averaged about 97% of net income over the past 10 years.

Quantitative Evaluations

S&P Quality Ranking **A+**

D	C	B-	B	B+	A-	A	A+

Relative Strength Rank **MODERATE**

46

LOWEST = 1 HIGHEST = 99

Revenue/Earnings Data

Revenue (Million $)

	1Q	2Q	3Q	4Q	Year
2006	3,297	3,579	3,538	--	--
2005	3,074	3,296	3,258	3,294	12,922
2004	2,710	3,002	2,967	3,052	11,731
2003	2,314	2,564	2,532	2,626	10,036
2002	2,205	2,435	2,401	2,427	9,468
2001	2,296	2,420	2,301	2,278	9,293

Earnings Per Share ($)

2006	0.65	**E**0.81	0.78	**E**0.79	**E**3.03
2005	0.53	0.65	0.72	0.71	2.60
2004	0.47	0.58	0.55	0.61	2.20
2003	0.33	0.46	0.44	0.47	1.69
2002	0.32	0.43	0.40	0.37	1.51
2001	0.30	0.38	0.33	0.31	1.31

Fiscal year ended Dec. 31. Next earnings report expected: Late January. EPS Estimates based on S&P Operating Earnings; historical GAAP earnings are as reported.

Dividend Data (Dates: mm/dd Payment Date: mm/dd/yy)

Amount ($)	Date Decl.	Ex-Div. Date	Stk. of Record	Payment Date
2-for-1 Stk.	03/06	05/26	05/18	05/25/06
0.330	05/05	06/28	06/30	07/17/06
0.210	08/04	09/27	09/30	10/16/06
0.210	10/27	12/27	12/31	01/22/07

Dividends have been paid since 1933. Source: Company reports.

Illinois Tool Works Inc.

Business Summary October 19, 2006

CORPORATE OVERVIEW. ITW operates about 700 small industrial businesses in a highly decentralized structure that places responsibility on managers at the lowest level possible, in order to focus each business unit on the needs of its particular customers. Each business unit manager is responsible, and is held strictly accountable, for the results of his or her individual business.

ITW is diversified not only by customer and industry, but also by geographic region, with about 40% of revenues derived overseas.

The Specialty Systems segment (49% of revenues in 2005, and 50% of operating income; 16% operating profit margins) produces longer lead time systems and related consumables for consumer and industrial packaging; marking, labeling and identification systems; welding equipment and metal consumables, industrial spray coating equipment and systems; and quality assurance equipment and systems. Important markets are food retail and service, general industrial, food and beverage, construction, and industrial capital goods. International sales and profits accounted for 38% and 28% of 2005 Specialty Systems revenues and earnings, respectively.

The Engineered Products segment (51%, 50%; 16% operating profit margins in 2005) produces short lead time plastic and metal components, fasteners and assemblies, industrial fluids and adhesives, fastening tools, and welding products. The largest markets served are construction, automotive, general industrial, consumer durables and electronics. International sales and profits accounted for 42% and 38% of 2005 Engineered Products revenues and earnings, respectively.

In late 2001, ITW classified its Consumer Products (CP) division as discontinued. The segment was made up of companies that make small electric appliances, physical fitness equipment, and ceramic tile.

Company Financials

Per Share Data ($) Year Ended Dec. 31	2005	2004	2003	2002	2001	2000	1999	1998	1997	1996
Tangible Book Value	6.89	7.59	8.22	6.90	5.42	4.82	4.64	4.30	4.07	3.40
Cash Flow	3.26	2.78	2.18	2.01	1.94	2.25	1.94	1.75	1.54	1.34
Earnings	2.60	2.20	1.69	1.51	1.31	1.58	1.38	1.34	1.17	0.98
S&P Core Earnings	2.60	2.13	1.63	1.38	1.13	NA	NA	NA	NA	NA
Dividends	0.61	0.52	0.47	0.45	0.42	0.38	0.34	0.26	0.23	0.18
Payout Ratio	23%	24%	28%	30%	32%	24%	25%	19%	20%	18%
Prices:High	47.32	48.35	42.35	38.90	36.00	34.50	41.00	36.59	30.06	21.81
Prices:Low	39.25	36.46	27.28	27.52	24.58	24.75	29.06	22.59	18.69	12.97
P/E Ratio:High	18	22	25	26	27	22	30	27	26	22
P/E Ratio:Low	15	17	16	18	19	16	21	17	16	13

Income Statement Analysis (Million $)	2005	2004	2003	2002	2001	2000	1999	1998	1997	1996
Revenue	12,922	11,731	10,036	9,468	9,293	9,984	9,333	5,648	5,220	4,997
Operating Income	2,558	2,410	1,940	1,812	1,692	1,977	1,830	1,291	1,113	979
Depreciation	383	353	307	306	386	413	343	212	185	178
Interest Expense	87.0	69.2	70.7	68.5	68.1	72.4	67.5	14.2	19.4	27.8
Pretax Income	2,182	1,999	1,576	1,434	1,231	1,478	1,353	1,060	924	770
Effective Tax Rate	31.5%	33.0%	34.0%	35.0%	34.8%	35.2%	37.8%	36.5%	36.5%	36.8%
Net Income	1,495	1,340	1,040	932	802	958	841	673	587	486
S&P Core Earnings	1,493	1,299	1,009	851	691	NA	NA	NA	NA	NA

Balance Sheet & Other Financial Data (Million $)	2005	2004	2003	2002	2001	2000	1999	1998	1997	1996
Cash	370	667	1,684	1,058	282	151	233	93.5	186	138
Current Assets	4,112	4,322	4,783	3,879	3,163	3,329	3,273	1,834	1,859	1,701
Total Assets	11,446	11,352	11,193	10,623	9,822	9,603	9,060	6,118	5,395	4,806
Current Liabilities	2,001	1,851	1,489	1,567	1,518	1,818	2,045	1,222	1,158	1,219
Long Term Debt	958	921	920	1,460	1,267	1,549	1,361	947	854	819
Common Equity	7,547	7,628	7,874	6,649	6,041	5,401	4,815	3,338	2,806	2,396
Total Capital	8,505	8,549	8,795	8,109	7,308	6,950	6,176	4,285	3,660	3,215
Capital Expenditures	293	283	258	271	257	314	336	208	179	169
Cash Flow	1,878	1,693	1,347	1,238	1,189	1,371	1,184	885	772	665
Current Ratio	2.1	2.3	3.2	2.5	2.1	1.8	1.6	1.5	1.6	1.4
% Long Term Debt of Capitalization	11.3	10.8	10.5	18.0	17.3	22.3	22.0	22.1	23.3	25.4
% Net Income of Revenue	11.6	11.4	10.4	9.8	8.6	9.6	9.0	11.9	11.3	9.7
% Return on Assets	13.1	11.9	9.5	9.1	8.3	10.3	9.7	11.7	11.5	11.6
% Return on Equity	19.7	17.3	14.3	14.7	14.0	18.8	18.6	21.9	22.6	22.5

Data as orig reptd.; bef. results of disc opers/spec. items. Per share data adj. for stk. divs.; EPS diluted. E-Estimated. NA-Not Available. NM-Not Meaningful. NR-Not Ranked. UR-Under Review.

Office: 3600 W. Lake Avenue, Glenview, IL 60026-1215.
Telephone: 847-724-7500.
Website: http://www.itwinc.com
Chrmn & CEO: D.B. Speer

VP, Secy & General Counsel: J.H. Wooten, Jr.
Investor Contact: J. Brooklier (847-657-4104)

Board of Directors: W. F. Aldinger, M. J. Birck, M. D. Brailsford, S. Crown, D. H. Davis, Jr., R. C. McCormack, R. S. Morrison, J. A. Skinner, H. B. Smith, D. B. Speer

Founded: 1912
Domicile: Delaware
Employees: 50,000

STANDARD &POOR'S

IMS Health Inc

S&P Recommendation HOLD ★★★★★	Price	12-Mo. Target Price	Investment Style
	$27.30 (as of Oct 27, 2006)	$28.00	Mid-Cap Growth

GICS Sector Health Care
Sub-Industry Health Care Technology

Comment IMS provides information solutions to the health care sector. In November 2005, IMS's agreement to be acquired by Dutch media group VNU N.V. was terminated.

Key Stock Statistics (Source S&P, Vickers, company reports)

52-Wk Range	$28.00–22.73	S&P Oper. EPS 2006E	1.40	P/E on S&P Oper. EPS 2006E	19.5	Dividend Rate/Share	$0.12
Trailing 12-Month EPS	$1.58	S&P Oper. EPS 2007E	1.55	Common Shares Outstg. (M)	201.5	Yield (%)	0.44
Trailing 12-Month P/E	17.3	S&P Core EPS 2006E	1.38	Market Capitalization(B)	$5.501	Beta	0.91
$10K Invested 5 Yrs Ago	$12,009	S&P Core EPS 2007E	1.52	Institutional Ownership (%)	87	S&P Credit Rating	NA

Price Performance

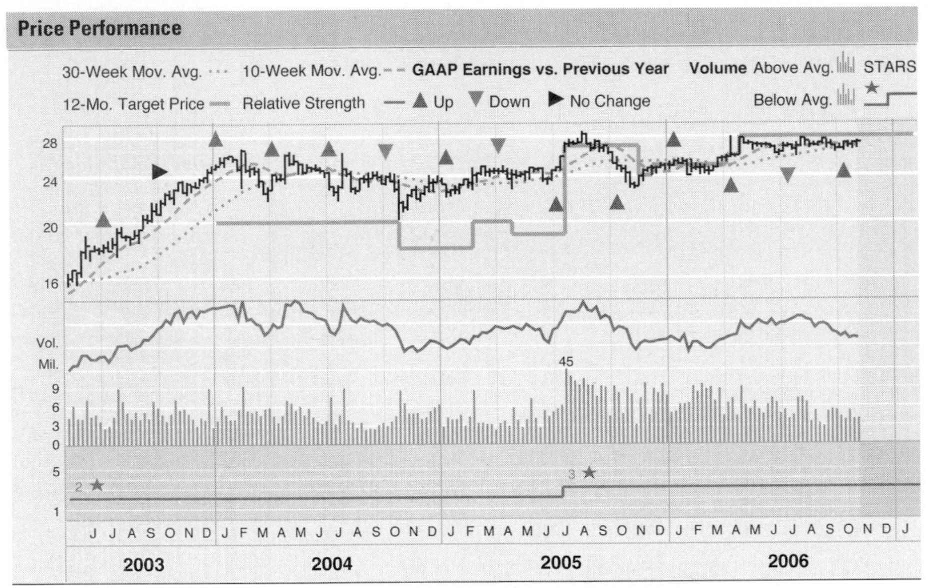

Options: ASE

Analysis prepared by **Michael W. Jaffe** on September 07, 2006, when the stock traded at **$ 26.69**.

Highlights

- We expect RX's revenues to increase 10% in 2006, followed by another 10% gain in 2007. We base that forecast on our outlook for a pickup in demand, plus RX's expansion efforts. We also think RX's aggressive program of new product introductions will aid revenues, despite somewhat slower than historical industry conditions, and that the company will gain market share in both years. In addition, we see revenues in 2006 being lifted somewhat by RX's full-year inclusion of several recent small acquisitions.
- We project relatively flat comparable operating margins in both 2006 and 2007. We expect margins to be aided by the pickup in demand that we forecast for RX's services, together with cost-cutting initiatives. We see those factors being offset by new product introduction costs and lower margins associated with acquisitions until they are completely integrated. We also think first quarter 2006 share repurchases will be accretive to EPS by $0.05.
- Our EPS estimates include $0.13 of forecast stock option expense in 2006 and 2007; stock option expense of $0.11 was excluded from 2005 EPS. Our 2006 forecast excludes $0.21 of net credits recorded in the first half.

Investment Rationale/Risk

- We believe IMS Health has been facing challenging business trends in its client base, as sales growth has slowed at many pharmaceutical companies in recent years. However, we have a favorable view of RX's ongoing efforts to design new products that should better enable its clients to prosper during difficult times. Based on these factors and valuation considerations, we believe the shares are near an appropriate valuation.
- Risks to our recommendation and target price include weaker than anticipated conditions in the health care and pharmaceutical markets served by RX, and a resultant weakening in demand for information and decision support services in these areas.
- The shares recently traded at about 18X our 2007 EPS forecast, a premium to the S&P 500, but at the low end of RX's historical norm. Based on our belief that RX will face challenging industry conditions for some time, but still manage to record moderate EPS growth, we think the stock is currently near an appropriate valuation. Our 12-month target price is $28.

Qualitative Risk Assessment

LOW | **MEDIUM** | HIGH

Our risk assessment reflects our view of RX's usually solid levels of free cash flow. However, we see that factor offset by the company's relatively high level of debt leverage and income statements that typically have numerous one-time items. We think that the latter factor raises questions about earnings quality.

Quantitative Evaluations

S&P Quality Ranking B+

D | C | B- | B | **B+** | A- | A | A+

Relative Strength Rank MODERATE

41

LOWEST = 1 HIGHEST = 99

Revenue/Earnings Data

Revenue (Million $)

	1Q	2Q	3Q	4Q	Year
2006	446.2	486.2	482.7	--	--
2005	411.0	433.3	432.8	477.7	1,755
2004	361.6	379.6	384.2	443.7	1,569
2003	313.9	337.8	346.0	384.1	1,382
2002	331.6	353.1	361.8	381.9	1,428
2001	329.6	334.4	328.1	340.9	1,333

Earnings Per Share ($)

2006	0.56	0.30	0.34	E0.39	E1.40
2005	0.13	0.41	0.30	0.38	1.22
2004	0.34	0.27	0.28	0.32	1.20
2003	-0.20	0.23	0.29	0.28	0.56
2002	0.20	0.21	0.29	0.22	0.93
2001	0.22	0.21	0.14	-0.11	0.46

Fiscal year ended Dec. 31. Next earnings report expected: Late January. EPS Estimates based on S&P Operating Earnings; historical GAAP earnings are as reported.

Dividend Data (Dates: mm/dd Payment Date: mm/dd/yy)

Amount ($)	Date Decl.	Ex-Div. Date	Stk. of Record	Payment Date
0.030	02/16	02/28	03/02	03/30/06
0.030	04/18	04/28	05/02	06/09/06
0.030	07/18	07/28	08/01	09/08/06
0.030	10/17	10/27	10/31	12/08/06

Dividends have been paid since 1997. Source: Company reports.

IMS Health Inc

Business Summary September 07, 2006

IMS Health provides information solutions to the pharmaceutical and health care industries, with operations in more than 100 countries (56% of revenues in 2005 from foreign operations). In November 2005, the company's planned agreement to be acquired by VNU N.V., a global information and media company, was mutually terminated. The cash and stock deal, valued at $7.0 billion at the time it was announced, was called off because of opposition from a group of major VNU shareholders.

IMS provides information and decision support services to the pharmaceutical and health care industries worldwide, including offerings in the areas of salesforce effectiveness (48% of revenues in 2005), portfolio optimization (29%), and launch, brand management and other (23%). During the first quarter of 2005, RX started to incorporate revenues from its consulting and services operations into its business lines.

The company's salesforce effectiveness services are used principally by pharmaceutical manufacturers to measure, forecast and optimize the effectiveness and efficiency of sales representatives, and to focus on sales and marketing efforts. They include sales territory and prescription tracking reports.

RX's principal portfolio optimization services consist of multinational integrated analytical tools, and syndicated pharmaceutical, medical and prescription audits. Clients use these services for strategic purposes, which include the identification of the optimum mix of products in their portfolios and pipelines, and the determination of which therapy classes to enter, which products to develop and license, and how to create the right marketing mix and identify the most promising acquisition targets.

In the area of launch, brand management and other services, RX's offerings combine information, analytical tools, services and expertise to address client needs relevant to each stage in the life of a pharmaceutical product. The areas covered include brand planning, pricing and market access, promotion management, and performance management.

Company Financials

Per Share Data ($) Year Ended Dec. 31	2005	2004	2003	2002	2001	2000	1999	1998	1997	1996
Tangible Book Value	NM	NM	NM	0.13	0.24	NM	0.51	1.45	2.21	1.84
Cash Flow	1.67	1.65	0.87	1.14	0.69	0.69	1.10	0.82	1.28	0.97
Earnings	1.22	1.20	0.56	0.93	0.46	0.39	0.78	0.53	1.40	0.75
S&P Core Earnings	1.09	0.95	0.47	0.82	0.52	NA	NA	NA	NA	NA
Dividends	0.08	0.08	0.08	0.08	0.08	0.08	0.08	0.06	0.06	Nil
Payout Ratio	7%	7%	14%	9%	17%	21%	10%	11%	4%	Nil
Prices:High	28.60	26.80	25.07	22.59	30.50	28.69	39.19	38.46	22.75	19.00
Prices:Low	22.01	20.16	13.68	12.90	17.30	14.25	21.50	21.34	14.00	15.25
P/E Ratio:High	23	22	45	24	66	74	50	73	16	26
P/E Ratio:Low	18	17	24	14	38	37	28	40	10	21

Income Statement Analysis (Million $)	2005	2004	2003	2002	2001	2000	1999	1998	1997	1996
Revenue	1,755	1,569	1,382	1,428	1,333	1,424	1,398	1,187	1,418	1,731
Operating Income	543	517	437	510	494	459	439	310	453	477
Depreciation	105	93.5	75.1	61.8	69.2	92.0	100	96.4	117	134
Interest Expense	22.7	19.5	15.4	14.4	18.1	17.6	7.59	1.17	2.29	1.34
Pretax Income	454	415	305	397	177	257	152	271	430	349
Effective Tax Rate	37.5%	31.2%	54.4%	32.9%	21.7%	54.7%	NM	34.1%	27.4%	44.0%
Net Income	284	285	139	266	138	116	250	178	312	195
S&P Core Earnings	252	226	116	236	155	NA	NA	NA	NA	NA

Balance Sheet & Other Financial Data (Million $)	2005	2004	2003	2002	2001	2000	1999	1998	1997	1996
Cash	363	460	385	415	268	119	116	206	318	429
Current Assets	821	937	779	827	657	569	607	634	694	994
Total Assets	1,973	1,891	1,644	1,619	1,368	1,243	1,451	1,732	1,580	1,875
Current Liabilities	549	554	837	679	635	827	723	550	441	680
Long Term Debt	611	627	152	325	150	Nil	Nil	Nil	Nil	Nil
Common Equity	415	256	190	222	218	147	494	825	802	873
Total Capital	1,126	984	443	727	513	282	619	972	915	978
Capital Expenditures	52.0	22.5	23.7	44.4	34.3	33.4	33.0	30.9	72.0	75.0
Cash Flow	389	379	214	328	208	208	351	275	430	329
Current Ratio	1.5	1.7	0.9	1.2	1.0	0.7	0.8	1.2	1.6	1.5
% Long Term Debt of Capitalization	54.3	63.7	34.3	44.7	29.2	Nil	Nil	Nil	Nil	Nil
% Net Income of Revenue	16.2	18.2	10.1	18.6	10.4	8.2	17.9	15.0	22.0	11.3
% Return on Assets	14.7	16.1	8.5	17.8	10.3	8.7	15.8	11.0	18.1	11.8
% Return on Equity	84.7	128.2	67.6	120.8	86.0	34.7	38.0	21.9	37.3	26.5

Data as orig reptd.; bef. results of disc opers/spec. items. Per share data adj. for stk. divs.; EPS diluted. E-Estimated. NA-Not Available. NM-Not Meaningful. NR-Not Ranked. UR-Under Review.

Office: 1499 Post Road, Fairfield, CT 06824.
Telephone: 203-319-4700.
Website: http://www.imshealth.com
Chrmn, Pres & CEO: D.R. Carlucci

SVP, Secy & General Counsel: R.H. Steinfeld
VP & Treas: J.J. Ford
VP & Cntlr: L.G. Katz
Investor Contact: D. Peck (203-319-4766)

Board of Directors: D. R. Carlucci, C. L. Clemente, J. D. Edwards, K. E. Giusti, J. P. Imlay, Jr., R. J. Kamerschen, H. E. Lockhart, M. B. Puckett, W. C. Van Faasen

Founded: 1998
Domicile: Delaware
Employees: 6,900

STANDARD &POOR'S

Ingersoll-Rand Co Ltd

S&P Recommendation HOLD ★★★★★

Price $37.45 (as of Oct 27, 2006)

12-Mo. Target Price $39.00

Investment Style Large-Cap Value

GICS Sector Industrials
Sub-Industry Industrial Machinery

Comment IR manufactures a wide range of industrial and commercial products, including refrigeration and construction equipment, compact vehicles and security products.

Key Stock Statistics (Source S&P, Vickers, company reports)

52-Wk Range	**$49.00–34.95**	S&P Oper. EPS 2006**E**	**3.35**	P/E on S&P Oper. EPS 2006**E**	**11.2**	Dividend Rate/Share	**$0.72**
Trailing 12-Month EPS	**$3.35**	S&P Oper. EPS 2007**E**	**3.50**	Common Shares Outstg. (M)	**321.7**	Yield (%)	**1.92**
Trailing 12-Month P/E	**11.2**	S&P Core EPS 2006**E**	**3.27**	Market Capitalization(B)	**$12.049**	Beta	**1.43**
$10K Invested 5 Yrs Ago	**$20,032**	S&P Core EPS 2007**E**	**3.41**	Institutional Ownership (%)	**75**	S&P Credit Rating	**NA**

Price Performance

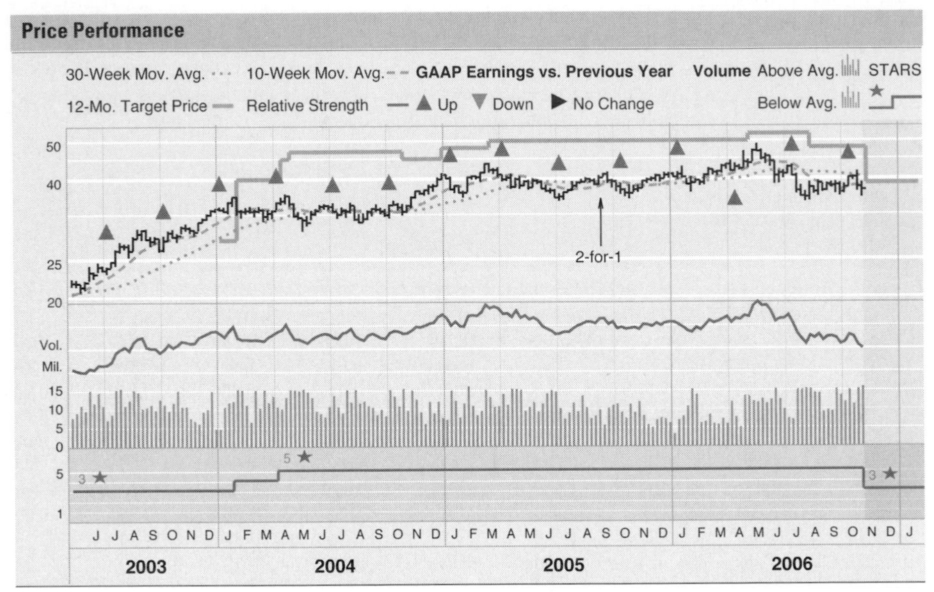

Options: ASE, CBOE, Ph

Highlights

- The STARS recommendation for IR has recently been changed to 3 (hold) from 5 (strong buy) and the 12-month target price has recently been changed to $39.00 from $48.00. The Highlights section of this Stock Report will be updated accordingly.

Investment Rationale/Risk

- The Investment Rationale/Risk section of this Stock Report will be updated shortly. For the latest News story on IR from MarketScope, see below.

- 10/27/06 09:16 am EDT... S&P DOWNGRADES SHARES OF INGERSOLL-RAND TO HOLD FROM STRONG BUY (IR 38.9***): Q3 EPS of $0.85 before charges versus $0.75 is $0.01 below our forecast. Profit gains were recorded in all segments except the compact vehicle division, where sales of Bobcat fell over 20% on a sharp drop in North American demand. The shares are set to open lower as IR guides to $0.74-$0.79 Q4 EPS versus our $0.96 estimate. Our '06 EPS estimate falls by $0.20 to $3.35, and '07's by $0.35 to $3.50. We are lowering our target price $9 to $39, or 11X our '07 forecast, closer in line with IR's historical valuation during moderating EPS periods. /M.Jaffe

Qualitative Risk Assessment

LOW | **MEDIUM** | HIGH

Our risk assessment reflects the cyclical nature of several of IR's major end markets, potential for change in status of its current low relative effective tax rate, and acquisition strategy, offset by an expanding recurring revenue base and an S&P Quality Ranking of A, which indicates above-average stability in earnings and dividends growth.

Quantitative Evaluations

S&P Quality Ranking **A**

D | C | B- | B | B+ | A- | **A** | A+

Relative Strength Rank **WEAK**

18

LOWEST = 1 HIGHEST = 99

Revenue/Earnings Data

Revenue (Million $)

	1Q	2Q	3Q	4Q	Year
2006	2,711	3,042	2,766	--	--
2005	2,459	2,760	2,615	2,713	10,547
2004	2,292	2,714	2,368	2,459	9,394
2003	2,182	2,509	2,520	2,666	9,876
2002	2,017	2,666	2,223	2,245	8,951
2001	2,120	2,286	2,383	2,557	9,682

Earnings Per Share ($)

	1Q	2Q	3Q	4Q	Year
2006	0.79	0.97	0.79	**E**0.79	**E**3.35
2005	0.67	0.86	0.75	0.81	3.09
2004	0.47	0.72	0.59	0.64	2.37
2003	0.28	0.45	0.44	0.56	1.72
2002	0.13	0.32	0.26	0.37	1.08
2001	0.16	0.19	0.10	0.29	0.74

Fiscal year ended Dec. 31. Next earnings report expected: Late January. EPS Estimates based on S&P Operating Earnings; historical GAAP earnings are as reported.

Dividend Data (Dates: mm/dd Payment Date: mm/dd/yy)

Amount ($)	Date Decl.	Ex-Div. Date	Stk. of Record	Payment Date
0.160	02/01	02/10	02/14	03/01/06
0.160	04/05	05/12	05/16	06/01/06
0.180	08/02	08/11	08/15	09/01/06
0.180	10/02	11/09	11/13	12/01/06

Dividends have been paid since 1910. Source: Company reports.

Ingersoll-Rand Co Ltd

Business Summary September 18, 2006

CORPORATE OVERVIEW. Ingersoll-Rand traces its roots to the merger of the Ingersoll-Sergeant Drill Co. and the Rand Drill Co. in the early 1870s. The company has since become a leading global provider of climate control equipment, compact vehicles, construction equipment, industrial solutions, and security and safety products. The Climate Control segment (27% of 2005 revenue; 22% of operating profits; 11.0% margin) makes transport temperature control units, HVAC systems, refrigerated display merchandisers, beverage coolers, and walk-in storage coolers and freezers. Its brand names include Hussmann and Thermo-King. Thermo-King is the world's largest maker of commercial refrigeration equipment used in truck trailers, seagoing containers, and railcars. Hussmann is one of the world's largest makers of refrigerated supermarket displays. The Compact Vehicle segment (25%; 29%; 15.5%) manufactures skid-steer loaders, all-wheel steer loaders, compact truck loaders, compact excavators, attachments and golf and utility vehicles. Brands include Bobcat and Club Car. The Construction Technologies division (11%; 7%; 8.9%) manufactures road construction and repair equipment, portable power products, portable light towers and compressors. The Industrial Solutions segment (17%; 16%; 12.9%) provides solutions to enhance customer industrial efficiency in the areas of air solutions, productivity solutions and energy systems, and makes air compressors, fluid products, energy generation systems, and industrial tools. The Security segment (20%; 26%; 18.1%) makes doors and locks for the commercial and do-it-yourself markets, electronic security products, and security and scheduling software. The segment makes products that include Schlage locks, door control hardware, and steel and power-operated doors.

Company Financials

Per Share Data ($) Year Ended Dec. 31	**2005**	**2004**	**2003**	**2002**	**2001**	**2000**	**1999**	**1998**	**1997**	**1996**
Tangible Book Value	1.60	2.54	NM	NM	NM	NM	NM	NM	NM	2.78
Cash Flow	3.66	2.81	2.28	1.68	1.83	2.60	2.46	2.39	1.80	1.74
Earnings	3.09	2.37	1.72	1.08	0.74	1.68	1.65	1.54	1.16	1.11
Dividends	0.57	0.44	0.36	0.34	0.34	0.34	0.32	0.30	0.29	0.26
Payout Ratio	18%	19%	21%	31%	46%	20%	19%	19%	25%	23%
Prices:High	43.96	41.45	34.10	27.20	25.14	28.88	36.91	27.00	23.13	15.88
Prices:Low	35.13	29.52	17.26	14.85	15.20	14.75	22.31	17.00	13.92	11.71
P/E Ratio:High	14	18	20	25	34	17	22	18	20	14
P/E Ratio:Low	11	12	10	14	21	9	14	11	12	11
Income Statement Analysis (Million $)										
Revenue	10,547	9,394	9,876	8,951	9,682	8,798	7,667	8,292	7,103	6,703
Operating Income	1,558	1,295	1,061	891	979	1,488	1,372	1,327	973	886
Depreciation	196	174	194	206	363	297	272	203	212	203
Interest Expense	144	153	177	230	253	254	203	226	140	120
Pretax Income	1,270	984	703	402	283	869	874	843	614	568
Effective Tax Rate	16.1%	14.1%	13.4%	5.05%	NM	32.6%	34.3%	33.2%	38.0%	37.0%
Net Income	1,053	830	594	367	246	546	545	509	381	358
Balance Sheet & Other Financial Data (Million $)										
Cash	1,037	1,704	460	342	121	200	223	77.6	112	192
Current Assets	4,248	4,610	3,539	4,112	3,188	3,323	2,868	2,428	2,545	2,536
Total Assets	11,756	11,415	10,665	10,810	11,064	10,529	8,400	8,310	8,416	5,622
Current Liabilities	3,200	2,877	3,053	3,798	2,851	3,967	1,739	1,849	2,328	1,290
Long Term Debt	1,184	1,268	1,519	2,092	2,901	1,943	2,516	2,569	2,528	1,164
Common Equity	5,762	5,734	4,493	3,478	3,917	3,495	3,083	2,708	2,341	2,091
Total Capital	6,946	7,001	6,133	5,685	7,098	5,548	5,695	5,410	4,997	3,368
Capital Expenditures	112	109	108	123	201	187	191	14.5	186	195
Cash Flow	1,249	1,004	788	573	609	843	817	792	593	561
Current Ratio	1.3	1.6	1.2	1.1	1.1	0.8	1.6	1.3	1.1	2.0
% Long Term Debt of Capitalization	17.0	18.1	24.8	36.8	40.9	35.0	44.2	47.5	50.5	34.5
% Net Income of Revenue	10.0	8.8	6.0	4.1	2.5	6.2	7.1	6.1	5.4	5.3
% Return on Assets	9.1	7.5	5.5	3.3	2.2	5.8	6.7	6.1	5.4	6.4
% Return on Equity	18.3	16.2	14.9	9.9	6.7	16.6	18.7	20.2	17.2	18.4

Data as orig reptd.; bef. results of disc opers/spec. items. Per share data adj. for stk. divs.; EPS diluted. E-Estimated. NA-Not Available. NM-Not Meaningful. NR-Not Ranked. UR-Under Review.

Office: Clarendon House, Hamilton, Bermuda HM 11.
Telephone: 441-295-2838.
Email: seekinfo@irco.com
Website: http://www.irco.com

Chrmn, Pres & CEO: H.L. Henkel
SVP & CFO: T.R. McLevish
SVP & General Counsel: P. Nachtigal
VP & Cntlr: R.W. Randall

Investor Contact: J. Fimbianti (201-573-3113)
Board of Directors: A. C. Berzin, P. C. Godsoe, H. L. Henkel, C. J. Horner, H. W. Lichtenberger, T. E. Martin, P. Nachtigal, O. R. Smith, R. J. Swift, T. L. White

Founded: 1905
Domicile: Bermuda
Employees: 40,000

STANDARD &POOR'S

Intel Corp

S&P Recommendation HOLD ★★★★★ | **Price** $21.10 (as of Oct 27, 2006) | **12-Mo. Target Price** $25.00 | **Investment Style** Large-Cap Growth

GICS Sector Information Technology
Sub-Industry Semiconductors

Comment INTC is the world's largest manufacturer of microprocessors, the central processing units of PCs, and also produces other semiconductor products.

Key Stock Statistics (Source S&P, Vickers, company reports)

52-Wk Range	$27.49–16.75	S&P Oper. EPS 2006E	0.86	P/E on S&P Oper. EPS 2006E	24.5	Dividend Rate/Share	$0.40
Trailing 12-Month EPS	$1.00	S&P Oper. EPS 2007E	1.18	Common Shares Outstg. (M)	5,768.0	Yield (%)	1.90
Trailing 12-Month P/E	21.1	S&P Core EPS 2006E	0.86	Market Capitalization(B)	$121.705	Beta	2.31
$10K Invested 5 Yrs Ago	$8,521	S&P Core EPS 2007E	1.18	Institutional Ownership (%)	56	S&P Credit Rating	A+

Price Performance

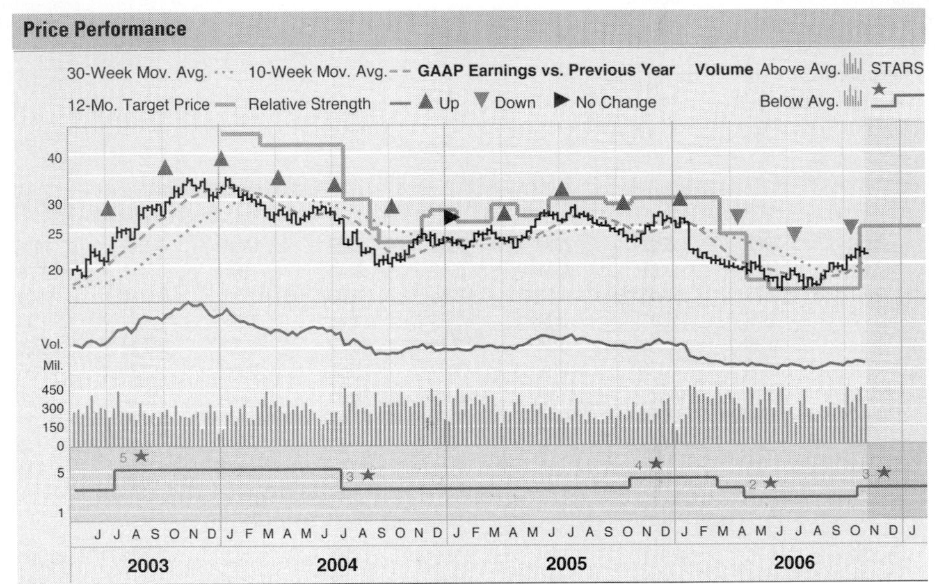

Options: ASE, CBOE, P, Ph

Analysis prepared by **Clyde Montevirgen** on October 24, 2006, when the stock traded at **$ 21.60**.

Highlights

- We project revenues will decrease 9.4% in 2006 and rise 10% in 2007. The company reported softening PC demand in the first half of the year, following record unit shipments in the fourth quarter of 2005. The rise in inventory to $4.5 billion in the third quarter from $2.8 billion in the third quarter of 2005 indicates a drag on revenue we think is apt to last through early 2007. We see results in the next few quarters aided by higher average selling prices from sales of new products.

- We see gross margins narrowing to 51.3% in 2006, from 59.4% in 2005, as lower sales volumes, plant expansion costs, new product ramp-up costs, and the incorporation of stock-based compensation expense hurt gross margins in the near term. In the third quarter, INTC announced a plan to cut 10,500 jobs, roughly 10% of its workforce. On June 27, INTC agreed to sell its communications and application processor business for about $600 million. Subject to approvals, the deal is expected to close in the fourth quarter.

- We estimate operating EPS of $0.86 for 2006 and $1.18 for 2007, including projected stock-based compensation.

Investment Rationale/Risk

- We see Intel continuing to benefit from scale-based strengths in R&D, manufacturing, and marketing. The company recently released a new lineup of leading edge chips, which we see gaining traction with customers. We also see Intel benefiting from lower per unit costs as it shifts to sub 65 nanometer production capabilities. However, we think INTC will suffer further share losses in certain processor markets and believe that its excess chip inventories are apt to be cleared at low prices or written off, limiting profitability.

- Risks to our recommendation and target price include possible downward swings in demand for PCs, a tougher than expected pricing environment, and less traction for its latest chips.

- Applying a price-to-sales (P/S) ratio of 4X our forward 12-month sales per share estimate of $6.63 indicates a value of $27. We estimate that this P/S multiple is near Intel's recent historical average P/S ratio. Applying a P/E of 20X, below its recent historical average P/E, to our 2007 EPS estimate of $1.18 indicates a value of $24. Blending these measures, we arrive at our 12-month target price of $25.

Qualitative Risk Assessment

LOW | **MEDIUM** | HIGH

Our view is that Intel's results reflect the sales cycles of the semiconductor industry and demand trends for personal computers. In addition, its above-average beta reflects high share price volatility. This is offset, in our opinion, by its large size, long corporate history, and what we see as its low debt levels compared to peers.

Quantitative Evaluations

S&P Quality Ranking **A**

D | C | B- | B | B+ | A- | **A** | A+

Relative Strength Rank **MODERATE**

68

LOWEST = 1 HIGHEST = 99

Revenue/Earnings Data

Revenue (Million $)

	1Q	2Q	3Q	4Q	Year
2006	8,940	8,009	8,739	--	--
2005	9,434	9,231	9,960	10,201	38,826
2004	8,091	8,049	8,471	9,598	34,209
2003	6,751	6,816	7,833	8,741	30,141
2002	6,781	6,319	6,504	7,160	26,764
2001	6,677	6,334	6,545	6,983	26,539

Earnings Per Share ($)

	1Q	2Q	3Q	4Q	Year
2006	0.23	0.15	0.22	**E**0.24	**E**0.86
2005	0.35	0.33	0.32	0.40	1.40
2004	0.26	0.27	0.30	0.33	1.16
2003	0.14	0.14	0.25	0.33	0.85
2002	0.14	0.07	0.10	0.16	0.46
2001	0.07	0.03	0.02	0.07	0.19

Fiscal year ended Dec. 31. Next earnings report expected: Mid January. EPS Estimates based on S&P Operating Earnings; historical GAAP earnings are as reported.

Dividend Data (Dates: mm/dd Payment Date: mm/dd/yy)

Amount ($)	Date Decl.	Ex-Div. Date	Stk. of Record	Payment Date
0.100	01/19	02/03	02/07	03/01/06
0.100	03/22	05/03	05/07	06/01/06
0.100	07/13	08/03	08/07	09/01/06
0.100	09/13	11/03	11/07	12/01/06

Dividends have been paid since 1992. Source: Company reports.

Please read the Required Disclosures and Analyst Certification on the last page of this report.

Intel Corp

Business Summary October 24, 2006

Intel is the world's largest semiconductor chip maker. It is well known for its dominant market share in microprocessors for personal computers (PCs). Although the PC processor is a mainstay, INTC has expanded its product lines to serve the networking and communications markets. The company's stated mission is to be the preeminent supplier of silicon chips and platform solutions to the worldwide digital economy, indicating ambitions beyond PCs.

In the first quarter of 2005, the company reorganized its operating segments to reflect a more customer-focused strategy. The Digital Enterprise Group or DEG (65% of 2005 total sales) designs and delivers computing and communications platforms for business and service providers. Revenues from microprocessors within DEG represented 50% of total sales in 2005, and chipsets, motherboards and other products were 15%. DEG serves the desktop computing market, including consumer desktops, as well as the networking and storage markets.

A microprocessor is the central processing unit (CPU) of a computer system. It processes system data and controls other devices in the system, acting as the "brains" of the computer. The chipset operates as the PC's "nervous system"--sending data from the processor to input, display, and storage devices. A motherboard is the principal board within a system that has connectors for attaching devices to the bus. Typically, the motherboard contains the CPU, memory, and the chipset.

Products within the DEG reflect a tiered branding approach. The Pentium 4 and Pentium D processors aim at the performance desktop market. The Celeron and Celeron D processors target the value market. For the server and workstation segments, Intel offers the Xeon processor line, which serves entry-level and high-end markets.

Company Financials

Per Share Data ($) Year Ended Dec. 31	2005	2004	2003	2002	2001	2000	1999	1998	1997	1996
Tangible Book Value	5.46	5.57	5.26	4.74	4.59	4.67	4.14	3.53	2.96	2.57
Cash Flow	2.15	1.91	1.62	1.25	1.13	2.20	1.57	0.63	1.27	0.99
Earnings	1.40	1.16	0.85	0.46	0.19	1.51	1.05	0.87	0.97	0.73
S&P Core Earnings	1.22	0.99	0.83	0.35	0.11	NA	NA	NA	NA	NA
Dividends	0.32	0.16	0.08	0.08	0.08	0.07	0.07	0.03	0.03	0.02
Payout Ratio	23%	14%	9%	17%	42%	4%	7%	4%	3%	3%
Prices:High	28.84	34.60	34.51	36.78	38.59	75.81	44.75	31.55	25.50	17.69
Prices:Low	21.94	19.64	14.88	12.95	18.96	29.81	25.06	16.41	15.72	6.23
P/E Ratio:High	21	30	41	80	NM	50	42	37	26	24
P/E Ratio:Low	16	17	18	28	NM	20	24	19	16	9
Income Statement Analysis (Million $)										
Revenue	38,826	34,209	30,141	26,764	26,539	33,726	29,389	26,273	25,070	20,847
Operating Income	16,685	15,019	13,225	9,740	8,923	15,339	13,756	11,351	12,079	9,441
Depreciation	4,595	4,889	5,070	5,344	6,469	4,835	3,597	2,807	2,192	1,888
Interest Expense	19.0	50.0	62.0	84.0	56.0	35.0	36.0	34.0	27.0	25.0
Pretax Income	12,610	10,417	7,442	4,204	2,183	15,141	11,228	9,137	10,659	7,934
Effective Tax Rate	31.3%	27.8%	24.2%	25.9%	40.9%	30.4%	34.9%	33.6%	34.8%	35.0%
Net Income	8,664	7,516	5,641	3,117	1,291	10,535	7,314	6,068	6,945	5,157
S&P Core Earnings	7,555	6,374	5,467	2,332	740	NA	NA	NA	NA	NA
Balance Sheet & Other Financial Data (Million $)										
Cash	7,324	8,407	7,971	7,404	7,970	2,976	3,695	2,038	4,102	4,165
Current Assets	21,194	24,058	22,882	18,925	17,633	21,150	17,819	13,475	15,867	13,684
Total Assets	48,314	48,143	47,143	44,224	44,395	47,945	43,849	31,471	28,880	23,765
Current Liabilities	9,234	8,006	6,879	6,595	6,570	8,650	7,099	5,804	6,020	4,863
Long Term Debt	2,106	703	936	929	1,050	707	955	702	448	728
Common Equity	36,182	38,579	37,846	35,468	35,830	37,322	32,535	23,377	19,295	16,872
Total Capital	38,991	40,137	40,264	37,629	37,825	39,295	36,750	25,667	22,860	18,872
Capital Expenditures	5,818	3,843	3,656	4,703	7,309	6,674	3,403	3,557	4,501	3,024
Cash Flow	13,259	12,405	10,711	8,461	7,760	15,370	10,911	8,875	9,137	7,045
Current Ratio	2.3	3.0	3.3	2.9	2.7	2.4	2.5	2.3	2.6	2.8
% Long Term Debt of Capitalization	5.4	1.8	2.3	2.5	2.8	1.8	2.6	2.7	1.9	3.8
% Net Income of Revenue	22.3	22.0	18.7	11.6	4.9	31.2	24.9	23.1	27.7	24.7
% Return on Assets	18.0	15.8	12.3	7.0	2.8	23.0	19.4	20.1	26.4	25.0
% Return on Equity	23.2	19.7	15.4	8.7	3.5	30.1	26.0	27.0	36.1	35.6

Data as orig reptd.; bef. results of disc opers/spec. items. Per share data adj. for stk. divs.; EPS diluted. E-Estimated. NA-Not Available. NM-Not Meaningful. NR-Not Ranked. UR-Under Review.

Office: 2200 Mission College Boulevard, Santa Clara, CA 95054-1549.
Telephone: 408-765-8080.
Website: http://www.intc.com
Chrmn: C.R. Barrett

Pres & CEO: P.S. Otellini
EVP & CFO: A.D. Bryant
SVP & General Counsel: D.B. Sewell
Investor Contact: N. Knupffer (408-653-5324)

Board of Directors: C. R. Barrett, C. Barshefsky, E. J. Browne, D. J. Guzy, R. E. Hundt, P. S. Otellini, J. D. Plummer, D. S. Pottruck, J. E. Shaw, J. L. Thornton, D. B. Yoffie

Founded: 1968
Domicile: Delaware
Employees: 99,900

STANDARD &POOR'S

International Business Machines Corp

S&P Recommendation BUY ★★★★★

Price $90.76 (as of Oct 27, 2006)

12-Mo. Target Price $102.00

Investment Style Large-Cap Growth

GICS Sector Information Technology
Sub-Industry Computer Hardware

Comment IBM, the world's largest technology company, offers a diversified line of computer hardware equipment, application and system software, and related services.

Key Stock Statistics (Source S&P, Vickers, company reports)

52-Wk Range	$92.04–72.73	S&P Oper. EPS 2006E	6.04	P/E on S&P Oper. EPS 2006E	15.0	Dividend Rate/Share	$1.20
Trailing 12-Month EPS	$5.80	S&P Oper. EPS 2007E	6.84	Common Shares Outstg. (M)	1,521.8	Yield (%)	1.32
Trailing 12-Month P/E	15.7	S&P Core EPS 2006E	5.90	Market Capitalization(B)	$138.122	Beta	1.63
$10K Invested 5 Yrs Ago	$8,524	S&P Core EPS 2007E	6.64	Institutional Ownership (%)	56	S&P Credit Rating	A+

Price Performance

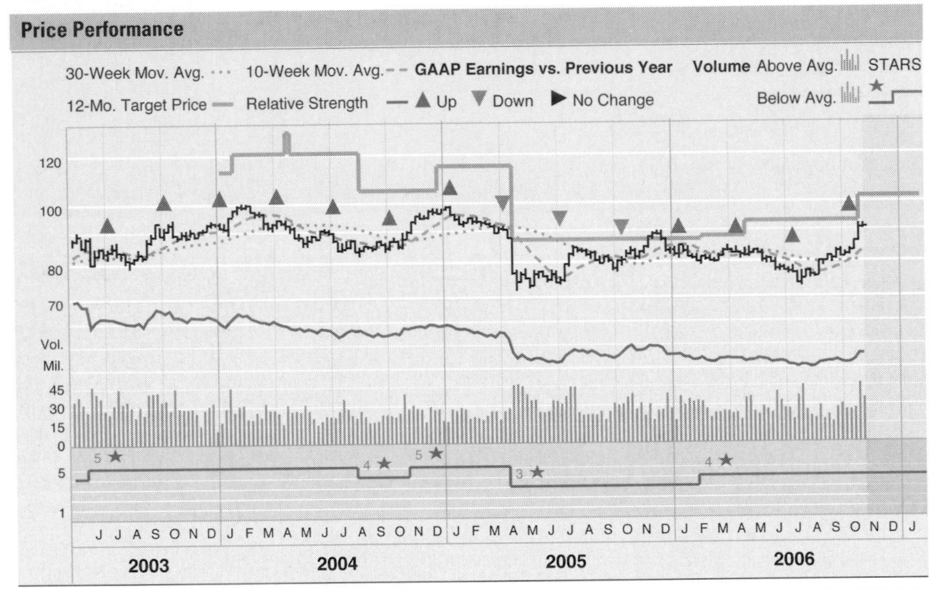

Options: ASE, CBOE, P, Ph

Analysis prepared by **Richard N. Stice, CFA** on October 19, 2006, when the stock traded at **$ 89.86**.

Highlights

- We see revenues advancing 5% in 2007, following our expectation of a modest decline in 2006. We expect market share gains in servers, and growth within its microelectronics business line, to offset the negative impact of a stiff pricing environment and a customer shift toward low-end systems. We anticipate growth in IBM's Software division as the company continues to capitalize on its middleware platform success, as well as an improvement in its Global Services unit. Finally, we believe revenue should also be aided by an ongoing push into emerging market economies.
- We look for the 2007 gross margin to widen modestly, to 42.0%, from 2006's expected 41.6%, as investments in Global Services are outweighed by ongoing cost reduction efforts. For both 2006 and 2007, we see SG&A expenses, as a percentage of revenues, remaining near 21%.
- We estimate 2007 EPS of $6.84, a 13% increase from 2006's anticipated $6.04, with both estimates including expected stock option expense. Our 2006 and 2007 S&P Core EPS estimates are $5.90 and $6.64, reflecting estimated pension costs.

Investment Rationale/Risk

- We believe IBM's results have benefited from margin improvement, enabled by cost cutting and the better margin profile of its portfolio lines, following the company's exit from the PC business. We believe revenue growth is improving, although we would like to see more consistency in IBM's Global Services unit. However, we think that broader strength in IBM's overall product offerings (both in services and software) is a positive catalyst for the shares.
- Risks to our opinion and target price include execution risks with regard to the Global Services business, further elongating of the sales cycle and pricing pressures. Regarding corporate governance practices, we are somewhat concerned that the roles of chairman and CEO are combined.
- Our 12-month target price of $102 is based on a blend of our discounted cash flow (DCF) and P/E analyses. Our DCF model assumes a WACC of 11.7% and expected terminal growth rate of 3%, implying an intrinsic value of $108. On a P/E basis, we equate the shares with the S&P 500's 2007 level of 14.1X, which implies a value of $96.

Qualitative Risk Assessment

LOW | **MEDIUM** | HIGH

Our risk assessment reflects what we view as IBM's competitively positioned solutions offerings, offset by what we see as an intensely competitive pricing environment.

Quantitative Evaluations

S&P Quality Ranking **A**

D | C | B- | B | B+ | A- | **A** | A+

Relative Strength Rank **STRONG**

83

LOWEST = 1 HIGHEST = 99

Revenue/Earnings Data

Revenue (Million $)

	1Q	2Q	3Q	4Q	Year
2006	20,659	21,890	22,617	--	--
2005	22,908	22,270	21,529	24,427	91,134
2004	22,175	23,098	23,349	27,671	96,293
2003	20,065	21,631	21,522	25,913	89,131
2002	18,030	19,651	19,821	23,684	81,186
2001	21,044	21,568	20,428	22,826	85,866

Earnings Per Share ($)

2006	1.08	1.30	1.45	**E**2.21	**E**6.04
2005	0.85	1.14	0.94	2.01	4.91
2004	0.93	1.16	1.06	1.81	4.94
2003	0.79	0.98	1.02	1.56	4.34
2002	0.73	0.25	0.99	1.11	3.07
2001	0.98	1.15	0.90	1.33	4.35

Fiscal year ended Dec. 31. Next earnings report expected: Mid January. EPS Estimates based on S&P Operating Earnings; historical GAAP earnings are as reported.

Dividend Data (Dates: mm/dd Payment Date: mm/dd/yy)

Amount ($)	Date Decl.	Ex-Div. Date	Stk. of Record	Payment Date
0.200	10/25	11/08	11/10	12/10/05
0.200	01/31	02/08	02/10	03/10/06
0.300	04/25	05/08	05/10	06/10/06
0.300	07/25	08/08	08/10	09/09/06

Dividends have been paid since 1916. Source: Company reports.

Please read the Required Disclosures and Analyst Certification on the last page of this report.

International Business Machines Corp

Business Summary October 19, 2006

CORPORATE OVERVIEW. In an information technology (IT) market, which is estimated at $1 trillion, International Business Machines, with about $90 billion in annual sales, is a major contributor to each major category that comprises the total IT market: hardware, software and services. The company is a leading server vendor, among the largest software vendors (behind Microsoft Corp. and Oracle Corp.), and has the largest global services organization.

CORPORATE STRATEGY. IBM has evolved its portfolio from a computer hardware vendor to a systems, services and software company. While computer hardware (included in the Systems & Technology Group) accounts for about 31% of sales in 2005, IBM has emphasized--through acquisitions and investments--services and software. These areas have gained momentum as IBM leverages these assets to offer total solutions to customers. IBM's focus on these higher value added areas such as services and software has caused these areas to represent some 64% of revenues and 71% of pretax profits in 2005.

The Systems group, once thought of principally as mainframes (zSeries) and minicomputers (AS/400), has made a transition to more open systems. IBM, a leader in UNIX systems (pSeries), also offers entry level servers. While IBM introduced the PC, it sold this business to Lenovo Group Ltd. in May, 2005, for $1.75 billion.

However, hardware remains a critical part of IBM's portfolio of businesses, and the company has tried to be innovative through its microelectronics division and early adoption of Linux to differentiate its products in a commoditizing market. The Hardware division, the Systems & Technology Group, includes IBM's Shark storage offering and its semiconductor unit (custom logic and communications, and with exposure to gaming consoles). The focus to improve the profitability of this business led to IBM's sale of its PC business, and its hard disk drive business in 2002 (to Hitachi for $2 billion).

Company Financials

Per Share Data ($) Year Ended Dec. 31	**2005**	**2004**	**2003**	**2002**	**2001**	**2000**	**1999**	**1998**	**1997**	**1996**
Tangible Book Value	13.97	11.86	12.36	10.84	12.96	11.08	10.65	9.84	9.62	10.00
Cash Flow	8.10	7.82	7.01	5.61	7.08	6.95	7.40	5.64	4.99	4.30
Earnings	4.91	4.94	4.34	3.07	4.35	4.44	4.12	3.28	3.01	2.56
S&P Core Earnings	3.93	4.06	3.00	0.08	1.33	NA	NA	NA	NA	NA
Dividends	0.78	0.70	0.63	0.59	0.55	0.51	0.47	0.44	0.39	0.33
Payout Ratio	16%	14%	15%	19%	13%	11%	11%	13%	13%	13%
Prices:High	99.10	100.43	94.54	126.39	124.70	134.94	139.19	94.97	56.75	41.50
Prices:Low	71.85	90.82	73.17	54.01	83.75	80.06	80.88	47.81	31.78	20.78
P/E Ratio:High	20	20	22	41	29	30	34	29	19	16
P/E Ratio:Low	15	18	17	18	19	18	20	15	11	8
Income Statement Analysis (Million $)										
Revenue	91,134	96,293	89,131	81,186	85,866	88,396	87,548	81,667	78,508	75,947
Operating Income	14,564	15,890	14,790	11,175	14,115	16,147	18,086	13,639	13,116	12,707
Depreciation	5,188	4,915	4,701	4,379	4,820	4,513	6,159	4,475	4,018	3,676
Interest Expense	220	139	145	145	238	717	727	713	760	716
Pretax Income	12,226	12,028	10,874	7,524	10,953	11,534	11,757	9,040	9,027	8,587
Effective Tax Rate	34.6%	29.8%	30.0%	29.1%	29.5%	29.8%	34.4%	30.0%	32.5%	36.8%
Net Income	7,994	8,448	7,613	5,334	7,723	8,093	7,712	6,328	6,093	5,429
S&P Core Earnings	6,395	6,923	5,270	111	2,302	NA	NA	NA	NA	NA
Balance Sheet & Other Financial Data (Million $)										
Cash	13,686	10,570	7,647	5,975	6,393	3,722	5,831	5,768	7,553	8,137
Current Assets	45,661	46,970	44,998	41,652	42,461	43,880	43,155	42,360	40,418	40,695
Total Assets	105,748	109,183	104,457	96,484	88,313	88,349	87,495	86,100	81,499	81,132
Current Liabilities	35,152	39,798	37,900	34,550	35,119	36,406	39,578	36,827	33,507	34,000
Long Term Debt	15,425	14,828	16,986	19,986	15,963	18,371	14,124	15,508	13,696	9,872
Common Equity	33,098	29,747	27,864	22,782	23,614	20,624	20,264	19,186	19,564	21,375
Total Capital	48,523	44,575	44,850	42,768	39,577	38,995	36,236	36,455	34,999	33,127
Capital Expenditures	3,842	4,368	4,393	4,753	5,660	5,616	5,959	6,520	6,793	5,883
Cash Flow	13,182	13,363	12,314	9,713	12,533	12,586	13,851	10,783	10,091	9,085
Current Ratio	1.3	1.2	1.2	1.2	1.2	1.2	1.1	1.2	1.2	1.2
% Long Term Debt of Capitalization	31.7	33.3	37.9	46.7	40.3	47.1	39.2	42.5	39.1	29.8
% Net Income of Revenue	8.8	8.8	8.5	6.6	9.0	9.2	8.8	7.7	7.8	7.2
% Return on Assets	7.4	7.9	7.6	5.7	8.7	9.2	8.9	7.6	7.5	6.8
% Return on Equity	24.7	29.3	30.1	23.1	35.1	39.7	39.0	32.7	29.8	24.9

Data as orig reptd.; bef. results of disc opers/spec. items. Per share data adj. for stk. divs.; EPS diluted. E-Estimated. NA-Not Available. NM-Not Meaningful. NR-Not Ranked. UR-Under Review.

Office: New Orchard Road, Armonk, NY 10504.
Telephone: 914-499-1900.
Website: http://www.ibm.com
Chrmn, Pres & CEO: S.J. Palmisano

SVP & CFO: M. Loughridge
SVP & General Counsel: D.J. Rosenberg
VP & Treas: J.J. Greene, Jr.
VP & Secy: D.E. O'Donnell

Board of Directors: C. Black, K. I. Chenault, J. Dormann, M. L. Eskew, S. A. Jackson, M. Makihara, L. A. Noto, J. W. Owens, S. J. Palmisano, J. E. Spero, S. Taurel, C. M. Vest, L. H. Zambrano

Founded: 1910
Domicile: New York
Employees: 329,373

STANDARD &POOR'S

International Flavors & Fragrances Inc.

S&P Recommendation HOLD ★★★★★	**Price** $41.70 (as of Oct 27, 2006)	**12-Mo. Target Price** $41.00	**Investment Style** Mid-Cap Growth

GICS Sector Materials
Sub-Industry Specialty Chemicals

Comment This leading producer of flavors and fragrances used in a wide variety of consumer goods derives over two-thirds of sales and earnings from operations outside the U.S.

Key Stock Statistics (Source S&P, Vickers, company reports)

52-Wk Range	$42.26–31.19	S&P Oper. EPS 2006**E**	2.25	P/E on S&P Oper. EPS 2006**E**	18.5	Dividend Rate/Share	$0.84
Trailing 12-Month EPS	$2.15	S&P Oper. EPS 2007**E**	2.45	Common Shares Outstg. (M)	90.7	Yield (%)	2.01
Trailing 12-Month P/E	19.4	S&P Core EPS 2006**E**	2.29	Market Capitalization(B)	$3.781	Beta	0.42
$10K Invested 5 Yrs Ago	$16,312	S&P Core EPS 2007**E**	2.49	Institutional Ownership (%)	81	S&P Credit Rating	BBB+

Price Performance

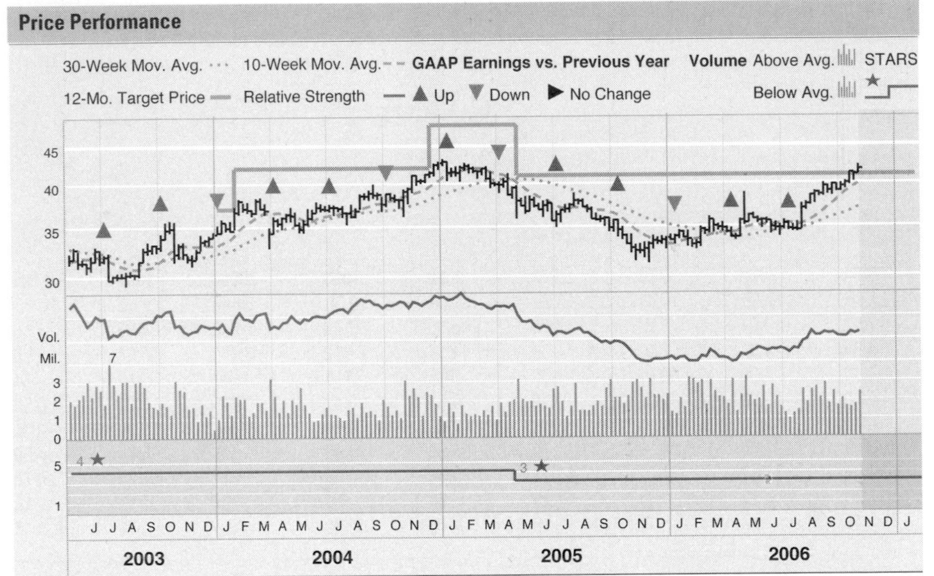

Options: CBOE

Analysis prepared by **Richard O'Reilly, CFA** on September 05, 2006, when the stock traded at **$ 39.53**.

Highlights

- We expect sales in 2006 to rise about 3%, on gains in both fragrances and flavors, aided by higher selling prices as well as favorable currency rates in the second half. Sales in the 2006 first half were flat, as a gain of 3% in local currencies was offset by the strength of the U.S. dollar. Flavor sales for 2005 were restricted by lower prices for naturals as well as $5 million of sales lost due to contaminated raw material.
- We see gross margins in 2006 recovering somewhat from 41.4% in 2005, despite expected higher costs for raw materials and freight. We do not expect any costs in addition to the $11 million in 2005 associated with the raw material contamination issue. We think that equity compensation expense for restricted stock units in 2006 will double to about $15 million. Interest expense should be similar to 2005, based on anticipated higher average rates.
- We project that the effective tax rate for 2006 will be about 28.5%, down from 2005's 31.6%, before a one-time tax charge. Reported EPS for 2005 includes a fourth quarter $0.17 restructuring charge.

Investment Rationale/Risk

- Our hold opinion reflects our view of a modest EPS recovery for 2006 as we see IFF continuing to renew sales growth with an improved win rate of new business, especially in fragrances. However, we think margins will remain restricted by higher raw material costs and a somewhat challenging selling price environment.
- Risks to our recommendation and target price include economic and political uncertainties in global markets, currency fluctuations, IFF's ability to maintain close relationships with customers, delays in customers' new product launches, and greater than expected increases in raw material costs.
- The shares were recently yielding about 2% and trading at a P/E of about 18X our 2006 EPS estimate, modestly lower than the corresponding multiples accorded to the shares of other major specialty chemical concerns, based on our estimates. Assuming that operating EPS growth continued into 2007, and a further narrowing of the stock's P/E multiple discount to the peer group, our 12-month target price is $41.

Qualitative Risk Assessment

LOW	**MEDIUM**	HIGH

Our risk assessment reflects our view of the stable nature of the company's businesses and end markets and its leadership positions, offset by a somewhat concentrated customer base.

Quantitative Evaluations

S&P Quality Ranking **B**

D	C	B-	**B**	B+	A-	A	A+

Relative Strength Rank **STRONG**

71

LOWEST = 1 HIGHEST = 99

Revenue/Earnings Data

Revenue (Million $)

	1Q	2Q	3Q	4Q	Year
2006	511.4	530.5	--	--	--
2005	523.1	515.6	493.1	461.7	1,993
2004	535.0	524.2	506.2	468.2	2,034
2003	466.2	482.6	480.9	471.8	1,902
2002	445.8	476.3	462.8	424.3	1,809
2001	483.7	478.2	462.7	419.2	1,844

Earnings Per Share ($)

2006	0.58	0.67	**E**0.54	**E**0.45	**E**2.25
2005	0.55	0.60	0.72	0.16	2.04
2004	0.59	0.59	0.44	0.43	2.05
2003	0.34	0.54	0.54	0.40	1.83
2002	0.44	0.47	0.52	0.41	1.84
2001	0.21	0.34	0.35	0.30	1.20

Fiscal year ended Dec. 31. Next earnings report expected: NA. EPS Estimates based on S&P Operating Earnings; historical GAAP earnings are as reported.

Dividend Data (Dates: mm/dd Payment Date: mm/dd/yy)

Amount ($)	Date Decl.	Ex-Div. Date	Stk. of Record	Payment Date
0.185	03/08	03/17	03/21	04/06/06
0.185	05/10	06/20	06/22	07/06/06
0.185	07/31	09/19	09/21	10/05/06
0.210	10/11	12/19	12/21	01/08/07

Dividends have been paid since 1956. Source: Company reports.

Please read the Required Disclosures and Analyst Certification on the last page of this report.

International Flavors & Fragrances Inc.

Business Summary September 05, 2006

CORPORATE OVERVIEW. International Flavors & Fragrances, founded in 1909, is a leading global maker of products used by other manufacturers to enhance the aromas and tastes of consumer products. The November 2000 purchase of Bush Boake Allen Inc. (BOA) for $970 million boosted annual sales to nearly $2 billion. With this purchase, IFF became the world's leading flavors company.

IFF receives about 70% of sales from outside the U.S. In 2005, North America contributed 31% of sales and 15% of operating profits; Europe 38% and 56%; India 3% and 4%; Latin America 12% and 8%; and Asia-Pacific 17% and 17%.

Fragrance products accounted for 57% of sales in 2005. Fragrances are used in the manufacture of soaps, detergents, cosmetic creams, lotions and powders, lipsticks, after shave lotions, deodorants, hair preparations, air fresheners, perfumes and colognes and other consumer products. Most major U.S. companies in these industries are IFF customers. Cosmetics (including perfumes and toiletries) and household products (soaps and detergents) are the two largest customer groups.

Flavor products account for IFF's remaining sales. Flavors are sold principally to the food, beverage and other industries for use in consumer products such as soft drinks, candies, cake mixes, desserts, prepared foods, dietary foods, dairy products, drink powders, pharmaceuticals, oral care products, alcoholic beverages and tobacco. Two of the largest customers for flavor products are major U.S. producers of prepared foods and beverages.

By category, 43% of sales in 2005 were from flavor compounds, 26% functional fragrances, 19% fine fragrances and toiletries, and 12% ingredients.

The company uses both synthetic and natural ingredients in its compounds. IFF manufactures most of the synthetic ingredients, of which a substantial portion (40% in 2005) is sold to others. It has had a consistent commitment to R&D spending, and anticipates that R&D expense will approximate 9% of annual sales over the next several years. R&D is conducted in 32 laboratories in 23 countries.

Company Financials

Per Share Data ($) Year Ended Dec. 31	**2005**	**2004**	**2003**	**2002**	**2001**	**2000**	**1999**	**1998**	**1997**	**1996**
Tangible Book Value	1.54	1.28	NM	NM	NM	NM	8.19	8.91	9.17	9.79
Cash Flow	3.07	3.01	2.77	2.72	2.47	1.90	2.06	2.35	2.45	2.15
Earnings	2.04	2.05	1.83	1.84	1.20	1.22	1.53	1.90	1.99	1.71
S&P Core Earnings	2.04	1.82	1.70	1.37	0.70	NA	NA	NA	NA	NA
Dividends	0.73	0.69	0.63	0.60	0.60	1.52	1.52	1.48	1.45	1.38
Payout Ratio	36%	33%	34%	33%	50%	125%	99%	78%	73%	81%
Prices:High	42.90	43.20	36.61	37.45	31.69	37.94	48.50	51.88	53.44	51.88
Prices:Low	31.19	32.77	29.18	26.05	19.75	14.69	33.63	32.06	39.88	40.75
P/E Ratio:High	21	21	20	20	26	31	32	27	27	30
P/E Ratio:Low	15	16	16	14	16	12	22	17	20	24
Income Statement Analysis (Million $)										
Revenue	1,993	2,034	1,902	1,809	1,844	1,463	1,439	1,407	1,427	1,436
Operating Income	382	433	415	396	409	322	338	356	382	388
Depreciation	91.9	91.0	86.7	84.5	123	69.3	56.4	49.0	50.3	47.7
Interest Expense	24.0	24.0	28.5	37.0	70.4	25.1	5.15	2.04	2.12	2.74
Pretax Income	246	281	252	266	188	184	243	311	340	299
Effective Tax Rate	21.6%	30.2%	31.5%	34.0%	38.2%	33.2%	33.5%	34.5%	35.9%	36.5%
Net Income	193	196	173	176	116	123	162	204	218	190
S&P Core Earnings	193	174	161	131	68.5	NA	NA	NA	NA	NA
Balance Sheet & Other Financial Data (Million $)										
Cash	273	32.6	12.1	14.9	48.5	129	62.1	116	217	318
Current Assets	1,191	961	903	867	896	1,019	835	848	935	1,006
Total Assets	2,638	2,363	2,307	2,233	2,268	2,489	1,401	1,388	1,422	1,507
Current Liabilities	1,203	400	526	359	560	1,179	370	273	265	280
Long Term Debt	131	669	690	1,007	939	417	3.83	4.34	5.11	8.29
Common Equity	915	910	743	575	524	631	858	945	1,000	1,077
Total Capital	1,047	1,579	1,433	1,582	1,508	1,152	895	1,084	1,029	1,102
Capital Expenditures	93.4	70.6	6.40	81.8	52.0	60.7	102	89.7	58.2	79.4
Cash Flow	285	287	259	260	239	192	218	253	269	238
Current Ratio	1.0	2.4	1.7	2.4	1.6	0.9	2.3	3.1	3.5	3.6
% Long Term Debt of Capitalization	12.5	42.4	48.2	63.7	62.3	36.2	0.4	0.4	0.5	0.8
% Net Income of Revenue	9.7	9.6	9.1	9.7	6.3	8.4	11.3	14.5	15.3	13.2
% Return on Assets	7.7	8.4	7.6	7.8	4.9	6.3	11.6	14.5	14.9	12.5
% Return on Equity	21.1	23.7	26.2	32.0	20.1	16.5	18.0	20.9	21.0	17.3

Data as orig reptd.; bef. results of disc opers/spec. items. Per share data adj. for stk. divs.; EPS diluted. E-Estimated. NA-Not Available. NM-Not Meaningful. NR-Not Ranked. UR-Under Review.

Office: 521 W 57th St, New York, NY 10019-2960.
Telephone: 212-765-5500.
Email: investor.relations@iff.com
Website: http://www.iff.com

Chrmn & CEO: R.M. Amen
COO: J.H. Dunsdon
SVP & CFO: D.J. Wetmore
SVP, Secy & General Counsel: D.M. Meany

Investor Contact: J. Fingeroth (212-521-4800)
Board of Directors: G. Blobel, J. M. Cook, P. A. Georgescu, M. Hayes Adame, A. A. Herzan, H. W. Howell, Jr., A. C. Martinez, B. M. Tansky

Founded: 1909
Domicile: New York
Employees: 5,160

STANDARD &POOR'S

International Game Technology

S&P Recommendation SELL ★★★★★

Price $42.36 (as of Oct 27, 2006)

12-Mo. Target Price $33.00

Investment Style Large-Cap Growth

GICS Sector Consumer Discretionary
Sub-Industry Casinos & Gaming

Comment This company is a leading maker of gaming machines and proprietary software systems for gaming machine networks.

Key Stock Statistics (Source S&P, Vickers, company reports)

52-Wk Range	$43.00–25.44	S&P Oper. EPS 2006E	1.35	P/E on S&P Oper. EPS 2006E	31.4	Dividend Rate/Share	$0.52
Trailing 12-Month EPS	$1.31	S&P Oper. EPS 2007E	1.55	Common Shares Outstg. (M)	339.4	Yield (%)	1.23
Trailing 12-Month P/E	32.3	S&P Core EPS 2006E	1.35	Market Capitalization(B)	$14.377	Beta	0.76
$10K Invested 5 Yrs Ago	$33,981	S&P Core EPS 2007E	1.55	Institutional Ownership (%)	83	S&P Credit Rating	BBB

Price Performance

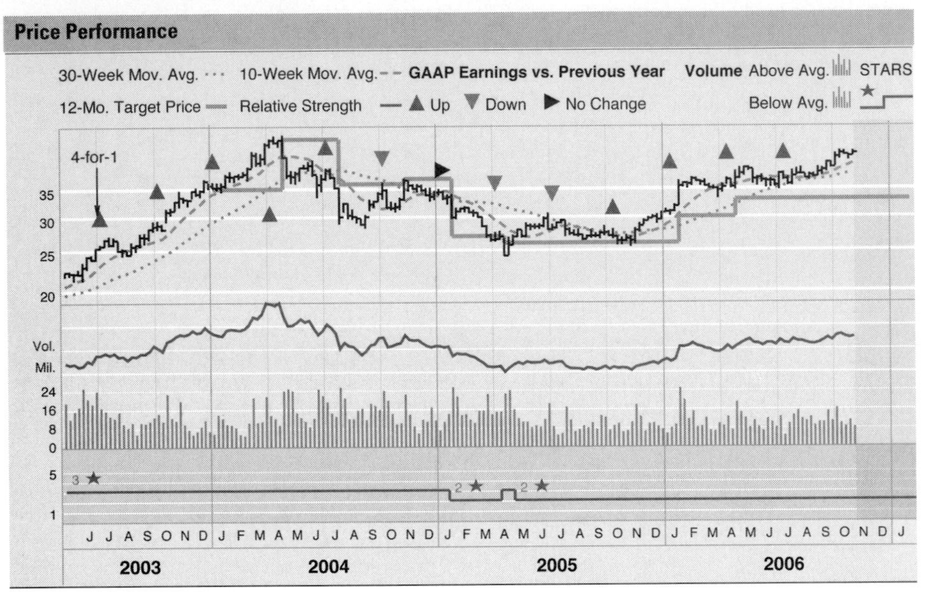

Options: ASE, CBOE

Analysis prepared by **Tom Graves, CFA** on July 27, 2006, when the stock traded at **$ 37.75**.

Highlights

- In FY 07 (Sep.), we look for revenues to be up moderately from the $2.5 billion projected for FY 06. We expect that contributors to FY 07 revenue growth will include sales of gaming machines for markets in Pennsylvania, and machine sales that will be part of a replacement cycle in Japan. Overall, during the next few years, we expect a shift toward sales or licensing of server-based games to become more evident, boosting revenue from replacement machines and games. However, we look for this impact to be larger in FY 08 than in FY 07.
- We estimate FY 07 net income of $506 million ($1.55 a share), versus the $471 million ($1.35) projected for FY 05. Our FY 07 and FY 06 EPS estimates include costs of $0.08 a share related to the initiation of stock option expensing. Our FY 07 forecast is based on an anticipated 5.0% fewer diluted shares, following a projected 4.4% decline in FY 06, reflecting expected stock repurchases.
- As of June 30, 2006, IGT had a remaining stock repurchase authorization totaling 17.7 million shares. The quarterly dividend was raised 4.2%, to $0.125 a share, with the October 2005 payment.

Investment Rationale/Risk

- We see some favorable prospects for sales of both replacement gaming machines and for sales to new gaming facilities. Also, we expect further growth in IGT's installed base of recurring revenue machines. However, in our view, the company's market leadership and longer-term growth prospects are amply reflected in the stock's premium P/E to the S&P 500.
- Risks to our recommendation and target price include the possibility that IGT's sales and profits will be stronger than expected, and that prospects for growth from new or expanded gaming markets will become more favorable than we anticipate.
- Our 12-month target price of $33 reflects our view that there will be a narrowing of the stock's P/E premium to the S&P 500. Based on our calendar 2006 EPS estimates, the stock recently had a P/E premium of about 90%. We expect support for the stock to be limited by its P/E multiple and by questions about the speed and scope at which demand for new gaming machines or systems will develop.

Qualitative Risk Assessment

LOW | **MEDIUM** | HIGH

In our view, this company has an industry-leading position as a supplier of gaming machines. We expect that IGT will continue to spend a sizable amount of money on research and development, which will likely help it to develop successful products. We expect the company to generate free cash flow, with at least some of it used for stock repurchases.

Quantitative Evaluations

S&P Quality Ranking B+

D | C | B- | B | **B+** | A- | A | A+

Relative Strength Rank MODERATE

70

LOWEST = 1 HIGHEST = 99

Revenue/Earnings Data

Revenue (Million $)

	1Q	2Q	3Q	4Q	Year
2006	616.2	644.4	612.4	--	--
2005	641.2	551.0	579.6	607.6	2,379
2004	608.1	636.1	618.9	621.7	2,485
2003	489.6	529.1	561.9	547.5	2,128
2002	301.5	500.9	522.4	522.8	1,848
2001	301.7	346.9	320.1	295.9	1,199

Earnings Per Share ($)

	1Q	2Q	3Q	4Q	Year
2006	0.34	0.35	0.33	E0.33	E1.35
2005	0.33	0.26	0.32	0.30	1.20
2004	0.33	0.32	0.38	0.15	1.18
2003	0.25	0.27	0.30	0.29	1.07
2002	0.18	0.20	0.23	0.20	0.80
2001	0.16	0.18	0.18	0.18	0.70

Fiscal year ended Sep. 30. Next earnings report expected: Early November. EPS Estimates based on S&P Operating Earnings; historical GAAP earnings are as reported.

Dividend Data (Dates: mm/dd Payment Date: mm/dd/yy)

Amount ($)	Date Decl.	Ex-Div. Date	Stk. of Record	Payment Date
0.125	12/08	12/20	12/22	01/05/06
0.125	03/07	03/17	03/21	04/04/06
0.125	06/13	06/23	06/27	07/11/06
0.130	09/26	10/04	10/09	10/23/06

Dividends have been paid since 2003. Source: Company reports.

International Game Technology

Business Summary July 27, 2006

CORPORATE OVERVIEW. International Game Technology (IGT) is a leading maker of gaming machines. In addition to selling machines, IGT's business includes the placement of machines from which it receives recurring revenues.

In FY 05 (Sep.), 50% of IGT revenues came from product sales, and the remainder from gaming operations, including progressive systems.

Product sales in FY 05 included the sale of 141,900 machines, down from 159,200 in FY 04. FY 05 sales included 50,500 machines for the North American market, versus 92,500 in FY 04. Shipments to international markets totaled 91,400 machines in FY 05, up from 66,700 in FY 04. International sales may include some lower-priced machines with relatively low-value prizes. In addition to machines for casinos, IGT has made video gaming terminals (VGTs) for government-sponsored programs, including lotteries.

IGT's gaming operations segment includes the placement of games in both casinos and government-sponsored gaming markets, under a variety of recurring revenue pricing arrangements, including wide-area progressive systems, standalone participation and flat fee, equipment leasing and rental, as well as hybrid pricing or premium products that include a product sale and a recurring fee.

CORPORATE STRATEGY. In FY 05, IGT's research and development spending totaled $138 million (5.8% of revenues), up from $129 million (5.2%) in FY 04. We expect that the company's ability to develop successful machines and games, with features that appeal to gamblers and casinos, will be a significant factor in the amount of product sales it has.

PRIMARY BUSINESS DYNAMICS. In our view, new market opportunities for IGT include the expected debut of slot machines at various locations in Pennsylvania, and the expected introduction of gaming machines at racetracks in Florida and New York. Also, in FY 07, we look for IGT to have increased sales of replacement machines for the Japanese market.

Overall, during the next few years, we expect a shift toward sales or licensing of server-based games to become more evident, creating opportunities for increased IGT revenues from sales or licensing of replacement machines or games for use in such locations as U.S. casinos.

Company Financials

Per Share Data ($) Year Ended Sep. 30	**2005**	**2004**	**2003**	**2002**	**2001**	**2000**	**1999**	**1998**	**1997**	**1996**
Tangible Book Value	1.56	1.98	1.42	0.55	0.40	NM	0.26	0.94	1.14	1.24
Cash Flow	1.78	1.56	1.45	1.23	0.91	0.67	0.29	0.42	0.35	0.29
Earnings	1.20	1.18	1.07	0.80	0.70	0.50	0.16	0.33	0.28	0.23
S&P Core Earnings	1.15	1.11	1.02	0.79	0.67	NA	NA	NA	NA	NA
Dividends	0.48	0.30	0.18	Nil	Nil	Nil	0.03	0.03	0.03	0.03
Payout Ratio	40%	25%	16%	Nil	Nil	Nil	18%	9%	11%	13%
Prices:High	34.63	47.12	37.00	20.03	17.99	12.34	6.03	7.17	6.72	5.88
Prices:Low	24.20	28.22	18.05	11.94	8.93	1.36	3.53	4.03	3.81	2.69
P/E Ratio:High	29	40	35	25	26	25	37	22	24	25
P/E Ratio:Low	20	24	17	15	13	9	22	12	13	12
Income Statement Analysis (Million $)										
Revenue	2,379	2,485	2,128	1,848	1,199	1,004	930	824	744	733
Operating Income	886	964	800	646	315	343	267	260	226	200
Depreciation	222	150	134	146	63.3	54.4	52.3	41.5	35.0	30.5
Interest Expense	58.1	90.5	117	117	102	102	72.8	41.0	30.4	23.5
Pretax Income	681	653	599	110	339	245	101	235	213	184
Effective Tax Rate	35.9%	34.2%	37.3%	NM	37.0%	36.0%	35.6%	35.0%	35.5%	36.0%
Net Income	437	430	375	277	214	157	65.3	152	137	118
S&P Core Earnings	415	405	357	273	204	NA	NA	NA	NA	NA
Balance Sheet & Other Financial Data (Million $)										
Cash	289	765	1,316	424	364	245	426	175	152	231
Current Assets	1,437	1,510	2,078	1,195	968	814	975	671	572	616
Total Assets	3,864	3,873	4,185	3,316	1,923	1,624	1,765	1,544	1,215	1,154
Current Liabilities	1,218	560	945	511	371	259	213	201	165	127
Long Term Debt	200	792	1,146	971	985	992	990	323	141	107
Common Equity	1,906	1,977	1,687	1,433	296	96.6	242	541	520	623
Total Capital	2,106	2,768	2,833	2,413	1,281	1,088	1,233	865	661	730
Capital Expenditures	239	211	30.8	33.8	34.7	18.5	17.8	16.8	33.1	71.6
Cash Flow	659	580	509	423	277	211	118	194	172	149
Current Ratio	1.2	2.7	2.2	2.3	2.6	3.1	4.6	3.3	3.5	4.9
% Long Term Debt of Capitalization	9.5	28.6	40.4	40.3	76.9	91.1	80.3	37.3	21.3	14.7
% Net Income of Revenue	18.3	17.3	17.6	15.0	17.8	15.6	7.0	18.5	18.4	16.1
% Return on Assets	11.3	10.7	10.0	10.6	12.1	9.3	3.9	11.1	11.6	11.1
% Return on Equity	22.5	23.5	24.1	32.0	109.0	92.6	16.7	28.7	24.0	42.1

Data as orig reptd.; bef. results of disc opers/spec. items. Per share data adj. for stk. divs.; EPS diluted. E-Estimated. NA-Not Available. NM-Not Meaningful. NR-Not Ranked. UR-Under Review.

Office: 9295 Prototype Drive, Reno, NV 89521.
Telephone: 775-448-7777.
Website: http://www.igt.com
Chrmn, Pres, CEO & COO: T.J. Matthews

EVP, CFO & Treas: M.T. Mullarkey
EVP, Secy & General Counsel: D.D. Johnson
Investor Contact: P. Cavanaugh (866-296-4232)

Board of Directors: N. Barsky, R. A. Bittman, R. R. Burt, P. S. Hart, L. S. Heisz, R. A. Mathewson, T. J. Matthews, R. Miller, F. B. Rentschler

Founded: 1980
Domicile: Nevada
Employees: 5,000

STANDARD &POOR'S

International Paper Co

S&P Recommendation BUY ★★★★★

Price $33.76 (as of Oct 27, 2006)

12-Mo. Target Price $41.00

Investment Style Large-Cap Value

GICS Sector Materials
Sub-Industry Paper Products

Comment This company is a leading worldwide producer and distributor of printing papers and packaging products.

Key Stock Statistics (Source S&P, Vickers, company reports)

52-Wk Range	**$37.98–28.60**	S&P Oper. EPS 2006**E**	**1.50**	P/E on S&P Oper. EPS 2006**E**	**22.5**	Dividend Rate/Share	**$1.00**
Trailing 12-Month EPS	**$-0.42**	S&P Oper. EPS 2007**E**	**1.90**	Common Shares Outstg. (M)	**454.9**	Yield (%)	**2.96**
Trailing 12-Month P/E	**NM**	S&P Core EPS 2006**E**	**1.36**	Market Capitalization(B)	**$15.358**	Beta	**1.01**
$10K Invested 5 Yrs Ago	**$10,229**	S&P Core EPS 2007**E**	**2.08**	Institutional Ownership (%)	**94**	S&P Credit Rating	**BBB**

Price Performance

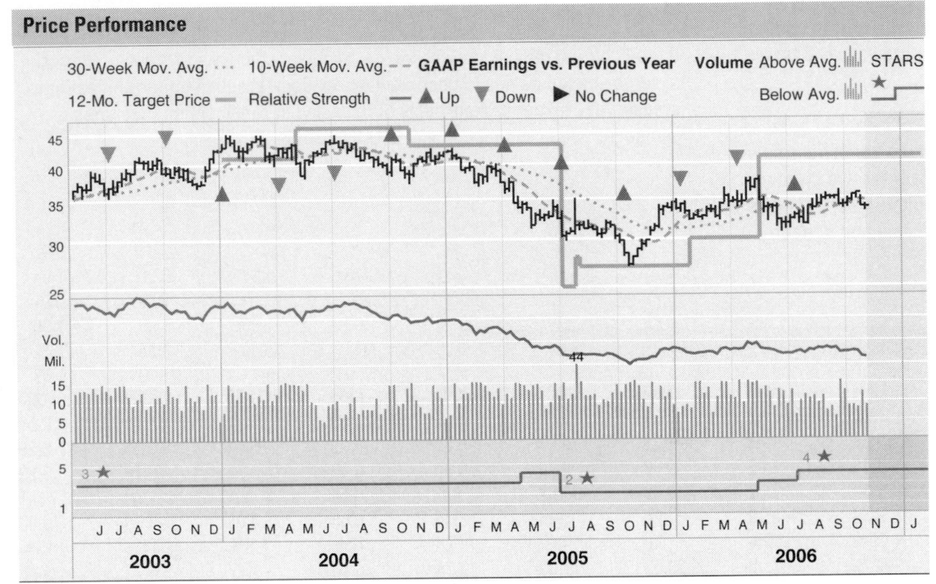

Options: ASE, CBOE, P, Ph

Analysis prepared by **Stuart J. Benway, CFA** on October 20, 2006, when the stock traded at **$ 33.96**.

Highlights

- With IP in the midst of a major corporate restructuring, forecasting sales remains difficult. As currently structured, we look for IP's revenues to benefit from higher prices for uncoated free sheet and containerboard and from higher volume in the distribution business. Lower lumber volume and prices, due to further projected declines in housing starts, should be a partial offset, in our view.
- We expect operating margins from continuing operations to improve slightly in 2006, following the 200 basis point drop in 2005, and a further improvement is seen in 2007. This projected widening should come from higher prices and lower input costs as we believe raw material and energy outlays will decline. We think debt reduction from the proceeds of asset sales will lead to lower interest expense.
- We see operating EPS of $1.50 for 2006 and $1.90 for 2007. Our Standard & Poor's Core EPS estimate of $1.36 for 2006 reflects restructuring charges, partially offset by pension adjustments, and our S&P Core EPS forecast of $2.08 for 2007 includes normalized pension expense.

Investment Rationale/Risk

- We have a generally positive view of IP's restructuring plan, from which it expects to generate $11 billion after taxes from asset sales. However, our outlook for the uncoated paper business is negative, due to what we see as slowing demand from the impact of electronic forms of communication and commerce. Based on our outlook for an ongoing expansion in the U.S. economy and limited supply growth, we think that the paper and packaging environment will improve modestly in 2007.
- Risks to our recommendation and target price include slower than expected economic strength, worse than projected demand and pricing trends for uncoated paper and packaging, and a renewed rise in energy and/or raw material costs.
- Given what we see as corporate changes ongoing at IP, we have adopted a sum-of-the-parts valuation model. The company estimates that it will generate about $11 billion in cash from asset sales, which equates to just over $22 per share. We believe the remaining businesses are worth about $19 per share on an operating basis. Our 12-month target price is $41.

Qualitative Risk Assessment

LOW | **MEDIUM** | HIGH

IP operates in a cyclical and capital intensive industry and is affected by changes in industrial production, interest rates, and economic growth. However, as one of the largest companies in the sector, IP has greater economies of scale than many of its competitors.

Quantitative Evaluations

S&P Quality Ranking **B**

D | C | B- | **B** | B+ | A- | A | A+

Relative Strength Rank **WEAK**

25

LOWEST = 1 HIGHEST = 99

Revenue/Earnings Data

Revenue (Million $)

	1Q	2Q	3Q	4Q	Year
2006	5,668	6,270	--	--	--
2005	6,011	5,916	6,036	6,134	24,097
2004	6,138	6,229	6,578	6,603	25,548
2003	6,075	6,264	6,373	6,500	25,179
2002	6,038	6,305	6,343	6,290	24,976
2001	6,894	6,686	6,529	6,254	26,363

Earnings Per Share ($)

2006	0.14	0.24	**E**0.45	**E**0.45	**E**1.50
2005	0.22	0.19	1.48	-0.17	1.74
2004	0.10	0.13	0.42	0.32	0.98
2003	0.11	0.19	0.25	0.11	0.66
2002	0.13	0.45	0.30	-0.27	0.61
2001	0.04	-0.65	-0.57	-1.19	-2.37

Fiscal year ended Dec. 31. Next earnings report expected: Early November. EPS Estimates based on S&P Operating Earnings; historical GAAP earnings are as reported.

Dividend Data (Dates: mm/dd Payment Date: mm/dd/yy)

Amount ($)	Date Decl.	Ex-Div. Date	Stk. of Record	Payment Date
0.250	02/14	02/15	02/17	03/15/06
0.250	05/08	05/17	05/19	06/15/06
0.250	07/11	08/16	08/18	09/15/06
0.250	10/10	11/15	11/17	12/15/06

Dividends have been paid since 1946. Source: Company reports.

International Paper Co

Business Summary October 20, 2006

CORPORATE OVERVIEW. International Paper is the world's largest paper and forest products company. According to Pulp & Paper magazine, its market share is about 25% in uncoated free sheet (UFS), used in copiers and for envelopes and forms, making it the market leader in that major category. It is the third largest linerboard producer, used to make corrugated boxes, with nearly 14% of the market. It also manufactures bleached paperboard used to package cosmetics, food, beverages, and pharmaceuticals, and is the top producer in this sector, with a share of around 34%.

MARKET PROFILE. IP operates in a highly cyclical and capital-intensive industry. Demand for the company's products are dependent on a number of factors, including industrial non-durable goods production, consumer spending, commercial printing and advertising activity, white collar employment levels, and new home construction and remodeling activity. Historical prices for paper and wood products have been volatile, and, despite its size, IP has had only a limited direct influence over the timing and extent of price changes for its products. Pricing is significantly affected by the relationship between supply and demand, and supply is mainly influenced by fluctuations in available manufacturing capacity. Technology seems to be having an impact on paper demand, especially in UFS, IP's largest category, where shipments have been down recently despite growth in the economy. We doubt the trend is likely to improve as industry forecaster Resource Information Systems Inc. (RISI) projects that demand for UFS is expected to grow at less than a 0.5% compound annual growth rate (CAGR) through 2009.

Company Financials

Per Share Data ($) Year Ended Dec. 31	**2005**	**2004**	**2003**	**2002**	**2001**	**2000**	**1999**	**1998**	**1997**	**1996**
Tangible Book Valuo	6.75	0.09	0.01	4.31	7.78	11.89	18.65	20.45	20.36	21.99
Cash Flow	4.38	4.19	4.07	3.90	1.51	4.28	4.16	4.65	3.68	5.12
Earnings	1.74	0.98	0.66	0.61	-2.37	0.82	0.48	0.77	-0.50	1.04
S&P Core Earnings	1.67	0.84	0.51	0.92	-2.25	NA	NA	NA	NA	NA
Dividends	1.00	1.00	1.00	1.00	1.00	1.00	1.00	1.00	1.00	1.00
Payout Ratio	57%	102%	152%	164%	NM	122%	NM	130%	NM	96%
Prices:High	42.59	45.01	43.32	46.20	43.31	60.00	59.50	55.25	61.00	44.63
Prices:Low	26.97	37.12	33.09	31.35	30.70	26.31	39.50	35.50	38.63	35.63
P/E Ratio:High	24	46	66	76	NM	73	NM	72	NM	43
P/E Ratio:Low	15	38	50	51	NM	32	NM	46	NM	34
Income Statement Analysis (Million $)										
Revenue	24,097	25,548	25,179	24,976	26,363	28,180	24,573	19,541	20,096	20,143
Operating Income	3,228	3,251	3,293	3,576	3,305	5,432	3,061	2,202	2,404	2,614
Depreciation	1,376	1,565	1,644	1,587	1,870	1,916	1,520	1,186	1,258	1,194
Interest Expense	593	743	766	783	929	791	541	496	490	530
Pretax Income	586	746	346	371	-1,265	497	448	392	16.0	002
Effective Tax Rate	NM	27.6%	NM	NM	NM	23.5%	19.2%	20.4%	237.5%	41.1%
Net Income	859	478	315	295	-1,142	142	199	236	-151	303
S&P Core Earnings	819	402	242	444	-1,091	NA	NA	NA	NA	NA
Balance Sheet & Other Financial Data (Million $)										
Cash	1,641	2,596	2,363	1,074	1,224	1,198	453	477	398	352
Current Assets	7,409	9,319	9,337	7,738	8,312	10,455	7,241	6,010	5,945	5,998
Total Assets	28,771	34,217	35,525	33,792	37,158	42,109	30,268	26,356	26,754	28,252
Current Liabilities	4,844	4,872	6,803	4,579	5,374	7,413	4,382	3,636	4,880	5,894
Long Term Debt	11,023	14,132	13,450	13,042	14,262	14,453	9,325	8,212	7,154	6,691
Common Equity	8,351	8,254	8,237	7,374	10,291	12,034	10,304	8,902	8,710	9,344
Total Capital	20,311	25,631	25,085	25,435	29,804	32,541	24,554	21,582	20,188	20,668
Capital Expenditures	1,155	1,262	1,166	1,009	1,049	1,352	1,139	1,049	1,111	1,394
Cash Flow	2,235	2,043	1,959	1,882	728	2,058	1,719	1,422	1,107	1,497
Current Ratio	1.5	1.9	1.4	1.7	1.5	1.4	1.7	1.7	1.2	1.0
% Long Term Debt of Capitalization	54.3	55.1	53.6	51.3	47.9	44.4	38.0	38.1	35.4	32.3
% Net Income of Revenue	3.6	1.9	1.3	1.2	NM	0.5	0.8	1.2	NM	1.5
% Return on Assets	2.7	1.4	0.9	0.8	NM	0.4	0.6	0.9	NM	1.2
% Return on Equity	10.3	5.8	4.0	3.3	NM	1.3	1.9	2.7	NM	3.5

Data as orig reptd.; bef. results of disc opers/spec. items. Per share data adj. for stk. divs.; EPS diluted. E-Estimated. NA-Not Available. NM-Not Meaningful. NR-Not Ranked. UR-Under Review.

Office: 400 Atlantic Street, Stamford, CT 06921.
Telephone: 203-541-8000.
Email: comm@ipaper.com
Website: http://www.internationalpaper.com

Chrmn & CEO: J.V. Faraci
Pres: R.M. Amen
EVP & CFO: M.M. Parrs
SVP, Secy & General Counsel: M.A. Smith

SVP & CIO: J.N. Balboni
Investor Contact: B.N. McDonald (203-541-8625)
Board of Directors: D. J. Bronczek, M. F. Brooks, J. V. Faraci, S. G. Gibara, J. A. Henderson, W. C. McClelland, D. F. McHenry, J. L. Townsend, III, J. F. Turner, W. G. Walter, A. Weisser

Founded: 1898
Domicile: New York
Employees: 68,700

Interpublic Group of Companies Inc. (The)

S&P Recommendation	Price	12-Mo. Target Price	Investment Style
HOLD ★★★★★	$10.71 (as of Oct 27, 2006)	$10.00	Mid-Cap Value

GICS Sector Consumer Discretionary
Sub-Industry Advertising

Comment Interpublic is one of the world's largest organizations of advertising agencies and marketing communications companies.

Key Stock Statistics (Source S&P, Vickers, company reports)

52-Wk Range	$11.25–7.79	S&P Oper. EPS 2006E	-0.11	P/E on S&P Oper. EPS 2006E	NM	Dividend Rate/Share	Nil
Trailing 12-Month EPS	$-0.62	S&P Oper. EPS 2007E	0.18	Common Shares Outstg. (M)	440.8	Yield (%)	Nil
Trailing 12-Month P/E	NM	S&P Core EPS 2006E	-0.11	Market Capitalization(B)	$4.721	Beta	1.85
$10K Invested 5 Yrs Ago	$4,882	S&P Core EPS 2007E	0.18	Institutional Ownership (%)	NA	S&P Credit Rating	B

Price Performance

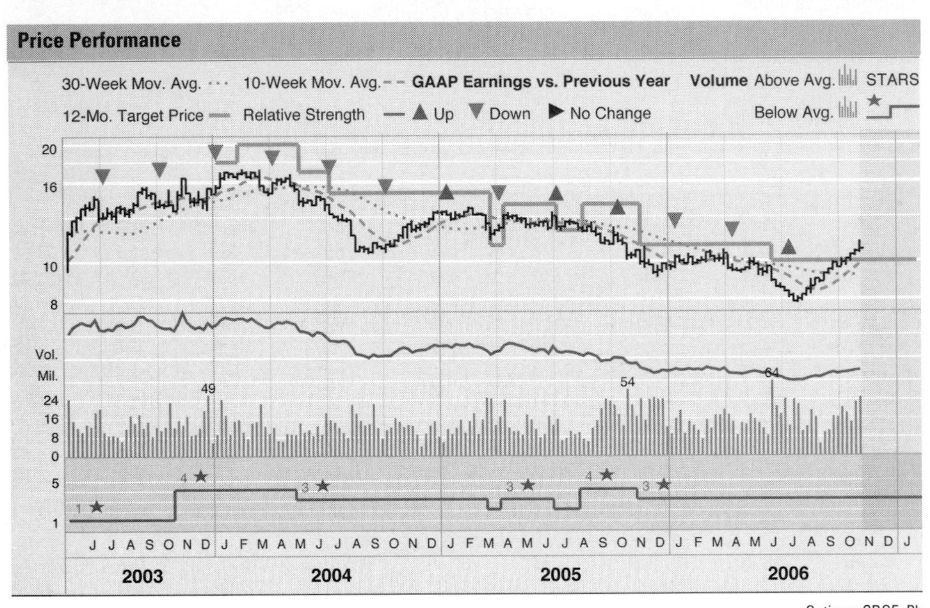

Options: CBOE, Ph

Analysis prepared by **James Peters, CFA** on August 31, 2006, when the stock traded at **$ 9.18**.

Highlights

- We see revenues declining about 2% in 2006, but we look for momentum to pick up late in the year after significant client losses in the second half of 2005. We believe new personnel in senior positions will be motivated by incentives that align company margins and revenue improvement with compensation, and we expect the company to focus its efforts on fostering organic revenue growth and streamlining internal operations.
- We anticipate continued high professional fees in 2006 as part of Sarbanes-Oxley compliance efforts; however, we think professional fees will begin to decrease in the latter half of 2006 as more system-based financial reporting systems are implemented. We see lower costs from about 3,000 recently completed layoffs, as well as from sharply lower severance costs. Overall, we foresee IPG's operating margin rising to about 5.7% in 2007, primarily on an anticipated further decline in professional fees, up from approximately 2.4% that we anticipate for 2006.
- Including restricted stock and stock option expense, we estimate a loss of $0.11 per share in 2006, which assumes a normalized tax rate of 40%.

Investment Rationale/Risk

- Given company comments on its May earnings call that IPG is unlikely to be Sarbanes-Oxley compliant in 2006, we think substantial investments will be made throughout the remainder of 2006 to create a more efficient operating and financial reporting structure, ultimately delaying a significant turnaround until 2007, in our view.
- Risks to our opinion and target price include significant business losses, additional adverse accounting-related developments, and the possibility that the implementation of corrective processes associated with Sarbanes-Oxley-related issues may take longer and/or cost more than anticipated to complete.
- Our 12-month target price of $10 is based on a applying a discount to peer average enterprise value/EBITDA multiple of 9.5X to $513 million, which is the average of our 2006 and 2007 EBITDA estimates. While we believe our 2007 EBITDA estimate is more representative of IPG's long-term potential, our valuation incorporates EBITDA estimates for both years to reflect significant uncertainty that we expect in the company's ability to execute a long anticipated turnaround.

Qualitative Risk Assessment

LOW | MEDIUM | **HIGH**

Our risk assessment reflects our view of a highly competitive advertising industry, economic cyclicality associated with advertising spending, and our expectation that the company should not be Sarbanes-Oxley compliant in 2006.

Quantitative Evaluations

S&P Quality Ranking C

D | **C** | B- | B | B+ | A- | A | A+

Relative Strength Rank STRONG

85

LOWEST = 1 HIGHEST = 99

Revenue/Earnings Data

Revenue (Million $)

	1Q	2Q	3Q	4Q	Year
2006	1,327	1,533	--	--	--
2005	1,328	1,611	1,440	1,896	6,274
2004	1,389	1,513	1,519	1,966	6,387
2003	1,316	1,499	1,419	1,629	5,863
2002	1,420	1,613	1,502	1,669	6,204
2001	1,658	1,743	1,606	1,720	6,727

Earnings Per Share ($)

2006	-0.43	0.11	E-0.14	E0.30	E-0.11
2005	-0.36	0.01	-0.25	-0.10	-0.70
2004	-0.21	-0.23	-1.22	0.22	-1.36
2003	-0.03	-0.06	-1.08	-0.26	-1.43
2002	0.16	0.29	-0.24	0.05	0.26
2001	-0.08	-0.30	-1.29	0.30	-1.37

Fiscal year ended Dec. 31. Next earnings report expected: NA. EPS Estimates based on S&P Operating Earnings; historical GAAP earnings are as reported.

Dividend Data

No cash dividends have been paid since 2002.

Interpublic Group of Companies Inc. (The)

Business Summary August 31, 2006

The Interpublic Group of Companies is one of the world's largest organizations of advertising agencies and marketing communications companies.

The company generates revenue from planning, creating and placing advertising in various media and from planning and executing other communications or marketing programs. IPG also receives commissions from clients for planning and supervising work done by outside contractors in the physical preparation of finished print advertisements and the production of TV and radio commercials and other forms of advertising. In addition, IPG derives revenue in a number of other ways, including the planning and placement in media of advertising produced by unrelated advertising agencies; the maintenance of specialized media placement facilities; the creation and publication of brochures, billboards, point of sale materials and direct marketing pieces for clients; the planning and carrying out of specialized marketing research; public relations campaigns; creating and managing special events at which client products are featured; and designing and carrying out interactive programs for special uses.

As of December 31, 2005, IPG organized its agencies into five global operating divisions and a group of stand-alone agencies. McCann WorldGroup, The FCB Group, The Lowe Group, and Draft Worldwide provide a comprehensive array of global communications and marketing services. The Constituent Management Group, including Weber Shandwick, FutureBrand, DeVries Public Relations, Golin Harris, Jack Morton and Octagon Worldwide, provides clients with diversified services, including public relations, meeting and event production, sports and entertainment marketing, corporate and brand identity, and strategic marketing consulting. In June 2006, IPG announced that it would merge the operations of FCB and Draft, with the integration expected to begin in the fall of 2006 and take six to 12 months to complete.

Company Financials

Per Share Data ($) Year Ended Dec. 31	**2005**	**2004**	**2003**	**2002**	**2001**	**2000**	**1999**	**1998**	**1997**	**1996**
Tangible Book Value	NM	NM	NM	NM	NM	NM	NM	NM	0.32	0.50
Cash Flow	-0.30	-0.91	-0.90	0.83	-0.36	1.99	1.77	1.67	1.21	1.10
Earnings	-0.70	-1.36	-1.43	0.26	-1.37	1.15	1.11	1.11	0.95	0.85
S&P Core Earnings	-0.62	-0.82	-0.84	0.36	-0.60	NA	NA	NA	NA	NA
Dividends	Nil	Nil	Nil	0.38	0.38	0.37	0.33	0.29	0.25	0.22
Payout Ratio	Nil	Nil	Nil	146%	NM	32%	30%	26%	26%	26%
Prices:High	13.80	17.31	16.50	34.98	47.44	57.69	58.38	40.31	26.50	16.75
Prices:Low	9.08	10.47	7.20	9.85	18.25	32.69	34.41	22.56	15.67	13.21
P/E Ratio:High	NM	NM	NM	NM	NM	50	53	36	28	20
P/E Ratio:Low	NM	NM	NM	NM	NM	28	31	20	16	15
Income Statement Analysis (Million $)										
Revenue	6,274	6,387	5,863	6,204	6,727	5,626	4,427	3,844	2,997	2,431
Operating Income	156	589	719	762	1,113	1,096	791	656	437	351
Depreciation	169	185	204	218	372	263	190	159	75.0	60.5
Interest Expense	182	172	173	146	165	109	66.4	58.7	49.4	40.7
Pretax Income	-173	-261	-330	271	-519	672	592	570	448	370
Effective Tax Rate	NM	NM	NM	51.8%	NM	40.7%	39.9%	40.7%	41.3%	40.5%
Net Income	-272	-545	-553	99.5	-505	359	322	310	239	205
S&P Core Earnings	-265	-363	-325	136	-217	NA	NA	NA	NA	NA
Balance Sheet & Other Financial Data (Million $)										
Cash	2,192	1,970	2,006	933	935	748	1,018	841	715	504
Current Assets	7,497	7,637	7,350	6,322	6,467	6,026	5,768	4,777	4,026	3,353
Total Assets	11,945	12,272	12,235	11,794	11,515	10,238	8,727	6,943	5,703	4,765
Current Liabilities	6,857	7,563	6,625	7,090	6,434	6,106	5,637	4,658	3,752	3,199
Long Term Debt	2,183	Nil	2,192	1,818	2,481	1,505	867	507	453	346
Common Equity	1,047	1,345	2,721	2,100	2,384	2,046	2,407	1,265	1,355	872
Total Capital	4,178	1,773	5,356	3,988	4,953	3,637	3,394	1,828	1,592	1,241
Capital Expenditures	141	194	160	183	268	202	150	137	96.9	79.1
Cash Flow	-129	-380	-349	317	-133	622	512	469	314	266
Current Ratio	1.1	1.0	1.1	0.9	1.0	1.0	1.0	1.0	1.1	1.1
% Long Term Debt of Capitalization	52.3	Nil	40.9	45.6	50.1	41.4	25.5	27.7	28.4	27.9
% Net Income of Revenue	NM	NM	NM	1.6	NM	6.4	7.3	8.1	8.0	8.4
% Return on Assets	NM	NM	NM	0.9	NM	3.7	4.1	4.9	4.6	4.5
% Return on Equity	NM	NM	NM	5.1	NM	18.8	14.7	23.7	19.6	25.3

Data as orig reptd.; bef. results of disc opers/spec. items. Per share data adj. for stk. divs., EPS diluted. E-Estimated. NA-Not Available. NM-Not Meaningful. NR-Not Ranked. UR-Under Review.

Office: 1271 Avenue of the Americas, New York, NY 10020-1300.
Telephone: 212-704-1200.
Website: http://www.interpublic.com
Chrmn & CEO: M.I. Roth

EVP & CFO: F. Mergenthaler
SVP, Chief Acctg Officer & Cntlr: C. Carroll
SVP, Secy & General Counsel: N.J. Camera
Investor Contact: J. Leshne (212-704-1439)

Board of Directors: F. J. Borelli, R. K. Brack, J. M. Considine, R. A. Goldstein, H. J. Greeniaus, W. T. Kerr, M. I. Roth, J. P. Samper, D. M. Thomas

Founded: 1902
Domicile: Delaware
Employees: 43,000

STANDARD &POOR'S

Intuit Inc

S&P Recommendation HOLD ★★★★★

Price
$34.43 (as of Oct 27, 2006)

12-Mo. Target Price
$33.00

Investment Style
Large-Cap Growth

GICS Sector Information Technology
Sub-Industry Application Software

Comment This company develops and markets small business accounting and management, tax preparation and personal finance software.

Key Stock Statistics (Source S&P, Vickers, company reports)

52-Wk Range	**$35.98–22.73**	S&P Oper. EPS 2007**E**	**1.28**	P/E on S&P Oper. EPS 2007**E**	**26.9**	Dividend Rate/Share	**Nil**
Trailing 12-Month EPS	**$1.16**	S&P Oper. EPS 2008**E**	**NA**	Common Shares Outstg. (M)	**345.2**	Yield (%)	**Nil**
Trailing 12-Month P/E	**29.7**	S&P Core EPS 2007**E**	**1.28**	Market Capitalization(B)	**$11.886**	Beta	**0.69**
$10K Invested 5 Yrs Ago	**$16,791**	S&P Core EPS 2008**E**	**NA**	Institutional Ownership (%)	**88**	S&P Credit Rating	**NA**

Price Performance

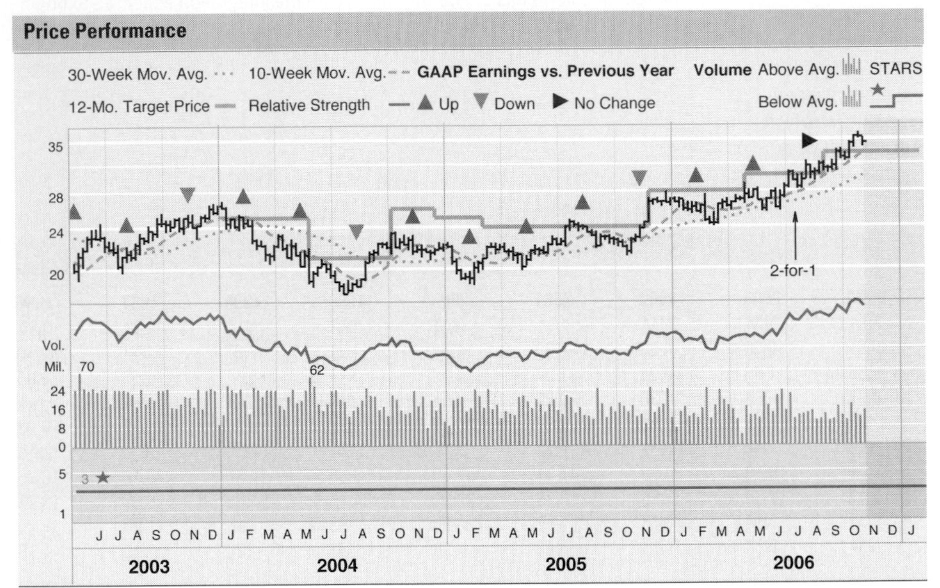

Options: ASE, CBOE, P, Ph

Analysis prepared by **Zaineb Bokhari** on September 06, 2006, when the stock traded at **$ 31.16**.

Highlights

- We forecast 9% revenue growth in FY 07 (Jul.), below the 15% pace reported for FY 06. We expect consumer tax sales to be a primary driver, rising 15% in FY 07. We see QuickBooks performing well, rising a likely 10% in FY 07, aided by a recent product upgrade to its flagship product. We expect payroll and payments revenues to rise by 16% in FY 07. We see other revenue declining by about 6% in FY 07, partly offsetting growth in INTU's core segments.
- Pro forma operating margins (excluding the impact of acquisition-related charges) have expanded significantly over the past several years, reflecting improved business processes and a more disciplined and effective allocation of resources, in our view. We expect pro forma operating margins to widen modestly in FY 07 as INTU invests in product development, particularly within its small business and tax segments.
- We forecast operating EPS (after a 2-for-1 stock split) of $1.28, including $0.12 of projected stock option expense, for FY 07; operating EPS (split adjusted) was $1.08 in FY 06, including $0.12 in stock option expense.

Investment Rationale/Risk

- INTU's profitability has improved notably over the past several years, and its balance sheet had nearly $1.2 billion in net cash, cash equivalents and short-term investments, as of July 31, 2006. Despite market share leadership in multiple areas, we believe INTU's biggest challenge is to reaccelerate revenue growth. The Internet offers significant growth potential, in our view, particularly for INTU's consumer tax franchise. INTU should be able to leverage its significant brand and market expertise to build share; however, we see this limited, to some extent, by competition.
- Risks to our opinion and target price include increasing competition in the small business market from Microsoft, which we believe would result in increased pricing pressure for INTU; and potential execution issues with respect to anticipated new product enhancements and introductions.
- Our 12-month target price of $33 is derived from our valuation of discounted free cash flow, assuming a weighted average cost of capital of 11.8% and a terminal growth rate of 4%. At recent prices, we view the shares as fairly valued.

Qualitative Risk Assessment

LOW | **MEDIUM** | HIGH

Our risk assessment reflects our view of the company's strong market position within the consumer tax and small business accounting software segments, and its liquid balance sheet. Our optimism is tempered by what we see as challenges that the company faces as it tries to grow beyond its core market segments as well as concerns regarding past stock option granting practices, which have become the subject of an informal inquiry by the SEC.

Quantitative Evaluations

S&P Quality Ranking **B**

D | C | B- | **B** | B+ | A- | A | A+

Relative Strength Rank **MODERATE**

69

LOWEST = 1 HIGHEST = 99

Revenue/Earnings Data

Revenue (Million $)

	1Q	2Q	3Q	4Q	Year
2006	304.1	742.7	952.6	342.9	2,342
2005	266.0	662.6	849.5	301.8	2,038
2004	242.5	636.3	713.0	275.9	1,868
2003	223.3	558.1	634.7	245.1	1,651
2002	168.7	490.8	501.7	197.2	1,358
2001	187.5	457.6	425.2	191.2	1,261

Earnings Per Share ($)

2006	-0.17	0.43	0.84	-0.06	1.05
2005	-0.11	0.39	0.81	-0.06	1.00
2004	-0.14	0.37	0.67	-0.11	0.79
2003	-0.13	0.29	0.53	-0.06	0.82
2002	-0.24	0.24	0.31	-0.16	0.16
2001	-0.12	0.06	-0.04	-0.15	-0.24

Fiscal year ended Jul. 31. Next earnings report expected: Mid November. EPS Estimates based on S&P Operating Earnings; historical GAAP earnings are as reported.

Dividend Data (Dates: mm/dd Payment Date: mm/dd/yy)

Amount ($)	Date Decl.	Ex-Div. Date	Stk. of Record	Payment Date
2-for-1 Stk.	05/17	07/07	06/21	07/06/06

Source: Company reports.

Business Summary September 06, 2006

Intuit aims to transform the way people run their businesses and manage their finances. Its growth strategy entails pursuing large and underserved markets where it can sustain competitive advantages, providing customer-driven innovation to address consumer needs, and using operational rigor and process excellence to execute effectively.

QuickBooks-related offerings (which accounted for about 36% of total net revenues in FY 05 (Jul.), up from 35% in FY 04) provide bookkeeping capabilities and business management tools. Products include QuickBooks Basic, QuickBooks Pro (for up to five simultaneous users), QuickBooks Premier (for small businesses needing more advanced accounting functionality), and QuickBooks Enterprise Solutions Business Management Software (for businesses with up to 250 employees). Premier and Enterprise offerings are also available in a variety of industry specific editions. Additional products are QuickBooks Point of Sale (for retail businesses) and QuickBooks Do-It-Yourself Payroll (for small business to prepare their own payrolls).

Intuit-Branded Small Business offerings (13% and 14%) consist of miscellaneous business management solutions. Outsourced payroll services include QuickBooks Assisted Payroll Service, Intuit Payroll Services Complete Payroll, Complete Payroll, and Premiere Payroll Service. INTU also offers Distribution Management Solutions (for wholesale durable goods companies), Real Estate Solutions (for residential, commercial and corporate property managers), and Construction Business Solutions (for construction companies).

The Consumer Tax segment (27% and 26%) is centered on TurboTax. TurboTax software enables individuals and small businesses to prepare and file income tax returns using computers. TurboTax for the Web allows individuals to prepare tax returns online. Versions of TurboTax Premier software are designed to address the special income tax needs of different types of users, including investors, those planning for retirement, and rental property owners. Electronic tax filing services are also provided.

Company Financials

Per Share Data ($) Year Ended Jul. 31	**2006**	**2005**	**2004**	**2003**	**2002**	**2001**	**2000**	**1999**	**1998**	**1997**
Tangible Book Value	3.41	3.61	2.75	3.44	4.02	4.15	4.00	2.75	2.01	1.31
Cash Flow	1.34	1.31	1.03	0.01	0.00	-0.09	1.23	1.36	0.14	0.20
Earnings	1.05	1.00	0.79	0.82	0.16	-0.24	0.73	0.99	-0.04	-0.01
S&P Core Earnings	1.04	0.86	0.61	0.41	NA	-0.32	NA	NA	NA	NA
Dividends	Nil	Nil	Nil	Nil	Nil	Nil	Nil	Nil	Nil	Nil
Payout Ratio	Nil	Nil	Nil	Nil	Nil	Nil	Nil	Nil	Nil	Nil
Prices:High	35.98	27.97	26.63	26.95	27.52	23.69	45.00	32.00	12.23	6.86
Prices:Low	23.99	18.62	17.92	16.65	17.26	11.31	12.88	11.25	5.65	3.48
P/E Ratio:High	34	28	34	33	NM	NM	62	32	NM	NM
P/E Ratio:Low	23	19	23	20	NM	NM	18	11	NM	NM
Income Statement Analysis (Million $)										
Revenue	2,342	2,038	1,868	1,651	1,358	1,261	1,094	848	593	599
Operating Income	677	659	561	461	343	265	200	254	70.5	107
Depreciation	104	118	97.0	76.5	59.9	59.9	213	141	53.2	58.7
Interest Expense	Nil	Nil	Nil	Nil	Nil	Nil	Nil	Nil	Nil	Nil
Pretax Income	610	556	453	393	84.9	-96.5	513	617	-19.8	9.81
Effective Tax Rate	38.0%	32.6%	30.0%	33.0%	17.9%	NM	40.4%	39.0%	NM	129.9%
Net Income	377	375	317	263	69.8	-97.1	306	377	-12.2	-2.93
S&P Core Earnings	372	323	245	172	-0.77	-129	NA	NA	NA	NA
Balance Sheet & Other Financial Data (Million $)										
Cash	180	83.8	27.2	1,207	452	535	643	950	138	46.8
Current Assets	1,817	1,614	1,517	1,669	1,995	2,148	2,129	1,586	980	455
Total Assets	2,770	2,716	2,696	2,790	2,963	2,962	2,879	2,328	1,499	664
Current Liabilities	1,016	1,003	857	796	733	788	807	781	375	212
Long Term Debt	15.4	17.5	5.77	29.3	14.6	12.4	0.54	36.3	35.6	36.4
Common Equity	1,738	1,695	1,822	1,965	2,216	2,170	4,143	1,511	1,088	415
Total Capital	1,754	1,713	1,828	1,994	2,230	2,182	4,143	1,547	1,124	452
Capital Expenditures	44.6	38.2	52.3	50.4	42.6	77.1	94.9	80.0	69.3	27.6
Cash Flow	482	493	414	340	130	-37.2	519	518	41.1	55.7
Current Ratio	1.8	1.6	1.8	2.1	2.7	2.7	2.6	2.0	2.6	2.1
% Long Term Debt of Capitalization	0.9	1.0	0.3	1.5	0.7	0.6	0.0	2.3	NA	8.1
% Net Income of Revenue	16.1	18.4	17.0	15.9	5.1	NM	27.9	44.4	NM	NM
% Return on Assets	13.8	13.8	11.6	9.2	2.4	NM	11.4	19.7	NM	NM
% Return on Equity	22.0	21.3	16.7	12.6	3.2	NM	8.4	29.0	NM	NM

Data as orig reptd.; bef. results of disc opers/spec. items. Per share data adj. for stk. divs.; EPS diluted. E-Estimated. NA-Not Available. NM-Not Meaningful. NR-Not Ranked. UR-Under Review.

Office: 2700 Coast Ave, Mountain View, CA 94043-1140.
Telephone: 650-944-6000.
Email: investor_relations@intuit.com
Website: http://www.intuit.com

Chrmn: W.V. Campbell
Pres & CEO: S.M. Bennett
SVP & CFO: K. Patel
SVP & CTO: R.W. Ihrie

VP, Secy & General Counsel: L.A. Fennell
Board of Directors: S. M. Bennett, C. W. Brody, W. V. Campbell, S. D. Cook, L. J. Doerr, D. L. Dubinsky, D. Greene, M. R. Hallman, D. Powell, S. D. Sclavos

Founded: 1984
Domicile: Delaware
Employees: 7,500

STANDARD &POOR'S

ITT Corp

S&P Recommendation STRONG BUY ★★★★★	Price $54.45 (as of Oct 27, 2006)	12-Mo. Target Price $68.00	Investment Style Large-Cap Growth

GICS Sector Industrials
Sub-Industry Industrial Machinery

Comment This diversified industrial manufacturer of advanced technology products is the legal successor to the old ITT Corp.

Key Stock Statistics (Source S&P, Vickers, company reports)

52-Wk Range	$58.73–45.34	S&P Oper. EPS 2006E	2.91	P/E on S&P Oper. EPS 2006E	18.7	Dividend Rate/Share	$0.44
Trailing 12-Month EPS	$1.94	S&P Oper. EPS 2007E	3.39	Common Shares Outstg. (M)	184.7	Yield (%)	0.81
Trailing 12-Month P/E	28.1	S&P Core EPS 2006E	2.77	Market Capitalization(B)	$10.056	Beta	0.60
$10K Invested 5 Yrs Ago	$22,383	S&P Core EPS 2007E	3.25	Institutional Ownership (%)	74	S&P Credit Rating	BBB+

Price Performance

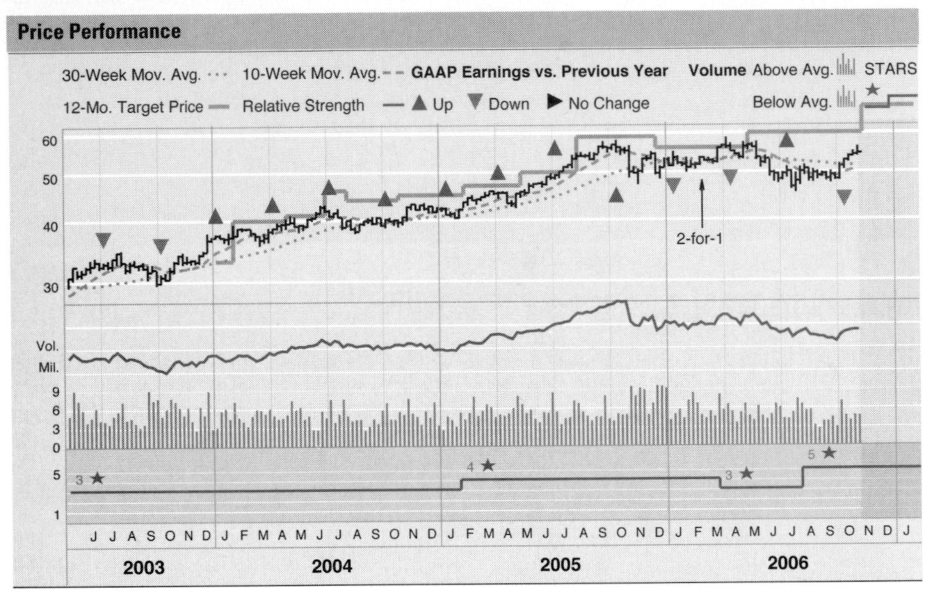

Options: CBOE, P

Qualitative Risk Assessment

LOW | **MEDIUM** | HIGH

Our risk assessment reflects our view of ITT's favorable growth prospects in most of the markets it serves and what we see as a strong management and a healthy balance sheet. This is offset by growth in U.S. defense spending, which may slow in coming years, in our opinion.

Quantitative Evaluations

S&P Quality Ranking B+

D | C | B- | B | **B+** | A- | A | A+

Relative Strength Rank STRONG

71

LOWEST = 1 HIGHEST = 99

Highlights

➤ The 12-month target price for ITT has recently been changed to $68.00 from $60.00. The Highlights section of this Stock Report will be updated accordingly.

Investment Rationale/Risk

➤ The Investment Rationale/Risk section of this Stock Report will be updated shortly. For the latest News story on ITT from MarketScope, see below.

➤ 10/27/06 11:41 am EDT... S&P REITERATES STRONG BUY OPINION ON SHARES OF ITT CORP. (ITT 55.23*****): Before special items, Q3 EPS from continuing operations of $0.77 vs. $0.67 is a penny above our estimate. Despite the shift of approximately $0.12 to discontinued operations, we are reducing our '06 EPS estimate by just $0.08, to $2.91. Q3 organic sales growth was 13%, very strong in our opinion. We think ITT's new $1 billion stock buyback program can be materially EPS accretive, depending on timing and prices of purchases. We are raising our '07 EPS estimate by $0.06, to $3.50, and boosting our 12-month target price by $8 to $68 on a blend of P/E and DCF analyses. / E.Levy-CFA

Revenue/Earnings Data

Revenue (Million $)

	1Q	2Q	3Q	4Q	Year
2006	1,887	2,068	2,001	--	--
2005	1,776	1,874	1,828	1,950	7,427
2004	1,511	1,647	1,663	1,943	6,764
2003	1,296	1,438	1,375	1,517	5,627
2002	1,186	1,320	1,235	1,244	4,985
2001	1,186	1,184	1,124	1,182	4,676

Earnings Per Share ($)

	1Q	2Q	3Q	4Q	Year
2006	0.57	0.76	0.75	E0.79	E2.91
2005	0.65	0.70	0.79	-0.48	1.67
2004	0.47	0.60	0.58	0.66	2.32
2003	0.46	0.49	0.55	0.58	2.08
2002	0.39	0.50	0.64	0.51	2.03
2001	0.33	0.42	0.38	0.08	1.20

Fiscal year ended Dec. 31. Next earnings report expected: Late January. EPS Estimates based on S&P Operating Earnings; historical GAAP earnings are as reported.

Dividend Data (Dates: mm/dd Payment Date: mm/dd/yy)

Amount ($)	Date Decl.	Ex-Div. Date	Stk. of Record	Payment Date
0.220	02/20	03/08	03/10	04/01/06
0.110	05/09	05/17	05/19	07/01/06
0.110	07/11	08/23	08/25	10/01/06
0.110	10/27	11/15	11/17	01/01/07

Dividends have been paid since 1996. Source: Company reports.

Business Summary August 02, 2006

CORPORATE OVERVIEW. ITT Industries (formerly ITT Corp.) is the legal successor to the old ITT Corp. In a restructuring completed in December 1995, old ITT was divided into three separate, publicly owned entities. ITT Industries retained old ITT's industrial units, and two companies were spun off: ITT Hartford Group (insurance), and New ITT Corp. (hotels, gaming, entertainment and education). After the discontinuation and spin off of ITT Hartford Group and New ITT Corp., ITT now produces mostly defense electronics and fluid technology products.

Fluid technology products (38% of 2005 sales) include pumps, valves, heat exchangers, mixers and fluid measuring instruments and controls for residential, agricultural, commercial, municipal and industrial applications. The fluid technology segment became the world's largest pump manufacturer (formerly third largest) following its 1997 acquisition of Goulds Pumps, Inc.

Defense electronics and services (43%) are sold to the military and government agencies. Products include traffic control systems, jamming devices that guard military planes against radar guided missiles, digital combat radios, night vision devices, radar, satellite instruments and other. About 83% of segment sales in 2005 were to the U.S. government.

Electronic components (10%) are marketed under the Cannon brand. These products include connectors, switches and cabling used in communications, computing, aerospace and industrial applications, as well as network services.

Motion and flow control (9%) products include switches and valves for industrial and aerospace applications, products for the marine and leisure markets, and fluid handling materials such as tubing systems and connectors for various automotive and industrial markets for the transportation industry.

CORPORATE STRATEGY. The company's strategy is to expand revenues through a combination of internal growth and acquisitions. We expect the company to continue its tradition of successful acquisition integrations.

At the same time, ITT plans to divest operations that do not fit its strategic goals or provide adequate returns. One current example is the planned divestiture of the switches components operations, which accounted for about half of the electronics components segment's 2005 revenues.

Company Financials

Per Share Data ($) Year Ended Dec. 31	**2005**	**2004**	**2003**	**2002**	**2001**	**2000**	**1999**	**1998**	**1997**	**1996**
Tangible Book Value	1.38	NM	0.78	NM	NM	NM	NM	2.27	NM	1.91
Cash Flow	2.71	3.37	3.08	2.94	2.37	2.59	2.25	0.43	2.03	2.83
Earnings	1.67	2.32	2.08	2.03	1.20	1.47	1.27	-0.43	0.47	0.93
S&P Core Earnings	2.28	2.13	1.94	0.69	-0.18	NA	NA	NA	NA	NA
Dividends	0.36	0.34	0.32	0.30	0.30	0.30	0.30	0.30	0.30	0.30
Payout Ratio	22%	15%	15%	15%	25%	20%	24%	NM	64%	32%
Prices:High	58.05	43.36	37.70	35.43	26.00	19.81	20.75	20.44	16.84	14.31
Prices:Low	40.24	35.52	25.06	22.80	17.78	11.19	15.25	14.00	11.00	10.75
P/E Ratio:High	35	19	18	17	22	13	16	NM	36	15
P/E Ratio:Low	24	15	12	11	15	8	12	NM	24	12
Income Statement Analysis (Million $)										
Revenue	7,427	6,764	5,627	4,985	4,676	4,829	4,632	4,493	8,777	8,718
Operating Income	985	871	559	706	707	695	592	525	904	941
Depreciation	197	199	188	171	213	202	181	196	378	433
Interest Expense	75.0	50.4	Nil	68.8	85.5	93.1	84.8	126	133	169
Pretax Income	448	610	531	509	333	420	370	-160	187	371
Effective Tax Rate	29.8%	28.3%	26.3%	25.3%	35.0%	37.0%	37.0%	NM	39.0%	40.0%
Net Income	314	438	391	380	217	265	233	-98.0	114	223
S&P Core Earnings	429	400	364	129	-31.7	NA	NA	NA	NA	NA
Balance Sheet & Other Financial Data (Million $)										
Cash	451	263	414	202	121	88.7	182	880	192	122
Current Assets	2,772	2,329	2,106	1,701	1,459	1,506	1,628	2,382	2,377	2,289
Total Assets	7,063	7,277	5,938	5,390	4,508	4,611	4,530	5,049	6,221	5,491
Current Liabilities	2,560	2,446	1,687	1,730	1,897	2,233	2,110	2,151	3,545	2,538
Long Term Debt	516	543	461	492	456	408	479	516	532	583
Common Equity	2,723	2,343	1,848	1,137	1,376	1,211	1,099	1,299	822	799
Total Capital	3,240	2,886	2,309	1,630	1,832	1,620	1,578	1,815	1,386	1,492
Capital Expenditures	179	165	154	153	174	181	228	213	460	406
Cash Flow	511	636	579	551	430	466	414	98.0	492	656
Current Ratio	1.1	1.0	1.2	1.0	0.8	0.7	0.8	1.1	0.7	0.9
% Long Term Debt of Capitalization	15.9	18.8	20.0	30.2	24.9	25.2	30.3	28.4	38.4	39.1
% Net Income of Revenue	4.2	6.5	6.9	7.6	4.6	5.5	5.0	NM	1.3	2.6
% Return on Assets	4.4	6.6	6.9	7.7	4.8	5.8	4.9	NM	1.9	3.9
% Return on Equity	12.4	20.9	26.2	30.2	16.8	22.9	19.4	NM	14.1	31.3

Data as orig reptd.; bef. results of disc opers/spec. items. Per share data adj. for stk. divs.; EPS diluted. E-Estimated. NA-Not Available. NM-Not Meaningful. NR-Not Ranked. UR-Under Review.

Office: 4 West Red Oak Lane, White Plains, NY 10604-3617.
Telephone: 914-641-2000.
Website: http://www.itt.com
Chrmn, Pres & CEO: S.R. Loranger

SVP & CFO: G.E. Minnich
SVP & CTO: B.L. Reichelderfer
SVP & Treas: D.E. Foley
SVP & General Counsel: V.A. Maffeo

Investor Contact: P.J. Milligan
Board of Directors: C. J. Crawford, C. A. Gold, R. F. Hake, J. J. Hamre, R. W. LeBoeuf, S. R. Loranger, F. T. MacInnis, L. S. Sanford, M. I. Tambakeras

Founded: 1920
Domicile: Indiana
Employees: 40,900

STANDARD &POOR'S

Jabil Circuit Inc

S&P Recommendation BUY ★★★★★

Price $28.71 (as of Oct 27, 2006)

12-Mo. Target Price $36.00

Investment Style Mid-Cap Growth

GICS Sector Information Technology
Sub-Industry Electronic Manufacturing Services

Comment This company manufactures circuit board assemblies for international OEMs in the PC, peripheral, communications and automotive markets.

Key Stock Statistics (Source S&P, Vickers, company reports)

52-Wk Range	$43.70–22.01	S&P Oper. EPS 2006E	1.37	P/E on S&P Oper. EPS 2006E	21.0	Dividend Rate/Share	$0.28
Trailing 12-Month EPS	$1.33	S&P Oper. EPS 2007E	1.77	Common Shares Outstg. (M)	212.3	Yield (%)	0.98
Trailing 12-Month P/E	21.6	S&P Core EPS 2006E	1.30	Market Capitalization(B)	$6.095	Beta	2.18
$10K Invested 5 Yrs Ago	$11,708	S&P Core EPS 2007E	1.77	Institutional Ownership (%)	86	S&P Credit Rating	BBB-

Price Performance

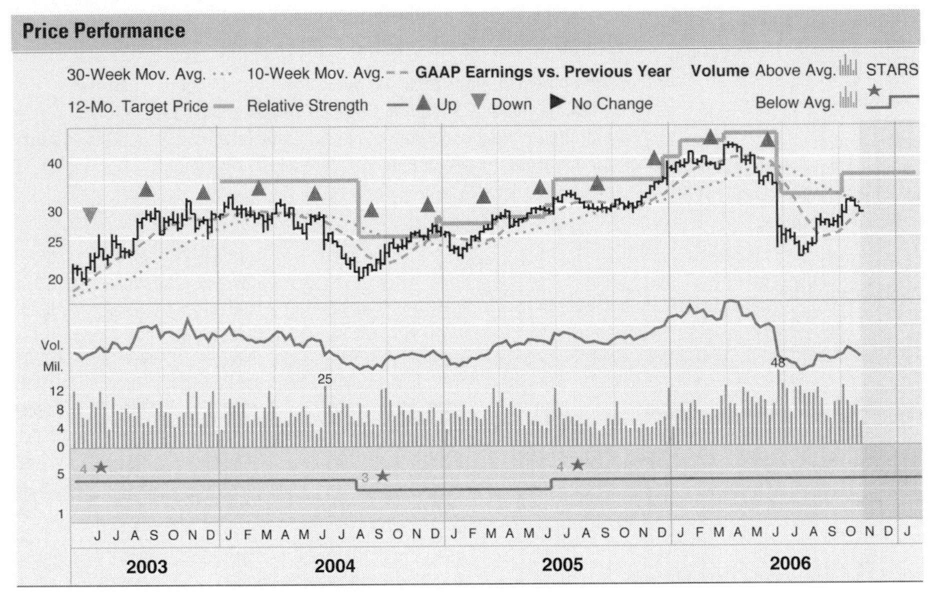

Options: ASE, CBOE, P, Ph

Analysis prepared by **Richard N. Stice, CFA** on September 28, 2006, when the stock traded at **$ 28.73**.

Highlights

- We forecast a 21% increase in FY 07 (Aug.) revenue, following a rise of 36% in FY 06. We anticipate that results will be driven by new business wins, at least a modest pickup in end-market demand, gains in market share, and an ongoing trend on the part of customers to outsource more of their production to primary industry participants such as JBL.
- We look for the FY 07 gross margin to remain near 8%, which exceeds the company's peer group average, as higher volumes are offset by costs associated with the buildout of its electromechanical business and restructuring activities at existing facilities. We expect the restructuring actions to be largely completed by the end of FY 07.
- We anticipate the effective tax rate at 15%, as we see JBL benefiting from favorable tax jurisdictions in offshore locations. We project FY 07 EPS of $1.77, which includes costs associated with projected stock option expense, up 29% from FY 06's anticipated EPS of $1.37 (excluding amortization charges of $0.07). Final FY 06 results are still being finalized due to an ongoing probe related to stock option grants.

Investment Rationale/Risk

- We believe the longer-term outlook for the electronic manufacturing services industry remains favorable, and we expect the company to benefit from further penetration of the outsourcing model. Moreover, we are encouraged by JBL's push to diversify its business mix into the automotive and instrumentation and medical sectors, and our view of relatively consistent free cash flow generation.
- Risks to our recommendation and target price include potential market share losses, delays in the implementation of new contracts and facilities and possible financial restatements resulting from an investigation into the company's stock option granting practices.
- Our 12-month target price of $36 is based on a combination of valuation metrics. The first is a relative P/E-to-growth measure that allocates JBL with a 10% premium to its peer group and results in a value of $39. The second utilizes discounted cash flow analysis, which leads to an intrinsic value of $33. Our assumptions include a weighted average cost of capital of 11% and an expected terminal growth rate of 3%.

Qualitative Risk Assessment

LOW	MEDIUM	HIGH

Our risk assessment reflects our view of the historically volatile nature of the electronic manufacturing services industry as well as what we see as the company's relatively high exposure to fluctuations in commodity prices.

Quantitative Evaluations

S&P Quality Ranking B

D	C	B-	B	B+	A-	A	A+

Relative Strength Rank MODERATE

38

LOWEST = 1 HIGHEST = 99

Revenue/Earnings Data

Revenue (Million $)

	1Q	2Q	3Q	4Q	Year
2006	2,404	2,315	2,592	--	--
2005	1,833	1,716	1,938	2,037	7,524
2004	1,509	1,492	1,626	1,626	6,253
2003	1,068	1,146	1,219	1,296	4,729
2002	884.6	822.1	850.6	988.2	3,545
2001	1,129	1,211	1,046	944.1	4,331

Earnings Per Share ($)

	1Q	2Q	3Q	4Q	Year
2006	0.37	0.32	0.30	E0.31	E1.37
2005	0.27	0.22	0.29	0.34	1.12
2004	0.20	0.19	0.19	0.22	0.81
2003	0.04	0.05	0.02	0.10	0.21
2002	0.04	0.02	0.10	0.01	0.17
2001	0.24	0.21	0.09	0.06	0.59

Fiscal year ended Aug. 31. Next earnings report expected: NA. EPS Estimates based on S&P Operating Earnings; historical GAAP earnings are as reported.

Dividend Data (Dates: mm/dd Payment Date: mm/dd/yy)

Amount ($)	Date Decl.	Ex-Div. Date	Stk. of Record	Payment Date
0.070	05/04	05/11	05/15	06/01/06
0.070	08/02	08/11	08/15	09/01/06

Dividends have been paid since 2006. Source: Company reports.

Jabil Circuit Inc

Business Summary September 28, 2006

CORPORATE OVERVIEW. This provider of electronic manufacturing services (EMS) works with customers in a variety of industries at facilities around the world. Between 2000 and 2005, sales doubled to more than $7.5 billion, with the vast majority of the growth generated internally.

In FY 05, 40 customers accounted collectively for approximately 90% of net revenue, with Royal Philips Electronics comprising 14%, Nokia Corp. 13% and Hewlett-Packard 10%. Also with respect to FY 05, JBL entered into 40 new customer relationships that it expects will account for 10% of FY 06 revenues.

MARKET PROFILE. We believe the EMS industry remains well positioned to capture new business from original equipment manufacturers (OEMs). This is due to our view that the cost advantages associated with the outsourcing model are beginning to be understood by potential participants. We think the benefits of this strategy are ample, with companies being able to reduce costs and reallocate resources toward their core competencies (e.g., marketing and research and development). We see the industry growing at a low double digit annual rate over the next several years and achieving nearly $180 billion in revenue by 2009.

We see a number of key trends emerging in the EMS landscape. For instance, OEMs have begun to limit the number of EMS providers with which they conduct business. We think this move results from the customer's desire to streamline its operations. While in the past, they may have utilized five or six vendors, many now seek to limit that total to just one or two. We believe this development bodes well for larger EMS companies such as JBL, as their broad range of service offerings and worldwide presence enable them to fulfill an entire slate of customer requests, in our opinion.

Company Financials

Per Share Data ($) Year Ended Aug. 31	**2005**	**2004**	**2003**	**2002**	**2001**	**2000**	**1999**	**1998**	**1997**	**1996**
Tangible Book Value	8.22	7.29	6.06	6.63	6.43	6.68	3.32	1.67	1.23	0.87
Cash Flow	2.18	1.89	1.32	1.11	1.35	1.31	0.90	0.60	0.51	0.29
Earnings	1.12	0.81	0.21	0.17	0.59	0.78	0.56	0.37	0.34	0.17
S&P Core Earnings	0.64	0.59	0.04	NA	0.46	NA	NA	NA	NA	NA
Dividends	Nil	Nil	Nil	Nil	Nil	Nil	Nil	Nil	Nil	Nil
Payout Ratio	Nil	Nil	Nil	Nil	Nil	Nil	Nil	Nil	Nil	Nil
Prices:High	39.00	32.40	31.66	26.79	40.99	68.00	38.97	18.72	18.00	5.33
Prices:Low	21.80	19.18	21.20	11.13	14.00	18.63	14.25	5.75	3.84	0.64
P/E Ratio:High	35	40	NM	NM	69	87	70	51	53	16
P/E Ratio:Low	19	24	NM	65	24	24	25	16	11	2

Income Statement Analysis (Million $)										
Revenue	7,524	6,253	4,729	3,545	4,331	3,558	2,000	1,277	978	863
Operating Income	507	439	369	296	353	317	197	142	107	63.6
Depreciation	220	222	224	188	155	99.3	56.0	35.7	24.9	18.2
Interest Expense	24.8	19.4	17.0	13.1	5.86	7.61	1.69	3.12	1.61	7.30
Pretax Income	276	198	37.0	44.8	166	213	140	82.0	80.2	38.1
Effective Tax Rate	16.1%	15.5%	NM	22.4%	28.7%	31.5%	34.4%	30.6%	34.6%	36.0%
Net Income	232	167	43.0	34.7	119	146	91.5	56.9	52.5	24.3
S&P Core Earnings	134	122	8.12	-0.11	93.4	NA	NA	NA	NA	NA

Balance Sheet & Other Financial Data (Million $)										
Cash	796	621	700	641	431	338	114	23.1	45.5	73.3
Current Assets	2,686	2,183	2,094	1,588	1,447	1,387	588	290	266	227
Total Assets	4,077	3,329	3,245	2,548	2,358	2,018	921	527	406	300
Current Liabilities	1,568	1,159	1,263	593	505	692	331	187	169	112
Long Term Debt	327	305	297	355	362	25.0	33.3	81.7	50.0	58.4
Common Equity	2,135	1,819	1,588	1,507	1,414	1,270	546	248	181	124
Total Capital	2,462	2,125	1,905	1,903	1,813	1,323	588	338	235	186
Capital Expenditures	257	218	117	85.5	309	333	150	99.8	93.8	27.3
Cash Flow	452	389	267	223	274	245	147	92.6	77.4	42.6
Current Ratio	1.7	1.9	1.7	2.7	2.9	2.0	1.8	1.6	1.6	2.0
% Long Term Debt of Capitalization	13.3	14.4	15.6	18.6	20.0	1.9	5.7	24.2	21.3	31.5
% Net Income of Revenue	3.1	2.7	0.9	1.0	2.7	4.1	4.6	4.5	5.4	2.8
% Return on Assets	6.3	5.1	1.5	1.4	5.4	9.5	12.7	12.2	14.9	8.4
% Return on Equity	11.7	9.8	2.8	2.4	8.8	15.8	23.0	26.5	34.3	26.5

Data as orig reptd.; bef. results of disc opers/spec. items. Per share data adj. for stk. divs.; EPS diluted. E-Estimated. NA-Not Available. NM-Not Meaningful. NR-Not Ranked. UR-Under Review.

Office: 10560 Dr. Martin Luther King Jr. Street North, St. Petersburg, FL 33716.
Telephone: 727-577-9749.
Email: investor_relations@jabil.com
Website: http://www.jabil.com

Chrmn: W.D. Morean
Pres & CEO: T.L. Main
Vice Chrmn: T.A. Sansone
COO: M. Mondello

Investor Contact: B. Walters (727-803-3349)
Board of Directors: L. S. Grafstein, M. S. Lavitt, T. L. Main, W. D. Morean, L. J. Murphy, F. A. Newman, S. A. Raymund, T. A. Sansone, K. A. Walters

Founded: 1969
Domicile: Delaware
Employees: 40,000

Janus Capital Group Inc.

STANDARD &POOR'S

S&P Recommendation SELL ★★★★★

Price $20.79 (as of Oct 27, 2006)

12-Mo. Target Price $18.00

Investment Style Mid-Cap Growth

GICS Sector Financials
Sub-Industry Asset Management & Custody Banks

Comment Janus is a U.S.-based investment management company that focuses on growth equity and quantitative strategies.

Key Stock Statistics (Source S&P, Vickers, company reports)

52-Wk Range	$24.20–15.50	S&P Oper. EPS 2006E	0.62	P/E on S&P Oper. EPS 2006E	33.5	Dividend Rate/Share	$0.04
Trailing 12-Month EPS	$0.52	S&P Oper. EPS 2007E	0.81	Common Shares Outstg. (M)	206.7	Yield (%)	0.19
Trailing 12-Month P/E	40.0	S&P Core EPS 2006E	0.62	Market Capitalization(B)	$4.297	Beta	2.20
$10K Invested 5 Yrs Ago	$9,767	S&P Core EPS 2007E	0.81	Institutional Ownership (%)	85	S&P Credit Rating	BBB+

Price Performance

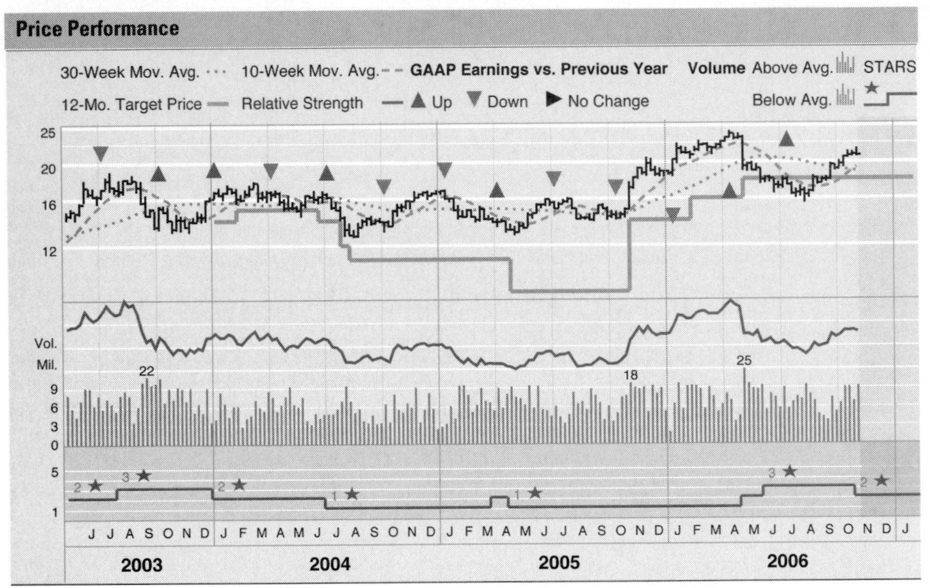

Options: ASE, CBOE, P, Ph

Highlights

➤ The STARS recommendation for JNS has recently been changed to 2 (sell) from 3 (hold). The Highlights section of this Stock Report will be updated accordingly.

Investment Rationale/Risk

➤ The Investment Rationale/Risk section of this Stock Report will be updated shortly. For the latest News story on JNS from MarketScope, see below.

➤ 10/26/06 10:09 am EDT... S&P DOWNGRADES SHARES OF JANUS CAPITAL TO SELL FROM HOLD (JNS 20.93**): Q3 EPS of $0.15 (on 7% lower shares) versus $0.15 is in line with our estimate. The benefits of share repurchases were offset by charges due to two sub-advised accounts and litigation fees. Assets under management came in shy our estimate, with 3.2% growth sequentially, and 14% growth year to year. We expect AUM to increase 10% in 2006 followed by 15% growth in 2007. Our 2006 EPS estimate declines to $0.62 from $0.64, and our 2007 estimate falls to $0.81 from $0.83. Our 12-month target price remains $18, 22.2X our 2007 EPS estimate, in line with peers. / M.Albrecht

Qualitative Risk Assessment

LOW | MEDIUM | **HIGH**

Our risk assessment reflects the company's lack of product diversification, previous regulatory issues, and turnover of investment personnel.

Quantitative Evaluations

S&P Quality Ranking NR

D | C | B- | B | B+ | A- | A | A+

Relative Strength Rank STRONG

76

LOWEST = 1 HIGHEST = 99

Revenue/Earnings Data

Revenue (Million $)

	1Q	2Q	3Q	4Q	Year
2006	256.1	254.6	--	--	--
2005	239.0	229.3	237.5	247.3	953.1
2004	274.4	258.8	237.8	239.8	1,011
2003	231.2	245.5	256.6	261.4	994.7
2002	328.3	310.4	257.8	248.3	1,145
2001	448.5	411.5	361.6	334.1	1,556

Earnings Per Share ($)

2006	0.17	0.15	E0.15	E0.15	E0.62
2005	0.09	0.12	0.15	0.05	0.40
2004	-0.10	0.54	0.20	0.08	0.73
2003	0.17	0.22	0.24	3.51	4.17
2002	0.42	0.30	-0.60	0.20	0.38
2001	0.48	0.39	0.11	0.32	1.31

Fiscal year ended Dec. 31. Next earnings report expected: Mid December. EPS Estimates based on S&P Operating Earnings; historical GAAP earnings are as reported.

Dividend Data (Dates: mm/dd Payment Date: mm/dd/yy)

Amount ($)	Date Decl.	Ex-Div. Date	Stk. of Record	Payment Date
0.040	04/25	05/11	05/15	05/31/06

Dividends have been paid since 2000. Source: Company reports.

Janus Capital Group Inc.

Business Summary September 05, 2006

CORPORATE OVERVIEW. Janus Capital Group, a single-branded global asset management company, was created through the January 1, 2003, merger of Janus Capital Corp. into its parent company, Stilwell Financial Inc., which had been spun off from Kansas City Southern Industries in July 2000 via a stock offering. The company had total assets under management of nearly $149 billion at the end of 2005, down from $193 billion at the end of 2001. The company distributes its products through one global distribution network directly to investors, and through advisers and financial intermediaries.

Wholly owned Janus Capital Management focuses on growth equities, and uses both fundamental and quantitative investment research. It also offers core, international, specialty fixed-income, and money market products. Its largest funds include Janus Fund (JANSX), Janus Worldwide (JAWWX) and Janus Twenty (JAVLX).

The company owns about 78% of Enhanced Investment Technologies, LLC (INTECH), which focuses on mathematically driven equity investing strategies. INTECH's assets under management totaled nearly $45 billion at the end of 2005, up from $7.3 billion at the end of 2002. INTECH, which manages assets for large institutions and endowments, seeks to achieve long-term returns that outperform a passive index, while controlling risks and trading costs.

JNS owns about 30% of Perkins, Wolf, McDonnell and Co., which focuses on value investing, and managed about $10 billion at the end of 2005, invested largely in REIT and value equities, through mutual funds and separate accounts. Bay Isle employs a bottom-up analysis, with a focus on what it believes to be quality companies that trade at discounts to their fair market value. Vontobel Asset Management is a sub-adviser for several Janus mutual funds and products, focusing on value equities.

The company owns about 9% of DST Systems, Inc., which provides information processing, printing and mailing, and computer software services and products to mutual funds, investment managers, communications concerns and other service providers. In December 2003, JNS exchanged 32.3 million DST Systems shares for all shares of a DST unit, referred to as JCG Partners, which owns a commercial printing business worth about $115 million, and has $999 million in cash. In December 2003, JNS said it would no longer use the equity method to account for its remaining investment.

Company Financials

Per Share Data ($) Year Ended Dec. 31	2005	2004	2003	2002	2001	2000	1999	1998	1997	1996
Tangible Book Value	0.88	1.43	1.00	NM	NM	3.50	NA	NA	NA	NA
Cash Flow	0.64	0.99	4.46	0.70	1.93	3.30	1.51	NA	NA	NA
Earnings	0.40	0.73	4.17	0.38	1.31	2.90	1.31	NA	NA	NA
S&P Core Earnings	0.42	0.32	1.60	0.42	1.18	NA	NA	NA	NA	NA
Dividends	0.04	0.04	0.04	0.05	0.04	0.01	NA	NA	NA	NA
Payout Ratio	10%	5%	1%	13%	3%	NM	NA	NA	NA	NA
Prices:High	20.59	17.90	19.00	29.24	46.63	54.50	NA	NA	NA	NA
Prices:Low	12.75	12.60	9.46	8.87	18.20	30.75	NA	NA	NA	NA
P/E Ratio:High	51	25	5	77	36	19	NA	NA	NA	NA
P/E Ratio:Low	32	17	2	24	14	11	NA	NA	NA	NA
Income Statement Analysis (Million $)										
Revenue	953	1,011	995	1,145	1,556	2,248	1,212	671	485	NA
Operating Income	224	264	396	441	872	1,118	554	297	212	NA
Depreciation	50.1	60.4	67.6	72.3	131	81.2	35.4	16.8	13.1	NA
Interest Expense	28.6	38.4	60.5	57.8	34.8	7.70	5.90	6.50	10.4	NA
Pretax Income	176	272	895	320	620	1,202	587	289	230	NA
Effective Tax Rate	38.6%	33.9%	NM	72.6%	35.1%	35.5%	38.8%	35.8%	37.8%	NA
Net Income	87.8	170	956	84.7	302	664	313	152	118	NA
S&P Core Earnings	92.5	74.1	367	92.4	276	NA	NA	NA	NA	NA
Balance Sheet & Other Financial Data (Million $)										
Cash	553	527	1,223	161	237	364	324	139	NA	NA
Current Assets	1,004	1,065	1,466	346	478	641	525	259	NA	NA
Total Assets	3,629	3,768	4,332	3,322	3,392	1,581	1,232	823	NA	NA
Current Liabilities	268	155	301	185	881	196	163	71.1	NA	NA
Long Term Debt	262	378	769	856	400	Nil	Nil	16.6	NA	NA
Common Equity	2,581	2,735	2,661	1,508	1,363	1,058	815	540	NA	NA
Total Capital	3,283	3,553	3,997	3,097	2,466	1,342	1,024	710	NA	NA
Capital Expenditures	23.6	26.5	23.9	16.3	34.3	107	50.5	35.0	NA	NA
Cash Flow	138	230	1,023	157	433	745	348	169	NA	NA
Current Ratio	3.7	6.9	4.9	1.9	0.5	3.3	3.2	3.6	NA	NA
% Long Term Debt of Capitalization	8.0	10.6	19.2	27.6	16.2	Nil	Nil	2.3	NA	NA
% Net Income of Revenue	9.2	16.8	96.1	7.4	19.4	29.5	25.8	22.7	NA	NA
% Return on Assets	2.4	4.2	25.0	2.5	12.2	47.2	30.5	NA	NA	NA
% Return on Equity	3.3	6.3	45.9	5.9	25.0	70.9	46.2	NA	NA	NA

Data as orig reptd.; bef. results of disc opers/spec. items. Per share data adj. for stk. divs.; EPS diluted. E-Estimated. NA-Not Available. NM-Not Meaningful. NR-Not Ranked. UR-Under Review.

Office: 151 Detroit St, Denver, CO 80206-4928.
Telephone: 303-333-3863.
Website: http://www.janus.com
Chrmn: S.L. Scheid

CEO: G.D. Black
EVP & CFO: D.R. Martin
EVP, Secy & General Counsel: J.H. Bluher
SVP & Treas: S.H. Belgrad

Board of Directors: P. F. Balser, M. D. Bills, G. D. Black, G. A. Cox, J. P. Craig, III, J. R. Fredericks, D. R. Gatzek, R. T. Parry, L. H. Rowland, S. L. Scheid, R. Skidelsky

Founded: 1998
Domicile: Delaware
Employees: 1,457

STANDARD &POOR'S

JDS Uniphase Corp

S&P Recommendation HOLD ★★★★★

Price $14.65 (as of Oct 27, 2006)

12-Mo. Target Price $20.00

Investment Style Mid-Cap Value

GICS Sector Information Technology
Sub-Industry Communications Equipment

Comment This company manufactures fiber optic products and communications test and measurement solutions.

Key Stock Statistics (Source S&P, Vickers, company reports)

52-Wk Range	**$34.40–13.98**	S&P Oper. EPS 2007**E**	**-0.24**	P/E on S&P Oper. EPS 2007**E**	**NM**	Dividend Rate/Share	**Nil**
Trailing 12-Month EPS	**$-0.72**	S&P Oper. EPS 2008**E**	**0.08**	Common Shares Outstg. (M)	**210.6**	Yield (%)	**Nil**
Trailing 12-Month P/E	**NM**	S&P Core EPS 2007**E**	**-0.24**	Market Capitalization(B)	**$3.085**	Beta	**3.06**
$10K Invested 5 Yrs Ago	**$2,088**	S&P Core EPS 2008**E**	**0.08**	Institutional Ownership (%)	**NA**	S&P Credit Rating	**NA**

Price Performance

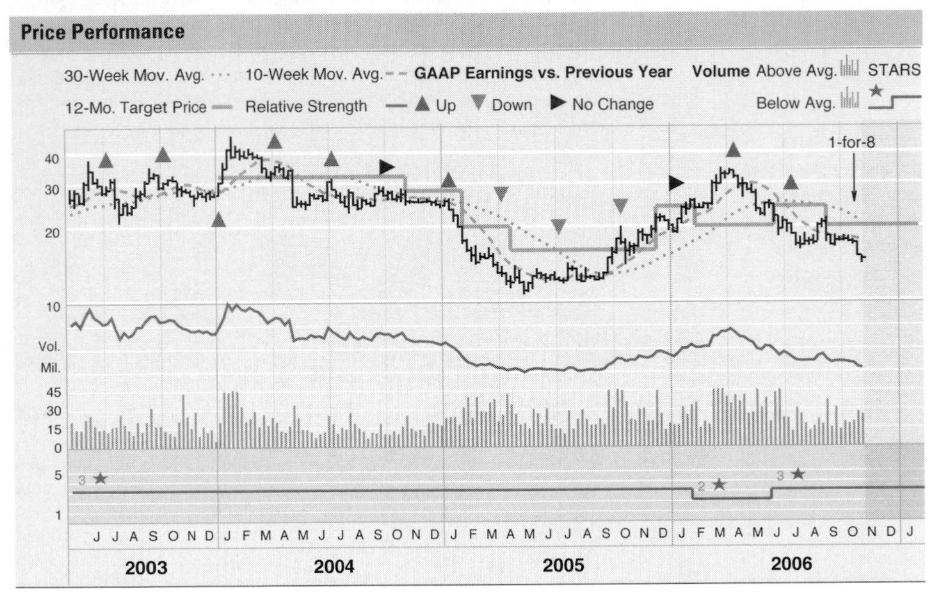

Options: ASE, CBOE, P, Ph

Analysis prepared by **Ari Bensinger** on September 01, 2006, when the stock traded at **$ 2.24**.

Highlights

- Following a 69% sales increase in FY 06 (Jun.), reflecting the full-year inclusion of the August 2005 Acterna acquisition, we see them advancing 12% in FY 06. We expect demand for optical communication products, particularly tunable laser and ROADMs, to benefit from accelerated buildouts of broadband networks. JDSU continues to expand its test and measurement business toward IP network services.
- The company is in the midst of a major restructuring program. As a result of the higher margin Acterna business and continued cost cutting, we believe FY 07 gross margins will widen to the 38% level, up from 35% in FY 06. We expect operating expenses as a percentage of sales to drop from the level of FY 06.
- After minimal taxes due to loss carryovers and factoring in a higher count in shares outstanding as a result of the Acterna purchase, we forecast a FY 07 loss of $0.03, including $0.08 of projected stock option expense, versus the $0.10 loss posted in FY 06.

Investment Rationale/Risk

- We believe demand for optical systems is strengthening as service operators look to expand their network bandwidth capabilities. While the operating environment seems to be improving operationally, we think JDSU needs to do a better job of reducing costs. We expect directors to execute the shareholder-authorized reverse stock split before the end of 2006.
- Risks to our recommendation and target price include decreased capital spending by telecom operators, integration issues related to the acquisition of Acterna, and the loss of a major customer.
- Our 12-month target price of $2.50 is largely based on a forward P/E of 28X applied to our FY 08 EPS estimate of $0.09 (excluding projected stock option expense of $0.08), which we view as a more normalized earnings number for the company given the restructuring initiatives under way. Our DCF model, assuming a weighted average cost of capital of 11.7% and terminal growth of free cash flow of 3%, indicates intrinsic value of slightly under $3.

Qualitative Risk Assessment

LOW | MEDIUM | **HIGH**

Our risk assessment reflects the highly competitive nature of the industry, the company's dependence on telecom carrier spending, which tends to be uneven due to the uncertain timing of network projects and upgrades, and the high degree of stock-price volatility.

Quantitative Evaluations

S&P Quality Ranking C

D | **C** | B- | B | B+ | A- | A | A+

Relative Strength Rank WEAK

5

LOWEST = 1 HIGHEST = 99

Revenue/Earnings Data

Revenue (Million $)

	1Q	2Q	3Q	4Q	Year
2006	258.3	312.9	314.9	318.2	1,204
2005	194.5	180.5	166.3	170.9	712.2
2004	147.4	152.6	161.4	174.5	635.9
2003	193.0	156.6	165.7	160.6	675.9
2002	328.6	286.1	261.8	221.7	1,098
2001	786.5	925.1	920.1	601.1	3,233

Earnings Per Share ($)

2006	-0.32	-0.24	Nil	-0.24	**E**-0.72
2005	-0.16	-0.24	-0.24	-0.80	-1.44
2004	-0.16	-0.32	-0.08	-0.16	-0.64
2003	-2.96	-1.20	-0.80	-0.32	-5.28
2002	-7.44	-12.80	-25.52	-6.08	-52.00
2001	-8.56	-7.44	-293.04	-75.12	-411.20

Fiscal year ended Jun. 30. Next earnings report expected: Early November. EPS Estimates based on S&P Operating Earnings; historical GAAP earnings are as reported.

Dividend Data (Dates: mm/dd Payment Date: mm/dd/yy)

Amount ($)	Date Decl.	Ex-Div. Date	Stk. of Record	Payment Date
1-for-8 REV.	--	10/17	--	10/17/06

Source: Company reports.

JDS Uniphase Corp

Business Summary September 01, 2006

CORPORATE OVERVIEW. JDS Uniphase supplies optical components, as well as communications test and measurement solutions for the communications market. The company also leverages its optical science capabilities on non-communications applications, offering products for display, security, medical environmental instrumentation, decorative, aerospace and defense applications. Net sales to customers in North America accounted for 66% of total sales in FY 05 (Jun.), up from 64% in FY 04. No single customer accounted for over 10% of sales in FY 05 and FY 04.

Products during FY 05 were grouped into two principal segments: communications and commercial and consumer products. As a result of the August 2005 acquisition of Acterna, JDSU reclassified its segments for FY 06 as optical communications, commercial and consumer, and communications test and measurement.

PRIMARY BUSINESS DYNAMICS. The communications product group, which accounted for 59% of total sales in FY 05, provides fiber optic components and modules, including source lasers, photodetectors and receivers, modulators, transmitters, transceivers, amplifiers, and add-drop multiplexers. The company supplies the basic building blocks for fiber optic networks, which, in turn, enable the rapid transmission of large amounts of data over long distances via light waves. Its fiber optic components and modules are deployed by system manufacturers for telecommunications, data communications and cable television. Division sales increased 33% in FY 05, reflecting improved market conditions, increased revenue from the sub-systems products group, and a full year's revenue from the E2O acquisition, which closed in May 2004.

The commercial and consumer segment provides high performance optics for application in commercial markets, including semiconductors, materials processing, and biotechnology. It also provides lasers for use in imaging, aerospace, and defense applications. On the consumer side, JDSU's optical technology protects approximately 100 currencies worldwide and has been introduced by leading pharmaceutical companies on prescription drug packaging.

Company Financials

Per Share Data ($) Year Ended Jun. 30	**2006**	**2005**	**2004**	**2003**	**2002**	**2001**	**2000**	**1999**	**1998**	**1997**
Tangible Book Value	2.72	5.76	7.12	7.92	11.44	22.24	20.88	2.16	4.56	8.20
Cash Flow	-0.46	-1.11	-0.32	-4.82	-42.21	-370.58	0.52	-3.52	-2.04	-0.86
Earnings	-0.72	-1.44	-0.64	-5.28	-52.00	-411.20	-10.08	-4.30	-2.34	-0.57
S&P Core Earnings	-0.88	-2.24	-2.56	-7.84	-32.88	-175.60	NA	NA	NA	NA
Dividends	Nil	Nil	Nil	Nil	Nil	Nil	Nil	Nil	Nil	Nil
Payout Ratio	Nil	Nil	Nil	Nil	Nil	Nil	Nil	Nil	Nil	Nil
Prices:High	34.40	26.08	47.08	37.68	82.72	519.50	1227	710.00	71.50	47.50
Prices:Low	13.98	10.56	22.72	19.84	12.64	40.96	296.00	59.25	31.25	15.63
P/E Ratio:High	NM	NM	NM	NM	NM	NM	NM	NM	NM	NM
P/E Ratio:Low	NM	NM	NM	NM	NM	NM	NM	NM	NM	NM

Income Statement Analysis (Million $)										
Revenue	1,204	712	636	676	1,098	3,233	1,430	283	176	107
Operating Income	-107	-83.9	-58.5	-306	-374	-62.5	446	94.6	36.7	21.2
Depreciation	57.4	61.3	55.9	79.2	1,645	5,542	951	30.7	10.1	4.70
Interest Expense	27.7	Nil	Nil	Nil	Nil	Nil	0.50	0.02	0.07	0.42
Pretax Income	152	-255	-128	-920	-8,501	-56,494	-830	-151	-69.8	-13.4
Effective Tax Rate	NM	NM	NM	NM	NM	NM	NM	NM	NM	NM
Net Income	-151	-261	-113	-934	-8,738	-56,122	-905	-171	-81.1	-18.9
S&P Core Earnings	-181	-394	-446	-1,399	-5,534	-23,966	NA	NA	NA	NA

Balance Sheet & Other Financial Data (Million $)										
Cash	365	511	328	242	412	763	319	75.4	39.8	29.2
Current Assets	1,805	1,588	1,866	1,515	1,857	3,036	1,973	928	165	134
Total Assets	3,065	2,080	2,422	2,138	3,005	12,245	26,389	8,192	269	178
Current Liabilities	422	240	350	423	483	848	647	298	45.8	25.3
Long Term Debt	900	467	465	Nil	5.50	12.8	41.0	Nil	Nil	Nil
Common Equity	1,584	1,335	1,571	1,671	2,471	10,706	24,779	3,619	218	150
Total Capital	2,484	1,802	2,063	1,699	2,519	11,392	25,722	3,937	218	150
Capital Expenditures	67.2	35.8	66.4	47.2	133	732	280	46.6	24.0	12.0
Cash Flow	-93.8	-200	-56.7	-855	-7,093	-50,580	46.0	-140	-71.0	-14.2
Current Ratio	4.3	6.6	5.3	3.6	3.8	3.6	3.0	3.1	3.6	5.3
% Long Term Debt of Capitalization	36.2	25.9	22.5	Nil	0.2	0.1	0.2	Nil	Nil	Nil
% Net Income of Revenue	NM	NM	NM	NM	NM	NM	NM	NM	NM	NM
% Return on Assets	NM	NM	NM	NM	NM	NM	NM	NM	NM	NM
% Return on Equity	NM	NM	NM	NM	NM	NM	NM	NM	NM	NM

Data as orig reptd.; bef. results of disc opers/spec. items. Per share data adj. for stk. divs.; EPS diluted. E-Estimated. NA-Not Available. NM-Not Meaningful. NR-Not Ranked. UR-Under Review.

Office: 430 N McCarthy Blvd, Milpitas, CA 95035-5116.
Telephone: 408-546-5000.
Email: investor.relations@jdsu.com
Website: http://www.jdsu.com

Chrmn: M.A. Kaplan
CEO: K.J. Kennedy
SVP & General Counsel: C.S. Dewees
CFO: D. Vellequette

Investor Contact: J. Ross (408-546-4445)
Board of Directors: R. E. Belluzzo, H. Covert, B. D. Day, K. A. DeNuccio, P. A. Guglielmi, M. Jabbar, M. A. Kaplan, K. J. Kennedy, R. T. Liebhaber, C. S. Skrzypczak

Founded: 1979
Domicile: Delaware
Employees: 7,099

STANDARD &POOR'S

Johnson Controls Inc.

S&P Recommendation HOLD ★★★★★

Price $82.63 (as of Oct 27, 2006)

12-Mo. Target Price $86.00

Investment Style Large-Cap Value

GICS Sector Consumer Discretionary
Sub-Industry Auto Parts & Equipment

Comment This company supplies building controls and energy management systems, automotive seating, and batteries.

Key Stock Statistics (Source S&P, Vickers, company reports)

52-Wk Range	**$90.00–66.36**	S&P Oper. EPS 2007**E**	**6.10**	P/E on S&P Oper. EPS 2007**E**	**13.5**	Dividend Rate/Share	**$1.12**
Trailing 12-Month EPS	**$5.26**	S&P Oper. EPS 2008**E**	**NA**	Common Shares Outstg. (M)	**195.6**	Yield (%)	**1.36**
Trailing 12-Month P/E	**15.7**	S&P Core EPS 2007**E**	**6.07**	Market Capitalization(B)	**$16.160**	Beta	**0.81**
$10K Invested 5 Yrs Ago	**$24,033**	S&P Core EPS 2008**E**	**NA**	Institutional Ownership (%)	**74**	S&P Credit Rating	**A-**

Price Performance

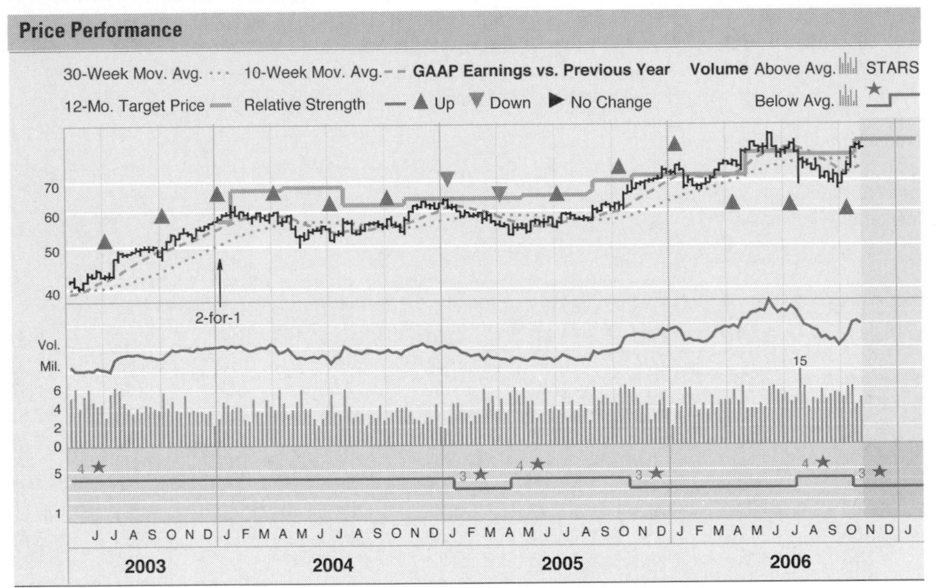

Options: Ph

Analysis prepared by **Efraim Levy, CFA** on October 20, 2006, when the stock traded at **$ 83.21**.

Highlights

- We expect FY 07 (Sep.) sales to advance about 10%, reflecting an expansion of the facilities management business, expected new automotive business, higher global automobile production, and acquisitions, partly offset by divestitures and lower U.S. production of certain high JCI content vehicles, especially in the December quarter. We see facilities management benefiting from new customers as outsourcing trends continue and the backlog of orders for installed systems continues to grow. Automotive revenues will likely benefit from new contracts and expanding business with Asian and European vehicle makers.
- We see operating margins widening modestly, as the company should benefit from the higher revenues that we see, plus restructuring activities, especially in Europe. We project a partial offset in higher health care expenses and pricing pressures from customers, and higher raw material costs.
- We estimate that FY 07 S&P Core EPS adjustments for net pension expenses will reduce reported EPS by less than 1%.

Investment Rationale/Risk

- We expect growth to exceed that of peers, and with greater earnings stability. We project that diversification in geography, products and customers will help JCI withstand weakness at the domestic auto manufacturers. The stock recently traded at a discount to the P/E multiple of the S&P 500. We view the balance sheet as strong, with long-term debt generally at 20% to 36% of capitalization over the past decade.
- Risks to our recommendation and target price include changes in cyclical demand, especially for automotive parts, higher raw material costs, a failure to achieve expected acquisition synergies, and pricing pressure from customers.
- Applying a P/E multiple of about 14X to our FY 07 estimate of $6.13, reflecting peer and historical comparisons, leads us to a value of about $86. Our DCF model, which assumes a weighted average cost of capital of 10.3%, a compound annual growth rate of 17% over the next 15 years and a terminal growth rate of 3%, also leads to an intrinsic value of about $86. Based on an equal weighting of our P/E and DCF analyses, our 12-month target price is $86. The cash dividend recently provided a 1.3% yield.

Qualitative Risk Assessment

LOW | **MEDIUM** | HIGH

Our risk assessment reflects favorable growth prospects in the building controls markets that JCI serves and what we view as a strong management team and a healthy balance sheet, offset by the challenges faced by automotive operations.

Quantitative Evaluations

S&P Quality Ranking A+

D | C | B- | B | B+ | A- | A | **A+**

Relative Strength Rank STRONG

76

LOWEST = 1 HIGHEST = 99

Revenue/Earnings Data

Revenue (Million $)

	1Q	2Q	3Q	4Q	Year
2006	7,528	8,167	8,390	8,150	32,235
2005	6,618	6,899	7,062	6,900	27,479
2004	6,384	6,620	6,792	6,757	26,553
2003	5,183	5,503	5,960	6,000	22,646
2002	4,818	4,811	5,257	5,218	20,103
2001	4,454	4,602	4,722	4,649	18,427

Earnings Per Share ($)

	1Q	2Q	3Q	4Q	Year
2006	0.86	0.83	1.70	1.86	5.25
2005	0.83	0.28	1.31	1.50	3.90
2004	0.86	0.82	1.15	1.41	4.24
2003	0.74	0.70	1.00	1.16	3.60
2002	0.64	0.61	0.93	1.01	3.18
2001	0.55	0.45	0.73	0.84	2.56

Fiscal year ended Sep. 30. Next earnings report expected: Mid January. EPS Estimates based on S&P Operating Earnings; historical GAAP earnings are as reported.

Dividend Data (Dates: mm/dd Payment Date: mm/dd/yy)

Amount ($)	Date Decl.	Ex-Div. Date	Stk. of Record	Payment Date
0.280	11/16	12/12	12/14	01/03/06
0.280	01/25	03/08	03/10	03/31/06
0.280	05/23	06/07	06/09	06/30/06
0.280	07/26	09/11	09/13	09/29/06

Dividends have been paid since 1887. Source: Company reports.

Johnson Controls Inc.

Business Summary October 20, 2006

CORPORATE OVERVIEW. Johnson Controls, founded in 1885, is a leading manufacturer of automotive interior systems, automotive batteries and automated building control systems. It also provides facility management services for commercial buildings. In FY 05 (Sep.), the automotive segment accounted for 79% of sales and 77% of income, with the balance coming from controls and facility management.

The automotive interior segment manufactures complete seats and seating components for North American and European car and light-truck manufacturers. The segment has grown rapidly in recent years, gaining contracts to produce seats formerly manufactured in-house by automakers, and expanding in Europe. Seating accounted for 68% of sales in FY 05.

The power solutions unit, the largest automotive battery operation in North America, makes lead-acid batteries primarily for the automotive replacement market and for OEMs. Batteries accounted for 11% of FY 05 sales and the unit is expanding operations in Europe.

The building efficiency (formerly called controls) segment manufactures, installs and services controls and control systems, principally for nonresidential buildings, which are used for temperature and energy management, and fire safety and security maintenance. The segment also includes custom engineering, installation and servicing of process control systems and a growing facilities management business. Building efficiency sales accounted for 21% of FY 05 revenues. At September 30, 2005, JCI had an unearned backlog of building systems and services contracts totaling $1.9 billion.

Government building trends promoting facility management outsourcing and energy efficiency programs are creating, in our view, additional opportunities.

GM, DaimlerChrysler and Ford accounted respectively for 14%, 11% and 11% of FY 05 sales. We expect the share of revenues from the largest three customers to shrink as the company expands its sales outside the U.S. and with non-domestic customers expanding in the U.S.

Company Financials

Per Share Data ($) Year Ended Sep. 30	2006	2005	2004	2003	2002	2001	2000	1999	1998	1997
Tangible Book Value	NA	10.56	5.78	3.80	2.23	3.52	1.83	0.23	NM	NM
Cash Flow	NA	7.22	7.45	6.52	5.90	5.30	5.37	4.65	3.87	3.33
Earnings	5.25	3.90	4.24	3.60	3.18	2.56	2.55	2.24	1.82	1.18
S&P Core Earnings	NA	3.93	4.26	3.47	2.67	2.10	NA	NA	NA	NA
Dividends	1.12	1.00	0.90	0.72	0.66	0.62	0.56	0.50	0.46	0.43
Payout Ratio	21%	26%	21%	20%	21%	24%	22%	22%	25%	36%
Prices:High	90.00	75.22	63.98	58.12	46.60	41.35	32.56	38.34	30.94	25.50
Prices:Low	66.36	52.57	49.57	35.88	34.55	25.97	22.91	24.50	20.25	17.69
P/E Ratio:High	17	19	15	16	15	16	13	17	17	22
P/E Ratio:Low	13	13	12	10	11	10	9	11	11	15
Income Statement Analysis (Million $)										
Revenue	NA	27,479	26,553	22,646	20,103	18,427	17,155	16,139	12,587	11,145
Operating Income	NA	1,913	1,918	1,720	1,639	1,477	1,427	1,300	1,048	951
Depreciation	NA	636	617	558	517	516	462	446	384	355
Interest Expense	NA	121	111	114	122	129	128	153	134	122
Pretax Income	NA	1,003	1,212	1,058	1,006	867	856	770	617	425
Effective Tax Rate	NA	20.4%	26.0%	31.0%	34.6%	38.7%	39.8%	40.5%	41.5%	42.4%
Net Income	NA	757	818	683	600	478	472	420	338	221
S&P Core Earnings	NA	764	818	650	497	385	NA	NA	NA	NA
Balance Sheet & Other Financial Data (Million $)										
Cash	NA	171	170	136	262	375	276	276	134	112
Current Assets	NA	7,139	6,377	5,620	4,946	4,544	4,277	3,849	3,404	2,529
Total Assets	NA	16,144	15,091	13,127	11,165	9,912	9,428	8,614	7,942	6,049
Current Liabilities	NA	6,841	6,602	5,584	4,806	4,580	4,510	4,267	4,288	2,973
Long Term Debt	NA	1,578	1,631	1,777	1,827	1,395	1,315	1,283	998	806
Common Equity	NA	6,058	5,206	4,164	3,396	2,862	2,447	2,135	1,801	1,545
Total Capital	NA	7,831	7,106	6,260	5,515	4,588	3,891	3,553	2,939	2,494
Capital Expenditures	NA	664	862	664	496	622	547	514	468	371
Cash Flow	NA	1,394	1,434	1,234	1,110	985	924	856	712	566
Current Ratio	NA	1.0	1.0	1.0	1.0	1.0	0.9	0.9	0.8	0.9
% Long Term Debt of Capitalization	NA	20.1	22.9	28.4	33.1	30.4	33.8	36.1	34.0	32.3
% Net Income of Revenue	NA	2.8	3.1	3.0	3.0	2.6	2.8	2.6	2.7	2.0
% Return on Assets	NA	4.9	5.8	5.6	5.7	4.9	5.2	5.1	4.8	4.0
% Return on Equity	NA	13.4	17.4	17.9	18.9	17.7	20.2	20.8	19.6	14.6

Data as orig reptd.; bef. results of disc opers/spec. items. Per share data adj. for stk. divs.; EPS diluted. E-Estimated. NA-Not Available. NM-Not Meaningful. NR-Not Ranked. UR-Under Review.

Office: 5757 N. Green Bay Avenue, Milwaukee, WI 53201-0591.
Telephone: 414-524-1200.
Website: http://www.johnsoncontrols.com
Chrmn & CEO: J.M. Barth

Pres & COO: K.E. Wandell
Vice Chrmn & EVP: S.A. Roell
VP & Treas: F.A. Voltolina
VP, Secy & General Counsel: J.D. Okarma

Investor Contact: D.M. Zutz
Board of Directors: D. W. Archer, R. L. Barnett, J. M. Barth, N. A. Black, P. A. Brunner, E. R. Clariond, R. A. Cornog, W. D. Davis, J. A. Joerres, W. H. Lacy, S. J. Morcott, S. A. Roell, R. F. Teerlink

Founded: 1900
Domicile: Wisconsin
Employees: 114,000

STANDARD &POOR'S

Johnson & Johnson

S&P Recommendation STRONG BUY ★★★★★

Price $68.17 (as of Oct 27, 2006)

12-Mo. Target Price $74.00

Investment Style Large-Cap Growth

GICS Sector Health Care
Sub-Industry Pharmaceuticals

Comment This company is a leader in the pharmaceutical, medical device and consumer products industries. Its stock has one of the largest market caps in the S&P 500.

Key Stock Statistics (Source S&P, Vickers, company reports)

52-Wk Range	$69.41–56.65	S&P Oper. EPS 2006E	3.73	P/E on S&P Oper. EPS 2006E	18.3	Dividend Rate/Share	$1.50
Trailing 12-Month EPS	$3.80	S&P Oper. EPS 2007E	4.10	Common Shares Outstg. (M)	2,925.0	Yield (%)	2.20
Trailing 12-Month P/E	17.9	S&P Core EPS 2006E	3.74	Market Capitalization(B)	$199.399	Beta	0.22
$10K Invested 5 Yrs Ago	$12,723	S&P Core EPS 2007E	4.12	Institutional Ownership (%)	63	S&P Credit Rating	AAA

Price Performance

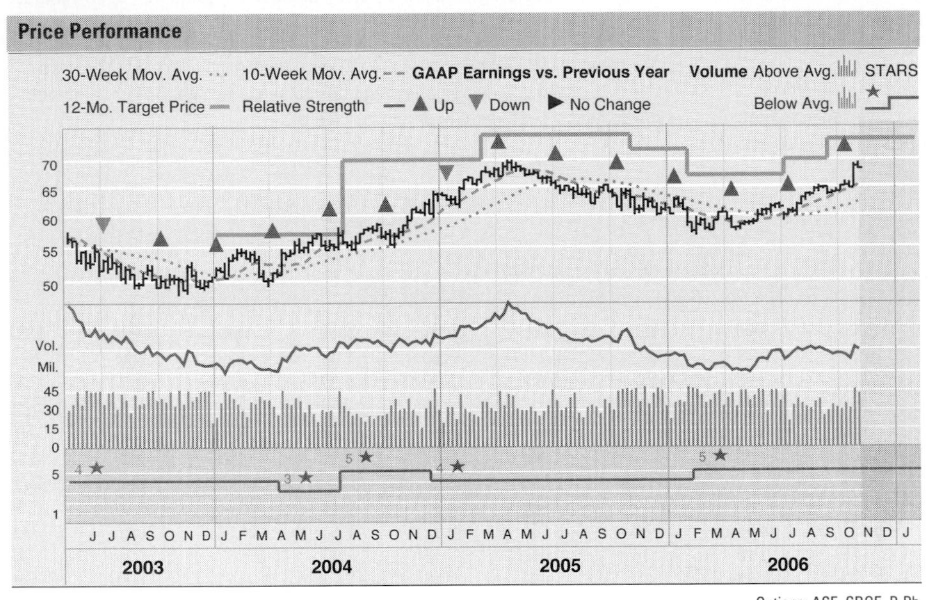

Options: ASE, CBOE, P, Ph

Analysis prepared by **Robert M. Gold** on October 18, 2006, when the stock traded at **$ 66.97**.

Highlights

➤ We see 2006 revenues of $53.5 billion. In the drug unit, we think patent expirations and pricing pressures make JNJ vulnerable to revenue weakness, but we believe the new product pipeline is promising and expect substantial contributions from new products into 2007. If the proposed deal to purchase Pfizer's (PFE: strong buy, $28) consumer products unit is consummated by year-end 2006, we see an incremental $4.0 billion in annual sales and $740 million in annual operating profits.

➤ We see a gross margin of 71.7% in 2006, with R&D costs consuming 13.8% of sales and SG&A expenses 33.3%. We foresee 2006 free cash flow of about $10.9 billion, and believe JNJ can generate sustained annual free cash flow growth of 5% to 7% over the next five years.

➤ We look for 2006 EPS of $3.73, including projected stock option expense of $0.10 but before a special gain related to the terminated Guidant acquisition and charges for acquired in-process R&D. For 2007, we estimate EPS of $4.10, after $0.14 of projected stock option expense. If consummated by year-end 2006, we think the proposed Pfizer transaction would lower EPS by about $0.11 in 2007.

Investment Rationale/Risk

➤ In June 2006, the company agreed to purchase the consumer products division of Pfizer Inc. for $16.6 billion in cash, subject to necessary approvals. In our opinion, the proposed deal fully values the operations at about 4.3X 2005 revenues of $3.9 billion, but we think JNJ has substantial revenue and cost synergies associated with the deal that could allow for some modest accretion to cash EPS by 2008.

➤ Risks to our opinion and target price include a faster than expected loss of branded pharmaceutical sales to generic drugs, unfavorable patent litigation, an inability to sustain growth in the device segment, and a failure to commercialize compounds in the research pipeline.

➤ Our 12-month target price of $74 represents a P/E of 18X our 2007 EPS estimate, and a forward P/E to earnings growth (PEG) ratio of 1.6X, in line with large cap pharmaceutical peers. In addition, our DCF analysis calculates intrinsic value at $76 per share, assuming 2006 free cash flow of $10.9 billion, with future growth ranging from 8% to 12%, a weighted average cost of capital of 7.7%, and a terminal growth rate of 3%.

Qualitative Risk Assessment

LOW | MEDIUM | HIGH

Our risk assessment reflects our belief that JNJ has products that are largely immune from economic cycles, the company's modest reliance on any single product category or customer for sustained growth, and competitive advantages owing to its large financial resources, business scale and expansive sales force.

Quantitative Evaluations

S&P Quality Ranking A+

D | C | B- | B | B+ | A- | A | A+

Relative Strength Rank MODERATE

67

LOWEST = 1 HIGHEST = 99

Revenue/Earnings Data

Revenue (Million $)

	1Q	2Q	3Q	4Q	Year
2006	12,992	13,363	13,287	--	--
2005	12,832	12,762	12,310	12,610	50,514
2004	11,559	11,484	11,553	12,752	47,348
2003	9,821	10,332	10,455	11,254	41,862
2002	8,743	9,073	9,079	9,403	36,298
2001	8,021	8,342	8,238	8,403	33,004

Earnings Per Share ($)

2006	1.10	0.95	0.94	E0.75	E3.73
2005	0.97	0.89	0.87	0.73	3.46
2004	0.83	0.82	0.78	0.41	2.84
2003	0.69	0.40	0.69	0.62	2.40
2002	0.59	0.54	0.57	0.46	2.16
2001	0.50	0.48	0.49	0.36	1.84

Fiscal year ended Dec. 31. Next earnings report expected: Late January. EPS Estimates based on S&P Operating Earnings; historical GAAP earnings are as reported.

Dividend Data (Dates: mm/dd Payment Date: mm/dd/yy)

Amount ($)	Date Decl.	Ex-Div. Date	Stk. of Record	Payment Date
0.330	01/04	02/24	02/28	03/14/06
0.375	04/27	05/25	05/30	06/13/06
0.375	07/17	08/25	08/29	09/12/06
0.375	10/18	11/24	11/28	12/12/06

Dividends have been paid since 1944. Source: Company reports.

Please read the Required Disclosures and Analyst Certification on the last page of this report.

Johnson & Johnson

Business Summary October 18, 2006

CORPORATE OVERVIEW. Johnson & Johnson ranks as one of the largest and most diversified health care firms, with products spanning across the pharmaceutical and medical device industries. The company is also a major participant in the global consumer products business, and recently agreed to purchase the consumer products unit of Pfizer (PFE: strong buy, $28) for $16.6 billion.

The pharmaceutical segment (44% of 2005 sales) focuses on the antifungal, anti-infective, cardiovascular, contraceptive, dermatology, gastrointestinal, hematology, immunology, neurology, oncology, pain management, central nervous system and urology fields. In 2005, eight products each generated over $1 billion of sales: Procrit/Eprex ($3.3 billion, down 7% from 2004, ex-currency), Risperdal ($3.6 billion, up 17%), Remicade ($2.5 billion, up 18%), Duragesic ($1.6 billion, down 24%), Topamax ($1.7 billion, up 19%), Levaquin/Floxin ($1.5 billion, up 15%), Aciphex/Pariet ($1.2 billion, up 5%) and hormonal contraceptives ($1.1 billion, down 11%).

The medical devices and diagnostics segment (38%) sells a wide range of products, including Ethicon's wound care, surgical sports medicine and women's health care products; Cordis's circulatory disease management products; Lifescan's blood glucose monitoring products; Ortho-Clinical Diagnostic's professional diagnostic products; Depuy's orthopaedic joint reconstruction and spinal products; and Vistakon's disposable contact lenses.

The consumer segment (18%) primarily sells personal care products including nonprescription drugs, adult skin and hair care products, baby care products, oral care products, first aid products, women's health products, and nutritional products. Major brands include Band-Aid Brand Adhesive Bandages, Imodium A-D antidiarrheal, Johnson's Baby line of products, Neutrogena skin and hair care products, and Tylenol pain reliever.

Company Financials

Per Share Data ($) Year Ended Dec. 31	2005	2004	2003	2002	2001	2000	1999	1998	1997	1996
Tangible Book Value	8.64	6.72	5.17	4.53	4.97	4.15	3.11	2.38	3.38	2.90
Cash Flow	4.20	3.58	3.01	2.67	2.35	2.23	1.98	1.57	1.59	1.47
Earnings	3.46	2.84	2.40	2.16	1.84	1.70	1.47	1.12	1.21	1.09
S&P Core Earnings	3.38	2.77	2.26	1.99	1.66	NA	NA	NA	NA	NA
Dividends	1.28	1.10	0.93	0.80	0.70	0.62	0.55	0.49	0.43	0.37
Payout Ratio	37%	39%	39%	37%	38%	36%	37%	43%	35%	34%
Prices:High	69.99	64.25	59.08	65.89	60.97	52.97	53.44	44.88	33.66	27.00
Prices:Low	59.76	49.25	48.05	41.40	40.25	33.06	38.50	31.69	24.31	20.78
P/E Ratio:High	20	23	25	31	33	31	36	40	28	25
P/E Ratio:Low	17	17	20	19	22	19	26	28	20	19

Income Statement Analysis (Million $)	2005	2004	2003	2002	2001	2000	1999	1998	1997	1996
Revenue	50,514	47,348	41,862	36,298	33,004	29,139	27,471	23,657	22,629	21,620
Operating Income	15,464	14,987	12,740	11,340	9,490	7,992	7,370	6,291	5,689	5,312
Depreciation	2,093	2,124	1,869	1,662	1,605	1,515	1,444	1,246	1,067	1,009
Interest Expense	54.0	187	207	160	153	146	197	110	120	125
Pretax Income	13,656	12,838	10,308	9,291	7,898	6,622	5,753	4,269	4,576	4,033
Effective Tax Rate	23.8%	33.7%	30.2%	29.0%	28.2%	27.5%	27.6%	28.3%	27.8%	28.4%
Net Income	10,411	8,509	7,197	6,597	5,668	4,800	4,167	3,059	3,303	2,887
S&P Core Earnings	10,161	8,263	6,785	6,052	5,090	NA	NA	NA	NA	NA

Balance Sheet & Other Financial Data (Million $)	2005	2004	2003	2002	2001	2000	1999	1998	1997	1996
Cash	16,138	12,884	9,523	7,596	8,941	6,013	4,320	2,994	3,284	2,487
Current Assets	31,394	27,320	22,995	19,266	18,473	15,450	13,200	11,132	10,563	9,370
Total Assets	58,025	53,317	48,263	40,556	38,488	31,321	29,163	26,211	21,453	20,010
Current Liabilities	12,635	13,927	13,448	11,449	8,044	7,140	7,454	8,162	5,283	5,184
Long Term Debt	2,017	2,565	2,955	2,022	2,217	2,037	2,450	1,269	1,126	1,410
Common Equity	37,871	31,813	26,869	22,697	24,233	18,808	16,213	13,590	12,359	10,836
Total Capital	40,099	34,781	30,604	25,362	26,943	21,100	18,950	15,437	13,660	12,416
Capital Expenditures	2,632	2,175	2,262	2,099	1,731	1,646	1,728	1,460	1,391	1,373
Cash Flow	12,504	10,633	9,066	8,259	7,273	6,315	5,611	4,305	4,370	3,896
Current Ratio	2.5	2.0	1.7	1.7	2.3	2.2	1.8	1.4	2.0	1.8
% Long Term Debt of Capitalization	5.0	7.4	9.7	8.0	8.2	9.7	12.9	8.2	8.2	11.4
% Net Income of Revenue	20.6	18.0	17.2	18.2	17.2	16.5	15.2	12.9	14.6	13.3
% Return on Assets	18.7	16.8	16.2	16.7	15.6	15.9	14.8	12.8	15.9	15.2
% Return on Equity	29.9	29.0	29.0	28.1	25.4	27.4	27.5	23.6	28.5	29.0

Data as orig reptd.; bef. results of disc opers/spec. items. Per share data adj. for stk. divs.; EPS diluted. E-Estimated. NA-Not Available. NM-Not Meaningful. NR-Not Ranked. UR-Under Review.

Office: One Johnson & Johnson Plaza, New Brunswick, NJ 08933.
Telephone: 732-524-0400.
Website: http://www.jnj.com
Chrmn & CEO: W.C. Weldon

Vice Chrmn: C.A. Poon
Vice Chrmn & CFO: R.J. Darretta
VP, General Counsel & CCO: R.C. Deyo
Secy: M.H. Ullmann

Investor Contact: L. Mehrotra (732-524-6491)
Auditor: Pricewaterhousecoopers
Board of Directors: M. Coleman, J. G. Cullen, R. J. Darretta, M. M. Johns, A. D. Jordan, A. G. Langbo, S. L. Lindquist, L. F. Mullin, C. A. Poon, C. Prince, S. S. Reinemund, D. Satcher, W. C. Weldon

Founded: 1887
Domicile: New Jersey
Employees: 115,600

STANDARD &POOR'S

Jones Apparel Group Inc.

S&P Recommendation HOLD ★★★★★ | **Price** $33.08 (as of Oct 27, 2006) | **12-Mo. Target Price** $36.00 | **Investment Style** Mid-Cap Value

GICS Sector Consumer Discretionary
Sub-Industry Apparel, Accessories & Luxury Goods

Comment JNY is a leading designer, marketer and wholesaler of women's apparel, footwear and accessories, with brands that include Jones New York, Nine West and Evan-Picone.

Key Stock Statistics (Source S&P, Vickers, company reports)

52-Wk Range	$36.10–27.25	S&P Oper. EPS 2006E	2.20	P/E on S&P Oper. EPS 2006E	15.0	Dividend Rate/Share	$0.56
Trailing 12-Month EPS	$1.57	S&P Oper. EPS 2007E	2.55	Common Shares Outstg. (M)	112.8	Yield (%)	1.69
Trailing 12-Month P/E	21.1	S&P Core EPS 2006E	2.20	Market Capitalization(B)	$3.732	Beta	1.15
$10K Invested 5 Yrs Ago	$12,867	S&P Core EPS 2007E	2.55	Institutional Ownership (%)	90	S&P Credit Rating	BBB-

Price Performance

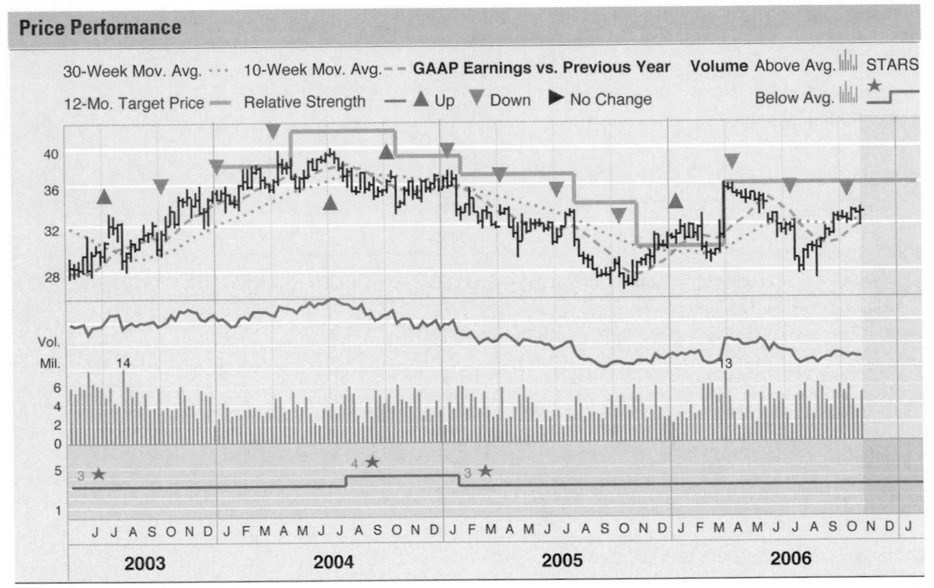

Options: CBOE

Analysis prepared by **Marie Driscoll, CFA** on July 31, 2006, when the stock traded at **$ 29.63**.

Highlights

- We expect a tough 2006 as JNY navigates its exposure to Federated (about 20% of 2005 revenues) and the broader challenges of retail channel shift. We project 2006 sales of $4.63 billion, down about 10% and including about $60 million in net licensing revenue. We believe JNY's weak receipts are a function of department stores' merchandise strategy that emphasizes differentiation and store or proprietary labels as well as reduced inventory commitments related to industry consolidation.
- We expect JNY's operating profits to decline 5%, a slower pace than sales, as JNY benefits from cost savings efforts implemented in 2005 (which are projected to save about $30 million in 2006). We project an operating margin of 10.4% up from 9.9% in 2005 (when it declined 160 basis points).
- We look for higher interest expense due to recent borrowings related to the Barney's acquisition, and an expected effective tax rate of 38% in 2006. We estimate operating EPS of $2.20 in 2006 vs. $2.48, (excluding $0.22 earnings related to recently sold Polo Jeans Company and a tax repatriation gain of $0.07).

Investment Rationale/Risk

- We regard many of JNY's 20-some apparel and footwear brands as mature. However, recently acquired businesses should provide growth opportunity along with potential cost synergies. We expect JNY to make further inroads into bridge apparel with multiple lines acquired with Kasper. Maxwell Shoe provides increased market penetration and line extension potential, in our opinion. We view the acquisition of Barney's as a plus, as JNY seeks to diversify and further penetrate specialty retail.
- Risks to our opinion and target price include changes in consumer spending, fashion and inventory risk, management's ability to integrate recent acquisitions, and the potential for reduced demand as a result of the proposed Federated/May merger.
- Our 12-month target price of $36 is derived by applying a 5% premium to the peer apparel and footwear group forward 2006 multiple of 15X to our 2006 EPS estimate. We note JNY has retained an advisor to explore the possible sale of the entire firm.

Qualitative Risk Assessment

LOW | **MEDIUM** | HIGH

Our medium risk assessment is based on exposure to department store channel contraction offset by a diversified brand portfolio spanning multiple channels.

Quantitative Evaluations

S&P Quality Ranking B+

D | C | B- | B | **B+** | A- | A | A+

Relative Strength Rank MODERATE

55

LOWEST = 1 HIGHEST = 99

Revenue/Earnings Data

Revenue (Million $)

	1Q	2Q	3Q	4Q	Year
2006	1,215	1,074	1,241	--	--
2005	1,349	1,176	1,328	1,221	5,074
2004	1,218	1,053	1,296	1,083	4,650
2003	1,234	980.4	1,181	980.2	4,375
2002	1,127	972.1	1,278	964.5	4,341
2001	1,071	879.9	1,236	887.1	4,073

Earnings Per Share ($)

2006	0.21	0.32	0.56	E0.60	E2.20
2005	0.71	0.46	0.65	0.48	2.30
2004	0.73	0.61	0.77	0.28	2.39
2003	0.90	0.54	0.71	0.33	2.48
2002	0.63	0.49	0.95	0.39	2.46
2001	0.75	0.43	0.41	0.25	1.82

Fiscal year ended Dec. 31. Next earnings report expected: Mid February. EPS Estimates based on S&P Operating Earnings; historical GAAP earnings are as reported.

Dividend Data (Dates: mm/dd Payment Date: mm/dd/yy)

Amount ($)	Date Decl.	Ex-Div. Date	Stk. of Record	Payment Date
0.120	02/15	03/01	03/03	03/17/06
0.120	04/26	05/10	05/12	05/26/06
0.120	07/26	08/09	08/11	08/25/06
0.140	10/25	11/15	11/17	12/01/06

Dividends have been paid since 2003. Source: Company reports.

Jones Apparel Group Inc.

Business Summary July 31, 2006

CORPORATE OVERVIEW. JNY is a multi-branded apparel and accessories company operating on both the wholesale and retail level.

MARKET PROFILE. JNY participates in the women's apparel market, which represented 56% of domestic apparel retail purchases, or $101 billion, in 2005, according to NPD Fashionworld consumer estimated data. The apparel market is fragmented, with national brands marketed by 20 companies accounting for about 30% of total apparel sales, and the remaining 70% comprised of smaller and/or private label "store" brands. The market is mature, in our view, with demand largely mirroring population growth and fashion trends accounting for a modicum of incremental volume. Deflationary pricing pressure is a function, we think, of channel competition and production steadily moving offshore to low-cost producers in India, Asia and China. S&P forecasts 2006 apparel sales increasing in the low single digits, generally in line with GDP growth. This compares with a 4% year-to-year advance in 2004 and 2005, and a 5% decline in 2003.

COMPETITIVE LANDSCAPE. By channel, specialty stores account for the largest share of apparel sales, at 30% in 2005, according to NPD. Mass merchants (Wal-Mart and Target) came in second at 18%, up 100 basis points and department stores, JNY's primary channel, came in third at 17%, down from their year ago number two spot and losing 200 basis points of market share. National chains (Sears and JC Penney) captured 15% of 2005 fourth quarter apparel sales and off-price retailers (TJX and Ross Stores) 8%. The remaining 12% is divided among factory outlets and direct and email pure plays. JNY holds meaningful market shares in department stores and national chains, where it competes with Liz Claiborne, Polo Ralph Lauren and VF Corp., as well as private label offerings, which garner about a third of total apparel purchases and are an important differentiator for retailers. JNY also sells directly to consumers through 398 specialty retail (391 located in the U.S.) and 674 (653 in the U.S.) outlet stores and participates in the luxury retail market via Barney's New York flagship store, three regional stores and eight Barney's New York CO-OP stores.

Company Financials

Per Share Data (3) Year Ended Dec. 31	2005	2004	2003	2002	2001	2000	1999	1998	1997	1996
Tangible Book Value	NM	NM	0.98	0.66	0.03	0.16	NM	2.33	3.98	3.41
Cash Flow	3.16	3.24	3.04	3.03	1.96	3.37	2.05	1.68	1.26	0.84
Earnings	2.30	2.39	2.48	2.46	1.82	2.48	1.60	1.47	1.13	0.75
S&P Core Earnings	2.32	2.34	2.40	2.35	1.63	NA	NA	NA	NA	NA
Dividends	0.44	0.36	0.16	Nil	Nil	Nil	Nil	Nil	Nil	Nil
Payout Ratio	19%	15%	6%	Nil	Nil	Nil	Nil	Nil	Nil	Nil
Prices:High	37.48	40.00	37.44	41.68	47.43	35.00	35.88	37.75	28.72	18.69
Prices:Low	26.47	33.00	25.61	26.18	23.75	20.13	21.50	15.88	16.06	8.91
P/E Ratio:High	16	17	15	17	26	14	22	26	25	25
P/E Ratio:Low	12	14	10	11	13	8	13	11	14	12
Income Statement Analysis (Million $)										
Revenue	5,074	4,650	4,375	4,341	4,073	4,143	3,151	1,685	1,387	1,034
Operating Income	600	636	664	679	506	714	431	283	211	139
Depreciation	103	108	84.3	88.8	25.7	109	53.1	21.2	14.6	8.90
Interest Expense	76.2	51.2	58.8	62.7	84.6	104	66.9	11.8	3.58	3.04
Pretax Income	425	483	529	534	400	503	315	252	195	128
Effective Tax Rate	35.5%	37.5%	37.5%	37.7%	40.9%	40.0%	40.1%	38.5%	37.5%	36.7%
Net Income	274	302	331	332	236	302	188	155	122	80.8
S&P Core Earnings	275	295	318	318	210	NA	NA	NA	NA	NA
Balance Sheet & Other Financial Data (Million $)										
Cash	34.9	45.0	350	283	76.5	60.5	47.0	129	51.3	30.1
Current Assets	1,284	1,296	1,456	1,318	1,141	1,182	1,131	632	441	390
Total Assets	4,578	4,551	4,188	3,853	3,374	2,979	2,792	1,189	581	488
Current Liabilities	836	684	629	427	378	887	661	174	110	96.0
Long Term Debt	790	1,017	835	978	977	576	834	415	27.3	12.1
Common Equity	2,666	2,654	2,538	2,304	1,905	1,477	1,241	594	436	377
Total Capital	3,632	3,806	3,503	3,380	2,963	2,053	2,075	1,009	463	389
Capital Expenditures	87.5	56.6	53.3	52.6	56.4	46.8	29.7	48.5	32.1	34.1
Cash Flow	377	410	415	421	262	411	242	176	136	89.8
Current Ratio	1.5	1.9	2.3	3.1	3.0	1.3	1.7	3.6	4.0	4.1
% Long Term Debt of Capitalization	21.7	26.7	23.8	28.9	33.0	28.1	40.2	41.1	5.9	3.1
% Net Income of Revenue	5.4	6.5	7.6	7.7	5.8	7.3	6.0	9.2	8.8	7.8
% Return on Assets	6.0	6.9	8.2	9.2	7.4	10.5	9.5	17.5	22.8	18.2
% Return on Equity	10.3	11.6	13.7	15.8	14.0	22.2	20.5	30.1	30.0	23.4

Data as orig reptd.; bef. results of disc opers/spec. items. Per share data adj. for stk. divs.; EPS diluted. E-Estimated. NA-Not Available. NM-Not Meaningful. NR-Not Ranked. UR-Under Review.

Office: 250 Rittenhouse Circle, Bristol, PA 19007.
Telephone: 215-785-4000.
Website: http://www.jny.com
Chrmn: S. Kimmel

Pres & CEO: P. Boneparth
COO: W.R. Card
EVP, Secy & General Counsel: I.M. Dansky
EVP & Cntlr: P.M. Farrell

Board of Directors: P. Boneparth, G. C. Crotty, H. Gittis, M. H. Kamens, J. R. Kerrey, S. Kimmel, A. I. Questrom, A. N. Reese, L. W. Robinson, A. F. Scarpa

Founded: 1975
Domicile: Pennsylvania
Employees: 18,430

STANDARD &POOR'S

JPMorgan Chase & Co.

S&P Recommendation HOLD ★★★★★

Price $47.29 (as of Oct 27, 2006)

12-Mo. Target Price $49.00

Investment Style Large-Cap Value

GICS Sector Financials
Sub-Industry Other Diversified Financial Services

Comment JPMorgan Chase is a leading global financial services firm with assets of $1.3 trillion and operations in more than 50 countries.

Key Stock Statistics (Source S&P, Vickers, company reports)

52-Wk Range	$48.57–36.40	S&P Oper. EPS 2006E	3.66	P/E on S&P Oper. EPS 2006E	12.9	Dividend Rate/Share	$1.36
Trailing 12-Month EPS	$3.54	S&P Oper. EPS 2007E	3.98	Common Shares Outstg. (M)	3,471.4	Yield (%)	2.88
Trailing 12-Month P/E	13.4	S&P Core EPS 2006E	3.61	Market Capitalization(B)	$164.164	Beta	1.73
$10K Invested 5 Yrs Ago	$15,374	S&P Core EPS 2007E	3.93	Institutional Ownership (%)	67	S&P Credit Rating	A+

Price Performance

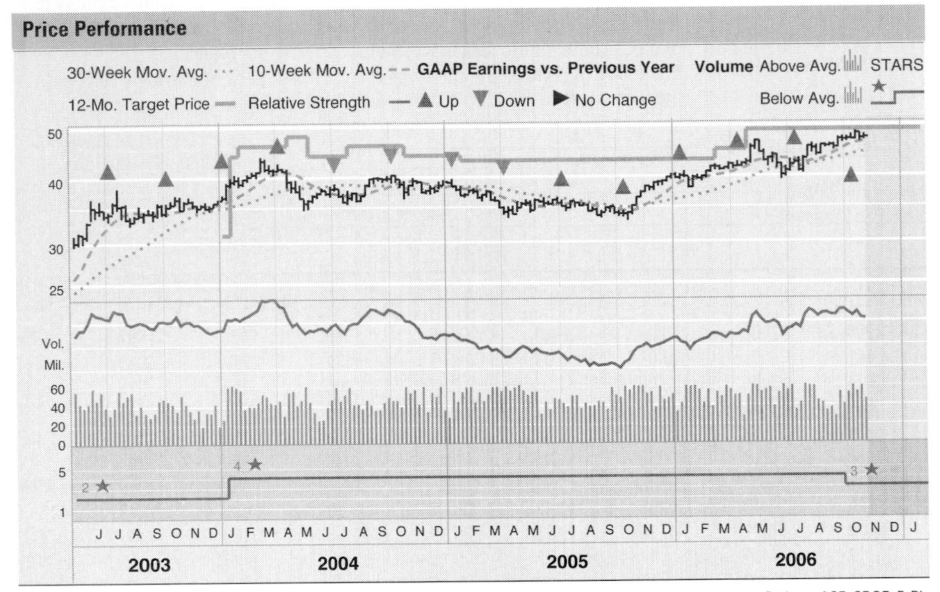

Options: ASE, CBOE, P, Ph

Analysis prepared by **Mark Hebeka, CFA** on October 25, 2006, when the stock traded at **$ 47.31**.

Highlights

- We look for continued healthy investment banking results in 2006 and 2007, partially offsetting potentially volatile trading results. We believe growth in commercial banking and treasury and security services should remain strong for the remainder of the year. We see earnings quality improving as the company makes further progress in the ongoing integration of Bank One, helping to offset more volatile businesses. While we view JPM's strategy of continued de novo branch building favorably, we believe it will take several years to make a material impact.
- In our view, favorable credit quality trends at the retail bank as well as in commercial lending, along with healthy capital markets activity in a stable economy plus merger-related cost savings, should offset higher technology related costs and position the company to show stable earnings growth in 2006 and 2007.
- Excluding merger-related charges, we estimate 2006 operating EPS of $3.66, up from $2.95 in 2005, followed by our EPS projection of $3.98 for 2007.

Investment Rationale/Risk

- We believe JPM has solid growth prospects and diverse geographic product lines. We think its large customer base and what we see as its strong fundamentals will allow it the flexibility to move toward higher growth products and markets as well as absorb potential challenges that may be ahead. However, we view market conditions as highly competitive, and see the interest rate environment as challenging.
- Risks to our recommendation and target price include legal and regulatory risk; a failure to realize projected cost savings; merger-related expenses in excess of our expectations; a severe economic downturn in combination with higher short-term interest rates that could result in a prolonged inverted yield curve; and any serious event that could adversely affect equity markets.
- Our 12-month target price of $49 is equal to a slightly above peer 12.3X our 2007 operating EPS estimate. We think this is a fair multiple, reflecting our view that JPM's earnings will become less volatile as it further integrates Bank One and works to stabilize its trading business.

Qualitative Risk Assessment

LOW | MEDIUM | HIGH

Our risk assessment of JPMorgan Chase reflects our view of strong fundamentals, solid credit quality, a large customer base, and a healthy economy. We also believe JPM's diversity in its geographic presence and product offerings provides significant protection from a local or regional downturn.

Quantitative Evaluations

S&P Quality Ranking **B**

D | C | B- | B | B+ | A- | A | A+

Relative Strength Rank **MODERATE**

49

LOWEST = 1 HIGHEST = 99

Revenue/Earnings Data

Revenue (Million $)

	1Q	2Q	3Q	4Q	Year
2006	23,477	24,175	--	--	--
2005	19,054	18,691	21,048	21,109	79,902
2004	11,625	11,227	16,546	17,483	56,931
2003	11,454	11,842	10,396	10,671	44,363
2002	10,957	11,190	7,301	--	43,372
2001	15,015	12,559	12,399	--	50,429

Earnings Per Share ($)

2006	0.86	0.98	0.90	E0.90	E3.66
2005	0.63	0.28	0.71	0.76	2.38
2004	0.92	-0.27	0.39	0.46	1.55
2003	0.69	0.89	0.78	0.89	3.24
2002	0.48	0.50	0.01	-0.20	0.80
2001	0.59	0.18	0.22	-0.18	0.81

Fiscal year ended Dec. 31. Next earnings report expected: Mid January. EPS Estimates based on S&P Operating Earnings; historical GAAP earnings are as reported.

Dividend Data (Dates: mm/dd Payment Date: mm/dd/yy)

Amount ($)	Date Decl.	Ex-Div. Date	Stk. of Record	Payment Date
0.340	12/13	01/04	01/06	01/31/06
0.340	03/21	04/04	04/06	04/30/06
0.340	05/16	07/03	07/06	07/31/06
0.340	09/21	10/04	10/06	10/31/06

Dividends have been paid since 1827. Source: Company reports.

JPMorgan Chase & Co.

Business Summary October 25, 2006

CORPORATE OVERVIEW. JP Morgan's operations are divided into six major business lines: Investment Banking, Retail Financial Services (RFS), Card Services (CS), Commercial Banking (CB), Treasury & Securities Services (TSS), and Asset & Wealth Management (AWM).

JPM is one of the world's leading investment banks, with clients consisting of corporations, financial institutions, governments, and institutional investors worldwide. Its products and services include advising on corporate strategy and structure, equity and debt capital raising, sophisticated risk management, research, and market making in cash securities and derivative instruments.

RFS includes Home Finance, Consumer & Small Business Banking, Auto & Education Finance and Insurance.

CS had over 98 million cards in circulation as of September 30, 2005. CS offers a wide variety of products to satisfy the needs of its cardmembers, including cards issued on behalf of many well-known partners, such as major airlines, hotels, universities, retailers, and other financial institutions.

Company Financials

Per Share Data ($) Year Ended Dec. 31	2005	2004	2003	2002	2001	2000	1999	1998	1997	1996
Tangible Book Value	15.88	14.77	14.77	15.82	12.54	12.95	18.59	17.93	15.84	14.16
Earnings	2.38	1.55	3.24	0.80	0.81	2.86	4.18	2.83	2.68	1.67
S&P Core Earnings	2.76	2.25	3.12	0.65	0.34	NA	NA	NA	NA	NA
Dividends	1.36	1.36	1.36	1.36	1.34	1.23	1.06	0.93	0.81	0.73
Payout Ratio	57%	88%	42%	170%	165%	43%	25%	33%	30%	43%
Prices:High	40.56	43.84	38.26	39.68	57.33	67.17	60.75	51.71	42.19	31.96
Prices:Low	32.92	34.62	20.13	15.26	29.04	32.38	43.87	23.71	28.21	17.38
P/E Ratio:High	17	28	12	50	71	23	15	18	16	19
P/E Ratio:Low	14	22	6	19	36	11	10	8	11	10

Income Statement Analysis (Million $)	2005	2004	2003	2002	2001	2000	1999	1998	1997	1996
Net Interest Income	19,831	16,761	12,337	11,526	10,802	9,512	8,744	8,566	8,158	8,340
Tax Equivalent Adjustment	NA	NA	NA	NA	NA	NA	NA	NA	NA	NA
Non Interest Income	34,702	26,336	19,473	16,525	17,382	23,193	13,372	9,692	8,313	7,377
Loan Loss Provision	3,483	NA	NA	4,331	3,185	1,377	1,621	1,343	804	897
% Expense/Operating Revenue	66.5%	85.6%	73.0%	81.2%	82.7%	69.8%	55.3%	63.5%	61.1%	59.4%
Pretax Income	12,215	6,194	10,028	2,519	2,566	8,733	8,375	5,930	5,910	3,811
Effective Tax Rate	30.6%	27.9%	33.0%	34.0%	33.0%	34.4%	35.0%	36.2%	37.6%	35.4%
Net Income	8,483	4,466	6,719	1,663	1,719	5,727	5,446	3,782	3,708	2,461
% Net Interest Margin	NA	NA	NA	2.09	1.99	1.87	2.98	2.89	2.86	3.21
S&P Core Earnings	9,802	6,456	6,439	1,290	698	NA	NA	NA	NA	NA

Balance Sheet & Other Financial Data (Million $)	2005	2004	2003	2002	2001	2000	1999	1998	1997	1996
Money Market Assets	432,358	390,168	329,739	314,110	265,875	293,429	115,168	83,391	106,207	97,266
Investment Securities	128,578	149,675	109,328	126,834	105,537	117,494	61,513	64,490	52,738	48,546
Commercial Loans	150,111	135,067	83,097	91,548	104,864	119,460	88,120	88,056	88,906	70,245
Other Loans	269,037	267,047	136,421	124,816	112,580	96,590	88,039	83,756	79,548	84,847
Total Assets	1,198,942	1,157,248	770,912	758,800	693,575	715,348	406,105	365,875	365,521	336,099
Demand Deposits	143,075	136,188	79,465	82,029	76,974	62,713	55,529	51,623	49,808	47,057
Time Deposits	411,916	385,268	247,027	222,724	216,676	216,652	186,216	160,814	143,880	133,864
Long Term Debt	119,886	105,718	54,782	45,190	44,172	47,788	20,690	18,375	15,127	13,314
Common Equity	107,072	105,314	45,145	41,297	40,090	40,818	22,689	22,810	20,002	20,444
% Return on Assets	0.7	0.5	0.9	0.2	0.2	0.8	1.4	1.0	1.1	0.8
% Return on Equity	8.0	5.9	15.4	4.0	4.1	15.2	23.6	17.2	18.4	12.3
% Loan Loss Reserve	1.7	1.8	2.1	2.5	2.1	1.7	2.0	2.1	2.2	2.3
% Loans/Deposits	75.5	77.1	67.2	71.0	74.0	77.3	72.9	84.0	87.0	85.7
% Equity to Assets	9.0	7.8	5.7	5.6	5.7	5.4	5.9	5.9	5.5	5.7

Data as orig reptd.; bef. results of disc opers/spec. items. Per share data adj. for stk. divs.; EPS diluted. E-Estimated. NA-Not Available. NM-Not Meaningful. NR-Not Ranked. UR-Under Review.

Office: 270 Park Ave, New York, NY 10017-2070.
Telephone: 212-270-6000.
Website: http://www.jpmorganchase.com
Chrmn: W.B. Harrison, Jr.

Pres & CEO: J. Dimon
EVP & CFO: M.J. Cavanagh
EVP & Cntlr: J.L. Sclafani
Chief Admin: F. Bisignano

Investor Contact: J. Bates (212-270-7318)
Board of Directors: J. H. Biggs, S. B. Burke, J. S. Crown, J. Dimon, E. V. Futter, W. H. Gray, III, W. B. Harrison, Jr., L. P. Jackson, Jr., J. W. Kessler, R. I. Lipp, R. A. Manoogian, D. C. Novak, L. R. Raymond, W. C. Weldon

Founded: 1823
Domicile: Delaware
Employees: 168,847

STANDARD &POOR'S

Juniper Networks Inc

S&P Recommendation SELL ★★★★★ | **Price** $16.93 (as of Oct 27, 2006) | **12-Mo. Target Price** $16.00 | **Investment Style** Large-Cap Growth

GICS Sector Information Technology
Sub-Industry Communications Equipment

Comment This company provides Internet Protocol networking products and services, with a specific emphasis on telecom routing solutions.

Key Stock Statistics (Source S&P, Vickers, company reports)

52-Wk Range	**$24.68–12.09**	S&P Oper. EPS 2006**E**	**0.60**	P/E on S&P Oper. EPS 2006**E**	**28.2**	Dividend Rate/Share	**Nil**
Trailing 12-Month EPS	**$0.59**	S&P Oper. EPS 2007**E**	**0.73**	Common Shares Outstg. (M)	**565.8**	Yield (%)	**Nil**
Trailing 12-Month P/E	**28.7**	S&P Core EPS 2006**E**	**0.60**	Market Capitalization(B)	**$9.578**	Beta	**3.02**
$10K Invested 5 Yrs Ago	**$6,772**	S&P Core EPS 2007**E**	**0.73**	Institutional Ownership (%)	**82**	S&P Credit Rating	**BB**

Price Performance

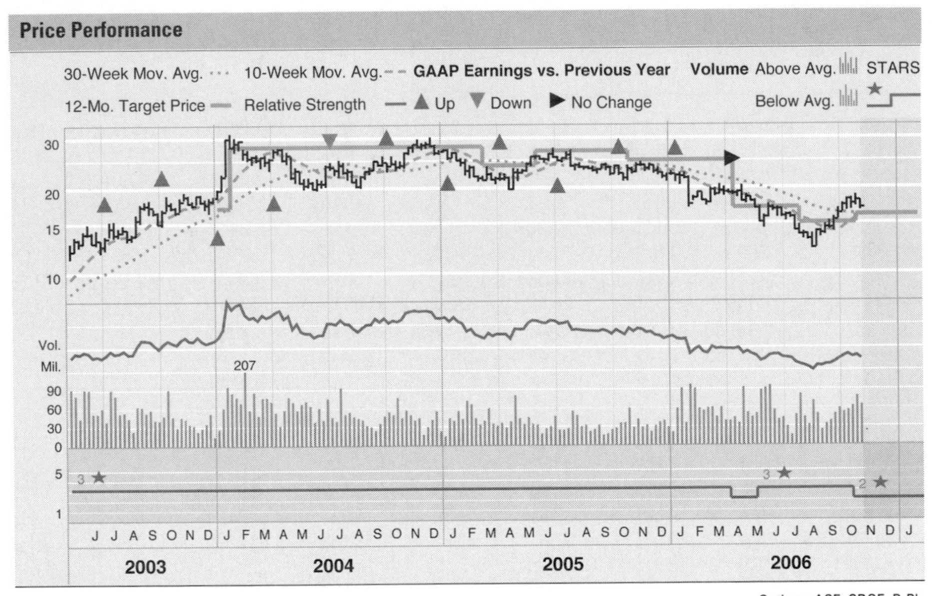

Options: ASE, CBOE, P, Ph

Analysis prepared by **Ari Bensinger** on October 20, 2006, when the stock traded at **$ 17.94**.

Highlights

- Following an estimated 12% increase in 2006, we see revenues advancing 18% in 2007, reflecting solid demand for network infrastructure products, as well as expanded revenue opportunities in the enterprise market due to the April 2004 acquisition of NetScreen Technologies. Revenue growth should benefit from our forecast of increased deployment of next generation networks by service operators during 2007.
- Despite the higher sales volume we foresee, we expect 2007 gross margins to narrow moderately from the prior year, to under 67%, owing to an increasing mix of lower-margin enterprise sales and continued industry pricing pressure. Operating expenses as a percentage of sales should decline, aided by the higher sales volumes.
- After higher interest income on an improved cash balance, we look for operating EPS of $0.73 in 2007, versus the $0.60 that we forecast for 2006. Estimates for both years include projected stock option expense of $0.15.

Investment Rationale/Risk

- We view the company's market position as attractive given its focus on the next generation networks, which, in our view, is gaining an increasing portion of service provider spending. However, we believe JNPR needs to expand its distribution base and product application features to better compete in the enterprise market. We also are concerned about recently discovered problems regarding stock option backdating.
- Risks to our recommendation and target price include increased carrier spending due to an acceleration in next generation network builds, material market share gains in the routing market, and better than expected sales traction into the enterprise sector.
- Our 12-month target price is $16. We believe JNPR should trade at a peer average 22X our 2007 EPS estimate of $0.73. Using our three-year earnings growth estimate of 16%, our target price represents a P/E to growth ratio of 1.4X--below peers--to account for our view of potential execution risks as the company expands its enterprise presence.

Qualitative Risk Assessment

LOW | MEDIUM | **HIGH**

Our risk assessment reflects the highly competitive nature of the industry and execution risks related to the company's planned expansion into the enterprise market.

Quantitative Evaluations

S&P Quality Ranking **NR**

D | C | B- | B | B+ | A- | A | A+

Relative Strength Rank **MODERATE**

61

LOWEST = 1 HIGHEST = 99

Revenue/Earnings Data

Revenue (Million $)

	1Q	2Q	3Q	4Q	Year
2006	566.7	--	--	--	--
2005	449.1	493.0	546.4	575.5	2,064
2004	224.1	306.9	375.0	430.1	1,336
2003	157.2	165.1	172.1	207.0	701.4
2002	122.2	117.0	152.0	155.3	546.6
2001	332.1	202.2	201.7	151.0	887.0

Earnings Per Share ($)

2006	0.13	**E**0.16	**E**0.15	**E**0.16	**E**0.60
2005	0.13	0.15	0.14	0.17	0.59
2004	0.08	-0.02	0.08	0.11	0.25
2003	0.01	0.03	0.02	0.04	0.10
2002	-0.14	0.02	-0.24	0.02	-0.34
2001	0.17	-0.12	-0.09	-0.02	-0.04

Fiscal year ended Dec. 31. Next earnings report expected: NA. EPS Estimates based on S&P Operating Earnings; historical GAAP earnings are as reported.

Dividend Data

No cash dividends have been paid.

Juniper Networks Inc

Business Summary October 20, 2006

Juniper Networks, founded in 1996, makes secure Internet Protocol (IP) networking solutions that are designed to address the needs at the core and at the edge of the network, and for wireless access. The company's core product is IP backbone routers for service providers. The acquisition of NetScreen in 2004 added a broad family of network security solutions aimed at enterprises, service providers, and government entities.

Service providers offer access to the Internet to consumers and corporations. Routers are devices that connect local area networks (LANS); the Internet uses routers to forward packets (a packet is a piece of a message) from one host to another. JNPR's Internet backbone routers are specifically designed to meet the requirements of the Internet, as they feature improved scalability.

Infrastructure products include the M-series and T-series routers, geared to service providers, offering carrier class reliability and scalability. The M-series, which can be deployed at the edge of operator networks, in small and medium core networks, includes the M320, M160, M40e, M20, M10i and M7i platforms. The T-series, T640 and T320, and TX Matrix are primarily designed for core IP infrastructures. Other product platforms include E-series and J-series (wireless router, developed through JNPR's joint venture with Ericsson). All routers run on JNPR's JUNOS Internet software, and are differentiated from their competition in that they also feature the company's high-performance, ASIC-based packet forwarding technology.

Through the acquisition of NetScreen, JNPR offers high performance security systems designed to provide integrated firewall, VPN, denial of service protection, secure-access secure sockets that layer VPN appliances, and intrusion detection and prevention capabilities for enterprise environments and carrier network infrastructures.

Company Financials

Per Share Data ($) Year Ended Dec. 31	2005	2004	2003	2002	2001	2000	1999	1998	1997	1996
Tangible Book Value	3.04	2.89	1.48	1.18	2.36	1.87	1.47	0.80	2.41	NA
Cash Flow	0.82	0.52	0.27	-0.16	0.42	0.53	-0.01	-1.35	-0.51	NA
Earnings	0.59	0.25	0.10	-0.34	-0.04	0.43	-0.05	-0.14	-0.20	NA
S&P Core Earnings	0.26	0.12	-0.06	-0.51	-0.38	NA	NA	NA	NA	NA
Dividends	Nil	Nil	Nil	Nil	Nil	Nil	Nil	NA	NA	NA
Payout Ratio	Nil	Nil	Nil	Nil	Nil	Nil	Nil	NA	NA	NA
Prices:High	27.65	31.25	19.38	23.01	145.00	244.50	64.06	NA	NA	NA
Prices:Low	19.65	18.75	6.88	4.15	8.90	48.83	5.67	NA	NA	NA
P/E Ratio:High	47	NM	NM	NM	NM	NM	NM	NA	NA	NA
P/E Ratio:Low	33	NM	NM	NM	NM	NM	NM	NA	NA	NA

Income Statement Analysis (Million $)	2005	2004	2003	2002	2001	2000	1999	1998	1997	1996
Revenue	2,064	1,336	701	547	887	674	103	3.81	Nil	NA
Operating Income	595	376	141	42.2	205	249	-9.31	-30.1	-10.9	NA
Depreciation	139	145	70.0	63.0	148	34.8	5.31	2.17	0.71	NA
Interest Expense	3.93	5.38	39.1	55.6	61.4	52.7	Nil	Nil	0.33	NA
Pretax Income	502	219	59.0	-115	16.5	230	-6.61	-31.0	-10.4	NA
Effective Tax Rate	29.5%	38.0%	33.6%	NM	NM	35.8%	NM	NM	NM	NA
Net Income	354	136	39.2	-120	13.4	140	-9.03	-31.0	-10.4	NA
S&P Core Earnings	156	65.9	-25.6	-180	-122	NA	NA	NA	NA	NA

Balance Sheet & Other Financial Data (Million $)	2005	2004	2003	2002	2001	2000	1999	1998	1997	1996
Cash	918	713	396	194	607	563	158	20.1	46.2	NA
Current Assets	1,818	1,414	691	681	1,126	1,349	378	28.8	46.8	NA
Total Assets	8,027	7,000	2,411	2,615	2,390	2,103	513	36.7	50.2	NA
Current Liabilities	627	503	291	242	242	216	55.7	14.4	2.08	NA
Long Term Debt	400	Nil	558	942	1,150	1,120	Nil	5.20	2.08	NA
Common Equity	6,900	5,993	1,562	1,431	997	730	458	17.1	46.0	NA
Total Capital	7,300	5,993	2,120	2,373	2,147	1,850	458	22.3	48.1	NA
Capital Expenditures	98.2	63.2	19.4	36.1	241	35.0	10.0	6.53	3.11	NA
Cash Flow	493	281	109	-56.6	134	183	-3.73	-28.8	-9.65	NA
Current Ratio	2.9	2.8	2.4	2.8	4.6	6.2	6.8	2.0	22.5	NA
% Long Term Debt of Capitalization	5.5	Nil	26.3	39.7	53.6	60.5	Nil	23.4	4.3	NA
% Net Income of Revenue	17.2	10.2	5.6	NM	NM	22.0	NM	NM	NM	NA
% Return on Assets	4.7	2.9	1.6	NM	NM	11.3	NM	NM	NM	NA
% Return on Equity	5.5	3.6	2.6	NM	NM	24.9	NM	NM	NM	NA

Data as orig reptd.; bef. results of disc opers/spec. items. Per share data adj. for stk. divs.; EPS diluted. E-Estimated. NA-Not Available. NM-Not Meaningful. NR-Not Ranked. UR-Under Review.

Office: 1194 North Mathilda Avenue, Sunnyvale, CA 94089.
Telephone: 408-745-2000.
Email: investor-relations@juniper.net
Website: http://www.juniper.net

Chrmn & CEO: S. Kriens
Vice Chrmn & CTO: P. Sindhu
EVP & CFO: R.R. Dykes
Investor Contact: M. Levine (408-936-2775)

Board of Directors: R. M. Calderoni, K. Goldman, W. R. Hearst, III, S. Kriens, K. Levy, F. Marshall, S. Sclavos, P. Sindhu, W. R. Stensrud

Founded: 1996
Domicile: Delaware
Employees: 4,145

KB Home

S&P Recommendation HOLD ★★★★★

Price $45.51 (as of Oct 27, 2006)

12-Mo. Target Price $48.00

Investment Style Mid-Cap Growth

GICS Sector Consumer Discretionary
Sub-Industry Homebuilding

Comment This large, diversified homebuilder has operations in most of the largest markets in the U.S., and also has a significant presence in France.

Key Stock Statistics (Source S&P, Vickers, company reports)

52-Wk Range	$81.99–37.89	S&P Oper. EPS 2006E	8.25	P/E on S&P Oper. EPS 2006E	5.5	Dividend Rate/Share	$1.00
Trailing 12-Month EPS	$10.54	S&P Oper. EPS 2007E	7.45	Common Shares Outstg. (M)	91.3	Yield (%)	2.20
Trailing 12-Month P/E	4.3	S&P Core EPS 2006E	8.25	Market Capitalization(B)	$4.156	Beta	0.85
$10K Invested 5 Yrs Ago	$31,661	S&P Core EPS 2007E	7.45	Institutional Ownership (%)	84	S&P Credit Rating	BB+

Price Performance

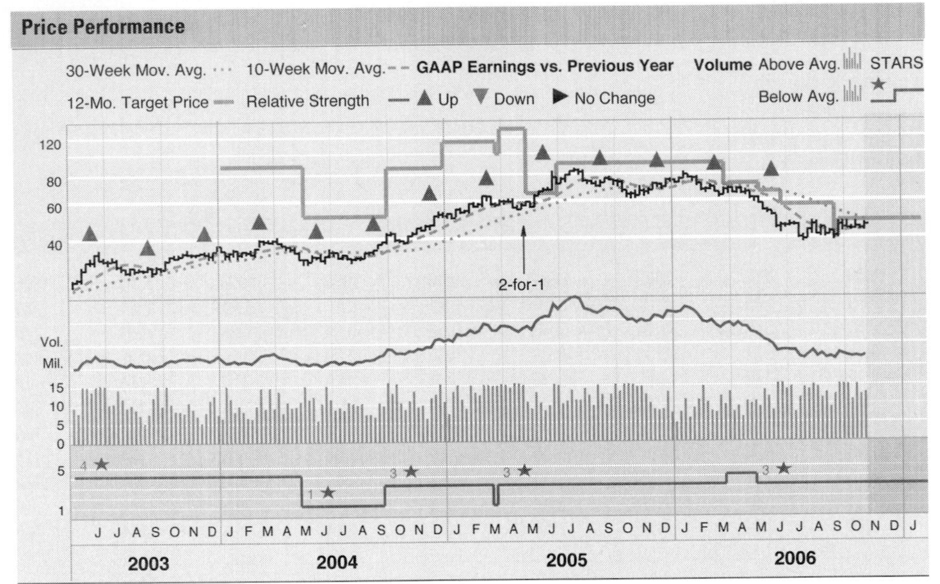

Options: Ph

Analysis prepared by **William R. Mack, CFA** on September 15, 2006, when the stock traded at **$ 45.70**.

Highlights

- We look for KB Home to increase its revenues by nearly 15% in FY 06 (Nov.). Nearly all of this projected jump is expected to arise from home price increases, which are seen slowing in the second half of the year from the mid-teens percentage levels recorded in the year's first half.
- The company is responding to broadly slower new home demand through a number of initiatives. It is reducing the time it takes to close on a home--which should also help minimize order cancellations--and reviewing terms of its land purchase agreements. As it relates to capital allocation decisions, the company is repurchasing shares and using a larger portion of cash flow to limit outstanding debt, rather than add to its base of land.
- As KBH adjusts to the recent turn in the cycle, we look for it to increasingly exploit its size to achieve better economies of scale, particularly in material costs. We continue to believe that market share gains will come at the expense of smaller builders, which we think are being more adversely affected by the current slowdown.

Investment Rationale/Risk

- Given a lack of earnings visibility since the homebuilding cycle's recent peak, we continue to favor an asset-based valuation model over one that's pegged to increasingly uncertain earnings (growth). We think stockholder's equity, currently at around $38 a share, will finish FY 06 above $40, modestly below KBH's recent trading price.
- Risks to our recommendation and target price include sharply higher mortgage rates and a broad slowdown in either the economy or employment gains. With KBH focused on entry-level and move-up products, its middle-income base of buyers is relatively sensitive to these economic factors.
- Our belief that KBH's secular earnings growth is relatively favorable and our view that its industry leadership position is becoming further established more than offsets its comparatively low pretax margins. We apply a multiple of 1.25X current book value, or alternatively a P/E of 6.4X--about in line with peers'--to our FY 07 EPS forecast to arrive at our 12-month target price of $48.

Qualitative Risk Assessment

LOW | **MEDIUM** | HIGH

Our risk assessment reflects that despite a leverage ratio that has recently spiked to almost 55%, we view KBH's investment grade balance sheet as healthy, and with a cost of capital of less than 6%, we judge its interest burden as relatively modest. Although most of KBH's discretionary cash flow is used to reinvest in land, it has, in our view, significant capacity to fund its relatively favorable dividend and to continue to repurchase shares.

Quantitative Evaluations

S&P Quality Ranking A

D | C | B- | B | B+ | A- | **A** | A+

Relative Strength Rank MODERATE

48

LOWEST = 1 HIGHEST = 99

Revenue/Earnings Data

Revenue (Million $)

	1Q	2Q	3Q	4Q	Year
2006	2,192	2,592	--	--	--
2005	1,636	2,130	2,525	3,150	9,442
2004	1,353	1,570	1,748	2,381	7,053
2003	1,095	1,440	1,442	1,873	5,851
2002	915.7	1,140	1,293	1,683	5,031
2001	821.1	1,067	1,235	1,451	4,574

Earnings Per Share ($)

2006	2.02	2.46	E1.90	E1.87	E8.25
2005	1.41	2.06	2.55	3.51	9.53
2004	0.88	1.20	1.42	2.21	5.70
2003	0.63	0.97	1.17	1.66	4.40
2002	0.48	0.71	0.98	1.46	3.58
2001	0.35	0.54	0.79	1.02	2.75

Fiscal year ended Nov. 30. Next earnings report expected: NA. EPS Estimates based on S&P Operating Earnings; historical GAAP earnings are as reported.

Dividend Data (Dates: mm/dd Payment Date: mm/dd/yy)

Amount ($)	Date Decl.	Ex-Div. Date	Stk. of Record	Payment Date
0.250	12/08	02/07	02/09	02/23/06
0.250	04/06	05/09	05/11	05/25/06
0.250	07/13	08/08	08/10	08/24/06
0.250	10/05	11/06	11/08	11/22/06

Dividends have been paid since 1986. Source: Company reports.

KB Home

Business Summary September 15, 2006

CORPORATE OVERVIEW. From its base in California, KB Home has become one of the five largest single-family homebuilders in the country. In doing so, it has helped establish what has become the industry model for rapid growth: using the acquisition of smaller builders as platforms for expansion into new markets. Since 1993, KBH has expanded into Nevada, Arizona, Colorado, New Mexico, Texas, Florida, Georgia, North Carolina, South Carolina, Illinois and Indiana.

KBH entered Georgia and North Carolina in March 2003, through the acquisition of Colony Homes; re-entered Illinois through the September 2003 takeover of Zale Homes in Chicago; South Carolina through the January 2004 purchase of Palmetto Traditional Homes; and Indiana through the June 2004 purchase of Dura Builders. KBH's French subsidiary, of which it owned about 53% in December 2005, expanded during 2004, acquiring Groupe Avantis, one of the leading property developer-builders in the Midi-Pyrenees region of France, and Foncier Investissement, a builder of apartment units for traditional home buyers and private and institutional investors, and vacation properties.

MANAGEMENT. We think KBH's management is the most progressive in the homebuilding industry. In early December 2005, the company announced the formation of KB HOME/Shaw Louisiana LLC, a joint venture aimed at building homes in and around New Orleans in the aftermath of recent hurricanes in Louisiana. To our knowledge, no other large builder has announced plans to seize what we believe is a significant opportunity in this currently under-served market.

In September 2005, the company sold its mortgage unit. This ancillary business generates significant pretax margins despite an increasingly competitive lending environment. By simultaneously striking a joint venture with Countrywide Financial Corp., the unit's acquiror, KBH should continue to see strategic and financial benefits from these operations while eliminating day to day management obligations, in our opinion. Moreover, we believe that KBH significantly reduces its exposure to consumer finance, where profitability is relatively volatile and hard to predict.

Company Financials

Per Share Data ($) Year Ended Nov. 30	**2005**	**2004**	**2003**	**2002**	**2001**	**2000**	**1999**	**1998**	**1997**	**1996**
Tangible Book Value	27.50	19.34	14.63	11.25	8.95	6.63	5.35	5.37	4.51	3.88
Cash Flow	9.79	5.96	4.65	3.77	3.32	3.14	1.95	1.38	0.87	-0.64
Earnings	9.53	5.70	4.40	3.58	2.75	2.62	1.54	1.16	0.73	-0.77
S&P Core Earnings	9.28	11.32	8.69	7.00	5.32	NA	NA	NA	NA	NA
Dividends	0.56	0.15	0.15	0.15	0.15	0.15	0.15	0.15	0.15	0.15
Payout Ratio	6%	3%	3%	4%	5%	6%	10%	13%	21%	NM
Prices:High	85.45	53.76	37.48	27.20	20.72	19.16	15.13	17.50	11.56	8.44
Prices:Low	40.26	30.14	21.20	18.57	12.34	8.41	8.38	8.56	6.38	5.63
P/E Ratio:High	9	9	9	8	8	7	10	15	16	NM
P/E Ratio:Low	5	5	5	5	4	3	5	7	9	NM
Income Statement Analysis (Million $)										
Revenue	9,442	7,053	5,851	5,031	4,574	3,931	3,836	2,449	1,876	1,787
Operating Income	1,390	796	584	539	448	373	333	203	141	136
Depreciation	23.4	21.8	21.5	17.2	43.9	41.3	40.0	18.1	11.9	10.8
Interest Expense	24.0	22.7	30.2	44.2	59.5	50.9	45.0	38.4	42.5	77.1
Pretax Income	1,374	787	580	486	352	329	257	154	91.5	-95.8
Effective Tax Rate	33.0%	30.1%	31.5%	31.9%	31.3%	26.6%	30.7%	33.4%	35.9%	NM
Net Income	842	481	371	314	214	210	147	95.3	58.2	-61.2
S&P Core Earnings	808	467	357	302	207	NA	NA	NA	NA	NA
Balance Sheet & Other Financial Data (Million $)										
Cash	145	234	138	330	281	33.1	28.0	63.4	68.2	9.78
Current Assets	NA	NA	NA	NA	NA	NA	NA	NA	NA	NA
Total Assets	7,747	5,836	4,236	4,026	3,693	2,829	2,664	1,860	1,419	1,243
Current Liabilities	NA	NA	NA	NA	NA	NA	NA	NA	NA	NA
Long Term Debt	2,433	2,048	1,393	1,181	1,111	1,208	1,308	800	698	578
Common Equity	2,852	2,056	1,593	1,274	1,092	655	676	475	383	340
Total Capital	5,429	4,231	3,075	2,530	2,267	1,919	1,994	1,472	1,083	919
Capital Expenditures	24.0	23.2	13.1	31.1	12.2	18.5	19.0	Nil	Nil	Nil
Cash Flow	866	503	392	332	258	251	187	113	70.1	-50.4
Current Ratio	NA	NA	NA	NA	NA	NA	NA	NA	NA	NA
% Long Term Debt of Capitalization	44.8	48.4	45.3	46.7	49.0	62.9	65.6	54.3	64.5	62.9
% Net Income of Revenue	8.9	6.8	6.3	6.2	4.7	5.3	3.8	3.9	3.1	NM
% Return on Assets	12.4	9.5	9.0	8.1	6.6	7.6	6.5	5.8	4.4	NM
% Return on Equity	34.3	26.4	25.9	26.6	24.5	31.6	25.6	22.2	16.1	NM

Data as orig reptd.; bef. results of disc opers/spec. items. Per share data adj. for stk. divs.; EPS diluted. E-Estimated. NA-Not Available. NM-Not Meaningful. NR-Not Ranked. UR-Under Review.

Office: 10990 Wilshire Boulevard, Los Angeles, CA 90024.
Telephone: 310-231-4000.
Website: http://www.kbhome.com
Chrmn & CEO: B. Karatz

COO & EVP: J.T. Mezger
EVP & Chief Lgl Officer: R.B. Hirst
SVP & CFO: D. Cecere
Investor Contact: K. Masuda (310-893-7434)

Board of Directors: R. Burkle, T. W. Finchem, R. R. Irani, K. M. Jastrow, II, J. A. Johnson, B. Karatz, J. T. Lanni, M. Lora, M. G. McCaffery, L. Moonves, L. G. Nogales

Founded: 1957
Domicile: Delaware
Employees: 6,700

STANDARD &POOR'S

Kellogg Co

S&P Recommendation BUY ★★★★★

Price $50.10 (as of Oct 30, 2006)

12-Mo. Target Price $55.00

Investment Style Large-Cap Growth

GICS Sector Consumer Staples
Sub-Industry Packaged Foods & Meats

Comment Kellogg is the world's leading producer of ready-to-eat cereal products, with a dominant 40% global volume share.

Key Stock Statistics (Source S&P, Vickers, company reports)

52-Wk Range	$50.87–42.41	S&P Oper. EPS 2006E	2.53	P/E on S&P Oper. EPS 2006E	19.8	Dividend Rate/Share	$1.16
Trailing 12-Month EPS	$2.53	S&P Oper. EPS 2007E	2.75	Common Shares Outstg. (M)	396.7	Yield (%)	2.32
Trailing 12-Month P/E	19.8	S&P Core EPS 2006E	2.51	Market Capitalization(B)	$19.875	Beta	0.10
$10K Invested 5 Yrs Ago	$18,888	S&P Core EPS 2007E	2.73	Institutional Ownership (%)	81	S&P Credit Rating	BBB+

Price Performance

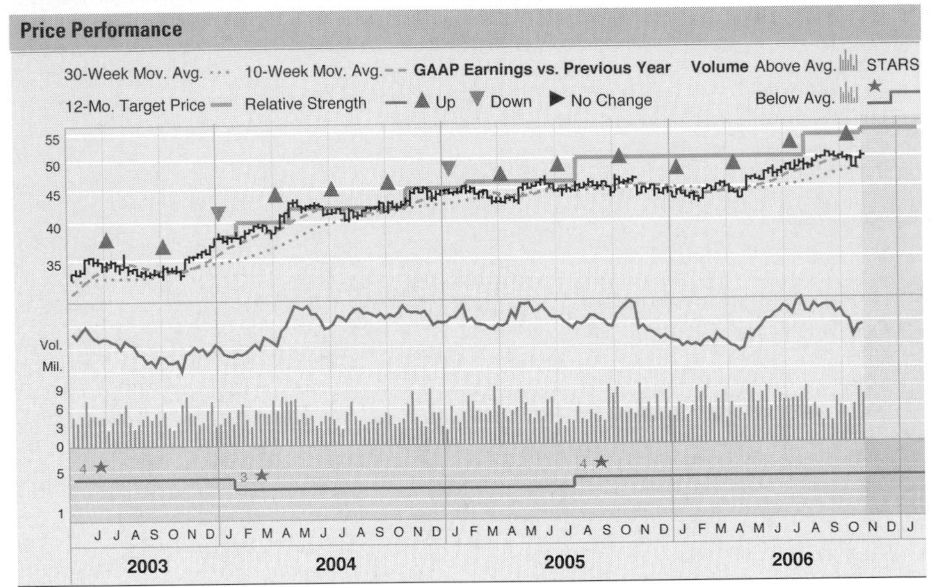

Options: ASE, CBOE

Analysis prepared by **Rick Joy** on October 27, 2006, when the stock traded at **$ 50.21**.

Highlights

- The company has stated that it expects to continue to increase its investments in brand building and innovation for the fourth quarter of 2006 and into 2007, which we believe will continue to fuel strong momentum for Kellogg products.
- We expect net sales to rise 4% to 5% in 2007, reflecting low single digit volume growth, new product introductions and pricing and product mix improvements. We see near-term results restricted by increased marketing and promotional activity to support new products, higher employee benefit expenses, and increased commodity and fuel costs. We think a combination of operating leverage, product mix improvement and productivity savings should help offset these higher costs, and allow operating profits to advance more than 7%.
- Following a modest reduction in shares outstanding, we project 2007 EPS of $2.75, up 8.7% from our 2006 EPS estimate of $2.53, which includes an estimated $0.11 for stock options expense. For the longer term, we expect EPS growth of 7% to 9%.

Investment Rationale/Risk

- Our buy recommendation reflects our belief that strong brand momentum and operating leverage will lead to improved EPS visibility and consistency. In our opinion, Kellogg is executing well in the marketplace and has done a good job managing through a difficult cost environment. We think the shares are attractive, based on our projections of solid earnings growth, strong free cash flows, and improving returns. The shares traded recently at approximately 18X our 2007 EPS estimate, a well deserved premium, in our view, to packaged food industry peers and the S&P 500.
- Risks to our recommendation and target price include competitive pressures in K's businesses, consumer acceptance of new product introductions, commodity cost inflation, and the company's ability to achieve sales and earnings growth forecasts.
- Our 12-month target price of $55 is based on our analysis of peer P/E and enterprise value to EBITDA multiples, and our discounted cash flow model, which assumes a weighted average cost of capital of 9% and a terminal growth rate of 3%.

Qualitative Risk Assessment

LOW	MEDIUM	HIGH

Our risk assessment for Kellogg Company reflects the relatively stable nature of the company's end markets, a strong balance sheet and cash flows, and corporate governance practices that we view as favorable versus peers.

Quantitative Evaluations

S&P Quality Ranking B+

D	C	B-	B	B+	A-	A	A+

Relative Strength Rank MODERATE

44

LOWEST = 1 HIGHEST = 99

Revenue/Earnings Data

Revenue (Million $)

	1Q	2Q	3Q	4Q	Year
2006	2,727	2,774	2,822	--	--
2005	2,572	2,587	2,623	2,394	10,177
2004	2,391	2,387	2,445	2,391	9,614
2003	2,148	2,247	2,282	2,135	8,812
2002	2,062	2,125	2,137	1,981	8,304
2001	1,707	2,343	2,590	2,213	8,853

Earnings Per Share ($)

	1Q	2Q	3Q	4Q	Year
2006	0.68	0.67	0.70	**E**0.49	**E**2.53
2005	0.61	0.62	0.66	0.47	2.36
2004	0.53	0.57	0.59	0.45	2.14
2003	0.40	0.50	0.56	0.46	1.92
2002	0.37	0.42	0.49	0.47	1.75
2001	0.23	0.28	0.37	0.31	1.18

Fiscal year ended Dec. 31. Next earnings report expected: NA. EPS Estimates based on S&P Operating Earnings; historical GAAP earnings are as reported.

Dividend Data (Dates: mm/dd Payment Date: mm/dd/yy)

Amount ($)	Date Decl.	Ex-Div. Date	Stk. of Record	Payment Date
0.278	02/17	02/27	03/01	03/15/06
0.278	04/21	05/30	06/01	06/15/06
0.291	04/21	08/30	09/01	09/15/06
0.291	10/20	11/29	12/01	12/15/06

Dividends have been paid since 1923. Source: Company reports.

Kellogg Co

Business Summary October 27, 2006

Kellogg Co., incorporated in 1922, is the world's leading producer of ready-to-eat cereal products, with an approximate 33% dollar market share in North America and nearly 40% globally. In recent years, the company has expanded its operations from ready-to-eat cereals to also include other grain-based convenience food products, such as Pop-Tarts toaster pastries, Eggo frozen waffles, Nutri-Grain cereal bars, and Rice Krispies Treats squares.

With the March 2001 acquisition of the Keebler Foods Co., the company also markets cookies, crackers and other convenience food products under brand names such as Keebler, Cheez-It, Murray and Famous Amos, and manufactures private label cookies, crackers and other products. These branded products will continue to be marketed through Keebler's direct store door (DSD) delivery system. K is also now marketing some of its other convenience foods products in the U.S. through this DSD system.

Products are manufactured in 17 countries and distributed in more than 180.

Ready-to-eat cereals include Corn Flakes, Rice Krispies, Special K, Frosted Flakes, All-Bran, Corn Pops, Raisin Bran, Frosted Mini-Wheats, and Low Fat Granola. Cereals are generally marketed under the Kellogg's name, and are sold principally to the grocery trade through direct sales forces for resale to consumers and through broker and distribution arrangements in less developed market areas.

Sales contributions by geographic region in 2005 were: North America 67%, Europe 20%, Latin America 8%, and Asia Pacific 5%. The company's largest customer, Wal-Mart Stores Inc. and its affiliates, accounted for approximately 17% of consolidated net sales during 2005, and 14% in 2004.

Company Financials

Per Share Data ($) Year Ended Dec. 31	**2005**	**2004**	**2003**	**2002**	**2001**	**2000**	**1999**	**1998**	**1997**	**1996**
Tangible Book Value	NM	NM	NM	NM	NM	1.21	1.28	1.26	2.42	2.15
Cash Flow	3.30	3.15	2.83	2.60	2.26	2.16	1.54	1.91	2.07	1.87
Earnings	2.36	2.14	1.92	1.75	1.18	1.46	0.83	1.20	1.32	1.25
S&P Core Earnings	2.29	2.10	1.86	1.24	0.77	NA	NA	NA	NA	NA
Dividends	1.06	1.01	1.01	1.01	1.01	1.00	0.96	0.92	0.87	0.81
Payout Ratio	45%	47%	53%	58%	86%	69%	116%	75%	66%	65%
Prices:High	46.99	45.32	38.57	37.00	34.00	32.00	42.25	50.19	50.50	40.31
Prices:Low	42.35	37.00	27.85	29.02	24.25	20.75	30.00	28.50	32.00	31.00
P/E Ratio:High	20	21	20	21	29	22	51	41	38	32
P/E Ratio:Low	18	17	15	17	21	14	36	23	24	25
Income Statement Analysis (Million $)										
Revenue	10,177	9,614	8,812	8,304	8,853	6,955	6,984	6,762	6,830	6,677
Operating Income	2,142	2,091	1,917	1,857	1,640	1,367	1,361	1,243	1,480	1,347
Depreciation	392	410	373	348	439	291	288	278	287	252
Interest Expense	300	309	371	391	352	138	119	119	108	70.0
Pretax Income	1,425	1,366	1,170	1,144	804	868	537	783	905	860
Effective Tax Rate	31.2%	34.8%	32.7%	37.0%	40.1%	32.3%	37.0%	35.8%	37.7%	38.3%
Net Income	980	891	787	721	482	588	338	503	564	531
S&P Core Earnings	953	875	763	510	312	NA	NA	NA	NA	NA
Balance Sheet & Other Financial Data (Million $)										
Cash	219	417	141	101	2,318	204	151	136	173	244
Current Assets	2,197	2,122	1,797	1,763	1,902	1,607	1,569	1,497	1,467	1,529
Total Assets	10,575	10,790	10,231	10,219	10,369	4,896	4,809	5,052	4,877	5,051
Current Liabilities	3,163	2,846	2,766	3,015	2,208	2,493	1,588	1,719	1,657	2,199
Long Term Debt	3,703	3,893	4,265	4,519	5,619	709	1,613	1,614	1,416	727
Common Equity	2,284	2,257	1,443	895	871	898	813	890	998	1,282
Total Capital	5,986	6,150	5,709	5,415	6,491	1,607	2,426	2,504	2,414	2,235
Capital Expenditures	374	279	247	254	277	231	266	344	312	307
Cash Flow	1,372	1,301	1,160	1,069	921	878	626	781	851	783
Current Ratio	0.7	0.7	0.6	0.6	0.9	0.6	1.0	0.9	0.9	0.7
% Long Term Debt of Capitalization	61.9	63.3	74.7	83.5	86.6	44.1	66.5	64.5	58.7	32.5
% Net Income of Revenue	9.6	9.3	8.9	8.7	5.4	8.5	4.8	7.4	8.3	8.0
% Return on Assets	9.3	8.5	7.7	7.0	6.3	12.1	6.9	10.1	11.4	11.2
% Return on Equity	43.2	48.1	67.3	81.6	54.5	68.7	39.7	53.3	49.5	37.0

Data as orig reptd.; bef. results of disc opers/spec. items. Per share data adj. for stk. divs.; EPS diluted. E-Estimated. NA-Not Available. NM-Not Meaningful. NR-Not Ranked. UR-Under Review.

Office: One Kellogg Square, Battle Creek, MI, USA 49016-3599.
Telephone: 269-961-2000.
Website: http://www.kelloggcompany.com
Chrmn & CEO: J.M. Jenness

Pres & COO: A.D. Mackay
SVP & CFO: J.M. Boromisa
SVP, Secy & General Counsel: G.H. Pilnick
VP & Cntlr: A.R. Andrews

Board of Directors: B. S. Carson, Sr., J. T. Dillon, C. X. Gonzalez, G. Gund, J. M. Jenness, D. A. Johnson, L. D. Jorndt, A. D. Mackay, A. McLaughlin Korologos, W. D. Perez, W. C. Richardson, J. L. Zabriskie

Founded: 1906
Domicile: Delaware
Employees: 25,606

STANDARD &POOR'S

KeyCorp

S&P Recommendation HOLD ★★★★★

Price $37.23 (as of Oct 27, 2006)

12-Mo. Target Price $39.00

Investment Style Large-Cap Value

GICS Sector Financials
Sub-Industry Regional Banks

Comment This multiregional bank holding company, headquartered in Cleveland, operates more than 900 branch offices.

Key Stock Statistics (Source S&P, Vickers, company reports)

52-Wk Range	$38.31–32.04	S&P Oper. EPS 2006E	2.96	P/E on S&P Oper. EPS 2006E	12.6	Dividend Rate/Share	$1.38
Trailing 12-Month EPS	$2.89	S&P Oper. EPS 2007E	3.22	Common Shares Outstg. (M)	403.3	Yield (%)	3.71
Trailing 12-Month P/E	12.9	S&P Core EPS 2006E	2.90	Market Capitalization(B)	$15.015	Beta	0.59
$10K Invested 5 Yrs Ago	$20,348	S&P Core EPS 2007E	3.18	Institutional Ownership (%)	54	S&P Credit Rating	A-

Price Performance

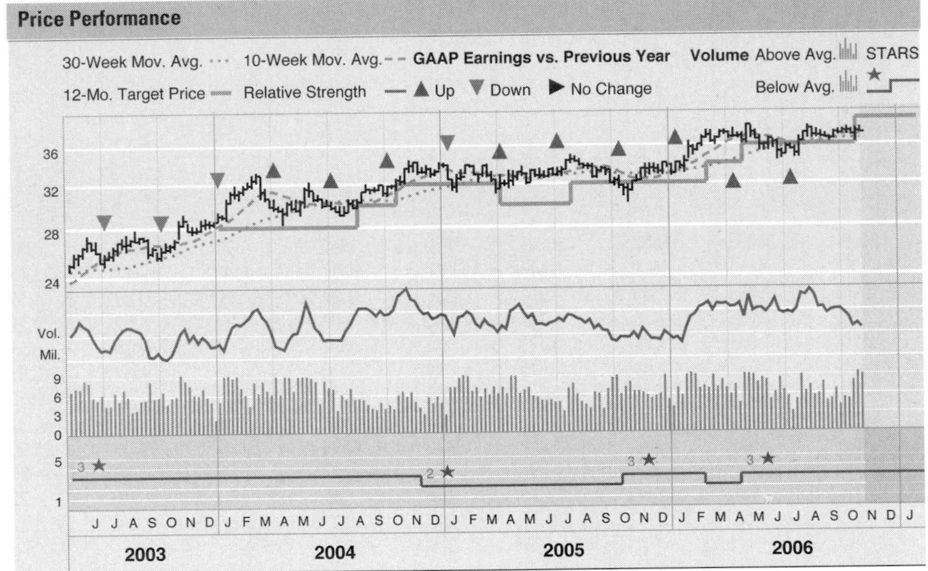

Options: ASE, P, Ph

Highlights

- The 12-month target price for KEY has recently been changed to $39.00 from $36.00. The Highlights section of this Stock Report will be updated accordingly.

Investment Rationale/Risk

- The Investment Rationale/Risk section of this Stock Report will be updated shortly. For the latest News story on KEY from MarketScope, see below.

- 10/17/06 11:03 am EDT... S&P MAINTAINS HOLD RECOMMENDATION ON SHARES OF KEYCORP (KEY 37.34***): Q3 EPS of $0.76 vs. $0.67 is $0.03 above our estimate. Non-interest income growth beat our projections, and provision for loan losses was below our forecast. Earning asset growth and net interest income before provision for loan losses both matched our estimates, but non-interest expense was slightly higher than we expected. We maintain our Q4 EPS estimate of $0.76, but we are raising our full '06 EPS estimate by $0.03 to $2.96. Although our '07 EPS estimate is unchanged at $3.22, we are raising our target price to $39 from $38, 12X our '07 estimate, a slight discount to peers. / E.Oja

Qualitative Risk Assessment

LOW | MEDIUM | HIGH

Our risk assessment reflects our view of the company's large-cap valuation, the strong credit quality of its loan portfolio, and its history of profitability. While the company operates in a highly competitive and fragmented industry, the industry tends to produce relatively stable financial results.

Quantitative Evaluations

S&P Quality Ranking A-

D | C | B- | B | B+ | A- | A | A+

Relative Strength Rank MODERATE

35

LOWEST = 1 HIGHEST = 99

Revenue/Earnings Data

Revenue (Million $)

	1Q	2Q	3Q	4Q	Year
2006	1,793	1,928	1,987	--	--
2005	1,565	1,602	1,705	1,823	6,695
2004	1,370	1,358	1,388	1,448	5,564
2003	1,418	1,456	1,434	1,422	5,730
2002	1,535	1,550	1,527	1,523	6,135
2001	2,025	1,865	1,834	1,628	7,352

Earnings Per Share ($)

2006	0.69	0.76	--	E0.76	E2.96
2005	0.64	0.70	0.67	0.72	2.73
2004	0.59	0.58	0.61	0.51	2.30
2003	0.51	0.53	0.53	0.55	2.12
2002	0.56	0.57	0.57	0.57	2.27
2001	0.51	-0.32	0.58	-0.41	0.37

Fiscal year ended Dec. 31. Next earnings report expected: Mid January. EPS Estimates based on S&P Operating Earnings; historical GAAP earnings are as reported.

Dividend Data (Dates: mm/dd Payment Date: mm/dd/yy)

Amount ($)	Date Decl.	Ex-Div. Date	Stk. of Record	Payment Date
0.325	11/17	11/25	11/29	12/15/05
0.345	01/19	02/24	02/28	03/15/06
0.345	05/15	05/25	05/30	06/15/06
0.345	07/21	08/25	08/29	09/15/06

Dividends have been paid since 1963. Source: Company reports.

KeyCorp

Business Summary July 19, 2006

CORPORATE OVERVIEW. KEY owns KeyBank located in Ohio, New York, Washington, Oregon, Maine, Colorado, Indiana, Utah, Idaho, Vermont, Alaska and Kentucky. The company has two reportable business segments: Consumer Banking, and Corporate and Investment Banking.

The Consumer Banking segment generates about 57% of total revenues. Consumer Banking houses Retail Banking, Small Business and McDonald Financial Group and provides individuals and small businesses with banking, investment and wealth and business advisory products and services.

The Corporate and Investment Banking generates about 43% of total revenues. Corporate and Investment Banking houses Corporate Banking, KeyBank Real Estate Capital and Key Equipment Finance and provides commercial and investment banking products, real estate construction and interim lending products, and equipment leasing products.

KEY's businesses expose it to interest rate, market, credit, liquidity and operational risks. The company uses securities, debt issuance and derivatives to manage interest rate and market risk, and has a credit policy in place to help mitigate credit risk.

MARKET PROFILE. KEY's wide footprint includes 224 branches in Ohio, 200 in New York, 154 in Washington, 65 in Maine, 65 in Indiana, 64 in Oregon, 47 in Colorado, 38 in Utah, 36 in Michigan, 31 in Idaho, and 35 in three other states. The projection for deposit weighted average population growth in the company's service territory is 4.1% from 2005 to 2010 according to SNL Financial. The projected national growth rate is 6.3% and the population weighted average growth rate of the states in the company's service territory is 4.1%.

COMPETITIVE LANDSCAPE. Competition for low cost deposits is fierce in the banking industry nationwide. Typically demand deposit (or checking) accounts are the cheapest, followed by interest bearing demand accounts and interest bearing time deposit accounts. Banks try to attract demand deposit accounts by offering everything from cash management services to businesses to free coolers for individuals who open accounts. In addition, bank's primary lending products are commodity type products and there are few ways to differentiate them.

Company Financials

Per Share Data ($) Year Ended Dec. 31	**2005**	**2004**	**2003**	**2002**	**2001**	**2000**	**1999**	**1998**	**1997**	**1996**
Tangible Book Value	15.05	13.91	13.87	13.34	11.85	12.39	11.13	10.28	9.14	8.95
Earnings	2.73	2.30	2.12	2.27	0.37	2.30	2.45	2.23	2.07	1.69
S&P Core Earnings	2.72	2.41	2.12	2.10	0.43	NA	NA	NA	NA	NA
Dividends	1.30	1.24	1.22	1.20	1.18	1.12	1.04	0.94	0.84	0.76
Payout Ratio	48%	54%	58%	53%	NM	49%	42%	42%	41%	45%
Prices:High	35.00	34.50	29.41	29.40	29.25	28.50	38.13	44.88	36.59	27.13
Prices:Low	30.10	28.23	22.31	20.98	20.49	15.56	21.00	23.38	23.94	16.69
P/E Ratio:High	13	15	14	13	79	12	16	20	18	16
P/E Ratio:Low	11	12	11	9	55	7	9	10	12	10

Income Statement Analysis (Million $)										
Net Interest Income	2,790	2,637	2,725	2,749	2,825	2,730	2,787	2,749	2,794	2,717
Tax Equivalent Adjustment	NA	94.0	71.0	120	45.0	28.0	32.0	34.0	44.0	50.0
Non Interest Income	2,077	1,742	1,749	1,763	1,690	2,222	2,265	1,566	1,305	1,086
Loan Loss Provision	143	185	501	553	1,350	490	348	297	320	197
% Expense/Operating Revenue	64.5%	62.8%	60.3%	57.3%	64.5%	58.6%	60.0%	58.6%	59.4%	71.7%
Pretax Income	1,588	1,388	1,242	1,312	259	1,517	1,684	1,479	1,345	1,143
Effective Tax Rate	28.9%	31.3%	27.3%	25.6%	39.4%	33.9%	34.3%	32.7%	31.7%	31.4%
Net Income	1,129	954	903	976	157	1,002	1,107	996	919	783
% Net Interest Margin	3.69	3.64	3.80	3.97	3.81	3.69	3.93	4.18	4.62	4.78
S&P Core Earnings	1,125	1,006	898	896	179	NA	NA	NA	NA	NA

Balance Sheet & Other Financial Data (Million $)										
Money Market Assets	NA	NA	NA	NA	NA	NA	NA	NA	NA	NA
Investment Securities	12,974	13,023	12,944	13,592	10,676	12,626	9,511	6,254	8,938	9,329
Commercial Loans	46,400	43,276	36,189	36,612	38,063	39,610	36,672	22,685	18,013	14,980
Other Loans	20,078	25,188	26,522	25,845	25,246	27,295	27,550	39,327	35,367	34,255
Total Assets	93,126	90,739	84,487	85,202	80,938	87,270	83,395	80,020	73,699	67,621
Demand Deposits	13,335	11,581	11,175	10,630	23,128	9,076	8,607	9,540	9,368	9,524
Time Deposits	45,430	46,261	39,683	38,716	21,667	39,573	34,626	33,043	35,705	35,793
Long Term Debt	13,939	14,846	15,294	16,865	15,842	15,404	17,124	13,964	7,446	4,213
Common Equity	7,598	7,117	6,969	6,835	6,155	6,623	6,389	6,167	5,223	4,881
% Return on Assets	1.2	1.1	1.1	1.2	0.2	1.2	1.4	1.3	1.3	1.2
% Return on Equity	15.3	13.5	13.1	15.0	2.5	15.4	17.6	17.5	18.1	15.6
% Loan Loss Reserve	1.4	1.7	2.2	2.3	2.7	1.5	1.4	1.5	1.7	1.8
% Loans/Deposits	118.9	118.4	123.3	126.6	138.0	137.5	148.5	145.6	118.4	94.9
% Equity to Assets	8.0	8.0	8.1	7.8	7.6	7.6	7.7	7.4	7.2	7.5

Data as orig reptd.; bef. results of disc opers/spec. items. Per share data adj. for stk. divs.; EPS diluted. E-Estimated. NA-Not Available. NM-Not Meaningful. NR-Not Ranked. UR-Under Review.

Office: 127 Public Square, Cleveland, OH 44114-1306.
Telephone: 216-689-6300.
Website: http://www.key.com
Chrmn, Pres & CEO: H.L. Meyer, III

Vice Chrmn: T.W. Bunn
Vice Chrmn: B. Mooney
Vice Chrmn & Chief Admin: T.C. Stevens
Sr EVP & CFO: J.B. Weeden

Board of Directors: R. Alvarez, W. G. Bares, E. P. Campbell, C. A. Cartwright, A. M. Cutler, H. J. Dallas, C. R. Hogan, L. E. Martin, D. J. McGregor, E. R. Menasce, H. L. Meyer, III, B. R. Sanford, T. C. Stevens, P. G. Ten Eyck, II

Founded: 1849
Domicile: Ohio
Employees: 19,485

STANDARD &POOR'S

Keyspan Corp.

S&P Recommendation HOLD ★★★★★

Price $40.56 (as of Oct 27, 2006)

12-Mo. Target Price $42.00

Investment Style Mid-Cap Value

GICS Sector Utilities
Sub-Industry Multi-Utilities

Comment This company is the fifth largest gas utility in the U.S., and has electric utility and power generation operations.

Key Stock Statistics (Source S&P, Vickers, company reports)

52-Wk Range	$41.52–33.27	S&P Oper. EPS 2006**E**	2.40	P/E on S&P Oper. EPS 2006**E**	16.9	Dividend Rate/Share	$1.86
Trailing 12-Month EPS	$2.26	S&P Oper. EPS 2007**E**	2.50	Common Shares Outstg. (M)	175.0	Yield (%)	4.59
Trailing 12-Month P/E	18.0	S&P Core EPS 2006**E**	2.56	Market Capitalization(B)	$7.099	Beta	0.48
$10K Invested 5 Yrs Ago	NA	S&P Core EPS 2007**E**	2.66	Institutional Ownership (%)	55	S&P Credit Rating	A

Price Performance

Options: CBOE, Ph

Analysis prepared by **Justin McCann** on September 19, 2006, when the stock traded at **$ 41.02**.

Highlights

- We expect a low single-digit increase in 2006 operating EPS, from 2005's EPS from continuing operations of $2.37. The modest increase should reflect an expected turnaround at energy services after a $2.7 million loss in the prior year, and lower interest expense on reduced debt levels. On a stand-alone basis, we project an approximate 4% increase in 2007 EPS.
- We expect slightly higher income from electric services in 2006 due to plant additions at Ravenswood. In December, KSE announced an agreement to extend the contract to operate the Long Island Power Authority's (LIPA) transmission and distribution system through 2013. The contract pricing includes a minimum annual base component of $224 million and a variable component based on electric sales exceeding a base threshold.
- We see gas distribution earnings falling as customer growth, which we believe will add about $50 million to gross profit, is outweighed by a drop in customer gas utilization. We also expect higher operating expenses from rising labor and pension costs and increased bad debt expense to impact profits, partly offset by lower marketing expenditures.

Investment Rationale/Risk

- In February, KSE agreed to be acquired by National Grid plc (NGG: hold, $60) for a total enterprise value of $11.8 billion. We expect the proposed transaction to be completed in early 2007, subject to necessary approvals. We think KSE's gas and electric assets should be a good fit with NGG's U.S. assets, which are also concentrated in New York and New England. On a stand-alone basis, we see KSE lagging peers in earnings growth.
- Risks to our opinion and target price include failure to close on the planned acquisition by National Grid, a slowdown in the economy, and higher than expected interest rates.
- Our 12-month target price of $42 is based on the $42 per share cash price offered by NGG for KSE shares. KSE's shares rose sharply on news of the proposed acquisition and we expect them to stay near the $42 level in the absence of any regulatory setbacks related to the purchase. Given a recent dividend yield of 4.5% and a dividend we think is secure, we recommend holding the shares.

Qualitative Risk Assessment

LOW | MEDIUM | HIGH

Our risk assessment reflects the fact that most of KSE's operating profits are derived from stable regulated gas and electric distribution operations.

Quantitative Evaluations

S&P Quality Ranking **B**

D | C | B- | B | B+ | A- | A | A+

Relative Strength Rank **MODERATE**

30

LOWEST = 1 HIGHEST = 99

Revenue/Earnings Data

Revenue (Million $)

	1Q	2Q	3Q	4Q	Year
2006	2,661	1,378	--	--	--
2005	2,481	1,343	1,303	2,536	7,662
2004	2,511	1,278	975.5	1,887	6,650
2003	2,513	1,408	1,132	1,863	6,915
2002	1,871	1,216	1,076	1,807	5,971
2001	2,575	1,339	1,102	1,616	6,633

Earnings Per Share ($)

2006	1.18	0.28	**E**0.23	**E**0.71	**E**2.40
2005	1.44	0.10	0.13	0.69	2.33
2004	1.53	0.80	-0.19	1.64	3.78
2003	1.53	-0.05	0.07	1.08	2.62
2002	1.51	0.20	0.02	1.03	2.75
2001	1.61	-0.09	-0.28	0.48	1.70

Fiscal year ended Dec. 31. Next earnings report expected: Early November. EPS Estimates based on S&P Operating Earnings; historical GAAP earnings are as reported.

Dividend Data (Dates: mm/dd Payment Date: mm/dd/yy)

Amount ($)	Date Decl.	Ex-Div. Date	Stk. of Record	Payment Date
0.465	12/14	01/10	01/12	02/01/06
0.465	03/23	04/10	04/12	05/01/06
0.465	06/30	07/10	07/12	08/01/06
0.465	10/04	10/16	10/18	11/01/06

Dividends have been paid since 1989. Source: Company reports.

Keyspan Corp.

Business Summary September 19, 2006

CORPORATE OVERVIEW. KeySpan Corporation (KSE) is the largest gas distribution company in the Northeast and the fifth largest in the US. KSE comprises core regulated natural gas and electric utilities and unregulated subsidiary companies and investments. It operates in four business segments: Gas Distribution, Electric Services, Energy Services, and Energy Investments. The Gas Distribution segment, which contributed 70.3% of KSE's revenues in 2005, operates through six regulated gas distribution subsidiaries in the states of New York, Massachusetts, and New Hampshire. The Electric Services segment, which accounted for 26.7% of the company's total revenue during the year, provides electric transmission and distribution as well as energy conversion services on a contractual basis. This segment also retails electricity to commercial customers. The Energy Services segment, which contributed 2.5% of KSE's 2005 revenues, provides energy-related services to customers that are primarily located within the northeastern United States. The Energy Investments segment, which contributed 0.5% of KSE's 2005 revenues, has investments in gas exploration and production, domestic pipelines, gas storage facilities, and LNG facilities and operations. In 2005, 61.1% of KSE's segment operating profit was derived from Gas Distribution operations (62.6% in 2004), 37.0% from Electric Services (31.3%), 2.2% from Energy Investments (11.3%), and -0.3% from Energy Services operations (-5.2%).

IMPACT OF MAJOR DEVELOPMENTS. On February 25, 2006, KSE entered into an agreement to merge with National Grid USA. Under the terms of the agreement, valued at $7.3 billion, National Grid would pay KSE shareholders $42 per share. If the transaction is completed, KSE would become a wholly owned subsidiary of National Grid but would continue to operate as KeySpan. The combined company would become the third-largest energy delivery utility company in the US. The proposed transaction is subject to necessary approvals, including the approval of the shareholders of both companies and certain federal and state regulatory approvals. On July 10, 2006, it cleared the review by the Federal Trade Commission under the Hart-Scott-Rodino Act. Assuming the required approvals, we expect the planned merger to be completed by early 2007. We believe the acquisition will provide adequate resources for KSE to pursue its proposed investments in energy infrastructure and other growth opportunities as well as result in cost synergies for the company.

Company Financials

Per Share Data ($) Year Ended Dec. 31	2005	2004	2003	2002	2001	2000	1999	1998	1997	1996
Tangible Book Value	16.04	13.79	11.60	8.11	7.95	7.09	22.79	19.50	20.45	19.16
Earnings	2.33	3.78	2.62	2.75	1.70	2.10	1.62	-1.34	2.56	2.20
S&P Core Earnings	2.70	2.74	3.09	1.85	0.32	NA	NA	NA	NA	NA
Dividends	1.82	1.78	1.78	1.78	1.78	1.78	1.78	1.19	1.78	1.78
Payout Ratio	78%	47%	68%	65%	105%	85%	110%	NM	70%	81%
Prices:High	41.03	41.53	38.14	38.20	41.94	43.63	31.31	34.19	30.50	17.75
Prices:Low	32.66	33.87	31.02	27.41	29.10	20.19	22.50	25.38	21.75	13.25
P/E Ratio:High	18	11	15	14	25	21	19	NM	12	8
P/E Ratio:Low	14	9	12	10	17	10	14	NM	8	6
Income Statement Analysis (Million $)										
Revenue	7,662	6,650	6,915	5,971	6,633	5,121	2,955	1,722	3,124	3,151
Depreciation	397	552	574	515	559	335	253	255	159	154
Maintenance	NA	NA	NA	NA	NA	NA	NA	114	NA	NA
Fixed Charges Coverage	3.34	2.83	3.35	3.04	2.33	3.58	3.23	-0.29	2.14	1.95
Construction Credits	NA	NA	NA	NA	NA	NA	NA	Nil	8.44	6.59
Effective Tax Rate	37.5%	33.3%	36.2%	34.8%	42.5%	39.8%	33.6%	NM	39.1%	39.9%
Net Income	399	615	424	397	244	301	259	-167	362	316
S&P Core Earnings	460	442	493	263	46.2	NA	NA	NA	NA	NA
Balance Sheet & Other Financial Data (Million $)										
Gross Property	10,369	9,868	12,673	8,191	9,936	6,974	4,761	5,706	5,692	5,425
Capital Expenditures	540	750	1,223	1,134	1,060	925	726	677	257	240
Net Property	7,337	7,068	8,894	7,218	6,606	6,358	4,240	3,778	3,814	3,695
Capitalization:Long Term Debt	3,921	4,419	5,611	5,224	4,698	4,275	1,683	1,619	4,396	4,457
Capitalization:% Long Term Debt	41.3	47.9	54.4	63.3	61.2	59.6	37.5	31.8	57.7	58.0
Capitalization:Preferred	Nil	19.7	83.6	83.8	84.1	84.2	84.3	448	563	702
Capitalization:% Preferred	Nil	0.21	0.81	1.02	1.10	1.17	1.88	8.80	7.40	9.10
Capitalization:Common	5,583	4,796	4,624	2,945	2,891	2,816	2,724	3,023	2,662	2,523
Capitalization:% Common	58.7	51.9	44.8	35.7	37.7	39.2	60.7	59.4	34.9	32.8
Total Capital	9,519	10,372	12,102	9,360	8,463	7,752	4,757	5,231	10,160	10,125
% Operating Ratio	91.5	91.0	89.4	88.6	91.1	88.7	88.3	99.2	75.4	76.6
% Earned on Net Property	12.4	11.0	12.6	13.1	12.7	13.8	8.6	0.3	20.4	20.2
% Return on Revenue	5.2	9.2	6.1	6.7	3.7	5.9	8.8	NM	11.6	10.0
% Return on Invested Capital	7.3	9.5	7.4	8.1	8.0	9.5	7.9	NM	7.6	9.6
% Return on Common Equity	7.6	12.9	10.0	13.4	8.3	10.2	7.8	NM	11.9	10.6

Data as orig reptd.; bef. results of disc opers/spec. items. Per share data adj. for stk. divs.; EPS diluted. E-Estimated. NA-Not Available. NM-Not Meaningful. NR-Not Ranked. UR-Under Review.

Office: One MetroTech Center, Brooklyn, NY 11201-3850.
Telephone: 718-403-1000.
Email: shareowner-svcs@email.bony.com
Website: http://www.keyspanenergy.com

Chrmn & CEO: R.B. Catell
Pres & COO: R.J. Fani
EVP & CFO: G. Luterman
EVP, Secy & General Counsel: J.J. Bishar, Jr.

SVP & Chief Acctg Officer: J.F. Bodanza, Jr.
Investor Contact: M.J. Taunton (718-403-3265)
Board of Directors: R. B. Catell, A. S. Christensen, R. Fani, A. H. Fishman, J. R. Jones, J. L. Larocca, G. C. Larson, S. W. McKessy, E. D. Miller, V. L. Pryor

Founded: 1895
Domicile: New York
Employees: 9,700

STANDARD &POOR'S

Kimberly-Clark Corp

S&P Recommendation BUY ★★★★☆

Price $66.25 (as of Oct 27, 2006)

12-Mo. Target Price $76.00

Investment Style Large-Cap Growth

GICS Sector Consumer Staples
Sub-Industry Household Products

Comment This leading consumer products company's global tissue, personal care and healthcare brands include Huggies, Pull-Ups, Kotex, Depend, Kleenex, Scott and Kimberly-Clark.

Key Stock Statistics (Source S&P, Vickers, company reports)

52-Wk Range	$67.67–55.60	S&P Oper. EPS 2006E	3.90	P/E on S&P Oper. EPS 2006E	17.0	Dividend Rate/Share	$1.96
Trailing 12-Month EPS	$3.03	S&P Oper. EPS 2007E	4.27	Common Shares Outstg. (M)	458.2	Yield (%)	2.96
Trailing 12-Month P/E	21.9	S&P Core EPS 2006E	4.03	Market Capitalization(B)	$30.356	Beta	0.39
$10K Invested 5 Yrs Ago	$13,764	S&P Core EPS 2007E	NA	Institutional Ownership (%)	77	S&P Credit Rating	AA-

Price Performance

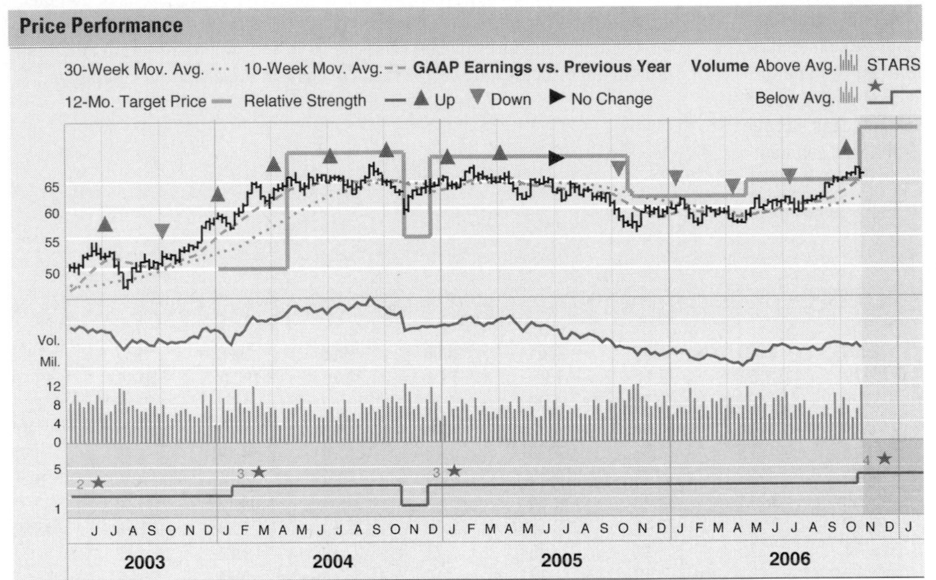

Options: ASE, CBOE, P

Analysis prepared by **Loran Braverman, CFA** on October 24, 2006, when the stock traded at **$ 67.19**.

Highlights

- We project sales growth of 4.7% for 2006, reflecting anticipated modest volume gains, higher prices, and slightly unfavorable currency translations. We expect personal care division revenues to advance approximately 6.1%, driven by new products and growth in developing markets. We see consumer tissue segment sales up 3.5%, driven by healthy demand in North America and developing markets, as well as price increases in the first half of 2006. Our sales growth forecast for 2007 is 5.2%.
- Based on our expectations of continuing difficult commodity and energy cost comparisons, we expect gross margins to be slightly lower than 2005's level of 33.2%. We believe that benefits from KMB's cost cutting program should offset our projected $47 million in stock option expense in 2006, allowing the selling, general and administrative expenses to be flat as a percentage of sales. For 2007, we expect the benefits of the strategic cost reduction program, begun in late 2005, to allow the operating margin to increase by 0.5 percentage points.
- We project that 2006 operating EPS will increase 3.2%, to $3.90, from 2005's $3.78.

Investment Rationale/Risk

- Although we continue to see intense competition in developed countries and in consumer tissue and personal care categories, we believe the company's efforts to expand in non-traditional (for KMB) categories and its focus on certain developing markets will support sales growth. In addition, we think KMB's earnings starting in 2007 will benefit from the strategic cost reduction program begun in late 2005.
- Risks to our recommendation and target price include increased promotional activity in the consumer paper category, higher commodity and energy costs, a lack of product innovation, and decreased consumer acceptance of KMB's products.
- Our 12-month target price is $76 and is a blend of our historical and relative analyses. Our historical analysis suggests a value of $77, using a P/E multiple slightly below the median of the last 10 years applied to our 2007 EPS forecast of $4.27. Our peer analysis uses a discount to the group average, implying a target price of $75.

Qualitative Risk Assessment

LOW | MEDIUM | HIGH

Our risk assessment reflects that demand for household and personal care products is generally static, and that demand is usually not affected by changes in the economy or geopolitical factors.

Quantitative Evaluations

S&P Quality Ranking A

D | C | B- | B | B+ | A- | A | A+

Relative Strength Rank MODERATE

53

LOWEST = 1 HIGHEST = 99

Revenue/Earnings Data

Revenue (Million $)

	1Q	2Q	3Q	4Q	Year
2006	4,068	4,161	4,210	--	--
2005	3,906	3,987	4,001	4,009	15,903
2004	3,712	3,687	3,783	3,901	15,083
2003	3,460	3,545	3,642	3,702	14,348
2002	3,331	3,409	3,487	3,340	13,566
2001	3,608	3,534	3,710	3,672	14,524

Earnings Per Share ($)

	1Q	2Q	3Q	4Q	Year
2006	0.60	0.82	0.79	**E**1.04	**E**3.90
2005	0.93	0.88	0.68	0.82	3.31
2004	0.88	0.88	0.87	0.92	3.55
2003	0.78	0.82	0.83	0.91	3.33
2002	0.86	0.81	0.85	0.72	3.24
2001	0.81	0.78	0.79	0.65	3.02

Fiscal year ended Dec. 31. Next earnings report expected: Late January. EPS Estimates based on S&P Operating Earnings; historical GAAP earnings are as reported.

Dividend Data (Dates: mm/dd Payment Date: mm/dd/yy)

Amount ($)	Date Decl.	Ex-Div. Date	Stk. of Record	Payment Date
0.450	11/16	12/07	12/09	01/04/06
0.490	02/22	03/08	03/10	04/04/06
0.490	04/27	06/07	06/09	07/05/06
0.490	08/01	09/06	09/08	10/03/06

Dividends have been paid since 1935. Source: Company reports.

Kimberly-Clark Corp

Business Summary October 24, 2006

Kimberly-Clark, best known for brand names such as Kleenex, Scott, Huggies and Kotex, sells consumer products in more than 150 countries. After operating as a broadly diversified enterprise, KMB made a major transition since the early 1990s, transforming itself into a global consumer products company. The company further developed its healthcare business through the acquisitions of Technol Medical Products, Ballard Medical Products, and Safeskin Corp. Reflecting more than 30 strategic acquisitions and 20 strategic divestitures since 1992, KMB has become a leading global manufacturer of tissue, personal care and healthcare products, manufactured in 42 countries.

KMB classifies its business into three segments: consumer tissue, personal care, and business-to-business. The consumer tissue segment includes facial and bathroom tissue, paper towels and napkins for household use; wet wipes; and related products. Products are sold under brand names that include Kleenex, Scott, Cottonelle, Viva, Andrex, Scottex, Page, Huggies and others.

The personal care segment includes disposable diapers, training and youth pants, and swimpants; feminine and incontinence care products; and related products. Products, primarily for household use, are sold under well known brand names that include Huggies, Pull-Ups, Little Swimmers, GoodNites, Kotex, Lightdays, Depend, Poise and others.

The business-to-business segment includes paper tissues, towels, napkins and wipers for away-from-home use; healthcare products, consisting of surgical gowns, drapes, infection control products, sterilization wraps, disposable face masks and exam gloves, respiratory products and other disposable medical products; specialty and technical papers; and other products. Products are sold under the Kimberly-Clark, Kimwipes, Wypall, Safeskin, Ballard and other brand names.

Company Financials

Per Share Data ($) Year Ended Dec. 31	**2005**	**2004**	**2003**	**2002**	**2001**	**2000**	**1999**	**1998**	**1997**	**1996**
Tangible Book Value	6.22	8.13	8.21	6.65	7.10	7.04	7.12	6.12	6.35	7.96
Cash Flow	5.08	5.32	4.80	4.60	1.39	4.55	4.17	3.11	2.46	3.49
Earnings	3.31	3.55	3.33	3.24	3.02	3.34	3.09	2.13	1.58	2.49
S&P Core Earnings	3.32	3.56	3.35	2.74	2.49	NA	NA	NA	NA	NA
Dividends	1.80	1.60	1.36	1.20	1.12	1.08	1.03	0.99	0.96	0.92
Payout Ratio	54%	45%	41%	37%	37%	32%	33%	46%	61%	37%
Prices:High	68.29	69.00	59.30	66.79	72.19	73.25	69.56	59.44	56.88	49.81
Prices:Low	55.60	56.19	42.92	45.30	52.06	42.00	44.81	35.88	43.25	34.31
P/E Ratio:High	21	19	18	21	24	22	23	28	36	20
P/E Ratio:Low	17	16	13	14	17	13	15	17	27	14
Income Statement Analysis (Million $)										
Revenue	15,903	15,083	14,348	13,566	14,524	13,982	13,007	12,298	12,547	13,149
Operating Income	3,155	3,358	3,158	3,170	3,162	3,203	2,815	2,320	2,276	2,615
Depreciation	844	800	746	707	740	673	586	542	491	561
Interest Expense	190	163	168	182	192	222	213	199	165	201
Pretax Income	2,106	2,328	2,153	2,411	2,319	2,622	2,441	1,763	1,345	2,154
Effective Tax Rate	20.8%	20.8%	23.9%	27.7%	27.8%	28.9%	29.9%	31.9%	32.2%	32.5%
Net Income	1,581	1,770	1,694	1,686	1,610	1,801	1,668	1,177	884	1,404
S&P Core Earnings	1,581	1,777	1,708	1,424	1,329	NA	NA	NA	NA	NA
Balance Sheet & Other Financial Data (Million $)										
Cash	364	594	291	495	405	207	323	144	91.0	83.0
Current Assets	4,783	4,962	4,438	4,274	3,922	3,790	3,562	3,367	3,489	3,539
Total Assets	16,303	17,018	16,780	15,586	15,008	14,480	12,816	11,510	11,266	11,846
Current Liabilities	4,643	4,537	3,919	4,038	4,168	4,574	3,846	3,791	3,706	3,687
Long Term Debt	3,352	3,021	3,301	3,398	2,962	Nil	1,927	2,068	1,804	1,739
Common Equity	5,558	6,630	6,766	5,650	5,647	5,767	5,093	3,887	4,125	4,483
Total Capital	9,878	10,859	10,366	10,158	9,923	7,036	8,101	6,819	6,673	7,233
Capital Expenditures	710	535	878	871	1,100	1,170	786	670	944	884
Cash Flow	2,425	2,571	2,440	2,393	740	2,474	2,254	1,719	1,375	1,965
Current Ratio	1.0	1.1	1.1	1.1	0.9	0.8	0.9	0.9	0.9	1.0
% Long Term Debt of Capitalization	33.9	27.8	31.8	33.4	29.9	Nil	23.8	30.3	27.0	24.0
% Net Income of Revenue	9.9	11.7	11.8	12.4	11.1	12.9	12.8	9.6	7.0	10.7
% Return on Assets	9.5	10.5	10.5	11.0	10.9	13.2	13.6	10.3	7.6	12.1
% Return on Equity	25.9	26.4	27.3	29.8	28.2	33.2	37.1	29.4	20.5	34.5

Data as orig reptd.; bef. results of disc opers/spec. items. Per share data adj. for stk. divs.; EPS diluted. E-Estimated. NA-Not Available. NM-Not Meaningful. NR-Not Ranked. UR-Under Review.

Office: P.O. Box 619100, Dallas, TX 75261-9100.
Telephone: 972-281-1200.
Website: http://www.kimberly-clark.com
Chrmn, Pres & CEO: T.J. Falk

SVP & CFO: M.A. Buthman
SVP & CCO: R.D. McCray
Investor Contact: M.D. Masseth (972-281-1478)

Board of Directors: J. R. Alm, D. R. Beresford, J. F. Bergstrom, A. E. Bru, P. S. Cafferty, R. W. Decherd, T. J. Falk, C. X. Gonzalez, M. C. Jemison, L. J. Rice, M. J. Shapiro, G. C. Sullivan

Founded: 1872
Domicile: Delaware
Employees: 57,000

STANDARD & POOR'S

Kimco Realty Corp

S&P Recommendation HOLD ★★★★★

Price $44.43 (as of Oct 31, 2006)

12-Mo. Target Price $47.00

Investment Style Large-Cap Value

GICS Sector Financials
Sub-Industry Retail REITS

Comment This REIT is one of the largest U.S. owners and operators of neighborhood and community shopping centers.

Key Stock Statistics (Source S&P, Vickers, company reports)

52-Wk Range	**$45.50–28.91**	S&P Oper. EPS 2006**E**	**1.35**	P/E on S&P Oper. EPS 2006**E**	**32.9**	Dividend Rate/Share	**$1.44**
Trailing 12-Month EPS	**$1.64**	S&P Oper. EPS 2007**E**	**1.46**	Common Shares Outstg. (M)	**252.0**	Yield (%)	**3.24**
Trailing 12-Month P/E	**27.1**	S&P Core EPS 2006**E**	**1.35**	Market Capitalization(B)	**$11.197**	Beta	**0.38**
$10K Invested 5 Yrs Ago	**$34,933**	S&P Core EPS 2007**E**	**1.46**	Institutional Ownership (%)	**67**	S&P Credit Rating	**A-**

Price Performance

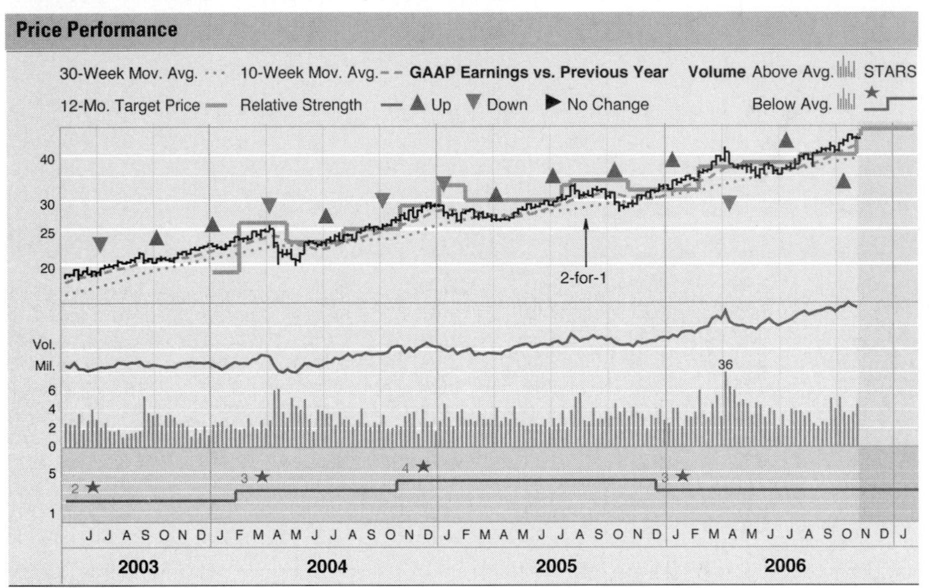

Options: ASE

Highlights

- The 12-month target price for KIM has recently been changed to $47.00 from $45.00. The Highlights section of this Stock Report will be updated accordingly.

Investment Rationale/Risk

- The Investment Rationale/Risk section of this Stock Report will be updated shortly. For the latest News story on KIM from MarketScope, see below.
- 10/30/06 11:55 am EST... S&P REITERATES HOLD OPINION ON SHARES OF KIMCO REALTY (KIM 44.04***): Q3 per-share funds from operations of $0.56 vs. $0.50 tops our $0.53 estimate, driven by a healthy retail environment and higher venture and real estate investment income. Revenues rose 20%. Occupancy rose to 95% at Q3-end from 94.8% last year, while rents on new leases jumped 23%. We expect robust conditions for KIM's tenant retailers, and contributions from acquisitions and ongoing international efforts to translate into solid growth. Our '06 FFO estimate rises to $2.20 from $2.18, '07's to $2.46 from $2.33, and our target price to $47 from $45 on our price-to-FFO analysis. / R.McMillan

Qualitative Risk Assessment

LOW	MEDIUM	HIGH

Our risk assessment of KIM reflects our view of strong fundamentals, a healthy credit quality, a diversified customer base, and a growing economy. We also believe KIM's diversity in geographic presence helps provide significant protection from a local or regional downturn.

Quantitative Evaluations

S&P Quality Ranking A+

D	C	B-	B	B+	A-	A	A+

Relative Strength Rank MODERATE

68

LOWEST = 1 HIGHEST = 99

Revenue/Earnings Data

Revenue (Million $)

	1Q	2Q	3Q	4Q	Year
2006	142.7	151.5	153.8	--	--
2005	129.3	126.7	129.6	137.0	580.6
2004	139.9	129.7	122.7	124.7	517.0
2003	119.7	115.0	118.5	126.6	479.7
2002	112.3	112.5	110.2	115.9	450.8
2001	121.6	117.9	114.3	114.9	468.6

Earnings Per Share ($)

	1Q	2Q	3Q	4Q	Year
2006	0.35	0.36	0.35	**E**0.35	**E**1.35
2005	0.36	0.33	0.32	0.40	1.40
2004	0.31	0.28	0.31	0.29	1.19
2003	0.32	0.23	0.40	0.36	1.04
2002	0.26	0.27	0.26	0.28	1.08
2001	0.26	0.27	0.27	0.28	1.08

Fiscal year ended Dec. 31. Next earnings report expected: Mid February. EPS Estimates based on S&P Operating Earnings; historical GAAP earnings are as reported.

Dividend Data (Dates: mm/dd Payment Date: mm/dd/yy)

Amount ($)	Date Decl.	Ex-Div. Date	Stk. of Record	Payment Date
0.330	12/15	12/29	01/03	01/17/06
0.330	03/15	04/03	04/05	04/17/06
0.330	06/15	07/03	07/06	07/17/06
0.360	07/25	10/02	10/04	10/16/06

Dividends have been paid since 1992. Source: Company reports.

Kimco Realty Corp

Business Summary July 27, 2006

Kimco Realty specializes in the acquisition, development and management of well located shopping centers with strong growth potential. At the end of 2005, KIM's real estate portfolio was comprised of interests in approximately 106.6 million square feet of GLA (not including 131 property interests comprising 10.8 million square feet of GLA related to the Preferred Equity program, 46 property interests comprising 0.8 million square feet of GLA related to FNC Realty and 15.0 million square feet of planned GLA for the 45 ground-up development projects) in 786 operating properties primarily consisting of neighborhood and community shopping centers, 22 retail store leases and six parcels of undeveloped land located in 44 states, Canada and Mexico. Kim's portfolio also includes equity interests in other shopping center properties.

The trust's investment objective has been to increase cash flow, current income and, consequently, the value of its existing portfolio of properties, and to seek continued growth through the strategic re-tenanting, renovation and expansion of its existing centers, and through the selective acquisition of established income-producing real estate properties and properties requiring significant re-tenanting and redevelopment. These properties are mainly located in neighborhood and community shopping centers in geographic regions in which it presently operates.

For KIM as well as other retail oriented REITS, we believe that location and the financial health and growth of its retail tenants are among the most important factors affecting the success of its portfolio. KIM's neighborhood and community shopping center properties are designed to attract local area customers and typically are anchored by a discount department store, a supermarket or a drugstore tenant offering day-to-day necessities rather than high-priced luxury items. The trust seeks to reduce operating and leasing risks through diversification achieved by the geographic distribution of its properties and a large tenant base. At December 31, 2005, the single largest neighborhood and community shopping center accounted for only 1.2% of annualized base rental revenues and only 0.8% of total shopping center gross leaseable area (GLA). At December 31, 2005, the five largest tenants were The Home Depot, TJX Companies, Sears Holdings, Kohl's, Kmart and Royal Ahold.

Company Financials

Per Share Data ($) Year Ended Dec. 31	2005	2004	2003	2002	2001	2000	1999	1998	1997	1996
Tangible Book Value	9.70	9.17	8.87	8.04	7.95	7.26	6.98	6.94	4.28	3.50
Earnings	1.40	1.19	1.04	1.10	1.08	0.96	0.82	0.67	0.59	0.54
S&P Core Earnings	1.40	1.18	1.03	1.08	1.07	NA	NA	NA	NA	NA
Dividends	1.27	1.16	1.10	1.05	0.98	0.91	0.79	0.66	0.59	0.53
Payout Ratio	91%	97%	105%	96%	91%	95%	96%	98%	99%	99%
Prices:High	33.35	29.64	22.93	16.94	17.03	14.92	13.58	13.88	12.06	11.63
Prices:Low	25.90	19.77	15.13	12.98	13.58	10.92	10.29	11.15	10.08	8.42
P/E Ratio:High	24	25	22	15	16	16	17	21	20	22
P/E Ratio:Low	18	17	14	12	13	11	13	17	17	16
Income Statement Analysis (Million $)										
Rental Income	523	517	480	451	469	459	434	339	199	168
Mortgage Income	Nil	Nil	Nil	Nil	Nil	Nil	Nil	Nil	Nil	Nil
Total Income	581	517	480	451	469	466	434	339	199	168
General Expenses	128	111	104	9.15	89.7	138	136	110	65.1	80.3
Interest Expense	128	108	103	86.9	89.4	92.1	83.6	64.9	31.7	27.0
Provision for Losses	Nil	Nil	Nil	Nil	Nil	Nil	Nil	Nil	Nil	Nil
Depreciation	106	102	86.2	76.7	74.2	71.1	67.4	51.3	30.1	27.1
Net Income	334	282	247	249	237	205	177	127	85.8	73.8
S&P Core Earnings	322	268	222	227	209	NA	NA	NA	NA	NA
Balance Sheet & Other Financial Data (Million $)										
Cash	1,018	757	581	36.0	93.8	19.1	28.1	43.9	31.0	37.4
Total Assets	5,535	4,747	4,604	3,757	3,385	3,171	3,007	3,051	1,344	1,023
Real Estate Investment	1,892	4,877	4,137	3,399	3,201	3,112	2,951	3,024	1,213	911
Loss Reserve	Nil	Nil	Nil	Nil	Nil	Nil	Nil	Nil	Nil	Nil
Net Investment	1,152	4,242	3,569	2,882	2,748	2,720	2,627	2,768	1,197	892
Short Term Debt	Nil	Nil	570	147	123	4.60	229	129	7.90	5.60
Capitalization:Debt	2,397	1,860	1,585	1,430	1,205	1,321	1,021	1,169	524	359
Capitalization:Equity	2,387	2,236	2,135	1,906	1,889	1,703	1,604	1,584	742	605
Capitalization:Total	4,907	4,203	3,820	3,431	3,103	3,039	2,640	2,759	1,272	968
% Earnings & Depreciation/Assets	8.5	8.2	8.0	9.1	9.5	8.9	8.1	8.1	9.8	10.6
Price Times Book Value:High	3.4	3.2	2.6	2.1	2.1	2.1	2.0	2.0	2.8	3.3
Price Times Book Value:Low	2.7	2.2	1.7	1.6	1.7	1.5	1.5	1.6	2.4	2.4

Data as orig reptd.; bef. results of disc opers/spec. items. Per share data adj. for stk. divs.; EPS diluted. E-Estimated. NA-Not Available. NM-Not Meaningful. NR-Not Ranked. UR-Under Review.

Office: 3333 New Hyde Park Road, New Hyde Park, NY 11042-0020.
Telephone: 800-285-4626.
Email: ir@kimcorealty.com
Website: http://www.kimcorealty.com

Chrmn & CEO: M. Cooper
Pres, Vice Chrmn & COO: M.J. Flynn
Vice Chrmn: D.B. Henry
EVP & CFO: M.V. Pappagallo

VP & Treas: G.G. Cohen
Investor Contact: S.G. Onufrey (516-869-7190)
Board of Directors: M. Cooper, R. G. Dooley, M. J. Flynn, J. Grills, D. B. Henry, F. P. Hughes, M. S. Kimmel, F. Lourenso, R. Saltzman

Founded: 1966
Domicile: Maryland
Employees: 503

STANDARD &POOR'S

Kinder Morgan Inc.

S&P Recommendation HOLD ★★★★★

Price $104.99 (as of Oct 27, 2006)

12-Mo. Target Price $108.00

Investment Style Large-Cap Value

GICS Sector Energy
Sub-Industry Oil & Gas Storage & Transportation

Comment KMI (formed through the 1999 merger of KN Energy and privately held Kinder Morgan) is one of the largest midstream energy companies in the U.S.

Key Stock Statistics (Source S&P, Vickers, company reports)

52-Wk Range	$106.19–81.00	S&P Oper. EPS 2006**E**	4.96	P/E on S&P Oper. EPS 2006**E**	21.2	Dividend Rate/Share	$3.50
Trailing 12-Month EPS	$5.09	S&P Oper. EPS 2007**E**	5.15	Common Shares Outstg. (M)	133.9	Yield (%)	3.33
Trailing 12-Month P/E	20.6	S&P Core EPS 2006**E**	4.95	Market Capitalization(B)	$14.060	Beta	0.72
$10K Invested 5 Yrs Ago	$24,014	S&P Core EPS 2007**E**	5.14	Institutional Ownership (%)	55	S&P Credit Rating	NA

Price Performance

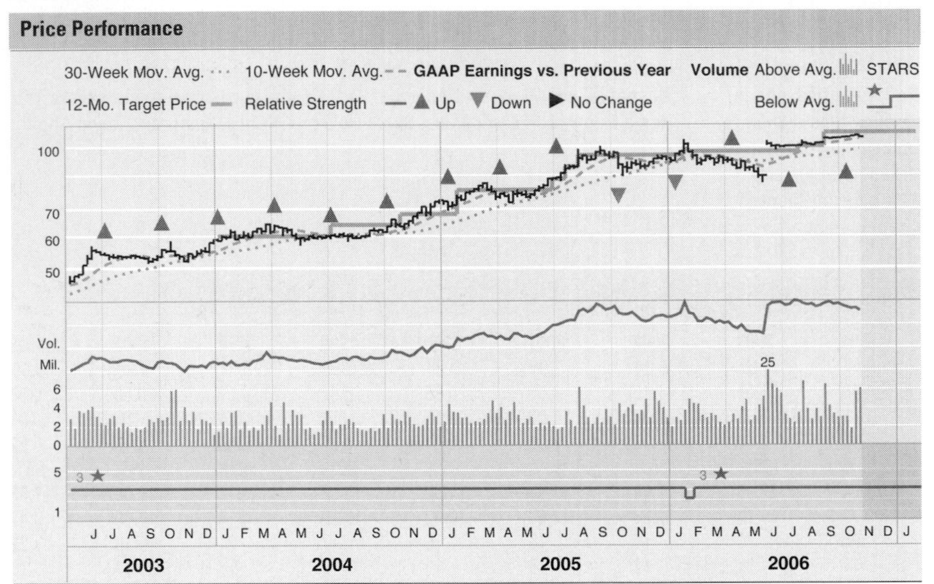

Options: P

Analysis prepared by **Michael Kay** on September 08, 2006, when the stock traded at **$ 104.05**.

Highlights

- For the first six months of 2006, KMI posted operating EPS of $2.59, versus $2.12 a year earlier, a 22% increase. Wholly owned Natural Gas Pipeline Co. of America (NGPL) has seen impressive growth, driven by expansion projects as well as signing new contracts at higher rates. KMI's integration of Terasen, Inc. is proceeding ahead of our forecasts on strong natural gas distribution. Partially offsetting NGPL's positive momentum has been lower than expected earnings at Kinder Morgan Energy Partners (KMP: buy, $45), reflecting lower rates on its pipelines.
- KMI is moving ahead with its multi-year expansion projects to serve Canadian oil sands production totaling about $1.1 billion on the Trans Mountain pipelines (TMX2). KMI remains positive on the prospects of its proposed 100,000 bbl. per day TMX2 expansion, a major future growth project for KMI.
- We continue to estimate 2006 EPS of $5.00, in line with management's recent guidance. In 2006, KMI increased its annual cash dividend to $3.50, from $3.00, in line with a targeted payout ratio of about 70%.

Investment Rationale/Risk

- On May 26, 2006, management proposed a $100 per share buyout, and on August 28th, KMI announced it has agreed to the management-led buyout worth $15 billion plus $7 billion of assumed debt. Pending required approvals, shareholders will receive $107.50 cash per share, representing a 27% premium to the closing price on May 26, the day the proposal was first made. CEO Richard Kinder will reinvest his 24 million shares, and the transaction will be financed through a combination of debt financing and equity by an investment group. KMI's equity investment in KMP offers a chance to participate indirectly in new midstream energy infrastructure, while NGPL has a leading market share serving the Chicago market.
- Risks to our recommendation and target price include failure to consummate the proposed deal; higher than expected interest rates; an inability to pass on increasing power, wage and benefits expenses; and a decline in economic activity that lowers demand for energy commodities.
- Our 12-month target price of $108 is based on our expectation that the proposed deal will be consummated in early 2007.

Qualitative Risk Assessment

LOW | MEDIUM | HIGH

Our risk assessment for KMI reflects its large and diverse asset base, stable, fee-based businesses, and low stock price volatility.

Quantitative Evaluations

S&P Quality Ranking **B**

D | C | B- | B | B+ | A- | A | A+

Relative Strength Rank **MODERATE**

42

LOWEST = 1 HIGHEST = 99

Revenue/Earnings Data

Revenue (Million $)

	1Q	2Q	3Q	4Q	Year
2006	3,433	2,838	2,828	--	--
2005	336.9	292.7	293.1	663.1	1,586
2004	352.6	236.9	249.6	325.8	1,165
2003	318.9	251.9	247.0	280.2	1,098
2002	291.4	213.7	225.1	285.0	1,015
2001	325.2	218.9	227.0	283.8	1,055

Earnings Per Share ($)

	1Q	2Q	3Q	4Q	Year
2006	1.46	1.17	1.06	**E**1.35	**E**4.96
2005	1.17	0.99	0.88	1.39	4.43
2004	1.02	0.84	0.90	1.48	4.23
2003	0.90	0.76	0.77	0.65	3.08
2002	0.71	0.59	0.66	0.55	2.50
2001	0.47	0.41	0.49	0.60	1.97

Fiscal year ended Dec. 31. Next earnings report expected: Mid January. EPS Estimates based on S&P Operating Earnings; historical GAAP earnings are as reported.

Dividend Data (Dates: mm/dd Payment Date: mm/dd/yy)

Amount ($)	Date Decl.	Ex-Div. Date	Stk. of Record	Payment Date
0.875	01/18	01/27	01/31	02/14/06
0.875	04/21	04/26	04/28	05/15/06
0.875	07/19	07/27	07/31	08/14/06
0.875	10/18	10/27	10/31	11/14/06

Dividends have been paid since 1937. Source: Company reports.

Please read the Required Disclosures and Analyst Certification on the last page of this report.

Kinder Morgan Inc.

Business Summary September 08, 2006

CORPORATE OVERVIEW. Kinder Morgan (KMI) is a major midstream energy company, operating 43,000 miles of gas and oil pipelines and 150 terminals for itself or on behalf of Kinder Morgan Energy Partners (KMP), in which it holds a 15.2% equity interest and acts as general partner. KMI also engages in natural gas utility and unregulated power generation operations.

KMI focuses on fee-based assets that generate consistent cash flow. The company has utilized KMP, a master limited partnership (MLP), as a tax-advantaged (no income tax) vehicle to hold and expand a significant portion of its portfolio. During 2005, KMP contributed 49.9% of KMI's segment earnings, derived primarily from quarterly cash distributions. In 2005, wholly owned Natural Gas Pipeline Company of America (NGPL) contributed 38.2% of KMI's segment operating earnings. NGPL owns two major interconnected transmission pipelines terminating in the Chicago metropolitan area and associated natural gas storage capacity of over 600 billion cubic feet. In 2005, remaining segment earnings were derived from domestic retail natural gas distribution (5.1%), Canadian natural gas distribution (4.0%), power generation facilities (1.7%), and Canadian pipeline operations (1.1%).

MARKET PROFILE. KMP is a leader in several core business segments. It is the largest independent U.S. operator of both refined products pipelines and liquid and bulk terminals. It is the largest independent U.S. owner and operator of pipelines transporting refined products as well as the largest independent operator of terminals. We believe KMP handles close to 25% of the nation's gasoline imports and over 15% of coal exports at its facilities. In addition, KMP is a leading transporter of carbon dioxide used for enhanced oil recovery projects, owns interests in two oil fields, and is a major transporter of natural gas.

NGPL is the largest transporter of natural gas to the Chicago, Illinois market. It competes with both interstate and intrastate pipelines accessing natural gas from domestic producers. Canadian-produced gas, including supplies transported by the Alliance Pipeline and the Northern Border Pipeline system, also provides a competitive alternative, in our opinion.

Company Financials

Per Share Data ($) Year Ended Dec. 31	2005	2004	2003	2002	2001	2000	1999	1998	1997	1996
Tangible Book Value	8.55	15.76	13.73	11.21	18.24	15.70	14.79	17.65	12.63	11.42
Earnings	4.43	4.23	3.08	2.50	1.97	1.60	1.92	0.92	1.63	1.43
S&P Core Earnings	3.95	4.12	3.01	2.21	1.68	NA	NA	NA	NA	NA
Dividends	2.90	2.25	1.10	0.30	0.20	0.20	0.65	0.76	0.73	0.70
Payout Ratio	65%	53%	36%	12%	10%	13%	34%	83%	44%	49%
Prices:High	99.97	73.82	59.27	57.50	60.00	54.25	24.69	40.33	36.00	27.50
Prices:Low	69.27	56.85	42.25	30.05	42.88	19.88	12.19	22.33	24.08	18.00
P/E Ratio:High	23	17	19	23	30	34	13	44	22	19
P/E Ratio:Low	16	13	14	12	22	12	6	24	15	13
Income Statement Analysis (Million $)										
Revenue	1,586	1,165	1,098	1,015	1,055	2,714	1,745	4,388	2,145	1,443
Depreciation	132	119	118	106	108	108	144	196	56.0	51.2
Maintenance	NA	NA	NA	NA	NA	NA	NA	NA	NA	NA
Fixed Charges Coverage	5.82	2.79	2.78	2.42	1.89	1.92	1.36	1.41	3.80	3.81
Construction Credits	NA	NA	NA	NA	NA	NA	Nil	Nil	Nil	NA
Effective Tax Rate	37.5%	27.9%	36.0%	27.1%	38.0%	37.1%	33.5%	33.4%	31.5%	36.0%
Net Income	552	529	382	309	239	104	155	60.0	77.5	63.8
S&P Core Earnings	493	514	373	273	204	NA	NA	NA	NA	NA
Balance Sheet & Other Financial Data (Million $)										
Gross Property	10,274	6,485	6,682	6,544	6,079	6,137	6,167	7,767	1,972	1,548
Capital Expenditures	187	164	161	175	124	137	94.3	257	311	120
Net Property	9,546	5,852	6,084	6,048	5,704	5,725	5,790	7,023	1,421	1,029
Capitalization:Long Term Debt	6,729	2,630	3,209	2,922	2,680	Nil	3,568	3,306	554	424
Capitalization:% Long Term Debt	63.2	47.9	54.6	55.4	54.2	Nil	68.2	73.0	47.4	44.6
Capitalization:Preferred	Nil	Nil	Nil	Nil	Nil	Nil	Nil	7.00	7.00	7.00
Capitalization:% Preferred	Nil	Nil	Nil	Nil	Nil	Nil	Nil	0.20	0.50	0.70
Capitalization:Common	3,924	2,865	2,666	2,355	2,265	1,797	1,666	1,217	606	520
Capitalization:% Common	36.8	52.1	45.4	44.6	45.8	100.0	31.8	26.8	51.9	54.7
Total Capital	15,057	9,130	9,363	8,680	8,191	4,082	7,472	6,567	1,383	1,099
% Operating Ratio	92.6	82.4	85.8	76.8	79.6	90.0	85.6	92.9	93.4	93.1
% Earned on Net Property	7.9	9.2	8.5	8.1	8.7	9.2	4.8	8.3	6.3	14.3
% Return on Revenue	34.8	45.4	34.8	30.5	22.6	6.8	8.9	1.4	3.6	4.4
% Return on Invested Capital	6.7	8.4	6.7	7.7	6.9	12.0	5.9	10.3	13.2	15.9
% Return on Common Equity	16.3	19.1	15.2	13.4	11.7	10.6	10.7	6.5	13.8	13.4

Data as orig reptd.; bef. results of disc opers/spec. items. Per share data adj. for stk. divs.; EPS diluted. E-Estimated. NA-Not Available. NM-Not Meaningful. NR-Not Ranked. UR-Under Review.

Office: 500 Dallas St. Ste 1000, Houston, TX 77002.
Telephone: 713-369-9000.
Email: ir@kindermorgan.com
Website: http://www.kindermorgan.com

Chrmn & CEO: R.D. Kinder
Pres: C.P. Shaper
COO & EVP: S.J. Kean
VP & CFO: K.A. Dang

VP & Treas: D.D. Kinder
Board of Directors: E. H. Austin, Jr., C. W. Battey, S. A. Bliss, T. A. Gardner, W. J. Hybl, R. D. Kinder, M. C. Morgan, E. Randall, III, F. Sarofim, J. M. Stanford, H. A. True, III, D. W. Whitehead

Auditor: PricewaterhouseCoopers
Founded: 1927
Domicile: Kansas
Employees: 8,481

King Pharmaceuticals Inc.

STANDARD &POOR'S

S&P Recommendation HOLD ★★★★★

Price $16.66 (as of Oct 27, 2006)

12-Mo. Target Price $21.00

Investment Style Mid-Cap Growth

GICS Sector Health Care
Sub-Industry Pharmaceuticals

Comment This company makes and markets a line of prescription pharmaceuticals. Altace, a treatment for hypertension and congestive heart failure, is the most important product.

Key Stock Statistics (Source S&P, Vickers, company reports)

52-Wk Range	**$20.00–14.20**	S&P Oper. EPS 2006**E**	**1.65**	P/E on S&P Oper. EPS 2006**E**	**10.1**	Dividend Rate/Share	**Nil**
Trailing 12-Month EPS	**$0.79**	S&P Oper. EPS 2007**E**	**1.40**	Common Shares Outstg. (M)	**243.1**	Yield (%)	**Nil**
Trailing 12-Month P/E	**21.1**	S&P Core EPS 2006**E**	**1.65**	Market Capitalization(B)	**$4.050**	Beta	**1.04**
$10K Invested 5 Yrs Ago	**$4,232**	S&P Core EPS 2007**E**	**1.40**	Institutional Ownership (%)	**96**	S&P Credit Rating	**BB**

Price Performance

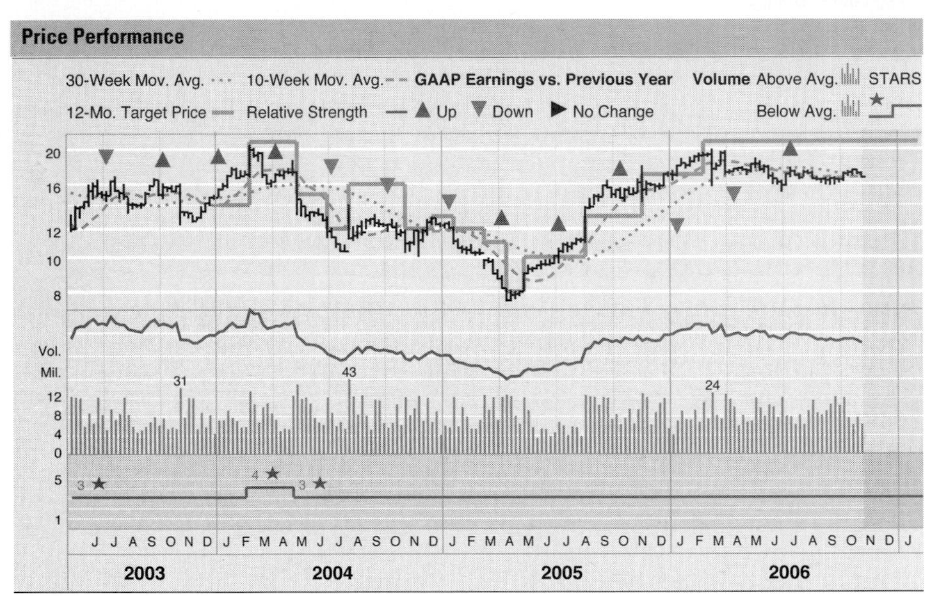

Options: ASE, CBOE, P, Ph

Analysis prepared by **Herman B. Saftlas** on August 31, 2006, when the stock traded at **$ 16.20**.

Highlights

- We expect net sales to increase 8% in 2006, to over $1.9 billion. Principal products such as Altace cardiovascular, Skelaxin muscle relaxant and Thrombin-JMI critical care treatment should show continued growth. However, these gains will probably be offset by generic erosion in the Levoxyl thyroid hormone replacement line, and increased competitive pressures in Sonata anti-insomnia. Sales in 2005 were significantly affected by fluctuations in wholesaler inventories. We expect sales this year to be more closely aligned with underlying demand.
- Gross margins are expected to slip to about 79.7%, from 81.3%, on a less profitable sales mix. SG&A costs will probably increase in line with sales, but R&D expenses should be sharply higher, inflated by anticipated costs to develop Remoxy and other R&D compounds.
- We project operating EPS of $1.65 in 2006, including an estimated $0.04 in stock option expense. Results exclude a special acquired R&D charge of $0.23 in the first quarter. Reflecting anticipated generic erosion in Skelaxin, we see EPS dipping to $1.40 in 2007.

Investment Rationale/Risk

- KG's second quarter operating EPS rose to $0.46 (well above our estimate), from $0.44, reflecting a 7.9% rise in sales, tight expense control, and reduced Altace co-promotion costs. However, we see less favorable comparisons over the balance of 2006, as results are likely to be affected by greater competitive pressures and higher R&D costs. We also think KG faces generic competition in its Skelaxin line in 2007. Longer term, we see much promise for Remoxy, an experimental antiabuse oxycontin pain drug.
- Risks to our recommendation and target price include greater than expected competitive pressures in key drug lines, generic erosion, and uncertainties related to Remoxy and other pipeline drugs.
- Our 12-month target price of $21 applies a discount to peers multiple of 15X our 2007 EPS estimate of $1.40. We think the discount is warranted due to expected generic erosion in key products over the next few years. Our DCF model, which assumes decelerating cash flow growth over the next 10 years, a WACC of 8.5%, and terminal growth of 1%, indicates intrinsic value of about $21.

Qualitative Risk Assessment

LOW | **MEDIUM** | HIGH

King's business model consists of in-licensing drugs from other companies, and growing its sales through aggressive marketing. With patents on older products expiring, KG is dependent on a constant flow of new licensing opportunities to facilitate growth. On the plus side, KG has a strong track record of successfully commercializing in-licensed drugs. In our view, it also has a fairly strong balance sheet.

Quantitative Evaluations

S&P Quality Ranking **NR**

D | C | B- | B | B+ | A- | A | A+

Relative Strength Rank **WEAK**

27

LOWEST = 1 HIGHEST = 99

Revenue/Earnings Data

Revenue (Million $)

	1Q	2Q	3Q	4Q	Year
2006	484.2	499.7	--	--	--
2005	368.6	462.9	518.0	423.3	1,773
2004	291.5	275.1	394.7	342.6	1,304
2003	343.8	370.7	424.2	382.6	1,521
2002	258.1	282.5	315.7	272.0	1,128
2001	181.3	206.5	230.1	254.4	872.3

Earnings Per Share ($)

	1Q	2Q	3Q	4Q	Year
2006	0.21	0.46	**E**0.40	**E**0.35	**E**1.65
2005	0.28	0.08	0.50	-0.39	0.48
2004	-0.01	-0.27	-0.01	0.06	-0.21
2003	-0.03	-0.15	0.44	0.17	0.44
2002	0.29	0.24	0.35	-0.13	0.74
2001	0.19	0.25	0.27	0.29	0.99

Fiscal year ended Dec. 31. Next earnings report expected: Early November. EPS Estimates based on S&P Operating Earnings; historical GAAP earnings are as reported.

Dividend Data

No cash dividends have been paid.

Please read the Required Disclosures and Analyst Certification on the last page of this report.

King Pharmaceuticals Inc.

Business Summary August 31, 2006

CORPORATE OVERVIEW. King Pharmaceuticals was formed by the Gregory family in 1994, with the purchase of a plant in Bristol, TN, to manufacture drug products under contract for major pharmaceutical companies such as GlaxoSmithKline and Novartis. A key part of its business strategy consists of the acquisition of branded prescription drugs being divested by large global pharmaceutical companies. To date, the company has successfully acquired and commercialized more than 35 branded products, and has introduced several product line extensions.

Sales of branded pharmaceuticals accounted for 87% of total net revenues in 2005, Meridian Medical Technologies (a maker of autoinjectors acquired in January 2003) 7%, royalties from licensed drugs 4%, and contract manufacturing and other 2%.

The company's most important product is Altace, a heart drug acquired together with two other products from Hoechst Marion Rousell in 1998, for $363 million. An angiotensin converting enzyme (ACE) inhibitor indicated for the treatment of hypertension and congestive heart failure, Altace had 2005 sales of $554 million, up from $347 million in 2004. Sales in 2004 were affected by wholesale inventory reductions estimated at about $180 million. Wyeth co-markets Altace. Other cardiovascular drugs include Corzide for high blood pressure, Procanbid treatment for arrhythmia, and Thalitone, a diuretic.

Other drugs include anti-infectives such as Bicillin, Cortisporin, and Neosporin, and Intal and Tilade oral multi-dose, nonsteroidal inhalers to treat asthma. King also provides contract manufacturing for leading drug companies such as Amgen, Pfizer, Johnson & Johnson, and Hoffmann-La Roche.

Through its purchase of Jones Pharma in mid-2000, KG acquired Levoxyl thyroid hormone replacement treatment (2005 sales of $140 million); Thrombin JMI ($221 million) and Brevital critical care drugs; as well as other treatments for thyroid disorders. In February 2000, the company purchased Medco Research, which derives royalties from two cardiovascular drugs, Adenocard and Adenoscan. Product acquisitions in recent years also included Corzide/Corgard heart drugs, Delestroge, an injectable estrogen, Florinef corticosteriod, Intal and Tilade asthma treatments, and Synercid, an injectable antibiotic.

Company Financials

Per Share Data ($) Year Ended Dec. 31	**2005**	**2004**	**2003**	**2002**	**2001**	**2000**	**1999**	**1998**	**1997**	**1996**
Tangible Book Value	3.66	7.67	0.68	2.90	3.47	0.85	NM	NM	NM	NA
Cash Flow	1.09	0.46	0.95	0.98	1.20	0.66	1.12	0.86	0.20	NA
Earnings	0.48	-0.21	0.44	0.74	0.99	0.47	0.47	0.28	0.09	NA
S&P Core Earnings	0.47	-0.06	0.41	0.71	0.94	NA	NA	NA	NA	NA
Dividends	Nil	Nil	Nil	Nil	Nil	Nil	Nil	Nil	NA	NA
Payout Ratio	Nil	Nil	Nil	Nil	Nil	Nil	Nil	Nil	NA	NA
Prices:High	17.99	20.62	18.13	42.13	46.06	41.63	31.00	0.68	NA	NA
Prices:Low	7.50	10.01	9.46	15.00	24.79	14.81	6.46	3.54	NA	NA
P/E Ratio:High	37	NM	41	57	47	88	72	34	NA	NA
P/E Ratio:Low	16	NM	22	20	25	31	14	13	NA	NA
Income Statement Analysis (Million $)										
Revenue	1,773	1,304	1,521	1,128	872	620	348	163	123	NA
Operating Income	551	272	403	426	429	326	155	64.7	35.4	NA
Depreciation	147	162	125	59.3	48.0	41.9	26.9	9.30	9.80	NA
Interest Expense	11.9	12.6	13.4	12.4	12.7	37.0	55.4	14.9	12.4	NA
Pretax Income	178	-58.0	177	268	371	192	73.0	40.7	13.1	NA
Effective Tax Rate	34.5%	NM	40.2%	31.8%	37.2%	45.4%	37.5%	37.8%	38.1%	NA
Net Income	117	-50.6	106	183	233	105	45.7	25.3	8.10	NA
S&P Core Earnings	115	-13.1	98.4	175	222	NA	NA	NA	NA	NA
Balance Sheet & Other Financial Data (Million $)										
Cash	48.5	359	146	815	924	76.4	8.50	1.16	12.5	NA
Current Assets	1,248	1,127	946	1,262	1,238	317	131	75.6	NA	NA
Total Assets	2,965	2,924	3,178	2,751	2,507	1,282	806	668	280	NA
Current Liabilities	971	689	669	370	151	105	89.8	44.5	NA	NA
Long Term Debt	Nil	345	345	345	346	99.0	553	514	150	NA
Common Equity	1,973	1,849	2,042	1,931	1,908	988	148	101	83.3	NA
Total Capital	1,973	2,194	2,387	2,310	2,292	1,104	716	623	NA	NA
Capital Expenditures	53.3	55.1	51.2	73.6	40.2	25.1	8.80	81.1	NA	NA
Cash Flow	264	111	230	242	281	147	22.6	34.6	17.9	NA
Current Ratio	1.3	1.6	1.4	3.4	8.2	3.0	1.5	1.7	NA	NA
% Long Term Debt of Capitalization	Nil	15.7	14.5	14.9	15.1	9.0	77.2	82.5	NA	NA
% Net Income of Revenue	6.6	NM	7.0	16.2	26.7	16.9	13.1	15.5	6.6	NA
% Return on Assets	4.0	NM	3.6	6.9	12.3	8.5	6.2	6.5	NA	NA
% Return on Equity	6.1	NM	5.3	9.5	16.1	14.1	36.7	38.9	NA	NA

Data as orig reptd.; bef. results of disc opers/spec. items. Per share data adj. for stk. divs.; EPS diluted. E-Estimated. NA-Not Available. NM-Not Meaningful. NR-Not Ranked. UR-Under Review.

Office: 501 Fifth Street, Bristol, TN 37620-2304.
Telephone: 423-989-8000.
Email: investorrelations@kingpharm.com
Website: http://www.kingpharm.com

Chrmn: T.G. Wood
Pres & CEO: B.A. Markison
Investor Contact: J.E. Green (423-989-8125)
CFO: J. Squicciarino

Secy & General Counsel: J.W. Elrod
Board of Directors: E. W. Deavenport, Jr., E. M. Greetham, G. D. Jordan, B. A. Markison, R. C. Moyer, P. M. Pfeffer, D. G. Rooker, T. G. Wood

Founded: 1993
Domicile: Tennessee
Employees: 2,799

STANDARD &POOR'S

KLA Tencor Corp

S&P Recommendation HOLD ★★★★★

Price $48.19 (as of Oct 27, 2006)

12-Mo. Target Price $50.00

Investment Style Large-Cap Growth

GICS Sector Information Technology
Sub-Industry Semiconductor Equipment

Comment This company is the world's leading manufacturer of yield monitoring and process control systems for the semiconductor industry.

Key Stock Statistics (Source S&P, Vickers, company reports)

52-Wk Range	**\$55.03–38.38**	S&P Oper. EPS 2006**E**	**1.68**	P/E on S&P Oper. EPS 2006**E**	**28.7**	Dividend Rate/Share	**\$0.48**
Trailing 12-Month EPS	**\$1.75**	S&P Oper. EPS 2007**E**	**2.52**	Common Shares Outstg. (M)	**199.1**	Yield (%)	**1.00**
Trailing 12-Month P/E	**27.5**	S&P Core EPS 2006**E**	**1.68**	Market Capitalization(B)	**\$9.594**	Beta	**2.53**
\$10K Invested 5 Yrs Ago	**\$11,084**	S&P Core EPS 2007**E**	**2.52**	Institutional Ownership (%)	**91**	S&P Credit Rating	**NA**

Price Performance

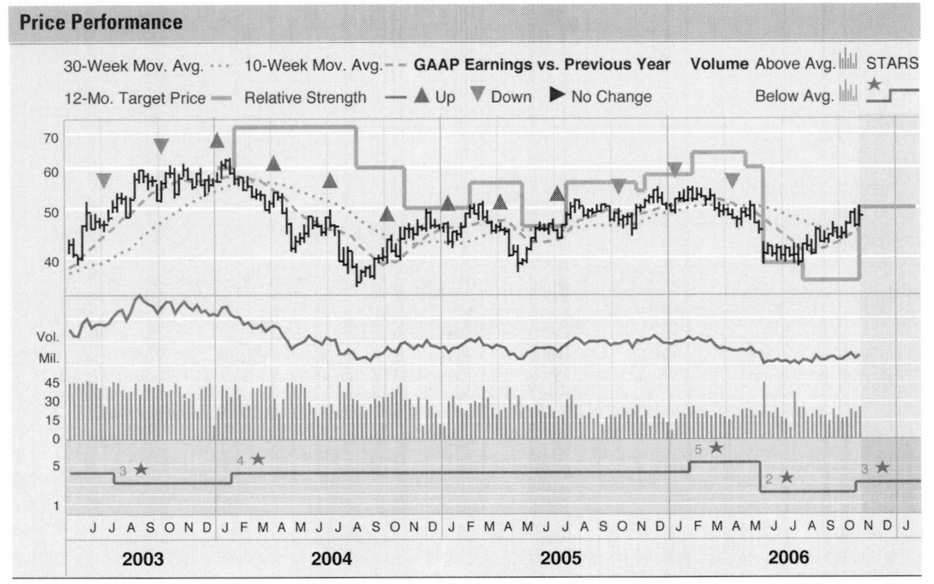

Options: ASE, CBOE, P, Ph

Highlights

➤ The STARS recommendation for KLAC has recently been changed to 3 (hold) from 2 (sell) and the 12-month target price has recently been changed to \$50.00 from \$36.00. The Highlights section of this Stock Report will be updated accordingly.

Investment Rationale/Risk

➤ The Investment Rationale/Risk section of this Stock Report will be updated shortly. For the latest News story on KLAC from MarketScope, see below.

➤ 10/25/06 10:59 am EDT... S&P UPGRADES SHARES OF KLA TENCOR TO HOLD FROM SELL (KLAC 49.76***): KLAC reported incomplete Sep-Q results due to ongoing restatements relating to retroactively priced stock options. Revenues grew 9% Q/Q, 6% above our view, despite weakness from NAND and memory customers. KLAC guided for Q/Q organic revenue growth of 5% in Dec-Q. We see secular growth in yield and process control, and believe share buybacks are likely in 2007. We are raising our FY 07 EPS estimate (Jun) by \$0.73 to \$2.62, including results from recently-acquired ADE Corp., and our target price by \$14 to \$50. However, we remain concerned about ongoing regulatory investigations. /D. Kaplan

Qualitative Risk Assessment

LOW | MEDIUM | **HIGH**

Our risk assessment reflects the company's exposure to the cyclicality of the semiconductor equipment industry and the amount of change in relevant technologies, only partially offset by limited pricing pressure and our view of KLAC's strong market position, size and financial condition.

Quantitative Evaluations

S&P Quality Ranking **B**

D | C | B- | **B** | B+ | A- | A | A+

Relative Strength Rank **STRONG**

73

LOWEST = 1 HIGHEST = 99

Revenue/Earnings Data

Revenue (Million \$)

	1Q	2Q	3Q	4Q	Year
2006	483.9	488.0	518.3	--	--
2005	518.8	532.9	541.6	491.9	2,085
2004	318.0	338.5	389.8	450.4	1,497
2003	375.5	334.9	304.3	308.3	1,323
2002	502.8	404.2	357.1	373.2	1,637
2001	382.8	500.8	612.6	602.6	2,104

Earnings Per Share (\$)

	1Q	2Q	3Q	4Q	Year
2006	0.38	0.38	0.48	**E**0.45	**E**1.68
2005	0.58	0.61	0.61	0.52	2.32
2004	0.18	0.22	0.33	0.48	1.21
2003	0.26	0.15	0.14	0.15	0.70
2002	0.44	0.25	0.17	0.23	1.10
2001	0.15	0.41	0.71	0.67	1.93

Fiscal year ended Jun. 30. Next earnings report expected: NA. EPS Estimates based on S&P Operating Earnings; historical GAAP earnings are as reported.

Dividend Data (Dates: mm/dd Payment Date: mm/dd/yy)

Amount (\$)	Date Decl.	Ex-Div. Date	Stk. of Record	Payment Date
0.120	01/24	02/13	02/15	03/01/06
0.120	05/05	05/11	05/15	06/01/06
0.120	08/03	08/11	08/15	09/01/06

Dividends have been paid since 2005. Source: Company reports.

KLA Tencor Corp

Business Summary September 20, 2006

CORPORATE OVERVIEW. KLA-Tencor is the world's leading manufacturer of yield management and process monitoring systems for the semiconductor industry. While overall semiconductor equipment sales fell 60% from calendar 2000 to 2002, KLAC's sales declined only 19%, indicating, in our view, less exposure to the semiconductor cycle than peers. We believe this is a function of the pivotal role KLAC's products have in reducing manufacturing costs.

Maximizing yields, or the number of good die (chips) per wafer, is a key goal in manufacturing integrated circuits (ICs). Higher yields increase revenues obtained for each semiconductor wafer processed. As IC linewidths decrease, yields become more sensitive to microscopic sized defects. KLAC's systems are used to improve yields by identifying defects, analyzing them to determine process problems and patterns, and facilitate corrective actions. These systems monitor subsequent results to ensure that problems have been contained. With in-line systems, corrections can be made while the wafer is still in the production line, rather than waiting for end-of-process testing and feedback.

KLAC offers a broad range of inspection and yield management tools. The company's wafer inspection systems include unpatterned and patterned wafer inspection tools used to find, count and characterize particles and pattern defects on wafers both in engineering applications and in-line at various stages during the semiconductor manufacturing process. Reticle inspection systems look for defects on the quartz plates used in copying circuit designs onto an IC during the photolithography process. Film measurement products measure a variety of optical and electrical properties of thin films. Finally, scanning electron beam microscopes (SEMs) can measure the critical dimensions (CDs) of tiny semiconductor features. For chip manufacturing below 90nm, e-beam inspection is becoming increasingly important, not only during the research and development phase, where the highest levels of sensitivity are needed to highlight and eradicate potential design problems, but also in production, where dedicated high-speed e-beam inspection systems.

Company Financials

Per Share Data ($) Year Ended Jun. 30	**2005**	**2004**	**2003**	**2002**	**2001**	**2000**	**1999**	**1998**	**1997**	**1996**
Tangible Book Value	15.49	13.34	11.56	10.70	9.38	9.11	6.95	6.85	6.05	5.28
Cash Flow	2.67	1.62	1.07	1.45	2.22	1.65	0.48	0.98	0.93	1.31
Earnings	2.32	1.21	0.70	1.10	1.93	1.32	0.22	0.76	0.62	1.16
S&P Core Earnings	1.88	0.77	0.12	0.49	1.45	NA	NA	NA	NA	NA
Dividends	0.12	Nil	Nil	Nil	Nil	Nil	Nil	Nil	Nil	Nil
Payout Ratio	5%	Nil	Nil	Nil	Nil	Nil	Nil	Nil	Nil	Nil
Prices:High	55.00	62.82	61.25	70.58	61.00	97.75	56.56	24.00	38.44	20.00
Prices:Low	37.39	35.02	31.20	25.16	28.61	25.50	21.19	10.38	16.81	8.75
P/E Ratio:High	24	52	88	64	32	74	NM	32	62	17
P/E Ratio:Low	16	29	45	23	15	19	99	14	27	8
Income Statement Analysis (Million $)										
Revenue	2,085	1,497	1,323	1,637	2,104	1,499	843	1,166	1,032	695
Operating Income	653	380	201	314	512	370	80.6	226	259	194
Depreciation	70.9	82.9	71.4	69.6	55.6	63.3	48.2	38.9	52.3	16.3
Interest Expense	Nil	Nil	0.39	Nil	Nil	Nil	Nil	Nil	Nil	1.36
Pretax Income	627	325	181	287	513	353	50.3	206	174	189
Effective Tax Rate	25.0%	24.9%	24.0%	24.8%	27.2%	28.1%	22.1%	35.0%	39.4%	36.0%
Net Income	467	244	137	216	373	254	39.2	134	105	121
S&P Core Earnings	377	156	22.4	96.5	281	NA	NA	NA	NA	NA
Balance Sheet & Other Financial Data (Million $)										
Cash	2,195	1,876	1,488	1,334	697	844	696	216	349	124
Current Assets	3,203	2,192	1,806	1,619	1,897	1,552	942	956	860	494
Total Assets	3,986	3,539	2,867	2,718	2,745	2,204	1,585	1,548	1,343	713
Current Liabilities	932	912	651	687	984	495	352	351	325	169
Long Term Debt	Nil	Nil	Nil	Nil	Nil	Nil	Nil	Nil	Nil	Nil
Common Equity	3,045	2,628	2,216	2,030	1,760	1,709	1,233	1,198	1,015	537
Total Capital	3,055	2,628	2,216	2,030	1,760	1,709	1,233	1,198	1,019	544
Capital Expenditures	59.7	55.5	134	68.7	162	78.7	56.8	64.4	56.8	39.1
Cash Flow	538	327	209	286	429	317	87.4	173	158	137
Current Ratio	3.4	2.4	2.8	2.4	1.9	3.1	2.7	2.7	2.6	2.9
% Long Term Debt of Capitalization	Nil	Nil	Nil	Nil	Nil	Nil	Nil	Nil	Nil	Nil
% Net Income of Revenue	22.4	16.3	10.4	13.2	17.7	16.9	4.7	11.5	10.2	17.5
% Return on Assets	12.4	7.6	4.9	7.9	15.1	13.4	2.5	9.3	11.5	19.2
% Return on Equity	16.5	10.1	6.5	11.4	21.5	17.3	3.2	12.1	15.3	25.7

Data as orig reptd.; bef. results of disc opers/spec. items. Per share data adj. for stk. divs.; EPS diluted. E-Estimated. NA-Not Available. NM-Not Meaningful. NR-Not Ranked. UR-Under Review.

Office: 160 Rio Robles, San Jose, CA 95134.
Telephone: 408-875-3000.
Website: http://www.tencor.com
Chrmn: E.W. Barnholt

Pres & COO: J.H. Kispert
CEO: R.P. Wallace
EVP & CTO: B. Tsai
CFO: J. Hall

Investor Contact: C. Halsted (408-875-2406)
Board of Directors: E. W. Barnholt, H. R. Bingham, R. T. Bond, R. J. Elkus, Jr., S. P. Kaufman, J. D. Tompkins, L. Urbanek, R. P. Wallace, D. C. Wang

Founded: 1975
Domicile: Delaware
Employees: 5,500

STANDARD &POOR'S

Kohl's Corp

S&P Recommendation	Price	12-Mo. Target Price	Investment Style
HOLD ★★★★★	$70.60 (as of Oct 31, 2006)	$75.00	Large-Cap Growth

GICS Sector Consumer Discretionary
Sub-Industry Department Stores

Comment This company operates about 750 specialty department stores in 43 states, featuring moderately priced apparel, shoes, accessories, and products for the home.

Key Stock Statistics (Source S&P, Vickers, company reports)

52-Wk Range	$74.44–42.78	S&P Oper. EPS 2007**E**	3.20	P/E on S&P Oper. EPS 2007**E**	22.1	Dividend Rate/Share	Nil
Trailing 12-Month EPS	$2.70	S&P Oper. EPS 2008**E**	3.85	Common Shares Outstg. (M)	327.4	Yield (%)	Nil
Trailing 12-Month P/E	26.2	S&P Core EPS 2007**E**	3.20	Market Capitalization(B)	$23.114	Beta	0.94
$10K Invested 5 Yrs Ago	$12,244	S&P Core EPS 2008**E**	3.85	Institutional Ownership (%)	87	S&P Credit Rating	BBB+

Price Performance

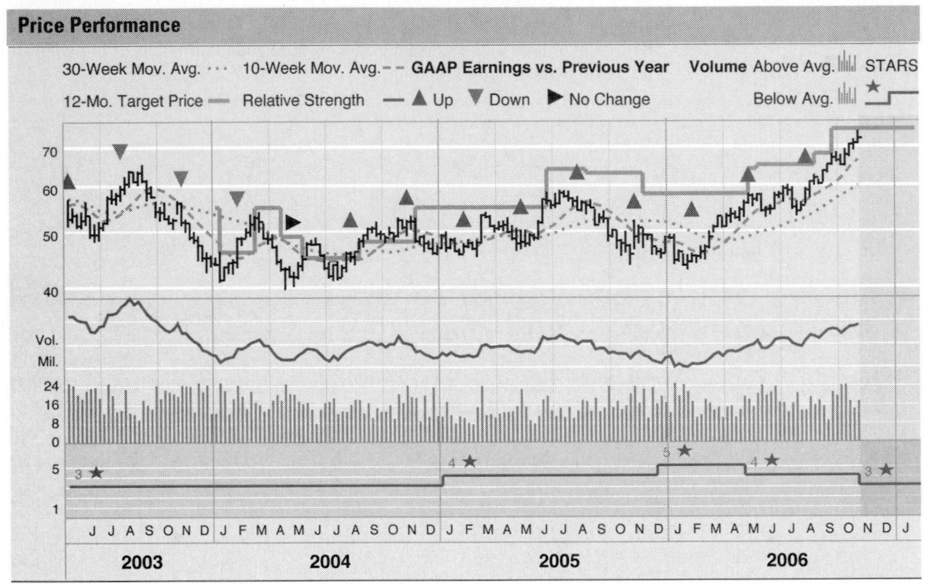

Options: ASE, CBOE, P, Ph

Highlights

- The STARS recommendation for KSS has recently been changed to 3 (hold) from 4 (buy). The Highlights section of this Stock Report will be updated accordingly.

Investment Rationale/Risk

- The Investment Rationale/Risk section of this Stock Report will be updated shortly. For the latest News story on KSS from MarketScope, see below.

- 10/31/06 12:16 pm EST... S&P DOWNGRADES SHARES OF KOHL'S TO HOLD FROM BUY, BASED ON VALUATION (KSS 72.14***): We see strength in KSS's growing stable of exclusive, higher quality brands and products sustaining its positive sales trend over the balance of FY 07 (Jan.) and through FY 08. We also look for operating margins to widen on the anticipated benefits of markdown optimization software and projected sales leverage on expenses. But we think these positive factors are well reflected in KSS's share price, which is up roughly 49% year-to-date. We are reiterating our $3.20 FY 07 and $3.85 FY 08 EPS estimates, and are keeping our 12-month target price of $75. / J.Asaeda

Qualitative Risk Assessment

LOW	**MEDIUM**	HIGH

Our risk assessment reflects our view of KSS's improving sales and profit margins, increasing market share in the moderate department store sector, and healthy balance sheet and cash flow, offset by uncertainty over consumer discretionary spending in light of rising interest rates and debt levels.

Quantitative Evaluations

S&P Quality Ranking B+

D	C	B-	B	**B+**	A-	A	A+

Relative Strength Rank STRONG

73

LOWEST = 1 HIGHEST = 99

Revenue/Earnings Data

Revenue (Million $)

	1Q	2Q	3Q	4Q	Year
2007	3,185	3,291	--	--	--
2006	2,743	2,888	3,119	4,652	13,402
2005	2,380	2,498	2,744	4,079	11,701
2004	2,118	2,208	2,394	3,562	10,282
2003	1,871	1,922	2,143	3,184	9,120
2002	1,488	1,516	1,760	2,724	7,489

Earnings Per Share ($)

	1Q	2Q	3Q	4Q	Year
2007	0.48	0.69	**E**0.59	**E**1.44	**E**3.20
2006	0.36	0.54	0.45	1.08	2.43
2005	0.32	0.45	0.41	0.94	2.12
2004	0.32	0.33	0.35	0.72	1.72
2003	0.31	0.36	0.39	0.81	1.87
2002	0.22	0.25	0.29	0.68	1.35

Fiscal year ended Jan. 31. Next earnings report expected: Early November. EPS Estimates based on S&P Operating Earnings; historical GAAP earnings are as reported.

Dividend Data

No cash dividends have been paid.

Kohl's Corp

Business Summary September 25, 2006

CORPORATE OVERVIEW. KSS, with its "Expect Great Things" line, has positioned itself as a preferred shopping destination for busy women. Its traditional customers are married women aged 25 to 54. The company's stores feature easy-to-shop layouts and emphasize moderately priced exclusive and national brand family apparel and shoes, accessories, cosmetics, home furnishings, and housewares. KSS uses a "nine-box grid" merchandising strategy. Product assortments fall into three categories, "good", "better" and "best", differentiated by price and quality, and also reflect three distinct customer styles: the "classic" customer who wants a coordinated look without bending the rules; the "updated" customer who likes classic styles with a twist; and the more fashion-forward "contemporary" customer.

PRIMARY BUSINESS DYNAMICS. KSS is one of the fastest growing retail chains in the U.S. From FY 01 through FY 06, the company increased its selling square footage at a compound annual growth rate (CAGR) of 19% as it expanded its store count from 320 to 732. In FY 06, KSS added 95 stores. By comparison, its closest peer, J.C. Penney Co., opened 18 new stores in FY 06. KSS expects to open about 500 new stores over the next five years, including 85 stores in FY 07, which we estimate will add approximately 11.5% to selling square footage. Based on this aggressive five-year growth plan, the company's store count will top 1,200 by the end of FY 11. As we see this level of expansion unlikely to be matched by other department stores, we think KSS is in a position to potentially capture market share, particularly as it enters untapped regional markets such as the Pacific Northwest.

Company Financials

Per Share Data ($) Year Ended Jan. 31	2006	2005	2004	2003	2002	2001	2000	1999	1998	1997
Tangible Book Value	16.62	13.78	11.60	9.85	7.78	6.21	4.70	3.55	2.88	1.57
Cash Flow	3.42	2.95	2.43	2.41	1.93	1.48	1.05	0.81	0.64	0.50
Earnings	2.43	2.12	1.72	1.87	1.35	1.10	0.78	0.59	0.46	0.35
S&P Core Earnings	2.43	2.04	1.62	1.78	1.38	1.04	NA	NA	NA	NA
Dividends	Nil	Nil	Nil	Nil	Nil	Nil	Nil	Nil	Nil	Nil
Payout Ratio	Nil	Nil	Nil	Nil	Nil	Nil	Nil	Nil	Nil	Nil
Calendar Year	2005	2004	2003	2002	2001	2000	1999	1998	1997	1996
Prices:High	58.90	54.10	65.44	78.83	72.24	66.50	40.63	30.75	18.84	10.50
Prices:Low	43.63	39.59	42.40	44.00	41.95	33.50	28.63	16.20	9.06	6.33
P/E Ratio:High	24	26	38	42	54	60	52	52	42	30
P/E Ratio:Low	18	19	25	24	31	30	37	27	20	18
Income Statement Analysis (Million $)										
Revenue	13,402	11,701	10,282	9,120	7,489	6,152	4,557	3,682	3,060	2,388
Operating Income	1,755	1,525	1,260	1,282	1,002	779	537	408	316	233
Depreciation	339	288	237	191	152	128	83.3	70.0	57.4	44.0
Interest Expense	72.1	64.1	75.2	59.4	57.4	Nil	29.5	22.9	24.6	17.9
Pretax Income	1,346	1,174	950	1,034	800	605	421	317	235	171
Effective Tax Rate	37.4%	37.8%	37.8%	37.8%	38.0%	38.5%	38.7%	39.3%	39.9%	40.2%
Net Income	842	730	591	643	496	372	258	192	141	102
S&P Core Earnings	842	703	557	608	471	349	NA	NA	NA	NA
Balance Sheet & Other Financial Data (Million $)										
Cash	127	117	113	90.1	107	124	12.6	29.6	44.2	8.90
Current Assets	4,266	3,643	3,025	3,284	2,464	1,922	1,367	939	811	465
Total Assets	9,153	7,979	6,698	6,316	4,930	3,855	2,915	1,936	1,620	1,122
Current Liabilities	1,746	1,456	1,122	1,508	880	723	634	380	286	236
Long Term Debt	1,046	1,103	1,076	1,059	1,095	803	495	311	310	312
Common Equity	5,957	4,967	4,191	3,512	2,791	2,203	1,686	1,163	955	517
Total Capital	7,221	6,367	5,504	4,743	4,001	3,090	2,247	1,527	1,310	868
Capital Expenditures	799	890	832	716	662	481	625	249	203	223
Cash Flow	1,181	1,019	828	835	648	500	341	262	199	146
Current Ratio	2.4	2.5	2.7	2.2	2.8	2.7	2.2	2.5	2.8	2.0
% Long Term Debt of Capitalization	14.5	17.3	19.5	22.3	27.4	26.0	22.0	20.4	23.6	35.9
% Net Income of Revenue	6.3	6.2	5.7	7.1	6.6	6.0	5.7	5.2	4.6	4.3
% Return on Assets	9.8	10.0	9.1	11.4	11.3	10.9	10.6	10.8	10.3	10.6
% Return on Equity	15.3	16.0	15.3	20.4	19.9	19.1	18.1	18.2	19.2	23.0

Data as orig reptd.; bef. results of disc opers/spec. items. Per share data adj. for stk. divs.; EPS diluted. E-Estimated. NA-Not Available. NM-Not Meaningful. NR-Not Ranked. UR-Under Review.

Office: N56W17000 Ridgewood Dr, Menomonee Falls, WI 53051-5660.
Telephone: 262-703-7000.
Website: http://www.kohls.com
Chrmn & CEO: R.L. Montgomery

Pres: K. Mansell
COO & Treas: A. Meier
Sr EVP: T.A. Kingsbury
Investor Contact: W.S. McDonald (262-703-1893)

Board of Directors: J. H. Baker, S. A. Burd, W. Embry, J. D. Ericson, J. F. Herma, W. S. Kellogg, K. Mansell, A. Meier, R. L. Montgomery, F. V. Sica, P. M. Sommerhauser, S. E. Watson, R. E. White

Founded: 1986
Domicile: Wisconsin
Employees: 107,000

STANDARD
&POOR'S

Kroger Co. (The)

S&P Recommendation BUY ★★★★★ | **Price** $22.80 (as of Oct 27, 2006) | **12-Mo. Target Price** $26.00 | **Investment Style** Large-Cap Growth

GICS Sector Consumer Staples
Sub-Industry Food Retail

Comment This supermarket operator, with about 2,500 stores in 31 states, also operates convenience stores, jewelry stores, supermarket fuel centers, and food processing plants.

Key Stock Statistics (Source S&P, Vickers, company reports)

52-Wk Range	$24.15–18.05	S&P Oper. EPS 2007E	1.42	P/E on S&P Oper. EPS 2007E	16.1	Dividend Rate/Share	$0.26
Trailing 12-Month EPS	$1.35	S&P Oper. EPS 2008E	1.55	Common Shares Outstg. (M)	717.4	Yield (%)	1.14
Trailing 12-Month P/E	16.9	S&P Core EPS 2007E	1.42	Market Capitalization(B)	$16.357	Beta	0.99
$10K Invested 5 Yrs Ago	$9,495	S&P Core EPS 2008E	1.55	Institutional Ownership (%)	82	S&P Credit Rating	BBB-

Price Performance

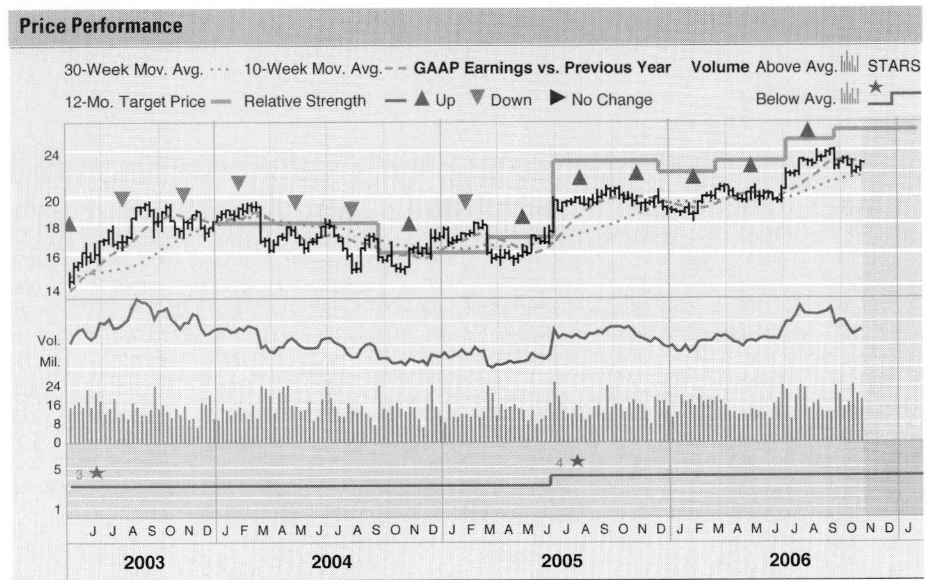

Options: ASE, CBOE, P

Analysis prepared by **Joseph Agnese** on September 20, 2006, when the stock traded at **$ 22.64**.

Highlights

- We expect sales growth of about 8% in FY 07 (Jan.), reflecting 2% square footage growth and mid-single digit comparable store sales gains. Total sales should benefit from increased gasoline sales, and from food cost inflation in the low single digits.
- Despite significant investments in pricing and promotions, we believe that margins will widen slightly on cost-saving opportunities that we see in areas such as administration, labor, shrinkage, warehousing and transportation, partially offset by increased promotional spending and higher sales of lower margin gasoline. We believe the company's sales growth strategy will focus on both service and merchandise improvements and price reductions. We believe these investments will help the company better compete against lower priced mass merchants.
- After benefits from lower interest expense and share repurchases, we expect FY 07 operating EPS to increase 8.4%, to $1.42 (including $0.05 in projected stock option expense), from $1.31 in FY 06.

Investment Rationale/Risk

- We have a buy recommendation on the shares as we believe the company's outlook is improving. We think results will continue to benefit from the company's strategy of boosting sales through price reductions, product differentiation, and improved service levels that, in our view, should limit downside risk despite intense competition in the food/retail industry.
- Risks to our recommendation and target price include potential weakness in the economy that could cause consumers to become more price conscious, and increased pricing competition.
- Our discounted cash flow analysis, which assumes a weighted average cost of capital of 8.5% and a terminal growth rate of 3%, calculates intrinsic value of $26. Based on our expectations of improving trends, we think the shares should trade at 16X our FY 08 EPS estimate of $1.55, in line with our estimated forward 12-month P/E multiple for the S&P 500, leading to an estimated value of $25. Blending our two valuation metrics, we arrive at our 12-month target price of $26.

Qualitative Risk Assessment

LOW | **MEDIUM** | HIGH

Our risk assessment reflects our view of the company's diversification through multiple format offerings, strong market share positions, and potential opportunities from industry consolidation, offset by a highly competitive environment.

Quantitative Evaluations

S&P Quality Ranking B

D | C | B- | **B** | B+ | A- | A | A+

Relative Strength Rank MODERATE

42

LOWEST = 1 HIGHEST = 99

Revenue/Earnings Data

Revenue (Million $)

	1Q	2Q	3Q	4Q	Year
2007	19,415	15,139	--	--	--
2006	17,948	13,865	14,021	14,720	60,553
2005	16,905	12,980	12,854	13,695	56,434
2004	16,266	12,351	12,141	13,034	53,791
2003	15,667	11,927	11,696	12,470	51,760
2002	15,102	11,485	11,382	12,129	50,098

Earnings Per Share ($)

2007	0.42	0.29	**E**0.28	**E**0.40	**E**1.42
2006	0.40	0.27	0.25	0.39	1.31
2005	0.35	0.19	0.19	-0.89	-0.14
2004	0.46	0.25	0.15	-0.45	0.42
2003	0.40	0.34	0.33	0.50	1.56
2002	0.36	0.31	0.16	0.43	1.26

Fiscal year ended Jan. 31. Next earnings report expected: Early December. EPS Estimates based on S&P Operating Earnings; historical GAAP earnings are as reported.

Dividend Data (Dates: mm/dd Payment Date: mm/dd/yy)

Amount ($)	Date Decl.	Ex-Div. Date	Stk. of Record	Payment Date
0.065	03/07	05/11	05/15	06/01/06
0.065	06/22	08/11	08/15	09/01/06
0.065	09/15	11/13	11/15	12/01/06

Dividends have been paid since 2006. Source: Company reports.

Kroger Co. (The)

Business Summary September 20, 2006

Kroger is one of the largest U.S. supermarket chains, with 2,483 supermarkets as of June 2006. The company's principal operating format is combination food and drug stores (combo stores). In addition to combo stores, KR also operates multi-department stores, price-impact warehouses, convenience stores, fuel centers, jewelry stores, and food processing plants. Total food store square footage exceeded 141 million as of June 2006.

Retail food stores are operated under three formats: combo stores, multi-department stores, and price-impact warehouse stores. Combo stores are considered neighborhood stores, and include many specialty departments, such as whole health sections, pharmacies, general merchandise, pet centers, and perishables, such as fresh seafood and organic produce. Combo banners include Kroger, Ralphs, King Soopers, City Market, Dillons, Smith's, Fry's, QFC, Hilander, Owen's, Jay C, Cala Foods, Bell Markets, Pay Less and Gerbes.

Multi-department stores offer one-stop shopping, are significantly larger in size than combo stores, and sell a wider selection of general merchandise items, including apparel, home fashion and furnishings, electronics, automotive, toys, and fine jewelry. Multi-department formats include Fred Meyer, Fry's Marketplace, Smith's Marketplace and Kroger Marketplace. Many combination and multi-department stores include a fuel center.

Price-impact warehouse stores offer everyday low prices, plus promotions for a wide selection of grocery and health and beauty care items. Price-impact warehouse stores include Food 4 Less and Foods Co.

Company Financials

Per Share Data ($) Year Ended Jan. 31	**2006**	**2005**	**2004**	**2003**	**2002**	**2001**	**2000**	**1999**	**1998**	**1997**
Tangible Book Value	3.04	1.85	1.18	0.36	NM	NM	NM	NM	NM	NM
Cash Flow	3.04	1.57	2.02	2.93	2.44	2.11	1.86	1.66	1.57	1.33
Earnings	1.31	-0.14	0.42	1.56	1.26	1.04	0.74	0.85	0.85	0.67
S&P Core Earnings	1.27	0.99	0.98	1.40	1.12	0.96	NA	NA	NA	NA
Dividends	Nil	Nil	Nil	Nil	Nil	Nil	Nil	Nil	Nil	Nil
Payout Ratio	Nil	Nil	Nil	Nil	Nil	Nil	Nil	Nil	Nil	Nil
Calendar Year	2005	2004	2003	2002	2001	2000	1999	1998	1997	1996
Prices:High	20.88	19.67	19.70	23.81	27.66	27.94	34.91	18.66	11.88	9.44
Prices:Low	15.15	14.65	12.05	11.00	19.60	14.06	14.88	11.34	8.38	5.84
P/E Ratio:High	16	NM	47	15	22	27	47	22	18	14
P/E Ratio:Low	12	NM	29	7	16	14	20	13	12	9

Income Statement Analysis (Million $)										
Revenue	60,553	56,434	53,791	51,760	50,098	49,000	45,352	28,203	26,567	25,171
Operating Income	3,300	3,003	3,147	3,676	3,567	3,397	3,125	1,410	1,377	1,212
Depreciation	1,265	1,256	1,209	1,087	973	907	961	430	380	344
Interest Expense	510	557	604	600	648	675	652	267	285	300
Pretax Income	1,525	290	770	1,973	1,711	1,508	1,129	713	712	568
Effective Tax Rate	37.2%	NM	59.1%	37.5%	39.0%	41.6%	43.5%	36.9%	37.6%	37.9%
Net Income	950	-100	315	1,233	1,043	880	638	450	444	353
S&P Core Earnings	928	720	745	1,105	914	816	NA	NA	NA	NA

Balance Sheet & Other Financial Data (Million $)										
Cash	210	144	159	171	161	161	281	122	65.0	Nil
Current Assets	6,466	6,406	5,619	5,566	5,512	5,416	5,531	2,673	2,641	2,353
Total Assets	20,482	20,491	20,184	20,102	19,087	18,190	17,966	6,700	6,301	5,825
Current Liabilities	6,715	6,316	5,586	5,608	5,485	5,591	5,728	3,192	2,944	2,713
Long Term Debt	6,678	7,900	8,116	8,222	8,412	8,210	8,045	3,229	3,493	3,479
Common Equity	4,390	3,540	4,011	3,850	3,502	3,089	2,683	-388	-784	-1,182
Total Capital	11,911	12,379	13,117	12,072	11,914	11,299	10,728	3,042	2,874	2,629
Capital Expenditures	1,306	1,634	2,000	1,891	2,139	1,623	1,701	923	612	734
Cash Flow	2,223	1,156	1,524	2,320	2,016	1,787	1,599	880	824	697
Current Ratio	1.0	1.0	1.0	1.0	1.0	1.0	1.0	0.8	0.9	0.9
% Long Term Debt of Capitalization	56.1	63.8	61.9	68.1	70.6	72.7	75.0	106.1	121.5	103.2
% Net Income of Revenue	1.6	NM	0.6	2.4	2.1	1.8	1.4	1.6	1.7	1.4
% Return on Assets	4.7	NM	1.6	6.3	5.6	4.9	3.7	6.9	7.3	6.5
% Return on Equity	23.9	NM	8.0	33.5	31.6	30.5	27.7	NM	NM	NM

Data as orig reptd.; bef. results of disc opers/spec. items. Per share data adj. for stk. divs.; EPS diluted. E-Estimated. NA Not Available. NM-Not Meaningful. NR-Not Ranked. UR-Under Review.

Office: 1014 Vine St, Cincinnati, OH 45202.
Telephone: 513-762-4000.
Email: investors@kroger.com
Website: http://www.kroger.com

Chrmn & CEO: D.B. Dillon
Pres & COO: D.W. McGeorge
Vice Chrmn: W.R. McMullen
EVP, Secy & General Counsel: P.W. Heldman

SVP & CFO: J.M. Schlotman
Investor Contact: C. Fike (513-762-4969)
Board of Directors: R. V. Anderson, R. D. Beyer, J. L. Clendenin, D. B. Dillon, J. T. LaMacchia, D. B. Lewis, D. W. McGeorge, W. R. McMullen, C. R. Moore, K. D. Ortega, S. M. Phillips, S. R. Rogel, J. A. Runde, B. S. Shackouls

Founded: 1883
Domicile: Ohio
Employees: 290,000

Laboratory Corporation of America Holdings

STANDARD &POOR'S

S&P Recommendation BUY ★★★★★

Price
$68.15 (as of Oct 27, 2006)

12-Mo. Target Price
$84.00

Investment Style
Mid-Cap Growth

GICS Sector Health Care
Sub-Industry Health Care Services

Comment This clinical laboratory organization offers a broad range of clinical tests through a national network of laboratories.

Key Stock Statistics (Source S&P, Vickers, company reports)

52-Wk Range	**$72.39–47.67**	S&P Oper. EPS 2006**E**	**3.19**	P/E on S&P Oper. EPS 2006**E**	**21.4**	Dividend Rate/Share	**Nil**
Trailing 12-Month EPS	**$3.07**	S&P Oper. EPS 2007**E**	**3.75**	Common Shares Outstg. (M)	**125.2**	Yield (%)	**Nil**
Trailing 12-Month P/E	**22.2**	S&P Core EPS 2006E	**3.19**	Market Capitalization(B)	**$8.532**	Beta	**0.13**
$10K Invested 5 Yrs Ago	**$15,685**	S&P Core EPS 2007E	**3.75**	Institutional Ownership (%)	**96**	S&P Credit Rating	**BBB**

Price Performance

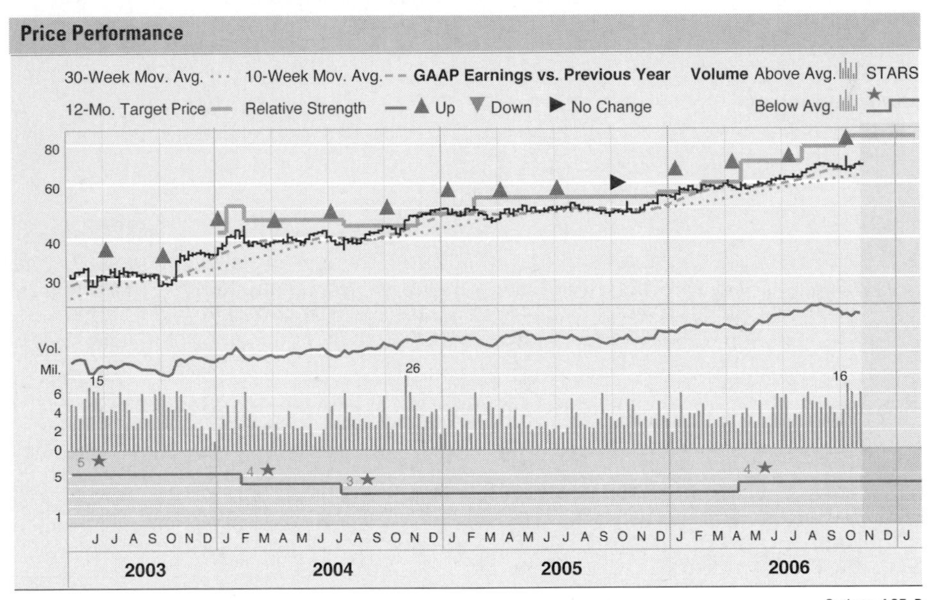

Options: ASE, P

Analysis prepared by **Jeffrey Loo, CFA** on October 09, 2006, when the stock traded at **$ 65.99**.

Highlights

- In October, LH entered into a 10-year agreement with United Healthcare (UNH: buy, $52) to become UNH's exclusive national laboratory effective January 1, 2007. We believe the contract will provide over $3 billion in sales over the life of the deal and is a significant win for LH. However, we think LH made significant concessions and will not realize meaningful margin expansion. LH agreed to reimburse UNH up to $200 million for transition costs related to developing an expanded lab network. We see LH adding several hundred patient service centers and establishing an expanded network with regional labs, particularly in the Northeast. We think it also increases LH's acquisition appetite.
- We expect sales to increase 8% and 12% in 2006 and 2007, respectively, to about $3.58 billion and $4 billion, on organic volume growth, higher price per accession, recent acquisitions and the UHN contract. We foresee operating margins improving 140 basis points in 2006 but see only a 40 basis rise in 2007 as we expect higher operating costs from expanding its network.
- After estimated stock option expense of $0.10, we forecast 2006 EPS of $3.22.

Investment Rationale/Risk

- We are encouraged by the UNH deal and believe LH will be able to expand faster than the industry's expected mid-single digit growth. However, we think it will take about 12-18 months for LH to fully establish its lab network required by the contract and we see Quest Diagnostics (DGX: $50, buy) retaining some business in the interim. Separate from the UNH deal, we foresee LH focusing on growing its esoteric and genetic tests business, which currently accounts for 34% of sales, and other managed care relationships. However, we are a bit concerned over potential margin pressure as additional managed care contracts are renewed.
- Risks to our recommendation and target price include greater than expected pricing pressures from regional labs and third-party payers; the inability to efficiently establish its lab network to absorb the UNH business; and a possible decline in the esoteric and genetic test mix.
- Our 12-month target price of $84 is based on our DCF analysis, assuming a WACC of 9.5% and a terminal growth rate of 3%, and on a P/E to earnings growth ratio of 1.5X applied to our 2007 EPS estimate, in line with peers.

Qualitative Risk Assessment

LOW	MEDIUM	HIGH

Our risk assessment reflects LH's leadership position in a large, mature industry, its broad geographic service area with clients in all 50 states, and our view of its diverse and balanced payer mix.

Quantitative Evaluations

S&P Quality Ranking B

D	C	B-	B	B+	A-	A	A+

Relative Strength Rank MODERATE

52

LOWEST = 1 HIGHEST = 99

Revenue/Earnings Data

Revenue (Million $)

	1Q	2Q	3Q	4Q	Year
2006	878.5	903.7	909.9	--	--
2005	799.1	853.3	852.9	822.3	3,328
2004	752.5	784.3	781.5	766.5	3,085
2003	712.2	743.7	752.0	731.5	2,939
2002	590.0	612.4	655.2	650.1	2,508
2001	525.4	549.7	560.9	563.8	2,200

Earnings Per Share ($)

2006	0.76	0.87	0.81	**E**0.74	**E**3.19
2005	0.67	0.74	0.66	0.64	2.71
2004	0.58	0.66	0.66	0.58	2.45
2003	0.51	0.60	0.58	0.54	2.22
2002	0.47	0.55	0.39	0.36	1.77
2001	0.31	0.37	0.31	0.29	1.29

Fiscal year ended Dec. 31. Next earnings report expected: Mid February. EPS Estimates based on S&P Operating Earnings; historical GAAP earnings are as reported.

Dividend Data

No cash dividends have been paid.

Laboratory Corporation of America Holdings

STANDARD &POOR'S

Business Summary October 09, 2006

CORPORATE OVERVIEW. Laboratory Corporation of America Holdings is the second largest independent U.S. clinical laboratory. Clinical laboratory tests are used by medical professionals in routine testing, patient diagnosis, and in the monitoring and treatment of disease. As of December 2005, LH had 36 primary testing facilities and more than 1,300 service sites consisting of branches, patient service centers, and STAT laboratories that have the ability to perform certain routine tests quickly and report results to the physician immediately. The company's laboratory services involve the testing of both bodily fluids and human tissues. LH offers more than 4,400 different tests, consisting of routine tests and specialty and niche testing (esoteric). The most frequently administered routine tests include blood chemistry analyses, urinalysis, blood cell counts, pap tests, HIV tests, microbiology cultures and procedures, and alcohol and other substance abuse tests. The company's esoteric tests include testing for infectious diseases, allergies, diagnostic genetics, identity, and oncology. An average of 360,000 specimens were being processed daily as of December 2005, with routine testing results generally available within 24 hours.

The company provides testing services to a broad range of health care providers, including independent physicians, hospitals, HMOs and other managed care groups, and governmental and other institutions. During 2005, no client accounted for over 4% of net sales. Most testing services are billed to a party other than the physician or other authorized person who ordered the test. Payers other than the direct patient include insurance companies, managed care organizations, Medicare and Medicaid. Client-billed accounted for 28% of revenue in 2005 (28% in 2004), and generated an average of $29.11 ($26.61 in 2004) in revenue per requisition; patients-billed 10% (9% in 2004) and $135.12 ($123.59 in 2004); managed care clients 40.0% (40.6% in 2004) and $34.98 ($33.67 in 2004); and Medicare, Medicaid and Insurance 23% (20.7% in 2004) and $38.49 ($34.84 in 2004). In May 2005, the company acquired Esoterix, Inc., a provider of specialty reference testing. In February 2005, LH bought US Labs, located in Irvine, CA. In March 2004, LH purchased laboratory operations in Poughkeepsie, NY, and Atlanta, GA, from MDS Diagnostic Services.

Company Financials

Per Share Data ($) Year Ended Dec. 31	**2005**	**2004**	**2003**	**2002**	**2001**	**2000**	**1999**	**1998**	**1997**	**1996**
Tangible Book Value	NM	1.04	0.27	2.67	0.83	0.09	NM	NM	NM	NM
Cash Flow	4.24	3.33	3.18	2.47	2.03	1.74	0.19	2.17	-0.89	-1.40
Earnings	2.71	2.45	2.22	1.77	1.29	0.81	0.29	0.50	-2.65	-3.13
S&P Core Earnings	2.53	2.25	2.04	1.56	1.15	NA	NA	NA	NA	NA
Dividends	Nil	Nil	Nil	Nil	Nil	Nil	Nil	Nil	Nil	Nil
Payout Ratio	Nil	Nil	Nil	Nil	Nil	Nil	Nil	Nil	Nil	Nil
Prices:High	55.00	50.03	37.72	52.38	45.68	45.75	9.69	6.88	10.00	23.44
Prices:Low	44.63	36.70	22.21	18.51	24.88	7.81	3.13	2.81	3.28	5.94
P/E Ratio:High	20	20	17	30	35	57	33	14	NM	NM
P/E Ratio:Low	16	15	10	10	19	10	11	6	NM	NM

Income Statement Analysis (Million $)	**2005**	**2004**	**2003**	**2002**	**2001**	**2000**	**1999**	**1998**	**1997**	**1996**
Revenue	3,328	3,085	2,939	2,508	2,200	1,919	1,699	1,613	1,519	1,608
Operating Income	785	736	671	554	472	340	234	212	17.5	174
Depreciation	150	139	136	102	104	89.6	84.5	84.2	86.8	84.5
Interest Expense	34.4	36.1	40.9	19.2	27.0	38.5	41.6	48.7	71.7	71.7
Pretax Income	641	615	540	432	332	208	106	81.5	-161	-188
Effective Tax Rate	39.7%	41.0%	40.6%	41.1%	45.0%	46.0%	38.0%	15.6%	NM	NM
Net Income	386	363	321	255	183	112	65.4	68.8	-107	-154
S&P Core Earnings	368	339	295	226	162	NA	NA	NA	NA	NA

Balance Sheet & Other Financial Data (Million $)	**2005**	**2004**	**2003**	**2002**	**2001**	**2000**	**1999**	**1998**	**1997**	**1996**
Cash	45.4	187	123	56.4	149	48.8	40.3	22.7	23.3	29.3
Current Assets	702	740	658	597	624	512	500	519	528	722
Total Assets	3,876	3,601	3,415	2,612	1,930	1,667	1,590	1,641	1,659	1,917
Current Liabilities	888	301	758	229	201	312	246	251	197	253
Long Term Debt	604	892	361	522	509	354	483	576	650	704
Common Equity	1,886	1,999	1,896	1,612	1,085	877	176	154	129	258
Total Capital	2,899	3,213	2,530	2,133	1,594	1,231	1,217	1,257	779	962
Capital Expenditures	93.6	95.0	83.6	74.3	88.1	55.5	69.4	58.7	34.5	54.1
Cash Flow	536	502	457	356	287	167	99.5	109	-44.0	-69.0
Current Ratio	0.8	2.5	0.9	2.6	3.1	1.6	2.0	2.1	2.7	2.9
% Long Term Debt of Capitalization	20.9	27.8	14.3	24.4	31.9	28.7	39.7	45.8	83.4	73.2
% Net Income of Revenue	11.6	11.8	10.9	10.2	8.3	5.8	3.9	4.3	NM	NM
% Return on Assets	10.3	10.3	10.7	11.2	10.2	6.9	4.0	4.2	NM	NM
% Return on Equity	19.9	18.6	18.3	18.9	18.6	14.8	9.1	17.2	NM	NM

Data as orig reptd.; bef. results of disc opers/spec. items. Per share data adj. for stk. divs.; EPS diluted. E-Estimated. NA-Not Available. NM-Not Meaningful. NR-Not Ranked. UR-Under Review.

Office: 358 South Main Street, Burlington, NC 27215.
Telephone: 336-229-1127.
Website: http://www.labcorp.com
Chrmn, Pres & CEO: T.P. Mac Mahon

COO & EVP: D.P. King
EVP, CFO & Treas: W.B. Hayes
EVP & CSO: M.P. Lai-Goldman
EVP, Secy & Chief Lgl Officer: B.T. Smith

Investor Contact: S. Fleming (336-436-4879)
Auditor: Pricewaterhousecoopers
Board of Directors: K. B. Anderson, J. Belingard, W. E. Lane, T. P. Mac Mahon, R. E. Mittelstaedt, Jr., A. H. Rubenstein, A. G. Wallace, M. K. Weikel

Founded: 1971
Domicile: Delaware
Employees: 24,000

STANDARD &POOR'S

Estee Lauder Companies Inc. (The)

S&P Recommendation HOLD ★★★★★

Price $40.00 (as of Oct 27, 2006)

12-Mo. Target Price $46.00

Investment Style Mid-Cap Growth

GICS Sector Consumer Staples
Sub-Industry Personal Products

Comment This company is one of the world's leading manufacturers and marketers of skin care, makeup and fragrance products.

Key Stock Statistics (Source S&P, Vickers, company reports)

52-Wk Range	**$43.60–32.25**	S&P Oper. EPS 2007E	**2.12**	P/E on S&P Oper. EPS 2007E	**18.9**	Dividend Rate/Share	**$0.50**
Trailing 12-Month EPS	**$1.13**	S&P Oper. EPS 2008E	**2.30**	Common Shares Outstg. (M)	**208.8**	Yield (%)	**1.25**
Trailing 12-Month P/E	**35.4**	S&P Core EPS 2007E	**2.07**	Market Capitalization(B)	**$4.958**	Beta	**0.61**
$10K Invested 5 Yrs Ago	**$12,355**	S&P Core EPS 2008E	**2.20**	Institutional Ownership (%)	**85**	S&P Credit Rating	**A+**

Price Performance

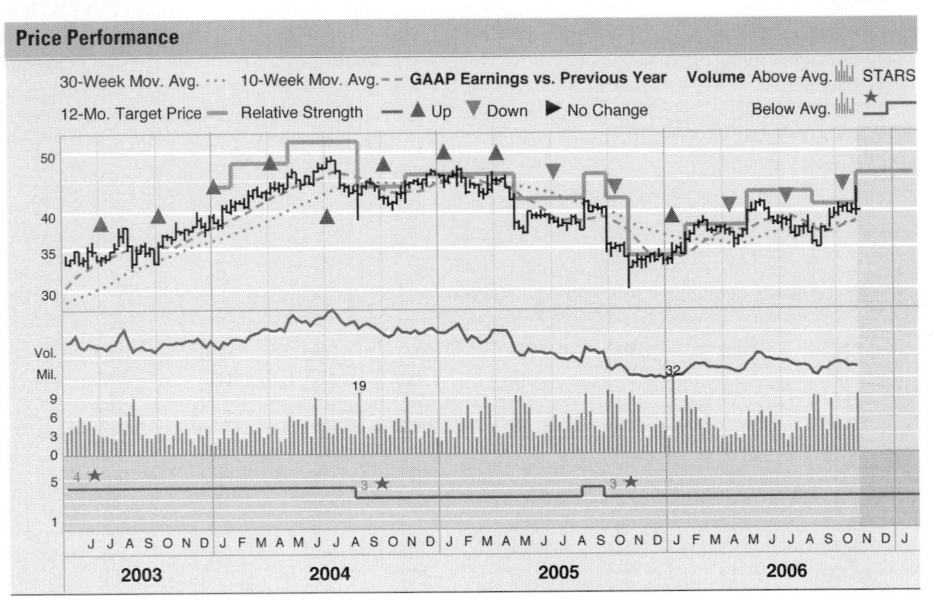

Options: ASE, CBOE, Ph

Highlights

- The 12-month target price for EL has recently been changed to $46.00 from $41.00. The Highlights section of this Stock Report will be updated accordingly.

Investment Rationale/Risk

- The Investment Rationale/Risk section of this Stock Report will be updated shortly. For the latest News story on EL from MarketScope, see below.

- 10/25/06 03:20 pm EDT... S&P REITERATES HOLD OPINION ON SHARES OF ESTEE LAUDER COMPANIES (EL 42.13***): EL reports Sep-Q EPS of $0.27 vs. $0.28, $0.05 above our estimate. The upside came from the gross margin, tax rate and share count, partially offset by a higher-than-expected SG&A expense ratio. We are increasing our full FY 07 (June) EPS estimate by $0.05 to $2.12. We are increasing our FY 08 EPS estimate by $0.10 to $2.30 largely to reflect higher projections from cost saving initiatives. We are raising our P/E-based 12-month target price by $5 to $46 to reflect our increased EPS estimates and higher peer multiples. /R.Mathis

Qualitative Risk Assessment

LOW | MEDIUM | HIGH

Our risk assessment reflects EL's market share advantage, leading brands and scale leverage. However, the company is exposed to short term events such as changes in the retail industry, geopolitical events, and consumer spending.

Quantitative Evaluations

S&P Quality Ranking A-

D | C | B- | B | B+ | **A-** | A | A+

Relative Strength Rank MODERATE

48

LOWEST = 1 HIGHEST = 99

Revenue/Earnings Data

Revenue (Million $)

	1Q	2Q	3Q	4Q	Year
2007	1,594	--	--	--	--
2006	1,497	1,784	1,578	1,605	6,464
2005	1,504	1,750	1,538	1,544	6,336
2004	1,352	1,619	1,422	1,403	5,790
2003	1,243	1,413	1,239	1,223	5,118
2002	1,195	1,298	1,122	1,129	4,744

Earnings Per Share ($)

2007	0.27	**E0.76**	**E0.54**	**E0.55**	**E2.12**
2006	0.28	0.70	0.28	0.23	1.49
2005	0.41	0.60	0.46	0.30	1.78
2004	0.34	0.54	0.43	0.31	1.62
2003	0.28	0.44	0.33	0.20	1.26
2002	0.38	0.35	0.19	-0.13	0.78

Fiscal year ended Jun. 30. Next earnings report expected: Late January. EPS Estimates based on S&P Operating Earnings; historical GAAP earnings are as reported.

Dividend Data (Dates: mm/dd Payment Date: mm/dd/yy)

Amount ($)	Date Decl.	Ex-Div. Date	Stk. of Record	Payment Date
0.400	11/10	12/07	12/09	12/28/05
0.500	10/25	12/06	12/08	12/27/06

Dividends have been paid since 1996. Source: Company reports.

Estee Lauder Companies Inc. (The)

STANDARD &POOR'S

Business Summary September 01, 2006

The Estee Lauder Companies was founded in 1946 by Estee and Joseph Lauder. The company has grown into one of the world's largest manufacturers and marketers of skin care, makeup and fragrance products, sold in more than 130 countries worldwide. EL has historically been a dominant player in the high end fragrance and cosmetic categories, with brand names such as Estee Lauder, Clinique, Aramis, Prescriptives, Origins, M.A.C, Bobbi Brown, La Mer, Aveda, Stila, Jo Malone, and Bumble and Bumble. The company is also the global licensee for fragrances and cosmetics sold under the Tommy Hilfiger, Donna Karan and Michael Kors brands. Each brand is distinctly positioned within the cosmetics market.

The Americas comprise EL's most important operating region, accounting for 53% of sales and 48% of profits in FY 06 (Jun.). Other regions include Europe, the Middle East and Africa (33% of sales and 42% of profits), and Asia-Pacific (14% and 10%).

The skin care division (37% of FY 06 net sales) addresses various skin care needs of women and men. Products include moisturizers, creams, lotions, cleansers, sun screens and self-tanning products. The makeup division (39%) manufactures, markets and sells a full array of makeup products, including lipsticks, mascaras, foundations, eyeshadows, nail polishes and powders. The fragrance division (19%) offers a variety of fragrance products, including eau de parfum sprays and colognes, as well as lotions, powders, creams and soaps that are based on a particular fragrance. The products of the hair care division (5%) are offered mainly in salons and in freestanding retail stores and include styling products, shampoos, conditioners and finishing sprays.

Company Financials

Per Share Data ($) Year Ended Jun. 30	**2006**	**2005**	**2004**	**2003**	**2002**	**2001**	**2000**	**1999**	**1998**	**1997**
Tangible Book Value	4.29	6.79	4.35	2.92	3.20	2.64	1.77	1.33	0.57	1.64
Cash Flow	2.41	2.64	2.45	2.01	1.46	1.82	1.73	1.45	1.22	0.98
Earnings	1.49	1.78	1.62	1.26	0.78	1.17	1.20	1.03	0.89	0.73
S&P Core Earnings	1.52	1.69	1.51	1.17	0.70	1.01	NA	NA	NA	NA
Dividends	0.40	0.40	0.30	0.20	0.20	0.20	0.15	0.18	0.17	0.17
Payout Ratio	27%	22%	19%	16%	26%	17%	12%	17%	19%	23%
Prices:High	43.60	47.50	49.34	40.20	38.80	44.35	55.88	56.50	43.25	28.19
Prices:Low	32.79	29.98	37.55	25.73	25.20	29.25	33.75	37.25	23.34	19.50
P/E Ratio:High	29	27	30	32	50	38	47	55	49	39
P/E Ratio:Low	22	17	23	20	32	25	28	36	26	27
Income Statement Analysis (Million $)										
Revenue	6,464	6,336	5,790	5,118	4,744	4,608	4,367	3,962	3,610	3,382
Operating Income	910	917	836	712	614	706	645	556	489	417
Depreciation	198	197	192	175	162	156	129	99.6	79.8	58.3
Interest Expense	23.8	13.9	27.1	8.10	9.80	12.3	17.1	16.7	6.30	Nil
Pretax Income	596	707	617	474	332	483	499	440	403	363
Effective Tax Rate	43.6%	41.2%	37.7%	33.9%	34.5%	36.0%	37.0%	38.0%	40.0%	42.0%
Net Income	325	406	375	320	213	307	314	273	237	198
S&P Core Earnings	332	390	351	274	171	245	NA	NA	NA	NA
Balance Sheet & Other Financial Data (Million $)										
Cash	369	553	612	364	547	347	320	348	278	256
Current Assets	2,177	2,303	2,199	1,845	1,928	1,739	1,619	1,570	1,455	1,311
Total Assets	3,784	3,886	3,708	3,350	3,417	3,219	3,043	2,747	2,513	1,873
Current Liabilities	1,438	1,498	1,322	1,054	960	857	902	862	837	760
Long Term Debt	432	451	462	284	404	411	418	423	425	Nil
Common Equity	1,622	1,693	1,733	1,424	1,462	1,352	1,160	924	696	548
Total Capital	2,079	2,160	2,211	2,080	2,226	2,123	1,939	1,707	1,481	908
Capital Expenditures	261	230	207	163	203	192	181	118	121	82.9
Cash Flow	523	603	567	471	351	440	420	349	293	233
Current Ratio	1.5	1.5	1.7	1.8	2.0	2.0	1.8	1.8	1.7	1.7
% Long Term Debt of Capitalization	20.8	20.9	20.9	13.6	18.1	19.4	21.6	24.8	28.6	NM
% Net Income of Revenue	5.0	6.4	6.5	6.2	4.5	6.7	7.2	6.9	6.5	5.9
% Return on Assets	8.5	10.7	10.6	9.5	6.4	9.8	10.8	10.4	10.7	10.8
% Return on Equity	19.6	23.7	23.8	20.5	13.4	22.6	27.9	30.8	34.3	37.0

Data as orig reptd.; bef. results of disc opers/spec. items. Per share data adj. for stk. divs.; EPS diluted. E-Estimated. NA-Not Available. NM-Not Meaningful. NR-Not Ranked. UR-Under Review.

Office: 767 5th Avenue, New York, NY 10153-0023.
Telephone: 212-572-4200.
Email: irdept@estee.com
Website: http://www.elcompanies.com

Chrmn: L.A. Lauder
Pres & CEO: W.P. Lauder
COO: D. Brestle
EVP & CFO: R.W. Kunes

EVP, Secy & General Counsel: S.E. Moss
Investor Contact: D. D'Andrea (212-572-4384)
Board of Directors: C. Barshefsky, R. M. Bravo, L. Forester de Rothschild, P. Fribourg, M. Hobson, I. O. Hockaday, Jr., A. Lauder, L. A. Lauder, R. S. Lauder, W. P. Lauder, R. D. Parsons, B. S. Sternlicht

Founded: 1946
Domicile: Delaware
Employees: 26,200

STANDARD & POOR'S

Leggett & Platt Inc

S&P Recommendation HOLD ★★★★★

Price $23.39 (as of Oct 27, 2006)

12-Mo. Target Price $25.00

Investment Style Mid-Cap Value

GICS Sector Consumer Discretionary
Sub-Industry Home Furnishings

Comment This company makes a broad line of bedding and furniture components and other home, office and commercial furnishings, as well as diversified products for non-furnishings markets.

Key Stock Statistics (Source S&P, Vickers, company reports)

52-Wk Range	$27.04–19.50	S&P Oper. EPS 2006E	1.65	P/E on S&P Oper. EPS 2006E	14.2	Dividend Rate/Share	$0.68
Trailing 12-Month EPS	$1.47	S&P Oper. EPS 2007E	1.80	Common Shares Outstg. (M)	180.7	Yield (%)	2.91
Trailing 12-Month P/E	15.9	S&P Core EPS 2006E	1.65	Market Capitalization(B)	$4.226	Beta	0.94
$10K Invested 5 Yrs Ago	$11,823	S&P Core EPS 2007E	1.80	Institutional Ownership (%)	68	S&P Credit Rating	A+

Price Performance

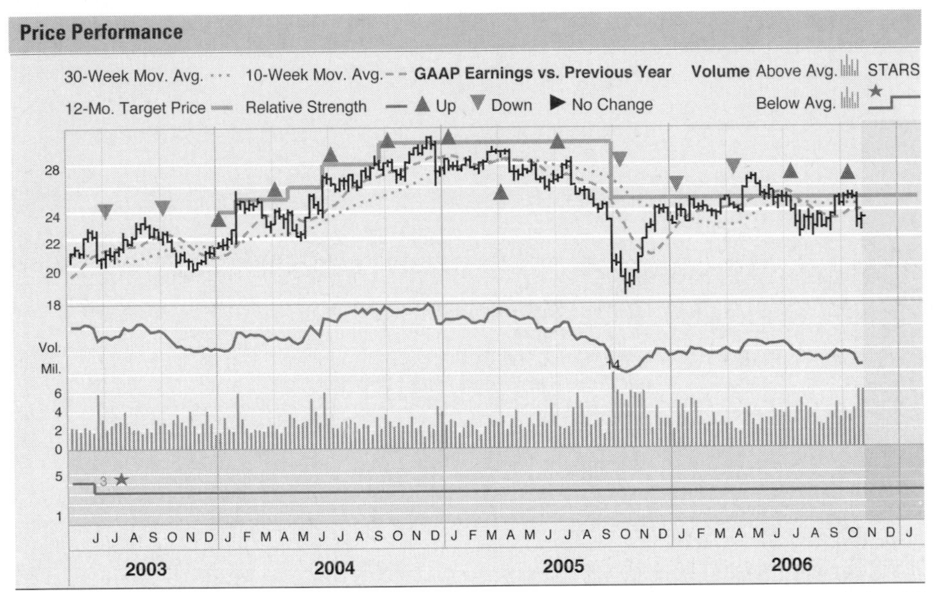

Options: ASE

Analysis prepared by **Amy F. Glynn, CFA** on August 02, 2006, when the stock traded at **$ 22.87**.

Highlights

- We see revenue growth of about 6% in 2006. We expect approximately 2% of organic growth and 5% from acquisitions to be partly offset by price deflation and some volume reductions due to the company's 2005 restructuring plan.
- Facing weak volumes, high and rising raw material costs and poor capacity utilization, LEG announced in September 2005 that it was seeking opportunities to consolidate, close or divest a number of production or warehouse facilities. As of April 2006, 36 eligible facilities had been identified, many of which have been closed, consolidated or divested. After the planned reduction in capacity, we think that LEG will have spare capacity remaining to support its expected sales growth when demand improves. Before related charges, we expect operating margins to widen in 2006 to 9%. We see operating EPS of $1.67 in 2006 and $1.90 in 2007.
- We think LEG will continue to focus on improving cash flow through effective working capital management. We believe restrained capital spending will enhance cash flow and help finance potential acquisitions, dividends and share repurchases.

Investment Rationale/Risk

- With our view of strong free cash flow, we think LEG can continue to pursue acquisitions and fund its share buyback program to help support its long-term goal of 15% EPS growth. However, in the near term, we think the company will be challenged by weak demand and rising costs, which should impede earnings growth. We think that margins over the longer term will benefit from LEG's recent plan to consolidate, close or divest a portion of its manufacturing base; however, with no near-term catalysts on the horizon, we would not add to positions.
- Risks to our opinion and target price include an unanticipated change in economic and market conditions; fluctuations in raw material, fuel and energy costs and wage rates; litigation risks; and management execution risk.
- Our 12-month target price of $25 is based on our historical P/E multiple model, and is derived by applying a P/E multiple of 13X to our 2007 operating EPS estimate of $1.90. This is a discount to LEG's five-year historical average, justified, in our view, by the lack of near-term catalysts.

Qualitative Risk Assessment

LOW | **MEDIUM** | HIGH

Our risk assessment takes into account LEG's long history of profitability and strong free cash flow, offset by our negative view of the cyclical industry in which the company operates.

Quantitative Evaluations

S&P Quality Ranking B+

D | C | B- | B | **B+** | A- | A | A+

Relative Strength Rank WEAK

19

LOWEST = 1 HIGHEST = 99

Revenue/Earnings Data

Revenue (Million $)

	1Q	2Q	3Q	4Q	Year
2006	1,378	1,403	1,415	--	--
2005	1,301	1,310	1,349	1,340	5,299
2004	1,187	1,278	1,338	1,282	5,086
2003	1,038	1,053	1,157	1,141	4,388
2002	1,023	1,115	1,121	1,013	4,272
2001	1,053	1,035	1,057	968.5	4,114

Earnings Per Share ($)

2006	0.33	0.45	0.45	**E**0.38	**E**1.65
2005	0.37	0.41	0.28	0.24	1.30
2004	0.32	0.39	0.41	0.33	1.45
2003	0.25	0.24	0.26	0.30	1.05
2002	0.28	0.35	0.29	0.25	1.17
2001	0.23	0.25	0.28	0.18	0.94

Fiscal year ended Dec. 31. Next earnings report expected: Late January. EPS Estimates based on S&P Operating Earnings; historical GAAP earnings are as reported.

Dividend Data (Dates: mm/dd Payment Date: mm/dd/yy)

Amount ($)	Date Decl.	Ex-Div. Date	Stk. of Record	Payment Date
0.160	02/23	03/13	03/15	04/14/06
0.170	05/10	06/13	06/15	07/14/06
0.170	08/02	09/13	09/15	10/13/06
0.170	08/02	09/13	09/15	10/13/06

Dividends have been paid since 1939. Source: Company reports.

Leggett & Platt Inc

Business Summary August 02, 2006

Leggett & Platt, founded in 1883, is a diversified manufacturer that conceives, designs and produces a wide range of engineered components and products that can be found in most homes, offices, retail stores and automobiles.

LEG's business is organized into five business segments. Residential Furnishings, which accounted for 45% of 2004 sales (47% in 2003), consists of the Bedding, Home Furniture & Consumer Products, and Fabric, Foam & Fiber Groups. The Commercial Fixturing and Components segment, 20% of 2004 sales (21%), consists of Fixture & Display and Office Furniture Components. Industrial Materials, 15% of 2004 sales (12%), consists of the Wire and Tubing Groups, while Aluminum Products, 10% (10%), and Specialized Products, 10% (10%), make up the balance.

In the past 20 years, about two-thirds of the company's sales growth has come from acquisitions. Over the past 10 years, the average acquisition target had revenues of $15 million to $20 million, which the company believes serves to minimize the risk of any single acquisition. The company has completed only four acquisitions of businesses with annual sales exceeding $100 million.

In 2004, LEG acquired nine businesses representing approximately $72 million in annualized sales. The acquired businesses added $22 million in sales to Residential Furnishings; $13 million to Commercial Fixturing & Components; and $37 million to Specialized Products, in 2004.

In July 2003, the company purchased the assets of RHC Spacemaster, one of its store fixture competitors. All told, it acquired 15 businesses in 2003, representing about $220 million of combined annualized sales. In addition, the company sold two businesses in 2003: a lumber company and a tubing fabrication facility. Annualized sales associated with the divested businesses were about $23 million. LEG purchased seven companies in 2002, with combined yearly sales of about $70 million, and 10 companies in 2001, with combined annual revenues of about $160 million. In 2002, it divested three concerns, with annual revenues aggregating about $40 million.

Company Financials

Per Share Data ($) Year Ended Dec. 31	2005	2004	2003	2002	2001	2000	1999	1998	1997	1996
Tangible Book Value	5.55	6.38	5.62	5.36	4.81	4.61	4.50	4.59	7.77	3.37
Cash Flow	2.18	2.35	1.89	1.99	1.92	2.18	2.19	1.87	3.25	1.34
Earnings	1.30	1.45	1.05	1.17	0.94	1.32	1.45	1.24	1.08	0.84
S&P Core Earnings	1.27	1.38	1.02	1.11	0.85	NA	NA	NA	NA	NA
Dividends	0.63	0.58	0.54	0.50	0.48	0.42	0.35	0.31	0.27	0.23
Payout Ratio	48%	40%	51%	43%	51%	32%	24%	25%	25%	28%
Prices:High	29.61	30.68	23.69	27.40	24.45	22.56	28.31	28.75	23.88	17.38
Prices:Low	18.19	21.19	17.16	18.60	16.85	14.19	18.63	16.88	15.75	10.31
P/E Ratio:High	23	21	23	23	26	17	20	23	22	21
P/E Ratio:Low	14	15	16	16	18	11	13	14	15	12
Income Statement Analysis (Million $)										
Revenue	5,299	5,086	4,388	4,272	4,114	4,276	3,779	3,370	2,909	2,466
Operating Income	605	622	520	582	558	660	650	555	467	396
Depreciation	171	177	167	165	197	173	149	128	106	92.2
Interest Expense	46.7	45.9	46.9	42.1	58.8	66.3	43.0	38.5	31.8	30.0
Pretax Income	356	423	315	364	297	419	463	396	333	250
Effective Tax Rate	29.4%	32.5%	34.7%	35.9%	36.9%	36.9%	37.2%	37.3%	37.5%	38.7%
Net Income	251	285	206	233	188	264	291	248	208	153
S&P Core Earnings	245	272	202	221	169	NA	NA	NA	NA	NA
Balance Sheet & Other Financial Data (Million $)										
Cash	64.9	491	444	225	187	37.3	20.6	83.5	7.70	3.70
Current Assets	1,763	2,065	1,819	1,488	1,422	1,405	1,256	1,137	945	763
Total Assets	4,053	4,197	3,890	3,501	3,413	3,373	2,978	2,535	2,106	1,713
Current Liabilities	738	960	626	598	457	477	432	401	373	293
Long Term Debt	922	779	1,012	809	978	988	787	574	466	389
Common Equity	2,249	2,313	2,114	1,977	1,867	1,794	1,646	1,437	1,174	941
Total Capital	3,230	3,178	3,221	2,865	2,909	2,854	2,502	2,086	1,693	1,384
Capital Expenditures	164	157	137	124	128	170	159	148	119	96.2
Cash Flow	422	463	373	398	384	437	440	376	314	245
Current Ratio	2.4	2.2	2.9	2.5	3.1	2.9	2.9	2.8	2.5	2.6
% Long Term Debt of Capitalization	28.5	24.5	31.4	28.2	33.6	34.6	31.5	27.5	27.5	28.1
% Net Income of Revenue	4.7	5.6	4.7	5.5	4.6	6.2	7.7	7.4	7.2	6.2
% Return on Assets	6.1	7.1	5.6	6.7	5.5	8.3	10.5	10.7	10.9	9.6
% Return on Equity	11.0	12.9	10.1	12.1	10.3	15.4	18.8	19.0	19.7	18.1

Data as orig reptd.; bef. results of disc opers/spec. items. Per share data adj. for stk. divs.; EPS diluted. E-Estimated. NA-Not Available. NM-Not Meaningful. NR-Not Ranked. UR-Under Review.

Office: No. 1 Leggett Road, Carthage, MO 64836-9649.
Telephone: 417-358-8131.
Email: invest@leggett.com
Website: http://www.leggett.com

Chrmn: F.E. Wright
Pres & CEO: D.S. Haffner
COO & EVP: K.G. Glassman
SVP & CFO: M.C. Flanigan

SVP, Secy & General Counsel: E.C. Jett
Investor Contact: S.R. McCoy (417-358-8131)
Board of Directors: R. F. Bentele, R. W. Clark, H. M. Cornell, Jr., R. T. Enloe, III, R. T. Fisher, K. G. Glassman, D. S. Haffner, J. W. McClanathan, J. C. Odom, M. E. Purnell, Jr., P. A. Wood, F. E. Wright

Founded: 1883
Domicile: Missouri
Employees: 33,000

STANDARD &POOR'S

Legg Mason Inc

S&P Recommendation HOLD ★★★★★ | **Price** $89.20 (as of Oct 27, 2006) | **12-Mo. Target Price** $95.00 | **Investment Style** Large-Cap Growth

GICS Sector Financials
Sub-Industry Asset Management & Custody Banks

Comment This diversified investment manager serves individual and institutional investors through offices around the United States.

Key Stock Statistics (Source S&P, Vickers, company reports)

52-Wk Range	$140.00–81.01	S&P Oper. EPS 2007E	4.30	P/E on S&P Oper. EPS 2007E	20.7	Dividend Rate/Share	$0.84
Trailing 12-Month EPS	$8.96	S&P Oper. EPS 2008E	5.29	Common Shares Outstg. (M)	131.1	Yield (%)	0.94
Trailing 12-Month P/E	10.0	S&P Core EPS 2007E	4.30	Market Capitalization(B)	$11.698	Beta	1.51
$10K Invested 5 Yrs Ago	$32,187	S&P Core EPS 2008E	5.29	Institutional Ownership (%)	82	S&P Credit Rating	BBB+

Price Performance

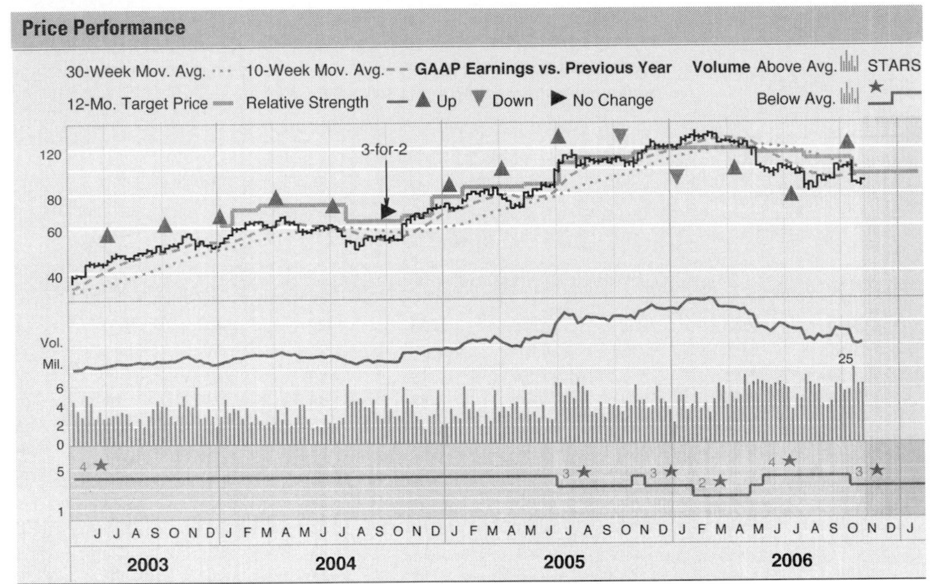

Options: CBOE

Analysis prepared by **Stuart Plesser** on October 13, 2006, when the stock traded at **$ 87.91**.

Highlights

- We think that over the next year, Legg Mason will gain market share due to its products' long history of strong relative investment performance. Although the company should benefit, in our view, from consistent net cash inflow, we look for a heavier concentration in lower revenue generating fixed income products, which should result in only modest sequential revenue growth for the remainder of FY 07 (Mar.)

- Assets under management likely totaled $890.0 billion at the end of the September quarter, 4% sequential growth, a trend that we believe will continue based on Legg Mason's strong historical fund performance. Cost synergies from recent acquisitions appear to be gaining traction, and we expect compensation to total roughly 36% of revenues by fiscal year end, compared to about 37% last year.

- We forecast EPS of $4.30 in FY 07 and $5.69 in FY 08, assuming consistent cash inflow, a mix shift back toward equity products, and prudent expense growth, partly offset by a higher share count.

Investment Rationale/Risk

- We believe that Legg Mason has a sustainable competitive advantage, based on our view of its consistent net client inflows, strong reputation, and impressive fund performance. However, the integration of its recent acquisition of Citigroup's asset management division is likely to continue to pose execution risk to these shares.

- Risks to our recommendation and target price include potential market depreciation, a deterioration in relative investment performance, and various regulatory issues. We believe that unsuccessful integrations and a lower than expected rate of retaining clients from recent acquisitions are secondary risks. We also view the retention of Bill Miller, a key portfolio manager, and his relatively concentrated investment strategy, as another risk.

- After strongly outperforming peers in 2005, the shares have underperformed peers, having declined over 25% thus far in calendar 2006. The shares recently traded at about 20X our FY 07 EPS estimate, a large discount to its peers, we believe justified by recent earnings misses. Our 12-month target price of $95 is equal to a P/E multiple of 22X applied to our FY 07 EPS estimate, in line with LM's five-year average.

Qualitative Risk Assessment

LOW | **MEDIUM** | HIGH

Our risk assessment reflects our view of the company's strong market share and impressive relative investment performance, offset by industry cyclicality and integration challenges we foresee from recent acquisitions.

Quantitative Evaluations

S&P Quality Ranking A

D | C | B- | B | B+ | A- | **A** | A+

Relative Strength Rank WEAK

16

LOWEST = 1 HIGHEST = 99

Revenue/Earnings Data

Revenue (Million $)

	1Q	2Q	3Q	4Q	Year
2007	1,038	1,031	--	--	--
2006	437.7	466.4	689.0	1,052	2,645
2005	554.9	585.5	658.3	690.8	2,490
2004	440.2	585.5	521.2	576.5	2,004
2003	417.4	395.5	401.0	401.5	1,615
2002	381.0	373.0	403.8	420.9	1,579

Earnings Per Share ($)

	1Q	2Q	3Q	4Q	Year
2007	1.08	1.00	**E**1.09	**E**1.13	**E**4.30
2006	0.93	0.75	0.77	1.04	3.30
2005	0.76	0.81	0.98	0.98	3.53
2004	0.55	0.81	0.71	0.81	2.64
2003	0.47	0.44	0.47	0.47	1.85
2002	0.35	0.30	0.40	0.45	1.49

Fiscal year ended Mar. 31. Next earnings report expected: Early February. EPS Estimates based on S&P Operating Earnings; historical GAAP earnings are as reported.

Dividend Data (Dates: mm/dd Payment Date: mm/dd/yy)

Amount ($)	Date Decl.	Ex-Div. Date	Stk. of Record	Payment Date
0.180	02/01	03/07	03/09	04/10/06
0.180	04/18	06/02	06/06	07/03/06
0.210	07/18	09/26	09/28	10/16/06
0.210	10/17	12/04	12/06	01/02/07

Dividends have been paid since 1983. Source: Company reports.

Legg Mason Inc

Business Summary October 13, 2006

CORPORATE OVERVIEW. Legg Mason is a holding company which, through subsidiaries, is principally engaged in providing asset management and other related financial services to individuals, institutions, corporations, government agencies. We are pleased with the company's recent efforts to focus on its asset management business, which we think makes LM a much larger, broader, and more focused asset management company. At the end FY 06 (Mar.), total assets under management were nearly $868 billion, up from $375 billion a year earlier. Headquartered in Baltimore, MD, LM's offices are mainly in the U.S., as well as in the U.K., Canada and Singapore. At the end of March 2006, fixed income assets represented 45% of total assets under management, equity assets 38%, and liquidity assets 17%. We are pleased with the company's success in diversifying its product offerings, but would like to see more sector and industry specific mutual funds.

We think LM has a diverse collection of asset management subsidiaries, which include Western Asset, Legg Mason Capital Management, Brandywine, and Permal. LM's Asset Management business provides asset management services to institutional and individual clients and investment advisory services to company-sponsored investment funds. Investment products include proprietary mutual funds ranging from money market and fixed income funds to equity funds managed in a wide variety of investing styles, non-U.S. funds, and a number of unregistered, alternative investment products. LM's mutual funds group sponsors domestic and international equity, fixed income and money market mutual funds, closed-end funds, and other proprietary funds. Legg Mason Value Trust (LMVTX), managed by Bill Miller, is the only equity mutual fund to have surpassed the S&P 500 Index for each of the past 15 calendar years.

Company Financials

Per Share Data ($) Year Ended Mar. 31	**2006**	**2005**	**2004**	**2003**	**2002**	**2001**	**2000**	**1999**	**1998**	**1997**
Tangible Book Value	NM	11.66	6.50	3.32	1.52	8.25	7.07	5.89	5.31	4.89
Cash Flow	3.90	3.83	2.62	1.85	1.49	1.53	1.56	1.03	0.87	NA
Earnings	3.30	3.53	2.64	1.85	1.49	1.53	1.55	1.03	0.88	0.78
S&P Core Earnings	3.25	3.41	2.57	1.63	1.35	1.44	NA	NA	NA	NA
Dividends	0.40	0.37	0.29	0.29	0.23	0.20	0.18	0.15	0.11	0.13
Payout Ratio	12%	11%	11%	15%	16%	13%	12%	15%	12%	16%
Calendar Year	2005	2004	2003	2002	2001	2000	1999	1998	1997	1996
Prices:High	129.00	73.70	56.77	38.10	37.99	40.17	28.58	21.52	18.77	9.84
Prices:Low	68.10	48.95	29.47	24.74	22.83	20.46	17.62	11.54	9.44	6.63
P/E Ratio:High	39	21	22	21	25	26	18	24	21	13
P/E Ratio:Low	21	14	11	13	15	13	11	13	11	8

Income Statement Analysis (Million $)	2006	2005	2004	2003	2002	2001	2000	1999	1998	1997
Commissions	Nil	358	344	317	331	359	363	279	241	190
Interest Income	48.0	119	84.3	109	168	282	223	160	127	84.1
Total Revenue	2,645	2,490	2,004	1,615	1,579	1,536	1,371	1,046	648	889
Interest Expense	52.6	80.8	63.2	87.1	127	175	134	94.9	73.7	43.4
Pretax Income	703	659	472	308	253	266	239	149	128	95.2
Effective Tax Rate	39.2%	38.0%	38.5%	38.1%	39.6%	41.2%	40.4%	40.0%	40.7%	40.6%
Net Income	434	408	291	191	153	156	143	89.3	76.1	56.6
S&P Core Earnings	421	394	283	168	138	146	NA	NA	NA	NA

Balance Sheet & Other Financial Data (Million $)	2006	2005	2004	2003	2002	2001	2000	1999	1998	1997
Total Assets	9,302	8,219	7,263	6,067	5,940	4,688	4,785	3,474	2,832	1,879
Cash Items	1,023	3,554	3,744	3,274	2,970	2,498	1,628	1,582	1,128	593
Receivables	850	1,564	1,458	1,155	1,230	1,333	1,652	921	713	527
Securities Owned	142	1,298	870	419	458	374	774	144	81.5	78.9
Securities Borrowed	Nil	588	488	220	280	253	688	309	448	264
Due Brokers & Customers	Nil	3,419	3,657	75.0	35.0	2,955	15.2	2,181	1,568	968
Other Liabilities	1,633	1,108	764	462	410	328	334	541	85.4	57.4
Capitalization:Debt	1,166	811	794	787	877	219	339	99.7	114	100
Capitalization:Equity	5,850	2,293	1,560	1,248	1,075	917	752	554	500	419
Capitalization:Total	7,016	3,104	2,354	2,035	1,952	1,136	1,091	654	600	519
% Return on Revenue	16.4	19.2	17.5	14.7	12.3	13.3	14.1	12.9	11.8	8.8
% Return on Assets	5.0	5.3	4.4	3.2	2.9	3.3	3.5	2.8	3.2	3.5
% Return on Equity	10.7	21.2	20.7	16.4	15.4	18.7	21.8	16.9	16.6	15.8

Data as orig reptd.; bef. results of disc opers/spec. items. Per share data adj. for stk. divs.; EPS diluted. E-Estimated. NA-Not Available. NM-Not Meaningful. NR-Not Ranked. UR-Under Review.

Office: 100 Light Street, Baltimore, MD 21202-1099.
Telephone: 410-539-0000.
Website: http://www.leggmason.com
Chrmn & CEO: R.A. Mason

Pres & COO: J.W. Hirschmann III
Sr EVP: M.R. Fetting
Sr EVP: P.L. Bain
Sr EVP & Chief Admin: T.C. Scheve

Board of Directors: H. L. Adams, D. R. Beresford, C. Bildt, J. E. Koerner, III, C. G. Krongard, R. A. Mason, E. I. O'Brien, W. A. Reed, M. M. Richardson, R. W. Schipke, K. L. Schmoke, N. J. St. George, J. E. Ukrop

Founded: 1899
Domicile: Maryland
Employees: 3,820

STANDARD &POOR'S

Lehman Brothers Holdings Inc.

S&P Recommendation	Price	12-Mo. Target Price	Investment Style
STRONG BUY ★★★★★	$76.56 (as of Oct 27, 2006)	$83.00	Large-Cap Value

GICS Sector Financials
Sub-Industry Investment Banking & Brokerage

Comment This major global investment bank serves institutional, corporate and government clients and high net worth individuals.

Key Stock Statistics (Source S&P, Vickers, company reports)

52-Wk Range	$78.89–58.37	S&P Oper. EPS 2006E	6.56	P/E on S&P Oper. EPS 2006E	11.7	Dividend Rate/Share	$0.48
Trailing 12-Month EPS	$6.40	S&P Oper. EPS 2007E	6.79	Common Shares Outstg. (M)	530.1	Yield (%)	0.63
Trailing 12-Month P/E	12.0	S&P Core EPS 2006E	6.56	Market Capitalization(B)	$40.581	Beta	1.29
$10K Invested 5 Yrs Ago	$24,016	S&P Core EPS 2007E	6.78	Institutional Ownership (%)	66	S&P Credit Rating	A+

Price Performance

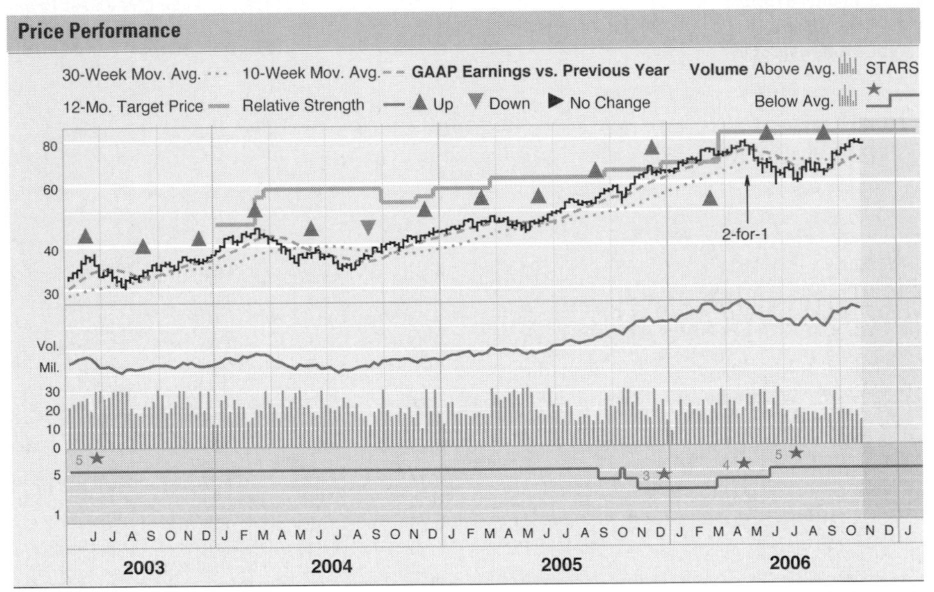

Options: ASE, CBOE, P, Ph

Analysis prepared by **Mark Hebeka, CFA** on September 14, 2006, when the stock traded at **$ 71.96**.

Highlights

- We think LEH has gained market share in its core fixed income business, but we are concerned that rising interest rates could result in fewer residential mortgage securitizations in FY 07 (Nov.). However, we are pleased with LEH's aggressive diversification efforts since its 1994 IPO, beyond its fixed income business, into the merger advisory, equity underwriting, and asset management businesses.
- We view third quarter results as strong, although not as impressive as the record first half results. We think the company's purchases of several mortgage companies will help securitization margins in FY 06. In asset management, we see improving fund performance and client inflows, and we believe that LEH will seek additional synergies at Neuberger in FY 06.
- We forecast EPS of $6.56 in FY 06 and $6.79 in FY 07, aided by slowing head count growth and a stable compensation to revenue ratio. We project strong growth in FY 06, notably in investment banking, equity capital markets, and asset management, augmented by more modest growth in fixed income revenue.

Investment Rationale/Risk

- We think our view of LEH's strong global competitive position, successful diversification efforts and significant scale merit a higher valuation. We believe LEH will grow faster than some of its closest peers, aided by recent growth initiatives. We believe executive compensation and stock option grants are generous, but view favorably significant insider ownership (about 30%) and strong growth in the asset management business.
- Risks to our recommendation and target price include widening credit spreads, stock and bond market depreciation, and potentially lower trading revenues. Finally, we remain concerned about increasing competition from the largest commercial banks, which are focused on gaining market share in investment banking.
- Our strong buy opinion is largely based on valuation. LEH shares were recently trading at 10X our FY 06 EPS estimate, a discount to peers on a P/E basis, but comparable on a price to book basis. Our 12-month target price is $83, which is 12.7X our FY 06 EPS estimate and a modest premium to the stock's average multiple over the past 10 years.

Qualitative Risk Assessment

LOW	MEDIUM	HIGH

Our risk assessment reflects our view of the company's long history of earnings growth, strong global competitive position, and successful diversification efforts, partially offset by industry cyclicality.

Quantitative Evaluations

S&P Quality Ranking A

D	C	B-	B	B+	A-	A	A+

Relative Strength Rank STRONG

74

LOWEST = 1 HIGHEST = 99

Revenue/Earnings Data

Revenue (Million $)

	1Q	2Q	3Q	4Q	Year
2006	10,307	11,515	11,727	--	--
2005	7,391	7,335	8,639	9,055	32,420
2004	5,125	5,228	5,051	5,846	21,250
2003	4,100	4,470	4,463	4,254	17,287
2002	4,226	4,347	4,075	4,133	16,781
2001	6,752	6,284	5,057	4,300	22,392

Earnings Per Share ($)

2006	1.75	1.69	1.57	E1.47	E6.56
2005	1.46	1.13	1.47	1.38	5.44
2004	1.11	1.01	0.86	0.98	3.95
2003	0.58	0.84	0.91	0.86	3.18
2002	0.50	0.54	0.35	0.35	1.74
2001	0.70	0.69	0.57	0.23	2.19

Fiscal year ended Nov. 30. Next earnings report expected: Mid December. EPS Estimates based on S&P Operating Earnings; historical GAAP earnings are as reported.

Dividend Data (Dates: mm/dd Payment Date: mm/dd/yy)

Amount ($)	Date Decl.	Ex-Div. Date	Stk. of Record	Payment Date
2-for-1 Stk.	04/06	05/01	04/18	04/28/06
0.120	04/27	05/11	05/15	05/23/06
0.120	08/01	08/11	08/15	08/24/06
0.120	10/26	11/13	11/15	11/22/06

Dividends have been paid since 1994. Source: Company reports.

The McGraw-Hill Companies

Lehman Brothers Holdings Inc.

Business Summary September 14, 2006

Lehman Brothers is an investment bank with operations worldwide. The company generated 63%, 25% and 12% of its FY 05 (Nov.) net revenues in the U.S., Europe, and the Asia/Pacific region, respectively. LEH serves institutional, corporate, government and high net worth individual clients through its world headquarters in New York, and regional headquarters in London and Tokyo. The company divides its operations into three segments: Capital Markets; Investment Banking; and Client Services. In FY 05, Capital Markets accounted for 67% of net revenues, Investment Banking 20%, and Client Services 13%. Lehman merged with American Express Co.'s Shearson brokerage unit in 1984, and was spun off as an independent public company 10 years later.

The company seeks to reduce risk through the diversification of its businesses, counterparties and activities in geographic regions by allocating the usage of capital to each of its businesses, establishing trading limits, and setting credit limits for individual counterparties, including regional concentrations. At the end of FY 05, the company's average Value at Risk (VaR), a principal tool used to measure market risk in trading positions, was $35.8 million, up from $27.9 million at the end of FY 04. We expect the company to continue to expand its Asian Capital Markets, prime brokerage and energy trading businesses.

Company Financials

Per Share Data ($) Year Ended Nov. 30	**2005**	**2004**	**2003**	**2002**	**2001**	**2000**	**1999**	**1998**	**1997**	**1996**
Tangible Book Value	22.92	18.78	16.05	17.38	15.95	14.60	12.81	9.55	8.26	7.91
Cash Flow	5.43	4.19	3.09	1.96	2.45	3.54	2.01	1.48	1.36	NA
Earnings	5.44	3.95	3.18	1.74	2.19	3.19	2.04	1.30	1.18	0.81
S&P Core Earnings	5.35	3.73	2.91	1.07	1.94	NA	NA	NA	NA	NA
Dividends	0.40	0.32	0.24	0.18	0.14	0.11	0.09	0.08	0.06	0.05
Payout Ratio	7%	8%	8%	10%	6%	3%	4%	6%	5%	6%
Prices:High	66.58	44.86	38.85	34.95	43.10	40.06	21.39	21.25	14.13	8.13
Prices:Low	42.71	33.63	25.08	21.24	21.75	15.16	10.95	5.66	7.13	5.16
P/E Ratio:High	12	11	12	20	20	13	10	16	12	10
P/E Ratio:Low	8	9	8	12	10	5	5	4	6	6
Income Statement Analysis (Million $)										
Commissions	1,728	1,537	1,210	1,286	1,091	944	651	513	423	362
Interest Income	19,043	11,032	9,942	11,728	16,470	19,440	14,251	16,542	13,635	11,298
Total Revenue	32,420	21,250	17,287	16,781	22,392	26,447	18,989	19,894	16,883	14,260
Interest Expense	17,790	9,698	8,712	10,682	15,712	18,796	13,691	15,781	13,010	10,816
Pretax Income	4,829	3,494	2,464	1,343	1,692	2,523	1,589	1,052	937	637
Effective Tax Rate	32.5%	32.2%	31.0%	27.4%	25.8%	29.6%	28.8%	30.0%	30.9%	34.7%
Net Income	3,260	2,369	1,699	975	1,255	1,775	1,132	736	647	416
S&P Core Earnings	3,124	2,149	1,488	558	1,027	NA	NA	NA	NA	NA
Balance Sheet & Other Financial Data (Million $)										
Total Assets	410,063	357,168	312,061	260,336	247,816	224,720	192,244	153,890	151,705	128,596
Cash Items	10,644	9,525	11,022	6,502	5,850	7,594	7,175	4,238	2,834	2,837
Receivables	21,643	18,763	15,310	13,964	17,057	10,382	12,360	11,965	12,838	9,944
Securities Owned	182,413	149,217	137,040	119,278	119,362	105,207	89,059	77,000	76,862	61,453
Securities Borrowed	13,154	115,188	89,870	8,137	12,541	7,242	127,693	96,533	93,284	82,483
Due Brokers & Customers	49,080	39,529	30,733	11,844	16,636	13,559	16,723	13,690	21,703	14,882
Other Liabilities	10,962	10,611	9,266	6,633	9,895	8,735	10,144	10,913	11,934	11,435
Capitalization:Debt	62,309	56,486	44,839	39,388	38,301	36,093	31,401	27,341	20,261	15,922
Capitalization:Equity	15,699	13,575	12,129	8,242	16,218	14,862	5,595	4,505	4,015	3,366
Capitalization:Total	79,103	71,406	58,013	48,330	55,219	51,655	37,684	32,754	24,276	19,796
% Return on Revenue	10.6	12.0	10.6	25.9	26.0	29.3	27.7	3.7	4.3	3.0
% Return on Assets	0.8	0.7	0.6	0.4	0.5	0.9	0.7	0.5	0.5	0.3
% Return on Equity	21.8	17.9	16.2	11.3	7.5	12.6	20.5	15.2	15.5	11.9

Data as orig reptd.; bef. results of disc opers/spec. items. Per share data adj. for stk. divs.; EPS diluted. E-Estimated. NA-Not Available. NM-Not Meaningful. NR-Not Ranked. UR-Under Review.

Office: 745 7th Ave, New York, NY 10019.
Telephone: 212-526-7000.
Email: inquiry@lehman.com
Website: http://www.lehman.com

Chrmn & CEO: R.S. Fuld, Jr.
Pres & COO: J.M. Gregory
CFO: C.M. O'Meara
Chief Admin: D. Goldfarb

CTO: J. Beyman
Investor Contact: S.K. Butler (212-526-3267)
Board of Directors: M. L. Ainslie, J. F. Akers, R. S. Berlind, T. H. Cruikshank, M. J. Evans, R. S. Fuld, Jr., C. Gent, R. A. Hernandez, H. Kaufman, J. D. Macomber

Founded: 1983
Domicile: Delaware
Employees: 22,919

STANDARD &POOR'S

Lennar Corp

S&P Recommendation HOLD ★★★★★

Price $47.65 (as of Oct 27, 2006)

12-Mo. Target Price $50.00

Investment Style Mid-Cap Growth

GICS Sector Consumer Discretionary
Sub-Industry Homebuilding

Comment One of the largest, most geographically diversified U.S. builders, this company concentrates on moderately priced homes.

Key Stock Statistics (Source S&P, Vickers, company reports)

52-Wk Range	$66.44–38.66	S&P Oper. EPS 2006E	6.05	P/E on S&P Oper. EPS 2006E	7.9	Dividend Rate/Share	$0.64
Trailing 12-Month EPS	$8.40	S&P Oper. EPS 2007E	4.50	Common Shares Outstg. (M)	158.5	Yield (%)	1.34
Trailing 12-Month P/E	5.7	S&P Core EPS 2006E	6.05	Market Capitalization(B)	$6.039	Beta	0.61
$10K Invested 5 Yrs Ago	$35,387	S&P Core EPS 2007E	4.50	Institutional Ownership (%)	99	S&P Credit Rating	BBB

Price Performance

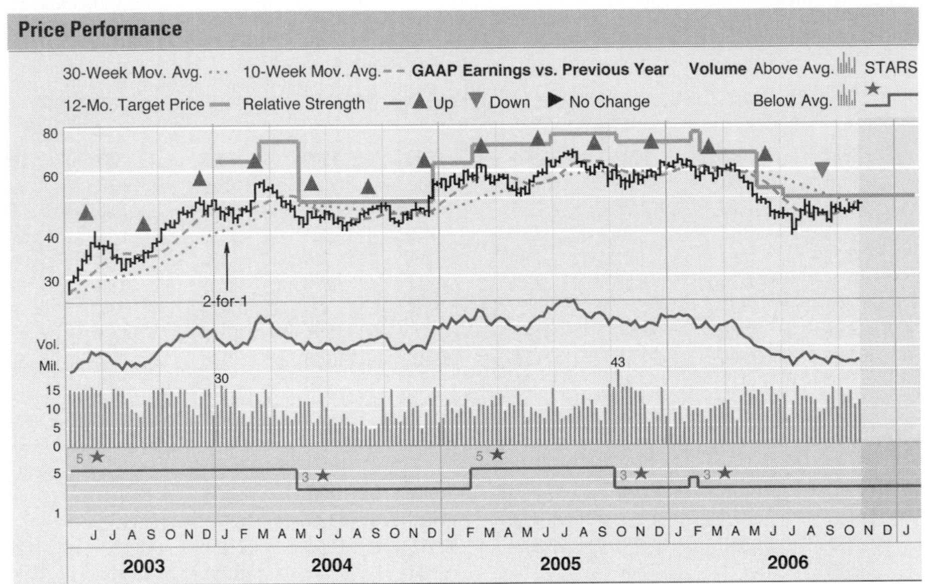

Options: ASE

Analysis prepared by **William R. Mack, CFA** on September 28, 2006, when the stock traded at **$ 45.85**.

Highlights

- Our projection for approximately a 20% jump in FY 06 (Nov.) revenues assumes that unit volume increases will outpace an average full year price increase of about 5%. We think unit order declines that began in the company's May quarter will give way to negative revenue comparisons beginning in FY 07.
- A material portion of costs associated with attracting potential buyers and retaining them in the company's backlog will be accrued and reflected in ongoing cost of sales. In addition, the August period's gross margin, which fell almost eight percentage points, also suggests to us that sales of recently purchased, higher priced land should put significant further pressure on FY 07's gross margin.
- We anticipate that most discretionary cash flows, after dividend payments, will be recycled into maintaining LEN's land bank -- which still comprises more than 300,000 controlled lots -- and share repurchases. Yet, option issuances are expected to approach buyback levels, and we look for the total share count to trend only modestly lower.

Investment Rationale/Risk

- Although acquisitions are an important part of LEN's growth strategy, we think enhanced disclosure of deals, regardless of size, would give investors a better handle on the company's fundamentals. Also, considering significant off-balance sheet activities, we see the broader issue of transparency as a concern that offsets our otherwise favorable view of its competitive position and leverage.
- Risks to our recommendation and target price include faster or larger increases than expected in 30-year mortgage rates and the possibility that large land positions in the markets that LEN serves may reduce its ability to weather a sustained downturn. In terms of corporate governance, we have some concerns over related-party transactions.
- Our 12-month target price of $50 is derived by applying a multiple of 1.25X to our estimated FY 06 book value of about $40. Alternatively, we apply about an 11X P/E to our FY 07 EPS forecast, above other builders to reflect LEN's "balance sheet first" approach.

Qualitative Risk Assessment

LOW | MEDIUM | **HIGH**

At about 32% debt to capital, LEN is among the least leveraged homebuilders in our coverage universe. However, the company's off balance sheet operations, including a 50%-owned development joint venture and a relatively significant proportion of land controlled through option contracts, suggest to us relatively limited financial transparency.

Quantitative Evaluations

S&P Quality Ranking A

D | C | B- | B | B+ | A- | **A** | A+

Relative Strength Rank MODERATE

58

LOWEST = 1 HIGHEST = 99

Revenue/Earnings Data

Revenue (Million $)

	1Q	2Q	3Q	4Q	Year
2006	3,241	4,578	4,182	--	--
2005	2,406	2,933	3,498	5,030	13,867
2004	1,863	2,343	2,748	3,551	10,505
2003	1,600	2,103	2,268	2,936	8,908
2002	1,248	1,572	1,861	2,640	7,320
2001	1,104	1,392	1,578	1,956	6,029

Earnings Per Share ($)

	1Q	2Q	3Q	4Q	Year
2006	1.58	2.00	1.30	**E**1.17	**E**6.05
2005	1.17	1.55	2.06	3.54	8.17
2004	0.84	1.22	1.36	2.29	5.70
2003	0.68	1.02	1.22	1.69	4.65
2002	0.52	0.76	1.01	1.58	3.86
2001	0.38	0.70	0.77	1.16	3.01

Fiscal year ended Nov. 30. Next earnings report expected: Mid December. EPS Estimates based on S&P Operating Earnings; historical GAAP earnings are as reported.

Dividend Data (Dates: mm/dd Payment Date: mm/dd/yy)

Amount ($)	Date Decl.	Ex-Div. Date	Stk. of Record	Payment Date
0.160	01/13	02/03	02/07	02/17/06
0.160	03/30	05/03	05/05	05/15/06
0.160	06/28	08/02	08/04	08/15/06
0.160	10/05	11/01	11/03	11/15/06

Dividends have been paid since 1978. Source: Company reports.

Lennar Corp

Business Summary September 28, 2006

CORPORATE OVERVIEW. Lennar Corp., the third largest homebuilder in the U.S. (based on FY 05 revenues), constructs homes for first-time, move-up, and active adult buyers, and also provides various financial services. It takes part in all phases of planning and building, and subcontracts nearly all development and construction work.

The financial services division provides mortgage financing, title insurance, closing services and insurance agency services for LEN homebuyers and others, and sells the loans it originates in the secondary mortgage market.

CORPORATE STRATEGY. Lennar greatly expanded its operations through the May 2000 purchase of U.S. Home Corp. (UH), and has maintained an active acquisition program since, in our opinion. The company entered the North Carolina and South Carolina markets, and extended its positions in Colorado and Arizona, through the acquisition of various operations of Fortress Group in two separate transactions in late 2001 and mid-2002. It expanded its California business by acquiring Pacific Century Homes and Cambridge Homes (combined annual deliveries of about 2,000 homes) in 2002. LEN entered the Chicago market through the late 2002 purchase of Concord Homes and the fall 2002 takeover of Summit Homes. LEN acquired Seppala Homes and Coleman Homes in 2003, expanding its operations in South Carolina and California.

In early 2004, a venture owned 50% by the company and 50% by LNR Property, LEN's former commercial real estate unit (which agreed in August 2004 to be acquired by Riley Property Holdings LLC), purchased Newhall Land and Farming Co., for about $1 billion. Newhall develops master-planned communities in and around Los Angeles.

In 2005, the company entered the metropolitan New York City and Boston markets by acquiring rights to develop a portfolio of properties in New Jersey facing mid-town Manhattan and waterfront properties near Boston. It also entered the Reno, NV, market through the acquisition of Barker Coleman. LEN also expanded its presence in Jacksonville through the acquisition of Admiral Homes that same year.

Company Financials

Per Share Data ($) Year Ended Nov. 30	**2005**	**2004**	**2003**	**2002**	**2001**	**2000**	**1999**	**1998**	**1997**	**1996**
Tangible Book Value	32.09	24.05	20.68	15.71	12.14	8.92	7.08	6.16	4.13	9.68
Cash Flow	8.60	5.98	5.11	4.32	3.45	2.23	1.69	1.44	0.79	1.38
Earnings	8.17	5.70	4.65	3.86	3.01	1.82	1.37	1.25	0.67	1.22
S&P Core Earnings	8.10	5.63	4.61	3.83	2.90	NA	NA	NA	NA	NA
Dividends	0.57	0.39	0.14	0.03	0.03	0.03	0.03	0.03	0.04	0.05
Payout Ratio	7%	7%	3%	1%	1%	1%	2%	2%	7%	4%
Prices:High	68.86	57.20	50.90	31.99	24.94	19.69	13.94	18.09	22.34	13.63
Prices:Low	50.30	40.30	24.10	21.60	15.52	7.63	6.53	7.44	7.50	10.81
P/E Ratio:High	8	10	11	8	8	11	10	15	33	11
P/E Ratio:Low	6	7	5	6	5	4	5	6	11	9

Income Statement Analysis (Million $)										
Revenue	13,867	10,505	8,908	7,320	6,029	4,707	3,119	2,417	1,303	1,181
Operating Income	2,124	1,426	1,158	1,094	868	533	382	NA	149	187
Depreciation	79.6	55.6	54.5	72.4	68.7	58.5	47.7	24.4	9.00	12.0
Interest Expense	Nil	Nil	141	146	120	98.6	48.9	47.6	25.0	31.3
Pretax Income	2,205	1,519	1,207	876	679	376	285	240	85.7	144
Effective Tax Rate	37.0%	37.0%	37.8%	37.8%	38.5%	39.0%	39.5%	40.0%	41.0%	39.0%
Net Income	1,344	946	751	545	418	229	173	144	50.6	88.0
S&P Core Earnings	1,331	934	744	541	404	NA	NA	NA	NA	NA

Balance Sheet & Other Financial Data (Million $)										
Cash	910	1,322	1,201	731	824	288	83.3	34.7	52.9	NA
Current Assets	NA	NA	NA	NA	NA	NA	NA	NA	NA	NA
Total Assets	12,541	9,165	6,775	5,756	4,714	3,778	2,058	1,918	1,343	1,766
Current Liabilities	NA	NA	NA	NA	NA	NA	NA	NA	NA	NA
Long Term Debt	2,565	2,918	1,552	1,521	1,488	1,240	524	799	614	858
Common Equity	5,251	4,053	3,264	2,229	1,659	1,229	881	716	439	695
Total Capital	7,895	6,971	4,816	3,751	3,147	2,468	1,405	1,515	1,053	1,553
Capital Expenditures	21.7	NA	29.6	4.09	13.1	16.0	15.3	13.2	70.8	26.3
Cash Flow	1,424	1,001	806	618	487	288	220	168	59.6	100
Current Ratio	NA	NA	NA	NA	NA	NA	NA	NA	NA	NA
% Long Term Debt of Capitalization	32.5	41.9	32.2	40.6	47.3	50.2	37.3	52.7	41.7	55.2
% Net Income of Revenue	9.7	9.0	8.4	7.4	6.9	4.9	5.5	6.0	3.9	7.5
% Return on Assets	12.4	11.9	12.0	10.4	9.8	7.9	8.7	8.8	3.3	5.5
% Return on Equity	28.9	25.8	27.4	28.0	28.9	21.7	21.6	25.0	8.9	6.2

Data as orig reptd.; bef. results of disc opers/spec. items. Per share data adj. for stk. divs.; EPS diluted. E-Estimated. NA-Not Available. NM-Not Meaningful. NR-Not Ranked. UR-Under Review.

Office: 700 NW 107th Ave , Miami, FL 33172.
Telephone: 305-559-4000.
Website: http://www.lennar.com
Chrmn: R.J. Strudler

Pres & CEO: S.A. Miller
COO & VP: J.M. Jaffe
VP & CFO: B.E. Gross
Investor Contact: M.H. Ames (800-741-4663)

Board of Directors: I. Bolotin, S. L. Gerard, R. K. Landon, S. Lapidus, S. A. Miller, D. E. Shalala, J. Sonnenfeld, R. J. Strudler

Founded: 1954
Domicile: Delaware
Employees: 13,687

STANDARD &POOR'S

Lexmark International Inc.

S&P Recommendation HOLD ★★★★★	**Price** $61.36 (as of Oct 27, 2006)	**12-Mo. Target Price** $63.00	**Investment Style** Mid-Cap Growth

GICS Sector Information Technology
Sub-Industry Computer Storage & Peripherals

Comment Lexmark develops, manufactures and supplies laser and inkjet printers and associated consumable supplies for the office and home markets.

Key Stock Statistics (Source S&P, Vickers, company reports)

52-Wk Range	$64.70–39.93	S&P Oper. EPS 2006E	3.89	P/E on S&P Oper. EPS 2006E	15.8	Dividend Rate/Share	Nil
Trailing 12-Month EPS	$3.08	S&P Oper. EPS 2007E	4.20	Common Shares Outstg. (M)	100.3	Yield (%)	Nil
Trailing 12-Month P/E	19.9	S&P Core EPS 2006E	3.83	Market Capitalization(B)	$6.154	Beta	1.30
$10K Invested 5 Yrs Ago	$13,739	S&P Core EPS 2007E	4.14	Institutional Ownership (%)	98	S&P Credit Rating	NA

Price Performance

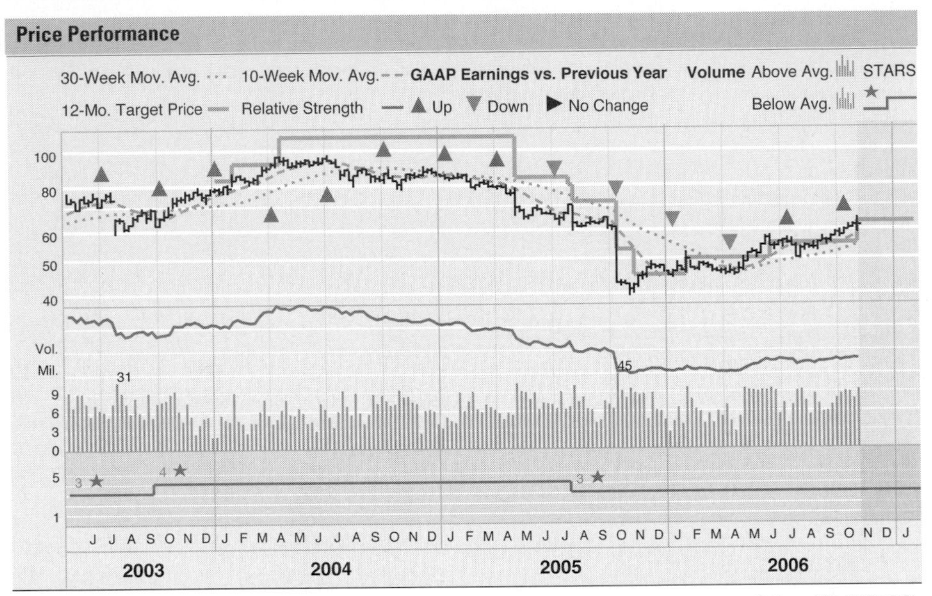

Options: ASE, CBOE, P, Ph

Analysis prepared by **Richard N. Stice, CFA** on October 25, 2006, when the stock traded at **$ 61.40**.

Highlights

- We project that revenues will increase modestly in 2007, following an anticipated decline of 2% in 2006. We believe results should benefit from new product introductions, an improving level of inkjet unit sales, and continued growth with its enterprise customer base. However, we expect pricing to remain intense, which should inhibit the overall rate of increase.

- We expect operating margins to widen in both 2006 and 2007, to 11.0% and 11.6%, respectively. This compares with 2005's 10.6%. We believe results will be aided by higher volumes as well as restructuring initiatives. We also see results benefiting from additional share buybacks. During the third quarter of 2006, LXK spent $130 million on repurchases and had about $600 million remaining in its authorization at the end of the period.

- We project 2007 EPS of $4.20, an 8% increase from our 2006 EPS estimate of $3.89 (excluding restructuring charges). Both estimates include our projections for stock option expense. Our Standard & Poor's Core EPS estimates for 2006 and 2007 are $3.83 and $4.14, respectively, which reflects our forecast for pension costs.

Investment Rationale/Risk

- We believe the company faces considerable challenges from Hewlett-Packard (HPQ: hold, $39), a leading producer of printers. While LXK has been innovative in its product line in the past and owns some important intellectual property, we think market conditions supporting low end systems will continue to pressure the company's growth in the near term. However, LXK has recently introduced plans to lower its cost structure and improve its product line in color laser and photo inkjet printers.

- Risks to our recommendation and target price include our view that LXK faces more of a threat from HPQ than in prior years. With respect to corporate governance practices, we are concerned that the positions of chairman and CEO are combined.

- Our 12-month target price of $63 reflects a combination of metrics. The first is relative P/E, in which we equate LXK with the S&P 500's 2007 P/E level of 14.2X. This leads to a value of $60. The second is discounted cash flow, which assumes a weighted average cost of capital of 11.7%, and a projected terminal growth rate of 3%, and results in an intrinsic value of $66.

Qualitative Risk Assessment

LOW | **MEDIUM** | HIGH

Our risk assessment reflects what we see as a difficult competitive pricing environment in the printer market, balanced by LXK's strides in improving its product portfolio and cost position.

Quantitative Evaluations

S&P Quality Ranking **B+**

D | C | B- | B | **B+** | A- | A | A+

Relative Strength Rank **STRONG**

71

LOWEST = 1 HIGHEST = 99

Revenue/Earnings Data

Revenue (Million $)

	1Q	2Q	3Q	4Q	Year
2006	1,275	1,229	1,235	--	--
2005	1,358	1,283	1,216	1,365	5,222
2004	1,256	1,248	1,266	1,544	5,314
2003	1,108	1,120	1,157	1,370	4,755
2002	1,050	1,058	1,041	1,207	4,356
2001	999.4	987.9	1,004	1,152	4,143

Earnings Per Share ($)

2006	0.78	0.74	0.85	**E**0.84	**E**3.89
2005	0.96	0.64	0.59	0.71	2.91
2004	0.91	1.02	1.17	1.18	4.28
2003	0.73	0.77	0.79	1.05	3.34
2002	0.53	0.67	0.70	0.90	2.79
2001	0.60	0.65	0.52	0.27	2.05

Fiscal year ended Dec. 31. Next earnings report expected: Late January. EPS Estimates based on S&P Operating Earnings; historical GAAP earnings are as reported.

Dividend Data

No cash dividends have been paid.

Lexmark International Inc.

Business Summary October 25, 2006

CORPORATE OVERVIEW. Lexmark shook up the printer industry with the introduction of the first desktop color printer priced under $100 with its November 1997 launch of the $99 color inkjet printer, aimed at building brand awareness and an installed base. We think LXK's competitive advantage in the past was its low cost structure and ability to price aggressively. However, in recent quarters it has been on the defensive, in our view, as peers have undercut its prices and LXK's product mix was not focused on some of the more compelling printer areas. Going forward, LXK management believes that its commitment to R&D should bear fruit and help revive unit growth and subsequently high margin supplies sales, but we view this as a multi-year process.

In addition to its core printer business, the company makes supplies for IBM branded printers, after-market supplies for OEM products, and typewriters and typewriter supplies sold under the IBM trademark. Lexmark also has an agreement with Dell under which Dell rebrands Lexmark printers, although this is not an exclusive agreement. (Dell accounted for 15% of LXK revenues in 2005.)

MARKET PROFILE. The total revenue market opportunity for laser and inkjet hardware units is expected to grow at a compound annual rate of growth of 4% from 2004 to 2009, to 135 million units, according to market research firm IDC, with growth in the laser market projected to be 6%. However, the revenue change over that period for laser and inkjets is projected at negative 0.5%. The key is that printer vendors are cutting prices on printers to expand their installed base and subsequently capitalize on the growth in margin-rich supplies sales. Revenue growth for supplies over the 2004 to 2009 time frame is expected to be at a compound annual growth rate of 7%, according to market research firm IDC.

Company Financials

Per Share Data ($) Year Ended Dec. 31	**2005**	**2004**	**2003**	**2002**	**2001**	**2000**	**1999**	**1998**	**1997**	**1996**
Tangible Book Value	12.77	NM	17.46	NM	8.25	6.11	6.24	5.22	4.07	3.72
Cash Flow	4.21	5.29	4.48	3.84	2.98	2.80	2.89	2.23	1.60	1.29
Earnings	2.91	4.28	3.34	2.79	2.05	2.13	2.32	1.70	1.09	0.85
S&P Core Earnings	2.52	3.94	3.04	2.27	1.57	NA	NA	NA	NA	NA
Dividends	Nil	Nil	Nil	Nil	Nil	Nil	Nil	Nil	Nil	Nil
Payout Ratio	Nil	Nil	Nil	Nil	Nil	Nil	Nil	Nil	Nil	Nil
Prices:High	86.62	97.50	79.65	69.50	70.75	135.88	104.00	51.00	19.00	13.88
Prices:Low	39.33	76.00	56.57	41.94	40.81	28.75	42.09	17.50	9.56	6.69
P/E Ratio:High	30	23	24	25	35	64	45	30	18	16
P/E Ratio:Low	14	18	17	15	20	13	18	10	9	8
Income Statement Analysis (Million $)										
Revenue	5,222	5,314	4,755	4,356	4,143	3,807	3,452	3,021	2,494	2,378
Operating Income	692	867	743	643	525	548	557	458	352	300
Depreciation	159	135	149	138	126	91.2	80.1	75.6	77.5	69.2
Interest Expense	11.2	12.3	12.5	9.00	14.8	12.8	10.7	11.0	10.8	20.9
Pretax Income	554	746	594	496	318	396	459	365	255	202
Effective Tax Rate	35.7%	23.8%	26.0%	26.0%	13.9%	28.0%	30.6%	33.5%	36.0%	36.6%
Net Income	356	569	439	367	274	285	319	243	163	128
S&P Core Earnings	308	524	399	298	210	NA	NA	NA	NA	NA
Balance Sheet & Other Financial Data (Million $)										
Cash	889	1,567	1,196	498	90.7	68.5	93.9	149	43.0	119
Current Assets	2,170	3,001	2,444	1,799	1,493	1,244	1,089	1,020	776	765
Total Assets	3,330	4,124	3,450	2,808	2,450	2,073	1,703	1,483	1,208	1,222
Current Liabilities	1,234	1,468	1,183	1,099	931	979	736	606	548	421
Long Term Debt	150	150	149	149	149	149	149	149	57.0	163
Common Equity	1,429	2,083	1,643	1,082	1,076	777	659	578	501	540
Total Capital	1,578	2,232	1,792	1,231	1,225	926	808	727	558	704
Capital Expenditures	201	198	93.8	112	214	297	220	102	69.5	145
Cash Flow	515	704	588	505	399	377	399	319	241	197
Current Ratio	1.8	2.0	2.1	1.6	1.6	1.3	1.5	1.7	1.4	1.8
% Long Term Debt of Capitalization	9.5	6.7	8.3	12.1	12.2	16.1	18.4	20.5	10.2	23.2
% Net Income of Revenue	6.8	10.7	9.2	8.4	6.6	7.5	9.2	8.0	6.5	5.4
% Return on Assets	9.6	15.0	14.0	13.9	12.1	15.1	20.0	18.1	13.4	10.8
% Return on Equity	20.3	30.5	32.2	34.0	29.5	39.7	51.5	45.1	31.3	27.5

Data as orig reptd.; bef. results of disc opers/spec. items. Per share data adj. for stk. divs.; EPS diluted. E-Estimated. NA-Not Available. NM-Not Meaningful. NR-Not Ranked. UR-Under Review.

Office: 740 West New Circle Road, Lexington, KY 40550.
Telephone: 859-232-2000.
Website: http://www.lexmark.com
Chrmn & CEO: P.J. Curlander

EVP & CFO: J.W. Gamble, Jr.
VP & Treas: R.A. Pelini
VP, Secy & General Counsel: V.J. Cole
VP & Cntlr: G.D. Stromquist

Board of Directors: B. C. Ames, T. Beck, P. J. Curlander, W. R. Fields, R. E. Gomory, S. R. Hardis, J. F. Hardymon, R. Holland, Jr., M. L. Mann, M. J. Maples, J. Montupet, K. P. Seifert, M. D. Walker

Founded: 1990
Domicile: Delaware
Employees: 13,600

Eli Lilly and Co

STANDARD &POOR'S

S&P Recommendation HOLD ★★★★★

Price $57.03 (as of Oct 27, 2006)

12-Mo. Target Price $62.00

Investment Style Large-Cap Growth

GICS Sector Health Care
Sub-Industry Pharmaceuticals

Comment Eli Lilly & Co. is a leading producer of prescription drugs, offering a wide range of treatments for neurological disorders, diabetes, cancer and other conditions. Animal health products are also sold.

Key Stock Statistics (Source S&P, Vickers, company reports)

52-Wk Range	$59.24–49.47	S&P Oper. EPS 2006E	3.14	P/E on S&P Oper. EPS 2006E	18.2	Dividend Rate/Share	$1.60
Trailing 12-Month EPS	$2.99	S&P Oper. EPS 2007E	3.40	Common Shares Outstg. (M)	1,130.4	Yield (%)	2.81
Trailing 12-Month P/E	19.1	S&P Core EPS 2006E	3.15	Market Capitalization(B)	$64.467	Beta	0.74
$10K Invested 5 Yrs Ago	$8,035	S&P Core EPS 2007E	3.40	Institutional Ownership (%)	72	S&P Credit Rating	AA

Price Performance

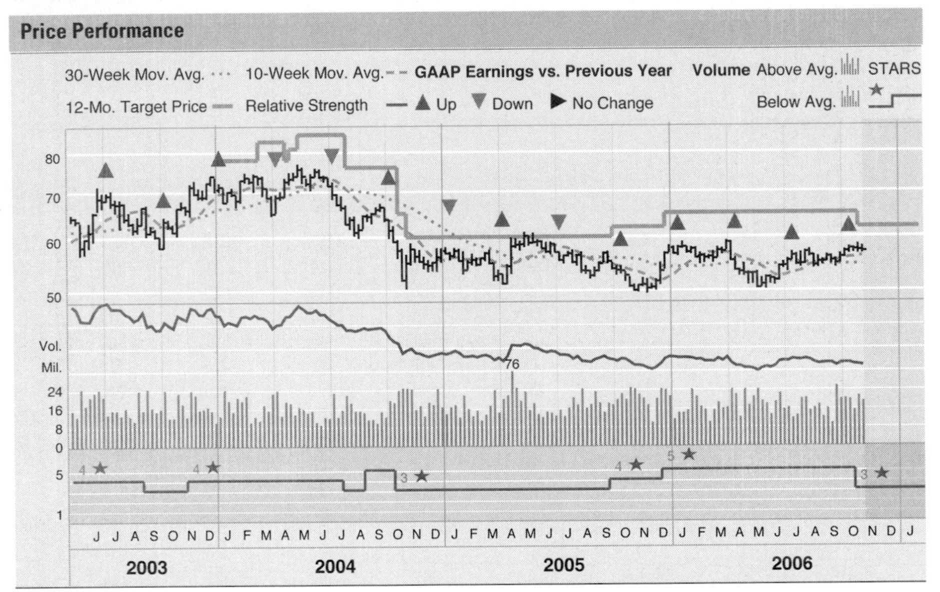

Options: ASE, CBOE, P, Ph

Analysis prepared by **Herman B. Saftlas** on October 24, 2006, when the stock traded at **$ 57.46**.

Highlights

- We expect revenues to grow about 5% in 2007, excluding the planned acquisition of ICOS. Sales growth should be augmented by an estimated 35% rise in sales of Cymbalta, an antidepressant, helped by an expanded direct to consumer advertising campaign, and greater managed care access. We also see volume gains for Symbyax for bipolar depression, and Forteo, an osteoporosis drug, but expect flat sales for Zyprexa anti-psychotic and continued weakness in LLY's diabetes lines. We believe the planned acquisition of ICOS (subject to necessary approvals), which would give LLY full ownership of Cialis erectile dysfunction drug, could add some $700 million to 2007 sales.
- Helped by manufacturing efficiencies, we expect a modest expansion in gross margins in 2007. Profitability should also benefit from a tight rein on SG&A and R&D costs, which should each account for a slightly lower percentage of revenues in 2007 than in 2006.
- We project operating EPS of $3.40 in 2007, up from an estimated $3.14 in 2006, excluding possible merger and plant closing charges.

Investment Rationale/Risk

- We recently lowered our recommendation on the shares to hold from strong buy. We attribute most of the 9.5% EPS gain in the third quarter to higher pricing, a one-time boost from shifting Zyprexa patients to Medicare, and cost economies. We are concerned about LLY's wide $0.77-$0.87 fourth quarter EPS guidance, as well as rising competition in key markets. On the plus side, we see promise in LLY's experimental Prasugrel anti-platelet compound and other pipeline drugs. Although we expect the planned $2.1 billion cash acquisition of ICOS (which will give LLY full ownership of Cialis) to be EPS dilutive in 2007, we project that it will be accretive in 2008.
- Risks to our recommendation and target price include possible greater than expected competitive pressures, as well as the failure to develop and commercialize new drugs.
- Our 12-month target price of $62 equals 18X our 2007 EPS estimate of $3.40. We think LLY's modest P/E premium relative to peers is justified by what we see as strong potential for its new drug pipeline and no material expiration losses until 2011.

Qualitative Risk Assessment

LOW | **MEDIUM** | HIGH

Our risk assessment reflects that LLY, along with other major drug companies, is subject to generic challenges to branded patents, and drug development and regulatory risks. This is offset by LLY's diverse drug portfolio, limited patent expiration exposure, and robust pipeline.

Quantitative Evaluations

S&P Quality Ranking B+

D | C | B- | B | **B+** | A- | A | A+

Relative Strength Rank MODERATE

42

LOWEST = 1 HIGHEST = 99

Revenue/Earnings Data

Revenue (Million $)

	1Q	2Q	3Q	4Q	Year
2006	3,715	3,867	3,864	--	--
2005	3,497	3,668	3,601	3,879	14,645
2004	3,377	3,556	3,280	3,644	13,858
2003	2,889	3,088	3,139	3,466	12,583
2002	2,561	2,775	2,786	2,956	11,078
2001	2,806	3,034	2,874	2,829	11,543

Earnings Per Share ($)

	1Q	2Q	3Q	4Q	Year
2006	0.77	0.76	0.80	**E**0.81	**E**3.14
2005	0.68	-0.23	0.73	0.66	1.83
2004	0.37	0.60	0.69	Nil	1.66
2003	0.38	0.64	0.66	0.69	2.37
2002	0.58	0.61	0.63	0.68	2.50
2001	0.74	0.76	0.54	0.54	2.58

Fiscal year ended Dec. 31. Next earnings report expected: Late January. EPS Estimates based on S&P Operating Earnings; historical GAAP earnings are as reported.

Dividend Data (Dates: mm/dd Payment Date: mm/dd/yy)

Amount ($)	Date Decl.	Ex-Div. Date	Stk. of Record	Payment Date
0.400	12/19	02/13	02/15	03/10/06
0.400	04/24	05/11	05/15	06/09/06
0.400	06/26	08/11	08/15	09/08/06
0.400	10/16	11/13	11/15	12/08/06

Dividends have been paid since 1885. Source: Company reports.

Eli Lilly and Co

Business Summary October 24, 2006

CORPORATE OVERVIEW. Eli Lilly and Co. is a leading maker of prescription drugs, offering a wide range of treatments for neurological disorders, diabetes, cancer and other conditions. Animal health products are also sold. Foreign operations accounted for 47% of sales in 2005. In October 2006, the company agreed to acquire ICOS Corp., subject to necessary approvals, which would give LLY full ownership of Cialis, a treatment for erectile dysfunction, presently marketed through a 50/50 venture with ICOS.

LLY's largest selling drug is Zyprexa, a treatment for schizophrenia and bipolar disorder that offers clinical advantages over older antipsychotic drugs. Sales of Zyprexa totaled $4.2 billion in 2005, down from $4.4 billion in 2004. Zyprexa accounted for about 13.6% of total U.S. antipsychotic prescriptions in September 2006, based on data from IMS Health, a pharmaceutical market intelligence firm. LLY also offers Symbyax, a combination of Zyprexa and Prozac, to treat bipolar depression. In August 2004, the company launched Cymbalta (sales of $680 million in 2005), a potent antidepressant. Cymbalta works on two body chemicals involved in depression--serotonin and norepinephrine--while most conventional antidepressants affect only serotonin.

Diabetes care products (sales of $2.8 billion in 2005) include Humulin, a human insulin produced through recombinant DNA technology; Humalog, a rapid-acting injectable human insulin analog; Iletin, an animal-source insulin; and Actos, an oral agent for Type 2 diabetes that is manufactured by Takeda Chemical Industries of Japan and co-marketed by Lilly and Takeda. In May 2005, the FDA approved Byetta (generically known as exenatide) for Type 2 diabetes. Lilly shares in the profits from Byetta with Amylin Pharmaceuticals, co-developer of the drug.

Other important drugs are Gemzar, a treatment for lung cancer and pancreatic cancer (sales of $1.3 billion); Evista, a drug used to prevent and treat osteoporosis in postmenopausal women ($1.0 billion); and Strattera, a treatment for attention deficit hyperactivity disorder ($552 million). LLY also offers Cialis for erectile dysfunction (sales of $747 million, partially booked by LLY); Forteo for severe osteoporosis ($389 million); Xigris for sepsis ($215 million); a line of anti-infectives such as Ceclor/cefaclor, Vancocin HCl, and Keflex; Humatrope, a recombinant human growth hormone; and Axid, a medication for excess stomach acid. Animal health products ($804 million) include cattle feed additives, antibiotics and related items.

Company Financials

Per Share Data ($) Year Ended Dec. 31	**2005**	**2004**	**2003**	**2002**	**2001**	**2000**	**1999**	**1998**	**1997**	**1996**
Tangible Book Value	9.55	9.51	8.69	7.37	6.32	5.37	4.49	2.66	2.83	1.87
Cash Flow	2.41	2.21	2.87	2.85	2.91	3.18	2.70	2.31	0.11	1.89
Earnings	1.83	1.66	2.37	2.50	2.58	2.79	2.30	1.87	-0.35	1.39
S&P Core Earnings	1.85	1.42	2.09	1.96	2.17	NA	NA	NA	NA	NA
Dividends	1.52	1.42	1.34	1.24	1.12	1.04	0.92	0.80	0.74	0.69
Payout Ratio	83%	86%	57%	50%	43%	37%	40%	43%	NM	49%
Prices:High	60.98	76.95	73.89	81.09	95.00	109.00	97.75	91.31	70.44	40.19
Prices:Low	49.47	50.34	52.77	43.75	70.01	54.00	60.56	57.69	35.56	24.69
P/E Ratio:High	33	46	31	32	37	39	42	49	NM	29
P/E Ratio:Low	27	30	22	17	27	19	26	31	NM	18
Income Statement Analysis (Million $)										
Revenue	14,645	13,858	12,583	11,078	11,543	10,862	10,003	9,237	8,518	7,347
Operating Income	4,375	4,256	4,050	3,821	4,185	3,996	3,803	3,315	2,968	2,591
Depreciation	726	598	548	493	455	436	440	490	510	544
Interest Expense	105	274	61.0	79.7	147	182	242	181	234	325
Pretax Income	2,718	2,942	3,262	3,458	3,552	3,859	3,245	2,665	510	2,032
Effective Tax Rate	26.3%	38.5%	21.5%	21.7%	20.9%	20.8%	21.5%	21.4%	175.5%	25.0%
Net Income	2,002	1,810	2,561	2,708	2,809	3,058	2,547	2,096	-385	1,524
S&P Core Earnings	2,016	1,558	2,261	2,128	2,359	NA	NA	NA	NA	NA
Balance Sheet & Other Financial Data (Million $)										
Cash	3,007	5,365	2,756	1,946	2,702	4,115	3,700	1,496	1,948	955
Current Assets	10,796	12,836	8,759	7,804	6,939	7,943	7,056	5,407	5,321	3,891
Total Assets	24,581	24,867	21,678	19,042	16,434	14,691	12,825	12,596	12,577	14,307
Current Liabilities	5,716	7,594	5,551	5,064	5,203	4,961	3,935	4,607	4,192	4,222
Long Term Debt	5,764	4,492	4,688	4,358	3,132	2,634	2,812	2,186	2,326	2,517
Common Equity	11,000	10,920	9,765	8,274	7,104	8,682	5,013	4,430	4,645	6,100
Total Capital	17,459	16,032	14,453	12,632	10,236	11,407	7,962	6,864	7,187	8,993
Capital Expenditures	1,298	1,898	1,707	1,131	884	678	528	420	366	444
Cash Flow	2,728	2,408	3,109	3,201	3,264	3,494	2,986	2,586	125	2,068
Current Ratio	1.9	1.7	1.6	1.5	1.3	1.6	1.8	1.2	1.3	0.9
% Long Term Debt of Capitalization	33.0	28.0	32.4	34.5	30.6	23.1	35.3	31.8	32.4	28.0
% Net Income of Revenue	13.7	13.1	20.4	24.4	24.3	28.2	25.5	22.7	NM	20.7
% Return on Assets	8.1	7.8	12.6	15.3	18.1	22.2	20.0	16.7	NM	10.6
% Return on Equity	18.1	17.5	28.4	35.2	42.7	44.7	53.9	46.2	NM	26.4

Data as orig reptd.; bef. results of disc opers/spec. items. Per share data adj. for stk. divs.; EPS diluted. E-Estimated. NA-Not Available. NM-Not Meaningful. NR-Not Ranked. UR-Under Review.

Office: Lilly Corporate Center, Indianapolis, IN 46285.
Telephone: 317-276-2000.
Website: http://www.lilly.com
Chrmn & CEO: S. Taurel

Pres & COO: J.C. Lechleiter
SVP & CFO: D. Rice
SVP & General Counsel: R.A. Armitage
Investor Contact: J.F. Greffet (317-433-1481)

Board of Directors: W. Bischoff, J. M. Cook, M. S. Feldstein, G. M. Fisher, J. E. Fyrwald, A. G. Gilman, K. N. Horn, J. C. Lechleiter, E. R. Marram, F. G. Prendergast, K. P. Seifert, S. Taurel

Founded: 1876
Domicile: Indiana
Employees: 42,600

STANDARD & POOR'S

Limited Brands Inc.

S&P Recommendation HOLD ★★★★★ | **Price** $29.23 (as of Oct 27, 2006) | **12-Mo. Target Price** $30.00 | **Investment Style** Large-Cap Value

GICS Sector Consumer Discretionary
Sub-Industry Apparel Retail

Comment This specialty retailer of women's apparel, lingerie and personal care and beauty products operates about 3,500 apparel and specialty stores.

Key Stock Statistics (Source S&P, Vickers, company reports)

52-Wk Range	$29.74–19.50	S&P Oper. EPS 2007E	1.70	P/E on S&P Oper. EPS 2007E	17.2	Dividend Rate/Share	$0.60
Trailing 12-Month EPS	$1.79	S&P Oper. EPS 2008E	1.85	Common Shares Outstg. (M)	395.0	Yield (%)	2.05
Trailing 12-Month P/E	16.3	S&P Core EPS 2007E	1.70	Market Capitalization(B)	$11.545	Beta	1.33
$10K Invested 5 Yrs Ago	$29,552	S&P Core EPS 2008E	1.85	Institutional Ownership (%)	77	S&P Credit Rating	BBB

Price Performance

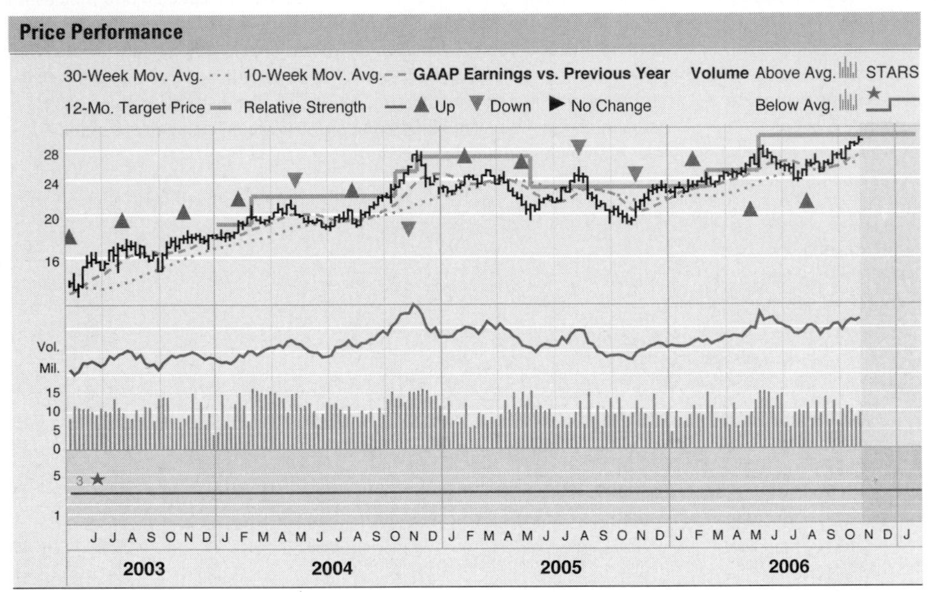

Options: ASE, CBOE, P, Ph

Analysis prepared by **Marie Driscoll, CFA** on October 04, 2006, when the stock traded at **$ 27.61**.

Highlights

- We expect low single digit sales growth in FY 07 (Jan.) and FY 08, reflecting same-store sales gains and little change in selling space. We look for apparel sales and profitability to improve modestly at Express as the year progresses and see continued sales momentum at Victoria's Secret.
- LTD's apparel business is beginning to win back the contemporary customer, in our view, as increased transactions offset lower prices and drive more full-price selling. We see this unit's turnaround gaining traction in FY 07 and we look for a mid-single digit sales gain and break-even division profits. However, we foresee LTD's future in its non-apparel brands. We view Victoria's Secret as the "jewel" in LTD's portfolio, and believe the brand will continue to provide growth opportunities via line extensions, sub-brands, and additional fragrance and beauty launches.
- We project a modest improvement in gross margins, reflecting an improvement in merchandise margins at Express and about 10 basis points of SG&A expense deleveraging in FY 07. We estimate FY 07 EPS of $1.70, benefiting from fewer shares outstanding.

Investment Rationale/Risk

- We see no near-term catalyst for share outperformance, given what we regard as a mature store base and retail concepts. We expect a modest incremental improvement in profitability and store productivity, but we seek signs of a tangible, sustainable improvement in apparel as well as LTD's various growth initiatives. Recent apparel results have improved at Express, but we believe a turnaround in apparel will take a number of years. The dividend recently provided a yield of 2.2%.
- Risks to our recommendation and target price include fashion and inventory risk, trends in consumer spending, and weak same-store sales trends.
- Our 12-month target price of $30 incorporates LTD's three-year historical forward P/E of 16X applied to our FY 08 EPS estimate of $1.85. Applying the peer forward P/E (16X as well) results in a $30 value.

Qualitative Risk Assessment

LOW | **MEDIUM** | HIGH

Our risk assessment reflects LTD's strong cash flow, offset by execution risk in the company's attempt to turn around its apparel businesses.

Quantitative Evaluations

S&P Quality Ranking B+

D | C | B- | B | **B+** | A- | A | A+

Relative Strength Rank STRONG

77

LOWEST = 1 HIGHEST = 99

Revenue/Earnings Data

Revenue (Million $)

	1Q	2Q	3Q	4Q	Year
2007	2,077	2,454	--	--	--
2006	1,975	2,291	1,892	3,542	9,699
2005	1,975	2,211	1,891	3,328	9,408
2004	1,842	2,014	1,847	3,231	8,934
2003	2,027	2,113	1,983	2,966	8,445
2002	2,127	2,192	1,906	3,138	9,363

Earnings Per Share ($)

2007	0.25	0.28	ENil	E1.15	E1.70
2006	0.16	0.20	Nil	1.28	1.62
2005	0.06	0.31	0.16	0.87	1.47
2004	0.19	0.19	0.25	0.74	1.36
2003	0.10	0.16	0.03	0.66	0.95
2002	0.07	0.17	-0.21	0.75	0.94

Fiscal year ended Jan. 31. Next earnings report expected: Mid November. EPS Estimates based on S&P Operating Earnings; historical GAAP earnings are as reported.

Dividend Data (Dates: mm/dd Payment Date: mm/dd/yy)

Amount ($)	Date Decl.	Ex-Div. Date	Stk. of Record	Payment Date
0.150	01/30	02/28	03/02	03/17/06
0.150	05/22	05/30	06/01	06/16/06
0.188	05/08	05/30	06/01	06/12/06
0.150	08/04	08/29	08/31	09/15/06

Dividends have been paid since 1970. Source: Company reports.

Limited Brands Inc.

Business Summary October 04, 2006

CORPORATE OVERVIEW. Limited Brands (formerly The Limited) is a specialty retailer that conducts its business in three primary segments: Victoria's Secret, a women's intimate apparel, personal care products and accessories retail brand; Bath & Body Works, a personal care and home fragrance products retail brand; and the Apparel segment, which operates Express and Limited Stores. At January 31, 2006, the store base consisted of 257 Express Women, 76 Express Men, 324 Express Dual Gender, 266 Limited Stores, 1,004 Victoria's Secret, and 1,536 Bath & Body Works locations. LTD also operates two Henri Bendel stores, and 11 C.O. Bigelows, an upscale apothecary. The company adopted its current name in May 2002.

The Apparel businesses accounted for 24% of total sales in FY 06 (Jan.), Victoria's Secret 46%, and Bath & Body Works 24%.

Victoria's Secret is the leading specialty retailer of women's intimate apparel and beauty products, with FY 06 sales of $4,448 million. Victoria's Secret Direct is a catalog and e-commerce retailer of women's intimate and other apparel and beauty products. Bath & Body Works is a specialty retailer of personal care and home fragrance products. FY 06 sales were $2,269 million, including White Barn Candle Company. Express, launched in 1980, seeks to offer cutting edge style for casual, professional and urban customers, both men and women. Express had sales of $1,780 million in FY 06. Limited stores focus on sophisticated sportswear for modern American women, with FY 06 sales of $545 million. Limited also owns Mast Industries, Inc., a contract manufacturer and apparel importer for its retail brands and third parties. Mast is a significant supplier for Victoria's Secret, Victoria's Secret Direct, Express and Limited stores. In 2005, Mast had external sales of $564 million.

Company Financials

Per Share Data ($) Year Ended Jan. 31	**2006**	**2005**	**2004**	**2003**	**2002**	**2001**	**2000**	**1999**	**1998**	**1997**
Tangible Book Value	1.69	1.31	6.78	5.93	6.40	5.43	5.00	4.92	3.75	3.55
Cash Flow	2.45	2.17	1.90	1.48	1.83	1.58	1.61	4.76	0.97	1.29
Earnings	1.62	1.47	1.36	0.95	0.94	0.96	1.00	4.16	0.40	0.77
S&P Core Earnings	1.57	1.27	1.03	0.94	0.80	0.91	NA	NA	NA	NA
Dividends	0.48	0.40	0.40	0.30	0.30	0.30	0.30	0.26	0.24	0.20
Payout Ratio	30%	27%	29%	32%	32%	31%	30%	6%	61%	26%
Calendar Year	2005	2004	2003	2002	2001	2000	1999	1998	1997	1996
Prices:High	25.50	27.89	18.46	22.34	21.29	27.88	25.31	18.25	12.88	11.25
Prices:Low	18.81	17.35	10.88	12.53	9.00	14.44	13.75	10.25	8.25	7.63
P/E Ratio:High	16	19	14	24	23	29	25	4	33	15
P/E Ratio:Low	12	12	8	13	10	15	14	2	21	10
Income Statement Analysis (Million $)										
Revenue	9,699	9,408	8,934	8,445	9,363	10,105	9,766	9,347	9,189	8,645
Operating Income	1,285	1,360	1,246	1,148	1,025	1,148	1,169	984	1,006	938
Depreciation	299	333	28.3	276	277	272	272	286	313	290
Interest Expense	94.0	58.0	62.0	30.0	34.0	58.0	78.0	69.0	69.0	75.4
Pretax Income	960	1,116	1,166	843	968	828	905	2,428	457	675
Effective Tax Rate	30.3%	36.8%	38.5%	40.5%	39.8%	40.0%	41.0%	12.8%	40.0%	35.7%
Net Income	669	705	717	496	519	428	461	2,054	217	434
S&P Core Earnings	638	609	540	492	352	406	NA	NA	NA	NA
Balance Sheet & Other Financial Data (Million $)										
Cash	1,208	1,161	3,129	2,262	1,375	563	817	1,222	1,098	313
Current Assets	2,784	2,684	4,433	3,606	2,682	2,068	2,285	2,318	2,031	1,545
Total Assets	6,346	6,089	7,873	7,246	4,719	4,088	4,126	4,550	4,301	4,120
Current Liabilities	1,575	1,451	1,392	1,259	1,319	1,000	1,236	1,248	1,093	907
Long Term Debt	1,669	1,646	648	547	250	400	400	550	650	650
Common Equity	2,471	2,335	5,266	4,860	2,744	2,317	2,147	2,233	2,044	1,923
Total Capital	4,319	4,191	6,048	5,532	3,171	2,860	2,666	2,894	2,797	2,810
Capital Expenditures	480	431	293	306	337	446	375	347	405	409
Cash Flow	968	1,038	1,000	772	796	700	733	2,340	530	724
Current Ratio	1.8	1.8	3.2	2.9	2.0	2.1	1.8	1.9	1.9	1.7
% Long Term Debt of Capitalization	38.6	39.3	10.7	9.9	7.9	14.0	15.0	19.0	23.2	23.1
% Net Income of Revenue	6.9	7.5	8.0	5.9	5.5	4.2	4.7	22.0	2.4	5.0
% Return on Assets	10.8	10.1	9.5	8.0	11.8	10.4	10.7	46.4	5.2	9.2
% Return on Equity	27.9	18.6	14.2	13.0	20.5	19.2	21.4	96.0	10.9	16.9

Data as orig reptd.; bef. results of disc opers/spec. items. Per share data adj. for stk. divs.; EPS diluted. E-Estimated. NA-Not Available. NM-Not Meaningful. NR-Not Ranked. UR-Under Review.

Office: Three Limited Parkway, Columbus, OH 43216.
Telephone: 614-415-7000.
Website: http://www.limited.com
Chrmn & CEO: L.H. Wexner

Vice Chrmn & COO: L.A. Schlesinger
EVP & CFO: K.T. Stevens
EVP & Chief Admin: M.R. Redgrave

Founded: 1967
Domicile: Delaware
Employees: 110,000

STANDARD &POOR'S

Lincoln National Corp

S&P Recommendation HOLD ★★★☆☆	**Price** $63.74 (as of Oct 27, 2006)	**12-Mo. Target Price** $64.00	**Investment Style** Large-Cap Value

GICS Sector Financials
Sub-Industry Life & Health Insurance

Comment This company offers annuities, life insurance, mutual funds, asset management and related advisory services to affluent individuals.

Key Stock Statistics (Source S&P, Vickers, company reports)

52-Wk Range	**$64.96–49.45**	S&P Oper. EPS 2006**E**	**4.93**	P/E on S&P Oper. EPS 2006**E**	**12.9**	Dividend Rate/Share	**$1.52**
Trailing 12-Month EPS	**$5.05**	S&P Oper. EPS 2007**E**	**5.45**	Common Shares Outstg. (M)	**287.1**	Yield (%)	**2.38**
Trailing 12-Month P/E	**12.6**	S&P Core EPS 2006**E**	**4.65**	Market Capitalization(B)	**$17.945**	Beta	**1.26**
$10K Invested 5 Yrs Ago	**$17,045**	S&P Core EPS 2007**E**	**5.25**	Institutional Ownership (%)	**70**	S&P Credit Rating	**A+**

Price Performance

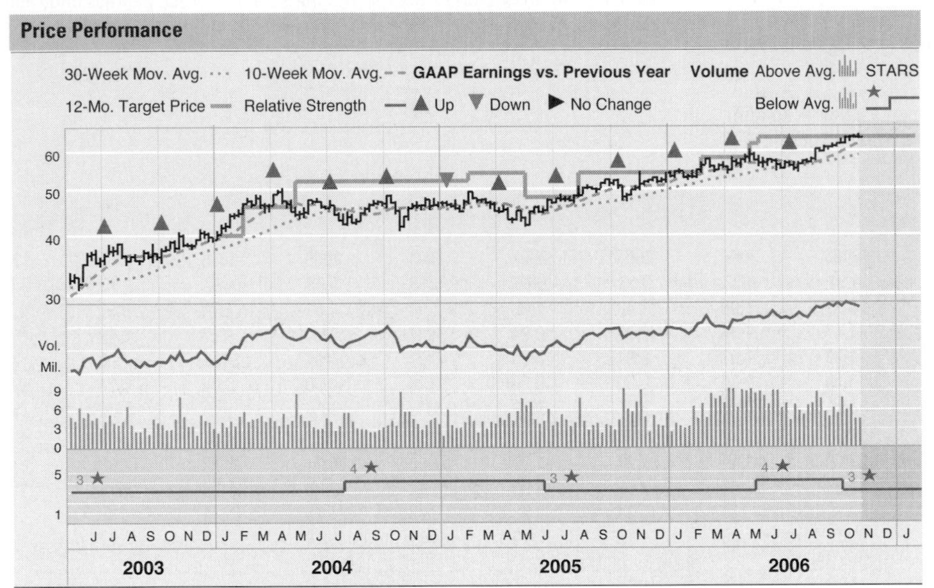

Options: ASE

Analysis prepared by **Frank Braden** on October 05, 2006, when the stock traded at **$ 63.29**.

Highlights

- We expect strong growth in premiums and operating earnings to be driven by the merger with Jefferson-Pilot, which closed April 3, 2006. We project strong sales growth in the individual markets segment, driven by new product introductions and variable annuity sales, but partially offset by a challenging life insurance market. We see the employer markets segment benefiting from demand for its retirement products.
- We anticipate that operating earnings for the smaller investment management segment will see strong growth in 2006, with improving margins partially offset by capacity issues with two large cap growth products. We forecast a modest decline in operating earnings of the small U.K. segment, to approximately $62 million. We expect the communications segment to post pretax operating earnings of around $63 million.
- Our operating EPS estimate for 2006 is $4.93, including projected stock option expense of approximately $0.15. Our operating EPS estimate for 2007 is $5.45.

Investment Rationale/Risk

- Over the short term, we think LNC will benefit from strong prepayment income and solid institutional investment inflows. Over the longer term, we see results benefiting from operational efficiencies following the merger with Jefferson-Pilot and continued stock repurchases. We further view the acquisition of Jefferson-Pilot as adding financial flexibility and distribution capabilities. Our view is somewhat tempered, however, by high levels of competition in the life insurance products segment.
- Risks to our recommendation and target price include difficulties integrating Jefferson-Pilot; dynamic hedging for guaranteed minimum benefits; sensitivity to volatile equity markets; pressures on product spreads due to low interest rates; difficulties in obtaining reinsurance for some products; currency risk; and potential unfavorable tax law changes lessening product competitiveness.
- Our 12-month target price of $64 is based on a P/E of 13X applied to our 2006 operating EPS estimate of $4.93, a slight premium to LNC's historical average.

Qualitative Risk Assessment

LOW | **MEDIUM** | HIGH

Our risk assessment reflects our view of the company's solid balance sheet with low debt-to-total capitalization and a stable dividend policy, tempered by risks associated with the acquisition of Jefferson-Pilot, and earnings volatility related to interest rate and equity market movements.

Quantitative Evaluations

S&P Quality Ranking **B+**

D | C | B- | B | **B+** | A- | A | A+

Relative Strength Rank **MODERATE**

58

LOWEST = 1 HIGHEST = 99

Revenue/Earnings Data

Revenue (Million $)

	1Q	2Q	3Q	4Q	Year
2006	1,417	2,496	--	--	--
2005	1,313	1,373	1,413	1,388	5,488
2004	1,259	1,359	1,406	1,347	5,371
2003	1,099	1,213	1,269	1,327	5,284
2002	1,126	1,145	1,141	1,189	4,635
2001	1,699	1,599	1,590	1,504	6,381

Earnings Per Share ($)

	1Q	2Q	3Q	4Q	Year
2006	1.24	1.23	**E**1.20	**E**1.24	**E**4.93
2005	1.01	1.13	1.30	1.28	4.72
2004	0.86	1.04	1.12	1.07	4.09
2003	0.23	0.80	0.74	1.08	2.85
2002	0.49	0.31	-0.68	0.35	0.49
2001	0.85	0.80	0.61	0.88	3.13

Fiscal year ended Dec. 31. Next earnings report expected: Early November. EPS Estimates based on S&P Operating Earnings; historical GAAP earnings are as reported.

Dividend Data (Dates: mm/dd Payment Date: mm/dd/yy)

Amount ($)	Date Decl.	Ex-Div. Date	Stk. of Record	Payment Date
0.380	11/10	01/06	01/10	02/01/06
0.380	03/09	04/11	04/14	05/01/06
0.380	06/09	07/06	07/10	08/01/06
0.380	09/14	10/10	10/12	11/01/06

Dividends have been paid since 1920. Source: Company reports.

Lincoln National Corp

Business Summary October 05, 2006

CORPORATE OVERVIEW. Lincoln National is a holding company with subsidiaries that operate multiple insurance and investment management businesses. Primary operating subsidiaries include The Lincoln National Life Insurance Company, First Penn-Pacific Life Insurance Company, Lincoln Life & Annuity Company of New York, Delaware Management Holdings, Inc., Lincoln National (UK) plc, Lincoln Financial Advisors (LFA), a retailing distribution unit, and Lincoln Financial Distributors (LFD), a wholesaling distribution unit.

Following the acquisition of Jefferson-Pilot in April 2006, LNC's segments were restructured and currently operations are divided into six business segments: individual markets (58% of second quarter 2006 operating revenue), employer markets (28%), investment management (5.4%), Lincoln U.K. (3.3%), Lincoln financial media (2.3%), and other operations (2.7%).

The individual markets segment encompasses the annuities and life insurance business lines. According to Variable Annuity Research and Data Services (VARDS), LNC ranked sixth in assets and fifth in individual variable annuity sales for 2005 in the U.S. The life insurance business targets the affluent market, and underwrites and sells universal life, variable universal life, interest sensitive whole life, corporate-owned life insurance (COLI), term-life insurance, and linked products such as universal life linked with long-term care benefits. The employer markets segment encompasses the retirement products, executive benefits, and benefit partners businesses.

The investment management segment offers retail and institutional mutual funds, separate and managed accounts, 529 college savings plans, and retirement plans and services, including 401(k) plans and administration services. Lincoln UK is licensed to do business throughout the U.K., and focuses primarily on retaining its existing customers and managing expenses for a closed block of business in the U.K., including accepting new deposits from, and offering new products to, existing policyholders. Offerings consist principally of unit-linked life and pension products, similar to U.S. variable life and annuity products. The other operations segment includes the financial data for the operations of Lincoln Financial Advisors (LFA) and Lincoln Financial Distributors (LFD), LNC's retail and wholesale distributors, operations that are not directly related to the business segments.

Company Financials

Per Share Data ($) Year Ended Dec. 31	**2005**	**2004**	**2003**	**2002**	**2001**	**2000**	**1999**	**1998**	**1997**	**1996**
Tangible Book Value	22.47	22.25	18.74	15.62	14.10	11.06	5.59	10.17	19.34	15.97
Operating Earnings	NA	NA	NA	2.56	3.56	3.27	2.32	2.61	-0.25	2.08
Earnings	4.72	4.09	2.85	0.49	3.13	3.19	2.30	2.51	0.11	2.46
S&P Core Earnings	4.71	3.78	4.36	1.16	3.10	NA	NA	NA	NA	NA
Dividends	1.46	1.40	1.34	1.28	1.22	1.16	1.10	1.30	0.98	0.92
Payout Ratio	31%	34%	47%	NM	39%	36%	48%	52%	NM	37%
Prices:High	54.41	50.38	41.32	53.65	52.75	56.38	57.50	49.44	39.06	28.50
Prices:Low	41.59	39.98	24.73	25.11	38.00	22.63	36.00	33.50	24.50	20.38
P/E Ratio:High	12	12	14	NM	17	18	25	20	NM	12
P/E Ratio:Low	9	10	9	NM	12	7	16	13	NM	8
Income Statement Analysis (Million $)										
Life Insurance in Force	338,500	NA	307,800	874	651,900	637,100	516,600	400,800	249,800	258,300
Premium Income:Life	NA	NA	1,694	1,730	2,907	3,064	2,721	2,260	1,588	1,408
Premium Income:A & H	NA	NA	3.98	20.3	341	410	698	635	573	793
Net Investment Income	2,702	2,704	2,639	2,608	2,680	2,747	2,808	2,681	2,251	2,366
Total Revenue	5,488	5,371	5,284	4,635	6,381	6,852	6,798	6,087	4,898	6,721
Pretax Income	1,075	1,036	1,048	1.62	764	836	570	697	34.0	712
Net Operating Income	NA	NA	NA	474	689	639	457	NA	257	434
Net Income	831	732	767	91.6	606	621	460	510	21.0	514
S&P Core Earnings	831	675	782	215	600	NA	NA	NA	NA	NA
Balance Sheet & Other Financial Data (Million $)										
Cash & Equivalent	2,838	2,187	2,234	2,227	3,659	2,474	2,429	2,433	3,795	1,715
Premiums Due	343	233	352	213	400	297	260	775	621	651
Investment Assets:Bonds	33,443	34,701	32,769	32,767	28,346	27,450	27,689	30,233	24,066	27,906
Investment Assets:Stocks	3,391	3,399	3,319	337	471	550	604	543	660	993
Investment Assets:Loans	5,525	5,728	6,119	6,151	6,475	6,624	6,628	6,233	4,051	4,031
Investment Assets:Total	43,168	44,507	42,778	40,000	36,113	35,369	35,578	37,929	25,212	34,045
Deferred Policy Costs	4,092	3,445	3,192	2,971	2,885	3,071	2,800	1,964	1,624	1,892
Total Assets	124,788	116,219	106,745	93,133	98,001	99,844	103,096	99,836	77,175	71,713
Debt	1,333	1,083	1,459	1,512	1,336	1,457	1,457	712	808	626
Common Equity	6,384	6,175	5,811	5,296	5,263	4,953	4,264	5,388	4,983	4,467
% Return on Revenue	15.1	13.6	14.5	2.0	9.5	9.1	6.8	28.6	0.7	7.6
% Return on Assets	0.1	0.1	0.1	0.1	0.6	0.6	0.5	0.6	0.0	0.8
% Return on Equity	13.2	12.2	13.8	1.7	11.9	13.5	0.4	9.8	0.4	11.6
% Investment Yield	6.1	6.8	7.1	6.9	7.5	7.7	7.6	7.9	7.5	7.2

Data as orig reptd.; bef. results of disc opers/spec. items. Per share data adj. for stk. divs.; EPS diluted. E-Estimated. NA-Not Available. NM-Not Meaningful. NR-Not Ranked. UR-Under Review.

Office: 1500 Market Street, Philadelphia, PA 19102.
Telephone: 215-448-1400.
Email: investorrelations@lnc.com
Website: http://www.lfg.com

Chrmn & CEO: J.A. Boscia
SVP & CFO: F.J. Crawford
SVP & General Counsel: D.L. Schoff

Board of Directors: W. J. Avery, J. P. Barrett, J. A. Boscia, W. H. Cunningham, D. R. Glass, G. W. Henderson, III, E. G. Johnson, M. L. Lachman, M. F. Mee, W. P. Payne, P. S. Pittard, J. S. Ruckelshaus, D. A. Stonecipher, I. Tidwell, G. F. Tilton

Founded: 1905
Domicile: Indiana
Employees: 5,259

STANDARD &POOR'S

Linear Technology Corp

S&P Recommendation BUY ★★★★★	Price	12-Mo. Target Price	Investment Style
	$30.97 (as of Oct 27, 2006)	$37.00	Large-Cap Growth

GICS Sector Information Technology
Sub-Industry Semiconductors

Comment This company manufactures high-performance linear integrated circuits.

Key Stock Statistics (Source S&P, Vickers, company reports)

52-Wk Range	$39.82–27.80	S&P Oper. EPS 2007E	1.55	P/E on S&P Oper. EPS 2007E	20.0	Dividend Rate/Share	$0.60
Trailing 12-Month EPS	$1.43	S&P Oper. EPS 2008E	1.82	Common Shares Outstg. (M)	301.2	Yield (%)	1.94
Trailing 12-Month P/E	21.7	S&P Core EPS 2007E	1.55	Market Capitalization(B)	$9.330	Beta	2.05
$10K Invested 5 Yrs Ago	$8,018	S&P Core EPS 2008E	1.82	Institutional Ownership (%)	97	S&P Credit Rating	NA

Price Performance

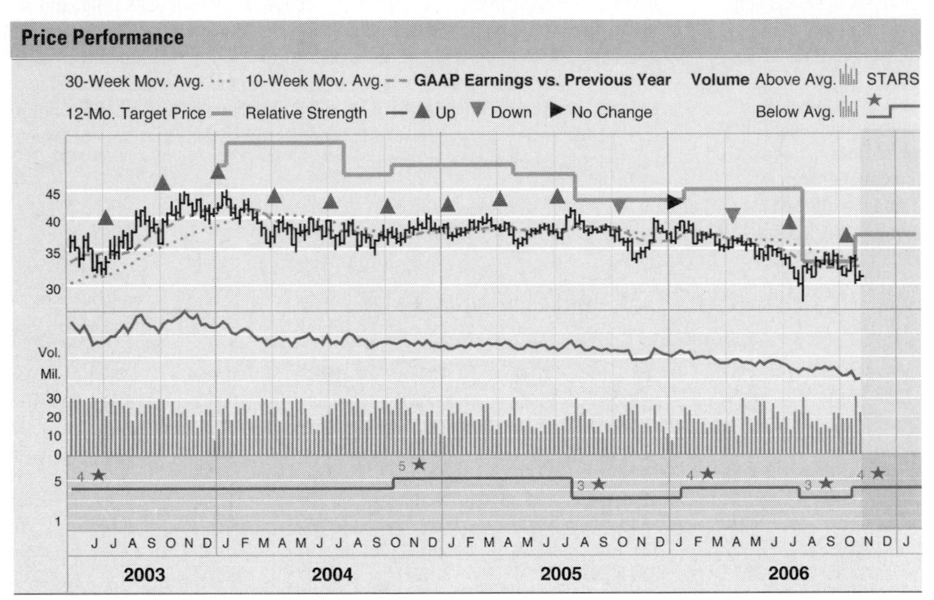

Options: ASE, CBOE, P, Ph

Analysis prepared by **Clyde Montevirgen** on October 24, 2006, when the stock traded at **$ 31.13**.

Highlights

- We forecast sales growth of 8.9% in FY 07 (Jun.) and 16.9% in FY 08, following 30% growth in FY 05 (including $40 million from a royalty settlement) and a slowdown to 4% growth in FY 06 (8% excluding the $40 million settlement). We believe that a possible slowdown in wireless infrastructure spending and more cautious consumer sentiment may limit near-term sales growth, but see demand for high-end products and power conversion semiconductors driving above-industry sales over the long run.
- We see gross margins widening slightly to 78.4% in FY 07, from 78.2% in FY 06. We view favorably the company's focus on high-end analog, as pricing should remain relatively stable, helping to preserve margins. Although we see R&D head count and related compensation costs increasing as the company takes on new projects, we think operating expenses will grow at a slower pace than sales, providing healthy operating leverage and supporting overall profitability.
- We expect EPS of $1.55 in FY 07, up from $1.37 in FY 06, and $1.82 in FY 08. Both estimates include stock option expense.

Investment Rationale/Risk

- We think the high-end analog chip category will grow faster than the overall semiconductor industry in the current fiscal year, and that LLTC can capitalize on its entrenched customer base after the expected near-term industrywide softening. Although we believe that our revenue forecast for LLTC has increasing risk as rising consumer interest and energy costs threaten to reduce spending on consumer electronics, we think its cost structure is more flexible than that of peers and can withstand negative near-term demand volatility. Although LLTC's shares trade at high multiples compared to peers, we believe that a premium is warranted in light of LLTC's attractive attributes; we think the shares are undervalued on a historical basis.
- Risks to our opinion and target price include the possibility of a sharp downturn in semiconductor demand. We are concerned about LLTC's corporate governance relating to its reliance on stock-based compensation.
- Our 12-month target price of $37 is based on a blend of relative metrics. We use multiples of 9.0X for price-to-sales and 22X for P/E, both around recent historical trough averages, implying values of $36 and $38, respectively.

Qualitative Risk Assessment

LOW	**MEDIUM**	HIGH

Linear is subject to the sales cycles of the semiconductor industry. Stabilizing factors include a high level of proprietary circuit design content, a diverse customer base, diverse end markets, an absence of long-term debt, and wider margins than most competitors.

Quantitative Evaluations

S&P Quality Ranking A

D	C	B-	B	B+	A-	**A**	A+

Relative Strength Rank WEAK

18

LOWEST = 1 HIGHEST = 99

Revenue/Earnings Data

Revenue (Million $)

	1Q	2Q	3Q	4Q	Year
2007	292.1	--	--	--	--
2006	256.0	265.2	278.9	292.9	1,093
2005	253.0	250.1	290.7	255.8	1,050
2004	174.1	186.0	209.1	238.1	807.3
2003	142.0	145.0	153.8	165.8	606.6
2002	120.1	121.3	130.2	140.8	512.3

Earnings Per Share ($)

2007	0.37	E0.36	E0.39	E0.44	E1.55
2006	0.31	0.33	0.35	0.37	1.37
2005	0.33	0.33	0.39	0.34	1.38
2004	0.22	0.23	0.27	0.31	1.02
2003	0.17	0.18	0.19	0.21	0.74
2002	0.14	0.14	0.16	0.17	0.60

Fiscal year ended Jun. 30. Next earnings report expected: Mid January. EPS Estimates based on S&P Operating Earnings; historical GAAP earnings are as reported.

Dividend Data (Dates: mm/dd Payment Date: mm/dd/yy)

Amount ($)	Date Decl.	Ex-Div. Date	Stk. of Record	Payment Date
0.150	01/18	01/25	01/27	02/15/06
0.150	04/18	04/26	04/28	05/17/06
0.150	07/27	08/02	08/04	08/23/06
0.150	10/17	10/25	10/27	11/15/06

Dividends have been paid since 1992. Source: Company reports.

Business Summary October 24, 2006

Linear Technology Corp. has grown rapidly since its incorporation in 1981. Annual revenues reached $100 million after 10 years of operations, approached $1 billion in the boom year of FY 01 (Jun.), and surpassed $1 billion in FY 05. LLTC designs, makes and markets a broad line of high-performance standard linear integrated circuits (ICs) that address a wide range of real-world signal processing applications. Real-world phenomena, such as temperature, pressure, sound, images, speed, acceleration, position and rotation, are specifically analog in nature, consisting of continuously varying information. According to LLTC, advantages offered by operating in the linear, as opposed to the digital, IC market, include smaller capital requirements, greater price stability and market diversity, and less Asian competition.

LLTC's products are used in a wide variety of applications, including wireless and wireline telecommunications, networking, satellite systems, notebook and desk-top PCs, computer peripherals, video/multimedia, industrial instrumentation, medical devices, and high-end consumer products such as digital cameras and MP3 players. The company has expanded its customer base throughout its history. LLTC initially served primarily an industrial customer base, with a high percentage of revenues from the military market. Since the late 1980s, new products led to growth in the PC and hand-held device markets, and communication and networking markets contributed to growth significantly in recent years. The company sells its products to more than 15,000 original equipment manufacturers.

By end market, FY 05 sales broke down as follows: 35% from communications, of which 11% was from handsets, 11% cell phone infrastructure, and 13% networking. About 32% of FY 05 business was derived from industrial markets, 16% computing, 9% high-end consumer, 5% automotive, and 3% satellite and military.

Company Financials

Per Share Data ($) Year Ended Jun. 30	**2006**	**2005**	**2004**	**2003**	**2002**	**2001**	**2000**	**1999**	**1998**	**1997**
Tangible Book Value	6.94	6.55	5.87	5.80	5.63	5.59	4.20	2.95	2.46	1.94
Cash Flow	1.53	1.53	1.17	0.88	0.74	1.39	0.95	0.68	0.63	0.47
Earnings	1.37	1.38	1.02	0.74	0.60	1.29	0.88	0.61	0.57	0.43
S&P Core Earnings	1.37	0.99	0.79	0.50	0.40	1.10	NA	NA	NA	NA
Dividends	0.50	0.36	0.28	0.21	0.17	0.13	0.08	0.08	0.06	0.05
Payout Ratio	36%	26%	27%	28%	28%	10%	9%	12%	11%	12%
Prices:High	39.35	41.67	45.09	44.80	47.50	65.13	74.75	41.59	22.63	18.75
Prices:Low	27.80	32.83	34.01	24.76	18.92	29.45	35.06	20.88	9.78	10.13
P/E Ratio:High	29	30	44	61	79	50	85	68	40	44
P/E Ratio:Low	20	24	33	33	32	23	40	34	17	24

Income Statement Analysis (Million $)										
Revenue	1,093	1,050	807	607	512	973	706	507	485	379
Operating Income	613	638	485	340	271	582	399	280	268	201
Depreciation	49.3	48.8	48.7	45.9	46.3	35.8	25.0	22.0	20.1	12.4
Interest Expense	Nil	Nil	Nil	Nil	Nil	Nil	Nil	Nil	Nil	Nil
Pretax Income	617	620	462	333	278	611	417	286	271	205
Effective Tax Rate	30.5%	30.0%	29.0%	29.0%	29.0%	30.0%	31.0%	32.0%	33.3%	34.3%
Net Income	429	434	328	237	198	427	288	194	181	134
S&P Core Earnings	429	311	253	161	132	366	NA	NA	NA	NA

Balance Sheet & Other Financial Data (Million $)										
Cash	541	323	204	136	212	321	230	787	638	443
Current Assets	2,077	2,007	1,832	1,776	1,728	1,728	1,310	905	768	559
Total Assets	2,391	2,286	2,088	2,057	1,988	2,017	1,507	1,047	893	680
Current Liabilities	237	208	203	162	169	202	169	125	123	89.0
Long Term Debt	Nil	Nil	Nil	Nil	Nil	Nil	Nil	Nil	Nil	Nil
Common Equity	2,104	2,007	1,811	1,815	1,781	1,782	1,322	907	756	589
Total Capital	2,104	2,007	1,811	1,815	1,819	1,815	1,339	922	770	591
Capital Expenditures	69.4	62.1	20.7	6.61	17.9	128	80.3	39.1	24.4	21.9
Cash Flow	478	483	377	282	244	463	313	216	201	147
Current Ratio	8.8	9.7	9.0	11.0	10.2	8.5	7.8	7.2	6.2	6.3
% Long Term Debt of Capitalization	Nil	Nil	Nil	Nil	Nil	Nil	Nil	Nil	Nil	Nil
% Net Income of Revenue	39.2	41.3	40.7	39.0	38.6	43.9	40.8	38.3	37.3	35.4
% Return on Assets	18.3	19.8	15.8	11.7	9.9	24.3	22.5	20.0	23.0	22.2
% Return on Equity	20.9	22.7	18.1	13.2	11.1	27.5	25.8	23.3	26.4	26.1

Data as orig reptd.; bef. results of disc opers/spec. items. Per share data adj. for stk. divs.; EPS diluted. E-Estimated. NA-Not Available. NM-Not Meaningful. NR-Not Ranked. UR-Under Review.

Office: 1630 McCarthy Boulevard, Milpitas, CA 95035-7487.
Telephone: 408-432-1900.
Website: http://www.linear.com
Exec Chrmn: R.H. Swanson, Jr.

Pres: D.B. Bell
CEO: L. Maier
COO & VP: A. McCann
Investor Contact: P. Coghlan (408-432-1900)

Board of Directors: D. S. Lee, L. Maier, R. M. Moley, R. H. Swanson, Jr., T. S. Volpe

Founded: 1981
Domicile: Delaware
Employees: 3,755

STANDARD &POOR'S

Liz Claiborne Inc.

S&P Recommendation HOLD ★★★★★

Price $40.93 (as of Oct 27, 2006)

12-Mo. Target Price $44.00

Investment Style Mid-Cap Growth

GICS Sector Consumer Discretionary
Sub-Industry Apparel, Accessories & Luxury Goods

Comment This company designs and markets women's and men's apparel that is made by independent suppliers and sold through department and specialty stores worldwide.

Key Stock Statistics (Source S&P, Vickers, company reports)

52-Wk Range	$42.00–33.40	S&P Oper. EPS 2006E	2.90	P/E on S&P Oper. EPS 2006E	14.1	Dividend Rate/Share	$0.23
Trailing 12-Month EPS	$2.49	S&P Oper. EPS 2007E	3.35	Common Shares Outstg. (M)	103.2	Yield (%)	0.55
Trailing 12-Month P/E	16.4	S&P Core EPS 2006E	2.80	Market Capitalization(B)	$4.223	Beta	1.05
$10K Invested 5 Yrs Ago	$18,119	S&P Core EPS 2007E	3.30	Institutional Ownership (%)	88	S&P Credit Rating	BBB

Price Performance

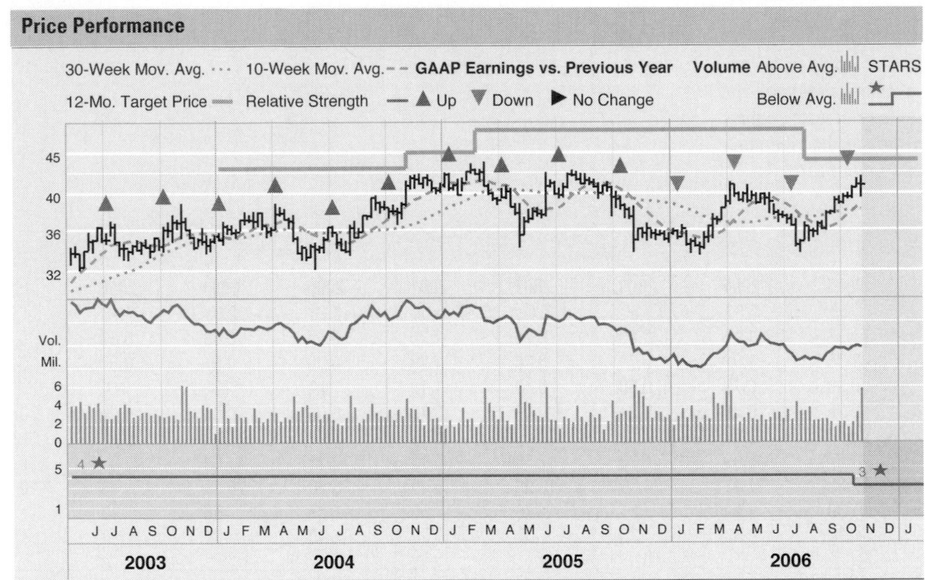

Options: CBOE, P

Analysis prepared by **Marie Driscoll, CFA** on October 20, 2006, when the stock traded at **$ 41.08**.

Highlights

- With its portfolio of 46 brands, a strong and flexible infrastructure and a seasoned management team, we think LIZ should be able to navigate a consolidating retail environment. We see specialty apparel retail expanding to 35%+ of sales over the next five years, based on new store openings and improved store productivity. Internationally, a platform is in place to nurture selected domestic apparel brands and drive market penetration. LIZ sees Juicy Couture as a billion dollar brand, and we concur.

- We estimate low single digit sales increases for 2006 and 2007, excluding acquisitions. We expect specialty retail via the power brands of Mexx, Juicy Couture and Lucky Brands to grow in the mid-teens. We project double digit growth in the non-apparel/accessories business, offset by a 5% drop in apparel wholesale revenues. We are looking for modest operating margin contraction in 2006 to about 10.6% of sales, before an estimated $60 million one-time streamlining expense.

- Our 2006 EPS estimate of $2.95 includes projected stock option expense of $0.10 per share, but excludes $0.36 of streamlining expense; for 2007, we project EPS of $3.35.

Investment Rationale/Risk

- With a new CEO taking the helm at LIZ this November, we are taking a more cautious stance on the shares. LIZ's broad diversification across brands, sales channels and demographics, and its consistently strong financial results, remain investment positives, and we see market share opportunities over the next few years as LIZ assimilates recent acquisitions and extends distribution and breadth of many of its 40-odd brands. We view LIZ's international opportunities as significant.

- Risks to our recommendation and target price include changes in consumer sentiment and spending trends, continued access to sourcing, as well as fashion and inventory risk.

- Our 12-month target price of $44 represents a P/E of 13X applied to our 2007 EPS estimate of $3.35, in line with the 13.5X average forward P/E that LIZ shares have traded at over the past 36 months, within a 9X-17X range. We believe that the growing proportion of retail sales in the overall sales mix should provide multiple expansion over the longer term.

Qualitative Risk Assessment

LOW | **MEDIUM** | HIGH

We assess LIZ's risk as medium based on our view of its exposure to department store consolidation, offset by its broad diversification and strong cash flows.

Quantitative Evaluations

S&P Quality Ranking A

D | C | B- | B | B+ | A- | **A** | A+

Relative Strength Rank MODERATE

64

LOWEST = 1 HIGHEST = 99

Revenue/Earnings Data

Revenue (Million $)

	1Q	2Q	3Q	4Q	Year
2006	1,171	1,125	1,370	--	--
2005	1,212	1,099	1,337	1,200	4,848
2004	1,103	1,026	1,307	1,198	4,633
2003	1,076	959.4	1,174	1,032	4,241
2002	892.9	789.5	1,041	993.9	3,718
2001	826.7	727.0	1,008	886.5	3,449

Earnings Per Share ($)

	1Q	2Q	3Q	4Q	Year
2006	0.45	0.38	0.93	E0.75	E2.90
2005	0.65	0.50	1.06	0.74	2.94
2004	0.62	0.46	1.03	0.75	2.85
2003	0.59	0.41	0.89	0.66	2.55
2002	0.48	0.36	0.78	0.54	2.16
2001	0.44	0.31	0.69	0.39	1.83

Fiscal year ended Dec. 31. Next earnings report expected: Early March. EPS Estimates based on S&P Operating Earnings; historical GAAP earnings are as reported.

Dividend Data (Dates: mm/dd Payment Date: mm/dd/yy)

Amount ($)	Date Decl.	Ex-Div. Date	Stk. of Record	Payment Date
0.056	01/24	02/22	02/24	03/15/06
0.056	05/18	05/30	06/01	06/15/06
0.056	07/11	08/23	08/25	09/15/06
0.056	10/05	11/17	11/21	12/15/06

Dividends have been paid since 1984. Source: Company reports.

Liz Claiborne Inc.

Business Summary October 20, 2006

CORPORATE OVERVIEW. Liz Claiborne is one of the largest U.S. apparel suppliers with a portfolio of approximately 46 apparel and accessory brands.

MARKET PROFILE. The women's apparel market represented 56% of 2005 domestic apparel retail purchases, or $101 billion, according to NPD Fashionworld consumer estimated data. The apparel market is fragmented, with national brands marketed by 20 companies accounting for about 30% of total apparel sales, and the remaining 70% comprised of smaller and/or private label "store" brands. The market is mature, with demand largely mirroring population growth and fashion trends accounting for a modicum of incremental volume. Deflationary pricing pressure is a function of channel competition and production steadily moving offshore to low-cost producers in India, Asia and China. S&P forecasts 2006 apparel sales increasing in the low single digits, generally in line with GDP growth, versus a 4% year-to-year advance in 2004 and 2005, and a 5% decline in 2003.

COMPETITIVE LANDSCAPE. By channel, specialty stores account for the largest share of apparel sales, at 30% in the fourth quarter of 2005, up from 29% in 2004's fourth quarter, according to NPD. Mass merchants (Wal-Mart and Target) came in second at 18%, up 100 basis points and department stores, came in third at 17%, down from their year ago number two spot and losing 200 basis points of market share. National chains (Sears and JC Penney) captured 15% of 2005 fourth quarter apparel sales and off-price retailers (TJX and Ross Stores) 8%. The remaining 12% is divided among factory outlets and direct and email pure plays. LIZ holds meaningful market shares in department stores and national chains, where it competes with Jones Apparel Group, Polo Ralph Lauren and VF Corp., as well as private label offerings, which garner about a third of total apparel purchases and are an important differentiator for retailers. LIZ also sells directly to consumers through 338 specialty retail stores and 321 outlet stores throughout the world as well as 646 international concession stores.

Company Financials

Per Share Data ($) Year Ended Dec. 31	**2005**	**2004**	**2003**	**2002**	**2001**	**2000**	**1999**	**1998**	**1997**	**1996**
Tangible Book Value	7.74	7.13	6.73	5.43	5.71	5.45	5.95	7.67	6.97	7.19
Cash Flow	4.12	3.95	3.51	3.06	2.79	2.43	2.11	1.71	1.64	1.37
Earnings	2.94	2.85	2.55	2.16	1.83	1.72	1.56	1.29	1.32	1.08
S&P Core Earnings	2.88	2.60	2.39	2.00	1.68	NA	NA	NA	NA	NA
Dividends	0.23	0.23	0.23	0.23	0.23	0.23	0.23	0.23	0.23	0.23
Payout Ratio	8%	8%	9%	10%	12%	13%	14%	18%	17%	21%
Prices:High	43.82	42.47	38.90	33.25	27.48	24.16	20.34	27.44	28.97	22.56
Prices:Low	33.70	32.09	26.23	23.55	18.00	15.47	15.44	12.50	19.06	13.13
P/E Ratio:High	15	15	15	15	15	14	13	21	22	21
P/E Ratio:Low	11	11	10	11	10	9	10	10	14	12
Income Statement Analysis (Million $)										
Revenue	4,848	4,633	4,241	3,718	3,449	3,104	2,807	2,535	2,413	2,218
Operating Income	652	628	575	493	780	402	368	340	323	278
Depreciation	128	116	105	96.4	101	77.0	67.8	55.8	46.0	42.9
Interest Expense	31.8	32.2	30.5	25.1	28.1	21.9	1.61	Nil	Nil	Nil
Pretax Income	491	480	438	362	300	288	302	267	293	249
Effective Tax Rate	35.4%	34.7%	36.2%	36.2%	36.0%	36.0%	36.2%	36.5%	37.0%	37.5%
Net Income	317	314	280	231	192	185	192	169	185	156
S&P Core Earnings	309	284	259	213	176	NA	NA	NA	NA	NA
Balance Sheet & Other Financial Data (Million $)										
Cash	343	393	344	276	161	54.4	37.9	230	138	529
Current Assets	1,457	1,509	1,348	1,203	1,106	911	859	1,075	1,057	1,142
Total Assets	3,152	3,030	2,607	2,296	1,951	1,512	1,412	1,393	1,305	1,383
Current Liabilities	608	638	527	591	447	358	352	363	328	326
Long Term Debt	418	485	440	378	387	269	116	Nil	Nil	1.00
Common Equity	2,003	1,812	1,600	1,286	1,056	834	902	981	922	1,020
Total Capital	2,478	2,359	2,094	1,705	1,480	1,139	1,044	999	932	1,030
Capital Expenditures	140	134	96.7	80.0	82.2	66.7	75.1	88.5	34.0	23.3
Cash Flow	445	429	385	328	294	262	260	225	231	199
Current Ratio	2.4	2.4	2.6	2.0	2.5	2.5	2.4	3.0	3.2	3.5
% Long Term Debt of Capitalization	16.9	20.6	21.0	22.2	26.1	23.6	11.1	Nil	Nil	0.1
% Net Income of Revenue	6.5	6.8	6.6	6.2	5.6	5.9	6.9	6.7	7.7	7.1
% Return on Assets	10.3	11.1	11.5	10.9	11.1	12.6	13.7	12.6	13.7	11.5
% Return on Equity	16.5	18.4	19.3	19.7	20.3	21.3	20.4	17.8	19.0	15.5

Data as orig reptd.; bef. results of disc opers/spec. items. Per share data adj. for stk. divs.; EPS diluted. E-Estimated. NA-Not Available. NM-Not Meaningful. NR-Not Ranked. UR-Under Review.

Office: 1441 Broadway, New York, NY 10018.
Telephone: 212-354-4900.
Email: investor_relations@liz.com
Website: http://www.lizclaiborne.com

Chrmn & CEO: P.R. Charron
Pres: T.F. Sullivan
SVP & CFO: M. Scarpa
SVP & CIO: J.J. Sullivan

Board of Directors: B. W. Aronson, D. A. Carp, P. R. Charron, R. J. Fernandez, M. Haben, N. J. Karch, K. P. Kopelman, K. Koplovitz, A. C. Martinez, O. R. Sockwell, P. E. Tierney, Jr.

Founded: 1976
Domicile: Delaware
Employees: 15,400

STANDARD &POOR'S

Lockheed Martin Corp

S&P Recommendation BUY ★★★★★

Price $84.61 (as of Oct 27, 2006)

12-Mo. Target Price $100.00

Investment Style Large-Cap Value

GICS Sector Industrials
Sub-Industry Aerospace & Defense

Comment This company is the world's largest military weapons manufacturer.

Key Stock Statistics (Source S&P, Vickers, company reports)

52-Wk Range	**$89.89–58.88**	S&P Oper. EPS 2006**E**	**5.50**	P/E on S&P Oper. EPS 2006**E**	**15.4**	Dividend Rate/Share	**$1.40**
Trailing 12-Month EPS	**$5.41**	S&P Oper. EPS 2007**E**	**5.70**	Common Shares Outstg. (M)	**423.9**	Yield (%)	**1.65**
Trailing 12-Month P/E	**15.6**	S&P Core EPS 2006**E**	**5.55**	Market Capitalization(B)	**$35.863**	Beta	**-0.31**
$10K Invested 5 Yrs Ago	**$18,146**	S&P Core EPS 2007**E**	**5.71**	Institutional Ownership (%)	**89**	S&P Credit Rating	**BBB+**

Price Performance

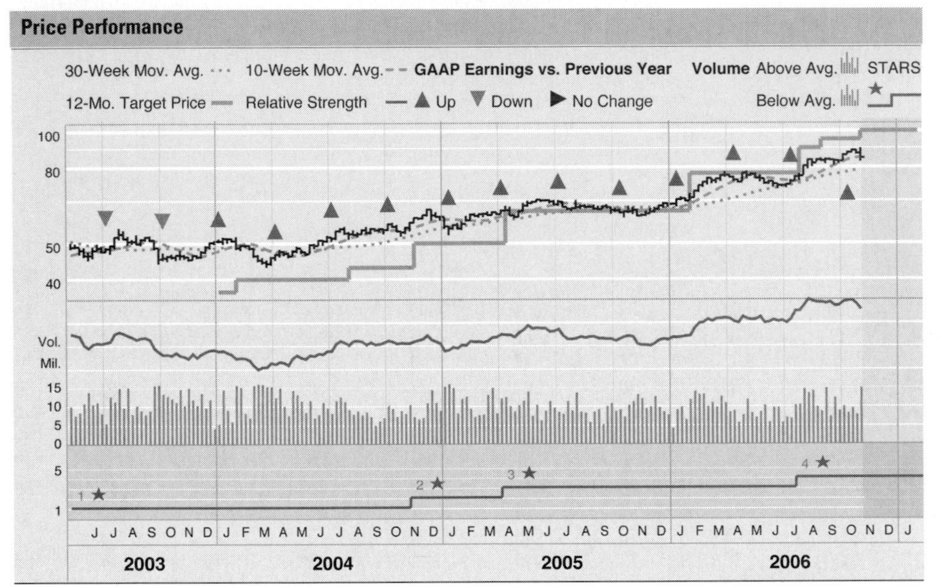

Options: ASE, CBOE, P, Ph

Highlights

- The 12-month target price for LMT has recently been changed to $100.00 from $95.00. The Highlights section of this Stock Report will be updated accordingly.

Investment Rationale/Risk

- The Investment Rationale/Risk section of this Stock Report will be updated shortly. For the latest News story on LMT from MarketScope, see below.

- 10/24/06 12:46 pm EDT... S&P REITERATES BUY RECOMMENDATION ON SHARES OF LOCKHEED MARTIN (LMT 89.59****): Q3 EPS of $1.46 after $0.16 in unusual gains, vs. year-ago $0.96, is well above our $1.15 estimate on a 4.4% sales rise. Backlog rose 4.1% and operating profit improved significantly in all segments. We continue to see strong prospects for LMT in electronics systems, IT outsourcing, aerospace, and space systems. We are raising our '06 EPS estimate by $0.33 to $5.50, and '07's by $0.40 to $5.70. We are also boosting our 12-month target price, by $5 to $100, based on a 17.5X P/E multiple applied to our '07 estimate, in line with LMT's 10-year historical average P/E. / R.Tortoriello

Qualitative Risk Assessment

LOW | **MEDIUM** | HIGH

Our risk assessment reflects the company's leading position in military markets and what we view as a healthy balance sheet, with long-term debt representing less than 40% of LMT's total capitalization at 2005 year end. However, our risk evaluation also factors in the highly cyclical nature of Lockheed's business, especially its dependence on government defense programs.

Quantitative Evaluations

S&P Quality Ranking **B**

D | C | B- | **B** | B+ | A- | A | A+

Relative Strength Rank **MODERATE**

37

LOWEST = 1 HIGHEST = 99

Revenue/Earnings Data

Revenue (Million $)

	1Q	2Q	3Q	4Q	Year
2006	9,214	9,961	9,605	--	--
2005	8,488	9,295	9,201	10,229	37,213
2004	8,347	8,776	8,438	9,965	35,526
2003	7,059	7,709	8,078	8,978	31,824
2002	5,966	6,290	6,542	7,780	26,578
2001	4,747	5,688	6,221	7,334	23,990

Earnings Per Share ($)

2006	1.34	1.34	1.46	**E**1.37	**E**5.50
2005	0.83	1.02	0.96	1.29	4.10
2004	0.65	0.66	0.69	0.83	2.83
2003	0.55	0.54	0.48	0.77	2.34
2002	0.50	0.78	0.66	-0.76	1.18
2001	0.30	0.34	-0.12	-0.34	0.18

Fiscal year ended Dec. 31. Next earnings report expected: Late January. EPS Estimates based on S&P Operating Earnings; historical GAAP earnings are as reported.

Dividend Data (Dates: mm/dd Payment Date: mm/dd/yy)

Amount ($)	Date Decl.	Ex-Div. Date	Stk. of Record	Payment Date
0.300	01/26	02/27	03/01	03/31/06
0.300	04/27	05/30	06/01	06/30/06
0.300	06/22	08/30	09/01	09/29/06
0.350	09/28	11/29	12/01	12/29/06

Dividends have been paid since 1995. Source: Company reports.

Lockheed Martin Corp

Business Summary August 29, 2006

CORPORATE OVERVIEW. Lockheed Martin is the world's largest military weapons maker. During 2005, the company derived 85% of its net sales from the U.S. government, including both Department of Defense and non-Department of Defense agencies.

Lockheed Martin conducts business through five operating segments. The Aeronautics segment (31% of gross revenues; 29% of operating profits; 8.5% profit margins in 2005) primarily makes fighter and military transport planes. Principal production programs consist of the C-130J military transport and the F-16 fighter. The segment's primary development programs include the F-35 Joint Strike fighter and the F-22 fighter. Electronic Systems (28%; 32%; 10.5%) primarily makes land-, sea- and air-based missiles. Other offerings include various electronic surveillance and reconnaissance systems. Space Systems (18%; 18%; 8.9%) mostly makes satellites, strategic and defensive missile systems and launch services. Integrated Systems & Solutions (11%; 11%; 8.8%) mainly provides networking systems that coordinate the U.S. military's various communications functions. Information & Technology Services (11%; 10%; 8.8%) primarily provides various management, engineering and information technology services to the U.S. government.

MARKET PROFILE. Customer requirements for defense and related advanced technology systems for 2006 and beyond will likely continue to be affected by the global war on terrorism. That effort has focused greater attention on homeland security and better communication and integration between law enforcement, civil government agencies and military services. However, U.S. defense posture has been moving toward a more joint capabilities-based structure, with greater force mobility, stronger space capabilities, enhanced missile defense and improved information systems capabilities and security.

In FY 07, President Bush is seeking to both reduce the federal budget and maintain the battle against global terrorism. As a result, the Department of Defense budget is slated to grow at a slower rate than the past few years. The Future Years Defense Plan for FY 07 through FY11 projects growth from the $439 billion Department of Defense budget for FY 07 to $502 billion in FY 11. These estimates do not include any allowance for ongoing military operations in Iraq, Afghanistan and the global war on terrorism, which are expected to be addressed through annual supplemental appropriations as required.

Company Financials

Per Share Data ($) Year Ended Dec. 31	2005	2004	2003	2002	2001	2000	1999	1998	1997	1996
Tangible Book Value	NM	NM	NM	NM	NM	NM	NM	NM	NM	NM
Cash Flow	5.68	4.39	3.69	2.40	2.08	1.36	3.30	5.27	5.37	6.73
Earnings	4.10	2.83	2.34	1.18	0.18	-1.05	1.92	2.63	3.05	3.40
S&P Core Earnings	4.11	3.23	2.20	-0.78	-2.29	NA	NA	NA	NA	NA
Dividends	1.05	0.91	0.58	0.44	0.44	0.44	0.88	0.82	0.80	0.78
Payout Ratio	26%	32%	25%	37%	NM	NM	46%	31%	26%	23%
Prices:High	65.46	61.77	58.95	71.52	52.98	37.58	46.00	58.94	56.72	48.31
Prices:Low	52.54	43.10	40.64	45.85	31.00	16.50	16.38	41.00	39.13	36.50
P/E Ratio:High	16	22	25	61	NM	NM	24	22	19	14
P/E Ratio:Low	13	15	17	39	NM	NM	9	16	13	11
Income Statement Analysis (Million $)										
Revenue	37,213	35,526	31,824	26,578	23,990	25,329	25,530	26,266	28,069	26,875
Operating Income	3,242	2,624	2,585	2,507	2,366	2,582	2,634	3,357	3,349	3,478
Depreciation	705	656	609	558	823	968	969	1,005	1,052	1,197
Interest Expense	370	425	487	581	700	919	809	861	842	700
Pretax Income	2,616	1,664	1,532	577	188	286	1,200	1,661	1,937	2,033
Effective Tax Rate	30.2%	23.9%	31.3%	7.63%	58.0%	NM	38.6%	39.7%	32.9%	33.7%
Net Income	1,825	1,266	1,053	533	79.0	-424	737	1,001	1,300	1,347
S&P Core Earnings	1,830	1,448	994	-353	-989	NA	NA	NA	NA	NA
Balance Sheet & Other Financial Data (Million $)										
Cash	2,244	1,060	1,010	2,738	912	1,505	455	285	Nil	Nil
Current Assets	10,529	8,953	9,401	10,626	10,778	11,259	10,696	10,611	10,105	9,940
Total Assets	27,744	25,554	26,175	25,758	27,654	30,349	30,012	28,744	28,361	29,257
Current Liabilities	9,428	8,566	8,893	9,821	9,689	10,175	8,812	10,267	9,189	8,704
Long Term Debt	4,784	5,104	6,072	6,217	7,422	9,065	11,427	8,957	10,528	10,188
Common Equity	7,867	7,021	6,756	5,865	6,443	7,160	6,361	6,137	5,176	5,856
Total Capital	12,651	12,125	12,828	12,082	14,857	16,961	17,788	15,094	15,704	17,044
Capital Expenditures	865	769	687	662	619	500	669	697	750	737
Cash Flow	2,530	1,922	1,662	1,091	902	544	1,266	2,006	2,299	2,544
Current Ratio	1.1	1.0	1.1	1.1	1.1	1.1	1.2	1.0	1.1	1.1
% Long Term Debt of Capitalization	37.8	42.1	47.3	51.5	50.0	53.4	64.2	59.3	67.0	59.7
% Net Income of Revenue	4.9	3.6	3.3	2.0	0.3	NM	2.9	3.8	4.6	5.0
% Return on Assets	6.8	4.9	4.0	2.0	0.3	NM	2.5	3.5	4.5	5.8
% Return on Equity	24.5	18.4	16.7	8.7	1.2	NM	11.8	17.7	22.6	22.8

Data as orig reptd.; bef. results of disc opers/spec. items. Per share data adj. for stk. divs.; EPS diluted. E-Estimated. NA-Not Available. NM-Not Meaningful. NR-Not Ranked. UR-Under Review.

Office: 6801 Rockledge Drive, Bethesda, MD 20817.
Telephone: 301-897-6000.
Website: http://www.lockheedmartin.com
Chrmn, Pres & CEO: R.J. Stevens

EVP & CFO: C.E. Kubasik
SVP & General Counsel: J.B. Comey
VP & Treas: A.G. Van Schaick
VP & Cntlr: M.T. Stanislav

Board of Directors: E. C. Aldridge, Jr., N. D. Archibald, M. C. Bennett, J. O. Ellis, Jr., G. S. King, J. M. Loy, D. H. McCorkindale, E. F. Murphy, J. W. Ralston, F. Savage, J. M. Schneider, A. Stevens, R. J. Stevens, J. R. Ukropina, D. C. Yearley

Founded: 1909
Domicile: Maryland
Employees: 135,000

STANDARD &POOR'S

Loews Corp

S&P Recommendation HOLD ★★★★★ **Price** $38.92 (as of Oct 31, 2006) **12-Mo. Target Price** $40.00 **Investment Style** Large-Cap Value

GICS Sector Financials
Sub-Industry Multi-line Insurance

Comment This conglomerate includes holdings in property/casualty insurance, tobacco, offshore drilling, hotels, and natural gas pipelines.

Key Stock Statistics (Source S&P, Vickers, company reports)

52-Wk Range	**$39.55–30.42**	S&P Oper. EPS 2006**E**	**3.68**	P/E on S&P Oper. EPS 2006**E**	**10.6**	Dividend Rate/Share	**$0.25**
Trailing 12-Month EPS	**$2.20**	S&P Oper. EPS 2007**E**	**4.30**	Common Shares Outstg. (M)	**550.7**	Yield (%)	**0.64**
Trailing 12-Month P/E	**17.7**	S&P Core EPS 2006**E**	**3.66**	Market Capitalization(B)	**$21.434**	Beta	**0.95**
$10K Invested 5 Yrs Ago	**$23,580**	S&P Core EPS 2007**E**	**4.27**	Institutional Ownership (%)	**66**	S&P Credit Rating	**A**

Price Performance

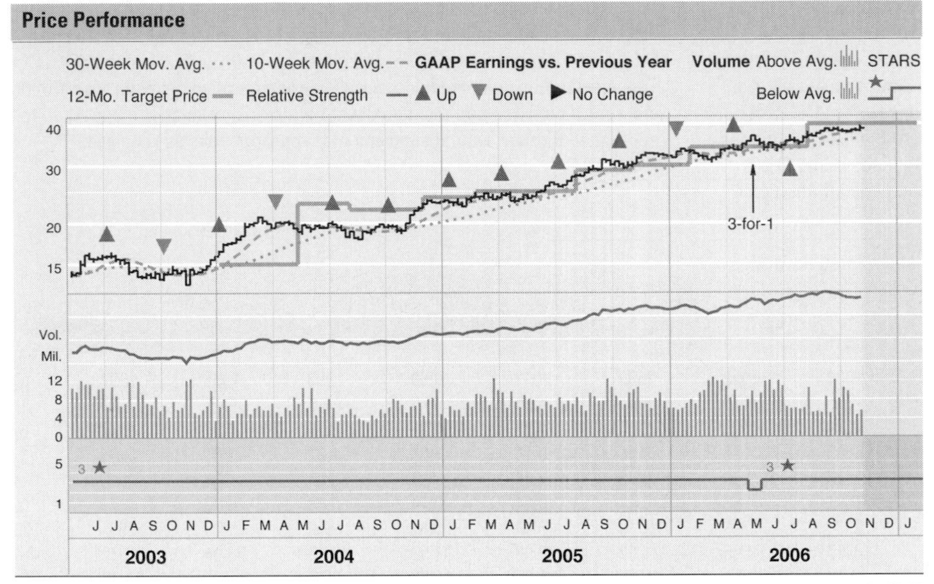

Options: ASE, CBOE

Analysis prepared by **Frank Braden** on September 28, 2006, when the stock traded at **$ 38.15**.

Highlights

- We project strong growth in operating earnings for the CNA Financial subsidiary in 2006, on a higher retention ratio, an increased focus on cross-selling opportunities, and a further reduction in the combined ratio due to continuing expense control efforts. We see 2006 revenues rising 4.9% at Lorillard, from expected moderate growth in discount volumes and higher average pricing for premium brands.
- We expect Diamond Offshore (DO) to benefit from the uptrend for dayrates in the deepwater and midwater semisubmersible markets, as near full effective utilization should benefit pricing. We forecast solid operating earnings growth for Boardwalk Pipeline Partners (BWP), primarily on our estimate of expanding natural gas storage capacity and improved operating efficiencies from the Gulf South acquisition. We see operating earnings for the hotels segment benefiting from a stronger travel and leisure market, leading to higher revenue per available room (RevPAR).
- Our operating EPS estimate for 2006 is $3.65, including projected stock option expense. For 2007, we see operating EPS of $4.30.

Investment Rationale/Risk

- Recent favorable court decisions in tobacco legislation have lowered the risk for potentially large payouts by the cigarette industry, in our view. We are encouraged by recent share repurchases and expect buybacks to continue throughout the year. We believe the company is well positioned to make opportunistic investments, with $3.9 billion in total cash and investments.
- Risks to our recommendation and target price include legal and regulatory risks associated with tobacco sales; extended periods of price promotions in the cigarette market; decreases in the global smoking population; falling oil prices; and higher-than-projected catastrophic, asbestos and environmental losses for CNA.
- Our 12-month target price of $40 is based on a sum-of-the-parts valuation in which we apply multiples of roughly 10.5X, 16X, 18X, 18X and 23X for the CNA, Lorillard (CG), BWP, DO and Loews Hotels' subsidiaries, respectively, to our 2006 operating EPS estimates. We adjust the combined value for net corporate debt, and apply a 15% discount to account for Tisch family control.

Qualitative Risk Assessment

LOW | **MEDIUM** | HIGH

Our risk assessment reflects LTR's diversified group of holdings, offset by risks inherent in the tobacco, offshore drilling, and insurance industries, including regulation risks, litigation risks, and catastrophic events. We are concerned about significant stock holdings, voting influence, and management control by members of the Tisch family.

Quantitative Evaluations

S&P Quality Ranking **B-**

D | C | **B-** | B | B+ | A- | A | A+

Relative Strength Rank **MODERATE**

54

LOWEST = 1 HIGHEST = 99

Revenue/Earnings Data

Revenue (Million $)

	1Q	2Q	3Q	4Q	Year
2006	4,245	4,277	--	--	--
2005	3,741	4,031	4,138	4,108	16,018
2004	3,491	3,915	3,785	4,051	15,242
2003	3,949	4,250	3,940	4,336	16,461
2002	4,792	4,652	4,079	3,972	17,495
2001	5,104	4,319	4,841	5,154	19,417

Earnings Per Share ($)

	1Q	2Q	3Q	4Q	Year
2006	0.86	0.85	**E**0.85	**E**0.99	**E**3.68
2005	0.53	0.68	0.42	0.07	1.69
2004	0.02	0.66	0.40	0.80	1.88
2003	0.29	0.34	-2.53	0.60	-1.30
2002	0.46	0.28	0.35	0.40	1.50
2001	0.89	-2.39	0.28	0.33	-0.92

Fiscal year ended Dec. 31. Next earnings report expected: NA. EPS Estimates based on S&P Operating Earnings; historical GAAP earnings are as reported.

Dividend Data (Dates: mm/dd Payment Date: mm/dd/yy)

Amount ($)	Date Decl.	Ex-Div. Date	Stk. of Record	Payment Date
0.150	11/15	11/29	12/01	12/12/05
0.150	02/15	02/27	03/01	03/13/06
3-for-1 Stk.	04/11	05/09	04/24	05/08/06
0.063	08/08	08/30	09/01	09/11/06

Dividends have been paid since 1967. Source: Company reports.

Loews Corp

Business Summary September 28, 2006

CORPORATE OVERVIEW. Loews Corp. is a holding company with interests in property/casualty insurance (CNA Financial Corp., 89% stake), cigarettes (Lorillard Inc.), hotels (Loews Hotels Holding Corp.), offshore oil and gas drilling (Diamond Offshore Drilling, Inc., 54% stake), interstate natural gas pipelines (Boardwalk Pipeline Partners, LP, 85% stake), watches and clocks (Bulova Corp.), and shipping (Majestic Shipping Corp., which holds a 49% stake in Hellespont Shipping Corp.).

Loews Corp. maintains a two class common stock structure. Carolina Group stock (NYSE: CG) is a tracking stock intended to reflect the economic performance of a defined group of assets and liabilities referred to as the Carolina Group, which includes Loews' equity interest in Lorillard Inc., $1.6 billion of notional intergroup debt owed by Carolina Group to the Loews Group, and any and all liabilities, costs and expenses arising out of or related to tobacco-related businesses. The Loews Group consists of all of the company's assets and liabilities other than the economic interest in the Carolina Group represented by the Carolina Group tracking stock and includes as an asset the notional intergroup debt of the Carolina Group. The Carolina Group and Loews Group are not separate legal entities, and holders of LTR's common stock and Carolina Group stock are both shareholders of Loews Corp. and are subject to the risks related to an equity investment in Loews Corp. At December 31, 2005, CG tracking stock represented a 45% economic interest in the Carolina Group.

CNA Financial Corp. (NYSE: CNA; 62% of consolidated total revenue in 2005) is an insurance holding company with subsidiaries that primarily consist of property and casualty insurance companies. Lorillard, Inc. (23%) is a leading U.S. producer of tobacco products, with principal products marketed under the brand names Newport, Kent, True, Maverick, and Old Gold. The Loews Hotels division (2.2%) owns and/or operates 18 hotels in the U.S. and Canada. Diamond Offshore (NYSE: DO; 8.1%) operates 44 offshore drilling rigs that are chartered on a contract basis for fixed terms by energy exploration companies. Boardwalk Pipeline (NYSE: BWP; 3.6%) owns and operates two interstate natural gas pipeline systems, Gulf South Pipeline and Texas Gas Transmission. Bulova (1.2%) distributes and sells watches and clocks. Other activities accounted for about 1.9% of consolidated total revenue in 2005.

Company Financials

Per Share Data ($) Year Ended Dec. 31	**2005**	**2004**	**2003**	**2002**	**2001**	**2000**	**1999**	**1998**	**1997**	**1996**
Tangible Book Value	68.86	21.35	NM	19.88	16.23	18.28	15.24	14.24	12.92	11.84
Operating Earnings	NA	NA	NA	1.71	-2.27	1.90	1.01	0.66	1.38	NA
Earnings	1.69	1.88	-1.30	1.50	-0.92	3.15	0.80	0.68	1.15	1.99
S&P Core Earnings	1.49	2.17	-2.00	2.63	-2.47	NA	NA	NA	NA	NA
Dividends	0.20	0.20	0.20	0.20	0.19	0.17	0.17	0.17	0.17	0.17
Relative Payout	12%	11%	NM	13%	NM	5%	21%	25%	14%	8%
Prices:High	32.90	23.87	16.49	20.77	24.17	34.98	17.42	18.04	19.27	15.98
Prices:Low	22.35	16.36	12.75	12.50	13.68	12.75	9.75	13.00	14.25	12.08
P/E Ratio:High	19	13	NM	14	NM	11	22	27	17	8
P/E Ratio:Low	13	9	NM	8	NM	4	12	19	12	6

Income Statement Analysis (Million $)										
Life Insurance in Force	20,548	56,645	388,968	437,751	497,732	534,781	469,990	394,394	311,598	237,009
Premium Income:Life A & H	704	901	2,275	3,382	4,351	4,549	4,502	4,391	3,431	3,347
Premium Income:Casualty/Property.	6,865	7,304	6,935	6,828	5,010	6,923	8,775	8,979	NA	10,127
Net Investment Income	2,099	1,869	1,732	1,867	2,145	2,388	2,175	2,558	2,442	2,476
Total Revenue	16,018	15,242	16,461	17,495	19,417	21,338	21,465	21,208	20,139	20,442
Pretax Income	1,847	1,822	-751	1,647	-813	3,206	945	1,078	1,593	2,408
Net Operating Income	NA	NA	NA	1,099	-1,328	1,134	658	452	954	14,491
Net Income	1,193	1,231	-468	983	-536	1,877	521	465	794	1,384
S&P Core Earnings	831	1,205	-1,112	1,594	-1,447	NA	NA	NA	NA	NA

Balance Sheet & Other Financial Data (Million $)										
Cash & Equivalent	153	220	1.90	185	181	195	184	287	498	306
Premiums Due	15,314	18,807	20,468	16,601	19,453	15,302	13,529	13,071	NA	NA
Investment Assets:Bonds	33,381	3,502	28,781	27,434	31,191	27,244	27,924	31,409	30,723	29,478
Investment Assets:Stocks	1,107	664	888	1,121	1,646	2,683	4,024	2,381	1,163	1,136
Investment Assets:Loans	Nil	Nil	Nil	NA	NA	NA	NA	NA	NA	NA
Investment Assets:Total	45,396	44,299	1,630	40,137	41,159	40,396	40,633	42,705	41,618	39,917
Deferred Policy Costs	1,197	1,268	2,533	2,551	2,424	2,418	2,436	2,422	2,142	1,854
Total Assets	70,676	73,750	2,725	70,520	75,251	70,877	69,464	70,906	69,577	67,683
Debt	4,609	5,980	2,032	5,652	5,920	6,040	5,706	5,967	5,906	4,371
Common Equity	45,525	45,428	-729	11,235	9,649	11,191	9,978	10,200	9,664	8,731
Combined Loss-Expense Ratio	120.3	105.9	146.6	110.3	158.6	113.6	120.9	114.2	108.2	108.4
% Return on Revenue	7.4	8.1	14.2	5.6	NM	8.8	2.4	2.2	4.5	6.8
% Return on Equity	2.6	2.8	NM	8.1	NM	4.9	5.2	4.7	8.6	16.3
% Investment Yield	2.6	4.3	4.2	4.6	5.2	5.9	5.2	6.1	5.9	6.2

Data as orig reptd.; bef. results of disc opers/spec. items. Per share data adj. for stk. divs.; EPS diluted. E-Estimated. NA-Not Available. NM-Not Meaningful. NR-Not Ranked. UR-Under Review.

Office: 667 Madison Ave, New York, NY 10021-8087.
Telephone: 212-521-2000.
Website: http://www.loews.com
Co-Chrmn: A.H. Tisch

Co-Chrmn: J.M. Tisch
Pres & CEO: J.S. Tisch
SVP & CFO: P.W. Keegan
SVP, Secy & General Counsel: G.W. Garson

Investor Contact: D. Daugherty (212-521-2788)
Board of Directors: A. E. Berman, J. L. Bower, C. M. Diker, P. J. Fribourg, W. L. Harris, P. A. Laskawy, G. R. Scott, A. H. Tisch, J. S. Tisch, J. M. Tisch

Founded: 1954
Domicile: Delaware
Employees: 21,600

Louisiana-Pacific Corp

STANDARD &POOR'S

S&P Recommendation HOLD ★★★★★	Price $20.31 (as of Oct 27, 2006)	12-Mo. Target Price $21.00	Investment Style Mid-Cap Value

GICS Sector Materials
Sub-Industry Forest Products

Comment This major forest products company produces oriented strand board, plywood, lumber and other building products.

Key Stock Statistics (Source S&P, Vickers, company reports)

52-Wk Range	$29.75–18.05	S&P Oper. EPS 2006E	1.40	P/E on S&P Oper. EPS 2006E	14.5	Dividend Rate/Share	$0.60
Trailing 12-Month EPS	$2.23	S&P Oper. EPS 2007E	0.30	Common Shares Outstg. (M)	105.2	Yield (%)	2.95
Trailing 12-Month P/E	9.1	S&P Core EPS 2006E	1.40	Market Capitalization(B)	$2.137	Beta	1.81
$10K Invested 5 Yrs Ago	$31,696	S&P Core EPS 2007E	0.30	Institutional Ownership (%)	90	S&P Credit Rating	BBB-

Price Performance

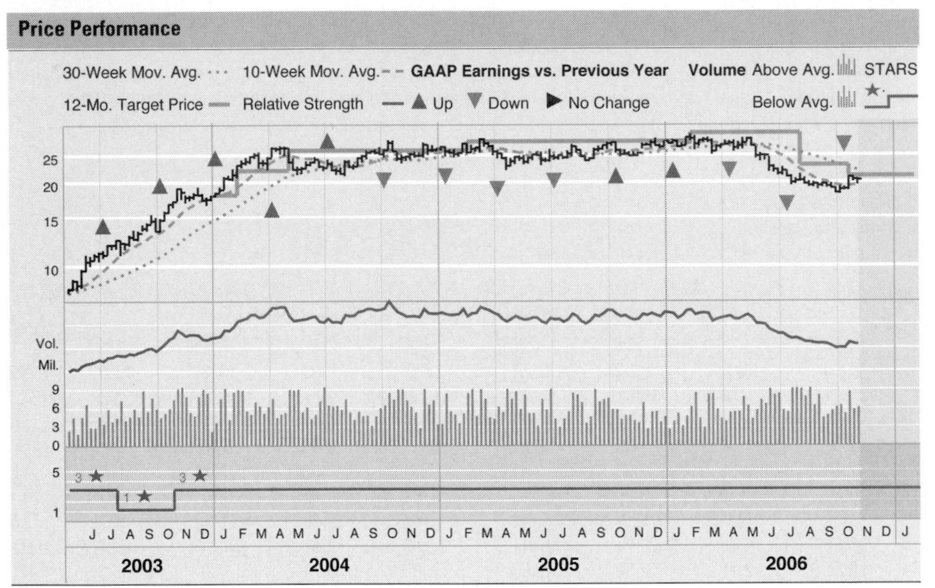

Options: ASE

Analysis prepared by **Stuart J. Benway, CFA** on October 11, 2006, when the stock traded at **$ 19.09**.

Highlights

- We project that revenues will fall about 15% in 2006, mainly due to lower price realizations for oriented strand board (OSB), as well as lower volumes in panels, decking, and laminated veneer lumber. These factors are expected to lead to a further 15%-20% revenue decline in 2007. A new oriented strand lumber product is unlikely to contribute meaningfully to revenues until 2008.
- For 2006, S&P's forecast is for an 11.6% decline in housing starts after several years of growth, and for 2007, we see an additional 14% decrease. OSB has steadily taken share from plywood in the structural panel market, and this trend is expected to continue. As a result, we believe producers will build additional capacity in the coming years, leading to an imbalance between supply and demand and lower prices for OSB. We believe LPX's effective tax rate will rise significantly this year due to the absence of repatriated foreign earnings.
- We estimate 2006 operating EPS of $1.50, and for 2007, we project $0.40. Our operating EPS estimates include projected stock option expense.

Investment Rationale/Risk

- As a major producer of OSB, siding, and engineered wood products, LPX results are closely tied to the residential construction sector, in which we expect a further downturn in coming quarters. OSB prices have slumped over 50% in the past year, and with significant additional capacity expected to come onstream in 2007, we see little recovery. Nevertheless, we consider LPX's balance sheet to be strong.
- Risks to our recommendation and target price include a greater than anticipated decline in housing starts and OSB prices and a renewed escalation in energy and raw material costs. In addition, since 40% of the company's cost of sales are in Canadian dollars, a further strengthening of that currency versus the U.S. dollar would hurt earnings.
- Our DCF model, which assumes a decline in free cash flow generation in both 2006 and 2007, before growth resumes in 2008, a 10% WACC, and 3% growth in perpetuity, shows intrinsic value of $21, which is our 12-month target price.

Qualitative Risk Assessment

LOW | **MEDIUM** | HIGH

LPX's business is concentrated in the residential construction market and it is therefore subject to movements in interest rates and employment growth. However, some of its business involves the remodeling sector, which is less cyclical, and it has high cash levels on its balance sheet, in our opinion.

Quantitative Evaluations

S&P Quality Ranking B

D | C | B- | **B** | B+ | A- | A | A+

Relative Strength Rank MODERATE

47

LOWEST = 1 HIGHEST = 99

Revenue/Earnings Data

Revenue (Million $)

	1Q	2Q	3Q	4Q	Year
2006	678.3	652.7	534.5	--	--
2005	680.0	692.0	621.3	624.2	2,599
2004	695.3	825.3	740.5	588.3	2,849
2003	413.1	478.5	674.8	733.8	2,300
2002	596.7	448.9	502.0	431.6	1,943
2001	558.5	649.8	635.5	515.9	2,360

Earnings Per Share ($)

2006	0.80	0.52	0.09	E-0.01	E1.40
2005	0.95	0.94	1.59	0.87	4.34
2004	1.03	1.72	0.96	0.16	3.87
2003	0.02	0.09	1.03	1.54	2.67
2002	-0.03	0.07	0.18	-0.44	-0.21
2001	-0.86	-0.09	-0.02	-0.68	-1.64

Fiscal year ended Dec. 31. Next earnings report expected: Early February. EPS Estimates based on S&P Operating Earnings; historical GAAP earnings are as reported.

Dividend Data (Dates: mm/dd Payment Date: mm/dd/yy)

Amount ($)	Date Decl.	Ex-Div. Date	Stk. of Record	Payment Date
0.125	11/07	11/16	11/18	12/01/05
0.150	02/06	02/13	02/15	03/01/06
0.150	05/05	05/15	05/17	06/01/06
0.150	08/07	08/15	08/17	09/01/06

Dividends have been paid since 2004. Source: Company reports.

Louisiana-Pacific Corp

Business Summary October 11, 2006

CORPORATE OVERVIEW. Louisiana-Pacific is one of North America's largest oriented strand board (OSB) producers, and also manufactures wood siding and engineered wood products. Its products are used primarily in new home construction, repair and remodeling, and manufactured housing. The company's main customers are wholesale distribution companies, building materials professional dealers, retail home centers, and manufactured housing producers. The OSB segment (60% of 2005 sales) had 14 plants with a combined annual capacity of 6.1 billion square feet at the end of 2004. The siding segment (17% of 2005 sales) produces and markets wood siding and related accessories, interior hardboard products and specialty OSB products. LPX's engineered wood segment (17% of sales) manufactures and distributes I-joists and laminated veneer lumber (LVL) and other related products. Other products (6% of sales) includes composite decking, decorative molding and Chilean OSB operations.

MARKET PROFILE. Most of the markets in which LPX competes are cyclical, capital-intensive and competitive. Demand for the company's products is dependent on a variety of factors, including new residential construction activity, home repair and remodeling activity, changes in economic conditions, interest rates, population growth, and weather conditions. Prices for the company's products have historically been volatile, and, despite its high market share, we believe the company has limited influence over the timing and extent of price changes for its products. OSB is made from wood strands arranged in layers and bonded with resin. It serves many of the same uses as unsanded plywood, including roof decking, sidewall sheathing and floor underlayment, but can be produced at a significantly lower cost. It is estimated that OSB accounts for approximately 58% of structural panel consumption, with plywood accounting for the remainder. LPX estimates the overall North American structural panel market at 45 billion square feet, of which the OSB market comprises an estimated 27 billion square feet. Based on its production capacity of 5.6 billion square feet, LPX accounted for 21% of the OSB market and 12% of the overall North American structural panel market in 2005.

Company Financials

Per Share Data ($) Year Ended Dec. 31	**2005**	**2004**	**2003**	**2002**	**2001**	**2000**	**1999**	**1998**	**1997**	**1996**
Tangible Book Value	16.66	13.47	9.46	6.73	7.49	9.29	9.65	10.84	11.09	12.70
Cash Flow	5.57	5.17	3.93	1.06	-0.01	1.64	3.51	1.73	0.76	-0.08
Earnings	4.34	3.87	2.67	-0.21	-1.64	-0.13	2.04	0.02	-0.94	-1.87
S&P Core Earnings	4.35	3.91	1.89	-0.63	-1.82	NA	NA	NA	NA	NA
Dividends	0.48	0.30	Nil	Nil	0.24	0.56	0.56	0.56	0.56	0.56
Payout Ratio	11%	8%	Nil	Nil	NM	NM	27%	NM	NM	NM
Prices:High	28.73	28.31	19.25	12.55	13.95	15.81	24.88	24.19	25.88	28.13
Prices:Low	22.00	17.50	7.10	5.35	5.46	7.06	11.38	16.38	17.00	19.63
P/E Ratio:High	7	7	7	NM	NM	NM	12	NM	NM	NM
P/E Ratio:Low	5	5	3	NM	NM	NM	6	NM	NM	NM
Income Statement Analysis (Million $)										
Revenue	2,599	2,849	2,300	1,943	2,360	2,933	2,879	2,297	2,403	2,486
Operating Income	667	913	602	142	280	284	533	260	95.4	223
Depreciation	135	144	135	132	170	184	156	185	184	192
Interest Expense	54.6	65.3	88.5	95.8	95.6	81.0	47.9	37.5	30.9	21.3
Pretax Income	537	703	517	-18.1	-289	-25.3	357	14.0	-150	-327
Effective Tax Rate	11.4%	39.8%	45.1%	NM	NM	NM	39.1%	112.9%	NM	NM
Net Income	476	424	284	-21.5	-172	-13.8	217	2.00	-102	-201
S&P Core Earnings	478	430	202	-63.8	-189	NA	NA	NA	NA	NA
Balance Sheet & Other Financial Data (Million $)										
Cash	608	545	926	137	61.6	38.1	116	127	31.9	27.8
Current Assets	1,797	1,604	1,325	491	493	654	739	612	597	579
Total Assets	3,598	3,451	3,204	2,773	3,017	3,375	3,488	2,519	2,578	2,589
Current Liabilities	346	440	290	273	310	378	541	367	319	345
Long Term Debt	735	622	1,021	1,070	1,152	1,184	1,015	460	572	459
Common Equity	2,086	1,780	1,410	1,132	1,081	2,590	1,360	1,223	1,286	1,428
Total Capital	3,198	2,920	2,838	2,418	2,469	4,108	2,375	1,886	2,037	2,050
Capital Expenditures	174	148	83.6	44.3	69.2	188	88.3	77.8	205	266
Cash Flow	611	567	419	110	-1.40	171	373	187	82.1	-9.00
Current Ratio	5.2	3.6	4.6	1.8	1.6	1.7	1.4	1.7	1.9	1.7
% Long Term Debt of Capitalization	23.0	21.3	36.0	44.3	46.7	28.8	42.7	24.4	28.1	22.4
% Net Income of Revenue	18.3	14.9	12.3	NM	NM	NM	7.5	0.1	NM	NM
% Return on Assets	13.5	12.7	9.5	NM	NM	NM	7.2	0.1	NM	NM
% Return on Equity	24.3	27.0	22.3	NM	NM	NM	16.8	0.2	NM	NM

Data as orig reptd.; bef. results of disc opers/spec. items. Per share data adj. for stk. divs.; EPS diluted. E-Estimated. NA-Not Available. NM-Not Meaningful. NR-Not Ranked. UR-Under Review.

Office: 414 Union St Ste 2000, Nashville, TN 37219-1711.
Telephone: 615-986-5600.
Website: http://www.lpcorp.com
Chrmn: E.G. Cook

CEO: R.W. Frost
EVP & CFO: C.M. Stevens
Investor Contact: B. Barckley (615-986-5600)

Board of Directors: E. G. Cook, A. W. Dunham, D. K. Frierson, R. W. Frost, P. W. Hansen, J. C. Kerr, K. M. Landgraf, D. E. McCoy, C. D. Watson

Founded: 1972
Domicile: Delaware
Employees: 5,600

STANDARD &POOR'S

Lowe's Companies Inc.

S&P Recommendation BUY ★★★★★

Price $30.34 (as of Oct 27, 2006)

12-Mo. Target Price $37.00

Investment Style Large-Cap Growth

GICS Sector Consumer Discretionary
Sub-Industry Home Improvement Retail

Comment This company retails building materials and supplies, lumber, hardware and appliances through more than 1,250 stores in 49 states.

Key Stock Statistics (Source S&P, Vickers, company reports)

52-Wk Range	$34.85–26.15	S&P Oper. EPS 2007E	2.01	P/E on S&P Oper. EPS 2007E	15.1	Dividend Rate/Share	$0.20
Trailing 12-Month EPS	$1.97	S&P Oper. EPS 2008E	2.26	Common Shares Outstg. (M)	1,527.9	Yield (%)	0.66
Trailing 12-Month P/E	15.4	S&P Core EPS 2007E	2.01	Market Capitalization(B)	$46.357	Beta	1.00
$10K Invested 5 Yrs Ago	$17,733	S&P Core EPS 2008E	2.26	Institutional Ownership (%)	85	S&P Credit Rating	A+

Price Performance

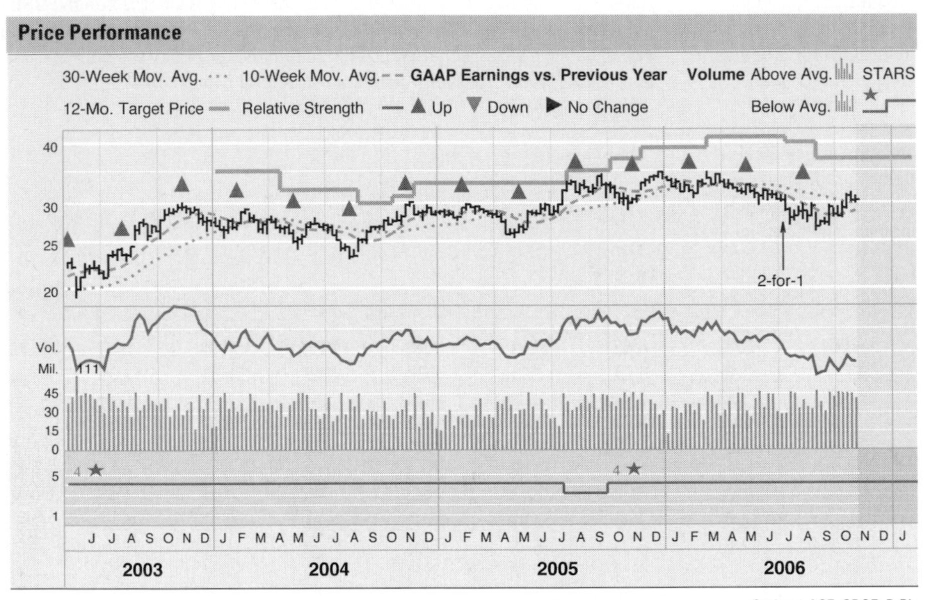

Options: ASE, CBOE, P, Ph

Analysis prepared by **Michael Souers** on October 04, 2006, when the stock traded at **$ 29.56**.

Highlights

- We forecast sales growth of between 10% and 12% in FY 07 (Jan.), driven by an estimated 155 net store openings, reflecting about a 12% increase in total square footage. We look for same-store sales to rise 2%-3%, on gains in average ticket, driven by improved merchandise assortments and healthy do-it-yourself (DIY) activity.
- We think lower sourcing costs and an improved product mix will largely be offset by higher distribution and payroll-related expenses. With economies of scale from continued sales growth only partly offset by increased compensation and advertising expenses, we see FY 07 operating margins widening by 10 to 30 basis points.
- We project slightly lower interest expense, taxes at an effective rate of 38.5%, and about 2% fewer shares outstanding, reflecting LOW's active share repurchase plan. Our FY 07 EPS estimate of $2.01 is a 16% increase from the $1.73 LOW earned in FY 06. We see FY 08 EPS of $2.26. Our FY 07 and FY 08 operating EPS estimates include stock option expense.

Investment Rationale/Risk

- We believe LOW will benefit strongly from the rebuilding efforts in New Orleans. In addition, we think the aging of homes and the increased net worth of baby boomers should nearly offset any slowdown in housing turnover in 2006. Despite higher interest rates and our projection of a slowdown in overall consumer spending, we believe consumers will continue to allocate a good portion of their discretionary income to home improvement projects, as they view their homes as investments.
- Risks to our recommendation and target price include a potential slowdown in the economy; a sharp rise in long-term interest rates; and the failure to execute LOW's metro market expansion strategy.
- At about 13X our FY 08 estimate, LOW's shares recently traded at a premium to key peer Home Depot (HD: strong buy, $37), but at a discount to the S&P 500. Our 12-month target price of $37 is derived from our discounted cash flow (DCF) analysis, which assumes a weighted average cost of capital of 9.4% and a terminal growth rate of 3%.

Qualitative Risk Assessment

LOW | **MEDIUM** | HIGH

Our risk assessment reflects the cyclical nature of the home improvement retail industry, which is reliant on economic growth, offset by our view of ample opportunities for retail growth both domestically and abroad, and an S&P Quality Ranking of A+, reflecting LOW's consistent historical earnings and dividend growth.

Quantitative Evaluations

S&P Quality Ranking A+

D | C | B- | B | B+ | A- | A | **A+**

Relative Strength Rank MODERATE

55

LOWEST = 1 HIGHEST = 99

Revenue/Earnings Data

Revenue (Million $)

	1Q	2Q	3Q	4Q	Year
2007	11,921	13,389	--	--	--
2006	9,913	11,929	10,592	10,808	43,243
2005	8,681	10,169	9,064	8,550	36,464
2004	7,118	8,666	7,802	7,252	30,838
2003	6,471	7,488	6,415	6,118	26,491
2002	5,276	6,127	5,454	5,253	22,111

Earnings Per Share ($)

	1Q	2Q	3Q	4Q	Year
2007	0.53	0.60	**E**0.45	**E**0.43	**E**2.01
2006	0.37	0.52	0.41	0.44	1.73
2005	0.28	0.44	0.32	0.32	1.36
2004	0.26	0.38	0.28	0.25	1.16
2003	0.22	0.29	0.22	0.20	0.93
2002	0.15	0.21	0.16	0.14	0.65

Fiscal year ended Jan. 31. Next earnings report expected: NA. EPS Estimates based on S&P Operating Earnings; historical GAAP earnings are as reported.

Dividend Data (Dates: mm/dd Payment Date: mm/dd/yy)

Amount ($)	Date Decl.	Ex-Div. Date	Stk. of Record	Payment Date
0.060	03/30	04/19	04/21	05/05/06
2-for-1 Stk.	05/25	07/03	06/16	06/30/06
0.050	05/25	07/19	07/21	08/04/06
0.050	08/21	10/18	10/20	11/03/06

Dividends have been paid since 1961. Source: Company reports.

Lowe's Companies Inc.

Business Summary October 04, 2006

CORPORATE OVERVIEW. Lowe's Companies is the world's second largest home improvement retailer. It focuses on retail do-it-yourself (DIY) customers, do-it-for-me (DIFM) customers who utilize LOW's installation services, and commercial business customers. Lowe's offers a complete line of products and services for home decorating, maintenance, repair, remodeling, and the maintenance of commercial buildings.

As of February 3, 2006, LOW operated 1,234 stores in 49 states, representing 140 million sq. ft. of selling space. The company has two prototype stores, a 116,000-square-foot store for larger markets and a 94,000-square-foot store used primarily to serve smaller markets. Both prototypes include a lawn and garden center, averaging an additional 31,000 square feet for larger stores and 26,000 square feet for smaller stores. Of the total stores operating at February 3, 2006, approximately 84% were owned, including stores on leased land, while the remaining 16% were leased from unaffiliated third parties. Typical LOW stores stock more than 40,000 items, with hundreds of thousands of items available through the company's special order system.

CORPORATE STRATEGY. LOW is focusing much of its future expansion on metropolitan markets with populations of 500,000 or more. Only 55% of LOW stores were in the top 100 metropolitan markets that comprise over 65% of the home improvement market. Approximately half of the 155 stores that LOW plans to open in FY 07 will be in the Northeast and West regions, which Lowe's believes are currently under-penetrated.

Lowe's is also planning to enter the home improvement market in Canada, and currently has plans to open between 6 and 10 stores in the greater Toronto area in 2007.

Company Financials

Per Share Data ($) Year Ended Jan. 31	**2006**	**2005**	**2004**	**2003**	**2002**	**2001**	**2000**	**1999**	**1998**	**1997**
Tangible Book Value	9.15	7.45	6.55	5.31	4.30	3.59	3.07	2.22	1.85	1.60
Cash Flow	2.44	1.92	1.68	1.32	0.98	0.79	0.66	0.53	0.43	0.37
Earnings	1.73	1.36	1.16	0.93	0.65	0.52	0.44	0.34	0.26	0.22
S&P Core Earnings	1.73	1.33	1.13	0.87	0.61	0.50	NA	NA	NA	NA
Dividends	0.08	0.06	0.06	0.04	0.04	0.04	0.03	0.03	0.03	0.03
Payout Ratio	4%	4%	5%	5%	0%	7%	7%	9%	11%	12%
Calendar Year	2005	2004	2003	2002	2001	2000	1999	1998	1997	1996
Prices:High	34.85	30.27	30.21	25.00	24.44	16.81	16.61	13.05	6.14	5.44
Prices:Low	25.36	22.95	16.69	16.25	10.94	8.56	10.75	5.40	3.95	3.58
P/E Ratio:High	20	22	26	27	38	32	38	38	24	26
P/E Ratio:Low	15	17	14	18	17	16	25	16	15	16

Income Statement Analysis (Million $)										
Revenue	43,243	36,464	30,838	26,491	22,111	18,779	15,906	12,245	10,137	8,600
Operating Income	5,715	4,878	3,959	3,186	2,332	1,811	1,511	1,105	865	701
Depreciation	1,051	920	781	645	534	409	337	272	241	198
Interest Expense	158	176	180	203	199	146	123	95.0	73.3	65.1
Pretax Income	4,506	3,536	2,998	2,359	1,624	1,283	1,065	758	559	454
Effective Tax Rate	38.5%	38.5%	37.9%	37.6%	37.0%	36.9%	36.8%	36.4%	36.0%	35.6%
Net Income	2,771	2,176	1,862	1,471	1,023	810	673	482	357	292
S&P Core Earnings	2,763	2,134	1,801	1,386	968	773	NA	NA	NA	NA

Balance Sheet & Other Financial Data (Million $)										
Cash	423	813	1,624	1,126	799	456	491	223	195	70.0
Current Assets	7,831	6,974	6,687	5,568	4,920	4,175	3,710	2,586	2,110	1,851
Total Assets	24,682	21,209	19,042	16,109	13,736	11,376	9,012	6,345	5,219	4,435
Current Liabilities	5,832	5,719	4,368	3,578	3,017	2,929	2,386	1,765	1,449	1,349
Long Term Debt	3,499	3,060	3,678	3,736	3,734	2,698	1,727	1,283	1,046	767
Common Equity	14,339	11,535	10,309	8,302	6,675	5,494	4,695	3,136	2,601	2,217
Total Capital	18,573	15,331	14,644	12,516	10,713	8,443	6,622	4,579	3,771	3,086
Capital Expenditures	3,379	2,927	2,444	2,362	2,199	2,332	1,472	928	773	677
Cash Flow	3,822	3,096	2,643	2,116	1,557	1,219	1,010	754	598	490
Current Ratio	1.3	1.2	1.5	1.6	1.6	1.4	1.6	1.5	1.5	1.4
% Long Term Debt of Capitalization	18.8	20.0	25.1	29.8	34.9	32.0	26.1	28.0	27.7	24.9
% Net Income of Revenue	6.4	6.0	6.0	5.6	4.6	4.3	4.2	3.9	3.5	3.4
% Return on Assets	12.1	10.9	10.6	9.9	8.2	7.9	8.4	8.3	7.4	7.3
% Return on Equity	21.4	20.0	20.0	19.6	16.8	15.9	16.2	16.8	14.8	15.1

Data as orig reptd.; bef. results of disc opers/spec. items. Per share data adj. for stk. divs.; EPS diluted. E-Estimated. NA-Not Available. NM-Not Meaningful. NR-Not Ranked. UR-Under Review.

Office: 1000 Lowes Blvd, Mooresville, NC 28117-8520.
Telephone: 704-758-1000.
Website: http://www.lowes.com
Chrmn, Pres & CEO: R.A. Niblock

Sr EVP: L.D. Stone
EVP & CFO: R.F. Hull, Jr.
SVP & Chief Acctg Officer: M.V. Hollifield
SVP, Secy & General Counsel: R.W. McCanless

Board of Directors: L. L. Berry, P. C. Browning, P. Fulton, D. E. Hudson, R. A. Ingram, R. L. Johnson, M. O. Larsen, R. K. Lochridge, R. A. Niblock, S. F. Page, O. T. Sloan, Jr.

Founded: 1952
Domicile: North Carolina
Employees: 185,000

STANDARD &POOR'S

L-3 Communications Holdings Inc

S&P Recommendation STRONG BUY ★★★★★

Price $80.52 (as of Oct 31, 2006)

12-Mo. Target Price $100.00

Investment Style Large-Cap Growth

GICS Sector Industrials
Sub-Industry Aerospace & Defense

Comment This company is a provider of intelligence, surveillance, and reconnaissance systems; secure communications systems; aircraft modernization, training and government services.

Key Stock Statistics (Source S&P, Vickers, company reports)

52-Wk Range	$88.50–66.50	S&P Oper. EPS 2006E	5.02	P/E on S&P Oper. EPS 2006E	16.0	Dividend Rate/Share	$0.75
Trailing 12-Month EPS	$4.09	S&P Oper. EPS 2007E	5.70	Common Shares Outstg. (M)	123.0	Yield (%)	0.93
Trailing 12-Month P/E	19.7	S&P Core EPS 2006E	4.90	Market Capitalization(B)	$9.906	Beta	0.04
$10K Invested 5 Yrs Ago	$17,704	S&P Core EPS 2007E	NA	Institutional Ownership (%)	82	S&P Credit Rating	BBB-

Price Performance

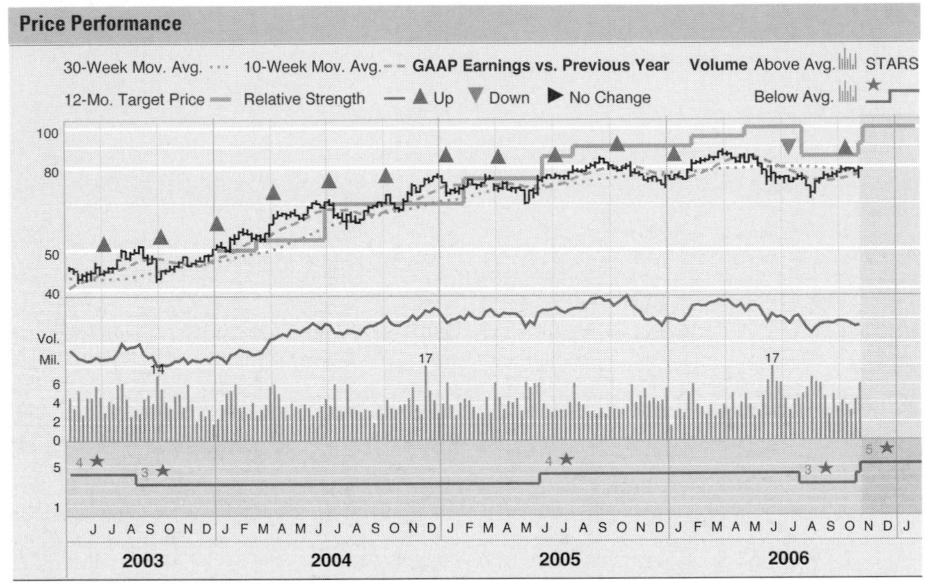

Options: ASE, CBOE, P

Highlights

➤ The STARS recommendation for LLL has recently been changed to 5 (strong buy) from 4 (buy) and the 12-month target price has recently been changed to $100.00 from $91.00. The Highlights section of this Stock Report will be updated accordingly.

Investment Rationale/Risk

➤ The Investment Rationale/Risk section of this Stock Report will be updated shortly. For the latest News story on LLL from MarketScope, see below.

➤ 10/30/06 11:37 am EST... S&P UPGRADES SHARES OF L-3 COMMUNICATIONS TO STRONG BUY FROM BUY (LLL 81.53*****): Given comments by CEO Mike Strianese reported in Financial Times today, we believe LLL plans to slow acquisitions, improve profit margins, and potentially offer itself for sale. Under a recently approved plan, senior officers would receive 1X-3X annual salaries and bonuses on termination in a takeover. Given our view of LLL's strong fundamentals, low valuations, and favorable markets, we view its shares as compelling. We are raising our target price to $100 from $91, based on 17.5X our '07 EPS estimate of $5.70, in line with LLL's 5-year average forward P/E. /R.Tortoriello

Qualitative Risk Assessment

LOW | **MEDIUM** | HIGH

Our risk assessment reflects our view of LLL's strong historical record of earnings growth, offset by the company's current low dividend payout ratio and relatively high financial leverage, and risks inherent in its dependence on government spending.

Quantitative Evaluations

S&P Quality Ranking NR

D | C | B- | B | B+ | A- | A | A+

Relative Strength Rank MODERATE

65

LOWEST = 1 HIGHEST = 99

Revenue/Earnings Data

Revenue (Million $)

	1Q	2Q	3Q	4Q	Year
2006	2,904	3,083	3,105	--	--
2005	1,963	2,076	2,506	2,900	9,445
2004	1,522	1,680	1,784	1,911	6,897
2003	1,089	1,227	1,265	1,481	5,062
2002	696.8	955.2	1,054	1,306	4,011
2001	461.9	561.6	618.2	705.8	2,347

Earnings Per Share ($)

2006	E1.13	0.40	1.31	E1.36	E5.02
2005	0.86	0.99	1.11	1.24	4.20
2004	0.67	0.81	0.93	1.01	3.33
2003	0.50	0.53	0.74	0.94	2.71
2002	0.36	0.49	0.62	0.79	2.29
2001	0.20	0.30	0.41	0.53	1.48

Fiscal year ended Dec. 31. Next earnings report expected: Late January. EPS Estimates based on S&P Operating Earnings; historical GAAP earnings are as reported.

Dividend Data (Dates: mm/dd Payment Date: mm/dd/yy)

Amount ($)	Date Decl.	Ex-Div. Date	Stk. of Record	Payment Date
0.188	02/07	02/17	02/22	03/15/06
0.188	04/25	05/15	05/17	06/15/06
0.188	07/11	08/15	08/17	09/15/06
0.188	10/10	11/15	11/17	12/15/06

Dividends have been paid since 2004. Source: Company reports.

Please read the Required Disclosures and Analyst Certification on the last page of this report.

L-3 Communications Holdings Inc

STANDARD &POOR'S

Business Summary August 09, 2006

CORPORATE OVERVIEW. L-3 Communications (LLL), an acquisitive maker of military and homeland security electronics, conducts business through four operating segments.

The Command, Control, Communications, Intelligence, Surveillance, and Reconnaissance (C3ISR) business segment (23% of sales and 25% of operating income in 2005), specializes in signals intelligence (SIGINT) and communications intelligence (COMINT) products. These products provide warfighters the ability to collect and analyze unknown electronic signals from command centers, communications nodes and air defense systems for real-time situation awareness and response. Major product lines are intelligence, surveillance and reconnaissance (ISR) systems, networked communications, C3ISR support services, and communications products.

The Government Services segment (19% of sales and 17% of operating profits) provides a full range of communications systems support, engineering services, information technology services, teaching and training services, marksmanship training systems and services, and intelligence support and analysis services. Services are sold primarily to the Department of Defense (DoD), U.S. Government intelligence agencies, and allied foreign governments.

The Aircraft Modernization & Maintenance segment (24% of sales and 23% of operating profits) provides specialized aircraft modernization and upgrades, maintenance, and logistics support services. Services are sold primarily to the U.S. DoD and the Canadian Department of National Defense.

The Specialized Products segment (34% of sales and 35% of operating profits) provides a broad range of products, including components, subsystem, and systems, to military and commercial customers in several diverse niche markets. Product lines include naval products, training devices and motion simulators, navigation & sensors, aviation products, premium fuzing products, and microwave components.

MARKET PROFILE. LLL's primary end-markets consist of the U.S. government (80% of 2005 revenues), commercial customers (12%) and foreign governments (8%). Sales to the DoD were distributed among the Armed Services and as a percentage of total sales as follows: U.S. Air Force 21%, Army 20%, Navy 15%, Marines 0.4%, and all other defense-wide customers 17%. Primary military contractor customers include Boeing, Lockheed Martin, Northrop Grumman, Raytheon and General Dynamics.

Company Financials

Per Share Data ($) Year Ended Dec. 31	2005	2004	2003	2002	2001	2000	1999	1998	1997	1996
Tangible Book Value	NM	NM	NM	NM	NM	NM	NM	NM	NM	NA
Cash Flow	5.46	4.27	3.52	2.96	2.37	2.25	16.75	1.41	NA	NA
Earnings	4.20	3.33	2.71	2.29	1.48	1.18	0.88	0.63	0.22	NA
S&P Core Earnings	4.07	3.22	2.66	1.87	1.08	NA	NA	NA	NA	NA
Dividends	0.50	0.40	Nil	Nil	Nil	Nil	Nil	Nil	NA	NA
Payout Ratio	12%	12%	Nil	Nil	Nil	Nil	Nil	Nil	NA	NA
Prices:High	84.84	77.26	51.83	66.78	49.04	39.66	27.13	24.75	NA	NA
Prices:Low	64.66	49.31	34.22	40.60	30.35	17.84	17.13	11.00	NA	NA
P/E Ratio:High	20	23	19	29	33	33	31	39	NA	NA
P/E Ratio:Low	15	15	13	18	21	15	20	17	NA	NA

Income Statement Analysis (Million $)	2005	2004	2003	2002	2001	2000	1999	1998	1997	1996
Revenue	9,445	6,897	5,062	4,011	2,347	1,910	1,405	1,037	894	NA
Operating Income	1,150	868	676	530	362	297	204	141	58.4	NA
Depreciation	153	119	95.4	75.9	87.0	74.3	53.7	40.4	NA	NA
Interest Expense	204	145	133	122	86.4	93.0	60.6	49.6	42.4	NA
Pretax Income	798	606	437	336	191	134	95.4	53.5	15.9	NA
Effective Tax Rate	35.1%	35.5%	35.7%	35.0%	37.1%	38.3%	38.5%	39.1%	30.0%	NA
Net Income	509	382	278	212	115	82.7	58.7	32.6	11.2	NA
S&P Core Earnings	493	370	274	171	82.0	NA	NA	NA	NA	NA

Balance Sheet & Other Financial Data (Million $)	2005	2004	2003	2002	2001	2000	1999	1998	1997	1996
Cash	394	653	135	135	361	32.7	42.8	26.1	50.0	NA
Current Assets	3,644	2,808	1,938	1,639	1,239	830	568	405	NA	NA
Total Assets	11,909	7,781	6,493	5,242	3,335	2,464	1,634	1,285	NA	NA
Current Liabilities	1,854	1,176	924	697	524	469	318	248	NA	NA
Long Term Debt	4,634	2,190	2,457	1,848	1,315	1,095	605	605	413	NA
Common Equity	4,491	3,800	2,574	2,202	1,214	693	583	300	235	NA
Total Capital	9,325	6,067	5,108	4,123	2,599	1,788	1,188	905	649	NA
Capital Expenditures	120	80.5	82.9	62.1	48.1	33.6	23.5	23.4	NA	NA
Cash Flow	661	501	373	288	202	157	112	72.9	NA	NA
Current Ratio	2.0	2.4	2.1	2.4	2.4	1.8	1.8	1.6	NA	NA
% Long Term Debt of Capitalization	49.7	36.1	48.1	44.8	50.6	61.3	50.9	66.9	63.7	NA
% Net Income of Revenue	5.4	5.5	5.5	5.3	4.9	4.3	4.2	3.1	NA	NA
% Return on Assets	5.2	5.3	4.7	5.0	4.0	4.0	4.0	3.3	NA	NA
% Return on Equity	12.3	12.0	11.6	12.4	12.1	13.0	13.3	15.0	NA	NA

Data as orig reptd.; bef. results of disc opers/spec. items. Per share data adj. for stk. divs.; EPS diluted. E-Estimated. NA-Not Available. NM-Not Meaningful. NR-Not Ranked. UR-Under Review.

Office: 600 3rd Ave, New York, NY 10016.
Telephone: 212-697-1111.
Website: http://www.L3com.com
Chrmn: R.B. Millard

Pres & CEO: M.T. Strianese
SVP, Secy & General Counsel: C.C. Cambria
VP & Chief Acctg Officer: R.G. D'Ambrosio
VP & Treas: S.M. Souza

Investor Contact: C. Mohrmann (212-850-5600)
Board of Directors: C. R. Canizares, P. A. Cohen, T. A. Corcoran, R. B. Millard, J. M. Shalikashvili, A. L. Simon, M. T. Strianese, A. H. Washkowitz, J. P. White

Founded: 1997
Domicile: Delaware
Employees: 59,500

STANDARD &POOR'S

LSI Logic Corp

S&P Recommendation HOLD ★★★★★

Price $9.88 (as of Oct 30, 2006)

12-Mo. Target Price $10.00

Investment Style Mid-Cap Value

GICS Sector Information Technology
Sub-Industry Semiconductors

Comment This California-based company is a leading supplier of complex, high-performance semiconductors and storage systems.

Key Stock Statistics (Source S&P, Vickers, company reports)

52-Wk Range	$11.81–7.41	S&P Oper. EPS 2006E	0.40	P/E on S&P Oper. EPS 2006E	24.7	Dividend Rate/Share	Nil
Trailing 12-Month EPS	$0.37	S&P Oper. EPS 2007E	0.50	Common Shares Outstg. (M)	399.6	Yield (%)	Nil
Trailing 12-Month P/E	26.7	S&P Core EPS 2006E	0.40	Market Capitalization(B)	$3.948	Beta	2.75
$10K Invested 5 Yrs Ago	$5,593	S&P Core EPS 2007E	0.50	Institutional Ownership (%)	72	S&P Credit Rating	BB-

Price Performance

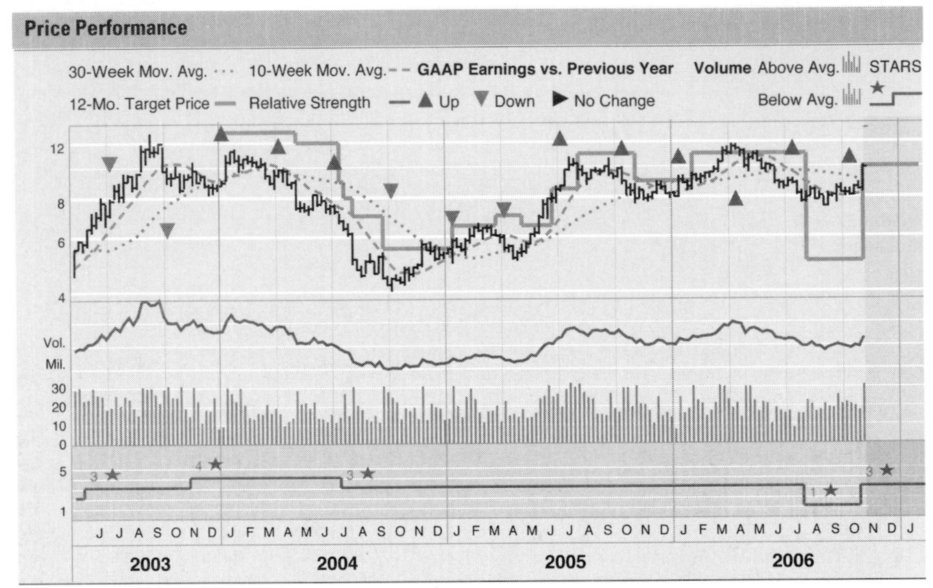

Options: ASE, CBOE, P, Ph

Analysis prepared by **Thomas W. Smith, CFA** on October 26, 2006, when the stock traded at **$ 9.53**.

Highlights

- We project sales growth of 3% for 2006 and 9% for 2007, in the context of our outlook for moderate growth near 8% for the chip industry in 2007. We expect new products such as serial attached SCSI (SAS) chips to continue to add to sales in the storage area. Consumer semiconductor products should reflect industry trends and any results from the company's efforts to attract new business.
- On May 15, 2006, the company sold its Gresham, OR, plant for $105 million to ON Semiconductor as part of a strategic shift to a fabless manufacturing model. A sale had been sought since September 2005. In March 2006, the company announced the redirection of its structured Application Specific Integrated Circuits (ASIC) R&D toward development of storage and consumer products, as part of a strategic agenda to build scale in key markets.
- We estimate operating EPS, including projected stock-based compensation expense, of $0.40 for 2006 and $0.50 for 2007.

Investment Rationale/Risk

- We recently upgraded our opinion on the shares to hold, from strong sell, as we believe there is sufficient strength in storage segments to outweigh weakness in semiconductor segments. On October 25, LSI announced an agreement to purchase StorageAge Networking Technologies for $50 million in cash, subject to necessary approvals. If completed, we think the acquisition would add expertise in SAN storage management and aid LSI's developing strength in storage. Meanwhile, the fading of consumer semiconductor revenue from the Sony Playstation and PortalPlayer accounts is apt to limit semiconductor segment growth.
- Risks to our opinion and target price include possible downturns in demand for semiconductors, and stock option expense that we view as high versus most S&P 500 companies.
- We arrive at our 12-month target price of $10 by applying a target price-to-sales per share ratio of 2X, near the middle of LSI's four-year historical range for P/S multiples, to our 2007 sales per share estimate of $4.96.

Qualitative Risk Assessment

LOW | MEDIUM | **HIGH**

LSI is subject to the sales cycles of the semiconductor industry and of consumer electronics and data storage end-markets. The company faces competition from makers of programmable logic devices as well as from many custom logic chip makers. We view the balance sheet as weaker than the peer group average.

Quantitative Evaluations

S&P Quality Ranking C

D | **C** | B- | B | B+ | A- | A | A+

Relative Strength Rank STRONG

94

LOWEST = 1 HIGHEST = 99

Revenue/Earnings Data

Revenue (Million $)

	1Q	2Q	3Q	4Q	Year
2006	475.9	489.6	493.0	--	--
2005	450.0	481.3	481.7	506.2	1,919
2004	452.4	447.9	380.2	419.7	1,700
2003	372.8	407.2	450.2	462.9	1,693
2002	412.5	437.8	487.0	479.7	1,817
2001	517.2	465.2	396.7	405.8	1,785

Earnings Per Share ($)

2006	0.03	0.13	0.11	**E**0.12	**E**0.40
2005	0.01	0.06	-0.19	0.09	-0.01
2004	0.02	0.02	-0.73	-0.51	-1.21
2003	-0.33	-0.43	-0.08	0.02	-0.82
2002	-0.47	-0.17	-0.07	-0.08	-0.79
2001	-0.10	-0.91	-1.09	-0.68	-2.84

Fiscal year ended Dec. 31. Next earnings report expected: Late January. EPS Estimates based on S&P Operating Earnings; historical GAAP earnings are as reported.

Dividend Data

No cash dividends have been paid.

LSI Logic Corp

Business Summary October 26, 2006

LSI Logic is best known as a leading supplier of application-specific and standard integrated circuits, although since 1998 it has diversified into storage components. In March 2006, the company announced plans to focus on growth opportunities in storage and consumer markets. Through 2005, principal markets served include storage components, storage systems, consumer, and communications. Customers are generally electronic original equipment manufacturers (OEMs). LSI focuses on larger companies that make products in high volume.

In 2005, the company operated in two main reporting segments: semiconductors, which accounted for 65% of revenues; and storage systems which represented 35%. Semiconductors posted a loss from operations in 2005, 2004, 2003 and 2002, while storage systems showed income.

Sales in 2005 by market segment were as follows: storage systems 35%, storage components 33%, consumer 18%, and communications 14%.

In August 2005, LSI announced a reorganization that created a four-segment structure: Custom Solutions Group addresses custom integrated circuits business; Consumer Products Group aims at standard product and custom solutions for consumer end markets, and employs LSI's digital media processing technology; Storage Components Group focuses on standard storage products, such as Ultra320 SCSI controllers; and Engenio Information Technologies offers storage system products, including RAID storage adaptors.

The company emphasizes complex system-on-a-chip products that employ its CoreWare design methodology. Using sophisticated electronic design automation tools, customers add product features to pre-wired cores of industry-standard architecture protocols and algorithms that are electronically stitched together on a single chip. CoreWare methodology is based on application-specific integrated circuit (ASIC) technology: semiconductors designed to satisfy particular customer requirements. LSI is a large player in the global ASIC market, competing with companies such as IBM, Agere Systems, Philips Electronics, Texas Instruments, and Broadcom.

Company Financials

Per Share Data ($) Year Ended Dec. 31	**2005**	**2004**	**2003**	**2002**	**2001**	**2000**	**1999**	**1998**	**1997**	**1996**
Tangible Book Value	1.66	1.38	2.39	2.80	3.15	5.96	5.21	4.17	5.59	5.09
Cash Flow	0.36	-0.75	-0.12	0.15	-1.32	1.81	1.62	0.41	1.14	1.13
Earnings	0.01	-1.21	-0.82	-0.79	-2.84	0.70	0.52	-0.47	0.56	0.56
S&P Core Earnings	-0.20	-1.51	-1.33	-1.36	-3.47	NA	NA	NA	NA	NA
Dividends	Nil	Nil	Nil	Nil	Nil	Nil	Nil	Nil	Nil	Nil
Payout Ratio	Nil	Nil	Nil	Nil	Nil	Nil	Nil	Nil	Nil	Nil
Prices:High	10.75	11.50	12.90	18.00	26.10	90.38	35.69	14.69	23.44	19.81
Prices:Low	4.92	4.01	3.78	3.97	9.70	16.30	8.06	5.25	9.31	8.50
P/E Ratio:High	NM	NM	NM	NM	NM	NM	69	NM	42	35
P/E Ratio:Low	NM	NM	NM	NM	NM	NM	16	NM	17	15
Income Statement Analysis (Million $)										
Revenue	1,919	1,700	1,693	1,817	1,785	2,738	2,089	1,491	1,290	1,239
Operating Income	283	172	171	155	-157	815	568	198	362	340
Depreciation	146	177	263	349	533	404	367	248	166	147
Interest Expense	25.3	25.3	30.7	52.0	44.6	41.6	40.0	8.48	1.50	13.6
Pretax Income	20.9	-439	-284	-291	-1,030	380	224	-124	224	205
Effective Tax Rate	NM	NM	NM	NM	NM	37.6%	29.0%	NM	28.0%	28.0%
Net Income	-5.62	-464	-309	-292	-992	237	159	-132	161	144
S&P Core Earnings	-80.0	-582	-505	-507	-1,214	NA	NA	NA	NA	NA
Balance Sheet & Other Financial Data (Million $)										
Cash	265	219	270	449	757	236	251	200	105	717
Current Assets	1,620	1,365	1,390	1,626	1,769	2,072	1,288	820	870	1,051
Total Assets	2,796	2,874	3,448	4,143	4,626	4,197	3,207	2,800	2,127	1,953
Current Liabilities	743	396	391	398	510	627	475	593	438	345
Long Term Debt	350	782	866	1,241	1,336	846	672	556	67.3	281
Common Equity	1,628	1,618	2,042	2,300	2,480	2,498	1,856	1,510	1,566	1,316
Total Capital	1,978	2,400	2,916	3,665	3,995	3,481	2,610	2,207	1,689	1,607
Capital Expenditures	48.1	52.8	78.2	39.0	224	277	205	329	513	362
Cash Flow	141	-287	-45.8	57.0	-459	641	526	116	327	294
Current Ratio	2.2	3.4	3.6	4.1	3.5	3.3	2.7	1.4	2.0	3.1
% Long Term Debt of Capitalization	17.7	32.6	29.7	33.8	33.4	24.3	25.7	25.2	4.0	17.5
% Net Income of Revenue	NM	NM	NM	NM	NM	8.6	7.6	NM	12.5	11.9
% Return on Assets	NM	NM	NM	NM	NM	6.4	5.3	NM	7.9	7.7
% Return on Equity	NM	NM	NM	NM	NM	10.9	9.4	NM	11.2	11.6

Data as orig reptd.; bef. results of disc opers/spec. items. Per share data adj. for stk. divs.; EPS diluted. E-Estimated. NA-Not Available. NM-Not Meaningful. NR-Not Ranked. UR-Under Review.

Office: 1621 Barber Lane, Milpitas, CA 95035.
Telephone: 408-433-8000.
Email: investorrelations@lsil.com
Website: http://www.lsilogic.com

Chrmn: J.H. Keyes
Pres & CEO: A.Y. Talwalkar
EVP & CFO: B. Look
SVP & CTO: R.L. Payne

VP, Secy & General Counsel: A.S. Hughes
Board of Directors: T. Y. Chen, M. R. Currie, C. A. Haggerty, J. H. Keyes, J. H. Miner, R. D. Norby, M. J. O'Rourke, G. Reyes, A. Y. Talwalkar

Founded: 1980
Domicile: Delaware
Employees: 4,322

STANDARD &POOR'S

Lucent Technologies Inc.

S&P Recommendation SELL ★★★★★	Price	12-Mo. Target Price	Investment Style
	$2.44 (as of Oct 27, 2006)	$2.00	Large-Cap Value

GICS Sector Information Technology
Sub-Industry Communications Equipment

Comment This former division of AT&T, one of the world's leading developers and manufacturers of telecommunications equipment, software and products, has agreed to merge with Alcatel.

Key Stock Statistics (Source S&P, Vickers, company reports)

52-Wk Range	$3.22–1.99	S&P Oper. EPS 2007E	0.15	P/E on S&P Oper. EPS 2007E	16.3	Dividend Rate/Share	Nil
Trailing 12-Month EPS	$0.11	S&P Oper. EPS 2008E	NA	Common Shares Outstg. (M)	4,482.0	Yield (%)	Nil
Trailing 12-Month P/E	22.2	S&P Core EPS 2007E	0.16	Market Capitalization(B)	$10.936	Beta	3.44
$10K Invested 5 Yrs Ago	$4,336	S&P Core EPS 2008E	NA	Institutional Ownership (%)	50	S&P Credit Rating	B

Price Performance

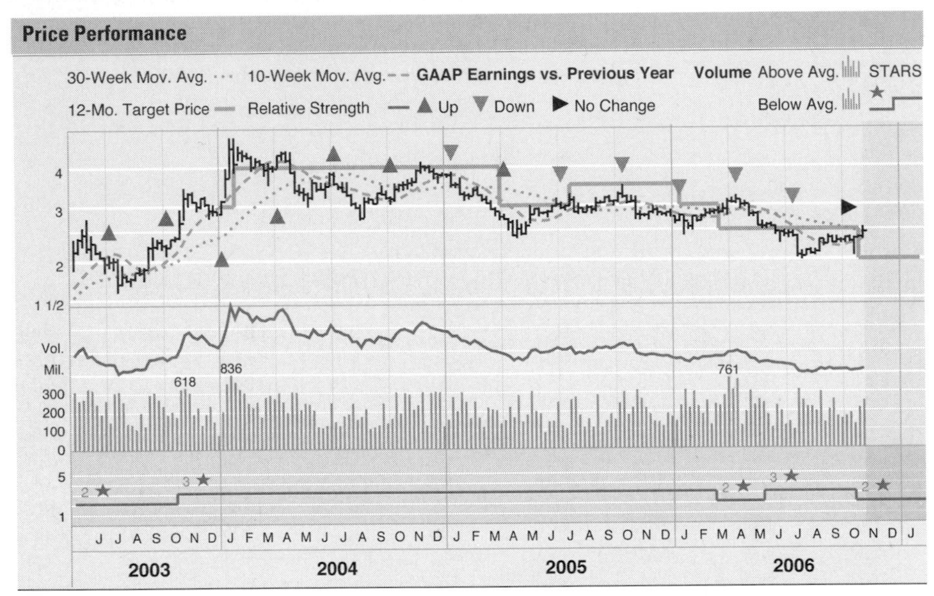

Options: ASE, CBOE, P, Ph

Analysis prepared by **Kenneth M. Leon, CPA** on October 25, 2006, when the stock traded at **$ 2.48**.

Highlights

- Following a 7% sales decline in FY 06 (Sep.), we forecast a 7% sales increase in FY 07 for LU as a stand-alone company. We believe LU's efforts in Internet Protocol (IP)-based multimedia systems will lead to narrower margins with increased new entrants from the IT industry. We believe most equipment suppliers, such as Ericsson, Nokia, Nortel and LU, are exposed to increased pricing pressure from fewer large telecom carriers that hold strong customer buying power.
- With the proposed merger of Alcatel and LU, which is expected to receive all necessary approvals by December 2006, we believe job security considerations may negatively affect the combined company's financial outlook in FY 07. We expect gross margins for LU to narrow to the 42% to 43% range in FY 06, from 44% in FY 05.
- In 2007, we expect LU to maintain operating expenses as a percentage of total sales, with flat R&D and marketing expenses. Following $0.14 in operating EPS for FY 06, we estimate $0.15 for FY 07; both years include $0.01 for projected stock option expense.

Investment Rationale/Risk

- Until the proposed merger with Alcatel (ALA: hold, $13) closes, we believe LU's share price is exposed to fundamental and stock market risks. Unlike its peers, neither LU nor Alcatel has a strong presence in faster growing markets such as handsets or enterprise networking. With a high customer mix of wireless and fixed-line carriers, we believe the combined company will be exposed to customer buying power and delayed broadband spending in its major markets.
- Risks to our recommendation and target price include better performance in its financial results until the Alcatel merger closes, increasing sales to LU's top five customers, which accounted for more than 20% of FY 05 total sales, and stronger capital spending.
- Our sell opinion reflects our viewpoint that LU will lose market share or realize delays in some new major orders in FY 07. Applying an enterprise value of 6.3X to our FY 07 EBITDA estimate, near the peer average, and a P/E ratio of 13.3X to our FY 07 earnings per share estimate, we arrive at our 12-month target price of $2.

Qualitative Risk Assessment

LOW	MEDIUM	HIGH

Terms of the proposed merger with Alcatel do not specify a guaranteed price range on LU shares, which means LU's share price is exposed to fundamental and stock market risks until the merger closes by December 2006, subject to necessary approvals. Assuming consummation, we see the combined firms still exposed to pricing pressure.

Quantitative Evaluations

S&P Quality Ranking B-

D	C	B-	B	B+	A-	A	A+

Relative Strength Rank MODERATE

65

LOWEST = 1 HIGHEST = 99

Revenue/Earnings Data

Revenue (Million $)

	1Q	2Q	3Q	4Q	Year
2006	2,047	2,138	2,050	2,561	8,796
2005	2,335	2,335	2,340	2,431	9,441
2004	2,259	2,194	2,190	2,402	9,045
2003	2,075	2,403	1,965	2,027	8,470
2002	3,579	3,516	2,949	2,277	12,321
2001	4,346	5,907	5,886	5,155	21,294

Earnings Per Share ($)

	1Q	2Q	3Q	4Q	Year
2006	-0.02	0.04	0.02	0.07	0.11
2005	0.04	0.06	0.07	0.07	0.24
2004	0.07	0.02	0.08	0.23	0.42
2003	-0.11	-0.14	-0.07	0.02	-0.29
2002	-0.14	-0.19	-2.34	-0.84	-3.51
2001	-0.47	-1.00	-0.55	-2.16	-4.18

Fiscal year ended Sep. 30. Next earnings report expected: Late January. EPS Estimates based on S&P Operating Earnings; historical GAAP earnings are as reported.

Dividend Data

No cash dividends have been paid since 2001.

Business Summary October 25, 2006

CORPORATE OVERVIEW. Lucent Technologies, formerly a unit of AT&T, is one of the world's leading communications equipment providers.

IMPACT OF MAJOR DEVELOPMENTS. On April 2, 2006, Alcatel and LU announced a definitive merger agreement whereby LU shareholders will receive 0.1952 of an ADS of Alcatel for every common share of LU currently held. Upon completion of the planned merger, which is subject to necessary approvals, Alcatel shareholders will own 60% of the combined company and LU shareholders will own the remaining 40%.

CORPORATE STRATEGY. We believe the combined company will be global in scale, have clear leadership in the areas that will define next-generation networks, have one of the largest R&D capabilities in communications, and employ the largest global services team in the industry. Alcatel and LU together will service most of the major fixed-line and wireless service providers in the world.

While Alcatel and LU believe the proposed merger will result in approximately $1.7 billion in new cash restructuring charges, with the charges to be recorded primarily in the first year, we are more skeptical on execution by the combined companies. A substantial majority of the restructuring is expected to be completed within 24 months after the closing date. Both companies believe the merger will be accretive to EPS in the first year after closing, reflecting synergies, but excluding restructuring charges and amortization of intangible assets. Management's goal is to realize pretax cost synergies savings of $1.7 billion within three years after the closing of the merger.

MARKET PROFILE. Prior to the planned merger, we think LU's wireless and worldwide services segment will show 3%-5% sales growth, with wireline products flat to modestly higher. In our opinion, the most important fundamental change in the company's business has been the rapid consolidation of service providers around the globe. We believe the balance of power resides with the service providers, with their concentrated buying power. Pricing power comes from the predominant buyer groups such as the RBOCs, large wireline carriers and wireless carriers.

Company Financials

Per Share Data ($) Year Ended Sep. 30	**2006**	**2005**	**2004**	**2003**	**2002**	**2001**	**2000**	**1999**	**1998**	**1997**
Tangible Book Value	NA	NM	NM	NM	NM	2.80	4.80	4.42	2.10	1.32
Cash Flow	NA	0.34	0.51	0.03	-3.07	-3.43	1.20	1.67	0.86	0.77
Earnings	0.11	0.24	0.42	-0.29	-3.51	-4.18	0.51	1.10	0.37	0.21
S&P Core Earnings	NA	0.06	0.19	-0.50	-4.86	-3.87	NA	NA	NA	NA
Dividends	Nil	Nil	Nil	Nil	Nil	0.06	0.08	0.08	0.08	0.08
Payout Ratio	Nil	Nil	Nil	Nil	Nil	NM	16%	7%	22%	35%
Prices:High	3.22	3.86	5.00	3.45	7.50	21.13	77.50	84.19	56.94	22.69
Prices:Low	1.99	2.35	2.70	1.24	0.55	5.00	12.19	47.00	18.36	11.19
P/E Ratio:High	29	16	12	NM	NM	NM	NM	77	NM	NM
P/E Ratio:Low	18	10	6	NM	NM	NM	NM	43	50	NM
Income Statement Analysis (Million $)										
Revenue	NA	9,441	9,045	8,470	12,321	21,294	33,813	38,303	30,147	26,360
Operating Income	NA	1,850	1,906	633	-3,257	-6,336	6,308	7,494	5,211	4,105
Depreciation	NA	599	693	978	1,470	2,536	2,318	1,806	1,334	1,450
Interest Expense	NA	341	398	353	382	518	348	406	318	305
Pretax Income	NA	1,034	1,063	-1,003	-7,057	-19,904	3,003	5,443	2,330	1,467
Effective Tax Rate	NA	NM	NM	NM	NM	NM	44.0%	36.5%	57.3%	63.1%
Net Income	NA	1,185	2,002	-770	-11,826	-14,170	1,681	3,458	970	541
S&P Core Earnings	NA	202	754	-1,980	-16,627	-13,160	NA	NA	NA	NA
Balance Sheet & Other Financial Data (Million $)										
Cash	NA	4,930	4,873	3,821	2,894	2,390	1,467	1,816	685	1,350
Current Assets	NA	5,583	8,231	7,833	9,155	16,103	21,490	21,931	14,078	12,501
Total Assets	NA	16,400	16,963	15,765	17,791	33,664	48,792	38,775	26,720	23,811
Current Liabilities	NA	3,820	4,466	5,015	6,326	10,169	10,877	11,778	10,428	10,738
Long Term Debt	NA	5,066	5,989	5,591	4,986	3,274	3,076	4,162	2,409	1,665
Common Equity	NA	375	-1,379	-4,239	-4,734	11,023	26,172	13,584	5,534	3,387
Total Capital	NA	5,441	4,610	2,220	1,932	16,283	30,514	17,746	7,943	5,052
Capital Expenditures	NA	221	157	291	449	1,390	2,701	2,215	1,626	1,635
Cash Flow	NA	1,784	2,695	105	-10,523	-11,662	3,999	5,264	2,304	1,991
Current Ratio	NA	1.5	1.8	1.6	1.4	1.6	2.0	1.9	1.4	1.2
% Long Term Debt of Capitalization	NA	93.1	129.9	251.8	258.1	20.1	10.1	23.5	30.3	33.0
% Net Income of Revenue	NA	12.6	22.1	NM	NM	NM	5.0	9.0	3.2	2.1
% Return on Assets	NA	7.1	12.2	NM	NM	NM	4.0	10.2	3.8	2.3
% Return on Equity	NA	NM	NM	NM	NM	NM	8.4	32.5	21.7	17.8

Data as orig reptd.; bef. results of disc opers/spec. items. Per share data adj. for stk. divs.; EPS diluted. E-Estimated. NA-Not Available. NM-Not Meaningful. NR-Not Ranked. UR-Under Review.

Office: 600 Mountain Avenue, New Providence, NJ 07974.
Telephone: 908-582-8500.
Website: http://www.lucent.com
Chrmn & CEO: P.F. Russo

COO: F. D'Amelio
SVP, Secy & General Counsel: W.R. Carapezzi, Jr.
CFO: J.A. Kritzmacher
Investor Contact: W. Zajack (973-509-0970)

Board of Directors: L. F. Deily, R. Denham, D. Goldin, E. Hagenlocker, C. A. Hills, K. J. Krapek, R. C. Levin, P. Russo, H. B. Schacht, F. A. Thomas, R. A. Williams

Founded: 1995
Domicile: Delaware
Employees: 30,500

STANDARD &POOR'S

Manor Care Inc.

S&P Recommendation HOLD ★★★★★

Price $47.99 (as of Oct 31, 2006)

12-Mo. Target Price $52.00

Investment Style Mid-Cap Growth

GICS Sector Health Care
Sub-Industry Health Care Facilities

Comment This company operates skilled nursing facilities, assisted living facilities, hospice and home health services, and outpatient therapy clinics.

Key Stock Statistics (Source S&P, Vickers, company reports)

52-Wk Range	**$53.68–37.30**	S&P Oper. EPS 2006**E**	**2.34**	P/E on S&P Oper. EPS 2006**E**	**20.5**	Dividend Rate/Share	**$0.64**
Trailing 12-Month EPS	**$1.91**	S&P Oper. EPS 2007**E**	**2.68**	Common Shares Outstg. (M)	**73.7**	Yield (%)	**1.33**
Trailing 12-Month P/E	**25.1**	S&P Core EPS 2006**E**	**2.34**	Market Capitalization(B)	**$3.535**	Beta	**0.48**
$10K Invested 5 Yrs Ago	**$21,022**	S&P Core EPS 2007**E**	**2.68**	Institutional Ownership (%)	**NA**	S&P Credit Rating	**BBB**

Price Performance

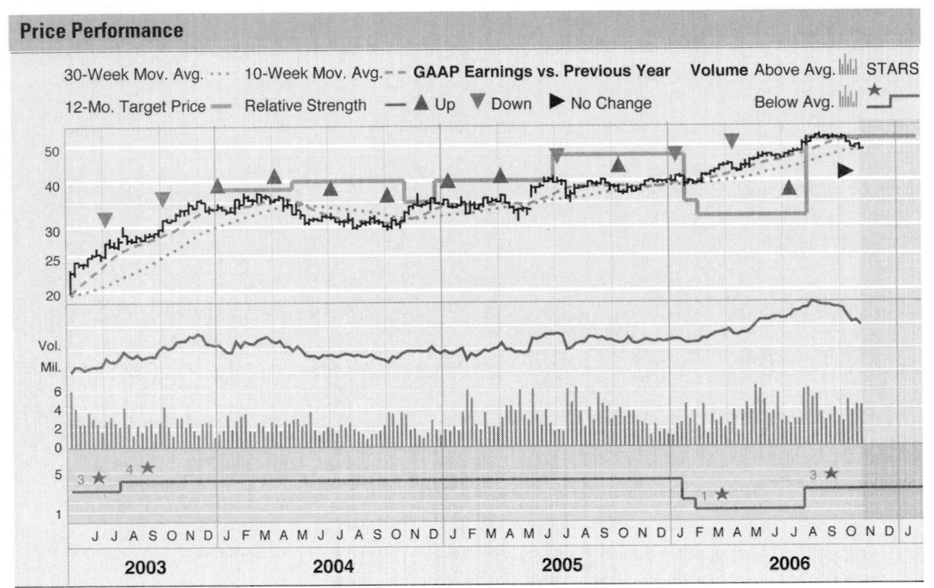

Options: CBOE, P, Ph

Analysis prepared by **Cameron Lavey** on October 31, 2006, when the stock traded at **$ 47.99**.

Highlights

- We look for revenues to grow about 6% in 2006. We think lower Medicare reimbursement rates for nursing homes will be partially offset by a more favorable payor mix and a shift to higher acuity patients. In 2007, we see revenue rising 5.8% on a slight increase in occupancy rates, a higher bed count, and an increase in acuity. We also expect revenues to benefit from average private pay per-diem price increases of 5%.
- In 2006, we anticipate that reduced labor costs, an improving payor mix, and a slight decline in operating expenses will drive modest EBITDA margin expansion. In 2007, we think EBITDA margins will widen due to lower G&A expenses as a percentage of revenue. We also expect lower interest expense, due to debt repurchases, and less general and professional liability costs to help boost earnings.
- We estimate 2006 EPS of $2.34, up about 14% from 2005's operating EPS of $2.05. In 2007, we see EPS rising 14.5%, to $2.68. Both estimates include projected stock option expense of $0.06. We think share buybacks will help HCR meet our EPS estimates.

Investment Rationale/Risk

- We think HCR will face a difficult reimbursement environment in 2007 and 2008. In our view, federal and state payors are likely to look for ways to cut reimbursement levels due to budget deficits. However, we believe the company can offset the reimbursement cuts by attracting higher acuity patients and increasing occupancy levels. Patient volumes at acute care hospitals, which drive admissions at many of HCR's facilities, have been weak, in our view.
- Risks to our recommendation and target price include the possibility that: Medicare and Medicaid reimbursement levels are lower than we project; patient volume growth is below our expectations; and HCR's cost reduction initiatives are not as effective as we anticipate. In addition, HCR may not be able to improve its quality mix of payors, which would adversely affect its reimbursement levels.
- Our 12-month target price of $52 is based on our relative value analysis. We assume that the shares will trade slightly above peers, at about 19X our 2007 EPS estimate of $2.68. We see this multiple as justified based on our view of HCR's above-average earnings growth potential.

Qualitative Risk Assessment

LOW | **MEDIUM** | HIGH

We think HCR will benefit from increased demand for skilled nursing and assisted living as the U.S. population ages. In our view, the company's diverse service offerings add to overall stability. However, HCR is highly dependent on third party reimbursement, which can be volatile.

Quantitative Evaluations

S&P Quality Ranking **B**

D | C | B- | **B** | B+ | A- | A | A+

Relative Strength Rank **WEAK**

18

LOWEST = 1 HIGHEST = 99

Revenue/Earnings Data

Revenue (Million $)

	1Q	2Q	3Q	4Q	Year
2006	869.3	894.2	915.5	--	--
2005	879.2	833.8	840.3	864.1	3,417
2004	797.3	799.1	806.8	805.6	3,209
2003	730.5	750.6	761.3	787.1	3,029
2002	716.0	728.4	732.9	728.1	2,905
2001	638.2	663.3	687.6	704.9	2,694

Earnings Per Share ($)

	1Q	2Q	3Q	4Q	Year
2006	0.33	0.58	0.60	**E**0.65	**E**2.34
2005	0.46	0.43	0.60	0.40	1.89
2004	0.45	0.45	0.45	0.55	1.90
2003	0.33	0.21	0.35	0.42	1.31
2002	0.33	0.38	0.38	0.24	1.33
2001	0.24	0.29	0.30	-0.18	0.66

Fiscal year ended Dec. 31. Next earnings report expected: Late January. EPS Estimates based on S&P Operating Earnings; historical GAAP earnings are as reported.

Dividend Data (Dates: mm/dd Payment Date: mm/dd/yy)

Amount ($)	Date Decl.	Ex-Div. Date	Stk. of Record	Payment Date
0.160	01/27	02/09	02/13	02/27/06
0.160	04/26	05/10	05/12	05/26/06
0.160	07/28	08/10	08/14	08/28/06
0.160	10/27	11/02	11/06	11/20/06

Dividends have been paid since 2003. Source: Company reports.

Manor Care Inc.

Business Summary October 31, 2006

CORPORATE OVERVIEW. Manor Care, formed via the September 1998 merger of Health Care and Retirement and the original Manor Care Inc., provides a range of health care services, including skilled nursing care, assisted living, subacute medical and rehabilitation care, rehabilitation therapy, home health care, and hospice care.

The most significant portion of the company's business is related to skilled nursing care and assisted living. At September 30, 2006, it operated 276 skilled nursing facilities and 65 assisted living facilities. The majority of facilities are located in Florida, Illinois, Michigan, Ohio and Pennsylvania. Certain centers have medical specialty units that provide subacute medical and rehabilitation care, and/or Alzheimer's care programs. The company's assisted living facilities operate under the brand names Arden Courts (54) and Springhouse (11). Arden Courts facilities specifically focus on providing care to persons suffering from early to middle-stage Alzheimer's disease and related memory impairment, while Springhouse facilities serve the general assisted living population of frail elderly. These facilities provide housing, personalized support and health care services in a non-institutional setting designed to address the needs of the elderly or Alzheimer's afflicted.

The home health care business specializes in all levels of home health, hospice care and rehabilitation therapy, with 114 offices, located in 24 states, as of September 30, 2006.

HCR provides rehabilitation therapy in its long-term care centers, other skilled nursing centers, hospitals, and 91 outpatient therapy clinics serving states in the Midwest and Mid-Atlantic, as well as Texas and Florida. The company provides program management services for subacute care and acute rehabilitation programs in hospitals and skilled nursing centers.

In the third quarter of 2006, private pay per diems (excluding assisted living) averaged $227.02, up from $213.70 a year earlier; Medicare averaged $383.16 ($361.13); Medicaid averaged $153.13 ($146.49), and private pay assisted living averaged $123.05 ($118.08).

Company Financials

Per Share Data ($) Year Ended Dec. 31	2005	2004	2003	2002	2001	2000	1999	1998	1997	1996
Tangible Book Value	8.26	10.26	9.87	9.68	9.28	8.87	8.72	10.35	6.78	NA
Cash Flow	3.53	3.34	2.72	2.59	1.90	1.55	0.57	0.67	2.32	NA
Earnings	1.89	1.90	1.31	1.33	0.66	0.38	-0.51	-0.42	1.40	NA
S&P Core Earnings	1.64	1.78	1.22	1.03	0.72	NA	NA	NA	NA	NA
Dividends	0.60	0.56	0.25	Nil	Nil	Nil	Nil	Nil	NA	NA
Payout Ratio	32%	29%	19%	Nil	Nil	Nil	Nil	Nil	NA	NA
Prices:High	41.16	37.25	35.83	27.01	34.50	21.19	33.50	35.00	NA	NA
Prices:Low	30.87	29.20	17.19	16.20	17.31	6.44	12.75	23.50	NA	NA
P/E Ratio:High	22	20	27	20	52	56	NM	NM	NA	NA
P/E Ratio:Low	16	15	13	12	26	17	NM	NM	NA	NA

Income Statement Analysis (Million $)										
Revenue	3,417	3,209	3,029	2,905	2,694	2,381	2,135	2,209	892	NA
Operating Income	433	561	348	372	307	260	362	397	151	NA
Depreciation	139	128	129	125	128	121	116	119	37.7	NA
Interest Expense	41.2	42.4	41.9	37.7	50.8	60.7	54.0	46.6	17.2	NA
Pretax Income	258	255	190	213	130	61.7	-102	-24.1	101	NA
Effective Tax Rate	37.5%	34.0%	37.5%	38.0%	47.3%	34.8%	NM	NM	30.7%	NA
Net Income	161	168	119	132	68.5	39.1	-55.2	-46.2	70.1	NA
S&P Core Earnings	141	158	111	101	74.0	NA	NA	NA	NA	NA

Balance Sheet & Other Financial Data (Million $)										
Cash	12.3	32.9	86.3	30.6	26.7	24.9	12.0	33.7	7.46	NA
Current Assets	531	540	585	511	590	505	431	418	171	NA
Total Assets	2,339	2,341	2,397	2,307	2,424	2,358	2,281	2,715	936	NA
Current Liabilities	452	402	388	642	391	473	409	504	121	NA
Long Term Debt	730	555	659	373	716	644	688	693	NA	NA
Common Equity	774	984	975	1,016	1,047	1,013	980	1,557	434	NA
Total Capital	1,607	1,674	1,771	1,468	1,865	1,766	1,795	2,496	NA	NA
Capital Expenditures	135	151	101	92.5	89.4	117	166	296	NA	NA
Cash Flow	300	296	248	257	197	160	60.8	73.1	108	NA
Current Ratio	1.2	1.3	1.5	0.8	1.5	1.1	1.1	0.8	1.4	NA
% Long Term Debt of Capitalization	45.5	33.2	37.2	25.4	38.4	36.5	38.3	27.8	NA	NA
% Net Income of Revenue	4.7	5.2	3.9	4.5	2.5	1.6	NM	NM	7.9	NA
% Return on Assets	6.9	7.1	5.0	5.6	2.9	1.7	NM	NM	8.1	NA
% Return on Equity	18.3	17.2	12.0	12.8	6.7	3.9	NM	NM	17.0	NA

Data as orig reptd.; bef. results of disc opers/spec. items. Per share data adj. for stk. divs.; EPS diluted. E-Estimated. NA-Not Available. NM-Not Meaningful. NR-Not Ranked. UR-Under Review.

Office: 333 N Summit St, Toledo, OH 43604-2617.
Telephone: 419-252-5500.
Email: info@hcr-manorcare.com
Website: http://www.hcr-manorcare.com

Chrmn, Pres & CEO: P.A. Ormond
COO & Sr EVP: M.K. Weikel
Investor Contact: S.C. Moler (419-252-5500)
VP & Chief Acctg Officer: S.C. Moler

VP, Secy & General Counsel: R.J. Bixler
Board of Directors: M. T. Behrens, J. F. Damico, W. H. Longfield, P. A. Ormond, J. T. Schwieters, R. C. Tuttle, M. K. Weikel, G. R. Wilensky, T. L. Young

Founded: 1991
Domicile: Delaware
Employees: 58,000

STANDARD &POOR'S

Marathon Oil Corp

S&P Recommendation BUY ★★★★★

Price $86.35 (as of Oct 27, 2006)

12-Mo. Target Price $93.00

Investment Style Large-Cap Value

GICS Sector Energy
Sub-Industry Integrated Oil & Gas

Comment MRO (formerly USX-Marathon Group, a part of USX Corp.) engages in worldwide oil and gas exploration and production, and domestic refining, marketing and transportation.

Key Stock Statistics (Source S&P, Vickers, company reports)

52-Wk Range	$93.28–56.10	S&P Oper. EPS 2006**E**	11.26	P/E on S&P Oper. EPS 2006**E**	7.7	Dividend Rate/Share	$1.60
Trailing 12-Month EPS	$12.54	S&P Oper. EPS 2007**E**	13.51	Common Shares Outstg. (M)	358.2	Yield (%)	1.85
Trailing 12-Month P/E	6.9	S&P Core EPS 2006E	11.31	Market Capitalization(B)	$30.928	Beta	0.59
$10K Invested 5 Yrs Ago	$35,227	S&P Core EPS 2007E	13.59	Institutional Ownership (%)	80	S&P Credit Rating	BBB+

Price Performance

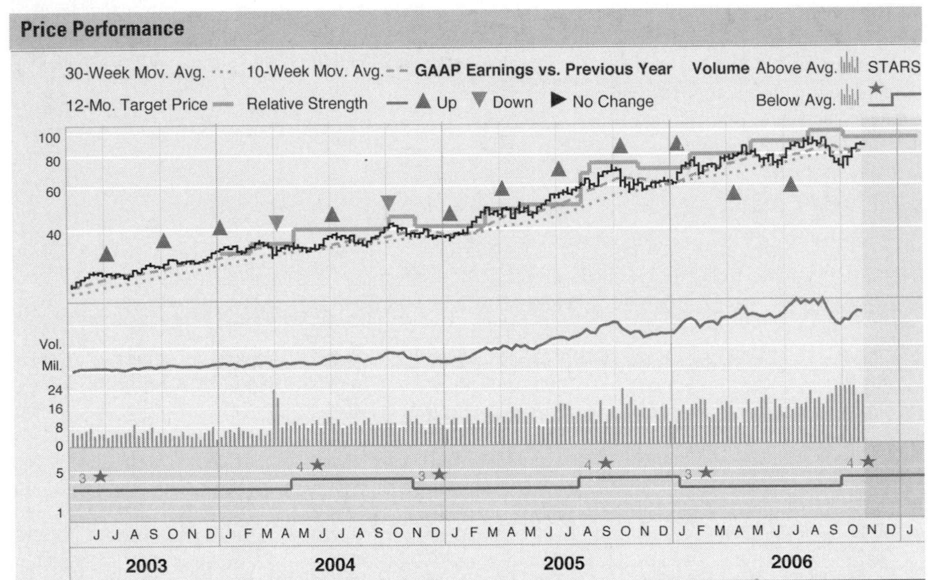

Options: ASE, CBOE, P, Ph

Analysis prepared by **Tina J. Vital** on October 10, 2006, when the stock traded at **$ 79.12**.

Highlights

- While U.S. refining margins have narrowed since the beginning of August 2006, we think this narrowing is temporary. We expect the switch to winter fuels to boost U.S. refining margins in the fourth quarter, and increased demand and the need to attract the necessary level of fuel imports to lead to wider margins in 2007.
- Oil and gas production rose 14% in the second quarter, but international volumes (particularly natural gas) were below our expectations. We project upstream volume growth of 2.5% in 2006, and over 6% per annum in 2006-2008 (in line with MRO's guidance range of 5%-9%), on start-ups in Equatorial Guinea, Angola, Norway, the U.K., the Gulf of Mexico and Libya. On June 2, 2006, MRO sold its Russian oil exploration and production businesses in Western Siberia to OAO Lukoil for $787 million plus working capital and other closing adjustments.
- Strong pricing and volumes boosted after-tax operating earnings by 143% in 2005, and we project increases of 26% in 2006 and 19% in 2007.

Investment Rationale/Risk

- We believe that MRO's January 2006 re-entry into Libya will raise its oil production by 40,000-45,000 barrels per day (b/d) at an attractive cost, which we estimate is nearly $4.58 per barrel, and that its June 2005 purchase of Ashland's (ASH: hold, $65) 38% interest in its refining joint venture should increase its earnings power by capitalizing on favorable refining fundamentals.
- Risks to our recommendation and target price include geopolitical risk, an inability to achieve upstream production targets, operational risk from development projects, and changes in market conditions affecting the oil and gas industry.
- Our discounted cash flow analysis (weighted average cost of capital of 7.1% and terminal growth of 3%) shows intrinsic value of $87. Blending our DCF model with peer multiple valuations, our 12-month target price is $93, representing an expected enterprise value of 4.2X our 2006 EBITDA estimate, a discount to peers.

Qualitative Risk Assessment

LOW	MEDIUM	HIGH

Our risk assessment reflects our view of the company's diversified and solid business profile in volatile and cyclical segments of the energy industry. We consider MRO's earnings stability as good, and its corporate governance practices as sound.

Quantitative Evaluations

S&P Quality Ranking B+

D	C	B-	B	B+	A-	A	A+

Relative Strength Rank STRONG

72

LOWEST = 1 HIGHEST = 99

Revenue/Earnings Data

Revenue (Million $)

	1Q	2Q	3Q	4Q	Year
2006	16,638	18,290	--	--	--
2005	12,932	16,019	17,248	17,314	63,673
2004	10,652	12,514	12,249	14,183	49,598
2003	10,033	9,643	10,253	11,034	40,963
2002	6,419	8,078	8,437	8,530	31,464
2001	8,607	9,113	8,496	6,803	33,019

Earnings Per Share ($)

2006	2.13	4.07	**E**2.99	**E**2.07	**E**11.26
2005	0.93	1.92	2.09	3.48	8.49
2004	0.83	1.01	0.64	1.23	3.72
2003	0.98	0.80	0.90	0.64	3.26
2002	0.22	0.54	0.23	0.62	1.72
2001	1.62	1.88	0.62	-2.90	4.26

Fiscal year ended Dec. 31. Next earnings report expected: NA. EPS Estimates based on S&P Operating Earnings; historical GAAP earnings are as reported.

Dividend Data (Dates: mm/dd Payment Date: mm/dd/yy)

Amount ($)	Date Decl.	Ex-Div. Date	Stk. of Record	Payment Date
0.330	01/30	02/14	02/16	03/10/06
0.400	04/26	05/15	05/17	06/12/06
0.400	07/26	08/14	08/16	09/11/06
0.400	10/25	11/14	11/16	12/11/06

Dividends have been paid since 1991. Source: Company reports.

Please read the Required Disclosures and Analyst Certification on the last page of this report.

Marathon Oil Corp

Business Summary October 10, 2006

In January 2002, the integrated oil and gas company Marathon Oil (MRO; formerly USX-Marathon Group, a part of USX Corp.) began trading as a standalone company after USX-Marathon shareholders voted to separate USX's steel and energy businesses via a tax free spin-off. On June 30, 2005, MRO acquired Ashland Inc.'s 38% interest in its Marathon Ashland Petroleum LLC (MAP) refining joint venture, ASH's maleic anhydride business, and 60 Valvoline Instant Oil Change retail outlets (located in Michigan and Ohio), for about $3.73 billion. As a result, the refining venture is now wholly owned by MRO. (MAP changed its name to Marathon Petroleum Co. LLC (MPC) on September 1, 2005.)

MRO is engaged in oil and gas exploration and production (E&P; 9% of 2005 revenues, 49% of 2005 segment income); refining, marketing and transportation (RM&T; 88%, 50%); and integrated gas (3%, 1%) in the U.S. (91% of 2005 revenues), the U.K. (4%), Equatorial Guinea (1%) and other (5%).

We estimate that the company organically replaced 159% of its oil and gas production in 2003-2005. At year-end 2005, net proved reserves increased to 1.295 billion barrels (71% developed, 54% liquids), versus 1.139 million (62%, 62%) in 2004, reflecting MRO's re-entry into Libya, extensions, discoveries, and other additions. MRO's production operations are focused in the U.S., Europe, West Africa, Libya, and Russia. In 2005, worldwide production averaged 346,000 barrels per day (b/d; 55% liquids), from 337,000 b/d (50%) in 2004. Key production investments continue in Norway, where the company is proceeding with the Alvheim/Vilje developments, and in the Gulf of Mexico, where the company is part of the Neptune development. Worldwide production costs rose to $7.26 per barrel oil equivalent (boe) in 2005, from $5.75 in 2004.

Company Financials

Per Share Data ($) Year Ended Dec. 31	**2005**	**2004**	**2003**	**2002**	**2001**	**2000**	**1999**	**1998**	**1997**	**1996**
Tangible Book Value	27.79	22.34	18.39	15.13	15.97	15.53	15.40	14.00	12.52	11.62
Cash Flow	12.28	7.13	7.05	5.60	8.24	5.38	5.17	4.27	3.89	4.74
Earnings	8.40	3.72	3.20	1.72	4.26	1.39	2.11	1.05	1.58	2.33
S&P Core Earnings	8.39	3.82	3.26	1.37	4.41	NA	NA	NA	NA	NA
Dividends	1.22	1.03	0.96	0.92	0.92	0.88	0.84	0.84	0.76	0.70
Payout Ratio	14%	28%	29%	53%	75%	63%	40%	80%	48%	30%
Prices:High	72.68	42.60	33.61	30.30	33.73	30.38	33.88	40.50	38.88	25.50
Prices:Low	35.52	30.30	19.85	18.82	24.95	20.69	19.63	25.00	23.75	17.25
P/E Ratio:High	9	11	10	18	28	22	16	39	25	11
P/E Ratio:Low	4	8	6	11	20	15	9	24	15	7
Income Statement Analysis (Million $)										
Revenue	63,673	49,598	40,963	31,464	33,019	34,487	24,212	21,726	15,668	16,332
Operating Income	6,660	8,379	2,988	2,253	4,215	3,521	1,997	1,530	1,510	1,927
Depreciation, Depletion and Amortization	1,358	1,217	1,175	1,201	1,236	1,245	950	941	664	693
Interest Expense	145	161	238	288	196	260	290	311	285	308
Pretax Income	5,157	2,509	1,898	1,098	2,781	1,412	1,425	701	672	991
Effective Tax Rate	33.5%	29.0%	30.8%	35.4%	27.3%	34.1%	22.7%	20.3%	32.1%	32.3%
Net Income	3,051	1,257	1,012	536	1,318	432	654	310	456	671
S&P Core Earnings	3,013	1,290	1,014	428	1,367	NA	NA	NA	NA	NA
Balance Sheet & Other Financial Data (Million $)										
Cash	2,617	3,369	1,396	488	657	340	111	137	36.0	32.0
Current Assets	9,383	8,867	6,040	4,479	4,411	4,985	4,102	2,976	2,018	2,046
Total Assets	28,498	23,423	19,482	17,812	16,129	15,232	15,705	14,544	10,565	10,151
Current Liabilities	8,154	5,253	4,207	3,659	3,468	4,012	3,149	2,610	2,262	2,142
Long Term Debt	3,698	4,057	4,085	4,410	3,432	4,196	3,504	3,640	2,476	2,642
Common Equity	11,705	8,111	6,075	5,082	4,940	4,845	4,800	4,312	3,618	3,340
Total Capital	17,868	16,411	12,171	12,908	11,632	12,235	11,552	10,992	7,596	7,342
Capital Expenditures	2,890	2,237	1,892	1,574	1,639	1,669	1,378	1,270	1,038	751
Cash Flow	4,409	2,474	2,187	1,737	2,546	1,677	1,604	1,251	1,120	1,364
Current Ratio	1.2	1.7	1.4	1.2	1.3	1.2	1.3	1.1	0.9	1.0
% Long Term Debt of Capitalization	20.7	24.7	33.6	34.2	29.5	34.3	30.3	33.1	32.6	36.0
% Return on Assets	11.8	5.9	5.4	3.2	7.9	2.8	4.3	2.5	4.4	6.6
% Return on Equity	30.8	17.7	18.1	10.7	22.4	9.0	14.4	7.8	13.1	21.6

Data as orig reptd.; bef. results of disc opers/spec. items. Per share data adj. for stk. divs.; EPS diluted. E-Estimated. NA-Not Available. NM-Not Meaningful. NR-Not Ranked. UR-Under Review.

Office: 5555 San Felipe Rd, Houston, TX 77056-2723.
Telephone: 713-629-6600.
Website: http://www.marathon.com
Chrmn: T.J. Usher

Pres & CEO: C.P. Cazalot, Jr.
SVP & CFO: J. Clark
VP & Treas: P.C. Reinbolt
VP, Secy & General Counsel: W.F. Schwind, Jr.

Investor Contact: K.L. Matheny (713-296-4114)
Board of Directors: C. F. Bolden, Jr., C. P. Cazalot, Jr., D. A. Daberko, W. L. Davis, S. Jackson, P. Lader, C. R. Lee, D. H. Reilley, S. E. Schofield, J. W. Snow, T. J. Usher, D. C. Yearley

Founded: 1901
Domicile: Delaware
Employees: 27,756

STANDARD &POOR'S

Marriott International Inc.

S&P Recommendation HOLD ★★★★★	Price	12-Mo. Target Price	Investment Style
	$41.50 (as of Oct 27, 2006)	$41.00	Large-Cap Growth

GICS Sector Consumer Discretionary
Sub-Industry Hotels, Resorts & Cruise Lines

Comment MAR's lodging brands include more than 2,600 properties, most of which are managed by the company or are operated by others through franchise relationships.

Key Stock Statistics (Source S&P, Vickers, company reports)

52-Wk Range	**$41.98–29.40**	S&P Oper. EPS 2006**E**	**1.65**	P/E on S&P Oper. EPS 2006**E**	**25.2**	Dividend Rate/Share	**$0.25**
Trailing 12-Month EPS	**$1.66**	S&P Oper. EPS 2007**E**	**1.90**	Common Shares Outstg. (M)	**395.4**	Yield (%)	**0.60**
Trailing 12-Month P/E	**25.0**	S&P Core EPS 2006**E**	**1.63**	Market Capitalization(B)	**$16.409**	Beta	**1.25**
$10K Invested 5 Yrs Ago	**$25,844**	S&P Core EPS 2007**E**	**1.90**	Institutional Ownership (%)	**55**	S&P Credit Rating	**BBB+**

Price Performance

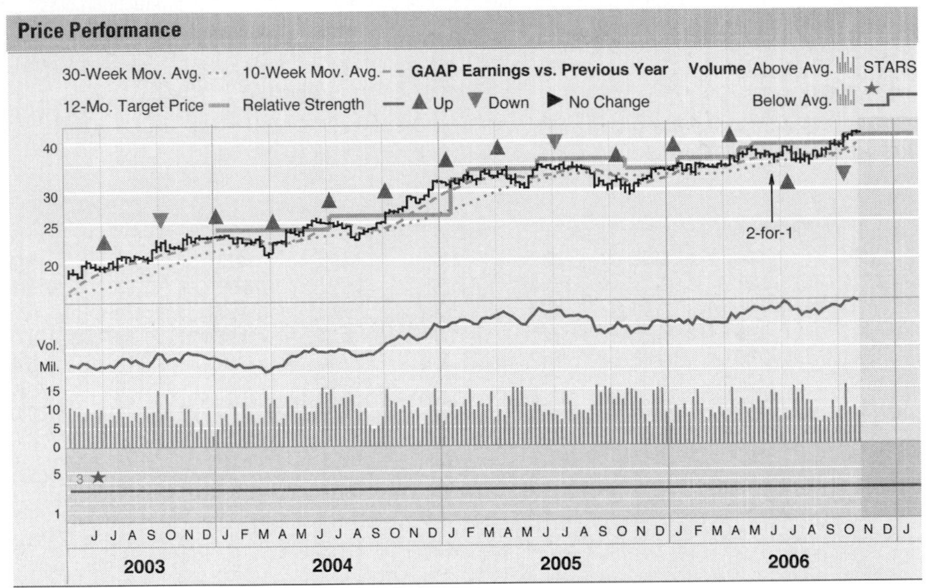

Options: ASE, CBOE, P, Ph

Highlights

- The 12-month target price for MAR has recently been changed to $41.00 from $39.00. The Highlights section of this Stock Report will be updated accordingly.

Investment Rationale/Risk

- The Investment Rationale/Risk section of this Stock Report will be updated shortly. For the latest News story on MAR from MarketScope, see below.

- 10/05/06 01:04 pm EDT... S&P REITERATES HOLD OPINION ON SHARES OF MARRIOTT INTERNATIONAL (MAR 39.89***): Before certain special items, Q3 EPS of $0.34 vs. about $0.28 tops our $0.30 estimate, with roughly $0.04 benefit from reserve reversal, and timeshare fees related to prior period profit. We are raising our '06 and '07 EPS estimates to $1.65 and $1.90, from $1.58 and $1.87. On estimated '07 EPS, MAR is at about a 51% P/E premium to the S&P 500. We expect its shares to get support from U.S. hotel industry upturn and our expectations for strong company cash flow, and we see further stock buybacks. With more favorable EPS outlook, our 12-month target price rises $2, to $41. /TGraves-CFA

Qualitative Risk Assessment

LOW | **MEDIUM** | HIGH

In our view, the company is subject to cyclical economic and industry changes. However, we believe that MAR's finances are relatively strong, and we expect that cash flow will be available to help finance future growth.

Quantitative Evaluations

S&P Quality Ranking **B+**

D | C | B- | B | **B+** | A- | A | A+

Relative Strength Rank **STRONG**

74

LOWEST = 1 HIGHEST = 99

Revenue/Earnings Data

Revenue (Million $)

	1Q	2Q	3Q	4Q	Year
2006	2,705	2,851	2,703	--	--
2005	2,534	2,661	2,714	3,641	11,550
2004	2,252	2,402	2,304	3,141	10,099
2003	2,023	2,016	2,109	2,866	9,014
2002	1,808	2,034	1,924	2,675	8,441
2001	2,461	2,450	2,373	2,868	10,152

Earnings Per Share ($)

2006	0.39	0.43	0.30	**E**0.51	**E**1.65
2005	0.31	0.29	0.33	0.54	1.45
2004	0.24	0.34	0.28	0.40	1.24
2003	0.18	0.26	0.19	0.35	0.97
2002	0.16	0.25	0.23	0.24	0.87
2001	0.24	0.25	0.20	-0.24	0.46

Fiscal year ended Dec. 31. Next earnings report expected: Mid February. EPS Estimates based on S&P Operating Earnings; historical GAAP earnings are as reported.

Dividend Data (Dates: mm/dd Payment Date: mm/dd/yy)

Amount ($)	Date Decl.	Ex-Div. Date	Stk. of Record	Payment Date
2-for-1	04/28	06/12	05/18	06/09/06
0.063	04/28	06/20	06/22	07/21/06
0.063	08/03	08/30	09/01	10/13/06

Dividends have been paid since 1998. Source: Company reports.

Marriott International Inc.

Business Summary July 19, 2006

CORPORATE OVERVIEW. As of fiscal year-end 2005, Marriott International's lodging and timeshare businesses included 2,741 properties, with 499,165 rooms or suites. Including the U.S. Virgin Islands and Puerto Rico, this included 2,356 U.S. properties with 400,435 rooms or suites.

At year-end 2005, MAR had 1,017 properties (261,800 rooms or suites) that MAR operated under long-term management or lease agreements, and had 17 owned hotels (5,317). With its management agreements, the company typically earns a base fee, and may receive an incentive management fee that is based on hotel profits. MAR also had 1,707 franchised properties, with 232,048 rooms, that were operated by other parties. With franchise properties, the company generally receives an initial application fee and continuing royalty fees.

By brand (including franchises), as of year end 2005, MAR's lodging business included 507 Marriott Hotels & Resorts, Marriott Conference Centers or JW Marriott Hotels & Resorts properties; 59 Ritz-Carlton hotels; 137 Renaissance hotels; 692 Courtyard hotels; 524 Fairfield Inn properties; 137 SpringHill Suites properties, 490 Residence Inn hotels; 122 TownPlace Suites properties; three Ramada International properties, one Bulgari Hotel & Resorts property, 52 timeshare properties; and 17 Marriott Executive Apartments. In 2005, MAR's full-service lodging segment, which largely consisted of the Marriott full-service, Ritz-Carlton, and Renaissance businesses, accounted for 65% of total revenues.

The company's international presence, as of year-end 2005, included 181 properties (37,485 rooms or suites) in Europe or the United Kingdom, 79 properties (28,724) in Asia, 26 (7,456) in the Middle East or Africa, 49 (10,914) in Canada, 10 (2,736) in Mexico, eight (2,354) in Australia, and 32 properties elsewhere.

CORPORATE STRATEGY. We look for MAR to continue an emphasis on managing and franchising, rather than owning, hotels. However, we expect that MAR will make loans and equity investments aimed at facilitating the growth and success of its lodging system. When MAR sells equity interests in hotels, it may hold management contracts for such properties.

Company Financials

Per Share Data ($) Year Ended Dec. 31	**2005**	**2004**	**2003**	**2002**	**2001**	**2000**	**1999**	**1998**	**1997**	**1996**
Tangible Book Value	4.52	5.85	5.17	4.57	3.56	2.81	2.13	1.68	NA	NA
Cash Flow	1.84	1.68	1.30	1.23	0.89	1.33	1.04	0.97	0.83	0.65
Earnings	1.45	1.24	0.97	0.87	0.46	0.95	0.76	0.73	0.60	0.50
S&P Core Earnings	1.25	1.00	0.68	0.77	0.35	NA	NA	NA	NA	NA
Dividends	0.20	0.17	0.15	0.14	0.13	0.12	0.11	0.07	NA	NA
Payout Ratio	14%	13%	15%	16%	28%	12%	13%	10%	NA	NA
Prices:High	35.39	32.00	23.60	23.23	25.25	21.75	22.25	18.97	NA	NA
Prices:Low	29.01	20.32	14.28	13.13	13.65	13.06	14.50	9.69	NA	NA
P/E Ratio:High	24	26	24	27	55	23	28	26	NA	NA
P/E Ratio:Low	20	16	15	15	30	14	18	13	NA	NA

Income Statement Analysis (Million $)	2005	2004	2003	2002	2001	2000	1999	1998	1997	1996
Revenue	11,550	10,099	9,014	8,441	10,152	10,017	8,739	7,968	9,046	7,267
Operating Income	739	643	537	634	779	997	828	766	647	525
Depreciation	184	166	160	187	222	195	162	140	126	89.0
Interest Expense	106	99.0	110	86.0	109	100	61.0	30.0	22.0	37.0
Pretax Income	717	654	488	471	370	757	637	632	531	436
Effective Tax Rate	13.1%	15.3%	NM	6.79%	36.2%	36.7%	37.2%	382.0%	39.0%	37.8%
Net Income	668	594	476	439	236	479	400	390	324	271
S&P Core Earnings	579	484	330	381	180	NA	NA	NA	NA	NA

Balance Sheet & Other Financial Data (Million $)	2005	2004	2003	2002	2001	2000	1999	1998	1997	1996
Cash	203	770	229	198	817	334	489	390	289	426
Current Assets	2,010	1,946	1,235	1,744	2,130	1,415	1,600	1,333	1,367	1,530
Total Assets	8,530	8,668	8,177	8,296	9,107	8,237	7,324	6,233	5,557	5,608
Current Liabilities	1,992	2,356	1,770	2,207	1,802	1,917	1,743	1,412	1,639	1,748
Long Term Debt	1,681	836	1,391	1,553	2,815	2,016	1,676	1,267	422	413
Common Equity	3,252	4,081	3,838	3,573	3,478	3,267	2,908	2,570	2,586	2,549
Total Capital	4,944	4,929	5,398	5,232	6,293	5,283	4,584	3,837	3,008	2,962
Capital Expenditures	780	181	210	292	560	1,095	929	937	520	NA
Cash Flow	852	760	636	626	458	674	562	530	450	360
Current Ratio	1.0	0.8	0.7	0.8	1.2	0.7	0.9	0.9	0.8	0.9
% Long Term Debt of Capitalization	34.0	16.9	25.7	29.7	44.7	38.2	36.6	33.0	14.0	13.9
% Net Income of Revenue	5.8	5.9	5.3	5.2	2.3	4.8	4.6	4.9	3.6	3.7
% Return on Assets	7.8	7.1	5.8	5.0	2.7	6.2	5.9	6.8	6.6	NA
% Return on Equity	18.2	15.0	12.8	12.5	7.0	15.5	14.6	15.1	16.1	NA

Data as orig reptd.; bef. results of disc opers/spec. items. Per share data adj. for stk. divs.; EPS diluted. E-Estimated. NA-Not Available. NM-Not Meaningful. NR-Not Ranked. UR-Under Review.

Office: 10400 Fernwood Road, Bethesda, MD 20817.
Telephone: 301-380-3000.
Website: http://www.marriott.com
Chrmn & CEO: J.W. Marriott, Jr.

Pres & COO: W.J. Shaw
EVP & CFO: A.M. Sorenson
EVP & General Counsel: J. Ryan
Secy: T.L. Turner

Investor Contact: T. Marder (301-380-2553)
Board of Directors: R. S. Braddock, L. W. Kellner, D. L. Lee, J. W. Marriott, III, J. W. Marriott, Jr., F. D. McKenzie, G. Munoz, H. J. Pearce, W. J. Shaw, L. M. Small

Founded: 1971
Domicile: Delaware
Employees: 143,000

STANDARD &POOR'S

Marshall & Ilsley Corp

S&P Recommendation BUY ★★★★★

Price $47.77 (as of Oct 27, 2006)

12-Mo. Target Price $53.00

Investment Style Large-Cap Growth

GICS Sector Financials
Sub-Industry Regional Banks

Comment This bank holding company operates mainly in Wisconsin, and also in Arizona, Nevada, Minnesota, Missouri, Florida, Kansas, and Oklahoma.

Key Stock Statistics (Source S&P, Vickers, company reports)

52-Wk Range	$49.10–40.83	S&P Oper. EPS 2006E	3.34	P/E on S&P Oper. EPS 2006E	14.3	Dividend Rate/Share	$1.08
Trailing 12-Month EPS	$3.23	S&P Oper. EPS 2007E	3.65	Common Shares Outstg. (M)	254.3	Yield (%)	2.26
Trailing 12-Month P/E	14.8	S&P Core EPS 2006E	3.25	Market Capitalization(B)	$12.148	Beta	0.54
$10K Invested 5 Yrs Ago	$17,854	S&P Core EPS 2007E	3.65	Institutional Ownership (%)	49	S&P Credit Rating	A

Price Performance

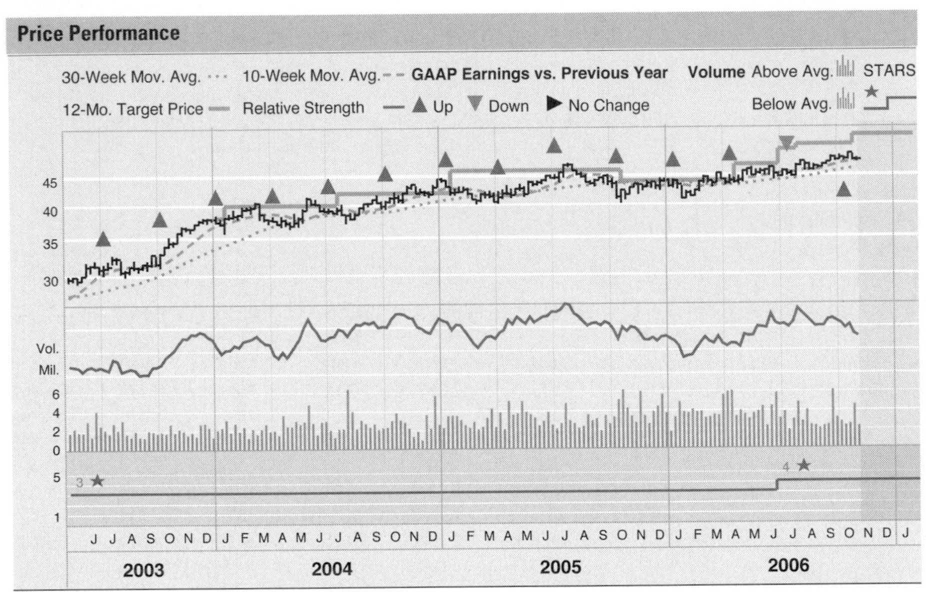

Options: ASE, Ph

Highlights

- The 12-month target price for MI has recently been changed to $53.00 from $51.00. The Highlights section of this Stock Report will be updated accordingly.

Investment Rationale/Risk

- The Investment Rationale/Risk section of this Stock Report will be updated shortly. For the latest News story on MI from MarketScope, see below.
- 10/16/06 04:04 pm EDT... S&P MAINTAINS BUY OPINION ON SHARES OF MARSHALL & ILSLEY (MI 48.16****): MI posts Q3 EPS of $0.92 vs. $0.75, $0.09 above our estimate. After $0.11 charge to terminate interest rate swaps not eligible for hedge accounting under FAS 133, core EPS is $0.81. Non-interest expense equal to 60.0% of revenues was better than our estimates, and provision for loan losses of $10.3M was below our projection. We are raising our '06 EPS estimate by $0.09 to $3.34, and still see $3.65 for '07. At 13.2X our '07 estimate, shares are at a discount to peers' 14.5X. We are raising our 12-month target price to $53 from $51, or 14.5X our '07 EPS estimate. /E.Oja

Qualitative Risk Assessment

LOW	MEDIUM	HIGH

Our risk assessment reflects our view of the company's large-cap valuation, good credit quality of its loan portfolio, and history of profitability. While the company operates in a highly competitive and fragmented industry, the industry tends to produce relatively stable financial results.

Quantitative Evaluations

S&P Quality Ranking A

D	C	B-	B	B+	A-	A	A+

Relative Strength Rank MODERATE

37

LOWEST = 1 HIGHEST = 99

Revenue/Earnings Data

Revenue (Million $)

	1Q	2Q	3Q	4Q	Year
2006	1,139	1,290	--	--	--
2005	895.1	975.8	1,014	--	3,963
2004	702.5	728.0	792.2	--	3,112
2003	548.7	682.2	696.3	818.5	2,746
2002	639.4	654.3	665.3	--	2,650
2001	699.4	559.3	678.9	--	2,712

Earnings Per Share ($)

	1Q	2Q	3Q	4Q	Year
2006	0.78	0.79	0.92	E0.85	E3.34
2005	0.73	0.81	0.78	0.78	3.10
2004	0.65	0.67	0.69	0.76	2.77
2003	0.56	0.59	0.61	0.62	2.38
2002	0.53	0.54	0.54	0.55	2.16
2001	0.40	0.28	0.38	0.49	1.54

Fiscal year ended Dec. 31. Next earnings report expected: Mid January. EPS Estimates based on S&P Operating Earnings; historical GAAP earnings are as reported.

Dividend Data (Dates: mm/dd Payment Date: mm/dd/yy)

Amount ($)	Date Decl.	Ex-Div. Date	Stk. of Record	Payment Date
0.240	02/16	02/27	03/01	03/10/06
0.270	04/25	05/24	05/26	06/09/06
0.270	08/17	08/29	08/31	09/08/06
0.270	10/19	11/28	11/30	12/08/06

Dividends have been paid since 1938. Source: Company reports.

Marshall & Ilsley Corp

Business Summary July 18, 2006

CORPORATE OVERVIEW. MI owns banking subsidiaries with operations in Wisconsin and the metropolitan areas of Phoenix and Tucson, AZ, Minneapolis/St. Paul, MN, St. Louis, MO, Las Vegas, NV, and Naples and Bonita Springs, FL. MI also owns nonbanking subsidiaries that are related or incidental to banking. The company has two reportable business segments: Banking (54% of total external revenues) and Data Services (37%). The company also has other business operations (8%) that include trust services, residential mortgage banking, capital markets, brokerage and insurance, commercial leasing, commercial mortgage banking, and community development investments.

The Banking segment consists of lending and deposit gathering as well as other banking-related products and services. As the company's products involve credit risk, the company aims to control and monitor this risk by active asset quality management, including the use of lending standards, potential borrower review, and establishment of collateral in certain cases.

The Data Services segment solely includes the Metavante subsidiary. Metavante delivers banking and payment technologies to financial services firms and businesses and organizes its business into two groups, Financial Solutions (FS) and Payment Solutions (PS). Metavante products and services drive account processing for deposit, loan and trust systems, image-based and conventional check processing, electronic funds transfer, consumer health care payments, and electronic presentment and payment.

MARKET PROFILE. MI's primary Midwestern footprint includes 200 branches in Wisconsin, 41 in Arizona, 21 in Missouri, 21 in Minnesota, 14 in Florida, 13 in Kansas, 3 in Oklahoma, and 1 in Nevada. The projection for deposit weighted average population growth in the company's service territory is 7.6% from 2005 to 2010 according to SNL Financial. The projected national growth rate is 6.3% and the population weighted average growth rate of the states in the company's service territory is 6.1%.

Company Financials

Per Share Data ($) Year Ended Dec. 31	2005	2004	2003	2002	2001	2000	1999	1998	1997	1996
Tangible Book Value	9.02	7.76	9.96	8.61	9.00	9.06	8.12	8.67	7.43	6.39
Earnings	3.10	2.77	2.38	2.16	1.54	1.45	1.57	1.31	1.21	1.04
S&P Core Earnings	2.99	2.66	2.28	2.07	1.49	NA	NA	NA	NA	NA
Dividends	0.93	0.81	0.70	0.55	0.57	0.52	0.47	0.43	0.39	0.36
Payout Ratio	30%	29%	29%	25%	37%	36%	30%	33%	32%	35%
Prices:High	47.40	44.70	38.46	32.12	32.12	31.13	36.38	31.13	31.13	17.81
Prices:Low	40.05	35.67	24.60	23.11	23.54	19.13	27.19	19.69	16.19	12.19
P/E Ratio:High	15	16	16	15	21	22	23	24	26	17
P/E Ratio:Low	13	13	10	11	15	13	17	15	13	12
Income Statement Analysis (Million $)										
Net Interest Income	1,233	1,132	1,057	1,006	843	673	705	676	564	506
Tax Equivalent Adjustment	33.3	NA	NA	32.2	31.2	31.0	28.7	26.2	22.8	13.9
Non Interest Income	1,704	1,411	1,194	1,089	1,020	978	850	726	596	488
Loan Loss Provision	44.8	38.0	63.0	74.4	54.1	30.4	25.4	27.1	17.3	15.2
% Expense/Operating Revenue	62.2%	62.7%	64.5%	61.9%	68.1%	65.4%	64.2%	67.1%	66.9%	67.5%
Pretax Income	1,090	945	758	719	501	470	528	465	370	313
Effective Tax Rate	33.3%	33.6%	28.3%	33.2%	32.6%	32.5%	32.9%	35.2%	33.8%	35.1%
Net Income	727	627	544	480	338	317	355	301	245	203
% Net Interest Margin	3.31	3.52	3.65	3.96	3.67	2.81	3.58	3.69	4.00	4.14
S&P Core Earnings	705	605	519	453	319	NA	NA	NA	NA	NA
Balance Sheet & Other Financial Data (Million $)										
Money Market Assets	330	191	163	250	947	163	175	146	81.0	85.4
Investment Securities	6,320	6,085	5,607	5,209	4,464	5,848	5,575	5,192	4,969	3,839
Commercial Loans	19,023	16,646	14,254	6,586	10,815	9,649	4,754	4,078	3,865	3,249
Other Loans	14,866	12,810	10,896	17,011	8,480	7,938	11,580	9,918	8,776	6,053
Total Assets	46,213	40,437	34,373	32,875	27,254	26,078	24,370	21,566	19,477	14,763
Demand Deposits	5,525	15,005	4,715	4,462	3,559	3,130	2,831	2,929	2,723	2,471
Time Deposits	22,149	11,450	17,555	15,932	12,934	16,119	13,604	12,991	11,633	8,481
Long Term Debt	6,669	5,027	2,735	2,284	1,560	921	665	794	791	336
Common Equity	4,769	3,970	3,329	3,037	2,536	3,200	2,117	2,282	1,919	1,261
% Return on Assets	1.7	1.7	1.6	1.6	1.3	1.3	1.5	1.5	1.4	1.5
% Return on Equity	16.6	17.1	17.1	17.4	13.8	10.6	13.8	14.0	15.1	15.9
% Loan Loss Reserve	1.1	1.2	1.4	1.4	1.4	1.3	1.4	1.6	1.6	1.7
% Loans/Deposits	123.5	111.6	113.1	117.2	117.0	91.4	99.4	88.0	87.4	85.0
% Equity to Assets	10.1	9.8	9.5	9.2	9.0	11.9	11.0	10.2	9.3	9.4

Data as orig reptd.; bef. results of disc opers/spec. items. Per share data adj. for stk. divs.; EPS diluted. E-Estimated. NA-Not Available. NM-Not Meaningful. NR-Not Ranked. UR-Under Review.

Office: 770 N Water St, Milwaukee, WI 53202.
Telephone: 414-765-7801.
Website: http://www.micorp.com
Chrmn & CEO: D.J. Kuester

Pres: M. Furlong
SVP & CFO: G.A. Smith
SVP & Treas: M.C. Smith
SVP, Secy & General Counsel: R.J. Erickson

Investor Contact: D.L. Urban
Board of Directors: M. M. Aslin, A. N. Baur, J. F. Chait, J. W. Daniels, Jr., M. F. Furlong, B. E. Jacobs, T. D. Kellner, D. J. Kuester, K. C. Lyall, J. A. Mellowes, E. L. Meyer, R. J. O'Toole, S. W. Orr, Jr., P. M. Platten III, J. S. Shiely, D. S. Waller, G. E. Wardeberg, J. B. Wigdale

Founded: 1959
Domicile: Wisconsin
Employees: 13,967

STANDARD &POOR'S

Marsh & McLennan Companies Inc.

S&P Recommendation	Price	12-Mo. Target Price	Investment Style
BUY ★★★★★	$29.40 (as of Oct 27, 2006)	$33.00	Large-Cap Growth

GICS Sector Financials
Sub-Industry Insurance Brokers

Comment This global professional services concern provides risk and insurance services, investment management, and consulting services through its operating companies.

Key Stock Statistics (Source S&P, Vickers, company reports)

52-Wk Range	$33.42–24.00	S&P Oper. EPS 2006E	1.63	P/E on S&P Oper. EPS 2006E	18.0	Dividend Rate/Share	$0.68
Trailing 12-Month EPS	$1.23	S&P Oper. EPS 2007E	1.85	Common Shares Outstg. (M)	550.4	Yield (%)	2.31
Trailing 12-Month P/E	23.9	S&P Core EPS 2006E	1.53	Market Capitalization(B)	$16.182	Beta	1.01
$10K Invested 5 Yrs Ago	$6,399	S&P Core EPS 2007E	1.73	Institutional Ownership (%)	77	S&P Credit Rating	BBB

Price Performance

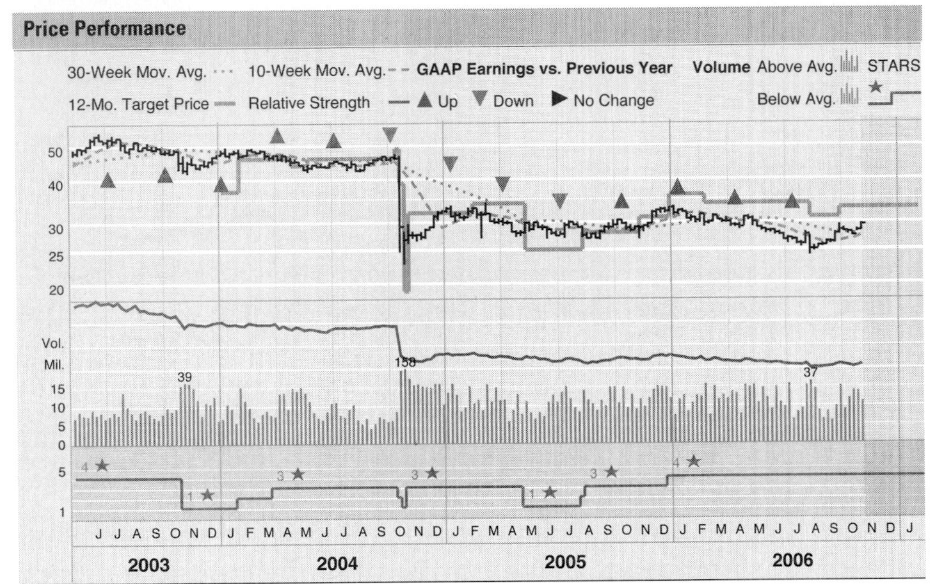

Options: CBOE, P

Analysis prepared by **Frank Braden** on September 22, 2006, when the stock traded at **$ 28.45**.

Highlights

- We estimate that total revenue will remain flat in 2006. We expect risk and insurance service revenue to decline 5%, largely due to the sale of Crump Group and Sedgwick. Marsh should benefit from better client retention, and we see margins improving on cost discipline. We project that revenues will rise 4% for the risk consulting and technology segment. Although we see net outflows at Putnam reversing in 2006, we do not expect growth in assets under management, nor do we see any material expense reduction. We estimate mid-single digit level growth for total consulting revenues, mostly on growth in specialty consulting.
- We estimate that adjusted pretax operating margins will rise roughly 80 basis points in 2006, primarily on our expectation that there will be significant improvements in adjusted operating margins for risk and insurance services and risk and consulting technology.
- Our 2006 operating EPS estimate is $1.63. Our EPS estimate excludes potential non-recurring charges, including additional restructuring, employee retention and settlement administration and legal expenses.

Investment Rationale/Risk

- We see visibility improving for financial results in late 2006 as management completes its efforts to right-size operations to contend with the loss of contingent commissions, as well as revenue pressures from a soft property and casualty market. Although we believe MMC faces a number of near-term challenges, we see management restructuring, higher retention rates, and improving results at Putnam leading to stronger results in late 2006 and 2007.
- Risks to our recommendation and target price include lower than expected revenue on rate increases and/or deteriorating client retention; less than projected cost savings from restructurings and layoffs; less than anticipated cost savings and growth at Kroll; and unfavorable legal and regulatory developments related to contingent commissions. Our corporate governance concerns include a "poison pill" anti-takeover plan that was not approved by shareholders.
- Our 12-month target price of $33 is based on a P/E multiple of 20X applied to our 2006 operating EPS estimate of $1.63, in line with MMC's historical multiple.

Qualitative Risk Assessment

LOW | **MEDIUM** | HIGH

Our risk assessment reflects the company's leading market share position, diversified businesses, and global scale, offset by regulatory scrutiny and business model changes as a result of contingent commissions.

Quantitative Evaluations

S&P Quality Ranking A-

D | C | B- | B | B+ | **A-** | A | A+

Relative Strength Rank STRONG

74

LOWEST = 1 HIGHEST = 99

Revenue/Earnings Data

Revenue (Million $)

	1Q	2Q	3Q	4Q	Year
2006	3,025	2,980	--	--	--
2005	3,070	2,977	2,779	2,826	11,652
2004	3,196	3,028	2,950	2,985	12,159
2003	2,852	2,865	2,837	3,034	11,588
2002	2,635	2,612	2,553	2,640	10,440
2001	2,594	2,505	2,371	2,473	9,943

Earnings Per Share ($)

2006	0.43	0.31	**E**0.33	**E**0.35	**E**1.63
2005	0.24	0.30	0.11	0.03	0.67
2004	0.83	0.73	0.04	-1.29	0.33
2003	0.81	0.66	0.65	0.69	2.81
2002	0.74	0.60	0.55	0.57	2.45
2001	0.64	0.51	0.29	0.26	1.70

Fiscal year ended Dec. 31. Next earnings report expected: Early November. EPS Estimates based on S&P Operating Earnings; historical GAAP earnings are as reported.

Dividend Data (Dates: mm/dd Payment Date: mm/dd/yy)

Amount ($)	Date Decl.	Ex-Div. Date	Stk. of Record	Payment Date
0.170	11/16	01/05	01/09	02/15/06
0.170	03/15	04/05	04/07	05/15/06
0.170	05/18	07/05	07/07	08/15/06
0.170	09/13	10/12	10/16	11/15/06

Dividends have been paid since 1923. Source: Company reports.

Marsh & McLennan Companies Inc.

Business Summary September 22, 2006

CORPORATE OVERVIEW. MMC is the world's largest insurance broker, based on 2005 revenues. The insurance brokerage industry has suffered in recent years from probes into bid rigging and contingent commissions. We believe recent settlements and corporate restructurings have improved the outlook at MMC, but ongoing legal and regulatory proceedings and uncertainty regarding implementing a new business model present weak near-term earnings visibility, in our view.

MMC operates in four main segments: risk and insurance, risk consulting and technology, consulting, and investment management. Risk and insurance (47% of segment revenues and 36% of segment operating profits in 2005; 52% and 14% in 2004) includes insurance services, reinsurance services and risk capital holdings, risk management and consulting, insurance broking, and insurance program management. Reinsurance broking and catastrophe and financial modeling services are done under the Guy Carpenter name. Risk consulting and technology (8% of segment revenues and 15% of segment operating profits in 2005; 3.4% and 8% in 2004) are performed under the Kroll name.

Investment management (13% of segment revenues and 31% of segment operating profits in 2005; 14% and 16% in 2004) is primarily carried out by Putnam Investments. At December 31, 2005, assets under management (AUM) amounted to $196 billion, a further decline from $217 billion at December 31, 2004, $240 billion at year-end 2003, and $251 billion at year-end 2002. We expect net outflows will gradually reverse in 2006. Consulting and human resource outsourcing (32% and 53%in 2005; 30% and 68% in 2004) is done under the Mercer name.

LEGAL/REGULATORY ISSUES. In April 2004, Putnam entered into the final settlements of charges by the SEC and the Massachusetts Secretary of the Commonwealth related to alleged short-term trading of Putnam mutual funds by employees in their personal accounts. Under the settlements, Putnam agreed, without admitting or denying the charges, to pay $110 million in penalties and restitution, and to implement a number of remedial actions. In March 2005, an independent consultant concluded that Putnam should pay fund shareholders $108.5 million, of which $83.5 million was in addition to previous settlement amounts.

Company Financials

Per Share Data ($) Year Ended Dec. 31	**2005**	**2004**	**2003**	**2002**	**2001**	**2000**	**1999**	**1998**	**1997**	**1996**
Tangible Book Value	NM	NM	NM	NM	NM	9.47	NM	NM	1.53	3.10
Cash Flow	1.58	1.18	3.52	3.10	2.61	2.94	2.07	1.98	1.19	1.38
Earnings	0.67	0.33	2.81	2.45	1.70	2.05	1.31	1.49	0.80	1.06
S&P Core Earnings	0.38	1.11	2.29	1.60	0.91	NA	NA	NA	NA	NA
Dividends	0.68	0.99	1.18	1.09	1.03	0.95	0.85	0.73	0.55	0.55
Payout Ratio	101%	NM	42%	44%	61%	46%	65%	49%	69%	52%
Prices:High	34.25	49.69	54.97	57.30	59.03	67.84	48.38	32.16	26.67	19.15
Prices:Low	26.67	22.75	38.27	34.61	39.50	35.25	28.56	21.69	17.10	14.04
P/E Ratio:High	51	NM	19	23	35	33	37	22	33	18
P/E Ratio:Low	40	NM	14	14	23	17	22	15	21	13

Income Statement Analysis (Million $)	2005	2004	2003	2002	2001	2000	1999	1998	1997	1996
Revenue	11,652	12,159	11,588	10,440	9,943	10,157	9,157	7,190	6,009	4,149
Operating Income	1,386	2,073	2,887	2,633	2,283	2,179	1,859	1,671	944	855
Depreciation	490	456	391	359	520	488	400	251	199	140
Interest Expense	332	219	185	160	196	247	233	140	106	61.6
Pretax Income	571	450	2,335	2,133	1,590	1,955	1,247	1,305	662	668
Effective Tax Rate	33.6%	57.6%	33.0%	35.0%	37.7%	38.5%	41.8%	39.0%	39.7%	31.3%
Net Income	369	176	1,540	1,365	974	1,181	726	796	399	459
S&P Core Earnings	211	590	1,254	890	525	NA	NA	NA	NA	NA

Balance Sheet & Other Financial Data (Million $)	2005	2004	2003	2002	2001	2000	1999	1998	1997	1996
Cash	2,020	1,396	665	546	537	240	428	610	424	300
Current Assets	5,262	4,887	3,901	3,664	3,792	3,639	3,283	3,245	2,569	1,749
Total Assets	17,892	18,337	15,053	13,855	13,293	13,769	13,021	11,871	7,914	4,545
Current Liabilities	4,351	4,735	4,089	3,863	3,938	4,119	4,318	5,002	2,379	1,556
Long Term Debt	5,044	4,691	2,910	2,891	2,334	2,347	2,357	1,590	1,240	458
Common Equity	5,360	5,056	5,451	5,018	5,173	5,228	4,170	3,659	3,199	1,889
Total Capital	10,404	9,747	8,361	7,909	7,507	7,575	6,527	5,249	4,439	2,347
Capital Expenditures	345	376	436	423	433	472	358	297	202	157
Cash Flow	859	632	1,931	1,724	1,494	1,669	1,126	1,047	598	599
Current Ratio	1.2	1.0	1.0	0.9	1.0	0.9	0.8	0.6	1.1	1.1
% Long Term Debt of Capitalization	48.5	48.1	34.8	36.6	31.1	31.0	36.1	30.3	27.9	19.6
% Net Income of Revenue	3.2	1.4	13.3	13.1	9.8	11.6	7.9	11.1	6.6	11.1
% Return on Assets	2.0	1.1	10.7	10.1	7.2	8.8	5.8	8.0	6.4	10.4
% Return on Equity	7.1	3.4	29.4	26.8	18.7	25.1	18.5	23.2	15.7	25.9

Data as orig reptd.; bef. results of disc opers/spec. items. Per share data adj. for stk. divs.; EPS diluted. E-Estimated. NA-Not Available. NM-Not Meaningful. NR-Not Ranked. UR-Under Review.

Office: 1166 Avenue Of The Americas, New York, NY 10036-2774.
Telephone: 212-345-5000.
Email: shareowner-svcs@email.bankofny.com
Website: http://www.mmc.com

Chrmn: S.R. Hardis
Pres & CEO: M.G. Cherkasky
EVP & General Counsel: P.J. Beshar
SVP & Chief Admin: M.A. Petrullo

SVP & CCO: E.S. Gilbert
Investor Contact: M. Bischoff (212-345-5470)
Board of Directors: L. M. Baker, Jr., L. W. Bernard, Z. W. Carter, M. G. Cherkasky, O. Fanjul, S. Hardis, G. S. King, M. D. Oken, D. A. Olsen, M. O. Schapiro, A. Simmons, L. of Monkton

Founded: 1923
Domicile: Delaware
Employees: 55,000

STANDARD &POOR'S

Masco Corp

S&P Recommendation BUY ★★★★★

Price $28.36 (as of Oct 27, 2006)

12-Mo. Target Price $32.00

Investment Style Large-Cap Value

GICS Sector Industrials
Sub-Industry Building Products

Comment MAS is one of the world's leading makers of faucets, cabinets, coatings and other consumer brand-name home improvement and building products.

Key Stock Statistics (Source S&P, Vickers, company reports)

52-Wk Range	$33.70–25.85	S&P Oper. EPS 2006E	2.30	P/E on S&P Oper. EPS 2006E	12.3	Dividend Rate/Share	$0.88
Trailing 12-Month EPS	$2.08	S&P Oper. EPS 2007E	2.45	Common Shares Outstg. (M)	398.1	Yield (%)	3.10
Trailing 12-Month P/E	13.6	S&P Core EPS 2006E	2.30	Market Capitalization(B)	$11.290	Beta	0.89
$10K Invested 5 Yrs Ago	$15,317	S&P Core EPS 2007E	2.45	Institutional Ownership (%)	91	S&P Credit Rating	BBB+

Price Performance

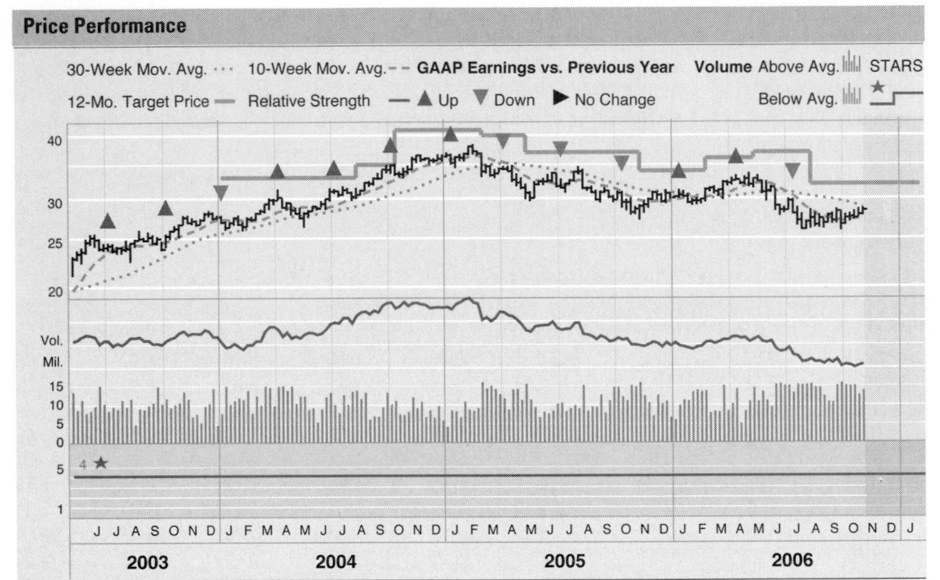

Options: ASE, P

Analysis prepared by **Michael W. Jaffe** on August 11, 2006, when the stock traded at **$ 26.55**.

Highlights

- We forecast a 6% sales gain in 2006, followed by a 5% increase in 2007. The slower housing market is limiting demand for MAS's products. A moderation in consumer spending, which we think has been driven by higher fuel prices and interest rates, has also restricted sales in its markets. We see much of the expected gains through 2007 coming from selling price increases, and to a lesser extent, from market share gains. We also look for flat sales in Europe, as we expect only modest economic growth in that region.
- We expect flat net margins in the second half of 2006 and in 2007. We see margins being aided by price hikes that we forecast and projected benefits from cost cutting initiatives put in place over the past year. However, we see these factors being offset by our view of a challenging market environment, and ongoing high materials, freight and energy costs.
- Our 2006 and 2007 EPS forecasts each include $0.05 a share of projected stock compensation expense. Our 2006 forecast excludes $0.24 a share of expected net one-time charges, of which $0.20 was recorded in the first half of the year. Operating EPS in 2005 was $2.19.

Investment Rationale/Risk

- We believe that macroeconomic factors and slower housing markets will limit Masco's growth in the coming periods, but that MAS's strong brand names and greater home center presence will enable it to gain market share. Despite what we view as softer business trends in Masco's markets, we think it will record moderate EPS gains through 2007. Based on these views and valuation considerations, we believe Masco is undervalued.
- Risks to our recommendation and target price include higher than expected interest rates in coming periods; an even larger than estimated impact from commodities prices; and a potential inability to put through anticipated price hikes to offset these higher costs.
- Recently trading at 10X our 2007 EPS forecast, MAS has been at a 21% discount to the S&P 500 and the low end of its range for the past decade. We believe that MAS's business has cyclical qualities, but think its very strong positions in many of the markets it serves should allow it to trade closer to a market multiple. Using a multiple of 12X our 2007 estimate, which is about a 9% discount to the S&P 500, we arrive at our 12-month target price of $32.

Qualitative Risk Assessment

LOW | MEDIUM | HIGH

Our low risk assessment for Masco reflects the company's relatively consistent generation of strong levels of free cash flow, and what we view as a very good business model. These factors have, in our view, been major contributors to MAS's 48 consecutive years of cash dividend increases.

Quantitative Evaluations

S&P Quality Ranking A-

D | C | B- | B | B+ | **A-** | A | A+

Relative Strength Rank MODERATE

49

LOWEST = 1 HIGHEST = 99

Revenue/Earnings Data

Revenue (Million $)

	1Q	2Q	3Q	4Q	Year
2006	3,186	3,389	--	--	--
2005	2,914	3,286	3,296	3,146	12,642
2004	2,806	3,061	3,173	3,034	12,074
2003	2,498	2,788	2,918	2,862	10,936
2002	2,100	2,314	2,518	2,487	9,419
2001	1,911	2,085	2,247	2,115	8,358

Earnings Per Share ($)

	1Q	2Q	3Q	4Q	Year
2006	0.51	0.54	E0.60	E0.45	E2.30
2005	0.47	0.62	0.60	0.34	2.03
2004	0.52	0.65	0.64	0.23	2.04
2003	0.32	0.46	0.53	0.19	1.51
2002	0.31	0.43	0.24	0.37	1.33
2001	0.25	0.30	-0.39	0.26	0.42

Fiscal year ended Dec. 31. Next earnings report expected: Early November. EPS Estimates based on S&P Operating Earnings; historical GAAP earnings are as reported.

Dividend Data (Dates: mm/dd Payment Date: mm/dd/yy)

Amount ($)	Date Decl.	Ex-Div. Date	Stk. of Record	Payment Date
0.200	12/07	01/04	01/06	02/06/06
0.220	03/29	04/10	04/12	05/08/06
0.220	06/23	07/05	07/07	08/07/06
0.220	09/15	10/04	10/06	11/06/06

Dividends have been paid since 1944. Source: Company reports.

Please read the Required Disclosures and Analyst Certification on the last page of this report.

Masco Corp

Business Summary August 11, 2006

Masco is one of the largest U.S. makers of brand name consumer products for home improvement and new construction markets; it derives most of its revenues from the sale of faucets, kitchen and bath cabinets, plumbing supplies and architectural coatings. Operations are focused on North America (83% of 2005 sales) and Europe (most of the rest). Home Depot contributed 21% of 2005 sales.

The plumbing products division (25% of 2005 sales) is a major global faucet maker. MAS revolutionized faucets in 1954 with the Delta, and also offers the Peerless, Brizo and Newport Brass brands and private label faucets. In addition, the division offers other bath products, including plumbing fittings and valves, bathtubs and shower enclosures, and spa items; brand names include Alsons, Aqua Glass, and HotSpring. It makes cabinets and related products (26%), including cabinetry for kitchen, bath, storage, home office and home entertainment applications, featuring the Kraftmaid, Merillat, and Mill's Pride brands. MAS believes it is the largest U.S. maker of kitchen and bath cabinetry.

MAS sells decorative architectural items (13%), including paints and stains, and decorative bath and shower accessories. Trade names include Behr in paints and stains and Franklin Brass in bath and shower. It also supplies and installs insulation products and other building products such as fireplaces, cabinetry, gutters, shelving and windows (24%); and sells other specialty products (11%), such as windows and patio doors, electric staple guns, radiators, and lock sets used mostly in the hospitality area.

An aggressive acquisition program enabled Masco to build large positions in the markets it serves. Since 2003, however, MAS has adopted a business plan that shifted it away from a focus on takeovers. It now plans to concentrate on internal growth, with an increased emphasis on cash flow and return on invested capital.

MAS raised net proceeds of $598 million from a May 2002 public offering of 22 million common shares. It also repurchased 37 million shares in 2003, at a total cost of $903 million, 31 million shares in 2004, for a sum of $779 million, and 31 million in 2005, for a total of $986 million. It bought back 24 million more shares in the first seven months of 2006.

Company Financials

Per Share Data ($) Year Ended Dec. 31	**2005**	**2004**	**2003**	**2002**	**2001**	**2000**	**1999**	**1998**	**1997**	**1996**
Tangible Book Value	0.88	1.54	1.36	1.31	1.30	2.78	3.14	4.99	4.53	4.30
Cash Flow	2.66	2.56	2.00	1.85	1.02	1.84	1.68	1.78	1.48	1.23
Earnings	2.03	2.04	1.51	1.33	0.42	1.31	1.28	1.39	1.17	0.92
S&P Core Earnings	2.17	2.25	1.67	1.52	1.12	NA	NA	NA	NA	NA
Dividends	0.78	0.66	0.58	0.55	0.52	0.49	0.45	0.43	0.40	0.38
Payout Ratio	38%	32%	38%	41%	125%	37%	35%	31%	34%	41%
Prices:High	38.43	37.02	28.44	29.43	26.94	27.00	33.69	33.00	26.91	18.44
Prices:Low	27.15	25.88	16.59	17.25	17.76	14.50	22.50	20.75	16.00	13.25
P/E Ratio:High	19	18	19	22	64	21	26	24	23	20
P/E Ratio:Low	13	13	11	13	42	11	18	15	14	14
Income Statement Analysis (Million $)										
Revenue	12,642	12,074	10,936	9,419	8,358	7,243	6,307	4,345	3,760	3,237
Operating Income	1,881	1,944	1,738	1,683	1,309	1,295	1,093	817	703	580
Depreciation	241	237	244	220	269	238	182	136	116	99.7
Interest Expense	247	217	262	237	239	191	120	85.3	79.9	74.7
Pretax Income	1,412	1,518	1,216	1,031	301	893	904	755	631	503
Effective Tax Rate	36.7%	37.5%	38.1%	33.8%	34.0%	33.8%	37.0%	37.0%	39.4%	41.3%
Net Income	872	930	740	682	199	592	570	476	382	295
S&P Core Earnings	936	1,027	816	779	528	NA	NA	NA	NA	NA
Balance Sheet & Other Financial Data (Million $)										
Cash	1,964	1,256	795	1,067	312	169	231	542	441	474
Current Assets	5,123	4,402	3,804	3,950	2,627	2,308	2,110	1,863	1,627	1,431
Total Assets	12,559	12,541	12,149	12,050	9,183	7,744	6,635	5,167	4,334	3,702
Current Liabilities	2,894	2,147	2,099	1,932	1,237	1,078	846	847	620	518
Long Term Debt	3,915	4,187	3,848	4,316	3,628	3,018	2,431	1,391	1,322	1,236
Common Equity	4,848	5,596	5,456	5,294	4,120	3,426	3,137	2,729	2,229	1,840
Total Capital	9,665	9,783	9,304	9,610	7,747	6,444	5,788	4,321	3,714	3,183
Capital Expenditures	282	310	271	285	274	388	351	189	167	138
Cash Flow	1,113	1,167	984	902	468	830	751	612	498	395
Current Ratio	1.8	2.1	1.8	2.0	2.1	2.1	2.5	2.2	2.6	2.8
% Long Term Debt of Capitalization	40.5	42.8	41.4	44.9	46.8	46.8	42.0	32.2	35.6	38.8
% Net Income of Revenue	6.9	7.7	6.8	7.2	2.4	8.2	9.0	11.0	10.2	9.1
% Return on Assets	6.9	7.5	6.1	6.5	2.3	8.2	9.3	10.0	9.5	7.9
% Return on Equity	17.0	16.6	13.8	14.7	5.3	18.0	19.3	19.2	18.8	16.9

Data as orig reptd.; bef. results of disc opers/spec. items. Per share data adj. for stk. divs.; EPS diluted. E-Estimated. NA-Not Available. NM-Not Meaningful. NR-Not Ranked. UR-Under Review.

Office: 21001 Van Born Road, Taylor, MI 48180.
Telephone: 313-274-7400.
Website: http://www.masco.com
Chrmn & CEO: R.A. Manoogian

Pres & COO: A.H. Barry
SVP & CFO: T. Wadhams
SVP & General Counsel: J.R. Leekley
VP & Treas: J.G. Sznewajs

Investor Contact: M.C. Duey (313-274-7400)
Board of Directors: D. W. Archer, T. G. Denomme, P. A. Dow, A. F. Earley, Jr., V. G. Istock, D. L. Johnston, J. M. Losh, R. A. Manoogian, M. Van Lokeren

Founded: 1929
Domicile: Delaware
Employees: 62,000

Mattel Inc.

S&P Recommendation HOLD ★★★★★

Price $22.50 (as of Oct 27, 2006)

12-Mo. Target Price $22.00

Investment Style Mid-Cap Value

GICS Sector Consumer Discretionary
Sub-Industry Leisure Products

Comment This large toy company's brands and products include Barbie dolls, Fisher-Price toys, and Hot Wheels.

Key Stock Statistics (Source S&P, Vickers, company reports)

52-Wk Range	$22.58–14.55	S&P Oper. EPS 2006E	1.32	P/E on S&P Oper. EPS 2006E	17.0	Dividend Rate/Share	$0.50
Trailing 12-Month EPS	$1.47	S&P Oper. EPS 2007E	1.39	Common Shares Outstg. (M)	378.0	Yield (%)	2.22
Trailing 12-Month P/E	15.3	S&P Core EPS 2006E	1.32	Market Capitalization(B)	$8.505	Beta	0.67
$10K Invested 5 Yrs Ago	$12,740	S&P Core EPS 2007E	1.39	Institutional Ownership (%)	89	S&P Credit Rating	BBB-

Price Performance

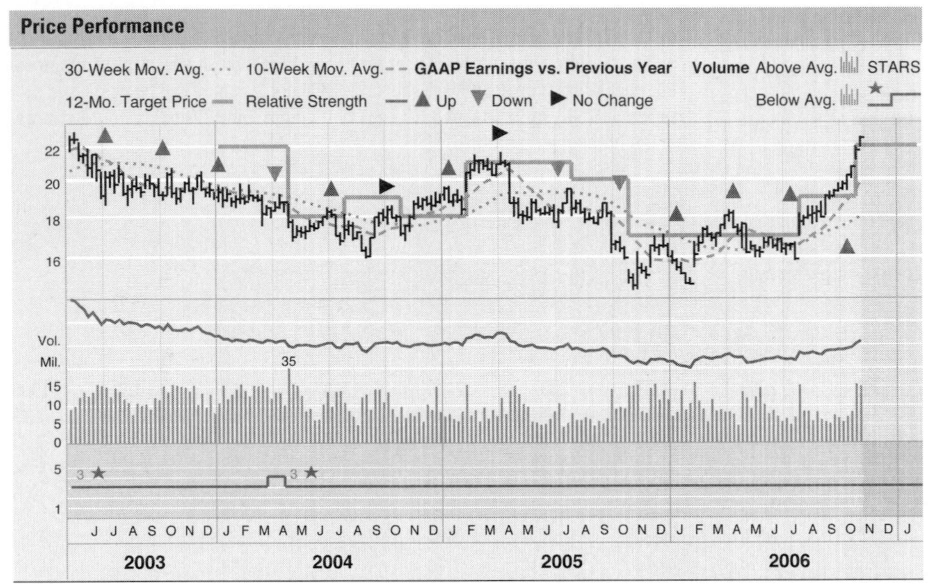

Options: ASE, CBOE, P, Ph

Qualitative Risk Assessment

LOW | **MEDIUM** | HIGH

Our risk assessment reflects our favorable view of MAT's leading market share position and strong balance sheet, offset by our negative view of the intense industry rivalry and concentrated buying power of U.S. toy retailers.

Quantitative Evaluations

S&P Quality Ranking B

D | C | B- | **B** | B+ | A- | A | A+

Relative Strength Rank STRONG

91

LOWEST = 1 HIGHEST = 99

Highlights

- The 12-month target price for MAT has recently been changed to $22.00 from $19.00. The Highlights section of this Stock Report will be updated accordingly.

Investment Rationale/Risk

- The Investment Rationale/Risk section of this Stock Report will be updated shortly. For the latest News story on MAT from MarketScope, see below.
- 10/16/06 01:18 pm EDT... S&P MAINTAINS HOLD RECOMMENDATION ON SHARES OF MATTEL (MAT 21.39***): Before a special item, Q3 EPS of about $0.66 versus $0.55 tops our estimate by $0.08, including stronger-than-anticipated sales and gross margin, and a lower-than-projected tax rate. In our view, Q3 shows Barbie sales stabilizing, as well as impressive gains in entertainment and Fisher-Price products. We are raising our full-year '06 EPS estimate to $1.32 from $1.21, and '07's to $1.39 from $1.27. With a more favorable EPS outlook, our target price increases to $22, about 16X our '07 EPS estimate, from $19. /T.Graves-CFA

Revenue/Earnings Data

Revenue (Million $)

	1Q	2Q	3Q	4Q	Year
2006	793.3	957.7	1,790	--	--
2005	783.1	886.8	1,666	1,843	5,179
2004	780.9	804.0	1,667	1,850	5,103
2003	745.3	769.0	1,705	1,741	4,960
2002	742.0	804.4	1,669	1,669	4,885
2001	732.0	854.3	1,613	1,605	4,804

Earnings Per Share ($)

	1Q	2Q	3Q	4Q	Year
2006	0.08	0.10	0.62	E0.66	E1.32
2005	0.02	-0.23	0.55	0.69	1.01
2004	0.02	0.06	0.61	0.68	1.35
2003	0.07	0.05	0.61	0.49	1.22
2002	-0.01	0.04	0.57	0.42	1.03
2001	-0.05	-0.01	0.46	0.32	0.71

Fiscal year ended Dec. 31. Next earnings report expected: Late January. EPS Estimates based on S&P Operating Earnings; historical GAAP earnings are as reported.

Dividend Data (Dates: mm/dd Payment Date: mm/dd/yy)

Amount ($)	Date Decl.	Ex-Div. Date	Stk. of Record	Payment Date
0.500	11/18	11/30	12/02	12/16/05

Dividends have been paid since 1990. Source: Company reports.

Mattel Inc.

Business Summary July 18, 2006

CORPORATE OVERVIEW. Mattel markets a wide variety of toy products on a worldwide basis. Brands are grouped in the following categories: Mattel Girls & Boys Brands, Fisher-Price Brands and American Girl Brands. Mattel brands include Barbie, Polly Pocket!, Disney Classics, Hot Wheels, Matchbox and Tyco R/C vehicles and playsets, Nickelodeon, Harry Potter, Yu-Gi-Oh!, Batman, Justice League, and Megaman, among others. Fisher-Price brands includes Fisher-Price, Power Wheels, Sesame Street, Little People, Winnie the Pooh, Rescue Heroes, Barney, See 'N Say, Dora the Explorer, BabyGear, and View-Master. American Girl Brands are sold directly to consumers, and its children's publications are sold to certain retailers. Brand names include American Girl Today, the American Girls Collection, and Bitty Baby.

MAT operates in the U.S. and internationally. Revenues from the international segment provided 44% of consolidated gross sales in 2005. In the international segment, the geographic breakdown was as follows: Europe 57% of 2005 sales; Latin America 26%; Canada 9%; and Asia Pacific 8%.

CORPORATE STRATEGY. We believe that two key elements of MAT's growth strategy are to build its brands and cut costs. With declining sales in its core Barbie brand, MAT has been focused on reinvigorating this product line, while driving growth in other key brands. In order to further leverage its brands, MAT also pursues licensing arrangements and strategic partnerships, which we think helps to extend its portfolio of brands into areas outside of traditional toys.

Faced with a challenging sales environment and inflationary pricing, MAT is also focused on reducing costs as a means to deliver bottom-line growth. In keeping with this strategy, in October 2005, MAT announced the consolidation of its domestic Mattel Girls & Boys Brands and Fisher-Price Brands divisions into one division. We think this consolidation will help MAT to better leverage its scale. In connection with this consolidation, MAT also recently completed a workforce reduction, eliminating approximately 200 positions.

Company Financials

Per Share Data ($) Year Ended Dec. 31	2005	2004	2003	2002	2001	2000	1999	1998	1997	1996
Tangible Book Value	4.48	3.97	3.49	2.92	1.46	0.59	1.36	1.64	4.06	3.84
Cash Flow	1.44	1.79	1.63	1.47	1.31	1.00	0.73	1.78	1.59	1.89
Earnings	1.01	1.35	1.22	1.03	0.71	0.40	-0.21	1.10	0.94	1.36
S&P Core Earnings	0.88	1.25	1.14	1.00	0.66	NA	NA	NA	NA	NA
Dividends	0.50	0.45	0.40	0.05	0.05	0.27	0.34	0.30	0.27	0.24
Payout Ratio	50%	33%	33%	5%	7%	67%	NM	27%	29%	18%
Prices:High	21.64	19.79	23.20	22.36	19.92	15.13	30.31	46.56	42.25	32.50
Prices:Low	14.52	15.94	18.57	15.05	13.52	8.94	11.69	21.25	23.38	21.63
P/E Ratio:High	21	15	19	22	20	38	NM	42	45	24
P/E Ratio:Low	14	12	15	15	19	22	NM	19	25	16
Income Statement Analysis (Million $)										
Revenue	5,179	5,103	4,960	4,885	4,804	4,670	5,515	4,782	4,835	3,786
Operating Income	840	913	974	934	881	652	671	841	1,014	796
Depreciation	175	182	184	192	263	256	390	215	190	149
Interest Expense	76.5	77.8	80.6	114	155	153	152	111	90.1	75.5
Pretax Income	652	696	741	621	430	225	-111	465	425	546
Effective Tax Rate	36.0%	17.7%	27.4%	26.8%	27.7%	24.5%	NM	28.6%	31.8%	30.8%
Net Income	417	573	538	455	311	170	-82.4	332	290	378
S&P Core Earnings	359	531	502	439	288	NA	NA	NA	NA	NA
Balance Sheet & Other Financial Data (Million $)										
Cash	998	1,157	1,153	1,267	617	232	275	212	695	501
Current Assets	2,413	2,637	2,395	2,389	2,093	1,751	2,420	2,058	2,462	1,771
Total Assets	4,372	4,756	4,511	4,460	4,541	4,313	5,127	4,262	3,804	2,894
Current Liabilities	1,463	1,727	1,468	1,649	1,597	1,502	1,818	1,317	1,173	960
Long Term Debt	525	400	589	640	1,021	1,242	1,184	984	664	364
Common Equity	2,102	2,386	2,216	1,979	1,738	1,403	1,963	1,819	1,726	1,448
Total Capital	2,627	2,786	2,805	2,619	2,759	2,645	3,147	2,804	2,486	1,812
Capital Expenditures	137	144	101	167	101	162	212	783	223	209
Cash Flow	592	755	721	647	573	427	304	539	469	527
Current Ratio	1.6	1.5	1.6	1.4	1.3	1.2	1.3	1.6	2.1	1.8
% Long Term Debt of Capitalization	20.0	14.4	21.0	24.4	37.0	47.0	37.6	35.1	26.7	20.1
% Net Income of Revenue	8.1	11.2	10.8	9.3	6.5	3.6	NM	6.9	6.0	10.0
% Return on Assets	9.1	12.4	12.0	10.1	7.0	3.8	NM	8.2	8.7	13.5
% Return on Equity	18.6	24.9	25.6	24.5	19.8	10.1	NM	17.8	17.1	27.7

Data as orig reptd.; bef. results of disc opers/spec. items. Per share data adj. for stk. divs.; EPS diluted. E-Estimated. NA-Not Available. NM-Not Meaningful. NR-Not Ranked. UR-Under Review.

Office: 333 Continental Boulevard, El Segundo, CA 90245-5012.
Telephone: 310-252-2000.
Website: http://www.mattel.com
Chrmn & CEO: R.A. Eckert

SVP & Treas: M.A. Salop
SVP, Secy & General Counsel: R. Normile
SVP & Cntlr: H.S. Topham
Investor Contact: D. Douglas (310-252-2703)

Board of Directors: E. P. Beard, K. Brittain White, M. J. Dolan, R. A. Eckert, F. D. Ferguson, T. M. Friedman, D. Ng, A. L. Rich, R. L. Sargent, C. A. Sinclair, G. C. Sullivan, J. L. Vogelstein

Founded: 1945
Domicile: Delaware
Employees: 26,000

Maxim Integrated Products Inc

STANDARD & POOR'S

S&P Recommendation HOLD ★★★★★

Price $29.43 (as of Oct 27, 2006)

12-Mo. Target Price $35.00

Investment Style Large-Cap Growth

GICS Sector Information Technology
Sub-Industry Semiconductors

Comment This company designs, develops and manufactures linear and mixed-signal integrated circuits used mainly in signal processing applications.

Key Stock Statistics (Source S&P, Vickers, company reports)

52-Wk Range	$42.99–26.09	S&P Oper. EPS 2007E	1.50	P/E on S&P Oper. EPS 2007E	19.6	Dividend Rate/Share	$0.62
Trailing 12-Month EPS	$1.37	S&P Oper. EPS 2008E	1.80	Common Shares Outstg. (M)	320.7	Yield (%)	2.12
Trailing 12-Month P/E	21.5	S&P Core EPS 2007E	1.50	Market Capitalization(B)	$9.438	Beta	2.40
$10K Invested 5 Yrs Ago	$6,256	S&P Core EPS 2008E	1.80	Institutional Ownership (%)	89	S&P Credit Rating	NA

Price Performance

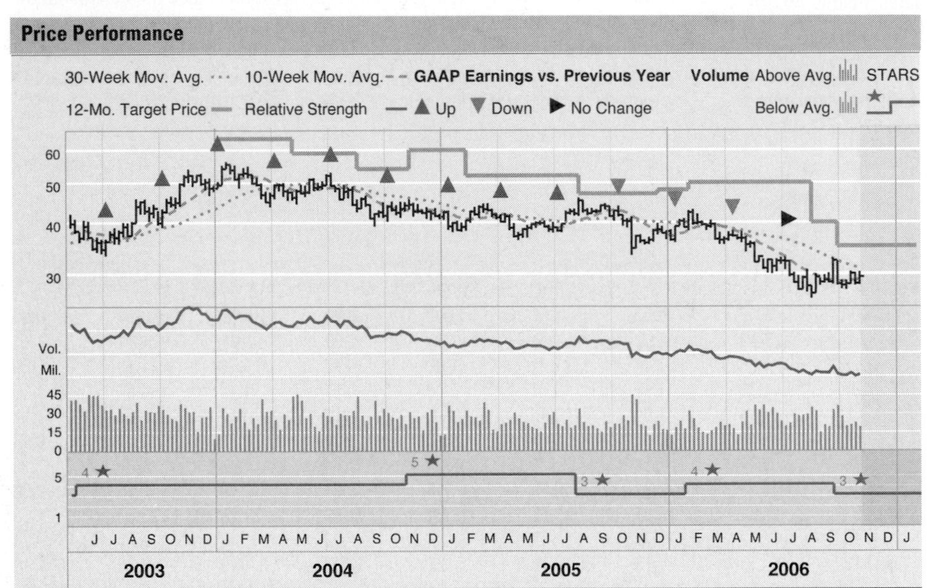

Options: ASE, CBOE, P, Ph

Analysis prepared by **Thomas W. Smith, CFA** on September 20, 2006, when the stock traded at **$ 29.67**.

Highlights

- We forecast that revenues will rise 13% in FY 07 (Jun.) and 14% in FY 08. A growth spurt in bookings in recent quarters has begun to fade, in our view. On September 19, the company lowered its September quarter revenue and EPS guidance, and described a mismatch of orders with inventory on hand, which suggests to us that inventory congestion is developing for some chip types at the same time that orders for some other chip types are not being filled in a timely manner.
- We project gross margins near 67% in FY 07 and FY 08, excluding projected stock option expense. This level is below the range of 69% to 72% in recent years because we expect Maxim to pursue some products in which attractive sales volumes may be possible, even if the margins are slightly below the company average. We expect R&D costs to grow slower than sales, contributing to operating margins near 43% in FY 07.
- Including projected stock option expense of $0.37 for FY 07 and $0.41 for FY 08, we estimate operating EPS of $1.50 for FY 07 and $1.80 for FY 08.

Investment Rationale/Risk

- We recently downgraded our opinion on MXIM shares to hold, from buy, given our view of slowing sales growth and limited near-term ability to improve margins that are already wide by industry standards. Positives we see for MXIM include a strong proprietary product portfolio, a diverse customer base and end markets, lack of debt, and cash and short-term investments of $1.3 billion.
- Risks to our opinion and target price include possible sudden downturns in demand for semiconductors, an informal inquiry by the SEC into past stock option grants and practices, and at least one stock option related shareholder lawsuit. We view MXIM's reliance on stock-based compensation as high versus most S&P 500 companies.
- Our 12-month target price for this highly volatile stock is $35, mainly derived by applying a price to sales ratio of 5.6X--at the low end of an historical range--to our FY 07 sales per share estimate of $6.21. We also apply a target P/E of 23X, in line with peers, to our FY 07 EPS estimate.

Qualitative Risk Assessment

LOW | **MEDIUM** | HIGH

Our risk assessment reflects that Maxim is subject to the sales cycles of the semiconductor industry. Gross margins are high relative to most peers, but as the company grows revenues, it faces some risk of diluting margins as it enters higher volume consumer markets, in our opinion. This is offset by a broad customer base and our view of a lack of debt.

Quantitative Evaluations

S&P Quality Ranking B+

D | C | B- | B | **B+** | A- | A | A+

Relative Strength Rank MODERATE

36

LOWEST = 1 HIGHEST = 99

Revenue/Earnings Data

Revenue (Million $)

	1Q	2Q	3Q	4Q	Year
2006	424.4	445.9	478.1	510.5	1,859
2005	435.1	436.1	400.2	400.4	1,672
2004	310.2	338.1	370.0	421.0	1,439
2003	285.9	286.1	286.2	295.0	1,153
2002	239.4	247.1	258.5	280.1	1,025
2001	422.3	438.3	306.8	318.2	1,577

Earnings Per Share ($)

	1Q	2Q	3Q	4Q	Year
2006	0.31	0.33	0.36	0.37	1.37
2005	0.42	0.42	0.37	0.37	1.58
2004	0.25	0.28	0.31	0.36	1.20
2003	0.22	0.23	0.23	0.24	0.91
2002	0.17	0.18	0.19	0.20	0.73
2001	0.33	0.34	0.33	-0.05	0.93

Fiscal year ended Jun. 30. Next earnings report expected: NA. EPS Estimates based on S&P Operating Earnings; historical GAAP earnings are as reported.

Dividend Data (Dates: mm/dd Payment Date: mm/dd/yy)

Amount ($)	Date Decl.	Ex-Div. Date	Stk. of Record	Payment Date
0.125	10/27	11/09	11/14	11/29/05
0.125	01/26	02/09	02/13	02/28/06
0.125	04/24	05/11	05/15	05/31/06
0.156	08/04	08/17	08/21	09/06/06

Dividends have been paid since 2002. Source: Company reports.

Maxim Integrated Products Inc

Business Summary September 20, 2006

Maxim Integrated Products designs, develops, makes, and markets a broad range of linear and mixed-signal integrated circuits known as analog circuits. Linear semiconductors handle continuously variable analog signals representing real-world phenomena (such as temperature, pressure, sound or speed). In contrast, digital semiconductors handle digital signals representing the zeroes and ones of binary arithmetic (the signal is either on or off, rather than continuous). Mixed-signal devices combine linear and digital functions. Compared to the digital integrated circuit market, the analog market is characterized by longer product life cycles, less foreign competition, lower capital requirements, and more stable growth rates that are less influenced by economic cycles.

In April 2001, the company expanded substantially by acquiring Dallas Semiconductor Corp. via an exchange of stock. The Dallas operations were similar to those of MXIM, and added complementary product lines in mixed-signal and digital chips. At April 2001, Dallas was selling 390 proprietary products to 15,000 customers worldwide.

MXIM serves a broad range of electronics end markets. Segments include automotive, communications, consumer, data processing, industrial control, instrumentation, and medical. Products include data converters, interface circuits, delay lines, microcontrollers, microprocessor supervisors, operational amplifiers, power supplies, multiplexers, switches, battery chargers, battery management circuits, RF circuits, fiber optic transceivers, sensors and voltage references. Applications for the company's products include global positioning systems, broadband networks, cable systems, PBX, video and wireless communications, flow control, robotics, automatic test equipment, data recorders, measuring instruments, bar code readers, disk drives, hand-held computers/PDAs, mainframes, servers, personal computers, point of sale terminals, and blood glucose meters.

Company Financials

Per Share Data ($) Year Ended Jun. 30	**2006**	**2005**	**2004**	**2003**	**2002**	**2001**	**2000**	**1999**	**1998**	**1997**
Tangible Book Value	NA	7.89	6.51	6.38	5.44	6.36	3.95	3.24	2.42	3.66
Cash Flow	NA	1.80	1.37	1.08	0.89	1.18	0.95	0.70	0.64	1.06
Earnings	1.37	1.58	1.20	0.91	0.73	0.93	0.88	0.65	0.59	0.47
S&P Core Earnings	NA	1.13	0.82	0.50	0.24	0.57	NA	NA	NA	NA
Dividends	0.48	0.38	0.32	0.08	Nil	Nil	Nil	Nil	Nil	Nil
Payout Ratio	35%	24%	27%	9%	Nil	Nil	Nil	Nil	Nil	Nil
Prices:High	42.99	45.91	56.25	53.95	61.36	70.13	90.13	48.31	22.75	19.09
Prices:Low	26.09	33.28	39.14	28.96	20.75	32.20	45.63	19.93	11.16	10.53
P/E Ratio:High	31	29	47	59	84	75	NM	55	39	41
P/E Ratio:Low	19	21	33	32	28	35	52	23	19	22
Income Statement Analysis (Million $)										
Revenue	NA	1,672	1,439	1,153	1,025	1,577	865	607	560	434
Operating Income	NA	858	668	507	402	699	405	294	270	216
Depreciation	NA	76.8	61.9	60.3	56.3	90.9	19.7	17.6	15.1	17.0
Interest Expense	NA	Nil	Nil	Nil	Nil	Nil	Nil	Nil	Nil	0.06
Pretax Income	NA	810	626	462	387	505	425	297	270	208
Effective Tax Rate	NA	33.2%	33.0%	33.0%	33.0%	33.7%	34.0%	34.0%	34.0%	34.0%
Net Income	NA	541	420	310	259	335	281	196	178	137
S&P Core Earnings	NA	385	285	170	84.7	205	NA	NA	NA	NA
Balance Sheet & Other Financial Data (Million $)										
Cash	NA	186	148	211	174	93.8	53.1	34.1	16.7	18.6
Current Assets	NA	1,974	1,578	1,565	1,236	1,699	931	729	508	377
Total Assets	NA	3,004	2,549	2,368	2,011	2,431	1,350	1,022	769	556
Current Liabilities	NA	285	319	216	229	325	208	121	130	85.2
Long Term Debt	NA	Nil	Nil	Nil	Nil	Nil	Nil	Nil	Nil	Nil
Common Equity	NA	2,584	2,112	2,070	1,741	2,101	1,118	879	631	466
Total Capital	NA	2,719	2,227	2,148	1,778	2,101	1,137	897	635	468
Capital Expenditures	NA	132	232	84.1	90.4	337	176	54.3	109	44.2
Cash Flow	NA	618	482	370	315	426	300	214	193	154
Current Ratio	NA	6.9	5.0	7.2	5.4	5.2	4.5	6.0	3.9	4.4
% Long Term Debt of Capitalization	NA	Nil	Nil	Nil	Nil	Nil	Nil	Nil	Nil	Nil
% Net Income of Revenue	NA	32.4	29.2	26.8	25.3	21.2	32.4	32.3	31.8	31.6
% Return on Assets	NA	19.5	17.1	14.1	11.7	14.8	23.7	21.9	26.9	28.1
% Return on Equity	NA	23.0	20.1	16.2	13.5	17.5	28.1	26.0	32.5	34.6

Data as orig reptd.; bef. results of disc opers/spec. items. Per share data adj. for stk. divs.; EPS diluted. E-Estimated. NA-Not Available. NM-Not Meaningful. NR-Not Ranked. UR-Under Review.

Office: 120 San Gabriel Drive, Sunnyvale, CA 94086.
Telephone: 408-737-7600.
Email: info@maxim-ic.com
Website: http://www.maxim-ic.com

Chrmn, Pres & CEO: J.F. Gifford
VP, CFO & Chief Acctg Officer: C.W. Jasper
Investor Contact: P. Maniar (408-737-7600)

Board of Directors: J. R. Bergman, M. J. Byrd, J. F. Gifford, B. K. Hagopian, A. F. Wazzan, P. de Roetth

Founded: 1983
Domicile: Delaware
Employees: 7,980

STANDARD &POOR'S

MBIA Inc.

S&P Recommendation HOLD ★★★★★

Price $62.71 (as of Oct 27, 2006)

12-Mo. Target Price $70.00

Investment Style Mid-Cap Value

GICS Sector Financials
Sub-Industry Property & Casualty Insurance

Comment This company is a leading provider of financial guarantee insurance and related services to public finance clients and financial institutions around the world.

Key Stock Statistics (Source S&P, Vickers, company reports)

52-Wk Range	**$64.42–56.00**	S&P Oper. EPS 2006**E**	**5.85**	P/E on S&P Oper. EPS 2006**E**	**10.7**	Dividend Rate/Share	**$1.24**
Trailing 12-Month EPS	**$6.01**	S&P Oper. EPS 2007**E**	**6.20**	Common Shares Outstg. (M)	**134.8**	Yield (%)	**1.98**
Trailing 12-Month P/E	**10.4**	S&P Core EPS 2006**E**	**5.76**	Market Capitalization(B)	**$8.451**	Beta	**1.12**
$10K Invested 5 Yrs Ago	**$14,205**	S&P Core EPS 2007**E**	**6.14**	Institutional Ownership (%)	**NA**	S&P Credit Rating	**AA**

Price Performance

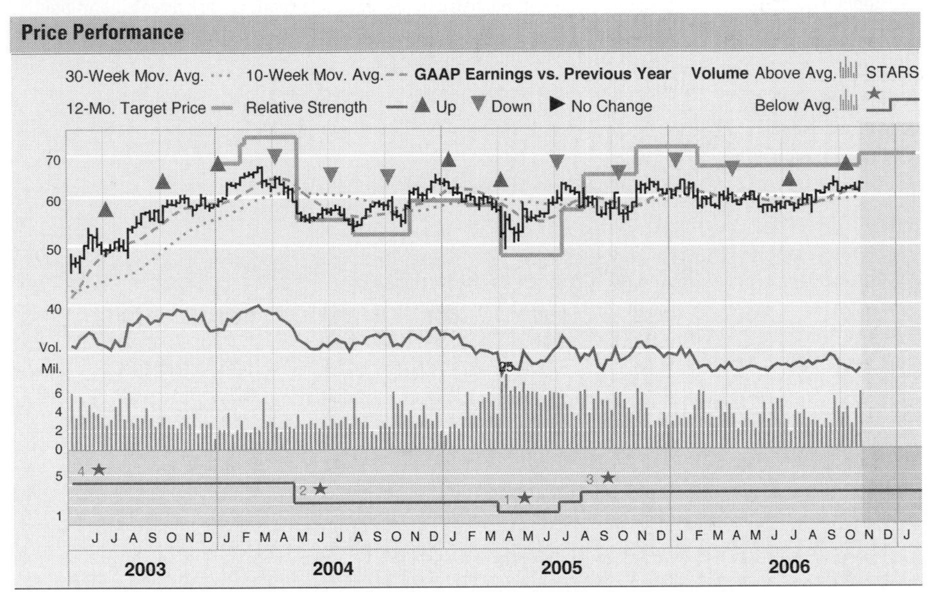

Options: ASE, Ph

Highlights

➤ The 12-month target price for MBI has recently been changed to $70.00 from $67.00. The Highlights section of this Stock Report will be updated accordingly.

Investment Rationale/Risk

➤ The Investment Rationale/Risk section of this Stock Report will be updated shortly. For the latest News story on MBI from MarketScope, see below.

➤ 10/27/06 07:20 am EDT... S&P MAINTAINS HOLD RECOMMENDATION ON SHARES OF MBIA INC. (MBI 62.99***): Q3 operating EPS of $1.55 vs. $1.39 exceeds our $1.40 estimate. Outperformance reflected higher revenues than expected, up 4.0% compared with our forecast of a modest decline, as 37% higher refunded premiums offset 1.8% lower earned premiums. Our outlook is tempered by the 16% drop in 9 months written premiums amid weakness in U.S. public finance and global structured finance. We are raising our '06 estimate by $0.15 to $5.85, but still see $6.20 in '07. Our 12-month target price of $70, raised $3 today, assumes shares trade at 11.3X our '07 estimate, nearer peer group average. /C.Seifert

Qualitative Risk Assessment

LOW | **MEDIUM** | HIGH

Our risk assessment reflects our view of the company as a market leader in municipal bond insurance and other financial guaranty products. This is offset, in our view, by issues related to certain regulatory related investigations under way.

Quantitative Evaluations

S&P Quality Ranking **A**

D | C | B- | B | B+ | A- | **A** | A+

Relative Strength Rank **MODERATE**

51

LOWEST = 1 HIGHEST = 99

Revenue/Earnings Data

Revenue (Million $)

	1Q	2Q	3Q	4Q	Year
2006	351.8	689.2	707.4	--	--
2005	326.0	339.3	605.2	600.0	2,285
2004	327.5	340.4	476.0	345.5	2,001
2003	280.9	310.7	313.0	325.8	1,230
2002	252.3	258.4	282.5	357.7	1,151
2001	229.0	206.6	246.5	256.1	1,134

Earnings Per Share ($)

	1Q	2Q	3Q	4Q	Year
2006	1.46	1.62	1.58	**E**1.35	**E**5.85
2005	1.52	1.37	1.05	1.34	5.19
2004	1.42	1.47	1.29	1.36	5.61
2003	1.54	1.51	1.31	1.25	5.61
2002	1.08	0.97	1.11	0.84	3.98
2001	0.87	0.96	1.03	1.05	3.91

Fiscal year ended Dec. 31. Next earnings report expected: Early February. EPS Estimates based on S&P Operating Earnings; historical GAAP earnings are as reported.

Dividend Data (Dates: mm/dd Payment Date: mm/dd/yy)

Amount ($)	Date Decl.	Ex-Div. Date	Stk. of Record	Payment Date
0.280	12/08	12/21	12/23	01/17/06
0.310	02/27	03/22	03/24	04/17/06
0.310	06/08	06/21	06/23	07/17/06
0.310	09/07	09/20	09/22	10/16/06

Dividends have been paid since 1987. Source: Company reports.

Business Summary October 02, 2006

MBIA Inc. (MBI), a dominant force in the municipal bond insurance market, has leveraged that strength and expanded into the structured finance market and into selected international markets. It is also engaged in asset management operations. At December 31, 2005, fixed income assets under management averaged $44.2 billion.

MBI offers insurance for new issues of municipal bonds, and for bonds traded in the secondary market, including bonds held in unit investment trusts and mutual funds. The economic value of municipal bond insurance to the governmental unit or agency offering bonds is a saving in interest costs reflecting the difference in yield on an insured bond from that on the same bond if uninsured. The company's guarantee also increases market acceptance for complex financings, and for municipal bonds of issuers that are not well known.

At December 31, 2005, the net par value of the company's insured debt obligations was $585 billion, of which general obligation municipal bonds accounted for 27%, utility bonds 12%, special revenue bonds 7%, transportation bonds 6%, health care bonds 5%, other U.S. municipal bonds 8%, non-U.S. municipal obligations 4%, U.S. structured finance obligations (asset/mortgage backed) 19%, and international structured finance 12%. Of the $585 billion of net outstanding insured debt obligations at December 31, 2005, 16% had been issued outside the U.S., 11% had been issued by California, 7% by New York, 4% by Florida, and about 3% each by Texas, New Jersey and Illinois.

MBI in recent years has expanded its presence in the structured finance (or asset-backed) markets. Gross written premiums (which include upfront and installment premiums) in the global public finance segment declined nearly 15% in 2005, to $569.0 million, from $665.6 million in 2004. Global structured finance gross written premiums (including upfront and installment premiums) declined 7.8% in 2005, to $415.9 million from $451.3 million in 2004.

Company Financials

Per Share Data ($) Year Ended Dec. 31	2005	2004	2003	2002	2001	2000	1999	1998	1997	1996
Tangible Book Value	48.36	46.63	42.87	37.32	31.66	27.86	23.01	24.50	21.01	10.27
Operating Earnings	NA	5.25	4.80	4.27	3.88	3.41	3.15	3.05	2.71	2.41
Earnings	5.19	5.61	5.61	3.98	3.91	3.55	2.13	2.88	2.81	2.48
S&P Core Earnings	5.75	5.33	5.25	3.91	3.81	NA	NA	NA	NA	NA
Dividends	1.12	0.96	0.80	0.68	0.60	0.55	0.53	0.52	0.51	0.48
Payout Ratio	22%	17%	14%	17%	15%	15%	25%	18%	18%	20%
Prices:High	64.00	67.34	60.72	60.11	57.49	50.79	47.92	53.96	44.92	34.88
Prices:Low	49.07	52.55	34.14	34.93	36.00	24.21	30.08	30.71	30.29	23.33
P/E Ratio:High	12	12	11	15	15	14	23	19	16	14
P/E Ratio:Low	9	9	6	9	9	7	14	11	11	9
Income Statement Analysis (Million $)										
Premium Income	843	822	733	589	524	440	443	425	297	252
Net Investment Income	492	474	447	442	413	394	359	332	281	248
Other Revenue	1,458	704	590	120	197	217	605	156	75.1	46.0
Total Revenue	2,301	2,001	1,770	1,151	1,134	1,057	964	912	654	546
Pretax Income	1,016	1,130	1,149	793	791	715	388	565	480	408
Net Operating Income	NA	NA	NA	NA	NA	NA	NA	NA	364	313
Net Income	712	813	814	587	583	529	321	433	374	322
S&P Core Earnings	789	773	761	577	568	NA	NA	NA	NA	NA
Balance Sheet & Other Financial Data (Million $)										
Cash & Equivalent	629	678	452	298	297	246	229	148	23.2	112
Premiums Due	408	505	536	522	507	NA	NA	NA	13.4	0.98
Investment Assets:Bonds	23,747	19,680	17,391	16,195	14,087	11,737	10,274	9,562	4,867	4,150
Investment Assets:Stocks	Nil	Nil	Nil	Nil	Nil	Nil	Nil	Nil	Nil	Nil
Investment Assets:Loans	Nil	Nil	Nil	Nil	Nil	Nil	Nil	Nil	Nil	205
Investment Assets:Total	40,562	41,556	27,707	17,095	14,516	12,233	10,694	10,080	8,470	7,648
Deferred Policy Costs	427	360	320	302	278	274	252	230	154	148
Total Assets	34,561	33,027	30,268	18,852	16,200	13,894	12,264	11,797	9,811	8,562
Debt	10,033	8,877	8,870	1,033	805	795	689	689	474	374
Common Equity	6,592	6,579	6,259	5,493	4,783	4,223	3,513	3,792	3,048	2,480
Property & Casualty:Loss Ratio	10.0	10.0	9.2	9.4	9.3	6.2	12.3	8.0	6.3	6.1
Property & Casualty:Expense Ratio	24.9	22.0	12.8	16.8	13.4	22.1	23.6	16.8	26.2	28.3
Property & Casualty Combined Ratio	34.9	32.0	22.0	26.2	22.7	28.3	35.9	24.8	32.5	34.4
% Return on Revenue	31.0	40.6	46.0	51.0	51.4	50.0	33.2	47.5	57.2	59.1
% Return on Equity	10.8	12.7	13.8	11.4	13.0	13.7	8.8	12.7	13.5	13.7

Data as orig reptd.; bef. results of disc opers/spec. items. Per share data adj. for stk. divs.; EPS diluted. E-Estimated. NA-Not Available. NM-Not Meaningful. NR-Not Ranked. UR-Under Review.

Office: 113 King Street, Armonk, NY 10504-1610.
Telephone: 914-273-4545.
Website: http://www.mbia.com
Chrmn: J.W. Brown

Pres & CEO: G.C. Dunton
VP & CTO: A.E. Randolph
VP, Secy & General Counsel: R.D. Wertheim
VP & CCO: W. Hill

Board of Directors: J. W. Brown, C. E. Chaplin, D. C. Clapp, G. C. Dunton, C. L. Gaudiani, D. P. Kearney, L. H. Meyer, D. J. Perry, J. A. Rolls, R. H. Walker, J. W. Yabuki

Founded: 1973
Domicile: Connecticut
Employees: 626

McCormick & Company Inc

S&P Recommendation HOLD ★★★★★

Price $36.70 (as of Oct 27, 2006)

12-Mo. Target Price $41.00

Investment Style Mid-Cap Growth

GICS Sector Consumer Staples
Sub-Industry Packaged Foods & Meats

Comment This company primarily produces spices, seasonings and flavorings for the retail food, foodservice and industrial markets. Trademarks include McCormick and Schilling.

Key Stock Statistics (Source S&P, Vickers, company reports)

52-Wk Range	$39.35–29.59	S&P Oper. EPS 2006E	1.70	P/E on S&P Oper. EPS 2006E	21.6	Dividend Rate/Share	$0.72
Trailing 12-Month EPS	$1.53	S&P Oper. EPS 2007E	1.85	Common Shares Outstg. (M)	131.4	Yield (%)	1.96
Trailing 12-Month P/E	24.0	S&P Core EPS 2006E	1.74	Market Capitalization(B)	$4.329	Beta	0.41
$10K Invested 5 Yrs Ago	$18,023	S&P Core EPS 2007E	1.89	Institutional Ownership (%)	72	S&P Credit Rating	A

Price Performance

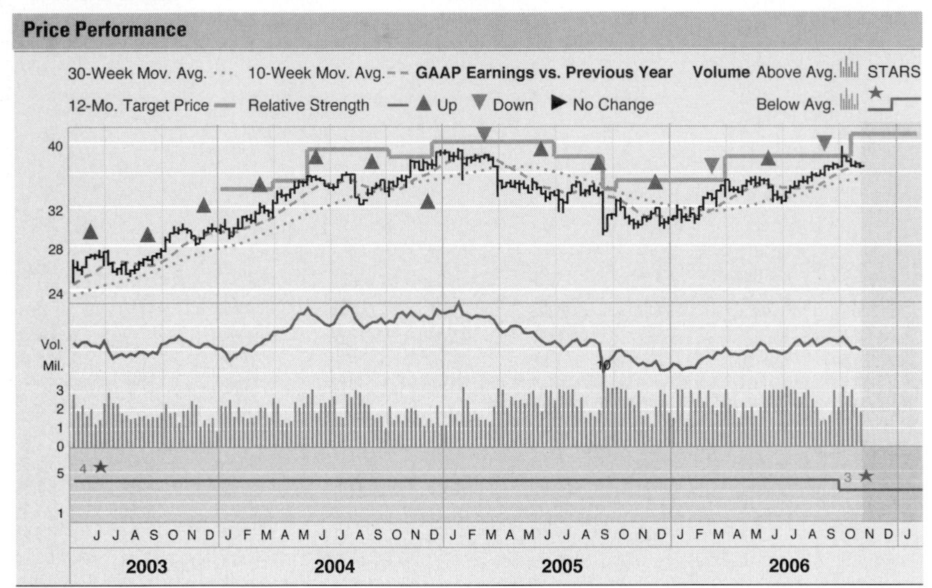

Options: Ph

Analysis prepared by **Rick Joy** on October 26, 2006, when the stock traded at **$ 36.99**.

Highlights

- We project net sales growth of 3% to 4% in FY 07 (Nov.), as core volume growth, higher prices and mix improvements outweigh a reduction in SKUs. We expect mid- to high single digit sales growth for the consumer business, and low single digit growth for the industrial segment on favorable comparisons and new product initiatives.
- We see operating profit margins widening, aided by modest price increases, a mix shift toward value-added products, the elimination of less profitable SKUs, a moderation of input cost inflation and supply chain improvements. Advertising and promotional spending will likely rise due to expected spending to support new products. We expect total operating profits to increase at a high single digit rate in FY 07.
- After higher interest expense and a modest reduction in shares outstanding, we see FY 07 EPS growing to $1.85, from anticipated FY 06 EPS of $1.70 (including an estimated $0.11 of stock option expense). For the longer term, we expect EPS growth of 8% to 10% a year.

Investment Rationale/Risk

- Our hold recommendation is primarily based on valuation, with the shares recently trading at a P/E multiple of about 20X our FY 07 EPS estimate, a premium to the P/E's for the S&P 500 index and MKC's packaged food peers. We expect that MKC's financial strength and free cash flow will continue to improve. New product and packaging initiatives should lead to strong growth for the consumer business and aid a continued rebound in the industrial business in FY 07, in our opinion.
- Risks to our recommendation and target price relate to competitive pressures in MKC's businesses, consumer acceptance of new product introductions, and commodity cost inflation. In terms of corporate governance, the company has a dual class capital structure with unequal voting rights, which we view unfavorably.
- Our 12-month target price of $41 is derived from our analysis of peer and historical multiples, and our discounted cash flow model, which assumes a weighted average cost of capital of 8.5% and a terminal growth rate for cash flows of 3.5%.

Qualitative Risk Assessment

LOW | MEDIUM | HIGH

Our risk assessment reflects the relatively stable nature of the company's end markets, a strong balance sheet and cash flows, and an S&P Quality Ranking of A+ that reflects historical stability of earnings and dividends.

Quantitative Evaluations

S&P Quality Ranking A+

D | C | B- | B | B+ | A- | A | A+

Relative Strength Rank MODERATE

37

LOWEST = 1 HIGHEST = 99

Revenue/Earnings Data

Revenue (Million $)

	1Q	2Q	3Q	4Q	Year
2006	609.7	639.9	663.1	--	--
2005	603.6	628.6	622.7	737.1	2,592
2004	572.4	596.2	613.5	744.1	2,526
2003	485.4	527.9	557.6	698.7	2,270
2002	518.9	552.6	545.0	703.4	2,320
2001	533.5	567.1	570.7	701.0	2,372

Earnings Per Share ($)

	1Q	2Q	3Q	4Q	Year
2006	0.11	0.46	0.32	E0.70	E1.70
2005	0.26	0.31	0.35	0.65	1.56
2004	0.27	0.30	0.33	0.62	1.52
2003	0.23	0.27	0.28	0.61	1.40
2002	0.24	0.24	0.25	0.54	1.26
2001	0.19	0.19	0.25	0.42	1.05

Fiscal year ended Nov. 30. Next earnings report expected: Late January. EPS Estimates based on S&P Operating Earnings; historical GAAP earnings are as reported.

Dividend Data (Dates: mm/dd Payment Date: mm/dd/yy)

Amount ($)	Date Decl.	Ex-Div. Date	Stk. of Record	Payment Date
0.180	11/22	12/28	12/30	01/20/06
0.180	03/22	03/30	04/03	04/17/06
0.180	06/27	07/05	07/07	07/21/06
0.180	09/26	10/04	10/06	10/20/06

Dividends have been paid since 1925. Source: Company reports.

McCormick & Company Inc

Business Summary October 26, 2006

Founded by Willoughby M. McCormick in 1889, McCormick & Co. is the world's largest spice company, with operations in the manufacture, marketing and distribution of spices, seasonings, flavorings and other specialty food products. The company markets its products to retail food, foodservice, and industrial markets under the McCormick and Schilling names.

McCormick operates in two business segments: consumer and industrial. The company formerly owned a packaging business, which was sold during the third quarter of 2003. The consumer segment, which accounted for 54% of sales and 73% of operating profits in FY 05 (Nov.), sells spices, herbs, extracts, proprietary seasoning blends, sauces and marinades to the consumer food market. The industrial segment (46%, 27%) sells spices, herbs, extracts, proprietary seasonings, condiments, coatings and compound flavors to food processors, restaurant chains, distributors, warehouse clubs, and institutional operations. Sales to McCormick's five largest customers represented approximately 29% of consolidated net sales in FY 05.

Many spices and herbs purchased by the company are imported into the U.S. from the country of origin, although significant quantities of some materials, such as paprika, dehydrated vegetables, onion and garlic, and food ingredients other than spices and herbs, originate in the U.S. McCormick is a direct importer of certain raw materials, mainly black pepper, vanilla beans, cinnamon, herbs and seeds. The raw materials most important to the company are onion, garlic and capsicums (paprika and chili peppers), which are produced in the U.S.; black pepper, most of which originates in India, Indonesia, Malaysia and Brazil; and vanilla beans, a large portion of which the company sources from the Malagasy Republic and Indonesia.

Company Financials

Per Share Data ($) Year Ended Nov. 30	**2005**	**2004**	**2003**	**2002**	**2001**	**2000**	**1999**	**1998**	**1997**	**1996**
Tangible Book Value	NM	0.45	0.28	0.62	NM	NM	1.70	1.57	1.59	1.82
Cash Flow	2.10	2.11	1.85	1.73	1.57	1.43	1.12	1.07	0.97	0.67
Earnings	1.56	1.52	1.40	1.26	1.05	0.99	0.72	0.71	0.65	0.27
S&P Core Earnings	1.51	1.43	1.28	1.12	0.90	NA	NA	NA	NA	NA
Dividends	0.64	0.56	0.46	0.37	0.40	0.38	0.34	0.32	0.30	0.28
Payout Ratio	41%	37%	33%	29%	38%	38%	48%	45%	47%	104%
Prices:High	39.14	38.94	30.21	27.25	23.27	18.88	17.31	18.22	14.19	12.69
Prices:Low	28.95	28.60	21.71	20.70	17.00	11.88	13.31	13.53	11.31	9.44
P/E Ratio:High	25	26	22	22	22	19	24	26	22	47
P/E Ratio:Low	19	19	16	16	16	12	19	19	18	35
Income Statement Analysis (Million $)										
Revenue	2,592	2,526	2,270	2,320	2,372	2,124	2,007	1,881	1,801	1,733
Operating Income	429	402	366	353	324	287	252	240	217	215
Depreciation	74.6	72.0	65.3	66.8	73.0	61.3	57.4	54.8	49.3	63.8
Interest Expense	48.2	41.0	38.6	43.6	52.9	39.7	32.4	36.9	36.3	33.8
Pretax Income	316	308	286	257	212	204	163	159	150	67.3
Effective Tax Rate	30.6%	28.9%	29.1%	28.9%	29.7%	32.6%	36.8%	34.6%	35.1%	35.4%
Net Income	215	215	199	180	147	138	103	104	97.4	43.5
S&P Core Earnings	208	202	182	158	126	NA	NA	NA	NA	NA
Balance Sheet & Other Financial Data (Million $)										
Cash	30.3	70.3	25.1	47.3	31.3	23.9	12.0	17.7	13.5	22.4
Current Assets	800	864	762	725	636	620	491	504	507	534
Total Assets	2,273	2,370	2,148	1,931	1,772	1,660	1,189	1,259	1,256	1,327
Current Liabilities	699	773	713	673	714	1,027	471	518	498	499
Long Term Debt	464	465	449	454	454	160	241	250	276	291
Common Equity	800	890	755	592	463	359	382	468	393	450
Total Capital	1,293	1,386	1,226	1,046	943	523	628	643	671	746
Capital Expenditures	73.8	69.8	91.6	111	112	53.6	49.3	54.8	43.9	74.7
Cash Flow	290	287	265	247	220	199	161	159	147	107
Current Ratio	1.1	1.1	1.1	1.1	0.9	0.6	1.0	1.0	1.0	1.1
% Long Term Debt of Capitalization	35.9	33.6	36.6	43.4	48.2	30.6	38.5	38.9	41.1	39.0
% Net Income of Revenue	8.3	8.5	8.8	7.8	6.2	6.5	5.1	5.5	5.4	2.5
% Return on Assets	9.3	9.5	9.8	9.7	8.5	9.7	8.4	8.3	7.5	3.0
% Return on Equity	25.4	26.1	29.6	34.1	35.7	37.1	26.8	24.1	23.1	9.0

Data as orig reptd.; bef. results of disc opers/spec. items. Per share data adj. for stk. divs.; EPS diluted. E-Estimated. NA-Not Available. NM-Not Meaningful. NR-Not Ranked. UR-Under Review.

Office: 18 Loveton Circle, Sparks, MD 21152-6000.
Telephone: 410-771-7301.
Website: http://www.mccormick.com
Chrmn, Pres & CEO: R.J. Lawless

EVP & CFO: F.A. Contino
SVP, Secy & General Counsel: R.W. Skelton
VP & Treas: P. Beard
Investor Contact: J. Brooks (410-771-7244)

Board of Directors: B. H. Beracha, J. P. Bilbrey, J. T. Brady, F. A. Contino, E. S. Dunn, Jr., J. M. Fitzpatrick, F. A. Hrabowski, III, R. J. Lawless, M. M. Preston, W. E. Stevens, K. D. Weatherholtz

Founded: 1889
Domicile: Maryland
Employees: 8,000

STANDARD &POOR'S

McDonald's Corp

S&P Recommendation HOLD ★★★★★

Price $41.47 (as of Oct 27, 2006)

12-Mo. Target Price $45.00

Investment Style Large-Cap Growth

GICS Sector Consumer Discretionary
Sub-Industry Restaurants

Comment MCD is the largest fast-food restaurant company in the world. At September 30, 2006, there were 13,728 McDonald's restaurants in the U.S., and 17,165 elsewhere.

Key Stock Statistics (Source S&P, Vickers, company reports)

52-Wk Range	**$42.48–31.55**	S&P Oper. EPS 2006E	**2.35**	P/E on S&P Oper. EPS 2006E	**17.6**	Dividend Rate/Share	**$1.00**
Trailing 12-Month EPS	**$2.31**	S&P Oper. EPS 2007E	**2.55**	Common Shares Outstg. (M)	**1,226.3**	Yield (%)	**2.41**
Trailing 12-Month P/E	**18.0**	S&P Core EPS 2006E	**2.80**	Market Capitalization(B)	**$50.856**	Beta	**1.26**
$10K Invested 5 Yrs Ago	**$15,441**	S&P Core EPS 2007E	**2.55**	Institutional Ownership (%)	**77**	S&P Credit Rating	**A**

Price Performance

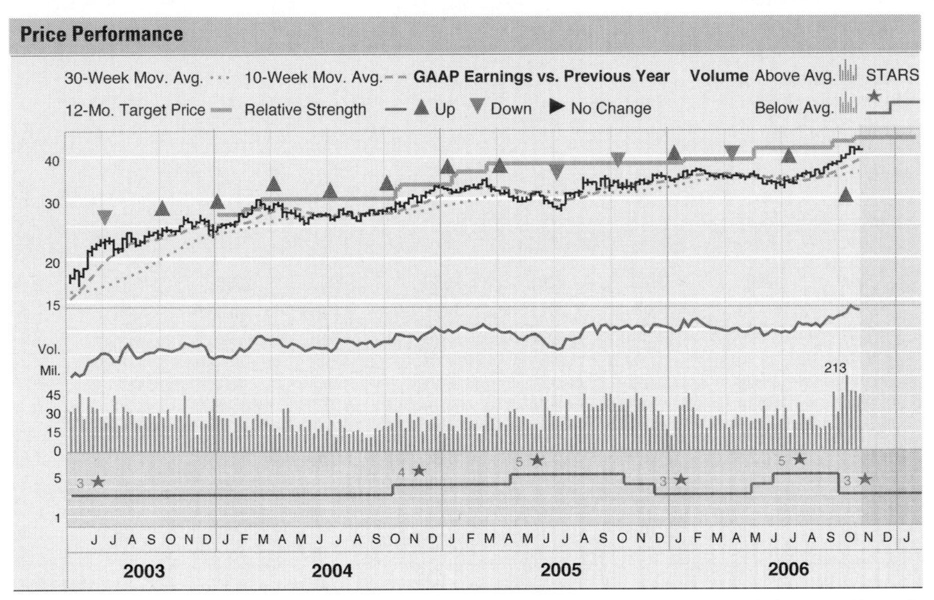

Options: ASE, CBOE, P, Ph

Analysis prepared by **Dennis P. Milton** on October 25, 2006, when the stock traded at **$ 42.00**.

Highlights

- In the first nine months of 2006, same-store sales increased 4.9%, year to year, in the U.S. and 5.5% worldwide. Results benefited from customer acceptance of new premium chicken sandwiches and improved breakfast sales, and extended hours of service at McDonald's stores. In 2005 and 2004, worldwide same-store sales rose 3.9% and 6.9%, respectively.
- We expect the company's U.S. rollout of new premium salad offerings and snack wraps to help sustain same-store sales momentum through the end of 2006. We look for a more value-driven menu to improve sales performance in Europe. We project revenue growth of 8% in 2006, reflecting same-store sales growth of about 6.2%, and international expansion.
- We see 2006 results benefiting from lower food prices, well-controlled corporate costs, reduced interest expense due to a lower debt balance, and share repurchases, partly offset by higher labor and utility costs. We project 2006 operating EPS of $2.35, up from $1.99, excluding one-time items, in 2005. Our 2007 EPS estimate of $2.55 reflects our projection of systemwide sales growth of 5% and significant share repurchases.

Investment Rationale/Risk

- At about 18X our 2006 EPS estimate, the shares recently traded in line with industry peers. We believe MCD's solid execution of its "Plan to Win" operating strategy has helped produce strong sales momentum over the past several years, and we expect healthy sales results over the next few years as the company shifts its menu focus to more upscale fare. However, we think that MCD has limited expansion prospects and faces strong competition from growing fast food and fast casual chains.
- Risks to our recommendation and target price include the potential for higher food costs; a lack of customer acceptance of MCD's new menu offerings; and exchange rate risk, in light of MCD's substantial international business.
- Our 12-month target price of $45 is based on a forward P/E of 17.5X, slightly below its current valuation, applied to our 2007 EPS estimate of $2.55. Our DCF model, which assumes revenue growth of 4% annually over the next several years, then gradually declining rates of growth thereafter, and a weighted average cost of equity of 9.8%, shows intrinsic value of $41.

Qualitative Risk Assessment

LOW	MEDIUM	HIGH

McDonald's competes in the relatively stable fast food industry, where it has a very strong brand name presence. However, results can vary widely due to fluctuations in food costs, competitive discounting, and exchange rate volatility.

Quantitative Evaluations

S&P Quality Ranking **A**

D	C	B-	B	B+	A-	A	A+

Relative Strength Rank **STRONG**

77

LOWEST = 1 HIGHEST = 99

Revenue/Earnings Data

Revenue (Million $)

	1Q	2Q	3Q	4Q	Year
2006	5,101	5,572	5,883	--	--
2005	4,803	5,096	5,327	5,235	20,460
2004	4,400	4,729	4,926	5,010	19,065
2003	3,800	4,281	4,505	4,555	17,141
2002	3,597	3,862	4,047	3,899	15,406
2001	3,512	3,708	3,879	3,772	14,870

Earnings Per Share ($)

	1Q	2Q	3Q	4Q	Year
2006	0.49	0.67	0.68	**E**0.56	**E**2.35
2005	0.56	0.42	0.58	0.48	2.04
2004	0.40	0.47	0.61	0.31	1.79
2003	0.29	0.37	0.43	0.10	1.18
2002	0.28	0.39	0.38	-0.27	0.77
2001	0.29	0.34	0.42	0.21	1.25

Fiscal year ended Dec. 31. Next earnings report expected: Late January. EPS Estimates based on S&P Operating Earnings; historical GAAP earnings are as reported.

Dividend Data (Dates: mm/dd Payment Date: mm/dd/yy)

Amount ($)	Date Decl.	Ex-Div. Date	Stk. of Record	Payment Date
0.670	09/21	11/10	11/15	12/01/05
1.000	09/27	11/13	11/15	12/01/06

Dividends have been paid since 1976. Source: Company reports.

McDonald's Corp

STANDARD &POOR'S

Business Summary October 25, 2006

CORPORATE OVERVIEW. With one of the world's most widely known brand names, McDonald's operates and franchises more than 30,000 restaurants in about 120 countries (at September 30, 2006, there were 13,728 McDonald's restaurants in the U.S., and 17,165 elsewhere). Systemwide sales totaled $54.3 billion in 2005, up from $51.2 billion in 2004. Systemwide sales by geographic area in 2005 were: the U.S., 47% (48% in 2004); Europe, 27% (28%); Asia/Pacific/Middle East/Africa, 16% (16%); Latin America, 3% (3%); Canada, 4% (4%), and Partner Brands 3% (2%). In the U.S., the McDonald's chain dominates the $120 billion quickservice restaurant industry. With U.S. systemwide sales of more than $25 billion in 2005, its domestic business was approximately three times larger than its closest competitors, Burger King and Wendy's Old Fashioned Hamburgers. MCD's international segment has supplied much of its earnings growth over the past two decades, and, in 2005, contributed 46% of operating income (before corporate expenses and one-time charges). All restaurants are operated by MCD, franchisees, or affiliates under joint venture agreements. At September 30, 2006, there were 18,469 franchised restaurants, 8,243 company-owned restaurants, and 4,181 affiliated restaurants.

Company Financials

Per Share Data ($) Year Ended Dec. 31	**2005**	**2004**	**2003**	**2002**	**2001**	**2000**	**1999**	**1998**	**1997**	**1996**
Tangible Book Value	10.45	9.74	8.18	6.88	6.30	5.86	6.20	6.26	5.86	5.49
Cash Flow	3.05	2.73	2.08	1.59	2.08	2.20	2.07	1.73	1.71	1.64
Earnings	2.04	1.79	1.18	0.77	1.25	1.46	1.39	1.10	1.15	1.11
S&P Core Earnings	2.00	1.66	0.96	0.51	1.01	NA	NA	NA	NA	NA
Dividends	0.67	0.55	0.40	0.24	0.23	0.22	0.20	0.18	0.16	0.15
Payout Ratio	33%	31%	34%	31%	18%	15%	14%	16%	14%	13%
Prices:High	35.69	32.96	27.01	30.72	35.06	43.63	49.56	39.75	27.44	27.13
Prices:Low	27.36	24.54	12.12	15.17	24.75	26.38	35.94	22.31	21.06	20.50
P/E Ratio:High	17	18	23	40	28	30	36	36	24	25
P/E Ratio:Low	13	14	10	20	20	18	26	20	18	19
Income Statement Analysis (Million $)										
Revenue	20,460	19,065	17,141	15,406	14,870	14,243	13,259	12,421	11,409	10,687
Operating Income	5,243	4,742	3,980	3,164	3,983	4,144	4,171	3,903	3,488	3,331
Depreciation	1,250	1,201	1,148	1,051	1,086	1,011	956	881	794	743
Interest Expense	356	358	388	360	452	430	396	414	363	365
Pretax Income	3,702	3,202	2,346	1,662	2,330	2,882	2,884	2,307	2,408	2,251
Effective Tax Rate	29.7%	28.9%	35.7%	40.3%	29.8%	31.4%	32.5%	32.8%	31.0%	30.2%
Net Income	2,602	2,279	1,508	992	1,637	1,977	1,948	1,550	1,643	1,573
S&P Core Earnings	2,540	2,100	1,226	667	1,328	NA	NA	NA	NA	NA
Balance Sheet & Other Financial Data (Million $)										
Cash	4,260	1,380	493	330	418	422	420	299	341	330
Current Assets	5,850	2,858	1,885	1,715	1,819	1,662	1,572	1,309	1,142	1,103
Total Assets	29,989	27,838	25,525	23,971	22,535	21,683	20,983	19,784	18,242	17,386
Current Liabilities	4,036	3,521	2,486	2,422	2,248	2,361	3,274	2,497	2,985	2,135
Long Term Debt	8,937	8,357	9,343	9,704	8,556	7,844	5,632	6,189	4,834	4,803
Common Equity	15,146	14,202	11,982	10,281	9,488	9,204	9,639	9,464	8,851	8,360
Total Capital	25,060	23,340	22,340	20,988	19,156	18,133	16,445	17,228	15,178	15,251
Capital Expenditures	1,607	1,419	1,307	2,004	1,906	1,945	1,868	1,879	2,111	2,375
Cash Flow	3,852	3,480	2,656	2,043	2,723	2,988	2,904	2,431	2,412	2,288
Current Ratio	1.4	0.8	0.8	0.7	0.8	0.7	0.5	0.5	0.4	0.5
% Long Term Debt of Capitalization	35.7	35.8	41.8	46.2	44.7	43.3	34.2	35.9	31.8	31.5
% Net Income of Revenue	12.7	12.0	8.8	6.4	11.0	13.9	14.7	12.5	14.4	14.8
% Return on Assets	9.0	8.5	6.1	4.3	7.4	9.3	9.6	8.2	9.2	9.6
% Return on Equity	17.7	17.4	13.5	10.0	17.5	21.0	20.4	16.9	18.8	19.5

Data as orig reptd.; bef. results of disc opers/spec. items. Per share data adj. for stk. divs.; EPS diluted. E-Estimated. NA-Not Available. NM-Not Meaningful. NR-Not Ranked. UR-Under Review.

Office: McDonald's Plaza, Oak Brook, IL 60523.
Telephone: 630-623-3000.
Website: http://www.mcdonalds.com
Chrmn: A.J. McKenna

Pres & COO: R. Alvarez
Vice Chrmn & CEO: J.A. Skinner
Sr EVP & CFO: M.H. Paull
EVP, Secy & General Counsel: G. Santona

Investor Contact: M. Shaw (630-623-7559)
Board of Directors: H. Adams, Jr., E. A. Brennan, R. A. Eckert, E. Hernandez, Jr., J. P. Jackson, R. H. Lenny, W. E. Massey, A. J. McKenna, C. D. McMillan, S. A. Penrose, M. J. Roberts, J. W. Rogers, J. A. Skinner, R. W. Stone

Founded: 1948
Domicile: Delaware
Employees: 447,000

McGraw-Hill Companies Inc. (The)

STANDARD &POOR'S

S&P Recommendation NOT RANKED

Price
$63.26 (as of Oct 27, 2006)

Investment Style
Large-Cap Growth

GICS Sector Consumer Discretionary
Sub-Industry Publishing

Comment MHP is a leading information services organization serving worldwide markets in education, business, industry, other professions and government.

Key Stock Statistics (Source S&P, Vickers, company reports)

52-Wk Range	$64.42–46.37	S&P Oper. EPS 2006E	NA	P/E on S&P Oper. EPS 2006E	NA	Dividend Rate/Share	$0.73
Trailing 12-Month EPS	$2.34	S&P Oper. EPS 2007E	NA	Common Shares Outstg. (M)	351.9	Yield (%)	1.15
Trailing 12-Month P/E	27.0	S&P Core EPS 2006E	NA	Market Capitalization(B)	$22.261	Beta	0.45
$10K Invested 5 Yrs Ago	$24,598	S&P Core EPS 2007E	NA	Institutional Ownership (%)	78	S&P Credit Rating	NR

Price Performance

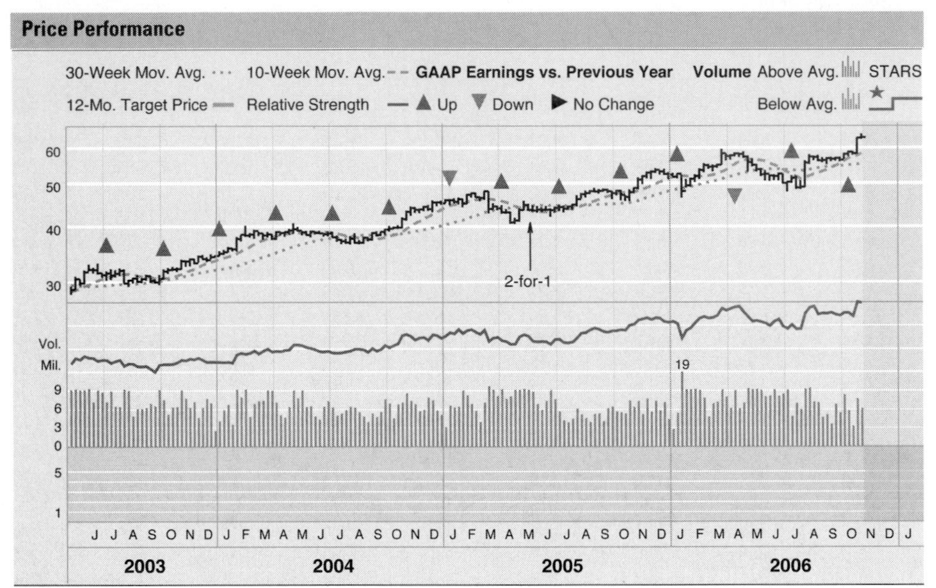

Options: Ph

Analysis prepared by **James Peters, CFA** on July 27, 2006, when the stock traded at **$ 54.29**.

Highlights

- For 2006, MHP expects Education segment revenues to be flat to down as much as 4%, Information and Media (I&M) revenues to rise in the single to low double digits, and Financial Services (FS) to post double digit growth, excluding revenues from the 2005 divestiture of Corporate Value Consulting.

- MHP expects a decline in Education segment operating profit of as much as 10%, a rise in I&M operating profit despite an estimated $15 million revenue shortfall from transitioning Sweet's to an online service, and FS operating margins at least equal to 2005's 42.5%.

- MHP said in July that it expects 2006 EPS of $2.44-$2.49, up from $2.21 in 2005. The EPS estimate includes projected dilution of $0.03-$0.04 from acquisitions, $0.02 from changes in pension plan assumptions, and $0.02-$0.03 from the Sweet's transition. The estimate excludes $0.13 of projected stock option expense and $0.04 for the elimination of a restoration stock option program.

Investment Rationale/Risk

- In July, MHP said it had completed the repurchase of 26.1 million shares to date in 2006, with an additional 3.1 million shares to be bought back in the second half of the year. The company anticipates increasing capital expenditures to about $200 million in 2006, from $120 million in 2005, driven by investments in data centers, where it is adding capacity to support increasing digitization in education, a new facility for MHP Education in Iowa, technology initiatives in Financial Services aimed at streamlining the ratings process, and leasehold improvements in India.

- MHP noted in its April 10-Q filed with the SEC that among the risks facing its businesses are the level of education funding both domestically and internationally, the pace of recovery in advertising, and the health of capital and equity markets, including future interest rate changes.

- EPS estimates for MHP from other analysts recently averaged about $2.35 for 2006 and $2.66 for 2007. Standard & Poor's is a division of MHP, and provides no EPS estimates, target price or recommendation for the company.

Qualitative Risk Assessment

A Qualitative Risk Assessment is not available for this company.

Quantitative Evaluations

S&P Quality Ranking NR

D	C	B-	B	B+	A-	A	A+

Relative Strength Rank STRONG

84

LOWEST = 1 HIGHEST = 99

Revenue/Earnings Data

Revenue (Million $)

	1Q	2Q	3Q	4Q	Year
2006	1,141	1,528	1,993	--	--
2005	1,029	1,456	1,977	1,541	6,004
2004	919.9	1,246	1,723	1,362	5,251
2003	830.8	1,172	1,603	1,222	4,828
2002	846.7	1,191	1,577	1,172	4,788
2001	846.4	1,149	1,535	1,115	4,646

Earnings Per Share ($)

	1Q	2Q	3Q	4Q	Year
2006	0.20	0.60	1.06	--	--
2005	0.21	0.51	1.00	0.50	2.21
2004	0.20	0.43	0.85	0.49	1.96
2003	0.11	0.37	0.76	0.56	1.79
2002	0.08	0.35	0.71	0.35	1.48
2001	0.05	0.31	0.61	-0.01	0.96

Fiscal year ended Dec. 31. Next earnings report expected: Late January. EPS Estimates based on S&P Operating Earnings; historical GAAP earnings are as reported.

Dividend Data (Dates: mm/dd Payment Date: mm/dd/yy)

Amount ($)	Date Decl.	Ex-Div. Date	Stk. of Record	Payment Date
0.182	01/24	02/22	02/24	03/10/06
0.182	04/26	05/24	05/26	06/12/06
0.182	07/26	08/24	08/28	09/12/06
0.182	10/25	11/24	11/28	12/12/06

Dividends have been paid since 1937. Source: Company reports.

McGraw-Hill Companies Inc. (The)

Business Summary July 27, 2006

The McGraw-Hill Companies, Inc. is a leading provider of information products and services to business, professional and educational markets worldwide. The company believes that through acquisitions, new product and service development and a strong commitment to customer service, many of its business units have grown to be leaders in their respective fields. Well known brands include BusinessWeek, Standard & Poor's, Platts, F.W. Dodge, and Sweet's. Operations are conducted through over 290 offices in 38 countries worldwide.

McGraw-Hill Education (45% of revenues and 28% of operating profit in 2005) is comprised of two operating groups, the School Education Group (SEG) and the Higher Education, Professional and International Group (HPI). SEG provides educational and professional materials in the U.S. to the pre-K to 12th grade market, and is a leading provider of assessment and reporting services. In July 2004, MHP acquired The Grow Network, a privately held company now part of SEG that provides assessment reporting and customized content for states and large school districts across the country.

HPI serves a global market offering e-books, on-line tutoring, customized course web sites and subscription services, as well as traditional materials to college, university and post-graduate fields. Professional operations focus on professional, reference and trade publishing for medical, business, engineering, and other professions. International operations cover markets worldwide with locally developed materials and English-language materials. The company believes that a number of global trends point to healthy demand for professional books over the long term, including favorable demographics, growth in the number of college-educated adults, and strong worldwide growth in professional services.

Company Financials

Per Share Data ($) Year Ended Dec. 31	**2005**	**2004**	**2003**	**2002**	**2001**	**2000**	**1999**	**1998**	**1997**	**1996**
Tangible Book Value	2.04	2.72	2.24	0.94	0.09	0.17	1.12	0.74	0.32	0.14
Cash Flow	3.21	2.98	2.84	1.71	2.04	2.13	1.85	1.61	1.46	1.84
Earnings	2.21	1.96	1.79	1.48	0.96	1.21	1.07	0.86	0.73	1.24
S&P Core Earnings	2.05	1.80	1.44	1.15	0.60	NA	NA	NA	NA	NA
Dividends	0.66	0.60	0.54	0.51	0.49	0.47	0.43	0.39	0.36	0.33
Payout Ratio	30%	31%	30%	34%	51%	39%	40%	46%	49%	27%
Prices:High	53.97	46.06	35.00	34.85	35.44	33.84	31.56	25.83	18.84	12.31
Prices:Low	40.51	34.55	25.87	25.36	24.35	20.94	23.56	17.13	11.22	9.31
P/E Ratio:High	24	23	20	24	37	28	29	30	26	10
P/E Ratio:Low	18	18	14	17	25	17	22	20	15	8

Income Statement Analysis (Million $)										
Revenue	6,004	5,251	4,828	4,788	4,646	4,281	3,992	3,729	3,534	3,075
Operating Income	1,749	1,467	1,369	1,037	1,044	1,128	984	851	779	662
Depreciation	385	393	403	89.6	421	362	308	299	294	239
Interest Expense	5.20	5.79	7.10	22.5	55.1	52.8	42.0	48.0	52.5	47.7
Pretax Income	1,360	1,169	1,130	905	615	767	698	560	471	815
Effective Tax Rate	37.9%	35.3%	39.1%	36.3%	38.7%	38.5%	39.0%	39.0%	38.3%	39.2%
Net Income	844	756	688	577	377	472	426	342	291	496
S&P Core Earnings	786	694	552	446	233	NA	NA	NA	NA	NA

Balance Sheet & Other Financial Data (Million $)										
Cash	749	681	696	58.2	53.5	3.17	6.49	10.5	4.77	3.43
Current Assets	2,591	2,448	2,256	1,674	1,813	1,802	1,554	1,429	1,464	1,350
Total Assets	6,396	5,863	5,394	5,032	5,161	4,931	4,089	3,788	3,724	3,642
Current Liabilities	2,225	1,969	1,994	1,775	1,876	1,781	1,525	1,291	1,206	1,219
Long Term Debt	0.34	0.51	0.39	459	834	818	355	452	607	557
Common Equity	3,113	4,952	2,557	2,202	1,884	1,761	1,691	1,565	1,435	1,361
Total Capital	3,432	5,185	2,758	2,861	2,908	2,742	2,182	2,147	2,153	2,068
Capital Expenditures	120	139	115	70.0	117	97.7	154	179	78.7	63.3
Cash Flow	1,230	1,149	1,091	666	798	834	734	641	584	734
Current Ratio	1.2	1.2	1.1	0.9	1.0	1.0	1.0	1.1	1.2	1.1
% Long Term Debt of Capitalization	0.0	0.0	0.0	16.0	28.7	29.8	16.3	21.1	28.2	26.9
% Net Income of Revenue	14.1	14.4	14.2	12.0	8.1	11.0	10.7	9.2	8.2	16.1
% Return on Assets	13.8	13.5	13.2	11.3	7.5	10.4	10.8	9.1	7.9	14.8
% Return on Equity	27.7	16.5	29.1	28.2	20.5	27.7	26.3	22.7	20.8	41.4

Data as orig reptd.; bef. results of disc opers/spec. items. Per share data adj. for stk. divs.; EPS diluted. E-Estimated. NA-Not Available. NM-Not Meaningful. NR-Not Ranked. UR-Under Review.

Office: 1221 Avenue of the Americas, New York, NY 10020-1095.
Telephone: 212-512-2000.
Email: investor_relations@mcgraw-hill.com
Website: http://www.mcgraw-hill.com

Chrmn, Pres & CEO: H. McGraw, III
EVP & CFO: R.J. Bahash
EVP & General Counsel: K.M. Vittor
EVP & CIO: B.D. Marcus

SVP & Secy: S.L. Bennett
Investor Contact: D.S. Rubin (212-512-4321)
Board of Directors: P. Aspe, W. F. Bischoff, W., D. N. Daft, L. K. Lorimer, R. P. McGraw, H. W. McGraw, III, H. W. McGraw, Jr., H. Ochoa-Brillembourg, J. H. Ross, E. B. Rust, Jr., K. L. Schmoke, S. Taurel

Founded: 1899
Domicile: New York
Employees: 19,600

STANDARD &POOR'S

McKesson Corp

S&P Recommendation HOLD ★★★★★

Price $50.90 (as of Oct 27, 2006)

12-Mo. Target Price $59.00

Investment Style Large-Cap Value

GICS Sector Health Care
Sub-Industry Health Care Distributors

Comment MCK (formerly McKesson HBOC) provides pharmaceutical supply management and information technologies to a broad range of health care customers.

Key Stock Statistics (Source S&P, Vickers, company reports)

52-Wk Range	$55.10–44.60	S&P Oper. EPS 2007**E**	2.70	P/E on S&P Oper. EPS 2007**E**	18.9	Dividend Rate/Share	$0.24
Trailing 12-Month EPS	$2.43	S&P Oper. EPS 2008**E**	3.10	Common Shares Outstg. (M)	299.3	Yield (%)	0.47
Trailing 12-Month P/E	21.0	S&P Core EPS 2007**E**	2.64	Market Capitalization(B)	$15.236	Beta	0.50
$10K Invested 5 Yrs Ago	$13,228	S&P Core EPS 2008**E**	3.08	Institutional Ownership (%)	85	S&P Credit Rating	BBB

Price Performance

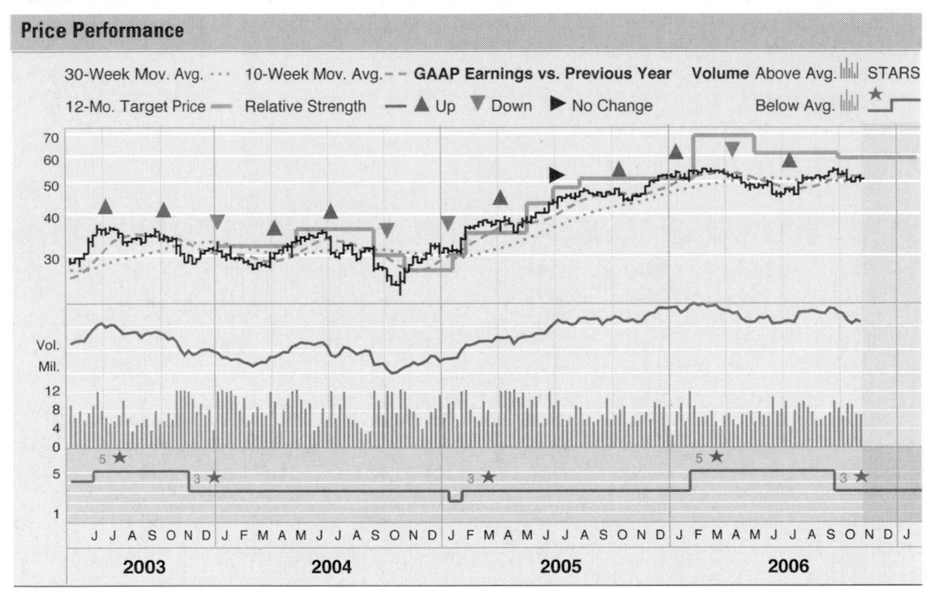

Options: ASE, CBOE, P, Ph

Analysis prepared by **Phillip M. Seligman** on September 26, 2006, when the stock traded at **$ 52.43**.

Highlights

- For FY 07 (Mar.), we look for Pharmaceutical Solutions' (P/S) operating (direct-store) revenue growth to decelerate from 10% in the June quarter to industry levels, on the lapping of the August 2005 D&K Healthcare acquisition, pricing pressures from higher generic drug volumes, and the loss of a large client. We see P/S operating margins modestly higher on increased generic sales and cost controls.
- We foresee low-double-digit revenue and earnings growth in the Medical-Surgical Solutions (M/S) segment, as MCK focuses on the high-growth alternate site market and plans to report its acute care business as a discontinued operation. Meanwhile, we expect high-margin Provider Technologies (P/T) revenues to grow in the mid- to high teens on hospitals' initiatives to convert medical records to electronic form.
- Our FY 07 operating EPS estimate of $2.70 includes stock option expense of $0.08, versus FY 06's $2.44, and we look for $3.10 in FY 08. Our FY 07 and FY 08 S&P Core EPS estimates of $2.64 and $3.08, respectively, take into account an expected nonrecurring restructuring charge and litigation gains in FY 07 only, and pension and post-retirement adjustments in both years.

Investment Rationale/Risk

- We see uncertainty surrounding a potential rise in sell-side pricing pressure on MCK's rapidly growing generic drug business from the decision by Wal-Mart (WMT: strong buy, $48) to slash generic drug prescription prices. While WMT is piloting the program in Tampa, Florida, and limiting it to 291 older, already deeply discounted generic drugs, we would not be surprised to see it expanded nationwide, copied by other drug retailers, and eventually pressuring prices on additional generic drugs. Elsewhere, however, we are encouraged by M/S's gains in the alternate site market and the pending sale of the group's acute-care business. We are also encouraged by what we see as P/T's robust growth, which is supported by hospitals desire to cut medical errors, and what we view as MCK's strong cash position and cash flow.
- Risks to our recommendation and target price include the loss of major accounts, unfavorable regulatory changes, and unfavorable changes in drugmaker-distributor agreements.
- Our estimated calendar 2007 P/E multiple is a peer-level 19.5X. Applying this multiple to our calendar 2007 EPS estimate of $3.05 yields our 12-month target price of $59.

Qualitative Risk Assessment

LOW | **MEDIUM** | HIGH

Our risk assessment reflects our view of MCK's improving profitability and the growing demand for its highly profitable IT products and services, offset by our belief that MCK is more price competitive than peers and that future drugmaker-distributor contract negotiations might be less favorable for distributors.

Quantitative Evaluations

S&P Quality Ranking **B**

D | C | B- | **B** | B+ | A- | A | A+

Relative Strength Rank **WEAK**

28

LOWEST = 1 HIGHEST = 99

Revenue/Earnings Data

Revenue (Million $)

	1Q	2Q	3Q	4Q	Year
2007	23,616	--	--	--	--
2006	20,968	21,515	22,510	23,057	88,050
2005	19,187	19,934	20,782	20,612	80,515
2004	16,524	16,810	18,232	17,940	69,506
2003	13,623	13,690	14,921	14,886	57,121
2002	11,654	12,159	13,197	12,991	50,006

Earnings Per Share ($)

2007	0.60	**E**0.60	**E**0.68	**E**0.79	**E**2.70
2006	0.55	0.49	0.61	0.70	2.34
2005	0.55	0.29	-2.26	0.85	-0.53
2004	0.53	0.53	0.41	0.73	2.19
2003	0.39	0.43	0.46	0.62	1.90
2002	0.36	0.27	0.37	0.42	1.43

Fiscal year ended Mar. 31. Next earnings report expected: Early November. EPS Estimates based on S&P Operating Earnings; historical GAAP earnings are as reported.

Dividend Data (Dates: mm/dd Payment Date: mm/dd/yy)

Amount ($)	Date Decl.	Ex-Div. Date	Stk. of Record	Payment Date
0.060	01/25	02/27	03/01	04/03/06
0.060	05/24	06/07	06/09	07/03/06
0.060	07/26	08/30	09/01	10/02/06
0.060	10/27	11/29	12/01	01/02/07

Dividends have been paid since 1995. Source: Company reports.

Please read the Required Disclosures and Analyst Certification on the last page of this report.

McKesson Corp

Business Summary September 26, 2006

CORPORATE OVERVIEW. McKesson Corp. is a leading distributor of medical products and supplies and health care information technology products and services.

Pharmaceutical Solutions (P/S), which accounted for 94.7% of FY 06 (Mar.) revenues, primarily distributes ethical and proprietary drugs, medical-surgical supplies and health and beauty care products in North America. The business focuses on three customer segments: retail independent pharmacies, retail chains, and institutions, in all 50 states and Canada. These customer categories accounted respectively for 13%, 22% and 32% of P/S's FY 06 March-quarter revenues, and direct sales to customers' warehouses accounted for 33%.

Medical-Surgical Solutions (M/S; 3.5%) provides medical-surgical supplies, equipment, logistics and related services to the continuum of health care providers: hospitals, physicians' offices, long-term care and home care. It also makes and markets automated pharmacy systems to hospitals and retail pharmacies.

Provider Technologies (P/T; 1.8%) provides patient care, clinical, financial, managed care and strategic management software solutions to the health care industry. Products and services are sold to integrated delivery networks, hospitals, physicians' offices, home health providers, pharmacies, reference labs, and HMOs. The products help automate individual hospital departments; provide care management services and medical call center management, data analysis and sharing and computer telephony and Internet links; document patient information for physicians and other clinicians; and offer practice management applications.

CORPORATE STRATEGY. Distribution agreements between distributors and most drugmakers have transitioned toward a more fee-based approach, with the distributors appropriately and predictably compensated for distribution and related logistic and administrative services and data, in our opinion. When completed, MCK and its peers see over 80% of their drugmaker compensation as fixed and not dependent upon drug price inflation.

Company Financials

Per Share Data ($) Year Ended Mar. 31	**2006**	**2005**	**2004**	**2003**	**2002**	**2001**	**2000**	**1999**	**1998**	**1997**
Tangible Book Value	13.36	12.47	12.66	10.57	9.81	8.55	8.40	5.89	7.11	5.74
Cash Flow	3.28	0.32	2.94	2.65	2.20	0.72	1.37	0.98	2.39	0.86
Earnings	2.34	-0.53	2.19	1.90	1.43	-0.15	0.66	0.31	1.59	0.06
S&P Core Earnings	2.07	1.93	1.29	1.24	0.87	-0.39	NA	NA	NA	NA
Dividends	0.24	0.24	0.24	0.24	0.24	0.24	0.31	0.50	0.50	0.50
Payout Ratio	10%	NM	11%	13%	17%	NM	46%	161%	31%	NM
Calendar Year	2005	2004	2003	2002	2001	2000	1999	1998	1997	1996
Prices:High	52.89	35.90	37.14	42.09	41.50	37.00	89.75	96.25	56.88	28.50
Prices:Low	30.13	22.61	22.61	24.99	23.40	16.00	18.56	47.88	25.88	19.50
P/E Ratio:High	23	NM	17	22	29	NM	NM	NM	36	NM
P/E Ratio:Low	13	NM	10	13	16	NM	NM	NM	16	NM

Income Statement Analysis (Million $)										
Revenue	88,050	80,515	69,506	57,121	50,006	42,010	36,734	30,382	20,857	12,887
Operating Income	1,425	1,260	1,216	1,134	923	454	359	531	449	165
Depreciation	266	251	232	204	208	246	201	199	86.0	72.0
Interest Expense	94.0	118	120	121	119	118	120	124	103	56.0
Pretax Income	1,158	-240	911	855	601	9.60	307	202	254	36.4
Effective Tax Rate	36.4%	NM	29.1%	34.3%	30.4%	NM	39.7%	57.9%	39.0%	86.0%
Net Income	737	-157	646	562	419	-42.7	185	85.0	155	5.00
S&P Core Earnings	650	565	380	364	255	-113	NA	NA	NA	NA

Balance Sheet & Other Financial Data (Million $)										
Cash	2,142	1,809	718	534	563	446	606	269	36.0	230
Current Assets	16,919	15,332	13,004	11,254	10,699	9,164	7,966	6,500	4,106	3,761
Total Assets	20,975	18,775	16,240	14,353	13,324	11,530	10,373	9,082	5,608	5,173
Current Liabilities	13,515	11,793	9,456	7,974	7,588	6,550	5,122	4,800	2,578	2,637
Long Term Debt	965	1,202	1,210	1,487	1,485	1,232	1,440	1,142	1,194	825
Common Equity	5,907	5,275	5,165	4,529	3,940	3,493	4,213	2,882	1,523	1,261
Total Capital	6,872	6,477	6,375	6,016	5,425	4,724	5,653	4,024	2,796	1,541
Capital Expenditures	167	140	115	116	132	159	145	251	130	76.9
Cash Flow	1,003	94.2	879	766	626	203	386	284	241	77.0
Current Ratio	1.3	1.3	1.4	1.4	1.4	1.4	1.6	1.4	1.6	1.4
% Long Term Debt of Capitalization	14.0	18.6	19.0	24.7	27.4	26.1	25.5	28.4	42.7	53.5
% Net Income of Revenue	0.8	NM	0.9	1.0	0.8	NM	0.5	0.3	0.7	Nil
% Return on Assets	3.7	NM	4.2	4.1	3.4	NM	1.9	1.2	2.9	0.1
% Return on Equity	13.2	NM	13.3	13.3	11.3	NM	4.8	3.9	10.7	0.4

Data as orig reptd.; bef. results of disc opers/spec. items. Per share data adj. for stk. divs.; EPS diluted. E-Estimated. NA-Not Available. NM-Not Meaningful. NR-Not Ranked. UR-Under Review.

Office: 1 Post St McKesson Plaza , San Francisco, CA 94104-5296.
Telephone: 415-983-8300.
Email: investors@mckesson.com
Website: http://www.mckesson.com

Chrmn, Pres & CEO: J.H. Hammergren
Investor Contact: J.C. Campbell (800-826-9360)
EVP & CFO: J.C. Campbell
EVP, Secy & General Counsel: L. Seeger

EVP & CIO: R.N. Spratt
Board of Directors: W. A. Budd, J. H. Hammergren, A. F. Irby, III, M. C. Jacobs, M. L. Knowles, D. M. Lawrence, R. W. Matshullat, J. V. Napier, J. E. Shaw

Founded: 1994
Domicile: Delaware
Employees: 26,400

STANDARD &POOR'S

MeadWestvaco Corp

S&P Recommendation BUY ★★★★★

Price $27.21 (as of Oct 27, 2006)

12-Mo. Target Price $33.00

Investment Style Mid-Cap Value

GICS Sector Materials
Sub-Industry Paper Products

Comment This company is primarily a major producer of paperboard packaging used in a variety of consumer markets.

Key Stock Statistics (Source S&P, Vickers, company reports)

52-Wk Range	$30.85–24.76	S&P Oper. EPS 2006E	0.95	P/E on S&P Oper. EPS 2006E	28.6	Dividend Rate/Share	$0.92
Trailing 12-Month EPS	$0.56	S&P Oper. EPS 2007E	1.40	Common Shares Outstg. (M)	181.2	Yield (%)	3.38
Trailing 12-Month P/E	48.6	S&P Core EPS 2006E	0.79	Market Capitalization(B)	$4.930	Beta	1.25
$10K Invested 5 Yrs Ago	$12,376	S&P Core EPS 2007E	1.40	Institutional Ownership (%)	81	S&P Credit Rating	BBB

Price Performance

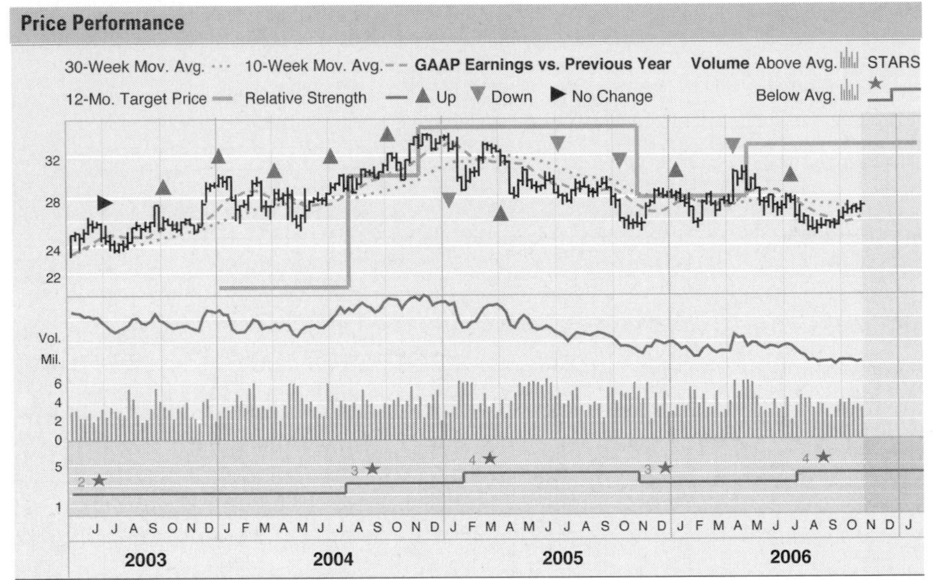

Options: CBOE, P

Analysis prepared by **Stuart J. Benway, CFA** on October 23, 2006, when the stock traded at **$ 26.90**.

Highlights

- We expect sales from continuing operations to rise about 3% in 2006 and 4%-6% in 2007. In our view, this improvement will be largely due to higher average prices across all of MWV's sectors. We look for a modest demand recovery in the beverage markets as well as share gains by coated natural kraft versus corrugated. The chemical segment is also poised for further growth, in our view.
- We anticipate moderately higher margins in 2006 and faster growth in 2007 because of the positive impact of the higher prices that we see, improved manufacturing efficiencies from the shutdown of high cost capacity, and the anticipated benefits of other cost cutting initiatives that MWV has implemented. We see these factors being partly offset by higher costs for manufacturing inputs such as energy, chemicals, and wood fiber.
- Our operating EPS forecast for 2006 is $0.95, up 8% from operating earnings of $0.88 in 2005. Our 2006 operating estimate differs from our S&P Core EPS projection of $0.79 due primarily to estimated restructuring charges. We see both operating and S&P Core EPS of $1.40 in 2007.

Investment Rationale/Risk

- We believe that MeadWestvaco is better positioned than most paper companies in our coverage universe, with its high market share in mostly non-commodity markets, its concentration in the growing packaging industry, and its geographic diversification. Although we are somewhat concerned that results in the near term will be hampered by high input costs, we expect a recent acquisition to add slightly to results in 2007.
- Risks to our recommendation and target price include a weaker than expected global economy, softer than projected demand and pricing trends for the company's packaging grades, and poor execution of MWV's planned cost cutting initiatives.
- The shares recently traded at about 19X our 2007 EPS forecast. This is a modest premium to the peer group, which we believe is justified due to the nature of the company's businesses. Our DCF model values the shares at $33 assuming a weighted average cost of capital of 9.1% and growth in perpetuity of 3%. This is the basis for our 12-month target price of $33.

Qualitative Risk Assessment

LOW | **MEDIUM** | HIGH

MWV operates in a moderately cyclical and seasonal sector and is subject to swings in certain commodity prices. However, it has some pricing power due to its high market share, and its debt levels are low relative to many of its peers.

Quantitative Evaluations

S&P Quality Ranking B-

D | C | **B-** | B | B+ | A- | A | A+

Relative Strength Rank MODERATE

51

LOWEST = 1 HIGHEST = 99

Revenue/Earnings Data

Revenue (Million $)

	1Q	2Q	3Q	4Q	Year
2006	1,434	1,570	--	--	--
2005	1,373	1,587	1,583	1,627	6,170
2004	1,833	2,095	2,148	2,151	8,227
2003	1,694	1,915	1,999	1,945	7,553
2002	1,461	2,012	2,023	1,893	7,242
2001	971.1	966.9	995.1	1,002	3,935

Earnings Per Share ($)

	1Q	2Q	3Q	4Q	Year
2006	0.02	-0.04	**E**0.37	**E**0.42	**E**0.95
2005	0.08	-0.06	0.30	0.33	0.62
2004	-0.01	0.24	0.52	-2.45	-1.73
2003	-0.36	-0.04	0.14	0.25	-0.01
2002	-0.37	-0.04	0.09	0.21	-0.01
2001	0.33	0.18	0.28	0.08	0.87

Fiscal year ended Dec. 31. Next earnings report expected: NA. EPS Estimates based on S&P Operating Earnings; historical GAAP earnings are as reported.

Dividend Data (Dates: mm/dd Payment Date: mm/dd/yy)

Amount ($)	Date Decl.	Ex-Div. Date	Stk. of Record	Payment Date
0.230	01/24	02/01	02/03	03/01/06
0.230	04/25	05/03	05/06	06/01/06
0.230	06/27	08/02	08/04	09/01/06
0.230	10/24	11/01	11/03	12/01/06

Dividends have been paid since 1892. Source: Company reports.

MeadWestvaco Corp

Business Summary October 23, 2006

CORPORATE OVERVIEW. Through a series of mergers and divestitures, MeadWestvaco has molded itself into one of the largest producers of packaging products in the world, and it is also a major supplier of consumer and office products and specialty chemicals. The packaging segment (75% of 2005 revenues) produces bleached paperboard, coated paperboard, kraft paperboard, linerboard and saturating kraft, and packaging for consumer products including media, beverage and dairy, cosmetics, tobacco, pharmaceuticals, and health care products. Some of the company's major customers include Altria, Anheuser-Busch, Coca-Cola and Procter & Gamble. The consumer and office products segment (16%) makes, markets and distributes school and office products, time management products, and envelopes. The specialty chemicals segment (9%) produces, markets and distributes specialty chemicals derived from sawdust and other by-products of the pulp and papermaking process. These chemicals include activated carbon, printing ink resins, emulsifiers used in asphalt paving, and dyestuffs. The company also owns about 1.1 million acres of forest lands in the U.S.

MARKET PROFILE. MeadWestvaco is the largest producer of paperboard, also known as folding boxboard or cartonboard, in North America, with a share of about 17%, according to Pulp & Paper magazine. The market is somewhat fragmented, with more than 15 companies accounting for at least a 1% share, although the top three producers control 38% of the industry. Unlike containerboard, paperboard has a bendable quality for creasing, scoring and shaping, and usually packages single items meant for consumer purchase. It is used in a variety of consumer applications where print quality, strength and customer appeal are important. Folding carton demand is driven primarily by consumer spending and industrial production. We believe the company's market position, technical expertise and product line diversity give it a moderate level of control over pricing.

Company Financials

Per Share Data ($) Year Ended Dec. 31	**2005**	**2004**	**2003**	**2002**	**2001**	**2000**	**1999**	**1998**	**1997**	**1996**
Tangible Book Value	14.58	18.44	19.89	20.44	17.34	23.17	21.65	22.39	22.35	21.69
Cash Flow	3.17	1.87	3.60	3.49	4.29	5.63	3.90	4.06	4.25	4.45
Earnings	0.62	-1.73	-0.01	-0.01	0.87	2.53	1.11	1.30	1.58	2.09
S&P Core Earnings	0.27	-2.67	-0.81	-1.37	-1.01	NA	NA	NA	NA	NA
Dividends	0.92	0.92	0.92	0.92	0.88	0.88	0.88	0.88	0.88	0.88
Payout Ratio	148%	NM	NM	NM	101%	35%	79%	68%	55%	42%
Prices:High	34.33	34.34	29.83	36.50	32.10	34.75	33.50	34.13	37.50	33.13
Prices:Low	25.06	25.16	21.37	15.57	22.68	24.06	20.81	21.00	25.00	25.38
P/E Ratio:High	55	NM	NM	NM	37	14	30	26	23	16
P/E Ratio:Low	40	NM	NM	NM	26	10	19	16	16	12

Income Statement Analysis (Million $)	2005	2004	2003	2002	2001	2000	1999	1998	1997	1996
Revenue	6,170	8,227	7,553	7,242	3,935	3,663	2,802	2,886	2,982	3,045
Operating Income	818	1,042	855	859	677	869	601	577	580	637
Depreciation	491	726	724	674	347	314	280	281	269	240
Interest Expense	208	278	291	309	208	192	124	110	93.3	105
Pretax Income	135	-454	-29.0	-15.0	119	404	148	204	247	336
Effective Tax Rate	11.9%	NM	NM	NM	25.6%	36.9%	24.9%	35.4%	34.0%	36.9%
Net Income	119	-349	-2.00	-3.00	88.2	255	111	132	163	212
S&P Core Earnings	50.6	-539	-164	-264	-104	NA	NA	NA	NA	NA

Balance Sheet & Other Financial Data (Million $)	2005	2004	2003	2002	2001	2000	1999	1998	1997	1996
Cash	297	270	225	372	81.2	255	109	105	175	115
Current Assets	2,030	2,562	2,426	2,431	1,016	1,064	738	739	805	716
Total Assets	8,908	11,681	12,487	12,921	6,787	6,570	4,897	5,009	4,899	4,437
Current Liabilities	1,042	1,751	1,501	1,620	701	567	425	467	406	419
Long Term Debt	2,417	3,427	3,969	4,233	2,660	2,687	1,502	1,526	1,513	1,153
Common Equity	3,483	4,317	4,768	4,831	2,341	2,333	2,171	2,246	2,279	2,210
Total Capital	7,052	9,249	10,415	10,821	6,009	5,927	4,472	4,541	4,494	4,018
Capital Expenditures	305	407	393	377	290	214	229	423	621	522
Cash Flow	610	377	722	671	436	569	392	413	432	453
Current Ratio	1.9	1.5	1.6	1.5	1.4	1.9	1.7	1.6	2.0	1.7
% Long Term Debt of Capitalization	34.3	37.1	38.1	39.1	44.3	45.3	33.6	33.6	33.7	28.7
% Net Income of Revenue	1.9	NM	NM	NM	2.2	7.0	4.0	4.6	5.5	7.0
% Return on Assets	1.2	NM	NM	NM	1.3	4.4	2.2	2.7	3.5	4.9
% Return on Equity	3.1	NM	NM	NM	3.8	11.3	5.0	5.8	7.3	9.9

Data as orig reptd.; bef. results of disc opers/spec. items. Per share data adj. for stk. divs.; EPS diluted. E-Estimated. NA-Not Available. NM-Not Meaningful. NR-Not Ranked. UR-Under Review.

Office: 1 High Ridge Park, Stamford, CT 06905-1330.
Telephone: 203-461-7400.
Website: http://www.meadwestvaco.com
Chrmn & CEO: J.A. Luke, Jr.

Pres: J.A. Buzzard
SVP & CFO: E.M. Rajkowski
SVP, Secy & General Counsel: W.L. Willkie, II
Treas: R.E. Birkenholz

Investor Contact: J. Thompson
Board of Directors: M. E. Campbell, T. W. Cole, Jr., J. G. Kaiser, R. B. Kelson, J. M. Kilts, J. A. Krol, S. J. Kropf, D. S. Luke, J. A. Luke, Jr., R. C. McCormack, T. H. Powers, E. M. Straw, J. L. Warner

Founded: 1846
Domicile: Delaware
Employees: 22,200

STANDARD &POOR'S

Medco Health Solutions Inc.

S&P Recommendation HOLD ★★★★★

Price $54.75 (as of Oct 27, 2006)

12-Mo. Target Price $63.00

Investment Style Large-Cap Growth

GICS Sector Health Care
Sub-Industry Health Care Services

Comment Medco, spun off from Merck & Co. in August 2003, is the largest U.S. pharmacy benefit manager (PBM) in terms of revenues and script count.

Key Stock Statistics (Source S&P, Vickers, company reports)

52-Wk Range	$64.13–46.40	S&P Oper. EPS 2006E	2.68	P/E on S&P Oper. EPS 2006E	20.4	Dividend Rate/Share	Nil
Trailing 12-Month EPS	$1.81	S&P Oper. EPS 2007E	3.10	Common Shares Outstg. (M)	293.9	Yield (%)	Nil
Trailing 12-Month P/E	30.3	S&P Core EPS 2006E	2.34	Market Capitalization(B)	$16.093	Beta	0.74
$10K Invested 5 Yrs Ago	NA	S&P Core EPS 2007E	2.78	Institutional Ownership (%)	77	S&P Credit Rating	BBB

Price Performance

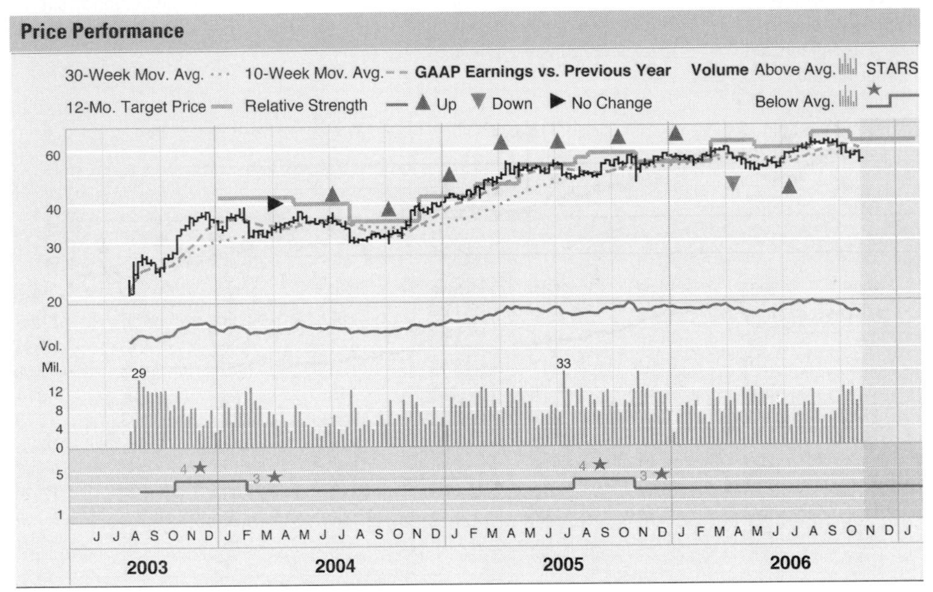

Analysis prepared by **Phillip M. Seligman** on October 11, 2006, when the stock traded at **$ 56.76**.

Highlights

- We forecast 2006 revenue of $42.5 billion, including $2.4 billion in net new business, $650 million in net new Medicare sales, and the August 2005 acquisition of specialty drug pharmacy Accredo Health. We see these gains partly offset by First DataBank's October 2006 decision to cut published average wholesale prices (AWPs) of branded drugs, which are used as reimbursement benchmarks, by 5%.
- We see EBITDA per adjusted prescription, which measures a pharmacy benefit manager's (PBMs) profitability, in the mid-teens in 2006, as the benefits of generic and specialty drug penetration are partly offset by the loss of large mail order clients, and a lower mail penetration rate among new, large state accounts.
- We estimate 2006 operating EPS of $2.68, including $0.21 of stock option expense but excluding an amortization charge of $0.36, versus 2005's $2.05 (excluding $0.21 of stock option expense), and we forecast EPS of $3.10 in 2007. Our 2006 and 2007 S&P Core EPS estimates of $2.34 and $2.78, respectively, reflect a one-time legal settlement in 2006 only, and amortization charges and modest pension and post-retirement plan adjustments in both years.

Investment Rationale/Risk

- We are encouraged by MHS's garnering of $3.6 billion in net new business on an annualized basis year to date as of June 30 and $900 million of new business so far for 2007. We are also pleased that MHS seems to be making progress in its account retention rates. We see Accredo enabling MHS to become a one-stop shop for a wide range of specialty needs. However, we think expansion of EBITDA per adjusted claim will slow at least temporarily in the fourth quarter and in most of 2007, assuming a one-time decline in AWPs without a concurrent decline in the cost of goods.
- Risks to our recommendation and target price include growing regulatory oversight, more stringent government regulations, and the potential loss of key client contracts, particularly that of the UnitedHealth Group. Our corporate governance concerns include what we believe to be excessively high hurdles faced by shareholders seeking to amend charters or bylaws.
- Our 12-month target price of $63 assumes a P/E to earnings growth ratio of 1.2X, reflecting an historical average valuation among PBM stocks, a three-year projected growth rate of 17%, and our 2007 operating EPS estimate.

Qualitative Risk Assessment

LOW | **MEDIUM** | HIGH

Our risk assessment reflects rising drug demand and our view of MHS's improving financial performance and declining debt leverage. However, we believe that intense competition and increased government regulation of pharmacy benefit managers, which we view as likely, could slow long-term progress in profits.

Quantitative Evaluations

S&P Quality Ranking NR

D | C | B- | B | B+ | A- | A | A+

Relative Strength Rank WEAK

13

LOWEST = 1 HIGHEST = 99

Revenue/Earnings Data

Revenue (Million $)

	1Q	2Q	3Q	4Q	Year
2006	10,564	10,589	--	--	--
2005	8,743	8,999	9,325	10,803	37,871
2004	8,906	8,836	8,697	8,913	35,352
2003	8,334	8,405	8,524	9,002	34,265
2002	--	--	--	--	32,959
2001	--	--	--	--	29,071

Earnings Per Share ($)

	1Q	2Q	3Q	4Q	Year
2006	0.15	0.56	E0.73	E0.75	E2.68
2005	0.47	0.48	0.53	0.57	2.05
2004	0.38	0.46	0.43	0.48	1.75
2003	0.38	0.39	0.37	0.43	1.57
2002	--	--	--	--	1.18
2001	--	--	--	--	0.95

Fiscal year ended Dec. 31. Next earnings report expected: Early November. EPS Estimates based on S&P Operating Earnings; historical GAAP earnings are as reported.

Dividend Data

No cash dividends have been paid.

Medco Health Solutions Inc.

Business Summary October 11, 2006

CORPORATE OVERVIEW. Medco Health Solutions was spun off to Merck & Co. (MRK) shareholders in a tax-free transaction on August 19, 2003. The company is one of the largest U.S. pharmacy benefit managers (PBMs). It provides programs and services to clients and members of PBMs, and to physicians and pharmacies that they use.

In 2005, MHS processed about 540 million prescriptions, compared to 503 million in 2004. Revenues and net income are derived from: rebates and discounts on prescription drugs from pharmaceutical manufacturers; competitive discounts from retail pharmacies; the negotiation of favorable client pricing, including rebate sharing terms; the shift in dispensing volumes from retail to home delivery; and the provision of services in a cost-efficient manner.

We believe that MHS is facing some risks, including pending lawsuits by plaintiffs alleging that MHS breached fiduciary obligations under the Employee Retirement Income Security Act (ERISA).

Gross rebates recorded as received from MRK totaled $301.1 million through the separation date of August 19, 2003, $443.9 million in 2002, and $439.4 million in 2001. According to MHS, effective as of the end of March 2006, the agreement entered into with MRK in July 2002 was terminated. Under that agreement, MRK provided MHS with rebates based, in part, on whether MRK products were included in formularies that MHS offers clients, and on whether MRK products achieve specified market share targets under MHS's plans. If MHS had failed to achieve the targets, it may have had to pay damages. That agreement was replaced with one that is similar to other rebate agreements that MHS has with other major drugmakers.

Company Financials

Per Share Data ($) Year Ended Dec. 31	2005	2004	2003	2002	2001	2000	1999	1998	1997	1996
Tangible Book Value	NM	0.98	NM	NM	1.70	1.31	NA	NA	NA	NA
Cash Flow	3.27	3.13	2.62	2.13	2.15	1.87	NA	NA	NA	NA
Earnings	2.05	1.75	1.57	1.18	0.95	0.80	NA	NA	NA	NA
S&P Core Earnings	1.86	1.48	1.03	1.07	0.71	NA	NA	NA	NA	NA
Dividends	Nil	Nil	Nil	NA	NA	NA	NA	NA	NA	NA
Payout Ratio	Nil	Nil	Nil	NA	NA	NA	NA	NA	NA	NA
Prices:High	57.95	41.90	38.00	NA	NA	NA	NA	NA	NA	NA
Prices:Low	40.55	29.40	20.20	NA	NA	NA	NA	NA	NA	NA
P/E Ratio:High	28	24	24	NA	NA	NA	NA	NA	NA	NA
P/E Ratio:Low	20	17	13	NA	NA	NA	NA	NA	NA	NA

Income Statement Analysis (Million $)	2005	2004	2003	2002	2001	2000	1999	1998	1997	1996
Revenue	37,871	35,352	34,265	32,959	29,071	22,266	NA	NA	NA	NA
Operating Income	1,350	1,244	1,025	886	837	731	NA	NA	NA	NA
Depreciation	358	378	283	257	323	289	NA	NA	NA	NA
Interest Expense	73.9	Nil	Nil	73.5	Nil	Nil	NA	NA	NA	NA
Pretax Income	953	806	729	547	518	448	NA	NA	NA	NA
Effective Tax Rate	36.8%	40.3%	41.6%	41.7%	50.5%	51.6%	NA	NA	NA	NA
Net Income	602	482	426	319	257	217	NA	NA	NA	NA
S&P Core Earnings	544	404	279	287	188	NA	NA	NA	NA	NA

Balance Sheet & Other Financial Data (Million $)	2005	2004	2003	2002	2001	2000	1999	1998	1997	1996
Cash	888	1,146	638	203	16.3	NA	NA	NA	NA	NA
Current Assets	5,061	4,320	3,760	3,044	2,534	NA	NA	NA	NA	NA
Total Assets	13,703	10,542	10,263	9,714	9,252	8,915	NA	NA	NA	NA
Current Liabilities	3,761	2,645	2,605	2,370	1,809	NA	NA	NA	NA	NA
Long Term Debt	944	1,093	1,346	1,385	Nil	Nil	NA	NA	NA	NA
Common Equity	7,724	5,719	5,080	4,738	6,268	6,358	NA	NA	NA	NA
Total Capital	9,882	6,812	7,604	7,305	7,423	7,502	NA	NA	NA	NA
Capital Expenditures	132	98.1	125	NA	322	251	NA	NA	NA	NA
Cash Flow	960	859	709	576	580	506	NA	NA	NA	NA
Current Ratio	1.3	1.6	1.4	1.3	1.4	NA	NA	NA	NA	NA
% Long Term Debt of Capitalization	9.6	16.0	17.7	19.0	Nil	Nil	NA	NA	NA	NA
% Net Income of Revenue	1.6	1.4	1.2	1.0	0.9	1.0	NA	NA	NA	NA
% Return on Assets	5.0	4.6	4.2	NA	2.8	NA	NA	NA	NA	NA
% Return on Equity	9.0	8.9	7.3	NA	4.1	NA	NA	NA	NA	NA

Data as orig reptd.; bef. results of disc opers/spec. items. Per share data adj. for stk. divs.; EPS diluted. E-Estimated. NA-Not Available. NM-Not Meaningful. NR-Not Ranked. UR-Under Review.

Office: 100 Parsons Pond Drive, Franklin Lakes, NJ 07417-2603.
Telephone: 201-269-3400.
Website: http://www.medco.com
Chrmn, Pres & CEO: D.B. Snow, Jr.

COO & EVP: K.O. Klepper
SVP & CFO: J.A. Reed
SVP, Secy & General Counsel: D.S. Machlowitz
Investor Contact: S. DeWitt (201-269-6187)

Board of Directors: H. W. Barker, Jr., J. L. Cassis, M. Goldstein, L. S. Lewin, C. M. Lillis, E. H. Shortliffe, D. B. Snow, Jr., B. L. Strom, T. G. Thompson, B. J. Wilson

Founded: 1983
Domicile: Delaware
Employees: 15,300

STANDARD &POOR'S

MedImmune Inc

S&P Recommendation HOLD ★★★★★

Price $31.74 (as of Oct 27, 2006)

12-Mo. Target Price $30.00

Investment Style Mid-Cap Growth

GICS Sector Health Care
Sub-Industry Biotechnology

Comment This biotech concern develops, manufactures and markets therapeutics and vaccines to treat and prevent certain infectious diseases and cancer.

Key Stock Statistics (Source S&P, Vickers, company reports)

52-Wk Range	**$37.58–24.87**	S&P Oper. EPS 2006**E**	**0.14**	P/E on S&P Oper. EPS 2006**E**	**NM**	Dividend Rate/Share	**Nil**
Trailing 12-Month EPS	**$-0.38**	S&P Oper. EPS 2007**E**	**0.72**	Common Shares Outstg. (M)	**239.4**	Yield (%)	**Nil**
Trailing 12-Month P/E	**NM**	S&P Core EPS 2006**E**	**0.14**	Market Capitalization(B)	**$7.600**	Beta	**0.89**
$10K Invested 5 Yrs Ago	**$7,808**	S&P Core EPS 2007**E**	**0.72**	Institutional Ownership (%)	**97**	S&P Credit Rating	**NA**

Price Performance

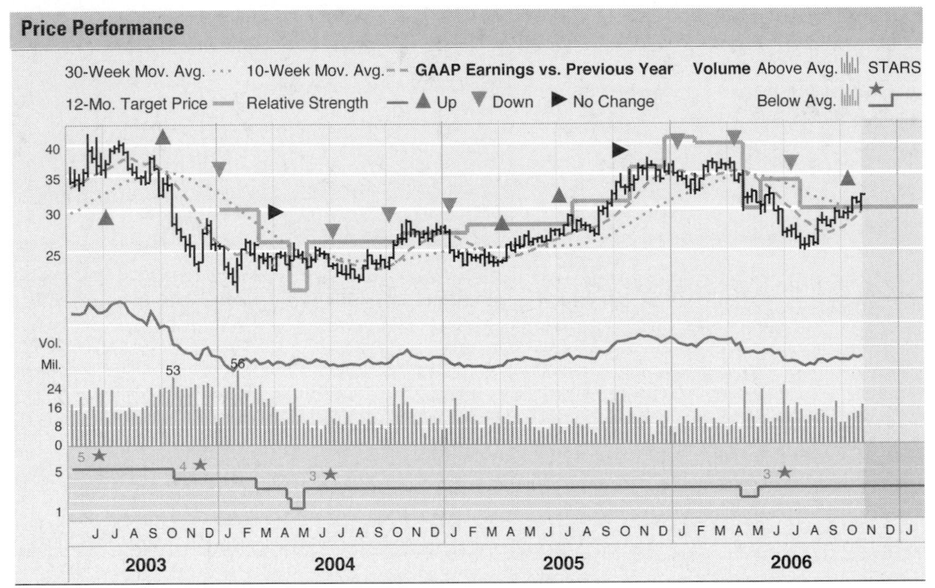

Options: ASE, CBOE, P, Ph

Analysis prepared by **Jeffrey Loo, CFA** on July 25, 2006, when the stock traded at **$ 25.92**.

Highlights

- We have lowered our 2006 revenue forecast for the second time this year following slower than expected second quarter seasonal sales of synagis. We now project total revenues of $1.27 billion in 2006, reduced from our prior forecasts of $1.34 billion and $1.45 billion. We estimate Synagis sales of $1.03 billion for 2006, down from our prior forecasts of $1.09 billion and $1.18 billion. But in June, the FDA approved Merck's Gardasil, a vaccine for the prevention of human papillomavirus (HPV). HPV could cause genital warts and cervical cancer. MEDI will be entitled to royalties on sales.
- We continue to assume that CAIV-T will be ready for commercial launch for the 2007/2008 flu season in the U.S. We also believe that MEDI has a healthy pipeline with 14 candidates in clinical trials and we see up to five investigational new drugs (INDs) by year-end.
- Including projected stock option expense and accounting for MEDI's stock buyback program, we estimate EPS for 2006 and 2007 at $0.14 and $0.72, respectively.

Investment Rationale/Risk

- On a forward PE and growth basis looking into 2007, we still do not consider the shares attractive relative to, in our view, top biotechs such as Genentech and Gilead Sciences. However, we do think the outlook for MEDI is improving and look for the second half of 2006 to show improvement. Potential second half catalysts include the potential launch of Merck's Gardasil, positive news for CAIV-T, and the potential new drug application (NDA) filing by Glaxo for approval of its HPV vaccine, Cervarix. MEDI would be entitled to royalties.
- Risks to our recommendation and target price include weak sales of Synagis, FDA rejection of CAIV-T, poor results for Numax and Abegrin, and a delay in Merck's Gardasil.
- Based on our net present value analysis (we assume combined Synagis/Numax sales of $1.8 billion by 2011; peak sales of CAIV-T of $420 million by 2011; and royalties approaching $250 million by 2017), our 12-month target price is $30.

Qualitative Risk Assessment

LOW | MEDIUM | **HIGH**

Currently, MedImmune is highly dependent on sales of Synagis, which represented about 87% of 2005 revenues. The company is also developing CAIV-T influenza vaccine and Numax, a follow-on product to Synagis. Negative clinical trial results for CAIV-T or Numax and weaker than expected sales of Synagis could adversely impact the shares.

Quantitative Evaluations

S&P Quality Ranking **C**

D | **C** | B- | B | B+ | A- | A | A+

Relative Strength Rank **STRONG**

81

LOWEST = 1 HIGHEST = 99

Revenue/Earnings Data

Revenue (Million $)

	1Q	2Q	3Q	4Q	Year
2006	498.0	72.90	177.2	--	--
2005	509.8	88.50	153.6	492.0	1,244
2004	489.0	93.68	92.58	465.8	1,141
2003	436.0	117.8	99.36	407.8	1,054
2002	329.6	63.72	72.63	381.8	848.0
2001	245.2	33.37	47.41	292.7	618.7

Earnings Per Share ($)

2006	0.18	-0.26	-0.23	**E**0.40	**E**0.14
2005	0.45	-0.18	-0.26	-0.09	-0.07
2004	0.43	-0.40	-0.26	0.20	-0.02
2003	0.43	0.05	-0.07	0.30	0.72
2002	-4.54	-0.12	-0.14	0.33	-4.40
2001	0.36	-0.04	-0.09	0.45	0.68

Fiscal year ended Dec. 31. Next earnings report expected: Early February. EPS Estimates based on S&P Operating Earnings; historical GAAP earnings are as reported.

Dividend Data

No cash dividends have been paid.

MedImmune Inc

Business Summary July 25, 2006

CORPORATE OVERVIEW. MedImmune, the seventh largest U.S. biotech company in terms of revenues, is developing and commercializing treatments for infectious diseases, autoimmune disorders, and cancer. In January 2002, it acquired Aviron by exchanging 1.075 MEDI shares for each Aviron share. The impetus for the deal was Aviron's FluMist, an influenza vaccine that was approved by the FDA in June 2003.

Synagis, an injectable humanized monoclonal antibody, is effective in neutralizing respiratory syncytial virus (RSV) infection. RSV, typically seen in the fall, winter and early spring, is the most common cause of lower respiratory infections in pediatric patients. More than 125,000 infants are hospitalized with severe RSV disease in the U.S. annually, with about 325,000 infants (primarily premature babies) in the U.S. and a similar number outside the U.S. at risk of acquiring severe RSV yearly. Synagis is the only drug with FDA clearance to treat RSV. MEDI recorded Synagis sales of $942 million in 2004, up from $849 million in 2003.

The company co-markets Synagis with Abbott Labs in the U.S. In August 2005, MEDI amended its agreement with Abbott. Abbott will continue to co-promote the drug through 2006. In 2007, MEDI will exclusively market the drug in the U.S. and will no longer make Synagis payments to Abbott. Overseas, Abbott will continue to have exclusive marketing rights to the drug, which it buys from MEDI. European sales began in 1999. Japanese approval was granted in January 2002. In September 2003, Synagis was granted FDA approval to treat pediatric congenital heart disease.

FluMist is a vaccine delivered as a nasal spray to prevent influenza in adults and children. It is based on cold-adapted influenza technology that weakens live influenza strains until the vaccine is safe for humans. The vaccine is a frozen product that must be stored in a proper environment. In June 2003, the FDA approved FluMist for the prevention of flu in healthy individuals ages 5 to 49. FluMist was launched in time for the 2003/2004 flu season. Henry Schein was the U.S. distributor for FluMist for the 2004/2005 flu season.

Company Financials

Per Share Data ($) Year Ended Dec. 31	**2005**	**2004**	**2003**	**2002**	**2001**	**2000**	**1999**	**1998**	**1997**	**1996**
Tangible Book Value	5.05	6.59	6.57	6.16	4.87	3.99	2.63	1.28	0.28	0.56
Cash Flow	0.25	0.15	0.87	-4.25	0.72	0.69	0.46	0.31	-0.25	-0.22
Earnings	-0.07	-0.02	0.72	-4.40	0.68	0.66	0.44	0.30	-0.26	-0.24
S&P Core Earnings	-0.22	-0.07	0.38	-4.73	0.31	NA	NA	NA	NA	NA
Dividends	Nil	Nil	Nil	Nil	Nil	Nil	Nil	Nil	Nil	Nil
Payout Ratio	Nil	Nil	Nil	Nil	Nil	Nil	Nil	Nil	Nil	Nil
Prices:High	37.58	28.70	42.09	48.35	54.56	86.13	58.60	16.90	7.25	3.35
Prices:Low	23.20	20.77	22.79	20.37	27.63	42.00	14.33	6.48	1.90	1.90
P/E Ratio:High	NM	NM	58	NM	80	NM	NM	56	NM	NM
P/E Ratio:Low	NM	NM	32	NM	41	NM	NM	21	NM	NM

Income Statement Analysis (Million $)										
Revenue	1,244	1,141	1,054	848	619	590	383	201	81.0	41.1
Operating Income	90.3	79.7	279	140	202	188	81.8	9.65	-34.7	-31.1
Depreciation	78.6	41.1	37.7	36.8	9.12	7.32	5.00	3.46	2.75	1.80
Interest Expense	9.20	8.40	10.3	9.11	0.59	0.47	3.18	4.04	3.48	2.26
Pretax Income	7.50	-9.20	291	-1,050	228	209	86.3	8.81	-36.9	-29.5
Effective Tax Rate	NM	NM	37.1%	NM	34.8%	30.8%	NM	NM	NM	NM
Net Income	-16.6	-3.80	183	-1,098	149	145	93.4	56.2	-36.9	-29.5
S&P Core Earnings	-54.3	-17.0	96.0	-1,180	69.1	NA	NA	NA	NA	NA

Balance Sheet & Other Financial Data (Million $)										
Cash	1,472	1,706	788	1,423	788	526	270	135	30.0	115
Current Assets	1,037	694	1,103	743	594	688	402	216	100	133
Total Assets	2,780	2,564	2,795	2,188	1,219	1,007	648	353	170	164
Current Liabilities	1,149	364	391	267	165	151	99.0	58.0	43.7	20.0
Long Term Debt	Nil	506	703	242	8.79	9.60	10.4	83.2	85.3	70.9
Common Equity	1,571	1,675	1,699	1,677	1,044	844	537	210	40.5	72.9
Total Capital	1,571	2,181	2,402	1,920	1,053	853	547	293	126	144
Capital Expenditures	91.5	79.8	113	80.9	18.3	8.29	12.2	10.1	36.7	22.7
Cash Flow	62.0	37.3	221	-1,061	158	152	98.4	59.7	-34.1	-27.7
Current Ratio	0.9	1.9	2.8	2.8	3.6	4.5	4.1	3.7	2.3	6.7
% Long Term Debt of Capitalization	Nil	23.2	29.3	12.6	0.8	1.1	1.9	28.4	67.7	49.3
% Net Income of Revenue	NM	NM	17.4	NM	24.1	26.8	24.4	28.0	NM	NM
% Return on Assets	NM	NM	7.4	NM	13.4	17.5	17.7	21.5	NM	NM
% Return on Equity	NM	NM	10.9	NM	15.8	21.0	23.8	44.9	NM	NM

Data as orig reptd.; bef. results of disc opers/spec. items. Per share data adj. for stk. divs.; EPS diluted. E-Estimated. NA-Not Available. NM-Not Meaningful. NR-Not Ranked. UR-Under Review.

Office: One MedImmune Way, Gaithersburg, MD 20878.
Telephone: 301-398-0000.
Email: ir@medimmune.com
Website: http://www.medimmune.com

Chrmn: W.T. Hockmeyer
Pres, Vice Chrmn & CEO: D.M. Mott
SVP & CFO: L.S. Zoth
SVP, Secy & General Counsel: W.C. Bertrand, Jr.

Investor Contact: W. Roberts (301-527-4358)
Board of Directors: D. Baltimore, M. J. Barrett, J. H. Cavanaugh, B. H. Franklin, W. T. Hockmeyer, G. S. Macklin, G. M. Milne, Jr., D. M. Mott, E. Wyatt

Founded: 1987
Domicile: Delaware
Employees: 2,215

STANDARD &POOR'S

Medtronic Inc.

S&P Recommendation HOLD ★★★★★

Price $48.67 (as of Oct 27, 2006)

12-Mo. Target Price $50.00

Investment Style Large-Cap Growth

GICS Sector Health Care
Sub-Industry Health Care Equipment

Comment This global medical device manufacturer has leadership positions in the pacemaker, defibrillator, orthopedic, diabetes management and other medical markets.

Key Stock Statistics (Source S&P, Vickers, company reports)

52-Wk Range	$59.87–42.37	S&P Oper. EPS 2007**E**	2.35	P/E on S&P Oper. EPS 2007**E**	20.7	Dividend Rate/Share	$0.44
Trailing 12-Month EPS	$2.34	S&P Oper. EPS 2008**E**	2.67	Common Shares Outstg. (M)	1,149.3	Yield (%)	0.90
Trailing 12-Month P/E	20.8	S&P Core EPS 2007**E**	2.35	Market Capitalization(B)	$55.939	Beta	0.41
$10K Invested 5 Yrs Ago	$11,902	S&P Core EPS 2008**E**	2.67	Institutional Ownership (%)	75	S&P Credit Rating	AA-

Price Performance

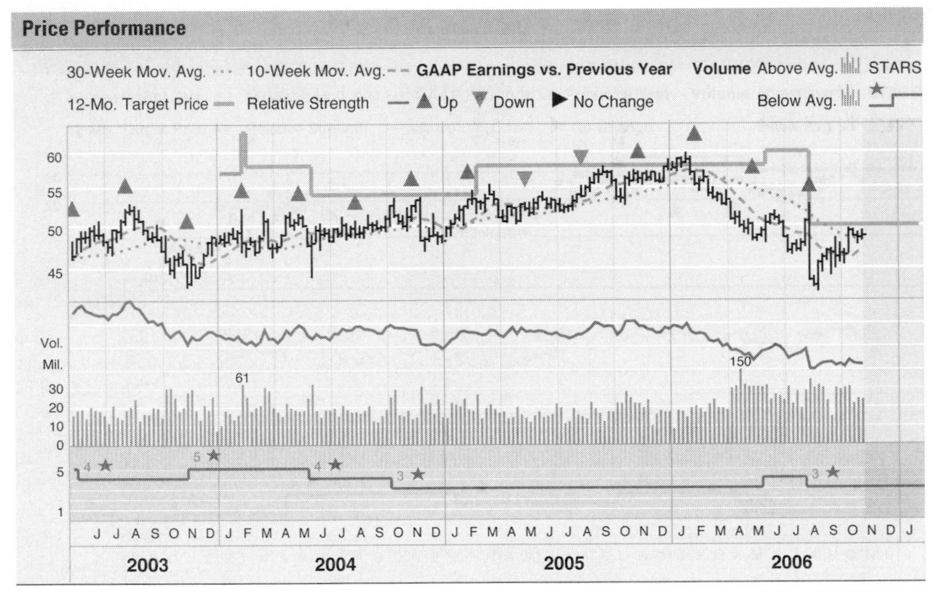

Options: ASE, CBOE, P, Ph

Analysis prepared by **Robert M. Gold** on September 01, 2006, when the stock traded at **$ 46.91**.

Highlights

- We project FY 07 (Apr.) sales of about $12.2 billion, including an approximate 6% gain in cardiac rhythm management, 16% in spinal surgery, 17% in neurology, 16% in vascular, 13% in diabetes, 8% in ENT and 3% in cardiac surgery. We think projections in the implantable cardioverter defibrillator (ICD) category has become more challenging, however, amid dramatically slowing growth within the domestic marketplace.
- We think FY 07 gross margins will suffer from reduced contributions from the U.S. ICD category, partially offset by manufacturing efficiencies. We expect R&D and SG&A costs to consume 10% and 32%, respectively, of sales. We see free cash flow at $2.0 billion, and think MDT may raise the dividend payment and/or pursue strategic acquisitions with the available cash.
- After $0.12 of projected stock option costs, which we expect to be spread evenly on a quarterly basis, our FY 07 EPS forecast is $2.35. We look for FY 08 EPS of $2.67, and think the long-term sustainable EPS growth rate is approximately 13%, assuming a resumption of more normal growth in the domestic ICD markets during calendars 2007 and 2008.

Investment Rationale/Risk

- We believe the recent Medicare decision to lower ICD reimbursements in 2007 by only about 3%, well below original proposals for a cut of up to 24%, bodes well for the overall market and should help reinvigorate procedure growth in 2007. However, we think some high profile product recalls and some inventory workdowns at the company's hospital customer base could limit ICD sales growth for several more quarters. Outside of the U.S., we think ICD demand has accelerated.
- Risks to our opinion and target price include loss of share in key markets, unfavorable patent litigation, adverse reimbursement rate changes and further weakness in the U.S. ICD market.
- In our view, the lack of near term visibility on the important ICD revenue stream will likely restrict the extent of valuation expansion, but we continue to believe the company's highly diversified product line justifies a forward PEG ratio in line with the device group. Our 12-month target price is $50, or 18.7X our FY 08 EPS estimate, translating into a forward PEG ratio of 1.4X, on par with other large cap names within our medical device coverage universe.

Qualitative Risk Assessment

LOW | **MEDIUM** | HIGH

The company operates within intensely competitive areas of the medical equipment markets, which are typically characterized by relatively short product life cycles, pricing pressures and the threat of new market entrants. However, we believe this is offset by MDT's many competitive advantages due to the scale of its operations and sales force, product breadth and what we see as its financial strength.

Quantitative Evaluations

S&P Quality Ranking A-

D | C | B- | B | B+ | **A-** | A | A+

Relative Strength Rank MODERATE

47

LOWEST = 1 HIGHEST = 99

Revenue/Earnings Data

Revenue (Million $)

	1Q	2Q	3Q	4Q	Year
2007	2,897	--	--	--	--
2006	2,690	2,765	2,770	3,077	11,292
2005	2,346	2,400	2,531	2,778	10,055
2004	2,064	2,164	2,194	2,665	9,087
2003	1,714	1,891	1,913	2,148	7,665
2002	1,456	1,571	1,592	1,792	6,411

Earnings Per Share ($)

2007	0.51	**E**0.57	**E**0.59	**E**0.65	**E**2.35
2006	0.26	0.67	0.55	0.62	2.09
2005	0.43	0.44	0.45	0.16	1.48
2004	0.37	0.39	0.38	0.47	1.60
2003	0.31	0.25	0.35	0.40	1.30
2002	0.25	0.05	0.26	0.25	0.80

Fiscal year ended Apr. 30. Next earnings report expected: Mid November. EPS Estimates based on S&P Operating Earnings; historical GAAP earnings are as reported.

Dividend Data (Dates: mm/dd Payment Date: mm/dd/yy)

Amount ($)	Date Decl.	Ex-Div. Date	Stk. of Record	Payment Date
0.096	01/19	04/05	04/07	04/28/06
0.110	06/22	07/05	07/07	07/28/06
0.110	08/24	10/04	10/06	10/27/06
0.110	10/20	01/03	01/05	01/26/07

Dividends have been paid since 1977. Source: Company reports.

Medtronic Inc.

Business Summary September 01, 2006

Medtronic has leading positions in medical device categories, including cardiac rhythm management, ear, nose and throat, spinal, vascular, neurological and cardiac surgery.

Cardiac rhythm management products (46% of FY 06 (Apr.) revenues) include implantable pacemakers to treat bradycardia (slow or irregular heartbeats). Bradycardia systems include pacemakers, leads and accessories. Some models are non-invasively programmed by a physician to adjust sensing, electrical pulse intensity, duration, rate and other factors, as well as pacers that can sense in both upper and lower heart chambers and produce appropriate impulses. In May 2005, FDA approval was received for EnRhythm, the company's newest dual-chamber pacemaker, and the first to offer an exclusive pacing mode, called Managed Ventricular Pacing, which enables the device to be programmed to minimize pacing pulses to the right ventricle.

Implantable cardioverter defibrillators (ICDs) treat abnormally fast heart beats (tachyarrhythmias) by monitoring the heart; when a rapid rhythm is detected, electrical impulses or shocks are delivered. Cardiac resynchronization therapy (CRT) devices synchronize contractions of multiple heart chambers. The company's InSynch ICD offers CRT for heart failure, as well as advanced defibrillation capabilities for patients also at risk for potentially lethal tachyarrhythmias that may lead to cardiac arrest. The Insynch Marquis system combines the cardiac resynchronization of InSynch devices with defibrillation therapies of the Marquis ICD platform. During FY 05, MDT launched its highest energy CRT-D device, the InSynch Maximo, and the InSynch Sentry CRT-D, which incorporates automatic fluid status monitoring. It also added a ventricle-to-ventricle feature to both InSynch Maximo and InSynch Sentry that allows physicians to separately adjust the timing of electrical therapy delivered to the two ventricles to optimize beating of the heart and enhance blood flow. MDT also sells external defibrillators.

Company Financials

Per Share Data ($) Year Ended Apr. 30	2006	2005	2004	2003	2002	2001	2000	1999	1998	1997
Tangible Book Value	2.98	4.26	3.18	2.21	1.10	3.53	2.61	1.99	1.68	1.34
Cash Flow	2.54	1.86	1.96	1.64	1.07	1.10	1.10	0.58	0.63	0.68
Earnings	2.09	1.48	1.60	1.30	0.80	0.85	0.90	0.40	0.48	0.56
S&P Core Earnings	2.00	1.65	1.46	1.10	0.76	0.91	NA	NA	NA	NA
Dividends	0.34	0.29	0.25	0.25	0.20	0.12	0.15	0.12	0.11	0.10
Payout Ratio	16%	20%	16%	19%	25%	14%	16%	30%	23%	17%
Calendar Year	2005	2004	2003	2002	2001	2000	1999	1998	1997	1996
Prices:High	58.91	53.70	52.92	50.69	60.81	62.00	44.63	38.38	26.38	17.47
Prices:Low	48.70	43.99	42.90	32.50	36.64	32.75	29.94	22.72	14.41	11.13
P/E Ratio:High	28	36	33	39	72	61	50	97	55	31
P/E Ratio:Low	23	30	27	25	43	32	33	58	30	20
Income Statement Analysis (Million $)										
Revenue	11,292	10,055	9,087	7,665	6,411	5,552	5,015	4,134	2,605	2,438
Operating Income	4,248	3,907	3,583	3,062	2,479	2,176	1,871	1,535	1,017	901
Depreciation	544	463	443	408	330	297	243	213	138	117
Interest Expense	Nil	55.1	56.5	7.20	Nil	74.0	13.0	28.8	8.16	9.38
Pretax Income	3,161	2,544	2,797	2,341	1,524	1,549	1,630	822	702	809
Effective Tax Rate	19.4%	29.1%	29.9%	31.7%	35.4%	32.5%	32.6%	43.0%	34.8%	34.5%
Net Income	2,547	1,804	1,959	1,600	984	1,046	1,099	468	457	530
S&P Core Earnings	2,450	2,006	1,790	1,347	936	1,121	NA	NA	NA	NA
Balance Sheet & Other Financial Data (Million $)										
Cash	2,994	2,232	1,594	1,470	411	1,030	448	376	383	251
Current Assets	10,377	7,422	5,313	4,606	3,488	3,757	3,013	2,395	1,552	1,238
Total Assets	19,665	16,617	14,111	12,321	10,905	7,039	5,669	4,870	2,775	2,409
Current Liabilities	4,406	3,380	4,241	1,813	3,985	1,359	992	990	572	519
Long Term Debt	5,486	1,973	1.10	1,980	9.50	13.0	14.0	17.6	16.2	13.9
Common Equity	9,383	10,450	9,077	7,906	6,431	5,510	4,491	3,655	2,044	1,746
Total Capital	14,891	12,901	9,486	10,191	6,674	5,523	4,520	3,703	2,074	1,762
Capital Expenditures	407	452	425	380	386	440	342	226	148	171
Cash Flow	3,090	2,267	2,402	2,008	1,314	1,343	1,342	681	595	647
Current Ratio	2.4	2.2	1.3	2.5	0.9	2.8	3.0	2.4	2.7	2.4
% Long Term Debt of Capitalization	36.8	15.3	0.0	19.4	0.1	0.2	0.3	0.5	0.8	0.7
% Net Income of Revenue	22.6	17.9	21.6	20.9	15.3	18.8	21.9	11.3	17.6	21.7
% Return on Assets	14.0	11.7	14.8	13.8	11.0	16.5	20.6	11.0	17.6	21.3
% Return on Equity	25.7	18.5	23.1	22.3	16.5	20.9	26.6	14.8	24.1	29.5

Data as orig reptd.; bef. results of disc opers/spec. items. Per share data adj. for stk. divs.; EPS diluted. E-Estimated. NA-Not Available. NM-Not Meaningful. NR-Not Ranked. UR-Under Review.

Office: 710 Medtronic Parkway, Minneapolis, MN 55432-5604.
Telephone: 763-514-4000.
Website: http://www.medtronic.com
Chrmn & CEO: A.D. Collins, Jr.

Pres & COO: W.A. Hawkins
Investor Contact: G.L. Ellis (763-505-2692)
SVP & CFO: G.L. Ellis
SVP, Secy & General Counsel: T.L. Carlson

Board of Directors: R. H. Anderson, M. R. Bonsignore, W. R. Brody, A. D. Collins, Jr., A. M. Gotto, Jr., S. A. Jackson, D. M. O'Leary, R. C. Pozen, J. Rosso, J. W. Schuler, G. M. Sprenger

Founded: 1957
Domicile: Minnesota
Employees: 36,000

STANDARD &POOR'S

Mellon Financial Corp

S&P Recommendation HOLD ★★★★★

Price $38.83 (as of Oct 27, 2006)

12-Mo. Target Price $43.00

Investment Style Large-Cap Value

GICS Sector Financials
Sub-Industry Asset Management & Custody Banks

Comment This Pittsburgh-based bank holding company (formerly Mellon Bank) provides a full range of banking, investment and trust products to individuals, businesses and institutions.

Key Stock Statistics (Source S&P, Vickers, company reports)

52-Wk Range	$39.73–31.31	S&P Oper. EPS 2006E	2.12	P/E on S&P Oper. EPS 2006E	18.3	Dividend Rate/Share	$0.88
Trailing 12-Month EPS	$2.10	S&P Oper. EPS 2007E	2.40	Common Shares Outstg. (M)	411.4	Yield (%)	2.27
Trailing 12-Month P/E	18.5	S&P Core EPS 2006E	2.10	Market Capitalization(B)	$15.976	Beta	1.37
$10K Invested 5 Yrs Ago	$12,315	S&P Core EPS 2007E	2.38	Institutional Ownership (%)	74	S&P Credit Rating	NA

Price Performance

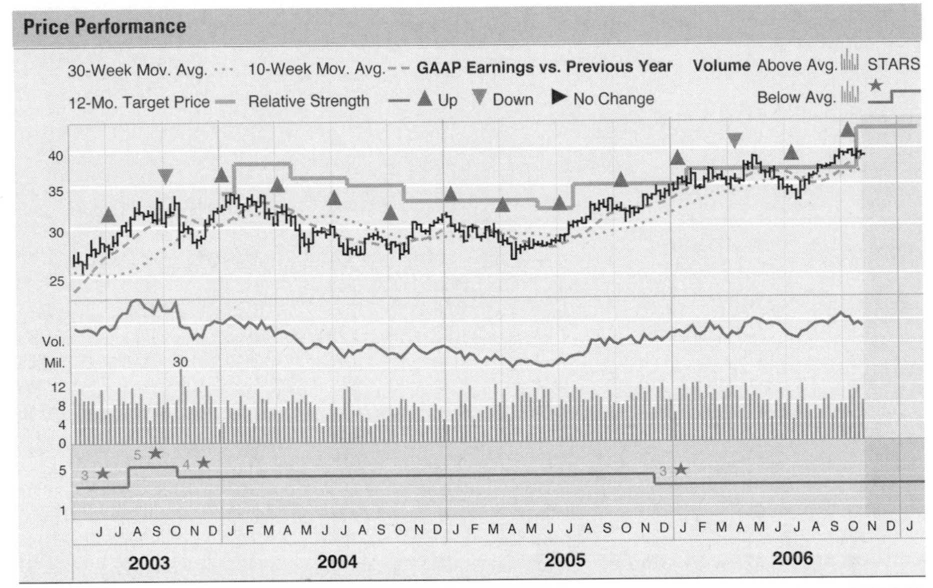

Options: CBOE, P, Ph

Analysis prepared by **Mark Hebeka, CFA** on October 24, 2006, when the stock traded at **$ 39.47**.

Highlights

- We believe MEL will experience strong performance from asset management and asset servicing businesses combined with expense control, which should help to boost EPS and profit margins for the next several quarters. Based on our expectations for equity market stability and healthy economic conditions, we believe MEL is well positioned to sustain its positive revenue growth momentum through 2007.
- Net interest income should continue to contribute approximately 8% to 10% of total revenue in 2006 and 2007. We see the primary risk to earnings as the company's ability to keep operating expenses under control and generate positive operating leverage, given that revenues are sensitive to market conditions and staff expenses account for a significant portion of operating expenses.
- We project 2006 operating EPS of $2.12, supported by expected share repurchases, up from $1.87 in 2005. Our 2007 EPS estimate is $2.40.

Investment Rationale/Risk

- We view MEL as having strong fundamentals, solid credit quality and good growth potential, combined with leverage to improving equity market conditions that we expect and a continued focus on expenses that we think should lead to slightly stronger EPS growth than peers. We believe MEL has good earnings momentum going into the next several quarters.
- Risks to our recommendation and target price include a significant decline in U.S. equity markets that would have a direct impact on the company's EPS, a failure to keep operating expenses under control, a rapid and significant deterioration in credit quality, and legislative, legal and regulatory risks.
- Our 12-month target price is $43, equal to about 17.9X our 2007 operating EPS estimate, in line with peers. We believe this valuation is justified due to a proven track record, strong fundamentals and good growth prospects.

Qualitative Risk Assessment

LOW | MEDIUM | HIGH

Our risk assessment reflects what we see as solid business fundamentals and a strong customer base. We view MEL as well diversified and able to withstand a major economic downturn.

Quantitative Evaluations

S&P Quality Ranking A-

D | C | B- | B | B+ | A- | A | A+

Relative Strength Rank MODERATE

47

LOWEST = 1 HIGHEST = 99

Revenue/Earnings Data

Revenue (Million $)

	1Q	2Q	3Q	4Q	Year
2006	1,475	1,538	1,567	--	--
2005	1,310	1,184	1,338	1,432	5,455
2004	1,265	1,169	1,132	1,360	4,926
2003	1,104	1,134	1,143	1,193	4,550
2002	1,212	1,198	1,152	1,077	4,737
2001	1,544	985.0	1,108	--	4,055

Earnings Per Share ($)

2006	0.49	0.56	0.53	E0.55	E2.12
2005	0.72	0.49	0.47	0.50	2.18
2004	0.57	0.42	0.43	0.47	1.89
2003	0.38	0.40	0.36	0.43	1.57
2002	0.47	0.24	0.43	0.38	1.52
2001	0.41	0.21	0.38	-0.09	0.91

Fiscal year ended Dec. 31. Next earnings report expected: Mid January. EPS Estimates based on S&P Operating Earnings; historical GAAP earnings are as reported.

Dividend Data (Dates: mm/dd Payment Date: mm/dd/yy)

Amount ($)	Date Decl.	Ex-Div. Date	Stk. of Record	Payment Date
0.200	01/18	01/27	01/31	02/15/06
0.220	04/18	04/26	04/28	05/15/06
0.220	07/19	07/27	07/31	08/15/06
0.220	10/19	10/27	10/31	11/15/06

Dividends have been paid since 1895. Source: Company reports.

Please read the Required Disclosures and Analyst Certification on the last page of this report.

Mellon Financial Corp

Business Summary October 24, 2006

Corporate Overview. Mellon Financial Corporation (MEL) is a global financial services company, which caters to corporations, institutions and high net worth individuals, mainly in the US and Europe. MEL's businesses are classified under three business groups; Asset Management, Payments and Securities Services, and Treasury Services/Other Activity.

The Asset Management business group comprises Mellon Asset Management (MAM) and Private Wealth Management (PWM) activities, while the Payments and Securities Services business group includes Asset Servicing and Payment Solutions & Investor Services. In 2005, MAM contributed approximately 40% to total revenues, while PWM accounted for 12%. Asset servicing division represented 22% of total revenues while Payment Solutions & Investor Services contributed 14%.

MEL's Treasury Services contributed 13% to total revenues in 2005. MAM provides equity, fixed-income, hedge, and liquidity management products through individual asset management companies and multiple distribution channels, including The Dreyfus Corporation and Mellon Global Investments. MEL has approximately $4.7 trillion in assets under management, custody and administration, including $781 billion under management as on December 31, 2005.

MEL provides PWM services such as investment management, wealth planning and comprehensive financial management services, and private banking. The PWM Services division had client assets worth $87 billion as on June 30, 2006. The division expanded geographically in December 2005 by acquiring City Capital Inc., an Atlanta-based investment management firm, which had approximately $800 million in client assets. MEL distributes Asset Servicing products through the franchise's sales organization along with its joint venture partners; CIBC Mellon and ABN AMRO Mellon. Through Payment Solutions & Investor Services business, MEL provides total working capital solutions and comprehensive shareholder and equity services, which would result in increased payments processing efficiency, improved cash flow, and better handling of complex company equity and shareholder services issues.

Company Financials

Per Share Data ($) Year Ended Dec. 31	**2005**	**2004**	**2003**	**2002**	**2001**	**2000**	**1999**	**1998**	**1997**	**1996**
Tangible Book Value	4.54	3.62	3.30	2.82	3.66	4.34	3.74	4.22	4.40	2.79
Earnings	2.18	1.89	1.57	1.52	0.91	2.03	1.90	1.63	1.44	1.29
S&P Core Earnings	1.80	1.63	1.38	1.09	0.52	NA	NA	NA	NA	NA
Dividends	0.78	0.70	0.57	0.49	0.82	0.86	0.78	0.71	0.65	0.59
Payout Ratio	36%	37%	36%	32%	90%	42%	41%	43%	45%	46%
Prices:High	35.15	34.13	33.83	40.80	51.63	51.94	40.19	40.19	32.41	18.69
Prices:Low	26.40	26.47	19.89	20.42	27.75	26.81	31.00	22.50	17.25	12.06
P/E Ratio:High	10	18	22	27	57	26	21	25	23	14
P/E Ratio:Low	12	14	13	13	30	13	16	14	12	9
Income Statement Analysis (Million $)										
Net Interest Income	485	458	569	610	574	1,328	1,430	1,491	1,467	1,478
Tax Equivalent Adjustment	18.0	16.0	17.0	12.0	8.00	10.0	NA	8.00	NA	10.0
Non Interest Income	4,295	3,114	3,571	3,622	2,658	3,072	3,100	2,921	2,418	2,019
Loan Loss Provision	19.0	-11.0	7.00	172	-4.00	45.0	45.0	60.0	148	155
% Expense/Operating Revenue	71.2%	94.1%	77.1%	73.7%	79.2%	64.8%	67.3%	68.2%	66.1%	62.6%
Pretax Income	1,345	1,157	988	993	675	1,582	1,563	1,340	1,169	1,151
Effective Tax Rate	32.2%	30.9%	31.5%	32.8%	35.4%	36.3%	36.7%	35.1%	34.0%	36.3%
Net Income	912	800	677	667	436	1,007	989	870	771	733
% Net Interest Margin	1.92	2.09	2.64	2.74	2.48	3.64	3.70	3.96	4.24	4.26
S&P Core Earnings	757	689	594	476	248	NA	NA	NA	NA	NA
Balance Sheet & Other Financial Data (Million $)										
Money Market Assets	3,354	4,935	3,694	4,791	5,683	4,193	1,502	945	1,083	1,076
Investment Securities	17,412	13,587	11,253	11,742	9,709	8,932	6,356	7,021	4,849	6,486
Commercial Loans	3,629	NA	NA	NA	NA	15,353	17,127	13,614	12,392	11,618
Other Loans	2,944	NA	NA	NA	NA	11,016	13,121	18,479	16,750	15,775
Total Assets	38,678	37,115	33,983	36,231	34,360	50,364	47,946	50,777	44,892	42,596
Demand Deposits	10,511	7,371	6,054	11,074	9,537	10,545	9,588	9,976	7,975	8,692
Time Deposits	15,563	16,220	14,789	11,583	11,178	26,345	23,833	24,407	23,330	22,682
Long Term Debt	4,404	5,624	5,266	5,541	5,036	4,512	3,529	4,294	2,573	2,518
Common Equity	4,202	4,102	3,702	3,395	3,482	4,152	4,016	4,521	3,652	3,456
% Return on Assets	2.4	2.3	1.9	1.9	1.3	2.0	2.0	1.8	1.8	1.8
% Return on Equity	22.0	20.5	19.1	19.4	11.4	24.7	23.2	21.1	21.1	18.4
% Loan Loss Reserve	1.0	-1.5	-1.4	1.5	1.5	1.5	1.3	1.5	1.6	1.9
% Loans/Deposits	25.2	28.6	35.8	37.2	41.2	71.5	90.5	93.3	93.1	87.3
% Equity to Assets	11.0	11.0	10.1	9.6	11.1	8.3	8.6	8.5	8.1	9.0

Data as orig reptd.; bef. results of disc opers/spec. items. Per share data adj. for stk. divs.; EPS diluted. E-Estimated. NA-Not Available. NM-Not Meaningful. NR-Not Ranked. UR-Under Review.

Office: One Mellon Center, Pittsburgh, PA 15258-0001.
Telephone: 412-234-5000.
Website: http://www.mellon.com
Chrmn, Pres & CEO: R.P. Kelly

Vice Chrmn: S.E. Canter
Vice Chrmn: D.F. Lamere
Vice Chrmn: R.P. O'Hanley
Vice Chrmn: S.G. Elliott

Investor Contact: S. Lackey (412-234-5601)
Board of Directors: R. E. Bruch, P. L. Cejas, J. L. Cohon, S. G. Elliott, I. J. Gumberg, E. F. Kelly, R. P. Kelly, R. Mehrabian, S. P. Mellon, M. A. Nordenberg, D. S. Shapira, W. E. Strickland, Jr., J. P. Surma, W. W. von Schack

Auditor: KPMG, Pittsburgh
Founded: 1869
Domicile: Pennsylvania
Employees: 16,700

STANDARD & POOR'S

Merck & Co Inc.

S&P Recommendation	Price	12-Mo. Target Price	Investment Style
BUY ★★★★★	$46.09 (as of Oct 27, 2006)	$49.00	Large-Cap Value

GICS Sector Health Care
Sub-Industry Pharmaceuticals

Comment Merck is one of the world's largest prescription pharmaceuticals concerns. The Medco pharmaceutical benefits management unit was spun off to shareholders in August 2003.

Key Stock Statistics (Source S&P, Vickers, company reports)

52-Wk Range	$46.37–27.65	S&P Oper. EPS 2006**E**	2.50	P/E on S&P Oper. EPS 2006**E**	18.4	Dividend Rate/Share	$1.52
Trailing 12-Month EPS	$2.32	S&P Oper. EPS 2007**E**	2.70	Common Shares Outstg. (M)	2,176.1	Yield (%)	3.30
Trailing 12-Month P/E	19.9	S&P Core EPS 2006**E**	2.50	Market Capitalization(B)	$100.297	Beta	0.76
$10K Invested 5 Yrs Ago	$8,836	S&P Core EPS 2007**E**	2.70	Institutional Ownership (%)	69	S&P Credit Rating	AA-

Price Performance

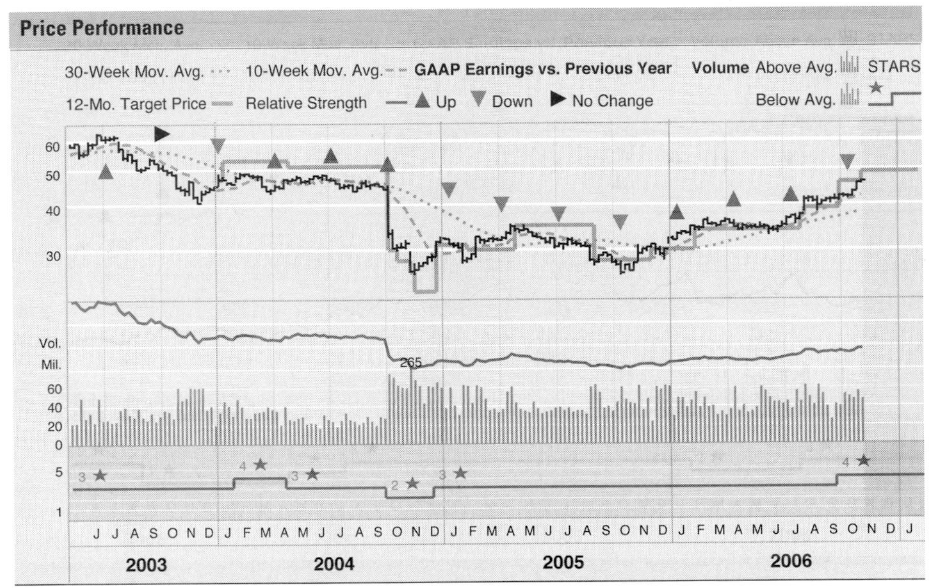

Options: ASE, CBOE, P, Ph

Analysis prepared by **Herman B. Saftlas** on October 24, 2006, when the stock traded at **$ 45.93**.

Highlights

- We expect revenues in 2007 to be flat with projected 2006 revenues, with volume impacted by the sharply lower sales of patent-expired Zocor cholesterol drug. We also see lower sales of Fosamax, an osteoporosis drug. On the plus side, we project another robust showing by Singulair, an asthma/allergic rhinitis treatment, which continues to be the market leader in the U.S. respiratory market. We also see a strong uptake for new products such as Gardasil, a vaccine for cervical cancer; and Januvia, a novel treatment for type 2 diabetes.
- Gross margins in 2007 are expected to narrow slightly from the 77% we see in 2006. However, results should benefit from controls over SG&A and R&D spending. We expect equity income from affiliates to increase by about 14%, largely on higher income from Vytorin and Zetia cholesterol drugs, which are sold through a joint venture with Schering-Plough.
- We project 2007 operating EPS of $2.70, up from an estimated $2.50 in 2006, after projected stock option expense in both years. Our EPS estimate for 2006 excludes restructuring charges.

Investment Rationale/Risk

- We commend Merck's new top management for its handling of daunting Vioxx litigation, new product development, and cost streamlining. On the new-product front, we see much promise for two recent approvals-Gardasil vaccine against cervical cancer, and Januvia for diabetes. Bolstered by aggressive restructuring moves (aggregate savings planned to reach $5 billion by 2010), we project compound annual operating EPS growth in low double digits over the coming years. While we think Merck is still vulnerable to negative Vioxx headlines, we note that MRK has so far won about half of litigated Vioxx actions. We also believe MRK has adequate financial resources to manage future liabilities.
- Risks to our recommendation and target price include much larger than expected Vioxx liabilities, and possible R&D pipeline disappointments.
- Our 12-month target price of $49 applies a modest premium to peers P/E of about 18X applied to our $2.70 EPS estimate for 2007. The $1.52 annual dividend recently provided a 3.3% yield.

Qualitative Risk Assessment

LOW | **MEDIUM** | HIGH

Along with risks common to other major pharmaceutical producers, we think MRK carries significant liability litigation risk from its former Vioxx pain medicine, which was removed from the market in 2004 after being found to be linked with heightened cardiac risk. However, we think Merck has done a commendable job in handling Vioxx cases to date, and we also believe MRK has adequate financial resources to manage future Vioxx liabilities.

Quantitative Evaluations

S&P Quality Ranking A

D | C | B- | B | B+ | A- | **A** | A+

Relative Strength Rank STRONG

86

LOWEST = 1 HIGHEST = 99

Revenue/Earnings Data

Revenue (Million $)

	1Q	2Q	3Q	4Q	Year
2006	5,410	5,772	5,410	--	--
2005	5,362	5,468	5,416	5,766	22,012
2004	5,631	6,022	5,538	5,748	22,939
2003	5,571	5,525	5,762	5,627	22,486
2002	12,169	12,810	12,893	13,918	51,790
2001	11,345	11,893	11,920	12,558	47,716

Earnings Per Share ($)

	1Q	2Q	3Q	4Q	Year
2006	0.69	0.69	0.43	**E**0.46	**E**2.50
2005	0.62	0.33	0.65	0.51	2.10
2004	1.06	1.26	1.28	0.50	2.61
2003	0.68	0.79	0.83	0.62	2.92
2002	0.71	0.77	0.83	0.83	3.14
2001	0.71	0.78	0.84	0.81	3.14

Fiscal year ended Dec. 31. Next earnings report expected: Late January. EPS Estimates based on S&P Operating Earnings; historical GAAP earnings are as reported.

Dividend Data (Dates: mm/dd Payment Date: mm/dd/yy)

Amount ($)	Date Decl.	Ex-Div. Date	Stk. of Record	Payment Date
0.380	11/22	11/30	12/02	01/03/06
0.380	02/28	03/08	03/10	04/03/06
0.380	05/23	05/31	06/02	07/03/06
0.380	07/25	08/30	09/01	10/02/06

Dividends have been paid since 1935. Source: Company reports.

Business Summary October 24, 2006

CORPORATE OVERVIEW. Merck & Co. is a leading global drugmaker, producing a wide range of prescription drugs in many therapeutic classes in the U.S. and abroad. Foreign operations accounted for 42% of total pharmaceutical and vaccine sales in 2005.

MRK's largest selling drug in 2005 was Zocor, a cholesterol lowering agent (sales of $4.3 billion). However, we expect sharply lower Zocor sales in 2006 and 2007 due to the expiration of Zocor's U.S patent in June 2006. Through a joint venture with Schering-Plough, MRK also markets Zetia--a new type of cholesterol therapy that works by blocking cholesterol absorption in the intestines--as well as Vytorin, a combination pill containing both Zocor and Zetia. Zetia had sales of $1.4 billion in 2005. Launched in July 2004, Vytorin had sales of $1.0 billion in 2005. MRK books only equity income from the Schering-Plough joint venture.

Other principal products include Cozaar/Hyzaar ($3.0 billion), a treatment for high blood pressure and congestive heart failure; Fosamax ($3.2 billion), a drug for osteoporosis (a bone-thinning disease that affects postmenopausal women); and Singulair ($3.0 billion), a treatment for asthma and seasonal allergic rhinitis. Other drugs include Vasotec/Vaseretic antihypertensives; Primaxin, an intravenous antibiotic; Crixivan, a protease inhibitor AIDS drug; and Proscar, a treatment for enlarged prostates. MRK is also a leading maker of vaccines.

OTC medications such as Pepcid AC are offered through a venture with Johnson & Johnson. Merial, a leading animal health products company, is owned jointly by MRK and Rhone-Poulenc SA. Through a venture with Astra AB of Sweden, MRK books sales of Prilosec and other Astra drugs.

MARKET PROFILE. The dollar value of the global pharmaceutical market was estimated at over $600 billion in 2005, based on data from IMS Health. Although drug sales continue to grow faster than most segments of the world economy, we expect industry growth to continue to decelerate over the balance of the decade, reflecting the loss of patent protection on many large selling drugs, tighter reimbursement from government and private health insurance payors, and relatively sluggish new product flow. For the U.S. market, we see industrywide pharmaceutical sales increasing by about 7% in 2006, helped by the new Medicare Part D prescription drug program.

Company Financials

Per Share Data ($) Year Ended Dec. 31	**2005**	**2004**	**2003**	**2002**	**2001**	**2000**	**1999**	**1998**	**1997**	**1996**
Tangible Book Value	7.48	7.03	6.13	4.88	3.77	3.23	2.43	1.91	2.45	2.17
Cash Flow	2.88	3.29	3.51	3.79	3.77	3.44	3.02	2.67	2.29	1.90
Earnings	2.10	2.61	2.92	3.14	3.14	2.90	2.45	2.15	1.87	1.60
S&P Core Earnings	2.09	2.56	2.71	2.81	2.87	NA	NA	NA	NA	NA
Dividends	1.52	1.49	1.45	1.41	1.37	1.26	1.10	0.95	0.87	0.74
Payout Ratio	72%	57%	50%	45%	44%	43%	45%	44%	47%	46%
Prices:High	35.36	49.33	63.50	64.50	95.25	96.69	87.38	80.88	54.09	42.13
Prices:Low	25.50	25.60	40.57	38.50	56.80	52.00	60.94	50.69	39.00	28.25
P/E Ratio:High	17	19	22	21	30	33	36	38	29	26
P/E Ratio:Low	12	10	14	12	18	18	25	24	21	18

Income Statement Analysis (Million $)	2005	2004	2003	2002	2001	2000	1999	1998	1997	1996
Revenue	22,012	22,939	22,486	51,790	47,716	40,363	32,714	26,898	23,637	19,829
Operating Income	7,567	8,074	9,912	11,361	11,192	10,686	9,056	7,655	6,701	5,912
Depreciation	1,708	1,451	1,314	1,488	1,464	1,277	1,145	1,279	1,034	731
Interest Expense	386	294	351	391	465	484	317	206	130	139
Pretax Income	7,486	8,129	9,220	10,428	10,693	10,133	8,842	8,295	6,594	5,685
Effective Tax Rate	36.5%	26.6%	26.7%	29.3%	29.2%	29.6%	30.9%	34.8%	28.0%	29.2%
Net Income	4,631	5,813	6,590	7,150	7,282	6,822	5,891	5,248	4,614	3,881
S&P Core Earnings	4,582	5,699	6,089	6,395	6,649	NA	NA	NA	NA	NA

Balance Sheet & Other Financial Data (Million $)	2005	2004	2003	2002	2001	2000	1999	1998	1997	1996
Cash	9,585	2,879	1,201	2,243	2,144	2,537	2,022	2,606	1,125	1,352
Current Assets	21,049	13,475	11,527	14,834	12,962	13,353	11,259	10,229	8,213	7,727
Total Assets	44,846	42,573	40,588	47,561	44,007	39,910	35,635	31,853	25,812	24,293
Current Liabilities	13,304	11,744	9,570	12,375	11,544	9,710	8,759	6,069	5,569	4,829
Long Term Debt	5,126	4,692	5,096	4,879	4,799	3,601	3,144	3,221	1,347	1,156
Common Equity	17,917	17,288	15,576	18,200	16,050	14,832	13,242	12,802	12,614	11,971
Total Capital	25,449	24,387	24,588	28,008	25,686	23,454	19,847	19,728	15,144	15,437
Capital Expenditures	1,403	1,726	1,916	2,370	2,725	2,728	2,561	1,973	1,449	1,197
Cash Flow	6,339	7,264	7,904	8,638	8,746	8,099	7,035	6,527	5,648	4,612
Current Ratio	1.6	1.1	1.2	1.2	1.1	1.4	1.3	1.7	1.5	1.6
% Long Term Debt of Capitalization	20.1	19.2	20.7	17.4	18.7	15.4	15.8	16.3	8.8	7.5
% Net Income of Revenue	21.0	25.3	29.3	13.8	15.3	16.9	18.0	19.5	19.5	19.6
% Return on Assets	10.6	14.0	15.0	15.6	17.3	18.1	17.4	18.2	18.4	16.1
% Return on Equity	26.3	35.4	39.0	41.7	47.2	48.6	20.1	41.3	37.5	33.1

Data as orig reptd.; bef. results of disc opers/spec. items. Per share data adj. for stk. divs.; EPS diluted. E-Estimated. NA-Not Available. NM-Not Meaningful. NR-Not Ranked. UR-Under Review.

Office: One Merck Drive, Whitehouse Station, NJ 08889-0100.
Telephone: 908-423-1000.
Website: http://www.merck.com
Pres & CEO: R.T. Clark

EVP & CFO: J.C. Lewent
SVP & General Counsel: K.C. Frazier
SVP & CIO: J.C. Scalet
VP & Cntlr: R.C. Henriques, Jr.

Board of Directors: L. A. Bossidy, W. G. Bowen, R. T. Clark, J. B. Cole, W. B. Harrison, Jr., W. N. Kelley, R. B. Lazarus, T. E. Shenk, A. M. Tatlock, S. O. Thier, W. P. Weeks, P. C. Wendell

Founded: 1891
Domicile: New Jersey
Employees: 61,500

STANDARD & POOR'S

Meredith Corp

S&P Recommendation BUY ★★★★★

Price $53.16 (as of Oct 27, 2006)

12-Mo. Target Price $58.00

Investment Style Mid-Cap Growth

GICS Sector Consumer Discretionary
Sub-Industry Publishing

Comment MDP derives the bulk of its earnings from publishing magazines (primarily Better Homes and Gardens and Ladies' Home Journal) and ownership of 14 TV stations.

Key Stock Statistics (Source S&P, Vickers, company reports)

52-Wk Range	$56.83–45.04	S&P Oper. EPS 2007E	3.27	P/E on S&P Oper. EPS 2007E	16.3	Dividend Rate/Share	$0.64
Trailing 12-Month EPS	$2.96	S&P Oper. EPS 2008E	3.54	Common Shares Outstg. (M)	47.8	Yield (%)	1.20
Trailing 12-Month P/E	18.0	S&P Core EPS 2007E	3.27	Market Capitalization(B)	$2.043	Beta	0.41
$10K Invested 5 Yrs Ago	$16,432	S&P Core EPS 2008E	3.54	Institutional Ownership (%)	90	S&P Credit Rating	NA

Price Performance

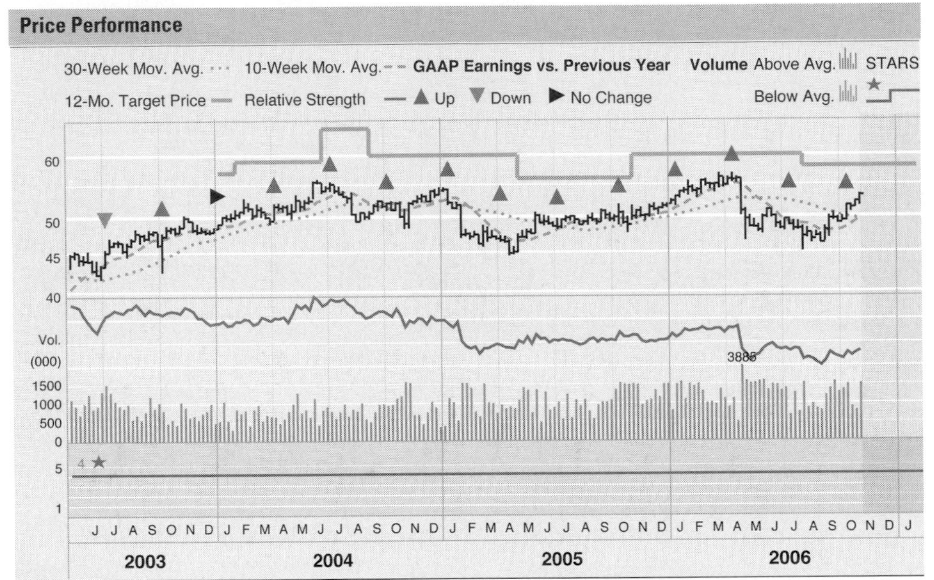

Options: ASE

Analysis prepared by **James Peters, CFA** on August 14, 2006, when the stock traded at **$ 46.71**.

Highlights

- For FY 07 (Jun.), we see revenues rising about 5.1%, including strong gains from election year political advertising in the broadcast segment, advances in interactive media as the company deploys resources to this high growth area, growth in integrated marketing, brand licensing and database marketing, and flat to slightly lower circulation revenues in the publishing segment.
- We anticipate MDP's operating margin widening to 17.5% from 16.7% in FY 06, primarily as a result of increased leverage from expected political revenues. We also see margin gains from integration of and lower costs for acquired properties as the acquisition integration process continues to gain traction.
- We see MDP using free cash flow in FY 07 for stock repurchases and paying down debt assumed with the Gruner & Jahr acquisition. We also believe the company will continue to supplement organic growth with special interest publication acquisitions. After slightly lower projected interest expense and sharecount, we forecast FY 07 EPS to grow about 14% to $3.27, up from $2.86 in FY 05.

Investment Rationale/Risk

- We view positively MDP's strategy of publishing special interest publications (SIPs) and developing new products that target growth segments of the U.S., including a growing Hispanic population, as we think this strategy will support a superior to peer rate of revenue growth over the next few years. We also expect the company to continue developing new revenue streams through brand licensing.
- Risks to our recommendation and target price include a rapid rise in paper prices, an economic slowdown that negatively affects advertising demand for MDP's print and broadcast properties, and a substantial decline in magazine circulation. We also are concerned about MDP's corporate governance, as we do not believe policies such as a dual class voting structure are in the best interest of common shareholders.
- Our 12-month target price of $58 is derived by applying a historical average and slight premium to peer 10.4X enterprise value/EBITDA ratio to our FY 07 EBITDA estimate of $339 million. We believe a premium is warranted based on superior growth prospects we foresee.

Qualitative Risk Assessment

LOW | **MEDIUM** | HIGH

Our risk assessment reflects what we view as a highly competitive environment for advertising among publishers and other media, offset by a consistent track record of earnings growth and the company's low beta and weighted average cost of capital.

Quantitative Evaluations

S&P Quality Ranking A-

D | C | B- | B | B+ | **A-** | A | A+

Relative Strength Rank STRONG

73

LOWEST = 1 HIGHEST = 99

Revenue/Earnings Data

Revenue (Million $)

	1Q	2Q	3Q	4Q	Year
2007	395.7	--	--	--	--
2006	390.3	386.0	394.9	426.4	1,598
2005	288.9	294.6	305.5	332.4	1,221
2004	272.7	280.4	299.6	309.1	1,162
2003	250.1	251.7	278.2	300.2	1,080
2002	236.6	228.0	256.2	267.2	987.8

Earnings Per Share ($)

	1Q	2Q	3Q	4Q	Year
2007	0.62	E0.71	E0.88	E1.06	E3.27
2006	0.52	0.58	0.97	0.97	2.86
2005	0.46	0.52	0.69	0.83	2.50
2004	0.37	0.38	0.67	0.76	2.14
2003	0.32	0.38	0.50	0.58	1.78
2002	0.17	0.17	0.35	1.10	1.79

Fiscal year ended Jun. 30. Next earnings report expected: Late January. EPS Estimates based on S&P Operating Earnings; historical GAAP earnings are as reported.

Dividend Data (Dates: mm/dd Payment Date: mm/dd/yy)

Amount ($)	Date Decl.	Ex-Div. Date	Stk. of Record	Payment Date
0.140	11/08	11/28	11/30	12/15/05
0.160	01/30	02/24	02/28	03/15/06
0.160	05/11	05/26	05/31	06/15/06
0.160	08/09	08/29	08/31	09/15/06

Dividends have been paid since 1930. Source: Company reports.

Meredith Corp

Business Summary August 14, 2006

Meredith Corp. is a diversified media and marketing company with operations in publishing (74% of FY 05 (Jun.) revenues) and broadcasting (26%).

The publishing segment includes magazine publishing, book publishing, interactive media and integrated marketing, with subscription based magazine Better Homes and Gardens accounting for a significant portion of segment and company revenues and operating profit. The company produces over 200 special-interest publications that are primarily sold on newsstands and issued from one to six times a year, and markets and publishes approximately 350 books directed at the home, family and child markets that are sold primarily through retail book and specialty stores, mass merchandisers, and other channels. Books are published under the Better Homes and Gardens trademark and under licensed trademarks such as The Home Depot books.

Meredith Interactive Media extends many of the company's brands to the Internet. The flagship site is bhg.com, which the company believes provides unique content and applications in its core content areas of decorating, food, home improvement, and remodeling. Meredith Integrated Marketing offers integrated promotional database management, relationship and direct marketing capabilities for corporate customers. Overall FY 05 publishing segment revenues were derived from advertising (47%), circulation (27%) and other (26%).

The broadcasting segment consists of 14 network-affiliated TV stations, including affiliations with CBS (6 stations), FOX (4), the WB (2), UPN (1) and NBC (1). Local and national advertising contributed approximately 98% of segment revenues in FY 05, and the company states that 30% to 40% of a market's television ad revenues are generated by local news on major network affiliated stations.

Company Financials

Per Share Data ($) Year Ended Jun. 30	**2006**	**2005**	**2004**	**2003**	**2002**	**2001**	**2000**	**1999**	**1998**	**1997**
Tangible Book Value	NM	NM	NM	NM	NM	NM	NM	NM	NM	1.01
Cash Flow	3.76	3.19	2.82	2.40	3.64	2.39	3.01	3.20	2.64	1.95
Earnings	2.86	2.50	2.14	1.78	1.79	1.39	1.35	1.67	1.46	1.22
S&P Core Earnings	2.84	2.49	2.01	1.64	0.92	0.92	NA	NA	NA	NA
Dividends	0.60	0.52	0.43	0.37	0.35	0.33	0.16	0.29	0.27	0.24
Payout Ratio	20%	21%	20%	22%	20%	24%	12%	17%	18%	20%
Prices:High	56.83	54.33	55.94	50.32	47.75	38.97	41.06	42.00	48.50	36.94
Prices:Low	45.04	44.51	48.24	47.09	33.42	26.50	22.38	30.63	26.69	22.13
P/E Ratio:High	19	22	26	28	27	28	30	25	33	30
P/E Ratio:Low	15	18	23	26	19	19	17	18	18	18
Income Statement Analysis (Million $)										
Revenue	1,598	1,221	1,162	1,080	988	1,053	1,097	1,036	1,010	855
Operating Income	312	263	238	209	212	204	249	254	217	155
Depreciation	45.7	35.3	35.2	31.4	93.8	51.6	87.6	82.6	64.5	40.4
Interest Expense	30.2	Nil	22.7	27.8	33.2	32.9	34.9	22.0	14.7	1.30
Pretax Income	237	209	181	149	149	116	128	152	139	118
Effective Tax Rate	39.0%	38.7%	38.7%	38.7%	38.7%	38.7%	44.3%	41.1%	42.6%	42.9%
Net Income	145	128	111	91.1	91.4	71.3	71.0	89.7	79.9	67.6
S&P Core Earnings	144	127	104	83.5	46.8	47.6	NA	NA	NA	NA
Balance Sheet & Other Financial Data (Million $)										
Cash	30.7	29.8	58.7	22.3	28.2	36.3	22.9	11.0	4.95	125
Current Assets	432	304	314	268	272	291	289	256	247	337
Total Assets	2,041	1,491	1,466	1,437	1,460	1,438	1,440	1,423	1,067	761
Current Liabilities	464	439	371	297	307	371	359	344	347	278
Long Term Debt	515	125	225	375	385	400	455	485	175	Nil
Common Equity	698	652	589	501	508	448	423	413	378	327
Total Capital	1,338	871	912	948	985	907	926	932	372	350
Capital Expenditures	29.2	23.8	24.5	26.6	23.4	56.0	39.4	25.7	46.2	23.3
Cash Flow	190	163	146	123	185	123	159	172	144	108
Current Ratio	0.9	0.7	0.8	0.9	0.9	0.8	0.8	0.7	0.7	1.2
% Long Term Debt of Capitalization	38.5	14.4	24.7	39.6	39.1	44.1	49.1	52.0	47.0	Nil
% Net Income of Revenue	9.1	10.5	9.5	8.4	9.3	6.8	6.5	8.7	7.9	7.9
% Return on Assets	8.2	8.7	7.6	6.3	6.3	5.0	5.0	7.2	8.7	9.0
% Return on Equity	21.5	20.3	20.4	18.1	19.1	16.4	17.0	22.7	22.7	23.0

Data as orig reptd.; bef. results of disc opers/spec. items. Per share data adj. for stk. divs.; EPS diluted. E-Estimated. NA-Not Available. NM-Not Meaningful. NR-Not Ranked. UR-Under Review.

Office: 1716 Locust Street, Des Moines, IA 50309-3023.
Telephone: 515-284-3000.
Website: http://www.meredith.com
Chrmn: W.T. Kerr

Pres & CEO: S.M. Lacy
Investor Contact: S.V. Radia (515-284-3357)
VP & CFO: S.V. Radia
VP, Secy & General Counsel: J.S. Zieser

Board of Directors: H. M. Baum, M. S. Coleman, J. R. Craigie, F. B. Henry, J. W. Johnson, W. T. Kerr, S. M. Lacy, R. E. Lee, D. J. Londoner, P. A. Marineau, M. Meredith Frazier, C. D. Peebler, Jr.

Founded: 1902
Domicile: Iowa
Employees: 3,161

STANDARD &POOR'S

Merrill Lynch & Co Inc

S&P Recommendation STRONG BUY ★★★★★

Price $86.97 (as of Oct 27, 2006)

12-Mo. Target Price $97.00

Investment Style Large-Cap Value

GICS Sector Financials
Sub-Industry Investment Banking & Brokerage

Comment Merrill Lynch is one of the world's largest and most diversified securities brokerage concerns.

Key Stock Statistics (Source S&P, Vickers, company reports)

52-Wk Range	**$87.86–63.99**	S&P Oper. EPS 2006**E**	**7.03**	P/E on S&P Oper. EPS 2006**E**	**12.4**	Dividend Rate/Share	**$1.00**
Trailing 12-Month EPS	**$6.59**	S&P Oper. EPS 2007**E**	**7.47**	Common Shares Outstg. (M)	**886.5**	Yield (%)	**1.15**
Trailing 12-Month P/E	**13.2**	S&P Core EPS 2006E	**7.03**	Market Capitalization(B)	**$77.097**	Beta	**1.71**
$10K Invested 5 Yrs Ago	**$20,026**	S&P Core EPS 2007E	**7.47**	Institutional Ownership (%)	**71**	S&P Credit Rating	**A+**

Price Performance

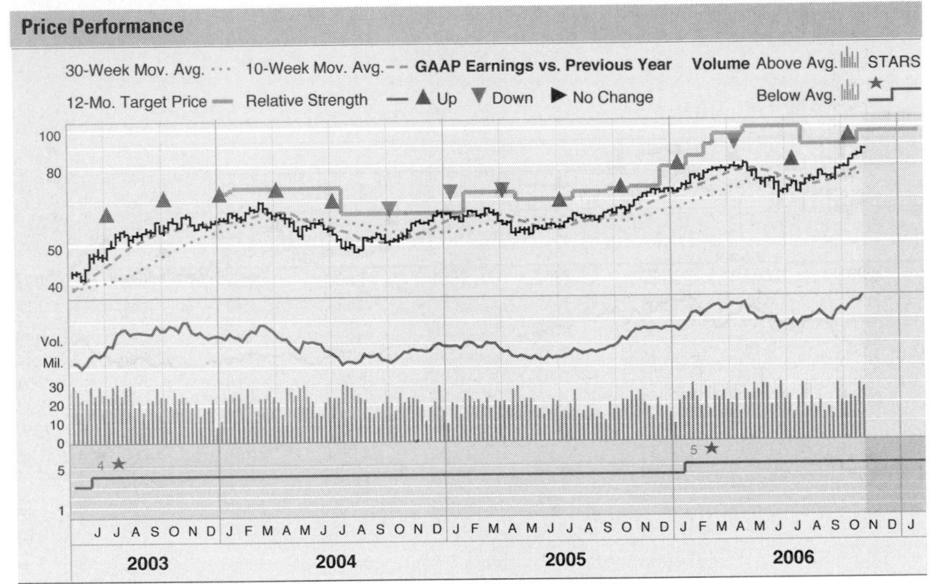

Options: ASE, CBOE, P, Ph

Analysis prepared by **Matthew Albrecht** on October 19, 2006, when the stock traded at **$ 83.94**.

Highlights

- We think Merrill Lynch is benefiting from a healthy economy and generally favorable investor confidence. Despite quarterly volatility in MER's various businesses, particularly in its sales and trading operations, we expect fundamentals to improve through 2007. We think MER's revenues are stabilizing, given the increasing percentage of fee-based revenue within its Global Private Client Group (GPC).
- Higher revenues across MER's businesses have fueled record results in 2006, and we expect revenues and earnings to trend higher in 2007. We expect continued net client inflows in GPC, aided by an increasing number of financial advisers around the globe. We think fixed income, currency and commodity trading revenues will lead the way in the Global Markets segment, and we believe that M&A advisory fees will be the strongest component of investment banking revenues.
- We see EPS of $7.03 in 2006, excluding a $1.2 billion non-cash charge in the first quarter and a $2.0 billion one-time gain from the merger of the asset management business with BlackRock, and EPS of $7.47 in 2007.

Investment Rationale/Risk

- Our recommendation is strong buy, given our view of Merrill's improving business momentum, broad business diversification, high financial adviser productivity, and prudent expense growth. We also are pleased with the company's common share repurchase program, which was recently extended to include another $5 billion, and which should benefit the company's return on equity.
- Risks to our recommendation and target price include stock and bond market depreciation, increased price competition, and various regulatory issues.
- The stock recently traded at a P/E of 12X our 2006 EPS estimate, which is a discount to the S&P 500 and to Merrill's historical average over the past decade. Our 12-month target price is $97, or 13X our 2007 EPS estimate. We think that its valuation multiple will expand as long as management continues to demonstrate that operating results are improving and that it is making the necessary investments in infrastructure and talent to maintain what we see as its strong franchise.

Qualitative Risk Assessment

LOW	MEDIUM	HIGH

Our risk assessment reflects the company's broad business diversification, strong customer relationships, and significant proportion of asset management and portfolio fees, only partly offset by industry cyclicality.

Quantitative Evaluations

S&P Quality Ranking A-

D	C	B-	B	B+	A-	A	A+

Relative Strength Rank STRONG

86

LOWEST = 1 HIGHEST = 99

Revenue/Earnings Data

Revenue (Million $)

	1Q	2Q	3Q	4Q	Year
2006	15,561	16,689	17,379	--	--
2005	6,221	6,317	12,344	13,500	47,783
2004	7,987	7,376	6,848	9,617	32,467
2003	6,923	7,292	6,857	6,673	27,745
2002	7,563	7,352	6,860	6,478	28,253
2001	11,934	10,320	8,929	7,574	38,757

Earnings Per Share ($)

2006	0.44	1.63	3.17	**E**1.75	**E**7.03
2005	1.21	1.14	1.40	1.41	5.16
2004	1.22	1.06	1.00	1.19	4.38
2003	0.72	1.05	1.04	1.23	4.05
2002	0.67	0.66	0.73	0.56	2.63
2001	0.92	0.56	0.44	-1.51	0.57

Fiscal year ended Dec. 31. Next earnings report expected: Mid January. EPS Estimates based on S&P Operating Earnings; historical GAAP earnings are as reported.

Dividend Data (Dates: mm/dd Payment Date: mm/dd/yy)

Amount ($)	Date Decl.	Ex-Div. Date	Stk. of Record	Payment Date
0.250	01/19	02/02	02/06	02/28/06
0.250	04/28	05/04	05/08	05/24/06
0.250	07/24	08/02	08/04	08/23/06
0.250	10/23	11/01	11/03	11/22/06

Dividends have been paid since 1961. Source: Company reports.

Merrill Lynch & Co Inc

STANDARD &POOR'S

Business Summary October 19, 2006

CORPORATE OVERVIEW. Merrill Lynch is one of the world's largest financial management and advisory companies, consistently ranking among the largest debt and equity underwriters and mergers and acquisitions advisers on a global basis. MER has three operating segments: Global Markets and Investment Banking (GMI); the Global Private Client Group (GPC); and Merrill Lynch Investment Managers (MLIM). In 2005, GMI accounted for 53% of total net revenues, GPC 41%, and MLIM 7%. GMI provides comprehensive investment banking and strategic advisory services, including debt and equity trading, underwriting and origination, and mergers and acquisitions. We remain concerned about rising competition from large commercial banks, which have been gaining market share in investment banking.

We think MER's Global Private Client Group is an undervalued franchise. We believe the company's Private Wealth and Wealth Management Advisors maintain strong relationships with MER's most affluent clients and high net worth individuals, respectively. MER's Financial Advisory Center serves more than a million clients who have more basic financial needs. At the end of 2005, MER had about 15,160 private client advisers in over 700 offices, with nearly $1.5 trillion in total client assets in GPC. We think MER is focused on attracting higher net worth clients and emphasizing asset-priced accounts.

In early October 2006, MER combined its asset management business (MLIM) with BlackRock Inc. Although MER did not receive a majority stake or voting control, it did obtain approximately a 49% equity stake and a 45% voting stake in a premier asset management company, which we think should see improved growth opportunities. BlackRock is now one of the world's largest investment managers, and we estimate it holds just under $1.1 trillion in assets under management following the merger. MER will report its share of earnings from the investment, net of expenses and taxes, as revenues on its income statement. Prior to the merger, more than 70% of MLIM's global assets under management were above the benchmark or category median for the three- and five-year periods ended December 2005.

Company Financials

Per Share Data ($) Year Ended Dec. 31	**2005**	**2004**	**2003**	**2002**	**2001**	**2000**	**1999**	**1998**	**1997**	**1996**
Tangible Book Value	29.37	26.48	23.69	20.76	18.38	16.67	10.67	6.09	3.66	9.47
Cash Flow	5.16	5.77	4.05	2.63	0.57	4.11	3.09	1.50	3.00	2.64
Earnings	5.16	4.38	4.05	2.63	0.57	4.11	3.09	1.50	2.42	2.05
S&P Core Earnings	5.18	4.41	3.79	1.80	-0.51	NA	NA	NA	NA	NA
Dividends	0.76	0.64	0.64	0.64	0.64	0.60	0.52	0.46	0.38	0.29
Payout Ratio	15%	15%	16%	24%	112%	15%	17%	31%	16%	14%
Prices:High	69.34	64.89	60.47	59.32	80.00	74.63	51.25	54.56	39.09	21.28
Prices:Low	52.00	47.35	30.75	28.21	33.50	36.31	31.00	17.88	19.63	12.34
P/E Ratio:High	13	15	15	23	NM	18	17	36	16	10
P/E Ratio:Low	10	11	8	11	NM	9	10	12	8	6
Income Statement Analysis (Million $)										
Commissions	5,371	4,877	4,396	4,657	5,266	6,977	6,334	5,779	4,667	3,786
Interest Income	26,571	14,973	11,678	13,178	20,143	21,196	15,097	19,314	17,087	12,899
Total Revenue	47,783	32,467	27,745	28,253	38,757	44,872	34,879	35,853	31,731	25,011
Interest Expense	21,774	10,444	7,782	9,836	17,072	18,280	13,205	18,306	16,109	11,895
Pretax Income	7,231	5,836	5,458	3,566	1,182	5,522	3,883	1,972	3,003	2,566
Effective Tax Rate	29.2%	24.0%	26.9%	29.5%	51.5%	31.5%	32.6%	36.2%	36.5%	36.9%
Net Income	5,116	4,436	3,988	2,513	573	3,784	2,618	1,259	1,906	1,619
S&P Core Earnings	5,066	4,418	3,689	1,694	-441	NA	NA	NA	NA	NA
Balance Sheet & Other Financial Data (Million $)										
Total Assets	681,015	648,059	494,518	447,928	419,419	407,200	328,071	299,804	292,819	213,016
Cash Items	26,535	44,302	25,321	17,586	15,537	29,297	16,707	19,120	17,416	9,003
Receivables	134,238	124,988	105,182	100,462	86,039	103,482	77,336	135,422	114,315	116,222
Securities Owned	148,710	181,950	134,309	100,216	92,883	91,514	106,734	107,845	106,778	75,524
Securities Borrowed	217,487	177,032	107,219	93,018	87,186	103,883	99,741	81,417	122,725	102,002
Due Brokers & Customers	55,147	60,750	47,968	45,110	40,636	34,276	34,119	28,871	20,631	15,000
Other Liabilities	108,053	137,028	109,720	95,804	79,654	72,765	71,880	117,432	98,044	62,855
Capitalization:Debt	135,501	119,576	85,969	59,070	79,267	72,937	56,190	78,869	43,090	26,721
Capitalization:Equity	32,927	30,740	27,226	22,450	19,583	17,879	12,377	9,707	7,904	6,273
Capitalization:Total	171,101	150,946	113,620	81,945	99,275	91,241	68,992	85,576	52,055	33,940
% Return on Revenue	10.7	13.7	14.4	10.7	1.7	10.0	9.2	3.5	6.0	6.5
% Return on Assets	0.8	1.0	0.8	0.6	0.1	1.1	0.8	0.4	0.8	0.8
% Return on Equity	15.9	14.8	15.9	11.8	2.9	24.6	23.4	13.9	26.3	26.8

Data as orig reptd.; bef. results of disc opers/spec. items. Per share data adj. for stk. divs.; EPS diluted. E-Estimated. NA-Not Available. NM-Not Meaningful. NR-Not Ranked. UR-Under Review.

Office: 4 World Financial Ctr , New York, NY 10080-0002.
Telephone: 212-449-1000.
Website: http://www.ml.com
Chrmn, Pres, CEO & COO: E.S. O'Neal

Vice Chrmn: R. McCormack
Vice Chrmn & EVP: R.J. McCann
Vice Chrmn & Chief Admin: A.L. Fakahany
EVP & General Counsel: R.T. Berkery

Investor Contact: L. Tosi (212-449-1000)
Board of Directors: A. Codina, V. Colbert, J. K. Conway, A. Cribiore, J. D. Finnegan, J. M. Jonas, H. Neuburger, D. K. Newbigging, E. S. O'Neal, A. L. Peters, J. W. Prueher, A. N. Reese, C. O. Rossotti

Founded: 1820
Domicile: Delaware
Employees: 54,600

STANDARD &POOR'S

Metlife Inc.

S&P Recommendation STRONG BUY ★★★★★

Price $57.13 (as of Oct 31, 2006)

12-Mo. Target Price $67.00

Investment Style Large-Cap Value

GICS Sector Financials
Sub-Industry Life & Health Insurance

Comment This company is a leading publicly traded diversified U.S. life insurance and financial services firm.

Key Stock Statistics (Source S&P, Vickers, company reports)

52-Wk Range	**$60.00–48.00**	S&P Oper. EPS 2006**E**	**5.05**	P/E on S&P Oper. EPS 2006**E**	**11.3**	Dividend Rate/Share	**$0.59**
Trailing 12-Month EPS	**$3.91**	S&P Oper. EPS 2007**E**	**5.45**	Common Shares Outstg. (M)	**759.4**	Yield (%)	**1.03**
Trailing 12-Month P/E	**14.6**	S&P Core EPS 2006**E**	**5.02**	Market Capitalization(B)	**$43.384**	Beta	**0.79**
$10K Invested 5 Yrs Ago	**$22,351**	S&P Core EPS 2007**E**	**5.42**	Institutional Ownership (%)	**56**	S&P Credit Rating	**A**

Price Performance

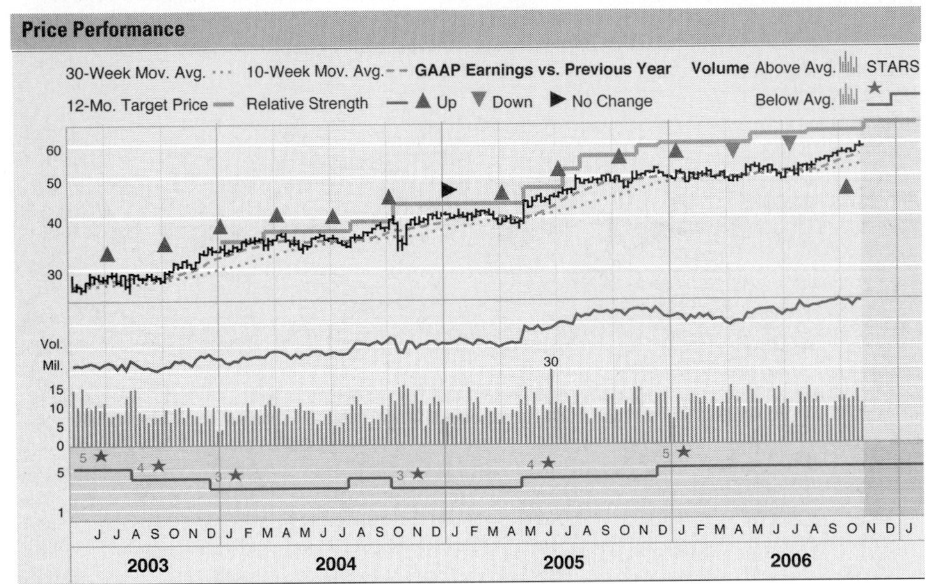

Options: ASE, CBOE, P

Highlights

- The 12-month target price for MET has recently been changed to $67.00 from $64.00. The Highlights section of this Stock Report will be updated accordingly.

Investment Rationale/Risk

- The Investment Rationale/Risk section of this Stock Report will be updated shortly. For the latest News story on MET from MarketScope, see below.

- 10/31/06 09:00 am EST... S&P REITERATES STRONG BUY RECOMMENDATION ON SHARES OF METLIFE (MET 58.95*****): Q3 operating EPS of $1.24 vs. $1.01 is $0.10 ahead of our estimate. Auto and home results were better than we expected, reflecting significantly lower catastrophe losses. International operating earnings increased 9%, led by strong performance in Latin American and Asian Pacific markets. We are encouraged by MET's resumption of share repurchases in Q4 '06. We are increasing our full-year '06 and '07 operating EPS estimate by $0.10 and $0.20, respectively to $5.05 and $5.45. Our target price rises to $67 from $64, 12.3X our '07 EPS estimate, a premium to historical average. /F. Braden

Qualitative Risk Assessment

LOW | MEDIUM | HIGH

Our risk assessment reflects the company's consistent earnings growth, strong brand identity, diversified product offerings and geographic footprint. MET has consistently been able to keep its long-term debt to total capital ratio below 30%.

Quantitative Evaluations

S&P Quality Ranking **NR**

D | C | B- | B | B+ | A- | A | A+

Relative Strength Rank **MODERATE**

47

LOWEST = 1 HIGHEST = 99

Revenue/Earnings Data

Revenue (Million $)

	1Q	2Q	3Q	4Q	Year
2006	11,585	11,409	12,551	--	--
2005	10,257	10,961	12,012	11,546	44,776
2004	9,426	9,479	10,047	10,062	39,014
2003	8,364	8,862	8,816	9,747	35,790
2002	7,973	8,244	8,120	8,810	33,147
2001	7,971	7,811	7,970	8,399	31,928

Earnings Per Share ($)

2006	0.93	0.76	1.19	**E**1.21	**E**5.05
2005	1.08	1.36	0.96	0.77	4.16
2004	0.86	1.11	0.93	0.68	3.59
2003	0.38	0.78	0.74	0.68	2.57
2002	0.41	0.50	0.43	0.24	1.58
2001	0.37	0.41	0.21	-0.41	0.62

Fiscal year ended Dec. 31. Next earnings report expected: Early February. EPS Estimates based on S&P Operating Earnings; historical GAAP earnings are as reported.

Dividend Data (Dates: mm/dd Payment Date: mm/dd/yy)

Amount ($)	Date Decl.	Ex-Div. Date	Stk. of Record	Payment Date
0.520	10/25	11/03	11/07	12/15/05
0.590	10/24	11/02	11/06	12/15/06

Dividends have been paid since 2000. Source: Company reports.

Metlife Inc.

Business Summary August 04, 2006

CORPORATE OVERVIEW. MetLife (MET) is one of the largest insurance and financial services companies in the U.S. MET benefits from a strong brand, a solid financial position and a large distribution network, in our view. According to A.M. Best Co., MET was the largest writer of group life insurance in 2004, based on net premiums written, and the second largest life and health company based on 2004 year-end assets. As of February 2006, MetLife had access to 71% of the world's life insurance markets, up from 36% in 2004. MET has also increased the number of customers outside of the U.S. from 9 million to 15 million. Formerly a mutual insurance company, MetLife demutualized and issued a publicly traded stock in 2000.

MET is organized into five business segments: institutional, individual, auto and home, international, and reinsurance. The institutional segment accounted for 42% of consolidated revenues in 2005 (42% in 2004), the individual segment accounted for 31% (32%), the auto and home segment accounted for 7.0% (8.1%), the international segment accounted for 8.1% (6.9%), and the reinsurance segment accounted for 10% (10%). Corporate and other activities, including MetLife Bank operations, accounted for 1.7% (0.7%) of consolidated revenues in 2005.

CORPORATE STRATEGY. On July 1, 2005, MET acquired Travelers Life & Annuity from Citigroup, Inc. and substantially all of Citigroup's international insurance businesses for $11.8 billion, including approximately $1 billion in MET shares and $10.8 billion in cash. The Travelers acquisition greatly enhances MET's size and scope in its core businesses, in our view. We also see the acquisition leading to strong top line growth in MET's international operations. We expect most of the expense savings to be achieved by the end of 2006 and expect $40 to $45 million in integration costs in 2006.

Company Financials

Per Share Data ($) Year Ended Dec. 31	2005	2004	2003	2002	2001	2000	1999	1998	1997	1996
Tangible Book Value	32.06	31.16	27.94	24.83	22.43	21.53	NA	NA	NA	NA
Operating Earnings	NA	NA	NA	NA	NA	NA	NA	NA	NA	NA
Earnings	4.16	3.59	2.57	1.58	0.62	1.49	1.21	NA	NA	NA
S&P Core Earnings	4.12	3.41	2.87	2.06	0.91	NA	NA	NA	NA	NA
Dividends	0.52	0.46	0.23	0.21	0.20	0.20	NA	NA	NA	NA
Payout Ratio	13%	13%	9%	13%	32%	13%	NA	NA	NA	NA
Prices:High	52.57	41.27	34.14	34.85	36.63	36.50	NA	NA	NA	NA
Prices:Low	37.29	32.30	23.51	20.60	24.70	14.25	NA	NA	NA	NA
P/E Ratio:High	13	11	13	22	59	24	NA	NA	NA	NA
P/E Ratio:Low	9	9	9	13	40	10	NA	NA	NA	NA
Income Statement Analysis (Million $)										
Life Insurance in Force	3,250,759	4,346,898	3,875,110	2,679,870	2,419,341	2,572,261	NA	NA	NA	NA
Premium Income:Life	24,860	15,341	14,065	13,070	11,611	11,224	NA	NA	NA	NA
Premium Income:A & H	NA	4,016	3,537	3,052	2,744	2,377	NA	NA	NA	NA
Net Investment Income	14,910	12,418	11,636	11,329	11,923	11,768	7,639	NA	NA	NA
Total Revenue	44,869	39,014	36,147	33,147	31,928	31,947	19,244	NA	NA	NA
Pretax Income	4,399	3,779	2,630	1,671	739	1,416	1,357	NA	NA	NA
Net Operating Income	NA	NA	NA	NA	NA	NA	NA	NA	NA	NA
Net Income	3,139	2,708	1,943	1,155	473	953	918	NA	NA	NA
S&P Core Earnings	3,123	2,574	2,144	1,512	697	NA	NA	NA	NA	NA
Balance Sheet & Other Financial Data (Million $)										
Cash & Equivalent	7,054	6,389	5,919	4,411	9,535	5,484	4,097	NA	NA	NA
Premiums Due	12,186	6,696	7,047	7,669	6,437	8,343	6,552	NA	NA	NA
Investment Assets:Bonds	230,050	176,763	167,752	140,553	115,398	112,979	75,252	NA	NA	NA
Investment Assets:Stocks	4,163	2,188	1,598	1,348	3,063	2,193	2,006	NA	NA	NA
Investment Assets:Loans	47,170	41,305	34,998	33,666	31,893	30,109	16,805	NA	NA	NA
Investment Assets:Total	301,709	234,985	218,099	188,335	162,222	156,527	105,187	NA	NA	NA
Deferred Policy Costs	19,641	14,336	12,943	11,727	11,167	10,618	4,416	NA	NA	NA
Total Assets	481,645	356,808	326,841	277,385	256,898	255,018	226,791	NA	NA	NA
Debt	12,022	5,944	5,703	5,690	4,884	3,516	3,350	NA	NA	NA
Common Equity	29,100	22,824	21,149	17,385	16,062	16,389	13,873	NA	NA	NA
% Return on Revenue	7.0	6.9	5.4	3.5	1.5	3.0	4.8	NA	NA	NA
% Return on Assets	0.7	0.8	0.6	0.4	0.2	0.4	NA	NA	NA	NA
% Return on Equity	11.8	12.3	10.1	6.9	2.9	6.3	NA	NA	NA	NA
% Investment Yield	5.6	6.8	5.7	6.5	7.5	8.0	NA	NA	NA	NA

Data as orig reptd.; bef. results of disc opers/spec. items. Per share data adj. for stk. divs.; EPS diluted. E-Estimated. NA-Not Available. NM-Not Meaningful. NR-Not Ranked. UR-Under Review.

Office: 200 Park Ave, New York, NY 10166-0005.
Telephone: 212-578-2211.
Website: http://www.metlife.com
Chrmn, Pres & CEO: C.R. Henrikson

Sr EVP & Chief Admin: C.A. Rein
EVP & CFO: W.J. Wheeler
EVP & General Counsel: J.L. Lipscomb

Board of Directors: C. H. Barnette, B. A. Dole, Jr., C. W. Grise, C. R. Henrikson, J. R. Houghton, H. P. Kamen, H. L. Kaplan, J. M. Keane, J. M. Kilts, C. M. Leighton, S. M. Mathews, H. B. Price, K. J. Sicchitano, W. C. Steere, Jr.

Founded: 1999
Domicile: Delaware
Employees: 65,500

STANDARD &POOR'S

MGIC Investment Corp

S&P Recommendation BUY ★★★★★

Price $59.26 (as of Oct 27, 2006)

12-Mo. Target Price $71.00

Investment Style Mid-Cap Growth

GICS Sector Financials
Sub-Industry Thrifts & Mortgage Finance

Comment Through its Mortgage Guaranty Insurance Corp. unit, this holding company is a leading U.S. provider of private mortgage insurance (PMI) coverage.

Key Stock Statistics (Source S&P, Vickers, company reports)

52-Wk Range	$72.73–53.96	S&P Oper. EPS 2006E	6.74	P/E on S&P Oper. EPS 2006E	8.8	Dividend Rate/Share	$1.00
Trailing 12-Month EPS	$6.62	S&P Oper. EPS 2007E	7.25	Common Shares Outstg. (M)	84.5	Yield (%)	1.69
Trailing 12-Month P/E	9.0	S&P Core EPS 2006E	6.70	Market Capitalization(B)	$5.005	Beta	1.38
$10K Invested 5 Yrs Ago	$11,141	S&P Core EPS 2007E	7.22	Institutional Ownership (%)	NA	S&P Credit Rating	NA

Price Performance

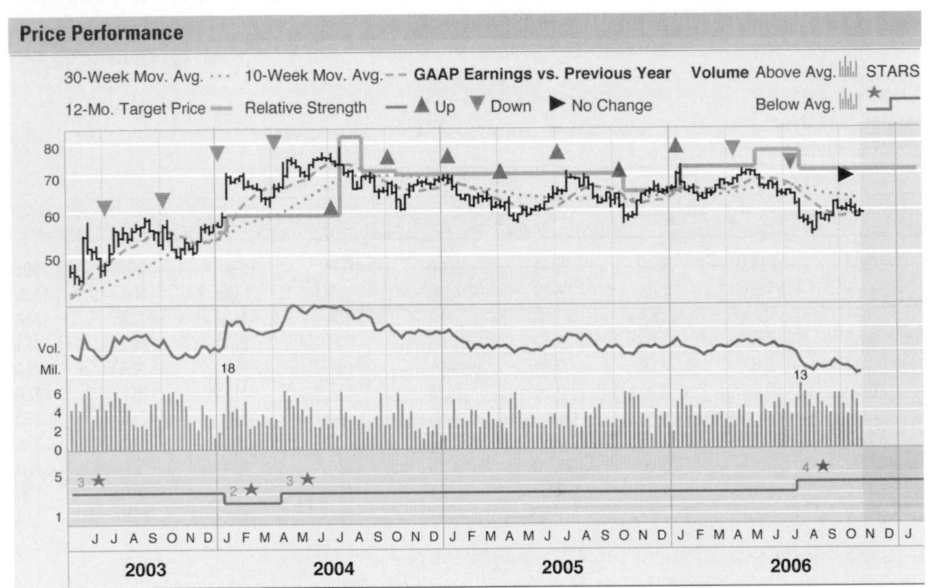

Options: ASE, CBOE, P

Analysis prepared by **Stuart Plesser** on October 17, 2006, when the stock traded at **$ 60.29**.

Highlights

- We project net premiums earned to decrease by about 4% in 2006 due largely to a modest decrease in new premiums written offset somewhat by a pickup in higher premium bulk business. We see persistency (insurance in force from one year prior) rising due to a flattening of the yield curve. We also see low single-digit growth in investment income. In the absence of any realized investment gains, we expect total revenues to decline moderately in 2006. Our forecast assumes mortgage rates will continue to rise in 2006 and home price appreciation will decelerate.
- We see net claims paid as relatively stable in 2006, but losses incurred to rise by about 7%. We also anticipate higher underwriting and other expenses, due to increased staffing in MTG's international operations as well as higher operating costs, causing operating margins to narrow moderately in 2006.
- Assuming a 7.6% decline in diluted shares, we estimate EPS of $6.74 in 2006 versus $6.78 in 2005. In 2007, we look for EPS of $7.25, an increase of 7.6%.

Investment Rationale/Risk

- We believe MTG will benefit from increasing volumes of low down-payment home mortgage originations. We think persistency rates will improve as mortgage rates rise and refinancing volumes decline, resulting in higher insurance in force. We also believe the company will benefit from higher short-term rates that have made piggyback loans more expensive relative to mortgage insurance. The possibility of new legislation allowing for the tax deductibility of mortgage insurance would also support these shares.
- Risks to our opinion and target price include higher than expected refinancing activity, which could hurt MTG's persistency rate; increased competition from other financial institutions, including captive reinsurance subsidiaries of mortgage lenders; insufficient loan reserves; and alternatives to mortgage insurance.
- Our 12-month target price of $71 equals a price to book multiple of about 1.3X, in line with peers, applied to our 12-month forward book value estimate of $54.40.

Qualitative Risk Assessment

LOW | MEDIUM | HIGH

Our risk assessment reflects our view of MTG as a leading provider of private mortgage insurance, with sound risk and capital management practice and a leading market share.

Quantitative Evaluations

S&P Quality Ranking A

D | C | B- | B | B+ | A- | A | A+

Relative Strength Rank WEAK

26

LOWEST = 1 HIGHEST = 99

Revenue/Earnings Data

Revenue (Million $)

	1Q	2Q	3Q	4Q	Year
2006	369.0	363.5	369.4	--	--
2005	384.9	395.0	375.7	370.9	1,527
2004	415.4	403.2	391.0	403.1	1,613
2003	422.9	459.6	445.6	401.6	1,685
2002	375.6	383.8	390.8	415.6	1,566
2001	320.5	339.5	339.8	358.0	1,358

Earnings Per Share ($)

2006	1.87	1.74	1.55	E1.56	E6.74
2005	1.90	1.87	1.55	1.44	6.78
2004	1.31	1.56	1.36	1.39	5.63
2003	1.42	1.46	1.06	1.05	4.99
2002	1.58	1.61	1.47	1.37	6.04
2001	1.46	1.49	1.47	1.50	5.93

Fiscal year ended Dec. 31. Next earnings report expected: Mid January. EPS Estimates based on S&P Operating Earnings; historical GAAP earnings are as reported.

Dividend Data (Dates: mm/dd Payment Date: mm/dd/yy)

Amount ($)	Date Decl.	Ex-Div. Date	Stk. of Record	Payment Date
0.250	01/26	02/08	02/10	03/01/06
0.250	05/11	05/22	05/24	06/09/06
0.250	07/27	08/09	08/11	09/01/06
0.250	10/26	11/08	11/10	12/01/06

Dividends have been paid since 1991. Source: Company reports.

MGIC Investment Corp

Business Summary October 17, 2006

COMPANY OVERVIEW. MTG is a leading provider of private mortgage insurance (PMI), which lets home buyers purchase homes with down payments of under 20% by reducing default risk borne by lenders. In addition, by improving the credit quality of the underlying loans, mortgage insurance facilitates the sale of mortgage loans in the secondary market.

PRIMARY BUSINESS DYNAMICS. There are two types of private mortgage insurance: primary and pool. Primary insurance provides default protection on individual loans and covers unpaid loan principal, interest, and certain expenses, with the insurer having the option to pay either the coverage percentage specified in the policy or 100% of the claim amount and acquire the title to the property. In general, a borrower may stop making mortgage insurance payments when the loan to value ratio (LTV) is scheduled to reach 80%. Primary insurance can be written on a flow basis, in which loans are insured in individual, loan-by-loan transactions, or on a bulk basis, in which a portfolio of loans is insured in a single bulk transaction. In 2005, new insurance written on a flow basis totaled $40.1 billion versus $47.1 billion in 2004; new insurance written for bulk transactions totaled $21.4 billion ($15.8 billion). We expect bulk business to remain strong in 2006.

Pool insurance is mortgage insurance that is supplemental to other insurance or that reduces a lender's credit risk to less than 50% of the property value, and is generally used as an additional credit enhancement for certain secondary market mortgage transactions. It covers the loss on a defaulted mortgage loan that exceeds the claim payment under the primary coverage as well as the total loss on a defaulted mortgage that did not require primary coverage.

Company Financials

Per Share Data ($) Year Ended Dec. 31	**2005**	**2004**	**2003**	**2002**	**2001**	**2000**	**1999**	**1998**	**1997**	**1996**
Tangible Book Value	47.30	43.05	38.58	33.87	28.47	23.07	16.79	15.05	13.07	11.59
Operating Earnings	NA	NA	NA	NA	NA	NA	NA	3.29	2.73	NA
Earnings	6.78	5.63	4.99	6.04	5.93	5.05	4.30	3.39	2.75	2.17
S&P Core Earnings	6.61	5.49	4.72	5.71	5.53	NA	NA	NA	NA	NA
Dividends	0.52	0.23	0.11	0.10	0.10	0.10	0.10	0.10	0.10	0.08
Payout Ratio	8%	4%	2%	2%	2%	2%	2%	3%	4%	4%
Prices:High	70.99	78.95	58.77	74.40	77.31	71.50	62.75	74.50	66.94	38.88
Prices:Low	56.70	56.20	35.30	33.60	50.56	31.94	30.13	24.25	34.94	25.25
P/E Ratio:High	10	14	12	12	13	14	15	22	24	18
P/E Ratio:Low	8	10	7	6	9	6	7	7	13	12
Income Statement Analysis (Million $)										
Premium Income	1,239	1,329	1,366	1,182	1,042	890	793	763	709	617
Net Investment Income	229	215	203	208	204	179	153	143	124	105
Other Revenue	288	68.2	117	176	111	41.7	51.1	65.4	35.0	23.2
Total Revenue	1,527	1,613	1,685	1,566	1,358	1,110	997	972	869	746
Pretax Income	804	713	640	898	932	789	681	555	465	365
Net Operating Income	NA	NA	NA	NA	NA	NA	NA	NA	NA	NA
Net Income	627	553	494	629	639	542	470	385	324	258
S&P Core Earnings	611	539	468	595	597	NA	NA	NA	NA	NA
Balance Sheet & Other Financial Data (Million $)										
Cash & Equivalent	71.0	70.1	83.2	69.5	85.4	57.0	49.0	46.1	40.4	37.2
Premiums Due	106	113	140	127	35.3	41.8	Nil	Nil	Nil	Nil
Investment Assets:Bonds	5,293	5,414	5,059	4,613	3,889	3,299	2,667	2,603	2,301	2,032
Investment Assets:Stocks	2.49	5.33	8.28	10.8	20.7	22.0	Nil	4.63	116	4.04
Investment Assets:Loans	Nil	Nil	Nil	Nil	Nil	Nil	Nil	Nil	Nil	Nil
Investment Assets:Total	5,968	5,997	5,513	5,069	4,231	3,472	2,790	2,780	2,417	2,036
Deferred Policy Costs	18.4	27.7	32.6	31.9	32.1	25.8	22.4	24.1	27.0	32.0
Total Assets	6,358	6,381	5,917	5,300	4,567	3,858	3,104	3,051	2,618	2,222
Debt	497	485	315	677	472	397	425	442	238	35.4
Common Equity	5,290	5,329	4,859	4,128	3,020	2,465	1,776	1,641	1,487	1,366
Property & Casualty:Loss Ratio	44.7	52.7	56.1	30.9	15.4	10.3	12.3	27.7	34.2	38.0
Property & Casualty:Expense Ratio	15.9	14.6	14.1	14.8	16.5	16.4	19.7	19.6	18.4	21.6
Property & Casualty Combined Ratio	60.6	67.3	70.2	45.7	31.9	26.7	32.0	47.3	52.6	59.6
% Return on Revenue	41.1	34.3	29.3	40.2	47.1	48.8	47.2	39.7	37.3	34.6
% Return on Equity	11.8	10.9	11.0	16.2	23.3	25.6	27.5	24.7	22.7	20.7

Data as orig reptd.; bef. results of disc opers/spec. items. Per share data adj. for stk. divs., EPS diluted. E-Estimated. NA-Not Available. NM-Not Meaningful. NR-Not Ranked. UR-Under Review.

Office: 250 East Kilbourn Avenue, Milwaukee, WI 53202.
Telephone: 414-347-6480.
Website: http://www.mgic.com
Chrmn & CEO: C.S. Culver

Pres & COO: P. Sinks
EVP & CFO: J.M. Lauer
SVP & Treas: J.A. Karpowicz
SVP, Secy & General Counsel: J.H. Lane

Investor Contact: M.J. Zimmerman (414-347-6596)
Board of Directors: J. A. Abbott, M. K. Bush, K. E. Case, C. S. Culver, D. S. Engelman, T. M. Hagerty, K. M. Jastrow, II, D. P. Kearney, M. E. Lehman, W. A. McIntosh, L. M. Muma

Founded: 1984
Domicile: Wisconsin
Employees: 1,200

STANDARD &POOR'S

Micron Technology Inc.

S&P Recommendation STRONG BUY ★★★★★

Price $14.17 (as of Oct 27, 2006)

12-Mo. Target Price $26.00

Investment Style Large-Cap Value

GICS Sector Information Technology
Sub-Industry Semiconductors

Comment MU is a manufacturer of semiconductor memory products, including DRAM, NAND flash memory and detachable memory, as well as image sensors.

Key Stock Statistics (Source S&P, Vickers, company reports)

52-Wk Range	$18.65–12.74	S&P Oper. EPS 2007E	1.20	P/E on S&P Oper. EPS 2007E	11.8	Dividend Rate/Share	Nil
Trailing 12-Month EPS	$0.57	S&P Oper. EPS 2008E	1.50	Common Shares Outstg. (M)	729.9	Yield (%)	Nil
Trailing 12-Month P/E	24.9	S&P Core EPS 2007E	1.20	Market Capitalization(B)	$10.342	Beta	2.84
$10K Invested 5 Yrs Ago	$5,916	S&P Core EPS 2008E	1.50	Institutional Ownership (%)	86	S&P Credit Rating	B+

Price Performance

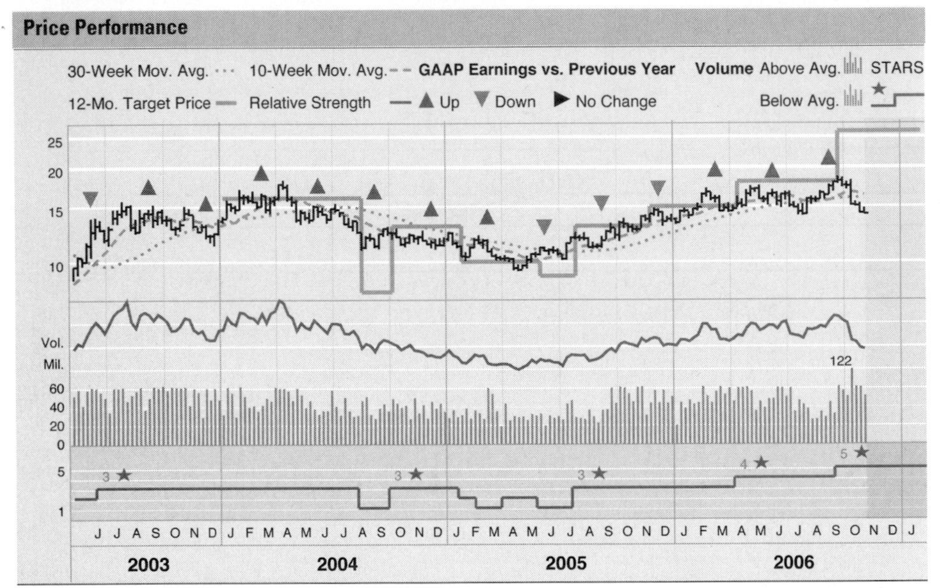

Options: ASE, CBOE, P, Ph

Analysis prepared by **Thomas W. Smith, CFA** on October 10, 2006, when the stock traded at **$ 15.32**.

Highlights

- We project that sales will increase about 30% in FY 07 (Aug.) and 11% in FY 08, reflecting acquisitions and moderate growth we see for the semiconductor industry. We believe that Micron's continuing diversification into NAND flash memories, CMOS image sensors, detachable memories and photomasks will help lift sales and aid overall gross margins.
- On June 21, 2006, MU completed the acquisition of Lexar Media, a maker of NAND flash controllers, for about $900 million. On May 8, MU became a 50.01% owner of a joint venture with Photronics (PLAB: buy, $15) called MP Mask Technology Center, located in Boise, ID. On January 6, 2006, the company began a joint venture with Intel (INTC: sell, 21) called IM Flash Technologies, LLC (IMFT).
- We anticipate that the gross margin will improve to 31% in FY 07 and 33% in FY 08, from the 23% achieved in FY 06, based on our view of a richer product mix and newer wafer plants. We estimate EPS of $1.20 in FY 07 and $1.50 for FY 08, including stock-based compensation expense.

Investment Rationale/Risk

- We have a strong buy recommendation on Micron shares, partly based on an improving trend that we see for DRAM pricing, as some industry capacity has been shifted from DRAM to NAND flash. Micron's collaboration with Intel should create some R&D savings and provide resources for factory upgrades. We think the acquisition of Lexar Media will further broaden the product mix. We see the shares as attractive based on the potential improvement in margins that we expect over the next 12 months, and the possibility of a higher valuation based on a rising, steadier gross margin.
- Risks to our opinion and target price include the possibilities of sudden downturns in end-market demand for PCs and downward fluctuations in DRAM pricing. Competition might prove more intense than we anticipate for DRAM or NAND flash memory.
- Our 12-month target price of $26 mainly reflects our price-to-sales model, and is derived by applying a multiple of 2.9X, toward the high end of a five-year historical range, to our projection for FY 07 sales per share.

Qualitative Risk Assessment

LOW | MEDIUM | **HIGH**

Micron is subject to semiconductor industry cyclicality and to sudden changes in pricing for commodity memory products. It is a relatively large semiconductor company and is the lone American survivor in the global DRAM industry, which has been consolidating in recent years.

Quantitative Evaluations

S&P Quality Ranking B-

D | C | **B-** | B | B+ | A- | A | A+

Relative Strength Rank WEAK

8

LOWEST = 1 HIGHEST = 99

Revenue/Earnings Data

Revenue (Million $)

	1Q	2Q	3Q	4Q	Year
2006	1,362	1,225	1,312	1,373	5,273
2005	1,260	1,308	1,054	1,258	4,880
2004	1,107	991.0	1,117	1,189	4,404
2003	685.1	785.0	732.7	888.5	3,091
2002	423.9	645.9	771.2	748.0	2,589
2001	1,572	1,066	818.3	480.3	3,936

Earnings Per Share ($)

	1Q	2Q	3Q	4Q	Year
2006	0.09	0.27	0.12	0.08	0.57
2005	0.23	0.17	-0.20	0.07	0.29
2004	Nil	-0.04	0.13	0.14	0.24
2003	-0.52	-1.02	-0.36	-0.20	-2.11
2002	-0.44	-0.05	-0.04	-0.97	-1.51
2001	0.59	-0.01	-0.50	-0.96	-0.88

Fiscal year ended Aug. 31. Next earnings report expected: Late December. EPS Estimates based on S&P Operating Earnings; historical GAAP earnings are as reported.

Dividend Data

The most recent cash dividend was a payment of $0.05 a share in May 1996.

Micron Technology Inc.

Business Summary October 10, 2006

Micron Technology is a global manufacturer and marketer of dynamic random access memory (DRAM), NAND flash memory, and complementary metal-oxide semiconductor (CMOS) image sensors. The company has been in the DRAM business since 1980, and is currently one of the world's largest DRAM suppliers. DRAM sales accounted for 87% of the total in FY 05 (Aug.), down from 92% in FY 04 and 96% in FY 03, reflecting an expansion into flash memory and CMOS image sensors over the last couple of years.

The company's products are used in an increasingly broad range of electronic devices, including personal computers, workstations, network servers, mobile phones, digital still cameras, MP3 players and other consumer electronics products. About 70% of FY 05 total sales were to the computing market, down from 75% in FY 04. Dell Computer and Hewlett-Packard together accounted for 23% of FY 05 sales, down from 27% in FY 04. Sales are made primarily through a direct salesforce, although distributors are also used. About 66% of sales were from outside the U.S. in FY 05.

DRAM products are high-density, low-cost per bit, random access memory devices that provide high-speed data storage and retrieval. Micron offers DRAM products with a variety of performance, pricing, and other characteristics. The company's DRAM products may be classified as core DRAM or specialty memory.

On January 6, 2006, the company began operating a joint venture with Intel called IM Flash Technologies, LLC (IMFT). The venture is 51% owned by Micron and 49% owned by Intel. Results for IMFT are included on Micron's statements. Micron contributed assets of about $995 million and $250 million in cash to the venture, and Intel added $1,196 million in cash and notes. The companies share in the output of IMFT approximately in proportion with their ownership stake. One large customer of NAND flash memory, Apple Computer, agreed to prepay $250 million to each of Micron and Intel.

Company Financials

Per Share Data ($) Year Ended Aug. 31	2006	2005	2004	2003	2002	2001	2000	1999	1998	1997
Tangible Book Value	NA	9.07	8.73	7.68	9.93	11.59	11.34	7.00	6.31	6.82
Cash Flow	NA	2.07	2.13	-0.10	0.45	1.00	4.13	1.49	0.88	1.84
Earnings	0.57	0.29	0.24	-2.11	-1.51	-0.88	2.56	-0.13	-0.55	0.77
S&P Core Earnings	NA	-0.12	-0.09	-2.60	-2.14	-1.06	NA	NA	NA	NA
Dividends	Nil	Nil	Nil	Nil	Nil	Nil	Nil	Nil	Nil	Nil
Payout Ratio	Nil	Nil	Nil	Nil	Nil	Nil	Nil	Nil	Nil	Nil
Prices:High	18.65	14.82	18.25	15.66	39.50	49.61	97.50	42.50	27.81	30.03
Prices:Low	13.34	9.32	10.89	6.60	9.50	16.39	28.00	17.13	10.03	11.00
P/E Ratio:High	33	51	76	NM	NM	NM	38	NM	NM	39
P/E Ratio:Low	23	32	45	NM	NM	NM	11	NM	NM	14

Income Statement Analysis (Million $)	2006	2005	2004	2003	2002	2001	2000	1999	1998	1997
Revenue	NA	4,880	4,404	3,091	2,589	3,936	7,336	3,764	3,012	3,516
Operating Income	NA	1,458	1,445	133	152	138	3,288	796	113	864
Depreciation	NA	1,265	1,218	1,210	1,177	1,114	994	843	607	462
Interest Expense	NA	46.9	36.0	36.5	17.1	16.7	104	130	49.4	39.9
Pretax Income	NA	199	232	-1,200	-998	-960	2,317	-91.5	-335	619
Effective Tax Rate	NA	5.34%	32.2%	NM	NM	NM	34.4%	NM	NM	43.2%
Net Income	NA	188	157	-1,273	-907	-521	1,504	-68.9	-234	332
S&P Core Earnings	NA	-75.8	-62.2	-1,578	-1,288	-626	NA	NA	NA	NA

Balance Sheet & Other Financial Data (Million $)	2006	2005	2004	2003	2002	2001	2000	1999	1998	1997
Cash	NA	525	486	570	398	469	702	295	559	620
Current Assets	NA	2,926	2,639	2,037	2,119	3,138	4,904	2,830	1,499	1,972
Total Assets	NA	8,006	7,760	7,158	7,555	8,363	9,632	6,965	4,688	4,851
Current Liabilities	NA	979	972	993	753	687	1,648	922	740	750
Long Term Debt	NA	1,020	1,028	997	361	445	934	1,528	757	762
Common Equity	NA	5,847	5,615	5,038	6,367	7,135	6,432	3,964	2,693	2,883
Total Capital	NA	6,902	6,685	6,035	6,727	7,599	7,899	5,969	3,887	3,885
Capital Expenditures	NA	1,065	1,081	822	760	1,489	1,188	804	707	517
Cash Flow	NA	1,453	1,375	-63.3	270	593	2,499	774	373	794
Current Ratio	NA	3.0	2.7	2.1	2.8	4.6	3.0	3.1	19.4	2.6
% Long Term Debt of Capitalization	NA	14.8	15.4	16.5	5.4	5.9	11.8	25.6	20.3	19.6
% Net Income of Revenue	NA	3.9	3.6	NM	NM	NM	20.5	NM	NM	9.2
% Return on Assets	NA	2.4	2.1	NM	NM	NM	18.1	NM	NM	7.7
% Return on Equity	NA	3.3	3.0	NM	NM	NM	28.9	NM	NM	12.3

Data as orig reptd.; bef. results of disc opers/spec. items. Per share data adj. for stk. divs.; EPS diluted. E-Estimated. NA-Not Available. NM-Not Meaningful. NR-Not Ranked. UR-Under Review.

Office: 8000 South Federal Way, Boise, ID 83716-7128.
Telephone: 208-368-4000.
Email: invrel@micron.com
Website: http://www.micron.com

Chrmn, Pres & CEO: S.R. Appleton
VP & CFO: W.G. Stover, Jr.
VP, Secy & General Counsel: R.W. Lewis
Investor Contact: K.A. Bedard (208-368-4400)

Auditor: PricewaterhouseCoopers
Board of Directors: T. Aoki, S. R. Appleton, J. W. Bagley, M. Johnson, R. A. Lothrop, L. N. Mondry, G. C. Smith, R. Switz, W. P. Weber

Founded: 1978
Domicile: Delaware
Employees: 18,800

STANDARD &POOR'S

Microsoft Corp

S&P Recommendation HOLD ★★★★★	Price	12-Mo. Target Price	Investment Style
	$28.71 (as of Oct 31, 2006)	$31.00	Large-Cap Growth

GICS Sector Information Technology
Sub-Industry Systems Software

Comment Microsoft, the world's largest software company, develops PC software, including the Windows operating system and the Office application suite.

Key Stock Statistics (Source S&P, Vickers, company reports)

52-Wk Range	$28.85–21.46	S&P Oper. EPS 2007E	1.46	P/E on S&P Oper. EPS 2007E	19.7	Dividend Rate/Share	$0.40
Trailing 12-Month EPS	$1.26	S&P Oper. EPS 2008E	1.66	Common Shares Outstg. (M)	9,830.5	Yield (%)	1.39
Trailing 12-Month P/E	22.8	S&P Core EPS 2007E	1.46	Market Capitalization(B)	$282.233	Beta	1.04
$10K Invested 5 Yrs Ago	$10,497	S&P Core EPS 2008E	1.66	Institutional Ownership (%)	57	S&P Credit Rating	NR

Price Performance

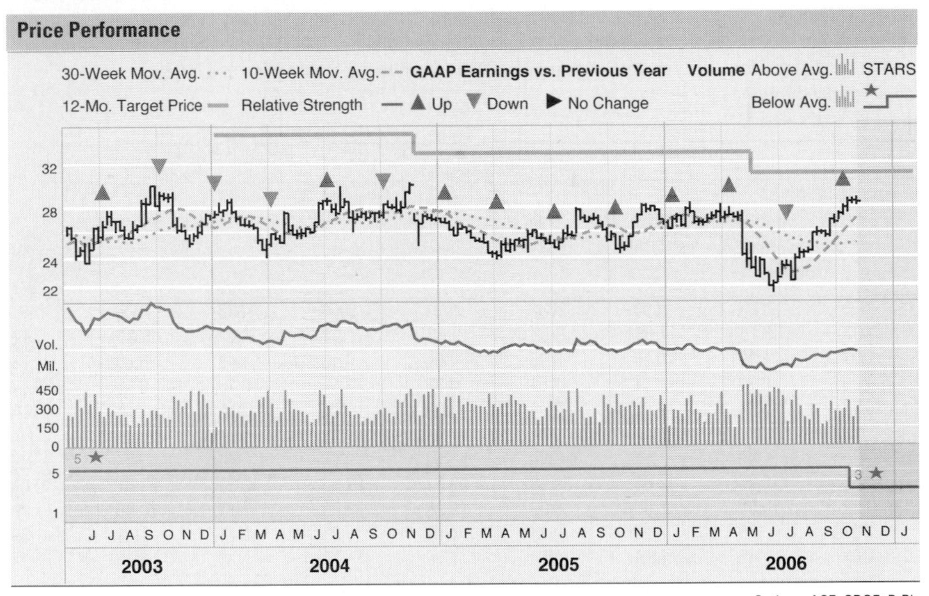

Options: ASE, CBOE, P, Ph

Analysis prepared by **Scott H. Kessler** on October 31, 2006, when the stock traded at **$ 28.53**.

Highlights

- We expect revenues to increase 13% in FY 07 (Jun.). We foresee that forthcoming new versions of operating system (Vista) and Office 2007 software, scheduled to be introduced in FY 07, will contribute to more notable growth in the second half. For FY 07, MSFT sees 8% to 10% growth in worldwide PC unit shipments, and a 10% to 12% increase in servers. We believe these forecasts will serve as baselines for the company's revenue gains.
- We look for operating margins to be hurt by notable development and marketing costs associated with new product launches. We think MSFT will continue to invest heavily in its entertainment and devices segment (which is responsible for Xbox and Xbox 360, as well as the upcoming Zune music and media system) and online services unit (largely consisting of MSN).
- Following the completion of a $30 billion share buyback program, and a $4 billion modified "Dutch auction" tender offer, as of September 2006, MSFT had some $35 billion in repurchase authorizations available through FY 11.

Investment Rationale/Risk

- We believe that MSFT's notable cash and investments, amounting to $32 billion as of September 2006, and its absence of debt provides flexibility for the company to continue repurchasing shares and increasing its dividend. We expect PC sales to remain healthy in FY 07, driven by solid corporate and consumer demand.
- Risks to our recommendation and target price include a slippage in any of the company's major product introductions, the adverse impact of regulatory or legal issues, and the more rapid adoption of open-source software than we currently anticipate.
- Our DCF model, assuming a weighted average cost of capital of 9.9%, a five-year growth rate for free cash flow of 12% and a terminal growth rate of 3%, yields an intrinsic value of $33. Peer-oriented P/E and P/E to growth considerations leads to a price of $29. Blending these methodologies results in our 12-month target price of $31. MSFT has an S&P Quality Ranking of B+, which is relatively high for a technology company.

Qualitative Risk Assessment

LOW	**MEDIUM**	HIGH

Our risk assessment reflects MSFT's ongoing antitrust related issues, the risk that its applications and operating systems may lose market share to open source rivals, and potential difficulties releasing new products in a timely manner, mitigated by the company's leading market positions and financial strength.

Quantitative Evaluations

S&P Quality Ranking **B+**

D	C	B-	B	**B+**	A-	A	A+

Relative Strength Rank **STRONG**

75

LOWEST = 1 HIGHEST = 99

Revenue/Earnings Data

Revenue (Million $)

	1Q	2Q	3Q	4Q	Year
2007	10,811	--	--	--	--
2006	9,741	11,837	10,900	11,804	44,282
2005	9,189	10,818	9,620	10,161	39,788
2004	8,215	10,153	9,175	9,292	36,835
2003	7,746	8,541	7,835	8,065	32,187
2002	6,126	7,741	7,245	7,253	28,365

Earnings Per Share ($)

2007	0.35	E0.35	E0.38	E0.42	E1.46
2006	0.29	0.34	0.29	0.28	1.20
2005	0.23	0.32	0.23	0.34	1.12
2004	0.24	0.14	0.12	0.25	0.75
2003	0.25	0.23	0.26	0.18	0.92
2002	0.12	0.21	0.25	0.14	0.71

Fiscal year ended Jun. 30. Next earnings report expected: Late January. EPS Estimates based on S&P Operating Earnings; historical GAAP earnings are as reported.

Dividend Data (Dates: mm/dd Payment Date: mm/dd/yy)

Amount ($)	Date Decl.	Ex-Div. Date	Stk. of Record	Payment Date
0.090	12/14	02/15	02/17	03/09/06
0.090	03/27	05/15	05/17	06/08/06
0.090	06/21	08/15	08/17	09/14/06
0.100	09/13	11/14	11/16	12/14/06

Dividends have been paid since 2003. Source: Company reports.

Please read the Required Disclosures and Analyst Certification on the last page of this report.

Microsoft Corp

Business Summary October 31, 2006

CORPORATE OVERVIEW. Microsoft is the world's largest software maker, primarily as a result of its dominant position in operating systems, which run 90% of all PCs currently in use, and business productivity applications, where its Office productivity suite has over 400 million users. The combination of these two strongholds provides MSFT with a strong barrier to entry for competitors, in our opinion. With MSFT generating over $1 billion every month in free cash flow, it had $31.8 billion in cash and investments as of September 2006, despite having paid out more than $60 billion for dividends and share buybacks from FY 04 to FY 06 (Jun.).

MARKET PROFILE. According to IDC, global spending on packaged software totaled $211.3 billion in 2005, with MSFT's share totaling $35.0 billion or 17% of the total market. IDC expects the system infrastructure market, which comprises roughly half of MSFT's software revenues, to grow at a compound annual growth rate (CAGR) of 9.1% from 2005 through 2010. The applications market, which constitutes more than a third of revenues, is expected to increase 7.0%, and the application development and deployment market, more than 10% of revenues, is expected to expand 7.1%. We expect MSFT to expand at slightly faster rates for the most part, as the Windows platform continues to gain market share.

CORPORATE STRATEGY. Ray Ozzie, when he was MSFT's Chief Technical Officer (he replaced Bill Gates as Chief Software Architect in June 2006), described the core of the company's business strategy as centered on software as a service rather than as a transactional purchase. This strategy is a further refinement of the .NET strategy described by Gates in 2002, and essentially is driven by three key themes: the power of advertising-supported business models, the effectiveness of online discovery and trial-version downloads as a model for new software adoption, and the demand from users for integrated user experiences that "just work."

Company Financials

Per Share Data ($) Year Ended Jun. 30	**2006**	**2005**	**2004**	**2003**	**2002**	**2001**	**2000**	**1999**	**1998**	**1997**
Tangible Book Value	3.55	4.14	6.55	5.34	2.05	4.39	3.92	2.69	1.59	1.02
Cash Flow	1.28	1.20	0.86	1.05	0.80	0.83	0.92	0.80	0.51	0.38
Earnings	1.20	1.12	0.75	0.92	0.71	0.66	0.85	0.71	0.42	0.33
S&P Core Earnings	1.27	1.20	0.83	0.75	0.65	0.58	NA	NA	NA	NA
Dividends	0.34	3.32	0.16	0.08	Nil	Nil	Nil	Nil	Nil	Nil
Payout Ratio	28%	NM	21%	9%	Nil	Nil	Nil	Nil	Nil	Nil
Prices:High	28.85	28.25	30.20	30.00	35.31	38.08	59.31	59.97	36.00	18.84
Prices:Low	21.46	23.82	24.86	22.55	20.71	21.44	20.13	34.00	15.55	10.09
P/E Ratio:High	24	25	40	33	50	58	70	84	86	57
P/E Ratio:Low	18	21	33	25	29	32	24	48	37	31
Income Statement Analysis (Million $)										
Revenue	44,282	39,788	36,835	32,187	28,365	25,296	22,956	19,747	14,484	11,358
Operating Income	17,375	15,416	10,220	14,656	12,994	13,256	11,685	10,938	7,734	5,687
Depreciation	903	855	1,186	1,439	1,084	1,536	748	1,010	1,024	557
Interest Expense	Nil	Nil	Nil	Nil	Nil	Nil	Nil	Nil	Nil	Nil
Pretax Income	18,262	16,628	12,196	14,726	11,513	11,525	14,275	11,891	7,117	5,314
Effective Tax Rate	31.0%	26.3%	33.0%	32.1%	32.0%	33.0%	34.0%	34.5%	36.9%	35.0%
Net Income	12,599	12,254	8,168	9,993	7,829	7,721	9,421	7,785	4,490	3,439
S&P Core Earnings	13,329	13,107	9,042	8,155	7,051	6,518	NA	NA	NA	NA
Balance Sheet & Other Financial Data (Million $)										
Cash	6,714	4,851	15,982	6,438	3,016	3,922	4,846	17,236	13,927	8,966
Current Assets	49,010	48,737	70,566	58,973	48,576	39,637	30,308	20,233	15,889	10,373
Total Assets	69,597	70,815	92,389	79,571	67,646	59,257	52,150	37,156	22,357	14,387
Current Liabilities	22,442	16,877	14,969	13,974	12,744	11,132	9,755	8,718	5,730	3,610
Long Term Debt	Nil	Nil	Nil	Nil	Nil	Nil	Nil	Nil	Nil	Nil
Common Equity	40,104	48,115	74,825	61,020	52,180	47,289	41,368	27,458	15,647	9,797
Total Capital	40,104	48,115	74,825	62,751	52,578	48,125	42,753	28,438	16,627	10,777
Capital Expenditures	1,578	812	1,109	891	770	1,103	879	583	656	499
Cash Flow	13,502	13,109	9,354	11,432	8,913	9,257	10,156	8,767	5,486	3,996
Current Ratio	2.2	2.9	4.7	4.2	3.8	3.6	3.1	2.3	2.8	2.9
% Long Term Debt of Capitalization	Nil	Nil	Nil	Nil	Nil	Nil	Nil	Nil	Nil	Nil
% Net Income of Revenue	28.5	30.8	22.2	31.0	27.6	30.5	41.0	39.4	31.0	30.3
% Return on Assets	17.9	14.8	9.4	13.6	12.4	13.9	20.8	26.2	24.4	28.2
% Return on Equity	28.6	19.9	11.7	17.7	15.7	17.4	27.3	36.0	35.1	41.2

Data as orig reptd.; bef. results of disc opers/spec. items. Per share data adj. for stk. divs.; EPS diluted. E-Estimated. NA-Not Available. NM-Not Meaningful. NR-Not Ranked. UR-Under Review.

Office: 1 Microsoft Way, Redmond, WA 98052-8300.
Telephone: 425-882-8080.
Email: msft@microsoft.com
Website: http://www.microsoft.com

Chrmn: W.H. Gates
CEO: S.A. Ballmer
COO: K. Turner
SVP, Secy & General Counsel: B. Smith

CFO: C. Liddell
Investor Contact: F. Brod (800-285-7772)
Board of Directors: S. A. Ballmer, J. I. Cash, Jr., D. Dublon, W. H. Gates III, R. V. Gilmartin, D. F. Marquardt, C. H. Noski, H. Panke, J. A. Shirley

Founded: 1975
Domicile: Washington
Employees: 71,000

Millipore Corp

STANDARD &POOR'S

S&P Recommendation BUY ★★★★★

Price $64.27 (as of Oct 30, 2006)

12-Mo. Target Price $79.00

Investment Style Mid-Cap Growth

GICS Sector Health Care
Sub-Industry Life Sciences Tools & Services

Comment This company provides technologies, tools and services for the development and production of new therapeutic drugs.

Key Stock Statistics (Source S&P, Vickers, company reports)

52-Wk Range	$76.95–59.58	S&P Oper. EPS 2006E	2.81	P/E on S&P Oper. EPS 2006E	22.9	Dividend Rate/Share	Nil
Trailing 12-Month EPS	$1.62	S&P Oper. EPS 2007E	3.40	Common Shares Outstg. (M)	53.3	Yield (%)	Nil
Trailing 12-Month P/E	39.7	S&P Core EPS 2006E	2.81	Market Capitalization(B)	$3.424	Beta	1.14
$10K Invested 5 Yrs Ago	$13,267	S&P Core EPS 2007E	3.40	Institutional Ownership (%)	NA	S&P Credit Rating	BB+

Price Performance

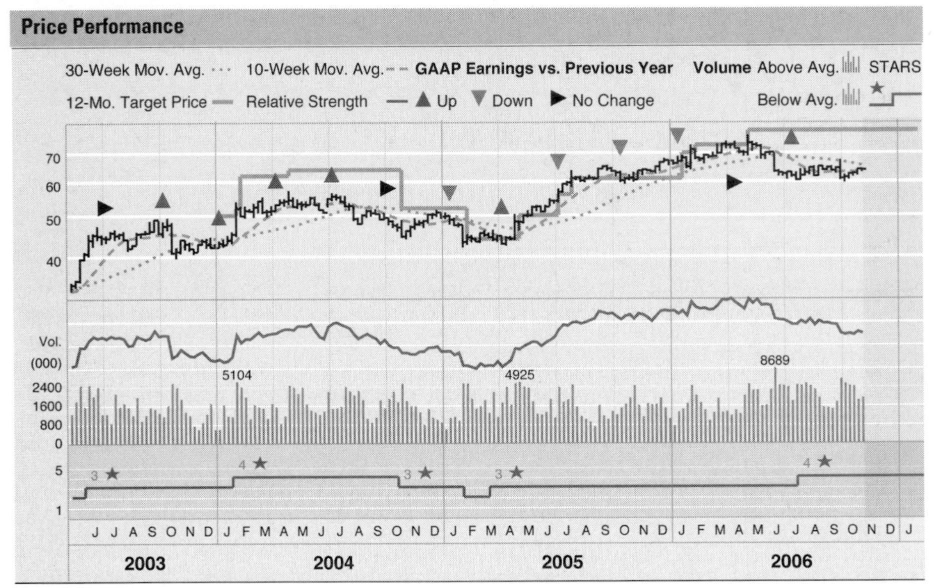

Options: ASE, CBOE

Analysis prepared by **Jeffrey Loo, CFA** on September 18, 2006, when the stock traded at **$ 64.63**.

Highlights

- In July 2006, MIL completed the acquisition of Serologicals Corp. for $1.4 billion. The combination expands MIL's product lines in both the BioScience and BioProcess segments, and MIL expects cost saving synergies of up to $10 million in 2007 and $17 million in 2008. We see the potential for attractive product line and geographic revenue synergies as the companies have minimal global sales overlap, particularly in Asia, where MIL has a strong presence.
- We see 2006 sales of $1.2 billion and about $1.5 billion in 2007. We expect operating margins to decline 40 basis points in 2006 after the inclusion of projected stock option expense, but increase 140 basis points in 2007 primarily due to operating leverage and an improvement in gross margins as a result of savings from its global supply chain initiative and the addition of higher margin Serologicals products. We see this partially offset by higher R&D costs.
- We estimate an effective 2006 tax rate of 28%, up from the 24% rate in 2005. Our 2006 EPS estimate, including projected stock option expense of $0.30, is $2.80.

Investment Rationale/Risk

- We believe MIL's share price has been depressed due to concerns over the premium paid for Serologicals and the potential dilution from MIL's $632.5 million convertible notes offering to finance the deal. Nevertheless, we believe the benefits from an expanding life sciences product line and geographic sales penetration outweigh the potential negatives. We are hopeful that MIL's acquisitions, product expansion and facilities consolidation will lead to long-term benefits and operational improvements. Still, we are cautious about MIL's ability to execute on all of its plans.
- Risks to our recommendation and target price include greater than expected integration challenges, failure to realize expected synergies, and deterioration in the pharmaceutical and biotech R&D spending environment.
- Based on our analyses of discounted cash flow, with assumptions that include a WACC of 9.7% and terminal growth of 3%, and relative valuation, assuming a P/E to growth (PEG) ratio of 1.45X, in line with peers, with a three-year EPS growth rate of 16%, applied to our 2007 EPS estimate, our 12-month target price is $79.

Qualitative Risk Assessment

LOW | **MEDIUM** | HIGH

Our risk assessment reflects MIL's broad product line and geographic reach, offset by its proactive acquisition strategy, which we believe increases its risk profile, along with its current restructuring program.

Quantitative Evaluations

S&P Quality Ranking B

D | C | B- | **B** | B+ | A- | A | A+

Relative Strength Rank MODERATE

44

LOWEST = 1 HIGHEST = 99

Revenue/Earnings Data

Revenue (Million $)

	1Q	2Q	3Q	4Q	Year
2006	268.4	273.8	--	--	--
2005	250.2	245.0	293.6	256.3	991.0
2004	222.5	224.7	210.7	225.4	883.3
2003	187.5	196.4	200.1	215.8	799.6
2002	166.6	176.1	175.6	185.9	704.3
2001	162.5	168.0	157.7	168.8	656.9

Earnings Per Share ($)

2006	0.64	0.54	**E**0.67	**E**0.80	**E**2.81
2005	0.64	0.47	0.44	0.02	1.55
2004	0.55	0.57	0.50	0.49	2.10
2003	0.44	0.46	0.50	0.66	2.06
2002	0.40	0.46	0.39	0.41	1.67
2001	0.15	0.43	0.33	0.41	1.32

Fiscal year ended Dec. 31. Next earnings report expected: NA. EPS Estimates based on S&P Operating Earnings; historical GAAP earnings are as reported.

Dividend Data

No cash dividends have been paid since January 2002.

Millipore Corp

Business Summary September 18, 2006

COMPANY OVERVIEW. Millipore provides tools and services for the development and production of therapeutic drugs. MIL focuses on solutions for drug manufacturing and other production processes, and on research and development tools for the life science industry. MIL's offerings include consumable products, capital equipment and services sold mainly to pharmaceutical, biotechnology and life science research companies. Consumables and services account for about 83% of sales, with the remaining 17% from hardware. The company sells more than 5,000 products, including process filtration and chromatography products, hardware components and systems used to manufacture and process biopharmaceuticals, process monitoring tools to test for contamination, laboratory sample preparation products, and laboratory water products used to create ultra pure water for laboratory analysis and clinical testing.

The company concentrates its in-house R&D on the development of new products. It has augmented its product offerings and research capabilities through acquisitions and alliances. Since 2005, MIL has made four acquisitions. MIL has said that its operations could be affected by an increasing number of biologic therapeutics being developed and approved over time, since its products are used in research laboratories, drug development programs, and drug manufacturing. According to the company, the drug industry is developing about 2,200 biologic compounds, including about 565 antibodies.

MIL sells its products through a global sales network. In the U.S., it mainly uses a direct sales force and website sales. Outside the U.S., MIL has subsidiaries and branches in more than 30 countries, and also employs independent distributors. Revenues by geographic region were as follows: the Americas 42% in 2005 (42% in 2004), Europe 40% (40%), and Asia Pacific (the majority derived from Japan) 18% (18%). Competitors include Amersham Biosciences, Apogent Technologies (now part of Fisher Scientific), Pall Corp., Qiagen, and United States Filter Corp.

Company Financials

Per Share Data ($) Year Ended Dec. 31	**2005**	**2004**	**2003**	**2002**	**2001**	**2000**	**1999**	**1998**	**1997**	**1996**
Tangible Book Value	12.74	12.24	8.72	5.16	7.60	5.25	2.36	1.37	1.64	3.67
Cash Flow	2.53	2.99	2.88	2.39	1.96	3.51	2.40	1.23	0.04	1.70
Earnings	1.55	2.10	2.06	1.67	1.32	2.53	1.42	0.22	-0.89	1.00
S&P Core Earnings	1.43	1.27	1.67	1.41	1.08	NA	NA	NA	NA	NA
Dividends	Nil	Nil	Nil	Nil	0.44	0.44	0.44	0.42	0.49	0.35
Payout Ratio	Nil	Nil	Nil	Nil	33%	17%	31%	191%	NM	35%
Prices:High	67.95	57.20	49.37	60.95	66.85	77.38	42.13	38.44	52.00	47.13
Prices:Low	42.01	42.13	29.90	27.25	42.65	36.25	23.44	17.25	33.50	33.63
P/E Ratio:High	44	27	24	36	51	31	30	NM	NM	47
P/E Ratio:Low	27	20	15	16	32	14	17	NM	NM	34
Income Statement Analysis (Million $)										
Revenue	991	883	800	704	657	954	771	699	759	619
Operating Income	195	182	166	160	150	216	149	89.2	41.8	92.0
Depreciation	50.7	44.5	40.5	35.0	30.7	46.1	44.3	44.4	40.7	30.6
Interest Expense	6.71	9.45	16.5	19.0	25.3	26.9	30.2	29.5	30.5	11.5
Pretax Income	138	130	112	104	78.4	154	82.4	8.54	-18.1	57.0
Effective Tax Rate	41.7%	19.1%	10.1%	22.0%	19.0%	22.4%	21.9%	NA	NM	23.5%
Net Income	80.2	106	101	80.8	63.5	119	64.3	9.86	-38.8	43.6
S&P Core Earnings	74.6	64.0	82.0	68.5	51.8	NA	NA	NA	NA	NA
Balance Sheet & Other Financial Data (Million $)										
Cash	651	152	147	101	62.5	58.4	51.1	36.0	2.24	46.9
Current Assets	1,067	541	516	390	312	465	359	305	352	312
Total Assets	1,647	1,014	951	786	916	875	793	762	766	683
Current Liabilities	243	163	222	134	134	235	270	299	305	216
Long Term Debt	552	147	216	334	320	300	313	299	287	224
Common Equity	792	639	461	288	394	305	177	137	149	218
Total Capital	1,350	793	677	622	759	605	490	436	436	442
Capital Expenditures	86.4	63.7	71.9	79.3	72.3	52.2	31.3	59.8	41.1	30.4
Cash Flow	131	150	141	116	94.2	165	109	54.3	1.88	74.2
Current Ratio	4.4	3.3	2.3	2.9	2.3	2.0	1.3	1.0	1.2	1.5
% Long Term Debt of Capitalization	40.9	18.5	31.9	53.7	42.1	49.6	63.9	68.6	65.8	50.7
% Net Income of Revenue	8.1	12.0	12.6	11.5	9.7	12.5	8.3	1.4	NM	7.1
% Return on Assets	6.0	10.7	11.5	9.3	7.3	14.3	8.3	1.3	NM	7.2
% Return on Equity	11.2	19.1	26.9	23.7	18.2	49.4	41.4	6.9	NM	19.7

Data as orig reptd.; bef. results of disc opers/spec. items. Per share data adj. for stk. divs.; EPS diluted. E-Estimated. NA-Not Available. NM-Not Meaningful. NR-Not Ranked. UR-Under Review.

Office: 290 Concord Road, Billerica, MA 01821.
Telephone: 978-715-4321 .
Website: http://www.millipore.com
Chrmn, Pres & CEO: M.D. Madaus

VP & CFO: K.B. Allen
VP, Secy & General Counsel: J. Rudin
Treas: G. Helliwell
Investor Contact: J. Young (800-225-3384)

Board of Directors: D. Bellus, R. C. Bishop, M. D. Booth, R. A. Classon, M. A. Hendricks, M. Hoffman, M. D. Madaus, J. F. Reno, E. M. Scolnick, K. E. Welke

Founded: 1954
Domicile: Massachusetts
Employees: 4,800

STANDARD &POOR'S

Molex Inc

S&P Recommendation HOLD ★★★★★

Price $35.30 (as of Oct 27, 2006)

12-Mo. Target Price $39.00

Investment Style Mid-Cap Value

GICS Sector Information Technology
Sub-Industry Electronic Manufacturing Services

Comment This company makes electrical and electronic devices primarily for OEMs in the computer, telecommunications, home appliance and home entertainment industries.

Key Stock Statistics (Source S&P, Vickers, company reports)

52-Wk Range	$40.10–24.84	S&P Oper. EPS 2007E	1.70	P/E on S&P Oper. EPS 2007E	20.8	Dividend Rate/Share	$0.30
Trailing 12-Month EPS	$1.42	S&P Oper. EPS 2008E	1.95	Common Shares Outstg. (M)	183.7	Yield (%)	0.85
Trailing 12-Month P/E	24.9	S&P Core EPS 2007E	1.70	Market Capitalization(B)	$3.509	Beta	1.57
$10K Invested 5 Yrs Ago	$11,813	S&P Core EPS 2008E	1.95	Institutional Ownership (%)	61	S&P Credit Rating	NA

Price Performance

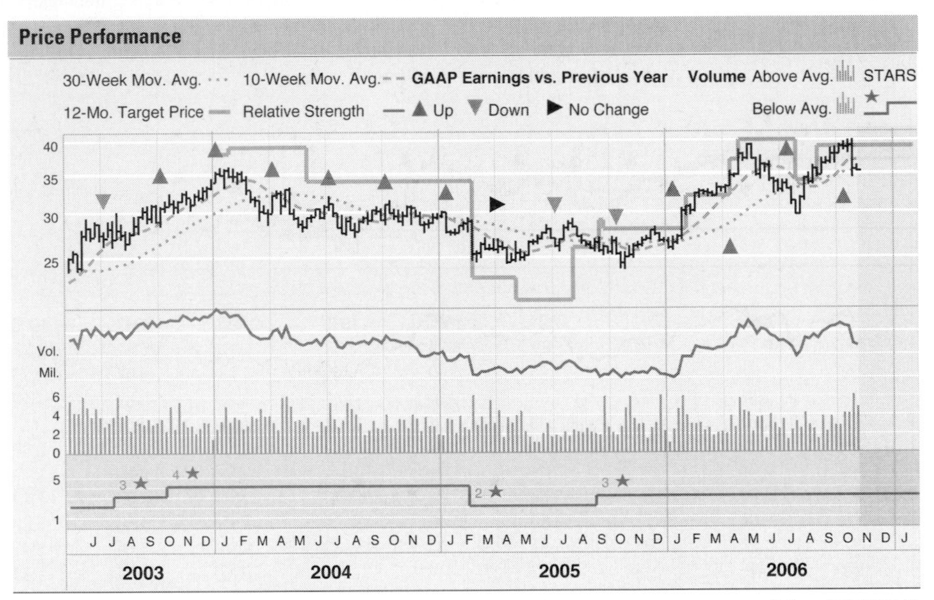

Options: ASE, CBOE, Ph

Analysis prepared by **Stewart Scharf** on October 24, 2006, when the stock traded at **$ 36.07**.

Highlights

- We expect organic revenues in FY 07 (Jun.) to advance 10%, led by increased global demand for digital consumer and telecom products. We also expect growth in the industrial and medical electronics markets. Revenues from the August 2006 acquisition of Woodhead Industries should bring total growth above 15%.

- We see gross margins widening slightly in FY 07 from 35% in FY 06, mainly back-end loaded, as a better product mix resulting from new product introductions, along with productivity improvements and price hikes, offset higher, albeit stabilizing, copper and gold costs. We expect the EBITDA margin to widen by nearly 100 basis points from FY 06's 19%, as MOLX continues to realign its manufacturing capacity and keeps SG&A expenses near 20% of sales (23% in FY 06). MOLX plans to close facilities and transfer production from Japan to China and eastern Europe.

- We estimate FY 07 operating EPS of $1.70, up 25% from $1.36 before a $0.10 restructuring charge in FY 06. We forecast FY 08 EPS of $1.95.

Investment Rationale/Risk

- We maintain our hold opinion, based on valuation and some concern regarding the global economy, especially for the consumer discretionary and information technology sectors. We note that there is an SEC investigation related to stock option grants.

- Risks to our recommendation and target price include a significant rise in raw material costs; a stronger dollar against the yen and the euro; adverse rulings in shareholder class action lawsuits; additional accounting errors; and possible difficulties integrating the Woodhead Industries acquisition. Corporate governance practices also concern us as MOLX has two classes of stock, and the board mainly consists of insiders.

- Utilizing our DCF model, assuming a 3.5% perpetuity growth rate and a 10% weighted average cost of capital, we see intrinsic value of $42. We also utilize a P/E to five year EPS growth (PEG) ratio of 1.5X, modestly above peers. The shares recently traded near 21X our FY 07 estimate, a premium to our projected P/E for the S&P 500 as well as MOLX's sub-industry group. Blending our relative and DCF analyses, we arrive at our 12-month target price of $39.

Qualitative Risk Assessment

LOW | **MEDIUM** | HIGH

Our risk assessment reflects the cyclicality in MOLX's global markets, price and product competition, volatile raw material costs, and weaker foreign currency exchange rates. However, we also consider the company's balance sheet, which we view as strong and virtually debt free.

Quantitative Evaluations

S&P Quality Ranking **B+**

D | C | B- | B | **B+** | A- | A | A+

Relative Strength Rank **WEAK**

17

LOWEST = 1 HIGHEST = 99

Revenue/Earnings Data

Revenue (Million $)

	1Q	2Q	3Q	4Q	Year
2007	829.6	--	--	--	--
2006	659.8	697.4	720.3	783.8	2,861
2005	640.2	651.8	612.8	643.8	2,549
2004	496.8	549.0	569.2	631.8	2,247
2003	469.3	454.6	443.2	476.1	1,843
2002	430.5	416.5	408.3	456.3	1,712

Earnings Per Share ($)

2007	0.41	**E**0.39	**E**0.47	**E**0.43	**E**1.70
2006	0.25	0.31	0.33	0.38	1.26
2005	0.29	0.27	0.24	0.03	0.81
2004	0.17	0.21	0.24	0.30	0.92
2003	0.15	0.15	0.13	0.01	0.44
2002	0.13	0.02	0.10	0.14	0.39

Fiscal year ended Jun. 30. Next earnings report expected: Mid January. EPS Estimates based on S&P Operating Earnings; historical GAAP earnings are as reported.

Dividend Data (Dates: mm/dd Payment Date: mm/dd/yy)

Amount ($)	Date Decl.	Ex-Div. Date	Stk. of Record	Payment Date
0.050	07/28	12/28	12/30	01/25/06
0.050	07/28	03/29	03/31	04/25/06
0.075	04/28	06/28	06/30	07/25/06
0.075	04/26	09/27	09/29	10/25/06

Dividends have been paid since 1976. Source: Company reports.

Molex Inc

STANDARD &POOR'S

Business Summary October 24, 2006

CORPORATE OVERVIEW. Molex is the world's second largest connector maker, operating 54 plants in 18 countries, and offering more than 100,000 products.

MOLX's products include electrical and electronic devices such as terminals, cable assemblies, interconnection systems, fiber-optic interconnection systems, and mechanical and electronic switches. In FY 06 (Jun.), these products were sold to the following industries: data products (22%), telecommunications (30%), consumer products (19%), automotive (18%), industrial (9%), and other (2%).

MOLX sells primarily to original equipment manufacturers (OEMs), subcontractors and suppliers. Customers include Arrow, Cisco, Dell, Delphi, Ford, Hewlett Packard, IBM, Matsushita, Motorola and Nokia.

Revenues outside the U.S. accounted for 73% of the FY 06 total, with 52% generated in Asia (19% in the Far East North and 33% in the Far East South), 18% in Europe and 2% in other regions.

At September 30, 2006, order backlog was $451 million, up 22% sequentially and 57% from a year ago (48% before the Woodhead acquisition). New orders in the September period were $865 million, up 10% sequentially and up nearly 25% from a year earlier.

In the first quarter of FY 07, MOLX repurchased 162,500 Class A common shares for $5 million. As of September 30, 2006, about $45 million remained available under the $250 million stock repurchase program. Previously, 4.5 million Class A and 1.5 million common shares had been bought back for $165 million.

In August 2006, following a review of stock option grant practices dating back to FY 95, MOLX and a special committee found that the dates of some grants to officers and other employees differed from the dates approved. Although no change to previously issued financial statements was required under GAAP, the company ordered 14 executives to return a total of $685,000 to compensate for backdated stock options over a 12 year period. In October 2006, the U.S. Justice Department subpoenaed MOLX, seeking documents related to the company's review of stock options.

Company Financials

Per Share Data ($) Year Ended Jun. 30	**2006**	**2005**	**2004**	**2003**	**2002**	**2001**	**2000**	**1999**	**1998**	**1997**
Tangible Book Value	11.60	10.78	10.05	9.10	8.64	8.25	7.83	6.94	6.47	6.30
Cash Flow	2.41	2.02	2.10	1.62	1.53	2.13	2.11	1.77	1.67	1.56
Earnings	1.26	0.81	0.92	0.44	0.39	1.03	1.12	0.91	0.92	0.85
S&P Core Earnings	1.27	0.76	0.85	0.39	0.39	1.01	NA	NA	NA	NA
Dividends	0.23	0.15	0.10	0.10	0.10	0.10	0.07	0.04	0.05	0.03
Payout Ratio	18%	19%	11%	23%	26%	10%	6%	4%	5%	4%
Prices:High	40.10	30.00	36.10	35.12	39.61	48.00	63.75	45.60	31.20	30.70
Prices:Low	25.63	23.75	27.07	19.98	19.43	25.76	34.19	20.40	18.40	17.28
P/E Ratio:High	32	37	39	80	NM	47	57	50	34	36
P/E Ratio:Low	20	29	29	45	50	25	31	22	20	20

Income Statement Analysis (Million $)	**2006**	**2005**	**2004**	**2003**	**2002**	**2001**	**2000**	**1999**	**1998**	**1997**
Revenue	2,861	2,549	2,247	1,843	1,712	2,366	2,217	1,712	1,623	1,540
Operating Income	552	481	450	-120	324	498	512	395	413	391
Depreciation	215	231	228	229	224	218	196	169	149	139
Interest Expense	Nil	Nil	Nil	Nil	Nil	Nil	Nil	Nil	Nil	Nil
Pretax Income	329	217	240	110	93.2	291	324	230	275	262
Effective Tax Rate	28.0%	28.8%	26.5%	22.5%	17.9%	30.0%	31.1%	22.7%	33.7%	36.4%
Net Income	237	154	176	84.9	76.5	204	222	178	182	167
S&P Core Earnings	239	143	164	76.1	76.7	200	NA	NA	NA	NA

Balance Sheet & Other Financial Data (Million $)	**2006**	**2005**	**2004**	**2003**	**2002**	**2001**	**2000**	**1999**	**1998**	**1997**
Cash	486	498	339	350	313	208	241	183	205	326
Current Assets	1,548	1,374	1,169	962	915	892	1,023	881	868	874
Total Assets	2,973	2,728	2,572	2,335	2,254	2,214	2,247	1,902	1,640	1,637
Current Liabilities	595	470	428	356	360	374	475	342	333	342
Long Term Debt	8.81	9.98	14.0	16.9	17.8	25.5	21.6	20.1	5.60	7.40
Common Equity	2,281	2,168	2,066	1,897	1,828	1,766	1,706	1,501	1,262	1,236
Total Capital	2,290	2,180	2,081	1,914	1,846	1,793	1,734	1,526	1,274	1,258
Capital Expenditures	277	231	190	171	172	376	337	229	227	209
Cash Flow	452	385	404	314	300	422	419	347	331	305
Current Ratio	2.6	2.9	2.7	2.7	2.5	2.4	2.2	2.6	2.6	2.6
% Long Term Debt of Capitalization	0.4	0.5	0.7	0.9	1.0	1.4	1.2	1.3	0.4	0.6
% Net Income of Revenue	8.3	6.1	7.8	4.6	4.5	8.6	10.0	10.4	11.2	10.8
% Return on Assets	8.3	5.8	7.2	3.7	3.4	9.1	10.7	10.1	11.1	10.8
% Return on Equity	10.7	7.3	8.9	4.6	4.3	11.7	13.9	12.9	14.6	14.1

Data as orig reptd.; bef. results of disc opers/spec. items. Per share data adj. for stk. divs.; EPS diluted. E-Estimated. NA-Not Available. NM-Not Meaningful. NR-Not Ranked. UR-Under Review.

Office: 2222 Wellington Court, Lisle, IL 60532.
Telephone: 630-969-4550.
Website: http://www.molex.com
Co-Chrmn: F.A. Krehbiel

Co-Chrmn: J.H. Krehbiel
Pres & COO: L. McCarthy
Vice Chrmn & CEO: M.P. Slark
Investor Contact: D.D. Johnson (630-969-4550)

Board of Directors: M. J. Birck, M. Collins, E. D. Jannotta, F. L. Krehbiel, F. A. Krehbiel, J. H. Krehbiel, Jr., D. L. Landsittel, J. W. Laymon, D. G. Lubin, M. Naitoh, R. J. Potter, M. P. Slark

Founded: 1938
Domicile: Delaware
Employees: 32,400

STANDARD &POOR'S

Molson Coors Brewing Co

S&P Recommendation HOLD ★★★★★

Price $71.18 (as of Oct 31, 2006)

12-Mo. Target Price $72.00

Investment Style Mid-Cap Value

GICS Sector Consumer Staples
Sub-Industry Brewers

Comment TAP, the fifth largest brewer in the world, was formed in early 2005 via the combination of Adolph Coors Co. and Molson, Inc.

Key Stock Statistics (Source S&P, Vickers, company reports)

52-Wk Range	$74.10–60.75	S&P Oper. EPS 2006E	3.91	P/E on S&P Oper. EPS 2006E	18.2	Dividend Rate/Share	$1.28
Trailing 12-Month EPS	$3.13	S&P Oper. EPS 2007E	4.60	Common Shares Outstg. (M)	86.1	Yield (%)	1.60
Trailing 12-Month P/E	22.7	S&P Core EPS 2006E	3.89	Market Capitalization(B)	$5.912	Beta	0.98
$10K Invested 5 Yrs Ago	$15,085	S&P Core EPS 2007E	4.40	Institutional Ownership (%)	63	S&P Credit Rating	BBB+

Price Performance

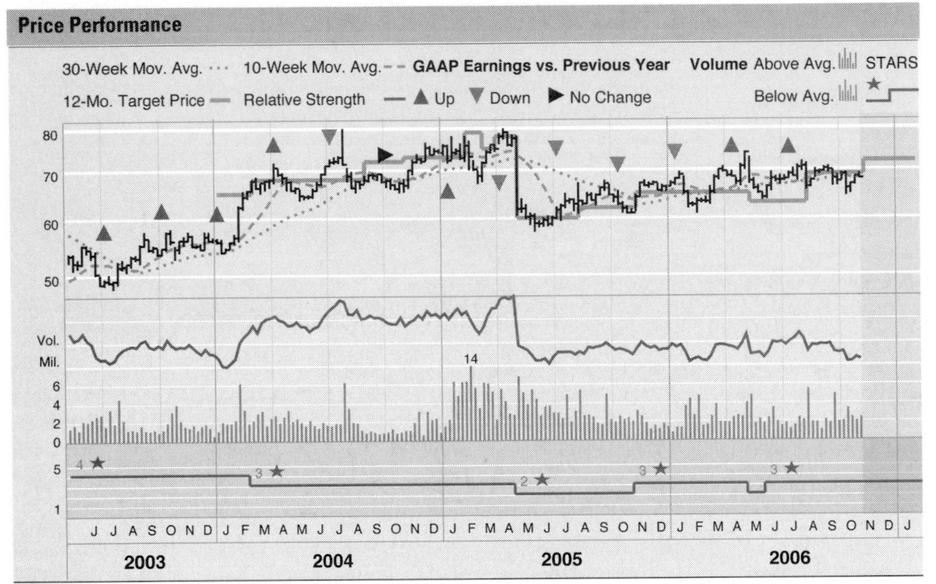

Options: P

Highlights

- The 12-month target price for TAP has recently been changed to $72.00 from $69.00. The Highlights section of this Stock Report will be updated accordingly.

Investment Rationale/Risk

- The Investment Rationale/Risk section of this Stock Report will be updated shortly. For the latest News story on TAP from MarketScope, see below.

- 10/31/06 04:52 pm EST... S&P REITERATES HOLD OPINION ON SHARES OF MOLSON COORS (TAP 71.18***): Q3 EPS of $1.56 vs. $1.26 is two cents shy of our estimate. However, excluding items such as discontinued operations, special charges, and tax benefits, TAP's operating EPS was $1.61 vs. $1.27. Volume remained flat, but revenue grew 3.3% on better-than-expected pricing. Although cost savings from merger synergies were more than offset by higher input costs, we expect margins to begin to recover. And with pricing trends becoming more favorable, we are raising our '07 EPS estimate by $0.20, to $4.60. Our 12-month target price rises $3, to $72, based on revised DCF analysis. / R.Mathis

Qualitative Risk Assessment

LOW | **MEDIUM** | HIGH

Our risk assessment reflects the stable revenue streams of the brewing industry, in which TAP is a major player. We have some corporate governance concerns with respect to TAP's multi-class stock structure and its more than 50% controlling family interest.

Quantitative Evaluations

S&P Quality Ranking A-

D | C | B- | B | B+ | **A-** | A | A+

Relative Strength Rank MODERATE

64

LOWEST = 1 HIGHEST = 99

Revenue/Earnings Data

Revenue (Million $)

	1Q	2Q	3Q	4Q	Year
2006	1,154	1,583	--	--	--
2005	1,048	1,547	1,527	1,385	5,507
2004	923.5	1,151	1,104	1,127	4,306
2003	828.1	1,100	1,049	1,023	4,000
2002	745.8	1,048	1,002	981.1	3,776
2001	543.7	692.7	634.7	558.4	2,429

Earnings Per Share ($)

2006	-0.22	1.82	**E**1.61	**E**0.91	**E**3.91
2005	-0.48	1.11	1.52	0.40	2.88
2004	0.13	1.90	1.68	1.45	5.19
2003	0.02	2.09	1.68	0.98	4.77
2002	0.75	1.84	1.28	0.55	4.42
2001	0.49	1.33	1.05	0.44	3.31

Fiscal year ended Dec. 31. Next earnings report expected: Early November. EPS Estimates based on S&P Operating Earnings; historical GAAP earnings are as reported.

Dividend Data (Dates: mm/dd Payment Date: mm/dd/yy)

Amount ($)	Date Decl.	Ex-Div. Date	Stk. of Record	Payment Date
0.320	11/10	11/28	11/30	12/15/05
0.320	02/17	02/24	02/28	03/15/06
0.320	05/18	05/26	05/31	06/15/06
0.320	07/26	08/29	08/31	09/15/06

Dividends have been paid since 1970. Source: Company reports.

Molson Coors Brewing Co

Business Summary August 31, 2006

CORPORATE OVERVIEW. Molson Coors Brewing Company was formed in February 2005 by the combination of Adolph Coors Co. and Canadian brewer Molson, Inc. Total combined sales are estimated at about 61 million hectoliters, making it the fifth largest brewer in the world. The transaction resulted in each Molson Class B voting share being converted to shares with 0.126 voting rights and 0.234 non-voting rights of Molson Coors stock, and each Molson Class A converted to shares with a 0.360 non-voting share of Molson Coors.

Molson Inc. was the world's 14th largest brewer in 2004, pre-merger, with operations in Canada, Brazil and the United States. A global brewer with C$3.5 billion in gross annual sales, Molson traces its roots back to 1786, making it North America's oldest beer brand. Adolph Coors Co. was the third largest U.S. brewer, with a 10.3% share of the U.S. beer market in 2004, selling 32.7 million barrels of beer and other malt beverage products, up 3% from the level of 2003. The company was founded in 1873.

TAP's stable of well known U.S. brands includes Coors Light, Original Coors, and Coors Non-Alcoholic premium beers; above-premium brews such as George Killian's Irish Red and Blue Moon Belgian White Ale; and lower priced beers, including Extra Gold, Keystone Premium, Keystone Light, and Keystone Ice. Coors produces Zima and Zima Citrus malt-based beverages. In 2004, the company introduced a new low-carbohydrate beer, Aspen Edge, to the U.S. market. Brands sold primarily in Canada include Molson Canadian, Molson Dry, Molson Export, Creemore Springs, Rickard's Red Ale, Carling and Pilsner. Brands sold primarily in the U.K. include Carling, Coors Fine Light Beer, Worthington's Caffrey's, Reef, Screamers, and Stones. Approximately 56% of TAP's 2005 volume was sold in the United States segment, 18% in the Canada segment, and 26% in the Europe segment. In 2005, Coors Light accounted for approximately 39% of reported volume, Carling for 17%, and Molson Canadian for 4%.

CORPORATE STRATEGY. We look favorably on TAP's strategy to gain market share in each area by cross marketing its products. We are particularly impressed with the gains seen for Coors Light brand in Canada, where it now has a 10% market share, making it the largest selling light-beer, and second largest-selling beer brand overall in Canada.

Company Financials

Per Share Data ($) Year Ended Dec. 31	**2005**	**2004**	**2003**	**2002**	**2001**	**2000**	**1999**	**1998**	**1997**	**1996**
Tangible Book Value	NM	3.43	NM	NM	24.06	24.32	22.06	20.51	19.36	18.30
Cash Flow	7.79	12.27	11.43	10.72	6.56	6.38	5.77	4.89	5.24	4.33
Earnings	2.88	5.19	4.77	4.42	3.31	2.93	2.46	1.81	2.16	1.14
S&P Core Earnings	2.14	4.25	4.20	1.53	1.36	NA	NA	NA	NA	NA
Dividends	1.28	0.82	0.82	0.82	0.80	0.72	0.65	0.60	0.55	0.50
Payout Ratio	44%	16%	17%	19%	24%	25%	26%	33%	25%	44%
Prices:High	79.99	80.11	64.81	70.15	81.19	82.31	65.81	56.75	41.25	24.25
Prices:Low	57.37	53.73	45.85	50.50	42.65	37.38	45.25	29.25	17.50	16.75
P/E Ratio:High	28	15	14	16	25	28	27	31	19	21
P/E Ratio:Low	20	10	10	11	13	13	18	16	8	15
Income Statement Analysis (Million $)										
Revenue	5,507	4,306	4,000	3,776	2,429	2,414	2,057	1,900	1,822	1,732
Operating Income	960	609	551	535	296	295	271	239	233	208
Depreciation	393	268	244	230	121	129	124	116	117	121
Interest Expense	131	72.4	81.2	70.9	2.01	6.41	4.36	9.80	13.6	17.1
Pretax Income	295	308	254	257	198	170	151	111	147	75.0
Effective Tax Rate	17.0%	30.9%	31.2%	37.0%	37.9%	35.3%	38.7%	39.0%	44.0%	42.1%
Net Income	230	197	175	162	123	110	92.3	67.8	82.3	43.4
S&P Core Earnings	172	161	154	56.1	50.7	NA	NA	NA	NA	NA
Balance Sheet & Other Financial Data (Million $)										
Cash	39.4	123	19.4	59.2	310	120	164	256	169	111
Current Assets	1,468	1,268	1,079	1,054	607	498	613	549	517	417
Total Assets	11,799	4,658	4,486	4,297	1,740	1,629	1,546	1,461	1,412	1,363
Current Liabilities	2,237	1,177	1,134	1,148	518	379	393	384	359	292
Long Term Debt	2,137	894	1,160	1,383	20.0	105	105	105	145	176
Common Equity	5,325	1,601	1,267	982	951	932	842	775	737	715
Total Capital	8,151	2,682	2,623	2,522	1,033	1,127	1,025	946	958	968
Capital Expenditures	406	212	240	240	245	154	134	105	60.3	65.0
Cash Flow	623	465	418	392	244	239	216	184	199	165
Current Ratio	0.7	1.1	1.0	0.9	1.2	1.3	1.6	1.4	1.4	1.4
% Long Term Debt of Capitalization	26.2	33.3	44.2	54.9	1.9	9.3	10.2	11.1	15.1	18.2
% Net Income of Revenue	4.2	4.6	4.4	4.3	5.1	4.5	4.5	3.6	4.5	2.5
% Return on Assets	2.8	4.3	4.0	5.4	7.3	6.9	6.1	4.7	5.9	3.2
% Return on Equity	6.7	13.7	15.5	16.7	13.1	12.4	11.4	9.0	11.3	6.2

Data as orig reptd.; bef. results of disc opers/spec. items. Per share data adj. for stk. divs.; EPS diluted. E-Estimated. NA-Not Available. NM-Not Meaningful. NR-Not Ranked. UR-Under Review.

Office: 1225 17th St, Denver, CO 80202-5534.
Telephone: 303-279-6565.
Website: http://www.molsoncoors.com
Chrmn: E.H. Molson

Pres & CEO: W.L. Kiely III
SVP, Secy & Chief Lgl Officer: S. Walker
VP & Chief Acctg Officer: M.L. Miller
CFO: T.V. Wolf

Investor Contact: D. Dunnewald (303-279-6565)
Board of Directors: F. Bellini, R. G. Brewer, J. E. Cleghorn, P. H. Coors, C. M. Herington, F. W. Hobbs IV, W. L. Kiely III, G. S. Matthews, A. T. Molson, E. H. Molson, D. P. O'Brien, M. C. Osborn, P. H. Patsley, H. S. Riley

Founded: 1873
Domicile: Delaware
Employees: 10,200

STANDARD & POOR'S

Monsanto Co

S&P Recommendation SELL ★★☆☆☆

Price $44.28 (as of Oct 27, 2006)

12-Mo. Target Price $39.00

Investment Style Large-Cap Value

GICS Sector Materials
Sub-Industry Fertilizers & Agricultural Chemicals

Comment This company is a global provider of agricultural products and integrated solutions for farmers.

Key Stock Statistics (Source S&P, Vickers, company reports)

52-Wk Range	$48.45–30.23	S&P Oper. EPS 2007E	1.59	P/E on S&P Oper. EPS 2007E	27.8	Dividend Rate/Share	$0.40
Trailing 12-Month EPS	$1.26	S&P Oper. EPS 2008E	1.84	Common Shares Outstg. (M)	542.8	Yield (%)	0.90
Trailing 12-Month P/E	35.1	S&P Core EPS 2007E	1.61	Market Capitalization(B)	$24.035	Beta	1.54
$10K Invested 5 Yrs Ago	$29,474	S&P Core EPS 2008E	1.84	Institutional Ownership (%)	88	S&P Credit Rating	A-

Price Performance

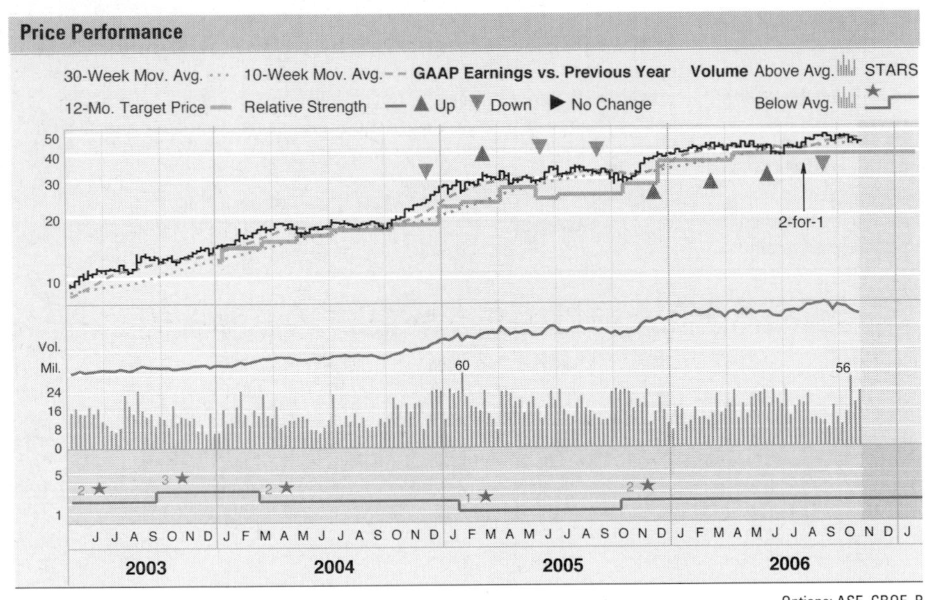

Options: ASE, CBOE, P

Analysis prepared by **Kevin Kirkeby** on October 17, 2006, when the stock traded at **$ 44.78**.

Highlights

- Following a 17% rise in FY 06 (Aug.), including acquisitions, we see FY 07 net sales increasing about 6%, to $7.8 billion, on higher volumes of genetically modified seeds and seed traits in the U.S., and a growing penetration of these products in global markets. We expect a continuing shift in the product mix and a strategic focus toward higher value added stacked traits in the seeds and genomics business. We project flat herbicide volumes at lower prices, amid increasing use of generic substitutes for Roundup.
- In MON's increasingly important seeds and genomics business, we look for widening margins on higher volumes. We see rising competition and costs pressuring chemical margins. We believe these trends, combined with modestly higher selling and administrative expenses, will support an operating margin, after depreciation, of approximately 18% in FY 07.
- Adjusting for multiple special gains and losses, FY 06 EPS rose 22%, to $1.27. For FY 07, we project 24% EPS growth, to $1.59, excluding the proposed acquisition of Delta & Pine Land Co. (DLP), subject to necessary approvals.

Investment Rationale/Risk

- We believe MON shares are overvalued, given our view of the company's business risks and industry concerns for the long term. We think MON has grown less dependent on its herbicide business, and should see its seeds and traits business driving near-term market share gains in global soy, corn and cotton markets. However, we foresee competition increasing longer term, with regulatory challenges remaining significant. We believe MON is likely to be mainly focused on achieving antitrust clearance over the next year for the planned purchase of DLP.
- Risks to our opinion and target price include the possibility of better than anticipated margin and market share growth, lower than expected legal and regulatory exposures, and favorable changes in planting volumes or exchange rates.
- Our DCF model, which assumes a 10% weighted cost of capital, annual free cash flow growth of 7% for 10 years, and 3.5% terminal growth, calculates intrinsic value of $36. Our relative valuation model targets a forward enterprise value (EV)/EBITDA multiple of 13X, and produces a value of $42. Blending these two metrics results in our 12-month target price of $39.

Qualitative Risk Assessment

LOW | **MEDIUM** | HIGH

Our risk assessment for MON reflects its exposure to global agricultural markets and currencies, adverse weather, legal, and regulatory developments, and risks relating to the enforcement of intellectual property rights, offset by relatively low exposure to economic cycles and our view of consistent cash flow generation.

Quantitative Evaluations

S&P Quality Ranking NR

D | C | B- | B | B+ | A- | A | A+

Relative Strength Rank WEAK

23

LOWEST = 1 HIGHEST = 99

Revenue/Earnings Data

Revenue (Million $)

	1Q	2Q	3Q	4Q	Year
2006	1,405	2,200	2,348	1,391	7,344
2005	1,072	1,908	2,040	1,274	6,294
2004	1,028	1,492	1,679	1,258	5,457
2003	--	--	--	--	3,373
2002	1,221	1,553	679.0	1,220	4,673
2001	1,306	2,011	936.0	1,209	5,462

Earnings Per Share ($)

	1Q	2Q	3Q	4Q	Year
2006	0.11	0.80	0.61	-0.25	1.27
2005	-0.24	0.68	0.08	-0.24	0.29
2004	-0.15	0.29	0.43	-0.07	0.51
2003	--	--	--	--	-0.02
2002	0.17	0.28	-0.32	0.12	0.25
2001	0.11	0.74	-0.09	-0.20	0.57

Fiscal year ended Aug. 31. Next earnings report expected: Early January. EPS Estimates based on S&P Operating Earnings; historical GAAP earnings are as reported.

Dividend Data (Dates: mm/dd Payment Date: mm/dd/yy)

Amount ($)	Date Decl.	Ex-Div. Date	Stk. of Record	Payment Date
0.200	01/17	04/05	04/07	04/28/06
0.200	06/27	07/05	07/07	07/28/06
2-for-1 Stk.	06/27	07/31	07/07	07/28/06
0.100	08/09	10/04	10/06	10/27/06

Dividends have been paid since 2001. Source: Company reports.

Monsanto Co

Business Summary October 17, 2006

CORPORATE OVERVIEW. MON produces leading seed brands and develops biotechnology traits that assist farmers in controlling insects and weeds, and provides other seed companies with genetic material and biotech traits. MON's Roundup herbicides are used for agricultural, industrial and residential weed control, and are sold in more than 80 countries.

MARKET PROFILE. MON operates in two segments: agricultural productivity, and seeds and genomics. The agricultural productivity segment (45% of sales and 31% of gross profits in FY 06 (Aug.)) consists of the company's crop protection products (Roundup herbicide and other glyphosate products), its animal agriculture, and the Roundup lawn and garden products. In the year ended August 31, 2006, Roundup and other glyphosate-based herbicides accounted for 31% of total sales. Patent protection for the active ingredient in Roundup herbicides expired in the U.S. in 2000. Since then, we believe herbicide pricing and margins have declined. MON's animal agriculture business focuses on improving animal productivity, producing the largest selling U.S. brand of recombinant bovine growth hormone, which increases milk production in dairy cows. We believe this business is in its maturity phase, moving toward a decline.

The seeds and genomics segment (55% of sales and 69% of gross profits) consists of the global seeds and related traits businesses, and technology platforms based on plant genomics, which increases the speed and power of genetic research. MON's seeds and genomics segment focuses on corn, soybeans and other oilseeds, cotton, and wheat. Given the loss of patent protection for Roundup, we believe MON has focused on capturing value and profitability in its patent-protected seeds and traits business, and expanded its product line through its acquisition of Seminis in 2005. Given this trend, we think that the growth and margin outlook for MON's seeds and genomics segment is superior to that of its agricultural productivity segment.

Company Financials

Per Share Data ($) Year Ended Aug. 31	2006	2005	2004	2003	2002	2001	2000	1999	1998	1997
Tangible Book Value	NA	5.99	7.71	7.26	7.24	7.84	7.24	NM	NA	NA
Cash Flow	NA	1.21	1.37	0.56	1.12	1.61	1.40	1.59	NA	NA
Earnings	1.27	0.29	0.51	-0.02	0.25	0.57	0.34	0.52	NA	NA
S&P Core Earnings	NA	0.67	0.68	0.61	0.01	0.52	NA	NA	NA	NA
Dividends	0.39	0.33	0.27	0.25	0.24	0.23	Nil	NA	NA	NA
Payout Ratio	30%	113%	53%	NM	98%	40%	Nil	NA	NA	NA
Prices:High	48.45	39.93	28.22	14.45	17.00	19.40	13.69	NA	NA	NA
Prices:Low	37.91	25.00	14.04	6.78	6.60	13.44	9.88	NA	NA	NA
P/E Ratio:High	38	NM	55	NM	69	34	40	NA	NA	NA
P/E Ratio:Low	30	86	28	NM	27	24	29	NA	NA	NA
Income Statement Analysis (Million $)										
Revenue	NA	6,294	5,457	3,373	4,673	5,462	5,493	5,248	NA	NA
Operating Income	NA	1,503	1,254	768	882	1,335	1,216	1,179	NA	NA
Depreciation	NA	488	452	302	460	554	546	547	NA	NA
Interest Expense	NA	115	91.0	57.0	59.0	99.0	214	269	NA	NA
Pretax Income	NA	261	402	-38.0	202	463	334	263	NA	NA
Effective Tax Rate	NA	39.8%	32.6%	NM	36.1%	35.9%	47.6%	43.0%	NA	NA
Net Income	NA	157	271	-11.0	129	297	175	150	NA	NA
S&P Core Earnings	NA	363	362	317	5.45	277	NA	NA	NA	NA
Balance Sheet & Other Financial Data (Million $)										
Cash	NA	525	1,037	511	428	307	131	26.0	NA	NA
Current Assets	NA	4,644	4,931	4,962	4,424	4,797	4,973	4,027	NA	NA
Total Assets	NA	10,579	9,164	9,461	8,890	11,429	11,726	11,101	NA	NA
Current Liabilities	NA	2,159	1,894	1,944	1,810	2,377	2,757	1,704	NA	NA
Long Term Debt	NA	1,458	1,075	1,258	851	893	962	4,278	NA	NA
Common Equity	NA	5,613	5,258	5,156	5,180	7,483	7,341	4,645	NA	NA
Total Capital	NA	7,071	6,333	6,414	6,031	8,376	8,303	8,923	NA	NA
Capital Expenditures	NA	281	210	114	224	382	582	632	NA	NA
Cash Flow	NA	645	723	291	589	851	721	697	NA	NA
Current Ratio	NA	2.2	2.6	2.6	2.4	2.0	1.8	2.4	NA	NA
% Long Term Debt of Capitalization	NA	20.6	17.0	19.6	14.1	10.7	11.6	47.9	NA	NA
% Net Income of Revenue	NA	2.5	5.0	NM	2.8	5.4	3.2	2.9	NA	NA
% Return on Assets	NA	1.6	2.9	NM	1.3	2.6	1.5	1.4	NA	NA
% Return on Equity	NA	2.9	5.2	NM	2.0	4.0	2.9	3.4	NA	NA

Data as orig reptd.; bef. results of disc opers/spec. items. Per share data adj. for stk. divs.; EPS diluted. E-Estimated. NA-Not Available. NM Not Meaningful. NR-Not Ranked. UR-Under Review.

Office: 800 North Lindbergh Boulevard, St. Louis, MO 63167.
Telephone: 314-694-1000.
Email: info@monsanto.com
Website: http://www.monsanto.com

Chrmn, Pres & CEO: H. Grant
EVP & CFO: T.K. Crews
EVP & CTO: R.T. Fraley
SVP, Secy & General Counsel: D.F. Snively

VP & Treas: R.A. Paley
Investor Contact: S. Foster (314-694-8148)
Board of Directors: F. V. AtLee, III, J. Bachmann, H. Grant, A. H. Harper, G. S. King, S. R. Long, C. S. McMillan, W. U. Parfet, G. H. Poste, R. J. Stevens

Founded: 2000
Domicile: Delaware
Employees: 17,000

STANDARD &POOR'S

Monster Worldwide Inc

S&P Recommendation STRONG SELL ★★★★★

Price $40.51 (as of Oct 31, 2006)

12-Mo. Target Price $30.00

Investment Style Mid-Cap Value

GICS Sector Industrials
Sub-Industry Human Resource & Employment Services

Comment Monster Worldwide operates a multinational online careers network, and is a provider of recruitment advertising services.

Key Stock Statistics (Source S&P, Vickers, company reports)

52-Wk Range	**$59.99–33.82**	S&P Oper. EPS 2006**E**	**1.19**	P/E on S&P Oper. EPS 2006**E**	**34.0**	Dividend Rate/Share	**Nil**
Trailing 12-Month EPS	**$0.28**	S&P Oper. EPS 2007**E**	**1.40**	Common Shares Outstg. (M)	**128.4**	Yield (%)	**Nil**
Trailing 12-Month P/E	**NM**	S&P Core EPS 2006**E**	**1.19**	Market Capitalization(B)	**$5.007**	Beta	**3.57**
$10K Invested 5 Yrs Ago	**$12,662**	S&P Core EPS 2007**E**	**1.40**	Institutional Ownership (%)	**93**	S&P Credit Rating	**NA**

Price Performance

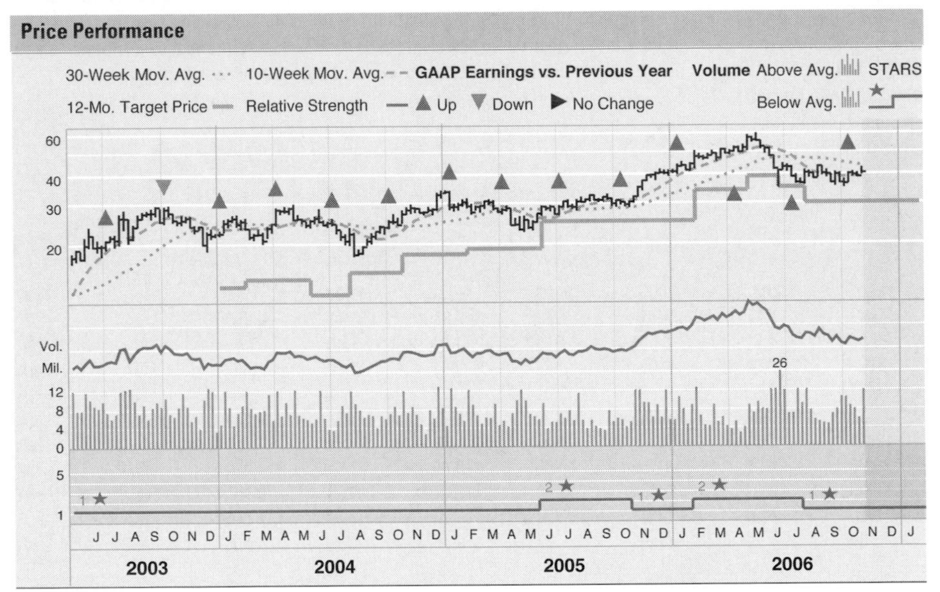

Options: ASE, CBOE, P

Analysis prepared by **Mark S. Basham** on July 27, 2006, when the stock traded at **$ 38.44**.

Highlights

- We estimate that 2006 revenues will increase 22%, to $1.2 billion, from $983 million in 2005, excluding divested operations. Revenue growth in the Monster division should be the stronger of MNST's two business segments, we think, with a 35% gain, as online recruitment continues to take share from newspaper and other recruiting channels. We look for international careers revenue growth of 55%, double the 27% we see for domestic careers.
- We think Monster has lost share in domestic job postings to its top rival, Careerbuilder.com. In addition, a second generation of online job sites, with more advanced features or a narrower focus on vertical markets, have begun to spring up. We see increasing competition, along with a slowing economy, resulting in a dramatic slowdown in 2007 revenue growth, to 9.6%.
- We think margins will continue to widen, albeit much less than in the past, on economies of scale across the company, with profitability rising faster than revenue. We estimate 2006 EPS of $1.29, a 40% increase from 2005's $0.92, followed by a 12% rise in 2007, to $1.45.

Investment Rationale/Risk

- We believe the current share price reflects online job listing growth expectations that are unrealistic over the long term, given our view that growth for this economic cycle peaked earlier this year. We think that MNST's S&P Quality Ranking of B- reflects the inherent cyclicality of employment services. Also, industry data show that competitors are gaining market share, albeit in a growing market, at MNST's expense. The unresolved issue of stock option backdating remains a risk, in our opinion.
- Risks to our recommendation and target price include the strengthening and extension of the current cyclical economic expansion beyond S&P's current expectations. Internationally, MNST could become more aggressive than it has been in pursuing industry consolidation through its active M&A program.
- Based on our discounted cash flow analysis, our 12-month target price is $30. Our DCF model assumes a weighted average cost of capital of 10.5%, two complete economic cycles over 14 years in which the rate of change in free cash ranges from -10% to 20%, and a terminal growth rate of 3%.

Qualitative Risk Assessment

LOW | MEDIUM | **HIGH**

Our risk assessment reflects the cyclicality of the help wanted industry, as it highly correlates with the economy. The company's domestic competitors have gained market share recently, reflecting, in our view, a commoditization of the online help wanted marketplace, where price has become a more important competitive factor. The company's foreign operations carry operating and foreign exchange rate risks that are not part of its domestic operations.

Quantitative Evaluations

S&P Quality Ranking **B-**

D | C | **B-** | B | B+ | A- | A | A+

Relative Strength Rank **MODERATE**

46

LOWEST = 1 HIGHEST = 99

Revenue/Earnings Data

Revenue (Million $)

	1Q	2Q	3Q	4Q	Year
2006	291.8	295.8	285.9	--	--
2005	232.1	239.0	249.3	266.6	986.9
2004	182.4	202.1	224.2	236.8	845.5
2003	168.5	166.7	173.7	170.8	679.6
2002	290.8	291.0	284.0	248.8	1,115
2001	362.8	383.6	361.2	326.1	1,448

Earnings Per Share ($)

2006	0.29	0.31	0.31	**E**0.34	**E**1.19
2005	0.19	0.21	0.25	0.28	0.92
2004	0.11	0.14	0.18	0.20	0.62
2003	-1.04	0.08	0.11	0.11	0.06
2002	0.06	-0.68	0.12	-0.46	-0.96
2001	0.05	0.17	0.23	0.16	0.61

Fiscal year ended Dec. 31. Next earnings report expected: Early February. EPS Estimates based on S&P Operating Earnings; historical GAAP earnings are as reported.

Dividend Data

No cash dividends have been paid.

Please read the Required Disclosures and Analyst Certification on the last page of this report.

Monster Worldwide Inc

Business Summary July 27, 2006

Monster Worldwide is a leading online recruitment and career management services provider through its Monster.com Web site. It also provides recruitment advertising and related services. MNST's clients include large global enterprises, including more than 90% of the Fortune 500, government organizations, and small to medium sized businesses in many markets in the U.S.

Among the most visited brands on the Internet, Monster (83% of revenue in 2005) at year-end 2005 had more than 61 million registered users (versus 56 million a year earlier) and 52 million resumes (46 million) in its database, according to company statistics. The Monster network connects companies with qualified job seekers, offering innovative technology and services that provide greater control over the recruiting process. The Monster.com global network consists of 26 local language and content sites in 24 countries, including the U.S., the U.K., Australia, Canada, Luxembourg, the Netherlands, Belgium, New Zealand, France, Singapore, Hong Kong, Germany, Spain, Ireland and India.

The company reports results for Monster in three segments: Careers North America (64% of division revenues), Careers International (23%), and Advertising & Fees (13%). Advertising & Fees collects revenues from display ads sold on Monster, click-throughs on links, advertiser leads and subscriptions to premium services.

Premium services include MonsterTRAK and Fastweb, which connect college students and alumni to college career centers and to college and scholarship sources. In 2004, the company expanded its product offerings through the acquisition of Tickle Inc. (www.tickle.com), a provider of career assessment and social networking services. Monster Government Solutions, which develops and markets recruitment portals and related tools for governments, expanded its offerings in 2004 with the purchase of Military Advantage, Inc. (www. military.com), with over four million members among Americans with military affinity.

Company Financials

Per Share Data ($) Year Ended Dec. 31	2005	2004	2003	2002	2001	2000	1999	1998	1997	1996
Tangible Book Value	1.47	0.27	0.18	2.02	2.61	5.16	0.18	NM	NM	NM
Cash Flow	1.22	0.92	0.31	-0.46	1.28	1.11	0.35	0.43	0.48	-0.93
Earnings	0.92	0.62	0.06	-0.90	0.81	0.53	-0.09	0.07	0.19	-1.36
S&P Core Earnings	0.36	0.37	-0.08	-1.48	0.10	NA	NA	NA	NA	NA
Dividends	Nil	Nil	Nil	Nil	Nil	Nil	Nil	Nil	Nil	Nil
Payout Ratio	Nil	Nil	Nil	Nil	Nil	Nil	Nil	Nil	Nil	Nil
Prices:High	42.03	34.25	29.65	48.13	68.73	94.69	80.50	21.31	14.38	7.13
Prices:Low	22.44	17.60	7.63	7.94	25.21	45.00	18.50	7.75	6.44	6.25
P/E Ratio:High	46	55	NM	NM	NM	NM	NM	NM	76	NM
P/E Ratio:Low	24	28	NM	NM	NM	NM	NM	NM	34	NM
Income Statement Analysis (Million $)										
Revenue	987	846	680	1,115	1,440	1,292	786	407	237	163
Operating Income	214	152	101	112	262	222	109	69.4	41.3	26.7
Depreciation	38.0	37.6	28.0	55.5	76.0	62.6	35.0	22.2	14.0	8.89
Interest Expense	Nil	Nil	Nil	4.90	10.6	9.49	17.0	13.7	11.0	14.6
Pretax Income	179	112	23.6	-130	125	114	-1.50	12.7	18.3	-48.5
Effective Tax Rate	35.8%	34.6%	69.0%	NM	46.1%	50.5%	NM	66.6%	46.7%	NM
Net Income	115	73.1	7.32	-107	69.0	56.9	-7.40	4.25	9.62	-52.2
S&P Core Earnings	45.7	44.0	-8.08	-165	11.4	NA	NA	NA	NA	NA
Balance Sheet & Other Financial Data (Million $)										
Cash	320	198	142	192	341	572	57.0	28.9	5.94	0.90
Current Assets	773	704	567	809	1,006	1,248	557	343	288	213
Total Assets	1,679	1,544	1,122	1,631	2,206	1,992	945	608	495	332
Current Liabilities	697	731	640	799	930	853	565	360	282	225
Long Term Debt	15.7	34.0	2.09	3.93	9.13	28.0	71.0	118	116	71.0
Common Equity	920	756	468	813	1,229	1,058	281	123	96.9	31.3
Total Capital	981	789	470	817	1,238	1,086	352	241	213	107
Capital Expenditures	39.8	24.3	21.6	46.7	73.6	78.9	NA	21.7	18.3	6.90
Cash Flow	153	111	35.4	-51.0	145	119	27.6	26.4	23.5	-43.6
Current Ratio	1.1	1.0	0.9	1.0	1.1	1.5	1.0	1.0	1.0	0.9
% Long Term Debt of Capitalization	1.6	4.3	0.4	0.5	0.7	2.6	NA	48.9	54.4	66.1
% Net Income of Revenue	11.7	8.6	1.1	NM	4.8	4.4	NM	1.0	4.1	NM
% Return on Assets	7.1	5.5	0.5	NM	3.2	3.7	NM	0.8	2.3	NM
% Return on Equity	13.7	11.9	1.1	NM	6.0	8.2	NM	3.9	14.8	NM

Data as orig reptd.; bef. results of disc opers/spec. items. Per share data adj. for stk. divs.; EPS diluted. E-Estimated. NA-Not Available. NM-Not Meaningful. NR-Not Ranked. UR-Under Review.

Office: 622 3rd Ave, New York, NY 10017-6707.
Telephone: 212-351-7000.
Email: corporate.communications@monsterworldwide.com
Website: http://www.monsterworldwide.com

Pres & CEO: W.M. Pastore
Investor Contact: C. Baker (212-351-7000)
SVP & CFO: C. Baker
SVP, Secy & General Counsel: M.F. Olesnyckyj

Board of Directors: G. R. Eisele, J. Gaulding, S. Iannuzzi, M. Kaufman, R. J. Kramer, W. M. Pastore, D. A. Stein, J. Swann

Founded: 1967
Domicile: Delaware
Employees: 4,800

STANDARD &POOR'S

Moody's Corp.

S&P Recommendation HOLD ★★★★★

Price $65.92 (as of Oct 27, 2006)

12-Mo. Target Price $67.00

Investment Style Large-Cap Value

GICS Sector Financials
Sub-Industry Specialized Finance

Comment Moody's is a leading global credit rating, research and risk analysis concern.

Key Stock Statistics (Source S&P, Vickers, company reports)

52-Wk Range	$73.29–49.76	S&P Oper. EPS 2006E	2.18	P/E on S&P Oper. EPS 2006E	30.2	Dividend Rate/Share	$0.28
Trailing 12-Month EPS	$2.11	S&P Oper. EPS 2007E	2.48	Common Shares Outstg. (M)	281.9	Yield (%)	0.42
Trailing 12-Month P/E	31.2	S&P Core EPS 2006E	2.18	Market Capitalization(B)	$18.583	Beta	0.21
$10K Invested 5 Yrs Ago	$37,453	S&P Core EPS 2007E	2.48	Institutional Ownership (%)	88	S&P Credit Rating	NA

Price Performance

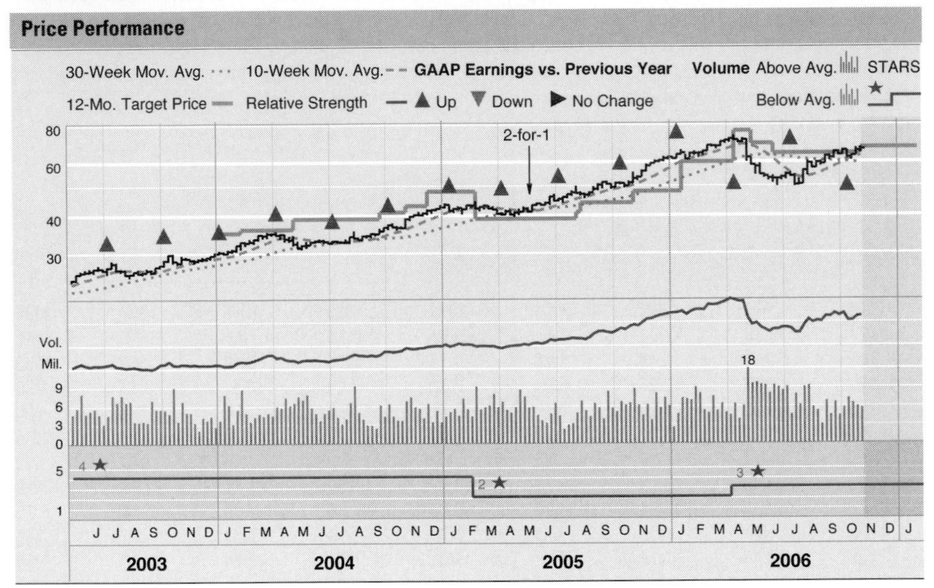

Options: ASE

Qualitative Risk Assessment

LOW | **MEDIUM** | HIGH

Our risk assessment reflects Moody's significant market share in what we view as a high barrier to entry ratings industry, and the company's net positive balance sheet cash position, offset by ratings business sensitivity to higher interest rates, and the possibility of regulatory reform designed to increase competition.

Quantitative Evaluations

S&P Quality Ranking B+

D | C | B- | B | **B+** | A- | A | A+

Relative Strength Rank STRONG

75

LOWEST = 1 HIGHEST = 99

Highlights

➤ The 12-month target price for MCO has recently been changed to $67.00 from $64.00. The Highlights section of this Stock Report will be updated accordingly.

Investment Rationale/Risk

➤ The Investment Rationale/Risk section of this Stock Report will be updated shortly. For the latest News story on MCO from MarketScope, see below.

➤ 10/25/06 12:04 pm EDT... S&P MAINTAINS HOLD RECOMMENDATION ON SHARES OF MOODY'S CORP. (MCO 64.5***): Excluding the impact of one-time items, MCO posts Q3 EPS of $0.55 vs. $0.44, $0.02 above our estimate. Revenues rose 18%, led by a 25% advance in structured finance. Operating margin declined 82 bps to 54.2% on higher option expense. While we see U.S. revenue growth moderating as the economy softens, we believe the impact will be cushioned by continued strong international growth. Thus, we are increasing our '06 and '07 EPS estimates to $2.18 and $2.48 from $2.11 and $2.36. We are raising our target price to $67 from $64 on revised blend of relative value and DCF analyses. /J.Peters-CFA

Revenue/Earnings Data

Revenue (Million $)

	1Q	2Q	3Q	4Q	Year
2006	440.2	511.4	495.5	--	--
2005	390.5	446.8	421.1	473.2	1,732
2004	331.2	357.6	357.9	391.6	1,438
2003	278.2	312.7	305.0	350.7	1,247
2002	231.6	271.5	248.3	271.9	1,023
2001	180.2	205.2	190.4	220.9	796.7

Earnings Per Share ($)

2006	0.49	0.59	0.55	E0.57	E2.18
2005	0.39	0.47	0.48	0.50	1.84
2004	0.34	0.34	0.32	0.40	1.40
2003	0.31	0.33	0.28	0.28	1.20
2002	0.23	0.25	0.22	0.23	0.92
2001	0.15	0.17	0.16	0.19	0.66

Fiscal year ended Dec. 31. Next earnings report expected: Early February. EPS Estimates based on S&P Operating Earnings; historical GAAP earnings are as reported.

Dividend Data (Dates: mm/dd Payment Date: mm/dd/yy)

Amount ($)	Date Decl.	Ex-Div. Date	Stk. of Record	Payment Date
0.070	12/13	02/15	02/20	03/10/06
0.070	04/25	05/17	05/20	06/10/06
0.070	08/01	08/16	08/20	09/10/06
0.070	10/24	11/16	11/20	12/10/06

Dividends have been paid since 1934. Source: Company reports.

Moody's Corp.

Business Summary September 05, 2006

Moody's Investors Service and the Dun & Bradstreet (D&B) operating company were separated into stand-alone entities on September 30, 2000. Old D&B changed its name to Moody's Corp. (MCO), and new D&B assumed the name Dun & Bradstreet Corp. (DNB).

Moody's is a provider of credit ratings, research and analysis covering debt instruments and securities in the global capital markets, and a provider of quantitative credit assessment services, credit training services and credit process software to banks and other financial institutions. Moody's credit ratings and research help investors analyze the credit risks associated with fixed-income securities. Beyond credit rating services for issuers, Moody's provides research services, data, and analytic tools that are utilized by institutional investors and other credit and capital markets professionals.

Moody's provides ratings and credit research on governmental and commercial entities in approximately 100 countries, and its customers include a wide range of corporate and governmental issuers of securities as well as institutional investors, depositors, creditors, investment banks, commercial banks, and other financial intermediaries. In 2005, no single customer accounted for 10% or more of total revenue.

Moody's operates in two reportable segments: Moody's Investors Service, and Moody's KMV. Moody's Investors Service consists of a research group (12% of 2005 revenues) and four ratings groups: structured finance (41%), corporate finance (19%), financial institutions and sovereign risk (15%), and public finance (5%). The research group primarily generates revenue from the sale of investor-oriented credit research, principally produced by the ratings groups. The ratings groups generate revenue principally from the assignment of credit ratings on fixed-income instruments in the debt markets.

Company Financials

Per Share Data ($) Year Ended Dec. 31	**2005**	**2004**	**2003**	**2002**	**2001**	**2000**	**1999**	**1998**	**1997**	**1996**
Tangible Book Value	0.30	0.39	NM	NM	NM	NM	NM	NM	NM	NM
Cash Flow	1.95	1.51	1.30	1.00	0.72	0.54	1.21	1.13	1.02	0.08
Earnings	1.84	1.40	1.20	0.92	0.66	0.49	0.78	0.72	0.64	-0.35
S&P Core Earnings	1.83	1.35	1.12	0.85	0.64	NA	NA	NA	NA	NA
Dividends	0.20	0.15	0.09	0.07	0.11	0.28	0.37	0.41	0.44	0.91
Payout Ratio	11%	11%	8%	7%	17%	57%	47%	56%	69%	NM
Prices:High	62.50	43.86	30.43	26.20	20.55	18.09	20.00	18.34	15.63	34.50
Prices:Low	39.55	29.85	19.75	17.90	12.78	11.31	11.69	10.88	11.56	9.63
P/E Ratio:High	34	31	25	29	31	37	26	25	36	NM
P/E Ratio:Low	21	21	17	20	19	23	15	15	18	NM

Income Statement Analysis (Million $)	2005	2004	2003	2002	2001	2000	1999	1998	1997	1996
Revenue	1,732	1,438	1,247	1,023	797	602	1,972	1,935	1,811	1,783
Operating Income	975	820	696	563	410	305	621	591	536	198
Depreciation	35.2	34.1	32.6	25.0	17.0	16.6	141	142	132	141
Interest Expense	21.0	16.2	21.8	21.0	16.5	3.60	5.00	12.0	53.0	37.0
Pretax Income	935	771	656	517	382	284	457	400	332	-14.0
Effective Tax Rate	40.0%	44.9%	44.6%	44.1%	44.4%	44.2%	39.1%	38.5%	34.0%	NM
Net Income	561	425	364	289	212	159	256	246	219	-116
S&P Core Earnings	558	413	340	269	203	NA	NA	NA	NA	NA

Balance Sheet & Other Financial Data (Million $)	2005	2004	2003	2002	2001	2000	1999	1998	1997	1996
Cash	486	606	269	40.0	163	119	113	91.0	82.0	128
Current Assets	1,052	1,023	569	272	371	278	785	764	806	760
Total Assets	1,457	1,376	941	631	505	398	1,786	1,789	2,225	2,294
Current Liabilities	579	837	432	462	359	253	1,415	1,353	1,497	2,008
Long Term Debt	300	Nil	300	300	300	300	Nil	Nil	Nil	Nil
Common Equity	309	318	-32.1	-327	-304	-283	-417	-371	-490	-455
Total Capital	609	318	268	-27.0	-4.10	17.5	-115	-70.0	-188	-455
Capital Expenditures	31.3	21.3	17.9	18.0	14.8	12.3	44.1	55.0	51.0	58.0
Cash Flow	596	459	397	314	229	175	397	388	351	25.0
Current Ratio	1.8	1.2	1.3	0.6	1.0	1.1	0.6	0.6	0.5	0.4
% Long Term Debt of Capitalization	49.2	Nil	112.0	NM	NM	NM	Nil	Nil	Nil	Nil
% Net Income of Revenue	32.4	29.6	29.2	28.2	26.6	26.3	13.0	12.7	12.1	NM
% Return on Assets	39.4	36.5	46.3	50.9	47.0	47.1	14.3	NA	10.2	NM
% Return on Equity	178.9	297.9	NM	NM	NM	NM	NM	NM	NM	NM

Data as orig reptd.; bef. results of disc opers/spec. items. Per share data adj. for stk. divs.; EPS diluted. E-Estimated. NA-Not Available. NM-Not Meaningful. NR-Not Ranked. UR-Under Review.

Office: 99 Church Street, New York, NY 10007-2707.
Telephone: 212-553-0300.
Website: http://www.moodys.com
Chrmn & CEO: R.W. McDaniel, Jr.

EVP & CFO: L. Huber
SVP & General Counsel: J.J. Goggins
SVP & Cntlr: J. McCabe
Investor Contact: M.D. Courtian (212-553-7194)

Board of Directors: B. L. Anderson, R. R. Glauber, E. Kist, C. Mack, R. W. McDaniel, Jr., H. A. McKinnell, Jr., N. S. Newcomb, J. K. Wulff

Founded: 1998
Domicile: Delaware
Employees: 2,900

STANDARD &POOR'S

Morgan Stanley

S&P Recommendation HOLD ★★★★★

Price $76.44 (as of Oct 27, 2006)

12-Mo. Target Price $75.00

Investment Style Large-Cap Value

GICS Sector Financials
Sub-Industry Investment Banking & Brokerage

Comment Morgan Stanley is among the largest securities firms in the United States, with operations in the brokerage, underwriting and credit card businesses.

Key Stock Statistics (Source S&P, Vickers, company reports)

52-Wk Range	$78.20–51.90	S&P Oper. EPS 2006E	6.58	P/E on S&P Oper. EPS 2006E	11.6	Dividend Rate/Share	$1.08
Trailing 12-Month EPS	$7.27	S&P Oper. EPS 2007E	6.53	Common Shares Outstg. (M)	1,058.6	Yield (%)	1.41
Trailing 12-Month P/E	10.5	S&P Core EPS 2006E	6.58	Market Capitalization(B)	$80.916	Beta	1.66
$10K Invested 5 Yrs Ago	$16,155	S&P Core EPS 2007E	6.53	Institutional Ownership (%)	68	S&P Credit Rating	A+

Price Performance

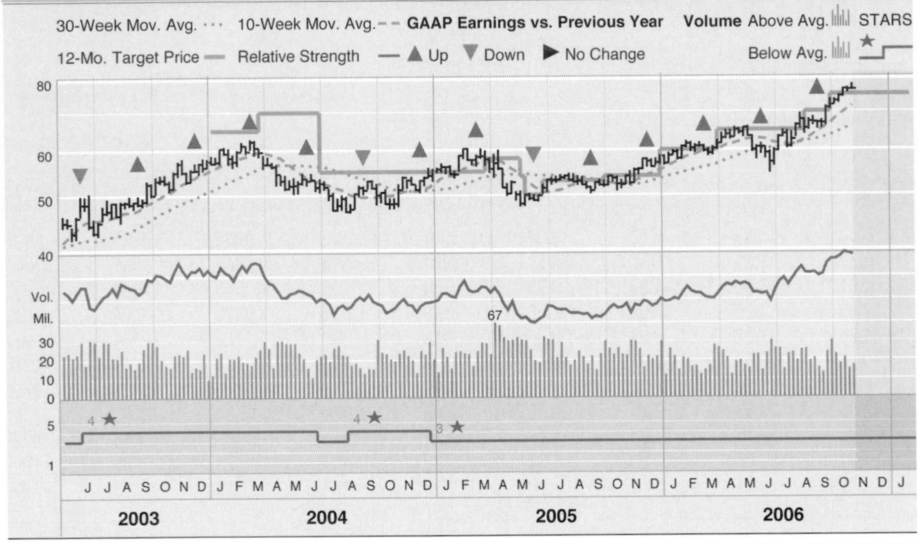

30-Week Mov. Avg. 10-Week Mov. Avg. GAAP Earnings vs. Previous Year Volume Above Avg. STARS
12-Mo. Target Price Relative Strength ▲ Up ▼ Down ▶ No Change Below Avg.

Vol. Mil.

J J A S O N D J F M A M J J A S O N D J F M A M J J A S O N D J F M A M J J A S O N D J
2003 2004 2005 2006

Options: ASE, CBOE, P, Ph

Analysis prepared by **Mark Hebeka, CFA** on September 21, 2006, when the stock traded at **$ 72.09**.

Highlights

- We think MS maintains a strong competitive position in its institutional securities business, its largest segment. However, we believe its retail brokerage, credit card and asset management businesses lack competitive advantages. We also expect an increase in compensation costs to hurt profitability as the company tries to retain and attract high profile executives.
- We see continued growth in MS's trading revenue in FY 06 (Nov.), and we expect the company to allocate additional capital to that business, notably to its prime brokerage and leveraged finance businesses. We look for competitive challenges to limit revenue growth in the Discover Credit Services segment, but expect the company to retain the business, despite industry consolidation.
- We forecast EPS of $6.58 for FY 06 and $6.53 in FY 07, aided by higher trading and investment banking revenues, but hurt by a flattened yield curve, increasing compensation costs, and higher credit card loan losses.

Investment Rationale/Risk

- We think the company's institutional securities business, its largest segment, is well positioned, but we see MS losing market share in its retail brokerage, credit card and asset management businesses. We have a hold opinion on the shares based on valuation.
- Risks to our recommendation and target price include stock market declines, wider credit spreads, and regulatory issues, notably in the brokerage segment. Trading revenue can be highly volatile from quarter to quarter, reducing earnings consistency. We also have concerns about corporate governance regarding generous compensation policies, and reserve adequacy in the Coleman Holdings lawsuit.
- The shares recently traded at a significant discount to the overall market and the stock's 10-year historical average of nearly 15X price to earnings. Although MS shares have underperformed peers in recent years, we view their valuation as appropriate. Our 12-month target price of $75 is equal to about 11.5X our FY 07 EPS estimate and is comparable to the company's largest peers.

Qualitative Risk Assessment

LOW | **MEDIUM** | HIGH

Our risk assessment reflects our favorable view of the company's diversification by product and by region, offset by our concerns about corporate governance and our view that certain segments lack competitive advantages.

Quantitative Evaluations

S&P Quality Ranking A-

D | C | B- | B | B+ | **A-** | A | A+

Relative Strength Rank STRONG

77

LOWEST = 1 HIGHEST = 99

Revenue/Earnings Data

Revenue (Million $)

	1Q	2Q	3Q	4Q	Year
2006	18,119	19,062	20,055	--	--
2005	11,641	11,845	13,157	15,525	52,081
2004	9,992	9,802	9,854	10,420	39,549
2003	8,502	8,418	8,929	9,092	34,933
2002	8,540	8,149	8,156	7,570	32,415
2001	12,644	12,569	10,296	8,218	43,727

Earnings Per Share ($)

2006	1.50	1.85	1.75	E1.43	E6.58
2005	1.23	0.86	1.09	1.69	4.81
2004	1.11	1.10	0.78	1.09	4.08
2003	0.82	0.55	1.15	0.92	3.45
2002	0.76	0.72	0.55	0.67	2.69
2001	0.94	0.82	0.65	0.78	3.19

Fiscal year ended Nov. 30. Next earnings report expected: Late December. EPS Estimates based on S&P Operating Earnings; historical GAAP earnings are as reported.

Dividend Data (Dates: mm/dd Payment Date: mm/dd/yy)

Amount ($)	Date Decl.	Ex-Div. Date	Stk. of Record	Payment Date
0.270	12/21	01/11	01/13	01/31/06
0.270	03/23	04/11	04/13	04/28/06
0.270	06/21	07/12	07/14	07/31/06
0.270	09/21	10/11	10/13	10/31/06

Dividends have been paid since 1993. Source: Company reports.

Morgan Stanley

Business Summary September 21, 2006

Morgan Stanley (MS) is a global financial services company that operates in four business segments: institutional securities, individual investor group, investment management and credit services. We are impressed with the company's institutional securities segment, which maintains high margins and strong market share in merger and acquisitions advisory, initial public equity offerings, and global debt issues. We remain concerned about increasing competition from the largest global commercial banks, which are focused on gaining market share in investment banking.

We expect legal costs for MS to remain at a high level. In April 2003, MS agreed to pay $125 million as part of a $1.4 billion settlement with regulators regarding allegations of conflicts of interest in investment research. In April 2005, MS increased its reserve with respect to the Coleman Holdings litigation to $360 million, and in May 2005, reaffirmed its intention to appeal the verdict and punitive damages.

We view the company's corporate governance policies negatively. Although we view favorably the replacement of chairman and CEO Philip Purcell, we think headcount reductions, continued media attention, and our view of diminished employee morale will negatively affect revenue growth in FY 06 (Nov.). We are disappointed that MS approved what we view as excessive, guaranteed compensation packages for certain current and former executives.

Company Financials

Per Share Data ($) Year Ended Nov. 30	**2005**	**2004**	**2003**	**2002**	**2001**	**2000**	**1999**	**1998**	**1997**	**1996**
Tangible Book Value	25.23	23.93	21.52	19.43	17.36	16.91	14.79	11.88	10.99	8.69
Earnings	4.81	4.08	3.45	2.69	3.19	4.73	4.10	2.76	2.13	1.40
S&P Core Earnings	5.00	4.18	3.48	2.38	2.84	NA	NA	NA	NA	NA
Dividends	1.08	1.00	0.92	0.92	0.92	0.80	0.48	0.40	0.28	0.22
Payout Ratio	22%	25%	27%	34%	29%	17%	12%	14%	13%	16%
Prices:High	60.51	62.83	58.78	60.02	90.49	110.00	71.44	48.75	29.75	17.25
Prices:Low	47.66	46.54	32.46	28.80	35.75	58.63	35.41	18.25	16.38	11.25
P/E Ratio:High	13	15	17	22	28	23	17	18	14	12
P/E Ratio:Low	10	11	9	11	11	12	9	7	8	8
Income Statement Analysis (Million $)										
Net Interest Income	3,750	3,731	2,935	3,896	3,348	3,058	2,365	2,922	2,777	2,021
Non Interest Income	23,906	20,959	19,189	16,549	19,600	24,179	20,110	14,656	13,549	5,441
Loan Loss Provision	878	925	1,267	1,336	1,052	810	529	1,173	1,493	1,232
Non Interest Expenses	20,857	18,333	16,636	15,725	17,264	18,746	14,281	15,530	12,052	5,917
% Expense/Operating Revenue	84.2%	80.8%	79.9%	81.3%	84.6%	79.5%	75.7%	81.1%	78.7%	69.2%
Pretax Income	7,050	6,312	5,334	4,633	5,684	8,526	7,728	5,385	4,274	1,545
Effective Tax Rate	26.4%	28.6%	29.0%	35.5%	36.5%	36.0%	38.0%	37.0%	39.5%	38.4%
Net Income	5,192	4,509	3,787	2,988	3,610	5,456	4,791	3,393	2,586	951
% Net Interest Margin	NA	NA	5.40	5.50	5.57	6.08	8.47	9.00	8.45	8.16
S&P Core Earnings	5,401	4,624	3,830	2,658	3,203	NA	NA	NA	NA	NA
Balance Sheet & Other Financial Data (Million $)										
Money Market Assets	174,330	123,041	78,205	76,910	54,618	50,992	70,366	90,101	6,890	4,044
Investment Securities	304,172	260,640	228,904	185,588	164,011	130,818	112,042	41,689	35,801	4,477
Earning Assets:Total Loans	23,754	21,169	20,384	24,322	20,955	21,870	20,229	22,388	24,499	23,177
Total Assets	898,523	775,410	602,843	529,499	482,628	426,794	366,967	317,590	302,287	42,414
Demand Deposits	2,629	1,117	1,264	1,441	1,741	1,589	1,458	1,355	1,210	1,716
Time Deposits	16,034	12,660	11,575	12,316	10,535	10,341	8,939	6,842	7,783	5,497
Long Term Debt	110,465	95,286	68,410	43,985	40,851	36,830	28,604	27,435	18,627	8,144
Common Equity	29,248	28,272	24,933	21,951	20,437	18,796	16,344	13,445	14,079	5,165
% Return on Assets	0.6	0.7	0.7	0.6	0.8	1.4	1.4	NA	1.5	2.4
% Return on Equity	18.9	16.9	16.2	14.1	18.2	30.3	30.3	25.2	26.2	19.0
% Loan Loss Reserve	3.5	4.5	4.9	3.8	4.0	3.6	3.7	NA	NA	3.5
% Loans/Deposits	127.3	153.7	158.8	176.8	170.7	183.3	229.2	272.8	294.2	322.4
% Loans/Assets	2.7	3.0	3.9	4.5	4.7	5.4	6.2	7.5	13.8	53.6
% Equity to Assets	3.3	3.9	4.1	4.2	4.3	4.5	4.4	4.3	5.6	12.4

Data as orig reptd.; bef. results of disc opers/spec. items. Per share data adj. for stk. divs.; EPS diluted. E-Estimated. NA-Not Available. NM-Not Meaningful. NR-Not Ranked. UR-Under Review.

Office: 1585 Broadway, New York, NY 10036.
Telephone: 212-761-4000.
Website: http://www.morganstanley.com
Chrmn & CEO: J.J. Mack

Vice Chrmn: R.A. Kindler
Vice Chrmn: J. Anda
EVP & Chief Admin: S. Crawford
EVP, Secy & General Counsel: D.G. Kempf, Jr.

Investor Contact: W. Pike (212-761-4472)
Board of Directors: R. J. Bostock, E. B. Bowles, H. J. Davies, C. R. Kidder, J. J. Mack, D. T. Nicolaisen, C. H. Noski, H. S. Olayan, C. E. Phillips, Jr., O. G. Sexton, L. D. Tyson, K. Zumwinkel

Auditor: Deloitte & Touche
Founded: 1981
Domicile: Delaware
Employees: 53,218

STANDARD &POOR'S

Motorola Inc.

S&P Recommendation HOLD ★★★★★	Price	12-Mo. Target Price	Investment Style
	$23.06 (as of Oct 31, 2006)	$25.00	Large-Cap Value

GICS Sector Information Technology
Sub-Industry Communications Equipment

Comment This leading supplier of cellular telephone systems, semiconductors, two-way radios and paging equipment also offers information systems and other electronics products.

Key Stock Statistics (Source S&P, Vickers, company reports)

52-Wk Range	$26.30–18.66	S&P Oper. EPS 2006E	1.27	P/E on S&P Oper. EPS 2006E	18.2	Dividend Rate/Share	$0.20
Trailing 12-Month EPS	$1.68	S&P Oper. EPS 2007E	1.45	Common Shares Outstg. (M)	2,450.0	Yield (%)	0.87
Trailing 12-Month P/E	13.7	S&P Core EPS 2006E	1.03	Market Capitalization(B)	$56.498	Beta	1.20
$10K Invested 5 Yrs Ago	$15,930	S&P Core EPS 2007E	1.45	Institutional Ownership (%)	72	S&P Credit Rating	A-

Price Performance

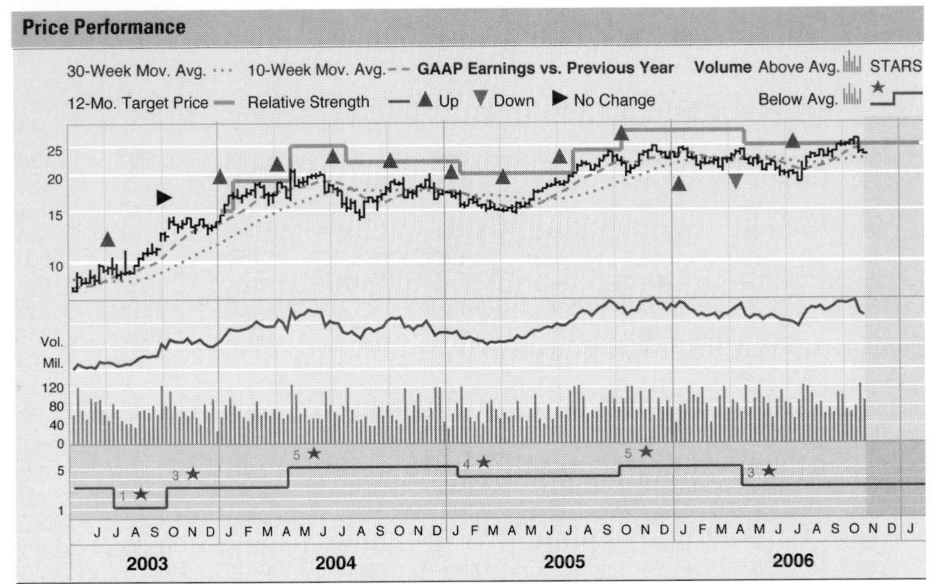

Options: ASE, CBOE, P, Ph

Analysis prepared by **Kenneth M. Leon, CPA** on October 18, 2006, when the stock traded at **$ 23.52**.

Highlights

- Following an estimated 21% sales increase in 2006, we expect sales to rise 10% to 12% in 2007, as we see MOT's leading businesses in mobile devices and homeland security systems supporting growth. MOT's 2006 first nine months sales of mobile devices advanced 38%, year to year, and accounted for more than two thirds of total sales. We continue to be disappointed with sales of MOT's networks and enterprise systems.
- For 2007, we forecast that the handset unit will realize an 11% sales advance, but we do not see growth above 7% for the Networks and Enterprise and Connected Home Solutions units. We foresee gross margins for 2006 and 2007 in the 31%-32% range. We expect MOT to control other operating costs.
- Our operating EPS estimates (excluding special items) are $1.27 for 2006 and $1.45 for 2007, which includes $0.08 for projected stock option expense in both years. With $16.1 billion in cash and cash equivalents with investments, the company may continue to repurchase its common shares.

Investment Rationale/Risk

- In our opinion, MOT is well positioned to grow its handset and broadband businesses and use its free cash flow to retire long-term debt, make some tactical acquisitions, and repurchase common shares. Our concerns rest with MOT's ability to achieve 10% or more sales growth from its Networks and Enterprise and Connected Home Solutions units.
- Risks to our recommendation and target price include failure to successfully introduce and ship new products and technologies; a slowdown in telecom equipment capital spending; and the growing purchasing power of MOT's largest customers.
- We think the shares, priced below peers at 1.1X our 2006 sales per share estimate, are benefiting from stronger global demand for wireless products, and from the company's momentum in handsets. Applying an assumed P/E multiple of 17.2X to our 2007 EPS estimate, or a price to sales ratio of 1.3X our 2007 sales per share estimate, near peers, we arrive at our 12-month target price of $25.

Qualitative Risk Assessment

LOW | **MEDIUM** | HIGH

The company is exposed to the economic health of the telecom and broadband industries and the risks related to high volume manufacturing and distribution to service providers. Despite intense vendor competition, our medium risk assessment takes into account our view of MOT's product leadership and strong balance sheet.

Quantitative Evaluations

S&P Quality Ranking **B+**

D | C | B- | B | **B+** | A- | A | A+

Relative Strength Rank **WEAK**

21

LOWEST = 1 HIGHEST = 99

Revenue/Earnings Data

Revenue (Million $)

	1Q	2Q	3Q	4Q	Year
2006	10,013	10,876	10,603	--	--
2005	8,161	8,825	9,424	10,433	36,843
2004	7,441	7,541	7,499	8,842	31,323
2003	6,043	6,163	6,829	8,023	27,058
2002	6,021	6,741	6,371	7,546	26,679
2001	7,752	7,522	7,406	7,324	30,004

Earnings Per Share ($)

2006	0.27	0.54	--	**E**0.39	**E**1.27
2005	0.28	0.38	0.69	0.47	1.82
2004	0.19	0.25	0.18	0.28	0.90
2003	0.07	0.05	0.05	0.20	0.38
2002	-0.20	-1.02	0.05	0.08	-1.09
2001	-0.24	-0.35	-0.64	-0.55	-1.78

Fiscal year ended Dec. 31. Next earnings report expected: Mid January. EPS Estimates based on S&P Operating Earnings; historical GAAP earnings are as reported.

Dividend Data (Dates: mm/dd Payment Date: mm/dd/yy)

Amount ($)	Date Decl.	Ex-Div. Date	Stk. of Record	Payment Date
0.040	11/15	12/13	12/15	01/13/06
0.040	02/14	03/13	03/15	04/14/06
0.050	05/01	06/13	06/15	07/15/06
0.050	07/26	09/13	09/15	10/13/06

Dividends have been paid since 1942. Source: Company reports.

Motorola Inc.

Business Summary October 18, 2006

CORPORATE OVERVIEW. Motorola is a leader in wireless and networking solutions for cable, fixed-line and wireless service providers. We believe all three markets are exposed to increased buyer's power with industry consolidation of service providers.

MARKET PROFILE. The Mobile Devices segment (66% of 2006 third quarter sales) primarily manufactures wireless handsets in all three major digital standards: GSM, TDMA and CDMA. Year over year, as of September 30, 2006, MOT increased its global handset market share to 22.4% from 18.6% in wireless handset shipments. We believe MOT's mobile device segment can sustain 2006 operating margins in the 11% to 12% range.

Networks and Enterprise (26%) encompasses the wireless and wireline infrastructure businesses, large enterprises and governments. Delayed spending from major carriers has slowed sales growth in the 2006 third quarter. We see price pressure from the largest service providers, which may lead to margins remaining in the 13%-15% range, compared to the historical levels in the mid- to upper teens. Connected Home Solutions (8%) consists of products such as digital set-top box converters, cable modems and other home devices. We believe key customers have slowed down capital spending.

IMPACT OF MAJOR DEVELOPMENTS. In March 2006, the company announced a reorganization to combine the Networks and Government and Enterprise Mobility Solutions Groups with financial reporting in the new format for the second quarter of 2006. We believe both businesses can attain synergy cost savings, but we are not confident the planned reorganization will produce faster sales growth.

In September 2006, MOT signed a definitive merger agreement to acquire all the outstanding shares of Symbol Technologies for $15 a share, or approximately $3.9 billion. We believe the merger will strengthen MOT's enterprise and government wireless business with Symbol's wide range of major customers around the world, particularly in vertical markets such as retail, travel and transportation, manufacturing, wholesale distribution and health care.

Company Financials

Per Share Data ($) Year Ended Dec. 31	**2005**	**2004**	**2003**	**2002**	**2001**	**2000**	**1999**	**1998**	**1997**	**1996**
Tangible Book Value	6.67	5.45	5.43	4.85	6.07	8.50	8.89	6.78	7.40	6.63
Cash Flow	2.06	1.15	1.09	-0.17	-0.63	1.70	1.60	0.69	1.91	1.89
Earnings	1.82	0.90	0.38	-1.09	-1.78	0.58	0.44	-0.54	0.65	0.63
S&P Core Earnings	1.18	0.78	0.08	-0.93	-2.23	NA	NA	NA	NA	NA
Dividends	0.16	0.16	0.16	0.16	0.16	0.16	0.16	0.16	0.16	0.15
Payout Ratio	9%	18%	42%	NM	NM	28%	37%	NM	25%	24%
Prices:High	24.99	20.89	14.40	17.12	25.13	61.54	49.83	21.96	30.17	22.83
Prices:Low	14.48	13.83	7.59	7.30	10.50	15.81	20.85	12.79	18.00	14.71
P/E Ratio:High	14	23	38	NM	NM	NM	NM	NM	47	36
P/E Ratio:Low	8	15	20	NM	NM	NM	NM	NM	28	23

Income Statement Analysis (Million $)	2005	2004	2003	2002	2001	2000	1999	1998	1997	1996
Revenue	36,843	31,323	27,058	26,679	30,004	37,580	30,931	29,398	29,794	27,973
Operating Income	4,851	3,887	2,694	2,059	-2,595	4,544	3,279	3,019	4,276	4,268
Depreciation	613	659	1,667	2,108	2,552	2,522	2,182	2,197	2,329	2,308
Interest Expense	325	199	295	668	645	494	305	301	216	249
Pretax Income	6,520	3,252	1,293	-3,446	-5,511	2,231	1,168	-1,374	1,816	1,775
Effective Tax Rate	29.5%	32.6%	30.9%	NM	NM	40.9%	30.1%	NM	35.0%	35.0%
Net Income	4,599	2,191	893	-2,485	-3,937	1,318	817	-962	1,180	1,154
S&P Core Earnings	2,964	1,899	164	-2,084	-4,893	NA	NA	NA	NA	NA

Balance Sheet & Other Financial Data (Million $)	2005	2004	2003	2002	2001	2000	1999	1998	1997	1996
Cash	14,641	10,556	7,877	6,507	6,082	3,301	3,345	1,453	1,445	1,811
Current Assets	27,869	21,082	17,907	17,134	17,149	19,885	16,503	13,531	13,236	11,319
Total Assets	35,649	30,889	32,098	31,152	33,398	42,343	37,327	28,728	27,278	24,076
Current Liabilities	12,488	10,573	9,433	9,810	9,698	16,257	12,416	11,440	9,055	7,995
Long Term Debt	3,806	4,578	7,161	7,674	8,857	4,778	3,573	2,633	2,144	1,931
Common Equity	16,673	13,331	12,689	11,239	13,691	18,612	16,344	12,222	13,272	11,795
Total Capital	20,479	17,909	19,850	18,913	22,548	24,894	23,398	16,043	17,038	14,834
Capital Expenditures	583	494	655	607	1,321	4,131	2,684	3,221	2,874	2,973
Cash Flow	5,212	2,850	2,560	-377	-1,385	3,840	2,999	1,235	3,509	3,462
Current Ratio	2.2	2.0	1.9	1.7	1.8	1.2	1.3	1.2	1.5	1.4
% Long Term Debt of Capitalization	18.6	25.6	36.1	40.6	39.3	19.2	15.3	16.4	12.6	13.0
% Net Income of Revenue	12.5	7.0	3.3	NM	NM	3.5	2.6	NM	4.0	4.1
% Return on Assets	13.8	7.0	2.8	NM	NM	3.2	2.5	NM	4.6	4.9
% Return on Equity	30.7	16.8	7.5	NM	NM	7.1	5.7	NM	9.4	10.1

Data as orig reptd.; bef. results of disc opers/spec. items. Per share data adj. for stk. divs.; EPS diluted. E-Estimated. NA-Not Available. NM-Not Meaningful. NR-Not Ranked. UR-Under Review.

Office: 1303 East Algonquin Road, Schaumburg, IL 60196.
Telephone: 800-262-8509.
Email: investors@motorola.com
Website: http://www.motorola.com

Chrmn & CEO: E.J. Zander
EVP & CFO: D. Devonshire
EVP & CTO: P. Warrior
EVP, Secy & General Counsel: A.P. Lawson

Investor Contact: E. Gams (847-576-6873)
Board of Directors: D. Dorman, H. L. Fuller, J. C. Lewent, T. J. Meredith, N. Negroponte, I. Nooyi, S. C. Scott III, R. Sommer, J. Stengel, D. A. Warner III, J. A. White, M. D. White, E. J. Zander

Founded: 1928
Domicile: Delaware
Employees: 69,000

STANDARD &POOR'S

M&T Bank Corp

S&P Recommendation HOLD ★★★★★

Price $121.20 (as of Oct 27, 2006)

12-Mo. Target Price $127.00

Investment Style Large-Cap Growth

GICS Sector Financials
Sub-Industry Regional Banks

Comment This New York bank holding company is the parent of M&T Bank and M&T Bank, N.A.

Key Stock Statistics (Source S&P, Vickers, company reports)

52-Wk Range	$124.98–105.64	S&P Oper. EPS 2006E	7.36	P/E on S&P Oper. EPS 2006E	16.5	Dividend Rate/Share	$2.40
Trailing 12-Month EPS	$7.27	S&P Oper. EPS 2007E	8.19	Common Shares Outstg. (M)	111.0	Yield (%)	1.98
Trailing 12-Month P/E	16.7	S&P Core EPS 2006E	7.37	Market Capitalization(B)	$13.454	Beta	0.37
$10K Invested 5 Yrs Ago	$19,129	S&P Core EPS 2007E	8.19	Institutional Ownership (%)	66	S&P Credit Rating	NA

Price Performance

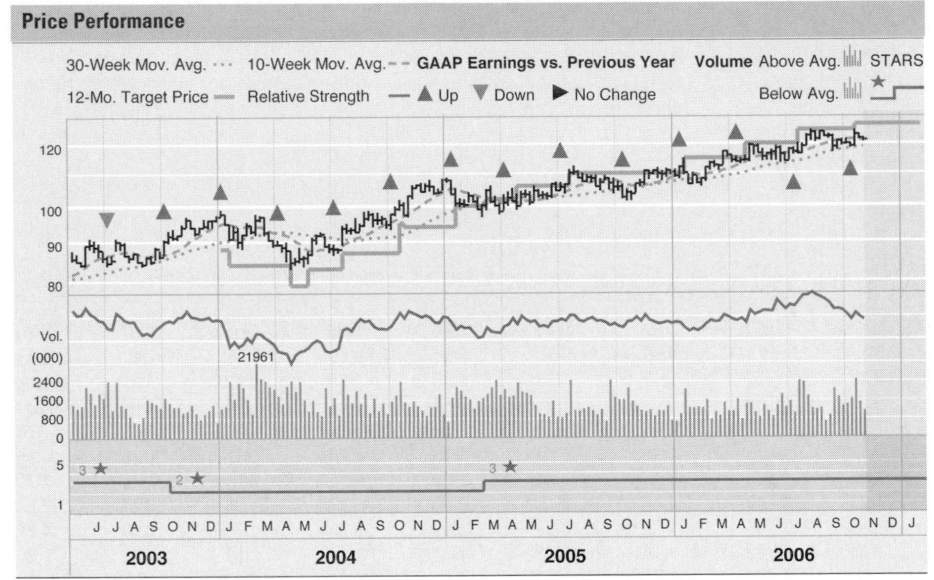

Options: P

Analysis prepared by **Christopher B. Muir** on October 12, 2006, when the stock traded at **$ 122.64**.

Highlights

- We expect that about average earning asset growth and solid fee income growth will help drive a revenue increase of around 3.3% in 2006. Our 2006 estimates include a net interest margin of 3.60% (down from 3.77% in 2005, due to our view of continued pressure from a relatively flat yield curve), average earning asset growth of 4.7%, and noninterest income growth of 6.2%.

- We expect the company's noninterest expense to increase in 2006 due mostly to the expensing of stock options and a relatively large charitable contribution. Our 2006 noninterest expense to total revenue forecast of 54.6% is only slightly worse than 2005's 54.1%, driven higher by the charitable contribution and the stock option expense in 2006, but partly offset by efficiency improvements. Credit quality remains strong, in our view, and we expect loan loss provisions to decrease to about $71 million in 2006, from $88 million in 2005.

- Assuming an effective tax rate of 32.1%, we see operating EPS rising to $7.36 in 2006, a 9.4% increase from 2005's $6.73. Our 2007 EPS estimate is $8.19, a further 11% increase.

Investment Rationale/Risk

- We believe MTB's entry into newer markets in Washington, DC, Maryland and northern Virginia could provide it with additional growth opportunities. We are also encouraged by the steady growth in the bank's diversified loan portfolio. The stock recently traded at 15X our 2007 EPS estimate, a 10% premium to the median for large-cap regional banking peers. In our view, the current valuation appropriately reflects MTB's business model.

- Risks to our opinion and target price include detrimental changes in the slope of the yield curve and operational performance that fails to meet our expectations.

- Our 12-month target price of $127 is based on our relative valuation analysis and our dividend discount model. Our target price is 15.3X our 2007 EPS estimate, or about a 13% premium to large cap regional banking peers, which we believe is warranted due to our EPS growth projections. Our dividend discount model, which estimates an intrinsic value of $127, assumes a terminal growth rate of 4% and a discount rate of 8.5%.

Qualitative Risk Assessment

LOW	MEDIUM	HIGH

Our risk assessment reflects the company's large-cap valuation, our view of the strong credit quality of its loan portfolio, and its history of profitability. While the company operates in a highly competitive and fragmented industry, the industry tends to produce relatively stable financial results.

Quantitative Evaluations

S&P Quality Ranking **A+**

D	C	B-	B	B+	A-	A	A+

Relative Strength Rank **MODERATE**

35

LOWEST = 1 HIGHEST = 99

Revenue/Earnings Data

Revenue (Million $)

	1Q	2Q	3Q	4Q	Year
2006	1,030	1,076	1,127	--	--
2005	872.6	921.9	942.3	1,002	3,738
2004	774.3	792.9	828.0	846.5	3,242
2003	568.4	809.3	795.7	784.2	2,958
2002	585.4	582.6	589.6	596.4	2,354
2001	664.7	662.3	646.4	623.5	2,579

Earnings Per Share ($)

	1Q	2Q	3Q	4Q	Year
2006	1.77	1.87	1.85	**E**1.87	**E**7.36
2005	1.62	1.69	1.64	1.78	6.73
2004	1.30	1.53	1.56	1.62	6.00
2003	1.23	1.10	1.28	1.35	4.95
2002	1.25	1.26	1.23	1.33	5.07
2001	0.85	0.94	0.98	1.05	3.82

Fiscal year ended Dec. 31. Next earnings report expected: Mid January. EPS Estimates based on S&P Operating Earnings; historical GAAP earnings are as reported.

Dividend Data (Dates: mm/dd Payment Date: mm/dd/yy)

Amount ($)	Date Decl.	Ex-Div. Date	Stk. of Record	Payment Date
0.450	11/16	11/29	12/01	12/30/05
0.450	02/22	02/24	02/28	03/31/06
0.600	04/18	05/30	06/01	06/30/06
0.600	07/25	08/30	09/01	09/29/06

Dividends have been paid since 1979. Source: Company reports.

M&T Bank Corp

Business Summary October 12, 2006

CORPORATE OVERVIEW. M&T Bank Corporation is a New York-based bank holding company with approximately $55 billion in assets as of December 31, 2005. Its primary subsidiaries are M&T Bank, a New York State chartered bank that focuses its lending on consumers and small and medium-sized businesses in the Mid-Atlantic region, and National Association (N.A.), a national banking association that offers selected deposit and loan products on a nationwide basis through direct mail and telephone marketing. MTB also operates other subsidiaries that provide insurance, securities, investments, leasing, mortgage, mortgage reinsurance, real estate and other financial products and services.

Following MTB's acquisition of Allfirst Financial Inc., a bank holding company in Baltimore, MD, from Allied Irish Banks, p.l.c. (AIB) on April 1, 2003, AIB gained a 22.5% stake in MTB. As of December 31, 2005, the foreign bank owned 23.8% of MTB's common stock. As long as AIB maintains a significant ownership in MTB, each bank will have representation on the other's board.

MARKET PROFILE. MTB operates branches in seven states: New York (where it is ranked seventh, based on a deposit market share of approximately 2.5% as of December 31, 2005), Pennsylvania (sixth, 3.5%), Maryland (third, 8.7%), Washington, D.C. (ninth, 1.8%), Virginia (92nd, 0.1%), West Virginia (68th, 0.2%) and Delaware (25th, 0.1%). Based on current and projected household income levels, we believe its markets are above average, although trends in population growth are below average.

Company Financials

Per Share Data ($) Year Ended Dec. 31	**2005**	**2004**	**2003**	**2002**	**2001**	**2000**	**1999**	**1998**	**1997**	**1996**
Tangible Book Value	25.56	24.52	21.43	20.23	17.84	16.10	14.88	13.72	15.59	13.55
Earnings	6.73	6.00	4.95	5.07	3.82	3.44	3.28	2.62	2.53	2.13
S&P Core Earnings	6.64	5.97	4.95	4.60	3.40	NA	NA	NA	NA	NA
Dividends	1.75	1.60	1.20	1.05	1.00	0.62	0.45	0.38	0.32	0.28
Payout Ratio	26%	27%	24%	21%	26%	18%	14%	15%	13%	13%
Prices:High	112.50	108.75	98.98	90.05	82.11	68.42	58.25	58.20	46.80	28.96
Prices:Low	96.71	82.90	74.71	67.70	59.80	35.70	40.60	40.00	28.10	20.90
P/E Ratio:High	17	18	20	18	21	20	18	22	19	14
P/E Ratio:Low	14	14	15	13	16	10	12	15	11	10

Income Statement Analysis (Million $)										
Net Interest Income	1,794	1,735	1,599	1,248	1,158	854	759	664	557	531
Tax Equivalent Adjustment	17.3	NA	16.3	14.0	17.5	10.5	7.71	7.19	5.84	4.50
Non Interest Income	978	940	831	513	476	325	282	269	161	170
Loan Loss Provision	88.0	95.0	131	122	104	NA	44.5	43.2	46.0	43.0
% Expense/Operating Revenue	53.2%	56.7%	59.6%	51.9%	57.4%	61.6%	59.4%	60.2%	58.7%	57.9%
Pretax Income	1,171	1,067	851	718	584	446	418	326	282	249
Effective Tax Rate	33.2%	32.3%	32.5%	32.3%	35.2%	35.9%	36.5%	36.1%	37.5%	39.3%
Net Income	782	723	574	485	378	286	266	208	176	151
% Net Interest Margin	3.77	3.88	4.09	4.36	4.23	4.02	4.02	3.97	4.38	4.45
S&P Core Earnings	772	718	574	440	336	NA	NA	NA	NA	NA

Balance Sheet & Other Financial Data (Million $)										
Money Market Assets	211	199	250	380	84.4	57.8	1,286	403	111	210
Investment Securities	8,400	8,475	7,259	3,955	3,024	3,310	1,901	2,786	1,725	1,572
Commercial Loans	23,940	22,886	20,869	14,522	14,071	13,399	6,141	3,657	2,542	2,364
Other Loans	16,614	15,758	15,169	11,415	11,117	9,571	11,431	12,348	9,224	8,756
Total Assets	55,146	52,939	49,826	33,175	31,450	28,949	22,409	20,584	14,003	12,944
Demand Deposits	9,044	9,246	10,150	5,101	4,634	4,218	2,844	2,576	1,458	1,352
Time Deposits	28,056	26,183	20,756	16,564	16,946	16,014	12,530	12,161	9,705	9,161
Long Term Debt	5,586	6,349	5,535	4,497	3,462	3,415	1,744	1,568	428	178
Common Equity	5,876	5,730	5,717	3,182	2,939	38.0	44.5	1,602	1,018	906
% Return on Assets	1.4	1.4	1.4	1.5	1.3	1.1	1.2	1.2	1.3	1.2
% Return on Equity	13.5	12.6	12.9	15.8	13.4	12.7	15.6	15.9	18.3	17.3
% Loan Loss Reserve	1.6	1.6	1.7	1.7	1.7	1.6	-2.0	1.9	2.4	2.5
% Loans/Deposits	108.7	108.4	108.0	119.7	116.7	112.4	115.4	107.2	105.4	99.4
% Equity to Assets	10.7	11.1	10.8	9.5	9.3	8.8	7.9	7.6	7.1	6.9

Data as orig reptd.; bef. results of disc opers/spec. items. Per share data adj. for stk. divs.; EPS diluted. E-Estimated. NA-Not Available. NM-Not Meaningful. NR-Not Ranked. UR-Under Review.

Office: 1 M And T Plz , Buffalo, NY 14203-2399.
Telephone: 716-842-5445.
Email: ir@mandtbank.com
Website: http://www.mandtbank.com

Chrmn: R.G. Wilmers
Pres & CEO: R.E. Sadler, Jr.
Vice Chrmn: J.G. Pereira
EVP & Treas: A.C. Kugler

EVP & CIO: M.P. Pinto
Board of Directors: W. F. Allyn, B. D. Baird, R. J. Bennett, C. A. Bontempo, R. T. Brady, M. D. Buckley, P. J. Callan, R. C. Carballada, T. J. Cunningham, III, C. E. Doherty, R. E. Garman, D. C. Hathaway, D. R. Hawbaker, P. W. Hodgson, R. G. King, R. B. Newman, II, J. G. Pereira, M. Pinto, R. E. Sadler, Jr., E. J. Sheehy, S. G. Sheetz, H. L. Washington, R. G. Wilmers

Founded: 1969
Domicile: New York
Employees: 13,525

STANDARD &POOR'S

Murphy Oil Corp

S&P Recommendation HOLD ★★★★★

Price $46.13 (as of Oct 30, 2006)

12-Mo. Target Price $55.00

Investment Style Mid-Cap Growth

GICS Sector Energy
Sub-Industry Integrated Oil & Gas

Comment This integrated oil company has exploration, production, refining and marketing interests in the U.S. and worldwide.

Key Stock Statistics (Source S&P, Vickers, company reports)

52-Wk Range	**$60.18–44.72**	S&P Oper. EPS 2006**E**	**3.60**	P/E on S&P Oper. EPS 2006**E**	**12.8**	Dividend Rate/Share	**$0.60**
Trailing 12-Month EPS	**$3.73**	S&P Oper. EPS 2007**E**	**5.25**	Common Shares Outstg. (M)	**186.8**	Yield (%)	**1.30**
Trailing 12-Month P/E	**12.4**	S&P Core EPS 2006**E**	**3.62**	Market Capitalization(B)	**$8.619**	Beta	**0.38**
$10K Invested 5 Yrs Ago	**$24,425**	S&P Core EPS 2007**E**	**5.27**	Institutional Ownership (%)	**77**	S&P Credit Rating	**BBB**

Price Performance

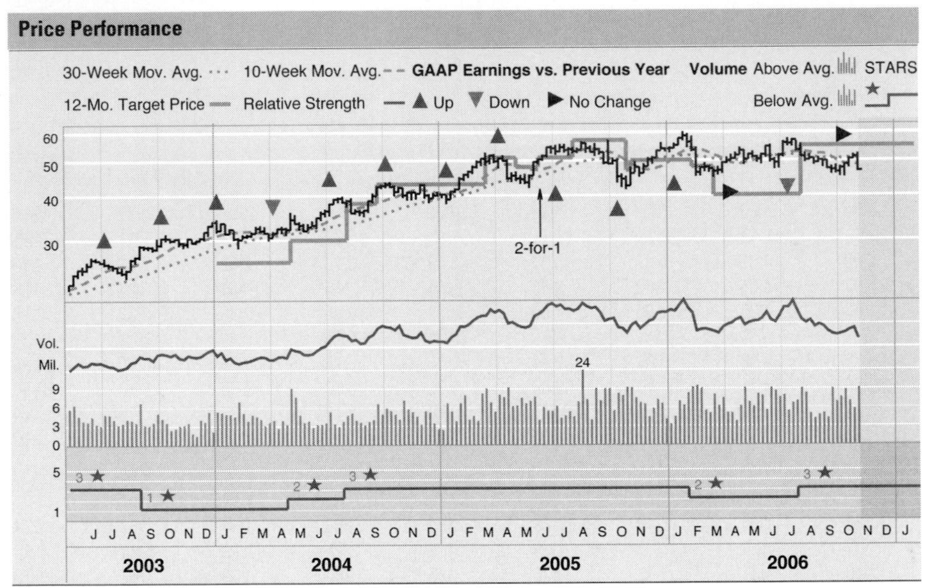

Options: ASE, CBOE, P

Analysis prepared by **Charles LaPorta, CFA** on October 27, 2006, when the stock traded at **$ 48.28**.

Highlights

- Third quarter EPS was $1.18, versus $1.59 last year and above our $0.62 EPS estimate, on a record quarterly profit from the refining segment. Production decreased 13% during the quarter due to the maintenance shutdown of the Terra Nova field, the shutdown of the Syncrude coker, and workovers at Front Runner and Medusa in the Gulf of Mexico. We expect a 12% production decline in 2006.
- The Mereaux, LA, refinery is back in operation, processing 110,000 bbl. per day in September. We believe that Meraux repair costs are largely behind the company now, including the settlement of oil spill class action litigation. We see narrowing refining margins offsetting sequential upstream production increases. We look for operating costs to increase below the industry trend in 2007, due to the additional volumes from the more prolific fields in Malaysia and deepwater Gulf of Mexico projects.
- Our 2006 EBITDAX (EBITDA before exploration expense) forecast is $1.8 billion, flat with 2005 levels, due to operational difficulties; interest expense should be $10 million higher than 2005 levels.

Investment Rationale/Risk

- We believe the Mereaux recommissioning went smoothly and should meaningfully contribute to earnings growth over the next 12 months. We believe the timing and the characteristics of the production ramp-up in the major Malaysian projects will drive the stock price over the next 18 months. Gulf of Mexico upstream operations are recovering less quickly than expected. MUR projects 2006 capital expenditures of $1.6 billion, 20% higher than last year. The balance sheet remains very strong, in our view, with debt representing 17% of total book capitalization as of September 30.
- Risks to our recommendation and target price include declining hydrocarbon prices, production delays for initial production of major Malaysian projects, and force majeure in the Gulf of Mexico.
- Based on a blend of our DCF and multiples analyses, and on our projections of upstream production growth and oil prices, our 12-month target price is $55. On a relative value basis, we believe the stock should trade at a premium to large capitalization peers, reflected by a P/E of 10.5X our 2007 EPS estimate and an enterprise value of 4.2X 2007 estimated EBITDAX.

Qualitative Risk Assessment

LOW	MEDIUM	**HIGH**

Our risk assessment reflects our view of MUR as a relatively small integrated oil company with aggressive exploration for its size, and refining operations that were significantly damaged by Hurricane Katrina.

Quantitative Evaluations

S&P Quality Ranking B+

D	C	B-	B	**B+**	A-	A	A+

Relative Strength Rank WEAK

13

LOWEST = 1 HIGHEST = 99

Revenue/Earnings Data

Revenue (Million $)

	1Q	2Q	3Q	4Q	Year
2006	2,991	3,799	4,153	--	--
2005	2,415	2,950	3,317	3,195	11,877
2004	1,628	2,096	2,291	2,301	8,360
2003	1,322	1,278	1,297	1,449	5,345
2002	748.4	1,035	1,044	1,139	3,967
2001	1,189	1,300	1,139	849.0	4,478

Earnings Per Share ($)

2006	0.60	1.13	1.18	**E**0.70	**E**3.60
2005	0.60	1.85	1.18	0.82	4.46
2004	0.43	0.90	0.62	0.71	2.66
2003	0.51	0.43	0.37	0.32	1.63
2002	0.02	0.07	0.20	0.25	0.53
2001	0.54	0.89	0.23	0.16	1.82

Fiscal year ended Dec. 31. Next earnings report expected: Early February. EPS Estimates based on S&P Operating Earnings; historical GAAP earnings are as reported.

Dividend Data (Dates: mm/dd Payment Date: mm/dd/yy)

Amount ($)	Date Decl.	Ex-Div. Date	Stk. of Record	Payment Date
0.113	02/01	02/09	02/13	03/01/06
0.113	04/05	05/10	05/12	06/01/06
0.150	08/02	08/11	08/15	09/01/06
0.150	10/02	11/08	11/10	12/01/06

Dividends have been paid since 1961. Source: Company reports.

Murphy Oil Corp

Business Summary October 27, 2006

CORPORATE OVERVIEW. As an integrated crude oil and natural gas company, Murphy Oil explores for oil and gas worldwide, and operates in refining and marketing and other businesses.

During 2005, MUR's principal exploration and production activities were conducted in the United States, Ecuador, Malaysia, the Republic of the Congo, Canada, the U.K. North Sea and Ecuador. MUR owns a 5% undivided interest in Syncrude Canada Ltd. in northern Alberta, the world's largest producer of synthetic crude oil.

MUR owns and operates two U.S. refineries (a 125,000 b/d capacity facility at Mereaux, LA, and a 35,000 b/d refinery at Superior, WI), and has a 30% stake in the 108,000 b/d U.K. Milford Haven refinery. In late August 2005, the Mereaux, Louisiana refinery was severely damaged by flooding and high winds caused by Hurricane Katrina. The plant has been down for repairs since the hurricane, and a restart of the plant is currently under way. Costs to repair the refinery have been estimated at $200 million. If the insurance recoveries and repair costs are as described, the company has estimated that uninsured repair costs could be up to $50 million in the first half of 2006.

MUR markets refined products through a network of retail gasoline stations and branded and unbranded wholesale customers in 23 states, primarily located in the parking areas of Wal-Mart stores in 21 states and using the brand name Murphy USA. At December 31, 2005, the company marketed products through 864 Murphy USA stations and 329 branded wholesale SPUR stations.

MARKET PROFILE. MUR operates from a global scope in a fragmented energy industry where an increasing proportion of the world's hydrocarbon reserves is inhabited by people in non-industrialized areas. Large government-owned national oil companies like Saudi Aramco have become more influential versus large publicly traded oil companies like ExxonMobil (XOM: strong buy, $60), in our view. As a relatively small integrated oil company, MUR has attempted to replicate its past success as an aggressive explorer for oil and gas resources. MUR has successfully found significant quantities of hydrocarbons in the deepwater Gulf of Mexico, and more recently in Malaysia (Kikeh field) and the Republic of the Congo. MUR booked proved oil reserves of 38.9 million bbl. in the Kikeh field at year-end 2005, with first production scheduled to begin in the second half of 2007.

Company Financials

Per Share Data ($) Year Ended Dec. 31	2005	2004	2003	2002	2001	2000	1999	1998	1997	1996
Tangible Book Value	18.38	14.16	10.27	8.41	7.99	6.72	5.87	5.44	6.02	5.73
Cash Flow	6.57	4.38	3.39	2.16	3.07	2.87	1.80	1.05	1.90	1.72
Earnings	4.46	2.66	1.63	0.53	1.82	1.69	0.67	-0.08	0.74	0.70
S&P Core Earnings	3.85	2.40	1.40	0.39	1.30	NA	NA	NA	NA	NA
Dividends	0.45	0.43	0.40	0.39	0.38	0.36	0.35	0.35	0.34	0.33
Payout Ratio	10%	16%	25%	73%	21%	21%	53%	NM	46%	46%
Prices:High	57.07	43.69	34.35	24.86	21.96	17.27	15.41	13.61	15.64	14.13
Prices:Low	37.80	28.45	19.27	15.95	13.81	12.05	8.22	8.63	10.75	10.16
P/E Ratio:High	13	16	21	47	12	10	23	NM	21	20
P/E Ratio:Low	8	11	12	30	8	7	12	NM	15	15

Income Statement Analysis (Million $)	2005	2004	2003	2002	2001	2000	1999	1998	1997	1996
Revenue	11,877	8,360	5,345	3,967	4,479	4,639	2,037	1,694	2,132	2,008
Operating Income	1,854	1,110	701	492	768	723	400	288	444	388
Depreciation, Depletion and Amortization	397	321	328	300	229	213	204	203	209	182
Interest Expense	8.77	34.1	20.5	27.0	19.0	16.3	20.3	10.5	0.62	13.1
Pretax Income	1,372	805	419	152	506	465	179	-8.28	212	216
Effective Tax Rate	38.9%	38.3%	28.1%	35.7%	34.6%	34.3%	32.9%	NM	37.4%	41.8%
Net Income	838	496	301	97.5	331	306	120	-14.4	132	126
S&P Core Earnings	725	448	259	71.4	236	NA	NA	NA	NA	NA

Balance Sheet & Other Financial Data (Million $)	2005	2004	2003	2002	2001	2000	1999	1998	1997	1996
Cash	585	536	252	165	82.7	133	34.1	28.3	24.3	110
Current Assets	1,839	1,629	1,039	854	599	817	593	437	518	610
Total Assets	6,369	5,458	4,713	3,886	3,259	3,134	2,446	2,164	2,238	2,244
Current Liabilities	1,287	1,205	810	718	560	745	488	381	469	554
Long Term Debt	610	613	1,090	863	521	525	393	333	206	202
Common Equity	3,461	2,649	1,951	1,594	1,498	1,260	1,057	978	1,079	1,027
Total Capital	4,685	3,263	3,463	2,784	2,322	2,014	1,604	1,436	1,422	1,356
Capital Expenditures	1,246	938	938	834	814	512	387	389	468	418
Cash Flow	1,235	818	630	398	560	519	324	188	342	308
Current Ratio	1.4	1.4	1.3	1.2	1.1	1.1	1.2	1.1	1.1	1.1
% Long Term Debt of Capitalization	13.0	18.8	31.5	31.0	22.4	26.1	24.5	23.2	14.5	14.9
% Return on Assets	14.2	9.8	7.0	2.7	10.4	11.0	5.2	NM	5.9	5.8
% Return on Equity	27.4	21.6	17.0	6.3	24.0	26.4	11.8	NM	12.6	11.8

Data as orig reptd.; bef. results of disc opers/spec. items. Per share data adj. for stk. divs.; EPS diluted. E-Estimated. NA-Not Available. NM-Not Meaningful. NR-Not Ranked. UR-Under Review.

Office: 200 Peach Street, El Dorado, AR 71730-7000.
Telephone: 870-862-6411.
Email: murphyoil@murphyoilcorp.com
Website: http://www.murphyoilcorp.com

Chrmn: W.C. Nolan, Jr.
Pres & CEO: C.P. Deming
EVP & General Counsel: S.A. Cosse
Treas: K.G. Fitzgerald

Secy: W.K. Compton
Investor Contact: M. West (870-864-6315)
Board of Directors: F. W. Blue, G. S. Dembroski, C. P. Deming, R. A. Hermes, J. V. Kelley, R. M. Murphy, W. C. Nolan, Jr., I. B. Ramberg, N. E. Schmale, D. J. Smith, C. G. Theus

Founded: 1950
Domicile: Delaware
Employees: 6,248

Mylan Laboratories Inc

S&P Recommendation HOLD ★★★★★

Price
$21.10 (as of Oct 27, 2006)

12-Mo. Target Price
$24.00

Investment Style
Mid-Cap Growth

GICS Sector Health Care
Sub-Industry Pharmaceuticals

Comment This leading manufacturer of generic pharmaceuticals produces a broad range of generic drugs in varying strengths, and also sells several proprietary drugs.

Key Stock Statistics (Source S&P, Vickers, company reports)

52-Wk Range	$25.00–18.65	S&P Oper. EPS 2007E	1.30	P/E on S&P Oper. EPS 2007E	16.2	Dividend Rate/Share	$0.24
Trailing 12-Month EPS	$0.98	S&P Oper. EPS 2008E	1.40	Common Shares Outstg. (M)	218.6	Yield (%)	1.14
Trailing 12-Month P/E	21.5	S&P Core EPS 2007E	1.30	Market Capitalization(B)	$4.613	Beta	0.02
$10K Invested 5 Yrs Ago	$13,412	S&P Core EPS 2008E	1.40	Institutional Ownership (%)	60	S&P Credit Rating	NA

Price Performance

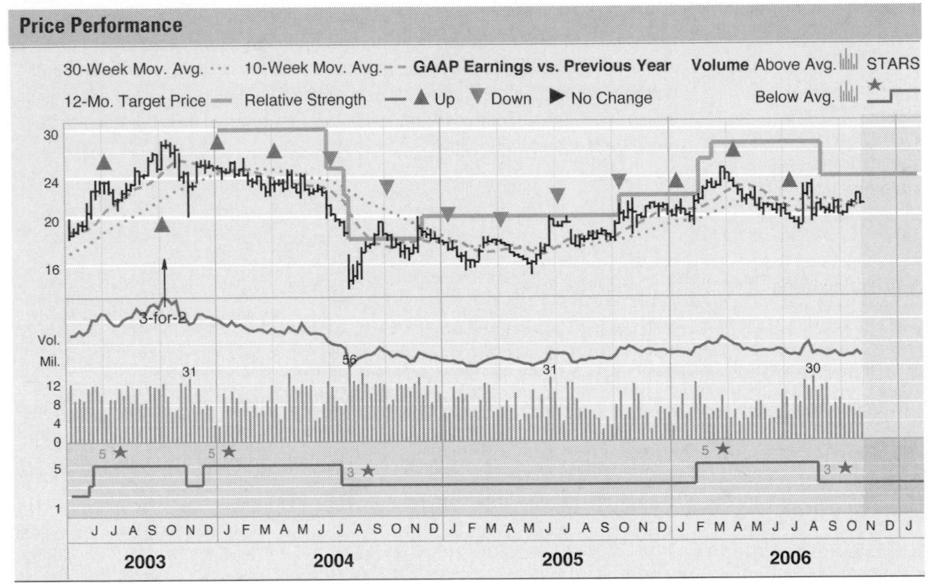

Options: ASE, CBOE, P

Analysis prepared by **Herman B. Saftlas** on August 21, 2006, when the stock traded at **$ 20.65**.

Highlights

➤ We expect revenues in FY 07 (Mar.) to increase about 9%, driven largely by new generic products. MYL expects to launch some 28 new generic drugs through the end of FY 07. Key opportunities, in our view, include generic versions of Ditropan XL incontinence drug, Risperdal anti-psychotic, Topamax anti-migraine, Levaquin antibiotic and Norvasc anti-hypertensive. Sales of most older generics, however, are expected to decline, reflecting heightened competitive pricing.

➤ We look for gross margins to benefit from the closing of the Bertek unit and other cost cutting measures. We expect SG&A expenses and R&D spending to account for lower percentages of total revenues in FY 07. MYL's recent stock buyback and corporate restructuring moves should also have a significant positive impact on bottom line results.

➤ We project FY 07 operating EPS of $1.30, including about $0.05 of estimated option expense. For FY 08, we see EPS climbing to $1.40, including projected option expense.

Investment Rationale/Risk

➤ We recently downgraded our recommendation to hold, from strong buy, based on new competition in the principal fentanyl (generic Duragesic) pain patch, which accounted for about 20% of sales, and probably more to EPS, in the June 2006 quarter. On the plus side, we think MYL has a fairly decent ANDA (generic filings) pipeline, including generic versions of Risperdal, Norvasc, Topamax, Ditropan XL and others. However, we believe that most of the key pipeline opportunities are subject to the outcome of litigation.

➤ Risks to our recommendation and target price include intense competitive pricing, and the need to obtain FDA approval of new drugs and mount legal challenges to branded patents.

➤ Our 12-month target price of $24 applies a peer multiple of 18.5X to our $1.30 EPS estimate for FY 07. Our DCF (discounted cash flow) model also supports an intrinsic valuation of $24, based on our projection of decelerating cash flow growth over the next 10 years, a WACC (weighted average cost of capital) of 8%, and perpetuity growth of 1%.

Qualitative Risk Assessment

LOW	**MEDIUM**	HIGH

Our risk assessment reflects risks inherent in the generic pharmaceutical business, which include the ability to successfully develop generic products, obtain regulatory approvals and legally challenge branded patents. However, we believe these risks are mitigated somewhat at Mylan, given the company's wide and diverse generic portfolio, expertise in patent litigation, and promising branded drug business.

Quantitative Evaluations

S&P Quality Ranking A-

D	C	B-	B	B+	**A-**	A	A+

Relative Strength Rank MODERATE

40

LOWEST = 1 HIGHEST = 99

Revenue/Earnings Data

Revenue (Million $)

	1Q	2Q	3Q	4Q	Year
2007	356.1	--	--	--	--
2006	323.4	298.0	311.3	324.6	1,257
2005	339.0	307.0	291.0	316.4	1,253
2004	331.4	360.1	349.8	333.4	1,375
2003	275.5	319.5	320.5	353.7	1,269
2002	237.9	286.3	297.2	282.6	1,104

Earnings Per Share ($)

2007	0.35	**E**0.32	**E**0.30	**E**0.33	**E**1.30
2006	0.16	0.16	0.22	0.27	0.79
2005	0.30	0.18	0.13	0.14	0.74
2004	0.31	0.33	0.31	0.27	1.21
2003	0.22	0.24	0.25	0.27	0.97
2002	0.18	0.22	0.27	0.24	0.91

Fiscal year ended Mar. 31. Next earnings report expected: Late October. EPS Estimates based on S&P Operating Earnings; historical GAAP earnings are as reported.

Dividend Data (Dates: mm/dd Payment Date: mm/dd/yy)

Amount ($)	Date Decl.	Ex-Div. Date	Stk. of Record	Payment Date
0.060	12/20	12/28	12/30	01/13/06
0.060	03/21	03/29	03/31	04/17/06
0.060	06/16	06/28	06/30	07/14/06
0.060	09/19	09/27	09/29	10/16/06

Dividends have been paid since 1983. Source: Company reports.

Mylan Laboratories Inc

Business Summary August 21, 2006

CORPORATE PROFILE. Mylan Laboratories is a leading manufacturer of generic pharmaceutical products in finished tablet, capsule and powder dosage forms. It began operations in 1961 as a privately owned company founded by Milan Puskar and an associate in White Sulphur Springs, WV. Generic drugs are the chemical equivalents of branded drugs, and are marketed after patents on the primary products expire. Generics are typically sold at prices significantly below those of comparable branded products.

MYL's product portfolio contains some 150 generic drugs, of which about 140 are in capsule or tablet form, in an aggregate of about 345 dosage strengths. These include 12 extended release products in 21 dosage strengths. MYL also markets four transdermal patches in 18 dosage strengths. In addition to manufactured drugs, Mylan markets 75 generic drugs in 128 dosage strengths under distribution agreements with other firms. MYL manufactures about 92% of all doses it sells. At the end of December 2005, Mylan hold first or second place market positions in new and refilled prescriptions dispensed among all U.S. drug companies, with respect to about 75% of the generics that MYL markets, excluding unit-dose products.

About 17% of revenues in FY 06 (Mar.) represented calcium channel blocker heart drugs, primarily nifedipine (generic Procardia). In addition, some 15% of net revenues comprised narcotic agonist analgesics, primarily fentanyl (generic Duragesic transdermal patch) used to treat chronic pain. MYL also produces antianxiety agents, antianginals, antibiotics, antidepressants, antihistamines, anti-inflammatories, antipsychotics and drugs that treat other conditions.

Eldepryl, a treatment for Parkinson's disease, is marketed by Somerset Pharmaceuticals, jointly owned by MYL and Watson Pharmaceuticals. Eldepryl is sold by Novartis under an agreement with Somerset. In February 2006, the FDA approved Somerset's Emsam selegiline patch for the treatment of depression, which is to be marketed by Bristol-Myers Squibb.

MYL markets its drugs directly to wholesalers and distributors, retail pharmacy chains, mail order pharmacies and others. Sales to key distributors AmerisourceBergen, Cardinal Health and McKesson represented about 16%, 14% and 17%, respectively, of net revenues in FY 06.

Company Financials

Per Share Data ($) Year Ended Mar. 31	**2006**	**2005**	**2004**	**2003**	**2002**	**2001**	**2000**	**1999**	**1998**	**1997**
Tangible Book Value	2.76	6.03	5.30	4.39	3.97	2.97	3.00	2.49	2.24	1.90
Cash Flow	0.99	0.91	1.37	1.11	1.07	0.28	0.65	0.50	0.44	0.29
Earnings	0.79	0.74	1.21	0.97	0.91	0.13	0.52	0.43	0.36	0.23
S&P Core Earnings	0.78	0.64	1.05	0.89	0.84	0.40	NA	NA	NA	NA
Dividends	0.12	0.10	0.08	0.08	0.07	0.07	0.07	0.07	0.07	0.07
Payout Ratio	15%	14%	7%	18%	8%	55%	14%	17%	20%	31%
Calendar Year	2005	2004	2003	2002	2001	2000	1999	1998	1997	1996
Prices:High	21.69	26.35	28.75	16.56	16.94	14.33	14.22	15.97	11.25	10.39
Prices:Low	15.21	14.24	15.56	11.15	8.96	7.11	7.58	7.58	5.11	6.22
P/E Ratio:High	27	36	24	17	19	NM	27	37	31	45
P/E Ratio:Low	19	19	13	12	12	NM	14	18	14	27

Income Statement Analysis (Million $)	2006	2005	2004	2003	2002	2001	2000	1999	1998	1997
Revenue	1,257	1,253	1,375	1,269	1,104	847	790	721	555	440
Operating Income	347	321	504	452	441	209	259	224	146	75.3
Depreciation	46.8	45.1	44.3	40.6	46.1	42.4	35.7	26.9	21.7	17.3
Interest Expense	31.3	Nil	Nil	Nil	Nil	Nil	Nil	Nil	Nil	Nil
Pretax Income	275	312	513	427	408	58.0	243	192	148	87.2
Effective Tax Rate	32.8%	34.8%	34.7%	36.1%	36.3%	36.0%	36.5%	40.0%	32.1%	27.6%
Net Income	185	204	335	272	260	37.1	154	115	101	63.1
S&P Core Earnings	184	175	286	247	241	113	NA	NA	NA	NA

Balance Sheet & Other Financial Data (Million $)	2006	2005	2004	2003	2002	2001	2000	1999	1998	1997
Cash	518	808	687	687	617	285	303	260	104	140
Current Assets	1,192	1,528	1,318	1,228	1,062	879	687	583	430	379
Total Assets	1,871	2,136	1,875	1,745	1,617	1,466	1,341	1,207	848	778
Current Liabilities	265	246	174	266	175	291	87.8	96.4	71.3	78.7
Long Term Debt	685	19.3	19.1	19.9	21.9	23.3	30.6	26.8	26.2	22.8
Common Equity	4,242	2,786	2,600	1,446	1,607	1,133	1,204	1,060	744	660
Total Capital	4,948	2,830	2,642	1,479	1,646	1,175	1,253	1,110	776	689
Capital Expenditures	104	90.7	118	32.6	20.6	24.7	28.8	16.7	28.9	26.9
Cash Flow	231	249	379	313	306	79.5	190	142	122	80.5
Current Ratio	4.5	6.2	7.6	4.6	6.1	3.0	7.8	6.0	6.0	4.8
% Long Term Debt of Capitalization	13.8	0.7	0.7	1.3	1.3	2.0	2.4	2.4	3.4	3.3
% Net Income of Revenue	14.7	16.2	24.3	21.5	23.6	4.4	19.5	16.0	18.1	14.4
% Return on Assets	9.2	10.1	18.5	16.2	16.9	2.6	12.1	11.2	12.4	8.6
% Return on Equity	5.3	7.6	14.1	19.1	17.7	3.2	13.6	12.8	14.4	9.9

Data as orig reptd.; bef. results of disc opers/spec. items. Per share data adj. for stk. divs.; EPS diluted. E-Estimated. NA-Not Available. NM-Not Meaningful. NR-Not Ranked. UR-Under Review.

Office: 1500 Corporate Dr, Canonsburg, PA 15317-8580.
Telephone: 724-514-1800.
Email: investor_relations@mylan.com
Website: http://www.mylan.com

Chrmn: M. Puskar
Pres & COO: L.J. DeBone
Vice Chrmn & CEO: R.J. Coury
VP & Cntlr: D.C. Rizzo, Jr.

CFO: E.J. Borkowski
Investor Contact: K. King (724-514-1800)
Board of Directors: W. Cameron, R. J. Coury, N. Dimick, D. J. Leech, J. C. Maroon, R. L. Piatt, M. Puskar, C. B. Todd, R. L. Vanderveen

Founded: 1970
Domicile: Pennsylvania
Employees: 2,900

STANDARD &POOR'S

Nabors Industries Ltd

S&P Recommendation BUY ★★★★★	Price $30.88 (as of Oct 31, 2006)	12-Mo. Target Price $41.00	Investment Style Large-Cap Growth

GICS Sector Energy
Sub-Industry Oil & Gas Drilling

Comment This Bermuda company, based in Barbados, is the world's largest oil and gas land drilling contractor.

Key Stock Statistics (Source S&P, Vickers, company reports)

52-Wk Range	**$41.35–27.26**	S&P Oper. EPS 2006**E**	**3.80**	P/E on S&P Oper. EPS 2006**E**	**8.1**	Dividend Rate/Share	**Nil**
Trailing 12-Month EPS	**$3.21**	S&P Oper. EPS 2007**E**	**4.91**	Common Shares Outstg. (M)	**316.0**	Yield (%)	**Nil**
Trailing 12-Month P/E	**9.6**	S&P Core EPS 2006**E**	**3.80**	Market Capitalization(B)	**$9.759**	Beta	**0.95**
$10K Invested 5 Yrs Ago	**$18,800**	S&P Core EPS 2007**E**	**4.91**	Institutional Ownership (%)	**74**	S&P Credit Rating	**A-**

Price Performance

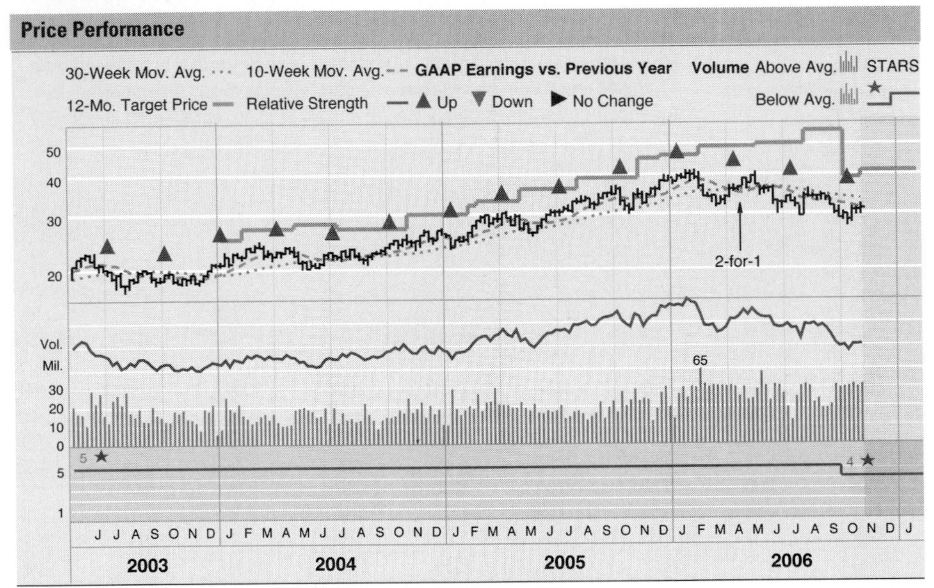

Options: ASE, CBOE, P, Ph

Analysis prepared by **Stewart Glickman, CFA** on October 31, 2006, when the stock traded at **$ 30.88**.

Highlights

- Dayrates for U.S. land drilling rose by $859 per day, to $21,045, in the third quarter, but cash margins rose by only $163 per day, to $11,023. Although both numbers represent record highs, we note that the implied 19% flowthrough of dayrate gains to the operating line is significantly lower than the 65% to 90% range seen over the prior six quarters. We believe that the current streak of 11 consecutive quarters of dayrate increases could end in 2007, and consequently, we expect that earnings growth in 2007 will largely be volume-driven. Overall for 2007, we see revenue growth of 15%, with operating margins in the mid-30% range.
- Unlike U.S. markets, we believe that considerable pricing power still exists in NBR's international markets, given that such markets typically have longer-term contracts and are slower to migrate customers to new leading edge dayrates. We see incremental operating income from international land drilling in 2007 rivaling that of U.S. Lower 48 land drilling.
- For 2006, we expect stock split-adjusted operating EPS of $3.80, rising to $4.91 in 2007. Estimates in both years include $0.07 of projected stock option expense.

Investment Rationale/Risk

- We are generally bullish on NBR, and view the company as better insulated than peers to potential U.S. land drilling dayrate erosion, given extensive use of long-term contracts and less exposure to smaller customers. In addition, we see strong fundamentals for international land drilling, and see improving growth prospects for the company's offshore and Alaskan operations. We expect the company's nascent joint venture with First Reserve Corporation to yield potential growth from exploration and production activities.
- Risks to our recommendation and target price include lower than expected land drilling activity; reduced oil and natural gas prices; reduced dayrates for land drilling work; and operating margin pressure due to rising cost inflation.
- Our DCF model, using free cash flow growth of 12%, and terminal growth of 3%, shows intrinsic value of about $41 per share. Assuming a 5.5X multiple on estimated 2006 EBITDA, 6.5X estimated 2006 cash flow (both premiums to peers), and our DCF model, our 12-month target price is $41 per share.

Qualitative Risk Assessment

LOW	MEDIUM	**HIGH**

Our risk assessment reflects NBR's sensitivity to volatile crude oil and natural gas prices (especially the latter), capital spending decisions made by oil and gas producing customers, and the rising number of newbuild land rigs on order. Partly offsetting these risks is NBR's diversified fleet, including overseas operations, and its leadership position in the industry.

Quantitative Evaluations

S&P Quality Ranking **B**

D	C	B-	**B**	B+	A-	A	A+

Relative Strength Rank **WEAK**

28

LOWEST = 1 HIGHEST = 99

Revenue/Earnings Data

Revenue (Million $)

	1Q	2Q	3Q	4Q	Year
2006	1,164	1,144	1,244	--	--
2005	783.7	786.1	893.3	1,016	3,551
2004	607.7	546.7	585.7	701.0	2,394
2003	455.7	433.4	476.0	524.6	1,880
2002	381.7	367.3	362.2	380.0	1,466
2001	546.6	613.6	621.2	428.9	2,121

Earnings Per Share ($)

2006	0.79	0.77	1.02	**E**1.22	**E**3.80
2005	0.40	0.41	0.56	0.65	2.00
2004	0.23	0.15	0.24	0.34	0.96
2003	0.16	0.10	0.17	0.21	0.63
2002	0.14	0.09	0.09	0.09	0.41
2001	0.26	0.32	0.34	0.18	1.09

Fiscal year ended Dec. 31. Next earnings report expected: Early February. EPS Estimates based on S&P Operating Earnings; historical GAAP earnings are as reported.

Dividend Data (Dates: mm/dd Payment Date: mm/dd/yy)

Amount ($)	Date Decl.	Ex-Div. Date	Stk. of Record	Payment Date
2-for-1 Stk.	12/13	04/18	03/31	04/17/06

Source: Company reports.

Nabors Industries Ltd

Business Summary October 31, 2006

CORPORATE OVERVIEW. The world's largest land drilling contractor, Nabors Industries Ltd. owns a fleet of about 600 land drilling rigs. Formed as a Bermuda-exempt company in December 2001, but operating continuously in the drilling sector since the early 1900s, Nabors conducts oil, gas and geothermal land drilling operations in the lower 48 U.S. states, Alaska and Canada, and internationally, mainly in South and Central America, the Middle East and Africa. NBR also owns approximately 565 land workover and well servicing rigs in the U.S. Southwest and West, and approximately 215 well servicing and workover rigs in Canada. In addition, it markets 43 platform, 19 jackup and three barge rigs in the Gulf of Mexico and international markets; these rigs provide well servicing, workover and drilling services.

The contract drilling segment (92% of 2005 revenues, and 95% of segment operating income) provides drilling, workover, well servicing and related services in the U.S. (including the lower 48, Alaska and offshore), Canada, and internationally. During 2005, 57% of contract drilling revenues served customers in the U.S., either for land drilling or land well-servicing. Well servicing and workover services are provided for existing wells where some form of artificial lift is required to bring oil to the surface. To supplement its primary business, NBR offers ancillary wellsite services, such as oilfield management, engineering, transportation, construction, maintenance, and well logging. As of March 2006, NBR had a fleet of 33 marine transportation and support vessels, primarily in the Gulf of Mexico, Trinidad, and the Middle East, providing marine transportation of drilling materials, supplies and crews for offshore rig operations and support for other offshore facilities. The supply vessels are used as freight-carrying vessels for bringing drill pipe, tubing, casing, drilling mud, and other equipment to drilling rigs and production platforms.

Company Financials

Per Share Data ($) Year Ended Dec. 31	**2005**	**2004**	**2003**	**2002**	**2001**	**2000**	**1999**	**1998**	**1997**	**1996**
Tangible Book Value	10.83	8.68	7.35	6.39	5.89	5.51	4.76	4.30	3.62	2.63
Cash Flow	3.04	1.84	1.36	1.06	1.59	0.94	0.53	0.93	0.80	0.63
Earnings	2.00	0.96	0.63	0.41	1.09	0.45	0.12	0.58	0.56	0.38
Dividends	Nil	Nil	Nil	Nil	Nil	Nil	Nil	Nil	Nil	Nil
Payout Ratio	Nil	Nil	Nil	Nil	Nil	Nil	Nil	Nil	Nil	Nil
Prices:High	39.94	27.13	22.93	24.99	31.56	30.24	15.63	15.78	23.41	10.75
Prices:Low	23.10	20.01	16.10	13.07	9.00	14.06	5.38	5.88	7.38	5.13
P/E Ratio:High	20	28	37	62	29	68	NM	27	42	28
P/E Ratio:Low	12	21	26	32	8	32	NM	10	13	13
Income Statement Analysis (Million $)										
Revenue	3,551	2,394	1,880	1,466	2,121	1,327	639	968	1,029	720
Operating Income	1,304	626	438	351	0.69	377	155	267	223	123
Depreciation, Depletion and Amortization	339	300	235	195	190	152	99.9	84.9	66.4	46.1
Interest Expense	44.8	48.5	70.7	67.1	60.7	35.4	30.4	15.5	16.5	11.9
Pretax Income	874	336	175	141	542	227	45.6	200	182	81.6
Effective Tax Rate	25.8%	9.94%	NM	13.7%	35.9%	40.2%	39.3%	37.5%	37.1%	13.6%
Net Income	649	302	192	121	348	135	27.7	125	115	70.6
Balance Sheet & Other Financial Data (Million $)										
Cash	565	1,253	1,532	1,331	919	551	112	47.3	3.92	104
Current Assets	2,617	1,581	1,516	1,370	1,031	1,018	461	266	306	329
Total Assets	7,230	5,863	5,603	5,064	4,152	3,137	2,398	1,450	1,234	871
Current Liabilities	1,352	1,199	598	751	330	279	265	244	235	156
Long Term Debt	1,252	1,202	1,986	1,615	1,568	855	483	217	230	230
Common Equity	3,758	2,929	2,490	2,158	1,858	1,806	1,470	867	728	458
Total Capital	5,727	4,517	4,849	4,175	3,711	2,759	2,046	1,157	986	706
Capital Expenditures	907	544	353	317	701	301	82.1	276	268	146
Cash Flow	987	603	427	317	538	288	128	210	181	117
Current Ratio	1.9	1.3	2.5	1.8	3.1	3.6	1.7	1.1	1.3	2.1
% Long Term Debt of Capitalization	21.9	26.6	41.0	38.7	42.2	31.0	23.6	18.8	23.3	32.6
% Return on Assets	9.9	5.3	3.6	2.6	9.5	4.9	1.4	9.3	10.9	9.7
% Return on Equity	19.4	11.2	8.3	6.0	19.0	8.3	2.4	15.7	19.4	17.1

Data as orig reptd.; bef. results of disc opers/spec. items. Per share data adj. for stk. divs.; EPS diluted. E-Estimated. NA-Not Available. NM-Not Meaningful. NR-Not Ranked. UR-Under Review.

Office: 8 Par-La_Ville Road, Hamilton, St. Michael, Barbados HM08.
Telephone: 441.292.1510.
Website: http://www.nabors.com
Chrmn & CEO: E.M. Isenberg

Pres & COO: A.G. Petrello
VP & CFO: B.P. Koch
VP & Secy: D. McLachlin
Investor Contact: D.A. Smith (281-874-0035)

Board of Directors: E. M. Isenberg, A. M. Knaster, J. L. Payne, A. G. Petrello, H. Schmidt, M. M. Sheinfeld, M. J. Whitman

Founded: 1968
Domicile: Bermuda
Employees: 19,714

STANDARD &POOR'S

National City Corp

S&P Recommendation HOLD ★★★★★

Price $36.94 (as of Oct 27, 2006)

12-Mo. Target Price $38.00

Investment Style Large-Cap Value

GICS Sector Financials
Sub-Industry Regional Banks

Comment The third largest Ohio bank holding company, NCC also has banking offices in Michigan, Kentucky, Indiana, Illinois, Missouri and Pennsylvania.

Key Stock Statistics (Source S&P, Vickers, company reports)

52-Wk Range	$40.00–32.00	S&P Oper. EPS 2006E	3.21	P/E on S&P Oper. EPS 2006E	11.5	Dividend Rate/Share	$1.56
Trailing 12-Month EPS	$3.05	S&P Oper. EPS 2007E	3.28	Common Shares Outstg. (M)	604.9	Yield (%)	4.22
Trailing 12-Month P/E	12.1	S&P Core EPS 2006E	3.14	Market Capitalization(B)	$22.344	Beta	0.55
$10K Invested 5 Yrs Ago	$16,548	S&P Core EPS 2007E	3.23	Institutional Ownership (%)	50	S&P Credit Rating	A

Price Performance

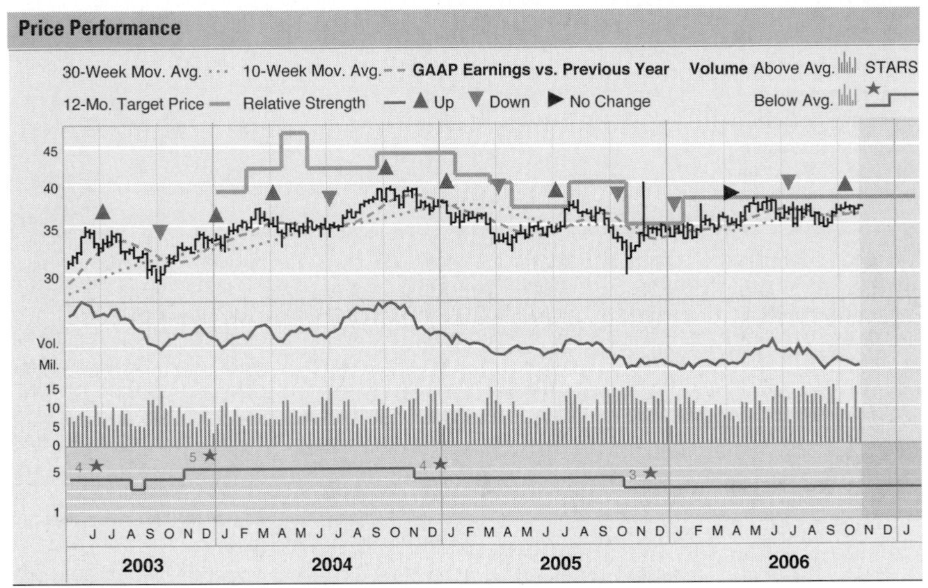

Options: ASE, CBOE, Ph

Analysis prepared by **Mark Hebeka, CFA** on August 14, 2006, when the stock traded at **$ 35.43**.

Highlights

- We believe NCC's net interest income will remain under pressure during 2006. We look for the revenue mix to improve as NCC moves away from its mortgage business and focuses on core banking operations. After initial charges associated with NCC's "Best In Class" program, we see an improvement in profitability. However, we continue to remain cautious as we see strong competition and an interest rate environment that remains challenging.
- We think credit quality metrics will remain solid, but based on NCC's significant progress in reducing the risk profile of its loan portfolio, we think levels may begin to deteriorate slightly. In our view, operating expenses (excluding merger-related and nonrecurring costs) should remain under control, as the benefits of recent investments in technology likely materialize with the completion of most of the company's investment program.
- We project 2006 operating EPS of $3.07 and $3.27 in 2007, supported by expected share repurchases, versus $3.09 in 2005.

Investment Rationale/Risk

- In our view, the stock's valuation and relative discount versus peers reflects the declining contribution from NCC's mortgage business and challenging markets due to increased competition and a difficult interest rate environment. We believe its valuation is likely to remain flat in coming quarters, but we see positive banking fundamentals and continue to view NCC as a potential acquisition candidate.
- Risks to our recommendation and target price include the possibility that long-term interest rates fall below short-term rates, creating an inverted yield curve; a deterioration in economic conditions; a rapid decline in credit quality; greater net hedging losses than we expect; and a further decrease in corporate loan demand.
- Our 12-month target price of $38 reflects a P/E of 11.6X our 2007 EPS estimate, which we see as justified by our view of NCC's sound banking fundamentals and long-term growth prospects.

Qualitative Risk Assessment

LOW | MEDIUM | HIGH

Our risk assessment reflects our view of NCC's solid fundamentals coupled with a strong customer base, strong credit quality and good diversification.

Quantitative Evaluations

S&P Quality Ranking A

D | C | B- | B | B+ | A- | A | A+

Relative Strength Rank MODERATE

44

LOWEST = 1 HIGHEST = 99

Revenue/Earnings Data

Revenue (Million $)

	1Q	2Q	3Q	4Q	Year
2006	2,801	3,020	--	--	--
2005	2,554	2,839	2,773	2,883	11,036
2004	2,462	2,261	2,639	3,198	10,560
2003	2,622	2,534	2,037	2,400	9,594
2002	2,248	2,209	2,064	2,207	8,728
2001	2,346	2,325	2,233	2,189	9,093

Earnings Per Share ($)

	1Q	2Q	3Q	4Q	Year
2006	0.74	0.77	0.90	E0.80	E3.21
2005	0.74	0.97	0.74	0.64	3.09
2004	1.16	0.83	0.86	1.46	4.31
2003	1.05	0.94	0.56	0.88	3.43
2002	0.73	0.63	0.61	0.62	2.59
2001	0.55	0.57	0.58	0.57	2.27

Fiscal year ended Dec. 31. Next earnings report expected: Mid January. EPS Estimates based on S&P Operating Earnings; historical GAAP earnings are as reported.

Dividend Data (Dates: mm/dd Payment Date: mm/dd/yy)

Amount ($)	Date Decl.	Ex-Div. Date	Stk. of Record	Payment Date
0.370	01/03	01/11	01/13	02/01/06
0.370	04/03	04/11	04/13	05/01/06
0.390	07/03	07/11	07/13	08/01/06
0.390	10/02	10/10	10/12	11/01/06

Dividends have been paid since 1936. Source: Company reports.

National City Corp

STANDARD &POOR'S

Business Summary August 14, 2006

CORPORATE OVERVIEW. NCC operates five major lines of business: consumer and small business financial services (CSB), wholesale banking, National City Mortgage (NCM), National Consumer Finance (NCF), and Asset Management. CSB provides banking services to consumers and small businesses within NCC's seven-state footprint. In addition to deposit gathering and direct lending services provided through the retail bank branch network, call centers, and the Internet, CSB's activities also include small business banking services, education finance, retail brokerage, and lending-related insurance services. Consumer lending products include home equity, government or privately guaranteed student loans, and credit cards and other unsecured personal and small business lines of credit.

Wholesale banking provides credit-related and treasury management services, as well as capital markets and international services, to large- and medium sized corporations. Major products and services include: lines of credit, term loans, leases, automobile floorplan lending, investment real estate lending, asset-based lending, structured finance, syndicated lending, equity and mezzanine capital, treasury management, and international payment and clearing services.

NCM primarily originates conventional residential mortgage and home equity loans both within NCC's banking footprint and nationally. NCM's activities also include servicing mortgage loans for third-party investors. Mortgage loans originated by NCM generally represent loans collateralized by one-to-four-family residential real estate and are made to borrowers in good credit standing. These loans are typically sold to primary mortgage market aggregators and jumbo loan investors.

NCF is comprised of four business units involved in the origination, sale and servicing of home equity loans, lines of credit, and nonconforming residential mortgage loans. Loans are originated nationally through correspondent relationships and a network of brokers. The National Home Equity business unit within NCF originates, primarily through brokers, prime-quality home equity loans outside NCC's banking footprint.

Company Financials

Per Share Data ($) Year Ended Dec. 31	**2005**	**2004**	**2003**	**2002**	**2001**	**2000**	**1999**	**1998**	**1997**	**1996**
Tangible Book Value	14.85	14.36	13.47	11.70	12.15	11.06	9.44	10.69	10.14	9.93
Earnings	3.09	4.31	3.43	2.59	2.27	2.13	2.22	1.61	1.83	1.65
S&P Core Earnings	2.99	3.44	3.30	2.31	1.95	NA	NA	NA	NA	NA
Dividends	1.44	1.34	1.25	1.20	1.16	1.14	1.06	0.94	0.84	0.74
Payout Ratio	47%	31%	36%	46%	51%	54%	48%	58%	46%	45%
Prices:High	40.00	39.66	34.97	33.75	32.70	29.75	37.81	38.75	33.78	23.63
Prices:Low	29.75	32.14	26.53	24.60	23.69	16.00	22.13	28.47	21.25	15.31
P/E Ratio:High	13	9	10	13	14	14	17	24	18	14
P/E Ratio:Low	10	7	8	9	10	8	10	18	12	9

Income Statement Analysis (Million $)										
Net Interest Income	4,696	4,504	4,368	4,005	3,439	2,958	3,000	2,912	1,943	1,943
Tax Equivalent Adjustment	NA	NA	28.0	30.4	33.3	33.7	36.9	40.3	19.4	20.9
Non Interest Income	3,225	4,444	3,549	2,731	2,533	2,427	2,242	1,695	899	1,165
Loan Loss Provision	287	323	638	682	605	287	250	201	140	146
% Expense/Operating Revenue	60.0%	51.0%	51.6%	55.4%	56.0%	59.1%	56.9%	73.3%	71.0%	66.6%
Pretax Income	2,961	4,078	3,237	2,406	2,167	1,972	2,149	1,647	1,169	1,058
Effective Tax Rate	33.0%	31.8%	34.6%	33.8%	35.9%	34.0%	34.6%	35.0%	31.0%	30.4%
Net Income	1,985	2,780	2,117	1,594	1,388	1,302	1,405	1,071	807	737
% Net Interest Margin	3.74	4.09	4.11	4.34	4.71	3.85	3.99	4.11	4.25	4.44
S&P Core Earnings	1,924	2,225	2,038	1,429	1,201	NA	NA	NA	NA	NA

Balance Sheet & Other Financial Data (Million $)										
Money Market Assets	301	303	162	136	171	81.0	556	930	600	342
Investment Securities	10,285	10,518	7,859	10,217	10,463	10,673	15,135	15,701	8,865	8,690
Commercial Loans	53,392	40,847	50,446	34,107	34,033	52,247	29,415	22,243	14,095	12,261
Other Loans	62,646	59,290	60,115	38,028	34,007	13,357	30,789	35,768	25,476	22,718
Total Assets	142,397	139,280	113,933	118,258	105,817	88,535	87,121	88,246	54,684	50,856
Demand Deposits	45,733	47,916	43,435	39,179	34,324	28,763	27,744	29,523	16,822	16,599
Time Deposits	38,253	38,039	20,495	25,940	28,806	26,494	22,322	28,724	20,039	19,401
Long Term Debt	19,370	28,444	23,666	22,730	17,316	18,145	15,038	9,009	4,810	2,994
Common Equity	12,613	12,804	9,329	8,308	7,381	6,740	5,698	6,977	4,281	4,432
% Return on Assets	1.4	2.2	1.8	1.4	1.4	1.5	1.6	1.5	1.5	1.5
% Return on Equity	15.6	25.1	24.2	20.3	19.7	20.9	22.2	18.7	18.5	17.7
% Loan Loss Reserve	10.3	1.2	1.2	1.1	1.2	1.3	1.5	1.7	1.8	2.0
% Loans/Deposits	126.3	116.5	148.0	141.7	130.0	125.3	114.9	106.3	103.5	102.0
% Equity to Assets	9.0	8.7	7.5	7.0	7.3	7.1	7.2	8.2	8.3	8.6

Data as orig reptd.; bef. results of disc opers/spec. items. Per share data adj. for stk. divs.; EPS diluted. E-Estimated. NA-Not Available. NM-Not Meaningful. NR-Not Ranked. UR-Under Review.

Office: 1900 E 9th St, Cleveland, OH, USA 44114-3484.
Telephone: 216-222-2000.
Email: investor.relation@nationalcity.com
Website: http://www.nationalcity.com

Chrmn & CEO: D.A. Daberko
Vice Chrmn: W.E. MacDonald III
Vice Chrmn: P.E. Raskind
Vice Chrmn & CFO: J.D. Kelly

EVP, Secy & General Counsel: D.L. Zoeller
Investor Contact: J. Hammarlund (800-622-4204)
Board of Directors: J. E. Barfield, J. S. Broadhurst, C. M. Connor, D. A. Daberko, J. T. Gorman, B. P. Healy, S. C. Lindner, P. A. Ormond, R. A. Paul, G. L. Shaheen, J. S. Thornton, M. Weiss

Founded: 1845
Domicile: Delaware
Employees: 34,270

STANDARD &POOR'S

National Oilwell Varco Inc

S&P Recommendation BUY ★★★★★

Price $59.87 (as of Oct 27, 2006)

12-Mo. Target Price $84.00

Investment Style Large-Cap Growth

GICS Sector Energy
Sub-Industry Oil & Gas Equipment & Services

Comment This provider of drill rig equipment and downhole tools and services changed its name to National Oilwell Varco, from National-Oilwell, after its March 2005 acquisition of Varco.

Key Stock Statistics (Source S&P, Vickers, company reports)

52-Wk Range	$77.60–51.62	S&P Oper. EPS 2006**E**	3.49	P/E on S&P Oper. EPS 2006**E**	17.2	Dividend Rate/Share	Nil
Trailing 12-Month EPS	$3.11	S&P Oper. EPS 2007**E**	4.47	Common Shares Outstg. (M)	175.4	Yield (%)	Nil
Trailing 12-Month P/E	19.3	S&P Core EPS 2006**E**	3.48	Market Capitalization(B)	$10.500	Beta	0.89
$10K Invested 5 Yrs Ago	$30,546	S&P Core EPS 2007**E**	4.46	Institutional Ownership (%)	93	S&P Credit Rating	NR

Price Performance

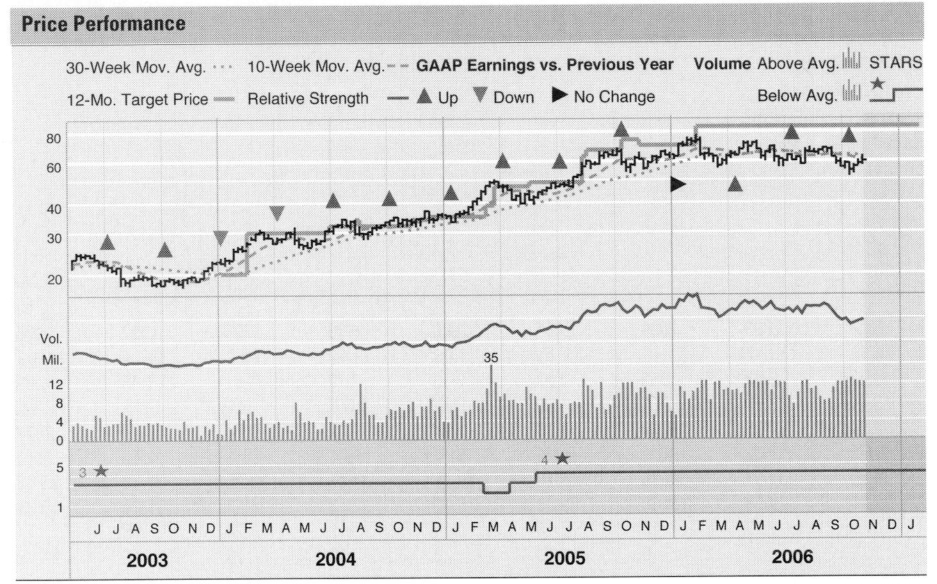

Options: ASE, CBOE, P

Analysis prepared by **Stewart Glickman, CFA** on August 11, 2006, when the stock traded at **$ 64.80**.

Highlights

- New orders for capital equipment reached a record $1.5 billion in the second quarter, up 14% over the first quarter of 2006, and total backlog at the end of the quarter stood at about $4.1 billion. A typical order for rig components for a newbuild jackup yields NOV approximately $48 million in revenue, while a similar order for a new floater typically yields about $150 million in revenue. Although a large number of jackup newbuild announcements have occurred over the last 12 months, we think there is potential for further newbuilds, particularly on the floater side.
- Second quarter 2006 operating margins widened in all three segments, with an overall margin of about 14.9%, versus 11.3% in 2005. For 2006, we see total revenue growth of approximately 44%, with a further 17% advance expected in 2007, and operating margins in the 16% range.
- For 2006, we see operating EPS of $3.49, and $3.48 on an S&P Core EPS basis, with the divergence reflecting adjustments for pension gains. For 2007, we estimate operating EPS of $4.47.

Investment Rationale/Risk

- With rising newbuild activity for drilling rigs, we think NOV merits a premium to peers given our view of its strong installed base of rig components. The stock recently traded at an enterprise value of 10.8X our 2006 EBITDA estimate, a bit above the 10.2X peer group average. The shares recently traded at about 12.8X estimated 2006 cash flow, below the 13.8X peer average.
- Risks to our recommendation and target price include lower than expected prices for crude oil and natural gas; a slowdown in drilling activity; and delays in meeting capital equipment orders.
- Our discounted cash flow model, assuming free cash flow growth of about 8% per year for 10 years, and 3% thereafter, discounted at a WACC of 10.8%, yields an intrinsic value of approximately $81. Based on an assumed 14X multiple of enterprise value to estimated 2006 EBITDA, 16.5X estimated 2006 cash flow, and our DCF model, our 12-month target price is $84.

Qualitative Risk Assessment

LOW | **MEDIUM** | HIGH

Our risk assessment reflects NOV's exposure to volatile crude oil and natural gas prices, and capital spending decisions made by its contract driller and exploration & production customers. Offsetting these risks is what we view as NOV's leading industry position as a manufacturer of rig capital equipment.

Quantitative Evaluations

S&P Quality Ranking **B**

D | C | B- | **B** | B+ | A- | A | A+

Relative Strength Rank **MODERATE**

32

LOWEST = 1 HIGHEST = 99

Revenue/Earnings Data

Revenue (Million $)

	1Q	2Q	3Q	4Q	Year
2006	1,512	1,657	1,778	--	--
2005	814.9	1,216	1,237	1,377	4,645
2004	496.2	533.5	618.9	669.5	2,318
2003	500.6	475.4	498.6	530.4	2,005
2002	389.0	372.4	366.9	393.6	1,522
2001	360.3	434.6	486.8	465.7	1,747

Earnings Per Share ($)

	1Q	2Q	3Q	4Q	Year
2006	0.68	0.84	1.00	**E**1.01	**E**3.49
2005	0.34	0.35	0.50	0.58	1.81
2004	0.13	0.25	0.32	0.58	1.27
2003	0.23	0.24	0.27	0.17	0.90
2002	0.26	0.21	0.22	0.21	0.89
2001	0.26	0.31	0.36	0.35	1.27

Fiscal year ended Dec. 31. Next earnings report expected: Late February. EPS Estimates based on S&P Operating Earnings; historical GAAP earnings are as reported.

Dividend Data

No cash dividends have been paid.

National Oilwell Varco Inc

Business Summary August 11, 2006

CORPORATE OVERVIEW. Formerly named National-Oilwell, this company changed its name to National Oilwell Varco (NOV) on March 14, 2005, following the completion of the merger with Varco International. NOV, a worldwide designer, manufacturer and marketer of comprehensive systems and components used in oil and gas drilling and production, as well as a provider of downhole tools and services, also provides supply chain integration services to the upstream oil and gas industry. The company estimates that more than 90% of the mobile offshore rig fleet and the majority of the world's larger land rigs (2,000 horsepower and greater) manufactured in the past 20 years use drawworks, mud pumps, and other drilling components manufactured by NOV.

The combined company generated 2005 revenues of about $4.65 billion, and operating income of $477 million, for an operating margin of approximately 10.3%. The company's Rig Technology segment ($2.22 billion of revenue in 2005, and $248 million of 2005 segment operating income) designs, manufactures and sells drilling systems and components for both land and offshore drilling rigs, as well as complete land drilling and well servicing rigs. The major mechanical components include drawworks, mud pumps, power swivels, SCR houses, solids control equipment, traveling equipment and rotary tables. Many of these components are designed specifically for applications in offshore, extended reach and deep land drilling. This equipment is installed on new rigs and is often replaced during the upgrade and refurbishment of existing rigs. As of June 30, 2006, total backlog in this segment was about $4.1 billion.

Company Financials

Per Share Data ($) Year Ended Dec. 31	2005	2004	2003	2002	2001	2000	1999	1998	1997	1996
Tangible Book Value	8.40	6.65	4.98	4.34	6.37	5.44	3.79	4.31	4.91	2.85
Cash Flow	2.54	1.78	1.37	1.20	1.75	0.60	0.42	1.66	1.27	0.03
Earnings	1.81	1.27	0.90	0.89	1.27	0.16	0.03	1.30	0.99	0.01
S&P Core Earnings	1.79	1.15	0.81	0.75	1.14	NA	NA	NA	NA	NA
Dividends	Nil	Nil	Nil	Nil	Nil	Nil	Nil	Nil	Nil	Nil
Payout Ratio	Nil	Nil	Nil	Nil	Nil	Nil	Nil	Nil	Nil	Nil
Prices:High	68.33	37.38	24.85	28.81	41.24	39.69	18.50	40.44	44.44	15.38
Prices:Low	33.08	21.66	17.50	15.19	12.40	14.00	8.50	7.63	14.00	8.50
P/E Ratio:High	38	29	28	32	32	NM	NM	31	45	NM
P/E Ratio:Low	18	17	19	17	10	NM	NM	6	14	NM
Income Statement Analysis (Million $)										
Revenue	4,645	2,318	2,005	1,522	1,747	1,150	745	1,172	1,006	649
Operating Income	623	213	198	159	228	97.6	45.1	157	113	91.7
Depreciation, Depletion and Amortization	115	44.0	39.2	25.0	38.9	35.0	23.2	19.2	14.7	0.41
Interest Expense	52.9	38.4	38.9	27.3	24.9	Nil	Nil	12.5	6.20	12.1
Pretax Income	430	132	117	112	168	27.0	4.52	109	82.5	0.39
Effective Tax Rate	32.3%	14.6%	28.9%	35.0%	38.1%	51.4%	66.4%	36.9%	37.8%	37.8%
Net Income	287	110	76.8	73.1	104	13.1	1.52	68.9	51.3	0.25
S&P Core Earnings	283	99.2	69.3	61.6	93.6	NA	NA	NA	NA	NA
Balance Sheet & Other Financial Data (Million $)										
Cash	209	143	74.2	118	43.2	42.5	12.4	11.4	19.8	4.32
Current Assets	2,998	1,537	1,246	1,115	909	743	478	558	464	233
Total Assets	6,679	2,599	2,243	1,969	1,472	1,279	782	818	568	267
Current Liabilities	1,187	800	452	346	277	263	176	211	211	103
Long Term Debt	836	350	594	595	300	222	196	206	61.6	36.4
Common Equity	4,194	1,296	1,090	933	868	767	395	387	278	109
Total Capital	5,428	1,767	1,753	1,592	1,188	1,006	597	597	342	145
Capital Expenditures	105	39.0	32.4	24.8	27.4	24.6	15.4	27.8	32.6	3.14
Cash Flow	402	154	116	98.1	143	48.2	24.8	88.1	66.0	0.70
Current Ratio	2.5	1.9	2.8	3.2	3.3	2.8	2.7	2.6	2.2	2.3
% Long Term Debt of Capitalization	15.4	19.8	33.9	37.3	25.3	22.1	32.8	34.5	18.0	25.1
% Return on Assets	6.2	4.6	3.6	4.2	7.6	1.2	0.2	9.9	12.3	0.1
% Return on Equity	10.5	9.2	7.6	8.1	12.7	1.9	0.4	20.7	26.5	0.2

Data as orig reptd.; bef. results of disc opers/spec. items. Per share data adj. for stk. divs.; EPS diluted. E-Estimated. NA-Not Available. NM-Not Meaningful. NR-Not Ranked. UR-Under Review.

Office: 10000 Richmond Avenue, Houston, TX 77042-4200.
Telephone: 713-346-7500.
Email: investor.relations@natoil.com
Website: http://www.natoil.com

Chrmn, Pres & CEO: M.A. Miller, Jr.
COO & EVP: J.C. Winkler
SVP & CFO: C.C. Williams
VP, Chief Acctg Officer & Cntlr: R. Blanchard

VP & General Counsel: D.W. Rettig
Board of Directors: G. L. Armstrong, R. E. Beauchamp, B. A. Guill, D. D. Harrison, R. L. Jarvis, E. L. Mattson, M. A. Miller, Jr., J. A. Smisek, J. D. Woods

Founded: 1987
Domicile: Delaware
Employees: 18,979

STANDARD &POOR'S

National Semiconductor Corp

S&P Recommendation HOLD ★★★★★

Price $24.47 (as of Oct 27, 2006)

12-Mo. Target Price $26.00

Investment Style Mid-Cap Value

GICS Sector Information Technology
Sub-Industry Semiconductors

Comment This company is a leading manufacturer of a broad line of semiconductors, including analog, digital and mixed-signal integrated circuits.

Key Stock Statistics (Source S&P, Vickers, company reports)

52-Wk Range	$30.93–20.56	S&P Oper. EPS 2007E	1.30	P/E on S&P Oper. EPS 2007E	18.8	Dividend Rate/Share	$0.16
Trailing 12-Month EPS	$1.37	S&P Oper. EPS 2008E	1.50	Common Shares Outstg. (M)	324.2	Yield (%)	0.65
Trailing 12-Month P/E	17.9	S&P Core EPS 2007E	1.30	Market Capitalization(B)	$7.934	Beta	2.77
$10K Invested 5 Yrs Ago	$17,336	S&P Core EPS 2008E	1.50	Institutional Ownership (%)	87	S&P Credit Rating	NA

Price Performance

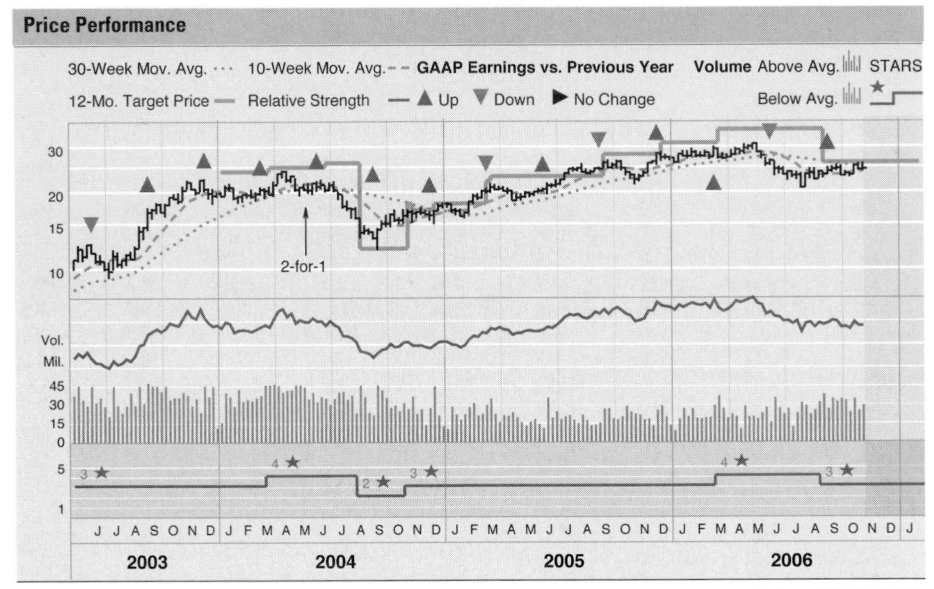

Options: ASE, CBOE, P, Ph

Analysis prepared by **Thomas W. Smith, CFA** on September 22, 2006, when the stock traded at **$ 23.11**.

Highlights

- We expect FY 07 (May) sales to be flat, and project 9% growth in FY 08. NSM is winding down activity for certain older product lines, and we expect the loss of revenues from these businesses to dampen total revenues in FY 07. However, we believe healthy sales growth in higher-margin analog businesses that the company is targeting for the long term should offset any lost sales. In the near term, sales stumbled on weak wireless handset markets and soft summer seasonal trends that have also affected several analog peers.
- We see gross margins improving to 61% in FY 07 and 63% in FY 08, from 59% in FY 06, due to continued focus on wider-margin analog products and better factory efficiency. We expect R&D costs and SG&A expenses to increase as a percentage of sales in FY 07, before declining in FY 08.
- Including stock-based compensation expenses, we forecast operating EPS of $1.30 for FY 07 and $1.50 for FY 08.

Investment Rationale/Risk

- We have a hold recommendation on the shares, given our projection of about 10% growth for the chip industry in calendar 2006 and our neutral outlook for the Semiconductors Sub-Industry. While we believe NSM is capable of gaining market share in the standard linear chip market, and is improving its gross margin, the sales dip in the first quarter makes us cautious on the time frame for progress.
- Risks to our recommendation and target price include the possibility of a sudden deterioration in demand for electronics goods that contain the company's chips and above-average share price volatility.
- We believe the shares are fairly valued. Our 12-month target price of $26 is based on a blend of our P/E and price-to-sales analyses. By applying a P/E multiple of 20X, near the middle of NSM's historical range, to our FY 07 EPS estimate of $1.30, we see potential value at $26. We see a slightly lower value of $25 by applying a price-to-sales ratio of 4X to our FY 07 sales per share estimate of $6.24.

Qualitative Risk Assessment

LOW | MEDIUM | **HIGH**

NSM operates in the semiconductor industry, which historically has experienced industry cycles of about four years. Sudden slowdowns can result from downturns in demand for electronics goods or from chip inventory buildup and industry overcapacity. Share price volatility for the stock is well above average.

Quantitative Evaluations

S&P Quality Ranking B-

D | C | **B-** | B | B+ | A- | A | A+

Relative Strength Rank MODERATE

43

LOWEST = 1 HIGHEST = 99

Revenue/Earnings Data

Revenue (Million $)

	1Q	2Q	3Q	4Q	Year
2007	541.4	--	--	--	--
2006	493.8	544.0	547.7	572.6	2,158
2005	548.0	448.9	449.2	467.0	1,913
2004	424.8	473.5	513.6	571.2	1,983
2003	420.6	422.3	404.3	425.3	1,673
2002	339.3	366.5	369.5	419.5	1,495

Earnings Per Share ($)

2007	0.35	E0.30	E0.31	E0.34	E1.30
2006	0.24	0.32	0.37	0.34	1.26
2005	0.31	0.24	0.21	0.36	1.11
2004	0.08	0.17	0.24	0.24	0.74
2003	0.01	0.02	-0.10	-0.01	-0.09
2002	-0.16	-0.13	-0.11	0.05	-0.34

Fiscal year ended May 31. Next earnings report expected: Early December. EPS Estimates based on S&P Operating Earnings; historical GAAP earnings are as reported.

Dividend Data (Dates: mm/dd Payment Date: mm/dd/yy)

Amount ($)	Date Decl.	Ex-Div. Date	Stk. of Record	Payment Date
0.030	03/09	03/16	03/20	04/10/06
0.030	06/12	06/15	06/19	07/10/06
0.030	09/07	09/14	09/18	10/10/06
0.040	10/06	12/14	12/18	01/08/07

Dividends have been paid since 2005. Source: Company reports.

National Semiconductor Corp

Business Summary September 22, 2006

National Semiconductor's CEO, Brian Halla, who joined the company in 1996, has led an effort to form a "new" NSM. The company's expertise has been primarily in analog intensive, digital, and mixed-signal complex integrated circuits. In 1996, NSM spun off its logic, memory and discrete products (considered commodity-type components) as a separate company, Fairchild Semiconductor. The company now focuses on high-end analog chips.

CEO Halla has often said that information is analog, a key NSM strength. Analog and mixed-signal products process analog information, and convert analog to digital and vice versa. Analog devices, controlling continuously variable functions (such as light, color, sound and power), are used in automotive, telecommunications and industrial applications. About 86% of sales come from the Analog Group in FY 06 (May). Analog sales rose 11% in FY 06, following a 1% increase in FY 05 and a 23% increase in FY 04. Power management demand has been spurred by growth in wireless handsets and other portable electronics where battery life can be a differentiating factor.

The company markets its products globally to original equipment manufacturers (OEMs) and original design manufacturers through a direct salesforce. In FY 06, 49% of sales were made directly to OEMs and 51% came from distributors. Leading distributors include Avnet (which accounted for 12% of NSM's FY 06 sales) and Arrow (12%). International sales accounted for 80% of total sales in FY 06.

Wafer fabrication is concentrated in two facilities in the U.S. and one in Scotland. Nearly all product assembly and final test operations are performed in several facilities in Asia. The Singapore assembly and test facility is scheduled for closure in FY 07 and most operations were transferred to the Malaysia and China plants during FY 06.

Company Financials

Per Share Data ($) Year Ended May 31	**2006**	**2005**	**2004**	**2003**	**2002**	**2001**	**2000**	**1999**	**1998**	**1997**
Tangible Book Value	5.57	5.65	4.21	4.18	4.46	4.70	4.63	2.67	5.62	6.03
Cash Flow	1.72	1.63	1.27	0.54	0.31	1.30	2.33	-1.81	0.59	0.91
Earnings	1.26	1.11	0.74	-0.09	-0.34	0.65	1.64	-3.02	-0.30	0.10
S&P Core Earnings	1.21	1.15	0.26	-0.59	-0.84	0.29	NA	NA	NA	NA
Dividends	0.04	Nil	Nil	Nil	Nil	Nil	Nil	Nil	Nil	Nil
Payout Ratio	3%	Nil	Nil	Nil	Nil	Nil	Nil	Nil	Nil	Nil
Calendar Year	2005	2004	2003	2002	2001	2000	1999	1998	1997	1996
Prices:High	28.75	24.35	22.63	18.65	17.55	42.97	25.94	14.13	21.44	13.81
Prices:Low	18.36	11.85	6.27	4.98	9.85	8.56	4.44	3.72	10.81	6.50
P/E Ratio:High	23	22	31	NM	NM	66	16	NM	NM	NM
P/E Ratio:Low	15	11	8	NM	NM	13	3	NM	NM	NM
Income Statement Analysis (Million $)										
Revenue	2,158	1,913	1,983	1,673	1,495	2,113	2,140	1,957	2,537	2,507
Operating Income	844	626	582	248	81.9	517	550	20.2	342	357
Depreciation	166	194	210	229	230	243	264	406	292	231
Interest Expense	Nil	Nil	Nil	Nil	3.90	5.00	17.9	Nil	26.3	13.8
Pretax Income	695	410	334	-23.3	-123	307	642	-1,085	-99.7	57.3
Effective Tax Rate	35.4%	NM	14.7%	NM	NM	19.4%	2.32%	NM	NM	52.0%
Net Income	449	415	285	-33.3	-122	246	628	-1,010	-98.6	27.5
S&P Core Earnings	433	430	102	-215	-298	108	NA	NA	NA	NA
Balance Sheet & Other Financial Data (Million $)										
Cash	932	867	643	802	681	818	850	419	461	890
Current Assets	1,541	1,514	1,246	1,281	1,073	1,275	1,468	989	1,308	1,553
Total Assets	2,511	2,504	2,280	2,245	2,289	2,362	2,382	2,044	3,101	2,914
Current Liabilities	398	285	461	367	404	472	628	665	794	791
Long Term Debt	21.1	23.0	Nil	19.9	20.4	26.0	48.6	416	391	324
Common Equity	1,926	2,062	1,681	1,706	1,781	1,768	1,643	701	1,859	1,749
Total Capital	1,947	2,085	1,681	1,726	1,802	1,794	1,692	1,317	2,254	2,082
Capital Expenditures	163	96.6	215	171	138	228	170	303	622	593
Cash Flow	616	610	495	195	109	489	891	-604	194	259
Current Ratio	3.9	5.3	2.7	3.5	2.7	2.7	2.3	1.5	1.6	2.0
% Long Term Debt of Capitalization	1.1	1.1	Nil	1.2	1.1	1.4	2.9	31.6	17.3	15.6
% Net Income of Revenue	20.8	21.7	14.4	NM	NM	11.6	29.3	NM	NM	1.1
% Return on Assets	17.9	17.4	12.6	NM	NM	10.3	28.4	NM	NM	1.0
% Return on Equity	22.6	22.1	16.8	NM	NM	14.4	49.3	NM	NM	1.7

Data as orig reptd.; bef. results of disc opers/spec. items. Per share data adj. for stk. divs.; EPS diluted. E-Estimated. NA-Not Available. NM-Not Meaningful. NR-Not Ranked. UR-Under Review.

Office: 2900 Semiconductor Dr, Santa Clara, CA 95051-0695.
Telephone: 408-721-5000.
Email: invest.group@nsc.com
Website: http://www.national.com

Chrmn & CEO: B.L. Halla
Pres & COO: D. Macleod
SVP & CFO: L. Chew
SVP, Secy & General Counsel: J.M. Clark, III

SVP & CIO: U. Seif
Board of Directors: S. R. Appleton, G. P. Arnold, R. J. Danzig, J. T. Dickson, R. J. Frankenberg, B. L. Halla, E. F. Kvamme, M. A. Maidique, E. R. McCracken

Founded: 1959
Domicile: Delaware
Employees: 8,500

STANDARD &POOR'S

Navistar International Corp

S&P Recommendation HOLD ★★★★★

Price $28.19 (as of Oct 27, 2006)

12-Mo. Target Price $30.00

Investment Style Mid-Cap Value

GICS Sector Industrials
Sub-Industry Construction & Farm Machinery & Heavy Trucks

Comment NAV is a global maker of trucks, buses, and diesel engines.

Key Stock Statistics (Source S&P, Vickers, company reports)

52-Wk Range	$30.55–20.53	S&P Oper. EPS 2005**E**	4.80	P/E on S&P Oper. EPS 2005**E**	5.9	Dividend Rate/Share	Nil
Trailing 12-Month EPS	$3.79	S&P Oper. EPS 2006**E**	5.30	Common Shares Outstg. (M)	70.1	Yield (%)	Nil
Trailing 12-Month P/E	7.4	S&P Core EPS 2005**E**	4.36	Market Capitalization(B)	$1.976	Beta	2.02
$10K Invested 5 Yrs Ago	$9,117	S&P Core EPS 2006**E**	5.06	Institutional Ownership (%)	99	S&P Credit Rating	BB-

Price Performance

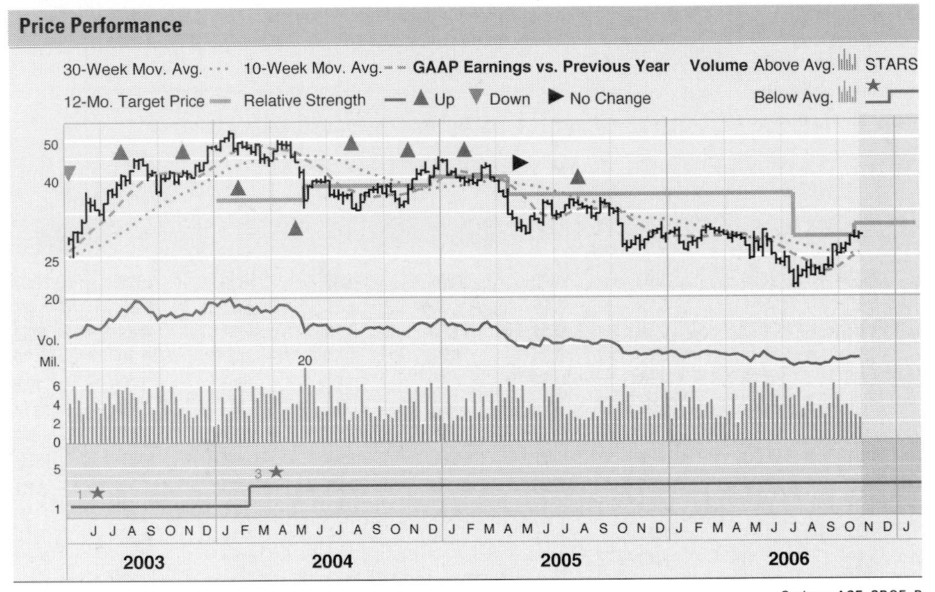

Options: ASE, CBOE, P

Analysis prepared by **Anthony M. Fiore, CFA** on October 18, 2006, when the stock traded at **$ 28.61**.

Highlights

- We think that a projected downturn in the truck manufacturing industry should result in a 10% to 15% decline in revenue in FY 07 (Oct.), following a projected advance of about 10% in FY 06. We anticipate that the replacement cycle, currently under way in our view, will result in higher unit volumes in FY 06. However, we believe that a significant portion of this demand is being generated from fleet owners seeking to purchase in advance of more stringent emission standards expected in 2007.
- We expect operating margins to narrow in FY 07, based largely on our outlook for lower volumes partly offset by benefits from ongoing cost reduction initiatives. However, in our view, higher steel prices and increased production costs related to emission standards are likely to continue to limit margin expansion in FY 06.
- Our FY 06 and FY 07 S&P Core EPS estimates are each $0.24 below our respective operating EPS forecasts, with the difference reflecting projected stock option expense and pension and post-retirement related cost adjustments. Our FY 06 and FY 07 operating EPS estimates each include $0.20 of projected stock option expense.

Investment Rationale/Risk

- We expect conditions in the medium- and heavy-duty truck markets to remain favorable in FY 06, before a projected downturn in FY 07. While we believe that NAV is making progress in improving its cost structure, we think higher product development expenses are likely to limit profitability gains in the near term. Given significant financial leverage, the SEC's investigation into NAV's restatement of financial results, and the growing maturity of the truck replacement cycle, we would not add to positions.
- Risks to our recommendation and target price include an unexpected downturn in the truck manufacturing market, continued raw material cost escalation, and further component shortages from suppliers.
- Our 12-month target price of $30 blends two valuation metrics. Our discounted cash flow model, which assumes a 5% to 6% average annual free cash flow growth rate over the next 10 years, 3.5% growth in perpetuity, and a 9% weighted average cost of capital, indicates intrinsic value of about $32. In terms of relative valuation, applying a target P/E multiple of 12X, in line with historical norms, to our FY 07 EPS estimate of $2.25 suggests a value of about $27.

Qualitative Risk Assessment

LOW | MEDIUM | **HIGH**

Our risk assessment for Navistar International reflects the cyclical nature of the company's business, limited accounting visibility due to delays in the filing of financial statements, significant postretirement benefit obligations, and our view of its relatively high financial leverage.

Quantitative Evaluations

S&P Quality Ranking C

D | **C** | B- | B | B+ | A- | A | A+

Relative Strength Rank STRONG

84

LOWEST = 1 HIGHEST = 99

Revenue/Earnings Data

Revenue (Million $)

	1Q	2Q	3Q	4Q	Year
2005	2,558	2,970	2,994	--	--
2004	1,943	2,354	2,348	3,079	9,724
2003	1,578	1,864	1,894	2,004	7,340
2002	1,465	1,672	1,591	2,056	6,784
2001	1,507	1,794	1,586	1,835	6,722
2000	2,166	2,388	1,924	1,973	8,451

Earnings Per Share ($)

2005	0.24	0.70	0.83	**E**3.06	**E**4.80
2004	-0.22	0.70	0.64	2.02	3.20
2003	-1.47	-0.18	0.26	1.00	-0.21
2002	-0.88	-0.04	-0.26	-6.67	-7.88
2001	-0.58	0.05	0.03	0.11	-0.39
2000	1.10	1.60	1.58	-1.77	2.58

Fiscal year ended Oct. 31. Next earnings report expected: NA. EPS Estimates based on S&P Operating Earnings; historical GAAP earnings are as reported.

Dividend Data

No cash dividends have been paid.

Navistar International Corp

Business Summary October 18, 2006

In April 2006, NAV said that it intends to restate results for FY 02 (Oct.) through FY 04 and for nine months of FY 05. It also says it has designated KPMG as its new independent auditor, replacing Deloitte & Touche. We think the change in auditors could further delay the filing of NAV's 10-K for FY 05. In June 2006, NAV also said it expects to file a 10-K for FY 06 by the middle of January 2007. Shortly before that time frame, NAV expects to complete the FY 02 through July FY 05 restatement.

Navistar International was created from the former International Harvester (IH). After shedding its construction and farm equipment businesses in the mid-1980s, the company's remaining truck and engine business was renamed Navistar International Corporation. NAV operates in three principal industry segments: trucks, engines, and financial services.

The truck-making segment accounted for 74% of FY 04 (Oct.) revenues. The segment primarily makes a full line of diesel powered medium and heavy-duty trucks, school buses, and severe service vehicles for the Class 6 through Class 8 truck markets in the U.S., Canada and Mexico. In general, these volatile and competitive end markets tend to move in response to cycles in the overall economy, and are particularly sensitive to fluctuations in the industrial sector. In FY 04, the company delivered 103,800 Class 6 through 8 trucks, including school buses, in the U.S., Canada and Mexico, an increase of 26% from the 82,200 units delivered in FY 03. Competitors in the Class 6 through Class 8 markets include PACCAR, Ford, GM, DaimlerChrysler (including Freightliner, Sterling, and Western Star), and Volvo Global (including Volvo Trucks and Mack Trucks). Margins for this segment over the last eight years averaged about 0.8%.

The company also makes diesel engines (23% of FY 04 revenues) for sale to third-party truck manufacturers, as well as for use in its own trucks and school buses. Under a 10-year agreement that began in 2003, NAV supplies V-8 diesel engines to Ford for use in Ford's diesel powered super duty trucks and vans. As of the end of FY 04, sales of mid-range diesel engines to Ford accounted for about 76% of total diesel engine unit volume. Primary competitors in the diesel engine manufacturing industry include Cummins, Caterpillar, and DaimlerChrysler's Detroit Diesel unit. Over the last eight years, segment margins averaged about 12%.

Company Financials

Per Share Data ($) Year Ended Oct. 31	**2004**	**2003**	**2002**	**2001**	**2000**	**1999**	**1998**	**1997**	**1996**	**1995**
Tangible Book Value	7.59	4.45	4.08	14.33	17.05	16.03	8.61	7.83	4.86	4.15
Cash Flow	6.28	2.60	-4.25	3.26	5.82	10.81	6.39	3.26	2.24	3.29
Earnings	3.20	-0.21	-7.88	-0.39	2.58	8.20	4.16	1.65	0.49	1.83
S&P Core Earnings	3.59	1.34	-10.38	-4.10	NA	NA	NA	NA	NA	NA
Dividends	Nil	Nil	Nil	Nil	Nil	Nil	Nil	Nil	Nil	Nil
Payout Ratio	Nil	Nil	Nil	Nil	Nil	Nil	Nil	Nil	Nil	Nil
Prices:High	52.95	48.71	47.38	41.20	48.00	56.25	35.88	29.50	12.13	17.50
Prices:Low	32.72	20.52	14.77	21.78	18.25	27.13	17.00	9.00	8.38	9.00
P/E Ratio:High	17	NM	NM	NM	19	7	9	18	25	10
P/E Ratio:Low	10	NM	NM	NM	7	3	4	5	17	5
Income Statement Analysis (Million $)										
Revenue	9,724	7,340	6,784	6,722	8,451	8,582	7,830	6,321	5,705	6,292
Operating Income	693	267	155	357	942	835	619	386	240	380
Depreciation	256	191	220	217	199	174	159	120	101	81.0
Interest Expense	127	272	154	161	146	135	105	74.0	83.0	87.0
Pretax Income	311	-45.0	-769	-47.0	224	591	410	242	105	262
Effective Tax Rate	20.6%	NM	NM	NM	29.0%	7.95%	27.1%	38.0%	38.1%	37.4%
Net Income	247	-14.0	-476	-23.0	159	544	299	150	65.0	164
S&P Core Earnings	279	91.4	-626	-245	NA	NA	NA	NA	NA	NA
Balance Sheet & Other Financial Data (Million $)										
Cash	860	1,042	736	1,085	501	576	440	609	881	485
Current Assets	3,167	2,210	2,608	2,736	2,467	2,842	NA	NA	NA	NA
Total Assets	7,592	6,900	6,943	7,067	6,945	6,928	6,178	5,516	5,326	5,566
Current Liabilities	3,250	2,204	2,399	2,273	2,409	2,502	NA	NA	NA	NA
Long Term Debt	2,045	2,396	2,398	2,468	2,148	2,075	2,122	1,316	1,420	1,279
Common Equity	527	306	247	1,123	1,310	1,287	765	776	672	626
Total Capital	2,576	2,706	2,649	3,595	3,462	3,366	3,891	2,336	2,092	1,905
Capital Expenditures	230	206	242	326	553	427	305	172	117	139
Cash Flow	503	177	-256	194	358	718	447	241	166	245
Current Ratio	1.0	1.0	1.1	1.2	1.0	1.1	NA	NA	NA	NA
% Long Term Debt of Capitalization	79.4	88.5	90.5	68.7	62.0	61.6	73.4	56.3	67.9	67.1
% Net Income of Revenue	2.5	NM	NM	NM	1.9	6.3	3.8	2.4	11.4	2.6
% Return on Assets	3.4	NM	NM	NM	2.3	8.3	5.1	2.8	1.2	3.1
% Return on Equity	60.6	NM	NM	NM	12.2	53.0	37.4	16.7	10.0	27.4

Data as orig reptd.; bef. results of disc opers/spec. items. Per share data adj. for stk. divs.; EPS diluted. E-Estimated. NA-Not Available. NM-Not Meaningful. NR-Not Ranked. UR-Under Review.

Office: 4201 Winfield Road, Warrenville, IL 60555.
Telephone: 630-753-5000.
Website: http://www.internationaldelivers.com
Chrmn, Pres & CEO: D.C. Ustian

Vice Chrmn: R.C. Lannert
EVP & CFO: B. Caton
SVP & Treas: T.M. Endsley
SVP & General Counsel: S.K. Covey

Investor Contact: M. Oberle (630-753-2406)
Board of Directors: Y. M. Belton, B. Caton, E. Clariond, J. D. Correnti, A. J. Griffin, M. N. Hammes, J. H. Keyes, D. McAllister, S. Morcott, D. C. Ustian

Founded: 1902
Domicile: Delaware
Employees: 14,800

STANDARD &POOR'S

NCR Corp

S&P Recommendation HOLD ★★★★★	**Price** $41.14 (as of Oct 27, 2006)	**12-Mo. Target Price** $42.00	**Investment Style** Mid-Cap Value

GICS Sector Information Technology
Sub-Industry Computer Hardware

Comment This Ohio-based company, spun off from AT&T in 1996, makes and services information technology products, services and solutions worldwide.

Key Stock Statistics (Source S&P, Vickers, company reports)

52-Wk Range	$44.45–29.10	S&P Oper. EPS 2006E	1.86	P/E on S&P Oper. EPS 2006E	22.1	Dividend Rate/Share	Nil
Trailing 12-Month EPS	$1.94	S&P Oper. EPS 2007E	2.11	Common Shares Outstg. (M)	180.2	Yield (%)	Nil
Trailing 12-Month P/E	21.2	S&P Core EPS 2006E	1.78	Market Capitalization(B)	$7.413	Beta	2.29
$10K Invested 5 Yrs Ago	$22,389	S&P Core EPS 2007E	2.03	Institutional Ownership (%)	82	S&P Credit Rating	BBB-

Price Performance

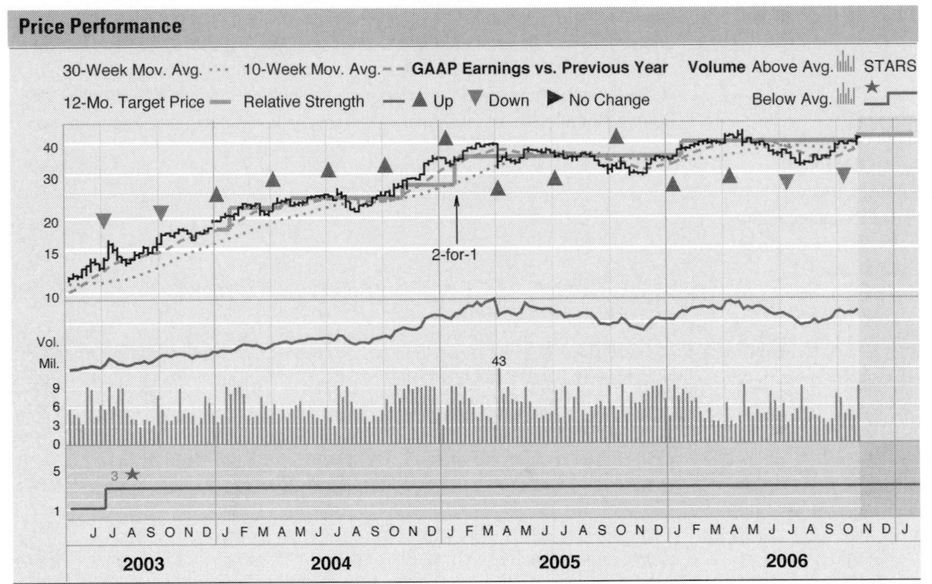

Options: ASE, CBOE

Highlights

- The 12-month target price for NCR has recently been changed to $42.00 from $40.00. The Highlights section of this Stock Report will be updated accordingly.

Investment Rationale/Risk

- The Investment Rationale/Risk section of this Stock Report will be updated shortly. For the latest News story on NCR from MarketScope, see below.

- 10/26/06 11:46 am EDT... S&P REITERATES HOLD RECOMMENDATION ON SHARES OF NCR CORP. (NCR 38.73***): NCR posts Q3 EPS of $0.49 vs. $0.45, $0.04 above our estimate. Revenue rose 1%, in line with our forecast, as the Data Warehousing and Retail Store Automation segments each expanded by 5%. We are raising our '06 EPS estimate by $0.12 to $1.98 and our 12-month target price by $2 to $42. We are pleased with NCR's ability to improve earnings despite limited revenue growth. In addition, share repurchases and free cash flow were also encouraging. But with shares trading at a P/E premium of 25% to the S&P 500, we believe these factors are already reflected in the stock. /R. Stice-CFA

Qualitative Risk Assessment

LOW | **MEDIUM** | HIGH

Our risk assessment reflects our view of NCR's improved margin profile over the past two years, offset by revenue growth challenges we see in its ATM and retail solutions businesses, reflecting pricing competition and maturing market opportunities.

Quantitative Evaluations

S&P Quality Ranking B

D | C | B- | **B** | B+ | A- | A | A+

Relative Strength Rank STRONG

85

LOWEST = 1 HIGHEST = 99

Revenue/Earnings Data

Revenue (Million $)

	1Q	2Q	3Q	4Q	Year
2006	1,283	1,531	1,517	--	--
2005	1,343	1,470	1,498	1,717	6,028
2004	1,290	1,452	1,454	1,788	5,984
2003	1,234	1,366	1,355	1,643	5,598
2002	1,247	1,380	1,377	1,581	5,585
2001	1,376	1,499	1,442	1,600	5,917

Earnings Per Share ($)

2006	0.22	0.42	0.49	E0.73	E1.86
2005	0.16	0.67	1.18	0.81	2.80
2004	-0.03	0.63	0.23	0.68	1.51
2003	-0.14	-0.07	0.10	0.42	0.30
2002	0.02	0.13	0.21	0.29	0.63
2001	0.61	0.18	-0.04	0.36	1.11

Fiscal year ended Dec. 31. Next earnings report expected: Late January. EPS Estimates based on S&P Operating Earnings; historical GAAP earnings are as reported.

Dividend Data

No cash dividends have been paid.

Please read the Required Disclosures and Analyst Certification on the last page of this report.

NCR Corp

Business Summary September 28, 2006

CORPORATE OVERVIEW. NCR Corp. provides technology and services that help businesses interact, connect and relate with their customers. The company categorizes its operations into six reportable segments: Data Warehousing (roughly 24% of total company revenue in 2005), Financial Self Service (22%), Retail Store Automation (14%), Customer Services (29%), Systemedia (8%) and Payment & Imaging and Other (3%).

Under the Teradata brand name, NCR provides data warehousing solutions for customers that combine software, data mining and analytical applications, hardware, and consulting and support services. The Financial Self Service business offers financial institutions, retailers and independent deployers Automated Teller Machines (ATMs), cash dispensers and software. Within the Retail Store Automation business, the company supplies point-of-sale terminals, self service kiosks and bar code scanners.

In 2005, revenue from outside of the U.S. accounted for 56% of the overall total, down from 57% in 2004. In addition, no single customer accounted for more than 10% of total revenue.

COMPETITIVE LANDSCAPE. Within the Teradata division, competition includes IBM and Oracle. NCR believes that the Teradata unit is one of only a few businesses that can provide complete, integrated and optimized data warehousing solutions. In the Financial Self Service market, the company competes directly with Diebold Inc. and Wincor Nixdorf GmbH.

In the Retail Store Automation business, NCR's competitors vary according to market segment, product, service and geography. Its primary rivals, however, are IBM, Wincor, Fujitsu, Hewlett-Packard, Dell, Metrologic and PSC Inc. Competition in the Customer Services unit is derived from other technology providers and service only firms. NCR believes that more global technology providers are becoming focused on this niche, which is increasing competitiveness in this segment.

In our estimation, Systemedia operates in a highly competitive market. Areas of differentiation are typically quality, logistics and supply chain management expertise, and total cost of ownership. Finally, in the Payment and Imaging business, NCR competes by product, service and geography. Other participants include IBM and Unisys Corp.

Company Financials

Per Share Data ($) Year Ended Dec. 31	2005	2004	2003	2002	2001	2000	1999	1998	1997	1996
Tangible Book Value	10.49	10.51	9.35	6.31	10.41	6.46	8.52	6.89	6.57	6.91
Cash Flow	4.10	2.95	1.94	2.28	3.23	2.75	3.45	2.38	1.91	1.37
Earnings	2.80	1.51	0.30	0.63	1.11	0.91	1.68	0.60	0.04	-0.54
S&P Core Earnings	2.93	1.47	0.29	-0.80	-0.54	NA	NA	NA	NA	NA
Dividends	Nil	Nil	Nil	Nil	Nil	Nil	Nil	Nil	Nil	Nil
Payout Ratio	Nil	Nil	Nil	Nil	Nil	Nil	Nil	Nil	Nil	Nil
Prices:High	39.84	35.50	19.74	22.75	25.00	26.84	27.88	20.94	20.69	20.38
Prices:Low	29.09	19.36	8.46	9.40	14.30	16.19	13.34	11.75	12.94	15.44
P/E Ratio:High	14	24	66	36	23	29	17	35	NM	NM
P/E Ratio:Low	10	13	28	15	13	18	8	20	NM	NM
Income Statement Analysis (Million $)										
Revenue	6,028	5,984	5,598	5,585	5,917	5,959	6,196	6,505	6,589	6,963
Operating Income	657	508	445	517	609	566	436	516	304	515
Depreciation	247	275	315	328	423	361	358	364	383	385
Interest Expense	23.0	23.0	26.0	19.0	18.0	13.0	12.0	13.0	15.0	56.0
Pretax Income	396	251	72.0	131	124	275	235	212	27.0	110
Effective Tax Rate	NM	NM	19.4%	2.29%	NM	35.3%	NM	42.5%	74.1%	NM
Net Income	529	290	58.0	128	221	178	337	122	7.00	-109
S&P Core Earnings	553	283	55.1	-159	-106	NA	NA	NA	NA	NA
Balance Sheet & Other Financial Data (Million $)										
Cash	810	750	689	526	336	357	763	514	1,129	1,203
Current Assets	2,693	2,633	2,422	2,186	1,963	2,234	2,541	2,632	3,271	3,318
Total Assets	5,287	5,554	5,480	4,672	4,855	5,106	4,895	4,892	5,293	5,280
Current Liabilities	1,645	1,724	1,579	1,417	1,518	1,836	1,662	1,700	1,964	1,967
Long Term Debt	305	307	307	306	10.0	11.0	40.0	33.0	35.0	48.0
Common Equity	2,035	2,086	1,875	1,325	2,027	1,758	1,596	1,447	1,353	1,396
Total Capital	2,361	2,411	2,204	1,651	2,059	1,796	1,685	1,524	1,652	1,733
Capital Expenditures	73.0	77.0	63.0	81.0	141	216	187	224	162	216
Cash Flow	776	565	373	456	644	539	695	486	390	276
Current Ratio	1.6	1.5	1.5	1.5	1.3	1.2	1.5	1.5	1.7	1.7
% Long Term Debt of Capitalization	12.9	12.7	13.9	18.5	0.5	0.6	2.4	2.2	2.1	2.8
% Net Income of Revenue	8.8	4.8	1.0	2.3	3.7	3.0	5.4	1.9	0.1	NM
% Return on Assets	9.8	5.4	1.1	2.7	4.4	3.6	6.9	2.4	0.1	NM
% Return on Equity	25.7	14.6	3.6	7.6	11.7	10.6	22.1	8.7	0.5	NM

Data as orig reptd.; bef. results of disc opers/spec. items. Per share data adj. for stk. divs.; EPS diluted. E-Estimated. NA-Not Available. NM-Not Meaningful. NR-Not Ranked. UR-Under Review.

Office: 1700 S Patterson Blvd, Dayton, OH 45479.
Telephone: 937-445-5000.
Email: investor.relations@ncr.com
Website: http://www.ncr.com

Chrmn: J. Ringler
Pres & CEO: W. Nuti
SVP & CFO: P. Bocian
SVP, Secy & General Counsel: P. Lieb

Investor Contact: G. Swearingen (937-445-4700)
Board of Directors: E. P. Boykin, G. Daichendt, M. Frissora, M. V. Hurd, L. F. Levinson, V. L. Lund, W. Nuti, L. Nyberg, C. K. Prahalad, J. M. Ringler, W. S. Stavropoulos

Founded: 1884
Domicile: Maryland
Employees: 28,200

STANDARD &POOR'S

Network Appliance Inc

S&P Recommendation HOLD ★★★★★

Price $35.78 (as of Oct 27, 2006)

12-Mo. Target Price $34.00

Investment Style Large-Cap Growth

GICS Sector Information Technology
Sub-Industry Computer Storage & Peripherals

Comment This company manufactures and supports high-performance network data storage devices that provide file service for data-intensive network environments.

Key Stock Statistics (Source S&P, Vickers, company reports)

52-Wk Range	**$39.73–25.85**	S&P Oper. EPS 2007**E**	**0.66**	P/E on S&P Oper. EPS 2007**E**	**54.2**	Dividend Rate/Share	**Nil**
Trailing 12-Month EPS	**$0.67**	S&P Oper. EPS 2008**E**	**0.99**	Common Shares Outstg. (M)	**372.4**	Yield (%)	**Nil**
Trailing 12-Month P/E	**53.4**	S&P Core EPS 2007**E**	**0.66**	Market Capitalization(B)	**$13.325**	Beta	**3.37**
$10K Invested 5 Yrs Ago	**$27,188**	S&P Core EPS 2008**E**	**0.99**	Institutional Ownership (%)	**88**	S&P Credit Rating	**NA**

Price Performance

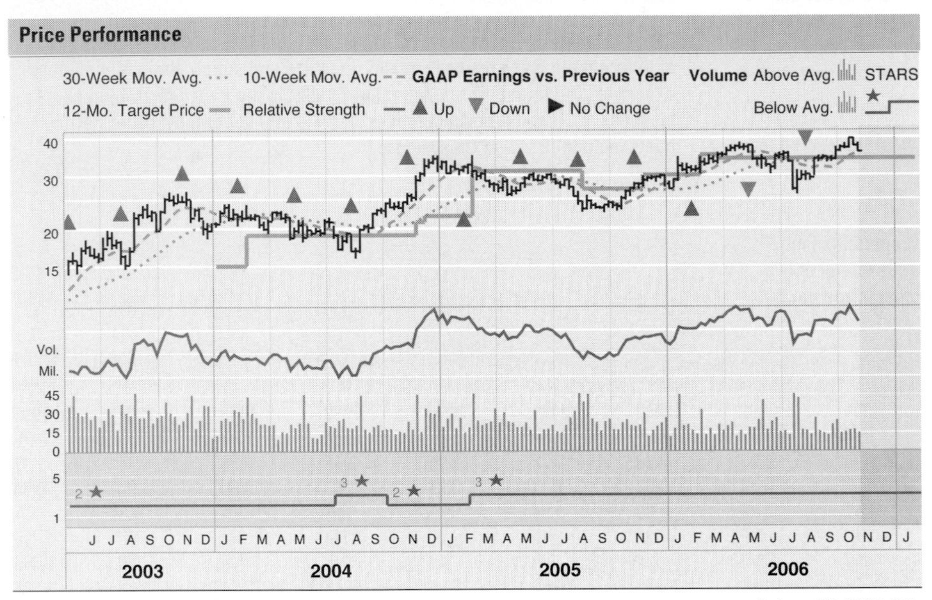

Options: ASE, CBOE, P, Ph

Analysis prepared by **Richard N. Stice, CFA** on August 23, 2006, when the stock traded at **$ 34.38**.

Highlights

- We expect revenues to advance about 32% in FY 07 (Apr.), following a rise of 29% in FY 06. This reflects our view that spending on products related to data storage will remain a high priority over the next 12 months, and that NTAP's new high-end product (Excelsior) offering, which began shipping during the April quarter, should stimulate additional demand. Moreover, we believe market share gains are likely to continue.
- We see gross margins narrowing, due to a shift in the business mix as NTAP's services revenue expands as a percentage of the overall total, and to an increasing focus on the small and mid-size business market. Conversely, we believe EPS will be aided by an acceleration in interest income as a result of what we expect to be continuing free cash flow generation. We also anticipate that additional share repurchases will take place during FY 07.
- We project FY 07 EPS of $0.66, down about 4% from FY 06's $0.69. We note that these totals include charges related to stock-based compensation expense.

Investment Rationale/Risk

- We believe the company possesses an attractive industry position within the data storage market. In addition, we think new product offerings such as the FAS6030 and the FAS6070 should help boost growth rates over the next few quarters. However, we think these factors are already reflected in the current share price. Moreover, based on our valuation analysis, we believe upside for the shares is limited.
- Risks to our recommendation and target price include demand for network storage products rising at a slower rate than we anticipate, a lengthening of the sales cycle, and a lack of execution associated with ongoing product transitions.
- Our 12-month target price of $34 is based on a combination of valuation metrics. The first is a relative P/E measure, in which we allocate a ratio of 50X our FY 07 EPS estimate of $0.66, within NTAP's three year average range. This results in a value of $33. The second metric, discounted cash flow (DCF) analysis, leads to an intrinsic value of $34. Our DCF assumptions include a weighted average cost of capital of 10.8% and an expected terminal growth rate of 3%.

Qualitative Risk Assessment

LOW | **MEDIUM** | HIGH

Our risk assessment takes into consideration the volatile nature of the data storage industry and the rapid pace of technological change. However, we believe these factors are offset by NTAP's market share position and earnings growth.

Quantitative Evaluations

S&P Quality Ranking **B**

D | C | B- | **B** | B+ | A- | A | A+

Relative Strength Rank **MODERATE**

37

LOWEST = 1 HIGHEST = 99

Revenue/Earnings Data

Revenue (Million $)

	1Q	2Q	3Q	4Q	Year
2007	621.3	--	--	--	--
2006	448.4	483.1	537.0	598.0	2,066
2005	358.4	375.2	412.7	451.8	1,598
2004	260.5	275.6	297.3	337.0	1,170
2003	206.8	215.2	228.5	241.6	892.1
2002	200.4	194.7	198.4	204.9	798.4

Earnings Per Share ($)

2007	0.14	**E**0.15	**E**0.17	**E**0.20	**E**0.66
2006	0.16	0.18	0.20	0.15	0.69
2005	0.13	0.15	0.16	0.16	0.59
2004	0.08	0.13	0.11	0.10	0.42
2003	0.05	0.05	0.06	0.07	0.22
2002	Nil	-0.03	0.02	0.02	0.01

Fiscal year ended Apr. 30. Next earnings report expected: Mid November. EPS Estimates based on S&P Operating Earnings; historical GAAP earnings are as reported.

Dividend Data

No cash dividends have been paid.

Network Appliance Inc

STANDARD &POOR'S

Business Summary August 23, 2006

Network Appliance supplies enterprise storage and data management software and hardware products and services. NTAP's solutions help global enterprises meet major information technology challenges such as managing the continued growth in the volume of data, scaling existing infrastructure, regulatory compliance and corporate security.

The NTAP family of modular, scalable, highly available, unified networked systems provides seamless access to a full range of enterprise data for users on a variety of platforms. These include Fibre Channel (FC), network-attached storage (NAS), storage area network (SAN), iSCSI environments, and Web data in central locations. NTAP refers to this as fabric-attached storage (FAS). Products include the 200, 900, 3000, and 6000 series.

NTAP's V-Series is a network-based solution that consolidates storage arrays from different suppliers enabling unified SAN and file access to data stored in heterogeneous FC SAN storage arrays. The V-Series family supports products from Hewlett-Packard, Hitachi Data Systems, and IBM.

NearStore products focus on optimizing data protection and retention applications. This system offers an alternative to customers by providing faster data access than offline storage at a significantly lower cost than primary storage. Offerings in this category include the Virtual Tape Library (VTL), a disk-to-disk backup appliance that appears as a tape library to a back-up software application.

The NetCache suite of solutions is designed to manage, control and improve access to Web-based information. Working with a range of software partners, NetCache gives large enterprises the ability to manage Internet access and security, thereby enabling IT managers to control who in their user base is going where on the Internet, when, and what content is being accessed.

Company Financials

Per Share Data ($) Year Ended Apr. 30	**2006**	**2005**	**2004**	**2003**	**2002**	**2001**	**2000**	**1999**	**1998**	**1997**
Tangible Book Value	3.62	3.67	2.91	2.75	2.39	2.21	1.54	1.02	0.64	0.41
Cash Flow	0.90	0.77	0.58	0.38	0.14	0.33	0.26	0.14	0.18	0.02
Earnings	0.69	0.59	0.42	0.22	0.01	0.21	0.21	0.12	0.07	Nil
S&P Core Earnings	0.45	0.39	0.16	-0.28	-0.77	-0.52	NA	NA	NA	NA
Dividends	Nil	Nil	Nil	Nil	Nil	Nil	Nil	Nil	Nil	Nil
Payout Ratio	Nil	Nil	Nil	Nil	Nil	Nil	Nil	Nil	Nil	Nil
Calendar Year	2005	2004	2003	2002	2001	2000	1999	1998	1997	1996
Prices:High	34.98	34.99	26.69	27.95	74.98	152.75	45.94	12.00	4.50	3.23
Prices:Low	22.50	15.92	9.26	5.18	6.00	33.88	9.53	3.25	1.33	1.25
P/E Ratio:High	51	59	64	NM	NM	NM	NM	NM	62	98
P/E Ratio:Low	33	27	22	NM	NM	NM	NM	NM	18	54

Income Statement Analysis (Million $)										
Revenue	2,066	1,598	1,170	892	798	1,006	579	289	166	93.3
Operating Income	395	319	228	146	76.5	179	121	63.3	38.2	20.7
Depreciation	81.8	65.6	59.5	57.4	65.3	42.3	15.7	8.15	5.55	2.78
Interest Expense	1.28	Nil	Nil	Nil	Nil	Nil	Nil	0.78	0.21	0.09
Pretax Income	350	276	170	97.8	2.53	133	114	57.0	33.5	4.04
Effective Tax Rate	23.9%	18.3%	10.8%	21.8%	NM	43.7%	35.5%	37.5%	37.5%	93.8%
Net Income	266	226	152	76.5	3.03	74.9	73.8	35.6	21.0	0.25
S&P Core Earnings	175	148	59.5	-98.0	-256	-167	NA	NA	NA	NA

Balance Sheet & Other Financial Data (Million $)										
Cash	461	194	241	284	211	272	279	221	37.3	21.5
Current Assets	2,033	1,576	1,089	853	679	636	533	315	98.9	56.6
Total Assets	3,261	2,373	1,877	1,319	1,109	1,036	592	346	116	68.9
Current Liabilities	917	520	344	265	216	219	113	50.5	29.3	14.7
Long Term Debt	138	4.47	4.86	3.10	3.73	0.15	0.05	0.09	0.16	0.21
Common Equity	1,923	1,661	1,416	987	858	804	479	296	86.3	54.0
Total Capital	2,061	1,665	1,421	990	862	805	479	296	86.4	54.2
Capital Expenditures	133	93.6	48.6	61.3	284	83.7	40.8	15.5	7.97	7.12
Cash Flow	348	291	212	134	47.4	117	89.5	43.8	26.5	3.03
Current Ratio	2.2	3.0	3.2	3.2	3.2	2.9	4.7	6.2	3.4	3.9
% Long Term Debt of Capitalization	6.7	0.3	0.3	0.3	0.4	0.0	0.0	0.0	Nil	Nil
% Net Income of Revenue	12.9	14.1	13.0	8.6	0.4	7.4	12.7	12.3	12.6	0.3
% Return on Assets	9.5	10.6	9.5	6.3	0.3	9.2	15.7	15.4	22.7	0.4
% Return on Equity	14.9	14.7	12.7	8.3	0.4	11.7	19.1	18.6	29.9	0.5

Data as orig reptd.; bef. results of disc opers/spec. items. Per share data adj. for stk. divs.; EPS diluted. E-Estimated. NA-Not Available. NM-Not Meaningful. NR-Not Ranked. UR-Under Review.

Office: 495 East Java Drive, Sunnyvale, CA 94089.
Telephone: 408-822-6000.
Email: investor_relations@netapp.com
Website: http://www.netapp.com

Chrmn: D.T. Valentine
Pres: T.F. Mendoza
CEO: D.J. Warmenhoven
EVP & CFO: S.J. Gomo

SVP & CTO: S. Kleinman
Investor Contact: K. McGaughey (408-822-3856)
Board of Directors: J. R. Allen, C. A. Bartz, A. L. Earhart, E. Kozel, M. Leslie, N. G. Moore, G. T. Shaheen, D. T. Valentine, R. T. Wall, D. J. Warmenhoven

Founded: 1992
Domicile: Delaware
Employees: 4,976

STANDARD &POOR'S

Newell Rubbermaid Inc.

S&P Recommendation HOLD ★★★★★

Price $28.78 (as of Oct 31, 2006)

12-Mo. Target Price $31.00

Investment Style Mid-Cap Value

GICS Sector Consumer Discretionary
Sub-Industry Housewares & Specialties

Comment This high-volume, brand-name consumer products concern has grown through acquisitions. Major product lines include housewares, home furnishings, office products and hardware.

Key Stock Statistics (Source S&P, Vickers, company reports)

52-Wk Range	$29.98–22.22	S&P Oper. EPS 2006**E**	1.85	P/E on S&P Oper. EPS 2006**E**	15.6	Dividend Rate/Share	$0.84
Trailing 12-Month EPS	$1.31	S&P Oper. EPS 2007**E**	1.93	Common Shares Outstg. (M)	276.9	Yield (%)	2.92
Trailing 12-Month P/E	22.0	S&P Core EPS 2006**E**	1.81	Market Capitalization(B)	$7.969	Beta	0.60
$10K Invested 5 Yrs Ago	$12,735	S&P Core EPS 2007**E**	1.89	Institutional Ownership (%)	82	S&P Credit Rating	BBB+

Price Performance

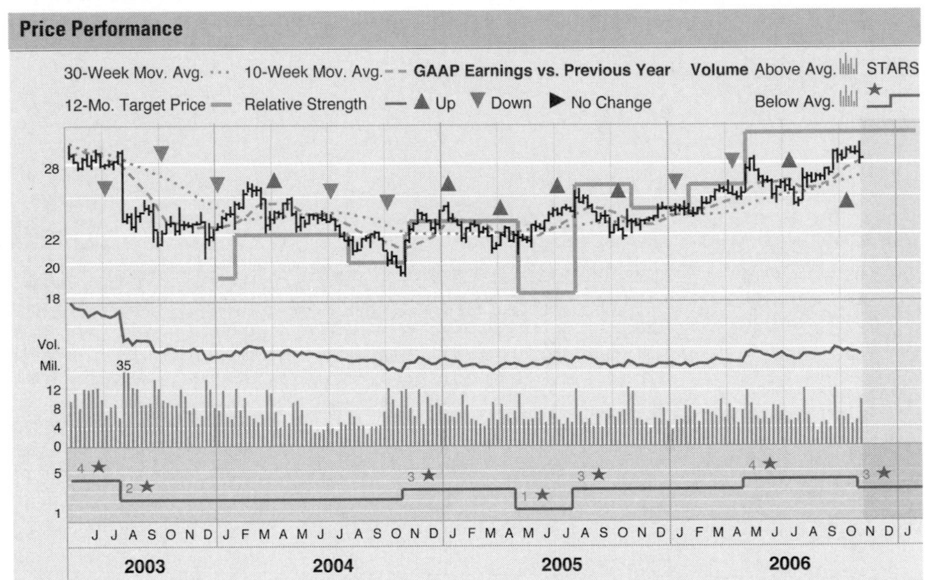

Options: CBOE, P

Analysis prepared by **Loran Braverman, CFA** on October 31, 2006, when the stock traded at **$ 28.78**.

Highlights

- We see net sales increasing approximately 5% in 2006, reflecting an acquisition, positive pricing and the elimination of non-strategic, low margin products. Sales growth should be led by the office products segment, largely due, in our view, to acquisitions. We look for growth in the tools and hardware division to be driven by new products. We expect sales eliminations to come from the Rubbermaid Home Products segment and the window fashions business in the U.K. Our 2007 sales growth forecast is 5%, again led by the Office Products segment.
- We expect the operating margin to widen by more than 100 basis points in 2006, as we see higher pricing, productivity gains, and the lapping of higher raw material and energy costs in the second half improving profitability. For 2007, we look for the benefits of the restructuring program to allow a further 200 basis point gain in the operating margin.
- We estimate that 2006 operating EPS will increase to $1.85, from $1.52 in 2005 (excluding charges but including stock option expense). We estimate S&P Core EPS of $1.81 for 2006, reflecting post-retirement adjustments.

Investment Rationale/Risk

- Our hold opinion reflects our view that, at the current price, the stock appropriately reflects what we view as better growth prospects. Under new leadership, we believe the company is poised for better innovation and efficiency. We think that NWL is shedding lower margin product lines and is investing in the more profitable categories. While the categories in which it competes are competitive, we believe NWL will be able to gain market share through better consumer research and greater product innovation.
- Risks to our recommendation and target price include a marked decline in sales, a low level of cost savings associated with the company's reorganization program, and a material increase in prices of key raw materials such as resin and steel.
- Our 12-month target price of $31 is a blend of our historical and relative analyses. Our historical model uses a P/E multiple of 16.4X our 2007 EPS estimate, a discount to the ten-year average, to arrive at a $32 valuation. Our relative analysis uses a 16.0X multiple, a slight premium to the peer average, implying a $31 value.

Qualitative Risk Assessment

LOW | **MEDIUM** | HIGH

We view the risk factors for housewares companies to be relatively low. The products are generally affordable, low-priced goods that are impacted at modest levels by swings in the economy. However, there is a greater level of import competition for commodity-type goods.

Quantitative Evaluations

S&P Quality Ranking B

D | C | B- | **B** | B+ | A- | A | A+

Relative Strength Rank MODERATE

49

LOWEST = 1 HIGHEST = 99

Revenue/Earnings Data

Revenue (Million $)

	1Q	2Q	3Q	4Q	Year
2006	1,485	1,697	1,586	--	--
2005	1,363	1,646	1,585	1,749	6,343
2004	1,541	1,736	1,672	1,809	6,748
2003	1,736	1,976	1,945	2,093	7,750
2002	1,597	1,895	1,948	2,014	7,454
2001	1,611	1,725	1,768	1,806	6,609

Earnings Per Share ($)

2006	0.21	0.49	0.41	**E**0.41	**E**1.85
2005	0.33	0.30	0.37	0.31	1.29
2004	0.12	0.21	-0.86	0.45	-0.07
2003	0.06	0.27	0.27	-0.77	-0.17
2002	0.19	0.33	0.29	0.36	1.16
2001	0.14	0.27	0.31	0.27	0.99

Fiscal year ended Dec. 31. Next earnings report expected: Late January. EPS Estimates based on S&P Operating Earnings; historical GAAP earnings are as reported.

Dividend Data (Dates: mm/dd Payment Date: mm/dd/yy)

Amount ($)	Date Decl.	Ex-Div. Date	Stk. of Record	Payment Date
0.210	11/10	11/17	11/21	12/07/05
0.210	02/09	02/17	02/22	03/09/06
0.210	05/11	05/26	05/31	06/15/06
0.210	08/10	08/29	08/31	09/15/06

Dividends have been paid since 1946. Source: Company reports.

Newell Rubbermaid Inc.

Business Summary October 31, 2006

CORPORATE OVERVIEW. Newell Rubbermaid is a global manufacturer and marketer of name-brand consumer products and their commercial extensions, serving a wide array of retail channels including department stores, warehouse clubs, home centers, hardware stores, commercial distributors, office superstores, contract stationers, automotive stores and baby superstores. Products are sold through five business segments: cleaning and organization (25% of 2005 sales, 17% of operating profits), office products (27%, 40%), tools & hardware (20%, 25%), home & family (15%, 15%) and home fashions (13%, 3%). About 28% of 2005 sales were made outside the U.S.

NWL's cleaning and organization segment is made up of several businesses all using the Rubbermaid name. These businesses collectively design, manufacture and distribute material handling, cleaning, refuse, indoor and outdoor organization, home storage, and food storage products. The office products segment primarily sells writing instruments, labeling solutions and office organization products. Brands include Sharpie, Paper-Mate, Waterman, Parker and Dymo. The tools & hardware business sells hand tools, power tool accessories, propane torches, manual paint applicator products, cabinet hardware, and window hardware under brand names such as Irwin, Lenox, and BernzOmatic. The home & family segment offers an extensive line of premium ktichenware (Calphalon brand), infant and juvenile products (Graco and Little Tikes) and hair care products (Goody). NWL's home fashion business consists of a global collection of window furnishing brands, including Levolor and Kirsch.

During 2005, the company acquired DYMO, a maker of labeling products and sold its Curver (home organization) business to Jardin International Holding BV. In January 2006, NWL sold its European cookware business. In September 2006, NWL announced that it entered into an agreement for the intended sale of its Little Tikes business unit. NWL has disclosed that Little Tikes contributed approximately $250 million in revenue in 2005; it expects to record a net gain of $15 to $25 million related to this transaction in the fourth quarter; and, due to the reclassifying of Little Tikes as a discontinued operation, it expects 2006 fully-diluted EPS to decline by $0.03 to $0.04, split evenly between the third and fourth quarters.

Company Financials

Per Share Data ($) Year Ended Dec. 31	**2005**	**2004**	**2003**	**2002**	**2001**	**2000**	**1999**	**1998**	**1997**	**1996**
Tangible Book Value	NM	NM	NM	NM	0.44	0.97	2.38	1.57	2.20	3.58
Cash Flow	2.07	0.84	0.84	2.21	2.22	2.57	1.30	3.14	2.82	2.35
Earnings	1.29	-0.07	-0.17	1.16	0.99	1.57	0.34	2.38	1.82	1.62
S&P Core Earnings	1.22	0.56	0.39	0.86	0.71	NA	NA	NA	NA	NA
Dividends	0.84	0.84	0.84	0.84	0.84	0.84	0.80	0.72	0.64	0.56
Payout Ratio	65%	NM	NM	72%	85%	54%	235%	30%	35%	35%
Prices:High	25.09	20.41	32.00	36.70	29.50	31.88	52.00	55.19	43.81	33.75
Prices:Low	20.50	19.05	20.27	26.11	20.50	18.25	25.25	35.69	30.13	25.00
P/E Ratio:High	20	NM	NM	32	30	20	NM	23	24	21
P/E Ratio:Low	16	NM	NM	23	21	12	NM	15	17	15
Income Statement Analysis (Million $)										
Revenue	6,343	6,748	7,750	7,454	6,909	6,935	6,413	3,720	3,234	2,873
Operating Income	843	870	992	1,033	966	1,173	862	736	702	602
Depreciation	214	249	278	281	329	293	272	148	162	116
Interest Expense	142	130	140	111	137	130	100	60.4	73.6	57.0
Pretax Income	418	86.3	20.1	495	443	685	231	685	482	425
Effective Tax Rate	14.8%	NM	NM	31.7%	34.2%	38.5%	58.7%	42.1%	39.5%	39.6%
Net Income	356	-19.1	-46.6	312	265	422	95.4	396	290	256
S&P Core Earnings	333	153	108	232	190	NA	NA	NA	NA	NA
Balance Sheet & Other Financial Data (Million $)										
Cash	116	506	144	55.1	6.80	31.7	102	57.5	36.1	4.36
Current Assets	2,473	3,012	3,000	3,080	2,851	2,897	2,739	1,591	1,382	1,108
Total Assets	6,446	6,666	7,481	7,389	7,266	7,262	6,724	4,328	3,944	3,005
Current Liabilities	1,798	1,871	2,022	2,614	2,534	1,551	1,630	821	664	637
Long Term Debt	2,430	2,424	2,869	2,357	1,865	2,815	1,956	1,366	784	672
Common Equity	1,643	1,764	2,016	2,064	2,433	2,449	2,697	1,912	1,714	1,492
Total Capital	4,073	4,189	4,887	4,426	4,373	5,358	4,738	3,300	3,096	2,211
Capital Expenditures	92.2	122	300	252	250	317	200	148	98.4	94.2
Cash Flow	570	230	232	592	593	714	367	544	452	373
Current Ratio	1.4	1.6	1.5	1.2	1.1	1.9	1.7	1.9	2.1	1.7
% Long Term Debt of Capitalization	59.7	57.9	58.7	53.2	42.7	52.5	41.3	41.3	25.4	30.4
% Net Income of Revenue	5.6	NM	NM	4.2	3.8	6.1	1.5	10.6	9.0	8.9
% Return on Assets	5.4	NM	NM	4.3	3.6	6.0	1.5	9.5	8.4	8.6
% Return on Equity	20.9	NM	NM	13.9	10.8	16.4	3.4	21.7	18.1	18.4

Data as orig reptd.; bef. results of disc opers/spec. items. Per share data adj. for stk. divs.; EPS diluted. E-Estimated. NA-Not Available. NM-Not Meaningful. NR-Not Ranked. UR-Under Review.

Office: 10B Glenlake Pkwy NE Ste 600, Atlanta, GA 30328-7266.
Telephone: 770-407-3800.
Email: investor.relations@newellco.com
Website: http://www.newellrubbermaid.com

Chrmn: W.D. Marohn
Pres & CEO: M.D. Ketchum
VP & CFO: J.P. Robinson
VP, Secy & General Counsel: D.L. Matschullat

Investor Contact: R.L. Hardnock (770-407-3994)
Board of Directors: T. E. Clarke, S. S. Cowen, M. T. Cowhig, M. D. Ketchum, W. D. Marohn, E. C. Millett, C. A. Montgomery, A. P. Newell, S. J. Strobel, G. R. Sullivan, R. G. Viault

Founded: 1903
Domicile: Delaware
Employees: 27,900

STANDARD &POOR'S

Newmont Mining Corp

S&P Recommendation BUY ★★★★★	Price	12-Mo. Target Price	Investment Style
	$44.32 (as of Oct 27, 2006)	$60.00	Large-Cap Growth

GICS Sector Materials
Sub-Industry Gold

Comment Newmont is the world's second largest gold producer.

Key Stock Statistics (Source S&P, Vickers, company reports)

52-Wk Range	$62.72–39.84	S&P Oper. EPS 2006E	1.80	P/E on S&P Oper. EPS 2006E	24.6	Dividend Rate/Share	$0.40
Trailing 12-Month EPS	$1.24	S&P Oper. EPS 2007E	2.15	Common Shares Outstg. (M)	449.7	Yield (%)	0.90
Trailing 12-Month P/E	35.7	S&P Core EPS 2006E	1.81	Market Capitalization(B)	$18.655	Beta	0.04
$10K Invested 5 Yrs Ago	$21,513	S&P Core EPS 2007E	2.16	Institutional Ownership (%)	74	S&P Credit Rating	BBB+

Price Performance

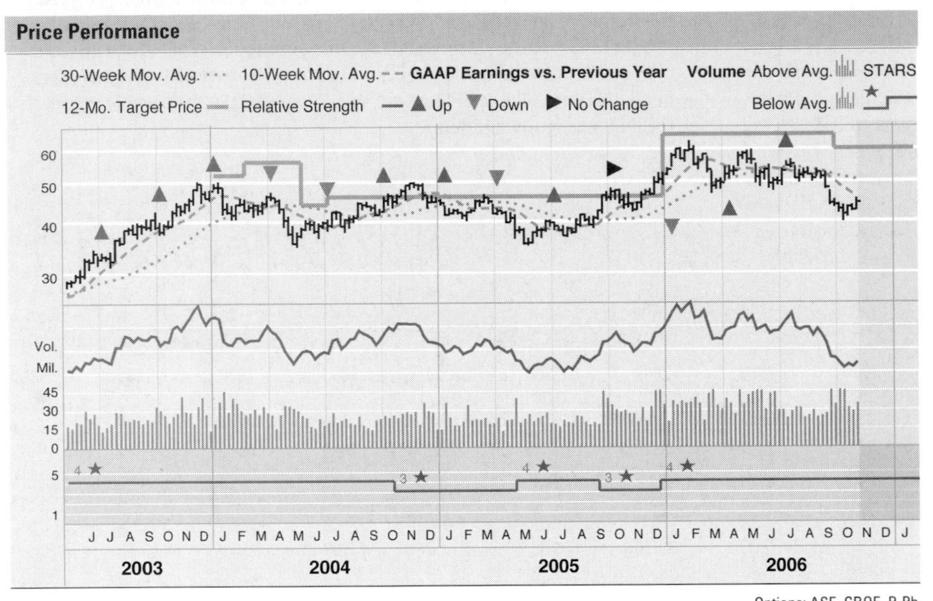

Options: ASE, CBOE, P, Ph

Analysis prepared by **Leo J. Larkin** on September 21, 2006, when the stock traded at **$ 43.69**.

Highlights

- Based on our forecast for an average gold price of $595 an ounce in 2006, versus 2005's average price of $445 an ounce, we project a 27% sales gain for NEM in 2006. In our view, a forecast increase in the average price of gold and copper will offset lower output for both metals. We think a likely decline in global gold production in 2006 and a strong global economy will support higher prices for gold and copper. Our estimated decline in NEM's gold production mostly reflects an expected decrease in ore grade at the Yanacocha mine in Peru. We expect copper output to decline in Indonesia as a result of lower ore grades, reduced recoveries, and a change in mine plans.
- Predicated on our expectation for less rapidly rising costs for energy and raw materials along with higher revenue per ounce, we look for increased operating profits, and we project operating earnings of $1.80 in 2006. Assuming a higher average gold price in 2007 and flat gold output, we estimate EPS of $2.15 in 2007.
- Long term, we see EPS aided by a projected rise in the price of gold, further industry consolidation, and continued strong profit contributions from copper.

Investment Rationale/Risk

- With most of NEM's output exposed to spot gold, we think it is well positioned for a higher gold price. We believe that gold is in a bull market for several reasons: we expect the gap between consumption and production to widen as production worldwide likely declines; given our view that financial asset returns in the first decade of the 21st century will trail the high levels seen in the late 1990s, we think that gold and gold shares will be viewed as attractive alternative investments; and we believe that currency instability will increase gold's role as a monetary reserve asset.
- Risks to our recommendation and target price include an end to the bull market in gold and lower than expected production from the Yanacocha mine.
- Given that the price of gold has risen steadily since May 2001, we anticipate that NEM will not command a high P/E on its 2007 EPS. In all likelihood, the length of the current gold bull market should produce a lower P/E. We expect NEM to trade at 28X our 2007 estimate, leading to our 12-month target price of $60. On our projected P/E, NEM would sell at the low end of its historical range.

Qualitative Risk Assessment

LOW | **MEDIUM** | HIGH

Our risk assessment is based on our belief that Newmont's production profile is stagnant through 2007 and could worsen if output from the Yanacocha mine declines more than currently expected. This is offset by our view of Newmont's strong balance sheet and favorable free cash flow generation.

Quantitative Evaluations

S&P Quality Ranking B-

D | C | **B-** | B | B+ | A- | A | A+

Relative Strength Rank WEAK

19

LOWEST = 1 HIGHEST = 99

Revenue/Earnings Data

Revenue (Million $)

	1Q	2Q	3Q	4Q	Year
2006	1,148	1,310	--	--	--
2005	945.0	998.0	1,158	1,305	4,406
2004	1,122	1,009	1,163	1,230	4,524
2003	748.5	747.2	897.0	821.4	3,214
2002	491.6	632.4	712.1	786.1	2,658
2001	424.1	362.4	424.4	445.2	1,656

Earnings Per Share ($)

	1Q	2Q	3Q	4Q	Year
2006	0.47	0.36	**E**0.44	**E**0.53	**E**1.80
2005	0.19	0.19	0.29	0.16	0.83
2004	0.30	0.08	0.29	0.43	1.10
2003	0.38	0.22	0.28	0.36	1.23
2002	-0.06	0.17	0.05	0.19	0.39
2001	-0.20	-0.17	0.11	0.10	-0.16

Fiscal year ended Dec. 31. Next earnings report expected: NA. EPS Estimates based on S&P Operating Earnings; historical GAAP earnings are as reported.

Dividend Data (Dates: mm/dd Payment Date: mm/dd/yy)

Amount ($)	Date Decl.	Ex-Div. Date	Stk. of Record	Payment Date
0.100	10/26	11/29	12/01	12/20/05
0.100	02/24	03/06	03/08	03/29/06
0.100	04/26	06/06	06/08	06/29/06
0.100	07/25	09/05	09/07	09/28/06

Dividends have been paid since 1934. Source: Company reports.

Please read the Required Disclosures and Analyst Certification on the last page of this report.

Newmont Mining Corp

Business Summary September 21, 2006

CORPORATE OVERVIEW. Newmont Mining Corp. is the world's second largest gold company. It has significant assets and operations in the United States, Australia, Peru, Indonesia, Canada, Uzbekistan, Bolivia, New Zealand, Ghana and Mexico. The company has two large development projects in Ghana, West Africa. Newmont is also engaged in the production of copper, principally through its Batu Hijau operation in Indonesia. Through its Merchant Banking unit, NEM manages a royalty portfolio, an equity portfolio, and a downstream gold refining business, and engages in portfolio management activities in oil and gas, iron ore, and coal properties.

Proven and probable gold reserves totaled 93.2 million oz. at the end of 2005, versus 92.4 million oz. at the end of 2004, using a gold price of $400 per oz., versus $350 per oz. for 2004.

At year-end 2005, 33.2 million oz. were located in Nevada, 16.8 million oz. in Peru, 10.7 million oz. in Ghana, 14.9 million oz. in Australia/New Zealand, 6.7 million oz. in Indonesia, and 2.9 million oz. in other operations located in Canada, Mexico, Bolivia, Turkey and Uzbekistan.

Copper reserves totaled 9.1 billion lbs. at the end of 2005, using a copper price assumption of $1.00 per lb., versus 8.9 billion lbs. at year-end 2004, using a copper price assumption of $0.90 per lb.

About 35% of Newmont's equity gold sales in 2005 came from the United States, 27% from Peru, 25% from Australia/New Zealand, 6% from Indonesia, and 7% from other operations. As of December 31, 2005, approximately 54% of the company's total long-lived assets were located in the U.S., with the balance located in Peru, Australia, Indonesia, Ghana, Canada, Mexico, Bolivia, Turkey and Uzbekistan.

CORPORATE STRATEGY. NEM's main strategy is to increase its portfolio of low cost, long-life mines. As a general policy, NEM engages in only limited hedging of its production, because it anticipates higher gold prices over the long term, and seeks to provide shareholders with greater leverage to the price of gold. NEM plans to spend $1.8 billion in capital development from 2006 to 2010 to offset the decline in production of mature operations. NEM estimates that its new mines will have project lives of over 16 years and add 2.6 million oz. of annual equity production at costs below the industry average.

Company Financials

Per Share Data ($) Year Ended Dec. 31	**2005**	**2004**	**2003**	**2002**	**2001**	**2000**	**1999**	**1998**	**1997**	**1996**
Tangible Book Value	12.27	11.02	8.39	2.77	7.49	8.58	8.66	8.62	10.17	10.30
Cash Flow	2.27	2.66	2.60	1.75	1.38	1.61	1.58	-0.45	2.14	2.11
Earnings	0.83	1.10	1.23	0.39	-0.16	-0.06	0.15	-2.27	0.44	0.86
S&P Core Earnings	0.79	1.22	1.05	0.25	-0.26	NA	NA	NA	NA	NA
Dividends	0.40	0.30	0.17	0.12	0.12	0.12	0.12	0.12	0.39	0.48
Payout Ratio	48%	28%	14%	31%	NM	NM	80%	NM	80%	50%
Prices:High	53.93	50.20	50.28	32.75	25.23	28.38	30.06	34.88	47.50	60.75
Prices:Low	34.90	34.70	24.08	18.52	14.00	12.75	16.38	13.25	26.56	43.88
P/E Ratio:High	65	46	41	84	NM	NM	NM	NM	NM	71
P/E Ratio:Low	42	32	20	47	NM	NM	NM	NM	NM	51
Income Statement Analysis (Million $)										
Revenue	4,406	4,524	3,214	2,658	1,656	1,555	1,399	1,454	1,573	768
Operating Income	1,621	1,878	1,219	852	435	502	493	500	582	172
Depreciation	644	697	564	506	300	293	240	289	266	125
Interest Expense	98.0	97.6	88.6	130	86.4	79.6	62.6	78.8	77.1	44.0
Pretax Income	1,068	1,102	890	268	-10.2	94.2	112	-471	132	74.6
Effective Tax Rate	29.4%	25.0%	23.2%	7.43%	NM	12.1%	12.9%	NM	48.2%	NM
Net Income	374	490	510	150	-23.3	-10.5	24.8	-360	68.4	85.1
S&P Core Earnings	356	540	435	96.7	-52.8	NA	NA	NA	NA	NA
Balance Sheet & Other Financial Data (Million $)										
Cash	1,899	1,726	1,459	402	149	60.3	55.3	79.1	146	186
Current Assets	3,036	2,721	2,360	1,113	709	512	534	513	641	456
Total Assets	13,992	12,771	11,050	10,155	4,062	3,510	3,383	3,187	3,614	2,081
Current Liabilities	1,350	1,101	834	693	486	291	274	212	395	224
Long Term Debt	1,733	1,311	887	1,701	1,090	976	1,014	1,201	1,179	585
Common Equity	8,376	7,938	7,385	5,419	1,469	1,466	1,452	1,440	1,591	1,025
Total Capital	11,489	10,500	9,251	8,132	2,955	2,695	2,627	2,733	2,938	1,716
Capital Expenditures	1,226	718	501	300	402	378	221	216	415	231
Cash Flow	1,018	1,187	1,075	652	269	283	264	-71.4	334	210
Current Ratio	2.2	2.5	2.8	1.6	1.5	1.8	2.0	2.4	1.6	2.0
% Long Term Debt of Capitalization	15.1	12.5	9.6	20.9	40.3	36.2	38.6	43.9	40.1	34.1
% Net Income of Revenue	8.5	10.8	15.9	5.7	NM	NM	1.8	NM	4.3	11.1
% Return on Assets	2.8	4.2	4.8	2.1	NM	NM	0.7	NM	2.4	4.4
% Return on Equity	4.5	6.4	8.0	4.4	NM	NM	1.7	NM	5.2	9.6

Data as orig reptd.; bef. results of disc opers/spec. items. Per share data adj. for stk. divs.; EPS diluted. E-Estimated. NA-Not Available. NM-Not Meaningful. NR-Not Ranked. UR-Under Review.

Office: 1700 Lincoln Street, Denver, CO 80203-4500.
Telephone: 303-863-7414.
Website: http://www.newmont.com
Chrmn & CEO: W.W. Murdy

Pres: P. Lassonde
SVP & CFO: R. O'Brien
SVP & General Counsel: B. Banks
VP & Treas: T.P. Mahoney

Board of Directors: G. A. Barton, V. A. Calarco, N. Doyle, V. Hagen, M. S. Hamson, L. I. Higdon, Jr., P. Lassonde, R. J. Miller, W. W. Murdy, R. A. Plumbridge, J. B. Prescott, D. C. Roth, S. Schulich, J. V. Taranik

Founded: 1916
Domicile: Delaware
Employees: 15,000

STANDARD
&POOR'S

New York Times Co (The)

S&P Recommendation HOLD ★★★★★	Price	12-Mo. Target Price	Investment Style
	$24.10 (as of Oct 27, 2006)	$24.00	Mid-Cap Growth

GICS Sector Consumer Discretionary
Sub-Industry Publishing

Comment This diversified communications company publishes newspapers, operates radio and television stations, and has equity holdings in newsprint and paper mills.

Key Stock Statistics (Source S&P, Vickers, company reports)

52-Wk Range	$29.49–21.54	S&P Oper. EPS 2006E	1.37	P/E on S&P Oper. EPS 2006E	17.6	Dividend Rate/Share	$0.70
Trailing 12-Month EPS	$1.25	S&P Oper. EPS 2007E	1.25	Common Shares Outstg. (M)	144.5	Yield (%)	2.90
Trailing 12-Month P/E	19.3	S&P Core EPS 2006E	1.42	Market Capitalization(B)	$3.462	Beta	0.68
$10K Invested 5 Yrs Ago	$6,170	S&P Core EPS 2007E	1.30	Institutional Ownership (%)	86	S&P Credit Rating	A-

Price Performance

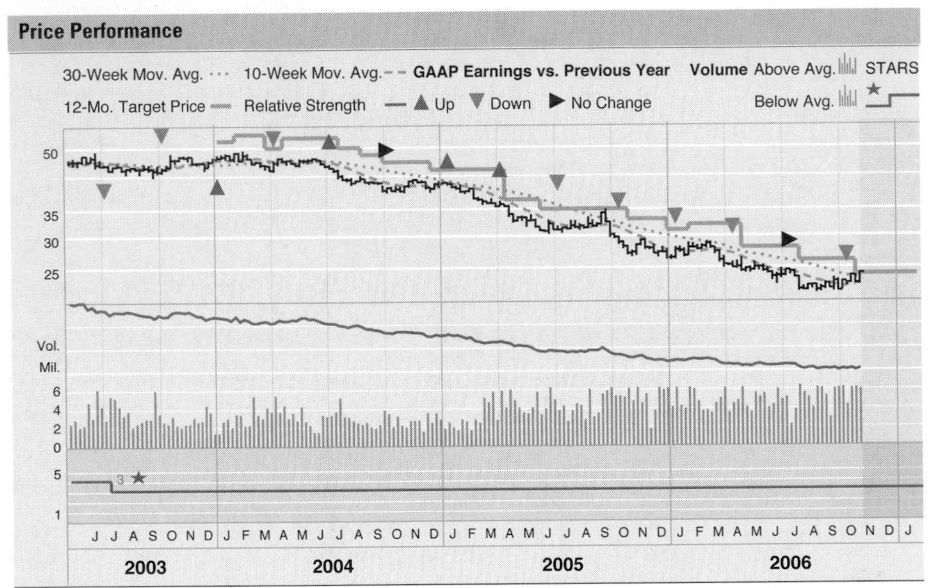

Options: ASE, CBOE, P, Ph

Highlights

➤ The 12-month target price for NYT has recently been changed to $24.00 from $26.00. The Highlights section of this Stock Report will be updated accordingly.

Investment Rationale/Risk

➤ The Investment Rationale/Risk section of this Stock Report will be updated shortly. For the latest News story on NYT from MarketScope, see below.

➤ 10/19/06 05:51 pm EDT... S&P MAINTAINS HOLD RECOMMENDATION ON SHARES OF NEW YORK TIMES COMPANY (NYT 22.74***): Before one-time items, NYT posts Q3 EPS from continuing operations of $0.13 vs. $0.21, in line with our estimate. The company says it will incur $78M-$90M of incremental accelerated depreciation expense over the next 18 months (about $0.06/qtr.) related to plant consolidation. We see a weak near-term print ad environment offsetting strong online revenue advances. Reflecting this outlook, along with depreciation adjustments, we are cutting our '06 and '07 EPS estimates to $1.37 and $1.25 from $1.46 and $1.51. We are also dropping our 12-month target price $2 to $24. /J.Peters-CFA

Qualitative Risk Assessment

LOW	**MEDIUM**	HIGH

Our risk assessment for New York Times reflects our view of a highly competitive advertising environment for publishers and other media, offset by the company's better than peer opportunity, in our opinion, to leverage its brand and NYT's low weighted average cost of capital.

Quantitative Evaluations

S&P Quality Ranking A-

D	C	B-	B	B+	**A-**	A	A+

Relative Strength Rank MODERATE

67

LOWEST = 1 HIGHEST = 99

Revenue/Earnings Data

Revenue (Million $)

	1Q	2Q	3Q	4Q	Year
2006	831.8	858.8	739.6	--	--
2005	805.6	845.1	791.1	931.0	3,373
2004	801.9	823.9	773.8	903.9	3,304
2003	783.7	801.9	759.3	882.3	3,227
2002	737.1	772.2	729.5	840.2	3,079
2001	778.2	760.3	696.9	780.6	3,016

Earnings Per Share ($)

2006	0.24	0.42	0.07	**E**0.50	**E**1.37
2005	0.76	0.42	0.16	0.49	1.82
2004	0.38	0.50	0.33	0.75	1.96
2003	0.45	0.47	0.33	0.73	1.98
2002	0.35	0.51	0.38	0.69	1.94
2001	0.36	0.15	0.28	0.49	1.26

Fiscal year ended Dec. 31. Next earnings report expected: Late January. EPS Estimates based on S&P Operating Earnings; historical GAAP earnings are as reported.

Dividend Data (Dates: mm/dd Payment Date: mm/dd/yy)

Amount ($)	Date Decl.	Ex-Div. Date	Stk. of Record	Payment Date
0.165	11/17	11/29	12/01	12/15/05
0.165	02/16	02/27	03/01	03/13/06
0.175	04/18	05/30	06/01	06/13/06
0.175	06/15	08/30	09/01	09/13/06

Dividends have been paid since 1958. Source: Company reports.

New York Times Co (The)

Business Summary October 02, 2006

The New York Times Company is a diversified media company including newspapers and related Internet businesses, television and radio stations, and forest products and other investments. NYT classifies its businesses into the News Media Group (95% of 2005 revenues), the Broadcast Media Group (4%), and About.com (1%). In March 2005, NYT completed the acquisition of About.com for approximately $410 million.

The News Media Group includes The New York Times Media Group, incorporating The New York Times, NYTimes.com, the International Herald Tribune, a newspaper distributor in the New York City metropolitan area, news, photo and graphics services and news and features syndication as part of NYT's two New York City radio stations; the New England Media Group, consisting of The Boston Globe, Boston.com and the Worcester Telegram & Gazette; and the Regional Group, consisting of 15 regional newspapers and related print and digital businesses. In 2005, about 66% of the News Media Group's revenues were derived from advertising sold in its newspapers and other publications and on its Web sites, 27% of revenues came from circulation, and 7% of revenues came from other sources. Around 45% of the Group's 2005 advertising revenues came from national advertising, 28% from classified, 24% from retail, and 3% from other.

Company Financials

Per Share Data ($) Year Ended Dec. 31	**2005**	**2004**	**2003**	**2002**	**2001**	**2000**	**1999**	**1998**	**1997**	**1996**
Tangible Book Value	NM	NM	NM	NM	NM	NM	0.83	1.12	1.77	0.90
Cash Flow	3.04	2.94	2.95	2.93	2.48	3.65	2.83	2.46	2.21	1.20
Earnings	1.02	1.96	1.98	1.94	1.26	2.32	1.73	1.49	1.33	0.44
S&P Core Earnings	1.41	1.62	1.77	1.35	0.72	NA	NA	NA	NA	NA
Dividends	0.65	0.61	0.57	0.53	0.49	0.45	0.41	0.37	0.32	0.29
Payout Ratio	36%	31%	29%	27%	39%	19%	24%	25%	24%	66%
Prices:High	40.90	49.23	49.06	53.00	47.98	49.88	49.94	40.69	33.25	19.94
Prices:Low	26.09	38.47	43.29	38.60	35.48	32.63	26.50	20.50	18.19	12.88
P/E Ratio:High	22	25	25	27	38	21	29	27	25	46
P/E Ratio:Low	14	20	22	20	28	14	15	14	14	30

Income Statement Analysis (Million $)										
Revenue	3,373	3,304	3,227	3,079	3,016	3,489	3,131	2,937	2,866	2,615
Operating Income	536	657	687	698	568	864	769	703	629	448
Depreciation	170	147	148	153	194	228	197	188	174	148
Interest Expense	49.2	44.2	44.8	48.7	51.4	64.1	52.5	46.9	45.0	50.3
Pretax Income	446	477	500	491	340	673	538	506	437	198
Effective Tax Rate	40.4%	38.5%	39.6%	39.0%	40.5%	40.9%	42.4%	43.3%	40.0%	57.3%
Net Income	266	293	303	300	202	398	310	287	262	84.5
S&P Core Earnings	205	242	268	208	116	NA	NA	NA	NA	NA

Balance Sheet & Other Financial Data (Million $)										
Cash	44.9	42.4	39.4	37.0	52.0	69.0	63.9	36.0	107	39.1
Current Assets	658	614	603	563	560	611	615	522	616	479
Total Assets	4,533	3,950	3,805	3,634	3,439	3,607	3,496	3,465	3,639	3,540
Current Liabilities	1,067	1,120	760	736	861	877	674	628	697	654
Long Term Debt	898	471	726	729	599	637	598	598	545	637
Common Equity	1,516	1,401	1,392	1,362	1,150	1,281	1,449	1,531	1,728	1,623
Total Capital	2,683	2,139	2,350	2,164	1,813	2,024	2,188	2,295	2,460	2,450
Capital Expenditures	221	154	121	161	90.4	85.3	73.4	82.6	153	211
Cash Flow	444	439	450	453	396	626	508	475	436	232
Current Ratio	0.6	0.5	0.8	0.8	0.7	0.7	0.9	0.8	0.9	0.7
% Long Term Debt of Capitalization	33.5	22.0	30.9	33.7	33.0	31.5	27.3	26.1	22.2	26.0
% Net Income of Revenue	7.9	8.9	9.4	9.7	6.7	11.4	9.9	9.8	9.2	3.2
% Return on Assets	6.3	7.5	8.1	8.5	5.7	11.2	8.9	8.1	7.3	2.4
% Return on Equity	18.2	21.0	22.7	23.9	16.6	29.1	20.8	17.6	15.6	5.2

Data as orig reptd.; bef. results of disc opers/spec. items. Per share data adj. for stk. divs.; EPS diluted. E-Estimated. NA-Not Available. NM-Not Meaningful. NR-Not Ranked. UR-Under Review.

Office: 229 W. 43rd St., New York, NY 10036.
Telephone: 212-556-1234.
Website: http://www.nytco.com
Chrmn: A. Sulzberger, Jr.

Pres & CEO: J. Robinson
Vice Chrmn: M. Golden
EVP & CFO: L.P. Forman
SVP & Chief Lgl Officer: S.B. Watson, IV

Investor Contact: C.J. Mathis (212-556-1981)
Board of Directors: J. F. Akers, B. C. Barnes, R. E. Cesan, L. G. Dolnick, M. Golden, W. E. Kennard, J. M. Kilts, D. E. Liddle, E. R. Marram, T. Middelhoff, J. Robinson, H. B. Schacht, C. J. Sulzberger, A. Sulzberger, Jr., D. A. Toben

Founded: 1896
Domicile: New York
Employees: 11,965

STANDARD &POOR'S

News Corp

S&P Recommendation	Price	12-Mo. Target Price	Investment Style
BUY ★★★★★	$20.86 (as of Oct 27, 2006)	$23.00	Large-Cap Value

GICS Sector Consumer Discretionary
Sub-Industry Movies & Entertainment

Comment This vertically integrated media and entertainment conglomerate has diversified global ownership interests in leading content and distribution assets, including Fox Entertainment, Sky Italia, DirecTV, BSkyB and STAR Asia.

Key Stock Statistics (Source S&P, Vickers, company reports)

52-Wk Range	$21.58–14.13	S&P Oper. EPS 2007**E**	1.02	P/E on S&P Oper. EPS 2007**E**	20.5	Dividend Rate/Share	$0.12
Trailing 12-Month EPS	$1.09	S&P Oper. EPS 2008**E**	NA	Common Shares Outstg. (M)	3,157.7	Yield (%)	0.58
Trailing 12-Month P/E	19.1	S&P Core EPS 2007**E**	1.02	Market Capitalization(B)	$45.290	Beta	1.56
$10K Invested 5 Yrs Ago	$17,491	S&P Core EPS 2008**E**	NA	Institutional Ownership (%)	71	S&P Credit Rating	BBB-

Price Performance

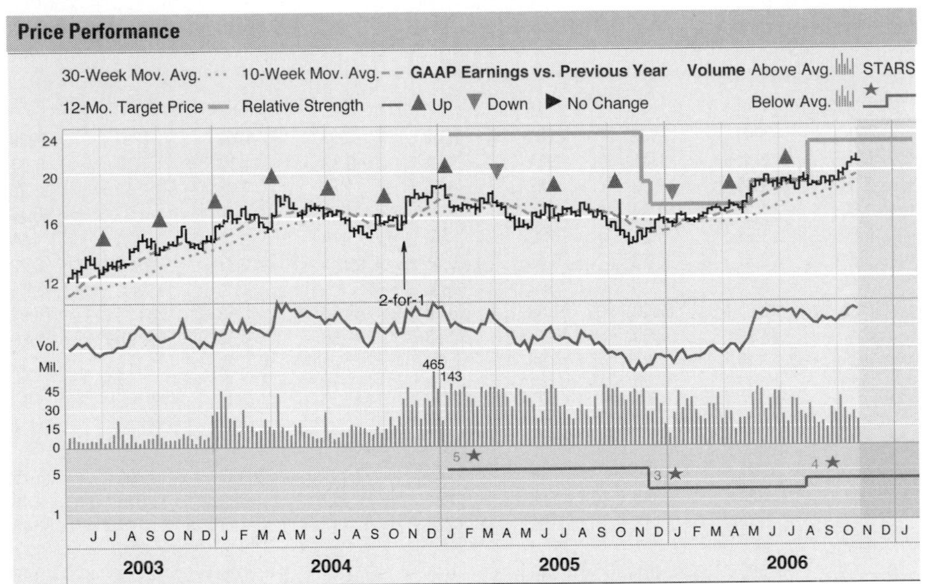

Options: ASE

Analysis prepared by **Tuna N. Amobi, CFA, CPA** on September 01, 2006, when the stock traded at **$ 19.02**.

Highlights

- We estimate that consolidated revenues will increase 8.5% in FY 07 (Jun.), mainly on advertising and affiliate revenues at the Fox News and FX networks, a strong DVD release slate, and internationally, continued solid growth at Sky Italia and STAR Asia. We see continued strong Fox ratings, which we think helped the network during the recent 2006-07 upfront, and expect the local stations to benefit from political advertising for the mid-term elections. We see relatively modest growth at the print businesses (magazines, inserts, newspapers and book publishing).
- We see operating margins aided by Fox News and FX, significantly improved Sky Italia profits, stronger contributions from BSkyB and DirecTV affiliates, and a continued ramp-up of higher-margin digital revenues at Fox Interactive Media (FIM).
- We estimate EBIT growth of approximately 16% in FY 07, to about $4.5 billion. With continued share buybacks under a $6 billion program, we forecast operating EPS of $1.02 in FY 07 (including $0.04 of stock option expense).

Investment Rationale/Risk

- We recently raised our opinion on the non-voting shares to buy, from hold, on continued momentum in fiscal fourth quarter results. We view the cable networks and Sky Italia as key catalysts, with Fox riding American Idol, Prison Break and 24, and we think filmed entertainment will see strong DVD sales of Ice Age 2 and X-Men 3. We also see solid growth at FIM and its leading social networking site MySpace, which recently signed a multi-year search deal with Google, with a minimum revenue guarantee of $900 million through the second quarter of 2010. We see ample financial flexibility for continued stock buybacks and a possible dividend increase.
- Risks to our recommendation and target price include competition from new media platforms; film volatility; corporate governance issues related to a pending vote on a "poison pill"; and foreign currency exposure.
- Our 12-month target price of $23 uses a blend of DCF analysis (assuming an 11.5% weighted average cost of capital and low to mid-teens long-term growth in free cash flow), and sum-of-the-parts valuation (including affiliates).

Qualitative Risk Assessment

LOW | **MEDIUM** | HIGH

Our risk assessment reflects the company's relatively large portfolio of leading businesses with well balanced business and geographic diversification, supported by what we view as a strong balance sheet, offset by exposure to cyclical ad and volatile film businesses, foreign currency risk, and some corporate governance issues.

Quantitative Evaluations

S&P Quality Ranking NR

D | C | B- | B | B+ | A- | A | A+

Relative Strength Rank STRONG

71

LOWEST = 1 HIGHEST = 99

Revenue/Earnings Data

Revenue (Million $)

	1Q	2Q	3Q	4Q	Year
2006	5,682	6,665	6,198	6,782	25,327
2005	5,191	6,562	6,043	6,108	23,859
2004	4,649	5,588	5,201	5,521	20,579
2003	3,813	4,681	4,388	4,592	20,157
2002	3,402	4,119	3,845	3,829	16,392
2001	3,240	3,850	3,270	3,442	13,802

Earnings Per Share ($)

	1Q	2Q	3Q	4Q	Year
2006	0.19	0.22	0.27	0.24	0.92
2005	0.16	0.56	0.14	0.23	0.73
2004	0.14	0.13	0.16	0.13	0.58
2003	0.06	0.09	0.11	0.13	0.46
2002	0.03	0.09	-1.58	-0.63	-2.75
2001	0.07	0.13	0.06	0.06	0.32

Fiscal year ended Jun. 30. Next earnings report expected: Early November. EPS Estimates based on S&P Operating Earnings; historical GAAP earnings are as reported.

Dividend Data (Dates: mm/dd Payment Date: mm/dd/yy)

Amount ($)	Date Decl.	Ex-Div. Date	Stk. of Record	Payment Date
0.060	03/03	03/13	03/15	04/19/06
0.060	09/06	09/11	09/13	10/18/06

Dividends have been paid since 1995. Source: Company reports.

News Corp

STANDARD &POOR'S

Business Summary September 01, 2006

CORPORATE OVERVIEW. News Corp., once a small publisher of Australian newspapers, has grown into one of the world's premier media conglomerates. In December 2004, the company moved its domicile to the U.S., followed in March 2005 by a tender offer for the public's 18% minority stake in its Fox Entertainment Group, which we believe helped to simplify its corporate structure.

Key U.S. assets include Fox film studio and 20th Century Fox TV; Fox broadcast network and TV stations; Fox News, FX and regional sports networks (FSN Ohio, FSN Florida and 40% of FSN Bay Area); HarperCollins (book publishers); the New York Post newspaper; a major inserts business; and a controlling 34% stake in DBS provider DirecTV. International assets include several newspaper businesses in the U.K. and Australia (including The Times, The Sun, News of the World and The Australian); the wholly owned DBS provider Sky Italia; a 37% controlling stake in U.K. DBS provider BSkyB; and several other associated entities in the U.S., Australia and Latin America. About 54% of FY 05 (Jun.) revenues were derived from the U.S., 31% from Europe, and 15% from Australasia.

CORPORATE STRATEGY. We see an increased focus to capitalize on higher growth Internet distribution. In August 2005, chairman Rupert Murdoch announced the formation of Fox Interactive Media (FIM), charged with increasing the company's presence across broadband and other newer media platforms. In 2005, the company make three key Internet acquisitions: Intermix, including MySpace.com, a leading social networking site, for about $650 million, IGN Entertainment for $650 million, and Scout Media for $65 million. FIM's properties have over 75 million unique monthly visitors.

We view MySpace as key to a multi-platform advertising strategy recently unveiled to media buyers during the 2006-07 TV upfront for the Fox broadcast network. The company recently reported that the fast-growing site, currently generating over 30 billion page views per month, was adding about 250,000 users per day, and in early August reached 100 million registered users. In August, MySpace signed a multi-year search deal with Google, with a minimum revenue guarantee of $900 million over the term of the deal. Other new media initiatives include a recent deal to provide 16 of the company's hit TV series on Apple's iTunes service, a separate download deal for American Idol, and a new destination for mobile content on mobile platforms named Mobizzo.

Company Financials

Per Share Data ($) Year Ended Jun. 30	2006	2005	2004	2003	2002	2001	2000	1999	1998	1997
Tangible Book Value	1.86	1.81	1.85	NM	0.68	3.34	0.76	1.67	NM	NM
Cash Flow	1.62	1.40	0.79	0.65	-2.39	-0.01	0.48	0.58	0.29	0.25
Earnings	0.92	0.73	0.58	0.46	-2.75	0.32	0.39	0.50	0.52	0.59
Dividends	0.13	0.11	0.10	0.08	0.07	0.07	0.07	0.08	0.04	Nil
Payout Ratio	14%	14%	17%	17%	NM	22%	18%	16%	8%	Nil
Prices:High	21.50	10.00	18.77	15.54	13.60	18.70	28.59	18.44	14.75	10.22
Prices:Low	15.17	13.94	14.57	9.33	7.54	9.80	13.44	11.47	9.06	7.00
P/E Ratio:High	23	26	32	34	NM	58	73	37	28	17
P/E Ratio:Low	16	19	25	20	NM	31	34	23	17	12

Income Statement Analysis (Million $)	2006	2005	2004	2003	2002	2001	2000	1999	1998	1997
Revenue	25,327	23,859	29,428	29,913	29,014	25,578	22,443	21,774	21,206	14,966
Operating Income	4,643	4,329	5,146	4,372	4,291	3,799	2,913	NA	3,066	2,033
Depreciation	775	765	844	776	749	706	562	510	415	320
Interest Expense	791	736	958	1,094	1,384	1,358	1,248	NA	898	723
Pretax Income	4,405	3,561	3,855	3,000	-10,959	-562	1,587	1,913	2,142	1,521
Effective Tax Rate	34.6%	34.3%	32.3%	25.8%	NM	NM	20.7%	15.0%	12.1%	8.68%
Net Income	2,812	2,128	2,312	1,808	-11,962	-746	1,259	1,471	1,800	1,342

Balance Sheet & Other Financial Data (Million $)	2006	2005	2004	2003	2002	2001	2000	1999	1998	1997
Cash	5,783	6,470	6,217	6,746	6,337	5,615	4,638	7,483	4,314	3,616
Current Assets	13,123	12,779	15,012	14,861	14,647	16,173	13,127	13,555	11,179	8,898
Total Assets	56,649	54,692	73,738	67,747	71,441	84,961	65,585	53,972	54,484	41,358
Current Liabilities	6,373	6,649	10,437	9,303	11,005	9,776	9,008	7,447	8,376	5,284
Long Term Debt	11,385	10,087	12,972	14,480	15,275	23,345	18,396	15,516	15,621	Nil
Common Equity	29,874	29,377	39,387	31,834	34,101	42,050	29,389	27,109	26,546	20,226
Total Capital	46,740	44,500	59,473	53,867	54,743	70,940	51,056	42,625	42,714	20,813
Capital Expenditures	976	901	517	551	505	1,113	671	702	848	401
Cash Flow	3,587	2,883	3,156	2,584	-11,213	-40.0	1,598	1,981	2,215	1,662
Current Ratio	2.1	1.9	1.4	1.6	1.3	1.7	1.5	1.8	1.3	1.7
% Long Term Debt of Capitalization	24.4	22.7	21.8	26.9	27.9	32.9	36.0	36.4	36.6	Nil
% Net Income of Revenue	11.1	8.9	7.9	6.0	NM	NM	5.6	6.8	8.5	9.0
% Return on Assets	5.1	4.1	3.3	2.6	NM	NM	2.1	2.7	3.8	3.7
% Return on Equity	9.5	8.4	6.5	5.5	NM	NM	4.0	4.4	7.7	7.3

Data as orig reptd.; bef. results of disc opers/spec. items. Per share data adj. for stk. divs.; EPS diluted. E-Estimated. NA-Not Available. NM-Not Meaningful. NR-Not Ranked. UR-Under Review.

Office: 1211 Avenue Of The Americas, New York, NY 10036-8701.
Telephone: 212-852-7000.
Website: http://www.newscorp.com
Chrmn & CEO: K.R. Murdoch

Pres & COO: P. Chernin
Sr EVP & CFO: D.F. DeVoe
Sr EVP & General Counsel: L.A. Jacobs
SVP & CCO: G. Gavenchak

Investor Contact: R. Nolte (212-852-7017)
Board of Directors: J. M. Aznar, P. Barnes, C. Carey, P. Cherin, K. E. Cowley, D. F. DeVoe, V. Dinh, R. I. Eddington, A. S. Knight, K. R. Murdoch, L. K. Murdoch, R. Paige, T. J. Perkins, A. M. Siskind, J. L. Thornton

Founded: 1922
Domicile: Delaware
Employees: 47,300

STANDARD &POOR'S

Nicor Inc.

S&P Recommendation HOLD ★★★★★

Price $45.91 (as of Oct 27, 2006)

12-Mo. Target Price $46.00

Investment Style Mid-Cap Value

GICS Sector Utilities
Sub-Industry Gas Utilities

Comment This holding company's Nicor Gas subsidiary is one of the largest U.S. distributors of natural gas.

Key Stock Statistics (Source S&P, Vickers, company reports)

52-Wk Range	**$46.54–38.72**	S&P Oper. EPS 2006**E**	**2.45**	P/E on S&P Oper. EPS 2006**E**	**18.7**	Dividend Rate/Share	**$1.86**
Trailing 12-Month EPS	**$2.51**	S&P Oper. EPS 2007**E**	**2.55**	Common Shares Outstg. (M)	**44.5**	Yield (%)	**4.05**
Trailing 12-Month P/E	**18.3**	S&P Core EPS 2006**E**	**2.13**	Market Capitalization(B)	**$2.045**	Beta	**0.78**
$10K Invested 5 Yrs Ago	**$15,100**	S&P Core EPS 2007**E**	**2.26**	Institutional Ownership (%)	**73**	S&P Credit Rating	**AA**

Price Performance

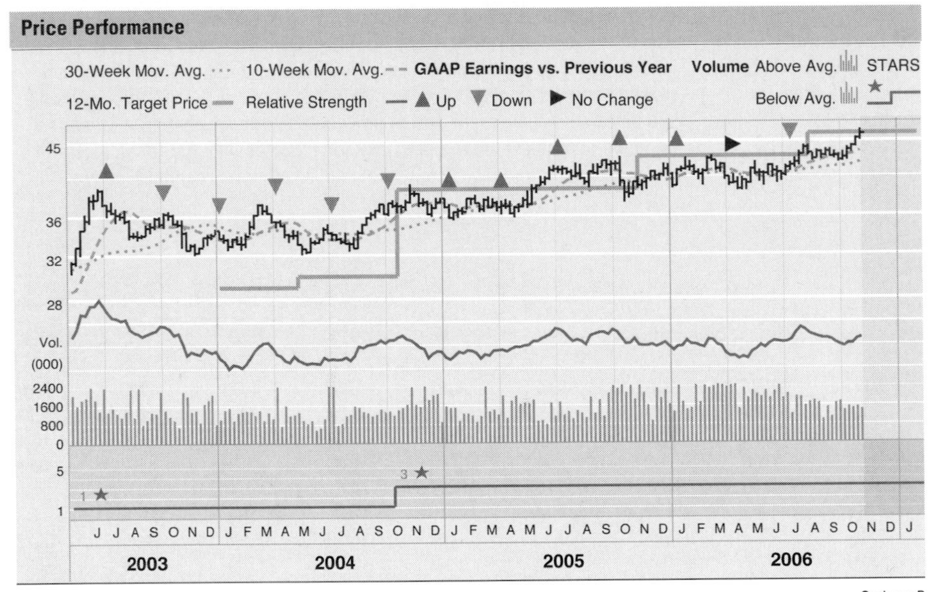

Options: P

Analysis prepared by **Scott H. Kessler** on August 22, 2006, when the stock traded at **$ 43.37**.

Highlights

- In 2006, we see a low single digit drop in gas distribution profits despite a $34.7 million rate hike received in November 2005 (reduced to $30.2 million in March 2006). We expect warmer than normal weather and high energy prices to depress demand. The operating margin should narrow on higher employee costs and bad debt expense. We expect lower legal expenses to partly offset rising costs.
- We see high single digit earnings growth from the shipping segment in 2006. Growth in income will likely be driven by higher volumes shipped and average rates, reflecting improving economic conditions throughout the Caribbean and Bahamas regions, partly offset by greater fuel costs.
- We expect mid-single digit growth in marketing and services, aided by gains in wholesale gas marketing and retail energy-related products and services businesses. With little change expected in interest expense, share count and the effective tax rate, we estimate EPS of $2.45 in 2006 and $2.55 in 2007, excluding one-time gains.

Investment Rationale/Risk

- We think GAS's prospects for additional rate relief are clouded by uncertainty related to outstanding regulatory issues. With the payout ratio over 80%, versus a peer average of about 66%, we see limited growth in dividends. However, we think that GAS's Chicago hub operations will see strong profit growth, on greater demand for natural gas. We expect continued volatility in the gas markets to benefit the wholesale and retail energy marketing and services business.
- Risks to our recommendation and target price include a potentially unfavorable resolution of ongoing regulatory issues and slower than projected growth in unregulated operations.
- The shares recently traded at about 18X our 2006 EPS estimate, above the level of 16X of certain components of the S&P 1500 Gas Utilities sub-industry. Our related P/E analysis yields a value of $46, which is our 12-month target price. The shares recently yielded 4.3%.

Qualitative Risk Assessment

LOW | MEDIUM | HIGH

Our risk assessment reflects the company's mid-size capitalization and our view of its balanced earnings sources, which include lower risk regulated gas distribution and unregulated tropical shipping.

Quantitative Evaluations

S&P Quality Ranking B

D | C | B- | **B** | B+ | A- | A | A+

Relative Strength Rank MODERATE

68

LOWEST = 1 HIGHEST = 99

Revenue/Earnings Data

Revenue (Million $)

	1Q	2Q	3Q	4Q	Year
2006	1,319	451.3	--	--	--
2005	1,180	484.4	336.0	1,358	3,358
2004	1,116	429.5	299.9	894.6	2,740
2003	1,171	452.8	294.8	743.9	2,663
2002	588.0	352.2	252.4	704.7	1,897
2001	1,474	373.0	244.4	453.0	2,544

Earnings Per Share ($)

2006	0.99	0.19	**E**0.01	**E**1.16	**E**2.45
2005	0.99	0.75	-0.06	1.40	3.07
2004	0.44	0.36	-0.26	1.08	1.70
2003	1.14	0.54	0.01	0.79	2.48
2002	0.82	0.50	0.67	0.89	2.88
2001	0.85	0.59	0.73	1.01	3.17

Fiscal year ended Dec. 31. Next earnings report expected: Early November. EPS Estimates based on S&P Operating Earnings; historical GAAP earnings are as reported.

Dividend Data (Dates: mm/dd Payment Date: mm/dd/yy)

Amount ($)	Date Decl.	Ex-Div. Date	Stk. of Record	Payment Date
0.465	11/17	12/28	12/30	02/01/06
0.465	03/16	03/29	03/31	05/01/06
0.465	04/20	06/28	06/30	08/01/06
0.465	07/20	09/27	09/29	11/01/06

Dividends have been paid since 1954. Source: Company reports.

Nicor Inc.

Business Summary August 22, 2006

CORPORATE OVERVIEW. Nicor Inc. is a holding company, whose principal subsidiaries are Northern Illinois Gas Company (doing business as Nicor Gas Company), one of the nation's largest distributors of natural gas, and Tropical Shipping, a transporter of containerized freight in the Bahamas and the Caribbean region. Nicor also owns several energy-related ventures, including Nicor Services and Nicor Solutions, which provide energy-related products and services to retail markets, and Nicor Enerchange, a wholesale natural gas marketing company.

PRIMARY BUSINESS DYNAMICS. Nicor seeks earnings growth through investment in unregulated operations, including its Tropical Shipping and Other Energy Ventures divisions. However, the company's main operating segment remains its regulated gas utility operations.

As of the end of 2005, Nicor Gas (68% of 2005 segment operating profits) served 2.1 million customers in a service area that covers most of northern Illinois, excluding Chicago. In 2005, gas deliveries declined to 470.6 billion cubic feet (Bcf) from 473.2 Bcf in 2004. The company has an extensive storage and transmission system that is directly connected to eight interstate pipelines, and includes eight owned underground gas storage facilities, with about 140 Bcf of top storage capacity. In addition, Nicor Gas has about 40 Bcf of purchased storage from an affiliated party under contracts that expire in 2006.

Nicor Gas is also engaged in non-traditional natural gas storage and transportation activities through its Chicago Hub, which serves marketers, other distributors, and electric power facilities.

GAS's Tropical Shipping unit (24% of EBIT) is one of the largest containerized cargo carriers in the Caribbean, with a fleet of 10 owned and 10 chartered vessels, with total container capacity of about 6,100 20-foot equivalent units (TEU), serving 25 ports. Total volumes shipped in 2005 were 214,200 TEU, up from 198,000 TEU in 2004 and 177,100 TEU in 2003.

Company Financials

Per Share Data ($) Year Ended Dec. 31	**2005**	**2004**	**2003**	**2002**	**2001**	**2000**	**1999**	**1998**	**1997**	**1996**
Tangible Book Value	18.36	16.99	17.15	16.55	16.39	15.56	16.76	15.97	15.43	14.75
Cash Flow	6.55	5.05	5.73	6.00	6.46	4.12	5.58	5.25	5.29	4.92
Earnings	3.07	1.70	2.48	2.88	3.17	1.00	2.62	2.42	2.61	2.42
S&P Core Earnings	2.47	1.97	2.45	2.30	1.99	NA	NA	NA	NA	NA
Dividends	1.86	1.86	1.86	1.84	1.76	1.66	1.54	1.46	1.40	1.32
Payout Ratio	61%	109%	75%	64%	56%	166%	59%	60%	54%	55%
Prices:High	42.97	39.65	39.30	49.00	42.38	43.88	42.94	44.44	42.94	37.13
Prices:Low	35.50	32.04	23.70	18.09	34.00	29.38	31.19	37.13	30.00	25.38
P/E Ratio:High	14	23	16	17	13	44	16	18	16	15
P/E Ratio:Low	12	19	10	6	11	29	12	15	11	10
Income Statement Analysis (Million $)										
Revenue	3,358	2,740	2,663	1,897	2,544	2,298	1,615	1,465	1,993	1,851
Operating Income	202	138	189	227	244	507	352	345	361	358
Depreciation	155	149	144	138	149	144	140	137	131	125
Interest Expense	48.0	41.6	37.3	38.5	44.9	48.6	45.1	46.6	49.1	47.8
Pretax Income	171	105	169	186	217	61.1	190	178	197	189
Effective Tax Rate	20.3%	28.7%	35.2%	31.0%	33.8%	23.6%	34.6%	34.4%	35.0%	35.8%
Net Income	136	75.1	110	128	144	46.7	124	116	128	121
S&P Core Earnings	110	87.7	108	102	90.4	NA	NA	NA	NA	NA
Balance Sheet & Other Financial Data (Million $)										
Cash	119	12.9	50.3	75.2	10.7	55.8	42.5	13.0	5.20	33.2
Current Assets	1,346	1,021	916	708	518	915	508	465	535	573
Total Assets	4,391	3,975	3,797	2,899	2,575	2,885	2,452	2,365	2,395	2,439
Current Liabilities	1,623	1,174	1,069	1,099	826	1,312	746	579	622	700
Long Term Debt	486	495	497	396	446	347	436	557	550	518
Common Equity	811	749	755	728	728	708	788	759	744	730
Total Capital	1,751	1,873	1,813	1,514	1,548	1,173	1,539	1,606	1,516	1,516
Capital Expenditures	202	190	181	193	186	158	154	136	113	120
Cash Flow	291	224	253	266	292	191	264	253	259	246
Current Ratio	0.8	0.9	0.9	0.6	0.6	0.7	0.7	0.8	0.9	1.3
% Long Term Debt of Capitalization	27.7	26.4	27.4	26.1	28.8	29.6	28.3	34.7	36.3	34.2
% Net Income of Revenue	4.5	2.7	4.1	6.7	5.6	2.0	7.7	7.9	6.4	6.5
% Return on Assets	11.4	7.8	3.3	4.7	5.3	1.8	5.1	4.9	5.3	5.2
% Return on Equity	17.4	9.9	14.8	12.3	20.0	6.2	16.0	15.4	17.3	17.1

Data as orig reptd.; bef. results of disc opers/spec. items. Per share data adj. for stk. divs.; EPS diluted. E-Estimated. NA-Not Available. NM-Not Meaningful. NR-Not Ranked. UR-Under Review.

Office: 1844 Ferry Road, Naperville, IL 60563-9600.
Telephone: 630-305-9500.
Website: http://www.nicorinc.com
Chrmn, Pres & CEO: R.M. Strobel

EVP & CFO: R.L. Hawley
VP & Treas: G.M. Behrens
VP, Secy & General Counsel: P.C. Gracey
Investor Contact: M. Knox (630-305-9500)

Board of Directors: R. M. Beavers, Jr., B. P. Bickner, J. H. Birdsall, III, T. A. Donahoe, R. A. Jean, J. E. Jones, D. J. Keller, R. E. Martin, G. R. Nelson, W. A. Osborn, J. Rau, J. F. Riordan, R. M. Strobel

Founded: 1953
Domicile: Illinois
Employees: 3,700

Stock Report | October 28, 2006 | NYS Symbol: **NKE** | **NKE** is in the S&P 500

STANDARD & POOR'S

NIKE Inc.

S&P Recommendation HOLD ★★★★★	**Price** $91.86 (as of Oct 27, 2006)	**12-Mo. Target Price** $90.00	**Investment Style** Large-Cap Growth

GICS Sector Consumer Discretionary
Sub-Industry Footwear

Comment NIKE is the world's leading designer and marketer of high-quality athletic footwear, athletic apparel, and accessories.

Key Stock Statistics (Source S&P, Vickers, company reports)

52-Wk Range	**$94.07–75.52**	S&P Oper. EPS 2007**E**	**5.50**	P/E on S&P Oper. EPS 2007**E**	**16.7**	Dividend Rate/Share	**$1.24**
Trailing 12-Month EPS	**$5.14**	S&P Oper. EPS 2008**E**	**5.70**	Common Shares Outstg. (M)	**250.7**	Yield (%)	**1.35**
Trailing 12-Month P/E	**17.9**	S&P Core EPS 2007**E**	**5.50**	Market Capitalization(B)	**$17.159**	Beta	**0.58**
$10K Invested 5 Yrs Ago	**$19,618**	S&P Core EPS 2008**E**	**5.70**	Institutional Ownership (%)	**82**	S&P Credit Rating	**A+**

Price Performance

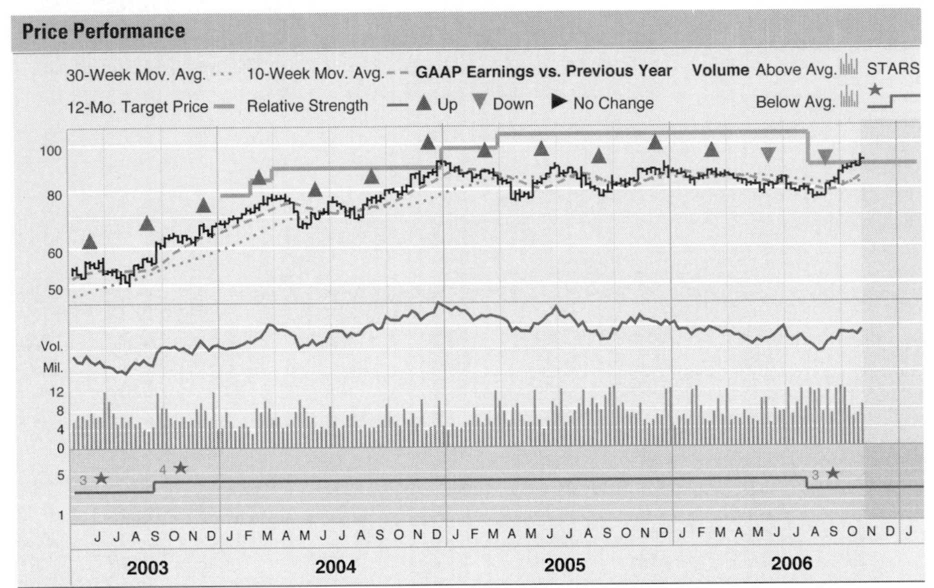

Options: ASE, CBOE, P, Ph

Analysis prepared by **Mark S. Basham** on October 02, 2006, when the stock traded at **$ 87.48**.

Highlights

- Our FY 07 (May) sales outlook has continued to weaken, as we now expect 6.8% sales growth, down from 8% when the fiscal year began. Bright spots include Nike Golf and the Asia-Pacific region. Our low single digit growth outlook for U.S. footwear sales reflects weaker retail sales of high priced, marquee shoes amid a shift to lower priced, casual footwear. Equipment sales surrounding the World Cup were disappointing to us.
- We look for FY 06 operating margins to narrow slightly, due to stock option expense and World Cup related marketing and promotion initiatives. Raw material costs should experience continued moderate pressure. Inventories as of August were up 15% from a year ago. We also believe inventories at NKE's major domestic accounts are up sharply, raising concerns about future orders.
- We anticipate that earnings growth in FY 07 will be entirely driven by share repurchases under a new four year, $3 billion stock repurchase program. We expect the diluted share count to decline by 4% to 5% in each year of the program.

Investment Rationale/Risk

- At about 17X our calendar 2006 EPS estimate of $5.22, NKE recently traded near the market multiple of the S&P 500. We think this is warranted by our expectation that consumer spending on footwear is likely to moderate. Europe remains soft, but consumer spending there may accelerate on job gains spurred by higher exports. Our different outlooks for consumer spending in Europe and the U.S. reflects the different points at which the two regions are in the economic cycle.
- Risks to our recommendation and target price include an economic slowdown domestically and a decline in consumer sentiment. International risks include economic weakness, supply disruptions, and unfavorable currency fluctuations.
- Our 12-month target price of $90 is equal to 17X our calendar 2006 EPS estimate of $5.22, nearer to the lower end of the 14X-26X range in which the stock has traded over the past five years. Our target price is based on our DCF analysis that assumes a WACC of 9.9%, and growth ranging from 9% to a perpetuity growth rate after 20 years of 3%.

Qualitative Risk Assessment

LOW	**MEDIUM**	HIGH

Our risk assessment reflects what we see as NKE's strong financial and operating metrics, offset by an increasingly competitive global marketplace and prospects for slowing consumer spending in the U.S.

Quantitative Evaluations

S&P Quality Ranking A+

D	C	B-	B	B+	A-	A	**A+**

Relative Strength Rank STRONG

78

LOWEST = 1 HIGHEST = 99

Revenue/Earnings Data

Revenue (Million $)

	1Q	2Q	3Q	4Q	Year
2007	4,194	--	--	--	--
2006	3,862	3,475	3,613	4,005	14,955
2005	3,562	3,148	3,308	3,721	13,740
2004	3,025	2,837	2,904	3,487	12,253
2003	2,796	2,515	2,401	2,985	10,697
2002	2,614	2,337	2,260	2,682	9,893

Earnings Per Share ($)

	1Q	2Q	3Q	4Q	Year
2007	1.47	**E**1.22	**E**1.34	**E**1.47	**E**5.50
2006	1.61	1.14	1.24	1.27	5.28
2005	1.21	0.97	1.01	1.30	4.48
2004	0.98	0.66	0.74	1.13	3.51
2003	0.81	0.57	0.47	0.92	2.77
2002	0.75	0.48	0.46	0.77	2.46

Fiscal year ended May 31. Next earnings report expected: Late December. EPS Estimates based on S&P Operating Earnings; historical GAAP earnings are as reported.

Dividend Data (Dates: mm/dd Payment Date: mm/dd/yy)

Amount ($)	Date Decl.	Ex-Div. Date	Stk. of Record	Payment Date
0.310	11/18	12/08	12/12	01/03/06
0.310	02/21	03/09	03/13	04/03/06
0.310	05/15	06/08	06/12	07/03/06
0.310	08/14	09/07	09/11	10/02/06

Dividends have been paid since 1984. Source: Company reports.

Business Summary October 02, 2006

CORPORATE OVERVIEW. Nike is the world's largest supplier of athletic footwear, with an estimated 33% of this $20 billion market. Sports apparel and equipment are also sold under the Nike banner, and the company's Other segment (13% of sales) houses its Cole Haan, Converse and Hurley businesses.

MARKET PROFILE. Innovation, marketing and the sports cycle drive the global footwear and athletic apparel markets, in our view. Technologically superior performance products, we think, convey the idea of extraordinary ability to the wearer and are the root of the marketing campaigns aimed at lifestyle consumers (individuals attracted to a brand's attributes of an active lifestyle regardless of sports participation). The global market for athletic apparel is about three times as large as the footwear market, and represents an approximate $44 billion U.S. retail market according to industry sources. An estimated 30% of this market consists of active sports apparel (purchased with the intent to be used in an active sport), and the remainder is lifestyle or casual wear. We see apparel representing a significant opportunity for NKE via its brand extensions and market penetration. According to NPD Fashionworld consumer estimated data, U.S. athletic footwear sales increased 7% in 2005, following several years of low single digit gains, with running and low performance shoes enjoying the strongest momentum. Frequent technological innovation enables manufacturers to hold and increase prices while building brand equity. S&P projects mid-single digit gains for these markets in 2006, aided by the 2006 World Cup.

COMPETITIVE LANDSCAPE. Both the athletic footwear and apparel markets are fragmented, providing opportunities for growing market share, in our view. Significant domestic retail channels include athletic footwear specialty shops (23% market share), sporting goods stores (16%), and discounters or mass merchants (14%). NKE's dominance will be tested by the recently completed Adidas-Reebok merger, in our view, but given the integration challenges we anticipate, we see a window of opportunity over the next 18-24 months for NKE to gain share. In fact, recent trends at athletic specialty stores show Reebok losing orders to Nike, and other footwear brands as retailers, we think, are taking a wait-and-see approach to the new combined entity.

Company Financials

Per Share Data ($) Year Ended May 31	**2006**	**2005**	**2004**	**2003**	**2002**	**2001**	**2000**	**1999**	**1998**	**1997**
Tangible Book Value	22.46	19.54	16.27	14.44	12.78	11.53	10.11	10.28	9.81	9.28
Cash Flow	6.35	5.43	4.44	3.66	7.01	2.88	2.75	2.25	1.98	3.15
Earnings	5.28	4.48	3.51	2.77	2.46	2.16	2.07	1.57	1.35	2.68
S&P Core Earnings	5.12	4.28	3.35	2.62	2.32	2.05	NA	NA	NA	NA
Dividends	0.90	0.90	0.68	0.52	0.48	0.48	0.48	0.48	0.44	0.35
Payout Ratio	17%	20%	19%	19%	20%	22%	23%	31%	33%	13%
Calendar Year	2005	2004	2003	2002	2001	2000	1999	1998	1997	1996
Prices:High	91.54	92.43	68.54	64.28	60.06	57.00	66.94	52.69	76.38	64.00
Prices:Low	75.10	65.81	42.38	38.53	35.50	25.81	38.75	31.00	37.75	31.75
P/E Ratio:High	17	21	20	26	24	26	32	34	57	24
P/E Ratio:Low	14	15	12	16	14	12	19	20	28	12
Income Statement Analysis (Million $)										
Revenue	14,955	13,740	12,253	10,697	9,893	9,489	8,995	8,777	9,553	9,187
Operating Income	23,912	2,151	1,802	1,485	1,291	1,212	1,150	1,054	1,049	1,518
Depreciation	282	257	252	239	224	197	188	198	185	138
Interest Expense	Nil	39.7	40.3	42.9	47.6	58.7	45.0	44.0	60.0	52.3
Pretax Income	2,142	1,860	1,450	1,123	2,035	921	919	745	653	1,295
Effective Tax Rate	35.0%	34.9%	34.8%	34.1%	17.2%	36.0%	37.0%	39.5%	38.7%	38.5%
Net Income	1,392	1,212	946	740	1,686	590	579	451	400	796
S&P Core Earnings	1,346	1,148	897	698	632	559	NA	NA	NA	NA
Balance Sheet & Other Financial Data (Million $)										
Cash	954	1,388	828	634	576	304	254	198	109	445
Current Assets	7,359	6,351	5,512	4,680	4,158	3,625	3,596	3,265	3,533	3,831
Total Assets	9,870	8,794	7,892	6,714	6,443	5,820	5,857	5,248	5,397	5,361
Current Liabilities	2,623	1,999	2,009	2,015	1,836	1,787	2,140	1,447	1,704	1,867
Long Term Debt	Nil	687	682	552	626	436	470	386	379	296
Common Equity	6,285	5,644	4,782	3,991	3,839	3,495	3,136	3,335	3,262	3,156
Total Capital	6,286	6,332	5,464	4,543	4,465	3,931	3,607	3,721	3,641	3,452
Capital Expenditures	334	257	214	186	283	318	420	384	506	466
Cash Flow	1,674	1,469	1,198	979	1,909	787	767	645	585	934
Current Ratio	2.8	3.2	2.7	2.3	2.3	2.0	1.7	2.3	2.1	2.1
% Long Term Debt of Capitalization	Nil	10.9	12.5	12.1	14.0	11.1	13.0	10.4	10.4	8.6
% Net Income of Revenue	9.3	8.8	7.7	6.9	17.0	6.2	6.4	5.1	4.2	8.7
% Return on Assets	14.9	14.5	12.9	11.3	27.5	10.1	10.4	8.5	7.4	17.1
% Return on Equity	23.3	23.2	21.6	18.9	46.0	17.8	17.9	13.7	12.5	28.5

Data as orig reptd.; bef. results of disc opers/spec. items. Per share data adj. for stk. divs.; EPS diluted. E-Estimated. NA-Not Available. NM-Not Meaningful. NR-Not Ranked. UR-Under Review.

Office: 1 Bowerman Dr, Beaverton, OR 97005-0979.
Telephone: 503-641-6453.
Website: http://www.nikebiz.com
Chrmn: P.H. Knight

Pres & CEO: M.G. Parker
VP & CFO: D.W. Blair
VP, Chief Lgl Officer & General Counsel: J.C. Carter
Investor Contact: P.M. Catlett (800-640-8007)

Board of Directors: J. G. Connors, J. K. Conway, T. D. Cook, R. D. DeNunzio, A. B. Graf, Jr., D. G. Houser, J. P. Jackson, P. H. Knight, M. G. Parker, O. C. Smith, J. R. Thompson, Jr.

Founded: 1964
Domicile: Oregon
Employees: 28,000

NiSource Inc.

STANDARD &POOR'S

S&P Recommendation HOLD ★★★★★ | **Price** $23.09 (as of Oct 27, 2006) | **12-Mo. Target Price** $22.00 | **Investment Style** Mid-Cap Value

GICS Sector Utilities
Sub-Industry Multi-Utilities

Comment NI, the third largest U.S. gas distribution utility and the fourth largest gas pipeline company, also provides electric utility services.

Key Stock Statistics (Source S&P, Vickers, company reports)

52-Wk Range	$23.73–19.51	S&P Oper. EPS 2006E	1.44	P/E on S&P Oper. EPS 2006E	16.0	Dividend Rate/Share	$0.92
Trailing 12-Month EPS	$0.93	S&P Oper. EPS 2007E	1.50	Common Shares Outstg. (M)	272.8	Yield (%)	3.98
Trailing 12-Month P/E	24.8	S&P Core EPS 2006E	1.44	Market Capitalization(B)	$6.299	Beta	0.60
$10K Invested 5 Yrs Ago	$12,860	S&P Core EPS 2007E	1.50	Institutional Ownership (%)	78	S&P Credit Rating	NA

Price Performance

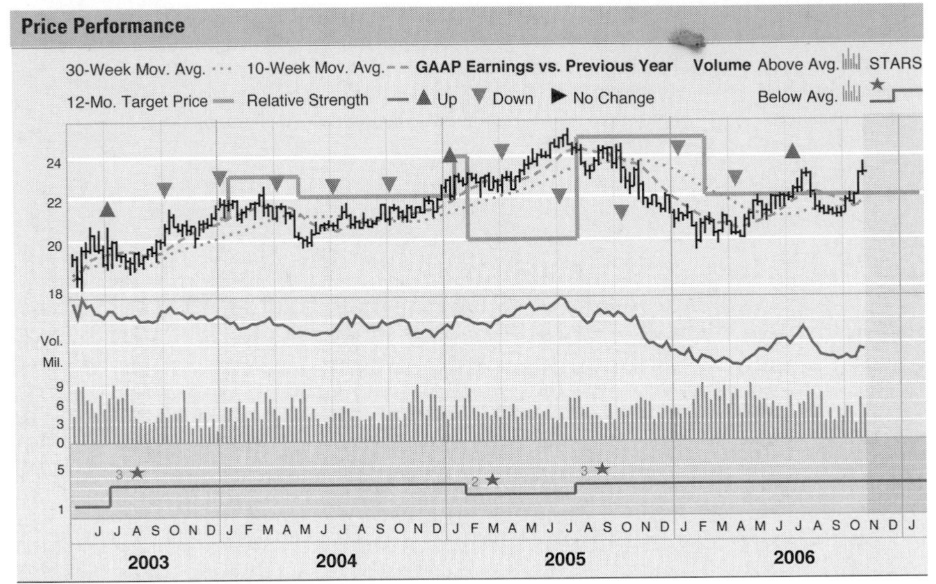

Options: CBOE, P

Analysis prepared by **Ari Bensinger** on August 25, 2006, when the stock traded at **$ 21.06**.

Highlights

- We expect low single digit gains in gas transmission and storage segment earnings in 2006, aided by higher capacity utilization. In 2005, this segment's profits fell due to, in our opinion, a restructuring of contracts and lower interruptible service revenues, partly offset by remarketing efforts and new firm contracts.
- We see 2%-4% higher electric utility earnings based on the positive impact of regulatory trackers and higher electrical revenues from the recovery of environmental costs and increased demand, partly offset by a return to milder temperatures. In addition, results should benefit from the deferral of costs related to participating in the Midwest Independent System Operator.
- We expect lower income from gas distribution operations based on reduced demand due to warmer weather and high gas prices, and on rising employee related costs, partly offset by the positive impact of regulatory trackers and restructuring. After lower interest expense, we see EPS of $1.44 in 2006, versus the $1.42 posted in 2005.

Investment Rationale/Risk

- Although the company faces rising labor costs, a new contract with IBM for back office services should help curtail cost inflation beyond 2006. Longer term, we believe NiSource can produce about 3% to 5% average annual EPS growth, slightly below the utility peer group average. We expect investments in Millennium Pipeline and Hardy Storage to contribute a significant portion of EPS growth starting in 2007.
- Risks to our recommendation and target price include a drop in power margins, unusually mild winter and summer weather, less than expected economic growth, a rise in natural gas prices, and sharply higher interest rates.
- The stock recently traded at a P/E of about 15X our 2006 EPS estimate, slightly below the utility group peer average. We believe below-peer EPS growth over the next couple of years will be balanced by NI's lower reliance on higher risk unregulated operations. Our 12-month target price of $22 implies a P/E of 15X applied to our 2007 EPS estimate, in the mid-range of peer valuations.

Qualitative Risk Assessment

LOW | MEDIUM | HIGH

Our risk assessment reflects the company's reliance on fairly stable regulated sources of earnings including gas distribution, gas transmission, and electric utility services.

Quantitative Evaluations

S&P Quality Ranking B

D | C | B- | B | B+ | A- | A | A+

Relative Strength Rank MODERATE

67

LOWEST = 1 HIGHEST = 99

Revenue/Earnings Data

Revenue (Million $)

	1Q	2Q	3Q	4Q	Year
2006	2,973	1,312	--	--	--
2005	2,683	1,356	1,165	2,695	7,899
2004	2,473	1,245	979.8	1,968	6,666
2003	2,525	1,141	898.3	1,683	6,247
2002	2,208	1,376	1,067	1,841	6,492
2001	3,798	1,875	1,756	2,029	9,459

Earnings Per Share ($)

2006	0.63	0.08	**E**0.10	**E**0.51	**E**1.44
2005	0.77	0.03	-0.02	0.27	1.04
2004	0.82	0.13	0.08	0.58	1.62
2003	0.87	0.15	0.09	0.53	1.63
2002	1.17	0.11	0.12	0.59	2.00
2001	0.85	-0.06	-0.10	0.32	1.01

Fiscal year ended Dec. 31. Next earnings report expected: Early November. EPS Estimates based on S&P Operating Earnings; historical GAAP earnings are as reported.

Dividend Data (Dates: mm/dd Payment Date: mm/dd/yy)

Amount ($)	Date Decl.	Ex-Div. Date	Stk. of Record	Payment Date
0.230	01/06	01/27	01/31	02/20/06
0.230	03/29	04/26	04/28	05/19/06
0.230	05/10	07/27	07/31	08/18/06
0.230	08/22	10/27	10/31	11/20/06

Dividends have been paid since 1987. Source: Company reports.

NiSource Inc.

Business Summary August 25, 2006

CORPORATE OVERVIEW. NiSource is the third largest U.S. natural gas distributor (measured by customers served), the fourth largest owner of U.S. natural gas interstate pipelines (by route miles), and one of the largest owners of underground natural gas storage. It also provides electric utility services in northern Indiana. The company's operating divisions include Gas Distribution (39% of year end-2005 segment operating profits), Gas Transmission and Storage (35%), Electric Operations (29%), Other Operations (-1.3%) and Corporate (1.9%).

Gas Distribution operations provide gas utility service to nearly 3.3 million customers in nine states. The division owns and operates over 56,000 miles of pipeline, 38,479 acres of underground storage, and eight storage wells. In 2005, total sales and transportation volumes were 864 MMDth, down from 898 MMDth in 2004.

Gas Transmission and Storage operates 16,021 miles of interstate natural gas pipelines and 877,144 acres of underground storage systems with a capacity of about 646 billion cubic feet (Bcf). In 2005, total throughput was 1,172.1 MMDth, about level with 2004. The division is working to develop the proposed Millennium Pipeline to access additional Canadian gas supply. Phase 1 of the Millennium project, a 186-mile section in New York state, is expected to be in service by November 2006.

NI's Northern Indiana subsidiary, NIPSCO, generates and distributes electricity for 450,397 electric utility customers. The utility operates four coal-fired plants (3,059 MW), six gas-fired plants (323 MW), and two hydroelectric plants (10 MW). In 2004, the utility generated 84.1% of its electric requirements, and purchased 15.9%. Other Operations include the Whiting Clean Energy project, a 525 MW gas-fired cogeneration plant. After being placed into service in 2002, Whiting was unable to deliver originally projected levels of steam. Whiting lost about $32.8 million after taxes in 2004 after losing about $30 million in 2003.

Company Financials

Per Share Data ($) Year Ended Dec. 31	**2005**	**2004**	**2003**	**2002**	**2001**	**2000**	**1999**	**1998**	**1997**	**1996**
Tangible Book Value	2.79	2.14	0.70	NM	NM	NM	9.88	9.20	9.59	9.17
Cash Flow	3.04	3.54	3.53	4.70	4.07	3.84	NA	NA	NA	NA
Earnings	1.04	1.62	1.63	2.00	1.01	1.08	1.27	1.59	1.53	1.44
S&P Core Earnings	1.20	1.62	1.67	1.43	0.32	NA	NA	NA	NA	NA
Dividends	0.92	0.92	1.10	1.16	1.16	1.08	1.02	0.96	0.90	0.84
Payout Ratio	88%	57%	67%	58%	115%	100%	80%	60%	59%	58%
Prices:High	25.50	22.82	21.97	24.99	32.55	31.50	30.94	33.75	24.94	20.13
Prices:Low	20.44	19.65	16.39	14.51	18.25	12.75	16.38	24.66	19.00	17.63
P/E Ratio:High	25	14	13	12	32	29	24	21	16	14
P/E Ratio:Low	20	12	10	7	18	12	13	16	12	12

Income Statement Analysis (Million $)	2005	2004	2003	2002	2001	2000	1999	1998	1997	1996
Revenue	7,899	6,666	6,247	6,492	9,459	6,031	3,145	2,933	2,587	1,822
Operating Income	1,520	1,072	1,116	1,203	1,009	568	773	678	660	612
Depreciation	545	510	497	574	642	374	311	256	250	215
Interest Expense	425	408	469	533	605	325	184	129	121	107
Pretax Income	433	671	662	680	416	298	NA	NA	NA	NA
Effective Tax Rate	34.5%	35.9%	35.4%	34.4%	44.1%	43.7%	33.5%	34.2%	35.5%	38.6%
Net Income	284	430	426	426	212	147	160	194	191	177
S&P Core Earnings	324	429	437	305	67.9	NA	NA	NA	NA	NA

Balance Sheet & Other Financial Data (Million $)	2005	2004	2003	2002	2001	2000	1999	1998	1997	1996
Cash	69.4	30.1	27.3	56.2	128	193	NA	NA	NA	NA
Current Assets	3,061	2,286	2,063	1,869	2,567	4,918	NA	NA	NA	NA
Total Assets	17,959	16,988	16,624	16,897	17,374	19,697	NA	NA	NA	NA
Current Liabilities	3,843	3,602	2,609	4,177	4,729	6,893	NA	NA	NA	NA
Long Term Debt	5,271	4,917	6,075	5,448	6,214	6,148	NA	NA	NA	NA
Common Equity	4,933	4,787	4,416	4,175	3,469	3,415	NA	NA	NA	NA
Total Capital	11,866	11,448	10,490	11,581	11,515	11,483	4,903	3,725	2,370	142
Capital Expenditures	590	517	575	622	668	366	NA	NA	NA	NA
Cash Flow	829	940	923	1,000	854	521	NA	NA	NA	NA
Current Ratio	0.8	0.6	0.8	0.4	0.5	0.7	NA	NA	NA	NA
% Long Term Debt of Capitalization	44.4	42.9	57.9	47.0	54.0	53.5	NA	NA	NA	NA
% Net Income of Revenue	3.6	6.5	6.8	6.6	2.2	2.4	NA	NA	NA	NA
% Return on Assets	1.6	2.6	2.5	2.5	1.1	1.1	NA	NA	NA	NA
% Return on Equity	5.8	9.3	9.9	11.1	6.2	6.2	NA	NA	NA	NA

Data as orig reptd.; bef. results of disc opers/spec. items. Per share data adj. for stk. divs.; EPS diluted. E-Estimated. NA-Not Available. NM-Not Meaningful. NR-Not Ranked. UR-Under Review.

Office: 801 East 86th Avenue, Merrillville, IN, USA 46410-6272.
Telephone: 877-647-5990.
Email: questions@nisource.com
Website: http://www.nisource.com

Chrmn: G.L. Neale
Pres & CEO: R.C. Skaggs, Jr.
EVP & CFO: M.W. O'Donnell
EVP & General Counsel: P.V. Fazio, Jr.

VP & Treas: D.J. Vajda
Investor Contact: R. Kozlowski (219-647-6083)
Board of Directors: S. C. Beering, D. E. Foster, S. R. McCracken, G. L. Neale, I. M. Rolland, R. C. Skaggs Jr., R. L. Thompson, R. J. Welsh, C. Y. Woo, R. A. Young

Founded: 1912
Domicile: Delaware
Employees: 7,822

Noble Corp

STANDARD &POOR'S

S&P Recommendation STRONG BUY ★★★★★

Price $68.72 (as of Oct 27, 2006)

12-Mo. Target Price $96.00

Investment Style Large-Cap Growth

GICS Sector Energy
Sub-Industry Oil & Gas Drilling

Comment This company principally provides contract drilling services for the oil and gas industry worldwide.

Key Stock Statistics (Source S&P, Vickers, company reports)

52-Wk Range	$86.16–58.51	S&P Oper. EPS 2006E	5.48	P/E on S&P Oper. EPS 2006E	12.5	Dividend Rate/Share	$0.16
Trailing 12-Month EPS	$4.60	S&P Oper. EPS 2007E	9.35	Common Shares Outstg. (M)	137.2	Yield (%)	0.23
Trailing 12-Month P/E	14.9	S&P Core EPS 2006E	5.45	Market Capitalization(B)	$9.425	Beta	0.83
$10K Invested 5 Yrs Ago	$20,823	S&P Core EPS 2007E	9.32	Institutional Ownership (%)	85	S&P Credit Rating	A-

Price Performance

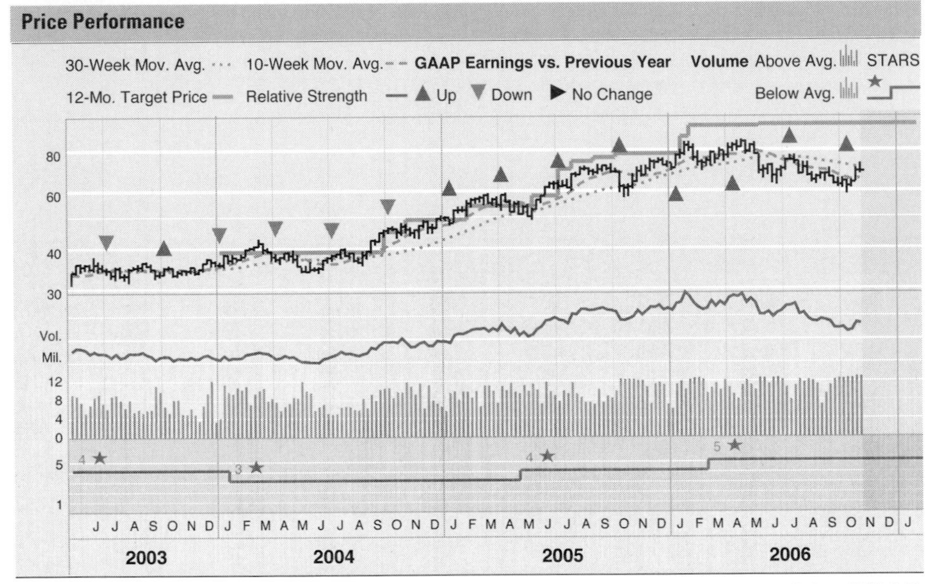

Options: CBOE, P, Ph

Analysis prepared by **Stewart Glickman, CFA** on September 29, 2006, when the stock traded at **$ 64.18**.

Highlights

- We think that NE's international jackup fleet, which generated an average dayrate of about $55,000 in 2005, should generate about $75,000 per day in 2006 and $114,000 in 2007. We see domestic semisubmersibles yielding average dayrates of $230,000 and $260,000 in 2006 and 2007, respectively, while international semisubmersibles should generate $145,000 per day and $260,000 per day, respectively. We expect overall rig utilization to be in the high 90% range in both years.
- All told, we estimate total revenue growth of 53% in 2006 and 35% in 2007, largely due to projected contract drilling revenue gains, with operating margins of about 45% in 2006 and 55% in 2007 (versus 25% in 2005). NE's two newbuild jackups under construction, the Noble Roger Lewis and Noble Hans Deul, are expected to be delivered in late 2007 and early 2008, respectively.
- We see EPS of $5.48 in 2006, rising to $9.35 in 2007. On a Standard & Poor's Core EPS basis, we project $5.45 and $9.32, respectively, with divergence from operating EPS estimates reflecting pension adjustments.

Investment Rationale/Risk

- We see further gains in rig dayrates, on anticipated supply deficits in several key drilling regions, including the Middle East, West Africa and Northwest Europe. NE has about half of its fleet in these three regions, and with dayrates expected to continue to rise through 2007, we think NE should be able to generate material dayrate gains.
- Risks to our recommendation and target price include reduced rig dayrates; lower exploration and production spending by oil and gas producers; and decreased oil and natural gas prices.
- Our net asset valuation, based on our estimates of daily operating margins for 10 years and 3% growth thereafter, discounted at a weighted average cost of capital of 9.1%, indicates an intrinsic value of approximately $97 per share. We think the shares merit a premium to peers, given NE's strong historical financial performance. Assuming multiples of 11X 2006 EBITDA and 12.5X estimated 2006 cash flow (both premiums to peers), and blending with our net asset value model, our 12-month target price is $96.

Qualitative Risk Assessment

LOW | **MEDIUM** | HIGH

Our risk assessment reflects NE's exposure to volatile crude oil and natural gas prices, capital spending decisions made by its oil and gas producing customers, and political risk associated with operating in frontier regions. Offsetting these risks is the company's strong historical financial performance relative to peers.

Quantitative Evaluations

S&P Quality Ranking B-

D | C | **B-** | B | B+ | A- | A | A+

Relative Strength Rank MODERATE

57

LOWEST = 1 HIGHEST = 99

Revenue/Earnings Data

Revenue (Million $)

	1Q	2Q	3Q	4Q	Year
2006	461.9	517.5	562.0	--	--
2005	310.3	344.0	367.2	360.6	1,382
2004	245.4	253.0	265.6	302.2	1,066
2003	245.0	247.9	254.7	239.8	987.4
2002	235.5	247.4	234.7	251.1	986.4
2001	222.4	246.7	272.8	260.5	1,002

Earnings Per Share ($)

	1Q	2Q	3Q	4Q	Year
2006	1.05	1.30	1.51	**E**1.61	**E**5.48
2005	0.33	0.53	0.55	0.73	2.16
2004	0.21	0.26	0.23	0.39	1.09
2003	0.30	0.33	0.40	0.23	1.25
2002	0.39	0.43	0.37	0.39	1.57
2001	0.40	0.50	0.58	0.48	1.97

Fiscal year ended Dec. 31. Next earnings report expected: Late January. EPS Estimates based on S&P Operating Earnings; historical GAAP earnings are as reported.

Dividend Data (Dates: mm/dd Payment Date: mm/dd/yy)

Amount ($)	Date Decl.	Ex-Div. Date	Stk. of Record	Payment Date
0.040	02/03	02/13	02/15	03/01/06
0.040	04/26	05/04	05/08	06/01/06
0.040	07/28	08/07	08/09	09/01/06
0.040	10/27	11/06	11/08	12/01/06

Dividends have been paid since 2005. Source: Company reports.

Noble Corp

STANDARD &POOR'S

Business Summary September 29, 2006

CORPORATE OVERVIEW. In April 2002, Noble Drilling Corp. shareholders approved a corporate restructuring that effectively changed the company's place of incorporation from Delaware to the Cayman Islands. The restructuring was completed April 30, 2002, upon the merger of an indirect subsidiary of Noble Corp., a newly formed Cayman Islands company, with Noble Drilling. Noble Corp. (NE) became the parent holding company of Noble Drilling and the other companies in the Noble corporate group.

NE provides contract drilling services in offshore markets worldwide. The company has a fleet of 62 offshore drilling rigs. Company owned rigs include floating deepwater units, including 13 semisubmersibles and three dynamically positioned drillships, 43 independent leg, cantilever jackup rigs (including two under construction), and three submersibles. As of March 2006, approximately 80% of the fleet was deployed in international markets, mainly in the Middle East, Mexico, the North Sea, Brazil, West Africa, India and the Mediterranean Sea. Contract drilling operations accounted for 93% of total revenues in 2005. The remaining 7% of revenues in 2005 was derived from labor contracts, under which NE provided services for drilling and workover activities on 13 third-party-owned rigs in the North Sea and two in Canada.

Within contract drilling operations, international activity accounted for 78% of revenues in 2005. PEMEX accounted for 12% of total revenues in 2005, and Petrobras contributed 10%; no other customer comprised more than 10% of revenues.

In 2005, average utilization for NE's international fleet rose to 97%, from 85% in 2004, while U.S. utilization rose to 91%, from 87%. Dayrates for the international fleet rose to $60,922, from $54,717, while for the U.S. fleet, dayrates rose to $74,056, from $65,239.

Company Financials

Per Share Data ($) Year Ended Dec. 31	**2005**	**2004**	**2003**	**2002**	**2001**	**2000**	**1999**	**1998**	**1997**	**1996**
Tangible Book Value	19.93	17.74	16.31	14.90	13.44	11.80	10.60	10.00	8.77	7.01
Cash Flow	3.93	2.64	2.36	2.51	2.85	2.04	1.39	1.77	2.56	1.19
Earnings	2.16	1.09	1.25	1.57	1.97	1.22	0.72	1.23	1.98	0.66
Dividends	0.10	Nil	Nil	Nil	Nil	Nil	Nil	Nil	Nil	Nil
Payout Ratio	5%	Nil	Nil	Nil	Nil	Nil	Nil	Nil	Nil	Nil
Prices:High	75.63	50.54	38.40	45.95	54.00	53.50	32.88	34.69	38.19	22.00
Prices:Low	47.04	33.53	30.46	27.00	20.80	27.25	12.00	10.75	15.50	8.00
P/E Ratio:High	35	46	31	29	27	44	46	28	19	33
P/E Ratio:Low	22	31	24	17	11	22	17	9	8	12
Income Statement Analysis (Million $)										
Revenue	1,382	1,066	987	986	1,002	883	706	788	713	514
Operating Income	585	396	366	400	503	379	245	301	261	128
Depreciation, Depletion and Amortization	242	209	148	125	119	111	89.0	72.0	77.9	52.2
Interest Expense	19.8	34.4	40.3	42.6	47.8	54.6	33.2	5.20	12.9	18.8
Pretax Income	364	162	187	243	350	226	124	231	380	102
Effective Tax Rate	18.5%	9.72%	11.0%	13.9%	24.6%	26.8%	24.3%	29.8%	30.5%	22.2%
Net Income	297	146	166	210	264	166	95.3	162	264	79.3
Balance Sheet & Other Financial Data (Million $)										
Cash	166	58.8	139	274	288	177	137	217	66.4	174
Current Assets	522	425	422	466	494	379	291	438	265	388
Total Assets	4,346	3,308	3,190	3,066	2,751	2,596	2,432	2,179	1,506	1,367
Current Liabilities	259	214	244	281	208	205	233	350	153	152
Long Term Debt	1,129	503	542	590	550	650	731	461	138	240
Common Equity	2,732	2,384	2,178	1,989	1,778	1,577	1,398	1,310	1,149	925
Total Capital	4,097	3,086	2,927	2,779	2,526	2,372	2,197	1,828	1,351	1,216
Capital Expenditures	434	261	307	268	134	125	422	541	391	217
Cash Flow	538	355	315	335	382	276	184	234	342	132
Current Ratio	2.0	2.0	1.7	1.7	2.4	1.8	1.2	1.3	1.7	2.6
% Long Term Debt of Capitalization	27.6	16.3	18.5	21.2	21.8	27.4	33.3	25.2	10.2	19.7
% Return on Assets	7.8	4.5	5.3	7.2	9.9	6.6	4.1	8.8	18.4	7.5
% Return on Equity	11.6	6.4	8.0	11.1	15.7	11.1	7.0	13.2	25.5	10.9

Data as orig reptd.; bef. results of disc opers/spec. items. Per share data adj. for stk. divs.; EPS diluted. E-Estimated. NA-Not Available. NM-Not Meaningful. NR-Not Ranked. UR-Under Review.

Office: 13135 South Dairy Ashford, Sugar Land, TX, USA 77478.
Telephone: 281-276-6100.
Website: http://www.noblecorp.com
Chrmn & CEO: J.C. Day

Pres & COO: M.A. Jackson
EVP & Secy: J.J. Robertson
SVP, CFO, Treas & Cntlr: T.L. Mitchell
SVP & General Counsel: R.D. Campbell

Investor Contact: L.M. Ahlstrom (281-276-6100)
Auditor: Pricewaterhousecoopers
Board of Directors: M. A. Cawley, L. J. Chazen, L. R. Corbett, J. C. Day, J. H. Edwards, M. A. Jackson, M. E. Leland, J. E. Little, M. P. Ricciardello, W. A. Sears

Founded: 1939
Domicile: Cayman Islands
Employees: 5,600

STANDARD & POOR'S

Nordstrom Inc.

S&P Recommendation HOLD ★★★★★

Price $46.83 (as of Oct 27, 2006)

12-Mo. Target Price $46.00

Investment Style Large-Cap Value

GICS Sector Consumer Discretionary
Sub-Industry Department Stores

Comment This Seattle-based specialty retailer of apparel and accessories, widely known for its emphasis on service, operates about 156 stores in 27 states.

Key Stock Statistics (Source S&P, Vickers, company reports)

52-Wk Range	**$49.52–31.77**	S&P Oper. EPS 2007**E**	**2.40**	P/E on S&P Oper. EPS 2007**E**	**19.5**	Dividend Rate/Share	**$0.42**
Trailing 12-Month EPS	**$2.22**	S&P Oper. EPS 2008**E**	**2.75**	Common Shares Outstg. (M)	**256.6**	Yield (%)	**0.90**
Trailing 12-Month P/E	**21.1**	S&P Core EPS 2007**E**	**2.40**	Market Capitalization(B)	**$12.018**	Beta	**1.65**
$10K Invested 5 Yrs Ago	**$64,733**	S&P Core EPS 2008**E**	**2.75**	Institutional Ownership (%)	**69**	S&P Credit Rating	**A**

Price Performance

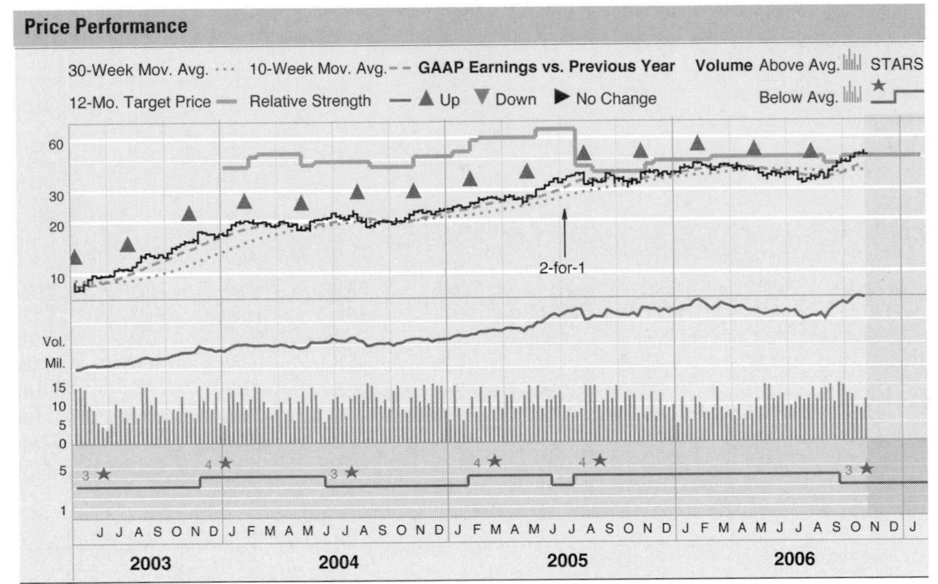

Options: ASE, P

Analysis prepared by **Jason N. Asaeda** on September 18, 2006, when the stock traded at **$ 41.60**.

Highlights

- We project net sales of $8.3 billion in FY 07 (Jan.). Retail sales are expected to reflect a 4% to 5% same-store sales rise and modest growth in retail square footage. Based on our view that JWN has well-edited luxury-focused assortments and superior customer service, we see potential for the company to increase its share of wallet among Baby Boomers that earn high salaries. We also look for a broader offering of designer apparel to attract a growing base of loyal younger customers.
- We see operating margins widening on increased full price sales across major categories, supported by JWN's leveraging of technology to better manage its merchandise assortments and inventory levels, as well as effective cost controls. This should be partly offset by markdowns on women's apparel, which has been a weaker performing business for the company since FY 06, incremental new store costs, and stock option expensing.
- After anticipated share buybacks, we estimate FY 07 operating and S&P Core EPS of $2.40.

Investment Rationale/Risk

- We recently lowered our opinion to hold from buy, based on valuation. While JWN will be up against its impressive FY 06 margin gains in FY 07, we see an opportunity for incremental operating margin improvement, as the company's merchant team is using systems investments to more accurately forecast sales trends and to better plan store-level inventory and expense. In our view, JWN's perpetual inventory management system has also enabled its sales associates to better anticipate and respond to customer needs. Given our expectation of strong fall and winter selling seasons and a gradually improving women's apparel mix, we look for JWN to sustain its positive sales and earnings momentum over the balance of FY 07 and into FY 08.
- Risks to our recommendation and target price include sales shortfalls due to unforeseen shifts in fashion trends, and cutbacks in consumer discretionary spending.
- Our 12-month target price of $46 is based on our discounted cash flow model, which assumes a weighted average cost of capital of 11.9% and a terminal growth rate of 2.5%.

Qualitative Risk Assessment

LOW | **MEDIUM** | HIGH

Our risk assessment reflects our view of JWN's improving sales and profit margins, increasing market share in the better department store sector, and healthy balance sheet and cash flow, offset by uncertainty over consumer discretionary spending in light of rising interest rates and debt levels.

Quantitative Evaluations

S&P Quality Ranking A-

D | C | B- | B | B+ | **A-** | A | A+

Relative Strength Rank STRONG

87

LOWEST = 1 HIGHEST = 99

Revenue/Earnings Data

Revenue (Million $)

	1Q	2Q	3Q	4Q	Year
2007	1,787	2,270	--	--	--
2006	1,654	2,106	1,666	2,296	7,723
2005	1,535	1,953	1,542	2,100	7,131
2004	1,344	1,795	1,421	1,933	6,492
2003	1,246	1,656	1,323	1,751	5,975
2002	1,218	1,546	1,239	1,632	5,634

Earnings Per Share ($)

2007	0.48	0.67	**E**0.43	**E**0.82	**E**2.40
2006	0.38	0.53	0.39	0.69	1.98
2005	0.24	0.38	0.27	0.50	1.39
2004	0.10	0.24	0.17	0.37	0.88
2003	-0.04	0.14	0.07	0.22	0.38
2002	0.09	0.15	0.04	0.19	0.46

Fiscal year ended Jan. 31. Next earnings report expected: Mid November. EPS Estimates based on S&P Operating Earnings; historical GAAP earnings are as reported.

Dividend Data (Dates: mm/dd Payment Date: mm/dd/yy)

Amount ($)	Date Decl.	Ex-Div. Date	Stk. of Record	Payment Date
0.085	11/17	11/28	11/30	12/15/05
0.105	02/22	02/24	02/28	03/15/06
0.105	05/18	05/26	05/31	06/15/06
0.105	08/22	08/29	08/31	09/15/06

Dividends have been paid since 1971. Source: Company reports.

Please read the Required Disclosures and Analyst Certification on the last page of this report.

Nordstrom Inc.

Business Summary September 18, 2006

CORPORATE OVERVIEW. In our view, JWN is the clear leader in the U.S. better department store sector, reflecting its focus on high-quality, differentiated merchandise; personalized customer service; and a consistent upscale shopping experience across its entire Nordstrom store base. The company derives its revenues from retail, credit and direct sales channels, as well as Faconnable, a wholly owned wholesaler and retailer of apparel and accessories. In FY 06 (Jan.), merchandise category sales were: women's apparel 35%; shoes 21%; women's accessories and cosmetics 20%; men's apparel 18%; children's apparel 3%; and other 3%.

IMPACT OF MAJOR DEVELOPMENTS. JWN spends about $150 million annually on information technology (IT). In FY 03, the company invested in a perpetual inventory system that has enabled its merchant teams to more accurately forecast sales trends and to better track and plan store-level inventory and expenses, resulting in improved sales performance and profitability, in our opinion. In FY 05, JWN put into place a new point of sales system that includes Personal Book, a tool that allows salespeople to tailor service to the needs of each customer by organizing and tracking customer preferences, purchases and contact information. The company has noted that Personal Book has driven incremental sales volume.

CORPORATE STRATEGY. JWN is pursuing a multi-channel retail strategy that included 99 full-line Nordstrom stores, 49 discount Nordstrom Rack stores, 32 Faconnable boutiques, catalogs and the Internet at www.nordstrom.com as of March 2006. Industry consolidation has presented the company with an opportunity to ramp up retail expansion. Growth plans for the next three years include opening 13 new stores and relocating or remodeling 18 existing stores. JWN opened one full-line store in March 2006 and plans to relocate one full-line store and to open one Nordstrom Rack clearance store in fall of 2006. In FY 07, the company is scheduled to open four full-line stores.

Company Financials

Per Share Data ($) Year Ended Jan. 31	**2006**	**2005**	**2004**	**2003**	**2002**	**2001**	**2000**	**1999**	**1998**	**1997**
Tangible Book Value	7.26	6.10	5.40	4.55	4.38	4.06	4.49	4.63	4.84	4.63
Cash Flow	2.98	2.31	1.78	1.24	1.27	1.16	1.44	1.32	1.11	0.94
Earnings	1.98	1.39	0.88	0.38	0.46	0.39	0.73	0.71	0.60	0.46
S&P Core Earnings	1.93	2.62	1.67	0.62	0.80	0.83	NA	NA	NA	NA
Dividends	0.24	0.21	0.21	0.19	0.18	0.16	0.18	0.15	0.13	0.13
Payout Ratio	12%	15%	23%	50%	38%	41%	24%	21%	22%	27%
Calendar Year	2005	2004	2003	2002	2001	2000	1999	1998	1997	1996
Prices:High	39.00	23.68	17.75	13.44	11.49	17.25	22.41	20.19	17.05	13.38
Prices:Low	22.71	16.55	7.50	7.80	6.90	7.06	10.84	10.71	8.47	8.56
P/E Ratio:High	20	17	20	35	25	44	31	29	28	29
P/E Ratio:Low	11	12	9	20	15	18	15	15	14	19

Income Statement Analysis (Million $)										
Revenue	7,723	7,131	6,492	5,975	5,634	5,529	5,124	5,028	4,852	4,453
Operating Income	1,010	817	585	424	363	335	467	458	393	310
Depreciation	276	265	251	234	218	203	194	180	160	156
Interest Expense	45.3	85.4	91.0	86.2	73.5	63.0	54.0	49.0	35.5	45.6
Pretax Income	885	647	398	196	204	167	332	338	307	244
Effective Tax Rate	37.7%	39.2%	39.0%	47.1%	39.0%	38.9%	38.9%	38.8%	39.4%	39.3%
Net Income	551	393	243	104	125	102	203	207	186	148
S&P Core Earnings	536	373	229	83.9	107	109	NA	NA	NA	NA

Balance Sheet & Other Financial Data (Million $)										
Cash	463	361	476	208	331	25.0	27.0	241	24.8	28.3
Current Assets	2,874	2,572	2,455	2,073	2,055	1,813	1,565	1,680	1,595	1,532
Total Assets	4,921	4,605	4,466	4,096	4,049	3,608	3,062	3,115	2,865	2,703
Current Liabilities	1,623	1,341	1,050	870	948	951	867	769	943	787
Long Term Debt	628	929	1,605	1,342	1,351	1,100	747	805	320	329
Common Equity	2,093	1,789	1,634	1,372	1,314	1,229	1,185	1,317	1,475	1,473
Total Capital	2,720	2,718	3,239	2,714	2,666	2,329	1,932	2,122	1,775	1,915
Capital Expenditures	272	247	258	328	390	321	305	291	260	204
Cash Flow	828	658	494	338	342	305	397	387	346	304
Current Ratio	1.8	1.9	2.3	2.4	2.2	1.9	1.8	2.2	1.7	2.0
% Long Term Debt of Capitalization	23.1	34.2	49.5	49.4	50.7	47.2	38.7	37.9	17.8	17.2
% Net Income of Revenue	7.1	5.5	3.7	1.7	2.2	1.8	4.0	4.1	3.8	3.3
% Return on Assets	11.6	8.6	5.7	2.5	3.3	3.1	6.6	6.9	6.7	5.4
% Return on Equity	28.4	23.0	16.2	7.7	9.8	8.5	16.3	14.8	12.6	10.2

Data as orig reptd.; bef. results of disc opers/spec. items. Per share data adj. for stk. divs.; EPS diluted. E-Estimated. NA-Not Available. NM-Not Meaningful. NR-Not Ranked. UR-Under Review.

Office: 1617 Sixth Avenue, Seattle, WA 98101-1707.
Telephone: 206-628-2111.
Email: invrelations@nordstrom.com
Website: http://www.nordstrom.com

Chrmn: B.A. Nordstrom
Pres: B.W. Nordstrom
EVP & CFO: M.G. Koppel
VP & Secy: D.L. Mackie

Chief Acctg Officer & Cntlr: P. Collins
Investor Contact: S. Allen (206-303-3200)
Board of Directors: P. Campbell, E. Hernandez, Jr., J. P. Jackson, R. G. Miller, B. W. Nordstrom, E. Nordstrom, P. Nordstrom, P. G. Satre, A. A. Winter

Founded: 1901
Domicile: Washington
Employees: 51,400

STANDARD & POOR'S

Norfolk Southern Corp

S&P Recommendation HOLD ★★★★★

Price $53.33 (as of Oct 27, 2006)

12-Mo. Target Price $54.00

Investment Style Large-Cap Value

GICS Sector Industrials
Sub-Industry Railroads

Comment This railroad operates 21,200 route miles serving 22 Eastern states and Canada.

Key Stock Statistics (Source S&P, Vickers, company reports)

52-Wk Range	$57.71–39.10	S&P Oper. EPS 2006E	3.53	P/E on S&P Oper. EPS 2006E	15.1	Dividend Rate/Share	$0.72
Trailing 12-Month EPS	$3.49	S&P Oper. EPS 2007E	3.97	Common Shares Outstg. (M)	413.8	Yield (%)	1.35
Trailing 12-Month P/E	15.3	S&P Core EPS 2006E	3.23	Market Capitalization(B)	$22.069	Beta	0.86
$10K Invested 5 Yrs Ago	$32,524	S&P Core EPS 2007E	3.74	Institutional Ownership (%)	68	S&P Credit Rating	BBB+

Price Performance

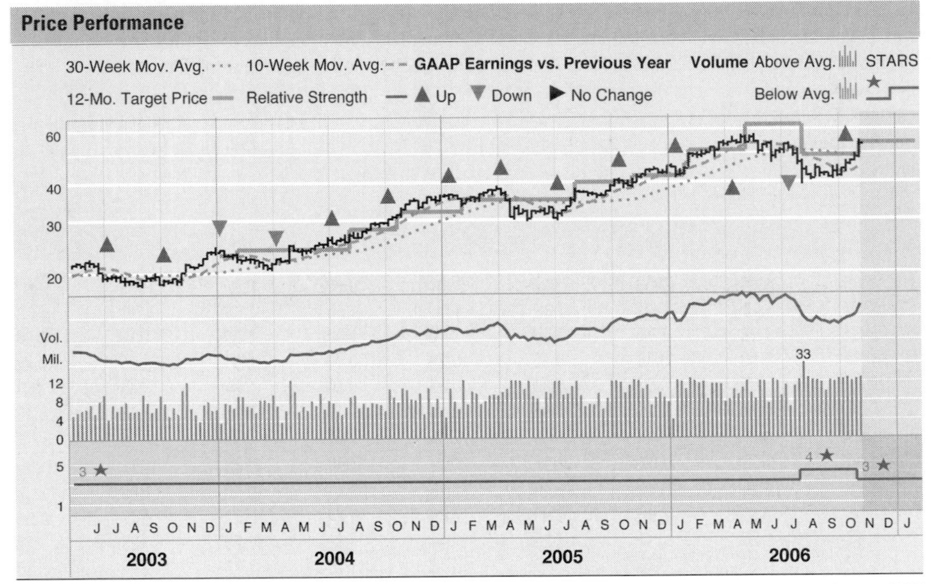

Options: CBOE

Highlights

- The STARS recommendation for NSC has recently been changed to 3 (hold) from 4 (buy) and the 12-month target price has recently been changed to $54.00 from $49.00. The Highlights section of this Stock Report will be updated accordingly.

Investment Rationale/Risk

- The Investment Rationale/Risk section of this Stock Report will be updated shortly. For the latest News story on NSC from MarketScope, see below.
- 10/25/06 11:06 am EDT... S&P DOWNGRADES OPINION ON SHARES OF NORFOLK SOUTHERN TO HOLD FROM BUY (NSC 54.12***): NSC posts Q3 EPS of $1.02 vs. $0.73 on an 11% rise in revenue and a 330 bps increase in operating margin, exceeding our $0.93 estimate. The company bought some 3% of its stock during the quarter for over $700M. While we expect further earnings growth in '07, we think momentum has peaked and that outsized price and volume gains will be harder to achieve. With about a 28% rise in share price since late July, we believe NSC is fairly valued. We are raising our '06 EPS estimate by $0.09 to $3.53, '07's by $0.06 to $3.97, and boosting our 12-month target price to $54 from $49. /KKirkeby-CFA

Qualitative Risk Assessment

LOW | **MEDIUM** | HIGH

Our risk assessment reflects what we see as NSC's exposure to economic cycles, regulations, labor and fuel costs, significant capital expenditure requirements, and challenges in maintaining system fluidity, offset by our view of a diverse customer base, historically positive free cash flow, and moderate financial leverage.

Quantitative Evaluations

S&P Quality Ranking B

D | C | B- | **B** | B+ | A- | A | A+

Relative Strength Rank STRONG

93

LOWEST = 1 HIGHEST = 99

Revenue/Earnings Data

Revenue (Million $)

	1Q	2Q	3Q	4Q	Year
2006	2,303	2,392	2,393	--	--
2005	1,961	2,154	2,155	2,257	8,527
2004	1,693	1,813	1,857	1,949	7,312
2003	1,561	1,633	1,598	1,676	6,468
2002	1,498	1,593	1,598	1,581	6,270
2001	1,540	1,592	1,508	1,530	6,170

Earnings Per Share ($)

2006	0.72	0.89	1.02	E0.93	E3.53
2005	0.47	1.04	0.73	0.87	3.11
2004	0.40	0.54	0.72	0.65	2.31
2003	0.54	0.35	0.35	0.13	1.05
2002	0.22	0.31	0.32	0.33	1.18
2001	0.16	0.28	0.20	0.30	0.94

Fiscal year ended Dec. 31. Next earnings report expected: Late January. EPS Estimates based on S&P Operating Earnings; historical GAAP earnings are as reported.

Dividend Data (Dates: mm/dd Payment Date: mm/dd/yy)

Amount ($)	Date Decl.	Ex-Div. Date	Stk. of Record	Payment Date
0.160	01/24	02/01	02/03	03/10/06
0.160	04/25	05/03	05/05	06/10/06
0.180	07/25	08/02	08/04	09/11/06
0.180	10/23	11/01	11/03	12/11/06

Dividends have been paid since 1901. Source: Company reports.

Please read the Required Disclosures and Analyst Certification on the last page of this report.

Norfolk Southern Corp

Business Summary August 01, 2006

CORPORATE OVERVIEW. Norfolk Southern provides rail transportation service in the eastern U.S., operating over 21,000 miles of road, with an extensive intermodal and coal service network and a significant general freight business, including an automotive business that is the largest in North America. NSC owns 58% of Conrail's shares, with CSX holding the remainder, and holds 50% voting rights. NSC and CSX operate separate portions of Conrail's rail routes and assets. NSC's non-rail activities includes real estate and natural resources.

MARKET PROFILE. We believe NSC's intermodal business, representing 21% of 2005 freight revenues, should be NSC's fastest growing segment longer term, driven by rising international trade and its cost savings over trucks for long-distance container movements. We believe the superior system fluidity of its most extensive intermodal network on the East Coast, supported by ongoing investment in facilities, should provide NSC with a continuing edge in garnering east coast intermodal traffic. Coal, which we believe is NSC's most profitable segment, accounted for 25% of 2005 freight revenues. Most of this traffic originates from the Appalachian coal fields, and is primarily delivered to power utilities. General merchandise, sensitive to U.S. GDP trends, provided 54% of freight revenues in 2005. We believe chemicals, agricultural products and automotive, representing 11%, 10% and 12% of 2005 freight revenues, respectively, are significant general merchandise subsegments that are facing low long-term volume growth prospects.

COMPETITIVE LANDSCAPE. The U.S. rail industry has an oligopoly-like structure, with over 80% of revenues generated by the four largest railroads: NSC and CSX Corp. operating on the East Coast, and Union Pacific Corp. and Burlington Northern Santa Fe Corp. operating on the West Coast. Railroads simultaneously compete for customers while cooperating by sharing assets, interfacing systems, and completing customer movements. Key suppliers include locomotive and rail equipment manufacturers, fuel suppliers, and labor. NSC's employees, about 85% of whom are unionized, enjoy above national average compensation due to their significant bargaining power.

Company Financials

Per Share Data ($) Year Ended Dec. 31	**2005**	**2004**	**2003**	**2002**	**2001**	**2000**	**1999**	**1998**	**1997**	**1996**
Tangible Book Value	22.66	19.98	17.83	16.71	15.78	15.17	15.53	15.61	14.44	13.27
Cash Flow	5.02	3.83	2.40	2.50	2.27	1.80	1.91	2.83	2.98	3.15
Earnings	3.11	2.31	1.05	1.18	0.94	0.45	0.63	1.65	1.84	2.03
S&P Core Earnings	2.97	2.13	0.95	0.70	0.41	NA	NA	NA	NA	NA
Dividends	0.48	0.46	0.30	0.26	0.24	0.80	0.80	0.80	0.80	0.75
Payout Ratio	15%	20%	29%	22%	26%	178%	127%	48%	43%	37%
Prices:High	45.81	36.69	24.62	26.98	24.11	22.75	36.44	41.75	38.13	32.21
Prices:Low	29.60	20.38	17.35	17.20	13.41	11.94	19.63	27.44	28.21	25.46
P/E Ratio:High	15	16	23	23	26	51	58	25	21	16
P/E Ratio:Low	10	9	17	15	14	27	31	17	15	13
Income Statement Analysis (Million $)										
Revenue	8,527	7,312	6,468	6,270	6,170	6,159	5,195	4,221	4,223	4,770
Operating Income	2,904	2,311	1,592	1,158	1,521	1,150	1,207	1,502	1,645	1,626
Depreciation	787	609	528	515	514	517	489	450	432	429
Interest Expense	500	506	497	518	553	551	561	516	385	159
Pretax Income	1,697	1,302	586	706	553	250	351	845	998	1,197
Effective Tax Rate	24.5%	29.1%	29.9%	34.8%	34.5%	31.2%	31.9%	25.4%	30.0%	35.6%
Net Income	1,281	923	411	460	362	172	239	630	699	770
S&P Core Earnings	1,224	849	365	270	155	NA	NA	NA	NA	NA
Balance Sheet & Other Financial Data (Million $)										
Cash	289	579	284	184	204	Nil	37.0	5.00	34.0	403
Current Assets	2,650	1,967	1,425	1,299	1,047	849	1,371	913	1,103	1,457
Total Assets	25,861	24,750	20,596	19,956	19,418	18,976	19,250	18,180	17,350	11,416
Current Liabilities	1,921	2,201	1,801	1,853	2,386	1,887	1,924	1,117	1,093	1,190
Long Term Debt	6,616	6,863	6,800	7,006	7,027	7,339	7,556	7,483	7,398	1,800
Common Equity	9,289	7,990	6,976	6,500	6,090	5,824	5,932	5,921	5,445	4,978
Total Capital	22,525	21,403	17,008	16,561	15,943	15,958	16,225	15,998	15,372	6,827
Capital Expenditures	1,025	1,041	720	689	746	731	912	956	875	688
Cash Flow	2,068	1,532	939	975	876	689	728	1,080	1,131	1,199
Current Ratio	1.4	0.9	0.8	0.7	0.4	0.4	0.7	0.8	1.0	1.2
% Long Term Debt of Capitalization	29.4	32.1	40.0	42.3	44.1	46.0	46.6	46.8	48.1	26.4
% Net Income of Revenue	15.0	12.6	6.4	7.3	5.9	2.8	4.6	14.9	16.6	16.1
% Return on Assets	5.1	4.1	2.0	2.3	1.9	0.9	1.3	3.5	4.9	6.9
% Return on Equity	14.8	12.3	6.1	7.3	6.1	2.9	4.0	11.1	13.4	15.7

Data as orig reptd.; bef. results of disc opers/spec. items. Per share data adj. for stk. divs.; EPS diluted. E-Estimated. NA-Not Available. NM-Not Meaningful. NR-Not Ranked. UR-Under Review.

Office: Three Commercial Place, Norfolk, VA 23510-2191.
Telephone: 757-629-2680.
Website: http://www.nscorp.com
Chrmn, Pres & CEO: C.W. Moorman

Vice Chrmn & COO: S.C. Tobias
Vice Chrmn & CFO: H.C. Wolf
VP & Cntlr: M.R. Stewart
General Counsel: J.C. Dimino

Investor Contact: L. Marilley (757-629-2861)
Board of Directors: G. L. Baliles, D. A. Carp, G. R. Carter, A. D. Correll, D. R. Goode, L. Hilliard, B. M. Joyce, S. F. Leer, C. W. Moorman, J. M. O'Brien, H. W. Pote, J. P. Reason, H. Wolf

Auditor: KPMG
Founded: 1980
Domicile: Virginia
Employees: 30,294

STANDARD &POOR'S

Northern Trust Corp

S&P Recommendation HOLD ★★★★★ | **Price** $58.10 (as of Oct 27, 2006) | **12-Mo. Target Price** $61.00 | **Investment Style** Large-Cap Growth

GICS Sector Financials
Sub-Industry Asset Management & Custody Banks

Comment Chicago-based Northern Trust is a leading provider of fiduciary, asset management and private banking services.

Key Stock Statistics (Source S&P, Vickers, company reports)

52-Wk Range	$60.80–49.12	S&P Oper. EPS 2006**E**	3.03	P/E on S&P Oper. EPS 2006**E**	19.2	Dividend Rate/Share	$1.00
Trailing 12-Month EPS	$2.90	S&P Oper. EPS 2007**E**	3.36	Common Shares Outstg. (M)	217.9	Yield (%)	1.72
Trailing 12-Month P/E	20.0	S&P Core EPS 2006**E**	3.02	Market Capitalization(B)	$12.661	Beta	1.32
$10K Invested 5 Yrs Ago	$12,045	S&P Core EPS 2007**E**	3.35	Institutional Ownership (%)	70	S&P Credit Rating	AA-

Price Performance

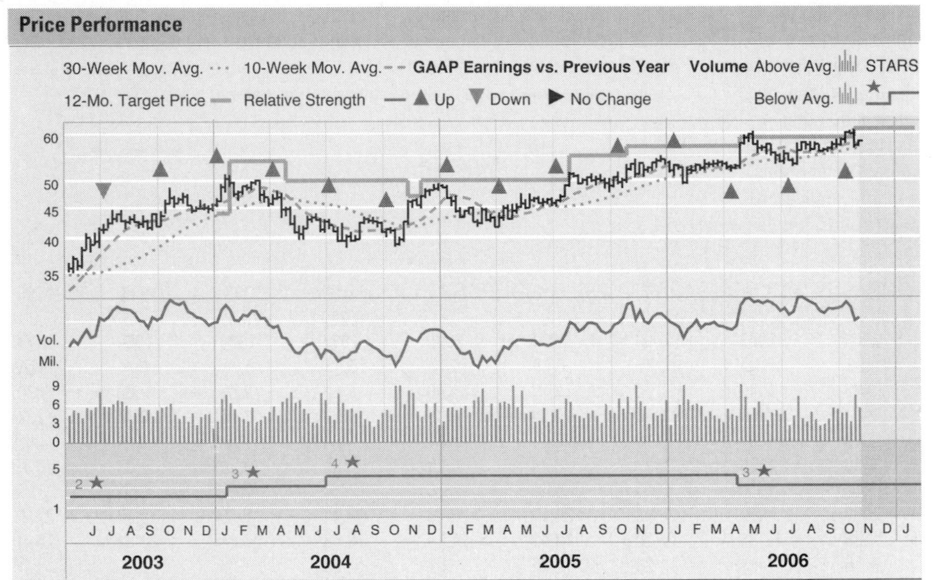

Options: CBOE, Ph

Analysis prepared by **Mark Hebeka, CFA** on October 25, 2006, when the stock traded at **$ 57.13**.

Highlights

- We continue to look for healthy investment asset growth, new business wins, and expense control to support operating earnings growth in the quarters ahead. We expect new business wins to continue to boost revenue, primarily from higher trust fees, under the assumption of modest equity market performance. Rising interest rates are likely to have a positive net impact on revenue, in our view.
- After the largest acquisition in its history, Baring Asset Management's Financial Services Group in March 2005, we believe NTRS will continue to see positive earnings momentum through 2007. While we foresee increasing loss provisions in the quarters ahead, we believe they will be moderate as we expect credit quality to remain solid, assuming that domestic and international economic growth maintains a healthy pace.
- We estimate that 2006 operating EPS will advance to $3.03, up from $2.64 in 2005, reflecting the benefits of a healthy economy that we see. We forecast 2007 operating EPS of $3.36.

Investment Rationale/Risk

- We have a hold recommendation on the shares on a total return basis, based on the stock's valuation compared to historical levels. We have a positive view of the company's product and geographic diversity, coupled with a good operating outlook. We believe the company's leading position in the affluent market, and its focus on ultra wealthy clients, should result in above peer average revenue and earnings growth in a stable or modestly rising equity market.
- Risks to our recommendation and target price include the failure to generate new business from existing and new clients, a significant decline in economic activity, and integration, legal and regulatory risks.
- Over the past three and five years, on average, the shares have traded at 19X and 24X 12-month forward EPS, respectively. Our 12-month target price of $61 is equal to approximately 18.2X our 2007 EPS estimate, a slight premium to peers.

Qualitative Risk Assessment

LOW | MEDIUM | HIGH

Our risk assessment reflects what we see as solid business fundamentals and a strong customer base. We view NTRS as well diversified geographically and able to withstand a major economic downturn.

Quantitative Evaluations

S&P Quality Ranking A-

D | C | B- | B | B+ | A- | A | A+

Relative Strength Rank MODERATE

38

LOWEST = 1 HIGHEST = 99

Revenue/Earnings Data

Revenue (Million $)

	1Q	2Q	3Q	4Q	Year
2006	1,030	1,134	--	--	--
2005	792.9	902.4	912.0	947.1	3,554
2004	680.9	695.9	686.7	765.6	2,829
2003	630.2	671.3	645.9	650.5	2,598
2002	714.2	719.3	678.6	663.0	2,775
2001	882.9	560.7	785.9	728.7	3,262

Earnings Per Share ($)

2006	0.74	0.76	0.74	**E**0.78	**E**3.03
2005	0.63	0.68	0.67	0.67	2.64
2004	0.57	0.59	0.52	0.59	2.26
2003	0.43	0.36	0.51	0.58	1.89
2002	0.56	0.56	0.43	0.43	1.97
2001	0.55	0.57	0.55	0.45	2.11

Fiscal year ended Dec. 31. Next earnings report expected: Mid January. EPS Estimates based on S&P Operating Earnings; historical GAAP earnings are as reported.

Dividend Data (Dates: mm/dd Payment Date: mm/dd/yy)

Amount ($)	Date Decl.	Ex-Div. Date	Stk. of Record	Payment Date
0.230	02/21	03/08	03/10	04/03/06
0.230	04/18	06/07	06/09	07/03/06
0.230	07/18	09/06	09/08	10/02/06
0.250	10/17	12/06	12/08	01/02/07

Dividends have been paid since 1896. Source: Company reports.

Please read the Required Disclosures and Analyst Certification on the last page of this report.

Northern Trust Corp

Business Summary October 25, 2006

CORPORATE OVERVIEW. NTRS organizes its services globally around its two principal business units: Corporate and Institutional Services (C&IS) and Personal Financial Services (PFS). C&IS is a leading worldwide provider of asset administration, asset management and related services to corporate and public entity retirement funds, foundation and endowment clients, fund managers, insurance companies and government funds. C&IS also offers a full range of commercial banking services through the bank, placing special emphasis on developing and supporting institutional relationships in two target markets: large U.S. corporations and financial institutions (both U.S. and non-U.S.). Asset administration, asset management and related services encompass a full range of capabilities including: worldwide master trust, asset servicing, fund administration, settlement and reporting; cash management; and investment risk and performance analytical services.

On March 31, 2005, NTRS completed its acquisition of the Financial Services Group Limited (FSG) from Baring Asset Management Holdings Limited. The purchase of FSG brought to C&IS expanded capabilities in institutional fund administration, custody, trust and related services as well as new capabilities in hedge fund and private equity administration, in our view.

PFS provides personal trust, custody and investment management services; individual retirement accounts; guardianship and estate administration; qualified retirement plans; banking (including private banking); personal lending; and residential real estate mortgage lending. PFS focuses on high net worth individuals, business owners, executives, retirees and established privately-held businesses in its target markets. PFS also includes the Wealth Management Group, which provides customized products and services to meet the complex financial needs of families and individuals in the U.S. and throughout the world, with assets typically exceeding $75 million.

Company Financials

Per Share Data ($) Year Ended Dec. 31	**2005**	**2004**	**2003**	**2002**	**2001**	**2000**	**1999**	**1998**	**1997**	**1996**
Tangible Book Value	14.72	14.14	13.88	13.04	11.97	10.54	9.25	7.54	6.62	5.93
Earnings	2.64	2.26	1.89	1.97	2.11	2.08	1.74	1.52	1.33	1.11
S&P Core Earnings	2.51	2.19	1.63	1.64	1.82	NA	NA	NA	NA	NA
Dividends	0.86	0.78	0.70	0.68	0.64	0.56	0.48	0.42	0.38	0.32
Payout Ratio	33%	35%	37%	35%	30%	27%	28%	28%	28%	29%
Prices:High	55.00	51.35	48.75	62.67	82.25	92.13	54.63	44.94	35.75	18.88
Prices:Low	41.60	38.40	27.64	30.41	41.40	46.75	40.16	27.88	17.00	12.31
P/E Ratio:High	21	23	26	32	39	44	31	30	27	17
P/E Ratio:Low	16	17	15	15	20	22	23	18	13	11
Income Statement Analysis (Million $)										
Net Interest Income	661	561	548	602	595	569	519	477	438	388
Tax Equivalent Adjustment	60.9	54.4	52.4	48.7	52.6	53.3	38.6	35.9	32.7	33.6
Non Interest Income	1,783	1,711	1,542	1,537	1,580	1,537	1,235	1,070	934	778
Loan Loss Provision	2.50	-15.0	2.50	37.5	66.5	24.0	12.5	9.00	9.00	12.0
% Expense/Operating Revenue	69.2%	65.9%	68.1%	67.2%	61.8%	62.6%	62.8%	63.0%	65.0%	64.0%
Pretax Income	1,776	754	631	669	732	730	616	543	472	387
Effective Tax Rate	17.1%	33.1%	32.9%	33.2%	33.4%	33.6%	34.3%	34.8%	34.4%	33.2%
Net Income	1,472	505	423	447	488	485	405	354	309	259
% Net Interest Margin	1.79	1.66	1.73	1.93	2.02	2.02	2.05	2.08	2.18	2.25
S&P Core Earnings	561	491	365	369	418	NA	NA	NA	NA	NA
Balance Sheet & Other Financial Data (Million $)										
Money Market Assets	16,036	13,168	9,565	9,332	10,546	5,865	3,439	1,174	5,275	3,197
Investment Securities	11,109	9,042	9,471	6,594	6,331	7,270	6,244	5,848	4,198	4,815
Commercial Loans	5,064	4,498	4,702	5,137	5,767	5,708	5,485	4,615	4,082	3,818
Other Loans	14,905	13,445	13,111	12,927	12,213	12,437	9,890	9,032	8,506	7,119
Total Assets	53,414	45,277	41,450	39,478	39,665	36,022	28,708	27,870	25,315	21,608
Demand Deposits	7,427	6,377	5,767	6,602	7,110	5,375	4,945	3,928	3,961	3,887
Time Deposits	31,093	24,681	20,503	19,460	17,909	17,453	16,426	14,275	12,399	9,909
Long Term Debt	2,791	1,340	1,341	1,284	1,485	1,356	1,427	1,426	1,225	733
Common Equity	3,601	3,296	3,055	2,880	2,653	2,342	2,055	1,820	1,619	1,424
% Return on Assets	3.0	1.2	1.0	1.1	1.3	1.5	1.4	1.3	1.3	1.2
% Return on Equity	42.7	15.9	14.2	16.1	19.4	21.8	20.7	20.3	20.0	18.8
% Loan Loss Reserve	0.6	0.7	0.8	0.9	0.9	0.9	1.0	1.1	1.2	1.4
% Loans/Deposits	51.8	57.8	67.8	69.3	71.9	79.5	71.9	75.0	76.9	79.3
% Equity to Assets	7.0	7.3	7.3	7.0	6.6	6.8	6.8	6.5	6.5	6.5

Data as orig reptd.; bef. results of disc opers/spec. items. Per share data adj. for stk. divs.; EPS diluted. E-Estimated. NA-Not Available. NM-Not Meaningful. NR-Not Ranked. UR-Under Review.

Office: 50 South LaSalle Street, Chicago, IL 60603-1003.
Telephone: 312-630-6000.
Website: http://www.northerntrust.com
Chrmn & CEO: W.A. Osborn

Pres & COO: F.H. Waddell
Vice Chrmn: P.R. Pero
Investor Contact: S.L. Fradkin (312-630-6000)
EVP & CFO: S.L. Fradkin

Board of Directors: D. L. Burnham, L. W. Bynoe, S. Crown, D. C. Jain, A. L. Kelly, R. C. McCormack, E. J. Mooney, W. A. Osborn, J. W. Rowe, H. B. Smith, W. D. Smithburg, C. A. Tribbett III

Founded: 1889
Domicile: Delaware
Employees: 9,008

STANDARD &POOR'S

North Fork Bancorporation Inc.

S&P Recommendation HOLD ★★★★★

Price $29.10 (as of Oct 27, 2006)

12-Mo. Target Price $33.00

Investment Style Large-Cap Value

GICS Sector Financials
Sub-Industry Regional Banks

Comment This regional bank holding company, with $58.9 billion in assets and more than 351 branches in the metro New York area, has agreed to be acquired by Capital One Financial.

Key Stock Statistics (Source S&P, Vickers, company reports)

52-Wk Range	**$30.64–24.75**	S&P Oper. EPS 2006**E**	**1.83**	P/E on S&P Oper. EPS 2006**E**	**15.9**	Dividend Rate/Share	**$1.00**
Trailing 12-Month EPS	**$1.85**	S&P Oper. EPS 2007**E**	**1.95**	Common Shares Outstg. (M)	**465.8**	Yield (%)	**3.44**
Trailing 12-Month P/E	**15.7**	S&P Core EPS 2006E	**1.82**	Market Capitalization(B)	**$13.556**	Beta	**0.31**
$10K Invested 5 Yrs Ago	**$17,753**	S&P Core EPS 2007E	**1.93**	Institutional Ownership (%)	**61**	S&P Credit Rating	**NA**

Price Performance

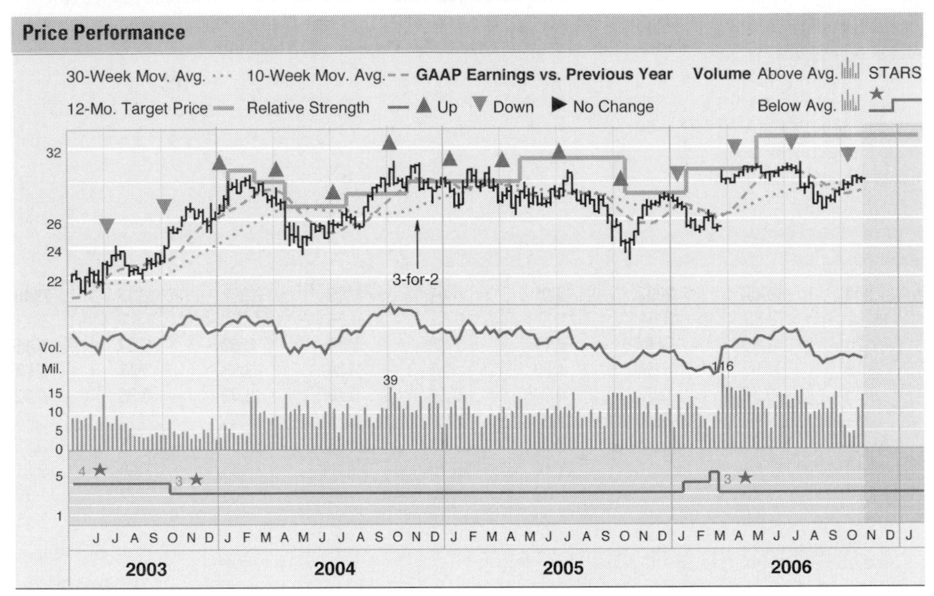

Options: P, Ph

Analysis prepared by **Mark Hebeka, CFA** on October 26, 2006, when the stock traded at **$ 29.11**.

Highlights

- NFB recently agreed to be acquired by Capital One Financial (COF: buy, $81) in a stock and cash transaction valued at approximately $14.6 billion. Subject to shareholder and regulatory approvals, the proposed deal is expected to close in the fourth quarter of 2006. For 2007, based on our expectations for slow asset growth, due to continued balance sheet restructuring, and slightly narrower net interest margins, we project net interest income to decline slightly, on a stand-alone basis.
- We see lower mortgage banking income due to slower originations, partly offset by stabilizing gain-on-sale margins and a recovery in mortgage servicing rights due to rising interest rates. We project moderate advances in service charges, reflecting growth in commercial products, partly offset by declines in personal fees due to competition, and stronger growth in investment fees.
- We forecast EPS of $1.83 in 2006 and $1.95 in 2007.

Investment Rationale/Risk

- We view NFB as a low-cost bank with a valuable franchise in the metro New York area, and we believe the GreenPoint integration is being executed as planned. We think the bank's focus on leveraging the existing GreenPoint branches will benefit growth in commercial loans and low-cost deposits while it continues to sell the majority of its mortgages. Given NFB's practice of selling its non-performing assets, option adjustable rate mortgages, and home equity products, we think its credit risk management is sound. However, we believe its proportions of mortgages and borrowings are still high.
- Risks to our opinion and target price include the possibility that the planned acquisition by COF will not close and a major economic downturn.
- Our 12-month target price of $33 is based on the terms of the proposed acquisition by COF.

Qualitative Risk Assessment

LOW	MEDIUM	HIGH

Our risk assessment reflects our positive view of NFB's diversified loan portfolio and funding sources and its large market share in a fast growing market.

Quantitative Evaluations

S&P Quality Ranking **A**

D	C	B-	B	B+	A-	**A**	A+

Relative Strength Rank **MODERATE**

45

LOWEST = 1 HIGHEST = 99

Revenue/Earnings Data

Revenue (Million $)

	1Q	2Q	3Q	4Q	Year
2006	866.2	892.6	953.1	--	--
2005	874.1	878.6	873.0	858.3	3,484
2004	309.4	338.6	379.4	799.3	1,827
2003	330.8	329.8	297.8	307.6	1,266
2002	314.5	322.9	336.8	339.4	1,313
2001	305.5	296.7	306.3	310.3	1,219

Earnings Per Share ($)

2006	0.46	0.48	0.44	**E**0.45	**E**1.83
2005	0.55	0.51	0.50	0.45	2.01
2004	0.45	0.45	0.47	0.48	1.85
2003	0.45	0.41	0.42	0.45	1.73
2002	0.41	0.43	0.44	0.45	1.72
2001	0.33	0.33	0.35	0.37	1.37

Fiscal year ended Dec. 31. Next earnings report expected: Mid January. EPS Estimates based on S&P Operating Earnings; historical GAAP earnings are as reported.

Dividend Data (Dates: mm/dd Payment Date: mm/dd/yy)

Amount ($)	Date Decl.	Ex-Div. Date	Stk. of Record	Payment Date
0.250	12/13	01/25	01/27	02/15/06
0.250	03/28	04/26	04/28	05/15/06
0.250	06/27	07/26	07/28	08/15/06
0.250	09/26	10/25	10/27	11/15/06

Dividends have been paid since 1994. Source: Company reports.

North Fork Bancorporation Inc.

Business Summary October 26, 2006

CORPORATE OVERVIEW. North Fork Bancorporation (NFB), a regional bank holding company, is one of the twenty largest banking organizations in the U.S. The bank offers a wide range of banking products and financial services to its retail and commercial customers. NFB operates its banking business through its primary subsidiary, North Fork Bank, and through GreenPoint Mortgage Funding Inc. (GPM), which it acquired in 2004. Superior Savings of New England, a subsidiary of NFB, focuses on telephonic and media-based generation of deposits. NFB's non-bank subsidiaries offer services such as asset management, securities brokerage, and sale of alternative investment products.

The bank conducts Retail Banking principally through North Fork Bank, which operates 353 retail bank branches in the New York metropolitan area. NFB offers deposit products to its customers through North Fork Bank's network of branches and online banking facility. The consumer lending operations focus on indirect automobile loans. NFB has a small presence in corporate lending in the form of commercial real estate, construction and land development loans, asset-based lending services, lease financing, and business credit services. NFB also offers trust, investment management, and custodial services through North Fork Bank's Trust Department and investment advisory services through its investment advisor.

The Mortgage Banking business is conducted nationwide through GPM, which originates, sells, and services a wide variety of mortgages secured by multi-family residences and small commercial properties. The bank originates most loans through a national wholesale loan broker and correspondent lender network. Originations are generally sold in the secondary market and from time to time securitized if market conditions warrant such execution. The bank retains certain products like commercial mortgages in its loan portfolio. GPM has established loan distribution channels in association with various financial institutions. GPM also engages in mortgage loan servicing, which includes customer service, escrow administration, default administration, payment processing, investor reporting, and other ancillary services related to the general administration of mortgage loans.

Company Financials

Per Share Data ($) Year Ended Dec. 31	**2005**	**2004**	**2003**	**2002**	**2001**	**2000**	**1999**	**1998**	**1997**	**1996**
Tangible Book Value	6.36	6.03	4.61	4.58	4.13	3.59	2.80	3.53	3.96	2.57
Earnings	2.01	1.85	1.73	1.72	1.37	0.93	1.08	0.79	0.80	0.43
S&P Core Earnings	1.98	1.83	1.69	1.66	1.33	NA	NA	NA	NA	NA
Dividends	0.88	0.82	0.72	0.65	0.54	0.48	0.48	0.32	0.25	0.17
Payout Ratio	44%	44%	42%	38%	40%	52%	45%	40%	31%	39%
Prices:High	30.27	30.81	27.34	28.49	22.49	16.67	17.83	18.36	15.00	8.06
Prices:Low	23.05	23.45	19.10	20.81	14.87	9.63	11.42	9.42	7.50	5.03
P/E Ratio:High	15	17	16	17	16	18	17	23	19	19
P/E Ratio:Low	11	13	11	12	11	10	11	12	9	12
Income Statement Analysis (Million $)										
Net Interest Income	1,810	1,175	816	842	687	592	449	425	278	231
Tax Equivalent Adjustment	47.9	NA	NA	22.2	19.4	14.5	8.75	5.51	7.40	3.82
Non Interest Income	695	236	140	120	100	99.4	59.4	54.9	35.4	29.2
Loan Loss Provision	36.0	27.2	26.3	25.0	17.8	17.0	6.00	15.5	6.00	6.80
% Expense/Operating Revenue	40.1%	39.4%	36.2%	31.7%	33.7%	42.7%	34.3%	47.5%	39.1%	32.9%
Pretax Income	1,455	841	599	636	506	376	339	243	191	112
Effective Tax Rate	34.8%	34.2%	33.9%	34.4%	34.5%	37.6%	35.0%	30.9%	37.6%	44.4%
Net Income	949	553	396	417	331	235	220	168	119	62.4
% Net Interest Margin	3.63	4.09	4.24	4.93	4.83	4.39	4.16	4.48	4.69	4.50
S&P Core Earnings	934	547	386	403	322	NA	NA	NA	NA	NA
Balance Sheet & Other Financial Data (Million $)										
Money Market Assets	1,062	1,063	531	27.6	351	310	63.8	17.0	11.8	2.30
Investment Securities	11,400	15,587	7,319	8,864	5,754	4,558	4,823	4,552	2,779	2,158
Commercial Loans	10,916	8,416	4,960	3,971	1,767	2,539	1,959	1,624	743	982
Other Loans	22,316	22,037	7,385	7,399	8,633	6,871	4,671	4,107	3,281	2,136
Total Assets	57,617	60,667	20,962	21,413	17,232	14,841	12,108	10,680	6,829	5,751
Demand Deposits	28,549	21,004	8,600	6,765	2,703	2,025	2,438	1,263	906	735
Time Deposits	8,067	13,809	6,517	6,428	8,601	7,144	4,107	2,214	1,385	3,391
Long Term Debt	4,211	16,099	1,486	1,918	1,794	795	199	199	36.0	35.0
Common Equity	9,002	8,881	1,478	1,514	1,437	1,214	619	831	602	458
% Return on Assets	1.6	1.4	1.9	2.2	2.1	1.6	1.9	1.9	1.9	1.1
% Return on Equity	10.6	10.7	26.5	28.3	25.0	21.2	30.4	23.4	22.5	14.5
% Loan Loss Reserve	0.6	0.7	1.0	1.0	1.0	1.0	1.0	1.3	1.5	1.7
% Loans/Deposits	102.7	87.5	81.7	86.2	92.0	102.5	101.1	88.9	79.8	69.8
% Equity to Assets	15.1	12.7	7.1	7.6	8.3	7.8	6.4	8.2	8.4	7.8

Data as orig reptd.; bef. results of disc opers/spec. items. Per share data adj. for stk. divs.; EPS diluted. E-Estimated. NA-Not Available. NM-Not Meaningful. NR-Not Ranked. UR-Under Review.

Office: 275 Broad Hollow Road, Melville, NY, USA 11747-4823.
Telephone: 631-531-2970.
Website: http://www.northforkbank.com
Chrmn, Pres & CEO: J.A. Kanas

Vice Chrmn: J. Bohlsen
EVP & CFO: D.M. Healy
Investor Contact: A. Campbell (631-531-2970)
VP & Secy: A. Campbell

Board of Directors: J. T. Austin, J. Bohlsen, K. M. Garrison, D. M. Healy, K. Heaviside, W. M. Jackson, T. S. Johnson, J. A. Kanas, R. A. Nielson, A. N. Puryear, J. F. Reeve, G. H. Rowsom, K. R. Schmeller, A. R. Towbin

Founded: 1980
Domicile: Delaware
Employees: 8,926

STANDARD &POOR'S

Northrop Grumman Corp

S&P Recommendation HOLD ★★★★★

Price $66.01 (as of Oct 27, 2006)

12-Mo. Target Price $72.00

Investment Style Large-Cap Value

GICS Sector Industrials
Sub-Industry Aerospace & Defense

Comment This company is one of the world's largest producers of military arms and equipment.

Key Stock Statistics (Source S&P, Vickers, company reports)

52-Wk Range	$71.37–53.18	S&P Oper. EPS 2006E	4.35	P/E on S&P Oper. EPS 2006E	15.2	Dividend Rate/Share	$1.20
Trailing 12-Month EPS	$4.01	S&P Oper. EPS 2007E	4.75	Common Shares Outstg. (M)	345.4	Yield (%)	1.82
Trailing 12-Month P/E	16.5	S&P Core EPS 2006E	3.80	Market Capitalization(B)	$22.801	Beta	-0.20
$10K Invested 5 Yrs Ago	$13,950	S&P Core EPS 2007E	4.17	Institutional Ownership (%)	87	S&P Credit Rating	BBB+

Price Performance

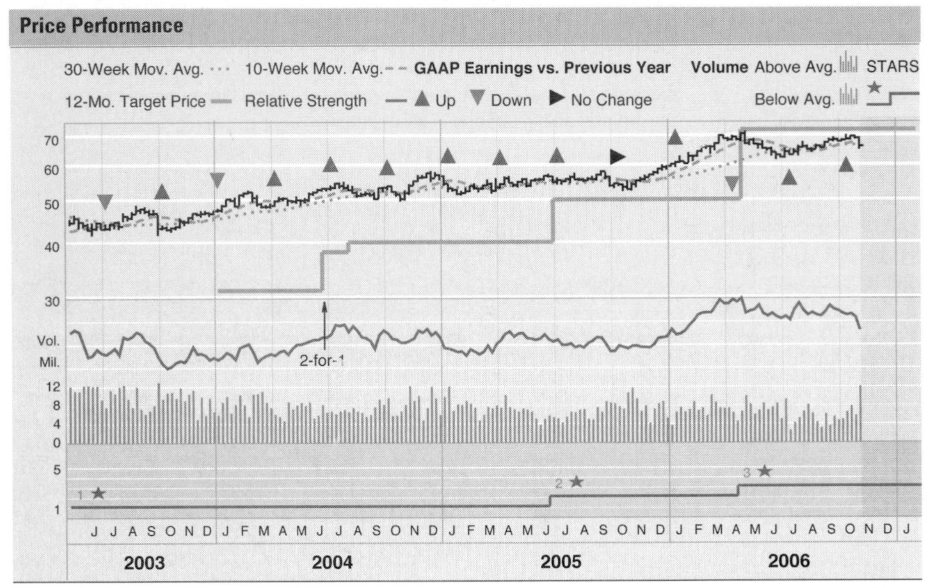

Options: ASE, CBOE, P

Analysis prepared by **Richard Tortoriello** on August 17, 2006, when the stock traded at **$ 66.29**.

Highlights

- We expect revenues to be flat in 2006. We see a number of positives in NOC's operating segments, including rising Mission Systems revenues, related to missile defense and Homeland Security, rising Integrated Systems revenues, and rising Electronics sales supporting a government move toward more advanced technologies. However, we see these expected gains mostly offset by NOC's strategic decision to exit its value-added reseller business, and weakness and lower volume in Ships, where work has been delayed by the ongoing impact of Hurricane Katrina, which brought massive damage to the U.S. Gulf Coast in late August 2005.
- We project wider margins in 2006, on the overall greater demand that we forecast for NOC, ongoing efforts to improve operating efficiencies, and our outlook for a reduction in interest charges. We also see margins in Ships recovering as the year goes on, as NOC works towards getting production back to pre-Katrina levels.
- We project EPS of $4.35 in 2006, excluding a $0.14 special tax gain recorded in the second quarter, and see growth to $4.75 in 2007.

Investment Rationale/Risk

- We expect NOC to record ongoing EPS gains through at least 2007, based on our outlook for modestly higher demand for advanced technology military products. We think NOC's large footprint in this area will enable it to record strong cash flow levels for an extended period. However, we believe these positive factors are already reflected in the shares.
- Risks to our recommendation and target price include a deterioration in the company's primary military electronics businesses, or reductions in the U.S. Defense Budget in some of NOC's major program areas.
- Our 12-month target price of $72 is based on a multiple of 15X our 2007 EPS estimate. This compares to a recent valuation of 14X 2007 EPS estimates for a group of 17 defense-related stocks in our coverage universe. Our target multiple is also slightly above NOC's 10-year historical average forward P/E of 13.5X. Given our view of NOC's continuing strong cash flows, we believe the quality of its earnings are high, and the shares should trade above their average P/E multiples.

Qualitative Risk Assessment

LOW | **MEDIUM** | HIGH

Our risk assessment reflects NOC's typically strong levels of cash flow and what we see as its strong balance sheet with a relatively low level of debt. We combine that with the highly cyclical nature of the company's business, particularly its dependence on government defense programs.

Quantitative Evaluations

S&P Quality Ranking B+

D | C | B- | B | **B+** | A- | A | A+

Relative Strength Rank WEAK

23

LOWEST = 1 HIGHEST = 99

Revenue/Earnings Data

Revenue (Million $)

	1Q	2Q	3Q	4Q	Year
2006	7,184	7,601	7,433	--	--
2005	7,453	7,962	7,446	7,860	30,721
2004	7,105	7,374	7,408	7,846	29,853
2003	5,866	6,627	6,619	7,094	26,206
2002	3,931	4,231	4,214	4,830	17,206
2001	1,986	3,663	3,605	4,304	13,558

Earnings Per Share ($)

2006	1.02	1.26	0.87	**E**1.15	**E**4.35
2005	1.08	1.00	0.80	0.92	3.81
2004	0.63	0.79	0.80	0.81	2.99
2003	0.46	0.55	0.61	0.56	2.16
2002	0.64	0.77	0.58	0.87	2.86
2001	0.71	0.64	0.42	0.64	2.40

Fiscal year ended Dec. 31. Next earnings report expected: Late January. EPS Estimates based on S&P Operating Earnings; historical GAAP earnings are as reported.

Dividend Data (Dates: mm/dd Payment Date: mm/dd/yy)

Amount ($)	Date Decl.	Ex-Div. Date	Stk. of Record	Payment Date
0.260	02/15	02/23	02/27	03/11/06
0.300	05/17	05/25	05/30	06/10/06
0.300	07/25	08/24	08/28	09/09/06
0.300	10/23	11/22	11/27	12/09/06

Dividends have been paid since 1951. Source: Company reports.

Northrop Grumman Corp

Business Summary August 17, 2006

This defense electronics- and warship-making giant, which operated through six segments in 2005, conducts most of its business with the U.S. Government, principally the Department of Defense. NOC also transacts with foreign governments and makes commercial sales both domestically and overseas.

The Electronics Systems segment (21% of revenues; 29% of earnings before interest and taxes/EBIT; and 10.7% EBIT margins in 2005) makes high performance sensors, intelligence, processing and navigation systems. Major competitors include Raytheon (RTN: buy, $48), Britain's BAE Systems, and France's Thales.

The Ships division (18%; 10%; 4.2%) primarily makes conventional battleships and nuclear-powered aircraft carriers. Its main competitor is General Dynamics (GD: hold, $69).

Information Technology (16%; 15%; 6.8%) develops and operates computer systems, mostly for various U.S. government agencies. Competitors include defense contractors Lockheed Martin (LMT: buy, $84) and General Dynamics, and civilian IT providers.

Mission Systems (17%; 16%; 7.1%) puts together complex information systems for the U.S. military. Competitors include Boeing (BA: buy, $79), Raytheon and Thales.

Integrated Systems (17%; 20%; 8.4%) designs and puts together highly sophisticated electronic battlefield surveillance and communications systems. Primary competitors include Boeing and Lockheed Martin.

The Space Technology segment (11%; 11%; 7.5%) mostly makes electronic components and systems for military satellites, rockets and missiles. Primary competitors include Lockheed Martin and Boeing.

Effective January 1, 2006, NOC created a Technical Services segment, to leverage existing business strengths and synergies in the logistics support, sustainment and technical services markets. In 2006, Mission Systems, Information Technology and Technical Services became part of an Information & Services segment. The Integrated Systems and Space Technology segments became part of Aerospace. The remaining segments are Electronics and Ships.

Company Financials

Per Share Data ($) Year Ended Dec. 31	**2005**	**2004**	**2003**	**2002**	**2001**	**2000**	**1999**	**1998**	**1997**	**1996**
Tangible Book Value	NM	NM	NM	NM	NM	NM	NM	NM	NM	NM
Cash Flow	5.94	5.01	4.05	5.29	6.31	7.08	6.23	4.25	6.16	5.57
Earnings	3.81	2.99	2.16	2.86	2.40	4.41	3.47	1.40	2.99	2.17
S&P Core Earnings	2.84	2.63	2.42	-0.95	-2.85	NA	NA	NA	NA	NA
Dividends	1.01	0.89	0.80	0.80	0.80	0.80	0.80	0.80	0.80	0.80
Payout Ratio	27%	30%	37%	28%	33%	18%	23%	57%	27%	37%
Prices:High	60.26	58.15	50.55	67.50	55.28	46.94	37.97	69.50	63.94	42.13
Prices:Low	51.10	46.91	41.50	43.60	38.20	21.31	23.50	29.66	35.69	28.88
P/E Ratio:High	16	19	23	24	23	11	11	50	21	19
P/E Ratio:Low	13	16	19	15	16	5	7	21	12	13
Income Statement Analysis (Million $)										
Revenue	30,721	29,853	26,206	17,206	13,558	7,618	8,995	8,902	9,153	8,071
Operating Income	2,951	2,740	1,538	1,391	1,649	1,479	1,358	1,149	1,298	1,025
Depreciation	773	734	682	525	645	381	389	393	418	367
Interest Expense	388	431	497	422	373	175	224	233	257	270
Pretax Income	2,044	1,615	1,131	1,009	699	975	762	312	651	384
Effective Tax Rate	32.3%	32.3%	28.6%	30.9%	38.9%	35.9%	36.6%	37.8%	37.5%	39.1%
Net Income	1,383	1,093	808	697	427	625	483	194	407	234
S&P Core Earnings	1,026	961	892	-223	-487	NA	NA	NA	NA	NA
Balance Sheet & Other Financial Data (Million $)										
Cash	1,605	1,230	342	1,412	464	319	142	44.0	63.0	44.0
Current Assets	7,549	6,907	5,745	15,835	4,589	2,526	2,793	3,033	2,936	2,597
Total Assets	34,214	33,361	33,009	42,266	20,886	9,622	9,285	9,536	9,677	9,422
Current Liabilities	7,974	6,223	6,361	11,373	5,132	2,688	2,464	2,367	2,715	2,600
Long Term Debt	3,881	5,116	5,410	9,398	5,033	1,605	2,000	2,562	2,500	2,950
Common Equity	16,825	16,970	15,785	14,322	7,391	3,919	3,257	2,850	2,623	2,128
Total Capital	21,651	22,942	22,067	24,209	13,443	5,800	5,321	5,412	5,198	5,139
Capital Expenditures	824	672	635	538	393	274	201	211	238	194
Cash Flow	2,156	1,827	1,490	1,222	1,072	1,006	872	587	825	601
Current Ratio	0.9	1.1	0.9	1.4	0.9	0.9	1.1	1.3	1.1	1.0
% Long Term Debt of Capitalization	17.9	22.3	24.5	38.8	37.4	27.7	37.6	47.3	48.1	57.4
% Net Income of Revenue	4.5	3.7	3.1	4.1	3.1	8.2	5.4	2.2	4.4	2.9
% Return on Assets	4.1	3.3	2.1	2.2	2.8	6.6	5.1	2.0	4.3	3.1
% Return on Equity	8.2	6.6	5.4	6.4	7.6	17.4	15.8	7.1	17.1	13.0

Data as orig reptd.; bef. results of disc opers/spec. items. Per share data adj. for stk. divs.; EPS diluted. E-Estimated. NA-Not Available. NM-Not Meaningful. NR-Not Ranked. UR-Under Review.

Office: 1840 Century Park East, Los Angeles, CA 90067-2199.
Telephone: 310-553-6262.
Email: investor_relations@mail.northgrum.com
Website: http://www.northropgrumman.com

Chrmn & CEO: R.D. Sugar
Pres & CFO: W.G. Bush
VP & Treas: J.L. Sanford
VP & Secy: J.H. Mullan

VP & General Counsel: W.B. Terry
Investor Contact: G. Kent (310-553-6262)
Board of Directors: J. T. Chain, Jr., L. W. Coleman, V. Fazio, S. E. Frank, P. Frost, C. R. Larson, R. B. Myers, P. A. Odeen, A. L. Peters, K. W. Sharer, J. B. Slaughter, R. D. Sugar

Founded: 1939
Domicile: Delaware
Employees: 125,000

STANDARD &POOR'S

Novell Inc

S&P Recommendation BUY ★★★★★

Price
$5.91 (as of Oct 27, 2006)

12-Mo. Target Price
$8.00

Investment Style
Mid-Cap Value

GICS Sector Information Technology
Sub-Industry Systems Software

Comment NOVL is a leading vendor of directory-enabled networking software, with its NetWare product line and Linux-based offerings.

Key Stock Statistics (Source S&P, Vickers, company reports)

52-Wk Range	**$9.83–5.73**	S&P Oper. EPS 2006**E**	**0.04**	P/E on S&P Oper. EPS 2006**E**	**NM**	Dividend Rate/Share	**Nil**
Trailing 12-Month EPS	**$0.02**	S&P Oper. EPS 2007**E**	**0.14**	Common Shares Outstg. (M)	**339.0**	Yield (%)	**Nil**
Trailing 12-Month P/E	**NM**	S&P Core EPS 2006**E**	**0.04**	Market Capitalization(B)	**$2.004**	Beta	**2.26**
$10K Invested 5 Yrs Ago	**$14,701**	S&P Core EPS 2007**E**	**0.12**	Institutional Ownership (%)	**80**	S&P Credit Rating	**NA**

Price Performance

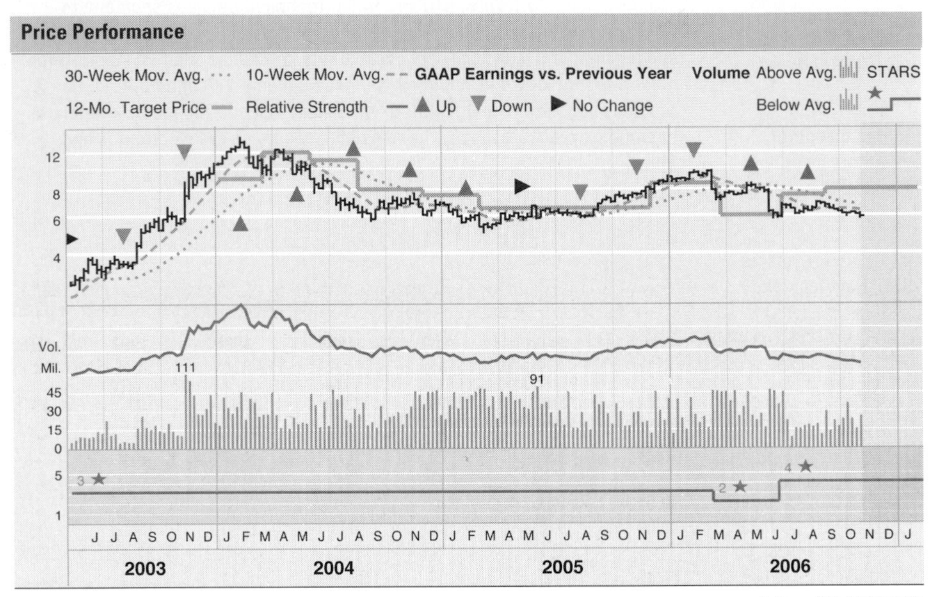

Options: ASE, CBOE, P, Ph

Analysis prepared by **Clyde Montevirgen** on August 31, 2006, when the stock traded at **$ 6.69**.

Highlights

- We expect revenues to decrease nearly 11% in FY 06 (Oct.) and 13% in FY 07, reflecting declining NetWare and Open Enterprise Server sales and the divestment of its Celerant consulting business. We believe NOVL is losing market share in the server market and that its legacy products will continue to experience double-digit decreases over the next year. However, we see above-industry growth from its Linux offerings, which grew 30% year-over-year in the third quarter, and from Identity and Access Management products, which grew 46%.
- We see gross margins widening to 64% and 66% in FY 06 and FY 07, respectively, on a shift in the revenue mix to more product and less service sales. We forecast that operating margins will widen as management continues to focus on cost cutting initiatives. However, NOVL's operating margins will still be lower than those of its peers over the midterm, in our opinion.
- We expect operating EPS of $0.04 in FY 06 and $0.14 in FY 07, including projected stock option expense of $0.10 and $0.07, respectively.

Investment Rationale/Risk

- We view NOVL's numerous strategy changes over the past few years as an indication of its struggle to capture market share in high growth niches within what we view as a mature networking software industry. Furthermore, we believe that NOVL is having problems transitioning customers from its NetWare to Linux-based products and is losing server market share as a result. However, we are encouraged by the recent appointment of Ronald Hovsepian, who was NOVL's COO, to the CEO post and think that he could accelerate restructuring and improve profitability. With shares down about 25% year to date, we have a buy recommendation on an expected operational turnaround and valuation.
- Risks to our opinion and target price include slower than expected progress in cost cutting initiatives, and negative repercussions from NOVL's internal options investigation.
- Our 12-month target price is $8 based on an enterprise value (EV) to free cash flow (FCF) of 19X our FY 07 FCF estimate, producing a value of about $8. At this price, the shares would be trading slightly under a 2X EV/Sales multiple, below that of NOVL's peers.

Qualitative Risk Assessment

LOW | MEDIUM | **HIGH**

Our risk assessment reflects the volatile market conditions in the Linux and open source software markets, the continuing decline in sales for NOVL's NetWare products, and our belief that NOVL is having difficulty gaining sufficient traction in Linux to offset the decrease in NetWare revenues.

Quantitative Evaluations

S&P Quality Ranking B-

D | C | **B-** | B | B+ | A- | A | A+

Relative Strength Rank WEAK

13

LOWEST = 1 HIGHEST = 99

Revenue/Earnings Data

Revenue (Million $)

	1Q	2Q	3Q	4Q	Year
2006	274.4	278.3	241.4	--	--
2005	290.1	297.1	290.2	320.3	1,198
2004	267.1	293.6	304.6	300.7	1,166
2003	260.0	276.0	282.8	286.8	1,105
2002	277.9	273.9	282.3	300.3	1,134
2001	245.0	240.8	246.7	307.6	1,040

Earnings Per Share ($)

2006	Nil	0.01	0.03	**E**Nil	**E**0.04
2005	0.90	-0.04	Nil	-0.01	0.86
2004	0.03	-0.04	0.06	0.03	0.08
2003	-0.03	-0.08	-0.03	-0.29	-0.44
2002	0.03	-0.08	0.03	-0.25	-0.28
2001	0.01	-0.48	-0.06	-0.26	-0.79

Fiscal year ended Oct. 31. Next earnings report expected: Early December. EPS Estimates based on S&P Operating Earnings; historical GAAP earnings are as reported.

Dividend Data

No cash dividends have been paid.

Please read the Required Disclosures and Analyst Certification on the last page of this report.

Novell Inc

Business Summary August 31, 2006

CORPORATE OVERVIEW. Novell is the second largest provider of Linux operating systems and subsystems, capturing 20% of the market by revenue in 2004 according to IDC, down from 25% in 2002. Novell offers solutions in three categories: identity-driven solutions, offering user authentication and provisioning and resource management capabilities; Linux and platform services solutions, which encompasses NOVL's two major operating systems, SUSE Linux and NetWare; and global services and support, including the Certified Novell Engineer, Certified Linux Engineer, and Certified Linux Professional programs.

CORPORATE STRATEGY. Novell relies on a series of alliances and partnerships to drive sales growth; its partners include IBM, HP, Dell, Intel, Oracle, SAP, AMD, Veritas, CA, EMC, and Adobe. Novell believes it has created an ecosystem around it to combine its strengths with those of its partners; however, these partners are also counted among the strategic partners of many other software firms, and we doubt the partnerships provide a significant competitive advantage. In addition, Novell's go-to market strategy embraces both a direct and indirect sales channel, with the indirect channel including independent distributors, value-added resellers, systems integrators, and hardware OEMs. NOVL does not share the proportion of business generated through the indirect channel, but has mentioned it as an area it is focusing on to drive growth. We believe the indirect channel provides the majority of NOVL's sales, and think this limits the company's control over how its offerings are sold and positioned.

According to IDC, the installed base of servers running Novell's NetWare operating system peaked in 2001 at 1.35 million, and new shipments fell at a 17% compound annual growth rate (CAGR) from 1999 to 2005. IDC expects shipments to decline at a 9% CAGR through 2009, and sees spending on services declining at a 12% CAGR. With revenues declining steadily, Novell needs to replace this revenue rapidly, in our opinion, and has focused on Linux as its replacement. Although we believe that Linux will capture a large portion of the NetWare market, we view Red Hat as a superior player in this space and consider it more likely to capture the lion's share of this opportunity.

Company Financials

Per Share Data ($) Year Ended Oct. 31	2005	2004	2003	2002	2001	2000	1999	1998	1997	1996
Tangible Book Value	2.42	1.39	1.89	2.31	2.98	3.80	4.57	4.42	4.46	4.67
Cash Flow	0.98	0.22	-0.27	-0.09	-0.53	0.39	0.75	0.50	0.04	0.65
Earnings	0.86	0.08	-0.44	-0.28	-0.79	0.15	0.55	0.29	-0.22	0.35
S&P Core Earnings	-0.11	-0.07	-0.45	-0.47	-1.27	NA	NA	NA	NA	NA
Dividends	Nil	Nil	Nil	Nil	Nil	Nil	Nil	Nil	Nil	Nil
Payout Ratio	Nil	Nil	Nil	Nil	Nil	Nil	Nil	Nil	Nil	Nil
Prices:High	9.27	14.24	10.77	5.64	9.13	44.56	41.19	19.00	13.00	15.63
Prices:Low	4.04	5.02	2.14	1.57	2.90	4.88	10.00	6.81	6.28	8.75
P/E Ratio:High	11	NM	NM	NM	NM	NM	75	66	NM	45
P/E Ratio:Low	6	NM	NM	NM	NM	33	29	23	NM	25
Income Statement Analysis (Million $)										
Revenue	1,198	1,166	1,105	1,134	1,040	1,162	1,273	1,084	1,007	1,375
Operating Income	99.3	140	52.3	103	46.1	98.2	293	175	-53.6	232
Depreciation	56.3	53.5	61.1	68.8	86.7	81.9	70.2	76.2	91.1	105
Interest Expense	9.63	Nil	Nil	Nil	Nil	Nil	Nil	Nil	Nil	Nil
Pretax Income	406	75.0	-55.0	-92.2	-277	70.7	244	142	-151	180
Effective Tax Rate	19.2%	23.7%	NM	NM	NM	30.0%	21.8%	28.0%	NM	30.0%
Net Income	377	57.2	-162	-103	-262	49.5	191	102	-78.3	126
S&P Core Earnings	-52.6	-30.8	-167	-172	-384	NA	NA	NA	NA	NA
Balance Sheet & Other Financial Data (Million $)										
Cash	811	434	752	636	705	698	895	1,007	1,033	1,025
Current Assets	2,009	1,535	1,031	920	1,027	1,007	1,336	1,436	1,470	1,591
Total Assets	2,762	2,292	1,568	1,665	1,904	1,712	1,942	1,924	1,911	2,049
Current Liabilities	753	693	626	592	611	455	440	415	322	365
Long Term Debt	600	600	Nil	Nil	Nil	Nil	Nil	Nil	Nil	Nil
Common Equity	1,386	963	934	1,066	1,271	1,245	1,492	1,493	1,565	1,616
Total Capital	2,004	1,599	941	1,074	1,293	1,257	1,503	1,509	1,589	1,685
Capital Expenditures	30.8	27.0	39.5	27.6	33.3	57.8	69.2	57.4	64.8	101
Cash Flow	433	84.6	-101	-34.3	-175	131	261	178	12.8	231
Current Ratio	2.7	2.2	1.6	1.6	1.7	2.2	3.0	3.5	4.6	4.4
% Long Term Debt of Capitalization	29.9	37.5	Nil	Nil	Nil	Nil	Nil	Nil	Nil	Nil
% Net Income of Revenue	31.5	4.9	NM	NM	NM	4.3	15.0	9.4	NM	9.2
% Return on Assets	14.9	3.0	NM	NM	NM	2.7	9.9	5.3	NM	5.7
% Return on Equity	32.1	3.3	NM	NM	NM	3.6	12.8	6.7	NM	7.1

Data as orig reptd.; bef. results of disc opers/spec. items. Per share data adj. for stk. divs.; EPS diluted. E-Estimated. NA-Not Available. NM-Not Meaningful. NR-Not Ranked. UR-Under Review.

Office: 404 Wyman St Ste 500, Waltham, MA 02451-1212.
Telephone: 781-464-8000.
Website: http://www.novell.com
Chrmn: T.G. Plaskett

Pres & CEO: R. Hovsepian
EVP & CTO: J. Jaffe
SVP, Secy & General Counsel: J.A. LaSala, Jr.
VP, CFO & Cntlr: D.C. Russell

Investor Contact: B. Smith (800-317-3195)
Board of Directors: A. Aiello, F. Corrado, R. Crandall, R. W. Hovsepian, C. Malone, J. L. Messman, R. L. Nolan, T. G. Plaskett, J. W. Poduska, Sr., J. D. Robinson, III, K. B. White

Founded: 1983
Domicile: Delaware
Employees: 4,800

STANDARD &POOR'S

Novellus Systems Inc

S&P Recommendation HOLD ★★★★★

Price $27.92 (as of Oct 27, 2006)

12-Mo. Target Price $29.00

Investment Style Mid-Cap Value

GICS Sector Information Technology
Sub-Industry Semiconductor Equipment

Comment This company manufactures, markets and services automated wafer fabrication systems for the deposition of thin films.

Key Stock Statistics (Source S&P, Vickers, company reports)

52-Wk Range	**$30.62–21.48**	S&P Oper. EPS 2006**E**	**1.66**	P/E on S&P Oper. EPS 2006**E**	**16.8**	Dividend Rate/Share	**Nil**
Trailing 12-Month EPS	**$1.33**	S&P Oper. EPS 2007**E**	**1.36**	Common Shares Outstg. (M)	**123.2**	Yield (%)	**Nil**
Trailing 12-Month P/E	**21.0**	S&P Core EPS 2006**E**	**1.66**	Market Capitalization(B)	**$3.441**	Beta	**2.80**
$10K Invested 5 Yrs Ago	**$7,865**	S&P Core EPS 2007**E**	**1.36**	Institutional Ownership (%)	**85**	S&P Credit Rating	**NA**

Price Performance

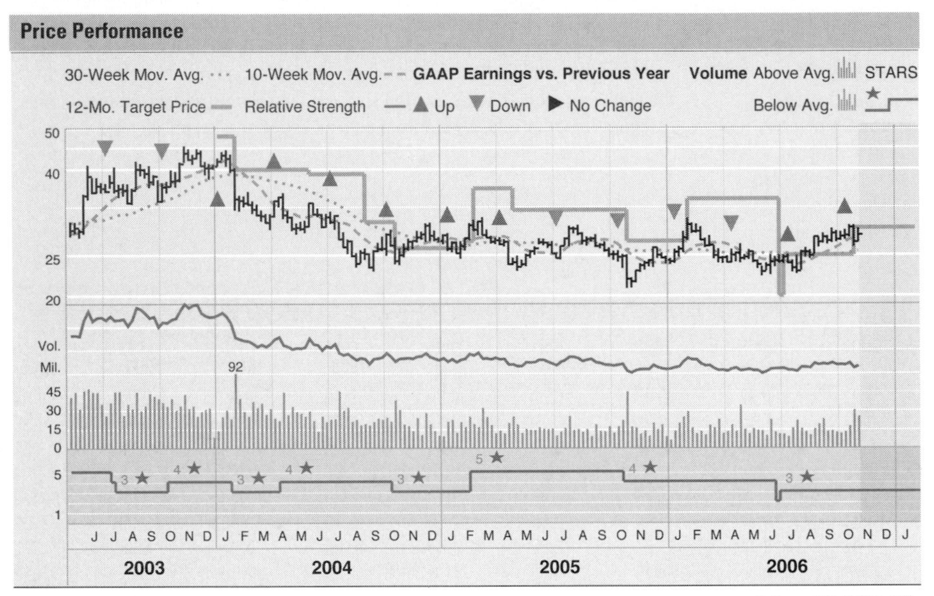

Options: ASE, CBOE, P, Ph

Analysis prepared by **David A Kaplan** on October 19, 2006, when the stock traded at **$ 26.45**.

Highlights

- Based on guidance from leading companies in the industry, we believe a period of softness for the sector is likely to begin in the final quarter of 2006. We expect industry sales to grow 20%-25% in calendar 2006, followed by flat revenues in 2007 as chip companies digest the strong capital investments of 2006, compounded by slower growth in the global economy. Third quarter sales rose 8% sequentially, and we see 5% sequential declines for each of the next few quarters.
- Third quarter gross margins rose to 51%, from 49% in the second quarter, and 37% in the fourth quarter of 2005. We expect gross margins to narrow as we enter the weaker environment ahead. We believe NVLS, as a low cost producer, can maintain profitability through the downturn, particularly based on our view that this downturn is likely to be more moderate than historical downturns.
- We forecast EPS of $1.66 for 2006, and $1.36 for 2007, compared with reported EPS of $0.80 in 2005.

Investment Rationale/Risk

- We view NVLS as a technology leader, but are concerned about the softening we see across the sector. While gross margins have widened substantially in recent quarters, we expect pricing pressure to increase in a softer environment as competitors likely cut prices to increase plant utilization to cover their fixed costs. We see strength returning in the second half of 2007, and view NVLS, trading at a discount to peers, as fairly valued.
- Risks to our recommendation and target price include a more severe than expected downturn and related pricing pressure, technological obsolescence, and greater than expected weakness in the global economy in 2007.
- NVLS recently traded at 16X our 2006 EPS estimate, at a discount to front-end peers trading at 18X, and at 2.0X our 2006 sales per share estimate, a discount to peers' 2.5X. Applying a peer-based target P/E of around 18X our 2006 EPS estimate, we derive our 12-month target price of $29.

Qualitative Risk Assessment

LOW | MEDIUM | **HIGH**

Our risk assessment reflects the historical cyclicality of the semiconductor equipment industry, the lack of visibility in the medium term, the dynamic nature of semiconductor technology, and intense competition. We believe these risks are only somewhat offset by our view of the company's strong market position, size, and current asset to liability ratio.

Quantitative Evaluations

S&P Quality Ranking **B-**

D | C | **B-** | B | B+ | A- | A | A+

Relative Strength Rank **MODERATE**

51

LOWEST = 1 HIGHEST = 99

Revenue/Earnings Data

Revenue (Million $)

	1Q	2Q	3Q	4Q	Year
2006	365.9	410.1	444.0	--	--
2005	339.7	329.6	338.9	332.3	1,340
2004	262.9	338.2	415.9	340.3	1,357
2003	238.4	239.1	221.1	226.5	925.1
2002	169.7	222.2	230.5	217.6	840.0
2001	458.7	376.9	303.7	200.0	1,339

Earnings Per Share ($)

2006	0.18	0.42	0.57	**E**0.49	**E**1.66
2005	0.22	0.24	0.17	0.17	0.80
2004	0.11	0.25	0.45	0.27	1.06
2003	0.08	0.05	-0.23	0.07	-0.03
2002	0.03	0.08	0.03	0.02	0.15
2001	0.55	0.40	-0.10	0.12	0.97

Fiscal year ended Dec. 31. Next earnings report expected: Late January. EPS Estimates based on S&P Operating Earnings; historical GAAP earnings are as reported.

Dividend Data

No cash dividends have been paid.

Novellus Systems Inc

Business Summary October 19, 2006

CORPORATE OVERVIEW. Novellus is the second largest maker of deposition equipment used to deposit conductive and insulating layers on semiconductor wafers to form integrated circuits (ICs). The company entered the market for wafer surface preparation equipment in 2001. NVLS also entered the chemical mechanical planarization (CMP) equipment market in 2002. These two types of equipment are complementary to deposition equipment.

NVLS's product line of deposition equipment includes chemical vapor deposition (CVD), physical vapor deposition (PVD) and electroplating (ECD) equipment, all of which are used to form the layers of wiring and insulation, known as the interconnect, of ICs. High-density plasma CVD (HDP) and plasma-enhanced CVD (PECVD) systems employ a chemical plasma to deposit all of the insulating layers and some of the conductive layers on the surface of a wafer. PVD systems deposit conductive layers through a process known as sputtering. ECD systems deposit conductive layers of copper on wafers, through a process known as electrochemical deposition.

Although NVLS's original tool sets established it as a leader in CVD, the company has centered its product strategy around the emergence of the copper interconnect market. Copper has lower resistance and capacitance values than aluminum, the conductive metal generally used in ICs, offering increased speed and decreased chip size. The company's SABRE tool offers a complete solution for the deposition of copper interconnects and holds the leading market share in copper.

Surface preparation products, including photoresist strip and clean, are becoming increasingly important with the industry's migration to copper interconnects. Surface preparation systems remove photoresist and other potential contaminants from a wafer before proceeding with the next deposition step. CMP systems polish the surface of a wafer after a deposition step to create a flat topography before moving on to subsequent manufacturing steps. Since copper is more difficult to polish and smooth than previous-generation aluminum interconnects, and low-k dielectrics are much more porous than their predecessors, NVLS's product offerings in this category have become very important, in our view.

Company Financials

Per Share Data ($) Year Ended Dec. 31	2005	2004	2003	2002	2001	2000	1999	1998	1997	1996
Tangible Book Value	11.29	11.06	12.42	12.69	13.04	11.49	6.47	3.63	2.98	3.83
Cash Flow	1.39	1.66	0.43	0.45	1.32	2.04	0.89	0.73	-0.78	1.06
Earnings	0.80	1.06	-0.03	0.15	0.97	1.75	0.64	0.50	-0.96	0.95
S&P Core Earnings	0.43	0.74	-0.42	-0.33	0.52	NA	NA	NA	NA	NA
Dividends	Nil	Nil	Nil	Nil	Nil	Nil	Nil	Nil	Nil	Nil
Payout Ratio	Nil	Nil	Nil	Nil	Nil	Nil	Nil	Nil	Nil	Nil
Prices:High	30.77	44.52	45.50	54.48	58.70	70.25	42.79	18.77	22.13	10.75
Prices:Low	20.83	22.89	24.93	19.40	25.37	24.94	14.96	6.96	7.96	5.25
P/E Ratio:High	38	42	NM	NM	61	40	67	39	NM	11
P/E Ratio:Low	26	22	NM	NM	26	14	23	14	NM	6

Income Statement Analysis (Million $)	2005	2004	2003	2002	2001	2000	1999	1998	1997	1996
Revenue	1,340	1,357	925	840	1,339	1,174	593	519	534	462
Operating Income	228	308	56.5	46.3	273	328	130	103	112	148
Depreciation	82.8	89.3	69.6	44.3	51.9	40.1	29.8	23.8	18.3	11.3
Interest Expense	3.51	2.13	0.91	1.02	1.15	2.34	1.70	4.07	2.74	0.47
Pretax Income	159	223	-15.3	22.9	209	342	114	80.0	-121	145
Effective Tax Rate	30.6%	29.8%	NM	NM	31.0%	31.0%	33.0%	34.0%	NM	35.0%
Net Income	110	157	-5.03	22.9	144	236	76.6	52.8	-95.7	94.0
S&P Core Earnings	59.8	108	-67.2	-50.7	81.6	NA	NA	NA	NA	NA

Balance Sheet & Other Financial Data (Million $)	2005	2004	2003	2002	2001	2000	1999	1998	1997	1996
Cash	649	106	497	616	551	571	182	81.2	59.3	177
Current Assets	1,364	1,369	1,572	1,634	2,517	1,827	733	399	351	374
Total Assets	2,290	2,402	2,339	2,494	3,010	2,015	910	552	493	460
Current Liabilities	344	324	221	382	1,138	505	140	111	127	86.1
Long Term Debt	125	161	Nil	Nil	Nil	Nil	Nil	65.0	65.0	Nil
Common Equity	1,779	1,862	2,072	2,056	1,872	1,511	770	375	301	374
Total Capital	1,904	2,023	2,072	2,075	1,872	1,511	770	440	366	374
Capital Expenditures	44.7	31.7	31.1	26.8	80.0	68.5	28.8	36.1	36.2	35.2
Cash Flow	193	246	64.5	67.2	196	276	106	76.7	-77.4	105
Current Ratio	4.0	4.2	7.1	4.3	2.2	3.6	5.2	3.6	2.8	4.3
% Long Term Debt of Capitalization	6.6	8.0	Nil	Nil	Nil	Nil	Nil	14.7	17.8	NM
% Net Income of Revenue	8.2	11.5	NM	2.7	10.8	20.1	12.9	10.2	NM	20.4
% Return on Assets	4.7	6.6	NM	0.8	5.5	16.1	10.5	10.1	NM	22.8
% Return on Equity	6.0	8.0	NM	1.2	8.2	20.7	13.4	15.6	NM	29.1

Data as orig reptd.; bef. results of disc opers/spec. items. Per share data adj. for stk. divs.; EPS diluted. E-Estimated. NA-Not Available. NM-Not Meaningful. NR-Not Ranked. UR-Under Review.

Office: 4000 North First Street, San Jose, CA 95134-1568.
Telephone: 408-943-9700.
Email: info@novellus.com
Website: http://www.novellus.com

Chrmn & CEO: R.S. Hill
Pres: S. Somekh
EVP & CFO: W.H. Kurtz
EVP & CTO: W. van den Hoek

Investor Contact: R.S. Yim (408-943-9700)
Board of Directors: N. R. Bonke, Y. A. El-Mansy, R. S. Hill, J. D. Litster, Y. Nishi, G. G. Possley, A. D. Rhoads, W. R. Spivey, D. A. Whitaker

Founded: 1984
Domicile: California
Employees: 3,550

STANDARD &POOR'S

Nucor Corp

S&P Recommendation HOLD ★★★★★

Price $58.36 (as of Oct 27, 2006)

12-Mo. Target Price $61.00

Investment Style Large-Cap Value

GICS Sector Materials
Sub-Industry Steel

Comment Nucor is the largest U.S. minimill and has one of the broadest product lines of any domestic steel producer.

Key Stock Statistics (Source S&P, Vickers, company reports)

52-Wk Range	$61.70–29.88	S&P Oper. EPS 2006E	5.74	P/E on S&P Oper. EPS 2006E	10.2	Dividend Rate/Share	$0.40
Trailing 12-Month EPS	$5.42	S&P Oper. EPS 2007E	4.90	Common Shares Outstg. (M)	308.3	Yield (%)	0.69
Trailing 12-Month P/E	10.8	S&P Core EPS 2006E	5.49	Market Capitalization(B)	$17.993	Beta	1.98
$10K Invested 5 Yrs Ago	$59,725	S&P Core EPS 2007E	4.89	Institutional Ownership (%)	82	S&P Credit Rating	AA-

Price Performance

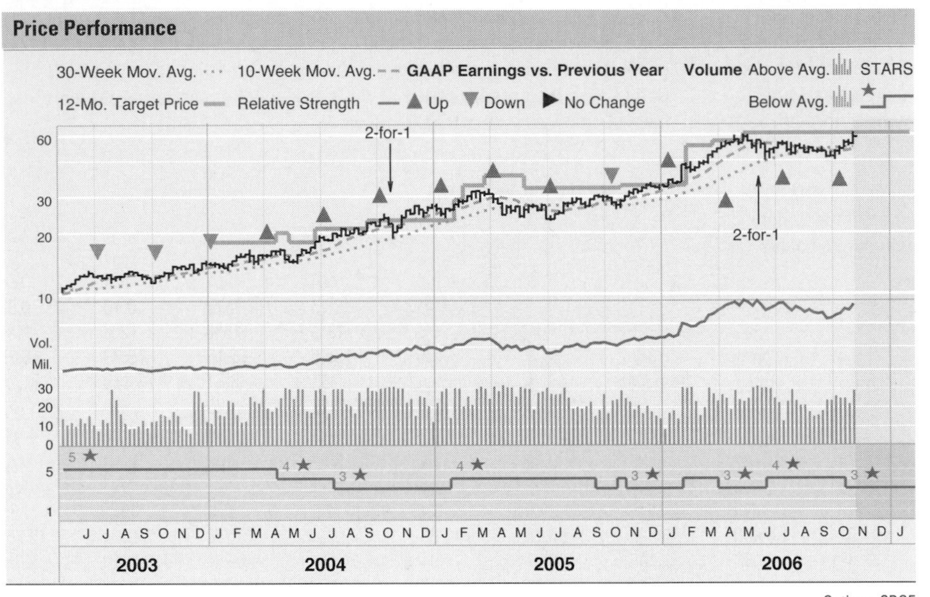

Options: CBOE

Analysis prepared by **Leo J. Larkin** on October 17, 2006, when the stock traded at **$ 54.35**.

Highlights

- Following a projected increase of 16% in 2006, we estimate a sales rise of 8% in 2007, reflecting acquisitions. Our expectation for a smaller rate of increase in sales reflects our forecast for lower prices stemming from less robust demand in 2007 compared with 2006. We believe this will be the case for two reasons. First, S&P projects GDP growth of 2.3% in 2007, versus growth of 3.4% estimated for 2006. Second, we anticipate that demand from distributors will be less robust compared with 2006. In our view, distributors may have overbuilt inventory in 2006 and will likely cut back on purchases in 2007.

- Penalized by a forecasted decrease in revenue per ton, we look for a decline in operating profits. Interest income will likely be higher in 2007 but not by enough to offset lower operating profit. On that basis, we project a decline in EPS to $4.90 in 2007, from $5.50 estimated for 2006.

- Longer term, we see EPS being aided by industry consolidation, the introduction of new steelmaking technology, an improvement in the product mix, and better control of raw material costs.

Investment Rationale/Risk

- We view Nucor as a vehicle for capitalizing on the consolidation of the global steel industry. With the global steel industry becoming more consolidated via mergers, the increased concentration of production among fewer companies should result in greater pricing discipline, in our view. Also, we see free cash flow growth accelerating in the future, on a combination of rising net income and moderate capital spending for the next several years. We believe that this could enable NUE to raise its dividend, make acquisitions and invest in new steelmaking technology. However, as the shares have only modest upside to our 12-month target price of $61, we would not add to positions.

- Risks to our opinion and target price include a decline in prices and distributor demand in 2007 in excess of what we currently project.

- The P/E of 12.4X that we apply to our 2007 EPS estimate of $4.90 is toward the low end of the stock's historical range of the past 10 years, but at a premium to that of peers. On this basis, our 12-month target price is $61.

Qualitative Risk Assessment

LOW | MEDIUM | HIGH

Our risk assessment reflects that although Nucor's earnings are exposed to cyclical markets such as non-residential construction, the company has a solid share of the markets in which it competes, has a very low ratio of total debt to assets, and generates what we view as substantial free cash flow.

Quantitative Evaluations

S&P Quality Ranking **B**

D | C | B- | B | B+ | A- | A | A+

Relative Strength Rank **STRONG**

89

LOWEST = 1 HIGHEST = 99

Revenue/Earnings Data

Revenue (Million $)

	1Q	2Q	3Q	4Q	Year
2006	3,545	3,806	3,931	--	--
2005	3,323	3,145	3,026	3,207	12,701
2004	2,286	2,762	3,240	3,089	11,376
2003	1,480	1,520	1,604	1,661	6,266
2002	1,028	1,142	1,166	1,233	4,802
2001	1,028	1,079	1,053	979.6	4,139

Earnings Per Share ($)

	1Q	2Q	3Q	4Q	Year
2006	1.21	1.45	1.68	E1.40	E5.74
2005	1.10	1.02	0.93	1.09	4.13
2004	0.36	0.79	1.30	1.06	3.51
2003	0.06	0.03	0.05	0.07	0.20
2002	0.07	0.19	0.13	0.14	0.52
2001	0.11	0.11	0.07	0.09	0.36

Fiscal year ended Dec. 31. Next earnings report expected: Late January. EPS Estimates based on S&P Operating Earnings; historical GAAP earnings are as reported.

Dividend Data (Dates: mm/dd Payment Date: mm/dd/yy)

Amount ($)	Date Decl.	Ex-Div. Date	Stk. of Record	Payment Date
.50 Ext.	06/06	06/28	06/30	08/11/06
0.100	06/06	06/28	06/30	08/11/06
.5 Ext.	09/06	09/27	09/29	11/10/06
0.100	09/06	09/27	09/29	11/10/06

Dividends have been paid since 1973. Source: Company reports.

Please read the Required Disclosures and Analyst Certification on the last page of this report.

Business Summary October 17, 2006

CORPORATE OVERVIEW. Nucor is the largest U.S. minimill steelmaker. In 2005, production was 20.3 million tons and shipments were 20.7 million tons.

MARKET PROFILE. The primary factor affecting demand for steel products is economic growth, in general, and growth in demand for durable goods, in particular. The two largest end markets for steel products in the U.S. are autos and construction. In 2005, these two markets accounted for 27.9% of shipments in the U.S. market. Other end markets include appliances, containers, machinery, and oil and gas. Distributors, also known as service centers, accounted for 22.4% of industry shipments in the U.S. market in 2005. Distributors are the largest single market for the steel industry in the U.S. Because distributors sell to a wide variety of OEMs, it is impossible to trace the final destination of much of the industry's shipments. Consequently, demand for steel from the auto, construction and other industries may be higher than the shipment data would suggest. Construction accounts for some 60% of the demand for Nucor's products, oil and gas 15%, autos and appliances 15%, and other markets 10%. In terms of production, the size of the U.S. market was 102.8 million tons in 2005, and Nucor's market share was 19.7%. In the U.S. market, consumption increased at a compound annual growth rate (CAGR) of 0.5% from 1996 through 2005. Global steel production was 1.19 billion tons in 2005. Consumption grew at a CAGR of 4.6% from 1995 through 2004.

Company Financials

Per Share Data ($) Year Ended Dec. 31	**2005**	**2004**	**2003**	**2002**	**2001**	**2000**	**1999**	**1998**	**1997**	**1996**
Tangible Book Value	13.80	10.84	7.45	7.43	7.07	6.87	6.49	5.93	5.33	4.58
Cash Flow	5.43	4.72	1.30	1.50	1.29	1.74	1.44	1.47	1.46	1.23
Earnings	4.13	3.51	0.20	0.52	0.36	0.95	0.70	0.75	0.84	0.71
S&P Core Earnings	4.09	3.49	0.15	0.46	0.33	NA	NA	NA	NA	NA
Dividends	0.30	0.24	0.20	0.19	0.17	0.15	0.13	0.12	0.10	0.08
Payout Ratio	7%	7%	100%	37%	47%	16%	18%	15%	12%	11%
Prices:High	35.11	27.74	14.70	17.54	14.13	14.11	15.45	15.16	15.73	15.75
Prices:Low	22.78	13.04	8.76	9.00	8.36	7.38	10.41	8.81	11.19	11.28
P/E Ratio:High	9	8	73	34	39	15	22	20	19	22
P/E Ratio:Low	6	4	44	17	23	8	15	12	13	16
Income Statement Analysis (Million $)										
Revenue	12,701	11,377	6,266	4,802	4,139	4,586	4,009	4,151	4,184	3,647
Operating Income	2,407	2,210	400	001	409	737	631	665	678	570
Depreciation	375	383	364	307	289	259	257	253	218	182
Interest Expense	4.20	22.4	24.6	22.9	22.0	24.1	20.5	10.0	9.28	8.11
Pretax Income	2,127	1,812	90.8	310	174	478	379	415	460	388
Effective Tax Rate	33.2%	33.6%	4.51%	22.0%	35.0%	35.0%	35.5%	36.5%	36.0%	36.0%
Net Income	1,310	1,121	62.8	162	113	311	245	264	294	248
S&P Core Earnings	1,296	1,114	47.9	143	101	NA	NA	NA	NA	NA
Balance Sheet & Other Financial Data (Million $)										
Cash	1,838	779	350	219	462	491	572	309	283	104
Current Assets	4,072	3,175	1,621	1,424	1,374	1,381	1,539	1,129	1,126	828
Total Assets	7,139	6,133	4,492	4,381	3,759	3,722	3,730	3,227	2,984	2,620
Current Liabilities	1,256	1,066	630	592	484	558	531	487	524	466
Long Term Debt	922	924	904	879	460	460	390	215	168	153
Common Equity	4,280	3,456	2,342	2,323	2,201	2,131	2,262	2,073	1,876	1,609
Total Capital	5,396	4,553	3,423	3,419	2,946	2,904	2,934	2,570	2,321	2,028
Capital Expenditures	331	286	215	244	261	415	375	503	307	537
Cash Flow	1,685	1,505	427	469	402	570	501	517	512	430
Current Ratio	3.2	3.0	2.6	2.4	2.8	2.5	2.9	2.3	2.1	1.8
% Long Term Debt of Capitalization	17.1	20.3	26.4	25.7	15.6	15.9	13.3	8.4	7.2	7.5
% Net Income of Revenue	10.3	9.9	1.0	3.4	2.7	6.8	6.1	6.4	7.0	6.8
% Return on Assets	19.7	21.1	1.4	4.0	3.0	8.3	7.0	8.5	10.5	10.1
% Return on Equity	33.9	38.7	2.7	5.1	5.2	14.2	11.3	13.4	16.9	16.6

Data as orig reptd.; bef. results of disc opers/spec. items. Per share data adj. for stk. divs.; EPS diluted. E-Estimated. NA-Not Available. NM-Not Meaningful. NR-Not Ranked. UR-Under Review.

Office: 2100 Rexford Road, Charlotte, NC 28211.
Telephone: 704-366-7000.
Email: info@nucor.com
Website: http://www.nucor.com

Chrmn, Pres & CEO: D.R. DiMicco
EVP, CFO & Treas: T.S. Lisenby
Cntlr: J. Frias

Board of Directors: P. C. Browning, C. C. Daley, Jr., D. R. DiMicco, H. B. Gantt, V. F. Haynes, J. D. Hlavacek, R. J. Milchovich

Founded: 1940
Domicile: Delaware
Employees: 10,300

STANDARD &POOR'S

NVIDIA Corp

S&P Recommendation HOLD ★★★★★	Price	12-Mo. Target Price	Investment Style
	$32.38 (as of Oct 27, 2006)	$31.00	Large-Cap Growth

GICS Sector Information Technology
Sub-Industry Semiconductors

Comment This company develops and markets 3D graphics processors and related software for personal computers, workstations and digital entertainment platforms.

Key Stock Statistics (Source S&P, Vickers, company reports)

52-Wk Range	$34.59–16.28	S&P Oper. EPS 2007**E**	1.04	P/E on S&P Oper. EPS 2007**E**	31.1	Dividend Rate/Share	Nil
Trailing 12-Month EPS	$0.88	S&P Oper. EPS 2008**E**	1.30	Common Shares Outstg. (M)	352.5	Yield (%)	Nil
Trailing 12-Month P/E	36.8	S&P Core EPS 2007**E**	1.04	Market Capitalization(B)	$11.414	Beta	4.15
$10K Invested 5 Yrs Ago	$14,143	S&P Core EPS 2008**E**	1.30	Institutional Ownership (%)	73	S&P Credit Rating	BB-

Price Performance

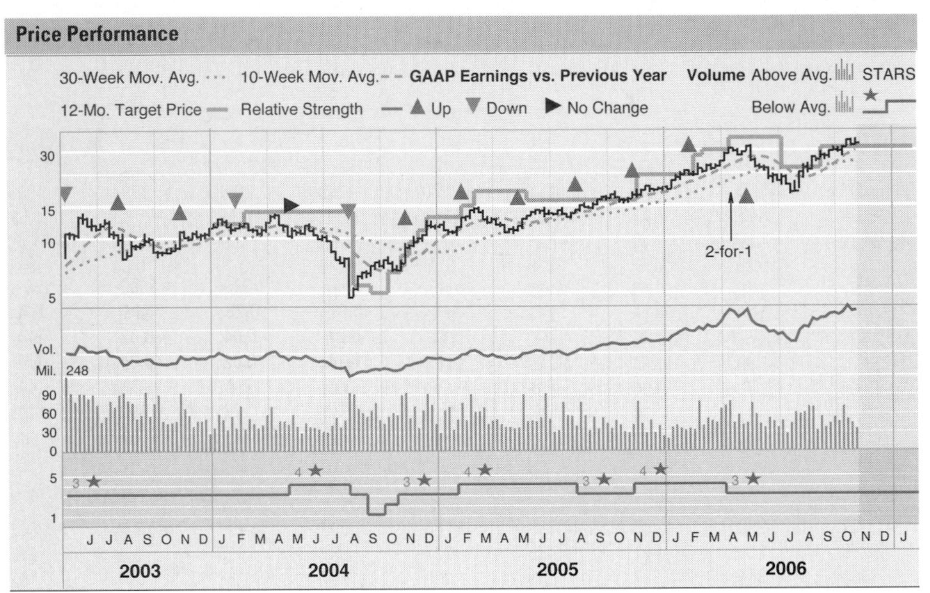

Analysis prepared by **Thomas W. Smith, CFA** on August 28, 2006, when the stock traded at **$ 27.40**.

Highlights

- We expect sales to advance 21% in FY 07 (Jan.) and 15% in FY 08, in the context of moderate growth we project for the semiconductor industry through calendar 2007. We also expect sales to benefit from acquisitions and market share gains in some graphics processor product categories.
- Gross margins have now fully recovered from their nadir in FY 03, when business for the Microsoft Xbox dropped off. In the FY 07 first quarter, NVDA's gross margins rose to 42.5%. We believe a more favorable product mix and operating cost controls contributed to the improvement. We project that gross margins will widen to an average of 43% in FY 07 and 44% in FY 08. We expect net margins to widen to 17% in FY 07, and 18% in FY 08.
- We estimate FY 07 operating EPS of $1.04, including projected stock option expense of about $0.21. For FY 08, we forecast EPS of $1.30. The company reported revenue but not EPS for the second quarter, as it awaits the conclusion of an internal review of stock option practices.

Investment Rationale/Risk

- We have a hold opinion on these volatile shares, reflecting our expectation for sales to exceed the pace of the overall semiconductor industry and for margins to improve, but with some caution about the industry possibly nearing a cyclical peak as economic growth slows. Increasing multimedia content is helping drive demand for graphics displays. On August 10, NVDA said it does not expect to make timely filing of its 10-Q for the second quarter, which we view as a bearish factor for investor sentiment, given an ongoing review by its audit committee of stock option practices since 1999.
- Risks to our opinion and target price include the possibility that slower economic growth might slow PC sales more than we expect. Other risks include repercussions from the review of stock option practices.
- Our 12-month target price of $31 is based mainly on our price-to-sales analysis. We apply a target price-to-sales ratio of 3.8X, in the upper half of the historical range, to our forward 12-month sales per share estimate.

Qualitative Risk Assessment

LOW | MEDIUM | **HIGH**

Our risk assessment reflects the cyclicality of the semiconductor industry and of demand trends for electronics goods that benefit from advanced visual displays, and revenue volatility resulting from wins and losses of deals with big accounts.

Quantitative Evaluations

S&P Quality Ranking B-

D | C | **B-** | B | B+ | A- | A | A+

Relative Strength Rank STRONG

88

LOWEST = 1 HIGHEST = 99

Revenue/Earnings Data

Revenue (Million $)

	1Q	2Q	3Q	4Q	Year
2007	681.8	--	--	--	--
2006	583.9	574.8	583.4	633.6	2,376
2005	471.9	456.1	515.6	566.5	2,010
2004	405.0	459.8	486.1	472.1	1,823
2003	582.9	427.3	430.3	469.0	1,909
2002	240.9	259.9	365.0	503.7	1,369

Earnings Per Share ($)

2007	0.23	**E**0.24	**E**0.27	**E**0.30	**E**1.04
2006	0.18	0.21	0.18	0.26	0.83
2005	0.06	0.02	0.08	0.14	0.29
2004	0.06	0.07	0.02	0.07	0.22
2003	0.24	0.02	-0.16	0.15	0.27
2002	0.08	0.10	0.12	0.22	0.52

Fiscal year ended Jan. 31. Next earnings report expected: NA. EPS Estimates based on S&P Operating Earnings; historical GAAP earnings are as reported.

Dividend Data (Dates: mm/dd Payment Date: mm/dd/yy)

Amount ($)	Date Decl.	Ex-Div. Date	Stk. of Record	Payment Date
2-for-1 Stk.	03/06	04/07	03/17	04/06/06

Source: Company reports.

Please read the Required Disclosures and Analyst Certification on the last page of this report.

NVIDIA Corp

Business Summary August 28, 2006

NVIDIA Corp. designs, develops and markets high-performance graphics processing units (GPUs), media and communications processors (MCPs), handheld GPUs, and related software for PCs and digital entertainment platforms, ranging from professional workstations to video game consoles to handheld electronic devices. It aims to be the leading supplier of performance GPUs, MCPs and handheld GPUs.

Interactive 3D graphics displays are an integral part of many computing applications for workstations, consumer and commercial desktop and laptop PCs, personal digital assistants, cellular phones, and gaming consoles. NVDA's products are designed into products offered by nearly all leading PC OEMs.

The company believes that PC interactive 3D graphics capability represents one of the primary means by which users differentiate between systems. NVDA thinks that PC users can easily differentiate the quality of graphics, and prefer displays that provide a superior visual experience.

NVDA's products provide high levels of visual quality, realistic imagery and motion, and complex object and scene interaction. The company offers a "top to bottom" family of graphics processors, serving various 3D and 2D submarkets in a full spectrum of price points. At the high end are the NVIDIA GeForce FX and GeForce4 GPUs (graphics processing units), which are designed to deliver high performance and cinematic quality graphics for interactive entertainment and digital image editing. The workstation market is addressed by the Quadro family of GPUs. The nForce family of MCPs offers a comprehensive set of multimedia capabilities and works with Advanced Micro Devices microprocessors. Products for handheld PDAs and wireless phones are available in the GoForce family of handheld GPUs.

Company Financials

Per Share Data ($) Year Ended Jan. 31	**2006**	**2005**	**2004**	**2003**	**2002**	**2001**	**2000**	**1999**	**1998**	**1997**
Tangible Book Value	3.78	3.12	2.75	2.72	2.28	1.40	0.51	0.28	NM	NA
Cash Flow	1.09	0.57	0.45	0.44	0.64	0.36	0.21	0.04	-0.02	NA
Earnings	0.83	0.29	0.22	0.27	0.52	0.31	0.14	0.02	-0.04	NA
S&P Core Earnings	0.65	0.04	-0.01	-0.33	0.15	0.17	NA	NA	NA	NA
Dividends	Nil	Nil	Nil	Nil	Nil	Nil	Nil	Nil	NA	NA
Payout Ratio	Nil	Nil	Nil	Nil	Nil	Nil	Nil	Nil	NA	NA
Calendar Year	2005	2004	2003	2002	2001	2000	1999	1998	1997	1996
Prices:High	19.25	13.68	13.88	36.33	35.13	22.00	5.94	NA	NA	NA
Prices:Low	10.23	4.65	4.67	3.60	7.06	4.38	1.50	NA	NA	NA
P/E Ratio:High	23	48	65	NM	68	71	42	NA	NA	NA
P/E Ratio:Low	12	16	22	NM	14	14	11	NA	NA	NA
Income Statement Analysis (Million $)										
Revenue	2,376	2,010	1,823	1,909	1,369	735	375	158	29.1	3.90
Operating Income	452	216	172	202	299	146	63.4	8.52	-2.10	-2.20
Depreciation	98.0	103	82.0	58.2	43.5	15.7	9.00	4.01	1.36	0.80
Interest Expense	0.07	0.16	12.0	Nil	16.2	4.85	Nil	Nil	Nil	NA
Pretax Income	360	125	86.7	151	253	147	56.2	4.49	-3.60	-3.10
Effective Tax Rate	16.0%	20.0%	14.1%	39.7%	30.0%	31.9%	32.1%	7.96%	Nil	Nil
Net Income	303	100	74.4	90.8	177	100	38.1	4.13	-3.60	-3.10
S&P Core Earnings	236	14.6	-1.44	-104	49.4	54.7	NA	NA	NA	NA
Balance Sheet & Other Financial Data (Million $)										
Cash	950	670	604	1,028	791	674	61.6	50.3	6.60	NA
Current Assets	1,549	1,305	1,053	1,352	1,234	930	173	101	19.3	NA
Total Assets	1,915	1,629	1,399	1,617	1,503	1,017	203	113	25.0	NA
Current Liabilities	439	421	334	379	433	110	76.2	47.1	3.20	NA
Long Term Debt	Nil	Nil	0.86	305	306	300	1.46	2.00	1.90	NA
Common Equity	1,458	1,178	1,051	933	764	406	125	64.2	6.90	NA
Total Capital	1,466	1,199	1,061	1,238	1,070	706	126	66.2	8.80	NA
Capital Expenditures	79.6	67.3	128	63.1	97.0	36.3	11.6	7.90	2.70	NA
Cash Flow	401	203	156	149	220	114	50.0	8.14	-2.24	NA
Current Ratio	3.5	3.1	3.2	3.6	2.8	8.4	2.3	2.1	6.0	NA
% Long Term Debt of Capitalization	Nil	Nil	0.1	24.6	28.6	42.4	1.2	3.0	21.5	NA
% Net Income of Revenue	12.7	5.0	4.1	4.8	12.9	13.4	10.9	2.6	NM	NA
% Return on Assets	17.1	6.6	4.9	5.8	14.0	16.1	25.9	5.8	NM	NA
% Return on Equity	23.0	9.0	7.5	10.7	30.2	36.9	42.9	11.3	NM	NA

Data as orig reptd.; bef. results of disc opers/spec. items. Per share data adj. for stk. divs.; EPS diluted. E-Estimated. NA-Not Available. NM-Not Meaningful. NR-Not Ranked. UR-Under Review.

Office: 2701 San Tomas Expressway, Santa Clara, CA 95050.
Telephone: 408-486-2000.
Email: ir@nvidia.com
Website: http://www.nvidia.com

Pres & CEO: J. Huang
SVP, Secy & General Counsel: D.M. Shannon
Investor Contact: M. Hara (408-486-2511)
CFO: M.D. Burkett

Board of Directors: S. Chu, T. Coxe, J. C. Gaither, J. Huang, H. C. Jones, W. J. Miller, M. L. Perry, A. B. Seawell, M. A. Stevens

Founded: 1993
Domicile: Delaware
Employees: 3,100

STANDARD & POOR'S

Occidental Petroleum Corp

S&P Recommendation HOLD ★★★★★ | **Price** $47.68 (as of Oct 27, 2006) | **12-Mo. Target Price** $50.00 | **Investment Style** Large-Cap Growth

GICS Sector Energy
Sub-Industry Integrated Oil & Gas

Comment This global oil and gas exploration and production company also has a chemicals division.

Key Stock Statistics (Source S&P, Vickers, company reports)

52-Wk Range	$55.45–35.79	S&P Oper. EPS 2006E	5.40	P/E on S&P Oper. EPS 2006E	8.8	Dividend Rate/Share	$0.88
Trailing 12-Month EPS	$5.13	S&P Oper. EPS 2007E	5.00	Common Shares Outstg. (M)	861.5	Yield (%)	1.85
Trailing 12-Month P/E	9.3	S&P Core EPS 2006E	5.88	Market Capitalization(B)	$41.078	Beta	0.49
$10K Invested 5 Yrs Ago	$41,056	S&P Core EPS 2007E	6.13	Institutional Ownership (%)	77	S&P Credit Rating	A-

Price Performance

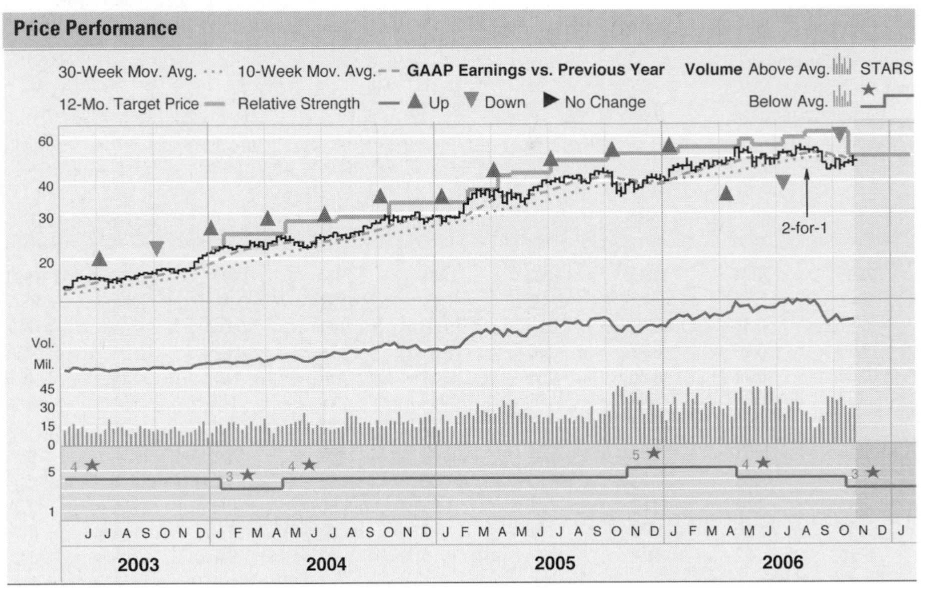

Options: ASE, CBOE, P, Ph

Analysis prepared by **Charles LaPorta, CFA** on October 23, 2006, when the stock traded at **$ 45.99**.

Highlights

- Third quarter operating EPS was $1.35, versus $0.91 last year. Chemical results were above expectations, due, we think, to higher than expected volumes in chlor-alkali and higher margins in chlorovinyl products. We expect OxyChem segment earnings of about $1.0 billion in 2006.
- Hydrocarbon production declined 3.7% sequentially in the second quarter, due to maintenance downtime at Horn Mountain, Qatar and Argentina. Drilling is expected to begin in Libya during the fourth quarter, and 16 wells are expected to be drilled in 2007. No volume from the Dolphin Project is expected in 2006, but we expect a quick production ramp in 2007. OXY's finding and development costs have risen markedly this year, due to recent acquisitions. Our 2006 and 2007 EBITDA estimates are each $10.0 billion.
- OXY has paid down $610 million in long-term debt year to date, but debt levels since the beginning of 2006 are about flat due to debt assumption from acquisitions. We expect interest expense to decline about $100 million in 2007. OXY has largely completed its stated share repurchase goals.

Investment Rationale/Risk

- We expect long-term upstream growth to be primarily driven by Middle East projects, due to Libya operations and the recent assumption of operations in a large field in Oman. However, we think inconsistent delivery of Libyan volumes and political difficulties surrounding Dolphin Project production starts and Phase II negotiations have removed significant near-term catalysts for share price appreciation. To fund upstream growth, capital spending in 2006 may be as high as $3.3 billion.
- Risks to our recommendation and target price include geopolitical risk associated with upstream growth in certain international regions (such as the Middle East and Libya), and the impact of high feedstock and energy costs on chemical operations.
- Given an anticipated choppy performance from new project start-ups such as Dolphin, Oman and Libya, we believe the stock will perform in line with peers. Our 12-month target price of $50 is based on a projected P/E of 10X our 2007 EPS estimate and an enterprise value of 4.4X our 2007 EBITDA estimate, premiums to our large-capitalization peers, reflecting OXY's high returns on invested capital.

Qualitative Risk Assessment

LOW | **MEDIUM** | HIGH

Our risk assessment reflects our view of the company's solid standing as a global exploration and production company. However, OXY is susceptible, in our opinion, to having its properties confiscated by governments in countries in which it operates. The stock is also exposed to substantial and sustained declines in oil and gas prices.

Quantitative Evaluations

S&P Quality Ranking B+

D | C | B- | B | **B+** | A- | A | A+

Relative Strength Rank MODERATE

30

LOWEST = 1 HIGHEST = 99

Revenue/Earnings Data

Revenue (Million $)

	1Q	2Q	3Q	4Q	Year
2006	4,570	4,599	4,522	--	--
2005	3,303	3,518	4,057	4,330	15,208
2004	2,557	2,724	3,005	3,082	11,368
2003	2,371	2,266	2,319	2,370	9,326
2002	1,523	1,867	1,963	1,985	7,338
2001	4,475	3,845	3,285	2,380	13,985

Earnings Per Share ($)

2006	1.42	1.39	1.35	**E**1.25	**E**5.40
2005	1.04	1.89	2.12	1.40	6.45
2004	0.62	0.73	0.94	0.96	3.25
2003	0.52	0.49	0.57	0.49	2.06
2002	0.17	0.32	0.63	0.42	1.54
2001	0.69	0.63	0.59	-0.33	1.59

Fiscal year ended Dec. 31. Next earnings report expected: Early February. EPS Estimates based on S&P Operating Earnings; historical GAAP earnings are as reported.

Dividend Data (Dates: mm/dd Payment Date: mm/dd/yy)

Amount ($)	Date Decl.	Ex-Div. Date	Stk. of Record	Payment Date
0.360	05/04	06/07	06/09	07/15/06
2-for-1 Stk.	07/20	08/16	08/01	08/15/06
0.220	07/20	09/06	09/08	10/15/06
0.220	10/12	12/06	12/08	01/15/07

Dividends have been paid since 1975. Source: Company reports.

Please read the Required Disclosures and Analyst Certification on the last page of this report.

Occidental Petroleum Corp

Business Summary October 23, 2006

CORPORATE OVERVIEW. Conducting business through subsidiaries, Occidental Petroleum is a global oil and gas exploration and production (68% of 2005 segment revenues; 91% of 2005 pretax operating profits) and chemical (32%; 9%) company. The oil and gas segment explores for, develops, produces and markets crude oil and natural gas. The company has active oil and gas operations in the U.S. (principally in California, the Hugoton area in Kansas and Oklahoma, the Permian field in West Texas and New Mexico, and the Gulf of Mexico) and internationally (Colombia, Ecuador, Oman, Pakistan, Qatar, Russia, the U.A.E., Yemen and Libya).

MARKET PROFILE. For a large exploration and production (E&P) company that produced 207 million barrels of oil equivalent (BOE) worldwide in 2005, OXY has a particularly narrow regional focus, in our opinion. We believe this is a source of competitive advantage for the company domestically, as it allows OXY to gather unique geographic and geologic knowledge within its operating areas, thus minimizing finding and development costs. The domestic market for hydrocarbon production in OXY's operating areas is fragmented, with major competitors including XTO Energy (XTO; buy, $46) and Apache (APA; buy, $68). Internationally, OXY relies heavily on its close business relationships in capturing development contracts from national oil companies of Middle Eastern countries. We believe this has been the major component in its success at minimizing finding and development costs.

OXY replaced 191% of worldwide oil and gas production from all sources in 2005. Excluding acquisitions, finding and development costs averaged $10.36 per BOE in 2005 versus an average finding and development cost of $7.05 per BOE in 2004. Excluding acquisitions, the three-year (2003-2005) average reserve replacement was 121%, at an average finding and development cost of $7.55 per BOE.

Company Financials

Per Share Data ($) Year Ended Dec. 31	2005	2004	2003	2002	2001	2000	1999	1998	1997	1996
Tangible Book Value	18.69	13.30	10.25	8.35	7.53	6.45	4.79	4.49	4.23	5.79
Cash Flow	8.26	4.93	3.56	2.87	2.88	3.35	1.92	1.63	1.39	2.50
Earnings	6.45	3.25	2.06	1.54	1.59	2.13	0.79	0.44	0.20	0.93
S&P Core Earnings	5.78	3.26	2.03	1.28	1.70	NA	NA	NA	NA	NA
Dividends	0.65	0.41	0.52	0.50	0.50	0.50	0.50	0.50	0.50	0.50
Payout Ratio	10%	13%	25%	33%	32%	23%	63%	114%	NM	54%
Prices:High	44.90	30.38	21.49	15.38	15.55	12.78	12.28	15.22	15.38	13.63
Prices:Low	27.09	20.98	13.59	11.49	10.94	7.88	7.31	8.31	10.88	10.06
P/E Ratio:High	7	9	10	10	10	6	16	35	79	15
P/E Ratio:Low	4	6	7	7	7	4	9	19	56	11

Income Statement Analysis (Million $)	2005	2004	2003	2002	2001	2000	1999	1998	1997	1996
Revenue	15,208	11,368	9,326	7,338	13,985	13,574	7,610	6,596	8,016	10,557
Operating Income	7,860	5,573	4,281	3,119	3,638	3,826	1,831	1,297	1,835	2,316
Depreciation, Depletion and Amortization	1,485	1,303	1,177	1,012	971	901	805	835	822	921
Interest Expense	293	260	332	295	392	518	498	559	434	484
Pretax Income	7,365	4,389	2,884	1,662	1,892	3,196	1,257	688	528	1,152
Effective Tax Rate	27.4%	38.9%	42.5%	25.4%	29.8%	45.1%	50.2%	52.8%	58.9%	39.4%
Net Income	5,272	2,600	1,595	1,163	1,186	1,569	568	325	217	698
S&P Core Earnings	4,729	2,607	1,568	963	1,273	NA	NA	NA	NA	NA

Balance Sheet & Other Financial Data (Million $)	2005	2004	2003	2002	2001	2000	1999	1998	1997	1996
Cash	2,189	1,449	683	146	199	97.0	214	96.0	113	279
Current Assets	6,574	4,431	2,474	1,873	1,483	2,067	1,688	2,795	1,916	2,190
Total Assets	26,108	21,391	18,168	16,548	17,850	19,414	14,125	15,252	15,282	17,634
Current Liabilities	4,280	3,423	2,526	2,235	1,890	2,740	1,967	2,931	1,870	2,470
Long Term Debt	2,873	3,345	3,993	4,452	4,528	5,658	4,854	5,367	4,925	4,511
Common Equity	15,032	10,550	7,929	6,318	5,634	4,774	3,523	3,120	2,304	3,809
Total Capital	19,207	15,470	13,235	12,085	13,489	13,977	9,372	9,555	10,239	12,211
Capital Expenditures	2,423	1,843	1,601	1,236	1,401	952	601	1,074	1,549	1,185
Cash Flow	6,757	3,909	2,772	2,175	2,157	2,470	1,366	1,143	951	1,619
Current Ratio	1.5	1.3	1.0	0.8	0.8	0.8	0.9	1.0	1.0	0.9
% Long Term Debt of Capitalization	15.0	21.6	30.2	36.8	33.6	40.5	51.8	56.2	48.1	36.9
% Return on Assets	22.2	13.2	9.2	6.8	6.4	9.4	3.9	2.1	1.3	3.9
% Return on Equity	41.2	28.2	22.4	19.5	22.8	37.8	16.9	12.6	6.2	17.0

Data as orig reptd.; bef. results of disc opers/spec. items. Per share data adj. for stk. divs.; EPS diluted. E-Estimated. NA-Not Available. NM-Not Meaningful. NR-Not Ranked. UR-Under Review.

Office: 10889 Wilshire Boulevard, Los Angeles, CA 90024-4201.
Telephone: 310-208-8800.
Email: investorrelations_newyork@oxy.com
Website: http://www.oxy.com

Chrmn, Pres & CEO: R.R. Irani
Sr EVP & CFO: S.I. Chazen
EVP, Secy & General Counsel: D.P. de Brier
VP & Treas: J.R. Havert

VP & Cntlr: J.A. Leonard
Investor Contact: K.J. Huffman (212-603-8183)
Board of Directors: S. Abraham, R. W. Burkle, J. S. Chalsty, E. P. Djerejian, R. C. Dreier, J. E. Feick, R. R. Irani, I. W. Maloney, R. Segovia, A. D. Syriani, R. Tomich, W. L. Weisman

Founded: 1920
Domicile: Delaware
Employees: 8,017

STANDARD &POOR'S

Officemax Inc

S&P Recommendation HOLD ★★★☆☆	Price	12-Mo. Target Price	Investment Style
	$47.52 (as of Oct 27, 2006)	$48.00	Mid-Cap Value

GICS Sector Consumer Discretionary
Sub-Industry Specialty Stores

Comment This retail and business to business office products distributor operates nearly 1,000 superstores.

Key Stock Statistics (Source S&P, Vickers, company reports)

52-Wk Range	$48.19–24.20	S&P Oper. EPS 2006E	2.05	P/E on S&P Oper. EPS 2006E	23.2	Dividend Rate/Share	$0.60
Trailing 12-Month EPS	$-0.15	S&P Oper. EPS 2007E	2.51	Common Shares Outstg. (M)	74.2	Yield (%)	1.26
Trailing 12-Month P/E	NM	S&P Core EPS 2006E	2.05	Market Capitalization(B)	$3.526	Beta	1.15
$10K Invested 5 Yrs Ago	$17,220	S&P Core EPS 2007E	2.51	Institutional Ownership (%)	96	S&P Credit Rating	BB

Price Performance

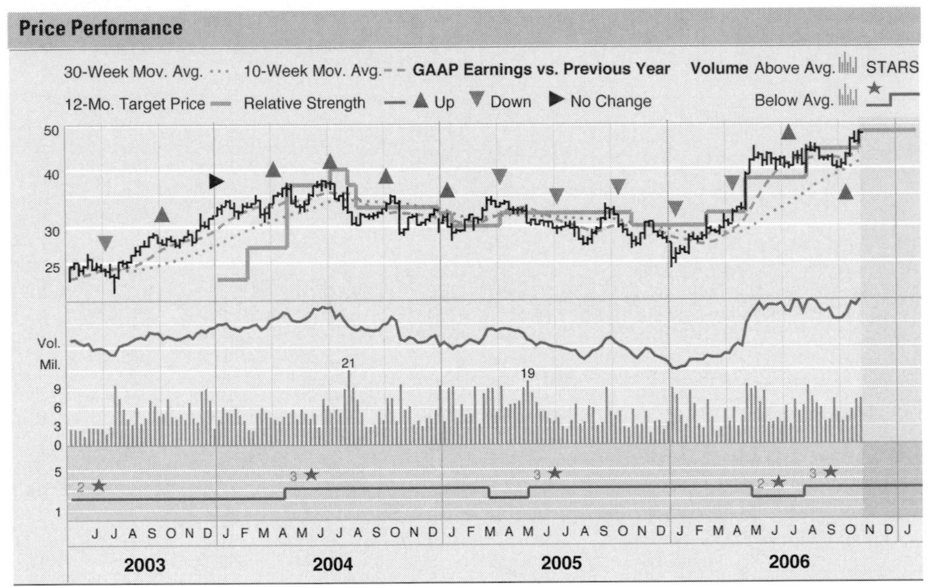

Options: ASE, CBOE

Highlights

- The 12-month target price for OMX has recently been changed to $48.00 from $44.00. The Highlights section of this Stock Report will be updated accordingly.

Investment Rationale/Risk

- The Investment Rationale/Risk section of this Stock Report will be updated shortly. For the latest News story on OMX from MarketScope, see below.

- 10/26/06 11:26 am EDT... S&P MAINTAINS HOLD RECOMMENDATION ON SHARES OF OFFICEMAX INC. (OMX 47.39***): Excluding special items, OMX posts Q3 EPS of $0.56 vs. $0.17, ahead of our estimate by $0.10 as strong cost discipline offset a 1.9% revenue decline. On a soft Q4 revenue outlook we are reducing our '06 EPS estimate to $2.05 from $2.12. But we are increasing '07's to $2.51 from $2.39 and raising our 12-month DCF-based target price to $48 from $44 on lower cost expectations. While we believe OMX is effectively streamlining its operations, we would not add to positions, based on our view that lackluster sales growth will limit long-term operating margin expansion opportunity. /M.Souers, J.Peters-CFA

Qualitative Risk Assessment

LOW | **MEDIUM** | HIGH

Our risk assessment reflects the rather cyclical nature of the office supply retailing industry, which is highly dependent on continued consumer and business spending, and what we view as a slightly weaker competitive position compared to peers in terms of buyer power with vendors, offset by what we see as a rational pricing environment that should help boost margins.

Quantitative Evaluations

S&P Quality Ranking B-

D | C | **B-** | B | B+ | A- | A | A+

Relative Strength Rank STRONG

86

LOWEST = 1 HIGHEST = 99

Revenue/Earnings Data

Revenue (Million $)

	1Q	2Q	3Q	4Q	Year
2006	2,424	2,041	2,244	--	--
2005	2,323	2,092	2,288	2,455	9,158
2004	3,530	3,401	3,651	2,688	13,270
2003	1,853	1,928	2,111	2,352	8,245
2002	1,788	1,888	1,935	1,801	7,412
2001	1,901	1,890	1,874	1,757	7,422

Earnings Per Share ($)

2006	-0.21	0.35	0.41	**E**0.41	**E**2.05
2005	-0.03	-0.23	-0.02	-0.33	-0.58
2004	0.67	0.58	0.69	0.51	2.44
2003	-0.38	-0.12	0.48	0.05	0.07
2002	-0.17	Nil	0.09	0.05	-0.03
2001	-0.68	0.28	0.20	-0.78	-0.96

Fiscal year ended Dec. 31. Next earnings report expected: Late February. EPS Estimates based on S&P Operating Earnings; historical GAAP earnings are as reported.

Dividend Data (Dates: mm/dd Payment Date: mm/dd/yy)

Amount ($)	Date Decl.	Ex-Div. Date	Stk. of Record	Payment Date
0.150	12/09	12/28	01/01	01/15/06
0.150	02/10	03/29	04/01	04/15/06
0.150	04/20	06/28	07/01	07/15/06
0.150	07/27	09/27	10/01	10/15/06

Dividends have been paid since 1935. Source: Company reports.

Officemax Inc

Business Summary August 08, 2006

CORPORATE OVERVIEW. OfficeMax (formerly Boise Cascade Corp.) is a leader in both business-to-business and retail office products distribution. It provides office supplies and paper, print and document services, technology products and solutions, and furniture to large, medium and small businesses, government offices, and consumers.

OfficeMax, Contract (51% of sales in 2005) distributes office supplies and paper, technology products and solutions and office furniture. The segment sells directly to large corporate and government offices, as well as to small and medium sized offices in the U.S., Canada, Australia, New Zealand and Mexico.

OfficeMax, Retail (49%) has operations in the U.S., Puerto Rico and the U.S. Virgin Islands. It also operates office products superstores in Mexico through a 51% owned joint venture. As of February 25, 2006, OMX's retail segment operated 970 stores, three large distribution centers and one small distribution center. Each superstore offers approximately 8,000 stock keeping units (SKUs) of name brand and OfficeMax private branded merchandise and a variety of business services targeted at serving the small business customer, including OfficeMax Print and Document Services.

In October 2004, the company sold its paper, forest products, and timberland assets for about $3.7 billion to affiliates of Boise Cascade, LLC. Prior to the sale, the company reported business results using five reportable segments.

Company Financials

Per Share Data ($) Year Ended Dec. 31	**2005**	**2004**	**2003**	**2002**	**2001**	**2000**	**1999**	**1998**	**1997**	**1996**
Tangible Book Value	4.41	13.20	9.55	14.72	18.07	21.81	18.10	14.93	17.47	21.88
Cash Flow	1.49	6.30	5.20	5.24	4.13	7.49	7.68	4.31	3.65	4.09
Earnings	-0.58	2.44	0.07	-0.03	-0.96	2.73	3.06	-0.85	-1.19	-0.63
S&P Core Earnings	-0.31	2.45	0.39	-1.15	-1.84	NA	NA	NA	NA	NA
Dividends	0.60	0.60	0.60	0.60	0.60	0.60	0.60	0.60	0.60	0.60
Payout Ratio	NM	25%	NM	NM	NM	22%	20%	NM	NM	NM
Prices:High	34.84	38.01	32.89	38.81	38.00	43.94	47.19	40.38	45.56	47.25
Prices:Low	24.20	28.58	20.72	19.61	26.99	21.75	28.75	22.25	27.75	27.38
P/E Ratio:High	NM	16	NM	NM	NM	16	15	NM	NM	NM
P/E Ratio:Low	NM	12	NM	NM	NM	8	9	NM	NM	NM

Income Statement Analysis (Million $)	2005	2004	2003	2002	2001	2000	1999	1998	1997	1996
Revenue	9,158	13,270	8,245	7,412	7,422	7,807	6,953	6,162	5,494	5,108
Operating Income	155	656	483	459	515	656	704	495	365	367
Depreciation	151	355	308	307	296	298	289	283	256	233
Interest Expense	129	152	133	118	128	151	145	160	137	146
Pretax Income	-37.6	379	19.3	1.01	-47.6	298	356	-15.0	28.0	31.3
Effective Tax Rate	NM	37.5%	11.5%	NM	NM	39.0%	40.0%	NM	NM	38.2%
Net Income	-41.2	234	17.1	11.3	-42.5	179	200	-25.7	-30.0	9.05
S&P Core Earnings	-24.4	223	22.6	-67.3	-106	NA	NA	NA	NA	NA

Balance Sheet & Other Financial Data (Million $)	2005	2004	2003	2002	2001	2000	1999	1998	1997	1996
Cash	72.2	1,243	125	65.2	56.7	62.8	66.9	74.4	64.0	261
Current Assets	1,942	3,259	2,501	1,296	1,245	1,577	1,531	1,368	1,354	1,355
Total Assets	6,272	7,543	7,376	4,947	4,934	5,267	5,138	4,967	4,970	4,711
Current Liabilities	1,588	1,857	1,977	1,054	1,266	1,014	1,125	1,130	894	933
Long Term Debt	1,877	2,055	2,191	1,611	1,144	1,823	1,717	1,734	1,903	1,526
Common Equity	1,681	2,549	2,157	1,258	1,458	1,654	1,523	1,187	1,251	1,323
Total Capital	3,640	4,689	4,598	3,176	3,203	3,973	3,774	3,535	3,852	3,538
Capital Expenditures	152	298	228	219	305	297	221	229	280	789
Cash Flow	106	577	312	305	238	460	472	241	190	197
Current Ratio	1.2	1.8	1.3	1.2	1.0	1.6	1.4	1.2	1.5	1.5
% Long Term Debt of Capitalization	51.6	43.8	47.7	50.7	35.7	45.9	45.5	49.1	49.4	43.1
% Net Income of Revenue	NM	1.8	0.2	0.2	NM	2.3	2.9	NM	NM	0.2
% Return on Assets	NM	3.1	0.3	0.2	NM	3.4	4.0	NM	NM	0.2
% Return on Equity	NM	9.5	0.2	0.8	NM	10.2	12.7	NM	NM	NM

Data as orig reptd.; bef. results of disc opers/spec. items. Per share data adj. for stk. divs.; EPS diluted. E-Estimated. NA-Not Available. NM-Not Meaningful. NR-Not Ranked. UR-Under Review.

Office: 150 E Pierce Rd, Itasca, IL 60143-1290.
Telephone: 630-773-5000.
Email: investor@bc.com
Website: http://www.officemax.com

Chrmn, Pres & CEO: S.K. Duncan
EVP & CFO: D. Civgin
SVP & Cntlr: P.P. DePaul
Investor Contact: J.S. Jennings (630-438-8760)

Board of Directors: D. J. Bern, W. F. Bryant, B. C. Cornell, J. M. DePinto, S. K. Duncan, R. Gangwal, M. R. Haymon, G. G. Michael, D. M. Szymanski, F. R. de Luzuriaga

Founded: 1931
Domicile: Delaware
Employees: 35,000

STANDARD &POOR'S

Office Depot Inc

S&P Recommendation SELL ★★★★★

Price $41.26 (as of Oct 27, 2006)

12-Mo. Target Price $39.00

Investment Style Large-Cap Growth

GICS Sector Consumer Discretionary
Sub-Industry Specialty Stores

Comment Office Depot is a leading operator of office products superstores and mail order catalogs.

Key Stock Statistics (Source S&P, Vickers, company reports)

52-Wk Range	$46.52–26.44	S&P Oper. EPS 2006E	1.95	P/E on S&P Oper. EPS 2006E	21.2	Dividend Rate/Share	Nil
Trailing 12-Month EPS	$1.65	S&P Oper. EPS 2007E	2.34	Common Shares Outstg. (M)	278.4	Yield (%)	Nil
Trailing 12-Month P/E	25.0	S&P Core EPS 2006E	1.95	Market Capitalization(B)	$11.487	Beta	1.54
$10K Invested 5 Yrs Ago	$27,860	S&P Core EPS 2007E	2.34	Institutional Ownership (%)	94	S&P Credit Rating	BBB-

Price Performance

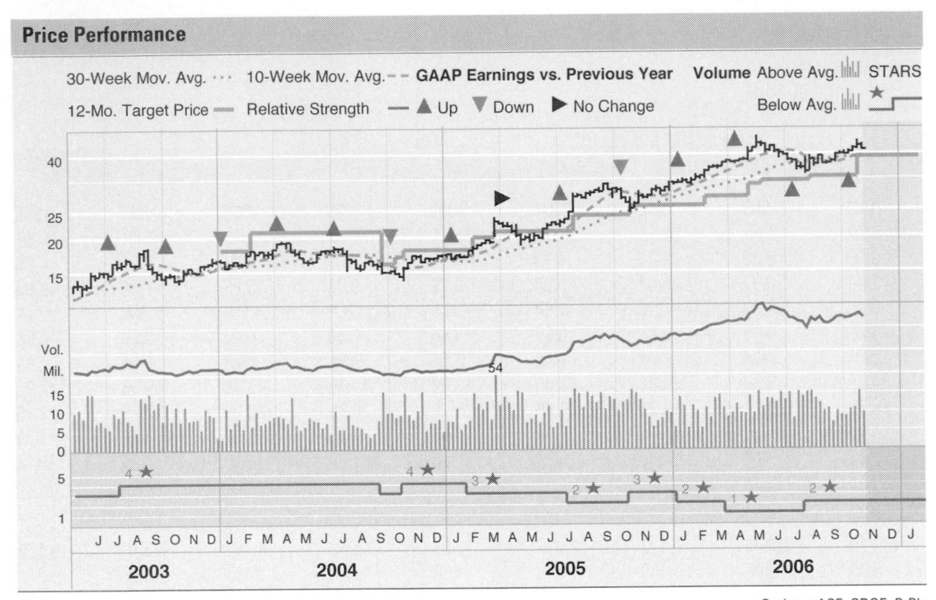

Options: ASE, CBOE, P, Ph

Analysis prepared by **Michael Souers** on October 18, 2006, when the stock traded at **$ 41.99**.

Highlights

- We expect sales to grow 6%-7% in 2006 on ODP's expansion of retail and delivery operations in the Northeast, modest gains in the U.S. contract business, and continued international penetration, mainly in Europe. We expect ODP to open 115 net new stores in 2006. In addition, we see same-store sales growth of 2%-3% on improved sales at remodeled locations as well as increases in the average ticket.

- We believe that ODP's aggressive cost-cutting efforts, combined with inventory optimization, improved sourcing, and a continued push toward selling higher-margin private label brands will yield a significant improvement in operating margins.

- We project slightly higher interest expense, an effective tax rate of 30.4%, and approximately 9% fewer shares as a result of ODP's aggressive share repurchase plan. Our 2006 operating EPS estimate of $1.95 is a 38% increase from the $1.41 the company earned in 2005, excluding extraordinary charges. We project 2007 EPS of $2.34. Our 2006 EPS estimate includes $0.06 of projected stock option expense.

Investment Rationale/Risk

- ODP shares have risen approximately 200% since October 2004, and we view that increase as excessive despite a substantial operational improvement. In essence, we believe the shares are already reflecting a significant further improvement that may not come to fruition. The stock recently traded at about 18X our 2007 EPS estimate, a premium to peers and the S&P 500. While we believe that additional cost cutting can be achieved over the near term, the lack of potential sales growth that we foresee for ODP may ultimately hurt the shares.

- Risks to our opinion and target price include a significant increase in capital spending by businesses, an ability to post mid-single digit or better same-store sales comps in its North America Retail division, and favorable currency fluctuations.

- At recent levels, ODP traded at a premium to its primary competitor, Staples (SPLS: hold, $26), with respect to P/E and P/E to growth ratios. Our 12-month target price of $39 is based on our DCF analysis, which assumes a weighted average cost of capital of 11.0% and a terminal growth rate of 4%.

Qualitative Risk Assessment

LOW | **MEDIUM** | HIGH

Our risk assessment for Office Depot reflects the cyclical nature of the office supply retailing industry, which is highly dependent on increased consumer and business spending, and a fairly large exposure to international markets, offset by what we view as a strong balance sheet.

Quantitative Evaluations

S&P Quality Ranking **B**

D | C | B- | **B** | B+ | A- | A | A+

Relative Strength Rank **MODERATE**

53

LOWEST = 1 HIGHEST = 99

Revenue/Earnings Data

Revenue (Million $)

	1Q	2Q	3Q	4Q	Year
2006	3,816	3,495	3,857	--	--
2005	3,703	3,364	3,493	3,719	14,279
2004	3,605	3,162	3,328	3,469	13,565
2003	3,056	2,816	3,236	3,251	12,359
2002	3,022	2,622	2,871	2,842	11,357
2001	3,018	2,554	2,782	2,800	11,154

Earnings Per Share ($)

	1Q	2Q	3Q	4Q	Year
2006	0.43	0.41	0.47	**E**0.55	**E**1.95
2005	0.37	0.31	-0.15	0.34	0.87
2004	0.37	0.25	0.28	0.17	1.06
2003	0.33	0.19	0.29	0.15	0.96
2002	0.32	0.18	0.27	0.21	0.98
2001	0.19	0.14	0.20	0.13	0.66

Fiscal year ended Dec. 31. Next earnings report expected: Mid February. EPS Estimates based on S&P Operating Earnings; historical GAAP earnings are as reported.

Dividend Data

No cash dividends have been paid.

Please read the Required Disclosures and Analyst Certification on the last page of this report.

Office Depot Inc

Business Summary October 18, 2006

CORPORATE OVERVIEW. Office Depot is a global supplier of office products and services. It generated net sales of nearly $14.3 billion in 2005 to customers and businesses of all sizes through three business segments: the North America Retail Division (46% of revenues in 2005), the North America Business Solutions Division (30%), and the International Group (24%). Sales by product group in 2005 were as follows: supplies 61%; technology 26%; and furniture and other 13%.

At December 31, 2005, ODP's North America Retail Division operated 1,047 office supply stores in 49 states, the District of Columbia and Canada. North America Retail sells a broad assortment of merchandise, including brand name and private brand office supplies, business machines and computers, computer software, office furniture and other business-related products through its chain of office supply stores. Most stores also contain a copy and print center that offers printing, reproduction mailing, shipping, and other services.

ODP's International Group served customers in 20 countries outside the U.S. and Canada through 70 company-owned stores and 153 additional stores operating under licensing and joint venture agreements as of December 31, 2005. In 2006, ODP plans to open between five and 20 company-owned stores.

MARKET PROFILE. The U.S. office products industry was approximately $312 billion in sales in 2004, according to the School, Home and Office Products Association (SHOPA). The market is mature, and S&P forecasts an industry growth rate of 3% for the next five years. Growth in the higher-margin commercial segment (36% of the total industry) will likely continue to outpace that of the retail segment (64%) over the next several years due to a solid macro environment for capital spending. While behemoths Staples, Office Depot and OfficeMax are often regarded as the dominant players, the office products industry remains quite fragmented, with the aforementioned trio comprising an approximate 11.5% share of U.S. sales in 2004, including only about 9% of the retail channel.

Company Financials

Per Share Data ($) Year Ended Dec. 31	2005	2004	2003	2002	2001	2000	1999	1998	1997	1996
Tangible Book Value	6.26	6.96	5.77	6.61	5.28	4.66	5.06	4.86	7.23	4.09
Cash Flow	1.72	1.92	1.75	1.59	1.27	0.86	1.08	0.93	1.49	0.89
Earnings	0.87	1.06	0.96	0.98	0.66	0.16	0.69	0.61	0.65	0.54
S&P Core Earnings	0.86	1.03	0.91	0.92	0.58	NA	NA	NA	NA	NA
Dividends	Nil	Nil	Nil	Nil	Nil	Nil	Nil	Nil	Nil	Nil
Payout Ratio	Nil	Nil	Nil	Nil	Nil	Nil	Nil	Nil	Nil	Nil
Prices:High	31.76	19.50	18.50	21.96	18.70	14.88	26.00	24.83	16.00	17.08
Prices:Low	16.50	13.87	10.28	10.60	7.13	5.88	9.00	10.58	8.42	8.58
P/E Ratio:High	37	18	19	22	28	93	38	41	25	32
P/E Ratio:Low	19	13	11	11	11	37	13	17	13	16

Income Statement Analysis (Million $)	2005	2004	2003	2002	2001	2000	1999	1998	1997	1996
Revenue	14,279	13,565	12,359	11,357	11,154	11,570	10,263	8,998	6,718	6,069
Operating Income	750	799	719	707	562	433	615	659	405	322
Depreciation	268	269	248	201	199	206	169	141	102	82.5
Interest Expense	32.4	61.1	54.8	46.2	44.3	33.9	26.1	22.4	21.6	26.1
Pretax Income	362	461	445	479	314	92.5	414	389	263	213
Effective Tax Rate	24.3%	27.3%	32.1%	35.0%	36.0%	46.6%	37.8%	40.0%	39.4%	39.3%
Net Income	274	336	302	311	201	49.3	258	233	160	129
S&P Core Earnings	270	327	286	292	178	NA	NA	NA	NA	NA

Balance Sheet & Other Financial Data (Million $)	2005	2004	2003	2002	2001	2000	1999	1998	1997	1996
Cash	703	794	791	877	563	151	219	705	200	51.4
Current Assets	3,530	3,916	3,577	3,210	2,806	2,699	2,631	2,780	2,021	1,822
Total Assets	6,099	6,767	6,145	4,766	4,332	4,196	4,276	4,113	2,981	2,740
Current Liabilities	2,469	2,618	2,277	1,992	2,102	1,908	1,944	1,531	1,138	1,128
Long Term Debt	569	584	829	412	318	598	321	471	447	417
Common Equity	2,739	3,223	2,794	2,297	1,848	1,601	1,908	2,029	1,329	1,156
Total Capital	3,308	3,957	3,868	2,774	2,230	2,200	2,229	2,500	1,777	1,573
Capital Expenditures	261	391	212	202	207	268	396	255	94.3	177
Cash Flow	542	605	550	512	400	255	426	374	262	212
Current Ratio	1.4	1.5	1.6	1.6	1.3	1.4	1.4	1.8	1.8	1.6
% Long Term Debt of Capitalization	17.2	14.8	21.4	14.9	14.2	27.2	14.4	18.8	25.2	26.5
% Net Income of Revenue	1.9	2.5	2.4	2.7	1.8	0.4	2.5	2.6	2.4	2.1
% Return on Assets	4.2	5.2	5.5	6.8	4.7	1.2	6.2	6.6	5.6	4.9
% Return on Equity	9.2	11.2	11.9	15.0	11.7	2.8	13.1	13.9	12.9	12.0

Data as orig reptd.; bef. results of disc opers/spec. items. Per share data adj. for stk. divs.; EPS diluted. E-Estimated. NA-Not Available. NM-Not Meaningful. NR-Not Ranked. UR-Under Review.

Office: 2200 Old Germantown Road, Delray Beach, FL 33445.
Telephone: 561-438-4800.
Email: investor.relations@officedepot.com
Website: http://www.officedepot.com

Chrmn & CEO: S. Odland
EVP & CFO: P.A. McKay
EVP, Secy & General Counsel: D.C. Fannin
Investor Contact: R. Tharpe (561-438-4800)

Board of Directors: L. A. Ault, III, N. R. Austrian, D. W. Bernauer, A. E. Bru, M. J. Evans, D. I. Fuente, B. J. Gaines, M. M. Hart, W. S. Hedrick, K. Mason, M. J. Myers, S. Odland

Founded: 1986
Domicile: Delaware
Employees: 47,000

Stock Report | October 31, 2006 | NYS Symbol: **OMC** | **OMC** is in the S&P 500

STANDARD &POOR'S

Omnicom Group Inc.

S&P Recommendation BUY ★★★★★

Price $101.45 (as of Oct 31, 2006)

12-Mo. Target Price $110.00

Investment Style Large-Cap Growth

GICS Sector Consumer Discretionary
Sub-Industry Advertising

Comment This company owns the DDB Worldwide, BBDO Worldwide and TBWA Worldwide advertising agency networks; it also owns more than 100 marketing and specialty services firms.

Key Stock Statistics (Source S&P, Vickers, company reports)

52-Wk Range	$102.44–78.75	S&P Oper. EPS 2006E	5.02	P/E on S&P Oper. EPS 2006E	20.2	Dividend Rate/Share	$1.00
Trailing 12-Month EPS	$4.79	S&P Oper. EPS 2007E	5.65	Common Shares Outstg. (M)	170.9	Yield (%)	0.99
Trailing 12-Month P/E	21.2	S&P Core EPS 2006E	5.02	Market Capitalization(B)	$17.338	Beta	1.35
$10K Invested 5 Yrs Ago	$13,173	S&P Core EPS 2007E	5.65	Institutional Ownership (%)	85	S&P Credit Rating	A-

Price Performance

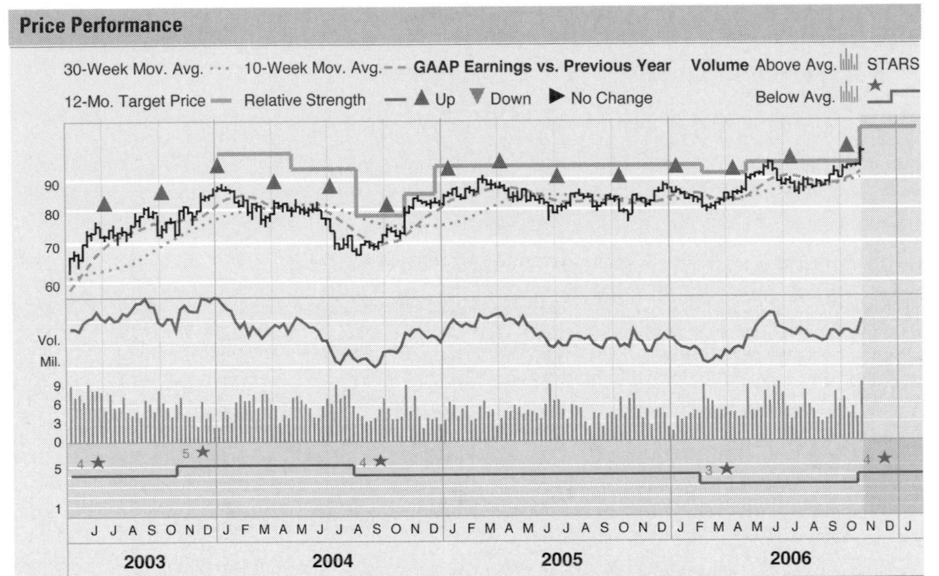

Options: CBOE, P

Analysis prepared by **James Peters, CFA** on October 27, 2006, when the stock traded at **$ 100.47**.

Highlights

- We forecast 2007 revenue growth of about 7.5%, following an 8.9% advance we project for 2006. We see overseas growth gaining momentum as European markets recover from a period of economic weakness and emerging markets continue to perform well. We also believe easier foreign exchange comparisons will boost international growth in the first half of the year. For the U.S., we see a strong but moderating advance given our outlook for lower GDP growth. We also expect OMC to be active in acquiring small and mid-sized non-traditional media agencies.
- We believe that fixed costs will continue to trend lower as a percentage of sales given our higher revenue forecast, and expect an overall operating margin improvement in 2007 to 13.4%, up from our 13.1% projection for 2006.
- After higher anticipated interest payments, we anticipate an operating EPS advance of about 13% in 2007, to $5.65, up from the $5.02 we forecast for 2006. We expect free cash flow to primarily be used for acquisitions, debt retirement and share repurchases.

Investment Rationale/Risk

- Aided by increased acquisition activity, we expect OMC over the next few years to post worldwide revenue, profitability and earnings growth superior to that of its peers. Over the longer term, we think a diversified revenue stream will benefit OMC, as we believe it positions the company to capture advertising and marketing spending regardless of the specific outlets and geographic locations clients utilize to engage their target audience.
- Risks to our recommendation and target price include a deterioration in global GDP, lost accounts through heightened merger activity, and possible stock dilution from convertible liquid yield options.
- Our 12-month target price of $110 is based on a blend of relative value and DCF analyses. Our DCF model yields a valuation of $106 and assumes an 8.7% WACC and 4.0% terminal growth. We derive a $114 valuation by applying a historical P/E multiple of 20.1X to our 2007 EPS estimate of $5.65. We arrive at a $110 valuation by applying a historical enterprise value/ EBITDA multiple of 11.4X to our 2007 EBITDA estimate of $1.84 billion.

Qualitative Risk Assessment

LOW | **MEDIUM** | HIGH

Our risk assessment reflects our view of a highly competitive advertising industry, offset by its diversified geographic and product revenue sources coupled with its position as the world's largest advertising agency by revenue, and the company's strong track record of EPS and free cash flow growth.

Quantitative Evaluations

S&P Quality Ranking A+

D | C | B- | B | B+ | A- | A | **A+**

Relative Strength Rank STRONG

82

LOWEST = 1 HIGHEST = 99

Revenue/Earnings Data

Revenue (Million $)

	1Q	2Q	3Q	4Q	Year
2006	2,563	2,823	2,774	--	--
2005	2,403	2,616	2,523	2,939	10,481
2004	2,231	2,408	2,319	2,789	9,747
2003	1,937	2,150	2,029	2,506	8,621
2002	1,732	1,917	1,768	2,119	7,536
2001	1,601	1,747	1,571	1,970	6,889

Earnings Per Share ($)

2006	0.93	1.42	1.04	**E**1.65	**E**5.02
2005	0.82	1.24	0.90	1.41	4.36
2004	0.72	1.10	0.79	1.28	3.88
2003	0.69	1.02	0.72	1.17	3.59
2002	0.68	1.00	0.68	1.08	3.44
2001	0.54	0.81	0.50	0.87	2.70

Fiscal year ended Dec. 31. Next earnings report expected: Mid February. EPS Estimates based on S&P Operating Earnings; historical GAAP earnings are as reported.

Dividend Data (Dates: mm/dd Payment Date: mm/dd/yy)

Amount ($)	Date Decl.	Ex-Div. Date	Stk. of Record	Payment Date
0.250	12/06	12/14	12/18	01/05/06
0.250	02/14	03/07	03/09	04/06/06
0.250	05/23	06/05	06/07	07/06/06
0.250	07/20	09/19	09/21	10/05/06

Dividends have been paid since 1986. Source: Company reports.

Omnicom Group Inc.

Business Summary October 27, 2006

Omnicom Group, a global advertising and marketing services company, is one of the world's largest corporate communications companies. OMC is comprised of more than 1,500 subsidiary agencies, operating in more than 100 countries. It operates as three independent global agency networks: the BBDO Worldwide Network, the DDB Worldwide Network, and the TBWA Worldwide Network. Each agency network has its own clients, and the networks compete with each other in the same markets.

OMC's companies provide an extensive range of services, which it groups into four disciplines: traditional media advertising (44% of 2005 revenues), customer relationship management (34%), public relations (10%), and specialty communications (12%) The services included in these categories are: advertising, brand consultancy, crisis communications, custom publishing, database management, digital and interactive marketing, direct marketing, directory advertising, entertainment marketing, environmental design, experiential marketing, field marketing, financial/corporate business-to-business advertising, graphic arts, health care communications, instore design, investor relations, marketing research, media planning and buying, multi-cultural marketing, non-profit marketing, organizational communications, package design, product placement, promotional marketing, public affairs, public relations, real estate advertising and marketing, recruitment communications, reputation consulting, retail marketing and sports and event marketing.

Company Financials

Per Share Data ($) Year Ended Dec. 31	**2005**	**2004**	**2003**	**2002**	**2001**	**2000**	**1999**	**1998**	**1997**	**1996**
Tangible Book Value	NM	NM	NM	NM	NM	NM	NM	NM	NM	NM
Cash Flow	5.42	4.80	4.20	4.07	3.75	3.63	2.59	2.38	1.92	1.70
Earnings	4.36	3.88	3.59	3.44	2.70	2.73	2.01	1.68	1.37	1.15
S&P Core Earnings	4.36	3.83	3.37	3.12	2.47	NA	NA	NA	NA	NA
Dividends	0.93	0.90	0.80	0.80	0.78	0.70	0.60	0.50	0.45	0.38
Payout Ratio	21%	23%	22%	23%	29%	26%	30%	30%	33%	33%
Prices:High	91.48	88.82	87.60	97.35	98.20	100.94	107.50	58.50	42.38	26.06
Prices:Low	75.75	66.43	46.50	36.50	59.10	68.13	55.94	37.00	22.25	17.75
P/E Ratio:High	21	23	24	28	36	37	53	35	31	23
P/E Ratio:Low	17	17	13	11	22	25	28	22	16	16
Income Statement Analysis (Million $)										
Revenue	10,481	9,747	8,621	7,536	6,889	6,154	5,131	4,092	3,125	2,642
Operating Income	1,515	1,388	1,289	1,224	1,179	1,065	821	693	506	412
Depreciation	175	172	124	120	211	187	97.1	133	103	85.8
Interest Expense	78.0	51.1	57.9	45.5	72.8	76.5	84.9	69.6	43.1	34.1
Pretax Income	1,308	1,196	1,137	1,087	908	923	689	545	411	326
Effective Tax Rate	33.3%	33.1%	33.5%	34.5%	38.8%	40.0%	39.7%	39.6%	38.0%	38.0%
Net Income	791	724	676	643	503	499	363	285	222	176
S&P Core Earnings	790	715	631	584	456	NA	NA	NA	NA	NA
Balance Sheet & Other Financial Data (Million $)										
Cash	836	1,166	1,529	667	472	517	576	648	556	523
Current Assets	7,967	8,095	7,286	5,637	5,234	5,367	4,712	3,981	2,988	2,425
Total Assets	15,920	16,002	14,499	11,820	10,617	9,891	9,018	6,910	4,966	4,056
Current Liabilities	8,700	8,744	7,762	6,840	6,644	6,625	6,009	4,796	3,579	2,863
Long Term Debt	2,357	2,358	2,537	1,945	1,340	1,245	712	716	342	205
Common Equity	3,948	4,079	3,466	2,569	2,178	1,548	1,553	1,086	981	801
Total Capital	6,921	6,949	6,394	4,687	3,677	2,970	2,708	1,893	1,273	1,068
Capital Expenditures	163	160	141	117	149	150	130	89.7	76.1	48.8
Cash Flow	966	896	800	763	714	685	460	418	325	262
Current Ratio	0.9	0.9	0.9	0.8	0.8	0.8	0.8	0.8	0.8	0.9
% Long Term Debt of Capitalization	34.1	33.9	39.7	41.5	36.4	41.9	26.3	37.8	68.1	19.2
% Net Income of Revenue	7.5	7.4	7.8	8.5	7.3	8.1	7.1	7.0	7.1	6.7
% Return on Assets	5.0	4.7	5.1	5.7	4.9	5.3	4.5	4.8	4.9	4.7
% Return on Equity	19.7	18.8	22.4	27.1	27.0	32.2	27.9	27.6	23.3	26.1

Data as orig reptd.; bef. results of disc opers/spec. items. Per share data adj. for stk. divs.; EPS diluted. E-Estimated. NA-Not Available. NM-Not Meaningful. NR-Not Ranked. UR-Under Review.

Office: 437 Madison Ave, New York, NY 10022-7000.
Telephone: 212-415-3600.
Email: IR@OmnicomGroup.com
Website: http://www.omnicomgroup.com

Chrmn: B. Crawford
Pres & CEO: J.D. Wren
Vice Chrmn: M. Birkin
Vice Chrmn: P. Mead

Investor Contact: R.J. Weisenburger (212-415-3600)
Board of Directors: R. C. Clark, L. Coleman, Jr., E. M. Cook, B. Crawford, S. S. Denison, M. A. Henning, J. R. Murphy, J. R. Purcell, L. J. Rice, G. L. Roubos, J. D. Wren

Founded: 1944
Domicile: New York
Employees: 62,000

STANDARD &POOR'S

Oracle Corp

S&P Recommendation BUY ★★★★★

Price $18.10 (as of Oct 27, 2006)

12-Mo. Target Price $22.00

Investment Style Large-Cap Growth

GICS Sector Information Technology
Sub-Industry Systems Software

Comment This company is a leading supplier of enterprise database management systems and business applications.

Key Stock Statistics (Source S&P, Vickers, company reports)

52-Wk Range	**$19.25–11.75**	S&P Oper. EPS 2007**E**	**0.93**	P/E on S&P Oper. EPS 2007**E**	**19.5**	Dividend Rate/Share	**Nil**
Trailing 12-Month EPS	**$0.67**	S&P Oper. EPS 2008**E**	**1.06**	Common Shares Outstg. (M)	**5,195.5**	Yield (%)	**Nil**
Trailing 12-Month P/E	**27.0**	S&P Core EPS 2007**E**	**0.93**	Market Capitalization(B)	**$94.038**	Beta	**1.03**
$10K Invested 5 Yrs Ago	**$13,328**	S&P Core EPS 2008**E**	**1.06**	Institutional Ownership (%)	**53**	S&P Credit Rating	**NA**

Price Performance

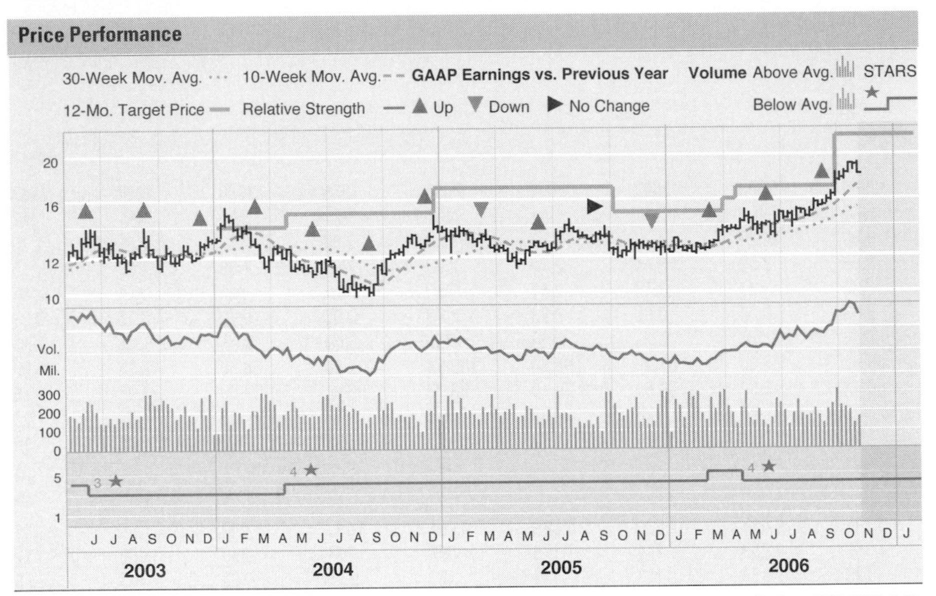

Options: ASE, CBOE, P, Ph

Analysis prepared by **Zaineb Bokhari** on September 21, 2006, when the stock traded at **$ 17.93**.

Highlights

- Although we forecast healthy organic growth rates for the company, we expect recent acquisitions (notably Siebel Systems) to help drive faster growth in ORCL's applications business in FY 07 (May) and FY 08 than its core database operations. We expect middleware to remain an area of strong growth for the company. We see non-GAAP revenue growth of nearly 19% in FY 07 to $17.5 billion; we forecast 8% higher revenues in FY 08, as year-to-year comparisons become tougher.
- Despite our strong revenue growth outlook, we expect operating margins to remain flat in FY 07 at 40.5%, comparable to 40.4% reported in FY 06, as management continues to integrate recent acquisitions. We expect operating margins to widen modestly in FY 08, as targeted cost synergies are achieved.
- After an effective tax rate of 30%, up from 29.7% reported in FY 06, we expect pro forma operating EPS to rise 16% to $0.93 in FY 07 and 14% to $1.06 in FY 08. Our EPS estimates for FY 07 and FY 08 include $0.03 of projected annual stock option expense. We expect EPS to be aided by what we expect to be notable share repurchases.

Investment Rationale/Risk

- We have a buy recommendation on the shares due to our view of ORCL's formidable market position, enviable operating margins, considerable free cash generation, and attractive relative valuation, based on its P/E. While we continue to foresee potential acquisition integration risks, we believe the current discount to peers is overdone.
- Risks to our recommendation and target price include potential delays with ORCL's Fusion suite (due in 2008) and acquisition integration risks. We have corporate governance concerns related to potential changes in board size without shareholder approval and related party transactions.
- Our 12-month target price of $22 is derived by using a blend of our relative and intrinsic valuation methods. Assumptions used in our valuation of discounted cash flow include a 10% WACC and a terminal growth rate of 4%, which leads to an intrinsic value of $22. At this level, the shares would trade at a P/E to growth ratio of about 1.6X our FY 07 non-GAAP EPS estimate of $0.93, assuming 15% growth, at the high end of the historical range for ORCL shares, warranted, we think, by our growth outlook.

Qualitative Risk Assessment

LOW | **MEDIUM** | HIGH

Our risk assessment reflects potential acquisition integration risks faced by the company, following a series of large purchases over the past two years. This is offset by our view of ORCL's strong balance sheet, considerable free cash flow, and what we see as a deep management bench.

Quantitative Evaluations

S&P Quality Ranking **B**

D | C | B- | **B** | B+ | A- | A | A+

Relative Strength Rank **MODERATE**

69

LOWEST = 1 HIGHEST = 99

Revenue/Earnings Data

Revenue (Million $)

	1Q	2Q	3Q	4Q	Year
2007	3,591	--	--	--	--
2006	2,768	3,292	3,470	4,851	14,380
2005	2,215	2,756	2,950	3,878	11,799
2004	2,072	2,498	2,509	3,076	10,156
2003	2,028	2,309	2,307	2,832	9,475
2002	2,265	2,380	2,254	2,774	9,673

Earnings Per Share ($)

2007	0.13	**E**0.21	**E**0.23	**E**0.32	**E**0.93
2006	0.10	0.15	0.14	0.24	0.64
2005	0.10	0.16	0.10	0.20	0.55
2004	0.08	0.12	0.12	0.19	0.50
2003	0.06	0.10	0.11	0.16	0.43
2002	0.09	0.10	0.09	0.12	0.39

Fiscal year ended May 31. Next earnings report expected: Mid December. EPS Estimates based on S&P Operating Earnings; historical GAAP earnings are as reported.

Dividend Data

No cash dividends have been paid.

Oracle Corp

Business Summary September 21, 2006

CORPORATE OVERVIEW. Oracle Corp. is a leading provider of enterprise software. The company is organized into two main businesses, software and services. The company further segments its software business into new software licenses (33% of revenue in FY 06 (May) and 34% in FY 05) and software license updates, and product support (48% and 47% of revenue in FY 06 and FY 05, respectively). The company's services business is divided into consulting (14%, 15%), On Demand (3%, 2%), and education (2%, 2%). Oracle's software products fall into two broad categories: database and middleware and application software. Database and middleware products accounted for about 67% of software revenues in FY 06 (75% in FY 05).

CORPORATE STRATEGY. ORCL has acquired companies that it believes offer complementary products and services. In January 2005, the company acquired PeopleSoft Inc., a provider of enterprise application software products, for about $11.1 billion. In January 2006, ORCL acquired Siebel Systems, a leading provider of customer relationship management software (CRM), for $5.85 billion in cash and stock. ORCL believes these acquisitions support its long-term strategy, strengthen its competitive position in the enterprise applications market, and expand its customer base. In addition to these large deals, ORCL has acquired several smaller companies that provide software solutions targeted at specific industries in an effort to gain expertise in what it considers to be key verticals such as retail and financial services. In April 2005, ORCL acquired Retek, Inc., a provider of software and services to the retail industry, for approximately $700 million. In December 2005, ORCL acquired a 43% stake in i-Flex Solutions, an India-based provider of software solutions for the banking and insurance industries. The company has continued to add to this stake in 2006. We have a favorable view of smaller acquisitions that extend ORCL's vertical industry expertise; however, we would be concerned by additional large acquisitions with significant product overlap.

Company Financials

Per Share Data ($) Year Ended May 31	**2006**	**2005**	**2004**	**2003**	**2002**	**2001**	**2000**	**1999**	**1998**	**1997**
Tangible Book Value	0.13	0.09	1.55	1.21	1.13	1.12	1.15	1.29	0.51	0.40
Cash Flow	0.79	0.63	0.55	0.49	0.45	0.50	1.10	0.43	0.19	0.18
Earnings	0.64	0.55	0.50	0.43	0.39	0.44	1.05	0.22	0.14	0.14
S&P Core Earnings	0.62	0.52	0.46	0.37	0.34	0.36	NA	NA	NA	NA
Dividends	Nil	Nil	Nil	Nil	Nil	Nil	Nil	Nil	Nil	Nil
Payout Ratio	Nil	Nil	Nil	Nil	Nil	Nil	Nil	Nil	Nil	Nil
Calendar Year	2005	2004	2003	2002	2001	2000	1999	1998	1997	1996
Prices:High	14.51	15.51	14.03	17.50	35.00	46.47	28.34	7.48	7.02	5.67
Prices:Low	11.25	9.78	10.64	7.25	10.16	21.50	5.25	2.96	3.49	2.93
P/E Ratio:High	23	20	28	41	90	NM	27	34	52	42
P/E Ratio:Low	18	18	21	17	26	NM	5	14	26	22
Income Statement Analysis (Million $)										
Revenue	14,380	11,799	10,156	9,475	9,673	10,860	10,130	8,827	7,144	5,684
Operating Income	5,764	4,802	4,098	3,767	3,934	4,124	3,472	2,248	1,740	1,528
Depreciation	806	425	234	327	363	347	391	375	329	265
Interest Expense	169	135	21.0	16.0	20.0	24.0	18.9	21.4	16.7	6.81
Pretax Income	4,810	4,051	3,945	3,425	3,408	3,971	10,123	1,982	1,328	1,284
Effective Tax Rate	29.7%	28.8%	32.0%	32.6%	34.7%	35.5%	37.8%	34.9%	38.7%	36.0%
Net Income	3,381	2,886	2,681	2,307	2,224	2,561	6,297	1,290	814	821
S&P Core Earnings	3,237	2,750	2,459	2,049	1,923	2,119	NA	NA	NA	NA
Balance Sheet & Other Financial Data (Million $)										
Cash	7,605	4,802	4,138	4,737	3,095	4,449	7,429	1,786	1,274	890
Current Assets	11,974	8,479	11,336	9,227	8,728	8,963	10,883	5,447	4,323	3,271
Total Assets	29,029	20,687	12,763	11,064	10,800	11,030	13,077	7,260	5,819	4,624
Current Liabilities	6,930	8,063	4,272	4,158	3,960	3,917	5,862	3,046	2,484	1,922
Long Term Debt	5,735	159	163	175	298	301	301	304	304	301
Common Equity	15,012	10,837	7,995	6,320	6,117	6,278	6,461	3,695	2,958	2,370
Total Capital	21,311	12,006	8,217	6,681	6,619	6,906	7,028	4,135	3,278	2,678
Capital Expenditures	236	188	189	291	278	313	263	347	328	391
Cash Flow	4,187	3,311	2,915	2,634	2,587	2,908	6,611	1,290	1,142	1,086
Current Ratio	1.7	1.1	2.7	2.2	2.2	2.3	1.9	1.8	1.7	1.7
% Long Term Debt of Capitalization	26.9	1.3	2.0	2.6	4.5	4.4	4.3	7.3	9.3	11.2
% Net Income of Revenue	23.5	24.4	26.4	24.3	23.0	23.6	62.2	14.6	11.4	14.5
% Return on Assets	13.6	17.3	22.6	21.1	20.4	21.2	61.9	19.7	15.6	20.6
% Return on Equity	26.2	30.7	37.5	37.1	35.9	40.2	124.0	19.4	30.5	38.7

Data as orig reptd.; bef. results of disc opers/spec. items. Per share data adj. for stk. divs.; EPS diluted. E-Estimated. NA-Not Available. NM-Not Meaningful. NR-Not Ranked. UR-Under Review.

Office: 500 Oracle Parkway, Redwood Shores, CA 94065-1675.
Telephone: 650-506-7000.
Email: investor_us@oracle.com
Website: http://www.oracle.com

Chrmn: J.O. Henley
CEO: L.J. Ellison
SVP, Secy & General Counsel: D. Cooperman
CFO & Co-Pres: S. Catz

Investor Contact: K. Bessinger (650-506-4073)
Board of Directors: J. Berg, H. R. Bingham, M. J. Boskin, S. A. Catz, L. J. Ellison, H. Garcia-Molina, J. O. Henley, J. F. Kemp, D. L. Lucas, C. E. Phillips, Jr., N. O. Seligman

Founded: 1977
Domicile: Delaware
Employees: 56,133

STANDARD & POOR'S

PACCAR Inc

S&P Recommendation HOLD ★★★★★

Price $59.21 (as of Oct 31, 2006)

12-Mo. Target Price $66.00

Investment Style Large-Cap Value

GICS Sector Industrials
Sub-Industry Construction & Farm Machinery & Heavy Trucks

Comment This heavy-duty truck manufacturer produces the well known Peterbilt and Kenworth brand heavy-duty highway trucks.

Key Stock Statistics (Source S&P, Vickers, company reports)

52-Wk Range	$62.53–45.19	S&P Oper. EPS 2006E	5.90	P/E on S&P Oper. EPS 2006E	10.0	Dividend Rate/Share	$0.80
Trailing 12-Month EPS	$5.65	S&P Oper. EPS 2007E	4.25	Common Shares Outstg. (M)	249.3	Yield (%)	1.35
Trailing 12-Month P/E	10.5	S&P Core EPS 2006E	5.90	Market Capitalization(B)	$14.762	Beta	1.36
$10K Invested 5 Yrs Ago	$42,480	S&P Core EPS 2007E	4.25	Institutional Ownership (%)	53	S&P Credit Rating	AA-

Price Performance

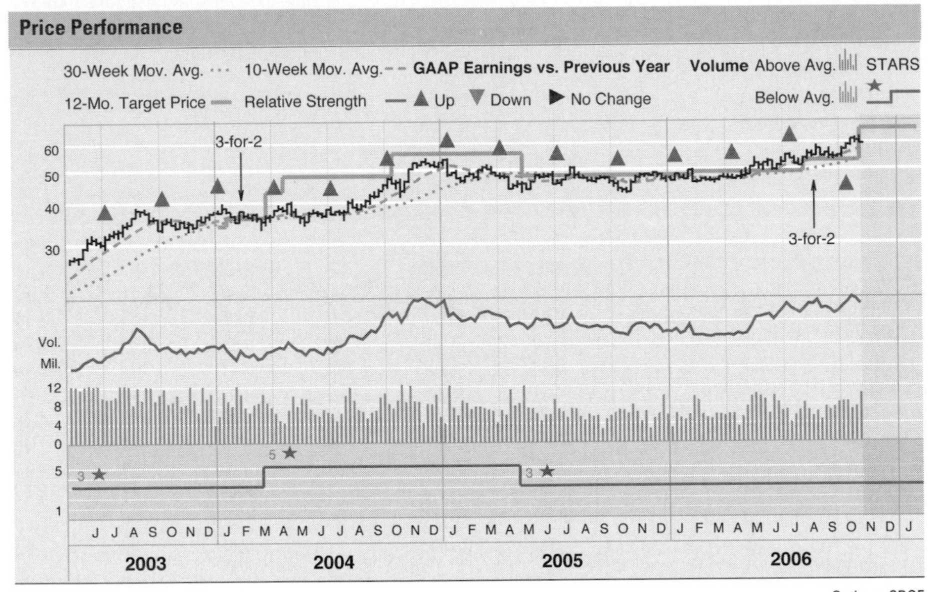

Options: CBOE

Analysis prepared by **Anthony M. Fiore, CFA** on October 31, 2006, when the stock traded at **$ 59.44**.

Highlights

- We see net sales declining about 25% in 2007, following a projected advance of 16% in 2006. We expect improved carrier profitability, coupled with an aging motor fleet, to drive strong replacement demand for heavy-duty trucks through 2006. However, we believe sales in 2007 will be limited by an emissions related pre-buy of trucks that we believe is occurring in 2006.
- We anticipate a narrowing of operating margins in 2007. We see significantly lower truck volumes contributing to a reduction in overall gross margins, partly offset by expected benefits from ongoing cost-control efforts. In addition, we believe raw material cost pressures should abate in 2007, which would provide support to margins. For the longer term, we think that earnings will continue to exhibit large swings, due to the highly cyclical nature of the global truck industry.
- We regard the company's quality of earnings as high versus peers, with no difference between our Standard & Poor's Core EPS estimates and our operating EPS forecasts.

Investment Rationale/Risk

- We would hold the shares based on total return. We believe PCAR is well positioned to benefit from continued strength in global truck demand, due to a cyclical upswing that we believe occurs on average every three to five years. Despite a projected industry downturn in 2007, we believe a rebound in industry demand is likely to begin to occur by early 2008.
- Risks to our recommendation and target price include a more severe than expected downturn in the North American and/or European truck markets; the potential for supply disruptions; and a continued escalation of raw material costs.
- Our 12-month target price of $66 combines two valuation metrics. Our discounted cash flow model, which assumes a 9% to 10% compound annual growth rate in free cash flow over the next 10 years, 3.5% growth in perpetuity, and a 9% discount rate, indicates intrinsic value of about $64. In terms of relative valuation, applying a target P/E multiple of about 16X, in line with historical norms, to our 2007 EPS estimate suggests a value of $68.

Qualitative Risk Assessment

LOW | **MEDIUM** | HIGH

Our risk assessment for Paccar reflects the highly cyclical nature of the heavy-duty (class 8) truck market, offset by our view of a strong balance sheet with a relatively low amount of debt and the company's above-average profitability. We estimate that over the past 10 years, the company has generated an average ROIC of 22% versus 9.2% for the S&P 1500 Industrials sector.

Quantitative Evaluations

S&P Quality Ranking B+

D | C | B- | B | **B+** | A- | A | A+

Relative Strength Rank MODERATE

58

LOWEST = 1 HIGHEST = 99

Revenue/Earnings Data

Revenue (Million $)

	1Q	2Q	3Q	4Q	Year
2006	3,852	3,937	3,959	--	--
2005	3,422	3,555	3,541	3,426	14,057
2004	2,501	2,787	2,775	3,190	11,396
2003	1,803	1,895	1,940	2,083	8,195
2002	1,502	1,802	1,996	1,919	7,219
2001	1,528	1,523	1,501	1,536	6,089

Earnings Per Share ($)

	1Q	2Q	3Q	4Q	Year
2006	1.35	1.47	1.61	**E**1.47	**E**5.90
2005	1.04	0.93	1.19	1.22	4.37
2004	0.69	0.89	0.94	0.92	3.44
2003	0.42	0.47	0.50	0.60	1.99
2002	0.18	0.28	0.49	0.47	1.42
2001	0.17	0.15	0.15	0.19	0.67

Fiscal year ended Dec. 31. Next earnings report expected: Late January. EPS Estimates based on S&P Operating Earnings; historical GAAP earnings are as reported.

Dividend Data (Dates: mm/dd Payment Date: mm/dd/yy)

Amount ($)	Date Decl.	Ex-Div. Date	Stk. of Record	Payment Date
0.300	04/25	05/16	05/18	06/05/06
3-for-2	07/11	08/11	07/27	08/10/06
0.200	07/11	08/16	08/18	09/05/06
0.200	09/12	11/15	11/17	12/05/06

Dividends have been paid since 1943. Source: Company reports.

Business Summary October 31, 2006

CORPORATE OVERVIEW. Originally incorporated in 1924 as the Pacific Car and Foundry Company, and tracing its roots back to the Seattle Car Manufacturing Company, PACCAR has grown into a multinational company with principal businesses that include the design, manufacture and distribution of high-quality light, medium and heavy-duty commercial trucks and related aftermarket parts. The company's heavy-duty (class 8) diesel trucks are marketed under the Peterbilt, Kenworth, DAF and Foden names. In addition, through its Peterbilt and Kenworth divisions, PCAR competes in the North American medium duty (class 6/7) markets and the European light/medium (6 to 15 metric ton) commercial vehicle market with DAF cab-over-engine trucks.

In 2005, the company's truck production and related aftermarket parts distribution businesses accounted for 94% of revenues and 86% of operating income. Segment profit margins in 2005, 2004 and 2003, were 11.5%, 10.6%, and 8.6%, respectively; in the boom years of 2000, 1999 and 1998, segment profit margins were 6.9%, 9.0% and 7.4%, respectively.

PCAR also manufactures industrial winches under the Braden, Carco and Gearmatic names. Sales of winches provided less than 1% of net sales in 2005, 2004 and 2003.

Like other big truck makers, the company aims to capitalize on a growing trend toward truck leasing and financing. The Finance Services segment accounted for 5.4% of 2005 revenues, but generated 11% of operating income; it posted 26%, 30% and 26% operating margins in 2005, 2004 and 2003, respectively. In 2005, 2004 and 2003, provisions for loan losses were $40 million, $18 million and $29 million, respectively.

Company Financials

Per Share Data ($) Year Ended Dec. 31	2005	2004	2003	2002	2001	2000	1999	1998	1997	1996
Tangible Book Value	15.40	14.42	11.04	9.12	8.45	8.46	7.70	6.69	5.69	5.17
Cash Flow	5.80	4.64	3.01	2.25	1.37	2.31	2.77	2.06	1.74	1.07
Earnings	4.37	3.44	1.99	1.42	0.67	1.70	2.20	1.57	1.31	0.77
S&P Core Earnings	4.38	3.37	1.98	1.33	0.56	NA	NA	NA	NA	NA
Dividends	0.58	0.50	0.69	0.43	0.36	0.36	0.71	0.62	0.62	0.37
Payout Ratio	13%	15%	35%	30%	53%	21%	32%	40%	47%	48%
Prices:High	54.25	54.28	38.92	23.55	20.53	16.07	18.67	19.78	17.63	10.83
Prices:Low	42.20	33.07	18.56	13.64	12.67	10.74	11.70	10.96	8.98	6.19
P/E Ratio:High	12	16	20	17	31	9	9	13	13	14
P/E Ratio:Low	10	10	9	10	19	6	5	7	7	8
Income Statement Analysis (Million $)										
Revenue	14,057	11,396	8,195	7,219	6,089	7,437	9,021	7,895	6,764	4,600
Operating Income	2,572	1,972	1,313	1,012	672	1,122	1,243	931	790	516
Depreciation	370	315	268	218	180	156	147	124	112	81.1
Interest Expense	445	331	3.50	249	275	294	223	192	170	152
Pretax Income	1,774	1,368	806	574	255	665	923	653	536	313
Effective Tax Rate	36.1%	33.7%	34.6%	35.2%	32.0%	33.6%	36.8%	36.1%	35.5%	35.8%
Net Income	1,133	907	527	372	174	442	584	417	346	201
S&P Core Earnings	1,134	889	523	349	145	NA	NA	NA	NA	NA
Balance Sheet & Other Financial Data (Million $)										
Cash	2,290	2,220	1,724	1,308	1,062	910	1,059	837	676	508
Current Assets	3,508	3,332	2,599	2,102	1,834	1,861	2,119	2,070	1,756	1,548
Total Assets	13,715	12,228	9,940	8,703	7,914	8,271	7,933	6,795	5,600	5,299
Current Liabilities	2,182	2,151	1,482	1,258	1,134	1,268	1,534	1,519	1,214	1,352
Long Term Debt	936	2,314	1,557	1,552	1,547	1,655	1,475	1,311	1,334	1,145
Common Equity	3,901	3,762	3,246	2,601	2,253	2,249	2,111	1,764	1,498	1,358
Total Capital	4,837	6,077	4,803	4,152	3,800	3,904	3,585	3,075	2,987	2,655
Capital Expenditures	300	232	111	78.8	83.9	143	256	193	133	123
Cash Flow	1,503	1,222	794	590	354	598	730	541	458	282
Current Ratio	1.6	1.5	1.8	1.7	1.6	1.5	1.4	1.4	1.4	1.1
% Long Term Debt of Capitalization	19.3	38.1	32.4	37.4	40.7	42.4	41.1	42.6	44.7	43.1
% Net Income of Revenue	8.1	8.0	6.4	5.2	2.9	5.9	6.5	5.3	5.1	4.4
% Return on Assets	8.7	8.2	5.6	4.5	2.1	5.5	7.9	6.7	6.4	4.1
% Return on Equity	29.6	25.9	18.0	15.3	7.7	20.3	30.1	25.6	24.2	15.4

Data as orig reptd.; bef. results of disc opers/spec. items. Per share data adj. for stk. divs.; EPS diluted. E-Estimated. NA-Not Available. NM-Not Meaningful. NR-Not Ranked. UR-Under Review.

Office: 777 106th Avenue NE, Bellevue, WA 98004-5027.
Telephone: 425-468-7400.
Website: http://www.paccar.com
Chrmn & CEO: M.C. Pigott

Pres: T.E. Plimpton
Vice Chrmn: M.A. Tembreull
VP & General Counsel: D.C. Anderson
VP & Cntlr: R.E. Armstrong

Board of Directors: A. J. Carnwath, J. M. Fluke, Jr., D. K. Newbigging, S. F. Page, R. T. Parry, J. C. Pigott, M. C. Pigott, W. G. Reed, Jr., M. A. Tembreull, H. A. Wagner, C. R. Williamson

Founded: 1905
Domicile: Delaware
Employees: 21,900

STANDARD &POOR'S

Pactiv Corp

S&P Recommendation BUY ★★★★★

Price $31.07 (as of Oct 30, 2006)

12-Mo. Target Price $35.00

Investment Style Mid-Cap Growth

GICS Sector Materials
Sub-Industry Metal & Glass Containers

Comment Pactiv Corp., spun off by Tenneco in 1999, is a leading provider of advanced packaging solutions for consumer, institutional and industrial markets.

Key Stock Statistics (Source S&P, Vickers, company reports)

52-Wk Range	$31.75–19.02	S&P Oper. EPS 2006E	1.60	P/E on S&P Oper. EPS 2006E	19.4	Dividend Rate/Share	Nil
Trailing 12-Month EPS	$1.80	S&P Oper. EPS 2007E	1.80	Common Shares Outstg. (M)	138.0	Yield (%)	Nil
Trailing 12-Month P/E	17.3	S&P Core EPS 2006E	1.32	Market Capitalization(B)	$4.287	Beta	0.88
$10K Invested 5 Yrs Ago	$18,647	S&P Core EPS 2007E	1.63	Institutional Ownership (%)	87	S&P Credit Rating	NA

Price Performance

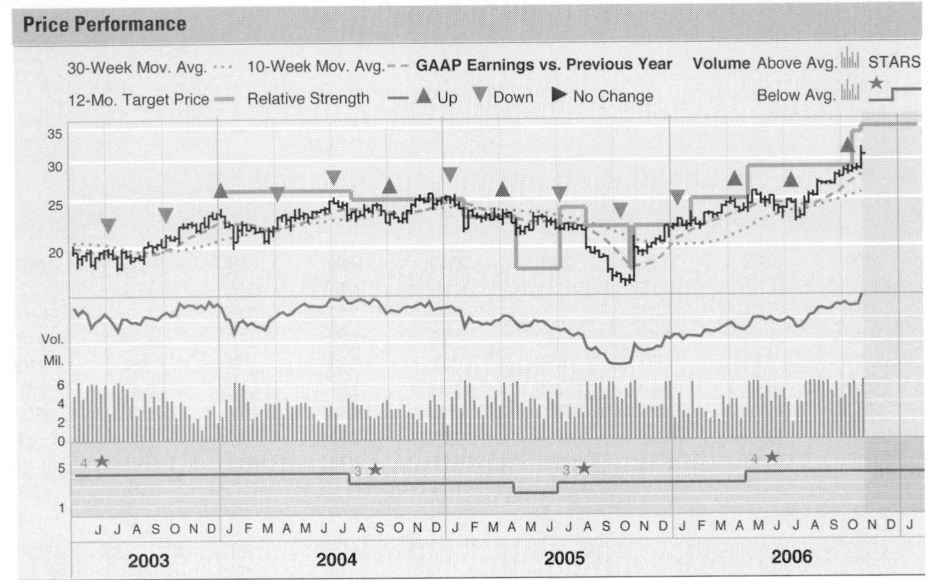

Options: ASE, Ph

Analysis prepared by **Stewart Scharf** on October 30, 2006, when the stock traded at **$ 30.90**.

Highlights

- We expect net sales to rise 7% in 2006, primarily based on pricing initiatives, which should offset soft volume, especially in food packaging. We see a sequential rebound based on demand for new consumer products, such as Hefty's foam tableware and waste bag products, while new business should aid food packaging volume.
- We expect gross margins (before D&A) to widen during 2006, to approach 31%, from 26% in 2005, reflecting a better product mix and pricing pass-throughs, and stabilizing resin costs later in the year. EBITDA margins should be about 20%, versus 2005's 16.6%, on price hikes, improved productivity and a sharp drop in launch costs. We think SG&A expenses will remain near 10% of sales, while pretax pension income should add $42 million to earnings.
- We estimate a tax rate of near 37% in 2006, and operating EPS of $1.60 (before $0.14 foreign exchange and $0.21 tax adjustment gains; on 6% few shares), advancing to $1.80 in 2007. Our S&P Core EPS estimates are $1.32 and $1.63, respectively, reflecting pension adjustments.

Investment Rationale/Risk

- We maintain our buy recommendation, based on our valuation models and our expectations of stabilizing resin costs following a recent decline in fuel prices.
- Risks to our recommendation and target price include a significant rise in resin prices, a soft global economy that may force some customers to shift to lower-priced private label products, and a negative effect from foreign currencies. Regarding corporate governance, we are concerned that the positions of chairman and CEO are held by the same person.
- We blend DCF with relative metrics to arrive at our 12-month target price of $35. Our DCF model, which assumes a 3% terminal growth rate and an 8.5% weighted average cost of capital (WACC), shows intrinsic value of $36. We apply a P/E of 21.5X to our 2006 EPS estimate to arrive at a value of $34. We think this P/E, which is above PTV's five-year historical average and other packaging companies, is justified due to strong demand for new consumer products, brand loyalty and well controlled operating expenses.

Qualitative Risk Assessment

LOW | **MEDIUM** | HIGH

Our risk assessment reflects increased foreign competition and demand for unbranded products, supplier and customer consolidation, and volatile energy costs. However, we believe the balance sheet is improving as it generates cash to pay down debt.

Quantitative Evaluations

S&P Quality Ranking NR

D | C | B- | B | B+ | A- | A | A+

Relative Strength Rank STRONG

89

LOWEST = 1 HIGHEST = 99

Revenue/Earnings Data

Revenue (Million $)

	1Q	2Q	3Q	4Q	Year
2006	680.0	750.0	749.0	--	--
2005	613.0	707.0	695.0	741.0	2,756
2004	775.0	858.0	865.0	884.0	3,382
2003	717.0	810.0	793.0	818.0	3,138
2002	647.0	728.0	727.0	778.0	2,880
2001	695.0	745.0	717.0	710.0	2,812

Earnings Per Share ($)

	1Q	2Q	3Q	4Q	Year
2006	0.35	0.49	0.75	E0.36	E1.60
2005	0.14	0.24	0.28	0.30	0.96
2004	Nil	0.33	0.37	0.31	1.01
2003	0.27	0.37	0.16	0.41	1.21
2002	0.26	0.38	0.37	0.37	1.37
2001	0.18	0.28	0.28	0.29	1.03

Fiscal year ended Dec. 31. Next earnings report expected: Late January. EPS Estimates based on S&P Operating Earnings; historical GAAP earnings are as reported.

Dividend Data

No cash dividends have been paid.

Pactiv Corp

Business Summary October 30, 2006

CORPORATE OVERVIEW. Pactiv Corp., a global supplier of specialty packaging and consumer products, derives more than 80% of its sales from markets in which it holds the No. 1 or No. 2 market-share position. It operates 40 manufacturing plants in four countries. In October 2005, PTV sold most of its protective and flexible packaging divisions to a unit of AEA Investors LLC, an international private equity company. PTV retained its European molded fiber business and Asian operations. In 2005, Wal-Mart accounted for over 15% of sales.

After discontinuing the protective and flexible packaging division during 2005, PTV operated two units: consumer products (Hefty) and foodservice/food packaging. Consumer products sales accounted for 36% of total sales in 2005 ($113 million of operating income, before restructuring charges), and foodservice/food packaging 64% ($191 million, before charges). In 2005, foreign sales accounted for about 10% of the total.

The company manufactures consumer products such as plastic storage bags and waste bags; foam and molded fiber disposable tableware; and disposable aluminum cookware. It sells many products under recognized brand names such as Hefty, Baggies, Hefty One-Zip, Zoo Pals, Kordite, The Gripper, and E-Z Foil. During 2005, PTV rolled out Hefty Serve 'n Store plates and bowls, Hefty Easy Grip part cups, and Hefty E-Z Ovenware disposable casserole pans. The company expects new product innovations in this group to generate $100 million in annual retail sales over the next few years.

PTV makes food packaging products for the food processing industry, including molded fiber egg cartons, foam meat trays, aluminum containers, and modified atmosphere packaging. The company also offers tableware products such as plates, bowls, cups, and takeout-service containers.

We believe the company will maintain its leading brand name position in the specialty packaging industry and will continue to develop new products.

Company Financials

Per Share Data ($) Year Ended Dec. 31	2005	2004	2003	2002	2001	2000	1999	1998	1997	1996
Tangible Book Value	0.23	0.98	0.77	1.79	4.91	3.79	2.19	NA	NA	NA
Cash Flow	1.94	2.10	2.24	2.35	2.14	1.84	0.43	1.43	NA	NA
Earnings	0.96	1.01	1.21	1.37	1.03	0.70	-0.67	0.39	NA	NA
S&P Core Earnings	0.56	0.64	1.00	-0.23	-0.57	NA	NA	NA	NA	NA
Dividends	Nil	Nil	Nil	Nil	Nil	Nil	Nil	NA	NA	NA
Payout Ratio	Nil	Nil	Nil	Nil	Nil	Nil	Nil	NA	NA	NA
Prices:High	25.58	25.73	24.03	24.47	18.10	13.31	14.50	NA	NA	NA
Prices:Low	16.50	19.80	17.55	15.35	11.26	7.50	9.31	NA	NA	NA
P/E Ratio:High	27	25	20	18	18	19	NM	NA	NA	NA
P/E Ratio:Low	17	20	15	11	11	11	NM	NA	NA	NA
Income Statement Analysis (Million $)										
Revenue	2,756	3,382	3,138	2,880	2,812	3,134	2,921	2,791	NA	NA
Operating Income	452	954	630	617	574	570	498	466	NA	NA
Depreciation	146	169	163	158	177	185	184	175	NA	NA
Interest Expense	82.0	101	96.0	96.0	107	134	146	164	NA	NA
Pretax Income	224	244	314	367	284	207	-159	124	NA	NA
Effective Tax Rate	36.2%	36.9%	37.6%	39.8%	41.5%	44.0%	NM	46.0%	NA	NA
Net Income	143	155	195	220	165	113	-112	66.0	NA	NA
S&P Core Earnings	82.3	96.9	160	-36.1	-91.1	NA	NA	NA	NA	NA
Balance Sheet & Other Financial Data (Million $)										
Cash	172	222	140	127	41.0	26.0	12.0	18.0	NA	NA
Current Assets	820	1,079	982	904	740	900	866	1,031	NA	NA
Total Assets	2,820	3,741	3,706	3,412	4,060	4,341	4,588	4,749	NA	NA
Current Liabilities	456	984	474	501	459	512	920	1,703	NA	NA
Long Term Debt	869	869	1,336	1,224	1,211	1,560	1,741	1,186	NA	NA
Common Equity	820	1,083	1,061	897	1,689	1,539	1,350	1,286	NA	NA
Total Capital	1,802	2,209	2,617	2,282	3,502	3,595	3,432	2,848	NA	NA
Capital Expenditures	121	100	112	126	145	135	1,129	NA	NA	NA
Cash Flow	289	324	358	378	342	298	72.0	241	NA	NA
Current Ratio	1.8	1.1	2.1	1.8	1.6	1.8	0.9	0.6	NA	NA
% Long Term Debt of Capitalization	48.2	39.3	51.1	53.6	34.6	43.4	50.7	41.6	NA	NA
% Net Income of Revenue	5.2	4.6	6.2	7.6	5.9	3.6	NM	2.4	NA	NA
% Return on Assets	4.4	4.2	5.5	5.9	4.0	2.5	NM	NA	NA	NA
% Return on Equity	15.0	14.5	19.9	17.0	10.2	7.8	NM	NA	NA	NA

Data as orig reptd.; bef. results of disc opers/spec. items. Per share data adj. for stk. divs.; EPS diluted. E-Estimated. NA-Not Available. NM-Not Meaningful. NR-Not Ranked. UR-Under Review.

Office: 1900 West Field Court, Lake Forest, IL 60045-4828.
Telephone: 847-482-2000.
Email: investorrelations@pactiv.com
Website: http://www.pactiv.com

Chrmn, Pres & CEO: R.L. Wambold
SVP & CFO: A.A. Campbell
VP, Secy & General Counsel: J.V. Faulkner, Jr.

Board of Directors: L. D. Brady, K. D. Brooksher, R. J. Darnall, M. R. Henderson, N. T. Linebarger, R. B. Porter, R. L. Wambold, N. H. Wesley

Founded: 1965
Domicile: Delaware
Employees: 11,100

STANDARD &POOR'S

Pall Corp

S&P Recommendation HOLD ★★★★★

Price $31.25 (as of Oct 27, 2006)

12-Mo. Target Price $32.00

Investment Style Mid-Cap Growth

GICS Sector Industrials
Sub-Industry Industrial Machinery

Comment This company is a leading producer of filters for the health care, aerospace, microelectronics and other industries.

Key Stock Statistics (Source S&P, Vickers, company reports)

52-Wk Range	$32.44–25.26	S&P Oper. EPS 2007E	1.50	P/E on S&P Oper. EPS 2007E	20.8	Dividend Rate/Share	$0.44
Trailing 12-Month EPS	$1.16	S&P Oper. EPS 2008E	1.70	Common Shares Outstg. (M)	122.2	Yield (%)	1.41
Trailing 12-Month P/E	26.9	S&P Core EPS 2007E	1.55	Market Capitalization(B)	$3.820	Beta	1.32
$10K Invested 5 Yrs Ago	$15,492	S&P Core EPS 2008E	1.75	Institutional Ownership (%)	91	S&P Credit Rating	A-

Price Performance

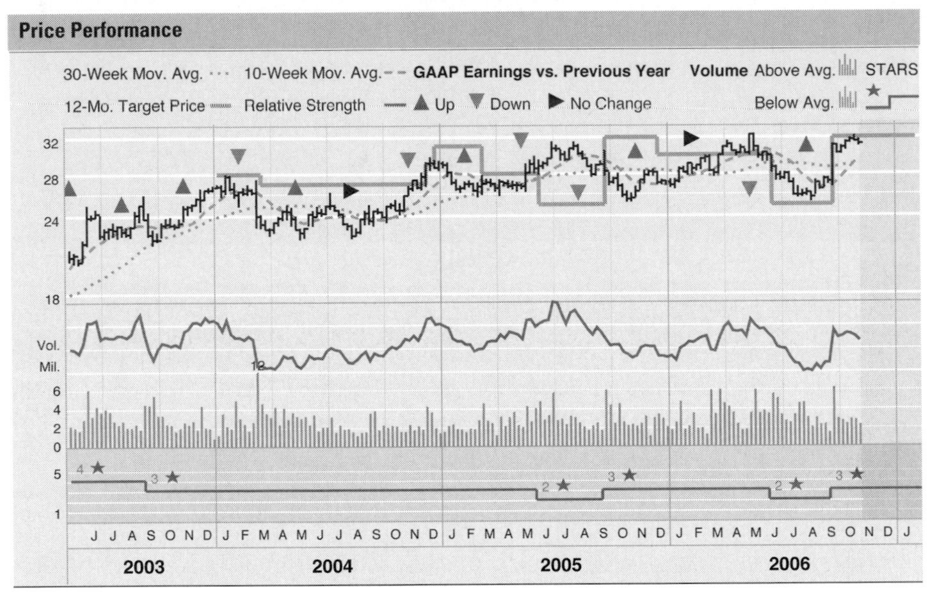

Options: CBOE

Analysis prepared by **Stewart Scharf** on September 15, 2006, when the stock traded at **$ 30.94**.

Highlights

- We expect sales to advance at least 5% in FY 07, driven by global strength in both general industrial and life sciences. In our view, sales of power generation, biopharm, and machinery and equipment will drive volume growth, while we see a slowdown in the microelectronics sector later in the fiscal year. We expect a slow but steady recovery in the blood filtration and hospital products segment.
- Gross margins should widen in FY 07 from FY 06's 46.8%, as price increases and improved productivity--especially later in the fiscal year--offset higher energy and commodities costs. We also see a gradual rebound in systems margins as replacement filters are ordered and systems become operational. We expect EBITDA margins to widen during FY 07, on cost-cutting initiatives in Europe and other regions, and we think SG&A expense will decline by 50 basis points, to about 31%.
- We forecast a tax rate of 24%, and project FY 07 EPS of $1.50 (before projected restructuring charges of $0.12), growing 13%, to $1.70 for FY 08.

Investment Rationale/Risk

- We recently upgraded our opinion on the shares to hold from sell, based on our valuation models and our view of favorable global market trends, and our belief that the company will continue to reduce costs during a transitional effort to reduce costs.
- Risks to our recommendation and target price include an extended cyclical downturn in the semiconductor sector, a weaker machinery and equipment business in Europe, negative foreign currencies against the U.S. dollar, and a further significant rise in raw material costs. In addition, corporate governance practices are a concern to us as one or more related party transactions involved the CEO.
- The stock recently traded at 20X our FY 07 EPS estimate, a modest premium to peers. However, the shares were at a discount to intrinsic value of $33, based on our DCF model, which assumes a terminal growth rate of 3.5% and a cost of capital of 8.3%. Blending our metrics, we apply a P/E of 21.5X to our FY 07 EPS projection, on par with PLL's five-year historical average forward P/E, and our 12-month target price is $32.

Qualitative Risk Assessment

LOW | **MEDIUM** | HIGH

Our risk assessment reflects the historically cyclical semiconductor sector, exposure to foreign markets and currency swings, and certain concerns that we have related to corporate governance practices. This is offset by our view of PLL's reduced debt levels and strong cash generation.

Quantitative Evaluations

S&P Quality Ranking B+

D | C | B- | B | **B+** | A- | A | A+

Relative Strength Rank MODERATE

66

LOWEST = 1 HIGHEST = 99

Revenue/Earnings Data

Revenue (Million $)

	1Q	2Q	3Q	4Q	Year
2006	431.2	478.4	510.0	597.3	2,017
2005	414.7	469.5	493.5	524.5	1,902
2004	374.3	428.1	463.9	504.5	1,771
2003	332.2	388.5	421.5	471.4	1,614
2002	274.1	285.4	302.4	428.9	1,291
2001	278.2	304.7	321.1	331.5	1,235

Earnings Per Share ($)

	1Q	2Q	3Q	4Q	Year
2006	0.20	0.26	0.20	0.50	1.16
2005	0.17	0.26	0.35	0.34	1.12
2004	0.19	0.20	0.37	0.44	1.20
2003	-0.19	0.25	0.33	0.44	0.83
2002	0.16	0.15	0.21	0.07	0.59
2001	0.21	0.24	0.30	0.21	0.95

Fiscal year ended Jul. 31. Next earnings report expected: Early December. EPS Estimates based on S&P Operating Earnings; historical GAAP earnings are as reported.

Dividend Data (Dates: mm/dd Payment Date: mm/dd/yy)

Amount ($)	Date Decl.	Ex-Div. Date	Stk. of Record	Payment Date
0.110	01/19	02/01	02/03	02/17/06
0.110	04/12	04/24	04/26	05/10/06
0.110	07/18	07/31	08/02	08/17/06
0.110	10/25	11/07	11/09	11/24/06

Dividends have been paid since 1974. Source: Company reports.

Pall Corp

Business Summary September 15, 2006

CORPORATE OVERVIEW. Pall Corp. is a global producer of filters for health care, aerospace and industrial markets. Pall divides these markets into the following subsegments: Medical and BioPharmaceuticals (Life Sciences), General Industrial, Aerospace, and Microelectronics (the Industrial business). The company's Industrial group includes machinery and equipment, food and beverage, fuels and chemicals, power generation, and municipal water.

The Industrial segment (61% of segment revenues in FY 06; $166 million in profits) makes filters and separation products for three markets. Aerospace (16% of the segment; $32 million in profits) includes both commercial and military markets. General Industrial (63%; $72 million in profits) produces filters for the aluminum, paper, automobile, oil, gas, chemical, petrochemical and power industries. Microelectronics (21%; $63 million in profits) makes products for the semiconductor, data storage and photographic film industries. PLL noted that over $300 million in FY 06 sales were derived from water filtration, with municipalities accounting for 22%.

The Life Sciences segment contributed 39% of total revenues ($142 million in operating profits) in FY 06 (Jul.). The BioPharmaceuticals division makes filter products used in the development of drugs, and food and beverage filters that help produce yeast- and bacteria-free water. The rapidly growing blood division offers hospitals and blood centers blood filters that reduce leukocyte (white cells) and other bloodborne viral contaminants, such as bacteria. Biopharmaceutical sales accounted for 44% of the segment's total sales in FY 06 ($88 million), while medical products (blood and cardiovascular filtration) accounted for 56% ($54 million). PLL estimates the market potential for medical filters at $4.3 billion.

In FY 06, sales were: Western Hemisphere, 40%; Europe 36%; and Asia 24%.

In June 2005, the company expanded its global strategic alliance with GE Infrastructure, Water & Process Technologies, a unit of General Electric (GE; NYSE). The companies should continue to combine their advanced membrane technologies and separation solutions to increase applications, including desalination, water reuse and municipal water. In our view, GE's June 2006 acquisition of ZENON Environmental Inc., a Canadian-based provider of membrane products and services, will not have an adverse effect on PLL's alliance with GE.

Company Financials

Per Share Data ($) Year Ended Jul. 31	2006	2005	2004	2003	2002	2001	2000	1999	1998	1997
Tangible Book Value	7.21	6.73	6.21	5.16	NM	6.29	5.41	5.09	5.32	5.84
Cash Flow	1.92	1.85	1.90	1.51	1.19	1.53	1.68	1.01	1.33	1.03
Earnings	1.16	1.12	1.20	0.83	0.59	0.95	1.18	0.41	0.75	0.53
S&P Core Earnings	1.22	1.13	1.16	0.70	0.42	0.83	NA	NA	NA	NA
Dividends	0.53	0.38	0.27	0.36	0.52	0.68	0.50	0.64	0.61	0.54
Payout Ratio	46%	34%	23%	43%	88%	71%	42%	156%	81%	102%
Prices:High	32.44	31.52	29.80	27.00	24.48	26.25	25.00	26.19	26.63	26.13
Prices:Low	25.26	25.21	22.00	15.01	14.68	17.50	17.13	15.75	19.38	19.50
P/E Ratio:High	28	28	25	33	41	28	21	64	36	49
P/E Ratio:Low	22	23	18	18	25	18	15	38	26	37
Income Statement Analysis (Million $)										
Revenue	2,017	1,902	1,771	1,614	1,291	1,235	1,224	1,147	1,087	1,062
Operating Income	341	337	320	299	215	256	274	160	216	182
Depreciation	95.7	90.9	88.9	83.9	74.0	71.5	63.4	74.8	73.1	62.8
Interest Expense	23.0	26.0	20.5	24.4	14.3	16.6	14.1	18.4	7.87	2.84
Pretax Income	210	181	198	143	100.0	150	188	58.9	135	86.1
Effective Tax Rate	30.8%	22.2%	23.4%	27.9%	26.7%	21.5%	22.2%	12.6%	30.6%	21.8%
Net Income	145	141	152	103	73.2	118	147	51.5	93.6	67.3
S&P Core Earnings	153	142	148	87.4	52.1	102	NA	NA	NA	NA
Balance Sheet & Other Financial Data (Million $)										
Cash	318	165	199	127	105	54.9	81.0	86.7	12.1	18.0
Current Assets	1,377	1,160	1,070	938	916	779	753	744	602	607
Total Assets	2,553	2,265	2,140	2,017	2,027	1,549	1,507	1,488	1,347	1,266
Current Liabilities	531	457	419	421	438	314	438	558	394	301
Long Term Debt	640	510	489	490	620	359	224	117	112	62.1
Common Equity	1,179	1,140	1,054	935	820	770	761	731	766	825
Total Capital	1,826	1,660	1,559	1,439	1,478	1,149	1,006	869	899	915
Capital Expenditures	96.0	86.2	61.3	62.2	69.9	77.8	66.5	71.2	85.1	88.6
Cash Flow	241	232	241	187	147	190	210	126	167	130
Current Ratio	2.6	2.5	2.6	2.2	2.1	2.5	1.7	1.3	1.5	2.0
% Long Term Debt of Capitalization	35.0	30.7	31.3	34.0	41.9	31.2	22.3	13.4	12.4	6.8
% Net Income of Revenue	7.2	7.4	8.6	6.4	5.7	9.6	12.0	4.5	8.6	6.3
% Return on Assets	6.0	6.3	7.3	5.1	NA	7.7	9.8	3.6	7.2	5.5
% Return on Equity	12.5	12.8	15.2	11.8	NA	15.4	19.7	6.9	11.8	8.6

Data as orig reptd.; bef. results of disc opers/spec. items. Per share data adj. for stk. divs.; EPS diluted. E-Estimated. NA-Not Available. NM-Not Meaningful. NR-Not Ranked. UR-Under Review.

Office: 2200 Northern Boulevard, Greenvale, NY 11548.
Telephone: 516-484-5400.
Email: invrel@pall.com
Website: http://www.pall.com

Chrmn & CEO: E. Krasnoff
Pres: M. Wilson
COO: D. Stevens
SVP, Secy & General Counsel: M. Bartlett

CFO & Treas: L. McDermott
Investor Contact: P. Iannucci (516-801-9848)
Board of Directors: D. J. Carroll, Jr., J. H. Haskell, Jr., U. Haynes, Jr., E. Krasnoff, D. Longstreet, E. W. Martin, Jr., K. L. Plourde, H. Shelley, E. L. Snyder, E. Travaglianti, J. D. Watson, M. Wilson

Founded: 1946
Domicile: New York
Employees: 10,828

Parametric Technology Corp

S&P Recommendation HOLD ★★★★★

Price $19.30 (as of Oct 27, 2006)

12-Mo. Target Price $20.00

Investment Style Mid-Cap Value

GICS Sector Information Technology
Sub-Industry Application Software

Comment This company, a leader in mechanical design automation, is attempting to shift its focus to collaborative product development software solutions.

Key Stock Statistics (Source S&P, Vickers, company reports)

52-Wk Range	**$20.27–11.66**	S&P Oper. EPS 2006**E**	**0.55**	P/E on S&P Oper. EPS 2006**E**	**35.1**	Dividend Rate/Share	**Nil**
Trailing 12-Month EPS	**$0.47**	S&P Oper. EPS 2007**E**	**0.78**	Common Shares Outstg. (M)	**111.6**	Yield (%)	**Nil**
Trailing 12-Month P/E	**41.1**	S&P Core EPS 2006**E**	**0.55**	Market Capitalization(B)	**$2.155**	Beta	**2.65**
$10K Invested 5 Yrs Ago	**$9,834**	S&P Core EPS 2007**E**	**0.78**	Institutional Ownership (%)	**91**	S&P Credit Rating	**NA**

Price Performance

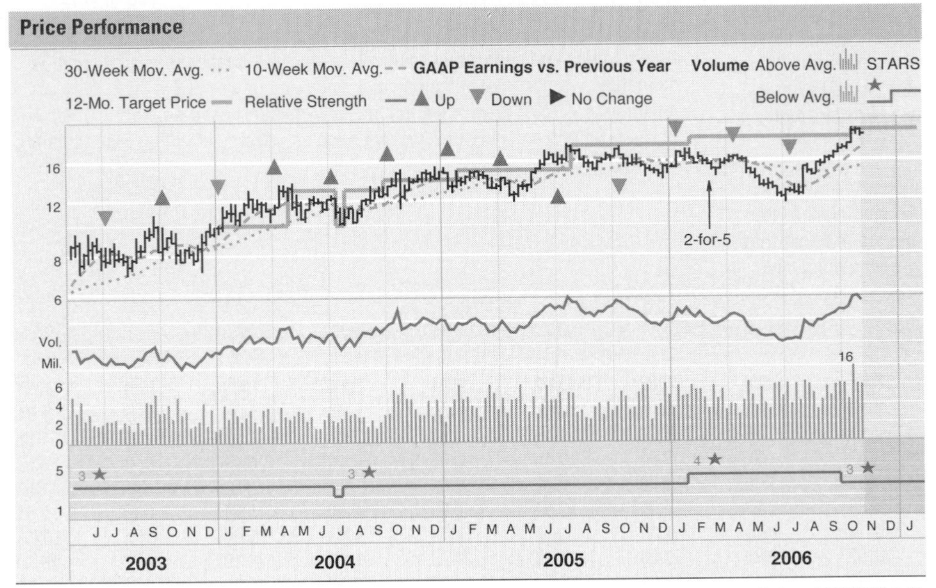

Options: ASE, CBOE, P, Ph

Analysis prepared by **Clyde Montevirgen** on October 13, 2006, when the stock traded at **$ 19.71**.

Highlights

- We see revenues increasing about 19% in FY 06 (Sep.), following 9% growth in FY 05. We project 10% growth in FY 07. We believe results for Windchill, PMTC's solution for product lifecycle management (PLM), have turned the corner with the release of version 8.0, and we expect continued solid growth from the application. We also believe PMTC is finding synergy through selling Windchill products to customers using Pro/E solutions.

- We see operating margins contracting in FY 06, largely due to the impact of stock option expense, but also as a result of PMTC's investments to flesh out its sales channels. Due to these factors, we see pretax margins declining to 9.0% in FY 06, from 12.8% in FY 05. As these investments likely begin to show results in the form of higher-margin sales, providing improved operating leverage, in the second half of FY 06 and into FY 07, we expect margins to recover, driving FY 07 pretax margins to 10.7%.

- We expect operating EPS of $0.55 in FY 06, including $0.35 of projected stock-based compensation expense. In FY 07, we look for EPS of $0.78, including $0.38 of estimated stock-based compensation expense.

Investment Rationale/Risk

- We believe PMTC's focus on small to medium businesses (SMB) and the Asia-Pacific segment should provide double-digit growth prospects. Spending for PLM products should remain strong as larger enterprises and SMBs look to simplify content management internally and across their growing supply chains, in our view. With an improved distribution channel, PMTC should be able to leverage its relationships with large businesses to sell PLM solutions to their suppliers. However, we have a hold recommendation because the stock is trading near our 12-month target price.

- Risks to our opinion and target price include rapidly changing technology, pricing pressures due to intense competition in the PLM and CAD software sectors, difficulty integrating Windchill with Pro/E, and weaker salesforce execution than we anticipate.

- Our 12-month target price of $20 is based on a blend of metrics. Our DCF model, which assumes a 12% weighted average cost of capital and a 3.5% terminal growth rate, shows intrinsic value of $19. An enterprise value to sales multiple of 2.5X, below that of peers, values the shares at $20.

Qualitative Risk Assessment

LOW | MEDIUM | **HIGH**

Our risk assessment reflects the historical cyclicality of the design software industry, the lack of visibility in the medium term, and intense competition.

Quantitative Evaluations

S&P Quality Ranking **B-**

D | C | **B-** | B | B+ | A- | A | A+

Relative Strength Rank **STRONG**

88

LOWEST = 1 HIGHEST = 99

Revenue/Earnings Data

Revenue (Million $)

	1Q	2Q	3Q	4Q	Year
2006	192.5	200.2	216.7	--	--
2005	169.2	176.1	180.3	195.1	720.7
2004	156.8	164.7	168.4	170.1	660.0
2003	172.0	171.0	165.2	163.7	671.9
2002	195.4	179.9	178.1	188.6	742.0
2001	234.9	245.1	229.1	225.4	934.6

Earnings Per Share ($)

2006	0.08	0.09	0.15	**E**0.18	**E**0.55
2005	0.18	0.18	0.25	0.15	0.75
2004	-0.25	0.03	0.15	0.38	0.33
2003	-0.10	-0.15	-0.33	-0.35	-0.93
2002	-0.05	-0.18	-0.25	-0.40	-0.90
2001	0.13	0.08	-0.03	-0.25	-0.08

Fiscal year ended Sep. 30. Next earnings report expected: Early November. EPS Estimates based on S&P Operating Earnings; historical GAAP earnings are as reported.

Dividend Data (Dates: mm/dd Payment Date: mm/dd/yy)

Amount ($)	Date Decl.	Ex-Div. Date	Stk. of Record	Payment Date
2-for-5 REV.	--	02/28	--	02/28/06

Source: Company reports.

Parametric Technology Corp

Business Summary October 13, 2006

Parametric Technology has been going through a product transition in recent years. As a result, the company is now organized into two business units, Design Solutions, which includes mechanical computer-aided design (MCAD) products, and Collaboration and Control Solutions, which includes the Windchill product line.

Historically, the company's core business has been developing mechanical CAD/CAM/CAE solutions through its Pro/ENGINEER design software. PMTC is now attempting to leverage its strength in mechanical design software to succeed in shifting its focus to product lifecycle management (PLM) software solutions.

PLM solutions include software and services that use the Internet to assist in the collaborative efforts in developing, building and managing products throughout their entire lifecycle. PLM combines many smaller, formerly isolated markets that address various phases of the product life cycle, including product data management, component and supplier management, visualization and digital mockup, computer-aided design, manufacturing and engineering, enterprise application integration, program and project management, manufacturing planning and maintenance, repair and overhaul.

PMTC reports its results in two product categories: Enterprise Solutions (30% of FY 05 (Sep.) revenues), which includes Windchill, Pro/INTRALINK 8.0, Arbortext Publishing Engine and all other solutions that help companies collaborate, manage and publish information across an extended enterprise; and Desktop Solutions (70%), which includes Pro/ENGINEER, Arbortext Editor and all other solutions that help companies create content and improve desktop productivity. The Windchill enterprise suite enables manufacturers to leverage the Internet in their product development and delivery process from customer driven engineer-to-order through development, manufacturing and retirement. Windchill Link solutions use a series of point solutions that employ the Web-based Windchill architecture; each is designed to address business-critical manufacturing functions.

Company Financials

Per Share Data ($) Year Ended Sep. 30	2005	2004	2003	2002	2001	2000	1999	1998	1997	1996
Tangible Book Value	0.60	1.73	1.35	2.25	2.95	3.68	3.28	3.05	6.31	5.03
Cash Flow	0.98	0.64	-0.54	-0.20	0.64	0.68	1.63	1.22	2.26	1.45
Earnings	0.75	0.33	-0.93	-0.90	-0.08	-0.03	1.08	0.95	2.05	1.30
S&P Core Earnings	0.60	0.03	-1.40	-1.93	-0.85	NA	NA	NA	NA	NA
Dividends	Nil	Nil	Nil	Nil	Nil	Nil	Nil	Nil	Nil	Nil
Payout Ratio	Nil	Nil	Nil	Nil	Nil	Nil	Nil	Nil	Nil	Nil
Prices:High	18.25	15.48	10.88	21.10	42.50	82.19	89.84	90.78	80.31	70.94
Prices:Low	11.83	9.63	4.50	4.10	9.93	18.44	29.22	21.25	46.88	32.34
P/E Ratio:High	24	48	NM	NM	NM	NM	84	96	39	55
P/E Ratio:Low	16	30	NM	NM	NM	NM	27	22	23	25
Income Statement Analysis (Million $)										
Revenue	721	660	672	742	935	928	1,058	1,018	809	600
Operating Income	111	116	-7.09	25.3	117	92.1	294	344	349	222
Depreciation	25.9	35.2	41.6	72.6	76.4	78.8	62.3	29.9	22.4	16.8
Interest Expense	Nil	Nil	Nil	Nil	Nil	0.37	0.62	13.3	Nil	Nil
Pretax Income	91.3	37.0	-82.4	-74.3	-10.9	-5.07	181	204	337	216
Effective Tax Rate	8.45%	6.01%	NM	NM	NM	NM	34.2%	48.2%	35.0%	36.2%
Net Income	83.6	34.8	-98.3	-93.6	-8.21	-3.98	119	106	219	138
S&P Core Earnings	65.2	2.80	-147	-201	-90.5	NA	NA	NA	NA	NA
Balance Sheet & Other Financial Data (Million $)										
Cash	204	295	205	179	217	326	240	206	154	434
Current Assets	424	523	416	501	516	628	705	594	691	562
Total Assets	787	666	578	675	798	925	1,017	833	832	659
Current Liabilities	345	333	298	316	360	362	457	420	187	146
Long Term Debt	Nil	Nil	Nil	Nil	Nil	Nil	Nil	Nil	Nil	Nil
Common Equity	324	242	195	290	400	529	521	327	645	512
Total Capital	324	243	197	290	400	529	521	359	645	512
Capital Expenditures	15.0	10.9	20.8	29.7	61.4	37.0	35.2	36.2	28.0	29.7
Cash Flow	109	70.0	-56.6	-21.0	68.2	74.8	182	136	242	155
Current Ratio	1.2	1.6	1.4	1.6	1.4	1.7	1.5	1.4	3.7	3.8
% Long Term Debt of Capitalization	Nil	Nil	Nil	Nil	Nil	Nil	Nil	Nil	Nil	NM
% Net Income of Revenue	11.6	5.3	NM	NM	NM	NM	11.3	10.4	27.1	23.0
% Return on Assets	11.4	5.5	NM	NM	NM	NM	13.1	12.7	29.4	24.8
% Return on Equity	29.5	15.9	NM	NM	NM	NM	27.9	21.7	37.9	31.2

Data as orig reptd.; bef. results of disc opers/spec. items. Per share data adj. for stk. divs.; EPS diluted. E-Estimated. NA-Not Available. NM-Not Meaningful. NR-Not Ranked. UR-Under Review.

Office: 140 Kendrick Street, Needham , MA, USA 02494.
Telephone: 781-370-5000.
Website: http://www.ptc.com
Chrmn: N. Posternak

Pres & CEO: C.R. Harrison
EVP & CFO: C.F. Moses
SVP, Clerk & General Counsel: A.C. von Staats
Investor Contact: M. Mendola (781-370-6151)

Board of Directors: R. N. Goldman, D. K. Grierson, C. R. Harrison, O. B. Marx, III, J. M. O'Donnell, M. E. Porter, N. G. Posternak

Founded: 1985
Domicile: Massachusetts
Employees: 3,751

STANDARD &POOR'S

Parker-Hannifin Corp

S&P Recommendation	Price	12-Mo. Target Price	Investment Style
HOLD ★★★★★	$82.53 (as of Oct 27, 2006)	$90.00	Large-Cap Value

GICS Sector Industrials
Sub-Industry Industrial Machinery

Comment This Ohio company is a global maker of industrial pumps, valves and hydraulics. Its products are used in everything from jet engines to trucks and autos and utility turbines.

Key Stock Statistics (Source S&P, Vickers, company reports)

52-Wk Range	$88.00–62.31	S&P Oper. EPS 2007E	6.35	P/E on S&P Oper. EPS 2007E	13.0	Dividend Rate/Share	$1.04
Trailing 12-Month EPS	$5.89	S&P Oper. EPS 2008E	6.50	Common Shares Outstg. (M)	120.2	Yield (%)	1.26
Trailing 12-Month P/E	14.0	S&P Core EPS 2007E	6.25	Market Capitalization(B)	$9.921	Beta	1.32
$10K Invested 5 Yrs Ago	$22,767	S&P Core EPS 2008E	6.45	Institutional Ownership (%)	77	S&P Credit Rating	A

Price Performance

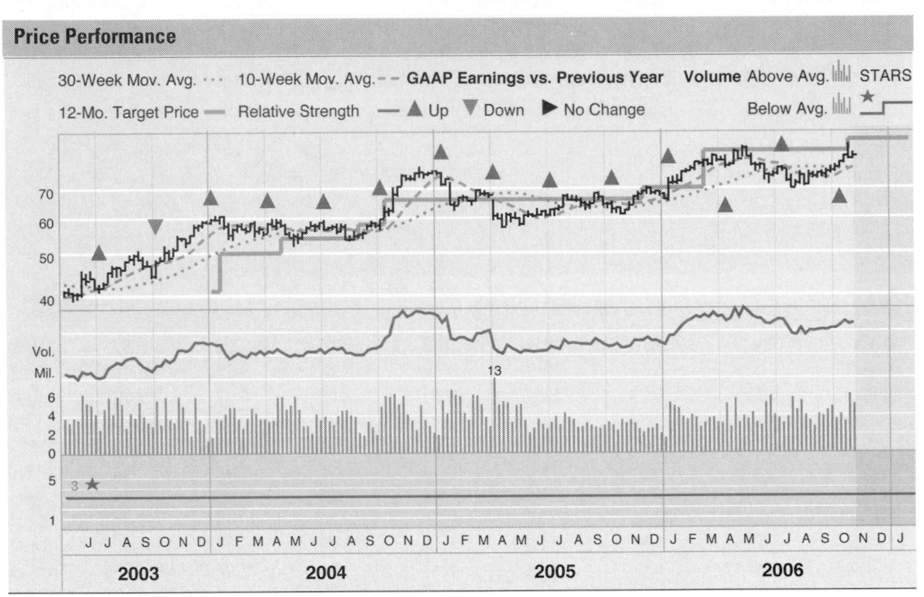

Options: Ph

Analysis prepared by **Richard Tortoriello** on October 25, 2006, when the stock traded at **$ 82.85**.

Highlights

- We anticipate that organic revenues will grow in the high single digits in FY 07 (Jun.), which we see driven by demand in the commercial aviation and international industrial markets. We forecast overall sales growth of 9.7%, excluding future acquisitions. We expect growth to slow in the second half of the fiscal year, due to our expectation of a continued weak automotive market and very tough comparisons in the Climate & Industrial Controls segment. For FY 08 we project 8% growth.
- Based on our projections of volume growth, a better product mix due to increased sales of higher-margin aircraft components, and improving operating efficiencies from ongoing cost containment programs, we expect operating margins to improve, to 14.0% in FY 07 from 13.4% in FY 06.
- We expect a tax rate of 30%, and project FY 07 EPS of $6.35; we project modest growth, to $6.50, in FY 08. We note that free cash flow (cash from operating activities less capital expenditures) per share totaled $6.26 in FY 06, well above reported EPS. We project continued strong free cash flow generation in FY 07.

Investment Rationale/Risk

- Although we expect PH's automotive business to continue to remain soft, we project strong growth for its industrial products, particularly outside the U.S. In addition, we see the current aerospace cycle as very strong, and with commercial airplane orders currently outpacing deliveries and backlogs at aerospace OEMs growing, we expect the strong cycle to continue for several years.
- Risks to our recommendation and target price include declines in global economic growth, leading to a decline in global capital spending, an unexpected downturn in the aerospace market, as well as the potential for production and other product-related problems at PH.
- Our 12-month target price of $90 is based on a P/E ratio of 14X our FY 08 EPS estimate of $6.50. This is slightly above PH's 10-year historical average forward P/E ratio of 13.5X, and well below historical highs of 21X. Given our belief that we are late in the industrial production economic cycle but still early in the aerospace cycle, we believe an average historical P/E ratio is appropriate for the shares.

Qualitative Risk Assessment

LOW | **MEDIUM** | HIGH

Our risk assessment reflects the highly cyclical nature of the company's industrial and aviation markets, volatile energy costs and a competitive environment. This is offset by our view of PH's favorable earnings and dividend track record.

Quantitative Evaluations

S&P Quality Ranking A-

D | C | B- | B | B+ | **A-** | A | A+

Relative Strength Rank MODERATE

68

LOWEST = 1 HIGHEST = 99

Revenue/Earnings Data

Revenue (Million $)

	1Q	2Q	3Q	4Q	Year
2007	2,552	--	--	--	--
2006	2,114	2,158	2,498	2,617	9,386
2005	1,947	1,943	2,142	2,211	8,215
2004	1,587	1,621	1,906	1,993	7,107
2003	1,586	1,517	1,647	1,661	6,411
2002	1,476	1,437	1,578	1,658	6,149

Earnings Per Share ($)

2007	1.75	E1.61	E1.51	E1.48	E6.35
2006	1.19	1.07	1.46	1.55	5.28
2005	1.11	0.94	1.18	1.34	4.55
2004	0.48	0.47	0.90	1.05	2.91
2003	0.52	0.32	0.42	0.42	1.68
2002	0.52	0.25	0.45	-0.10	1.12

Fiscal year ended Jun. 30. Next earnings report expected: Mid January. EPS Estimates based on S&P Operating Earnings; historical GAAP earnings are as reported.

Dividend Data (Dates: mm/dd Payment Date: mm/dd/yy)

Amount ($)	Date Decl.	Ex-Div. Date	Stk. of Record	Payment Date
0.230	01/26	02/14	02/16	03/03/06
0.230	04/20	05/16	05/18	06/02/06
0.260	08/17	08/24	08/28	09/08/06
0.260	10/25	11/14	11/16	12/01/06

Dividends have been paid since 1949. Source: Company reports.

Parker-Hannifin Corp

Business Summary October 25, 2006

CORPORATE OVERVIEW. With $10 billion in annual revenues (our projection for FY 07 (Jun.)), Parker-Hannifin is one of the world's largest makers of components that control the flow of industrial fluids. It is also a major global maker of components that move and/or control the operation of a variety of machinery and equipment. In addition to motion control products, PH also produces fluid purification, fluid and fuel control, process instrumentation, air conditioning, refrigeration, electromagnetic shielding, and thermal management products and systems. PH's offerings include a wide range of valves, pumps, hydraulics, filters and related products. The company's components are used in everything from jet engines to medical devices, farm tractors and utility turbines.

Although U.S. markets still account for most of the company's revenues, PH is expanding its overseas presence; in FY 06 (Jun.), international sales accounted for 34% of total revenues.

PH's Industrial segment (73% of FY 06 revenues; 76% of earnings before interest and taxes (EBIT); and 14% EBIT margins) makes valves, pumps, filters, seals and hydraulic components for a broad range of industries, as well as pneumatic and electromechanical components and systems. The company's industrial components are sold to manufacturers (as part of original equipment) and to end users (as replacement parts). Replacement part sales are generally more profitable than original equipment sales. PH's industrial components are designed for both standard and custom specifications. Custom-made components are typically more profitable than standard components.

Aerospace, PH's most profitable segment (16%; 17%; 15%) primarily makes hydraulic, pneumatic and fuel equipment used in civilian and military airframes and jet engines. It also makes aircraft wheels and brakes for small planes and military aircraft. PH sells aircraft components to aircraft manufacturers as new equipment, and to end-users (such as airlines) as replacement parts. As with industrial components, aircraft-related replacement parts sales are generally more profitable than are original equipment sales.

PH's Climate & Industrial Controls unit (11%; 7%; 9%) makes refrigeration and air conditioning systems and components and fluid control process systems used primarily in the mobile and stationary refrigeration and air conditioning industry.

Company Financials

Per Share Data ($) Year Ended Jun. 30	**2006**	**2005**	**2004**	**2003**	**2002**	**2001**	**2000**	**1999**	**1998**	**1997**
Tangible Book Value	14.63	13.84	14.08	11.45	12.27	13.43	14.94	12.62	11.68	11.32
Cash Flow	7.60	6.75	5.01	3.85	3.55	5.29	5.17	4.68	4.52	3.98
Earnings	5.28	4.55	2.91	1.68	1.12	2.99	3.31	2.83	2.88	2.46
S&P Core Earnings	5.74	4.62	3.00	0.91	0.56	1.78	NA	NA	NA	NA
Dividends	0.92	0.78	0.76	0.74	0.72	0.70	0.51	0.64	0.60	0.51
Payout Ratio	17%	17%	26%	44%	64%	23%	16%	23%	21%	21%
Prices:High	88.00	76.23	78.42	59.80	54.88	50.10	54.00	51.44	52.63	51.25
Prices:Low	65.16	56.80	51.73	35.82	34.52	30.40	31.00	29.50	26.56	24.92
P/E Ratio:High	17	17	27	36	49	17	16	18	18	21
P/E Ratio:Low	12	12	18	21	31	10	9	10	9	10
Income Statement Analysis (Million $)										
Revenue	9,386	8,215	7,107	6,411	6,149	5,980	5,355	4,959	4,633	4,091
Operating Income	1,263	1,100	817	639	628	836	829	741	733	633
Depreciation	281	265	253	259	282	265	206	202	183	170
Interest Expense	75.8	67.0	73.4	81.6	82.0	90.4	59.2	63.7	52.8	46.7
Pretax Income	900	756	494	297	218	534	562	478	504	425
Effective Tax Rate	29.1%	27.6%	30.0%	34.0%	40.3%	35.5%	34.5%	35.0%	35.9%	35.5%
Net Income	638	548	346	196	130	344	368	311	323	274
S&P Core Earnings	694	557	357	107	65.0	204	NA	NA	NA	NA
Balance Sheet & Other Financial Data (Million $)										
Cash	172	336	184	246	46.0	23.7	68.5	33.3	30.5	69.0
Current Assets	3,139	2,786	2,537	2,397	2,236	2,196	2,153	1,775	1,780	1,500
Total Assets	8,173	6,899	6,257	5,986	5,733	5,338	4,646	3,706	3,525	2,999
Current Liabilities	1,681	1,336	1,260	1,424	1,360	1,413	1,186	755	989	716
Long Term Debt	1,059	938	954	966	1,089	857	702	725	513	433
Common Equity	4,241	3,340	2,982	2,521	2,584	2,529	2,309	1,854	1,683	1,547
Total Capital	5,419	4,314	4,015	3,508	3,750	3,518	3,089	2,610	2,226	2,006
Capital Expenditures	198	157	142	158	207	345	230	230	237	189
Cash Flow	919	813	599	455	412	609	575	513	506	444
Current Ratio	1.9	2.1	2.0	1.7	1.6	1.6	1.8	2.3	1.8	2.1
% Long Term Debt of Capitalization	19.6	21.8	23.8	27.5	29.0	24.4	22.7	27.8	23.0	21.6
% Net Income of Revenue	6.8	6.7	4.9	3.1	2.1	5.8	6.9	6.3	7.0	6.7
% Return on Assets	8.5	8.3	5.6	3.3	2.3	6.9	8.8	8.6	9.9	9.3
% Return on Equity	16.8	17.3	12.6	7.7	5.1	14.2	17.7	17.6	20.0	18.7

Data as orig reptd.; bef. results of disc opers/spec. items. Per share data adj. for stk. divs.; EPS diluted. E-Estimated. NA-Not Available. NM-Not Meaningful. NR-Not Ranked. UR-Under Review.

Office: 6035 Parkland Boulevard, Cleveland, OH 44124-4141.
Telephone: 216-896-3000.
Website: http://www.parker.com
Chrmn & CEO: D.E. Washkewicz

Pres & COO: N.W. Vande Steeg
EVP & CFO: T.K. Pistell
VP & Treas: P. Huggins
VP, Secy & General Counsel: T.A. Piraino, Jr.

Investor Contact: C. Groudle (216-896-3000)
Board of Directors: W. E. Kassling, R. J. Kohlhepp, G. Mazzaupi, K. Mueller, C. Obourn, J. Scaminace, W. R. Schmitt, M. I. Tambakeras, N. W. Vande Steeg, D. E. Washkewicz

Founded: 1924
Domicile: Ohio
Employees: 57,073

STANDARD &POOR'S

Patterson Companies Inc

S&P Recommendation STRONG SELL ★★★★★

Price $33.21 (as of Oct 27, 2006)

12-Mo. Target Price $27.00

Investment Style Mid-Cap Growth

GICS Sector Health Care
Sub-Industry Health Care Distributors

Comment PDCO is one of the largest distributors of dental supplies in North America and also sells veterinary supplies and rehabilitative equipment.

Key Stock Statistics (Source S&P, Vickers, company reports)

52-Wk Range	**$43.15–29.61**	S&P Oper. EPS 2007**E**	**1.50**	P/E on S&P Oper. EPS 2007**E**	**22.1**	Dividend Rate/Share	**Nil**
Trailing 12-Month EPS	**$1.42**	S&P Oper. EPS 2008**E**	**1.60**	Common Shares Outstg. (M)	**139.0**	Yield (%)	**Nil**
Trailing 12-Month P/E	**23.4**	S&P Core EPS 2007**E**	**1.50**	Market Capitalization(B)	**$4.615**	Beta	**-0.30**
$10K Invested 5 Yrs Ago	**$17,571**	S&P Core EPS 2008**E**	**1.60**	Institutional Ownership (%)	**78**	S&P Credit Rating	**NA**

Price Performance

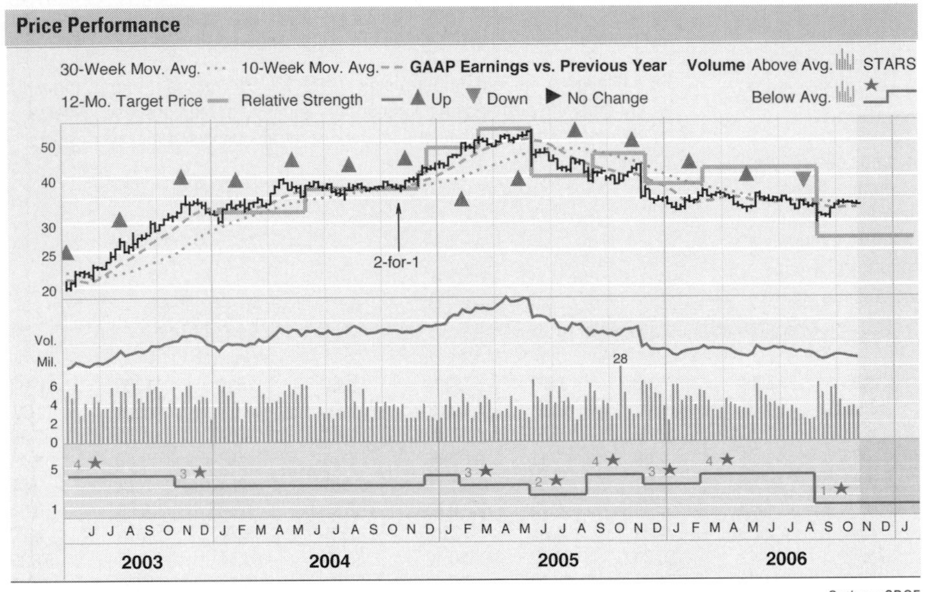

Options: CBOE

Analysis prepared by **Richard Tortoriello** on August 29, 2006, when the stock traded at **$ 30.98**.

Highlights

- We see a strong dental supply market, driven by various trends, including aging baby boomers, increased cosmetic dentistry, and a shortage of dentists (creating a need for equipment that increases their productivity). Although PDCO's sales growth in FY 06 (Apr.) declined to 3%, from 23% in FY 05 and FY 04, we see sales growth recovering to 10% in FY 07, and we estimate further growth of 9% in FY 08.
- However, we are concerned about PDCO's recent trend toward declining growth in net income, reflecting deteriorating trends in margins, in our view. Operating margins fell to 10.5% in the first quarter of FY 07, from an average of 12.4% in FY 06 and 13.6% in FY 05. We project an operating margin of 11.3% in FY 07. We believe that risk factors include slower sales of higher-margin advanced dental equipment, including CEREC; slow growth and the need for investment in the Patterson Medical business (12% of FY 06 sales); and continued weak margins in the Webster Veterinary business (13%).
- We estimate EPS of $1.50 in FY 07, including projected stock option expense of $0.04, and we project $1.60 for FY 08.

Investment Rationale/Risk

- We believe PDCO's past growth was derived, to a large extent, from a strong dental salesforce (now totaling over 1,500), with an excellent training program and good compensation. However, eroding margins lead us to believe that this salesforce may no longer be enough to drive strong growth amid a competitive dental market. In addition, we see a drag on profit growth from the 2004 acquisitions of the Patterson Medical and Webster Veterinary units. We expect a multiple contraction in the shares until corrective actions begin to produce renewed bottom-line growth.
- Risks to our recommendation and target price primarily include a better than expected performance in PDCO's operating segments, leading to improved profit margins and EPS growth.
- Our 12-month target price of $27 is based on a P/E of 17X our FY 08 EPS estimate of $1.60, significantly below PDCO's 10-year average historical forward P/E of 22X, with a low of 14X. This P/E ratio is in line with the current 2006 P/E for the S&P MidCap 400 Index of 17X, based on S&P EPS estimates.

Qualitative Risk Assessment

LOW | **MEDIUM** | HIGH

Our risk assessment is based on our view of PDCO's strong long-term record of earnings growth, offset by its record of high valuation multiples relative to the overall stock market. Because of these high multiples, we view the company as vulnerable to price declines in the event of an earnings disappointment.

Quantitative Evaluations

S&P Quality Ranking **B+**

D | C | B- | B | **B+** | A- | A | A+

Relative Strength Rank **MODERATE**

34

LOWEST = 1 HIGHEST = 99

Revenue/Earnings Data

Revenue (Million $)

	1Q	2Q	3Q	4Q	Year
2007	655.5	--	--	--	--
2006	595.9	641.7	682.4	695.2	2,615
2005	577.9	578.2	638.0	627.3	2,421
2004	433.3	477.5	521.2	537.4	1,969
2003	387.7	400.8	421.1	447.3	1,657
2002	303.3	355.0	357.4	399.9	1,416

Earnings Per Share ($)

2007	0.30	**E**0.34	**E**0.40	**E**0.46	**E**1.50
2006	0.31	0.32	0.39	0.41	1.43
2005	0.29	0.31	0.36	0.36	1.32
2004	0.22	0.26	0.29	0.33	1.09
2003	0.19	0.20	0.22	0.25	0.85
2002	0.15	0.17	0.18	0.20	0.70

Fiscal year ended Apr. 30. Next earnings report expected: Late November. EPS Estimates based on S&P Operating Earnings; historical GAAP earnings are as reported.

Dividend Data

No cash dividends have been paid.

Patterson Companies Inc

Business Summary August 29, 2006

Patterson Companies (formerly Patterson Dental), one of two large distributors of dental products in North America, is a full-service supplier to dentists, dental laboratories, institutions, physicians, and other health care professionals. Through the July 2001 acquisition of J.A. Webster, PDCO became the second largest U.S. distributor of companion-pet veterinary supplies. Also, through the August 2003 acquisition of AbilityOne Products Corp. (now Patterson Medical), PDCO became the largest distributor of non-wheelchair assistive products for patient rehabilitation in the U.S. and the U.K.

The company's strategy is to emphasize its value-added, full-service capabilities--using technology to enhance customer service--improve operating efficiencies, and grow through internal expansion and acquisitions. PDCO plans to grow its businesses, through both internal growth and acquisitions, at four percentage points higher than market growth. The company estimates that the U.S. dental market is increasing at 7%-9% per year, the rehabilitation market (which includes the U.K.) is growing at 6%-8%, and the veterinary market is growing at 5%-7%. PDCO also seeks to lower its operating margin, through cost efficiencies, by 0.5% per year.

PDCO's Patterson Dental subsidiary, 76% of FY 05 (Apr.) sales, provides a broad range of consumables (X-ray film, restorative materials, and sterilization products), advanced technology dental equipment, practice management software, and office forms and stationery.

Consumables and printed products accounted for 54% of dental supply sales in FY 05, down from 57% in FY 04. The company offers its own private label line of anesthetics, instruments, preventative and restorative products, as well as brand name supplies, including X-ray film, protective clothing, toothbrushes, and other dental accessories. Printed products include insurance and billing forms, stationery, appointment books, and other stock office supply products.

PDCO offers a wide range of dental equipment, which accounted for 37% of dental supply sales in FY 05, up from 34% in FY 04. The product line includes X-ray machines, sterilizers, dental chairs, dental lights and diagnostic equipment. Two of PDCO's fastest growing product lines are the CEREC chairside ceramic dental-restorative system and digital radiography (X-ray) systems.

Company Financials

Per Share Data ($) Year Ended Apr. 30	**2006**	**2005**	**2004**	**2003**	**2002**	**2001**	**2000**	**1999**	**1998**	**1997**
Tangible Book Value	2.73	1.95	0.76	3.66	2.85	2.64	2.08	1.62	1.22	0.91
Cash Flow	1.60	1.52	1.27	0.94	0.80	0.65	0.55	0.43	0.36	0.30
Earnings	1.43	1.32	1.09	0.85	0.70	0.57	0.48	0.37	0.31	0.25
S&P Core Earnings	1.39	1.30	1.08	0.84	0.70	0.57	NA	NA	NA	NA
Dividends	Nil	Nil	Nil	Nil	Nil	Nil	Nil	Nil	Nil	Nil
Payout Ratio	Nil	Nil	Nil	Nil	Nil	Nil	Nil	Nil	Nil	Nil
Calendar Year	2005	2004	2003	2002	2001	2000	1999	1998	1997	1996
Prices:High	53.85	44.20	35.75	27.56	21.03	17.25	12.53	11.59	7.63	6.15
Prices:Low	33.21	29.70	17.71	19.00	13.75	8.13	8.28	7.03	4.46	3.33
P/E Ratio:High	38	33	33	32	30	31	26	31	25	25
P/E Ratio:Low	23	22	16	22	20	14	17	19	14	13
Income Statement Analysis (Million $)										
Revenue	2,615	2,421	1,969	1,657	1,416	1,156	1,040	879	778	662
Operating Income	347	329	262	192	161	391	205	86.6	72.7	56.8
Depreciation	23.7	20.9	19.4	12.8	14.3	11.1	10.2	8.20	7.46	6.19
Interest Expense	13.4	15.1	9.60	0.07	0.11	0.12	0.13	0.52	0.67	0.56
Pretax Income	317	293	240	186	152	122	103	79.7	65.7	52.0
Effective Tax Rate	37.4%	37.4%	37.6%	37.6%	37.4%	37.4%	37.4%	37.4%	38.0%	37.6%
Net Income	198	184	150	116	95.3	76.5	64.5	49.9	40.8	32.4
S&P Core Earnings	194	180	147	115	95.3	76.5	NA	NA	NA	NA
Balance Sheet & Other Financial Data (Million $)										
Cash	224	233	287	195	126	160	113	78.7	35.6	9.10
Current Assets	847	800	778	606	529	443	351	287	228	164
Total Assets	1,912	1,685	1,589	824	718	549	452	373	316	244
Current Liabilities	410	322	264	184	198	133	113	98.7	94.4	69.8
Long Term Debt	210	302	480	0.13	Nil	Nil	Nil	1.68	2.74	2.79
Common Equity	1,243	1,015	802	634	514	409	330	265	210	163
Total Capital	1,502	1,363	1,325	634	514	409	330	269	215	167
Capital Expenditures	49.2	31.5	19.6	11.4	11.1	10.0	15.4	7.09	5.96	4.94
Cash Flow	222	211	169	129	110	87.6	74.7	58.1	48.2	38.6
Current Ratio	2.1	2.5	2.9	3.3	2.7	3.3	3.1	2.9	2.4	2.4
% Long Term Debt of Capitalization	14.0	22.1	36.2	Nil	Nil	Nil	Nil	0.6	1.2	1.7
% Net Income of Revenue	7.6	7.6	7.6	7.0	6.7	6.6	6.2	5.7	5.2	4.9
% Return on Assets	11.0	11.2	12.4	15.1	15.0	15.3	15.6	14.5	14.5	14.5
% Return on Equity	17.6	20.2	20.8	20.3	20.7	20.7	21.6	21.0	21.9	24.2

Data as orig reptd.; bef. results of disc opers/spec. items. Per share data adj. for stk. divs.; EPS diluted. E-Estimated. NA-Not Available. NM-Not Meaningful. NR-Not Ranked. UR-Under Review.

Office: 1031 Mendota Heights Road, St. Paul, MN 55120-1419.
Telephone: 612-686-1600.
Email: investors@pattersondental.com
Website: http://www.pattersondental.com

Chrmn: P.L. Frechette
Pres & CEO: J.W. Wiltz
Investor Contact: R.S. Armstrong (651-686-1600)
EVP, CFO & Treas: R.S. Armstrong

Secy & General Counsel: M.L. Levitt
Board of Directors: R. E. Ezerski, P. L. Frechette, A. B. Lacy, C. Reich, E. A. Rudnick, H. C. Slavkin, J. W. Wiltz

Founded: 1877
Domicile: Minnesota
Employees: 6,440

STANDARD &POOR'S

Paychex Inc

S&P Recommendation HOLD ★★★★★

Price $39.45 (as of Oct 27, 2006)

12-Mo. Target Price $39.00

Investment Style Large-Cap Growth

GICS Sector Information Technology
Sub-Industry Data Processing & Outsourced Services

Comment Paychex provides payroll accounting services to small and medium size concerns throughout the U.S.

Key Stock Statistics (Source S&P, Vickers, company reports)

52-Wk Range	$43.37–32.98	S&P Oper. EPS 2007E	1.39	P/E on S&P Oper. EPS 2007E	28.4	Dividend Rate/Share	$0.84
Trailing 12-Month EPS	$1.27	S&P Oper. EPS 2008E	1.58	Common Shares Outstg. (M)	380.4	Yield (%)	2.13
Trailing 12-Month P/E	31.1	S&P Core EPS 2007E	1.39	Market Capitalization(B)	$15.008	Beta	1.08
$10K Invested 5 Yrs Ago	$12,164	S&P Core EPS 2008E	1.58	Institutional Ownership (%)	68	S&P Credit Rating	NA

Price Performance

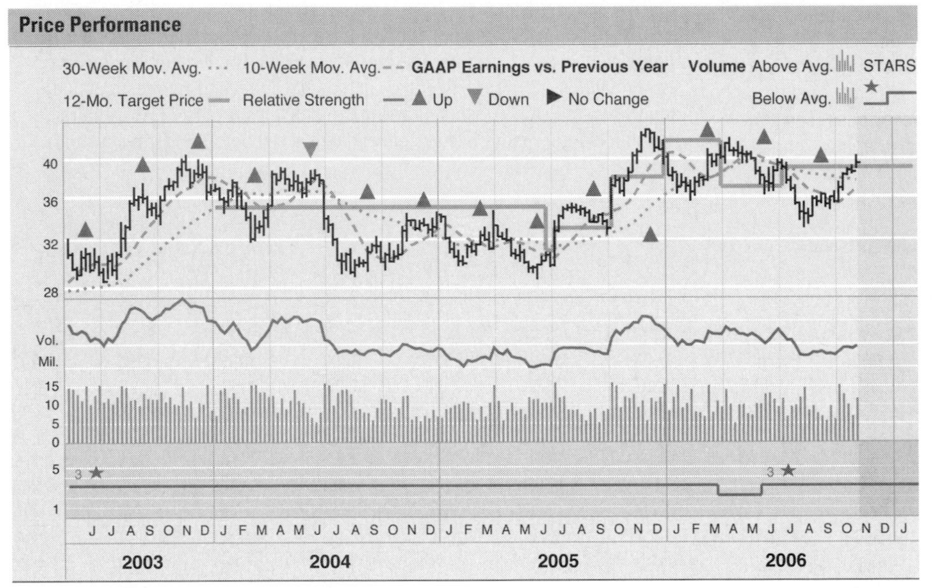

Options: CBOE, P, Ph

Analysis prepared by **Dylan Cathers** on September 29, 2006, when the stock traded at **$ 36.82**.

Highlights

- We look for revenues to increase 13% in FY 07 (May) and 11% in FY 08, versus a 16% advance in FY 06. We expect revenue growth to be aided by increased income on funds held for clients, which has risen due to higher short-term interest rates.
- We project FY 07 growth in the core payroll client base in the low single digits, including further penetration of add-on services such as Taxpay and direct deposit. We expect the HR business to increase 21%, versus 31% growth in FY 06. We look for payroll, which is PAYX's largest segment, at 79% of service revenue in the August quarter, to increase around 9% in FY 07, versus 14% last year.
- We foresee operating margins in FY 07 at 39%, roughly in line with those seen in FY 06, as we believe expenses from rising personnel levels and promotion of new products will largely offset solid cost controls, reduced attrition levels, and high customer retention rates. We estimate EPS in FY 07 of $1.39, including projected stock option expense. For FY 08, we forecast EPS of $1.58, which also includes estimated stock option expense.

Investment Rationale/Risk

- Our hold recommendation is based on valuation. We see the company's earnings benefiting from solid execution, higher retention rates, falling attrition, increased interest earned on funds held for clients, and strong profitability levels.
- Risks to our recommendation and target price stem from volatility in the small to medium-sized business environment; and the impact of competition on pricing and margins. Automatic Data Processing (ADP: strong buy, $47) is the leader in the payroll processing space, and is promoting a payroll processing and tax filing software solution coupled with Microsoft's small business software. We see this product potentially affecting Paychex's growth in the small office market.
- Using our calendar 2006 EPS estimate of $1.31, we blend valuations based on a peer-based P/E multiple of 30X and a P/E to growth (PEG) ratio of 1.65X to arrive at our 12-month target price of $39, a slight premium to its peers. The peer group includes comparable data processing and outsourcing companies that offer solutions that compete with PAYX.

Qualitative Risk Assessment

LOW | **MEDIUM** | HIGH

Our risk assessment reflects what we see as the company's strong balance sheet and regular cash inflows, offset by the highly competitive nature of the outsourcing industry as well as the threat of new entrants into the human resources segment.

Quantitative Evaluations

S&P Quality Ranking A+

D | C | B- | B | B+ | A- | A | **A+**

Relative Strength Rank MODERATE

70

LOWEST = 1 HIGHEST = 99

Revenue/Earnings Data

Revenue (Million $)

	1Q	2Q	3Q	4Q	Year
2007	459.4	--	--	--	--
2006	403.7	399.8	430.6	440.5	1,675
2005	345.0	347.3	373.9	379.0	1,445
2004	309.3	312.1	342.6	330.4	1,294
2003	252.7	268.8	287.8	289.8	1,099
2002	234.8	233.0	242.8	244.3	954.9

Earnings Per Share ($)

2007	0.35	E0.33	E0.35	E0.36	E1.39
2006	0.30	0.30	0.30	0.32	1.22
2005	0.23	0.23	0.24	0.27	0.97
2004	0.21	0.21	0.21	0.16	0.80
2003	0.20	0.20	0.19	0.19	0.78
2002	0.19	0.18	0.18	0.18	0.73

Fiscal year ended May 31. Next earnings report expected: Late December. EPS Estimates based on S&P Operating Earnings; historical GAAP earnings are as reported.

Dividend Data (Dates: mm/dd Payment Date: mm/dd/yy)

Amount ($)	Date Decl.	Ex-Div. Date	Stk. of Record	Payment Date
0.160	01/13	01/30	02/01	02/15/06
0.160	04/13	04/27	05/01	05/15/06
0.160	07/13	07/28	08/01	08/15/06
0.210	10/05	10/30	11/01	11/15/06

Dividends have been paid since 1988. Source: Company reports.

Paychex Inc

Business Summary September 29, 2006

CORPORATE OVERVIEW. Paychex is a leading provider of payroll processing, human resources and benefits services. The company was founded in 1971, and began by serving the payroll accounting services of businesses with fewer than 200 employees. It currently has more than 100 locations and serves more than 522,000 clients throughout the U.S.

The company's payroll segment prepares payroll checks, earnings statements, internal accounting records, all federal, state and local payroll tax returns, and provides collection and remittance of payroll obligations. PAYX's tax filing and payment services provide automatic tax filing and payment, preparation and submission of tax returns, plus deposit of funds with tax authorities. Employee Payment Services provides a variety of ways for businesses to pay employees.

In our opinion, PAYX has shown an ability to expand its client base (up 3.4% in FY 05 (May)) and increase the use of ancillary services, which we believe will lead to consistent growth for its mainstay payroll segment.

The Human Resources/Professional Employer Organization (HRS/PEO) segment provides employee benefits, management and human resources services. The Paychex Administrative Services (PAS) product offers businesses a bundled package that includes payroll, employer compliance, and human resource and employee benefit administration. PAYX also offers 401(k) plan services.

MARKET PROFILE. PAYX's primary market is the payroll service market, which, according to market researcher IDC, totaled about $10.1 billion in calendar 2004 (latest available). With payroll-related revenue of about $990 million in 2004, IDC estimates that the company captured 9.8% of the market, a slight decline from 2003. It is the second-largest payroll-outsourcing provider behind Automatic Data Processing.

Company Financials

Per Share Data ($) Year Ended May 31	**2006**	**2005**	**2004**	**2003**	**2002**	**2001**	**2000**	**1999**	**1998**	**1997**
Tangible Book Value	3.12	2.40	1.88	1.55	2.43	2.00	1.50	1.18	0.90	0.69
Cash Flow	1.39	1.13	1.02	0.89	0.80	0.75	0.57	0.43	0.33	0.25
Earnings	1.22	0.97	0.80	0.78	0.73	0.68	0.51	0.37	0.28	0.20
S&P Core Earnings	1.17	0.93	0.80	0.72	0.66	0.65	NA	NA	NA	NA
Dividends	0.51	0.47	0.44	0.33	0.33	0.22	0.18	0.12	0.08	0.07
Payout Ratio	42%	48%	55%	56%	45%	32%	35%	32%	29%	35%
Calendar Year	2005	2004	2003	2002	2001	2000	1999	1998	1997	1996
Prices:High	43.37	39.12	40.54	42.15	51.00	61.25	29.92	24.47	15.33	12.57
Prices:Low	28.60	28.83	23.76	20.39	28.27	24.17	15.71	13.37	7.56	6.02
P/E Ratio:High	36	40	51	54	70	90	59	66	55	63
P/E Ratio:Low	23	30	30	26	39	36	31	36	27	30
Income Statement Analysis (Million $)										
Revenue	1,675	1,445	1,294	1,099	955	870	728	597	494	400
Operating Income	716	596	516	444	393	700	283	210	153	112
Depreciation	66.5	62.0	82.8	43.4	29.5	26.4	23.9	22.1	18.8	15.3
Interest Expense	Nil	Nil	Nil	Nil	Nil	Nil	Nil	Nil	Nil	Nil
Pretax Income	675	546	450	432	395	364	275	200	144	104
Effective Tax Rate	31.1%	32.5%	32.6%	32.0%	30.5%	30.0%	31.0%	30.5%	29.1%	27.5%
Net Income	465	369	303	293	275	255	190	139	102	75.2
S&P Core Earnings	445	353	304	272	252	243	NA	NA	NA	NA
Balance Sheet & Other Financial Data (Million $)										
Cash	137	281	219	79.9	61.9	45.8	47.1	343	251	183
Current Assets	4,444	3,689	3,280	3,033	2,815	2,791	2,363	1,793	1,479	1,141
Total Assets	5,549	4,379	3,950	3,691	2,953	2,907	2,456	1,873	1,550	1,201
Current Liabilities	3,838	2,942	2,722	2,588	2,023	2,144	1,887	1,432	1,216	946
Long Term Debt	Nil	Nil	Nil	Nil	Nil	Nil	Nil	Nil	Nil	Nil
Common Equity	1,670	1,411	1,235	1,077	924	745	563	436	330	252
Total Capital	1,686	1,429	1,249	1,084	924	745	563	436	330	252
Capital Expenditures	81.1	70.7	50.6	60.2	54.4	45.3	32.9	22.1	28.2	18.0
Cash Flow	531	431	386	337	304	281	214	161	121	90.5
Current Ratio	1.2	1.3	1.2	1.2	1.4	1.3	1.3	1.3	1.2	1.2
% Long Term Debt of Capitalization	Nil	Nil	Nil	Nil	Nil	Nil	Nil	Nil	Nil	Nil
% Net Income of Revenue	27.8	25.5	23.4	26.7	28.7	29.3	26.1	23.3	20.7	18.8
% Return on Assets	9.1	8.9	7.9	8.8	9.4	9.5	8.8	8.1	7.4	7.4
% Return on Equity	30.2	27.9	26.2	29.3	32.6	38.7	38.0	36.3	35.2	34.0

Data as orig reptd.; bef. results of disc opers/spec. items. Per share data adj. for stk. divs.; EPS diluted. E-Estimated. NA-Not Available. NM-Not Meaningful. NR-Not Ranked. UR-Under Review.

Office: 911 Panorama Trail South, Rochester, NY 14625-2396.
Telephone: 585-385-6666.
Website: http://www.paychex.com
Chrmn: B.T. Golisano

Pres & CEO: J.J. Judge
SVP, CFO & Secy: J.M. Morphy
VP & Cntlr: M. Janik
Investor Contact: T.J. Allen (585-383-3406)

Board of Directors: D. J. Flaschen, B. T. Golisano, P. Horsley, G. M. Inman, P. A. Joseph, J. J. Judge, J. M. Tucci

Founded: 1979
Domicile: Delaware
Employees: 10,900

STANDARD &POOR'S

J. C. Penney Company Inc.

S&P Recommendation HOLD ★★★★★ | **Price** $76.25 (as of Oct 27, 2006) | **12-Mo. Target Price** $70.00 | **Investment Style** Large-Cap Value

GICS Sector Consumer Discretionary
Sub-Industry Department Stores

Comment JCP is the leading mall-based family department store operator in the U.S., with about 1,021 retail locations and catalog/Internet operations.

Key Stock Statistics (Source S&P, Vickers, company reports)

52-Wk Range	$77.76–49.51	S&P Oper. EPS 2007E	4.58	P/E on S&P Oper. EPS 2007E	16.6	Dividend Rate/Share	$0.72
Trailing 12-Month EPS	$4.78	S&P Oper. EPS 2008E	5.15	Common Shares Outstg. (M)	224.2	Yield (%)	0.94
Trailing 12-Month P/E	16.0	S&P Core EPS 2007E	4.48	Market Capitalization(B)	$17.096	Beta	1.21
$10K Invested 5 Yrs Ago	$34,750	S&P Core EPS 2008E	5.05	Institutional Ownership (%)	94	S&P Credit Rating	BBB-

Price Performance

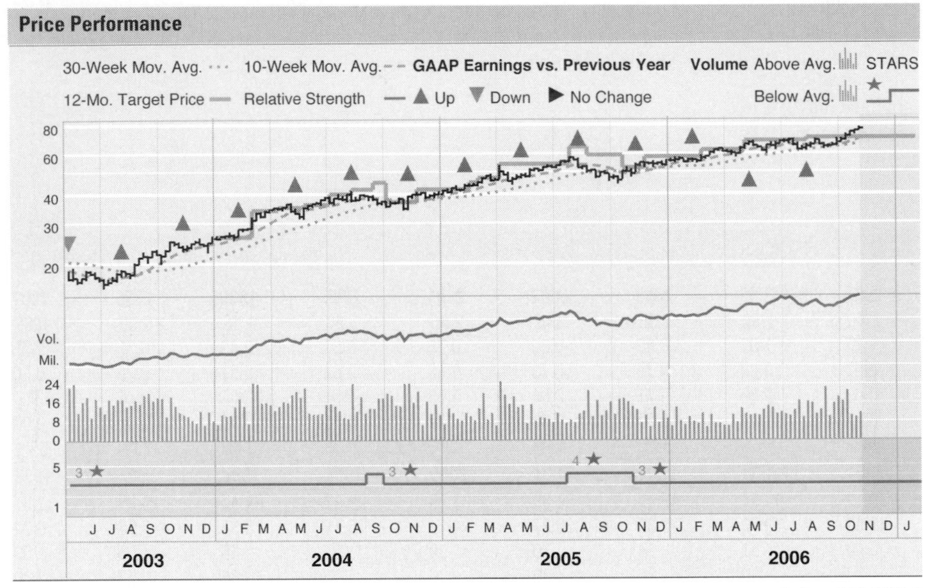

Options: ASE, CBOE, P

Analysis prepared by **Jason N. Asaeda** on August 15, 2006, when the stock traded at **$ 67.45**.

Highlights

- In FY 07 (Jan.), we expect net sales of $19.7 billion, with $16.8 billion in retail sales and over $2.9 billion in direct sales. At retail, we look for same-store sales to increase 3% to 4%, supported by increased newness in assortments and a promotional calendar. We expect fine jewelry, children's apparel, and women's accessories to be among JCP's best performing categories. We also look for sales of women's apparel to improve on pay off of the company's investments in new brands such as a.n.a, which have generated significant marketing buzz.
- We project operating margins to widen 70 basis points, to 9.1%, on increased sales penetration of higher-margin private brands, expense controls, and efficiencies in JCP's growing direct business, partly offset by promotional markdowns and stock option expensing.
- Factoring in likely share buybacks, we estimate FY 07 operating EPS of $4.58 and S&P Core EPS of $4.48, with the difference reflecting projected pension and post-retirement costs.

Investment Rationale/Risk

- In an effort to broaden its consumer appeal, JCP recently announced a partnership with cosmetics retailer Sephora to open Sephora shops within JCP stores, as well as plans to reduce the cycle time of new merchandise, particularly fashion assortments. We see the planned addition of brand name cosmetics and the promise of faster turning assortments as pluses for JCP's business, but we do not expect much near-term benefit, as we think the company will roll out both initiatives slowly to reduce execution risk. We do see an appreciable lift to sales and earnings from FY 08 on, especially as JCP plans to accelerate its off-mall expansion.
- Risks to our recommendation and target price include sales shortfalls due to unforeseen shifts in fashion trends and consumer discretionary spending patterns, as well as competitive pressures.
- Our 12-month target price of $70 is derived from our DCF analysis, which assumes a weighted average cost of capital of 9.6% and a terminal growth rate of 2.5%.

Qualitative Risk Assessment

LOW | **MEDIUM** | HIGH

Our risk assessment reflects our view of JCP's improving sales and profit margins, increasing market share in the moderate department store sector, and what we see as a healthy balance sheet and cash flow, offset by uncertainty over consumer discretionary spending in light of rising interest rates and debt levels.

Quantitative Evaluations

S&P Quality Ranking B-

D | C | **B-** | B | B+ | A- | A | A+

Relative Strength Rank STRONG

85

LOWEST = 1 HIGHEST = 99

Revenue/Earnings Data

Revenue (Million $)

	1Q	2Q	3Q	4Q	Year
2007	4,220	4,238	--	--	--
2006	4,192	3,981	4,479	6,203	18,781
2005	4,033	3,857	4,461	6,073	18,424
2004	7,493	7,313	7,985	6,098	17,786
2003	7,728	7,198	7,872	9,549	32,347
2002	7,522	7,211	7,729	9,542	32,004

Earnings Per Share ($)

	1Q	2Q	3Q	4Q	Year
2007	0.90	0.75	E1.08	E1.85	E4.58
2006	0.63	0.46	0.94	1.92	3.83
2005	0.38	0.23	0.53	1.16	2.23
2004	0.05	-0.03	0.31	0.83	1.21
2003	0.29	-0.05	0.30	0.68	1.25
2002	0.13	-0.23	0.09	0.32	0.32

Fiscal year ended Jan. 31. Next earnings report expected: Mid November. EPS Estimates based on S&P Operating Earnings; historical GAAP earnings are as reported.

Dividend Data (Dates: mm/dd Payment Date: mm/dd/yy)

Amount ($)	Date Decl.	Ex-Div. Date	Stk. of Record	Payment Date
0.125	12/07	01/06	01/10	02/01/06
0.180	03/22	04/06	04/10	05/01/06
0.180	05/19	07/06	07/10	08/01/06
0.180	09/22	10/05	10/10	11/01/06

Dividends have been paid since 1922. Source: Company reports.

J. C. Penney Company Inc.

Business Summary August 15, 2006

CORPORATE OVERVIEW. Over the past decade, JCP has shed its image as a mass merchandiser, transforming itself into what we consider to be the leading mall-based family department store operator, with 1,021 JCPenney stores in 49 states and Puerto Rico, as of July 29, 2006. The company has also adeptly responded to the needs of time-strapped shoppers, in our view, with the improved shopping convenience afforded by its direct business, comprised of JCPenney catalogs and the jcpenney.com Web site, as well as its growing off-mall retail presence.

CORPORATE STRATEGY. From 2000 to 2005, JCP executed a turnaround plan to improve the profitability of its JCPenney stores. The company focused on delivering competitive, fashionable merchandise assortments; developing a compelling and appealing marketing program; improving store environments; reducing its expense structure; and attracting and retaining an experienced and professional work force. In support of these objectives, JCP moved from decentralized to centralized merchandising, marketing and operating functions, and invested in a new store distribution network and in new merchandise planning, allocation and replenishment systems.

With what we view as the success of its turnaround, JCP has mapped out a new 2005-2009 plan for making JCPenney the preferred shopping choice for "Middle America", which it defines as customers aged 35 to 54 with annual household incomes of $35,000 to $85,000. Key strategies include offering styles that make an emotional connection with the customer; making it easier for the customer to shop seamlessly across store/catalog/Internet channels; creating and sustaining a customer-focused culture; and using the off-mall store format to expand the company's presence in high-potential markets.

Company Financials

Per Share Data ($) Year Ended Jan. 31	**2006**	**2005**	**2004**	**2003**	**2002**	**2001**	**2000**	**1999**	**1998**	**1997**
Tangible Book Value	17.20	17.92	18.54	12.04	11.46	NM	14.28	15.04	15.50	15.73
Cash Flow	5.79	3.33	2.68	3.45	3.00	0.36	3.87	4.40	4.46	4.13
Earnings	3.83	2.23	1.21	1.25	0.32	-2.29	1.16	2.19	2.10	2.29
S&P Core Earnings	3.77	2.26	1.24	0.66	0.15	-2.47	NA	NA	NA	NA
Dividends	0.50	0.50	0.50	0.50	0.50	0.50	2.19	2.18	2.14	2.08
Payout Ratio	13%	22%	41%	40%	156%	NM	188%	100%	102%	91%
Calendar Year	2005	2004	2003	2002	2001	2000	1999	1998	1997	1996
Prices:High	57.99	41.82	26.42	27.75	29.50	22.50	54.44	78.75	68.25	57.00
Prices:Low	40.26	25.29	15.57	14.07	10.50	8.63	17.69	42.63	44.88	44.00
P/E Ratio:High	15	19	22	22	92	NM	47	36	32	25
P/E Ratio:Low	11	11	10	11	33	NM	15	19	21	19

Income Statement Analysis (Million $)	2006	2005	2004	2003	2002	2001	2000	1999	1998	1997
Revenue	18,781	18,424	17,786	32,347	32,004	31,846	32,510	30,678	30,546	22,653
Operating Income	1,949	1,600	1,184	1,881	1,473	873	1,681	2,253	1,687	1,075
Depreciation	372	368	394	667	717	695	710	637	584	381
Interest Expense	169	233	261	388	386	427	673	663	648	414
Pretax Income	1,444	1,020	546	584	203	-886	531	955	925	909
Effective Tax Rate	32.3%	34.6%	33.3%	36.5%	43.8%	NM	36.7%	37.8%	38.8%	37.8%
Net Income	977	667	345	371	114	-568	336	594	566	565
S&P Core Earnings	960	662	345	171	41.0	-650	NA	NA	NA	NA

Balance Sheet & Other Financial Data (Million $)	2006	2005	2004	2003	2002	2001	2000	1999	1998	1997
Cash	3,016	4,687	2,994	2,474	2,840	944	1,233	96.0	287	131
Current Assets	6,702	8,427	6,515	8,353	8,677	7,257	8,472	11,125	11,484	11,712
Total Assets	12,461	14,127	18,300	17,867	18,048	19,742	20,888	23,638	23,493	22,088
Current Liabilities	2,762	3,447	3,754	4,159	4,499	4,235	4,465	5,970	6,137	7,966
Long Term Debt	3,444	3,464	5,114	4,940	5,179	5,448	5,844	7,143	6,986	4,565
Common Equity	4,007	4,856	5,121	6,037	5,766	5,860	6,782	6,694	6,831	5,526
Total Capital	8,738	9,638	11,756	12,701	12,539	12,843	14,087	15,829	15,668	11,879
Capital Expenditures	535	412	373	658	631	648	631	744	824	704
Cash Flow	1,349	1,023	733	1,011	802	94.0	1,010	1,193	1,110	946
Current Ratio	2.4	2.4	1.7	2.0	1.9	1.7	1.9	1.9	1.9	1.5
% Long Term Debt of Capitalization	39.4	35.9	43.5	38.9	41.3	42.4	41.5	45.1	44.6	38.4
% Net Income of Revenue	5.2	3.6	2.0	1.1	0.4	NM	1.0	1.9	1.9	2.5
% Return on Assets	7.3	4.1	2.0	2.1	0.1	NM	1.5	2.5	2.5	2.9
% Return on Equity	22.0	13.1	6.1	5.8	1.9	NM	4.5	8.2	8.6	9.5

Data as orig reptd.; bef. results of disc opers/spec. items. Per share data adj. for stk. divs.; EPS diluted. E-Estimated. NA-Not Available. NM-Not Meaningful. NR-Not Ranked. UR-Under Review.

Office: 6501 Legacy Drive, Plano, TX 75024-3698.
Telephone: 972-431-1000.
Website: http://www.jcpenney.net
Chrmn & CEO: M.E. Ullman, III

Pres: K.C. Hicks
COO & EVP: C.G. West
EVP & CFO: R.B. Cavanaugh
EVP, Secy & General Counsel: J.L. Bober

Investor Contact: R. Johnson (972-431-8167)
Board of Directors: C. C. Barrett, A. Burns, M. Clark, T. J. Engibous, K. B. Foster, V. E. Jordan, Jr., B. Osborne, L. H. Roberts, M. Stone West, A. M. Tallman, R. G. Turner, M. C. Ullman, III

Founded: 1902
Domicile: Delaware
Employees: 151,000

STANDARD &POOR'S

Peoples Energy Corp

S&P Recommendation HOLD ★★★★★

Price $43.49 (as of Oct 27, 2006)

12-Mo. Target Price $43.00

Investment Style Mid-Cap Value

GICS Sector Utilities
Sub-Industry Gas Utilities

Comment This diversified energy company focuses on gas distribution, power generation, oil and gas production, asset-based gas wholesaling, and retail energy services.

Key Stock Statistics (Source S&P, Vickers, company reports)

52-Wk Range	**$44.00–34.88**	S&P Oper. EPS 2006**E**	**1.47**	P/E on S&P Oper. EPS 2006**E**	**29.6**	Dividend Rate/Share	**$2.18**
Trailing 12-Month EPS	**$0.03**	S&P Oper. EPS 2007**E**	**2.00**	Common Shares Outstg. (M)	**38.5**	Yield (%)	**5.01**
Trailing 12-Month P/E	**NM**	S&P Core EPS 2006**E**	**1.47**	Market Capitalization(B)	**$1.673**	Beta	**0.44**
$10K Invested 5 Yrs Ago	**$14,416**	S&P Core EPS 2007**E**	**2.00**	Institutional Ownership (%)	**67**	S&P Credit Rating	**A-**

Price Performance

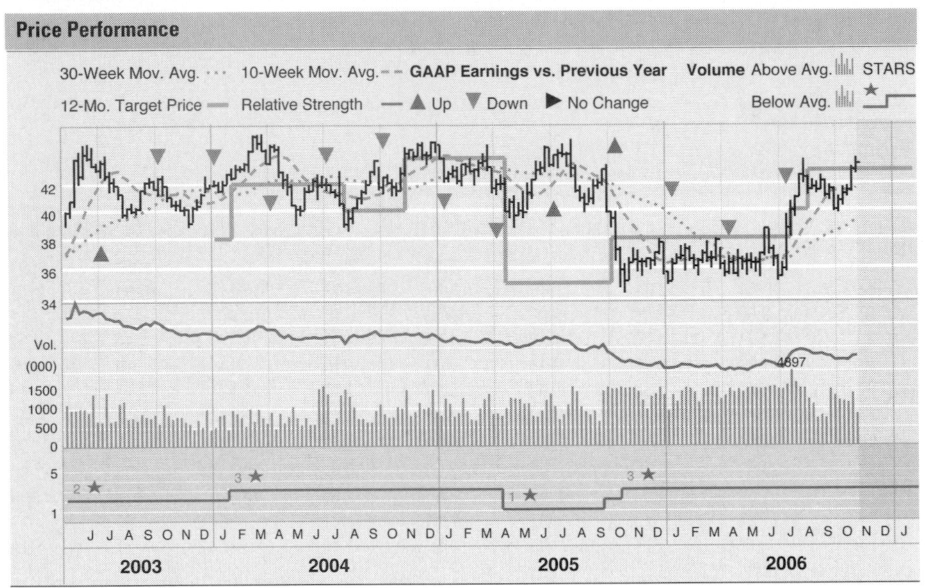

Options: P

Analysis prepared by **Ari Bensinger** on August 11, 2006, when the stock traded at **$ 41.48**.

Highlights

- We expect lower gas deliveries in FY 06 (Sep.), reflecting warmer than normal weather and less weather-normalized demand due to high natural gas prices. Weather insurance recoveries should partly offset the impact of projected lower demand. We see results restricted by higher labor costs and bad debt expense.

- We project high single digit growth in oil and gas production despite slightly higher production costs and lower production volumes on increased realized prices as lower priced hedges roll off. Power generation and midstream services should see a slight improvement in earnings, aided by a better market for wholesale power and gas and natural gas liquids. Retail energy services should see 10%-12% growth, spurred by greater marketing efforts an and expansion into new service areas, as well as increased energy marketing margins.

- With higher pension expense and an increased share count, but less interest expense and a lower effective tax rate, we see FY 06 EPS of $1.47, below the $2.26 operating EPS posted in FY 05.

Investment Rationale/Risk

- In July 2006, PGL announced an agreement to merge with WPS Resources Corp. (WPS: $51; hold). The planned merger is expected to be completed by the end of the second quarter of FY 07, pending necessary approvals. We see PGL's utility operations facing a near-term earnings squeeze due to high natural gas prices, which we think will pressure its ability to secure in full any proposed rate hikes. Although we expect PGL to resume earnings growth in FY 07, based on favorable trends in its E&P business, we think its long-term EPS prospects are weaker than peers in our coverage universe.

- Risks to our recommendation and target price include a prolonged rise in natural gas prices, lower than expected oil and gas production, sharply higher interest rates, and milder than normal winter weather.

- Our 12-month target price of $43 is based on our view that the proposed deal with WPS is likely to be consummated. Under the terms of the planned transaction, each PGL share would be converted into 0.825 shares of WPS.

Qualitative Risk Assessment

LOW | MEDIUM | HIGH

Our risk assessment is based on our view that most of the company's earnings are derived from less volatile regulated businesses. We think the company's diversification into upstream and midstream operations also contributes to a lower risk profile.

Quantitative Evaluations

S&P Quality Ranking **B**

D | C | B- | B | B+ | A- | A | A+

Relative Strength Rank **MODERATE**

67

LOWEST = 1 HIGHEST = 99

Revenue/Earnings Data

Revenue (Million $)

	1Q	2Q	3Q	4Q	Year
2006	1,052	1,180	400.5	--	--
2005	737.4	1,027	455.9	379.3	2,600
2004	604.9	927.0	401.1	327.2	2,260
2003	549.1	903.8	398.2	287.3	2,138
2002	377.6	522.8	347.2	235.0	1,483
2001	717.0	1,074	318.5	161.0	2,270

Earnings Per Share ($)

	1Q	2Q	3Q	4Q	Year
2006	-0.51	0.87	-0.35	**E**-0.29	**E**1.47
2005	0.59	1.34	0.18	-0.06	2.05
2004	0.85	1.46	0.15	-0.27	2.18
2003	0.87	1.77	0.22	0.04	2.87
2002	0.87	1.55	0.04	0.05	2.51
2001	1.03	1.76	0.33	0.38	2.74

Fiscal year ended Sep. 30. Next earnings report expected: Late October. EPS Estimates based on S&P Operating Earnings; historical GAAP earnings are as reported.

Dividend Data (Dates: mm/dd Payment Date: mm/dd/yy)

Amount ($)	Date Decl.	Ex-Div. Date	Stk. of Record	Payment Date
0.545	01/31	03/20	03/22	04/13/06
0.545	06/07	06/20	06/22	07/14/06
0.545	08/02	09/20	09/22	10/13/06
0.545	08/02	09/20	09/22	10/13/06

Dividends have been paid since 1937. Source: Company reports.

Please read the Required Disclosures and Analyst Certification on the last page of this report.

Peoples Energy Corp

Business Summary August 11, 2006

CORPORATE OVERVIEW. Peoples Energy is a Chicago-based utility with diverse unregulated operations in power generation, midstream natural gas services, oil and gas production and retail energy services. PGL's regulated gas utilities (Peoples Gas and North Shore Gas) purchase, store, distribute, sell and transport natural gas through a 6,000-mile distribution system that serves Chicago and 54 communities in northeastern Illinois. At the end of FY 05 (Sep.), the utilities served about 969,000 customers.

The Power Generation segment partly owns two natural gas fired power plants near Chicago, representing 1,750 megawatts (MW) of generating capacity. Midstream Services provides wholesale natural gas services to utilities, marketers, pipelines and electric generators in the Midwest. The segment operates a natural gas hub near Chicago, a 2 billion cubic feet (Bcf) per day pipeline and a propane peaking facility. The Retail Energy Services segment provides competitive retail natural gas and electricity supply to over 25,000 customers in the deregulated Illinois energy market.

Oil and Gas Production operations engage in onshore drilling (primarily for natural gas), by acquiring proved reserves with upside potential (realized through drilling, production enhancements and reservoir optimization). During FY 05, daily production dropped to 66.6 million cubic feet equivalent (MMcfe) from 76.1 MMcfe in the prior year.

In July 2006, PGL agreed to merge with WPS. Under the terms of the proposed agreement, scheduled to close during the second quarter of FY 07 pending necessary approvals, each PGL share would be exchanged for 0.825 shares of WPS. The planned transaction is expected to be accretive in calendar year 2008.

Company Financials

Per Share Data ($) Year Ended Sep. 30	**2005**	**2004**	**2003**	**2002**	**2001**	**2000**	**1999**	**1998**	**1997**	**1996**
Tangible Book Value	20.97	23.06	23.11	22.74	22.76	22.02	21.66	20.94	20.43	19.48
Earnings	2.05	2.18	2.87	2.51	2.74	2.44	2.61	2.25	2.81	2.96
S&P Core Earnings	2.22	2.11	2.55	1.08	1.97	NA	NA	NA	NA	NA
Dividends	2.18	2.15	2.11	2.07	2.03	1.99	1.95	1.91	1.87	1.83
Payout Ratio	106%	99%	74%	82%	74%	82%	75%	85%	67%	62%
Prices:High	45.52	46.03	45.25	40.45	44.63	46.94	40.25	40.13	39.88	37.38
Prices:Low	34.34	38.50	34.93	27.80	34.35	26.19	31.75	32.13	31.25	29.63
P/E Ratio:High	22	21	16	16	16	19	15	18	14	13
P/E Ratio:Low	17	18	12	11	13	11	12	14	11	10
Income Statement Analysis (Million $)										
Revenue	2,600	2,260	2,138	1,483	2,270	1,418	1,194	1,138	1,274	1,199
Depreciation	111	125	112	98.9	95.0	101	83.5	77.2	74.1	70.6
Maintenance	NA	NA	NA	NA	NA	NA	NA	44.0	47.6	45.6
Fixed Charges Coverage	3.01	3.35	3.95	3.21	2.46	3.10	4.40	6.71	8.32	7.34
Construction Credits	NA	NA	NA	NA	NA	1.12	1.96	Nil	Nil	Nil
Effective Tax Rate	36.4%	31.7%	36.3%	34.2%	34.6%	33.4%	36.2%	64.8%	31.3%	32.7%
Net Income	78.1	81.6	104	89.1	97.1	86.4	92.6	79.4	98.4	103
S&P Core Earnings	84.4	78.8	92.5	38.7	69.7	NA	NA	NA	NA	NA
Balance Sheet & Other Financial Data (Million $)										
Gross Property	3,214	3,124	2,962	2,972	2,890	2,682	2,462	2,254	2,134	2,046
Capital Expenditures	73.0	189	187	201	266	248	229	116	89.4	85.6
Net Property	1,947	1,904	1,838	1,952	1,940	1,810	1,650	1,490	1,419	1,391
Capitalization:Long Term Debt	896	897	744	554	644	420	522	517	527	527
Capitalization:% Long Term Debt	52.8	50.8	46.7	40.7	44.4	35.1	40.4	41.0	42.4	43.6
Capitalization:Preferred	Nil	Nil	Nil	Nil	Nil	Nil	Nil	Nil	Nil	Nil
Capitalization:% Preferred	Nil	Nil	Nil	Nil	Nil	Nil	Nil	Nil	Nil	Nil
Capitalization:Common	800	870	848	806	806	777	769	741	716	681
Capitalization:% Common	47.2	49.2	53.3	59.3	55.6	64.9	59.6	58.9	57.7	56.4
Total Capital	1,696	2,217	2,028	1,767	1,814	1,570	1,621	1,561	1,527	1,474
% Operating Ratio	96.1	100.2	93.8	91.6	95.1	91.8	91.3	86.2	89.7	88.9
% Earned on Net Property	8.7	15.2	10.6	8.8	24.0	9.2	9.9	7.8	9.4	9.6
% Return on Revenue	3.0	3.6	4.9	6.0	4.3	6.1	7.8	7.0	7.7	8.6
% Return on Invested Capital	8.2	6.7	8.1	8.2	10.0	8.7	8.3	17.0	6.6	9.8
% Return on Common Equity	9.4	9.5	12.6	11.1	12.3	11.2	12.3	10.9	14.1	15.6

Data as orig reptd.; bef. results of disc opers/spec. items. Per share data adj. for stk. divs.; EPS diluted. E-Estimated. NA-Not Available. NM-Not Meaningful. NR-Not Ranked. UR-Under Review.

Office: 130 East Randolph Street, Chicago, IL 60601-6207.
Telephone: 312-240-4000.
Email: corporatecommunications@pecorp.com
Website: http://www.peoplesenergy.com

Chrmn, Pres & CEO: T.M. Patrick
EVP & CFO: T.A. Nardi
VP & Treas: D.M. Ruschau
VP & Cntlr: L.M. Kallas

Secy: P.H. Kauffman
Investor Contact: J. Chiti (312-240-4730)
Board of Directors: K. E. Bailey, J. R. Boris, W. J. Brodsky, P. S. Cafferty, D. S. Ferguson, J. Higgins, D. C. Jain, M. E. Lavin, H. J. Livingston, Jr., T. M. Patrick, R. P. Toft, A. R. Velasquez

Founded: 1855
Domicile: Illinois
Employees: 2,182

STANDARD &POOR'S

PepsiCo Inc

S&P Recommendation STRONG BUY ★★★★★

Price $63.53 (as of Oct 30, 2006)

12-Mo. Target Price $72.00

Investment Style Large-Cap Growth

GICS Sector Consumer Staples
Sub-Industry Soft Drinks

Comment This company is a major international producer of branded beverage and snack food products.

Key Stock Statistics (Source S&P, Vickers, company reports)

52-Wk Range	$65.99–56.00	S&P Oper. EPS 2006E	2.99	P/E on S&P Oper. EPS 2006E	21.2	Dividend Rate/Share	$1.20
Trailing 12-Month EPS	$2.93	S&P Oper. EPS 2007E	3.32	Common Shares Outstg. (M)	1,642.1	Yield (%)	1.89
Trailing 12-Month P/E	21.7	S&P Core EPS 2006E	3.01	Market Capitalization(B)	$104.321	Beta	0.52
$10K Invested 5 Yrs Ago	$14,121	S&P Core EPS 2007E	3.35	Institutional Ownership (%)	68	S&P Credit Rating	A+

Price Performance

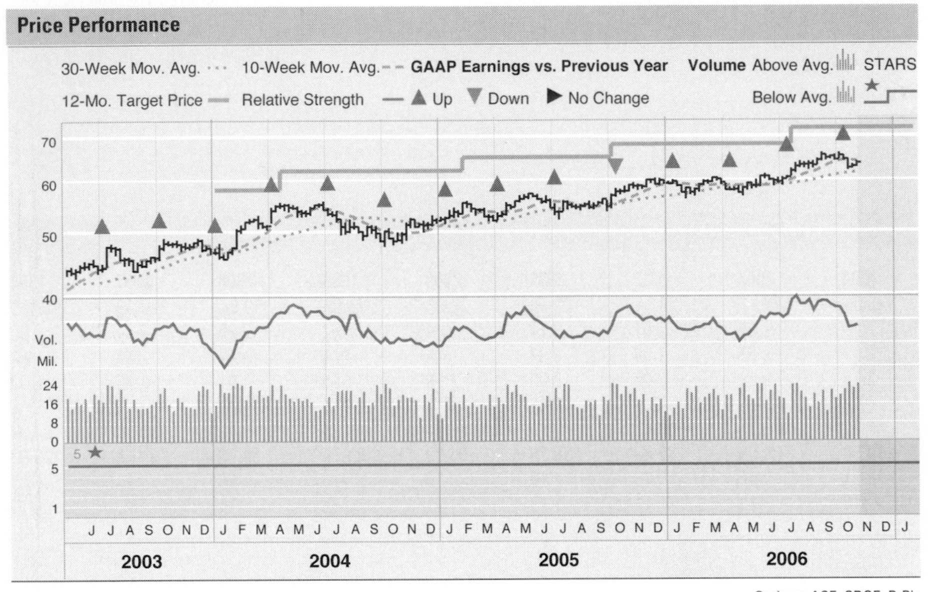

Options: ASE, CBOE, P, Ph

Analysis prepared by **Rick Joy** on October 26, 2006, when the stock traded at **$ 63.85**.

Highlights

- We expect net sales to grow 7% to 8% in 2007 from new products, a favorable pricing environment, strong gains in international markets and a modest foreign currency benefit. We see segment operating income rising 9% to 10% on favorable pricing and product mix benefits, operating efficiencies, and productivity gains. While fuel, energy and PET resin costs will likely remain at elevated levels during 2007, we expect PEP's total input cost inflation to ease through the year.
- By segment, we see operating profits for North American beverages rising 8% to 9%, and expect profits for Frito-Lay North America to grow 6% to 7%. For the PepsiCo International segment, we believe profits will climb more than 14%, while we think the Quaker Foods business will see profits rise in the mid-single digits.
- With 1% to 2% fewer shares outstanding, we estimate 2007 operating EPS of $3.32, an 11% gain from our operating EPS estimate of $2.99 for 2006. For the longer term, we expect annual EPS growth of 11% to 12%.

Investment Rationale/Risk

- Our strong buy recommendation reflects our view of strong volume trends and cash flow growth, and what we see as solid EPS visibility and consistency. Based on the company's leading market positions, we believe PEP will deliver 11% to 12% annual EPS growth for the longer term. We view the shares as very attractive, in light of what we see as the company's high degree of earnings visibility and promising longer-term growth prospects in the growing worldwide packaged beverage and snack industries.
- Risks to our recommendation and target price include unfavorable weather conditions in the company's markets, increased competitive activity, and weak consumer acceptance of new product introductions.
- Our DCF model, which assumes a cost of capital of 8.5% and a terminal growth rate of 4%, calculates intrinsic value of $75. Our relative valuation model, derived from an analysis of peer P/E and enterprise value (EV)/EBITDA multiples, targets a value of $69. Blending our valuations, our 12-month target price is $72.

Qualitative Risk Assessment

LOW | MEDIUM | HIGH

Our risk assessment reflects the relatively stable nature of the company's end markets, strong cash flow, leading global market positions, corporate governance practices that we view as favorable versus peers, and an S&P Quality Rank that reflects historical growth and stability of earnings and dividends.

Quantitative Evaluations

S&P Quality Ranking A+

D | C | B- | B | B+ | A- | A | A+

Relative Strength Rank MODERATE

33

LOWEST = 1 HIGHEST = 99

Revenue/Earnings Data

Revenue (Million $)

	1Q	2Q	3Q	4Q	Year
2006	7,205	8,599	8,950	--	--
2005	6,585	7,697	8,184	10,096	32,562
2004	6,131	7,070	7,257	8,803	29,261
2003	5,530	6,538	6,830	8,073	26,971
2002	5,101	6,178	6,376	7,457	25,112
2001	5,330	6,713	6,906	7,986	26,935

Earnings Per Share ($)

2006	0.60	0.80	0.88	E0.73	E2.99
2005	0.53	0.70	0.51	0.65	2.39
2004	0.46	0.61	0.79	0.55	2.41
2003	0.45	0.58	0.62	0.52	2.05
2002	0.36	0.49	0.54	0.46	1.85
2001	0.32	0.44	0.34	0.37	1.47

Fiscal year ended Dec. 31. Next earnings report expected: Early February. EPS Estimates based on S&P Operating Earnings; historical GAAP earnings are as reported.

Dividend Data (Dates: mm/dd Payment Date: mm/dd/yy)

Amount ($)	Date Decl.	Ex-Div. Date	Stk. of Record	Payment Date
0.260	11/18	12/07	12/09	01/03/06
0.260	02/03	03/08	03/10	03/31/06
0.300	05/03	06/07	06/09	06/30/06
0.300	07/21	09/06	09/08	09/29/06

Dividends have been paid since 1952. Source: Company reports.

PepsiCo Inc

Business Summary October 26, 2006

Originally incorporated in 1919, PepsiCo is a leader in the global snack and beverage industry. The company manufactures, markets and sells a variety of salty, convenient, sweet and grain-based snacks, carbonated and non-carbonated beverages, and foods. PepsiCo is organized into four business segments: Frito-Lay North America (FLNA), PepsiCo Beverages North America (PBNA), PepsiCo International (PI) and Quaker Foods North America (QFNA). The company's North American divisions operate in the U.S. and Canada. PepsiCo's international divisions operate in more than 200 countries, with its largest operations in Mexico and the United Kingdom.

FLNA (32% of 2005 net revenue, 38% of division operating profits) produces the best-selling line of snack foods in the U.S., including Fritos brand corn chips, Lay's and Ruffles potato chips, Doritos and Tostitos tortilla chips, Cheetos cheese-flavored snacks, Rold Gold pretzels, Sunchips multigrain snacks, Grandma's cookies, Quaker Fruit and Oatmeal bars, Quaker Chewy granola bars, Lay's Stax potato crisps, Cracker Jack candy-coated popcorn and Quaker Quakes corn and rice snacks. FLNA branded products are sold to independent distributors and retailers. Products are transported from Frito-Lay's manufacturing plants to major distribution centers, principally by company-owned trucks.

PBNA (28%, 30%) manufactures or uses contract manufacturers, markets and sells beverage concentrates, fountain syrups and finished goods, under the brands Pepsi, Mountain Dew, Sierra Mist, Mug, SoBe, Gatorade, Slice, Tropicana Juice Drinks, Tropicana Pure Premium, Dole, Tropicana Season's Best, Tropicana Twister and Propel. PBNA also manufactures, markets and sells ready-to-drink tea and coffee products through joint ventures with Lipton and Starbucks. In addition, it markets the Aquafina water brand and licenses it to its bottlers. Pepsi-Cola bottlers are licensed by PepsiCo to manufacture, sell and distribute, within defined territories, beverages and syrups bearing the Pepsi-Cola beverage trademarks.

Company Financials

Per Share Data ($) Year Ended Dec. 31	**2005**	**2004**	**2003**	**2002**	**2001**	**2000**	**1999**	**1998**	**1997**	**1996**
Tangible Book Value	2.17	1.96	3.82	2.37	1.90	1.91	1.48	NM	0.72	NM
Cash Flow	3.25	2.45	2.75	2.47	2.07	2.13	2.06	2.12	1.65	1.79
Earnings	2.39	2.41	2.05	1.85	1.47	1.48	1.37	1.31	0.95	0.72
S&P Core Earnings	2.37	2.44	2.03	1.54	1.20	NA	NA	NA	NA	NA
Dividends	1.01	0.85	0.63	0.60	0.58	0.56	0.53	0.51	0.49	0.45
Payout Ratio	42%	35%	31%	32%	39%	38%	39%	39%	52%	62%
Prices:High	60.34	55.71	48.88	53.50	50.46	49.94	42.56	44.81	41.31	35.88
Prices:Low	51.34	45.30	36.24	34.00	40.25	29.69	30.13	27.56	28.25	27.25
P/E Ratio:High	25	23	24	29	34	34	31	34	43	50
P/E Ratio:Low	21	19	18	18	27	20	22	21	30	38
Income Statement Analysis (Million $)										
Revenue	32,562	29,261	26,971	25,112	26,935	20,438	20,367	22,348	20,917	31,645
Operating Income	7,230	6,673	6,208	6,066	5,490	4,185	3,915	4,106	4,058	5,087
Depreciation	1,308	1,264	1,221	1,112	1,082	960	1,032	1,234	1,106	1,719
Interest Expense	256	167	163	178	219	221	363	395	478	600
Pretax Income	6,382	5,546	4,992	4,868	4,029	3,210	3,656	2,263	2,309	2,047
Effective Tax Rate	36.1%	24.7%	28.5%	31.9%	33.9%	32.0%	43.9%	11.9%	35.4%	43.9%
Net Income	4,078	4,174	3,568	3,313	2,662	2,183	2,050	1,993	1,491	1,149
S&P Core Earnings	4,028	4,191	3,543	2,749	2,164	NA	NA	NA	NA	NA
Balance Sheet & Other Financial Data (Million $)										
Cash	1,716	1,280	820	1,638	683	864	964	311	2,883	786
Current Assets	10,454	8,639	6,930	6,413	5,853	4,604	4,173	4,362	6,251	5,139
Total Assets	31,727	27,987	25,327	23,474	21,695	18,339	17,551	22,660	20,101	24,512
Current Liabilities	9,406	6,752	6,415	6,052	4,998	3,935	3,788	7,914	4,257	5,139
Long Term Debt	2,313	2,397	1,702	2,187	2,651	2,346	2,812	4,028	4,946	8,439
Common Equity	14,210	13,572	11,896	9,250	8,648	7,249	6,881	6,401	6,939	6,623
Total Capital	17,998	17,226	14,837	13,196	12,821	10,956	10,902	12,432	13,582	16,840
Capital Expenditures	1,736	1,387	1,345	1,437	1,324	1,067	1,118	1,405	1,506	2,287
Cash Flow	5,384	4,109	4,786	4,421	3,744	3,143	3,082	3,227	2,597	2,868
Current Ratio	1.1	1.3	1.1	1.1	1.2	1.2	1.1	0.6	1.5	1.0
% Long Term Debt of Capitalization	12.9	13.9	11.5	16.6	20.7	21.4	25.8	32.4	36.4	50.1
% Net Income of Revenue	12.5	14.3	13.2	13.2	9.9	10.7	10.1	8.9	7.1	3.6
% Return on Assets	13.7	15.7	14.6	14.7	12.5	12.2	10.2	9.3	7.1	4.6
% Return on Equity	29.4	22.3	33.3	37.0	32.8	30.9	30.9	29.9	22.0	16.5

Data as orig reptd.; bef. results of disc opers/spec. items. Per share data adj. for stk. divs.; EPS diluted. E-Estimated. NA-Not Available. NM-Not Meaningful. NR-Not Ranked. UR-Under Review.

Office: 700 Anderson Hill Road, Purchase, NY 10577.
Telephone: 914-253-2000.
Website: http://www.pepsico.com
Chrmn: S.S. Reinemund

Pres & CEO: I.K. Nooyi
Vice Chrmn: M. White
SVP & Treas: L.L. Nowell, III
SVP, Secy & General Counsel: L.D. Thompson

Investor Contact: J. Caulfield (914-253-3035)
Board of Directors: J. F. Akers, R. E. Allen, D. Dublon, V. J. Dzau, R. L. Hunt, A. Ibarguen, A. C. Martinez, I. K. Nooyi, S. S. Reinemund, S. P. Rockefeller, J. J. Schiro, F. A. Thomas, C. M. Trudell, D. Vasella

Founded: 1916
Domicile: North Carolina
Employees: 157,000

STANDARD &POOR'S

Pepsi Bottling Group Inc.

S&P Recommendation BUY ★★★★★

Price $31.71 (as of Oct 30, 2006)

12-Mo. Target Price $39.00

Investment Style Mid-Cap Growth

GICS Sector Consumer Staples
Sub-Industry Soft Drinks

Comment This company is the world's largest manufacturer, seller and distributor of carbonated and non-carbonated Pepsi-Cola beverages.

Key Stock Statistics (Source S&P, Vickers, company reports)

52-Wk Range	$35.83–27.99	S&P Oper. EPS 2006**E**	1.88	P/E on S&P Oper. EPS 2006**E**	16.9	Dividend Rate/Share	$0.44
Trailing 12-Month EPS	$1.92	S&P Oper. EPS 2007**E**	2.07	Common Shares Outstg. (M)	236.0	Yield (%)	1.39
Trailing 12-Month P/E	16.5	S&P Core EPS 2006**E**	1.97	Market Capitalization(B)	$7.484	Beta	0.96
$10K Invested 5 Yrs Ago	$13,662	S&P Core EPS 2007**E**	2.16	Institutional Ownership (%)	57	S&P Credit Rating	A

Price Performance

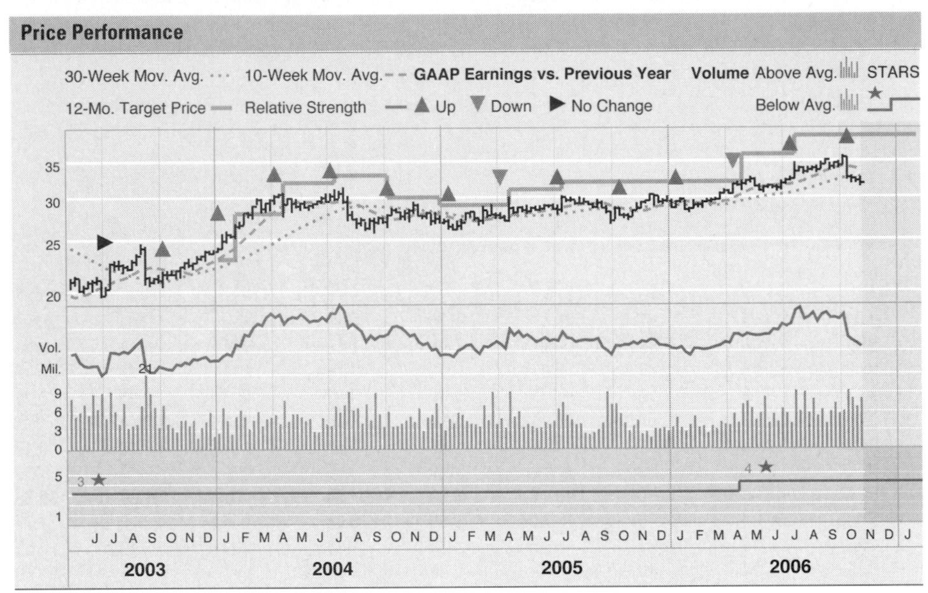

Options: ASE, CBOE, P, Ph

Analysis prepared by **Rick Joy** on October 26, 2006, when the stock traded at **$ 31.98**.

Highlights

- We expect net revenues to rise 5% to 6% in 2007, primarily reflecting 3% comparable worldwide volume growth and a 2% to 3% increase in net revenues per case. Volume comparisons should benefit from strong bottled water growth and the addition of new beverage products, but we think carbonated soft drink trends will remain sluggish. By geographic segment, we see volume growth of 2% for the U.S., 3% for Mexico and a 6% gain for Europe.
- We expect net revenues per case to benefit from new products and higher pricing, and from channel and package mix improvements. However, we think that higher raw material and packaging costs will likely lead to a 4% to 5% increase in cost of goods sold per case.
- After expected higher interest expense, balanced against share repurchases that we see reducing the number of shares outstanding by 1% to 2%, we forecast 2007 EPS of $2.07, a 10% increase from our 2006 EPS estimate of $1.88. For the longer term, we project 8% to 10% annual EPS growth.

Investment Rationale/Risk

- Our buy recommendation reflects our expectation for strong brand momentum, cost structure improvements and better EPS visibility in coming quarters. We expect to see modest market share gains behind new product introductions, improving revenue per case growth, and continuing improvement in the Mexican business during 2007.
- Risks to our recommendation and target price include rising competitive pressures for PBG's business in Mexico, increasing commodity cost pressures, an inability to meet volume and revenue growth targets, and unfavorable weather conditions in the company's markets. In terms of corporate governance, the company has a dual class capital structure with unequal voting rights, which we view unfavorably.
- Our 12-month target price of $39 is derived from our analysis of comparable peer multiples and discounted free cash flows. Our DCF assumptions include a weighted average cost of capital of 9% and an expected terminal growth rate for cash flows of 3%.

Qualitative Risk Assessment

LOW | MEDIUM | HIGH

Our risk assessment reflects the relatively stable nature of the company's end markets, strong cash flows and market share positions, and its relationship with corporate partner PepsiCo.

Quantitative Evaluations

S&P Quality Ranking NR

D | C | B- | B | B+ | A- | A | A+

Relative Strength Rank WEAK

17

LOWEST = 1 HIGHEST = 99

Revenue/Earnings Data

Revenue (Million $)

	1Q	2Q	3Q	4Q	Year
2006	2,367	3,138	3,460	--	--
2005	2,147	2,862	3,214	3,662	11,885
2004	2,067	2,675	2,934	3,230	10,906
2003	1,874	2,532	2,810	3,049	10,265
2002	1,772	2,209	2,455	2,780	9,216
2001	1,647	2,060	2,274	2,462	8,443

Earnings Per Share ($)

2006	0.14	0.61	0.86	**E**0.33	**E**1.88
2005	0.15	0.59	0.82	0.30	1.86
2004	0.19	0.53	0.73	0.29	1.73
2003	0.14	0.47	0.67	0.26	1.52
2002	0.19	0.47	0.61	0.20	1.46
2001	0.09	0.39	0.51	0.05	1.03

Fiscal year ended Dec. 31. Next earnings report expected: Late January. EPS Estimates based on S&P Operating Earnings; historical GAAP earnings are as reported.

Dividend Data (Dates: mm/dd Payment Date: mm/dd/yy)

Amount ($)	Date Decl.	Ex-Div. Date	Stk. of Record	Payment Date
0.110	03/23	06/07	06/09	06/30/06
0.110	03/23	06/07	06/09	06/30/06
0.110	07/26	09/06	09/08	09/29/06
0.110	10/25	12/06	12/08	01/02/07

Dividends have been paid since 1999. Source: Company reports.

Pepsi Bottling Group Inc.

Business Summary October 26, 2006

The Pepsi Bottling Group is the world's largest manufacturer, seller and distributor of carbonated and non-carbonated Pepsi-Cola beverages. The company has exclusive rights to manufacture, sell and distribute Pepsi-Cola beverages in all or a portion of 41 states, the District of Columbia, nine Canadian provinces, Spain, Greece, Turkey, Mexico and Russia. In 2005, approximately 71% of PBG's net revenues were generated in the U.S., 10% were generated in Mexico and the remaining 19% were generated in Canada, Spain, Greece, Russia and Turkey.

The company's brands include some of the world's best recognized trademarks, and include Pepsi-Cola, Diet Pepsi, Mountain Dew, Lipton Brisk, Lipton's Iced Tea, 7UP outside the U.S., Pepsi Max, Pepsi One, Slice, Sierra Mist, Mug, Aquafina, Starbucks Frappaccino and Miranda, which are bottled under licenses from PepsiCo or PepsiCo joint ventures.

According to PBG, market shares for carbonated soft drinks sold under trademarks owned by PepsiCo in its U.S. territories range from approximately 21% to approximately 37%. The company's market share for carbonated soft drinks sold under PepsiCo trademarks for each country outside of the U.S. where PBG does business is as follows: Canada 38%; Russia 25%; Turkey 19%; Spain 12%; and Greece 9%. In addition, market share for PBG's territories and the territories of other Pepsi bottlers in Mexico is 13% for carbonated soft drinks sold under trademarks owned by PepsiCo.

The company has established an extensive production and distribution system to deliver products directly to stores without using wholesalers or middlemen. At December 31, 2005, it operated 95 soft drink production facilities worldwide, as well as 546 distribution facilities. PBG also owns or leases and operates approximately 41,000 vehicles, and owns more than 2 million coolers and soft drink dispensing and vending machines.

Company Financials

Per Share Data ($) Year Ended Dec. 31	**2005**	**2004**	**2003**	**2002**	**2001**	**2000**	**1999**	**1998**	**1997**	**1996**
Tangible Book Value	NM	NM	NM	NM	NM	NM	NM	NM	NA	NA
Cash Flow	4.38	3.99	3.57	3.00	2.77	2.23	2.43	2.96	NA	NA
Earnings	1.86	1.73	1.52	1.46	1.03	0.77	0.46	-0.39	NA	NA
S&P Core Earnings	1.71	1.64	1.42	1.18	0.78	NA	NA	NA	NA	NA
Dividends	0.29	0.16	0.04	0.04	0.04	0.04	0.02	NA	NA	NA
Payout Ratio	16%	9%	3%	3%	4%	5%	4%	NA	NA	NA
Prices:High	30.35	31.40	27.62	34.80	25.00	21.25	12.63	NA	NA	NA
Prices:Low	26.00	24.00	17.00	21.65	15.81	8.13	7.75	NA	NA	NA
P/E Ratio:High	16	18	18	24	24	28	27	NA	NA	NA
P/E Ratio:Low	14	14	11	15	15	11	17	NA	NA	NA

Income Statement Analysis (Million $)										
Revenue	11,885	10,906	10,265	9,216	8,443	7,982	7,505	7,041	NA	NA
Operating Income	1,653	1,568	1,524	1,349	1,190	1,025	901	749	NA	NA
Depreciation	630	593	568	451	514	435	505	472	NA	NA
Interest Expense	250	230	239	191	194	192	202	221	NA	NA
Pretax Income	772	745	710	700	482	397	209	-192	NA	NA
Effective Tax Rate	32.0%	31.1%	33.5%	31.6%	28.2%	34.0%	33.5%	NM	NA	NA
Net Income	466	457	422	428	305	229	118	-146	NA	NA
S&P Core Earnings	431	435	394	347	229	NA	NA	NA	NA	NA

Balance Sheet & Other Financial Data (Million $)										
Cash	502	305	1,235	222	277	318	190	36.0	NA	NA
Current Assets	2,412	2,039	3,039	1,737	1,548	1,584	1,493	1,318	NA	NA
Total Assets	11,524	10,793	11,544	10,027	7,857	7,736	7,619	7,322	NA	NA
Current Liabilities	2,598	1,581	2,478	1,248	1,081	967	947	1,025	NA	NA
Long Term Debt	3,939	4,489	4,493	4,523	3,285	3,271	3,268	3,361	NA	NA
Common Equity	2,043	1,949	1,881	1,824	1,601	1,646	1,563	-238	NA	NA
Total Capital	7,899	8,298	8,191	7,960	6,226	6,295	6,287	4,325	NA	NA
Capital Expenditures	715	717	644	623	593	515	560	507	NA	NA
Cash Flow	1,096	1,050	990	879	819	664	623	326	NA	NA
Current Ratio	0.9	1.3	1.2	1.4	1.4	1.6	1.6	1.3	NA	NA
% Long Term Debt of Capitalization	49.9	54.1	54.9	56.8	52.8	52.0	51.9	77.7	NA	NA
% Net Income of Revenue	3.9	4.2	4.1	4.6	3.6	2.9	1.6	NM	NA	NA
% Return on Assets	4.1	4.1	3.9	4.8	3.9	3.0	1.6	NM	NA	NA
% Return on Equity	23.3	23.9	22.8	25.0	18.8	14.3	17.8	NM	NA	NA

Data as orig reptd.; bef. results of disc opers/spec. items. Per share data adj. for stk. divs.; EPS diluted. E-Estimated. NA-Not Available. NM-Not Meaningful. NR-Not Ranked. UR-Under Review.

Office: One Pepsi Way, Somers, NY 10589-2204.
Telephone: 914-767-6000.
Email: shareholder.relations@pepsi.com
Website: http://www.pbg.com

Exec Chrmn: J.T. Cahill
Pres & CEO: E.J. Foss
SVP & CFO: A.H. Drewes
SVP, Secy & General Counsel: S.M. Rapp

SVP & CIO: N.A. Bronzo
Investor Contact: M. Settino (914-767-7216)
Board of Directors: L. G. Alvarado, B. H. Beracha, J. T. Cahill, E. J. Foss, I. D. Hall, T. E. Kean, S. Kronick, B. J. McGarvie, M. D. Moore, J. Quelch, C. G. Small

Founded: 1999
Domicile: Delaware
Employees: 66,900

STANDARD &POOR'S

PerkinElmer Inc.

S&P Recommendation HOLD ★★★★★	Price	12-Mo. Target Price	Investment Style
	$21.42 (as of Oct 27, 2006)	$23.00	Mid-Cap Value

GICS Sector Health Care
Sub-Industry Life Sciences Tools & Services

Comment This diversified technology company provides advanced scientific and technical products and services worldwide to the pharmaceutical and industrial industries.

Key Stock Statistics (Source S&P, Vickers, company reports)

52-Wk Range	$24.17–16.31	S&P Oper. EPS 2006E	1.12	P/E on S&P Oper. EPS 2006E	19.1	Dividend Rate/Share	$0.28
Trailing 12-Month EPS	$2.03	S&P Oper. EPS 2007E	1.30	Common Shares Outstg. (M)	125.6	Yield (%)	1.31
Trailing 12-Month P/E	10.6	S&P Core EPS 2006E	1.12	Market Capitalization(B)	$2.690	Beta	2.08
$10K Invested 5 Yrs Ago	$8,588	S&P Core EPS 2007E	1.30	Institutional Ownership (%)	81	S&P Credit Rating	BBB-

Price Performance

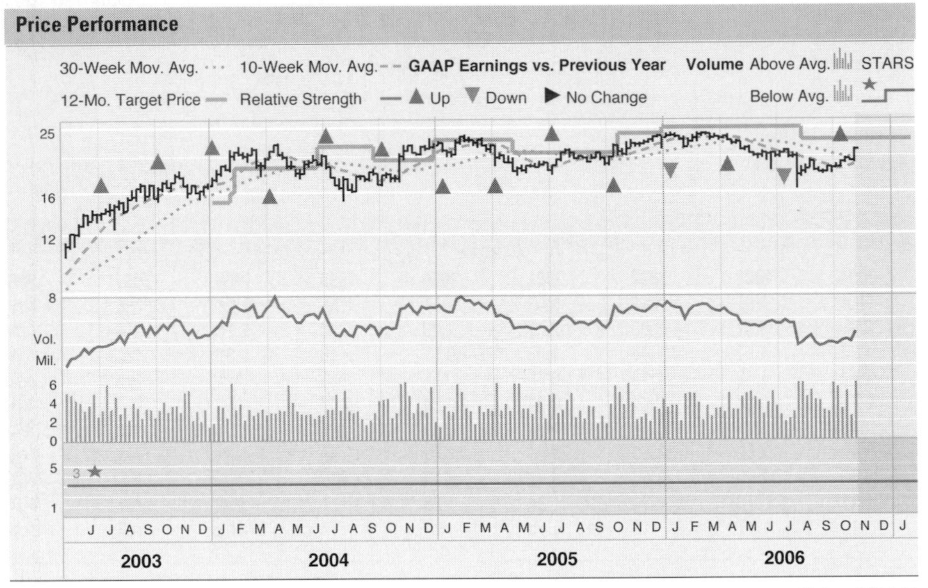

Options: CBOE, Ph

Analysis prepared by **Jeffrey Loo, CFA** on September 21, 2006, when the stock traded at **$ 18.76**.

Highlights

- Following a soft first half where organic sales were in the low single digits, we lowered our 2006 sales estimate, and now see 4% organic sales growth in 2006, down from our initial 6% estimate. However, acquisitions should aid 2006 sales, to $1.5 billion, while recent divestitures narrowed PKI's portfolio and should enable the company to focus on higher margin and faster growing products. We expect continued double digit growth in genetic screening and medical imaging, partially offset by slow growth in biopharmaceuticals. Genetic screening, which represents 12% of PKI's Life and Analytical Sciences unit, will continue to be a significant growth driver for several years, in our view.
- We see operating margins declining 90 basis points, as manufacturing improvements and operating leverage in SG&A costs are offset by increasing R&D costs and the inclusion of stock options.
- After projected stock option expense of $0.05, excluding intangible amortization, and with an expected lower tax rate of 24.5% due to the divestiture of Fluid Sciences, our 2006 operating EPS estimate is $1.15.

Investment Rationale/Risk

- We believe the shares are fairly valued at about 18X-20X our 2006 EPS estimate, in line with peers. Our 2006 EPS estimate accounts for the divestiture of the Fluid Sciences unit, which we see adversely affecting earnings by 7%. Despite the expected adverse earnings impact, we view PKI's recent divestitures positively, as we believe they will allow PKI to focus on the faster growing, higher margin health sciences end market, which should account for about 80% of sales. We believe the health sciences proportion will increase, as PKI has completed several acquisitions, and we see PKI making more acquisitions.
- Risks to our recommendation and target price include slower than anticipated growth in health sciences end markets, particularly in genetic screening, and a possible greater than expected slowing of the Chinese economy.
- Our 12-month target price of $23 is based on our DCF analysis, using a weighted average cost of capital (WACC) of 9.9% and a terminal growth rate of 3%, and our relative valuation analysis, using an in-line peer P/E multiple of 20X our 2006 EPS estimate.

Qualitative Risk Assessment

LOW | **MEDIUM** | HIGH

Our risk assessment reflects PKI's broad product mix and diverse global client base. However, the company has been actively restructuring its business units and product portfolio, which we believe could increase operating risks.

Quantitative Evaluations

S&P Quality Ranking B

D | C | B- | **B** | B+ | A- | A | A+

Relative Strength Rank STRONG

85

LOWEST = 1 HIGHEST = 99

Revenue/Earnings Data

Revenue (Million $)

	1Q	2Q	3Q	4Q	Year
2006	355.5	377.0	386.9	--	--
2005	358.2	368.0	360.0	387.7	1,474
2004	392.6	412.6	403.4	478.6	1,687
2003	358.5	377.1	367.1	432.6	1,535
2002	346.3	383.1	366.0	409.6	1,505
2001	334.9	331.8	302.1	361.2	1,330

Earnings Per Share ($)

	1Q	2Q	3Q	4Q	Year
2006	0.17	0.21	0.23	**E**0.37	**E**1.12
2005	0.12	0.23	0.20	-0.05	0.51
2004	0.11	0.17	0.19	0.29	0.75
2003	0.03	0.08	0.11	0.21	0.43
2002	-0.23	0.03	0.08	0.01	-0.03
2001	0.13	0.30	0.21	-0.49	-0.01

Fiscal year ended Dec. 31. Next earnings report expected: Late January. EPS Estimates based on S&P Operating Earnings; historical GAAP earnings are as reported.

Dividend Data (Dates: mm/dd Payment Date: mm/dd/yy)

Amount ($)	Date Decl.	Ex-Div. Date	Stk. of Record	Payment Date
0.070	10/21	01/18	01/20	02/10/06
0.070	01/24	04/19	04/21	05/12/06
0.070	05/16	07/19	07/21	08/11/06
0.070	07/25	10/18	10/20	11/10/06

Dividends have been paid since 1965. Source: Company reports.

PerkinElmer Inc.

Business Summary September 21, 2006

CORPORATE OVERVIEW. PerkinElmer is a global technology company with operations in more than 125 countries. It develops, manufactures and provides scientific instruments, consumables and services to the pharmaceutical, biomedical, environmental testing and general industrial markets. Collectively, these markets are commonly referred to as the health sciences and industrial sciences markets. In 2005, PKI operated three business segments within its end-markets: Life and Analytical Sciences, Optoelectronics, and Fluid Sciences. However, in 2005 and 2006, PKI divested its Fluid Sciences unit in an effort to focus on the health sciences market, which PKI believes has greater growth and profitability potential. The health sciences markets include all of the businesses in the Life and Analytical Sciences unit and the medical imaging, medical sensors and lighting business in the Optoelectronics unit. The industrial sciences markets include the remaining businesses in Optoelectronics.

Life and Analytical Sciences provides drug discovery, genetic screening and environmental and chemical analysis tools, including instruments, reagents, consumables and services. Its instruments are used for scientific research and clinical applications. For drug discovery, PKI offers a wide range of instrumentation, software and consumables, including reagents, based on its core expertise in fluorescent, chemiluminescent and radioactive labeling, and the detection of nucleic acids and proteins. For genetic screening laboratories, it provides software, reagents and analysis tools to test for various inherited disorders. For chemical analysis, the company offers analytical tools employing technologies such as molecular and atomic spectroscopy, high-pressure liquid chromatography, gas chromatography and thermal analysis.

Company Financials

Per Share Data ($) Year Ended Dec. 31	**2005**	**2004**	**2003**	**2002**	**2001**	**2000**	**1999**	**1998**	**1997**	**1996**
Tangible Book Value	1.91	NM	NM	NM	NM	NM	NM	0.92	2.75	2.75
Cash Flow	1.03	1.35	1.07	0.58	0.77	1.62	1.01	1.66	0.82	1.01
Earnings	0.51	0.75	0.43	-0.03	-0.01	1.32	0.31	1.11	0.34	0.58
S&P Core Earnings	0.40	0.63	0.25	-0.34	-0.68	NA	NA	NA	NA	NA
Dividends	0.28	0.28	0.28	0.28	0.28	0.28	0.28	0.28	0.28	0.28
Payout Ratio	55%	37%	65%	NM	NM	21%	92%	25%	84%	49%
Prices:High	24.02	23.28	18.71	36.30	52.31	60.50	22.50	16.88	12.31	12.56
Prices:Low	17.92	15.05	7.22	4.28	21.28	19.00	12.75	9.44	9.00	8.13
P/E Ratio:High	47	31	44	NM	NM	46	74	15	37	22
P/E Ratio:Low	35	20	17	NM	NM	14	42	9	27	14

Income Statement Analysis (Million $)	2005	2004	2003	2002	2001	2000	1999	1998	1997	1996
Revenue	1,474	1,687	1,535	1,505	1,330	1,695	1,363	1,408	1,461	1,427
Operating Income	229	253	211	131	196	263	177	144	132	129
Depreciation	67.0	76.2	80.2	76.6	80.5	79.1	66.1	50.4	44.6	40.9
Interest Expense	74.3	38.0	Nil	Nil	Nil	Nil	28.3	11.4	12.5	13.4
Pretax Income	66.7	137	80.9	-8.55	34.2	144	44.9	156	54.0	80.4
Effective Tax Rate	0.19%	28.2%	32.0%	NM	NM	40.4%	36.8%	34.6%	43.3%	32.2%
Net Income	66.5	98.3	55.0	-4.14	-0.62	86.1	28.4	102	30.6	54.5
S&P Core Earnings	53.8	81.3	31.2	-43.1	-71.3	NA	NA	NA	NA	NA

Balance Sheet & Other Financial Data (Million $)	2005	2004	2003	2002	2001	2000	1999	1998	1997	1996
Cash	502	208	202	317	138	126	127	95.6	57.9	47.8
Current Assets	999	748	766	991	997	893	815	565	488	455
Total Assets	2,693	2,576	2,608	2,836	2,919	2,260	1,715	1,185	832	823
Current Liabilities	495	446	452	698	708	718	852	524	286	260
Long Term Debt	243	365	544	614	598	583	115	130	114	115
Common Equity	1,651	1,460	1,349	1,252	1,364	728	551	400	328	365
Total Capital	1,894	1,825	1,893	1,866	1,962	1,312	666	530	443	480
Capital Expenditures	25.1	19.0	16.6	37.8	88.7	70.6	41.1	NA	48.7	80.5
Cash Flow	134	174	135	72.4	79.9	165	94.5	152	75.3	95.4
Current Ratio	2.0	1.7	1.7	1.4	1.4	1.2	1.0	1.1	1.7	1.8
% Long Term Debt of Capitalization	12.8	20.0	28.7	32.9	30.5	44.5	17.3	24.5	25.9	24.0
% Net Income of Revenue	4.5	5.8	3.6	NM	NM	5.1	2.1	7.2	2.1	3.8
% Return on Assets	2.5	3.8	2.0	NM	NM	4.3	2.0	10.1	3.7	6.7
% Return on Equity	4.3	7.0	4.2	NM	NM	13.5	6.0	28.0	8.8	14.9

Data as orig reptd.; bef. results of disc opers/spec. items. Per share data adj. for stk. divs.; EPS diluted. E-Estimated. NA-Not Available. NM-Not Meaningful. NR-Not Ranked. UR-Under Review.

Office: 45 William St, Wellesley, MA 02481-4008.
Telephone: 781-237-5100.
Website: http://www.perkinelmer.com
Chrmn, Pres & CEO: G.L. Summe

Vice Chrmn: R.F. Friel
SVP, CFO & Chief Acctg Officer: J.D. Capello
SVP, Secy & General Counsel: K.A. O'Hara
Investor Contact: S. Delahunt (781-431-4258)

Auditor: Deloitte & Touche
Board of Directors: T. J. Erickson, N. A. Lopardo, A. P. Michas, J. C. Mullen, V. L. Sato, G. Schmergel, K. J. Sicchitano, G. L. Summe, G. R. Tod

Founded: 1947
Domicile: Massachusetts
Employees: 8,000

Pfizer Inc.

STANDARD &POOR'S

S&P Recommendation STRONG BUY ★★★★★	Price $26.65 (as of Oct 31, 2006)	12-Mo. Target Price $31.00	Investment Style Large-Cap Growth

GICS Sector Health Care
Sub-Industry Pharmaceuticals

Comment Pfizer, the world's largest drugmaker, with about 11% of the global market, acquired Pharmacia in April 2003, in exchange for 1.8 billion PFE shares.

Key Stock Statistics (Source S&P, Vickers, company reports)

52-Wk Range	$28.60–20.27	S&P Oper. EPS 2006E	2.00	P/E on S&P Oper. EPS 2006E	13.3	Dividend Rate/Share	$0.96
Trailing 12-Month EPS	$1.72	S&P Oper. EPS 2007E	2.16	Common Shares Outstg. (M)	7,291.5	Yield (%)	3.60
Trailing 12-Month P/E	15.5	S&P Core EPS 2006E	2.00	Market Capitalization(B)	$194.317	Beta	0.53
$10K Invested 5 Yrs Ago	$7,148	S&P Core EPS 2007E	2.16	Institutional Ownership (%)	65	S&P Credit Rating	AAA

Price Performance

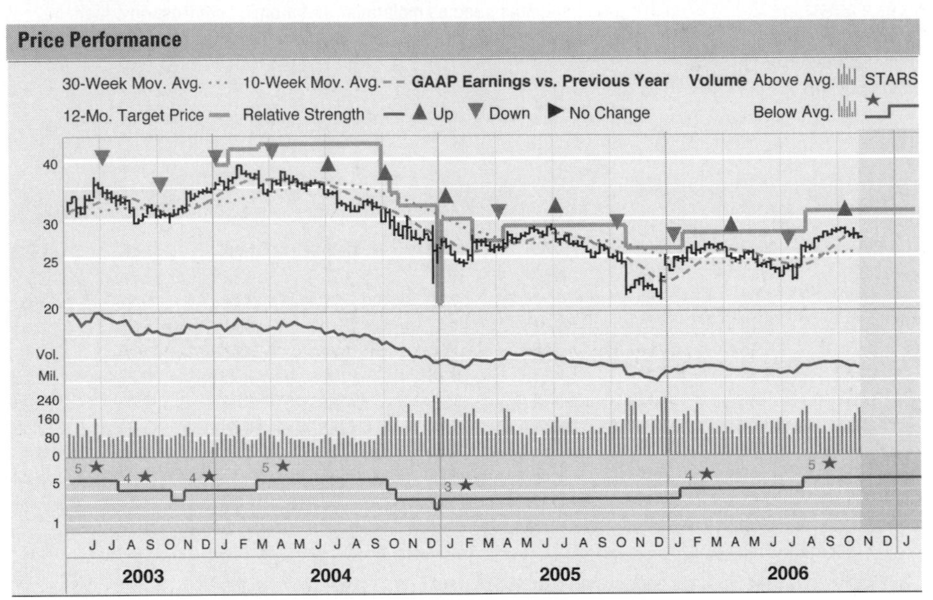

Options: ASE, CBOE, P, Ph

Analysis prepared by **Herman B. Saftlas** on October 25, 2006, when the stock traded at **$ 27.23**.

Highlights

- We project that revenues in 2007 will be comparable with the $48 billion we estimate for 2006, excluding the consumer products business that PFE has agreed to sell to Johnson & Johnson. We expect sales of Lipitor (PFE's largest selling drug) to hold steady with 2006, while further gains are seen for Celebrex and Viagra. Sales of newer products such as Lyrica, Exubera and Sutent should increase. Alliance revenues and animal health sales should also rise. These gains should roughly offset the effects of expiration losses on Zoloft, Zithromax, and Norvasc.
- We expect gross margins to expand modestly in 2007, benefiting from plant rationalization measures. Helped by extensive cost streamlining measures in R&D and SG&A spending, Pfizer believe total operating expenses in 2007 will be lower than those of 2006.
- We project EPS of $2.16 in 2007, up from a forecast $2.00 in 2006, after estimated stock option expense in each year. EPS in 2007 should benefit from an indicated 4% decline in average shares outstanding.

Investment Rationale/Risk

- PFE is one of the leading companies in the global pharmaceutical space. We expect the company to continue to benefit from an investor rotation to large-capitalization, high quality (S&P's Quality Ranking for PFE is A-), defensive drug names. We see the new CEO, Jeff Kindler, as likely to take strategic initiatives to enhance shareholder value. PFE expects to generate $34 billion in cash flow, after capital expenditures and dividends, in the 30 months through the end of 2008, with half slated for stock buybacks and half for acquisitions. We project PFE's EPS rising at a mid- to high-single digit rate over the 2006-2010 period. PFE also recently offered a 3.5% dividend yield.
- Risks to our recommendation and target price include competitive pressures in key drug lines, and possible pipeline setbacks.
- Our 12-month target price of $31 roughly applies a peer level P/E of 14.4X to our 2007 EPS estimate. Our target price is also close to our calculation of intrinsic value, derived from our DCF model, which assumes decelerating cash flow growth over 10 years and a weighted average cost of capital of 7.2%.

Qualitative Risk Assessment

LOW	**MEDIUM**	HIGH

Our risk assessment reflects PFE's lead position in the global pharmaceutical market, which we believe affords the company significant competitive advantages in terms of marketing and R&D. We also think PFE has unmatched financial flexibility in the pharmaceutical sector. However, we see these pluses offset by the effects of patent expirations and pipeline uncertainties.

Quantitative Evaluations

S&P Quality Ranking A-

D	C	B-	B	B+	**A-**	A	A+

Relative Strength Rank WEAK

24

LOWEST = 1 HIGHEST = 99

Revenue/Earnings Data

Revenue (Million $)

	1Q	2Q	3Q	4Q	Year
2006	12,660	11,741	12,280	--	--
2005	13,091	12,425	12,189	13,592	51,298
2004	12,487	12,274	12,831	14,924	52,516
2003	8,525	9,993	12,504	14,167	45,188
2002	7,747	7,296	7,996	9,333	32,373
2001	7,645	7,686	7,898	9,030	32,259

Earnings Per Share ($)

2006	0.56	0.31	0.44	E0.46	E2.00
2005	0.04	0.47	0.22	0.37	1.09
2004	0.30	0.38	0.43	0.39	1.49
2003	0.40	-0.49	0.29	0.08	0.22
2002	0.37	0.30	0.37	0.43	1.47
2001	0.30	0.29	0.33	0.30	1.22

Fiscal year ended Dec. 31. Next earnings report expected: Mid January. EPS Estimates based on S&P Operating Earnings; historical GAAP earnings are as reported.

Dividend Data (Dates: mm/dd Payment Date: mm/dd/yy)

Amount ($)	Date Decl.	Ex-Div. Date	Stk. of Record	Payment Date
0.240	12/12	02/08	02/10	03/07/06
0.240	04/27	05/10	05/12	06/06/06
0.240	06/22	08/09	08/11	09/05/06
0.240	10/26	11/08	11/10	12/05/06

Dividends have been paid since 1901. Source: Company reports.

Please read the Required Disclosures and Analyst Certification on the last page of this report.

Pfizer Inc.

Business Summary October 25, 2006

CORPORATE OVERVIEW. Pfizer towers over its peers in the $600 billion global pharmaceutical sector. Growth over the past 10 years was augmented by two major acquisitions--Warner-Lambert Co. in 2000 and Pharmacia Corp. in 2003--as well as through internal product development. In June 2006, PFE announced plans to sell its consumer health care products business (sales of $3.9 billion in 2005) to Johnson & Johnson for $16.6 billion in cash, subject to necessary approvals.

MARKET PROFILE. After expanding rapidly at double digit rates for close to a decade, worldwide pharmaceutical industry revenue growth slowed to about 7% over the 2004-2005 period, reflecting the effects of tighter reimbursements from key managed care markets, the loss of patent protection on blockbuster drugs, and relatively sluggish new product flow stemming from reduced R&D productivity. However, we expect new Medicare Part D drug coverage, plus new products, to provide some impetus for growth during 2006 and 2007.

COMPETITIVE LANDSCAPE. We think Pfizer's size gives it important competitive advantages over peers, especially in terms of marketing prowess in managed care and Medicare markets. In our opinion, the company's size and financial resources also empower it with a greater ability to make acquisitions and form strategic alliances with smaller pharmaceutical and biotechnology companies. PFE's drug portfolio is unmatched in terms of breadth and depth in the global drug market. Foreign sales accounted for 48% of total revenues in 2005.

Principal cardiovasculars include Lipitor, the world's largest selling cholesterol-lowering agent as well as the biggest drug in any therapeutic category in 2005 (sales of $12.2 billion in 2005), and antihypertensives such as Norvasc ($4.7 billion) and Cardura ($586 million). Infectious disease drugs consist of Zithromax, a now off-patent broad spectrum antibiotic ($2.0 billion), and Zyvox ($618 million), a treatment for severe bacterial infections. Key central nervous system medicines include Zoloft, an antidepressant ($3.3 billion), and off-patent Neurontin, an anticonvulsant ($639 million).

Company Financials

Per Share Data ($) Year Ended Dec. 31	2005	2004	2003	2002	2001	2000	1999	1998	1997	1996
Tangible Book Value	1.91	1.48	0.85	3.04	2.64	2.26	2.11	2.06	2.03	1.43
Cash Flow	1.84	2.16	0.78	1.64	1.39	0.74	0.96	0.63	0.69	0.61
Earnings	1.09	1.49	0.22	1.47	1.22	0.59	0.82	0.49	0.57	0.50
S&P Core Earnings	1.02	1.45	0.29	1.35	1.09	NA	NA	NA	NA	NA
Dividends	0.76	0.68	0.60	0.52	0.44	0.36	0.31	0.25	0.23	0.20
Payout Ratio	70%	46%	273%	35%	36%	61%	37%	51%	40%	40%
Prices:High	29.21	38.89	36.92	42.46	46.75	49.25	50.04	42.98	26.67	15.21
Prices:Low	20.27	21.99	27.90	25.13	34.00	30.00	31.54	23.69	13.44	10.04
P/E Ratio:High	27	26	NM	29	38	83	61	87	47	31
P/E Ratio:Low	19	15	NM	17	28	51	38	48	24	20
Income Statement Analysis (Million $)										
Revenue	51,298	52,516	45,188	32,373	32,259	29,574	16,204	13,544	12,504	11,306
Operating Income	20,501	22,117	17,061	13,436	12,147	9,758	5,091	4,092	3,848	3,510
Depreciation	5,576	5,093	4,078	1,036	1,068	968	542	489	502	430
Interest Expense	488	359	290	279	432	401	236	143	149	165
Pretax Income	11,534	14,007	3,263	11,796	10,329	5,781	4,448	2,594	3,000	2,804
Effective Tax Rate	29.7%	19.0%	49.7%	22.1%	24.8%	35.4%	28.0%	24.7%	28.0%	31.0%
Net Income	8,094	11,332	1,639	9,181	7,752	3,718	3,199	1,950	2,213	1,929
S&P Core Earnings	7,588	11,030	2,147	8,441	6,862	NA	NA	NA	NA	NA
Balance Sheet & Other Financial Data (Million $)										
Cash	2,247	1,808	1,520	1,878	1,036	1,099	739	1,552	877	1,150
Current Assets	41,896	39,694	29,741	24,781	18,450	17,187	11,191	9,931	6,820	6,468
Total Assets	117,565	123,684	116,775	46,356	39,153	33,510	20,574	18,302	15,336	14,667
Current Liabilities	28,448	26,458	23,657	18,555	13,640	11,981	9,185	7,192	5,305	5,640
Long Term Debt	6,347	7,279	5,755	3,140	2,609	1,123	525	527	729	687
Common Equity	65,458	68,085	65,158	19,950	18,293	16,076	8,887	8,810	7,933	6,954
Total Capital	82,214	88,189	84,370	23,454	21,354	17,579	9,713	9,534	8,818	7,944
Capital Expenditures	2,106	2,601	2,641	1,758	2,203	2,191	1,561	1,198	943	774
Cash Flow	13,661	16,417	5,710	10,217	8,820	4,686	3,741	2,484	2,715	2,359
Current Ratio	1.5	1.5	1.3	1.3	1.4	1.4	1.2	1.4	1.3	1.1
% Long Term Debt of Capitalization	7.7	8.3	6.8	13.4	12.2	6.4	5.4	5.5	8.3	8.6
% Net Income of Revenue	15.8	21.6	3.6	28.4	24.0	12.6	19.7	14.4	17.7	17.1
% Return on Assets	6.7	9.4	2.0	21.5	21.3	11.5	16.5	11.6	14.8	14.1
% Return on Equity	12.1	17.0	3.8	48.0	45.1	24.8	36.2	23.3	29.7	31.0

Data as orig reptd.; bef. results of disc opers/spec. items. Per share data adj. for stk. divs.; EPS diluted. E-Estimated. NA-Not Available. NM-Not Meaningful. NR-Not Ranked. UR-Under Review.

Office: 235 East 42nd Street, New York, NY 10017-5703.
Telephone: 212-573-2323.
Website: http://www.pfizer.com
Chrmn: H.A. McKinnell

Vice Chrmn: D.L. Shedlarz
CEO: J.B. Kindler
General Counsel: A. Waxman
Investor Contact: A. Naj

Board of Directors: D. A. Ausiello, M. S. Brown, M. A. Burns, R. N. Burt, W. D. Cornwell, W. H. Gray III, C. J. Horner, W. R. Howell, S. O. Ikenberry, J. B. Kindler, G. A. Lorch, H. A. McKinnell, D. G. Mead, R. J. Simmons, W. C. Steere, Jr.

Founded: 1849
Domicile: Delaware
Employees: 106,000

PG&E Corp

STANDARD &POOR'S

S&P Recommendation SELL ★★★★★

Price $43.14 (as of Oct 31, 2006)

12-Mo. Target Price $41.00

Investment Style Large-Cap Value

GICS Sector Utilities
Sub-Industry Multi-Utilities

Comment This energy holding company is the parent of Pacific Gas and Electric Co., which emerged from bankruptcy reorganization in April 2004.

Key Stock Statistics (Source S&P, Vickers, company reports)

52-Wk Range	$43.65–34.54	S&P Oper. EPS 2006**E**	2.45	P/E on S&P Oper. EPS 2006**E**	17.6	Dividend Rate/Share	$1.32
Trailing 12-Month EPS	$2.39	S&P Oper. EPS 2007**E**	2.70	Common Shares Outstg. (M)	348.1	Yield (%)	3.06
Trailing 12-Month P/E	18.1	S&P Core EPS 2006**E**	2.48	Market Capitalization(B)	$15.016	Beta	0.97
$10K Invested 5 Yrs Ago	$25,182	S&P Core EPS 2007**E**	2.74	Institutional Ownership (%)	65	S&P Credit Rating	NR

Price Performance

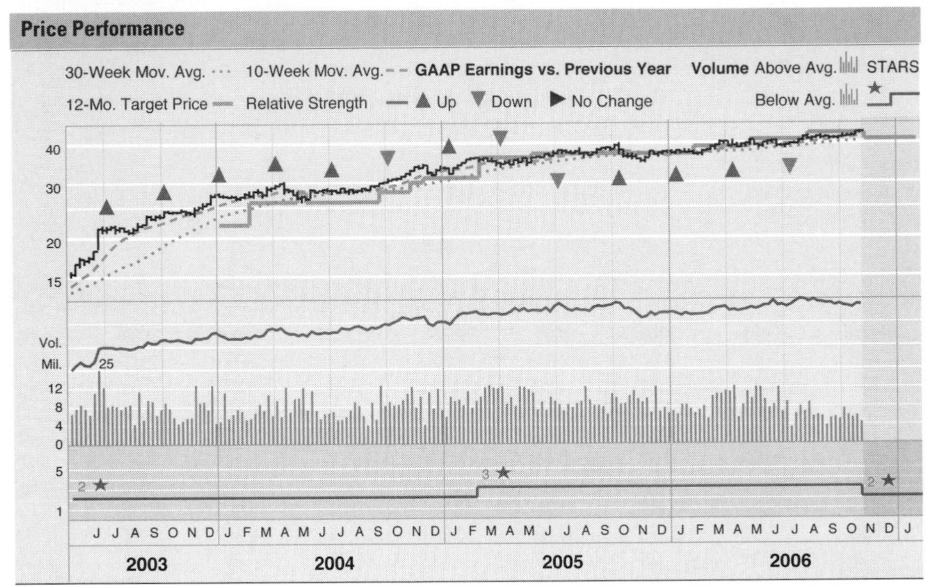

Options: ASE, CBOE, P

Highlights

➤ The STARS recommendation for PCG has recently been changed to 2 (sell) from 3 (hold) and the 12-month target price has recently been changed to $41.00 from $43.00. The Highlights section of this Stock Report will be updated accordingly.

Investment Rationale/Risk

➤ The Investment Rationale/Risk section of this Stock Report will be updated shortly. For the latest News story on PCG from MarketScope, see below.

➤ 10/30/06 02:55 pm EST... S&P DOWNGRADES SHARES OF PG&E CORP TO SELL FROM HOLD (PCG 43.25**): Given the rise in the share price, more than 16% year-to-date, we believe PCG stock is overvalued at its current level. We expect the company to report Q3 earnings November 8th, and we still expect EPS of $0.69. We are also maintaining our EPS estimates of $2.45 for full-year '06 and $2.70 for '07. However, with the yield from PCG's dividend having declined to around 3.0%, compared to a peer average of about 3.1%, we believe the shares are more fairly valued at a more modest premium-to-peers P/E of 15.2X our '07 estimate. Our 12-month target price falls $2 to $41. /J.McCann

Qualitative Risk Assessment

LOW	MEDIUM	HIGH

Our risk assessment reflects our view of the company's strong and steady cash flow from the regulated Pacific Gas & Electric subsidiary, a much improved balance sheet and credit profile, a healthy economy in its service territory, and a greatly improved regulatory environment.

Quantitative Evaluations

S&P Quality Ranking **B**

D	C	B-	B	B+	A-	A	A+

Relative Strength Rank **MODERATE**

54

LOWEST = 1 HIGHEST = 99

Revenue/Earnings Data

Revenue (Million $)

	1Q	2Q	3Q	4Q	Year
2006	3,148	3,017	--	--	--
2005	2,669	2,498	2,804	3,732	11,703
2004	2,722	2,749	2,623	2,986	11,080
2003	2,065	2,729	3,103	2,538	10,435
2002	2,935	2,938	3,654	2,968	12,495
2001	6,675	5,013	6,301	4,978	22,959

Earnings Per Share ($)

2006	0.60	0.65	**E**0.69	**E**0.52	**E**2.45
2005	0.54	0.70	0.62	0.49	2.34
2004	7.15	0.88	0.53	0.44	8.97
2003	-0.21	0.81	1.24	0.09	1.96
2002	1.71	0.75	1.17	-3.72	-0.15
2001	-2.62	2.07	2.12	1.42	2.99

Fiscal year ended Dec. 31. Next earnings report expected: Early November. EPS Estimates based on S&P Operating Earnings; historical GAAP earnings are as reported.

Dividend Data (Dates: mm/dd Payment Date: mm/dd/yy)

Amount ($)	Date Decl.	Ex-Div. Date	Stk. of Record	Payment Date
0.330	12/21	12/28	12/30	01/16/06
0.330	02/15	03/29	03/31	04/15/06
0.330	06/21	06/29	07/03	07/15/06
0.330	09/20	09/28	10/02	10/15/06

Dividends have been paid since 2005. Source: Company reports.

PG&E Corp

Business Summary August 07, 2006

CORPORATE OVERVIEW. PG&E Corporation (PCG) is an energy-based holding company that conducts its business through Pacific Gas and Electric Company, a public utility operating in northern and central California. The utility's business consists of four main operational units: electricity and natural gas distribution, electricity generation, gas transmission, and electricity transmission. The utility is primarily regulated by the California Public Utilities Commission (CPUC) and the Federal Energy Regulatory Commission (FERC).

CORPORATE STRATEGY. During 2005, the utility identified and undertook various initiatives to improve its business processes and systems to provide better, faster and more cost-effective service to its customers. It also defined the performance metrics against which the initiatives would be benchmarked. The company has drawn up a five-year transformation program by defining business priorities such as providing attractive shareholder returns, increasing investment in utility infrastructure, implementing an effective energy procurement plan, developing effective communication and scouting for investment opportunities.

Company Financials

Per Share Data ($) Year Ended Dec. 31	2005	2004	2003	2002	2001	2000	1999	1998	1997	1996
Tangible Book Value	19.67	20.60	10.11	8.92	11.87	8.74	19.13	21.06	21.28	20.60
Earnings	2.34	8.97	1.96	-0.15	2.99	-9.18	0.04	1.88	1.75	1.75
S&P Core Earnings	2.45	9.00	2.05	-1.08	1.59	NA	NA	NA	NA	NA
Dividends	1.23	Nil	Nil	Nil	Nil	1.20	1.20	1.20	1.20	1.77
Payout Ratio	53%	Nil	Nil	Nil	Nil	NM	NM	64%	69%	101%
Prices:High	40.10	34.46	27.98	23.75	20.94	31.81	34.00	35.06	30.94	28.38
Prices:Low	31.83	25.90	11.69	8.00	6.50	17.00	20.25	29.06	20.88	19.50
P/E Ratio:High	17	4	14	NM	7	NM	NM	19	18	16
P/E Ratio:Low	14	3	6	NM	2	NM	NM	15	12	11
Income Statement Analysis (Million $)										
Revenue	11,703	11,080	10,435	12,495	22,959	26,232	20,820	19,942	15,400	9,610
Depreciation	1,735	1,497	1,222	1,309	1,068	3,659	1,780	1,609	1,889	1,222
Maintenance	NA	NA	NA	NA	NA	NA	NA	NA	NA	NA
Fixed Charges Coverage	3.48	2.75	2.23	2.94	2.48	3.01	2.99	2.65	2.90	2.90
Construction Credits	NA	NA	NA	NA	NA	NA	Nil	Nil	Nil	Nil
Effective Tax Rate	37.6%	39.2%	36.7%	NM	35.8%	NM	95.0%	44.2%	43.4%	42.4%
Net Income	904	3,820	791	-57.0	1,090	-3,324	13.0	719	716	755
S&P Core Earnings	974	3,828	830	-404	580	NA	NA	NA	NA	NA
Balance Sheet & Other Financial Data (Million $)										
Gross Property	32,030	30,509	29,222	31,179	33,012	28,469	28,067	29,844	20,472	33,310
Capital Expenditures	1,804	1,559	1,698	3,032	2,665	1,758	1,584	1,619	1,822	1,230
Net Property	19,955	18,989	18,107	16,928	19,167	16,591	16,776	17,633	20,472	19,008
Capitalization:Long Term Debt	9,794	8,311	9,924	11,590	9,527	5,516	9,484	10,523	7,659	7,821
Capitalization:% Long Term Debt	57.5	49.0	70.2	76.2	68.8	63.5	57.9	56.6	35.7	46.0
Capitalization:Preferred	Nil	Nil	Nil	Nil	Nil	Nil	Nil	Nil	539	840
Capitalization:% Preferred	Nil	Nil	Nil	Nil	Nil	Nil	Nil	Nil	2.71	4.90
Capitalization:Common	7,240	8,633	4,215	3,613	4,322	3,172	6,886	8,066	8,897	8,363
Capitalization:% Common	42.5	51.0	29.8	23.8	31.2	36.5	42.1	43.4	41.5	49.1
Total Capital	20,238	20,596	15,122	16,786	15,668	10,536	19,748	22,733	21,424	21,345
% Operating Ratio	87.8	102.2	80.4	67.2	90.3	84.1	90.9	92.8	92.3	86.0
% Earned on Net Property	10.1	38.4	14.6	31.2	15.0	34.7	5.1	5.0	8.8	7.1
% Return on Revenue	7.7	34.5	7.6	NM	4.7	NM	0.1	3.6	4.6	7.9
% Return on Invested Capital	7.3	15.6	13.9	22.8	16.7	29.1	9.7	6.4	9.0	6.5
% Return on Common Equity	11.4	59.5	20.2	NM	29.1	NM	0.2	8.5	8.3	8.5

Data as orig reptd.; bef. results of disc opers/spec. items. Per share data adj. for stk. divs.; EPS diluted. E-Estimated. NA-Not Available. NM-Not Meaningful. NR-Not Ranked. UR-Under Review.

Office: 1 Market Spear Tower Ste 2400, San Francisco, CA 94105.
Telephone: 415-267-7000.
Email: invrel@pg-corp.com
Website: http://www.pgecorp.com

Chrmn, Pres & CEO: P.A. Darbee
SVP, CFO & Treas: C.P. Johns
SVP & General Counsel: B.R. Worthington
Investor Contact: G.B. Togneri (415-267-7080)

Board of Directors: D. R. Andrews, D. A. Coulter, C. L. Cox, P. A. Darbee, M. C. Herringer, M. S. Metz, B. L. Rambo, B. L. Williams

Founded: 1995
Domicile: California
Employees: 19,800

STANDARD &POOR'S

Phelps Dodge Corp

S&P Recommendation HOLD ★★★★★

Price $100.58 (as of Oct 27, 2006)

12-Mo. Target Price $110.00

Investment Style Large-Cap Value

GICS Sector Materials
Sub-Industry Diversified Metals & Mining

Comment Phelps Dodge is the world's second largest producer of copper and a large producer of molybdenum.

Key Stock Statistics (Source S&P, Vickers, company reports)

52-Wk Range	$102.80–58.85	S&P Oper. EPS 2006E	12.60	P/E on S&P Oper. EPS 2006E	8.0	Dividend Rate/Share	$0.80
Trailing 12-Month EPS	$8.97	S&P Oper. EPS 2007E	10.40	Common Shares Outstg. (M)	204.0	Yield (%)	0.80
Trailing 12-Month P/E	11.2	S&P Core EPS 2006E	12.55	Market Capitalization(B)	$20.517	Beta	1.98
$10K Invested 5 Yrs Ago	$73,123	S&P Core EPS 2007E	10.34	Institutional Ownership (%)	86	S&P Credit Rating	BBB

Price Performance

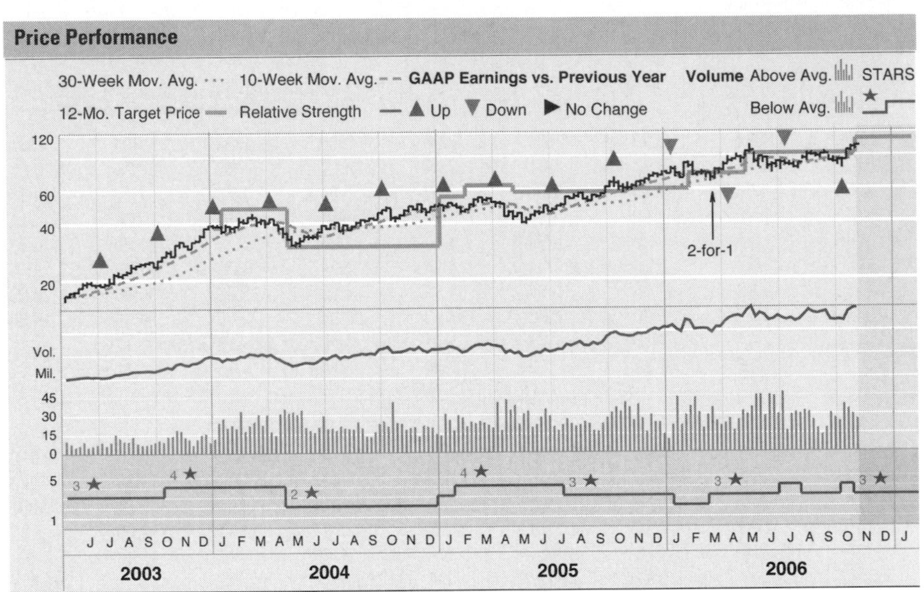

Options: ASE, CBOE, P

Analysis prepared by **Leo J. Larkin** on October 25, 2006, when the stock traded at **$ 99.91**.

Highlights

- Following an estimated sales gain of 48% in 2006, we look for a 7% decline in 2007 as an expected increase in copper production should be offset by a projected decline in the average price of copper. We also look for a lower average price for molybdenum and flat molybdenum production versus 2006. Our expectation for a lower copper price assumes the absence of strike-related disruption along with less vibrant global demand in 2007. In our view, there will be a larger copper surplus in 2007 compared with 2006. It appears to us that a combination of strikes and investment fund demand led to 2006's record high copper price, even though there was a small supply glut for most of 2006, following a deficit in 2005.
- We look for a small contraction in margins in 2007 as the benefit of higher copper output is offset by reduced revenue per pound. On that basis, we project EPS of $10.40 versus operating EPS of $12.60 estimated for 2006.
- Longer term, we believe that EPS will benefit from a secular rise in copper demand from Asia, less rapid growth of global copper production, and consolidation of the global mining industry.

Investment Rationale/Risk

- We believe that 2006 will likely represent a peak for both EPS and copper prices. However, with the shares recently trading at just 9.4X our EPS estimate for 2007, we think the stock is worth holding. Also, our secular outlook for copper remains positive. Increased growth in China and India should keep demand higher than in the previous cycle. Also, we expect the global copper supply to rise less rapidly as mine output levels off. We see this keeping the average copper price higher than in the previous cycle. In turn, this should lead to higher EPS and free cash flow over the course of the next cycle.
- Risks to our recommendation and target price include a decline in the price of copper in 2007 in excess of what we currently expect.
- Based on our expectation that sales, EPS and free cash flow in the current cycle will be stronger than in the prior one, we believe that PD will sell at 10.6X our 2007 EPS estimate, which is toward the low end of its historical range but above the P/E following the last copper price peak. On that basis, our 12-month target price is $110.

Qualitative Risk Assessment

LOW | **MEDIUM** | HIGH

Our risk assessment reflects the cyclicality of the construction industry and other end markets for copper, and the company's stagnant reserve profile, offset by our view of PD's reduced debt, strengthened balance sheet, and substantial free cash flow.

Quantitative Evaluations

S&P Quality Ranking B-

D | C | **B-** | B | B+ | A- | A | A+

Relative Strength Rank STRONG

90

LOWEST = 1 HIGHEST = 99

Revenue/Earnings Data

Revenue (Million $)

	1Q	2Q	3Q	4Q	Year
2006	2,225	2,992	3,458	--	--
2005	1,887	1,966	2,179	2,256	8,287
2004	1,597	1,651	1,847	1,995	7,089
2003	978.0	962.2	1,031	1,171	4,143
2002	918.5	966.8	941.2	895.5	3,722
2001	1,101	1,064	937.0	901.2	4,002

Earnings Per Share ($)

2006	1.72	2.32	4.37	**E**4.20	**E**12.60
2005	1.87	3.34	1.78	0.85	7.82
2004	0.95	1.15	1.48	1.70	5.29
2003	-0.15	-0.11	-0.02	0.35	0.03
2002	-0.02	-0.23	-0.17	-1.29	-1.77
2001	0.11	-0.71	-0.64	-0.50	-1.74

Fiscal year ended Dec. 31. Next earnings report expected: Late January. EPS Estimates based on S&P Operating Earnings; historical GAAP earnings are as reported.

Dividend Data (Dates: mm/dd Payment Date: mm/dd/yy)

Amount ($)	Date Decl.	Ex-Div. Date	Stk. of Record	Payment Date
2.0 Spl.	04/05	05/12	05/16	06/02/06
0.200	04/05	05/12	05/16	06/02/06
0.200	06/07	08/10	08/14	09/01/06
0.200	10/24	11/14	11/16	12/01/06

Dividends have been paid since 2004. Source: Company reports.

Please read the Required Disclosures and Analyst Certification on the last page of this report.

Phelps Dodge Corp

Business Summary October 25, 2006

CORPORATE OVERVIEW. Phelps Dodge is the world's second largest copper producer and is also a large producer of molybdenum. PD has mines and processing facilities in North and South America, Europe and China. It also processes other minerals as byproducts, such as gold, silver and rhenium.

Consolidated copper production was 1,228,000 metric tons in 2005, versus 1,260,600 metric tons in 2004. Commercially recoverable copper reserves totaled 23.7 million metric tons at the end of 2005, versus 26.1 million metric tons at the end of 2004, and 21.1 million metric tons at the end of 2003 and 2002.

Molybdenum production totaled 62.3 million pounds in 2005, versus 57.5 million pounds in 2004.

CORPORATE STRATEGY. PD's strategy is to position the company to prosper throughout all phases of the copper cycle. To that end, PD invests to improve the quality of its existing assets in an effort to lower costs and improve productivity. It also seeks to increase reserves through exploration.

Company Financials

Per Share Data ($) Year Ended Dec. 31	2005	2004	2003	2002	2001	2000	1999	1998	1997	1996
Tangible Book Value	27.42	22.07	14.52	15.82	17.20	18.62	19.50	20.11	19.62	19.96
Cash Flow	10.21	7.79	2.39	0.72	1.22	3.12	0.60	4.10	5.59	5.40
Earnings	7.82	5.29	0.03	-1.77	-1.74	0.19	-2.07	1.63	3.32	3.49
S&P Core Earnings	4.91	5.20	-0.03	-1.89	-2.80	NA	NA	NA	NA	NA
Dividends	0.63	0.25	Nil	Nil	0.38	1.00	1.00	1.00	1.00	0.98
Payout Ratio	8%	5%	Nil	Nil	NM	NM	NM	62%	30%	28%
Prices:High	74.63	50.78	39.71	21.26	27.84	36.50	35.31	35.88	44.81	38.81
Prices:Low	39.10	29.90	15.06	11.45	12.87	18.03	20.94	21.94	29.94	27.31
P/E Ratio:High	10	10	NM	NM	NM	NM	NM	22	14	11
P/E Ratio:Low	5	6	NM	NM	NM	NM	NM	13	9	8
Income Statement Analysis (Million $)										
Revenue	8,287	7,089	4,143	3,722	4,002	4,525	3,114	3,063	3,914	3,786
Operating Income	2,749	2,078	658	437	389	753	468	525	940	973
Depreciation	491	507	423	410	465	464	329	293	284	250
Interest Expense	62.3	126	145	187	226	213	120	94.0	62.0	68.0
Pretax Income	2,351	1,390	74.1	-394	-263	55.0	-422	333	594	698
Effective Tax Rate	24.5%	10.2%	65.2%	NM	NM	34.5%	NM	40.2%	30.3%	31.6%
Net Income	1,584	1,046	18.1	-289	-273	29.0	-255	191	409	462
S&P Core Earnings	988	1,013	5.29	-316	-440	NA	NA	NA	NA	NA
Balance Sheet & Other Financial Data (Million $)										
Cash	1,917	1,200	684	350	387	250	234	222	158	471
Current Assets	4,071	2,662	1,790	1,428	1,504	1,508	1,693	980	1,051	1,422
Total Assets	10,358	8,594	7,273	7,029	7,619	7,031	8,229	5,037	4,965	4,816
Current Liabilities	1,609	1,168	1,015	784	1,014	1,418	1,418	651	701	686
Long Term Debt	678	972	1,704	1,948	2,522	1,963	2,172	836	857	555
Common Equity	5,602	4,341	3,062	2,812	2,707	3,106	3,278	2,588	2,511	2,756
Total Capital	7,753	6,319	5,248	5,193	5,730	5,600	5,932	4,026	3,806	3,821
Capital Expenditures	686	304	151	130	263	397	201	318	662	513
Cash Flow	2,068	1,540	427	121	192	493	74.0	484	693	712
Current Ratio	2.5	2.3	1.8	1.8	1.5	1.1	1.2	1.5	1.5	2.1
% Long Term Debt of Capitalization	8.7	15.4	32.5	37.5	44.0	35.1	36.6	20.8	22.5	14.5
% Net Income of Revenue	19.1	14.8	0.4	NM	NM	0.6	NM	6.2	10.4	12.2
% Return on Assets	16.7	13.2	0.3	NM	NM	0.4	NM	3.8	8.4	9.8
% Return on Equity	31.7	27.9	0.2	NM	NM	0.9	NM	7.5	15.5	17.0

Data as orig reptd.; bef. results of disc opers/spec. items. Per share data adj. for stk. divs.; EPS diluted. E-Estimated. NA-Not Available. NM-Not Meaningful. NR-Not Ranked. UR-Under Review.

Office: 1 N Central Ave , Phoenix, AZ, USA 85004-4464.
Telephone: 602-366-8100.
Website: http://www.phelpsdodge.com
Chrmn & CEO: J.S. Whisler

Pres & COO: T.R. Snider
EVP & CFO: R.G. Peru
SVP & General Counsel: S.D. Colton
Investor Contact: S.K. Rideout (602-366-8589)

Board of Directors: A. W. Dunham, W. A. Franke, R. D. Johnson, M. L. Knowles, C. C. Krulak, J. C. Madonna, D. E. McCoy, G. R. Parker, W. J. Post, M. Richenhagen, J. E. Thompson, J. S. Whisler

Founded: 1885
Domicile: New York
Employees: 15,000

STANDARD &POOR'S

Pinnacle West Capital Corp

S&P Recommendation HOLD ★★★★★

Price $48.08 (as of Oct 27, 2006)

12-Mo. Target Price $47.00

Investment Style Mid-Cap Value

GICS Sector Utilities
Sub-Industry Electric Utilities

Comment This utility holding company is the parent of Arizona Public Service (APS), Arizona's largest electric utility.

Key Stock Statistics (Source S&P, Vickers, company reports)

52-Wk Range	$48.93–38.31	S&P Oper. EPS 2006E	3.08	P/E on S&P Oper. EPS 2006E	15.6	Dividend Rate/Share	$2.10
Trailing 12-Month EPS	$3.29	S&P Oper. EPS 2007E	3.30	Common Shares Outstg. (M)	99.5	Yield (%)	4.37
Trailing 12-Month P/E	14.6	S&P Core EPS 2006E	2.88	Market Capitalization(B)	$4.783	Beta	0.86
$10K Invested 5 Yrs Ago	$14,594	S&P Core EPS 2007E	3.02	Institutional Ownership (%)	81	S&P Credit Rating	BBB-

Price Performance

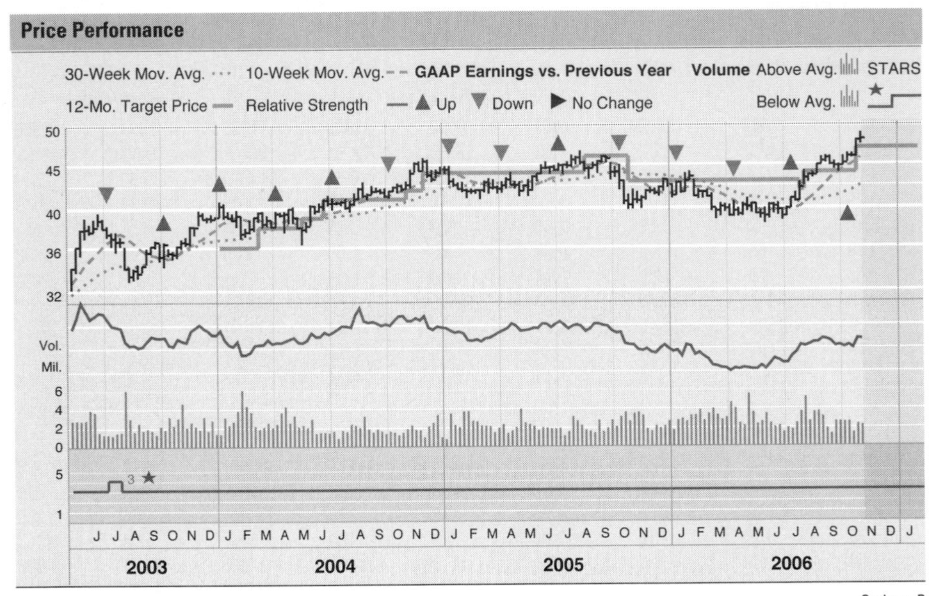

Options: P

Analysis prepared by **Justin McCann** on October 17, 2006, when the stock traded at **$ 46.38**.

Highlights

- Following an anticipated 33% advance in 2006 operating EPS (from 2005 EPS from continuing operations of $2.31), we expect operating EPS in 2007 to increase about 7%. Operating results in the first half of 2006 were aided by customer growth well above the industry average, fuel and purchased power cost deferrals, and the hottest June on record.
- We see 2006 EPS benefiting from strong customer growth at Arizona Public Service (APS) and about $0.45 from SunCor real estate. EPS should also benefit from the stronger than expected second quarter, which was aided by fuel and purchased power cost deferrals (that are expected to be recovered through commission approved adjustors and surcharges) and the hottest June on record. However, we believe earnings from the marketing and trading operations will remain negligible.
- In May 2006, the Arizona Corporation Commission approved APS's request for an emergency interim rate increase of $232 million to recover the undercollection of higher fuel and purchased power costs. APS would be subject to a refund pending a final ruling on its prior $409 million (19.1%) rate increase request.

Investment Rationale/Risk

- After underperforming the S&P Electric Utility Index for the past two years, the shares were recently up about 12% year to date. While the year-to-date increase is roughly in line with PNW's peers, we believe the stock will continue to trade at a discount to the peer P/E on our EPS estimates for 2007. However, with the 15% federal tax rate on dividends having been extended through 2010, the shares should be partly supported by PNW's dividend growth, which has been faster than that of peers.
- Risks to our recommendation and target price include worse than expected earnings from the real estate subsidiary, and a significant decline in the average P/E multiple of the group as a whole.
- Following the last $0.10 increase in the annual dividend (implemented with the December quarterly payment), and with the dividend payout ratio of 65% of our EPS estimate for 2006 only slightly above the industry average, we expect PNW to maintain its dividend policy of $0.10 annual increases. We see the shares trading at a discount to peers' P/E of about 14.2X our EPS estimate for 2007. Our 12-month target price is $47.

Qualitative Risk Assessment

LOW | MEDIUM | HIGH (rating: LOW)

Our risk assessment reflects the steady cash flow that we project from the electric utility operations of Arizona Public Service, which has one of the fastest growing service territories in the U.S. While the regulatory environment has often been difficult, we do not expect to see the general strength of the utility severely impeded by regulatory rulings. This should help to offset the less predictable earnings stream from the real estate business and the power marketing and trading operations.

Quantitative Evaluations

S&P Quality Ranking A-

D | C | B- | B | B+ | **A-** | A | A+

Relative Strength Rank STRONG

72

LOWEST = 1 HIGHEST = 99

Revenue/Earnings Data

Revenue (Million $)

	1Q	2Q	3Q	4Q	Year
2006	670.2	925.0	1,076	--	--
2005	585.4	755.3	955.6	691.7	2,988
2004	574.4	722.7	886.8	734.7	2,900
2003	552.6	683.3	847.7	734.2	2,818
2002	380.2	496.8	719.4	416.6	2,637
2001	938.8	1,294	1,574	744.7	4,551

Earnings Per Share ($)

	1Q	2Q	3Q	4Q	Year
2006	0.12	1.11	1.84	E0.35	E3.08
2005	0.32	0.88	0.86	0.24	2.31
2004	0.33	0.78	1.14	0.32	2.57
2003	0.22	0.60	1.20	0.50	2.52
2002	0.63	0.89	1.19	-0.17	2.53
2001	0.73	0.79	1.91	0.42	3.85

Fiscal year ended Dec. 31. Next earnings report expected: Early February. EPS Estimates based on S&P Operating Earnings; historical GAAP earnings are as reported.

Dividend Data (Dates: mm/dd Payment Date: mm/dd/yy)

Amount ($)	Date Decl.	Ex-Div. Date	Stk. of Record	Payment Date
0.500	01/18	01/30	02/01	03/01/06
0.500	03/22	04/27	05/01	06/01/06
0.500	07/19	07/28	08/01	09/01/06
0.525	10/18	10/30	11/01	12/01/06

Dividends have been paid since 1993. Source: Company reports.

Pinnacle West Capital Corp

Business Summary October 17, 2006

CORPORATE OVERVIEW. Pinnacle West Capital, formed in 1985, is the holding company for Arizona Public Service (APS), which, with about 1,033,500 customers, is Arizona's largest electric utility. PNW's other major subsidiaries are APS Energy Services, which provides competitive energy services, including wholesale marketing and trading, and SunCor, which is engaged in real estate development and investment activities. In 2005, the regulated electricity segment accounted for 74.9% of PNW's consolidated revenues (also 74.9% of net income), the real estate segment, 11.3% (15.7%); the marketing and trading segment, 11.8% (7.2%); and other, 2.0% (2.2%).

MARKET PROFILE. APS provides vertically integrated retail and wholesale service to the entire state, with the exception of Tucson and about 50% of the Phoenix area. In 2005, residential customers accounted for 48.3% of the utility's regulated electric sales (48.4% in 2004); business customers, 46.5% (48.1%); and wholesale and other, 5.2% (3.5%). APS has a 29.1% owned or leased interest in the Palo Verde Nuclear Generating Station's Units 1 and 3, and a 17.0% interest in Unit 2. It has a 100% interest in Units 1, 2 and 3; a 15% interest in Units 4 and 5 of the coal-fueled Four Corners Steam Generating Station; and a 14.0% in Units 1, 2 and 3 of the coal-fueled Navajo Steam Generating Station (NGS). Consolidated fuel sources for APS in 2005 were: purchased power and net interchange, 51.8% (56.9% in 2004); coal, 26.3% (20.8%); nuclear, 15.1% (13.5%); gas, 6.8% (8.7%); and other, 0.1% (0.1%). With APS dependent on purchased power for so much of its fuel sources, we believe that it has been hurt by the sharp rise in natural gas prices and by the time lags involved in being authorized to recover the difference between its actual fuel costs and the rates the company is allowed to charge its customers.

SunCor develops residential, commercial and industrial real estate projects in Arizona, Idaho, New Mexico and Utah. The company, which had total assets of $487 million at the end of 2005, intends to continue its focus on the development of master-planned communities. Although SunCor's operating revenues declined to $338 million in 2005, from $350 million in 2004, its net income rose by $11 million, to $56 million. We believe the company will continue to be an important source of PNW's earnings and cash flow.

Company Financials

Per Share Data ($) Year Ended Dec. 31	**2005**	**2004**	**2003**	**2002**	**2001**	**2000**	**1999**	**1998**	**1997**	**1996**
Tangible Book Value	34.58	30.99	29.81	28.23	29.46	28.09	26.00	25.50	23.90	22.51
Earnings	2.31	2.57	2.52	2.53	3.85	3.56	1.97	2.85	2.76	2.41
S&P Core Earnings	2.00	2.15	2.43	1.65	3.00	NA	NA	NA	NA	NA
Dividends	1.93	1.83	1.73	1.63	1.53	1.43	1.33	1.23	1.13	1.03
Payout Ratio	83%	71%	68%	64%	40%	40%	67%	43%	41%	43%
Prices:High	46.68	45.84	40.48	46.68	50.70	52.69	43.38	49.25	42.75	32.25
Prices:Low	39.81	36.30	28.34	21.70	37.65	25.69	30.19	39.38	27.63	26.25
P/E Ratio:High	20	18	16	18	13	15	22	17	15	13
P/E Ratio:Low	17	14	11	9	10	7	15	14	10	11

Income Statement Analysis (Million $)	2005	2004	2003	2002	2001	2000	1999	1998	1997	1996
Revenue	2,988	2,900	2,818	2,637	4,551	3,690	2,423	2,131	1,995	1,818
Depreciation	348	401	438	425	428	394	386	380	368	300
Maintenance	NA	NA	NA	NA	NA	NA	NA	NA	NA	NA
Fixed Charges Coverage	2.77	2.75	2.43	2.64	3.80	3.95	3.61	3.17	2.93	2.80
Construction Credits	11.2	4.89	14.2	NA	NA	NA	11.7	18.6	16.2	14.7
Effective Tax Rate	36.2%	35.4%	31.4%	39.1%	39.5%	42.5%	38.4%	40.4%	38.9%	37.8%
Net Income	223	235	231	215	327	302	270	243	236	211
S&P Core Earnings	193	197	223	140	255	NA	NA	NA	NA	NA

Balance Sheet & Other Financial Data (Million $)	2005	2004	2003	2002	2001	2000	1999	1998	1997	1996
Gross Property	11,200	18,280	10,470	16,316	9,285	8,383	7,805	7,876	7,730	7,145
Capital Expenditures	634	538	693	896	1,041	659	343	319	308	259
Net Property	7,577	14,914	7,310	12,842	5,907	5,133	4,779	5,062	5,043	4,655
Capitalization:Long Term Debt	2,608	2,585	2,898	2,882	2,673	1,955	2,206	2,144	2,244	2,372
Capitalization:% Long Term Debt	43.2	46.7	50.6	51.8	51.7	45.1	50.0	49.8	50.5	52.0
Capitalization:Preferred	Nil	Nil	Nil	Nil	Nil	Nil	Nil	Nil	171	219
Capitalization:% Preferred	Nil	Nil	Nil	Nil	Nil	Nil	Nil	Nil	3.80	4.80
Capitalization:Common	3,425	2,950	2,830	2,686	2,499	2,383	2,206	2,163	2,027	1,970
Capitalization:% Common	56.8	53.3	49.4	48.2	48.3	54.9	50.0	50.2	45.6	43.2
Total Capital	7,259	6,763	7,057	6,777	6,237	5,481	5,599	5,678	5,856	5,995
% Operating Ratio	82.4	85.8	86.6	81.7	89.9	87.7	83.1	75.7	74.0	77.1
% Earned on Net Property	6.8	3.4	6.8	4.2	24.6	13.6	12.2	11.2	11.0	11.7
% Return on Revenue	7.5	8.1	8.2	8.2	7.2	8.2	11.1	11.4	11.8	11.6
% Return on Invested Capital	8.0	6.9	6.2	7.7	7.9	8.2	7.5	13.9	7.0	6.8
% Return on Common Equity	7.0	8.1	8.4	8.3	13.4	13.2	12.3	11.6	11.8	11.0

Data as orig reptd.; bef. results of disc opers/spec. items. Per share data adj. for stk. divs.; EPS diluted. E-Estimated. NA-Not Available. NM-Not Meaningful. NR-Not Ranked. UR-Under Review.

Office: 400 North 5th Street, Phoenix, AZ 85004-3902.
Telephone: 602-250-1000.
Website: http://www.pinnaclewest.com
Chrmn & CEO: W.J. Post

Pres & COO: J.E. Davis
EVP & CFO: D. Brandt
VP & Treas: B.M. Gomez
VP, Secy & General Counsel: N.C. Loftin

Investor Contact: R. Hickman (602-250-5668)
Board of Directors: E. N. Basha, Jr., J. E. Davis, M. L. Gallagher, P. Grant, R. A. Herberger, Jr., M. O. Hesse, W. S. Jamieson, Jr., H. S. Lopez, K. L. Munro, B. J. Nordstrom, W. J. Post, W. L. Stewart

Founded: 1920
Domicile: Arizona
Employees: 7,300

STANDARD &POOR'S

Pitney Bowes Inc.

S&P Recommendation HOLD ★★★★★ | **Price** $46.26 (as of Oct 27, 2006) | **12-Mo. Target Price** $49.00 | **Investment Style** Large-Cap Growth

GICS Sector Industrials
Sub-Industry Office Services & Supplies

Comment PBI, the world's largest maker of mailing systems, also provides production and document management equipment and facilities management services.

Key Stock Statistics (Source S&P, Vickers, company reports)

52-Wk Range	$47.10–40.18	S&P Oper. EPS 2006E	2.68	P/E on S&P Oper. EPS 2006E	17.3	Dividend Rate/Share	$1.28
Trailing 12-Month EPS	$0.23	S&P Oper. EPS 2007E	2.97	Common Shares Outstg. (M)	221.5	Yield (%)	2.77
Trailing 12-Month P/E	NM	S&P Core EPS 2006E	2.63	Market Capitalization(B)	$10.248	Beta	0.95
$10K Invested 5 Yrs Ago	$15,768	S&P Core EPS 2007E	2.91	Institutional Ownership (%)	78	S&P Credit Rating	A+

Price Performance

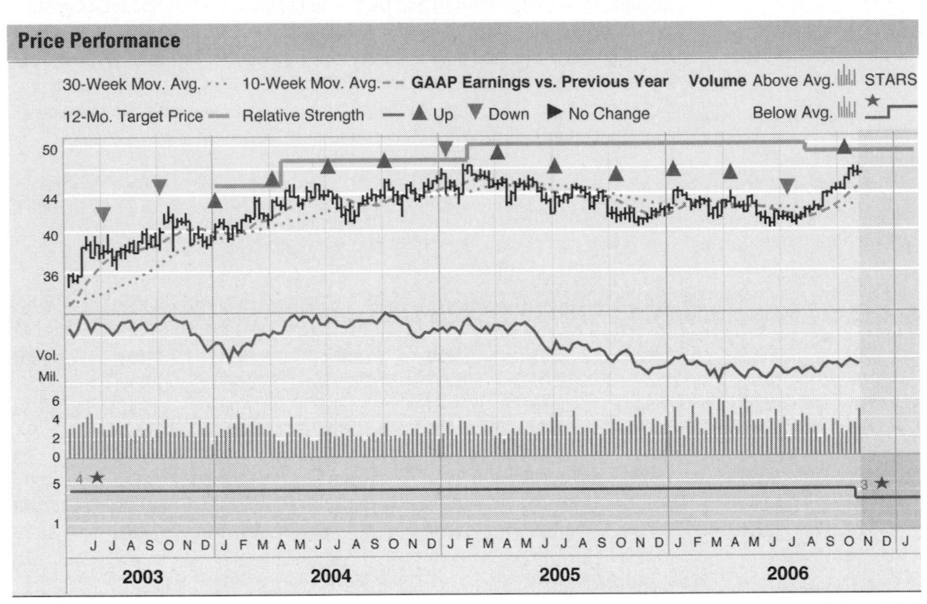

Options: ASE, P

Analysis prepared by **Richard N. Stice, CFA** on October 24, 2006, when the stock traded at **$ 46.26**.

Highlights

- We look for 2006 and 2007 revenues to rise 6% and 5%, respectively, aided by continued economic growth, a migration to digital meters, strengthening international markets, and further acquisition activity. We believe that the July 2006 sale of the company's Capital Services division should allow for a greater focus on its core businesses.
- We see gross margins remaining near the 55% level through 2007, as higher volumes are offset by a less favorable business mix. We believe PBI will maintain SG&A expenses at about 31% of total revenue. Results should continue to be favorably affected by share buybacks. Through the first three quarters of 2006, the company utilized $312 million for repurchases and ended the period with $229 million remaining in its program.
- We forecast 2007 EPS of $2.97, up 11% from our 2006 EPS estimate of $2.68 (excluding $0.04 of special items). Both estimates include projected stock option expense. Our S&P Core EPS estimates for 2006 and 2007 are $2.63 and $2.91, respectively, reflecting our projection of pension costs.

Investment Rationale/Risk

- We believe PBI has a large recurring revenue stream and leadership position within its market, as well as an above-average dividend yield of 2.7%. We see synergies from recent acquisitions, and new product introductions focusing on digital technology leading to steady growth in future periods. However, with the shares trading at a premium to the S&P 500, we think these attributes are already reflected in the current price.
- Risks to our recommendation and target price include increased competition in the document management outsourcing market, which would have an impact on pricing within PBI's Management Services, a contributor of nearly 20% of revenues.
- Our 12-month target price of $49 is based on a combination of metrics. The first, its P/E, allocates PBI a level of 16.9X, which is in line with its three year, monthly historical average. Combined with our 2007 EPS estimate, this results in a value of $50. The second, discounted cash flow, assumes a weighted average cost of capital of 8.0% and an expected terminal growth rate of 3%. This leads to an intrinsic value of $48.

Qualitative Risk Assessment

LOW | **MEDIUM** | HIGH

Our risk assessment reflects our view of PBI's steady cash flow, recurring revenue streams, and history of a consistent dividend policy and share buyback programs. However, we think these factors are offset by a lackluster rate of revenue growth and integration risk associated with recent acquisitions.

Quantitative Evaluations

S&P Quality Ranking A-

D | C | B- | B | B+ | **A-** | A | A+

Relative Strength Rank MODERATE

60

LOWEST = 1 HIGHEST = 99

Revenue/Earnings Data

Revenue (Million $)

	1Q	2Q	3Q	4Q	Year
2006	1,404	1,389	1,433	--	--
2005	1,318	1,360	1,356	1,458	5,492
2004	1,172	1,206	1,218	1,362	4,957
2003	1,091	1,134	1,137	1,215	4,577
2002	1,050	1,081	1,114	1,165	4,410
2001	966.3	1,021	1,044	1,091	4,122

Earnings Per Share ($)

	1Q	2Q	3Q	4Q	Year
2006	0.67	0.54	0.64	E0.76	E2.68
2005	0.64	0.60	0.62	0.41	2.27
2004	0.54	0.58	0.58	0.35	2.05
2003	0.48	0.50	0.50	0.61	2.10
2002	0.53	0.59	0.61	0.08	1.81
2001	0.42	0.76	0.49	0.41	2.08

Fiscal year ended Dec. 31. Next earnings report expected: Early February. EPS Estimates based on S&P Operating Earnings; historical GAAP earnings are as reported.

Dividend Data (Dates: mm/dd Payment Date: mm/dd/yy)

Amount ($)	Date Decl.	Ex-Div. Date	Stk. of Record	Payment Date
0.310	11/07	11/16	11/18	12/12/05
0.320	02/01	02/15	02/17	03/12/06
0.320	04/10	05/17	05/19	06/12/06
0.320	07/10	08/16	08/18	09/12/06

Dividends have been paid since 1934. Source: Company reports.

Pitney Bowes Inc.

Business Summary October 24, 2006

CORPORATE OVERVIEW. Pitney Bowes is a provider of global, integrated mail and document management offerings. The company operates in the following business groups: Global Mailstream Solutions and Global Business Services. A third division, Capital Services, was divested in July 2006.

The Global Mailstream Solutions segment, which accounted for 71% of 2005 revenue (68% in 2004), is comprised of three units. The first, Inside the U.S., includes U.S. revenue and related expenses from the sale, rental and financing of mail finishing, and mail creation and shipping equipment. The second, Document Messaging Technologies (DMT), includes U.S. revenue and related expenses from the sale, service and financing of high speed, production mail systems, sorting equipment, incoming mail systems, and electronic statement, billing and payment solutions. The third unit, Outside the U.S., encompasses the above mentioned products and services relative to overseas markets.

The Global Business Services segment (27%, 30%) is made up of three divisions: Management Services (PBMS), Mail Services and Marketing Services. The PBMS unit focuses on facilities management contracts for advanced mailing, secure mail services, reprographic, document management and other high value services. The Mail Services group offers presort mail services and international outbound mail services. The Marketing Services business is comprised of direct mail and marketing campaign services.

IMPACT OF MAJOR DEVELOPMENTS. In April 2005, PBI entered into a definitive agreement with an affiliate of Cerberus Capital Management, L.P. for a sponsored spin-off of its Capital Services business. The transaction was completed in July 2006, with the unit becoming an independent company called EntreCap Financial Corp. PBI received a net amount of approximately $750 million as well as relinquished debt obligations of $470 million. PBI applied the proceeds toward a $1.1 billion tax settlement, about $900 million of which resulted from the Capital Services sale.

Company Financials

Per Share Data ($) Year Ended Dec. 31	**2005**	**2004**	**2003**	**2002**	**2001**	**2000**	**1999**	**1998**	**1997**	**1996**
Tangible Book Value	NM	NM	NM	0.10	1.05	4.34	5.28	5.26	5.06	6.06
Cash Flow	3.70	3.36	3.32	2.98	3.44	3.55	4.05	3.31	2.21	2.48
Earnings	2.27	2.05	2.10	1.81	2.08	2.18	2.42	2.03	1.80	1.56
S&P Core Earnings	2.09	1.94	1.87	1.34	0.81	NA	NA	NA	NA	NA
Dividends	1.24	1.22	1.20	1.18	1.16	1.14	1.02	0.90	0.80	0.69
Payout Ratio	55%	60%	57%	65%	56%	52%	42%	44%	44%	44%
Prices:High	47.50	46.97	42.75	44.41	44.70	54.13	73.31	66.38	45.75	30.69
Prices:Low	40.34	38.88	29.45	28.55	32.00	24.00	40.88	42.22	26.81	20.94
P/E Ratio:High	21	23	20	25	21	25	30	33	25	20
P/E Ratio:Low	18	19	14	16	15	11	17	21	15	13
Income Statement Analysis (Million $)										
Revenue	5,492	4,957	4,577	4,410	4,122	3,881	4,433	4,221	4,100	3,859
Operating Income	1,435	1,352	1,291	1,276	1,046	1,316	1,526	1,375	1,303	1,160
Depreciation	332	307	289	264	317	321	412	361	300	278
Interest Expense	214	172	168	185	193	201	184	169	209	204
Pretax Income	867	699	721	619	766	803	985	864	803	684
Effective Tax Rate	39.3%	31.3%	31.4%	29.3%	32.9%	29.9%	33.1%	34.3%	34.3%	31.4%
Net Income	527	481	495	438	514	563	659	568	526	469
S&P Core Earnings	485	456	440	324	199	NA	NA	NA	NA	NA
Balance Sheet & Other Financial Data (Million $)										
Cash	244	316	294	315	232	198	254	129	139	137
Current Assets	2,742	2,693	2,513	2,553	2,557	2,627	3,343	2,509	2,464	2,222
Total Assets	10,621	9,821	8,891	8,732	8,318	7,901	8,223	7,661	7,893	8,156
Current Liabilities	2,911	3,294	2,647	3,350	3,083	2,882	2,873	2,722	3,373	3,305
Long Term Debt	3,850	3,109	3,151	2,317	2,419	2,192	2,308	2,023	1,068	1,300
Common Equity	1,301	1,289	1,086	852	890	1,283	1,624	1,734	1,870	2,237
Total Capital	7,074	4,399	5,898	4,706	4,584	4,704	5,015	4,680	4,146	4,260
Capital Expenditures	292	317	286	225	256	269	305	298	244	272
Cash Flow	858	787	784	702	832	884	1,071	929	646	747
Current Ratio	0.9	0.8	0.9	0.8	0.8	0.9	1.2	0.9	0.7	0.7
% Long Term Debt of Capitalization	54.4	70.7	53.4	49.2	52.8	46.6	46.0	43.2	25.8	30.5
% Net Income of Revenue	11.2	9.7	10.8	9.9	12.5	14.5	14.9	13.5	12.8	12.2
% Return on Assets	5.1	5.1	5.6	5.1	6.3	7.0	8.3	7.3	6.6	5.9
% Return on Equity	40.7	40.5	51.1	50.3	47.3	38.7	40.3	31.5	25.6	21.8

Data as orig reptd.; bef. results of disc opers/spec. items. Per share data adj. for stk. divs.; EPS diluted. E-Estimated. NA-Not Available. NM-Not Meaningful. NR-Not Ranked. UR-Under Review.

Office: 1 Elmcroft Rd, Stamford, CT 06926-0700.
Telephone: 203-351-6858.
Email: investorrelations@pb.com
Website: http://www.pb.com

Chrmn & CEO: M.J. Critelli
Pres & COO: M.D. Martin
EVP & CFO: B.P. Nolop
SVP & General Counsel: M.C. Mayes

SVP & CIO: G.E. Buoncontri
Investor Contact: C.F. McBride (203-351-6349)
Board of Directors: L. G. Alvarado, C. G. Campbell, M. J. Critelli, A. S. Fuchs, E. Green, J. H. Keyes, J. S. McFarlane, E. R. Menasce, M. I. Roth, D. L. Shedlarz, D. B. Snow, Jr., R. E. Weissman

Founded: 1920
Domicile: Delaware
Employees: 34,165

STANDARD &POOR'S

Plum Creek Timber Co Inc.

S&P Recommendation HOLD ★★★★★

Price $35.85 (as of Oct 30, 2006)

12-Mo. Target Price $38.00

Investment Style Mid-Cap Value

GICS Sector Financials
Sub-Industry Specialized REITS

Comment Plum Creek Timber Co., a real estate investment trust (REIT), is the largest private timberland owner in the United States, with about 8.2 million acres of timberlands in 18 states.

Key Stock Statistics (Source S&P, Vickers, company reports)

52-Wk Range	**$39.63–31.21**	S&P Oper. EPS 2006**E**	**1.70**	P/E on S&P Oper. EPS 2006**E**	**21.1**	Dividend Rate/Share	**$1.60**
Trailing 12-Month EPS	**$1.71**	S&P Oper. EPS 2007**E**	**1.75**	Common Shares Outstg. (M)	**179.2**	Yield (%)	**4.46**
Trailing 12-Month P/E	**21.0**	S&P Core EPS 2006**E**	**1.70**	Market Capitalization(B)	**$6.425**	Beta	**0.80**
$10K Invested 5 Yrs Ago	**$16,471**	S&P Core EPS 2007**E**	**1.75**	Institutional Ownership (%)	**51**	S&P Credit Rating	**NA**

Price Performance

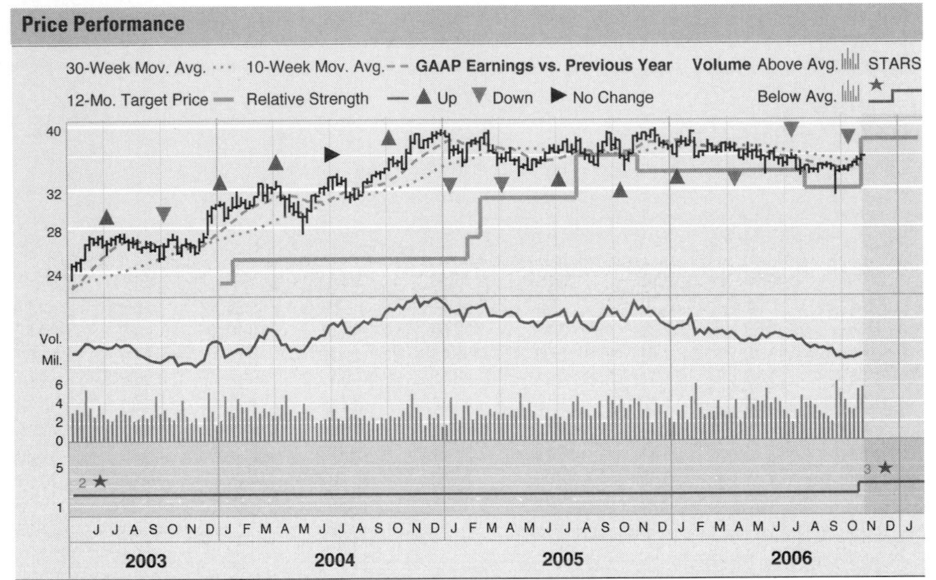

Options: ASE, Ph

Analysis prepared by **Stuart J. Benway, CFA** on October 30, 2006, when the stock traded at **$ 35.72**.

Highlights

- S&P projects that housing starts will decline 11.6% in 2006 and fall an additional 14.2% in 2007. We expect this to prevent any meaningful recovery in lumber and sawlog prices, which have fallen in recent quarters. However, we look for revenues of this timber REIT to be essentially unchanged due to an increase in harvest volumes and higher real estate sales.
- We believe that average wood product prices in late 2006 and early 2007 will be below year-earlier levels, as demand from the housing market slows. In our view, this will put some pressure on margins in the timberland operations. We see PCL capturing improved market prices for its higher and better use land sales, although the timing is uncertain, and the impact should be more significant in 2007 and beyond.
- Corporate spending, interest expense and taxes are all expected to increase in 2006, and we estimate that earnings will decline about 5% as a result. Our operating EPS estimate for 2006 is $1.70, and for 2007 we project $1.75.

Investment Rationale/Risk

- We believe Plum Creek has significant value in its land holdings and expect real estate transactions to become a more significant source of earnings in coming years. PCL has identified 225,000 acres of land that it plans to develop over the next 15 years, and we estimate that these properties can be sold at high margin levels. In our view, this will allow PCL to continue to pay a high and moderately rising dividend.
- Risks to our recommendation and target price include further declines in log demand and prices than we expect due to weakness in the U.S. housing market, and lower than projected profits on sales of higher and better use land.
- Our first valuation metric, which applies a forward P/E of 22.4X to our 2007 EPS estimate of $1.75, in line with peers, indicates a potential value of $39. Our dividend discount model, which assumes a 96% payout ratio in 2007, a required rate of return of 10%, and constant dividend growth of 5.5%, indicates that the stock has an intrinsic value of about $37. Using an equal-weighted blend of these metrics, our 12-month target price is $38.

Qualitative Risk Assessment

LOW	**MEDIUM**	HIGH

Plum Creek operates in a cyclical industry, with demand for its products tied to residential construction and paper manufacturing. It is subject to movements in interest rates, economic conditions and currency, and prices for its products have historically been volatile. However, it is a major landowner, and its debt levels are relatively low.

Quantitative Evaluations

S&P Quality Ranking **NR**

D	C	B-	B	B+	A-	A	A+

Relative Strength Rank **MODERATE**

54

LOWEST = 1 HIGHEST = 99

Revenue/Earnings Data

Revenue (Million $)

	1Q	2Q	3Q	4Q	Year
2006	414.0	380.0	454.0	--	--
2005	400.0	358.0	427.0	391.0	1,576
2004	497.0	341.0	363.0	327.0	1,528
2003	273.0	318.0	290.0	315.0	1,196
2002	275.0	271.0	310.0	281.0	1,137
2001	117.0	100.0	141.0	240.0	598.0

Earnings Per Share ($)

	1Q	2Q	3Q	4Q	Year
2006	0.50	0.34	0.51	**E**0.35	**E**1.70
2005	0.56	0.37	0.52	0.34	1.79
2004	0.84	0.31	0.42	0.28	1.84
2003	0.18	0.31	0.25	0.30	1.04
2002	0.30	0.29	0.38	0.29	1.26
2001	0.32	0.24	0.42	1.25	2.58

Fiscal year ended Dec. 31. Next earnings report expected: Late January. EPS Estimates based on S&P Operating Earnings; historical GAAP earnings are as reported.

Dividend Data (Dates: mm/dd Payment Date: mm/dd/yy)

Amount ($)	Date Decl.	Ex-Div. Date	Stk. of Record	Payment Date
0.380	11/01	11/14	11/16	11/30/05
0.400	02/07	02/15	02/17	03/03/06
0.400	05/02	05/11	05/15	05/31/06
0.400	08/01	08/14	08/16	08/31/06

Dividends have been paid since 1989. Source: Company reports.

Please read the Required Disclosures and Analyst Certification on the last page of this report.

Plum Creek Timber Co Inc.

Business Summary October 30, 2006

CORPORATE OVERVIEW. Plum Creek Timber Co., a real estate investment trust (REIT), is the largest private timberland owner in the United States, with about 8.2 million acres of timberlands in 18 states. In addition, the trust operates several wood products manufacturing facilities and is actively involved in land purchases and sales. The company conducts operations through four business segments: the timber operation accounted for 48% of 2005 revenues, manufacturing (32%), real estate (19%), and other (1%). The Northern Resources portion of the timber segment encompasses 3.9 million acres of timberlands, mostly in Maine, Michigan, Montana, and Wisconsin. The Southern Resources portion of the timber segment consists of 4.3 million acres of timberlands primarily in Arkansas, Florida, Georgia, Louisiana, and Mississippi.

MARKET PROFILE. The timber industry provides raw materials and manages resources for the paper and forest products industry. Harvested logs are sold to third party mills that produce lumber, plywood, oriented strand board, and pulp and paper products. There are five primary end markets for most of the timber harvested in the United States: new housing construction, home repair and remodeling, products for industrial uses, raw material for the manufacture of pulp and paper, and logs for export.

The demand for timber is directly related to the underlying demand for pulp and paper products, lumber, panels, and other wood products. The demand for pulp and paper is largely driven by population growth and per-capita income levels. The demand for lumber and manufactured wood products is affected primarily by the level of new residential construction activity and repair and remodeling activity, which, in turn, is affected by changes in general economic and demographic factors, including population growth and interest rates for home mortgages and construction loans. The market for wood fiber used in paper production and wood products manufacturing is very diverse, with many manufacturers of various sizes. We therefore believe that Plum Creek has only limited control over the prices that it can charge for timber and wood products. However, due to growing demand and limitations on supply caused by, among other factors, environmental restrictions and urban sprawl, prices for softwood timber have exhibited a compound annual growth rate of about 4% from 1982 through 2005.

Company Financials

Per Share Data ($) Year Ended Dec. 31	**2005**	**2004**	**2003**	**2002**	**2001**	**2000**	**1999**	**1998**	**1997**	**1996**
Tangible Book Value	12.62	12.19	11.57	12.04	12.21	7.46	7.70	8.78	10.14	10.58
Cash Flow	NA	2.46	1.63	1.82	3.00	2.47	3.10	3.12	3.93	6.74
Earnings	1.79	1.84	1.04	1.26	2.58	1.91	1.72	0.90	1.72	4.71
S&P Core Earnings	1.80	1.82	1.04	1.24	2.57	NA	NA	NA	NA	NA
Dividends	1.52	1.42	1.40	1.49	2.85	2.28	2.28	2.26	2.16	2.00
Payout Ratio	85%	77%	135%	118%	110%	119%	133%	NM	126%	42%
Prices:High	39.63	39.45	30.75	31.98	30.00	29.81	32.13	34.88	36.00	27.75
Prices:Low	33.40	27.30	20.88	18.92	23.30	21.50	23.13	23.44	25.75	22.88
P/E Ratio:High	22	21	30	25	12	16	19	39	21	6
P/E Ratio:Low	19	15	20	15	9	11	13	26	15	5
Income Statement Analysis (Million $)										
Revenue	1,576	1,528	1,196	1,137	598	209	461	699	726	634
Operating Income	561	586	410	443	305	166	206	210	244	222
Depreciation	113	114	107	105	55.0	38.9	59.7	69.3	70.2	56.9
Interest Expense	109	111	117	103	54.0	46.8	63.5	60.6	60.4	50.1
Pretax Income	339	366	186	235	196	132	100	76.0	112	225
Effective Tax Rate	2.30%	7.40%	NM	0.85%	NM	NM	NM	0.68%	0.07%	0.60%
Net Income	331	339	192	233	338	132	113	75.4	112	224
S&P Core Earnings	332	336	193	229	336	NA	NA	NA	NA	NA
Balance Sheet & Other Financial Data (Million $)										
Cash	395	376	260	246	193	181	115	114	135	124
Current Assets	574	499	405	378	306	195	133	210	232	222
Total Assets	4,812	4,378	4,387	4,289	4,122	1,250	1,251	1,438	1,301	1,356
Current Liabilities	375	184	168	155	149	180	74.2	80.9	74.0	69.0
Long Term Debt	1,524	1,853	2,031	1,839	1,667	560	643	943	745	763
Common Equity	2,325	2,240	2,119	2,222	2,247	507	533	405	470	490
Total Capital	3,888	4,138	4,187	4,105	3,952	1,066	1,176	1,348	1,215	1,253
Capital Expenditures	89.0	70.0	246	231	59.0	21.7	25.6	54.9	28.3	19.3
Cash Flow	444	453	299	338	393	171	173	145	182	281
Current Ratio	1.5	2.7	2.4	2.4	2.1	1.1	1.8	2.6	3.1	3.2
% Long Term Debt of Capitalization	39.1	44.8	48.5	44.8	42.2	52.5	54.7	69.9	61.3	60.9
% Net Income of Revenue	21.0	22.2	16.1	20.5	56.5	63.1	24.6	10.8	15.4	35.3
% Return on Assets	7.2	7.7	4.4	5.5	11.8	10.5	8.4	5.5	8.5	20.7
% Return on Equity	14.5	15.6	8.8	10.4	28.3	25.4	24.2	17.2	23.2	61.7

Data as orig reptd.; bef. results of disc opers/spec. items. Per share data adj. for stk. divs.; EPS diluted. E-Estimated. NA-Not Available. NM-Not Meaningful. NR-Not Ranked. UR-Under Review.

Office: 999 3rd Ave Ste 4300, Seattle, WA 98104-4096.
Telephone: 206-467-3600.
Email: info@plumcreek.com
Website: http://www.plumcreek.com

Chrmn: D.D. Leland
Pres & CEO: R.R. Holley
SVP & CFO: D.W. Lambert
SVP, Secy & General Counsel: J.A. Kraft

Treas: L.B. Smith
Investor Contact: J. Hobbs (800-858-5347)
Board of Directors: I. B. Davidson, R. R. Holley, R. Josephs, J. G. McDonald, R. B. McLeod, H. R. Moghadam, J. H. Scully, S. C. Tobias, C. B. Webb, m. A. White

Founded: 1989
Domicile: Delaware
Employees: 2,100

STANDARD &POOR'S

PMC Sierra Inc

S&P Recommendation HOLD ★★★★★	Price	12-Mo. Target Price	Investment Style
	$6.41 (as of Oct 27, 2006)	$8.00	Mid-Cap Value

GICS Sector Information Technology
Sub-Industry Semiconductors

Comment This company designs, develops, markets and supports high-performance semiconductor networking solutions for advanced communications markets.

Key Stock Statistics (Source S&P, Vickers, company reports)

52-Wk Range	$13.77–4.78	S&P Oper. EPS 2006E	0.21	P/E on S&P Oper. EPS 2006E	30.5	Dividend Rate/Share	Nil
Trailing 12-Month EPS	$-0.19	S&P Oper. EPS 2007E	0.32	Common Shares Outstg. (M)	209.0	Yield (%)	Nil
Trailing 12-Month P/E	NM	S&P Core EPS 2006E	0.21	Market Capitalization(B)	$1.340	Beta	4.54
$10K Invested 5 Yrs Ago	$3,569	S&P Core EPS 2007E	0.32	Institutional Ownership (%)	NA	S&P Credit Rating	NA

Price Performance

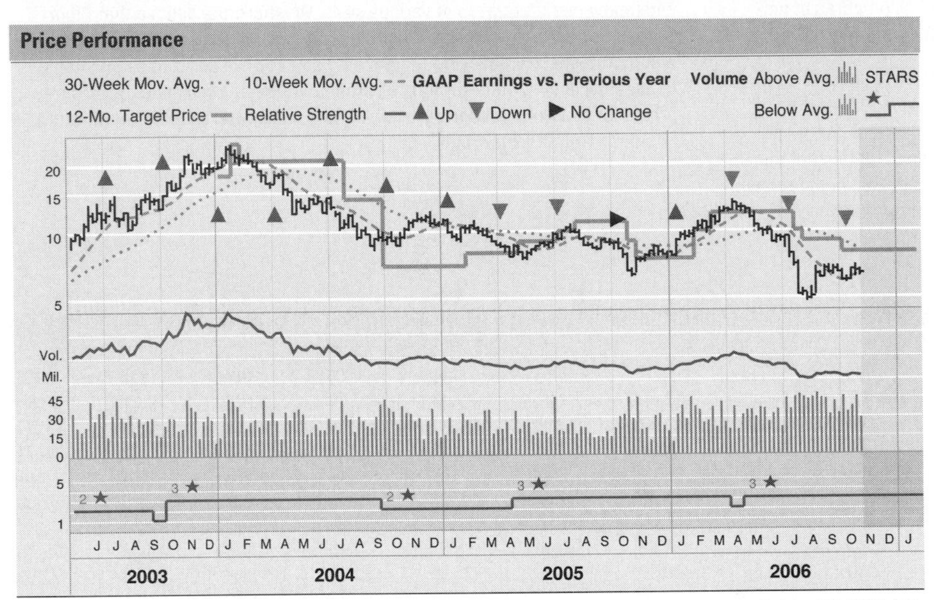

Options: ASE, CBOE, P, Ph

Analysis prepared by **Jawahar Hingorani** on October 25, 2006, when the stock traded at **$ 6.50**.

Highlights

- Our forecast of 49% revenue growth for 2006 reflects contributions from the company's recent acquisitions. We expect enterprise storage to continue to show growth during the second half of 2006 but see lower fiber-to-the-home deployments. We project nearly 20% revenue growth in 2007.

- Despite our outlook for rising sales volumes and PMCS's ongoing focus on managing supply chain costs, we expect pro forma gross margins to narrow to approximately 66% from 72% reported in 2005, hurt by recent acquisitions; we see modestly wider pro forma gross margins in 2007. We look for wider operating margins (excluding stock option expense) in 2006 and 2007 as revenue growth likely outpaces expenses and PMCS benefits from a lower cost structure following past restructurings. We expect additional restructuring in future periods following recent acquisitions.

- We expect pro forma EPS, excluding noncash items, of $0.21 and $0.32 in 2006 and 2007, respectively, compared to $0.20 in 2005. Our EPS estimates for 2006 and 2007 include $0.12 of projected stock option expense in both years.

Investment Rationale/Risk

- We think customer inventory levels remain reasonable. We have a favorable view of the company's acquisition of the storage semiconductor business of Avago Technologies (March 2006) and Passave (fiber-to-the-home; closed May 2006), which should help expand PMCS's presence in key end-markets. Our optimism is tempered, however, by our outlook for narrowing gross margins, integration risks and restructuring charges ahead.

- Risks to our opinion and target price include the rising proportion of 2006 revenues that we forecast from PMCS's volatile "turns business," which represents orders placed and shipped in the same quarter. Driven by PMCS's supply agreements with certain key customers and a high proportion of turns for recent acquisitions, we see this affecting already low forward visibility. Regarding corporate governance, we have concerns about the company's compensation practices.

- We derive our 12-month target price of $8 by applying a 3.3X price to sales multiple to our 2007 revenue per share estimate of $2.42, at the low end of the historical average range for the shares of 3.3X-10.4X.

Qualitative Risk Assessment

LOW | MEDIUM | **HIGH**

Our risk assessment reflects our outlook for future integration risks and restructuring charges after recent acquisitions. We also believe that the company remains vulnerable to volatile demand for communications equipment, although we think customer inventory levels remain reasonable, and that there is poor visibility into the future.

Quantitative Evaluations

S&P Quality Ranking B-

D | C | **B-** | B | B+ | A- | A | A+

Relative Strength Rank WEAK

22

LOWEST = 1 HIGHEST = 99

Revenue/Earnings Data

Revenue (Million $)

	1Q	2Q	3Q	4Q	Year
2006	87.78	118.8	116.5	--	--
2005	66.11	71.54	76.20	77.56	291.4
2004	78.66	85.70	71.17	61.85	297.4
2003	55.39	60.38	63.10	70.62	249.5
2002	51.44	54.51	59.58	52.56	218.1
2001	119.9	94.13	61.56	47.16	322.7

Earnings Per Share ($)

2006	-0.08	-0.16	-0.05	**E**0.05	**E**0.21
2005	0.02	Nil	0.03	0.10	0.15
2004	0.09	0.08	0.03	0.07	0.27
2003	-0.07	-0.05	0.02	0.05	-0.05
2002	-0.08	-0.07	-0.05	-0.18	-0.38
2001	-0.38	-1.39	-0.20	-1.82	-3.80

Fiscal year ended Dec. 31. Next earnings report expected: Late January. EPS Estimates based on S&P Operating Earnings; historical GAAP earnings are as reported.

Dividend Data

No cash dividends have been paid.

PMC Sierra Inc

Business Summary October 25, 2006

CORPORATE OVERVIEW. PMC-Sierra designs, develops, markets and supports high-performance semiconductor integrated circuits that are used for telecommunications and data networking applications. PMCS offers more than 250 semiconductor devices in network infrastructure for the Metro, Access, Storage, Enterprise and Consumer Premise segments.

Access has traditionally accounted for a majority of sales (about 70% in 2005), while Storage, Enterprise and Customer Premise, collectively, have represented a smaller portion of revenues (about 30% in 2005). PMCS's recent acquisition of the storage semiconductor business from Avago Technologies is expected to shift the mix of the company's revenues to approximately 50% telecommunications-related and 50% from enterprise and storage end-markets.

The majority of PMCS's products are incorporated into networking equipment by original equipment manufacturers (OEMs) who then sell the equipment to telecommunications service providers. The company aims to profitably expand its overall business by strengthening its market position within its traditional service provider market while expanding its presence in newer markets such as enterprise and storage. To support these goals, PMCS is focusing its R&D resources on developing solutions for the growth areas of its service provider customers' businesses and on broadening its storage and enterprise product offerings. The company also aims to increase its presence in Asian markets from 50% and 46% in 2005 and 2004, respectively.

PMCS sells its products to end-customers directly and through distributors and independent manufacturer representatives. In 2005, approximately 40% of orders were shipped through distributors, approximately 50% were sent by the company directly to contract manufacturers selected by OEMs, and the balance were sent directly to OEM customers. The company's two largest distributors, Memec Group (acquired by Avnet Inc. in 2005) and Macnica, accounted for 27% and 10% of total revenues in 2005, respectively, down from 32% and 12%, respectively in 2004.

Company Financials

Per Share Data ($) Year Ended Dec. 31	2005	2004	2003	2002	2001	2000	1999	1998	1997	1996
Tangible Book Value	1.86	1.60	1.25	1.14	1.59	3.24	1.61	0.85	0.69	0.34
Cash Flow	0.21	0.35	0.12	-0.13	-3.22	0.82	0.74	0.09	0.33	-0.31
Earnings	0.15	0.27	-0.05	-0.38	-3.80	0.41	0.60	-0.02	0.26	-0.41
S&P Core Earnings	-0.10	-0.09	-0.43	-0.94	-3.35	NA	NA	NA	NA	NA
Dividends	Nil	Nil	Nil	Nil	Nil	Nil	Nil	Nil	Nil	Nil
Payout Ratio	Nil	Nil	Nil	Nil	Nil	Nil	Nil	Nil	Nil	Nil
Prices:High	11.45	24.91	22.81	26.80	111.75	255.50	80.56	16.41	8.78	6.19
Prices:Low	6.20	8.22	4.64	2.70	9.37	60.00	15.67	5.72	3.47	1.97
P/E Ratio:High	76	92	NM	NM	NM	NM	NM	NM	33	NM
P/E Ratio:Low	41	30	NM	NM	NM	NM	NM	NM	13	NM
Income Statement Analysis (Million $)										
Revenue	291	297	249	218	323	695	262	162	127	188
Operating Income	47.4	57.8	23.5	-33.0	-93.1	251	119	74.7	56.7	36.5
Depreciation	11.9	15.3	28.4	42.4	98.0	74.2	21.2	14.2	9.20	10.9
Interest Expense	Nil	Nil	Nil	Nil	Nil	Nil	Nil	0.96	1.90	1.28
Pretax Income	30.1	48.4	-15.8	-83.9	-657	178	132	20.0	50.0	-38.4
Effective Tax Rate	7.00%	NM	NM	NM	NM	57.6%	31.6%	NM	31.5%	NM
Net Income	28.0	51.7	-7.99	-65.0	-639	75.3	90.0	-2.88	34.3	-48.1
S&P Core Earnings	-20.3	-14.0	-74.5	-159	-563	NA	NA	NA	NA	NA
Balance Sheet & Other Financial Data (Million $)										
Cash	406	121	290	75.8	152	256	84.1	33.9	69.2	42.1
Current Assets	687	327	464	476	494	571	254	123	93.5	68.3
Total Assets	733	507	553	729	855	1,126	342	197	149	130
Current Liabilities	121	175	147	247	280	230	89.1	54.9	34.9	47.9
Long Term Debt	225	Nil	175	275	275	0.56	1.08	5.22	9.10	18.4
Common Equity	354	299	226	199	272	851	236	126	90.6	48.4
Total Capital	608	299	401	476	576	896	246	134	115	79.3
Capital Expenditures	5.16	9.92	11.7	3.14	27.8	104	30.7	21.5	8.20	4.00
Cash Flow	39.9	67.0	20.4	-22.6	-541	149	111	11.3	43.5	-37.2
Current Ratio	5.7	1.9	3.2	1.9	1.8	2.5	2.9	2.2	2.7	1.4
% Long Term Debt of Capitalization	37.0	Nil	43.6	57.7	47.8	0.1	0.4	3.9	7.9	23.2
% Net Income of Revenue	9.6	17.4	NM	NM	NM	10.8	34.3	NM	27.0	NM
% Return on Assets	4.5	9.8	NM	NM	NM	9.9	32.9	NM	24.6	NM
% Return on Equity	8.6	19.7	NM	NM	NM	14.0	49.1	NM	49.4	NM

Data as orig reptd.; bef. results of disc opers/spec. items. Per share data adj. for stk. divs.; EPS diluted. E-Estimated. NA-Not Available. NM-Not Meaningful. NR-Not Ranked. UR-Under Review.

Office: 3975 Freedom Circle, Santa Clara, CA 95054-1241.
Telephone: 408-239-8000.
Email: investor_relations@pmc-sierra.com
Website: http://www.pmc-sierra.com

Chrmn, Pres & CEO: R.L. Bailey
VP & CTO: R. Young

Board of Directors: R. Bailey, R. Belluzzo, J. V. Diller, M. Farese, J. Judge, W. Kurtz, F. J. Marshall

Founded: 1983
Domicile: Delaware
Employees: 875

STANDARD &POOR'S

PNC Financial Services Group Inc.

S&P Recommendation BUY ★★★★★

Price $70.03 (as of Oct 31, 2006)

12-Mo. Target Price $82.00

Investment Style Large-Cap Value

GICS Sector Financials
Sub-Industry Regional Banks

Comment This bank holding company (formerly PNC Bank Corp.) conducts regional banking, wholesale banking and asset management businesses.

Key Stock Statistics (Source S&P, Vickers, company reports)

52-Wk Range	$74.00–60.27	S&P Oper. EPS 2006**E**	5.07	P/E on S&P Oper. EPS 2006**E**	13.8	Dividend Rate/Share	$2.20
Trailing 12-Month EPS	$8.66	S&P Oper. EPS 2007**E**	5.92	Common Shares Outstg. (M)	294.5	Yield (%)	3.14
Trailing 12-Month P/E	8.1	S&P Core EPS 2006**E**	4.98	Market Capitalization(B)	$20.621	Beta	0.87
$10K Invested 5 Yrs Ago	$14,206	S&P Core EPS 2007**E**	5.82	Institutional Ownership (%)	65	S&P Credit Rating	A

Price Performance

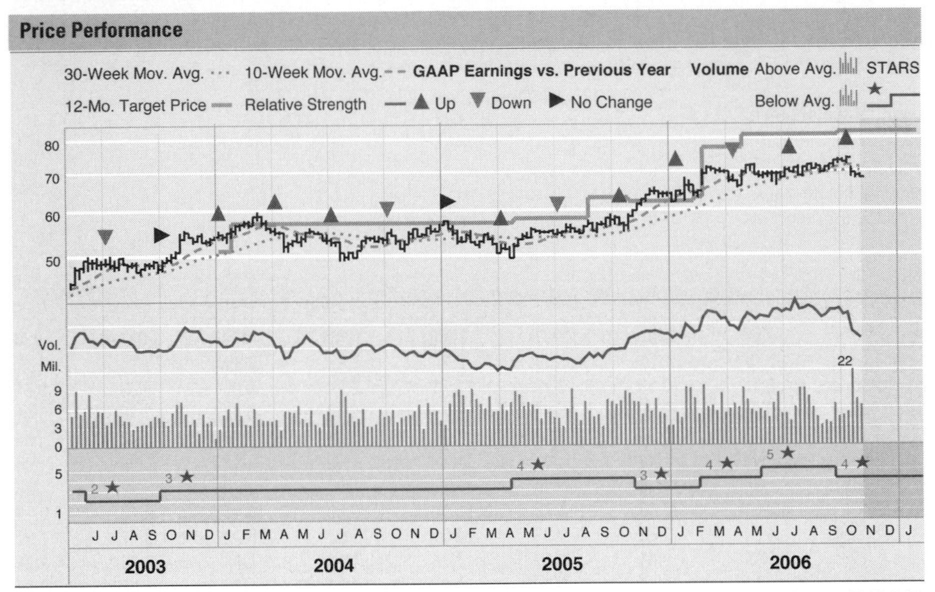

Options: CBOE, P, Ph

Analysis prepared by **Christopher B. Muir** on September 25, 2006, when the stock traded at **$ 72.71**.

Highlights

- We believe 2006 revenue growth of an estimated 16% will be driven mostly by growth in non-interest income. We expect earning asset growth will be partly offset by a lower net interest margin. Our 2006 estimates include a net interest margin of 2.83% (down from 2005, due to our view of continued pressure from a relatively flat yield curve), earning asset growth of 14%, and non-interest income growth of 19%.
- We expect non-interest expense to remain high, but to improve as cost savings from the One PNC expense reduction initiatives start to be realized. Our non-interest expense to total revenue forecast of 65.3% indicates a solid improvement from 2005's 67.1%. We think asset quality has stabilized, with strong improvement achieved in 2004 and 2005. However, we look for higher loan loss provisions of about $200 million in 2006, up from about $20 million in 2005.
- We expect 2006 operating EPS of $5.07, an 11% increase from the $4.55 earned in 2005. Our 2007 EPS estimate is $5.92, a further 17% increase.

Investment Rationale/Risk

- In February, BlackRock, 70%-owned by PNC, announced a deal to buy Merrill Lynch's asset management business. We think this planned deal should create significant value for PNC. Also, PNC's cost reduction program is expected to capture $400 million by 2007, more than PNC originally anticipated. We think PNC stock, recently trading at 12.3X our 2007 EPS estimate, or an 8.2% discount to the median of its large-cap peers, has significant room for multiple expansion.
- Risks to our recommendation and target price include detrimental changes in the slope of the yield curve and operating performance that fails to meet our expectations.
- Our 12-month target price of $82 is based on our relative valuation analysis and dividend discount model. Our target price implies a P/E ratio of 13.9X our 2007 EPS estimate, or a slight premium to the peer multiple of 13.3X. We think this valuation is warranted by our strong growth outlook for PNC. Our dividend discount model, which assumes a terminal growth rate of 4% and a discount rate of 9.4%, estimates an intrinsic value of $83.

Qualitative Risk Assessment

LOW | MEDIUM | HIGH

Our risk assessment for PNC reflects our view of the company's large-cap valuation, strong loan portfolio credit quality, and history of profitability. While the industry in which PNC operates is highly competitive and fragmented, it tends to produce relatively stable financial results.

Quantitative Evaluations

S&P Quality Ranking B+

D | C | B- | B | **B+** | A- | A | A+

Relative Strength Rank WEAK

29

LOWEST = 1 HIGHEST = 99

Revenue/Earnings Data

Revenue (Million $)

	1Q	2Q	3Q	4Q	Year
2006	2,251	2,356	--	--	--
2005	1,777	1,826	2,108	2,185	7,896
2004	1,577	1,395	1,523	1,413	6,315
2003	1,487	1,468	1,493	1,521	5,969
2002	1,648	1,674	1,540	1,507	6,369
2001	1,873	1,799	1,691	1,317	6,680

Earnings Per Share ($)

	1Q	2Q	3Q	4Q	Year
2006	1.19	1.28	5.01	**E**1.32	**E**5.07
2005	1.24	0.98	1.14	1.20	4.55
2004	1.15	1.07	0.91	1.08	4.21
2003	0.92	0.65	1.00	1.08	3.65
2002	1.11	1.12	1.00	0.97	4.20
2001	0.89	1.00	0.84	-1.52	1.26

Fiscal year ended Dec. 31. Next earnings report expected: Mid January. EPS Estimates based on S&P Operating Earnings; historical GAAP earnings are as reported.

Dividend Data (Dates: mm/dd Payment Date: mm/dd/yy)

Amount ($)	Date Decl.	Ex-Div. Date	Stk. of Record	Payment Date
0.500	01/05	01/11	01/13	01/24/06
0.550	04/06	04/11	04/14	04/24/06
0.550	07/06	07/12	07/14	07/24/06
0.550	10/05	10/11	10/13	10/24/06

Dividends have been paid since 1865. Source: Company reports.

PNC Financial Services Group Inc.

Business Summary September 25, 2006

CORPORATE OVERVIEW. PNC is a bank holding company that operates businesses engaged in retail banking, corporate and institutional banking, asset management, and global fund processing services. The company has four primary reportable business segments: Retail Banking, Corporate and Institutional Banking, BlackRock, and PFPC.

The Retail Banking and Corporate and Institutional Banking segments generate an estimated 66% of total revenues. Retail Banking (45%) provides deposit, lending, brokerage, trust, investment management and cash management services to consumers and small businesses. Corporate and Institutional Banking (21%) offers lending, treasury management and capital markets products and services to mid-sized corporations, government entities and selectively to large corporations.

The BlackRock segment (19%) includes the operations of 70%-owned BlackRock, Inc. (BLK). BLK, with $453 billion in assets under management, provides diversified investment management services to institutional and individual investors worldwide through a variety of fixed income, cash management, equity and alternative investment products.

PFPC (13%) provides mutual fund transfer agency and accounting and administration services.

The company attempts to measure, control and monitor risks on a corporate wide basis. The company's risk management program includes credit risk management, operational risk management, liquidity risk management, and market risk management. The company uses various derivative instruments and insurance contracts in an effort to reduce some of these risks.

MARKET PROFILE. PNC's footprint includes 363 branches in Pennsylvania, 302 in New Jersey, 58 in Kentucky, 45 in Ohio, 39 in Delaware, 30 in Washington, DC, 16 in Virginia, 10 in Maryland, and 10 branches in other states. The projection for deposit-weighted average population growth in the company's service territory is 0.4% from 2005 to 2010 according to SNL Financial. The projected national growth rate is 6.3%, and the population weighted average growth rate of the states in the company's service territory is 2.7%.

Company Financials

Per Share Data ($) Year Ended Dec. 31	2005	2004	2003	2002	2001	2000	1999	1998	1997	1996
Tangible Book Value	13.98	14.55	14.22	14.78	12.19	13.37	12.07	11.49	12.47	13.08
Earnings	4.55	4.21	3.65	4.20	1.26	4.09	4.15	3.60	3.28	2.90
S&P Core Earnings	4.43	4.00	3.53	3.83	0.92	NA	NA	NA	NA	NA
Dividends	2.00	2.00	1.94	1.92	1.92	1.83	1.68	1.58	1.50	1.42
Payout Ratio	44%	48%	53%	46%	152%	45%	40%	44%	46%	49%
Prices:High	65.66	59.79	55.55	62.80	75.81	75.00	62.00	66.75	58.75	39.75
Prices:Low	49.35	48.90	41.63	32.70	51.14	36.00	43.00	38.75	36.50	27.50
P/E Ratio:High	14	14	15	15	60	18	15	19	18	14
P/E Ratio:Low	11	12	11	8	41	9	10	11	11	9
Income Statement Analysis (Million $)										
Net Interest Income	2,154	1,969	1,996	2,197	2,262	2,164	2,433	2,573	2,495	2,444
Tax Equivalent Adjustment	33.0	NA	NA	NA	NA	18.0	22.0	49.0	99.0	35.0
Non Interest Income	4,203	3,508	3,141	3,108	2,412	2,871	2,723	2,503	1,759	1,373
Loan Loss Provision	21.0	52.0	177	309	903	136	163	225	70.0	Nil
% Expense/Operating Revenue	48.6%	68.2%	67.7%	60.8%	71.4%	60.8%	60.3%	63.6%	61.5%	60.0%
Pretax Income	1,962	1,745	1,600	1,858	564	1,848	1,891	1,710	1,618	1,527
Effective Tax Rate	30.8%	30.8%	33.7%	33.4%	33.2%	34.3%	33.2%	34.8%	35.0%	35.0%
Net Income	1,325	1,197	1,029	1,200	377	1,214	1,264	1,115	1,052	992
% Net Interest Margin	3.00	3.22	3.64	3.99	3.84	3.64	3.68	3.85	3.94	3.83
S&P Core Earnings	1,294	1,134	993	1,093	270	NA	NA	NA	NA	NA
Balance Sheet & Other Financial Data (Million $)										
Money Market Assets	350	1,635	50.0	3,658	1,335	1,151	1,148	1,014	1,526	774
Investment Securities	23,253	18,609	16,409	17,421	15,243	7,053	8,759	8,088	8,522	11,917
Commercial Loans	26,115	19,418	15,987	22,335	23,134	28,635	24,198	25,182	19,989	18,062
Other Loans	22,986	24,077	18,093	13,115	14,840	21,966	26,572	32,468	34,668	33,736
Total Assets	91,954	79,723	68,168	66,377	69,568	69,844	75,413	77,207	75,120	73,260
Demand Deposits	14,988	12,915	11,505	9,538	10,124	8,490	8,441	9,943	10,158	10,937
Time Deposits	45,287	40,354	33,736	35,444	37,180	39,174	38,227	37,553	37,491	34,739
Long Term Debt	6,797	8,684	7,667	9,112	8,922	7,266	9,395	10,994	11,523	11,744
Common Equity	8,563	7,548	6,735	6,943	5,822	6,649	5,939	6,036	5,377	5,862
% Return on Assets	1.5	1.6	1.5	1.8	0.5	1.7	1.7	1.5	1.4	1.4
% Return on Equity	16.5	16.8	15.0	18.7	5.9	19.0	20.8	19.2	18.4	17.0
% Loan Loss Reserve	1.2	1.3	1.8	1.8	1.5	1.3	1.2	1.3	1.8	2.3
% Loans/Deposits	123.7	84.8	78.4	82.4	89.1	109.6	119.7	121.4	111.8	113.4
% Equity to Assets	9.3	9.7	10.2	9.4	8.9	9.0	7.8	7.5	7.6	7.9

Data as orig reptd.; bef. results of disc opers/spec. items. Per share data adj. for stk. divs.; EPS diluted. E-Estimated. NA-Not Available. NM-Not Meaningful. NR-Not Ranked. UR-Under Review.

Office: 249 5th Ave, 1 PNC Plz, Pittsburgh, PA 15222-2707.
Telephone: 412-762-2000.
Email: corporate.communiations@pncbank.com
Website: http://www.pnc.com

Chrmn & CEO: J.E. Rohr
Pres: J. Guyaux
Vice Chrmn: W.C. Mutterperl
Vice Chrmn & CFO: W.S. Demchak

SVP & General Counsel: H.P. Pudlin
Investor Contact: W. Callihan (800-843-2206)
Board of Directors: P. W. Chellgren, R. N. Clay, J. G. Cooper, G. A. Davidson, Jr., K. C. James, R. Kelson, B. C. Lindsay, A. Massaro, T. H. O'Brien, J. G. Pepper, J. E. Rohr, L. K. Steffes, D. F. Strigl, S. G. Thieke, T. J. Usher, G. H. Walls, H. H. Wehmeier

Founded: 1922
Domicile: Pennsylvania
Employees: 25,348

STANDARD &POOR'S

PPG Industries Inc.

S&P Recommendation HOLD ★★★★★

Price $68.96 (as of Oct 30, 2006)

12-Mo. Target Price $72.00

Investment Style Large-Cap Value

GICS Sector Materials
Sub-Industry Diversified Chemicals

Comment PPG is a leading manufacturer of coatings and resins, flat and fiber glass, and industrial and specialty chemicals.

Key Stock Statistics (Source S&P, Vickers, company reports)

52-Wk Range	$69.80–56.11	S&P Oper. EPS 2006E	5.00	P/E on S&P Oper. EPS 2006E	13.8	Dividend Rate/Share	$1.92
Trailing 12-Month EPS	$4.01	S&P Oper. EPS 2007E	5.50	Common Shares Outstg. (M)	165.2	Yield (%)	2.78
Trailing 12-Month P/E	17.2	S&P Core EPS 2006E	5.66	Market Capitalization(B)	$11.390	Beta	1.00
$10K Invested 5 Yrs Ago	$15,527	S&P Core EPS 2007E	5.92	Institutional Ownership (%)	61	S&P Credit Rating	A

Price Performance

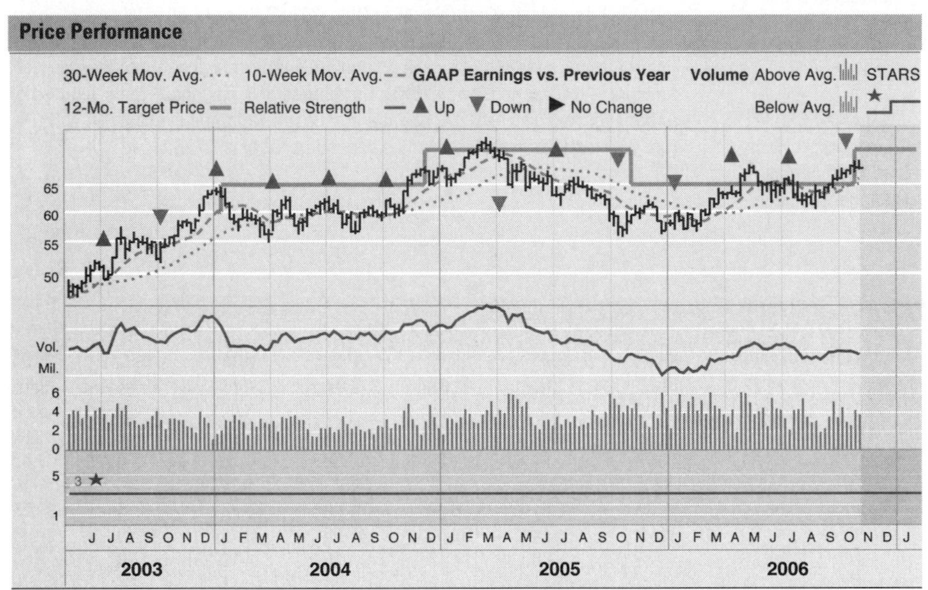

Options: Ph

Analysis prepared by **Richard O'Reilly, CFA** on October 30, 2006, when the stock traded at **$ 68.96**.

Highlights

- We expect sales to rise in 2007 on top of a 7% gain projected for 2006. We see coatings sales advancing strongly in 2007, boosted by recent acquisitions that should add nearly $800 million to annual sales. Coatings and glass should be limited by downturns in domestic auto and residential construction markets. We believe industrial, packaging, and aerospace coatings will benefit from strong industrial activity, and architectural coatings should grow along with its key home center customer.
- We forecast that margins for the coatings unit will continue to recover back to 2004's levels as additional price increases help to offset the climb in raw material costs since mid-2004 (including $245 million in 2005). We think that chemicals margins will benefit from current favorable energy costs, and optical products should continue to post good sales growth.
- We expect the effective tax rate before special items to remain at about 31.5%. We forecast that quarterly charges of a couple of cents related to PPG's asbestos settlement obligation will continue into 2007. Our EPS forecast for 2006 excludes special charges totaling $0.79.

Investment Rationale/Risk

- We would hold the shares, based on valuation and an above average yield. The stock was recently trading at a P/E multiple, based on our 2006 EPS estimate, which was about 15% below the S&P 500. We view PPG as a well-run company with an attractive strategy of investing globally in several growth businesses to help provide greater earnings consistency, while remaining a low-cost producer in its glass and commodity chemicals operations.
- Risks to our recommendation and target price include slower than projected industrial activity, unplanned production outages and interruptions, exposure to domestic auto makers, and unexpected weakness in selling prices for commodity chemicals.
- Our 12-month target price of $72 assumes that the stock's P/E multiple of 13X, based on our 2007 operating EPS estimate of $5.50, will remain below that of the S&P 500 due to the unusually high profit contribution from cyclical commodity chemicals. Dividends have increased for 35 consecutive years, and the recent yield is well above that of the S&P 500.

Qualitative Risk Assessment

LOW | **MEDIUM** | HIGH

Our risk assessment reflects the company's diversified business mix, large market shares in key products, and what we see as a strong balance sheet, offset by the cyclical nature of the commodity chemicals business and the auto and construction related end markets.

Quantitative Evaluations

S&P Quality Ranking B

D | C | B- | **B** | B+ | A- | A | A+

Relative Strength Rank MODERATE

58

LOWEST = 1 HIGHEST = 99

Revenue/Earnings Data

Revenue (Million $)

	1Q	2Q	3Q	4Q	Year
2006	2,638	2,824	2,802	--	--
2005	2,493	2,656	2,547	2,505	10,201
2004	2,264	2,429	2,409	2,411	9,513
2003	2,071	2,304	2,206	2,175	8,756
2002	1,875	2,134	2,068	1,990	8,067
2001	2,099	2,164	1,999	1,907	8,169

Earnings Per Share ($)

	1Q	2Q	3Q	4Q	Year
2006	1.11	1.68	0.54	**E**1.11	**E**5.00
2005	0.55	1.34	0.92	0.68	3.49
2004	0.69	1.08	1.12	1.06	3.95
2003	0.49	0.89	0.83	0.71	2.92
2002	0.25	-2.03	0.87	0.55	-0.36
2001	0.33	0.92	0.55	0.49	2.29

Fiscal year ended Dec. 31. Next earnings report expected: Mid January. EPS Estimates based on S&P Operating Earnings; historical GAAP earnings are as reported.

Dividend Data (Dates: mm/dd Payment Date: mm/dd/yy)

Amount ($)	Date Decl.	Ex-Div. Date	Stk. of Record	Payment Date
0.470	01/19	02/15	02/17	03/10/06
0.480	04/20	05/08	05/10	06/12/06
0.480	07/20	08/08	08/10	09/12/06
0.480	10/20	11/08	11/10	12/12/06

Dividends have been paid since 1899. Source: Company reports.

Business Summary October 30, 2006

CORPORATE OVERVIEW. PPG Industries is a diversified chemical company. Sales and operating profits by product group in 2005 were: coatings (55% and 55%), glass (22% and 5%) and chemicals (23% and 40%). International operations contributed 36% of sales and 31% of operating profits in 2005.

PPG Industries is one of the world's leading producers of original and refinish automotive and industrial coatings (used in appliance, industrial equipment and packaging markets) and is a major North American supplier of architectural coatings (Pittsburgh, Olympic, Porter and Lucite brands). The architectural finishes business operated 378 company-owned service centers at year-end 2005, which represented an increase of 68 over the prior year. The company is a global supplier of aircraft coatings and sealants. PPG also produces metal pretreatments, adhesives and sealants for the automotive industry, and sealants for architectural insulating glass. The coatings industry is highly competitive and consists of a few large firms with a global presence and many smaller firms serving local or regional markets.

The company is also one of the world's largest producers of flat glass and fabricated glass, with 13 plants located in North America. Major markets include original and replacement glass for automobiles, commercial and residential construction, aircraft transparencies, furniture, and various industrial uses. These businesses aim for cash generation and earnings growth. PPG notes that profits for its auto OEM glass business declined in 2005 partly due to lower sales volumes to domestic auto customers. With plants in North America and Europe, PPG is the world's third largest producer of continuous strand and chopped strand fiberglass, including plastic reinforcement yarns and electronic and specialty materials, for transportation, construction, electronics, recreational and industrial uses. It also provides claims processing services to insurance companies and the automotive after-market through LYNX Services.

PPG is the world's third largest producer of chlorine and caustic soda (used in a wide variety of industrial applications), vinyl chloride monomer (for use in polyvinyl chloride resins) and chlorinated solvents. These commodity chemicals are highly cyclical; PPG volumes fell 11% in 2005 due to a plant disruption caused by hurricanes. The company's electrochemical unit (ECU) prices in 2005 were higher than in 2004.

Company Financials

Per Share Data ($) Year Ended Dec. 31	**2005**	**2004**	**2003**	**2002**	**2001**	**2000**	**1999**	**1998**	**1997**	**1996**
Tangible Book Value	8.46	10.81	7.36	3.49	9.10	8.57	8.30	13.09	14.10	13.49
Cash Flow	5.66	6.19	5.23	1.99	4.93	6.20	12.99	6.69	6.04	5.89
Earnings	3.49	3.95	2.92	-0.36	2.29	3.57	3.23	4.48	3.94	3.96
S&P Core Earnings	4.57	4.42	3.48	1.76	1.17	NA	NA	NA	NA	NA
Dividends	1.86	1.79	1.73	1.70	1.68	1.60	1.52	1.42	1.33	1.26
Payout Ratio	53%	45%	59%	NM	73%	45%	47%	32%	34%	32%
Prices:High	74.73	68.79	64.42	62.86	59.75	65.06	70.75	76.63	67.50	62.25
Prices:Low	55.64	54.81	42.61	41.39	38.99	36.00	47.94	49.13	48.63	42.88
P/E Ratio:High	21	17	22	NM	26	18	22	17	17	16
P/E Ratio:Low	16	14	15	NM	17	10	15	11	12	11
Income Statement Analysis (Million $)										
Revenue	10,201	9,513	8,756	8,067	8,169	8,629	7,757	7,510	7,379	7,218
Operating Income	1,648	1,496	1,367	1,309	1,371	1,649	1,528	1,659	1,689	1,658
Depreciation	372	388	394	398	447	447	419	383	373	364
Interest Expense	81.0	90.0	107	128	169	161	133	110	105	108
Pretax Income	947	1,063	843	-28.0	666	1,017	973	1,294	1,175	1,240
Effective Tax Rate	29.8%	30.3%	34.8%	NM	37.1%	36.3%	38.7%	36.0%	37.0%	37.9%
Net Income	596	683	500	-60.0	387	620	568	801	714	744
S&P Core Earnings	780	765	597	300	197	NA	NA	NA	NA	NA
Balance Sheet & Other Financial Data (Million $)										
Cash	466	709	499	117	108	111	158	128	129	70.0
Current Assets	4,019	4,054	3,537	2,945	2,703	3,093	3,062	2,660	2,584	2,296
Total Assets	8,681	8,932	8,424	7,863	8,452	9,125	8,914	7,387	6,868	6,441
Current Liabilities	2,349	2,221	2,139	1,920	1,955	2,543	2,384	1,912	1,662	1,796
Long Term Debt	1,169	1,184	1,339	1,699	1,699	1,810	1,836	1,081	1,257	834
Common Equity	3,053	3,572	2,911	2,150	3,080	3,097	3,106	2,880	2,509	2,483
Total Capital	4,420	4,997	4,475	4,044	5,453	5,578	5,560	4,488	4,254	3,393
Capital Expenditures	288	244	217	238	291	561	490	487	466	476
Cash Flow	968	1,071	894	338	834	1,067	987	1,184	1,087	1,108
Current Ratio	1.7	1.8	1.7	1.5	1.4	1.2	1.3	1.4	1.6	1.3
% Long Term Debt of Capitalization	26.4	23.7	29.9	42.0	31.2	32.4	33.0	24.0	29.5	24.6
% Net Income of Revenue	5.8	7.2	5.7	NM	4.7	7.2	7.3	10.7	9.7	10.3
% Return on Assets	6.8	7.9	6.1	NM	4.4	6.9	7.0	11.2	10.7	11.8
% Return on Equity	18.0	21.1	19.8	NM	12.5	20.0	19.0	29.7	28.6	29.4

Data as orig reptd.; bef. results of disc opers/spec. items. Per share data adj. for stk. divs.; EPS diluted. E-Estimated. NA-Not Available. NM-Not Meaningful. NR-Not Ranked. UR-Under Review.

Office: 1 PPG Place, Pittsburgh, PA 15272.
Telephone: 412-434-3131.
Website: http://www.ppg.com
Chrmn & CEO: C.E. Bunch

Investor Contact: W.H. Hernandez (412-434-3131)
SVP & CFO: W.H. Hernandez
SVP & General Counsel: J.C. Diggs

Board of Directors: J. G. Berges, C. E. Bunch, E. B. Davis, Jr., H. Grant, V. F. Haynes, M. J. Hooper, R. Mehrabian, R. Ripp, T. J. Usher, D. R. Whitwam

Founded: 1883
Domicile: Pennsylvania
Employees: 0

STANDARD &POOR'S

PPL Corp

S&P Recommendation BUY ★★★★★

Price $34.52 (as of Oct 31, 2006)

12-Mo. Target Price $40.00

Investment Style Large-Cap Value

GICS Sector Utilities
Sub-Industry Electric Utilities

Comment This Pennsylvania-based holding company for PPL Utilities also has holdings in the U.K. and Latin America.

Key Stock Statistics (Source S&P, Vickers, company reports)

52-Wk Range	$35.50–27.83	S&P Oper. EPS 2006E	2.28	P/E on S&P Oper. EPS 2006E	15.1	Dividend Rate/Share	$1.10
Trailing 12-Month EPS	$2.21	S&P Oper. EPS 2007E	2.42	Common Shares Outstg. (M)	381.0	Yield (%)	3.19
Trailing 12-Month P/E	15.6	S&P Core EPS 2006E	2.20	Market Capitalization(B)	$13.152	Beta	0.54
$10K Invested 5 Yrs Ago	$24,651	S&P Core EPS 2007E	2.33	Institutional Ownership (%)	64	S&P Credit Rating	NA

Price Performance

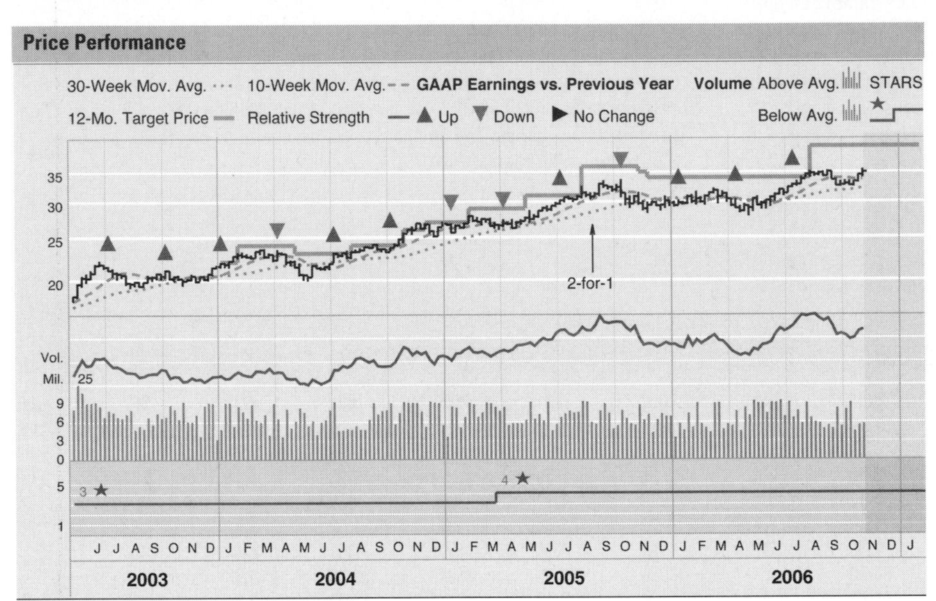

Options: P, Ph

Analysis prepared by **Justin McCann** on August 10, 2006, when the stock traded at **$ 34.54**.

Highlights

- We expect operating EPS in 2006 to increase about 12% from 2005's EPS from ongoing operations of $2.08. EPS in 2005 benefited from a combined 7.1% increase in distribution rates and transmission charges for the Pennsylvania utilities, unusually warm weather, higher electric delivery revenues in the U.K. and Latin America, and lower taxes on foreign earnings.
- We expect EPS in 2006 to benefit from higher power supply margins, driven by the 8.4% increase in generation prices agreed to in the commission-approved contract between PPL's competitive energy business and its regulated utility. We see the power supply segment accounting for about 55% of EPS in 2006; the international delivery segment, about 25%; and the Pennsylvania delivery segment, about 20%.
- We expect lower earnings from the Pennsylvania delivery business in 2006 due to increased operating and maintenance expenses and a return to normal weather. We expect higher earnings from the international delivery segment due to higher electricity margins in the U.K. and Latin America, partially offset by higher operating costs in the U.K, unfavorable currency effects and higher taxes on foreign earnings.

Investment Rationale/Risk

- After having outperformed the S&P Index of Electric Utilities for each of the past three years, we expect the shares to continue to outperform over the next 12 months on a total return basis. We believe that after nearly 4% anticipated EPS growth in 2007, PPL can realize low double digit growth for the remainder of the decade, as expired energy contracts are replaced by higher margin contracts. The stock's dividend yield (recently about 3.2%) remains below the peer average (4.1%), but the effective payout ratio (53% of 2005 operating EPS) is also below that of peers (67%).
- Risks to our recommendation and target price include potential unfavorable regulatory rulings, significantly lower results from the unregulated operations, and a major shift in the average P/E multiple of the peer group as a whole.
- Our 12-month target price is $40. In light of PPL's strength in a strong wholesale power market and its well-above-peer projected earnings growth rate, we expect the shares to trade at about 17.2X our 2006 EPS estimate of $2.33, reflecting a nearly 5% premium to the average projected peer P/E multiple, based on our EPS estimates for 2006.

Qualitative Risk Assessment

LOW | **MEDIUM** | HIGH

Our risk assessment reflects a balance between the steady cash flows expected from the regulated Pennsylvania and U.K. distribution segments, which operate within supportive regulatory environments, offset by the highly profitable but less predictable earnings and cash flow from the power supply segment, as well as the currency risks related to the U.K. and Latin American businesses.

Quantitative Evaluations

S&P Quality Ranking **B**

D | C | B- | **B** | B+ | A- | A | A+

Relative Strength Rank **MODERATE**

52

LOWEST = 1 HIGHEST = 99

Revenue/Earnings Data

Revenue (Million $)

	1Q	2Q	3Q	4Q	Year
2006	1,783	1,642	--	--	--
2005	1,602	1,476	1,643	1,498	6,219
2004	1,520	1,362	1,465	1,465	5,812
2003	1,487	1,338	1,456	1,296	5,587
2002	1,351	1,288	1,476	1,314	5,429
2001	1,566	1,409	1,438	1,312	5,725

Earnings Per Share ($)

2006	0.73	0.51	E0.63	E0.52	E2.28
2005	0.44	0.47	0.51	0.50	1.92
2004	0.50	0.41	0.52	0.47	1.89
2003	0.53	0.34	0.49	0.72	2.08
2002	0.50	-0.09	0.40	0.36	1.17
2001	0.76	0.40	0.52	-1.10	0.58

Fiscal year ended Dec. 31. Next earnings report expected: Early November. EPS Estimates based on S&P Operating Earnings; historical GAAP earnings are as reported.

Dividend Data (Dates: mm/dd Payment Date: mm/dd/yy)

Amount ($)	Date Decl.	Ex-Div. Date	Stk. of Record	Payment Date
0.250	11/18	12/07	12/09	01/01/06
0.275	02/24	03/08	03/10	04/01/06
0.275	05/26	06/07	06/09	07/01/06
0.275	08/25	09/06	09/08	10/01/06

Dividends have been paid since 1946. Source: Company reports.

PPL Corp

Business Summary August 10, 2006

CORPORATE OVERVIEW. PPL Corporation (PPL) is an energy and utility holding company organized into three operating segments: the supply segment, the Pennsylvania delivery segment, and the international delivery segment. PPL's subsidiaries PPL Generation and PPL EnergyPlus comprise the supply segment. These units are involved in electricity generation and marketing of electricity and other power purchases to deregulated wholesale and retail markets. The Pennsylvania delivery segment operates through its subsidiaries PPL Electric and PPL Gas Utilities, which provide electric and gas utility services in the regulated Pennsylvania market. The international delivery segment is focused on electricity distribution in the U.K and Latin America through its subsidiary PPL Global.

CORPORATE STRATEGY. The company's business strategy is to achieve stable growth in the regulated delivery business. It plans to achieve long-term growth in delivery through efficient and low-cost operations while working to enhance strong customer and regulatory relations. In the unregulated supply business, PPL intends to reduce the volatility in both its cash flows and earnings and to ensure disciplined growth. The company's strategy for its electricity generation and marketing business is to build an effective risk management framework to handle energy price risk and counterparty risk. It will work to reduce risk by entering into supply contracts of varying duration, which should reflect fluctuations in demand.

Company Financials

Per Share Data ($) Year Ended Dec. 31	**2005**	**2004**	**2003**	**2002**	**2001**	**2000**	**1999**	**1998**	**1997**	**1996**
Tangible Book Value	7.73	7.50	5.53	5.87	6.98	6.65	5.60	5.94	8.39	8.37
Earnings	1.92	1.89	2.00	1.17	0.58	1.08	1.57	1.15	0.90	1.03
S&P Core Earnings	1.87	1.74	1.95	0.79	0.90	NA	NA	NA	NA	NA
Dividends	1.21	0.82	0.77	0.68	0.53	0.53	0.50	0.67	0.84	0.84
Payout Ratio	63%	43%	37%	57%	92%	32%	32%	59%	93%	81%
Prices:High	33.68	27.08	22.17	19.98	31.18	23.06	16.00	14.47	12.13	13.00
Prices:Low	25.52	19.92	15.83	13.00	15.50	9.19	10.19	10.44	9.50	10.81
P/E Ratio:High	18	14	11	17	54	14	10	13	13	13
P/E Ratio:Low	13	11	8	11	27	5	6	9	11	11
Income Statement Analysis (Million $)										
Revenue	6,219	5,812	5,587	5,429	5,725	5,683	4,590	3,786	3,049	2,910
Depreciation	420	412	380	367	254	261	257	338	374	363
Maintenance	NA	NA	NA	314	209	201	215	182	184	191
Fixed Charges Coverage	2.70	2.72	2.72	2.49	3.08	2.95	3.20	3.45	3.25	3.77
Construction Credits	NA	NA	NA	NA	NA	NA	NA	Nil	NA	NA
Effective Tax Rate	14.0%	21.6%	18.5%	29.5%	54.4%	36.3%	26.1%	39.3%	42.7%	45.4%
Net Income	737	700	748	425	221	513	478	379	296	329
S&P Core Earnings	716	645	674	240	262	NA	NA	NA	NA	NA
Balance Sheet & Other Financial Data (Million $)										
Gross Property	18,615	18,692	17,775	16,406	12,477	11,418	10,717	10,489	10,336	10,242
Capital Expenditures	811	703	771	648	565	460	318	304	310	360
Net Property	10,916	11,209	10,446	9,566	6,135	5,948	5,644	4,363	6,766	6,905
Capitalization:Long Term Debt	6,095	6,881	8,145	6,562	5,906	4,717	4,103	3,092	2,698	2,968
Capitalization:% Long Term Debt	58.0	61.6	71.1	74.0	75.3	69.1	71.8	60.3	47.0	48.0
Capitalization:Preferred	Nil	51.0	51.0	82.0	82.0	97.0	Nil	347	347	466
Capitalization:% Preferred	Nil	0.46	0.45	0.92	1.05	1.42	Nil	6.70	6.10	7.50
Capitalization:Common	4,418	4,239	3,259	2,224	1,857	2,012	1,613	1,790	2,809	2,745
Capitalization:% Common	42.0	37.9	28.5	25.1	23.7	29.5	28.2	34.9	49.0	44.4
Total Capital	12,766	13,653	13,710	11,274	9,332	6,880	7,328	5,317	8,075	8,075
% Operating Ratio	80.3	79.5	78.9	76.8	81.1	84.0	84.8	79.8	82.1	80.9
% Earned on Net Property	12.2	12.7	13.4	17.5	14.2	28.6	22.3	10.3	8.0	8.0
% Return on Revenue	11.9	12.0	13.4	7.8	3.9	9.0	10.4	10.0	9.7	11.3
% Return on Invested Capital	9.5	9.0	10.0	12.6	12.4	14.3	11.3	13.1	9.4	6.5
% Return on Common Equity	17.0	18.6	26.2	17.5	8.7	28.3	28.1	16.5	10.7	12.3

Data as orig reptd.; bef. results of disc opers/spec. items. Per share data adj. for stk. divs.; EPS diluted. E-Estimated. NA-Not Available. NM-Not Meaningful. NR-Not Ranked. UR-Under Review.

Office: 2 N 9th St, Allentown, PA, USA 18101-1170.
Telephone: 610-774-5151.
Email: invrel@pplweb.com
Website: http://www.pplweb.com

Chrmn, Pres & CEO: J.H. Miller
COO & EVP: W.H. Spence
EVP & CFO: J.R. Biggar
SVP, Secy & General Counsel: R.J. Grey

VP & Treas: J.E. Abel
Investor Contact: T.J. Paukovits (610-774-4124)
Board of Directors: F. M. Bernthal, J. R. Biggar, J. W. Conway, E. A. Deaver, L. K. Goeser, S. Heydt, J. H. Miller, C. A. Rogerson, W. K. Smith, S. M. Stalnecker, K. H. Williamson

Founded: 1920
Domicile: Pennsylvania
Employees: 12,276

STANDARD &POOR'S

Praxair Inc.

S&P Recommendation SELL ★★★★★

Price $60.61 (as of Oct 30, 2006)

12-Mo. Target Price $52.00

Investment Style Large-Cap Growth

GICS Sector Materials
Sub-Industry Industrial Gases

Comment This company is the largest producer of industrial gases in North and South America, and the second largest worldwide. It also provides ceramic and metallic coatings.

Key Stock Statistics (Source S&P, Vickers, company reports)

52-Wk Range	$60.68–47.50	S&P Oper. EPS 2006E	2.93	P/E on S&P Oper. EPS 2006E	20.7	Dividend Rate/Share	$1.00
Trailing 12-Month EPS	$2.85	S&P Oper. EPS 2007E	3.25	Common Shares Outstg. (M)	322.9	Yield (%)	1.65
Trailing 12-Month P/E	21.3	S&P Core EPS 2006E	2.87	Market Capitalization(B)	$19.571	Beta	0.89
$10K Invested 5 Yrs Ago	$25,626	S&P Core EPS 2007E	3.16	Institutional Ownership (%)	83	S&P Credit Rating	A

Price Performance

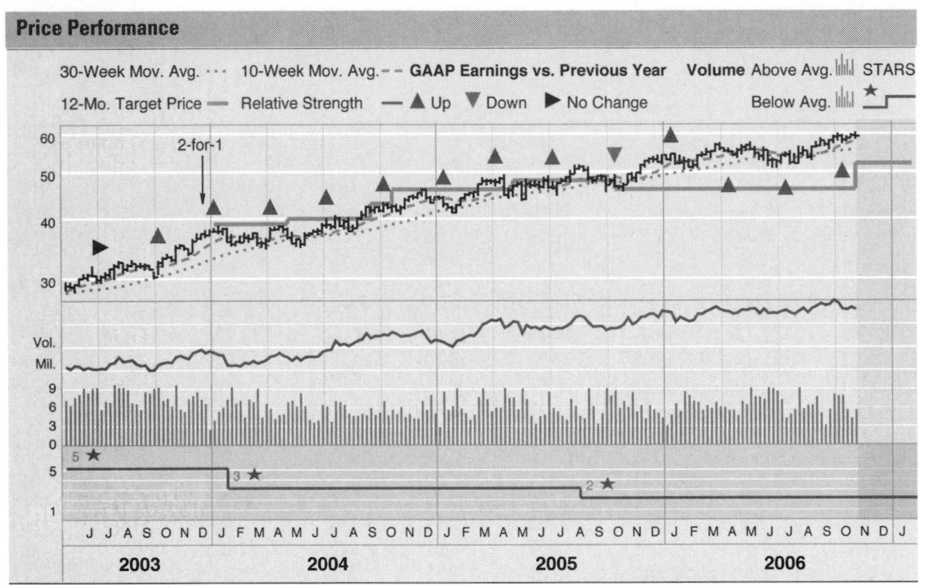

Options: ASE

Analysis prepared by **Richard O'Reilly, CFA** on October 30, 2006, when the stock traded at **$ 60.56**.

Highlights

- We project that sales will continue to grow about 10% annually into 2007, as PX has over 35 new major projects scheduled to start up through 2008. We expect that U.S. gases volumes will continue to show mid-single digit growth, aided by the start-up of two new hydrogen plants in the 2006 second half.
- We also see the European and South American regions posting modest sales gains, while Asian growth should continue in the double digits, driven by new projects. We expect healthy increases in selling prices in most regions. We look for Surface Technologies' ongoing sales to grow close to 10% on stronger demand in coatings services for industrial equipment and OEM aircraft engines.
- We project that 2007 operating profit margins will remain at about 18%, aided by the pass-through of expected lower natural gas costs to hydrogen customers. We look for the effective tax rate to remain at about 26.5%; 2005's tax rate included a special $0.28 per share charge in the third quarter. The expensing of stock options should reduce annual EPS by about $0.08 beginning in 2006.

Investment Rationale/Risk

- We have a sell opinion on the shares based on what we view as an excessive valution. The stock recently traded at 20.3X our 2006 EPS estimate of $2.93, a sharp premium to the S&P 500. PX typically had sold at a discount prior to 2004. We believe that the company's longer-term fundamentals remain sound and that it is concentrating on several less capital intensive, faster growing global markets such as health care, as well as hydrogen for use by petroleum refiners.
- Risks to our recommendation and target price include an unexpected pickup in industrial activity, especially metals related markets, lower than projected power and natural gas costs, and a more rapid ability to develop and successfully introduce new products and applications for industrial gases.
- We believe the shares are trading at a steep premium to the overall chemical industry and the S&P 500. Our 12-month target price of $52 assumes a narrowing of the P/E multiple to about 16X to our 2007 EPS forecast of $3.25. The stock's S&P Quality Ranking is A (the dividend has been raised for 13 consecutive years).

Qualitative Risk Assessment

LOW | **MEDIUM** | HIGH

Our risk assessment reflects the relatively stable growth and cash flow nature of the industrial gases industry versus commodity chemicals, and PX's S&P Quality Ranking of A that reflects the company's growing dividend. This is offset by its exposure to volatile energy costs.

Quantitative Evaluations

S&P Quality Ranking A

D | C | B- | B | B+ | A- | **A** | A+

Relative Strength Rank MODERATE

65

LOWEST = 1 HIGHEST = 99

Revenue/Earnings Data

Revenue (Million $)

	1Q	2Q	3Q	4Q	Year
2006	2,026	2,076	2,099	--	--
2005	1,827	1,919	1,890	2,020	7,656
2004	1,531	1,603	1,674	1,786	6,594
2003	1,337	1,401	1,414	1,461	5,613
2002	1,232	1,307	1,292	1,297	5,128
2001	1,335	1,314	1,271	1,238	5,158

Earnings Per Share ($)

	1Q	2Q	3Q	4Q	Year
2006	0.68	0.75	0.75	**E**0.75	**E**2.93
2005	0.59	0.63	0.33	0.67	2.22
2004	0.49	0.53	0.53	0.55	2.10
2003	0.40	0.46	0.46	0.47	1.77
2002	0.39	0.46	0.40	0.43	1.66
2001	0.39	0.39	0.19	0.36	1.32

Fiscal year ended Dec. 31. Next earnings report expected: Late January. EPS Estimates based on S&P Operating Earnings; historical GAAP earnings are as reported.

Dividend Data (Dates: mm/dd Payment Date: mm/dd/yy)

Amount ($)	Date Decl.	Ex-Div. Date	Stk. of Record	Payment Date
0.250	01/25	03/03	03/07	03/15/06
0.250	04/25	06/05	06/07	06/15/06
0.250	07/25	09/05	09/07	09/15/06
0.250	10/24	12/05	12/07	12/15/06

Dividends have been paid since 1992. Source: Company reports.

Praxair Inc.

Business Summary October 30, 2006

CORPORATE OVERVIEW. Since its 1992 spin-off from Union Carbide Corp., PX, the largest producer of industrial gases in North and South America, has expanded its operations to 40 countries. Foreign sales accounted for 52% of the total in 2005, with Brazil alone providing 13%.

PX conducts its industrial gases business through four operating segments: North America (59% of sales and 53% of profits in 2005); South America (14%, 16%); Europe (14%, 20%); and Asia (7%, 7%). The capital intensive industrial gases business involves the production, distribution and sale of atmospheric gases (oxygen, nitrogen, argon and rare gases), carbon dioxide, hydrogen, helium, acetylene, and specialty and electronic gases. Atmospheric gases are produced through air separation processes, primarily cryogenic, while other gases are produced by various methods. PX also produces specialty products (sputtering targets, mechanical planarization slurries and polishing pads, and coatings) for use in semiconductor manufacturing. In addition, the business includes the construction and sale of equipment to produce industrial gases.

Industrial gases are supplied to customers through three basic methods: on-site/pipeline (26% of total 2005 sales, sold under long-term contracts), merchant (30%, with three to five year contracts) and packaged (33%). At the end of 2005, the company had 284 cryogenic air separation plants worldwide (178 in North America), 85 carbon dioxide plants (51), and 38 hydrogen plants (32). S.A. White Martins (Brazil, 99.2% owned) is the largest producer of industrial gases in South America, with a 60% market share.

The Surface Technologies business (6%, 4%) applies metallic and ceramic coatings and powders to parts and equipment provided by customers, including aircraft engine, printing, power generation and other industrial markets, and manufactures electric arc, plasma and oxygen fuel spray equipment. In July 2006 PX sold its aviation services business (annual sales of $80 million).

Company Financials

Per Share Data ($) Year Ended Dec. 31	**2005**	**2004**	**2003**	**2002**	**2001**	**2000**	**1999**	**1998**	**1997**	**1996**
Tangible Book Value	7.05	6.08	6.00	4.03	7.59	3.97	3.70	3.36	2.89	2.39
Cash Flow	4.23	3.85	3.33	3.12	2.84	2.59	2.73	2.73	2.62	2.21
Earnings	2.22	2.10	1.77	1.66	1.32	1.13	1.37	1.30	1.27	0.89
S&P Core Earnings	2.16	2.02	1.67	1.38	1.04	NA	NA	NA	NA	NA
Dividends	0.72	0.60	0.46	0.38	0.34	0.31	0.28	0.25	0.22	0.19
Payout Ratio	32%	29%	26%	23%	26%	28%	21%	19%	17%	21%
Prices:High	54.31	46.25	38.26	30.56	27.96	27.47	29.06	26.94	29.00	25.06
Prices:Low	41.06	34.52	25.02	22.28	18.25	15.16	16.00	15.34	19.63	15.75
P/E Ratio:High	24	22	22	18	21	24	21	21	23	28
P/E Ratio:Low	18	16	14	13	14	13	12	12	16	18
Income Statement Analysis (Million $)										
Revenue	7,656	6,594	5,613	5,128	5,158	5,043	4,639	4,833	4,735	4,449
Operating Income	1,948	1,681	1,444	1,358	1,333	1,220	1,199	1,310	1,230	1,125
Depreciation	665	578	517	483	499	471	445	467	444	420
Interest Expense	163	155	151	206	224	224	204	260	216	220
Pretax Income	1,145	959	735	726	585	493	638	607	633	350
Effective Tax Rate	32.8%	24.2%	23.7%	21.8%	23.1%	20.9%	23.8%	20.9%	23.9%	31.4%
Net Income	732	697	585	548	432	363	441	425	416	282
S&P Core Earnings	711	671	552	454	343	NA	NA	NA	NA	NA
Balance Sheet & Other Financial Data (Million $)										
Cash	173	25.0	50.0	39.0	39.0	31.0	76.0	34.0	43.0	63.0
Current Assets	2,133	1,744	1,449	1,286	1,276	1,361	1,335	1,394	1,497	1,666
Total Assets	10,491	9,878	8,305	7,401	7,715	7,762	7,722	8,096	7,810	7,538
Current Liabilities	2,001	1,875	1,117	1,100	1,194	1,439	1,725	1,289	1,366	2,550
Long Term Debt	2,926	2,876	2,661	2,510	2,725	2,641	2,111	2,895	2,874	1,703
Common Equity	3,902	3,608	3,088	2,340	2,477	2,357	2,290	2,332	2,122	2,122
Total Capital	6,828	6,709	5,944	5,014	5,363	5,156	4,835	5,789	5,592	4,195
Capital Expenditures	877	668	983	498	595	704	653	781	902	893
Cash Flow	1,397	1,275	1,102	1,031	931	834	886	892	860	696
Current Ratio	1.1	0.9	1.3	1.2	1.1	0.9	0.8	1.1	1.1	0.7
% Long Term Debt of Capitalization	42.9	42.9	44.8	50.1	50.8	51.2	43.7	50.0	51.4	40.6
% Net Income of Revenue	9.6	10.6	10.4	10.7	8.4	7.2	9.5	8.8	8.8	6.3
% Return on Assets	7.2	7.7	7.4	7.3	5.6	4.7	5.6	5.3	5.4	4.9
% Return on Equity	19.5	20.8	21.6	22.8	17.9	15.6	19.1	19.1	20.6	18.5

Data as orig reptd.; bef. results of disc opers/spec. items. Per share data adj. for stk. divs.; EPS diluted. E-Estimated. NA-Not Available. NM-Not Meaningful. NR-Not Ranked. UR-Under Review.

Office: 39 Old Ridgebury Rd, Danbury, CT 06810-5113.
Telephone: 203-837-2000.
Website: http://www.praxair.com
Chrmn, Pres & CEO: D.H. Reilley
Pres & COO: S.F. Angel
EVP & CFO: J.S. Sawyer
VP & Treas: M.J. Allan
VP, Secy & General Counsel: D.H. Chaifetz
Investor Contact: E.T. Hirsch (203-837-2354)
Board of Directors: S. F. Angel, C. W. Gargalli, I. D. Hall, R. L. Kuehn, Jr., R. W. LeBoeuf, G. J. Ratcliffe, Jr., D. H. Reilley, W. T. Smith, H. M. Watson, Jr., R. L. Wood
Founded: 1988
Domicile: Delaware
Employees: 27,306

Principal Financial Group Inc.

S&P Recommendation HOLD ★★★★★

Price $56.49 (as of Oct 31, 2006)

12-Mo. Target Price $59.00

Investment Style Large-Cap Value

GICS Sector Financials
Sub-Industry Life & Health Insurance

Comment PFG offers businesses, individuals, and other clients various financial products and services, including insurance and retirement and investment services.

Key Stock Statistics (Source S&P, Vickers, company reports)

52-Wk Range	$56.86–45.91	S&P Oper. EPS 2006E	3.49	P/E on S&P Oper. EPS 2006E	16.2	Dividend Rate/Share	$0.65
Trailing 12-Month EPS	$3.47	S&P Oper. EPS 2007E	3.87	Common Shares Outstg. (M)	269.3	Yield (%)	1.15
Trailing 12-Month P/E	16.3	S&P Core EPS 2006E	3.38	Market Capitalization(B)	$15.212	Beta	0.42
$10K Invested 5 Yrs Ago	$27,389	S&P Core EPS 2007E	3.84	Institutional Ownership (%)	54	S&P Credit Rating	NA

Price Performance

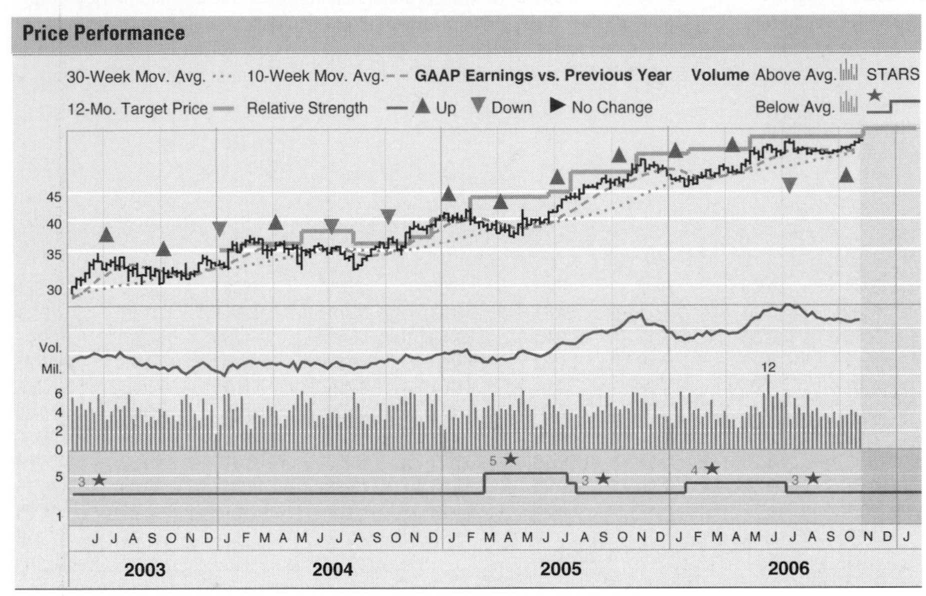

Qualitative Risk Assessment

LOW | **MEDIUM** | HIGH

Our risk assessment reflects our view of PFG's consistent earnings growth, diversified products, geographic scope, conservative debt to total capital ratio, and large excess capital. This is offset by several macroeconomic factors that affect the company, including decelerating job growth and rising interest rates.

Quantitative Evaluations

S&P Quality Ranking **NR**

D | C | B- | B | B+ | A- | A | A+

Relative Strength Rank **MODERATE**

60

LOWEST = 1 HIGHEST = 99

Revenue/Earnings Data

Revenue (Million $)

	1Q	2Q	3Q	4Q	Year
2006	2,392	2,448	2,439	--	--
2005	2,144	2,200	2,218	2,445	9,008
2004	1,997	1,980	2,089	2,239	8,304
2003	2,297	2,412	2,266	2,479	9,404
2002	2,228	2,336	1,996	2,424	9,223
2001	--	--	2,457	--	8,818

Earnings Per Share ($)

2006	1.01	0.76	0.94	E0.88	E3.49
2005	0.68	0.77	0.74	0.83	3.02
2004	0.62	0.40	0.62	0.71	2.23
2003	0.47	0.62	0.68	0.60	2.23
2002	0.68	0.33	0.12	0.64	1.77
2001	--	--	0.32	--	1.02

Fiscal year ended Dec. 31. Next earnings report expected: Early February. EPS Estimates based on S&P Operating Earnings; historical GAAP earnings are as reported.

Dividend Data (Dates: mm/dd Payment Date: mm/dd/yy)

Amount ($)	Date Decl.	Ex-Div. Date	Stk. of Record	Payment Date
0.650	11/02	11/15	11/17	12/16/05

Dividends have been paid since 2002. Source: Company reports.

Highlights

- The 12-month target price for PFG has recently been changed to $59.00 from $57.00. The Highlights section of this Stock Report will be updated accordingly.

Investment Rationale/Risk

- The Investment Rationale/Risk section of this Stock Report will be updated shortly. For the latest News story on PFG from MarketScope, see below.
- 10/31/06 03:23 pm EST... S&P MAINTAINS HOLD OPINION ON SHARES OF PRINCIPAL FINANCIAL (PFG 56.22***): Q3 operating EPS of $0.94 vs. $0.75 is $0.11 above our estimate. The U.S. asset management and accumulation segment benefitted from a 15% rise in assets under management. We expect the Pension Protection Act to add considerable deposit growth to this segment over the long term. Growth in the international segment was driven by Brazil and Hong Kong, partly offset by a slowdown in Mexico. We are raising our '06 and '07 operating EPS estimates by $0.11 and $0.05, to $3.49 and $3.87. Our 12-month target price rises $2 to $59, 15.2X our '07 estimate, in line with PFG's past average. /F. Braden

Principal Financial Group Inc.

Business Summary August 07, 2006

CORPORATE OVERVIEW. The Principal Financial Group is a leading provider of retirement savings, investment and insurance products and services, with more than 15 million customers and $195 billion in assets under management at December 31, 2005. According to Treasury and Risk magazine, PFG ranked #1 in bundled 401(k) plans, and according to PLANSPONSOR magazine, the company ranked #1 in both nonqualified deferred compensation plans and employee stock ownership plans.

PFG's businesses are organized into four operating segments. The U.S. Asset Management and Accumulation segment (USAMA), which accounted for 45% of operating revenue from continuing operations in 2005, provides retirement savings and related investment products and services, and asset management operations, with a concentration on small and medium-sized businesses with fewer than 1,000 employees. At year-end 2005, USAMA account values totaled $120.3 billion.

The International Asset Management and Accumulation segment (IAMA) consists of Principal International and offers retirement products and services, annuities, mutual funds and life insurance through operations in Brazil, Chile, Mexico, China, Hong Kong and India. IAMA accounted for 6.7% of operating revenues from continuing operations in 2005.

The life and health insurance segment, which accounted for 49% of operating revenues from continuing operations in 2005, offers individual and group life and disability insurance, as well as group health, dental and vision insurance. The corporate and other segment includes, among other things, intersegment eliminations, income on capital not allocated to other segments, and the company's financing activities.

Company Financials

Per Share Data ($) Year Ended Dec. 31	2005	2004	2003	2002	2001	2000	1999	1998	1997	1996
Tangible Book Value	24.14	23.67	22.12	19.32	10.59	14.89	NA	NA	NA	NA
Operating Earnings	NA	NA	NA	2.46	1.96	NA	NA	NA	NA	NA
Earnings	3.02	2.23	2.23	1.77	1.02	1.74	NA	NA	NA	NA
S&P Core Earnings	3.02	2.36	2.38	1.85	1.69	NA	NA	NA	NA	NA
Dividends	0.65	0.55	0.45	0.25	Nil	NA	NA	NA	NA	NA
Payout Ratio	22%	25%	20%	14%	Nil	NA	NA	NA	NA	NA
Prices:High	52.00	41.26	34.67	31.50	24.75	NA	NA	NA	NA	NA
Prices:Low	36.80	32.00	25.21	22.00	18.50	NA	NA	NA	NA	NA
P/E Ratio:High	17	19	16	18	24	NA	NA	NA	NA	NA
P/E Ratio:Low	12	14	11	12	18	NA	NA	NA	NA	NA
Income Statement Analysis (Million $)										
Life Insurance in Force	197,690	180,344	136,530	137,794	62,309	60,389	NA	NA	NA	NA
Premium Income:Life	3,975	3,710	1,500	1,824	2,089	1,792	NA	NA	NA	NA
Premium Income:A & H	NA	NA	2,135	2,058	2,033	2,205	NA	NA	NA	NA
Net Investment Income	3,361	3,227	3,420	3,305	3,395	3,172	NA	NA	NA	NA
Total Revenue	9,008	8,304	9,404	9,223	8,818	8,885	NA	NA	NA	NA
Pretax Income	1,124	882	954	666	449	872	NA	NA	NA	NA
Net Operating Income	NA	NA	NA	864	711	NA	NA	NA	NA	NA
Net Income	892	702	728	620	370	627	NA	NA	NA	NA
S&P Core Earnings	871	742	778	647	608	NA	NA	NA	NA	NA
Balance Sheet & Other Financial Data (Million $)										
Cash & Equivalent	2,324	1,131	2,344	1,685	1,218	940	NA	NA	NA	NA
Premiums Due	593	628	720	460	531	572	NA	NA	NA	NA
Investment Assets:Bonds	42,117	40,916	37,553	34,287	30,030	29,328	NA	NA	NA	NA
Investment Assets:Stocks	815	763	712	379	834	579	NA	NA	NA	NA
Investment Assets:Loans	12,312	12,529	14,312	11,900	11,898	12,359	NA	NA	NA	NA
Investment Assets:Total	57,583	57,012	55,578	48,996	44,773	44,403	NA	NA	NA	NA
Deferred Policy Costs	2,174	1,838	1,572	1,414	1,373	1,338	NA	NA	NA	NA
Total Assets	127,035	113,798	107,754	89,861	88,351	86,838	NA	NA	NA	NA
Debt	899	844	2,767	1,333	1,378	1,391	NA	NA	NA	NA
Common Equity	7,807	7,544	7,400	13,314	6,820	6,624	NA	NA	NA	NA
% Return on Revenue	9.9	8.5	7.7	7.0	4.2	7.1	NA	NA	NA	NA
% Return on Assets	0.7	0.6	0.7	0.7	0.4	NA	NA	NA	NA	NA
% Return on Equity	11.4	9.4	10.4	4.6	5.7	NA	NA	NA	NA	NA
% Investment Yield	5.9	5.8	6.5	7.0	7.8	NA	NA	NA	NA	NA

Data as orig reptd.; bef. results of disc opers/spec. items. Per share data adj. for stk. divs.; EPS diluted. E-Estimated. NA-Not Available. NM-Not Meaningful. NR-Not Ranked. UR-Under Review.

Office: 711 High Street, Des Moines, IA 50392.
Telephone: 515-247-5111.
Website: http://www.principal.com
Chrmn & CEO: J.B. Griswell

Pres & COO: L.D. Zimpleman
EVP & CFO: M.H. Gersie
EVP & General Counsel: K.E. Shaff
SVP & CIO: G.P. Scholten

Investor Contact: T. Graf (515-235-9500)
Board of Directors: B. J. Bernard, J. Carter-Miller, G. E. Costley, M. T. Dan, D. J. Drury, C. D. Gelatt, Jr., J. B. Griswell, S. L. Helton, C. S. Johnson, W. T. Kerr, R. L. Keyser, A. K. Mathrani, F. F. Pena, E. E. Tallett, T. M. Vaughan, L. D. Zimpleman

Founded: 1998
Domicile: Delaware
Employees: 14,507

STANDARD &POOR'S

Procter & Gamble Co (The)

S&P Recommendation STRONG BUY ★★★★★

Price $63.39 (as of Oct 31, 2006)

12-Mo. Target Price $74.00

Investment Style Large-Cap Growth

GICS Sector Consumer Staples
Sub-Industry Household Products

Comment This leading consumer products company markets household and personal care products in more than 160 countries.

Key Stock Statistics (Source S&P, Vickers, company reports)

52-Wk Range	$64.02–52.75	S&P Oper. EPS 2007E	3.00	P/E on S&P Oper. EPS 2007E	21.1	Dividend Rate/Share	$1.24
Trailing 12-Month EPS	$2.66	S&P Oper. EPS 2008E	NA	Common Shares Outstg. (M)	3,179.0	Yield (%)	1.96
Trailing 12-Month P/E	23.8	S&P Core EPS 2007E	2.90	Market Capitalization(B)	$201.517	Beta	0.23
$10K Invested 5 Yrs Ago	$19,243	S&P Core EPS 2008E	NA	Institutional Ownership (%)	59	S&P Credit Rating	AA-

Price Performance

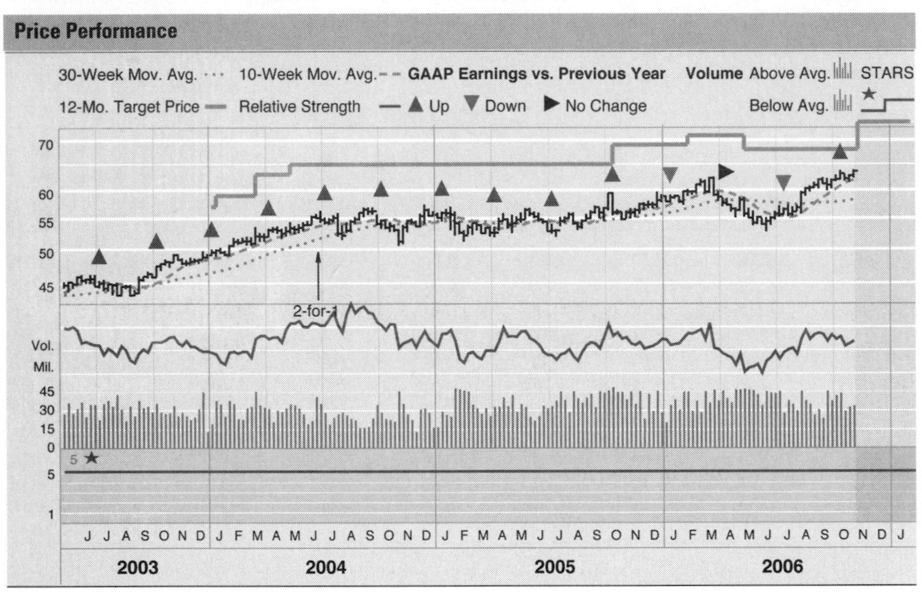

Options: ASE, CBOE, P, Ph

Highlights

- The 12-month target price for PG has recently been changed to $74.00 from $68.00. The Highlights section of this Stock Report will be updated accordingly.

Investment Rationale/Risk

- The Investment Rationale/Risk section of this Stock Report will be updated shortly. For the latest News story on PG from MarketScope, see below.
- 10/31/06 08:36 am EST... S&P REITERATES STRONG BUY OPINION ON SHARES OF PROCTER & GAMBLE (PG 63.81*****): PG posts Sep-Q EPS of $0.79 vs. $0.77, in line with our estimate. Included is an estimated $0.05-0.06 of dilution related to Gillette, slightly above our forecast. Sales rose 27%, a little ahead of our estimate, including 6% organic sales growth. We are increasing our full-year FY 07 (Jun.) EPS estimate by $0.02 to $3.00, with minor reductions in our forecasts for net other expense and share count. We are raising our P/E-based 12-month target price by $6 to $74 to reflect increased peer multiples and greater visibility of earnings growth. /L.Braverman-CFA

Qualitative Risk Assessment

LOW | MEDIUM | HIGH

Demand for household and personal care products is generally stable and not affected by changes in the economy or geopolitical factors, except for select categories such as fragrances.

Quantitative Evaluations

S&P Quality Ranking A

D | C | B- | B | B+ | A- | A | A+

Relative Strength Rank MODERATE

56

LOWEST = 1 HIGHEST = 99

Revenue/Earnings Data

Revenue (Million $)

	1Q	2Q	3Q	4Q	Year
2007	18,785	--	--	--	--
2006	14,793	18,337	17,250	17,842	68,222
2005	13,744	14,452	14,287	14,258	56,741
2004	12,195	13,221	13,029	12,962	51,407
2003	10,796	11,005	10,656	10,920	43,377
2002	9,766	10,403	9,900	10,169	40,238

Earnings Per Share ($)

2007	0.79	E0.83	E0.73	E0.65	E3.00
2006	0.77	0.72	0.63	0.55	2.64
2005	0.73	0.74	0.63	0.56	2.66
2004	0.63	0.65	0.55	0.50	2.32
2003	0.52	0.53	0.46	0.34	1.85
2002	0.40	0.32	0.37	0.32	1.54

Fiscal year ended Jun. 30. Next earnings report expected: Late January. EPS Estimates based on S&P Operating Earnings; historical GAAP earnings are as reported.

Dividend Data (Dates: mm/dd Payment Date: mm/dd/yy)

Amount ($)	Date Decl.	Ex-Div. Date	Stk. of Record	Payment Date
0.280	01/10	01/18	01/20	02/15/06
0.310	03/13	04/19	04/21	05/15/06
0.310	07/11	07/19	07/21	08/15/06
0.310	10/10	10/18	10/20	11/15/06

Dividends have been paid since 1891. Source: Company reports.

Procter & Gamble Co (The)

Business Summary August 17, 2006

CORPORATE OVERVIEW. Procter & Gamble's business is focused on providing branded products of what it considers superior quality and value to improve the lives of the world's consumers. By doing so successfully, the company believes this will result in leadership sales, profits, and value creation for employees, shareholders and the communities in which it operates. PG markets over 300 brands in more than 160 countries. The Family Health segment, with brands such as Bounty, Crest and Iams, accounted for 34% of sales in FY 05 (Jun.). The Beauty segment, with brands such as Cover Girl, Pantene and Secret, also accounted for 34% of sales. The Household Care segment, with brands such as Tide, Folgers and Pringles, contributed 32% of sales in FY 05 (Jun.). In FY 05, North America accounted for 48% of total sales, Western Europe 24%, Northeast Asia 5%, and developing markets 23%.

IMPACT OF MAJOR DEVELOPMENTS. On October 1, 2005, PG acquired The Gillette Company for approximately $54 billion. The Gillette Company is the world leader in the male and female grooming categories. Gillette also holds the number one position worldwide in alkaline batteries and toothbrushes. We expect the acquisition to add to shareholder value over time through cost synergies and sales growth opportunities.

COMPETITIVE LANDSCAPE. We believe PG's competitive strengths are a diverse portfolio of businesses, scale, strong brands, and a strong focus on product innovation. Combined with geographic diversity, category diversity provides PG with a consistent revenue stream, in our view. With approximately $68 billion in sales, PG (including Gillette) has the benefit of scale, which provides greater sales opportunities and cost savings compared to its peers, in our view. PG also has great brand strength, in our opinion, across the globe, with 22 brands generating over $1 billion in sales. Product innovation is a key growth driver in this industry, and we believe PG has delivered on this front in recent years, generating about $5 billion in retail sales from product categories in which it did not operate four years ago. Similarly, Gillette generated $5 billion of retail sales from new products over the past five years, and was set to introduce its next generation male shaver (Fusion) in 2006.

Company Financials

Per Share Data ($) Year Ended Jun. 30	**2006**	**2005**	**2004**	**2003**	**2002**	**2001**	**2000**	**1999**	**1998**	**1997**
Tangible Book Value	NM	NM	NM	0.43	NM	0.78	0.68	1.31	1.28	3.00
Cash Flow	3.56	3.30	2.90	2.41	2.11	1.85	2.01	2.00	1.80	1.77
Earnings	2.64	2.66	2.32	1.85	1.54	1.04	1.24	1.30	1.28	1.22
S&P Core Earnings	2.60	2.45	2.17	1.58	1.28	0.81	NA	NA	NA	NA
Dividends	1.15	1.03	0.93	0.82	0.76	0.70	0.64	0.57	0.51	0.45
Payout Ratio	44%	39%	40%	44%	49%	68%	52%	44%	39%	37%
Prices:High	64.02	59.70	57.40	49.97	47.38	40.86	59.19	57.81	47.41	41.69
Prices:Low	52.75	51.16	48.80	39.70	37.04	27.00	26.30	41.00	32.50	25.91
P/E Ratio:High	24	22	25	27	31	39	48	45	37	34
P/E Ratio:Low	20	19	21	22	24	27	21	32	25	21

Income Statement Analysis (Million $)										
Revenue	68,222	56,741	51,407	43,377	40,238	39,244	39,951	38,125	37,154	35,764
Operating Income	15,876	12,811	11,560	9,556	8,371	7,007	8,145	8,401	7,653	6,975
Depreciation	2,627	1,884	1,733	1,703	1,693	2,271	2,191	2,148	1,598	1,487
Interest Expense	1,119	834	629	561	603	794	722	650	548	457
Pretax Income	12,413	10,439	9,350	7,530	6,383	4,616	5,536	5,838	5,708	5,249
Effective Tax Rate	30.0%	30.5%	30.7%	31.1%	31.8%	36.7%	36.0%	35.5%	33.8%	34.9%
Net Income	8,684	7,257	6,481	5,186	4,352	2,922	3,542	3,763	3,780	3,415
S&P Core Earnings	8,420	6,552	5,922	4,313	3,486	2,165	NA	NA	NA	NA

Balance Sheet & Other Financial Data (Million $)										
Cash	6,693	6,389	5,469	5,912	3,427	2,306	1,415	2,294	1,549	2,350
Current Assets	24,329	20,329	17,115	15,220	12,166	10,889	10,146	11,358	10,577	10,786
Total Assets	135,695	61,527	57,048	43,706	40,776	34,387	34,366	32,113	30,966	27,544
Current Liabilities	19,985	25,039	22,147	12,358	12,704	9,846	10,141	10,761	9,250	7,798
Long Term Debt	35,976	12,887	12,554	11,475	11,201	9,792	8,916	6,231	5,765	4,143
Common Equity	61,457	15,994	15,752	14,606	12,072	10,309	10,550	10,277	10,415	10,187
Total Capital	111,238	33,258	32,093	29,057	25,984	22,696	21,828	18,651	16,608	14,889
Capital Expenditures	2,667	2,181	2,024	1,482	1,679	2,486	3,018	2,828	2,559	2,129
Cash Flow	11,311	9,005	8,083	6,764	5,921	5,193	5,733	5,802	5,274	4,798
Current Ratio	1.2	0.8	0.8	1.2	1.0	1.1	1.0	1.1	1.1	1.4
% Long Term Debt of Capitalization	32.3	38.7	39.1	39.5	43.1	43.1	40.8	33.4	34.7	27.8
% Net Income of Revenue	12.7	12.8	12.6	12.0	10.8	7.4	8.9	9.9	10.2	9.5
% Return on Assets	8.8	12.2	12.9	12.3	11.6	8.5	10.7	11.9	12.9	12.4
% Return on Equity	22.1	45.7	41.8	37.9	37.8	28.0	34.0	35.3	35.7	33.1

Data as orig reptd.; bef. results of disc opers/spec. items. Per share data adj. for stk. divs.; EPS diluted. E-Estimated. NA-Not Available. NM-Not Meaningful. NR-Not Ranked. UR-Under Review.

Office: One Procter & Gamble Plaza, Cincinnati, OH 45202.
Telephone: 513-983-1100.
Website: http://www.pg.com
Chrmn, Pres & CEO: A.G. Lafley

Vice Chrmn: S. Arnold
Vice Chrmn: B.L. Byrnes
Vice Chrmn: R. McDonald
VP & Cntlr: V.L. Sheppard

Investor Contact: C. Peterson (800-742-6253)
Board of Directors: N. R. Augustine, B. L. Byrnes, S. Cook, J. T. Gorman, A. G. Lafley, C. R. Lee, L. M. Martin, W. J. McNerney, Jr., J. A. Rodgers, J. F. Smith, Jr., R. Snyderman, M. v. Whitman, E. Zedillo

Founded: 1837
Domicile: Ohio
Employees: 138,000

STANDARD &POOR'S

Progressive Corp (The)

S&P Recommendation HOLD ★★★★★

Price $23.98 (as of Oct 27, 2006)

12-Mo. Target Price $28.00

Investment Style Large-Cap Growth

GICS Sector Financials
Sub-Industry Property & Casualty Insurance

Comment This leading underwriter of nonstandard auto and other lines of coverage has expanded its product line and evolved into a full-service auto insurer.

Key Stock Statistics (Source S&P, Vickers, company reports)

52-Wk Range	$31.23–22.18	S&P Oper. EPS 2006**E**	1.90	P/E on S&P Oper. EPS 2006**E**	12.6	Dividend Rate/Share	$0.04
Trailing 12-Month EPS	$1.80	S&P Oper. EPS 2007**E**	2.00	Common Shares Outstg. (M)	772.2	Yield (%)	0.15
Trailing 12-Month P/E	13.3	S&P Core EPS 2006**E**	1.90	Market Capitalization(B)	$18.518	Beta	0.67
$10K Invested 5 Yrs Ago	$19,602	S&P Core EPS 2007**E**	2.00	Institutional Ownership (%)	73	S&P Credit Rating	A+

Price Performance

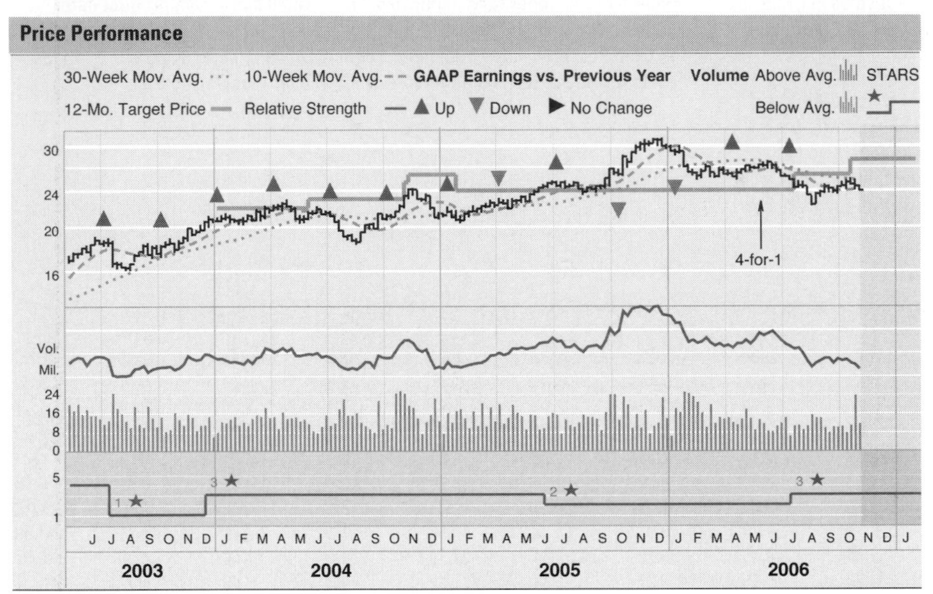

Options: CBOE, P, Ph

Analysis prepared by **Cathy A. Seifert** on October 13, 2006, when the stock traded at **$ 24.73**.

Highlights

- We believe earned premium growth in 2006 will likely be less than 5%, in line with the nearly 5% rise reported for 2005, but down sharply from 16% reported for 2004.
- Underwriting margins in recent periods have benefited from favorable claim trends, particularly in the personal auto line. However, we question the sustainability of this trend. PGR's underwriting results in 2005 eroded somewhat, as evidenced by the combined ratio of 88.1%, versus 85.1% in 2004. We expect PGR's underwriting margins to contract further in 2006.
- Our operating EPS estimates of $1.90 for 2006 and $2.00 for 2007 assume that slowing growth in earned premiums and single digit net investment income growth will be exacerbated by erosion in underwriting margins, amid an uptick in some competitive pressures and slight deterioration in unusually favorable claim trends. We also expect PGR to incur higher marketing-related expenses.

Investment Rationale/Risk

- We acknowledge PGR's historically above average rate of premium growth and its historically superior (to peers) underwriting results; however, we remain concerned about the sustainability of these trends. At current levels, the shares trade at a premium to peers, both on a forward price/earnings and a price/book basis. We do not believe this premium is warranted, particularly in light of the emerging evidence that indicates to us that PGR's rates of growth are slowing.
- Risks to our recommendation and target price include a slowdown in premium growth. Increased competitive pressures in PGR's core personal auto line could also pressure results.
- Our 12-month target price of $28 assumes that PGR shares will continue to trade at a premium to peers, albeit a smaller one, both on a forward price/book basis and forward P/E basis.

Qualitative Risk Assessment

LOW | **MEDIUM** | HIGH

Our risk assessment reflects our view of PGR's position as a leading underwriter of personal lines coverage, combined with what we see as its superior financial strength. As primarily an auto insurer, PGR is less exposed to catastrophe losses than a number of its peers, in our view. Nonetheless, exposure to catastrophe losses always exists.

Quantitative Evaluations

S&P Quality Ranking **B+**

D | C | B- | B | **B+** | A- | A | A+

Relative Strength Rank **WEAK**

23

LOWEST = 1 HIGHEST = 99

Revenue/Earnings Data

Revenue (Million $)

	1Q	2Q	3Q	4Q	Year
2006	3,661	3,708	--	--	--
2005	3,492	3,590	3,623	3,599	14,303
2004	3,280	3,367	3,438	3,696	13,782
2003	2,720	2,921	3,081	3,170	11,892
2002	2,069	2,259	2,419	--	9,373
2001	1,774	1,863	1,860	1,988	7,488

Earnings Per Share ($)

2006	0.55	0.51	**E**0.43	**E**0.45	**E**1.90
2005	0.51	0.49	0.39	0.36	1.75
2004	0.52	0.44	0.44	0.50	1.91
2003	0.33	0.32	0.36	0.41	1.42
2002	0.20	0.18	0.20	0.17	0.75
2001	0.10	0.12	0.11	0.14	0.46

Fiscal year ended Dec. 31. Next earnings report expected: NA. EPS Estimates based on S&P Operating Earnings; historical GAAP earnings are as reported.

Dividend Data (Dates: mm/dd Payment Date: mm/dd/yy)

Amount ($)	Date Decl.	Ex-Div. Date	Stk. of Record	Payment Date
4-for-1 Stk.	04/21	05/19	05/08	05/18/06
0.030	04/21	06/07	06/09	06/30/06
0.009	08/18	09/06	09/08	09/30/06
0.009	10/13	12/06	12/08	12/31/06

Dividends have been paid since 1965. Source: Company reports.

Progressive Corp (The)

Business Summary October 13, 2006

CORPORATE OVERVIEW. This regional auto insurer has expanded from a specialty writer of nonstandard coverage into a full-service insurer. Net written premiums totaled $14.0 billion in 2005, of which personal lines accounted for 87% and commercial and other lines for the remaining 13%.

PGR's core business (92% of 2005's $12.2 billion in personal lines net premiums written) consists of underwriting private passenger automobile insurance. Based on 2004 year-end industry net written premium data (latest available), the company was the third largest private U.S. passenger auto insurer, a position PGR believes it retained in 2005. PGR's other lines of business include recreational vehicle, motorcycle and small commercial vehicle insurance, and to a lesser degree, commercial indemnity insurance. PGR believes it is the market leader in providing coverage for watercraft vehicles and for motorcycles.

PGR distributes its core personal lines products through the Drive channel, which includes a network of more than 30,000 including independent agents, as well as brokers in New York and California, and strategic alliance business relationships with an array of financial institutions. During 2005 approximately 66% of total net written premiums were distributed through the Drive channel (68% in 2004). Distribution through direct channels, including a toll free telephone line and the Internet, accounted for 34% of net written premiums in 2005 (32% in 2004).

The company conducts business throughout the United States and the District of Columbia. In 2004 (latest available), Florida accounted for nearly 13% of net premiums written, Texas 8%, New York 7%, California 7%, Georgia 5%, Pennsylvania 5%, Ohio 5%, and all other states the remaining 50%.

Company Financials

Per Share Data ($) Year Ended Dec. 31	**2005**	**2004**	**2003**	**2002**	**2001**	**2000**	**1999**	**1998**	**1997**	**1996**
Tangible Book Value	7.74	6.43	5.85	4.32	3.69	3.25	3.14	2.94	2.46	1.95
Operating Earnings	NA	NA	NA	0.81	0.54	0.06	0.30	0.50	0.37	0.34
Earnings	1.75	1.91	1.42	0.75	0.46	0.05	0.33	0.51	0.44	0.35
S&P Core Earnings	1.77	1.85	1.40	0.79	0.52	NA	NA	NA	NA	NA
Dividends	0.03	0.04	0.03	0.02	0.02	0.02	0.02	0.02	0.02	0.02
Payout Ratio	2%	2%	2%	3%	5%	44%	7%	4%	5%	6%
Prices:High	31.23	24.32	21.17	15.12	12.65	9.25	14.52	14.33	10.07	6.02
Prices:Low	20.34	18.28	11.56	11.19	6.84	3.75	5.71	7.83	5.13	3.36
P/E Ratio:High	18	13	15	20	28	NM	44	28	23	17
P/E Ratio:Low	12	10	8	15	15	NM	17	15	12	10
Income Statement Analysis (Million $)										
Premium Income	13,764	13,170	11,341	8,884	7,162	6,348	5,684	4,948	4,190	3,199
Net Investment Income	537	484	465	455	414	385	341	295	275	226
Other Revenue	539	612	54.5	34.3	24.7	37.4	99.0	49.6	144	53.0
Total Revenue	14,303	13,782	11,892	9,373	7,488	6,771	6,124	5,292	4,608	3,478
Pretax Income	2,059	2,451	1,860	981	588	31.8	412	661	578	442
Net Operating Income	NA	NA	NA	718	486	55.4	267	449	336	309
Net Income	1,394	1,649	1,255	667	411	46.1	295	457	400	314
S&P Core Earnings	1,415	1,591	1,234	702	469	NA	NA	NA	NA	NA
Balance Sheet & Other Financial Data (Million $)										
Cash & Equivalent	139	124	110	94.8	86.4	73.1	68.2	71.7	23.3	62.0
Premiums Due	2,906	2,669	2,351	1,959	1,497	1,567	1,761	1,456	1,161	821
Investment Assets:Bonds	10,222	9,084	9,133	7,713	5,949	4,784	4,533	4,219	4,301	3,568
Investment Assets:Stocks	3,279	2,621	2,751	2,004	2,050	2,012	1,666	1,013	970	882
Investment Assets:Loans	Nil	Nil	Nil	Nil	Nil	Nil	Nil	Nil	Nil	Nil
Investment Assets:Total	14,275	13,082	12,532	10,284	8,226	6,983	6,428	5,674	5,270	4,450
Deferred Policy Costs	445	432	412	364	317	310	343	299	260	200
Total Assets	18,899	17,184	16,282	13,564	11,122	10,052	9,705	8,463	7,560	6,184
Debt	1,285	1,284	1,490	1,489	1,096	749	1,049	777	776	776
Common Equity	6,108	5,155	5,060	3,768	3,251	2,870	2,753	2,557	2,136	1,677
Property & Casualty:Loss Ratio	68.1	65.0	67.4	70.9	73.6	83.2	75.0	68.5	71.1	70.2
Property & Casualty:Expense Ratio	87.4	19.6	18.8	20.4	21.0	21.0	22.1	22.4	20.7	19.8
Property & Casualty Combined Ratio	19.3	84.6	86.2	91.3	94.7	104.2	97.1	90.9	91.8	90.0
% Return on Revenue	9.7	12.0	10.6	7.1	5.4	0.7	4.8	8.6	278.2	9.0
% Return on Equity	24.8	32.4	28.4	19.3	13.4	1.6	11.1	19.5	21.0	20.5

Data as orig reptd.; bef. results of disc opers/spec. items. Per share data adj. for stk. divs.; EPS diluted. E-Estimated. NA-Not Available. NM-Not Meaningful. NR-Not Ranked. UR-Under Review.

Office: 6300 Wilson Mills Road, Mayfield Village, OH 44143.
Telephone: 440-461-5000.
Website: http://www.progressive.com
Chrmn: P.B. Lewis

Pres & CEO: G.M. Renwick
VP & CFO: W.T. Forrester
Investor Contact: J.W. Basch (440-446-2851)
VP & Chief Acctg Officer: J.W. Basch

Board of Directors: M. N. Allen, S. Hardis, B. Healy, J. D. Kelly, A. F. Kohnstamm, P. Laskawy, P. Lewis, N. Matthews, P. Nettles, G. M. Renwick, D. B. Shackelford, B. T. Sheares

Founded: 1965
Domicile: Ohio
Employees: 28,336

STANDARD &POOR'S

Progress Energy Inc.

S&P Recommendation HOLD ★★★★★

Price $45.90 (as of Oct 27, 2006)

12-Mo. Target Price $44.00

Investment Style Large-Cap Value

GICS Sector Utilities
Sub-Industry Electric Utilities

Comment This diversified energy company owns two electric utilities serving approximately 2.9 million customers in North Carolina, South Carolina and Florida.

Key Stock Statistics (Source S&P, Vickers, company reports)

52-Wk Range	$46.31–40.27	S&P Oper. EPS 2006**E**	2.52	P/E on S&P Oper. EPS 2006**E**	18.2	Dividend Rate/Share	$2.42
Trailing 12-Month EPS	$2.44	S&P Oper. EPS 2007**E**	2.70	Common Shares Outstg. (M)	253.3	Yield (%)	5.27
Trailing 12-Month P/E	18.8	S&P Core EPS 2006E	2.49	Market Capitalization(B)	$11.629	Beta	0.56
$10K Invested 5 Yrs Ago	$14,249	S&P Core EPS 2007E	2.67	Institutional Ownership (%)	63	S&P Credit Rating	BBB

Price Performance

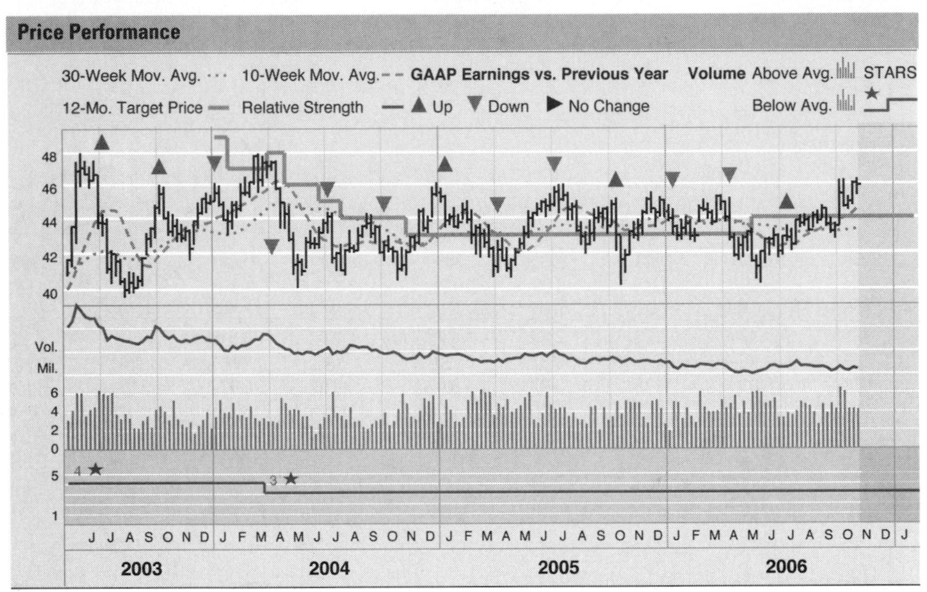

Options: ASE, P, Ph

Analysis prepared by **Justin McCann** on August 18, 2006, when the stock traded at **$ 44.07**.

Highlights

- Excluding synfuel-related earnings, which contributed $0.63 to 2005's operating EPS of $3.33, we expect 2006 EPS to decline to $2.50. With the surge in oil prices likely to phase out or eliminate synfuel tax credits, PGN idled its production facilities on May 22, 2006. It is difficult to predict what impact on earnings these operations will have in 2006 or, if resumed, in 2007.
- We see 2006 EPS declining due to the unfavorable weather and higher fuel and purchased power expenses in the first half, as well as the absence of earnings from divested operations, as PGN accelerates its plans for asset sales and debt reduction. However, we do not expect major equity issuances over the next several years. An agreement with regulators in Florida has provided rate certainty through 2009, and the utility will be allowed to recover about 90% of its $252 million in storm-related costs.
- In February 2006, PGN announced the IRS had determined that four of its Earthco synfuel facilities had met the "placed-in-service" requirements that had been disputed by an IRS field auditors' report, and that it would be eligible for the $1.25 billion in tax credits generated from these facilities through the end of 2005.

Investment Rationale/Risk

- We expect the shares, which have underperformed the company's electric utility peers for the past two years, to remain relatively flat in 2006. With the favorable IRS ruling on PGN's prior synfuel tax credits, we believe a major uncertainty was removed. We also believe the EPS decline we see in 2006 and the uncertainty regarding synfuel tax credits in 2006 and 2007 have been largely discounted by the market. Given the stock's above-average yield from a dividend that we view as secure, we would hold existing positions for total return.
- Risks to our recommendation and target price include a sharp decline in the average P/E multiple of the group as a whole, as well as the implementation of a significant phase-out or complete elimination of the company's synthetic fuel-related tax credits in 2006 and 2007.
- We expect the stock to be supported by a well-above-peer dividend yield. However, based on the recent rise in interest rates and our expectation that the average peer P/E will contract modestly, we see the shares trading at a premium-to-peers P/E of about 16.3X our 2007 EPS estimate (excluding any potential synfuel-related earnings). Our 12-month target price is $44.

Qualitative Risk Assessment

LOW | **MEDIUM** | HIGH

Our risk assessment reflects a balance between the strong and steady cash flow that we expect from the regulated utilities in both the Carolinas and Florida, which we believe have well above average customer growth and operate within a generally supportive regulatory environment, and the higher risk and much less predictable contribution that we anticipate from the synthetic fuel business.

Quantitative Evaluations

S&P Quality Ranking B+

D | C | B- | B | **B+** | A- | A | A+

Relative Strength Rank MODERATE

55

LOWEST = 1 HIGHEST = 99

Revenue/Earnings Data

Revenue (Million $)

	1Q	2Q	3Q	4Q	Year
2006	2,433	2,499	--	--	--
2005	2,198	2,333	3,097	2,578	10,108
2004	2,234	2,430	2,775	2,358	9,772
2003	2,187	2,050	2,458	2,048	8,743
2002	1,787	1,959	2,277	1,922	7,945
2001	1,908	2,316	2,331	1,907	8,461

Earnings Per Share ($)

2006	0.19	0.06	**E**1.15	**E**0.49	**E**2.52
2005	0.43	0.02	1.81	0.63	2.94
2004	0.45	0.63	1.24	0.78	3.10
2003	0.89	0.65	1.40	0.47	3.40
2002	0.58	0.56	0.72	0.66	2.53
2001	0.77	0.56	1.77	-0.42	2.64

Fiscal year ended Dec. 31. Next earnings report expected: NA. EPS Estimates based on S&P Operating Earnings; historical GAAP earnings are as reported.

Dividend Data (Dates: mm/dd Payment Date: mm/dd/yy)

Amount ($)	Date Decl.	Ex-Div. Date	Stk. of Record	Payment Date
0.605	12/14	01/06	01/10	02/01/06
0.605	03/15	04/06	04/10	05/01/06
0.605	05/10	07/06	07/10	08/01/06
0.605	09/22	10/05	10/10	11/01/06

Dividends have been paid since 1937. Source: Company reports.

Please read the Required Disclosures and Analyst Certification on the last page of this report.

Progress Energy Inc.

Business Summary August 18, 2006

CORPORATE OVERVIEW. Headquartered in Raleigh, North Carolina, Progress Energy operates in retail utility markets in the southeastern U.S., and in competitive electricity, gas and other fuel markets in the eastern U.S. It is the holding company for the fully integrated regulated utilities Progress Energy Carolinas and Progress Energy Florida. It is also the holding company for the non-regulated Progress Ventures, which is involved in various energy-related businesses and a Coal and Synthetic Fuels segment. In 2005, the regulated utility operations accounted for 78.6% of PGN's consolidated revenues (79.7% of operating income), while the unregulated businesses accounted for 21.4% (20.2%).

CORPORATE STRATEGY. As an integrated energy company, PGN has stated that its primary focus will be on the end-use and wholesale electricity markets in its service territory and region. It is intent on enhancing its operational excellence, strengthening its financial flexibility and growth, preparing for future power generating capacity, and improving the return on its Progress Ventures business. It aims to achieve sustainable earnings growth at both Progress Ventures and its regulated utilities, and to continue its track record of having increased its dividend for 18 consecutive years. We believe the ability of PGN to realize these objective will be largely dependent on its ability to reduce its debt and related interest expense through selected asset sales, increased cash flows from its utility operations, and whatever synthetic fuel tax credits it will be able to obtain. The company plans to reduce its year-end 2005 debt by $1.3 billion by the end of 2007 and, through May 9, 2006, had announced over $500 million in asset sales.

Company Financials

Per Share Data ($) Year Ended Dec. 31	**2005**	**2004**	**2003**	**2002**	**2001**	**2000**	**1999**	**1998**	**1997**	**1996**
Tangible Book Value	15.94	14.48	13.78	12.43	10.58	7.48	19.43	19.20	18.18	17.16
Earnings	2.94	3.10	3.40	2.53	2.64	3.03	2.55	2.75	2.66	2.66
S&P Core Earnings	2.94	2.93	3.44	2.04	2.59	NA	NA	NA	NA	NA
Dividends	2.36	2.30	2.24	2.18	2.12	2.06	2.00	1.94	1.88	1.82
Payout Ratio	80%	74%	66%	86%	80%	68%	78%	71%	71%	68%
Prices:High	46.00	47.95	48.00	52.70	49.25	49.38	47.88	49.63	42.69	38.75
Prices:Low	40.19	40.09	37.45	32.84	38.78	28.25	29.25	39.19	32.75	33.75
P/E Ratio:High	16	15	14	21	19	16	19	18	16	15
P/E Ratio:Low	14	13	11	13	15	9	11	14	12	13
Income Statement Analysis (Million $)										
Revenue	10,108	9,772	8,743	7,945	8,461	4,119	3,358	3,130	3,024	2,996
Depreciation	1,074	1,068	1,040	820	1,090	740	496	487	482	387
Maintenance	NA	NA	NA	NA	NA	NA	NA	NA	NA	NA
Fixed Charges Coverage	1.93	2.21	2.16	1.64	1.75	2.60	4.23	4.50	4.25	4.13
Construction Credits	13.0	6.00	7.00	8.13	18.0	20.7	11.5	6.82	4.92	6.42
Effective Tax Rate	NM	13.5%	NM	NM	NM	29.8%	40.3%	39.2%	37.6%	40.8%
Net Income	727	753	811	552	542	478	382	399	388	391
S&P Core Earnings	726	712	819	445	532	NA	NA	NA	NA	NA
Balance Sheet & Other Financial Data (Million $)										
Gross Property	26,401	25,602	25,172	23,021	22,541	21,028	12,233	10,797	10,475	10,197
Capital Expenditures	1,286	998	1,018	2,109	1,216	950	765	527	450	457
Net Property	16,799	16,819	17,056	12,541	12,445	11,677	7,257	6,300	6,294	6,400
Capitalization:Long Term Debt	10,539	9,650	10,027	9,840	9,577	5,983	3,029	2,614	2,416	2,526
Capitalization:% Long Term Debt	56.7	55.8	57.4	59.6	61.5	52.4	46.6	46.5	45.6	47.1
Capitalization:Preferred	Nil	Nil	Nil	Nil	Nil	Nil	59.4	59.4	59.4	144
Capitalization:% Preferred	Nil	Nil	Nil	Nil	Nil	Nil	0.91	1.06	1.10	2.70
Capitalization:Common	8,038	7,633	7,444	6,677	6,004	5,424	3,413	2,949	2,819	2,690
Capitalization:% Common	43.3	44.2	42.6	40.4	38.5	47.6	52.5	52.4	53.2	50.2
Total Capital	19,061	18,058	18,398	17,656	17,241	13,476	8,337	7,514	7,239	7,420
% Operating Ratio	87.2	86.7	66.8	85.4	83.5	87.1	82.4	79.3	80.6	82.8
% Earned on Net Property	7.7	8.8	8.2	8.3	10.3	7.6	12.1	10.2	8.9	8.1
% Return on Revenue	7.2	7.7	9.3	6.9	6.4	11.6	11.4	12.8	12.8	13.1
% Return on Invested Capital	7.3	7.6	8.2	7.2	9.2	7.1	7.3	7.8	7.7	7.8
% Return on Common Equity	9.3	10.0	11.5	8.7	9.4	10.8	11.9	13.7	13.9	14.5

Data as orig reptd.; bef. results of disc opers/spec. items. Per share data adj. for stk. divs.; EPS diluted. E-Estimated. NA-Not Available. NM-Not Meaningful. NR-Not Ranked. UR-Under Review.

Office: 410 S Wilmington St, Raleigh, NC 27601-1849.
Telephone: 919-546-6111.
Email: shareholder.relations@progress-energy.com
Website: http://www.progress-energy.com

Chrmn & CEO: R.B. McGehee
Pres & COO: W.D. Johnson
SVP, Secy & General Counsel: J.R. McArthur
VP & Treas: T.R. Sullivan

VP & General Counsel: F.A. Schiller
Investor Contact: B. Drennan (919-546-7474)
Board of Directors: E. B. Borden, J. E. Bostic, Jr., D. L. Burner, R. L. Daugherty, H. E. DeLoach Jr., W. D. Frederick, Jr., S. Jones, R. B. McGehee, E. M. McKee, J. H. Mullin, III, C. A. Saladrigas, T. M. Stone, A. C. Tollison Jr., J. G. Wittner

Founded: 1926
Domicile: North Carolina
Employees: 11,600

ProLogis

STANDARD &POOR'S

S&P Recommendation BUY ★★★★★	Price	12-Mo. Target Price	Investment Style
	$63.27 (as of Oct 31, 2006)	$70.00	Large-Cap Value

GICS Sector Financials
Sub-Industry Industrial REITS

Comment This REIT (formerly ProLogis Trust) is the largest publicly held, U.S.-based owner and operator of distribution facilities, with operations in North America, Europe and Asia.

Key Stock Statistics (Source S&P, Vickers, company reports)

52-Wk Range	$64.02–40.36	S&P Oper. EPS 2006E	2.23	P/E on S&P Oper. EPS 2006E	28.4	Dividend Rate/Share	$1.60
Trailing 12-Month EPS	$2.47	S&P Oper. EPS 2007E	2.55	Common Shares Outstg. (M)	245.1	Yield (%)	2.53
Trailing 12-Month P/E	25.6	S&P Core EPS 2006E	2.23	Market Capitalization(B)	$15.508	Beta	0.36
$10K Invested 5 Yrs Ago	$40,249	S&P Core EPS 2007E	2.55	Institutional Ownership (%)	94	S&P Credit Rating	BBB+

Price Performance

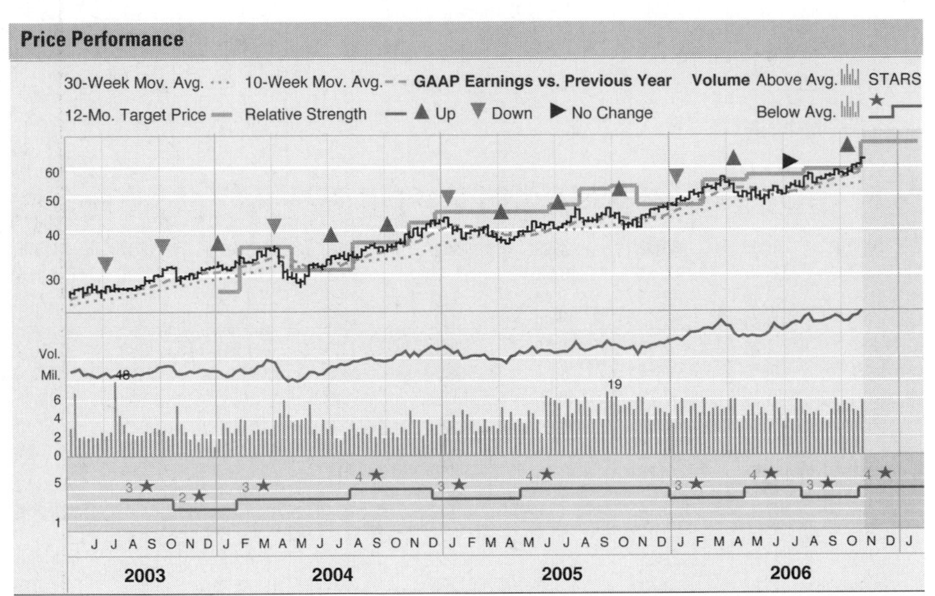

Analysis prepared by **Robert McMillan** on October 31, 2006, when the stock traded at **$ 63.27**.

Highlights

- We see rental income rising about 50% in 2006, driven by our expectations of a moderate increase in demand for industrial real estate, contributions from acquisitions and development activities, and income from its property funds business. We see rental income advancing a more modest 9% in 2007.
- We believe that a moderately expanding economy, accompanied by a rise in worldwide trading levels, will contribute to an increase in demand for PLD's properties, and eventually rent growth. At September 30, 2006, the trust's stabilized operating portfolio was 94.7% leased, up from 94.5% a year earlier. We were encouraged that rents rose 2.1%, with rent growth accelerating in many markets. We look for the company's acquisition and development program, particularly in Asia, to continue to benefit operations by enhancing PLD's economies of scale and geographic presence around the world.
- We project EPS of $2.23 in 2006 and $2.55 in 2007; we see funds from operations (FFO) per share of $3.61 and $3.90 in 2006 and 2007, respectively. We estimate fourth quarter FFO of $1.03.

Investment Rationale/Risk

- We think PLD deserves to trade at a premium to peers due to its position as one of the largest owners of global distribution facilities, which are increasingly important, in our view, to global companies looking to increase efficiency by concentrating their business among fewer space providers. We view PLD's success in the property funds business, which allows it to expand its portfolio and collect management fees while using capital from institutional investors, as a positive factor in our valuation.
- Risks to our recommendation and target price include slower than expected growth in demand and rental rates for industrial space, a non-renewal of leases by customers, and sharper than projected increases in interest rates.
- The shares recently traded at about 20X PLD's trailing 12-month FFO. Our 12-month target price of $70 is equal to 18.5X our forward 12-month FFO estimate of $3.80. With the shares trading near peak valuation levels, we believe that the multiple will narrow to a more sustainable level over the next 12 months.

Qualitative Risk Assessment

LOW	MEDIUM	HIGH

Our risk assessment reflects our view of PLD's position as one of the largest owners of industrial space in the world, its broad geographic and customer diversification, and what we view as its healthy balance sheet.

Quantitative Evaluations

S&P Quality Ranking A-

D	C	B-	B	B+	A-	A	A+

Relative Strength Rank STRONG

83

LOWEST = 1 HIGHEST = 99

Revenue/Earnings Data

Revenue (Million $)

	1Q	2Q	3Q	4Q	Year
2006	580.8	689.1	580.9	--	--
2005	431.9	469.6	532.0	434.6	1,868
2004	151.0	150.1	148.8	150.0	598.1
2003	159.9	169.4	116.8	213.1	734.1
2002	172.3	174.5	135.0	193.3	675.0
2001	162.2	163.5	150.8	76.94	574.3

Earnings Per Share ($)

2006	0.62	0.47	0.46	E0.74	E2.23
2005	0.34	0.47	0.42	0.22	1.39
2004	0.19	0.39	0.27	0.23	1.09
2003	0.21	0.26	-0.04	0.72	1.16
2002	0.31	0.31	0.14	0.44	1.20
2001	0.25	0.26	0.28	-0.27	0.52

Fiscal year ended Dec. 31. Next earnings report expected: Mid February. EPS Estimates based on S&P Operating Earnings; historical GAAP earnings are as reported.

Dividend Data (Dates: mm/dd Payment Date: mm/dd/yy)

Amount ($)	Date Decl.	Ex-Div. Date	Stk. of Record	Payment Date
0.370	11/01	11/14	11/16	11/30/05
0.400	02/01	02/13	02/15	02/28/06
0.400	05/01	05/12	05/16	05/31/06
0.400	08/01	08/14	08/16	08/31/06

Dividends have been paid since 1994. Source: Company reports.

ProLogis

Business Summary October 31, 2006

ProLogis (formerly ProLogis Trust, and prior to that Security Capital Industrial Trust) is a REIT that owns and operates industrial distribution and temperature-controlled distribution facilities in North America, Europe and Japan. The trust's investment strategy focuses on generic industrial distribution facilities in markets that PLD thinks offer attractive long-term growth prospects, and in which it believes it can achieve a strong market position by acquiring and developing flexible facilities for warehousing and light manufacturing uses.

PLD's business is organized into three main operating segments: property operations, fund management, and corporate distribution facilities services and other (CDFS). The property operations segment (55% of 2005 operating income) is involved in long-term ownership, management and leasing of industrial distribution facilities, usually adaptable for both distribution and light manufacturing or assembly uses. The trust earns income from rents and reimbursement of property operating expenses from unaffiliated customers, and management fees from entities in which it has an ownership interest. At December 31, 2005, PLD's property operations segment consisted of 1,461 operating properties aggregating 186.7 million square feet in North America, Europe and Asia. Included in this segment were 124 operating properties aggregating 29.4 million square feet at a total investment of $1.4 billion that were developed or acquired in the CDFS business segment but are included in the property operations segment's assets pending contribution or sale.

The fund management segment (14% of 2005 operating income) is involved in the long-term investment management of unconsolidated property funds, and the properties they own, with the objective of generating a high level of returns for PLD and its fund partners. It allows PLD, as the manager of the property funds, to maintain the market presence and customer relationships that are the key drivers of the ProLogis Operating System, and it enables the company to realize a portion of the development profits from its CDFS business activities by contributing its stabilized development properties to property funds. It also allows PLD to earn fees and incentives for providing services to the property funds and enables PLD to maintain a long-term ownership position in the properties.

Company Financials

Per Share Data ($) Year Ended Dec. 31	**2005**	**2004**	**2003**	**2002**	**2001**	**2000**	**1999**	**1998**	**1997**	**1996**
Tangible Book Value	21.08	14.82	14.35	13.96	12.94	13.53	13.86	12.83	13.13	12.41
Earnings	1.39	1.09	1.16	1.20	0.52	0.96	0.81	0.51	0.04	0.63
S&P Core Earnings	1.39	1.06	1.14	1.17	0.49	NA	NA	NA	NA	NA
Dividends	1.48	1.46	1.44	1.42	1.38	1.34	1.30	1.24	1.07	1.01
Payout Ratio	106%	134%	124%	118%	NM	140%	160%	267%	245%	160%
Prices:High	47.62	43.33	32.62	26.00	23.30	24.69	22.19	26.50	25.50	22.50
Prices:Low	36.50	27.62	23.63	20.96	19.35	17.56	16.75	19.75	18.88	16.50
P/E Ratio:High	34	40	28	22	45	26	27	52	NM	36
P/E Ratio:Low	26	25	20	17	37	18	20	39	NM	26
Income Statement Analysis (Million $)										
Rental Income	635	527	Nil	449	466	480	492	345	285	227
Mortgage Income	Nil	Nil	Nil	Nil	Nil	Nil	Nil	Nil	18.0	6.46
Total Income	1,868	598	734	675	574	644	567	368	302	233
General Expenses	1,210	224	210	91.0	83.0	78.0	76.7	58.1	51.7	112
Interest Expense	178	153	155	153	164	172	172	104	52.7	38.8
Provision for Losses	Nil	Nil	Nil	Nil	Nil	Nil	Nil	Nil	Nil	Nil
Depreciation	199	172	165	153	143	151	152	101	76.6	59.9
Net Income	318	234	251	249	128	214	182	111	39.7	79.4
S&P Core Earnings	292	199	208	210	86.8	NA	NA	NA	NA	NA
Balance Sheet & Other Financial Data (Million $)										
Cash	1,241	1,145	1,009	111	28.0	57.9	69.3	63.1	25.0	4.77
Total Assets	13,114	7,098	6,369	5,924	5,604	5,946	5,848	4,331	3,034	2,462
Real Estate Investment	11,875	6,334	5,854	5,396	4,588	4,689	4,975	3,658	3,006	2,509
Loss Reserve	Nil	Nil	Nil	Nil	Nil	Nil	Nil	Nil	Nil	Nil
Net Investment	10,757	5,345	5,007	4,683	4,013	4,213	4,608	3,403	2,835	2,400
Short Term Debt	Nil	Nil	Nil	222	49.3	69.7	43.5	42.9	20.0	56.9
Capitalization:Debt	6,678	3,414	2,991	2,510	2,529	2,555	2,413	1,796	857	652
Capitalization:Equity	5,138	2,752	2,586	2,486	2,276	2,236	2,243	1,583	1,542	1,163
Capitalization:Total	12,225	6,583	6,089	5,439	5,251	5,574	5,428	4,104	2,379	2,264
% Earnings & Depreciation/Assets	5.1	6.0	6.8	7.0	4.7	6.2	6.6	5.7	4.2	6.5
Price Times Book Value:High	2.3	2.9	2.3	1.9	1.8	1.8	1.6	4.0	1.9	1.8
Price Times Book Value:Low	1.7	1.9	1.6	1.5	1.5	1.3	1.2	3.0	1.4	1.3

Data as orig reptd.; bef. results of disc opers/spec. items. Per share data adj. for stk. divs.; EPS diluted. E-Estimated. NA-Not Available. NM-Not Meaningful. NR-Not Ranked. UR-Under Review.

Office: 4545 Airport Way, Denver, CO 80239.
Telephone: 303-567-5000.
Email: info@prologis.com
Website: http://www.prologis.com

Chrmn: K.D. Brooksher
Pres & COO: W.C. Rakowich
CEO: J.H. Schwartz
EVP & CFO: D.M. Bokides

SVP & Treas: M.G. Keiser, Jr.
Investor Contact: M. Marsden (303-567-5622)
Trustees: K. D. Brooksher, S. L. Feinberg, G. L. Fotiades, C. Garvey, D. P. Jacobs, W. C. Rakowich, N. C. Rising, J. H. Schwartz, D. M. Steuert, J. A. Teixeira, W. D. Zollars, A. Zulberti

Founded: 1991
Domicile: Maryland
Employees: 1,050

STANDARD &POOR'S

Prudential Financial Inc

S&P Recommendation STRONG BUY ★★★★★

Price $77.58 (as of Oct 27, 2006)

12-Mo. Target Price $87.00

Investment Style Large-Cap Growth

GICS Sector Financials
Sub-Industry Life & Health Insurance

Comment Through its subsidiaries, Prudential Financial provides a wide range of insurance, investment management and other financial products and services to customers in the U.S. and overseas.

Key Stock Statistics (Source S&P, Vickers, company reports)

52-Wk Range	$80.30–71.10	S&P Oper. EPS 2006E	5.75	P/E on S&P Oper. EPS 2006E	13.5	Dividend Rate/Share	$0.78
Trailing 12-Month EPS	$5.65	S&P Oper. EPS 2007E	6.53	Common Shares Outstg. (M)	485.0	Yield (%)	1.01
Trailing 12-Month P/E	13.7	S&P Core EPS 2006E	5.10	Market Capitalization(B)	$37.626	Beta	0.54
$10K Invested 5 Yrs Ago	NA	S&P Core EPS 2007E	5.92	Institutional Ownership (%)	53	S&P Credit Rating	A

Price Performance

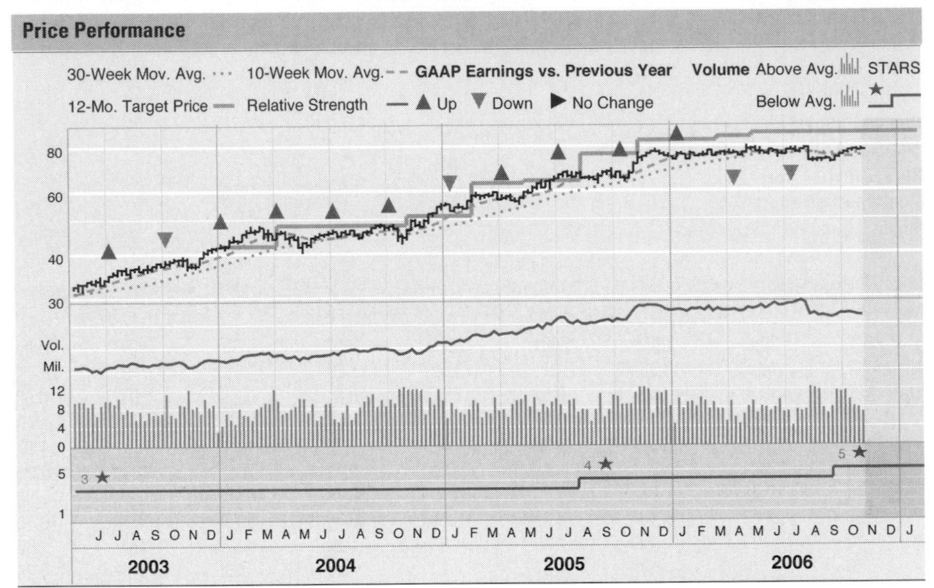

Analysis prepared by **Frank Braden** on September 29, 2006, when the stock traded at **$ 76.28**.

Highlights

- We expect pretax adjusted operating income in the insurance division to remain relatively flat in 2006, with unfavorable mortality experience offset by increased cost control measures driven by reduced head count. We project that sales in this division will benefit from new annuity products and an expanded distribution network. We forecast strong growth in pretax adjusted operating income for the investment division, helped by our expectation for more than $110 million in expense savings from the CIGNA retirement division acquisition and the Wachovia joint venture. We expect demand for total retirement services and earnings from stable value products to help drive growth.
- We estimate that pretax adjusted operating income will see mid- to high single digit growth in 2006 for the international insurance and investments division, on improving retention rates, expanded distribution and strategic acquisitions, partially offset by higher expenses relating to recruiting and client servicing.
- Our operating EPS estimate is $5.75 in 2006 and $6.53 in 2007, including projected stock option expense.

Investment Rationale/Risk

- We believe PRU has several sources of potential growth in 2006, including the June 1, 2006 acquisition of Allstate Financial's variable annuity business; the Wachovia joint venture; the completion of the integration of the CIGNA retirement division; and the potential to increase overall debt leverage, which should also help ROE improve, in our view. Furthermore, we believe new annuity products should support continued earnings growth at the U.S. insurance division in 2006.
- Risks to our recommendation and target price include currency risk; lower than expected investment income in a continued low interest rate environment; reserving risks for new guaranteed minimum benefits; the pricing and availability of reinsurance for some products; integration risks from acquisitions; regulatory risks; and litigation resulting from market timing issues related to the joint venture with Wachovia.
- Our 12-month target price of $87 is based on a P/E of 13.3X applied to our 2007 operating EPS estimate of $6.53, in line with our underlying EPS growth estimate.

Qualitative Risk Assessment

LOW	MEDIUM	HIGH

Our risk assessment reflects PRU's varied product offerings, geographic diversification, disciplined capital management, prominent market position and high risk-based capital ratio.

Quantitative Evaluations

S&P Quality Ranking NR

D	C	B-	B	B+	A-	A	A+

Relative Strength Rank MODERATE

48

LOWEST = 1 HIGHEST = 99

Revenue/Earnings Data

Revenue (Million $)

	1Q	2Q	3Q	4Q	Year
2006	7,927	7,432	--	--	--
2005	7,721	8,318	7,787	7,882	31,708
2004	6,743	6,904	7,346	7,355	28,348
2003	6,785	7,304	6,693	7,125	27,907
2002	6,684	6,637	6,679	6,675	26,675
2001	6,747	7,168	6,356	6,906	27,177

Earnings Per Share ($)

2006	1.38	0.92	**E**1.48	**E**1.52	**E**5.75
2005	1.47	1.56	2.61	0.78	6.46
2004	0.72	0.98	1.09	0.64	3.45
2003	0.42	0.21	0.48	0.95	2.06
2002	0.47	0.20	0.68	Nil	1.36
2001	--	--	--	--	0.07

Fiscal year ended Dec. 31. Next earnings report expected: Early November. EPS Estimates based on S&P Operating Earnings; historical GAAP earnings are as reported.

Dividend Data (Dates: mm/dd Payment Date: mm/dd/yy)

Amount ($)	Date Decl.	Ex-Div. Date	Stk. of Record	Payment Date
0.780	11/08	11/18	11/22	12/19/05

Dividends have been paid since 2002. Source: Company reports.

Please read the Required Disclosures and Analyst Certification on the last page of this report.

Prudential Financial Inc

Business Summary September 29, 2006

CORPORATE OVERVIEW. Prudential Financial is one of the largest U.S. financial services companies, with $532 billion in assets under management and more than $2 trillion of life insurance in force at 2005 year end, and serves customers in roughly 30 other countries.

Financial services operates through insurance (36% of 2005 operating revenues, 38% in 2004), investments (27%, 25%), international insurance and investments (35%, 34%), as well as a corporate and other segment (2.4%, 2.6%). The insurance segment consists of the individual life and annuities unit (49% of the division's 2005 operating revenues) and the group insurance unit (51%), which distributes group life, disability and related insurance products through employee and member benefit plans.

The asset management segment (27% of the division's 2005 operating revenues), the financial advisory segment (7.3%) and the retirement services segment (65%) comprise the investment division. International insurance and investments consists of insurance (94% of the division's 2005 operating revenues) and investments (6.0%).

The closed block businesses represent some insurance products no longer offered, including certain participating insurance and annuity policies. At December 31, 2005, PRU had reinsurance agreements covering about 90% of the closed block policies.

Company Financials

Per Share Data ($) Year Ended Dec. 31	**2005**	**2004**	**2003**	**2002**	**2001**	**2000**	**1999**	**1998**	**1997**	**1996**
Tangible Book Value	45.53	42.40	39.65	37.89	31.80	NA	NA	NA	NA	NA
Operating Earnings	NA	NA	NA	NA	NA	NA	NA	NA	NA	NA
Earnings	6.46	3.45	2.06	1.36	0.07	0.82	NA	NA	NA	NA
S&P Core Earnings	4.96	1.91	1.79	1.13	NA	NA	NA	NA	NA	NA
Dividends	0.78	0.63	0.50	0.40	Nil	NA	NA	NA	NA	NA
Payout Ratio	12%	18%	24%	29%	Nil	NA	NA	NA	NA	NA
Prices:High	78.62	55.62	42.21	36.00	33.74	NA	NA	NA	NA	NA
Prices:Low	52.07	40.14	27.03	25.25	27.50	NA	NA	NA	NA	NA
P/E Ratio:High	12	16	20	26	NM	NA	NA	NA	NA	NA
P/E Ratio:Low	8	12	13	19	NM	NA	NA	NA	NA	NA
Income Statement Analysis (Million $)										
Life Insurance in Force	NA	NA	1,928,650	1,800,788	1,768,038	NA	NA	NA	NA	NA
Premium Income:Life	13,685	12,580	10,972	10,897	10,078	NA	NA	NA	NA	NA
Premium Income:A & H	NA	NA	806	586	515	NA	NA	NA	NA	NA
Net Investment Income	10,560	9,079	8,681	8,832	9,151	9,467	NA	NA	NA	NA
Total Revenue	31,708	28,348	27,907	26,675	27,177	26,514	NA	NA	NA	NA
Pretax Income	4,471	3,287	1,958	64.0	-227	525	NA	NA	NA	NA
Net Operating Income	NA	NA	NA	NA	NA	NA	NA	NA	NA	NA
Net Income	3,602	2,332	1,308	256	-170	304	NA	NA	NA	NA
S&P Core Earnings	2,580	1,022	981	650	-403	NA	NA	NA	NA	NA
Balance Sheet & Other Financial Data (Million $)										
Cash & Equivalent	9,866	10,100	9,746	11,688	20,364	19,994	NA	NA	NA	NA
Premiums Due	3,548	32,790	Nil	Nil	Nil	NA	NA	NA	NA	NA
Investment Assets:Bonds	158,515	153,715	132,011	128,075	110,316	NA	NA	NA	NA	NA
Investment Assets:Stocks	18,792	4,283	6,703	2,807	2,272	NA	NA	NA	NA	NA
Investment Assets:Loans	32,811	32,761	27,621	22,094	28,299	NA	NA	NA	NA	NA
Investment Assets:Total	221,401	216,624	181,041	183,094	165,834	169,251	NA	NA	NA	NA
Deferred Policy Costs	9,438	8,847	7,826	7,031	6,868	6,751	NA	NA	NA	NA
Total Assets	417,776	401,058	321,274	292,746	293,030	298,414	NA	NA	NA	NA
Debt	8,270	7,627	5,610	4,757	5,304	14,812	NA	NA	NA	NA
Common Equity	22,763	22,344	21,292	21,330	20,453	20,692	NA	NA	NA	NA
% Return on Revenue	11.4	8.2	4.7	1.0	NM	1.1	NA	NA	NA	NA
% Return on Assets	0.9	0.6	0.4	0.1	NM	NA	NA	NA	NA	NA
% Return on Equity	16.0	10.7	6.1	1.2	NM	NA	NA	NA	NA	NA
% Investment Yield	4.8	4.6	4.8	5.1	5.8	NA	NA	NA	NA	NA

Data as orig reptd.; bef. results of disc opers/spec. items. Per share data adj. for stk. divs.; EPS diluted. E-Estimated. NA-Not Available. NM-Not Meaningful. NR-Not Ranked. UR-Under Review.

Office: 751 Broad St, Newark, NJ 07102.
Telephone: 973-802-6000.
Email: investor.relations@prudential.com
Website: http://www.investor.prudential.com

Chrmn, Pres & CEO: A.F. Ryan
Vice Chrmn: V.L. Banta
Vice Chrmn: M.B. Grier
Vice Chrmn: J.R. Strangfeld, Jr.

Vice Chrmn: R.A. Lawson
Board of Directors: F. K. Becker, G. M. Bethune, G. Caperton, G. F. Casellas, J. G. Cullen, W. H. Gray, III, J. F. Hanson, C. J. Horner, K. J. Krapek, C. Poon, A. F. Ryan, J. A. Unruh

Founded: 1875
Domicile: New Jersey
Employees: 38,853

STANDARD &POOR'S

Public Storage Inc

S&P Recommendation BUY ★★★★★

Price $88.36 (as of Oct 27, 2006)

12-Mo. Target Price $91.00

Investment Style Large-Cap Value

GICS Sector Financials
Sub-Industry Specialized REITS

Comment This real estate investment trust invests primarily in self-service storage facilities (mini-warehouses), but also in commercial and industrial properties.

Key Stock Statistics (Source S&P, Vickers, company reports)

52-Wk Range	$89.76–64.47	S&P Oper. EPS 2006E	2.23	P/E on S&P Oper. EPS 2006E	39.6	Dividend Rate/Share	$2.00
Trailing 12-Month EPS	$2.15	S&P Oper. EPS 2007E	2.34	Common Shares Outstg. (M)	168.1	Yield (%)	2.26
Trailing 12-Month P/E	41.1	S&P Core EPS 2006E	2.19	Market Capitalization(B)	$11.426	Beta	0.17
$10K Invested 5 Yrs Ago	$32,686	S&P Core EPS 2007E	2.29	Institutional Ownership (%)	60	S&P Credit Rating	A-

Price Performance

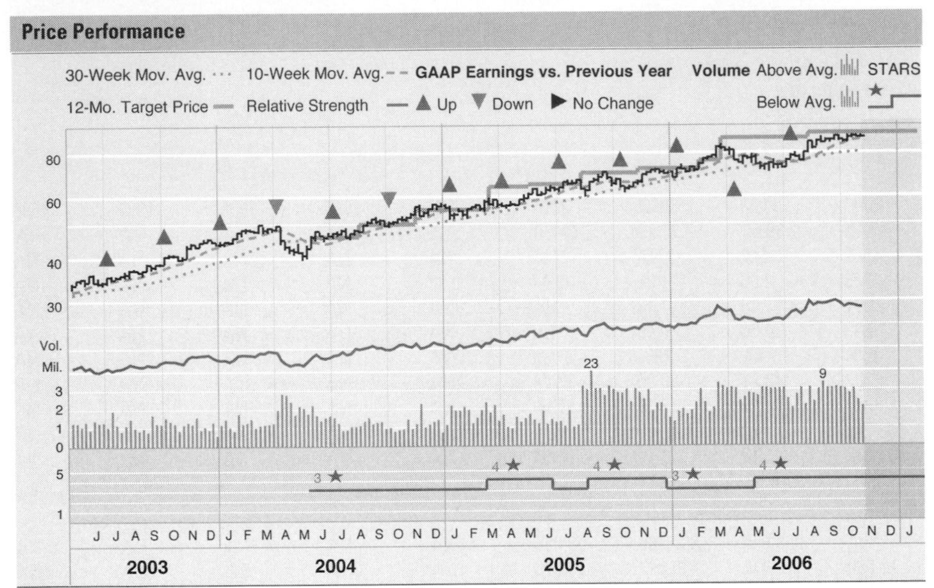

Options: Ph

Analysis prepared by **Robert McMillan** on August 08, 2006, when the stock traded at **$ 83.46**.

Highlights

- We expect PSA to benefit from an expanding economy in the U.S., which we see generating increased jobs and greater moving and relocation activity, and should translate into more demand for self-storage space.
- After an 11% rise in 2005, we look for revenues to increase about 8% in 2006, on continued organic growth as well as contributions from acquisitions. We look for a growing economy to contribute to higher occupancy and rental rates well into 2006. Same-store occupancy remained healthy, at 92.1%, as of June 30, 2006, unchanged from the year-earlier level. During the second quarter, realized annual rent per occupied square foot increased 5.5%, year to year, to $12.05, and revenue per available square foot rose 5.5%, to $11.10. This helped net operating income in the same-store portfolio increase 8.5%, year to year, during the second quarter.
- We project EPS of $2.23 in 2006 and $2.34 in 2007; we look for FFO of $4.00 and $4.30 in 2006 and 2007, respectively. We see third quarter FFO of $1.00.

Investment Rationale/Risk

- We believe that a healthy economy will continue to stimulate moving activity at a rapid pace. We see PSA benefiting from its ability to continue gaining share at the expense of smaller competitors by creating customer awareness in its markets and offering an array of customer services, such as container services, which many small competitors cannot provide.
- Risks to our recommendation and target price include slower than expected growth in rental rates, higher than projected vacancy levels, a significant drop in employment levels or relocation activity, and a greater than expected rise in interest rates.
- The shares recently traded at 22.3X trailing 12-month FFO, well above their historical average of about 13.4X, which has been rising in recent quarters. Our 12-month target price of $91 is equal to 22X our 12-month FFO estimate of $4.10. Although we expect operating results and dividends to continue growing, we think the multiple will narrow slightly over the next 12 months, after recent gains in the shares.

Qualitative Risk Assessment

LOW | MEDIUM | HIGH (LOW)

Our risk assessment reflects PSA's position as one of the largest providers of self storage space in a consolidating industry, as well as our view of its consistent growth and healthy balance sheet.

Quantitative Evaluations

S&P Quality Ranking B+

D | C | B- | B | B+ | A- | A | A+

Relative Strength Rank MODERATE

52

LOWEST = 1 HIGHEST = 99

Revenue/Earnings Data

Revenue (Million $)

	1Q	2Q	3Q	4Q	Year
2006	278.7	298.0	--	--	--
2005	243.8	254.3	264.9	273.6	1,061
2004	222.7	231.6	237.2	240.3	928.0
2003	206.9	217.1	228.0	223.1	875.1
2002	203.8	205.7	215.8	207.6	841.5
2001	197.8	207.4	215.7	231.7	834.7

Earnings Per Share ($)

	1Q	2Q	3Q	4Q	Year
2006	0.48	0.55	**E**0.57	**E**0.63	**E**2.23
2005	0.37	0.47	0.58	0.49	1.92
2004	0.17	0.38	0.39	0.46	1.39
2003	0.27	0.34	0.40	0.26	1.27
2002	0.37	0.30	0.36	0.20	1.28
2001	0.34	0.39	0.41	0.38	1.51

Fiscal year ended Dec. 31. Next earnings report expected: Late October. EPS Estimates based on S&P Operating Earnings; historical GAAP earnings are as reported.

Dividend Data (Dates: mm/dd Payment Date: mm/dd/yy)

Amount ($)	Date Decl.	Ex-Div. Date	Stk. of Record	Payment Date
0.500	11/01	12/13	12/15	12/29/05
0.500	02/23	03/13	03/15	03/30/06
0.500	05/04	05/31	06/02	06/29/06
0.500	08/02	09/13	09/15	09/28/06

Dividends have been paid since 1981. Source: Company reports.

Public Storage Inc

Business Summary August 08, 2006

Public Storage is an equity real estate investment trust that was organized as a corporation under the laws of California on July 10, 1980. It is a fully integrated, self-administered and self-managed REIT that acquires, develops, owns and operates storage facilities.

PSA is the largest U.S. owner and operator of storage space, with direct and indirect equity investments in 1,501 storage facilities containing about 92 million sq. ft. of net rentable space as of December 31, 2005, located in 37 states. The largest concentration of properties was in California (21%), Texas (11%) and Florida (10%). The trust's facilities are generally operated to maximize cash flow through the regular review, and, when warranted by market conditions, an adjustment of scheduled rents.

The trust's primary objective is to increase shareholder value through internal growth (by increasing funds from operations and cash available for distribution) and acquisitions of additional real estate investments. PSA believes that its access to capital, geographic diversification, and operating efficiencies resulting from its size will enhance the company's ability to achieve its objective.

PSA's growth strategies consist of improving the operating performance of stabilized existing traditional self-storage properties; acquiring additional interests in entities that own properties operated by the trust; purchasing interests in properties that are owned or operated by others; developing properties in selected markets; improving the operating performance of the containerized storage operations; and participating in the growth of PS Business Parks, Inc.

Company Financials

Per Share Data ($) Year Ended Dec. 31	**2005**	**2004**	**2003**	**2002**	**2001**	**2000**	**1999**	**1998**	**1997**	**1996**
Tangible Book Value	16.72	16.69	17.03	16.16	28.37	18.24	21.43	16.65	15.71	13.10
Earnings	1.90	1.39	1.27	1.28	1.51	1.41	1.52	1.30	0.91	1.10
S&P Core Earnings	1.91	1.38	1.25	1.26	1.48	NA	NA	NA	NA	NA
Dividends	1.85	1.80	1.80	1.80	1.69	1.48	0.88	0.88	0.88	0.88
Payout Ratio	97%	129%	142%	1%	112%	105%	58%	68%	97%	80%
Prices:High	72.02	57.64	45.81	39.29	35.15	26.93	29.38	33.63	30.88	31.38
Prices:Low	51.50	39.50	28.25	27.98	24.13	20.87	20.81	22.63	25.88	18.75
P/E Ratio:High	38	41	36	33	23	19	19	26	34	29
P/E Ratio:Low	27	28	22	24	16	15	14	17	28	17
Income Statement Analysis (Million $)										
Rental Income	980	894	844	813	782	703	628	536	434	294
Mortgage Income	Nil	Nil	Nil	Nil	Nil	Nil	Nil	Nil	Nil	Nil
Total Income	1,061	928	875	841	835	757	677	582	471	341
General Expenses	400	349	336	311	297	273	229	223	182	170
Interest Expense	8.22	0.76	1.12	3.81	3.23	3.29	7.97	4.51	6.79	8.48
Provision for Losses	Nil	Nil	Nil	Nil	Nil	Nil	Nil	Nil	Nil	Nil
Depreciation	196	183	186	180	168	149	138	107	91.5	65.0
Net Income	450	367	335	319	324	297	288	227	179	154
S&P Core Earnings	247	179	157	156	183	NA	NA	NA	NA	NA
Balance Sheet & Other Financial Data (Million $)										
Cash	329	708	205	103	49.3	89.5	55.1	51.2	41.5	26.9
Total Assets	5,552	5,205	4,968	4,844	4,626	4,514	4,214	3,404	3,312	2,572
Real Estate Investment	6,314	5,908	5,544	5,424	5,062	4,822	4,421	3,496	3,346	2,572
Loss Reserve	Nil	Nil	Nil	Nil	Nil	Nil	Nil	Nil	Nil	Nil
Net Investment	4,814	4,588	4,391	4,436	4,242	4,154	3,887	3,085	2,968	2,274
Short Term Debt	Nil	Nil	Nil	39.8	Nil	Nil	Nil	Nil	15.1	11.2
Capitalization:Debt	134	130	76.0	76.1	144	156	167	81.4	104	97.2
Capitalization:Equity	2,319	2,328	2,353	2,342	2,369	2,569	2,534	2,250	1,927	1,471
Capitalization:Total	5,205	4,989	4,722	4,675	4,508	4,413	4,043	3,340	3,225	2,402
% Earnings & Depreciation/Assets	12.0	10.8	10.6	10.5	7.1	10.2	11.2	7.6	9.2	9.7
Price Times Book Value:High	4.3	3.5	2.7	2.4	1.2	1.5	1.4	2.0	2.0	2.4
Price Times Book Value:Low	3.1	2.4	1.7	1.7	0.9	1.1	1.0	1.4	1.7	1.4

Data as orig reptd.; bef. results of disc opers/spec. items. Per share data adj. for stk. divs.; EPS diluted. E-Estimated. NA-Not Available. NM-Not Meaningful. NR-Not Ranked. UR-Under Review.

Office: 701 Western Ave, Glendale, CA 91201-2349.
Telephone: 818-244-8080.
Email: investor@publicstorage.com
Website: http://www.publicstorage.com

Chrmn: B.W. Hughes
Pres, Vice Chrmn & CEO: R.L. Havner, Jr.
SVP & CFO: J. Reyes
SVP & Chief Lgl Officer: J.S. Baumann

Investor Contact: C. Teng (818-244-8080)

Founded: 1980
Domicile: California
Employees: 4,030

STANDARD &POOR'S

Public Service Enterprise Group Inc

S&P Recommendation HOLD ★★★★★

Price $60.85 (as of Oct 27, 2006)

12-Mo. Target Price $66.00

Investment Style Large-Cap Value

GICS Sector Utilities
Sub-Industry Multi-Utilities

Comment PEG is the holding company for Public Service Electric and Gas (PSE&G), with a service area that encompasses 70% of New Jersey.

Key Stock Statistics (Source S&P, Vickers, company reports)

52-Wk Range	$72.61–59.00	S&P Oper. EPS 2006E	3.65	P/E on S&P Oper. EPS 2006E	16.7	Dividend Rate/Share	$2.28
Trailing 12-Month EPS	$3.58	S&P Oper. EPS 2007E	4.60	Common Shares Outstg. (M)	251.7	Yield (%)	3.75
Trailing 12-Month P/E	17.0	S&P Core EPS 2006E	3.64	Market Capitalization(B)	$15.317	Beta	0.65
$10K Invested 5 Yrs Ago	$19,500	S&P Core EPS 2007E	4.58	Institutional Ownership (%)	54	S&P Credit Rating	BBB

Price Performance

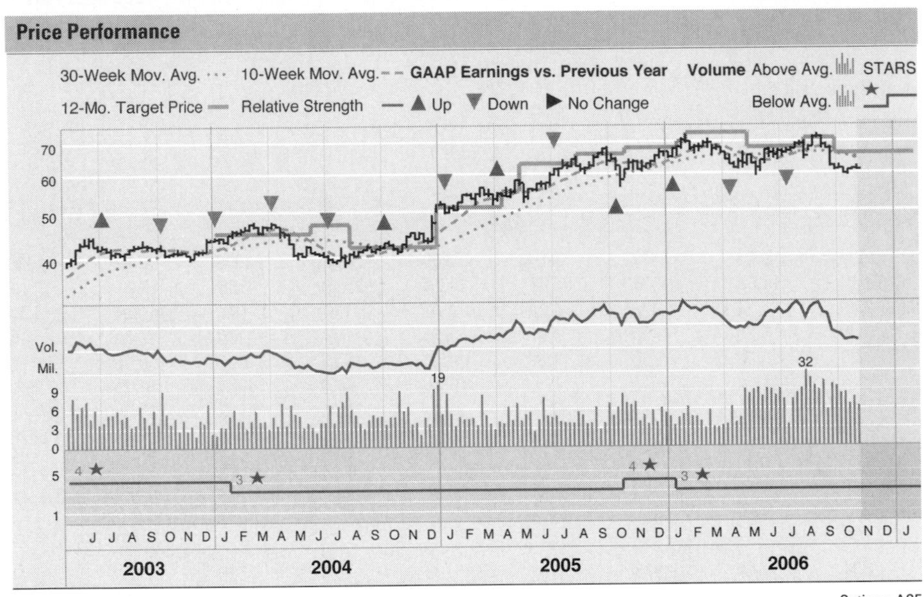

Options: ASE

Analysis prepared by **Justin McCann** on September 20, 2006, when the stock traded at **$ 61.30**.

Highlights

- Although the termination of the planned merger with Exelon (EXC: buy, $59) has eliminated the long-term strategic benefit of being an integral part of one of the largest utilities and power generators in the U.S., we believe the company's prospects on a stand-alone basis are positive. With the reduction of its international exposure, PEG has, in our view, improved its financial stability, and we expect it to benefit from the favorable pricing in energy markets.
- We expect EPS in 2006 to increase about 4% from 2005 EPS from continuing operations of $3.51. We expect higher earnings at the Power division, driven by higher prices and sales, and a full year of eased transmission constraints due to a nuclear services contract with Exelon. This contract expires in January 2007, but PEG has options to renew it for up to three years.
- For 2007, we expect EPS to advance about 25% from anticipated operating results in 2006. This will be driven, in our view, by the renewal of power contracts at higher commodity prices, which could result in double-digit earnings growth for the next few years.

Investment Rationale/Risk

- With PEG's share price having been in an approximate correlation with the 1.225 exchange ratio for EXC shares, the stock dropped sharply after the announced termination of the proposed merger with Exelon. We believe PEG's troubled nuclear power plants have benefited greatly from EXC's nuclear expertise and, if their service contract is renewed, should continue to do so. With natural gas prices high, the company should continue to have a major cost advantage in the Northeast power markets.
- Risks to our opinion and target price include failure to complete plants under construction on time, an inability to continue hedging over 75% of electric generating capacity, and narrower wholesale power margins.
- With the recent decline in the shares, the yield from the dividend has increased from around 3.4% to 3.7%. While this is still below the recent peer average of about 4.0%, we believe the shares should benefit from a projected growth rate that is well above peers. Our target price of $66 reflects a modest discount-to-peers P/E of about 14.3X our 2007 EPS estimate.

Qualitative Risk Assessment

LOW | MEDIUM | HIGH

Our risk assessment reflects strong and steady cash flows from the regulated electric and gas utility operations of PSE&G, as well as the strong but less predictable earnings and cash flows from the non-regulated power generating operations. It also reflects a lowering of the company's risk profile through the divestiture of its non-core international investments.

Quantitative Evaluations

S&P Quality Ranking B+

D | C | B- | B | **B+** | A- | A | A+

Relative Strength Rank WEAK

17

LOWEST = 1 HIGHEST = 99

Revenue/Earnings Data

Revenue (Million $)

	1Q	2Q	3Q	4Q	Year
2006	3,521	2,606	--	--	--
2005	3,310	2,442	3,376	3,472	12,430
2004	3,221	2,290	2,747	2,731	10,996
2003	3,364	2,419	2,805	--	11,116
2002	1,914	1,469	2,328	2,679	8,390
2001	2,814	2,171	2,401	2,429	9,815

Earnings Per Share ($)

2006	0.79	-0.05	**E**1.27	**E**0.93	**E**3.65
2005	1.18	0.42	1.06	0.89	3.51
2004	1.14	0.50	1.03	0.38	3.03
2003	1.42	0.66	0.93	0.69	3.72
2002	0.87	-1.10	1.00	1.19	1.99
2001	1.22	0.67	0.82	0.95	3.67

Fiscal year ended Dec. 31. Next earnings report expected: Early December. EPS Estimates based on S&P Operating Earnings; historical GAAP earnings are as reported.

Dividend Data (Dates: mm/dd Payment Date: mm/dd/yy)

Amount ($)	Date Decl.	Ex-Div. Date	Stk. of Record	Payment Date
0.560	11/15	12/06	12/08	12/30/05
0.570	01/17	03/06	03/08	03/31/06
0.570	04/18	06/06	06/08	06/30/06
0.570	07/18	09/06	09/08	09/29/06

Dividends have been paid since 1907. Source: Company reports.

Public Service Enterprise Group Inc

Business Summary September 20, 2006

CORPORATE OVERVIEW. Headquartered in Newark, NJ, Public Service Enterprise Group has three primary operating units: Public Service Electric and Gas Co. - PSE&G ($348 million of net income in 2005), Power ($406 million), and Energy Holdings ($199 million). The parent company and intersegment eliminations accounted for a loss of $95 million. PEG has sought to minimize its earnings and cash flow volatility by entering into long-term contracts for most of its competitive wholesale power generation, and by reducing its exposure to international operations over time.

IMPACT OF MAJOR DEVELOPMENTS. On September 14, 2006, the company and Exelon Corp.(EXC) announced the termination of the merger agreement they had announced on December 20, 2004. While we view the termination of the merger as a negative for PEG shareholders (who would have received 1.225 shares of EXC for each PEG share), we believe the rate concessions and additional power plant divestitures demanded by the New Jersey regulators would have significantly diluted many of the expected benefits of the proposed transaction.

Company Financials

Per Share Data ($) Year Ended Dec. 31	**2005**	**2004**	**2003**	**2002**	**2001**	**2000**	**1999**	**1998**	**1997**	**1996**
Tangible Book Value	21.57	21.41	20.84	14.78	16.93	19.21	18.50	21.86	21.72	21.60
Earnings	3.51	3.03	3.72	1.99	3.67	3.55	3.29	2.79	2.41	2.42
S&P Core Earnings	3.40	2.97	4.03	3.06	3.16	NA	NA	NA	NA	NA
Dividends	2.24	2.20	2.16	2.16	2.16	2.16	2.16	2.16	2.16	2.16
Payout Ratio	64%	73%	58%	109%	59%	61%	66%	77%	90%	89%
Prices:High	68.47	52.64	44.50	47.25	51.55	50.00	42.63	42.75	31.81	32.13
Prices:Low	49.32	38.10	32.09	20.00	36.88	25.69	32.00	30.31	22.88	25.13
P/E Ratio:High	20	17	12	24	14	14	13	15	13	13
P/E Ratio:Low	14	13	9	10	10	7	10	11	9	10
Income Statement Analysis (Million $)										
Revenue	12,430	10,996	11,116	8,390	9,815	6,848	6,497	5,931	6,370	6,041
Depreciation	748	719	527	571	522	362	536	669	630	607
Maintenance	NA	NA	NA	NA	NA	NA	NA	NA	281	318
Fixed Charges Coverage	2.55	2.21	2.43	2.38	2.46	2.88	3.20	2.87	2.69	2.97
Construction Credits	NA	NA	NA	NA	NA	NA	NA	13.0	20.0	18.0
Effective Tax Rate	38.7%	38.2%	35.3%	37.3%	NM	39.1%	43.8%	39.5%	37.0%	33.1%
Net Income	858	721	852	416	763	764	723	644	560	612
S&P Core Earnings	834	708	925	638	656	NA	NA	NA	NA	NA
Balance Sheet & Other Financial Data (Million $)										
Gross Property	18,896	19,121	17,406	16,562	14,886	11,968	11,156	18,386	17,982	16,400
Capital Expenditures	1,024	1,255	1,351	1,814	2,053	959	582	535	542	586
Net Property	13,336	13,750	12,422	11,449	10,064	7,702	7,078	11,026	11,217	11,179
Capitalization:Long Term Debt	11,359	13,005	13,025	12,391	11,061	6,505	5,783	4,813	4,925	4,622
Capitalization:% Long Term Debt	65.4	69.4	70.2	75.7	72.8	60.2	59.1	43.3	45.5	44.2
Capitalization:Preferred	Nil	Nil	Nil	Nil	Nil	Nil	Nil	1,208	683	681
Capitalization:% Preferred	Nil	Nil	Nil	Nil	Nil	Nil	Nil	10.9	6.30	6.50
Capitalization:Common	6,022	5,739	5,529	3,987	4,137	4,294	3,996	5,098	5,211	5,213
Capitalization:% Common	34.6	30.6	29.8	24.3	27.2	39.8	40.9	45.8	48.2	49.8
Total Capital	21,629	23,091	22,750	19,302	18,403	13,906	12,707	14,825	14,556	14,128
% Operating Ratio	88.6	87.5	86.5	78.8	76.9	79.6	80.4	80.0	82.5	82.5
% Earned on Net Property	15.9	14.9	17.3	14.3	21.3	18.9	20.4	10.7	9.9	5.5
% Return on Revenue	6.9	6.6	7.7	5.0	7.8	11.2	11.1	10.9	8.8	10.2
% Return on Invested Capital	7.6	6.9	8.1	9.3	9.6	10.8	9.5	8.1	10.1	7.5
% Return on Common Equity	14.6	12.8	18.1	10.2	18.8	18.4	15.9	12.5	10.7	11.5

Data as orig reptd.; bef. results of disc opers/spec. items. Per share data adj. for stk. divs.; EPS diluted. E-Estimated. NA-Not Available. NM-Not Meaningful. NR-Not Ranked. UR-Under Review.

Office: 80 Park Plaza, Newark, NJ 07102-4109.
Telephone: 973-430-7000.
Email: stkserv@pseg.com
Website: http://www.pseg.com

Chrmn & CEO: E.J. Ferland
Pres & COO: R. Izzo
EVP & CFO: T.M. O'Flynn
SVP & General Counsel: R.E. Selover

VP & Cntlr: P.A. Rado
Investor Contact: M. Plawner (973-430-6474)
Board of Directors: C. Dorsa, E. H. Drew, E. J. Ferland, A. R. Gamper, Jr., C. K. Harper, W. V. Hickey, R. Izzo, S. A. Jackson, T. A. Renyi, R. J. Swift

Founded: 1985
Domicile: New Jersey
Employees: 10,025

STANDARD &POOR'S

Pulte Homes Inc.

S&P Recommendation HOLD ★★★★★	Price	12-Mo. Target Price	Investment Style
	$31.27 (as of Oct 30, 2006)	$36.00	Mid-Cap Value

GICS Sector Consumer Discretionary
Sub-Industry Homebuilding

Comment This builder of a wide range of single-family homes and condominiums throughout the country is the leading U.S. developer of active adult communities, and has a mortgage banking unit.

Key Stock Statistics (Source S&P, Vickers, company reports)

52-Wk Range	$44.70–26.02	S&P Oper. EPS 2006E	3.11	P/E on S&P Oper. EPS 2006E	10.1	Dividend Rate/Share	$0.16
Trailing 12-Month EPS	$4.88	S&P Oper. EPS 2007E	3.25	Common Shares Outstg. (M)	255.0	Yield (%)	0.51
Trailing 12-Month P/E	6.4	S&P Core EPS 2006E	3.11	Market Capitalization(B)	$7.975	Beta	1.09
$10K Invested 5 Yrs Ago	$38,053	S&P Core EPS 2007E	3.25	Institutional Ownership (%)	79	S&P Credit Rating	BBB

Price Performance

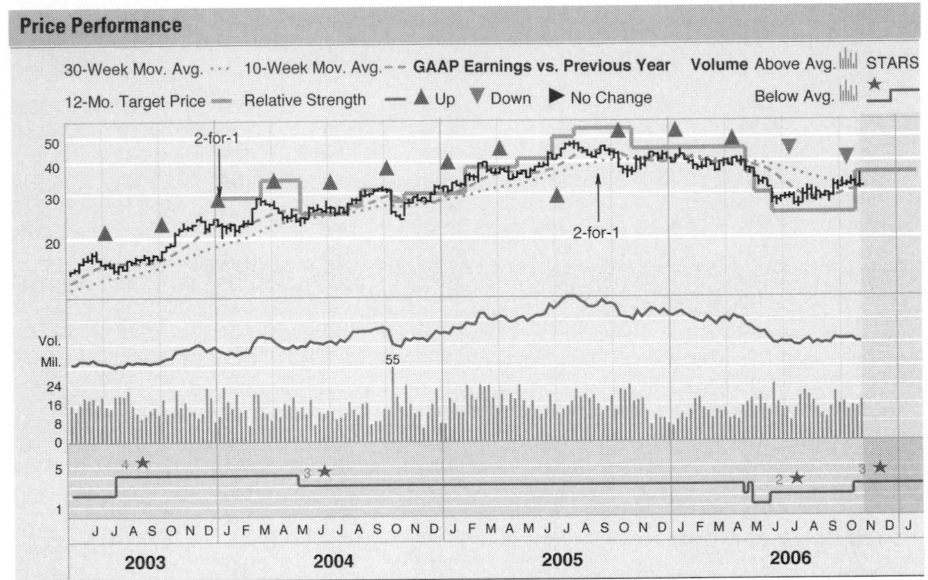

Analysis prepared by **William R. Mack, CFA** on October 19, 2006, when the stock traded at **$ 31.94**.

Highlights

- Even after a dramatic 30% unit order decline in the June quarter, we think the current industry-wide downturn has only just begun. Despite recent interest rates that we consider to be more stable, potentially slower job growth could prompt further downward revisions in profit guidance by management, which, in our view, has been slow to respond to the cyclical turn under way. Although we believe the company has modestly reduced its supply of lots in the past year, PHM still controls five to six years of available land.
- Helped by about a $50 million windfall from the sale of its Mexican mortgage banking operations, a portion of its discretionary cash is being spent to repurchase shares and reduce debt. However, even as its equity-based capital declines, we believe that PHM's debt is growing apace.
- We anticipate that the homebuilding gross margin will fall by close to 250 basis points this year, as higher accrued land costs meet moderating home prices. We look for overhead improvements to mitigate the impact from some of these higher expected costs.

Investment Rationale/Risk

- We recently raised our recommendation on the shares to hold from sell, following declines in the price of the stock. PHM's recent sales pace appears no better than its peers', in our opinion; however, we think much of that weakness is now embedded in the stock's reduced valuation. We believe the company's size connotes significant advantages, including a low cost of capital and a broad geographic diversification.
- Risks to our recommendation and target price include steep downward revaluations of its land inventory, which includes about 350,000 homesites, about half of which are owned outright.
- We believe trough earnings at Pulte could be below our recently reduced 2007 EPS forecast. In light of the great uncertainty in new home demand in what we view as the first year of a multi-period downcycle, we believe shareholders' equity is the best approximation of the company's intrinsic value. Our 12-month target price of $36 represents about a 20% premium to our mid-2007 book value forecast of almost $30 a share.

Qualitative Risk Assessment

LOW	**MEDIUM**	HIGH

Our risk assessment reflects that as the largest U.S. builder based on 2005 revenues, we believe PHM's size and geographic diversity suggest favorable access to capital and operations that are relatively well balanced among its numerous markets. As an offset, PHM has what we consider a relative abundance of land on its balance sheet, which increases its inventory risk.

Quantitative Evaluations

S&P Quality Ranking **A+**

D	C	B-	B	B+	A-	A	**A+**

Relative Strength Rank **MODERATE**

30

LOWEST = 1 HIGHEST = 99

Revenue/Earnings Data

Revenue (Million $)

	1Q	2Q	3Q	4Q	Year
2006	2,963	3,359	3,564	--	--
2005	2,518	3,251	3,794	5,132	14,695
2004	2,032	2,515	2,960	4,205	11,711
2003	1,553	1,958	2,400	3,138	9,049
2002	1,379	1,686	1,860	2,548	7,472
2001	839.8	1,058	1,482	2,002	5,382

Earnings Per Share ($)

	1Q	2Q	3Q	4Q	Year
2006	1.01	0.94	0.74	**E**0.50	**E**3.11
2005	0.83	1.16	1.45	2.03	5.47
2004	0.51	0.73	1.00	1.60	3.84
2003	0.35	0.49	0.64	0.97	2.46
2002	0.28	0.36	0.46	0.70	1.80
2001	0.23	0.35	0.38	0.50	1.50

Fiscal year ended Dec. 31. Next earnings report expected: Early February. EPS Estimates based on S&P Operating Earnings; historical GAAP earnings are as reported.

Dividend Data (Dates: mm/dd Payment Date: mm/dd/yy)

Amount ($)	Date Decl.	Ex-Div. Date	Stk. of Record	Payment Date
0.040	12/08	12/21	12/23	01/03/06
0.040	02/08	03/10	03/14	04/03/06
0.040	05/11	06/15	06/19	07/03/06
0.040	09/14	09/21	09/25	10/02/06

Dividends have been paid since 1977. Source: Company reports.

Pulte Homes Inc.

Business Summary October 19, 2006

CORPORATE OVERVIEW. Pulte Homes focuses on building single-family detached homes, which account for about 80% to 85% of unit volume. PHM's average price for U.S. homes sold in 2005 was $315,000, with about 70% of closings ranging in price from $100,000 to $350,000.

PHM targets buyers in nearly all home categories, but has recently concentrated its expansion efforts on affordable housing and on mature buyers (age 50 and over). In July 2001, it acquired Del Webb Corp., the leading U.S. builder of active adult communities, for a total of $1.9 billion in stock, cash, and the assumption of debt. This active adult segment accounted for nearly 35% of revenues at year-end 2005, according to management.

CORPORATE STRATEGY. At December 31, 2005 and December 31, 2004, PHM controlled about 363,000 and 343,000 lots, respectively. Approximately 174,000 and 158,000 lots were owned, and about 189,000 and 185,000 lots were under option at December 31, 2005 and December 31, 2004. The total purchase price applicable to approved land under option approximated $4.1 billion at December 31, 2004. At that time, land option agreements--which may be canceled at PHM's discretion, and are generally non-refundable--totaled $327.6 million.

To assist its home sales effort, PHM offers mortgage banking and title insurance services through Pulte Mortgage and other units for the benefit of its domestic home buyers, but also services the general public. In addition, it engages in the sale of loans and the related servicing rights. Mortgage underwriting, processing and closing functions are centralized in Denver using a mortgage operations center (MOC) concept.

PHM delivered approximately 7,000 homes in 2005. In late 2005, the company announced the divestiture of Pulte Mexico, sharply reducing its international presence; we think this sale occurred at about the unit's $116 million book value. In the fourth quarter of 2005, PHM reported these ongoing results as discontinued operations. As of early 2006, the company was continuing to evaluate long-term strategies for its remaining international operations (e.g., Puerto Rico).

Company Financials

Per Share Data ($) Year Ended Dec. 31	**2005**	**2004**	**2003**	**2002**	**2001**	**2000**	**1999**	**1998**	**1997**	**1996**
Tangible Book Value	21.49	15.95	12.13	9.41	7.64	7.51	6.32	5.34	4.78	4.46
Cash Flow	5.70	4.01	2.61	1.92	1.67	1.38	1.09	0.61	0.33	0.35
Earnings	5.47	3.84	2.46	1.80	1.50	1.30	1.02	0.58	0.29	0.32
S&P Core Earnings	5.46	3.82	2.45	1.76	1.43	NA	NA	NA	NA	NA
Dividends	0.09	0.10	0.04	0.04	0.04	0.04	0.04	0.04	0.03	0.03
Payout Ratio	2%	3%	2%	2%	3%	3%	4%	6%	11%	10%
Prices:High	48.23	32.50	24.71	14.94	12.56	11.25	7.81	9.05	5.31	4.33
Prices:Low	30.01	20.00	11.36	9.05	6.53	3.81	4.19	4.98	3.41	3.00
P/E Ratio:High	9	8	10	8	8	9	8	16	19	14
P/E Ratio:Low	5	5	5	5	4	3	4	9	12	10
Income Statement Analysis (Million $)										
Revenue	14,695	11,711	9,049	7,472	5,382	4,159	3,730	2,867	2,524	2,384
Operating Income	244	1,587	997	746	601	429	350	222	135	145
Depreciation	62.0	46.3	40.2	29.8	32.9	14.2	13.5	5.04	7.81	6.75
Interest Expense	180	56.4	Nil	Nil	81.6	65.1	56.8	51.1	26.6	53.3
Pretax Income	2,277	1,601	996	729	492	355	286	166	81.0	102
Effective Tax Rate	36.8%	37.6%	38.0%	39.0%	38.5%	38.5%	37.8%	39.0%	38.5%	38.3%
Net Income	1,437	998	617	445	302	218	178	101	49.8	63.2
S&P Core Earnings	1,435	993	615	436	288	NA	NA	NA	NA	NA
Balance Sheet & Other Financial Data (Million $)										
Cash	1,002	315	404	613	72.1	184	51.7	125	245	190
Current Assets	NA	NA	NA	NA	NA	NA	NA	NA	NA	NA
Total Assets	13,048	10,407	8,063	6,888	5,714	2,886	2,597	2,350	2,151	1,985
Current Liabilities	NA	NA	NA	NA	NA	NA	NA	NA	NA	NA
Long Term Debt	3,387	2,737	1,962	1,913	1,738	678	526	570	584	436
Common Equity	5,957	4,522	3,448	2,760	2,277	1,248	1,093	921	813	829
Total Capital	9,352	7,274	5,418	4,674	4,015	1,926	1,619	1,492	1,397	1,265
Capital Expenditures	88.9	75.2	39.1	NA	NA	NA	NA	NA	Nil	Nil
Cash Flow	1,499	1,044	657	474	335	233	192	106	57.6	70.0
Current Ratio	NA	NA	NA	NA	NA	NA	NA	NA	NA	NA
% Long Term Debt of Capitalization	36.2	37.6	36.2	40.9	43.3	35.2	32.5	38.2	41.8	34.5
% Net Income of Revenue	9.7	8.5	6.8	6.0	5.6	5.3	4.8	3.5	2.0	2.7
% Return on Assets	12.2	10.8	8.3	7.1	7.0	8.1	7.2	4.5	2.4	3.2
% Return on Equity	27.4	25.0	19.9	17.7	17.2	18.7	17.7	11.7	6.1	8.0

Data as orig reptd.; bef. results of disc opers/spec. items. Per share data adj. for stk. divs.; EPS diluted. E-Estimated. NA-Not Available. NM-Not Meaningful. NR-Not Ranked. UR-Under Review.

Office: 100 Bloomfield Hills Pkwy Ste 300, Bloomfield Hills, MI 48304-2950.
Telephone: 248-647-2750.
Website: http://www.pulte.com
Chrmn: W.J. Pulte

Pres & CEO: R.J. Dugas, Jr.
COO & EVP: S.C. Petruska
EVP & CFO: R.A. Cregg
VP & Treas: B.E. Robinson

Investor Contact: J. Zeumer (248-433-4597)
Board of Directors: B. P. Anderson, D. K. Anderson, R. J. Dugas, Jr., D. Kelly-Ennis, D. N. McCammon, P. J. O'Leary, W. J. Pulte, B. W. Reznicek, A. E. Schwartz, F. J. Sehn, J. J. Shea, W. B. Smith

Founded: 1969
Domicile: Michigan
Employees: 13,400

STANDARD &POOR'S

QLogic Corp

S&P Recommendation BUY ★★★★★	**Price** $20.58 (as of Oct 31, 2006)	**12-Mo. Target Price** $25.00	**Investment Style** Mid-Cap Growth

GICS Sector Information Technology
Sub-Industry Computer Storage & Peripherals

Comment This company designs and supplies semiconductor and board-level I/O (input/output) and enclosure management products.

Key Stock Statistics (Source S&P, Vickers, company reports)

52-Wk Range	**$21.62–15.01**	S&P Oper. EPS 2007**E**	**0.85**	P/E on S&P Oper. EPS 2007**E**	**24.2**	Dividend Rate/Share	**Nil**
Trailing 12-Month EPS	**$1.49**	S&P Oper. EPS 2008**E**	**0.99**	Common Shares Outstg. (M)	**159.3**	Yield (%)	**Nil**
Trailing 12-Month P/E	**13.8**	S&P Core EPS 2007E	**0.69**	Market Capitalization(B)	**$3.279**	Beta	**2.67**
$10K Invested 5 Yrs Ago	**$9,806**	S&P Core EPS 2008E	**0.83**	Institutional Ownership (%)	**81**	S&P Credit Rating	**NA**

Price Performance

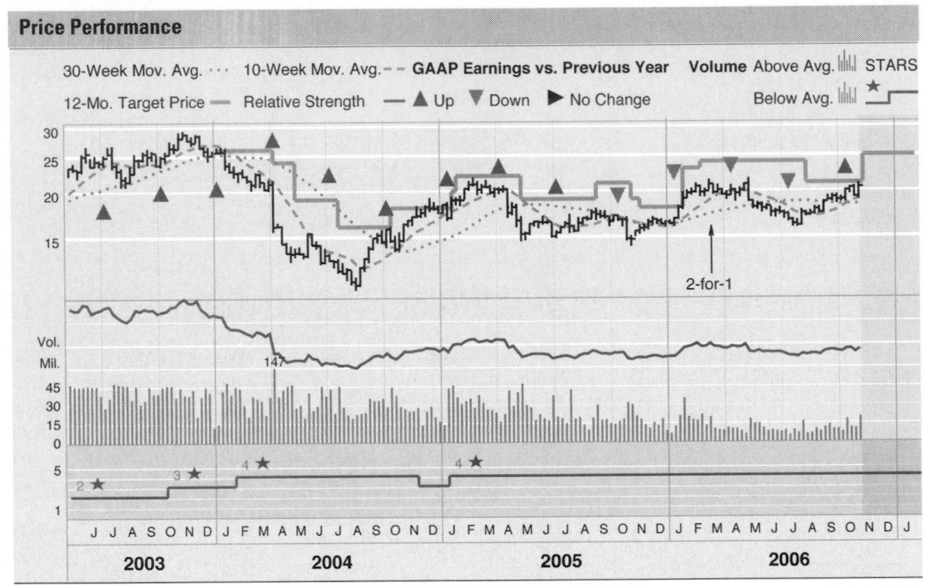

Options: ASE, CBOE, P, Ph

Highlights

- The 12-month target price for QLGC has recently been changed to $25.00 from $21.00. The Highlights section of this Stock Report will be updated accordingly.

Investment Rationale/Risk

- The Investment Rationale/Risk section of this Stock Report will be updated shortly.

Qualitative Risk Assessment

LOW | **MEDIUM** | HIGH

Our risk assessment reflects the volatile nature of the data storage industry and the rapid pace of technological change. Offsetting these factors is our view of the company's significant market share position and financial structure.

Quantitative Evaluations

S&P Quality Ranking B+

D | C | B- | B | **B+** | A- | A | A+

Relative Strength Rank STRONG

79

LOWEST = 1 HIGHEST = 99

Revenue/Earnings Data

Revenue (Million $)

	1Q	2Q	3Q	4Q	Year
2007	136.7	145.3	--	--	--
2006	158.8	119.0	129.2	130.5	494.1
2005	129.8	134.6	150.3	157.2	571.9
2004	126.2	132.3	137.1	128.3	523.9
2003	98.96	107.1	114.2	120.6	440.8
2002	89.90	80.88	83.63	92.26	344.2

Earnings Per Share ($)

2007	0.13	0.19	**E**0.26	**E**0.26	**E**0.85
2006	0.23	0.17	0.20	0.19	0.70
2005	0.17	0.19	0.23	0.25	0.84
2004	0.17	0.18	0.18	0.17	0.70
2003	0.12	0.12	0.15	0.16	0.55
2002	0.10	0.09	0.09	0.10	0.37

Fiscal year ended Mar. 31. Next earnings report expected: Mid January. EPS Estimates based on S&P Operating Earnings; historical GAAP earnings are as reported.

Dividend Data (Dates: mm/dd Payment Date: mm/dd/yy)

Amount ($)	Date Decl.	Ex-Div. Date	Stk. of Record	Payment Date
2-for-1	--	03/03	02/16	03/02/06

Source: Company reports.

QLogic Corp

Business Summary August 04, 2006

CORPORATE OVERVIEW. QLogic Corp. designs and develops storage networking infrastructure components sold to OEMs and distributors. QLGC produces host bus adapters (HBAs), fabric switches and management controller chips that provide the connectivity infrastructure for storage networks. The company serves customers with solutions based on various storage connectivity technologies, including Small Computer Systems Interface (SCSI), Internet SCSI (iSCSI), Fibre Channel and Infiniband.

International revenues accounted for 55% of net revenues in FY 06 (Mar.), up from 53% in FY 05. IBM, Hewlett-Packard and Sun Microsystems each accounted for over 10% of FY 06 sales. The 10 largest customers accounted for 77% of FY 06 revenues, down from 78% in FY 05. QLGC works closely with independent hardware and software vendors, as well as with developers and integrators who create, test and evaluate complementary storage networking products. Key alliance partners include Cisco Systems, Microsoft, and Symantec.

MARKET PROFILE. According to research firm IDC, external storage area network (SAN) storage capacity shipped in 2005 was 660 Petabytes (one Petabyte is roughly equivalent to one billion books), which was an increase of 74% from 2004. Moreover, IDC projects that total capacity shipments will exceed 5,680 Petabytes in 2009.

While QLGC sees storage capacity and revenue opportunities continuing to expand in North America, storage growth is expected to grow even more rapidly in emerging countries such as China, India and Russia. The company expects these markets to move ahead of older direct attached infrastructures by deploying storage networks from the start. Another area of focus for SAN vendors is the medium sized business market. The total number of businesses in this category, with between 100 and 1,000 employees, are estimated to exceed 500,000, and the vast majority still deploy direct attached storage architectures.

Company Financials

Per Share Data ($) Year Ended Mar. 31	**2006**	**2005**	**2004**	**2003**	**2002**	**2001**	**2000**	**1999**	**1998**	**1997**
Tangible Book Value	5.10	5.19	4.61	4.00	3.33	2.84	1.64	1.06	1.71	0.26
Cash Flow	0.81	0.92	0.77	0.62	0.44	0.42	0.38	0.19	0.24	0.09
Earnings	0.70	0.84	0.70	0.55	0.37	0.36	0.35	0.17	0.10	0.06
S&P Core Earnings	0.49	0.67	0.52	0.35	0.22	0.16	NA	NA	NA	NA
Dividends	Nil	Nil	Nil	Nil	Nil	Nil	Nil	Nil	Nil	Nil
Payout Ratio	Nil	Nil	Nil	Nil	Nil	Nil	Nil	Nil	Nil	Nil
Calendar Year	2005	2004	2003	2002	2001	2000	1999	1998	1997	1996
Prices:High	21.83	26.57	29.36	28.55	49.56	101.63	41.88	8.41	2.84	1.77
Prices:Low	14.10	10.72	16.07	9.87	8.60	10.81	6.01	1.50	1.10	0.41
P/E Ratio:High	31	32	42	52	NM	NM	NM	49	27	30
P/E Ratio:Low	20	13	23	18	NM	NM	NM	9	11	7
Income Statement Analysis (Million $)										
Revenue	494	572	524	441	344	358	203	117	81.4	68.9
Operating Income	196	240	214	157	99.5	132	78.8	36.7	20.9	12.4
Depreciation	17.9	15.6	14.8	14.7	13.0	10.8	4.80	3.37	2.43	3.02
Interest Expense	Nil	Nil	Nil	Nil	Nil	Nil	0.02	0.08	0.11	0.13
Pretax Income	200	242	216	159	106	117	81.7	38.9	21.8	9.83
Effective Tax Rate	39.2%	35.0%	38.0%	35.0%	33.0%	41.2%	34.0%	34.0%	38.6%	40.5%
Net Income	122	158	134	103	70.7	68.8	54.0	25.7	13.4	5.85
S&P Core Earnings	85.6	126	99.4	67.0	42.1	30.5	NA	NA	NA	NA
Balance Sheet & Other Financial Data (Million $)										
Cash	125	166	157	138	76.1	128	64.1	43.2	64.1	19.1
Current Assets	819	940	854	748	587	490	177	131	108	31.1
Total Assets	938	1,026	929	817	670	571	267	173	136	37.0
Current Liabilities	78.4	68.8	60.8	66.7	51.0	47.8	24.2	20.2	17.6	11.3
Long Term Debt	Nil	Nil	Nil	Nil	Nil	Nil	Nil	Nil	0.14	0.35
Common Equity	859	956	868	751	619	524	243	153	118	24.4
Total Capital	859	958	868	751	619	524	243	153	118	24.7
Capital Expenditures	28.3	25.7	22.3	15.7	14.5	16.7	40.0	6.77	3.92	3.90
Cash Flow	140	173	149	118	83.7	79.6	58.8	29.1	15.8	8.87
Current Ratio	10.5	13.7	14.0	11.2	11.5	10.3	7.3	6.5	6.2	2.7
% Long Term Debt of Capitalization	Nil	Nil	Nil	Nil	Nil	Nil	Nil	Nil	0.1	1.4
% Net Income of Revenue	24.7	27.6	25.5	23.5	20.5	19.2	26.6	21.9	16.5	8.5
% Return on Assets	12.4	16.1	15.3	13.9	11.4	14.2	24.5	16.6	15.5	17.9
% Return on Equity	13.4	17.3	16.5	15.1	12.4	15.6	27.3	19.0	18.8	28.8

Data as orig reptd.; bef. results of disc opers/spec. items. Per share data adj. for stk. divs.; EPS diluted. E-Estimated. NA-Not Available. NM-Not Meaningful. NR-Not Ranked. UR-Under Review.

Office: 26650 Aliso Viejo Pkwy, Aliso Viejo, CA 92656-2674.
Telephone: 949-389-6000.
Website: http://www.qlogic.com
Chrmn, Pres & CEO: H.K. Desai

Investor Contact: A.J. Massetti (949-389-7533)
SVP & CFO: A.J. Massetti
VP, Secy & General Counsel: M.L. Hawkins

Board of Directors: J. S. Birnbaum, L. R. Carter, H. K. Desai, J. R. Fiebiger, B. S. Iyer, C. L. Miltner, G. D. Wells

Auditor: KPMG
Founded: 1992
Domicile: Delaware
Employees: 923

QUALCOMM Inc

STANDARD &POOR'S

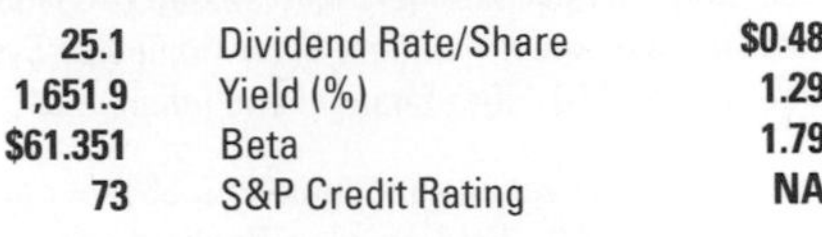

S&P Recommendation STRONG BUY ★★★★★

Price $37.14 (as of Oct 27, 2006)

12-Mo. Target Price $50.00

Investment Style Large-Cap Growth

GICS Sector Information Technology
Sub-Industry Communications Equipment

Comment This company focuses on developing products and services based on its advanced wireless broadband technology.

Key Stock Statistics (Source S&P, Vickers, company reports)

52-Wk Range	$53.01–32.76	S&P Oper. EPS 2006**E**	1.48	P/E on S&P Oper. EPS 2006**E**	25.1	Dividend Rate/Share	$0.48
Trailing 12-Month EPS	$1.39	S&P Oper. EPS 2007**E**	1.70	Common Shares Outstg. (M)	1,651.9	Yield (%)	1.29
Trailing 12-Month P/E	26.7	S&P Core EPS 2006**E**	1.47	Market Capitalization(B)	$61.351	Beta	1.79
$10K Invested 5 Yrs Ago	$13,833	S&P Core EPS 2007**E**	1.70	Institutional Ownership (%)	73	S&P Credit Rating	NA

Price Performance

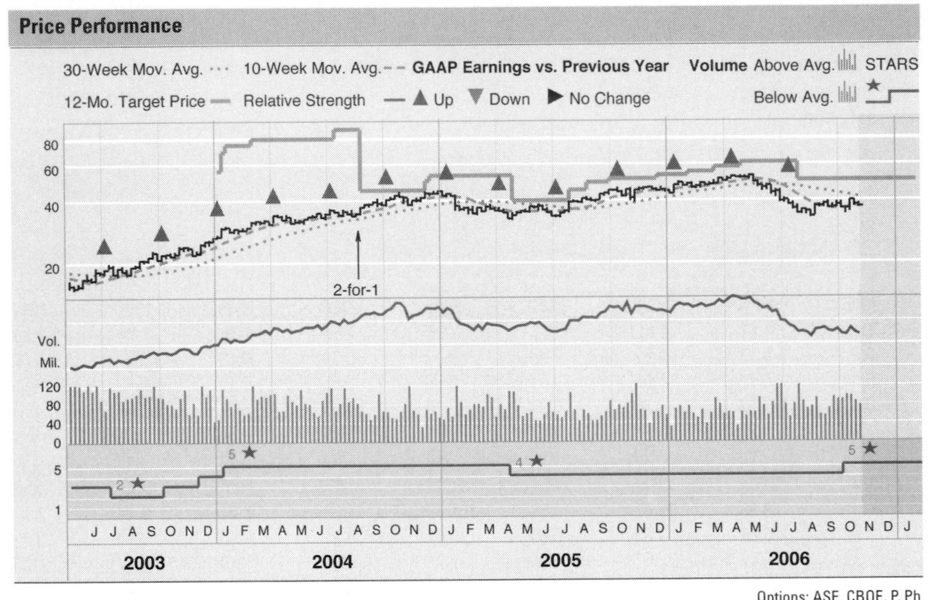

Options: ASE, CBOE, P, Ph

Analysis prepared by **Kenneth M. Leon, CPA** on October 04, 2006, when the stock traded at **$ 35.48**.

Highlights

- Following estimated revenue growth of 32% in FY 06 (Sep.), we forecast 12% to 15% growth in FY 07, driven by code division multiple access (CDMA) chipset shipments and license fees. For the CDMA chipset business, we expect FY 06 sales to be up 31%, with improving volume shipments and some price erosion per unit compared to the prior year, while the very profitable licensing business continues to grow at a rate of 43%.
- We estimate CDMA chipset shipments to reach 206 million in FY 06 from 152 million in FY 05, followed by an expected 231 million in FY 07. Despite market share loss from its leading handset licensees, we believe Samsung and LG Electronics will rebound in FY 07 with new CDMA handsets that are currently available for wireless carriers.
- We forecast gross margins of 71% to 72% in FY 06 and FY 07 and estimate net margins to remain flat in the 33% to 35% area in FY 06 and FY 07. We estimate operating EPS of $1.48 for FY 06 and $1.70 for FY 07, including $0.20 of projected stock option expense in both years.

Investment Rationale/Risk

- CDMA handset demand is outpacing the overall handset market, in our opinion, and we believe the company, unlike its peers, has strong pricing power with its CDMA patents. We see QCOM's addressable market for license fees and chipset sales growing from the upper 20% area of the global handset market in 2005, to 35% or more by 2008.
- Risks to our opinion and target price include the possibility that developed countries will not keep up with the replacement rate expected for more advanced CDMA handsets; lower ASPs for handsets in emerging markets; customer terminations; and litigation risks related to QCOM's intellectual property rights.
- We view QCOM as having a very attractive financial model, with 33% to 35% net margins, no long-term debt, and $9.5 billion in cash and investments at June 30, 2006. Applying a P/E multiple of 29.4X to our FY 07 EPS estimate, a premium to peers that we think is warranted by QCOM's strong franchise in CDMA-related technologies, we arrive at our 12-month target price of $50.

Qualitative Risk Assessment

LOW	**MEDIUM**	HIGH

We believe QCOM's intellectual property rights and strong service provider relations give the company one of the strongest business models in the industry. However, despite its strong cash flow and no debt, we believe QCOM is exposed to litigation risks related to equipment vendors that are challenging its CDMA patents.

Quantitative Evaluations

S&P Quality Ranking **B**

D	C	B-	**B**	B+	A-	A	A+

Relative Strength Rank **WEAK**

24

LOWEST = 1 HIGHEST = 99

Revenue/Earnings Data

Revenue (Million $)

	1Q	2Q	3Q	4Q	Year
2006	1,741	1,834	1,951	--	--
2005	1,390	1,365	1,358	1,560	5,673
2004	1,207	1,216	1,341	1,118	4,880
2003	1,097	1,043	921.6	908.8	3,971
2002	698.6	696.1	770.9	873.9	3,040
2001	684.0	713.3	640.0	650.8	2,680

Earnings Per Share ($)

	1Q	2Q	3Q	4Q	Year
2006	0.36	0.34	0.37	**E**0.37	**E**1.48
2005	0.30	0.31	0.33	0.32	1.26
2004	0.25	0.26	0.29	0.23	1.03
2003	0.15	0.07	0.12	0.18	0.51
2002	0.09	0.03	-0.01	0.12	0.22
2001	-0.24	0.09	-0.18	-0.03	-0.36

Fiscal year ended Sep. 30. Next earnings report expected: Early November. EPS Estimates based on S&P Operating Earnings; historical GAAP earnings are as reported.

Dividend Data (Dates: mm/dd Payment Date: mm/dd/yy)

Amount ($)	Date Decl.	Ex-Div. Date	Stk. of Record	Payment Date
0.090	01/12	02/22	02/24	03/24/06
0.120	04/07	05/24	05/26	06/23/06
0.120	07/07	08/23	08/25	09/22/06
0.120	10/05	12/05	12/07	01/04/07

Dividends have been paid since 2003. Source: Company reports.

QUALCOMM Inc

Business Summary October 04, 2006

CORPORATE OVERVIEW. The company is organized by these operating segments: CDMA technology (QCT), technology licensing (QTL), wireless and Internet (QWI), and strategic initiatives (QSI). The QCT segment, which accounted for about 58% of total sales in the third quarter of FY 06 (Sep.), provides integrated circuits and system software solutions to many of the world's leading wireless handset and infrastructure manufacturers. QCOM uses a fabless business model, employing several independent semiconductor foundries to manufacture all of its semiconductor products.

The technology licensing business (QTL) accounted for about 35% of third quarter FY 06 total sales, with 91% operating margins. QCOM holds a number of patents related to CDMA, and derives royalties from licensing its technology. Royalties are paid when manufacturers earn revenue from the sale of CDMA-based equipment. Entry barriers are high, with QCOM's global franchise protected by legal patents. Even firms in China are signing license agreements with the company, but in October 2005, six competitors filed complaint suits against QCOM with the European Commission.

The QWI segment accounted for about 7% of third quarter FY 06 sales. QWI provides satellite-based two-way data messaging and position reporting equipment to transportation companies. It shipped 10,700 OmniTRAC units in the third quarter of FY 06, bringing the total to 597,000 units shipped. QWI also includes the BREW product for software developers and interface device suppliers.

CORPORATE STRATEGY. We believe QCOM has become adept at evolving its CDMA intellectual property into wireless data and web-based applications. QCOM expects to invest $800 million over five years to build and operate MediaFLO. In December 2005, Verizon Wireless said it will launch MediaFLO in about 50% of its U.S. covered markets to offer real-time mobile TV services.

In April 2006, MediaFLO USA and Network LIVE, a joint venture between AOL, XM Satellite Radio and AEG, announced an agreement to provide LIVE content and programming for MediaFLOW USA's wireless multimedia service offering.

Company Financials

Per Share Data ($) Year Ended Sep. 30	**2005**	**2004**	**2003**	**2002**	**2001**	**2000**	**1999**	**1998**	**1997**	**1996**
Tangible Book Valuo	6.43	5.09	4.54	2.77	2.82	3.14	2.22	0.83	0.92	0.78
Cash Flow	1.38	1.13	0.62	0.47	-0.14	0.57	0.28	0.21	0.16	0.07
Earnings	1.26	1.03	0.51	0.22	-0.36	0.43	0.16	0.09	0.08	0.02
S&P Core Earnings	1.03	0.83	0.74	0.34	-0.68	NA	NA	NA	NA	NA
Dividends	0.32	0.19	0.09	Nil	Nil	Nil	Nil	Nil	Nil	Nil
Payout Ratio	25%	18%	17%	Nil	Nil	Nil	Nil	Nil	Nil	Nil
Prices:High	46.60	44.99	27.43	26.67	41.60	100.00	92.52	4.21	4.50	3.41
Prices:Low	32.08	26.67	14.79	11.61	19.16	25.75	3.27	2.36	2.45	1.90
P/E Ratio:High	37	44	54	NM	NM	NM	NM	46	57	NM
P/E Ratio:Low	25	26	29	NM	NM	NM	21	26	31	NM
Income Statement Analysis (Million $)										
Revenue	5,673	4,880	3,971	3,040	2,680	3,197	3,937	3,348	2,096	814
Operating Income	2,586	2,266	1,684	1,068	877	1,105	564	385	191	49.4
Depreciation	200	163	180	394	320	244	158	142	93.6	56.8
Interest Expense	3.00	2.00	30.7	25.7	10.2	4.92	14.7	8.06	11.0	3.40
Pretax Income	2,809	2,313	1,285	461	-426	1,197	307	197	111	39.8
Effective Tax Rate	23.7%	25.4%	35.6%	22.0%	NM	44.0%	34.5%	20.4%	14.8%	14.0%
Net Income	2,143	1,725	827	360	-531	670	201	109	91.9	21.0
S&P Core Earnings	1,733	1,395	610	274	-512	NA	NA	NA	NA	NA
Balance Sheet & Other Financial Data (Million $)										
Cash	6,548	5,982	4,561	2,795	2,283	1,772	660	176	249	110
Current Assets	7,791	7,227	5,949	3,941	3,055	2,730	2,978	1,537	1,550	751
Total Assets	12,479	10,820	8,822	6,510	5,747	6,063	4,535	2,567	2,275	1,185
Current Liabilities	1,070	894	808	675	521	472	876	882	567	326
Long Term Debt	Nil	Nil	123	94.3	Nil	Nil	660	664	667	10.9
Common Equity	11,119	9,664	7,599	5,392	4,890	5,516	2,872	958	1,024	845
Total Capital	11,119	9,664	7,722	5,530	4,896	5,563	3,584	1,661	1,691	856
Capital Expenditures	576	332	231	142	114	163	180	322	163	217
Cash Flow	2,343	1,888	1,007	754	-211	914	359	250	186	77.8
Current Ratio	7.3	8.1	7.4	5.8	5.9	5.8	3.4	1.7	2.7	2.3
% Long Term Debt of Capitalization	Nil	Nil	1.6	1.7	Nil	Nil	18.4	39.9	39.4	1.3
% Net Income of Revenue	37.8	35.3	20.8	11.8	NM	21.0	5.1	3.2	4.4	2.6
% Return on Assets	18.4	17.6	10.8	5.9	NM	12.6	5.7	4.5	5.3	2.0
% Return on Equity	20.6	20.0	12.7	7.1	NM	16.0	10.5	11.0	9.8	2.6

Data as orig reptd.; bef. results of disc opers/spec. items. Per share data adj. for stk. divs.; EPS diluted. E-Estimated. NA-Not Available. NM-Not Meaningful. NR-Not Ranked. UR-Under Review.

Office: 5775 Morehouse Drive, San Diego, CA 92121-1714.
Telephone: 858-587-1121.
Email: ir@qualcomm.com
Website: http://www.qualcomm.com

Chrmn: I.M. Jacobs
Pres: S.R. Altman
CEO: P.E. Jacobs
Investor Contact: W.E. Keitel (858-587-1121)

EVP & CFO: W.E. Keitel
Board of Directors: B. T. Alexander, R. C. Atkinson, A. A. Coffman, D. Cruickshank, R. V. Dittamore, D. L. Dougan, I. M. Jacobs, R. E. Kahn, S. Lansing, D. A. Nelles, P. M. Sacerdote, B. Scowcroft, M. I. Stern, R. J. Sulpizio

Founded: 1985
Domicile: Delaware
Employees: 9,300

STANDARD &POOR'S

Quest Diagnostics Inc

S&P Recommendation BUY ★★★★★

Price $49.70 (as of Oct 27, 2006)

12-Mo. Target Price $65.00

Investment Style Large-Cap Growth

GICS Sector Health Care
Sub-Industry Health Care Services

Comment This company provides diagnostic testing, information and services to physicians, hospitals, managed care organizations, employers and government agencies.

Key Stock Statistics (Source S&P, Vickers, company reports)

52-Wk Range	$64.69–46.00	S&P Oper. EPS 2006E	3.06	P/E on S&P Oper. EPS 2006E	16.2	Dividend Rate/Share	$0.40
Trailing 12-Month EPS	$2.78	S&P Oper. EPS 2007E	3.38	Common Shares Outstg. (M)	197.1	Yield (%)	0.80
Trailing 12-Month P/E	17.9	S&P Core EPS 2006E	3.06	Market Capitalization(B)	$9.798	Beta	0.30
$10K Invested 5 Yrs Ago	$14,566	S&P Core EPS 2007E	3.38	Institutional Ownership (%)	72	S&P Credit Rating	BBB+

Price Performance

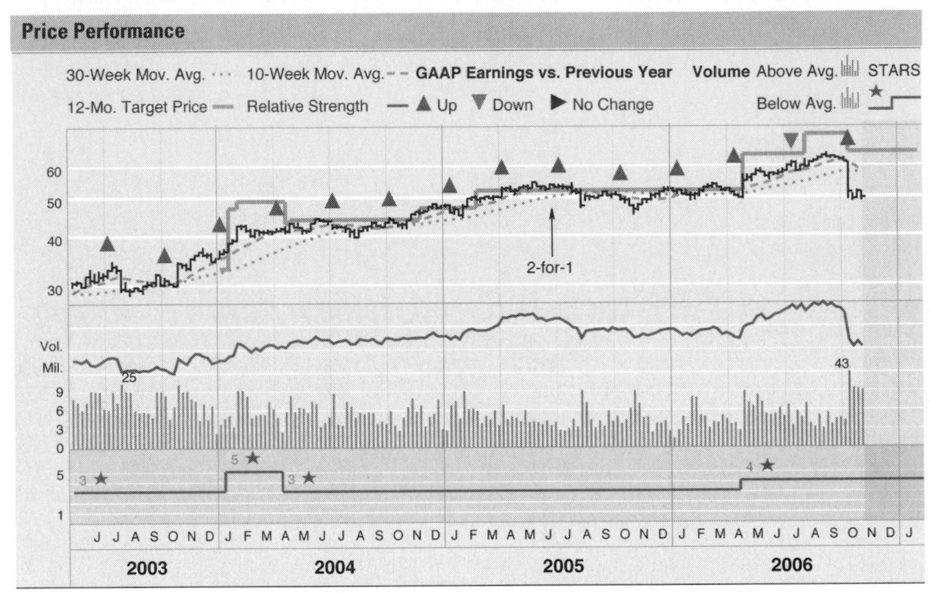

Analysis prepared by **Jeffrey Loo, CFA** on October 11, 2006, when the stock traded at **$ 49.97**.

Highlights

- In October, DGX announced it will no longer be a national contracted lab provider for UnitedHealth Group (UNH: buy, $52) as UNH awarded Laboratory Corp. of America (LH: buy, $66) with a 10-year exclusive national contract, effective January 1, 2007. We believe this is a major loss for DGX as UNH was its largest client, representing about 7% of sales. Although we expect DGX to lose most of the UNH sales, we believe DGX will retain some business, particularly in the northeast, for the next 12-18 months as DGX has established relationships and infrastructure. LH plans to expand its lab network and develop hundreds of patient service centers.
- We see 2006 sales growing 16%, to $6.4 billion, however, with the loss of UNH, we see sales growth of only 5% in 2007. We believe DGX will need to cut costs and staff in certain locations due to the related volume decline from the UNH loss. But we see increased esoteric tests and more tests ordered aiding revenue per requisition and gross margins.
- Including projected stock option expense of $0.24 and aided by stock buybacks, our 2006 EPS forecast is $3.01.

Investment Rationale/Risk

- Although we believe the UNH contract was a major loss, we believe the decline in share price was overdone. DGX remains the largest provider of clinical lab services, and we are encouraged by what we see as better-than-expected price increases and the contribution from LabOne. We believe that an improved esoteric test mix and price increases have aided its revenue per requisition, and that these increases should be sustainable. However, we believe the lab industry's growth prospects are limited, and we see only mid-single digit organic growth and are cautious over potential margin compression as more managed care contracts are up for renewal.
- Risks to our recommendation and target price include greater pricing pressure from third-party payers resulting in a decline in revenue per requisition and increased competition.
- Our 12-month target price of $65 is based on a blend of our DCF analysis, assuming a WACC of 9.8% and terminal growth of 3% leading to an intrinsic value of $64, and a P/E-to-growth ratio of 1.5X, applied to our 2007 EPS estimate and three year EPS growth rate of 13%, in line with peers.

Qualitative Risk Assessment

LOW | MEDIUM | HIGH

Our risk assessment reflects our view of DGX's leadership position in this large, mature industry; its broad geographic service area; its diverse and balanced payer mix; and the growing recognition of the importance and significance of diagnostic testing.

Quantitative Evaluations

S&P Quality Ranking B

D | C | B- | B | B+ | A- | A | A+

Relative Strength Rank WEAK

8

LOWEST = 1 HIGHEST = 99

Revenue/Earnings Data

Revenue (Million $)

	1Q	2Q	3Q	4Q	Year
2006	1,555	1,584	1,583	--	--
2005	1,319	1,378	1,372	1,435	5,504
2004	1,256	1,298	1,290	1,283	5,127
2003	1,093	1,220	1,221	1,204	4,738
2002	946.8	1,069	1,059	1,034	4,108
2001	882.6	931.6	903.2	910.4	3,628

Earnings Per Share ($)

2006	0.72	0.66	0.82	E0.79	E3.06
2005	0.64	0.72	0.66	0.64	2.66
2004	0.54	0.59	0.62	0.60	2.35
2003	0.43	0.56	0.56	0.51	2.06
2002	0.34	0.44	0.44	0.41	1.62
2001	0.19	0.24	0.26	0.26	0.94

Fiscal year ended Dec. 31. Next earnings report expected: Late January. EPS Estimates based on S&P Operating Earnings; historical GAAP earnings are as reported.

Dividend Data (Dates: mm/dd Payment Date: mm/dd/yy)

Amount ($)	Date Decl.	Ex-Div. Date	Stk. of Record	Payment Date
0.090	12/13	01/09	01/11	01/25/06
0.100	01/26	04/03	04/05	04/19/06
0.100	05/10	07/05	07/07	07/21/06
0.100	08/09	10/02	10/04	10/18/06

Dividends have been paid since 2004. Source: Company reports.

Quest Diagnostics Inc

Business Summary October 11, 2006

CORPORATE OVERVIEW. Quest Diagnostics is the largest independent U.S. clinical lab provider. The clinical laboratory market is estimated to be about a $40 billion market, with hospital-based labs accounting for about 60% of the market, independent commercial labs, such as DGX, accounting for 33%, and physician-office labs the rest. DGX offers a broad range of clinical laboratory testing services used by physicians in the detection, diagnosis, and treatment of diseases and other medical conditions. Tests range from routine (such as blood cholesterol tests) to highly complex esoteric (such as gene-based testing and molecular diagnostics testing). At the end of 2005, DGX had a network of 35 principal laboratories throughout the U.S., 150 smaller "rapid response" (STAT) laboratories, and over 2,000 patient service centers, along with facilities in Mexico, Puerto Rico, and England. DGX also operates two esoteric testing laboratories and R&D facilities at its Nichols Institute unit.

The company processes more than 144 million requisitions (order forms completed by physicians indicating tests to be performed) annually. Routine testing generated 78% of net sales in 2005 (82% in 2004), esoteric testing 17% (14% in 2004), clinical trials 3% (3%) and risk assessment services from recently acquired LabOne (acquired in November 2005), less than 1%. Routine tests measure important health parameters such as the function of the kidney, heart, liver, thyroid and other organs. Esoteric tests are performed less frequently than routine tests, and/or require more sophisticated equipment and materials, professional hands-on attention, and more highly skilled personnel. As a result, they are generally priced substantially higher than routine tests.

Company Financials

Per Share Data ($) Year Ended Dec. 31	**2005**	**2004**	**2003**	**2002**	**2001**	**2000**	**1999**	**1998**	**1997**	**1996**
Tangible Book Value	NM	NM	NM	NM	NM	NM	NM	0.60	0.23	NA
Cash Flow	3.51	3.12	2.79	2.31	1.70	1.27	0.64	0.79	0.45	NA
Earnings	2.66	2.35	2.06	1.62	0.94	0.56	-0.01	0.22	-0.19	NA
S&P Core Earnings	2.57	2.13	1.80	1.42	0.83	NA	NA	NA	NA	NA
Dividends	0.26	0.30	Nil	Nil	Nil	Nil	Nil	Nil	Nil	Nil
Payout Ratio	10%	13%	Nil	Nil	Nil	Nil	Nil	Nil	Nil	Nil
Prices:High	54.80	48.41	37.50	48.07	37.88	36.56	8.23	5.77	5.22	3.94
Prices:Low	44.32	35.94	23.68	24.55	18.30	7.28	4.44	3.63	3.56	3.31
P/E Ratio:High	21	21	18	30	40	66	NM	26	NM	NA
P/E Ratio:Low	17	15	11	15	19	13	NM	16	NM	NA
Income Statement Analysis (Million $)										
Revenue	5,504	5,127	4,738	4,108	3,628	3,421	2,205	1,459	1,529	1,616
Operating Income	1,144	1,060	950	724	559	452	243	163	151	166
Depreciation	176	169	154	131	148	134	90.8	68.8	76.4	99.1
Interest Expense	61.4	57.9	59.8	53.7	70.5	120	69.8	44.0	46.0	74.9
Pretax Income	930	854	755	557	343	210	19.8	53.9	-19.1	-676
Effective Tax Rate	39.2%	39.3%	39.9%	39.5%	43.4%	45.7%	NM	50.1%	NM	NM
Net Income	546	499	437	322	184	105	-1.27	26.9	-22.3	-626
S&P Core Earnings	531	456	377	279	162	NA	NA	NA	NA	NA
Balance Sheet & Other Financial Data (Million $)										
Cash	92.1	73.3	155	96.8	122	171	27.3	203	162	42.0
Current Assets	1,069	931	996	824	877	981	873	578	572	511
Total Assets	5,306	4,204	4,301	3,324	2,931	2,865	2,878	1,360	1,401	1,395
Current Liabilities	1,101	1,044	724	636	659	955	701	309	295	249
Long Term Debt	1,255	724	1,029	797	820	761	1,171	413	482	515
Common Equity	2,763	2,289	2,397	1,769	1,336	1,031	862	567	541	538
Total Capital	4,018	3,013	3,426	2,565	2,156	1,793	2,046	2,034	1,024	1,054
Capital Expenditures	224	176	175	155	149	116	76.0	39.6	30.8	70.4
Cash Flow	722	668	591	454	332	239	89.6	95.7	54.1	-527
Current Ratio	1.0	0.9	1.4	1.3	1.3	1.0	1.2	1.9	1.9	2.1
% Long Term Debt of Capitalization	31.2	24.0	30.0	31.0	38.0	42.4	57.6	42.1	47.1	48.9
% Net Income of Revenue	9.9	9.7	9.2	7.8	5.1	3.1	NM	1.8	NM	NM
% Return on Assets	11.5	11.7	11.5	10.3	6.3	3.7	NM	1.9	NM	NM
% Return on Equity	21.6	21.3	20.9	20.8	15.5	11.1	NM	4.9	NM	NM

Data as orig reptd.; bef. results of disc opers/spec. items. Per share data adj. for stk. divs.; EPS diluted. E-Estimated. NA-Not Available. NM-Not Meaningful. NR-Not Ranked. UR-Under Review.

Office: 1290 Wall St W, Lyndhurst, NJ 07071-3683.
Telephone: 201-393-5000.
Email: investor@questdiagnostics.com
Website: http://www.questdiagnostics.com

Chrmn, Pres & CEO: S.N. Mohapatra
SVP & CFO: R.A. Hagemann
SVP & General Counsel: M.E. Prevoznik
Investor Contact: L. Park (201-393-5030)

Board of Directors: J. C. Baldwin, J. K. Britell, W. F. Buehler, J. F. Flaherty, III, W. R. Grant, R. Haggerty, S. N. Mohapatra, G. M. Pfeiffer, D. C. Stanzione, G. R. Wilensky, J. B. Ziegler

Founded: 1967
Domicile: Delaware
Employees: 41,500

STANDARD & POOR'S

Qwest Communications International Inc.

S&P Recommendation SELL ★★★★★	Price	12-Mo. Target Price	Investment Style
	$8.63 (as of Oct 31, 2006)	$7.00	Large-Cap Value

GICS Sector Telecommunication Services
Sub-Industry Integrated Telecommunication Services

Comment This company provides wireline and wireless services, primarily serving customers in 14 western and midwestern U.S. states.

Key Stock Statistics (Source S&P, Vickers, company reports)

52-Wk Range	$9.22–4.14	S&P Oper. EPS 2006E	0.26	P/E on S&P Oper. EPS 2006E	33.2	Dividend Rate/Share	Nil
Trailing 12-Month EPS	$-0.07	S&P Oper. EPS 2007E	0.29	Common Shares Outstg. (M)	1,905.2	Yield (%)	Nil
Trailing 12-Month P/E	NM	S&P Core EPS 2006E	0.20	Market Capitalization(B)	$16.442	Beta	3.26
$10K Invested 5 Yrs Ago	$4,924	S&P Core EPS 2007E	0.25	Institutional Ownership (%)	82	S&P Credit Rating	BB-

Price Performance

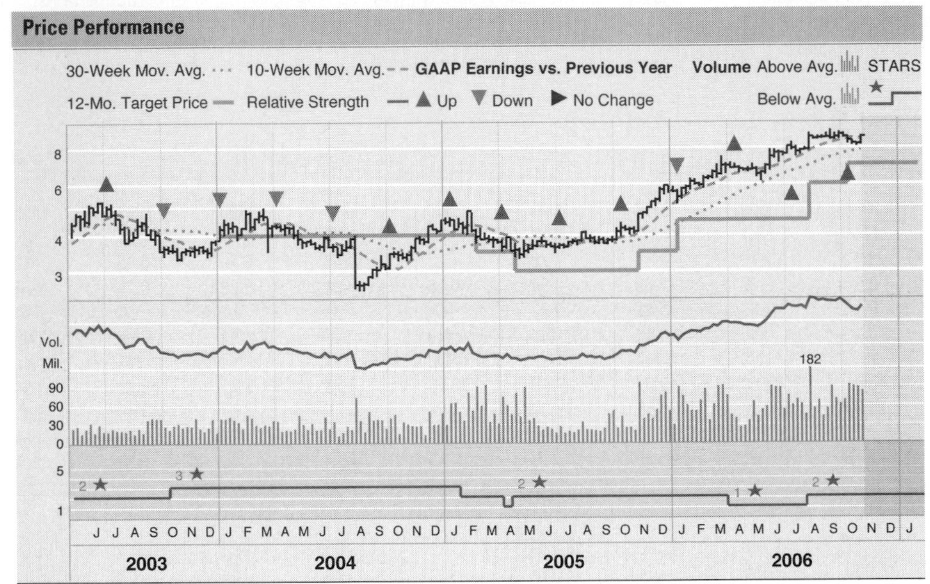

Options: ASE, CBOE, P, Ph

Analysis prepared by **Todd Rosenbluth** on October 05, 2006, when the stock traded at **$ 8.35**.

Highlights

- We believe Q's wireline customer retention and revenues in 2006 will perform in a similar fashion to 2005, even as the company further bundles services, given increasing cable and wireless competition. We project that revenues will rise 1% in 2006 and 1.5% in 2007, aided by DSL gains. Over the longer term, we think Q will face greater competition from wireline providers, as the industry is consolidating.
- We expect EBITDA margins to expand to 31% in 2006 and 32% in 2007, from 28.5% in 2005, a level still below peers, as the launch of new lower-margin services should be outweighed by work force reductions, improving facilities costs, and lower wireless service costs. We see less depreciation charges and think interest expense will be down 22% in 2006, as some debt has been repurchased.
- We estimate operating EPS of $0.19 in 2006, including $0.02 for projected stock option expense, and we see $0.25 in 2007, aided by share buybacks. Our Standard & Poor's Core EPS projections incorporate pension adjustments.

Investment Rationale/Risk

- We believe the shares are overvalued, based on our view of Q's high debt leverage, the absence of a dividend, and the limited benefit from wireless operations. Despite improvements in the first half of 2006, with its higher percentage of access line losses and weak margins, we think Q is not a peer of rural telecom providers. However, we believe Q's planned share buybacks should provide some downside support, even though its cash usage is hefty.
- Risks to our recommendation and target price include strong wireless growth, significant debt reduction, asset sales, and stronger than expected demand for Q's bundled wireline services that improves margins.
- With the operational challenges that we foresee, we believe Q does not warrant its current premium to its Bell peers using our enterprise value (EV)/EBITDA multiple analysis. We utilize a 6X peer group multiple of EV to our 2007 estimated EBITDA to arrive at our 12-month target price of $7. We think that due to its lack of a dividend, Q has less downside support than its peers.

Qualitative Risk Assessment

LOW | MEDIUM | **HIGH**

Our risk assessment reflects the highly competitive nature of the industry, our view of the above average debt load that Q carries, and the lack of a dividend to lend support to the share price.

Quantitative Evaluations

S&P Quality Ranking C

D | **C** | B- | B | B+ | A- | A | A+

Relative Strength Rank MODERATE

49

LOWEST = 1 HIGHEST = 99

Revenue/Earnings Data

Revenue (Million $)

	1Q	2Q	3Q	4Q	Year
2006	3,476	3,472	3,487	--	--
2005	3,449	3,470	3,504	3,480	13,903
2004	3,481	3,442	3,449	3,437	13,809
2003	3,624	3,596	3,570	3,498	14,288
2002	3,985	3,915	3,776	3,709	15,385
2001	5,051	5,222	4,766	4,656	19,695

Earnings Per Share ($)

2006	0.05	0.06	0.09	E0.06	E0.26
2005	0.03	-0.09	-0.08	-0.27	-0.41
2004	-0.17	-0.43	-0.31	-0.09	-1.00
2003	-0.07	-0.07	-0.39	-0.22	-0.76
2002	-0.59	-10.48	-0.07	0.62	-10.48
2001	0.01	-1.99	-0.09	-0.32	-2.38

Fiscal year ended Dec. 31. Next earnings report expected: Mid February. EPS Estimates based on S&P Operating Earnings; historical GAAP earnings are as reported.

Dividend Data

A dividend of $0.05 a share was paid in June 2001.

Qwest Communications International Inc.

Business Summary October 05, 2006

CORPORATE OVERVIEW. Following the June 2000 acquisition of Baby Bell U.S. WEST, Inc., Qwest Communications International (Q) provides telecommunications services in 14 Midwestern and Western states. Q had 14.3 million local access lines for consumers and businesses, including 4.8 million long-distance customers, and 1.8 million DSL broadband customers as of June 2006. In March 2004, Q began offering wireless services under the Qwest name using Sprint's network but retaining control of all marketing, customer services, pricing and promotional offerings. In 2005, 66% of Q's revenues were derived from a declining wireline voice services segment, a higher percentage than most peers.

COMPETITIVE LANDSCAPE. We believe Q faces competitive challenges partly due to low barriers to entry and characteristics unique to the company. As of June 2006, Q's access line count was 5.3% lower than a year earlier, as wireless substitution was intense, with national carriers offering 1,500 whenever minutes for $40. As a reseller of wireless services, we believe Q is at a competitive disadvantage to the telecom providers that own their own wireless networks and can more easily bundle wireline and wireless services. In addition, we believe Q will face added competition from cable providers such as Cox Communications and Comcast that offer broadband services and are rolling out telephony products in 2006. To offset possible customer migration to cable, Q is offering a triple-play package of voice, data and video services through a partnership with satellite provider Direct TV. As of June 2006, 54% of its retail customers were receiving a bundle of two or more services from the company.

CORPORATE STRATEGY. In early 2005, Q aggressively pursued MCI Inc., making multiple acquisition bids. Q's last stock and cash offer of $30 a share, in April 2005, included $16 a share in cash and financing commitments of $7.25 billion. In early May, MCI agreed to merge with Verizon Communications. During the first half of 2006, Q focused on reducing its operating expenses, aiming to improve its below average EBITDA margin. Q's headcount was reduced by 5% during 2005, and the company has lowered its wireline facility costs.

Company Financials

Per Share Data ($) Year Ended Dec. 31	2005	2004	2003	2002	2001	2000	1999	1998	1997	1996
Tangible Book Value	NM	NM	NM	NM	1.28	5.37	4.95	0.82	0.93	1.36
Cash Flow	1.26	0.74	1.07	-7.65	0.83	2.56	1.13	-1.15	0.09	0.03
Earnings	-0.41	-1.00	-0.76	-10.48	-2.38	-0.06	0.60	-1.51	0.04	-0.02
S&P Core Earnings	-0.68	-0.81	-0.81	-7.38	-1.39	NA	NA	NA	NA	NA
Dividends	Nil	Nil	Nil	Nil	0.05	Nil	Nil	Nil	Nil	NA
Payout Ratio	Nil	Nil	Nil	Nil	NM	Nil	Nil	Nil	Nil	NA
Prices:High	5.95	5.00	6.15	15.19	48.19	66.00	52.38	25.66	17.22	NA
Prices:Low	3.30	2.60	0.01	1.07	11.00	32.13	25.03	11.00	5.50	NA
P/E Ratio:High	NM	NM	NM	NM	NM	NM	87	NM	NM	NA
P/E Ratio:Low	NM	NM	NM	NM	NM	NM	42	NM	NM	NA
Income Statement Analysis (Million $)										
Revenue	13,903	13,809	14,288	15,385	19,695	16,610	3,928	2,243	697	231
Depreciation	3,065	3,123	3,167	3,847	5,335	3,342	404	202	20.3	16.2
Maintenance	NA	NA	NA	NA	NA	NA	NA	NA	NA	NA
Construction Credits	NA	NA	NA	NA	NA	NA	NA	NA	NA	NA
Effective Tax Rate	NM	NM	NM	NM	NM	NM	21.4%	NM	38.4%	NM
Net Income	-757	-1,794	-1,313	-17,625	-3,958	-81.0	459	-844	14.5	-6.97
S&P Core Earnings	-1,154	-1,465	-1,382	-12,411	-2,327	NA	NA	NA	NA	NA
Balance Sheet & Other Financial Data (Million $)										
Gross Property	45,954	45,428	45,094	44,580	55,099	48,318	4,469	2,811	657	NA
Net Property	15,568	16,853	18,149	18,995	29,977	25,583	4,109	2,655	615	NA
Capital Expenditures	1,613	1,731	2,088	2,764	8,543	6,597	1,900	1,413	346	NA
Total Capital	11,751	14,078	14,744	16,924	59,046	58,493	9,370	6,545	1,012	NA
Fixed Charges Coverage	0.6	NM	NM	0.2	1.3	2.5	4.9	1.0	2.2	NA
Capitalization:Long Term Debt	14,968	16,690	15,639	19,754	20,197	15,421	2,368	2,307	630	NA
Capitalization:Preferred	Nil	Nil	Nil	Nil	Nil	Nil	Nil	Nil	Nil	NA
Capitalization:Common	-3,217	-2,612	-1,016	-2,830	36,655	41,304	7,001	4,238	382	NA
% Return on Revenue	NM	NM	NM	NM	NM	NM	11.7	NM	2.1	NA
% Return on Invested Capital	8.1	NM	NM	12.4	NM	7.6	9.3	0.0	NA	NA
% Return on Common Equity	NM	NM	NM	NM	NM	NM	8.2	NM	NA	NA
% Earned on Net Property	24.2	NM	17.5	16.9	26.4	32.9	22.4	18.0	NA	NA
% Long Term Debt of Capitalization	127.4	118.6	106.9	116.7	34.2	27.2	25.3	35.2	62.3	NA
Capital % Preferred	Nil	Nil	Nil	Nil	Nil	Nil	Nil	Nil	Nil	NA
Capitalization:% Common	-27.4	-18.6	-6.9	-16.7	62.0	72.8	74.7	64.8	37.7	NA

Data as orig reptd.; bef. results of disc opers/spec. items. Per share data adj. for stk. divs.; EPS diluted. E-Estimated. NA-Not Available. NM-Not Meaningful. NR-Not Ranked. UR-Under Review.

Office: 1801 California St, Denver, CO 80202-5555.
Telephone: 303-992-1400.
Email: investor.relations@qwest.com
Website: http://www.qwest.com

Chrmn & CEO: R.C. Notebaert
Vice Chrmn & CFO: O.G. Shaffer
EVP, Secy & General Counsel: R.N. Baer
SVP & Cntlr: J.W. Richardson

VP & CIO: G.K. Varma
Board of Directors: L. G. Alvarado, P. F. Anschutz, C. L. Biggs, K. D. Brooksher, C. Y. Harvey, P. S. Hellman, R. D. Hoover, P. J. Martin, C. Matthews, W. W. Murdy, R. C. Notebaert, F. Popoff, J. A. Unruh, A. Welters

Founded: 1983
Domicile: Delaware
Employees: 39,000

STANDARD &POOR'S

RadioShack Corp

S&P Recommendation SELL ★★★★★

Price $17.67 (as of Oct 27, 2006)

12-Mo. Target Price $15.00

Investment Style Mid-Cap Growth

GICS Sector Consumer Discretionary
Sub-Industry Computer & Electronics Retail

Comment This consumer electronics retailer operates the RadioShack chain, which has nearly 7,000 outlets (including dealers/franchises).

Key Stock Statistics (Source S&P, Vickers, company reports)

52-Wk Range	**$23.95–13.73**	S&P Oper. EPS 2006E	**0.73**	P/E on S&P Oper. EPS 2006E	**24.2**	Dividend Rate/Share	**$0.25**
Trailing 12-Month EPS	**$0.32**	S&P Oper. EPS 2007E	**0.93**	Common Shares Outstg. (M)	**135.8**	Yield (%)	**1.41**
Trailing 12-Month P/E	**55.2**	S&P Core EPS 2006E	**0.73**	Market Capitalization(B)	**$2.400**	Beta	**1.07**
$10K Invested 5 Yrs Ago	**$6,609**	S&P Core EPS 2007E	**0.93**	Institutional Ownership (%)	**89**	S&P Credit Rating	**BB**

Price Performance

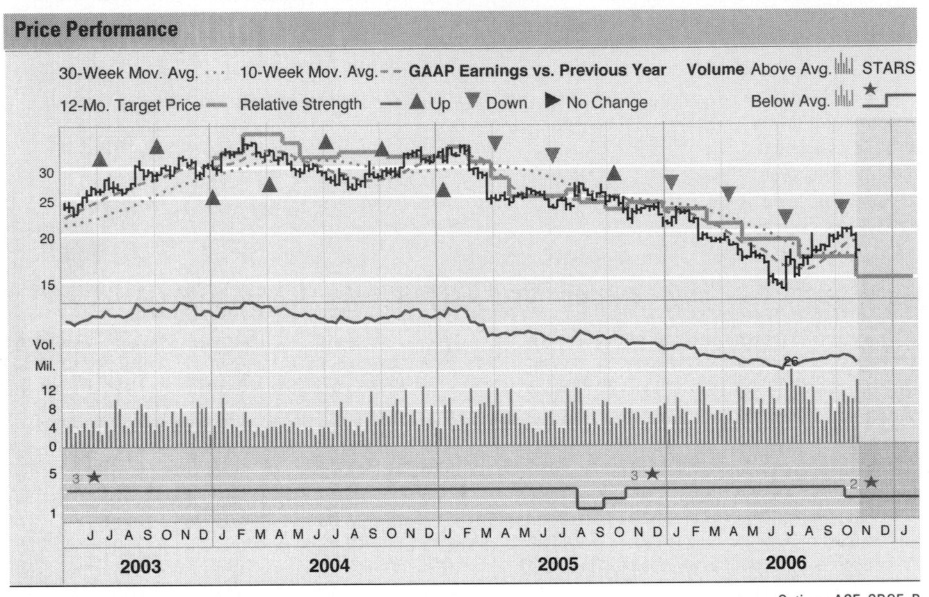

Options: ASE, CBOE, P

Analysis prepared by **Michael Souers** on October 26, 2006, when the stock traded at **$ 17.77**.

Highlights

- Following a 5% increase in 2005, we expect sales to decline 3%-4% in 2006, partly due to the expected closing of 500 to 700 stores, or up to approximately 10% of RSH's store base. We look for kiosk expansion and RSH's more recent focus on faster-moving categories, such as satellite radio, MP3 players and digital cameras, to partly offset lost sales from anticipated store closures and weakness in wireless in RSH's core retail operations.

- We think potential cost savings from a recently announced 18-month turnaround plan will be more than offset by margin pressure related to clearance sales, inventory writedowns and greater investment in store labor hours. As a result, we project a significant narrowing of operating margins. In addition, as RSH focuses on faster-moving, but typically lower-margin, categories, we think it will struggle to achieve historical gross margin levels going forward.

- After taxes forecast at 38.0% and a modestly lower share count, we project operating EPS of $0.73 in 2006, a significant decline from the $1.41 earned in 2005, excluding a one-time gain. We see EPS of $0.93 in 2007.

Investment Rationale/Risk

- We view the company as in the early stages of a turnaround plan, which is focused on increasing average unit volume, rationalizing its cost structure, and growing profitable square footage. We view positively the recent appointment of Julian Day as CEO, as he has extensive experience with successful retail turnarounds. However, we think the next couple of quarters are more likely to yield unsatisfactory results as RSH focuses on clearing out inventory and improving sales of its ailing in-store wireless business. We think the risk/reward quotient for owning the shares remains negative, with the stock recently trading at about 19X our 2007 EPS estimate.

- Risks to our recommendation and target price include management's ability to rapidly execute on its turnaround plan and macroeconomic factors that could boost higher than anticipated consumer spending levels.

- Our 12-month target price of $15 is derived by applying a 16X P/E to our 2007 EPS estimate. This multiple is in line with RSH's three-year historical average and is a warranted discount to peers, in our view, due to near-term concerns.

Qualitative Risk Assessment

LOW | **MEDIUM** | HIGH

The company is the fifth largest player in a fragmented industry, with numerous suppliers and buyers, and a history of profitability. However, we view consumer electronics retailing as highly competitive, with numerous rivals and strong price competition.

Quantitative Evaluations

S&P Quality Ranking B+

D | C | B- | B | **B+** | A- | A | A+

Relative Strength Rank WEAK

16

LOWEST = 1 HIGHEST = 99

Revenue/Earnings Data

Revenue (Million $)

	1Q	2Q	3Q	4Q	Year
2006	1,160	1,100	1,060	--	--
2005	1,123	1,092	1,195	1,672	5,082
2004	1,093	1,054	1,102	1,593	4,841
2003	1,070	1,025	1,064	1,490	4,649
2002	1,034	998.1	1,047	1,498	4,577
2001	1,140	1,040	1,081	1,516	4,776

Earnings Per Share ($)

	1Q	2Q	3Q	4Q	Year
2006	0.06	-0.02	-0.12	**E**0.43	**E**0.73
2005	0.34	0.33	0.75	0.40	1.81
2004	0.41	0.42	0.43	0.81	2.08
2003	0.33	0.34	0.34	0.77	1.77
2002	0.31	0.28	0.25	0.63	1.45
2001	0.23	0.21	0.23	0.18	0.85

Fiscal year ended Dec. 31. Next earnings report expected: Mid February. EPS Estimates based on S&P Operating Earnings; historical GAAP earnings are as reported.

Dividend Data (Dates: mm/dd Payment Date: mm/dd/yy)

Amount ($)	Date Decl.	Ex-Div. Date	Stk. of Record	Payment Date
0.250	10/03	11/29	12/01	12/19/05

Dividends have been paid since 1987. Source: Company reports.

RadioShack Corp

Business Summary October 26, 2006

CORPORATE OVERVIEW. As of December 31, 2005, this consumer electronics retailer had 4,972 company-operated stores located through the U.S., including Puerto Rico and the U.S. Virgin Islands. RSH also had a network of 1,686 dealer/franchise stores, including 37 located outside the U.S. At the end of 2005, RSH also operated 777 non-RadioShack branded kiosks, which offer product lines such as wireless phones and associated accessories.

Each store carries an assortment of electronic parts, batteries and accessories; wireless and conventional phones; audio/video equipment; direct-to-home (DTH) satellite systems; PCs; and specialized products such as home air cleaners and unique toys. RSH also provides access to third-party services, such as cellular and PCS phone and DTH satellite activation, long-distance telephone service, prepaid wireless airtime, and extended service plans. We believe that RSH is focusing on revamping its product offerings in order to enhance its competitive position within the consumer electronics industry. For example, in the second half of 2005, RSH began dedicating floor space to Apple's iPod and accessories, a rapidly growing consumer electronics category.

MARKET PROFILE. The domestic consumer electronics industry generated $112.9 billion of sales in 2004. The Consumer Electronics Association (CEA) projected an 8.9% increase in 2005, to $122.9 billion, and a preliminary increase of 7.2% in 2006, for total industry sales of $131.8 billion. For 2006, we estimate that RSH will have a market share of approximately 4%, trailing competitors such as Best Buy, Wal-Mart, Circuit City, and Dell. We expect pure-play electronic retailers to see increased competition from discounters and mass merchants as these companies have been ramping up their consumer electronics offerings to take advantage of what we view as a strong technology cycle. We believe that, historically, RSH has differentiated itself from big box competitors, due to its heavy emphasis on high margin, smaller ticket items such as batteries and accessories. Along these lines, RSH's smaller store format does not afford the company the opportunity to capitalize on the strong demand for advanced televisions.

Company Financials

Per Share Data ($) Year Ended Dec. 31	2005	2004	2003	2002	2001	2000	1999	1998	1997	1996
Tangible Book Value	4.36	5.83	4.73	4.24	4.04	4.46	3.70	3.84	4.69	5.11
Cash Flow	2.65	2.70	2.31	1.97	1.41	2.38	1.87	0.73	1.24	0.07
Earnings	1.81	2.08	1.77	1.45	0.85	1.84	1.43	0.27	0.82	-0.41
S&P Core Earnings	1.69	1.94	1.49	1.18	1.06	NA	NA	NA	NA	NA
Dividends	0.25	0.25	0.25	0.22	0.22	0.22	0.15	0.20	0.20	0.20
Payout Ratio	14%	12%	14%	15%	25%	12%	10%	74%	25%	NM
Prices:High	34.48	36.24	32.48	36.21	56.50	72.94	79.50	31.94	23.00	14.78
Prices:Low	20.55	26.04	18.74	16.99	20.10	35.06	20.59	15.19	10.16	8.53
P/E Ratio:High	19	17	18	25	66	40	56	NM	28	NM
P/E Ratio:Low	11	13	11	12	24	19	14	NM	12	NM
Income Statement Analysis (Million $)										
Revenue	5,082	4,841	4,649	4,577	4,776	4,795	4,126	4,788	5,372	6,286
Operating Income	474	660	576	510	583	736	597	424	434	261
Depreciation	124	101	92.0	94.7	108	107	90.2	99.0	97.2	109
Interest Expense	44.5	29.6	35.7	43.4	50.8	53.9	37.2	45.4	46.1	36.0
Pretax Income	322	542	473	425	292	591	481	99.7	304	-146
Effective Tax Rate	16.0%	37.8%	36.9%	38.0%	42.8%	38.0%	38.0%	38.5%	38.5%	NM
Net Income	270	337	299	263	167	368	298	61.3	187	-91.6
S&P Core Earnings	251	315	252	211	200	NA	NA	NA	NA	NA
Balance Sheet & Other Financial Data (Million $)										
Cash	224	438	635	447	401	131	165	64.5	106	122
Current Assets	1,627	1,775	1,667	1,707	1,714	1,818	1,403	1,299	1,716	1,940
Total Assets	2,205	2,517	2,244	1,707	2,245	2,577	2,142	1,994	2,318	2,583
Current Liabilities	986	957	858	829	826	1,232	925	880	976	1,194
Long Term Debt	495	507	541	591	565	303	319	235	236	104
Common Equity	589	922	769	729	714	812	758	748	959	1,165
Total Capital	1,084	1,429	1,311	1,320	1,344	1,284	1,150	1,083	1,295	1,369
Capital Expenditures	171	229	190	107	139	120	102	132	118	175
Cash Flow	394	439	391	354	270	470	383	155	278	17.0
Current Ratio	1.6	1.9	1.9	2.1	2.1	1.5	1.5	1.5	1.8	1.6
% Long Term Debt of Capitalization	45.7	35.5	41.3	44.8	42.1	23.6	27.8	21.7	18.2	7.6
% Net Income of Revenue	5.3	7.0	6.4	5.8	3.5	7.7	7.2	1.3	3.5	NM
% Return on Assets	11.4	14.2	13.4	13.3	6.9	15.6	14.4	2.8	7.6	NM
% Return on Equity	35.7	39.9	39.9	35.9	21.2	46.2	38.8	6.5	17.0	NM

Data as orig reptd.; bef. results of disc opers/spec. items. Per share data adj. for stk. divs.; EPS diluted. E-Estimated. NA-Not Available. NM-Not Meaningful. NR-Not Ranked. UR-Under Review.

Office: 300 Radioshack Cir, Fort Worth, TX 76102-1964.
Telephone: 817-415-3700.
Email: investor.relations@radioshack.com
Website: http://www.radioshack.com

Chrmn & CEO: J. Day
Pres & COO: C. Babrowski
EVP & CFO: J. Gooch
Investor Contact: J. Grant (817-415-7833)

Board of Directors: F. J. Belatti, R. E. Elmquist, R. S. Falcone, D. R. Feehan, R. J. Hernandez, R. J. Kamerschen, H. E. Lockhart, J. L. Messman, W. G. Morton, Jr., T. G. Plaskett, E. D. Woodbury

Founded: 1899
Domicile: Delaware
Employees: 47,000

STANDARD &POOR'S

Raytheon Co.

S&P Recommendation BUY ★★★★★	**Price** $49.62 (as of Oct 27, 2006)	**12-Mo. Target Price** $54.00	**Investment Style** Large-Cap Value

GICS Sector Industrials
Sub-Industry Aerospace & Defense

Comment Raytheon, one of the world's largest U.S. military contractors, specializes in making high-tech missiles and electronics.

Key Stock Statistics (Source S&P, Vickers, company reports)

52-Wk Range	$50.95–36.86	S&P Oper. EPS 2006**E**	2.68	P/E on S&P Oper. EPS 2006**E**	18.5	Dividend Rate/Share	$0.96
Trailing 12-Month EPS	$2.65	S&P Oper. EPS 2007**E**	3.00	Common Shares Outstg. (M)	448.7	Yield (%)	1.93
Trailing 12-Month P/E	18.7	S&P Core EPS 2006**E**	2.80	Market Capitalization(B)	$22.265	Beta	0.72
$10K Invested 5 Yrs Ago	$16,413	S&P Core EPS 2007**E**	2.90	Institutional Ownership (%)	76	S&P Credit Rating	BBB

Price Performance

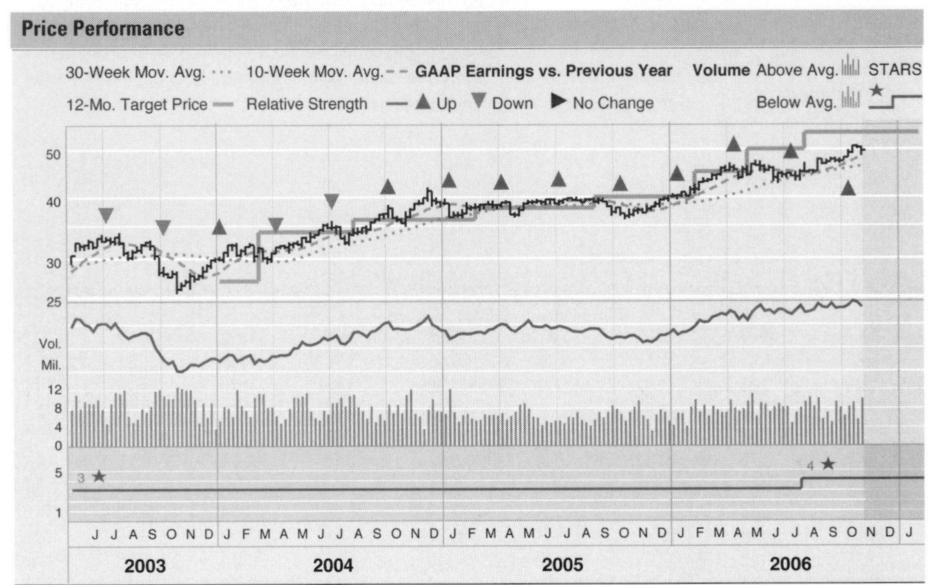

Options: ASE, CBOE, P

Analysis prepared by **Richard Tortoriello** on September 29, 2006, when the stock traded at **$ 48.01**.

Highlights

- We anticipate that increased Pentagon demand for RTN's missiles and military electronics (75% of revenues) will lead to a 7% rise in 2006 revenues. For 2007, we are projecting slower growth of about 5%, due to anticipated slower military spending.
- We believe that both increased sales volumes and productivity improvements will allow RTN to expand operating profit margin to 8.4% in 2006, from 7.7% in 2005, and project a further increase to 8.9% in 2007. Combining our expectation of increased earnings with our projection for decreased share counts, as RTN has been using excess cash to repurchase shares, we project EPS of $2.68 in 2006, up from $2.08 in 2005, and see further growth to $3.00 in 2007.
- We note that RTN generated free cash flow (cash flow from operating activities less capital expenses) per share of about $4.80 in 2005, well above reported EPS. We project free cash flow per share of over $4.00 in 2006, and see excess cash being used for share repurchases and dividend increases. In late July, RTN said that it was considering strategic alternatives, including possible sale, of its Raytheon Aircraft business.

Investment Rationale/Risk

- Given ongoing military conflicts and potential military threats, we view the outlook for RTN as positive. The 2007 defense budget submitted for Congressional review proposes a 7% increase in defense spending. We believe that RTN's leading positions in both missiles and defense electronics situate it well to provide products for defense against current and potential future threats.
- Risks to our recommendation and target price include lower than expected increases in future U.S. defense budgets, competitive threats to RTN from other large defense contractors, and production or other operational problems affecting RTN's output and project costs.
- Our 12-month target price of $54 is based on a P/E ratio of 18X our 2007 EPS estimate. This valuation is above RTN's 10-year average historical forward P/E ratio of 16X, with the upside due to our positive view of the defense market in general and RTN's product portfolio in particular. We note that RTN recently traded at 10X price to free cash flow versus a 10-year average of 13X.

Qualitative Risk Assessment

LOW	**MEDIUM**	HIGH

Our risk assessment reflects RTN's exposure to economic cycles and changes in defense spending, significant off-balance-sheet liabilities, and historically below-average earnings stability, offset by its leading defense contractor status and significant project backlog.

Quantitative Evaluations

S&P Quality Ranking B-

D	C	**B-**	B	B+	A-	A	A+

Relative Strength Rank MODERATE

55

LOWEST = 1 HIGHEST = 99

Revenue/Earnings Data

Revenue (Million $)

	1Q	2Q	3Q	4Q	Year
2006	5,152	5,711	5,693	--	--
2005	4,944	5,409	5,331	6,210	21,894
2004	4,676	4,929	4,936	5,704	20,245
2003	4,201	4,429	4,378	5,101	18,109
2002	3,911	4,095	4,092	4,662	16,760
2001	3,968	4,307	3,961	4,631	16,867

Earnings Per Share ($)

2006	0.64	0.69	0.72	**E**0.71	**E**2.68
2005	0.43	0.51	0.51	0.63	2.08
2004	0.24	-0.22	0.41	0.54	0.99
2003	0.27	0.45	0.05	0.52	1.29
2002	0.37	0.54	0.56	0.38	1.85
2001	0.28	0.33	-0.73	0.15	0.01

Fiscal year ended Dec. 31. Next earnings report expected: Early February. EPS Estimates based on S&P Operating Earnings; historical GAAP earnings are as reported.

Dividend Data (Dates: mm/dd Payment Date: mm/dd/yy)

Amount ($)	Date Decl.	Ex-Div. Date	Stk. of Record	Payment Date
0.220	12/14	12/29	01/03	01/31/06
0.240	03/30	04/07	04/11	05/09/06
0.240	06/30	07/13	07/17	08/14/06
0.240	09/22	10/02	10/04	11/01/06

Dividends have been paid since 1964. Source: Company reports.

Raytheon Co.

Business Summary September 29, 2006

CORPORATE OVERVIEW. Raytheon, a leading missile and military electronics manufacturer, conducts business through seven business segments.

Integrated Defense Systems (16% of sales and 24% of operating profits in 2005) is a leader in mission systems integration, providing integrated air defense, maritime, and joint battlespace solutions. Customers include the U.S. Missile Defense Agency (MDA) and the U.S. Armed Forces. Business areas include Future Naval Capability, focusing on the DD(X), the Navy's next-generation naval destroyer; Integrated Air Defense; Missile Defense; international operations; maritime mission systems; and joint battlespace integration.

Intelligence Information Systems (11% of sales and 10% of profits) provides systems, subsystems, and software engineering services for national and tactical intelligence systems, as well as for homeland security and information technology (IT) solutions. Areas of concentration include processing, analysis, and dissemination of signals and imagery, production of geospatial intelligence, command and control of airborne, and space borne platforms, and integrated ground systems for weather and environmental programs.

Missile Systems (18% of sales and 19% of profits) makes and supports a broad range of leading-edge solutions and products for the armed forces of the U.S. and other countries. Business areas include Naval weapon systems, which provides defensive missiles and guided projectiles to the navies of over 30 countries; Strike, with products focused on ground-based targets, including the Tomahawk cruise missile; Air-to-Air missiles; Land Combat, which includes the Javelin anti-tank missile; and other programs.

Network Centric Systems (14% of sales and 14% of profits) makes net-centric mission solutions for network sensors, command and control, communications and air traffic management, and homeland security. Customers include all branches of the Department of Defense, the Department of Homeland Security, the Federal Aviation Administration, and other customers.

Company Financials

Per Share Data ($) Year Ended Dec. 31	**2005**	**2004**	**2003**	**2002**	**2001**	**2000**	**1999**	**1998**	**1997**	**1996**
Tangible Book Value	NM	NM	NM	NM	NM	NM	NM	NM	NM	6.44
Cash Flow	3.19	1.93	2.22	2.74	2.03	3.50	3.46	4.75	4.07	4.77
Earnings	2.08	0.99	1.29	1.85	0.01	1.46	1.34	2.53	2.18	3.21
S&P Core Earnings	2.57	1.96	1.11	-0.25	-2.68	NA	NA	NA	NA	NA
Dividends	0.86	0.80	0.80	0.80	0.80	0.80	0.80	0.80	0.80	0.79
Payout Ratio	41%	81%	62%	43%	NM	55%	60%	32%	37%	25%
Prices:High	40.57	41.89	33.97	45.70	37.44	35.81	76.56	60.75	60.50	56.13
Prices:Low	35.96	29.28	24.31	26.30	23.95	17.50	22.19	40.69	41.75	43.38
P/E Ratio:High	21	42	26	25	NM	25	57	24	28	17
P/E Ratio:Low	19	30	19	14	NM	12	17	16	19	14
Income Statement Analysis (Million $)										
Revenue	21,894	20,245	18,109	16,760	16,867	16,895	19,841	19,530	13,673	12,331
Operating Income	2,131	1,822	1,709	2,118	1,488	2,319	2,251	2,797	2,036	1,602
Depreciation	444	434	393	364	729	694	724	761	457	369
Interest Expense	312	418	537	497	660	736	713	739	397	256
Pretax Income	1,440	579	762	1,074	117	877	828	1,467	790	1,083
Effective Tax Rate	34.6%	24.2%	29.8%	29.7%	95.7%	43.2%	44.8%	41.1%	33.3%	29.8%
Net Income	942	439	535	755	5.00	498	457	864	527	761
S&P Core Earnings	1,161	866	460	-105	-970	NA	NA	NA	NA	NA
Balance Sheet & Other Financial Data (Million $)										
Cash	1,202	556	661	544	1,214	871	230	421	296	139
Current Assets	7,567	7,124	6,585	7,190	8,362	8,013	8,931	8,637	9,233	5,604
Total Assets	24,381	24,153	23,668	23,946	26,636	26,777	28,110	27,939	28,598	11,126
Current Liabilities	5,900	5,644	3,849	5,107	5,753	4,865	7,886	6,680	11,886	4,692
Long Term Debt	3,969	4,637	7,376	7,138	6,875	9,054	7,298	8,163	4,406	1,500
Common Equity	10,798	10,611	9,162	8,870	11,290	10,823	10,959	10,856	10,425	4,598
Total Capital	15,011	15,345	16,538	16,008	18,743	20,650	18,810	19,580	15,617	6,098
Capital Expenditures	75.0	363	428	458	486	431	532	509	459	406
Cash Flow	1,386	873	928	1,119	734	1,192	1,181	1,625	984	1,130
Current Ratio	1.3	1.3	1.7	1.4	1.5	1.6	1.1	1.3	0.8	1.2
% Long Term Debt of Capitalization	26.4	30.2	44.6	44.6	36.7	43.8	38.8	41.7	28.2	24.6
% Net Income of Revenue	4.3	2.2	3.0	4.5	0.0	2.9	2.3	4.4	3.9	6.2
% Return on Assets	3.9	1.8	2.2	3.0	0.0	1.8	1.6	3.1	2.7	7.3
% Return on Equity	8.8	4.4	5.9	7.5	0.0	4.6	4.2	8.1	7.0	17.2

Data as orig reptd.; bef. results of disc opers/spec. items. Per share data adj. for stk. divs.; EPS diluted. E-Estimated. NA-Not Available. NM-Not Meaningful. NR-Not Ranked. UR-Under Review.

Office: 870 Winter St, Waltham, MA 02451-1449.
Telephone: 781-522-3000.
Email: invest@raytheon.com
Website: http://www.raytheon.com

Chrmn & CEO: W.H. Swanson
SVP & CFO: D.C. Wajsgras
SVP & General Counsel: J.B. Stephens
VP & Chief Acctg Officer: M.J. Wood

VP & Treas: R.A. Goglia
Investor Contact: T. Rutledge (781-522-3000)
Board of Directors: B. M. Barrett, V. Clark, F. Colloredo-Mansfeld, J. M. Deutch, F. M. Poses, M. C. Ruettgers, R. L. Skates, W. R. Spivey, L. G. Stuntz, W. H. Swanson

Founded: 1928
Domicile: Delaware
Employees: 79,900

STANDARD &POOR'S

Realogy Corp

S&P Recommendation HOLD ★★★★★ | **Price** $26.64 (as of Oct 27, 2006) | **12-Mo. Target Price** $23.00 | **Investment Style** Mid-Cap Growth

GICS Sector Financials
Sub-Industry Real Estate Management & Development

Comment This company is the world's largest real estate brokerage franchisor, the largest U.S. residential real estate brokerage firm, the largest U.S. provider and a leading global provider of outsourced employee relocation services, and a provider of title and settlement services.

Key Stock Statistics (Source S&P, Vickers, company reports)

52-Wk Range	$27.67–19.90	S&P Oper. EPS 2006E	1.57	P/E on S&P Oper. EPS 2006E	17.0	Dividend Rate/Share	Nil
Trailing 12-Month EPS	$1.77	S&P Oper. EPS 2007E	1.54	Common Shares Outstg. (M)	213.5	Yield (%)	Nil
Trailing 12-Month P/E	15.1	S&P Core EPS 2006E	1.52	Market Capitalization(B)	$5.686	Beta	1.00
$10K Invested 5 Yrs Ago	NA	S&P Core EPS 2007E	1.54	Institutional Ownership (%)	1	S&P Credit Rating	NA

Price Performance

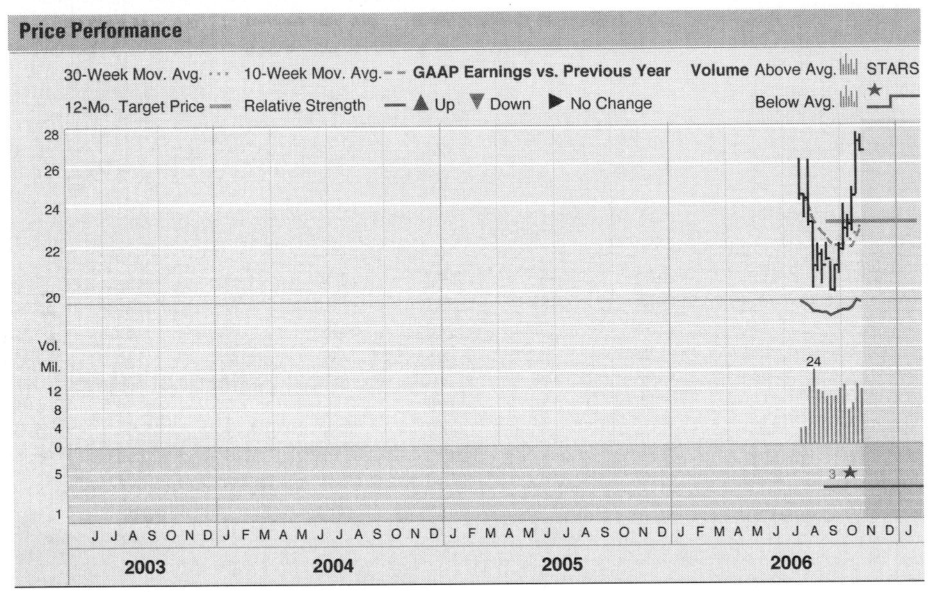

Analysis prepared by **Tom Graves, CFA** on August 29, 2006, when the stock traded at **$ 21.37**.

Highlights

- Ownership of Realogy was spun off from Cendant Corp. in July 2006, with one share of Realogy common stock distributed for every four Cendant common shares outstanding as of the close of business July 21.
- We look for revenue to decline 9% in 2006, to $6.5 billion, with fewer real estate transactions contributing to lower revenues from the real estate franchise and brokerage businesses. We expect this to be partly offset by higher revenue from the title and settlement business, with growth there primarily from an acquisition.
- Excluding special items, we estimate 2006 net income at $376 million ($1.57 a share), which includes about five months of Realogy as a standalone company. This assumes that Realogy repurchases about 48 million of its common shares in the second half of 2006. In 2007, we look for revenue and segment EBITDA to decline modestly, for unallocated corporate expense and interest expense to rise, and for net income to be down 16%, to $316 million. With about 15% fewer shares outstanding, we estimate 2007 EPS of $1.54.

Investment Rationale/Risk

- We expect that the August 2006 announcement of an authorization to repurchase up to 48 million common shares (about 19% of the total outstanding) will help provide near-term support for the stock. However, we also expect that concern about the prospect of continued softness in the U.S. residential real estate market, following a period of strong growth, will weigh on the shares.
- Risks to our opinion and target price include the possibility that the U.S. residential real estate market will be weaker than expected.
- Although Realogy has some well known brands and leading market positions, we expect the stock's valuation to be limited by the company's dependence on the U.S. residential real estate market. Our 12-month target price of $23 reflects a blend of our DCF analysis, assuming a weighted average cost of capital of 9.3% and perpetuity annual cash flow growth of 2%, and relative valuation, in which we assign a P/E multiple (14.9X) to our 2007 EPS estimate that is about 12% above the current P/E of the S&P 500.

Qualitative Risk Assessment

LOW | **MEDIUM** | HIGH

Our risk assessment reflects our view that the company's business is sensitive to the strength of the U.S. residential housing market, including the volume and prices of home sales. Much of the company's profit comes from fee-based, high-margin operations of its real estate franchise business.

Quantitative Evaluations

S&P Quality Ranking NR

D | C | B- | B | B+ | A- | A | A+

Relative Strength Rank STRONG

89

LOWEST = 1 HIGHEST = 99

Revenue/Earnings Data

Revenue (Million $)

	1Q	2Q	3Q	4Q	Year
2006	--	1,902	--	--	--
2005	--	--	--	--	7,139
2004	--	--	--	--	--
2003	--	--	--	--	--
2002	--	--	--	--	--
2001	--	--	--	--	--

Earnings Per Share ($)

	1Q	2Q	3Q	4Q	Year
2006	--	0.65	E0.60	E0.06	E1.57
2005	--	--	--	--	2.08
2004	--	--	--	--	--
2003	--	--	--	--	--
2002	--	--	--	--	--
2001	--	--	--	--	--

Fiscal year ended Dec. 31. Next earnings report expected: NA. EPS Estimates based on S&P Operating Earnings; historical GAAP earnings are as reported.

Dividend Data

No cash dividends have been paid.

Realogy Corp

Business Summary August 29, 2006

CORPORATE OVERVIEW. Realogy is the world's largest real estate brokerage franchisor, the largest U.S. residential real estate brokerage firm, the largest U.S. provider and a leading global provider of outsourced employee relocation services, and a provider of title and settlement services.

The company has about 15,000 offices and 310,000 sales associates operating under its real estate franchise brands, including more than 1,000 company-owned and operated brokerage offices. Realogy's real estate brands include Century 21 (about 7,900 offices), Coldwell Banker (about 4,000), ERA (about 2,800), Sotheby's International (about 220), and Coldwell Banker Commercial (about 160).

Through its NRT Inc. business, Realogy owns and operates a full-service real estate brokerage business in more than 35 of the largest metropolitan areas of the U.S. This includes operations under Realogy's franchised brands as well as proprietary brands that Realogy owns, but does not currently franchise to third parties, such as The Corcoran Group. Realogy has nearly 1,100 company-owned brokerage offices. Looking ahead, we expect Realogy to acquire additional brokerage operations and to seek to expand its real estate franchise business with additional affiliations to brokerage businesses that it does not own.

Realogy has a title and settlement services business that was formed in 2002 in conjunction with Cendant's acquisition of 100% of NRT. In addition, through its Cartus Corp. subsidiary, Realogy offers a broad range of employee relocation services.

Company Financials

Per Share Data ($) Year Ended Dec. 31	2005	2004	2003	2002	2001	2000	1999	1998	1997	1996
Tangible Book Value	NM	NA	NA	NA	NA	NA	NA	NA	NA	NA
Cash Flow	2.61	NA	NA	NA	NA	NA	NA	NA	NA	NA
Earnings	2.08	NA	NA	NA	NA	NA	NA	NA	NA	NA
S&P Core Earnings	2.37	NA	NA	NA	NA	NA	NA	NA	NA	NA
Dividends	Nil	NA	NA	NA	NA	NA	NA	NA	NA	NA
Payout Ratio	Nil	NA	NA	NA	NA	NA	NA	NA	NA	NA
Prices:High	NA	NA	NA	NA	NA	NA	NA	NA	NA	NA
Prices:Low	NA	NA	NA	NA	NA	NA	NA	NA	NA	NA
P/E Ratio:High	NA	NA	NA	NA	NA	NA	NA	NA	NA	NA
P/E Ratio:Low	NA	NA	NA	NA	NA	NA	NA	NA	NA	NA
Income Statement Analysis (Million $)										
Revenue	7,139	NA	NA	NA	NA	NA	NA	NA	NA	NA
Operating Income	1,102	NA	NA	NA	NA	NA	NA	NA	NA	NA
Depreciation	142	NA	NA	NA	NA	NA	NA	NA	NA	NA
Interest Expense	49.0	NA	NA	NA	NA	NA	NA	NA	NA	NA
Pretax Income	911	NA	NA	NA	NA	NA	NA	NA	NA	NA
Effective Tax Rate	39.2%	NA	NA	NA	NA	NA	NA	NA	NA	NA
Net Income	550	NA	NA	NA	NA	NA	NA	NA	NA	NA
S&P Core Earnings	627	NA	NA	NA	NA	NA	NA	NA	NA	NA
Balance Sheet & Other Financial Data (Million $)										
Cash	91.0	NA	NA	NA	NA	NA	NA	NA	NA	NA
Current Assets	1,413	NA	NA	NA	NA	NA	NA	NA	NA	NA
Total Assets	5,801	NA	NA	NA	NA	NA	NA	NA	NA	NA
Current Liabilities	2,035	NA	NA	NA	NA	NA	NA	NA	NA	NA
Long Term Debt	750	NA	NA	NA	NA	NA	NA	NA	NA	NA
Common Equity	2,826	NA	NA	NA	NA	NA	NA	NA	NA	NA
Total Capital	3,576	NA	NA	NA	NA	NA	NA	NA	NA	NA
Capital Expenditures	131	NA	NA	NA	NA	NA	NA	NA	NA	NA
Cash Flow	692	NA	NA	NA	NA	NA	NA	NA	NA	NA
Current Ratio	0.7	NA	NA	NA	NA	NA	NA	NA	NA	NA
% Long Term Debt of Capitalization	20.9	NA	NA	NA	NA	NA	NA	NA	NA	NA
% Net Income of Revenue	7.7	NA	NA	NA	NA	NA	NA	NA	NA	NA
% Return on Assets	NA	NA	NA	NA	NA	NA	NA	NA	NA	NA
% Return on Equity	NA	NA	NA	NA	NA	NA	NA	NA	NA	NA

Data as orig reptd.; bef. results of disc opers/spec. items. Per share data adj. for stk. divs.; EPS diluted. E-Estimated. NA-Not Available. NM-Not Meaningful. NR-Not Ranked. UR-Under Review.

Office: One Campus Drive, Parsippany, NJ 07054.
Telephone: 973-496-6700.
Website: http://www.realogy.com
Chrmn & CEO: H.R. Silverman

Pres & Vice Chrmn: R.A. Smith
EVP, CFO & Treas: A.E. Hull
EVP & Chief Admin: D.J. Weaving
EVP, Secy & General Counsel: C.P. Cardwell, IV

Investor Contact: H.A. Diamond (973-407-2710)
Board of Directors: M. L. Edelman, K. Fisher, C. D. Mills, R. E. Nederlander, R. W. Pittman, H. R. Silverman, R. A. Smith, R. F. Smith

Auditor: Deloitte and Touche, Parsippany, NJ
Founded: 2006
Domicile: Delaware
Employees: 15,000

Regions Financial Corp

S&P Recommendation BUY ★★★★★

Price $37.94 (as of Oct 27, 2006)

12-Mo. Target Price $43.00

Investment Style Large-Cap Value

GICS Sector Financials
Sub-Industry Regional Banks

Comment This major southeastern bank holding company operates more than 1,300 offices in 15 states.

Key Stock Statistics (Source S&P, Vickers, company reports)

52-Wk Range	$39.15–32.37	S&P Oper. EPS 2006**E**	2.93	P/E on S&P Oper. EPS 2006**E**	12.9	Dividend Rate/Share	$1.40
Trailing 12-Month EPS	$2.71	S&P Oper. EPS 2007**E**	3.15	Common Shares Outstg. (M)	454.7	Yield (%)	3.69
Trailing 12-Month P/E	14.0	S&P Core EPS 2006**E**	2.94	Market Capitalization(B)	$17.249	Beta	0.46
$10K Invested 5 Yrs Ago	$20,192	S&P Core EPS 2007**E**	3.13	Institutional Ownership (%)	34	S&P Credit Rating	A

Price Performance

Options: Ph

Analysis prepared by **Christopher B. Muir** on October 16, 2006, when the stock traded at **$ 38.56**.

Highlights

- We expect that gains (versus losses in 2005) on sales of securities, coupled with some growth in earning assets and non-interest income, will help drive revenue growth of 7.6% in 2006. Our 2006 estimates include a net interest margin of 4.20% (up from 3.91% in 2005, despite our view of continued pressure from a relatively flat yield curve), average earning asset growth of 1.8%, and non-interest income growth of 3.9%.
- We think that operating expense will improve and that consolidation expense will continue to moderate in 2006, but that the expensing of stock options will partly offset these benefits. Our 2006 non-interest expense to total revenue forecast of 58.6% is much better than 2005's 61.9%. We believe credit quality will remain solid in 2006. We project that loan loss provisions will decrease to $118 million, from $165 million in 2005.
- Assuming an effective tax rate of 30.8% and continued share repurchases, we estimate 2006 operating EPS of $2.93, an 18% increase from operating EPS of $2.48 in 2005. Our 2007 EPS forecast is $3.15, a further increase of 7.5%.

Investment Rationale/Risk

- We think the proposed acquisition of AmSouth (ASO: buy, $31), subject to necessary approvals, will benefit RF through merger savings and a much larger presence in the fast growing Florida market. We believe it remains well positioned in the faster growing areas of the Southeast and that the effect from Katrina will continue to be muted. RF recently traded at 12.3X our 2007 EPS estimate, a 10% discount to its large-cap regional banking peers, which we view as too wide a discount.
- Risks to our opinion and target price include detrimental changes in the yield curve and an operational performance that fails to meet our forecast.
- Our 12-month target price of $43 is based on our relative valuation analysis, which we think reflects the true value of the company. Our target price implies a P/E multiple of 13.6X our 2007 EPS estimate, even with its peers, which we think is warranted based on our forecast for EPS growth and expected benefits from the proposed merger with ASO. We see an intrinsic value of $40, if the planned merger agreement is dissolved.

Qualitative Risk Assessment

LOW | MEDIUM | HIGH

Our risk assessment reflects the company's large-cap valuation, our view of the strong credit quality of its loan portfolio, and its history of profitability. While the company operates in a highly competitive and fragmented industry, the industry tends to produce relatively stable financial results.

Quantitative Evaluations

S&P Quality Ranking B+

D | C | B- | B | **B+** | A- | A | A+

Relative Strength Rank MODERATE

51

LOWEST = 1 HIGHEST = 99

Revenue/Earnings Data

Revenue (Million $)

	1Q	2Q	3Q	4Q	Year
2006	1,666	1,756	--	--	--
2005	1,423	1,565	1,564	1,572	6,124
2004	893.7	868.8	1,432	1,416	4,610
2003	917.6	940.1	888.6	871.7	3,618
2002	920.2	929.4	967.4	978.9	3,796
2001	956.0	1,063	1,014	1,004	4,038

Earnings Per Share ($)

	1Q	2Q	3Q	4Q	Year
2006	0.64	0.75	0.77	**E**0.77	**E**2.93
2005	0.51	0.53	0.55	0.55	2.15
2004	0.61	0.58	0.55	0.50	2.19
2003	0.58	0.59	0.59	0.59	2.35
2002	0.53	0.54	0.57	0.57	2.20
2001	0.46	0.40	0.48	0.49	1.81

Fiscal year ended Dec. 31. Next earnings report expected: Mid January. EPS Estimates based on S&P Operating Earnings; historical GAAP earnings are as reported.

Dividend Data (Dates: mm/dd Payment Date: mm/dd/yy)

Amount ($)	Date Decl.	Ex-Div. Date	Stk. of Record	Payment Date
0.350	04/20	04/27	05/01	05/15/06
0.350	07/20	07/28	08/01	08/15/06
0.350	10/19	10/30	11/01	11/15/06
0.350	10/19	11/13	11/15	11/01/06

Dividends have been paid since 1968. Source: Company reports.

Regions Financial Corp

Business Summary October 16, 2006

CORPORATE OVERVIEW. Regions Financial is a bank holding company that operates primarily in the southeastern U.S., with operations consisting of banking, brokerage and investment services, mortgage banking, insurance brokerage, credit life insurance, commercial accounts receivable factoring and specialty financing. RF conducts its banking operations through Regions Bank, an Alabama chartered commercial bank that is a member of the Federal Reserve System, and Union Planters Bank, National Association (UPBNA), a national bank.

Banking operations also include Regions Mortgage (RMI) and EquiFirst Corp. (EFC), which are involved in mortgage banking. RMI's primary business is the origination and servicing of mortgage loans for long-term investors. EFC typically originates mortgage loans that are sold to third-party investors with servicing released. RMI and EFC generally provide services in the same states in which RF has banking operations.

Financial services operations include Morgan Keegan (acquired in 2001), a regional full-service brokerage and investment bank. Morgan Keegan, which operates 281 offices, offers products and services, including securities brokerage, asset management, financial planning, mutual funds, securities underwriting, sales, trading, and investment banking.

MARKET PROFILE. RF's Southern footprint includes 192 branches in Alabama, 149 branches in Florida, 206 branches in Tennessee, 143 branches in Georgia, 121 branches in Arkansas, 108 branches in Louisiana, 79 branches in Illinois, 80 branches in Texas, 109 branches in Mississippi, 73 branches in Missouri, 72 branches in Indiana, and 82 branches in four other states. The projection for deposit-weighted average population growth in the company's service territory is 7.3% from 2005 to 2010, according to SNL Financial, a financial information provider. The projected national growth rate is 6.3% and the population-weighted average growth rate of the states in the company's service territory is 6.0%.

Company Financials

Per Share Data ($) Year Ended Dec. 31	**2005**	**2004**	**2003**	**2002**	**2001**	**2000**	**1999**	**1998**	**1997**	**1996**
Tangible Book Value	11.55	11.58	16.25	15.29	10.58	11.00	9.75	9.72	9.56	8.75
Earnings	2.15	2.19	2.35	2.20	1.81	1.93	1.90	1.52	1.74	1.50
S&P Core Earnings	2.11	2.17	2.32	2.11	1.63	NA	NA	NA	NA	NA
Dividends	1.36	0.93	1.00	0.94	0.91	0.87	0.79	0.72	0.62	0.57
Payout Ratio	63%	43%	43%	43%	50%	45%	42%	47%	36%	38%
Prices:High	35.54	35.97	30.70	31.10	26.72	22.68	33.72	36.96	36.45	21.87
Prices:Low	29.16	27.26	24.16	21.95	20.84	14.83	18.78	23.39	20.81	16.40
P/E Ratio:High	17	16	13	14	15	12	18	24	21	15
P/E Ratio:Low	14	12	10	10	11	8	10	15	12	11

Income Statement Analysis (Million $)										
Net Interest Income	2,821	2,113	1,475	1,498	1,425	1,389	1,426	1,325	829	700
Tax Equivalent Adjustment	NA	NA	NA	NA	NA	NA	NA	NA	NA	13.3
Non Interest Income	1,832	1,591	1,373	1,207	950	641	537	468	258	221
Loan Loss Provision	165	129	122	128	165	127	114	60.5	41.8	29.0
% Expense/Operating Revenue	65.5%	66.5%	64.6%	65.1%	64.2%	55.2%	54.2%	61.6%	55.2%	59.3%
Pretax Income	1,422	1,176	912	869	718	742	785	635	445	338
Effective Tax Rate	29.6%	29.9%	28.5%	28.7%	29.1%	28.9%	33.1%	33.6%	32.7%	32.1%
Net Income	1,001	824	652	620	509	528	525	422	300	230
% Net Interest Margin	3.91	3.66	3.49	3.73	3.66	3.55	3.94	4.25	4.20	4.27
S&P Core Earnings	903	811	647	592	458	NA	NA	NA	NA	NA

Balance Sheet & Other Financial Data (Million $)										
Money Market Assets	1,794	1,761	1,491	1,424	1,502	112	90.3	427	127	54.0
Investment Securities	11,979	12,617	9,088	8,995	7,847	8,994	10,913	7,969	4,451	3,901
Commercial Loans	14,728	15,180	9,914	10,842	9,912	9,070	8,230	7,144	3,856	2,830
Other Loans	43,677	42,556	22,501	20,144	21,225	22,402	19,992	17,286	12,572	10,505
Total Assets	84,786	84,106	48,598	47,939	45,383	43,688	42,714	36,832	23,034	18,930
Demand Deposits	13,699	11,424	5,718	5,148	5,085	4,513	4,420	4,577	2,368	1,909
Time Deposits	46,679	47,243	27,015	27,779	26,463	27,510	25,569	23,773	15,383	13,139
Long Term Debt	11,938	7,240	5,712	5,386	4,748	4,478	1,751	571	400	447
Common Equity	10,614	10,749	4,452	4,178	4,036	3,458	3,065	3,000	1,913	1,599
% Return on Assets	1.2	1.2	1.4	1.3	1.1	1.2	1.3	1.4	1.4	1.3
% Return on Equity	9.4	10.8	15.1	15.1	13.6	16.2	17.3	17.2	17.1	15.2
% Loan Loss Reserve	1.3	1.3	1.4	1.3	1.3	1.2	1.2	1.3	1.2	1.3
% Loans/Deposits	99.3	101.1	102.1	98.7	100.7	98.7	95.7	85.9	91.5	85.9
% Equity to Assets	12.6	11.5	8.9	8.8	8.4	7.5	7.6	8.2	8.4	8.5

Data as orig reptd.; bef. results of disc opers/spec. items. Per share data adj. for stk. divs.; EPS diluted. E-Estimated. NA-Not Available. NM-Not Meaningful. NR-Not Ranked. UR-Under Review.

Office: 417 20th St N, Birmingham, AL 35203-3203.
Telephone: 205-944-1300.
Email: askus@regionsbank.com
Website: http://www.regions.com

Chrmn, Pres & CEO: J.W. Moore
Vice Chrmn: R.D. Horsley
Vice Chrmn: A.B. Morgan, Jr.
EVP & CFO: D.B. Jordan

Investor Contact: J.G. Kimbrough (205-244-2823)
Board of Directors: S. W. Bartholomew, Jr., G. W. Bryan, J. S. French, M. H. Greene, J. E. Harwood, R. D. Horsley, P. S. Lewis, Jr., S. W. Matlock, J. W. Moore, A. B. Morgan, Jr., J. M. Perez, M. Portera, J. R. Roberts, M. S. Starnes, W. W. Stewart, L. J. Styslinger, III, R. A. Trippeer, Jr., R. W. Waller, J. H. Watson, S. L. Wilson, H. W. Witt

Founded: 1970
Domicile: Delaware
Employees: 25,000

STANDARD &POOR'S

Reynolds American Inc

S&P Recommendation HOLD ★★★★★

Price $63.50 (as of Oct 30, 2006)

12-Mo. Target Price $67.00

Investment Style Large-Cap Value

GICS Sector Consumer Staples
Sub-Industry Tobacco

Comment RAI, the second largest U.S. cigarette manufacturer, was formed via the mid-2004 merger of R.J. Reynolds and Brown & Williamson.

Key Stock Statistics (Source S&P, Vickers, company reports)

52-Wk Range	$67.09–42.31	S&P Oper. EPS 2006E	4.25	P/E on S&P Oper. EPS 2006E	14.9	Dividend Rate/Share	$3.00
Trailing 12-Month EPS	$4.05	S&P Oper. EPS 2007E	4.35	Common Shares Outstg. (M)	295.5	Yield (%)	4.72
Trailing 12-Month P/E	15.7	S&P Core EPS 2006E	3.75	Market Capitalization(B)	$18.767	Beta	0.71
$10K Invested 5 Yrs Ago	$27,297	S&P Core EPS 2007E	3.90	Institutional Ownership (%)	65	S&P Credit Rating	BB+

Price Performance

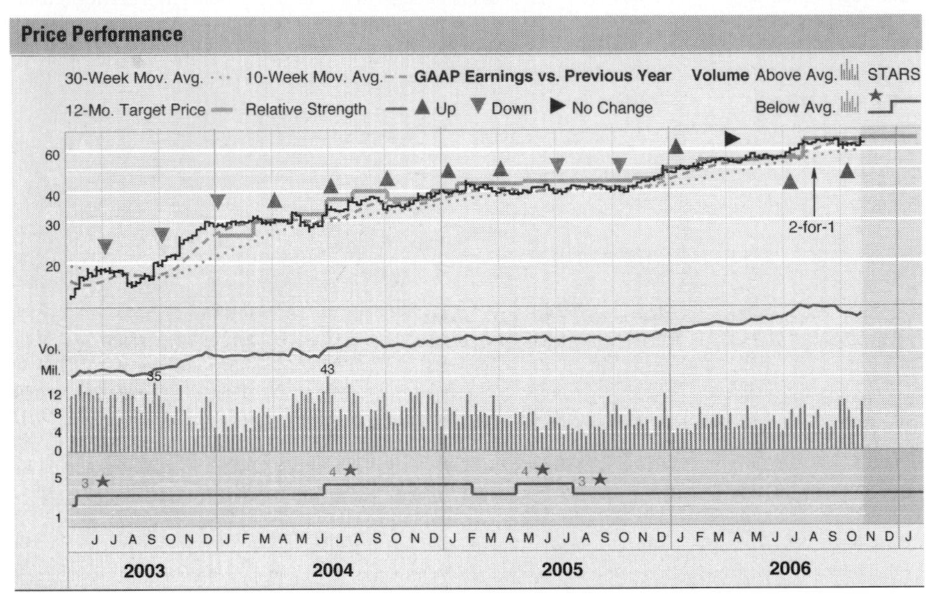

Options: ASE, CBOE, P, Ph

Analysis prepared by **Raymond Mathis** on October 30, 2006, when the stock traded at **$ 63.67**.

Highlights

- We expect revenues to rise about 6% in 2006, on a product mix shift, price increases and the Conwood acquisition. We see a likely rise in volumes for focus brands Camel and Kool, but anticipate continued volume declines for select-support and non-support brands, as marketing efforts are reduced or eliminated. Further, we see increased competitive pressures in the menthol category limiting growth for RAI's menthol brands. RAI recently acquired Conwood, the second largest maker of smokeless tobacco, for $3.5 billion.
- We anticipate a faster realization of cost synergies from the merger than we previously expected, and see a likely improvement in gross margins. Cost savings at the SG&A level are likely to continue in 2006. We look for savings from changes to sales programs, increased outsourcing and facility consolidation to boost operating margins.
- We see higher interest expense in 2006, and an effective tax rate of 38%. We project operating EPS of $4.25 in 2006. In 2007, we see EPS rising to $4.35, reflecting further merger related cost savings. The Conwood acquisition could add $0.05 to quarterly EPS.

Investment Rationale/Risk

- Our fundamental outlook for Reynolds has improved. We are encouraged by the new marketing strategy, as price increases have held and focus brands continue to gain share. Although we expect overall industry volumes to decline, we see a favorable mix shift, new product launches and acquisitions supporting the top line. Further, we believe RAI will achieve its $600 million of anticipated synergies in two years, and see wider margins in the longer term. With the Price and Engle cases dismissed, we are more confident of a favorable litigation environment for Big Tobacco.
- Risks to our recommendation and target price include near-term pressure on trading multiples due to ongoing litigation. Also, we believe RAI's anti-takeover "poison pill" is not in its shareholders' best interests.
- Assuming a perpetuity growth rate of 1% and a weighted average cost of capital of 9%, our discounted cash flow analysis calculates intrinsic value of $62 a share. Applying a forward P/E multiple of about 17X, slightly above peers, to our 2007 EPS estimate, we arrive at a relative valuation of $72. Blending these values, we arrive at our 12-month target price of $67.

Qualitative Risk Assessment

LOW | MEDIUM | **HIGH**

The tobacco industry is currently involved in significant litigation, which could affect RAI and its peers negatively. Also, we think the "poison pill," RAI's anti-takeover provision, is not in its shareholders' best interests.

Quantitative Evaluations

S&P Quality Ranking NR

D | C | B- | B | B+ | A- | A | A+

Relative Strength Rank MODERATE

44

LOWEST = 1 HIGHEST = 99

Revenue/Earnings Data

Revenue (Million $)

	1Q	2Q	3Q	4Q	Year
2006	1,960	2,291	2.19	--	--
2005	1,957	2,103	2,149	2,047	8,256
2004	1,218	1,352	1,866	2,001	6,437
2003	1,218	1,431	1,384	1,234	5,267
2002	1,515	1,705	1,585	1,406	6,211
2001	1,950	2,269	2,273	2,093	8,585

Earnings Per Share ($)

	1Q	2Q	3Q	4Q	Year
2006	0.95	1.25	1.05	E0.96	E4.25
2005	0.95	0.85	0.72	0.82	3.34
2004	0.72	0.88	1.14	0.22	2.81
2003	0.42	0.42	-20.66	-2.27	-22.04
2002	0.90	1.15	0.78	-0.58	2.32
2001	0.49	0.63	0.66	0.47	2.24

Fiscal year ended Dec. 31. Next earnings report expected: Early February. EPS Estimates based on S&P Operating Earnings; historical GAAP earnings are as reported.

Dividend Data (Dates: mm/dd Payment Date: mm/dd/yy)

Amount ($)	Date Decl.	Ex-Div. Date	Stk. of Record	Payment Date
1.250	02/01	06/07	06/09	07/03/06
2-for-1 Stk.	--	08/15	--	08/15/06
2-for-1 Stk.	07/19	08/15	07/31	08/14/06
0.750	07/19	09/07	09/11	10/02/06

Dividends have been paid since 1999. Source: Company reports.

The McGraw-Hill Companies

Reynolds American Inc

Business Summary October 30, 2006

CORPORATE OVERVIEW. On July 30, 2004, R.J. Reynolds Tobacco Co. (RJRT) merged with Brown & Williamson (B&W), the U.S. operations of British American Tobacco (BTI), to form a new publicly traded company, Reynolds American, Inc. Shareholders of RJRT received a 58% interest in the new entity, and shareholders of B&W received 42%. Combining RJRT and B&W, the second and third largest players, RAI is the second largest U.S. cigarette manufacturer, having a combined market share of over 30.8% during 2004.

RAI is the parent company of RJRT, Santa Fe Natural Tobacco, which RJRT acquired in 2002, and Lane Limited, which was purchased from BTI for $400 million as part of the merger. RJRT is the only reportable segment of RAI. In 2003, prior to the merger, RJRT began a significant restructuring plan, targeting cost savings of $1 billion by the end of 2005 through a significant work force reduction, asset divestitures and associated exit activities. Full integration of RJRT and B&W is expected to be completed in 2006. The business combination is expected to result in approximately $600 million in annualized savings by the end of 2006, including headcount reductions and operations consolidation, when compared with a separate entity basis.

In May 2006, RAI completed the acquisition of Conwood, the second largest manufacturer of smokeless tobacco products in the U.S., for $3.5 billion. RAI plans to combine Conwood with its Lane Limited subsidiary into an Other Tobacco Products division by mid-2007.

The company's leading products are its Camel and Salem brand cigarettes. The company's other brands include Winston, Doral, Vantage, More, Eclipse, American Spirit, and Now. Eclipse, a cigarette that primarily heats rather than burns tobacco in an effort to reduce second-hand smoke, is offered in selected retail chain outlets.

CORPORATE STRATEGY. At the start of 2005, RAI implemented a new portfolio strategy, designed to improve profitability, which established three categories for the combined brands of RJRT and B&W. The investment brand category, which includes Camel and Kool, receive the majority of resources to promote market share growth. The selective support brands, which includes Winston, Salem, Doral and Pall Mall, receive limited support to optimize profitability; and the remaining brands are called non-support brands, which are managed to maximize profitability.

Company Financials

Per Share Data ($) Year Ended Dec. 31	**2005**	**2004**	**2003**	**2002**	**2001**	**2000**	**1999**	**1998**	**1997**	**1996**
Tangible Book Value	NM	NM	NM	NM	NM	NM	NM	NM	NA	NA
Cash Flow	4.00	2.65	-20.81	3.34	4.72	4.10	3.11	NA	NA	NA
Earnings	3.34	2.81	-22.04	2.32	2.24	1.73	0.90	-1.38	NA	NA
S&P Core Earnings	9.69	9.96	9.44	10.79	10.00	NA	NA	NA	NA	NA
Dividends	2.10	0.95	1.90	1.86	1.65	1.55	0.39	NA	NA	NA
Payout Ratio	63%	34%	NM	80%	74%	90%	43%	NA	NA	NA
Prices:High	51.19	40.27	30.07	35.95	31.35	25.13	17.00	NA	NA	NA
Prices:Low	38.24	26.69	13.76	17.42	22.09	7.88	8.00	NA	NA	NA
P/E Ratio:High	15	14	NM	15	14	15	19	NA	NA	NA
P/E Ratio:Low	11	9	NM	8	10	5	9	NA	NA	NA

Income Statement Analysis (Million $)	**2005**	**2004**	**2003**	**2002**	**2001**	**2000**	**1999**	**1998**	**1997**	**1996**
Revenue	8,256	6,437	5,267	6,211	8,585	8,167	7,567	5,716	NA	NA
Operating Income	1,880	1,239	873	1,200	1,409	1,399	1,368	NA	NA	NA
Depreciation	195	153	151	184	491	485	482	NA	NA	NA
Interest Expense	113	85.0	111	147	150	168	268	176	NA	NA
Pretax Income	1,416	829	-3,918	683	892	748	510	-340	NA	NA
Effective Tax Rate	30.4%	24.4%	NM	38.8%	50.2%	52.9%	61.8%	NM	NA	NA
Net Income	985	627	-3,689	418	444	352	195	-299	NA	NA
S&P Core Earnings	2,857	2,221	1,615	1,947	1,980	NA	NA	NA	NA	NA

Balance Sheet & Other Financial Data (Million $)	**2005**	**2004**	**2003**	**2002**	**2001**	**2000**	**1999**	**1998**	**1997**	**1996**
Cash	1,333	1,499	1,523	1,584	2,020	2,543	1,177	3,036	NA	NA
Current Assets	5,065	4,624	3,331	3,992	3,856	3,871	2,468	4,138	NA	NA
Total Assets	14,519	14,428	9,677	14,651	15,050	15,554	14,377	16,301	NA	NA
Current Liabilities	4,149	4,055	2,865	3,427	2,792	2,776	3,068	3,885	NA	NA
Long Term Debt	1,558	1,595	1,671	1,755	1,631	1,674	1,653	2,065	NA	NA
Common Equity	6,553	6,176	3,057	6,716	8,026	8,436	7,064	7,555	NA	NA
Total Capital	8,750	8,576	5,534	9,707	11,383	11,966	10,347	11,073	NA	NA
Capital Expenditures	105	92.0	70.0	111	74.0	60.0	55.0	NA	NA	NA
Cash Flow	1,180	780	-3,538	602	935	837	677	NA	NA	NA
Current Ratio	1.2	1.1	1.2	1.2	1.4	1.4	0.8	1.1	NA	NA
% Long Term Debt of Capitalization	17.8	18.6	30.2	18.1	14.3	14.0	16.0	18.6	NA	NA
% Net Income of Revenue	11.9	9.7	NM	6.7	5.2	4.3	2.6	NM	NA	NA
% Return on Assets	6.8	5.2	NM	2.8	2.9	2.4	1.2	NM	NA	NA
% Return on Equity	15.5	13.6	NM	5.7	5.4	4.5	2.3	NM	NA	NA

Data as orig reptd.; bef. results of disc opers/spec. items. Per share data adj. for stk. divs.; EPS diluted. E-Estimated. NA-Not Available. NM-Not Meaningful. NR-Not Ranked. UR-Under Review.

Office: 401 North Main Street, Winston-Salem, NC 27102-2866.
Telephone: 336-741-2000.
Email: talktorjrt@rjrt.com
Website: http://www.reynoldsamerican.com

Chrmn, Pres & CEO: S.M. Ivey
EVP & CFO: D.M. Neal
EVP & General Counsel: E.J. Lambeth
SVP & Chief Acctg Officer: M.S. Desmond

SVP & Treas: D.A. Fawley
Board of Directors: B. Atkins, J. T. Chain, Jr., M. D. Feinstein, E. V. Goings, S. M. Ivey, N. Mensah, A. Monteiro de Castro, H. G. Powell, J. P. Viviano, T. C. Wajnert, N. R. Withington

Founded: 1875
Domicile: Delaware
Employees: 8,200

STANDARD &POOR'S

Robert Half International Inc.

S&P Recommendation STRONG BUY ★★★★★

Price $36.71 (as of Oct 27, 2006)

12-Mo. Target Price $46.00

Investment Style Mid-Cap Growth

GICS Sector Industrials
Sub-Industry Human Resource & Employment Services

Comment RHI is the world's largest specialized provider of temporary and permanent personnel in the fields of accounting and finance.

Key Stock Statistics (Source S&P, Vickers, company reports)

52-Wk Range	$43.94–29.91	S&P Oper. EPS 2006E	1.65	P/E on S&P Oper. EPS 2006E	22.2	Dividend Rate/Share	$0.32
Trailing 12-Month EPS	$1.57	S&P Oper. EPS 2007E	1.95	Common Shares Outstg. (M)	171.3	Yield (%)	0.87
Trailing 12-Month P/E	23.4	S&P Core EPS 2006E	1.65	Market Capitalization(B)	$6.289	Beta	1.88
$10K Invested 5 Yrs Ago	$16,938	S&P Core EPS 2007E	1.95	Institutional Ownership (%)	84	S&P Credit Rating	NA

Price Performance

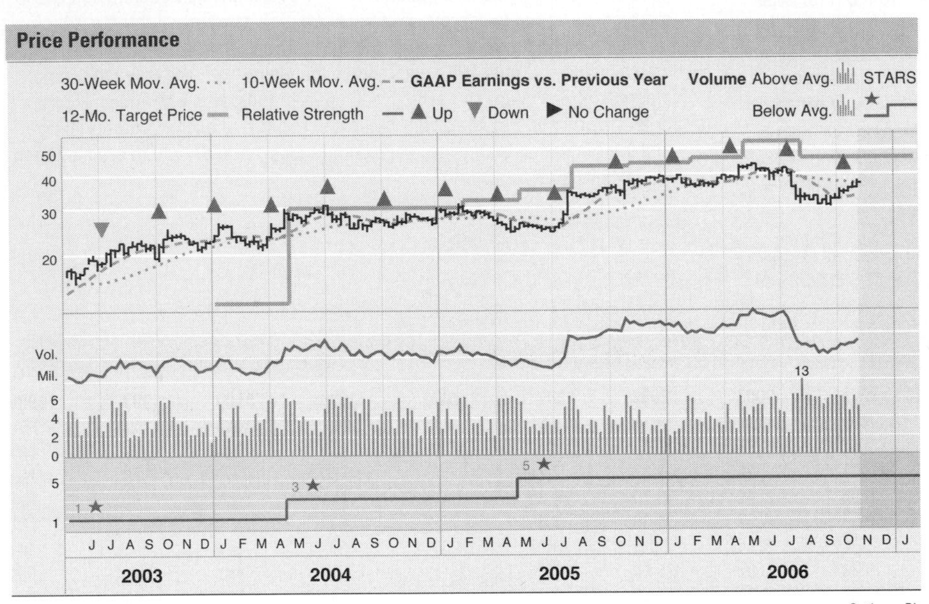

Options: Ph

Analysis prepared by **Michael W. Jaffe** on October 25, 2006, when the stock traded at **$ 37.34**.

Highlights

- We expect revenues to grow 12% in 2007, on our outlook for ongoing U.S. economic gains. We expect RHI to benefit from demand related to a heightened focus on internal accounting controls and other corporate governance requirements, in light of the well publicized corporate governance problems in the business world over the past few years. We also see a solid rise in revenues from the Protiviti unit, where volume should be raised by office additions.
- Operating margins should widen in 2007. We see these expected gains being driven by the increased demand we anticipate for RHI's services, higher billing rates, an increased proportion of permanent placements (which have better margins than the temporary placement business), and operating leverage. We see these factors outweighing the costs of RHI's continuing investments in Protiviti's international operations.
- Our 2006 and 2007 EPS estimates each include $0.06 of projected stock-based compensation. RHI's reported earnings for 2005 excluded $0.07 of stock option expense.

Investment Rationale/Risk

- RHI's operating performance has been in an uptrend since early 2004, as temporary worker markets picked up, and we believe the greater need for internal accounting controls in U.S. corporations also began to assist its performance. Although job growth in the U.S. has slowed in recent months, we expect ongoing economic gains to lead to further solid levels of job additions in coming periods. Based on these factors and valuation considerations, we believe the shares are considerably undervalued.
- Risks to our recommendation and target price include a downturn in the U.S. economy and a worse than expected impact from competition.
- The shares recently traded at 19X our 2007 EPS forecast, a small discount to RHI's peer group but at the low end of the company's valuation of the past decade. However, in light of our outlook for ongoing growth in labor markets and our belief that current corporate trends will keep demand strong for the accounting and finance personnel on which RHI concentrates, we think a higher P/E multiple is warranted. We have a 12-month target price of $46, or nearly 24X our 2007 EPS estimate.

Qualitative Risk Assessment

LOW | **MEDIUM** | HIGH

Our risk assessment reflects what we view as RHI's strong position in accounting and finance placements and a healthy balance sheet. This is offset by the highly cyclical nature of the company's business, which is largely dependent on the U.S. economy and the health of labor markets.

Quantitative Evaluations

S&P Quality Ranking B

D | C | B- | **B** | B+ | A- | A | A+

Relative Strength Rank STRONG

74

LOWEST = 1 HIGHEST = 99

Revenue/Earnings Data

Revenue (Million $)

	1Q	2Q	3Q	4Q	Year
2006	943.9	981.8	1,028	--	--
2005	770.0	816.7	867.0	884.8	3,338
2004	572.3	641.2	708.0	754.2	2,676
2003	473.2	483.0	501.1	517.7	1,975
2002	468.5	473.1	484.8	478.6	1,905
2001	719.3	648.4	574.7	510.5	2,453

Earnings Per Share ($)

2006	0.38	0.39	0.43	**E**0.45	**E**1.65
2005	0.29	0.33	0.37	0.37	1.36
2004	0.09	0.18	0.24	0.28	0.79
2003	-0.02	Nil	0.03	0.03	0.04
2002	0.05	0.02	-0.02	-0.04	0.01
2001	0.26	0.21	0.13	0.07	0.67

Fiscal year ended Dec. 31. Next earnings report expected: Late January. EPS Estimates based on S&P Operating Earnings; historical GAAP earnings are as reported.

Dividend Data (Dates: mm/dd Payment Date: mm/dd/yy)

Amount ($)	Date Decl.	Ex-Div. Date	Stk. of Record	Payment Date
0.070	11/01	11/22	11/25	12/15/05
0.080	02/15	02/23	02/27	03/15/06
0.080	05/02	05/23	05/25	06/15/06
0.080	08/01	08/23	08/25	09/15/06

Dividends have been paid since 2004. Source: Company reports.

Please read the Required Disclosures and Analyst Certification on the last page of this report.

Robert Half International Inc.

Business Summary October 25, 2006

Robert Half International is the world's largest specialized staffing service in the fields of accounting and finance. In May 2002, RHI expanded its offerings to include risk consulting and internal audit services through its Protiviti unit. In 2005, the company derived 79% of its revenue base from activities in temporary and consultant staffing, 7% from permanent placement staffing, and the remaining 14% from risk consulting and internal audit services. Foreign operations accounted for 19% of RHI's revenues in 2005. At March 1, 2006, the company's staffing businesses had more than 330 offices in 42 states, the District of Columbia, and 13 foreign nations, while Protiviti had 50 offices in 22 states and 11 foreign nations.

RHI's Accountemps temporary services division offers customers an economical means of dealing with uneven or peak work loads for accounting, tax and finance personnel. The temporary workers are employees of Accountemps, and are paid by Accountemps only when working on customer assignments. The customer pays a fixed rate for hours worked. If the client converts the temporary hire to a permanent worker, it typically pays a one-time fee for the conversion.

RHI offers permanent placement services through Robert Half Finance & Accounting, which specializes in accounting, financial, tax and banking personnel. Fees for successful permanent placements are paid only by the employer and are usually a percentage of the new employee's annual salary.

Since the early 1990s, the company has expanded into additional specialty fields. OfficeTeam, formed in 1991, provides skilled temporary and full-time administrative and office personnel. In 1992, RHI acquired Robert Half Legal (formerly The Affiliates), which places temporary and regular employees in attorney, paralegal, legal administrative and other legal support positions. In 1994, Robert Half Technology (formerly RHI Consulting) was created to concentrate on the placement of temporary and contract information technology professionals. In 1997, the company established Robert Half Management Resources (formerly RHI Management Resources) to provide senior level project professionals specializing in the accounting and finance fields. The Creative Group, which started up in 1999, provides project staffing in the advertising, marketing ,and Web design fields. In 2005, Accountemps provided 37% of revenues, OfficeTeam 20%, other placement businesses 29%, and Protiviti 14%.

Company Financials

Per Share Data ($) Year Ended Dec. 31	**2005**	**2004**	**2003**	**2002**	**2001**	**2000**	**1999**	**1998**	**1997**	**1996**
Tangible Book Value	4.72	4.30	3.65	3.41	3.69	3.13	2.28	1.89	1.33	0.75
Cash Flow	1.66	1.07	0.42	0.42	1.07	1.30	0.98	0.82	0.59	0.40
Earnings	1.36	0.79	0.04	0.01	0.67	1.00	0.77	0.70	0.50	0.33
S&P Core Earnings	1.29	0.71	-0.11	-0.17	0.51	NA	NA	NA	NA	NA
Dividends	0.28	0.18	Nil	Nil	Nil	Nil	Nil	Nil	Nil	Nil
Payout Ratio	21%	23%	Nil	Nil	Nil	Nil	Nil	Nil	Nil	Nil
Prices:High	39.86	30.98	25.18	30.90	30.90	38.63	24.19	30.13	21.53	13.83
Prices:Low	23.95	20.69	11.44	11.94	18.50	12.34	10.22	14.50	11.13	6.50
P/E Ratio:High	29	39	NM	NM	46	39	32	43	43	41
P/E Ratio:Low	18	26	NM	NM	28	12	13	21	22	19
Income Statement Analysis (Million $)										
Revenue	3,338	2,676	1,975	1,905	2,453	2,699	2,081	1,793	1,303	899
Operating Income	433	280	75.0	71.2	261	348	268	240	172	113
Depreciation	51.3	49.1	65.9	72.3	73.1	56.6	39.1	24.6	17.7	11.9
Interest Expense	Nil	Nil	Nil	Nil	Nil	Nil	Nil	Nil	Nil	0.71
Pretax Income	392	235	11.7	3.50	196	302	235	221	159	104
Effective Tax Rate	39.3%	40.1%	45.5%	38.0%	38.3%	38.3%	39.7%	40.5%	41.0%	41.1%
Net Income	238	141	6.39	2.17	121	186	141	132	93.7	61.1
S&P Core Earnings	224	125	-18.4	-30.2	91.1	NA	NA	NA	NA	NA
Balance Sheet & Other Financial Data (Million $)										
Cash	458	437	377	317	347	239	151	166	131	80.2
Current Assets	1,017	916	699	643	686	672	491	430	334	218
Total Assets	1,319	1,199	980	936	994	971	777	704	561	416
Current Liabilities	337	280	189	184	177	237	176	153	122	86.6
Long Term Debt	2.70	2.27	2.34	2.40	2.48	2.54	2.60	3.40	4.53	5.07
Common Equity	971	912	789	745	806	719	576	522	419	308
Total Capital	974	914	791	747	808	721	601	551	439	329
Capital Expenditures	61.8	32.9	36.5	48.3	84.7	74.0	52.6	67.2	32.0	18.0
Cash Flow	289	190	72.3	74.5	194	243	181	156	111	73.0
Current Ratio	3.0	3.3	3.7	3.5	3.9	2.8	2.8	2.8	2.7	2.5
% Long Term Debt of Capitalization	0.3	0.2	0.3	0.3	0.3	0.4	0.4	0.6	1.1	1.6
% Net Income of Revenue	7.1	5.3	0.3	0.1	4.9	6.9	6.8	7.3	7.2	6.8
% Return on Assets	18.9	12.9	0.7	0.2	12.3	21.3	19.1	20.8	19.2	17.1
% Return on Equity	25.3	16.5	0.8	0.3	15.9	28.7	25.7	28.0	25.8	22.8

Data as orig reptd.; bef. results of disc opers/spec. items. Per share data adj. for stk. divs.; EPS diluted. E-Estimated. NA-Not Available. NM-Not Meaningful. NR-Not Ranked. UR-Under Review.

Office: 2884 Sand Hill Rd Ste 200, Menlo Park, CA 94025-7072.
Telephone: 650-234-6000.
Website: http://www.rhi.com
Chrmn & CEO: H.M. Messmer, Jr.

Pres, Vice Chrmn & CFO: M.K. Waddell
COO: P.F. Gentzkow
VP & Treas: M. Buckley
VP, Secy & General Counsel: S. Karel

Board of Directors: A. S. Berwick, Jr., F. P. Furth, E. W. Gibbons, H. M. Messmer, Jr., T. J. Ryan, J. S. Schaub, M. K. Waddell

Founded: 1967
Domicile: Delaware
Employees: 230,000

STANDARD &POOR'S

Rockwell Automation Inc.

S&P Recommendation HOLD ★★★★★

Price $63.22 (as of Oct 27, 2006)

12-Mo. Target Price $65.00

Investment Style Large-Cap Value

GICS Sector Industrials
Sub-Industry Electrical Components & Equipment

Comment This former aerospace and defense contractor (formerly Rockwell International) now primarily manufactures automated industrial equipment and power generators.

Key Stock Statistics (Source S&P, Vickers, company reports)

52-Wk Range	$79.47–52.15	S&P Oper. EPS 2007E	3.75	P/E on S&P Oper. EPS 2007E	16.9	Dividend Rate/Share	$0.90
Trailing 12-Month EPS	$3.47	S&P Oper. EPS 2008E	NA	Common Shares Outstg. (M)	175.9	Yield (%)	1.42
Trailing 12-Month P/E	18.2	S&P Core EPS 2007E	3.74	Market Capitalization(B)	$11.123	Beta	1.14
$10K Invested 5 Yrs Ago	$48,279	S&P Core EPS 2008E	NA	Institutional Ownership (%)	64	S&P Credit Rating	A

Price Performance

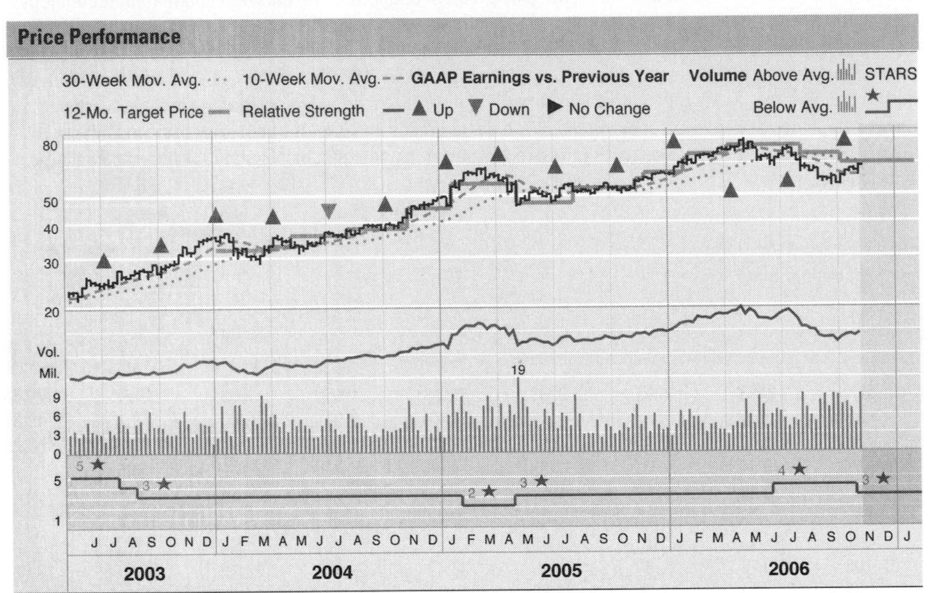

Options: CBOE

Highlights

➤ The STARS recommendation for ROK has recently been changed to 3 (hold) from 4 (buy). The Highlights section of this Stock Report will be updated accordingly.

Investment Rationale/Risk

➤ The Investment Rationale/Risk section of this Stock Report will be updated shortly. For the latest News story on ROK from MarketScope, see below.

➤ 10/24/06 02:57 pm EDT... S&P DOWNGRADES SHARES OF ROCKWELL AUTOMATION TO HOLD FROM BUY (ROK 59.53***): ROK posts Sep-Q EPS of $0.97, excluding $0.07 unusual gain, vs. $0.70, above our estimate of $0.84, on a 7.7% sales rise. Sales and operating income were below our estimate, but were more than offset by a lower-than-expected tax rate and lower share count. ROK says it is moving ahead with plans to sell the Power Systems business. We are maintaining our FY 08 (Sep.) EPS estimate of $3.75, and our 12-month target price of $65. However, with signs of slower growth and the share price within 10% of our target price, we prefer a more cautious stance on the shares. /R.Tortoriello

Qualitative Risk Assessment

LOW | **MEDIUM** | HIGH

Our risk assessment reflects the company's highly-cyclical end market demand, offset by corporate governance practices that we view as favorable and an S&P Quality Ranking of B+, reflecting stability in earnings and dividend growth.

Quantitative Evaluations

S&P Quality Ranking B+

D | C | B- | B | **B+** | A- | A | A+

Relative Strength Rank MODERATE

64

LOWEST = 1 HIGHEST = 99

Revenue/Earnings Data

Revenue (Million $)

	1Q	2Q	3Q	4Q	Year
2006	1,301	1,378	1,428	1,454	5,561
2005	1,185	1,218	1,265	1,335	5,003
2004	990.3	1,080	1,135	1,206	4,411
2003	984.0	1,029	1,033	1,058	4,104
2002	939.0	958.0	995.0	1,017	3,909
2001	1,107	1,171	1,027	974.0	4,279

Earnings Per Share ($)

	1Q	2Q	3Q	4Q	Year
2006	0.80	0.83	0.83	1.04	3.49
2005	0.65	0.75	0.68	0.69	2.77
2004	0.30	0.39	0.66	0.51	1.85
2003	0.22	0.26	0.67	0.33	1.49
2002	0.16	0.31	0.47	0.26	1.20
2001	0.38	0.38	-0.15	0.07	0.68

Fiscal year ended Sep. 30. Next earnings report expected: Late January. EPS Estimates based on S&P Operating Earnings; historical GAAP earnings are as reported.

Dividend Data (Dates: mm/dd Payment Date: mm/dd/yy)

Amount ($)	Date Decl.	Ex-Div. Date	Stk. of Record	Payment Date
0.225	11/02	11/09	11/14	12/05/05
0.225	02/01	02/09	02/13	03/06/06
0.225	04/05	05/11	05/15	06/05/06
0.225	06/02	08/10	08/14	09/05/06

Dividends have been paid since 1948. Source: Company reports.

Rockwell Automation Inc.

Business Summary September 29, 2006

CORPORATE OVERVIEW. In the early 1990s, Rockwell Automation (formerly Rockwell International) operated a broad range of manufacturing businesses. Following a series of divestitures that included the 2001 spinoff of Rockwell Collins, it now operates two business segments: Control Systems and Power Systems. The Control Systems (CS) segment accounted for 82% of FY 05 (Sep.) total revenues and 87% of total operating profits, with 18.4% profit margins. CS supplies industrial automation products, systems, software and services focused on helping customers control, monitor and improve manufacturing processes. Products include industrial components, power control and motor management products, programmable logic controllers (PLCs), input/output devices, sensors and software. Major markets served include consumer products, food and beverage, transportation, metals, mining, pulp and paper, and oil and gas. Competitors include Emerson Electric, GE, and Schneider Electric.

The Power Systems (PS) segment (18% of total sales and 13% of operating profits; 12.5% operating margins) makes power transmission components, gear reducers, speed drives, shaft mounted reducers, conveyor pulleys, shaft couplings, clutches, motor brakes, mounted bearings and motors. Products are marketed mainly under the Dodge and Reliance Electric brand names. Major markets served include mining, aggregate, food/beverage, forestry, petrochemicals, metals, unit handling, air handling and environmental. Competitors include Baldor Electric, Emerson, and Regal-Beloit. In 2005, 62% of total sales were in the U.S.

Company Financials

Per Share Data ($) Year Ended Sep. 30	**2006**	**2005**	**2004**	**2003**	**2002**	**2001**	**2000**	**1999**	**1998**	**1997**
Tangible Book Value	NA	2.95	3.95	2.41	2.61	2.23	6.90	6.56	10.05	14.67
Cash Flow	NA	3.68	2.83	2.53	2.29	5.39	4.80	4.74	0.99	5.00
Earnings	3.49	2.77	1.85	1.49	1.20	0.68	3.35	3.01	-0.55	2.97
S&P Core Earnings	NA	2.68	1.88	1.16	0.75	-0.06	NA	NA	NA	NA
Dividends	0.90	0.78	0.66	0.66	0.66	0.93	1.02	1.02	1.02	1.16
Payout Ratio	26%	28%	36%	44%	55%	137%	30%	34%	NM	42%
Prices:High	79.47	63.30	49.97	36.10	22.79	49.45	54.50	64.94	61.63	70.63
Prices:Low	53.49	45.40	28.45	18.75	14.71	11.78	27.69	39.94	32.13	44.38
P/E Ratio:High	23	23	27	24	19	73	16	22	NM	26
P/E Ratio:Low	15	16	15	13	12	17	8	13	NM	16

Income Statement Analysis (Million $)	**2006**	**2005**	**2004**	**2003**	**2002**	**2001**	**2000**	**1999**	**1998**	**1997**
Revenue	NA	5,003	4,411	4,104	3,000	4,270	7,151	7,040	0,752	7,702
Operating Income	NA	944	691	543	488	1,079	1,223	1,203	1,001	1,367
Depreciation	NA	171	187	198	206	872	276	337	306	484
Interest Expense	NA	45.8	41.7	52.0	66.0	83.0	73.0	84.0	58.0	27.0
Pretax Income	NA	737	438	299	233	168	943	890	25.0	923
Effective Tax Rate	NA	29.7%	19.2%	5.69%	3.00%	25.6%	32.6%	34.6%	536.0%	36.5%
Net Income	NA	518	354	282	226	125	636	582	-109	586
S&P Core Earnings	NA	498	361	221	142	-12.0	NA	NA	NA	NA

Balance Sheet & Other Financial Data (Million $)	**2006**	**2005**	**2004**	**2003**	**2002**	**2001**	**2000**	**1999**	**1998**	**1997**
Cash	NA	464	474	226	289	121	190	356	103	283
Current Assets	NA	2,187	2,026	1,736	1,775	1,697	3,206	3,582	4,096	3,684
Total Assets	NA	4,525	4,201	3,986	4,024	4,074	6,390	6,704	7,170	7,971
Current Liabilities	NA	941	864	820	966	867	1,820	2,108	1,983	1,970
Long Term Debt	NA	748	758	764	767	922	924	911	908	156
Common Equity	NA	1,649	1,861	1,587	1,609	1,600	2,669	2,637	3,245	4,811
Total Capital	NA	2,397	2,708	2,388	2,534	2,693	3,593	3,548	4,153	4,967
Capital Expenditures	NA	124	98.0	109	104	157	315	377	408	683
Cash Flow	NA	690	541	480	432	997	912	919	197	1,070
Current Ratio	NA	2.3	2.3	2.1	1.8	2.0	1.8	1.7	2.1	1.9
% Long Term Debt of Capitalization	NA	31.2	28.0	32.0	30.3	34.2	25.7	25.7	21.9	3.2
% Net Income of Revenue	NA	10.4	8.0	6.9	5.8	2.9	8.9	8.3	NM	7.5
% Return on Assets	NA	11.9	8.7	7.1	5.6	2.7	9.8	8.4	NM	6.5
% Return on Equity	NA	29.5	20.5	17.6	14.1	5.9	24.4	19.8	NM	12.9

Data as orig reptd.; bef. results of disc opers/spec. items. Per share data adj. for stk. divs.; EPS diluted. E-Estimated. NA-Not Available. NM-Not Meaningful. NR-Not Ranked. UR-Under Review.

Office: 777 East Wisconsin Avenue, Milwaukee, WI 53202-5317.
Telephone: 414-212-5200.
Website: http://www.rockwellautomation.com
Chrmn, Pres & CEO: K.D. Nosbusch

SVP & CFO: J. Gelly
SVP, Secy & General Counsel: D.M. Hagerman

Board of Directors: B. C. Alewine, D. H. Davis, Jr., V. Istock, B. C. Johnson, W. T. McCormick, Jr., K. Nosbusch, B. M. Rockwell, D. Speer, J. F. Toot, Jr., K. F. Yontz

Founded: 1928
Domicile: Delaware
Employees: 21,000

STANDARD &POOR'S

Rockwell Collins Inc.

S&P Recommendation HOLD ★★★★★

Price $57.90 (as of Oct 27, 2006)

12-Mo. Target Price $60.00

Investment Style Large-Cap Growth

GICS Sector Industrials
Sub-Industry Aerospace & Defense

Comment This company is one of the world's largest makers of military and commercial electronics, including cockpit controls, communications and navigation systems, and in-flight entertainment systems.

Key Stock Statistics (Source S&P, Vickers, company reports)

52-Wk Range	$60.41–43.25	S&P Oper. EPS 2006E	2.67	P/E on S&P Oper. EPS 2006E	21.7	Dividend Rate/Share	$0.64
Trailing 12-Month EPS	$2.55	S&P Oper. EPS 2007E	3.05	Common Shares Outstg. (M)	171.4	Yield (%)	1.11
Trailing 12-Month P/E	22.7	S&P Core EPS 2006E	2.35	Market Capitalization(B)	$9.925	Beta	0.92
$10K Invested 5 Yrs Ago	$42,233	S&P Core EPS 2007E	2.74	Institutional Ownership (%)	68	S&P Credit Rating	NA

Price Performance

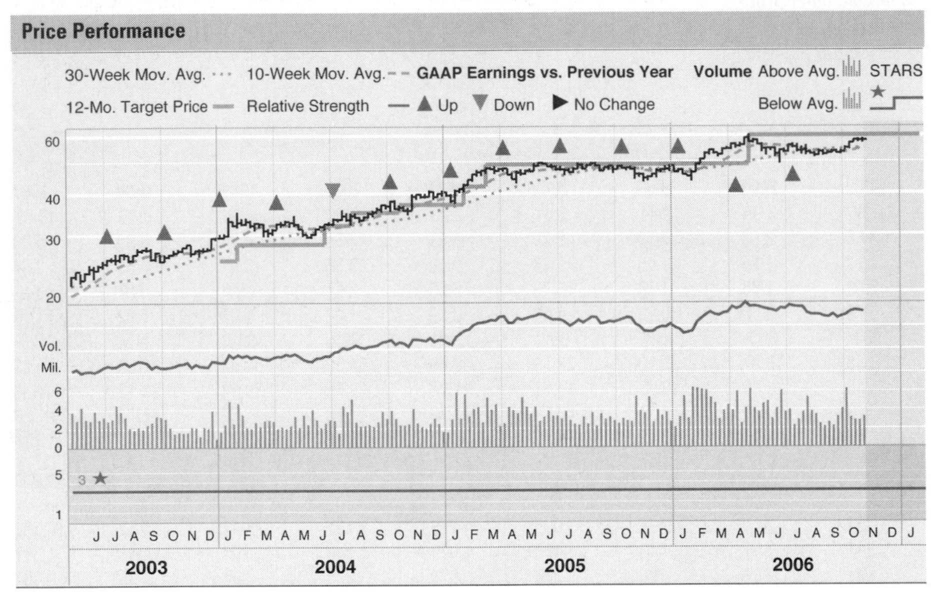

Analysis prepared by **Richard Tortoriello** on August 14, 2006, when the stock traded at **$ 52.49**.

Highlights

- We estimate that revenues will rise about 12% in FY 06 (Sep.), driven by expected advances in higher-margin government/military aircraft-related component sales (54% of estimated 2006 revenues) and commercial aerospace-related component sales (46%). We project a 13% revenue increase in FY 07.
- We project that improved operating leverage from the expected volume sales hikes, as well as increased sales of COL's higher-margin military electronics offerings, should allow operating profit margins to expand to 19.7%, from 18.1% in FY 05. For FY 06, we forecast a modest improvement in profit margins, to 20.5%.
- Based on these projections and assuming a 31% tax rate, we project EPS of $2.67 for FY 06, rising 14%, to $3.05, in FY 07. We expect free cash flow (cash flow from operating activities less capital expenditures) per share to total about $2.45 in FY 06, and expect COL to continue to use excess cash to repurchase shares.

Investment Rationale/Risk

- Our hold opinion is based primarily on our positive outlook for the aerospace market, the company's strong market position in its primary offerings, and its recent relatively high earnings yield of 5.1%.
- Risks to our recommendation and target price include unanticipated deterioration in COL's primary commercial and military avionics end markets. Other major risks include loss of government contracts, other competitive threats, and the possibility of manufacturing and other operational mis-steps.
- Our 12-month target price of $60 is based primarily on our discounted free cash flow model, which values COL by adding the discounted sum of cash earnings expanding at projected 10-year compound annual growth rates (CAGRs) of 11%-15%, and at 3.0% thereafter. We calculate our CAGR assumptions by multiplying our sustainable 15%-20% average ROE estimates by our projected 75% earnings retention rate. Our weighted average cost of capital is 9%.

Qualitative Risk Assessment

LOW | **MEDIUM** | HIGH

Our risk assessment reflects the company's exposure to the airline industry, dependence on U.S. military procurement and R&D budgets and high fixed-cost structure, offset by what we view as a solid balance sheet, strong returns, and corporate governance practices that we consider favorable versus peers.

Quantitative Evaluations

S&P Quality Ranking NR

D | C | B- | B | B+ | A- | A | A+

Relative Strength Rank MODERATE

63

LOWEST = 1 HIGHEST = 99

Revenue/Earnings Data

Revenue (Million $)

	1Q	2Q	3Q	4Q	Year
2006	881.0	957.0	964.0	--	--
2005	763.0	829.0	890.0	963.0	3,445
2004	628.0	719.0	744.0	839.0	2,930
2003	561.0	618.0	620.0	743.0	2,542
2002	563.0	608.0	623.0	698.0	2,492
2001	587.0	690.0	727.0	816.0	2,820

Earnings Per Share ($)

2006	0.59	0.65	0.70	E0.73	E2.67
2005	0.50	0.52	0.56	0.62	2.20
2004	0.38	0.39	0.42	0.48	1.67
2003	0.27	0.33	0.43	0.40	1.43
2002	0.26	0.31	0.33	0.38	1.28
2001	0.30	0.31	0.36	-0.26	0.72

Fiscal year ended Sep. 30. Next earnings report expected: Early November. EPS Estimates based on S&P Operating Earnings; historical GAAP earnings are as reported.

Dividend Data (Dates: mm/dd Payment Date: mm/dd/yy)

Amount ($)	Date Decl.	Ex-Div. Date	Stk. of Record	Payment Date
0.120	11/01	11/09	11/14	12/05/05
0.120	01/23	02/09	02/13	03/06/06
0.160	04/28	05/11	05/15	06/05/06
0.160	07/31	08/10	08/14	09/05/06

Dividends have been paid since 2001. Source: Company reports.

Rockwell Collins Inc.

STANDARD &POOR'S

Business Summary August 14, 2006

CORPORATE OVERVIEW. This global $3.5 billion revenue aircraft electronics (avionics) maker conducts its business through two segments: Commercial Systems and Government Systems. CS (47% of revenues and 51% of earnings before interest and taxes (EBIT), and EBIT margins of 18% in FY 05 (Sep.)) primarily makes cockpit control equipment and inflight entertainment systems. CS also provides a range of repair and overhaul services. GS (53%; 49%; 16%) primarily makes communication radios and cockpit displays installed in military jets. GS also makes navigation equipment embedded in guided missiles.

MARKET PROFILE. COL's primary large-jet manufacturing customers include Boeing and Airbus. Principal small-jet making customers include Canada's Bombardier, Brazil's Embraer, the General Dynamics Gulfstream unit, and Textron's Cessna division. The commercial aviation electronics equipment market totals about $5 billion. GS primarily sells its wares to defense industry giants Lockheed Martin, Raytheon and Northrop Grumman. COL's served military market totals about $6 billion. Demand for commercial aviation electronics (avionics) is ultimately driven by airline profitability and air traffic growth. Based on the latest Air Transport Association statistics, from 1994 through 2004 the U.S. airline industry generated annual operating earnings as high as $9.3 billion, and losses of as much as $10.3 billion. Based on the latest statistics provided by independent aviation research firm Avitas, Inc., from 1994 through 2004, passenger air traffic grew at a 5.9% annual rate. Regarding COL's commercial avionics end markets, from 1994 through 2004, demand for commercial aircraft cockpit controls grew at a 1.9% average annual rate (AAR), based on statistics provided by the Aerospace Industries Association (AIA). Demand for COL's military cockpit controls is driven by growth in the procurement and research and development segments of the U.S. military budget (40% of global military spending). In turn, growth in procurement and R&D budgets is driven by the U.S. military's anticipated long-term needs, the current geopolitical environment, and U.S. government budget allocations. Based on U.S. Defense Department statistics, in the past 10 years (government FY 94 (Oct.) through FY 04), procurement and R&D budgets grew at 5.3% and 5.1% AARs, respectively. From 1994 through 2004, defense-related cockpit controls equipment grew at a 4.7% AAR, based on statistics provided by the AIA.

Company Financials

Per Share Data ($) Year Ended Sep. 30	**2005**	**2004**	**2003**	**2002**	**2001**	**2000**	**1999**	**1998**	**1997**	**1996**
Tangible Book Value	2.13	3.29	2.21	2.93	4.48	NA	NA	NA	NA	NA
Cash Flow	2.86	2.28	2.02	1.85	1.47	1.87	NA	NA	NA	NA
Earnings	2.20	1.67	1.43	1.28	0.72	1.35	NA	NA	NA	NA
S&P Core Earnings	2.04	1.47	0.82	0.46	NA	NA	NA	NA	NA	NA
Dividends	0.48	0.39	0.36	0.36	Nil	NA	NA	NA	NA	NA
Payout Ratio	22%	23%	25%	28%	Nil	NA	NA	NA	NA	NA
Prices:High	49.80	40.94	30.10	28.00	27.12	NA	NA	NA	NA	NA
Prices:Low	37.22	29.16	17.20	18.50	11.80	NA	NA	NA	NA	NA
P/E Ratio:High	23	25	21	22	38	NA	NA	NA	NA	NA
P/E Ratio:Low	17	17	12	14	16	NA	NA	NA	NA	NA
Income Statement Analysis (Million $)										
Revenue	3,445	2,930	2,542	2,492	2,820	2,510	NA	NA	NA	NA
Operating Income	660	539	440	427	492	492	NA	NA	NA	NA
Depreciation	119	109	105	105	131	99.0	NA	NA	NA	NA
Interest Expense	11.0	8.00	3.00	6.00	3.00	20.0	NA	NA	NA	NA
Pretax Income	547	430	368	341	224	381	NA	NA	NA	NA
Effective Tax Rate	27.6%	30.0%	29.9%	30.8%	37.9%	32.5%	NA	NA	NA	NA
Net Income	396	301	258	236	139	257	NA	NA	NA	NA
S&P Core Earnings	367	264	148	86.8	59.2	NA	NA	NA	NA	NA
Balance Sheet & Other Financial Data (Million $)										
Cash	145	196	66.0	49.0	60.0	20.0	NA	NA	NA	NA
Current Assets	1,775	1,663	1,427	1,438	1,639	1,531	NA	NA	NA	NA
Total Assets	3,140	2,874	2,591	2,560	2,628	2,628	NA	NA	NA	NA
Current Liabilities	1,177	964	901	1,043	1,135	1,073	NA	NA	NA	NA
Long Term Debt	200	201	Nil	Nil	Nil	Nil	NA	NA	NA	NA
Common Equity	939	1,133	833	987	1,110	1,086	NA	NA	NA	NA
Total Capital	1,139	1,334	833	987	1,110	1,086	NA	NA	NA	NA
Capital Expenditures	111	94.0	72.0	62.0	110	NA	NA	NA	NA	NA
Cash Flow	515	410	363	341	270	356	NA	NA	NA	NA
Current Ratio	1.5	1.7	1.6	1.4	1.4	1.4	NA	NA	NA	NA
% Long Term Debt of Capitalization	17.6	15.1	Nil	Nil	Nil	Nil	NA	NA	NA	NA
% Net Income of Revenue	11.5	10.3	10.1	9.5	4.9	10.2	NA	NA	NA	NA
% Return on Assets	13.2	11.0	10.0	9.1	5.9	NA	NA	NA	NA	NA
% Return on Equity	38.2	30.6	28.4	22.5	13.8	NA	NA	NA	NA	NA

Data as orig reptd.; bef. results of disc opers/spec. items. Per share data adj. for stk. divs.; EPS diluted. E-Estimated. NA-Not Available. NM-Not Meaningful. NR-Not Ranked. UR-Under Review.

Office: 400 Collins Rd NE, Cedar Rapids, IA 52498-0503.
Telephone: 319-295-1000.
Email: investorrelations@rockwellcollins.com
Website: http://www.rockwellcollins.com

Chrmn, Pres & CEO: C.M. Jones
COO & EVP: G.S. Churchill
SVP & CFO: P.E. Allen
SVP, Secy & General Counsel: G.R. Chadick

VP & Cntlr: D. Brehm
Investor Contact: D. Crookshank (319-295-7575)
Board of Directors: D. R. Beall, A. J. Carbone, M. P. Carns, C. A. Davis, M. Donegan, R. J. Ferris, C. M. Jones, A. J. Policano, C. L. Shavers, J. F. Toot, Jr.

Employees: 17,100

STANDARD &POOR'S

Rohm and Haas Co

S&P Recommendation HOLD ★★★★★

Price $52.15 (as of Oct 27, 2006)

12-Mo. Target Price $54.00

Investment Style Large-Cap Value

GICS Sector Materials
Sub-Industry Specialty Chemicals

Comment One of the world's largest producers of specialty chemicals and plastics, this company also supplies salt products.

Key Stock Statistics (Source S&P, Vickers, company reports)

52-Wk Range	$53.00–41.92	S&P Oper. EPS 2006**E**	3.41	P/E on S&P Oper. EPS 2006**E**	15.3	Dividend Rate/Share	$1.32
Trailing 12-Month EPS	$3.12	S&P Oper. EPS 2007**E**	3.50	Common Shares Outstg. (M)	218.4	Yield (%)	2.53
Trailing 12-Month P/E	16.7	S&P Core EPS 2006**E**	3.46	Market Capitalization(B)	$11.391	Beta	1.05
$10K Invested 5 Yrs Ago	$17,154	S&P Core EPS 2007**E**	3.53	Institutional Ownership (%)	55	S&P Credit Rating	A-

Price Performance

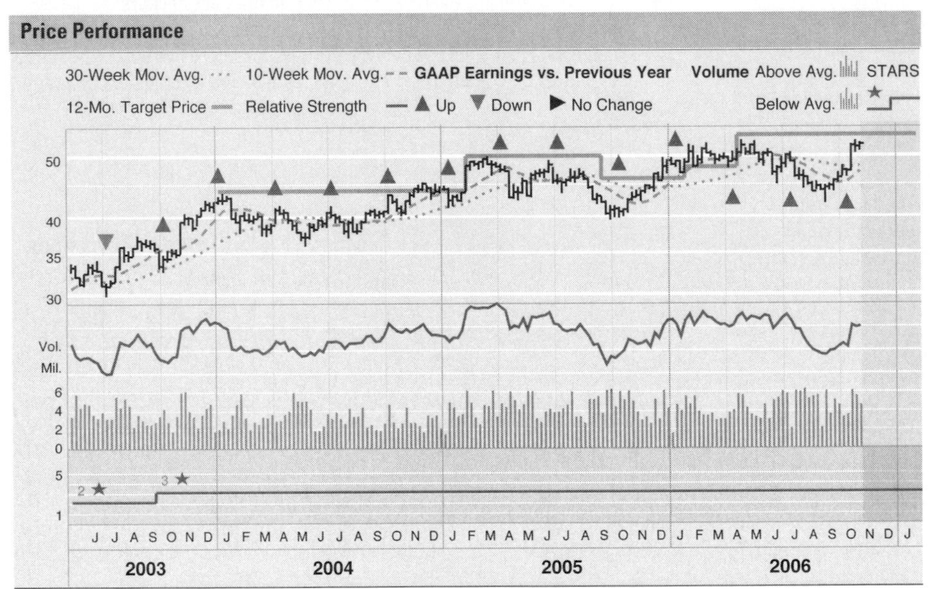

Options: ASE

Analysis prepared by **Richard O'Reilly, CFA** on October 03, 2006, when the stock traded at **$ 46.75**.

Highlights

- We expect sales to grow 5% in 2006, followed by a similar gain in 2007, aided by price increases in the chemicals units in response to high raw material costs. We see volume growth of about 3%-4% in 2006 on better demand in the chemicals segments. New global supplies should put downward pressure on monomer pricing and margins. We look for gains in electronic materials sales to slow in the latter half of 2006, for a full year rise of about 16%. We see salt sales declining, reflecting a significant reduction in demand for ice control salt in early 2006 due to unusually mild winter weather.
- We estimate a gross margin of about 30%--similar to 2005--helped by a continued shift in the product mix. We believe raw material costs will remain historically high in 2006, with price initiatives designed to offset increased costs. ROH suffered only minimal damage from Hurricane Rita, posting $0.03 a share of shut-down costs in the 2005 third quarter.
- We expect interest expense to be lower in 2006 due to debt reduction of $445 million in 2005, including $400 million in March 2005. We see the effective tax rate at about 29.5% versus 25.7% in 2005.

Investment Rationale/Risk

- We have a hold opinion on the shares based on total return potential. We view the company's fundamentals as favorable as we expect volume growth to continue into 2007. We project that the company will largely recover through price increases the recent surge in raw material and energy costs. Based on our 2006 EPS estimate, the shares were recently trading at a P/E multiple of 14X, modestly below the S&P 500 and below specialty chemicals peers (17X).
- Risks to our recommendation and target price include unexpected cost increases and/or supply shortages for raw materials, unsuccessful new product introductions, unusually mild winter weather and soft demand for ice-control salt, and unscheduled plant outages and interruptions by the company and/or its suppliers.
- Our 12-month target price of $54 is based on a P/E multiple of 16X, which is closer to peers, applied to our 2006 EPS estimate. The dividend, increased in 2006 for the 29th consecutive year, provides an above market yield, and we expect the dividend to continue to rise over the long term.

Qualitative Risk Assessment

LOW | **MEDIUM** | HIGH

Our risk assessment reflects our view of the broad mix and cash flow generation ability of the company's business segments, offset by the cyclical nature of many of the product lines and exposure to volatile raw material and energy costs.

Quantitative Evaluations

S&P Quality Ranking A

D | C | B- | B | B+ | A- | **A** | A+

Relative Strength Rank STRONG

81

LOWEST = 1 HIGHEST = 99

Revenue/Earnings Data

Revenue (Million $)

	1Q	2Q	3Q	4Q	Year
2006	2,083	2,081	2,065	--	--
2005	2,022	2,007	1,953	2,012	7,994
2004	1,832	1,801	1,803	1,864	7,300
2003	1,613	1,570	1,591	1,647	6,421
2002	1,381	1,457	1,454	1,435	5,727
2001	1,572	1,408	1,346	1,340	5,666

Earnings Per Share ($)

2006	0.93	0.87	0.86	**E**0.75	**E**3.41
2005	0.70	0.80	0.76	0.59	2.86
2004	0.51	0.52	0.61	0.56	2.21
2003	0.37	-0.02	0.45	0.49	1.30
2002	0.38	0.42	0.35	0.16	0.98
2001	0.22	-0.94	0.24	0.17	-0.31

Fiscal year ended Dec. 31. Next earnings report expected: Early February. EPS Estimates based on S&P Operating Earnings; historical GAAP earnings are as reported.

Dividend Data (Dates: mm/dd Payment Date: mm/dd/yy)

Amount ($)	Date Decl.	Ex-Div. Date	Stk. of Record	Payment Date
0.290	02/06	02/15	02/17	03/01/06
0.330	05/01	05/10	05/12	06/01/06
0.330	07/24	08/09	08/11	09/01/06
0.330	09/21	11/01	11/03	12/01/06

Dividends have been paid since 1927. Source: Company reports.

Rohm and Haas Co

Business Summary October 03, 2006

CORPORATE OVERVIEW. Rohm & Haas is one of the world's largest specialty chemical companies, with annual sales of about $8.0 billion. As a result of the 1999 purchase of Morton International Inc., the company is now a leading global maker of chemicals used in coatings, adhesives, sealants, plastics, and electronic materials. International operations accounted for 52% of sales in 2005.

Coatings (29% of sales and 27% of income in 2005) include polymers and resins (including opaque polymers, emulsions, rheology modifiers, binders, thickeners, dispersants) for paints, coatings, inks, paper, textile, nonwoven materials, construction products and leather finishes. Decorative paints account for over 50% of end use. The segment also includes powder coatings (4% of total sales) for automobile parts, appliances, furniture and equipment. ROH has agreed to sell its automotive liquids coatings (1%, reported as discontinued operations in 2006) business for $230 million. Adhesives and sealants (8%, 2%) consist of materials for use in pressure sensitive tapes and labels, laminated food packaging, graphic arts, and industrial products.

Performance chemicals (20%, 21%) include plastic additives (impact modifiers, processing aids, thermal stabilizers and lubricants); consumer and industrial specialties (biocides, water-soluble polymers, dispersants, antimicrobials, and scale inhibitors for industrial, household cleaning and personal care products); and process chemicals (ion exchange and fluid process chemicals for water treatment and food and chemical processing and inorganic chemicals (sodium borohydride)).

The monomer segment (18%, 25%) produces methyl methacrylate, acrylic acid and specialty monomers. ROH uses these products in many of its acrylic technologies in other segments and they are also sold externally (one-third of sales) for use in superabsorbent polymers and acrylic resins and sheet.

Company Financials

Per Share Data ($) Year Ended Dec. 31	**2005**	**2004**	**2003**	**2002**	**2001**	**2000**	**1999**	**1998**	**1997**	**1996**
Tangible Book Value	3.11	1.07	0.13	NM	NM	NM	NM	8.77	8.51	7.84
Cash Flow	5.00	4.36	3.44	3.04	2.24	4.39	5.87	4.04	3.67	3.19
Earnings	2.86	2.21	1.30	0.98	-0.31	1.61	1.27	2.52	2.13	1.82
S&P Core Earnings	2.81	1.98	0.90	0.23	-0.91	NA	NA	NA	NA	NA
Dividends	1.12	0.97	0.86	0.82	0.80	0.78	0.74	0.69	0.63	0.57
Payout Ratio	39%	44%	66%	84%	NM	48%	58%	27%	30%	32%
Prices:High	50.00	45.41	43.05	42.60	38.70	49.44	49.25	38.88	33.75	27.50
Prices:Low	39.47	35.90	26.26	30.19	24.90	24.38	28.13	26.00	23.54	18.29
P/E Ratio:High	17	21	33	43	NM	31	39	15	16	15
P/E Ratio:Low	14	16	20	31	NM	15	22	10	11	10
Income Statement Analysis (Million $)										
Revenue	7,994	7,300	6,421	5,727	5,666	6,879	5,339	3,720	3,999	3,986
Operating Income	1,522	1,291	1,264	1,066	973	1,395	1,220	898	896	839
Depreciation	481	481	478	457	562	613	902	276	279	262
Interest Expense	117	133	126	132	182	241	159	34.0	39.0	54.0
Pretax Income	872	692	415	320	-64.0	576	465	690	616	530
Effective Tax Rate	25.7%	29.9%	30.6%	31.9%	NM	39.4%	46.2%	34.1%	32.6%	31.5%
Net Income	638	496	288	218	-70.0	354	249	453	410	363
S&P Core Earnings	627	446	209	50.9	202	NA	NA	NA	NA	NA
Balance Sheet & Other Financial Data (Million $)										
Cash	566	625	196	295	92.0	92.0	57.0	16.0	40.0	11.0
Current Assets	3,205	3,247	2,527	2,543	2,421	2,781	2,497	1,287	1,397	1,456
Total Assets	9,727	10,095	9,445	9,706	10,350	11,267	11,256	3,648	3,900	3,933
Current Liabilities	1,694	1,740	1,797	1,621	1,624	2,194	2,510	875	850	886
Long Term Debt	2,074	2,563	2,468	2,872	2,720	3,225	3,122	409	509	562
Common Equity	3,917	3,697	3,357	3,333	3,815	3,693	3,475	1,488	1,671	1,597
Total Capital	7,089	7,423	6,775	7,402	7,831	8,228	7,847	2,157	2,510	2,501
Capital Expenditures	333	5.00	339	407	401	391	323	229	254	334
Cash Flow	1,119	977	766	675	492	967	1,149	723	682	625
Current Ratio	1.9	1.9	1.4	1.6	1.5	1.3	1.0	1.5	1.6	1.6
% Long Term Debt of Capitalization	29.3	34.5	36.4	38.8	34.7	39.2	39.8	19.0	20.2	22.5
% Net Income of Revenue	8.0	6.8	4.5	3.8	NM	5.1	4.7	12.2	10.3	9.1
% Return on Assets	6.4	5.1	3.0	2.2	NM	3.1	3.3	12.0	10.5	9.2
% Return on Equity	16.8	14.1	8.9	5.9	NM	9.8	10.0	28.3	24.7	21.9

Data as orig reptd.; bef. results of disc opers/spec. items. Per share data adj. for stk. divs.; EPS diluted. E-Estimated. NA-Not Available. NM-Not Meaningful. NR-Not Ranked. UR-Under Review.

Office: 100 Independence Mall W, Philadelphia, PA 19106.
Telephone: 215-592-3000.
Website: http://www.rohmhaas.com
Chrmn & CEO: R.L. Gupta

VP & CFO: J.M. Croisetiere
VP, Secy & General Counsel: R.A. Lonergan
Investor Contact: G.S. O'Brien (215-592-3409)

Board of Directors: W. J. Avery, R. L. Gupta, D. W. Haas, T. W. Haas, R. L. Keyser, R. J. Mills, J. P. Montoya, S. O. Moose, G. S. Omenn, G. L. Rogers, R. H. Schmitz, G. M. Whitesides, M. C. Whittington

Founded: 1909
Domicile: Delaware
Employees: 16,519

STANDARD &POOR'S

Rowan Companies Inc.

S&P Recommendation HOLD ★★★★★	Price $33.38 (as of Oct 31, 2006)	12-Mo. Target Price $37.00	Investment Style Mid-Cap Growth

GICS Sector Energy
Sub-Industry Oil & Gas Drilling

Comment This company performs contract oil and natural gas drilling, and builds heavy equipment and offshore drilling rigs.

Key Stock Statistics (Source S&P, Vickers, company reports)

52-Wk Range	$48.15–29.03	S&P Oper. EPS 2006E	3.71	P/E on S&P Oper. EPS 2006E	9.0	Dividend Rate/Share	$0.40
Trailing 12-Month EPS	$2.91	S&P Oper. EPS 2007E	4.76	Common Shares Outstg. (M)	110.4	Yield (%)	1.20
Trailing 12-Month P/E	11.5	S&P Core EPS 2006E	3.69	Market Capitalization(B)	$3.685	Beta	1.21
$10K Invested 5 Yrs Ago	$19,023	S&P Core EPS 2007E	4.74	Institutional Ownership (%)	85	S&P Credit Rating	NR

Price Performance

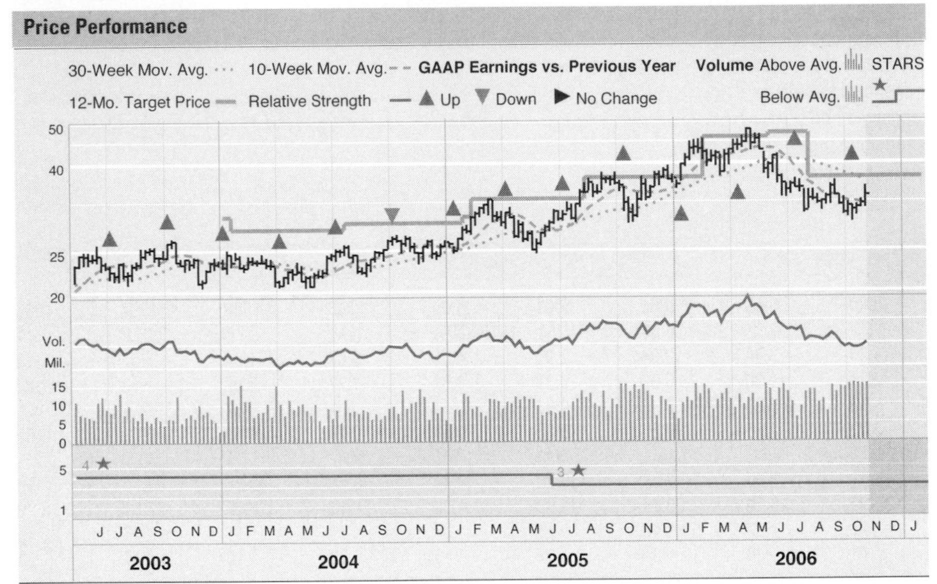

Options: ASE, CBOE, P

Analysis prepared by **Stewart Glickman, CFA** on July 27, 2006, when the stock traded at **$ 34.12**.

Highlights

- One of RDC's newbuild jackup rigs on order, the Hank Boswell, is slated for delivery in September 2006. The next newbuild jackup, the Tarzan IV, is due in September 2007. Two other newbuilds are due in June 2008 and January 2009, respectively.
- The GOM (Gulf of Mexico) jackup market remains very tight, which has pushed dayrates upward. We see this trend continuing in the near term, and we think RDC, which typically commands a higher average dayrate than the industry due to a larger number of premium jackups, will benefit. In the longer term, the approximately 60 newbuild jackups currently on order could reduce regional dayrates and utilization. However, we do not expect most such newbuilds to begin operating until the 2007-2009 time frame.
- We estimate EPS of $3.71 in 2006, rising to $4.76 in 2007. On a Standard & Poor's Core Earnings basis, we project EPS of $3.69 and $4.74 for the respective years, with divergence from operating EPS in 2006 due to estimated pension adjustments.

Investment Rationale/Risk

- With premium rigs focused in the GOM, a tightening market for jackups, we think RDC is well positioned for growth in 2006. The migration of competing rigs out of the GOM to other regions, expected to continue in 2006, should enable dayrates for jackups in the region to remain strong. While newbuild jackup deliveries loom on the horizon, mainly in 2007-2008, we believe the potential for delays in deliveries, natural rig attrition, and rising demand for rigs, if realized, would mitigate this concern.
- Risks to our recommendation and target price include lower than expected dayrates and utilization; reduced drilling activity in the GOM; and faster than expected deliveries of new premium jackups.
- Our net asset valuation model, assuming terminal growth of 3% per year and a weighted average cost of capital of 11.1%, indicates that the shares have an intrinsic value of $37. Assuming relative multiples of 6X estimated 2006 EBITDA and 10X projected 2006 cash flow (modest discounts to peers), and blending with our NAV model, our 12-month target price is $37.

Qualitative Risk Assessment

LOW	**MEDIUM**	HIGH

Our risk assessment reflects RDC's exposure to volatile crude oil and natural gas prices, capital spending decisions made by its oil and gas producing customers, and risks associated with operating in frontier regions. Offsetting these risks is the company's relatively higher specification jackup rig fleet than peers.

Quantitative Evaluations

S&P Quality Ranking B-

D	C	**B-**	B	B+	A-	A	A+

Relative Strength Rank MODERATE

47

LOWEST = 1 HIGHEST = 99

Revenue/Earnings Data

Revenue (Million $)

	1Q	2Q	3Q	4Q	Year
2006	299.8	382.9	417.1	--	--
2005	222.4	244.6	284.4	317.4	1,069
2004	170.5	190.9	234.6	202.2	708.5
2003	131.4	158.1	193.9	195.8	679.1
2002	137.8	148.5	184.2	146.8	617.3
2001	193.5	210.4	191.3	135.8	731.1

Earnings Per Share ($)

2006	0.53	0.98	0.77	**E**1.28	**E**3.71
2005	0.28	0.39	0.67	0.63	1.97
2004	-0.11	-0.02	0.09	0.15	0.25
2003	-0.18	-0.07	0.12	0.05	-0.08
2002	0.92	-0.09	0.11	-0.03	0.90
2001	0.33	0.36	0.22	-0.10	0.80

Fiscal year ended Dec. 31. Next earnings report expected: Early March. EPS Estimates based on S&P Operating Earnings; historical GAAP earnings are as reported.

Dividend Data (Dates: mm/dd Payment Date: mm/dd/yy)

Amount ($)	Date Decl.	Ex-Div. Date	Stk. of Record	Payment Date
0.25 Spl.	01/27	02/06	02/08	02/24/06
0.100	05/02	05/10	05/12	05/26/06
0.100	07/25	08/02	08/04	08/18/06

Dividends have been paid since 2005. Source: Company reports.

Rowan Companies Inc.

Business Summary July 27, 2006

CORPORATE OVERVIEW. Rowan Companies, a major provider of international and domestic contract drilling and aviation services, also operates a mini-steel mill, a manufacturing facility that produces heavy equipment, and a marine construction division. At March 15, 2006, RDC owned 16 cantilever jackups, four conventional jackups, and a fleet of 17 land rigs. Of the 20 jackups in the fleet, 13 were in the GOM, four were in the Middle East, two were in the North Sea, and one was in Eastern Canada. Drilling operations generated 73% of total revenues and 98% of total segment operating income in 2005. The company's jackup rigs perform both exploratory and development drilling and, in certain areas, well workover operations. Its larger, deepwater jackups can drill to depths of 20,000 ft. to 30,000 ft. in maximum water depths of 250 ft. to 490 ft. Of the 16 cantilever jackup rigs, three are harsh environment Gorilla Class rigs, four are enhanced Super Gorilla Class rigs, and two are Tarzan Class rigs. The Gorilla Class rigs (Gorillas II, III and IV) are heavier duty rigs intended to drill up to 30,000 ft. in water depths up to 328 ft. in extreme hostile environments (winds up to 100 miles per hour and seas up to 90 ft.). During 1998, RDC launched the first of three Super Gorilla Class rigs, Rowan Gorilla V, an enhanced Gorilla Class rig; it completed the Rowan Gorilla VI in 2000 and the Super Gorilla VII in 2001. The Super Gorilla VIII was completed in the 2003 third quarter. The Tarzan class jackup rigs are designed specifically for deeper drilling (more than 25,000 ft.) in water depths less than 300 ft. in the GOM. The first such rig, the Scooter Yeargain, was delivered in April 2004, and the second, the Bob Keller, was delivered in August 2005.

RDC's worldwide rig utilization rate increased to 96% in 2005, from 92% in 2004; average dayrates increased about 60%, to $78,100. Land rig utilization was 98% in 2005 (versus 97% in 2004), with an average day rate of $18,400 ($12,200). The manufacturing division (27% of total revenues, 2% of segment operating income) operates a mini-steel mill that recycles scrap and produces steel plate; a manufacturing facility that produces heavy equipment such as front-end loaders; and a marine group that built the Gorilla V in late 1998, the Gorilla VI in June 2000, the Gorilla VII in December 2001, the Bob Palmer in August 2003, the Scooter Yeargain in April 2004, and the Bob Keller in August 2005. This division is also constructing the Hank Boswell and the first 240C jackup.

Company Financials

Per Share Data ($) Year Ended Dec. 31	**2005**	**2004**	**2003**	**2002**	**2001**	**2000**	**1999**	**1998**	**1997**	**1996**
Tangible Book Value	14.75	12.97	11.95	12.09	11.84	11.17	8.69	8.77	7.53	5.80
Cash Flow	2.71	1.14	0.84	1.72	1.52	1.36	0.54	2.00	2.28	1.25
Earnings	1.97	0.25	-0.08	0.90	0.80	0.74	-0.12	1.43	1.76	0.70
S&P Core Earnings	1.63	0.28	-0.05	-0.31	0.65	NA	NA	NA	NA	NA
Dividends	Nil	Nil	Nil	Nil	Nil	Nil	Nil	Nil	Nil	Nil
Payout Ratio	Nil	Nil	Nil	Nil	Nil	Nil	Nil	Nil	Nil	Nil
Prices:High	39.50	27.26	26.72	27.03	33.89	34.25	21.69	32.50	43.93	24.50
Prices:Low	24.53	20.44	17.70	16.04	11.10	19.06	8.50	9.00	16.75	8.88
P/E Ratio:High	20	NM	NM	30	42	46	NM	23	25	35
P/E Ratio:Low	12	NM	NM	18	14	26	NM	6	10	13
Income Statement Analysis (Million $)										
Revenue	1,069	709	679	617	731	646	461	706	695	571
Operating Income	355	152	89.0	65.1	193	170	45.1	232	230	127
Depreciation, Depletion and Amortization	81.3	95.7	86.0	78.1	68.5	58.9	54.7	49.7	47.1	47.9
Interest Expense	22.0	18.7	15.9	15.9	13.1	12.1	11.5	1.24	16.2	27.5
Pretax Income	345	42.8	-12.0	133	120	111	-14.5	194	173	60.5
Effective Tax Rate	36.9%	38.4%	NM	35.0%	35.9%	36.7%	NM	35.7%	9.73%	NM
Net Income	218	26.4	-7.77	86.3	77.0	70.2	-9.67	124	156	61.3
S&P Core Earnings	181	28.9	-4.74	-30.2	62.8	NA	NA	NA	NA	NA
Balance Sheet & Other Financial Data (Million $)										
Cash	676	466	58.2	179	237	193	87.1	149	108	97.2
Current Assets	1,208	815	444	470	507	483	325	366	412	317
Total Assets	2,975	2,492	2,191	2,055	1,939	1,678	1,356	1,249	1,122	899
Current Liabilities	341	235	150	116	201	104	202	79.6	81.5	85.3
Long Term Debt	550	574	569	513	438	372	297	310	256	267
Common Equity	1,620	1,409	1,137	1,132	1,108	1,053	724	730	653	496
Total Capital	2,485	2,147	1,924	1,811	1,674	1,516	1,099	1,116	984	765
Capital Expenditures	200	137	250	243	305	216	205	248	181	118
Cash Flow	299	122	79.1	164	145	129	45.0	174	204	109
Current Ratio	3.5	3.5	3.0	4.1	2.5	4.6	1.6	4.6	5.1	3.7
% Long Term Debt of Capitalization	22.1	26.8	29.6	28.3	26.2	24.5	27.0	27.8	26.0	34.9
% Return on Assets	8.0	1.1	NM	4.3	4.3	4.6	NM	10.5	15.5	7.2
% Return on Equity	14.4	2.1	NM	7.7	7.1	7.9	NM	18.0	27.2	13.3

Data as orig reptd.; bef. results of disc opers/spec. items. Per share data adj. for stk. divs.; EPS diluted. E-Estimated. NA-Not Available. NM-Not Meaningful. NR-Not Ranked. UR-Under Review.

Office: 2800 Post Oak Blvd Ste 5450, Houston, TX 77056-6127.
Telephone: 713-621-7800.
Email: ir@rowancompanies.com
Website: http://www.rowancompanies.com

Chrmn, Pres & CEO: D.F. McNease
Vice Chrmn & Chief Admin: R.G. Croyle
Investor Contact: W.C. Provine (713-960-7575)
Secy & CCO: M. Trent

Cntlr: G. Hatfield
Board of Directors: R. G. Croyle, W. T. Fox III, G. Hearne, F. R. Lausen, H. E. Lentz, D. F. McNease, L. Moynihan, C. R. Palmer, P. D. Peacock

Founded: 1923
Domicile: Delaware
Employees: 4,577

STANDARD & POOR'S

Ryder System Inc

S&P Recommendation HOLD ★★★★★

Price $54.77 (as of Oct 30, 2006)

12-Mo. Target Price $55.00

Investment Style Mid-Cap Value

GICS Sector Industrials
Sub-Industry Trucking

Comment This company provides truck leasing and rental, logistics, and supply chain management solutions worldwide.

Key Stock Statistics (Source S&P, Vickers, company reports)

52-Wk Range	$59.93–39.54	S&P Oper. EPS 2006E	4.07	P/E on S&P Oper. EPS 2006E	13.5	Dividend Rate/Share	$0.72
Trailing 12-Month EPS	$3.93	S&P Oper. EPS 2007E	4.20	Common Shares Outstg. (M)	60.7	Yield (%)	1.31
Trailing 12-Month P/E	13.9	S&P Core EPS 2006E	3.33	Market Capitalization(B)	$3.326	Beta	0.69
$10K Invested 5 Yrs Ago	$29,759	S&P Core EPS 2007E	3.89	Institutional Ownership (%)	95	S&P Credit Rating	BBB+

Price Performance

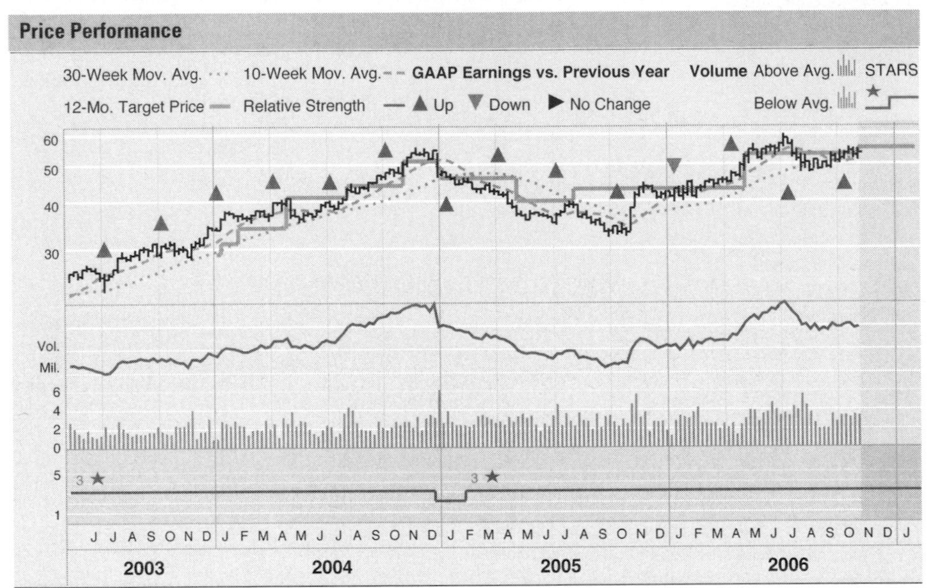

Options: ASE, CBOE, P

Analysis prepared by **Kevin Kirkeby** on October 26, 2006, when the stock traded at **$ 53.92**.

Highlights

- We forecast revenue growth of 10% in 2006, slowing to 6% in 2007, as fuel price increases--which are passed along to clients--are likely to flatten. For R's largest segment, fleet management solutions, we expect firm demand and moderate price increases in both years, supported by new customer wins and improved retention of existing customers. We see higher growth rates in the smaller supply chain solutions and contract carriage segments.
- We expect operating margins to widen modestly in 2007, primarily due to higher rates and larger revenue contributions relative to fixed costs. Interest expenses should increase due to higher debt levels in both years and rising effective rates. We see gross capital expenditures in 2006 rising to $1.8 billion, as R purchases more vehicles to support replacement initiatives and an increase in new customer leases. We also see pretax profit growth slowing in 2007 to 4%.
- We forecast EPS of $4.07 in 2006, including $0.05 per share of non-recurring items, and $4.20 in 2007. Included in our respective EPS figures are $3.6 million and $4.0 million for stock option expense.

Investment Rationale/Risk

- After a number of restructurings in the past decade, we believe R has passed the peak of its cost-cutting phase, and expect the company to focus more on a strategy of profitable revenue growth, supported by increased capital spending, leverage, and acquisitions. We forecast earnings growth to average 5% over the next five years. We see free cash flow turning positive in 2007, following two years of substantial capital expenditures, and growing at a double digit rate over the next five years.
- Risks to our opinion and target price include weaker than expected economic growth; declining leasing demand and lease rates; increased competition from traditional truckload providers; sharply rising interest rates, to which R is exposed in light of its financial leverage; and declining used vehicle prices.
- Our discounted cash flow model assumes a 7.7% cost of capital and 3.5% terminal growth, and calculates intrinsic value of $58. Our relative valuation model, which relates historical peer group valuations to profitability and leverage, estimates a forward P/E multiple of about 12X (equal to $52). Blending these models, we arrive at our 12-month target price of $55.

Qualitative Risk Assessment

LOW | **MEDIUM** | HIGH

Our risk assessment reflects our view of the company's significant financial leverage, exposure to low-margin businesses, and heavy capital spending needs to maintain its fleet, offset by its strong market position in truck leasing and what we see as steady cash flow generated by multi-year lease contracts.

Quantitative Evaluations

S&P Quality Ranking B+

D | C | B- | B | **B+** | A- | A | A+

Relative Strength Rank MODERATE

65

LOWEST = 1 HIGHEST = 99

Revenue/Earnings Data

Revenue (Million $)

	1Q	2Q	3Q	4Q	Year
2006	1,496	1,596	1,621	--	--
2005	1,316	1,390	1,491	1,545	5,741
2004	1,212	1,269	1,306	1,363	5,150
2003	1,194	1,197	1,194	1,217	4,802
2002	1,150	1,209	1,212	1,205	4,776
2001	1,282	1,294	1,243	1,188	5,006

Earnings Per Share ($)

2006	0.77	1.13	1.06	E1.08	E4.07
2005	0.64	0.98	0.98	0.93	3.53
2004	0.53	0.97	0.83	0.96	3.28
2003	0.33	0.55	0.63	0.61	2.12
2002	0.27	0.47	0.54	0.52	1.80
2001	0.07	0.33	-0.09	Nil	0.31

Fiscal year ended Dec. 31. Next earnings report expected: Early February. EPS Estimates based on S&P Operating Earnings; historical GAAP earnings are as reported.

Dividend Data (Dates: mm/dd Payment Date: mm/dd/yy)

Amount ($)	Date Decl.	Ex-Div. Date	Stk. of Record	Payment Date
0.180	02/09	02/15	02/20	03/17/06
0.180	05/05	05/18	05/22	06/16/06
0.180	07/14	08/17	08/21	09/15/06
0.180	10/06	11/16	11/20	12/15/06

Dividends have been paid since 1976. Source: Company reports.

Ryder System Inc

Business Summary October 26, 2006

Ryder System has undertaken a series of corporate restructurings and asset divestitures in the past. During the 1990s, it sold assets accounting for over 50% of revenues. A reorganizational plan was implemented in January 2000 that was designed to make the company's earnings less cyclical and seasonal and its business less capital intensive, and to allow for better client service. Business operations are currently full-service leasing, short-term truck rental, truck maintenance services, logistics services, and dedicated contract carriage.

Fleet management solutions (FMS; 64% of revenues and 83% of pretax profits in 2005) provides full service truck leasing to more than 13,300 customers worldwide, ranging from large national enterprises to small companies, with a fleet of 137,000 trucks, tractors and trailers at December 31, 2005. Under a full service lease, the company provides customers with vehicles, maintenance, supplies and related equipment necessary for operation, while customers furnish and supervise their own drivers, and dispatch and exercise control over the vehicles. R leased approximately 100,100 vehicles under full service leases in 2005.

FMS also services customer vehicles under maintenance contracts, and provides short-term truck rental to commercial customers to supplement their fleets during peak periods. A range of vehicles, from heavy-duty tractors and trailers to light-duty trucks, is available for commercial short-term rental. FMS provides additional services, including fleet management, freight management, and insurance programs. In 2005, the commercial rental fleet of about 35,000 units had an average age of 5.1 years, and a utilization rate of 75%.

Supply chain solutions (SCS; 27%, 9.2%) provides global integrated logistics support of entire customer supply chains, from inbound raw materials supply through finished goods distribution, management of carriers, and inventory deployment and overall supply chain design and management. Services include combinations of logistics systems and information technology design, the provision of vehicles and equipment (including maintenance and drivers), warehouse and transportation management, vehicle dispatch, and just-in-time delivery.

The dedicated contract carriage segment (DCC; 8.9%, 8.2%) combines the equipment, maintenance and administrative services of a full-service lease with additional services, including driver hiring and training, routing and scheduling, fleet sizing, and other technical support.

Company Financials

Per Share Data ($) Year Ended Dec. 31	**2005**	**2004**	**2003**	**2002**	**2001**	**2000**	**1999**	**1998**	**1997**	**1996**
Tangible Book Value	21.81	20.65	18.09	14.97	17.51	17.43	16.87	11.51	11.17	11.01
Cash Flow	15.65	14.03	11.90	10.65	9.30	11.20	10.12	11.12	10.29	9.20
Earnings	3.53	3.28	2.12	1.80	0.31	1.49	1.06	2.16	2.05	-0.39
S&P Core Earnings	3.09	2.80	2.26	0.84	-0.76	NA	NA	NA	NA	NA
Dividends	0.64	0.60	0.60	0.60	0.60	0.60	0.60	0.60	0.60	0.60
Payout Ratio	18%	18%	28%	33%	194%	40%	57%	28%	29%	NM
Prices:High	47.82	55.55	34.65	31.09	23.19	25.13	28.75	40.56	37.13	31.13
Prices:Low	32.00	33.61	20.00	21.05	16.06	14.81	18.81	19.44	27.13	22.63
P/E Ratio:High	14	17	16	17	75	17	27	19	18	NM
P/E Ratio:Low	9	10	9	12	52	10	18	9	13	NM
Income Statement Analysis (Million $)										
Revenue	5,741	5,150	4,802	4,776	5,006	5,337	4,952	5,189	4,894	5,519
Operating Income	1,165	1,076	905	854	798	906	997	1,115	1,097	943
Depreciation	740	706	625	552	545	580	623	665	654	779
Interest Expense	120	100	96.2	91.7	119	154	184	199	189	207
Pretax Income	357	331	212	176	30.7	141	117	258	264	-17.6
Effective Tax Rate	36.3%	34.9%	36.2%	36.0%	39.2%	37.0%	37.9%	38.4%	39.4%	NM
Net Income	228	216	136	113	18.7	89.0	72.9	159	160	-31.3
S&P Core Earnings	200	184	145	53.1	-46.3	NA	NA	NA	NA	NA
Balance Sheet & Other Financial Data (Million $)										
Cash	129	101	141	104	118	122	113	138	78.0	191
Current Assets	1,164	1,228	1,107	1,024	982	928	1,209	1,110	1,092	1,148
Total Assets	6,033	5,638	5,279	4,767	4,924	5,475	5,770	5,709	5,509	5,645
Current Liabilities	1,253	1,455	1,074	862	1,014	1,302	1,450	1,363	1,090	1,155
Long Term Debt	1,916	1,394	1,449	1,389	1,392	1,604	1,819	2,100	2,268	2,237
Common Equity	1,527	1,510	1,344	1,108	1,231	1,253	1,205	1,095	1,061	1,106
Total Capital	4,293	3,775	3,688	3,431	3,625	3,874	4,035	4,003	4,054	4,029
Capital Expenditures	1,399	1,092	725	600	657	1,289	1,734	1,369	1,042	1,303
Cash Flow	968	922	760	665	564	669	696	824	813	748
Current Ratio	0.9	0.8	1.0	1.2	1.0	0.7	0.8	0.8	1.0	1.0
% Long Term Debt of Capitalization	44.6	36.9	39.3	40.5	38.4	41.4	45.1	52.5	55.9	55.6
% Net Income of Revenue	4.0	4.2	2.8	2.4	0.4	1.7	1.5	3.1	3.3	NM
% Return on Assets	3.9	3.9	2.7	2.3	0.4	1.6	1.3	2.8	2.9	NM
% Return on Equity	15.0	15.1	11.1	9.6	1.5	7.2	1.1	14.7	14.8	NM

Data as orig reptd.; bef. results of disc opers/spec. items. Per share data adj. for stk. divs.; EPS diluted. E-Estimated. NA-Not Available. NM-Not Meaningful. NR-Not Ranked. UR-Under Review.

Office: 11690 NW 105th St, Medley, FL 33178-1103.
Telephone: 305-593-3726.
Email: ryderforinvestor@ryder.com
Website: http://www.ryder.com

Chrmn, Pres & CEO: G.T. Swienton
EVP & CFO: M.T. Jamieson
EVP, Secy & General Counsel: R.D. Fatovic

Board of Directors: J. M. Berra, D. I. Fuente, L. P. Hassey, L. M. Martin, D. Mudd, E. A. Renna, A. J. Smith, E. F. Smith, G. Swienton, H. E. Tookes, II, C. A. Varney

Founded: 1955
Domicile: Florida
Employees: 27,000

STANDARD &POOR'S

Sabre Holdings Corp

S&P Recommendation HOLD ★★★★★

Price $25.21 (as of Oct 27, 2006)

12-Mo. Target Price $25.00

Investment Style Mid-Cap Value

GICS Sector Information Technology
Sub-Industry Data Processing & Outsourced Services

Comment Spun off from AMR (the parent of American Airlines) in March 2000, this company offers a variety of electronic travel-related services.

Key Stock Statistics (Source S&P, Vickers, company reports)

52-Wk Range	$25.86–19.34	S&P Oper. EPS 2006E	1.58	P/E on S&P Oper. EPS 2006E	16.0	Dividend Rate/Share	$0.52
Trailing 12-Month EPS	$0.92	S&P Oper. EPS 2007E	1.73	Common Shares Outstg. (M)	131.8	Yield (%)	2.06
Trailing 12-Month P/E	27.4	S&P Core EPS 2006E	1.58	Market Capitalization(B)	$3.323	Beta	2.01
$10K Invested 5 Yrs Ago	$9,761	S&P Core EPS 2007E	1.73	Institutional Ownership (%)	96	S&P Credit Rating	BBB

Price Performance

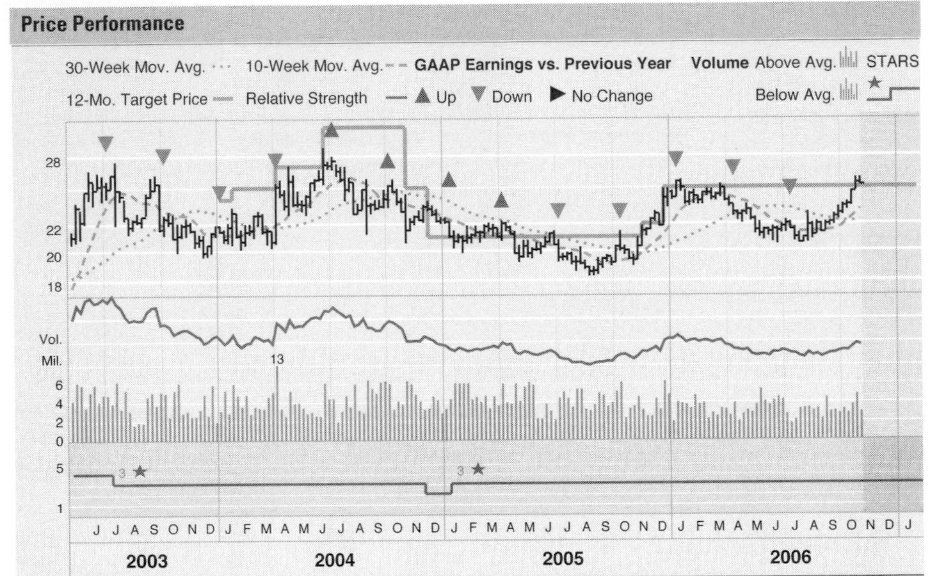

Options: ASE, CBOE

Analysis prepared by **Scott H. Kessler** on August 23, 2006, when the stock traded at **$ 21.96**.

Highlights

- We project 2006 revenue growth of 15%, reflecting the July 2005 acquisition of lastminute.com, solid performance from Travelocity, and a relatively healthy airline industry. We see growth of 4% in 2007. Our forecasts account for what we view as challenges related to access to inventory and the competitive environment.
- TSG has been taking actions intended to improve profitability. In June 2005, Sabre announced a restructuring of its product and system delivery group that is expected to deliver expense reductions of up to $16 million in 2006. In early 2004, TSG revised the terms of its relationship with AOL, yielding material cost savings. We believe margins have benefited from these actions, and will be aided in 2006 and 2007 by a more favorable revenue mix, despite notable marketing spending for Travelocity.
- In July 2005, TSG acquired lastminute.com, one of Europe's largest providers of online travel services, for about $1.2 billion. Lastminute.com has become Travelocity's lead brand in the region.

Investment Rationale/Risk

- We expect favorable travel spending to contribute to growth in 2006 revenues and profits. However, in our opinion, TSG faces notable competition from Expedia (EXPE: hold, $16), priceline.com (PCLN: hold, $33), and Orbitz, as well as airline and hotel company websites, and emerging travel search offerings.
- Risks to our recommendation and target price include the potential expirations of a number of global distribution system (GDS) contracts, renewals of such agreements on less favorable terms, and increasing competition in the online travel agency and GDS businesses.
- P/E analysis involving the S&P 500 Data Processing & Outsourced Services sub-industry yields a price of $28. Similar P/E-to-growth considerations leads to a price of $20. With assumptions including a WACC of 10%, and free cash flow increasing from $318 million in 2006 to $408 million in 2010, our DCF-based intrinsic value calculation is $38. Blending these methodologies, and accounting for a modest discount due to what we consider are numerous challenges, leads to our 12-month target price of $25.

Qualitative Risk Assessment

LOW | **MEDIUM** | HIGH

Our risk assessment reflects what we view as the company's relatively large base of revenues and profits, solid market position in certain segments, and flexible balance sheet, offset by notable competitive pressures.

Quantitative Evaluations

S&P Quality Ranking **B**

D | C | B- | **B** | B+ | A- | A | A+

Relative Strength Rank **STRONG**

80

LOWEST = 1 HIGHEST = 99

Revenue/Earnings Data

Revenue (Million $)

	1Q	2Q	3Q	4Q	Year
2006	700.2	722.6	--	--	--
2005	581.9	619.3	699.7	620.4	2,521
2004	539.8	550.9	544.4	495.9	2,131
2003	543.8	507.2	526.8	467.4	2,045
2002	549.4	536.8	517.4	453.0	2,056
2001	573.4	582.0	524.8	422.8	2,103

Earnings Per Share ($)

2006	0.13	0.26	**E**0.59	**E**0.28	**E**1.58
2005	0.44	0.34	0.45	0.09	1.32
2004	0.31	0.42	0.49	0.16	1.38
2003	0.45	0.05	0.18	-0.10	0.58
2002	0.64	0.47	0.40	0.01	1.50
2001	Nil	0.04	0.13	-0.52	-0.35

Fiscal year ended Dec. 31. Next earnings report expected: Early November. EPS Estimates based on S&P Operating Earnings; historical GAAP earnings are as reported.

Dividend Data (Dates: mm/dd Payment Date: mm/dd/yy)

Amount ($)	Date Decl.	Ex-Div. Date	Stk. of Record	Payment Date
0.100	01/31	02/08	02/10	02/28/06
0.100	05/02	05/09	05/11	05/25/06
0.100	08/01	08/09	08/11	08/28/06
0.130	10/11	10/19	10/23	11/10/06

Dividends have been paid since 2003. Source: Company reports.

Please read the Required Disclosures and Analyst Certification on the last page of this report.

Sabre Holdings Corp

Business Summary August 23, 2006

CORPORATE OVERVIEW. Sabre Holdings is one of the world's largest providers (based on revenues) of travel-related commerce, marketing travel offerings, and distribution and technology solutions for the travel industry.

The Sabre global distribution system (often referred to as a GDS) and other similar systems are a principal means of air travel distribution. Through the Sabre GDS, online and off-line travel agencies and corporate travel departments can access information about, and can book reservations for a variety of travel needs, including, airline trips, hotel stays, car rentals, cruises, and tour packages. TSG has estimated that nearly $80 billion in travel-related offerings were sold through the Sabre GDS in 2005. During 2005, more airline and hotel booking were made through the Sabre GDS than through any other GDS.

The Sabre Travel Network, which markets the Sabre GDS, accounts for a majority of TSG's segment revenues (64% and 73% in 2005 and 2004, respectively). As of December 2005, travel agencies with about 50,000 locations in more than 113 countries subscribed to the Sabre system. Subscribers could make reservations with 410 airlines, 30 car rental companies, 40 tour operators, 11 cruise lines, 6 railroads, and 261 hotel companies.

Travelocity (33%, 20%) is a leading provider (based on gross bookings and revenues) of consumer-direct travel services for leisure and business travelers. Through Travelocity.com, its international websites, its contact centers, travel agency partners, and the Travelocity Partner Network (including Yahoo Travel, AOL, American Express, Southwest Airlines, US Airways, and AARP) offering, travelers can shop, compare prices, and make travel arrangements online with airlines, car rental companies, hoteliers, and cruise and tour providers. Travelocity acts as an agency by receiving fees from travel providers for sales of their offerings. It also purchases wholesale inventory from travel suppliers, and sells it independently or as part of packages. Travelocity also garners revenues from advertising on its websites.

The Sabre Airline Solutions segment (10%, 11%) provides passenger management solutions, software, and related services. The segment's offerings are designed to help airlines and other travel providers increase their revenues, streamline their operations, improve workflow, and raise productivity.

Company Financials

Per Share Data ($) Year Ended Dec. 31	**2005**	**2004**	**2003**	**2002**	**2001**	**2000**	**1999**	**1998**	**1997**	**1996**
Tangible Book Value	NM	4.80	5.60	5.51	2.83	NM	9.72	7.35	5.79	4.36
Cash Flow	2.32	2.23	1.55	2.32	2.95	3.77	4.52	3.68	2.94	2.69
Earnings	1.32	1.38	0.58	1.50	-0.35	1.11	2.54	1.78	1.53	1.44
S&P Core Earnings	1.06	1.24	0.15	1.18	-0.75	NA	NA	NA	NA	NA
Dividends	0.36	0.30	0.21	Nil	Nil	5.20	Nil	Nil	Nil	Nil
Payout Ratio	27%	22%	30%	Nil	Nil	NM	Nil	Nil	Nil	Nil
Prices:High	24.90	28.85	27.50	49.98	54.98	53.50	72.00	44.88	37.00	33.38
Prices:Low	18.26	20.10	14.00	14.85	21.22	22.31	38.25	23.00	23.25	25.63
P/E Ratio:High	19	21	47	33	NM	48	28	25	24	23
P/E Ratio:Low	14	15	24	10	NM	20	15	13	15	18

Income Statement Analysis (Million $)										
Revenue	2,521	2,131	2,045	2,056	2,103	2,617	2,435	2,306	1,784	1,622
Operating Income	392	375	302	434	429	596	631	598	493	492
Depreciation	131	117	136	117	438	346	258	248	185	165
Interest Expense	53.1	26.9	24.1	23.4	41.2	31.7	10.00	19.5	21.7	27.4
Pretax Income	245	257	127	339	11.5	236	528	371	324	306
Effective Tax Rate	29.7%	25.9%	34.7%	36.8%	NM	52.1%	37.1%	37.6%	38.3%	39.0%
Net Income	172	190	83.3	214	-47.0	144	332	232	200	187
S&P Core Earnings	137	170	22.3	169	-99.8	NA	NA	NA	NA	NA

Balance Sheet & Other Financial Data (Million $)										
Cash	512	837	923	912	667	145	6.63	8.01	11.3	443
Current Assets	1,248	1,280	1,368	1,312	1,092	693	976	944	874	695
Total Assets	4,374	3,018	2,956	2,757	2,376	2,650	1,951	1,927	1,524	1,287
Current Liabilities	1,892	608	503	500	564	1,266	525	401	317	290
Long Term Debt	585	600	588	436	400	149	Nil	318	318	318
Common Equity	1,643	1,626	1,680	1,642	1,042	791	1,262	954	757	570
Total Capital	2,267	2,232	2,279	2,101	1,662	1,227	1,262	1,285	1,087	931
Capital Expenditures	91.7	78.0	71.5	62.7	158	190	168	320	218	186
Cash Flow	303	307	219	331	391	490	590	480	385	352
Current Ratio	0.7	2.1	2.7	2.6	1.9	0.5	1.9	2.4	2.8	2.4
% Long Term Debt of Capitalization	25.8	26.9	25.8	20.7	24.1	12.1	Nil	24.7	29.3	34.2
% Net Income of Revenue	6.8	8.9	4.1	10.4	NM	5.5	13.6	10.1	11.2	11.5
% Return on Assets	4.7	6.4	2.9	8.3	NM	6.3	17.1	13.4	14.2	18.5
% Return on Equity	10.5	11.5	5.0	16.0	NM	14.0	30.0	27.1	30.1	NM

Data as orig reptd.; bef. results of disc opers/spec. items. Per share data adj. for stk. divs.; EPS diluted. E-Estimated. NA-Not Available. NM-Not Meaningful. NR-Not Ranked. UR-Under Review.

Office: 3150 Sabre Drive, Southlake, TX 76092-2199.
Telephone: 682-605-1000.
Email: contact.us@sabre.com
Website: http://www.sabre-holdings.com

Chrmn, Pres & CEO: S. Gilliland
EVP, CFO & Treas: J.M. Jackson
EVP & General Counsel: D. Schwarte
Investor Contact: M. Berman (682 605 2397)

Board of Directors: R. S. Caldwell, P. C. Ely, Jr., M. S. Gilliland, R. G. Lindner, B. L. Martin, P. B. Strobel, M. A. Taylor, R. L. Thomas

Founded: 1996
Domicile: Delaware
Employees: 8,800

STANDARD & POOR'S

SAFECO Corp

S&P Recommendation HOLD ★★★★★

Price $58.19 (as of Oct 31, 2006)

12-Mo. Target Price $64.00

Investment Style Mid-Cap Value

GICS Sector Financials
Sub-Industry Property & Casualty Insurance

Comment This Seattle-based property and casualty insurance company sells insurance to drivers, homeowners and owners of small- and medium-sized businesses.

Key Stock Statistics (Source S&P, Vickers, company reports)

52-Wk Range	$61.39–49.09	S&P Oper. EPS 2006E	6.30	P/E on S&P Oper. EPS 2006E	9.2	Dividend Rate/Share	$1.20
Trailing 12-Month EPS	$7.08	S&P Oper. EPS 2007E	5.75	Common Shares Outstg. (M)	116.4	Yield (%)	2.06
Trailing 12-Month P/E	8.2	S&P Core EPS 2006E	5.80	Market Capitalization(B)	$6.771	Beta	0.36
$10K Invested 5 Yrs Ago	$20,379	S&P Core EPS 2007E	5.29	Institutional Ownership (%)	71	S&P Credit Rating	BBB+

Price Performance

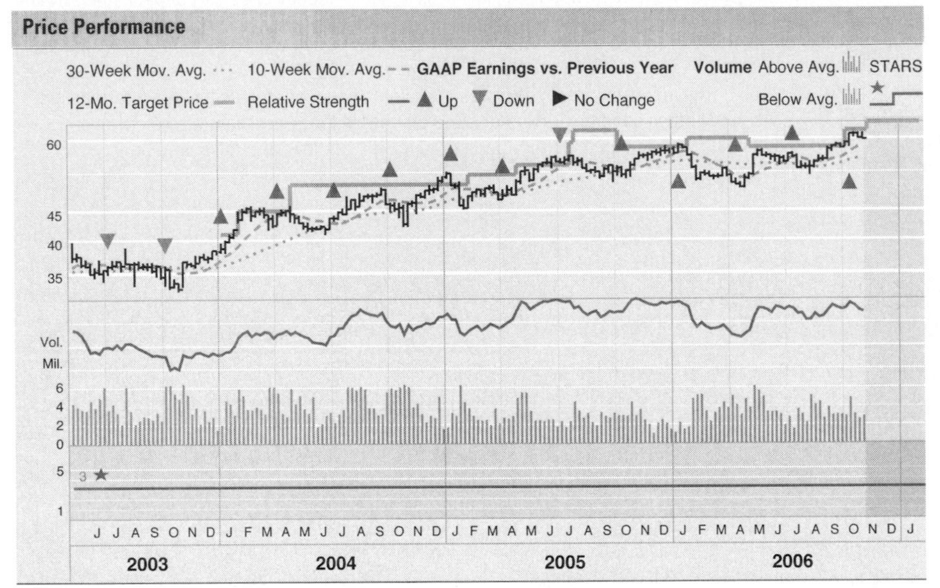

Options: CBOE

Highlights

- The 12-month target price for SAFC has recently been changed to $64.00 from $62.00. The Highlights section of this Stock Report will be updated accordingly.

Investment Rationale/Risk

- The Investment Rationale/Risk section of this Stock Report will be updated shortly. For the latest News story on SAFC from MarketScope, see below.
- 10/31/06 12:40 pm EST... S&P MAINTAINS HOLD RECOMMENDATION ON SHARES OF SAFECO CORP. (SAFC 58.41***): SAFC posts $1.46 vs. $0.77 Q3 operating EPS amid sharply lower catastrophe losses. Q3 results also exclude $0.69 per-share gain on sale of real estate. That aside, underwriting results were subpar, in our view, with Q3 net written premiums down 3.8%. Underwriting results in Q3 (excluding catastrophes) also deteriorated, as evidenced by the 87.1% vs. 86.1% combined ratio. We are raising our '06 operating EPS estimate by $0.30 to $6.30 and our '07 estimate by $0.15 to $5.75. Our 12-month target price, raised $2 today to $64, is 11.1X our '07 estimate, in line with peers. / C.Seifert

Qualitative Risk Assessment

LOW | **MEDIUM** | HIGH

Our risk assessment reflects our view of SAFC as a sound underwriter with acceptable risk and capital management practices. Offsetting this is our concern over SAFC's exposure to catastrophe losses and the execution risk we see as SAFC attempts a turnaround under a new management team.

Quantitative Evaluations

S&P Quality Ranking **B**

D | C | B- | **B** | B+ | A- | A | A+

Relative Strength Rank **MODERATE**

31

LOWEST = 1 HIGHEST = 99

Revenue/Earnings Data

Revenue (Million $)

	1Q	2Q	3Q	4Q	Year
2006	1,562	1,536	--	--	--
2005	1,581	1,591	1,586	1,594	6,351
2004	1,498	1,556	1,567	1,574	6,195
2003	1,763	1,872	1,781	1,943	7,358
2002	1,713	1,798	1,795	1,760	7,065
2001	1,733	1,716	1,708	1,706	6,863

Earnings Per Share ($)

	1Q	2Q	3Q	4Q	Year
2006	1.69	1.68	2.20	**E**1.51	**E**6.30
2005	1.65	1.46	0.80	1.53	5.43
2004	1.33	1.78	0.04	1.41	4.59
2003	0.65	0.81	-0.21	1.19	2.44
2002	0.50	0.82	0.59	0.42	2.33
2001	-6.89	-0.11	-1.22	0.06	-8.18

Fiscal year ended Dec. 31. Next earnings report expected: Late January. EPS Estimates based on S&P Operating Earnings; historical GAAP earnings are as reported.

Dividend Data (Dates: mm/dd Payment Date: mm/dd/yy)

Amount ($)	Date Decl.	Ex-Div. Date	Stk. of Record	Payment Date
0.250	11/02	01/04	01/06	01/23/06
0.250	02/01	04/05	04/07	04/24/06
0.300	05/03	07/05	07/07	07/24/06
0.300	08/11	10/04	10/06	10/23/06

Dividends have been paid since 1933. Source: Company reports.

SAFECO Corp

Business Summary September 28, 2006

Seattle-based insurer SAFECO has undergone a number of transitions in recent years, culminating in the sale of its non-core operations to better focus on the property-casualty insurance business. SAFC was the 17th largest U.S. property-casualty (p-c) insurance company, based on 2004 net written premiums (latest available data). Earned premiums exceeded $5.8 billion in 2005, up 5.5% from earned premiums of over $5.5 billion in 2004. Through a network of independent agents and brokers and through the Internet, most major lines of personal and commercial p-c coverage are offered in nearly all states, although much of SAFC's business is concentrated in the Pacific Northwest.

Safeco Personal Insurance (66% of 2005 earned premiums) primarily underwrites personal auto insurance and homeowners' coverage. The division also offers an array of umbrella, earthquake, dwelling fire, inland marine, recreational vehicle, motorcycle and boat insurance coverage for individuals. Underwriting results (as measured by the combined loss and expense ratio) in this line have been profitable in recent years. The combined ratio equaled 91.0% in 2005, versus 89.1% in 2004. (A combined ratio of under 100% indicates an underwriting profit, while one in excess of 100% points to an underwriting loss).

Safeco Business Insurance (29% of 2005 earned premiums) offers a line of commercial insurance products designed for small to medium sized businesses. Principal products offered include commercial multi-peril, workers' compensation, property, general liability, and commercial auto. Underwriting results here were profitable in 2005, with a combined ratio of 91.2%, versus 95.6% in 2004. The Surety and Other segment (5% of earned premiums in 2005) provides surety bonds for construction, performance, and legal matters that include appeals, probate and bankruptcies; and includes businesses being run-off. The surety line's combined ratio was 78.9% in 2005, versus 79.1% in 2004.

Company Financials

Per Share Data ($) Year Ended Dec. 31	**2005**	**2004**	**2003**	**2002**	**2001**	**2000**	**1999**	**1998**	**1997**	**1996**
Tangible Book Value	33.37	30.87	34.92	30.69	27.70	26.48	22.80	31.01	29.28	32.58
Operating Earnings	NA	NA	NA	NA	NA	0.19	1.32	2.07	3.02	3.02
Earnings	5.43	4.59	2.44	2.33	-8.18	0.90	1.90	2.51	3.31	3.48
S&P Core Earnings	5.02	3.60	2.80	1.77	-1.43	NA	NA	NA	NA	NA
Dividends	0.94	0.78	0.74	0.74	0.93	1.48	1.44	1.34	1.22	1.11
Relative Payout	17%	17%	30%	32%	NM	164%	76%	53%	37%	32%
Prices:High	58.35	52.65	39.79	38.00	32.95	35.88	46.75	56.00	55.38	42.25
Prices:Low	45.18	37.95	32.50	24.99	21.50	18.00	21.81	38.25	36.50	30.88
P/E Ratio:High	11	11	16	16	NM	40	25	22	17	12
P/E Ratio:Low	8	8	13	11	NM	20	11	15	11	9
Income Statement Analysis (Million $)										
Life Insurance in Force	Nil	Nil	66,738	67,001	57,511	55,262	48,175	45,206	NA	NA
Premium Income:Life A & H	5,805	Nil	868	778	637	503	361	353	290	266
Premium Income:Casualty/Property.	NA	5,529	4,902	4,521	4,473	4,563	4,383	4,208	2,817	2,275
Net Investment Income	485	465	1,680	1,672	1,649	1,627	1,585	1,519	1,245	1,117
Total Revenue	6,351	6,195	7,358	7,065	6,863	7,118	31.0	6,547	4,709	3,965
Pretax Income	986	893	441	418	-1,458	114	287	418	573	578
Net Operating Income	NA	NA	NA	27.8	-1,062	69.0	221	335	366	380
Net Income	691	620	339	301	-1,045	115	252	352	430	439
S&P Core Earnings	639	485	388	229	-184	NA	NA	NA	NA	NA
Balance Sheet & Other Financial Data (Million $)										
Cash & Equivalent	688	382	550	3,482	593	529	440	398	728	296
Premiums Due	1,085	1,147	1,640	1,626	973	1,063	1,058	978	954	467
Investment Assets:Bonds	9,362	9,294	26,207	24,278	21,444	20,830	19,564	20,576	19,987	14,530
Investment Assets:Stocks	1,124	1,101	1,279	1,083	1,597	1,816	2,005	2,037	1,880	1,299
Investment Assets:Loans	Nil	Nil	936	926	924	823	861	630	584	506
Investment Assets:Total	1,124	11,506	28,807	26,771	24,875	23,811	22,931	24,160	22,451	16,889
Deferred Policy Costs	376	382	639	626	627	605	599	521	545	396
Total Assets	14,887	14,586	35,845	34,656	30,093	31,512	30,573	30,892	29,468	19,918
Debt	1,307	1,333	1,966	1,968	1,592	1,617	3,159	3,458	2,360	1,233
Common Equity	4,125	3,921	5,023	4,432	3,635	4,695	4,295	5,576	5,462	4,115
Combined Loss-Expense Ratio	78.3	77.3	100.1	105.3	118.7	111.4	108.4	102.6	98.7	98.3
% Return on Revenue	10.9	10.0	4.6	4.3	NM	1.6	3.8	5.4	9.1	11.1
% Return on Equity	17.2	13.9	7.2	7.5	NM	2.6	5.1	12.6	0.0	9.4
% Investment Yield	4.7	4.2	6.0	5.1	6.8	7.0	6.7	12.6	6.5	6.7

Data as orig reptd.; bef. results of disc opers/spec. items. Per share data adj. for stk. divs.; EPS diluted. E-Estimated. NA-Not Available. NM-Not Meaningful. NR-Not Ranked. UR-Under Review.

Office: Safeco Plaza, Seattle, WA 98185.
Telephone: 206-545-5000.
Website: http://www.safeco.com
Chrmn: J.W. Brown

Pres & CEO: P.R. Reynolds
EVP & CFO: R. Kari
EVP & General Counsel: A. Chong
SVP & Cntlr: C.F. Horne, Jr.

Investor Contact: N. Fuller (206-545-5537)
Board of Directors: J. W. Brown, R. S. Cline, P. Currie, M. S. Eitel, J. Green, III, J. Hamlin, G. T. Hutton, K. Killinger, G. Locke, W. G. Reed, Jr., P. R. Reynolds, J. M. Runstad

Founded: 1929
Domicile: Washington
Employees: 9,181

STANDARD &POOR'S

Safeway Inc

S&P Recommendation BUY ★★★★★	Price	12-Mo. Target Price	Investment Style
	$29.02 (as of Oct 27, 2006)	$34.00	Large-Cap Value

GICS Sector Consumer Staples
Sub-Industry Food Retail

Comment This major food retailer operates about 1,800 stores in the U.S. and Canada.

Key Stock Statistics (Source S&P, Vickers, company reports)

52-Wk Range	$31.42–21.67	S&P Oper. EPS 2006E	1.73	P/E on S&P Oper. EPS 2006E	16.8	Dividend Rate/Share	$0.23
Trailing 12-Month EPS	$1.64	S&P Oper. EPS 2007E	1.94	Common Shares Outstg. (M)	443.3	Yield (%)	0.79
Trailing 12-Month P/E	17.7	S&P Core EPS 2006E	1.73	Market Capitalization(B)	$12.865	Beta	0.95
$10K Invested 5 Yrs Ago	$6,842	S&P Core EPS 2007E	1.94	Institutional Ownership (%)	92	S&P Credit Rating	BBB-

Price Performance

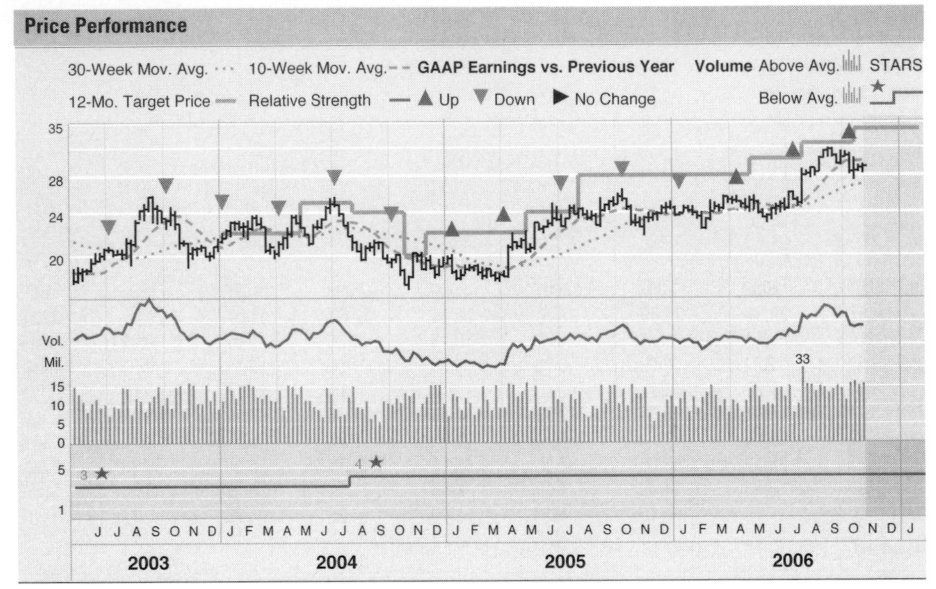

Options: ASE, CBOE, P

Analysis prepared by **Joseph Agnese** on October 13, 2006, when the stock traded at **$ 28.38**.

Highlights

- We expect sales to rise about 5% in 2006 as benefits from the new Lifestyle remodeling campaign are expected to help fuel identical-store sales growth of around 3%. We project that square footage will grow about 1% to 2%, reflecting the completion of around 275 store remodelings and the opening of 20 new stores in 2006.
- Gross margins should be flat to up slightly, reflecting reduced shrink expense, despite increased levels of advertising spending and lower pricing. We look for operating margins to widen as a significant restructuring of labor contracts, coupled with efficiency gains stemming from centralized marketing and procurement functions, should help the company leverage growth in sales while offsetting increased operating expenses associated with the expansion of new store formats coupled with higher energy prices.
- Interest expense should be flat, in our opinion, as a reduction in debt levels is offset by higher interest rates. We project 2006 operating EPS of $1.73, up 24% from $1.40 in 2005.

Investment Rationale/Risk

- We expect earnings trends to improve, reflecting the company's aggressive rollout of its Lifestyle stores and better sales leverage because of the restructuring of labor contracts.
- Risks to our recommendation and target price include a more intense competitive environment in Southern California than we anticipate and a slowdown in the economy. In addition, we are concerned about corporate governance because the CEO and chairman of the board positions are not separate.
- With the stock recently trading at 15X our 2007 EPS estimate of $1.94, inl ine with its five-year historical average forward P/E multiple of 15X, we believe the shares are attractively valued. Due to improved employee costs and favorable sales comparisons that we foresee, we project five-year annual EPS growth of at least 12%. Our 12-month target price of $34, equal to 17.4X our 2008 EPS estimate of $1.95, is based on our assumption that the shares will trade 15% above their historical forward 12-month P/E, as we expect favorable trends to continue.

Qualitative Risk Assessment

LOW	**MEDIUM**	HIGH

Our risk assessment reflects our view of an improved shopping experience associated with new Lifestyle store remodelings as well as potential opportunities to gain market share following the consolidation of a major rival, offset by a continued intense competitive environment as new entrants enter the company's markets.

Quantitative Evaluations

S&P Quality Ranking **B**

D	C	B-	**B**	B+	A-	A	A+

Relative Strength Rank **MODERATE**

35

LOWEST = 1 HIGHEST = 99

Revenue/Earnings Data

Revenue (Million $)

	1Q	2Q	3Q	4Q	Year
2006	8,895	9,367	9,420	--	--
2005	8,621	8,803	8,946	12,046	38,416
2004	7,639	8,361	8,297	11,390	35,823
2003	8,043	8,248	8,277	10,985	35,553
2002	7,367	7,514	7,508	10,011	32,399
2001	7,666	7,986	7,962	10,686	34,301

Earnings Per Share ($)

2006	0.32	0.55	0.39	**E**0.59	**E**1.73
2005	0.29	0.30	0.27	0.39	1.25
2004	0.10	0.35	0.35	0.45	1.25
2003	0.36	0.36	0.45	-1.57	-0.38
2002	0.66	0.62	0.60	-0.77	1.20
2001	0.55	0.59	0.60	0.70	2.44

Fiscal year ended Dec. 31. Next earnings report expected: Late February. EPS Estimates based on S&P Operating Earnings; historical GAAP earnings are as reported.

Dividend Data (Dates: mm/dd Payment Date: mm/dd/yy)

Amount ($)	Date Decl.	Ex-Div. Date	Stk. of Record	Payment Date
0.050	12/09	12/28	12/30	01/20/06
0.050	03/10	03/29	03/31	04/21/06
0.058	05/25	06/14	06/16	07/07/06
0.058	08/28	09/11	09/13	10/05/06

Dividends have been paid since 2005. Source: Company reports.

Safeway Inc

Business Summary October 13, 2006

CORPORATE OVERVIEW. Safeway is one of the largest U.S. food and drug retailers, operating about 1,800 stores principally in California, Oregon, Washington, Alaska, Colorado, Arizona, Texas, and the Mid-Atlantic region. To support its store network, SWY has a network of distribution, manufacturing and food processing facilities. The company seeks to provide value to customers by maintaining high store standards and a wide selection of high quality produce and meat at competitive prices.

MARKET PROFILE. The U.S. grocery industry was a $863 billion business in 2005, according to Progressive Grocer. Supermarkets generated $479 billion, or 55% of total grocery industry sales, followed by convenience stores ($279 billion, 32%) and warehouse clubs ($9.9 billion, 10%). When supermarkets are broken down by format, conventional supermarkets have the largest market share, holding 73% of the supermarket category, with $351 billion in sales. However, supercenters are quickly gaining market share, and generated a 21% market share in 2005 ($102 billion in sales).

With $38.4 billion in sales in 2005, Safeway held an 8% market share within the supermarket category and 4.5% of total grocery sales. Not only does the average size of Safeway's stores (over 45,000 square feet) exceed the industry average (34,000 square feet) but so does the company's sales per square foot ($474 per square foot for Safeway versus the supermarket average of $434 per square foot in 2005).

Company Financials

Per Share Data ($) Year Ended Dec. 31	**2005**	**2004**	**2003**	**2002**	**2001**	**2000**	**1999**	**1998**	**1997**	**1996**
Tangible Book Value	5.60	4.24	2.79	1.77	1.67	1.35	NM	NM	0.68	1.98
Cash Flow	3.32	3.24	1.57	2.91	4.29	3.77	3.24	2.63	2.38	1.68
Earnings	1.25	1.25	-0.38	1.20	2.44	2.13	1.88	1.59	1.25	0.97
S&P Core Earnings	1.26	1.15	1.21	2.42	2.19	NA	NA	NA	NA	NA
Dividends	0.15	Nil	Nil	Nil	Nil	Nil	Nil	Nil	Nil	Nil
Payout Ratio	12%	Nil	Nil	Nil	Nil	Nil	Nil	Nil	Nil	Nil
Prices:High	26.46	25.64	25.83	46.90	61.38	62.69	62.44	61.38	31.72	22.69
Prices:Low	17.85	17.26	16.20	18.45	37.44	30.75	29.31	30.50	21.06	11.22
P/E Ratio:High	21	21	NM	39	25	29	33	39	25	24
P/E Ratio:Low	14	14	NM	15	15	14	16	19	17	12

Income Statement Analysis (Million $)	2005	2004	2003	2002	2001	2000	1999	1998	1997	1996
Revenue	38,416	35,823	35,553	32,399	34,301	31,977	28,860	24,484	22,484	17,269
Operating Income	2,147	2,067	2,167	3,190	3,535	3,119	2,698	2,134	1,841	1,231
Depreciation	933	895	864	812	946	838	700	533	561	339
Interest Expense	403	411	442	369	447	457	362	244	247	183
Pretax Income	849	794	141	1,320	2,095	1,867	1,674	1,397	1,076	768
Effective Tax Rate	33.9%	29.4%	NM	56.9%	40.1%	41.5%	42.0%	42.2%	42.3%	40.0%
Net Income	561	560	-170	568	1,254	1,092	971	807	622	461
S&P Core Earnings	566	517	538	1,140	1,122	NA	NA	NA	NA	NA

Balance Sheet & Other Financial Data (Million $)	2005	2004	2003	2002	2001	2000	1999	1998	1997	1996
Cash	373	267	175	73.7	68.5	91.7	106	46.0	77.0	79.7
Current Assets	3,702	3,598	3,508	4,259	3,312	3,224	3,052	2,320	2,030	1,654
Total Assets	15,757	15,377	15,097	16,047	17,463	15,965	14,900	11,390	8,494	5,545
Current Liabilities	4,264	3,792	3,464	3,936	3,883	3,780	3,583	2,894	2,539	2,030
Long Term Debt	5,605	6,124	7,072	7,522	6,712	5,822	6,357	4,651	3,041	1,729
Common Equity	4,920	4,307	3,644	3,628	5,890	5,390	4,086	3,082	2,149	1,187
Total Capital	10,748	10,894	11,139	11,727	13,100	11,721	10,822	7,950	5,487	2,915
Capital Expenditures	1,384	1,213	936	1,371	1,793	1,573	1,334	1,075	758	542
Cash Flow	1,494	1,455	694	1,381	2,200	1,930	1,671	1,340	1,183	800
Current Ratio	0.9	0.9	1.0	1.1	0.9	0.9	0.9	0.8	0.8	0.8
% Long Term Debt of Capitalization	52.2	56.2	63.5	64.1	51.2	49.7	58.7	58.5	55.4	59.3
% Net Income of Revenue	1.5	1.6	NM	1.8	3.7	3.4	3.4	3.3	2.8	2.7
% Return on Assets	3.6	3.7	NM	3.4	7.5	7.1	7.4	8.1	8.9	8.6
% Return on Equity	12.2	14.1	NM	11.9	22.2	23.0	27.1	30.9	37.3	46.5

Data as orig reptd.; bef. results of disc opers/spec. items. Per share data adj. for stk. divs.; EPS diluted. E-Estimated. NA-Not Available. NM-Not Meaningful. NR-Not Ranked. UR-Under Review.

Office: 5918 Stoneridge Mall Road, Pleasanton, CA 94588-3229.
Telephone: 925-467-3000.
Website: http://www.safeway.com
Chrmn, Pres & CEO: S.A. Burd

EVP & CFO: R.L. Edwards
SVP & General Counsel: R.A. Gordon
Investor Contact: M.C. Plaisance (925-467-3790)

Board of Directors: S. A. Burd, J. E. Grove, M. Gyani, P. Hazen, R. I. MacDonnell, D. J. Mackenzie, R. A. Stirn, W. Y. Tauscher, R. G. Viault

Founded: 1915
Domicile: Delaware
Employees: 201,000

STANDARD &POOR'S

St. Jude Medical Inc.

S&P Recommendation	Price	12-Mo. Target Price	Investment Style
HOLD ★★★★★	$34.09 (as of Oct 27, 2006)	$38.00	Large-Cap Growth

GICS Sector Health Care
Sub-Industry Health Care Equipment

Comment St. Jude, the leading maker of mechanical heart valves, also produces pacemakers, defibrillators and other cardiac devices.

Key Stock Statistics (Source S&P, Vickers, company reports)

52-Wk Range	$54.75–31.20	S&P Oper. EPS 2006E	1.43	P/E on S&P Oper. EPS 2006E	23.8	Dividend Rate/Share	Nil
Trailing 12-Month EPS	$1.06	S&P Oper. EPS 2007E	1.70	Common Shares Outstg. (M)	352.6	Yield (%)	Nil
Trailing 12-Month P/E	32.2	S&P Core EPS 2006E	1.43	Market Capitalization(B)	$12.022	Beta	0.28
$10K Invested 5 Yrs Ago	$19,071	S&P Core EPS 2007E	1.70	Institutional Ownership (%)	76	S&P Credit Rating	BBB+

Price Performance

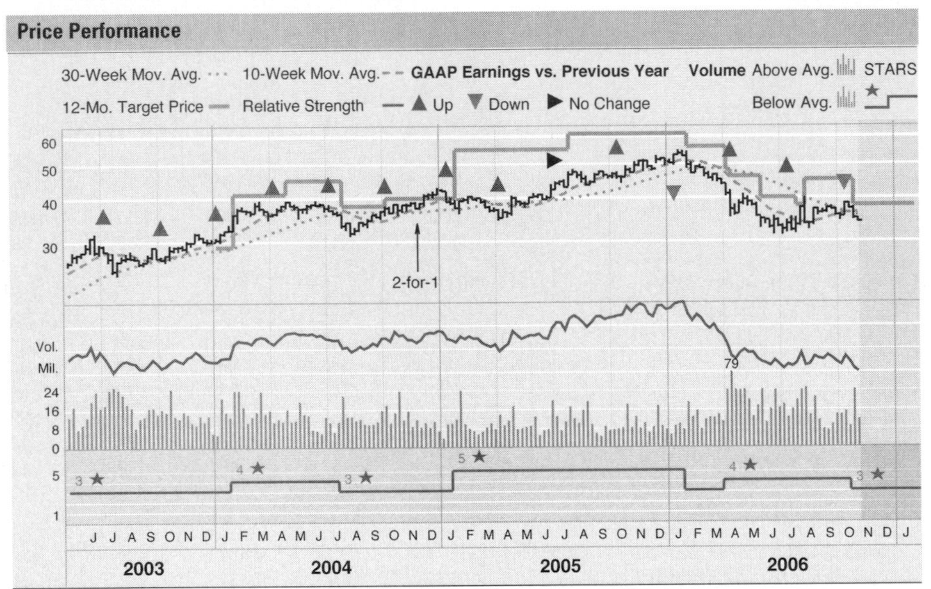

Options: ASE, CBOE

Analysis prepared by **Robert M. Gold** on October 19, 2006, when the stock traded at **$ 34.81**.

Highlights

- We think St. Jude will capture share in the global implantable cardioverter defibrillator (ICD) market in 2006 and 2007, but we believe that the ICD market growth rate will slow to about 5% in 2006, versus an estimated 21% in 2005, as product recalls by some competitors drive down overall procedure levels. We think ICD market growth in 2007 will approximate 10% to 13%, but visibility remains low, in our view. We see 2006 revenues of $3.2 billion, and 2007 revenues of $3.6 billion.
- Our 2006 revenue forecast assumes $1.0 billion in sales of ICDs; $955 million for pacemakers; $315 million of atrial fibrillation-related products; $445 million of cardiology products; $285 million from cardiac surgery; and $175 million from Advanced Neuromodulation. We expect 2006 gross margins to approximate 73.0%, with SG&A expenses consuming 36% of sales and R&D outlays at 13.5% of sales. The 2006 effective tax rate is expected to be 26.6%.
- We project 2006 operating EPS of $1.43, including $0.15 of projected stock option expense. Our 2007 EPS estimate is $1.70, which includes $0.20 of estimated stock option expense.

Investment Rationale/Risk

- We are concerned about the possibility of stagnant ICD market conditions through the first half of 2007, and believe the company's 2006 fourth quarter guidance is at risk should the domestic ICD market continue to exhibit contraction that was evident in the third quarter. Although we continue to believe the recent release of revised Medicare reimbursement guidelines to hospitals for ICDs--which call for an approximate 3% reimbursement reduction versus an earlier proposal for a cut of up to 23%--was a positive and could spur some incremental ICD implantations in 2007, we think the market will be challenged to resume growth in excess of 15% in the foreseeable future.
- Risks to our recommendation and target price include the failure to successfully commercialize new products, adverse changes to Medicare and private pay reimbursement rates, and negative patent litigation outcomes.
- Our 12-month target price of $38 applies a peer average P/E to growth (PEG) ratio of about 1.5X to our 2007 EPS estimate of $1.70. We estimate three-year EPS growth of 15%, which is approximately in line with the level of peers in our coverage universe.

Qualitative Risk Assessment

LOW	**MEDIUM**	HIGH

The company operates in a highly competitive industry characterized by relatively short product life cycles and volatile market share fluctuations. However, there are significant barriers to entry in the company's core markets, as products must obtain FDA approval prior to launch and they require a large investment in both research and development, and sales.

Quantitative Evaluations

S&P Quality Ranking **B**

D	C	B-	**B**	B+	A-	A	A+

Relative Strength Rank **WEAK**

15

LOWEST = 1 HIGHEST = 99

Revenue/Earnings Data

Revenue (Million $)

	1Q	2Q	3Q	4Q	Year
2006	784.4	832.9	821.3	--	--
2005	663.9	723.7	737.8	789.9	2,915
2004	548.6	556.6	578.3	610.7	2,294
2003	441.4	495.1	477.5	518.6	1,933
2002	371.2	404.4	404.9	409.5	1,590
2001	326.1	336.1	337.0	348.2	1,347

Earnings Per Share ($)

	1Q	2Q	3Q	4Q	Year
2006	0.36	0.38	0.32	**E**0.38	**E**1.43
2005	0.32	0.27	0.44	0.01	1.04
2004	0.26	0.27	0.25	0.33	1.10
2003	0.22	0.22	0.23	0.26	0.92
2002	0.17	0.19	0.20	0.20	0.76
2001	0.13	0.12	0.09	0.14	0.48

Fiscal year ended Dec. 31. Next earnings report expected: Late January. EPS Estimates based on S&P Operating Earnings; historical GAAP earnings are as reported.

Dividend Data

No cash dividends have been paid since 1994.

Please read the Required Disclosures and Analyst Certification on the last page of this report.

St. Jude Medical Inc.

Business Summary October 19, 2006

CORPORATE OVERVIEW. St. Jude Medical sells medical devices in the cardiac rhythm management (CRM), cardiology, cardiac surgery, atrial fibrillation, and pain management categories. Although the company has a diversified product line, the principal driver of growth in recent years has been the CRM segment, where it sells pacemakers and defibrillators.

CRM products (66% of 2005 sales) include implantable cardioverter defibrillators (ICDs) that are used to treat hearts that beat too fast (tachycardia) by monitoring the heartbeat and delivering high energy electrical impulses to terminate ventricular tachychardia and ventricular fibrillation. ICD products include the Atlas, Photon, and Contour lines, as well as the Epic HF and Atlas+ HF ICDs with the ventricle-to-ventricle (V-to-V) timing feature.

Also within the CRM division, pacemakers and related systems are sold to treat patients with hearts that beat too slowly (bradycardia). Current pacemakers include the Victory and Victory XL models that provide the enhancements of earlier STJ models, plus new capabilities such as automatic P-wave and R-wave measurements with trends, lead monitoring and automatic polarity switch, follow-up electrograms, and Ventricular Intrinsic Preference (VIP) to reduce right ventricle pacing and a ventricular rate during an automatic mode switch histogram.

Company Financials

Per Share Data ($) Year Ended Dec. 31	**2005**	**2004**	**2003**	**2002**	**2001**	**2000**	**1999**	**1998**	**1997**	**1996**
Tangible Book Value	1.84	4.27	3.02	3.27	2.28	1.50	1.02	1.44	1.75	1.47
Cash Flow	1.38	1.34	1.12	0.96	0.74	0.65	0.32	0.57	0.33	0.42
Earnings	1.04	1.10	0.92	0.76	0.48	0.38	0.07	0.38	0.15	0.28
S&P Core Earnings	0.90	1.03	0.82	0.63	0.38	NA	NA	NA	NA	NA
Dividends	Nil	Nil	Nil	Nil	Nil	Nil	Nil	Nil	Nil	Nil
Payout Ratio	Nil	Nil	Nil	Nil	Nil	Nil	Nil	Nil	Nil	Nil
Prices:High	52.80	42.90	32.00	21.56	19.52	15.63	10.19	9.92	10.73	11.50
Prices:Low	34.48	29.90	19.38	15.26	11.11	5.91	5.73	4.80	6.75	7.41
P/E Ratio:High	51	39	35	29	41	41	NM	26	73	41
P/E Ratio:Low	33	27	21	20	23	16	NM	13	46	26

Income Statement Analysis (Million $)										
Revenue	2,915	2,294	1,933	1,590	1,347	1,179	1,115	1,016	994	809
Operating Income	911	672	533	445	347	326	300	263	212	260
Depreciation	130	85.8	76.7	74.9	90.3	92.3	85.7	68.9	66.1	44.9
Interest Expense	Nil	Nil	Nil	Nil	Nil	Nil	Nil	23.7	14.4	3.54
Pretax Income	621	537	459	373	228	177	67.0	186	88.2	142
Effective Tax Rate	36.7%	23.7%	26.0%	26.0%	24.3%	27.2%	63.8%	30.5%	38.0%	35.0%
Net Income	393	410	339	276	173	129	24.2	129	54.7	92.2
S&P Core Earnings	341	377	302	231	136	NA	NA	NA	NA	NA

Balance Sheet & Other Financial Data (Million $)										
Cash	535	688	461	402	148	108	88.9	88.0	28.5	185
Current Assets	1,941	1,863	1,492	1,114	798	705	690	682	743	665
Total Assets	4,845	3,231	2,556	1,951	1,629	1,533	1,554	1,385	1,459	1,301
Current Liabilities	1,534	605	510	375	322	297	283	203	252	293
Long Term Debt	177	235	352	Nil	123	295	477	375	220	172
Common Equity	2,883	2,334	1,604	1,577	1,184	941	794	806	987	836
Total Capital	3,217	2,625	2,046	1,577	1,307	1,235	1,272	1,181	1,207	1,008
Capital Expenditures	159	89.5	49.6	62.2	63.1	39.7	69.4	74.2	94.0	95.0
Cash Flow	524	496	416	351	263	221	110	198	121	137
Current Ratio	1.3	3.1	2.9	3.0	2.5	2.4	2.4	3.4	3.0	2.3
% Long Term Debt of Capitalization	5.5	8.9	17.2	Nil	9.4	23.8	37.6	31.7	18.2	17.1
% Net Income of Revenue	13.5	17.9	17.6	17.4	12.8	11.0	2.2	12.7	5.5	11.4
% Return on Assets	9.7	14.2	15.1	15.4	10.9	8.4	1.6	9.1	4.0	7.9
% Return on Equity	15.1	20.8	21.3	20.0	16.2	14.9	3.0	14.4	6.0	11.8

Data as orig reptd.; bef. results of disc opers/spec. items. Per share data adj. for stk. divs.; EPS diluted. E-Estimated. NA-Not Available. NM-Not Meaningful. NR-Not Ranked. UR-Under Review.

Office: One Lillehei Plaza, St. Paul, MN 55117.
Telephone: 651-483-2000.
Website: http://www.sjm.com
Chrmn, Pres & CEO: D.J. Starks

Investor Contact: J.C. Heinmiller (651-483-2000)
EVP, CFO & Treas: J.C. Heinmiller
VP, Secy & General Counsel: K.T. O'Malley
VP & Cntlr: D. Zurbay

Board of Directors: J. W. Brown, R. Devenuti, S. M. Essig, T. H. Garrett, III, M. A. Rocca, D. A. Thompson, S. Widensohler, W. Yarno, F. Yin

Founded: 1976
Domicile: Minnesota
Employees: 10,000

St. Paul Travelers Companies Inc. (The)

STANDARD &POOR'S

S&P Recommendation	Price	12-Mo. Target Price	Investment Style
BUY ★★★★★	$49.92 (as of Oct 27, 2006)	$58.00	Large-Cap Value

GICS Sector Financials
Sub-Industry Property & Casualty Insurance

Comment Formed via the 2004 merger of Travelers Property Casualty Corp. and Saint Paul Cos., STA is a leading provider of commercial property-liability and homeowners and auto insurance.

Key Stock Statistics (Source S&P, Vickers, company reports)

52-Wk Range	$51.18–40.23	S&P Oper. EPS 2006E	5.60	P/E on S&P Oper. EPS 2006E	8.9	Dividend Rate/Share	$1.04
Trailing 12-Month EPS	$4.49	S&P Oper. EPS 2007E	5.85	Common Shares Outstg. (M)	690.9	Yield (%)	2.08
Trailing 12-Month P/E	11.1	S&P Core EPS 2006E	5.48	Market Capitalization(B)	$34.491	Beta	1.16
$10K Invested 5 Yrs Ago	NA	S&P Core EPS 2007E	5.73	Institutional Ownership (%)	85	S&P Credit Rating	A-

Price Performance

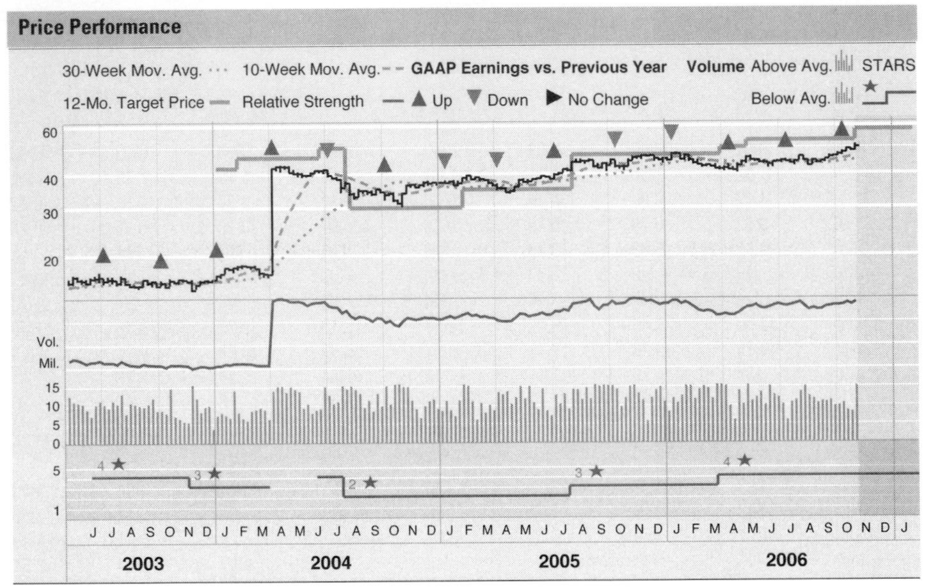

Qualitative Risk Assessment

LOW | **MEDIUM** | HIGH

Our risk assessment reflects our view of STA as a leading property-casualty underwriter with a diversified mix of business and sound capital management practices. Offsetting this is our view that STA may have to add to loss reserves for certain "long tail" liability lines of coverage.

Quantitative Evaluations

S&P Quality Ranking NR

D | C | B- | B | B+ | A- | A | A+

Relative Strength Rank STRONG

76

LOWEST = 1 HIGHEST = 99

Revenue/Earnings Data

Revenue (Million $)

	1Q	2Q	3Q	4Q	Year
2006	6,050	6,255	6,316	--	--
2005	6,105	6,037	6,042	6,181	24,365
2004	4,128	6,181	6,261	6,365	22,934
2003	3,603	3,749	3,746	4,042	15,139
2002	3,233	3,320	3,564	4,153	14,270
2001	3,058	2,983	3,012	3,178	12,231

Earnings Per Share ($)

2006	1.41	1.36	1.47	**E**1.38	**E**5.60
2005	1.25	1.33	0.11	0.26	2.95
2004	1.34	-0.42	0.50	0.44	1.53
2003	0.34	0.44	0.42	0.49	1.68
2002	0.43	0.33	0.33	-0.79	0.23
2001	--	--	--	--	1.06

Fiscal year ended Dec. 31. Next earnings report expected: Early February. EPS Estimates based on S&P Operating Earnings; historical GAAP earnings are as reported.

Dividend Data (Dates: mm/dd Payment Date: mm/dd/yy)

Amount ($)	Date Decl.	Ex-Div. Date	Stk. of Record	Payment Date
0.230	10/25	12/07	12/09	12/30/05
0.230	02/07	03/08	03/10	03/31/06
0.260	05/02	06/07	06/09	06/30/06
0.260	08/03	09/06	09/08	09/29/06

Dividends have been paid since 2003. Source: Company reports.

Highlights

- The 12-month target price for STA has recently been changed to $58.00 from $53.00. The Highlights section of this Stock Report will be updated accordingly.

Investment Rationale/Risk

- The Investment Rationale/Risk section of this Stock Report will be updated shortly. For the latest News story on STA from MarketScope, see below.
- 10/26/06 11:34 am EDT... S&P MAINTAINS BUY RECOMMENDATION ON SHARES OF SAINT PAUL TRAVELERS COS. (STA 50.75****): STA reports $1.46 vs. $0.07 Q3 operating EPS, besting our $1.10 estimate. Though results were aided by sharply lower catastrophe losses, we are encouraged that STA used the favorable loss development in certain casualty lines to offset a prudent boost to its asbestos reserves. We are also encouraged by 4% rise in YTD written premiums, which is above many peers. We are increasing our '06 EPS estimate by $0.60 to $5.60, '07's by $0.50 to $5.85. We are raising our target price by $5 to $58, 1.8X estimated '07 tangible book, the upper end of STA's historical range. / C.Seifert

St. Paul Travelers Companies Inc. (The)

Business Summary September 27, 2006

CORPORATE OVERVIEW. STA is a leading property-casualty underwriter. Net written premiums of $20.4 billion in 2005 were divided as follows: commercial lines 41%, personal lines 31%, and specialty lines 28%.

The commercial lines segment offers a broad array of coverages that are distributed through approximately 6,300 independent brokers and agencies throughout the United States. Commercial lines net written premiums totaled $8.4 billion in 2005 and were divided as follows: commercial multi-peril 34%, commercial auto 20%, workers' compensation 20%, commercial property 17%, and general liability 9%. More than half of this unit's premium volume in 2005 was derived from STA's commercial accounts unit, which targets the sale of casualty products to mid-sized companies and property-based products to firms of various sizes.

The specialty lines segment underwrites a number of specialized lines of business, including lines of coverage related to the surety bond business, the construction industry, and certain types of professional and managerial liability lines of coverage. This unit operates throughout the U.S. and in the United Kingdom, Canada and Ireland. Net written premiums totaled $5.7 billion in 2005 and were divided as follows: general liability 37%, fidelity and surety 18%, international 19%, workers' compensation 8%, commercial auto 6%, property 10%, and commercial multi-peril 2%. During 2005, the bond business (primarily surety bonds) accounted for 23% of this unit's premium volume, construction for 16%, financial and professional services for 15%, international for 19%, and other for 27%.

The personal lines segment underwrites an array of coverage covering personal risks (primarily personal automobile and homeowners' coverage) via a network of independent agencies. Net premiums written of $6.2 billion in 2005 were divided as follows: personal auto 58% and homeowners' and other 44%. Business in New York state accounted for more than 16% of this unit's premium volume in 2005.

Company Financials

Per Share Data ($) Year Ended Dec. 31	2005	2004	2003	2002	2001	2000	1999	1998	1997	1996
Tangible Book Value	25.66	20.93	9.52	10.29	6.66	NA	NA	NA	NA	NA
Operating Earnings	NA	NA	NA	NA	NA	NA	NA	NA	NA	NA
Earnings	2.95	1.53	1.68	0.23	1.06	NA	NA	NA	NA	NA
S&P Core Earnings	2.87	1.50	3.71	0.14	2.42	NA	NA	NA	NA	NA
Dividends	0.91	0.74	0.28	Nil	NA	NA	NA	NA	NA	NA
Payout Ratio	31%	48%	17%	Nil	NA	NA	NA	NA	NA	NA
Prices:High	46.97	43.31	17.42	19.50	NA	NA	NA	NA	NA	NA
Prices:Low	33.70	16.55	12.98	12.09	NA	NA	NA	NA	NA	NA
P/E Ratio:High	16	28	10	85	NA	NA	NA	NA	NA	NA
P/E Ratio:Low	11	11	8	53	NA	NA	NA	NA	NA	NA

Income Statement Analysis (Million $)										
Premium Income	20,341	19,038	12,545	11,155	9,411	NA	NA	NA	NA	NA
Net Investment Income	3,165	2,663	1,869	1,881	2,034	NA	NA	NA	NA	NA
Other Revenue	21,200	20,271	725	1,234	786	NA	NA	NA	NA	NA
Total Revenue	24,365	22,934	15,139	14,270	12,231	NA	NA	NA	NA	NA
Pretax Income	2,671	1,128	2,229	-260	1,389	NA	NA	NA	NA	NA
Net Operating Income	NA	NA	NA	NA	NA	NA	NA	NA	NA	NA
Net Income	2,061	955	1,696	216	1,062	NA	NA	NA	NA	NA
S&P Core Earnings	2,001	937	1,615	41.1	803	NA	NA	NA	NA	NA

Balance Sheet & Other Financial Data (Million $)										
Cash & Equivalent	2,420	2,467	714	432	NA	NA	NA	NA	NA	NA
Premiums Due	19,574	25,255	4,090	3,861	NA	NA	NA	NA	NA	NA
Investment Assets:Bonds	58,983	54,256	33,046	30,003	NA	NA	NA	NA	NA	NA
Investment Assets:Stocks	579	791	733	852	NA	NA	NA	NA	NA	NA
Investment Assets:Loans	145	191	211	258	32,843	NA	NA	NA	NA	NA
Investment Assets:Total	68,287	64,710	38,652	38,425	NA	NA	NA	NA	NA	NA
Deferred Policy Costs	1,527	1,559	925	873	NA	NA	NA	NA	NA	NA
Total Assets	113,187	111,815	64,872	64,138	57,599	NA	NA	NA	NA	NA
Debt	5,850	5,709	2,675	2,744	3,755	NA	NA	NA	NA	NA
Common Equity	33,077	32,323	11,987	10,137	9,729	NA	NA	NA	NA	NA
Property & Casualty:Loss Ratio	71.9	NA	NA	NA	80.7	NA	NA	NA	NA	NA
Property & Casualty:Expense Ratio	29.4	NA	NA	NA	27.3	NA	NA	NA	NA	NA
Property & Casualty Combined Ratio	101.3	107.7	96.9	117.4	108.0	NA	NA	NA	NA	NA
% Return on Revenue	8.5	4.2	11.2	1.6	8.7	NA	NA	NA	NA	NA
% Return on Equity	6.3	3.7	15.3	NA	NA	NA	NA	NA	NA	NA

Data as orig reptd.; bef. results of disc opers/spec. items. Per share data adj. for stk. divs.; EPS diluted. E-Estimated. NA-Not Available. NM-Not Meaningful. NR-Not Ranked. UR-Under Review.

Office: 385 Washington Street, Saint Paul, MN 55102.
Telephone: 651-310-7911.
Website: http://www.stpaultravelers.com
Chrmn, Pres & CEO: J.S. Fishman

Vice Chrmn: C.J. Clarke
Vice Chrmn: I.R. Ettinger
Vice Chrmn: J.A. MacColl
Vice Chrmn: W.H. Heyman

Investor Contact: M. Parr (860-277-0779)
Board of Directors: J. H. Dasburg, L. B. Disharoon, J. M. Dolan, K. M. Duberstein, J. S. Fishman, L. G. Graev, T. R. Hodgson, R. I. Lipp, B. J. McGarvie, G. D. Nelson, C. Otis, Jr., L. J. Thomsen

Auditor: KPMG, Minneapolis, MN
Founded: 1853
Domicile: Minnesota
Employees: 31,900

STANDARD &POOR'S

SanDisk Corp

S&P Recommendation HOLD ★★★★★

Price
$48.10 (as of Oct 31, 2006)

12-Mo. Target Price
$53.00

Investment Style
Large-Cap Growth

GICS Sector Information Technology
Sub-Industry Computer Storage & Peripherals

Comment This company designs, makes and markets flash memory storage products used in a wide variety of electronic systems.

Key Stock Statistics (Source S&P, Vickers, company reports)

52-Wk Range	$79.80–37.34	S&P Oper. EPS 2006E	1.82	P/E on S&P Oper. EPS 2006E	26.4	Dividend Rate/Share	Nil
Trailing 12-Month EPS	$1.83	S&P Oper. EPS 2007E	2.20	Common Shares Outstg. (M)	196.0	Yield (%)	Nil
Trailing 12-Month P/E	26.3	S&P Core EPS 2006E	1.82	Market Capitalization(B)	$9.426	Beta	3.37
$10K Invested 5 Yrs Ago	$76,680	S&P Core EPS 2007E	2.20	Institutional Ownership (%)	92	S&P Credit Rating	BB-

Price Performance

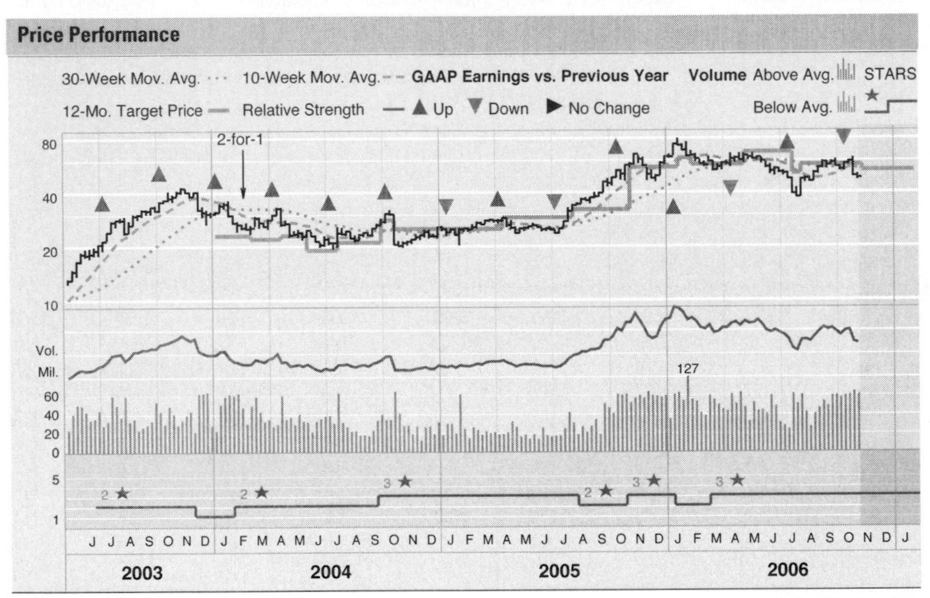

Options: ASE, CBOE, P, Ph

Highlights

➤ The 12-month target price for SNDK has recently been changed to $53.00 from $57.00. The Highlights section of this Stock Report will be updated accordingly.

Investment Rationale/Risk

➤ The Investment Rationale/Risk section of this Stock Report will be updated shortly.

Qualitative Risk Assessment

LOW | MEDIUM | **HIGH**

Our risk assessment takes into consideration the volatile nature of the flash memory space, an intensifying competitive environment, and what we deem to be significant price erosion within the industry.

Quantitative Evaluations

S&P Quality Ranking **B**

D | C | B- | **B** | B+ | A- | A | A+

Relative Strength Rank **WEAK**

9

LOWEST = 1 HIGHEST = 99

Revenue/Earnings Data

Revenue (Million $)

	1Q	2Q	3Q	4Q	Year
2006	623.3	719.2	751.4	--	--
2005	451.0	514.9	589.6	750.6	2,306
2004	386.9	433.3	408.0	548.9	1,777
2003	174.5	234.6	281.4	389.3	1,080
2002	92.62	127.7	141.1	179.8	541.3
2001	101.3	107.2	65.89	91.94	366.3

Earnings Per Share ($)

2006	0.17	0.47	0.51	**E**0.70	**E**1.82
2005	0.39	0.37	0.55	0.68	2.00
2004	0.34	0.38	0.29	0.42	1.44
2003	0.17	0.26	0.09	0.47	1.02
2002	-0.03	0.07	0.08	0.13	0.26
2001	-1.05	-0.08	-1.25	0.18	-2.19

Fiscal year ended Dec. 31. Next earnings report expected: Late January. EPS Estimates based on S&P Operating Earnings; historical GAAP earnings are as reported.

Dividend Data

No cash dividends have been paid.

Please read the Required Disclosures and Analyst Certification on the last page of this report.

SanDisk Corp

Business Summary October 24, 2006

CORPORATE OVERVIEW. SanDisk Corp. designs, makes and markets flash storage card products used in a wide variety of consumer electronics products such as digital cameras, mobile phones, Universal Serial Bus, or USB, drives, gaming devices and MP3 players. Flash storage allows data to be stored in a compact format that retains the data for an extended period of time after the power has been turned off. The company's strategy focuses on identifying and developing current and emerging mass consumer markets for flash storage products and -- through its vertical integration supply strategy -- selling all major card formats in high volumes.

CORPORATE STRATEGY. SNDK focuses primarily on five consumer electronics markets: imaging, mobile phones, USB flash drives, gaming devices and digital audio players. In the imaging market, the company makes cards used in all major brands of digital cameras. For mobile phones, SNDK's cards are experiencing increasing demand as multimedia features such as video and Internet access become more prevalent. USB flash drives allow consumers to store computer files and transfer them between laptops, desktops and other devices. More robust portable game consoles have expanded the need for storage capabilities. Finally, SNDK offers a number of digital audio players, which allow consumers to download, store and play music.

Products are available to end users at approximately 200,000 retail storefronts around the globe and as data storage cards bundled with host products by SNDK's OEM customers. In 2005, the retail market accounted for 78% of product revenues, compared with 77% in 2004, while the OEM channel comprised 22% (23%). Also in 2005, SNDK's top 10 customers and licensees accounted for 50% of total revenues, down from 55% in 2004. Best Buy (BBY: buy, $48) was the only customer during 2005 that accounted for more than 10% of total revenues.

SNDK develops and owns leading edge technology and patents for flash memory and data storage cards. One key technology patented and successfully commercialized by the company is multi-level cell technology, or MLC, which allows a flash memory cell to be programmed to store two or more bits of data in about the same area of silicon that is typically required to store one bit of data. SNDK has an extensive patent portfolio that has been licensed by three of the four largest semiconductor companies based on revenues. Over the past three years, on a cumulative basis, the company's license and royalty revenues have exceeded $500 million.

Company Financials

Per Share Data ($) Year Ended Dec. 31	**2005**	**2004**	**2003**	**2002**	**2001**	**2000**	**1999**	**1998**	**1997**	**1996**
Tangible Book Value	13.41	10.78	9.32	4.54	4.93	6.40	4.38	1.95	1.85	0.98
Cash Flow	2.34	1.62	1.12	0.40	-2.04	2.17	0.26	0.17	0.23	0.19
Earnings	2.00	1.44	1.02	0.26	-2.19	2.06	0.22	0.11	0.20	0.15
S&P Core Earnings	1.76	1.29	0.89	0.18	-1.05	NA	NA	NA	NA	NA
Dividends	Nil	Nil	Nil	Nil	Nil	Nil	Nil	Nil	Nil	Nil
Payout Ratio	Nil	Nil	Nil	Nil	Nil	Nil	Nil	Nil	Nil	Nil
Prices:High	65.49	36.35	43.15	14.60	24.34	84.81	25.16	6.56	10.00	5.44
Prices:Low	20.25	19.28	7.39	4.80	4.30	13.75	3.31	1.28	2.22	2.19
P/E Ratio:High	33	25	42	57	NM	41	NM	61	51	36
P/E Ratio:Low	10	13	7	19	NM	7	NM	12	11	14
Income Statement Analysis (Million $)										
Revenue	2,306	1,777	1,080	541	366	602	247	136	125	97.6
Operating Income	642	457	280	79.5	-124	141	37.2	18.6	23.7	14.8
Depreciation	65.8	38.9	23.0	21.3	20.5	15.9	7.15	5.84	3.99	2.35
Interest Expense	0.57	5.95	6.75	6.70	Nil	Nil	Nil	Nil	NA	0.00
Pretax Income	613	423	242	40.0	-442	492	39.6	18.5	23.3	15.6
Effective Tax Rate	37.0%	37.0%	30.2%	9.35%	NM	39.3%	33.0%	36.0%	15.0%	7.30%
Net Income	386	267	169	36.2	-298	299	26.6	11.8	19.8	14.5
S&P Core Earnings	339	239	149	25.7	-144	NA	NA	NA	NA	NA
Balance Sheet & Other Financial Data (Million $)										
Cash	762	464	734	267	254	106	146	15.4	20.9	19.3
Current Assets	2,576	1,880	1,725	757	542	697	568	186	188	97.5
Total Assets	3,120	2,320	2,024	976	932	1,108	658	256	245	108
Current Liabilities	571	353	347	173	127	171	85.6	47.9	54.1	20.5
Long Term Debt	Nil	Nil	150	150	125	Nil	Nil	Nil	Nil	Nil
Common Equity	2,524	1,940	1,501	628	675	863	572	208	191	87.8
Total Capital	2,524	1,940	1,651	778	800	863	572	208	191	87.8
Capital Expenditures	134	126	52.5	16.6	26.2	26.6	21.4	7.49	9.60	8.40
Cash Flow	452	305	192	57.6	-277	315	33.7	17.7	23.8	16.8
Current Ratio	4.5	5.3	5.0	4.4	4.3	4.1	6.6	3.9	3.5	4.8
% Long Term Debt of Capitalization	Nil	Nil	9.1	19.3	15.6	Nil	Nil	Nil	Nil	Nil
% Net Income of Revenue	16.8	15.0	15.6	6.7	NM	49.6	10.7	8.7	15.8	14.8
% Return on Assets	14.2	12.2	11.3	3.8	NM	33.8	5.8	4.7	11.2	14.5
% Return on Equity	17.3	15.4	15.9	5.6	NM	41.6	6.8	5.9	14.2	18.1

Data as orig reptd.; bef. results of disc opers/spec. items. Per share data adj. for stk. divs.; EPS diluted. E-Estimated. NA-Not Available. NM-Not Meaningful. NR-Not Ranked. UR-Under Review.

Office: 140 Caspian Court, Sunnyvale, CA 94089.
Telephone: 408-542-0500.
Email: investor_relations@sandisk.com
Website: http://www.sandisk.com

Chrmn & CEO: E. Harari
Pres & COO: S. Mehrotra
Vice Chrmn: I. Federman
EVP, CFO & Chief Acctg Officer: J. Bruner

Investor Contact: L.B. Padon (408-542-0585)
Board of Directors: I. Federman, S. J. Gomo, E. Harari, E. W. Hartenstein, C. P. Lego, M. Marks, J. D. Meindl, A. F. Shugart

Auditor: Ernst & Young
Founded: 1988
Domicile: Delaware
Employees: 1,083

STANDARD &POOR'S

Sanmina SCI Corporation

S&P Recommendation HOLD ★★★★★

Price $3.81 (as of Oct 27, 2006)

12-Mo. Target Price $4.00

Investment Style Mid-Cap Value

GICS Sector Information Technology
Sub-Industry Electronic Manufacturing Services

Comment This company provides customized integrated manufacturing services to OEMs in the electronics industry.

Key Stock Statistics (Source S&P, Vickers, company reports)

52-Wk Range	$5.85–3.04	S&P Oper. EPS 2006E	0.27	P/E on S&P Oper. EPS 2006E	14.1	Dividend Rate/Share	Nil
Trailing 12-Month EPS	$-0.14	S&P Oper. EPS 2007E	0.41	Common Shares Outstg. (M)	532.8	Yield (%)	Nil
Trailing 12-Month P/E	NM	S&P Core EPS 2006E	0.16	Market Capitalization(B)	$2.030	Beta	3.31
$10K Invested 5 Yrs Ago	$2,337	S&P Core EPS 2007E	0.41	Institutional Ownership (%)	81	S&P Credit Rating	BB-

Price Performance

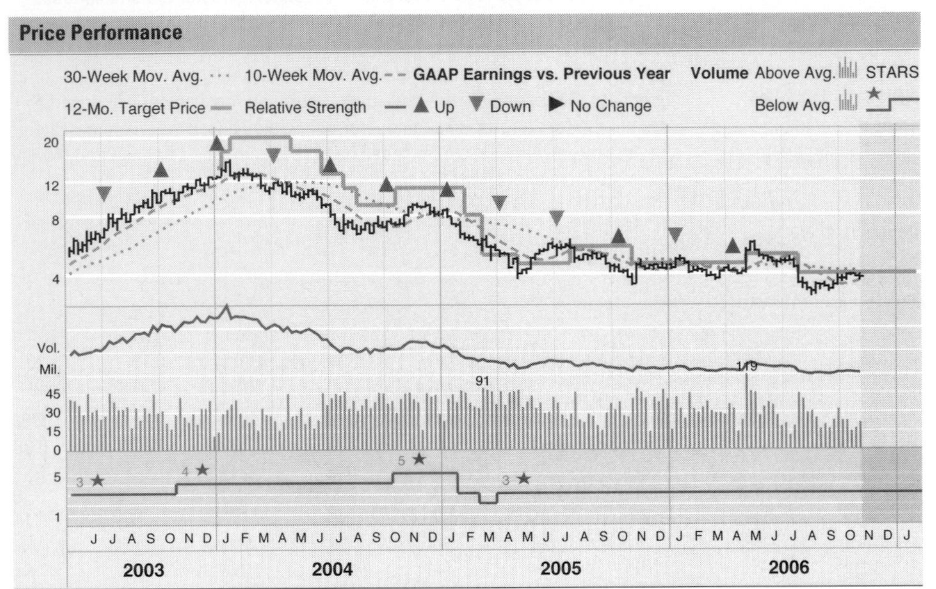

Options: CBOE

Analysis prepared by **Richard N. Stice, CFA** on August 07, 2006, when the stock traded at **$ 3.27**.

Highlights

- We expect revenues to increase 3.5% in FY 07 (Sep.), following a projected decline of 6% in FY 06. We think results should benefit from an acceleration in demand for outsourcing services, an increasing focus on non-traditional markets, and benefits from the company's original design manufacturing business, where we see a developing interest by customers to collaborate on product creation.

- We see gross margins as likely to widen due to a more favorable business mix and ongoing efficiency improvements, including the expected completion of its major restructuring initiatives. We anticipate SG&A costs will remain relatively constant, at about 3% of revenues. Interest expense should decline significantly, in our estimation, following the early retirement of $750 million of high yield notes.

- We forecast FY 07 operating EPS of $0.41, which includes projected stock option expense, a 52% increase from our FY 06 estimate of $0.27. The FY 06 total excludes special charges of $0.43.

Investment Rationale/Risk

- We think the company continues to face limited near-term demand and visibility. Moreover, we believe that an ongoing internal investigation related to its stock option granting practices adds an element of uncertainty. However, we believe recent execution difficulties are being addressed, and anticipate beneficial results to emerge over the next several quarters as restructuring efforts are completed.

- Risks to our recommendation and target price include a financial restatement or filing delays stemming from the company's stock option probe. Regarding SANM's corporate governance practices, we are concerned that the positions of chairman and CEO are held by the same individual.

- Our 12-month target price of $4 is based on a blend of metrics. The first is a calendar 2006 P/E measure, equated to the S&P 500 Index, that results in a value of $4.00. The second relates to discounted cash flow analysis with a calculated intrinsic value of $3. Our DCF model assumes a weighted average cost of capital of 12.4%.

Qualitative Risk Assessment

LOW | MEDIUM | **HIGH**

Our risk assessment reflects the volatility of SANM's business model, the ongoing reduction of its market share, its high debt level relative to its peer group, and net losses in each of the past four fiscal years.

Quantitative Evaluations

S&P Quality Ranking **C**

D | **C** | B- | B | B+ | A- | A | A+

Relative Strength Rank **MODERATE**

40

LOWEST = 1 HIGHEST = 99

Revenue/Earnings Data

Revenue (Million $)

	1Q	2Q	3Q	4Q	Year
2006	2,862	2,668	--	--	--
2005	3,253	2,885	2,831	2,765	11,735
2004	2,970	2,862	3,070	3,302	12,205
2003	2,537	2,444	2,649	2,732	10,361
2002	1,130	2,411	2,618	2,602	8,762
2001	1,390	1,191	776.6	600.7	4,054

Earnings Per Share ($)

2006	0.04	-0.20	**E**0.06	**E**0.08	**E**0.27
2005	0.05	-1.99	Nil	0.01	-1.93
2004	0.03	-0.09	0.02	Nil	-0.03
2003	-0.01	-0.06	-0.02	-0.17	-0.27
2002	-0.12	-0.08	-0.01	-5.10	-5.60
2001	0.34	0.19	0.09	-0.52	0.12

Fiscal year ended Sep. 30. Next earnings report expected: NA. EPS Estimates based on S&P Operating Earnings; historical GAAP earnings are as reported.

Dividend Data

No cash dividends have been paid.

Sanmina SCI Corporation

Business Summary August 07, 2006

CORPORATE OVERVIEW. This provider of electronics manufacturing services (EMS) works with customers in a number of industries including the communications, computing and storage markets. SANM operates in a number of locations around the world, with manufacturing facilities in both China and Mexico exceeding 1.5 million square feet of space.

In 2005, one customer, International Business Machines Corp. (IBM: buy, $73) accounted for greater than 10% of total revenues (23.2%). A substantial portion of SANM's business with IBM relates to personal computer (PC) products. In December 2004, IBM sold this portion of its business to Lenovo Group, Ltd., a Chinese manufacturer of PCs.

MARKET PROFILE. We believe the EMS industry remains well positioned to capture new business from original equipment manufacturers (OEMs). This is due to our view that the cost advantages associated with the outsourcing model are beginning to be understood by potential participants. We think the benefits of this strategy are ample, with companies being able to reduce costs and reallocate resources toward their core competencies (e.g., marketing and research and development). According to research firm IDC, the industry is projected to grow at a low double digit annual rate over the next several years and achieve nearly $180 billion in revenue by 2009.

We see a number of key trends emerging in the EMS landscape. For instance, OEMs have begun to limit the number of EMS providers with which they conduct business. We think this move results from customers' desire to streamline their operations. While in the past, they may have utilized five or six vendors, many now seek to limit that total to one or two. We believe this development bodes well for larger EMS companies such as SANM, as their broad range of service offerings and worldwide presence enable them to fulfill an entire slate of customer requests, in our opinion.

Company Financials

Per Share Data ($) Year Ended Sep. 30	**2005**	**2004**	**2003**	**2002**	**2001**	**2000**	**1999**	**1998**	**1997**	**1996**
Tangible Book Value	1.24	2.10	2.23	2.50	4.85	4.54	2.46	1.70	1.08	0.71
Cash Flow	-1.59	0.34	0.17	5.00	0.07	1.14	0.50	0.47	0.37	0.28
Earnings	-1.93	-0.03	-0.27	-5.60	0.12	0.64	0.38	0.36	0.17	0.20
S&P Core Earnings	-1.48	-0.12	-0.37	-2.11	-0.01	NA	NA	NA	NA	NA
Dividends	Nil	Nil	Nil	Nil	Nil	Nil	Nil	Nil	Nil	Nil
Payout Ratio	Nil	Nil	Nil	Nil	Nil	Nil	Nil	Nil	Nil	Nil
Prices:High	8.68	15.51	12.81	23.80	54.75	60.50	27.31	15.63	11.34	7.09
Prices:Low	3.45	6.30	3.43	1.52	11.64	21.06	12.38	4.91	4.75	2.53
P/E Ratio:High	NM	NM	NM	NM	NM	95	72	44	41	35
P/E Ratio:Low	NM	NM	NM	NM	NM	33	33	14	17	13
Income Statement Analysis (Million $)										
Revenue	11,735	12,205	10,361	8,762	4,054	3,912	1,215	723	405	265
Operating Income	430	438	357	331	456	545	220	139	81.5	53.4
Depreciation	178	191	223	250	181	157	48.8	27.3	12.9	8.10
Interest Expense	142	133	130	98.0	55.2	Nil	Nil	0.69	5.10	5.16
Pretax Income	-594	-15.6	-198	-2,814	82.8	330	148	107	67.1	45.3
Effective Tax Rate	NM	NM	NM	NM	51.1%	40.3%	36.6%	36.5%	39.0%	38.0%
Net Income	-1,000	-15.0	-137	-2,697	40.4	197	93.7	68.2	40.9	28.1
S&P Core Earnings	-772	-64.6	-193	-1,018	-1.97	NA	NA	NA	NA	NA
Balance Sheet & Other Financial Data (Million $)										
Cash	1,068	1,116	1,083	1,065	568	993	136	153	122	115
Current Assets	3,747	4,263	4,169	4,159	2,583	2,585	885	342	234	185
Total Assets	6,242	7,547	7,450	7,518	3,640	3,639	1,202	468	303	231
Current Liabilities	2,074	2,786	2,036	2,054	492	712	217	115	60.3	40.0
Long Term Debt	1,645	1,311	1,926	1,975	1,219	1,144	355	5.77	86.3	86.3
Common Equity	2,379	3,355	3,323	3,415	1,841	1,701	626	344	156	104
Total Capital	4,024	4,666	5,339	5,407	3,121	2,907	982	350	242	190
Capital Expenditures	74.5	87.2	70.7	93.0	188	199	65.3	29.0	30.2	21.8
Cash Flow	-828	176	85.4	-2,447	221	355	142	95.4	53.8	36.2
Current Ratio	1.8	1.5	2.0	2.0	5.2	3.6	4.1	3.0	3.9	4.6
% Long Term Debt of Capitalization	40.9	28.1	36.1	36.5	39.1	39.3	36.2	1.6	35.6	45.4
% Net Income of Revenue	NM	NM	NM	NM	1.0	5.0	7.7	9.4	10.1	10.6
% Return on Assets	NM	NM	NM	NM	1.1	7.0	10.1	17.7	15.3	13.4
% Return on Equity	NM	NM	NM	NM	2.2	15.4	16.9	27.3	31.5	32.9

Data as orig reptd.; bef. results of disc opers/spec. items. Per share data adj. for stk. divs.; EPS diluted. E-Estimated. NA-Not Available. NM-Not Meaningful. NR-Not Ranked. UR-Under Review.

Office: 2700 North First Street, San Jose, CA 95134.
Telephone: 408-964-3500.
Email: info@sanmina-sci.com
Website: http://www.sanmina-sci.com

Chrmn & CEO: J. Sola
EVP & CFO: D.L. White
Investor Contact: P. Bombino (408-964-3610)

Auditor: KPMG, Mountain View, CA
Board of Directors: N. R. Bonke, A. Couder, M. M. Rosati, A. E. Sapp, Jr., W. Shortridge, P. J. Simone, J. Sola, J. M. Ward

Founded: 1989
Domicile: Delaware
Employees: 48,621

STANDARD &POOR'S

Sara Lee Corp

S&P Recommendation SELL ★★★★★

Price $17.19 (as of Oct 30, 2006)

12-Mo. Target Price $15.00

Investment Style Large-Cap Growth

GICS Sector Consumer Staples
Sub-Industry Packaged Foods & Meats

Comment This diversified producer of branded food products (meats, fresh and frozen baked goods and coffee products) also makes personal apparel and household care products.

Key Stock Statistics (Source S&P, Vickers, company reports)

52-Wk Range	**$19.64–14.08**	S&P Oper. EPS 2007**E**	**0.80**	P/E on S&P Oper. EPS 2007**E**	**21.5**	Dividend Rate/Share	**$0.40**
Trailing 12-Month EPS	**$0.72**	S&P Oper. EPS 2008**E**	**0.85**	Common Shares Outstg. (M)	**770.5**	Yield (%)	**2.33**
Trailing 12-Month P/E	**23.9**	S&P Core EPS 2007**E**	**0.86**	Market Capitalization(B)	**$13.244**	Beta	**0.58**
$10K Invested 5 Yrs Ago	**$10,718**	S&P Core EPS 2008**E**	**0.92**	Institutional Ownership (%)	**60**	S&P Credit Rating	**BBB+**

Price Performance

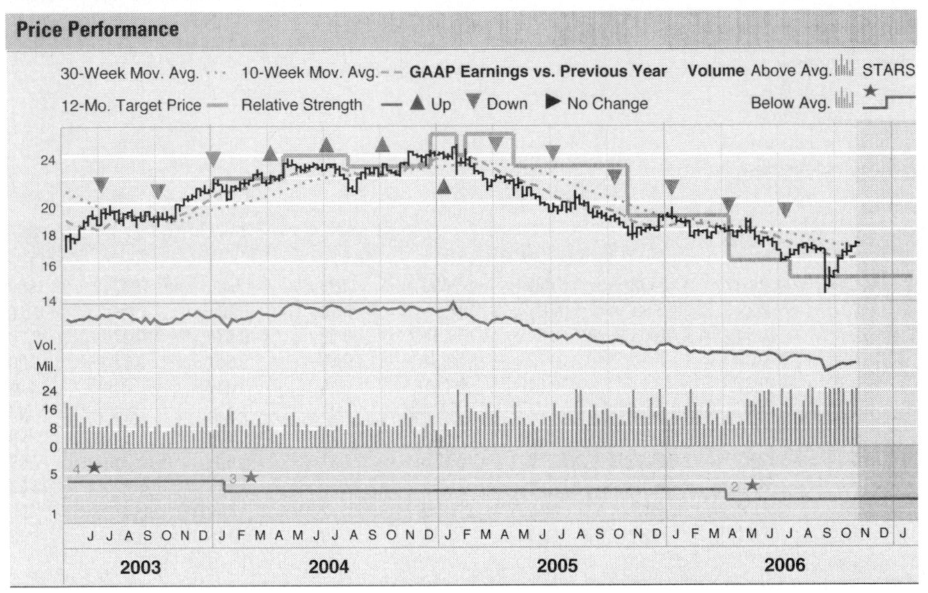

Options: ASE, CBOE, P

Analysis prepared by **Rick Joy** on October 27, 2006, when the stock traded at **$ 17.13**.

Highlights

- Sara Lee has made significant progress with its transformation plan, completing the spinoff of the Hanesbrands apparel business on September 5, 2006, and the sale of its European meats business in August 2006. During FY 06 (Jun.), the company disposed of its direct selling, European branded apparel, U.K. apparel, U.S. retail coffee, European snacks & nuts and U.S. meat snacks businesses.
- We see FY 07 net sales declining approximately 25%, as modest volume growth and higher prices are outweighed by divestitures. We anticipate that input cost inflation (coffee, fuel, energy and packaging) will continue to drag on earnings. We expect operating profit gains for the meats and beverage divisions, while profits for the bakery and household products segments should be even with the prior year.
- Following recent divestitures and the apparel business spinoff, and a reduction in shares outstanding, we project FY 07 operating EPS of $0.80, down from FY 06 operating EPS of $1.19.

Investment Rationale/Risk

- Our sell recommendation primarily reflects our belief that a turnaround for SLE's businesses is several quarters away. Results in recent quarters have been affected by mixed operating results for the company's businesses, and by higher commodity costs that we see continuing in FY 07. The company cut its dividend by more than 49% following the spinoff of its branded apparel business in September 2006.
- Risks to our recommendation and target price include a rapid improvement in the commodity cost environment, better than expected sales trends for key businesses, and the realization of cost savings from restructuring actions at a faster than expected pace.
- Our 12-month target price of $15 is based on our analysis of peer P/E multiples and enterprise value to EBITDA ratios, and our discounted cash flow analysis, which assumes a weighted average cost of capital of 9% and a terminal growth rate for cash flows of 3%.

Qualitative Risk Assessment

LOW	MEDIUM	HIGH

Our risk assessment for Sara Lee reflects the relatively stable nature of the company's end markets, strong cash flows and corporate governance practices that we view as favorable relative to peers.

Quantitative Evaluations

S&P Quality Ranking B+

D	C	B-	B	B+	A-	A	A+

Relative Strength Rank MODERATE

65

LOWEST = 1 HIGHEST = 99

Revenue/Earnings Data

Revenue (Million $)

	1Q	2Q	3Q	4Q	Year
2006	3,900	4,155	3,789	4,100	15,944
2005	4,861	5,199	4,785	4,754	19,254
2004	4,666	5,017	4,745	5,138	19,566
2003	4,534	4,776	4,350	4,631	18,291
2002	4,518	4,990	4,200	4,495	17,628
2001	4,455	4,757	4,308	4,227	17,747

Earnings Per Share ($)

	1Q	2Q	3Q	4Q	Year
2006	0.25	0.24	0.18	-0.15	0.53
2005	0.44	0.41	0.24	-0.14	0.92
2004	0.29	0.39	0.47	0.44	1.59
2003	0.38	0.42	0.33	0.37	1.50
2002	0.30	0.20	0.31	0.43	1.23
2001	0.27	0.17	0.28	1.15	1.87

Fiscal year ended Jun. 30. Next earnings report expected: Early November. EPS Estimates based on S&P Operating Earnings; historical GAAP earnings are as reported.

Dividend Data (Dates: mm/dd Payment Date: mm/dd/yy)

Amount ($)	Date Decl.	Ex-Div. Date	Stk. of Record	Payment Date
0.198	04/27	05/30	06/01	07/10/06
Stk.	08/08	08/16	08/18	09/05/06
0.100	08/08	09/11	09/13	10/06/06
0.100	10/26	11/29	12/01	01/08/07

Dividends have been paid since 1946. Source: Company reports.

Sara Lee Corp

Business Summary October 27, 2006

Sara Lee, best known for its familiar baked goods, also boasts many other branded food and non-food products, ranging from Sara Lee baked goods and Ball Park franks to Kiwi shoe polish. The company aims to build leadership brands in three highly focused global businesses: food, beverages and household products.

In February 2005, the company announced a comprehensive restructuring program, involving a reorganization of business units and plans to dispose of businesses with annual sales of $8.2 billion. The key components of the this plan are to transform the company's portfolio, reorganize continuing operations, improve operational efficiency and consolidate the North American and European headquarters. The company expects the transformation plan to be completed by 2010, and expects restructuring charges to total $1 billion over the next five years, with estimated annual cost savings of $575 million to $800 million by 2010.

During FY 06 (Jun.), Sara Lee disposed of its direct selling, European branded apparel, U.K. apparel, U.S. retail coffee, European nuts and snacks, and U.S. meat snacks businesses. In August 2006, Sara Lee completed the sale of its European meats business, and on September 5, 2006, the company completed the spinoff of its branded apparel Americas/Asia business. This business was spun off as an independent company named Hanesbrands Inc.

At the beginning of FY 06, Sara Lee reorganized its businesses around distinct customers and geographic markets. The company's new structure was organized around seven business segments; North American Retail Meats (16% of FY 06 sales), North American Retail Bakery (12%), Foodservice (14%), International Beverage (15%), International Bakery (5%), Household and Body Care (11%) and Branded Apparel (28%). As noted above, the Branded Apparel business was spun off in September 2006.

Company Financials

Per Share Data ($) Year Ended Jun. 30	**2006**	**2005**	**2004**	**2003**	**2002**	**2001**	**2000**	**1999**	**1998**	**1997**
Tangible Book Value	NM	NM	NM	NM	NM	NM	NM	NM	NM	0.35
Cash Flow	1.46	1.87	2.53	2.44	1.94	2.80	1.92	1.83	0.08	1.72
Earnings	0.53	0.92	1.59	1.50	1.23	1.87	1.27	1.26	-0.57	0.99
S&P Core Earnings	0.44	0.86	1.67	1.30	1.00	0.92	NA	NA	NA	NA
Dividends	0.79	0.78	0.60	0.62	0.60	0.57	0.54	0.49	0.45	0.41
Payout Ratio	149%	85%	38%	41%	48%	30%	43%	39%	NM	40%
Prices:High	19.64	25.00	24.49	23.13	23.84	24.75	25.31	28.75	31.81	28.88
Prices:Low	14.08	17.31	20.17	16.25	16.15	18.26	13.38	21.06	22.16	18.25
P/E Ratio:High	37	27	15	15	19	13	20	23	NM	28
P/E Ratio:Low	27	19	13	11	13	10	11	17	NM	18

Income Statement Analysis (Million $)										
Revenue	15,944	19,254	19,566	18,291	17,628	17,747	17,511	20,012	20,011	19,734
Operating Income	1,779	2,183	2,386	2,345	2,138	2,191	2,345	2,304	2,391	2,323
Depreciation	701	737	734	674	582	599	602	553	618	680
Interest Expense	308	290	271	276	304	270	252	237	224	202
Pretax Income	683	934	1,542	1,484	1,185	1,851	1,567	1,671	-443	1,484
Effective Tax Rate	40.0%	21.7%	17.5%	17.7%	14.8%	13.4%	26.1%	28.7%	NM	32.0%
Net Income	410	731	1,272	1,221	1,010	1,603	1,158	1,191	-523	1,009
S&P Core Earnings	339	684	1,336	1,047	806	768	NA	NA	NA	NA

Balance Sheet & Other Financial Data (Million $)										
Cash	2,231	545	638	942	298	548	314	279	273	272
Current Assets	6,774	5,811	5,746	5,953	4,986	5,083	5,974	4,987	5,220	5,391
Total Assets	14,522	14,412	14,883	15,084	13,753	10,167	11,611	10,521	10,989	12,953
Current Liabilities	6,277	4,968	5,423	5,199	5,463	4,958	6,759	5,953	5,733	5,016
Long Term Debt	3,807	4,115	4,171	5,157	4,326	2,640	2,248	1,892	2,270	1,933
Common Equity	2,449	2,938	2,948	1,870	1,534	899	1,007	1,034	1,561	4,280
Total Capital	6,324	7,134	7,194	7,806	7,252	4,646	4,271	3,866	4,718	7,394
Capital Expenditures	625	538	530	746	669	532	647	535	474	547
Cash Flow	1,111	1,468	2,006	1,895	1,592	2,191	1,748	1,732	71.0	1,663
Current Ratio	1.1	1.2	1.1	1.1	0.9	1.0	0.9	0.8	0.9	1.1
% Long Term Debt of Capitalization	60.2	57.6	58.0	66.1	59.7	56.8	52.6	48.9	48.1	26.1
% Net Income of Revenue	2.6	3.8	6.5	6.7	5.7	9.0	6.6	6.0	NM	5.1
% Return on Assets	2.8	5.0	8.4	8.5	8.4	14.7	10.6	11.1	NM	7.9
% Return on Equity	15.2	24.7	52.8	71.7	83.0	167.1	112.3	90.9	NM	22.9

Data as orig reptd.; bef. results of disc opers/spec. items. Per share data adj. for stk. divs.; EPS diluted. E Estimated. NA-Not Available. NM-Not Meaningful. NR-Not Ranked. UR-Under Review.

Office: 3 First National Plz, Chicago, IL 60602-5010.
Telephone: 312-726-2600.
Website: http://www.saralee.com
Chrmn & CEO: B.C. Barnes

EVP, CFO & Chief Admin: L.M. de Kool
EVP, Secy & General Counsel: R.A. Palmore
SVP, Chief Acctg Officer & Cntlr: W. Szypulski
Investor Contact: D. Ferguson (312-726-2600)

Auditor: Pricewaterhousecoopers
Board of Directors: B. C. Barnes, J. T. Battenberg, III, C. B. Begley, C. B. Carroll, V. Colbert, J. S. Crown, W. D. Davis, L. T. Koellner, I. Prosser, R. L. Ridgway, J. P. Ward, C. J. van Lede

Founded: 1941
Domicile: Maryland
Employees: 109,000

STANDARD &POOR'S

Schering-Plough

S&P Recommendation	Price	12-Mo. Target Price	Investment Style
BUY ★★★★	$22.70 (as of Oct 27, 2006)	$27.00	Large-Cap Growth

GICS Sector Health Care
Sub-Industry Pharmaceuticals

Comment This leading producer of prescription and OTC pharmaceuticals also has important interests in sun care, animal health and foot care products.

Key Stock Statistics (Source S&P, Vickers, company reports)

52-Wk Range	$23.28–17.88	S&P Oper. EPS 2006E	0.76	P/E on S&P Oper. EPS 2006E	29.9	Dividend Rate/Share	$0.22
Trailing 12-Month EPS	$0.64	S&P Oper. EPS 2007E	0.90	Common Shares Outstg. (M)	1,481.3	Yield (%)	0.97
Trailing 12-Month P/E	35.5	S&P Core EPS 2006E	0.76	Market Capitalization(B)	$33.626	Beta	0.41
$10K Invested 5 Yrs Ago	$6,633	S&P Core EPS 2007E	0.90	Institutional Ownership (%)	77	S&P Credit Rating	A-

Price Performance

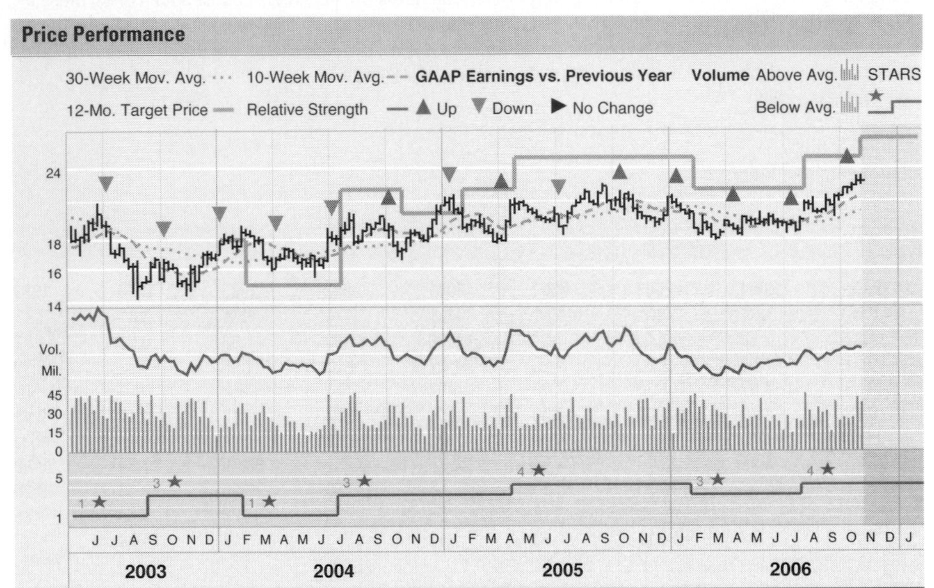

Options: ASE, CBOE, P, Ph

Analysis prepared by **Herman B. Saftlas** on October 26, 2006, when the stock traded at **$ 22.44**.

Highlights

- We project revenue growth of about 6% in 2007, helped by continued strength in Remicade for rheumatoid arthritis, Nasonex nasal asthma treatment, and Temodar, an anticancer agent. However, we see relatively flat sales in the Claritin/Clarinex franchise and lower sales in the PEG-Intron/Rebetol hepatitis C franchise, with the latter affected by increased competitive pressures.

- SGP's gross margins are well below those of peer drugmakers because most of its earnings are derived from equity income. In addition, ongoing plant remediation costs continue to inflate manufacturing expenses. However, we see overall profitability benefiting from cost-cutting measures, as well as from increased equity income from SGP's joint venture with Merck. The latter reflects projected higher sales of the venture's Zetia and Vytorin cholesterol-lowering drugs.

- We project operating EPS of $0.90 for 2007, up from an estimated $0.76 in 2006. Results in both years include expected option expense, but exclude litigation reserves, plant consolidation costs and other nonrecurring items.

Investment Rationale/Risk

- We see SGP delivering on its turnaround strategy, as sales and earnings trends in recent quarters have exceeded our forecasts. Key sales growth drivers were Remicade, Nasonex and PEG-Intron, while royalties from the important Vytorin/Zetia joint venture advanced 81%, to $390 million, in the third quarter. Despite the recent entry of generic versions of Zocor and Pravachol, we still see dual-action Vytorin (a combination Zocor and Zetia) continuing to gain market share in the $20 billion cholesterol drug market, helped by competitive advantages. We think EPS could reach $1.20 by 2008. We also think SGP has takeover appeal at current levels.

- Risks to our recommendation and target price include failure by Vytorin to live up to expectations, worsening competitive pressures in other lines, and possible pipeline disappointments.

- Our 12-month target price of $27 is based on our discounted cash flow model, which assumes steady free cash flow growth over 10 years, a weighted average cost of capital of 7.3%, and terminal growth of 2%.

Qualitative Risk Assessment

LOW	MEDIUM	HIGH

Our risk assessment incorporates our view that SGP's turnaround phase will continue for several more years. We also think the company is dependent on a relatively small number of drugs to support future growth.

Quantitative Evaluations

S&P Quality Ranking A-

D	C	B-	B	B+	A-	A	A+

Relative Strength Rank STRONG

71

LOWEST = 1 HIGHEST = 99

Revenue/Earnings Data

Revenue (Million $)

	1Q	2Q	3Q	4Q	Year
2006	2,551	2,818	2,574	--	--
2005	2,369	2,532	2,284	2,324	9,508
2004	1,963	2,147	1,978	2,184	8,272
2003	2,082	2,338	1,998	1,948	8,334
2002	2,556	2,833	2,421	2,370	10,180
2001	2,319	2,630	2,382	2,471	9,802

Earnings Per Share ($)

2006	0.22	0.16	0.19	**E**0.19	**E**0.76
2005	0.07	-0.05	0.03	0.07	0.12
2004	-0.05	-0.04	0.01	-0.58	-0.67
2003	0.12	0.12	-0.18	-0.12	-0.06
2002	0.41	0.43	0.29	0.21	1.34
2001	0.38	0.43	0.41	0.10	1.32

Fiscal year ended Dec. 31. Next earnings report expected: Late January. EPS Estimates based on S&P Operating Earnings; historical GAAP earnings are as reported.

Dividend Data (Dates: mm/dd Payment Date: mm/dd/yy)

Amount ($)	Date Decl.	Ex-Div. Date	Stk. of Record	Payment Date
0.055	12/06	02/01	02/03	02/28/06
0.055	02/28	05/03	05/05	05/30/06
0.055	06/27	08/02	08/04	08/29/06
0.055	09/19	11/01	11/03	11/28/06

Dividends have been paid since 1952. Source: Company reports.

Schering-Plough

Business Summary October 26, 2006

Schering-Plough is a leading maker of niche-oriented prescription pharmaceuticals. It also has interests in animal health products, over-the-counter (OTC) medications, and consumer products. In mid-April 2003, Fred Hassan (formerly chairman and CEO of Pharmacia Corp.) was elected chairman and CEO of SGP.

Prescription pharmaceuticals accounted for about 80% of total sales in 2005, consumer health care products for 11%, and animal health items for 9%. Sales outside of the U.S. represented 62% of total sales in 2005.

Through a joint venture with Merck & Co., Schering-Plough shares in the profits of two new cholesterol-lowering drugs. These are Zetia, a novel lipid-lowering agent that works by blocking the absorption of cholesterol in the intestines; and Vytorin, a combination of Zetia with Merck's Zocor statin cholesterol agent that was introduced in July 2004. SGP booked equity income from this venture of $873 million in 2005, up from $347 million in 2004. Sales of Zetia and Vytorin (not booked by SGP) totaled $2.4 billion in 2005. As of August 2006, combined sales of Zetia and Vytorin accounted for close to 16.4% of total U.S. cholesterol drug sales, up from some 11% in July 2005, based on IMS data.

SGP is a global leader in treatments for hepatitis C with its PEG-Intron (sales of $751 million in 2005), a once-weekly alpha interferon, combined with Rebetol antiviral agent ($331 million). In the anti-inflammatory area, SGP offers Remicade ($942 million), a TNF-alpha treatment for rheumatoid arthritis and Crohn's disease. Other important products are Temodar ($588 million), a treatment for brain tumors; Integrilin ($315 million) for cardiovascular problems; Intron A for cancer and viral infections; Subutex for opiate dependence; Caelyx for skin cancer; Cipro, an antibiotic; and Elocon, for inflammatory skin conditions.

A longtime leader in the U.S. respiratory/allergy market, SGP's most important prescription drugs in that area are Nasonex corticosteroid nasal spray ($737 million) and Clarinex/Aerius nonsedating antihistamine ($646 million). Other important allergy/respiratory drugs include Asmanex and Foradil.

Company Financials

Per Share Data ($) Year Ended Dec. 31	2005	2004	2003	2002	2001	2000	1999	1998	1997	1996
Tangible Book Value	3.64	4.73	4.57	4.07	4.41	3.75	3.11	2.33	1.60	1.41
Cash Flow	0.45	-0.36	0.22	1.28	1.54	1.84	1.60	0.44	1.11	0.94
Earnings	0.12	-0.67	-0.06	1.34	1.32	1.64	1.42	1.18	0.98	0.83
S&P Core Earnings	0.19	-0.72	0.16	1.17	1.41	NA	NA	NA	NA	NA
Dividends	0.22	0.22	0.57	0.67	0.62	0.55	0.49	0.43	0.55	0.32
Payout Ratio	183%	NM	NM	50%	47%	33%	34%	36%	56%	39%
Prices:High	22.53	21.37	23.75	36.25	57.25	60.00	60.81	57.75	32.00	18.28
Prices:Low	17.67	15.45	14.16	16.10	32.35	30.50	40.25	30.34	15.88	12.63
P/E Ratio:High	NM	NM	NM	27	43	37	43	49	33	22
P/E Ratio:Low	NM	NM	NM	12	25	19	28	26	16	15

Income Statement Analysis (Million $)	2005	2004	2003	2002	2001	2000	1999	1998	1997	1996
Revenue	9,508	8,272	8,334	10,180	9,802	9,815	9,176	8,077	6,778	5,656
Operating Income	409	237	975	2,941	3,248	3,394	3,015	2,566	2,159	1,820
Depreciation	486	453	417	372	320	299	264	238	200	173
Interest Expense	Nil	Nil	81.0	Nil	Nil	44.0	29.0	19.0	40.0	56.0
Pretax Income	497	-168	-46.0	2,563	2,523	3,188	2,795	2,326	1,913	1,606
Effective Tax Rate	45.9%	NM	NM	23.0%	23.0%	24.0%	24.5%	24.5%	24.5%	24.6%
Net Income	269	-947	-92.0	1,974	1,943	2,423	2,110	1,756	1,444	1,213
S&P Core Earnings	279	-1,052	247	1,717	2,070	NA	NA	NA	NA	NA

Balance Sheet & Other Financial Data (Million $)	2005	2004	2003	2002	2001	2000	1999	1998	1997	1996
Cash	4,767	4,984	4,218	3,521	2,716	2,397	1,876	1,259	714	536
Current Assets	9,732	10,003	9,147	8,272	6,519	5,720	4,909	3,958	2,920	2,365
Total Assets	15,469	15,911	15,102	14,136	12,174	10,805	9,375	7,840	6,507	5,398
Current Liabilities	4,659	5,208	4,609	4,729	3,917	3,645	3,209	3,032	2,891	2,599
Long Term Debt	2,399	2,392	2,410	Nil	Nil	Nil	Nil	4.00	46.0	47.0
Common Equity	16,825	6,118	7,337	8,142	7,125	6,119	5,165	4,002	2,821	2,060
Total Capital	20,779	10,059	9,981	8,500	7,427	6,333	5,449	4,297	3,145	2,374
Capital Expenditures	478	489	701	770	759	763	543	389	405	325
Cash Flow	669	-528	325	2,346	2,263	2,722	2,374	1,994	1,644	1,386
Current Ratio	2.1	1.9	2.0	1.7	1.7	1.6	1.5	1.3	1.0	0.9
% Long Term Debt of Capitalization	11.5	23.8	24.1	Nil	Nil	Nil	Nil	0.1	1.4	2.0
% Net Income of Revenue	2.8	NM	NM	19.4	19.8	24.7	23.0	21.7	21.3	21.5
% Return on Assets	1.7	NM	NM	15.0	16.9	24.0	24.5	24.5	24.3	24.1
% Return on Equity	1.1	NM	NM	25.9	29.3	42.9	46.0	51.5	59.2	65.9

Data as orig reptd.; bef. results of disc opers/spec. items. Per share data adj. for stk. divs.; EPS diluted. E-Estimated. NA-Not Available. NM-Not Meaningful. NR-Not Ranked. UR-Under Review.

Office: 2000 Galloping Hill Road, Kenilworth, NJ 07033.
Telephone: 908-298-4000.
Website: http://www.schering-plough.com
Chrmn & CEO: F. Hassan

EVP & CFO: R.J. Bertolini
EVP & General Counsel: T.J. Sabatino, Jr.
VP & Treas: E.K. Moore
VP & Secy: S. Wolf

Investor Contact: A. Kelly (908-298-7436)
Board of Directors: H. W. Becherer, T. J. Colligan, F. Hassan, C. R. Kidder, P. Leder, E. R. McGrath, C. E. Mundy, Jr., P. F. Russo, K. C. Turner, A. Weinbach, R. F. van Oordt

Founded: 1970
Domicile: New Jersey
Employees: 32,600

STANDARD &POOR'S

Schlumberger Ltd

S&P Recommendation STRONG BUY ★★★★★

Price
$62.81 (as of Oct 27, 2006)

12-Mo. Target Price
$83.00

Investment Style
Large-Cap Value

GICS Sector Energy
Sub-Industry Oil & Gas Equipment & Services

Comment This leading oilfield services company provides equipment and technology to the oil and gas industry worldwide.

Key Stock Statistics (Source S&P, Vickers, company reports)

52-Wk Range	$74.75–44.35	S&P Oper. EPS 2006E	2.97	P/E on S&P Oper. EPS 2006E	21.1	Dividend Rate/Share	$0.50
Trailing 12-Month EPS	$2.63	S&P Oper. EPS 2007E	3.91	Common Shares Outstg. (M)	1,178.2	Yield (%)	0.80
Trailing 12-Month P/E	23.9	S&P Core EPS 2006E	2.93	Market Capitalization(B)	$74.004	Beta	1.10
$10K Invested 5 Yrs Ago	$25,221	S&P Core EPS 2007E	3.85	Institutional Ownership (%)	79	S&P Credit Rating	A+

Price Performance

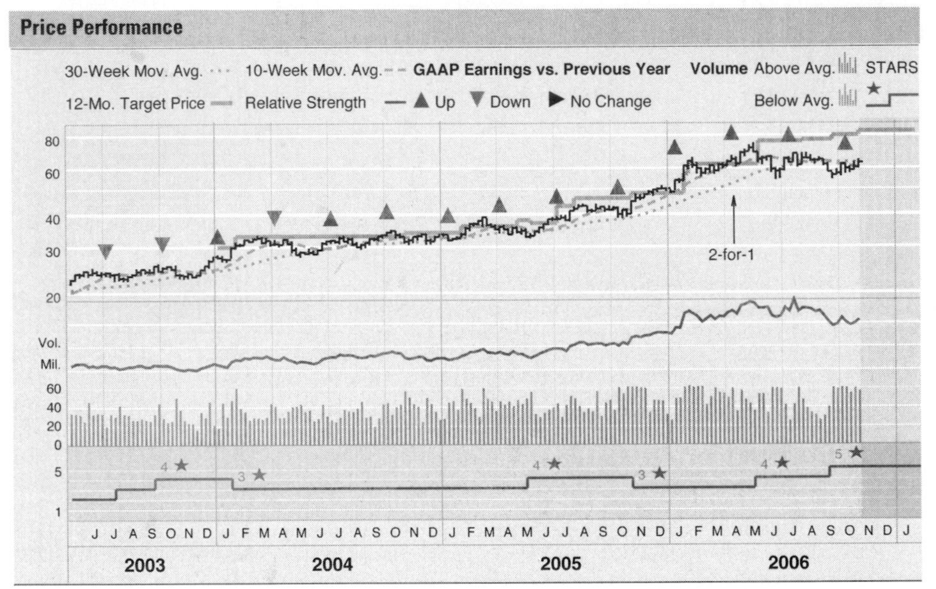

Options: ASE, CBOE, P, Ph

Analysis prepared by **Stewart Glickman, CFA** on October 26, 2006, when the stock traded at **$ 64.11**.

Highlights

- For 2006, we expect oilfield services revenues to improve about 31%, rising an additional 19% in 2007. We look for operating margins of about 28% in 2006, and 30% in 2007.
- In April 2006, SLB acquired Baker Hughes's (BHI: buy, $71) 30% stake in their WesternGeco joint venture for $2.4 billion in cash. We like the deal strategically for SLB, as it should enable the company to capture the full value of rising demand for reservoir seismic services and management. WesternGeco reported revenue growth of 17% in the third quarter, with operating margins of about 37%, nearly double the 19% recorded in 2005.
- With a majority of revenues from outside North America, we forecast that 2007 will be a strong year for international operations, reflecting our expectations of strong capital spending by state owned oil companies and an industrywide emphasis on low cost drilling opportunities. For 2006, we see EPS of $2.97, rising to $3.91 in 2007. Our S&P Core EPS estimates for 2006 and 2007 are $2.93 and $3.85, respectively, reflecting adjustments for pension gains.

Investment Rationale/Risk

- We believe SLB is well positioned to benefit from growing demand for oilfield services technology, particularly in frontier regions such as the Middle East, Africa, and Eastern Europe. Worldwide, we anticipate a growing trend toward new oil and gas development opportunities that require higher levels of technology content, which we believe plays to the benefit of larger oilfield service providers.
- Risks to our recommendation and target price include a decline in oil and gas exploration and production activity; reduced demand for integrated systems in oilfield services; and political risk in emerging markets.
- Our DCF model, assuming free cash flow growth of about 11% per year for 10 years, and 3% thereafter, discounted by a WACC of 10.2%, shows the shares to have an intrinsic value of about $83 per share. On a relative basis, we think the shares merit a premium to peers on the strength of SLB's leadership position. Applying an enterprise value of 14X to our 2007 EBITDA estimate, a multiple of 15X projected 2007 cash flow (both premiums to peer averages), and blending with our DCF model, our 12-month target price is $83.

Qualitative Risk Assessment

LOW | **MEDIUM** | HIGH

Our risk assessment reflects exposure to volatile crude oil and natural gas prices; capital spending decisions by SLB's oil and gas producing customers; and political risk associated with operating in frontier regions around the world. This is offset by the company's leading industry position.

Quantitative Evaluations

S&P Quality Ranking **B**

D | C | B- | **B** | B+ | A- | A | A+

Relative Strength Rank **MODERATE**

55

LOWEST = 1 HIGHEST = 99

Revenue/Earnings Data

Revenue (Million $)

	1Q	2Q	3Q	4Q	Year
2006	4,239	4,687	4,955	--	--
2005	3,159	3,429	3,698	4,023	14,309
2004	2,673	2,833	2,906	3,068	11,480
2003	3,263	3,485	3,474	3,671	14,059
2002	3,257	3,337	3,446	3,434	13,474
2001	2,910	3,635	3,624	3,577	13,746

Earnings Per Share ($)

2006	0.59	0.69	0.81	**E**0.88	**E**2.97
2005	0.44	0.39	0.45	0.54	1.81
2004	0.09	0.22	0.25	0.29	0.85
2003	0.13	0.12	-0.05	0.20	0.41
2002	0.15	0.17	0.15	-2.46	-2.09
2001	0.21	-0.08	0.17	0.16	0.46

Fiscal year ended Dec. 31. Next earnings report expected: Mid January. EPS Estimates based on S&P Operating Earnings; historical GAAP earnings are as reported.

Dividend Data (Dates: mm/dd Payment Date: mm/dd/yy)

Amount ($)	Date Decl.	Ex-Div. Date	Stk. of Record	Payment Date
2-for-1	01/19	04/10	03/01	04/07/06
0.125	04/20	06/05	06/07	07/07/06
0.125	07/20	09/01	09/06	10/06/06
0.125	10/19	12/04	12/06	01/05/07

Dividends have been paid since 1957. Source: Company reports.

Schlumberger Ltd

Business Summary October 26, 2006

CORPORATE OVERVIEW. As a global oilfield and information services company with major activity in the energy industry, Schlumberger operates in two primary business segments: Oilfield Services (88% of 2005 revenues; 90% of 2005 segment operating income), and WesternGeco (12%, 11%). Oilfield Services provides exploration and production services, solutions and technology to the petroleum industry. It is managed through four geographic areas (North America, South America, Europe/CIS/Africa, and the Middle East/Asia). The company is largely focused on international operations; North America generated only 30% of oilfield services' total revenues in 2005, and only 33% of the segment's pre-tax operating income. The Middle East/Asia region generated the highest operating margins in 2005, at 28.7%, with North America second, at 24.8%. Operations within oilfield services are organized into six technology segments: wireline services, providing information technology to evaluate the reservoir, plan and monitor wells, and evaluate and monitor production; drilling and measurements, including directional drilling, measurement while drilling and logging while drilling services; well services, constructing mostly oil and gas wells; well completions and productivity; data and consulting services; and Schlumberger Information Solutions. Supporting these six technologies are 23 R&D centers.

In addition, SLB operates its WesternGeco seismic segment. WesternGeco provides worldwide comprehensive reservoir imaging, monitoring and development services, with seismic crews and data processing centers, as well as a large multiclient seismic library. Services include 3D and time-lapse (4D) seismic surveys, and multi-component surveys for delineating prospects and reservoir management. Backlog in this segment reached $790 million at the end of 2005, up from $670 million at the end of 2004; the company expects most of the backlog to be completed during 2006.

Company Financials

Per Share Data ($) Year Ended Dec. 31	**2005**	**2004**	**2003**	**2002**	**2001**	**2000**	**1999**	**1998**	**1997**	**1996**
Tangible Book Value	3.63	2.54	1.87	0.70	1.14	5.87	5.65	6.24	5.55	4.46
Cash Flow	2.89	1.89	1.74	-0.75	2.08	1.73	1.20	1.91	2.21	1.77
Earnings	1.81	0.85	0.41	-2.09	0.46	0.64	0.29	0.91	1.26	0.87
Dividends	0.42	0.38	0.38	0.38	0.38	0.38	0.38	0.38	0.56	0.38
Payout Ratio	23%	44%	93%	NM	82%	59%	129%	41%	45%	43%
Prices:High	51.49	34.95	28.12	31.22	41.41	44.44	35.34	43.22	47.22	27.06
Prices:Low	31.57	26.27	17.81	16.70	20.42	26.75	22.72	20.03	24.50	16.34
P/E Ratio:High	28	41	69	NM	91	70	NM	48	37	31
P/E Ratio:Low	17	31	44	NM	45	42	NM	22	19	19

Income Statement Analysis (Million $)										
Revenue	14,309	11,480	14,059	13,474	13,746	9,611	8,395	11,816	10,648	8,956
Operating Income	4,520	2,895	2,474	-456	3,165	2,084	1,327	2,428	2,622	1,895
Depreciation, Depletion and Amortization	1,351	1,308	1,571	1,545	1,896	1,271	1,021	1,137	973	885
Interest Expense	197	272	334	368	385	276	193	150	87.0	0.72
Pretax Income	2,972	1,327	568	-2,230	1,126	959	470	1,323	1,669	675
Effective Tax Rate	22.9%	20.9%	36.9%	NM	51.1%	23.8%	29.9%	23.4%	22.3%	NM
Net Income	2,199	1,014	473	-2,418	522	733	329	1,014	1,296	851

Balance Sheet & Other Financial Data (Million $)										
Cash	191	224	234	168	178	3,040	4,390	3,957	1,761	1,359
Current Assets	8,554	7,060	10,369	7,185	7,705	7,493	8,606	8,805	6,071	5,043
Total Assets	18,077	16,001	20,041	19,435	22,326	17,173	15,081	16,078	12,097	10,325
Current Liabilities	5,515	4,701	6,795	6,451	6,218	3,991	3,474	3,919	3,630	3,474
Long Term Debt	3,591	3,944	6,097	6,029	6,216	3,573	3,183	3,285	1,069	637
Common Equity	7,592	6,117	5,881	5,606	8,378	8,295	7,721	8,119	6,695	5,626
Total Capital	11,688	10,477	12,376	12,188	15,231	12,474	10,904	11,404	7,764	6,263
Capital Expenditures	1,593	1,216	1,025	1,366	2,053	1,323	792	1,887	1,496	1,158
Cash Flow	3,550	2,322	2,044	-872	2,418	2,003	1,350	2,151	2,269	1,736
Current Ratio	1.6	1.5	1.5	1.1	1.2	1.9	2.5	2.2	1.7	1.5
% Long Term Debt of Capitalization	30.7	37.6	49.3	49.5	40.8	28.6	29.2	28.8	13.8	10.1
% Return on Assets	12.9	5.6	2.4	NM	2.6	4.5	2.1	7.2	11.6	8.8
% Return on Equity	32.1	16.9	8.2	NM	6.3	9.1	4.2	13.7	21.0	16.0

Data as orig reptd.; bef. results of disc opers/spec. items. Per share data adj. for stk. divs.; EPS diluted. E-Estimated. NA-Not Available. NM-Not Meaningful. NR-Not Ranked. UR-Under Review.

Office: 153 East 53rd Street, New York, NY 10022-4624.
Telephone: 212-350-9400.
Email: irsupport@slb.com
Website: http://www.slb.com

Chrmn & CEO: A. Gould
EVP & CFO: J. Perraud
VP & Treas: S. Ayat
Investor Contact: D. Pferdehirt (212-350-9432)

Chief Acctg Officer: H. Guild
Board of Directors: J. Deutch, J. S. Gorelick, A. Gould, T. Isaac, A. Lajous, A. Levy-Lang, M. E. Marks, D. Primat, T. Sandvold, N. Seydoux, L. G. Stuntz, R. Talwar

Founded: 1956
Domicile: Netherlands Antilles
Employees: 60,000

STANDARD &POOR'S

Schwab (Charles) Corp

S&P Recommendation HOLD ★★★★★

Price $17.81 (as of Oct 27, 2006)

12-Mo. Target Price $18.00

Investment Style Large-Cap Growth

GICS Sector Financials
Sub-Industry Investment Banking & Brokerage

Comment This company's Charles Schwab & Co. subsidiary is among the largest brokerage companies in the U.S., primarily serving retail clients.

Key Stock Statistics (Source S&P, Vickers, company reports)

52-Wk Range	$18.53–13.64	S&P Oper. EPS 2006E	0.80	P/E on S&P Oper. EPS 2006E	22.3	Dividend Rate/Share	$0.20
Trailing 12-Month EPS	$0.73	S&P Oper. EPS 2007E	0.98	Common Shares Outstg. (M)	1,276.7	Yield (%)	1.12
Trailing 12-Month P/E	24.4	S&P Core EPS 2006E	0.80	Market Capitalization(B)	$22.738	Beta	1.67
$10K Invested 5 Yrs Ago	$13,204	S&P Core EPS 2007E	0.98	Institutional Ownership (%)	60	S&P Credit Rating	A-

Price Performance

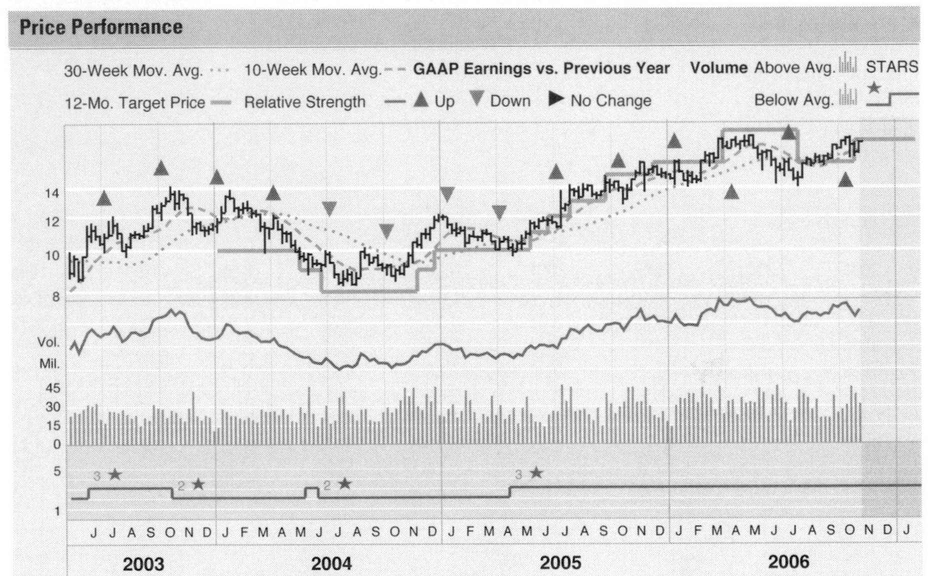

Options: ASE, CBOE, P, Ph

Analysis prepared by **Matthew Albrecht** on October 17, 2006, when the stock traded at **$ 16.80**.

Highlights

- We think that Schwab is regaining its competitive differentiation as a discount broker, largely due to several major reductions in its commission rates since June 2004, as well as the elimination of order handling and account service fees, which have brought its pricing closer to that of its competitors. We expect that cost reductions, increased trading activity, and growth in asset-based fees will offset the revenue impact in 2006 from the reduced commission rates.

- We look for trading volumes to trend higher in the fourth quarter of 2006 and into 2007, given that we see generally improving investor confidence, but caution that a challenging market environment, including seasonality and trading volatility, could result in significant variability. We believe SCHW is getting traction from its "Talk to Chuck" advertising push, and we expect advertising costs to come in at just under 4% of revenues for 2006 and 2007.

- We estimate EPS of $0.80 in 2006 and $0.98 in 2007, aided by client inflows, higher asset-based revenues, increased profitability in the banking segment, and additional cost reductions, specifically related to compensation.

Investment Rationale/Risk

- We think the premium on the shares is appropriate in view of the company's brand recognition, affluent client base, and high proportion of recurring asset-based fees. We also see SCHW's success servicing the rapidly growing independent investment adviser channel as a positive in our valuation of the shares. However, recent management changes and our view of the company's unsuccessful acquisition strategy temper our enthusiasm. We also think that the banking segment, although growing, merits a lower valuation.

- Risks to our recommendation and target price include reduced trading volumes, equity market declines, and a potentially more onerous regulatory environment. We think Mr. Schwab will continue to serve as both chairman and CEO through 2007, despite our concerns regarding management succession and corporate governance issues.

- Our 12-month target price of $18 is based on about 18X our 2007 EPS estimate. This represents a moderate premium to on-line brokerage peers, reflecting our positive assessment of SCHW's leading market position and recurrent revenue from asset-based fees.

Qualitative Risk Assessment

LOW | **MEDIUM** | HIGH

Our risk assessment reflects our view of the company's strong competitive position, brand recognition, and affluent client base, offset by industry cyclicality and our concerns about corporate governance.

Quantitative Evaluations

S&P Quality Ranking B+

D | C | B- | B | **B+** | A- | A | A+

Relative Strength Rank MODERATE

67

LOWEST = 1 HIGHEST = 99

Revenue/Earnings Data

Revenue (Million $)

	1Q	2Q	3Q	4Q	Year
2006	1,491	1,546	1,552	--	--
2005	1,059	1,087	1,138	1,180	5,151
2004	1,108	1,034	1,000	1,060	4,479
2003	900.0	1,018	1,051	1,118	4,328
2002	1,059	1,049	1,031	996.0	4,480
2001	1,200	1,071	1,023	1,059	5,281

Earnings Per Share ($)

2006	0.19	0.19	0.21	**E**0.21	**E**0.80
2005	0.11	0.14	0.16	0.14	0.56
2004	0.12	0.08	-0.03	0.04	0.30
2003	0.05	0.09	0.09	0.11	0.35
2002	0.07	0.07	Nil	-0.06	0.07
2001	0.07	-0.01	0.01	-0.01	0.06

Fiscal year ended Dec. 31. Next earnings report expected: Mid January. EPS Estimates based on S&P Operating Earnings; historical GAAP earnings are as reported.

Dividend Data (Dates: mm/dd Payment Date: mm/dd/yy)

Amount ($)	Date Decl.	Ex-Div. Date	Stk. of Record	Payment Date
0.030	04/26	05/04	05/08	05/22/06
0.030	07/25	08/04	08/08	08/22/06
0.050	10/19	11/06	11/08	11/22/06
0.050	10/19	11/06	11/08	11/20/06

Dividends have been paid since 1989. Source: Company reports.

Schwab (Charles) Corp

Business Summary October 17, 2006

CORPORATE OVERVIEW. SCHW is a financial holding company that provides securities brokerage and related financial services through three segments, including Individual Investor, Institutional Investor, and U.S. Trust. Other subsidiaries include Charles Schwab Investment Management, the investment adviser for Schwab's proprietary mutual funds; and CyberTrader, Inc., an electronic trading technology and brokerage concern, acquired in 2000, which provides services to highly active, online traders.

Through the Individual Investor segment (61% of 2005 operating revenue), the company provides retail brokerage and banking services. Through various types of brokerage accounts, Schwab offers the purchase and sale of securities, including Nasdaq, exchange-listed and other equity securities, options, mutual funds, unit investment trusts, variable annuities and fixed income investments. At the end of 2005, the company, through subsidiaries, served 7.1 million active client accounts, and held client assets of $1.2 trillion.

Through its Institutional Investor segment (18%), SCHW provides custodial, trade execution and support services to investment advisers, serves company 401(k) plan sponsors and third-party administrators, and supports company stock option plans. The company's Institutional segment had more than $439 billion in assets under management on behalf of over 5,000 adviser firms and their over 1 million accounts as of March 31, 2006. SCHW launched Schwab Advisor Network in May 2002, which refers affluent investors to local investment advisers.

U.S. Trust Corp. (19%), founded in 1853, provides fiduciary services and private banking services. In October 2003, U.S. Trust acquired the Private Asset Management group of State Street Corp., which had $12 billion in assets under management, for about $365 million in cash. At the end of 2005, U.S. Trust had nearly $149 billion in client assets, up 5% year over year. We think high net worth clients are increasing their allocations to hedge funds and other alternative investments, an area where we think U.S. Trust lacks a competitive product offering. We expect the company to sell its U.S. Trust asset management division, given our view of its poor relative investment performance.

Company Financials

Per Share Data ($) Year Ended Dec. 31	**2005**	**2004**	**2003**	**2002**	**2001**	**2000**	**1999**	**1998**	**1997**	**1996**
Tangible Book Value	2.71	2.57	2.56	0.55	2.58	2.69	1.81	1.15	0.91	0.67
Cash Flow	0.72	0.47	0.35	0.30	0.30	0.70	0.59	0.39	0.32	0.27
Earnings	0.56	0.30	0.35	0.07	0.06	0.51	0.47	0.28	0.22	0.19
S&P Core Earnings	0.53	0.23	0.27	-0.02	-0.09	NA	NA	NA	NA	NA
Dividends	0.09	0.07	0.05	0.04	0.04	0.04	0.04	0.04	0.03	0.03
Payout Ratio	16%	25%	14%	63%	73%	8%	8%	13%	13%	14%
Prices:High	16.14	13.92	14.20	19.00	33.00	44.75	51.67	22.83	9.83	4.87
Prices:Low	0.05	0.25	0.25	7.22	8.13	22.46	16.96	6.17	4.50	2.67
P/E Ratio:High	29	46	41	NM	NM	88	NM	81	45	25
P/E Ratio:Low	17	28	18	NM	NM	44	NM	22	20	14

Income Statement Analysis (Million $)										
Commissions	779	936	1,207	1,206	1,355	2,294	1,863	1,309	1,174	954
Interest Income	1,944	1,213	970	1,186	1,857	2,589	1,471	1,127	900	681
Total Revenue	5,151	4,479	4,328	4,480	5,281	7,139	4,713	3,388	2,845	2,277
Interest Expense	687	277	241	345	928	1,352	768	652	546	426
Pretax Income	1,185	645	710	168	135	1,231	971	577	447	394
Effective Tax Rate	38.4%	35.8%	33.5%	42.3%	42.2%	41.7%	39.4%	39.6%	39.6%	40.7%
Net Income	730	414	472	97.0	78.0	718	589	348	270	234
S&P Core Earnings	678	314	357	-31.5	-131	NA	NA	NA	NA	NA

Balance Sheet & Other Financial Data (Million $)										
Total Assets	47,351	47,133	45,866	39,705	40,464	38,154	29,299	22,264	16,482	13,779
Cash Items	17,589	21,797	24,175	24,119	22,148	14,300	10,547	11,399	7,571	7,869
Receivables	11,600	10,323	9,137	7,067	10,066	16,680	17,543	9,980	8,019	5,244
Securities Owned	6,857	5,335	4,023	1,716	1,700	1,603	340	242	283	128
Securities Borrowed	Nil	Nil	Nil	Nil	Nil	Nil	Nil	Nil	Nil	Nil
Due Brokers & Customers	25,994	28,622	29,845	27,877	27,822	26,785	25,171	19,867	14,228	12,054
Other Liabilities	1,388	1,396	1,330	1,302	1,327	1,277	931	618	478	361
Capitalization:Debt	514	585	772	642	730	770	455	351	361	284
Capitalization:Equity	4,450	4,386	4,461	4,011	4,163	4,230	2,274	1,429	1,145	855
Capitalization:Total	4,964	4,971	5,233	4,653	4,893	5,000	2,729	1,780	1,506	1,139
% Return on Revenue	14.2	9.2	15.1	3.0	2.0	14.8	20.7	10.3	9.4	10.2
% Return on Assets	1.5	0.9	1.1	0.2	0.2	2.0	2.3	1.8	1.8	2.0
% Return on Equity	16.5	9.4	11.1	2.4	1.9	21.1	31.8	27.5	27.0	31.5

Data as orig reptd.; bef. results of disc opers/spec. items. Per share data adj. for stk. divs.; EPS diluted. E-Estimated. NA-Not Available. NM-Not Meaningful. NR-Not Ranked. UR-Under Review.

Office: 120 Kearny Street, San Francisco, CA 94108.
Telephone: 415-627-7000.
Email: investor.relations@schwab.com
Website: http://www.schwab.com

Chrmn & CEO: C.R. Schwab
EVP & CFO: C.V. Dodds
EVP, Secy & General Counsel: C.E. Dwyer
Investor Contact: R.G. Fowler (415-636-9869)

Board of Directors: W. F. Adlinger III, N. H. Bechtle, C. P. Butcher, D. G. Fisher, F. C. Herringer, M. Magner, S. T. McLin, C. R. Schwab, P. A. Sneed, R. O. Walther, R. N. Wilson, D. B. Yoffie

Founded: 1971
Domicile: Delaware
Employees: 14,200

STANDARD &POOR'S

Scripps (E.W.) Co. (The)

S&P Recommendation BUY ★★★★★

Price $49.30 (as of Oct 27, 2006)

12-Mo. Target Price $58.00

Investment Style Mid-Cap Growth

GICS Sector Consumer Discretionary
Sub-Industry Broadcasting & Cable TV

Comment This diversified media concern operates in the broadcasting, entertainment, publishing and interactive media industries.

Key Stock Statistics (Source S&P, Vickers, company reports)

52-Wk Range	**$51.09–40.86**	S&P Oper. EPS 2006E	**2.28**	P/E on S&P Oper. EPS 2006E	**21.6**	Dividend Rate/Share	**$0.48**
Trailing 12-Month EPS	**$1.33**	S&P Oper. EPS 2007E	**2.54**	Common Shares Outstg. (M)	**163.4**	Yield (%)	**0.97**
Trailing 12-Month P/E	**37.1**	S&P Core EPS 2006E	**2.27**	Market Capitalization(B)	**$6.253**	Beta	**0.50**
$10K Invested 5 Yrs Ago	**$15,990**	S&P Core EPS 2007E	**2.53**	Institutional Ownership (%)	**66**	S&P Credit Rating	**A**

Price Performance

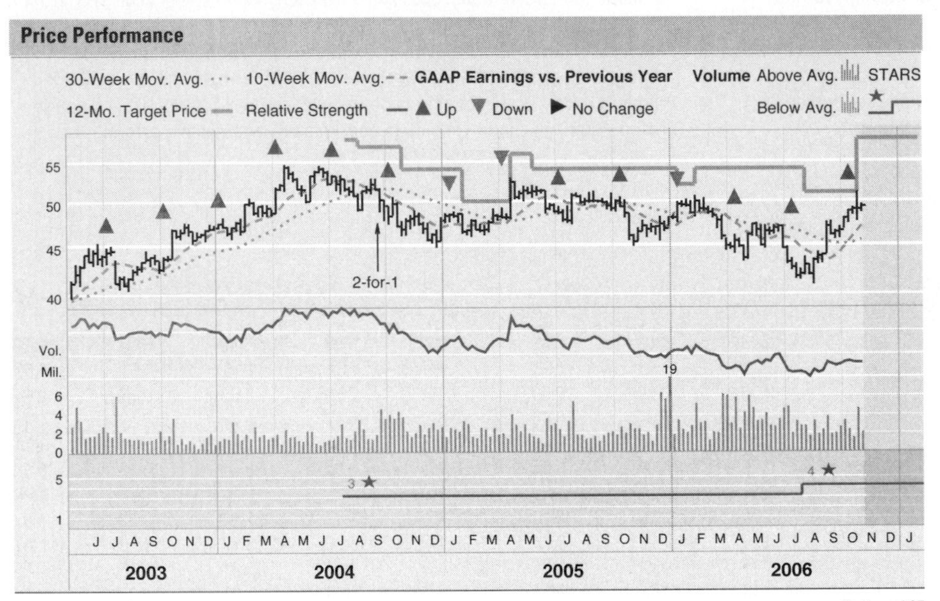

Options: ASE

Analysis prepared by **James Peters, CFA** on October 24, 2006, when the stock traded at **$ 48.75.**

Highlights

- We expect revenue growth in 2007 of about 10%, following a rise of 16% that we forecast for 2006. We see growth led by strong gains in the interactive media segment, including from Shopzilla, acquired in June 2005, and from uSwitch, acquired in March 2006. We anticipate an advance of approximately 10% for Scripps Networks, and for the Broadcast segment, we expect modest growth of about 2.6%, following strong political advertising gains in 2006. In September, the company reached an agreement to sell its five Shop at Home affiliates for $170 million, and the planned sale is expected to be completed in the first half of 2007, subject to necessary approvals.
- We forecast a slight operating margin improvement in 2007 to 27.3%, up from the 27.1% we project for 2006. We believe SSP will generate operating leverage from higher revenues, mostly offset by slightly rising newsprint costs and investments in its interactive media division.
- We see 2007 EPS of $2.54, versus the $2.28 we project for 2006. EPS in 2006 includes $0.09 of projected stock option related expense and dilution of $0.10-$0.15 from the acquisition of uSwitch.

Investment Rationale/Risk

- We view SSP's strategy of transforming itself from a newspaper company to a cable network and interactive media company favorably, as long-term opportunities for revenue and profit growth appear greater, in our opinion, for these businesses. Scripps currently garners about 14% of its total revenues from its online operations, which compares favorably with peer newspaper, local television and radio company figures of about 5.5%, 1.5% and 1.0% of advertising revenues generated from online sources, respectively.
- Risks to our recommendation and target price include lower than expected advertising spending, acquisition integration risks, and limited success at the smaller networks--DIY, Fine Living or GAC.
- Our 12-month target price of $58 is based on our sum of the parts analysis. By applying peer average EBITDA multiples of 8.1X for newspapers, 11.2X for broadcasting and 19.9X for interactive media, we arrive at a blended peer-average EBITDA multiple of 11.4X. Applying an 11.4X multiple to our 2007 EBITDA estimate of $926 million, we derive a $58 valuation.

Qualitative Risk Assessment

LOW | **MEDIUM** | HIGH

Our risk assessment reflects our view of a highly competitive environment for advertising among newspapers, television networks and other media and below industry average financial leverage, offset by what we see as better growth prospects than its peers and a low beta.

Quantitative Evaluations

S&P Quality Ranking A-

D | C | B- | B | B+ | **A-** | A | A+

Relative Strength Rank MODERATE

67

LOWEST = 1 HIGHEST = 99

Revenue/Earnings Data

Revenue (Million $)

	1Q	2Q	3Q	4Q	Year
2006	589.7	641.9	583.5	--	--
2005	585.1	627.3	594.7	706.8	2,514
2004	513.7	547.3	499.8	606.7	2,168
2003	445.2	474.9	440.5	514.3	1,875
2002	359.8	399.9	371.5	478.1	1,536
2001	362.1	368.4	336.1	370.6	1,437

Earnings Per Share ($)

2006	0.49	0.64	0.48	**E**0.71	**E**2.28
2005	0.42	0.58	0.35	-0.01	1.35
2004	0.43	0.52	0.34	0.55	1.84
2003	0.33	0.40	0.32	0.62	1.66
2002	0.25	0.17	0.29	0.47	1.17
2001	0.42	0.25	0.14	0.06	0.87

Fiscal year ended Dec. 31. Next earnings report expected: Early February. EPS Estimates based on S&P Operating Earnings; historical GAAP earnings are as reported.

Dividend Data (Dates: mm/dd Payment Date: mm/dd/yy)

Amount ($)	Date Decl.	Ex-Div. Date	Stk. of Record	Payment Date
0.110	02/14	02/24	02/28	03/10/06
0.120	05/12	05/26	05/31	06/09/06
0.120	08/02	08/23	08/25	09/08/06
0.120	10/27	11/21	11/24	12/08/06

Dividends have been paid since 1922. Source: Company reports.

Please read the Required Disclosures and Analyst Certification on the last page of this report.

Scripps (E.W.) Co. (The)

Business Summary October 24, 2006

CORPORATE OVERVIEW. The E.W. Scripps Co. is a diversified media company that has interests in national television networks (Scripps Networks), newspaper publishing (in 18 markets), broadcast television (10 stations), interactive media, including online comparison shopping (Shopzilla) and an online site for comparing and switching essential home services (uSwitch), and licensing and syndication. All of the media businesses provide content and advertising services on the Web. The Scripps Networks segment includes Home and Garden Television (HGTV), the Food Network (TFN), the Do It Yourself (DIY) Network, Fine Living, Great American Country (GAC), and a 12% interest in FOX Sports Net South, a regional television network. The Shop At Home television retailing network was reclassified as a discontinued operation in April 2006 and sold in June 2006 for $17 million.

In 2004, Scripps Networks surpassed Newspapers as the largest reportable segment in both revenues and profits. In 2005, it accounted for 36% of revenues in 2005 and 33% in 2004 and 55% of segment profits (49% in 2004). Newspapers accounted for 29% (33%) of revenues and 30% (40%) of profits, broadcast television 13% (12%) and 12% (18%), Shop At Home 14% (14%) and a loss equal to 4% (-4%), Shopzilla 4% (Nil) and 4% (Nil), and licensing and other media 4% (5%) and 3% (3%).

Advertising remains the most important source of revenue to SSP, accounting, we believe, for close to 65% of overall revenues. In 2005, advertising provided about 80% of the revenues of both the Scripps Network and the Newspaper segments and 96% of the revenues of the Broadcast TV segment. Substantially all of Shop At Home's revenues are derived from the sale of merchandise and related shipping and handling charges. Shopzilla earns revenues primarily from lead referrals provided to participating online merchants. Approximately 95% of the licensing revenues are provided by Peanuts.

IMPACT OF MAJOR DEVELOPMENTS. Management has changed the profile of SSP significantly in the last 10 years, primarily through internal development and acquisitions. In 1995, Newspapers accounted for over half of total revenues and 60% of profits, with Broadcast TV accounting for most of the rest. The Licensing and other media segment was a similarly small contributor then as it is now. Scripps Network had only $19 million in revenues then and reported a loss of $17 million in segment profits.

Company Financials

Per Share Data ($) Year Ended Dec. 31	**2005**	**2004**	**2003**	**2002**	**2001**	**2000**	**1999**	**1998**	**1997**	**1996**
Tangible Book Value	NM	0.72	1.22	NM	0.23	0.44	NM	NM	NM	1.98
Cash Flow	1.90	2.28	2.05	1.56	1.48	1.72	1.34	1.45	1.44	1.24
Earnings	1.35	1.84	1.66	1.17	0.87	1.03	0.93	0.81	0.97	0.81
S&P Core Earnings	1.78	1.63	1.61	1.31	0.48	NA	NA	NA	NA	NA
Dividends	0.43	0.39	0.30	0.30	0.30	0.28	0.28	0.27	0.26	0.26
Payout Ratio	32%	21%	18%	26%	35%	27%	30%	33%	27%	32%
Prices:High	52.91	54.65	47.58	43.75	35.85	31.63	26.50	29.25	24.47	26.19
Prices:Low	44.85	44.73	36.95	32.56	27.35	21.19	20.25	19.25	16.13	16.38
P/E Ratio:High	39	30	29	37	41	31	28	36	25	32
P/E Ratio:Low	33	24	22	28	32	21	22	24	17	20

Income Statement Analysis (Million $)										
Revenue	2,514	2,168	1,875	1,536	1,437	1,719	1,571	1,455	1,242	1,122
Operating Income	638	538	435	401	374	454	400	380	328	275
Depreciation	91.2	71.8	63.5	62.8	99.1	109	65.3	104	77.6	69.4
Interest Expense	38.8	30.9	31.6	28.3	39.2	51.9	45.2	47.1	18.5	10.3
Pretax Income	472	543	423	309	241	276	255	229	280	220
Effective Tax Rate	40.5%	36.1%	32.6%	37.4%	41.3%	39.2%	40.7%	40.6%	41.9%	39.2%
Net Income	223	304	271	188	138	163	147	131	158	130
S&P Core Earnings	293	269	263	211	76.8	NA	NA	NA	NA	NA

Balance Sheet & Other Financial Data (Million $)										
Cash	19.2	12.3	18.2	15.5	17.4	14.1	10.5	14.4	14.3	12.8
Current Assets	797	643	562	500	451	524	477	407	379	309
Total Assets	4,033	3,425	3,009	2,870	2,644	2,573	2,520	2,345	2,281	1,464
Current Liabilities	348	375	331	426	906	533	577	532	430	323
Long Term Debt	826	533	509	650	110	502	502	502	602	31.8
Common Equity	2,287	2,096	1,823	1,515	1,352	1,278	1,164	1,065	1,049	945
Total Capital	3,562	2,629	2,524	2,308	1,609	1,910	1,810	1,682	1,739	1,041
Capital Expenditures	72.1	76.8	89.3	88.4	68.2	74.6	79.8	67.0	56.6	53.3
Cash Flow	314	376	334	251	237	273	212	235	235	200
Current Ratio	2.3	1.7	1.7	1.2	0.5	1.0	0.8	0.8	0.9	1.0
% Long Term Debt of Capitalization	23.2	20.3	20.2	28.2	6.8	26.3	27.7	29.8	34.6	0.3
% Net Income of Revenue	8.9	14.0	14.4	12.3	9.6	9.5	9.4	9.0	12.7	11.6
% Return on Assets	6.0	9.4	9.2	6.8	5.3	6.4	6.0	5.7	8.4	8.4
% Return on Equity	10.2	15.5	16.2	13.1	10.5	13.4	13.2	12.4	15.8	12.2

Data as orig reptd.; bef. results of disc opers/spec. items. Per share data adj. for stk. divs.; EPS diluted. E-Estimated. NA-Not Available. NM-Not Meaningful. NR-Not Ranked. UR-Under Review.

Office: 312 Walnut Street, Cincinnati, OH 45201.
Telephone: 513-977-3000.
Email: ir@scripps.com
Website: http://www.scripps.com

Chrmn: W.R. Burleigh
Pres & CEO: K.W. Lowe
COO & EVP: R.A. Boehne
EVP & CFO: J.G. NeCastro

SVP & General Counsel: A.B. Cruz, III
Investor Contact: T.E. Stautberg (513-977-3826)
Board of Directors: W. R. Burleigh, J. H. Burlingame, D. A. Galloway, K. W. Lowe, J. Mohn, N. B. Paumgarten, J. Sagansky, N. E. Scagliotti, E. W. Scripps, P. K. Scripps, R. W. Tysoe, J. A. Wrigley

Founded: 1878
Domicile: Ohio
Employees: 9,600

STANDARD &POOR'S

Sealed Air Corp

S&P Recommendation BUY ★★★★★

Price $59.09 (as of Oct 27, 2006)

12-Mo. Target Price $67.00

Investment Style Mid-Cap Value

GICS Sector Materials
Sub-Industry Paper Packaging

Comment This company is a leading global manufacturer of a wide range of food and protective packaging materials and systems.

Key Stock Statistics (Source S&P, Vickers, company reports)

52-Wk Range	$59.80–45.62	S&P Oper. EPS 2006E	3.02	P/E on S&P Oper. EPS 2006E	19.6	Dividend Rate/Share	$0.60
Trailing 12-Month EPS	$2.81	S&P Oper. EPS 2007E	3.45	Common Shares Outstg. (M)	81.1	Yield (%)	1.02
Trailing 12-Month P/E	21.0	S&P Core EPS 2006E	3.05	Market Capitalization(B)	$4.791	Beta	2.05
$10K Invested 5 Yrs Ago	$14,256	S&P Core EPS 2007E	3.48	Institutional Ownership (%)	90	S&P Credit Rating	BBB

Price Performance

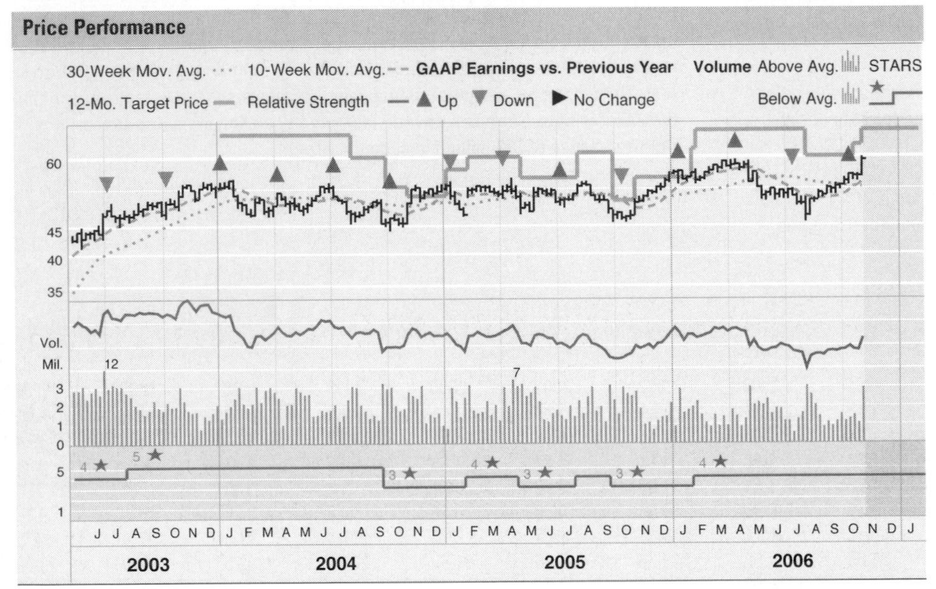

Options: ASE, CBOE, Ph

Highlights

- The 12-month target price for SEE has recently been changed to $67.00 from $63.00. The Highlights section of this Stock Report will be updated accordingly.

Investment Rationale/Risk

- The Investment Rationale/Risk section of this Stock Report will be updated shortly. For the latest News story on SEE from MarketScope, see below.

- 10/25/06 09:52 am EDT... S&P REITERATES BUY RECOMMENDATION ON SHARES OF SEALED AIR (SEE 56.35****): SEE posts Q3 EPS of $0.82 vs. $0.68, $0.02 below our estimate. Sales grew 6% on a better product mix and pricing. We project 4%-plus organic revenue growth through '07, driven by prior food packaging acquisitions and price hikes. We think margins will widen in '07 on stabilizing resin costs and a global restructuring. The shares are nearly 20% below intrinsic value of $69 based on our DCF model. Blending metrics, we think the stock warrants near-average-historical P/E of 19.5X our '07 EPS estimate of $3.45. We are raising our 12-mo. target price by $4 to $67. /S.Scharf

Qualitative Risk Assessment

LOW | **MEDIUM** | HIGH

Our risk assessment reflects asbestos litigation, volatile energy prices, food-related health issues that could lead to restrictions on imports and exports, and some corporate governance concerns. This is offset by our view of the company's sound balance sheet and cash flow generation.

Quantitative Evaluations

S&P Quality Ranking NR

D | C | B- | B | B+ | A- | A | A+

Relative Strength Rank STRONG

85

LOWEST = 1 HIGHEST = 99

Revenue/Earnings Data

Revenue (Million $)

	1Q	2Q	3Q	4Q	Year
2006	1,019	1,082	1,081	--	--
2005	969.8	1,020	1,020	1,076	4,085
2004	913.1	923.7	944.2	1,017	3,798
2003	822.9	865.6	908.7	934.8	3,532
2002	746.1	786.3	825.8	846.1	3,204
2001	758.3	761.6	766.2	781.4	3,067

Earnings Per Share ($)

	1Q	2Q	3Q	4Q	Year
2006	0.60	0.62	0.82	**E**0.88	**E**3.02
2005	0.58	0.66	0.68	0.77	2.69
2004	0.62	0.64	0.69	0.33	2.25
2003	0.52	0.56	0.41	0.50	2.00
2002	0.56	0.61	0.62	-6.13	-4.30
2001	0.25	0.30	0.37	0.30	1.22

Fiscal year ended Dec. 31. Next earnings report expected: Late January. EPS Estimates based on S&P Operating Earnings; historical GAAP earnings are as reported.

Dividend Data (Dates: mm/dd Payment Date: mm/dd/yy)

Amount ($)	Date Decl.	Ex-Div. Date	Stk. of Record	Payment Date
0.150	01/30	03/01	03/03	03/17/06
0.150	04/07	05/31	06/02	06/16/06
0.150	08/11	08/30	09/01	09/15/06

Dividends have been paid since 2006. Source: Company reports.

Sealed Air Corp

Business Summary October 18, 2006

CORPORATE OVERVIEW. Sealed Air Corp., with a broader global presence following its merger with the Cryovac packaging business of W.R. Grace in 1998, is a leading protective and specialty packaging company. It expects an increasing proportion of sales to come from outside the U.S. Foreign operations (excluding Canada, with about 3%) accounted for 48% of sales in 2005, with Europe accounting for 29% of total sales, Latin America 7.3%, and Asia Pacific 12%.

The company operates in two business segments: protective packaging products (38% of net sales in 2005; 37% of operating profits) and food packaging products (62%; 63%). Food packaging products primarily consist of flexible materials and related systems marketed mainly under the Cryovac trademark for a broad range of perishable food applications. The segment also manufactures polystyrene foam trays that are used by supermarkets and food processors to protect and display fresh meat, poultry and produce. In our view, the late 2005 lifting of U.S. restrictions on imports of beef from Canada, and Japan opening its borders to beef imports during the first half of 2006, should gradually aid meat packaging volume. The U.S. Department of Agriculture (USDA) projects increases in U.S. protein consumption. The protective packaging products segment includes surface protection and other cushioning products such as air cellular packaging materials, and plastic sheets containing encapsulated air bubbles that protect products from damage during shipment, under the Bubble Wrap and Air Cap brand names. SEE's engineered products include Instapak foam-in-place packaging systems and void-fill packaging. The company also makes Jiffy protective mailers.

In 2006, the company was evaluating the effects of the repatriation provision based on the American Jobs Creation Act (AJCA), which was signed into law in October 2004. The deduction would produce the equivalent of a 5.25% effective tax rate on repatriated foreign earnings. SEE qualifies to repatriate up to $500 million.

A loss of $6.13 per share in the 2002 fourth quarter reflected an asbestos settlement and restructuring charges totaling $6.81 a share related to its 1998 acquisition of W.R. Grace's Cryovac unit. SEE has a current liability for an asbestos settlement of nearly $513 million, which will be paid when Grace emerges from bankruptcy.

Company Financials

Per Share Data ($) Year Ended Dec. 31	**2005**	**2004**	**2003**	**2002**	**2001**	**2000**	**1999**	**1998**	**1997**	**1996**
Tangible Book Value	NM	NM	NM	NM	NM	NM	NM	NM	5.69	NA
Cash Flow	5.28	3.98	3.91	-2.34	3.84	4.33	3.41	2.44	2.38	NA
Earnings	2.69	2.25	2.00	-4.30	1.22	1.93	1.68	0.12	1.17	NA
S&P Core Earnings	2.73	2.28	2.06	2.58	1.25	NA	NA	NA	NA	NA
Dividends	Nil	Nil	Nil	Nil	Nil	Nil	Nil	Nil	NA	NA
Payout Ratio	Nil	Nil	Nil	Nil	Nil	Nil	Nil	Nil	NA	NA
Prices:High	56.64	54.90	54.47	48.39	47.10	61.88	68.44	68.00	NA	NA
Prices:Low	45.55	44.06	35.00	12.70	28.80	26.38	44.50	27.38	NA	NA
P/E Ratio:High	21	24	27	NM	39	32	41	NM	NA	NA
P/E Ratio:Low	17	20	17	NM	24	14	26	NM	NA	NA

Income Statement Analysis (Million $)										
Revenue	4,085	3,798	3,532	3,204	3,067	3,068	2,840	2,507	1,480	NA
Operating Income	687	716	693	1,766	641	687	648	524	155	NA
Depreciation	175	180	154	166	221	220	147	178	93.0	NA
Interest Expense	150	154	134	65.3	76.4	64.5	58.1	53.6	19.0	NA
Pretax Income	377	323	377	-392	297	413	396	199	143	NA
Effective Tax Rate	32.1%	33.2%	36.2%	NM	47.3%	45.5%	46.6%	63.3%	38.5%	NA
Net Income	256	216	240	-309	157	225	211	73.0	88.0	NA
S&P Core Earnings	259	219	192	227	111	NA	NA	NA	NA	NA

Balance Sheet & Other Financial Data (Million $)										
Cash	456	412	365	127	13.8	11.2	13.7	45.0	48.0	NA
Current Assets	1,695	1,611	1,428	1,056	776	877	803	845	2,176	NA
Total Assets	4,864	4,855	4,704	4,261	3,908	4,048	3,855	4,040	3,773	NA
Current Liabilities	1,534	1,304	1,190	1,153	627	675	582	535	1,358	NA
Long Term Debt	1,813	2,088	2,260	868	788	944	665	997	48.5	NA
Common Equity	1,392	1,334	1,124	813	850	753	551	437	468	NA
Total Capital	3,229	3,448	3,418	3,039	3,215	3,301	3,193	3,425	322	NA
Capital Expenditures	96.9	103	124	91.6	146	114	75.1	82.4	24.3	NA
Cash Flow	430	395	366	-197	322	381	287	179	181	NA
Current Ratio	1.1	1.2	1.2	0.9	1.2	1.3	1.4	1.6	1.6	NA
% Long Term Debt of Capitalization	56.1	60.5	66.1	28.6	24.5	28.6	20.8	29.1	15.1	NA
% Net Income of Revenue	6.3	5.7	6.8	NM	5.1	7.3	7.4	2.9	5.9	NA
% Return on Assets	5.3	4.5	5.4	NM	3.9	5.7	5.3	1.9	2.0	NA
% Return on Equity	18.8	17.5	21.9	NM	12.7	24.7	28.3	0.2	16.0	NA

Data as orig reptd.; bef. results of disc opers/spec. items. Per share data adj. for stk. divs.; EPS diluted. E-Estimated. NA-Not Available. NM-Not Meaningful. NR-Not Ranked. UR-Under Review.

Office: Park 80 East, Saddle Brook, NJ 07663-5291.
Telephone: 201-791-7600.
Website: http://www.sealedair.com
Pres & CEO: W.V. Hickey

SVP & CFO: D. Kelsey
VP, Secy & General Counsel: H.K. White
Treas: T.S. Christie
Investor Contact: E.D. Burrell (201-791-7600)

Board of Directors: H. Brown, M. Chu, L. R. Codey, T. D. Dunphy, C. F. Farrell, Jr., W. V. Hickey, J. B. Kosecoff, K. P. Manning, W. J. Marino

Auditor: KPMG
Founded: 1996
Domicile: Delaware
Employees: 17,000

STANDARD & POOR'S

Sears Holdings Corp

S&P Recommendation HOLD ★★★★★

Price $176.93 (as of Oct 27, 2006)

12-Mo. Target Price $165.00

Investment Style Large-Cap Growth

GICS Sector Consumer Discretionary
Sub-Industry Department Stores

Comment Through its wholly owned Sears and Kmart subsidiaries, Sears Holdings is the third largest broadline retailer in the U.S.

Key Stock Statistics (Source S&P, Vickers, company reports)

52-Wk Range	$182.38–111.64	S&P Oper. EPS 2007E	8.65	P/E on S&P Oper. EPS 2007E	20.5	Dividend Rate/Share	Nil
Trailing 12-Month EPS	$7.52	S&P Oper. EPS 2008E	10.60	Common Shares Outstg. (M)	154.0	Yield (%)	Nil
Trailing 12-Month P/E	23.5	S&P Core EPS 2007E	8.49	Market Capitalization(B)	$27.254	Beta	-0.14
$10K Invested 5 Yrs Ago	NA	S&P Core EPS 2008E	10.46	Institutional Ownership (%)	94	S&P Credit Rating	NA

Price Performance

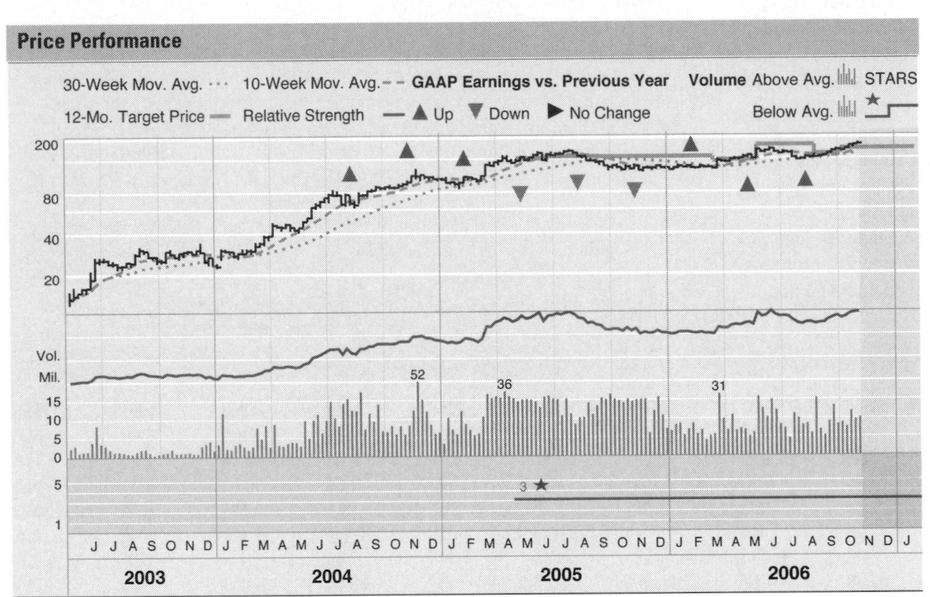

Analysis prepared by **Jason N. Asaeda** on September 27, 2006, when the stock traded at **$ 160.18.**

Highlights

- Factoring a full year of sales contribution from Sears, we look for revenues to rise modestly in FY 07 (Jan.), to $52.2 billion. At Kmart, we anticipate a sales benefit from fashion-right apparel, strong demand for food and consumables, store remodels, and sales of select Sears products and home services. We expect to see continued sales declines at Sears, as SHLD has indicated that new fashion-forward brands launched in FY 06 have been met with lackluster customer response. We also look for the company to slow conversion of Kmart stores to Sears this year, based on what we believe were disappointing results from Sears Essentials test stores.
- We look for consolidated same-store sales to decline 3% to 4%. However, we project that operating margins will widen on anticipated expense reductions from the integration of Sears and Kmart operations.
- Factoring in likely share buybacks, we see FY 07 operating EPS of $8.65 and S&P Core EPS of $8.49. The difference reflects projected pension and post-retirement costs.

Investment Rationale/Risk

- We are seeing positive mix changes at Kmart, particularly in apparel and home fashions, which we think are helping improve its competitive positioning, but with Sears executing unevenly across most major merchandise categories, we do not anticipate a near-term reversal of SHLD's negative same-sales trend. However, we look for merger-related cost synergies and the repurchase of up to $618 million of shares (authorized as of September 12, 2006) to offer earnings support in FY 07.
- Risks to our recommendation and target price include revenue shortfalls due to poor merchandising or competitive pressures. Our corporate governance concerns include cash-only payments to directors and non-disclosure of specific hurdle rates for performance-based equity awards.
- We derive our 12-month target price of $165 from our P/E-to-growth (PEG) valuation, which applies a peer-median forward PEG ratio of 1.1, expected forward EPS growth of 14% over the next five years, and our FY 08 operating EPS estimate of $10.60.

Qualitative Risk Assessment

LOW	**MEDIUM**	HIGH

Our risk assessment reflects our view of SHLD's significant opportunity to leverage Kmart's and Sears's best practices and brands, as well as merger-related cost synergies, and to strengthen its competitive positioning, partly offset by the two units' long records of inconsistent sales and earnings, in our opinion.

Quantitative Evaluations

S&P Quality Ranking NR

D	C	B-	B	B+	A-	A	A+

Relative Strength Rank STRONG

87

LOWEST = 1 HIGHEST = 99

Revenue/Earnings Data

Revenue (Million $)

	1Q	2Q	3Q	4Q	Year
2007	11,998	12,785	--	--	--
2006	7,626	13,192	12,202	16,086	49,124
2005	4,615	4,785	4,392	5,909	19,701
2004	--	5,652	5,092	6,328	17,072
2003	--	--	--	--	30,762
2002	--	--	--	--	--

Earnings Per Share ($)

	1Q	2Q	3Q	4Q	Year
2007	1.14	1.88	**E**0.95	**E**4.82	**E**8.65
2006	0.65	0.98	0.35	4.03	6.17
2005	0.94	1.54	5.45	3.09	11.00
2004	--	-0.06	-0.26	2.78	2.52
2003	--	--	--	--	NA
2002	--	--	--	--	--

Fiscal year ended Jan. 31. Next earnings report expected: Early December. EPS Estimates based on S&P Operating Earnings; historical GAAP earnings are as reported.

Dividend Data

No cash dividends have been paid.

Sears Holdings Corp

Business Summary September 27, 2006

CORPORATE OVERVIEW. Through the March 2005 merger of Kmart Holding Corp. and Sears, Roebuck and Co., which continue to operate under their separate brand names, Sears Holdings has emerged as the third largest broadline retailer in the U.S. based on FY 06 (Jan.) reported revenues. As of January 2006, the company operated about 2,400 Sears-branded full line and specialty stores in the U.S. and Canada (operated by Sears Canada, a 54%-owned subsidiary at the time), and over 1,400 Kmart-branded discount stores and supercenters across the U.S. SHLD completed the integration of the Sears and Kmart supply chain, IT, finance, legal, human resources, marketing, and merchandising functions during FY 06, and the combination of store operations in February 2006.

CORPORATE STRATEGY. SHLD believes it has an opportunity to leverage Kmart's off-mall locations to expand the distribution of Sears products and services at a more rapid pace and at a lower cost than Sears would have been able to accomplish on its own. The company also sees the potential for Kmart to improve its value proposition and competitive positioning through the addition of Sears-owned brands and services (cross-selling).

In FY 06, SHLD introduced select Sears private label branded products, including Kenmore appliances and Craftsman tools, into about 100 Kmart stores. The company further completed a national roll-out of Sears credit card acceptance to all Kmart locations, and tested certain Sears customer services at select Kmart locations. Based on Kmart's initial success with leveraging Sears's best brand assets that have driven incremental sales, we look for SHLD to continue to roll out Sears brand products into Kmart locations in FY 07.

Company Financials

Per Share Data ($) Year Ended Jan. 31	**2006**	**2005**	**2004**	**2003**	**2002**	**2001**	**2000**	**1999**	**1998**	**1997**
Tangible Book Value	41.80	50.21	24.36	NA	NA	NA	NA	NA	NA	NA
Cash Flow	12.24	11.59	2.81	NA	NA	NA	NA	NA	NA	NA
Earnings	6.17	11.00	2.52	NA	NA	NA	NA	NA	NA	NA
S&P Core Earnings	4.53	4.51	-4.53	-6.80	-5.74	-0.55	NA	NA	NA	NA
Dividends	Nil	Nil	Nil	NA	NA	NA	NA	NA	NA	NA
Payout Ratio	Nil	Nil	Nil	NA	NA	NA	NA	NA	NA	NA
Calendar Year	2005	2004	2003	2002	2001	2000	1999	1998	1997	1996
Prices:High	163.50	119.69	34.55	NA	NA	NA	NA	NA	NA	NA
Prices:Low	84.51	22.41	12.00	NA	NA	NA	NA	NA	NA	NA
P/E Ratio:High	26	11	14	NA	NA	NA	NA	NA	NA	NA
P/E Ratio:Low	14	2	5	NA	NA	NA	NA	NA	NA	NA
Income Statement Analysis (Million $)										
Revenue	49,124	19,701	17,072	30,762	NA	NA	NA	NA	NA	NA
Operating Income	2,901	944	442	-1,303	NA	NA	NA	NA	NA	NA
Depreciation	932	69.0	31.0	737	NA	NA	NA	NA	NA	NA
Interest Expense	322	146	105	155	NA	NA	NA	NA	NA	NA
Pretax Income	1,965	1,775	400	-3,286	NA	NA	NA	NA	NA	NA
Effective Tax Rate	36.4%	37.7%	38.0%	NM	NA	NA	NA	NA	NA	NA
Net Income	948	1,106	248	-3,262	NA	NA	NA	NA	NA	NA
S&P Core Earnings	696	448	-405	-3,439	-2,840	-260	NA	NA	NA	NA
Balance Sheet & Other Financial Data (Million $)										
Cash	4,440	3,435	2,088	613	NA	NA	NA	NA	NA	NA
Current Assets	15,207	7,541	5,811	6,102	NA	NA	NA	NA	NA	NA
Total Assets	30,573	8,651	6,084	11,238	NA	NA	NA	NA	NA	NA
Current Liabilities	10,350	2,086	1,776	2,120	NA	NA	NA	NA	NA	NA
Long Term Debt	3,268	661	819	623	NA	NA	NA	NA	NA	NA
Common Equity	11,611	4,469	2,192	-301	NA	NA	NA	NA	NA	NA
Total Capital	14,879	5,130	3,011	322	NA	NA	NA	NA	NA	NA
Capital Expenditures	546	230	108	252	NA	NA	NA	NA	NA	NA
Cash Flow	1,880	1,175	279	-2,525	NA	NA	NA	NA	NA	NA
Current Ratio	1.5	3.6	3.3	2.9	NA	NA	NA	NA	NA	NA
% Long Term Debt of Capitalization	22.0	12.9	27.2	NM	NA	NA	NA	NA	NA	NA
% Net Income of Revenue	1.9	5.6	1.5	NM	NA	NA	NA	NA	NA	NA
% Return on Assets	4.8	15.0	3.9	NM	NA	NA	NA	NA	NA	NA
% Return on Equity	11.8	33.1	12.7	NM	NA	NA	NA	NA	NA	NA

Data as orig reptd.; bef. results of disc opers/spec. items. Per share data adj. for stk. divs.; EPS diluted. E-Estimated. NA-Not Available. NM-Not Meaningful. NR-Not Ranked. UR-Under Review.

Office: 3333 Beverly Rd, Hoffman Estates, IL 60179-0001.
Telephone: 847-286-2500.
Website: http://www.searsholdings.com
Chrmn: E.S. Lampert

Pres & CEO: A. Lewis
EVP & Chief Admin: W.C. Crowley
EVP & CIO: K.A. Austin
VP, Chief Acctg Officer & Cntlr: W.K. Phelan

Board of Directors: D. J. Carty, W. C. Crowley, J. C. Day, E. S. Lampert, A. Lewis, M. A. Miles, S. T. Mnuchin, R. C. Perry, A. N. Reese, T. J. Tisch

Founded: 1899
Domicile: Delaware
Employees: 355,000

STANDARD &POOR'S

Sempra Energy

S&P Recommendation BUY ★★★★★

Price $53.10 (as of Oct 27, 2006)

12-Mo. Target Price $54.00

Investment Style Large-Cap Value

GICS Sector Utilities
Sub-Industry Multi-Utilities

Comment This gas and electric utility is also engaged in unregulated power, liquefied natural gas and international energy projects.

Key Stock Statistics (Source S&P, Vickers, company reports)

52-Wk Range	$53.85–41.85	S&P Oper. EPS 2006E	3.70	P/E on S&P Oper. EPS 2006E	14.4	Dividend Rate/Share	$1.20
Trailing 12-Month EPS	$4.67	S&P Oper. EPS 2007E	3.80	Common Shares Outstg. (M)	261.2	Yield (%)	2.26
Trailing 12-Month P/E	11.4	S&P Core EPS 2006E	3.70	Market Capitalization(B)	$13.870	Beta	0.80
$10K Invested 5 Yrs Ago	$28,115	S&P Core EPS 2007E	3.80	Institutional Ownership (%)	62	S&P Credit Rating	BBB+

Price Performance

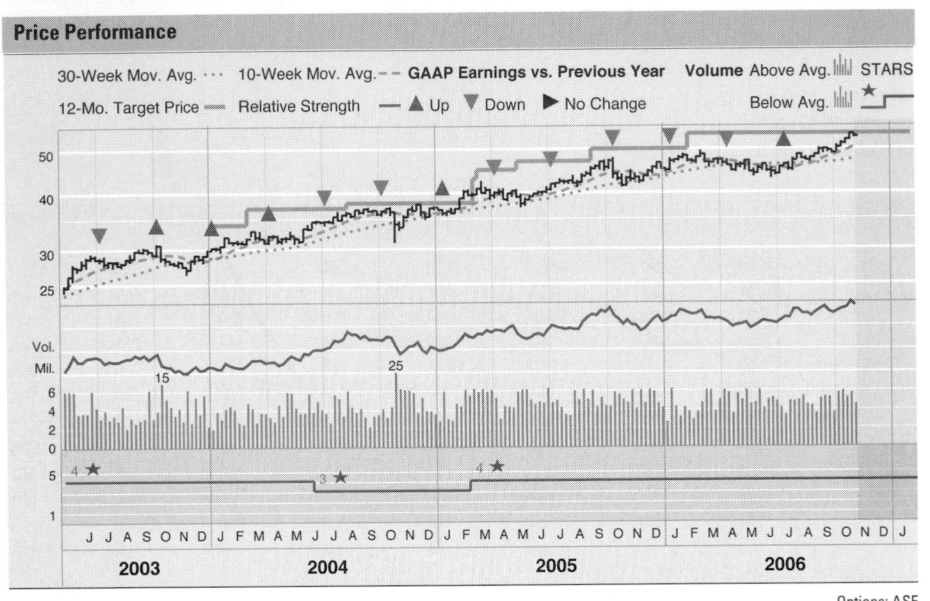

Options: ASE

Analysis prepared by **Ari Bensinger** on August 31, 2006, when the stock traded at **$ 49.72**.

Highlights

- The commodities segment should see improved growth on higher natural gas and power sales in North America and Europe. We think continued volatility and high prices for natural gas and petroleum will drive modest margin expansion and volume gains for trading operations. The company's generation operations should see lower earnings, as improved pricing in wholesale power markets and the full-year impact of 2005 acquisitions are outweighed by the absence of income from divested Texas power assets.
- We see utility income growing 3%-5% in 2006, reflecting expansion in the rate base, 1%-2% customer growth, and improved cost control. The addition of the Palomar power plant in 2006 is expected to add $500 million to the rate base. We project high single digit income gains at the pipelines and storage segment on improved Latin American operations, but expect LNG operations to see a wider loss.
- With lower interest expense, we estimate 2006 EPS of $3.70, compared to $3.98 earned in 2005, before one-time charges and gains.

Investment Rationale/Risk

- A more constructive regulatory environment in California, favorable regulatory decisions, and legal and regulatory settlements related to the 2001 California energy crisis have led to improved earnings clarity, in our opinion. We expect two LNG projects under construction to add $0.30 to $0.35 per share to earnings, starting in 2008. We think SRE will outpace its targeted 5% annual EPS growth through 2008.
- Risks to our recommendation and target price include a failure to complete LNG projects, declining wholesale power margins, potential losses from energy and metals trading, and a weaker economy.
- Although SRE still has greater earnings exposure to more volatile commodity trading operations compared to more regulated multi-utility peers, in our view, this is balanced by its stronger EPS growth prospects. The stock recently traded at a P/E of 13X our 2006 EPS estimate, below 14.5X for multi-utility peers. Our 12-month target price of $54 implies a peer average P/E of about 14.5X to our 2006 EPS estimate.

Qualitative Risk Assessment

LOW | **MEDIUM** | HIGH

Our risk assessment reflects a balance between stable and steady earnings provided by SRE's regulated gas and electric utility operations and cyclical and volatile earnings from unregulated businesses, including power generation, energy marketing and trading, and international energy investments.

Quantitative Evaluations

S&P Quality Ranking B

D | C | B- | **B** | B+ | A- | A | A+

Relative Strength Rank MODERATE

70

LOWEST = 1 HIGHEST = 99

Revenue/Earnings Data

Revenue (Million $)

	1Q	2Q	3Q	4Q	Year
2006	3,349	2,486	--	--	--
2005	2,697	2,276	2,770	3,994	11,737
2004	2,360	1,996	2,165	2,889	9,410
2003	1,923	1,840	2,058	2,066	7,887
2002	1,460	1,488	1,384	1,688	6,020
2001	3,242	1,900	1,510	1,377	8,029

Earnings Per Share ($)

	1Q	2Q	3Q	4Q	Year
2006	0.91	0.73	E0.93	E1.01	E3.70
2005	0.92	0.49	0.86	1.40	3.69
2004	0.96	0.55	0.98	1.43	3.93
2003	0.56	0.56	1.00	1.11	3.24
2002	0.71	0.70	0.73	0.65	2.79
2001	0.88	0.66	0.46	0.52	2.52

Fiscal year ended Dec. 31. Next earnings report expected: Early November. EPS Estimates based on S&P Operating Earnings; historical GAAP earnings are as reported.

Dividend Data (Dates: mm/dd Payment Date: mm/dd/yy)

Amount ($)	Date Decl.	Ex-Div. Date	Stk. of Record	Payment Date
0.290	12/06	12/20	12/22	01/15/06
0.300	02/21	03/21	03/23	04/15/06
0.300	06/06	06/20	06/22	07/15/06
0.300	09/12	09/26	09/28	10/15/06

Dividends have been paid since 1998. Source: Company reports.

Sempra Energy

Business Summary August 31, 2006

CORPORATE OVERVIEW. Sempra Energy (SRE) is a holding company with diverse interests in the energy domain. The company's principal business segments include California Utilities (CU), which contributed 60% of the revenues in 2005, and the Sempra Global and parent division (SG), which contributed the remaining 40%. The CU segment consists of regulated public utilities, including Southern California Gas Company (SCG) and San Diego Gas & Electric Company (SDGE), which provide electricity and natural gas services in California from the state's Central Valley to the Mexican border. The unregulated business of SG includes Sempra Generation, which develops and operates power plants and energy infrastructure; Sempra Commodities, which provides marketing and risk management services for energy products and base metals; Sempra LNG, which constructs and operates LNG receipt terminals in North America; and Sempra Pipelines & Storage, which operates natural gas pipelines and storage facilities in Mexico and the US.

CORPORATE STRATEGY. Sempra seeks to increase earnings through a mix of moderate growth at its regulated utilities and faster growth in non-regulated businesses. In the utility segment, the company focuses on managing regulatory risk as well as operating and capital expenditures.

Over the past three years, SRE has focused on acquisitions as well as on new construction in generation, LNG, and pipelines and storage segments. In 2004, SRE paid $430 million for a 50% interest in six active Texas power plants (975 MW net) and four inactive plants (930 MW net). During 2003, Generation finished building three new power plants (2,125 MW net). In July 2005, Generation purchased the remaining 50% interest in a 480 MW natural gas fired, combined-cycle power plant in Nevada for about $132 million. However, in late 2005, the company changed course, agreeing to sell a 380 MW coal-fired plant in Texas for $480 million. In addition, SRE announced that it was exploring a potential sale of the 50% stake in Texas assets acquired in 2004.

Company Financials

Per Share Data ($) Year Ended Dec. 31	2005	2004	2003	2002	2001	2000	1999	1998	1997	1996
Tangible Book Value	23.97	20.79	17.14	13.78	13.17	12.27	12.60	12.14	12.56	12.21
Cash Flow	6.25	6.59	6.12	5.68	5.35	NA	NA	NA	NA	NA
Earnings	3.69	3.93	3.24	2.79	2.52	2.06	1.66	1.24	1.82	1.77
S&P Core Earnings	3.44	3.65	3.29	2.16	1.76	NA	NA	NA	NA	NA
Dividends	1.16	1.00	1.00	1.00	1.00	1.00	1.56	1.56	1.27	1.24
Payout Ratio	31%	25%	31%	36%	40%	49%	94%	126%	70%	NA
Prices:High	47.86	37.93	30.90	26.25	28.61	24.88	26.00	29.31	NA	NA
Prices:Low	35.53	29.51	22.25	15.50	17.31	16.19	17.13	23.75	NA	NA
P/E Ratio:High	13	10	10	9	11	12	10	24	NA	NA
P/E Ratio:Low	10	8	7	6	7	8	10	19	NA	NA
Income Statement Analysis (Million $)										
Revenue	11,737	9,410	7,887	6,020	8,029	7,143	5,360	5,481	5,069	4,496
Operating Income	1,111	1,272	939	987	993	NA	1,617	1,536	1,503	1,508
Depreciation	646	621	615	596	579	563	879	929	604	586
Interest Expense	321	332	327	323	352	301	229	207	107	103
Pretax Income	971	1,113	742	721	731	NA	NA	NA	NA	NA
Effective Tax Rate	4.33%	17.3%	6.33%	20.2%	29.1%	38.0%	31.2%	31.9%	41.1%	41.3%
Net Income	929	920	695	575	518	429	394	294	432	427
S&P Core Earnings	866	855	708	445	362	NA	NA	NA	NA	NA
Balance Sheet & Other Financial Data (Million $)										
Cash	772	419	432	455	605	NA	NA	NA	NA	NA
Current Assets	13,318	8,776	7,886	7,010	4,808	NA	NA	NA	NA	NA
Total Assets	29,213	23,643	22,009	17,757	15,156	NA	NA	NA	NA	NA
Current Liabilities	12,157	9,082	8,348	7,247	5,524	NA	NA	NA	NA	NA
Long Term Debt	5,002	4,371	4,199	4,487	3,840	NA	NA	NA	NA	NA
Common Equity	6,160	4,865	3,890	2,825	2,692	NA	NA	NA	NA	NA
Total Capital	11,480	9,734	8,807	8,202	7,474	7,093	6,813	6,489	7,309	6,859
Capital Expenditures	1,404	1,083	1,049	1,214	1,068	NA	NA	NA	NA	NA
Cash Flow	1,575	1,541	1,310	1,171	1,097	NA	NA	NA	NA	NA
Current Ratio	1.1	1.0	0.9	1.0	0.9	NA	NA	NA	NA	NA
% Long Term Debt of Capitalization	43.6	44.9	47.7	54.7	51.4	NA	NA	NA	NA	NA
% Net Income of Revenue	7.9	9.8	8.8	9.6	6.5	NA	NA	NA	NA	NA
% Return on Assets	3.5	4.0	3.3	3.5	3.4	NA	NA	NA	NA	NA
% Return on Equity	16.9	21.0	20.7	20.8	20.0	NA	NA	NA	NA	NA

Data as orig reptd.; bef. results of disc opers/spec. items. Per share data adj. for stk. divs.; EPS diluted. E-Estimated. NA-Not Available. NM-Not Meaningful. NR-Not Ranked. UR-Under Review.

Office: 101 Ash Street, San Diego, CA 92101-3017.
Telephone: 619-696-2000.
Email: investor@sempra.com
Website: http://www.sempra.com

Chrmn & CEO: D.E. Felsinger
Pres & COO: N.E. Schmale
EVP & CFO: M. Snell
EVP & General Counsel: M.J. Chaudhri

SVP & Cntlr: F.H. Ault
Investor Contact: D.V. Arriola (619-696-2901)
Board of Directors: J. G. Brocksmith, Jr., R. A. Collato, D. E. Felsinger, D. K. Fletcher, W. D. Godbold, Jr., W. D. Jones, R. G. Newman, W. G. Ouchi, W. C. Rusnack, W. P. Rutledge, N. E. Schmale

Founded: 1998
Domicile: California
Employees: 14,000

Sherwin-Williams Co (The)

STANDARD &POOR'S

S&P Recommendation HOLD ★★★★★

Price $57.96 (as of Oct 27, 2006)

12-Mo. Target Price $60.00

Investment Style Mid-Cap Value

GICS Sector Consumer Discretionary
Sub-Industry Home Improvement Retail

Comment This company, the largest U.S. producer of paints, is also a major seller of wallcoverings and related products.

Key Stock Statistics (Source S&P, Vickers, company reports)

52-Wk Range	**$60.28–37.40**	S&P Oper. EPS 2006E	**4.12**	P/E on S&P Oper. EPS 2006E	**14.1**	Dividend Rate/Share	**$1.00**
Trailing 12-Month EPS	**$4.01**	S&P Oper. EPS 2007E	**4.40**	Common Shares Outstg. (M)	**134.8**	Yield (%)	**1.73**
Trailing 12-Month P/E	**14.5**	S&P Core EPS 2006E	**4.12**	Market Capitalization(B)	**$7.814**	Beta	**0.92**
$10K Invested 5 Yrs Ago	**$24,923**	S&P Core EPS 2007E	**4.40**	Institutional Ownership (%)	**70**	S&P Credit Rating	**A-**

Price Performance

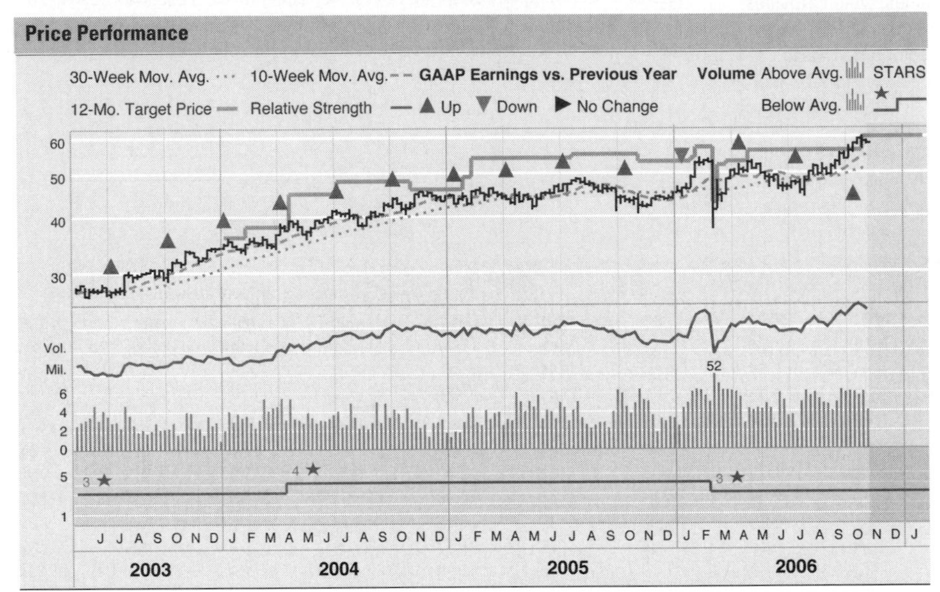

Options: CBOE

Analysis prepared by **Michael Souers** on October 23, 2006, when the stock traded at **$ 58.54**.

Highlights

- We expect sales growth of between 8% and 10% in 2006, following an 18% increase in 2005. Paint store segment sales gains will likely be driven by the addition of approximately 100 net new stores and high single-digit same-store sales increases, benefiting from strong architectural paint sales to commercial customers.
- We expect a modest improvement in gross margins as SHW should be able to pass on the majority of raw material cost increases to end consumers. We see operating margins widening by approximately 100 basis points, as cost cutting initiatives and the leveraging of expenses are only partially offset by continuing investments in new stores and the inclusion of stock options.
- After slightly higher expected interest expense, taxes at 32.3%, and about 2% fewer shares, reflecting SHW's buyback program, we estimate 2006 EPS of $4.12, representing a 26% increase from the $3.28 earned in 2005. We project 2007 EPS of $4.40. Our 2006 EPS estimate includes $0.08 of projected stock option expense.

Investment Rationale/Risk

- Our favorable view of the company's fundamentals is offset by litigation overhang, most notably a negative court ruling against SHW in Rhode Island. SHW was found liable for creating a public nuisance by selling lead paint decades ago. We believe industry fundamentals remain strong despite our projections of a slowing housing market in 2006, as we believe that DIY activity will continue as consumers view their homes as investments.
- Risks to our opinion and target price include a significant slowdown in economic growth; a sharper than expected rise in interest rates, which could dampen home-related spending; and any negative rulings on other lead pigment litigation cases outside of Rhode Island.
- At about 13X our 2007 EPS estimate, SHW shares recently traded at a multiple roughly in line with peers but below the S&P 500, which we regard as appropriate. Our 12-month DCF-based target price of $60, about 13.6X our 2007 EPS estimate, assumes a weighted average cost of capital of 10.6% and a terminal growth rate of 3%.

Qualitative Risk Assessment

LOW | **MEDIUM** | HIGH

Our risk assessment for Sherwin-Williams reflects the cyclical nature of the company, which is reliant on new housing starts and remodeling, and lead pigment litigation risk, offset by an S&P Earnings & Dividend Rank of A.

Quantitative Evaluations

S&P Quality Ranking A

D | C | B- | B | B+ | A- | **A** | A+

Relative Strength Rank STRONG

71

LOWEST = 1 HIGHEST = 99

Revenue/Earnings Data

Revenue (Million $)

	1Q	2Q	3Q	4Q	Year
2006	1,769	2,130	2,117	--	--
2005	1,539	1,965	1,977	1,710	7,191
2004	1,320	1,618	1,677	1,499	6,114
2003	1,148	1,472	1,503	1,285	5,408
2002	1,149	1,453	1,426	1,156	5,185
2001	1,158	1,408	1,367	1,133	5,067

Earnings Per Share ($)

	1Q	2Q	3Q	4Q	Year
2006	0.82	1.33	1.30	E0.66	E4.12
2005	0.58	1.08	1.07	0.54	3.28
2004	0.35	0.87	0.92	0.57	2.72
2003	0.21	0.75	0.82	0.48	2.26
2002	0.23	0.70	0.74	0.38	2.04
2001	0.23	0.58	0.58	0.29	1.68

Fiscal year ended Dec. 31. Next earnings report expected: Late January. EPS Estimates based on S&P Operating Earnings; historical GAAP earnings are as reported.

Dividend Data (Dates: mm/dd Payment Date: mm/dd/yy)

Amount ($)	Date Decl.	Ex-Div. Date	Stk. of Record	Payment Date
0.250	02/22	03/01	03/03	03/17/06
0.250	04/19	05/17	05/19	06/09/06
0.250	07/19	08/16	08/18	09/01/06
0.250	10/18	11/15	11/17	12/08/06

Dividends have been paid since 1979. Source: Company reports.

Sherwin-Williams Co (The)

Business Summary October 23, 2006

CORPORATE PROFILE. Sherwin-Williams manufactures, distributes and sells paints, coatings and related products to professional, industrial, commercial and retail customers primarily in North and South America. The company is structured into five reportable segments: Paint Stores, Consumer, Automotive Finishes, International Coatings and Administrative.

Paint Stores (67% of revenues in 2005) offer Sherwin-Williams branded architectural and industrial paints, stains and related products. Its diverse customer base includes architectural and industrial painting contractors, residential and commercial builders, property owners and managers, OEM product finishers and do-it-yourself (DIY) homeowners. In 2005, SHW opened 98 net new stores, bringing the North America Paint Stores store count to 3,081.

The Consumer segment (19%) makes architectural paints, stains, varnishes, industrial maintenance products, wood finishing products, paint applicators, corrosion inhibitors and paint related products. Brands include Dutch Boy, Krylon, Minwax, Thompson's Water Seal and Pratt & Lambert, as well as private label brands.

Automotive Finishes (8%) develops, makes and distributes various motor vehicle finish, refinish, and touch-up products to a diverse market, including automotive jobbers, wholesale distributors and collision repair facilities. SHW sells its products in over 200 company-operated branches in the U.S., Canada, Jamaica, Chile and Peru, and other operations throughout North and South America, the Caribbean Islands, Europe and China.

The International Coatings segment (5%) manufactures and licenses architectural paints, stains, varnishes, industrial maintenance products, product finishes, wood finishing products and paint-related products worldwide. A majority of segment sales come from South America, as the company has 74 stores in Chile, Brazil, Uruguay and Argentina.

Company Financials

Per Share Data ($) Year Ended Dec. 31	**2005**	**2004**	**2003**	**2002**	**2001**	**2000**	**1999**	**1998**	**1997**	**1996**
Tangible Book Value	3.83	3.12	2.95	4.06	3.60	3.10	2.32	1.70	0.80	2.19
Cash Flow	4.30	3.59	3.13	2.86	2.39	0.77	2.42	2.17	2.48	1.09
Earnings	3.28	2.72	2.26	2.04	1.68	0.10	1.80	1.57	1.50	1.33
S&P Core Earnings	3.24	2.60	2.15	1.81	1.62	NA	NA	NA	NA	NA
Dividends	0.82	0.68	0.62	0.60	0.58	0.54	0.48	0.45	0.50	0.35
Payout Ratio	25%	25%	27%	29%	35%	NM	27%	29%	33%	26%
Prices:High	48.84	45.61	34.77	33.24	28.23	27.63	32.88	37.88	33.38	28.88
Prices:Low	40.47	32.95	24.42	21.75	19.73	17.13	18.75	19.44	24.13	19.50
P/E Ratio:High	15	17	16	16	17	NM	10	24	22	22
P/E Ratio:Low	12	12	11	11	12	NM	10	12	16	15
Income Statement Analysis (Million $)										
Revenue	7,191	6,114	5,408	5,105	5,067	5,212	5,004	4,934	4,881	4,133
Operating Income	898	758	690	670	599	676	680	629	613	495
Depreciation	144	126	117	116	109	109	105	97.8	90.2	76.0
Interest Expense	49.6	39.9	38.7	40.5	54.6	62.0	61.2	72.0	80.8	25.0
Pretax Income	656	580	523	497	424	143	490	440	427	375
Effective Tax Rate	29.2%	32.0%	36.5%	37.5%	38.0%	88.8%	38.0%	38.0%	39.0%	38.9%
Net Income	463	393	332	311	263	16.0	304	273	261	229
S&P Core Earnings	458	376	317	276	254	NA	NA	NA	NA	NA
Balance Sheet & Other Financial Data (Million $)										
Cash	36.0	45.9	303	164	119	2.90	18.6	19.1	3.53	1.90
Current Assets	1,891	1,782	1,715	1,506	1,507	1,552	1,597	1,547	1,532	1,416
Total Assets	4,369	4,274	3,683	3,432	3,628	3,751	4,052	4,065	4,036	2,995
Current Liabilities	1,554	1,520	1,154	1,083	1,141	1,115	1,190	1,112	1,116	1,051
Long Term Debt	487	488	503	507	504	624	624	730	844	143
Common Equity	1,696	1,475	1,174	1,300	1,319	1,472	1,699	1,716	1,592	1,401
Total Capital	2,218	2,139	1,962	1,849	1,991	2,095	2,323	2,446	2,436	1,544
Capital Expenditures	143	107	117	127	82.6	133	134	146	164	123
Cash Flow	607	519	449	426	372	125	409	371	351	305
Current Ratio	1.2	1.2	1.5	1.4	1.3	1.4	1.3	1.4	1.4	1.4
% Long Term Debt of Capitalization	22.0	22.8	25.6	27.4	25.3	29.8	26.9	29.9	34.6	9.3
% Net Income of Revenue	6.4	6.4	6.1	6.0	5.2	0.3	6.1	5.5	5.3	5.5
% Return on Assets	10.7	9.9	9.3	8.8	7.1	0.4	7.5	6.7	7.4	8.9
% Return on Equity	29.2	29.7	26.8	23.7	18.9	1.0	17.8	16.5	17.4	17.5

Data as orig reptd.; bef. results of disc opers/spec. items. Per share data adj. for stk. divs.; EPS diluted. E-Estimated. NA-Not Available. NM-Not Meaningful. NR-Not Ranked. UR-Under Review.

Office: 101 Prospect Avenue N.W., Cleveland, OH 44115-1075.
Telephone: 216-566-2000.
Website: http://www.sherwin.com
Chrmn & CEO: C.M. Connor

Pres & COO: J.G. Morikis
SVP, CFO & Treas: S. Hennessy
Investor Contact: C.G. Ivy (216-566-2140)
VP, Secy & General Counsel: L.E. Stellato

Founded: 1866
Domicile: Ohio
Employees: 29,434

STANDARD &POOR'S

Sigma Aldrich Corporation

S&P Recommendation HOLD ★★★★★

Price $74.32 (as of Oct 27, 2006)

12-Mo. Target Price $75.00

Investment Style Mid-Cap Growth

GICS Sector Materials
Sub-Industry Specialty Chemicals

Comment This company makes and sells a wide range of biochemicals, organic chemicals and chromatography products.

Key Stock Statistics (Source S&P, Vickers, company reports)

52-Wk Range	$77.47–62.53	S&P Oper. EPS 2006E	4.00	P/E on S&P Oper. EPS 2006E	18.6	Dividend Rate/Share	$0.84
Trailing 12-Month EPS	$3.88	S&P Oper. EPS 2007E	4.20	Common Shares Outstg. (M)	66.4	Yield (%)	1.13
Trailing 12-Month P/E	19.2	S&P Core EPS 2006E	3.83	Market Capitalization(B)	$4.933	Beta	0.50
$10K Invested 5 Yrs Ago	$20,960	S&P Core EPS 2007E	4.18	Institutional Ownership (%)	82	S&P Credit Rating	NA

Price Performance

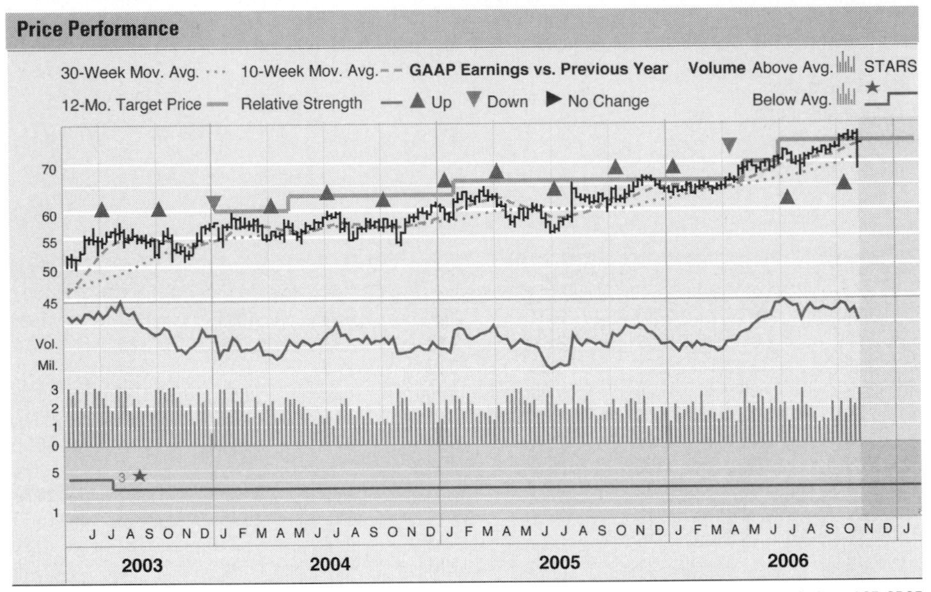

Options: ASE, CBOE

Analysis prepared by **Richard O'Reilly, CFA** on September 05, 2006, when the stock traded at **$ 72.82**.

Highlights

- We expect sales to rise about 8% in 2006, before contributions from any possible acquisitions. The acquisition of JRH Biosciences in February 2005 should add about 1% to full year sales growth, all in the first quarter, by our estimation. Currency exchange rates should have about a 2% favorable impact in the second half but be neutral for the full year. We expect volumes in 2006 to show continued mid-single digit growth after improved performance in 2005 (following flat results in 2004 and a nearly 3% decline in 2003), on new products and marketing initiatives.
- We see annual price increases of 2%, slower than in 2005. We expect pretax margins in 2006 of about 21% versus 20.6% reported for 2005, should be aided by additional process improvements. 2006 results include projected stock option expense of about $0.16 a share, while the first quarter included a $0.03 a share acquisition related charge, versus $0.16 for all of 2005.
- We foresee an effective tax rate of 30.0% for 2006, up from the 24.8% rate in 2005, which included a one-time first quarter $0.16 a share tax benefit. We think EPS comparisons will benefit from additional modest share repurchases.

Investment Rationale/Risk

- Since early 2005, the company has achieved its strongest organic revenue growth (about 7%-8%) in several years, boosted by new marketing initiatives and an expanded sales force, and we expect this trend to continue through 2006. The early 2005 purchase of JRH Biosciences has boosted sales in the company's fine chemicals business, in our opinion. The company is reemphasizing an annual sales growth target of 10%, including 3% contributions from acquisitions.
- Risks to our recommendation and target price include unexpected weakness in key markets such as pharmaceutical and academia, greater price competition, adverse currency exchange movements, an inability to successfully introduce new products, and the failure to successfully integrate future acquisitions.
- The shares have advanced about 15% year to date, and traded recently at about 18.6X our 2006 EPS estimate of $3.95, below the life science peer average of 21X. Our 12-month target price of $75 assumes a P/E multiple of 19X our 2006 EPS estimate. We think a premium to the S&P 500 is justified in view of what we believe is an attractive EPS record.

Qualitative Risk Assessment

LOW	MEDIUM	HIGH

Our risk assessment reflects the stable nature of the company's laboratory chemicals business, broad geographic sales mix, and a strong balance sheet.

Quantitative Evaluations

S&P Quality Ranking A+

D	C	B-	B	B+	A-	A	A+

Relative Strength Rank MODERATE

36

LOWEST = 1 HIGHEST = 99

Revenue/Earnings Data

Revenue (Million $)

	1Q	2Q	3Q	4Q	Year
2006	443.1	448.5	441.4	--	--
2005	399.8	444.0	412.2	410.5	1,667
2004	368.1	348.6	340.6	351.9	1,409
2003	334.7	327.1	314.2	322.2	1,298
2002	301.6	304.3	304.8	296.3	1,207
2001	305.7	293.7	287.7	292.3	1,179

Earnings Per Share ($)

2006	0.98	1.04	1.02	E0.96	E4.00
2005	1.07	0.91	0.94	0.84	3.76
2004	0.89	0.85	0.81	0.79	3.34
2003	0.72	0.67	0.66	0.67	2.68
2002	0.54	-0.30	0.63	0.92	1.78
2001	0.48	0.49	0.45	0.45	1.87

Fiscal year ended Dec. 31. Next earnings report expected: Mid February. EPS Estimates based on S&P Operating Earnings; historical GAAP earnings are as reported.

Dividend Data (Dates: mm/dd Payment Date: mm/dd/yy)

Amount ($)	Date Decl.	Ex-Div. Date	Stk. of Record	Payment Date
0.190	11/08	11/29	12/01	12/15/05
0.210	02/14	02/27	03/01	03/15/06
0.210	05/02	05/30	06/01	06/15/06
0.210	08/09	08/30	09/01	09/15/06

Dividends have been paid since 1970. Source: Company reports.

Please read the Required Disclosures and Analyst Certification on the last page of this report.

Sigma Aldrich Corporation

Business Summary September 05, 2006

CORPORATE OVERVIEW. Sigma-Aldrich, well known for its extensive catalog business, is one of the world's largest providers of research chemicals, reagents, chromatography products, and related products.

Foreign sales accounted for 59% of the total in 2005, with about 40% from Europe.

SIAL distributes more than 100,000 chemical products, under the Sigma, Aldrich, Fluka and Supelco brands names, for use primarily in research and development, diagnosis of disease, and as specialty chemicals for manufacturing. About 75% of sales are to customers in the life sciences, with the remaining 25% used in high technology applications. Customer sectors include pharmaceutical (40% of sales), academia and government (30%), chemical industry (20%), and hospitals and commercial laboratories (10%). The company itself produces about 40,000 products, accounting for 60% of 2005 net sales of chemical products. Remaining products are purchased from outside sources. The company also supplies 30,000 equipment products.

The Scientific Research unit (53% of sales in 2005) supplies biochemicals, organic and inorganic compounds, reagents, and related equipment for use in university, governmental, non-profit agencies, and pharmaceutical industry research. The Biotechnology unit (21%) supplies products used in biotechnology, genomic and proteomics research and chromatography. Sigma-Genosys (acquired in 1998) is a major maker of custom synthetic DNA products, synthetic peptides and genes to the life science product categories. SIAL believes it is the leading supplier of products used in cell signaling and neuroscience. The JRH Biosciences acquisition in early 2005 made the Fine Chemicals unit (26%) the tenth largest global supplier of bulk quantities of organic, inorganic and biochemicals to pharmaceutical, biotechnology and industrial customers.

SIAL also offers about 80,000 esoteric chemicals (less than 1% of total sales) as a special service to customers that screen them for potential applications.

Company Financials

Per Share Data ($) Year Ended Dec. 31	2005	2004	2003	2002	2001	2000	1999	1998	1997	1996
Tangible Book Value	11.42	15.34	12.83	10.90	6.75	7.34	11.58	10.96	10.56	9.42
Cash Flow	5.07	4.39	3.65	3.45	2.82	2.47	2.13	2.26	2.08	1.93
Earnings	3.76	3.34	2.68	1.78	1.87	1.66	1.47	1.64	1.62	1.48
S&P Core Earnings	3.62	3.16	2.55	2.10	1.76	NA	NA	NA	NA	NA
Dividends	0.76	0.68	0.50	0.35	0.33	0.32	0.29	0.28	0.26	0.23
Payout Ratio	20%	20%	19%	19%	18%	19%	20%	17%	16%	16%
Prices:High	67.10	61.62	57.91	52.80	51.49	40.88	35.25	42.75	41.13	32.06
Prices:Low	55.34	53.22	40.94	38.16	36.25	20.19	24.50	25.75	26.88	23.75
P/E Ratio:High	18	18	22	30	28	25	24	26	25	22
P/E Ratio:Low	15	16	15	21	19	12	17	16	17	16
Income Statement Analysis (Million $)										
Revenue	1,667	1,409	1,298	1,207	1,179	1,096	1,038	1,194	1,127	1,035
Operating Income	452	392	353	323	291	284	275	305	302	277
Depreciation	90.1	73.4	69.3	66.3	71.4	67.6	66.9	61.8	48.1	45.2
Interest Expense	18.1	7.20	10.1	13.8	18.2	10.2	Nil	0.92	0.73	1.82
Pretax Income	343	312	273	272	202	203	204	243	253	230
Effective Tax Rate	24.8%	25.3%	30.2%	31.4%	30.2%	31.5%	27.1%	31.4%	34.3%	35.6%
Net Income	258	233	190	187	141	139	149	166	166	148
S&P Core Earnings	249	221	180	155	133	NA	NA	NA	NA	NA
Balance Sheet & Other Financial Data (Million $)										
Cash	98.6	169	128	52.4	37.6	31.1	43.8	24.3	46.2	104
Current Assets	950	893	815	695	727	714	775	773	707	667
Total Assets	2,131	1,745	1,548	1,390	1,440	1,348	1,432	1,433	1,244	1,100
Current Liabilities	461	231	257	266	398	335	106	142	119	110
Long Term Debt	283	177	176	177	178	101	0.21	0.42	0.55	3.79
Common Equity	1,233	1,212	999	882	810	859	1,259	1,216	1,073	942
Total Capital	1,597	1,389	1,176	1,059	987	960	1,260	1,217	1,061	946
Capital Expenditures	92.2	70.3	57.7	60.7	110	69.2	91.8	130	109	93.8
Cash Flow	348	306	260	253	212	207	216	228	214	193
Current Ratio	2.1	3.9	3.2	2.6	1.8	2.1	7.3	5.4	5.9	6.0
% Long Term Debt of Capitalization	17.7	12.8	15.0	16.7	18.0	10.5	0.0	0.0	0.0	0.4
% Net Income of Revenue	15.5	16.5	14.7	15.5	11.9	12.7	14.3	13.9	14.7	14.3
% Return on Assets	13.3	14.1	12.7	13.2	10.1	10.0	10.4	12.4	14.2	14.2
% Return on Equity	21.1	21.1	20.2	22.1	16.9	13.1	12.0	14.5	16.4	16.7

Data as orig reptd.; bef. results of disc opers/spec. items. Per share data adj. for stk. divs.; EPS diluted. E-Estimated. NA-Not Available. NM-Not Meaningful. NR-Not Ranked. UR-Under Review.

Office: 3050 Spruce Street, St. Louis, MO 63103.
Telephone: 314-771-5765.
Website: http://www.sigma-aldrich.com
Chrmn: D.R. Harvey

Pres & CEO: J.P. Nagarkatti
VP, Secy & General Counsel: R. Keffer
Investor Contact: M.R. Hogan (314-771-5765)
CFO & Chief Admin: M.R. Hogan

Board of Directors: N. V. Fedoroff, D. R. Harvey, W. L. McCollum, J. Nagarkatti, A. M. Nash, W. C. O'Neil, Jr., J. P. Reinhard, T. R. Sear, D. D. Spatz, B. A. Toan

Founded: 1951
Domicile: Delaware
Employees: 6,849

STANDARD &POOR'S

Simon Property Group Inc.

S&P Recommendation BUY ★★★★★

Price $97.10 (as of Oct 31, 2006)

12-Mo. Target Price $105.00

Investment Style Large-Cap Value

GICS Sector Financials
Sub-Industry Retail REITS

Comment Simon Property Group owns, develops and manages retail real estate, primarily regional malls, Premium Outlet centers and community/lifestyle centers, across the U.S.

Key Stock Statistics (Source S&P, Vickers, company reports)

52-Wk Range	$97.87–69.46	S&P Oper. EPS 2006E	1.70	P/E on S&P Oper. EPS 2006E	57.1	Dividend Rate/Share	$3.04
Trailing 12-Month EPS	$1.70	S&P Oper. EPS 2007E	2.25	Common Shares Outstg. (M)	221.2	Yield (%)	3.13
Trailing 12-Month P/E	57.1	S&P Core EPS 2006E	1.70	Market Capitalization(B)	$21.474	Beta	0.30
$10K Invested 5 Yrs Ago	$46,200	S&P Core EPS 2007E	2.25	Institutional Ownership (%)	88	S&P Credit Rating	A-

Price Performance

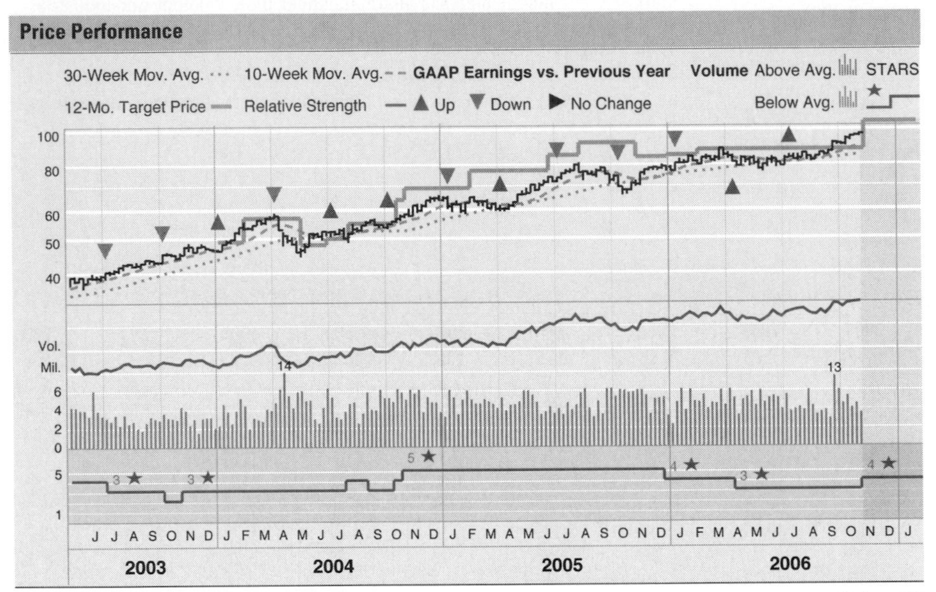

Options: ASE

Qualitative Risk Assessment

LOW | MEDIUM | HIGH

Our risk assessment reflects SPG's position as one of the largest owners of shopping centers with a diverse tenant and geographic mix and a variety of shopping center formats. The majority of SPG's customers are under long-term leases, which helps lessen short-term volatility. The company also has a healthy balance sheet, in our view.

Quantitative Evaluations

S&P Quality Ranking B+

D | C | B- | B | **B+** | A- | A | A+

Relative Strength Rank STRONG

75

LOWEST = 1 HIGHEST = 99

Highlights

➤ The STARS recommendation for SPG has recently been changed to 4 (buy) from 3 (hold) and the 12-month target price has recently been changed to $105.00 from $88.00. The Highlights section of this Stock Report will be updated accordingly.

Investment Rationale/Risk

➤ The Investment Rationale/Risk section of this Stock Report will be updated shortly. For the latest News story on SPG from MarketScope, see below.

➤ 10/31/06 11:06 am EST... S&P UPGRADES SHARES OF SIMON PROPERTY GROUP TO BUY FROM HOLD (SPG 96.54****): Q3 per-share funds from operations of $1.30 vs. $1.19 tops our $1.29 estimate, on 4.5% revenue rise. Though occupancy dipped at Q3-end, we still view it as healthy, and average rents per square foot rose 3.8%. We look for continued healthy retail conditions and retailer expansion to benefit SPG occupancy and rent growth. Also, the addition of mixed-use components to its portfolio should help future growth. We are keeping our '06 FFO estimate at $5.37, increasing '07's by $0.06 to $5.80, and raising our target price to $105 from $88 on updated price/FFO and peer analyses. / R.McMillan

Revenue/Earnings Data

Revenue (Million $)

	1Q	2Q	3Q	4Q	Year
2006	787.7	798.7	--	--	--
2005	756.9	756.3	786.8	889.8	3,167
2004	582.1	600.6	623.0	836.1	2,642
2003	547.8	566.3	566.6	659.9	2,314
2002	495.0	517.5	550.8	622.6	2,186
2001	487.2	488.3	500.7	569.2	2,045

Earnings Per Share ($)

2006	0.47	1.37	E0.38	E0.66	E1.70
2005	0.26	0.27	0.30	0.44	1.27
2004	0.24	0.34	0.36	0.49	1.44
2003	0.29	0.33	0.27	0.64	1.53
2002	0.17	0.91	0.33	0.52	1.93
2001	0.19	0.21	0.21	0.25	0.87

Fiscal year ended Dec. 31. Next earnings report expected: NA. EPS Estimates based on S&P Operating Earnings; historical GAAP earnings are as reported.

Dividend Data (Dates: mm/dd Payment Date: mm/dd/yy)

Amount ($)	Date Decl.	Ex-Div. Date	Stk. of Record	Payment Date
0.760	02/06	02/15	02/17	02/28/06
0.760	04/28	05/15	05/17	05/31/06
0.760	07/31	08/15	08/17	08/31/06
0.760	10/30	11/14	11/16	11/30/06

Dividends have been paid since 1994. Source: Company reports.

Please read the Required Disclosures and Analyst Certification on the last page of this report.

Simon Property Group Inc.

Business Summary August 24, 2006

CORPORATE OVERVIEW. Simon Property Group owns, develops, manages, leases and acquires primarily regional malls and community shopping centers. It is one of the largest owners of shopping centers in the world. At December 31, 2005, SPG owned 297 income-producing properties in the U.S. SPG also had ownership interests in 57 shopping centers and premium outlet centers in Europe, Japan, Canada and Mexico. The company's other properties include office space, hotel components as well as interests in land held for future development.

SPG's regional malls typically contain at least one traditional department store anchor or a combination of anchors and big box retailers with a wide variety of smaller stores located in enclosed malls connecting the anchors. Additional freestanding stores are usually located along the perimeter of the parking area. SPG's 171 regional malls range in size from approximately 400,000 to 2.0 million square feet of gross leasable area (GLA) and contain more than 18,300 occupied stores, including approximately 700 anchors, which are mostly national retailers. The regional mall totals include certain lifestyle centers when the center contains a traditional department store anchor.

SPG's premium outlet centers generally contain a wide variety of retailers located in open-air manufacturer's outlet centers. The company's 33 Premium Outlet centers range in size from approximately 200,000 to 600,000 square feet of GLA and are generally located near metropolitan areas .

SPG's 71 community and lifestyle shopping centers are generally unenclosed and smaller than its regional malls. The community and lifestyle centers generally range in size from approximately 100,000 to 600,000 square feet of GLA and are designed to serve a larger trade area and typically contain at least two anchors and other tenants that are usually national retailers among the leaders in their markets. These tenants generally occupy a significant portion of the GLA of the center. The company also owns traditional community shopping centers that focus primarily on value-oriented and convenience goods and services. These centers are usually anchored by a supermarket, discount retailer, or drugstore and are designed to service a neighborhood area. Finally, the company owns open-air centers adjacent to its regional malls designed to take advantage of the drawing power of the mall.

Company Financials

Per Share Data ($) Year Ended Dec. 31	2005	2004	2003	2002	2001	2000	1999	1998	1997	1996
Tangible Book Value	14.64	16.21	14.66	13.87	13.00	14.29	15.36	15.70	11.11	10.45
Earnings	1.27	1.44	1.53	1.93	0.87	1.13	1.00	1.01	1.08	1.02
S&P Core Earnings	1.12	1.44	1.55	2.07	0.97	NA	NA	NA	NA	NA
Dividends	2.80	2.60	2.40	2.18	2.08	2.02	2.02	2.02	2.01	2.12
Payout Ratio	NM	181%	157%	113%	NM	179%	202%	200%	186%	208%
Prices:High	80.97	65.87	48.59	36.95	30.97	27.13	30.94	34.88	34.38	31.00
Prices:Low	58.29	44.39	31.70	28.80	23.75	21.50	20.44	25.81	27.88	21.13
P/E Ratio:High	64	46	32	19	36	24	31	34	32	30
P/E Ratio:Low	46	31	21	15	27	19	20	26	26	21
Income Statement Analysis (Million $)										
Rental Income	2,920	2,411	1,423	1,386	1,320	1,284	1,207	900	680	469
Mortgage Income	Nil	Nil	Nil	Nil	Nil	Nil	Nil	Nil	Nil	Nil
Total Income	3,167	2,642	2,314	2,186	2,045	2,013	1,895	1,405	1,054	748
General Expenses	820	675	611	788	712	674	655	495	228	409
Interest Expense	799	662	615	603	622	667	580	420	288	208
Provision for Losses	8.10	17.7	Nil	8.97	8.41	9.64	8.50	6.60	Nil	3.46
Depreciation	850	623	498	423	453	420	382	268	201	136
Net Income	457	450	339	1,109	201	242	210	160	137	88.8
S&P Core Earnings	247	301	288	371	169	NA	NA	NA	NA	NA
Balance Sheet & Other Financial Data (Million $)										
Cash	19,836	520	536	397	255	214	155	130	787	70.4
Total Assets	21,131	22,070	15,685	14,905	13,794	13,911	14,199	13,277	7,663	5,896
Real Estate Investment	23,307	23,175	14,972	14,250	13,187	13,038	12,794	11,850	6,867	5,301
Loss Reserve	Nil	Nil	Nil	20.5	24.7	20.1	14.6	14.5	Nil	Nil
Net Investment	19,499	20,012	12,415	12,027	11,311	11,558	11,697	11,127	6,406	5,022
Short Term Debt	Nil	Nil	1,481	940	665	1,164	1,162	1,030	390	49.8
Capitalization:Debt	14,106	13,044	8,786	8,606	8,176	7,904	9,109	7,973	5,078	3,632
Capitalization:Equity	3,227	3,580	2,971	2,653	2,327	2,515	3,246	3,409	2,465	1,012
Capitalization:Total	19,681	19,065	13,241	12,074	11,381	10,958	12,355	11,382	6,939	4,937
% Earnings & Depreciation/Assets	6.0	5.7	5.5	10.7	4.7	4.7	4.3	4.1	5.0	5.3
Price Times Book Value:High	5.5	4.1	3.3	2.7	2.4	1.9	2.0	2.2	3.1	3.0
Price Times Book Value:Low	4.0	2.7	2.2	2.1	1.8	1.5	1.3	1.6	2.5	2.0

Data as orig reptd.; bef. results of disc opers/spec. items. Per share data adj. for stk. divs.; EPS diluted. E-Estimated. NA-Not Available. NM-Not Meaningful. NR-Not Ranked. UR-Under Review.

Office: 115 W Washington St Ste 15, Indianapolis, IN 46204.
Telephone: 317-636-1600.
Website: http://www.simon.com
Co-Chrmn: M. Simon

Co-Chrmn: H. Simon
Pres & COO: R.S. Sokolov
CEO: D. Simon
EVP & CFO: S.E. Sterrett

Investor Contact: S.J. Doran (317-685-7330)
Trustees: B. Bayh, M. E. Bergstein, L. W. Bynoe, M. D. DeBartolo York, K. N. Horn, R. S. Leibowitz, F. W. Petri, D. Simon, H. Simon, M. Simon, J. A. Smith, Jr., R. S. Sokolov, P. S. van den Berg

Founded: 1993
Domicile: Delaware
Employees: 4,700

STANDARD & POOR'S

SLM Corp

S&P Recommendation HOLD ★★★★★

Price $48.03 (as of Oct 27, 2006)

12-Mo. Target Price $56.00

Investment Style Large-Cap Growth

GICS Sector Financials
Sub-Industry Consumer Finance

Comment This company (formerly USA Education) is the leading U.S. provider of post-secondary educational financial services.

Key Stock Statistics (Source S&P, Vickers, company reports)

52-Wk Range	$58.35–45.76	S&P Oper. EPS 2006E	2.84	P/E on S&P Oper. EPS 2006E	16.9	Dividend Rate/Share	$1.00
Trailing 12-Month EPS	$3.51	S&P Oper. EPS 2007E	3.41	Common Shares Outstg. (M)	410.0	Yield (%)	2.08
Trailing 12-Month P/E	13.7	S&P Core EPS 2006E	2.85	Market Capitalization(B)	$19.694	Beta	0.25
$10K Invested 5 Yrs Ago	$18,596	S&P Core EPS 2007E	3.42	Institutional Ownership (%)	96	S&P Credit Rating	A

Price Performance

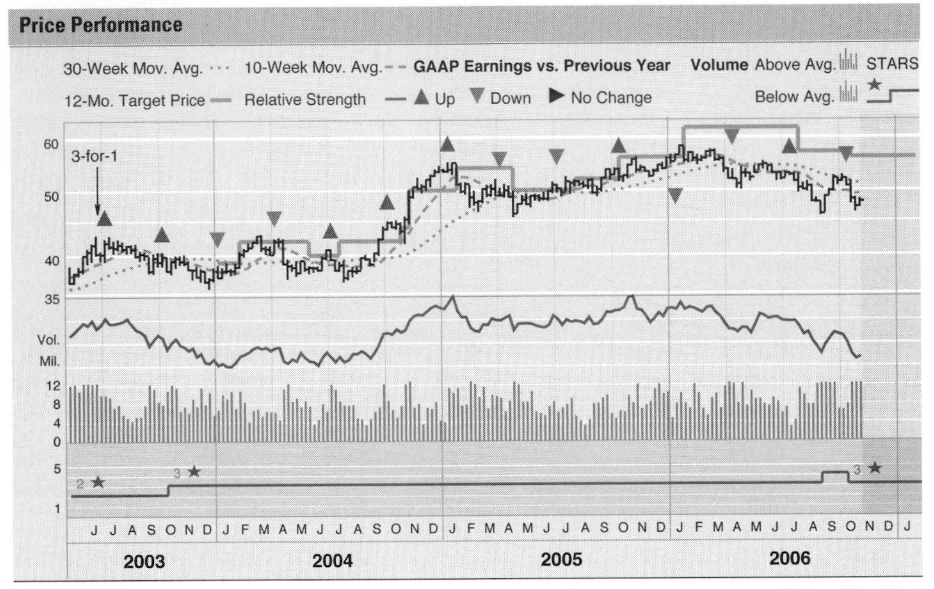

Options: ASE, CBOE, P

Analysis prepared by **Stuart Plesser** on October 11, 2006, when the stock traded at **$ 50.32**.

Highlights

- We believe that SLM's student loan yields will rise in the near term, partially offset by a growing cost of funds. Based on our expectations for a stabilization in student loan spreads and continued strength in loan origination volumes, we see SLM's net interest income rising by about 12% in 2006. We believe loan loss provisions will increase, due largely to growth of the private education loan portfolio as well as SLM's establishment of a risk-sharing allowance for losses on federal student loans, as default insurance coverage on such loans fell by 1%, to 99%, on loans originated after July 1, 2006.
- We project continued double-digit increases in other income in 2006, reflecting strong organic growth as well as SLM's acquisition of GRP Financial Services during the third quarter of 2005. Due to the company's focus on controlling costs, we expect modest improvements in operating margins.
- Taking into account moderate share repurchase activity and the impact of expensing stock options, we forecast operating EPS of $2.84 in 2006 and $3.41 in 2007, reflecting 20% growth.

Investment Rationale/Risk

- As a market leader in education finance, we believe SLM is in a strong position to benefit from what we see as increasing demand for post-secondary education and rising tuition costs. We also see income from the Debt Management Operations segment, which collects payments on SLM's behalf as well as external clients, increasing due to recent acquisitions, which should allow the company to service most types of consumer debt. But the possibility of adverse legislation, particularly as it applies to a reduction in subsidies and guarantees for the Federal Family Education Loan program, makes us cautious about these shares.
- Risks to our recommendation and target price include a potentially negative impact from the reauthorization of the Higher Education Act (HEA) as well as competitive threats to SLM's market share.
- Our 12-month target price of $56 is equal to a P/E multiple of roughly 18.2X applied to our 12-month forward EPS estimate of $3.08, a slight discount to the stock's five-year average P/E of 18.6X.

Qualitative Risk Assessment

LOW | MEDIUM | HIGH

Our risk assessment for SLM reflects its leading position in education finance and its participation in the Federal Family Education Loan Program. Also, the company has maintained consistent earnings and dividend growth.

Quantitative Evaluations

S&P Quality Ranking B+

D | C | B- | B | **B+** | A- | A | A+

Relative Strength Rank WEAK

19

LOWEST = 1 HIGHEST = 99

Revenue/Earnings Data

Revenue (Million $)

	1Q	2Q	3Q	4Q	Year
2006	1,766	2,695	2,252	--	--
2005	1,285	1,506	1,715	2,012	6,518
2004	915.1	1,509	1,047	1,525	4,997
2003	1,109	1,047	1,013	955.9	4,160
2002	1,158	702.2	404.0	968.1	3,232
2001	929.2	1,191	411.6	983.4	3,515

Earnings Per Share ($)

	1Q	2Q	3Q	4Q	Year
2006	0.34	1.52	0.60	E0.73	E2.84
2005	0.49	0.66	0.95	0.96	3.05
2004	0.64	1.36	0.80	1.40	4.04
2003	0.88	0.80	0.76	0.57	3.01
2002	0.88	0.26	-0.14	0.64	1.64
2001	0.05	0.56	-0.42	0.56	0.76

Fiscal year ended Dec. 31. Next earnings report expected: Mid January. EPS Estimates based on S&P Operating Earnings; historical GAAP earnings are as reported.

Dividend Data (Dates: mm/dd Payment Date: mm/dd/yy)

Amount ($)	Date Decl.	Ex-Div. Date	Stk. of Record	Payment Date
0.220	01/26	03/01	03/03	03/17/06
0.250	05/18	05/31	06/02	06/16/06
0.250	07/27	08/30	09/01	09/15/06
0.250	10/26	11/29	12/01	12/15/06

Dividends have been paid since 1983. Source: Company reports.

SLM Corp

Business Summary October 11, 2006

COMPANY OVERVIEW. SLM Corp., formerly USA Education Inc., is the largest U.S. private source of funding, delivery and service support for higher education loans, primarily through its participation in the Federal Family Education Loan Program (FFELP). The company's main business is to originate, acquire and hold student loans with the net interest income and gains on the sales of student loans in securitization, the primary source of earnings. The company funds its operation through student loan asset-backed securities and unsecured debt securities. SLM was chartered by an Act of Congress in 1972, but in 1996 it was rechartered as a private sector corporation and completed its privatization process in December 2004.

The company is divided into two business segments: Lending and Debt Management Operations (DMO). According to the company, SLM Lending segment manages the largest portfolio of FFELP and Private Education Loans in the student loan industry. As of December 31, 2005, the company served nine million borrowers, and managed $122.5 billion in student loans, of which 87% were federally insured. In 2005, its Preferred Channel Originations totaled $14.9 billion, which according to SLM represented a 27% market share. Its DMO segment provides a wide range of accounts receivable and collections services.

PRIMARY BUSINESS DYNAMICS. There are two competing programs that divide student loans where the ultimate risk lies with the federal government: the FFELP and the Federal Direct Lending program (FDLP). FFELP loans are provided by private sector institutions, such as SLM, and are ultimately guaranteed by the U.S. Department of Education (ED). FDLP loans are funded by taxpayers and provided to borrowers directly by ED. Private Education Loans are originated by financial institutions where the lender assumes the credit risk of the borrower. SLM's position as an Exceptional Performer enables the company to receive a guarantee of 100% and 99% for student loans and accrued interest, originated before and after July 1, 2006, respectively.

Company Financials

Per Share Data ($) Year Ended Dec. 31	**2005**	**2004**	**2003**	**2002**	**2001**	**2000**	**1999**	**1998**	**1997**	**1996**
Tangible Book Value	5.13	4.81	4.55	3.08	3.59	2.54	1.43	1.33	1.30	1.48
Earnings	3.05	4.04	3.01	1.64	0.76	0.92	1.02	0.98	0.93	0.71
S&P Core Earnings	2.98	3.95	2.75	1.40	0.53	NA	NA	NA	NA	NA
Dividends	0.85	0.74	0.59	0.28	0.24	0.22	0.20	0.19	0.17	0.16
Payout Ratio	28%	18%	20%	17%	32%	24%	20%	19%	19%	23%
Prices:High	56.48	54.44	42.92	35.65	29.33	22.75	17.98	17.13	15.73	9.36
Prices:Low	45.56	36.43	33.73	25.67	18.63	9.27	13.17	9.17	8.48	6.02
P/E Ratio:High	19	13	14	22	39	25	18	17	17	13
P/E Ratio:Low	15	9	11	16	25	10	13	9	9	9
Income Statement Analysis (Million $)										
Interest on:Mortgages	4,233	2,500	2,197	2,124	2,625	2,977	2,569	2,293	2,711	2,900
Interest on:Investment	277	233	151	07.9	373	501	240	295	573	543
Interest Expense	3,059	1,434	1,022	1,203	2,124	2,837	2,115	1,925	2,526	2,577
Guaranty Fees	Nil	Nil	Nil	Nil	Nil	Nil	Nil	Nil	Nil	Nil
Loan Loss Provision	203	111	147	117	66.0	32.1	34.4	Nil	Nil	Nil
Administration Expenses	1,138	895	808	690	708	586	359	361	269	199
Pretax Income	2,117	2,557	2,103	1,223	617	712	752	750	765	608
Effective Tax Rate	34.4%	25.1%	35.7%	35.3%	36.2%	33.1%	31.9%	31.7%	31.8%	30.2%
Net Income	1,382	1,913	1,404	792	384	465	501	501	511	424
S&P Core Earnings	1,324	1,853	1,276	664	261	NA	NA	NA	NA	NA
Balance Sheet & Other Financial Data (Million $)										
Mortgages	83,980	66,161	51,078	43,541	42,037	38,635	34,852	29,825	32,765	38,016
Investment	4,775	3,579	5,268	4,231	5,072	5,206	5,185	3,990	5,076	7,436
Cash & Equivalent	2,499	3,395	1,652	758	715	734	590	116	54.0	271
Total Assets	99,339	84,094	64,611	53,175	52,874	48,792	44,025	37,210	39,909	47,630
Short Term Debt	3,810	2,208	18,735	25,619	31,065	30,464	37,491	26,588	23,176	22,517
Long Term Debt	88,119	75,915	23,211	22,242	17,285	14,911	4,496	8,811	14,541	22,606
Equity	3,226	2,937	3,564	1,833	1,507	1,250	676	654	675	834
% Return on Assets	1.5	2.6	2.4	1.5	0.8	1.0	1.2	1.3	1.2	0.9
% Return on Equity	44.1	70.4	25.8	47.4	27.8	48.2	75.1	75.5	67.7	49.9
Equity/Assets Ratio	29.8	27.5	10.9	3.1	2.7	2.1	1.6	1.7	1.7	1.7
Price Times Book Value:High	11.0	11.3	9.4	11.6	8.2	8.9	12.6	12.9	12.1	6.3
Price Times Book Value:Low	8.9	7.6	7.4	8.3	5.2	3.6	9.2	6.9	6.5	4.1

Data as orig reptd.; bef. results of disc opers/spec. items. Per share data adj. for stk. divs.; EPS diluted. E-Estimated. NA-Not Available. NM-Not Meaningful. NR-Not Ranked. UR-Under Review.

Office: 12061 Bluemont Way, Reston, VA 20190-5684.
Telephone: 703-810-3000.
Website: http://www.salliemae.com
Chrmn: E.A. Fox

Vice Chrmn & CEO: T. Fitzpatrick
EVP & CIO: R. Auter
CFO: C.E. Andrews
Investor Contact: S. McGarry (703-810-7746)

Board of Directors: C. L. Daley, W. M. Diefenderfer, III, T. J. Fitzpatrick, D. S. Gilleland, E. A. Goode, R. F. Hunt, B. J. Lambert, III, A. L. Lord, B. A. Munitz, A. A. Porter, Jr., W. Schoellkopf, S. L. Shapiro, A. Torre Bates, B. L. Williams

Founded: 1972
Domicile: Delaware
Employees: 11,000

STANDARD &POOR'S

Smith International Inc.

S&P Recommendation BUY ★★★★★

Price $38.77 (as of Oct 30, 2006)

12-Mo. Target Price $51.00

Investment Style Mid-Cap Growth

GICS Sector Energy
Sub-Industry Oil & Gas Equipment & Services

Comment This Houston-based company is an international supplier of products and services primarily used in drilling for oil and gas.

Key Stock Statistics (Source S&P, Vickers, company reports)

52-Wk Range	$46.48–31.50	S&P Oper. EPS 2006E	2.46	P/E on S&P Oper. EPS 2006E	15.8	Dividend Rate/Share	$0.32
Trailing 12-Month EPS	$2.21	S&P Oper. EPS 2007E	2.92	Common Shares Outstg. (M)	200.5	Yield (%)	0.83
Trailing 12-Month P/E	17.5	S&P Core EPS 2006E	2.46	Market Capitalization(B)	$7.772	Beta	0.70
$10K Invested 5 Yrs Ago	$31,270	S&P Core EPS 2007E	2.92	Institutional Ownership (%)	91	S&P Credit Rating	BBB+

Price Performance

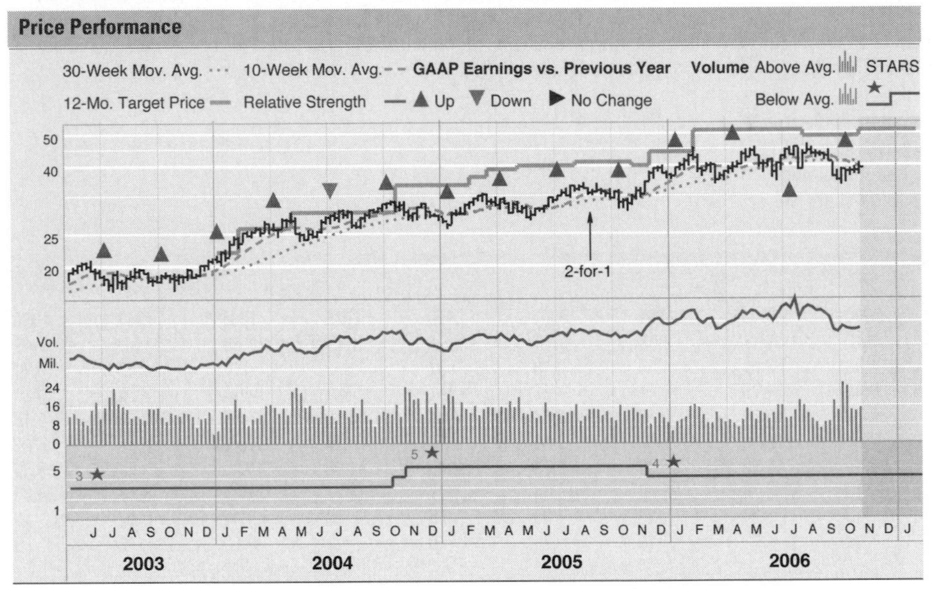

Options: ASE, CBOE, P, Ph

Analysis prepared by **Stewart Glickman, CFA** on October 30, 2006, when the stock traded at **$ 39.21**.

Highlights

- We see higher drilling activity in deepwater fields in the near term, and expect SII to benefit, given a strong position in drilling fluids and drill bit technology. Typically, deepwater drilling and completion projects demand more advanced equipment, given the relatively harsh environments found in such projects.

- We expect total revenues to increase about 31% in 2006 (with a 34% gain in oilfield services) and to grow a further 14% in 2007. In addition, we anticipate a gradual improvement in margins, especially in oilfield services, with overall margins of about 14% to 15% in 2006 and 2007, versus 12% in 2005. While margins at Wilson are markedly lower than those in oilfield services, we note that Wilson's margins were 5.1% in the third quarter of 2006, up modestly from 4.0% in 2005.

- For 2006, we estimate operating EPS of $2.46, rising to $2.92 in 2007. Our EPS estimates in both years include a projected $0.06 per share deduction for stock option expensing.

Investment Rationale/Risk

- We believe SII is well positioned to benefit from ongoing trends in oil and gas exploration and production. Given that much of the shallower reservoirs around the world are in mature production, we believe that significant growth opportunities lie mainly in deeper waters.

- Risks to our recommendation and target price include political risk in frontier regions; reduced demand for drilling fluids and drill bits; and increased competition from larger companies in the drilling fluids business.

- Our DCF model, assuming free cash flow growth of 15% per year for 10 years, and a WACC of 10.5%, indicates intrinsic value of about $50. On a relative valuation basis, we think the shares should trade in line with peers, as we project return on capital employed of 19% in 2006, versus a 19% peer average. Assuming a 9X multiple on projected 2007 EBITDA and a 12X multiple on estimated 2007 cash flow (both in line with peers), and blending with our DCF model, we derive our 12-month target price of $51.

Qualitative Risk Assessment

LOW | **MEDIUM** | HIGH

Our risk assessment reflects SII's exposure to volatile crude oil and natural gas prices, capital spending decisions made by its oil and gas producing customers, and political risk associated with operating in frontier regions. Offsetting these risks is SII's strong position in drill bits and drilling fluids.

Quantitative Evaluations

S&P Quality Ranking **B**

D | C | B- | **B** | B+ | A- | A | A+

Relative Strength Rank **WEAK**

23

LOWEST = 1 HIGHEST = 99

Revenue/Earnings Data

Revenue (Million $)

	1Q	2Q	3Q	4Q	Year
2006	1,682	1,738	1,914	--	--
2005	1,288	1,350	1,410	1,530	5,579
2004	1,018	1,064	1,119	1,218	4,419
2003	808.8	877.7	924.8	983.5	3,595
2002	827.4	801.0	777.2	764.4	3,170
2001	865.3	872.4	909.7	903.8	3,551

Earnings Per Share ($)

2006	0.53	0.59	0.66	E0.69	E2.46
2005	0.33	0.33	0.39	0.44	1.48
2004	0.22	0.14	0.26	0.29	0.89
2003	0.11	0.15	0.18	0.19	0.62
2002	0.15	0.14	0.10	0.09	0.47
2001	0.17	0.19	0.21	0.19	0.76

Fiscal year ended Dec. 31. Next earnings report expected: Late January. EPS Estimates based on S&P Operating Earnings; historical GAAP earnings are as reported.

Dividend Data (Dates: mm/dd Payment Date: mm/dd/yy)

Amount ($)	Date Decl.	Ex-Div. Date	Stk. of Record	Payment Date
0.080	03/01	03/13	03/15	04/14/06
0.080	04/20	06/13	06/15	07/14/06
0.080	07/21	09/13	09/15	10/16/06
0.080	10/23	12/13	12/15	01/15/07

Dividends have been paid since 2005. Source: Company reports.

Smith International Inc.

Business Summary October 30, 2006

CORPORATE OVERVIEW. Driven by exploration and production activities worldwide, Smith International manufactures and markets technologically advanced products and services to the oil and gas industry. Approximately 55% of total 2005 revenues were derived from equipment sold or services provided to customers outside the United States (versus 55% in 2004). In 2005, top non-U.S. regions included Europe/Africa (21%), Canada (13%), the Middle East (8.5%), Latin America (8.1%), and the Far East (4.1%). The Oilfield Products and Services segment (71% of 2005 revenues, and 91% of segment operating profits) consists of three businesses: M-I SWACO (48% of 2005 revenues); Smith Technologies (11%); and Smith Services (12%).

M-I SWACO provides drilling and completion fluid systems and services, solids control equipment and waste management services. Drilling fluid products and systems are used to cool and lubricate the bit during drilling, contain formation pressures, remove rock cuttings, and maintain the stability of the wellbore. Engineering services ensure that products are applied to optimize operations.

Smith Technologies is a worldwide leader in the design, manufacture and marketing of drilling bits primarily used in drilling oil and natural gas wells. In addition, Smith Technologies is the leading provider of downhole turbine products and services that enhance the operating performance of drillbits.

Smith Services manufactures and markets products used in the oil and gas industry for drilling, workover, well completion, and well re-entry. Drilling Optimization Solutions provides a broad range of downhole impact tools for drilling applications. Fishing and Remedial Solutions removes obstructions from the wellbore that may arise during drilling, completion or workover activities, and manufactures and markets hole openers and underreamers that create larger hole diameters in certain sections of the wellbore. Casing Exit and Multilateral Solutions manufactures proprietary casing exit tools. Completion Solutions specializes in providing fit-for-purpose liner hangers, liner cementing equipment, isolation packers, retrievable and permanent packers, packer products and multilateral completion equipment.

The Distribution segment (29% of total 2005 revenues, and 9% of total segment operating profits) consists of Wilson, a supply-chain management company that markets pipe, valves, fittings, and mill and safety products.

Company Financials

Per Share Data ($) Year Ended Dec. 31	**2005**	**2004**	**2003**	**2002**	**2001**	**2000**	**1999**	**1998**	**1997**	**1996**
Tangible Book Value	3.40	3.06	2.72	2.23	1.90	1.83	1.89	1.79	1.64	1.32
Cash Flow	2.05	1.41	1.12	0.91	1.22	0.76	0.67	0.54	0.93	0.60
Earnings	1.48	0.89	0.62	0.47	0.76	0.36	0.29	0.18	0.64	0.41
S&P Core Earnings	1.41	0.94	0.57	0.42	0.72	NA	NA	NA	NA	NA
Dividends	0.24	Nil	Nil	Nil	Nil	Nil	Nil	Nil	Nil	Nil
Payout Ratio	16%	Nil	Nil	Nil	Nil	Nil	Nil	Nil	Nil	Nil
Prices:High	40.08	31.49	21.59	19.36	21.13	22.13	13.02	16.13	21.97	12.00
Prices:Low	25.80	20.03	14.75	11.60	8.08	11.25	5.89	4.31	9.63	4.97
P/E Ratio:High	27	35	35	42	28	61	45	92	34	30
P/E Ratio:Low	17	23	24	25	11	31	20	25	15	12
Income Statement Analysis (Million $)										
Revenue	5,579	4,419	3,595	3,170	3,551	2,761	1,806	2,119	1,563	1,157
Operating Income	788	545	430	345	464	280	310	278	264	993
Depreciation, Depletion and Amortization	118	106	102	89.3	92.9	80.7	76.0	70.3	46.7	31.6
Interest Expense	44.4	38.8	41.0	40.9	45.4	36.8	40.8	46.0	26.9	18.6
Pretax Income	628	401	290	218	329	164	111	81.9	193	116
Effective Tax Rate	32.3%	32.3%	32.2%	30.6%	32.3%	33.5%	43.2%	32.1%	26.3%	23.1%
Net Income	302	182	125	93.2	152	72.8	56.7	34.1	102	64.4
S&P Core Earnings	290	192	115	84.6	145	NA	NA	NA	NA	NA
Balance Sheet & Other Financial Data (Million $)										
Cash	62.5	53.6	51.3	86.8	44.7	36.5	24.1	22.7	29.0	25.5
Current Assets	2,437	2,020	1,680	1,427	1,523	1,310	1,055	997	851	665
Total Assets	4,060	3,507	3,097	2,750	2,736	2,295	1,895	1,759	1,396	1,075
Current Liabilities	933	887	631	595	666	643	457	693	373	301
Long Term Debt	611	388	489	442	539	375	347	369	306	228
Common Equity	1,365	1,401	1,236	1,064	949	817	720	634	469	369
Total Capital	2,827	2,537	2,392	2,087	2,019	1,615	1,422	1,012	999	752
Capital Expenditures	178	111	98.9	97.1	128	94.6	57.2	119	82.8	73.0
Cash Flow	420	289	226	183	245	153	133	104	149	96.0
Current Ratio	2.6	2.3	2.7	2.4	2.3	2.0	2.3	1.4	2.3	2.2
% Long Term Debt of Capitalization	21.6	15.3	20.4	21.2	26.7	23.2	24.4	36.4	30.7	30.3
% Return on Assets	8.0	5.5	4.3	3.4	6.0	3.5	3.1	2.2	8.3	7.2
% Return on Equity	21.9	13.8	10.8	9.3	17.2	9.5	8.4	6.2	24.4	19.2

Data as orig reptd.; bef. results of disc opers/spec. items. Per share data adj. for stk. divs.; EPS diluted. E-Estimated. NA-Not Available. NM-Not Meaningful. NR-Not Ranked. UR-Under Review.

Office: 411 N Sam Houston Pkwy Ste 600, Houston, TX 77060-3545.
Telephone: 281-443-3370.
Website: http://www.smith.com
Chrmn, Pres, CEO & COO: D.L. Rock

Investor Contact: M.K. Dorman (281-443-3370)
SVP, CFO & Treas: M.K. Dorman
VP & General Counsel: R.E. Chandler, Jr.

Board of Directors: B. J. Bailar, G. C. Buck, L. K. Carroll, D. A. Fraser, J. R. Gibbs, R. Kelley, J. W. Neely, D. L. Rock

Founded: 1937
Domicile: Delaware
Employees: 14,697

STANDARD & POOR'S

Snap-On Inc

S&P Recommendation HOLD ★★★★★

Price $47.03 (as of Oct 31, 2006)

12-Mo. Target Price $46.00

Investment Style Mid-Cap Value

GICS Sector Consumer Discretionary
Sub-Industry Household Appliances

Comment This company is the largest manufacturer and distributor of hand tools, storage units and diagnostic equipment for professional mechanics.

Key Stock Statistics (Source S&P, Vickers, company reports)

52-Wk Range	$48.35–35.18	S&P Oper. EPS 2006E	1.96	P/E on S&P Oper. EPS 2006E	24.0	Dividend Rate/Share	$1.08
Trailing 12-Month EPS	$1.52	S&P Oper. EPS 2007E	2.25	Common Shares Outstg. (M)	58.4	Yield (%)	2.30
Trailing 12-Month P/E	30.9	S&P Core EPS 2006E	1.96	Market Capitalization(B)	$2.745	Beta	1.47
$10K Invested 5 Yrs Ago	$20,002	S&P Core EPS 2007E	2.25	Institutional Ownership (%)	86	S&P Credit Rating	A

Price Performance

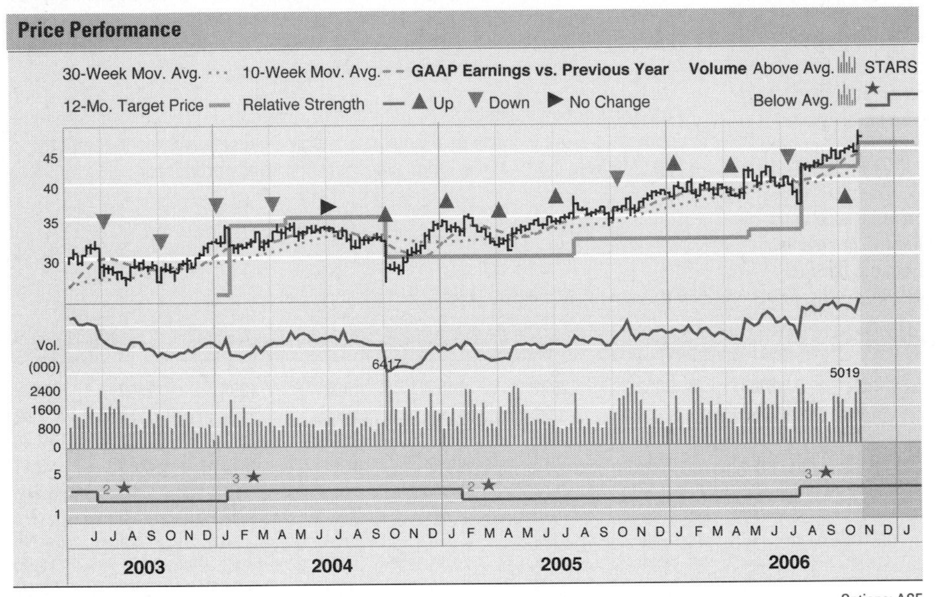

Options: ASE

Analysis prepared by **Efraim Levy, CFA** on October 31, 2006, when the stock traded at **$ 46.94**.

Highlights

- SNA continues to focus on improving its dealer business, which we think will ultimately benefit from the addition of new dealers and improved service levels. We see Dealer Group sales rising modestly in 2007. We see mid-single digit increases in the Commercial and Industrial and Diagnostics and Information segments. Overall, we expect sales to rise 5% in 2007. We estimate that, assuming consummation, the planned purchase of the business solutions unit of ProQuest should add 15% more.
- We think SNA has done a good job of improving its cost structure, particularly while facing external cost pressures. For 2006, in the Dealer Group, we expect that investments to improve the franchise system will pressure the segment's margins. We believe that investment spending in SNA's other segments will be offset by expected productivity gains, resulting in better segment operating earnings. SNA's goal is to improve operating margins to 10% over the next three years.
- We forecast operating EPS of $1.96 in 2006 and $2.25 in 2007, before the planned ProQuest deal.

Investment Rationale/Risk

- We believe SNA is undergoing a transformation to become a leaner organization, with a high priority on bettering customer responsiveness and top-line growth. We think these ongoing improvements will ultimately restore margins to prior levels. We think the planned acquisition of ProQuest's business solutions unit will help the company expand revenues and profits. However, with the shares recently trading at nearly 21X our 2007 EPS estimate, a premium to peers, and given our concerns about tempered growth in the industry, we would not add to positions.
- Risks to our opinion and target price include weaker than expected results in SNA's major markets, a failure to successfully introduce new products into the pipeline or failure to achieve set goals for revenue growth and/or productivity initiatives.
- Our 12-month target price of $46 is based on our historical P/E model, which applies a target P/E of 20.5X to our 2007 operating EPS estimate.

Qualitative Risk Assessment

LOW	**MEDIUM**	HIGH

Our risk assessment is based on our view of SNA's strong brand equity and clean balance sheet with little debt, offset by intense competition.

Quantitative Evaluations

S&P Quality Ranking B

D	C	B-	**B**	B+	A-	A	A+

Relative Strength Rank STRONG

73

LOWEST = 1 HIGHEST = 99

Revenue/Earnings Data

Revenue (Million $)

	1Q	2Q	3Q	4Q	Year
2006	593.5	624.4	599.5	--	--
2005	612.8	608.6	567.2	573.6	2,362
2004	616.3	612.1	568.8	610.0	2,407
2003	543.1	565.2	525.6	599.3	2,233
2002	510.0	547.2	502.4	549.5	2,109
2001	527.4	525.6	508.1	534.6	2,096

Earnings Per Share ($)

2006	0.37	0.20	0.48	**E**0.50	**E**1.96
2005	0.31	0.46	0.36	0.47	1.59
2004	0.22	0.38	0.39	0.42	1.40
2003	0.37	0.38	0.30	0.30	1.35
2002	0.37	0.50	0.33	0.56	1.76
2001	0.51	0.15	0.01	-0.30	0.37

Fiscal year ended Dec. 31. Next earnings report expected: Early February. EPS Estimates based on S&P Operating Earnings; historical GAAP earnings are as reported.

Dividend Data (Dates: mm/dd Payment Date: mm/dd/yy)

Amount ($)	Date Decl.	Ex-Div. Date	Stk. of Record	Payment Date
0.250	08/26	11/16	11/18	12/09/05
0.270	02/01	02/15	02/17	03/10/06
0.270	04/27	05/17	05/19	06/09/06
0.270	08/04	08/17	08/21	09/11/06

Dividends have been paid since 1939. Source: Company reports.

Snap-On Inc

Business Summary October 31, 2006

CORPORATE OVERVIEW. SNA is a leading global manufacturer and marketer of high-quality tool, diagnostic, service and equipment solutions for professional tool and equipment users under various brands and trade names. Product lines include a broad range of hand and power tools, tool storage, saws and cutting tools, pruning tools, vehicle service diagnostics equipment, vehicle service equipment, including wheel service, safety testing and collision repair equipment, vehicle service information, business management systems, equipment repair services, and other tool and equipment solutions. SNA's customers include automotive technicians, vehicle service centers, manufacturers, industrial tool and equipment users, and those involved in commercial applications such as construction, electrical and agriculture. SNA services these customers through three primary channels of distribution: the mobile dealer van channel, including the company's technical representatives, company direct sales, and distributors.

SNA has four reportable business segments. The Snap-on Dealer Group (38% of 2005 sales, 38% of operating profits) consists of SNA's business operations serving the worldwide franchised dealer van channel. The Commercial and Industrial Group (43%, 33%) provides tools, equipment products and equipment repair services to industrial and commercial customers worldwide through direct, distributor and other non-franchised distribution channels. The Diagnostics and Information Group (17%, 22%) provides diagnostic equipment, vehicle service information, business management systems and other solutions for customers in the vehicle service and repair marketplace. Financial Services (2%, 7%) is a relatively new business segment, which was originated in 2004. It consists of Snap-on Credit LLC, a consolidated 50%-owned joint venture between SNA and The CIT Group, and SNA's wholly owned finance subsidiaries in international markets where SNA has dealer operations. SNA groups its products and services into two categories: tools (61% of 2004 sales) and equipment (39%).

Company Financials

Per Share Data ($) Year Ended Dec. 31	**2005**	**2004**	**2003**	**2002**	**2001**	**2000**	**1999**	**1998**	**1997**	**1996**
Tangible Book Value	8.17	9.67	8.29	6.27	6.01	6.53	6.69	9.60	12.74	12.30
Cash Flow	2.48	2.45	2.38	2.65	1.54	3.23	3.10	0.68	3.06	2.68
Earnings	1.59	1.40	1.35	1.76	0.37	2.10	2.16	-0.08	2.44	2.16
S&P Core Earnings	1.56	1.35	1.31	0.92	0.09	NA	NA	NA	NA	NA
Dividends	1.00	1.00	1.00	0.97	0.96	0.94	0.90	0.86	0.82	0.76
Payout Ratio	63%	71%	74%	55%	NM	45%	42%	NM	34%	35%
Prices:High	38.71	34.67	32.38	35.15	34.40	32.44	37.81	46.44	46.31	38.25
Prices:Low	30.57	27.15	22.60	20.71	21.15	20.88	26.44	25.50	34.25	27.33
P/E Ratio:High	24	25	24	20	93	15	18	NM	19	18
P/E Ratio:Low	19	19	17	12	57	10	12	NM	14	13

Income Statement Analysis (Million $)	2005	2004	2003	2002	2001	2000	1999	1998	1997	1996
Revenue	2,362	2,407	2,233	2,109	2,096	2,176	1,946	1,773	1,672	1,485
Operating Income	220	203	167	217	168	270	220	102	232	188
Depreciation	52.2	61.0	60.3	51.7	68.0	66.2	55.4	45.0	38.4	31.9
Interest Expense	21.7	23.0	24.4	28.7	35.5	40.7	27.4	21.3	17.7	12.6
Pretax Income	148	120	117	161	47.6	193	198	10.8	239	209
Effective Tax Rate	37.2%	32.1%	32.6%	36.0%	54.8%	36.1%	35.7%	NM	37.0%	37.3%
Net Income	92.9	81.7	78.7	103	21.5	123	127	-4.78	150	131
S&P Core Earnings	91.6	78.3	76.6	53.9	5.49	NA	NA	NA	NA	NA

Balance Sheet & Other Financial Data (Million $)	2005	2004	2003	2002	2001	2000	1999	1998	1997	1996
Cash	170	150	96.1	18.4	6.70	6.10	17.6	15.0	25.7	15.4
Current Assets	1,073	1,193	1,132	1,051	1,139	1,186	1,206	1,080	1,022	1,017
Total Assets	2,008	2,290	2,139	1,994	1,974	2,050	2,150	1,675	1,641	1,521
Current Liabilities	506	674	567	552	549	538	453	458	353	341
Long Term Debt	202	203	303	304	446	473	247	247	151	150
Common Equity	962	1,111	1,011	830	868	844	825	762	892	828
Total Capital	1,239	1,390	1,348	1,168	1,339	1,342	1,099	1,018	1,055	985
Capital Expenditures	40.1	38.7	29.4	45.8	53.6	57.6	35.4	46.8	55.4	52.3
Cash Flow	145	143	139	155	89.5	189	183	40.2	189	163
Current Ratio	2.1	1.8	2.0	1.9	2.1	2.2	2.7	2.4	2.9	3.0
% Long Term Debt of Capitalization	16.3	14.6	22.5	26.0	33.3	35.3	22.4	24.2	14.3	15.2
% Net Income of Revenue	3.9	3.4	3.5	4.9	1.0	5.7	6.5	NM	9.0	8.9
% Return on Assets	4.3	3.7	3.8	5.2	1.1	5.9	6.7	NM	9.5	9.1
% Return on Equity	9.0	7.7	8.5	12.9	2.4	14.7	16.0	NM	17.5	16.7

Data as orig reptd.; bef. results of disc opers/spec. items. Per share data adj. for stk. divs.; EPS diluted. E-Estimated. NA-Not Available. NM-Not Meaningful. NR-Not Ranked. UR-Under Review.

Office: 2801 80th St, Kenosha, WI 53143-5656.
Telephone: 262-656-5200.
Website: http://www.snapon.com
Chrmn, Pres & CEO: J.D. Michaels

Investor Contact: M.M. Ellen (262-656-5200)
SVP & CFO: M.M. Ellen
VP, Secy & Chief Lgl Officer: S.F. Marrinan
VP & Cntlr: C.R. Johnsen

Board of Directors: B. S. Chelberg, K. L. Daniel, R. J. Decyk, J. F. Fiedler, A. L. Kelly, W. D. Lehman, J. D. Michaels, L. Nyberg, E. H. Rensi, R. F. Teerlink

Founded: 1920
Domicile: Delaware
Employees: 11,400

STANDARD &POOR'S

Solectron Corp

S&P Recommendation HOLD ★★★★★

Price $3.40 (as of Oct 27, 2006)

12-Mo. Target Price $3.50

Investment Style Mid-Cap Value

GICS Sector Information Technology
Sub-Industry Electronic Manufacturing Services

Comment This company is a major provider of electronic manufacturing services to OEMs in the computer, telecom, datacom, consumer and other industries.

Key Stock Statistics (Source S&P, Vickers, company reports)

52-Wk Range	$4.13–2.81	S&P Oper. EPS 2007E	0.18	P/E on S&P Oper. EPS 2007E	18.9	Dividend Rate/Share	Nil
Trailing 12-Month EPS	$0.15	S&P Oper. EPS 2008E	NA	Common Shares Outstg. (M)	914.6	Yield (%)	Nil
Trailing 12-Month P/E	22.7	S&P Core EPS 2007E	0.18	Market Capitalization(B)	$3.110	Beta	3.21
$10K Invested 5 Yrs Ago	$2,329	S&P Core EPS 2008E	NA	Institutional Ownership (%)	84	S&P Credit Rating	B+

Price Performance

Options: ASE, CBOE, P, Ph

Analysis prepared by **Jawahar Hingorani** on October 18, 2006, when the stock traded at **$ 3.33**.

Highlights

- We expect revenues to increase 6% in FY 07 (Aug.), following a 1% rise in FY 06. We look for SLR's end markets to improve, and believe the company's push into non-traditional segments is likely to aid results. Moreover, we think that longer-term trends in the electronic manufacturing services (EMS) space remain attractive and expect original equipment manufacturers (OEMs) to expand their use of the outsourcing model over the next several years.
- We look for gross margins to widen in FY 07. Higher volumes and a shift of production to lower cost regions should outweigh a less favorable business mix, as a larger proportion of consumer products is being manufactured. We expect SG&A expenses to decline, given our expectations of benefits associated with the streamlining of manufacturing activities. We also anticipate results being aided by additional share repurchases.
- We forecast FY 07 EPS from continuing operations of $0.18, a 64% increase from FY 06's comparable $0.11. Both estimates include our projections for stock-based compensation expense.

Investment Rationale/Risk

- Although we believe revenue growth is improving, we think SLR continues to lose share in the EMS space. Moreover, in our estimation, near-term visibility remains limited. However, we are encouraged by the company's broadening customer base and lower operating expenses. In addition, we believe SLR's position within the EMS industry provides it with an advantage over smaller competitors.
- Risks to our recommendation and target price include a prolonged slowdown in the computing and storage and networking markets, an inability to gain significant traction in new business segments, a decline in demand for outsourcing services, and integration difficulties related to the establishment of facilities in lower-cost geographies.
- Our 12-month target price of $3.50 is based on a combination of valuation metrics. The first, relative P/E, equates the S&P 500's forward P/E of 14.1X with our calendar 2007 EPS estimated of $0.20 and results in a value of about $3. The second, discounted cash flow analysis, leads to an intrinsic value of $4.50. Our assumptions include a weighted average cost of capital of 12.4% and a terminal growth rate of 3%.

Qualitative Risk Assessment

LOW | MEDIUM | **HIGH**

Our risk assessment reflects the volatile nature of the electronic manufacturing services industry, the company's recent market share erosion, and five consecutive years of reported losses.

Quantitative Evaluations

S&P Quality Ranking C

D | **C** | B- | B | B+ | A- | A | A+

Relative Strength Rank MODERATE

57

LOWEST = 1 HIGHEST = 99

Revenue/Earnings Data

Revenue (Million $)

	1Q	2Q	3Q	4Q	Year
2006	2,456	2,500	2,703	2,902	10,561
2005	2,691	2,756	2,596	2,399	10,441
2004	2,697	2,887	3,040	3,014	11,638
2003	2,943	2,637	2,655	2,778	11,014
2002	3,152	2,975	3,033	3,117	12,276
2001	5,696	5,419	3,983	3,595	18,692

Earnings Per Share ($)

	1Q	2Q	3Q	4Q	Year
2006	0.02	0.02	0.05	0.04	0.13
2005	0.05	Nil	-0.07	0.01	-0.01
2004	-0.06	-0.11	-0.08	-0.05	-0.29
2003	-0.09	-0.13	-3.74	-0.21	-3.75
2002	-0.08	-0.19	-0.35	-3.21	-3.98
2001	0.29	0.18	-0.28	-0.38	-0.19

Fiscal year ended Aug. 31. Next earnings report expected: Late December. EPS Estimates based on S&P Operating Earnings; historical GAAP earnings are as reported.

Dividend Data

No cash dividends have been paid.

Solectron Corp

Business Summary October 18, 2006

CORPORATE OVERVIEW. Solectron Corp. provides electronic manufacturing services (EMS) to a variety of companies in the technology industry. SLR experienced declining revenues in FY 05 (Aug.), which we believe was largely due to market share erosion, followed by a modest improvement of 1.1% in FY 06. We anticipate a rise in FY 07, as the outsourcing model gathers additional momentum. We believe this projection is supported by growth in the company's business pipeline during 2005. The company also expects restructuring efforts undertaken in 2005 to result in $20 million in annual savings.

MARKET PROFILE. Given what we see as the limited margin potential within the EMS space, industry participants are expanding their addressable market in order to supplement growth. One trend that has become more prevalent as a result, in our view, is the push toward servicing more non-traditional markets, such as the automotive, aerospace and defense, industrial and medical fields. Examples of products offered in these segments by SLR include audio and navigation systems, wafer fabrication equipment tools and X-ray equipment. While these segments are a small portion of the company's revenue total at present, we expect them to become a much more relevant contributor to growth in the years ahead.

In FY 05, Cisco Systems and Nortel Networks accounted for 15.7% and 10.8%, respectively, of revenues. Some transfer of existing Nortel business to an SLR competitor recently occurred. The 10 largest customers contributed a total of 61.6% of net sales in FY 05. The top three end markets served in FY 05, based on revenue, were computing and storage, networking, and communications.

International sales contributed 70% of revenues in FY 05, down from 72% in FY 04. In terms of square footage from continuing operations, non-U.S. facilities accounted for 66% of the overall total as of the end of FY 05. Asia made up the largest share of the international footprint, with both China and Malaysia each containing over one million square feet of space.

Company Financials

Per Share Data ($) Year Ended Aug. 31	2006	2005	2004	2003	2002	2001	2000	1999	1998	1997
Tangible Book Value	NA	2.40	2.32	1.48	3.16	4.81	6.28	5.16	5.02	2.01
Cash Flow	NA	0.19	-0.03	-3.43	-3.50	0.64	1.21	0.91	1.28	0.57
Earnings	0.13	-0.01	-0.29	-3.75	-3.98	-0.19	0.80	0.57	0.41	0.34
S&P Core Earnings	NA	-0.08	-0.34	-2.57	-1.93	-0.15	NA	NA	NA	NA
Dividends	Nil	Nil	Nil	Nil	Nil	Nil	Nil	Nil	Nil	Nil
Payout Ratio	Nil	Nil	Nil	Nil	Nil	Nil	Nil	Nil	Nil	Nil
Prices:High	4.13	5.39	8.20	6.89	12.42	41.95	52.63	49.00	23.38	11.84
Prices:Low	2.81	3.08	4.39	2.80	1.39	9.65	24.54	18.64	8.86	5.89
P/E Ratio:High	32	NM	NM	NM	NM	NM	66	87	57	35
P/E Ratio:Low	22	NM	NM	NM	NM	NM	31	33	21	17

Income Statement Analysis (Million $)	2006	2005	2004	2003	2002	2001	2000	1999	1998	1997
Revenue	NA	10,441	11,638	11,014	12,276	18,692	14,138	8,391	5,288	3,694
Operating Income	NA	353	-366	145	204	984	994	622	423	345
Depreciation	NA	193	227	264	377	536	251	183	124	105
Interest Expense	NA	56.5	144	210	244	176	71.6	36.5	24.8	26.6
Pretax Income	NA	5.20	-252	-2,524	-3,578	-158	740	432	299	238
Effective Tax Rate	NA	NM	NM	NM	NM	NM	32.3%	32.0%	33.5%	33.7%
Net Income	NA	-10.5	-252	-3,105	-3,110	-124	501	294	199	158
S&P Core Earnings	NA	-74.3	-297	-2,129	-1,506	-96.9	NA	NA	NA	NA

Balance Sheet & Other Financial Data (Million $)	2006	2005	2004	2003	2002	2001	2000	1999	1998	1997
Cash	NA	1,683	1,430	1,519	1,918	2,482	1,476	1,326	225	225
Current Assets	NA	4,223	4,666	4,954	6,660	8,704	8,628	3,994	1,888	1,476
Total Assets	NA	5,258	5,817	6,530	11,014	12,930	10,376	4,835	2,411	1,852
Current Liabilities	NA	2,214	2,159	3,235	3,005	2,689	3,217	1,113	841	544
Long Term Debt	NA	541	1,221	1,818	3,184	5,028	3,320	923	386	386
Common Equity	NA	2,444	2,379	1,422	4,773	5,151	3,802	2,793	1,181	919
Total Capital	NA	2,985	3,600	3,240	7,957	10,178	7,122	3,716	1,567	1,305
Capital Expenditures	NA	150	150	137	242	537	506	426	244	188
Cash Flow	NA	183	-24.9	-2,841	-2,733	413	752	477	323	263
Current Ratio	NA	1.9	2.2	1.5	2.2	3.2	2.7	3.6	2.2	2.7
% Long Term Debt of Capitalization	NA	18.1	33.9	56.1	40.0	49.4	46.6	24.8	24.6	29.6
% Net Income of Revenue	NA	NM	NM	NM	NM	NM	3.5	3.5	3.8	4.3
% Return on Assets	NA	NM	NM	NM	NM	NM	6.3	8.1	9.3	9.6
% Return on Equity	NA	NM	NM	NM	NM	NM	14.4	14.8	18.9	19.5

Data as orig reptd.; bef. results of disc opers/spec. items. Per share data adj. for stk. divs.; EPS diluted. E-Estimated. NA-Not Available. NM-Not Meaningful. NR-Not Ranked. UR-Under Review.

Office: 847 Gibraltar Dr, Milpitas, CA 95035-6332.
Telephone: 408-957-8500.
Website: http://www.solectron.com
Pres & CEO: M. Cannon

Investor Contact: P. Hayes (408-957-8500)
SVP & Treas: P. Hayes
SVP & Cntlr: W. Ligan
CFO: P.J. Tufano

Board of Directors: M. Cannon, R. A. D'Amore, P. Eberhart, H. Fridrich, W. R. Graber, W. Hasler, P. Low, C. W. Scott, C. Yansouni

Founded: 1977
Domicile: Delaware
Employees: 53,000

STANDARD &POOR'S

Southern Co (The)

S&P Recommendation HOLD ★★★★★	Price $36.40 (as of Oct 31, 2006)	12-Mo. Target Price $36.00	Investment Style Large-Cap Value

GICS Sector Utilities
Sub-Industry Electric Utilities

Comment This Atlanta-based energy holding company is one of the largest producers of electricity in the U.S.

Key Stock Statistics (Source S&P, Vickers, company reports)

52-Wk Range	$36.60–30.48	S&P Oper. EPS 2006E	2.08	P/E on S&P Oper. EPS 2006E	17.5	Dividend Rate/Share	$1.55
Trailing 12-Month EPS	$2.07	S&P Oper. EPS 2007E	2.17	Common Shares Outstg. (M)	742.3	Yield (%)	4.26
Trailing 12-Month P/E	17.6	S&P Core EPS 2006E	1.93	Market Capitalization(B)	$27.019	Beta	-0.14
$10K Invested 5 Yrs Ago	$18,860	S&P Core EPS 2007E	2.00	Institutional Ownership (%)	41	S&P Credit Rating	A

Price Performance

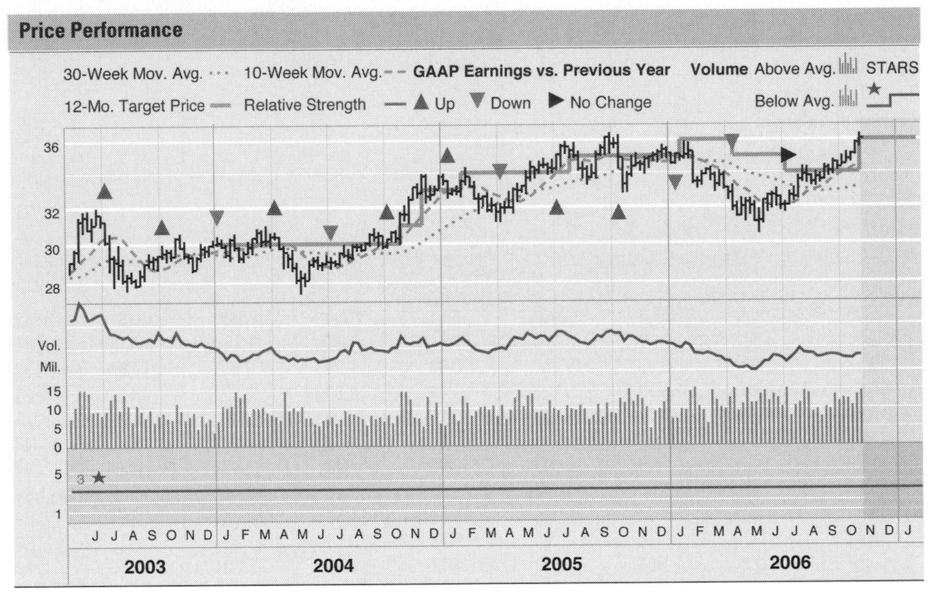

Options: CBOE

Analysis prepared by **Justin McCann** on October 31, 2006, when the stock traded at **$ 36.22**.

Highlights

- Due to the phasing out of Southern's synfuel operations and related tax credits, which contributed $0.12 to 2005 EPS, we expect EPS to decline approximately 3% in 2006. SO recorded EPS of $1.86 for the first three quarters of 2006, with results benefiting from a strong economy and sustained hot weather in the third quarter. We expect EPS in 2007 to increase around 4.3% from anticipated results in 2006.
- With long-term contracts seen reducing risk, we believe the competitive generation business will increase its net income of $270 million in 2005 by approximately 5% to about $284 million in 2006 and by nearly 4% to around $295 million by the end of 2007. We see the utilities recording annual customer growth of about 1.7% and demand growth of about 2%, and expect SO to post average annual EPS growth of 4% to 5% for the longer term.
- SO merged its Savannah Electric unit into its Georgia Power subsidiary on July 1, 2006. We believe Savannah Electric customers will benefit from Georgia Power's more diverse and lower-cost generating facilities, while consolidated results should be enhanced by the operational efficiencies expected to result from the merger.

Investment Rationale/Risk

- The stock has underperformed SO's electric utility peers year-to-date, and we expect it to remain relatively flat over the next 12 months. This reflects, in our view, the projected loss of synfuel-related tax credits. Long term, we expect SO to trade at a premium-to-peers multiple, reflecting, in part, the relative predictability of SO's earnings and dividend stream (with a high S&P Quality ranking of A-).
- Risks to our recommendation and target price include the possible failure of a counterparty to a purchase power agreement to fulfill its contract, and a significant decline in the average P/E of the group as a whole.
- SO increased its dividend 4.0% with the June 2006 payment. This roughly equaled the prior increase, and with the payout ratio (75% of our EPS estimate for 2006) within SO's targeted range of 70% to 75%, we expect future dividends to also grow at around 4% annually, which would approximate our projected long-term average annual EPS growth rate of 4% to 5%. While there could be a contraction in the peer P/Es on our EPS estimates for 2007, we believe the stock will trade at a premium to its peers. Our 12-month target price is $36.

Qualitative Risk Assessment

LOW	MEDIUM	HIGH

Our risk assessment reflects our view of the company's strong and steady cash flows from the regulated electric utility operations, strong balance sheet, a healthy economy in most of its service territories and a generally supportive regulatory environment.

Quantitative Evaluations

S&P Quality Ranking A-

D	C	B-	B	B+	**A-**	A	A+

Relative Strength Rank MODERATE

67

LOWEST = 1 HIGHEST = 99

Revenue/Earnings Data

Revenue (Million $)

	1Q	2Q	3Q	4Q	Year
2006	3,063	3,592	--	--	--
2005	2,864	3,144	4,378	3,287	13,552
2004	2,732	3,009	3,441	2,720	11,902
2003	2,553	2,859	3,319	2,564	11,251
2002	2,214	2,631	3,248	2,457	10,549
2001	2,270	2,561	3,165	2,159	10,155

Earnings Per Share ($)

	1Q	2Q	3Q	4Q	Year
2006	0.35	0.52	E0.95	E0.22	E2.08
2005	0.43	0.52	0.97	0.21	2.14
2004	0.45	0.47	0.87	0.27	2.06
2003	0.41	0.59	0.84	0.17	2.02
2002	0.32	0.46	0.83	0.23	1.85
2001	0.26	0.40	0.79	0.16	1.61

Fiscal year ended Dec. 31. Next earnings report expected: NA. EPS Estimates based on S&P Operating Earnings; historical GAAP earnings are as reported.

Dividend Data (Dates: mm/dd Payment Date: mm/dd/yy)

Amount ($)	Date Decl.	Ex-Div. Date	Stk. of Record	Payment Date
0.373	01/13	02/02	02/06	03/06/06
0.388	04/17	04/27	05/01	06/06/06
0.388	07/17	08/03	08/07	09/06/06
0.388	10/16	11/02	11/06	12/06/06

Dividends have been paid since 1948. Source: Company reports.

Southern Co (The)

Business Summary October 31, 2006

CORPORATE OVERVIEW. The Southern Company is one of the largest producers of electricity in the U.S. Based in Atlanta, GA, this utility holding company has more than 40,000 megawatts of generating capacity and provides electricity to nearly 4.2 million customers in the Southeast through five integrated utilities: Alabama Power, Georgia Power, Gulf Power (located in the northwestern portion of Florida), Mississippi Power, and Savannah Electric & Power.

MARKET PROFILE. Southern Power Company (SPC) was formed by SO in January 2001 to own, manage and finance wholesale generating assets in the Southeast. It serves both the utility units and the wholesale power market. Energy from SPC's assets, which included 5,403 megawatts of generating capacity at the end of 2005, was to be marketed to wholesale customers through the Southern Company Generation and Energy Marketing unit. SPC and the utility units enter into contracts for power purchases, sales and exchange among themselves, as well as with other utilities in the Southeast. Southern Company Gas was formed by SO in June 2002 as a retail gas marketer in Georgia, and began operations in August 2002. In January 2006, SO sold nearly all the assets of Southern Company Gas to Gas South.

With all of SPC's counterparties having investment grade credit ratings and with its long-term bi-lateral contracts having a weighted average life of 13 years, we consider this to be a relatively low-risk business. SO is also the parent company for Southern Telecom, which provides wholesale fiber optic solutions to telecommunication providers in the Southeast; Southern Communications Services (Southern LINC), which provides digital, wireless communications services to SO's five utility units, as well as to the general public within the Southeast; and Southern Nuclear, which provides services to SO's nuclear power plants.

Company Financials

Per Share Data ($) Year Ended Dec. 31	**2005**	**2004**	**2003**	**2002**	**2001**	**2000**	**1999**	**1998**	**1997**	**1996**
Tangible Book Value	14.19	13.65	12.92	11.56	10.87	15.12	6.14	8.77	10.52	12.49
Earnings	2.14	2.06	2.02	1.85	1.61	1.52	1.86	1.40	1.42	1.00
S&P Core Earnings	2.04	1.93	1.85	1.35	1.12	NA	NA	NA	NA	NA
Dividends	1.48	1.77	1.39	1.36	1.34	1.34	1.34	1.34	1.30	1.26
Payout Ratio	69%	86%	69%	74%	83%	88%	72%	96%	92%	75%
Prices:High	36.47	33.96	32.00	31.14	35.72	35.00	29.63	31.56	26.25	25.88
Prices:Low	31.14	27.44	27.00	23.22	20.89	20.38	22.06	23.94	19.88	21.13
P/E Ratio:High	17	16	16	17	22	23	16	23	18	15
P/E Ratio:Low	15	13	13	13	13	13	12	17	14	13
Income Statement Analysis (Million $)										
Revenue	13,554	11,902	11,251	10,549	10,155	10,066	11,585	11,403	12,611	10,358
Depreciation	1,176	955	1,027	1,047	1,173	1,171	1,307	1,539	1,246	996
Maintenance	1,116	1,027	837	961	909	852	945	887	783	782
Fixed Charges Coverage	3.90	4.11	4.21	3.80	3.25	2.87	2.71	2.63	2.68	3.77
Construction Credits	51.0	47.0	25.0	22.0	NA	NA	NA	NA	20.0	23.0
Effective Tax Rate	27.2%	27.7%	29.3%	28.6%	33.3%	37.2%	33.2%	38.8%	42.7%	39.9%
Net Income	1,591	1,532	1,474	1,318	1,119	994	1,276	977	972	1,127
S&P Core Earnings	1,532	1,436	1,351	964	776	NA	NA	NA	NA	NA
Balance Sheet & Other Financial Data (Million $)										
Gross Property	47,580	45,585	43,722	41,764	38,104	35,972	38,620	37,363	34,044	34,190
Capital Expenditures	2,370	2,110	2,002	2,717	2,617	2,225	2,560	2,005	1,859	1,229
Net Property	31,853	30,634	29,418	26,315	23,084	21,622	24,544	24,124	22,110	23,269
Capitalization:Long Term Debt	13,442	13,010	10,587	8,956	10,941	10,457	14,443	13,020	10,274	7,935
Capitalization:% Long Term Debt	55.7	55.9	52.3	50.7	57.8	49.4	60.8	57.1	46.3	42.7
Capitalization:Preferred	Nil	Nil	Nil	Nil	Nil	Nil	Nil	Nil	2,237	1,402
Capitalization:% Preferred	Nil	Nil	Nil	Nil	Nil	Nil	Nil	Nil	10.0	7.60
Capitalization:Common	10,689	10,278	9,648	8,710	7,984	10,690	9,296	9,797	9,647	9,216
Capitalization:% Common	44.3	44.1	47.7	49.3	42.2	50.6	39.2	42.9	43.5	49.7
Total Capital	30,394	29,077	25,809	22,937	24,147	26,436	29,662	24,790	27,997	24,454
% Operating Ratio	82.5	81.2	79.7	80.5	81.9	82.0	81.7	82.6	84.6	82.1
% Earned on Net Property	9.5	9.4	10.0	10.1	10.7	11.4	8.5	7.3	8.6	8.0
% Return on Revenue	11.7	12.9	13.1	12.5	11.0	9.9	11.0	8.6	7.7	10.9
% Return on Invested Capital	8.0	7.9	8.9	8.5	7.4	7.3	9.6	13.8	10.4	7.9
% Return on Common Equity	15.2	15.4	16.1	15.8	12.0	10.0	13.4	10.0	10.3	12.5

Data as orig reptd.; bef. results of disc opers/spec. items. Per share data adj. for stk. divs.; EPS diluted. E-Estimated. NA-Not Available. NM-Not Meaningful. NR-Not Ranked. UR-Under Review.

Office: 30 Ivan Allen Jr. Blvd, N.W., Atlanta, GA 30308.
Telephone: 404-506-5000.
Email: investors@southerncompany.com
Website: http://www.southernco.com

Chrmn, Pres & CEO: D. Ratcliffe
EVP, CFO & Treas: T.A. Fanning
Investor Contact: G. Kundert (404-506-5135)

Board of Directors: J. P. Baranco, D. J. Bern, F. S. Blake, T. F. Chapman, D. M. James, Z. T. Pate, J. N. Purcell, D. M. Ratcliffe, W. G. Smith, Jr., G. J. St. Pe

Founded: 1945
Domicile: Delaware
Employees: 25,554

Southwest Airlines Co.

S&P Recommendation BUY ★★★★★

Price $15.27 (as of Oct 27, 2006)

12-Mo. Target Price $20.00

Investment Style Large-Cap Growth

GICS Sector Industrials
Sub-Industry Airlines

Comment LUV, the sixth largest U.S. airline, offers discounted fares, primarily for short-haul, point-to-point flights.

Key Stock Statistics (Source S&P, Vickers, company reports)

52-Wk Range	$18.20–15.10	S&P Oper. EPS 2006E	0.79	P/E on S&P Oper. EPS 2006E	19.3	Dividend Rate/Share	$0.02
Trailing 12-Month EPS	$0.68	S&P Oper. EPS 2007E	1.02	Common Shares Outstg. (M)	791.8	Yield (%)	0.12
Trailing 12-Month P/E	22.5	S&P Core EPS 2006E	0.95	Market Capitalization(B)	$12.091	Beta	1.17
$10K Invested 5 Yrs Ago	$9,605	S&P Core EPS 2007E	1.05	Institutional Ownership (%)	77	S&P Credit Rating	A

Price Performance

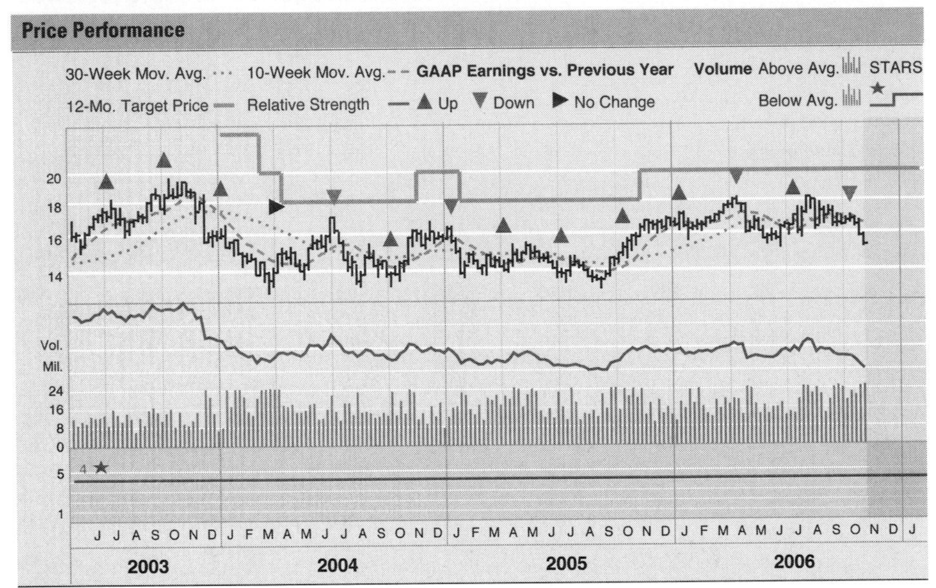

Options: ASE, CBOE, P, Ph

Analysis prepared by **Jim Corridore** on July 25, 2006, when the stock traded at **$ 17.70**.

Highlights

- We look for 2006 revenues to grow about 20%. We expect 8%-10% capacity growth, along with higher load factors and airfares. We think passenger demand is likely to remain strong. LUV is increasing its flights out of Chicago, is expanding service in Philadelphia and Pittsburgh, and recently added Ft. Meyers, FL and Denver as new cities.

- We see margins likely to benefit from increased revenue yields, efficiency gains and cost savings that outweigh higher fuel costs. LUV is 70% hedged on oil prices in 2006 at an average of $36 a barrel. We think this is substantially better than any other U.S. airline, and will help mitigate the effects of high oil prices. However, we note that 2006's average price of $36 a barrel is 38% higher than 2005's average of $26 a barrel for about 85% of consumption, which is one reason why we see LUV's fuel costs rising about 42% in 2006.

- We estimate 2006 EPS of $0.95 (including projected stock option expense of $0.06), up 42% from the $0.67 LUV reported in 2005. On a Standard & Poor's Core Earnings basis, we also project 2006 EPS of $0.95.

Investment Rationale/Risk

- We believe LUV is the financially strongest U.S. airline. LUV has posted 33 consecutive years and 61 consecutive quarters of profitable operations, and we see the quality of those earnings as high. In our view, LUV has ample cash, and its debt to total capitalization is significantly below peer levels. We think these measures warrant a premium valuation to the S&P 500. We believe the stock should also benefit from LUV's strong oil hedge position, somewhat insulating the shares from current high oil prices.

- Risks to our recommendation and target price include a possible pricing war with one of its competitors, and that high oil prices could drive investor sentiment away from airline stocks. We are concerned about LUV's corporate governance relating to its use of affiliated outsiders on its nominating and compensation committees.

- Our 12-month target price of $20 is equal to about 19X our 2007 EPS estimate of $1.05, toward the low end of LUV's five-year historical P/E range. We expect the shares to be volatile due to difficult industry conditions and fluctuating oil prices, but less so than peers.

Qualitative Risk Assessment

LOW | **MEDIUM** | HIGH

Even though Southwest participates in the highly volatile airline industry, its conservative balance sheet with low debt to total capitalization, track record of 33 consecutive years of profitability, and the industry's leading fuel hedge position support our risk assessment.

Quantitative Evaluations

S&P Quality Ranking A-

D | C | B- | B | B+ | **A-** | A | A+

Relative Strength Rank WEAK

12

LOWEST = 1 HIGHEST = 99

Revenue/Earnings Data

Revenue (Million $)

	1Q	2Q	3Q	4Q	Year
2006	2,019	2,449	2,342	--	--
2005	1,663	1,944	1,989	1,987	7,584
2004	1,484	1,716	1,674	1,633	6,530
2003	1,351	1,515	1,553	1,517	5,937
2002	1,257	1,473	1,391	1,401	5,522
2001	1,429	1,554	1,335	1,238	5,555

Earnings Per Share ($)

2006	0.07	0.40	0.06	**E**0.13	**E**0.79
2005	0.09	0.20	0.28	0.10	0.67
2004	0.03	0.14	0.15	0.07	0.38
2003	0.03	0.30	0.13	0.08	0.54
2002	0.03	0.13	0.09	0.05	0.30
2001	0.15	0.22	0.19	0.08	0.63

Fiscal year ended Dec. 31. Next earnings report expected: Mid January. EPS Estimates based on S&P Operating Earnings; historical GAAP earnings are as reported.

Dividend Data (Dates: mm/dd Payment Date: mm/dd/yy)

Amount ($)	Date Decl.	Ex-Div. Date	Stk. of Record	Payment Date
0.005	11/17	12/06	12/08	01/05/06
0.005	01/19	02/28	03/02	03/23/06
0.005	05/17	06/06	06/08	06/29/06
0.005	07/20	08/29	08/31	09/21/06

Dividends have been paid since 1976. Source: Company reports.

Southwest Airlines Co.

Business Summary July 25, 2006

CORPORATE OVERVIEW. Southwest Airlines was the sixth largest U.S. airline in 2005, based on revenue passenger miles. At December 31, 2005, it served 61 cities in 31 states. LUV specializes in low fare, point-to-point, short-haul, high-frequency service. Since 1993, it has concentrated its expansion program on markets in the East. Although 80% of its work force belongs to unions, the company believes that it has generally enjoyed harmonious labor relations. LUV began service to Philadelphia in May 2004, and started service to Pittsburgh in May 2005 and Ft. Meyers, FL in October 2005, and Denver in January 2006.

MARKET PROFILE. The U.S. airline industry is a $132 billion market, according to 2004 data from the Department of Transportation. With 2004 revenues of $6.5 billion (which grew about 17% to $7.5 billion in 2005), LUV comprised about 5% of total industry revenues. Southwest also has an approximate 8.7% market share when measured by RPMs. While Southwest was profitable in 2005 for the 33rd consecutive year and is likely to be profitable again in 2006, S&P believes the ten largest U.S. airlines as a whole lost about $27.2 billion (including about $23.2 billion in reorganization charges at airlines in bankruptcy). Total losses over the past five years by the top ten U.S. airlines approximates $58.6 billion. Over the same time period, LUV's net income totaled $2.1 billion.

Company Financials

Per Share Data ($) Year Ended Dec. 31	**2005**	**2004**	**2003**	**2002**	**2001**	**2000**	**1999**	**1998**	**1997**	**1996**
Tangible Book Value	8.38	7.04	6.40	5.69	5.23	4.57	3.79	3.21	2.69	2.24
Cash Flow	1.25	0.91	1.00	0.74	1.03	1.14	0.90	0.83	0.67	0.51
Earnings	0.67	0.38	0.54	0.30	0.63	0.79	0.59	0.55	0.41	0.27
S&P Core Earnings	0.62	0.30	0.48	0.23	0.61	NA	NA	NA	NA	NA
Dividends	0.02	0.02	0.02	0.02	0.01	0.01	0.01	0.01	0.01	0.01
Payout Ratio	3%	5%	3%	6%	2%	1%	2%	2%	2%	3%
Prices:High	16.95	17.06	19.69	22.00	23.32	23.32	15.72	10.56	7.78	6.57
Prices:Low	13.05	12.88	11.72	10.90	11.25	10.00	9.58	6.81	4.20	4.07
P/E Ratio:High	25	45	36	73	37	30	26	19	19	24
P/E Ratio:Low	19	34	22	36	18	13	16	12	10	15
Income Statement Analysis (Million $)										
Revenue	7,584	6,530	5,937	5,522	5,555	5,650	4,736	4,164	3,817	3,406
Operating Income	1,200	005	007	774	949	1,302	1,030	909	720	534
Depreciation	469	431	384	356	318	281	249	225	196	183
Interest Expense	83.0	49.0	58.0	89.3	49.3	42.3	22.9	30.7	43.7	59.3
Pretax Income	874	489	708	393	828	1,017	774	705	517	341
Effective Tax Rate	37.3%	36.0%	37.6%	38.6%	38.2%	38.5%	38.7%	38.5%	38.5%	39.3%
Net Income	548	313	442	241	511	625	474	433	318	207
S&P Core Earnings	506	239	385	188	486	NA	NA	NA	NA	NA
Balance Sheet & Other Financial Data (Million $)										
Cash	2,280	1,305	1,865	1,815	2,280	523	419	379	623	582
Current Assets	3,620	2,172	2,313	2,232	2,520	832	631	574	806	751
Total Assets	14,218	11,337	9,878	8,954	8,997	6,670	5,652	4,716	4,246	3,723
Current Liabilities	3,848	2,142	172	1,434	2,239	1,298	960	851	869	765
Long Term Debt	1,394	1,700	1,332	1,553	1,327	761	872	623	628	650
Common Equity	6,675	5,524	5,052	4,422	4,014	3,451	2,836	2,398	2,009	1,648
Total Capital	9,965	8,834	7,804	7,202	6,399	5,065	4,400	3,570	3,076	2,749
Capital Expenditures	1,210	1,775	1,238	603	998	1,135	1,168	947	689	677
Cash Flow	1,017	744	826	597	829	906	723	659	513	391
Current Ratio	0.9	1.0	13.4	1.6	1.1	0.6	0.7	0.7	0.9	1.0
% Long Term Debt of Capitalization	14.0	19.2	17.1	21.6	20.7	15.0	19.8	17.5	20.4	24.5
% Net Income of Revenue	7.2	4.8	7.4	4.4	9.2	11.1	10.0	10.4	8.3	6.1
% Return on Assets	4.3	3.0	4.7	2.7	6.5	10.1	9.2	9.7	8.0	5.9
% Return on Equity	9.0	5.9	9.3	5.7	13.7	19.9	18.1	19.7	17.4	13.5

Data as orig reptd.; bef. results of disc opers/spec. items. Per share data adj. for stk. divs.; EPS diluted. E-Estimated. NA-Not Available. NM-Not Meaningful. NR-Not Ranked. UR-Under Review.

Office: P.O. Box 36611, Dallas, TX 75235-1611.
Telephone: 214-792-4000.
Website: http://www.southwest.com
Chrmn: H.D. Kelleher

Pres, COO & Secy: C.C. Barrett
Vice Chrmn & CEO: G.C. Kelly
Investor Contact: L. Wright (214-792-4415)
SVP & CFO: L. Wright

Board of Directors: C. C. Barrett, D. Biegler, L. Caldera, C. W. Crockett, W. H. Cunningham, W. P. Hobby, T. C. Johnson, H. D. Kelleher, G. Kelly, N. Loeffler, J. T. Montford

Founded: 1967
Domicile: Texas
Employees: 31,729

STANDARD &POOR'S

Sovereign Bancorp Inc.

S&P Recommendation HOLD ★★★★★

Price $23.02 (as of Oct 27, 2006)

12-Mo. Target Price $26.00

Investment Style Large-Cap Value

GICS Sector Financials
Sub-Industry Thrifts & Mortgage Finance

Comment This $89 billion bank holding company has branches in Pennsylvania, New Jersey, Connecticut, New Hampshire, Rhode Island, Massachusetts, New York, Maryland and Delaware.

Key Stock Statistics (Source S&P, Vickers, company reports)

52-Wk Range	$24.98–19.47	S&P Oper. EPS 2006E	1.45	P/E on S&P Oper. EPS 2006E	15.9	Dividend Rate/Share	$0.32
Trailing 12-Month EPS	$1.04	S&P Oper. EPS 2007E	1.76	Common Shares Outstg. (M)	471.9	Yield (%)	1.39
Trailing 12-Month P/E	22.1	S&P Core EPS 2006E	1.45	Market Capitalization(B)	$10.863	Beta	1.03
$10K Invested 5 Yrs Ago	$25,397	S&P Core EPS 2007E	1.76	Institutional Ownership (%)	49	S&P Credit Rating	BBB

Price Performance

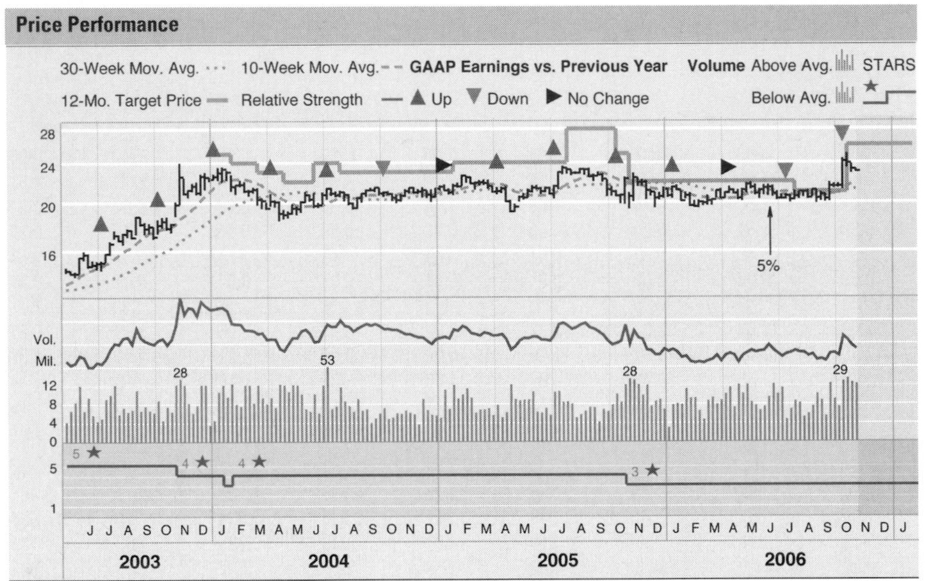

Options: ASE, CBOE, P, Ph

Analysis prepared by **Stuart Plesser** on October 13, 2006, when the stock traded at **$ 23.72**.

Highlights

- We believe SOV's total revenue is likely to grow 7.3% in 2006, helped by the acquisition of Independence Community Bancorp (ICBC) and growth in net interest income, partly offset by declines in mortgage banking fees. Our 2006 estimates include a net interest margin of 2.90% (down from 2.98% in 2005, due to pressure from a relatively flat yield curve), earning asset growth of 17.6%, and a 14.6% decline in non-interest income.
- We believe that the Independence acquisition should lead to expense reduction, and look for SOV's efficiency ratio to improve in the remaining quarters of 2006 to 50% from 52% in the first two quarters of the year. In 2007, we look for an efficiency ratio of roughly 49%. Credit quality appears to be strong, and charge-off levels remain relatively low. However, we expect loan loss provisions to increase to $146 million in 2006, from $90 million in 2005, largely due to the addition of ICBC's loan portfolio.
- Assuming an effective tax rate of 15.5% for 2006 and continued share repurchases, we estimate 2006 operating EPS of $1.45, an 18% decline from $1.77 in 2005. Our 2007 estimate is $1.76.

Investment Rationale/Risk

- The company's long-time CEO, Jay Sidhu, recently resigned. We think his departure may open the door for the board putting the company up for sale over the near term instead of waiting for June 2008, when Banco Santander (STD: hold, $17) has an option to buy the company at $40 a share. Regardless, we don't believe that a buyer can be found at a price that would interest the board until SOV improves its operating performance.
- Risks to our recommendation and target price include detrimental changes in the slope of the yield curve, and operating performance that fails to meet our expectations. Regarding corporate governance, we are concerned about SOV's practice of staggering annual elections for directors and bypassing shareholders on significant strategic decisions. We believe that SOV's corporate governance issues will improve under new leadership.
- Our 12-month target price of $26 is derived by applying a P/E multiple of roughly 14.8X to our 2007 EPS estimate, a slight premium to SOV's three-year average P/E, justified by the possibility of a buyout.

Qualitative Risk Assessment

LOW	MEDIUM	HIGH

Our risk assessment reflects our view of SOV's mid-cap valuation, the strong credit quality of its loan portfolio, and its history of profitability. While the industry in which the company operates is highly competitive and fragmented, it tends to produce relatively stable financial results.

Quantitative Evaluations

S&P Quality Ranking A-

D	C	B-	B	B+	A-	A	A+

Relative Strength Rank MODERATE

66

LOWEST = 1 HIGHEST = 99

Revenue/Earnings Data

Revenue (Million $)

	1Q	2Q	3Q	4Q	Year
2006	973.9	829.0	1,442	--	--
2005	802.5	872.0	921.2	969.6	3,565
2004	627.6	639.7	714.1	726.0	2,706
2003	621.6	621.5	601.8	607.2	2,452
2002	602.4	622.1	634.5	633.1	2,492
2001	687.9	681.8	665.5	613.3	2,649

Earnings Per Share ($)

2006	0.36	-0.15	0.37	E0.38	E1.45
2005	0.36	0.45	0.46	0.42	1.69
2004	0.31	0.40	0.23	0.36	1.30
2003	0.26	0.35	0.35	0.36	1.31
2002	0.24	0.30	0.31	0.31	1.17
2001	0.05	0.11	0.03	0.29	0.46

Fiscal year ended Dec. 31. Next earnings report expected: Mid January. EPS Estimates based on S&P Operating Earnings; historical GAAP earnings are as reported.

Dividend Data (Dates: mm/dd Payment Date: mm/dd/yy)

Amount ($)	Date Decl.	Ex-Div. Date	Stk. of Record	Payment Date
0.080	03/15	04/27	05/01	05/15/06
5%	03/15	06/13	06/15	07/06/06
0.080	06/22	07/28	08/01	08/15/06
0.080	10/17	10/30	11/01	11/15/06

Dividends have been paid since 1987. Source: Company reports.

Please read the Required Disclosures and Analyst Certification on the last page of this report.

Sovereign Bancorp Inc.

Business Summary October 13, 2006

CORPORATE OVERVIEW. Sovereign Bancorp, once a small thrift, has grown into a large banking franchise, with over $89 billion in assets as of October 2006. The company has grown largely through acquisitions. From 1990 through December 2005, SOV acquired 27 financial institutions, branch networks and/or related businesses. From 1995, 17 of these acquisitions had assets totaling approximately $35 billion.

The company has more than 650 community banking offices, and over 1,000 ATMs located principally in Pennsylvania, New Jersey, Connecticut, New Hampshire, Rhode Island, Massachusetts New York and Maryland. SOV, which gathers substantially all of its deposits in these market areas, uses them, as well as other financing sources, to fund its loan and investment portfolios. SOV earns interest on its loan portfolio. In addition, the company generates non-interest income from a number of sources, including deposit and loan services, sales of residential loans and investment securities, capital markets products and bank-owned life insurance. SOV's principal non-interest expense includes employee compensation and benefits, occupancy and facility-related costs, technology and other administrative expenses.

PRIMARY BUSINESS DYNAMICS. SOV's financial results are highly correlated to the economic environment, including interest rates, consumer and business confidence and spending, as well as competitive conditions. The company believes its major strengths are: strong franchise value in terms of market share and demographics; a stable low-cost core deposit base; a diversified loan portfolio and products; a strong service culture; and the ability to cross-sell multiple product lines.

As of December 31, 2005, total loans of $43.8 billion were 28% residential real estate loans, 38% commercial loans, and 34% consumer loans (mostly home equity and auto loans). We look for consumer loans to decline over the next year due to higher short-term interest rates. As of December 31, 2005, deposits totaling $38.0 billion consisted of 14% demand accounts, 23% NOW accounts, 3% customer repurchase agreements, 9% savings accounts, 21% money markets, and 30% CDs. The company is attempting to attract more low-cost deposits by launching new products and services such as remote image capture, remote check clearing, and health savings accounts. This should help widen net margins, in our view. The allowance for loan losses at December 31, 2005, was $419.6 million (equal to 2X total non-performing assets), up from $408.7 million (2.6X) a year earlier. Net chargeoffs in 2005 totaled $81.7 million (0.20 of average loans), compared to $110.3 million (0.36) in 2004. Nonperforming assets totaled $205.6 million (0.32% of total assets) at December 31, 2005, versus $160.1 million (0.29%).

Company Financials

Per Share Data ($) Year Ended Dec. 31	**2005**	**2004**	**2003**	**2002**	**2001**	**2000**	**1999**	**1998**	**1997**	**1996**
Tangible Book Value	7.60	7.11	6.30	5.02	3.24	2.04	5.74	4.51	4.78	3.57
Earnings	1.69	1.30	1.31	1.17	0.46	-0.17	0.96	0.81	0.60	0.57
S&P Core Earnings	1.68	1.28	1.31	1.15	0.38	NA	NA	NA	NA	NA
Dividends	0.16	0.11	0.10	0.10	0.10	0.10	0.09	0.07	0.07	0.06
Payout Ratio	10%	8%	7%	8%	21%	NM	9%	9%	11%	10%
Prices:High	23.61	23.57	24.00	15.14	12.86	9.49	25.00	21.67	17.56	9.18
Prices:Low	19.10	18.39	12.00	10.67	6.82	5.95	6.67	8.33	8.52	6.06
P/E Ratio:High	14	18	18	13	28	NM	26	27	29	16
P/E Ratio:Low	11	14	9	9	15	NM	7	10	14	11

Income Statement Analysis (Million $)	2005	2004	2003	2002	2001	2000	1999	1998	1997	1996
Net Interest Income	1,588	1,405	1,206	1,160	1,054	855	615	494	341	217
Loan Loss Provision	90.0	127	162	147	97.1	56.5	30.0	28.0	37.2	2.50
Non Interest Income	635	468	456	381	411	230	130	106	38.5	26.7
Non Interest Expenses	2,319	2,100	968	979	1,175	1,013	446	360	212	158
Pretax Income	915	603	598	467	209	-106	269	211	130	83.0
Effective Tax Rate	23.6%	21.2%	25.6%	26.7%	12.7%	NM	33.3%	35.4%	40.3%	38.0%
Net Income	676	454	402	342	123	-41.0	179	136	77.6	51.5
% Net Interest Margin	3.09	3.24	3.42	3.61	3.57	3.19	2.86	2.56	2.68	2.59
S&P Core Earnings	669	450	401	336	101	NA	NA	NA	NA	NA

Balance Sheet & Other Financial Data (Million $)	2005	2004	2003	2002	2001	2000	1999	1998	1997	1996
Total Assets	63,679	54,471	43,505	39,524	35,475	33,458	26,607	21,914	14,336	9,433
Loans	43,384	36,222	25,821	22,829	20,135	21,656	14,094	11,152	9,833	9,096
Deposits	37,978	32,556	27,344	26,785	23,298	24,499	11,720	12,323	7,890	5,052
Capitalization:Debt	9,330	9,642	12,124	6,240	6,869	5,367	316	4,108	858	1,092
Capitalization:Equity	5,811	4,988	3,260	2,764	2,202	1,949	1,821	1,204	682	376
Capitalization:Total	15,347	14,834	15,587	9,205	2,202	7,315	2,138	5,312	1,733	1,568
% Return on Assets	1.1	0.9	1.0	0.9	0.4	NM	19.2	82.7	12.6	5.5
% Return on Equity	12.5	11.0	13.3	13.8	5.9	NM	11.9	13.8	13.5	12.9
% Loan Loss Reserve	1.0	1.1	1.3	1.3	1.3	1.2	-0.9	1.2	0.9	0.4
% Risk Based Capital	10.7	11.6	12.1	7.6	10.7	10.3	14.9	10.3	12.2	15.1
Price Times Book Value:High	3.1	3.3	3.8	3.0	2.9	4.6	4.4	4.8	4.4	2.0
Price Times Book Value:Low	2.5	2.6	1.9	2.1	1.8	2.9	1.2	1.9	2.1	1.3

Data as orig reptd.; bef. results of disc opers/spec. items. Per share data adj. for stk. divs.; EPS diluted. E-Estimated. NA-Not Available. NM-Not Meaningful. NR-Not Ranked. UR-Under Review.

Office: 1500 Market St, Philadelphia, PA 19102-2100.
Telephone: 215-557-4630.
Email: investor@sovereignbank.com
Website: http://www.sovereignbank.com

Chrmn: J.S. Sidhu
Pres, Vice Chrmn & CEO: J.P. Campanelli
Vice Chrmn: J.J. Lynch
Vice Chrmn & Chief Admin: L.M. Thompson, Jr.

CFO: M.R. McCollum
Investor Contact: S. Weikel (610-208-6112)
Board of Directors: E. Botin, P. M. Ehlerman, B. Hard, M. L. Heard, A. C. Hove, Jr., W. J. Moran, M. F. Ramirez, J. Rodriguez-Inciarte, D. K. Rothermel, J. S. Sidhu, C. C. Troilo, Sr., R. V. Whitworth

Founded: 1984
Domicile: Pennsylvania
Employees: 10,174

STANDARD &POOR'S

Sprint Nextel Corp

S&P Recommendation BUY ★★★★★

Price $18.89 (as of Oct 30, 2006)

12-Mo. Target Price $22.00

Investment Style Large-Cap Value

GICS Sector Telecommunication Services
Sub-Industry Wireless Telecommunication Services

Comment This leading provider of wireless and other telecommunications services was formed in August 2005 via the merger of Sprint Corp. and Nextel Communications, Inc.

Key Stock Statistics (Source S&P, Vickers, company reports)

52-Wk Range	$26.89–15.92	S&P Oper. EPS 2006E	1.20	P/E on S&P Oper. EPS 2006E	15.7	Dividend Rate/Share	$0.10
Trailing 12-Month EPS	$0.31	S&P Oper. EPS 2007E	1.35	Common Shares Outstg. (M)	2,987.4	Yield (%)	0.53
Trailing 12-Month P/E	60.9	S&P Core EPS 2006E	1.27	Market Capitalization(B)	$55.722	Beta	1.67
$10K Invested 5 Yrs Ago	$11,870	S&P Core EPS 2007E	1.35	Institutional Ownership (%)	85	S&P Credit Rating	BBB+

Price Performance

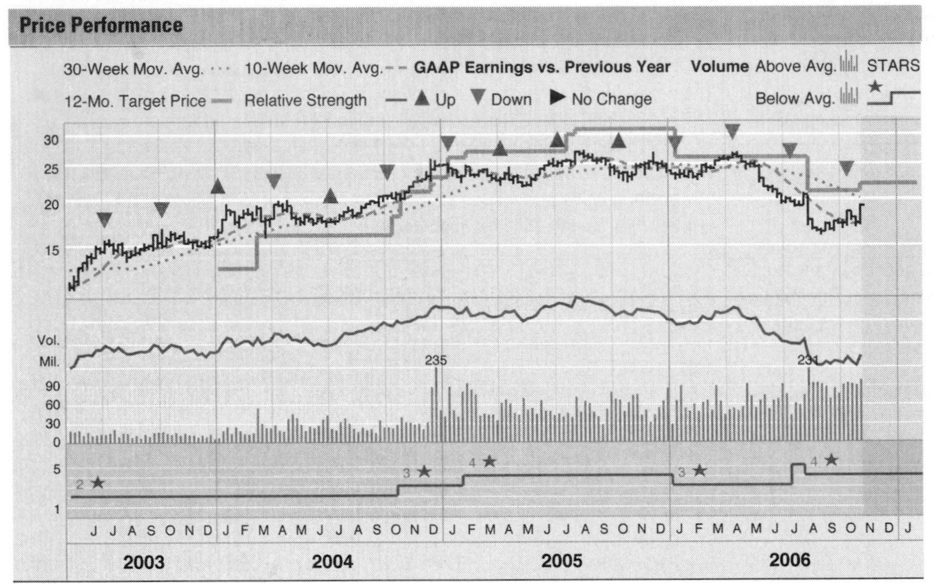

Options: ASE, CBOE, P, Ph

Analysis prepared by **Kenneth M. Leon, CPA** on October 30, 2006, when the stock traded at **$ 18.92**.

Highlights

- Following an estimated 5.2% revenue increase in 2006, we project 9% to 10% growth in 2007 as S begins to execute better on its combined wireless operations. We believe the wireless unit is in transition as S has taken measures to tighten credit policy, which has reduced net new subscriber additions. In our opinion, S should begin to improve subscriber growth with improving monthly customer churn in early 2007.
- We estimate total 2006 and 2007 EBITDA margins in the 29% to 30% area, versus 30.4% in 2005, as S should need time to realize cost savings from multiple acquisitions. We believe controlling marketing costs will also be a key driver for improving margins.
- We believe S can realize annualized EBITDA growth of 6% to 10% in the next three years from improved top-line growth and cost controls. In our opinion, S has the potential to grow faster than its Regional Bell Operating Company (RBOC) peers. We estimate operating EPS of $1.20 for 2006 and $1.35 in 2007, which include $0.02 for stock option expense in each year.

Investment Rationale/Risk

- As one of the largest U.S. wireless carriers, we believe S should realize higher revenue growth and wider margins as it executes better. While 2006 is in transition for integrating Nextel Partners, Alamosa Holdings and UbiquiTel, we believe S will begin to realize cost savings in 2007 from the $1 billion savings it has targeted from these acquisitions.
- Risks to our opinion and target price include execution risks in realizing merger cost savings and new revenues from the new acquisitions. Also, increased competition from nationwide peers may pressure S's net subscriber additions.
- With the stock down 40% from its April high, the shares are trading below our 12-month target price of $22. A newly authorized $6 billion common stock repurchase plan will benefit the share price, in our opinion. Our 12-month target price assumes an enterprise value of 6.3X our 2007 EBITDA estimate, in line with RBOC peers. Over the long term, we believe S will grow faster than peers to support a higher valuation compared to peers.

Qualitative Risk Assessment

LOW | **MEDIUM** | HIGH

As one of the four leading U.S. wireless service providers, S generates strong operating cash flow to meet its working capital, capital expenditure and debt requirements. While the U.S. wireless market is maturing, we believe the company will continue to grow free cash flow, which may be used for stock repurchases.

Quantitative Evaluations

S&P Quality Ranking B

D | C | B- | **B** | B+ | A- | A | A+

Relative Strength Rank STRONG

71

LOWEST = 1 HIGHEST = 99

Revenue/Earnings Data

Revenue (Million $)

	1Q	2Q	3Q	4Q	Year
2006	11,548	10,014	10,496	--	--
2005	6,936	7,113	9,335	11,296	34,680
2004	6,707	6,869	6,922	6,930	27,428
2003	3,581	3,530	3,538	3,536	14,185
2002	4,029	3,965	3,805	3,659	15,182
2001	4,358	4,310	4,244	4,012	16,924

Earnings Per Share ($)

	1Q	2Q	3Q	4Q	Year
2006	0.14	0.10	0.08	E0.32	E1.20
2005	0.32	0.40	0.23	0.07	0.87
2004	0.16	0.16	-1.32	0.29	-0.71
2003	0.31	0.10	-0.48	0.40	0.33
2002	0.32	0.12	0.54	0.28	1.18
2001	0.36	0.33	0.18	-1.02	-0.16

Fiscal year ended Dec. 31. Next earnings report expected: Late February. EPS Estimates based on S&P Operating Earnings; historical GAAP earnings are as reported.

Dividend Data (Dates: mm/dd Payment Date: mm/dd/yy)

Amount ($)	Date Decl.	Ex-Div. Date	Stk. of Record	Payment Date
0.025	04/18	05/15	05/17	06/30/06
Stk.	05/02	05/18	05/08	05/17/06
0.025	07/25	09/06	09/08	09/29/06
0.025	09/25	12/06	12/08	12/29/06

Dividends have been paid since 1939. Source: Company reports.

Sprint Nextel Corp

Business Summary October 30, 2006

CORPORATE OVERVIEW. On August 15, 2005, shares of Sprint Nextel Corp., a leading telecommunications provider, began trading on the New York Stock Exchange under the symbol S. The company has a balanced mix of consumer, business and government customers. S spun off to shareholders the local telephone business in May 2006. As of the 2006 third quarter, S provided nationwide service to 51 million wireless subscribers, with 82% of revenues from its direct postpaid customers, 7% from prepaid, and 11% from wholesale customers like Virgin Mobile.

MARKET PROFILE. We believe S has national brand name recognition, and an above average reputation for network quality and service reliability. S, like its wireless peers, has large-scale distribution channels through its own sales force for the enterprise and government markets, company-owned retail stores, kiosks in shopping malls, and Internet websites.

In the U.S. market, wireless is perceived more as a necessity than a luxury service as it once was in the early adoption years. More than 70% of the total U.S. population has subscribed to mobile wireless services, extending from the workplace to family members. Affordable service plans such as prepaid services may enable wireless to reach higher market penetration rates. Network reliability may drive higher penetration of wireline substitution.

COMPETITIVE LANDSCAPE. In most major U.S. metropolitan markets, four national carriers offer competing wireless services to customers. Wireless carriers such as S have adjusted to potential substitutes by integrating the service features into the handsets. Until recently, S had a unique service with push-to-talk service through Nextel's iDEN network, but Cingular has launched a competing nationwide service aimed at the consumer segment, in contrast to S's dominant position with small business and enterprise firms. In our opinion, S needs to better integrate Nextel and other affiliates into a unified brand and improved quality of service to its customers. We believe management's initiatives should begin to show better sales traction and wider margins in 2007.

Company Financials

Per Share Data ($) Year Ended Dec. 31	**2005**	**2004**	**2003**	**2002**	**2001**	**2000**	**1999**	**1998**	**1997**	**1996**
Tangible Book Value	0.88	3.85	14.40	11.45	11.41	13.95	10.42	10.45	10.52	9.91
Cash Flow	3.93	2.56	3.12	4.14	2.60	4.00	-4.35	7.19	3.07	3.27
Earnings	0.87	-0.71	0.33	1.18	-0.16	1.45	1.97	1.78	1.09	1.40
S&P Core Earnings	0.86	-0.72	1.20	1.26	-0.12	NA	NA	NA	NA	NA
Dividends	0.30	0.50	0.50	0.50	0.50	0.50	0.50	0.50	0.50	0.50
Payout Ratio	34%	NM	152%	42%	NM	34%	25%	28%	46%	36%
Prices:High	27.20	25.80	16.76	20.47	29.31	67.81	75.94	42.66	30.31	22.75
Prices:Low	21.57	15.74	10.22	6.65	18.50	19.63	36.88	27.63	19.19	16.94
P/E Ratio:High	31	NM	51	17	NM	47	39	24	28	16
P/E Ratio:Low	25	NM	31	6	NM	14	19	16	18	12
Income Statement Analysis (Million $)										
Revenue	34,680	27,428	14,185	15,182	16,924	17,688	17,016	17,135	14,874	14,045
Operating Income	10,220	8,148	4,376	4,488	4,238	5,101	-5,059	3,075	4,178	3,858
Depreciation	6,269	4,720	2,519	2,645	2,449	2,267	2,129	2,705	1,726	1,591
Interest Expense	1,351	1,248	236	295	57.0	76.0	182	895	280	301
Pretax Income	2,906	-1,603	434	1,453	-129	2,170	-2,797	698	1,583	1,912
Effective Tax Rate	38.0%	NM	32.3%	28.0%	NM	40.5%	37.9%	56.2%	39.8%	37.7%
Net Income	1,801	-1,012	294	1,046	-146	1,292	-1,736	457	953	1,191
S&P Core Earnings	1,772	-1,036	1,096	1,132	-112	NA	NA	NA	NA	NA
Balance Sheet & Other Financial Data (Million $)										
Cash	10,665	4,556	1,635	641	134	122	104	605	102	1,151
Current Assets	19,092	9,975	4,378	3,327	3,485	4,512	4,282	4,388	3,773	4,353
Total Assets	102,580	41,321	21,862	23,043	24,164	23,649	21,803	33,231	18,185	16,953
Current Liabilities	14,050	6,902	2,359	4,320	6,298	5,004	4,301	4,551	3,077	3,314
Long Term Debt	Nil	15,916	2,627	2,736	3,258	3,482	4,531	11,942	3,755	2,981
Common Equity	51,937	13,521	13,372	11,814	11,704	12,343	10,514	12,202	9,025	8,520
Total Capital	52,184	29,684	17,632	16,385	16,514	17,101	15,980	26,221	13,809	12,360
Capital Expenditures	5,057	3,980	1,674	2,181	5,295	4,105	3,534	42,311	2,863	2,434
Cash Flow	8,063	3,701	2,821	3,698	2,310	3,566	-3,858	3,156	2,678	2,781
Current Ratio	1.4	1.4	1.9	0.8	0.6	0.9	1.0	1.0	1.2	1.3
% Long Term Debt of Capitalization	Nil	53.6	14.9	16.7	19.7	20.4	28.4	45.5	27.1	24.1
% Net Income of Revenue	5.2	NM	2.1	6.9	NM	7.3	10.2	2.6	6.4	8.5
% Return on Assets	2.5	NM	1.3	4.4	NM	5.7	8.5	1.8	5.4	7.4
% Return on Equity	5.5	NM	2.3	8.8	NM	11.2	17.7	4.2	10.8	18.1

Data as orig reptd.; bef. results of disc opers/spec. items. Per share data adj. for stk. divs.; EPS diluted. E-Estimated. NA-Not Available. NM-Not Meaningful. NR-Not Ranked. UR-Under Review.

Office: 2001 Edmund Halley Dr, Reston, VA 20191-3436.
Telephone: 703-433-4000.
Email: investorrelation.sprintcom@mail.sprint.com
Website: http://www.sprint.com

Exec Chrmn: T.M. Donahue
Pres & CEO: G.D. Forsee
COO: L. Lauer
VP & Treas: R.S. Lindahl

Investor Contact: K. Fawkes (913-794-1140)
Board of Directors: K. J. Bane, R. R. Bennett, G. M. Bethune, T. M. Donahue, F. M. Drendel, G. D. Forsee, J. H. Hance, Jr., V. J. Hill, I. O. Hockaday, Jr., W. E. Kennard, L. K. Lorimer, S. M. Shern, W. H. Swanson

Founded: 1925
Domicile: Kansas
Employees: 79,900

Stanley Works (The)

STANDARD &POOR'S

S&P Recommendation HOLD ★★★★★

Price $47.36 (as of Oct 27, 2006)

12-Mo. Target Price $53.00

Investment Style Mid-Cap Value

GICS Sector Consumer Discretionary
Sub-Industry Household Appliances

Comment This company is a worldwide producer of tools, hardware and specialty hardware for home improvement, consumer, industrial and professional use.

Key Stock Statistics (Source S&P, Vickers, company reports)

52-Wk Range	$54.59–41.60	S&P Oper. EPS 2006E	3.80	P/E on S&P Oper. EPS 2006E	12.5	Dividend Rate/Share	$1.20
Trailing 12-Month EPS	$3.13	S&P Oper. EPS 2007E	4.11	Common Shares Outstg. (M)	80.9	Yield (%)	2.53
Trailing 12-Month P/E	15.1	S&P Core EPS 2006E	3.80	Market Capitalization(B)	$3.832	Beta	1.02
$10K Invested 5 Yrs Ago	$13,681	S&P Core EPS 2007E	4.11	Institutional Ownership (%)	73	S&P Credit Rating	A

Price Performance

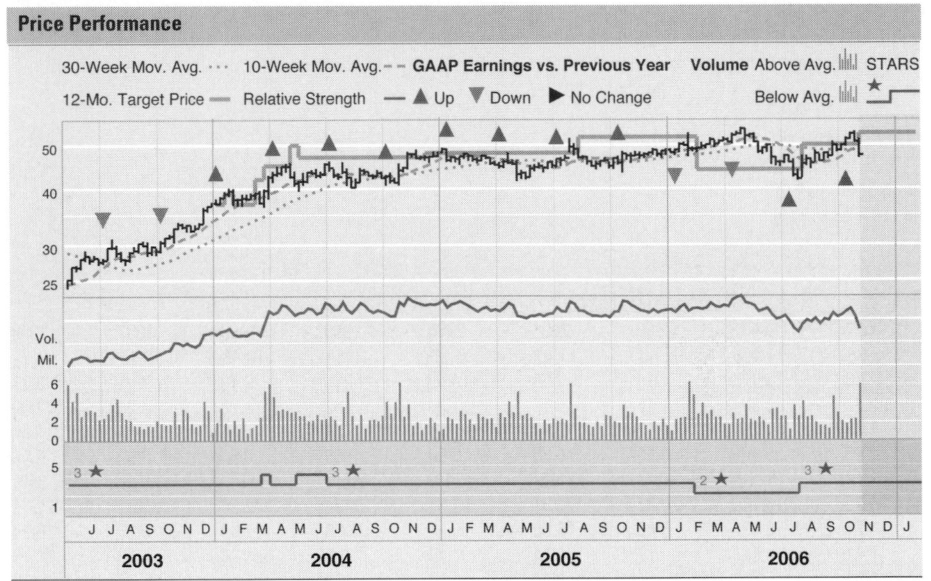

Options: P

Highlights

- The 12-month target price for SWK has recently been changed to $53.00 from $50.00. The Highlights section of this Stock Report will be updated accordingly.

Investment Rationale/Risk

- The Investment Rationale/Risk section of this Stock Report will be updated shortly. For the latest News story on SWK from MarketScope, see below.

- 10/25/06 03:14 pm EDT... S&P REITERATES HOLD OPINION ON SHARES OF STANLEY WORKS (SWK 48.25***): Q3 EPS before special items of $1.10, vs. $0.89, is above our $1.06 estimate. We are raising our '06 EPS estimate by $0.27 to $3.80 to exclude restructuring and inventory step-up charges. Although we are reducing our '07 sales estimate by $170 million to $4.17 billion, we are keeping our '07 EPS estimate at $4.11 to reflect our improved margin projections and a lower tax rate and share count that we expect. We are raising our target price by $3 to $53, applying a 13X P/E to our '07 EPS estimate. Trading below that target, we would hold shares for total return potential. / E.Levy-CFA

Qualitative Risk Assessment

LOW | **MEDIUM** | HIGH

Our risk assessment takes into account our positive view of SWK's strong brand name and solid competitive position, offset by our negative view of industry cyclicality.

Quantitative Evaluations

S&P Quality Ranking B+

D | C | B- | B | **B+** | A- | A | A+

Relative Strength Rank WEAK

18

LOWEST = 1 HIGHEST = 99

Revenue/Earnings Data

Revenue (Million $)

	1Q	2Q	3Q	4Q	Year
2006	968.7	1,018	1,013	--	--
2005	796.3	814.7	834.9	839.4	3,285
2004	734.8	753.9	751.8	802.9	3,043
2003	632.2	652.6	665.6	727.7	2,678
2002	616.7	649.1	665.5	661.7	2,594
2001	626.2	676.5	676.1	645.6	2,624

Earnings Per Share ($)

2006	0.45	0.90	1.09	**E**1.05	**E**3.80
2005	0.78	0.77	0.89	0.75	3.18
2004	0.66	0.70	0.73	0.77	2.85
2003	0.22	0.11	0.46	0.38	1.14
2002	0.56	0.72	0.62	0.20	2.10
2001	0.54	0.58	0.62	0.07	1.81

Fiscal year ended Dec. 31. Next earnings report expected: Late January. EPS Estimates based on S&P Operating Earnings; historical GAAP earnings are as reported.

Dividend Data (Dates: mm/dd Payment Date: mm/dd/yy)

Amount ($)	Date Decl.	Ex-Div. Date	Stk. of Record	Payment Date
0.290	02/22	03/06	03/08	03/28/06
0.290	04/26	06/05	06/07	06/27/06
0.300	07/25	09/06	09/08	09/26/06
0.300	10/24	12/06	12/08	12/19/06

Dividends have been paid since 1877. Source: Company reports.

Stanley Works (The)

Business Summary August 04, 2006

The Stanley Works is a worldwide supplier of industrial tools and security solutions for professional, industrial and consumer use. SWK's operations are classified into three business segments: Consumer Products (35% of 2004 sales), Industrial Tools (42%), and Security Solutions (22%).

In Consumer Products, SWK manufactures and markets hand tools, consumer mechanics tools and storage units, and hardware. Products are distributed directly to retailers (including home centers, mass merchants, hardware stores, and retail lumber yards) as well as third party distributors, and include measuring instruments, hammers, knives and blades, screwdrivers, sockets and tool boxes. Products are marketed under the Stanley, FatMax, Powerlock, IntelliTools, Goldblatt, Husky and ZAG brands.

The Industrial Tools segment manufactures and markets professional mechanics tools, pneumatic tools and fasteners, hydraulic tools and accessories, assembly tools and systems, and electronic measuring tools. Products are distributed primarily through third party distributors and a direct salesforce. Brands include Stanley, Proto, Mac, Jensen, Bostick, CST/Berger and David White.

The Security Solutions segment is a provider of access and security solutions primarily for retailers, educational and healthcare institutions, government, financial institutions, and commercial and industrial customers. Products include security integration systems, software, related installation and maintenance services, automatic doors, and locking mechanisms, and are sold on a direct sales basis. Brands include Best, Blick, Frisco Bay and ISR.

A large portion of SWK's products in the Consumer Products and Industrial Tools segments are sold through home centers and mass merchant distribution channels in the U.S. In 2004, sales to Home Depot accounted for 12% of total sales.

Company Financials

Per Share Data ($) Year Ended Dec. 31	2005	2004	2003	2002	2001	2000	1999	1998	1997	1996
Tangible Book Value	4.59	3.56	2.65	5.05	7.05	6.59	6.18	5.33	5.67	7.68
Cash Flow	4.40	4.07	2.16	2.90	2.76	3.17	2.62	2.41	0.34	1.93
Earnings	3.18	2.85	1.14	2.10	1.81	2.22	1.67	1.53	-0.47	1.09
S&P Core Earnings	3.16	2.49	1.12	1.43	1.30	NA	NA	NA	NA	NA
Dividends	1.14	1.08	1.03	0.99	0.94	0.90	0.87	0.83	0.77	0.73
Payout Ratio	36%	38%	90%	47%	52%	41%	52%	54%	NM	67%
Prices:High	51.75	49.33	37.87	52.00	46.97	31.88	35.00	57.25	47.38	32.81
Prices:Low	41.51	36.42	20.84	27.31	28.06	18.44	22.00	23.50	28.00	23.63
P/E Ratio:High	16	17	33	25	26	14	21	37	NM	30
P/E Ratio:Low	13	13	18	13	16	8	13	15	NM	22
Income Statement Analysis (Million $)										
Revenue	3,285	3,043	2,678	2,594	2,624	2,749	2,752	2,729	2,670	2,671
Operating Income	493	513	342	360	412	424	321	331	331	342
Depreciation	96.5	95.0	86.5	71.2	82.9	83.3	86.0	79.7	72.4	74.7
Interest Expense	40.4	38.6	34.2	28.5	18.9	34.6	33.0	31.0	24.7	28.0
Pretax Income	358	329	133	273	237	294	231	215	-18.6	174
Effective Tax Rate	24.1%	27.0%	27.3%	32.1%	33.1%	33.8%	35.1%	36.0%	NM	44.4%
Net Income	272	240	96.7	185	158	194	150	138	-41.9	96.9
S&P Core Earnings	270	209	94.7	127	113	NA	NA	NA	NA	NA
Balance Sheet & Other Financial Data (Million $)										
Cash	658	250	204	122	115	93.6	88.0	110	152	84.0
Current Assets	1,826	1,372	1,201	1,190	1,141	1,094	1,091	1,086	1,005	911
Total Assets	3,545	2,851	2,424	2,418	2,056	1,885	1,891	1,933	1,759	1,660
Current Liabilities	875	819	754	681	826	707	693	702	623	382
Long Term Debt	895	482	535	564	197	249	290	345	284	343
Common Equity	1,946	1,388	1,032	1,165	844	933	737	669	608	780
Total Capital	2,925	1,960	1,567	1,729	1,041	1,181	1,027	1,014	892	1,123
Capital Expenditures	53.3	47.6	31.4	37.2	55.7	59.8	78.0	56.9	73.3	78.7
Cash Flow	368	335	183	256	241	278	236	218	30.5	172
Current Ratio	2.1	1.7	1.6	1.7	1.4	1.5	1.6	1.5	1.6	2.4
% Long Term Debt of Capitalization	30.6	24.6	34.1	32.6	18.9	21.1	28.2	34.0	31.8	30.6
% Net Income of Revenue	8.3	7.9	3.6	7.1	6.0	7.1	5.5	5.0	NM	3.7
% Return on Assets	8.5	9.1	4.0	8.3	8.0	10.3	7.8	7.5	NM	5.9
% Return on Equity	14.4	19.8	8.8	16.9	20.0	20.8	20.8	21.6	NM	12.8

Data as orig reptd.; bef. results of disc opers/spec. items. Per share data adj. for stk. divs.; EPS diluted. E-Estimated. NA-Not Available. NM-Not Meaningful. NR-Not Ranked. UR-Under Review.

Office: 1000 Stanley Dr Ste, New Britain, CT 06053.
Telephone: 860-225-5111.
Website: http://www.stanleyworks.com
Chrmn & CEO: J.F. Lundgren

EVP & CFO: J.M. Loree
VP, Secy & General Counsel: B.H. Beatt
VP & CIO: H. Davis, Jr.
Investor Contact: G. Gould (860-827-3833)

Board of Directors: J. G. Breen, S. B. Brown, V. W. Colbert, E. A. Kampouris, E. S. Kraus, J. F. Lundgren, K. D. Wriston, L. A. Zimmerman

Founded: 1843
Domicile: Connecticut
Employees: 20,000

Staples Inc

STANDARD &POOR'S

S&P Recommendation HOLD ★★★★★

Price $25.77 (as of Oct 27, 2006)

12-Mo. Target Price $28.00

Investment Style Large-Cap Growth

GICS Sector Consumer Discretionary
Sub-Industry Specialty Stores

Comment This leading operator of office products superstores has about 1,800 units in the U.S. and internationally.

Key Stock Statistics (Source S&P, Vickers, company reports)

52-Wk Range	$27.71–21.08	S&P Oper. EPS 2007E	1.27	P/E on S&P Oper. EPS 2007E	20.3	Dividend Rate/Share	$0.22
Trailing 12-Month EPS	$1.21	S&P Oper. EPS 2008E	1.46	Common Shares Outstg. (M)	726.5	Yield (%)	0.85
Trailing 12-Month P/E	21.3	S&P Core EPS 2007E	1.27	Market Capitalization(B)	$18.722	Beta	1.42
$10K Invested 5 Yrs Ago	$25,441	S&P Core EPS 2008E	1.46	Institutional Ownership (%)	87	S&P Credit Rating	BBB

Price Performance

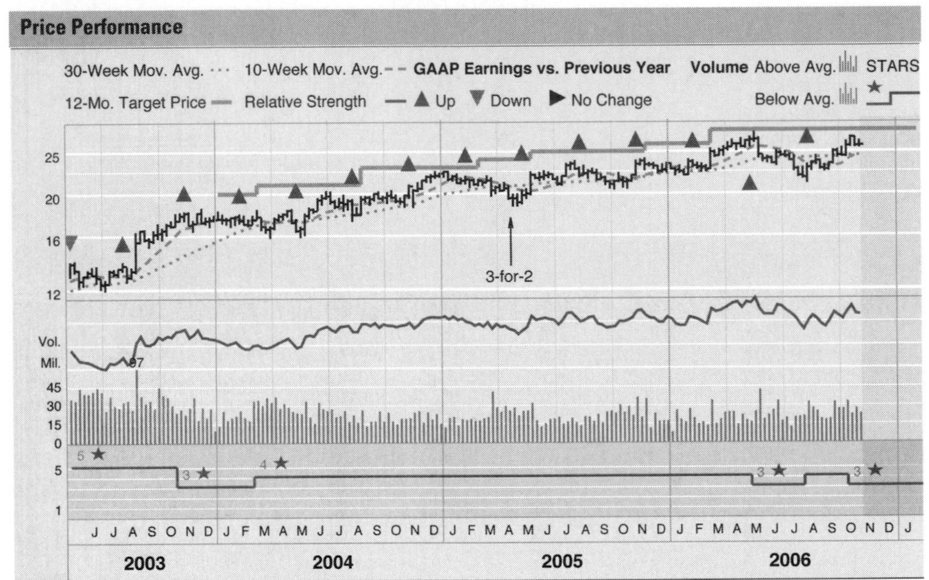

Options: ASE, CBOE, P, Ph

Analysis prepared by **Michael Souers** on October 13, 2006, when the stock traded at **$ 26.99**.

Highlights

- We project sales growth of between 10% and 11% in FY 07 (Jan.), following an 11% rise in FY 06. Sales growth should be achieved by account growth in the delivery business, continued international penetration, and about 100 store additions in North America. We see same-store sales gains of approximately 3%, on modest increases in customer traffic and average ticket.
- We think gross margins will widen on benefits from a growing private label business, supply chain initiatives, lower sourcing costs, and modest leverage from occupancy costs. We see operating margins widening slightly despite higher expected payroll-related expenses and the inclusion of stock options.
- We project slightly lower interest expense, taxes at an effective rate of 36.0%, and approximately 1% fewer shares outstanding. We estimate FY 07 EPS of $1.27, a 13% increase from the $1.12 the company earned in FY 06. We see $1.46 in FY 08. Our FY 07 EPS estimate includes an $0.08 charge for the expensing of projected stock options.

Investment Rationale/Risk

- We believe business spending trends and a solid job market bode well for SPLS. Recent performance in the North American Delivery division has been stellar, in our opinion, and we anticipate continued strong results throughout the remainder of the year. In addition, we think strong early results from new Chicago stores indicate further growth in untapped domestic metropolitan areas. Longer term, we believe China and South America provide SPLS with additional growth avenues. However, at over 18X our FY 08 EPS estimate, the shares recently traded at a significant premium to the S&P 500, though at a slight discount to its slower-growing key peer Office Depot (ODP: sell, $42).
- Risks to our recommendation and target price include a slowdown in economic growth and slower than expected capital spending and hiring by businesses. International risks include economic instability and unfavorable currency movements.
- Our 12-month target price of $28, about 19X our FY 08 EPS estimate, is also derived from our DCF model, which assumes a weighted average cost of capital of 10.0% and a terminal growth rate of 3.5%.

Qualitative Risk Assessment

LOW | **MEDIUM** | HIGH

Our risk assessment reflects the rather cyclical nature of the company, which relies on consumer as well as business spending, and investment in emerging markets for future growth, offset by untapped growth areas in major domestic metro markets.

Quantitative Evaluations

S&P Quality Ranking B+

D | C | B- | B | **B+** | A- | A | A+

Relative Strength Rank MODERATE

57

LOWEST = 1 HIGHEST = 99

Revenue/Earnings Data

Revenue (Million $)

	1Q	2Q	3Q	4Q	Year
2007	4,238	3,881	--	--	--
2006	3,899	3,472	4,246	4,462	16,079
2005	3,452	3,089	3,830	4,077	14,448
2004	3,147	2,869	3,485	3,681	13,181
2003	2,745	2,426	3,090	3,335	11,596
2002	2,667	2,314	2,834	2,929	10,744

Earnings Per Share ($)

2007	0.25	0.22	E0.36	E0.44	--
2006	0.20	0.20	0.32	0.39	1.12
2005	0.17	0.16	0.27	0.33	0.93
2004	0.03	0.12	0.22	0.28	0.66
2003	0.13	0.09	0.18	0.23	0.63
2002	0.06	0.06	0.13	0.13	0.42

Fiscal year ended Jan. 31. Next earnings report expected: Mid November. EPS Estimates based on S&P Operating Earnings; historical GAAP earnings are as reported.

Dividend Data (Dates: mm/dd Payment Date: mm/dd/yy)

Amount ($)	Date Decl.	Ex-Div. Date	Stk. of Record	Payment Date
0.220	02/28	03/29	03/31	04/20/06

Dividends have been paid since 2004. Source: Company reports.

Please read the Required Disclosures and Analyst Certification on the last page of this report.

Staples Inc

Business Summary October 13, 2006

CORPORATE OVERVIEW. Staples is the world's leading office products company, with net sales of nearly $16.1 billion in FY 06 (Jan.). Staples operates under three segments: North American Retail (56% of total revenues in FY 06); North American Delivery (31%); and International Operations (13%). Sales by product line were: office supplies and services 41%; business machines and related products 30%; computers and related products 22%; and office furniture 7%.

At January 28, 2006, SPLS operated 1,780 superstores, mostly in North America (1,522 stores), but also in five European countries: the U.K. (137), Germany (55), the Netherlands (44), Portugal (19) and Belgium (3).

SPLS has approximately 8,000 stock keeping units (SKUs) stocked in each of its typical North American retail stores and approximately 15,000 SKUs stocked in its North American Delivery fulfillment centers. On Staples.com, the company's Internet site, approximately 50,000 SKUs are available to customers.

CORPORATE STRATEGY. Staples seeks to maintain its leadership position in the office products industry by differentiating itself from the competition, delivering industry-best execution and expanding its market share. In FY 07, it plans to add 100 new stores in North America, filling in existing markets along with expansion into untapped metro markets. Staples entered Chicago in March 2005, and initial results exceeded expectations, according to the company. We believe significant growth opportunities remain in other metropolitan markets where SPLS has yet to venture, and expect the company to establish a strong Midwest presence over the next several years. SPLS also plans to open approximately 10 stores in Europe in FY 07.

South America and Asia potentially represent longer-term growth markets. In 2004, SPLS acquired Officenet S.A. to gain access to Brazil and Argentina. Also in 2004, the company entered China through a joint venture with a delivery business based in Shanghai, and it has expanded its presence by launching operations in Beijing. We view Staples' growth in emerging markets positively due to the size and potential of those markets.

Company Financials

Per Share Data ($) Year Ended Jan. 31	**2006**	**2005**	**2004**	**2003**	**2002**	**2001**	**2000**	**1999**	**1998**	**1997**
Tangible Book Value	3.84	3.45	3.01	1.74	2.63	2.19	1.99	2.18	1.46	1.24
Cash Flow	1.56	1.33	1.03	1.01	0.73	0.42	0.67	0.69	0.35	0.29
Earnings	1.12	0.93	0.66	0.63	0.42	0.10	0.45	0.27	0.23	0.19
S&P Core Earnings	1.05	0.88	0.61	0.58	0.32	0.21	NA	NA	NA	NA
Dividends	0.17	0.13	Nil	Nil	Nil	Nil	Nil	Nil	Nil	Nil
Payout Ratio	15%	14%	Nil	Nil	Nil	Nil	Nil	Nil	Nil	Nil
Calendar Year	2005	2004	2003	2002	2001	2000	1999	1998	1997	1996
Prices:High	24.14	22.57	18.58	14.97	12.97	19.17	23.96	20.53	8.93	6.70
Prices:Low	18.64	15.79	10.49	7.79	7.35	6.83	10.96	7.06	5.07	3.73
P/E Ratio:High	22	24	28	24	31	NM	54	76	39	35
P/E Ratio:Low	17	17	16	12	17	NM	25	26	22	20
Income Statement Analysis (Million $)										
Revenue	16,079	14,448	13,181	11,596	10,744	10,674	8,937	7,123	5,181	3,968
Operating Income	1,617	1,405	1,081	950	768	719	708	514	355	260
Depreciation	304	279	283	267	249	231	174	99.2	83.4	56.0
Interest Expense	56.8	39.9	20.2	20.6	27.2	45.2	17.1	17.4	23.1	20.1
Pretax Income	1,314	1,116	778	662	431	244	516	306	213	173
Effective Tax Rate	36.5%	36.5%	37.0%	32.6%	38.5%	75.5%	39.0%	39.5%	38.5%	38.5%
Net Income	834	708	490	446	265	59.7	315	185	131	106
S&P Core Earnings	784	667	450	413	221	147	NA	NA	NA	NA
Balance Sheet & Other Financial Data (Million $)										
Cash	978	997	457	596	395	264	110	358	355	106
Current Assets	4,145	3,782	3,479	2,717	2,403	2,356	2,192	2,064	1,666	1,151
Total Assets	7,677	7,071	6,503	5,721	4,093	3,989	3,814	3,179	2,455	1,788
Current Liabilities	2,480	2,197	2,123	2,175	1,596	1,711	1,455	1,265	941	603
Long Term Debt	528	558	567	732	350	441	501	205	509	391
Common Equity	4,425	4,115	3,663	2,659	2,054	1,764	1,829	1,657	967	762
Total Capital	4,963	4,696	4,230	3,441	2,411	2,205	2,330	1,862	1,476	1,153
Capital Expenditures	456	335	278	265	340	450	355	322	183	200
Cash Flow	1,138	987	773	713	514	291	489	285	214	162
Current Ratio	1.7	1.7	1.6	1.2	1.5	1.4	1.5	1.6	1.8	1.9
% Long Term Debt of Capitalization	10.6	11.9	13.4	21.3	14.5	20.0	21.5	11.0	34.5	33.9
% Net Income of Revenue	5.2	4.9	3.7	3.8	2.5	0.6	3.5	2.6	2.5	2.7
% Return on Assets	11.3	10.4	8.0	9.1	6.6	1.5	9.0	6.6	6.2	6.7
% Return on Equity	19.5	18.2	15.5	18.9	13.9	3.3	18.1	14.1	15.1	15.5

Data as orig reptd.; bef. results of disc opers/spec. items. Per share data adj. for stk. divs.; EPS diluted. E-Estimated. NA-Not Available. NM-Not Meaningful. NR-Not Ranked. UR-Under Review.

Office: Five Hundred Staples Dr, Framingham , MA 01702.
Telephone: 508-253-5000.
Email: investor@staples.com
Website: http://www.staples.com

Chrmn & CEO: R.L. Sargent
Pres & COO: M.A. Miles
Vice Chrmn & CFO: J.J. Mahoney
EVP, Secy & General Counsel: J.A. VanWoerkom

SVP & Cntlr: C.T. Komola
Investor Contact: L. Lefebvre (508-253-4080)
Board of Directors: B. L. Anderson, B. C. Barnes, A. M. Blank, M. E. Burton, G. L. Crittenden, R. J. Currie, G. J. Mitchell, R. T. Moriarty, R. C. Nakasone, R. L. Sargent, M. Trust, P. F. Walsh

Founded: 1985
Domicile: Delaware
Employees: 68,533

STANDARD &POOR'S

Starbucks Corp

S&P Recommendation HOLD ★★★★★	Price $38.02 (as of Oct 27, 2006)	12-Mo. Target Price $40.00	Investment Style Large-Cap Growth

GICS Sector Consumer Discretionary
Sub-Industry Restaurants

Comment SBUX purchases and roasts high-quality whole bean coffees, which it sells--together with fresh, rich-brewed coffees--primarily through the company's 12,400 retail stores.

Key Stock Statistics (Source S&P, Vickers, company reports)

52-Wk Range	$39.88–27.70	S&P Oper. EPS 2006E	0.74	P/E on S&P Oper. EPS 2006E	51.4	Dividend Rate/Share	Nil
Trailing 12-Month EPS	$0.72	S&P Oper. EPS 2007E	0.91	Common Shares Outstg. (M)	756.1	Yield (%)	Nil
Trailing 12-Month P/E	52.8	S&P Core EPS 2006E	0.78	Market Capitalization(B)	$28.746	Beta	0.61
$10K Invested 5 Yrs Ago	$42,576	S&P Core EPS 2007E	0.91	Institutional Ownership (%)	72	S&P Credit Rating	NA

Price Performance

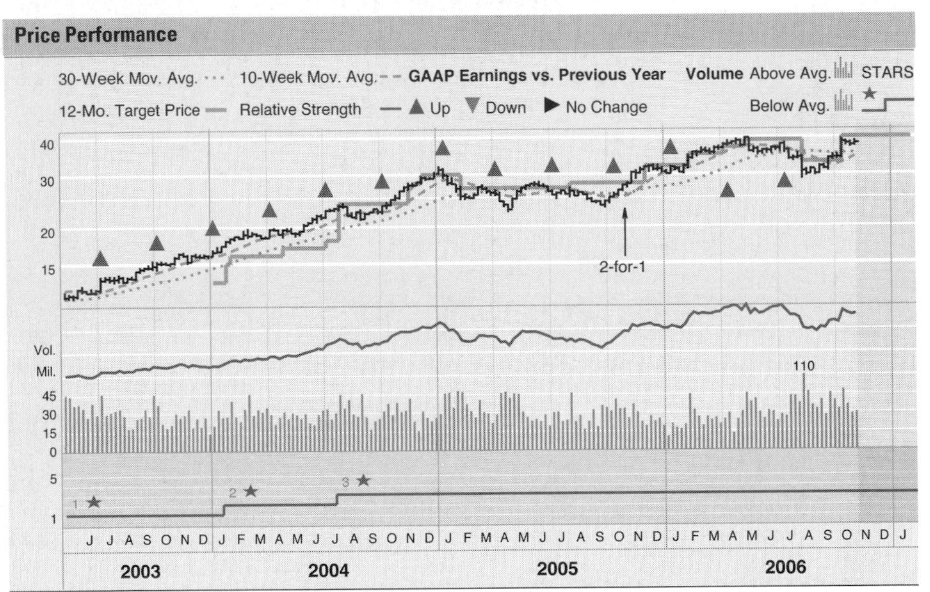

Options: ASE, CBOE, P, Ph

Analysis prepared by **Dennis P. Milton** on October 09, 2006, when the stock traded at **$ 38.35**.

Highlights

- SBUX plans to add at least 2,000 retail units annually for the next several years as it expands operations worldwide, and has a long-term global target of 40,000 locations. It anticipates annual revenue growth of 20%, with EPS gains of 20% to 25%, over the next three years. In FY 06 (Sep.), SBUX opened nearly 2,000 new stores, with more than 1,530 openings in the U.S. and another 660 internationally.
- We expect retail revenues to increase about 23% in FY 07, due to expansion and average unit growth of about 4.0%. We see specialty revenues growing about 20%, primarily due to increased royalty revenues and a further significant increase in licensee stores.
- Our FY 07 EPS estimate is $0.91, versus our FY 06 EPS estimate of $0.74. We believe operating margins will narrow slightly, primarily due to higher labor and coffee costs, and expenses related to what we view as the company's aggressive expansion, partly offset by the leverage of a larger sales base over fixed costs. We expect results to benefit from share repurchases.

Investment Rationale/Risk

- At 50X our calendar 2006 EPS estimate of $0.77, the shares recently traded at a significant premium to industry peers and the S&P 500, but in line with the company's historical valuation. We believe this valuation is appropriate, given what we view as SBUX's strong growth prospects, its demonstrated ability to achieve impressive same-store sales growth and, more recently, its significant operating margin expansion. We expect expansion to fuel revenue growth at a compound annual growth rate (CAGR) of 20% over the next several years.
- Risks to our opinion and target price include a potentially negative impact on customer traffic from price increases, a lack of customer acceptance of the company's food initiatives, and the possibility that aggressive expansion in the U.S. will increase cannibalization rates.
- Our 12-month target price of $40 applies a P/E multiple of 41X--below the share's historical range due to brand maturation--to our calendar 2007 EPS estimate of $0.97. We believe investors will continue to reward what we view as the company's strong sales execution, despite a significant valuation premium to peers.

Qualitative Risk Assessment

LOW | MEDIUM | **HIGH**

Our risk assessment reflects SBUX's relatively high P/E multiple, which we believe suggests that much of the company's value rests on its growth prospects. Failure to properly execute its expansion program could have a significant impact on the share price, in our view. This is partially offset as the company has only $205 million in debt, and nearly $500 million in cash and marketable securities, resulting in a strong balance sheet, in our opinion.

Quantitative Evaluations

S&P Quality Ranking **B+**

D | C | B- | B | **B+** | A- | A | A+

Relative Strength Rank **STRONG**

79

LOWEST = 1 HIGHEST = 99

Revenue/Earnings Data

Revenue (Million $)

	1Q	2Q	3Q	4Q	Year
2006	1,934	1,886	1,964	--	--
2005	1,590	1,519	1,602	1,659	6,369
2004	1,281	1,241	1,319	1,453	5,294
2003	1,004	954.2	1,037	1,081	4,076
2002	805.3	783.2	835.2	865.2	3,289
2001	667.4	629.3	662.8	689.5	2,649

Earnings Per Share ($)

2006	0.22	0.16	0.18	**E**0.19	**E**0.74
2005	0.17	0.12	0.16	0.16	0.61
2004	0.14	0.10	0.12	0.13	0.48
2003	0.10	0.07	0.09	0.09	0.34
2002	0.09	0.04	0.07	0.08	0.27
2001	0.06	0.04	0.06	0.07	0.23

Fiscal year ended Sep. 30. Next earnings report expected: Mid November. EPS Estimates based on S&P Operating Earnings; historical GAAP earnings are as reported.

Dividend Data

No Dividend Data Available

Starbucks Corp

Business Summary October 09, 2006

Starbucks Corp.'s rapid growth in retail outlets throughout the U.S. has made its name synonymous with specialty coffee. A caffeine-fueled expansion has brought the number of Starbucks retail stores to 12,440 at October 1, 2006, from 165 stores at the end of FY 92 (Sep.). Company revenues grew 22% in FY 06, to nearly $6.4 billion, and have posted a CAGR of about 28% over the past five years.

The company's objective is to rapidly expand its retail operations, expand its specialty operations, and selectively pursue new product introduction and the development of new channels of distribution.

Retail stores accounted for 85% of FY 05 net sales (latest available, up from 84% in FY 04). Stores are typically clustered in high-traffic, high-visibility locations in each market. They are located in office buildings, downtown and suburban retail centers, and kiosks placed in building lobbies, airport terminals and supermarkets. In FY 05, the retail store sales mix by product type was 77% beverages, 15% food items, 4% whole bean coffees, and 4% coffee-related hardware items. The company is currently expanding its food menu at many of its U.S. retail locations.

SBUX seeks to expand its retail business by increasing its share in existing markets and opening stores in new markets in which it sees an opportunity to become the leading specialty coffee retailer. It opened a total of 1,040 company-owned stores in FY 06, and plans to open a similar number in FY 07. At October 1, 2006, SBUX operated 5,668 stores in the U.S., and 1,434 stores in international markets including Canada, the U.K., Germany, Australia, and China.

Specialty operations, which accounted for 15% of total revenues in FY 05 (16% in FY 04), aims to develop the Starbucks brand outside the company-owned retail store environment through a number of channels. SBUX has licensing agreements (69% of specialty revenues in FY 05, 68% in FY 04) with prominent retailers in North America, Central America, Europe, the Middle East, Africa and Asia. As of October 1, 2006, there were 5,338 licensed retail stores worldwide.

Company Financials

Per Share Data ($) Year Ended Sep. 30	**2005**	**2004**	**2003**	**2002**	**2001**	**2000**	**1999**	**1998**	**1997**	**1996**
Tangible Book Value	2.56	3.00	2.52	2.20	1.78	1.50	1.29	1.11	0.84	0.73
Cash Flow	1.06	0.85	0.66	0.55	0.45	0.48	0.28	0.20	0.18	0.13
Earnings	0.61	0.48	0.34	0.27	0.23	0.12	0.14	0.09	0.09	0.07
S&P Core Earnings	0.53	0.42	0.29	0.23	0.18	NA	NA	NA	NA	NA
Dividends	Nil	Nil	Nil	Nil	Nil	Nil	Nil	Nil	Nil	Nil
Payout Ratio	Nil	Nil	Nil	Nil	Nil	Nil	Nil	Nil	Nil	Nil
Prices:High	32.40	32.13	10.72	12.85	12.83	12.70	10.25	7.49	5.59	5.03
Prices:Low	22.29	16.45	9.81	9.22	6.73	5.78	4.97	3.59	3.27	1.81
P/E Ratio:High	53	68	50	48	56	NM	76	80	64	75
P/E Ratio:Low	37	35	29	34	29	NM	37	38	37	27

Income Statement Analysis (Million $)	2005	2004	2003	2002	2001	2000	1999	1998	1997	1996
Revenue	6,369	5,294	4,076	3,289	2,649	2,169	1,680	1,309	967	696
Operating Income	1,071	854	646	504	430	334	264	199	146	96.4
Depreciation	367	305	259	221	177	142	108	80.9	58.2	39.4
Interest Expense	Nil	Nil	Nil	Nil	Nil	Nil	1.36	1.38	7.27	8.70
Pretax Income	796	624	436	341	289	161	164	116	93.3	68.5
Effective Tax Rate	37.9%	37.2%	38.5%	37.0%	37.3%	41.1%	38.0%	41.2%	38.5%	38.5%
Net Income	494	392	268	215	181	94.6	102	68.4	57.4	42.1
S&P Core Earnings	437	346	231	181	143	NA	NA	NA	NA	NA

Balance Sheet & Other Financial Data (Million $)	2005	2004	2003	2002	2001	2000	1999	1998	1997	1996
Cash	174	299	201	175	113	70.8	66.4	102	70.1	126
Current Assets	1,209	1,368	924	848	594	460	387	337	317	340
Total Assets	3,514	3,328	2,730	2,293	1,851	1,493	1,253	993	851	727
Current Liabilities	1,227	783	609	537	445	313	252	179	139	101
Long Term Debt	2.87	3.62	4.35	5.08	5.79	6.48	7.02	Nil	167	167
Common Equity	2,091	2,487	2,082	1,727	1,376	1,148	961	794	532	452
Total Capital	2,094	2,537	2,120	1,754	1,406	1,180	1,001	813	712	626
Capital Expenditures	644	386	357	375	384	316	262	202	170	162
Cash Flow	862	697	528	436	358	367	209	149	116	81.5
Current Ratio	1.0	1.7	1.5	1.6	1.3	1.5	1.5	1.9	2.3	3.4
% Long Term Debt of Capitalization	0.1	0.1	0.2	0.3	0.4	0.5	0.7	Nil	23.4	26.6
% Net Income of Revenue	7.8	7.4	6.6	6.5	6.8	4.4	6.1	5.2	5.9	6.0
% Return on Assets	14.3	12.9	10.9	10.4	10.8	6.9	9.1	7.4	7.3	7.1
% Return on Equity	21.7	17.1	14.1	13.9	14.4	9.0	11.6	10.3	11.7	11.0

Data as orig reptd.; bef. results of disc opers/spec. items. Per share data adj. for stk. divs.; EPS diluted. E-Estimated. NA-Not Available. NM-Not Meaningful. NR-Not Ranked. UR-Under Review.

Office: 2401 Utah Avenue South, Seattle, WA 98134.
Telephone: 206-447-1575.
Email: investorrelations@starbucks.com
Website: http://www.starbucks.com

Chrmn: H. Schultz
Pres & CEO: O.C. Smith
EVP, CFO & Chief Admin: M. Casey
EVP, Secy & General Counsel: P.E. Boggs

CIO: B. Crynes
Auditor: Deloitte & Touche
Board of Directors: B. Bass, H. P. Behar, W. W. Bradley, J. Donald, M. Hobson, O. Lee, G. B. Maffei, H. Schultz, J. G. Shennan, Jr., J. G. Teruel, M. E. Ullman, III, C. E. Weatherup

Founded: 1985
Domicile: Washington
Employees: 115,000

STANDARD &POOR'S

Starwood Hotels & Resorts Worldwide Inc.

S&P Recommendation HOLD ★★★★★

Price $59.47 (as of Oct 27, 2006)

12-Mo. Target Price $62.00

Investment Style Large-Cap Growth

GICS Sector Consumer Discretionary
Sub-Industry Hotels, Resorts & Cruise Lines

Comment Starwood is one of the world's largest lodging companies, with more than 850 hotels, including the Sheraton, Westin, St. Regis, W, and Four Points by Sheraton brands.

Key Stock Statistics (Source S&P, Vickers, company reports)

52-Wk Range	$68.87–49.68	S&P Oper. EPS 2006E	2.60	P/E on S&P Oper. EPS 2006E	22.9	Dividend Rate/Share	$0.84
Trailing 12-Month EPS	$4.44	S&P Oper. EPS 2007E	2.48	Common Shares Outstg. (M)	217.8	Yield (%)	1.41
Trailing 12-Month P/E	13.4	S&P Core EPS 2006E	2.60	Market Capitalization(B)	$12.953	Beta	1.44
$10K Invested 5 Yrs Ago	$35,489	S&P Core EPS 2007E	2.48	Institutional Ownership (%)	93	S&P Credit Rating	BBB-

Price Performance

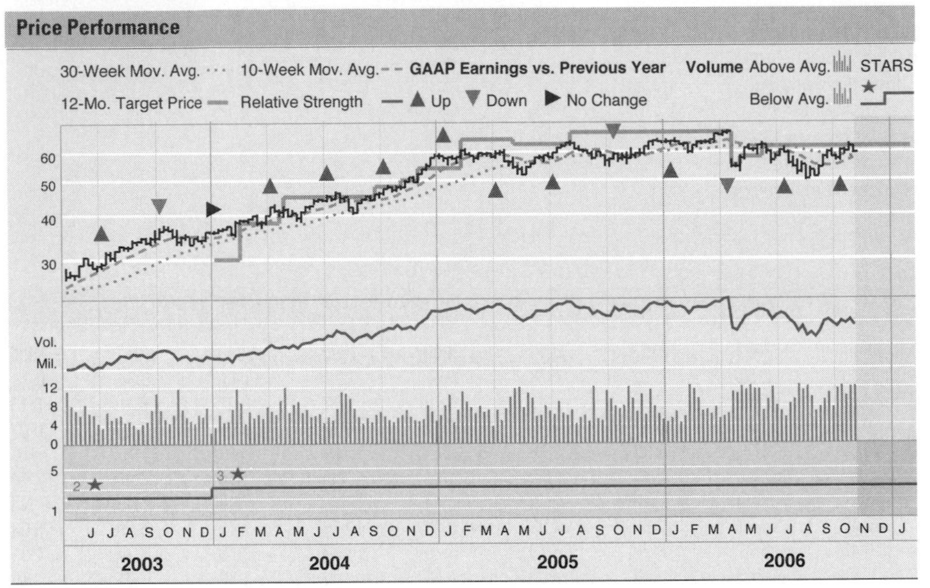

Options: CBOE, Ph

Analysis prepared by **Tom Graves, CFA** on September 27, 2006, when the stock traded at **$ 57.52**.

Highlights

- In 2006's second quarter, HOT sold 33 hotels to Host Hotels & Resorts (HST: hold, $23) or an affiliate. The multi-phase transaction was valued at about $4.1 billion, including debt assumption. Of this, a distribution of Host common stock valued at $2.68 billion, plus $119 million of cash, was paid directly to HOT shareholders. Based on Host's stock price in early April, we value this distribution at about $13 per HOT share. The remaining consideration from the asset sale, which was paid to HOT, included $1.2 billion of cash, $77 million of debt assumption, and Host common stock valued at $61 million.
- Before some special items, we estimate 2006 EPS of $2.40, versus $2.34 in 2005. Our 2006 estimate includes projected dilution from asset sales to Host Hotels & Resorts or an affiliate, and a distribution of much of the proceeds to HOT shareholders. Our estimate includes a $0.13 impact from initiation of stock option expensing. For 2007, we estimate EPS of $2.60.
- Year to date, through July 26, 2006, HOT repurchased about 13.2 million of its shares at a total cost of about $810 million. Authorization for about $833 million of stock repurchase remained.

Investment Rationale/Risk

- Our hold recommendation reflects our belief that the stock will benefit from expectations of a further hotel industry upturn, profit growth, and cash generation. We expect that the stock will receive at least near-term support from the prospect that there will be further share repurchases by the company. In addition, even if HOT's acquisition of assets related to the Le Meridien hotel business results in some transition costs (excluded from our 2006 EPS estimate), we believe that the acquisition will enhance longer-term growth prospects for Starwood.
- Risks to our recommendation and target price include the possibility that terrorism fears could heighten further, leading to lower than expected demand for hotel rooms.
- Based on our 2006 EPS estimates, the stock is trading at a sharp P/E premium to the S&P 500. However, we expect the stock to be bolstered by expectations of improving hotel industry fundamentals, asset sales, a distribution to shareholders, and share repurchases. Our 12-month target price of $62 reflects a premium-to-peers 24X P/E multiple of our 2007 EPS estimate.

Qualitative Risk Assessment

LOW | **MEDIUM** | HIGH

In our view, Starwood's recent divestiture of various hotels has moved the company's business mix more toward management and franchising of hotels, with less emphasis on real estate ownership. We view the company's operations as being sensitive to macroeconomic conditions. However, over the long term, we expect the company to generate a sizable amount of cash flow, some of which we expect will be used for growth initiatives, payment of dividends, and possibly stock repurchases.

Quantitative Evaluations

S&P Quality Ranking NR

D | C | B- | B | B+ | A- | A | A+

Relative Strength Rank MODERATE

47

LOWEST = 1 HIGHEST = 99

Revenue/Earnings Data

Revenue (Million $)

	1Q	2Q	3Q	4Q	Year
2006	1,441	1,505	1,461	--	--
2005	1,406	1,559	1,496	1,516	5,977
2004	1,227	1,363	1,336	1,442	5,368
2003	1,073	1,220	1,140	1,197	4,630
2002	1,096	1,232	1,157	1,174	4,659
2001	1,014	1,110	965.0	878.0	3,967

Earnings Per Share ($)

2006	0.34	3.01	0.71	E0.74	E2.60
2005	0.36	0.65	0.18	0.72	1.88
2004	0.16	0.56	0.49	0.51	1.72
2003	-0.58	0.42	0.23	0.42	0.51
2002	0.16	0.37	0.26	0.42	1.20
2001	0.30	0.55	0.14	-0.28	0.73

Fiscal year ended Dec. 31. Next earnings report expected: Early February. EPS Estimates based on S&P Operating Earnings; historical GAAP earnings are as reported.

Dividend Data (Dates: mm/dd Payment Date: mm/dd/yy)

Amount ($)	Date Decl.	Ex-Div. Date	Stk. of Record	Payment Date
0.840	12/20	12/28	12/31	01/20/06
0.210	02/21	02/24	02/28	03/10/06
0.210	03/16	03/23	03/27	04/07/06

Dividends have been paid since 1995. Source: Company reports.

Starwood Hotels & Resorts Worldwide Inc.

Business Summary September 27, 2006

CORPORATE OVERVIEW. Starwood Hotels is one of the world's largest hotel companies, with owned, leased, managed or franchised hotels in more than 95 countries. At June 30, 2006, the company's business included 851 hotels, with 261,191 rooms. Also, including an unconsolidated joint venture, HOT had 15 vacation ownership resorts in operation. Some of these resorts, plus some additional HOT-related resorts were actively selling inventory.

HOT's business includes owned, managed and franchised properties. Its brands include St. Regis (luxury full-service hotels and resorts), The Luxury Collection (luxury full-service hotels and resorts), Westin (luxury and upscale full-service hotels and resorts), Sheraton (full-service hotels and resorts), W (boutique full-service urban hotels), and Four Points (moderately priced full-service hotels). At June 30, 2006, the company's hotel business included 391 Sheratons (134,837 rooms), 123 Westins (52,176 rooms), 57 properties (9,097 rooms) in the St. Regis or Luxury Collection groups, 124 Four Points (21,755 rooms), 20 hotels (5,942 rooms) in the W chain, 122 Le Meridien (31,597 rooms), and 14 other hotels (5,787 rooms).

CORPORATE STRATEGY. In our view, HOT has moved toward placing more of an emphasis on managing and franchising hotels, with less of an emphasis on hotel ownership. As of June 30, 2006, HOT owned (at least a majority interest) or leased, 91 hotels, down from 137 such properties one year earlier. Meanwhile, HOT's number of managed and/or unconsolidated joint venture hotels had increased to 413 properties, from 272, with some of the increase coming from HOT's November 2005 acquisition of the Le Meridien management business, and from HOT continuing to manage various hotels that it has sold. Also, as of June 30, 2006, HOT had 347 franchised hotels, up from 319 one year earlier.

We expect some further asset sales by HOT, but we also believe that the company may acquire some properties with such objectives as hotel redevelopment or rebranding.

We expect that HOT's efforts to expand its hotel system will include the development of a new hotel concept called aloft and a Westin extended-stay hotel concept.

Company Financials

Per Share Data ($) Year Ended Dec. 31	**2005**	**2004**	**2003**	**2002**	**2001**	**2000**	**1999**	**1998**	**1997**	**1996**
Tangible Book Value	13.59	10.73	4.55	3.57	2.35	2.50	2.16	1.43	NA	NA
Cash Flow	3.69	3.72	2.58	2.28	3.29	4.30	-0.86	3.73	NA	NA
Earnings	1.88	1.72	0.51	1.20	0.73	1.96	-3.41	0.67	NA	NA
S&P Core Earnings	1.66	1.37	0.12	0.77	0.52	NA	NA	NA	NA	NA
Dividends	0.84	0.84	0.84	0.84	0.80	0.69	0.60	2.04	NA	NA
Payout Ratio	45%	49%	165%	70%	110%	35%	NM	NM	NA	NA
Prices:High	65.22	59.50	37.60	39.94	40.89	37.50	37.75	57.88	61.50	36.92
Prices:Low	51.50	34.81	21.68	19.00	17.10	19.75	19.50	18.75	33.50	19.67
P/E Ratio:High	35	35	74	33	56	19	NM	86	NA	NA
P/E Ratio:Low	27	20	43	16	23	10	NM	28	NA	NA

Income Statement Analysis (Million $)	2005	2004	2003	2002	2001	2000	1999	1998	1997	1996
Revenue	5,977	5,368	4,630	4,659	3,967	4,345	3,862	4,710	NA	NA
Operating Income	1,242	1,047	1,698	1,856	1,191	1,509	1,329	1,361	NA	NA
Depreciation	407	431	429	222	526	481	476	556	NA	NA
Interest Expense	258	257	287	338	369	439	516	639	NA	NA
Pretax Income	642	412	-5.00	252	200	610	533	43.0	NA	NA
Effective Tax Rate	34.1%	10.4%	NM	1.59%	23.0%	33.0%	NM	NM	NA	NA
Net Income	423	369	105	246	151	401	-638	141	NA	NA
S&P Core Earnings	376	291	27.7	157	107	NA	NA	NA	NA	NA

Balance Sheet & Other Financial Data (Million $)	2005	2004	2003	2002	2001	2000	1999	1998	1997	1996
Cash	897	326	508	216	157	189	436	290	NA	NA
Current Assets	2,283	1,683	1,245	950	897	1,048	1,176	1,077	NA	NA
Total Assets	12,454	12,298	11,894	12,259	12,461	12,660	12,923	16,101	NA	NA
Current Liabilities	2,879	2,128	1,644	2,199	1,587	1,805	2,303	2,074	NA	NA
Long Term Debt	2,926	3,823	4,393	4,449	5,269	5,074	4,779	8,111	NA	NA
Common Equity	5,211	4,788	4,326	6,357	3,756	3,851	3,690	4,202	NA	NA
Total Capital	8,724	9,518	9,676	11,882	10,380	10,417	10,167	13,580	NA	NA
Capital Expenditures	464	333	307	82.0	477	544	521	832	NA	NA
Cash Flow	830	800	534	468	677	882	-162	697	NA	NA
Current Ratio	0.8	0.8	0.8	0.4	0.6	0.6	0.5	0.5	NA	NA
% Long Term Debt of Capitalization	33.5	40.2	45.4	37.4	50.8	48.7	47.0	59.7	NA	NA
% Net Income of Revenue	7.1	6.9	NM	5.3	3.8	9.2	NM	3.0	NA	NA
% Return on Assets	3.4	3.1	NM	2.0	1.2	3.1	NM	NA	NA	NA
% Return on Equity	8.5	8.1	NM	3.9	4.0	10.6	NM	NA	NA	NA

Data as orig reptd.; bef. results of disc opers/spec. items. Per share data adj. for stk. divs.; EPS diluted. E-Estimated. NA-Not Available. NM-Not Meaningful. NR-Not Ranked. UR-Under Review.

Office: 1111 Westchester Avenue, White Plains, NY 10604.
Telephone: 914-640-8100.
Website: http://www.starwoodhotels.com
Chrmn: B.W. Duncan

CEO: S.J. Heyer
EVP & CFO: V.M. Prabhu
EVP & CTO: T. Conophy
EVP, Secy & General Counsel: K.S. Siegal

Investor Contact: F.D. Gibson (914-640-8100)
Board of Directors: A. M. Aron, C. Barshefsky, J. Chapus, B. W. Duncan, L. Galbreath, S. J. Heyer, E. Hippeau, S. R. Quazzo, T. O. Ryder, D. W. Yih, K. C. Youngblood

Founded: 1969
Domicile: Maryland
Employees: 145,000

State Street Corp

S&P Recommendation HOLD ★★★★★ | **Price** $63.01 (as of Oct 27, 2006) | **12-Mo. Target Price** $66.00 | **Investment Style** Large-Cap Growth

GICS Sector Financials
Sub-Industry Asset Management & Custody Banks

Comment This bank holding company, with about $11 trillion in assets under custody, is a leading servicer of financial assets worldwide.

Key Stock Statistics (Source S&P, Vickers, company reports)

52-Wk Range	$66.47–54.39	S&P Oper. EPS 2006E	3.39	P/E on S&P Oper. EPS 2006E	18.6	Dividend Rate/Share	$0.80
Trailing 12-Month EPS	$3.12	S&P Oper. EPS 2007E	3.70	Common Shares Outstg. (M)	331.1	Yield (%)	1.27
Trailing 12-Month P/E	20.2	S&P Core EPS 2006E	3.38	Market Capitalization(B)	$20.865	Beta	1.25
$10K Invested 5 Yrs Ago	$14,195	S&P Core EPS 2007E	3.69	Institutional Ownership (%)	80	S&P Credit Rating	AA-

Price Performance

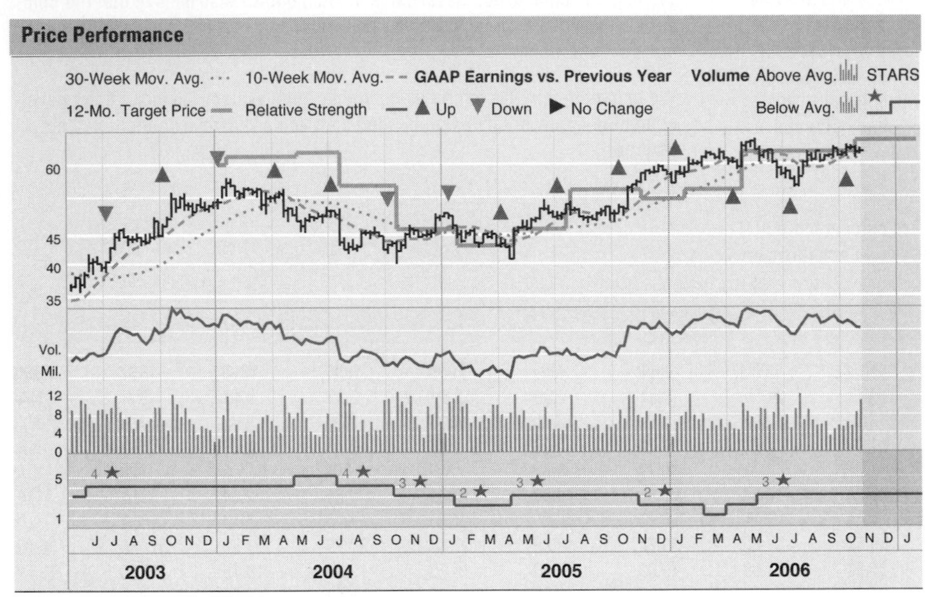

Options: Ph

Analysis prepared by **Mark Hebeka, CFA** on October 25, 2006, when the stock traded at **$ 62.66**.

Highlights

- We believe that long-term macro trends affecting STT remain intact, including outsourcing of custody services, growth of worldwide pension systems, development of more complex investment vehicles, consolidation among financial processing providers, and increasing pressure on public retirement systems. We believe the company's long-term reserve growth prospects are positive, based on our assumptions regarding economic conditions and equity market stability, combined with what we view as STT's success in gaining new assets both in the U.S. and internationally from existing and new clients in recent quarters.
- We remain confident in management's ability to better align operating expenses with its market-sensitive revenue model in a challenging interest rate environment through 2007.
- We project operating EPS of $3.39 in 2006 and $3.70 in 2007, up from $2.82 reported for 2005, assuming a healthy and stable economy.

Investment Rationale/Risk

- We have a hold recommendation on the shares, based on valuation. In our view, the shares are fairly valued relative to those of asset management and custody bank peers. While we do not believe cost-cutting initiatives are hurting longer term growth prospects, we continue to monitor spending levels needed to sustain growth.
- Risks to our recommendation and target price include a significant slowdown in capital markets; a longer-than-anticipated period of short-term interest rate increases; unexpected decreases in the pricing of the company's service offerings; and slower-than-expected implementation of announced cost-cutting initiatives.
- Our 12-month target price is $66, or approximately 18X our 2007 EPS estimate, a slight premium to peers. We believe this multiple is appropriate based on our view of the company's short-term operating outlook and the progress it has reported in reducing its expenses.

Qualitative Risk Assessment

LOW	MEDIUM	HIGH

Our risk assessment reflects our view of solid fundamentals coupled with a strong customer base and good diversification. We believe STT has a well established business and has maintained healthy earnings growth.

Quantitative Evaluations

S&P Quality Ranking A

D	C	B-	B	B+	A-	**A**	A+

Relative Strength Rank MODERATE

40

LOWEST = 1 HIGHEST = 99

Revenue/Earnings Data

Revenue (Million $)

	1Q	2Q	3Q	4Q	Year
2006	2,218	2,423	2,349	--	--
2005	1,699	1,837	1,925	2,035	7,496
2004	1,400	1,469	1,424	1,604	5,897
2003	1,213	1,290	1,287	1,673	5,463
2002	1,225	1,265	1,208	1,697	5,395
2001	1,491	1,463	1,413	1,270	5,637

Earnings Per Share ($)

	1Q	2Q	3Q	4Q	Year
2006	0.84	0.68	0.83	**E**0.83	**E**3.39
2005	0.67	0.66	0.75	0.74	2.82
2004	0.63	0.65	0.52	0.55	2.35
2003	0.29	-0.07	0.60	1.33	2.15
2002	0.54	0.54	0.56	1.46	3.10
2001	0.37	0.50	0.51	0.52	1.90

Fiscal year ended Dec. 31. Next earnings report expected: Mid January. EPS Estimates based on S&P Operating Earnings; historical GAAP earnings are as reported.

Dividend Data (Dates: mm/dd Payment Date: mm/dd/yy)

Amount ($)	Date Decl.	Ex-Div. Date	Stk. of Record	Payment Date
0.190	12/15	12/29	01/03	01/17/06
0.190	03/16	03/30	04/03	04/17/06
0.200	06/15	06/29	07/03	07/17/06
0.200	09/20	09/28	10/02	10/16/06

Dividends have been paid since 1910. Source: Company reports.

State Street Corp

Business Summary October 25, 2006

CORPORATE OVERVIEW: STT is a leading specialist in meeting the needs of institutional investors worldwide. Its customers include mutual funds and other collective investment funds, corporate and public pension funds, investment managers, and others. STT operates in the U.S., Australia, Austria, Belgium, Canada, Cayman Islands, Chile, France, Germany, India, Ireland, Italy, Japan, Luxembourg, Mauritius, Netherlands, New Zealand, China, Singapore, South Africa, South Korea, Switzerland, Taiwan, Thailand, United Arab Emirates and the United Kingdom.

STT reports two lines of business: Investment Servicing and Investment Management. Investment Servicing provides services for mutual funds and collective investment funds, corporate and public retirement plans, insurance companies, foundations, endowments, and other investment pools worldwide. Products include custody, product- and participant-level accounting, daily pricing and administration; master trust and master custody, recordkeeping; foreign exchange, brokerage and other trading services; securities finance; deposit and short-term investment facilities; loans and lease financing; investment manager and hedge fund manager operations outsourcing; and performance, risk and compliance analytics to support institutional investors.

Investment Management offers a broad array of services for managing financial assets, including investment management and investment research services, primarily for institutional investors worldwide. These services include passive and active U.S. and non-U.S. equity and fixed income strategies, and other related services, such as securities finance.

Company Financials

Per Share Data ($) Year Ended Dec. 31	**2005**	**2004**	**2003**	**2002**	**2001**	**2000**	**1999**	**1998**	**1997**	**1996**
Tangible Book Value	13.73	12.49	11.66	12.92	11.87	10.13	8.31	7.19	6.20	5.47
Earnings	2.82	2.35	2.15	3.10	1.90	1.82	1.89	1.33	1.16	0.90
S&P Core Earnings	2.80	2.30	1.41	2.01	1.83	NA	NA	NA	NA	NA
Dividends	0.72	0.64	0.56	0.48	0.41	0.35	0.29	0.25	0.22	0.19
Payout Ratio	26%	27%	26%	15%	21%	19%	15%	19%	19%	21%
Prices:High	59.80	56.90	53.63	58.36	63.93	68.40	47.63	37.16	31.84	17.13
Prices:Low	40.62	39.91	30.37	32.11	36.25	31.22	27.75	23.94	15.66	10.44
P/E Ratio:High	21	24	25	19	34	38	25	28	27	19
P/E Ratio:Low	14	17	14	10	19	17	15	18	13	12

Income Statement Analysis (Million $)	2005	2004	2003	2002	2001	2000	1999	1998	1997	1996
Net Interest Income	907	859	810	979	1,025	894	781	745	641	551
Tax Equivalent Adjustment	42.0	45.0	51.0	61.0	67.0	65.0	40.0	40.0	44.0	37.0
Non Interest Income	4,566	4,074	3,925	3,421	2,782	2,665	2,255	1,997	1,673	1,292
Loan Loss Provision	Nil	-18.0	Nil	4.00	10.0	9.00	80.0	17.0	16.0	8.00
% Expense/Operating Revenue	73.8%	76.2%	76.5%	64.6%	75.3%	74.3%	76.9%	75.4%	73.5%	74.4%
Pretax Income	1,432	1,192	1,112	1,555	930	906	968	657	564	447
Effective Tax Rate	34.0%	33.1%	35.1%	34.7%	32.5%	34.3%	36.1%	33.6%	32.6%	34.5%
Net Income	945	798	722	1,015	628	595	619	436	380	293
% Net Interest Margin	1.08	1.08	1.17	1.42	1.66	1.66	1.66	1.90	2.18	2.23
S&P Core Earnings	939	782	473	658	604	NA	NA	NA	NA	NA

Balance Sheet & Other Financial Data (Million $)	2005	2004	2003	2002	2001	2000	1999	1998	1997	1996
Money Market Assets	12,039	26,829	31,694	46,342	37,991	44,083	35,616	26,399	16,450	16,952
Investment Securities	59,870	37,571	38,215	28,071	20,781	13,740	14,703	9,737	10,375	9,387
Commercial Loans	4,152	2,352	2,768	2,052	3,289	3,476	2,326	4,721	3,919	3,701
Other Loans	2,312	2,277	2,253	2,122	2,052	1,797	1,967	1,588	1,643	1,012
Total Assets	97,968	94,040	87,534	85,794	69,896	69,298	60,896	47,082	37,975	36,524
Demand Deposits	9,402	13,671	7,893	7,279	9,390	10,009	8,943	8,386	7,785	6,395
Time Deposits	50,244	41,458	39,623	38,189	29,169	27,928	25,202	19,153	17,093	13,124
Long Term Debt	2,659	2,458	2,222	1,270	1,217	1,219	921	922	774	511
Common Equity	6,367	6,159	5,747	4,787	3,845	3,262	2,652	2,311	1,995	1,775
% Return on Assets	1.0	0.9	0.8	1.3	0.9	0.9	1.1	1.0	1.1	1.1
% Return on Equity	15.1	13.4	13.7	23.5	17.7	20.1	24.9	20.3	20.2	17.5
% Loan Loss Reserve	0.3	0.4	1.2	1.5	1.1	1.1	1.1	1.3	1.5	1.6
% Loans/Deposits	10.9	8.4	10.6	9.2	13.9	13.9	12.6	22.9	22.4	24.2
% Equity to Assets	6.5	6.6	6.1	5.5	5.1	4.5	4.6	5.1	5.4	5.9

Data as orig reptd.; bef. results of disc opers/spec. items. Per share data adj. for stk. divs.; EPS diluted. E-Estimated. NA-Not Available. NM-Not Meaningful. NR-Not Ranked. UR-Under Review.

Office: 1 Lincoln St, Boston, MA 02111-2901.
Telephone: 617-786-3000.
Email: ir@statestreet.com
Website: http://www.statestreet.com

Chrmn & CEO: R.E. Logue
EVP & CFO: E.J. Resch
EVP & Treas: E.J. O'Brien
EVP, Secy & General Counsel: C.C. Cutrell, III

EVP & Chief Lgl Officer: J.N. Carp
Investor Contact: S.K. MacDonald (617-664-2888)
Board of Directors: T. E. Albright, K. F. Burnes, N. F. Darehshori, A. L. Goldstein, D. P. Gruber, L. A. Hill, C. R. LaMantia, R. E. Logue, R. P. Sergel, R. L. Skates, G. L. Summe, D. C. Walsh, R. E. Weissman

Founded: 1832
Domicile: Massachusetts
Employees: 21,375

STANDARD &POOR'S

Stryker Corp

S&P Recommendation STRONG BUY ★★★★★

Price $52.65 (as of Oct 27, 2006)

12-Mo. Target Price $65.00

Investment Style Large-Cap Growth

GICS Sector Health Care
Sub-Industry Health Care Equipment

Comment SYK makes specialty surgical and medical products such as orthopedic implants, endoscopic items, and hospital beds, and operates a chain of physical therapy clinics.

Key Stock Statistics (Source S&P, Vickers, company reports)

52-Wk Range	**$54.35–39.77**	S&P Oper. EPS 2006**E**	**2.02**	P/E on S&P Oper. EPS 2006**E**	**26.1**	Dividend Rate/Share	**$0.11**
Trailing 12-Month EPS	**$1.85**	S&P Oper. EPS 2007**E**	**2.43**	Common Shares Outstg. (M)	**406.6**	Yield (%)	**0.21**
Trailing 12-Month P/E	**28.5**	S&P Core EPS 2006**E**	**2.02**	Market Capitalization(B)	**$21.405**	Beta	**0.48**
$10K Invested 5 Yrs Ago	**$17,985**	S&P Core EPS 2007**E**	**2.43**	Institutional Ownership (%)	**45**	S&P Credit Rating	**A**

Price Performance

Options: ASE, CBOE, Ph

Analysis prepared by **Robert M. Gold** on October 20, 2006, when the stock traded at **$ 52.73**.

Highlights

- We see 2007 sales of $6.2 billion, up from a projected $5.4 billion in 2006, as 12% growth in the implant (knees, hips and extremities) category joins with similar growth in the medical/surgical (arthroscopy, endoscopy, surgical instrument, hospital beds and stretchers) segment and 1% to 2% growth in physical therapy revenues. Based on recent trends and our expectation of new product launches, we think the company will not experience meaningful unit price decreases through 2008.

- We anticipate steady gross margin expansion to occur through 2008, driven by manufacturing efficiencies and new product introductions. We expect that SG&A costs will absorb about 37% of sales over the coming three years, and we see R&D costs consuming between 5% and 6% of sales, though R&D outlays in 2006 alone could approach the high end of this range.

- Our 2006 operating EPS estimate (excluding in-process R&D charges) is $2.02, including $0.10 of projected stock option expense. In our view, the company's exposure to stock option expense is modest relative to peers. Looking into 2007, we see EPS of $2.43, which also includes $0.10 of estimated stock option expense.

Investment Rationale/Risk

- We think Stryker has the ability to sustain high double-digit earnings growth through 2008, driven by new product launches, rising gross margins, and well-managed operating costs. We believe the company can meaningfully expand its implant segment operating margins, in particular, and expect that SYK will generate sales and EPS growth at the high end of the orthopedic device peer group.

- Risks to our opinion and target price include unfavorable patent litigation outcomes, Medicare reimbursement rate reductions, and greater than expected price erosion in core markets.

- We believe the orthopedics group offers sustainable unit growth of about 11%, and that global pricing pressures will be relatively benign through 2009, aided by new product introductions and strong underlying demand for existing technologies. Our 12-month target price of $65 is based on a forward P/E to earnings growth ratio of about 1.5--in line with our large cap medical device coverage universe--applied to our 2007 EPS estimate, and assuming three-year EPS growth of 18%.

Qualitative Risk Assessment

LOW	**MEDIUM**	HIGH

Stryker operates in very competitive areas of the global medical device industry, characterized by rapid technological innovation and relatively high levels of market share volatility. However, we believe demand for the company's orthopedic products is largely immune from economic cycles, and long-term unit demand drivers are more closely related to an aging global population.

Quantitative Evaluations

S&P Quality Ranking B+

D	C	B-	B	**B+**	A-	A	A+

Relative Strength Rank STRONG

73

LOWEST = 1 HIGHEST = 99

Revenue/Earnings Data

Revenue (Million $)

	1Q	2Q	3Q	4Q	Year
2006	1,321	1,328	1,294	--	--
2005	1,203	1,219	1,172	1,279	4,872
2004	1,035	1,043	1,029	1,156	4,262
2003	846.9	891.7	885.4	1,001	3,625
2002	702.9	733.9	745.6	829.2	3,012
2001	634.2	639.0	619.3	709.8	2,602

Earnings Per Share ($)

2006	0.36	0.52	0.46	**E**0.55	**E**2.02
2005	0.42	0.45	0.32	0.45	1.64
2004	0.33	0.37	0.04	0.40	1.14
2003	0.26	0.26	0.26	0.33	1.12
2002	0.20	0.21	0.18	0.26	0.85
2001	0.16	0.16	0.15	0.20	0.67

Fiscal year ended Dec. 31. Next earnings report expected: Late January. EPS Estimates based on S&P Operating Earnings; historical GAAP earnings are as reported.

Dividend Data (Dates: mm/dd Payment Date: mm/dd/yy)

Amount ($)	Date Decl.	Ex-Div. Date	Stk. of Record	Payment Date
0.110	12/07	12/28	12/30	01/31/06

Dividends have been paid since 1992. Source: Company reports.

Stryker Corp

Business Summary October 20, 2006

Stryker Corp. traces its origins to a business founded in 1941 by Dr. Homer H. Stryker, a leading orthopedic surgeon and the inventor of several orthopedic products. The company has significant exposure to the artificial hip, prosthetic knee, and trauma product areas. International sales accounted for 35% of the total in 2004 and 2005.

Orthopedic implants (59% of 2005 sales) consist of products such as hip, knee, shoulder and spinal implants, associated implant instrumentation, trauma-related products, and bone cement. Artificial joints are made of cobalt chromium, titanium alloys, ceramics, or ultra-high molecular weight polyethylene, and are implanted in patients whose natural joints have been damaged by arthritis, osteoporosis, other diseases, or injury. SYK also sells trauma-related products, used primarily in the fixation of fractures resulting from sudden injury, including internal fixation devices such as nails, plates and screws, and external fixation devices such as pins, wires and connection bars. The division also sells Simplex bone cement, a material used to secure cemented implants to bone, and the OP-1 Bone Growth Device. Composed of recombinant human osteogenic protein-1 and a bioresorbable collagen matrix, the product induces the formation of new bone when implanted into existing bone, and is approved to treat long bone fractures in patients in whom use of autograft treatments has failed or is not a feasible option. Stryker continues to develop OP-1 for spinal indications, including spinal stenosis.

Company Financials

Per Share Data ($) Year Ended Dec. 31	**2005**	**2004**	**2003**	**2002**	**2001**	**2000**	**1999**	**1998**	**1997**	**1996**
Tangible Book Value	5.75	4.44	2.98	1.42	0.65	0.01	NM	NM	1.40	1.25
Cash Flow	2.34	1.78	1.71	1.30	1.09	0.97	0.46	0.20	0.40	0.36
Earnings	1.64	1.14	1.12	0.85	0.67	0.55	0.05	0.10	0.32	0.27
S&P Core Earnings	1.57	1.08	1.08	0.80	0.63	NA	NA	NA	NA	NA
Dividends	0.11	0.09	0.07	0.06	0.05	0.03	0.03	0.03	0.03	0.03
Payout Ratio	7%	8%	6%	7%	7%	5%	60%	27%	9%	9%
Prices:High	56.32	57.66	42.68	33.74	31.60	28.88	18.31	13.94	11.33	8.03
Prices:Low	39.74	40.30	29.83	21.93	21.65	12.22	11.11	7.75	6.06	4.97
P/E Ratio:High	34	51	38	40	47	52	NM	NM	35	30
P/E Ratio:Low	24	35	27	26	32	22	NM	NM	19	18
Income Statement Analysis (Million $)										
Revenue	4,872	4,262	3,625	3,012	2,602	2,200	2,104	1,103	980	910
Operating Income	1,305	1,092	901	751	645	600	329	226	217	169
Depreciation	290	251	230	186	172	169	163	37.6	33.3	34.7
Interest Expense	7.70	6.80	22.6	40.3	67.9	96.6	123	12.2	4.12	4.35
Pretax Income	1,003	717	652	507	406	335	29.8	60.0	196	160
Effective Tax Rate	32.7%	35.0%	30.5%	31.8%	33.0%	34.0%	34.9%	34.0%	35.7%	38.4%
Net Income	675	466	454	346	272	221	19.4	39.6	125	104
S&P Core Earnings	645	441	436	324	257	NA	NA	NA	NA	NA
Balance Sheet & Other Financial Data (Million $)										
Cash	1,057	349	65.9	37.8	50.1	54.0	80.0	142	351	368
Current Assets	2,870	2,143	1,398	1,151	993	997	1,110	1,312	757	754
Total Assets	4,944	4,084	3,159	2,816	2,424	2,431	2,581	2,886	985	994
Current Liabilities	1,249	1,114	850	708	533	617	670	699	303	252
Long Term Debt	184	0.70	18.8	491	721	876	1,181	1,488	4.45	90.0
Common Equity	3,252	2,752	2,155	1,498	1,056	855	672	643	657	530
Total Capital	3,436	2,753	2,174	1,989	1,777	1,731	1,853	2,148	653	706
Capital Expenditures	272	188	145	139	162	80.7	76.2	51.2	35.2	26.7
Cash Flow	965	717	683	532	444	390	182	77.2	159	139
Current Ratio	2.3	1.9	1.6	1.6	1.9	1.6	1.7	1.9	2.5	3.0
% Long Term Debt of Capitalization	5.4	0.0	0.9	24.7	40.6	50.6	63.8	69.3	0.7	12.7
% Net Income of Revenue	13.9	10.9	12.5	11.5	10.4	9.7	0.9	3.6	12.8	11.5
% Return on Assets	15.0	12.9	15.2	13.2	11.2	8.8	0.7	2.0	12.7	11.3
% Return on Equity	22.5	19.0	24.8	27.1	28.4	29.0	2.9	6.1	20.5	21.2

Data as orig reptd.; bef. results of disc opers/spec. items. Per share data adj. for stk. divs.; EPS diluted. E-Estimated. NA-Not Available. NM-Not Meaningful. NR-Not Ranked. UR-Under Review.

Office: 2725 Fairfield Rd, Kalamazoo, MI 49002-1752.
Telephone: 269-385-2600.
Website: http://www.strykercorp.com
Chrmn: J.W. Brown

Pres & CEO: S.P. MacMillan
Investor Contact: D.H. Bergy (269-385-2600)
VP, CFO & Secy: D.H. Bergy
VP & General Counsel: C.E. Hall

Board of Directors: J. W. Brown, H. E. Cox, Jr., D. M. Engelman, L. L. Francesconi, J. H. Grossman, S. P. MacMillan, W. U. Parfet, R. E. Stryker

Founded: 1946
Domicile: Michigan
Employees: 17,265

STANDARD &POOR'S

Sunoco Inc.

S&P Recommendation BUY ★★★★★

Price $66.40 (as of Oct 27, 2006)

12-Mo. Target Price $86.00

Investment Style Mid-Cap Value

GICS Sector Energy
Sub-Industry Oil & Gas Refining & Marketing

Comment As the seventh largest refiner in the U.S., Sunoco has diversified operations in refining, marketing, chemicals, logistics and cokemaking.

Key Stock Statistics (Source S&P, Vickers, company reports)

52-Wk Range	**$97.25–57.50**	S&P Oper. EPS 2006**E**	**8.93**	P/E on S&P Oper. EPS 2006**E**	**7.4**	Dividend Rate/Share	**$1.00**
Trailing 12-Month EPS	**$8.30**	S&P Oper. EPS 2007**E**	**7.89**	Common Shares Outstg. (M)	**130.4**	Yield (%)	**1.51**
Trailing 12-Month P/E	**8.0**	S&P Core EPS 2006**E**	**8.99**	Market Capitalization(B)	**$8.659**	Beta	**0.60**
$10K Invested 5 Yrs Ago	**$38,227**	S&P Core EPS 2007**E**	**7.97**	Institutional Ownership (%)	**76**	S&P Credit Rating	**BBB**

Price Performance

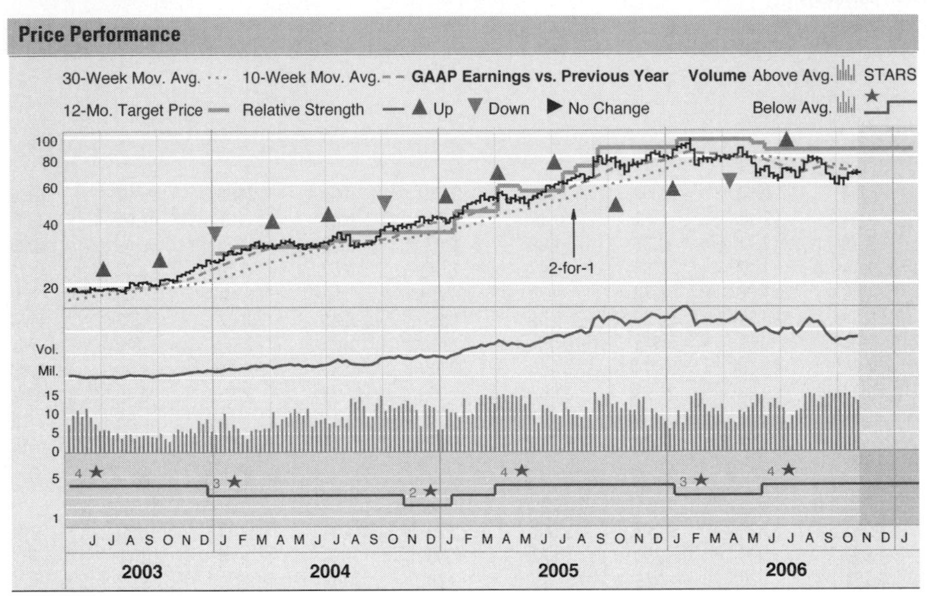

Options: CBOE, Ph

Analysis prepared by **Tina J. Vital** on August 17, 2006, when the stock traded at **$ 75.47**.

Highlights

- Second quarter after-tax operating earnings rose 76% to $426 million, or $3.22 per share. Results beat our estimate by $0.13 per share, reflecting better-than-expected volumes and reformulated gasoline and low-sulfur diesel margins.
- Refining throughputs declined 1.4% in the second quarter on maintenance turnarounds, but were above our expectations. We expect refinery throughputs to decline 1.8% in 2006 from the prior year's levels.
- Strong refining margins boosted after-tax operating earnings by 70% in 2005, reflecting tight industry fundamentals. We expect refining margins for all crude slates to remain strong over the next twelve months, and project SUN's after-tax operating earnings will increase 17% in 2006, before declining 12% in 2007 on lower projected pricing. We expect solid free cash flow will support buybacks and dividend hikes in 2006. During the 2006 first half, share repurchases totaled $198 million and the authorization stood at $609 million.

Investment Rationale/Risk

- While we believe SUN's focus on light sweet crude oil feedstocks has limited its ability to lower costs, it has permitted a relatively high volume of higher grade products. We think its strong East Coast and Midwest retail distribution provides long-term earnings stability, and its stake in Sunoco Logistics Partners L.P. (SXL: buy, $45) provides a stable source of distributions. We see limited internal growth opportunities, and expect SUN will pursue acquisitions across all of its business lines.
- Risks to our recommendation and target price include changes in economic, industry and operating conditions, earnings volatility from its increased exposure to chemicals, and an aggressive spending program.
- Our DCF analysis, based on a weighted average cost of capital of 8.7% and a terminal growth rate of 3%, yields an intrinsic value of about $93. A blend of our DCF and relative valuations leads to our 12-month target price of $86, representing an enterprise value of 6.3X our 2006 EBITDA estimate, a premium to peers.

Qualitative Risk Assessment

LOW	MEDIUM	HIGH

Our risk assessment reflects the company's solid business profile in a volatile and competitive refining industry.

Quantitative Evaluations

S&P Quality Ranking A-

D	C	B-	B	B+	A-	A	A+

Relative Strength Rank MODERATE

32

LOWEST = 1 HIGHEST = 99

Revenue/Earnings Data

Revenue (Million $)

	1Q	2Q	3Q	4Q	Year
2006	8,593	10,590	--	--	--
2005	7,209	7,990	9,295	9,270	33,764
2004	5,245	6,276	6,558	7,429	25,508
2003	4,570	4,189	4,594	4,576	17,929
2002	2,931	3,556	3,812	4,085	14,384
2001	3,627	3,916	3,588	2,932	14,063

Earnings Per Share ($)

2006	0.59	3.22	**E**2.85	**E**2.26	**E**8.93
2005	0.84	1.75	2.39	2.12	7.08
2004	0.58	1.54	0.70	1.24	4.04
2003	0.56	0.52	0.70	0.24	2.02
2002	-0.70	0.06	-0.07	0.40	-0.31
2001	0.62	1.17	0.50	0.03	2.43

Fiscal year ended Dec. 31. Next earnings report expected: Early November. EPS Estimates based on S&P Operating Earnings; historical GAAP earnings are as reported.

Dividend Data (Dates: mm/dd Payment Date: mm/dd/yy)

Amount ($)	Date Decl.	Ex-Div. Date	Stk. of Record	Payment Date
0.200	01/05	02/07	02/09	03/10/06
0.250	02/02	05/06	05/09	06/09/06
0.250	07/06	08/04	08/08	09/08/06
0.250	10/05	11/06	11/08	12/08/06

Dividends have been paid since 1904. Source: Company reports.

STANDARD &POOR'S

Sunoco Inc.

Business Summary August 17, 2006

Sunoco Inc. (SUN) has been active in the petroleum industry since 1886, and conducts its business through five operating segments: Refining and Supply (49% of 2005 revenues; 83% of 2005 after-tax segment income); Retail Marketing (35%; 3%); Chemicals (7%; 8%); Logistics (8%; 2%); and Coke (1%; 4%).

Refining and Supply manufactures petroleum products and commodity petrochemicals. As of December 31, 2005, SUN owned and operated five refineries with a crude unit capacity of about 900,000 barrels per day (b/d), located in the Northeast (655,000 b/d; in Marcus Hook, PA, Philadelphia, PA, and "Eagle Point" in Westville, NJ), and the MidContinent (245,000 b/d; Toledo, OH, and Tulsa, OK). Products manufactured rose 2.8% to 975,700 b/d in 2005 (gasoline 45%, middle distillates 33%, residual fuels 8%, petrochemicals 4%, lubricants 1%, and other 9%).

SUN meets all of its crude oil requirements through purchases from third parties. Approximately 70% of SUN's 2005 crude oil supply came from West Africa (40% from Nigeria), 16% from the U.S., 7% from Canada, 1% from the North Sea, 5% from South and Central America, and 1% from lubes extracted gasoil/naphtha intermediate feedstock. In the 2004 second half, the company began processing limited amounts of lower value high acid sweet crude oils in some of its Northeast refineries; during 2005, about 56,000 b/d of high acid crude oil was processed.

Retail Marketing consists of the retail sale of gasoline and middle distillates, and the operation of convenience stores in 24 states, primarily on the East Coast and in the Midwest region of the U.S. Retail Marketing is one of the largest providers of heating products in the U.S. As of December 31, 2005, SUN had 4,763 retail gasoline outlets (62% distributor outlets - a distributor takes delivery at a terminal where branded products are available; and 38% direct outlets - owned by SUN or an independent dealer).

Company Financials

Per Share Data ($) Year Ended Dec. 31	**2005**	**2004**	**2003**	**2002**	**2001**	**2000**	**1999**	**1998**	**1997**	**1996**
Tangible Book Value	15.42	11.65	10.23	9.05	10.88	10.03	8.37	8.41	5.21	4.73
Cash Flow	10.20	9.50	4.35	1.85	4.38	4.05	2.05	2.72	2.46	-0.40
Earnings	7.08	4.04	2.02	-0.31	2.43	2.35	0.54	1.48	1.35	-2.21
S&P Core Earnings	7.56	4.19	2.13	-0.70	1.88	NA	NA	NA	NA	NA
Dividends	0.75	0.58	0.51	0.50	0.50	0.50	0.50	0.50	0.50	0.50
Payout Ratio	11%	14%	25%	NM	21%	21%	93%	34%	37%	NM
Prices:High	85.29	42.26	26.30	21.13	21.37	17.28	19.72	22.16	23.19	16.31
Prices:Low	38.10	25.26	14.84	13.51	14.56	10.97	11.44	14.75	12.00	10.94
P/E Ratio:High	12	10	13	NM	9	7	37	15	17	NM
P/E Ratio:Low	5	6	7	NM	6	5	21	10	9	NM
Income Statement Analysis (Million $)										
Revenue	33,764	25,508	17,929	14,384	14,063	14,300	10,068	8,413	10,464	11,233
Operating Income	2,078	1,501	934	313	954	948	331	605	680	225
Depreciation, Depletion and Amortization	429	818	363	329	321	298	276	257	259	267
Interest Expense	69.0	97.0	111	108	103	78.0	82.0	71.0	71.0	79.0
Pretax Income	1,580	995	495	-73.0	587	596	150	389	385	-408
Effective Tax Rate	38.4%	39.2%	37.0%	NM	32.2%	31.0%	35.3%	28.0%	31.7%	NM
Net Income	974	605	312	-47.0	398	411	97.0	280	263	-281
S&P Core Earnings	1,040	626	330	-106	307	NA	NA	NA	NA	NA
Balance Sheet & Other Financial Data (Million $)										
Cash	919	405	431	390	42.0	239	87.0	38.0	33.0	67.0
Current Assets	3,687	2,551	2,068	1,898	1,510	1,683	1,456	1,180	1,248	1,535
Total Assets	9,931	8,079	6,922	6,441	5,932	5,426	5,196	4,849	4,667	5,025
Current Liabilities	4,210	3,022	2,170	1,776	1,778	1,646	1,766	1,384	1,464	1,817
Long Term Debt	1,234	1,379	1,350	1,453	1,142	933	878	823	824	835
Common Equity	2,051	1,607	1,556	1,394	1,642	1,702	4,782	1,514	739	690
Total Capital	4,749	4,271	3,940	3,816	3,335	2,885	5,897	2,512	2,359	2,273
Capital Expenditures	970	832	425	385	331	465	374	457	380	408
Cash Flow	1,403	1,423	675	282	719	709	373	517	478	-59.0
Current Ratio	0.9	0.8	1.0	1.1	0.8	1.0	0.8	0.9	0.9	0.9
% Long Term Debt of Capitalization	26.0	32.3	34.3	38.1	34.2	32.3	14.9	32.8	34.9	36.8
% Return on Assets	10.8	8.0	4.7	NM	7.0	7.7	1.9	5.9	5.4	NM
% Return on Equity	53.3	38.3	21.2	NM	23.8	25.6	2.0	23.1	30.7	NM

Data as orig reptd.; bef. results of disc opers/spec. items. Per share data adj. for stk. divs.; EPS diluted. E-Estimated. NA-Not Available. NM-Not Meaningful. NR-Not Ranked. UR-Under Review.

Office: 1735 Market St, Suite LL, Philadelphia, PA 19103-7501.
Telephone: 215-977-3000.
Email: sunocoonline@sunocoinc.com
Website: http://www.sunocoinc.com

Chrmn, Pres & CEO: J.G. Drosdick
SVP & CFO: T.W. Hofmann
SVP & Chief Admin: C.K. Valutas
SVP & General Counsel: M.S. Kuritzkes

Investor Contact: T.P. Delaney (215-977-6106)
Board of Directors: R. J. Darnall, J. G. Drosdick, U. F. Fairbairn, T. P. Gerrity, R. Greco, J. P. Jones, J. G. Kaiser, R. Lenny, R. A. Pew, G. J. Ratcliffe, J. G. Rowe, J. K. Wulff

Founded: 1886
Domicile: Pennsylvania
Employees: 13,800

STANDARD &POOR'S

Sun Microsystems Inc

S&P Recommendation HOLD ★★★★★

Price $5.43 (as of Oct 31, 2006)

12-Mo. Target Price $5.50

Investment Style Large-Cap Value

GICS Sector Information Technology
Sub-Industry Computer Hardware

Comment This company makes high-performance servers, workstations and operating system software, and invented the Java programming language.

Key Stock Statistics (Source S&P, Vickers, company reports)

52-Wk Range	**$5.62–3.62**	S&P Oper. EPS 2007**E**	**-0.02**	P/E on S&P Oper. EPS 2007**E**	**NM**	Dividend Rate/Share	**Nil**
Trailing 12-Month EPS	**$-0.23**	S&P Oper. EPS 2008**E**	**0.07**	Common Shares Outstg. (M)	**3,509.3**	Yield (%)	**Nil**
Trailing 12-Month P/E	**NM**	S&P Core EPS 2007**E**	**-0.02**	Market Capitalization(B)	**$19.055**	Beta	**3.04**
$10K Invested 5 Yrs Ago	**$5,288**	S&P Core EPS 2008**E**	**0.07**	Institutional Ownership (%)	**64**	S&P Credit Rating	**BB+**

Price Performance

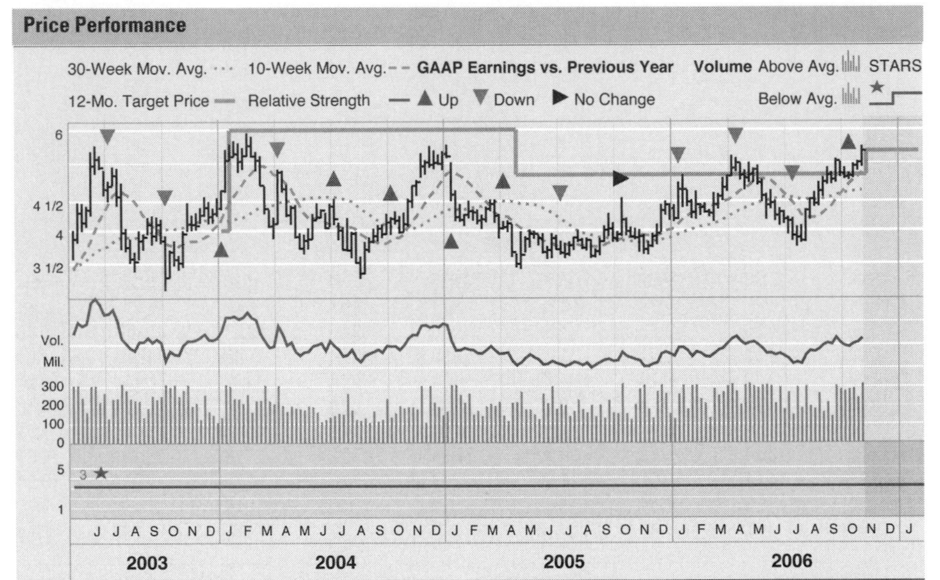

Options: ASE, CBOE, P, Ph

Analysis prepared by **Richard N. Stice, CFA** on October 31, 2006, when the stock traded at **$ 5.45**.

Highlights

➤ We expect a 10% increase in revenue in FY 07 (Jun.), following an 18% gain in FY 06. In our opinion, revenues continue to reflect a relatively consistent level of IT spending overall, as well as benefits from various international markets. However, we think these factors are likely to be somewhat offset by continued pricing pressures in the server market, as well as a negative impact from the mix shift, reflecting Sun's new lower-end product offerings. For FY 08, we also anticipate growth of 10%.

➤ We expect strong pricing competition and the impact of Sun's increased low-end sales mix to be outweighed by higher volumes and manufacturing efficiencies. As a result, we anticipate the gross margin to widen to 43.4% in FY 07, from 43.1% in FY 06. We see SG&A expenses declining as a percentage of revenue due to SUNW's restructuring efforts.

➤ We expect a loss per share of $0.02 for FY 07 and EPS of $0.07 in FY 08. Both estimates include projected stock option expense.

Investment Rationale/Risk

➤ While we believe the company faces competitive threats from the Windows and Linux operating systems, we think that Sun's relatively recent entry into the Linux-based server market may offset these pressures over the longer term. In addition, an expected work force reduction of up to 5,000 employees during FY 07, should help to realign SUNW's cost structure.

➤ Risks to our opinion and target price include the possibility of an accelerated migration away from UNIX systems, which still account for the majority of Sun's sales.

➤ Our 12-month target price of $5.50 is based on our price to sales and DCF analyses. We believe a ratio of 1.3X our FY 07 revenue per share estimate is appropriate, based on our review of the stock's three year, monthly historical average. This leads to a value of $5.50. Our DCF model assumes a weighted average cost of capital (WACC) of 13% and an expected terminal growth rate of 3%. This results in an intrinsic value of $6.

Qualitative Risk Assessment

LOW | MEDIUM | **HIGH**

Our risk assessment reflects the losses the company has sustained over the past several years, our view of its reliance on high-end systems sales, and the difficult pricing pressures we see in the computer hardware industry.

Quantitative Evaluations

S&P Quality Ranking **C**

D | **C** | B- | B | B+ | A- | A | A+

Relative Strength Rank **STRONG**

83

LOWEST = 1 HIGHEST = 99

Revenue/Earnings Data

Revenue (Million $)

	1Q	2Q	3Q	4Q	Year
2007	3,189	--	--	--	--
2006	2,726	3,337	3,177	3,828	13,068
2005	2,628	2,841	2,627	2,974	11,070
2004	2,536	2,888	2,651	3,110	11,185
2003	2,747	2,915	2,790	2,982	11,434
2002	2,861	3,108	3,107	3,420	12,496

Earnings Per Share ($)

2007	-0.02	**E**Nil	**E**0.01	**E**-0.01	**E**-0.02
2006	-0.04	-0.07	-0.06	-0.09	-0.25
2005	-0.04	Nil	-0.01	0.01	-0.03
2004	-0.09	-0.04	-0.23	0.23	-0.12
2003	-0.04	-0.72	Nil	-0.32	-1.07
2002	-0.06	-0.13	-0.01	0.02	-0.18

Fiscal year ended Jun. 30. Next earnings report expected: Late January. EPS Estimates based on S&P Operating Earnings; historical GAAP earnings are as reported.

Dividend Data

No cash dividends have been paid.

Sun Microsystems Inc

Business Summary October 31, 2006

CORPORATE OVERVIEW. Sun Microsystems, founded in 1982, invented the workstation, but is mostly known in recent years for its higher-end systems, which experienced significant growth in demand during the build out of the Internet in the late 1990s. The company continues to focus on a single vision--that the network is the computer. Sun's systems power the infrastructure underlying a range of business and technical processes, from webserving, to high performance technical computing, to enterprise wide resource planning, as well as customer relationship and database management. The company serves a variety of markets including financial services, government, manufacturing, retail and telecommunications.

Sun is a primary supplier of networked computing products, including workstations, servers and storage products, which had primarily used the company's own Scaleable Processor Architecture (SPARC) microprocessors and its Solaris software, but this has been expanded to include other chips and operating system software. Computer systems accounted for 46% of net revenues in FY 06 (Jun.), data management products 18%, support services 28%, and client solutions and educational services 8%. In FY 06, General Electric accounted for 15% of total revenue.

CORPORATE STRATEGY. We believe the company has undertaken a number of restructuring initiatives over the past several years in an effort to offset slowing demand trends. Total revenues declined nearly 40% between 2001 and 2005. Sun's most recent plan, Restructuring Plan VI, was initiated in May 2006 and has a goal of reducing its employee base by an additional 4,000 to 5,000 employees. Through the end of FY 06, Sun had cut its work force by about 300 and recognized charges of $138 million.

Company Financials

Per Share Data ($) Year Ended Jun. 30	**2006**	**2005**	**2004**	**2003**	**2002**	**2001**	**2000**	**1999**	**1998**	**1997**
Tangible Book Value	0.80	1.80	1.77	1.88	2.32	2.63	2.22	1.55	1.17	0.93
Cash Flow	-0.08	0.17	0.10	-0.79	0.12	0.65	0.78	0.51	0.38	0.36
Earnings	-0.25	-0.03	-0.12	-1.07	-0.18	0.29	0.55	0.32	0.24	0.25
S&P Core Earnings	-0.26	-0.25	-0.67	-0.81	-0.38	0.14	NA	NA	NA	NA
Dividends	Nil	Nil	Nil	Nil	Nil	Nil	Nil	Nil	Nil	Nil
Payout Ratio	Nil	Nil	Nil	Nil	Nil	Nil	Nil	Nil	Nil	Nil
Prices:High	5.62	5.26	5.93	5.64	14.41	35.13	64.66	41.51	11.05	6.66
Prices:Low	3.74	3.42	3.29	3.02	2.34	7.52	25.13	10.89	4.70	3.23
P/E Ratio:High	NM	NM	NM	NM	NM	NM	NM	NM	46	27
P/E Ratio:Low	NM	NM	NM	NM	NM	26	46	34	19	13

Income Statement Analysis (Million $)										
Revenue	13,068	11,070	11,185	11,434	12,496	18,250	15,721	11,726	9,791	8,598
Operating Income	119	556	3.00	694	239	2,617	3,181	2,269	1,746	1,391
Depreciation	575	671	730	918	970	1,229	776	627	440	342
Interest Expense	55.0	49.0	37.0	43.0	58.0	100	84.0	0.68	1.57	7.46
Pretax Income	-675	-184	437	-2,653	-1,048	1,584	2,771	1,606	1,176	1,121
Effective Tax Rate	NM	NM	NM	NM	NM	38.1%	33.1%	35.8%	35.1%	32.0%
Net Income	-864	-107	-388	-3,429	-587	981	1,854	1,031	763	762
S&P Core Earnings	-904	-864	-2,166	-2,581	-1,253	471	NA	NA	NA	NA

Balance Sheet & Other Financial Data (Million $)										
Cash	4,065	3,396	3,601	3,062	2,885	1,472	1,849	1,089	822	660
Current Assets	8,273	7,191	7,303	6,779	7,777	7,934	6,877	6,116	4,148	3,728
Total Assets	15,082	14,190	14,503	12,985	16,522	18,181	14,152	8,420	5,711	4,697
Current Liabilities	6,165	4,766	5,113	4,129	5,057	5,146	4,759	3,227	2,123	1,849
Long Term Debt	575	1,123	1,175	1,531	1,449	1,705	1,720	Nil	Nil	106
Common Equity	6,344	6,674	6,438	6,491	9,801	10,586	7,309	4,812	3,514	2,742
Total Capital	6,919	7,797	7,613	8,022	11,250	13,035	9,393	4,812	3,514	2,848
Capital Expenditures	315	257	249	373	559	1,292	982	739	830	554
Cash Flow	-289	564	342	-2,511	383	2,210	2,630	1,658	1,203	1,104
Current Ratio	1.3	1.5	1.4	1.6	1.5	1.5	1.4	1.9	2.0	2.0
% Long Term Debt of Capitalization	8.3	14.4	15.4	19.1	12.8	13.1	18.3	Nil	Nil	3.9
% Net Income of Revenue	NM	NM	NM	NM	NM	5.4	11.8	8.8	7.8	8.9
% Return on Assets	NM	NM	NM	NM	NM	6.1	16.4	14.6	14.7	17.9
% Return on Equity	NM	NM	NM	NM	NM	11.0	30.5	24.8	24.4	30.5

Data as orig reptd.; bef. results of disc opers/spec. items. Per share data adj. for stk. divs.; EPS diluted. E-Estimated. NA-Not Available. NM-Not Meaningful. NR-Not Ranked. UR-Under Review.

Office: 4150 Network Circle, Santa Clara, CA 95054.
Telephone: 650-960-1300.
Email: investor-relations@sun.com
Website: http://www.sun.com

Chrmn: S.G. McNealy
Pres & CEO: J.I. Schwartz
EVP & CFO: M. Lehman
EVP & CTO: G.M. Papadopoulos

EVP, Secy & General Counsel: M.A. Dillon
Board of Directors: J. L. Barksdale, S. Bennett, R. Finocchio, Jr., S. G. McNealy, P. E. Mitchell, M. K. Oshman, J. I. Schwartz, N. O. Seligman

Founded: 1982
Domicile: Delaware
Employees: 38,000

STANDARD &POOR'S

SunTrust Banks Inc.

S&P Recommendation	Price	12-Mo. Target Price	Investment Style
BUY ★★★★★	$78.60 (as of Oct 27, 2006)	$87.00	Large-Cap Value

GICS Sector Financials
Sub-Industry Regional Banks

Comment This Atlanta-based bank holding company has about $180 billion in assets and $122 billion in deposits.

Key Stock Statistics (Source S&P, Vickers, company reports)

52-Wk Range	$81.59–69.68	S&P Oper. EPS 2006E	5.93	P/E on S&P Oper. EPS 2006E	13.3	Dividend Rate/Share	$2.44
Trailing 12-Month EPS	$5.85	S&P Oper. EPS 2007E	6.46	Common Shares Outstg. (M)	364.8	Yield (%)	3.10
Trailing 12-Month P/E	13.4	S&P Core EPS 2006E	5.99	Market Capitalization(B)	$28.674	Beta	0.42
$10K Invested 5 Yrs Ago	$14,636	S&P Core EPS 2007E	6.65	Institutional Ownership (%)	55	S&P Credit Rating	AA-

Price Performance

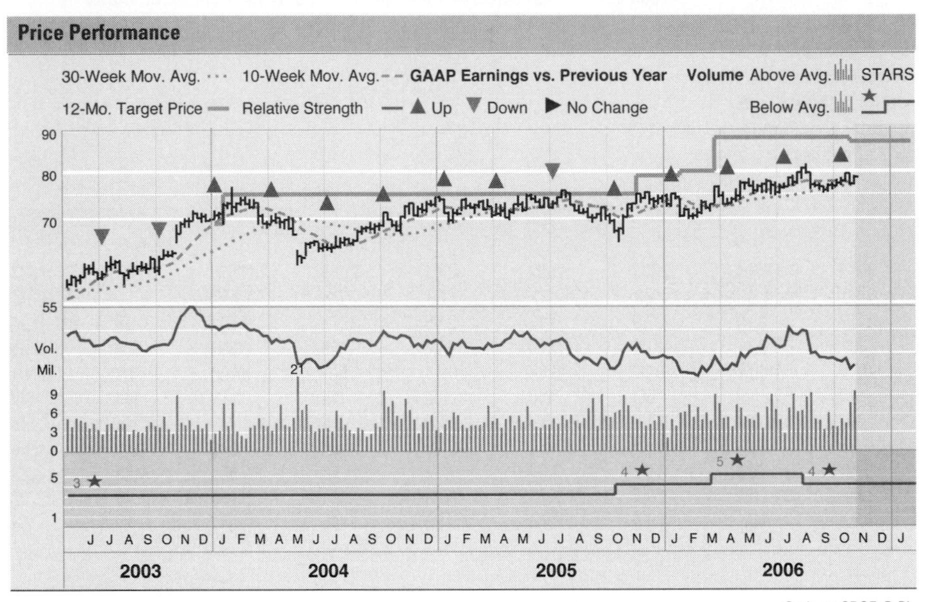

Options: CBOE, P, Ph

Highlights

- The 12-month target price for STI has recently been changed to $87.00 from $88.00. The Highlights section of this Stock Report will be updated accordingly.

Investment Rationale/Risk

- The Investment Rationale/Risk section of this Stock Report will be updated shortly. For the latest News story on STI from MarketScope, see below.

- 10/17/06 01:57 pm EDT... S&P MAINTAINS BUY OPINION ON SHARES OF SUNTRUST BANKS (STI 78.89****): STI posts Q3 EPS of $1.47 versus $1.40, $0.05 below our estimate. Net-interest income was below our projection; the provision for loan losses was above our forecast. The company expects upper single-digit loan growth in '07, which is below our estimate, and '07 commercial and consumer deposit growth in the mid-single digits, slightly above our projection. We are lowering our '06 EPS estimate $0.08 to $5.93, and our '07 estimate $0.22 to $6.46. We are reducing our target price to $87 from $88, 13.5X our '07 EPS estimate, about even with regional banking peers. /E.Oja

Qualitative Risk Assessment

LOW	MEDIUM	HIGH

Our risk assessment reflects the company's large-cap valuation, the strong credit quality of its loan portfolio, and its history of profitability. While the company operates in a highly competitive and fragmented industry, the industry tends to produce relatively stable financial results.

Quantitative Evaluations

S&P Quality Ranking **A+**

D	C	B-	B	B+	A-	A	**A+**

Relative Strength Rank **MODERATE**

43

LOWEST = 1 HIGHEST = 99

Revenue/Earnings Data

Revenue (Million $)

	1Q	2Q	3Q	4Q	Year
2006	3,130	3,298	3,384	--	--
2005	2,470	2,614	2,829	2,973	10,886
2004	1,769	1,811	1,880	2,363	7,823
2003	1,766	1,771	1,752	1,783	7,072
2002	1,913	1,918	1,852	1,845	7,527
2001	2,270	2,156	2,060	1,949	8,435

Earnings Per Share ($)

	1Q	2Q	3Q	4Q	Year
2006	1.46	1.49	1.47	**E**1.51	**E**5.93
2005	1.36	1.28	1.40	1.43	5.47
2004	1.26	1.29	1.30	1.26	5.19
2003	1.17	1.17	1.18	1.21	4.73
2002	1.06	1.20	1.21	1.20	4.66
2001	1.14	1.25	1.15	1.16	4.70

Fiscal year ended Dec. 31. Next earnings report expected: Mid January. EPS Estimates based on S&P Operating Earnings; historical GAAP earnings are as reported.

Dividend Data (Dates: mm/dd Payment Date: mm/dd/yy)

Amount ($)	Date Decl.	Ex-Div. Date	Stk. of Record	Payment Date
0.550	11/08	11/29	12/01	12/15/05
0.610	02/14	02/27	03/01	03/15/06
0.610	04/18	05/30	06/01	06/15/06
0.610	08/08	08/30	09/01	09/15/06

Dividends have been paid since 1985. Source: Company reports.

SunTrust Banks Inc.

Business Summary August 08, 2006

CORPORATE OVERVIEW. STI owns SunTrust Bank, an organization aligned by geographic region: the Carolinas Group (North and South Carolina), the Central Group (Georgia, Tennessee), the Florida Group, and the Mid-Atlantic Group (D.C., Maryland, Virginia and West Virginia). The company has six reportable business segments: Retail Banking, Commercial Banking, Corporate and Investment Banking, Mortgage Banking, Wealth and Investment Management, and Corporate/Other.

The Retail and Commercial Banking segments generate about 60% of total segment revenues. Retail Banking (43%) provides lending and deposit gathering as well as other banking-related products and services to consumers and small businesses with sales up to $10 million. Commercial Banking (17%) offers financial products and services, including commercial lending, treasury management, financial risk management, and corporate bankcard services, to enterprises with sales up to $250 million.

The Corporate and Investment Banking segment (12%) houses the company's corporate banking, investment banking, capital markets, commercial leasing, and merchant banking activities. This segment focuses on companies with sales in excess of $250 million, and concentrates on small-cap and mid-cap growth companies, raising public and private equity, and providing merger and acquisition advisory services for investment banking.

The Mortgage Banking segment (11%) offers residential mortgage products nationally through its retail, broker and correspondent channels. The Wealth and Investment Management segment (17%) provides wealth management products and professional services to both individual and institutional clients.

The company has adapted an enterprise risk management model, which seeks to synthesize, assess, report and mitigate the full set of risks at the enterprise level and to provide management with an overall picture of the company's risk profile. The model incorporates an analysis of credit risk, organizational risk, market risk from trading activities, market risk from non-trading activities and market liquidity risk.

Company Financials

Per Share Data ($) Year Ended Dec. 31	**2005**	**2004**	**2003**	**2002**	**2001**	**2000**	**1999**	**1998**	**1997**	**1996**
Tangible Book Value	24.67	23.13	29.73	25.46	26.67	25.07	22.13	22.99	23.38	20.88
Earnings	5.47	5.19	4.73	4.66	4.70	4.30	3.50	3.04	3.13	2.76
S&P Core Earnings	5.39	5.17	4.80	4.38	4.50	NA	NA	NA	NA	NA
Dividends	2.20	2.00	1.80	1.72	1.60	1.48	1.38	1.00	0.93	0.83
Payout Ratio	40%	39%	38%	37%	34%	34%	39%	33%	30%	30%
Prices:High	75.77	76.65	71.73	70.20	72.35	68.06	79.81	87.75	75.25	52.50
Prices:Low	65.32	61.27	51.44	51.48	57.29	41.63	60.44	54.00	44.13	32.00
P/E Ratio:High	14	15	15	15	15	16	23	26	24	19
P/E Ratio:Low	12	12	11	11	12	10	17	16	14	12

Income Statement Analysis (Million $)										
Net Interest Income	4,579	3,685	3,320	3,244	3,253	3,108	3,145	2,929	1,894	1,784
Tax Equivalent Adjustment	NA	NA	45.0	39.5	40.8	40.4	42.5	46.4	36.6	40.1
Non Interest Income	3,162	2,646	2,179	2,187	2,003	1,767	1,769	1,708	933	804
Loan Loss Provision	177	136	314	470	275	134	170	215	117	116
% Expense/Operating Revenue	60.6%	67.3%	68.4%	61.5%	59.2%	58.0%	59.3%	62.8%	59.6%	61.5%
Pretax Income	2,866	2,257	1,909	1,823	2,020	1,920	1,690	1,498	1,026	903
Effective Tax Rate	30.7%	30.3%	30.2%	27.0%	32.2%	32.6%	33.7%	35.2%	35.0%	31.7%
Net Income	1,987	1,573	1,332	1,332	1,369	1,294	1,124	971	667	617
% Net Interest Margin	3.16	3.15	3.08	3.41	NA	3.55	3.88	3.97	4.11	4.40
S&P Core Earnings	1,957	1,570	1,351	1,253	1,310	NA	NA	NA	NA	NA

Balance Sheet & Other Financial Data (Million $)										
Money Market Assets	4,457	3,796	3,243	2,820	3,025	2,223	1,869	2,027	1,180	1,815
Investment Securities	26,526	28,941	25,607	23,445	19,656	18,810	18,317	17,559	11,729	10,551
Commercial Loans	33,764	31,824	30,682	28,694	28,946	30,781	26,933	24,590	14,387	11,966
Other Loans	80,791	69,602	50,050	44,474	40,013	41,459	39,069	40,496	25,749	23,428
Total Assets	179,714	158,870	125,393	117,323	104,741	103,496	95,390	93,170	57,983	52,468
Demand Deposits	41,973	30,979	24,185	21,250	19,200	15,064	14,201	14,066	8,928	8,900
Time Deposits	80,081	72,382	57,004	58,456	48,337	54,469	45,900	44,968	29,270	27,990
Long Term Debt	20,779	22,127	15,314	11,880	12,661	8,945	6,017	5,808	3,172	1,565
Common Equity	16,887	15,987	9,731	16,030	15,064	14,536	13,691	8,179	5,199	4,880
% Return on Assets	1.2	1.1	1.1	1.2	1.3	1.3	1.2	1.3	1.2	1.2
% Return on Equity	12.1	12.2	14.4	8.6	9.3	9.2	8.0	14.5	13.2	13.5
% Loan Loss Reserve	0.5	1.0	1.1	1.1	1.2	1.2	1.3	1.5	1.9	2.1
% Loans/Deposits	171.3	104.5	106.3	101.5	108.5	106.4	112.4	110.3	137.1	96.0
% Equity to Assets	9.7	9.1	7.6	14.0	14.2	14.2	14.8	8.9	9.1	9.3

Data as orig reptd.; bef. results of disc opers/spec. items. Per share data adj. for stk. divs.; EPS diluted. E-Estimated. NA-Not Available. NM-Not Meaningful. NR-Not Ranked. UR-Under Review.

Office: 303 Peachtree St NE, Atlanta, GA 30308-3201.
Telephone: 404-588-7711.
Website: http://www.suntrust.com
Chrmn & CEO: L.P. Humann

Pres, Vice Chrmn & COO: J.M. Wells III
Vice Chrmn: W. Reed
Sr EVP: R.H. Coords
Sr EVP & CFO: M.A. Chancy

Investor Contact: J.T. Lienhard, II (866-639-4994)
Board of Directors: R. M. Beall II, J. H. Brown, A. D. Correll, J. C. Crowe, T. Farnsworth, Jr., P. C. Frist, B. Garrett, Jr., T. Garrott, D. H. Hughes, L. P. Humann, E. N. Isdell, M. D. Ivester, J. H. Lanier, G. G. Minor III, L. L. Prince, F. S. Royal, K. H. Williams, P. Wynn, Jr.

Founded: 1891
Domicile: Georgia
Employees: 33,406

STANDARD &POOR'S

SUPERVALU INC.

S&P Recommendation HOLD ★★★★★

Price $33.64 (as of Oct 27, 2006)

12-Mo. Target Price $34.00

Investment Style Mid-Cap Value

GICS Sector Consumer Staples
Sub-Industry Food Retail

Comment SVU, one of the largest U.S. food wholesalers, is also one of the largest supermarket retailers in the U.S.

Key Stock Statistics (Source S&P, Vickers, company reports)

52-Wk Range	$34.75–26.14	S&P Oper. EPS 2007E	2.57	P/E on S&P Oper. EPS 2007E	13.1	Dividend Rate/Share	$0.66
Trailing 12-Month EPS	$1.79	S&P Oper. EPS 2008E	2.85	Common Shares Outstg. (M)	205.9	Yield (%)	1.96
Trailing 12-Month P/E	18.8	S&P Core EPS 2007E	2.57	Market Capitalization(B)	$6.926	Beta	1.18
$10K Invested 5 Yrs Ago	$16,604	S&P Core EPS 2008E	2.85	Institutional Ownership (%)	84	S&P Credit Rating	BB-

Price Performance

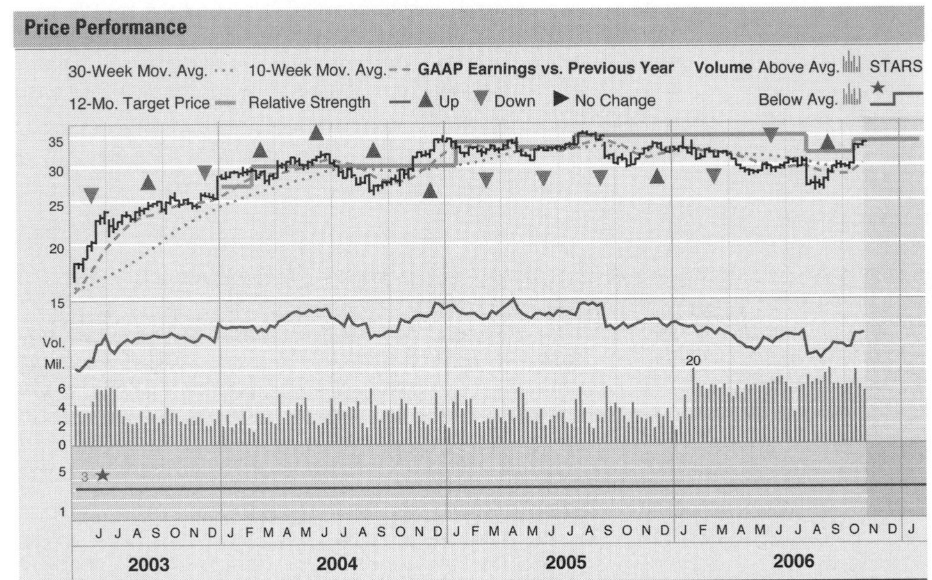

Options: Ph

Analysis prepared by **Joseph Agnese** on October 16, 2006, when the stock traded at **$ 32.76**.

Highlights

- We see FY 07 (Feb.) revenues increasing to nearly $38 billion from $19.9 billion, reflecting the acquisition of Albertson's stores, the opening of 40 standard stores, 50 to 75 limited assortment stores and 80 major remodels. We think food distribution sales should increase in the low-single digits, as a result of new business wins offset by continued customer attrition.

- We view FY 07 as a transitional year as the company begins to integrate the acquisition of Albertson's stores. Margins should widen as we look for the company to start to experience synergies due to leveraging its larger scale through better purchasing, the removal of duplicate administrative expenses, leveraging Albertson's advanced information technology investments, and the rationalization of its current supply chain network. However, interest expense and shares outstanding are expected to rise significantly due to the inclusion of debt from the Albertson's acquisition.

- Excluding $0.27 in one-time transaction costs following the acquisition of Albertson's stores, we look for FY 07 operating EPS of $2.57, up 15% from $2.23 in FY 06.

Investment Rationale/Risk

- We believe SVU is well positioned with strong regional market share positions despite an intensely competitive environment. We see significant benefits from synergies over the next three years as well as from an increased focus on improving the in-store shopping experience at newly acquired stores.

- Risks to our recommendation and target price include difficulty integrating newly acquired stores, deterioration in the economic environment, and slower than expected improvement in results due to increased competition.

- The shares traded recently at 12.8X our FY 07 operating EPS estimate of $2.57, slightly below the two-year historical average of 13X. Although we see potential significant synergy savings from acquisitions, we believe the stock will continue to trade below its historical average multiple of about 13X due to potential integration risks. Applying a forward P/E multiple of 12X to our calendar 2007 EPS estimate of $2.80, we arrive at our 12-month target price of $34. We would hold existing positions in the shares, which recently offered a 2% dividend yield.

Qualitative Risk Assessment

LOW | **MEDIUM** | HIGH

Our risk assessment for SUPERVALU reflects the company's strong market share positions, and S&P's Quality Ranking of B+, partially offset by an intense competitive environment and threats of new entrants into its markets.

Quantitative Evaluations

S&P Quality Ranking B+

D | C | B- | B | **B+** | A- | A | A+

Relative Strength Rank STRONG

85

LOWEST = 1 HIGHEST = 99

Revenue/Earnings Data

Revenue (Million $)

	1Q	2Q	3Q	4Q	Year
2007	5,783	10,666	--	--	--
2006	5,972	4,556	4,695	4,640	19,864
2005	5,911	4,487	4,555	4,591	19,543
2004	5,836	4,591	4,739	5,044	20,210
2003	5,654	4,340	4,553	4,613	19,160
2002	6,932	4,715	4,610	4,651	20,909

Earnings Per Share ($)

2007	0.57	0.61	E0.70	E0.72	E2.57
2006	0.64	0.24	0.53	0.04	1.46
2005	1.04	0.55	0.46	0.65	2.71
2004	0.55	0.46	0.36	0.70	2.07
2003	0.57	0.44	0.43	0.48	1.91
2002	0.45	0.39	0.44	0.26	1.53

Fiscal year ended Feb. 28. Next earnings report expected: Early January. EPS Estimates based on S&P Operating Earnings; historical GAAP earnings are as reported.

Dividend Data (Dates: mm/dd Payment Date: mm/dd/yy)

Amount ($)	Date Decl.	Ex-Div. Date	Stk. of Record	Payment Date
0.163	02/08	02/27	03/01	03/15/06
0.163	04/12	05/26	05/31	06/15/06
0.165	08/09	08/30	09/01	09/15/06
0.165	10/12	11/29	12/01	12/15/06

Dividends have been paid since 1936. Source: Company reports.

SUPERVALU INC.

Business Summary October 16, 2006

CORPORATE OVERVIEW. SUPERVALU, organized in 1925 as the successor to two wholesale grocery concerns established in the 1870s, has grown into the largest U.S. food distributor to supermarkets, and the second largest conventional food retailer in the U.S. Retail operations are conducted through extreme value stores, price superstores, and supermarkets. As of July 2006, the company operated about 2,500 multi-format retail food stores and served more than 5,000 primary customer sites in addition to its own retail operations.

CORPORATE STRATEGY. SVU operates national and regional grocery retail banners in more than 34 million square feet of space. Nationally, the company operates stores under the Save-A-Lot banner. Through over 1,100 stores in 39 states, the company differentiates Save-A-Lot from competitors by targeting low income consumers. The company positions itself to offer low prices by carrying a limited selection of the most frequently purchased goods and by also carrying an assortment of $1.00 priced general merchandise. In early 2006, the company began to roll out its second national banner, Sunflower Market. The Sunflower Market banner is a limited assortment, fresh food focused banner also aimed at price conscious consumers. The majority of national stores are found in small town/rural communities as opposed to urban and suburban locations.

Excluding recently acquired operations, the company operates 258 regional food banners in 15 states under 14 million square feet of space. Banners under operation include Cub Foods, Shop n' Save, bigg's, Shoppers Food and Pharmacy, Scott's, Hornbacher's and Farm Fresh Markets. The company operates regional banners as traditional supermarket chains with a focus on fresh foods and low prices.

Supply chain services offer traditional wholesale and retail, as well as third party logistics services. The company targets the approximately $150 billion retail grocery industry that is supplied by wholesalers. The company aims to win business through consistent high service levels with over 95% on-time delivery and in-stock positions and through its capability of offering tailored food programs. The company supports both national and independent retailers and regional banners.

Company Financials

Per Share Data ($) Year Ended Feb. 28	**2006**	**2005**	**2004**	**2003**	**2002**	**2001**	**2000**	**1999**	**1998**	**1997**
Tangible Book Value	7.37	6.52	4.84	3.24	2.54	1.43	1.40	6.10	5.81	6.05
Cash Flow	3.55	4.75	4.34	4.14	4.08	3.20	4.03	3.48	3.66	3.04
Earnings	1.46	2.71	2.07	1.91	1.53	0.62	1.87	1.57	1.82	1.30
S&P Core Earnings	1.90	2.21	2.03	1.61	1.24	0.39	NA	NA	NA	NA
Dividends	0.60	0.58	0.57	0.56	0.55	0.54	0.54	0.52	0.52	0.50
Payout Ratio	41%	21%	27%	29%	36%	87%	29%	33%	29%	38%
Calendar Year	2005	2004	2003	2002	2001	2000	1999	1998	1997	1996
Prices:High	35.88	35.15	28.84	30.81	24.10	22.88	28.88	28.94	21.13	16.50
Prices:Low	29.55	25.70	12.60	14.75	12.60	11.75	16.81	20.19	14.06	13.56
P/E Ratio:High	25	13	14	16	16	37	15	18	12	13
P/E Ratio:Low	20	9	6	8	8	19	9	13	8	10
Income Statement Analysis (Million $)										
Revenue	19,864	19,543	20,210	19,160	20,909	23,194	20,339	17,421	17,201	16,552
Operating Income	750	936	919	870	904	860	800	652	636	613
Depreciation	311	303	302	297	341	344	277	234	230	232
Interest Expense	139	138	166	182	194	213	154	124	134	137
Pretax Income	329	601	455	408	344	154	448	316	385	281
Effective Tax Rate	37.4%	35.8%	38.4%	37.0%	40.1%	46.8%	45.8%	39.6%	40.0%	37.6%
Net Income	206	386	280	257	206	82.0	243	191	231	175
S&P Core Earnings	269	313	276	217	166	51.2	NA	NA	NA	NA
Balance Sheet & Other Financial Data (Million $)										
Cash	686	464	292	29.2	12.0	11.0	11.0	8.00	6.00	6.54
Current Assets	2,168	2,127	2,037	1,647	1,604	2,092	2,178	1,583	1,612	1,601
Total Assets	6,038	6,278	6,153	5,896	5,825	6,407	6,495	4,266	4,093	4,283
Current Liabilities	1,507	1,632	1,872	1,525	1,701	2,341	2,510	1,522	1,457	1,369
Long Term Debt	1,406	1,579	1,634	2,020	1,875	2,008	1,954	1,246	1,261	1,420
Common Equity	2,619	2,511	2,210	2,009	1,918	1,793	1,821	1,300	1,196	1,301
Total Capital	4,079	4,240	3,986	4,146	3,873	3,831	3,778	2,606	2,499	2,765
Capital Expenditures	308	233	328	383	293	398	408	240	231	245
Cash Flow	517	689	582	554	547	426	520	425	461	407
Current Ratio	1.4	1.3	1.1	1.1	0.9	0.9	0.9	1.0	1.1	1.2
% Long Term Debt of Capitalization	34.5	37.2	41.0	48.7	48.4	52.4	51.7	47.8	50.5	51.4
% Net Income of Revenue	1.0	2.0	1.4	1.3	1.0	0.4	1.2	1.1	1.3	1.1
% Return on Assets	3.3	6.2	4.6	4.4	3.4	1.3	4.5	4.6	5.5	4.2
% Return on Equity	8.0	16.3	13.3	13.2	11.1	4.5	15.6	15.3	18.5	14.0

Data as orig reptd.; bef. results of disc opers/spec. items. Per share data adj. for stk. divs.; EPS diluted. E-Estimated. NA-Not Available. NM-Not Meaningful. NR-Not Ranked. UR-Under Review.

Office: 11840 Valley View Road, Eden Prairie, MN 55344.
Telephone: 952-828-4000.
Website: http://www.supervalu.com
Chrmn & CEO: J. Noddle

Pres & COO: M.L. Jackson
EVP & CFO: P.K. Knous
SVP & CIO: P. Singer
VP & Cntlr: D.M. Oliver

Investor Contact: Y. Scharton (952-828-4540)
Board of Directors: A. G. Ames, I. Cohen, R. E. Daly, L. A. Del Santo, S. E. Engel, P. L. Francis, E. C. Gage, G. L. Keith, Jr., C. M. Lillis, J. Noddle, M. Peterson, S. S. Rogers, W. Sales, K. P. Seifert

Founded: 1871
Domicile: Delaware
Employees: 52,400

STANDARD &POOR'S

Symantec Corp

S&P Recommendation HOLD ★★★★★

Price $18.82 (as of Oct 27, 2006)

12-Mo. Target Price $19.00

Investment Style Large-Cap Growth

GICS Sector Information Technology
Sub-Industry Systems Software

Comment This company provides content security solutions, including antivirus software.

Key Stock Statistics (Source S&P, Vickers, company reports)

52-Wk Range	$24.01–14.78	S&P Oper. EPS 2007E	0.94	P/E on S&P Oper. EPS 2007E	20.0	Dividend Rate/Share	Nil
Trailing 12-Month EPS	$-0.03	S&P Oper. EPS 2008E	1.11	Common Shares Outstg. (M)	989.2	Yield (%)	Nil
Trailing 12-Month P/E	NM	S&P Core EPS 2007E	0.91	Market Capitalization(B)	$18.617	Beta	0.91
$10K Invested 5 Yrs Ago	$26,189	S&P Core EPS 2008E	1.05	Institutional Ownership (%)	89	S&P Credit Rating	NR

Price Performance

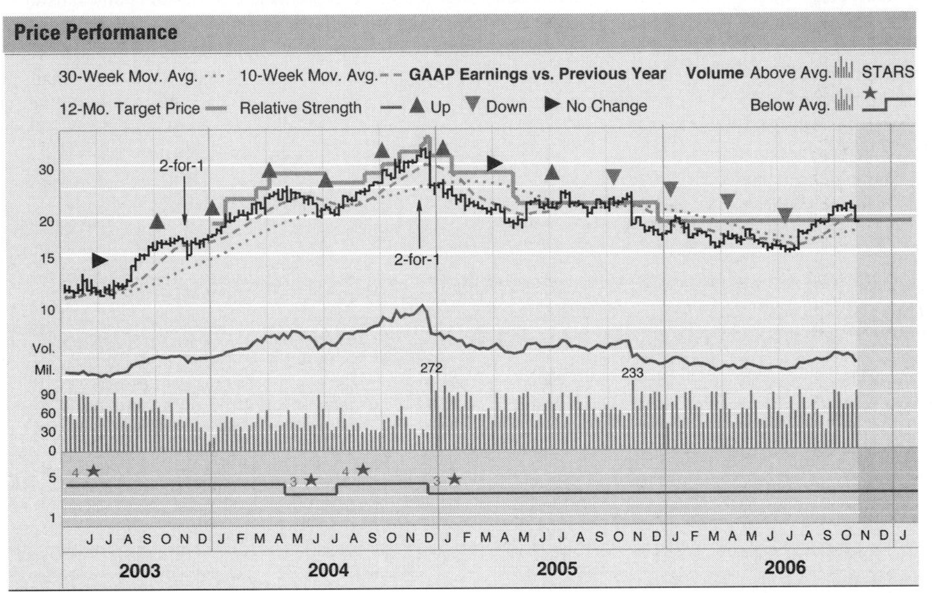

Options: ASE, CBOE, P, Ph

Analysis prepared by **Clyde Montevirgen** on August 17, 2006, when the stock traded at **$ 18.26**.

Highlights

- On July 2, 2005, SYMC acquired Veritas Software in exchange for approximately $13.5 billion of stock. On a pro forma basis, FY 06 (Mar.) revenues grew 8%, to $5.0 billion. In FY 07, we see revenues increasing 6%, as marketing synergies of both companies continue to gain traction. We think SYMC's Norton Confidential and Norton 360 launches should support sales growth as its latest storage and server management and data protection products gain popularity. In FY 08, we project sales growth of 8%.
- Given the major changes at SYMC following the Veritas acquisition, we expect operating margins to decline to about 24% in FY 07, from 31.6% in FY 06, as the company continues to digest this large acquisition. In addition, we expect higher R&D costs to depress margins as the firm works to integrate its combined offerings. We expect SYMC to make progress on integration by mid-FY 07, enabling operating margins to increase in the second half of the year.
- We expect operating EPS of $0.94 in FY 07 and $1.11 in FY 08, including projected stock option expense of $0.12 and $0.09 in the respective years.

Investment Rationale/Risk

- Our hold recommendation reflects our concerns over SYMC's acquisition of Veritas for $13.5 billion in stock. We continue to see significant integration risk as a result of the size and scope of the transaction, and we are cautious of slow product synergy. We also believe the transaction may pressure sales and margin expansion as enterprise spending may decelerate and as its consumer security products face formidable competition. However, we see SYMC's latest storage management offerings gaining traction among enterprises. Furthermore, we think company guidance could prove conservative.
- Risks to our recommendation and target price include intense competition in the Internet security software industry, a potential slowdown in corporate information technology (IT) spending, and integration risk associated with the recent Veritas acquisition.
- Using a blend of methodologies, including a PEG ratio of 1.5X and an enterprise value to sales ratio of 3.4X, in line with peers, we arrive at our 12-month target price of $19.

Qualitative Risk Assessment

LOW | MEDIUM | **HIGH**

Our risk assessment for Symantec reflects our concern regarding the highly competitive market in which the company operates, integration risk from the Veritas purchase, and the company's high proportion of revenue stemming from relatively few product lines.

Quantitative Evaluations

S&P Quality Ranking **B**

D | C | B- | **B** | B+ | A- | A | A+

Relative Strength Rank **WEAK**

17

LOWEST = 1 HIGHEST = 99

Revenue/Earnings Data

Revenue (Million $)

	1Q	2Q	3Q	4Q	Year
2007	1,259	--	--	--	--
2006	699.9	1,056	1,149	1,239	4,143
2005	556.6	618.3	695.2	712.7	2,583
2004	391.1	428.7	493.9	556.4	1,870
2003	316.0	325.2	375.6	390.0	1,407
2002	228.0	242.4	290.3	310.8	1,071

Earnings Per Share ($)

	1Q	2Q	3Q	4Q	Year
2007	0.09	E0.22	E0.25	E0.26	E0.94
2006	0.27	-0.21	0.08	0.11	0.15
2005	0.16	0.19	0.22	0.16	0.74
2004	0.09	0.12	0.16	0.16	0.54
2003	0.09	0.08	0.11	0.10	0.38
2002	-0.04	-0.02	Nil	0.01	-0.05

Fiscal year ended Mar. 31. Next earnings report expected: Early November. EPS Estimates based on S&P Operating Earnings; historical GAAP earnings are as reported.

Dividend Data

No cash dividends have been paid.

The McGraw·Hill Companies

Symantec Corp

Business Summary August 17, 2006

Symantec, a world leader in Internet security technology, provides a broad range of content and network security solutions to individuals and enterprises. The company is a leading provider of virus protection, firewall, virtual private network, vulnerability management, intrusion detection, remote management technologies, and security services to consumers and enterprises worldwide.

The company is organized into five operating segments: Consumer Products, Enterprise Security, Enterprise Administration, Services, and Other.

The Consumer Products segment accounted for 51% of net revenues in FY 05 (Mar.), up from 47% in FY 04. The segment's charter is to ensure that consumers and their information are secure and protected in a connected world. Primary product lines include Norton AntiVirus software for protection against, and detection and elimination of, computer viruses, and Norton Internet Security, a fully integrated suite that provides total Internet protection for the home computer. Other products include Norton SystemWorks, Norton Utilities, and Norton CleanSweep.

The Enterprise Security and Administration segments accounted for 36% and 11% of total net revenues in FY 05, respectively, versus 39% and 12% in FY 04. The objective of the Enterprise Security segment is to provide a broad range of security solutions for SYMC's enterprise customers. The segment focuses on two areas: content and network security. The Enterprise Administration segment offers products that enable companies to be more effective and efficient within their Information Technology (IT) departments. Products include pcAnywhere and Ghost Corporate Edition.

Company Financials

Per Share Data ($) Year Ended Mar. 31	**2006**	**2005**	**2004**	**2003**	**2002**	**2001**	**2000**	**1999**	**1998**	**1997**
Tangible Book Value	0.63	3.07	1.97	2.89	1.26	0.97	1.11	0.59	0.70	0.49
Cash Flow	0.48	0.86	0.62	0.45	0.37	0.18	0.43	0.16	0.23	0.01
Earnings	0.15	0.74	0.54	0.38	-0.05	0.12	0.34	0.11	0.18	0.06
S&P Core Earnings	-0.06	0.59	0.43	0.26	-0.19	0.03	NA	NA	NA	NA
Dividends	Nil	Nil	Nil	Nil	Nil	Nil	Nil	Nil	Nil	Nil
Payout Ratio	Nil	Nil	Nil	Nil	Nil	Nil	Nil	Nil	Nil	Nil
Calendar Year	2005	2004	2003	2002	2001	2000	1999	1998	1997	1996
Prices:High	26.60	34.05	17.50	11.55	9.19	10.20	8.66	4.08	3.47	2.89
Prices:Low	16.32	17.27	9.09	6.80	3.90	3.42	1.56	1.09	1.50	1.09
P/E Ratio:High	NM	46	33	30	78	NM	25	38	20	49
P/E Ratio:Low	NM	23	17	18	33	NM	5	10	8	19

Income Statement Analysis (Million $)										
Revenue	4,143	2,583	1,870	1,407	1,071	854	746	593	578	472
Operating Income	942	926	611	417	269	240	191	90.0	126	57.6
Depreciation	340	96.3	78.8	59.6	238	105	42.9	30.2	25.2	22.8
Interest Expense	18.0	12.3	21.2	21.2	9.17	Nil	0.02	1.80	1.22	1.40
Pretax Income	363	858	542	364	45.5	141	257	83.2	112	30.4
Effective Tax Rate	56.8%	37.5%	31.6%	31.7%	NM	54.6%	33.9%	39.6%	24.1%	14.2%
Net Income	157	536	371	248	-28.2	63.9	170	50.2	85.1	26.0
S&P Core Earnings	-51.0	423	284	157	-106	14.8	NA	NA	NA	NA

Balance Sheet & Other Financial Data (Million $)										
Cash	2,316	1,091	2,410	1,706	1,375	557	432	193	226	160
Current Assets	3,908	3,688	2,842	1,988	1,563	782	546	316	329	238
Total Assets	17,913	5,614	4,456	3,266	2,503	1,792	846	563	476	342
Current Liabilities	3,478	1,701	1,287	895	579	413	227	217	153	109
Long Term Debt	24.9	4.41	606	607	604	2.36	1.55	1.50	6.00	15.0
Common Equity	13,668	3,705	2,426	1,764	1,320	1,377	618	345	318	218
Total Capital	14,187	3,798	3,077	2,371	1,924	1,379	620	347	323	233
Capital Expenditures	267	91.5	111	192	141	61.2	28.5	25.1	26.3	27.2
Cash Flow	497	633	453	308	210	95.9	213	74.2	110	48.8
Current Ratio	1.1	2.2	2.2	2.2	31.3	1.9	2.4	1.5	2.1	2.2
% Long Term Debt of Capitalization	0.2	0.1	19.7	25.6	0.3	0.2	0.3	2.1	1.8	6.4
% Net Income of Revenue	3.8	20.8	19.8	17.7	NM	7.5	22.8	8.5	14.7	5.5
% Return on Assets	1.3	10.6	9.6	8.6	NM	4.8	24.1	9.7	20.8	8.2
% Return on Equity	1.8	17.5	17.7	16.1	NM	6.4	35.3	15.2	31.8	13.0

Data as orig reptd.; bef. results of disc opers/spec. items. Per share data adj. for stk. divs.; EPS diluted. E-Estimated. NA-Not Available. NM-Not Meaningful. NR-Not Ranked. UR-Under Review.

Office: 20330 Stevens Creek Boulevard, Cupertino, CA 95014-2132.
Telephone: 408-517-8000.
Email: investor-relations@symantec.com
Website: http://www.symantec.com

Chrmn & CEO: J.W. Thompson
EVP & CFO: J.A. Beer
EVP, Secy & General Counsel: A.F. Courville
EVP & CIO: D. Thompson

VP & Chief Acctg Officer: S.C. Markowski
Investor Contact: H. Corcos (408-517-8324)
Board of Directors: M. Brown, W. T. Coleman, D. L. Mahoney, R. S. Miller, G. Reyes, D. J. Roux, D. H. Schulman, J. W. Thompson, V. P. Unruh

Founded: 1983
Domicile: Delaware
Employees: 16,000

STANDARD &POOR'S

Symbol Technologies Inc.

S&P Recommendation HOLD ★★★★★

Price $14.93 (as of Oct 31, 2006)

12-Mo. Target Price $15.00

Investment Style Mid-Cap Value

GICS Sector Information Technology
Sub-Industry Electronic Equipment Manufacturers

Comment This company develops, makes and sells portable bar-code scanning equipment that uses laser technology to read data encoded in bar-code symbols.

Key Stock Statistics (Source S&P, Vickers, company reports)

52-Wk Range	**$15.37–8.01**	S&P Oper. EPS 2006E	**0.46**	P/E on S&P Oper. EPS 2006E	**32.5**	Dividend Rate/Share	**$0.02**
Trailing 12-Month EPS	**$0.42**	S&P Oper. EPS 2007E	**0.56**	Common Shares Outstg. (M)	**253.9**	Yield (%)	**0.13**
Trailing 12-Month P/E	**35.6**	S&P Core EPS 2006E	**0.46**	Market Capitalization(B)	**$3.791**	Beta	**2.40**
$10K Invested 5 Yrs Ago	**$11,138**	S&P Core EPS 2007E	**0.56**	Institutional Ownership (%)	**85**	S&P Credit Rating	**NA**

Price Performance

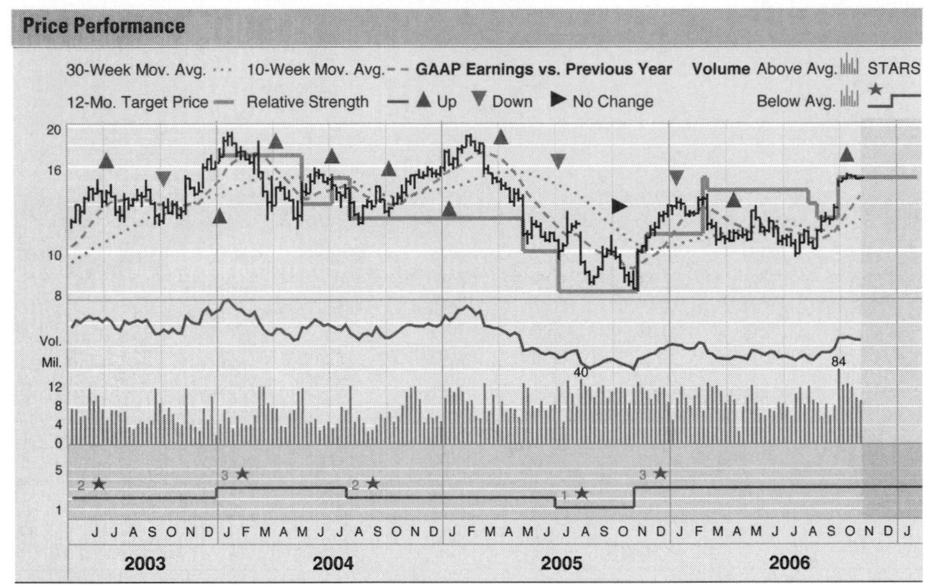

Options: ASE, CBOE, Ph

Analysis prepared by **Dylan Cathers** on September 21, 2006, when the stock traded at **$ 14.62**.

Highlights

- We see revenues rising 2% and 6% in 2006 and 2007, respectively. We believe increases in IT spending related to warehouse and shipping logistics, route accounting and wireless mobility will likely drive product revenue growth, as the company has been focusing on new product launches in these areas. In services, we look for revenues to be flat while SBL focuses on building its Global Services program.
- We estimate a gross margin for 2006 of 45.5%, on higher volumes and cost efficiencies, versus 43.5% in 2005. We believe SBL will continue at its current R&D spending rate in the high single digits as a percent of sales, due to a strong emphasis on new product development. We look for the operating margin to widen to 10% in 2006, on lower operating expenses. A restructuring effort under way could further bolster operating margins in the longer term after related charges.
- For 2006 and 2007, we expect EPS of $0.46 and $0.56, respectively. Both our 2006 and 2007 EPS estimates include projected stock option expense.

Investment Rationale/Risk

- Our hold recommendation is based on valuation. SBL recently agreed to be acquired by Motorola (MOT: $25, hold) for $15 a share, for a total value of about $3.9 billion. Subject to shareholder and regulatory approval, the planned deal is expected to close in late 2006 or early 2007.
- Risks to our recommendation and target price include a failure to get the appropriate merger approvals, more aggressive competition than expected, and a slower shift to alternate technologies such as radio frequency identification technology, which is being adopted by Wal-Mart, among others. We have corporate governance concerns about: the poison pill in place; the board's ability to amend bylaws without shareholder approval; and stock-based incentive plans that were adopted without shareholder approval.
- Our 12-month target price of $15 is based on the planned transaction price and reflects a P/E of about 33X our 2006 EPS estimate and 27X our 2007 EPS estimate.

Qualitative Risk Assessment

LOW	MEDIUM	**HIGH**

Our risk assessment for Symbol reflects the competitive nature of the industry, being overseen by the SEC due to alleged actions of the former management team, and pending litigation against the former management team.

Quantitative Evaluations

S&P Quality Ranking B-

D	C	**B-**	B	B+	A-	A	A+

Relative Strength Rank STRONG

84

LOWEST = 1 HIGHEST = 99

Revenue/Earnings Data

Revenue (Million $)

	1Q	2Q	3Q	4Q	Year
2006	444.9	453.1	458.2	--	--
2005	457.5	427.8	441.5	438.9	1,766
2004	419.7	432.8	429.2	450.5	1,732
2003	386.4	373.8	377.1	393.0	1,530
2002	317.6	329.1	382.0	372.9	1,402
2001	450.2	340.2	331.2	331.1	1,453

Earnings Per Share ($)

	1Q	2Q	3Q	4Q	Year
2006	0.12	--	0.09	**E**0.12	**E**0.46
2005	0.09	-0.12	0.07	0.09	0.13
2004	0.03	0.12	0.07	0.11	0.33
2003	-0.13	0.03	0.05	0.07	0.01
2002	0.02	-0.11	0.14	-0.30	-0.25
2001	0.12	-0.27	-0.16	0.06	-0.24

Fiscal year ended Dec. 31. Next earnings report expected: Late February. EPS Estimates based on S&P Operating Earnings; historical GAAP earnings are as reported.

Dividend Data (Dates: mm/dd Payment Date: mm/dd/yy)

Amount ($)	Date Decl.	Ex-Div. Date	Stk. of Record	Payment Date
0.010	09/26	10/05	10/10	10/28/05
0.010	03/02	03/29	03/31	04/14/06

Dividends have been paid since 1997. Source: Company reports.

Symbol Technologies Inc.

Business Summary September 21, 2006

CORPORATE OVERVIEW. Symbol Technologies has grown from being a manufacturer of bar-code scanning products to become a global provider of wireless networking and information systems that allow access to information over local area networks (LANs), wide area networks (WANs), and the Internet. The company makes scanner integrated mobile and wireless information management systems that consist of mobile computing devices, wireless local area networks (WLAN), bar code readers, network appliances, peripherals, software, and programming tools.

The company's bar-code reading devices are designed to capture and decode one- and two-dimensional bar code symbols, and to store, process and transmit information. SBL's mobile computing devices are microprocessor-based, lightweight and battery-operated hand-held computers. Information may be captured by a bar-code reader, or may be manually entered via a keyboard, touch screen, or pen computer display/entry device, and transmitted instantly by a host computer across a WLAN, or in some cases, via a modem.

SBL's wireless communication solutions connect its mobile computing devices to wireless WANs and LANs. Based on spread spectrum RF technology, the company's WLAN products provide real-time wireless data communication at data rates of up to 11 Mbps, and in combination with its telephony products, can provide wireless voice and data over TCP/IP data networks.

SBL's global services organization provides a full range of professional and customer support services, from project planning and network design, through integration and installation, to ongoing service and support. Management's strategy for the service segment focuses on leveraging the repair business into more advanced solutions that can be linked to sales of their extensive product line.

Company Financials

Per Share Data ($) Year Ended Dec. 31	**2005**	**2004**	**2003**	**2002**	**2001**	**2000**	**1999**	**1998**	**1997**	**1996**
Tangible Book Value	2.65	2.19	2.53	2.38	3.35	3.64	2.56	2.09	1.71	1.45
Cash Flow	0.41	0.65	0.30	0.05	-0.01	0.06	0.86	0.70	0.56	0.44
Earnings	0.13	0.33	0.01	-0.25	-0.24	-0.33	0.54	0.44	0.34	0.24
S&P Core Earnings	-0.21	0.19	0.15	-0.15	-0.35	NA	NA	NA	NA	NA
Dividends	0.02	0.02	0.02	0.02	0.02	0.01	0.01	0.01	0.01	Nil
Payout Ratio	15%	6%	NM	NM	NM	NM	2%	2%	2%	Nil
Prices:High	19.12	19.37	17.70	17.50	37.33	46.03	28.89	19.07	8.88	6.52
Prices:Low	8.01	11.30	8.01	4.98	9.50	17.08	11.56	7.25	5.63	4.20
P/E Ratio:High	NM	59	NM	NM	NM	NM	53	43	26	27
P/E Ratio:Low	NM	34	NM	NM	NM	NM	21	16	17	17
Income Statement Analysis (Million $)										
Revenue	1,766	1,732	1,530	1,402	1,453	1,449	1,139	978	774	657
Operating Income	168	217	149	139	-8.90	171	243	200	158	136
Depreciation	70.8	77.8	68.8	69.3	53.5	82.1	66.2	55.2	45.3	39.5
Interest Expense	12.1	20.0	10.6	16.8	20.7	16.4	8.14	5.82	5.50	4.89
Pretax Income	32.8	124	3.90	-82.6	-80.4	-79.6	171	139	110	81.1
Effective Tax Rate	1.70%	33.9%	15.5%	NM	NM	NM	32.0%	33.0%	36.0%	38.0%
Net Income	32.2	81.8	3.30	-57.8	-54.7	-69.0	116	93.0	70.2	50.3
S&P Core Earnings	-53.5	48.3	38.0	-33.7	-80.3	NA	NA	NA	NA	NA
Balance Sheet & Other Financial Data (Million $)										
Cash	139	218	150	76.1	81.0	63.4	30.1	16.3	60.0	34.3
Current Assets	730	743	734	690	1,000	1,078	584	480	400	352
Total Assets	1,816	1,930	1,647	1,572	1,893	2,093	1,048	838	679	614
Current Liabilities	497	607	536	474	340	458	233	184	158	131
Long Term Debt	44.5	176	99.0	136	310	308	99.6	64.6	40.3	50.5
Common Equity	1,207	1,073	921	888	1,181	1,202	640	531	454	400
Total Capital	1,252	1,249	1,020	1,023	1,491	1,598	740	596	494	450
Capital Expenditures	72.0	91.6	60.6	34.7	98.5	79.7	70.0	89.3	42.7	34.7
Cash Flow	103	160	72.1	11.6	-1.20	13.1	183	148	116	89.8
Current Ratio	1.5	1.2	1.4	1.5	2.9	2.4	2.5	2.6	2.5	2.7
% Long Term Debt of Capitalization	3.6	14.1	9.7	13.3	20.8	19.3	13.5	10.8	8.2	11.2
% Net Income of Revenue	1.8	4.7	0.2	NM	NM	NM	10.2	9.5	9.1	7.7
% Return on Assets	1.7	4.6	0.2	NM	NM	NM	12.3	12.3	10.9	8.7
% Return on Equity	2.8	8.2	0.4	NM	NM	NM	19.9	18.9	16.5	13.4

Data as orig reptd.; bef. results of disc opers/spec. items. Per share data adj. for stk. divs.; EPS diluted. E-Estimated. NA-Not Available. NM-Not Meaningful. NR-Not Ranked. UR-Under Review.

Office: 1 Symbol Plz, Holtsville, NY 11742-1300.
Telephone: 631-738-2400.
Email: info@symbol.com
Website: http://www.symbol.com

Chrmn: R. Chrenc
Pres & CEO: S. Iannuzzi
SVP & CFO: T.T. Yates
VP & Chief Acctg Officer: J.M. Langrock

Investor Contact: L.C. Chaitman (631-738-2400)
Board of Directors: R. Chrenc, S. Iannuzzi, J. M. Lawrie, G. Samenuk, T. T. Yates, M. A. Yellin

Founded: 1973
Domicile: Delaware
Employees: 5,200

STANDARD &POOR'S

Synovus Financial Corp.

S&P Recommendation HOLD ★★★★★	Price	12-Mo. Target Price	Investment Style
	$29.34 (as of Oct 27, 2006)	$31.00	Large-Cap Growth

GICS Sector Financials
Sub-Industry Regional Banks

Comment Synovus owns about 40 community banks in Georgia and four other southern states, and has an 81% interest in one of the world's largest bank payment processing companies.

Key Stock Statistics (Source S&P, Vickers, company reports)

52-Wk Range	$30.05–25.74	S&P Oper. EPS 2006E	1.85	P/E on S&P Oper. EPS 2006E	15.9	Dividend Rate/Share	$0.78
Trailing 12-Month EPS	$1.81	S&P Oper. EPS 2007E	2.07	Common Shares Outstg. (M)	324.0	Yield (%)	2.66
Trailing 12-Month P/E	16.2	S&P Core EPS 2006E	1.85	Market Capitalization(B)	$9.507	Beta	0.81
$10K Invested 5 Yrs Ago	$13,734	S&P Core EPS 2007E	2.07	Institutional Ownership (%)	48	S&P Credit Rating	A

Price Performance

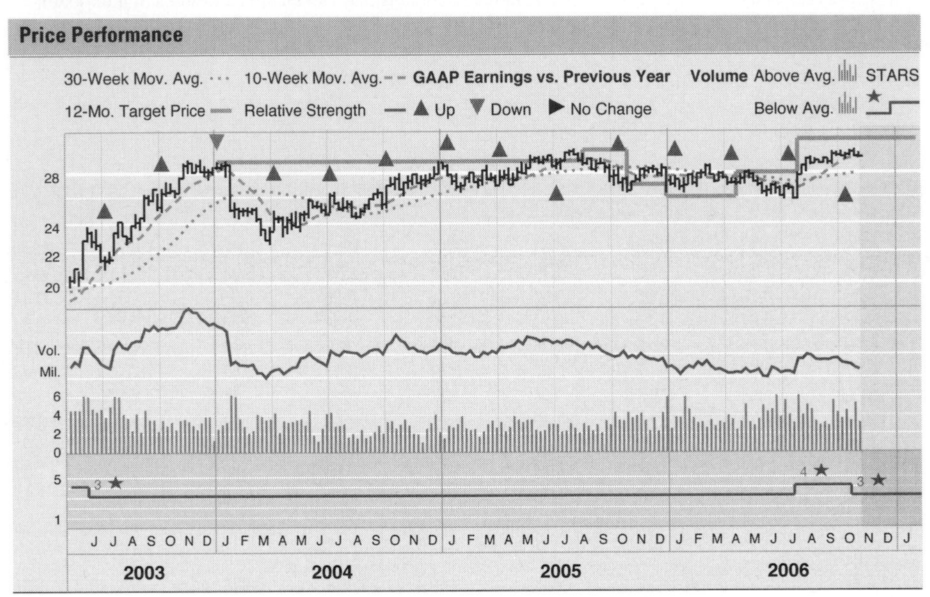

Options: CBOE

Highlights

- The STARS recommendation for SNV has recently been changed to 3 (hold) from 4 (buy). The Highlights section of this Stock Report will be updated accordingly.

Investment Rationale/Risk

- The Investment Rationale/Risk section of this Stock Report will be updated shortly. For the latest News story on SNV from MarketScope, see below.

- 10/19/06 09:21 am EDT... S&P DOWNGRADES SHARES OF SYNOVUS FINANCIAL TO HOLD FROM BUY (SNV 30.02***): Our downgrade is based on valuation following the shares' recent rise. SNV reports Q3 EPS of $0.47 vs. $0.43, a penny below our estimate. Core deposits grew 16.9% from a year ago and loans rose 11.8%. The company raises its guidance for '06 EPS growth to 15%, above our 13% projection. We are increasing our '06 EPS estimate to $1.89 from $1.85. However, because of our concerns about expected deposit growth and pricing trends in '07, we are leaving our '07 EPS estimate at $2.07, and our 12-month target price remains at $31, 15X that estimate. /E.Oja

Qualitative Risk Assessment

LOW | **MEDIUM** | HIGH

Our risk assessment for SNV reflects our view of the company's large investment in its payment processing subsidiary, offset by its mid-cap valuation, good credit quality of its loan portfolio, and history of profitability. While the company operates in a highly competitive and fragmented industry, the industry tends to produce relatively stable financial results, in our view.

Quantitative Evaluations

S&P Quality Ranking A+

D | C | B- | B | B+ | A- | A | **A+**

Relative Strength Rank MODERATE

39

LOWEST = 1 HIGHEST = 99

Revenue/Earnings Data

Revenue (Million $)

	1Q	2Q	3Q	4Q	Year
2006	932.9	1,015	1,060	--	--
2005	756.4	845.5	891.8	921.0	3,415
2004	646.8	648.6	684.0	700.7	2,680
2003	585.0	612.0	613.4	620.3	2,431
2002	547.4	558.1	580.7	603.7	2,290
2001	516.6	550.8	513.8	487.5	2,069

Earnings Per Share ($)

2006	0.43	0.47	0.47	E0.47	E1.85
2005	0.37	0.41	0.43	0.44	1.64
2004	0.34	0.34	0.35	0.38	1.41
2003	0.30	0.32	0.33	0.34	1.28
2002	0.28	0.29	0.31	0.35	1.21
2001	0.25	0.26	0.27	0.29	1.05

Fiscal year ended Dec. 31. Next earnings report expected: Mid January. EPS Estimates based on S&P Operating Earnings; historical GAAP earnings are as reported.

Dividend Data (Dates: mm/dd Payment Date: mm/dd/yy)

Amount ($)	Date Decl.	Ex-Div. Date	Stk. of Record	Payment Date
0.183	11/15	12/20	12/22	01/02/06
0.195	02/22	03/21	03/23	04/01/06
0.195	05/16	06/20	06/22	07/01/06
0.195	08/15	09/19	09/21	10/02/06

Dividends have been paid since 1930. Source: Company reports.

Synovus Financial Corp.

Business Summary August 25, 2006

CORPORATE OVERVIEW. Synovus is a bank holding company with 39 wholly owned bank subsidiaries in five southeastern states. The company has seven non-bank financial services subsidiaries that provide securities, trust, mortgage banking, insurance, financial planning, asset management and investment advisory services, and an 80% stake in a transaction processing company. The company's two segments are Financial Services and Transaction Processing Services. The company operates in Georgia, South Carolina, Florida, Alabama and Tennessee.

The Financial Services segment accounted for 45% of 2005 revenues. Banking operations consist of lending and deposit gathering as well as other banking-related products and services, including investment, trust, insurance, and mortgage services. SNV's banking subsidiaries operate independently, with decentralized decision-making processes in place that allow each subsidiary to act independently.

The Transaction Processing Services segment (55% of revenues) owns 81% of the common stock of Total System Services (TSS: hold, $23), which provides electronic payment processing and associated services to financial and non-financial institutions in the U.S., Canada, Mexico, Honduras, Puerto Rico and Europe. Services provided include processing for consumer, debit, commercial, stored value and retail cards, as well as for student loans. The company divides its services into three operating segments: domestic-based support services (75% of 2005 revenues), international-based support services (9% of 2005 revenues), and merchant processing services (16% of 2005 revenues).

SNV uses derivative instruments, including commitments to sell fixed-rate mortgage loans and interest rate swaps, to manage its exposure to various types of interest rate risks and to meet the financing and interest rate risk management needs of its customers. When using derivative instruments on behalf of its customers, SNV enters into offsetting transactions to minimize its risk.

Company Financials

Per Share Data ($) Year Ended Dec. 31	**2005**	**2004**	**2003**	**2002**	**2001**	**2000**	**1999**	**1998**	**1997**	**1996**
Tangible Book Value	7.82	7.04	6.50	6.40	5.75	4.98	4.35	3.96	3.43	3.00
Earnings	1.64	1.41	1.28	1.21	1.05	0.92	0.80	0.70	0.62	0.53
S&P Core Earnings	1.60	1.33	1.23	1.17	0.97	NA	NA	NA	NA	NA
Dividends	0.73	0.69	0.66	0.59	0.51	0.44	0.34	0.28	0.24	0.20
Payout Ratio	45%	49%	52%	49%	49%	48%	43%	40%	39%	37%
Prices:High	30.10	29.09	29.25	31.93	34.74	27.38	25.13	25.92	22.42	14.83
Prices:Low	26.30	22.50	17.24	16.48	22.75	14.00	17.25	17.25	13.11	7.78
P/E Ratio:High	18	21	23	26	33	30	31	37	36	28
P/E Ratio:Low	16	16	13	14	22	15	22	25	21	15
Income Statement Analysis (Million $)										
Net Interest Income	969	861	763	718	630	562	513	441	412	375
Tax Equivalent Adjustment	6.44	6.96	7.39	7.27	7.25	6.00	5.30	4.54	4.42	4.60
Non Interest Income	1,918	1,521	1,592	1,009	936	833	739	561	489	426
Loan Loss Provision	82.5	75.3	71.8	65.3	51.7	44.3	34.0	26.7	32.3	31.8
% Expense/Operating Revenue	67.2%	66.5%	50.7%	62.1%	64.0%	66.2%	68.4%	67.0%	66.7%	66.7%
Pretax Income	861	718	638	588	510	428	363	302	268	219
Effective Tax Rate	35.7%	35.1%	34.9%	33.8%	35.0%	34.8%	34.2%	34.6%	34.9%	36.3%
Net Income	516	437	389	365	312	263	225	187	165	140
% Net Interest Margin	4.19	4.22	NA	4.65	4.65	4.70	5.07	5.22	5.26	5.19
S&P Core Earnings	502	413	375	351	286	NA	NA	NA	NA	NA
Balance Sheet & Other Financial Data (Million $)										
Money Market Assets	99.2	140	177	97.8	27.6	380	94.0	54.1	93.3	38.2
Investment Securities	2,958	2,696	2,529	2,238	2,088	2,078	1,994	1,818	1,655	1,639
Commercial Loans	18,091	16,340	13,686	11,791	9,809	8,495	6,789	5,225	4,411	4,002
Other Loans	3,301	3,140	2,779	2,673	2,609	2,257	2,289	2,195	2,204	2,073
Total Assets	27,621	25,050	21,633	19,036	16,658	14,908	12,547	10,498	9,260	8,612
Demand Deposits	3,701	3,338	2,834	2,303	1,985	1,727	1,625	1,362	2,385	2,212
Time Deposits	17,084	15,240	13,108	11,625	10,162	9,435	7,815	7,180	5,323	4,991
Long Term Debt	1,252	1,880	1,576	1,336	1,053	841	319	127	126	97.0
Common Equity	2,949	2,641	2,245	2,041	1,695	1,417	1,227	1,071	904	784
% Return on Assets	2.0	3.3	1.9	2.0	2.0	1.9	1.9	1.9	1.8	1.7
% Return on Equity	18.5	17.9	18.1	19.6	20.0	19.9	19.3	19.0	19.6	19.1
% Loan Loss Reserve	1.3	1.4	1.4	1.4	1.3	1.4	1.4	1.5	1.6	1.6
% Loans/Deposits	103.6	105.5	104.1	105.6	105.5	96.3	97.1	86.8	85.8	82.9
% Equity to Assets	10.6	18.3	10.5	10.5	9.9	9.6	10.0	10.0	9.4	8.9

Data as orig reptd.; bef. results of disc opers/spec. items. Per share data adj. for stk. divs.; EPS diluted. E-Estimated. NA-Not Available. NM-Not Meaningful. NR-Not Ranked. UR-Under Review.

Office: 1111 Bay Ave Ste 500, Columbus, GA 31901-5269.
Telephone: 706-649-5220.
Website: http://www.synovus.com
Chrmn & CEO: R.E. Anthony

Pres & COO: F.L. Green III
Vice Chrmn & CIO: E.R. James
Sr EVP, Secy & General Counsel: G.S. Griffith, III
EVP & CFO: T.J. Prescott

Investor Contact: P.A. Reynolds (706-649-5220)
Board of Directors: D. P. Amos, R. E. Anthony, J. H. Blanchard, R. Y. Bradley, F. W. Brumley, E. W. Camp, C. E. Floyd, G. W. Garrard, Jr., T. M. Goodrich, V. N. Hansford, J. P. Illges, III, A. W. Jones, III, M. H. Lampton, E. C. Ogie, H. L. Page, J. N. Purcell, M. T. Stith, W. B. Turner, Jr., J. D. Yancey

Founded: 1888
Domicile: Georgia
Employees: 12,691

Stock Report | October 31, 2006 | NYS Symbol: **SYY** | **SYY** is in the S&P 500

STANDARD &POOR'S

Sysco Corp

S&P Recommendation HOLD ★★★★★

Price $34.98 (as of Oct 31, 2006)

12-Mo. Target Price $35.00

Investment Style Large-Cap Growth

GICS Sector Consumer Staples
Sub-Industry Food Distributors

Comment This company is the largest U.S. marketer and distributor of foodservice products, serving more than 400,000 customers.

Key Stock Statistics (Source S&P, Vickers, company reports)

52-Wk Range	$35.00–26.50	S&P Oper. EPS 2007E	1.54	P/E on S&P Oper. EPS 2007E	22.7	Dividend Rate/Share	$0.68
Trailing 12-Month EPS	$1.35	S&P Oper. EPS 2008E	NA	Common Shares Outstg. (M)	619.6	Yield (%)	1.94
Trailing 12-Month P/E	25.9	S&P Core EPS 2007E	1.54	Market Capitalization(B)	$21.674	Beta	0.56
$10K Invested 5 Yrs Ago	$14,921	S&P Core EPS 2008E	NA	Institutional Ownership (%)	71	S&P Credit Rating	AA-

Price Performance

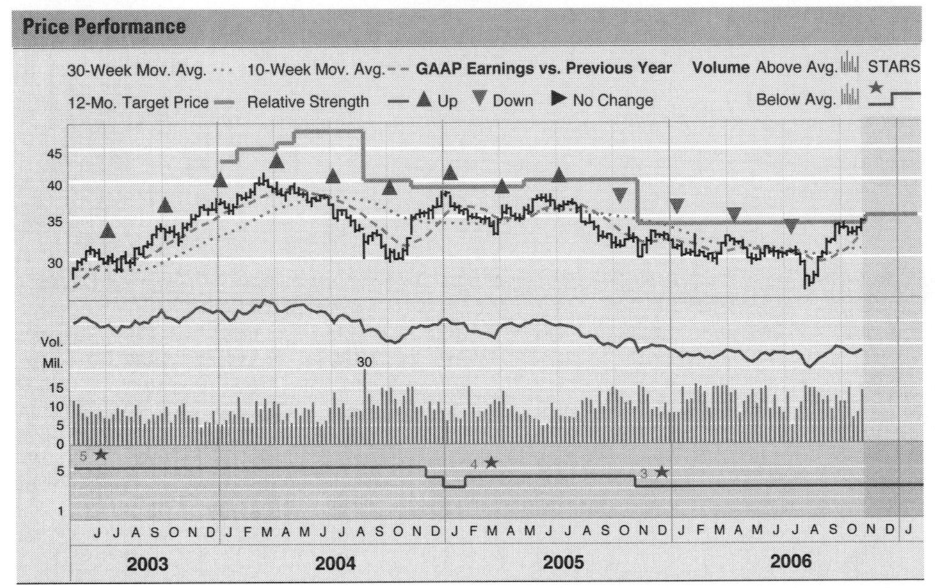

Options: ASE, CBOE, P

Qualitative Risk Assessment

LOW | MEDIUM | HIGH

Our risk assessment reflects that SYY operates in a relatively stable industry, in which we believe it has the largest market share. It is a large cap company and its shares exhibit a relatively low beta, in our opinion.

Quantitative Evaluations

S&P Quality Ranking A+

D | C | B- | B | B+ | A- | A | A+

Relative Strength Rank STRONG

79

LOWEST = 1 HIGHEST = 99

Highlights

- The 12-month target price for SYY has recently been changed to $35.00 from $34.00. The Highlights section of this Stock Report will be updated accordingly.

Investment Rationale/Risk

- The Investment Rationale/Risk section of this Stock Report will be updated shortly. For the latest News story on SYY from MarketScope, see below.
- 10/30/06 05:13 pm EST... S&P REITERATES HOLD OPINION ON SHARES OF SYSCO CORP. (SYY 34.58***): SYY posts Sep-Q EPS of $0.30 vs. $0.33. Excluding 2 accounting changes, EPS would have been $0.37, matching our estimate. The co. continued to gain market share, growing revenue ahead of the industry pace. However, gross margin contracted on an unfavorable sales mix shift. We view new distribution facilities coming on line and declining fuel costs as positives for upcoming quarters. We are raising our 12-month target price by $1, to $35, giving heavier weighting to our P/E analysis of 23X our FY 07 (June) EPS estimate of $1.54, a justifiable premium to peers, in our view. /R.Mathis

Revenue/Earnings Data

Revenue (Million $)

	1Q	2Q	3Q	4Q	Year
2006	8,010	7,971	8,138	8,509	32,628
2005	7,532	7,331	7,437	7,981	30,282
2004	7,134	7,037	7,026	8,139	29,335
2003	6,424	6,349	6,395	6,972	26,140
2002	5,829	5,591	5,620	6,311	23,351
2001	5,360	5,291	5,345	5,789	21,784

Earnings Per Share ($)

	1Q	2Q	3Q	4Q	Year
2006	0.31	0.33	0.30	0.41	1.35
2005	0.35	0.36	0.34	0.44	1.47
2004	0.32	0.34	0.30	0.43	1.37
2003	0.28	0.28	0.26	0.37	1.18
2002	0.24	0.24	0.23	0.31	1.01
2001	0.22	0.21	0.21	0.26	0.88

Fiscal year ended Jun. 30. Next earnings report expected: Early November. EPS Estimates based on S&P Operating Earnings; historical GAAP earnings are as reported.

Dividend Data (Dates: mm/dd Payment Date: mm/dd/yy)

Amount ($)	Date Decl.	Ex-Div. Date	Stk. of Record	Payment Date
0.170	11/11	01/04	01/06	01/27/06
0.170	02/17	04/05	04/07	04/28/06
0.170	05/12	07/05	07/07	07/28/06
0.170	09/08	10/04	10/06	10/27/06

Dividends have been paid since 1970. Source: Company reports.

Sysco Corp

Business Summary September 28, 2006

Sysco is the largest marketer and distributor of foodservice products in the U.S. and Canada, holding a 14% share of the foodservice industry. Since its formation in 1970, Sysco has grown significantly, with sales increasing from $115 million to over $30 billion, via internal expansion and acquisitions. From inception through the end of FY 05 (Jun.), the company made 130 such acquisitions. Its long-term goal is to attain: real sales growth in the upper single digits; minimum growth in EPS of 500 basis points above the real sales growth rate; 37% return on equity; and long-term debt equal to 35% to 40% of capitalization.

As of June 2005, SYY operated a fleet of about 8,550 delivery vehicles, from 166 distribution facilities and self-serve centers throughout the continental U.S., Alaska, and parts of Canada, providing products and services to more than 390,000 restaurants, hotels, schools, hospitals, retirement homes, and other foodservice operations--nearly anywhere a meal is prepared away from home.

The company stresses prompt and accurate delivery of orders, close contact with customers, and offers a full array of products and services. Sysco also provides ancillary services related to foodservice distribution such as data services, menu-planning, food safety, and inventory control.

Sysco distributes food products, including frozen foods such as meats, fully prepared entrees, fruits, vegetables and desserts; canned and dry foods; fresh meats; imported specialties and fresh produce. The company also distributes non-food products. These include paper products, tableware (china and silverware), restaurant and kitchen supplies, and cleaning supplies. All the products are either nationally branded merchandise or Sysco's own brands.

Company Financials

Per Share Data ($) Year Ended Jun. 30	**2006**	**2005**	**2004**	**2003**	**2002**	**2001**	**2000**	**1999**	**1998**	**1997**
Tangible Book Value	2.67	2.35	2.11	1.68	1.85	2.07	1.90	1.71	1.57	1.68
Cash Flow	1.89	1.96	1.80	1.59	1.47	1.27	1.02	0.84	0.74	0.66
Earnings	1.35	1.47	1.37	1.18	1.01	0.88	0.68	0.54	0.48	0.43
S&P Core Earnings	1.38	1.39	1.31	1.08	0.92	0.82	NA	NA	NA	NA
Dividends	0.49	0.58	0.61	0.40	0.32	0.26	0.18	0.20	0.17	0.14
Payout Ratio	36%	39%	45%	34%	32%	30%	26%	36%	35%	33%
Prices:High	35.00	38.04	41.27	37.57	32.58	30.12	30.44	20.56	14.34	11.81
Prices:Low	26.50	29.98	29.48	22.90	21.25	21.75	13.06	12.47	9.97	7.31
P/E Ratio:High	26	26	30	32	32	34	45	38	30	28
P/E Ratio:Low	20	20	22	19	21	25	19	23	21	17

Income Statement Analysis (Million $)										
Revenue	32,628	30,282	29,335	26,140	23,351	21,784	19,303	17,423	15,328	14,455
Operating Income	1,840	1,906	1,816	1,597	1,439	1,286	1,030	873	772	703
Depreciation	345	317	284	273	278	248	220	206	181	160
Interest Expense	109	75.0	69.9	72.2	62.9	71.0	71.0	73.0	58.0	47.0
Pretax Income	1,395	1,525	1,475	1,260	1,101	967	738	594	533	496
Effective Tax Rate	39.3%	37.0%	38.5%	38.3%	38.3%	38.3%	38.5%	39.1%	39.0%	39.0%
Net Income	846	961	907	778	680	597	454	362	325	303
S&P Core Earnings	866	890	868	710	618	559	NA	NA	NA	NA

Balance Sheet & Other Financial Data (Million $)										
Cash	202	192	200	421	230	136	159	149	110	118
Current Assets	4,400	4,002	3,851	3,630	3,185	2,985	2,733	2,409	2,180	1,964
Total Assets	8,992	8,268	7,848	6,937	5,990	5,469	4,814	4,097	3,780	3,437
Current Liabilities	3,226	3,458	3,127	2,701	2,239	2,090	1,783	1,428	1,324	1,114
Long Term Debt	1,627	956	1,231	1,249	1,176	961	1,024	998	867	686
Common Equity	3,052	2,759	2,565	2,198	2,133	2,148	1,762	1,427	1,357	1,400
Total Capital	5,403	4,440	4,483	3,945	3,750	3,379	3,032	2,669	2,456	2,323
Capital Expenditures	515	390	530	436	416	341	266	287	259	211
Cash Flow	1,191	1,278	1,191	1,051	958	845	674	567	506	463
Current Ratio	1.4	1.2	1.2	1.3	1.4	1.4	1.5	1.7	1.6	1.8
% Long Term Debt of Capitalization	30.1	21.5	27.4	31.7	31.4	28.4	33.8	37.4	35.3	29.6
% Net Income of Revenue	2.6	3.2	3.1	3.0	2.9	2.7	2.4	2.1	2.1	2.1
% Return on Assets	9.8	11.9	12.3	12.0	12.0	11.6	10.2	9.2	9.0	9.0
% Return on Equity	29.1	36.1	38.1	35.9	32.1	30.5	28.5	26.0	23.6	21.1

Data as orig reptd.; bef. results of disc opers/spec. items. Per share data adj. for stk. divs.; EPS diluted. E-Estimated. NA-Not Available. NM-Not Meaningful. NR-Not Ranked. UR-Under Review.

Office: 1390 Enclave Parkway, Houston, TX, USA 77077-2099.
Telephone: 281-584-1390.
Website: http://www.sysco.com
Chrmn, Pres & CEO: R.J. Schneiders

EVP & CFO: J.K. Stubblefield
EVP & Chief Admin: K.J. Carrig
SVP & Treas: D.D. Sanders
SVP & CIO: K.G. Drummond

Board of Directors: J. M. Cassaday, J. B. Craven, M. A. Fernandez, J. Golden, J. A. Hafner, R. G. Merrill, N. S. Newcomb, R. J. Schnieders, P. S. Sewell, J. K. Stubblefield, Jr., R. G. Tilghman, J. M. Ward

Founded: 1969
Domicile: Delaware
Employees: 49,600

STANDARD &POOR'S

Target Corp

S&P Recommendation BUY ★★★★★	Price	12-Mo. Target Price	Investment Style
	$58.56 (as of Oct 27, 2006)	$62.00	Large-Cap Growth

GICS Sector Consumer Discretionary
Sub-Industry General Merchandise Stores

Comment This company operates about 1,282 Target and 162 SuperTarget general merchandise stores across the U.S.

Key Stock Statistics (Source S&P, Vickers, company reports)

52-Wk Range	$59.85–44.70	S&P Oper. EPS 2007E	3.12	P/E on S&P Oper. EPS 2007E	18.8	Dividend Rate/Share	$0.48
Trailing 12-Month EPS	$2.88	S&P Oper. EPS 2008E	3.58	Common Shares Outstg. (M)	858.7	Yield (%)	0.82
Trailing 12-Month P/E	20.3	S&P Core EPS 2007E	3.11	Market Capitalization(B)	$50.285	Beta	1.26
$10K Invested 5 Yrs Ago	$19,285	S&P Core EPS 2008E	3.57	Institutional Ownership (%)	86	S&P Credit Rating	A+

Price Performance

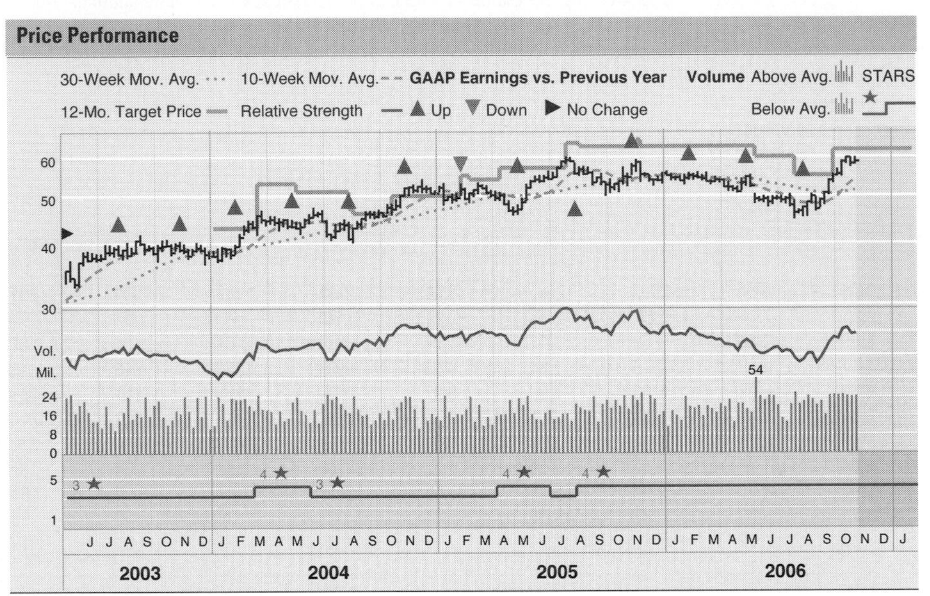

Options: ASE, CBOE, Ph

Analysis prepared by **Jason N. Asaeda** on September 21, 2006, when the stock traded at **$ 54.53**.

Highlights

- In FY 07 (Jan.), we look for sales to rise 11.7%, to $57.3 billion, on 4.5% same-store sales growth and the net addition of about 8% retail square footage. Combined with credit revenues of $1.6 billion, we see total FY 07 revenues of $58.9 billion. While food/consumables carry lower margins versus discretionary items, we think improved in-stock levels, merchandising differentiation, and an increase focus on food/consumables will drive shopping frequency ahead.
- Operating margins should widen modestly on higher merchandise markups and reduced inventory shrinkage, supported by direct imports and better inventory management, and cycling of stock option expensing initiated in FY 06, and should be partly offset by investments in new distribution centers, increases in store payroll and utilities costs, and higher marketing spending.
- Factoring in likely share buybacks, we see FY 07 operating EPS of $3.12 and S&P Core EPS of $3.11, with the difference reflecting projected pension costs.

Investment Rationale/Risk

- In FY 07, we look for expanded food and consumables assortments and marketing efforts that better convey TGT's "Expect More. Pay Less." brand message to provide a sales lift. Also, we see opportunity for the company to capture more of customers' discretionary dollars with further refinement of its home assortments, lifestyle merchandising with the Isaac Mizrahi brand, and introduction of new women's fashion apparel and accessories lines such as the "GO International" series of capsule collections from designers Luella Bartley, Tara Jarmon and Sophie Albou.
- Risks to our recommendation and target price include sales shortfalls due to lackluster customer response to new home assortments, reduced consumer discretionary spending, and increased competition in apparel from Wal-Mart Stores, Inc. (WMT: strong buy, $49).
- Our 12-month target price of $62 is based on our discounted cash flow model, which assumes a weighted average cost of capital of 8.8% and a terminal growth rate of 3.0%.

Qualitative Risk Assessment

LOW | **MEDIUM** | HIGH

Our risk assessment reflects our view of TGT's improving sales and profit margins, and healthy balance sheet and cash flow, partly offset by uncertainty over consumer discretionary spending in light of rising interest rates and debt levels.

Quantitative Evaluations

S&P Quality Ranking A+

D | C | B- | B | B+ | A- | A | **A+**

Relative Strength Rank STRONG

79

LOWEST = 1 HIGHEST = 99

Revenue/Earnings Data

Revenue (Million $)

	1Q	2Q	3Q	4Q	Year
2007	12,863	13,347	--	--	--
2006	11,477	11,990	12,206	16,947	52,620
2005	11,587	10,556	10,909	15,194	46,839
2004	10,322	10,984	11,286	15,571	48,163
2003	9,594	10,068	10,194	14,061	43,917
2002	8,345	8,952	9,354	13,237	39,888

Earnings Per Share ($)

	1Q	2Q	3Q	4Q	Year
2007	0.63	0.70	**E**0.54	**E**1.25	**E**3.12
2006	0.55	0.61	0.49	1.06	2.71
2005	0.48	0.40	0.37	0.90	2.07
2004	0.38	0.39	0.33	0.91	2.01
2003	0.38	0.38	0.30	0.75	1.81
2002	0.28	0.30	0.20	0.73	1.51

Fiscal year ended Jan. 31. Next earnings report expected: Early November. EPS Estimates based on S&P Operating Earnings; historical GAAP earnings are as reported.

Dividend Data (Dates: mm/dd Payment Date: mm/dd/yy)

Amount ($)	Date Decl.	Ex-Div. Date	Stk. of Record	Payment Date
0.100	01/12	02/15	02/20	03/10/06
0.100	03/09	05/17	05/20	06/10/06
0.120	06/15	08/16	08/20	09/10/06
0.120	09/14	11/16	11/20	12/10/06

Dividends have been paid since 1965. Source: Company reports.

Target Corp

Business Summary September 21, 2006

CORPORATE PROFILE. In FY 05 (Jan.), TGT shed its non-core legacy department store operations, retaining only its eponymous chain of upscale general merchandise stores that cater to middle- and upper-income consumers. As of August 31, 2006, the company operated 1,444 locations, including 162 SuperTarget stores. SuperTarget stores combine a full line of groceries with the fashion apparel, electronics, home furnishings and other general merchandise found in Target stores. TGT's Web site serves as both a sales driver and a marketing vehicle. Target.com offers a more extensive selection of merchandise than the company's physical stores, including exclusive online products. To support sales and earnings growth, TGT offers credit to qualified customers. In FY 06, its credit card operations contributed $1.2 billion of revenues.

CORPORATE STRATEGY. The monetizing of assets has provided TGT with cash to invest in its core business and to fund capital repositioning - actions that improve shareholder value. TGT sold its entire Marshall Field's business unit, including about $600 million of credit card receivables, as well as its Mervyn's stores in Minnesota, to The May Department Stores Co. in July 2004 and August 2004, respectively, for a total of $3.24 billion in cash. Also in August 2004, TGT sold the balance of its Mervyn's stores to an investment consortium that includes Sun Capital Partners, Inc., Cerberus Capital Management, L.P., and Lubert-Adler/Klaff and Partners, L.P., and Mervyn's credit card receivables unit to GE Consumer Finance for a total of $1.65 billion in cash.

Company Financials

Per Share Data ($) Year Ended Jan. 31	**2006**	**2005**	**2004**	**2003**	**2002**	**2001**	**2000**	**1999**	**1998**	**1997**
Tangible Book Value	16.25	14.63	12.14	10.38	8.68	7.27	6.43	5.71	4.78	4.05
Cash Flow	4.29	3.45	3.45	3.14	2.70	2.41	2.19	1.87	1.61	1.29
Earnings	2.71	2.07	2.01	1.81	1.51	1.38	1.27	1.02	0.85	0.52
S&P Core Earnings	2.68	2.06	1.95	1.70	1.42	1.37	NA	NA	NA	NA
Dividends	0.30	0.26	0.26	0.24	0.21	0.20	0.20	0.18	0.17	0.15
Payout Ratio	11%	13%	13%	13%	14%	14%	16%	18%	19%	30%
Calendar Year	2005	2004	2003	2002	2001	2000	1999	1998	1997	1996
Prices:High	60.00	54.14	41.80	46.15	41.74	39.19	38.50	27.13	18.50	10.16
Prices:Low	45.55	36.63	25.60	24.90	26.00	21.63	25.03	15.72	8.97	5.76
P/E Ratio:High	22	26	21	25	28	28	30	27	22	20
P/E Ratio:Low	17	18	13	14	17	16	20	15	11	11

Income Statement Analysis (Million $)										
Revenue	52,620	46,839	48,163	43,917	39,888	36,903	33,702	30,951	27,757	25,371
Operating Income	5,732	4,860	4,839	4,476	3,759	3,418	3,183	2,734	2,435	2,009
Depreciation	1,409	1,259	1,320	1,212	1,079	940	854	780	693	650
Interest Expense	532	674	559	588	464	425	393	398	416	442
Pretax Income	3,860	3,031	2,960	2,676	2,216	2,053	1,936	1,556	1,326	783
Effective Tax Rate	37.6%	37.8%	37.8%	38.2%	38.0%	38.4%	38.8%	38.2%	39.5%	39.5%
Net Income	2,408	1,885	1,841	1,654	1,374	1,264	1,185	962	802	474
S&P Core Earnings	2,383	1,876	1,791	1,553	1,289	1,247	NA	NA	NA	NA

Balance Sheet & Other Financial Data (Million $)										
Cash	1,648	2,245	716	758	499	356	220	255	211	201
Current Assets	14,405	13,922	12,928	11,935	9,648	7,304	6,483	6,005	5,561	5,440
Total Assets	34,995	32,293	31,392	28,603	24,154	19,490	17,143	15,666	14,191	13,389
Current Liabilities	9,588	8,220	8,314	7,523	7,054	6,301	5,850	5,057	4,556	4,111
Long Term Debt	9,119	9,034	10,217	10,186	8,088	5,634	4,521	4,452	4,425	4,808
Common Equity	14,205	13,029	11,065	9,443	7,860	6,519	5,862	5,043	4,180	3,519
Total Capital	24,175	23,036	21,282	21,080	15,948	12,153	10,383	10,585	9,635	9,278
Capital Expenditures	3,388	3,068	3,004	3,221	3,163	2,528	1,918	1,657	1,354	1,301
Cash Flow	3,817	3,144	3,161	2,866	2,453	2,204	2,039	1,742	1,495	1,124
Current Ratio	1.5	1.7	1.6	1.6	1.4	1.2	1.1	1.2	1.2	1.3
% Long Term Debt of Capitalization	37.7	39.2	48.0	48.3	50.7	46.4	43.5	42.1	45.9	51.8
% Net Income of Revenue	4.5	4.0	3.8	3.8	3.4	3.4	3.5	3.1	2.9	1.9
% Return on Assets	7.1	5.9	6.1	6.3	6.3	6.9	7.2	6.4	6.0	3.7
% Return on Equity	17.6	15.6	18.0	19.1	19.1	20.4	21.7	20.8	20.8	14.2

Data as orig reptd.; bef. results of disc opers/spec. items. Per share data adj. for stk. divs.; EPS diluted. E-Estimated. NA-Not Available. NM-Not Meaningful. NR-Not Ranked. UR-Under Review.

Office: 1000 Nicollet Mall, Minneapolis, MN 55403-2467.
Telephone: 612-304-6073.
Website: http://www.target.com
Chrmn & CEO: R.J. Ulrich

Pres: G.W. Steinhafel
EVP & CFO: D.A. Scovanner
SVP, Secy & General Counsel: T.R. Baer

Board of Directors: R. Austin, C. Darden, J. A. Johnson, R. M. Kovacevich, M. E. Minnick, A. M. Mulcahy, S. W. Sanger, W. R. Staley, G. W. Tamke, S. D. Trujillo, R. J. Ulrich

Founded: 1902
Domicile: Minnesota
Employees: 338,000

TECO Energy Inc.

S&P Recommendation SELL ★★★★★

Price $16.49 (as of Oct 27, 2006)

12-Mo. Target Price $15.00

Investment Style Mid-Cap Value

GICS Sector Utilities
Sub-Industry Multi-Utilities

Comment TE owns Tampa Electric Co., which serves the Tampa Bay region in west central Florida, and has significant diversified operations related to its core business.

Key Stock Statistics (Source S&P, Vickers, company reports)

52-Wk Range	**$17.99–14.40**	S&P Oper. EPS 2006**E**	**0.94**	P/E on S&P Oper. EPS 2006**E**	**17.5**	Dividend Rate/Share	**$0.76**
Trailing 12-Month EPS	**$1.19**	S&P Oper. EPS 2007**E**	**1.05**	Common Shares Outstg. (M)	**208.9**	Yield (%)	**4.61**
Trailing 12-Month P/E	**13.9**	S&P Core EPS 2006**E**	**0.87**	Market Capitalization(B)	**$3.445**	Beta	**0.66**
$10K Invested 5 Yrs Ago	**$8,453**	S&P Core EPS 2007**E**	**1.04**	Institutional Ownership (%)	**52**	S&P Credit Rating	**BB**

Price Performance

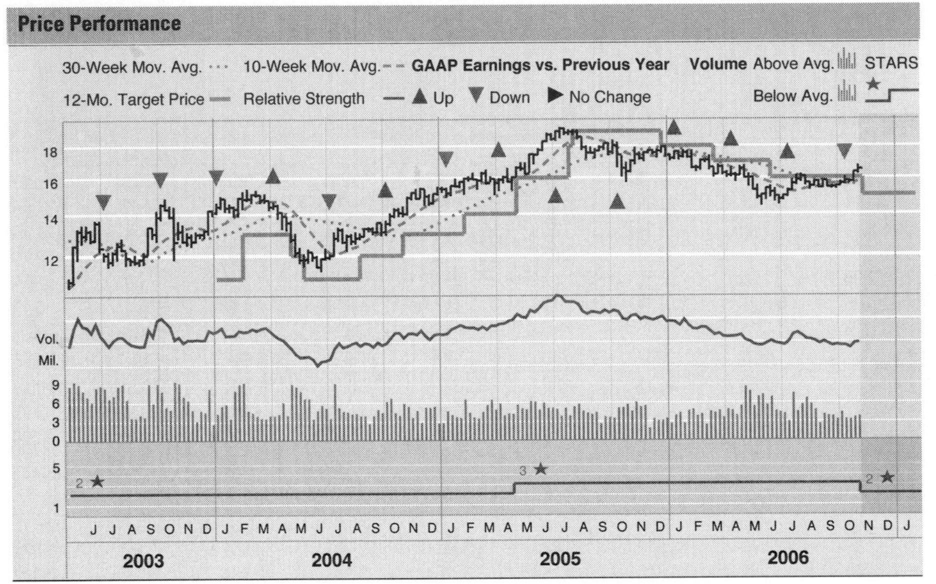

Options: Ph

Highlights

➤ The STARS recommendation for TE has recently been changed to 2 (sell) from 3 (hold) and the 12-month target price has recently been changed to $15.00 from $16.00. The Highlights section of this Stock Report will be updated accordingly.

Investment Rationale/Risk

➤ The Investment Rationale/Risk section of this Stock Report will be updated shortly. For the latest News story on TE from MarketScope, see below.

➤ 10/27/06 01:34 pm EDT... S&P DOWNGRADES SHARES OF TECO ENERGY TO SELL FROM HOLD (TE 16.61**): Given the recent rise in the shares, over 6% since the start of October, we believe the stock is overvalued at its current level. Before synfuel-related tax credits, Q3 operating EPS of $0.30 vs. $0.34 is in line with our estimate. Weather-related decline at Tampa Electric and lower volume at Teco Coal more than offset the benefit of higher river barge rates at the Transport unit. Before synfuel, our EPS estimates fall by $0.06 to $0.94 in '06 and by $0.01 to $1.05 in '07. We are also lowering our 12-month target price by $1 to $15, an about peer P/E of 14.3X our '07 estimate. /J.McCann

Qualitative Risk Assessment

LOW | **MEDIUM** | HIGH

Our risk assessment reflects the steady cash flow that we expect from the regulated electric and gas utilities, which operate within a generally supportive regulatory environment, offset by our view of the much less predictable earnings and cash flow from the unregulated coal and transport operations, particularly given the uncertainties concerning the tax credits related to the synthetic fuel operations.

Quantitative Evaluations

S&P Quality Ranking **B-**

D | C | **B-** | B | B+ | A- | A | A+

Relative Strength Rank **MODERATE**

63

LOWEST = 1 HIGHEST = 99

Revenue/Earnings Data

Revenue (Million $)

	1Q	2Q	3Q	4Q	Year
2006	836.4	862.6	922.9	--	--
2005	684.7	719.0	836.4	770.0	3,010
2004	642.3	713.0	742.3	660.2	2,669
2003	651.8	695.3	759.1	633.8	2,740
2002	606.6	677.7	731.0	660.5	2,676
2001	671.1	641.9	677.8	657.8	2,649

Earnings Per Share ($)

2006	0.26	0.29	0.38	**E**0.15	**E**0.94
2005	0.25	0.04	0.45	0.24	1.00
2004	0.15	-0.44	0.27	-2.05	-2.10
2003	-0.12	0.03	0.03	-0.02	-0.08
2002	0.50	0.56	0.72	0.20	1.95
2001	0.53	0.52	0.71	0.47	2.24

Fiscal year ended Dec. 31. Next earnings report expected: Late January. EPS Estimates based on S&P Operating Earnings; historical GAAP earnings are as reported.

Dividend Data (Dates: mm/dd Payment Date: mm/dd/yy)

Amount ($)	Date Decl.	Ex-Div. Date	Stk. of Record	Payment Date
0.190	01/25	02/01	02/03	02/15/06
0.190	04/26	05/03	05/05	05/15/06
0.190	07/26	08/02	08/04	08/15/06
0.190	10/24	11/01	11/03	11/15/06

Dividends have been paid since 1900. Source: Company reports.

Please read the Required Disclosures and Analyst Certification on the last page of this report.

TECO Energy Inc.

Business Summary September 05, 2006

CORPORATE OVERVIEW. TECO Energy (TE) is a holding company for a diverse set of energy companies including the regulated utility subsidiary Tampa Electric Company, which provides retail electric service in West Central Florida. TE's other regulated utility is People Gas System, which distributes natural gas in Florida's metropolitan areas. TE's unregulated businesses include TECO Coal, which has coal-mining operations and synthetic fuel facilities; TECO transport, which provides shipping and storage services for coal and other dry-bulk commodities; and TECO Guatemala, which participates in independent power projects and electric distribution in Guatemala. In 2005, Tampa Electric accounted for 56.6% of TE's consolidated revenues; Peoples Gas System, 17.8%; TECO Coal, 16.4%; TECO Transport, 9.0%; and TECO Guatemala, 0.2%.

CORPORATE STRATEGY. Since 2003, TE's business strategy has been to reduce the risk to cash flow and earnings from its involvement in the merchant power sector, and to focus its attention on the growth prospects for both of the regulated Florida utilities, as well as the unregulated coal, transportation and Guatemalan operations. By January 2006, TE completed the divestiture of its non-core operations, and has now eliminated its exposure to the merchant power sector. With this process behind it, TE is planning to strengthen its balance sheet and to retire the debt that is maturing in 2007. We believe this will be a major step in reducing the company's business risk, improving its cash flows, and eventually restoring its investment grade credit rating.

Company Financials

Per Share Data ($) Year Ended Dec. 31	**2005**	**2004**	**2003**	**2002**	**2001**	**2000**	**1999**	**1998**	**1997**	**1996**
Tangible Book Value	7.36	6.13	8.55	13.75	12.94	11.93	11.19	11.42	11.04	10.73
Earnings	1.00	-2.10	-0.08	1.95	2.24	1.97	1.53	1.52	1.61	1.71
S&P Core Earnings	1.00	-1.58	0.24	1.75	2.04	NA	NA	NA	NA	NA
Dividends	0.76	0.76	0.93	1.41	1.37	1.33	1.29	1.23	1.17	1.11
Payout Ratio	76%	NM	NM	72%	61%	68%	84%	81%	72%	65%
Prices:High	19.30	15.49	17.00	29.05	32.97	33.19	28.00	30.63	28.19	27.00
Prices:Low	14.87	11.30	9.47	10.02	24.75	17.25	18.38	24.75	22.75	23.00
P/E Ratio:High	19	NM	NM	15	15	17	18	20	18	16
P/E Ratio:Low	15	NM	NM	5	11	9	12	16	14	13
Income Statement Analysis (Million $)										
Revenue	3,010	2,669	2,740	2,676	2,640	2,205	1,000	1,050	1,002	1,470
Depreciation	282	282	326	303	298	268	232	228	225	185
Maintenance	168	141	152	162	151	140	125	129	114	92.2
Fixed Charges Coverage	1.25	1.26	2.30	2.43	2.51	2.59	3.30	3.95	3.88	3.69
Construction Credits	Nil	1.00	27.4	9.60	2.60	0.70	0.50	Nil	0.20	22.9
Effective Tax Rate	45.1%	NM	NM	NM	NM	6.87%	30.2%	28.8%	30.9%	26.1%
Net Income	211	-404	-14.7	298	304	251	201	200	211	201
S&P Core Earnings	212	-306	44.4	267	277	NA	NA	NA	NA	NA
Balance Sheet & Other Financial Data (Million $)										
Gross Property	6,755	6,723	8,040	8,215	7,544	6,560	8,501	5,601	5,360	4,722
Capital Expenditures	295	273	591	1,065	966	688	426	296	213	268
Net Property	4,567	4,658	5,679	5,464	4,838	3,970	6,064	3,308	3,237	2,957
Capitalization:Long Term Debt	3,709	3,880	4,393	3,973	2,043	1,575	1,208	1,280	1,080	996
Capitalization:% Long Term Debt	70.0	75.1	73.0	43.2	50.9	51.1	46.0	45.9	42.8	43.7
Capitalization:Preferred	Nil	Nil	Nil	Nil	Nil	Nil	Nil	Nil	Nil	20.0
Capitalization:% Preferred	Nil	Nil	Nil	Nil	Nil	Nil	Nil	Nil	Nil	0.90
Capitalization:Common	1,592	1,284	1,622	5,223	1,972	1,507	1,418	1,508	1,445	1,262
Capitalization:% Common	30.0	24.9	27.0	56.8	49.1	48.9	54.0	54.1	57.2	55.4
Total Capital	5,318	5,691	6,537	9,719	4,545	3,564	3,284	3,334	3,048	2,761
% Operating Ratio	91.4	80.2	83.7	84.0	83.7	82.8	83.0	82.6	82.9	81.5
% Earned on Net Property	7.7	NA	0.3	7.6	9.6	10.9	7.3	12.1	13.3	9.3
% Return on Revenue	7.0	NA	NM	11.1	11.5	10.9	10.1	10.2	11.4	13.6
% Return on Invested Capital	9.3	14.2	9.6	6.4	11.9	12.4	9.7	11.3	10.9	10.6
% Return on Common Equity	14.7	NA	NM	6.5	17.5	17.2	13.7	13.6	15.6	16.5

Data as orig reptd.; bef. results of disc opers/spec. items. Per share data adj. for stk. divs.; EPS diluted. E-Estimated. NA-Not Available. NM-Not Meaningful. NR-Not Ranked. UR-Under Review.

Office: 702 North Franklin Street, Tampa, FL 33602.
Telephone: 813-228-4111.
Website: http://www.tecoenergy.com
Chrmn & CEO: S. Hudson

Pres & COO: J.B. Ramil
EVP & CFO: G.L. Gillette
SVP & General Counsel: S.M. McDevitt
Investor Contact: M.M. Kane (813-228-1772)

Board of Directors: C. D. Ausley, S. L. Baldwin, J. L. Ferman, Jr., L. Guinot, Jr., S. Hudson, J. P. Lacher, L. A. Penn, T. L. Rankin, W. D. Rockford, W. P. Sovey, J. T. Touchton, J. O. Welch, Jr., P. L. Whiting

Founded: 1899
Domicile: Florida
Employees: 4,998

STANDARD &POOR'S

Tektronix Inc.

S&P Recommendation BUY ★★★★★

Price $30.18 (as of Oct 27, 2006)

12-Mo. Target Price $33.00

Investment Style Mid-Cap Value

GICS Sector Information Technology
Sub-Industry Electronic Equipment Manufacturers

Comment This test, measurement and monitoring company provides measurement solutions to the semiconductor, computer, telecommunications and other industries.

Key Stock Statistics (Source S&P, Vickers, company reports)

52-Wk Range	$36.89–22.64	S&P Oper. EPS 2007E	1.35	P/E on S&P Oper. EPS 2007E	22.4	Dividend Rate/Share	$0.24
Trailing 12-Month EPS	$1.16	S&P Oper. EPS 2008E	1.50	Common Shares Outstg. (M)	82.5	Yield (%)	0.80
Trailing 12-Month P/E	26.0	S&P Core EPS 2007E	1.35	Market Capitalization(B)	$2.489	Beta	1.32
$10K Invested 5 Yrs Ago	$15,390	S&P Core EPS 2008E	1.50	Institutional Ownership (%)	88	S&P Credit Rating	BB+

Price Performance

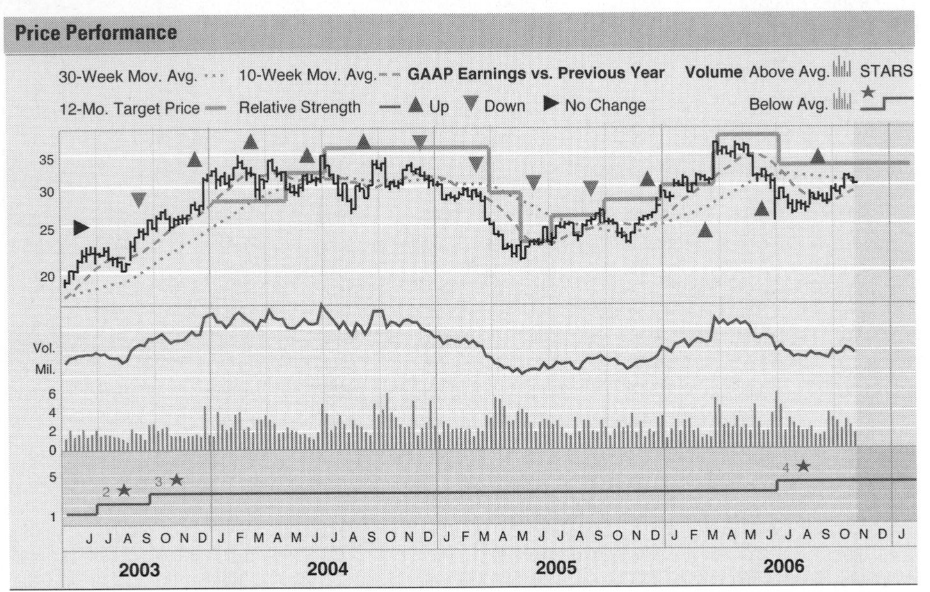

Options: ASE, CBOE, P

Analysis prepared by **Stuart J. Benway, CFA** on September 19, 2006, when the stock traded at **$ 28.88**.

Highlights

- We look for sales in FY 07 to rebound about 10% as the company rolls out new products throughout the fiscal year. Demand for spectrum analyzers should remain strong, in our view, as the company's real-time technology is a significant innovation. These products provide new capabilities for digital radio frequency (RF) applications. We also expect demand for network management products from communications providers to be a source of sales growth in coming quarters.
- We expect gross margins will narrow somewhat in FY 07 as higher non-cash amortization charges and less absorption of overhead are only partially offset by a more favorable product mix. Operating margins should benefit from the growing demand for higher-margin products and increased overall sales, although higher R&D costs to support new product introductions will likely offset most of this improvement.
- We see FY 07 operating and S&P Core EPS of $1.35, following $1.08 in FY 06. These estimates include costs that the company classifies as unusual, but we consider to be ongoing.

Investment Rationale/Risk

- We think TEK has growth opportunities in several product categories, including radio frequency identification software, signal sources, real-time spectrum analyzers, and video test products for high-definition TV. Demand for equipment to improve the reliability of next-generation telecommunications equipment should also be strong. We expect TEK to continue to use its balance sheet for share buybacks and niche acquisitions.
- Risks to our recommendation and target price include a slowdown in the global economy, especially in Japan and China; slow acceptance of new products; canceled orders; and weakness in the electronics and communications sectors.
- Our discounted cash flow (DCF) model indicates intrinsic value of $30, using a weighted average cost of capital (WACC) of 11.1% and a terminal growth rate of 3.5%. Blending this metric with a value of $35 based on a forward peer P/E multiple of 26X applied to our FY 07 EPS estimate, we arrive at our 12-month target price of $33.

Qualitative Risk Assessment

LOW | **MEDIUM** | HIGH

Our risk assessment reflects that TEK's customer base consists primarily of cyclical companies, and it sells its products into rapidly changing high technology markets, which can lead to sharp swings in demand. This is offset as the company has what we view as a strong balance sheet and significant geographic diversification.

Quantitative Evaluations

S&P Quality Ranking **B**

D | C | B- | **B** | B+ | A- | A | A+

Relative Strength Rank **MODERATE**

50

LOWEST = 1 HIGHEST = 99

Revenue/Earnings Data

Revenue (Million $)

	1Q	2Q	3Q	4Q	Year
2007	268.1	--	--	--	--
2006	235.1	253.4	262.1	289.3	1,040
2005	250.5	266.8	256.3	261.0	1,035
2004	201.4	217.9	243.5	257.8	920.6
2003	198.5	203.6	186.7	202.3	791.1
2002	216.6	214.6	203.6	208.5	843.3

Earnings Per Share ($)

2007	0.24	E0.30	E0.35	E0.46	E1.35
2006	0.17	0.24	0.30	0.37	1.08
2005	0.43	-0.03	0.26	0.24	0.89
2004	0.13	0.42	0.50	0.31	1.37
2003	0.24	0.10	0.01	0.05	0.40
2002	0.08	0.09	0.11	0.05	0.33

Fiscal year ended May 31. Next earnings report expected: Mid December. EPS Estimates based on S&P Operating Earnings; historical GAAP earnings are as reported.

Dividend Data (Dates: mm/dd Payment Date: mm/dd/yy)

Amount ($)	Date Decl.	Ex-Div. Date	Stk. of Record	Payment Date
0.060	12/15	01/04	01/06	01/23/06
0.060	03/17	04/05	04/07	04/24/06
0.060	06/22	07/05	07/07	07/24/06
0.060	09/14	10/04	10/06	10/23/06

Dividends have been paid since 2003. Source: Company reports.

Tektronix Inc.

Business Summary September 19, 2006

CORPORATE OVERVIEW. Tektronix develops, manufactures, markets, and services test, measurement, and monitoring products to a wide variety of customers in many industries. These products include a broad range of instruments designed to measure, test or calibrate electrical and optical circuits, mechanical motion, sound or radio waves. Oscilloscopes are TEK's primary measurement product, and they are used when an electrical signal needs to be viewed, measured, analyzed, tested, or verified. Logic Analyzers are debugging tools used to capture, display and analyze streams of digital data that occur simultaneously over many channels. Signal sources are general purpose stimulus products used in the design and manufacturing of a variety of electronic products. TEK's real-time spectrum analyzers enable customers to perform simultaneous frequency, time, and modulation measurements on radio frequency signals.

TEK also produces video test products, which include waveform monitors, MPEG test products, and video signal generators as well as network monitoring and protocol testing products. TEK conducts operations in the Americas (38% of FY 06 (May) sales), Europe--including the Middle East and Africa (28%), the Pacific (19%), and Japan (15%).

CORPORATE STRATEGY. TEK's primary strategy is to focus its efforts on those product areas where the company believes it has either a market leadership position or where it can attain a leading position. TEK seeks to achieve long-term growth from three strategies: increasing market share in core areas where it already has a strong presence; expanding the addressable market for core categories; and applying its technical expertise to penetrate adjacent product lines. The sectors where Tektronix has the strongest positions are oscilloscopes, logic analyzers, video test, network management, and network diagnostics. The company is seeking to broaden the market in these categories by introducing products targeted at specific applications, focusing on market segments with faster growth, and investing in geographic expansion, particularly in emerging markets. It is also striving to develop a solid market position in signal sources and spectrum analyzers. Tektronix has boosted its R&D spending in recent years, from 12.8% of sales in FY 03 to 17.6% in FY 06, and it has a full pipeline of new products that it will be introducing over the next 12 to 18 months.

Company Financials

Per Share Data ($) Year Ended May 31	2006	2005	2004	2003	2002	2001	2000	1999	1998	1997
Tangible Book Value	10.52	8.03	9.39	8.32	9.48	10.41	10.28	6.63	7.18	7.70
Cash Flow	1.69	1.23	1.72	0.79	0.77	1.92	0.59	0.25	1.44	1.77
Earnings	1.08	0.89	1.37	0.40	0.33	1.46	0.13	-0.54	0.80	1.15
S&P Core Earnings	0.92	0.70	0.65	-0.25	-0.23	0.83	NA	NA	NA	NA
Dividends	0.22	0.12	Nil	Nil	Nil	0.18	0.24	0.24	0.23	0.20
Payout Ratio	20%	13%	Nil	Nil	Nil	12%	185%	NM	29%	17%
Calendar Year	2005	2004	2003	2002	2001	2000	1999	1998	1997	1996
Prices:High	30.20	35.00	32.25	28.60	40.50	43.66	20.00	24.09	23.21	17.42
Prices:Low	20.97	26.26	15.65	14.64	16.75	17.19	8.78	6.84	16.08	9.92
P/E Ratio:High	20	39	24	70	NM	30	NM	NM	29	15
P/E Ratio:Low	19	30	11	42	NM	12	NM	NM	20	9

Income Statement Analysis (Million $)	2006	2005	2004	2003	2002	2001	2000	1999	1998	1997
Revenue	1,040	1,035	921	791	843	1,235	1,121	1,861	2,086	1,940
Operating Income	188	184	144	90.5	104	220	115	99.7	219	223
Depreciation	52.1	29.2	29.8	33.5	41.0	44.8	44.1	74.8	65.9	59.6
Interest Expense	0.48	0.82	2.21	6.87	10.0	13.0	15.8	15.7	10.1	12.1
Pretax Income	128	124	167	33.3	47.0	220	19.6	-75.2	123	169
Effective Tax Rate	29.2%	36.5%	29.3%	NM	35.0%	36.4%	35.0%	NM	33.0%	32.0%
Net Income	90.9	78.9	118	35.1	30.5	140	12.7	-51.2	82.3	115
S&P Core Earnings	77.0	61.7	55.5	-21.9	-22.0	79.5	NA	NA	NA	NA

Balance Sheet & Other Financial Data (Million $)	2006	2005	2004	2003	2002	2001	2000	1999	1998	1997
Cash	216	132	149	190	263	292	684	39.7	121	143
Current Assets	737	619	545	588	747	936	1,112	720	749	752
Total Assets	1,634	1,460	1,331	1,391	1,384	1,542	1,535	1,359	1,377	1,317
Current Liabilities	272	252	249	237	273	336	330	497	350	304
Long Term Debt	Nil	Nil	0.50	55.0	57.0	128	150	151	151	152
Common Equity	1,188	986	871	779	927	1,013	978	622	785	771
Total Capital	1,254	986	871	834	984	1,141	1,128	772	936	923
Capital Expenditures	36.3	32.5	18.6	17.2	16.4	31.5	42.3	108	155	112
Cash Flow	143	108	148	68.7	71.5	185	56.9	23.6	148	174
Current Ratio	2.7	2.5	2.2	2.5	2.7	2.8	3.4	1.4	2.1	2.5
% Long Term Debt of Capitalization	Nil	Nil	0.1	6.6	5.8	11.2	13.3	19.5	19.2	16.5
% Net Income of Revenue	8.7	7.6	12.8	4.4	3.6	11.3	1.1	NM	3.9	5.9
% Return on Assets	5.9	5.6	8.7	2.5	2.1	9.2	0.9	NM	6.1	8.7
% Return on Equity	8.4	8.5	14.3	4.1	3.1	14.1	1.6	NM	10.6	15.9

Data as orig reptd.; bef. results of disc opers/spec. items. Per share data adj. for stk. divs.; EPS diluted. E-Estimated. NA-Not Available. NM-Not Meaningful. NR-Not Ranked. UR-Under Review.

Office: 14200 S.W. Karl Braun Drive, Beaverton, OR 97077.
Telephone: 503-627-7111.
Email: investor-relations@tektronix.com
Website: http://www.tek.com

Chrmn, Pres & CEO: R.H. Wills
Investor Contact: C.L. Slade (503-627-4027)
SVP & CFO: C.L. Slade
SVP, Secy & General Counsel: J.F. Dalton

Board of Directors: P. L. Alker, A. G. Ames, G. B. Cameron, D. N. Campbell, F. C. Gill, R. L. Washington, R. H. Wills, C. J. Yansouni

Founded: 1946
Domicile: Oregon
Employees: 4,359

STANDARD &POOR'S

Tellabs Inc

S&P Recommendation BUY ★★★★★

Price $10.34 (as of Oct 27, 2006)

12-Mo. Target Price $14.00

Investment Style Mid-Cap Value

GICS Sector Information Technology
Sub-Industry Communications Equipment

Comment This company manufactures voice and data equipment used in public and private communications networks worldwide.

Key Stock Statistics (Source S&P, Vickers, company reports)

52-Wk Range	**$17.28–8.73**	S&P Oper. EPS 2006**E**	**0.58**	P/E on S&P Oper. EPS 2006**E**	**17.8**	Dividend Rate/Share	**Nil**
Trailing 12-Month EPS	**$0.57**	S&P Oper. EPS 2007**E**	**0.68**	Common Shares Outstg. (M)	**447.7**	Yield (%)	**Nil**
Trailing 12-Month P/E	**18.1**	S&P Core EPS 2006E	**0.58**	Market Capitalization(B)	**$4.629**	Beta	**3.10**
$10K Invested 5 Yrs Ago	**$6,745**	S&P Core EPS 2007E	**0.68**	Institutional Ownership (%)	**73**	S&P Credit Rating	**NA**

Price Performance

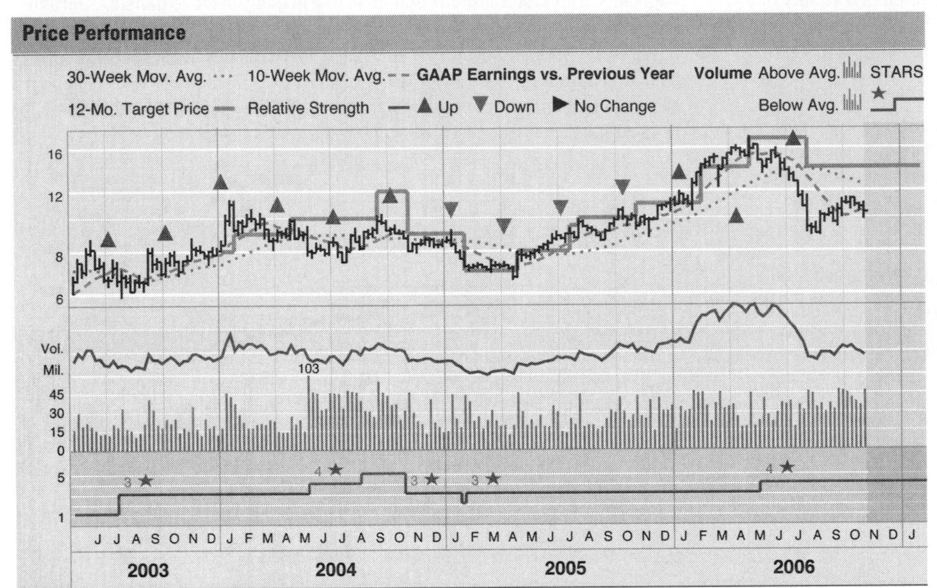

Options: ASE, CBOE, P, Ph

Analysis prepared by **Todd Rosenbluth** on October 27, 2006, when the stock traded at **$ 10.29**.

Highlights

- We forecast 16% sales growth in 2006 and a modest slowdown to 13% growth in 2007. We expect TLAB to experience growth in its access products and services, and we see continued gains in wireless transport products as national carriers further roll out their 3G technology. We believe access product revenue from fiber deployments by key wireline customers will be key drivers for TLAB. We think broadband capital spending will comprise a larger portion of customer budgets than in the past, though we expect quarter to quarter fluctuations as customers deal with inventory levels.
- We expect TLAB's gross margin to widen to 47% in 2006 and 47.5% in 2007, from 45% in 2005, due to a product mix that favors transport products. We assume the operating margin will rise to 17% by the end of 2006 and average 18% in 2007, aided by well contained SG&A expenses.
- A lower effective tax rate helped 2005 results, but we see a 35% rate for 2006 and 2007. We project EPS of $0.58 in 2006, followed by $0.68 in 2007. Both estimates include $0.05 of projected stock option expense.

Investment Rationale/Risk

- We project that sales will continue to improve, driven by transport and access products. In the third quarter of 2006, TLAB surpassed our EPS estimate for the second straight quarter, but we view its revenue guidance as reflecting limited visibility regarding a traditional budget flush. We think TLAB is well positioned to take share of carrier customer spending as new services are launched, but expect the shares to remain volatile.
- Risks to our recommendation and target price include a slower pace of market penetration of the company's new broadband products; slow to no growth for its core transport products; and a slowdown in spending by major customers in advance of merger activity.
- Applying a P/E of 20X to our 2007 EPS estimate, in line with peers despite its wider portfolio of broadband products, we arrive at our 12-month target price of $14. Our target price values TLAB at 2.5X our 2007 sales per share estimate, near its wireline equipment peers.

Qualitative Risk Assessment

LOW | MEDIUM | **HIGH**

Our risk assessment reflects the competitive pressure the company faces, and its dependence on a consolidating telecom industry.

Quantitative Evaluations

S&P Quality Ranking C

D | **C** | B- | B | B+ | A- | A | A+

Relative Strength Rank WEAK

16

LOWEST = 1 HIGHEST = 99

Revenue/Earnings Data

Revenue (Million $)

	1Q	2Q	3Q	4Q	Year
2006	514.7	549.3	522.5	--	--
2005	435.6	462.5	463.9	521.4	1,883
2004	263.8	304.3	284.3	379.4	1,232
2003	222.5	234.1	244.5	279.3	980.4
2002	371.5	344.6	288.1	312.8	1,317
2001	772.1	509.4	448.2	470.0	2,200

Earnings Per Share ($)

	1Q	2Q	3Q	4Q	Year
2006	0.11	0.12	--	**E**0.16	**E**0.58
2005	Nil	0.09	0.09	0.20	0.39
2004	0.03	0.12	0.11	-0.32	-0.07
2003	-0.10	-0.27	-0.16	-0.06	-0.58
2002	0.01	-0.35	-0.22	-0.21	-0.76
2001	0.29	-0.43	-0.12	-0.20	-0.44

Fiscal year ended Dec. 31. Next earnings report expected: Late January. EPS Estimates based on S&P Operating Earnings; historical GAAP earnings are as reported.

Dividend Data

No cash dividends have been paid.

Tellabs Inc

Business Summary October 27, 2006

CORPORATE OVERVIEW. Tellabs designs, manufactures, markets and services optical networking, next-generation switching and broadband access solutions. The company's transport systems (39% of sales in the first nine months of 2006) are designed to help service providers lower their costs, generate more revenues, and efficiently manage bandwidth as the end-user demand for communication services grows. TLAB's managed access solutions (15%) provide seamless integration of circuit-switched voice and data, IP-data and voice-over-Internet protocol (VoIP) services, and access capacity expansion through digital subscriber line (DSL) technology.

MARKET PROFILE. In our opinion, one of the most important fundamental changes in the telecom sector has been the rapid consolidation of service providers. The largest single group of customers for TLAB in 2005 was the Incumbent Local Exchange Carriers (ILECs), which include AT&T, BellSouth, Verizon, and Qwest Communications. We believe the balance of power resides with the service provider. In our view, due to their size, these large ILECs and their respective wireless segments have pricing power over suppliers, with a decision to slow down spending putting pressure on TLAB's projected revenue in the fourth quarter of 2006. We expect flat- to mid-single digit capital spending growth in 2006 to be largely focused on broadband and fiber-based initiatives. We project that Verizon will spend 39% of its wireline budget on its fiber initiative in 2006, up from 34% in 2005; BellSouth should spend 50% of its budget on DSL and fiber in 2006, up from 44% in 2005.

COMPETITIVE LANDSCAPE. Competition for new telecom customers as well as for new infrastructure deployments is particularly intense and increasingly focused on price, in our view. We believe customer concentration has raised customer buying power, with more demanding requirements from the largest service providers. It seems to us that capital spending decisions are also more challenging and more competitive from service providers that use an open standard platform in which to choose network solutions from different equipment suppliers, leading to longer sales cycles. For example, after conducting a supplier search for a year, in July 2006, Verizon selected TLAB as a supplier of its reconfigurable optical add/drop multiplexer (ROADM) service, helping Verizon reshape its metro core optical network.

Company Financials

Per Share Data ($) Year Ended Dec. 31	**2005**	**2004**	**2003**	**2002**	**2001**	**2000**	**1999**	**1998**	**1997**	**1996**
Tangible Book Value	3.53	3.34	3.76	4.45	5.55	6.26	4.85	3.40	2.40	1.47
Cash Flow	0.66	0.12	-0.32	-0.41	-0.06	2.09	1.56	1.18	0.83	0.41
Earnings	0.39	-0.07	-0.58	-0.76	-0.44	1.82	1.36	1.03	0.71	0.32
S&P Core Earnings	0.38	-0.14	-0.71	-1.03	-0.68	NA	NA	NA	NA	NA
Dividends	Nil	Nil	Nil	Nil	Nil	Nil	Nil	Nil	Nil	Nil
Payout Ratio	Nil	Nil	Nil	Nil	Nil	Nil	Nil	Nil	Nil	Nil
Prices:High	11.49	11.37	9.73	17.47	67.13	76.94	77.25	46.56	32.50	23.38
Prices:Low	6.56	7.40	5.07	4.00	8.98	37.63	32.38	15.69	16.00	7.63
P/E Ratio:High	29	NM	NM	NM	NM	42	57	45	46	73
P/E Ratio:Low	17	NM	NM	NM	NM	21	24	15	23	24
Income Statement Analysis (Million $)										
Revenue	1,883	1,232	980	1,317	2,200	3,387	2,319	1,660	1,204	869
Operating Income	330	152	-77.1	-12.7	70.9	1,117	832	593	410	276
Depreciation	126	82.3	110	143	158	116	84.6	56.1	46.9	32.0
Interest Expense	Nil	Nil	0.70	0.90	0.51	0.63	0.58	0.29	0.41	1.17
Pretax Income	213	-10.2	-245	-328	-245	1,109	816	590	400	175
Effective Tax Rate	17.5%	NM	NM	NM	NM	31.5%	31.5%	32.5%	34.0%	32.6%
Net Income	176	-29.8	-242	-313	-182	760	559	398	264	118
S&P Core Earnings	171	-58.9	-295	-427	-277	NA	NA	NA	NA	NA
Balance Sheet & Other Financial Data (Million $)										
Cash	1,371	293	246	1,019	1,102	1,022	966	643	109	90.4
Current Assets	1,873	1,819	1,499	1,534	1,945	2,322	1,786	1,253	863	475
Total Assets	3,515	3,523	2,608	2,623	2,866	3,073	2,353	1,628	1,183	744
Current Liabilities	525	524	208	257	320	412	274	218	226	132
Long Term Debt	Nil	Nil	Nil	Nil	3.39	2.85	2.85	2.85	2.90	2.85
Common Equity	2,815	2,797	2,219	2,290	2,466	2,628	2,048	1,377	933	591
Total Capital	2,815	2,797	2,319	2,290	2,490	2,637	2,058	1,391	936	601
Capital Expenditures	61.8	41.4	9.50	34.1	208	208	98.9	75.9	84.7	64.8
Cash Flow	302	52.5	-131	-171	-24.5	876	644	454	311	151
Current Ratio	3.6	3.5	7.2	6.0	6.1	5.6	6.5	5.7	3.8	5.6
% Long Term Debt of Capitalization	Nil	Nil	Nil	Nil	0.1	0.1	0.1	0.2	0.0	0.5
% Net Income of Revenue	9.3	NM	NM	NM	NM	22.4	24.1	24.0	21.9	13.6
% Return on Assets	5.0	NM	NM	NM	NM	28.0	28.0	28.3	27.4	18.2
% Return on Equity	6.3	NM	NM	NM	NM	32.5	32.5	34.5	34.6	23.0

Data as orig reptd.; bef. results of disc opers/spec. items. Per share data adj. for stk. divs.; EPS diluted. E-Estimated. NA-Not Available. NM-Not Meaningful. NR-Not Ranked. UR-Under Review.

Office: 1415 W Diehl Rd, Naperville, IL 60563-2349.
Telephone: 630-798-8800.
Website: http://www.tellabs.com
Chrmn: M.J. Birck

Pres & CEO: K.A. Prabhu
EVP & CFO: T.J. Wiggins
EVP & CTO: T. Gruenwald
Chief Admin, Secy & General Counsel: J. Sheehan

Investor Contact: T. Scottino (630-798-3602)
Board of Directors: L. Beck, M. J. Birck, B. Hedfors, F. Ianna, F. A. Krehbiel, M. E. Lavin, S. P. Marshall, K. A. Prabhu, W. F. Souders, J. H. Suwinski

Founded: 1974
Domicile: Delaware
Employees: 3,609

STANDARD
&POOR'S

Temple-Inland Inc.

S&P Recommendation BUY ★★★★★

Price $39.99 (as of Oct 27, 2006)

12-Mo. Target Price $48.00

Investment Style Mid-Cap Value

GICS Sector Materials
Sub-Industry Paper Packaging

Comment This major producer of corrugated containers and containerboard also makes building products and provides financial services.

Key Stock Statistics (Source S&P, Vickers, company reports)

52-Wk Range	$47.92–36.00	S&P Oper. EPS 2006E	3.35	P/E on S&P Oper. EPS 2006E	11.9	Dividend Rate/Share	$1.00
Trailing 12-Month EPS	$3.47	S&P Oper. EPS 2007E	3.40	Common Shares Outstg. (M)	108.8	Yield (%)	2.50
Trailing 12-Month P/E	11.5	S&P Core EPS 2006E	3.38	Market Capitalization(B)	$4.349	Beta	1.71
$10K Invested 5 Yrs Ago	$17,735	S&P Core EPS 2007E	3.48	Institutional Ownership (%)	80	S&P Credit Rating	BBB

Price Performance

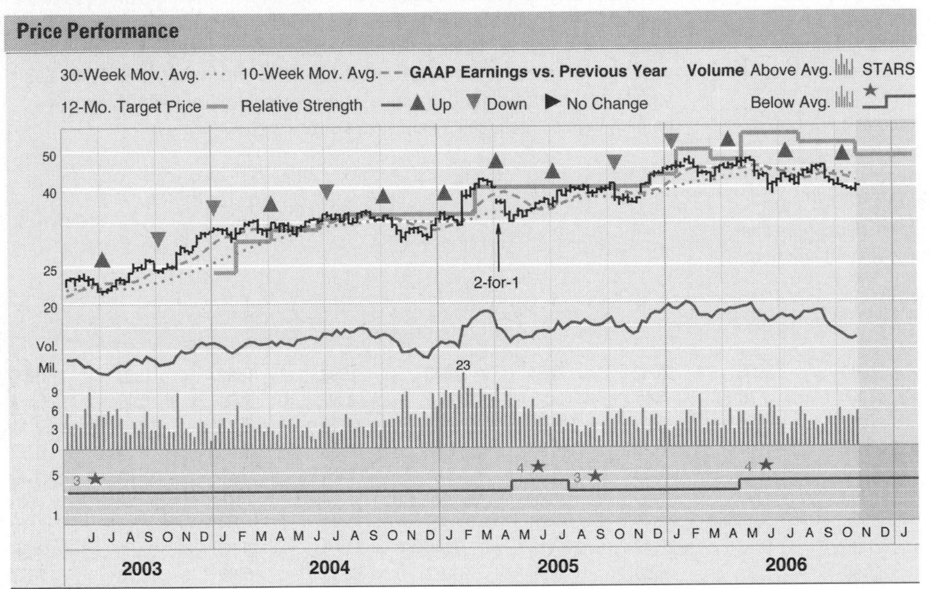

Options: ASE

Qualitative Risk Assessment

LOW | **MEDIUM** | HIGH

Our risk assessment reflects our view that Temple-Inland's manufacturing businesses are cyclical and capital intensive, while its financial services unit is subject to interest rate risk. While we believe that both businesses are economically sensitive, this unusual mix of operations reduces Temple-Inland's overall business risk, in our opinion.

Quantitative Evaluations

S&P Quality Ranking B+

D | C | B- | B | **B+** | A- | A | A+

Relative Strength Rank WEAK

22

LOWEST = 1 HIGHEST = 99

Revenue/Earnings Data

Revenue (Million $)

	1Q	2Q	3Q	4Q	Year
2006	1,384	1,433	1,409	--	--
2005	1,203	1,255	1,218	1,212	4,888
2004	1,148	1,218	1,194	1,190	4,750
2003	1,135	1,182	1,170	1,166	4,653
2002	1,020	1,190	1,157	1,151	4,518
2001	1,053	1,062	1,057	1,000	4,172

Earnings Per Share ($)

2006	0.67	1.71	0.87	E0.75	E3.35
2005	0.39	0.59	0.32	0.23	1.54
2004	0.12	0.49	0.36	0.47	1.44
2003	-0.16	1.43	-0.03	-0.35	0.89
2002	0.15	0.16	0.14	0.18	0.62
2001	0.12	0.29	0.45	0.27	1.13

Fiscal year ended Dec. 31. Next earnings report expected: Early February. EPS Estimates based on S&P Operating Earnings; historical GAAP earnings are as reported.

Dividend Data (Dates: mm/dd Payment Date: mm/dd/yy)

Amount ($)	Date Decl.	Ex-Div. Date	Stk. of Record	Payment Date
0.225	11/04	11/29	12/01	12/15/05
0.250	02/03	02/27	03/01	03/15/06
0.250	05/05	05/30	06/01	06/15/06
0.250	08/04	08/30	09/01	09/15/06

Dividends have been paid since 1984. Source: Company reports.

Highlights

- The 12-month target price for TIN has recently been changed to $48.00 from $52.00. The Highlights section of this Stock Report will be updated accordingly.

Investment Rationale/Risk

- The Investment Rationale/Risk section of this Stock Report will be updated shortly. For the latest News story on TIN from MarketScope, see below.

- 10/24/06 01:08 pm EDT... S&P MAINTAINS BUY RECOMMENDATION ON SHARES OF TEMPLE-INLAND (TIN 39.54****): TIN posts sharply higher Q3 EPS of $0.93 vs. $0.47, beating our estimate of $0.83. Most of the gain came from the company's corrugated packaging unit, where prices increased sharply and operating profits rose nearly five-fold. The forest products and real estate units also posted higher results. We are raising our '06 EPS estimate to $3.35 from $3.25. However, in '07, we expect a lower housing market to hurt the forest products segment, and we are reducing our EPS forecast to $3.40 from $3.50. We have also cut our 12-month target price $4 to $48, based on a lower '07 peer P/E. /S. Benway-CFA

Temple-Inland Inc.

Business Summary August 01, 2006

CORPORATE OVERVIEW. With its operations in the areas of forest products and financial services, Temple-Inland has a diverse combination of businesses. Its corrugated packaging segment (58% of 2005 sales, 21% of operating income) makes containerboard and converts it into boxes. The forest products segment (21%, 41%) produces wood products, including lumber, particleboard, medium density fiberboard, gypsum wallboard and fiberboard. The financial services segment (21%, 38%) includes Guaranty Bank, which has $17 billion in assets and conducts business in Texas and California, where some of the fastest growing markets in the country are located. It also owns an insurance agency and a real estate development unit.

MARKET PROFILE. TIN's corrugated containers range from commodity brown boxes to intricate die-cut packages that can be printed with multi-color graphics. Sales of corrugated packaging follow changing population patterns and other demographic trends. Historically, there has been a correlation between the demand for corrugated packaging and orders for nondurable goods. With its 13.5% of total industry shipments, we believe TIN is the third largest producer of corrugated packaging in the United States. However, because of the fragmented and commodity-oriented nature of the packaging industry, TIN has little control over the pricing or demand for its products. TIN's building products are used primarily in home construction, remodeling and repair, and cabinet and furniture production. The forest products business is heavily dependent on the level of residential housing expenditures, and, like the packaging sector, the forest products industry is fairly fragmented and commodity oriented, and pricing varies with the supply and demand balance.

Company Financials

Per Share Data ($) Year Ended Dec. 31	**2005**	**2004**	**2003**	**2002**	**2001**	**2000**	**1999**	**1998**	**1997**	**1996**
Tangible Book Value	14.90	15.22	14.67	14.42	17.45	18.71	17.84	17.97	18.15	18.17
Cash Flow	3.71	3.71	3.40	3.13	3.34	4.12	3.71	3.06	2.84	3.49
Earnings	1.54	1.44	0.89	0.62	1.13	1.92	1.72	0.61	0.45	1.20
S&P Core Earnings	1.77	1.53	0.92	0.10	0.48	NA	NA	NA	NA	NA
Dividends	0.90	0.72	0.85	0.64	0.64	0.64	0.64	0.64	0.64	0.62
Payout Ratio	58%	50%	96%	103%	57%	33%	37%	106%	142%	52%
Prices:High	45.28	35.01	31.43	30.00	31.08	33.84	38.75	33.63	34.72	27.69
Prices:Low	31.58	28.63	18.43	16.34	20.17	17.31	26.81	21.34	24.81	19.88
P/E Ratio:High	29	24	35	48	27	18	23	56	77	23
P/E Ratio:Low	21	20	21	26	18	9	16	35	55	17
Income Statement Analysis (Million $)										
Revenue	4,888	4,750	4,653	4,518	4,172	4,286	3,682	3,740	3,625	3,460
Operating Income	620	612	316	511	491	654	610	546	467	515
Depreciation	249	254	270	260	216	225	225	275	268	254
Interest Expense	109	125	135	133	98.0	104	95.0	106	110	113
Pretax Income	262	233	-97.0	107	177	320	306	124	95.0	156
Effective Tax Rate	32.8%	30.5%	NM	39.3%	37.3%	39.1%	37.6%	46.0%	46.3%	14.8%
Net Income	176	162	97.0	65.0	111	195	191	67.0	51.0	133
S&P Core Earnings	203	171	99.4	10.9	46.0	NA	NA	NA	NA	NA
Balance Sheet & Other Financial Data (Million $)										
Cash	444	372	399	455	590	322	284	244	188	228
Current Assets	NA	NA	NA	NA	NA	NA	NA	NA	NA	NA
Total Assets	21,633	20,119	21,143	21,760	18,687	18,142	16,186	15,990	14,364	12,947
Current Liabilities	NA	NA	NA	NA	NA	NA	NA	NA	NA	NA
Long Term Debt	8,906	1,996	2,155	6,124	1,859	1,897	1,691	2,018	1,605	1,791
Common Equity	2,080	2,092	1,968	1,949	1,896	1,833	1,927	1,998	2,045	2,015
Total Capital	11,129	4,167	4,130	8,309	4,059	4,002	3,814	4,258	3,873	3,871
Capital Expenditures	265	264	159	125	210	257	204	214	251	290
Cash Flow	425	416	367	325	327	420	416	342	319	387
Current Ratio	NA	NA	NA	NA	NA	NA	NA	NA	NA	NA
% Long Term Debt of Capitalization	80.0	47.9	52.2	73.7	45.8	47.4	44.3	47.4	41.4	42.8
% Net Income of Revenue	3.6	3.4	NM	1.4	2.7	4.5	5.2	1.8	1.4	3.9
% Return on Assets	0.8	0.8	NM	0.3	0.6	1.1	1.2	0.4	0.4	1.1
% Return on Equity	8.4	8.0	NM	3.4	6.0	10.4	9.7	3.3	2.5	6.7

Data as orig reptd.; bef. results of disc opers/spec. items. Per share data adj. for stk. divs.; EPS diluted. E-Estimated. NA-Not Available. NM-Not Meaningful. NR-Not Ranked. UR-Under Review.

Office: 1300 MoPac Expressway South, Austin, TX 78746.
Telephone: 512-434-5800.
Email: investorrelations@templeinland.com
Website: http://www.temple-inland.com

Chrmn & CEO: K.M. Jastrow, II
VP & Chief Acctg Officer: L.R. Brill
VP & Secy: L.K. O' Neal
CFO: R.D. Levy

Chief Admin & General Counsel: J.B. Johnston
Investor Contact: C.L. Nines (512-434-5587)
Board of Directors: A. M. Beschloss, D. M. Carlton, C. C. Carr, E. L. Draper, Jr., L. R. Faulkner, J. T. Hackett, J. M. Heller, K. M. Jastrow, II, J. A. Johnson, W. A. Reed, L. E. Temple, A. Temple, III

Founded: 1983
Domicile: Delaware
Employees: 15,500

Tenet Healthcare Corp

STANDARD &POOR'S

S&P Recommendation HOLD ★★★★★

Price $7.42 (as of Oct 30, 2006)

12-Mo. Target Price $8.00

Investment Style Mid-Cap Value

GICS Sector Health Care
Sub-Industry Health Care Facilities

Comment This Dallas-based company is the second largest U.S. for-profit hospital manager.

Key Stock Statistics (Source S&P, Vickers, company reports)

52-Wk Range	$9.27–5.77	S&P Oper. EPS 2006E	-0.08	P/E on S&P Oper. EPS 2006E	NM	Dividend Rate/Share	Nil
Trailing 12-Month EPS	$-2.13	S&P Oper. EPS 2007E	0.10	Common Shares Outstg. (M)	471.3	Yield (%)	Nil
Trailing 12-Month P/E	NM	S&P Core EPS 2006E	-0.08	Market Capitalization(B)	$3.497	Beta	-0.42
$10K Invested 5 Yrs Ago	$2,144	S&P Core EPS 2007E	0.10	Institutional Ownership (%)	94	S&P Credit Rating	B

Price Performance

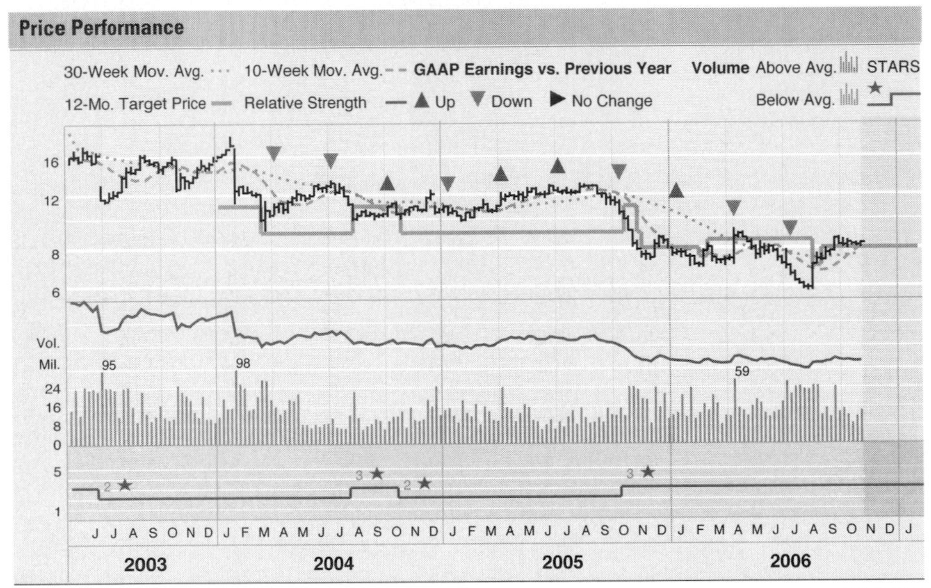

Options: ASE, CBOE, P

Analysis prepared by **Cameron Lavey** on August 22, 2006, when the stock traded at **$ 7.38**.

Highlights

- We look for 2006 revenues to decline 7%, after a 3.2% decrease in 2005. Our forecast includes mid-single digit increases in Medicare and managed care reimbursement rates and a flat Medicaid environment. We also see a slight decline in inpatient and outpatient volumes as physicians refer patients to competing facilities. In 2007, we expect revenue to remain flat as higher pricing is offset by an increase in discounts for uninsured patients and higher charity care write-offs.
- We expect EBITDA margins to widen slightly in 2006, mainly due to lower bad debt expense. However, patient discounts distort reported bad debt expense, in our view, and reduce the validity of comparisons in prior years. We see EBITDA margins widening in 2007 due to lower supplies expense and a slight decline in bad debt expense.
- We estimate a loss of $0.03 per share in 2006, significantly improved from 2005's operating loss of $1.32 per share. Our forecast assumes an average share count of 465 million and includes projected stock option expense of $0.08. In 2007, we see EPS of $0.10.

Investment Rationale/Risk

- We believe that industry conditions, including a rise in self-pay admissions, remain challenging. In addition, we think THC faces company-specific challenges, including inconsistent volume statistics, lack of operating margin improvement in several core hospitals, and strained relationships with physicians. On the positive side, second quarter results came in slightly ahead of our expectations, and we think results will continue to improve over the next several quarters.
- Risks to our opinion and target price include potential reimbursement cuts in Medicare and/or Medicaid, continued difficulty in managed care negotiations, and the potential for physicians to refer patients to competing facilities. In addition, the rising number of uninsured patients could negatively affect bad debt expense beyond our expectations.
- Given THC's negative free cash flow and EPS, we use a price to book analysis to derive our target price. We apply a price to book of 2.6X, slightly above peers; our model incorporates only THC's 57 core hospitals. On this basis, our 12-month target price is $8.

Qualitative Risk Assessment

LOW | **MEDIUM** | HIGH

Our risk assessment for THC reflects our view of stable demand for healthcare services and THC's favorable corporate governance practices. This is offset by the company's strong dependence on third-party reimbursements, including Medicare and Medicaid, which can be unpredictable.

Quantitative Evaluations

S&P Quality Ranking C

D | **C** | B- | B | B+ | A- | A | A+

Relative Strength Rank WEAK

15

LOWEST = 1 HIGHEST = 99

Revenue/Earnings Data

Revenue (Million $)

	1Q	2Q	3Q	4Q	Year
2006	2,414	2,195	--	--	--
2005	2,501	2,420	2,394	2,299	9,614
2004	2,574	2,505	2,428	2,412	9,919
2003	3,417	3,346	3,268	3,181	13,212
2002	--	--	--	--	8,743
2001	3,297	3,394	3,484	3,738	13,913

Earnings Per Share ($)

2006	-0.03	-0.95	**E**-0.06	**E**-0.05	**E**-0.08
2005	0.04	Nil	-0.82	-0.54	-1.32
2004	-0.04	-0.45	-0.11	-3.43	-3.85
2003	0.03	-0.28	-0.50	-2.34	-3.01
2002	--	--	--	--	0.93
2001	0.45	0.38	0.57	0.64	2.04

Fiscal year ended Dec. 31. Next earnings report expected: Early November. EPS Estimates based on S&P Operating Earnings; historical GAAP earnings are as reported.

Dividend Data

Dividends, initiated in 1973, were omitted beginning in 1993. A special dividend of $0.01 a share was paid in March 2000.

Tenet Healthcare Corp

Business Summary August 22, 2006

CORPORATE OVERVIEW. Tenet Healthcare ranks as the second largest U.S. for-profit hospital manager. At June 30, 2006, it owned or operated 57 hospitals in continuing operations, with 15,047 licensed beds. The largest concentrations of hospital beds were in California, Florida, and Texas. THC also owns and operates a small number of rehabilitation hospitals, a specialty hospital, skilled nursing facilities, and medical office buildings located on or near the general hospital properties. In the first six months of 2006, on a same-facility basis, admissions fell 2.8% and equivalent admissions declined 2.0%. In 2005, total admissions were down 2.8% and equivalent admissions decreased 2.4%.

In January 2003, THC was sued by the U.S. Justice Department for allegedly submitting false claims to Medicare. In October 2003, the Justice Department served THC with a subpoena related to its investigation of Medicare outlier payments. In September 2003, the U.S. Senate launched an investigation into the company's corporate governance practices with respect to federal health care programs. In October 2004, additional investigations were announced into THC's medical directorship arrangements and physician relocation agreements.

In January 2006, THC reached an agreement to settle federal securities class action lawsuits as well as shareholder derivative litigation for $215 million in cash. The company expects insurance proceeds to cover $75 million of the total amount. The lawsuits were filed against the company beginning in 2002 and were consolidated in January 2003. In June 2006, THC and the U.S. Department of Justice reached an agreement to settle the ongoing investigation into Medicare outlier billing. The company agreed to pay $725 million over a period of four years, plus interest, and to waive its right to collect $175 million in Medicare payments for past services. THC also agreed to sell 11 hospitals by mid-2007. The settlement does not involve the Securities and Exchange Commission, which is investigating THC's financial disclosures surrounding the Medicare outlier payments. In our view, the Justice Department settlement removes some risk in the stock, but we expect its valuation to continue to be driven by the company's underlying operating fundamentals.

Company Financials

Per Share Data ($) Year Ended Dec. 31	2005	2004	2003	2002	2001	2000	1999	1998	1997	1996
Tangible Book Value	NM	1.63	4.85	4.40	4.40	3.45	1.57	1.01	0.31	0.17
Cash Flow	-0.51	-3.02	-2.00	1.54	3.24	2.51	1.85	1.71	1.79	0.81
Earnings	-1.32	-3.85	-3.01	0.93	2.04	1.39	0.72	0.53	0.81	-0.16
S&P Core Earnings	-1.14	-2.28	0.27	1.54	1.24	NA	NA	NA	NA	NA
Dividends	Nil	Nil	Nil	Nil	Nil	Nil	0.01	Nil	Nil	Nil
Payout Ratio	Nil	Nil	Nil	Nil	Nil	Nil	1%	Nil	Nil	Nil
Prices:High	13.06	18.73	19.25	52.50	41.85	30.50	18.12	27.29	23.25	15.83
Prices:Low	7.27	9.15	11.32	13.70	24.67	11.29	10.25	15.83	14.25	12.08
P/E Ratio:High	NM	NM	NM	56	21	22	25	52	29	NM
P/E Ratio:Low	NM	NM	NM	15	12	8	14	30	18	NM

Income Statement Analysis (Million $)	2005	2004	2003	2002	2001	2000	1999	1998	1997	1996
Revenue	9,614	9,919	13,212	8,743	13,913	12,053	11,414	10,880	9,895	8,691
Operating Income	571	434	1,072	1,676	2,797	2,244	1,935	1,858	1,809	1,597
Depreciation	382	388	471	302	604	554	533	556	460	443
Interest Expense	405	333	296	147	327	456	479	485	464	417
Pretax Income	-701	-1,616	-1,829	777	1,799	1,156	639	481	669	-21.0
Effective Tax Rate	NM	NM	NM	38.5%	40.9%	40.1%	43.5%	46.8%	40.2%	NM
Net Income	-621	-1,797	-1,404	459	1,025	678	340	249	378	-73.0
S&P Core Earnings	-561	-1,061	123	760	607	NA	NA	NA	NA	NA

Balance Sheet & Other Financial Data (Million $)	2005	2004	2003	2002	2001	2000	1999	1998	1997	1996
Cash	1,373	654	619	210	38.0	62.0	135	29.0	155	151
Current Assets	3,508	3,992	4,248	3,792	3,394	3,226	3,594	3,962	2,890	2,391
Total Assets	9,812	10,078	12,298	13,780	13,814	12,995	13,161	13,771	12,833	11,705
Current Liabilities	2,292	2,130	2,394	2,381	2,584	2,166	1,912	2,022	1,767	1,869
Long Term Debt	4,784	4,395	4,039	3,872	3,919	4,202	5,668	6,391	5,829	5,022
Common Equity	1,760	2,460	4,361	5,723	5,619	5,079	4,066	3,870	3,558	3,224
Total Capital	6,756	7,166	8,404	10,121	10,227	9,835	10,225	10,701	9,810	8,678
Capital Expenditures	568	454	753	490	889	601	619	592	534	406
Cash Flow	-239	-1,409	-933	761	1,629	1,232	873	805	838	370
Current Ratio	1.5	1.9	1.8	1.6	1.3	1.5	1.9	2.0	1.6	1.3
% Long Term Debt of Capitalization	70.8	61.3	48.1	38.3	38.3	42.7	55.4	59.7	59.4	57.9
% Net Income of Revenue	NM	NM	NM	5.2	7.4	5.6	3.0	2.3	3.8	NM
% Return on Assets	NM	NM	NM	NM	7.6	5.2	2.5	1.9	3.1	NM
% Return on Equity	NM	NM	NM	NM	19.2	14.8	8.6	6.7	11.1	NM

Data as orig reptd.; bef. results of disc opers/spec. items. Per share data adj. for stk. divs.; EPS diluted. E-Estimated. NA-Not Available. NM-Not Meaningful. NR-Not Ranked. UR-Under Review.

Office: 13737 Noel Rd, Dallas, TX 75240-2019.
Telephone: 469-893-2200.
Email: feedback@tenethealth.com
Website: http://www.tenethealth.com

Chrmn: E.A. Kangas
Pres & CEO: T. Fetter
COO: R.J. Jennings
CFO: B.C. Porter

Chief Acctg Officer: T. Pullen
Investor Contact: T. Rice (805-563-7188)
Board of Directors: T. Fetter, B. J. Gaines, K. M. Garrison, E. A. Kangas, J. R. Kerrey, F. D. Loop, R. R. Pettingill, J. A. Unruh, J. M. Williams

Founded: 1967
Domicile: Nevada
Employees: 73,434

STANDARD &POOR'S

Teradyne Inc.

S&P Recommendation HOLD ★★★★★

Price $14.02 (as of Oct 31, 2006)

12-Mo. Target Price $15.00

Investment Style Mid-Cap Value

GICS Sector Information Technology
Sub-Industry Semiconductor Equipment

Comment This maker of automatic test equipment (ATE), used primarily by the semiconductor and telecommunications industries, recently sold its connection systems business.

Key Stock Statistics (Source S&P, Vickers, company reports)

52-Wk Range	$18.08–11.50	S&P Oper. EPS 2006E	0.87	P/E on S&P Oper. EPS 2006E	16.1	Dividend Rate/Share	Nil
Trailing 12-Month EPS	$2.08	S&P Oper. EPS 2007E	0.42	Common Shares Outstg. (M)	197.0	Yield (%)	Nil
Trailing 12-Month P/E	6.7	S&P Core EPS 2006E	0.87	Market Capitalization(B)	$2.762	Beta	3.34
$10K Invested 5 Yrs Ago	$5,847	S&P Core EPS 2007E	0.42	Institutional Ownership (%)	99	S&P Credit Rating	NR

Price Performance

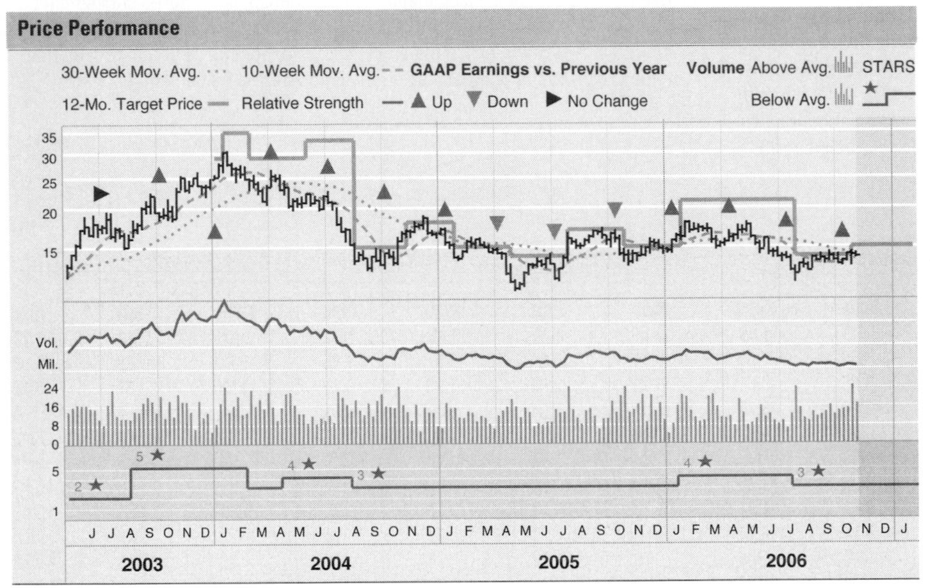

Options: ASE, CBOE, P, Ph

Analysis prepared by **David A Kaplan** on October 31, 2006, when the stock traded at **$ 13.92**.

Highlights

- We expect sales growth of 29% in 2006, and a decline of around 10% in 2007. September quarter sales were down 8% sequentially, and TER expects December quarter sales to decline around 25%. We believe sales will trough in the coming quarter and slowly regain strength over 2007, assuming continued growth in the global economy, which would result in a more moderate slowdown than historically seen in this sector.
- TER recorded a 50 basis point decline in gross margins, to around 49% in the third quarter of 2006, as fixed costs were spread over declining revenues. TER recently announced a $400 million share buyback program.
- TER reduced its break-even quarterly sales rate to $330 million, enabling it to be profitable through most of the cycle. We forecast 2006 operating EPS of $0.87 (including $0.12 of projected stock option expense) and 2007 EPS of $0.42, compared with a loss per share of $0.31 for 2005.

Investment Rationale/Risk

- We have a hold recommendation on these volatile shares, based on valuation. Incorporated in our view is TER's leadership position in the business, its strong cash position, and potential share buybacks, offset by the weaker environment that we foresee.
- Risks to our recommendation and target price include intensified pricing pressures, technological obsolescence, weakness in the global economy, and some customer concentration issues, with 18% of sales coming from three customers.
- TER shares recently traded at around 2.6X trailing 2005 sales, a 20% premium to back-end peers, and in the lower half of the peer group's historical price to sales (P/S) range of 1.8X to 4.2X. Applying a target P/S of 2.2X to our 2006 sales estimate, a 20% premium to peers, we derive our 12-month target price of $15.

Qualitative Risk Assessment

LOW | MEDIUM | **HIGH**

Our risk assessment reflects the historical cyclicality of the semiconductor equipment industry, the lack of visibility in the mid-term, the dynamic nature of the change in technology, and intense competition; moderately offset by Teradyne's market position and current asset to liability ratio.

Quantitative Evaluations

S&P Quality Ranking C

D | **C** | B- | B | B+ | A- | A | A+

Relative Strength Rank MODERATE

46

LOWEST = 1 HIGHEST = 99

Revenue/Earnings Data

Revenue (Million $)

	1Q	2Q	3Q	4Q	Year
2006	362.9	391.6	359.1	--	--
2005	210.4	226.2	293.6	345.2	1,075
2004	430.6	526.5	457.8	377.0	1,792
2003	334.6	331.5	329.2	357.6	1,353
2002	248.0	309.9	330.7	333.6	1,222
2001	605.2	365.8	249.4	220.2	1,441

Earnings Per Share ($)

	1Q	2Q	3Q	4Q	Year
2006	0.23	0.40	0.33	**E**0.04	**E**0.87
2005	-0.28	-0.26	-0.22	0.44	-0.31
2004	0.20	0.39	0.21	0.02	0.84
2003	-0.41	-0.28	-0.28	-0.06	-1.03
2002	-0.42	-0.28	-0.91	-2.31	-3.93
2001	0.30	-0.23	-0.59	-0.63	-1.15

Fiscal year ended Dec. 31. Next earnings report expected: Mid January. EPS Estimates based on S&P Operating Earnings; historical GAAP earnings are as reported.

Dividend Data

No cash dividends have been paid.

Teradyne Inc.

Business Summary October 31, 2006

CORPORATE OVERVIEW. Founded in 1960, Teradyne is a leading global supplier of automatic test equipment (ATE) for the electronics industry. As electronic systems have become more complex, the need for products to test the systems has grown dramatically. TER's product segments include systems to test semiconductors (76% of 2005 revenue, 81% in 2004), assemble test systems (14%, 11%), and other test systems (10%, 8%).

Semiconductor test systems products test SOC (system on a chip) semiconductor devices during the manufacturing process. These systems are used both for wafer level and device packaging testing and span a broad range of end users and functionality. TER's systems help customers improve and control quality, reduce time to market, increase production yields, and improve product performance. TER's FLEX Test platform is designed for scalability and allows for simultaneous parallel testing, reducing costs. The versatility of the FLEX system to handle a wide range of devices makes it attractive to subcontracting test-houses. Other systems include the J750 system for higher volume and the Catalyst system for higher performance SOC devices.

The Assembly test systems group of products test and inspect printed circuit boards (PCBs), which are thin plates or cards on which semiconductor chips and other electronic components are placed. In-circuit test systems assess electrical interconnections, verify inter-operation on PCBs, and are used both in prototype testing and high volume board manufacturing. Imaging inspection systems, such as the Xstation MX, use a 3-dimensional X-ray system for higher density double sided boards where half of all solder connections are invisible to optical inspection systems. Military/aerospace test systems are used by department of defense programs across U.S. military branches and allied military services worldwide.

Company Financials

Per Share Data ($) Year Ended Dec. 31	**2005**	**2004**	**2003**	**2002**	**2001**	**2000**	**1999**	**1998**	**1997**	**1996**
Tangible Book Value	5.75	5.00	4.33	4.97	8.69	9.89	6.77	6.13	5.63	5.11
Cash Flow	0.16	1.47	-0.22	-3.06	-0.36	3.42	1.56	1.04	1.08	0.85
Earnings	-0.31	0.84	-1.03	-3.93	-1.15	2.86	1.07	0.60	0.74	0.55
S&P Core Earnings	-0.80	0.37	-1.44	-4.25	-1.65	NA	NA	NA	NA	NA
Dividends	Nil	Nil	Nil	Nil	Nil	Nil	Nil	Nil	Nil	Nil
Payout Ratio	Nil	Nil	Nil	Nil	Nil	Nil	Nil	Nil	Nil	Nil
Prices:High	17.33	30.70	26.31	40.20	47.21	115.44	66.00	24.22	29.59	13.88
Prices:Low	10.80	12.53	8.75	7.10	18.43	23.00	20.63	7.50	11.81	5.56
P/E Ratio:High	NM	37	NM	NM	NM	40	62	41	40	25
P/E Ratio:Low	NM	15	NM	NM	NM	8	19	13	16	10

Income Statement Analysis (Million $)	**2005**	**2004**	**2003**	**2002**	**2001**	**2000**	**1999**	**1998**	**1997**	**1996**
Revenue	1,075	1,792	1,353	1,222	1,441	3,044	1,791	1,489	1,266	1,172
Operating Income	27.1	318	47.3	-192	-1.54	813	345	210	234	174
Depreciation	91.2	124	152	160	139	102	86.4	76.3	59.2	50.9
Interest Expense	16.2	18.8	20.9	21.8	4.09	1.84	1.66	1.57	2.24	2.43
Pretax Income	-80.1	188	-186	-561	-326	740	274	146	193	140
Effective Tax Rate	NM	12.1%	NM	NM	NM	30.0%	30.0%	30.0%	34.0%	33.0%
Net Income	-60.5	165	-194	-718	-202	518	192	102	128	93.5
S&P Core Earnings	-161	73.3	-270	-777	-290	NA	NA	NA	NA	NA

Balance Sheet & Other Financial Data (Million $)	**2005**	**2004**	**2003**	**2002**	**2001**	**2000**	**1999**	**1998**	**1997**	**1996**
Cash	695	285	586	541	586	464	387	298	74.7	250
Current Assets	1,095	806	769	809	1,207	1,378	908	759	727	617
Total Assets	1,860	1,923	1,785	1,895	2,542	2,356	1,568	1,313	1,252	1,097
Current Liabilities	515	277	281	279	296	619	392	256	278	225
Long Term Debt	1.82	399	408	451	452	8.35	8.95	13.2	13.1	15.6
Common Equity	1,243	1,134	950	1,028	1,764	1,707	1,153	1,026	937	842
Total Capital	1,244	1,532	1,357	1,479	2,216	1,737	1,176	1,057	974	872
Capital Expenditures	113	165	30.8	46.4	198	235	120	119	106	59.4
Cash Flow	30.7	290	-41.5	-559	-63.5	620	278	178	187	144
Current Ratio	2.1	2.9	2.7	2.9	4.1	2.2	2.3	3.0	2.6	2.7
% Long Term Debt of Capitalization	0.1	26.0	30.0	30.5	20.4	0.5	0.8	1.2	1.4	1.8
% Net Income of Revenue	NM	9.2	NM	NM	NM	17.0	10.7	6.9	10.1	8.0
% Return on Assets	NM	8.9	NM	NM	NM	26.4	13.3	8.0	10.9	8.8
% Return on Equity	NM	15.9	NM	NM	NM	36.2	17.6	10.4	14.3	11.7

Data as orig reptd.; bef. results of disc opers/spec. items. Per share data adj. for stk. divs.; EPS diluted. E-Estimated. NA-Not Available. NM-Not Meaningful. NR-Not Ranked. UR-Under Review.

Office: 321 Harrison Avenue, Boston, MA 02118.
Telephone: 617-482-2700.
Email: investorrelations@teradyne.com
Website: http://www.teradyne.com

Chrmn: G. Chamillard
Pres & CEO: M.A. Bradley
VP, CFO & Treas: G.R. Beecher
VP, Secy & General Counsel: E. Casal

Investor Contact: T.B. Newman, Jr. (617-422-2425)
Board of Directors: J. W. Bagley, M. A. Bradley, A. Carnesale, G. W. Chamillard, E. J. Gillis, V. M. O'Reilly, P. J. Tufano, R. A. Vallee, P. S. Wolpert

Founded: 1960
Domicile: Massachusetts
Employees: 4,400

STANDARD &POOR'S

Texas Instruments Inc

S&P Recommendation STRONG BUY ★★★★★

Price $29.90 (as of Oct 27, 2006)

12-Mo. Target Price $39.00

Investment Style Large-Cap Growth

GICS Sector Information Technology
Sub-Industry Semiconductors

Comment One of the world's largest manufacturers of semiconductors, this company also produces handheld graphing calculator products.

Key Stock Statistics (Source S&P, Vickers, company reports)

52-Wk Range	$36.40–26.77	S&P Oper. EPS 2006E	1.68	P/E on S&P Oper. EPS 2006E	17.8	Dividend Rate/Share	$0.16
Trailing 12-Month EPS	$2.63	S&P Oper. EPS 2007E	1.78	Common Shares Outstg. (M)	1,532.6	Yield (%)	0.54
Trailing 12-Month P/E	11.4	S&P Core EPS 2006E	1.68	Market Capitalization(B)	$45.824	Beta	2.15
$10K Invested 5 Yrs Ago	$9,893	S&P Core EPS 2007E	1.78	Institutional Ownership (%)	72	S&P Credit Rating	A

Price Performance

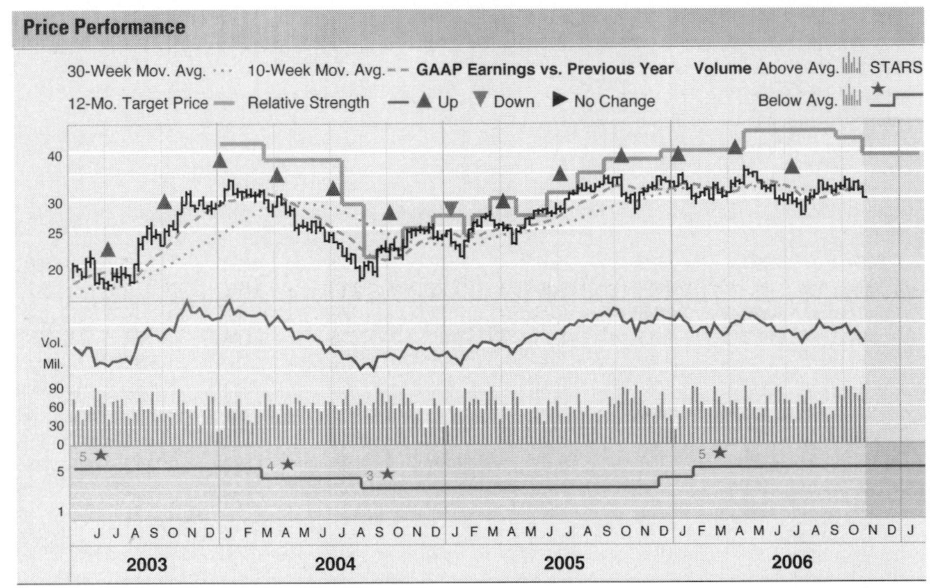

Options: ASE, CBOE, P, Ph

Analysis prepared by **Clyde Montevirgen** on October 25, 2006, when the stock traded at **$ 30.69**.

Highlights

- We estimate sales will rise 7.8% in 2006 and 4.6% in 2007. Since the January 9, 2006, announcement of TXN's plans to sell its Sensors & Controls segment for $3 billion in cash, we have followed the company's lead in modeling the segment as discontinued operations. The deal closed on April 27, and TXN recorded an after-tax gain of about $1.65 billion in the second quarter. Sensors & Controls had 2005 revenues of almost $1.2 billion. Revenue for the second quarter included $70 million from a royalty settlement with Conexant and about $57 million from a state tax refund.
- We project that gross margins will widen to 51.1% in 2006 and 51.8% in 2007, from 47.5% in 2005, as the company focuses on enriching its product mix. The cash from the Sensors division sale should provide TXN greater financial flexibility to make acquisitions, continue a share buyback campaign that reduced the share count by about 5% in 2005, or increase the dividend.
- We estimate operating EPS (including projected stock option expense) of $1.68 for 2006, and $1.78 for 2007.

Investment Rationale/Risk

- We believe the company's technology leadership position in semiconductors for wireless communication, advanced television sets, and analog functions, plus scale-based advantages in R&D and in manufacturing and marketing, should help it prosper over the long term. We view the shares as attractively valued compared to TXN's historical average multiples.
- Risks to our recommendation and target price include possible sudden downturns in demand for semiconductors, competition in chip design and price, and the challenges of operating wafer plants.
- Applying a target P/E of 22X, below historical norms (which we believe is appropriate, given our outlook for moderate industry growth near 10% in 2006), to our 12-month forward operating EPS estimate of $1.78, we see an indicated value of $39. Applying a price to sales ratio of 4.1X, near the middle of the historical range, to our 12-month forward sales per share estimate of $9.45, we also derive a value of $39, which is our 12-month target price.

Qualitative Risk Assessment

LOW | **MEDIUM** | HIGH

Our risk assessment reflects the cyclicality of the industry in which TXN operates and the high beta of its shares, offset by the large number of company operations, and TXN's mixed line of semiconductor products with exposure to many end-markets and customers, low debt levels and long corporate history.

Quantitative Evaluations

S&P Quality Ranking **B**

D | C | B- | **B** | B+ | A- | A | A+

Relative Strength Rank **WEAK**

15

LOWEST = 1 HIGHEST = 99

Revenue/Earnings Data

Revenue (Million $)

	1Q	2Q	3Q	4Q	Year
2006	3,334	3,697	--	--	--
2005	2,972	3,239	3,590	3,591	13,392
2004	2,936	3,241	3,250	3,153	12,580
2003	2,192	2,339	2,533	2,770	9,834
2002	1,827	2,162	2,248	2,146	8,383
2001	2,528	2,037	1,849	1,786	8,201

Earnings Per Share ($)

2006	0.33	0.47	**E**0.45	**E**0.43	**E**1.68
2005	0.24	0.38	0.38	0.40	1.39
2004	0.21	0.25	0.32	0.28	1.05
2003	0.07	0.07	0.25	0.29	0.68
2002	-0.02	0.05	0.11	-0.34	-0.20
2001	0.13	-0.11	-0.07	-0.07	-0.12

Fiscal year ended Dec. 31. Next earnings report expected: Late November. EPS Estimates based on S&P Operating Earnings; historical GAAP earnings are as reported.

Dividend Data (Dates: mm/dd Payment Date: mm/dd/yy)

Amount ($)	Date Decl.	Ex-Div. Date	Stk. of Record	Payment Date
0.030	01/19	01/27	01/31	02/13/06
0.030	04/19	04/27	05/01	05/22/06
0.030	07/20	07/27	07/31	08/21/06
0.040	09/21	10/27	10/31	11/20/06

Dividends have been paid since 1962. Source: Company reports.

Texas Instruments Inc

Business Summary October 25, 2006

CORPORATE OVERVIEW. Texas Instruments is the world's third-largest semiconductor company, in terms of 2005 revenues. It has design, sales or manufacturing operations in more than 25 countries. The company has increasingly concentrated on digital signal processors (DSPs), and on analog and mixed-signal integrated circuits. Semiconductors grew from less than 60% of revenues in 1996 to 87% in the boom year of 2000, and accounted for 87% in 2005 (85% in 2004).

In addition to Semiconductors, the company had two other principal segments in 2005. The Sensors & Controls segment accounted for 9% of 2005 sales (10% in 2004) and sold electrical and electronic controls, sensors, and radio frequency identification systems to the commercial and industrial markets. The Educational & Productivity Solutions segment represented 4% of 2005 sales (5%) and is a leading supplier of graphing calculators used in education, science and business.

On April 27, 2006, the company closed on its sale of the Sensors & Control segment to Bain Capital for $3 billion in cash (about $1.6 billion to $1.7 billion after tax). The company began treating the Sensors segment earnings as discontinued operations as of the first quarter of 2006. Sensors & Controls had 2005 revenue of almost $1.2 billion and about 5,400 employees. The radio frequency identification (RFID) operations included within the Sensors segment were not part of the sale and were transferred to the Semiconductors segment.

TXN sells its semiconductor products to original equipment manufacturers (OEMs), original design manufacturers (ODMs), contract manufacturers, and distributors. Direct sales to its OEM customer Nokia accounted for slightly less than 10% of revenue in 2005. Distributors handled 25% of 2005 semiconductor sales.

End markets for TXN's chips in 2005 included communications at 50% of Semiconductor sales, computing 30%, consumer electronics 10%, industrial 5%, and automotive 5%.

Company Financials

Per Share Data ($) Year Ended Dec. 31	**2005**	**2004**	**2003**	**2002**	**2001**	**2000**	**1999**	**1998**	**1997**	**1996**
Tangible Book Value	6.99	7.13	6.35	5.73	6.42	6.71	5.39	4.19	3.80	2.69
Cash Flow	2.32	1.93	1.54	0.78	0.94	2.49	1.47	0.97	0.89	0.56
Earnings	1.39	1.05	0.68	-0.20	-0.12	1.73	0.84	0.26	0.19	-0.03
S&P Core Earnings	1.26	0.86	0.40	-0.16	-0.34	NA	NA	NA	NA	NA
Dividends	0.11	0.09	0.09	0.09	0.09	0.09	0.09	0.06	0.09	0.09
Payout Ratio	8%	9%	13%	NM	NM	5%	10%	24%	45%	NM
Prices:High	34.68	33.98	31.67	35.94	54.69	99.78	55.75	22.61	17.81	8.55
Prices:Low	20.70	18.06	13.90	13.10	20.10	35.00	21.50	10.06	7.77	5.06
P/E Ratio:High	25	32	47	NM	NM	58	66	89	94	NM
P/E Ratio:Low	15	17	20	NM	NM	20	26	39	41	NM
Income Statement Analysis (Million $)										
Revenue	13,392	12,580	9,834	8,383	8,201	11,875	9,468	8,460	9,750	9,940
Operating Income	4,222	3,756	2,493	1,977	1,246	3,715	2,751	1,568	1,724	878
Depreciation	1,431	1,549	1,528	1,689	1,828	1,376	1,055	1,169	1,109	904
Interest Expense	9.00	21.0	39.0	57.0	61.0	75.0	75.0	75.0	94.0	108
Pretax Income	2,988	2,421	1,250	-346	-426	4,578	2,019	617	713	-23.0
Effective Tax Rate	22.2%	23.1%	4.16%	NM	NM	32.6%	30.4%	34.0%	57.6%	NM
Net Income	2,324	1,861	1,198	-344	-201	3,087	1,406	407	302	-46.0
S&P Core Earnings	2,110	1,516	701	-275	-587	NA	NA	NA	NA	NA
Balance Sheet & Other Financial Data (Million $)										
Cash	1,219	2,668	1,818	949	431	745	662	540	1,015	964
Current Assets	9,185	10,190	7,709	6,126	5,775	8,115	6,055	4,846	6,103	4,454
Total Assets	15,063	16,299	15,510	14,679	15,779	17,720	15,028	11,250	10,849	9,360
Current Liabilities	2,346	1,925	2,200	1,934	1,580	2,813	2,628	2,196	2,496	2,486
Long Term Debt	360	368	395	833	1,211	1,216	1,097	1,027	1,286	1,697
Common Equity	11,937	13,063	11,864	10,734	11,879	12,588	9,255	6,527	5,914	4,097
Total Capital	12,320	13,471	12,318	11,696	13,421	14,273	11,346	7,935	7,200	5,794
Capital Expenditures	1,330	1,298	800	802	1,790	2,762	1,373	1,031	1,238	2,063
Cash Flow	3,882	3,410	2,726	1,345	1,627	4,463	2,461	1,551	1,411	858
Current Ratio	3.9	5.3	3.5	3.2	3.7	2.9	2.3	2.2	2.4	1.8
% Long Term Debt of Capitalization	2.9	2.7	3.2	7.1	9.0	8.5	9.7	12.9	17.9	29.3
% Net Income of Revenue	17.4	14.8	12.2	NM	NM	26.0	14.9	4.8	3.1	NM
% Return on Assets	14.8	11.7	7.9	NM	NM	18.6	10.6	3.7	3.0	NM
% Return on Equity	18.6	14.9	10.6	NM	NM	27.9	17.6	6.5	6.0	NM

Data as orig reptd.; bef. results of disc opers/spec. items. Per share data adj. for stk. divs.; EPS diluted. E-Estimated. NA-Not Available. NM-Not Meaningful. NR-Not Ranked. UR-Under Review.

Office: 12500 Ti Blvd, Dallas, TX 75243-0592.
Telephone: 972-995-3773.
Website: http://www.ti.com
Chrmn: T.J. Engibous

Pres & CEO: R.K. Templeton
SVP & CFO: K. March
SVP, Secy & General Counsel: J.F. Hubach
Investor Contact: T. West

Board of Directors: J. R. Adams, D. L. Boren, D. A. Carp, C. S. Cox, T. J. Engibous, G. W. Fronterhouse, D. R. Goode, P. H. Patsley, W. R. Sanders, R. J. Simmons, R. K. Templeton, C. Whitman

Founded: 1938
Domicile: Delaware
Employees: 35,207

STANDARD & POOR'S

Textron Inc.

S&P Recommendation BUY ★★★★★

Price $88.67 (as of Oct 27, 2006)

12-Mo. Target Price $104.00

Investment Style Large-Cap Value

GICS Sector Industrials
Sub-Industry Industrial Conglomerates

Comment This conglomerate primarily makes industrial bolts and screws, and industrial equipment and components, as well as Cessna business jets and Bell helicopters.

Key Stock Statistics (Source S&P, Vickers, company reports)

52-Wk Range	$98.96–71.00	S&P Oper. EPS 2006E	5.32	P/E on S&P Oper. EPS 2006E	16.7	Dividend Rate/Share	$1.55
Trailing 12-Month EPS	$3.97	S&P Oper. EPS 2007E	6.25	Common Shares Outstg. (M)	126.3	Yield (%)	1.75
Trailing 12-Month P/E	22.3	S&P Core EPS 2006E	5.03	Market Capitalization(B)	$11.195	Beta	1.49
$10K Invested 5 Yrs Ago	$29,539	S&P Core EPS 2007E	5.96	Institutional Ownership (%)	70	S&P Credit Rating	A-

Price Performance

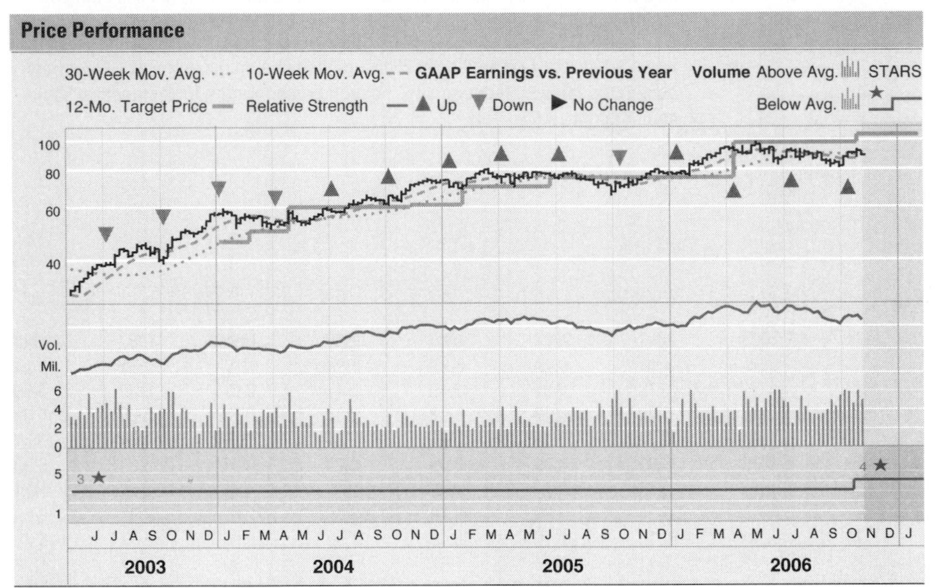

Options: Ph

Highlights

- The STARS recommendation for TXT has recently been changed to 4 (buy) from 3 (hold) and the 12-month target price has recently been changed to $104.00 from $98.00. The Highlights section of this Stock Report will be updated accordingly.

Investment Rationale/Risk

- The Investment Rationale/Risk section of this Stock Report will be updated shortly. For the latest News story on TXT from MarketScope, see below.
- 10/19/06 10:50 am EDT... S&P UPGRADES SHARES OF TEXTRON TO BUY FROM HOLD (TXT 92.3****): Q3 EPS of $1.36 vs. $1.07 is above our $1.27 estimate. TXT saw continued strength at Cessna where deliveries are sold out through '07. With strong demand for business jets, we see a solid order book and profitability at Cessna going forward. We also see a strong outlook for Bell's military/commercial helicopters, with profits constrained near term by high research & development. We are raising our '06 EPS estimate $0.12 to $5.32, and '07 $0.15 to $6.25. Our 12-month target price rises $6 to $104, or 16.6X our '07 EPS estimate, below a current PE of 17 for peers. /R.Tortoriello

Qualitative Risk Assessment

LOW | **MEDIUM** | HIGH

Our risk assessment reflects our view of TXT's cyclical earnings and that the company's stock is more volatile than average, with a recent beta of 1.73, offset by a stable dividend over the past 10 years.

Quantitative Evaluations

S&P Quality Ranking B+

D | C | B- | B | **B+** | A- | A | A+

Relative Strength Rank MODERATE

38

LOWEST = 1 HIGHEST = 99

Revenue/Earnings Data

Revenue (Million $)

	1Q	2Q	3Q	4Q	Year
2006	2,632	2,820	2,837	--	--
2005	2,791	3,188	2,862	2,701	10,043
2004	2,354	2,547	2,569	2,833	10,242
2003	2,399	2,530	2,231	2,699	9,859
2002	2,418	2,824	2,554	2,862	10,658
2001	3,040	3,288	2,810	3,183	12,321

Earnings Per Share ($)

2006	1.19	1.34	1.36	**E**1.42	**E**5.32
2005	0.57	0.94	-1.25	1.25	3.78
2004	0.26	0.71	0.73	0.87	2.66
2003	0.49	0.62	0.34	0.60	2.05
2002	0.40	0.74	0.51	0.95	2.60
2001	0.79	0.88	-2.34	1.81	1.16

Fiscal year ended Dec. 31. Next earnings report expected: Late January. EPS Estimates based on S&P Operating Earnings; historical GAAP earnings are as reported.

Dividend Data (Dates: mm/dd Payment Date: mm/dd/yy)

Amount ($)	Date Decl.	Ex-Div. Date	Stk. of Record	Payment Date
0.388	01/26	03/08	03/10	04/01/06
0.388	04/26	06/07	06/09	07/01/06
0.388	07/26	09/13	09/15	10/01/06
0.388	10/25	12/13	12/15	01/01/07

Dividends have been paid since 1942. Source: Company reports.

Textron Inc.

Business Summary July 31, 2006

CORPORATE OVERVIEW. This $10 billion in revenue industrial and finance conglomerate conducts business through the following operating segments.

TXT's Bell Helicopter segment (29% of 2005 revenues and 32% of operating profits, with a 12.8% operating profit margin), is comprised of Bell Helicopter and Textron Systems. Based on 2004 revenues, Bell Helicopter was the world's third largest helicopter maker. EADS's Eurocopter unit, AgustaWestland, United Technologies' Sikorsky unit, and Boeing's helicopter operations were the world's first-, second-, fourth- and fifth-largest helicopter manufacturers, respectively. The $15 billion-revenue helicopter-making industry is oligopolistic; the five largest helicopter makers account for about 85% of industry revenues.

Bell Helicopter manufactures both military and commercial helicopters, and accounted for about 21% of TXT's revenues in 2005. Bell supplies advanced military helicopters and support (including spare parts, support equipment, technical data, trainers, etc.) to the U.S. government and to military customers outside the U.S. Bell is also a leading supplier of commercially certified helicopters to corporate, offshore petroleum exploration and development, utility, charter, police, fire, rescue, and emergency medical helicopter operators. The Textron Systems sub-segment makes "smart" weapons, airborne and ground-based surveillance systems, aircraft landing systems, hovercraft, search and rescue vessels, armored vehicles and turrets, reciprocating piston aircraft engines, and aircraft and missile control actuators, valves, and related components.

Company Financials

Per Share Data ($) Year Ended Dec. 31	**2005**	**2004**	**2003**	**2002**	**2001**	**2000**	**1999**	**1998**	**1997**	**1996**
Tangible Book Value	16.05	14.69	16.18	12.92	12.40	11.60	10.56	5.54	9.10	9.42
Cash Flow	6.30	5.38	4.65	5.23	4.76	5.28	6.90	4.87	5.84	5.05
Earnings	3.78	2.66	2.05	2.60	1.16	1.90	4.05	2.68	3.29	2.80
S&P Core Earnings	4.12	2.01	1.18	0.27	-1.40	NA	NA	NA	NA	NA
Dividends	1.40	1.33	1.30	1.30	1.30	1.30	1.26	1.11	1.00	0.88
Payout Ratio	37%	50%	63%	50%	NM	68%	9%	41%	30%	31%
Prices:High	80.71	74.92	57.99	53.60	60.47	77.50	98.00	80.94	70.75	48.88
Prices:Low	65.20	50.59	26.00	32.20	31.29	40.69	65.88	52.06	45.00	34.56
P/E Ratio:High	21	28	28	21	52	41	24	30	22	17
P/E Ratio:Low	17	19	13	12	27	21	16	19	14	12
Income Statement Analysis (Million $)										
Revenue	10,043	10,242	9,859	10,658	12,321	13,090	11,579	9,683	10,544	9,274
Operating Income	1,450	1,260	1,171	1,285	1,461	2,074	1,702	1,439	2,109	1,945
Depreciation	303	353	356	368	514	494	440	361	435	387
Interest Expense	290	248	283	330	459	492	260	315	726	731
Pretax Income	739	528	388	464	393	585	1,004	737	922	827
Effective Tax Rate	30.2%	29.4%	27.6%	21.6%	57.8%	52.6%	37.9%	39.9%	39.5%	38.9%
Net Income	516	373	281	364	166	277	623	443	558	482
S&P Core Earnings	565	282	161	38.6	-202	NA	NA	NA	NA	NA
Balance Sheet & Other Financial Data (Million $)										
Cash	796	732	843	307	260	289	209	53.0	87.0	47.0
Current Assets	4,975	4,168	3,592	3,887	4,017	3,914	3,735	4,355	NA	NA
Total Assets	16,499	15,875	15,090	15,505	16,052	16,370	16,393	13,721	18,610	18,235
Current Liabilities	3,147	2,975	2,256	2,239	3,075	3,263	3,256	3,919	NA	NA
Long Term Debt	7,079	6,141	6,144	7,038	5,962	6,648	6,142	4,192	10,496	10,346
Common Equity	3,266	3,642	3,680	3,395	3,923	3,982	4,365	2,984	3,215	3,169
Total Capital	10,816	10,246	10,224	10,842	10,253	10,957	10,826	7,511	14,207	14,012
Capital Expenditures	365	302	301	296	532	527	532	475	412	343
Cash Flow	819	726	637	732	680	771	1,062	803	992	869
Current Ratio	1.6	1.4	1.6	1.7	1.3	1.2	1.1	1.1	NA	NA
% Long Term Debt of Capitalization	65.4	59.9	60.1	64.9	58.1	60.7	56.7	55.8	73.9	73.8
% Net Income of Revenue	5.1	3.6	2.9	3.4	1.3	2.1	5.4	4.6	5.3	2.0
% Return on Assets	3.2	2.4	1.8	2.3	1.0	1.7	4.1	2.7	3.0	2.7
% Return on Equity	14.9	10.2	7.9	9.9	4.2	6.6	16.9	14.3	17.4	14.7

Data as orig reptd.; bef. results of disc opers/spec. items. Per share data adj. for stk. divs.; EPS diluted. E-Estimated. NA-Not Available. NM-Not Meaningful. NR-Not Ranked. UR-Under Review.

Office: 40 Westminster Street, Providence, RI 02903-2525.
Telephone: 401-421-2800.
Website: http://www.textron.com
Chrmn, Pres & CEO: L.B. Campbell

EVP & CFO: T.R. French
EVP & General Counsel: T. O'Donnell
VP & CIO: G. Cantrell
Investor Contact: D.R. Wilburne (401-457-3606)

Board of Directors: H. J. Arnelle, K. M. Bader, L. B. Campbell, R. K. Clark, I. J. Evans, L. K. Fish, J. T. Ford, P. E. Gagne, D. M. Hancock, B. H. Rowe, T. B. Wheeler, L. of Bayswater

Founded: 1928
Domicile: Delaware
Employees: 37,000

STANDARD &POOR'S

Thermo Electron Corp

S&P Recommendation STRONG BUY ★★★★★

Price $43.16 (as of Oct 27, 2006)

12-Mo. Target Price $52.00

Investment Style Mid-Cap Value

GICS Sector Health Care
Sub-Industry Life Sciences Tools & Services

Comment This leading maker of analytical instruments provides scientific and measurement equipment and services for life science, drug discovery and industrial applications.

Key Stock Statistics (Source S&P, Vickers, company reports)

52-Wk Range	**$44.65–29.33**	S&P Oper. EPS 2006**E**	**1.76**	P/E on S&P Oper. EPS 2006**E**	**24.5**	Dividend Rate/Share	**Nil**
Trailing 12-Month EPS	**$1.22**	S&P Oper. EPS 2007**E**	**2.03**	Common Shares Outstg. (M)	**157.6**	Yield (%)	**Nil**
Trailing 12-Month P/E	**35.4**	S&P Core EPS 2006**E**	**1.76**	Market Capitalization(B)	**$6.802**	Beta	**1.16**
$10K Invested 5 Yrs Ago	**$21,604**	S&P Core EPS 2007**E**	**2.03**	Institutional Ownership (%)	**92**	S&P Credit Rating	**BBB+**

Price Performance

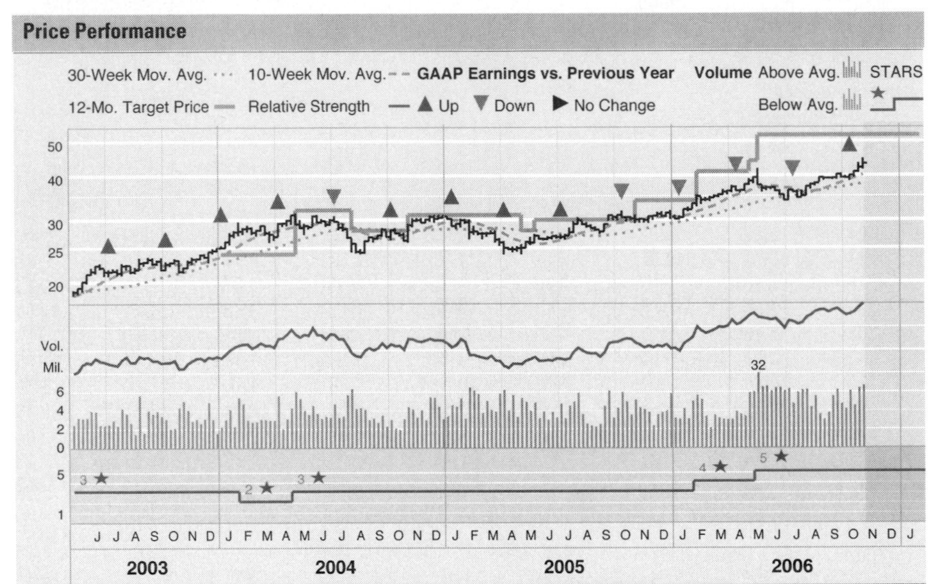

Options: CBOE, P

Analysis prepared by **Jeffrey Loo, CFA** on August 10, 2006, when the stock traded at **$ 37.29.**

Highlights

- In May 2006, TMO agreed to acquire Fisher Scientific (FSH: strong buy, $76) in a stock-for-stock reverse merger for about $10.6 billion based on TMO's closing price on May 5, 2006, subject to necessary approvals. TMO will issue two shares for each FSH share and will own 39% of the combined entity to be named Thermo Fisher Scientific, with expected revenues exceeding $9 billion. The proposed deal is expected to close in the fourth quarter of 2006 and achieve $150 million in cost saving synergies and $50 million in revenue synergies.
- Separately, we see 2006 sales growth of 9% to $2.88 billion, including a contribution from Kendro Laboratory Products, acquired in May 2005. We estimate gross margins improving 80 basis points despite the lower margin distribution business of Kendro and see operating margins improving 90 basis points despite stock option costs, due to operating leverage and improved efficiency.
- Including estimated stock option expense of $0.10, we anticipate 2006 operating EPS of $1.76, before accounting for the amortization of acquisition-related intangible assets.

Investment Rationale/Risk

- We think TMO's agreement to acquire FSH makes sense, as we see the integration of products resulting in the most comprehensive life sciences product offering. We think the companies can use their extensive global sales and distribution network to drive cost and revenue synergies, enabling potential operating margin expansion of about 300 basis points. We also see some integration risks lessened as both companies have integrated numerous companies. We expect TMO to retain its measurement and control unit as it contributes solid profit margins and provides diversification.
- Risks to our recommendation and target price include failure to consummate the planned deal with FSH; a prolonged slowdown in pharmaceutical R&D spending; adverse regulatory actions; and a potential larger than expected negative foreign currency impact.
- Our 12-month target price of $52 is based a P/E-to-growth (PEG) analysis using a PEG ratio of 1.4X, based on our 2007 pro forma EPS estimate of $2.30, slightly below peers, as we take some integration risks into account.

Qualitative Risk Assessment

LOW | **MEDIUM** | HIGH

Our risk assessment reflects TMO's broad product lines, spread across the life sciences and industrial marketplaces, which we believe reduces risk. However, TMO has a proactive acquisition strategy that we believe raises its risk profile.

Quantitative Evaluations

S&P Quality Ranking B-

D | C | **B-** | B | B+ | A- | A | A+

Relative Strength Rank STRONG

81

LOWEST = 1 HIGHEST = 99

Revenue/Earnings Data

Revenue (Million $)

	1Q	2Q	3Q	4Q	Year
2006	684.3	713.5	725.0	--	--
2005	559.2	653.6	679.4	740.8	2,633
2004	525.0	525.3	542.3	613.3	2,206
2003	500.2	516.4	497.1	583.4	2,097
2002	491.3	509.1	517.2	568.8	2,086
2001	573.1	542.5	512.9	559.7	2,188

Earnings Per Share ($)

2006	0.26	0.30	0.30	**E**0.52	**E**1.76
2005	0.28	0.35	0.25	0.34	1.21
2004	0.24	0.30	0.26	0.52	1.31
2003	0.19	0.32	0.24	0.30	1.04
2002	0.34	0.23	0.23	0.25	1.12
2001	0.12	0.05	0.14	-0.04	0.27

Fiscal year ended Dec. 31. Next earnings report expected: Early February. EPS Estimates based on S&P Operating Earnings; historical GAAP earnings are as reported.

Dividend Data

No cash dividends have been paid.

Please read the Required Disclosures and Analyst Certification on the last page of this report.

The McGraw-Hill Companies

Thermo Electron Corp

Business Summary August 10, 2006

Thermo Electron Corp. develops and manufactures analytical systems, instruments and components, and provides solutions used to monitor, collect and analyze data. These instruments are used primarily in life science, drug discovery, clinical, environmental and industrial laboratory applications.

In January 2000, TMO embarked on a major reorganization that ultimately resulted in taking private all of its public subsidiaries (approximately 22 public entities), selling non-core businesses and spinning off its paper recycling and medical products businesses. As part of the reorganization, TMO divested businesses with aggregate revenues of over $2 billion. This reorganization was substantially completed in February 2002. In July 2004, TMO further streamlined its business by divesting its optical technologies segment, Spectra-Physics. TMO's continuing operations are comprised solely of its instrument businesses.

After its reorganization, TMO has two principal segments: Life and Laboratory Sciences and Measurement and Control.

The Life and Laboratory Sciences segment, accounting for 71.3% of 2004 revenue (68.1% in 2003), serves the pharmaceutical, biotechnology, academic, government, and other research and industrial laboratory markets, as well as the clinical laboratory and health care industries. This segment has four principal products and groupings: Bioscience Technologies, Scientific Instruments, Informatics and Services, and Clinical Diagnostics. Bioscience Technologies products consist primarily of sample preparation and handling equipment; Scientific Instruments products include analytical instrumentation that analyzes the prepared samples; Informatics and Services provides software interpretation tools and development support for that data generated by the instruments; and Clinical Diagnostics products are used by health care and other laboratories to prepare and analyze patient samples.

Company Financials

Per Share Data ($) Year Ended Dec. 31	**2005**	**2004**	**2003**	**2002**	**2001**	**2000**	**1999**	**1998**	**1997**	**1996**
Tangible Book Value	2.32	6.19	5.00	3.79	1.33	6.34	5.03	1.51	1.60	1.60
Cash Flow	1.95	1.70	1.35	1.35	0.81	0.94	0.63	1.90	2.13	2.13
Earnings	1.21	1.31	1.04	1.12	0.27	0.36	-0.11	1.04	1.41	1.35
S&P Core Earnings	1.01	1.18	0.79	0.50	0.02	NA	NA	NA	NA	NA
Dividends	Nil	Nil	Nil	Nil	Nil	Nil	Nil	Nil	Nil	Nil
Payout Ratio	Nil	Nil	Nil	Nil	Nil	Nil	Nil	Nil	Nil	Nil
Prices:High	31.87	31.40	25.40	24.60	30.62	31.24	20.25	44.25	44.50	44.38
Prices:Low	23.94	24.00	16.89	14.33	16.55	14.00	12.50	13.56	28.38	29.75
P/E Ratio:High	26	24	24	22	NM	87	NM	43	32	33
P/E Ratio:Low	20	18	16	13	NM	39	NM	13	20	22

Income Statement Analysis (Million $)										
Revenue	2,633	2,206	2,097	2,086	2,100	2,201	2,471	3,868	3,558	3,558
Operating Income	404	319	292	264	265	296	362	538	543	543
Depreciation	123	66.1	58.5	56.4	98.5	97.5	114	162	136	136
Interest Expense	26.7	11.0	18.7	Nil	71.8	Nil	Nil	104	93.1	93.1
Pretax Income	286	259	219	288	70.7	185	37.5	392	488	488
Effective Tax Rate	30.6%	15.8%	21.0%	32.3%	30.1%	60.7%	NM	43.6%	35.8%	35.8%
Net Income	198	218	173	195	49.6	62.0	-14.6	177	239	239
S&P Core Earnings	164	196	131	79.3	5.63	NA	NA	NA	NA	NA

Balance Sheet & Other Financial Data (Million $)										
Cash	214	327	304	339	298	506	282	397	594	594
Current Assets	1,354	1,470	1,395	1,772	1,965	2,466	2,517	3,301	3,094	3,094
Total Assets	4,252	3,577	3,389	3,647	3,825	4,863	5,182	6,332	5,796	5,796
Current Liabilities	792	579	685	1,104	1,142	729	1,066	1,138	1,092	1,092
Long Term Debt	469	226	230	451	728	1,528	1,566	2,026	1,743	1,550
Common Equity	2,793	2,666	2,383	2,033	1,908	2,534	2,014	2,248	1,998	1,998
Total Capital	3,327	2,907	2,624	2,495	2,650	4,098	4,026	5,025	3,925	4,065
Capital Expenditures	43.5	50.0	46.1	51.2	84.8	74.0	87.2	148	112	125
Cash Flow	322	285	231	252	148	160	99.1	339	375	375
Current Ratio	1.7	2.5	2.0	1.6	1.7	3.4	2.4	2.9	2.8	2.8
% Long Term Debt of Capitalization	14.1	7.8	8.7	18.1	27.4	37.3	38.9	40.3	44.4	38.1
% Net Income of Revenue	7.5	9.9	8.2	9.4	2.3	2.7	NM	4.6	6.7	6.7
% Return on Assets	5.1	6.3	4.9	5.2	1.1	1.2	NM	2.9	4.1	5.0
% Return on Equity	7.3	8.7	7.8	9.9	2.2	2.7	NM	8.3	12.0	14.5

Data as orig reptd.; bef. results of disc opers/spec. items. Per share data adj. for stk. divs.; EPS diluted. E-Estimated. NA-Not Available. NM-Not Meaningful. NR-Not Ranked. UR-Under Review.

Office: 81 Wyman Street, Waltham, MA 02254-9046.
Telephone: 781-622-1000.
Website: http://www.thermo.com
Chrmn: J.P. Manzi

Pres & CEO: M.E. Dekkers
VP & CFO: P.M. Wilver
VP, Secy & General Counsel: S.H. Hoogasian
Chief Acctg Officer & Cntlr: P.E. Hornstra

Investor Contact: K.J. Apicerno (781-622-1111)
Board of Directors: M. E. Dekkers, J. L. LaMattina, P. J. Manning, J. P. Manzi, R. A. McCabe, R. W. O'Leary, M. E. Porter, E. S. Ullian

Auditor: PricewaterhouseCoopers
Founded: 1956
Domicile: Delaware
Employees: 11,500

3M Co

STANDARD &POOR'S

S&P Recommendation HOLD ★★★★★

Price $78.95 (as of Oct 27, 2006)

12-Mo. Target Price $84.00

Investment Style Large-Cap Growth

GICS Sector Industrials
Sub-Industry Industrial Conglomerates

Comment This diversified global company has operations in electronics, health care, industrial, consumer and office, telecommunications, safety and security, and other markets.

Key Stock Statistics (Source S&P, Vickers, company reports)

52-Wk Range	$88.35–67.05	S&P Oper. EPS 2006E	4.50	P/E on S&P Oper. EPS 2006E	17.5	Dividend Rate/Share	$1.84
Trailing 12-Month EPS	$4.65	S&P Oper. EPS 2007E	5.05	Common Shares Outstg. (M)	753.2	Yield (%)	2.33
Trailing 12-Month P/E	17.0	S&P Core EPS 2006E	4.47	Market Capitalization(B)	$59.468	Beta	0.62
$10K Invested 5 Yrs Ago	$15,918	S&P Core EPS 2007E	5.02	Institutional Ownership (%)	68	S&P Credit Rating	AA

Price Performance

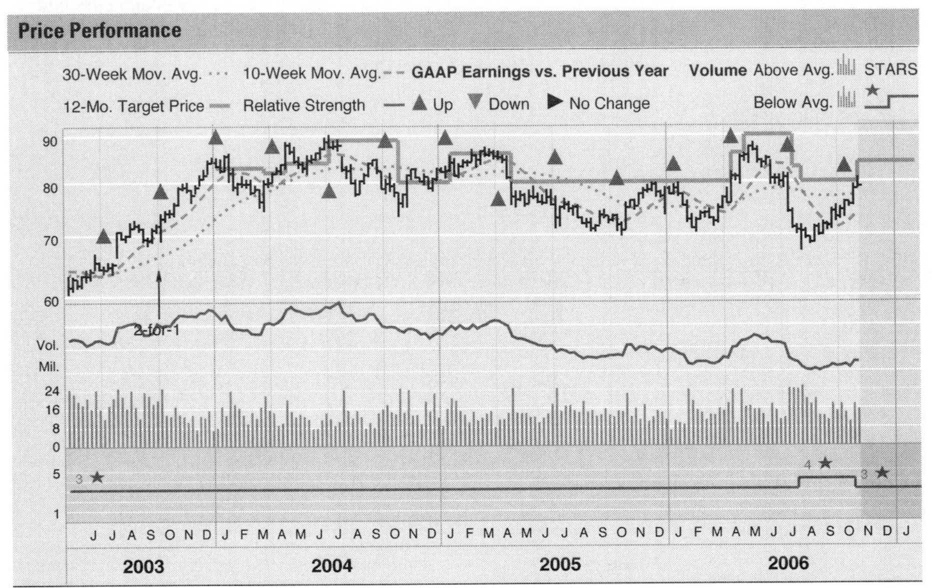

Options: ASE, CBOE, P, Ph

Analysis prepared by **Anthony M. Fiore, CFA** on October 24, 2006, when the stock traded at **$ 79.89**.

Highlights

- We see revenues increasing about 5% in 2007. We expect top-line growth in 2007 to benefit from further penetration of the Asia-Pacific and Latin America regions, the development of adjacent market opportunities, an expanding pipeline of new products, and contributions from acquisitions.
- We see operating margins remaining about flat in 2007, as projected benefits from Six Sigma and improving volumes are largely offset by an expected decline in profitability in the Display and Graphics segment. MMM's operating margin (before one-time items), which averaged about 19% from 1995 to 2004, was 23% in 2005. Over the next few years, we believe that continued efforts to streamline this diverse company will enable MMM to maintain above-average profitability.
- Our Standard & Poor's Core EPS estimate for 2007 is $0.03 a share below our operating EPS projection, with the difference reflecting pension and post-retirement related cost adjustments. Our S&P Core EPS and operating EPS estimates for 2007 each include $0.17 of projected stock option expense.

Investment Rationale/Risk

- We expect favorable end market conditions to continue over the next 12 months, based on our outlook for ongoing global economic growth. We think 3M's global footprint positions the company well to participate in markets that are likely to grow faster than the U.S. over the next several years.
- Risks to our recommendation and target price include an unexpected downturn in the global economy; a greater than projected moderation of growth in the optical display business; execution risk associated with acquisitions and/or cost saving initiatives; and weaker than anticipated commercialization of the R&D pipeline.
- Our 12-month target price of $84 is based on a blend of valuations. Our DCF model, which assumes a 7% average annual free cash flow growth rate over the next 10 years, 3.5% growth in perpetuity, and a 9.3% WACC, indicates intrinsic value of about $82. In terms of relative valuation, we believe MMM should be able to command a P/E ratio that is 20% above the S&P 500 P/E of 14.2X, due to the company's above-average profitability. Applying a P/E of 17X to our 2007 EPS estimate suggests a value of $86.

Qualitative Risk Assessment

LOW	MEDIUM	HIGH

Our risk assessment reflects our view of the company's historical stability in earnings and dividends, its leading position in many of the end markets that it serves, a strong balance sheet with a relatively low amount of debt, and free cash flow that has averaged about 95% of net income over the past 10 years.

Quantitative Evaluations

S&P Quality Ranking A

D	C	B-	B	B+	A-	A	A+

Relative Strength Rank MODERATE

68

LOWEST = 1 HIGHEST = 99

Revenue/Earnings Data

Revenue (Million $)

	1Q	2Q	3Q	4Q	Year
2006	5,595	5,688	5,858	--	--
2005	5,166	5,294	5,382	5,325	21,167
2004	4,939	5,012	4,969	5,091	20,011
2003	4,318	4,580	4,616	4,718	18,232
2002	3,890	4,161	4,143	4,138	16,332
2001	4,170	4,079	3,967	3,863	16,079

Earnings Per Share ($)

	1Q	2Q	3Q	4Q	Year
2006	1.17	1.15	1.18	E1.11	E4.50
2005	1.03	1.00	1.10	1.04	4.16
2004	0.90	0.97	0.97	0.91	3.75
2003	0.63	0.78	0.83	0.77	3.02
2002	0.57	0.59	0.69	0.65	2.49
2001	0.57	0.25	0.50	0.48	1.79

Fiscal year ended Dec. 31. Next earnings report expected: Late January. EPS Estimates based on S&P Operating Earnings; historical GAAP earnings are as reported.

Dividend Data (Dates: mm/dd Payment Date: mm/dd/yy)

Amount ($)	Date Decl.	Ex-Div. Date	Stk. of Record	Payment Date
0.420	11/14	11/22	11/25	12/12/05
0.460	02/13	02/22	02/24	03/12/06
0.460	05/09	05/17	05/19	06/12/06
0.460	08/15	08/23	08/25	09/12/06

Dividends have been paid since 1916. Source: Company reports.

Business Summary October 24, 2006

CORPORATE OVERVIEW. During the first quarter of 2006, 3M combined its Industrial and Transportation segments. The new reportable business units are Industrial and Transportation; Health Care; Display and Graphics; Consumer and Office; Electro and Communications; and Safety, Security and Protection Services.

The Industrial and Transportation segment (29% of 2005 revenues and 20% operating margin) serves a broad range of markets, from appliances and electronics to paper and packaging, food and beverages, automotive, automotive aftermarket, aerospace and marine, and other transportation-related industries. Products include pressure-sensitive tapes, abrasives, adhesives, specialty materials, supply chain management software and solutions, insulation components, films, masking tapes, fasteners, adhesives and abrasives used in the repair and maintenance of automotive, marine, aircraft and other specialty vehicles.

The Health Care segment (18% and 30%) serves markets worldwide, including medical and surgical, pharmaceutical, dental, health information systems and personal care. Products provided include medical and surgical, infection prevention, pharmaceuticals, drug delivery systems, dental products, health information systems, personal care and other products.

The Display and Graphics segment (17% and 33%) serves markets that include electronic display, touch screen, commercial graphics and traffic control materials. Optical products include Vikkuiti display enhancement films for electronic displays, lens systems for projection televisions, and 3M MicroTouch touch screens and touch monitors. Other products include 3M Scotchlite reflective sheeting for transportation safety and Scotchprint commercial graphics systems.

The Consumer and Office segment (14% and 18%) serves markets that include consumer, office, education, home improvement, building maintenance, food service and other markets. Offerings consist of office supplies, construction and home improvement products, protective materials, and visual systems.

Company Financials

Per Share Data ($) Year Ended Dec. 31	**2005**	**2004**	**2003**	**2002**	**2001**	**2000**	**1999**	**1998**	**1997**	**1996**
Tangible Book Value	8.13	9.62	6.62	4.91	6.23	7.17	7.06	7.39	7.32	7.54
Cash Flow	5.43	5.01	4.23	3.70	3.15	3.60	3.28	2.55	3.57	2.87
Earnings	4.16	3.75	3.02	2.49	1.79	2.32	2.17	1.49	2.53	1.82
S&P Core Earnings	4.13	3.66	2.91	1.71	0.94	NA	NA	NA	NA	NA
Dividends	1.68	1.44	1.32	1.24	1.20	1.16	1.12	1.10	1.06	0.96
Payout Ratio	40%	38%	44%	50%	67%	50%	52%	74%	42%	53%
Prices:High	87.45	90.29	85.40	65.78	63.50	61.47	51.69	48.94	52.75	42.94
Prices:Low	69.71	73.31	59.73	50.00	42.93	39.09	34.66	32.81	40.00	30.63
P/E Ratio:High	21	24	28	26	35	26	24	33	21	24
P/E Ratio:Low	17	20	20	20	24	17	16	22	16	17

Income Statement Analysis (Million $)	**2005**	**2004**	**2003**	**2002**	**2001**	**2000**	**1999**	**1998**	**1997**	**1996**
Revenue	21,167	20,011	18,232	16,332	16,079	16,724	15,659	15,021	15,070	14,236
Operating Income	5,995	5,577	4,677	4,000	3,274	3,898	3,828	3,398	3,545	3,374
Depreciation	986	999	964	954	1,089	1,025	900	866	870	883
Interest Expense	82.0	69.0	84.0	80.0	124	111	109	139	94.0	79.0
Pretax Income	4,983	4,555	3,657	3,005	2,186	2,974	2,880	1,952	3,440	2,479
Effective Tax Rate	34.0%	33.0%	32.9%	32.1%	32.1%	34.5%	35.8%	35.1%	36.1%	35.7%
Net Income	3,234	2,990	2,403	1,974	1,430	1,857	1,763	1,213	2,121	1,516
S&P Core Earnings	3,227	2,918	2,319	1,356	750	NA	NA	NA	NA	NA

Balance Sheet & Other Financial Data (Million $)	**2005**	**2004**	**2003**	**2002**	**2001**	**2000**	**1999**	**1998**	**1997**	**1996**
Cash	1,072	2,757	1,836	618	616	302	387	448	477	744
Current Assets	7,115	8,720	7,720	6,059	6,296	6,379	6,066	6,318	6,168	6,486
Total Assets	20,513	20,708	17,600	15,329	14,606	14,522	13,896	14,153	13,238	13,364
Current Liabilities	5,238	6,071	5,082	4,457	4,509	4,754	3,819	4,386	3,983	3,789
Long Term Debt	1,309	727	1,735	2,140	1,520	971	1,480	1,614	1,015	851
Common Equity	10,100	10,378	7,885	5,993	6,086	6,531	6,289	5,936	5,926	6,294
Total Capital	11,409	11,105	9,620	8,133	7,606	7,502	7,769	7,550	6,941	7,135
Capital Expenditures	943	937	677	763	980	1,115	1,039	1,430	1,406	1,109
Cash Flow	4,220	3,989	3,367	2,928	2,519	2,882	2,663	2,079	2,991	2,399
Current Ratio	1.4	1.4	1.5	1.4	1.4	1.3	1.6	1.4	1.5	1.7
% Long Term Debt of Capitalization	11.5	6.5	18.0	26.3	20.0	12.9	19.1	21.3	14.6	11.9
% Net Income of Revenue	15.3	14.9	13.2	12.1	8.9	11.1	11.3	8.1	14.1	10.6
% Return on Assets	15.7	15.6	14.6	13.2	9.8	13.1	12.6	8.9	15.9	11.0
% Return on Equity	31.6	32.7	34.6	32.7	22.7	29.0	28.8	20.5	34.7	23.0

Data as orig reptd.; bef. results of disc opers/spec. items. Per share data adj. for stk. divs.; EPS diluted. E-Estimated. NA-Not Available. NM-Not Meaningful. NR-Not Ranked. UR-Under Review.

Office: 3M Center, St. Paul, MN 55144-1000.
Telephone: 651-733-1110.
Email: innovation@mmm.com
Website: http://www.3m.com

Chrmn, Pres & CEO: G.W. Buckley
EVP & CTO: F.J. Palensky
SVP & CFO: P.D. Campbell
SVP & General Counsel: R.F. Ziegler

Investor Contact: M. Colin (651-733-8206)
Board of Directors: L. G. Alvarado, E. A. Brennan, G. W. Buckley, V. D. Coffman, M. L. Eskew, W. J. Farrell, E. M. Liddy, R. S. Morrison, A. L. Peters, R. L. Ridgway, K. W. Sharer, L. W. Sullivan

Founded: 1902
Domicile: Delaware
Employees: 69,315

STANDARD &POOR'S

Tiffany & Co.

S&P Recommendation HOLD ★★★★★	Price $35.88 (as of Oct 27, 2006)	12-Mo. Target Price $37.00	Investment Style Mid-Cap Growth

GICS Sector Consumer Discretionary
Sub-Industry Specialty Stores

Comment Tiffany is a leading international retailer, designer, manufacturer and distributor of fine jewelry and gift items.

Key Stock Statistics (Source S&P, Vickers, company reports)

52-Wk Range	$43.80–29.63	S&P Oper. EPS 2007E	1.80	P/E on S&P Oper. EPS 2007E	19.9	Dividend Rate/Share	$0.40
Trailing 12-Month EPS	$1.72	S&P Oper. EPS 2008E	2.03	Common Shares Outstg. (M)	138.1	Yield (%)	1.11
Trailing 12-Month P/E	20.9	S&P Core EPS 2007E	1.81	Market Capitalization(B)	$4.957	Beta	1.65
$10K Invested 5 Yrs Ago	$14,567	S&P Core EPS 2008E	2.05	Institutional Ownership (%)	90	S&P Credit Rating	NR

Price Performance

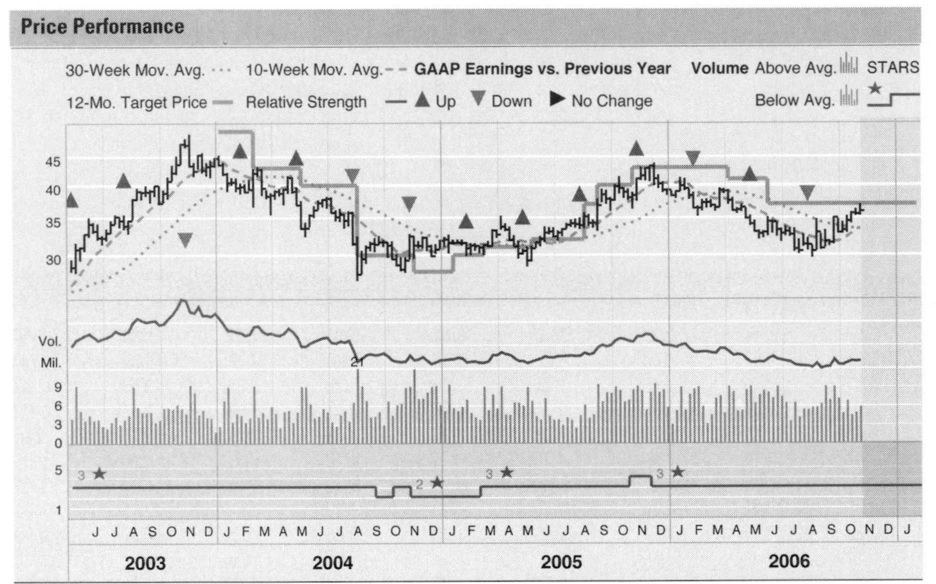

Options: CBOE, P, Ph

Analysis prepared by **Jason N. Asaeda** on September 07, 2006, when the stock traded at **$ 31.50**.

Highlights

- We see about an 8% increase in FY 07 (Jan.) retail sales, to $2.3 billion, from $2.1 billion in FY 06, with sales strength in the U.S., despite projected weakness in tourist spending in Hawaii, and across all international markets, including Japan, due to turnaround initiatives. Combined with estimated direct marketing and other sales of $317 million, versus $274 million in FY 06, we look for TIF's net sales to advance 9% in FY 07, to $2.6 billion.
- We expect operating margins to widen, on expense controls and efficiencies from the company's expanded internal manufacturing and diamond sourcing capabilities, partly offset by an anticipated increase in wholesale diamond sales and marketing costs tied to the recent launch of the new Frank Gehry jewelry collection. We also see TIF adjusting retail prices to reflect higher precious metal costs.
- Factoring in anticipated share buybacks, we see FY 07 operating EPS of $1.80 and S&P Core EPS of $1.81. The difference reflects projected pension income.

Investment Rationale/Risk

- In the second quarter of FY 07, U.S. retail same-store sales rose a healthy 5%, with strong sales of higher-priced jewelry, due to, we think, its favorable U.S. market position as a premier luxury brand. In Japan, same-store sales rose a better than expected 6% on a constant exchange basis, reflecting a payoff of investments in new products, marketing, and selling, in our view. We look for TIF to achieve further sales productivity gains in Japan this year.
- Risks to our recommendation and target price include weaker than expected sales growth due to a downturn in consumer spending and/or increased competition from European luxury brands and independent high-end jewelers. Our corporate governance concerns include a lack of performance reviews of individual directors and the non-disclosure of specific hurdle rates for performance-based equity incentive awards.
- We derive our 12-month target price of $37 from our discounted cash flow analysis, which assumes a weighted average cost of capital of 11% and a terminal growth rate of 2.5%.

Qualitative Risk Assessment

LOW | **MEDIUM** | HIGH

Our risk assessment reflects TIF's favorable market position as a premier global luxury brand, as well as its improving profit margin trends, offset by our view of the company's inconsistent sales and earnings records, and an uncertain outlook for U.S. consumer discretionary spending.

Quantitative Evaluations

S&P Quality Ranking A

D | C | B- | B | B+ | A- | **A** | A+

Relative Strength Rank MODERATE

69

LOWEST = 1 HIGHEST = 99

Revenue/Earnings Data

Revenue (Million $)

	1Q	2Q	3Q	4Q	Year
2007	539.2	574.9	--	--	--
2006	509.9	526.7	500.1	858.5	2,395
2005	457.0	476.6	461.2	810.1	2,205
2004	395.8	442.5	430.1	731.6	2,000
2003	347.1	374.4	366.0	619.0	1,707
2002	336.4	371.3	333.1	565.8	1,607

Earnings Per Share ($)

2007	0.30	0.29	E0.16	E1.05	E1.80
2006	0.27	0.35	0.16	0.97	1.75
2005	0.25	0.22	0.12	1.48	2.05
2004	0.24	0.28	0.19	0.74	1.45
2003	0.22	0.22	0.24	0.60	1.28
2002	0.20	0.24	0.16	0.55	1.15

Fiscal year ended Jan. 31. Next earnings report expected: Late November. EPS Estimates based on S&P Operating Earnings; historical GAAP earnings are as reported.

Dividend Data (Dates: mm/dd Payment Date: mm/dd/yy)

Amount ($)	Date Decl.	Ex-Div. Date	Stk. of Record	Payment Date
0.080	11/17	12/16	12/20	01/10/06
0.080	02/16	03/16	03/20	04/10/06
0.100	05/18	06/16	06/20	07/10/06
0.100	08/17	09/18	09/20	10/10/06

Dividends have been paid since 1988. Source: Company reports.

Please read the Required Disclosures and Analyst Certification on the last page of this report.

Business Summary September 07, 2006

BUSINESS SUMMARY. Charles Lewis Tiffany founded Tiffany & Co. in 1837. Jewelry is the company's primary sales driver, accounting for 82% of FY 06 (Jan.) net sales. The Tiffany & Co. brand also encompasses timepieces, sterling silver merchandise, china, crystal, stationery, fragrances, and personal accessories. TIF additionally sells other brands of timepieces and tableware in its U.S. stores.

Products are sold via four distribution channels: U.S. retail, comprised of company-owned stores and non-Internet, business-to-business sales (51% of FY 06 net sales); international retail (38%), including both retail and wholesale sales and a limited amount of business-to-business and Internet sales; U.S. direct marketing (less than 7%), consisting of Internet, direct mail catalog and business-to-business Internet sales; and other (under 5%), which reflects sales transacted under trademarks and trade names other than Tiffany & Co., as well as wholesale sales of diamonds that do not meet the company's quality standards.

CORPORATE STRATEGY. Diamonds are at the heart of TIF's merchandise offering, which also includes colored gemstones and silver and gold fashion jewelry. In FY 06, the company produced 65% of its jewelry merchandise, based on cost, and purchased almost all non-jewelry merchandise from third-party vendors. To drive sales, TIF introduces new products annually. This year, the company added architect Frank Gehry to its list of outside designers (which includes Jean Schlumberger, Elsa Peretti and Paloma Picasso) whose jewelry is licensed and sold exclusively under the Tiffany & Co. brand.

TIF believes that its multi-channel distribution represents a competitive advantage in a large and fragmented industry. In recent years, the company has expanded its direct marketing business, with a focus on e-commerce. TIF offers over 2,800 products through its U.S. consumer Web site, www.tiffany.com, which was launched in FY 00. The company extended e-commerce purchase capabilities to the U.K. in FY 02 and to both Japan and Canada in FY 06, and launched an informational Web site for China in FY 07.

Company Financials

Per Share Data ($) Year Ended Jan. 31	2006	2005	2004	2003	2002	2001	2000	1999	1998	1997
Tangible Book Value	12.85	11.77	10.01	8.34	7.15	6.34	5.23	3.72	3.18	2.74
Cash Flow	2.50	2.79	2.06	1.80	1.58	1.56	1.25	0.83	0.66	0.57
Earnings	1.75	2.05	1.45	1.28	1.15	1.26	0.98	0.63	0.51	0.42
S&P Core Earnings	1.80	1.22	1.37	1.16	1.09	1.20	NA	NA	NA	NA
Dividends	0.30	0.23	0.19	0.16	0.16	0.15	0.11	0.09	0.07	0.05
Payout Ratio	17%	11%	13%	13%	14%	12%	11%	14%	13%	11%
Calendar Year	2005	2004	2003	2002	2001	2000	1999	1998	1997	1996
Prices:High	43.80	45.22	49.45	41.00	38.25	45.38	45.00	13.00	12.16	10.56
Prices:Low	28.60	27.00	21.60	19.40	19.90	27.09	12.63	6.75	8.44	6.17
P/E Ratio:High	25	22	34	32	33	36	46	21	24	25
P/E Ratio:Low	16	13	15	15	17	22	13	11	17	15
Income Statement Analysis (Million $)										
Revenue	2,395	2,205	2,000	1,707	1,607	1,668	1,462	1,169	1,018	922
Operating Income	492	403	446	397	375	374	298	191	155	130
Depreciation	109	108	90.4	78.0	64.6	46.7	41.5	29.7	22.1	20.8
Interest Expense	23.1	22.0	14.9	15.1	19.8	16.2	15.0	9.33	8.04	9.50
Pretax Income	368	472	343	300	289	318	248	156	128	103
Effective Tax Rate	30.8%	35.6%	37.1%	36.6%	40.0%	40.0%	41.3%	42.1%	43.0%	43.2%
Net Income	255	304	216	190	174	191	146	90.1	72.8	58.4
S&P Core Earnings	261	181	204	173	164	181	NA	NA	NA	NA
Balance Sheet & Other Financial Data (Million $)										
Cash	394	188	276	156	174	196	217	189	107	117
Current Assets	1,699	1,608	1,348	1,070	954	1,005	892	816	631	569
Total Assets	2,777	2,666	2,391	1,924	1,630	1,568	1,344	1,057	827	739
Current Liabilities	365	400	395	300	341	337	281	293	250	226
Long Term Debt	427	398	393	297	179	242	250	194	91.0	93.0
Common Equity	1,831	1,701	1,468	1,208	1,037	925	757	516	444	378
Total Capital	2,257	2,132	1,884	1,505	1,216	1,168	1,007	711	535	471
Capital Expenditures	157	142	273	220	171	108	171	62.8	51.0	40.0
Cash Flow	364	412	306	268	238	237	187	120	94.9	79.0
Current Ratio	4.7	4.0	3.4	3.6	2.8	3.0	3.2	2.8	2.5	2.5
% Long Term Debt of Capitalization	18.9	18.7	20.9	19.7	14.7	20.7	24.8	27.3	17.0	19.7
% Net Income of Revenue	10.6	13.8	10.8	11.1	10.8	11.4	10.0	7.7	7.2	6.3
% Return on Assets	9.4	12.0	10.0	10.7	10.9	13.1	12.1	9.6	9.3	8.4
% Return on Equity	14.4	19.2	16.1	16.9	17.7	22.7	22.9	18.8	17.7	18.2

Data as orig reptd.; bef. results of disc opers/spec. items. Per share data adj. for stk. divs.; EPS diluted. E-Estimated. NA-Not Available. NM-Not Meaningful. NR-Not Ranked. UR-Under Review.

Office: 727 Fifth Avenue, New York, NY 10022.
Telephone: 212-755-8000.
Website: http://www.tiffany.com
Chrmn & CEO: M.J. Kowalski

Pres: J.E. Quinn
EVP & CFO: J.N. Fernandez
SVP, Secy & General Counsel: P.B. Dorsey
Investor Contact: M.L. Aaron (212-230-5301)

Board of Directors: R. Bravo, W. R. Chaney, S. L. Hayes, III, A. F. Kohnstamm, M. J. Kowalski, C. K. Marquis, J. T. Presby, J. E. Quinn, W. A. Shutzer

Founded: 1837
Domicile: Delaware
Employees: 8,000

STANDARD &POOR'S

Time Warner Inc.

S&P Recommendation HOLD ★★★★★ | **Price** $19.91 (as of Oct 27, 2006) | **12-Mo. Target Price** $20.00 | **Investment Style** Large-Cap Growth

GICS Sector Consumer Discretionary
Sub-Industry Movies & Entertainment

Comment The world's largest media company, TWX has diversified interests in web properties, filmed entertainment content, cable systems, television networks and publishing.

Key Stock Statistics (Source S&P, Vickers, company reports)

52-Wk Range	$20.08–15.70	S&P Oper. EPS 2006E	0.86	P/E on S&P Oper. EPS 2006E	23.2	Dividend Rate/Share	$0.22
Trailing 12-Month EPS	$1.07	S&P Oper. EPS 2007E	1.00	Common Shares Outstg. (M)	4,067.0	Yield (%)	1.10
Trailing 12-Month P/E	18.6	S&P Core EPS 2006E	0.86	Market Capitalization(B)	$79.129	Beta	1.92
$10K Invested 5 Yrs Ago	$6,031	S&P Core EPS 2007E	1.00	Institutional Ownership (%)	76	S&P Credit Rating	BBB+

Price Performance

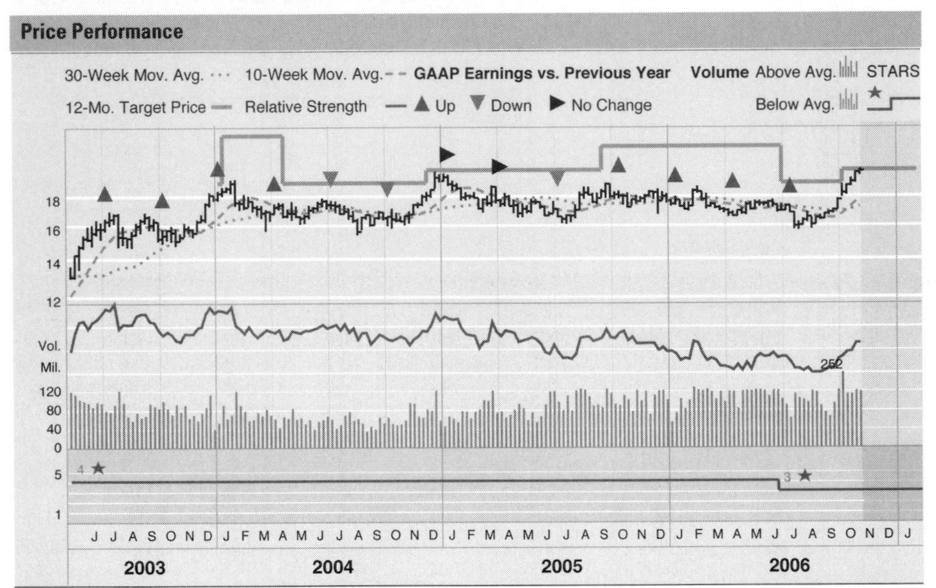

Options: ASE, CBOE, P, Ph

Analysis prepared by **Tuna N. Amobi, CFA, CPA** on September 29, 2006, when the stock traded at **$ 18.23**.

Highlights

- We see total revenues essentially flat in 2006 (including the effect of a discontinued book publishing business), and rising about 6% in 2007. This reflects continued strong low double-digit growth at the cable segment (on bundled phone and high-speed data services), and high single-digit increase in cable networks advertising and affiliate revenues. We see potentially robust gains in AOL advertising, partly offset by sharply declining dial-up subscriptions. We think 2007 should reflect easier comparisons with film/DVD titles, as well as relatively modest gains in print advertising.
- Including newly acquired Adelphia, TWX sees low double-digit growth in 2006 adjusted EBITDA, which we project at about $11.2 billion, likely growing about 10% in 2007, with a targeted $1 billion of restructuring-related cost savings.
- Assuming share buybacks under a $20 billion program (consistent with TWX's plans to spend $15 billion in 2006 and the remainder in 2007), we forecast EPS of $0.86 and $1.00 for the respective years, including $0.05 of option expense in each year.

Investment Rationale/Risk

- In recent weeks the stock has rallied modestly higher than large media peers on improved AOL outlook, in our view, as the online unit seems to be addressing potential kinks in its new ad-centric strategy. With likely sharp subscriptions declines, offset by about $1 billion in cost cuts by the end of 2007, AOL sees its new ad-centric strategy as EBITDA neutral in 2006, with EBITDA growth in 2007-2009. Separately, we think TWX's lackluster summer box office could limit 2006 holiday DVD sales, but see continued strong unit growth in the second half for Time Warner Cable, driven by digital phone, with further potential upside on the Adelphia integration and a likely cable IPO in 2007.
- Risks to our recommendation and target price include uncertainties with AOL's strategy, increased competition for cable's triple-play offerings, a soft ad market, and film volatility.
- Our 12-month target price of $20 is based on a blend of our DCF model, which shows intrinsic value of $18 (using a 12% WACC, low double digit growth in free cash flow, and 3% terminal growth), and a $22 sum-of-the-parts value (using divisional cash flow multiples and corporate overhead).

Qualitative Risk Assessment

LOW | **MEDIUM** | HIGH

Our risk assessment reflects our view of the company's leading content and distribution businesses and ample financial flexibility, offset by a relatively volatile stock, and exposure to the potentially adverse impact of continued fragmentation of traditional media platforms.

Quantitative Evaluations

S&P Quality Ranking B-

D | C | **B-** | B | B+ | A- | A | A+

Relative Strength Rank STRONG

86

LOWEST = 1 HIGHEST = 99

Revenue/Earnings Data

Revenue (Million $)

	1Q	2Q	3Q	4Q	Year
2006	10,455	10,708	--	--	--
2005	10,483	10,744	10,538	11,887	43,652
2004	10,126	10,888	9,965	11,110	42,089
2003	9,236	9,922	9,503	10,904	39,565
2002	9,407	10,203	9,963	11,388	40,961
2001	9,080	9,202	9,320	10,632	38,234

Earnings Per Share ($)

2006	0.26	0.20	**E**0.19	**E**0.24	**E**0.86
2005	0.20	-0.07	0.19	0.29	0.62
2004	0.20	0.17	0.11	0.24	0.68
2003	0.09	0.23	0.12	0.24	0.68
2002	Nil	0.09	0.01	-10.04	-10.01
2001	-0.31	-0.17	-0.22	-0.41	-1.11

Fiscal year ended Dec. 31. Next earnings report expected: Early November. EPS Estimates based on S&P Operating Earnings; historical GAAP earnings are as reported.

Dividend Data (Dates: mm/dd Payment Date: mm/dd/yy)

Amount ($)	Date Decl.	Ex-Div. Date	Stk. of Record	Payment Date
0.050	01/26	02/24	02/28	03/15/06
0.050	04/27	05/26	05/31	06/15/06
0.055	07/27	08/29	08/31	09/15/06
0.055	10/26	11/28	11/30	12/15/06

Dividends have been paid since 2005. Source: Company reports.

Time Warner Inc.

Business Summary September 29, 2006

CORPORATE OVERVIEW. In January 2001, online access and content company America Online (AOL) merged with cable systems and media concern Time Warner, forming AOL Time Warner (later changed to Time Warner in October 2003), in a $106 billion transaction. Revenues consist of subscriptions (51% of 2005 revenues), content (29%), advertising (17%), and other (3%).

AOL had 17.7 million subscribers in the U.S. and 5.7 million in Europe at June 30, 2006. It owns AOL, CompuServe and Netscape access brands, and AOL.com, AIM and MapQuest portals and websites. Time Warner Cable serves about 11 million basic subscribers, also offering high speed data, digital video (including SVOD/VOD, DVRs, HDTV), and digital (VoIP) phone. In July 2006, Time Warner Cable closed on the Adelphia/Comcast transactions to consolidate its position as the second largest U.S. cable multiple system operator (MSO), with about 14.4 million subscribers.

Filmed Entertainment includes the Warner Bros. and New Line Cinema (independent) studios and home entertainment businesses, with key franchises such as Harry Potter, Lord of the Rings and Batman. The Networks segment includes cable networks CNN, HBO/Cinemax and Turner (TNT, TBS). In January 2006, TWX's WB broadcast network agreed to join with CBS's UPN to create CW network. Publishing includes Time Inc. with over 130 magazine titles worldwide, including Time, People, Sports Illustrated and Fortune (77 titles in the U.K. and Australia).

CORPORATE STRATEGY. Under CEO Richard Parsons and COO Jeffrey Bewkes, we believe TWX aims for market-leading positions in its various businesses. In August 2006, AOL unveiled a new strategy to capitalize on the rapid growth in online advertising, enticing its broadband users with free access services such as software and e-mail. In March 2006, AOL and Google significantly expanded their search partnership, and Google invested $1 billion for a 5% stake in AOL.

Company Financials

Per Share Data ($) Year Ended Dec. 31	**2005**	**2004**	**2003**	**2002**	**2001**	**2000**	**1999**	**1998**	**1997**	**1996**
Tangible Book Value	NM	NM	NM	NM	NM	2.51	2.44	1.17	0.12	0.03
Cash Flow	2.06	1.99	1.92	-8.62	0.97	0.62	0.61	0.42	0.11	-0.25
Earnings	0.62	0.68	0.68	-10.01	-1.11	0.45	0.48	0.30	0.05	-0.33
S&P Core Earnings	0.83	0.62	0.42	-3.44	-1.08	NA	NA	NA	NA	NA
Dividends	0.10	Nil	Nil	Nil	Nil	Nil	Nil	Nil	Nil	Nil
Payout Ratio	16%	Nil	Nil	Nil	Nil	Nil	Nil	Nil	Nil	Nil
Prices:High	19.64	19.90	18.32	32.92	58.51	83.38	83.38	95.81	40.00	5.70
Prices:Low	16.10	15.41	9.90	8.70	27.40	32.75	32.75	32.50	5.16	1.98
P/E Ratio:High	32	29	27	NM	NM	NM	NM	NM	NM	NM
P/E Ratio:Low	26	23	15	NM	NM	NM	NM	NM	NM	NM
Income Statement Analysis (Million $)										
Revenue	43,652	42,089	39,565	40,961	38,234	7,703	6,886	4,777	2,600	1,685
Operating Income	14,292	12,846	11,502	11,593	11,864	2,271	1,776	851	341	101
Depreciation	6,790	6,132	5,724	5,595	11,583	444	363	298	132	124
Interest Expense	1,622	1,754	1,926	1,900	1,576	55.0	40.0	20.0	13.0	1.60
Pretax Income	4,377	5,153	4,731	-44,156	-4,465	1,884	2,014	1,096	92.0	-499
Effective Tax Rate	27.1%	33.0%	29.0%	NM	NM	38.9%	38.8%	30.5%	NM	NM
Net Income	2,905	3,209	3,146	-44,574	-4,921	1,152	1,232	762	92.0	-499
S&P Core Earnings	3,929	2,938	1,999	-15,240	-4,771	NA	NA	NA	NA	NA
Balance Sheet & Other Financial Data (Million $)										
Cash	4,220	6,139	3,040	1,730	719	2,610	2,490	887	631	125
Current Assets	13,463	14,639	12,268	11,155	10,274	4,671	4,428	1,979	930	323
Total Assets	122,475	123,339	121,783	115,450	208,559	10,827	10,673	5,348	2,214	847
Current Liabilities	12,588	14,624	15,518	13,395	12,972	2,328	2,395	1,725	894	554
Long Term Debt	20,238	20,703	23,458	27,354	22,792	1,411	1,630	348	372	50.0
Common Equity	62,715	60,771	56,038	52,817	152,071	6,778	6,161	3,033	598	100
Total Capital	103,875	103,431	99,688	96,042	189,714	8,189	7,791	3,381	970	205
Capital Expenditures	3,246	3,024	2,761	3,023	3,634	485	642	301	297	150
Cash Flow	9,695	9,341	8,870	-38,979	4,282	1,596	1,595	1,060	224	-375
Current Ratio	1.1	1.0	0.8	0.8	0.8	2.0	1.8	1.1	1.0	0.6
% Long Term Debt of Capitalization	19.5	20.0	23.5	28.5	12.0	17.2	20.9	10.3	38.4	24.4
% Net Income of Revenue	6.7	7.6	8.0	NM	NM	15.0	17.9	16.0	3.5	NM
% Return on Assets	2.4	2.6	2.7	NM	NM	10.9	15.3	18.5	6.0	NM
% Return on Equity	4.7	5.5	5.8	NM	NM	17.6	26.6	37.8	25.3	NM

Data as orig reptd.; bef. results of disc opers/spec. items. Per share data adj. for stk. divs.; EPS diluted. E-Estimated. NA-Not Available. NM-Not Meaningful. NR-Not Ranked. UR-Under Review.

Office: 1 Time Warner Ctr, New York, NY 10019-6038.
Telephone: 212-484-8000.
Email: aoltwir@aoltw.com
Website: http://www.timewarner.com

Chrmn & CEO: R.D. Parsons
Pres & COO: J. Bewkes
EVP & CFO: W.H. Pace
EVP, Secy & General Counsel: P.T. Cappuccio

Investor Contact: J.E. Burtson
Board of Directors: J. L. Barksdale, S. F. Bollenbach, F. J. Caufield, R. C. Clark, M. Dopfner, J. P. Einhorn, R. Mark, M. A. Miles, K. J. Novack, R. D. Parsons, F. T. Vincent, Jr., D. C. Wright

Founded: 1985
Domicile: Delaware
Employees: 87,850

TJX Companies Inc. (The)

STANDARD &POOR'S

S&P Recommendation HOLD ★★★★★

Price $28.82 (as of Oct 27, 2006)

12-Mo. Target Price $30.00

Investment Style Large-Cap Growth

GICS Sector Consumer Discretionary
Sub-Industry Apparel Retail

Comment TJX operates seven chains of off-price apparel and home fashion specialty stores in the U.S., Canada, Ireland and the U.K.

Key Stock Statistics (Source S&P, Vickers, company reports)

52-Wk Range	$29.74–21.17	S&P Oper. EPS 2007E	1.58	P/E on S&P Oper. EPS 2007E	18.2	Dividend Rate/Share	$0.28
Trailing 12-Month EPS	$1.54	S&P Oper. EPS 2008E	1.84	Common Shares Outstg. (M)	449.5	Yield (%)	0.97
Trailing 12-Month P/E	18.7	S&P Core EPS 2007E	1.59	Market Capitalization(B)	$12.955	Beta	0.96
$10K Invested 5 Yrs Ago	$17,016	S&P Core EPS 2008E	1.85	Institutional Ownership (%)	95	S&P Credit Rating	A

Price Performance

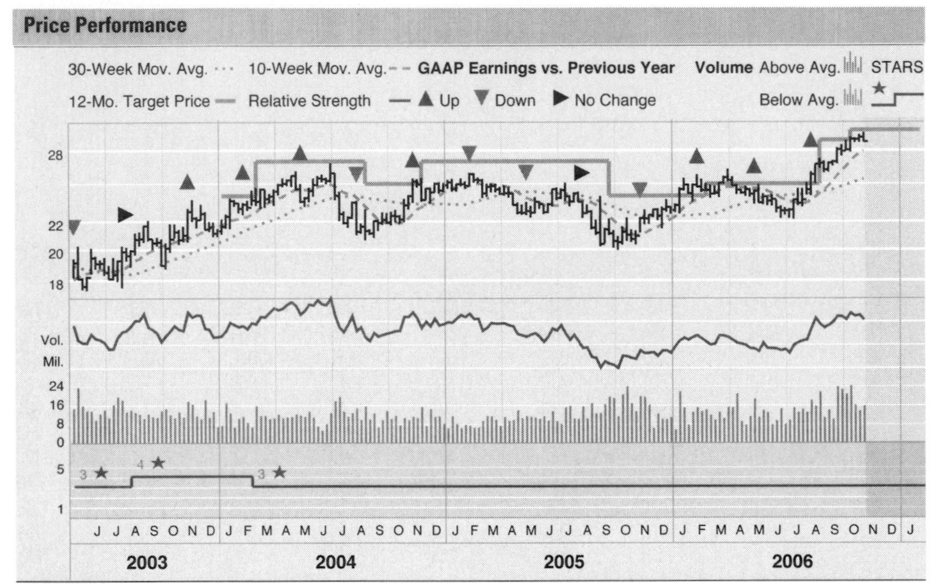

Options: ASE, CBOE

Analysis prepared by **Jason N. Asaeda** on October 11, 2006, when the stock traded at **$ 28.92**.

Highlights

- In FY 07 (Jan.), we see net sales up nearly 9%, to $17.5 billion, on expected contributions from new stores and a low single digit consolidated same-store sales increase. In TJX's core Marmaxx division, we believe that planned shifts in the apparel mix from upfront buys (purchases made before or early in a season) to off-price buys (purchases made opportunistically and closer to need during a season), as well as from moderate to better brands, will drive improved sales productivity, particularly in women's sportswear, which has been a challenging category.
- Balancing what we see as improving merchandise margins, supported by an increase in off-price buys, which carry higher mark-ups than upfront buys, and effective expense management against the likely deleveraging of occupancy costs on modest same-store sales growth and stock option expensing, we look for operating margins to widen in FY 07.
- We see FY 07 operating EPS of $1.58 and S&P Core EPS of $1.59, with the difference reflecting projected pension income.

Investment Rationale/Risk

- In FY 07, we expect TJX to benefit from increased demand for better apparel, although the maturity of the core Marmaxx division tempers our enthusiasm. We also see ample operating cash flow funding business expansion, investments in infrastructure, and additional share buybacks. We also look for the expansion of promising growth categories at A.J. Wright, TK Maxx and Winners, and "treasure hunt" assortments at HomeGoods and HomeSense, to support improving operations.
- Risks to our recommendation and target price include declining consumer confidence, changes in spending habits and buying preferences, as well as merchandise availability.
- Based on our FY 08 operating EPS estimate of $1.84 and expected forward EPS growth of 15% over the next five years, the stock's P/E-to-growth (PEG) ratio was recently about 1.1X versus a peer-median 1.0X. Our 12-month target price of $30 applies a peer-median forward P/E multiple of 16.1X to our FY 08 operating EPS estimate.

Qualitative Risk Assessment

LOW | **MEDIUM** | HIGH

Our risk assessment reflects our view of TJX's leadership position in off-price retail and promising new merchandising and productivity initiatives that could boost sales and profit margins, offset by an inconsistent earnings track record and an uncertain outlook for consumer discretionary spending, in our opinion.

Quantitative Evaluations

S&P Quality Ranking A+

D | C | B- | B | B+ | A- | A | **A+**

Relative Strength Rank MODERATE

62

LOWEST = 1 HIGHEST = 99

Revenue/Earnings Data

Revenue (Million $)

	1Q	2Q	3Q	4Q	Year
2007	3,896	3,988	--	--	--
2006	3,652	3,648	4,042	4,716	16,058
2005	3,353	3,414	3,817	4,329	14,913
2004	2,789	3,046	3,387	4,106	13,328
2003	2,666	2,765	3,045	3,505	11,981
2002	2,271	2,488	2,742	3,209	10,709

Earnings Per Share ($)

2007	0.34	0.29	**E**0.45	**E**0.49	**E**1.58
2006	0.28	0.23	0.32	0.60	1.41
2005	0.32	0.23	0.40	0.35	1.30
2004	0.22	0.24	0.36	0.47	1.28
2003	0.27	0.24	0.28	0.29	1.08
2002	0.22	0.20	0.27	0.28	0.97

Fiscal year ended Jan. 31. Next earnings report expected: Mid November. EPS Estimates based on S&P Operating Earnings; historical GAAP earnings are as reported.

Dividend Data (Dates: mm/dd Payment Date: mm/dd/yy)

Amount ($)	Date Decl.	Ex-Div. Date	Stk. of Record	Payment Date
0.060	12/06	02/07	02/09	03/02/06
0.070	04/04	05/09	05/11	06/01/06
0.070	06/06	08/08	08/10	08/31/06
0.070	09/07	11/07	11/09	11/30/06

Dividends have been paid since 1980. Source: Company reports.

TJX Companies Inc. (The)

Business Summary October 11, 2006

COMPANY PROFILE. With $16 billion in annual revenues, TJX is the largest U.S. off-price family apparel and home fashion retailer via its seven retail concepts. As of October 5, 2006, the company's core Marmaxx Group division operated 817 T.J. Maxx and 741 Marshalls stores. TJX also operated 161 A.J. Wright, 36 Bob's Stores, and 264 HomeGoods stores in the U.S. The company's international operations were comprised of 207 T.K. Maxx stores in Europe, and 183 Winners and 67 HomeSense stores in Canada.

TJX believes it derives a competitive advantage by offering rapidly changing assortments of affordable, quality brand name and designer merchandise. Prices at T.J. Maxx and Marshalls are usually 20% to 60% below department and specialty store regular prices. With over 2,400 stores, the company has substantial buying power with more than 10,000 vendors worldwide. TJX purchases later in the buying cycle than department and specialty stores. Generally, purchases are for current selling seasons, with a limited quantity of pack-away inventory intended for a future selling season. A combination of opportunistic buying, an expansive distribution infrastructure, and a low expense structure enable the company to offer everyday savings to its customers.

MARKET PROFILE. U.S. apparel sales at retail totaled $181.2 billion in 2005, up about 4% from 2004 levels, according to NDP Fashionworld estimated data. Sales of women's apparel accounted for 56% of all apparel sales, followed by men's at 29%, and children's, at 15%. The apparel market is mature, with demand mirroring population growth, and it is fragmented, with national brands marketed by 20 companies accounting for approximately 30% of total apparel sales, and the remaining 70% comprised of smaller and/or private label "store" brands. Standard & Poor's forecasts that 2006 apparel sales will increase in the low single digits, about in line with its GDP growth, versus 4% growth in 2004 and 2005 and a 5% decline in 2003.

Company Financials

Per Share Data ($) Year Ended Jan. 31	**2006**	**2005**	**2004**	**2003**	**2002**	**2001**	**2000**	**1999**	**1998**	**1997**
Tangible Book Value	3.71	3.06	2.74	2.36	2.14	1.85	1.55	1.59	1.39	1.20
Cash Flow	2.23	1.86	1.75	1.46	1.34	1.23	1.08	0.85	0.60	0.47
Earnings	1.41	1.30	1.28	1.08	0.97	0.93	0.83	0.65	0.44	0.29
S&P Core Earnings	1.40	1.22	1.21	1.01	0.91	0.90	NA	NA	NA	NA
Dividends	0.17	0.14	0.13	0.12	0.11	0.07	0.07	0.06	0.07	0.04
Payout Ratio	12%	10%	10%	11%	11%	7%	8%	9%	15%	12%
Calendar Year	2005	2004	2003	2002	2001	2000	1999	1998	1997	1996
Prices:High	25.96	26.82	23.70	22.45	20.30	15.75	18.50	15.00	9.64	6.03
Prices:Low	19.95	20.64	15.54	15.30	13.56	6.97	8.25	7.75	4.78	2.13
P/E Ratio:High	18	21	19	21	21	17	22	23	22	20
P/E Ratio:Low	14	16	12	14	14	7	10	12	11	7

Income Statement Analysis (Million $)										
Revenue	16,058	14,913	13,328	11,981	10,709	9,579	8,795	7,949	7,389	6,689
Operating Income	1,444	1,394	1,334	1,171	1,104	1,064	1,022	842	652	530
Depreciation	405	288	238	208	204	176	160	137	125	127
Interest Expense	39.0	33.5	27.3	25.4	25.6	34.7	20.4	1.69	4.50	37.4
Pretax Income	1,009	1,080	1,068	938	874	865	854	704	522	366
Effective Tax Rate	31.6%	38.5%	38.4%	38.3%	38.2%	37.8%	38.3%	38.5%	41.3%	41.6%
Net Income	690	664	658	578	540	538	527	433	307	214
S&P Core Earnings	687	615	619	546	506	519	NA	NA	NA	NA

Balance Sheet & Other Financial Data (Million $)										
Cash	466	307	246	492	493	133	372	461	404	475
Current Assets	3,140	2,905	2,452	2,241	2,116	1,722	1,701	1,743	1,683	1,662
Total Assets	5,496	5,075	4,397	3,940	3,596	2,932	2,805	2,748	2,610	2,561
Current Liabilities	2,252	2,204	1,691	1,566	1,315	1,229	1,366	1,307	1,218	1,182
Long Term Debt	807	599	692	694	702	319	319	220	221	244
Common Equity	1,893	1,653	1,552	1,409	1,341	1,219	1,119	1,221	1,091	977
Total Capital	2,700	2,405	2,369	2,145	2,043	1,538	1,439	1,441	1,392	1,379
Capital Expenditures	496	429	409	397	449	257	239	208	192	119
Cash Flow	1,096	953	897	786	744	714	687	566	420	341
Current Ratio	1.4	1.3	1.5	1.4	1.6	1.4	1.2	1.3	1.4	1.4
% Long Term Debt of Capitalization	29.9	24.9	29.2	32.3	34.4	20.8	22.2	15.3	15.8	17.7
% Net Income of Revenue	4.3	4.5	4.9	4.8	5.0	5.6	6.0	5.4	4.1	3.2
% Return on Assets	13.1	14.0	15.8	15.3	16.6	18.8	19.0	16.2	11.9	8.2
% Return on Equity	37.9	41.4	44.5	42.1	42.2	46.0	45.0	37.2	28.5	29.3

Data as orig reptd.; bef. results of disc opers/spec. items. Per share data adj. for stk. divs.; EPS diluted. E-Estimated. NA-Not Available. NM-Not Meaningful. NR-Not Ranked. UR-Under Review.

Office: 770 Cochituate Road, Framingham, MA 01701-4666.
Telephone: 508-390-1000.
Website: http://www.tjx.com
Chrmn & CEO: B. Cammarata

Pres: C. Meyrowitz
Vice Chrmn: D. Cambell
Sr EVP: P.A. Maich
Sr EVP: A. Smith

Investor Contact: S. Lang (508-390-2323)
Board of Directors: D. Brandon, B. Cammarata, G. L. Crittenden, G. Deegan, D. F. Hightower, A. .. Lane, R. G. Lesser, C. Meyrowitz, J. F. O'Brien, R. F. Shapiro, W. B. Shire, F. H. Wiley

Founded: 1956
Domicile: Delaware
Employees: 119,000

STANDARD &POOR'S

Torchmark Corp

S&P Recommendation	Price	12-Mo. Target Price	Investment Style
SELL ★★★★★	$62.18 (as of Oct 27, 2006)	$62.00	Mid-Cap Growth

GICS Sector Financials
Sub-Industry Life & Health Insurance

Comment This financial services company derives most of its earnings from life and health insurance operations.

Key Stock Statistics (Source S&P, Vickers, company reports)

52-Wk Range	$64.51–52.31	S&P Oper. EPS 2006E	4.96	P/E on S&P Oper. EPS 2006E	12.5	Dividend Rate/Share	$0.52
Trailing 12-Month EPS	$4.90	S&P Oper. EPS 2007E	5.45	Common Shares Outstg. (M)	98.9	Yield (%)	0.84
Trailing 12-Month P/E	12.7	S&P Core EPS 2006E	4.93	Market Capitalization(B)	$6.152	Beta	0.59
$10K Invested 5 Yrs Ago	$16,971	S&P Core EPS 2007E	5.42	Institutional Ownership (%)	73	S&P Credit Rating	A+

Price Performance

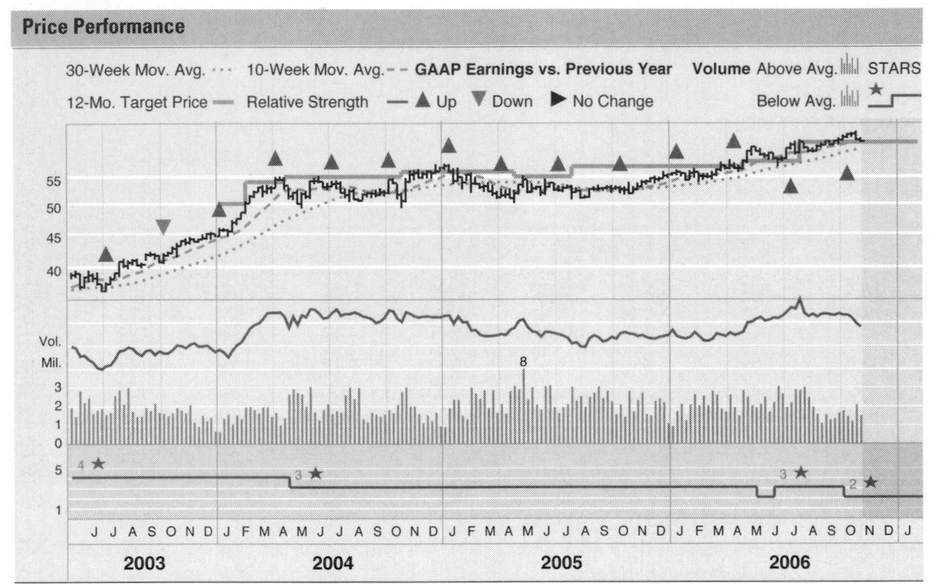

Options: ASE

Analysis prepared by **Frank Braden** on October 24, 2006, when the stock traded at **$ 62.56**.

Highlights

- We expect premium revenue in the life insurance segment to rise 4.1% in 2006 and 5.3% in 2007. We look for future premium growth to be limited by the recent decline in life insurance first-year premiums. We project that health insurance premiums, excluding Medicare Part D, will remain flat in 2006 and see a modest improvement in 2007, and the underwriting margin will experience a slight decline. We foresee strong underwriting margin growth in the Medicare Part D prescription drug program on lower benefit costs. We estimate that net investment income will grow 3% in 2007, with a modest increase in the portfolio investment yield.
- We believe the hostilities in the Middle East could continue to adversely affect claims in the company's military distribution channel, and we see first-year premiums continuing to decline sharply in that business.
- Our 2006 EPS estimate is $4.96, including approximately $0.04 of projected stock option expense, on nearly 5% fewer shares due to share repurchases. Our operating EPS estimate for 2007 is $5.45.

Investment Rationale/Risk

- We expect TMK to benefit from less competition in its niche distribution channels. A decline in sales in 2006 has largely been the result of a shrinking agent count. Recent efforts to improve agent recruiting have seen mixed results, but we expect a higher agent count to boost sales in 2007. The Medicare Part D program has supported earnings thus far in 2006, in our opinion, but we expect competitive pricing pressures to lead to slightly lower profitability in this segment in 2007.
- Risks to our recommendation and target price include decreased competition for some products; possible market trends in senior health care that promote TMK's Medicare supplemental policies; improved recruitment and motivation of sales agents; lower claims for policies covering U.S. military personnel; and better trends for TMK's Medicare Part D program's loss ratio.
- Our 12-month target price of $62 is based on a P/E of 12.5X our 2006 EPS estimate, in line with TMK's historical multiples.

Qualitative Risk Assessment

LOW	MEDIUM	HIGH

Our risk assessment for Torchmark reflects our view of its varied product lineup and diversified distribution network. TMK generates strong cash flow growth, in our opinion, and uses excess cash flow to repurchase shares and pay its dividend.

Quantitative Evaluations

S&P Quality Ranking A

D	C	B-	B	B+	A-	A	A+

Relative Strength Rank MODERATE

32

LOWEST = 1 HIGHEST = 99

Revenue/Earnings Data

Revenue (Million $)

	1Q	2Q	3Q	4Q	Year
2006	857.0	869.0	837.9	--	--
2005	783.0	804.8	769.0	769.1	3,126
2004	772.5	764.0	774.2	760.8	3,072
2003	718.4	734.3	730.4	747.5	2,931
2002	689.7	633.5	715.8	699.0	2,738
2001	674.8	689.0	686.7	656.6	2,707

Earnings Per Share ($)

	1Q	2Q	3Q	4Q	Year
2006	1.16	1.26	1.28	E1.28	E4.96
2005	1.09	1.25	1.14	1.21	4.68
2004	1.05	1.04	1.12	1.05	4.25
2003	0.85	0.95	0.94	0.98	3.73
2002	0.80	0.52	0.98	0.89	3.18
2001	0.79	0.78	0.82	0.67	3.11

Fiscal year ended Dec. 31. Next earnings report expected: Early December. EPS Estimates based on S&P Operating Earnings; historical GAAP earnings are as reported.

Dividend Data (Dates: mm/dd Payment Date: mm/dd/yy)

Amount ($)	Date Decl.	Ex-Div. Date	Stk. of Record	Payment Date
0.110	02/22	04/05	04/07	05/01/06
0.130	05/01	07/05	07/07	08/01/06
0.130	09/25	10/04	10/06	11/01/06
0.130	10/26	01/03	01/05	02/01/07

Dividends have been paid since 1933. Source: Company reports.

Torchmark Corp

Business Summary October 24, 2006

CORPORATE OVERVIEW. TMK's subsidiaries offer a full line of nonparticipating ordinary individual life products and health insurance, as well as fixed and variable annuities. Traditional whole life insurance constituted 58% of life insurance in force at the end of 2005, as measured by annualized premiums, with interest-sensitive whole life 8%, term life 31%, and other life products 2.9%. Medicare supplemental insurance accounted for 58% of supplemental health insurance in force at the end of 2005, as measured by annualized premiums, and limited-benefit plans accounted for 42% of premiums in force. The number of individual health policies in force was 1.70 million at December 31, 2005, up 3.7% from the year-earlier level. Annuity separate account assets totaled $1.56 billion at December 31, 2005, down 2.2% from the year-earlier level.

Life segment premium revenue accounted for 59% of total premium revenue in 2005 (56% in 2004), with the health segment at 40% (42%) and the annuity segment at 1.0% (1.1%).

CORPORATE STRATEGY. A key corporate strategy for TMK is to improve its distribution system. Distribution is through direct solicitation, independent agents, and exclusive agents. The Liberty National exclusive agency markets products to middle-income families in the Southeastern U.S. through full-time sales representatives. The American Income exclusive agency focuses on members of labor unions, credit unions, and other associations in the U.S., Canada, and New Zealand. The United Investors agency markets to middle-income Americans through independent agents. The military agency consists of a nationwide independent agency comprised of former commissioned and noncommissioned military officers who sell exclusively to military officers and their families. The United American independent agency focuses primarily on health insurance in the U.S. and Canada to individuals over the age of 50. The United American branch office agency also focuses on health insurance to over-age 50 individuals through exclusive producing agents.

Company Financials

Per Share Data ($) Year Ended Dec. 31	**2005**	**2004**	**2003**	**2002**	**2001**	**2000**	**1999**	**1998**	**1997**	**1996**
Tangible Book Value	29.49	28.16	25.39	20.91	17.24	14.34	12.05	13.48	10.05	7.81
Operating Earnings	NA	NA	3.87	3.51	3.12	2.85	2.45	2.29	NA	2.21
Earnings	4.68	4.25	3.73	3.18	3.11	2.82	1.93	1.81	2.56	2.23
S&P Core Earnings	4.29	4.03	3.68	3.39	2.73	NA	NA	NA	NA	NA
Dividends	0.44	0.44	0.38	0.36	0.36	0.36	0.36	0.58	0.59	0.58
Payout Ratio	9%	10%	10%	11%	12%	13%	19%	32%	23%	26%
Prices:High	57.50	57.57	45.75	42.17	43.25	41.19	38.00	49.81	42.81	26.06
Prices:Low	50.05	44.61	33.00	30.02	32.56	18.75	24.56	31.81	25.00	20.13
P/E Ratio:High	12	14	12	13	14	15	20	28	17	12
P/E Ratio:Low	11	10	9	9	10	7	13	18	10	9
Income Statement Analysis (Million $)										
Life Insurance in Force	137,668	133,084	128,737	118,660	113,055	108,319	101,846	96,339	91,870	86,948
Premium Income:Life	2,508	2,472	1,246	1,221	1,144	1,082	1,018	960	910	855
Premium Income:A & H	NA	NA	1,034	1,019	1,011	911	825	760	739	733
Net Investment Income	603	577	557	519	492	472	447	460	434	405
Total Revenue	3,126	3,072	2,931	2,738	2,707	2,516	2,220	2,158	1,849	2,206
Pretax Income	732	721	655	580	597	553	393	410	516	495
Net Operating Income	NA	NA	446	424	393	365	328	324	336	316
Net Income	495	476	430	383	391	362	259	256	338	319
S&P Core Earnings	455	452	424	408	343	NA	NA	NA	NA	NA
Balance Sheet & Other Financial Data (Million $)										
Cash & Equivalent	178	164	155	140	129	154	127	104	126	110
Premiums Due	67.3	73.4	80.7	70.4	67.5	75.0	53.5	130	127	112
Investment Assets:Bonds	8,837	8,715	8,103	7,194	6,526	5,950	5,680	5,768	5,860	5,328
Investment Assets:Stocks	48.0	36.9	57.4	24.5	0.57	0.54	29.0	10.0	12.0	8.86
Investment Assets:Loans	317	338	704	401	393	374	245	358	301	271
Investment Assets:Total	9,649	9,405	8,795	7,784	7,154	6,471	6,399	6,413	6,538	5,940
Deferred Policy Costs	2,768	2,506	2,330	2,184	2,066	1,942	1,742	1,503	1,371	1,254
Total Assets	14,769	14,252	13,461	12,361	12,428	12,963	12,132	11,249	10,967	9,801
Debt	353	540	693	552	681	366	372	383	564	792
Common Equity	3,433	6,840	3,240	2,851	2,497	2,202	1,993	2,260	1,933	1,629
% Return on Revenue	15.8	15.5	14.7	14.0	14.4	14.4	11.7	11.9	18.3	14.4
% Return on Assets	3.4	3.4	3.3	3.1	3.1	2.9	2.2	2.3	3.3	3.3
% Return on Equity	14.5	7.1	14.1	14.3	16.6	17.2	12.2	12.2	19.0	19.8
% Investment Yield	6.3	6.4	6.7	7.0	7.2	7.5	6.8	7.1	7.0	6.9

Data as orig reptd.; bef. results of disc opers/spec. items. Per share data adj. for stk. divs.; EPS diluted. E-Estimated. NA-Not Available. NM-Not Meaningful. NR-Not Ranked. UR-Under Review.

Office: 2001 Third Avenue South, Birmingham, AL 35233.
Telephone: 205-325-4200.
Website: http://www.torchmarkcorp.com
Chrmn & CEO: M.S. McAndrew

EVP & CFO: G.L. Coleman
EVP & Chief Admin: T.G. Brill
EVP & General Counsel: L.M. Hutchison
VP & Secy: C.A. McCoy

Investor Contact: J.L. Lane (972-569-3627)
Board of Directors: C. E. Adair, D. L. Boren, J. Buchan, R. W. Ingram, J. L. Lanier, Jr., M. S. McAndrew, H. T. McCormick, L. W. Newton, S. R. Perry, L. C. Smith, P. J. Zucconi

Founded: 1900
Domicile: Delaware
Employees: 4,530

STANDARD & POOR'S

Transocean Inc

S&P Recommendation HOLD ★★★★★	**Price** $72.11 (as of Oct 27, 2006)	**12-Mo. Target Price** $77.00	**Investment Style** Large-Cap Value

GICS Sector Energy
Sub-Industry Oil & Gas Drilling

Comment RIG is a leading provider of contract drilling services for the oil and gas industry, with the world's largest fleet of mobile offshore drilling units.

Key Stock Statistics (Source S&P, Vickers, company reports)

52-Wk Range	**$90.16–56.45**	S&P Oper. EPS 2006**E**	**3.01**	P/E on S&P Oper. EPS 2006**E**	**24.0**	Dividend Rate/Share	**Nil**
Trailing 12-Month EPS	**$2.31**	S&P Oper. EPS 2007**E**	**7.15**	Common Shares Outstg. (M)	**315.1**	Yield (%)	**Nil**
Trailing 12-Month P/E	**31.2**	S&P Core EPS 2006**E**	**3.01**	Market Capitalization(B)	**$22.720**	Beta	**1.25**
$10K Invested 5 Yrs Ago	**$21,909**	S&P Core EPS 2007**E**	**7.15**	Institutional Ownership (%)	**79**	S&P Credit Rating	**NA**

Price Performance

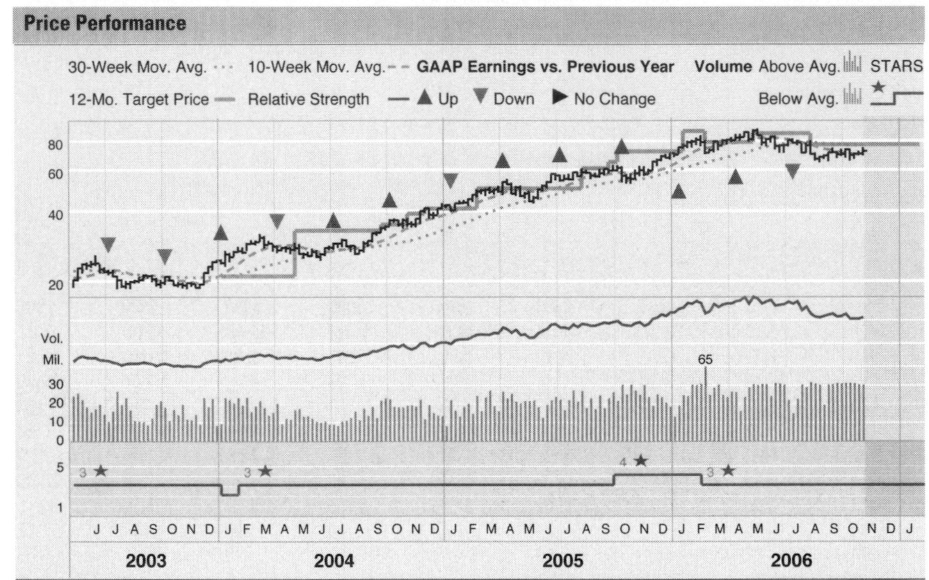

Options: ASE, CBOE, P, Ph

Analysis prepared by **Stewart Glickman, CFA** on August 09, 2006, when the stock traded at **$ 66.80**.

Highlights

- We believe that prospects for the company's high-specification semisubmersibles will continue to improve in 2006, as the deepwater rig market is expected to remain strong. The Northwest Europe, West Africa and Southeast Asia markets have been improving, and we think they could see rig shortages later in the year. With deepwater rigs almost fully utilized, the mid-water market is enjoying a resurgence in utilization, and we also project this market will continue its recent upward momentum in late 2006.
- We project RIG will generate an average dayrate of about $143,000 per day in 2006, with utilization in the mid-80% range. However, we note that operating expenses have been on the rise of late, reflecting both increased labor costs as well as greater than expected shipyard time for repairs and maintenance.
- For 2006, we see operating EPS of $3.01, rising to $7.15 in 2007 (include projected stock option expense of $0.02 in each year).

Investment Rationale/Risk

- We see the dearth of available deepwater rigs putting upward pressure on floater dayrates. While newbuild activity is on the rise, with approximately 90 rigs due for delivery by 2009, the majority of these rigs are jackups, not floaters. With the largest set of deepwater drilling assets in the world, we believe RIG should benefit from strong utilization and rising dayrates.
- Risks to our recommendation and target price include less than anticipated drilling activity in Northwest Europe, West Africa and Southeast Asia; lower oil and natural gas prices; and reduced utilization and dayrates in mid-water and deepwater markets.
- Our net asset value model, using terminal growth of 3% and a WACC of 10.6%, indicates an intrinsic value of about $73. On a relative basis, we think RIG shares merit a premium to their offshore drilling peers given the company's greater exposure to deepwater drilling. Using a 16.0X multiple on estimated 2006 EBITDA, and 16.0X estimated 2006 cash flow (both premiums to peers), and blending with our NAV model, our 12-month target price is $77.

Qualitative Risk Assessment

LOW | **MEDIUM** | HIGH

Our risk assessment reflects RIG's exposure to volatile crude oil and natural gas prices, capital spending decisions by oil and gas producing customers, and risks associated with operating in frontier regions. Offsetting these risks is RIG's leadership position in deepwater drilling.

Quantitative Evaluations

S&P Quality Ranking **B-**

D | C | **B-** | B | B+ | A- | A | A+

Relative Strength Rank **MODERATE**

42

LOWEST = 1 HIGHEST = 99

Revenue/Earnings Data

Revenue (Million $)

	1Q	2Q	3Q	4Q	Year
2006	817.3	853.3	--	--	--
2005	630.5	727.4	762.6	771.2	2,892
2004	652.0	633.2	651.8	676.9	2,614
2003	616.0	603.9	622.9	591.5	2,434
2002	667.9	646.2	695.2	664.6	2,674
2001	550.1	752.2	770.2	747.6	2,820

Earnings Per Share ($)

2006	0.61	0.75	**E**0.83	**E**1.16	**E**3.01
2005	0.28	0.90	0.50	0.45	2.13
2004	0.07	0.15	0.48	-0.23	0.47
2003	0.15	-0.14	0.03	0.02	0.06
2002	0.24	0.25	0.79	-8.71	-7.42
2001	0.11	0.26	0.30	0.19	0.86

Fiscal year ended Dec. 31. Next earnings report expected: Early November. EPS Estimates based on S&P Operating Earnings; historical GAAP earnings are as reported.

Dividend Data

Dividends, paid since 1993, were discontinued in June 2002.

The McGraw-Hill Companies

Transocean Inc

Business Summary August 09, 2006

CORPORATE OVERVIEW. Transocean (formerly Transocean Sedco Forex), the world's largest offshore drilling company, acquired R&B Falcon (FLC) on January 31, 2001, for about $9.6 billion. In May 2002, the company adopted its current name. Transocean Sedco Forex had been formed in December 1999, upon the merger of Transocean Offshore and Sedco Forex Holdings (the former offshore contract drilling unit of Schlumberger). RIG focuses mainly on deepwater drilling activity, where the deepwater sector is defined by the company as that which begins in water depths of 4,500 ft., and extending to practical maximum depth, which is currently at about 10,000 ft. of water. The mid-water market typically covers water depths of 400 ft. to 4,500 ft., while the shallow water market covers water depths of up to 400 ft.

COMPETITIVE LANDSCAPE. RIG's addressable market for offshore drilling rigs is global in nature, given that rigs can be mobilized from region to region. Active offshore drilling regions around the globe include the U.S. Gulf of Mexico, the North Sea, West Africa, Southeast Asia, the Mediterranean, the Caspian Sea, and the Middle East. With 90 mobile offshore drilling rigs as of December 31, 2005, RIG is the leading player in this market. Of the 90 rigs, 55 are "floater" rigs -- semisubmersibles and drillships -- of which 28 are rated for deepwater drilling. The company has the vast majority of its drilling rigs located in seven regions: Northwest Europe (14 rigs), the U.S. Gulf of Mexico (12), Southeast Asia (12), India (11) West Africa (11), South America (10), and the Egypt/Middle East/Mediterranean (6). The company's 14 rigs in Northwest Europe and 11 rigs in West Africa represented 21% and 25%, respectively, of these regions' total rig supply.

Company Financials

Per Share Data ($) Year Ended Dec. 31	**2005**	**2004**	**2003**	**2002**	**2001**	**2000**	**1999**	**1998**	**1997**	**1996**
Tangible Book Value	17.78	15.99	15.55	15.42	13.94	14.08	18.61	12.96	9.29	8.39
Cash Flow	3.30	2.08	1.65	-5.85	2.85	1.73	0.90	4.56	2.38	1.74
Earnings	2.13	0.47	0.06	-7.42	0.86	0.50	0.53	3.41	1.38	1.09
Dividends	Nil	Nil	Nil	0.06	0.12	0.12	0.12	0.12	0.12	0.12
Payout Ratio	Nil	Nil	Nil	NM	14%	24%	23%	4%	9%	11%
Prices:High	70.93	43.25	25.90	39.30	57.69	65.50	36.50	59.94	60.50	35.69
Prices:Low	39.79	23.10	18.40	18.10	23.05	29.25	19.63	23.00	26.13	20.56
P/E Ratio:High	33	92	NM	NM	67	NM	69	18	44	33
P/E Ratio:Low	19	49	NM	NM	27	NM	37	7	19	19
Income Statement Analysis (Million $)										
Revenue	2,892	2,614	2,434	2,674	2,820	1,230	648	1,090	892	529
Operating Income	1,096	821	759	1,114	1,159	375	181	577	320	154
Depreciation, Depletion and Amortization	406	525	508	500	625	259	132	117	103	46.6
Interest Expense	111	172	202	212	224	3.03	10.3	23.9	22.9	7.22
Pretax Income	802	240	21.6	-2,489	361	144	48.8	487	207	122
Effective Tax Rate	10.8%	38.0%	13.9%	NM	23.8%	25.4%	NM	29.5%	31.5%	35.9%
Net Income	716	152	18.4	-2,368	272	107	58.1	343	142	78.0
Balance Sheet & Other Financial Data (Million $)										
Cash	445	451	474	1,214	853	34.5	166	69.5	54.2	24.2
Current Assets	1,279	1,109	1,179	1,912	1,737	448	559	362	307	252
Total Assets	10,457	10,758	11,663	12,665	17,020	6,359	6,140	3,251	2,755	2,443
Current Liabilities	924	430	511	1,504	1,144	495	529	192	185	231
Long Term Debt	1,197	2,462	3,612	3,630	4,539	1,430	1,188	814	728	392
Common Equity	7,982	7,393	7,193	7,141	10,910	4,004	3,910	1,979	1,621	1,628
Total Capital	9,247	9,983	10,848	10,879	15,767	5,794	5,482	3,023	2,521	2,172
Capital Expenditures	182	127	496	141	506	575	537	573	406	213
Cash Flow	1,121	677	527	-1,868	897	367	190	460	245	125
Current Ratio	1.4	2.6	2.3	1.3	1.5	0.9	1.1	1.9	1.7	1.1
% Long Term Debt of Capitalization	12.9	24.7	33.3	33.4	28.7	24.7	21.7	26.9	28.9	18.1
% Return on Assets	6.7	1.4	0.2	NM	2.3	1.7	1.5	11.4	5.5	5.3
% Return on Equity	9.3	2.1	0.3	NM	3.6	2.7	2.6	19.1	8.7	7.9

Data as orig reptd.; bef. results of disc opers/spec. items. Per share data adj. for stk. divs.; EPS diluted. E-Estimated. NA-Not Available. NM-Not Meaningful. NR-Not Ranked. UR-Under Review.

Office: 4 Greenway Plaza, Houston, TX 77046.
Telephone: 713-232-7500.
Email: info@houston.deepwater.com
Website: http://www.deepwater.com

Chrmn: J.M. Talbert
Pres: J.P. Cahuzac
CEO: R.L. Long
COO & EVP: S.L. Newman

SVP & CFO: G.L. Cauthen
Investor Contact: J.L. Chastain (713-232-7551)
Board of Directors: V. E. Grijalva, J. J. Kelly, A. Lindenauer, R. Long, M. B. McNamara, R. L. Monti, K. Siem, R. M. Sprague, I. C. Strachan, J. M. Talbert

Founded: 1953
Domicile: Cayman Islands
Employees: 12,000

STANDARD & POOR'S

Tribune Co

S&P Recommendation HOLD ★★★★★	**Price** $33.47 (as of Oct 27, 2006)	**12-Mo. Target Price** $34.00	**Investment Style** Mid-Cap Value

GICS Sector Consumer Discretionary
Sub-Industry Publishing

Comment This leading media company has interests in radio and television broadcasting, newspaper publishing and the Internet.

Key Stock Statistics (Source S&P, Vickers, company reports)

52-Wk Range	**$34.28–27.09**	S&P Oper. EPS 2006**E**	**2.02**	P/E on S&P Oper. EPS 2006**E**	**16.6**	Dividend Rate/Share	**$0.72**
Trailing 12-Month EPS	**$1.65**	S&P Oper. EPS 2007**E**	**2.12**	Common Shares Outstg. (M)	**257.6**	Yield (%)	**2.15**
Trailing 12-Month P/E	**20.3**	S&P Core EPS 2006**E**	**2.00**	Market Capitalization(B)	**$8.623**	Beta	**0.74**
$10K Invested 5 Yrs Ago	**$11,157**	S&P Core EPS 2007**E**	**2.09**	Institutional Ownership (%)	**62**	S&P Credit Rating	**BB+**

Price Performance

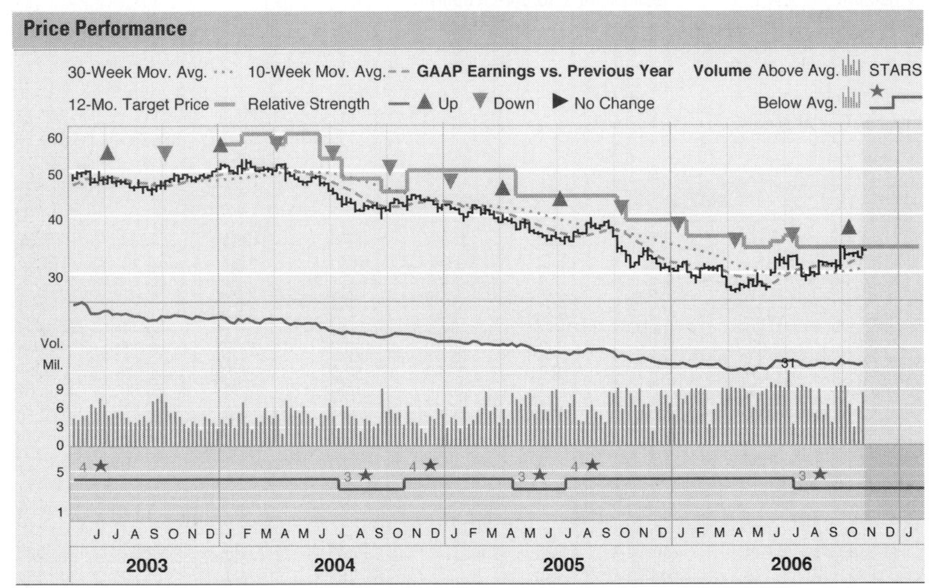

Options: CBOE, P

Analysis prepared by **James Peters, CFA** on September 19, 2006, when the stock traded at **$ 30.48**.

Highlights

- We look for total revenues to rise about 0.5% in 2006, boosted by a 53-week reporting period. We forecast growth of 0.7% in the publishing division, including a 4.8% rise in classified advertising and a 4.3% decline in circulation revenues. Longer term, we are encouraged by the company's plan to derive at least 12% of its revenues from high growth online operations within three years.
- In addition to about $65 million of cost savings we anticipate in 2006 from layoffs announced in 2005 and recently concluded union negotiations, we see TRB continuing to focus on reducing its cost structure and redeploying resources to areas of growth within the company, such as its Internet operations. However, we expect TRB's operating margins to narrow to about 20.1% in 2006, from 21.6% in 2005, due to estimated incremental stock option expense of about $32 million and higher paper costs.
- After substantially higher estimated interest expenses to fund recent and anticipated stock repurchases and excluding derivative gains or losses, we forecast 2006 operating EPS of $2.02, down from $2.12 in 2005.

Investment Rationale/Risk

- We expect the CW network to combine the best programming from the WB and UPN networks, which we think should result in stronger ratings for 16 of the 19 TRB stations affected by the change. We are in favor of TRB's plan to sell at least $500 million of non-core assets, and expect proceeds to be used to pay down debt. We also view positively continued cost cutting actions. However, we are concerned about what we see as TRB's slow pace of revenue growth, especially given the challenging near-term advertising environment we foresee.
- Risks to our opinion and target price include a slower than expected recovery in the Chicago, New York and Los Angeles markets, and the potential for adverse media cross-ownership regulatory rulings.
- We derive our 12-month target price of $34 from a blend of our relative valuation and DCF analyses. Our DCF model yields an intrinsic value of $36 and includes assumptions of a 6.8% WACC and a 3.0% terminal growth rate. Applying a premium to peer but discount to historical average EBITDA multiple of 9.4X to $1.37 billion--which is the average of our 2006 and 2007 EBIDTA estimates--yields a value of $31.

Qualitative Risk Assessment

LOW | **MEDIUM** | HIGH

Our risk assessment reflects a highly competitive environment for advertising among broadcasters, publishers and other media, and an uncertain regulatory outlook for cross-media ownership, offset by our view of the company's strong free cash flow, low beta and low cost of capital.

Quantitative Evaluations

S&P Quality Ranking **B**

D | C | B- | **B** | B+ | A- | A | A+

Relative Strength Rank **MODERATE**

64

LOWEST = 1 HIGHEST = 99

Revenue/Earnings Data

Revenue (Million $)

	1Q	2Q	3Q	4Q	Year
2006	1,299	1,432	1,349	--	--
2005	1,316	1,462	1,403	1,415	5,596
2004	1,332	1,496	1,414	1,484	5,726
2003	1,290	1,450	1,386	1,470	5,595
2002	1,234	1,381	1,340	1,430	5,384
2001	1,293	1,367	1,276	1,318	5,253

Earnings Per Share ($)

	1Q	2Q	3Q	4Q	Year
2006	0.33	0.53	0.65	**E**0.65	**E**2.02
2005	0.44	0.73	0.07	0.43	1.67
2004	0.35	0.29	0.37	0.72	1.72
2003	0.41	0.67	0.53	1.00	2.61
2002	0.18	0.33	0.71	0.57	1.80
2001	0.20	0.21	-0.49	0.32	0.28

Fiscal year ended Dec. 31. Next earnings report expected: Early February. EPS Estimates based on S&P Operating Earnings; historical GAAP earnings are as reported.

Dividend Data (Dates: mm/dd Payment Date: mm/dd/yy)

Amount ($)	Date Decl.	Ex-Div. Date	Stk. of Record	Payment Date
0.180	02/14	02/21	02/23	03/09/06
0.180	05/02	05/23	05/25	06/08/06
0.180	07/19	08/29	08/31	09/14/06
0.180	10/18	11/28	11/30	12/14/06

Dividends have been paid since 1902. Source: Company reports.

Please read the Required Disclosures and Analyst Certification on the last page of this report.

The McGraw·Hill Companies

Tribune Co

Business Summary September 19, 2006

Tribune Company is a media and entertainment company engaged through its subsidiaries in newspaper publishing, television and radio broadcasting and entertainment. The company's operations are divided into two segments: publishing (73% of 2005 revenues) and broadcasting and entertainment (27%).

In September 2005, TRB announced an adverse U.S. tax court ruling on its 1998 tax-free reorganization; the company appealed the decision but also issued commercial paper to cover an estimated net cash liability of $840 million for this and a similar transaction.

About 79% of 2005 publishing segment revenues came from the sale of advertising in newspapers and interactive Web sites, 15% from the sale of newspapers, and about 6% from a variety of other activities. Tribune Publishing's primary daily newspapers include the Los Angeles Times, Chicago Tribune, Newsday (New York), The Baltimore Sun, South Florida Sun-Sentinel, the Orlando Sentinel, The Morning Call (Pennsylvania), The Hartford Courant, The Advocate (Stamford), Greenwich Time, and Daily Press (VA). The publishing segment also manages the Web sites of the company's daily newspapers and television stations, as well as other branded sites targeting specific communities of interest.

Company Financials

Per Share Data ($) Year Ended Dec. 31	**2005**	**2004**	**2003**	**2002**	**2001**	**2000**	**1999**	**1998**	**1997**	**1996**
Tangible Book Value	NM	NM	NM	NM	NM	NM	NM	NM	NA	NM
Cash Flow	2.51	2.52	3.20	2.43	1.82	2.27	6.44	2.21	2.02	2.02
Earnings	1.67	1.72	2.61	1.80	0.28	0.99	5.62	1.51	1.41	1.08
S&P Core Earnings	1.35	1.64	2.02	1.06	0.05	NA	NA	NA	NA	NA
Dividends	0.72	0.48	0.44	0.44	0.44	0.40	0.36	0.34	0.32	0.30
Payout Ratio	43%	28%	17%	24%	157%	40%	6%	23%	23%	28%
Prices:High	42.17	53.00	51.77	49.49	45.90	55.19	60.88	37.53	31.34	22.06
Prices:Low	30.05	39.20	41.60	35.66	29.71	27.88	30.16	22.38	17.75	14.16
P/E Ratio:High	25	31	20	27	NM	56	11	25	22	21
P/E Ratio:Low	18	23	16	20	NM	28	5	15	13	13
Income Statement Analysis (Million $)										
Revenue	5,596	5,726	5,595	5,384	5,253	4,910	3,222	2,981	2,720	2,406
Operating Income	1,391	1,451	1,589	1,499	1,244	1,404	993	898	815	633
Depreciation	244	233	228	223	442	371	222	196	173	143
Interest Expense	155	153	198	213	255	241	113	88.5	86.5	47.8
Pretax Income	1,110	941	1,415	940	269	597	526	705	659	474
Effective Tax Rate	51.8%	39.1%	37.0%	35.3%	58.7%	45.3%	NM	41.2%	40.3%	40.4%
Net Income	535	573	891	609	111	310	1,483	414	394	283
S&P Core Earnings	424	536	669	337	17.1	NA	NA	NA	NA	NA
Balance Sheet & Other Financial Data (Million $)										
Cash	151	124	248	106	65.8	116	631	12.4	66.6	274
Current Assets	1,493	1,452	1,605	1,525	1,364	1,491	2,085	945	848	887
Total Assets	14,546	14,168	14,280	14,078	14,505	14,676	8,798	5,936	4,778	3,701
Current Liabilities	1,447	1,370	1,264	1,154	1,533	1,449	861	828	706	673
Long Term Debt	2,959	2,318	2,350	3,227	3,685	4,007	2,694	1,616	1,521	980
Common Equity	6,619	6,730	6,941	5,806	5,294	5,513	3,189	2,063	1,522	1,227
Total Capital	12,037	11,433	11,635	11,448	11,479	12,039	7,415	4,675	3,710	2,397
Capital Expenditures	206	217	194	187	266	302	135	140	104	93.3
Cash Flow	770	798	1,095	807	553	681	1,687	591	547	496
Current Ratio	1.0	1.1	1.3	1.3	0.9	1.0	2.4	1.1	1.2	1.3
% Long Term Debt of Capitalization	24.6	20.3	20.2	28.2	32.1	33.3	36.3	34.6	41.0	40.9
% Net Income of Revenue	9.6	10.0	15.9	11.3	2.1	6.3	46.0	13.9	14.5	11.8
% Return on Assets	3.7	4.0	6.3	4.3	0.8	2.7	20.1	7.7	9.3	8.1
% Return on Equity	7.9	8.3	13.6	10.5	2.1	7.1	55.8	22.1	27.3	23.2

Data as orig reptd.; bef. results of disc opers/spec. items. Per share data adj. for stk. divs.; EPS diluted. E-Estimated. NA-Not Available. NM-Not Meaningful. NR-Not Ranked. UR-Under Review.

Office: 435 North Michigan Avenue, Chicago, IL 60611.
Telephone: 312-222-9100.
Website: http://www.tribune.com
Chrmn, Pres & CEO: D. FitzSimons

SVP, Secy & General Counsel: C.H. Kenney
Investor Contact: R. Musil (312-222-3787)
VP & Cntlr: R.M. Mallory

Board of Directors: J. Chandler, D. J. FitzSimons, R. Goodan, B. D. Holden, W. A. Osborn, D. S. Taft, K. C. Turner

Founded: 1847
Domicile: Delaware
Employees: 22,400

STANDARD &POOR'S

T. Rowe Price Group Inc

S&P Recommendation BUY ★★★★★

Price $46.81 (as of Oct 27, 2006)

12-Mo. Target Price $53.00

Investment Style Large-Cap Growth

GICS Sector Financials
Sub-Industry Asset Management & Custody Banks

Comment This company (formerly T. Rowe Price Associates) operates one of the largest no-load mutual fund complexes in the United States.

Key Stock Statistics (Source S&P, Vickers, company reports)

52-Wk Range	$48.50–32.29	S&P Oper. EPS 2006E	1.86	P/E on S&P Oper. EPS 2006E	25.2	Dividend Rate/Share	$0.56
Trailing 12-Month EPS	$1.80	S&P Oper. EPS 2007E	2.20	Common Shares Outstg. (M)	263.6	Yield (%)	1.20
Trailing 12-Month P/E	26.0	S&P Core EPS 2006E	1.86	Market Capitalization(B)	$12.341	Beta	1.57
$10K Invested 5 Yrs Ago	$36,434	S&P Core EPS 2007E	2.20	Institutional Ownership (%)	62	S&P Credit Rating	NA

Price Performance

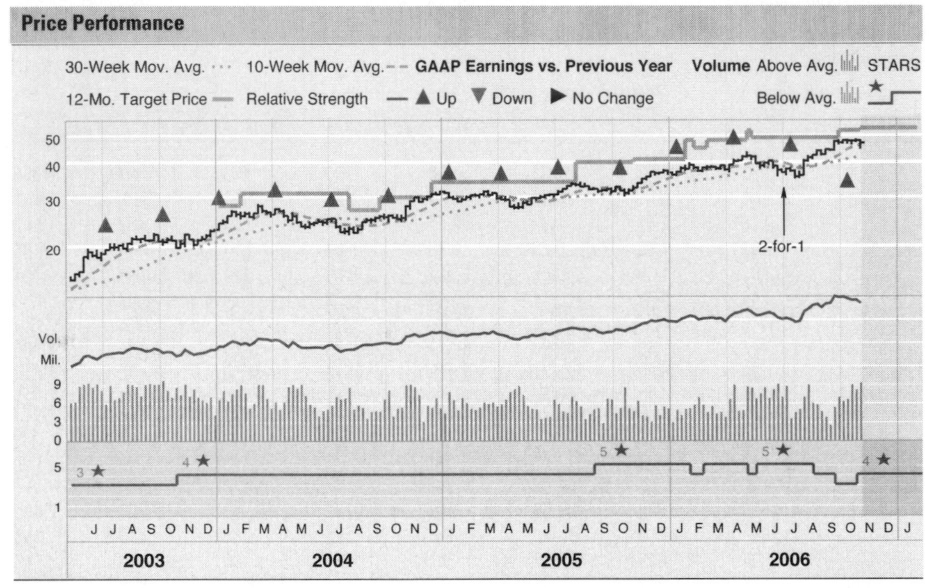

Options: CBOE

Qualitative Risk Assessment

LOW | MEDIUM | HIGH

Our risk assessment reflects the company's strong market share, consistent net client inflows, and impressive relative investment performance, taking into account industry cyclicality.

Quantitative Evaluations

S&P Quality Ranking A

D | C | B- | B | B+ | A- | A | A+

Relative Strength Rank MODERATE

56

LOWEST = 1 HIGHEST = 99

Revenue/Earnings Data

Revenue (Million $)

	1Q	2Q	3Q	4Q	Year
2006	430.3	446.0	451.8	--	--
2005	358.0	364.5	389.6	403.8	1,516
2004	306.5	310.5	317.0	346.4	1,280
2003	219.5	238.3	259.1	364.5	996.5
2002	242.0	240.3	221.6	219.6	925.8
2001	280.5	262.1	243.6	241.3	1,028

Earnings Per Share ($)

2006	0.42	0.49	0.46	E0.49	E1.86
2005	0.35	0.38	0.43	0.43	1.58
2004	0.29	0.30	0.31	0.36	1.26
2003	0.16	0.21	0.26	0.26	0.89
2002	0.21	0.20	0.17	0.19	0.76
2001	0.19	0.20	0.20	0.18	0.76

Fiscal year ended Dec. 31. Next earnings report expected: Late January. EPS Estimates based on S&P Operating Earnings; historical GAAP earnings are as reported.

Dividend Data (Dates: mm/dd Payment Date: mm/dd/yy)

Amount ($)	Date Decl.	Ex-Div. Date	Stk. of Record	Payment Date
0.280	03/10	03/22	03/24	04/07/06
0.140	06/08	06/22	06/26	07/11/06
2-for-1 Stk.	06/08	06/26	06/19	06/23/06
0.140	09/07	09/26	09/28	10/12/06

Dividends have been paid since 1986. Source: Company reports.

Highlights

➤ The STARS recommendation for TROW has recently been changed to 4 (buy) from 3 (hold) and the 12-month target price has recently been changed to $53.00 from $52.00. The Highlights section of this Stock Report will be updated accordingly.

Investment Rationale/Risk

➤ The Investment Rationale/Risk section of this Stock Report will be updated shortly. For the latest News story on TROW from MarketScope, see below.

➤ 10/25/06 11:09 am EDT... S&P UPGRADES OPINION ON SHARES OF T. ROWE PRICE TO BUY FROM HOLD, ON VALUATION (TROW 46.17****): TROW's Q3 EPS of $0.46 vs. $0.43 is $0.02 below our estimate. Revenues rose 16%, but expenses grew 20% and the effective tax rate was 41.1%, up from 36.9%. Assets under management were up 20% year-over-year and 4.9% sequentially, as flows to target date retirement funds and mutual funds were up. We expect this trend to continue based on fund performance and international sales efforts. Our '06 EPS estimate falls a penny, to $1.86, but our '07 estimate rises $0.06 to $2.20. Our 12-month target price rises $1 to $53, based on 24X our new '07 EPS estimate. /M.Albrecht

STANDARD &POOR'S

T. Rowe Price Group Inc

Business Summary September 20, 2006

CORPORATE OVERVIEW. T. Rowe Price Group (TROW) is the successor to an investment counseling business formed by the late Thomas Rowe Price, Jr. in 1937. It is now the investment adviser to the T. Rowe Price family of no-load mutual funds, and is one of the largest publicly held U.S. mutual fund complexes. At the end of 2005, TROW had nearly $270 billion in assets under management, up from $235 billion at the end of 2004. At the end of 2005, 77% of assets under management were invested in equity securities, and 23% were invested in bond and money market securities.

T. Rowe Price offers mutual funds that employ a broad range of investment styles, including growth, value, sector-focused, tax-efficient, and quantitative index-oriented approaches. The company's investment approach is based upon a strong commitment to proprietary research, sophisticated risk-management processes, and strict adherence to stated investment objectives. The company employs both fundamental and quantitative methods in performing security analyses, using internal equity and fixed income investment research capabilities. We believe T. Rowe Price's broad line of no-load mutual funds makes it easy for investors to reallocate assets among funds (which is not the case at some smaller fund companies), contributing to increased client retention, in our opinion.

All of the company's funds are sold without a sales commission, known as no-load funds. TROW also manages private accounts for individuals and institutions. At the end of 2005, assets under management were sourced about 20%-30% from each of the following: individual U.S. investors, U.S. defined contribution retirement plans, third-party distributors, and institutional investors. Revenues primarily come from investment advisory fees for managing portfolios, which depend largely on the total value and composition of assets under management. At December 31, 2005, the five largest Price funds, Equity Income, Mid-Cap Growth, Growth Stock, Blue Chip Growth, and Small-Cap Stock, accounted for 24% of assets under management and nearly 30% of 2005 investment advisory revenues.

Company Financials

Per Share Data ($) Year Ended Dec. 31	**2005**	**2004**	**2003**	**2002**	**2001**	**2000**	**1999**	**1998**	**1997**	**1996**
Tangible Book Value	5.21	3.98	2.66	1.91	1.68	1.21	3.18	2.53	2.05	1.48
Cash Flow	1.80	1.48	1.11	0.96	20.71	1.33	1.13	0.80	1.36	0.40
Earnings	1.58	1.26	0.89	0.76	0.76	1.04	0.93	0.67	0.56	0.40
S&P Core Earnings	1.43	1.16	0.78	0.67	0.65	NA	NA	NA	NA	NA
Dividends	0.49	0.40	0.35	0.33	0.31	0.27	0.20	0.17	0.14	0.11
Payout Ratio	31%	32%	40%	43%	40%	26%	22%	25%	25%	28%
Prices:High	37.70	31.70	23.80	21.35	21.97	24.97	21.63	21.44	18.44	11.41
Prices:Low	27.10	21.92	19.19	10.63	11.72	15.03	12.94	10.44	9.13	5.33
P/E Ratio:High	24	25	27	28	29	24	23	32	33	29
P/E Ratio:Low	17	17	22	14	15	14	14	16	16	13
Income Statement Analysis (Million $)										
Income Interest	Nil	Nil	1.54	3.06	32.8	59.1	37.5	28.5	22.0	17.0
Income Other	Nil	Nil	995	923	995	1,153	999	858	733	569
Total Income	1,516	1,280	996	926	1,028	1,212	1,036	886	755	586
General Expenses	814	638	585	552	603	690	589	540	461	381
Interest Expense	4.03	3.30	3.29	4.96	12.7	9.72	Nil	Nil	Nil	Nil
Depreciation	42.0	40.0	45.3	50.6	80.5	53.7	32.6	32.6	29.0	18.1
Net Income	431	337	227	194	196	269	239	174	144	98.5
S&P Core Earnings	391	309	198	169	167	NA	NA	NA	NA	NA
Balance Sheet & Other Financial Data (Million $)										
Cash	804	500	237	111	79.7	80.5	358	284	200	115
Receivables	175	158	121	96.8	104	131	122	101	86.8	73.2
Cost of Investments	378	329	273	216	154	250	279	220	193	169
Total Assets	2,311	1,929	1,547	1,370	1,313	1,469	998	797	646	479
Loss Reserve	Nil	Nil	Nil	Nil	Nil	Nil	Nil	Nil	Nil	Nil
Short Term Debt	Nil	Nil	Nil	Nil	Nil	Nil	Nil	Nil	NA	Nil
Capitalization:Debt	Nil	Nil	Nil	Nil	104	312	17.7	Nil	Nil	Nil
Capitalization:Equity	2,036	1,697	1,329	1,189	1,078	991	770	614	487	346
Capitalization:Total	2,036	1,697	1,329	1,189	1,181	1,304	848	667	537	384
Price Times Book Value:High	7.2	7.9	9.0	11.2	13.1	20.6	6.8	8.5	9.0	7.7
Price Times Book Value:Low	5.2	5.5	7.2	5.6	7.0	12.4	4.1	4.1	4.5	3.6
Cash Flow	473	377	273	245	276	323	272	207	173	117
% Expense/Operating Revenue	56.7	63.8	65.8	65.7	67.8	62.2	60.0	64.7	64.9	68.0
% Earnings & Depreciation/Assets	22.3	21.7	18.7	18.3	19.9	26.2	30.3	28.6	30.8	27.6

Data as orig reptd.; bef. results of disc opers/spec. items. Per share data adj. for stk. divs.; EPS diluted. E-Estimated. NA-Not Available. NM-Not Meaningful. NR-Not Ranked. UR-Under Review.

Office: 100 East Pratt Street, Baltimore, MD 21202.
Telephone: 410-345-2000.
Email: info@troweprice.com
Website: http://www.troweprice.com

Chrmn & Pres: G.A. Roche
VP & CFO: K.V. Moreland
Investor Contact: J.P. Croteau (410-345-2000)
VP & Treas: J.P. Croteau

Board of Directors: E. C. Bernard, J. T. Brady, J. A. Broaddus, Jr., D. B. Hebb, Jr., J. A. Kennedy, C., J. S. Riepe, G. A. Roche, B. C. Rogers, A. Sommer, D. S. Taylor, A. M. Whittemore

Founded: 1937
Domicile: Maryland
Employees: 4,372

STANDARD &POOR'S

TXU Corp.

S&P Recommendation HOLD ★★★★★

Price $63.13 (as of Oct 31, 2006)

12-Mo. Target Price $68.00

Investment Style Large-Cap Value

GICS Sector Utilities
Sub-Industry Independent Power Producers & Energy Traders

Comment This Dallas-based energy holding company provides energy services to customers in Texas.

Key Stock Statistics (Source S&P, Vickers, company reports)

52-Wk Range	$67.21–44.10	S&P Oper. EPS 2006E	5.60	P/E on S&P Oper. EPS 2006E	11.3	Dividend Rate/Share	$1.65
Trailing 12-Month EPS	$4.31	S&P Oper. EPS 2007E	5.50	Common Shares Outstg. (M)	461.4	Yield (%)	2.61
Trailing 12-Month P/E	14.7	S&P Core EPS 2006E	5.60	Market Capitalization(B)	$29.127	Beta	-0.31
$10K Invested 5 Yrs Ago	$32,032	S&P Core EPS 2007E	5.50	Institutional Ownership (%)	71	S&P Credit Rating	BBB-

Price Performance

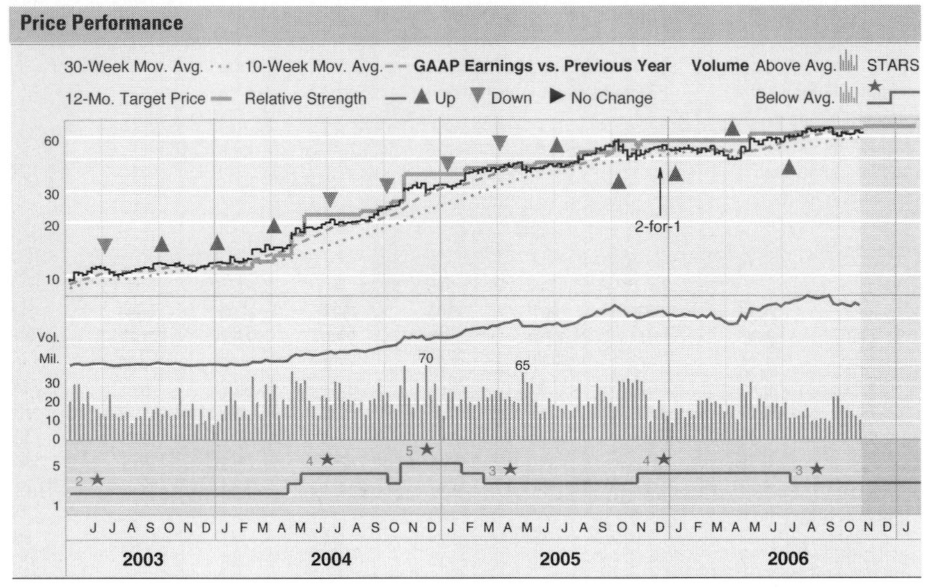

Options: ASE, CBOE, P

Highlights

➤ The 12-month target price for TXU has recently been changed to $68.00 from $67.00. The Highlights section of this Stock Report will be updated accordingly.

Investment Rationale/Risk

➤ The Investment Rationale/Risk section of this Stock Report will be updated shortly. For the latest News story on TXU from MarketScope, see below.

➤ 10/30/06 03:51 pm EST... S&P REITERATES HOLD OPINION ON SHARES OF TXU CORP (TXU 62.61***): TXU has filed an event report with the Nuclear Regulatory Commission following yesterday's manual shutdown of the 1,150 megawatt Unit 2 at the company's Comanche Peak nuclear facility. The shutdown was due to a lowering steam generator level and was completed without incident. We expect TXU to report Q3 earnings on November 9, and are raising our EPS estimates for Q3 and '06 both by $0.05, to $1.94 and $5.60, but we maintain our '07 estimate of $5.50. We are also raising our 12-month target price $1 to $68, reflecting a discount-to-peers P/E of 12.4X our '07 estimate. / J.McCann

Qualitative Risk Assessment

LOW | **MEDIUM** | HIGH

Our risk assessment reflects a balance between the low risk of the regulated electric transmission and delivery business and the high commodity price exposure of the unregulated generation and retail marketing operations. While the earnings and cash flow of the unregulated business have strongly benefited from the sharp rise in gas prices, they could be adversely affected by a sharp decline.

Quantitative Evaluations

S&P Quality Ranking **B**

D | C | B- | **B** | B+ | A- | A | A+

Relative Strength Rank **MODERATE**

38

LOWEST = 1 HIGHEST = 99

Revenue/Earnings Data

Revenue (Million $)

	1Q	2Q	3Q	4Q	Year
2006	2,304	2,667	--	--	--
2005	2,040	2,486	3,191	2,720	10,437
2004	2,132	2,303	2,743	2,130	9,308
2003	2,760	2,617	3,104	2,527	11,008
2002	2,453	2,505	2,918	2,158	10,034
2001	8,375	6,127	6,603	6,822	27,927

Earnings Per Share ($)

2006	1.09	1.07	**E**1.94	**E**1.18	**E**5.60
2005	-0.13	0.71	1.17	0.86	2.61
2004	0.18	-1.48	0.19	-0.65	-1.32
2003	0.17	0.25	0.51	0.10	1.02
2002	0.51	0.32	0.44	-0.91	0.28
2001	0.38	0.39	0.64	0.16	1.56

Fiscal year ended Dec. 31. Next earnings report expected: NA. EPS Estimates based on S&P Operating Earnings; historical GAAP earnings are as reported.

Dividend Data (Dates: mm/dd Payment Date: mm/dd/yy)

Amount ($)	Date Decl.	Ex-Div. Date	Stk. of Record	Payment Date
0.413	11/07	12/15	12/19	01/03/06
0.413	02/16	03/01	03/03	04/03/06
0.413	05/18	05/31	06/02	07/03/06
0.413	08/17	08/30	09/01	10/02/06

Dividends have been paid since 1946. Source: Company reports.

TXU Corp.

Business Summary August 04, 2006

CORPORATE OVERVIEW. TXU Corp. (TXU) is a holding company, which operates a portfolio of regulated and competitive unregulated subsidiaries. TXU Electric Delivery (TED), the regulated subsidiary that provides transmission and distribution services, contributed to 20% of consolidated revenues in 2005. The company's unregulated operations are reported under TXU Energy Holdings and include TXU Energy, TXU Power and TXU Wholesale. TXU Energy provides competitive retail electric services while TXU Power owns and operates diversified generation capacity. TXU Wholesale provides trading and energy marketing services for the company's electric services and generation units, as well as for other utility operators. TXU Energy Holdings contributed to 80% of 2005 revenues.

CORPORATE STRATEGY. TXU's goal over the next five years is to be an industry leader in energy generation and energy infrastructure. The company has outlined three core principles for achieving these objectives: a continuous improvement in the core businesses, organic growth in existing regions, and leveraging transactions to gain scale in operations outside Texas. In the generation segment, the company plans to be the most productive and lowest cost operator of solid fuel plants in the U.S., and launched the TXU Operating System to drive lean operations in mining and generation activities. The company is also investing in energy infrastructure and new technologies such as automated meter reading and remote system monitoring to achieve high network reliability and service quality.

Company Financials

Per Share Data ($) Year Ended Dec. 31	**2005**	**2004**	**2003**	**2002**	**2001**	**2000**	**1999**	**1998**	**1997**	**1996**
Tangible Book Value	NM	NM	5.85	4.94	0.77	NM	1.48	2.46	10.98	NA
Earnings	2.61	-1.32	1.02	0.28	1.56	1.72	1.77	1.40	1.43	NA
S&P Core Earnings	2.47	0.09	1.02	0.27	1.28	NA	NA	NA	NA	NA
Dividends	1.26	0.47	0.25	0.96	1.20	1.20	1.16	1.11	1.06	NA
Payout Ratio	48%	NM	25%	NM	77%	70%	66%	79%	75%	NA
Prices:High	58.30	33.50	11.98	28.53	25.00	22.63	23.59	24.03	21.00	NA
Prices:Low	30.22	11.68	7.50	5.05	17.41	12.97	16.38	19.19	15.75	NA
P/E Ratio:High	22	NM	12	NM	16	13	13	17	15	NA
P/E Ratio:Low	12	NM	7	NM	11	8	9	14	11	NA

Income Statement Analysis (Million $)										
Revenue	10,437	9,308	11,008	10,034	27,927	22,009	17,118	14,736	7,946	NA
Depreciation	836	826	959	949	1,418	1,419	1,448	1,340	839	NA
Maintenance	NA	NA	NA	NA	NA	NA	NA	NA	NA	NA
Fixed Charges Coverage	3.87	1.12	1.90	1.18	1.48	1.76	1.82	1.90	2.20	NA
Construction Credits	17.0	12.0	12.0	12.0	23.0	11.0	10.0	9.00	8.90	NA
Effective Tax Rate	26.3%	34.1%	29.9%	34.9%	NM	26.9%	31.3%	41.5%	36.3%	NA
Net Income	1,775	81.0	737	175	831	916	985	740	660	NA
S&P Core Earnings	1,698	48.6	716	153	661	NA	NA	NA	NA	NA

Balance Sheet & Other Financial Data (Million $)										
Gross Property	29,054	27,902	32,754	30,759	33,443	33,587	33,054	31,110	25,743	NA
Capital Expenditures	1,047	912	956	996	1,626	NA	1,632	1,173	586	NA
Net Property	17,192	16,676	20,920	19,642	22,480	23,301	23,640	22,867	18,571	NA
Capitalization:Long Term Debt	11,332	12,450	13,629	12,426	17,049	16,986	17,875	16,537	9,959	NA
Capitalization:% Long Term Debt	96.0	95.1	69.7	71.0	68.2	68.6	68.2	66.8	59.2	NA
Capitalization:Preferred	Nil	300	300	300	300	300	Nil	Nil	Nil	NA
Capitalization:% Preferred	Nil	2.30	1.50	1.70	1.20	1.20	Nil	Nil	Nil	NA
Capitalization:Common	475	339	5,619	4,766	7,656	7,476	8,334	8,246	6,843	NA
Capitalization:% Common	4.02	2.60	28.8	27.3	30.6	30.2	31.8	33.2	40.7	NA
Total Capital	15,888	16,215	23,917	21,552	29,280	29,274	30,671	29,049	20,362	NA
% Operating Ratio	70.7	80.5	82.3	84.3	91.8	88.7	84.8	83.3	76.0	NA
% Earned on Net Property	18.0	10.8	9.5	8.1	10.0	10.6	11.2	11.9	10.5	NA
% Return on Revenue	17.0	0.9	6.7	1.7	3.0	4.2	5.8	5.0	8.3	NA
% Return on Invested Capital	11.0	4.1	7.5	4.7	8.1	8.4	8.5	8.6	7.6	NA
% Return on Common Equity	4.4	NM	13.8	2.5	10.7	11.4	11.9	9.8	10.3	NA

Data as orig reptd.; bef. results of disc opers/spec. items. Per share data adj. for stk. divs.; EPS diluted. E-Estimated. NA-Not Available. NM-Not Meaningful. NR-Not Ranked. UR-Under Review.

Office: 1601 Bryan St, Dallas, TX 75201-3411.
Telephone: 214-812-4600.
Email: investor@txu.com
Website: http://www.txu.com

Chrmn, Pres & CEO: C.J. Wilder
EVP & General Counsel: D. Poole
SVP & Treas: A. Horton
SVP & Secy: K.K. Rucker

SVP & Cntlr: S. Szlauderbach
Investor Contact: T. Hogan (214-812-4641)
Board of Directors: L. E. Echols, K. Laday, J. E. Little, G. I. Lopez, J. E. Oesterreicher, M. W. Ranger, L. H. Roberts, G. F. Tilton, J. Wilder, E. G. de Planque

Founded: 1944
Domicile: Texas
Employees: 7,615

STANDARD &POOR'S

Tyco International Ltd

S&P Recommendation HOLD ★★★★★	Price	12-Mo. Target Price	Investment Style
	$29.18 (as of Oct 27, 2006)	$28.00	Large-Cap Value

GICS Sector Industrials
Sub-Industry Industrial Conglomerates

Comment In January 2006, directors approved a plan to separate this global conglomerate into three separate publicly traded companies.

Key Stock Statistics (Source S&P, Vickers, company reports)

52-Wk Range	$31.28–24.65	S&P Oper. EPS 2006E	1.82	P/E on S&P Oper. EPS 2006E	16.0	Dividend Rate/Share	$0.40
Trailing 12-Month EPS	$1.62	S&P Oper. EPS 2007E	2.00	Common Shares Outstg. (M)	2,036.6	Yield (%)	1.37
Trailing 12-Month P/E	18.0	S&P Core EPS 2006E	1.84	Market Capitalization(B)	$59.428	Beta	2.12
$10K Invested 5 Yrs Ago	$5,988	S&P Core EPS 2007E	2.02	Institutional Ownership (%)	83	S&P Credit Rating	BBB+

Price Performance

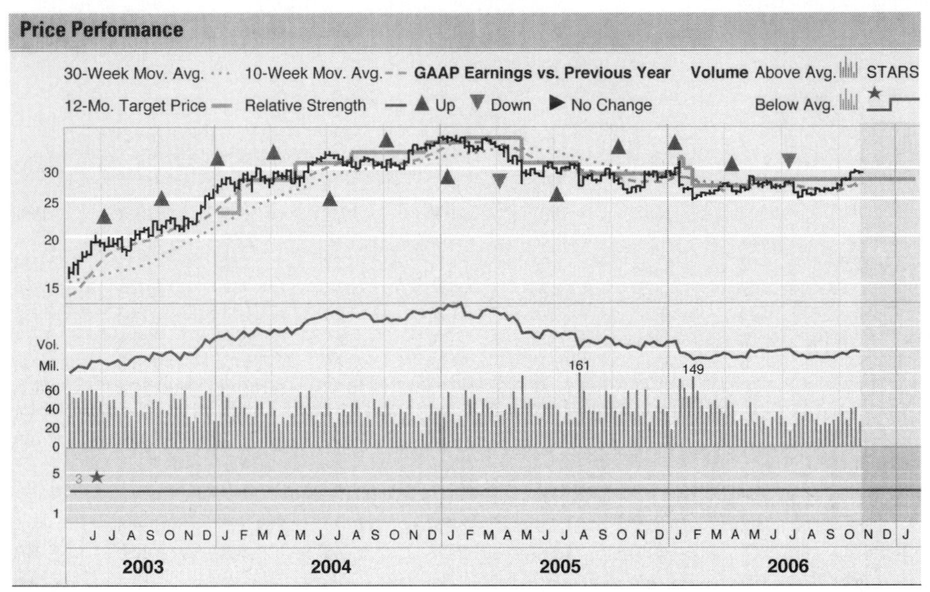

Options: ASE, CBOE, P, Ph

Analysis prepared by **Michael W. Jaffe** on August 22, 2006, when the stock traded at **$ 26.12**.

Highlights

- In January 2006, directors approved the division of Tyco into three separate companies, which we think will close as expected in early 2007. As a whole, we see sales from continuing operations rising slightly to that point. We see the expected gains driven by price hikes in certain areas and a likely modest pickup in demand for electronics and engineered products. We see these factors being partly offset by much lower sales of retail health care products, where demand for TYC's products has slowed in recent periods, and by TYC's recall of several imaging and respiratory products.
- We expect net margins to narrow slightly in coming periods, on the relatively soft revenues we see in certain Healthcare businesses, and the likely ongoing impact of high materials costs. We see these factors slightly outweighing the expected positive impact of the expected higher pricing and TYC's cost reduction actions.
- Our FY 06 and FY 07 forecasts each include $0.06 a share of projected stock option expense; an equal amount was excluded in FY 05. Operating income in FY 05 was $1.86.

Investment Rationale/Risk

- We think that TYC's overall business is operating inefficiently, and that its plan to divide into three separate companies should allow for better management focus. In addition, since we believe there are limited synergies among TYC's businesses, we do not think a split-up would cause it to sacrifice much operating leverage. We also think TYC's financial footing has greatly improved since Edward Breen's July 2002 appointment as chairman and CEO, but we still see TYC's operating performance as unexceptional in coming periods.
- Risks to our recommendation and target price include a worse than expected global economy, and negative consequences related to certain actions of TYC's former leaders.
- The stock recently traded at 13X our calendar 2007 EPS forecast of $2.03, which is in line with the S&P 500. We think Tyco's operating performance will be lackluster in coming periods, and in light of the cyclicality of most of its businesses, and shareholder lawsuits still pending against the company, we view its valuation as appropriate. Using a multiple of 14X our calendar 2007 EPS estimate, we arrive at our 12-month target price of $28.

Qualitative Risk Assessment

LOW	**MEDIUM**	HIGH

Our risk assessment reflects our view of Tyco's strong levels of free cash flow in recent years. However, the company's recent operating performance has been lackluster, in our opinion, and it also still faces the possible consequences of shareholder litigation related to the actions of former Tyco executives.

Quantitative Evaluations

S&P Quality Ranking B

D	C	B-	**B**	B+	A-	A	A+

Relative Strength Rank MODERATE

69

LOWEST = 1 HIGHEST = 99

Revenue/Earnings Data

Revenue (Million $)

	1Q	2Q	3Q	4Q	Year
2006	9,706	10,206	10,504	--	--
2005	10,065	10,456	10,562	10,030	39,727
2004	9,665	9,821	10,225	10,442	40,153
2003	8,927	8,989	9,413	9,473	36,801
2002	8,579	8,611	9,104	9,350	35,644
2001	8,029	8,810	8,680	8,517	34,037

Earnings Per Share ($)

2006	0.39	0.52	0.43	**E**0.49	**E**1.82
2005	0.35	0.11	0.56	0.42	1.51
2004	0.34	0.34	0.43	0.27	1.41
2003	0.28	0.06	0.27	-0.11	0.52
2002	0.47	-1.03	-0.23	-0.75	-1.54
2001	0.57	0.63	0.64	0.70	2.55

Fiscal year ended Sep. 30. Next earnings report expected: Mid November. EPS Estimates based on S&P Operating Earnings; historical GAAP earnings are as reported.

Dividend Data (Dates: mm/dd Payment Date: mm/dd/yy)

Amount ($)	Date Decl.	Ex-Div. Date	Stk. of Record	Payment Date
0.100	12/08	12/29	01/03	02/02/06
0.100	03/09	03/30	04/03	05/03/06
0.100	06/14	06/29	07/03	08/01/06
0.100	09/27	10/04	10/09	11/09/06

Dividends have been paid since 1975. Source: Company reports.

Please read the Required Disclosures and Analyst Certification on the last page of this report.

Tyco International Ltd

Business Summary August 22, 2006

Tyco International, a global conglomerate, is in the process of separating its portfolio of businesses into three separate publicly traded companies. Under a plan that was approved by directors in January 2006, the company was to break up into Tyco Healthcare, a diversified health care company; Tyco Electronics, the world's largest passive electronic components manufacturer; and Tyco Fire & Security and Engineered Products & Services, with positions in residential and commercial security, fire protection, and industrial products and services. TYC planned to accomplish the planned separation through tax-free stock dividends to its shareholders, who would own 100% of the equity in each of the three new companies. Tyco derived 51% of its revenues outside the U.S. in FY 05 (Sep.).

These planned changes were announced some 3 1/2 years after Tyco underwent an executive upheaval, which was largely related to charges that Dennis Kozlowski, its former chairman and CEO, and Mark Swartz, its former CFO, had misused company funds. In June 2005, Mr. Kozlowski and Mr. Swartz were found guilty of nearly all charges filed by the Manhattan District Attorney, which centered around them being the main recipients of over $600 million of unauthorized bonuses, interest-free loans, and forgiveness of these loans.

Tyco Healthcare (24% of TYC's sales and 38% of operating profits in FY 05) provides advanced surgical instruments and supplies, respiratory care products, contrast media and diagnostic imaging products, needles and syringes, vascular therapies, sutures and wound care products, and generic pharmaceuticals.

Tyco Electronics (31% and 31%, respectively) supplies electronic components, including connectors, switches, relays, circuit protection devices, touch screens, magnetics, resistors, wire and cable, as well as fiber-optic and wireless components and systems.

The combination of Tyco's Fire & Security and Engineered Products & Services divisions (45% of sales and 31% of profits) provides electronic security solutions for residential, business and governmental customers, fire protection and sprinkler systems, and industrial valves and controls.

In FY 06's third quarter, Tyco repurchased 41 million of its common shares, for a total of $1.1 billion. It bought back an additional five million shares in July, for $134 million, bringing total repurchases through that point in FY 06 to 76 million shares (3.5% of diluted outstanding shares).

Company Financials

Per Share Data ($) Year Ended Sep. 30	2005	2004	2003	2002	2001	2000	1999	1998	1997	1996
Tangible Book Value	1.39	NM	NM	NM	NM	0.42	0.10	NM	1.30	1.15
Cash Flow	2.45	2.34	1.25	-0.52	3.72	3.60	1.40	1.49	0.84	0.64
Earnings	1.51	1.41	0.52	-1.54	2.55	2.64	0.62	1.01	0.65	0.51
Dividends	0.40	0.05	0.05	0.05	0.05	0.05	0.05	0.05	0.05	0.05
Payout Ratio	26%	4%	10%	NM	2%	2%	8%	5%	8%	10%
Prices:High	36.58	36.42	27.18	58.81	63.21	59.19	53.88	39.09	22.75	14.00
Prices:Low	25.66	26.01	11.20	6.98	39.24	32.00	22.50	20.13	12.94	8.09
P/E Ratio:High	24	26	52	NM	25	22	87	39	35	28
P/E Ratio:Low	17	18	22	NM	15	12	36	20	20	16

Income Statement Analysis (Million $)	2005	2004	2003	2002	2001	2000	1999	1998	1997	1996
Revenue	39,727	40,153	36,801	35,644	34,037	28,932	22,497	12,311	6,598	5,090
Operating Income	7,637	7,957	5,568	6,509	8,865	7,393	4,977	2,490	899	666
Depreciation	2,100	2,176	1,472	2,033	2,141	1,644	1,322	566	120	83.0
Interest Expense	815	963	1,148	1,077	776	845	547	236	90.8	62.0
Pretax Income	4,192	4,159	1,803	-2,811	6,004	6,465	1,651	1,718	688	524
Effective Tax Rate	23.5%	27.4%	42.4%	NM	21.4%	29.8%	37.6%	31.5%	39.1%	40.8%
Net Income	3,199	3,005	1,035	-3,070	4,671	4,520	1,031	1,177	419	310

Balance Sheet & Other Financial Data (Million $)	2005	2004	2003	2002	2001	2000	1999	1998	1997	1996
Cash	3,196	4,467	4,329	6,383	2,587	1,265	1,762	820	171	69.4
Current Assets	18,537	18,545	17,240	19,765	NA	12,816	11,163	5,743	2,447	1,696
Total Assets	62,621	63,667	63,545	66,414	111,287	40,404	32,362	16,527	5,888	3,954
Current Liabilities	11,835	11,152	10,572	19,632	NA	11,679	9,179	5,048	1,735	1,292
Long Term Debt	10,600	14,617	18,251	16,487	38,503	9,462	9,109	4,652	919	512
Common Equity	32,450	30,292	26,369	24,791	31,737	17,033	12,333	6,137	3,052	1,938
Total Capital	43,111	44,977	44,733	41,320	70,542	27,630	21,946	10,847	3,996	2,469
Capital Expenditures	1,272	1,015	1,170	1,709	1,798	1,704	1,633	781	199	123
Cash Flow	5,299	5,181	2,507	-1,037	6,812	6,165	2,353	1,743	539	393
Current Ratio	1.6	1.7	1.6	1.0	NA	1.1	1.2	1.1	1.4	1.3
% Long Term Debt of Capitalization	24.6	32.5	40.8	39.9	54.6	34.2	41.5	42.9	23.0	20.7
% Net Income of Revenue	8.1	7.5	2.8	NM	13.7	15.6	4.6	9.6	6.4	6.1
% Return on Assets	5.1	4.7	1.6	NM	6.2	12.4	3.7	8.7	8.5	8.5
% Return on Equity	10.2	10.6	4.1	NM	19.2	30.7	9.3	24.6	16.8	17.4

Data as orig reptd.; bef. results of disc opers/spec. items. Per share data adj. for stk. divs.; EPS diluted. E-Estimated. NA-Not Available. NM-Not Meaningful. NR-Not Ranked. UR-Under Review.

Office: 90 Pitts Bay Road, Pembroke, Bermuda HM 08.
Telephone: 441-292-8674.
Email: info@tyco.com
Website: http://www.tyco.com

Chrmn & CEO: E. Breen
EVP & CFO: C.J. Coughlin
EVP & General Counsel: W.B. Lytton
SVP & Chief Acctg Officer: C.A. Davidson

SVP & Treas: M. Hund-Mejean
Investor Contact: E.C. Arditte (609-720-4621)
Board of Directors: D. C. Blair, E. D. Breen, B. Duperreault, B. Gordon, R. L. Gupta, J. A. Krol, H. C. McCall, M. J. McDonald, B. R. O'Neill, S. S. Wijnberg, J. B. York

Founded: 1960
Domicile: Bermuda
Employees: 247,900

STANDARD &POOR'S

Tyson Foods Inc.

S&P Recommendation	Price	12-Mo. Target Price	Investment Style
BUY ★★★★★	$14.33 (as of Oct 27, 2006)	$17.00	Mid-Cap Value

GICS Sector Consumer Staples
Sub-Industry Packaged Foods & Meats

Comment Tyson is the world's largest supplier of beef, chicken and pork products.

Key Stock Statistics (Source S&P, Vickers, company reports)

52-Wk Range	**$19.50–12.57**	S&P Oper. EPS 2006**E**	**-0.30**	P/E on S&P Oper. EPS 2006**E**	**NM**	Dividend Rate/Share	**$0.16**
Trailing 12-Month EPS	**$-0.13**	S&P Oper. EPS 2007**E**	**1.00**	Common Shares Outstg. (M)	**354.9**	Yield (%)	**1.12**
Trailing 12-Month P/E	**NM**	S&P Core EPS 2006**E**	**-0.41**	Market Capitalization(B)	**$3.812**	Beta	**0.68**
$10K Invested 5 Yrs Ago	**$16,887**	S&P Core EPS 2007**E**	**1.00**	Institutional Ownership (%)	**76**	S&P Credit Rating	**BBB-**

Price Performance

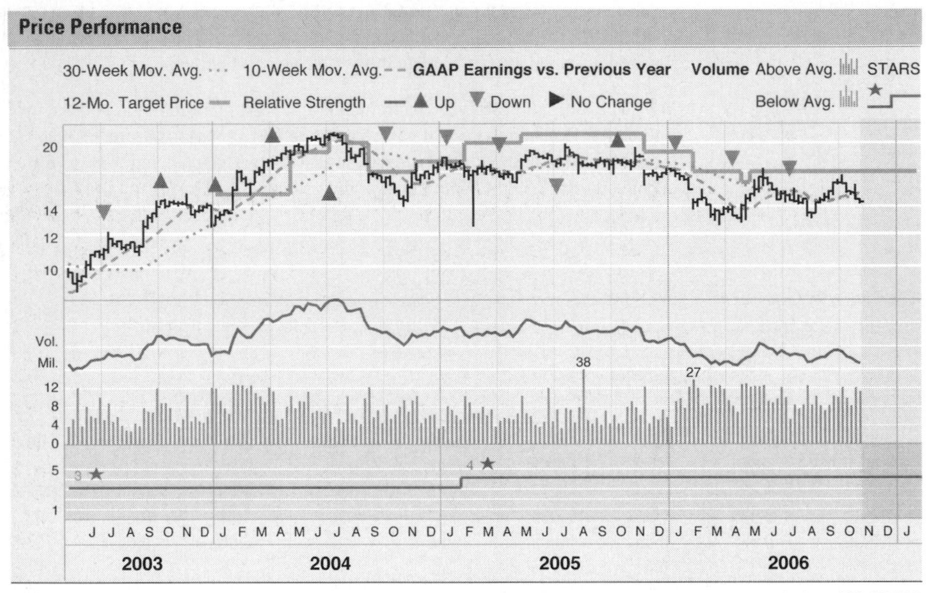

Options: ASE, CBOE, P

Analysis prepared by **Joseph Agnese** on August 16, 2006, when the stock traded at **$ 13.51**.

Highlights

- We expect sales to decline slightly in FY 06 (Sep.), reflecting weak international demand. We believe beef exports will begin to accelerate at the end of FY 06 as bans on U.S. beef begin to be lifted. We believe gains will be offset by depressed chicken prices, as fears regarding the spread of avian influenza in international markets result in decreased demand.
- We expect chicken margins to narrow significantly as lower selling prices offset benefits from decreased feed costs. However, we believe beef margins will see improvement in the fourth quarter as the opening of the Canadian border to live cattle imports should result in decreased raw material costs, while the opening of export markets increases demand. We believe pork segment results will be pressured by lower demand and pricing as consumers switch purchasing to other meat products. We expect interest expense to decline, as TSN remains focused on paying down debt.
- We see an FY 06 operating loss of $0.30 per share, down from operating EPS of $1.01 in FY 05. For FY 07, we see EPS of $1.00.

Investment Rationale/Risk

- We believe margins will improve in FY 07, reflecting continued low feed costs, strengthening chicken demand, and improved live cattle supplies. Longer term, we believe the company is well positioned to benefit from reduced commodity exposure due to a strategy focused on growing value added prepared food products.
- Risks to our recommendation and target price include significant uncertainty regarding resumption of trade in international markets and corporate governance concerns that we have, which are related to board issues.
- Our analysis of discounted cash flows, assuming a weighted average cost of capital of 9.0% and a terminal growth rate of 3.0%, suggests an intrinsic value of $16 a share. Our P/E analysis, assuming the shares trade at a multiple of 15X our calendar year 2007 EPS estimate of $1.15, at the midpoint of the company's historical trading range of 8X-22X, suggests a value of $17 a share. Using a blend of these valuation metrics, our 12-month target price is $17.

Qualitative Risk Assessment

LOW | MEDIUM | **HIGH**

Our risk assessment reflects the company's cyclical operations, which are significantly affected by exposure to commodity crop and meat markets, and international trade restrictions.

Quantitative Evaluations

S&P Quality Ranking **B**

D | C | B- | **B** | B+ | A- | A | A+

Relative Strength Rank **WEAK**

17

LOWEST = 1 HIGHEST = 99

Revenue/Earnings Data

Revenue (Million $)

	1Q	2Q	3Q	4Q	Year
2006	6,454	6,251	6,383	--	--
2005	6,452	6,359	6,708	6,495	26,014
2004	6,505	6,153	6,634	7,149	26,441
2003	5,802	5,845	6,330	6,572	24,549
2002	5,865	5,839	5,902	5,761	23,367
2001	1,743	1,828	1,894	5,088	10,751

Earnings Per Share ($)

2006	0.11	-0.37	-0.15	**E**Nil	**E**-0.30
2005	0.14	0.21	0.36	0.28	0.99
2004	0.16	0.33	0.45	0.19	1.13
2003	0.11	0.20	0.23	0.42	0.96
2002	0.36	0.18	0.30	0.24	1.08
2001	0.12	-0.03	0.09	0.22	0.40

Fiscal year ended Sep. 30. Next earnings report expected: NA. EPS Estimates based on S&P Operating Earnings; historical GAAP earnings are as reported.

Dividend Data (Dates: mm/dd Payment Date: mm/dd/yy)

Amount ($)	Date Decl.	Ex-Div. Date	Stk. of Record	Payment Date
0.040	11/18	02/27	03/01	03/15/06
0.040	03/08	05/30	06/01	06/15/06
0.040	05/19	08/30	09/01	09/15/06
0.040	08/08	11/29	12/01	12/15/06

Dividends have been paid since 1976. Source: Company reports.

Tyson Foods Inc.

Business Summary August 16, 2006

Tyson Foods is the world's largest supplier of beef, chicken and pork products. The company holds about 27% of the U.S. beef market, 23% of the chicken market, and 19% of the pork market. Its goal is to become the primary protein provider for its customers. The company exports to more than 80 countries including Canada, China, Europe, Japan, Mexico, Russia and South Korea. Operations are conducted through five segments: beef, chicken, pork, prepared foods, and other.

The beef segment (45% of FY 05 (Sep.) revenues) includes the slaughter of live cattle and fabrication into primal and sub-primal meat cuts and case-ready products. Operations reduce live cattle to dressed carcasses and allied products for sales to further processors. The company markets its products to food retailers, distributors, wholesalers, restaurants and hotel chains, and other food processors. Allied products are marketed to manufacturers of pharmaceuticals and animal feeds. The company's primary supply of live cattle is purchased on a daily basis.

The chicken segment (32%) includes fresh, frozen and value-added chicken products sold through domestic foodservice, domestic retail markets for at-home consumption, wholesale club markets targeted to small food service operations, and individuals and distributors that deliver to restaurants, schools and international markets throughout the world. Also included in this segment are sales from allied products and TSN's chicken breeding stock subsidiary. The segment's primary raw material is live chickens that are raised by independent contractors. Profitability is partially dependent on corn and soybean meal, representing 39% of the cost of growing a chicken.

Company Financials

Per Share Data ($) Year Ended Sep. 30	**2005**	**2004**	**2003**	**2002**	**2001**	**2000**	**1999**	**1998**	**1997**	**1996**
Tangible Book Value	5.66	4.49	3.17	2.92	1.71	NM	5.09	4.05	4.16	3.70
Cash Flow	2.39	2.50	2.26	2.39	1.91	-1.97	2.26	1.32	1.91	1.51
Earnings	0.99	1.13	0.96	1.08	0.40	0.68	1.00	0.11	0.85	0.40
S&P Core Earnings	1.06	1.10	0.64	1.02	0.39	NA	NA	NA	NA	NA
Dividends	0.16	0.16	0.16	0.16	0.16	0.16	0.13	0.10	0.10	0.08
Payout Ratio	16%	14%	17%	15%	40%	24%	13%	91%	11%	20%
Prices:High	19.91	21.28	15.10	15.71	14.20	17.38	23.75	26.00	24.25	23.08
Prices:Low	12.50	12.97	7.25	9.27	8.10	8.50	14.88	16.31	17.38	13.83
P/E Ratio:High	20	19	16	15	35	26	24	NM	29	58
P/E Ratio:Low	13	11	8	9	20	13	15	NM	20	35

Income Statement Analysis (Million $)										
Revenue	26,014	26,441	24,549	23,367	10,751	7,268	7,363	7,414	6,356	6,454
Operating Income	1,266	1,415	837	1,407	650	643	854	622	631	510
Depreciation	501	490	458	467	335	294	291	276	231	240
Interest Expense	227	275	592	305	144	116	124	139	110	133
Pretax Income	528	635	523	593	165	234	371	71.0	330	133
Effective Tax Rate	33.1%	36.5%	35.6%	35.4%	35.2%	35.5%	34.9%	64.8%	43.6%	36.8%
Net Income	353	403	337	383	88.0	151	230	25.0	186	87.0
S&P Core Earnings	379	392	224	365	87.5	NA	NA	NA	NA	NA

Balance Sheet & Other Financial Data (Million $)										
Cash	40.0	33.0	25.0	51.0	70.0	43.0	30.0	47.0	24.0	37.0
Current Assets	3,485	3,532	3,371	3,144	3,290	1,576	1,727	1,765	1,573	1,810
Total Assets	10,504	10,464	10,486	10,372	10,632	4,854	5,083	5,243	4,411	4,544
Current Liabilities	2,157	2,293	2,475	2,093	2,416	886	987	831	721	686
Long Term Debt	2,869	3,024	3,114	3,733	4,016	1,357	1,515	1,967	1,558	1,806
Common Equity	4,615	4,912	3,954	3,662	3,354	2,175	2,128	1,971	1,622	1,542
Total Capital	8,141	8,631	7,790	8,038	7,979	3,917	4,041	4,371	3,686	3,844
Capital Expenditures	571	486	402	433	261	196	363	310	291	214
Cash Flow	854	893	795	850	423	445	521	301	417	327
Current Ratio	1.6	1.5	1.4	1.5	1.4	1.8	1.7	2.1	2.2	2.6
% Long Term Debt of Capitalization	35.2	35.0	40.0	46.4	50.3	34.6	37.5	45.0	42.3	47.0
% Net Income of Revenue	1.4	1.5	1.4	1.6	0.8	2.1	3.1	0.3	2.9	1.3
% Return on Assets	3.4	3.8	3.2	3.6	1.1	3.0	4.5	0.5	4.2	1.9
% Return on Equity	7.9	8.5	8.8	10.9	3.2	7.0	11.2	1.4	11.8	5.8

Data as orig reptd.; bef. results of disc opers/spec. items. Per share data adj. for stk. divs.; EPS diluted. E-Estimated. NA-Not Available. NM-Not Meaningful. NR-Not Ranked. UR-Under Review.

Office: 2210 West Oaklawn Drive, Springdale, AR 72762-6999.
Telephone: 479-290-4000.
Email: tysonir@tysonfoodinc.com
Website: http://www.tysonfoodsinc.com

Chrmn: J.H. Tyson
Pres & CEO: R.L. Bond
EVP & CFO: W.D. Miquelon
EVP & General Counsel: J.A. Gonzalez-Pita

SVP, Chief Acctg Officer & Cntlr: C.J. Hart
Investor Contact: R.A. Wisener (479 290 4000)
Auditor: Ernst & Young
Board of Directors: R. L. Bond, S. Ford, L. V. Hackley, J. Kever, J. R. Smith, L. E. Tollett, B. A. Tyson, D. Tyson, J. H. Tyson, A. C. Zapanta

Founded: 1935
Domicile: Delaware
Employees: 114,000

STANDARD &POOR'S

Union Pacific Corp

S&P Recommendation HOLD ★★★★★ | **Price** $90.86 (as of Oct 27, 2006) | **12-Mo. Target Price** $99.00 | **Investment Style** Large-Cap Value

GICS Sector Industrials
Sub-Industry Railroads

Comment Union Pacific operates the largest U.S. railroad, with over 32,000 miles of rail serving the western two-thirds of the country.

Key Stock Statistics (Source S&P, Vickers, company reports)

52-Wk Range	$97.49–68.19	S&P Oper. EPS 2006E	5.62	P/E on S&P Oper. EPS 2006E	16.2	Dividend Rate/Share	$1.20
Trailing 12-Month EPS	$5.23	S&P Oper. EPS 2007E	6.36	Common Shares Outstg. (M)	269.4	Yield (%)	1.32
Trailing 12-Month P/E	17.4	S&P Core EPS 2006E	5.37	Market Capitalization(B)	$24.473	Beta	0.70
$10K Invested 5 Yrs Ago	$19,164	S&P Core EPS 2007E	6.11	Institutional Ownership (%)	84	S&P Credit Rating	BBB

Price Performance

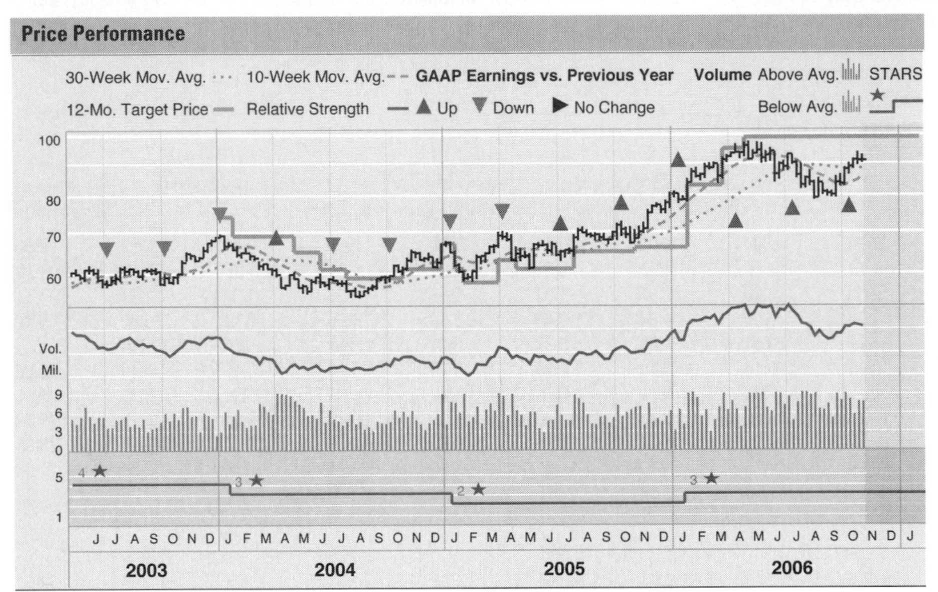

Options: CBOE, Ph

Analysis prepared by **Kevin Kirkeby** on October 23, 2006, when the stock traded at **$ 91.14**.

Highlights

- We see revenue growth slowing to 7% in 2007, following an anticipated 16% rise in 2006, as fewer customer contracts are up for renewal and fuel surcharges stabilize. We expect the intermodal and agricultural segments to be the primary contributors to volume gains in 2007, while infrastructure constraints in the Powder River Basin are expected to limit growth in coal. In July, UNP announced it was considering a 15% increase to its capital spending program for 2007 to accelerate capacity expansions.
- We expect operating margins to rise to about 18% in 2006, on pricing gains, net of fuel costs, along with improved asset utilization and efforts to shed low-margin businesses. For 2007, we see a modest widening of margins, coming largely from service improvements. We also see the effective tax rate returning to a more historical level of 37.5% in both years, up from the unusually low 28.6% in 2005.
- We forecast 2006 operating EPS of $5.62, up 64% from adjusted operating EPS of $3.42 in 2005. We estimate a 13% increase in 2007, to $6.36. Our 2006 S&P Core EPS of $5.37 reflects adjustments to remove gains on asset sales and insurance recoveries.

Investment Rationale/Risk

- Given our expectation for slowing volume growth and limited pricing gains, we view current valuations as fair. For the period 2007-2012, we forecast compound annual revenue and EPS growth to slow to 3.7% and 8.0%, respectively. Among the drivers are expansion in international trade with Asia and in NAFTA and a shifting of long-haul volumes from trucking companies to the railroads.
- Risks to our opinion and target price include weaker than expected economic growth, capacity constraints in parts of the rail network, a rapid increase in fuel prices that leads to slower than anticipated cost recovery, wage pressures, and unusually severe weather.
- Our relative valuation model suggests a forward price to sales multiple of about 1.4X, reflecting the current stage of economic and sector expansion, and a value of $91. Our discounted cash flow model, which assumes an 8% weighted average cost of capital and a 3% terminal growth rate, estimates an intrinsic value of $108. Blending these models, we arrive at our 12-month target price of $99.

Qualitative Risk Assessment

LOW | **MEDIUM** | HIGH

Our risk assessment reflects UNP's exposure to economic cycles, regulations, labor and fuel costs, coupled with significant capital expenditure requirements, and challenges in maintaining system fluidity, offset by the company's historically positive cash flow generation and moderate financial leverage.

Quantitative Evaluations

S&P Quality Ranking B+

D | C | B- | B | **B+** | A- | A | A+

Relative Strength Rank MODERATE

61

LOWEST = 1 HIGHEST = 99

Revenue/Earnings Data

Revenue (Million $)

	1Q	2Q	3Q	4Q	Year
2006	3,710	3,923	3,983	--	--
2005	3,152	3,344	3,461	3,621	13,578
2004	2,893	3,029	3,076	3,217	12,215
2003	2,736	2,894	2,956	2,965	11,551
2002	2,967	3,154	3,199	3,171	12,491
2001	2,943	2,998	3,026	3,006	11,973

Earnings Per Share ($)

	1Q	2Q	3Q	4Q	Year
2006	1.15	1.43	1.54	E1.54	E5.62
2005	0.48	0.88	1.38	1.10	3.85
2004	0.63	0.60	0.77	0.30	2.30
2003	0.60	1.10	1.21	1.28	4.07
2002	0.86	1.15	1.63	1.41	5.05
2001	0.72	0.95	1.04	1.06	3.77

Fiscal year ended Dec. 31. Next earnings report expected: Mid January. EPS Estimates based on S&P Operating Earnings; historical GAAP earnings are as reported.

Dividend Data (Dates: mm/dd Payment Date: mm/dd/yy)

Amount ($)	Date Decl.	Ex-Div. Date	Stk. of Record	Payment Date
0.300	11/17	12/12	12/14	01/02/06
0.300	02/23	03/06	03/08	04/03/06
0.300	05/04	05/26	05/31	07/03/06
0.300	07/27	08/29	08/31	10/02/06

Dividends have been paid since 1900. Source: Company reports.

Please read the Required Disclosures and Analyst Certification on the last page of this report.

Union Pacific Corp

Business Summary October 23, 2006

CORPORATE OVERVIEW. We believe Union Pacific, operating the largest U.S. railroad, will focus on improving service levels, system fluidity, and removing bottlenecks, challenges which we believe hampered its results in 2004 and 2005. UNP's system spans about 33,000 miles, linking Pacific Coast and Gulf Coast ports to midwestern and eastern gateways, and schedules are coordinated with other carriers.

MARKET PROFILE. We believe UNP's intermodal business, representing 19% of 2005 revenue, should be UNP's fastest growing segment longer term, driven by rising international trade and the outsourcing of manufacturing to Asia. However, weak service and timeliness levels in 2004 and 2005 hampered its ability to effectively compete with other railroad and trucking companies, in our view. Industrial products, sensitive to GDP trends, provided 22% of freight revenues in 2005, and included building products, metals and minerals. Energy, which we believe is UNP's most profitable segment, accounted for 20% of 2005 freight revenues. UNP is a major transporter of low-sulfur coal, with 67% of its energy traffic consisting of coal originating in the Powder River Basin of Wyoming and Montana, primarily delivered to power utilities. We believe chemicals, agricultural products and automotive, representing 14%, 15% and 10% of 2005 freight revenues, respectively, all face low long-term volume growth prospects.

COMPETITIVE LANDSCAPE. The U.S. rail industry has an oligopoly-like structure, with over 80% of revenues generated by the four largest railroads: UNP and Burlington Northern Santa Fe Corp. operating on the West Coast, and CSX Corp. and Norfolk Southern Corp. operating on the East Coast. Railroads simultaneously compete for customers while cooperating by sharing assets, interfacing systems, and completing customer movements. Key suppliers include locomotive and rail equipment manufacturers, fuel suppliers, and labor. UNP's employees, about 85% of whom are unionized, enjoy above national average compensation due to their significant bargaining power.

Company Financials

Per Share Data ($) Year Ended Dec. 31	**2005**	**2004**	**2003**	**2002**	**2001**	**2000**	**1999**	**1998**	**1997**	**1996**
Tangible Book Value	51.15	48.49	47.85	41.99	38.30	35.07	32.29	29.93	30.79	30.51
Cash Flow	8.26	6.54	7.92	9.19	7.87	7.34	6.91	1.78	5.97	6.86
Earnings	3.85	2.30	4.07	5.05	3.77	3.34	3.12	-2.57	1.74	3.36
S&P Core Earnings	3.32	2.11	3.76	3.83	2.82	NA	NA	NA	NA	NA
Dividends	1.20	1.20	0.99	0.83	0.80	0.80	0.80	1.03	1.72	1.72
Payout Ratio	31%	52%	24%	16%	21%	24%	26%	NM	99%	51%
Prices:High	81.26	69.56	69.50	65.15	60.70	52.81	67.88	63.75	72.98	74.50
Prices:Low	58.18	54.80	50.90	53.00	43.75	34.25	39.00	37.31	56.25	48.25
P/E Ratio:High	21	30	17	13	16	16	22	NM	42	22
P/E Ratio:Low	15	24	13	10	12	10	13	NM	32	14

Income Statement Analysis (Million $)	2005	2004	2003	2002	2001	2000	1999	1998	1997	1996
Revenue	13,578	12,215	11,551	12,491	11,973	11,878	11,273	10,553	11,079	8,786
Operating Income	2,970	2,406	3,200	3,530	2,072	2,043	2,887	1,446	2,296	2,295
Depreciation	1,175	1,111	1,067	1,206	1,174	1,140	1,083	1,070	1,043	762
Interest Expense	504	527	574	633	701	723	733	714	605	501
Pretax Income	1,436	856	1,637	2,016	1,533	1,310	1,202	-696	676	1,113
Effective Tax Rate	28.6%	29.4%	35.5%	33.5%	37.0%	35.7%	34.9%	NM	36.1%	34.1%
Net Income	1,026	604	1,056	1,341	966	842	783	-633	432	733
S&P Core Earnings	886	551	972	1,003	708	NA	NA	NA	NA	NA

Balance Sheet & Other Financial Data (Million $)	2005	2004	2003	2002	2001	2000	1999	1998	1997	1996
Cash	773	977	527	369	113	105	175	176	90.0	191
Current Assets	2,325	2,290	2,089	2,152	1,542	1,285	1,314	1,502	1,415	1,334
Total Assets	35,620	34,589	33,460	32,764	31,551	30,499	29,888	29,374	28,764	27,914
Current Liabilities	3,384	2,516	2,456	2,701	2,692	2,962	2,885	2,932	3,247	3,056
Long Term Debt	6,760	7,981	7,822	8,928	9,386	9,644	9,926	10,011	8,285	7,900
Common Equity	13,707	12,655	12,354	10,651	9,575	8,662	8,001	7,393	8,225	8,225
Total Capital	29,949	29,816	29,345	28,057	26,843	25,449	24,642	23,712	22,762	22,064
Capital Expenditures	2,169	1,876	1,752	1,887	1,736	1,783	1,834	2,111	2,101	1,360
Cash Flow	2,201	1,715	2,123	2,547	2,140	1,982	1,866	437	1,475	1,495
Current Ratio	0.7	0.9	0.9	0.8	0.6	0.4	0.5	0.5	0.4	0.4
% Long Term Debt of Capitalization	22.6	26.8	26.7	31.8	35.0	37.9	40.3	42.2	36.3	35.8
% Net Income of Revenue	7.6	4.9	9.1	10.7	8.1	7.1	6.9	NM	3.9	8.3
% Return on Assets	2.9	1.8	3.2	4.2	3.1	2.8	2.6	NM	1.5	3.1
% Return on Equity	7.8	4.8	9.2	13.3	10.6	10.1	10.2	NM	5.3	10.0

Data as orig reptd.; bef. results of disc opers/spec. items. Per share data adj. for stk. divs.; EPS diluted. E-Estimated. NA-Not Available. NM-Not Meaningful. NR-Not Ranked. UR-Under Review.

Office: 1400 Douglas St, Omaha, NE 68179-1001.
Telephone: 402-544-5000.
Website: http://www.up.com
Chrmn: R.K. Davidson

Pres & CEO: J.R. Young
EVP & CFO: R. Knight, Jr.
SVP & General Counsel: J.M. Hemmer
SVP & CIO: L. Tennison

Investor Contact: M.S. Jones (402-544-6111)
Board of Directors: A. Card, R. K. Davidson, E. B. Davis, Jr., T. J. Donohue, A. W. Dunham, J. R. Hope, C. C. Krulak, M. McConnell, S. R. Rogel, J. R. Young

Founded: 1862
Domicile: Utah
Employees: 49,747

STANDARD &POOR'S

Unisys Corp

S&P Recommendation HOLD ★★★★★	**Price** $6.56 (as of Oct 27, 2006)	**12-Mo. Target Price** $7.00	**Investment Style** Mid-Cap Value

GICS Sector Information Technology
Sub-Industry IT Consulting & Other Services

Comment Unisys is a leading worldwide supplier of information services and technology solutions to more than 60,000 customers in 100 countries.

Key Stock Statistics (Source S&P, Vickers, company reports)

52-Wk Range	**$7.20–4.72**	S&P Oper. EPS 2006**E**	**-0.10**	P/E on S&P Oper. EPS 2006**E**	**NM**	Dividend Rate/Share	**Nil**
Trailing 12-Month EPS	**$-0.95**	S&P Oper. EPS 2007**E**	**0.18**	Common Shares Outstg. (M)	**343.8**	Yield (%)	**Nil**
Trailing 12-Month P/E	**NM**	S&P Core EPS 2006**E**	**-0.87**	Market Capitalization(B)	**$2.255**	Beta	**2.40**
$10K Invested 5 Yrs Ago	**$7,130**	S&P Core EPS 2007**E**	**0.18**	Institutional Ownership (%)	**76**	S&P Credit Rating	**B+**

Price Performance

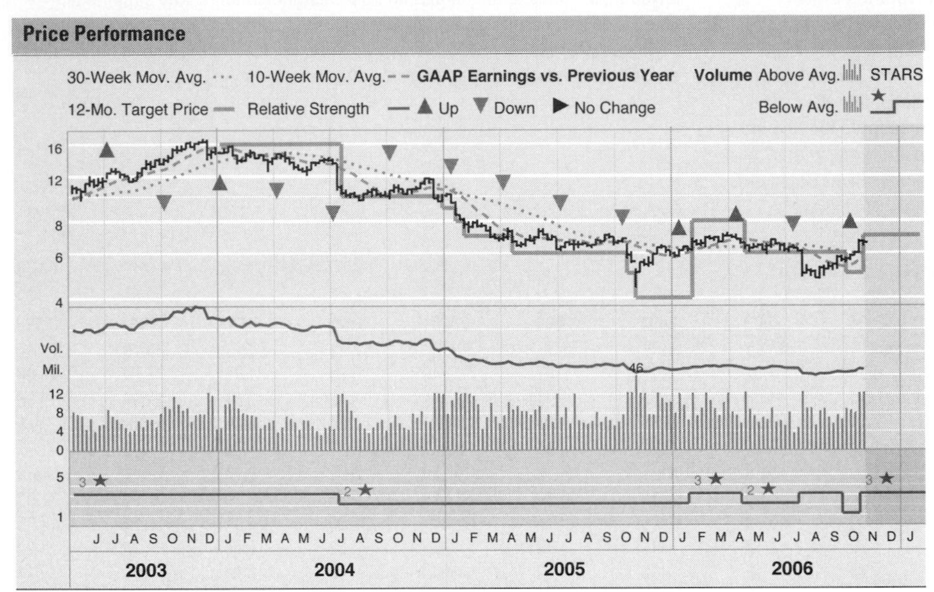

Options: ASE, CBOE, P, Ph

Analysis prepared by **Dylan Cathers** on October 27, 2006, when the stock traded at **$ 6.41**.

Highlights

- We expect revenues to be up 1% and 3% in 2006 and 2007, respectively, following a 1% decline in 2005. We think momentum in UIS's services business has begun to pick up, as it increased by 4% in the third quarter, but we see weakness persisting in its hardware segment, which we project will decline by roughly 10% this year. Revenues should also be affected by the gradual divestiture of non-core operations.
- We expect gross margins to narrow this year to about 16.5%, from 20% in 2005, due to expenses incurred from the company's cost-cutting activities, including the lay-off of 5,600 employees, and the inclusion of stock option expense. We look for cost savings, including the increased use of global sourcing, to help widen gross margins to 22% in 2007.
- We project an operating loss of $0.10 in 2006, excluding pension expenses. On an S&P Core EPS basis, we see a loss of $0.87 in 2006. In 2007, we expect earnings of $0.18 per share, including pension expenses. All estimates include the effect of stock option expense.

Investment Rationale/Risk

- We recently raised our opinion to hold, from strong sell, based on valuation. We believe the pace of UIS's contract wins is improving. We anticipate cost reductions materializing next year, though we expect UIS's high retirement expenses to persist, particularly in Europe. We think demand in the tech segment will continue to be a drag on revenues, although margins in the segment are improving. Further, UIS intends to expand its offshore presence to 6,000 workers by 2008.
- Risks to our recommendation and target price include more intense competition in the outsourcing and IT services space, a further slackening in demand for the company's server and software offerings, and a slower-than-expected reduction in costs from the ongoing restructuring program.
- Our 12-month target price of $7 is based on our discounted cash flow (DCF) analysis. Our DCF assumptions include a weighted average cost of capital of 11%, a free cash outflow in 2006 and 2007, but growth of about 9% over the next 15 years, and a terminal growth rate of 3%.

Qualitative Risk Assessment

LOW	MEDIUM	**HIGH**

Our risk assessment for Unisys centers around the highly competitive nature of the IT consulting and services market, as well as the weak demand for the company's technology offerings.

Quantitative Evaluations

S&P Quality Ranking **C**

D	**C**	B-	B	B+	A-	A	A+

Relative Strength Rank **STRONG**

90

LOWEST = 1 HIGHEST = 99

Revenue/Earnings Data

Revenue (Million $)

	1Q	2Q	3Q	4Q	Year
2006	1,388	1,407	1,410	--	--
2005	1,367	1,436	1,387	1,570	5,759
2004	1,463	1,388	1,446	1,524	5,821
2003	1,399	1,425	1,450	1,638	5,911
2002	1,363	1,360	1,332	1,553	5,607
2001	1,624	1,461	1,376	1,557	6,018

Earnings Per Share ($)

2006	-0.08	-0.57	-0.23	**E**0.09	**E**-0.10
2005	-0.13	-0.08	-4.78	-0.09	-5.09
2004	0.09	0.06	0.07	-0.10	0.11
2003	0.12	0.16	0.17	0.33	0.78
2002	0.10	0.13	0.18	0.27	0.69
2001	0.22	0.09	0.07	-0.53	-0.16

Fiscal year ended Dec. 31. Next earnings report expected: Late January. EPS Estimates based on S&P Operating Earnings; historical GAAP earnings are as reported.

Dividend Data

Common dividends, paid since 1895, were omitted in September 1990.

Unisys Corp

Business Summary October 27, 2006

CORPORATE OVERVIEW. Unisys is a technology services and solutions company, which operates through two business units: services and technology.

The services segment provides end-to-end services and solutions designed to help clients improve their competitiveness and efficiency in the global marketplace. UIS's portfolio of offerings includes systems integration and consulting; outsourcing, which includes the management of a customer's internal information systems and specific business processes such as payment processing, mortgage administration, and cargo management; infrastructure services involving the design, management and support of customer desktops, servers, mobile and wireless systems, and networks; and enterprise-wide security solutions to protect systems, networks, applications and data. Services revenue provide over 80% of total revenue.

The technology group develops servers and related products designed to operate in transaction intensive, mission critical environments. Major offerings include enterprise class servers; operating system software and middleware to power high-end servers; and specialized technologies, including payment systems, chip testing, and peripheral support products. The company has entered into a series of agreements with NEC in an effort to cut costs by sharing server technology, research and development, manufacturing, and solutions delivery. Revenues from the technology group account for less than one-fifth of the company's total revenues.

The primary vertical markets served by the company worldwide include financial services, communications, transportation, commercial, and the public sector, including the U.S. federal government. Products and services are marketed primarily through a direct sales force.

Company Financials

Per Share Data ($) Year Ended Dec. 31	**2005**	**2004**	**2003**	**2002**	**2001**	**2000**	**1999**	**1998**	**1997**	**1996**
Tangible Book Value	NM	3.88	3.65	2.12	6.06	6.89	6.29	0.38	NM	NM
Cash Flow	-3.99	1.27	1.81	1.16	0.79	1.63	2.51	2.04	1.39	0.91
Earnings	-5.09	0.11	0.78	0.69	-0.16	0.77	1.63	1.06	-5.30	-0.34
S&P Core Earnings	-5.21	-0.02	0.39	-0.56	-1.46	NA	NA	NA	NA	NA
Dividends	Nil	Nil	Nil	Nil	Nil	Nil	Nil	Nil	Nil	Nil
Payout Ratio	Nil	Nil	Nil	Nil	Nil	Nil	Nil	Nil	Nil	Nil
Prices:High	10.24	15.88	16.85	13.84	19.70	36.06	49.69	35.38	16.50	9.13
Prices:Low	4.38	9.50	8.25	5.92	7.70	9.13	20.94	13.31	5.75	5.38
P/E Ratio:High	NM	NM	22	20	NM	47	30	33	NM	NM
P/E Ratio:Low	NM	NM	11	9	NM	12	13	13	NM	NM

Income Statement Analysis (Million $)										
Revenue	5,759	5,821	5,911	5,607	6,018	6,885	7,545	7,208	6,636	6,371
Operating Income	212	359	770	578	298	698	1,226	1,076	1,722	556
Depreciation	374	394	343	155	302	271	265	266	1,218	228
Interest Expense	64.7	69.0	69.6	66.5	70.0	79.8	128	172	233	250
Pretax Income	-171	-76.0	381	333	-46.5	379	770	604	-759	93.7
Effective Tax Rate	NM	NM	32.0%	33.0%	NM	35.4%	32.1%	35.9%	NM	34.1%
Net Income	-1,732	38.6	259	223	-49.9	245	523	387	-854	61.8
S&P Core Earnings	-1,772	-7.26	132	-183	-463	NA	NA	NA	NA	NA

Balance Sheet & Other Financial Data (Million $)										
Cash	642	660	636	302	326	378	464	605	803	1,035
Current Assets	2,153	2,418	2,258	1,946	2,204	2,587	2,846	2,817	2,887	3,133
Total Assets	4,029	5,621	5,475	4,981	5,769	5,718	5,890	5,578	5,591	6,967
Current Liabilities	1,815	2,023	2,054	2,185	2,323	2,686	2,619	2,583	2,577	2,465
Long Term Debt	1,049	898	1,048	748	745	536	950	1,105	1,438	2,271
Common Equity	-32.6	1,507	1,395	856	2,113	2,186	1,953	97.0	-214	187
Total Capital	1,016	2,405	2,444	1,604	2,858	2,722	2,904	2,622	2,644	4,027
Capital Expenditures	256	315	251	196	199	198	220	207	302	162
Cash Flow	-1,358	433	601	378	252	516	751	546	253	157
Current Ratio	1.2	1.2	1.1	0.9	0.9	1.0	1.1	1.1	1.1	1.3
% Long Term Debt of Capitalization	103.2	37.4	42.9	46.6	26.1	19.7	32.7	42.1	54.4	56.4
% Net Income of Revenue	NM	NM	4.4	4.0	NM	3.6	6.9	5.4	NM	0.1
% Return on Assets	NM	NM	4.9	4.1	NM	4.2	9.1	6.9	NM	NM
% Return on Equity	NM	NM	23.0	15.0	NM	11.8	47.6	NA	NM	NM

Data as orig reptd.; bef. results of disc opers/spec. items. Per share data adj. for stk. divs.; EPS diluted. E-Estimated. NA-Not Available. NM-Not Meaningful. NR-Not Ranked. UR-Under Review.

Office: Unisys Way, Blue Bell, PA 19424
Telephone: 215-986-4011.
Website: http://www.unisys.com
Chrmn: H.C. Duques

Pres & CEO: J.W. McGrath
Vice Chrmn: G.R. Gazerwitz
SVP & CFO: J.B. Haugen
SVP, Secy & General Counsel: N.S. Sundheim

Investor Contact: J.F. McHale (215-986-4011)
Board of Directors: J. P. Bolduc, J. J. Duderstadt, H. C. Duques, M. J. Espe, D. K. Fletcher, R. J. Hogan, E. A. Huston, C. M. Jones, L. F. Kenne, T. E. Martin, J. W. McGrath, L. A. Weinbach

Founded: 1886
Domicile: Delaware
Employees: 36,100

UnitedHealth Group Inc

S&P Recommendation STRONG BUY ★★★★★

Price $48.78 (as of Oct 31, 2006)

12-Mo. Target Price $60.00

Investment Style Large-Cap Growth

GICS Sector Health Care
Sub-Industry Managed Health Care

Comment This leading health care services company provides health benefit services to more than 28.1 million individuals across the U.S.

Key Stock Statistics (Source S&P, Vickers, company reports)

52-Wk Range	$64.61–41.44	S&P Oper. EPS 2006E	2.80	P/E on S&P Oper. EPS 2006E	17.4	Dividend Rate/Share	$0.03
Trailing 12-Month EPS	$2.86	S&P Oper. EPS 2007E	3.42	Common Shares Outstg. (M)	1,347.0	Yield (%)	0.06
Trailing 12-Month P/E	17.1	S&P Core EPS 2006E	2.80	Market Capitalization(B)	$65.706	Beta	0.22
$10K Invested 5 Yrs Ago	$29,379	S&P Core EPS 2007E	3.42	Institutional Ownership (%)	86	S&P Credit Rating	A

Price Performance

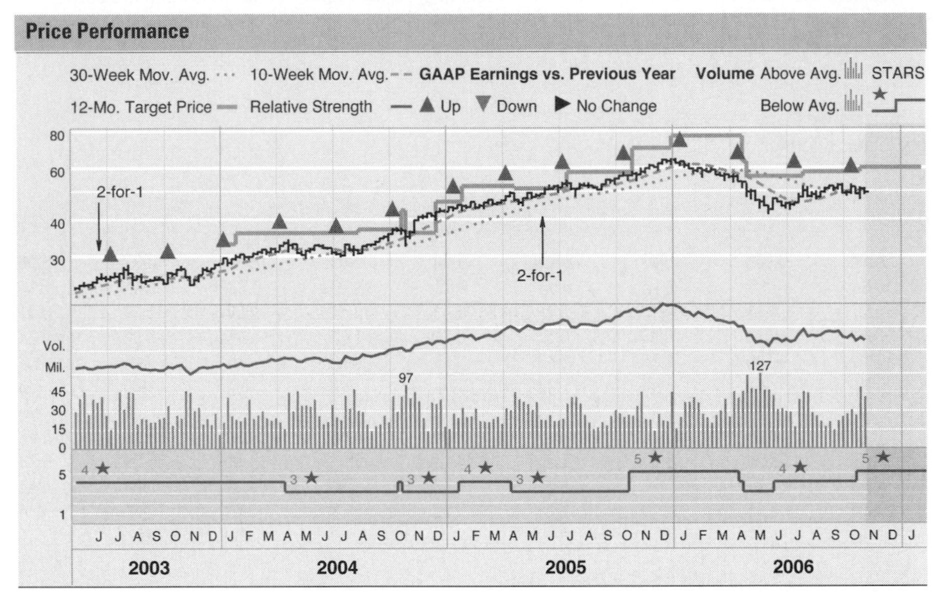

Options: ASE, CBOE, P

Analysis prepared by **Phillip M. Seligman** on October 23, 2006, when the stock traded at **$ 50.64**.

Highlights

- We project 2007 operating revenue (excluding investment and other income) of almost $79 billion, up from $71 billion we expect in 2006, driven by a premium yield that is above medical cost trends seen by UNH at 7% to 8%, strong growth of the Medicare and Medicaid businesses, and at least 3% self-funded commercial enrollment growth, offset by weak risk-based commercial enrollment growth.
- We expect 2007 medical cost trends to continue to moderate, mainly on increased generic drug usage, and assuming no health care provider (e.g., doctor or hospital) utilization run-up. We also expect the SG&A cost ratio to decline, with savings realized mainly on consolidation synergies and technology upgrades of almost $300 million in 2006 and another $300-plus million in 2007.
- For 2007, we see EPS of $3.42. That is 22% above our 2006 operating EPS estimate of $2.80, which is before $0.16 of favorable prior-year reserve development but includes $0.13 of projected stock option expense. In 2005, UNH reported operating EPS of $2.32, which excluded $0.19 of favorable prior-year reserve development and $0.12 of stock option expense.

Investment Rationale/Risk

- We are encouraged by UNH's strong operating performance and organic enrollment gains since year-end 2005 in all markets but risk-based commercial, partly due to competition and the repricing of PacifiCare accounts. We are also positive on UNH's cost-control focus, pricing discipline amid competition, and its strongly growing presence in the Medicare and Medicaid markets. Our corporate governance concerns have mostly dissipated with the board's recent moves to strengthen internal controls. We also view the stock option backdating overhang, and any legal and/or regulatory action against UNH that might stem from it, as one-time, and unlikely to hurt operations.
- Risks to our recommendation and target price include an unexpected medical cost rise, unfavorable regulatory changes, and unfavorable rulings from the investigations by the SEC, the IRS, the U.S. Attorney for the Southern District of New York, and the Minnesota attorney general concerning past stock option grants.
- By applying a peer-level 1.1X P/E to growth ratio, assuming 3-year EPS growth of 16%, to our 2007 EPS estimate, we derive our 12-month target price of $60.

Qualitative Risk Assessment

LOW | **MEDIUM** | HIGH

Our risk assessment reflects UNH's leadership in the highly fragmented managed care market and its wide geographic, market and product diversity that we believe permit stable operational performance even during periods of economic downturn. However, we see slowing commercial enrollment growth on an enlarging base and intensifying competition.

Quantitative Evaluations

S&P Quality Ranking A+

D | C | B- | B | B+ | A- | A | **A+**

Relative Strength Rank WEAK

25

LOWEST = 1 HIGHEST = 99

Revenue/Earnings Data

Revenue (Million $)

	1Q	2Q	3Q	4Q	Year
2006	17,586	17,917	18,008	--	--
2005	10,887	11,111	11,322	12,045	45,365
2004	8,144	8,704	9,859	10,511	37,218
2003	6,975	7,087	7,238	7,523	28,823
2002	6,013	6,078	6,247	6,682	25,020
2001	5,680	5,813	5,941	6,020	23,454

Earnings Per Share ($)

	1Q	2Q	3Q	4Q	Year
2006	0.63	0.70	0.79	**E**0.81	**E**2.80
2005	0.58	0.61	0.64	0.65	2.48
2004	0.44	0.47	0.52	0.55	1.97
2003	0.33	0.36	0.39	0.42	1.48
2002	0.23	0.25	0.28	0.30	1.07
2001	0.16	0.17	0.18	0.19	0.70

Fiscal year ended Dec. 31. Next earnings report expected: Mid January. EPS Estimates based on S&P Operating Earnings; historical GAAP earnings are as reported.

Dividend Data (Dates: mm/dd Payment Date: mm/dd/yy)

Amount ($)	Date Decl.	Ex-Div. Date	Stk. of Record	Payment Date
0.030	02/01	03/30	04/03	04/17/06

Dividends have been paid since 1990. Source: Company reports.

UnitedHealth Group Inc

Business Summary October 23, 2006

CORPORATE OVERVIEW. UnitedHealth Group, a U.S. leader in health care management, provides a broad range of health care products and services, including health maintenance organizations (HMOs), point of service (POS) plans, preferred provider organizations (PPOs), and managed fee for service programs.

The company reports results in four business segments, organized by product and/or market basis:

The Health Care Services segment (84% of 2005 revenues and 71% of operating earnings) consists of the following business units: UnitedHealthcare coordinates network-based health and well-being services on behalf of multistate mid-sized and local employers and for consumers. AmeriChoice facilitates and manages health care services for state Medicaid programs and their beneficiaries. Ovations delivers health and well-being services to Americans over the age of 50. At September 30, 2006, risk and fee-based health plan enrollment totaled 17,340,000 versus 16,495,000 on December 31, 2005, including risk-based commercial (9,850,000 versus 10,105,000), fee-based commercial (4,670,000 versus 3,990,000), Medicare Advantage (1,415,000 versus 1,150,000) and Medicaid (1,405,000 versus 1,250,000) members.

Uniprise (8% and 15%) provides network-based health services, consumer connectivity, and technology support services to large, self-insured accounts in return for administrative fees; it generally assumes no responsibility for health care costs. At September 30, 2006, segment enrollment was 10,990,000 versus 10,480,000.

Specialized Care Services (6% and 11%) offers a comprehensive array of specialized benefits, networks, services and resources.

Ingenix (2% and 3%) is a leader in the field of health care data, analysis and application, serving pharmaceutical companies, health insurers and other payers, physicians and other health care providers, large employers and governments. We view Ingenix as key to the other segments' competitive strengths.

Company Financials

Per Share Data ($) Year Ended Dec. 31	2005	2004	2003	2002	2001	2000	1999	1998	1997	1996
Tangible Book Value	NM	0.04	1.24	0.79	0.88	0.61	0.75	1.03	1.47	1.14
Cash Flow	2.82	2.26	1.72	1.26	0.90	0.73	0.56	-0.01	0.38	0.31
Earnings	2.48	1.97	1.48	1.07	0.70	0.55	0.40	-0.14	0.28	0.22
S&P Core Earnings	2.36	1.86	1.37	0.99	0.62	NA	NA	NA	NA	NA
Dividends	0.02	0.02	0.01	0.01	0.01	0.00	0.00	0.00	0.00	0.00
Payout Ratio	1%	1%	1%	1%	1%	1%	1%	NM	1%	2%
Prices:High	64.61	44.38	29.34	25.25	18.20	15.86	8.75	9.24	7.52	8.63
Prices:Low	42.63	27.73	19.60	16.96	12.63	5.80	4.92	3.70	5.30	3.75
P/E Ratio:High	26	23	20	24	26	29	22	NM	27	39
P/E Ratio:Low	17	14	13	16	18	11	12	NM	19	17

Income Statement Analysis (Million $)	2005	2004	2003	2002	2001	2000	1999	1998	1997	1996
Revenue	45,365	37,218	28,823	25,020	23,454	21,122	19,343	17,106	11,563	9,889
Operating Income	5,826	4,475	3,234	2,441	1,831	1,215	957	619	657	544
Depreciation	453	374	299	255	265	247	233	185	146	133
Interest Expense	241	128	95.0	90.0	94.0	72.0	49.0	4.00	NM	0.59
Pretax Income	5,132	3,973	2,840	2,096	1,472	1,155	894	-46.0	742	581
Effective Tax Rate	35.7%	34.9%	35.7%	35.5%	38.0%	36.3%	36.5%	NM	38.0%	38.7%
Net Income	3,300	2,587	1,825	1,352	913	736	568	-166	460	356
S&P Core Earnings	3,137	2,443	1,689	1,260	812	NA	NA	NA	NA	NA

Balance Sheet & Other Financial Data (Million $)	2005	2004	2003	2002	2001	2000	1999	1998	1997	1996
Cash	5,421	3,991	2,262	1,130	1,540	1,419	1,605	1,644	750	1,037
Current Assets	10,640	8,241	6,120	5,174	4,946	4,405	4,568	4,280	2,193	2,740
Total Assets	41,374	27,879	17,634	14,164	12,486	11,053	10,273	9,701	7,623	6,997
Current Liabilities	16,644	11,329	8,768	8,379	7,491	6,570	5,892	5,342	2,570	2,643
Long Term Debt	3,850	3,350	1,750	950	900	650	400	249	19.0	31.0
Common Equity	17,733	10,717	5,128	4,428	3,891	3,688	3,863	4,038	4,534	3,823
Total Capital	21,583	14,067	6,878	5,378	4,791	4,338	4,263	4,287	4,553	4,354
Capital Expenditures	5,876	350	352	419	425	245	196	210	187	165
Cash Flow	3,753	2,961	2,124	1,607	1,178	983	801	-9.00	577	460
Current Ratio	0.6	0.7	0.7	0.6	0.7	0.7	0.8	0.8	0.9	1.0
% Long Term Debt of Capitalization	17.8	23.8	25.4	17.7	18.8	15.0	9.4	5.8	0.4	0.7
% Net Income of Revenue	7.3	7.0	6.3	5.4	3.9	3.5	2.9	NM	4.0	3.6
% Return on Assets	9.5	11.4	11.5	10.1	7.8	6.9	5.7	NM	6.3	5.4
% Return on Equity	23.2	32.7	38.2	32.5	24.1	19.5	14.4	NM	10.3	9.3

Data as orig reptd.; bef. results of disc opers/spec. items. Per share data adj. for stk. divs.; EPS diluted. E-Estimated. NA-Not Available. NM-Not Meaningful. NR-Not Ranked. UR-Under Review.

Office: 9900 Bren Rd E, Minnetonka, MN 55343.
Telephone: 952-936-1300.
Website: http://www.unitedhealthgroup.com
Chrmn: R.T. Burke

Pres & COO: S.J. Hemsley
CEO: W.W. McGuire
Investor Contact: P.J. Erlandson (952-936-1300)

Board of Directors: W. C. Ballard, Jr., R. T. Burke, S. Hemsley, J. A. Johnson, T. H. Kean, D. W. Leatherdale, M. O. Mundinger, R. L. Ryan, D. E. Shalala, G. R. Wilensky

Founded: 1974
Domicile: Minnesota
Employees: 55,000

STANDARD &POOR'S

United Parcel Service Inc.

S&P Recommendation BUY ★★★★★

Price $74.87 (as of Oct 27, 2006)

12-Mo. Target Price $85.00

Investment Style Large-Cap Growth

GICS Sector Industrials
Sub-Industry Air Freight & Logistics

Comment UPS is the world's largest express delivery company, and has established itself as a facilitator of e-commerce.

Key Stock Statistics (Source S&P, Vickers, company reports)

52-Wk Range	$83.99–65.50	S&P Oper. EPS 2006E	3.85	P/E on S&P Oper. EPS 2006E	19.4	Dividend Rate/Share	$1.52
Trailing 12-Month EPS	$3.77	S&P Oper. EPS 2007E	4.30	Common Shares Outstg. (M)	1,081.0	Yield (%)	2.03
Trailing 12-Month P/E	19.9	S&P Core EPS 2006E	3.78	Market Capitalization(B)	$49.535	Beta	0.49
$10K Invested 5 Yrs Ago	$15,932	S&P Core EPS 2007E	4.22	Institutional Ownership (%)	65	S&P Credit Rating	AAA

Price Performance

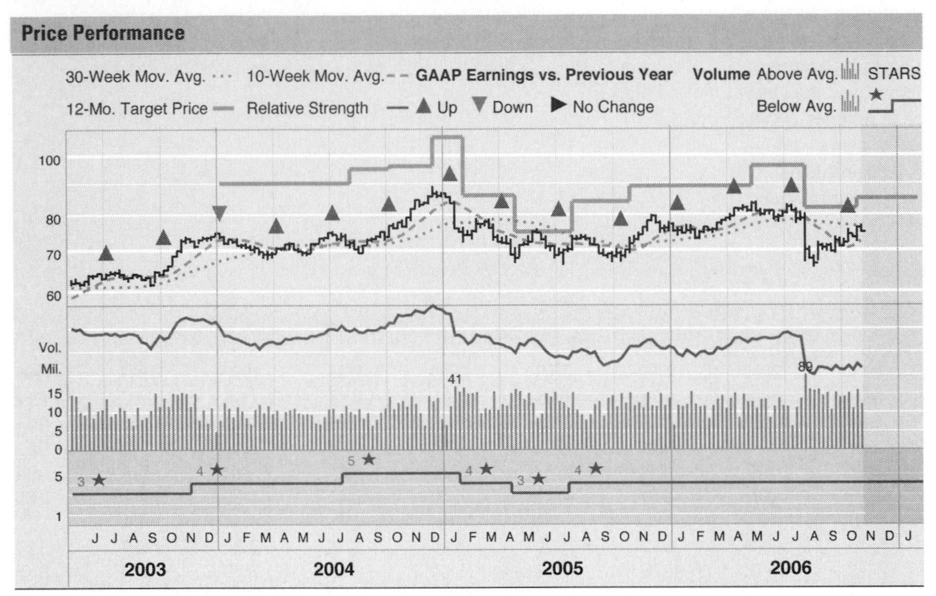

Options: ASE, CBOE, P, Ph

Analysis prepared by **Jim Corridore** on October 26, 2006, when the stock traded at **$ 75.50**.

Highlights

- We expect 2007 revenues to rise 10%, on top of the 12% growth we see for 2006. We expect international revenues to be up 15%, aided by strong export activity from China and other Asian regions. We see 5% domestic revenue growth, about equally distributed through express, deferred, and ground. We look for a general rate increase of about 2% for 2007. We foresee about 20% growth in the supply chain and freight segment.

- We expect operating margins to widen. We look for reduced workers compensation expense to partially offset rising wages and benefits. We also anticipate improved productivity and a better package mix. UPS's implementation of its package flow technology should be complete in 2007, and is targeted to save the company about $700 million annually. UPS is also implementing a restructuring program in its supply chain business, designed to save $100 million annually.

- We estimate 2007 EPS of $4.30 (including $0.05 of projected option expense), up 12% from our 2006 EPS estimate of $3.85. On a Standard & Poor's Core EPS basis, we forecast 2007 EPS of $4.22 and 2006 EPS of $3.78.

Investment Rationale/Risk

- We believe UPS will benefit from a strong global economy and export activity out of Asia. In our view, the company has a healthy balance sheet and generates a great deal of cash from operations, which it has used historically to increase its dividend rate and make acquisitions. An ongoing stock repurchase program has been successful in reducing the share count.

- Risks to our recommendation and target price include an economic slowdown, and a possible price war with competitors. Regarding corporate governance, we are concerned that Class A shareholders have 10 votes per share on many matters.

- Our 12-month target price is $85, valuing the stock at 20X our 2007 EPS estimate, near the low end of the company's five year historical P/E range of 18.9X-30.4X earnings, due to our concerns about a potential P/E contraction related to the later stage of the economic cycle. This is still a premium to the S&P 500, which we see as warranted by UPS's high returns on assets and what we view as strong cash flow from operations.

Qualitative Risk Assessment

LOW	MEDIUM	HIGH

Our risk assessment reflects what we see as: UPS's geographically diversified and growing revenue base, a strong balance sheet with ample cash, low debt relative to total capitalization, and a track record of earnings and cash flow growth.

Quantitative Evaluations

S&P Quality Ranking NR

D	C	B-	B	B+	A-	A	A+

Relative Strength Rank MODERATE

45

LOWEST = 1 HIGHEST = 99

Revenue/Earnings Data

Revenue (Million $)

	1Q	2Q	3Q	4Q	Year
2006	11,521	11,736	11,662	--	--
2005	9,886	10,191	10,550	11,954	42,581
2004	8,919	8,871	8,952	9,840	36,582
2003	8,015	8,226	8,312	8,932	33,485
2002	7,579	7,682	7,754	8,257	31,272
2001	7,510	7,566	7,481	8,089	30,646

Earnings Per Share ($)

	1Q	2Q	3Q	4Q	Year
2006	0.89	0.97	0.96	E1.03	E3.85
2005	0.78	0.88	0.86	0.95	3.47
2004	0.67	0.72	0.78	0.76	2.93
2003	0.54	0.61	0.65	0.75	2.55
2002	0.50	0.54	0.51	1.32	2.87
2001	0.48	0.55	0.50	0.57	2.12

Fiscal year ended Dec. 31. Next earnings report expected: Late January. EPS Estimates based on S&P Operating Earnings; historical GAAP earnings are as reported.

Dividend Data (Dates: mm/dd Payment Date: mm/dd/yy)

Amount ($)	Date Decl.	Ex-Div. Date	Stk. of Record	Payment Date
0.330	11/16	11/23	11/28	01/04/06
0.380	02/09	02/16	02/21	03/07/06
0.380	05/04	05/11	05/15	05/31/06
0.380	08/10	08/17	08/21	09/06/06

Dividends have been paid since 2000. Source: Company reports.

Please read the Required Disclosures and Analyst Certification on the last page of this report.

United Parcel Service Inc.

Business Summary October 26, 2006

United Parcel Service is the world's largest express and package delivery company. It is also a leading commerce facilitator, offering various logistics and financial services. The company, which was privately held since its founding in 1907, had its IPO of Class B stock in November 1999.

The company seeks to position itself as the primary coordinator of the flow of goods, information and funds throughout the entire supply chain (the movement from the raw materials and parts stage through final consumption of the finished product).

Domestic package delivery services accounted for 67% of revenues in 2005. About 84% of the 13.2 million daily domestic shipments handled by the company in 2005 was moved by its ground delivery service, which is available to every address in the 48 contiguous states in the U.S. Domestic air delivery is provided throughout the U.S., including next-day air, which is guaranteed by 10:30 a.m. to more than 75% of the U.S. population, and by noon to an additional 15% of the population.

UPS entered the international arena in 1975. In 2005, it handled 1.5 million international shipments per day. Its international package delivery service (19% of total revenues in 2005) is growing faster than its domestic business. UPS delivers international shipments to more than 200 countries and territories worldwide and provides delivery within one to two business days to the world's major business centers. Services include export (packages that cross national borders), and domestic (packages that stay within a single country's boundaries). UPS has a portfolio of domestic services in 20 major countries. Transborder services within the European Union is expected to continue to be a growth engine for the company. Asia continues to be an area in which UPS is investing in infrastructure and technology.

Company Financials

Per Share Data ($) Year Ended Dec. 31	**2005**	**2004**	**2003**	**2002**	**2001**	**2000**	**1999**	**1998**	**1997**	**1996**
Tangible Book Value	12.44	12.84	12.03	11.09	9.14	8.58	10.31	13.10	5.42	NA
Cash Flow	4.94	4.33	3.91	4.20	3.41	3.50	1.77	5.15	1.77	1.87
Earnings	3.47	2.93	2.55	2.87	2.12	2.50	0.77	1.57	0.81	1.01
S&P Core Earnings	3.40	2.87	2.46	2.48	1.70	NA	NA	NA	NA	NA
Dividends	1.32	1.12	0.92	0.76	0.76	0.81	Nil	NA	NA	NA
Payout Ratio	38%	38%	36%	26%	36%	32%	Nil	NA	NA	NA
Prices:High	85.84	89.11	74.87	67.10	62.50	69.75	76.94	NA	NA	NA
Prices:Low	66.10	67.51	53.00	54.25	46.15	49.50	50.00	NA	NA	NA
P/E Ratio:High	25	30	29	23	29	28	NM	NA	NA	NA
P/E Ratio:Low	19	23	21	19	22	20	NM	NA	NA	NA
Income Statement Analysis (Million $)										
Revenue	42,581	36,582	33,485	31,272	30,646	29,771	27,052	24,788	22,458	22,368
Operating Income	7,787	6,532	5,994	5,560	5,358	5,685	5,127	4,202	2,761	2,993
Depreciation	1,644	1,543	1,549	1,464	1,396	1,173	1,139	1,112	1,063	964
Interest Expense	172	149	121	173	184	205	228	227	187	95.0
Pretax Income	6,075	4,922	4,370	5,009	3,937	4,834	2,088	2,902	1,553	1,910
Effective Tax Rate	36.3%	32.3%	33.7%	35.0%	38.4%	39.3%	57.7%	40.0%	41.5%	40.0%
Net Income	3,870	3,333	2,898	3,254	2,425	2,934	883	1,741	909	1,146
S&P Core Earnings	3,784	3,261	2,790	2,820	1,948	NA	NA	NA	NA	NA
Balance Sheet & Other Financial Data (Million $)										
Cash	1,369	5,197	2,951	2,211	1,616	1,952	6,278	1,629	460	NA
Current Assets	11,003	12,605	9,853	8,738	7,597	7,124	11,138	5,425	4,477	NA
Total Assets	35,222	33,026	28,909	26,357	24,636	21,662	23,043	17,067	15,912	14,954
Current Liabilities	6,793	6,483	5,518	5,555	4,629	4,501	4,198	3,717	3,398	NA
Long Term Debt	3,159	3,261	3,149	3,495	4,648	2,981	1,912	2,191	2,583	2,573
Common Equity	16,884	16,384	14,852	12,455	10,248	9,735	12,474	7,598	6,087	5,901
Total Capital	20,043	25,027	18,001	15,950	14,896	12,716	14,386	9,789	8,676	8,474
Capital Expenditures	2,187	2,127	1,947	1,658	2,372	2,147	1,476	1,645	1,984	2,333
Cash Flow	5,514	4,876	4,447	4,718	3,821	4,107	2,022	2,853	1,972	2,110
Current Ratio	1.6	1.9	1.8	1.6	1.6	1.6	2.7	1.5	1.3	NA
% Long Term Debt of Capitalization	15.8	13.0	17.5	21.9	31.2	23.4	13.3	22.4	29.8	30.4
% Net Income of Revenue	9.1	9.1	8.7	10.4	7.9	9.9	3.3	7.0	4.0	5.1
% Return on Assets	11.3	10.6	10.5	12.8	10.5	13.1	4.4	10.6	5.9	8.3
% Return on Equity	23.3	21.3	21.2	28.7	24.3	26.4	8.8	25.4	21.0	20.7

Data as orig reptd.; bef. results of disc opers/spec. items. Per share data adj. for stk. divs.; EPS diluted. E-Estimated. NA-Not Available. NM-Not Meaningful. NR-Not Ranked. UR-Under Review.

Office: 55 Glenlake Parkway N.E., Atlanta, GA 30328.
Telephone: 404-828-6000.
Website: http://www.shareholder.com/ups
Chrmn & CEO: M. Eskew

COO & SVP: J. Beystehner
Investor Contact: D.S. Davis (404-828-6000)
SVP, CFO & Treas: D.S. Davis
SVP, Secy & General Counsel: T.P. McClure

Board of Directors: J. Beystehner, M. J. Burns, S. Davis, S. E. Eizenstat, M. L. Eskew, J. P. Kelly, A. M. Livermore, G. E. MacDougal, V. A. Pelson, J. W. Thompson, C. B. Tome, B. Verwaayen

Founded: 1907
Domicile: Delaware
Employees: 407,000

U.S. Bancorp

STANDARD &POOR'S

S&P Recommendation HOLD ★★★★★

Price $34.00 (as of Oct 27, 2006)

12-Mo. Target Price $35.00

Investment Style Large-Cap Value

GICS Sector Financials
Sub-Industry Diversified Banks

Comment This bank holding company was formed through the February 2001 merger of Minneapolis-based U.S. Bancorp and Milwaukee-based Firstar Corp.

Key Stock Statistics (Source S&P, Vickers, company reports)

52-Wk Range	$34.15–28.54	S&P Oper. EPS 2006E	2.63	P/E on S&P Oper. EPS 2006E	12.9	Dividend Rate/Share	$1.32
Trailing 12-Month EPS	$2.57	S&P Oper. EPS 2007E	2.85	Common Shares Outstg. (M)	1,777.2	Yield (%)	3.88
Trailing 12-Month P/E	13.2	S&P Core EPS 2006E	2.61	Market Capitalization(B)	$60.424	Beta	0.96
$10K Invested 5 Yrs Ago	$22,506	S&P Core EPS 2007E	2.84	Institutional Ownership (%)	56	S&P Credit Rating	AA-

Price Performance

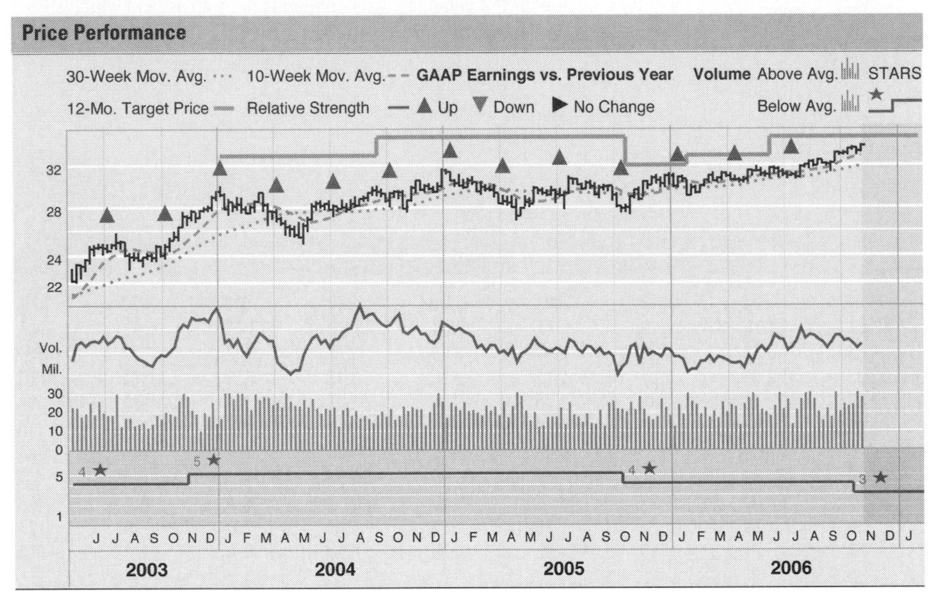

Options: ASE, CBOE, Ph

Analysis prepared by **Mark Hebeka, CFA** on October 24, 2006, when the stock traded at **$ 33.54**.

Highlights

- We expect continued healthy loan growth to drive net interest income growth through 2007. We believe that USB is one of the most profitable large cap banks in terms of returns on equity and assets. This reflects, in our view, the company's focus on revenue growth and cost controls, and what we see as its attractive mix of high-margin fee businesses.
- We look for revenues and earnings to grow steadily in 2006 and 2007, in line with the higher middle market and corporate commercial loan growth that we expect. We think that USB is likely to remain an active acquirer of its common stock based on announced stock repurchase authorizations, excess levels of capital, and the company's stated commitment to return at least 80% of earnings to shareholders.
- We see operating EPS increasing to an estimated $2.63 in 2006 from $2.42 in 2005, and to $2.85 for 2007, aided by what we expect to be a healthy U.S. economy and growing commercial loan demand.

Investment Rationale/Risk

- We believe that the company's diversified revenue model of economically sensitive businesses, combined with our projection of accelerating growth in commercial lending and USB's strong focus on expense management, should generate above industry average profitability, revenue and earnings growth in a strong economy.
- Risks to our recommendation and target price include a severe economic downturn in combination with higher short-term interest rates that could result in an inverted yield curve, a marked decline in consumer spending, a significant deterioration in credit quality, legal and regulatory risks, and any serious event that could hurt U.S. equity markets.
- Our 12-month target price of $35 is supported by our multi-stage dividend discount model, which assumes longer-term EPS growth of 8.5% annually and a discount rate of approximately 8.7%. Our target price is equivalent to a P/E of about 12.3X our 2007 EPS estimate.

Qualitative Risk Assessment

LOW	MEDIUM	HIGH

Our risk assessment for U.S. Bancorp reflects our view of the company's solid fundamentals, along with good geographic and product diversification. We think USB may sustain a downturn in the U.S. economy better than many peers.

Quantitative Evaluations

S&P Quality Ranking B+

D	C	B-	B	B+	A-	A	A+

Relative Strength Rank MODERATE

56

LOWEST = 1 HIGHEST = 99

Revenue/Earnings Data

Revenue (Million $)

	1Q	2Q	3Q	4Q	Year
2006	4,505	4,773	4,897	--	--
2005	3,817	4,106	4,294	4,379	16,596
2004	3,576	3,478	3,827	3,825	14,706
2003	3,697	3,801	3,489	3,584	14,571
2002	3,690	3,813	3,978	3,492	15,422
2001	4,420	4,154	4,026	3,843	16,443

Earnings Per Share ($)

2006	0.63	0.66	--	E0.68	E2.63
2005	0.57	0.60	0.62	0.62	2.42
2004	0.52	0.54	0.56	0.56	2.18
2003	0.46	0.48	0.49	0.50	1.92
2002	0.41	0.43	0.45	0.44	1.73
2001	0.21	0.29	0.02	0.36	0.88

Fiscal year ended Dec. 31. Next earnings report expected: Mid January. EPS Estimates based on S&P Operating Earnings; historical GAAP earnings are as reported.

Dividend Data (Dates: mm/dd Payment Date: mm/dd/yy)

Amount ($)	Date Decl.	Ex-Div. Date	Stk. of Record	Payment Date
0.330	12/20	12/28	12/30	01/16/06
0.330	03/21	03/29	03/31	04/17/06
0.330	06/20	06/28	06/30	07/17/06
0.330	09/19	09/27	09/30	10/16/06

Dividends have been paid since 1863. Source: Company reports.

U.S. Bancorp

Business Summary October 24, 2006

CORPORATE OVERVIEW. USB consists of several major lines of business, which include wholesale banking, consumer banking, private client, trust and asset management, payment services, and treasury and corporate support. Wholesale banking offers lending, depository, treasury management and other financial services to middle market, large corporate and public sector clients. Consumer banking delivers products and services through banking offices, telephone servicing and sales, on-line services, direct mail and ATMs. It encompasses community banking, metropolitan banking, in-store banking, small business banking, including lending guaranteed by the Small Business Administration, small-ticket leasing, consumer lending, mortgage banking, consumer finance, workplace banking, student banking, 24-hour banking and investment product and insurance sales.

Private client, trust and asset management provides trust, custody, private banking, financial advisory, investment management and mutual fund servicing through five businesses: private client group, corporate trust, FAF Advisors, institutional trust and custody and fund services. Payment services includes consumer and business credit cards, stored-value cards, debit cards, corporate and purchasing card services, consumer lines of credit, ATM processing and merchant processing.

CORPORATE STRATEGY. USB has several goals in order to achieve long-term success, including: 10% plus EPS growth, a 20% plus ROE, reducing credit and earnings volatility, providing high-quality customer service, investing in future growth, and targeting 80% return of earnings to shareholders. In banking, USB is maintaining what we view as its low-cost, highly efficient model and plans to grow organically and through smaller, fill-in acquisitions in higher growth markets.

Company Financials

Per Share Data ($) Year Ended Dec. 31	**2005**	**2004**	**2003**	**2002**	**2001**	**2000**	**1999**	**1998**	**1997**	**1996**
Tangible Book Value	5.62	5.87	5.77	4.93	4.64	7.11	4.66	5.38	NA	NA
Earnings	2.42	2.18	1.92	1.73	0.88	1.32	0.87	0.65	0.78	0.64
S&P Core Earnings	2.41	2.16	1.89	1.59	0.66	NA	NA	NA	NA	NA
Dividends	1.23	1.02	0.86	0.78	0.75	0.65	0.40	Nil	NA	NA
Payout Ratio	51%	47%	45%	45%	85%	49%	46%	Nil	NA	NA
Prices:High	31.36	31.65	30.00	24.50	26.06	28.00	35.33	31.31	NA	NA
Prices:Low	26.80	24.89	18.56	16.05	16.50	15.38	19.56	23.50	NA	NA
P/E Ratio:High	13	15	16	14	30	21	41	48	NA	NA
P/E Ratio:Low	11	11	10	9	19	12	22	36	NA	NA

Income Statement Analysis (Million $)	2005	2004	2003	2002	2001	2000	1999	1998	1997	1996
Net Interest Income	7,055	7,111	7,189	6,840	6,409	2,699	2,643	1,413	1,366	1,243
Tax Equivalent Adjustment	33.0	28.6	28.2	36.6	55.9	45.1	54.3	43.3	40.6	39.1
Non Interest Income	6,151	5,624	5,068	5,569	5,030	1,505	1,388	859	770	643
Loan Loss Provision	666	670	1,254	1,349	2,529	222	187	114	124	97.0
% Expense/Operating Revenue	44.3%	45.3%	45.7%	83.7%	57.5%	55.0%	59.9%	65.7%	57.3%	61.6%
Pretax Income	6,571	6,176	5,651	5,103	2,634	1,927	1,413	638	785	624
Effective Tax Rate	31.7%	32.5%	34.4%	34.8%	35.2%	31.4%	38.0%	32.6%	34.0%	33.4%
Net Income	4,489	4,167	3,710	3,326	1,707	1,284	875	430	519	415
% Net Interest Margin	3.97	4.25	4.49	4.61	4.45	4.73	4.83	4.46	NA	NA
S&P Core Earnings	4,470	4,135	3,655	3,062	1,280	NA	NA	NA	NA	NA

Balance Sheet & Other Financial Data (Million $)	2005	2004	2003	2002	2001	2000	1999	1998	1997	1996
Money Market Assets	Nil	Nil	Nil	1,332	1,607	200	897	2.75	150	NA
Investment Securities	39,768	41,481	43,334	28,488	26,608	13,866	13,114	6,432	7,196	NA
Commercial Loans	71,405	67,758	65,768	68,811	71,703	28,498	26,198	15,241	NA	NA
Other Loans	66,401	58,557	52,467	47,440	42,702	25,208	24,428	10,627	NA	NA
Total Assets	209,465	195,104	189,286	180,027	171,390	77,585	72,788	38,476	37,100	NA
Demand Deposits	32,214	30,756	32,470	35,106	31,212	10,980	10,300	10,498	6,181	NA
Time Deposits	92,495	89,985	86,582	80,428	74,007	45,298	41,586	18,353	21,658	NA
Long Term Debt	37,069	22,807	33,816	31,582	28,542	3,877	5,038	1,709	1,371	NA
Common Equity	20,086	19,539	19,242	18,101	16,461	6,528	6,309	3,530	3,185	NA
% Return on Assets	2.2	2.2	2.0	1.9	1.0	1.7	1.2	1.2	NA	NA
% Return on Equity	22.7	21.5	19.7	19.2	10.8	20.0	13.6	13.7	NA	NA
% Loan Loss Reserve	1.5	1.6	2.0	2.0	2.1	1.3	1.4	1.5	1.6	NA
% Loans/Deposits	111.9	105.8	100.5	100.6	111.4	95.4	98.8	89.7	NA	NA
% Equity to Assets	9.8	10.1	10.2	9.8	9.4	8.5	8.8	8.8	NA	NA

Data as orig reptd.; bef. results of disc opers/spec. items. Per share data adj. for stk. divs.; EPS diluted. E-Estimated. NA-Not Available. NM-Not Meaningful. NR-Not Ranked. UR-Under Review.

Office: 800 Nicollet Mall, Minneapolis, MN 55402-7000.
Telephone: 651-466-3000.
Website: http://www.usbank.com
Chrmn & CEO: J.A. Grundhofer

Pres, Vice Chrmn & COO: R.K. Davis
Vice Chrmn: A. Cecere
Vice Chrmn: R. Hartnack
Vice Chrmn: J. Otting

Investor Contact: J.T. Murphy (612-303-0783)
Board of Directors: A. D. Collins, Jr., P. H. Coors, R. K. Davis, V. B. Gluckman, J. A. Grundhofer, J. W. Johnson, O. F. Kirtley, J. W. Levin, D. B. O'Maley, O. M. Owens, R. G. Reiten, C. D. Schnuck, W. R. Staley, P. T. Stokes

Founded: 1929
Domicile: Delaware
Employees: 49,684

STANDARD &POOR'S

United States Steel Corp

S&P Recommendation BUY ★★★★★

Price $67.60 (as of Oct 31, 2006)

12-Mo. Target Price $84.00

Investment Style Mid-Cap Value

GICS Sector Materials
Sub-Industry Steel

Comment This company, based in Pittsburgh, manufactures and sells a wide variety of steel sheet, plate, tubular and tin products, coke, and taconite pellets.

Key Stock Statistics (Source S&P, Vickers, company reports)

52-Wk Range	$77.77–36.68	S&P Oper. EPS 2006E	10.92	P/E on S&P Oper. EPS 2006E	6.2	Dividend Rate/Share	$0.80
Trailing 12-Month EPS	$9.54	S&P Oper. EPS 2007E	8.25	Common Shares Outstg. (M)	123.1	Yield (%)	1.18
Trailing 12-Month P/E	7.1	S&P Core EPS 2006E	11.42	Market Capitalization(B)	$8.320	Beta	2.63
$10K Invested 5 Yrs Ago	$45,876	S&P Core EPS 2007E	NA	Institutional Ownership (%)	92	S&P Credit Rating	BB

Price Performance

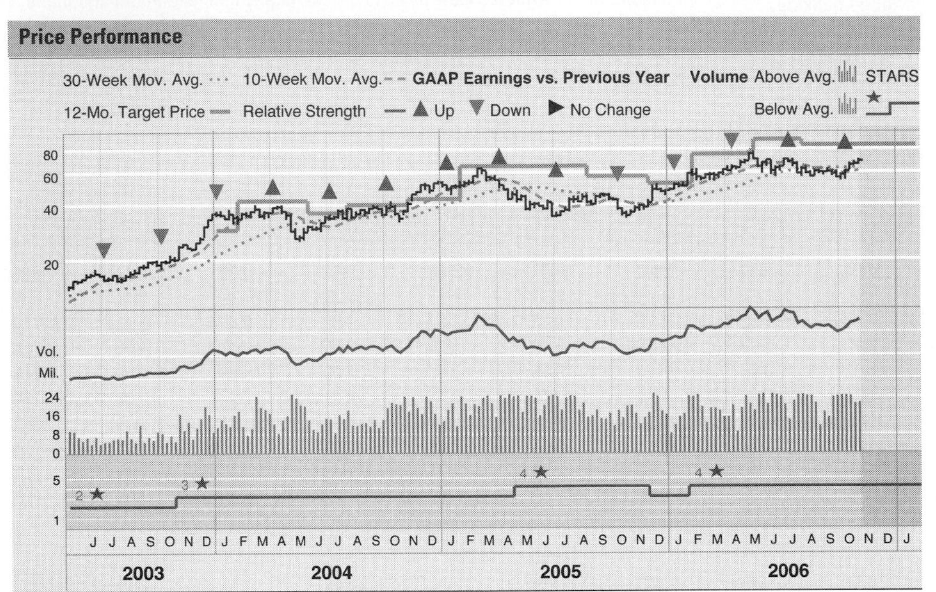

Options: ASE, CBOE

Analysis prepared by **Leo J. Larkin** on July 28, 2006, when the stock traded at **$ 62.21**.

Highlights

- We look for a 9.0% sales gain in 2006, reflecting a forecasted rebound in shipments of domestic flat roll steel, continued strength in tubular goods, another increase in European volume and a small gain in average realized price per ton. We expect that rebuilding of inventories by distributors in the U.S. and stronger demand in Europe will lift volume from 2005's depressed levels. In our view, inventory liquidation in 2005 was excessive, and we look for distributors to add to inventories through most of 2006. Also, shipments in 2005 were constrained by scheduled outages in both the U.S. and Europe. We do not expect this situation to recur in 2006, and this should boost volume.

- Aided by higher volume, much lower costs for maintenance outages, less rapidly rising costs for raw materials and lower interest expense, we look for an increase in EPS to $10.70 in 2006.

- We think X's long-term sales and EPS will benefit from consolidation of the global steel industry and a gradual decline in costs for employee pension and health care.

Investment Rationale/Risk

- Since 2003, X has made substantial progress in regaining profitability and becoming free cash flow positive. While a rebound in steel prices helped X return to the black, EPS and free cash flow in 2004 were far above the most recent industry peak in 1995. Also, despite lower EPS, X remained solidly free cash flow positive in 2005 even with higher capital spending and implementation of a share buyback. This improvement is a function, we think, of well executed mergers and more efficient use of capital.

- Risks to our recommendation and target price include asbestos liabilities. In 2003, X incurred litigation expenses totaling $25 million to settle an asbestos-related lawsuit. While the 2003 settlement could prove to be an aberration, we see it as a cause for some caution.

- We believe that X should trade at about 7.9X our 2006 estimate of $10.70. At 7.9X, the P/E would be at the lower end of the historical range. In our view, 2006 could represent peak of cycle EPS and we believe that this perception will result in a low multiple. Based on our projected P/E, our 12-month target price is $84.

Qualitative Risk Assessment

LOW | MEDIUM | **HIGH**

Our risk assessment reflects the exposure of X's sales and EPS to highly cyclical industries such as autos and construction. While X has reduced debt and improved its free cash flow generation, the company's unfunded pension and heath care liabilities totaled $2.9 billion at the end of 2005.

Quantitative Evaluations

S&P Quality Ranking B-

D | C | **B-** | B | B+ | A- | A | A+

Relative Strength Rank STRONG

78

LOWEST = 1 HIGHEST = 99

Revenue/Earnings Data

Revenue (Million $)

	1Q	2Q	3Q	4Q	Year
2006	3,728	4,107	4,106	--	--
2005	3,787	3,582	3,200	3,470	14,039
2004	2,963	3,466	3,729	3,932	14,108
2003	1,907	2,362	2,508	2,681	9,458
2002	1,434	1,807	1,914	1,899	7,054
2001	1,564	1,737	1,660	1,414	6,375

Earnings Per Share ($)

2006	2.04	3.22	3.42	**E**2.14	**E**10.92
2005	3.51	1.91	0.71	0.85	7.00
2004	0.36	1.62	2.72	3.59	8.37
2003	-0.35	-0.01	-3.47	-0.26	-4.09
2002	-0.93	0.28	1.04	0.10	0.62
2001	-0.10	-0.34	-0.26	-1.95	-2.45

Fiscal year ended Dec. 31. Next earnings report expected: Early February. EPS Estimates based on S&P Operating Earnings; historical GAAP earnings are as reported.

Dividend Data (Dates: mm/dd Payment Date: mm/dd/yy)

Amount ($)	Date Decl.	Ex-Div. Date	Stk. of Record	Payment Date
0.100	10/25	11/14	11/16	12/10/05
0.100	01/31	02/13	02/15	03/10/06
0.150	04/25	05/15	05/17	06/10/06
0.200	07/25	11/13	11/15	12/09/06

Dividends have been paid since 1991. Source: Company reports.

United States Steel Corp

Business Summary July 28, 2006

CORPORATE OVERVIEW. U.S. Steel is the second largest integrated steel company in the U.S. and has operations in Central Europe. In 2005, X produced 15.3 million tons in the U.S. and 5.9 million in Europe.

MARKET PROFILE. The primary factor affecting demand for steel products is economic growth in general, and growth in demand for durable goods in particular. The two largest end markets for steel products in the U.S. are autos and construction, which together accounted for 27.9% of shipments in 2005. Other end markets include appliances, containers, machinery, and oil and gas. Distributors, also known as service centers, accounted for 22.4% of industry shipments in the U.S. in 2005. Distributors are the largest single market for the steel industry in the U.S. Because distributors sell to a wide variety of OEMs, it is impossible to trace the final destination of much of the industry's shipments. Consequently, consumption of steel by the auto, construction and other industries may be higher than the shipment data would suggest. U.S. production was 102.8 million tons in 2005, and X's market share was 15%. X's largest end markets were distributors (22% of revenues), converters (24%), construction (11%), automotive (14%), containers (9%), oil and gas (6%), and other (16%). U.S. consumption in 1996-2005 increased at a compound annual growth rate (CAGR) of 0.5%. Global steel production was 1.19 billion tons in 2005, and consumption in 1995-2004 grew at a CAGR of 4.6%.

Company Financials

Per Share Data ($) Year Ended Dec. 31	**2005**	**2004**	**2003**	**2002**	**2001**	**2000**	**1999**	**1998**	**1997**	**1996**
Tangible Book Value	25.63	32.30	7.98	15.81	28.16	21.54	23.22	22.22	18.78	14.38
Cash Flow	11.54	11.17	0.57	4.24	1.42	3.72	3.03	6.72	7.09	6.49
Earnings	7.00	8.37	-4.09	0.62	-2.45	-0.33	0.48	3.92	4.88	3.00
S&P Core Earnings	6.64	8.74	-1.06	-4.10	-8.47	NA	NA	NA	NA	NA
Dividends	0.28	0.20	0.20	0.20	0.55	1.00	1.00	1.00	1.00	1.00
Payout Ratio	4%	2%	NM	32%	NM	NM	NM	26%	20%	33%
Prices:High	63.90	54.06	37.05	22.00	22.00	32.94	34.25	43.06	40.75	37.88
Prices:Low	33.59	25.22	9.61	10.66	13.00	12.69	21.75	20.44	25.38	24.13
P/E Ratio:High	9	6	NM	35	NM	NM	71	11	8	13
P/E Ratio:Low	5	3	NM	17	NM	NM	45	5	5	8

Income Statement Analysis (Million $)										
Revenue	14,039	14,108	9,458	7,054	6,375	6,090	5,380	6,189	6,814	6,547
Operating Income	1,740	1,064	316	470	61.0	422	520	703	940	852
Depreciation	366	382	363	350	344	360	304	283	303	292
Interest Expense	107	138	148	136	153	115	75.0	53.0	98.0	128
Pretax Income	1,312	1,461	-860	13.0	-546	-1.00	76.0	537	686	367
Effective Tax Rate	27.8%	24.0%	NM	NM	NM	NM	32.9%	32.2%	34.1%	25.1%
Net Income	910	1,077	-406	61.0	-218	-21.0	51.0	364	452	275
S&P Core Earnings	847	1,104	-109	-398	-755	NA	NA	NA	NA	NA

Balance Sheet & Other Financial Data (Million $)										
Cash	1,479	1,037	316	243	147	219	22.0	9.00	18.0	23.0
Current Assets	4,831	4,243	3,107	2,440	2,073	2,717	1,981	1,275	1,531	1,428
Total Assets	9,822	10,956	7,838	7,977	8,337	8,711	7,525	6,693	6,694	6,580
Current Liabilities	2,749	2,531	2,130	1,372	1,259	1,391	1,266	1,016	1,334	1,299
Long Term Debt	1,363	1,363	1,890	1,408	1,434	2,485	1,151	712	456	1,014
Common Equity	3,108	3,754	867	2,027	2,506	1,917	2,053	2,090	1,634	1,559
Total Capital	4,719	5,959	2,989	3,658	4,672	5,070	3,555	2,805	2,486	2,644
Capital Expenditures	741	579	316	258	287	244	287	310	261	337
Cash Flow	1,258	1,441	-59.0	411	126	331	346	638	742	545
Current Ratio	1.8	1.7	1.5	1.8	1.6	2.0	1.6	1.3	1.1	1.1
% Long Term Debt of Capitalization	28.9	22.9	63.2	38.5	30.7	49.0	32.4	25.4	18.3	38.4
% Net Income of Revenue	6.5	7.8	NM	0.9	NM	NM	0.9	5.9	6.6	4.2
% Return on Assets	8.7	11.5	NM	0.7	NM	NM	0.7	5.4	6.8	4.2
% Return on Equity	25.6	45.8	NM	2.7	NM	NM	2.0	18.4	31.7	17.5

Data as orig reptd.; bef. results of disc opers/spec. items. Per share data adj. for stk. divs.; EPS diluted. E-Estimated. NA-Not Available. NM-Not Meaningful. NR-Not Ranked. UR-Under Review.

Office: 600 Grant Street, Pittsburgh, PA 15219-2800.
Telephone: 412-433-1121.
Email: shareholderservices@uss.com
Website: http://www.ussteel.com

Chrmn, Pres & CEO: J.P. Surma, Jr.
Vice Chrmn, Chief Admin, Secy & General Counsel: D.D. Sandman
COO & EVP: J.H. Goodish
EVP & CFO: G.R. Haggerty

VP & Treas: L.T. Brockway
Investor Contact: N. Harper (412-433-1184)
Board of Directors: J. G. Cooper, R. J. Darnall, J. Drosdick, R. A. Gephardt, C. R. Lee, F. Lucchino, D. D. Sandman, S. E. Schofield, J. P. Surma, D. C. Yearley

Founded: 2001
Domicile: Delaware
Employees: 46,000

United Technologies Corp

STANDARD &POOR'S

S&P Recommendation HOLD ★★★★★

Price $64.94 (as of Oct 27, 2006)

12-Mo. Target Price $70.00

Investment Style Large-Cap Value

GICS Sector Industrials
Sub-Industry Aerospace & Defense

Comment This company's business portfolio includes Pratt & Whitney jet engines, Sikorsky helicopters, Otis elevators and Carrier air conditioners.

Key Stock Statistics (Source S&P, Vickers, company reports)

52-Wk Range	$67.47–50.69	S&P Oper. EPS 2006E	3.70	P/E on S&P Oper. EPS 2006E	17.6	Dividend Rate/Share	$1.06
Trailing 12-Month EPS	$3.56	S&P Oper. EPS 2007E	4.04	Common Shares Outstg. (M)	1,003.7	Yield (%)	1.63
Trailing 12-Month P/E	18.2	S&P Core EPS 2006E	3.62	Market Capitalization(B)	$65.177	Beta	1.01
$10K Invested 5 Yrs Ago	$24,642	S&P Core EPS 2007E	3.95	Institutional Ownership (%)	80	S&P Credit Rating	A

Price Performance

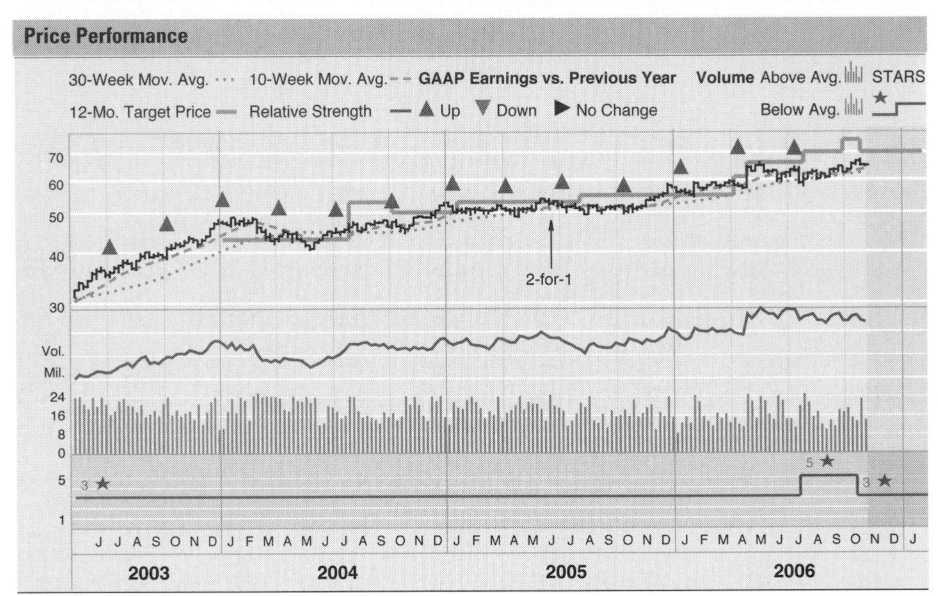

Options: ASE, CBOE, P, Ph

Analysis prepared by **Richard Tortoriello** on October 18, 2006, when the stock traded at **$ 65.27**.

Highlights

- We believe a combination of organic growth and acquisitions will lead to a 10% increase in 2006 revenues, following a 14% rise in 2005. We project further sales growth of about 8% for 2007. For 2007 we project strong, but slower, sales growth from Pratt & Whitney and Hamilton Sunstrand, healthy growth from Otis, UTC Fire & Security and Sikorsky, and much slower growth from Carrier, due to a slowdown in sales of U.S. residential housing.

- We see total segment operating margins rising to 13.1% in 2006, from 12.1% in 2005, aided by sales volume increases at UTX's operating segments. We believe that UTX has done a good job of passing along commodity price increases to customers without losing contracts. For 2007, we project stable or slightly higher margins for each of UTX's business segments.

- We project EPS of $3.70 in 2006, with growth to $4.04 in 2007. UTX had double-digit EPS growth in each of the past seven quarters. We note that free cash flow generation has been strong, with free cash flow per share near or above EPS for each of the past five years. We expect UTX to post cash flow per share in line with EPS in 2006.

Investment Rationale/Risk

- Given recent strong earnings gains and cash flow generation and continued share repurchases, we view UTX's fundamental position as positive. However, with valuations close to the high end of UTX's historical range, and our projection of much slower growth at Carrier and projected slower growth from very high levels at Pratt & Whitney and Hamilton Sundstrand, we believe the shares are likely to consolidate for some time before heading higher. As a result, we recently lowered our recommendation to hold from strong buy.

- Risks to our recommendation and target price include any unanticipated slowdown in growth of the global economy, competitive pressures in UTX's core businesses, as well as industry-specific slowdowns.

- Our 12-month target price of $70 is based on a P/E of about 17X our 2007 EPS estimate of $4.04. This is above an historical 10-year average forward P/E ratio of 16X, with a high of 22X and a low of 11X. Based on our three-year EPS growth projection of 15%, our target price implies a P/E to growth (PEG) ratio of 1.2X. This compares to our estimated PEG of about 1.2X for the S&P 500 based on 2007 estimates.

Qualitative Risk Assessment

LOW	MEDIUM	HIGH

Our risk assessment is based on our view of UTX's history of steady growth in both earnings and dividends over the past 10 years, as reflected in an S&P Quality Ranking of A+. We also consider UTX's balance sheet as clean, with 26% long-term debt to total capital and 6% cash to assets as of September 2006.

Quantitative Evaluations

S&P Quality Ranking A+

D	C	B-	B	B+	A-	A	A+

Relative Strength Rank MODERATE

46

LOWEST = 1 HIGHEST = 99

Revenue/Earnings Data

Revenue (Million $)

	1Q	2Q	3Q	4Q	Year
2006	10,615	12,264	12,163	--	--
2005	9,309	10,974	10,832	11,172	42,725
2004	8,646	9,622	9,339	8,938	37,445
2003	6,702	7,790	7,954	8,588	31,034
2002	6,374	7,324	7,299	7,215	28,212
2001	6,671	7,332	6,920	6,974	27,897

Earnings Per Share ($)

	1Q	2Q	3Q	4Q	Year
2006	0.76	1.09	E0.99	E0.86	E3.70
2005	0.64	0.95	0.81	0.71	3.12
2004	0.57	0.83	0.72	0.65	2.76
2003	0.50	0.63	0.64	0.58	2.35
2002	0.46	0.62	0.61	0.53	2.21
2001	0.43	0.58	0.56	0.35	1.92

Fiscal year ended Dec. 31. Next earnings report expected: Late January. EPS Estimates based on S&P Operating Earnings; historical GAAP earnings are as reported.

Dividend Data (Dates: mm/dd Payment Date: mm/dd/yy)

Amount ($)	Date Decl.	Ex-Div. Date	Stk. of Record	Payment Date
0.220	02/06	02/15	02/17	03/10/06
0.265	04/12	05/17	05/19	06/10/06
0.265	06/14	08/16	08/18	09/10/06
0.265	10/11	11/15	11/17	12/10/06

Dividends have been paid since 1936. Source: Company reports.

United Technologies Corp

Business Summary October 18, 2006

CORPORATE OVERVIEW. This multi-industry holding company conducts business through six business segments: Otis, Carrier, Pratt & Whitney, UTC Fire & Security, Hamilton Sundstrand, and Sikorsky.

Otis (22% of 2005 sales, 32% of operating profits, 18% operating margins) is the world's largest maker of elevators and escalators. Otis designs, manufactures, sells and installs a wide range of passenger and freight elevators for low-, medium-, and high-speed applications, as well as a broad line of escalators and moving walkways. International revenues were 80% of total segment revenues in 2005.

Carrier (29% of sales, 20% of operating profits, 9% operating margins) is the world's largest maker of commercial and residential heating, ventilating and air-conditioning (HVAC) systems. It also offers refrigeration and food service equipment, and related controls for residential, commercial, industrial and transportation applications. International sales, including U.S. export sales, accounted for 55% of segment sales in 2005.

Pratt & Whitney (22%, 27%, 6%), one of the world's "Big Three" jet engine makers, which generates about 22% of segment revenues from jet engine sales to Boeing and Airbus, also makes engines for military jet fighters and transports. Sales to Boeing and Airbus were about 9% and 13%, respectively, of segment sales in 2005. Aircraft spare parts and overhaul service operations are an important source of high-margin, recurring revenues. International revenues were 54% of total segment revenues in 2005.

UTC Fire & Security (10%, 4%, 6%) is a global provider of fire safety products and services. This segment was created in the second quarter of 2005 following the acquisition of Kidde plc, a provider of fire safety products and services to commercial, industrial, aerospace and retail customers in 29 countries. International sales accounted for 87% of total segment sales in 2005.

Company Financials

Per Share Data ($) Year Ended Dec. 31	**2005**	**2004**	**2003**	**2002**	**2001**	**2000**	**1999**	**1998**	**1997**	**1996**
Tangible Book Value	0.91	1.84	2.32	1.46	1.66	0.95	0.80	2.92	3.37	3.81
Cash Flow	4.09	3.73	3.14	2.93	2.81	2.63	1.66	2.13	1.86	1.68
Earnings	3.12	2.76	2.35	2.21	1.92	1.78	0.83	1.26	1.05	0.86
S&P Core Earnings	3.05	2.59	2.16	1.32	1.14	NA	NA	NA	NA	NA
Dividends	0.88	0.70	0.57	0.49	0.45	0.41	0.38	0.35	0.31	0.28
Payout Ratio	28%	25%	24%	22%	23%	23%	46%	28%	29%	32%
Prices:High	58.89	53.14	48.38	38.88	43.75	39.88	37.98	28.13	22.23	17.63
Prices:Low	48.43	40.34	26.76	24.42	20.05	23.25	25.81	16.75	16.28	11.31
P/E Ratio:High	19	19	21	18	23	22	46	22	21	20
P/E Ratio:Low	16	15	11	11	10	13	31	13	15	13

Income Statement Analysis (Million $)	2005	2004	2003	2002	2001	2000	1999	1998	1997	1996
Revenue	42,725	37,445	31,034	28,212	27,897	26,583	23,844	25,687	24,495	23,273
Operating Income	6,166	5,448	4,644	4,384	4,138	3,999	2,361	2,993	2,598	2,395
Depreciation	984	978	799	727	905	859	844	854	848	853
Interest Expense	498	363	375	381	426	382	260	204	195	237
Pretax Income	4,684	4,107	3,470	3,276	2,807	2,758	1,257	1,963	1,764	1,560
Effective Tax Rate	26.8%	26.4%	27.1%	27.1%	26.9%	30.9%	25.9%	31.7%	32.5%	33.5%
Net Income	3,164	2,788	2,361	2,236	1,938	1,808	841	1,255	1,072	906
S&P Core Earnings	3,089	2,619	2,147	1,298	1,113	NA	NA	NA	NA	NA

Balance Sheet & Other Financial Data (Million $)	2005	2004	2003	2002	2001	2000	1999	1998	1997	1996
Cash	2,247	2,265	1,623	2,080	1,558	748	957	550	755	1,127
Current Assets	17,206	15,522	12,364	11,751	11,263	10,662	10,627	9,355	9,248	9,611
Total Assets	45,925	40,035	34,648	29,090	26,969	25,364	24,366	18,375	16,719	16,745
Current Liabilities	15,345	12,947	10,295	7,903	8,371	9,344	9,215	7,735	7,311	7,390
Long Term Debt	5,935	4,231	4,257	4,632	4,237	3,476	3,086	1,575	1,275	1,437
Common Equity	16,991	14,008	11,707	10,506	8,369	7,662	7,117	3,998	3,658	4,306
Total Capital	23,704	19,149	16,673	16,445	13,899	12,514	11,664	6,994	6,362	6,810
Capital Expenditures	929	795	530	586	793	937	762	866	843	794
Cash Flow	4,148	3,766	3,160	2,963	2,843	2,667	1,685	2,109	1,888	1,753
Current Ratio	1.1	1.2	1.2	1.5	1.3	1.1	1.2	1.2	1.3	1.3
% Long Term Debt of Capitalization	25.0	22.1	25.5	28.2	30.5	27.8	26.5	22.5	20.0	21.1
% Net Income of Revenue	7.4	7.4	7.6	7.9	6.9	6.8	3.5	4.9	4.4	3.9
% Return on Assets	7.3	7.4	7.4	8.0	7.4	7.3	4.0	7.2	6.4	5.5
% Return on Equity	20.2	21.7	23.9	23.0	24.2	24.5	14.6	32.8	27.7	21.6

Data as orig reptd.; bef. results of disc opers/spec. items. Per share data adj. for stk. divs.; EPS diluted. E-Estimated. NA-Not Available. NM-Not Meaningful. NR-Not Ranked. UR-Under Review.

Office: 1 Financial Plz, Hartford, CT 06103.
Telephone: 860-728-7000.
Email: invrelations@corphq.utc.com
Website: http://www.utc.com

Chrmn, Pres & CEO: G.A. David
Pres & COO: L. Chenevert
Investor Contact: T. Rogan (860-728-7912)
VP & Treas: T. Rogan

VP & Secy: D. Valentine
Board of Directors: L. Chenevert, G. A. David, J. V. Faraci, J. Garnier, J. S. Gorelick, C. R. Lee, R. D. McCormick, H. McGraw III, R. B. Myers, F. P. Popoff, H. P. Swygert, A. Villeneuve, H. A. Wagner, C. T. Whitman

Founded: 1934
Domicile: Delaware
Employees: 222,200

Univision Communications Inc.

STANDARD &POOR'S

S&P Recommendation	Price	12-Mo. Target Price	Investment Style
HOLD ★★★★★	$35.01 (as of Oct 27, 2006)	$37.00	Mid-Cap Growth

GICS Sector Consumer Discretionary
Sub-Industry Broadcasting & Cable TV

Comment Univision Communications is the nation's leading U.S. Spanish-language television and radio broadcasting media company, with other growing related music and online assets.

Key Stock Statistics (Source S&P, Vickers, company reports)

52-Wk Range	$36.67–25.69	S&P Oper. EPS 2006E	1.08	P/E on S&P Oper. EPS 2006E	32.4	Dividend Rate/Share	Nil
Trailing 12-Month EPS	$0.79	S&P Oper. EPS 2007E	1.25	Common Shares Outstg. (M)	306.0	Yield (%)	Nil
Trailing 12-Month P/E	44.3	S&P Core EPS 2006E	1.08	Market Capitalization(B)	$8.318	Beta	1.87
$10K Invested 5 Yrs Ago	$12,634	S&P Core EPS 2007E	1.25	Institutional Ownership (%)	83	S&P Credit Rating	BB-

Price Performance

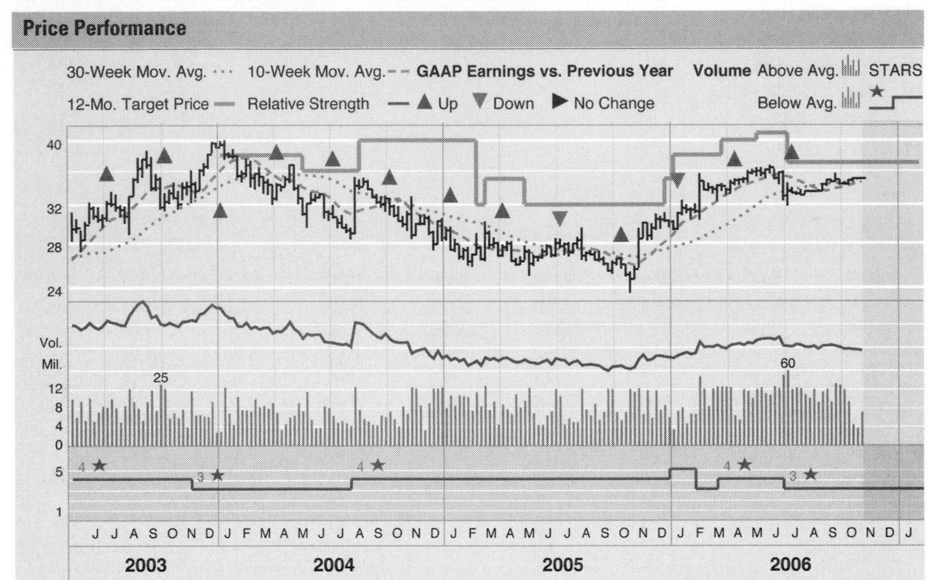

Options: ASE, CBOE

Analysis prepared by **Tuna N. Amobi, CFA, CPA** on August 08, 2006, when the stock traded at **$ 33.44**.

Highlights

➤ We estimate that 2006 consolidated revenues will rise about 15%, fueled by incremental gains from the soccer World Cup. We see 12% total revenue growth in 2007, helped by likely strong gains for the Univision network at the 2006-07 upfront. We see continued strong ratings across the TV and radio properties, and expect UVN to further outpace the broadcast industry in both local and national advertising sales, with gains in several key categories such as packaged goods, automotive, retail and pharmaceuticals. We also see steady growth at the smaller music and nascent online businesses.

➤ We expect margins to benefit from a TV segment restructuring in late 2005, and from new cross-platform deals across TV and radio assets. We forecast adjusted EBITDA of about $800 million in 2006 (with about neutral impact for the World Cup), and $900 million in 2007.

➤ With a projected 40% effective tax rate, we forecast EPS of $1.08 and $1.25 in 2006 and 2007, respectively, including about $0.05 of estimated stock option expense in each year.

Investment Rationale/Risk

➤ In late June 2006, UVN accepted a $13.7 billion buyout offer for $36.25 per share in cash (a 13% premium on the previous day's close), plus $1.6 billion of assumed debt, pending approvals. We saw a valuation somewhat shy of UVN's target, but noted a key milestone on the auction of this leading Spanish media conglomerate. In early August, UVN reported what we saw as strong second quarter results, fueled by record TV ratings for the soccer World Cup, some of which should carry over into the third quarter.

➤ Risks to our recommendation and target price include uncertainties due to the pending bid for the company and pending litigation with UVN's key partner and shareholder Grupo Televisa (TV: buy, $19), which had lost a rival bid; stagnant growth in Spanish-language advertising; and governance issues related to a controlling shareholder.

➤ Our 12-month target price is $37. Our calculation assumes that the pending acquisition will be consummated at an ample 20X enterprise value to trailing 12-month EBITDA, or 35%-40% above recent private auctions of English-language broadcasters.

Qualitative Risk Assessment

LOW | **MEDIUM** | HIGH

Our risk assessment reflects what we view as UVN's dominant position in the attractive Hispanic segment and a strong balance sheet, offset by exposure to cyclical advertising businesses and uncertainties with the final outcome of a pending buyout of the company.

Quantitative Evaluations

S&P Quality Ranking **B**

D | C | B- | **B** | B+ | A- | A | A+

Relative Strength Rank **MODERATE**

43

LOWEST = 1 HIGHEST = 99

Revenue/Earnings Data

Revenue (Million $)

	1Q	2Q	3Q	4Q	Year
2006	449.8	634.0	--	--	--
2005	433.0	508.5	497.5	513.5	1,953
2004	352.9	495.3	477.4	462.0	1,787
2003	261.7	320.2	321.1	408.1	1,311
2002	214.5	322.8	269.8	284.2	1,091
2001	194.9	237.5	221.7	233.8	887.9

Earnings Per Share ($)

2006	0.16	0.32	E0.29	E0.32	E1.08
2005	0.13	0.10	0.23	0.08	0.54
2004	0.09	0.24	0.21	0.19	0.72
2003	0.05	0.16	0.16	0.17	0.55
2002	0.03	0.09	0.08	0.14	0.34
2001	0.03	0.12	0.04	0.05	0.23

Fiscal year ended Dec. 31. Next earnings report expected: Early November. EPS Estimates based on S&P Operating Earnings; historical GAAP earnings are as reported.

Dividend Data

No cash dividends have been paid.

Univision Communications Inc.

Business Summary August 08, 2006

Univision Communications strengthened its position as the leading U.S. Spanish language media conglomerate after its acquisition of the former Hispanic Broadcasting in 2003. The company aims to benefit from rapid expansion of the Hispanic population and advertiser awareness of Hispanic buying power. In late June 2006, the company agreed to be acquired, subject to necessary approvals, by an investment consortium comprised of Madison Dearborn Partners, Providence Equity Partners, Texas Pacific Group, Thomas H. Lee Partners and Saban Capital Group, for $36.25 per share in cash, plus $1.6 billion of assumed debt, in a transaction valued at $13.7 billion.

UVN's principal business, television broadcasting (68% of 2005 revenues), consists of the Univision, Galavision and Telefutura TV networks, 72 owned and operated broadcast television stations (37 full power and 35 low power) largely affiliated with the Univision and Telefutura networks, and a TV production business.

The Univision network is the most popular U.S. Spanish language broadcast network, reaching more than 98% of all U.S. Hispanic households. Galavision is the leading U.S. Spanish general entertainment cable network, reaching about 5.9 million Hispanic households. The Telefutura, whose signal covers about 86% of U.S. Hispanic households, was launched in January 2002 (with assets received from the $1.1 billion cash acquisition of USA Broadcasting in December 2001) as a general interest Spanish language broadcast network, in a move to counter-program traditional lineups and draw new Spanish TV viewers. That deal instantly gave UVN duopolies in seven of the eight leading Hispanic markets.

UVN television broadcasting has program license agreements through 2017 with Mexico's Televisa and Venezuela's Venevision, to provide UVN's three television networks with a substantial amount of programming. In return, UVN pays a license fee of about 15% of TV net revenues to Televisa and Venevision combined, subject to certain upward adjustments. Televisa and Venevision currently own a 15% equity stake in UVN, with warrants to increase their stake to 25%.

Company Financials

Per Share Data ($) Year Ended Dec. 31	**2005**	**2004**	**2003**	**2002**	**2001**	**2000**	**1999**	**1998**	**1997**	**1996**
Tangible Book Value	NM	NM	NM	NM	NM	0.77	NM	NM	NM	NM
Cash Flow	0.81	1.01	0.85	0.64	0.58	0.60	0.62	0.32	0.61	0.25
Earnings	0.54	0.72	0.55	0.34	0.23	0.57	0.36	0.05	0.36	0.16
S&P Core Earnings	0.57	0.62	0.43	0.20	0.09	NA	NA	NA	NA	NA
Dividends	Nil	Nil	Nil	Nil	Nil	Nil	Nil	Nil	Nil	Nil
Payout Ratio	Nil	Nil	Nil	Nil	Nil	Nil	Nil	Nil	Nil	Nil
Prices:High	31.15	40.05	39.95	47.00	52.25	62.69	51.59	21.00	17.84	10.06
Prices:Low	23.52	27.30	21.83	16.40	16.30	24.00	17.06	10.53	7.94	5.75
P/E Ratio:High	58	56	73	NM	NM	NM	NM	NM	50	64
P/E Ratio:Low	44	38	40	NM	NM	NM	NM	NM	22	37
Income Statement Analysis (Million $)										
Revenue	1,953	1,787	1,311	1,091	888	863	693	577	460	370
Operating Income	663	595	434	332	300	289	267	196	163	107
Depreciation	93.2	101	84.9	78.8	84.1	28.0	64.0	64.4	58.6	39.5
Interest Expense	87.4	69.5	75.2	91.1	56.0	31.5	27.5	37.5	41.8	41.7
Pretax Income	373	428	261	148	118	225	175	50.3	63.7	24.3
Effective Tax Rate	48.8%	38.5%	40.4%	41.5%	53.5%	48.0%	52.3%	80.3%	NM	23.5%
Net Income	187	256	155	86.5	54.7	117	83.5	9.93	83.2	18.6
S&P Core Earnings	201	219	122	49.8	20.3	NA	NA	NA	NA	NA
Balance Sheet & Other Financial Data (Million $)										
Cash	99.4	190	76.7	35.7	381	54.5	22.6	13.0	10.7	11.6
Current Assets	634	665	521	385	596	250	178	154	139	112
Total Assets	8,128	8,227	7,643	3,402	3,164	1,448	974	938	968	884
Current Liabilities	910	292	289	223	270	363	142	153	144	120
Long Term Debt	969	1,228	1,368	1,432	1,662	378	303	377	461	498
Common Equity	5,091	5,388	5,103	1,558	813	695	514	395	346	262
Total Capital	7,138	7,851	7,265	3,106	2,850	1,079	826	781	819	760
Capital Expenditures	103	67.6	56.3	92.3	130	64.7	39.0	41.0	35.2	12.6
Cash Flow	280	357	240	165	139	144	147	73.8	141	58.1
Current Ratio	0.7	2.3	1.8	1.7	2.2	0.7	1.3	1.0	1.0	0.9
% Long Term Debt of Capitalization	13.6	15.6	18.8	46.1	58.3	35.0	36.7	48.3	56.3	65.5
% Net Income of Revenue	9.6	14.3	11.9	7.9	6.2	13.5	12.1	1.7	18.1	7.6
% Return on Assets	2.3	3.2	2.8	2.6	2.4	9.7	8.7	1.0	9.0	2.1
% Return on Equity	3.6	4.9	4.7	7.3	7.2	19.3	18.3	2.5	27.2	7.6

Data as orig reptd.; bef. results of disc opers/spec. items. Per share data adj. for stk. divs.; EPS diluted. E-Estimated. NA-Not Available. NM-Not Meaningful. NR-Not Ranked. UR-Under Review.

Office: 1999 Avenue of the Stars, Los Angeles, CA 90067-4613.
Telephone: 310-556-7676.
Website: http://www.univision.net
Chrmn & CEO: A.J. Perenchio

Pres & COO: R. Rodriguez
Vice Chrmn & Secy: R.V. Cahill
Sr EVP & CFO: A.W. Hobson
EVP & General Counsel: C.D. Kranwinkle

Investor Contact: D.M. Vesga (310-556-7665)
Board of Directors: A. Cassara, G. A. Cisneros R., H. Gaba, A. Horn, M. O. Johnson, A. J. Perenchio, J. G. Perenchio, A. Rivera, R. Rodriguez, M. T. Tichenor, Jr.

Founded: 1992
Domicile: Delaware
Employees: 4,219

STANDARD &POOR'S

UnumProvident Corp

S&P Recommendation BUY ★★★★★	Price	12-Mo. Target Price	Investment Style
	$20.08 (as of Oct 27, 2006)	$22.00	Mid-Cap Value

GICS Sector Financials
Sub-Industry Life & Health Insurance

Comment This leading provider of individual and group disability coverage was formed through the June 1999 merger of Provident Cos. and UNUM Corp.

Key Stock Statistics (Source S&P, Vickers, company reports)

52-Wk Range	$24.44–16.15	S&P Oper. EPS 2006E	1.70	P/E on S&P Oper. EPS 2006E	11.8	Dividend Rate/Share	$0.30
Trailing 12-Month EPS	$1.20	S&P Oper. EPS 2007E	1.85	Common Shares Outstg. (M)	342.5	Yield (%)	1.49
Trailing 12-Month P/E	16.7	S&P Core EPS 2006E	1.70	Market Capitalization(B)	$6.878	Beta	0.99
$10K Invested 5 Yrs Ago	$9,559	S&P Core EPS 2007E	1.85	Institutional Ownership (%)	98	S&P Credit Rating	BB+

Price Performance

Options: ASE, CBOE, P

Analysis prepared by **Frank Braden** on August 31, 2006, when the stock traded at **$ 18.95**.

Highlights

- We see 2006 pretax operating earnings for the U.S. brokerage segment remaining flat, excluding an $86 million regulatory reassessment charge, on weak but improving profitability in the group long-term income protection line, partially offset by higher net investment income. We see pretax operating earnings for the Unum Limited segment rising about 18%, on strong premium growth, a steady benefit ratio, and a declining expense ratio.
- We foresee operating earnings for the Colonial segment growing 9% in 2006, to about $183 million, on strong sales activity and an improving combined ratio. For the run-off closed block individual income protection segment, we estimate a modest decline in pretax operating earnings for 2006. We expect the company to use its excess capital to continue to deleverage its balance sheet back down to a 25% debt-to-total capital ratio, in an attempt to improve its standing with the credit rating agencies.
- We project that adjusted EPS from continuing operations will remain flat in 2006, at $1.70, including projected stock option expense. Our estimate excludes any one-time charges.

Investment Rationale/Risk

- In our view, the settlement with the California Department of Insurance removes a major uncertainty regarding the claims handling lawsuits in one of UNM's major markets. Although further legal and regulatory actions are possible, we expect UNM to maintain its capital management discipline and reach its goal of ROE expansion to 10% to 12% over the next three years, from its current 9%.
- Risks to our recommendation and target price include unfavorable outcomes to legal and regulatory actions; worse than expected client retention and sales following income protection product price increases; poor claims handling in the group income protection area; and higher than expected costs for reassessed claims under recent market conduct exam settlements.
- Our 12-month target price of $22 is based on an assumed price to book multiple of roughly 1.1X our 2006 book value per share estimate, in line with UNM's long-term historical average. This target price is equal to a multiple of 12.9X applied to our 2006 operating EPS estimate, a premium to its historical multiple.

Qualitative Risk Assessment

LOW | MEDIUM | **HIGH**

Our risk assessment for UnumProvident reflects regulatory scrutiny surrounding certain claims practices. Although the largest suits have been settled, UNM faces the possibility of additional suits and increased reserving for benefit costs in its claims reassessment.

Quantitative Evaluations

S&P Quality Ranking B-

D | C | **B-** | B | B+ | A- | A | A+

Relative Strength Rank MODERATE

59

LOWEST = 1 HIGHEST = 99

Revenue/Earnings Data

Revenue (Million $)

	1Q	2Q	3Q	4Q	Year
2006	2,646	2,668	--	--	--
2005	2,572	2,657	2,544	2,665	10,437
2004	2,624	2,509	2,655	2,677	10,465
2003	2,395	2,529	2,556	2,511	9,992
2002	2,331	2,402	2,450	2,431	9,613
2001	2,341	2,363	2,377	2,314	9,395

Earnings Per Share ($)

2006	0.23	0.38	**E**0.42	**E**0.45	**E**1.70
2005	0.49	0.55	0.17	0.43	1.64
2004	-1.93	0.25	0.55	0.45	-0.65
2003	-1.02	0.36	0.36	-0.71	-0.96
2002	0.30	0.40	0.45	0.39	1.68
2001	0.75	0.60	0.52	0.52	2.39

Fiscal year ended Dec. 31. Next earnings report expected: Early November. EPS Estimates based on S&P Operating Earnings; historical GAAP earnings are as reported.

Dividend Data (Dates: mm/dd Payment Date: mm/dd/yy)

Amount ($)	Date Decl.	Ex-Div. Date	Stk. of Record	Payment Date
0.075	01/09	01/26	01/30	02/17/06
0.075	04/11	04/20	04/24	05/19/06
0.075	07/18	07/27	07/31	08/18/06
0.075	10/16	10/26	10/30	11/17/06

Dividends have been paid since 1925. Source: Company reports.

Please read the Required Disclosures and Analyst Certification on the last page of this report.

UnumProvident Corp

Business Summary August 31, 2006

CORPORATE OVERVIEW. As of February 2006, UNM believed it was the largest provider of group and individual income protection insurance in North America and the U.K. through its subsidiaries. The company also offers other products, including long-term care insurance, life insurance, group benefits, and related services.

Effective July 1, 2005, UNM modified its reporting segments to separate its United States business from that of its United Kingdom subsidiary, Unum Limited. Operations are now organized into six business segments: U.S. brokerage; Unum Limited; Colonial; individual income protection - closed block; other; and corporate. Income protection accounted for 61% of operating revenue in 2005, Unum Limited 9.1%, Colonial 8.5%, individual income protection - closed block 18%, other 3.2%, and corporate 0.6%. In 2005, annualized premiums and fees on new sales of U.S. brokerage segment products declined 1.2%, Unum Limited segment new sales declined 28%, and Colonial segment new sales rose 2.8%.

The U.S. brokerage segment includes group income protection insurance, group life and accidental death and dismemberment products, and supplemental and voluntary lines of business. The Unum Limited segment includes group long-term income protection insurance, group life products, and individual income protection products issued by Unum Limited and sold primarily in the United Kingdom through field sales personnel and independent brokers and consultants. The Colonial segment includes a broad line of products sold mainly to employees at their workplaces, including income protection, life, and cancer and critical illness products. The other segment includes products that are no longer actively marketed, with the exception of the closed block business, including individual life and corporate-owned life insurance, reinsurance pools and management operations, group pension, health insurance, and individual annuities. The corporate segment includes investment income on unallocated corporate assets, interest expense, and certain unallocated corporate income and expense items.

Company Financials

Per Share Data ($) Year Ended Dec. 31	**2005**	**2004**	**2003**	**2002**	**2001**	**2000**	**1999**	**1998**	**1997**	**1996**
Tangible Book Value	23.76	23.45	22.94	25.58	21.74	20.29	17.82	20.05	17.69	17.34
Operating Earnings	NA	NA	NA	2.52	2.44	2.37	-1.00	2.14	1.77	1.52
Earnings	1.64	-0.65	-0.96	1.68	2.39	2.33	-0.77	1.82	1.84	1.46
S&P Core Earnings	1.81	-0.26	-0.54	2.35	2.30	NA	NA	NA	NA	NA
Dividends	0.30	0.30	0.37	0.59	0.59	0.59	0.35	0.40	0.38	0.36
Payout Ratio	18%	NM	NM	35%	25%	25%	NM	22%	21%	25%
Prices:High	22.90	18.25	19.54	29.70	33.75	31.94	56.88	42.44	39.06	25.75
Prices:Low	15.50	11.41	5.91	16.30	22.25	11.94	26.00	26.13	23.19	14.25
P/E Ratio:High	14	NM	NM	18	14	14	NM	23	21	18
P/E Ratio:Low	9	NM	NM	10	9	5	NM	14	13	10
Income Statement Analysis (Million $)										
Life Insurance in Force	833,363	908,034	787,199	712,826	642,988	583,848	567,215	158,317	138,341	102,665
Premium Income:Life	7,816	5,985	1,800	1,683	1,554	1,448	1,452	503	1,287	646
Premium Income:A & H	1,787	1,855	5,816	5,770	5,524	5,608	5,391	1,845	NA	501
Net Investment Income	2,188	2,159	2,158	2,086	2,003	2,060	2,060	1,374	1,355	1,090
Total Revenue	10,437	10,465	9,992	9,613	9,395	9,432	9,330	3,938	3,553	2,292
Pretax Income	710	-260	-435	1,019	825	866	-166	403	380	226
Net Operating Income	NA	NA	NA	614	593	NA	NA	368	NA	151
Net Income	514	-192	-265	817	582	564	-183	254	247	146
S&P Core Earnings	570	-77.1	-150	568	564	NA	NA	NA	NA	NA
Balance Sheet & Other Financial Data (Million $)										
Cash & Equivalent	688	719	663	734	2,515	1,958	836	366	401	288
Premiums Due	5,609	6,969	6,243	5,986	6,224	6,047	765	98.4	73.9	72.3
Investment Assets:Bonds	34,857	32,488	31,187	27,486	24,393	22,589	22,357	15,142	17,342	11,145
Investment Assets:Stocks	13.6	12.9	39.1	27.9	10.9	24.5	38.0	2.10	10.0	4.90
Investment Assets:Loans	3,941	3,572	3,353	3,344	3,510	3,679	3,595	2,107	1,984	1,749
Investment Assets:Total	39,357	36,588	35,028	31,152	28,324	26,604	26,549	17,333	19,434	13,317
Deferred Policy Costs	2,913	2,883	3,052	2,982	2,675	2,424	2,391	465	363	422
Total Assets	51,867	50,832	49,718	45,260	42,443	40,364	38,448	23,088	23,178	14,993
Debt	3,262	2,862	2,789	1,914	2,304	1,915	1,467	900	725	200
Common Equity	7,364	7,224	7,271	9,398	5,940	5,576	4,983	3,409	3,123	1,582
% Return on Revenue	4.9	NM	NM	8.5	6.2	6.0	NM	6.5	7.0	6.4
% Return on Assets	1.0	NM	NM	1.9	1.4	1.4	NM	1.1	1.3	0.9
% Return on Equity	7.0	NM	NM	9.1	10.1	10.7	NM	7.7	10.0	9.5
% Investment Yield	5.8	6.0	6.5	7.0	7.3	7.8	NM	7.9	7.6	7.8

Data as orig reptd.; bef. results of disc opers/spec. items. Per share data adj. for stk. divs.; EPS diluted. E-Estimated. NA-Not Available. NM-Not Meaningful. NR-Not Ranked. UR-Under Review.

Office: 1 Fountain Square, Chattanooga, TN 37402-1307.
Telephone: 423.294.1011.
Website: http://www.unumprovident.com
Chrmn: C.W. Pollard

Pres & CEO: T.R. Watjen
Sr EVP & CFO: J.M. Zubretsky
EVP & General Counsel: C. Glick
Investor Contact: T.A. White (423-755-8996)

Board of Directors: J. S. Fossel, P. H. Godwin, R. E. Goldsberry, T. A. Kinser, G. C. Larson, A. S. MacMillan, Jr., H. O. Maclellan, Jr., E. J. Muhl, M. J. Passarella, C. W. Pollard, W. J. Ryan, T. R. Watjen

Founded: 1887
Domicile: Delaware
Employees: 11,300

UST Inc.

S&P Recommendation	Price	12-Mo. Target Price	Investment Style
HOLD ★★★★★	$53.31 (as of Oct 27, 2006)	$55.00	Mid-Cap Growth

GICS Sector Consumer Staples
Sub-Industry Tobacco

Comment UST is a leading producer of moist smokeless tobacco products, marketed under such leading brand names as Copenhagen and Skoal. It also imports and produces wines.

Key Stock Statistics (Source S&P, Vickers, company reports)

52-Wk Range	$57.42–37.61	S&P Oper. EPS 2006E	3.10	P/E on S&P Oper. EPS 2006E	17.2	Dividend Rate/Share	$2.28
Trailing 12-Month EPS	$3.15	S&P Oper. EPS 2007E	3.20	Common Shares Outstg. (M)	160.8	Yield (%)	4.28
Trailing 12-Month P/E	16.9	S&P Core EPS 2006E	3.08	Market Capitalization(B)	$8.574	Beta	0.92
$10K Invested 5 Yrs Ago	$20,568	S&P Core EPS 2007E	3.21	Institutional Ownership (%)	95	S&P Credit Rating	A

Price Performance

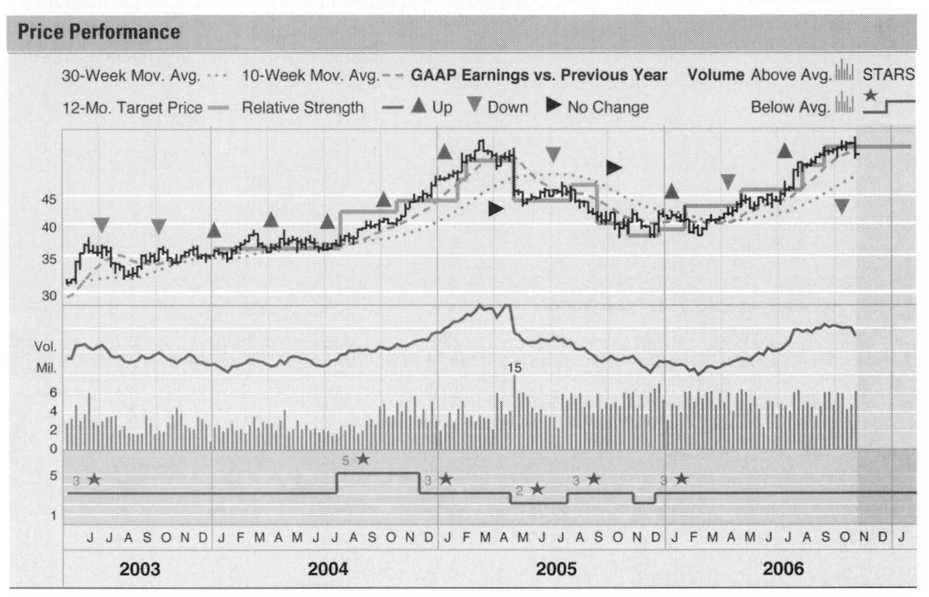

Options: ASE, CBOE, P

Analysis prepared by **Raymond Mathis** on September 11, 2006, when the stock traded at **$ 54.23**.

Highlights

➤ We see a net sales increase of 1.5% in 2006. We expect the majority of growth to come from the price-value segment, as double-digit volume gains will likely outweigh pricing pressure in this category and volume pressure in the premium category. With planned marketing increases in 2006, we see volume trends improving for premium brands in the second half. However, we are wary of planned price increases on premium products, which we believe contributed to weak volumes early in the year. We look for new line extensions, and pouches, to aid sales volumes.

➤ We look for a narrowing of gross margins, as premium products likely decline and as increased promotional activity offsets possible volume growth in the price-value brand. Also, as momentum in wine volume builds, we see a negative impact on margins. More importantly, we anticipate that significantly higher marketing expenses will lead to a net margin of 26.2% in 2006, down from 29.3% in 2005.

➤ Aided by lower interest expense due to reduced debt levels, we estimate 2006 operating EPS of $3.07, down from 2005's $3.28.

Investment Rationale/Risk

➤ With increased marketing efforts on premium products in 2006, we look for a recovery in this category over the long term. Furthermore, we see UST's efforts to build the smokeless category supporting long-term industry growth. However, we remain concerned about competitive discounting in the price-value category, which may continue to widen price gaps. We are wary of continued trading down to the price-value category, and although we expect the sub-price value category to remain buoyant, we look for a negative impact on margins.

➤ Risks to our recommendation and target price include continued volume declines in the premium category, despite increased marketing efforts, which would pressure margins further. Also, the Project Momentum restructuring plan could fail to achieve the expected cost benefits.

➤ Our 12-month target price of $55 is based on a weighted blend of two metrics. Our DCF model, which assumes five-year annual sales growth of 3% and a weighted average cost of capital of 8%, derives an intrinsic value of $57. By applying a forward peer P/E multiple of 16X to our 2006 EPS estimate, we see a value of $49. The stock recently yielded 4.2%.

Qualitative Risk Assessment

LOW | MEDIUM | **HIGH**

Our risk assessment reflects that the tobacco industry is typified by relatively stable revenue streams, while tobacco company stocks typically have below average betas. Although the smokeless tobacco industry is not subject to as much litigation as cigarette manufacturers, there is a risk, in our opinion, that future litigation could affect cash flow. Also, due to its large market share, UST has been subject to antitrust actions.

Quantitative Evaluations

S&P Quality Ranking A-

D | C | B- | B | B+ | **A-** | A | A+

Relative Strength Rank MODERATE

34

LOWEST = 1 HIGHEST = 99

Revenue/Earnings Data

Revenue (Million $)

	1Q	2Q	3Q	4Q	Year
2006	433.6	472.9	458.7	--	--
2005	440.5	480.1	456.8	474.4	1,852
2004	433.3	464.7	462.0	478.3	1,838
2003	420.0	438.9	437.6	446.2	1,743
2002	375.2	432.3	451.3	424.0	1,683
2001	383.0	422.2	417.8	447.4	1,670

Earnings Per Share ($)

2006	0.71	0.83	0.71	**E**0.81	**E**3.10
2005	0.73	0.82	0.80	0.88	3.23
2004	0.73	0.92	0.80	0.77	3.23
2003	0.66	0.77	0.74	-0.27	1.90
2002	0.61	0.80	0.77	-3.82	-1.61
2001	0.66	0.74	0.75	0.82	2.97

Fiscal year ended Dec. 31. Next earnings report expected: Late January. EPS Estimates based on S&P Operating Earnings; historical GAAP earnings are as reported.

Dividend Data (Dates: mm/dd Payment Date: mm/dd/yy)

Amount ($)	Date Decl.	Ex-Div. Date	Stk. of Record	Payment Date
0.550	11/03	12/13	12/15	12/30/05
0.570	02/23	03/13	03/15	03/31/06
0.570	05/02	06/13	06/15	06/30/06
0.570	08/03	09/13	09/15	09/29/06

Dividends have been paid since 1912. Source: Company reports.

UST Inc.

Business Summary September 11, 2006

CORPORATE OVERVIEW. UST is the holding company for United States Smokeless Tobacco Company, which was formed in 1911. The company's three segments include Smokeless Tobacco Products, Wine, and Other operations including international tobacco.

The company's moist smokeless tobacco products include Copenhagen and Skoal, the world's two best selling brands of moist smokeless tobacco. Moist brands also include Skoal Long Cut, Skoal Bandits, Copenhagen Long Cut, Rooster, and Husky. Dry tobacco products carry the names Bruton, CC, and Red Seal. The company's tobacco products (84.3% of 2005 revenues) are sold throughout the U.S., principally to chain stores and tobacco and grocery wholesalers.

In addition to its smokeless tobacco offerings, UST is also a significant importer and producer of wines, and has other operations. Wines (13.4% of 2005 revenues) consist of premium varietal and blended wines dominated by Washington State-produced Chateau Ste. Michelle and Columbia Crest, and Villa Mt. Eden, a premium-quality California wine. Case volume for Columbia Crest and Chateau Ste. Michelle accounted for 75.3% of the company's premium wine case volume in 2005.

Other businesses (2.3% of 2005 revenues) include UST's international operation, which markets moist smokeless tobacco, and formerly included the manufacture and marketing of premium cigars (Don Tomas, Astral, and Hellix). In March 2004, UST paid $200 million and transferred its cigar operations to Swedish Match North America, to dismiss a case brought by that company.

CORPORATE STRATEGY. UST's objective in the Smokeless Tobacco segment is to continue to grow the moist smokeless tobacco category by building awareness and social acceptability of smokeless tobacco products among adult smokers, and by being competitive in every moist smokeless tobacco category segment. The company believes its future growth and profitability is in attracting growing numbers of adult consumers, primarily smokers, as approximately every 1% of adult smokers who convert to moist smokeless tobacco represents a 10% increase in the segment's adult consumer base. In addition to advertising initiatives, in 2004 and 2005 UST began a direct mail program to over 1 million adult smokers and began an advertising campaign to promote the convenience of smokeless tobacco relative to cigarettes.

Company Financials

Per Share Data ($) Year Ended Dec. 31	**2005**	**2004**	**2003**	**2002**	**2001**	**2000**	**1999**	**1998**	**1997**	**1996**
Tangible Book Value	0.46	0.06	NM	NM	3.47	1.66	1.20	2.57	2.37	1.53
Cash Flow	3.51	3.52	2.15	-1.31	3.23	2.94	2.89	2.61	2.53	2.57
Earnings	3.23	3.23	1.90	-1.61	2.97	2.70	2.68	2.44	2.37	2.42
S&P Core Earnings	3.20	3.24	1.93	3.13	2.84	NA	NA	NA	NA	NA
Dividends	2.20	2.08	2.00	1.92	1.84	1.76	1.68	1.62	1.62	1.48
Payout Ratio	68%	64%	105%	NM	62%	65%	63%	66%	68%	61%
Prices:High	56.90	48.97	37.79	41.35	36.00	28.88	34.94	36.88	36.94	35.88
Prices:Low	37.59	34.00	26.73	25.30	23.38	13.88	24.06	24.56	25.50	28.25
P/E Ratio:High	18	15	20	NM	12	11	13	15	16	15
P/E Ratio:Low	12	11	14	NM	8	5	9	10	11	12
Income Statement Analysis (Million $)										
Revenue	1,852	1,838	1,743	1,683	1,670	1,548	1,512	1,423	1,402	1,397
Operating Income	936	960	958	912	876	792	813	764	742	779
Depreciation	46.4	47.6	41.6	49.7	43.2	39.6	37.0	31.7	30.5	28.3
Interest Expense	50.6	75.0	76.9	46.1	66.2	47.4	13.5	4.42	8.40	7.29
Pretax Income	828	838	515	-444	799	718	763	734	704	745
Effective Tax Rate	35.4%	35.8%	38.1%	NM	38.5%	38.5%	38.5%	38.0%	37.6%	37.7%
Net Income	534	538	319	-271	492	442	469	455	439	464
S&P Core Earnings	529	540	323	528	470	NA	NA	NA	NA	NA
Balance Sheet & Other Financial Data (Million $)										
Cash	202	510	438	382	272	96.0	75.0	33.2	6.93	54.5
Current Assets	890	1,173	1,248	2,291	892	691	580	507	442	444
Total Assets	1,367	1,659	1,726	2,765	2,012	1,646	1,016	913	827	807
Current Liabilities	259	619	521	1,462	222	170	261	197	167	307
Long Term Debt	840	840	1,140	1,140	863	869	411	100	100	100
Common Equity	2,983	2,918	-115	-47.0	581	271	201	468	438	282
Total Capital	3,835	3,768	-47.0	1,093	1,627	1,326	612	568	538	382
Capital Expenditures	89.9	70.3	45.1	57.2	47.2	51.1	59.3	56.3	58.1	44.7
Cash Flow	581	586	360	-222	535	481	506	487	470	492
Current Ratio	3.4	1.9	2.4	1.6	4.0	4.1	2.2	2.6	2.7	1.4
% Long Term Debt of Capitalization	21.9	22.3	110.8	104.3	53.0	65.5	67.2	17.6	18.6	26.2
% Net Income of Revenue	28.9	29.3	18.3	NM	29.4	28.6	31.0	32.0	31.3	33.2
% Return on Assets	35.3	31.8	14.2	NM	26.9	33.2	48.7	52.3	53.7	58.3
% Return on Equity	18.1	20.3	NM	NM	115.4	187.5	19.3	100.5	122.0	161.2

Data as orig reptd.; bef. results of disc opers/spec. items. Per share data adj. for stk. divs.; EPS diluted. E-Estimated. NA-Not Available. NM-Not Meaningful. NR-Not Ranked. UR-Under Review.

Office: 100 West Putnam Ave, Greenwich, CT 06830.
Telephone: 203-661-1100.
Website: http://www.ustinc.com
Chrmn & CEO: V.A. Gierer, Jr.

Pres & COO: M.S. Kessler
SVP & CFO: R.T. D'Alessandro
SVP, Secy & General Counsel: R.A. Kohlberger
Investor Contact: M. Rozelle (203-622-3520)

Board of Directors: J. Barr, J. P. Clancey, E. H. DeHority, Jr., P. Diaz Dennis, V. A. Gierer, Jr., J. E. Heid, M. S. Kessler, P. J. Mannelly, P. J. Neff, A. J. Parsons, R. J. Rossi

Founded: 1911
Domicile: Delaware
Employees: 5,111

STANDARD &POOR'S

Valero Energy Corp

S&P Recommendation STRONG BUY ★★★★★

Price $53.08 (as of Oct 27, 2006)

12-Mo. Target Price $78.00

Investment Style Large-Cap Growth

GICS Sector Energy
Sub-Industry Oil & Gas Refining & Marketing

Comment Valero is the largest refiner in North America, one of the largest U.S. independent retailers, and operates refineries that can process sour and acidic crude oils.

Key Stock Statistics (Source S&P, Vickers, company reports)

52-Wk Range	$70.75–46.84	S&P Oper. EPS 2006E	7.69	P/E on S&P Oper. EPS 2006E	6.9	Dividend Rate/Share	$0.32
Trailing 12-Month EPS	$7.90	S&P Oper. EPS 2007E	7.43	Common Shares Outstg. (M)	612.9	Yield (%)	0.60
Trailing 12-Month P/E	6.7	S&P Core EPS 2006E	7.56	Market Capitalization(B)	$32.531	Beta	0.94
$10K Invested 5 Yrs Ago	$55,313	S&P Core EPS 2007E	7.43	Institutional Ownership (%)	70	S&P Credit Rating	BBB-

Price Performance

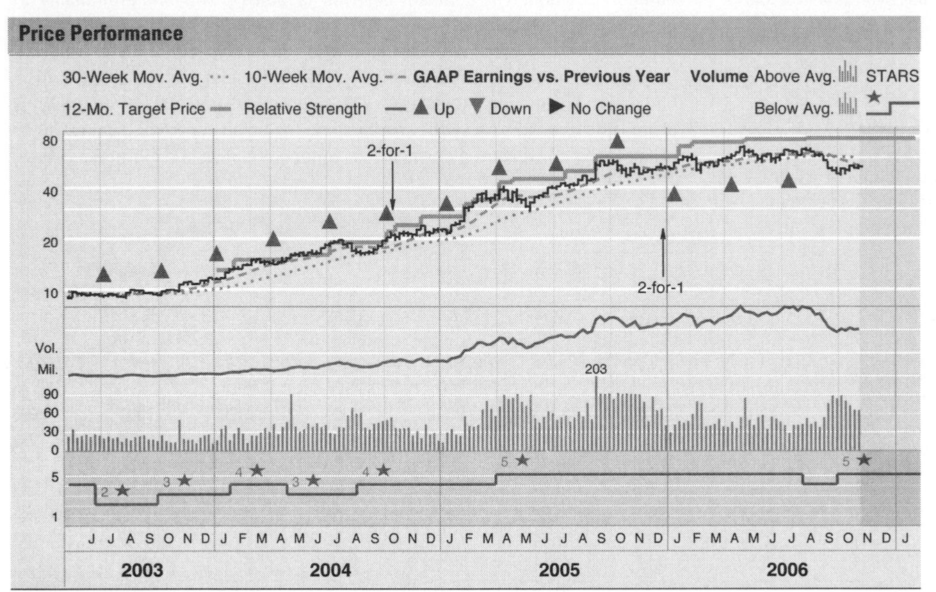

Options: ASE

Analysis prepared by **Tina J. Vital** on October 04, 2006, when the stock traded at **$ 48.49**.

Highlights

- While U.S. refining margins have narrowed since the beginning of August 2006, we believe this decline is temporary and we expect the switch to winter fuels combined with scheduled industry maintenance will boost U.S. refining margins in the fourth quarter. In addition, increased demand and the need to attract the necessary level of fuel imports should lead to stronger pricing in 2007.

- On August 6, 2006, BP (BP: buy, $64) began a partial shut-down of its Prudhoe Bay, Alaska oilfield due to unexpected corrosion in its Eastern Operating Area pipelines; as of mid-September, about 200,000 b/d remained shut-in. On September 22, BP received permission from the U.S. Department of Transportation to restart 150,000 b/d of shut-in production, and we expect production will ramp up to normal levels by October. VLO uses about 60,000 b/d of Alaskan crude (or 1.8% of VLO's crude supply) at its 185,000 b/d Benicia, CA refinery.

- While after-tax operating earnings rose 117% in 2005, we expect that strong industry fundamentals will boost operating earnings by 24% in 2006, before declining about 4% in 2007.

Investment Rationale/Risk

- As VLO is the largest refiner in North America, we believe its size and ability to refine heavy sour crude feedstocks offer strategic and economic advantages. With the majority of refining costs focused on feedstocks, we think VLO's ability to refine lower quality crudes (about 55% of its 2005 feedstocks were sour or acidic) is a major competitive advantage. We estimate VLO holds an above-average level of conversion capacity (near 1.6 million b/d), and the company is expanding its upgrading capacity at its Aruba refinery and Port Arthur, TX crude unit .

- Risks to our recommendation and target price include relatively high environmental spending through 2007, and changes in economic and industry conditions that could lead to a narrowing of refining margins.

- Using a blend of our discounted cash flow (assuming a weighted average cost of capital of 10.3% and terminal growth of 3%) and relative valuations, we derive our 12-month target price of $78. Our target price represents an enterprise value of 6.3X our 2006 EBITDA estimate, a premium to peers.

Qualitative Risk Assessment

LOW | MEDIUM | HIGH

Our risk assessment reflects our view of VLO's strong business profile in a volatile and competitive refining industry. The company is the largest refiner in the U.S. and holds above-average refining complexity, which allows it to process a large amount of lower cost heavy and sour crudes.

Quantitative Evaluations

S&P Quality Ranking **B+**

D | C | B- | B | B+ | A- | A | A+

Relative Strength Rank **WEAK**

20

LOWEST = 1 HIGHEST = 99

Revenue/Earnings Data

Revenue (Million $)

	1Q	2Q	3Q	4Q	Year
2006	20,941	26,781	--	--	--
2005	14,943	18,032	23,283	25,894	82,162
2004	11,082	13,808	14,339	15,390	54,619
2003	9,693	8,844	9,922	9,509	37,969
2002	5,122	6,522	7,192	8,110	26,976
2001	3,769	4,499	3,859	2,861	14,988

Earnings Per Share ($)

	1Q	2Q	3Q	4Q	Year
2006	1.32	2.98	E2.35	E1.04	E7.69
2005	0.96	1.53	1.47	2.06	6.10
2004	0.46	1.14	0.79	0.88	3.27
2003	0.38	0.27	0.38	0.25	1.27
2002	-0.09	0.03	0.07	0.20	0.21
2001	0.53	1.06	0.40	0.21	2.21

Fiscal year ended Dec. 31. Next earnings report expected: Late October. EPS Estimates based on S&P Operating Earnings; historical GAAP earnings are as reported.

Dividend Data (Dates: mm/dd Payment Date: mm/dd/yy)

Amount ($)	Date Decl.	Ex-Div. Date	Stk. of Record	Payment Date
0.060	01/19	02/13	02/15	03/15/06
0.080	04/27	05/15	05/17	06/14/06
0.080	07/27	08/14	08/16	09/14/06
0.080	10/19	11/06	11/08	12/13/06

Dividends have been paid since 1997. Source: Company reports.

Please read the Required Disclosures and Analyst Certification on the last page of this report.

Valero Energy Corp

Business Summary October 04, 2006

Incorporated in 1981 under the name Valero Refining and Marketing Co., the company changed its name to Valero Energy Co. (VLO) in 1997. In 2001, VLO merged with Ultramar Diamond Shamrock, and in September 2005 with Premcor Inc., creating the largest refiner in North America, based on atmospheric distillation capacity.

The company's business segments are refining (91% of 2005 revenues, 98% of operating income) and retail (9%, 2%). VLO serves customers in the U.S. (87% of 2005 revenues), Canada (9%), and other countries (4%); no single customer accounted for over 10% of consolidated operating revenues.

The refining segment includes refining operations, wholesale marketing, product supply and distribution, and transportation operations. As of September 2006, the company owned and operated 18 refineries in the U.S., Canada and Aruba, with a combined throughput capacity of 3.3 million barrels per day (b/d). The refining segment by region consisted of the Gulf Coast (nine refineries, 53% of 2005 throughput capacity), the Mid-Continent (four, 19%), the West Coast (two, 9%) and the Northeast (three, 19%). As of the 2005 fourth quarter, sour crude oils represented 53% of VLO's throughput volumes, acidic sweet crude oils 2%, sweet crude oil 16%, residual fuel oil 13%, other feedstocks 6%, and the remaining 10% was composed of blendstocks. About 65% of VLO's current crude oil feedstock requirements were purchased through term contracts, with the remainder generally purchased on the spot market. About 75% of these crude oil feedstocks are imported from foreign sources, and about 25% are domestic.

Company Financials

Per Share Data ($) Year Ended Dec. 31	2005	2004	2003	2002	2001	2000	1999	1998	1997	1996
Tangible Book Value	15.82	9.55	5.86	3.24	3.90	6.28	4.84	4.85	5.16	NA
Cash Flow	7.57	3.24	2.31	1.23	2.75	1.86	0.47	0.14	0.78	NA
Earnings	6.10	3.27	1.27	0.21	2.21	1.40	0.06	-0.21	0.51	0.13
S&P Core Earnings	6.02	3.25	1.25	0.14	2.14	NA	NA	NA	NA	NA
Dividends	0.19	0.15	0.15	0.10	0.09	0.08	0.08	0.06	0.04	NA
Payout Ratio	3%	4%	11%	48%	4%	6%	128%	NM	8%	NA
Prices:High	58.63	23.91	11.77	12.49	13.15	9.66	6.33	9.13	8.78	NA
Prices:Low	21.01	11.43	8.05	5.79	7.88	4.63	4.17	4.41	6.73	NA
P/E Ratio:High	10	7	9	60	6	7	NM	NM	17	NA
P/E Ratio:Low	3	3	6	28	4	3	NM	NM	13	NA

Income Statement Analysis (Million $)										
Revenue	82,162	54,619	37,969	26,976	14,988	14,671	7,961	5,539	5,756	2,758
Operating Income	6,334	2,979	1,733	920	1,139	723	162	198	276	145
Depreciation, Depletion and Amortization	875	NA	511	449	138	112	92.4	78.7	65.2	55.0
Interest Expense	266	260	278	256	102	83.0	55.4	32.5	42.5	41.4
Pretax Income	5,287	2,710	989	164	895	528	20.2	-83.1	176	39.1
Effective Tax Rate	32.1%	33.4%	36.9%	35.5%	37.0%	35.8%	29.2%	NM	36.3%	42.5%
Net Income	3,590	1,804	622	91.5	564	339	14.3	-47.3	112	22.5
S&P Core Earnings	3,534	1,785	604	60.0	547	NA	NA	NA	NA	NA

Balance Sheet & Other Financial Data (Million $)										
Cash	436	864	369	409	346	14.6	60.1	11.2	9.94	NA
Current Assets	8,276	5,264	3,817	3,536	4,113	1,285	829	640	789	352
Total Assets	32,728	19,392	15,664	14,465	14,337	4,308	2,979	2,726	2,493	1,986
Current Liabilities	7,305	4,534	3,064	3,007	4,730	1,039	719	498	597	301
Long Term Debt	5,156	3,901	4,245	4,867	2,805	1,042	785	822	430	353
Common Equity	14,982	7,590	5,535	4,308	4,203	1,527	1,085	1,085	1,159	1,076
Total Capital	20,206	13,710	11,585	10,592	8,884	3,149	2,146	2,117	1,846	1,655
Capital Expenditures	2,133	1,292	976	628	394	195	101	166	69.2	NA
Cash Flow	4,452	1,791	1,128	541	701	451	107	31.4	172	66.2
Current Ratio	1.1	1.2	1.2	1.2	0.9	1.2	1.2	1.3	1.3	1.2
% Long Term Debt of Capitalization	25.5	28.5	36.6	45.9	31.6	33.0	36.5	NM	62.8	21.3
% Return on Assets	13.8	10.3	4.1	0.6	6.0	9.3	0.5	NM	4.9	NA
% Return on Equity	31.7	27.3	12.5	2.2	19.7	26.0	1.3	NM	10.0	NA

Data as orig reptd.; bef. results of disc opers/spec. items. Per share data adj. for stk. divs.; EPS diluted. E-Estimated. NA-Not Available. NM-Not Meaningful. NR-Not Ranked. UR-Under Review.

Office: One Valero Place, San Antonio, TX 78212.
Telephone: 210-370-2000.
Email: investorrelations@valero.com
Website: http://www.valero.com

Chrmn: W.E. Greehey
Pres: G.C. King
Vice Chrmn & CEO: W.R. Klesse
EVP & CFO: M.S. Ciskowski

EVP & Chief Admin: K.D. Booke
Investor Contact: E. Fisher (210-345-2896)
Board of Directors: E. G. Biggs, W. E. Bradford, R. K. Calgaard, J. D. Choate, I. F. Engelhardt, R. M. Escobedo, W. E. Greehey, S. Kaufman Purcell, W. Klesse, B. Marbut, D. L. Nickles, R. A. Profusek

Founded: 1955
Domicile: Delaware
Employees: 22,068

VeriSign Inc

STANDARD &POOR'S

S&P Recommendation STRONG SELL ★★★★★	**Price** $20.90 (as of Oct 27, 2006)	**12-Mo. Target Price** $18.00	**Investment Style** Mid-Cap Growth

GICS Sector Information Technology
Sub-Industry Internet Software & Services

Comment This company is a leading provider of infrastructure services that enable secure digital communications and commerce.

Key Stock Statistics (Source S&P, Vickers, company reports)

52-Wk Range	$25.45–15.95	S&P Oper. EPS 2006E	0.81	P/E on S&P Oper. EPS 2006E	25.8	Dividend Rate/Share	Nil
Trailing 12-Month EPS	$2.70	S&P Oper. EPS 2007E	0.93	Common Shares Outstg. (M)	245.1	Yield (%)	Nil
Trailing 12-Month P/E	7.7	S&P Core EPS 2006E	0.81	Market Capitalization(B)	$5.123	Beta	3.33
$10K Invested 5 Yrs Ago	$4,881	S&P Core EPS 2007E	0.93	Institutional Ownership (%)	83	S&P Credit Rating	NA

Price Performance

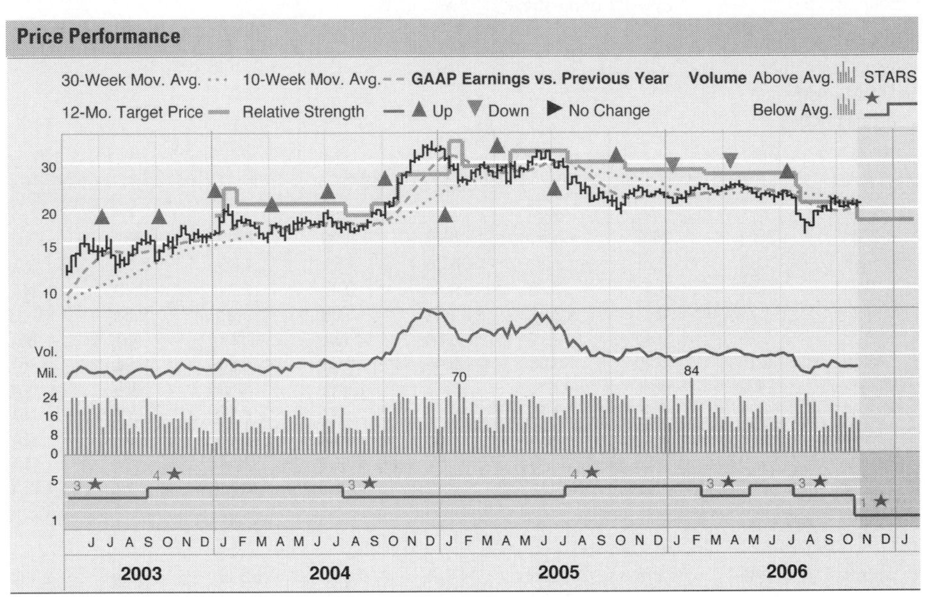

Options: ASE, CBOE, P, Ph

Analysis prepared by **Scott H. Kessler** on October 23, 2006, when the stock traded at **$ 20.49**.

Highlights

- We believe VRSN stands to benefit from increasing spending on Internet security, online naming services, and certain telecommunications offerings. We see 2006 revenues declining 4%, reflecting the November 2005 sale of the payments business. Excluding the impact of this transaction, we foresee mid-teens growth. We project 2007 revenues will increase 16%.
- We expect the share count to decline in 2006 and 2007, aided by a $1 billion stock repurchase program announced in May 2006. Our EPS forecasts for 2006 and 2007 reflect the impact of projected stock option expense of $64 million ($0.18 per share) and $69 million ($0.20), respectively, which is considerably lower than the $137 million accrued in 2004. In December 2005, VRSN accelerated the vesting of certain stock options, and indicated this action would reduce related 2006 expenses by $28 million.
- VRSN has actively acquired companies since mid-2004, and has made more than $1 billion in purchases over the past two years or so. In November 2005, VRSN sold its security gateway business to eBay (EBAY: strong buy, $30) for $370 million.

Investment Rationale/Risk

- We view VRSN as a diversified play on the continuing secular growth in Internet and wireless users and usage. However, we believe transactional efforts since the summer of 2004 have been excessive, detracting from VRSN's focus, transparency, and balance sheet. We also think issues associated with alleged stock option backdating are notable, and have temporarily limited financial disclosures and forestalled buyback activity.
- Risks to our opinion and target price include unexpected strength in technology and telecommunications spending, and matters concerning alleged stock option backdating being resolved more quickly and easily than we foresee.
- VRSN's P/E was recently well below that of the S&P 500 Internet Software & Services sub-industry, and its P/E-to-growth (PEG) ratio was much lower. Associated relative analyses yielded a value of $19. The stock's P/E and PEG were notably above that of S&P 500 Technology Sector, leading to a value estimate of $16. Blending these considerations results in our 12-month target price of $18.

Qualitative Risk Assessment

LOW	MEDIUM	**HIGH**

Our risk assessment reflects what we consider the emerging nature of, and notable competition in, many of the company's businesses, and substantial acquisition activity since 2004, in terms of the number and value of transactions.

Quantitative Evaluations

S&P Quality Ranking **B-**

D	C	**B-**	B	B+	A-	A	A+

Relative Strength Rank **MODERATE**

46

LOWEST = 1 HIGHEST = 99

Revenue/Earnings Data

Revenue (Million $)

	1Q	2Q	3Q	4Q	Year
2006	373.6	391.9	--	--	--
2005	401.0	444.8	414.8	392.1	1,609
2004	229.1	256.1	325.3	356.0	1,166
2003	269.8	265.3	268.1	251.6	1,055
2002	327.8	317.4	301.4	275.0	1,222
2001	213.4	231.2	255.2	283.8	983.6

Earnings Per Share ($)

2006	0.08	1.42	**E**0.19	**E**0.23	**E**0.81
2005	0.17	0.14	0.17	0.07	0.53
2004	0.04	0.09	0.16	0.43	0.72
2003	-0.22	-0.60	-0.13	-0.13	-1.08
2002	-0.17	-20.31	-0.34	-0.17	-20.97
2001	-6.90	-55.49	-1.91	-1.91	-65.64

Fiscal year ended Dec. 31. Next earnings report expected: NA. EPS Estimates based on S&P Operating Earnings; historical GAAP earnings are as reported.

Dividend Data

No cash dividends have been paid.

VeriSign Inc

Business Summary October 23, 2006

CORPORATE OVERVIEW. VeriSign provides infrastructure services intended to enable secure digital communications and commerce. Core offerings include security services, naming and directory services, and telecommunications services. The company has two primary operating units: the Internet Services Group (40% and 46% of revenues in 2005 and 2004, respectively), and the Communications Services Group (60%, 54%). In November 2003, VRSN sold 85% of its Network Solutions to a private equity company, in a transaction valued at $98 million, consisting of $58 million in cash and a $40 million senior subordinated note.

The Internet Services Group consists of two businesses: Security Services, and Information Services. Security Services includes network and applications security services (including managed security and global security consulting services), authentication services, commerce site services, and digital certificate services. Information Services (largely associated with VRSN being the exclusive registry of the .com and .net domain names) includes domain name registry services (VRSN owns and maintains the shared registration system for second-level domains), intelligent supply chain services, real-time publisher services, and digital brand management services. The Communications Services Group provides communications services to wireline, broadband and mobile operators, and enterprise customers. They include network connectivity and interoperability services, intelligent database services, content and application services, messaging services, clearing and settlement services, and billing and payment services.

Company Financials

Per Share Data ($) Year Ended Dec. 31	**2005**	**2004**	**2003**	**2002**	**2001**	**2000**	**1999**	**1998**	**1997**	**1996**
Tangible Book Value	2.98	2.92	3.16	1.89	3.60	4.16	2.88	0.88	NA	NA
Cash Flow	1.25	1.05	-0.61	0.16	1.63	0.64	0.08	-0.38	-0.58	NA
Earnings	0.53	0.72	-1.08	-20.97	-65.64	-19.57	0.03	-0.24	NA	NA
S&P Core Earnings	NA	0.01	-1.75	-8.79	-35.05	NA	NA	NA	NA	NA
Dividends	Nil	Nil	Nil	Nil	Nil	Nil	Nil	Nil	NA	NA
Payout Ratio	Nil	Nil	Nil	Nil	Nil	Nil	Nil	Nil	NA	NA
Prices:High	33.67	36.09	17.55	39.23	97.75	258.50	212.00	19.38	NA	NA
Prices:Low	19.01	14.94	6.55	3.92	26.25	65.38	13.50	3.50	NA	NA
P/E Ratio:High	64	50	NM	NM	NM	NM	NM	NM	NA	NA
P/E Ratio:Low	36	21	NM	NM	NM	NM	NM	NM	NA	NA
Income Statement Analysis (Million $)										
Revenue	1,609	1,166	1,055	1,222	984	475	84.8	38.9	9.38	NA
Operating Income	416	242	304	287	277	70.0	2.09	-15.6	-16.5	NA
Depreciation	191	85.6	114	5,000	13,687	3,217	5.40	3.95	2.61	NA
Interest Expense	Nil	Nil	Nil	149	20.7	Nil	Nil	Nil	NA	NA
Pretax Income	248	214	-237	-4,951	-13,433	-3,114	3.12	-21.0	-20.7	NA
Effective Tax Rate	42.2%	12.9%	NM	NM	NM	NM	NM	NM	NA	NA
Net Income	139	186	-260	-4,961	-13,356	-3,115	3.96	-19.7	-19.2	NA
S&P Core Earnings	-1.39	2.76	-421	-2,080	-7,134	NA	NA	NA	NA	NA
Balance Sheet & Other Financial Data (Million $)										
Cash	477	331	394	282	306	460	70.4	22.8	3.94	NA
Current Assets	1,228	1,006	880	604	1,091	1,186	183	53.7	14.9	NA
Total Assets	3,173	2,593	2,100	2,391	7,538	19,195	341	64.3	24.4	NA
Current Liabilities	938	700	555	665	834	665	42.7	22.6	9.69	NA
Long Term Debt	Nil	Nil	Nil	Nil	Nil	Nil	Nil	Nil	NA	NA
Common Equity	2,032	1,692	1,414	1,579	6,506	18,471	299	40.7	12.5	NA
Total Capital	2,092	1,728	1,443	1,579	6,533	18,471	299	41.7	NA	NA
Capital Expenditures	140	92.5	108	176	380	58.8	6.02	4.41	NA	NA
Cash Flow	330	272	-145	38.9	331	101	9.36	-15.8	-16.6	NA
Current Ratio	1.3	1.4	1.6	0.9	1.3	1.8	4.3	2.4	1.5	NA
% Long Term Debt of Capitalization	Nil	Nil	Nil	Nil	Nil	Nil	Nil	Nil	NA	NA
% Net Income of Revenue	8.6	16.0	NM	NM	NM	NM	4.7	NM	NA	NA
% Return on Assets	4.8	7.9	NM	NM	NM	NM	2.0	NM	NA	NA
% Return on Equity	7.4	12.1	NM	NM	NM	NM	2.3	NM	NA	NA

Data as orig reptd.; bef. results of disc opers/spec. items. Per share data adj. for stk. divs.; EPS diluted. E-Estimated. NA-Not Available. NM-Not Meaningful. NR-Not Ranked. UR-Under Review.

Office: 487 East Middlefield Road, Mountain View, CA 94043.
Telephone: 650-961-7500.
Website: http://www.verisign.com
Chrmn, Pres & CEO: S.D. Sclavos

Vice Chrmn: D.J. Bidzos
Investor Contact: D.L. Evan (866-447-8776)
EVP & CFO: D.L. Evan
SVP, Secy & General Counsel: J.M. Ulam

Board of Directors: D. J. Bidzos, W. L. Chenevich, M. Guthrie, S. G. Kriens, L. J. Lauer, R. H. Moore, E. A. Mueller, G. Reyes, W. A. Roper, Jr., S. D. Sclavos, L. A. Simpson

Founded: 1995
Domicile: Delaware
Employees: 4,076

STANDARD &POOR'S

Verizon Communications Inc

S&P Recommendation HOLD ★★★★★

Price $37.00 (as of Oct 31, 2006)

12-Mo. Target Price $38.00

Investment Style Large-Cap Value

GICS Sector Telecommunication Services
Sub-Industry Integrated Telecommunication Services

Comment VZ offers wireline, wireless and broadband services primarily in the northeastern part of the United States. In January 2006, VZ acquired MCI Inc.

Key Stock Statistics (Source S&P, Vickers, company reports)

52-Wk Range	$38.95–30.00	S&P Oper. EPS 2006E	2.55	P/E on S&P Oper. EPS 2006E	14.5	Dividend Rate/Share	$1.62
Trailing 12-Month EPS	$2.39	S&P Oper. EPS 2007E	2.66	Common Shares Outstg. (M)	2,898.7	Yield (%)	4.38
Trailing 12-Month P/E	15.5	S&P Core EPS 2006E	2.22	Market Capitalization(B)	$107.253	Beta	1.25
$10K Invested 5 Yrs Ago	$9,505	S&P Core EPS 2007E	2.45	Institutional Ownership (%)	60	S&P Credit Rating	NR

Price Performance

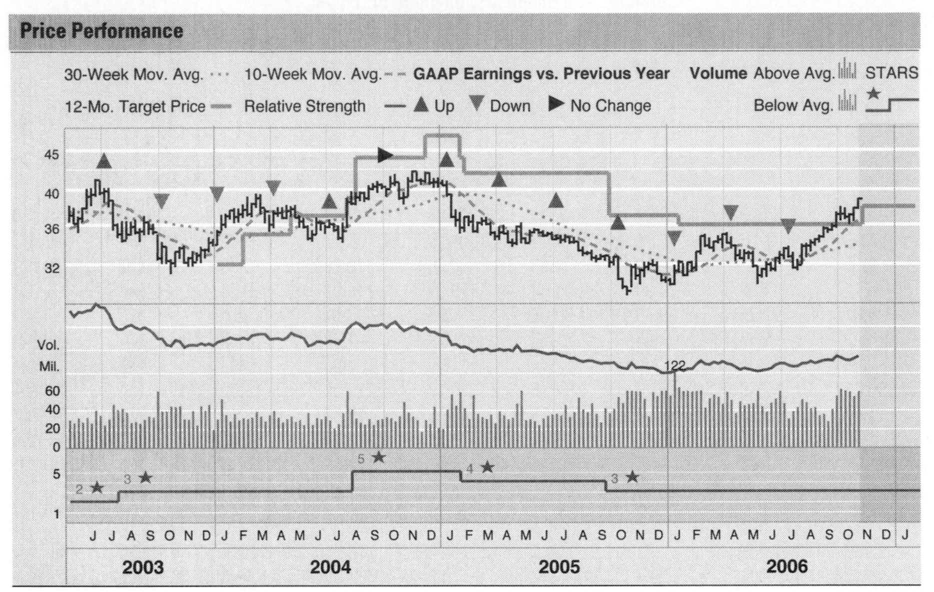

Options: ASE, CBOE, P, Ph

Highlights

➤ The 12-month target price for VZ has recently been changed to $38.00 from $36.00. The Highlights section of this Stock Report will be updated accordingly.

Investment Rationale/Risk

➤ The Investment Rationale/Risk section of this Stock Report will be updated shortly. For the latest News story on VZ from MarketScope, see below.

➤ 10/30/06 09:04 am EST... S&P MAINTAINS HOLD OPINION ON SHARES OF VERIZON COMMUNICATIONS (VZ 38.84***): VZ posts Q3 EPS of $0.66 vs $0.68, $0.04 ahead of our estimate. Revenues were stronger than expected, driven largely by wireless, though wireline was more stable than we had projected. EBITDA margins were wider, even with dilution from the fiber buildout, aided by merger integration benefits. We see access line losses being offset by broadband growth and business gains. We are raising our 12-month target price by $2 to $38, based on relative P/E and enterprise value/EBITDA analyses that reflects our increasing confidence. VZ also provides a 4.2% dividend yield. /T.Rosenbluth

Qualitative Risk Assessment

LOW | **MEDIUM** | HIGH

Our risk assessment reflects our view of VZ's strong cash flow generation, the pricing power it has over its suppliers, and the competitive landscape it faces offering telecom services.

Quantitative Evaluations

S&P Quality Ranking B

D | C | B- | **B** | B+ | A- | A | A+

Relative Strength Rank MODERATE

50

LOWEST = 1 HIGHEST = 99

Revenue/Earnings Data

Revenue (Million $)

	1Q	2Q	3Q	4Q	Year
2006	22,743	22,678	--	--	--
2005	18,179	18,569	19,038	19,326	75,112
2004	17,056	17,758	18,206	18,263	71,283
2003	16,490	16,829	17,155	17,278	67,752
2002	16,375	16,835	17,201	17,214	67,625
2001	16,266	16,909	17,004	17,011	67,190

Earnings Per Share ($)

	1Q	2Q	3Q	4Q	Year
2006	0.57	0.51	**E**0.62	**E**0.64	**E**2.55
2005	0.63	0.75	0.67	0.59	2.65
2004	0.42	0.64	0.64	0.90	2.59
2003	0.63	0.46	0.64	-0.53	1.27
2002	Nil	-0.78	1.60	0.83	1.67
2001	0.65	-0.38	0.69	-0.75	0.22

Fiscal year ended Dec. 31. Next earnings report expected: NA. EPS Estimates based on S&P Operating Earnings; historical GAAP earnings are as reported.

Dividend Data (Dates: mm/dd Payment Date: mm/dd/yy)

Amount ($)	Date Decl.	Ex-Div. Date	Stk. of Record	Payment Date
0.405	03/02	04/06	04/10	05/01/06
0.405	06/01	07/06	07/10	08/01/06
0.405	09/07	10/05	10/10	11/01/06
Stk.	10/18	11/20	11/01	11/17/06

Dividends have been paid since 1984. Source: Company reports.

Verizon Communications Inc

Business Summary August 03, 2006

CORPORATE OVERVIEW. Verizon Communications was formed through the $60 billion merger of Bell Atlantic Corp. and GTE Corp. in June 2000. As of June 2006, VZ provided wireline service to 47 million access lines (down 7.4% from a year earlier) and, through its joint venture with the Vodafone Group, was the second largest wireless carrier, with 54.8 million wireless customers (up 16%). About 65% of VZ's residential local service customers had also purchased DSL and/or long-distance from VZ. In January 2006, VZ completed its $8.5 billion acquisition of MCI Inc. for $2.74 a share in cash and 0.5743 of a share of VZ, adding consumer long distance operations and telecom services targeted to government and medium and large enterprise customers that combined with VZ's operations have been renamed Verizon Business.

MARKET PROFILE. By March 2006, consumers were spending approximately $175 a month on wireline, wireless, Internet, and television services. With spending on wireline services, which Verizon has long dominated, declining in the past 12 months, the company has focused on growing its share of the other communications categories.

In the first half of 2006, Verizon Wireless added an industry leading 3.5 million net subscribers and has what we estimate to be a more than 27% share of the market. Strong industrywide wireless rivalry has raised the level of competition, in our view, with new service plans and data services. As of June 2006, Verizon Wireless had a better-than-average 1.2% monthly churn rate, and 10 million retail customers had access to its BroadbandAccess EV-DO service, which offers made-for-mobile video clips and games. Wireless data service revenues doubled in the second quarter of 2006 and comprised 13% of service revenues.

Similar to its telecom peers, Verizon serves the Internet market through its broadband offerings (6.1 million connections) and has lowered prices and increased the speed of its connectivity in what we view as an effort to upgrade dial-up customers. As of December 2005, cable companies continued to lead the telecom providers, owning a 57% share of the residential broadband market.

Company Financials

Per Share Data ($) Year Ended Dec. 31	**2005**	**2004**	**2003**	**2002**	**2001**	**2000**	**1999**	**1998**	**1997**	**1996**
Tangible Book Value	NM	NM	NM	NM	NM	12.79	10.22	8.39	8.23	8.48
Cash Flow	7.61	7.67	6.14	6.56	5.22	8.43	6.59	5.62	5.29	4.93
Earnings	2.65	2.59	1.27	1.67	0.22	3.95	2.66	1.87	1.57	1.98
S&P Core Earnings	2.42	2.76	1.76	1.91	0.58	NA	NA	NA	NA	NA
Dividends	1.60	1.54	1.54	1.54	1.54	1.54	1.54	1.54	1.49	1.43
Payout Ratio	60%	60%	121%	92%	NM	39%	58%	82%	95%	72%
Prices:High	41.06	42.27	44.31	51.09	57.40	66.00	69.50	61.19	45.88	37.44
Prices:Low	29.13	34.13	31.10	26.01	43.80	39.06	50.63	40.44	28.38	27.56
P/E Ratio:High	15	16	35	31	NM	17	26	33	29	19
P/E Ratio:Low	11	13	24	16	NM	10	19	22	18	14
Income Statement Analysis (Million $)										
Revenue	75,112	71,283	67,752	67,625	67,190	64,707	33,174	31,566	30,194	13,081
Depreciation	14,047	13,910	13,617	13,423	13,657	12,261	6,221	5,870	5,864	2,595
Maintenance	NA	NA	NA	NA	NA	NA	NA	NA	NA	NA
Construction Credits	NA	NA	NA	NA	NA	NA	NA	NA	NA	NA
Effective Tax Rate	23.5%	22.8%	19.7%	21.7%	64.2%	38.9%	37.8%	40.2%	38.4%	36.8%
Net Income	7,397	7,261	3,509	4,584	590	10,810	4,208	2,991	2,455	1,739
S&P Core Earnings	6,774	7,724	4,859	5,250	1,557	NA	NA	NA	NA	NA
Balance Sheet & Other Financial Data (Million $)										
Gross Property	193,610	185,522	180,975	178,028	169,586	158,957	89,238	83,065	77,437	34,758
Net Property	75,305	74,124	75,316	74,496	74,419	69,504	39,299	36,816	35,039	15,916
Capital Expenditures	15,324	13,259	11,884	11,984	17,371	17,633	8,675	7,447	6,638	2,553
Total Capital	120,714	120,819	118,935	122,120	116,888	115,923	39,091	33,678	29,522	14,881
Fixed Charges Coverage	6.7	5.1	2.5	5.5	3.6	3.7	6.9	5.1	4.3	6.1
Capitalization:Long Term Debt	31,869	35,674	39,413	44,791	45,657	42,491	18,664	17,846	13,265	5,960
Capitalization:Preferred	Nil	Nil	Nil	Nil	Nil	Nil	Nil	Nil	200	145
Capitalization:Common	39,680	37,560	33,466	33,720	32,539	36,342	15,880	13,026	12,789	7,423
% Return on Revenue	9.8	10.2	5.2	6.8	0.9	16.7	12.7	9.5	8.1	13.3
% Return on Invested Capital	10.5	8.6	5.1	7.6	4.0	15.4	16.9	18.3	17.2	19.7
% Return on Common Equity	19.2	20.4	10.6	13.5	1.8	33.5	29.1	23.2	24.3	24.7
% Earned on Net Property	37.9	36.2	28.1	34.5	50.5	38.3	22.3	18.4	21.0	18.5
% Long Term Debt of Capitalization	44.5	48.7	54.1	36.6	58.4	53.9	54.0	57.8	50.5	44.1
Capital % Preferred	Nil	Nil	Nil	Nil	Nil	Nil	Nil	Nil	0.8	1.1
Capitalization:% Common	55.5	51.3	45.9	42.9	41.6	46.1	46.0	42.2	48.7	54.9

Data as orig reptd.; bef. results of disc opers/spec. items. Per share data adj. for stk. divs.; EPS diluted. E-Estimated. NA-Not Available. NM-Not Meaningful. NR-Not Ranked. UR-Under Review.

Office: 1095 Avenue of the Americas, New York, NY 10036.
Telephone: 212-395-2121.
Website: http://www.verizon.com
Chrmn & CEO: I.G. Seidenberg

Pres & Vice Chrmn: L.T. Babbio, Jr.
EVP & CFO: D. Toben
EVP & General Counsel: W.P. Barr
SVP & Treas: T.A. Bartlett

Investor Contact: C. Webster
Board of Directors: J. R. Barker, R. L. Carrion, R. W. Lane, S. O. Moose, J. Neubauer, D. T. Nicolaisen, T. H. O'Brien, C. Otis Jr., H. B. Price, I. G. Seidenberg, W. V. Shipley, J. R. Stafford, R. D. Storey

Founded: 1983
Domicile: Delaware
Employees: 217,000

V.F. Corp

S&P Recommendation BUY ★★★★★

Price $74.63 (as of Oct 27, 2006)

12-Mo. Target Price $88.00

Investment Style Mid-Cap Value

GICS Sector Consumer Discretionary
Sub-Industry Apparel, Accessories & Luxury Goods

Comment VFC is a global apparel company with leading shares in denim and intimate apparel that is transforming into a designer and marketer of lifestyle apparel brands.

Key Stock Statistics (Source S&P, Vickers, company reports)

52-Wk Range	$78.57–51.80	S&P Oper. EPS 2006E	5.10	P/E on S&P Oper. EPS 2006E	14.6	Dividend Rate/Share	$2.20
Trailing 12-Month EPS	$4.88	S&P Oper. EPS 2007E	5.70	Common Shares Outstg. (M)	110.9	Yield (%)	2.95
Trailing 12-Month P/E	15.3	S&P Core EPS 2006E	5.20	Market Capitalization(B)	$8.278	Beta	0.88
$10K Invested 5 Yrs Ago	$24,029	S&P Core EPS 2007E	5.80	Institutional Ownership (%)	89	S&P Credit Rating	A-

Price Performance

Analysis prepared by **Marie Driscoll, CFA** on October 23, 2006, when the stock traded at **$ 75.05**.

Highlights

- We look for about 7% sales growth in 2006 and 2007, driven by high single to low double digit growth in VFC's lifestyle brands and flat to modest increases in its heritage businesses. We see organic growth at Nautica in tandem with its women's product launch. At Vans, we look for increased international market penetration and continued gains for The North Face brand of outdoor products.

- We project modest EBIT margin expansion in 2006 and 2007 from the 12.7% achieved in 2004 and 2005, with VFC increasing marketing spending to support the lifestyle emphasis, funded by sourcing savings. VFC's move to centralize supply chain functions across the organization should lead to improved efficiencies longer term, in our view.

- We project 2006 EPS of $5.10, up 12% from 2005's $4.54 operating EPS (excludes a one-time $0.10 cumulative adjustment charge). Our 2006 estimate includes projected stock option expense of $0.17. We estimate EPS of $5.70 for 2007.

Investment Rationale/Risk

- We believe that a number of VFC's recent acquisitions have superior growth potential, as does further penetration of the international market, and, given our view of the acumen of the company's management team, we anticipate market share gains and improving profitability. At VFC's mature denim and intimates brands, we are seeing a turnaround that we believe will gain traction in the 2006-2008 period. VFC plans to open about 75 to 100 retail store annually (up from the current 560), supporting its Vans, The North Face, Napapiri, Kipling, and Lee brands.

- Risks to our recommendation and target price include fashion and inventory risk, and integration risk from recent acquisitions.

- Our 12-month target price of $88 is derived by incorporating a peer group forward P/E multiple of 15X applied to our 2007 EPS estimate of $5.70. The dividend was recently increased 90%, to yield 2.9%.

Qualitative Risk Assessment

LOW | **MEDIUM** | HIGH

Our risk assessment reflects our view of VFC's strong cash flow, offset by integration risk as VFC pursues growth via acquisitions.

Quantitative Evaluations

S&P Quality Ranking A-

D | C | B- | B | B+ | **A-** | A | A+

Relative Strength Rank MODERATE

54

LOWEST = 1 HIGHEST = 99

Revenue/Earnings Data

Revenue (Million $)

	1Q	2Q	3Q	4Q	Year
2006	1,656	1,567	2,015	--	--
2005	1,582	1,452	1,822	1,646	6,502
2004	1,433	1,270	1,793	1,560	6,055
2003	1,250	1,135	1,435	1,387	5,207
2002	1,212	1,160	1,400	1,311	5,084
2001	1,423	1,323	1,477	1,295	5,519

Earnings Per Share ($)

2006	1.14	0.88	1.75	E1.30	E5.10
2005	1.00	0.85	1.57	1.13	4.54
2004	0.93	0.80	1.38	1.10	4.21
2003	0.83	0.68	1.14	0.96	3.61
2002	0.67	0.79	1.15	0.69	3.24
2001	0.67	0.60	0.90	-1.03	1.19

Fiscal year ended Dec. 31. Next earnings report expected: Early February. EPS Estimates based on S&P Operating Earnings; historical GAAP earnings are as reported.

Dividend Data (Dates: mm/dd Payment Date: mm/dd/yy)

Amount ($)	Date Decl.	Ex-Div. Date	Stk. of Record	Payment Date
0.290	02/08	03/08	03/10	03/20/06
0.550	04/25	06/07	06/09	06/19/06
0.550	07/19	09/06	09/08	09/18/06
0.550	10/20	12/06	12/08	12/18/06

Dividends have been paid since 1941. Source: Company reports.

Business Summary October 23, 2006

CORPORATE OVERVIEW. VF Corp. is the world's largest apparel manufacturer, and holds the leading position in several market categories, including jeanswear, intimate apparel, workwear and daypacks. In early 2004, VFC developed a growth plan to support its long-term sales growth target of 6% to 8% annually, its 14% operating margin goal, and a 17% return on invested capital goal. The growth strategy consists of five drivers: building new growing lifestyle brands; expanding share with successful retailers; growing internationally; leveraging supply chain and information technology; and identifying, developing and recruiting qualified leaders.

MARKET PROFILE. VFC participates in the broad apparel market, spanning product categories from women's intimate apparel to denim, as well as the outdoor market for apparel and accessories via its lifestyle brands. Apparel is a mature market, with demand mirroring population growth and a modicum related to fashion; it is fragmented, with national brands marketed by 20 companies accounting for about 30% of total apparel sales and the remaining 70% comprised of smaller and/or private label "store"brands. Deflationary pricing pressure is a function, we think, of channel competition and production steadily moving offshore to low-cost producers in India, Asia and China. S&P forecasts a low single digit increase in 2006 apparel sales, generally in line with GDP growth, versus a 4% year-to-year-advance in 2004 and 2005, and a 5% decline in 2003.

The outdoor market is reaching a broader audience, in our view, as more Americans are attracted to a healthy lifestyle. According to the Outdoor Industry Foundation, during 2004 (latest data available), more than 70% of Americans, or 159 million people, 16 and older participated in at least one outdoor sport (26% of which were in the 16-24 year old age group), with a mean household income of $60,000. Hiking and biking are the most popular activities, with more than 75 million participants. The Outdoor Industry Association estimated retail sales of products (apparel, footwear and equipment) used in outdoor activities at $33 billion for the 12 months ended July 2005. Spurring growth is the increase in participants as well as enthusiasts.

Company Financials

Per Share Data ($) Year Ended Dec. 31	**2005**	**2004**	**2003**	**2002**	**2001**	**2000**	**1999**	**1998**	**1997**	**1996**
Tangible Book Value	8.78	7.56	8.61	10.91	9.97	9.71	10.08	9.36	8.69	8.67
Cash Flow	5.56	5.53	4.64	4.35	0.00	3.73	5.71	4.39	3.87	3.57
Earnings	4.54	4.21	3.61	3.24	1.19	2.27	2.99	3.10	2.70	2.32
S&P Core Earnings	4.67	4.36	3.70	2.75	0.77	NA	NA	NA	NA	NA
Dividends	1.10	1.05	1.01	0.97	0.93	0.89	0.85	0.81	0.77	0.73
Payout Ratio	24%	25%	28%	30%	78%	39%	28%	26%	29%	31%
Prices:High	61.61	55.61	44.08	45.64	42.70	36.90	55.00	54.69	48.25	34.94
Prices:Low	50.44	42.06	32.62	31.50	28.15	20.94	27.44	33.44	32.25	23.81
P/E Ratio:High	14	13	12	14	36	16	18	18	18	15
P/E Ratio:Low	11	10	9	10	24	9	9	11	12	10

Income Statement Analysis (Million $)										
Revenue	6,502	6,055	5,207	5,084	5,519	5,748	5,552	5,479	5,222	5,137
Operating Income	944	874	718	729	516	683	820	845	761	718
Depreciation	116	141	104	107	169	173	335	161	156	161
Interest Expense	70.6	76.1	61.4	71.3	93.4	88.7	71.4	62.0	50.0	62.8
Pretax Income	771	712	599	562	263	432	596	631	585	508
Effective Tax Rate	32.7%	33.3%	33.5%	35.1%	47.6%	38.1%	38.5%	38.5%	40.0%	41.1%
Net Income	519	475	398	364	138	267	366	388	351	300
S&P Core Earnings	532	490	406	303	84.6	NA	NA	NA	NA	NA

Balance Sheet & Other Financial Data (Million $)										
Cash	297	486	515	496	332	119	79.9	63.0	124	271
Current Assets	2,365	2,379	2,209	2,075	2,031	2,110	1,877	1,848	1,601	1,706
Total Assets	5,171	5,004	4,246	3,503	4,103	4,358	4,027	3,837	3,323	3,450
Current Liabilities	1,152	1,372	872	875	814	1,006	1,113	1,033	766	766
Long Term Debt	648	557	956	602	904	905	518	522	516	519
Common Equity	2,808	2,513	1,951	1,658	2,113	2,192	2,164	2,046	1,841	1,974
Total Capital	3,479	3,096	2,938	2,297	3,062	3,145	2,733	2,622	2,439	2,562
Capital Expenditures	110	81.4	86.6	64.5	81.6	125	150	189	154	139
Cash Flow	635	615	502	472	304	437	698	549	503	457
Current Ratio	2.1	1.7	2.5	2.4	2.5	2.1	1.7	1.8	2.1	2.2
% Long Term Debt of Capitalization	18.6	18.0	32.6	26.2	29.5	28.8	18.9	19.9	21.1	20.3
% Net Income of Revenue	7.9	7.8	7.6	7.2	2.5	4.6	6.6	7.1	6.7	5.9
% Return on Assets	10.2	10.3	10.3	9.6	3.3	6.4	9.3	10.8	10.4	8.6
% Return on Equity	19.5	21.3	22.1	19.3	6.3	12.1	17.1	20.0	18.3	15.8

Data as orig reptd.; bef. results of disc opers/spec. items. Per share data adj. for stk. divs.; EPS diluted. E-Estimated. NA-Not Available. NM-Not Meaningful. NR-Not Ranked. UR-Under Review.

Office: 105 Corporate Center Boulevard , Greensboro, NC 27408.
Telephone: 336-424-6000.
Email: irrequest@vfc.com
Website: http://www.vfc.com

Chrmn & CEO: M.J. McDonald
Pres & COO: E.C. Wiseman
SVP & CFO: R.K. Shearer
VP & Treas: F. Pickard, III

VP, Secy & General Counsel: C.S. Cummings
Investor Contact: C. Knoebel (336-424-6189)
Board of Directors: E. E. Crutchfield, J. Ernesto de Bedout, U. F. Fairbairn, B. S. Feigin, G. Fellows, D. Hesse, R. J. Hurst, W. A. McCollough, M. J. McDonald, C. Otis, Jr., M. R. Sharp, R. G. Viault, E. C. Wiseman

Founded: 1899
Domicile: Pennsylvania
Employees: 52,300

Viacom Inc

STANDARD &POOR'S

S&P Recommendation HOLD ★★★★★

Price $39.93 (as of Oct 27, 2006)

12-Mo. Target Price $38.00

Investment Style Large-Cap Value

GICS Sector Consumer Discretionary
Sub-Industry Movies & Entertainment

Comment Among the key brands of this entertainment content provider, one of the two companies that emerged after the January 2006 split of "old" Viacom into two companies, are MTV Networks and Paramount Pictures (which acquired DreamWorks studios).

Key Stock Statistics (Source S&P, Vickers, company reports)

52-Wk Range	$44.95–32.42	S&P Oper. EPS 2006E	1.95	P/E on S&P Oper. EPS 2006E	20.5	Dividend Rate/Share	Nil
Trailing 12-Month EPS	$1.76	S&P Oper. EPS 2007E	2.26	Common Shares Outstg. (M)	709.5	Yield (%)	Nil
Trailing 12-Month P/E	22.7	S&P Core EPS 2006E	1.95	Market Capitalization(B)	$25.890	Beta	1.00
$10K Invested 5 Yrs Ago	NA	S&P Core EPS 2007E	2.26	Institutional Ownership (%)	75	S&P Credit Rating	NA

Price Performance

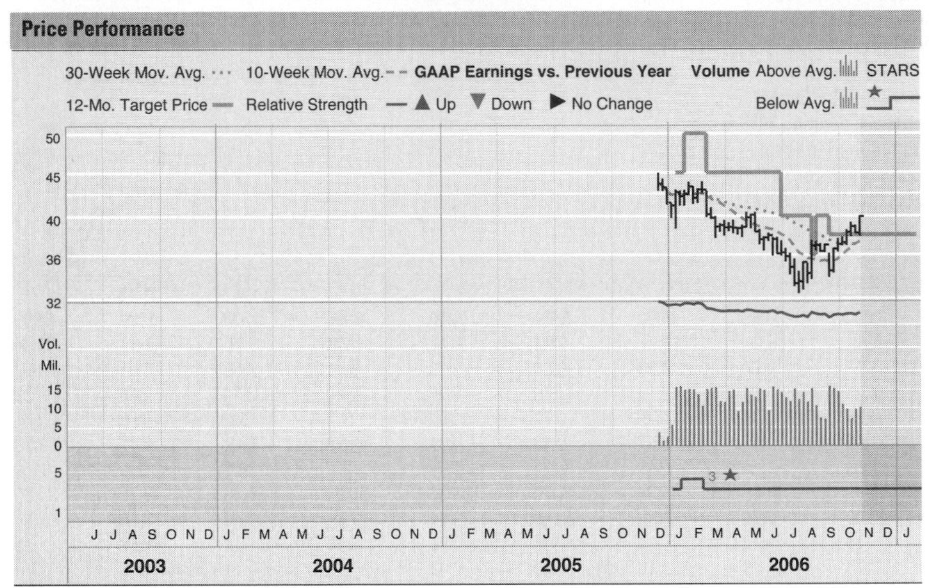

Analysis prepared by **Tuna N. Amobi, CFA, CPA** on September 29, 2006, when the stock traded at **$ 37.50**.

Highlights

- We estimate that total revenues will rise 19% in 2006 (including DreamWorks, acquired in February), and 7% in 2007. We view MTV Networks as the primary driver, with a relatively steady base of ad revenues and worldwide affiliate fees, and growing consumer licensing business at Nickelodeon. We are cautious on Paramount Pictures (where VIA.B plans 14 to 16 films per year, including four to six at DreamWorks), but we see some upside in home video with more catalog and current releases.
- We see cable networks cash flow margins above 40%, aided by stronger ancillary contributions, and despite likely higher programming expenses and continued digital investments. However, the entertainment segment's margins could be depressed by higher film amortization and marketing costs at Paramount.
- We project total EBITDA of $3.3 billion and $3.7 billion in 2006 and 2007, respectively, and after significantly higher interest expense, we forecast EPS of $1.95 and $2.26 (including $0.04 of projected option expense), assuming continued stock buybacks under a $3 billion program set earlier in January.

Investment Rationale/Risk

- After what we view as relatively strong 2006 second quarter results, we were somewhat surprised by the abrupt ouster of former CEO Tom Freston in early September. However, we are encouraged by comments from new CEO Philippe Dauman, who sees no major shift in strategy, but plans to foster a more entrepreneurial culture. Our outlook is tempered by what we consider a lackluster 2006-07 cable upfront market. We see multi-faceted digital initiatives, including MTV's content syndication deal with Google, which should help drive management's targeted double digit revenue and earnings growth over the next few years.
- Risks to our recommendation and target price include an ad slowdown, potentially dilutive acquisitions, uncertainties with Paramount's turnaround strategy, film volatility, post-separation governance issues, and foreign exchange exposure.
- Our 12-month target price of $38 is 17X-18X projected free cash flow of $1.5 billion and $1.6 billion in 2006 and 2007, respectively. We view the stock's 1.5X forward P/E-to-growth ratio as ample relative to peers and the S&P 500.

Qualitative Risk Assessment

LOW | **MEDIUM** | HIGH

Our risk assessment of this pure content player reflects what we view as its leading demographically targeted brands, relatively strong growth prospects and ample financial flexibility, offset by its exposure to cyclical advertising, a volatile film business, and post-separation governance issues.

Quantitative Evaluations

S&P Quality Ranking NR

D | C | B- | B | B+ | A- | A | A+

Relative Strength Rank STRONG

76

LOWEST = 1 HIGHEST = 99

Revenue/Earnings Data

Revenue (Million $)

	1Q	2Q	3Q	4Q	Year
2006	2,368	2,847	--	--	--
2005	2,107	2,302	2,478	2,724	9,610
2004	--	--	--	--	8,132
2003	--	--	--	--	--
2002	--	--	--	--	--
2001	--	--	--	--	--

Earnings Per Share ($)

	1Q	2Q	3Q	4Q	Year
2006	0.43	0.58	E0.46	E0.58	E1.95
2005	--	--	--	0.29	1.73
2004	--	--	--	--	1.48
2003	--	--	--	--	--
2002	--	--	--	--	--
2001	--	--	--	--	--

Fiscal year ended Dec. 31. Next earnings report expected: NA. EPS Estimates based on S&P Operating Earnings; historical GAAP earnings are as reported.

Dividend Data

No cash dividends have been paid.

Please read the Required Disclosures and Analyst Certification on the last page of this report.

The McGraw·Hill Companies

Viacom Inc

Business Summary September 29, 2006

CORPORATE OVERVIEW. In its present form, the "new" Viacom is one of the two public companies created after the January 2006 separation of the "old" Viacom into two independent public entities (the "old" Viacom was renamed CBS Corp.). Each Class A and B shareholder of the "old" Viacom got 0.5 of a share of the corresponding A or B stock of each of the new entities. We believe that the company is the faster growing of the two companies resulting from the separation, and specifically targeted to growth-oriented investors.

The company's cable networks segment (70% of 2005 revenues) mainly comprises MTV Networks (including MTV, Nickelodeon, VH1, Comedy Central, Country Music Television, Spike TV, TV Land, Logo, Neopets, Xfire and VIVA) and BET Networks. The entertainment segment (30%) includes Paramount Pictures film studio (and home entertainment) and Famous Music (publishing). About 40% of 2005 revenues were derived from ad sales, 21% from affiliate fees, 30% from feature films, and 9% from other ancillary sources (including merchandise licensing).

CORPORATE STRATEGY. We expect a new management team led by Philippe Dauman to remain focused on digital initiatives across various broadband and wireless platforms, aided by partnerships with telecom and technology companies. In August, MTV signed a content syndication deal to distribute its video across dozens of websites under Google's ad network. Since the start of 2006, the company has made selective digital acquisitions (mostly in online gaming and films), including Xfire, Y2M, Atom Entertainment and, most recently, a pending deal for Harmonic Music Systems. The company's global footprint traverses Europe and emerging markets (India and China), with nearly 125 channels (including over 95 MTV channels) across 169 territories in 28 languages, reaching nearly 450 million homes.

Company Financials

Per Share Data ($) Year Ended Dec. 31	2005	2004	2003	2002	2001	2000	1999	1998	1997	1996
Tangible Book Value	NM	NM	NA	NA	NA	NA	NA	NA	NA	NA
Cash Flow	2.08	1.78	NA	NA	NA	NA	NA	NA	NA	NA
Earnings	1.73	1.48	NA	NA	NA	NA	NA	NA	NA	NA
S&P Core Earnings	1.46	1.47	NA	NA	NA	NA	NA	NA	NA	NA
Dividends	Nil	NA	NA	NA	NA	NA	NA	NA	NA	NA
Payout Ratio	Nil	NA	NA	NA	NA	NA	NA	NA	NA	NA
Prices:High	44.95	NA	NA	NA	NA	NA	NA	NA	NA	NA
Prices:Low	39.78	NA	NA	NA	NA	NA	NA	NA	NA	NA
P/E Ratio:High	26	NA	NA	NA	NA	NA	NA	NA	NA	NA
P/E Ratio:Low	23	NA	NA	NA	NA	NA	NA	NA	NA	NA

Income Statement Analysis (Million $)	2005	2004	2003	2002	2001	2000	1999	1998	1997	1996
Revenue	9,610	8,132	NA	NA	NA	NA	NA	NA	NA	NA
Operating Income	2,625	2,534	NA	NA	NA	NA	NA	NA	NA	NA
Depreciation	259	2,522	NA	NA	NA	NA	NA	NA	NA	NA
Interest Expense	23.0	20.0	NA	NA	NA	NA	NA	NA	NA	NA
Pretax Income	2,328	2,017	NA	NA	NA	NA	NA	NA	NA	NA
Effective Tax Rate	43.8%	36.4%	NA	NA	NA	NA	NA	NA	NA	NA
Net Income	1,304	1,281	NA	NA	NA	NA	NA	NA	NA	NA
S&P Core Earnings	1,165	1,282	NA	NA	NA	NA	NA	NA	NA	NA

Balance Sheet & Other Financial Data (Million $)	2005	2004	2003	2002	2001	2000	1999	1998	1997	1996
Cash	361	99.2	NA	NA	NA	NA	NA	NA	NA	NA
Current Assets	3,513	2,384	NA	NA	NA	NA	NA	NA	NA	NA
Total Assets	19,116	18,400	NA	NA	NA	NA	NA	NA	NA	NA
Current Liabilities	3,269	2,617	NA	NA	NA	NA	NA	NA	NA	NA
Long Term Debt	5,702	3,718	NA	NA	NA	NA	NA	NA	NA	NA
Common Equity	7,788	9,905	NA	NA	NA	NA	NA	NA	NA	NA
Total Capital	13,534	13,623	NA	NA	NA	NA	NA	NA	NA	NA
Capital Expenditures	193	NA	NA	NA	NA	NA	NA	NA	NA	NA
Cash Flow	1,563	1,533	NA	NA	NA	NA	NA	NA	NA	NA
Current Ratio	1.1	0.9	NA	NA	NA	NA	NA	NA	NA	NA
% Long Term Debt of Capitalization	42.1	27.3	NA	NA	NA	NA	NA	NA	NA	NA
% Net Income of Revenue	13.6	15.8	NA	NA	NA	NA	NA	NA	NA	NA
% Return on Assets	6.9	NA	NA	NA	NA	NA	NA	NA	NA	NA
% Return on Equity	12.3	NA	NA	NA	NA	NA	NA	NA	NA	NA

Data as orig reptd.; bef. results of disc opers/spec. items. Per share data adj. for stk. divs.; EPS diluted. E-Estimated. NA-Not Available. NM-Not Meaningful. NR-Not Ranked. UR-Under Review.

Office: 51 W 52nd St, New York, NY 10019-6188.
Telephone: 212-975-4321.
Website: http://www.viacom.com
Exec Chrmn: S.M. Redstone

Pres & CEO: P. Dauman
Sr EVP & Chief Admin: T.E. Dooley
EVP & CFO: M.J. Dolan
EVP, Secy & General Counsel: M.D. Fricklas

Investor Contact: J. Bombassei
Board of Directors: G. S. Abrams, P. P. Dauman, T. E. Dooley, T. E. Freston, E. V. Futter, A. C. Greenberg, R. K. Kraft, C. E. Phillips, Jr., S. Redstone, S. M. Redstone, F. V. Salerno, W. Schwartz

Founded: 2005
Domicile: Delaware
Employees: 9,500

Vornado Realty Trust

STANDARD &POOR'S

S&P Recommendation HOLD ★★★★★

Price $119.25 (as of Oct 31, 2006)

12-Mo. Target Price $116.00

Investment Style Large-Cap Growth

GICS Sector Financials
Sub-Industry Diversified REITS

Comment This REIT owns a diverse group of properties, including Northeast retail properties, New York City office buildings, and interests in a cold-storage company and Alexander's, Inc.

Key Stock Statistics (Source S&P, Vickers, company reports)

52-Wk Range	$119.39–78.35	S&P Oper. EPS 2006E	3.10	P/E on S&P Oper. EPS 2006E	38.5	Dividend Rate/Share	$3.40
Trailing 12-Month EPS	$2.77	S&P Oper. EPS 2007E	3.65	Common Shares Outstg. (M)	141.7	Yield (%)	2.85
Trailing 12-Month P/E	43.1	S&P Core EPS 2006E	2.69	Market Capitalization(B)	$16.900	Beta	0.48
$10K Invested 5 Yrs Ago	$39,722	S&P Core EPS 2007E	3.65	Institutional Ownership (%)	79	S&P Credit Rating	BBB+

Price Performance

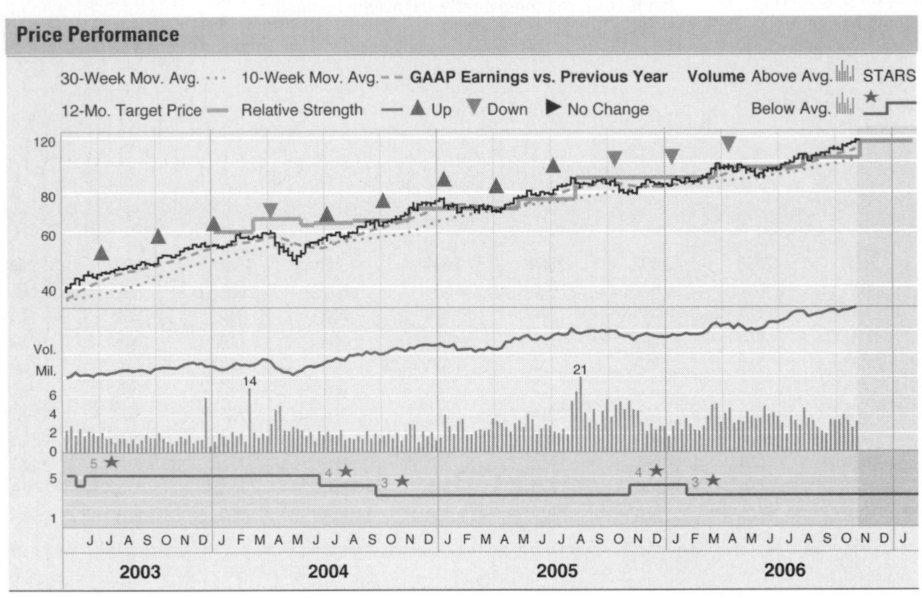

Highlights

➤ The 12-month target price for VNO has recently been changed to $116.00 from $103.00. The Highlights section of this Stock Report will be updated accordingly.

Investment Rationale/Risk

➤ The Investment Rationale/Risk section of this Stock Report will be updated shortly. For the latest News story on VNO from MarketScope, see below.

➤ 10/31/06 02:15 pm EST... S&P MAINTAINS HOLD RECOMMENDATION ON SHARES OF VORNADO REALTY TRUST (VNO 118.55***): Sep-Q EPS from continuing ops. of $0.76 trails our $0.80 estimate but compares to $0.19 a year ago on greater investment gains. Per-share FFO of $1.31 exceeds $1.25 consensus. Results reflect strong demand for office space in New York and Washington and higher retail rental income. We are increasing our '06 EPS estimate by $0.10 to $3.10, while keeping our FFO est. at $5.15. On positive office market trends, we initiate a '07 FFO forecast of $5.65. Our new $116 target price, up $13, is based on 20.5X our '07 FFO est., comparable to office peers. VNO currently yields 2.9%. /R. Shepard

Qualitative Risk Assessment

LOW	MEDIUM	HIGH

Our risk assessment of VNO reflects its large market capitalization, what we see as its financial strength, diversified asset portfolio, and low stock volatility as measured by beta.

Quantitative Evaluations

S&P Quality Ranking A

D	C	B-	B	B+	A-	A	A+

Relative Strength Rank STRONG

82

LOWEST = 1 HIGHEST = 99

Revenue/Earnings Data

Revenue (Million $)

	1Q	2Q	3Q	4Q	Year
2006	647.6	663.0	--	--	--
2005	598.7	594.8	657.0	697.2	2,548
2004	391.4	397.8	413.4	504.7	1,707
2003	365.0	371.1	380.2	386.8	1,503
2002	346.3	353.3	361.2	366.8	1,435
2001	242.6	246.1	250.3	246.8	985.8

Earnings Per Share ($)

	1Q	2Q	3Q	4Q	Year
2006	0.79	--	**E**0.76	**E**0.66	**E**3.10
2005	1.38	1.03	0.19	0.71	3.27
2004	0.59	0.69	0.72	1.72	3.75
2003	0.75	0.66	0.56	1.66	2.29
2002	0.40	0.57	0.52	0.36	2.18
2001	0.52	0.64	0.74	0.57	2.50

Fiscal year ended Dec. 31. Next earnings report expected: Early November. EPS Estimates based on S&P Operating Earnings; historical GAAP earnings are as reported.

Dividend Data (Dates: mm/dd Payment Date: mm/dd/yy)

Amount ($)	Date Decl.	Ex-Div. Date	Stk. of Record	Payment Date
0.800	04/27	05/03	05/05	05/17/06
0.800	07/27	08/07	08/09	08/22/06
.54 Spl.	10/26	11/03	11/07	11/21/06
0.850	10/26	11/03	11/07	11/21/06

Dividends have been paid since 1990. Source: Company reports.

Vornado Realty Trust

Business Summary August 14, 2006

CORPORATE OVERVIEW. Vornado Realty Trust is a diversified REIT that has interests in a wide range of properties, including office buildings, retail properties, refrigerated warehouses, a hotel, and dry warehouses, among others, primarily in the Northeast. The company conducts its business through, was the sole general partner of, and, as of June 30, 2006, owned 89.7% of the limited partnership interests, in Vornado Realty L.P.

MARKET PROFILE. During 2005, VNO derived 59% of operating segment EBITDA from office properties. The market for office leases is inherently cyclical. The U.S. office market tends to track the overall economy on a lagged basis. As of June 30 2006, we believe the national vacancy rate was approximately 14%, reflecting improvement since cyclical lows in 2002-2003.

Local economic conditions, particularly the employment level, play an important role in determining competitive dynamics. In our opinion, VNO's principal target markets, the New York City metropolitan area and Washington DC, have among the lowest vacancy rates in the nation at less than 10%. In addition, unlike many markets, rates on new or renewed leases are often at higher rates than those previously in place. At June 30, 2006, VNO owned or had an interest in 111 office properties totaling 31.7 million sq. ft. The New York portfolio was 96.6% occupied at June 30, 2006; the Washington, DC, portfolio was 92.2% occupied.

In 2005, VNO derived about 19% of EBITDA from its retail segment. As of June 30, 2006, the retail portfolio included about 14.8 million sq. ft. in nine states and Washington DC. For VNO, as well as other retail oriented REITS, location and the financial health and growth of its retail tenants are among the most important factors affecting the success of its portfolio. Further, the companies in this industry enjoy relatively high barriers to entry, since developing new shopping centers requires large amounts of capital as well as time-consuming regulatory approvals which have been difficult to obtain in the recent past amid concerns about traffic and pollution. We expect VNO to focus on the re-development of recently acquired properties, including the Broadway Mall on Long Island and the Springfield Mall in Fairfax County, Virginia.

Company Financials

Per Share Data ($) Year Ended Dec. 31	**2005**	**2004**	**2003**	**2002**	**2001**	**2000**	**1999**	**1998**	**1997**	**1996**
Tangible Book Value	31.38	26.86	24.15	21.68	21.15	18.31	18.14	17.55	14.19	5.21
Earnings	3.27	3.75	2.29	2.18	2.50	2.21	1.94	1.59	0.79	1.25
S&P Core Earnings	3.09	3.62	3.63	2.15	2.58	NA	NA	NA	NA	NA
Dividends	3.85	2.89	2.91	2.97	2.31	1.97	1.81	1.64	1.36	1.22
Payout Ratio	118%	77%	127%	136%	92%	89%	93%	103%	172%	98%
Prices:High	89.70	76.99	55.84	47.20	42.03	40.75	40.00	49.81	47.38	26.44
Prices:Low	68.25	47.00	33.25	33.20	34.47	29.87	29.69	26.00	25.38	17.81
P/E Ratio:High	27	21	24	22	17	18	21	31	60	21
P/E Ratio:Low	21	13	15	15	14	14	15	16	32	14
Income Statement Analysis (Million $)										
Rental Income	1,397	1,345	1,261	1,249	842	695	591	426	168	87.4
Mortgage Income	Nil	Nil	Nil	Nil	Nil	Nil	Nil	Nil	Nil	Nil
Total Income	2,548	1,707	1,503	1,435	986	827	697	510	209	117
General Expenses	1,488	825	706	668	472	366	322	295	88.3	55.3
Interest Expense	341	242	230	240	173	170	142	115	42.9	16.7
Provision for Losses	Nil	Nil	Nil	Nil	Nil	Nil	Nil	Nil	Nil	Nil
Depreciation	335	243	215	206	124	99.8	83.6	59.2	45.9	11.6
Net Income	507	514	285	263	267	235	203	153	61.0	61.0
S&P Core Earnings	435	476	421	236	238	NA	NA	NA	NA	NA
Balance Sheet & Other Financial Data (Million $)										
Cash	1,941	1,390	1,464	1,512	1,867	1,931	1,565	4,206	2,291	117
Total Assets	13,637	11,581	9,519	9,018	6,777	6,370	5,479	4,426	2,524	565
Real Estate Investment	11,449	9,757	7,748	7,560	4,690	4,295	3,922	3,316	1,564	397
Loss Reserve	Nil	Nil	Nil	Nil	Nil	Nil	Nil	Nil	Nil	Nil
Net Investment	9,776	8,349	6,879	6,822	4,184	3,901	3,613	3,089	1,391	246
Short Term Debt	398	Nil	Nil	Nil	Nil	425	681	268	120	1.05
Capitalization:Debt	5,857	4,937	3,768	3,622	1,643	2,232	1,368	1,783	957	241
Capitalization:Equity	4,260	3,301	2,827	2,362	2,101	1,597	1,577	1,782	1,025	1,025
Capitalization:Total	12,208	8,238	8,767	8,287	5,693	5,767	4,645	2,216	2,330	517
% Earnings & Depreciation/Assets	6.6	7.1	5.4	5.9	5.9	5.6	5.8	6.1	6.9	13.8
Price Times Book Value:High	2.9	2.9	2.3	2.2	2.0	2.2	2.2	2.8	3.3	5.1
Price Times Book Value:Low	2.2	1.7	1.4	1.5	1.6	1.6	1.6	1.5	1.8	3.4

Data as orig reptd.; bef. results of disc opers/spec. items. Per share data adj. for stk. divs.; EPS diluted. E-Estimated. NA-Not Available. NM-Not Meaningful. NR-Not Ranked. UR-Under Review.

Office: 888 Seventh Avenue, New York , NY 10019-4308.
Telephone: 212-894-7000.
Website: http://www.vno.com
Chrmn & CEO: S. Roth

Pres: M.D. Fascitelli
Investor Contact: J. Macnow (201-587-1000)
EVP & CFO: J. Macnow

Founded: 1941
Domicile: Maryland
Employees: 3,015

Vulcan Materials Co

STANDARD &POOR'S

S&P Recommendation BUY ★★★★☆	**Price** $81.48 (as of Oct 31, 2006)	**12-Mo. Target Price** $96.00	**Investment Style** Mid-Cap Growth

GICS Sector Materials
Sub-Industry Construction Materials

Comment This company is the largest U.S. producer of construction aggregates and a major producer of other construction materials.

Key Stock Statistics (Source S&P, Vickers, company reports)

52-Wk Range	$93.85–63.40	S&P Oper. EPS 2006E	4.65	P/E on S&P Oper. EPS 2006E	17.5	Dividend Rate/Share	$1.48
Trailing 12-Month EPS	$4.38	S&P Oper. EPS 2007E	5.15	Common Shares Outstg. (M)	96.5	Yield (%)	1.82
Trailing 12-Month P/E	18.6	S&P Core EPS 2006E	4.53	Market Capitalization(B)	$7.862	Beta	1.05
$10K Invested 5 Yrs Ago	$20,818	S&P Core EPS 2007E	NA	Institutional Ownership (%)	77	S&P Credit Rating	A+

Price Performance

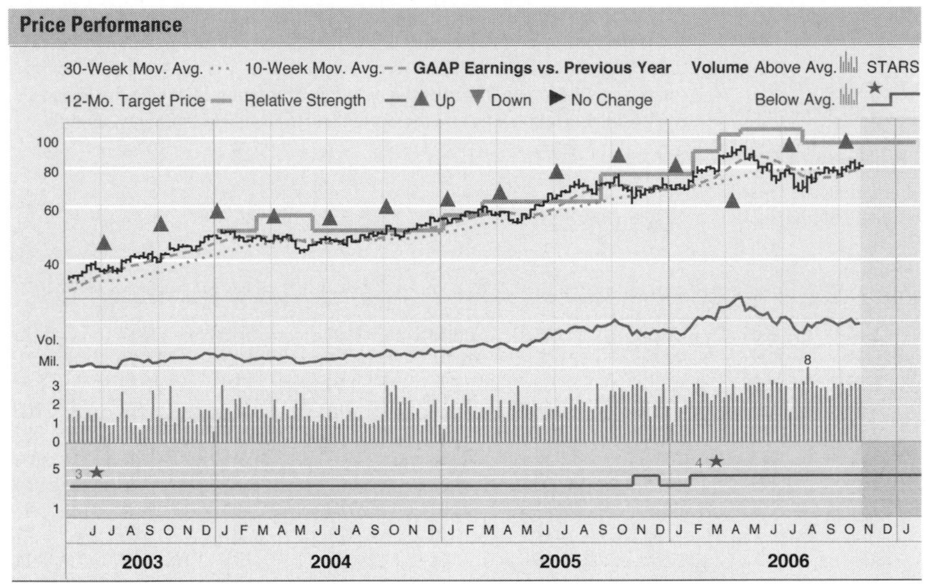

Options: P

Analysis prepared by **Leo J. Larkin** on July 28, 2006, when the stock traded at **$ 68.73**.

Highlights

- We expect sales from continuing operations to advance 24% in 2006, reflecting higher average revenue per ton and another increase in tons shipped. Our expectation for increased volume and prices assumes 3.5% GDP growth for 2006, versus 2005's 3.5% growth. We also believe private nonresidential construction spending troughed in 2003, and will continue to rise in 2006. In addition, we look for increased highway spending to boost construction aggregates, reflecting passage of a new federal highway funding bill and improved finances of state governments.
- Aided by our outlook for increased volume, a higher capacity utilization rate and less rapidly rising costs for energy, we look for an expansion in operating margins. Benefiting further from lower interest expense, we project an EPS gain in 2006 to $4.65, despite a higher expected tax rate.
- For the longer term, we see sales and EPS benefiting from continued consolidation of the construction materials industry, acquisitions and the rebuilding of hurricane damaged areas in the southeastern United States.

Investment Rationale/Risk

- We see VMC as a beneficiary of consolidation of the construction aggregates industry, implementation of the highway spending bill, and the rebuilding of the U.S. Gulf Coast. With what we see as a strong balance sheet and rising EPS, we believe that VMC will continue to grow via acquisitions. Also, with its rising free cash flow, we think VMC will be able to continue to increase the dividend and buy back shares while still making acquisitions or new investments to enhance existing plants.
- Risks to our recommendation and target price include the possibility of weaker than expected end markets for aggregates, leading to a decline, rather than an increase in EPS.
- We look for VMC to trade at about 20.6X our 2006 EPS estimate. This is at the upper end of the historical range of the past 10 years. Following the sale of its chemical unit, VMC will be a purer play on construction materials. That, together with an improving return on equity, rising free cash flow and higher operating margins we see, should lead to a higher P/E. On that basis, our 12-month target price is $96.

Qualitative Risk Assessment

LOW	MEDIUM	HIGH

Our risk assessment reflects that while VMC's earnings are exposed to the construction industry, about 44% of the aggregates' revenue comes from public construction, which is more stable than commercial construction. Our assessment also reflects VMC's low debt levels and free cash flow generation.

Quantitative Evaluations

S&P Quality Ranking A-

D	C	B-	B	B+	**A-**	A	A+

Relative Strength Rank MODERATE

60

LOWEST = 1 HIGHEST = 99

Revenue/Earnings Data

Revenue (Million $)

	1Q	2Q	3Q	4Q	Year
2006	708.7	888.2	929.3	--	--
2005	528.6	782.1	830.0	754.6	2,895
2004	617.5	816.3	891.2	608.7	2,454
2003	566.7	766.8	829.9	728.7	2,892
2002	587.1	681.4	785.8	676.0	2,797
2001	569.1	825.3	843.1	728.1	3,020

Earnings Per Share ($)

2006	0.70	1.47	1.45	**E**1.14	**E**4.65
2005	0.21	0.98	1.23	0.89	3.30
2004	0.14	0.85	0.96	0.62	2.52
2003	0.01	0.65	0.91	0.59	2.18
2002	0.11	0.64	0.75	0.36	1.86
2001	0.06	0.78	0.90	0.44	2.17

Fiscal year ended Dec. 31. Next earnings report expected: Early February. EPS Estimates based on S&P Operating Earnings; historical GAAP earnings are as reported.

Dividend Data (Dates: mm/dd Payment Date: mm/dd/yy)

Amount ($)	Date Decl.	Ex-Div. Date	Stk. of Record	Payment Date
0.370	02/10	02/22	02/24	03/10/06
0.370	05/12	05/24	05/26	06/09/06
0.370	07/14	08/23	08/25	09/11/06
0.370	10/13	11/22	11/27	12/11/06

Dividends have been paid since 1934. Source: Company reports.

Vulcan Materials Co

Business Summary July 28, 2006

Vulcan Materials is the nation's largest producer of construction aggregates and a major producer of asphalt and ready-mixed concrete.

Construction materials consists of the production, distribution and sale of construction aggregates and other construction materials and related services. Construction aggregates include crushed stone, sand and gravel, rock asphalt and recrushed concrete. Aggregates are employed in virtually all types of construction, including highway construction and maintenance, and in the production of asphaltic and portland cement concrete mixes. Aggregates also are widely used as railroad track ballast.

Construction aggregates constituted approximately 72% of the dollar volume of Construction Materials' 2005 net sales, as compared to 73% in 2004 and 72% in 2003. The remaining sales in Construction Materials result primarily from other products and services including asphalt mix and related products, ready-mixed concrete, trucking services, and water transportation services.

Shipments of aggregates totaled about 260 million tons in 2005, versus 243.1 million tons in 2004, 232.8 million tons in 2003, and 217.3 million tons in 2002.

Company Financials

Per Share Data ($) Year Ended Dec. 31	**2005**	**2004**	**2003**	**2002**	**2001**	**2000**	**1999**	**1998**	**1997**	**1996**
Tangible Book Value	15.05	13.77	12.01	11.04	10.02	9.00	8.63	11.47	9.81	8.60
Cash Flow	5.43	4.88	4.87	4.47	4.89	4.43	4.37	3.86	3.21	2.85
Earnings	3.30	2.52	2.18	1.86	2.17	2.29	2.35	2.50	2.03	1.79
S&P Core Earnings	3.17	2.29	1.89	1.51	1.81	NA	NA	NA	NA	NA
Dividends	1.16	1.04	0.97	0.94	0.90	0.84	0.78	0.69	0.63	0.56
Payout Ratio	35%	41%	44%	51%	41%	37%	33%	28%	31%	31%
Prices:High	76.31	55.53	48.60	49.95	55.30	48.88	51.25	44.67	34.65	22.17
Prices:Low	52.36	41.94	28.75	32.35	37.50	36.50	34.31	31.33	18.42	17.71
P/E Ratio:High	23	22	22	27	25	21	22	18	17	12
P/E Ratio:Low	16	17	13	17	17	16	15	13	9	10
Income Statement Analysis (Million $)										
Revenue	2,895	2,454	2,892	2,797	3,020	2,492	2,356	1,776	1,679	1,569
Operating Income	690	623	618	560	649	573	565	481	409	387
Depreciation	221	216	277	268	278	232	207	138	121	113
Interest Expense	37.1	40.3	54.1	55.0	61.3	48.1	48.6	7.23	6.91	8.64
Pretax Income	480	376	311	260	324	312	352	375	301	286
Effective Tax Rate	28.4%	30.4%	28.3%	25.8%	31.3%	29.6%	31.8%	31.7%	30.4%	33.9%
Net Income	344	261	223	190	223	220	240	256	209	189
S&P Core Earnings	328	236	194	155	186	NA	NA	NA	NA	NA
Balance Sheet & Other Financial Data (Million $)										
Cash	275	271	417	171	101	55.3	52.8	181	129	50.8
Current Assets	1,165	1,418	1,050	700	730	605	625	576	407	394
Total Assets	3,589	3,665	3,637	3,448	3,398	3,229	2,839	1,659	1,449	1,321
Current Liabilities	579	427	543	298	344	572	387	211	208	195
Long Term Debt	323	605	339	858	906	685	699	76.5	81.9	85.5
Common Equity	2,127	2,014	1,803	1,697	1,604	1,471	1,324	1,154	1,025	884
Total Capital	2,725	2,967	2,573	2,993	2,829	2,426	2,273	1,329	1,162	1,056
Capital Expenditures	216	204	194	249	287	340	315	203	161	152
Cash Flow	565	506	501	458	501	452	447	394	330	301
Current Ratio	2.0	3.3	1.9	2.7	2.1	1.2	1.6	2.7	2.3	2.0
% Long Term Debt of Capitalization	11.9	20.4	13.2	28.7	32.0	28.3	30.7	5.8	7.0	8.1
% Net Income of Revenue	11.9	10.6	7.7	6.8	7.4	8.8	10.2	14.4	12.5	12.0
% Return on Assets	9.5	7.2	6.3	5.6	6.7	7.2	10.7	16.5	15.1	14.9
% Return on Equity	16.6	13.7	12.8	11.5	14.5	15.7	19.4	23.5	21.6	22.5

Data as orig reptd.; bef. results of disc opers/spec. items. Per share data adj. for stk. divs.; EPS diluted. E-Estimated. NA-Not Available. NM-Not Meaningful. NR-Not Ranked. UR-Under Review.

Office: 1200 Urban Center Drive, Birmingham, AL 35242.
Telephone: 205-298-3000.
Email: ir@vmcmail.com
Website: http://www.vulcanmaterials.com

Chrmn & CEO: D.M. James
SVP, CFO & Treas: D.F. Sansone
SVP, Secy & General Counsel: W.F. Denson, III
VP, Cntlr & CIO: E.A. Khan

Treas: P. Alford
Investor Contact: M. Warren (205-298-3191)
Board of Directors: P. J. Carroll, Jr., L. D. DeSimone, P. W. Farmer, H. A. Franklin, D. M. James, D. J. McGregor, J. V. Napier, D. B. Rice, O. R. Smith, V. J. Trosino

Founded: 1910
Domicile: New Jersey
Employees: 8,051

Wachovia Corp

STANDARD &POOR'S

S&P Recommendation STRONG BUY ★★★★★

Price $55.25 (as of Oct 27, 2006)

12-Mo. Target Price $67.00

Investment Style Large-Cap Value

GICS Sector Financials
Sub-Industry Diversified Banks

Comment This bank holding company, the fourth largest in the U.S., operates banking offices in 16 states and Washington, DC.

Key Stock Statistics (Source S&P, Vickers, company reports)

52-Wk Range	$60.04–49.53	S&P Oper. EPS 2006E	4.70	P/E on S&P Oper. EPS 2006E	11.8	Dividend Rate/Share	$2.24
Trailing 12-Month EPS	$4.52	S&P Oper. EPS 2007E	5.05	Common Shares Outstg. (M)	1,914.3	Yield (%)	4.05
Trailing 12-Month P/E	12.2	S&P Core EPS 2006E	4.66	Market Capitalization(B)	$105.767	Beta	0.76
$10K Invested 5 Yrs Ago	$21,523	S&P Core EPS 2007E	5.01	Institutional Ownership (%)	44	S&P Credit Rating	A+

Price Performance

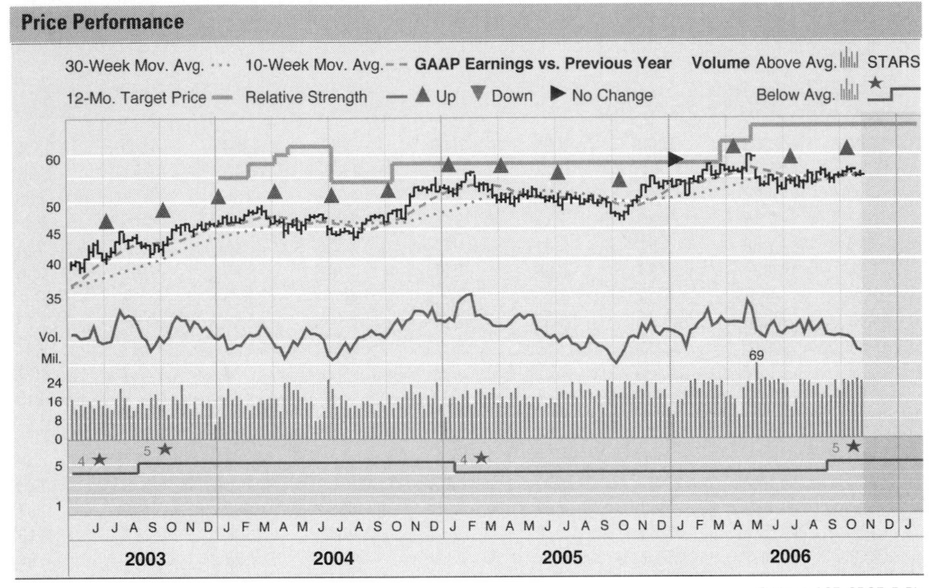

Options: ASE, CBOE, P, Ph

Analysis prepared by **Mark Hebeka, CFA** on October 17, 2006, when the stock traded at **$ 54.90**.

Highlights

- While we expect fee income to maintain healthy growth through 2007, we see net interest income coming under pressure. We foresee this projected increase in fee income mitigating some of the negative effects of a highly competitive pricing environment and an inverted yield curve. We continue to believe that revenue growth will be driven by commercial and consumer loan growth and fee income growth from market sensitive businesses, which should offset our expectations for a relatively flat to slightly narrower net interest margin.
- We believe provisions are likely to increase at a slightly faster rate than loan growth, assuming stable credit quality for the next several quarters. In our view, the company will continue to aggressively target planned expense reductions in its attempt to continue to post above industry average EPS growth with the assistance of stock repurchases.
- We estimate 2006 operating EPS (including the recent merger with Golden West Financial) of $4.70, up from $4.30 reported for 2005, followed by EPS of $5.05 projected for 2007.

Investment Rationale/Risk

- Our strong buy recommendation reflects our view of the company's focus on expense control, credit quality, and productivity improvements, which should allow for balanced above peer average long-term growth in a variety of economic and interest rate scenarios. On October 1, 2006, WB acquired Golden West Financial for about $25.5 billion in stock and cash. We believe the deal will add a larger presence in key markets and increased product distribution capabilities that we think will create significant revenue synergies.
- Risks to our recommendation and target price include a severe economic downturn; greater credit losses than we expect; integration risk; and a serious geopolitical event affecting equity markets.
- Our 12-month target price of $67 equates to 13.3X our 2007 operating EPS estimate, and is at the middle range of our multi-stage dividend discount model, which is mainly based on the assumption of a five-year EPS growth rate of about 10%, and a discount rate of 8.5%.

Qualitative Risk Assessment

LOW | MEDIUM | HIGH (rated: LOW)

Our risk assessment reflects our view of Wachovia's solid fundamentals coupled with a diversity in business lines and geography. In our opinion, it has consistent earnings and a well-established business, which should allow it to maintain healthy earnings levels during a prolonged economic downturn.

Quantitative Evaluations

S&P Quality Ranking A-

D | C | B- | B | B+ | A- | A | A+

Relative Strength Rank MODERATE

32

LOWEST = 1 HIGHEST = 99

Revenue/Earnings Data

Revenue (Million $)

	1Q	2Q	3Q	4Q	Year
2006	10,224	10,987	11,249	--	--
2005	8,448	8,679	9,302	9,479	35,908
2004	6,766	6,626	6,902	7,773	28,067
2003	5,776	5,841	6,315	6,542	24,474
2002	5,930	6,004	5,802	5,855	23,591
2001	5,599	5,450	4,976	6,371	22,396

Earnings Per Share ($)

	1Q	2Q	3Q	4Q	Year
2006	1.09	1.17	1.17	E1.18	E4.70
2005	1.01	1.04	1.06	0.95	4.05
2004	0.94	0.95	0.96	0.95	3.81
2003	0.76	0.77	0.82	0.83	3.17
2002	0.66	0.62	0.66	0.66	2.60
2001	0.59	0.64	-0.31	0.54	1.45

Fiscal year ended Dec. 31. Next earnings report expected: Mid January. EPS Estimates based on S&P Operating Earnings; historical GAAP earnings are as reported.

Dividend Data (Dates: mm/dd Payment Date: mm/dd/yy)

Amount ($)	Date Decl.	Ex-Div. Date	Stk. of Record	Payment Date
0.510	04/18	05/26	05/31	06/15/06
0.560	08/22	08/29	08/31	09/15/06
0.510	08/22	08/29	08/31	09/15/06
0.560	10/17	11/28	11/30	12/15/06

Dividends have been paid since 1914. Source: Company reports.

Wachovia Corp

Business Summary October 17, 2006

CORPORATE OVERVIEW. WB consists of several reporting segments: general bank (GB); capital management (CM); wealth management (WM); corporate and investment bank (CIB); and parent. GB provides a broad range of banking products and services to individuals, small businesses, commercial enterprises and governmental institutions in 16 states and Washington, D.C. It focuses on small business customers with annual revenues of up to $3 million; business banking customers with annual revenues between $3 million and $15 million; and commercial customers with revenues between $15 million and $250 million. CM leverages its multi-channel distribution to provide a full line of proprietary and nonproprietary investment and retirement products and services to retail and institutional clients. Retail brokerage services are offered through the 2,700 offices of Wachovia Securities in 49 states and Washington, D.C., and in Latin America. Evergreen Investments, a large and diversified asset management company, manages investments for a broad range of retail and institutional investors.

WM provides private banking, trust and investment management and financial planning services to high net worth individuals, their families and businesses. Relationship managers and specialty advisors focus on serving clients with $2 million or more in investable assets, while family offices focus on families with $25 million or more in investable assets. Wachovia Insurance Services provides commercial insurance brokerage and risk management services, employee benefits, life insurance, executive benefits and personal insurance services to businesses and individuals. The CIB division serves domestic and global corporate and institutional clients typically with revenues in excess of $250 million, and primarily in these key industry sectors: healthcare; media and communications; technology and services; finance; real estate; consumer and retail; industrial growth; defense and aerospace; and energy and power. CIB includes corporate lending, investment banking, and treasury and international trade finance lines of business. CIB also serves an institutional client base of money managers, hedge funds, insurance companies, pension funds, banks and broker dealers.

Company Financials

Per Share Data ($) Year Ended Dec. 31	**2005**	**2004**	**2003**	**2002**	**2001**	**2000**	**1999**	**1998**	**1997**	**1996**
Tangible Book Value	15.76	15.25	15.27	14.48	11.50	11.92	11.22	12.36	14.71	12.46
Earnings	4.05	3.81	3.17	2.60	1.45	0.12	3.33	2.95	2.99	2.68
S&P Core Earnings	4.02	3.75	3.09	2.32	1.14	NA	NA	NA	NA	NA
Dividends	1.94	1.66	1.25	1.00	0.96	1.92	1.88	1.58	1.22	1.10
Payout Ratio	48%	44%	39%	38%	66%	NM	56%	54%	41%	41%
Prices:High	56.28	55.01	46.74	39.88	36.60	38.88	65.75	65.94	53.00	38.88
Prices:Low	46.30	43.05	32.12	28.57	25.22	23.50	32.00	40.94	36.31	25.56
P/E Ratio:High	14	14	15	15	25	NM	20	22	18	15
P/E Ratio:Low	11	11	10	11	17	NM	10	11	12	10
Income Statement Analysis (Million $)										
Net Interest Income	13,681	11,961	10,607	9,823	7,775	7,277	7,452	7,277	5,743	4,996
Tax Equivalent Adjustment	219	250	256	218	159	117	118	117	Nil	84.0
Non Interest Income	12,130	10,789	9,309	7,836	7,003	5,682	6,995	6,198	3,362	2,322
Loan Loss Provision	249	257	586	1,479	1,947	691	692	691	840	375
% Expense/Operating Revenue	60.9%	63.8%	65.4%	65.3%	65.8%	89.6%	60.8%	67.5%	61.4%	63.1%
Pretax Income	9,804	7,633	6,080	4,667	2,293	703	4,831	3,965	2,710	2,310
Effective Tax Rate	30.9%	31.7%	30.1%	23.3%	29.4%	80.4%	33.3%	27.1%	30.0%	35.1%
Net Income	6,429	5,214	4,247	3,579	1,619	138	3,223	2,891	1,896	1,499
% Net Interest Margin	3.24	3.41	3.72	3.92	3.57	3.81	3.79	3.81	4.36	4.21
S&P Core Earnings	6,386	5,141	4,144	3,187	1,255	NA	NA	NA	NA	NA
Balance Sheet & Other Financial Data (Million $)										
Money Market Assets	65,257	72,809	61,747	45,827	46,180	36,109	27,542	12,675	13,907	11,274
Investment Securities	114,889	110,597	100,445	75,804	58,467	49,246	53,035	53,988	23,590	16,683
Commercial Loans	112,695	141,226	107,466	109,097	61,258	87,447	80,619	79,689	28,111	23,639
Other Loans	146,320	82,614	58,105	54,000	102,543	36,313	54,947	59,720	72,148	72,219
Total Assets	520,755	493,324	401,032	341,839	330,452	254,170	253,024	237,363	157,274	157,274
Demand Deposits	67,587	64,197	48,683	44,640	43,464	30,315	31,375	35,614	21,753	18,632
Time Deposits	257,407	230,856	172,542	146,878	143,989	112,353	109,672	106,853	81,136	76,183
Long Term Debt	48,971	46,759	36,730	39,662	41,733	35,809	31,975	22,949	8,042	7,660
Common Equity	47,561	47,317	32,428	32,078	28,438	15,347	16,709	17,173	12,032	10,008
% Return on Assets	1.3	1.2	1.1	1.1	0.6	0.1	1.3	1.5	1.3	1.1
% Return on Equity	13.6	13.1	13.2	11.8	7.4	0.9	19.2	19.8	17.2	16.5
% Loan Loss Reserve	1.0	1.2	1.5	1.7	-1.8	1.4	1.3	1.3	1.3	1.4
% Loans/Deposits	81.7	80.3	74.8	85.2	87.4	86.7	96.1	97.7	94.2	101.1
% Equity to Assets	9.4	8.9	8.7	9.0	7.5	6.3	6.9	7.4	7.4	6.6

Data as orig reptd.; bef. results of disc opers/spec. items. Per share data adj. for stk. divs.; EPS diluted. E-Estimated. NA-Not Available. NM-Not Meaningful. NR-Not Ranked. UR-Under Review.

Office: One Wachovia Center, Charlotte, NC 28288-0013.
Telephone: 704-374-6565.
Website: http://www.wachovia.com
Chrmn, Pres & CEO: G.K. Thompson

Vice Chrmn: B.P. Jenkins, III
Sr EVP: D.M. Carroll
Sr EVP: S.E. Cummings
Sr EVP: J.E. Davis

Board of Directors: J. D. Baker, II, J. S. Balloun, R. J. Brown, P. C. Browning, J. T. Casteen, III, J. Gitt, W. H. Goodwin, Jr., M. Herringer, R. A. Ingram, D. M. James, M. J. McDonald, J. Neubauer, T. Proctor, E. S. Rady, V. L. Richey, R. G. Shaw, L. L. Smith, G. K. Thompson, J. C. Whitaker, Jr., D. D. Young

Auditor: KPMG
Founded: 1879
Domicile: North Carolina
Employees: 93,980

STANDARD &POOR'S

Walgreen Co

S&P Recommendation BUY ★★★★★

Price $42.84 (as of Oct 27, 2006)

12-Mo. Target Price $51.00

Investment Style Large-Cap Growth

GICS Sector Consumer Staples
Sub-Industry Drug Retail

Comment The largest U.S. retail drug chain in terms of revenues, this company operates over 5,400 drug stores in 47 states and Puerto Rico.

Key Stock Statistics (Source S&P, Vickers, company reports)

52-Wk Range	$51.60–39.55	S&P Oper. EPS 2007E	2.00	P/E on S&P Oper. EPS 2007E	21.4	Dividend Rate/Share	$0.31
Trailing 12-Month EPS	$1.72	S&P Oper. EPS 2008E	NA	Common Shares Outstg. (M)	1,008.0	Yield (%)	0.72
Trailing 12-Month P/E	24.9	S&P Core EPS 2007E	2.00	Market Capitalization(B)	$43.183	Beta	0.37
$10K Invested 5 Yrs Ago	$12,873	S&P Core EPS 2008E	NA	Institutional Ownership (%)	64	S&P Credit Rating	A+

Price Performance

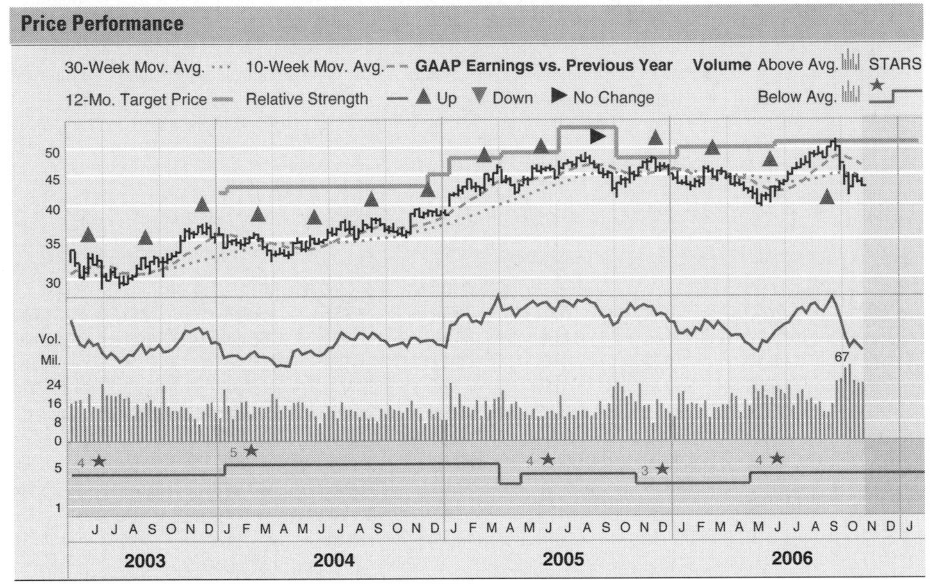

Options: ASE, CBOE, P

Analysis prepared by **Joseph Agnese** on September 28, 2006, when the stock traded at **$ 44.91**.

Highlights

- We see sales advancing about 11% in FY 07 (Aug.), fueled by the expected opening of about 500 new stores (at least 400 net new stores after closings and relocations), pharmacy same-store sales gains of 10%, and front-end same-store sales growth of 5%. We see front-end growth benefiting from improved traffic trends and improved convenience levels as the company expands store operating hours and the number of freestanding locations while improving product assortment.
- We expect margins to benefit from increased sales of generic drugs, improved sales leverage from new stores, and improved volumes from new Medicare Part D recipients, partially offset by a shift in mix as pharmacy becomes a larger portion of product mix. WAG's investment in in-store digital photo finishing labs should continue to benefit sales and gross margins by increasing traffic flow despite increased operating costs.
- We look for FY 07 operating EPS to increase 16% to $2.00, from operating EPS of $1.72 in FY 06.

Investment Rationale/Risk

- We believe the company will benefit from new store growth and increased generic drug sales despite near-term costs associated with implementation of new Medicare legislation in FY 06.
- Risks to our recommendation and target price include a weaker than expected economy, increased competition from peers and other retail formats, and legislative changes that may affect drug reimbursements.
- Our 12-month target price of $51 is based on a blend of our DCF and P/E analyses. The stock recently traded at about 22X our FY 07 EPS estimate, about 1.6X our projected longer-term EPS growth rate of 14%, and a premium to the shares of other drug chains we cover. We believe the above-average multiple is justified by what we see as WAG's long history of stable earnings growth, strong balance sheet, and leadership position in its industry. Applying a P/E multiple of 25X to our FY 07 EPS estimate of $2.00 results in a value of $50. Our DCF assumptions include a weighted average cost of capital of 9.0% and a terminal growth rate of 3.0% and result in intrinsic value of $52.

Qualitative Risk Assessment

LOW | **MEDIUM** | HIGH

Our risk assessment reflects the company's leadership position, resulting in what we see as strong market share positions, in a relatively stable U.S. retail drug industry, offset by growth of non-traditional competitors and potential legislation changes.

Quantitative Evaluations

S&P Quality Ranking A+

D | C | B- | B | B+ | A- | A | **A+**

Relative Strength Rank WEAK

14

LOWEST = 1 HIGHEST = 99

Revenue/Earnings Data

Revenue (Million $)

	1Q	2Q	3Q	4Q	Year
2006	10,900	12,163	12,175	12,170	47,409
2005	9,889	10,987	10,831	10,495	42,202
2004	8,721	9,782	9,579	9,427	37,508
2003	7,485	8,446	8,328	8,246	32,505
2002	6,559	7,489	7,398	7,235	28,681
2001	5,614	6,429	6,296	6,284	24,623

Earnings Per Share ($)

2006	0.34	0.51	0.46	0.41	1.72
2005	0.32	0.48	0.40	0.32	1.52
2004	0.25	0.42	0.33	0.32	1.32
2003	0.22	0.36	0.29	0.27	1.14
2002	0.18	0.32	0.25	0.24	0.99
2001	0.15	0.29	0.21	0.21	0.86

Fiscal year ended Aug. 31. Next earnings report expected: Early January. EPS Estimates based on S&P Operating Earnings; historical GAAP earnings are as reported.

Dividend Data (Dates: mm/dd Payment Date: mm/dd/yy)

Amount ($)	Date Decl.	Ex-Div. Date	Stk. of Record	Payment Date
0.065	01/11	02/15	02/17	03/11/06
0.065	04/11	05/17	05/19	06/12/06
0.078	07/12	08/16	08/18	09/12/06
0.078	10/11	11/09	11/13	12/12/06

Dividends have been paid since 1933. Source: Company reports.

Walgreen Co

Business Summary September 28, 2006

CORPORATE OVERVIEW. Walgreen Co. is one of the largest drug store chains in the U.S., based on sales and store count. In 1909, the company's founder, Charles Rudolph Walgreen Sr., purchased one of the busiest drug stores on Chicago's South Side, and transformed it by constructing an ice cream fountain that featured his own brand of ice cream. The ice cream fountain was the forerunner of the famous Walgreen's soda fountain, which became the main attraction for customers from the 1920s through the 1950s. People lined up to buy a product that WAG invented in the early 1920s: the milkshake. The company continued to be innovative by pioneering computerized pharmacies connected by satellite in 1981, completing chain-wide point-of-sale scanning in 1991, and introducing freestanding stores with drive-thru pharmacies in 1992.

MARKET PROFILE. Walgreen operates the largest U.S. drugstore chain based on sales, generating $47.4 billion in sales in FY 06 (Aug.). According to our analysis, filling 529 million prescriptions in FY 06, the company accounts for about 15% of the U.S. retail market. The company experienced an 8.1% growth rate in prescription volume in FY 06, outpacing our estimate of a low single digit growth rate for the industry. On a dollar basis, WAG pharmacy sales rose 13% in FY 06 to $30 billion, versus our estimate of upper single digit growth rate for the total industry, on comparable prescription sales growth of 9.2%. Sales of non-pharmacy items also outperformed competitors with the company increasing market share in 58 out of its top 60 core categories versus, drugstore, grocery and mass merchant competition. Based on store count, Walgreen is the second largest chain store operator in the U.S. As of September 25, 2006, the company operated 5,461 drug stores in 47 states and Puerto Rico, up 9.5% from 4,985 a year earlier. The company's goal is to operate 7,000 total stores by FY 10.

Company Financials

Per Share Data ($) Year Ended Aug. 31	**2006**	**2005**	**2004**	**2003**	**2002**	**2001**	**2000**	**1999**	**1998**	**1997**
Tangible Book Value	NA	8.69	8.04	7.02	6.08	5.11	4.19	3.47	2.86	2.40
Cash Flow	NA	1.99	1.71	1.47	1.29	1.12	0.99	0.82	0.72	0.60
Earnings	1.72	1.52	1.32	1.14	0.99	0.86	0.76	0.62	0.54	0.44
S&P Core Earnings	NA	1.44	1.27	1.07	0.93	0.80	NA	NA	NA	NA
Dividends	0.27	0.22	0.18	0.16	0.15	0.14	0.14	0.13	0.13	0.12
Payout Ratio	16%	15%	14%	14%	15%	16%	18%	21%	23%	27%
Prices:High	51.60	49.01	39.51	37.42	40.70	45.29	45.75	33.94	30.22	16.81
Prices:Low	39.55	39.66	32.00	26.90	27.70	28.70	22.06	22.69	14.78	9.63
P/E Ratio:High	30	32	30	33	41	53	60	55	56	38
P/E Ratio:Low	23	26	24	24	28	33	29	37	28	22

Income Statement Analysis (Million $)										
Revenue	NA	42,202	37,508	32,505	28,681	24,623	21,207	17,839	15,307	13,363
Operating Income	NA	2,906	2,546	2,194	1,932	1,668	1,454	1,226	1,024	872
Depreciation	NA	482	403	346	307	269	230	210	189	164
Interest Expense	NA	Nil	Nil	Nil	Nil	3.10	0.40	0.40	1.00	2.00
Pretax Income	NA	2,456	2,176	1,889	1,637	1,423	1,263	1,027	877	712
Effective Tax Rate	NA	36.5%	37.5%	37.8%	37.8%	37.8%	38.5%	39.2%	38.8%	38.8%
Net Income	NA	1,560	1,360	1,176	1,019	886	777	624	537	436
S&P Core Earnings	NA	1,478	1,302	1,104	955	820	NA	NA	NA	NA

Balance Sheet & Other Financial Data (Million $)										
Cash	NA	577	1,696	1,017	450	16.9	12.8	142	144	73.0
Current Assets	NA	8,317	7,764	6,358	5,167	4,394	3,550	3,222	2,623	2,326
Total Assets	NA	14,609	13,342	11,406	9,879	8,834	7,104	5,907	4,902	4,207
Current Liabilities	NA	4,481	4,078	3,421	2,955	3,012	2,304	1,924	1,580	1,439
Long Term Debt	NA	Nil	Nil	Nil	Nil	Nil	Nil	Nil	Nil	Nil
Common Equity	NA	8,890	8,228	7,196	6,230	5,207	4,234	3,484	2,849	2,373
Total Capital	NA	9,130	8,556	7,424	6,407	5,344	4,336	3,559	2,938	2,486
Capital Expenditures	NA	1,238	940	795	934	1,237	1,119	696	641	485
Cash Flow	NA	2,042	1,763	1,522	1,327	1,155	1,007	834	726	600
Current Ratio	NA	1.9	1.9	1.9	1.7	1.5	1.5	1.7	1.7	1.6
% Long Term Debt of Capitalization	NA	Nil	Nil	Nil	Nil	Nil	Nil	Nil	Nil	Nil
% Net Income of Revenue	NA	3.7	3.6	3.6	3.6	3.6	3.7	3.5	3.5	3.3
% Return on Assets	NA	11.2	10.9	11.0	10.9	11.1	11.9	11.5	11.8	11.1
% Return on Equity	NA	18.3	17.6	17.5	17.8	18.8	20.1	19.7	20.6	19.7

Data as orig reptd.; bef. results of disc opers/spec. items. Per share data adj. for stk. divs.; EPS diluted. E-Estimated. NA-Not Available. NM-Not Meaningful. NR-Not Ranked. UR-Under Review.

Office: 200 Wilmot Road, Deerfield, IL 60015.
Telephone: 847-940-2500.
Email: investor.relations@walgreens.com
Website: http://www.walgreens.com

Chrmn: D.W. Bernauer
Pres & CEO: J.A. Rein
SVP & CFO: W. Rudolphsen
SVP & Treas: J.W. Gleeson

SVP, Secy & General Counsel: D. Green
Investor Contact: R. Hans (847-940-2500)
Board of Directors: D. W. Bernauer, W. C. Foote, J. J. Howard, A. G. McNally, C. Reed, J. Rein, N. M. Schlichting, D. Y. Schwartz, J. B. Schwemm, J. Skinner, C. R. Walgreen, III, M. M. von Ferstel

Founded: 1901
Domicile: Illinois
Employees: 179,000

STANDARD &POOR'S

Wal-Mart Stores

S&P Recommendation STRONG BUY ★★★★★	Price	12-Mo. Target Price	Investment Style
	$50.73 (as of Oct 27, 2006)	$59.00	Large-Cap Growth

GICS Sector Consumer Staples
Sub-Industry Hypermarkets & Super Centers

Comment WMT, the largest retailer in North America, operates a chain of discount department stores, wholesale clubs, and combination discount stores and supermarkets.

Key Stock Statistics (Source S&P, Vickers, company reports)

52-Wk Range	$52.15–42.31	S&P Oper. EPS 2007E	2.92	P/E on S&P Oper. EPS 2007E	17.4	Dividend Rate/Share	$0.67
Trailing 12-Month EPS	$2.56	S&P Oper. EPS 2008E	3.30	Common Shares Outstg. (M)	4,169.0	Yield (%)	1.32
Trailing 12-Month P/E	19.8	S&P Core EPS 2007E	2.92	Market Capitalization(B)	$211.495	Beta	0.52
$10K Invested 5 Yrs Ago	$9,943	S&P Core EPS 2008E	NA	Institutional Ownership (%)	37	S&P Credit Rating	AA

Price Performance

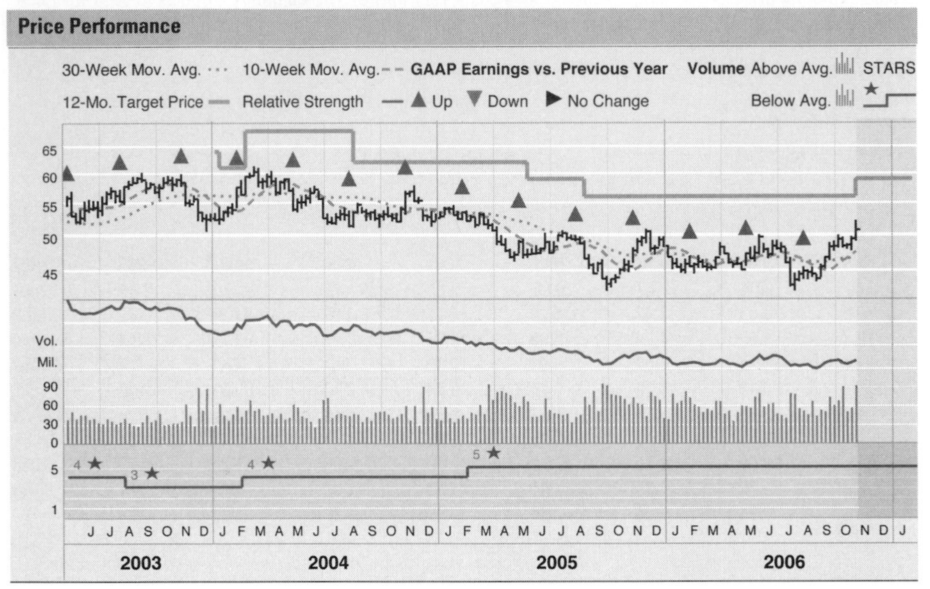

Options: ASE, CBOE, P, Ph

Highlights

- The 12-month target price for WMT has recently been changed to $59.00 from $56.00. The Highlights section of this Stock Report will be updated accordingly.

Investment Rationale/Risk

- The Investment Rationale/Risk section of this Stock Report will be updated shortly. For the latest News story on WMT from MarketScope, see below.

- 10/25/06 10:17 am EDT... S&P REITERATES STRONG BUY OPINION ON SHARES OF WAL-MART STORES (WMT 51.71*****): After WMT's 2-day analyst meeting, we are raising our target price by $3 to $59 on our updated DCF and P/E analysis. We believe a change in domestic expansion philosophy is likely to result in improved comp-store sales growth trends and increased cash flow increases. We expect comp-sales growth will gradually benefit from a reduction in new-store cannibalization, as well as completion of significant remodeling efforts. We see lower growth in capital spending on a slowdown in square footage additions, lower building material costs and reduced distribution expansion needs. /J.Agnese

Qualitative Risk Assessment

LOW	MEDIUM	HIGH

Our risk assessment of Wal-Mart Stores reflects our view of the company's: high quality earnings, as reflected in its Standard & Poor's Earnings & Dividend Rank of A+, dominant market share positions, continued price leadership, and strong cash flow generation.

Quantitative Evaluations

S&P Quality Ranking A+

D	C	B-	B	B+	A-	A	**A+**

Relative Strength Rank STRONG

72

LOWEST = 1 HIGHEST = 99

Revenue/Earnings Data

Revenue (Million $)

	1Q	2Q	3Q	4Q	Year
2007	79,613	84,524	--	--	--
2006	71,680	76,811	75,436	89,273	312,427
2005	64,763	69,722	68,520	82,216	285,222
2004	56,718	62,637	62,480	74,494	256,329
2003	54,960	59,694	58,797	71,073	244,524
2002	48,052	52,799	52,738	64,210	217,799

Earnings Per Share ($)

	1Q	2Q	3Q	4Q	Year
2007	0.63	0.72	E0.61	E0.96	E2.92
2006	0.58	0.67	0.57	0.86	2.68
2005	0.50	0.62	0.54	0.75	2.41
2004	0.41	0.52	0.46	0.63	2.03
2003	0.37	0.46	0.41	0.57	1.81
2002	0.31	0.36	0.33	0.49	1.50

Fiscal year ended Jan. 31. Next earnings report expected: NA. EPS Estimates based on S&P Operating Earnings; historical GAAP earnings are as reported.

Dividend Data (Dates: mm/dd Payment Date: mm/dd/yy)

Amount ($)	Date Decl.	Ex-Div. Date	Stk. of Record	Payment Date
0.168	03/02	03/15	03/17	04/03/06
0.168	03/02	05/17	05/19	06/05/06
0.168	03/02	08/16	08/18	09/05/06
0.168	03/02	12/13	12/15	01/02/07

Dividends have been paid since 1973. Source: Company reports.

Wal-Mart Stores

Business Summary August 21, 2006

CORPORATE OVERVIEW. Wal-Mart, the largest retailer in North America, has set its sights on other parts of the world. The company's operations are divided into three divisions: Wal-Mart, Sam's Club, and International. In FY 06 (Jan.), the Wal-Mart segment, comprised of discount stores, Supercenters and Neighborhood Markets, had sales of $209.9 billion, up 9% from the level of FY 05. Sam's Club sales totaled $39.8 billion, up 7.3%. In international markets, in which WMT operates a variety of formats, some via joint ventures, sales were up 18%, to $62.7 billion, up 11% from FY 05. Internationally, WMT operated 11 units in Argentina, 295 in Brazil, 278 in Canada, 56 in China (through joint ventures), 88 in Germany, 16 in Korea, 774 in Mexico, 54 in Puerto Rico, and 315 in the U.K.

MARKET PROFILE. With over 138 million people walking into Wal-Mart stores every week, the company is a dominant player in many of the markets in which it competes. With FY 06 sales of about $97 billion within supermarket related categories (grocery, candy and tobacco; pharmaceuticals, health and beauty aids; photo processing), the Wal-Mart division is the largest supermarket operator in the U.S., commanding an estimated 20% market share of the $479 billion supermarket industry, in our view. Other major product categories within the Wal-Mart division include hardgoods ($40 billion in estimated sales in FY 06), softgoods ($32 billion), electronics ($21 billion) and sporting goods ($11 billion). Sam's Club is the second largest warehouse club in the U.S., with sales of $39.8 billion in FY 06.

Company Financials

Per Share Data ($) Year Ended Jan. 31	**2006**	**2005**	**2004**	**2003**	**2002**	**2001**	**2000**	**1999**	**1998**	**1997**
Tangible Book Value	9.84	9.12	7.83	6.78	5.95	4.99	3.69	4.75	4.13	3.75
Cash Flow	3.81	3.44	2.91	2.58	2.22	2.04	1.78	1.41	1.15	0.99
Earnings	2.68	2.41	2.03	1.81	1.50	1.40	1.25	0.99	0.78	0.67
S&P Core Earnings	2.66	2.41	2.03	1.79	1.47	1.39	NA	NA	NA	NA
Dividends	0.60	0.52	0.36	0.30	0.28	0.24	0.20	0.16	0.14	0.11
Payout Ratio	22%	22%	18%	17%	19%	17%	16%	16%	17%	16%
Calendar Year	2005	2004	2003	2002	2001	2000	1999	1998	1997	1996
Prices:High	54.60	61.31	60.20	63.94	58.75	69.00	70.25	41.38	20.97	14.13
Prices:Low	42.31	51.08	46.25	43.72	42.00	41.44	38.68	18.78	11.00	9.55
P/E Ratio:High	20	25	30	35	39	49	56	42	27	21
P/E Ratio:Low	16	21	23	24	28	30	31	19	14	14

Income Statement Analysis (Million $)										
Revenue	312,427	285,222	256,329	244,524	217,799	191,329	165,013	137,634	117,958	104,859
Operating Income	23,247	18,729	16,525	15,075	15,367	12,392	10,684	8,418	6,796	5,871
Depreciation	4,717	4,405	3,852	3,432	3,290	2,868	2,375	1,872	1,634	1,463
Interest Expense	1,420	1,187	996	1,063	1,326	1,374	1,022	797	784	889
Pretax Income	17,358	16,105	14,193	12,719	10,751	10,116	9,083	7,323	5,719	4,850
Effective Tax Rate	33.4%	34.7%	36.1%	35.3%	36.2%	36.5%	36.8%	37.4%	37.0%	37.0%
Net Income	11,231	10,267	8,861	8,039	6,671	6,295	5,575	4,430	3,526	3,056
S&P Core Earnings	11,134	10,267	8,861	7,955	6,592	6,235	NA	NA	NA	NA

Balance Sheet & Other Financial Data (Million $)										
Cash	6,414	5,488	5,199	2,758	2,161	2,054	1,856	1,879	1,447	883
Current Assets	43,824	38,491	34,421	30,483	28,246	26,555	24,356	21,132	19,352	17,993
Total Assets	138,187	120,223	104,912	94,685	83,451	78,130	70,349	49,996	45,384	39,604
Current Liabilities	48,826	42,888	37,418	32,617	27,282	28,949	25,803	16,762	14,460	10,957
Long Term Debt	30,171	23,669	20,099	19,608	18,732	15,655	16,674	9,607	9,674	10,016
Common Equity	53,171	49,396	43,623	39,337	35,102	31,343	25,834	21,112	18,503	17,143
Total Capital	84,809	74,388	65,206	60,307	55,041	48,138	43,987	32,518	30,115	28,647
Capital Expenditures	14,563	12,893	10,308	9,355	8,383	8,042	6,183	3,734	2,636	2,643
Cash Flow	15,948	14,672	12,713	11,471	9,961	9,163	7,950	6,302	5,160	4,519
Current Ratio	0.9	0.9	0.9	0.9	1.0	0.9	0.9	1.3	1.3	1.6
% Long Term Debt of Capitalization	35.6	31.8	30.8	32.5	34.0	32.5	38.0	29.5	32.1	35.0
% Net Income of Revenue	3.5	3.6	3.5	3.3	3.1	3.3	3.4	3.2	3.0	2.9
% Return on Assets	8.7	9.1	8.9	9.0	8.3	8.5	9.3	9.3	8.3	7.9
% Return on Equity	21.9	22.1	21.3	21.6	20.1	22.0	23.8	22.4	19.8	19.2

Data as orig reptd.; bef. results of disc opers/spec. items. Per share data adj. for stk. divs.; EPS diluted. E-Estimated. NA-Not Available. NM-Not Meaningful. NR-Not Ranked. UR-Under Review.

Office: 702 S.W. 8th Street, Bentonville, AR 72716.
Telephone: 479-273-4000.
Website: http://www.walmartstores.com
Chrmn: S.R. Walton

Pres & CEO: H.L. Scott, Jr.
Vice Chrmn: J. Menzer
Investor Contact: T.M. Schoewe (479-273-4000)
EVP & CFO: T.M. Schoewe

Board of Directors: J. Breyer, M. M. Burns, D. N. Daft, D. Glass, R. A. Hernandez, J. D. Opie, J. P. Reason, H. L. Scott, Jr., J. C. Shewmaker, J. H. Villarreal, J. Walton, S. R. Walton, C. J. Williams, L. S. Wolf

Founded: 1945
Domicile: Delaware
Employees: 1,800,000

Washington Mutual Inc

STANDARD &POOR'S

S&P Recommendation BUY ★★★★★

Price $42.33 (as of Oct 27, 2006)

12-Mo. Target Price $48.00

Investment Style Large-Cap Value

GICS Sector Financials
Sub-Industry Thrifts & Mortgage Finance

Comment Washington Mutual is the largest U.S. savings and loan company and the seventh largest among all U.S.-based bank and thrift holding companies, based on assets.

Key Stock Statistics (Source S&P, Vickers, company reports)

52-Wk Range	$47.01–38.89	S&P Oper. EPS 2006**E**	3.60	P/E on S&P Oper. EPS 2006**E**	11.8	Dividend Rate/Share	$2.12
Trailing 12-Month EPS	$3.38	S&P Oper. EPS 2007**E**	4.09	Common Shares Outstg. (M)	963.5	Yield (%)	5.01
Trailing 12-Month P/E	12.5	S&P Core EPS 2006**E**	3.57	Market Capitalization(B)	$40.784	Beta	0.51
$10K Invested 5 Yrs Ago	$16,829	S&P Core EPS 2007**E**	4.06	Institutional Ownership (%)	81	S&P Credit Rating	A-

Price Performance

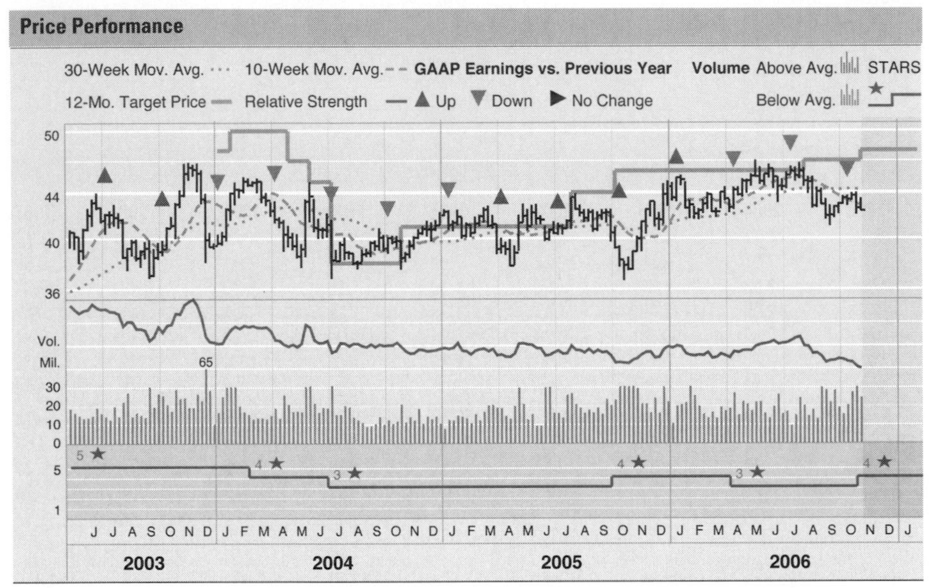

Options: ASE, CBOE, P, Ph

Highlights

- The STARS recommendation for WM has recently been changed to 4 (buy) from 3 (hold) and the 12-month target price has recently been changed to $48.00 from $47.00. The Highlights section of this Stock Report will be updated accordingly.

Investment Rationale/Risk

- The Investment Rationale/Risk section of this Stock Report will be updated shortly. For the latest News story on WM from MarketScope, see below.

- 10/25/06 09:18 am EDT... S&P UPGRADES SHARES OF WASHINGTON MUTUAL TO BUY OPINION FROM HOLD (WM 43.11****): Although we see WM's operating EPS declining moderately to $3.60 in '06, we look for '07 EPS growth of roughly 14% to $4.09 (both estimates reduced today). Growth will likely be driven by net interest margin expansion reflecting repositioning of balance sheet toward higher-margin loans. Headcount reduction, totalling 22% year-to-date, will likely lead to 5% lower '07 non-interest expense. We are raising our target price by $1 to $48, 12X our '07 EPS estimate, in line with larger thrifts. The stock also provides a dividend yield of close to 5%. /S. Plesser

Qualitative Risk Assessment

LOW	**MEDIUM**	HIGH

Our risk assessment reflects that as one of the top mortgage originators and servicers in the U.S., WM is exposed to the cyclicality of the mortgage industry. However, we see this offset by an increasingly diversified balance sheet as well as earnings from its retail banking and card services businesses.

Quantitative Evaluations

S&P Quality Ranking **A**

D	C	B-	B	B+	A-	**A**	A+

Relative Strength Rank **WEAK**

22

LOWEST = 1 HIGHEST = 99

Revenue/Earnings Data

Revenue (Million $)

	1Q	2Q	3Q	4Q	Year
2006	6,382	6,513	6,675	--	--
2005	4,768	4,973	5,314	6,174	21,820
2004	3,958	3,646	4,075	4,283	15,962
2003	4,523	4,664	4,562	4,264	18,013
2002	4,690	4,793	4,793	4,760	19,037
2001	4,664	4,741	4,428	3,859	17,692

Earnings Per Share ($)

2006	0.98	0.78	0.76	**E**0.85	**E**3.60
2005	1.01	0.95	0.92	0.85	3.73
2004	0.73	0.55	0.76	0.76	2.81
2003	1.05	1.10	1.09	0.91	4.12
2002	0.98	1.01	1.01	1.03	4.05
2001	0.77	0.91	0.85	0.62	3.15

Fiscal year ended Dec. 31. Next earnings report expected: Mid January. EPS Estimates based on S&P Operating Earnings; historical GAAP earnings are as reported.

Dividend Data (Dates: mm/dd Payment Date: mm/dd/yy)

Amount ($)	Date Decl.	Ex-Div. Date	Stk. of Record	Payment Date
0.500	01/18	01/27	01/31	02/15/06
0.510	04/18	04/26	04/28	05/15/06
0.520	07/21	07/27	07/31	08/15/06
0.530	10/18	10/27	10/31	11/15/06

Dividends have been paid since 1986. Source: Company reports.

Washington Mutual Inc

Business Summary September 01, 2006

CORPORATE PROFILE. Washington Mutual, Inc. is a retailer of financial services to consumers and small businesses. WM has four operating segments: Retail Banking and Financial Services, which provides non-mortgage consumer loans and other banking and investment products to individuals and small businesses; Home Loans, which originates, services, purchases and sells home loans and includes its subprime subsidiary, Long Beach Mortgage Co.; Commercial, which provides multi-family, commercial real estate and construction loans; and Card Services, which was newly formed following WM's acquisition of Providian Financial Corp. (PVN) on October 1, 2005. Effective January 1, 2006, WM reorganized its single-family residential mortgage lending operations by combining Long Beach and Mortgage Banker Finance, its warehouse lending unit, within the Home Loans group from the Commercial group. Due to the unpredictable nature of mortgage banking activities, we believe WM's earnings volatility is greater than that of a traditional thrift, but we see some of this mitigated by efforts to diversify its assets away from residential mortgages.

MARKET PROFILE. At the end of 2005, WM operated in 15 states: California (ranked second, based on a deposit market share of approximately 16.8%), New York (eighth, 2.1%), Washington (second, 13.8%), Florida (fourth, 3.4%), Texas (sixth, 2.6%), Oregon (third, 12.8%), New Jersey (14th, 1.4%), Nevada (eighth, 2.9%), Arizona (ninth, 1.2%), Illinois (51st, 0.3%), Utah (sixth, 2.4%), Georgia (22nd, 0.4%), Idaho (sixth, 3.6%), Colorado (27th, 0.5%) and Connecticut (66th, NA). Based on current income levels and projected changes in population and household income, we believe the prospects for its markets are above average.

Company Financials

Per Share Data ($) Year Ended Dec. 31	**2005**	**2004**	**2003**	**2002**	**2001**	**2000**	**1999**	**1998**	**1997**	**1996**
Tangible Book Value	19.43	17.20	16.38	14.36	13.44	11.21	9.16	9.37	9.09	7.98
Earnings	3.73	2.81	4.12	4.05	3.15	2.36	2.11	1.71	0.83	0.38
S&P Core Earnings	3.70	2.77	4.05	3.94	3.03	NA	NA	NA	NA	NA
Dividends	1.90	1.74	1.40	1.06	0.90	0.76	0.65	0.55	0.47	0.40
Payout Ratio	51%	62%	34%	26%	29%	32%	31%	37%	57%	106%
Prices:High	45.06	45.47	46.85	39.98	42.99	37.29	30.50	34.44	32.28	20.39
Prices:Low	36.64	36.80	32.40	27.80	26.52	14.42	16.46	17.83	18.78	11.61
P/E Ratio:High	12	16	11	10	14	16	14	20	39	54
P/E Ratio:Low	10	13	8	7	8	6	8	10	23	31

Income Statement Analysis (Million $)										
Net Interest Income	7,886	7,116	7,629	8,341	6,876	4,311	4,452	4,292	2,656	1,191
Loan Loss Provision	316	209	42.0	595	575	185	167	162	207	202
Non Interest Income	8,272	6,994	5,174	4,022	1,883	1,985	1,509	1,524	751	259
Non Interest Expenses	7,870	5,014	7,408	6,382	4,167	3,126	2,910	3,284	2,300	1,025
Pretax Income	5,438	3,984	6,029	6,154	4,311	2,984	2,884	2,369	901	223
Effective Tax Rate	36.9%	37.8%	37.1%	36.7%	36.6%	36.4%	37.0%	37.2%	46.5%	42.8%
Net Income	3,432	2,479	3,793	3,896	2,732	1,899	1,817	1,487	482	114
% Net Interest Margin	2.67	2.82	3.11	3.48	3.32	2.38	2.63	2.88	3.03	2.89
S&P Core Earnings	3,400	2,446	3,735	3,788	2,616	NA	NA	NA	NA	NA

Balance Sheet & Other Financial Data (Million $)										
Total Assets	343,839	307,918	275,178	268,298	242,506	194,716	186,514	165,493	96,981	44,552
Loans	227,937	205,770	174,394	145,875	131,587	118,612	113,497	108,371	67,140	30,467
Deposits	193,167	173,658	153,181	155,516	107,182	79,574	81,130	85,492	50,986	24,080
Capitalization:Debt	55,166	34,442	22,123	22,198	23,883	29,951	28,313	45,198	23,791	7,918
Capitalization:Equity	27,616	21,226	19,742	20,134	14,063	10,166	9,053	9,344	5,191	2,398
Capitalization:Total	82,782	21,226	41,865	42,332	38,048	40,117	37,366	54,542	29,100	10,316
% Return on Assets	1.1	0.9	1.4	1.5	1.2	1.0	1.0	1.0	0.5	0.3
% Return on Equity	14.1	12.1	19.1	22.8	22.5	19.8	19.8	20.2	9.3	3.9
% Loan Loss Reserve	0.6	0.5	0.6	0.9	0.9	-0.8	0.9	1.0	1.0	1.2
% Risk Based Capital	11.6	12.4	10.8	11.4	10.9	11.4	11.2	12.1	NA	NA
Price Times Book Value:High	2.3	2.6	2.0	2.8	3.2	3.3	3.3	3.7	3.9	2.6
Price Times Book Value:Low	1.9	2.1	2.1	1.9	2.0	1.3	1.8	1.9	2.3	1.5

Data as orig reptd.; bef. results of disc opers/spec. items. Per share data adj. for stk. divs.; EPS diluted. E-Estimated. NA-Not Available. NM-Not Meaningful. NR-Not Ranked. UR-Under Review.

Office: 1201 3rd Ave, Seattle, WA 98101.
Telephone: 206-461-2000.
Website: http://www.wamu.com
Chrmn & CEO: K.K. Killinger

Pres & COO: S. Rotella
Vice Chrmn: W.A. Longbrake
Sr EVP & General Counsel: F.L. Chapman
EVP & CFO: T.W. Casey

Investor Contact: A. Magleby (212-326-6019)
Board of Directors: A. V. Farrell, S. E. Frank, K. K. Killinger, T. C. Leppert, C. M. Lillis, P. D. Matthews, R. Montoya, R. Montoya, M. K. Murphy, M. Osmer-McQuade, M. E. Pugh, W. G. Reed, Jr., O. C. Smith, J. H. Stever, W. B. Wood, Jr.

Founded: 1889
Domicile: Washington
Employees: 60,798

STANDARD &POOR'S

Waste Management Inc.

S&P Recommendation HOLD ★★★★★ | **Price** $37.32 (as of Oct 27, 2006) | **12-Mo. Target Price** $41.00 | **Investment Style** Large-Cap Growth

GICS Sector Industrials
Sub-Industry Environmental & Facilities Services

Comment This Houston-based company is the largest U.S. trash hauling/disposal concern.

Key Stock Statistics (Source S&P, Vickers, company reports)

52-Wk Range	$38.35–29.00	S&P Oper. EPS 2006E	1.80	P/E on S&P Oper. EPS 2006E	20.7	Dividend Rate/Share	$0.88
Trailing 12-Month EPS	$2.17	S&P Oper. EPS 2007E	2.00	Common Shares Outstg. (M)	540.5	Yield (%)	2.36
Trailing 12-Month P/E	17.2	S&P Core EPS 2006E	1.80	Market Capitalization(B)	$20.171	Beta	1.00
$10K Invested 5 Yrs Ago	$14,137	S&P Core EPS 2007E	2.00	Institutional Ownership (%)	84	S&P Credit Rating	BBB

Price Performance

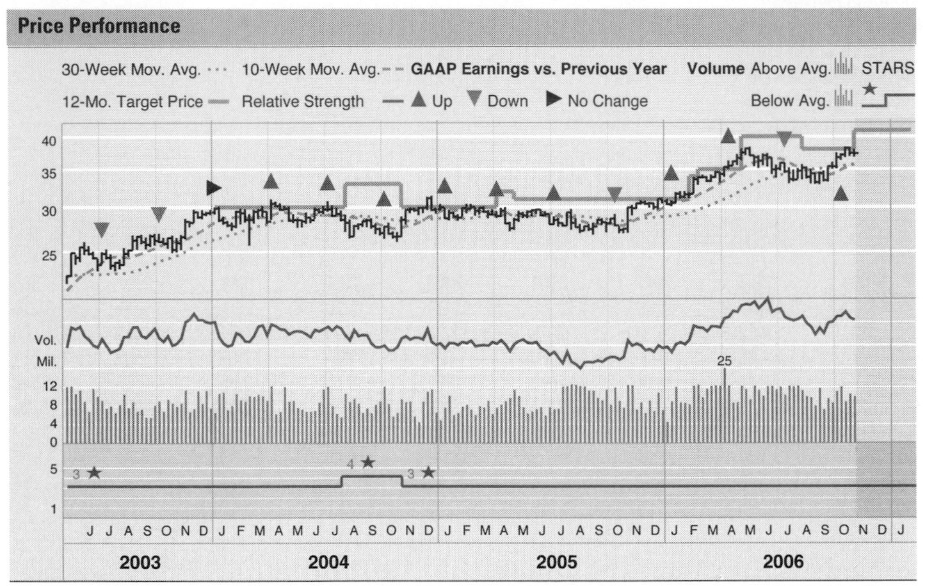

Options: ASE, CBOE, P, Ph

Qualitative Risk Assessment

LOW | MEDIUM | HIGH

Our risk assessment reflects broad-based pricing initiatives and fuel surcharges geared to reducing volatile fuel costs, stable economic conditions, and what we view as a strong balance sheet with declining debt levels and solid return on equity. Additionally, we view corporate governance practices as sound.

Quantitative Evaluations

S&P Quality Ranking **B**

D | C | B- | **B** | B+ | A- | A | A+

Relative Strength Rank **MODERATE**

56

LOWEST = 1 HIGHEST = 99

Revenue/Earnings Data

Revenue (Million $)

	1Q	2Q	3Q	4Q	Year
2006	3,229	3,410	3,441	--	--
2005	3,038	3,289	3,375	3,372	13,074
2004	2,896	3,138	3,274	3,208	12,516
2003	2,716	2,915	2,975	2,968	11,574
2002	2,609	2,825	2,896	2,812	11,142
2001	2,719	2,915	2,897	2,791	11,322

Earnings Per Share ($)

2006	0.34	0.76	0.55	**E**0.45	**E**1.80
2005	0.26	0.92	0.38	0.52	2.09
2004	0.25	0.37	0.52	0.47	1.60
2003	0.18	0.30	0.35	0.39	1.21
2002	0.22	0.35	0.38	0.39	1.33
2001	0.20	0.30	0.05	0.25	0.80

Fiscal year ended Dec. 31. Next earnings report expected: Mid February. EPS Estimates based on S&P Operating Earnings; historical GAAP earnings are as reported.

Dividend Data (Dates: mm/dd Payment Date: mm/dd/yy)

Amount ($)	Date Decl.	Ex-Div. Date	Stk. of Record	Payment Date
0.200	10/07	11/29	12/01	12/23/05
0.220	12/15	03/02	03/06	03/24/06
0.220	05/05	06/01	06/05	06/23/06
0.220	08/25	08/31	09/05	09/22/06

Dividends have been paid since 1998. Source: Company reports.

Highlights

- The 12-month target price for WMI has recently been changed to $41.00 from $38.00. The Highlights section of this Stock Report will be updated accordingly.

Investment Rationale/Risk

- The Investment Rationale/Risk section of this Stock Report will be updated shortly. For the latest News story on WMI from MarketScope, see below.

- 10/25/06 09:38 am EDT... S&P REITERATES HOLD OPINION ON SHARES OF WASTE MANAGEMENT (WMI 37.14***): WMI posts Q3 EPS of $0.55 vs. $0.45 before $0.07 net charge, $0.07 above our estimate. Core internal revenues grew 1.8%, as an increase of 3.6% due to price was partially offset by lower volume. We expect '06 EBITDA margins to expand on pricing initiatives and cost reductions, and free cash flow exceeding $1.2B; we see additional share buybacks. Although we think collection volume will remain soft, our '06 EPS estimate rises by $0.07 to $1.80. We apply a near historical P/E of 20.5X our '07 estimate of $2.00 (raised today from $1.90), and our target price rises by $3 to $41. /S. Scharf

Waste Management Inc.

Business Summary September 19, 2006

CORPORATE OVERVIEW. Waste Management, the largest U.S. waste disposal company in North America, provides collection, transfer, recycling and resource recovery, as well as disposal services. It also owns U.S. waste-to-energy facilities. Recently, it had more than 430 collection operations. In 2005, revenues from the North American solid waste (NASW) business were: 56% collection; 20% landfill; 5.9% waste-to-energy (Wheelabrator Technologies unit); 11% transfer; and 7.3% recycling and other. WMI's average remaining landfill life was recently about 27 years (36 years when considering remaining permitted capacity, probable expansion capacity at 73 landfills, and projected annual disposal volume).

WMI sees no material impact on EPS related to the expensing of stock options as it accelerated the vesting of options in the 2005 fourth quarter, eliminating $55 million in pretax compensation charges for 2006 through 2008. However, WMI projects $10 million in expenses in 2006 due to equity compensation plans.

We project free cash flow above $1.2 billion for 2006, targeted for share buybacks and dividend payments. As of late July 2006, WMI had bought back $710 million of stock (over 21 million shares) year to date, and authorized the repurchase of up to an additional $350 million during the balance of 2006. The company projects capital expenditures of near $1.5 billion, slated mainly for buying land around landfills and for a new revenue management system, as well as for fleet upgrades to meet new diesel regulations mandated for 2007; we also expect WMI to invest in landfill gas-to-energy, medical waste projects, and other initiatives.

Company Financials

Per Share Data ($) Year Ended Dec. 31	**2005**	**2004**	**2003**	**2002**	**2001**	**2000**	**1999**	**1998**	**1997**	**1996**
Tangible Book Value	1.10	0.91	0.24	0.21	0.43	NM	NM	NM	4.51	4.57
Cash Flow	4.50	3.90	3.44	5.29	2.97	2.14	1.99	1.25	2.47	1.33
Earnings	2.09	1.60	1.21	1.33	0.80	-0.16	-0.64	-1.31	1.26	0.24
S&P Core Earnings	1.00	1.48	1.00	1.17	1.04	NA	NA	NA	NA	NA
Dividends	0.80	0.75	0.01	0.01	0.01	0.01	0.02	0.02	Nil	Nil
Payout Ratio	38%	47%	1%	1%	1%	NM	NM	NM	Nil	Nil
Prices:High	31.03	31.42	29.72	31.25	32.50	28.31	60.00	58.19	44.13	34.25
Prices:Low	26.80	25.67	19.39	20.20	22.51	13.00	14.00	34.44	28.63	17.25
P/E Ratio:High	15	20	25	23	41	NM	NM	NM	35	NM
P/E Ratio:Low	13	16	16	15	28	NM	NM	NM	23	NM

Income Statement Analysis (Million $)										
Revenue	13,074	12,516	11,574	11,142	11,322	12,492	13,127	12,703	2,614	1,313
Operating Income	3,167	3,021	2,841	2,870	3,034	3,216	2,154	4,010	983	448
Depreciation	1,361	1,336	1,265	2,444	1,371	1,429	1,614	1,499	303	153
Interest Expense	496	455	439	462	541	740	770	601	104	45.5
Pretax Income	1,140	1,214	1,129	1,240	792	344	-139	-676	463	78.1
Effective Tax Rate	NM	20.3%	35.8%	34.2%	35.9%	NM	NM	NM	41.0%	57.8%
Net Income	1,182	931	719	823	503	-97.0	-395	-767	273	32.9
S&P Core Earnings	1,072	864	643	725	653	NA	NA	NA	NA	NA

Balance Sheet & Other Financial Data (Million $)										
Cash	666	443	135	264	730	94.0	181	88.7	51.2	23.5
Current Assets	3,451	2,819	2,588	2,700	3,124	2,457	6,221	3,881	655	340
Total Assets	21,135	20,905	20,656	19,631	19,490	18,565	22,681	22,715	6,623	2,831
Current Liabilities	3,257	3,205	3,332	3,173	3,721	2,937	7,489	4,294	569	320
Long Term Debt	8,165	8,182	7,997	8,062	7,709	8,372	8,399	11,114	2,724	1,158
Common Equity	6,121	5,971	5,563	5,308	5,392	4,801	4,403	4,372	2,629	1,155
Total Capital	15,931	14,435	15,473	13,389	14,241	14,067	13,540	16,069	5,674	2,322
Capital Expenditures	1,180	1,258	1,200	1,287	1,328	1,313	1,327	1,651	436	348
Cash Flow	2,543	2,267	1,984	3,267	1,874	1,332	1,219	732	577	186
Current Ratio	1.1	0.9	0.8	0.9	0.8	0.8	0.8	0.9	1.2	1.1
% Long Term Debt of Capitalization	51.3	56.7	51.7	60.2	54.1	59.5	62.0	69.2	48.0	49.9
% Net Income of Revenue	9.0	7.4	6.2	7.4	4.4	NM	NM	NM	10.5	2.5
% Return on Assets	5.6	4.5	3.5	4.2	2.6	NM	NM	NM	4.1	1.4
% Return on Equity	19.6	16.1	13.2	15.4	9.9	NM	NM	NM	10.4	3.2

Data as orig reptd.; bef. results of disc opers/spec. items. Per share data adj. for stk. divs.; EPS diluted. E-Estimated. NA-Not Available. NM-Not Meaningful. NR-Not Ranked. UR-Under Review.

Office: 1001 Fannin Street, Houston, TX 77002.
Telephone: 713-512-6200.
Website: http://www.wm.com
Chrmn: J. Pope

Pres & COO: L. O'Donnell, III
CEO: D.P. Steiner
SVP & CFO: R.G. Simpson
SVP, General Counsel & CCO: R.L. Wittenbraker

Investor Contact: G. Nikkel (713-265-1358)
Board of Directors: P. S. Cafferty, F. M. Clark, Jr., J. C. Pope, W. R. Reum, S. G. Rothmeier, D. P. Steiner, T. Weidemeyer

Founded: 1894
Domicile: Delaware
Employees: 50,000

STANDARD &POOR'S

Waters Corp

S&P Recommendation HOLD ★★★★★

Price $49.43 (as of Oct 27, 2006)

12-Mo. Target Price $50.00

Investment Style Mid-Cap Growth

GICS Sector Health Care
Sub-Industry Life Sciences Tools & Services

Comment This company manufactures scientific and industrial analytical equipments such as liquid chromatography, thermal analysis and mass spectrometry products.

Key Stock Statistics (Source S&P, Vickers, company reports)

52-Wk Range	$50.10–35.55	S&P Oper. EPS 2006E	2.20	P/E on S&P Oper. EPS 2006E	22.5	Dividend Rate/Share	Nil
Trailing 12-Month EPS	$2.03	S&P Oper. EPS 2007E	2.50	Common Shares Outstg. (M)	102.4	Yield (%)	Nil
Trailing 12-Month P/E	24.4	S&P Core EPS 2006E	2.20	Market Capitalization(B)	$5.064	Beta	1.03
$10K Invested 5 Yrs Ago	$13,381	S&P Core EPS 2007E	2.50	Institutional Ownership (%)	91	S&P Credit Rating	NA

Price Performance

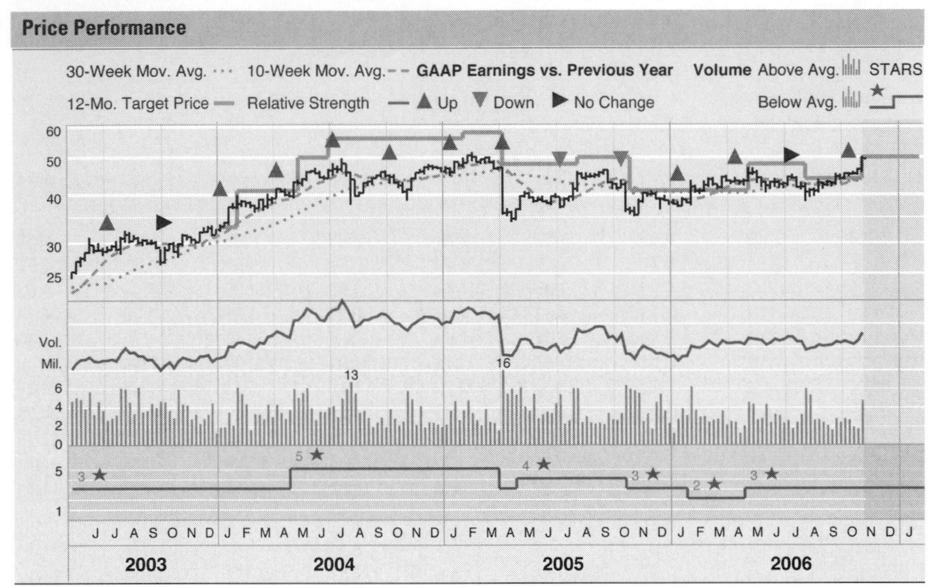

Options: CBOE, Ph

Highlights

- The 12-month target price for WAT has recently been changed to $50.00 from $44.00. The Highlights section of this Stock Report will be updated accordingly.

Investment Rationale/Risk

- The Investment Rationale/Risk section of this Stock Report will be updated shortly. For the latest News story on WAT from MarketScope, see below.

- 10/24/06 11:49 am EDT... S&P MAINTAINS HOLD RECOMMENDATION ON SHARES OF WATERS CORP. (WAT 48.0***): Q3 EPS of $0.49 after stock options, vs. $0.43, both adjusted, is $0.03 above our estimate. Sales grew 10%, despite soft thermal analysis segment sales, reflecting improved sales to large U.S. pharmaceutical firms, continued strong sales in Asia, and better sales in Europe. We see U.S. sales improving over the next several quarters, since we think capital budgets are improving, leading to both new and replacement equipment purchases. We also see thermal analysis rebounding, based on strength in Q3 order flow. We are raising our target price by $6 to $50 on revised DCF analysis. /J.Loo-CFA

Qualitative Risk Assessment

LOW | **MEDIUM** | HIGH

Our risk assessment reflects WAT's strong market share in the liquid chromatography and mass spectrometry markets, offset by a highly competitive marketplace and a reliance on customer demand for expensive instruments.

Quantitative Evaluations

S&P Quality Ranking B

D | C | B- | **B** | B+ | A- | A | A+

Relative Strength Rank STRONG

87

LOWEST = 1 HIGHEST = 99

Revenue/Earnings Data

Revenue (Million $)

	1Q	2Q	3Q	4Q	Year
2006	290.2	301.9	301.2	--	--
2005	268.3	284.6	273.0	332.3	1,158
2004	255.1	260.5	264.8	324.2	1,105
2003	221.0	231.8	230.4	275.1	958.2
2002	200.3	217.2	216.1	256.4	890.0
2001	201.0	206.8	202.7	248.7	859.2

Earnings Per Share ($)

	1Q	2Q	3Q	4Q	Year
2006	0.42	0.46	0.49	E0.78	E2.20
2005	0.38	0.46	0.22	0.71	1.74
2004	0.33	0.49	0.42	0.58	1.82
2003	0.26	0.33	0.29	0.47	1.34
2002	0.27	0.28	0.29	0.30	1.12
2001	0.28	0.29	0.28	-0.01	0.84

Fiscal year ended Dec. 31. Next earnings report expected: Late January. EPS Estimates based on S&P Operating Earnings; historical GAAP earnings are as reported.

Dividend Data

No cash dividends have been paid.

Waters Corp

Business Summary August 14, 2006

CORPORATE OVERVIEW. Waters manufactures, distributes and services analytical instruments to the pharmaceutical, life sciences, biochemical, industrial, academic and government end-markets. Analytical instruments and components manufactured include high performance liquid chromatography (HPLC) instruments, columns and other consumables, mass spectrometry (MS) instruments that can be integrated with other analytical instruments; and thermal analysis (TA) and rheology instruments. HPLC is the standard technique to identify and analyze constituent components of various chemicals and materials. Its unique performance capabilities let it separate and identify 80% of known chemicals and materials. HPLC is used to analyze substances in a variety of industries for R&D, quality control, and process engineering applications. Pharmaceutical and life science industries use HPLC primarily to identify new drugs.

In March 2004, WAT introduced a novel technology that it describes as Ultra Performance Chromatography, the Acquity UPLC. WAT believes the Acquity UPLC provides more comprehensive chemical separation and faster analysis times compared to the HPLC. MS is an analytical technique used to identify unknown compounds, quantify known materials, and elucidate the structural and chemical properties of molecules by measuring the masses of individual molecules that have been converted into ions. These products serve diverse markets, including pharmaceutical and environmental industries. The TA Instruments division makes and services thermal analysis and rheology instruments used for the physical characterization of polymers and related materials. Thermal analysis measures physical characteristics of materials as a function of temperature. Changes in temperature affect several characteristics of materials, such as their physical state, weight, dimension and mechanical and electrical properties, which may be measured using thermal analysis techniques. As a result, thermal analysis is widely used to develop, produce and characterize materials in industries such as plastics, chemicals and pharmaceuticals.

WAT has supplemented its internal growth with various strategic acquisitions. In January 2003, WAT acquired the rheology instruments and services business of Rheometric Scientific, Inc. In July 2003, the company purchased privately held Creon Lab Control, which provides scientific data management solutions. In March 2004, WAT acquired NuGenesis Technologies Corp. for about $43 million. NuGenesis and Creon Lab formed the company's new Lab Informatics market segment.

Company Financials

Per Share Data ($) Year Ended Dec. 31	**2005**	**2004**	**2003**	**2002**	**2001**	**2000**	**1999**	**1998**	**1997**	**1996**
Tangible Book Value	NM	3.05	2.67	NM	3.19	2.21	0.98	NM	NM	NM
Cash Flow	2.12	2.16	1.60	1.40	1.08	1.36	1.14	0.78	0.09	0.28
Earnings	1.74	1.82	1.34	1.12	0.84	1.14	0.92	0.57	-0.08	0.15
S&P Core Earnings	1.57	1.45	1.18	0.99	1.07	NA	NA	NA	NA	NA
Dividends	Nil	Nil	Nil	Nil	Nil	Nil	Nil	Nil	Nil	Nil
Payout Ratio	Nil	Nil	Nil	Nil	Nil	Nil	Nil	Nil	Nil	Nil
Prices:High	51.57	49.80	33.42	39.25	85.38	90.94	33.84	21.88	12.11	8.41
Prices:Low	33.99	33.10	19.79	17.86	22.33	21.97	18.13	9.13	5.78	4.19
P/E Ratio:High	30	27	25	35	NM	80	37	39	NM	56
P/E Ratio:Low	20	18	15	16	NM	19	20	16	NM	28
Income Statement Analysis (Million $)										
Revenue	1,158	1,105	958	890	859	795	704	619	465	391
Operating Income	330	321	271	251	258	240	205	164	113	87.9
Depreciation	43.7	41.9	33.8	37.2	34.0	29.4	28.9	27.2	20.0	16.7
Interest Expense	24.7	10.1	2.37	2.48	1.26	Nil	8.95	18.3	13.7	14.7
Pretax Income	275	286	224	195	147	211	168	102	7.47	31.1
Effective Tax Rate	26.4%	21.6%	23.6%	22.1%	22.3%	26.0%	27.0%	26.7%	211.0%	36.1%
Net Income	202	224	171	152	115	156	122	74.4	-8.29	19.9
S&P Core Earnings	183	179	150	134	147	NA	NA	NA	NA	NA
Balance Sheet & Other Financial Data (Million $)										
Cash	494	539	357	313	227	75.5	3.80	5.50	3.11	0.60
Current Assets	913	974	715	636	523	344	247	252	213	144
Total Assets	1,429	1,460	1,131	1,011	887	692	584	578	552	366
Current Liabilities	604	493	379	320	281	221	198	186	171	83.0
Long Term Debt	500	250	125	Nil	Nil	Nil	81.1	218	305	210
Common Equity	284	679	590	665	582	452	292	150	62.3	57.8
Total Capital	784	929	715	665	582	452	373	377	376	275
Capital Expenditures	51.0	66.2	34.6	37.9	42.4	35.4	19.4	15.0	18.2	10.1
Cash Flow	246	266	205	189	148	186	151	101	10.8	35.6
Current Ratio	1.5	2.0	1.9	2.0	1.9	1.6	1.3	1.4	1.2	1.7
% Long Term Debt of Capitalization	63.8	26.9	17.5	Nil	Nil	Nil	21.7	57.8	81.1	76.4
% Net Income of Revenue	17.4	20.3	17.8	17.1	13.3	19.6	17.4	12.0	NM	5.1
% Return on Assets	14.0	17.3	15.9	16.0	14.5	24.4	21.1	13.2	NM	6.0
% Return on Equity	42.0	35.3	27.2	24.3	22.2	42.0	55.3	69.1	NM	32.7

Data as orig reptd.; bef. results of disc opers/spec. items. Per share data adj. for stk. divs.; EPS diluted. E-Estimated. NA-Not Available. NM-Not Meaningful. NR-Not Ranked. UR-Under Review.

Office: 34 Maple Street, Milford, MA 01757-3696.
Telephone: 508-478-2000.
Email: info@waters.com
Website: http://www.waters.com

Chrmn & CEO: D.A. Berthiaume
VP & CFO: J.A. Ornell
VP, Secy & General Counsel: M. Beaudouin
Investor Contact: E.G. Cassis (508-482-2349)

Board of Directors: J. Bekenstein, M. J. Berendt, D. A. Berthiaume, E. Conard, L. H. Glimcher, W. J. Miller, T. P. Salice

Founded: 1991
Domicile: Delaware
Employees: 4,503

STANDARD &POOR'S

Watson Pharmaceuticals Inc.

S&P Recommendation	Price	12-Mo. Target Price	Investment Style
HOLD ★★★★★	$26.67 (as of Oct 27, 2006)	$28.00	Mid-Cap Growth

GICS Sector Health Care
Sub-Industry Pharmaceuticals

Comment This company produces generic and branded drugs. In June 2006, shareholders of rival drugmaker Andrx Corp. approved a plan for that firm to be acquired by Watson for about $1.9 billion in cash.

Key Stock Statistics (Source S&P, Vickers, company reports)

52-Wk Range	$35.27–21.35	S&P Oper. EPS 2006E	1.25	P/E on S&P Oper. EPS 2006E	21.3	Dividend Rate/Share	Nil
Trailing 12-Month EPS	$0.63	S&P Oper. EPS 2007E	1.55	Common Shares Outstg. (M)	102.2	Yield (%)	Nil
Trailing 12-Month P/E	42.3	S&P Core EPS 2006E	1.25	Market Capitalization(B)	$2.726	Beta	0.45
$10K Invested 5 Yrs Ago	$5,307	S&P Core EPS 2007E	1.55	Institutional Ownership (%)	83	S&P Credit Rating	BBB-

Price Performance

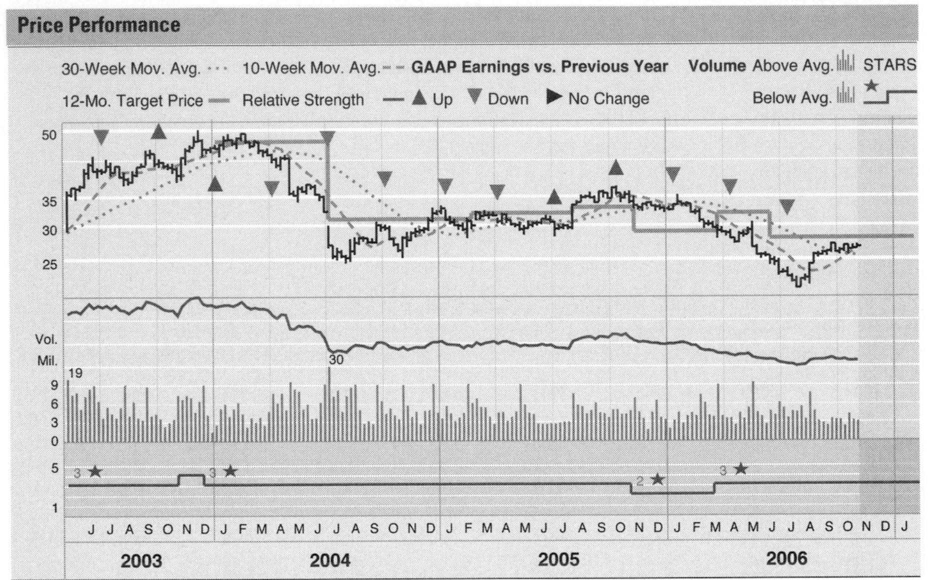

Options: ASE, CBOE, Ph

Analysis prepared by **Herman B. Saftlas** on August 31, 2006, when the stock traded at **$ 25.58**.

Highlights

- Based on Watson's present operations (excluding the planned acquisition of rival drugmaker Andrx), we project revenue growth of 12% in 2006. The estimated gain should be driven by new generic versions of Pravachol and Oxycontin, as well as anticipated launches of generic equivalents of Duragesic, Flonase and Seasonale. However, we see lower sales for WPI's generic oral contraceptives. Branded product sales are also expected to decline.
- We foresee a contraction in the gross margin, to about 41% in 2006, from 48.2% in 2005, reflecting an ongoing product mix shift to lower-margin generics. On the plus side, we see better SG&A and R&D cost ratios, higher other income and reduced interest expense.
- We look for 2006 operating EPS of $1.25, including projected stock option expense of about $0.05, but excluding estimated nonrecurring expense of $0.05 related to the closure of facilities in Puerto Rico. Boosted by greater contributions from new generic products, we see EPS rising to $1.55 in 2007, including estimated stock option expense.

Investment Rationale/Risk

- We think the planned acquisition of rival drugmaker Andrx (ADRX: hold, $24) for $1.9 billion in cash should provide operating and cost synergies to drive revenue and earnings growth for WPI over the coming years. In June 2006, Andrx shareholders approved the deal, which we expect to be completed before the end of 2006 (subject to regulatory approvals). We expect the transaction, if consummated, to be dilutive initially but accretive in 2007, helped by an estimated $30 million of cost synergies.
- Risks to our recommendation and target price include failure to gain necessary approvals for the planned Andrx deal. Competitive pressures in key generic and specialty drugs and pipeline disappointments are additional concerns.
- We have a 12-month target price of $28, which applies a modest premium-to-peers P/E of about 18X to our 2007 EPS estimate of $1.55. Our DCF model, which assumes decelerated cash flow growth over the next 10 years, a weighted average cost of capital of 7%, and perpetuity growth of 1%, also supports our target price.

Qualitative Risk Assessment

LOW | **MEDIUM** | HIGH

Our risk assessment reflects risks common to the generic pharmaceutical business, which include the ability to successfully develop generic products, obtain regulatory approvals and legally challenge branded patents. However, we believe these risks are offset by the company's wide and diverse generic portfolio and the balance afforded by WPI's branded drug business.

Quantitative Evaluations

S&P Quality Ranking **B**

D | C | B- | **B** | B+ | A- | A | A+

Relative Strength Rank **MODERATE**

55

LOWEST = 1 HIGHEST = 99

Revenue/Earnings Data

Revenue (Million $)

	1Q	2Q	3Q	4Q	Year
2006	407.2	510.4	--	--	--
2005	400.8	416.3	410.3	418.8	1,646
2004	409.7	399.4	408.0	423.5	1,641
2003	336.9	355.9	358.8	406.2	1,458
2002	285.7	300.1	307.9	329.6	1,223
2001	296.9	299.0	270.9	293.9	1,161

Earnings Per Share ($)

2006	0.23	-0.15	E0.34	E0.35	E1.25
2005	0.32	0.35	0.35	0.19	1.21
2004	0.39	0.29	0.13	0.46	1.27
2003	0.44	0.47	0.47	0.48	1.86
2002	0.30	0.56	0.38	0.40	1.64
2001	0.58	0.61	-0.55	0.43	1.07

Fiscal year ended Dec. 31. Next earnings report expected: Early November. EPS Estimates based on S&P Operating Earnings; historical GAAP earnings are as reported.

Dividend Data

No cash dividends have been paid.

Please read the Required Disclosures and Analyst Certification on the last page of this report.

Watson Pharmaceuticals Inc.

Business Summary August 31, 2006

CORPORATE PROFILE. Watson Pharmaceuticals is a leading maker of generic pharmaceuticals. WPI targets difficult to produce niche off-patent drugs in an effort to minimize competition with traditional commodity-oriented generic drug companies. To reduce its dependence on the volatile generic market, the company is building up its branded drug business. Many WPI pharmaceuticals incorporate the company's novel proprietary drug delivery systems, such as transmucosal, vaginal and transdermal systems that allow for defined rates of drug release. Total revenues in 2005 were 76% from generic drugs, and 24% from branded drugs.

WPI currently markets more than 125 generic drug products, which comprise a broad cross section of therapeutic categories. Key segments include oral contraceptives, analgesics, antihypertensives, diuretics, antiulcers, antipsychotics, anti-inflammatories, analgesics, hormone replacements, antispasmodics and antidiarrheals.

During 2005, WPI expanded its generic product line with the launch of six new generic products. In November 2005, the company launched oxycodone HCL controlled-release tablets, a narcotic analgesic used for moderate to severe pain. In 2005, WPI filed 22 Abbreviated New Drug Applications (ANDAs). As of mid-August 2006, WPI had 49 ANDAs on file at the FDA, including 12 that have received tentative approval and nine that are potential first-to-file or shared exclusivity opportunities.

Branded pharmaceuticals comprise specialty drugs and nephrology products. Specialty drugs includes urology; antihypertensive, psychiatry, pain management and dermatology products; and a genital warts treatment. Key products include Trelstar, a treatment for prostate cancer; Oxytrol, an oxybutynin transdermal patch to treat urinary incontinence; and Androderm, a testosterone transdermal patch.

The nephrology product line consists of products used to treat iron deficiency anemia. The primary product is Ferrlecit, which is indicated for patients undergoing hemodialysis in conjunction with erythropoietin therapy. Ferrlecit accounted for about 9% of revenues in 2005. Branded products are marketed to urologists, primary care physicians, endocrinologists, obstetricians and gynecologists.

Company Financials

Per Share Data ($) Year Ended Dec. 31	**2005**	**2004**	**2003**	**2002**	**2001**	**2000**	**1999**	**1998**	**1997**	**1996**
Tangible Book Value	8.81	7.97	5.54	4.33	3.79	0.98	5.00	3.08	3.14	5.20
Cash Flow	2.87	2.07	2.78	2.45	2.01	2.34	2.28	1.66	1.17	1.05
Earnings	1.21	1.27	1.86	1.64	1.07	1.65	1.83	1.32	1.01	0.98
S&P Core Earnings	1.09	1.16	1.64	1.36	0.52	NA	NA	NA	NA	NA
Dividends	Nil	Nil	Nil	Nil	Nil	Nil	Nil	Nil	Nil	Nil
Payout Ratio	Nil	Nil	Nil	Nil	Nil	Nil	Nil	Nil	Nil	Nil
Prices:High	36.93	49.19	50.12	33.25	66.39	71.50	62.94	63.00	34.13	24.75
Prices:Low	27.99	24.50	26.90	17.95	26.50	33.69	26.50	30.50	16.00	13.00
P/E Ratio:High	31	39	27	20	62	43	34	48	34	25
P/E Ratio:Low	23	19	14	11	25	20	14	23	16	13

Income Statement Analysis (Million $)	2005	2004	2003	2002	2001	2000	1999	1998	1997	1996
Revenue	1,646	1,641	1,458	1,223	1,161	812	689	556	338	194
Operating Income	450	419	439	386	404	227	281	237	152	89.0
Depreciation	207	107	100	86.6	101	71.4	44.0	31.3	14.8	8.25
Interest Expense	14.5	13.3	25.8	22.1	27.8	24.3	11.1	7.06	NA	Nil
Pretax Income	219	237	318	279	199	355	273	199	145	109
Effective Tax Rate	37.0%	36.1%	36.2%	37.0%	41.5%	52.0%	34.4%	39.3%	37.6%	32.8%
Net Income	138	151	203	176	116	171	179	121	90.2	73.3
S&P Core Earnings	123	137	178	146	56.3	NA	NA	NA	NA	NA

Balance Sheet & Other Financial Data (Million $)	2005	2004	2003	2002	2001	2000	1999	1998	1997	1996
Cash	630	680	574	273	329	238	116	72.7	82.8	211
Current Assets	1,360	1,370	1,323	921	890	831	435	293	247	280
Total Assets	3,080	3,244	3,283	2,663	2,528	2,580	1,439	1,070	755	420
Current Liabilities	246	256	339	375	245	280	129	94.8	99.8	21.4
Long Term Debt	588	588	723	332	416	438	150	150	2.39	2.90
Common Equity	2,104	2,243	2,057	1,798	1,672	1,548	1,055	750	565	383
Total Capital	2,692	2,831	2,924	2,282	2,274	2,242	1,292	955	604	398
Capital Expenditures	78.8	69.2	151	87.5	62.0	34.3	26.8	26.5	14.6	10.2
Cash Flow	345	258	303	262	218	242	223	152	105	79.5
Current Ratio	5.5	5.4	3.9	2.5	3.6	3.0	3.4	3.1	2.5	13.1
% Long Term Debt of Capitalization	21.8	20.8	24.7	14.5	18.3	19.6	11.6	15.7	0.4	0.1
% Net Income of Revenue	8.4	9.2	13.9	14.4	10.0	21.0	26.0	21.7	26.7	37.8
% Return on Assets	4.4	4.6	6.8	6.8	4.6	8.4	13.9	13.2	15.4	19.8
% Return on Equity	6.4	7.0	10.5	10.1	7.2	13.1	19.3	18.4	19.0	21.8

Data as orig reptd.; bef. results of disc opers/spec. items. Per share data adj. for stk. divs.; EPS diluted. E-Estimated. NA-Not Available. NM-Not Meaningful. NR-Not Ranked. UR-Under Review.

Office: 311 Bonnie Circle, Corona, CA 92880-2882.
Telephone: 951-493-5300.
Website: http://www.watsonpharm.com
Chrmn, Pres & CEO: A.Y. Chao

SVP, Secy & General Counsel: D.A. Buchen
VP, CFO, Chief Acctg Officer & Cntlr: R.T. Joyce
Investor Contact: P. Eisenhaur (951-493-5300)

Board of Directors: A. Y. Chao, M. J. Fedida, M. J. Feldman, A. F. Hummel, C. M. Klema, J. Michelson, R. R. Taylor, A. L. Turner, F. G. Weiss

Founded: 1983
Domicile: Nevada
Employees: 3,844

Weatherford International Ltd.

S&P Recommendation BUY ★★★★★

Price $42.27 (as of Oct 27, 2006)

12-Mo. Target Price $61.00

Investment Style Large-Cap Growth

GICS Sector Energy
Sub-Industry Oil & Gas Equipment & Services

Comment This company is one of the leading global providers of equipment and services used for the drilling, completion and production of oil and natural gas wells.

Key Stock Statistics (Source S&P, Vickers, company reports)

52-Wk Range	$58.73–30.75	S&P Oper. EPS 2006E	2.53	P/E on S&P Oper. EPS 2006E	16.7	Dividend Rate/Share	Nil
Trailing 12-Month EPS	$2.48	S&P Oper. EPS 2007E	3.78	Common Shares Outstg. (M)	346.0	Yield (%)	Nil
Trailing 12-Month P/E	17.0	S&P Core EPS 2006E	2.53	Market Capitalization(B)	$14.626	Beta	0.92
$10K Invested 5 Yrs Ago	$22,942	S&P Core EPS 2007E	3.78	Institutional Ownership (%)	78	S&P Credit Rating	BBB+

Price Performance

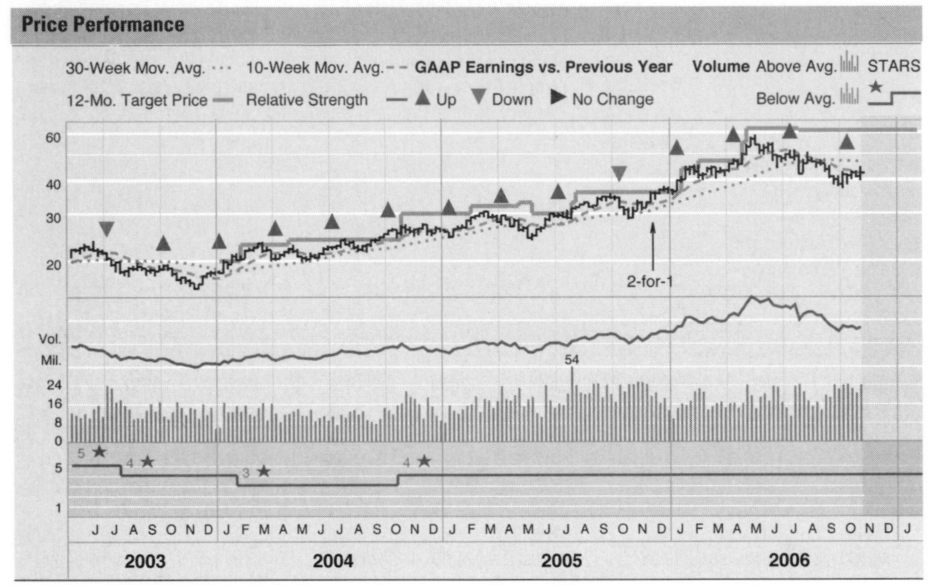

Options: CBOE

Analysis prepared by **Stewart Glickman, CFA** on July 31, 2006, when the stock traded at **$ 46.84**.

Highlights

- In the second quarter, total revenues advanced $601 million, or 64%, year-over-year, due in large part to the August 2005 Precision acquisition.
- The company has increased its presence in a number of frontier regions over the past few years, including the Caspian Sea, the Middle East and North Africa. While we think such regions carry higher operational risks than those in mature areas, we believe that growth opportunities in such regions typically can benefit greatly from newer drilling and completion technologies. We expect well construction and production optimization businesses to perform strongly in the near term.
- For 2006, we project total revenue growth of 51%, due mainly to the August 2005 acquisition of Precision Energy Services and Precision Drilling International, and see revenues rising a further 28% in 2007. We see operating margins in the low 20% range in both years, compared to about 14% in 2005. Overall, we see EPS of $2.53 in 2006, rising in 2007 to $3.78.

Investment Rationale/Risk

- We think WFT's strategy of focusing its oilfield services growth opportunities in the Eastern Hemisphere is a sound one, given our view that frontier regions offer strong growth potential. We believe the Precision Drilling oilfield services, previously marketed mainly in North America, could be expanded to the Eastern Hemisphere with WFT's greater breadth.
- Risks to our recommendation and target price include reduced drilling activity in key geographic markets; reduced oil and natural gas prices; and business risks associated with operating in frontier regions.
- Our DCF model, assuming free cash flow growth of 6% to 7% per year for 10 years, 3% thereafter, and a WACC of 10.2%, indicates intrinsic value of $69. While we estimate that WFT has historically had a lower return on capital employed than peers, we think a par valuation with peers is still appropriate, given our view that WFT has above-average growth prospects. Based on a 12.5X multiple to estimated 2006 EBITDA, and 16X estimated 2006 cash flow (both in line with peers), and our DCF model, we arrive at our blended 12-month target price of $61.

Qualitative Risk Assessment

LOW | **MEDIUM** | HIGH

Our risk assessment reflects this company's exposure to crude oil and natural gas prices, capital spending decisions made by oil and gas producers, its commitment to technological innovation in oilfield services, and geographic risk associated with operating in frontier regions around the globe. This is offset by leading edge technology.

Quantitative Evaluations

S&P Quality Ranking B-

D | C | **B-** | B | B+ | A- | A | A+

Relative Strength Rank WEAK

26

LOWEST = 1 HIGHEST = 99

Revenue/Earnings Data

Revenue (Million $)

	1Q	2Q	3Q	4Q	Year
2006	1,536	1,539	1,697	--	--
2005	857.7	937.3	1,077	1,461	4,333
2004	712.6	742.2	794.3	882.6	3,132
2003	589.3	617.7	660.5	723.9	2,591
2002	568.3	593.9	584.9	581.9	2,329
2001	526.2	573.0	608.6	620.9	2,329

Earnings Per Share ($)

	1Q	2Q	3Q	4Q	Year
2006	0.57	0.52	0.66	**E**0.74	**E**2.53
2005	0.28	0.32	0.15	0.69	1.47
2004	0.19	0.29	0.25	0.45	1.18
2003	0.14	0.11	0.12	0.18	0.55
2002	0.18	0.16	-0.51	0.13	-0.03
2001	0.19	0.23	0.25	0.22	0.88

Fiscal year ended Dec. 31. Next earnings report expected: Early February. EPS Estimates based on S&P Operating Earnings; historical GAAP earnings are as reported.

Dividend Data (Dates: mm/dd Payment Date: mm/dd/yy)

Amount ($)	Date Decl.	Ex-Div. Date	Stk. of Record	Payment Date
2-for-1 Stk.	10/27	12/01	11/14	11/30/05

Source: Company reports.

Please read the Required Disclosures and Analyst Certification on the last page of this report.

Weatherford International Ltd.

Business Summary July 31, 2006

CORPORATE OVERVIEW. Weatherford International is one of the world's leading providers of equipment and services for the drilling, completion and production of oil and natural gas wells. As of December 31, 2005, it had more than 750 manufacturing and service locations in over 100 countries. North America contributed 55% of 2005 revenues (U.S. 37% and Canada 18%), while International operations contributed 45%. Internationally, the Europe/CIS/West Africa region generated 15% of total revenues; Middle East and North Africa added 12%; Latin America 10%; and Asia Pacific 8%.

CORPORATE STRATEGY. WFT has focused its long-term strategy on geographic expansion of its products and services to the Eastern Hemisphere (Europe, Africa, the Middle East, Russia, and Asia), and on product and service expansion that assists in the drilling of new oilfields or efficiently producing oil and gas from existing oilfields. We view this strategy as consistent with ongoing secular trends in the energy industry, as oil and gas producers - including supermajors, large independents, and nationalized oil companies - seek low-cost, high-growth opportunities. Frequently, such opportunities tend to be located in such frontier regions, and/or are found in challenging geological conditions that demand improved technologies.

IMPACT OF MAJOR DEVELOPMENTS. Following the April 2000 spinoff of the Grant Prideco Drilling Products division and the February 2001 merger of the Compression Services division into a subsidiary of Universal Compression Holdings, Inc., WFT's business was divided into three principal operating divisions: Drilling and Intervention Services; Completion Systems; and Artificial Lift Systems. In April 2003, the company restructured its reporting divisions, and reported results in two segments: Drilling Services and Production Systems. In August 2005, WFT completed the acquisition of Precision Energy Services (PES) and Precision Drilling International. Following these acquisitions, the company reorganized into three operating segments: Evaluation, Drilling & Intervention Services (EDI); Completion & Production Services (CPS); and Other Operations.

Company Financials

Per Share Data ($) Year Ended Dec. 31	**2005**	**2004**	**2003**	**2002**	**2001**	**2000**	**1999**	**1998**	**1997**	**1996**
Tangible Book Value	6.45	4.95	3.11	0.90	1.94	1.17	3.89	3.51	1.32	3.85
Cash Flow	2.48	1.99	1.43	0.87	1.59	0.73	0.89	1.20	1.24	0.50
Earnings	1.47	1.18	0.55	-0.03	0.88	-0.21	0.08	0.33	0.89	0.30
Dividends	Nil	Nil	Nil	Nil	Nil	Nil	Nil	Nil	Nil	Nil
Payout Ratio	Nil	Nil	Nil	Nil	Nil	Nil	Nil	Nil	Nil	Nil
Prices:High	37.94	27.62	23.85	27.13	30.18	31.00	21.06	29.22	36.50	12.88
Prices:Low	23.82	17.91	15.65	16.28	11.36	15.88	8.38	7.50	11.69	5.56
P/E Ratio:High	26	24	44	NM	34	NM	NM	89	41	43
P/E Ratio:Low	16	15	29	NM	13	NM	NM	23	13	19
Income Statement Analysis (Million $)										
Revenue	4,333	3,132	2,591	2,329	2,329	1,814	1,240	2,011	892	478
Operating Income	977	649	499	488	596	372	231	461	176	53.8
Depreciation, Depletion and Amortization	334	256	233	215	208	199	167	171	33.7	7.50
Interest Expense	80.3	63.6	76.7	85.5	74.0	59.3	44.9	54.5	23.1	16.5
Pretax Income	626	431	195	-9.84	339	71.3	28.4	99.4	129	31.5
Effective Tax Rate	25.4%	21.5%	26.0%	NM	36.3%	NM	29.9%	34.8%	34.9%	22.3%
Net Income	466	337	143	-6.03	215	-38.9	16.2	64.8	83.7	24.5
Balance Sheet & Other Financial Data (Million $)										
Cash	134	317	56.1	48.8	88.8	154	44.4	40.2	31.9	248
Current Assets	2,639	1,943	1,436	1,259	1,231	1,242	869	1,082	631	559
Total Assets	8,580	5,543	5,000	4,495	4,296	3,462	3,514	2,832	1,366	1,366
Current Liabilities	1,998	660	782	877	760	463	666	557	314	233
Long Term Debt	632	1,404	1,380	1,514	1,500	1,133	629	632	446	127
Common Equity	5,667	3,313	2,708	1,974	1,838	1,338	1,833	1,494	527	454
Total Capital	6,387	4,748	4,107	3,523	3,437	2,834	2,661	2,126	1,052	581
Capital Expenditures	527	311	303	269	339	267	174	206	62.6	89.0
Cash Flow	801	593	376	209	423	160	183	236	117	41.0
Current Ratio	1.3	2.9	1.8	1.4	1.6	2.7	1.3	1.9	2.0	2.4
% Long Term Debt of Capitalization	9.9	29.6	33.6	43.0	43.6	40.0	23.6	29.7	42.4	21.9
% Return on Assets	6.6	6.4	3.0	NM	5.5	NM	0.5	3.1	7.5	3.8
% Return on Equity	10.4	11.2	6.1	NM	13.5	NM	1.0	6.4	17.1	7.2

Data as orig reptd.; bef. results of disc opers/spec. items. Per share data adj. for stk. divs.; EPS diluted. E-Estimated. NA-Not Available. NM-Not Meaningful. NR-Not Ranked. UR-Under Review.

Office: 515 Post Oak Boulevard, Houston, TX 77027-3415.
Telephone: 713-693-4000.
Email: investor.relations@weatherford.com
Website: http://www.weatherford.com

Chrmn, Pres & CEO: B.J. Duroc-Danner
Investor Contact: A.P. Becnel (713-693-4136)
SVP & CFO: A.P. Becnel
SVP & CTO: S.E. Ferguson

SVP, Secy & General Counsel: B.M. Martin
Board of Directors: N. F. Brady, D. J. Butters, B. J. Duroc-Danner, S. B. Lubar, W. E. Macaulay, R. B. Millard, R. K. Moses, Jr., R. A. Rayne

Founded: 1972
Domicile: Bermuda
Employees: 25,100

Stock Report | October 31, 2006 | NYS Symbol: **WLP** | **WLP** is in the S&P 500

STANDARD &POOR'S

WellPoint Inc

S&P Recommendation BUY ★★★★★

Price $76.32 (as of Oct 31, 2006)

12-Mo. Target Price $91.00

Investment Style Large-Cap Value

GICS Sector Health Care
Sub-Industry Managed Health Care

Comment This Indiana-based Blue Cross and Blue Shield licensee is the largest managed health organization in the U.S., serving more than 34 million members in 14 states.

Key Stock Statistics (Source S&P, Vickers, company reports)

52-Wk Range	$80.40–65.50	S&P Oper. EPS 2006E	4.78	P/E on S&P Oper. EPS 2006E	16.0	Dividend Rate/Share	Nil
Trailing 12-Month EPS	$4.58	S&P Oper. EPS 2007E	5.50	Common Shares Outstg. (M)	620.0	Yield (%)	Nil
Trailing 12-Month P/E	16.7	S&P Core EPS 2006E	4.67	Market Capitalization(B)	$47.320	Beta	0.13
$10K Invested 5 Yrs Ago	NA	S&P Core EPS 2007E	5.38	Institutional Ownership (%)	80	S&P Credit Rating	BBB+

Price Performance

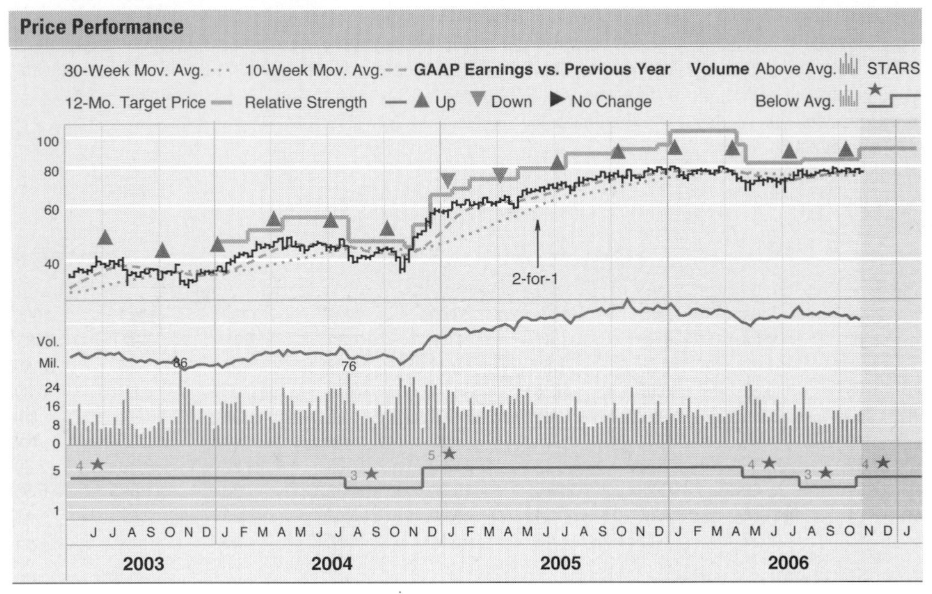

Analysis prepared by **Phillip M. Seligman** on October 31, 2006, when the stock traded at **$ 76.32**.

Highlights

- We look for 2007 operating revenues to rise by 6%, to about $60 billion, from the approximately $56.1 billion we forecast for 2006. Such growth is well below the 26% we see in 2006, owing to the WellChoice (WC) acquisition in late 2005. We see 2007 growth mainly driven by higher prices and 3% to 5% higher enrollment, with healthy gains in national accounts, Medicare and Medicaid, tempered by continued softness in the large account sector.
- We expect the 2007 benefits expense ratio to rise 20 basis points (bps), on a change in revenue mix, as growth of the Medicaid and Medicare businesses outweighs companywide benefits from continued medical cost moderation. We expect the SG&A cost ratio to decline by 60 bps, on IT development and on synergies from the Anthem-WellPoint Health Networks merger and the WC merger.
- For 2007, we look for EPS of $5.50, versus our 2006 estimate of $4.78. Operating EPS in 2005 was $4.01, before $0.18 of stock option expense. Our 2006 and 2007 S&P Core EPS estimates of $4.67 and $5.38, respectively, reflect pension and post-retirement adjustments. We see share repurchases aiding EPS growth.

Investment Rationale/Risk

- We are encouraged by the 7.7% rise in national enrollment year to date as of September 30, and see similarly robust growth in this sector in 2007. We are also encouraged by the company's four recent state Medicaid contract wins. Meanwhile, we believe that, excluding the exit of two states' employee accounts, large-account enrollment grew, albeit modestly. We think that WLP lost accounts on disciplined pricing, which we view favorably. But we see this strategy, and our view that groupwide retention rates have increased, making it difficult to grow risk-based enrollment meaningfully. We also think that the recent consolidation among large managed care firms ratcheted up competition. In this environment, we believe that its increasing product and market diversification and especially its Blue Cross/Blue Shield tie are competitive strengths.
- Risks to our recommendation and target price include competition, higher than expected medical costs, and a weakened job market.
- Our 12-month target price of $91 is derived by utilizing a peer-level PEG ratio of 1.1X, assuming three-year growth of 15% and our 2007 EPS estimate of $5.50.

Qualitative Risk Assessment

LOW | **MEDIUM** | HIGH

Our risk assessment reflects WLP's leadership in the highly fragmented managed care market, strong cash flow, and history of improving financial performance. We also view its geographic, market and product diversity as enabling these trends to be sustainable in most economic conditions. Even so, we think that enrollment growth going forward will be limited by heightened competition we see following consolidation in the managed care sub-sector.

Quantitative Evaluations

S&P Quality Ranking NR

D | C | B- | B | B+ | A- | A | A+

Relative Strength Rank MODERATE

30

LOWEST = 1 HIGHEST = 99

Revenue/Earnings Data

Revenue (Million $)

	1Q	2Q	3Q	4Q	Year
2006	13,820	13,942	14,426	--	--
2005	11,100	11,299	11,305	11,432	45,136
2004	4,574	4,608	4,807	6,826	20,815
2003	4,100	4,114	4,262	4,295	16,771
2002	2,812	2,900	3,579	3,900	13,282
2001	2,561	2,558	2,664	2,662	10,445

Earnings Per Share ($)

2006	1.09	1.17	1.29	**E**1.27	**E**4.78
2005	0.98	0.90	1.02	1.04	3.94
2004	1.04	0.83	0.85	0.46	3.05
2003	0.68	0.63	0.69	0.74	2.73
2002	0.48	0.51	0.65	0.60	2.26
2001	0.34	0.35	5.35	0.43	1.65

Fiscal year ended Dec. 31. Next earnings report expected: Late January. EPS Estimates based on S&P Operating Earnings; historical GAAP earnings are as reported.

Dividend Data

No cash dividends have been paid.

WellPoint Inc

Business Summary October 31, 2006

CORPORATE OVERVIEW. WellPoint, Inc. was formed by the merger consummated on November 30, 2004 between publicly traded managed care giants Anthem, Inc. and WellPoint Health Networks Inc. (WHN). Consequently, all historical data in this stock report are for Anthem. WLP is the largest publicly traded commercial health benefits company in the U.S., serving 34.2 million members as of June 30, 2006 (versus 33.9 million on December 31, 2005), and an independent licensee of the Blue Cross and Blue Shield Association. It serves members as the Blue Cross licensee for California and the Blue Cross or Blue Cross and Blue Shield (BCBS) licensee in all or parts of 13 other states. WLP also serves members in various parts of the U.S. as UniCare and conducts insurance operations in all 50 states and Puerto Rico through an affiliate.

WLP's network-based managed care plans include preferred provider organizations (PPOs), health maintenance organizations (HMOs), point-of-service plans (POS), traditional indemnity plans and other hybrid plans, including consumer-driven health plans (CDHPs), hospital only, and limited benefit products. It also provides managed care services to self-funded customers. WLP also provides specialty and other products and services including pharmacy benefit management, group life and disability insurance, dental, vision, behavioral health, workers compensation and long-term care insurance. Approximately 93% of 2005 operating revenue was derived from premium income and 7% from administrative services and other revenues.

The customer base includes large groups with 51 to 4,999 eligible employees (15,959,000 members as of June 30, 2006, versus 16,362,000 as of December 31, 2005); individuals under age 65 and small groups of one to 50 employees (ISG, 5,651,000 versus 5,645,000); National Accounts (multi-state employer groups with 5,000 or more employees, 5,142,000 versus 4,776,000), BlueCard Host (enrollees of non-owned BCBS plans who receive benefits in WLP's BCBS markets, 4,104,000 versus 3,915,000); Senior (over age 65 individuals in Medicare Supplement or Medicare Advantage policies, 1,246,000 versus 1,224,000); and State Sponsored Programs (Medicaid and State Children's Health Insurance Plans, 1,971,000 versus 1,934,000).

Company Financials

Per Share Data ($) Year Ended Dec. 31	**2005**	**2004**	**2003**	**2002**	**2001**	**2000**	**1999**	**1998**	**1997**	**1996**
Tangible Book Value	2.78	2.03	8.44	5.76	7.71	7.66	NA	NA	NA	NA
Cash Flow	3.94	2.05	3.59	2.90	2.23	1.55	NA	NA	NA	NA
Earnings	3.94	3.05	2.73	2.26	1.65	1.05	NA	NA	NA	NA
S&P Core Earnings	3.82	2.69	2.49	1.93	1.16	NA	NA	NA	NA	NA
Dividends	Nil	Nil	Nil	Nil	Nil	NA	NA	NA	NA	NA
Payout Ratio	Nil	Nil	Nil	Nil	Nil	NA	NA	NA	NA	NA
Prices:High	80.40	58.88	41.45	37.75	25.95	NA	NA	NA	NA	NA
Prices:Low	54.50	00.10	20.50	23.20	10.00	NA	NA	NA	NA	NA
P/E Ratio:High	20	19	15	17	16	NA	NA	NA	NA	NA
P/E Ratio:Low	14	12	10	10	11	NA	NA	NA	NA	NA
Income Statement Analysis (Million $)										
Revenue	45,136	20,815	16,771	13,282	10,445	8,771	NA	NA	NA	NA
Operating Income	4,750	2,072	1,595	1,093	733	487	NA	NA	NA	NA
Depreciation	634	279	245	157	121	102	NA	NA	NA	NA
Interest Expense	226	142	131	98.5	60.2	69.6	NA	NA	NA	NA
Pretax Income	3,890	1,443	1,219	808	525	315	NA	NA	NA	NA
Effective Tax Rate	36.7%	33.5%	36.1%	31.6%	35.0%	30.8%	NA	NA	NA	NA
Net Income	2,464	960	774	549	342	216	NA	NA	NA	NA
S&P Core Earnings	2,402	842	708	467	240	NA	NA	NA	NA	NA
Balance Sheet & Other Financial Data (Million $)										
Cash	2,897	1,457	523	744	406	421	NA	NA	NA	NA
Current Assets	25,945	19,358	8,865	7,877	5,300	5,025	NA	NA	NA	NA
Total Assets	51,405	39,738	13,439	12,293	6,277	6,021	NA	NA	NA	NA
Current Liabilities	14,857	11,571	4,772	4,449	2,963	2,784	NA	NA	NA	NA
Long Term Debt	6,325	4,277	1,663	1,659	818	789	NA	NA	NA	NA
Common Equity	25,755	20,331	6,000	5,362	2,060	2,055	NA	NA	NA	NA
Total Capital	35,386	27,204	8,188	7,412	2,878	2,844	NA	NA	NA	NA
Capital Expenditures	162	137	111	123	70.4	NA	NA	NA	NA	NA
Cash Flow	2,464	1,239	1,019	706	463	318	NA	NA	NA	NA
Current Ratio	1.7	1.7	1.9	1.8	1.8	1.8	NA	NA	NA	NA
% Long Term Debt of Capitalization	17.9	15.7	20.3	22.4	28.4	27.7	NA	NA	NA	NA
% Net Income of Revenue	5.5	4.7	4.6	50.8	35.6	2.5	NA	NA	NA	NA
% Return on Assets	5.4	3.6	6.0	5.9	5.7	NA	NA	NA	NA	NA
% Return on Equity	10.7	7.2	13.6	14.8	17.2	NA	NA	NA	NA	NA

Data as orig reptd.; bef. results of disc opers/spec. items. Per share data adj. for stk. divs.; EPS diluted. E-Estimated. NA-Not Available. NM-Not Meaningful. NR-Not Ranked. UR-Under Review.

Office: 120 Monument Circle, Indianapolis, IN 46204-4903.
Telephone: 317-488-6000.
Email: anthem.corporate.communications@anthem.com
Website: http://www.wellpoint.com

Chrmn, Pres & CEO: L.C. Glasscock
EVP, CFO & Chief Acctg Officer: D.C. Colby
EVP, Secy & General Counsel: A. Braly
SVP & Chief Acctg Officer: W.S. DeVeydt

Investor Contact: T. Durle (317-488-6390)
Board of Directors: L. D. Baker, Jr., S. B. Bayh, S. P. Burke, W. H. Bush, L. C. Glasscock, J. A. Hill, W. Y. Jobe, V. S. Liss, L. B. Lytle, W. G. Mays, R. G. Peru, J. G. Pisano, D. W. Riegle, Jr., W. J. Ryan, E. A. Sanders, G. A. Schaefer, Jr., J. M. Ward

Founded: 1944
Domicile: Indiana
Employees: 42,000

STANDARD &POOR'S

Wells Fargo & Co

S&P Recommendation HOLD ★★★★★

Price $36.32 (as of Oct 27, 2006)

12-Mo. Target Price $37.00

Investment Style Large-Cap Value

GICS Sector Financials
Sub-Industry Diversified Banks

Comment This San Francisco-based bank holding company provides banking, insurance, investment, mortgage and consumer finance services throughout North America.

Key Stock Statistics (Source S&P, Vickers, company reports)

52-Wk Range	$36.99–29.64	S&P Oper. EPS 2006E	2.51	P/E on S&P Oper. EPS 2006E	14.5	Dividend Rate/Share	$1.12
Trailing 12-Month EPS	$2.42	S&P Oper. EPS 2007E	2.75	Common Shares Outstg. (M)	3,367.2	Yield (%)	3.08
Trailing 12-Month P/E	15.0	S&P Core EPS 2006E	2.44	Market Capitalization(B)	$122.297	Beta	0.35
$10K Invested 5 Yrs Ago	$20,473	S&P Core EPS 2007E	2.71	Institutional Ownership (%)	68	S&P Credit Rating	AA

Price Performance

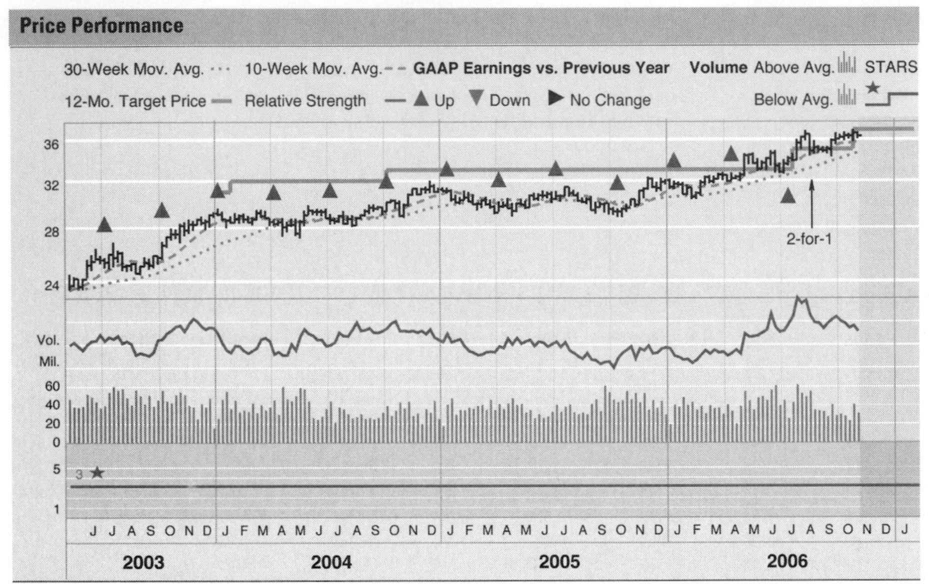

Options: ASE, CBOE, P, Ph

Analysis prepared by **Mark Hebeka, CFA** on October 24, 2006, when the stock traded at **$ 36.67**.

Highlights

- We continue to think that WFC's strong sales culture, proven ability to cross-sell its diverse product mix to its customer base, high credit quality standards, and exposure to attractive growth regions should support its ability to achieve above-average revenue and earnings growth for the long term. However, we believe that a potential slowdown in mortgage business growth would keep revenue and earnings growth below historical levels into 2007.
- We estimate 2006 total loan growth of 5%, following 8% growth reported in 2005, on lower residential mortgage originations, partly offset by stronger commercial loans. We believe that WFC's large mortgage servicing portfolio should offset some of the expected decline in mortgage origination fees and loan sale gains. We see an average net interest margin of 4.81% in 2006, down slightly from 4.86% in 2005.
- We project EPS of $2.51 for 2006 and $2.75 in 2007, up from $2.25 in 2005.

Investment Rationale/Risk

- Our hold recommendation is based on the stock's valuation versus peers and what we consider a mixed operating outlook; we expect the shares to perform in line with the S&P 500 in the year ahead. We view WFC as having solid banking fundamentals and a diverse customer base, and we look for continued growth through 2007, albeit slower.
- Risks to our recommendation and target price include a severe economic downturn in combination with higher short-term interest rates that could result in an inverted yield curve; litigation and regulatory risks; and a serious event that could affect equity markets. We are concerned about WFC's corporate governance relating to the presence of affiliated outsiders on a number of board committees.
- The stock's average P/E multiples were 16X and 14X in the past five years and three years, respectively. Our 12-month target price of $37 is about 13.5X our FY 07 EPS estimate, a slight premium to peers, based on our view of strong earnings momentum.

Qualitative Risk Assessment

LOW | MEDIUM | HIGH

Our risk assessment reflects what we see as solid business fundamentals and a strong customer base. We view WFC as well diversified and able to withstand a major global or U.S. economic downturn.

Quantitative Evaluations

S&P Quality Ranking A

D | C | B- | B | B+ | A- | A | A+

Relative Strength Rank MODERATE

44

LOWEST = 1 HIGHEST = 99

Revenue/Earnings Data

Revenue (Million $)

	1Q	2Q	3Q	4Q	Year
2006	11,217	11,882	12,286	--	--
2005	9,509	9,529	10,427	10,897	40,407
2004	7,955	8,269	8,305	9,347	33,876
2003	7,561	7,637	8,170	8,257	31,800
2002	6,982	7,005	7,044	7,443	28,473
2001	7,295	5,361	7,099	7,137	26,891

Earnings Per Share ($)

	1Q	2Q	3Q	4Q	Year
2006	0.60	0.62	--	E0.66	E2.51
2005	0.54	0.56	0.58	0.57	2.25
2004	0.52	0.50	0.51	0.52	2.05
2003	0.44	0.45	0.46	0.48	1.83
2002	0.40	0.41	0.42	0.43	1.66
2001	0.34	-0.03	0.34	0.35	0.99

Fiscal year ended Dec. 31. Next earnings report expected: Mid January. EPS Estimates based on S&P Operating Earnings; historical GAAP earnings are as reported.

Dividend Data (Dates: mm/dd Payment Date: mm/dd/yy)

Amount ($)	Date Decl.	Ex-Div. Date	Stk. of Record	Payment Date
0.520	04/25	05/03	05/05	06/01/06
0.560	06/27	08/02	08/04	09/01/06
2-for-1 Stk.	06/27	08/14	08/04	08/11/06
0.280	10/24	11/01	11/03	12/01/06

Dividends have been paid since 1939. Source: Company reports.

Wells Fargo & Co

Business Summary October 24, 2006

CORPORATE OVERVIEW. WFC has three lines of business for management reporting: community banking, wholesale banking, and Wells Fargo Financial. The community banking group offers a complete line of banking and diversified financial products and services to consumers and small businesses with annual sales generally up to $20 million, in which the owner generally is the financial decision maker. Community banking also offers investment management and other services to retail customers and high net worth individuals, insurance, securities brokerage through affiliates and venture capital financing.

Community banking serves customers through a wide range of channels, which include traditional banking stores, in-store banking centers, business centers and ATMs. Also, Phone Bank centers and the National Business Banking Center provide 24-hour telephone service. Online banking services include single sign-on to online banking, bill pay and brokerage, as well as online banking for small business.

The wholesale banking group serves businesses across the United States with annual sales generally in excess of $10 million. Wholesale banking provides a complete line of commercial, corporate and real estate banking products and services. These include traditional commercial loans and lines of credit, letters of credit, asset-based lending, equipment leasing, mezzanine financing, high-yield debt, international trade facilities, foreign exchange services, treasury management, investment management, institutional fixed income and equity sales, interest rate, commodity and equity risk management, online/electronic products, insurance brokerage services and investment banking services.

Wholesale banking manages and administers institutional investments, employee benefit trusts and mutual funds, including the Wells Fargo Advantage Funds. Wholesale banking includes the majority ownership interest in the Wells Fargo HSBC Trade Bank, which provides trade financing, letters of credit, and collection services, and is sometimes supported by the Export-Import Bank of the United States.

Company Financials

Per Share Data ($) Year Ended Dec. 31	**2005**	**2004**	**2003**	**2002**	**2001**	**2000**	**1999**	**1998**	**1997**	**1996**
Tangible Book Value	8.81	7.95	7.04	6.11	4.90	4.59	3.96	3.39	4.51	3.99
Earnings	2.25	2.05	1.83	1.66	0.99	1.17	1.12	0.58	0.88	0.77
S&P Core Earnings	2.18	1.96	1.78	1.57	0.84	NA	NA	NA	NA	NA
Dividends	1.00	0.93	0.75	0.55	0.50	0.45	0.39	0.35	0.31	0.26
Payout Ratio	44%	45%	41%	33%	51%	39%	35%	60%	35%	34%
Prices:High	32.35	32.02	29.59	26.72	27.41	28.19	24.97	21.94	19.75	11.72
Prices:Low	28.81	27.16	21.64	21.65	19.13	15.69	16.09	13.75	10.69	7.63
P/E Ratio:High	14	16	16	16	28	24	22	37	23	15
P/E Ratio:Low	13	13	12	13	19	13	14	24	12	10
Income Statement Analysis (Million $)										
Net Interest Income	18,504	17,150	16,007	14,855	12,460	10,865	9,355	8,990	4,033	3,701
Tax Equivalent Adjustment	110	104	NA	NA	NA	65.0	64.0	59.0	44.5	32.2
Non Interest Income	14,054	12,530	12,323	9,348	7,227	9,565	6,653	6,427	2,924	2,612
Loan Loss Provision	2,383	1,717	1,722	1,733	1,780	1,329	1,045	1,545	525	395
% Expense/Operating Revenue	58.2%	64.8%	60.7%	52.2%	65.5%	57.7%	60.9%	68.4%	63.5%	64.5%
Pretax Income	11,548	10,769	9,477	8,854	5,479	6,549	5,948	3,293	2,050	1,782
Effective Tax Rate	33.6%	34.9%	34.6%	35.5%	37.5%	38.5%	37.0%	40.8%	34.1%	35.2%
Net Income	7,671	7,014	6,202	5,710	3,423	4,026	3,747	1,950	1,351	1,154
% Net Interest Margin	4.86	4.89	5.08	5.57	5.36	5.35	5.66	5.79	5.74	5.63
S&P Core Earnings	7,423	6,722	6,055	5,374	2,894	NA	NA	NA	NA	NA
Balance Sheet & Other Financial Data (Million $)										
Money Market Assets	16,211	14,020	2,745	3,174	2,530	1,598	1,554	1,517	1,501	2,701
Investment Securities	41,834	33,717	32,953	27,947	40,308	38,655	38,518	31,997	18,731	16,959
Commercial Loans	108,903	98,515	48,729	47,292	47,547	60,541	46,538	41,830	12,878	12,125
Other Loans	201,934	189,071	204,344	149,342	124,952	10,583	72,926	66,164	31,757	29,029
Total Assets	481,741	427,849	387,798	349,259	307,569	272,426	218,102	202,475	88,540	80,175
Demand Deposits	87,712	81,082	74,387	74,094	65,362	55,096	42,916	43,732	16,253	14,296
Time Deposits	226,738	193,776	173,140	142,822	121,904	114,463	89,792	90,056	39,204	35,834
Long Term Debt	79,668	73,580	63,642	50,205	38,530	32,981	24,160	19,709	12,767	13,082
Common Equity	40,335	37,596	34,255	30,107	26,996	26,103	21,860	20,296	6,755	5,875
% Return on Assets	1.7	1.7	1.7	1.7	1.2	1.6	1.8	1.0	1.6	1.5
% Return on Equity	19.7	19.5	19.3	20.0	12.8	16.2	17.6	14.2	21.2	20.0
% Loan Loss Reserve	1.1	1.2	1.3	1.5	1.8	2.1	2.5	2.9	2.9	2.6
% Loans/Deposits	111.9	118.6	117.0	117.3	110.9	104.7	93.8	79.0	76.7	78.6
% Equity to Assets	8.6	8.8	8.7	8.7	9.2	9.7	10.0	10.2	7.4	7.5

Data as orig reptd.; bef. results of disc opers/spec. items. Per share data adj. for stk. divs.; EPS diluted. E-Estimated. NA-Not Available. NM-Not Meaningful. NR-Not Ranked. UR-Under Review.

Office: 420 Montgomery St, San Francisco, CA 94163.
Telephone: 1-866-878-5865.
Website: http://www.wellsfargo.com
Chrmn & CEO: R.M. Kovacevich

Pres & COO: J.G. Stumpf
Sr EVP: M.C. Oman
Sr EVP: D.A. Hoyt
Investor Contact: H.I. Atkins (888-662-7865)

Board of Directors: J. S. Chen, L. H. Dean, S. E. Engel, E. Hernandez, Jr., R. L. Joss, R. M. Kovacevich, R. D. McCormick, C. H. Milligan, N. G. Moore, P. J. Quigley, D. B. Rice, J. M. Runstad, S. W. Sanger, J. G. Stumpf, S. G. Swenson, M. W. Wright

Founded: 1929
Domicile: Delaware
Employees: 153,500

Wendy's International Inc.

S&P Recommendation SELL ★★★★★

Price $34.97 (as of Oct 27, 2006)

12-Mo. Target Price $29.00

Investment Style Mid-Cap Growth

GICS Sector Consumer Discretionary
Sub-Industry Restaurants

Comment Wendy's operates or franchises about 6,700 Wendy's, about 2,900 Tim Horton's, and about 300 Baja Fresh restaurants, mainly in the U.S. and Canada.

Key Stock Statistics (Source S&P, Vickers, company reports)

52-Wk Range	$67.19–31.75	S&P Oper. EPS 2006E	0.61	P/E on S&P Oper. EPS 2006E	57.3	Dividend Rate/Share	$0.34
Trailing 12-Month EPS	$1.05	S&P Oper. EPS 2007E	1.34	Common Shares Outstg. (M)	117.7	Yield (%)	0.97
Trailing 12-Month P/E	33.3	S&P Core EPS 2006E	0.08	Market Capitalization(B)	$4.115	Beta	0.43
$10K Invested 5 Yrs Ago	$28,141	S&P Core EPS 2007E	1.34	Institutional Ownership (%)	84	S&P Credit Rating	BB+

Price Performance

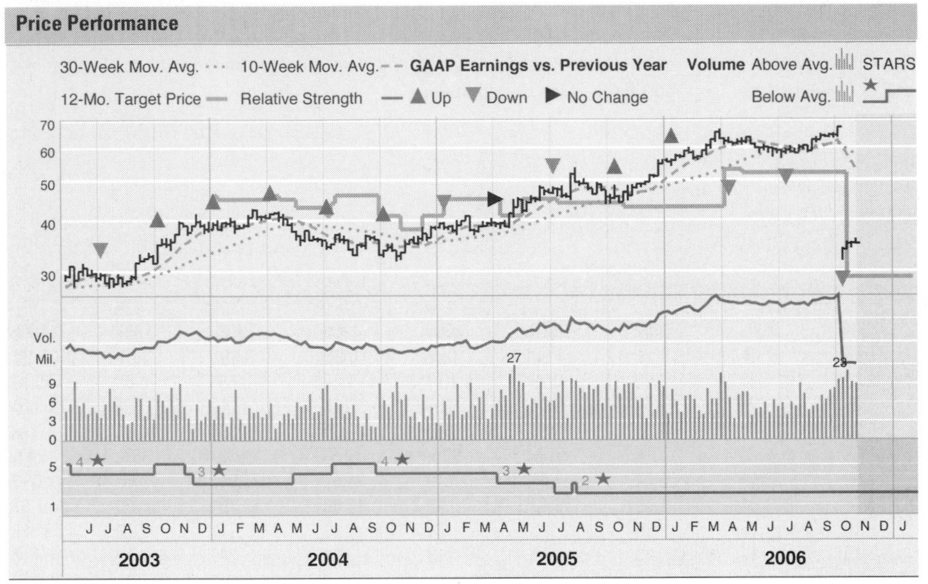

Options: CBOE, P

Qualitative Risk Assessment

LOW | **MEDIUM** | HIGH

Wendy's and Tim Hortons compete in the relatively stable fast food industry, in which they possess a very strong brand name presence, in our view. However, operating margins can vary widely due to fluctuations in food costs and competitive discounting.

Quantitative Evaluations

S&P Quality Ranking A-

D | C | B- | B | B+ | **A-** | A | A+

Relative Strength Rank WEAK

2

LOWEST = 1 HIGHEST = 99

Highlights

- The 12-month target price for WEN has recently been changed to $29.00 from $52.00. The Highlights section of this Stock Report will be updated accordingly.

Investment Rationale/Risk

- The Investment Rationale/Risk section of this Stock Report will be updated shortly. For the latest News story on WEN from MarketScope, see below.

- 10/26/06 04:52 pm EDT... S&P REITERATES SELL OPINION ON SHARES OF WENDY'S INTERNATIONAL (WEN 35.5**): Sep-Q EPS was $0.21 before one-time items, vs. $0.17. Including discontinued operations, EPS was $0.66 vs. our estimate of $0.68. Results benefited from same-store sales growth of 4.1% at Wendy's units and lower beef prices. We are lowering our '06 EPS estimate to $0.61 from $2.08, to account for the spin-off of Tim Horton's and the sale of Baja Fresh. We are keeping our '07 EPS estimate of $1.34 and our 12-month target price of $29. At 26.5X our '07 estimate, WEN is trading at a significant premium to peers, which we think overvalues the company's potential growth prospects. /D.Milton

Revenue/Earnings Data

Revenue (Million $)

	1Q	2Q	3Q	4Q	Year
2006	931.5	1,030	623.8	--	--
2005	894.2	951.0	960.6	977.3	3,783
2004	834.8	908.9	914.0	972.8	3,635
2003	694.0	786.0	806.5	862.4	3,149
2002	612.4	684.1	722.1	711.7	2,730
2001	555.5	609.6	610.4	615.7	2,391

Earnings Per Share ($)

2006	0.44	-0.25	0.16	**E**0.22	**E**0.61
2005	0.45	0.61	0.61	0.25	1.92
2004	0.45	0.62	0.60	-1.20	0.45
2003	0.38	0.53	0.58	0.56	2.05
2002	0.39	0.54	0.52	0.44	1.89
2001	0.33	0.47	0.44	0.41	1.65

Fiscal year ended Dec. 31. Next earnings report expected: Early February. EPS Estimates based on S&P Operating Earnings; historical GAAP earnings are as reported.

Dividend Data (Dates: mm/dd Payment Date: mm/dd/yy)

Amount ($)	Date Decl.	Ex-Div. Date	Stk. of Record	Payment Date
0.170	04/27	05/04	05/08	05/22/06
0.170	07/27	08/03	08/07	08/21/06
Stk.	08/31	10/02	09/15	09/29/06
0.085	10/26	11/02	11/06	11/20/06

Dividends have been paid since 1976. Source: Company reports.

Wendy's International Inc.

Business Summary September 29, 2006

COMPANY OVERVIEW. Wendy's International operates Wendy's Old Fashioned Hamburgers, the world's third largest quick service restaurant (QSR) chain. Systemwide sales were $8.3 billion in 2005, up 5.5% from 2004. At July 2, 2006, the chain totaled 6,743 restaurants, predominantly in the U.S. and Canada. Of these restaurants, 1,475 were operated by the company and 5,268 by franchisees. Franchisees pay monthly royalty fees, typically 4% of sales.

In addition to Wendy's, the company also owns the Tim Hortons and Baja Fresh restaurant concepts. Tim Hortons location offers coffee, fresh baked goods, and, in some units, sandwiches and soups. The concept has a 75% market share of the coffee and fresh baked goods market in Canada. Systemwide sales totaled about $3.1 billion in 2005, up 16.3% from 2004. As of July 2, 2006, there were 2,625 Tim Horton's units in Canada and 297 units in the U.S. About 97% of the units were operated by franchisees. Baja Fresh is a "fast-casual" concept specializing in fresh Mexican food. The company's food offerings are more upscale and expensive than traditional fast food selections. The average check per customer is between $7 and $8, compared with Wendy's average check of $5.25 to $5.50. At July 2, 2006, there were 298 Baja Fresh units, predominantly in the western U.S.

MARKET PROFILE. According to the National Restaurant Association, sales at limited service restaurants totaled $135.6 billion in 2005. Wendy's main competitors in the hamburger segment of the fast-food industry are McDonald's (2005 systemwide sales of $25.6 billion), and Burger King ($7.9 billion). Strong regional competitors include Sonic Drive-In ($3.0 billion) and Jack In The Box ($2.7 billion). Driven by new product development and higher menu prices, sales rose 4.8% at limited service restaurants in 2005 and 7.4% in 2004, significantly higher than in previous years. We expect growth rates to slow to 3.0% to 3.5% over the next several years, mainly due to increasing price competition and lower rates of expansion.

Company Financials

Per Share Data ($) Year Ended Dec. 31	**2005**	**2004**	**2003**	**2002**	**2001**	**2000**	**1999**	**1998**	**1997**	**1996**
Tangible Book Value	16.02	13.41	12.15	9.84	9.40	9.48	8.60	9.37	9.78	8.89
Cash Flow	3.63	2.02	3.51	3.10	2.62	2.31	2.06	1.63	1.68	1.91
Earnings	1.92	0.45	2.05	1.89	1.65	1.44	1.32	0.95	0.97	1.20
S&P Core Earnings	1.48	1.92	1.94	1.74	1.54	NA	NA	NA	NA	NA
Dividends	0.75	0.48	0.24	0.24	0.24	0.24	0.24	0.24	0.24	0.24
Payout Ratio	39%	107%	12%	13%	15%	17%	18%	25%	25%	20%
Prices:High	56.40	42.75	41.55	41.60	30.50	27.13	31.69	25.19	27.94	23.00
Prices:Low	36.73	31.74	23.97	26.15	20.00	14.00	19.69	18.13	19.63	16.75
P/E Ratio:High	29	95	20	22	18	19	24	27	29	19
P/E Ratio:Low	19	71	12	14	12	10	15	10	20	14

Income Statement Analysis (Million $)	2005	2004	2003	2002	2001	2000	1999	1998	1997	1996
Revenue	3,783	3,635	3,149	2,730	2,391	2,237	2,072	1,948	2,037	1,897
Operating Income	603	599	586	531	453	424	389	346	335	350
Depreciation	200	182	168	143	123	113	103	100	105	95.0
Interest Expense	46.4	47.0	45.8	41.5	30.2	28.9	10.2	19.8	18.9	20.3
Pretax Income	338	184	378	346	307	271	269	208	219	255
Effective Tax Rate	33.7%	71.7%	37.5%	36.8%	37.0%	37.5%	38.0%	40.6%	40.5%	38.8%
Net Income	224	52.0	236	219	194	170	167	123	131	156
S&P Core Earnings	173	222	221	200	181	NA	NA	NA	NA	NA

Balance Sheet & Other Financial Data (Million $)	2005	2004	2003	2002	2001	2000	1999	1998	1997	1996
Cash	393	177	171	172	111	170	211	161	234	224
Current Assets	757	459	463	331	266	319	350	314	382	337
Total Assets	3,440	3,198	3,164	2,667	2,076	1,958	1,884	1,838	1,942	1,781
Current Liabilities	583	688	528	360	297	296	284	249	213	208
Long Term Debt	616	594	693	682	651	448	449	446	250	242
Common Equity	2,059	1,716	1,980	1,449	1,030	1,126	1,065	1,068	1,184	1,057
Total Capital	2,753	2,419	2,805	2,239	1,763	1,647	1,584	1,575	1,715	1,562
Capital Expenditures	371	341	342	331	301	276	248	242	295	307
Cash Flow	424	234	404	362	317	283	270	224	236	251
Current Ratio	1.3	0.7	0.9	0.9	0.9	1.1	1.2	1.3	1.8	1.6
% Long Term Debt of Capitalization	22.4	24.5	24.7	30.4	36.9	27.2	28.3	28.3	14.6	15.5
% Net Income of Revenue	5.9	1.4	7.5	8.0	8.1	7.6	8.0	6.3	6.4	8.2
% Return on Assets	6.8	1.6	8.0	9.2	9.6	8.8	9.0	6.5	7.0	9.5
% Return on Equity	11.9	3.0	13.8	17.7	18.0	15.5	15.6	11.0	11.7	16.6

Data as orig reptd.; bef. results of disc opers/spec. items. Per share data adj. for stk. divs.; EPS diluted. E-Estimated. NA-Not Available. NM-Not Meaningful. NR-Not Ranked. UR-Under Review.

Office: 4288 West Dublin-Granville Road, Dublin, OH 43017-0256.
Telephone: 614-764-3100.
Email: investor_relations@wendys.com
Website: http://www.wendys-invest.com

Chrmn: J.V. Pickett
Pres & CEO: K.B. Anderson
EVP & Treas: J.F. Catherwood
EVP, Secy & General Counsel: L.M. McCorkle, Jr.

SVP & Cntlr: D.L. Boone
Investor Contact: M. Gordon (614-764-3019)
Board of Directors: K. B. Anderson, A. B. Crane, J. Hill, P. D. House, T. F. Keller, W. E. Kirwan, D. P. Lauer, J. R. Lewis, J. F. Millar, J. V. Pickett, J. T. Schuessler, J. R. Thompson

Auditor: PricewaterhouseCoopers
Founded: 1969
Domicile: Ohio
Employees: 57,000

Western Union Co

S&P Recommendation HOLD ★★★★★ | **Price** $22.05 (as of Oct 31, 2006) | **12-Mo. Target Price** $25.00 | **Investment Style** Large-Cap Growth

GICS Sector Information Technology
Sub-Industry Data Processing & Outsourced Services

Comment Spun off from First Data Corp. in September 2006, Western Union is a leading independent provider of consumer money transfer services.

Key Stock Statistics (Source S&P, Vickers, company reports)

52-Wk Range	$23.04–16.85	S&P Oper. EPS 2006E	1.12	P/E on S&P Oper. EPS 2006E	19.7	Dividend Rate/Share	Nil
Trailing 12-Month EPS	$0.91	S&P Oper. EPS 2007E	1.15	Common Shares Outstg. (M)	765.2	Yield (%)	Nil
Trailing 12-Month P/E	24.2	S&P Core EPS 2006E	1.12	Market Capitalization(B)	$16.872	Beta	1.00
$10K Invested 5 Yrs Ago	NA	S&P Core EPS 2007E	1.15	Institutional Ownership (%)	NA	S&P Credit Rating	NA

Price Performance

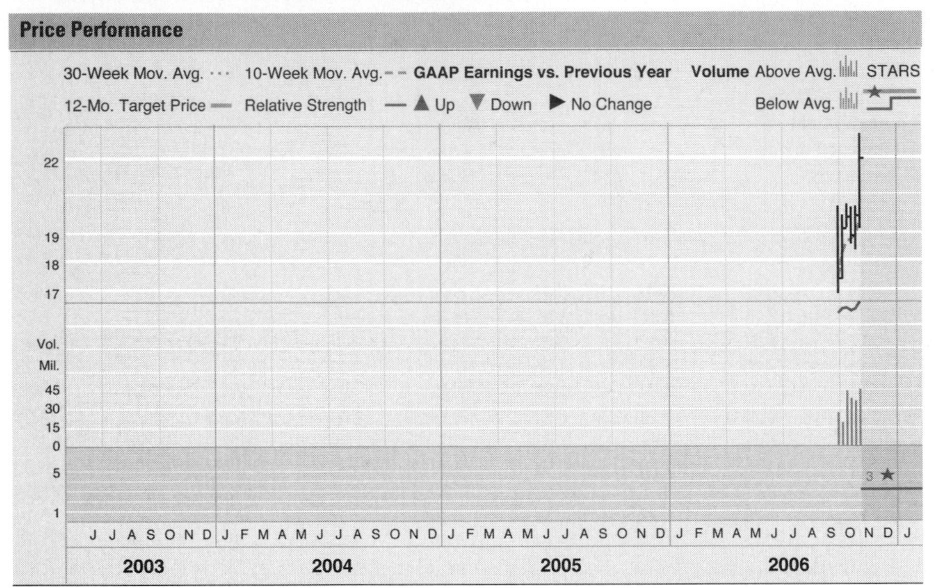

Analysis prepared by **Zaineb Bokhari** on October 31, 2006, when the stock traded at **$ 22.33**.

Highlights

- We forecast that revenues will rise 12% in 2006, with growth paced by an 11% increase in transaction fees. We expect this transaction fee growth to be driven by a 23%-24% rise in consumer-to-consumer (C2C) transactions and a 14% increase in C2C segment revenues, reflecting ongoing price declines within the segment. We look for WU's consumer-to business (C2B) segment to post transaction growth in the low teens, with revenue growth in the mid-single digit range. We expect total revenues to rise by 11% in 2007.

- We expect gross and operating margins to narrow modestly in both 2006 and 2007, reflecting our outlook for ongoing price declines within WU's money transfer business. We also look for SG&A to rise in both years, as a percentage of revenues, reflecting WU's ongoing investment in its brand as well as additional expenses related to its structure as an independent public company.

- Our 2006 and 2007 operating EPS estimates are $1.12 and $1.15, respectively. We expect WU to pay down up to $500 million in 2007 and repurchase shares of up to $400 million in 2007, aiding EPS.

Investment Rationale/Risk

- We recently initiated coverage with a hold recommendation. WU recently noted a slowdown in its U.S. to Mexico business, hurt by uncertainty in U.S. immigration policy. We believe WU's market leadership and geographic diversity (excluding the U.S. and Mexico) will enable it to weather headwinds related to future immigration policy changes. However, we look for near-term financial results to be restrained by this slowdown and by price competition from smaller competitors who are attempting to win market share.

- Risks to our recommendation and target price include accelerating consumer adoption of digital alternatives to WU's money transfer offerings, competition from traditional financial institutions and money transfer peers, and the potential for a negative impact from the U.S. government's anti-money laundering and anti-terrorism measures.

- Our DCF model, which assumes a WACC of 10.1% and a perpetuity growth rate of 3%, leads to an intrinsic value of $25, which is our 12-month target price. At this level, the shares would trade slightly above peers at a P/E of about 21.7X our 2007 EPS estimate.

Qualitative Risk Assessment

LOW	**MEDIUM**	HIGH

Our risk assessment reflects what we see as relatively high barriers to entry in WU's businesses and its market leadership, offset by risks related to consolidation in the financial services area, and the uncertainty related to the ongoing immigration debate in the U.S.

Quantitative Evaluations

S&P Quality Ranking **NR**

D	C	B-	B	B+	A-	A	A+

Relative Strength Rank **WEAK**

-1

LOWEST = 1 HIGHEST = 99

Revenue/Earnings Data

Revenue (Million $)

	1Q	2Q	3Q	4Q	Year
2006	--	--	1,140	--	--
2005	919.6	980.8	1,019	1,068	3,988
2004	--	--	--	--	--
2003	--	--	--	--	--
2002	--	--	--	--	--
2001	--	--	--	--	--

Earnings Per Share ($)

	1Q	2Q	3Q	4Q	Year
2006	--	--	0.34	E0.20	E1.12
2005	--	--	--	--	0.96
2004	--	--	--	--	--
2003	--	--	--	--	--
2002	--	--	--	--	--
2001	--	--	--	--	--

Fiscal year ended Dec. 31. Next earnings report expected: NA. EPS Estimates based on S&P Operating Earnings; historical GAAP earnings are as reported.

Dividend Data

No cash dividends have been paid.

Western Union Co

Business Summary October 31, 2006

CORPORATE OVERVIEW. Spun off from First Data Corp. in September 2006, Western Union is a leading independent provider of consumer money transfer services. WU offers its services through a network of over 285,000 agent locations spanning more than 200 countries and territories. The company provides its services globally, mainly under the Western Union brand name and also under the Orlandi Valuta and Vigo brands. WU derives the majority of revenues from fees that consumers pay when they send money. The company's main segments include consumer-to-consumer (C2C; 82% of 2005 revenues) and consumer-to-business (C2B; 18%).

WU's core C2C services allow customers to transfer money to other individuals. The majority of these transfers are originated in cash at Western Union agent locations, although consumers can also send money via the Internet, telephone, credit or debit card and, in some cases, through bank debits. In 2005, C2C transactions increased 23% to 119 million while C2C transaction fees rose about 14%.

Through its C2B segment, consumers can make payments to businesses electronically, over the telephone, via the Internet, or at one of WU's agent locations. The company has long-standing relationships with billers such as utilities, auto finance companies, mortgage servicers, financial service providers and government agencies who accept such payments. In 2005, WU's C2B transactions increased 12% to over 215 million while C2B transaction fees rose about 4%.

CORPORATE STRATEGY. The pursuit of growth through international expansion is a key tenet of Western Union's growth strategy. The company estimates that about 80% of its C2C transactions involve at least one non-U.S. location. The U.S. accounted for 19% of 2005 total revenues (21% in 2004) while Mexico accounted for 9% (8%). Outside of these two countries, WU's revenue base is well-diversified geographically. Building on and maintaining its well-recognized consumer brand is another key element to the company's strategy. WU has spent 7% of revenues on marketing, advertising and developing customer loyalty programs in each of 2003, 2004 and 2005. The company has also invested about 3% of annual revenues in selective price reductions on its C2C services in individual markets depending on the dynamics within those markets. We think the difference in growth between transaction fees and transaction volumes is evidence of this strategy.

Company Financials

Per Share Data ($) Year Ended Dec. 31	2005	2004	2003	2002	2001	2000	1999	1998	1997	1996
Tangible Book Value	NM	NA	NA	NA	NA	NA	NA	NA	NA	NA
Cash Flow	NA	NA	NA	NA	NA	NA	NA	NA	NA	NA
Earnings	0.96	NA	NA	NA	NA	NA	NA	NA	NA	NA
S&P Core Earnings	1.10	0.95	NA	NA	NA	NA	NA	NA	NA	NA
Dividends	NA	NA	NA	NA	NA	NA	NA	NA	NA	NA
Payout Ratio	NA	NA	NA	NA	NA	NA	NA	NA	NA	NA
Prices:High	NA	NA	NA	NA	NA	NA	NA	NA	NA	NA
Prices:Low	NA	NA	NA	NA	NA	NA	NA	NA	NA	NA
P/E Ratio:High	NA	NA	NA	NA	NA	NA	NA	NA	NA	NA
P/E Ratio:Low	NA	NA	NA	NA	NA	NA	NA	NA	NA	NA
Income Statement Analysis (Million $)										
Revenue	3,988	NA	NA	NA	NA	NA	NA	NA	NA	NA
Operating Income	NA	NA	NA	NA	NA	NA	NA	NA	NA	NA
Depreciation	NA	NA	NA	NA	NA	NA	NA	NA	NA	NA
Interest Expense	202	NA	NA	NA	NA	NA	NA	NA	NA	NA
Pretax Income	1,063	NA	NA	NA	NA	NA	NA	NA	NA	NA
Effective Tax Rate	29.5%	NA	NA	NA	NA	NA	NA	NA	NA	NA
Net Income	749	NA	NA	NA	NA	NA	NA	NA	NA	NA
S&P Core Earnings	859	734	NA	NA	NA	NA	NA	NA	NA	NA
Balance Sheet & Other Financial Data (Million $)										
Cash	1,186	NA	NA	NA	NA	NA	NA	NA	NA	NA
Current Assets	NA	NA	NA	NA	NA	NA	NA	NA	NA	NA
Total Assets	4,659	NA	NA	NA	NA	NA	NA	NA	NA	NA
Current Liabilities	NA	NA	NA	NA	NA	NA	NA	NA	NA	NA
Long Term Debt	3,500	NA	NA	NA	NA	NA	NA	NA	NA	NA
Common Equity	-687	NA	NA	NA	NA	NA	NA	NA	NA	NA
Total Capital	2,183	NA	NA	NA	NA	NA	NA	NA	NA	NA
Capital Expenditures	NA	NA	NA	NA	NA	NA	NA	NA	NA	NA
Cash Flow	NA	NA	NA	NA	NA	NA	NA	NA	NA	NA
Current Ratio	NA	NA	NA	NA	NA	NA	NA	NA	NA	NA
% Long Term Debt of Capitalization	160.3	NA	NA	NA	NA	NA	NA	NA	NA	NA
% Net Income of Revenue	18.8	NA	NA	NA	NA	NA	NA	NA	NA	NA
% Return on Assets	NA	NA	NA	NA	NA	NA	NA	NA	NA	NA
% Return on Equity	NA	NA	NA	NA	NA	NA	NA	NA	NA	NA

Data as orig reptd.; bef. results of disc opers/spec. items. Per share data adj. for stk. divs.; EPS diluted. Pro forma data in 2005, balance sheet and book value as of Jun. 30, 2006. E-Estimated. NA-Not Available. NM-Not Meaningful. NR-Not Ranked. UR-Under Review.

Office: 12500 East Belford Avenue, Englewood, CO 80112.
Telephone: 866-405-5012.
Website: http://www.westernunion.com
Chrmn: J.M. Greenberg

Pres & CEO: C.A. Gold
EVP & CFO: S. Scheirman
EVP, Secy & General Counsel: D. Schlapbach
Investor Contact: G. Kohn (720-332-8276)

Board of Directors: D. S. Devitre, C. A. Gold, J. M. Greenberg, B. D. Holden, A. J. Lacy, L. F. Levinson, R. G. Mendoza, M. A. Miles, D. Stevenson

Auditor: Ernst & Young, Denver, CO
Founded: 1851
Domicile: Delaware
Employees: 4,700

STANDARD &POOR'S

Weyerhaeuser Co

S&P Recommendation HOLD ★★★★★

Price $64.04 (as of Oct 30, 2006)

12-Mo. Target Price $72.00

Investment Style Large-Cap Value

GICS Sector Materials
Sub-Industry Forest Products

Comment One of the world's largest integrated forest products companies, WY grows timber; makes and sells forest products, paper, and packaging; and engages in real estate construction and development.

Key Stock Statistics (Source S&P, Vickers, company reports)

52-Wk Range	$75.50–54.25	S&P Oper. EPS 2006E	3.60	P/E on S&P Oper. EPS 2006E	17.8	Dividend Rate/Share	$2.40
Trailing 12-Month EPS	$-1.09	S&P Oper. EPS 2007E	3.50	Common Shares Outstg. (M)	243.2	Yield (%)	3.75
Trailing 12-Month P/E	NM	S&P Core EPS 2006E	3.17	Market Capitalization(B)	$15.577	Beta	1.10
$10K Invested 5 Yrs Ago	$14,048	S&P Core EPS 2007E	3.10	Institutional Ownership (%)	81	S&P Credit Rating	BBB

Price Performance

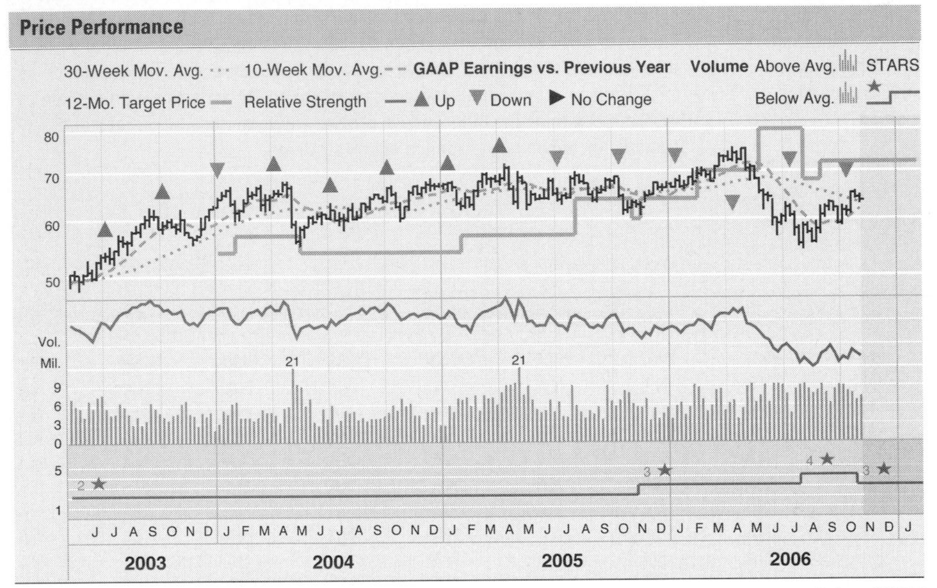

Options: CBOE, P

Analysis prepared by **Stuart J. Benway, CFA** on October 30, 2006, when the stock traded at **$ 64.01**.

Highlights

- We look for about a 2% decline in revenues from continuing operations in both 2006 and 2007. Our forecast is for housing starts to fall 11.6% this year and a further 14% in 2007. We believe this projected downturn will prevent a recovery in prices for lumber and panels, which have fallen sharply in recent months. However, we expect higher prices for paper and packaging products due to a balanced supply and demand environment in those sectors.
- We believe the cost reductions that the company is making in its packaging operations, as well as improving prices, will lead to higher margins in that segment in 2006 and 2007. Nevertheless, an expected continuation in the downturn in the housing market is likely to lead to reduced profits at the company's wood products and home building businesses. We estimate that operating margins will narrow to 8.5% in 2006, from 10.6% in 2005.
- Our EPS estimate for 2006 is $3.60, and for 2007, we project EPS of $3.50. Our Standard & Poor's Core EPS forecasts of $3.17 for 2006 and $3.10 for 2007 reflect expected pension costs and restructuring charges.

Investment Rationale/Risk

- WY has taken several steps to bolster its performance, in our view, either by cutting costs at underperforming businesses or divesting them, and by expanding the home building operation. While we expect a downturn in the housing market to hurt profits, we think a combination of good cost control and improved conditions in the paper and packaging segments will prevent a major drop in earnings in coming quarters.
- Risks to our recommendation and target price include greater than expected declines in wood product prices, a renewed escalation in energy costs, a more severe than forecast downturn in the housing market, or a sudden drop in paper and packaging prices.
- Our discounted cash flow (DCF) model, which assumes a weighted average cost of capital of 8.5%, a cyclical pattern of cash flow through 2010, and a 3% growth rate in perpetuity, derives intrinsic value of $73. Applying a peer forward premium P/E of 20.3X to our 2007 EPS estimate of $3.50, we value the shares at $71. Using a blend of these metrics, we arrive at our 12-month target price of $72.

Qualitative Risk Assessment

LOW | **MEDIUM** | HIGH

Our risk assessment reflects that Weyerhaeuser operates in a cyclical industry, with large capital requirements and significant variability in both costs and prices. However, the company is one of the largest companies in the industry, and we believe it has a major base of assets and modest debt levels.

Quantitative Evaluations

S&P Quality Ranking B

D | C | B- | **B** | B+ | A- | A | A+

Relative Strength Rank MODERATE

54

LOWEST = 1 HIGHEST = 99

Revenue/Earnings Data

Revenue (Million $)

	1Q	2Q	3Q	4Q	Year
2006	5,376	5,687	5,328	--	--
2005	5,404	5,838	5,604	5,868	22,629
2004	5,037	5,893	5,849	5,886	22,665
2003	4,614	4,930	5,184	5,145	19,873
2002	3,991	4,922	4,890	4,718	18,521
2001	3,553	3,842	3,752	3,398	14,545

Earnings Per Share ($)

2006	-2.36	1.20	0.75	E0.93	E3.60
2005	0.98	1.22	1.16	-1.00	2.36
2004	0.54	1.57	2.45	0.82	5.43
2003	-0.19	0.71	0.37	0.41	1.30
2002	0.24	0.32	0.06	0.57	1.09
2001	0.49	0.78	0.41	-0.07	1.61

Fiscal year ended Dec. 31. Next earnings report expected: Early February. EPS Estimates based on S&P Operating Earnings; historical GAAP earnings are as reported.

Dividend Data (Dates: mm/dd Payment Date: mm/dd/yy)

Amount ($)	Date Decl.	Ex-Div. Date	Stk. of Record	Payment Date
0.500	01/12	02/01	02/03	02/27/06
0.500	04/20	05/03	05/05	05/30/06
0.600	06/15	08/02	08/04	08/28/06
0.600	10/19	11/08	11/10	12/04/06

Dividends have been paid since 1933. Source: Company reports.

Weyerhaeuser Co

Business Summary October 30, 2006

CORPORATE OVERVIEW. Weyerhaeuser, one of the world's largest integrated forest products companies, is primarily engaged in growing and harvesting timber; the production, distribution and sale of wood and paper products; and real estate development. Through its timberlands segment (5% of 2005 sales), WY manages 5.7 million acres of company-owned timberlands and leases 700,000 acres of timberlands in eight states. The wood products businesses (42%) produce and sell softwood and hardwood lumber, plywood and veneer, composite panels, oriented strand board, and engineered lumber. Products made by the pulp and paper unit (19%) include paper grade, absorbent, dissolving and specialty pulp grades. Paper products include coated and uncoated papers, which are used in the printing and publishing industries as well as for office use. The containerboard, packaging and recycling segment (21%) manufactures corrugating medium, linerboard and kraft paper. Through Weyerhaeuser Real Estate Company (13%), the company is involved in the development of single-family housing and residential lots, including the development of master-planned communities.

MARKET PROFILE. Weyerhaeuser operates in a highly cyclical and capital-intensive industry. Demand for the company's products is dependent on a number of factors, including industrial non-durable goods production, consumer spending, commercial printing and advertising activity, white collar employment levels, domestic and Japanese new home construction and repair and remodeling activity, and movements in currency exchange rates. Historical prices for paper and wood products have been volatile, and, despite its size, WY has had only a limited direct influence over the timing and extent of price changes for its products. Pricing is significantly affected by the relationship between supply and demand, and supply is influenced primarily by fluctuations in available manufacturing capacity.

Company Financials

Per Share Data ($) Year Ended Dec. 31	**2005**	**2004**	**2003**	**2002**	**2001**	**2000**	**1999**	**1998**	**1997**	**1996**
Tangible Book Value	27.81	24.84	17.44	15.80	25.45	25.95	27.15	22.74	23.31	23.25
Cash Flow	7.80	10.76	7.23	6.63	5.94	7.52	6.07	4.55	4.85	5.45
Earnings	2.36	5.43	1.30	1.09	1.61	3.72	2.98	1.47	1.71	2.34
S&P Core Earnings	1.79	4.37	0.70	-0.75	NA	NA	NA	NA	NA	NA
Dividends	1.90	1.60	1.60	1.60	1.60	1.60	1.60	1.60	1.60	1.60
Payout Ratio	81%	29%	123%	147%	99%	43%	54%	109%	94%	68%
Prices:High	71.85	68.59	64.70	68.09	63.50	74.50	73.94	62.00	63.94	49.88
Prices:Low	60.62	55.06	45.40	37.35	42.77	36.06	49.56	36.75	42.63	39.50
P/E Ratio:High	30	13	50	62	39	20	25	42	37	21
P/E Ratio:Low	26	10	35	34	27	10	17	25	25	17

Income Statement Analysis (Million $)										
Revenue	22,629	22,665	19,873	18,521	14,545	15,980	12,262	10,766	11,210	11,114
Operating Income	3,443	4,028	2,716	2,455	1,689	2,536	1,902	1,385	1,480	1,887
Depreciation	1,337	1,322	1,318	1,225	876	859	640	616	628	617
Interest Expense	730	829	796	771	344	351	277	273	297	405
Pretax Income	906	1,945	436	371	516	1,323	970	463	539	720
Effective Tax Rate	35.8%	34.0%	33.9%	35.0%	31.4%	36.5%	36.5%	36.5%	36.5%	35.7%
Net Income	582	1,283	288	241	354	840	616	294	342	463
S&P Core Earnings	444	1,029	156	-168	2.35	NA	NA	NA	NA	NA

Balance Sheet & Other Financial Data (Million $)										
Cash	1,104	1,197	202	122	204	123	1,643	35.0	122	33.0
Current Assets	4,876	5,293	4,021	3,888	3,061	3,288	4,543	2,170	2,294	2,225
Total Assets	28,229	29,954	28,109	28,219	18,293	18,195	18,339	12,834	13,075	13,596
Current Liabilities	3,255	3,149	2,525	2,994	1,863	2,704	2,934	1,499	1,384	1,483
Long Term Debt	8,262	10,144	12,397	12,721	5,715	5,114	4,453	4,662	4,743	5,328
Common Equity	9,800	9,255	7,109	6,623	6,695	6,832	7,173	4,526	4,649	4,604
Total Capital	22,097	23,932	23,800	23,400	14,787	14,323	13,611	10,592	10,931	11,369
Capital Expenditures	861	492	608	930	660	848	487	615	656	879
Cash Flow	1,919	2,605	1,606	1,466	1,230	1,699	1,256	910	970	1,080
Current Ratio	1.5	1.7	1.6	1.3	1.6	1.2	1.5	1.4	1.7	1.5
% Long Term Debt of Capitalization	37.4	42.4	52.1	54.4	38.6	35.7	32.7	44.0	43.4	40.5
% Net Income of Revenue	2.6	5.7	1.4	1.3	2.4	5.3	5.0	2.7	3.1	4.2
% Return on Assets	2.0	4.4	1.0	1.0	1.9	4.6	4.0	2.3	2.6	3.5
% Return on Equity	6.1	15.7	4.2	3.6	5.2	12.0	10.5	6.4	7.4	10.2

Data as orig reptd.; bef. results of disc opers/spec. items. Per share data adj. for stk. divs.; EPS diluted. E-Estimated. NA-Not Available. NM-Not Meaningful. NR-Not Ranked. UR-Under Review.

Office: 33663 Weyerhaeuser Way South, Federal Way, WA 98003.
Telephone: 253-924-2345.
Email: invrelations@weyerhaeuser.com
Website: http://www.weyerhaeuser.com

Chrmn, Pres & CEO: S.R. Rogel
COO & EVP: R.E. Hanson
EVP & CFO: R.J. Taggart
SVP & CTO: M.P. Drake

SVP & General Counsel: S.D. McDade
Investor Contact: K.F. McAuley (253-924-2058)
Board of Directors: R. F. Haskayne, S. Hillyard, M. R. Ingram, J. I. Kieckhefer, A. G. Langbo, D. F. Mazankowski, N. W. Piasecki, S. R. Rogel, R. H. Sinkfield, D. M. Steuert, J. N. Sullivan, K. Williams, K. Williams, C. R. Williamson

Founded: 1900
Domicile: Washington
Employees: 49,887

STANDARD &POOR'S

Whirlpool Corp

S&P Recommendation HOLD ★★★★★	Price	12-Mo. Target Price	Investment Style
	$86.24 (as of Oct 27, 2006)	$95.00	Mid-Cap Value

GICS Sector Consumer Discretionary
Sub-Industry Household Appliances

Comment WHR, which recently merged with Maytag, is the world's largest manufacturer of home appliances. Sears, Roebuck is its largest customer.

Key Stock Statistics (Source S&P, Vickers, company reports)

52-Wk Range	$96.00–74.07	S&P Oper. EPS 2006E	6.25	P/E on S&P Oper. EPS 2006E	13.8	Dividend Rate/Share	$1.72
Trailing 12-Month EPS	$6.14	S&P Oper. EPS 2007E	9.00	Common Shares Outstg. (M)	78.2	Yield (%)	1.99
Trailing 12-Month P/E	14.1	S&P Core EPS 2006E	6.25	Market Capitalization(B)	$6.746	Beta	1.28
$10K Invested 5 Yrs Ago	$15,824	S&P Core EPS 2007E	9.00	Institutional Ownership (%)	NA	S&P Credit Rating	BBB

Price Performance

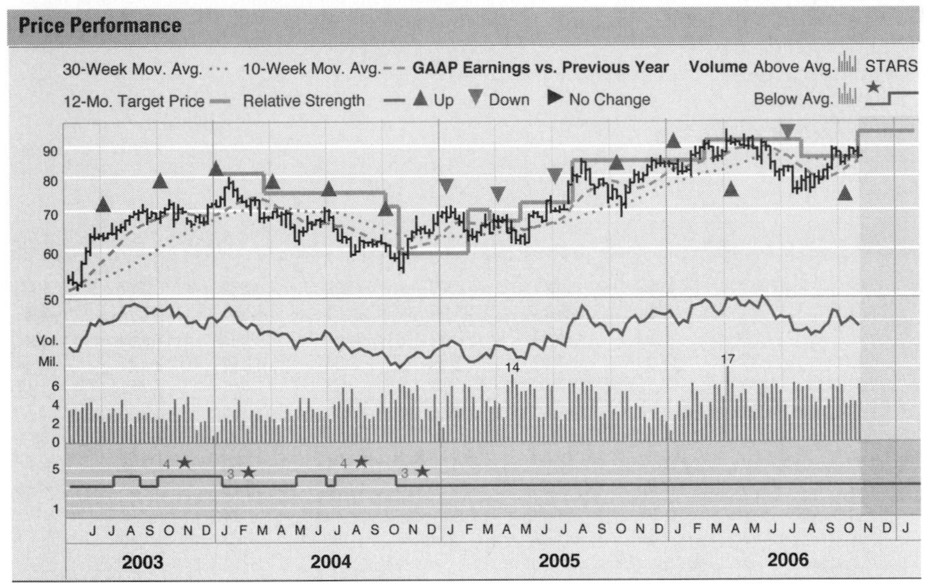

Options: CBOE, P

Highlights

- The 12-month target price for WHR has recently been changed to $95.00 from $86.00. The Highlights section of this Stock Report will be updated accordingly.

Investment Rationale/Risk

- The Investment Rationale/Risk section of this Stock Report will be updated shortly. For the latest News story on WHR from MarketScope, see below.

- 10/24/06 01:02 pm EDT... S&P REITERATES HOLD OPINION ON SHARES OF WHIRLPOOL CORP. (WHR 85.69***): Q3 EPS of $1.47, vs. $1.66, is two cents below our estimate. EPS from continuing operations is $1.68. Revenues rose 35%, reflecting 8% organic growth plus the Maytag acquisition. The appliance maker expects global industry unit shipment growth near 1%-2% in 2007. We project WHR to grow similarly while improving margins. We are raising our '06 operating EPS estimate to $6.25 from $6.17, and maintaining $9.00 for '07. Now applying a higher target P/E of 10.5X, near middle of historical range, to our '07 EPS estimate, we are raising our 12-month target price by $9 to $95. /T.Smith-CFA

Qualitative Risk Assessment

LOW | **MEDIUM** | HIGH

Our risk assessment reflects WHR's leading market share, offset by intense industry rivalry and heightened competition from foreign companies.

Quantitative Evaluations

S&P Quality Ranking B+

D | C | B- | B | **B+** | A- | A | A+

Relative Strength Rank MODERATE

45

LOWEST = 1 HIGHEST = 99

Revenue/Earnings Data

Revenue (Million $)

	1Q	2Q	3Q	4Q	Year
2006	3,536	4,734	4,843	--	--
2005	3,208	3,556	3,599	3,954	14,317
2004	3,007	3,264	3,318	3,632	13,220
2003	2,716	2,988	3,113	3,359	12,176
2002	2,574	2,737	2,759	2,947	11,016
2001	2,517	2,585	2,594	2,647	10,343

Earnings Per Share ($)

2006	1.70	1.26	1.68	E1.62	E6.25
2005	1.26	1.42	1.66	1.83	6.19
2004	1.43	1.53	1.50	1.44	5.90
2003	1.32	1.35	1.48	1.76	5.91
2002	1.21	0.91	1.46	0.20	3.78
2001	0.49	1.10	-1.40	0.31	0.50

Fiscal year ended Dec. 31. Next earnings report expected: Early February. EPS Estimates based on S&P Operating Earnings; historical GAAP earnings are as reported.

Dividend Data (Dates: mm/dd Payment Date: mm/dd/yy)

Amount ($)	Date Decl.	Ex-Div. Date	Stk. of Record	Payment Date
0.430	02/21	03/01	03/03	03/15/06
0.430	04/18	05/17	05/19	06/15/06
0.430	08/14	08/24	08/28	09/15/06
0.430	10/16	11/15	11/17	12/15/06

Dividends have been paid since 1929. Source: Company reports.

Whirlpool Corp

Business Summary July 27, 2006

Whirlpool manufactures and markets a full line of major appliances and related products, primarily for home use. Products are manufactured in 12 countries and marketed in more than 170. The company's growth strategy over the past several years has been to introduce innovative new products, strengthen customer loyalty, expand its global footprint, enhance distribution channels, and make strategic acquisitions where appropriate.

Major product categories include home laundry appliances (31% of 2004 sales); home refrigerators and freezers (29%); home cooking appliances (15%); and other appliances (25%). Other appliances include home dishwashers, room air-conditioning equipment, and mixers, among others. The total number of units sold in 2004 increased 4.9% over 2003, following a 5.6% increase in the prior year.

Under the Kenmore brand name, WHR has been the principal supplier of home laundry appliances to Sears, Roebuck and Co. for more than 80 years. WHR also sells Whirlpool and KitchenAid brand products through Sears. In total, Sears accounted for 17% of WHR's 2004 sales, down from 18% in 2003.

In 2004, 61% of total sales were made in North America. Major brands in the U.S. include Whirlpool, KitchenAid, Roper and Estate. Major brands in Canada are Inglis, Admiral, Speed Queen, Roper, Whirlpool and KitchenAid. In Mexico, major brands are Whirlpool, Acros, KitchenAid, Estate, Roper and Supermatic. WHR is the market share leader in North America. In Europe, which generated 23% of sales, products are marketed under the Whirlpool, Bauknecht, Ignis, Laden and Polar brand names.

Markets also include Latin America and Asia. About 13% of total sales were in Latin America, where WHR distributes its major home appliances under the Whirlpool, Brastemp, Consul, and Eslabon de Lugo brand names. About 3% of sales were in Asia.

Company Financials

Per Share Data ($) Year Ended Dec. 31	**2005**	**2004**	**2003**	**2002**	**2001**	**2000**	**1999**	**1998**	**1997**	**1996**
Tangible Book Value	21.49	19.85	15.23	5.82	11.10	13.07	14.29	14.01	11.25	14.08
Cash Flow	12.65	12.35	12.00	9.62	6.32	10.39	9.64	9.71	4.13	6.32
Earnings	6.19	5.90	5.91	3.78	0.50	5.20	4.56	4.06	-0.62	2.08
S&P Core Earnings	5.99	5.58	5.71	2.12	-1.91	NA	NA	NA	NA	NA
Dividends	1.72	1.72	1.36	1.36	1.02	1.36	1.36	1.36	1.36	1.36
Payout Ratio	28%	29%	23%	36%	NM	26%	30%	33%	NM	65%
Prices:High	86.52	80.00	73.35	79.80	74.20	68.31	78.25	75.25	69.50	61.38
Prices:Low	60.78	54.53	42.80	39.23	45.88	31.50	40.94	43.69	45.25	44.25
P/E Ratio:High	11	11	12	21	NM	13	17	19	NM	30
P/E Ratio:Low	10	9	7	10	NM	6	9	11	NM	21
Income Statement Analysis (Million $)										
Revenue	14,317	13,220	12,176	11,016	10,343	10,325	10,511	10,323	8,617	8,696
Operating Income	1,291	1,218	1,219	1,207	1,147	1,178	1,261	1,126	710	754
Depreciation	442	445	427	405	396	371	386	438	356	318
Interest Expense	130	128	137	143	162	180	166	260	168	236
Pretax Income	598	615	652	468	89.0	580	510	565	-104	223
Effective Tax Rate	28.6%	34.0%	35.0%	41.2%	48.3%	34.5%	38.6%	37.0%	NM	36.4%
Net Income	422	406	414	262	34.0	367	347	310	-46.0	156
S&P Core Earnings	408	384	401	147	-130	NA	NA	NA	NA	NA
Balance Sheet & Other Financial Data (Million $)										
Cash	524	243	249	192	316	114	261	636	578	129
Current Assets	4,710	4,514	3,865	3,327	3,311	3,237	3,177	3,882	4,281	3,812
Total Assets	8,248	8,181	7,361	6,631	6,967	6,902	6,826	7,935	8,270	8,015
Current Liabilities	4,301	3,985	3,589	3,505	3,082	3,303	2,892	3,267	3,676	4,022
Long Term Debt	745	1,160	1,134	1,092	1,295	795	714	1,087	1,074	955
Common Equity	1,745	1,606	1,301	796	2,126	1,684	1,867	2,001	1,771	1,926
Total Capital	2,749	3,074	2,734	2,083	3,725	2,801	2,738	3,854	3,035	3,269
Capital Expenditures	484	511	423	430	378	375	437	523	378	336
Cash Flow	864	851	841	667	430	738	733	748	310	474
Current Ratio	1.1	1.1	1.1	0.9	1.1	1.0	1.1	1.2	1.2	1.0
% Long Term Debt of Capitalization	27.1	37.8	41.5	52.4	34.8	28.4	26.1	28.2	35.4	29.3
% Net Income of Revenue	2.9	3.1	3.4	2.4	0.3	3.6	3.3	3.0	NM	NM
% Return on Assets	5.1	5.2	5.9	3.9	0.5	5.3	4.7	3.8	NM	2.0
% Return on Equity	25.2	27.9	40.6	22.8	1.5	20.7	17.9	16.4	NM	8.2

Data as orig reptd.; bef. results of disc opers/spec. items. Per share data adj. for stk. divs.; EPS diluted. E-Estimated. NA-Not Available. NM-Not Meaningful. NR-Not Ranked. UR-Under Review.

Office: 2000 N M 63, Benton Harbor, MI 49022-2692.
Telephone: 269-923-5000.
Email: info@whirlpool.com
Website: http://www.whirlpool.com

Chrmn & CEO: J.M. Fettig
EVP & CFO: R.W. Templin
EVP & CTO: M.D. Thieneman
Investor Contact: L. Venturelli (269-923-4678)

Co-Pres: M.A. Todman
Board of Directors: G. T. DiCamillo, J. M. Fettig, A. D. Gilmour, K. J. Hempel, M. F. Johnston, W. T. Kerr, A. G. Langbo, P. G. Stern, J. D. Stoney, D. L. Swift, M. A. Todman, M. D. White

Founded: 1906
Domicile: Delaware
Employees: 65,682

STANDARD &POOR'S

Whole Foods Market Inc

S&P Recommendation BUY ★★★★★

Price $64.75 (as of Oct 27, 2006)

12-Mo. Target Price $65.00

Investment Style Mid-Cap Growth

GICS Sector Consumer Staples
Sub-Industry Food Retail

Comment WFMI owns and operates the largest U.S. chain of natural foods supermarkets, with about 180 stores.

Key Stock Statistics (Source S&P, Vickers, company reports)

52-Wk Range	$79.90–46.91	S&P Oper. EPS 2006E	1.42	P/E on S&P Oper. EPS 2006E	45.6	Dividend Rate/Share	$0.60
Trailing 12-Month EPS	$1.19	S&P Oper. EPS 2007E	1.68	Common Shares Outstg. (M)	141.2	Yield (%)	0.93
Trailing 12-Month P/E	54.4	S&P Core EPS 2006E	1.39	Market Capitalization(B)	$9.141	Beta	1.02
$10K Invested 5 Yrs Ago	$37,540	S&P Core EPS 2007E	1.65	Institutional Ownership (%)	86	S&P Credit Rating	BBB-

Price Performance

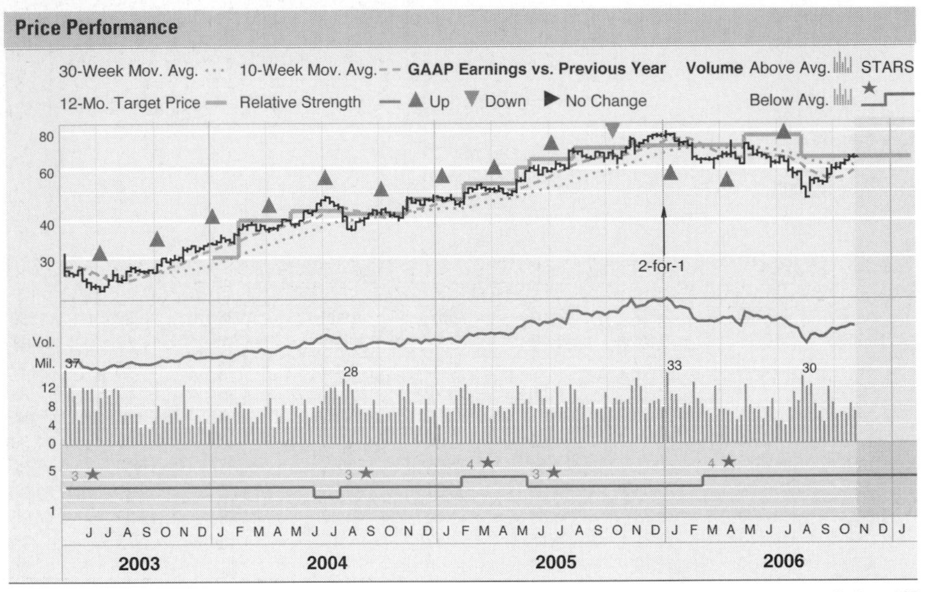

Options: ASE

Analysis prepared by **Joseph Agnese** on August 16, 2006, when the stock traded at **$ 52.91**.

Highlights

- We expect FY 07 (Sep.) sales to grow about 18%, fueled by 17% square footage growth, projected comparable-store sales gains of about 9% to 10%, and an extra week of sales versus the prior year.
- We believe the company will generate gross margins near the midpoint of its historical range of 34% to 35% in FY 07, as it maintains pricing flexibility, offsetting improved product mix and procurement. However, margins should be pressured, in our view, reflecting an acceleration of new store growth and the lack of leverage within new stores. We think G&A expenses are likely to stabilize as a percentage of sales as improved sales leverage offsets increased costs of investment in marketing and infrastructure. We estimate that pre-opening and relocation expenses will rise about 20% as square footage growth accelerates.
- We project that FY 07 operating EPS will advance 18%, to $1.68, from our estimate of $1.42 in FY 06.

Investment Rationale/Risk

- We view the company as favorably positioned to achieve strong long-term earnings growth as the acceptance of its branded natural and organic food stores increases, and its new store expansion program remains strong.
- Risks to our recommendation and target price include intensifying competition, particularly in the company's California markets, as conventional supermarkets promote aggressively to win back market share.
- Our 12-month target price of $65 is based on a blend of our P/E and DCF analyses. Our DCF assumptions include a WACC of 10.0% and a terminal growth rate of 3.0%, resulting in an intrinsic value of $70. Our P/E to growth (PEG) analysis derives a value of $60. Given that WFMI is the fastest growing public retail food chain in the U.S. under our coverage, we expect its shares to trade at a significant premium PEG multiple to supermarket peers and the S&P 500. Our target price is equal to about 36X our FY 07 EPS estimate of $1.68, based on a PEG ratio of 1.8X our estimated long-term growth rate of 20%, in line with high growth retail company peers.

Qualitative Risk Assessment

LOW | **MEDIUM** | HIGH

Our risk assessment for Whole Foods Markets incorporates our view of a strong balance sheet position and growing natural and organic food industry sales momentum, moderated by an intense competitive environment in the retail food industry.

Quantitative Evaluations

S&P Quality Ranking B

D | C | B- | **B** | B+ | A- | A | A+

Relative Strength Rank STRONG

78

LOWEST = 1 HIGHEST = 99

Revenue/Earnings Data

Revenue (Million $)

	1Q	2Q	3Q	4Q	Year
2006	1,667	1,312	1,338	--	--
2005	1,368	1,085	1,133	1,115	4,701
2004	1,118	902.1	917.4	927.3	3,865
2003	923.8	725.1	749.0	750.7	3,149
2002	780.8	622.8	648.8	638.1	2,690
2001	643.4	516.7	535.6	576.6	2,272

Earnings Per Share ($)

2006	0.40	0.36	0.37	**E**0.32	**E**1.42
2005	0.35	0.29	0.29	0.07	0.99
2004	0.30	0.27	0.25	0.23	1.05
2003	0.21	0.21	0.23	0.19	0.83
2002	0.17	0.17	0.18	0.18	0.70
2001	0.14	0.25	0.15	0.09	0.61

Fiscal year ended Sep. 30. Next earnings report expected: Early November. EPS Estimates based on S&P Operating Earnings; historical GAAP earnings are as reported.

Dividend Data (Dates: mm/dd Payment Date: mm/dd/yy)

Amount ($)	Date Decl.	Ex-Div. Date	Stk. of Record	Payment Date
2.0 Spl.	11/09	01/11	01/13	01/23/06
0.150	04/05	04/11	04/14	04/24/06
0.150	06/14	07/12	07/14	07/24/06
0.150	09/28	10/11	10/13	10/23/06

Dividends have been paid since 2004. Source: Company reports.

Whole Foods Market Inc

Business Summary August 16, 2006

Whole Foods Market, established in 1980, has grown into the largest U.S. retailer of natural and organic foods, with $4.7 billion in sales in FY 05 (Sep.). Reflecting a series of store openings and acquisitions, the company has expanded from a single Austin, TX, store in 1980 to a chain of more than 180 stores in 28 states plus Washington, DC, Canada and the United Kingdom. The company strives to differentiate its stores from those of its competitors by tailoring its product mix, customer service attitude, and store environment to appeal to health conscious and gourmet customers. By 2010, the company's goal is to have over $12 billion in sales and about 300 stores.

Stores average about 33,000 sq. ft., and offer a selection of some 26,000 food and non-food products. Each store contributes approximately $25 million in annual sales, with sales per gross sq. ft. of $869 ($751 in FY 04). Products sold include natural and organic foods and beverages; dietary supplements; natural personal care products; natural household goods; and educational products. Natural foods can be defined as foods that are minimally processed, largely or completely free of artificial ingredients, preservatives and other non-naturally occurring chemicals, and as near as possible to their whole, natural state. Organic foods are based on the minimal use of off-farm inputs and on management practices that restore, maintain and enhance the ecology.

The company opens or acquires stores in existing regions, and in metropolitan areas in which it believes it can become the leading natural foods supermarket retailer. In developing new stores, WFMI seeks to open large format units of 50,000 sq. ft. to 80,000 sq. ft., located on premium sites, often in urban, highly populated areas. Although approximately 33% of its store base consists of acquired stores, the company expects more of its future growth to come from developing new stores. As of November 2005, WFMI had signed leases for 64 stores averaging approximately 55,000 square feet in size, which is more than 50% larger than its existing store base average. As of July 2006, the company operated about 6.2 million square feet of retail space. There were 86 stores representing 4.8 million square feet (78% of existing sq. ft.) of retail space that were under development at that time.

Company Financials

Per Share Data ($) Year Ended Sep. 30	**2005**	**2004**	**2003**	**2002**	**2001**	**2000**	**1999**	**1998**	**1997**	**1996**
Tangible Book Value	9.06	6.82	5.57	4.21	2.98	2.11	2.35	2.16	1.62	1.34
Cash Flow	1.93	1.84	1.54	1.34	1.16	0.85	0.87	0.79	0.60	0.11
Earnings	0.99	1.04	0.83	0.70	0.61	0.26	0.39	0.41	0.26	-0.23
S&P Core Earnings	-0.21	0.85	0.70	0.58	0.38	NA	NA	NA	NA	NA
Dividends	0.42	0.23	Nil	Nil	Nil	Nil	Nil	Nil	Nil	Nil
Payout Ratio	42%	22%	Nil	Nil	Nil	Nil	Nil	Nil	Nil	Nil
Prices:High	79.90	48.74	33.81	27.30	23.25	15.94	12.41	17.53	12.84	9.28
Prices:Low	44.14	32.96	22.39	17.74	9.73	8.60	7.06	8.00	4.30	3.00
P/E Ratio:High	81	47	41	39	38	60	32	43	49	NM
P/E Ratio:Low	45	32	27	25	16	32	18	20	17	NM

Income Statement Analysis (Million $)										
Revenue	4,701	3,865	3,149	2,690	2,272	1,839	1,568	1,390	1,117	892
Operating Income	363	341	285	248	209	181	144	125	89.5	50.0
Depreciation	134	112	98.0	85.9	78.8	63.9	53.3	42.3	34.5	25.5
Interest Expense	2.22	7.25	8.11	10.4	17.9	15.1	8.25	7.69	6.04	4.67
Pretax Income	237	229	173	141	89.8	63.5	69.1	72.1	39.4	-20.6
Effective Tax Rate	42.5%	40.0%	40.0%	40.0%	42.5%	54.5%	39.0%	37.0%	32.3%	NM
Net Income	136	137	104	84.5	51.6	28.9	42.2	45.4	26.6	-17.2
S&P Core Earnings	-28.0	109	85.0	70.4	43.0	NA	NA	NA	NA	NA

Balance Sheet & Other Financial Data (Million $)										
Cash	309	198	166	12.6	1.84	0.40	9.02	36.7	13.4	1.70
Current Assets	673	485	364	172	145	152	141	184	114	61.6
Total Assets	1,889	1,520	1,197	943	829	760	660	545	400	311
Current Liabilities	418	331	240	176	156	143	121	91.0	77.3	56.7
Long Term Debt	12.9	165	163	162	251	298	209	159	92.7	84.3
Common Equity	1,366	988	776	589	409	307	311	277	205	146
Total Capital	1,379	1,173	942	751	660	605	525	439	306	237
Capital Expenditures	116	110	84.1	61.4	49.0	111	75.0	41.2	31.1	18.2
Cash Flow	270	249	202	170	130	92.8	95.5	87.7	61.1	8.30
Current Ratio	1.6	1.5	1.5	1.0	0.9	1.1	1.2	2.0	1.5	1.1
% Long Term Debt of Capitalization	0.9	14.0	17.3	21.6	38.0	49.2	39.8	36.2	30.3	35.6
% Net Income of Revenue	2.9	3.5	3.3	3.1	2.3	1.6	2.7	3.3	2.4	NM
% Return on Assets	8.0	10.1	9.7	9.5	6.5	4.1	7.0	9.6	7.5	NM
% Return on Equity	11.8	15.5	15.2	16.9	14.4	9.4	14.3	18.8	15.1	NM

Data as orig reptd.; bef. results of disc opers/spec. items. Per share data adj. for stk. divs.; EPS diluted. E-Estimated. NA-Not Available. NM-Not Meaningful. NR-Not Ranked. UR-Under Review.

Office: 550 Bowie St, Austin, TX 78703.
Telephone: 512-477-4455.
Website: http://www.wholefoods.com
Chrmn & CEO: J.P. Mackey

COO & Co-Pres: A.C. Gallo
COO & Co-Pres: W. Robb
EVP & CFO: G.F. Chamberlain
Investor Contact: C. McCann (512-477-4455)

Board of Directors: D. W. Dupree, J. B. Elstrott, G. Greene, H. Hassan, J. Mackey, L. A. Mason, M. Siegel, R. Z. Sorenson

Founded: 1978
Domicile: Texas
Employees: 38,000

STANDARD &POOR'S

Williams Cos Inc. (The)

S&P Recommendation BUY ★★★★★	Price	12-Mo. Target Price	Investment Style
	$24.51 (as of Oct 27, 2006)	$28.00	Large-Cap Value

GICS Sector Energy
Sub-Industry Oil & Gas Storage & Transportation

Comment This Oklahoma-based company, which primarily finds, produces, gathers, processes and transports natural gas, also manages a wholesale power business.

Key Stock Statistics (Source S&P, Vickers, company reports)

52-Wk Range	$25.58–19.35	S&P Oper. EPS 2006E	1.26	P/E on S&P Oper. EPS 2006E	19.5	Dividend Rate/Share	$0.36
Trailing 12-Month EPS	$0.21	S&P Oper. EPS 2007E	1.45	Common Shares Outstg. (M)	595.8	Yield (%)	1.47
Trailing 12-Month P/E	NM	S&P Core EPS 2006E	1.22	Market Capitalization(B)	$14.603	Beta	2.87
$10K Invested 5 Yrs Ago	$9,503	S&P Core EPS 2007E	1.41	Institutional Ownership (%)	73	S&P Credit Rating	BB-

Price Performance

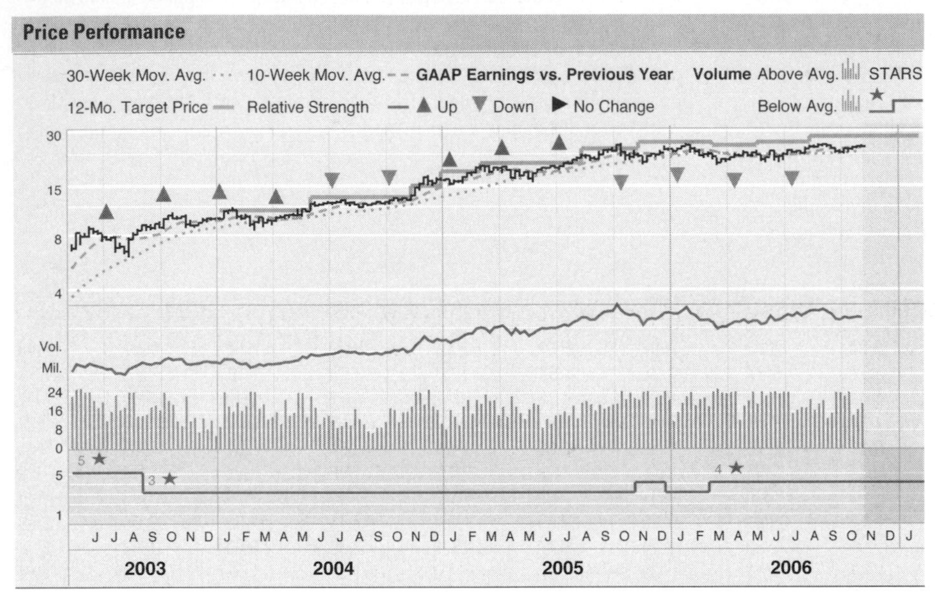

Options: ASE, CBOE, P

Analysis prepared by **Michael Kay** on August 08, 2006, when the stock traded at **$ 24.42**.

Highlights

- EPS in the first six months of 2006 was $0.59. Second quarter operating EPS of $0.33 surpassed our $0.25 estimate. E&P volumes grew 20%, year to year, and should continue this pace through 2006. WMB currently operates 23 rigs in the Piceance Basin and expects to add four more this year. Given WMB's repeatable drilling inventory in this basin, and a focus by WMB to increase the pace of developing natural gas reserves, we anticipate significant long-term segment profit growth.
- Continuing with its success in the initial public offering of part of its midstream assets via the master limited partnership Williams Partners (WPZ: $34), WMB has completed the sale of a 25% stake in its Four Corners facilities to the MLP. Our optimistic outlook on WMB's gas pipeline segment is driven by expansion projects in both the Gulfstream and Transco systems, and the expected filing of rate cases by the end of 2006.
- We expect debt levels to remain flat with 2005, as WMB commits capital to growth projects. We expect an effective tax rate of 40% in 2006, but cash taxes should be minimal due to the availability of net operating loss carryforwards.

Investment Rationale/Risk

- A softening in natural gas prices following a mild winter have benefited WMB's midstream business, in our opinion, as sales margins for natural gas liquids have escalated rapidly. WMB has been very active in drilling for natural gas and is benefiting from deepwater investments. New pipeline rates are expected to become effective in early 2007. Thus far in 2006, WMB has invested $1 billion and plans to spend between $2.2 billion and $2.4 billion.
- Risks to our recommendation and target price include reductions in power margins and natural gas prices, divestitures of power trading contracts, lower rates for WMB's FERC regulated pipelines, and reduced natural gas production growth rates.
- As a large pipeline company with other operations experiencing improved fundamentals, we believe WMB should trade roughly in line with its pipeline and multi-industry peers. Our 12-month target price of $28 reflects a price to tangible book value of 3.2X, a discount to peers, and an enterprise value to EBITDA multiple of 8X, a premium to peers. We believe that blending both metrics reflects the most accurate representation of appropriate value.

Qualitative Risk Assessment

LOW | **MEDIUM** | HIGH

Our risk assessment reflects that although WMB has an E&P segment that can be very volatile, we believe the company is involved in several complementary industries. Its business portfolio is overweight in regulated industries with largely proscribed returns, in our opinion.

Quantitative Evaluations

S&P Quality Ranking B

D | C | B- | **B** | B+ | A- | A | A+

Relative Strength Rank MODERATE

52

LOWEST = 1 HIGHEST = 99

Revenue/Earnings Data

Revenue (Million $)

	1Q	2Q	3Q	4Q	Year
2006	3,028	2,715	--	--	--
2005	2,954	2,871	3,082	3,676	12,584
2004	3,070	3,052	3,375	2,964	12,461
2003	4,833	3,657	4,795	3,549	16,834
2002	1,622	1,057	1,266	1,703	5,608
2001	3,096	2,815	2,805	2,319	11,035

Earnings Per Share ($)

2006	0.22	-0.11	**E**0.30	**E**0.37	**E**1.26
2005	0.34	0.07	0.01	0.12	0.53
2004	Nil	-0.03	0.03	0.17	0.18
2003	-0.09	0.17	0.04	-0.16	-0.03
2002	0.05	-0.59	-0.35	-0.26	-1.14
2001	0.78	0.69	0.44	-0.20	1.67

Fiscal year ended Dec. 31. Next earnings report expected: Early November. EPS Estimates based on S&P Operating Earnings; historical GAAP earnings are as reported.

Dividend Data (Dates: mm/dd Payment Date: mm/dd/yy)

Amount ($)	Date Decl.	Ex-Div. Date	Stk. of Record	Payment Date
0.075	11/17	12/07	12/09	12/26/05
0.075	01/27	03/08	03/10	03/27/06
0.090	05/18	06/07	06/09	06/26/06
0.090	07/20	08/23	08/25	09/11/06

Dividends have been paid since 1974. Source: Company reports.

Please read the Required Disclosures and Analyst Certification on the last page of this report.

Williams Cos Inc. (The)

STANDARD &POOR'S

Business Summary August 08, 2006

CORPORATE OVERVIEW. In February 2003, WMB announced a business strategy focused on migrating to an integrated natural gas business comprised of a smaller portfolio of natural gas businesses, reducing debt and increasing liquidity via asset sales, strategic levels of financing and reductions in operating costs.

Having largely achieved these objectives in mid-2005, WMB has transitioned its corporate strategy towards aggressively attacking the market in the segments where it perceives a sustainable competitive advantage, primarily its exploration and production (E&P) segment and its Midstream segment. With about 3.0 Tcfe of proved reserves (99% natural gas, 51% proved undeveloped), natural gas is produced from tight sands formations and coal bed methane reserves in the Piceance (64% of total reserves), San Juan (20%), Powder River (10%), Arkoma and other basins (6%).

The midstream division provides natural gas gathering, processing and treating, and natural gas liquid fractionation, storage and marketing, with primary service areas concentrated in the western states of Wyoming, Colorado, and New Mexico, and the onshore and offshore shelf and deepwater areas in and around the Gulf Coast states of Texas, Louisiana, Mississippi and Alabama.

Geographically, Midstream natural gas assets are positioned to maximize commercial and operational synergies with other WMB assets (e.g., offshore gathering and processing assets attach and process or condition natural gas supplies delivered to the Transco pipeline; WMB gathering and processing facilities in the San Juan basin handle about 80% of the group's wellhead production in the basin).

MARKET PROFILE. The gas pipeline division has 14,700 miles of pipeline, with total annual throughput of 2,600 trillion BTUs, including the Transcontinental Gas Pipeline (Transco), Northwest Pipeline, and a 50% ownership interest in the Gulfstream Pipeline. Each pipeline system operates under Federal Energy Regulatory Commission (FERC) approved tariffs that establish rates, cost recovery mechanisms, and service terms and conditions. The established rates are a function of WMB's cost of providing services, including a "reasonable" return on invested capital.

Company Financials

Per Share Data ($) Year Ended Dec. 31	**2005**	**2004**	**2003**	**2002**	**2001**	**2000**	**1999**	**1998**	**1997**	**1996**
Tangible Book Value	7.70	7.06	5.96	7.15	9.43	13.26	11.69	8.34	9.35	10.35
Cash Flow	1.75	1.37	1.27	0.53	3.17	3.80	2.04	1.82	2.49	2.36
Earnings	0.53	0.18	-0.03	-1.14	1.67	1.95	0.36	0.32	1.04	1.09
S&P Core Earnings	0.64	0.05	-0.26	-1.34	1.40	NA	NA	NA	NA	NA
Dividends	0.25	0.08	0.04	0.42	0.68	0.60	0.60	0.60	0.54	0.47
Payout Ratio	47%	44%	NM	NM	41%	31%	167%	171%	52%	43%
Prices:High	25.72	17.18	10.73	26.35	46.44	49.75	53.75	36.94	28.63	19.50
Prices:Low	15.18	8.49	2.51	0.78	20.80	29.50	28.00	20.00	18.13	14.17
P/E Ratio:High	49	95	NM	NM	28	26	NM	NM	28	18
P/E Ratio:Low	29	47	NM	NM	12	15	NM	NM	17	13

Income Statement Analysis (Million $)	2005	2004	2003	2002	2001	2000	1999	1998	1997	1996
Revenue	12,584	12,461	16,834	5,608	11,035	10,398	8,593	7,658	4,410	3,531
Operating Income	1,972	1,903	1,849	1,566	3,389	2,602	1,591	1,372	1,414	1,271
Depreciation	740	668	671	775	798	832	742	646	500	411
Interest Expense	664	833	1,241	1,325	747	1,010	668	515	405	360
Pretax Income	557	246	71.0	-617	1,533	1,415	316	247	542	545
Effective Tax Rate	38.4%	53.4%	51.3%	NM	41.1%	39.1%	51.0%	44.6%	32.8%	33.6%
Net Income	317	93.2	15.2	-502	835	873	162	147	351	362
S&P Core Earnings	388	27.3	-144	-699	703	NA	NA	NA	NA	NA

Balance Sheet & Other Financial Data (Million $)	2005	2004	2003	2002	2001	2000	1999	1998	1997	1996
Cash	1,597	930	2,316	2,019	1,301	1,211	1,092	503	81.3	115
Current Assets	9,697	6,044	8,795	12,886	12,938	15,477	6,517	3,532	2,256	1,890
Total Assets	29,443	23,993	27,022	34,989	38,906	40,197	25,289	18,647	13,879	12,419
Current Liabilities	8,450	5,146	6,270	11,309	13,495	16,804	5,772	4,439	3,027	2,199
Long Term Debt	7,591	7,712	11,040	11,896	10,621	10,532	9,746	6,366	4,565	4,377
Common Equity	5,428	4,956	4,102	4,778	6,044	5,892	5,585	4,155	3,430	3,260
Total Capital	15,741	15,238	17,595	20,723	21,532	20,693	18,475	13,193	9,973	9,425
Capital Expenditures	1,299	787	957	1,824	1,922	4,904	3,513	1,708	1,162	819
Cash Flow	1,057	762	657	274	1,633	1,705	901	786	840	763
Current Ratio	1.1	1.2	1.4	1.1	1.0	0.9	1.1	0.8	0.7	0.9
% Long Term Debt of Capitalization	48.2	50.6	62.7	57.4	49.3	50.9	52.8	48.3	45.8	46.4
% Net Income of Revenue	2.5	0.7	0.1	NM	7.6	8.4	1.9	1.9	7.9	10.3
% Return on Assets	1.2	0.4	0.0	NM	2.3	2.7	0.7	0.9	2.7	3.2
% Return on Equity	6.1	2.1	0.0	NM	14.0	15.2	3.3	3.7	10.2	11.2

Data as orig reptd.; bef. results of disc opers/spec. items. Per share data adj. for stk. divs.; EPS diluted. E-Estimated. NA-Not Available. NM-Not Meaningful. NR-Not Ranked. UR-Under Review.

Office: 1 Williams Ctr, Tulsa, OK 74172-0140.
Telephone: 918-573-2000.
Website: http://www.williams.com
Chrmn, Pres & CEO: S.J. Malcolm

SVP & CFO: D. Chappel
SVP & Chief Admin: M.P. Johnson, Sr.
SVP & General Counsel: J.J. Bender
Investor Contact: R. George (918-573-3679)

Board of Directors: K. B. Cooper, I. F. Engelhardt, W. R. Granberry, W. E. Green, J. H. Hinshaw, W. R. Howell, C. M. Lillis, G. A. Lorch, W. G. Lowrie, F. T. MacInnis, S. J. Malcolm, J. D. Stoney

Founded: 1908
Domicile: Delaware
Employees: 3,913

Quantitative Stock Report
Oct 28,2006
NYSE SYMBOL:**WIN**

Windstream Corp

S&P Quality Ranking: **NR** Standard & Poor's Fair Value Rank : **NR**

WIN has an approximate 0.05% weighting in the **S&P 500**

Sector: Telecommunication Services
Sub-Industry: Integrated Telecommunication Services

Summary: This company provides voice, broadband and entertainment services to customers in 16 states. It has about 3.4 million access lines.

Quantitative Evaluations

S&P Quality Ranking : NR

S&P Fair Value Rank: NR

Fair Value Calc: NA

S&P Investability Quotient Percentile

60%

1 Lowest Highest 100

WIN scored higher than 60% of all companies for which an S&P Report is available.

Volatility: Average

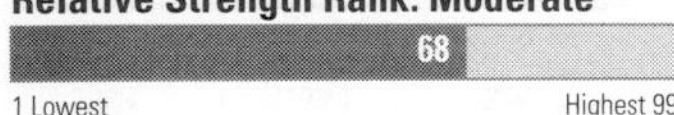

Technical Evaluation: NA

Relative Strength Rank: Moderate

68

1 Lowest Highest 99

Price as of Oct 27,2006: $13.85 | **52-Week Range: $14.02 - $ 11.13**

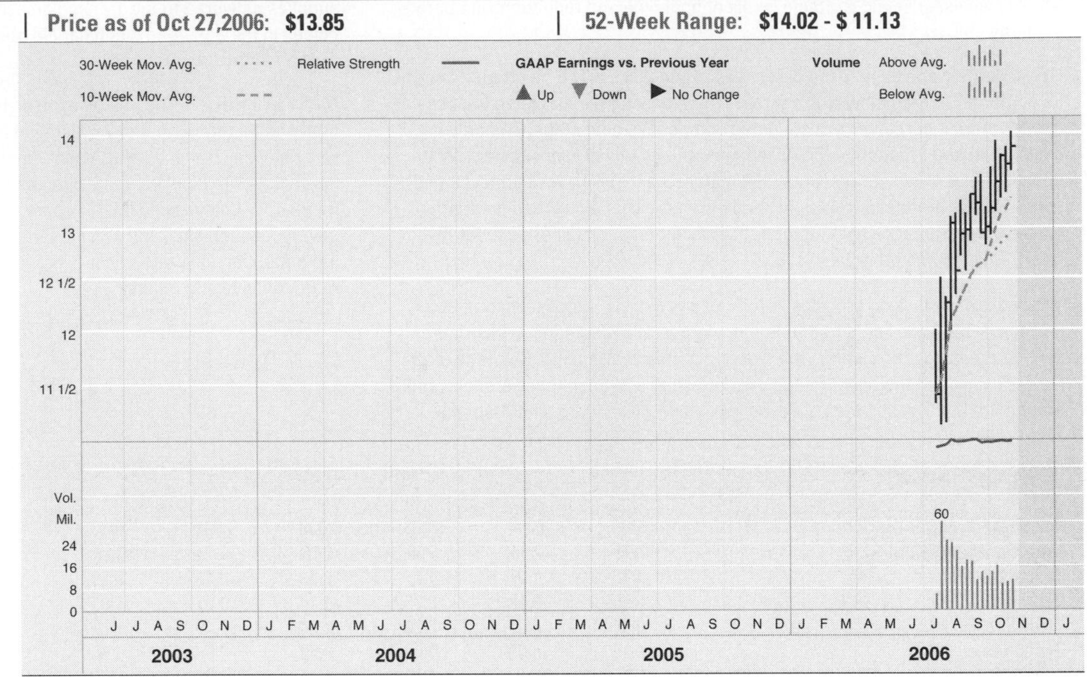

Investment Strategy

Key financial variables to consider in assessing the investment merits of an industrial company are the following:

Sales: What is the trend? Is future sales growth expected to be greater than the past 5-year and 9-year growth average? Accelerating sales growth ultimately provides the fuel behind earnings growth.

Net Margin: As a key measure of company profitabilty, a rising net margin assesses management capability to wring out more net income from incremental sales.

% LT Debt of Capitalization: A rising percentage implies greater financial risk, all else being equal. Rising debt leverage without a concomitant rise in Return on Equity should raise warning signals of potential cash flow problems. Percentages above 40%-50% should also be considered a warning.

% Return on Equity: A key perfomance measurement of capital efficiency assesses what investment returns management can earn on a company's existing capital base. A sustained percentage above 20% is considered above average.

Revenues/Earnings Data Fiscal year ending Dec. 31

Revenues (Million $)

	2006	2005	2004	2003	2002	2001
1Q	--	--	--	--	--	--
2Q	125.5	--	--	--	--	--
3Q	--	--	--	--	--	--
4Q	--	--	--	--	--	--
Year	--	3,414	--	--	--	--

Earnings per Share ($)

	2006	2005	2004	2003	2002	2001
1Q	--	--	--	--	--	--
2Q	0.22	--	--	--	--	--
3Q	--	--	--	--	--	--
4Q	--	--	--	--	--	--
Year	--	0.83	--	--	--	--

Next earnings report expected: NA

Historical GAAP earnings are as reported.

Key Growth Rates and Averages

Past Growth Rate (%)	1 Year	3 Year	5 Year	9 Year
Sales	NA	NA	NA	NA
Net Income	NA	NA	NA	NA
Ratio Analysis (Average)				
Net Margin	11.54	NA	NA	NA
% LTD of Capitalization	78.21	NA	NA	NA
% Return on Equity	NA	NA	NA	NA

Key Stock Statistics

Average Daily Volume	**2.340 mil.**	Beta	**1.00**
Market Capitalization	**$6.566 Bil.**	Trailing 12 Month EPS	**$0.00**
Institutional Holdings	**9%**	12 Month P/E	**NM**
Shareholders of Record	**NA**	Current Yield	**Nil**

Value of $10,000 Invested five yrs Ago : **NA**

Please read the required disclosures and Reg. AC certification on the last page of this report.

This report was prepared by Standard & Poor's Quantitative Services.

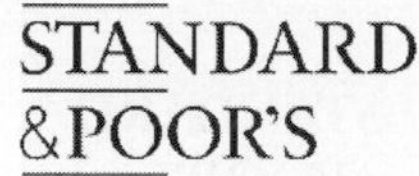

Windstream Corp

Quantitative Stock Report
Oct 28,2006
NYSE SYMBOL:**WIN**

S&P Quality Ranking: **NR** Standard & Poor's Fair Value Rank : **NR**

Wall Street Opinions/Average (Mean) Opinion: Buy/Hold

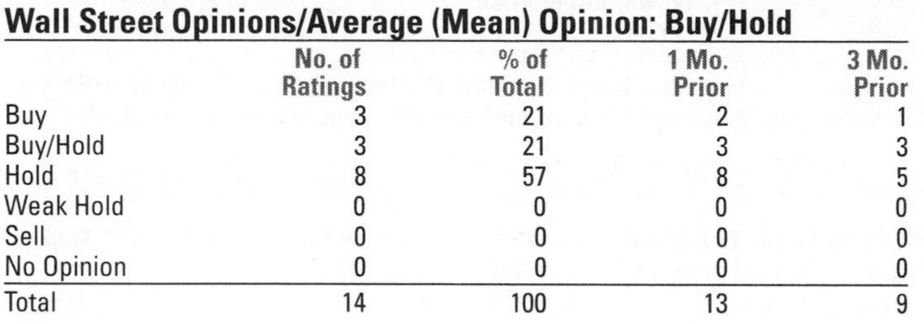

	No. of Ratings	% of Total	1 Mo. Prior	3 Mo. Prior
Buy	3	21	2	1
Buy/Hold	3	21	3	3
Hold	8	57	8	5
Weak Hold	0	0	0	0
Sell	0	0	0	0
No Opinion	0	0	0	0
Total	14	100	13	9

Insider Moves

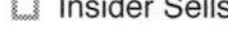

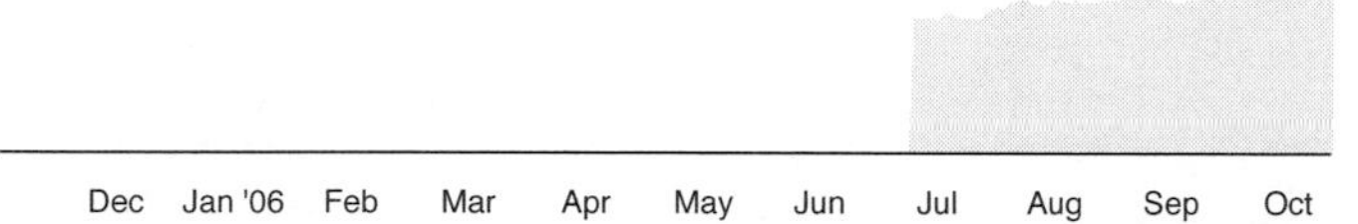

Stock Performance

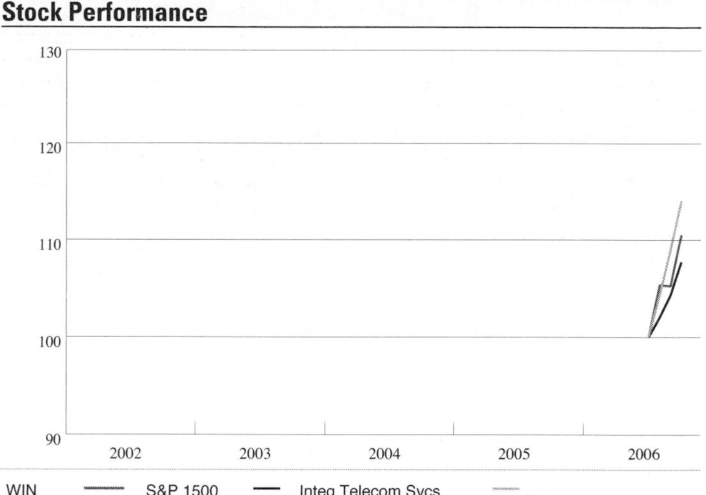

Dividend Data Dividend have been paid since 2006

Amount($)	Date Decl.	Ex. Div. Date	Stock of Record	Payment Date
0.125	Jul.20	Sep.6	Sep.8	Oct.03 '06
.204	Aug.3	Sep.27	Sep.29	Oct.16 '06

	Company(%)	Industry(%)	S&P 1500(%)
YTD Return (% Annualized)	--	50.8	12.4
One Year Return	--	43.9	16.9
Three Year Return	--	14.4	10.7
Five Year Return	--	-2.2	5.3
Value of $10,000 Invested 5 Years Ago	NA	$8,955	$12,961

Company Financials Fiscal year ending Dec. 31

Per Share Data ($) (Year Ended Dec. 31)	2005	2004	2003	2002	2001	2000	1999	1998	1997	1996
Tangible Book Value	NM	NA	NA	NA	NA	NA	NA	NA	NA	NA
Cash Flow	2.08	NA	NA	NA	NA	NA	NA	NA	NA	NA
Earnings	0.83	NA	NA	NA	NA	NA	NA	NA	NA	NA
Dividends	NA	NA	NA	NA	NA	NA	NA	NA	NA	NA
Payout Ratio	NA	NA	NA	NA	NA	NA	NA	NA	NA	NA
Prices:High	NA	NA	NA	NA	NA	NA	NA	NA	NA	NA
Prices:Low	NA	NA	NA	NA	NA	NA	NA	NA	NA	NA
P/E Ratio:High	NA	NA	NA	NA	NA	NA	NA	NA	NA	NA
P/E Ratio:Low	NA	NA	NA	NA	NA	NA	NA	NA	NA	NA
Income Statement Analysis (Million $)										
Revenue	3,414	NA	NA	NA	NA	NA	NA	NA	NA	NA
Operating Income	1,617	NA	NA	NA	NA	NA	NA	NA	NA	NA
Depreciation	593	NA	NA	NA	NA	NA	NA	NA	NA	NA
Interest Expense	391	NA	NA	NA	NA	NA	NA	NA	NA	NA
Pretax Income	662	NA	NA	NA	NA	NA	NA	NA	NA	NA
Effective Tax Rate	40%	NA	NA	NA	NA	NA	NA	NA	NA	NA
Net Income	394	NA	NA	NA	NA	NA	NA	NA	NA	NA
Balance Sheet & Other Financial Data (Million $)										
Cash	119	NA	NA	NA	NA	NA	NA	NA	NA	NA
Current Assets	533	NA	NA	NA	NA	NA	NA	NA	NA	NA
Total Assets	7,751	NA	NA	NA	NA	NA	NA	NA	NA	NA
Current Liabilities	459	NA	NA	NA	NA	NA	NA	NA	NA	NA
Long Term Debt	5,525	NA	NA	NA	NA	NA	NA	NA	NA	NA
Common Equity	533	NA	NA	NA	NA	NA	NA	NA	NA	NA
Total Capital	7,064	NA	NA	NA	NA	NA	NA	NA	NA	NA
Capital Expenditures	NA	NA	NA	NA	NA	NA	NA	NA	NA	NA
Cash Flow	987	NA	NA	NA	NA	NA	NA	NA	NA	NA
Current Ratio	1.2	NA	NA	NA	NA	NA	NA	NA	NA	NA
% Long Term Debt of Capitalization	78.2	NA	NA	NA	NA	NA	NA	NA	NA	NA
% Net Income of Revenue	11.5	NA	NA	NA	NA	NA	NA	NA	NA	NA
% Return on Assets	NA	NA	NA	NA	NA	NA	NA	NA	NA	NA
% Return on Equity	NA	NA	NA	NA	NA	NA	NA	NA	NA	NA

Data as orig. reptd; bef. results of disc opers/spec. items. Per share data adj. for stk. divs. as of ex-div date. NA-Not Available. NM-Not Meaningful. NR-Not Ranked.

Office: **4001 Rodney Parham Road, Little Rock, AR, 72212**
Tel: **501-748-7578**
Website: **http://www.windstream.com**
Chrmn: **F. X. Frantz**
Pres & CEO: **J. R. Gardner**

Dirs: **A. J. de Nicola, D. E. Foster, F. X. Frantz, J. R. Gardner, J. T. Hinson, J. K. Jones, W. A. Montgomery, F. E. Reed**
EVP & CFO: **B. K. Whittington**
COO: **K. D. Paglusch**
EVP & General Counsel: **J. P. Fletcher**
SVP & Treas: **R. G. Clancy, Jr.**

Investor Contact: **Mary Michaels(501-748-7578)**
Auditor: **Deloitte & Touche, Dallas, TX**
Founded: **2000**
Domicile: **Delaware**
Employees: **8,000**

WM. Wrigley Jr. Co

STANDARD &POOR'S

S&P Recommendation STRONG BUY ★★★★★

Price $52.36 (as of Oct 27, 2006)

12-Mo. Target Price $62.00

Investment Style Large-Cap Growth

GICS Sector Consumer Staples
Sub-Industry Packaged Foods & Meats

Comment This company is the world's largest producer of chewing gum, with approximately 60% of the U.S. market. The Wrigley family controls 51% of the supervoting Class B stock.

Key Stock Statistics (Source S&P, Vickers, company reports)

52-Wk Range	$57.25–43.00	S&P Oper. EPS 2006E	2.00	P/E on S&P Oper. EPS 2006E	26.2	Dividend Rate/Share	$1.02
Trailing 12-Month EPS	$1.77	S&P Oper. EPS 2007E	2.22	Common Shares Outstg. (M)	277.5	Yield (%)	1.96
Trailing 12-Month P/E	29.6	S&P Core EPS 2006E	2.01	Market Capitalization(B)	$11.263	Beta	0.17
$10K Invested 5 Yrs Ago	$17,065	S&P Core EPS 2007E	2.23	Institutional Ownership (%)	63	S&P Credit Rating	NA

Price Performance

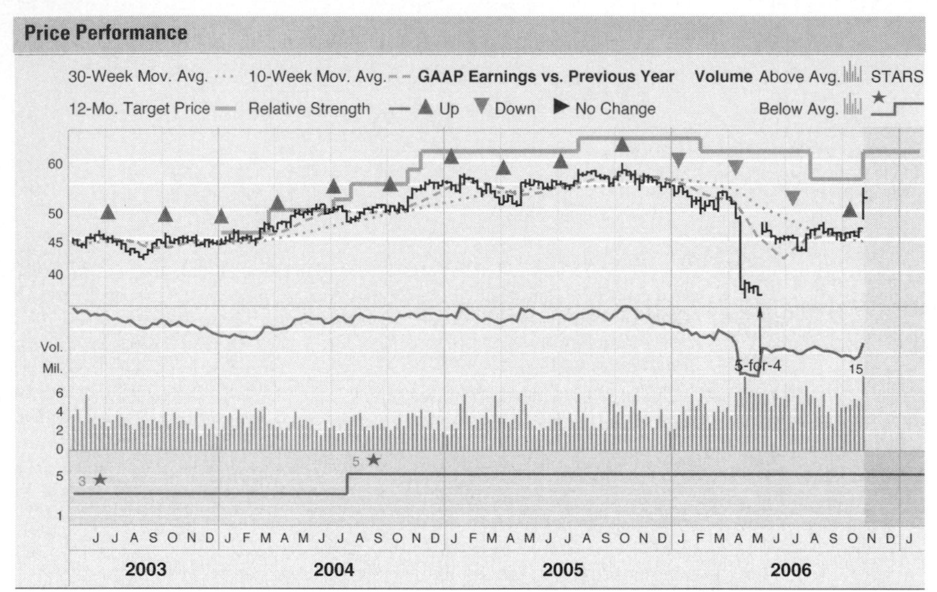

Options: ASE

Analysis prepared by **Rick Joy** on October 25, 2006, when the stock traded at **$ 52.48**.

Highlights

- We project that net sales will rise 7% to 8% in 2007, reflecting volume growth, product mix improvements and distribution gains in fast growing international markets. We believe new products should help North American sales advance 5% to 6% in 2007, while we expect international sales growth to exceed 10% on new product contributions and strong volume gains in Eastern Europe, Russia and Asia.
- We see gross margins benefiting from modestly higher prices and an improved product mix, though likely restricted somewhat by the inclusion of acquired brands and costs from new product introductions. We expect advertising and promotional spending to increase to support new gum products and the Lifesavers and Altoids brands acquired from Kraft. We see the acquired brands beginning to add to earnings in 2007.
- We expect EPS in 2007 to increase 11%, to $2.22, from anticipated EPS of $2.00 (including an estimated $0.11 in stock option expense) in 2006. For the longer term, we project annual EPS growth of 9% to 11%.

Investment Rationale/Risk

- We believe the shares are attractive, in light of our view of WWY's relatively high and improving operating profitability, strong balance sheet, dominant and growing U.S. market share (about 60%), and impressive global distribution infrastructure. We believe free cash flow will continue to grow and will likely continue to fund niche acquisitions and share repurchases.
- Risks to our recommendation and target price include consumer acceptance of new product introductions, slowing economies in key foreign markets such as China, and foreign currency movements. In terms of corporate governance, the company has a dual class capital structure with unequal voting rights and a non-shareholder approved poison pill in place, both of which we view unfavorably.
- Our 12-month target price of $62 is based on our analyses of discounted cash flow (DCF) and comparable peer multiples. Our DCF assumptions include a weighted average cost of capital of 8.5% and an expected terminal growth rate for cash flow of 4%.

Qualitative Risk Assessment

LOW | MEDIUM | HIGH

Our risk assessment for Wm. Wrigley Jr. Company reflects the relatively stable nature of the company's end markets, our view of a strong balance sheet and cash flow, leading global market shares, and an S&P Quality Ranking of A+ that reflects above-average growth and stability of earnings and dividends.

Quantitative Evaluations

S&P Quality Ranking **A+**

D | C | B- | B | B+ | A- | A | **A+**

Relative Strength Rank **STRONG**

89

LOWEST = 1 HIGHEST = 99

Revenue/Earnings Data

Revenue (Million $)

	1Q	2Q	3Q	4Q	Year
2006	1,076	1,207	1,179	--	--
2005	950.4	1,040	1,062	1,106	4,159
2004	812.2	957.9	916.7	961.9	3,649
2003	672.4	792.6	782.9	821.2	3,069
2002	599.0	708.5	699.5	739.3	2,746
2001	561.6	623.9	597.6	646.6	2,430

Earnings Per Share ($)

2006	0.32	0.51	0.53	**E**0.50	**E**2.00
2005	0.46	0.58	0.46	0.34	1.83
2004	0.39	0.50	0.45	0.42	1.75
2003	0.34	0.45	0.40	0.39	1.58
2002	0.30	0.39	0.35	0.38	1.42
2001	0.29	0.35	0.33	0.32	1.29

Fiscal year ended Dec. 31. Next earnings report expected: Early February. EPS Estimates based on S&P Operating Earnings; historical GAAP earnings are as reported.

Dividend Data (Dates: mm/dd Payment Date: mm/dd/yy)

Amount ($)	Date Decl.	Ex-Div. Date	Stk. of Record	Payment Date
5-for-4	04/04	04/12	04/17	05/01/06
0.256	05/19	07/12	07/14	08/01/06
0.256	08/15	10/11	10/13	11/01/06
0.256	10/23	01/10	01/12	02/01/07

Dividends have been paid since 1913. Source: Company reports.

Please read the Required Disclosures and Analyst Certification on the last page of this report.

WM. Wrigley Jr. Co

Business Summary October 25, 2006

Since 1891, Wrigley has concentrated its operations essentially on one line of business: the manufacture and marketing of chewing gum. The company is the world's largest gum manufacturer, accounting for more than 40% of total chewing gum sales volume worldwide. Principal products include: Wrigley's Spearmint; Doublemint; Juicy Fruit; Big Red; Winterfresh; and Extra. Other products include: Airwaves; Freedent; Ice White; Orbit; P.K.; and Hubba Bubba (bubble gum). Chewing gum and other confectionery products account for over 90% of total worldwide sales and earnings.

Finished gum is manufactured in four factories in the U.S. and 15 factories in other countries. Three wholly owned associated domestic companies also manufacture products other than finished chewing gum: L. A. Dreyfus Co. produces chewing gum base for Wrigley and other customers; Northwestern Flavors, Inc. processes flavorings and rectifies mint oil for Wrigley and ingredients for other food-related industries; and The Wrico Packaging division produces a large portion of the company's domestic printed and other wrapping supplies.

The Amurol Confections subsidiary, which manufactures and markets children's bubble gum items (Big League Chew, Bubble Tape) and other uniquely packaged confections, also includes various non-gum items, such as a line of suckers, dextrose candy, liquid gel candy, and hard roll candies as an important part of its total business.

By geographic area, sales contributions in 2005 were: North America, consisting of the U.S. and Canada, 37%; the EMEAI region, consisting of Europe, the Middle East, Africa and India, 45.5%; Asia, 12%; and all other, 5.5%. In alphabetical order, WWY's 10 largest revenue producing countries outside of the U.S. in 2005 were Australia, Canada, China, France, Germany, Poland, Russia, Spain, Taiwan, and the United Kingdom. WWY brands are sold in more than 180 countries and territories. Asia is the company's fastest growing region.

Company Financials

Per Share Data ($) Year Ended Dec. 31	**2005**	**2004**	**2003**	**2002**	**2001**	**2000**	**1999**	**1998**	**1997**	**1996**
Tangible Book Value	2.66	7.01	6.48	5.42	4.54	2.01	3.98	3.98	3.40	3.10
Cash Flow	2.49	2.26	2.01	1.73	1.53	1.36	1.27	1.24	1.11	0.96
Earnings	1.83	1.75	1.58	1.42	1.29	1.16	1.06	1.05	0.94	0.80
S&P Core Earnings	1.80	1.73	1.56	1.33	1.20	NA	NA	NA	NA	NA
Dividends	0.86	0.74	0.69	0.64	0.60	0.56	0.53	0.52	0.47	0.41
Payout Ratio	47%	42%	44%	45%	46%	48%	50%	49%	50%	51%
Prices:High	59.48	55.99	47.12	47.12	42.64	38.65	40.25	41.72	32.82	25.15
Prices:Low	50.62	43.84	40.84	35.37	34.35	23.94	26.60	28.37	21.82	19.35
P/E Ratio:High	32	32	30	33	33	33	38	40	35	32
P/E Ratio:Low	28	25	26	25	27	21	25	27	23	24
Income Statement Analysis (Million $)										
Revenue	4,159	3,649	3,069	2,746	2,430	2,146	2,062	2,005	1,937	1,836
Operating Income	952	862	769	671	582	521	489	468	432	412
Depreciation	175	142	120	85.6	68.3	57.9	61.3	55.8	50.4	47.3
Interest Expense	31.6	Nil	Nil	Nil	Nil	Nil	0.71	0.62	0.96	1.10
Pretax Income	755	720	652	583	527	479	444	441	394	359
Effective Tax Rate	31.5%	31.6%	31.6%	31.2%	31.2%	31.4%	30.7%	30.9%	31.1%	35.9%
Net Income	517	493	446	402	363	329	308	305	272	230
S&P Core Earnings	508	488	438	374	336	NA	NA	NA	NA	NA
Balance Sheet & Other Financial Data (Million $)										
Cash	258	629	505	279	308	301	288	215	207	301
Current Assets	1,306	1,506	1,291	1,006	914	829	804	843	798	729
Total Assets	4,460	3,167	2,520	2,108	1,766	1,575	1,548	1,521	1,343	1,234
Current Liabilities	981	718	465	386	332	288	252	219	226	218
Long Term Debt	1,000	Nil	Nil	Nil	Nil	Nil	Nil	Nil	Nil	Nil
Common Equity	2,214	2,179	1,821	1,523	1,276	1,133	1,139	1,157	985	897
Total Capital	3,325	2,267	1,904	1,593	1,319	1,173	1,184	1,197	1,016	922
Capital Expenditures	282	220	220	217	182	125	128	148	127	102
Cash Flow	693	635	566	487	431	387	369	360	322	278
Current Ratio	1.3	2.1	2.8	2.6	2.7	2.9	3.2	3.9	3.5	3.3
% Long Term Debt of Capitalization	30.1	Nil	Nil	Nil	Nil	Nil	Nil	Nil	Nil	Nil
% Net Income of Revenue	12.4	13.5	14.5	14.6	14.9	15.3	14.9	15.2	14.0	12.5
% Return on Assets	13.6	17.3	19.3	20.7	21.7	21.1	20.1	21.3	21.1	19.7
% Return on Equity	23.5	24.7	26.7	28.7	30.1	29.0	26.8	28.4	28.9	27.2

Data as orig reptd.; bef. results of disc opers/spec. items. Per share data adj. for stk. divs.; EPS diluted. E-Estimated. NA-Not Available. NM-Not Meaningful. NR-Not Ranked. UR-Under Review.

Office: 410 North Michigan Avenue, Chicago, IL, USA 60611.
Telephone: 312-644-2121.
Website: http://www.wrigley.com
Exec Chrmn: W. Wrigley, Jr.

Pres & CEO: W.D. Perez
SVP & CFO: R. Gamoran
SVP & Chief Admin: D. Petrovich
Investor Contact: A.J. Schneider (312-644-2121)

Board of Directors: J. F. Bard, H. B. Bernick, T. A. Knowlton, W. D. Perez, J. Rau, M. R. Rich, S. B. Sample, A. Shumate, R. K. Smucker, W. Wrigley, Jr.

Founded: 1910
Domicile: Delaware
Employees: 14,300

Wyeth

STANDARD &POOR'S

S&P Recommendation BUY ★★★★★

Price $52.00 (as of Oct 27, 2006)

12-Mo. Target Price $58.00

Investment Style Large-Cap Growth

GICS Sector Health Care
Sub-Industry Pharmaceuticals

Comment Wyeth (formerly American Home Products Corp.) is a leading maker of prescription drugs and OTC medications.

Key Stock Statistics (Source S&P, Vickers, company reports)

52-Wk Range	$54.13–40.90	S&P Oper. EPS 2006E	3.15	P/E on S&P Oper. EPS 2006E	16.5	Dividend Rate/Share	$1.04
Trailing 12-Month EPS	$2.99	S&P Oper. EPS 2007E	3.50	Common Shares Outstg. (M)	1,345.7	Yield (%)	2.00
Trailing 12-Month P/E	17.4	S&P Core EPS 2006E	3.15	Market Capitalization(B)	$69.974	Beta	1.09
$10K Invested 5 Yrs Ago	$9,997	S&P Core EPS 2007E	3.50	Institutional Ownership (%)	77	S&P Credit Rating	A

Price Performance

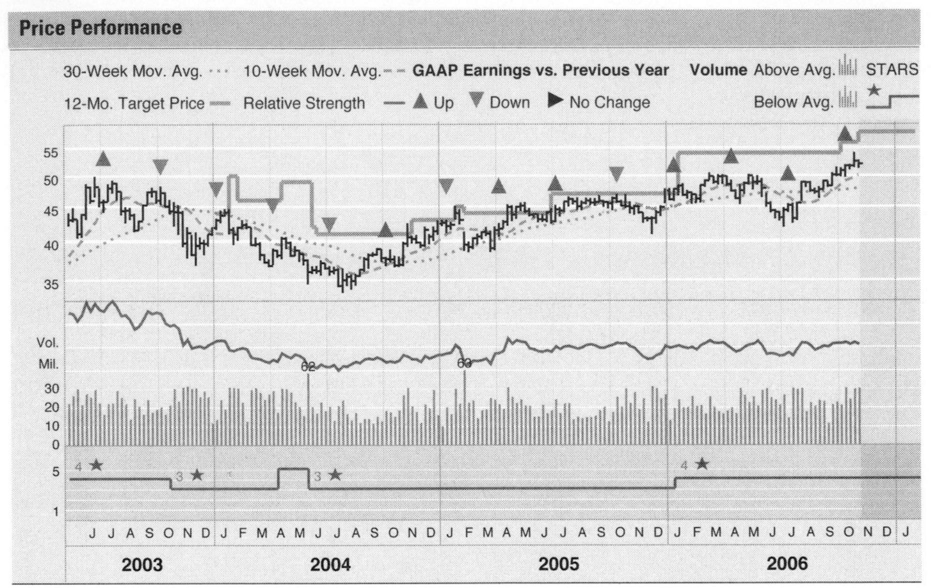

Options: ASE, CBOE, P, Ph

Analysis prepared by **Herman B. Saftlas** on October 26, 2006, when the stock traded at **$ 52.60**.

Highlights

- We project revenues to advance about 7% in 2007, comparable to growth estimated for 2006. The gain seen for 2007 should be driven largely by growth in Prevnar pediatric vaccine, and Enbrel, an anti-inflammatory agent. Both products should continue to benefit from strong consumer demand, increased manufacturing capacity and greater penetration of foreign markets. We see more modest gains for Effexor, Protonix, and Premarin. Sales of animal health products and consumer medications should both post modest increases.
- Helped by manufacturing efficiencies, we expect the gross margin to rise to about 74% in 2007, from an estimated 73.3% in 2006. We see increases in SG&A and R&D costs in the mid-single digits. Interest expense could also be higher, depending on the timing and magnitude of diet drug related payments. Other income will probably decline.
- We project operating EPS of $3.50 for 2007, up from an estimated $3.15 in 2006, after option expense in both years. Helped by new drugs, we see EPS rising to $3.85 in 2008.

Investment Rationale/Risk

- Supported by strength in key lines, a robust pipeline, and cost economies, we think WYE has the potential to rank among the top earnings performers in the drug sector among the companies we follow. In addition, we believe WYE has made significant progress in resolving diet drug liabilities. At present levels, we think the stock is attractively valued, given its modest discount to peer P/E multiples, and a P/E to earnings (PEG) ratio of 1.6X projected three-year EPS growth, versus 1.8X for the big pharma sector.
- Risks to our recommendation and target price include the possibility of significantly greater diet drug liabilities, the failure to resolve recent manufacturing issues in Puerto Rico, and possible R&D pipeline setbacks.
- Our 12-month target price of $58 is derived by applying a peer level P/E multiple of 16.6X to our 2007 EPS estimate. Our target price approximates our calculation of WYE's intrinsic value based on our DCF model, which assumes decelerating free cash flow growth over 10 years and a weighted average cost of capital of 7.3%. The shares recently yielded 2.0%.

Qualitative Risk Assessment

LOW | **MEDIUM** | HIGH

Our risk assessment reflects that Wyeth is subject to the inherent risks associated with the pharmaceuticals business, which include generic threats to branded drugs, as well as pipeline and regulatory risks. However, although WYE still has significant potential diet drug liability risk, we believe it has made meaningful progress in resolving diet drug litigation, with planned agreements to settle most of the remaining outstanding cases.

Quantitative Evaluations

S&P Quality Ranking B

D | C | B- | **B** | B+ | A- | A | A+

Relative Strength Rank MODERATE

60

LOWEST = 1 HIGHEST = 99

Revenue/Earnings Data

Revenue (Million $)

	1Q	2Q	3Q	4Q	Year
2006	4,838	5,157	5,136	--	--
2005	4,579	4,714	4,716	4,747	18,756
2004	4,015	4,223	4,472	4,648	17,358
2003	3,689	3,747	4,082	4,333	15,851
2002	3,644	3,503	3,624	3,814	14,584
2001	3,449	3,216	3,736	3,727	14,129

Earnings Per Share ($)

	1Q	2Q	3Q	4Q	Year
2006	0.82	0.78	0.85	**E**0.78	**E**3.15
2005	0.80	0.72	0.64	0.54	2.70
2004	0.56	0.62	1.06	-1.32	0.91
2003	0.96	0.65	-0.32	0.25	1.54
2002	0.65	0.45	1.05	1.18	3.33
2001	0.55	0.36	0.19	0.62	1.72

Fiscal year ended Dec. 31. Next earnings report expected: Late January. EPS Estimates based on S&P Operating Earnings; historical GAAP earnings are as reported.

Dividend Data (Dates: mm/dd Payment Date: mm/dd/yy)

Amount ($)	Date Decl.	Ex-Div. Date	Stk. of Record	Payment Date
0.250	01/27	02/09	02/13	03/01/06
0.250	04/27	05/10	05/12	06/01/06
0.250	06/22	08/09	08/11	09/01/06
0.260	09/28	11/09	11/13	12/01/06

Dividends have been paid since 1919. Source: Company reports.

Business Summary October 26, 2006

CORPORATE OVERVIEW. Wyeth (formerly American Home Products) is a leading producer of prescription pharmaceuticals, as well as consumer medications and animal health products. WYE's corporate strategy in recent years has focused on higher-margin products, while divesting less profitable businesses. Human prescription pharmaceuticals accounted for 82% of total sales in 2005, consumer health care products 13%, and animal health products 5%. Foreign operations are significant, accounting for 45% of sales in 2005.

WYE's largest selling product is Effexor (sales of $3.5 billion in 2005), an antidepressant that works on both serotonin and norepinephrine. Other key products include Protonix ($1.7 billion), a treatment for heartburn caused by gastroesophageal erosive reflux disease; Prevnar ($1.5 billion), a broad-based pediatric vaccine; Enbrel ($1.1 billion), a treatment for rheumatoid arthritis that is marketed in conjunction with Amgen, Inc.; and Zosyn/Tazocin ($892 million), an injectable penicillin antibiotic. The company also offers Cordarone, Veralan and Ziac cardiovasculars; Lodine, Oruvail and Naprelan antiarthritics; Suprax, and Minocin anti-infectives; and Refacto, a factor VIII treatment for hemophilia A. WYE markets Altace, a cardiovascular, through a co-marketing pact with King Pharmaceuticals.

WYE remains a leader in women's drugs, with its line of Premarin estrogen and PremPro/Premphase estrogen/progestin hormone replacement therapy (HRT) products (sales of $909 million in 2005), and oral contraceptives ($525 million) such as Triphasal, Lo/Ovral and Alesse. The HRT business has been negatively affected by clinical studies released in mid-2002 that highlighted cardiovascular and cancer risks with HRT products.

A full line of pediatric and adult nutritional products (sales of $1.0 billion) is offered, including infant formulas and adult supplements. The Whitehall and A.H. Robins divisions offer a broad range of OTC medications such as Advil and Anacin analgesics, Dimetapp and Robitussin for coughs and colds, Primatene for asthma, Preparation H for hemorrhoids, and Centrum and Solgar vitamins.

Company Financials

Per Share Data ($) Year Ended Dec. 31	**2005**	**2004**	**2003**	**2002**	**2001**	**2000**	**1999**	**1998**	**1997**	**1996**
Tangible Book Value	6.23	4.33	4.01	3.22	0.17	NM	NM	1.23	NM	NM
Cash Flow	3.26	1.37	1.94	3.72	2.17	-0.28	-0.42	2.35	4.18	2.00
Earnings	2.70	0.91	1.54	3.33	1.72	-0.69	-0.94	1.85	1.56	1.48
S&P Core Earnings	2.55	2.62	1.78	1.73	1.92	NA	NA	NA	NA	NA
Dividends	0.94	0.92	0.92	0.92	0.92	0.92	0.91	0.87	0.83	0.78
Payout Ratio	35%	101%	60%	28%	53%	NM	NM	47%	53%	53%
Prices:High	47.88	44.70	49.95	66.51	63.80	65.25	70.25	58.75	42.44	33.25
Prices:Low	38.48	33.50	32.75	28.25	52.00	39.38	36.50	37.75	28.50	23.53
P/E Ratio:High	18	49	32	20	37	NM	NM	32	27	22
P/E Ratio:Low	14	37	21	8	30	NM	NM	20	18	16
Income Statement Analysis (Million $)										
Revenue	18,756	17,358	15,851	14,584	14,129	13,263	13,550	13,463	14,196	14,088
Operating Income	5,244	4,773	4,450	4,060	4,299	3,808	3,759	3,931	3,946	3,634
Depreciation	787	622	538	485	608	534	682	665	701	658
Interest Expense	357	110	103	202	146	239	343	323	462	563
Pretax Income	4,781	-130	2,362	6,097	2,869	-1,101	-1,926	3,585	2,815	2,755
Effective Tax Rate	23.5%	NM	13.1%	27.1%	20.3%	NM	NM	31.0%	27.4%	31.6%
Net Income	3,656	1,234	2,051	4,447	2,285	-901	-1,227	2,474	2,043	1,883
S&P Core Earnings	3,455	3,542	2,379	2,313	2,551	NA	NA	NA	NA	NA
Balance Sheet & Other Financial Data (Million $)										
Cash	8,235	6,489	7,180	3,947	3,027	2,985	2,413	1,301	1,051	1,544
Current Assets	18,045	14,438	14,962	11,596	9,767	10,181	9,738	7,956	7,361	7,470
Total Assets	35,841	33,630	31,032	25,995	22,968	21,092	23,906	21,079	20,825	20,785
Current Liabilities	9,948	8,536	8,430	5,476	7,257	9,742	7,110	4,211	4,327	4,338
Long Term Debt	9,231	7,792	8,076	7,546	7,357	2,395	3,669	3,859	5,032	6,021
Common Equity	11,994	9,848	9,294	8,156	4,073	2,818	6,216	9,615	8,176	6,962
Total Capital	21,226	17,640	17,371	15,702	11,430	5,213	9,885	13,695	13,415	13,179
Capital Expenditures	1,081	1,255	1,909	1,932	1,924	1,682	1,000	810	830	652
Cash Flow	4,443	1,856	2,589	4,932	2,893	-367	-545	3,139	2,744	2,541
Current Ratio	1.8	1.7	1.8	2.1	1.3	1.0	1.4	1.9	1.7	1.7
% Long Term Debt of Capitalization	43.5	44.2	46.5	48.1	64.4	45.9	37.1	28.2	37.5	45.7
% Net Income of Revenue	19.5	NM	12.9	30.5	16.2	NM	NM	18.4	14.4	13.4
% Return on Assets	10.5	NM	7.2	18.2	10.4	NM	NM	11.8	9.8	8.9
% Return on Equity	33.5	NM	23.5	72.7	66.3	NM	NM	27.8	27.0	30.1

Data as orig reptd.; bef. results of disc opers/spec. items. Per share data adj. for stk. divs.; EPS diluted. E-Estimated. NA-Not Available. NM-Not Meaningful. NR-Not Ranked. UR-Under Review.

Office: 5 Giralda Farms, Madison, NJ 07940-1021.
Telephone: 973-660-5000.
Website: http://www.wyeth.com
Chrmn & CEO: R. Essner

Pres & Vice Chrmn: B.J. Poussot
Vice Chrmn & CFO: K.J. Martin
SVP & General Counsel: L.V. Stein
VP & Treas: J. O' Connor

Investor Contact: J.R. Victoria (973-660-5000)
Board of Directors: R. Essner, J. D. Feerick, F. D. Fergusson, V. F. Ganzi, R. S. Langer, J. P. Mascotte, R. J. McGuire, M. L. Polan, G. L. Rogers, I. G. Seidenberg, W. V. Shipley, J. R. Torell, III

Founded: 1926
Domicile: Delaware
Employees: 49,732

Wyndham Worldwide Corp

STANDARD &POOR'S

S&P Recommendation HOLD ★★★★★	Price	12-Mo. Target Price	Investment Style
	$29.27 (as of Oct 27, 2006)	$30.00	Mid-Cap Value

GICS Sector Consumer Discretionary
Sub-Industry Hotels, Resorts & Cruise Lines

Comment This company's operations include the sale of interests in vacation ownership resorts; facilitating the exchange and rental of access to vacation properties; and the franchising of hotels.

Key Stock Statistics (Source S&P, Vickers, company reports)

52-Wk Range	**$34.87–25.48**	S&P Oper. EPS 2006**E**	**1.90**	P/E on S&P Oper. EPS 2006**E**	**15.4**	Dividend Rate/Share	**Nil**
Trailing 12-Month EPS	**$1.15**	S&P Oper. EPS 2007**E**	**1.95**	Common Shares Outstg. (M)	**200.4**	Yield (%)	**Nil**
Trailing 12-Month P/E	**25.5**	S&P Core EPS 2006**E**	**1.78**	Market Capitalization(B)	**$5.865**	Beta	**1.00**
$10K Invested 5 Yrs Ago	**NA**	S&P Core EPS 2007**E**	**1.95**	Institutional Ownership (%)	**1**	S&P Credit Rating	**NA**

Price Performance

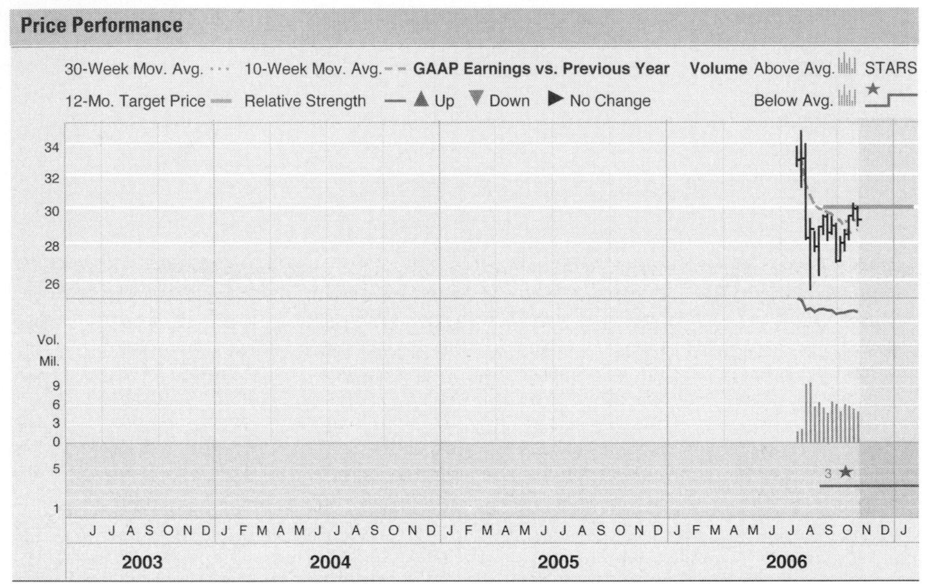

Analysis prepared by **Tom Graves, CFA** on August 29, 2006, when the stock traded at **$ 28.94**.

Highlights

- Ownership of WYN was spun off from Cendant Corp. in July 2006, with Cendant distributing one share of WYN common stock for every five shares of Cendant common stock outstanding as of the close of business July 21, 2006.
- We look for WYN to have revenue in 2006 of about $3.7 billion, up some 6% from $3.5 billion in 2005. We project that revenue from WYN's vacation ownership will rise 8%, to $2.0 billion, and account for 54% of total revenue. We look for revenue from WYN's lodging business to rise 27%, to $675 million, including more than $100 million related to the October 2005 acquisition of the Wyndham hotel management and franchising business.
- Excluding second quarter special charges of about $0.12 a share, and excluding separation costs related to Cendant, we estimate 2006 EPS of $1.90 a share. This includes higher corporate and interest costs in the second half, following the separation from Cendant. For 2007, with high corporate costs and increased interest expense, we estimate EPS of $1.95, which assumes some stock repurchase activity in the latter part of 2006 and in 2007.

Investment Rationale/Risk

- We look for the stock to be bolstered by prospects of the company generating cash flow that can be used to help fund expansion of WYN's vacation ownership business, and for stock repurchases. Our hold recommendation reflects our view that the shares are appropriately valued.
- Risks to our opinion and target price include weaker-than-expected consumer confidence and a related impact on vacation spending by consumers. Also, future travel activity could be negatively affected by fears of terrorism.
- Due to the large portion of WYN's profit that is expected to come from its vacation ownership business (before special items, about 39% of segment EBITDA in 2006), we believe that the stock should have lower P/E and enterprise value multiples than some of its lodging industry peers in our coverage universe. Our 12-month target price of $30 reflects a blend of sum-of-the-parts and discounted cash flow analyses, with the latter assuming a weighted average cost of capital of 9.0% and perpetuity annual cash flow growth of 3%.

Qualitative Risk Assessment

LOW | **MEDIUM** | HIGH

Our risk assessment reflects our view that the company's business is likely to be sensitive to changes in consumer confidence, travel conditions (including threats of terrorism), and the company's ability to retain and attract affiliated properties.

Quantitative Evaluations

S&P Quality Ranking **NR**

D | C | B- | B | B+ | A- | A | A+

Relative Strength Rank **MODERATE**

32

LOWEST = 1 HIGHEST = 99

Revenue/Earnings Data

Revenue (Million $)

	1Q	2Q	3Q	4Q	Year
2006	--	0.96	--	--	--
2005	--	--	--	--	3,471
2004	--	--	--	--	--
2003	--	--	--	--	--
2002	--	--	--	--	--
2001	--	--	--	--	--

Earnings Per Share ($)

	1Q	2Q	3Q	4Q	Year
2006	--	0.37	**E**0.53	**E**0.42	**E**1.90
2005	--	--	--	--	1.73
2004	--	--	--	--	--
2003	--	--	--	--	--
2002	--	--	--	--	--
2001	--	--	--	--	--

Fiscal year ended Dec. 31. Next earnings report expected: NA. EPS Estimates based on S&P Operating Earnings; historical GAAP earnings are as reported.

Dividend Data

No cash dividends have been paid.

Wyndham Worldwide Corp

Business Summary August 29, 2006

CORPORATE OVERVIEW. This company, which operates lodging, vacation exchange and rental and vacation ownership businesses, was previously part of Cendant Corp. On July 31, 2006, Cendant distributed one share of WYN common stock for every five shares of Cendant common stock outstanding as of the close of business July 21.

The Wyndham Hotel Group franchises hotels in various segments of the lodging industry and provides property management services to owners of upscale branded hotels. WYN's lodging business has more than 6,300 franchised hotels with about 525,000 rooms.

WYN's RCI Global Vacation Network provides vacation exchange products and services to developers, managers and owners of intervals of vacation ownership interests, and markets vacation rental properties. WYN's vacation exchange and rental business has access for specified periods, often on an exclusive basis, to about 55,000 vacation properties, which are comprised of approximately 4,000 vacation ownership resorts around the world and approximately 51,000 vacation rental properties located principally in Europe.

WYN's vacation ownership segment includes marketing and sales of vacation ownership interests, consumer financing in connection with the purchase by individuals of vacation ownership interests, property management services for property owners' associations, and development and acquisition of vacation ownership resorts. WYN's vacation ownership business is operated primarily through its Fairfield and Trendwest brands. WYN has developed or acquired more than 140 vacation ownership resorts that represent more than 18,000 individual vacation ownership units and more than 750,000 owners of vacation ownership interests and other real estate interests.

CORPORATE STRATEGY. We expect WYN's growth strategy to include efforts to add more properties to its hotel systems, especially outside of North America and in the middle and upscale segments of the North American market; to add more vacation rental properties in North America; and to leverage the Wyndham name in the higher-end vacation ownership market.

Company Financials

Per Share Data ($) Year Ended Dec. 31	2005	2004	2003	2002	2001	2000	1999	1998	1997	1996
Tangible Book Value	NM	NA	NA	NA	NA	NA	NA	NA	NA	NA
Cash Flow	2.37	NA	NA	NA	NA	NA	NA	NA	NA	NA
Earnings	1.73	NA	NA	NA	NA	NA	NA	NA	NA	NA
S&P Core Earnings	1.97	NA	NA	NA	NA	NA	NA	NA	NA	NA
Dividends	Nil	NA	NA	NA	NA	NA	NA	NA	NA	NA
Payout Ratio	Nil	NA	NA	NA	NA	NA	NA	NA	NA	NA
Prices:High	NA	NA	NA	NA	NA	NA	NA	NA	NA	NA
Prices:Low	NA	NA	NA	NA	NA	NA	NA	NA	NA	NA
P/E Ratio:High	NA	NA	NA	NA	NA	NA	NA	NA	NA	NA
P/E Ratio:Low	NA	NA	NA	NA	NA	NA	NA	NA	NA	NA
Income Statement Analysis (Million $)										
Revenue	3,471	NA	NA	NA	NA	NA	NA	NA	NA	NA
Operating Income	699	NA	NA	NA	NA	NA	NA	NA	NA	NA
Depreciation	135	NA	NA	NA	NA	NA	NA	NA	NA	NA
Interest Expense	41.0	NA	NA	NA	NA	NA	NA	NA	NA	NA
Pretax Income	523	NA	NA	NA	NA	NA	NA	NA	NA	NA
Effective Tax Rate	29.8%	NA	NA	NA	NA	NA	NA	NA	NA	NA
Net Income	367	NA	NA	NA	NA	NA	NA	NA	NA	NA
S&P Core Earnings	419	NA	NA	NA	NA	NA	NA	NA	NA	NA
Balance Sheet & Other Financial Data (Million $)										
Cash	106	NA	NA	NA	NA	NA	NA	NA	NA	NA
Current Assets	1,874	NA	NA	NA	NA	NA	NA	NA	NA	NA
Total Assets	8,590	NA	NA	NA	NA	NA	NA	NA	NA	NA
Current Liabilities	2,212	NA	NA	NA	NA	NA	NA	NA	NA	NA
Long Term Debt	1,733	NA	NA	NA	NA	NA	NA	NA	NA	NA
Common Equity	3,464	NA	NA	NA	NA	NA	NA	NA	NA	NA
Total Capital	5,987	NA	NA	NA	NA	NA	NA	NA	NA	NA
Capital Expenditures	134	NA	NA	NA	NA	NA	NA	NA	NA	NA
Cash Flow	502	NA	NA	NA	NA	NA	NA	NA	NA	NA
Current Ratio	0.9	NA	NA	NA	NA	NA	NA	NA	NA	NA
% Long Term Debt of Capitalization	28.9	NA	NA	NA	NA	NA	NA	NA	NA	NA
% Net Income of Revenue	10.5	NA	NA	NA	NA	NA	NA	NA	NA	NA
% Return on Assets	NA	NA	NA	NA	NA	NA	NA	NA	NA	NA
% Return on Equity	NA	NA	NA	NA	NA	NA	NA	NA	NA	NA

Data as orig reptd.; bef. results of disc opers/spec. items. Per share data adj. for stk. divs.; EPS diluted. E-Estimated. NA-Not Available. NM-Not Meaningful. NR-Not Ranked. UR-Under Review.

Office: Seven Sylvan Way, Parsippany, NJ 07054.
Telephone: 973-496-8900.
Website: http://www.wyndhamworldwide.com
Chrmn & CEO: S.P. Holmes

EVP & CFO: V.M. Wilson
EVP & General Counsel: S.G. McLester
SVP & Chief Acctg Officer: N. Rossi
Investor Contact: M.C. Happer (973-496-2705)

Board of Directors: M. J. Biblowit, J. E. Buckman, G. Herrera, S. P. Holmes, B. Mulroney, P. D. Richards, M. H. Wargotz

Auditor: Deloitte & Touche, Parsippany, NY
Employees: 28,800

STANDARD &POOR'S

Xcel Energy Inc.

S&P Recommendation HOLD ★★★☆☆	Price $21.88 (as of Oct 27, 2006)	12-Mo. Target Price $22.00	Investment Style Mid-Cap Value

GICS Sector Utilities
Sub-Industry Multi-Utilities

Comment This energy holding company was created through the August 2000 merger of Minneapolis-based Northern States Power and Denver-based New Century Energies.

Key Stock Statistics (Source S&P, Vickers, company reports)

52-Wk Range	$22.15–17.80	S&P Oper. EPS 2006E	1.36	P/E on S&P Oper. EPS 2006E	16.1	Dividend Rate/Share	$0.89
Trailing 12-Month EPS	$1.39	S&P Oper. EPS 2007E	1.43	Common Shares Outstg. (M)	406.0	Yield (%)	4.07
Trailing 12-Month P/E	15.7	S&P Core EPS 2006E	1.30	Market Capitalization(B)	$8.883	Beta	1.34
$10K Invested 5 Yrs Ago	$9,964	S&P Core EPS 2007E	1.36	Institutional Ownership (%)	61	S&P Credit Rating	BBB

Price Performance

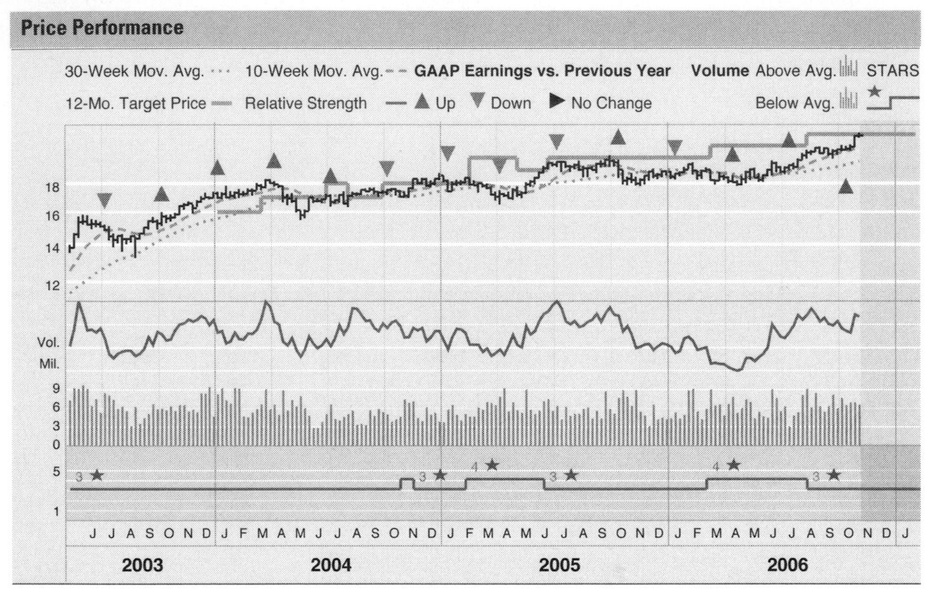

Options: ASE, CBOE

Analysis prepared by **Justin McCann** on August 10, 2006, when the stock traded at **$ 20.46**.

Highlights

- We expect EPS from continuing operations in 2006 to increase nearly 11% from 2005 EPS from continuing operations of $1.20. Despite higher operating margins, 2005 EPS from continuing operations was down 5.5% from the prior year due to a higher effective tax rate (25.8% versus 23.7%) and a sharp rise in fuel costs, as well as increased operating and maintenance expense. We expect EPS in 2007 to increase more than 6% from our EPS estimate for 2006.
- For 2006, we expect utility operations (aided by fewer nuclear outages) to earn about $1.31 a share, and for holding company costs of around $0.10 to be offset by a tax benefit of about $0.10. We expect earnings in both 2006 and 2007 to benefit from electric and gas rate hikes in Wisconsin, a gas rate increase in Colorado, and a pending gas rate case in Minnesota.
- EPS in 2006 should also benefit from a 6.5% interim electric rate increase for NSP Minnesota that became effective in January. However, this may be subject to a refund pending the outcome of a regulatory decision (expected in September 2006) on the utility's rate increase request of 8.05%. Our EPS estimate for 2006 assumes an effective tax rate of about 28%.

Investment Rationale/Risk

- Given the recent rise in the price of the shares, we recently downgraded our recommendation to hold from buy. Although the stock underperformed XEL's electric and gas utility peers in 2005, it has performed roughly in line year to date. We believe that investors should note the above-peer yield from the dividend.
- Risks to our recommendation and target price include the possibility of an adverse ruling by the Internal Revenue Service on the company's potential tax liabilities, unfavorable legislative or regulatory decisions, and a major decline in the average P/E of the group as a whole.
- XEL recently traded at a 2% to 3% premium to the electric and gas peer average P/E of about 15.2X our EPS estimates for 2006. With the dividend recently providing a yield of 4.4%, we see the shares benefiting from the 15% tax rate on dividends. While the shares could be pressured by concerns over an IRS dispute, with our projection that the annual dividend will be increased at a rate similar to our estimate of long-term annual EPS growth of 2% to 4%, we see the stock trading at an approximate peer P/E of 15.5X our EPS estimate for 2007. Our 12-month target price is $22.

Qualitative Risk Assessment

LOW	MEDIUM	HIGH

Our risk assessment reflects the steady cash flow that we expect from the regulated electric and gas utility operations, which have a relatively low-cost power supply, our view of a generally healthy economy in most of the company's service territories, and a relatively supportive regulatory environment.

Quantitative Evaluations

S&P Quality Ranking **B**

D	C	B-	**B**	B+	A-	A	A+

Relative Strength Rank **MODERATE**

70

LOWEST = 1 HIGHEST = 99

Revenue/Earnings Data

Revenue (Million $)

	1Q	2Q	3Q	4Q	Year
2006	2,888	2,074	2,412	--	--
2005	2,381	2,074	2,289	2,882	9,625
2004	2,280	1,797	2,009	2,259	8,345
2003	2,086	1,722	2,020	2,110	7,938
2002	2,371	2,227	2,473	2,454	9,524
2001	4,231	3,699	3,763	3,336	15,028

Earnings Per Share ($)

2006	0.36	0.24	0.53	E0.23	E1.36
2005	0.31	0.18	0.47	0.24	1.20
2004	0.35	0.21	0.40	0.30	1.27
2003	0.31	0.14	0.43	0.36	1.23
2002	0.26	0.22	-4.10	-0.54	-4.36
2001	0.61	0.49	0.79	0.38	2.27

Fiscal year ended Dec. 31. Next earnings report expected: Early February. EPS Estimates based on S&P Operating Earnings; historical GAAP earnings are as reported.

Dividend Data (Dates: mm/dd Payment Date: mm/dd/yy)

Amount ($)	Date Decl.	Ex-Div. Date	Stk. of Record	Payment Date
0.215	12/14	12/29	01/03	01/20/06
0.215	02/22	03/28	03/30	04/20/06
0.223	05/17	06/27	06/29	07/20/06
0.223	08/22	09/26	09/28	10/20/06

Dividends have been paid since 1910. Source: Company reports.

Xcel Energy Inc.

Business Summary August 10, 2006

CORPORATE OVERVIEW. Xcel Energy Inc. (XEL) is a holding company with a diverse portfolio of regulated and nonregulated subsidiaries. The company's utility subsidiaries are Northern States Power Company at Minnesota and Wisconsin (NSPM and NSPW respectively), Public Services Company of Colorado (PSCo) and Southwestern Public Service Co. (SPS), which provide electric and gas services in 10 western and Midwestern states, and WestGas Interstate Inc. (WGI), an interstate natural gas pipeline. XEL's nonregulated subsidiaries include Eloigne Co., which operates rental housing projects. In 2005, the electric utility operations contributed 75% of the operating revenues while the natural gas utility operations contributed 24%. The nonregulated operations and others contributed the rest.

CORPORATE STRATEGY. XEL's strategy is to continue investing in the core utility business and to earn the authorized returns, and to divest those businesses not linked to the electric and natural gas operations. In its most significant transaction, the company divested its ownership interest in NRG Energy, which was involved in independent power projects in the U.S. and internationally, in December 2003. XEL had divested its ownership interest in nearly all of its non-utility subsidiaries as of December 31, 2005. XEL's other remaining non-regulated non-utility business is Eloigne, which invests in projects qualifying for low income housing tax credits. XEL expects the demand for energy to increase in the future, especially in Colorado and Minnesota, and plans to invest $7 billion over the next five years in its core operations. The company also has a strong focus on system reliability and continues to invest in transmission and distribution systems. To recover the cost without the delay caused by the filing of rate cases, XEL gets regulatory approval for rate riders. This ensures fair returns on the company's investment.

Company Financials

Per Share Data ($) Year Ended Dec. 31	**2005**	**2004**	**2003**	**2002**	**2001**	**2000**	**1999**	**1998**	**1997**	**1996**
Tangible Book Value	13.11	12.99	12.95	11.44	17.91	15.79	15.67	15.58	15.23	15.42
Earnings	1.20	1.27	1.23	-4.36	2.27	1.54	1.43	1.84	1.70	1.91
S&P Core Earnings	1.15	1.21	1.03	-4.57	1.68	NA	NA	NA	NA	NA
Dividends	0.85	0.81	0.75	1.13	1.50	1.47	1.44	1.42	1.40	1.37
Payout Ratio	71%	64%	61%	NM	66%	96%	101%	77%	82%	72%
Prices:High	20.19	18.78	17.40	28.49	31.85	30.00	27.94	30.81	29.44	26.69
Prices:Low	16.50	15.48	10.40	5.12	24.19	16.13	19.31	25.69	22.25	22.25
P/E Ratio:High	17	15	14	NM	14	19	20	17	17	14
P/E Ratio:Low	14	12	8	NM	11	10	14	14	13	12
Income Statement Analysis (Million $)										
Revenue	9,625	8,345	7,938	9,524	15,028	11,592	2,869	2,819	2,734	2,654
Depreciation	782	708	756	1,037	949	792	356	338	326	306
Maintenance	NA	NA	NA	NA	NA	NA	179	181	165	156
Fixed Charges Coverage	2.43	2.36	2.50	1.54	2.37	2.54	1.86	2.64	7.80	3.33
Construction Credits	0.88	33.6	NA	NA	NA	NA	7.00	15.8	16.6	18.9
Effective Tax Rate	25.8%	23.2%	23.7%	NM	28.2%	34.2%	22.8%	27.1%	29.0%	37.0%
Net Income	499	527	510	-1,661	785	546	224	282	237	275
S&P Core Earnings	472	498	417	-1,745	579	NA	NA	NA	NA	NA
Balance Sheet & Other Financial Data (Million $)										
Gross Property	24,054	23,160	22,371	29,119	31,770	25,000	13,478	11,049	10,460	8,741
Capital Expenditures	1,304	1,274	951	1,503	5,366	2,196	462	411	433	412
Net Property	14,696	14,096	13,667	18,816	21,165	15,273	8,146	6,020	5,759	4,338
Capitalization:Long Term Debt	5,898	6,493	6,519	7,044	12,612	8,060	3,653	2,051	1,879	1,593
Capitalization:% Long Term Debt	51.3	55.0	55.0	59.6	66.7	58.7	57.8	44.2	42.2	40.1
Capitalization:Preferred	105	105	105	105	105	105	104	105	200	240
Capitalization:% Preferred	0.91	0.89	0.89	0.89	0.56	0.76	1.65	2.26	4.50	6.10
Capitalization:Common	5,484	5,203	5,222	4,665	6,194	5,562	2,558	2,482	2,372	2,136
Capitalization:% Common	47.7	44.1	44.1	39.5	32.8	40.5	40.5	53.5	53.3	53.8
Total Capital	13,813	14,019	14,017	13,303	22,040	15,996	7,246	5,581	5,382	4,923
% Operating Ratio	98.6	88.8	88.1	78.0	87.1	87.0	85.9	85.6	85.0	86.2
% Earned on Net Property	13.0	7.8	8.0	13.0	10.7	11.2	4.8	6.2	NA	8.5
% Return on Revenue	5.2	6.3	6.4	NM	5.2	4.7	7.8	10.0	8.7	10.3
% Return on Invested Capital	6.9	7.0	7.3	12.4	10.9	10.3	7.5	11.5	9.2	10.5
% Return on Common Equity	9.2	10.1	10.1	NM	13.5	10.0	8.7	11.4	NA	12.6

Data as orig reptd.; bef. results of disc opers/spec. items. Per share data adj. for stk. divs.; EPS diluted. E-Estimated. NA-Not Available. NM-Not Meaningful. NR-Not Ranked. UR-Under Review.

Office: 800 Nicollet Mall, Minneapolis, MN 55402-5667.
Telephone: 612-330-5500.
Website: http://www.xcelenergy.com
Chrmn, Pres & CEO: R.C. Kelly

VP & CFO: B.G. Fowke, III
VP & Treas: G.E. Tyson, II
VP & Secy: C.J. Hart
VP & General Counsel: G.R. Johnson

Investor Contact: R.J. Kolkmann (612-215-4559)
Board of Directors: R. H. Anderson, C. C. Burgess, R. R. Hemminghaus, A. B. Hirschfeld, R. C. Kelly, D. W. Leatherdale, A. F. Moreno, M. R. Preska, A. P. Sampson, R. H. Truly

Founded: 1909
Domicile: Minnesota
Employees: 9,781

Xerox Corp

STANDARD &POOR'S

S&P Recommendation HOLD ★★★★★	Price	12-Mo. Target Price	Investment Style
	$16.70 (as of Oct 27, 2006)	$17.00	Large-Cap Value

GICS Sector Information Technology
Sub-Industry Office Electronics

Comment This company serves the document processing market worldwide, offering a complete line of copiers, electronic printers, and other office and computer equipment.

Key Stock Statistics (Source S&P, Vickers, company reports)

52-Wk Range	$16.95–13.16	S&P Oper. EPS 2006E	1.03	P/E on S&P Oper. EPS 2006E	16.2	Dividend Rate/Share	Nil
Trailing 12-Month EPS	$1.27	S&P Oper. EPS 2007E	1.12	Common Shares Outstg. (M)	993.1	Yield (%)	Nil
Trailing 12-Month P/E	13.2	S&P Core EPS 2006E	1.02	Market Capitalization(B)	$16.584	Beta	2.10
$10K Invested 5 Yrs Ago	$24,029	S&P Core EPS 2007E	1.10	Institutional Ownership (%)	80	S&P Credit Rating	BB+

Price Performance

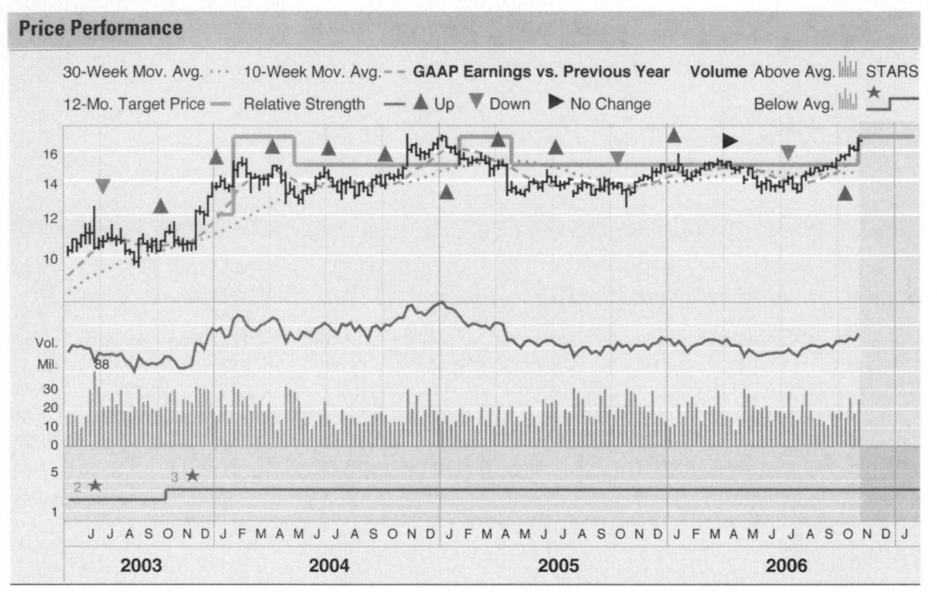

Options: ASE, CBOE, P, Ph

Analysis prepared by **Richard N. Stice, CFA** on October 25, 2006, when the stock traded at **$ 16.74**.

Highlights

- For 2007, we believe revenues should grow about 2%, and exceed $16 billion for the first time since 2001, compared with a projected 1% rise in 2006. We see this gradual turnaround as likely to result from a number of new product offerings, increasing penetration of color-based systems and documents and improving business conditions in developing markets.
- We see gross margins remaining near 41% in both 2006 and 2007. We expect benefits from higher volumes and new products to be largely offset by pricing and a less favorable business mix. We also anticipate results benefiting from additional share buybacks. At the end of the third quarter of 2006, XRX had $400 million remaining in its repurchase program.
- We forecast 2007 EPS of $1.12, up 8.7% from 2006's expected $1.03. Both estimates include our projection for stock option expense. Our 2006 and 2007 Standard & Poor's Core Earnings estimates are $1.02 and $1.10, respectively, reflecting anticipated pension costs.

Investment Rationale/Risk

- We believe the company's turnaround efforts have yielded positive results, with XRX having strengthened its balance sheet, reduced expenses, and bolstered its product offerings. However, we believe that there are several hurdles that the company needs to overcome. We think demand for office products, specifically high-end systems, remains lackluster, and we expect competition to intensify over the next 12 months. In addition, we still view debt levels as relatively high. As a result, we would not add to positions.
- Risks to our recommendation and target price include a more aggressive pricing environment and delays in the deployment of new products.
- Our 12-month target price of $17 is based on a combination of metrics. The first equates XRX with the S&P 500's 2007 P/E ratio and leads to a value of $16. The second, discounted cash flow analysis, calculates an intrinsic value of $19. Our assumptions include a weighted average cost of capital (WACC) of 10.7% and an expected terminal growth rate of 3%.

Qualitative Risk Assessment

LOW | **MEDIUM** | HIGH

Our risk assessment reflects XRX's strides in lowering its debt exposure, coupled with efforts to improve the balance of profitability in the company's product portfolio, in our opinion. However, in our view, this is offset by ongoing lackluster revenue growth.

Quantitative Evaluations

S&P Quality Ranking B

D | C | B- | **B** | B+ | A- | A | A+

Relative Strength Rank STRONG

81

LOWEST = 1 HIGHEST = 99

Revenue/Earnings Data

Revenue (Million $)

	1Q	2Q	3Q	4Q	Year
2006	3,695	3,977	3,844	--	--
2005	3,771	3,921	3,759	4,250	15,701
2004	3,827	3,853	3,716	4,326	15,722
2003	3,757	3,920	3,732	4,292	15,701
2002	3,858	3,952	3,793	4,246	15,849
2001	4,291	4,283	4,052	4,382	17,008

Earnings Per Share ($)

	1Q	2Q	3Q	4Q	Year
2006	0.20	0.26	0.54	E0.33	E1.03
2005	0.20	0.35	0.06	0.27	0.90
2004	0.17	0.21	0.17	0.24	0.78
2003	-0.10	0.09	0.11	0.22	0.36
2002	-0.07	0.12	0.04	0.01	0.10
2001	0.27	0.14	-0.05	-0.23	-0.17

Fiscal year ended Dec. 31. Next earnings report expected: Late January. EPS Estimates based on S&P Operating Earnings; historical GAAP earnings are as reported.

Dividend Data

Cash dividends were suspended in 2001.

Xerox Corp

Business Summary October 25, 2006

CORPORATE OVERVIEW. XRX competes in the monochrome (black and white) and color segments, and believes it can differentiate itself versus peers by providing what it believes to be the industry's broadest range of document products, solutions and services. In addition, XRX also provides software and solutions intended to help businesses easily print books or create personalized documents for customers. The company's services include operating in-house production centers, developing on-line document repositories and analyzing how customers can most efficiently create and share documents in the office.

In 2005, revenues from major segments were as follows: production 29%, office 49%, developing markets 11% and other 11%. These percentages were largely unchanged from 2004's breakdown.

The company has, and is likely to continue to have, a substantial amount of debt, partly because like other large technology hardware companies, it provides customer financing. By year-end 2005, XRX had more than $7 billion in total debt with more than $3 billion secured by finance receivables.

MARKET PROFILE. Xerox participates in an estimated $112 billion total market opportunity, which includes digital multifunction devices, as well as traditional copiers, printers, faxes, software, and supplies, and services. While the company has been experiencing what we view as lackluster revenue growth over the past several years, Xerox hopes to capitalize on a transition in the document industry away from older light lens devices to digital technology, a transition from black and white to color, and the management of publishing and printing jobs over the Internet. XRX has targeted key areas for growth, including color systems, the replacement of multiple single-function office devices with multifunction systems, and the transition of low-end offset printing to digital technology.

Company Financials

Per Share Data ($) Year Ended Dec. 31	**2005**	**2004**	**2003**	**2002**	**2001**	**2000**	**1999**	**1998**	**1997**	**1996**
Tangible Book Value	4.68	4.29	1.57	NM	0.52	2.86	4.79	4.76	5.54	5.79
Cash Flow	1.62	1.45	1.25	1.38	1.72	0.96	3.13	2.00	2.96	2.95
Earnings	0.90	0.78	0.36	0.10	-0.17	-0.44	1.96	0.80	2.02	1.75
S&P Core Earnings	0.88	0.75	0.53	-0.17	-1.33	NA	NA	NA	NA	NA
Dividends	Nil	Nil	Nil	Nil	0.05	0.65	0.78	0.70	0.64	0.58
Payout Ratio	Nil	Nil	Nil	Nil	NM	NM	40%	87%	32%	33%
Prices:High	17.02	17.24	13.89	11.45	11.35	29.31	63.94	60.81	44.00	29.13
Prices:Low	12.40	12.55	7.90	4.20	4.69	3.75	19.00	33.09	25.75	19.90
P/E Ratio:High	19	22	39	NM	NM	NM	33	76	22	17
P/E Ratio:Low	14	16	22	NM	NM	NM	10	41	13	11

Income Statement Analysis (Million $)										
Revenue	15,701	15,722	15,701	15,849	17,008	18,701	19,228	19,449	18,166	17,378
Operating Income	2,159	2,451	2,585	2,803	3,011	1,946	3,815	3,685	3,400	3,161
Depreciation	637	686	748	1,035	1,332	948	935	821	739	715
Interest Expense	326	708	362	401	457	605	547	570	520	513
Pretax Income	928	1,116	494	306	418	-323	2,104	837	2,268	1,821
Effective Tax Rate	NM	30.5%	27.1%	19.6%	NM	NM	30.0%	24.7%	32.1%	38.4%
Net Income	933	776	360	154	-109	-257	1,424	585	1,452	1,206
S&P Core Earnings	862	666	434	-128	-931	NA	NA	NA	NA	NA

Balance Sheet & Other Financial Data (Million $)										
Cash	1,322	3,218	2,477	2,887	3,990	1,741	126	79.0	75.0	104
Current Assets	8,736	10,928	10,335	11,019	12,600	13,022	11,985	12,475	10,766	10,152
Total Assets	21,953	24,884	24,591	25,458	27,689	29,475	28,814	30,024	27,732	26,818
Current Liabilities	4,346	6,300	7,569	7,787	10,260	6,268	7,950	8,507	7,692	7,204
Long Term Debt	6,765	7,767	8,739	11,485	11,815	16,042	11,632	11,505	9,416	8,424
Common Equity	6,319	6,244	3,291	1,893	1,820	3,493	4,911	4,857	4,985	4,985
Total Capital	13,973	14,900	13,418	14,001	14,313	20,323	17,339	17,173	15,233	14,355
Capital Expenditures	181	204	197	146	219	452	594	566	520	510
Cash Flow	1,512	1,389	1,037	1,116	1,209	638	2,305	1,350	2,134	1,921
Current Ratio	2.0	1.7	1.4	1.4	1.2	2.1	1.5	1.5	1.4	1.4
% Long Term Debt of Capitalization	48.4	52.1	65.1	82.0	82.5	78.9	67.1	67.0	61.8	58.7
% Net Income of Revenue	5.9	4.9	2.3	1.0	NM	NM	7.4	3.0	8.0	6.9
% Return on Assets	4.0	3.1	1.4	0.6	NM	NM	4.8	2.0	5.3	4.6
% Return on Equity	13.9	14.7	11.1	4.4	NM	NM	28.1	10.7	29.8	27.8

Data as orig reptd.; bef. results of disc opers/spec. items. Per share data adj. for stk. divs.; EPS diluted. E-Estimated. NA-Not Available. NM-Not Meaningful. NR-Not Ranked. UR-Under Review.

Office: 800 Long Ridge Road, Stamford, CT 06904-1600.
Telephone: 203-968-3000.
Website: http://www.xerox.com
Chrmn & CEO: A.M. Mulcahy

SVP & CFO: L.A. Zimmerman
VP & Chief Acctg Officer: G.R. Kabureck
VP & Treas: R.L. Seegal
VP, Secy & General Counsel: J.M. Farren

Investor Contact: J.H. Lesco
Board of Directors: G. A. Britt, R. Harrington, W. Hunter, V. E. Jordan, Jr., H. Kopper, R. S. Larsen, R. A. McDonald, A. M. Mulcahy, N. J. Nicholas, Jr., A. Reese, S. Robert

Founded: 1906
Domicile: New York
Employees: 55,220

Xilinx Inc

STANDARD &POOR'S

S&P Recommendation HOLD ★★★★★ | **Price** $25.51 (as of Oct 31, 2006) | **12-Mo. Target Price** $29.00 | **Investment Style** Mid-Cap Growth

GICS Sector Information Technology
Sub-Industry Semiconductors

Comment This California-based company is the world's largest supplier of programmable logic chips and related development system software.

Key Stock Statistics (Source S&P, Vickers, company reports)

52-Wk Range	**$29.98–18.35**	S&P Oper. EPS 2007**E**	**1.09**	P/E on S&P Oper. EPS 2007**E**	**23.4**	Dividend Rate/Share	**$0.36**
Trailing 12-Month EPS	**$1.06**	S&P Oper. EPS 2008**E**	**1.26**	Common Shares Outstg. (M)	**339.9**	Yield (%)	**1.41**
Trailing 12-Month P/E	**24.1**	S&P Core EPS 2007**E**	**1.08**	Market Capitalization(B)	**$8.670**	Beta	**2.59**
$10K Invested 5 Yrs Ago	**$7,823**	S&P Core EPS 2008**E**	**1.25**	Institutional Ownership (%)	**89**	S&P Credit Rating	**NA**

Price Performance

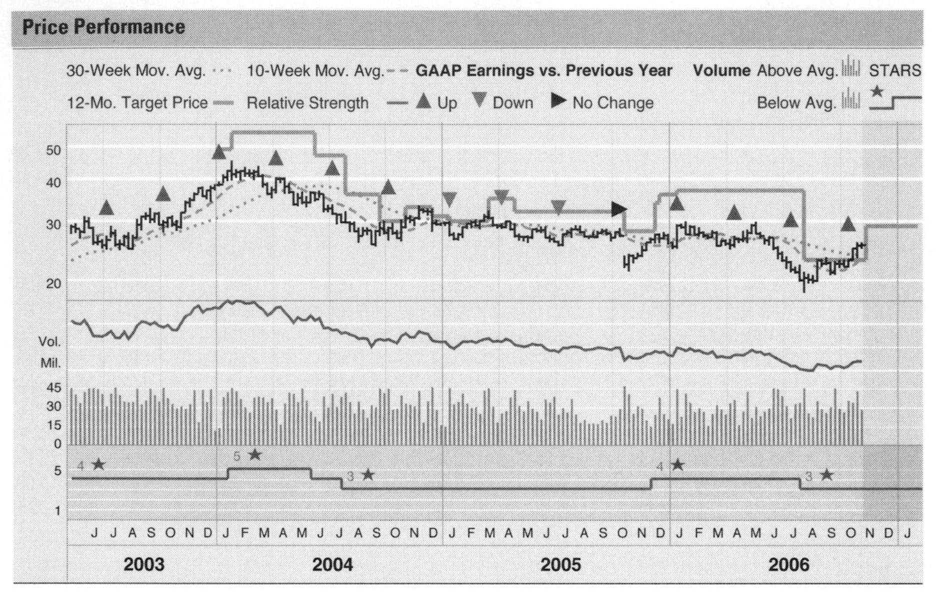

Options: ASE, CBOE, P

Analysis prepared by **Clyde Montevirgen** on October 31, 2006, when the stock traded at **$ 25.45**.

Highlights

- We project revenue growth of 12% in FY 07 (Mar.) and 13% in FY 08. We see some weak spots beginning to develop, especially for communication products, in a generally healthy sales environment. The company recently cautioned of lower visibility for the remainder of 2006 and of its relatively high level of expected turns-based business required to meet its guidance. Although we think that its guarded outlook and potential pricing pressure for older products indicate slower sales growth, we expect new products to yield above-industry growth over the next few years.
- We project gross margins of 61% in FY 07 and 62% in FY 08, versus 62% to 63% in the past three years. The company generally maintains fairly steady gross margins at relatively high levels compared to most semiconductor peers, partly reflecting its effective management of fixed cost by partnering with chip foundries, in our opinion. We look for operating margins of nearly 21% for FY 07 and 24% in FY 08.
- Including projected stock option expense, we forecast EPS of $1.09 for FY 07 and $1.26 for FY 08.

Investment Rationale/Risk

- We view the company as the market share leader in a category of semiconductors, namely programmable chips, that we expect to grow faster than the overall semiconductor industry growth pace of 8% that we project for calendar 2006. However, given the lackluster revenue performance in the first half of FY 07 and forecast risks from reduced visibility, we think valuation multiples will be subdued near term.
- Risks to our recommendation and target price include industry cyclicality, dependence on chip foundry partners for production, fluctuation in chip inventories, and reliance on stock-based compensation that we view as moderately high versus peers.
- Our 12-month target price of $29 is derived by applying a price to sales (P/S) multiple of 5X, at the low end of the historical range, to our 12-month forward sales estimate of $5.82. The shares generally trade at a premium P/S to most stocks in the S&P 500 but approximately in line with peers operating in rapid growth semiconductor niches.

Qualitative Risk Assessment

LOW | **MEDIUM** | HIGH

Our risk assessment reflects the cyclicality of the semiconductor industry, offset by the company's position as the largest competitor in a fast-growing niche, our view of its debt-free position, its diverse end markets, and its sharing of factory operations risk with chip foundry partners.

Quantitative Evaluations

S&P Quality Ranking **B**

D | C | B- | **B** | B+ | A- | A | A+

Relative Strength Rank **STRONG**

83

LOWEST = 1 HIGHEST = 99

Revenue/Earnings Data

Revenue (Million $)

	1Q	2Q	3Q	4Q	Year
2007	481.4	467.2	--	--	--
2006	405.4	398.9	449.6	472.3	1,726
2005	423.6	403.3	355.4	391.0	1,573
2004	313.3	315.6	365.6	403.4	1,398
2003	289.9	277.9	282.7	305.5	1,156
2002	289.3	224.7	228.1	273.5	1,016

Earnings Per Share ($)

	1Q	2Q	3Q	4Q	Year
2007	0.24	0.27	**E**0.28	**E**0.30	**E**1.09
2006	0.21	0.24	0.23	0.32	1.00
2005	0.26	0.24	0.18	0.19	0.87
2004	0.13	0.16	0.19	0.36	0.85
2003	0.12	0.11	-0.01	0.14	0.36
2002	0.05	-0.53	0.03	0.10	-0.34

Fiscal year ended Mar. 31. Next earnings report expected: Mid January. EPS Estimates based on S&P Operating Earnings; historical GAAP earnings are as reported.

Dividend Data (Dates: mm/dd Payment Date: mm/dd/yy)

Amount ($)	Date Decl.	Ex-Div. Date	Stk. of Record	Payment Date
0.070	01/19	02/06	02/08	03/01/06
0.090	04/26	05/08	05/10	05/31/06
0.090	07/25	08/14	08/16	09/06/06
0.090	10/20	11/13	11/15	12/06/06

Dividends have been paid since 2004. Source: Company reports.

Xilinx Inc

Business Summary October 31, 2006

Founded in 1984, Xilinx is the world's leading supplier of programmable logic devices based on market share. These devices, commonly known as PLD chips, include field programmable gate arrays (FPGAs) and complex programmable logic devices (CPLDs). They are standard integrated circuits (ICs) that are programmed by customers to perform desired logic operations. The company believes it provides high levels of integration and creates significant time and cost savings for electronic equipment manufacturers in the telecommunications, networking, computing and industrial markets.

FPGAs account for the vast majority of sales, but the company also derives revenue from development and system software tools, and field engineering support. In FY 06 (Mar.), revenues were derived 41% from North America (42% in FY 05), 20% (21%) from Europe, 15% (14%) from Japan, and 24% (23%) from Asia Pacific and other regions.

XLNX's FPGAs are proprietary ICs designed by the company; they provide a combination of the high logic density usually associated with custom gate arrays, the time-to-market advantages of programmable logic, and the availability of a standard product. The company has several product families, including the XC4000, Coolrunner, Spartan and Virtex lines. The Virtex-II Pro product line, introduced in March 2002, is a platform for programmable systems, enabling very high-bandwidth system-on-a-chip designs with the flexibility and low development cost of programmable logic.

Company products are classified as new, mainstream, base and support. New products accounted for 32% of FY 06 sales (18% in FY 05), mainstream products 47% (58%), base products 15% (18%), and support products 6% (6%).

Company Financials

Per Share Data ($) Year Ended Mar. 31	**2006**	**2005**	**2004**	**2003**	**2002**	**2001**	**2000**	**1999**	**1998**	**1997**
Tangible Book Value	7.53	7.24	6.79	5.44	5.26	5.82	5.68	2.82	1.89	1.67
Cash Flow	1.19	1.05	1.05	0.57	-0.02	0.36	2.03	0.52	0.50	0.43
Earnings	1.00	0.87	0.85	0.36	-0.34	0.10	1.90	0.42	0.40	0.35
S&P Core Earnings	0.78	0.58	0.57	0.05	-0.31	0.35	NA	NA	NA	NA
Dividends	0.28	0.20	Nil	Nil	Nil	Nil	Nil	Nil	Nil	Nil
Payout Ratio	28%	23%	Nil	Nil	Nil	Nil	Nil	Nil	Nil	Nil
Calendar Year	2005	2004	2003	2002	2001	2000	1999	1998	1997	1996
Prices:High	32.30	45.40	39.20	47.15	59.25	98.31	48.56	16.75	14.63	11.63
Prices:Low	21.25	25.21	18.50	13.50	19.52	35.25	15.31	7.44	7.13	6.13
P/E Ratio:High	32	47	46	NM	NM	NM	26	40	37	33
P/E Ratio:Low	21	26	22	NM	NM	NM	8	18	18	18
Income Statement Analysis (Million $)										
Revenue	1,726	1,573	1,398	1,156	1,016	1,659	1,021	662	614	568
Operating Income	489	442	412	283	87.3	568	371	214	207	192
Depreciation	69.5	63.1	67.9	72.5	106	93.5	44.2	32.1	32.7	28.0
Interest Expense	Nil	Nil	Nil	Nil	0.06	0.17	Nil	11.9	13.9	14.6
Pretax Income	457	401	351	170	-193	61.1	1,030	184	183	166
Effective Tax Rate	22.4%	21.9%	13.6%	26.0%	NM	42.3%	36.7%	29.8%	30.9%	33.4%
Net Income	354	313	303	126	-114	35.3	652	129	127	110
S&P Core Earnings	277	205	204	18.1	-103	132	NA	NA	NA	NA
Balance Sheet & Other Financial Data (Million $)										
Cash	783	449	337	214	230	209	85.5	53.6	167	216
Current Assets	1,648	1,466	1,302	1,175	999	1,102	1,041	658	600	602
Total Assets	3,174	3,039	2,937	2,422	2,335	2,502	2,349	1,070	941	848
Current Liabilities	345	298	381	314	196	350	245	167	126	97.3
Long Term Debt	Nil	Nil	Nil	Nil	Nil	Nil	Nil	Nil	250	250
Common Equity	2,729	2,674	2,483	1,951	1,904	1,918	1,777	879	550	491
Total Capital	2,821	2,741	2,556	2,108	2,140	2,152	2,104	903	816	751
Capital Expenditures	67.0	61.4	41.0	46.0	94.9	223	144	40.9	29.7	26.8
Cash Flow	424	376	371	198	-7.51	129	697	161	159	138
Current Ratio	4.8	4.9	3.4	3.7	5.1	3.1	4.3	3.9	4.8	6.2
% Long Term Debt of Capitalization	Nil	Nil	Nil	Nil	Nil	Nil	Nil	Nil	30.6	33.3
% Net Income of Revenue	20.5	19.8	21.7	10.9	NM	2.1	63.9	19.5	20.6	19.4
% Return on Assets	11.4	10.5	11.3	5.3	NM	1.5	38.2	12.9	14.2	14.1
% Return on Equity	13.1	12.1	13.7	6.5	NM	1.9	49.1	18.1	24.3	25.7

Data as orig reptd.; bef. results of disc opers/spec. items. Per share data adj. for stk. divs.; EPS diluted. E-Estimated. NA-Not Available. NM-Not Meaningful. NR-Not Ranked. UR-Under Review.

Office: 2100 Logic Drive, San Jose, CA, USA 95124-3400.
Telephone: 408-559-7778.
Email: ir@xilinx.com
Website: http://www.xilinx.com

Chrmn, Pres & CEO: W.P. Roelandts
VP & CFO: J.A. Olson
VP, Secy & General Counsel: T.R. Lavelle

Auditor: Ernst & Young
Board of Directors: J. L. Doyle, J. G. Fishman, P. T. Gianos, W. G. Howard, Jr., J. M. Patterson, W. P. Roelandts, E. W. Vanderslice

Founded: 1984
Domicile: Delaware
Employees: 3,295

STANDARD &POOR'S

XL Capital Ltd

S&P Recommendation HOLD ★★★★★	Price	12-Mo. Target Price	Investment Style
	$70.82 (as of Oct 27, 2006)	$72.00	Large-Cap Value

GICS Sector Financials
Sub-Industry Property & Casualty Insurance

Comment Bermuda-based XL, which originally provided excess liability coverage, has expanded into providing reinsurance and other risk management services.

Key Stock Statistics (Source S&P, Vickers, company reports)

52-Wk Range	$74.44–59.82	S&P Oper. EPS 2006E	8.45	P/E on S&P Oper. EPS 2006E	8.4	Dividend Rate/Share	$1.52
Trailing 12-Month EPS	$1.23	S&P Oper. EPS 2007E	9.05	Common Shares Outstg. (M)	180.4	Yield (%)	2.15
Trailing 12-Month P/E	57.6	S&P Core EPS 2006E	8.02	Market Capitalization(B)	$12.777	Beta	0.68
$10K Invested 5 Yrs Ago	$9,032	S&P Core EPS 2007E	8.87	Institutional Ownership (%)	99	S&P Credit Rating	NA

Price Performance

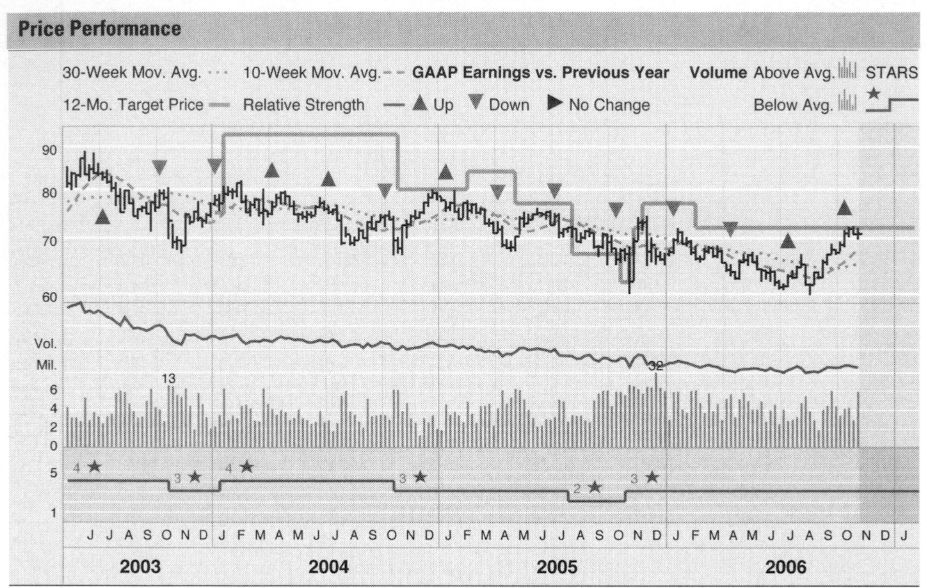

Options: CBOE, P, Ph

Analysis prepared by **Cathy A. Seifert** on September 28, 2006, when the stock traded at **$ 69.07**.

Highlights

- We believe earned premium growth in 2006 will be driven by a sharp rise in life and annuity premiums and increased contributions from the (smaller) financial operations unit, partly offset by an expected decline in core property-casualty earned premiums amid a competitive pricing environment. Premium growth in 2007 in the property-casualty space is predicated on XL's ability to leverage opportunities for growth, particularly in certain property-based and energy lines.
- Net investment income growth in 2006 will likely not be as strong as the 43% rise in 2005, but should remain in the double digits.
- The turnaround in per share operating results that we see for 2006 (an $8.45 profit, versus the $10.86 a share loss in 2005) is skewed by after-tax catastrophe losses of nearly $1.9 billion in 2005; and by an after-tax, fourth quarter charge of $834.2 million related to certain post-closing actuarial adjustments related to its 2001 acquisition of Winterthur International.

Investment Rationale/Risk

- Our hold opinion on the shares reflects our concern that XL's level and exposure to catastrophe losses appears outsized to its market share. Despite this exposure to storm losses, XL's book of business remains skewed toward casualty lines of coverage, where pricing remains competitive. We are also concerned that reserves levels in certain lines may not be adequate.
- Risks to our opinion and target price include a deterioration in underwriting results; and the uncertainty over the numerous regulatory investigations of the industry currently under way.
- Our 12-month target price of $72 assumes that the shares continue to trade at a discount of approximately 20% to 30% from the peer group average. Our target price also assumes the shares trade at 1.5X estimated 2006 tangible book. This represents a discount to the overall peer group average. We believe this discount is warranted, in light of our view of the relatively higher than industry average risk profile of XL's business mix.

Qualitative Risk Assessment

LOW	MEDIUM	HIGH

Our risk assessment reflects our view of XL as an opportunistic underwriter capable of leveraging opportunities for growth, offset by our concerns about XL's exposure to catastrophe losses and the adequacy of its loss reserves in certain liability lines of business.

Quantitative Evaluations

S&P Quality Ranking B-

D	C	B-	B	B+	A-	A	A+

Relative Strength Rank MODERATE

61

LOWEST = 1 HIGHEST = 99

Revenue/Earnings Data

Revenue (Million $)

	1Q	2Q	3Q	4Q	Year
2006	2,473	2,499	2,364	--	--
2005	2,401	4,108	2,296	2,479	11,285
2004	2,157	3,179	2,370	2,390	10,028
2003	1,792	1,892	1,969	2,363	8,017
2002	1,165	1,168	2,340	1,942	6,578
2001	767.1	791.7	845.0	1,654	4,057

Earnings Per Share ($)

2006	2.56	2.10	2.32	E2.27	E8.45
2005	3.18	0.97	-7.53	-5.51	-9.14
2004	3.25	2.62	0.16	2.07	8.13
2003	1.74	2.51	0.71	-2.29	2.69
2002	0.65	-0.68	1.34	1.56	2.88
2001	1.73	1.01	-6.70	-0.64	-4.55

Fiscal year ended Dec. 31. Next earnings report expected: Early February. EPS Estimates based on S&P Operating Earnings; historical GAAP earnings are as reported.

Dividend Data (Dates: mm/dd Payment Date: mm/dd/yy)

Amount ($)	Date Decl.	Ex-Div. Date	Stk. of Record	Payment Date
0.380	01/27	03/13	03/15	03/31/06
0.380	04/28	06/08	06/12	06/30/06
0.380	07/26	09/07	09/11	09/29/06
0.380	10/27	12/07	12/11	12/29/06

Dividends have been paid since 1992. Source: Company reports.

XL Capital Ltd

Business Summary September 28, 2006

Bermuda-based XL was formed in 1986 by a consortium of Fortune 500 companies to provide excess liability coverage. Since then, XL has expanded (mostly via acquisitions) to include insurance, reinsurance, and other financial services. Insurance net written premiums of $4.25 billion were divided: professional liability 36%, casualty 27%, marine/energy/aviation/satellite 17%, property 14%, property catastrophe 2%, and other 4%. Reinsurance net written premiums of $5.01 billion were divided: life and annuity 45%, casualty 16%, property 14%, professional liability 7%, catastrophe 6%, marine/energy/aviation/satellite 4%, and other 8%. Financial services neat earned premiums of $254.1 million were divided: financial guaranty 68%, political risk 10%, and other 22%.

Insurance business written includes general liability, as well as other specialized types of liability coverage, such as directors' and officers' liability and professional and employment practices liability. An array of property coverage, as well as marine and aviation insurance, and surety coverage, is also underwritten. Reinsurance business written includes treaty and facultative reinsurance to primary insurers of casualty risk. The financial services unit provides insurance and reinsurance solutions for complex financial risks.

In July 2001, the company acquired Winterthur International, for about $330.2 million in cash (as adjusted). As part of the transaction, XL received certain post-closing arrangements protecting it against (among other things) certain types of adverse loss development. XL valued the post-closing payment at $1.45 billion and Winterthur Swiss Insurance Co. (the seller) believed the post-closing payment is $541 million. In December 2005, an independent actuarial review concluded that Winterthur's estimate were closer than those submitted by XL. As a result of this difference, XL recorded a fourth quarter 2005 after-tax charge of $834.2 million.

Company Financials

Per Share Data ($) Year Ended Dec. 31	**2005**	**2004**	**2003**	**2002**	**2001**	**2000**	**1999**	**1998**	**1997**	**1996**
Tangible Book Value	37.08	42.55	37.07	36.13	28.35	31.86	30.91	29.67	26.20	24.27
Operating Earnings	NA	NA	NA	5.10	-3.67	4.52	3.63	4.36	3.95	3.14
Earnings	-9.14	8.13	2.69	2.88	-4.55	4.03	3.62	6.20	7.84	5.39
Dividends	2.00	1.96	1.92	1.88	1.84	1.80	1.76	1.64	1.36	0.95
Payout Ratio	NM	24%	71%	65%	NM	45%	49%	26%	17%	18%
Prices:High	79.80	82.00	88.87	98.48	96.50	89.25	75.75	84.00	65.19	40.25
Prices:Low	60.03	66.70	63.49	58.45	61.50	39.00	41.94	59.13	36.88	29.81
P/E Ratio:High	NM	10	33	34	NM	22	21	14	8	7
P/E Ratio:Low	NM	8	24	20	NM	10	12	10	5	6

Income Statement Analysis (Million $)										
Premium Income	2,238	1,406	6,969	5,990	3,476	2,035	1,750	685	541	518
Net Investment Income	1,475	995	780	735	563	542	525	279	217	199
Other Revenue	8,064	7,426	268	-147	18.0	140	236	253	402	265
Total Revenue	11,285	10,028	8,017	6,578	4,057	2,717	2,511	1,218	1,159	982
Pretax Income	-1,194	1,260	451	442	-764	451	431	594	682	497
Net Operating Income	NA	NA	NA	701	-465	NA	NA	NA	NA	288
Net Income	-1,252	1,167	412	406	-576	506	471	588	677	494

Balance Sheet & Other Financial Data (Million $)										
Cash & Equivalent	4,085	2,631	2,698	3,785	2,044	1,074	669	503	395	308
Premiums Due	4,842	4,934	4,847	4,833	2,182	1,120	1,126	690	363	345
Investment Assets:Bonds	32,310	25,100	19,494	14,483	10,832	8,605	7,581	5,213	3,417	2,961
Investment Assets:Stocks	869	963	583	575	548	557	1,136	1,129	838	812
Investment Assets:Loans	Nil	Nil	Nil	Nil	Nil	Nil	Nil	Nil	Nil	Nil
Investment Assets:Total	38,171	30,066	22,821	17,956	13,741	10,472	9,768	6,616	4,255	3,733
Deferred Policy Costs	866	845	778	688	394	309	276	98.0	22.0	30.0
Total Assets	58,455	49,015	40,764	35,647	27,963	16,942	15,091	10,109	6,088	5,032
Debt	3,413	2,721	1,905	1,878	1,605	450	411	Nil	Nil	Nil
Common Equity	14,078	12,286	10,171	6,569	5,437	5,574	5,577	4,818	2,479	2,116
Property & Casualty:Loss Ratio	107.1	68.6	75.3	68.0	105.0	70.4	69.1	57.0	67.6	78.3
Property & Casualty:Expense Ratio	25.8	27.4	27.3	29.0	34.9	36.4	34.3	26.3	18.2	15.3
Property & Casualty Combined Ratio	132.9	96.0	102.6	97.0	139.9	106.8	103.4	83.3	85.8	93.6
% Return on Revenue	NM	11.9	5.2	6.0	NM	18.6	19.9	48.3	77.2	50.3
% Return on Equity	NM	10.0	3.9	6.6	NM	9.1	8.4	16.1	29.5	24.0

Data as orig reptd.; bef. results of disc opers/spec. items. Per share data adj. for stk. divs.; EPS diluted. E-Estimated. NA-Not Available. NM-Not Meaningful. NR-Not Ranked. UR-Under Review.

Office: XL House, One Bermudiana Rd, Hamilton, Bermuda HM 11.
Telephone: 441-292-8515.
Website: http://www.xlcapital.com
Chrmn: M.P. Esposito, Jr.

Pres & CEO: B.M. O'Hara
COO: H.C. Keeling
EVP, CFO & Treas: J.M. de St. Paer
EVP & General Counsel: C.F. Barr

Investor Contact: D.R. Radulski (441-294-7460)
Board of Directors: D. Comey, M. P. Esposito, Jr., R. R. Glauber, H. Haag, J. Mauriello, E. M. McQuade, B. M. O'Hara, R. S. Parker, C. E. Rance, A. Z. Senter, J. T. Thornton, E. E. Thrower

Founded: 1986
Domicile: Cayman Islands
Employees: 3,600

STANDARD &POOR'S

XTO Energy Inc.

S&P Recommendation BUY ★★★★★

Price $46.52 (as of Oct 27, 2006)

12-Mo. Target Price $52.00

Investment Style Large-Cap Growth

GICS Sector Energy
Sub-Industry Oil & Gas Exploration & Production

Comment This producer of natural gas, coal bed methane and crude oil is engaged in the acquisition and development of long-lived properties across the U.S.

Key Stock Statistics (Source S&P, Vickers, company reports)

52-Wk Range	$50.01–36.51	S&P Oper. EPS 2006E	4.00	P/E on S&P Oper. EPS 2006E	11.6	Dividend Rate/Share	$0.30
Trailing 12-Month EPS	$5.10	S&P Oper. EPS 2007E	5.15	Common Shares Outstg. (M)	365.7	Yield (%)	0.64
Trailing 12-Month P/E	9.1	S&P Core EPS 2006E	4.00	Market Capitalization(B)	$17.014	Beta	0.53
$10K Invested 5 Yrs Ago	$59,585	S&P Core EPS 2007E	5.15	Institutional Ownership (%)	78	S&P Credit Rating	BBB

Price Performance

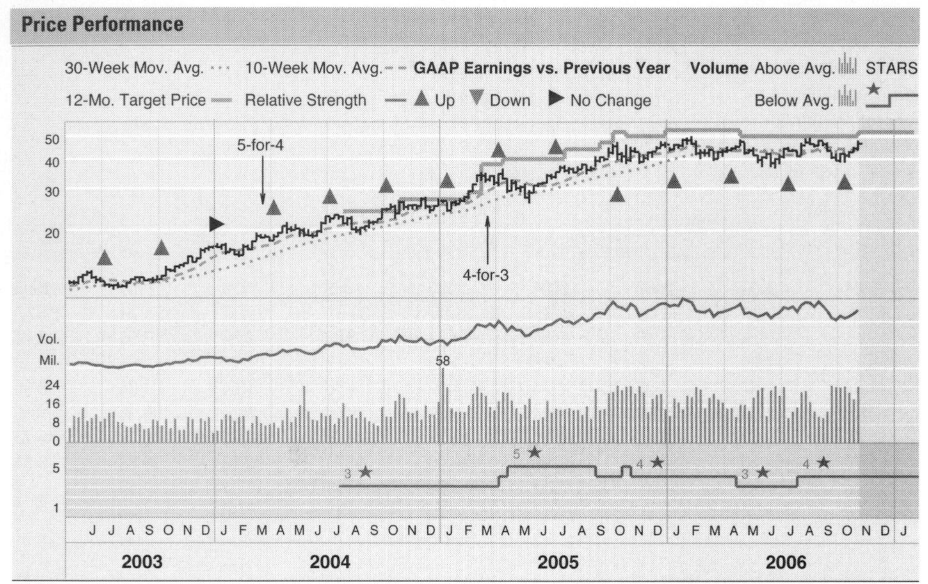

Options: ASE, CBOE, P, Ph

Analysis prepared by **Charles LaPorta, CFA** on October 26, 2006, when the stock traded at **$ 47.27**.

Highlights

- Third quarter operating EPS was $0.94, versus $0.85 last year, above our estimate of $0.80. Production increased 3.6% sequentially and is expected to grow about 14% in 2006. This strong performance is being driven by tremendous success in the Freestone Trend and Barnett Shale Texas plays. In addition, XTO continues to increase production in its long-held Permian Basin assets.
- Per-unit production costs declined sequentially, due to lower severance taxes, lower power and field fuel costs. The company has continued a high level of drilling activity, currently operating about 72 rigs, with particular emphasis on the Freestone Trend in East Texas and the Barnett Shale. SG&A expenses were down to normalized levels this quarter, after large option expenses in the second quarter, but should trend back to first quarter levels for the remainder of the year.
- EBITDA before exploration expenses (EBITDAX) is expected to total $3.5 billion in 2006, on strong volume growth and with attractive hedges. We expect interest expense to increase about $30 million versus last year, due to continued acquisition activity.

Investment Rationale/Risk

- In our view, XTO continues to grow successfully through acquisitions, maintains above-average production growth at a relatively low cost, and has long-lived reserves with a strong replacement rate. At year end, natural gas represented 80% of total reserves, and 69% of reserves were proved developed. XTO's 2006 development capital budget is $1.7 billion. Long-term debt was 40.4% of total book capitalization as of September 30, 2006.
- Risks to our recommendation and target price include the possibility that XTO could make an aggressively priced and financed acquisition. In addition, the purchase of coal bed methane properties from ChevronTexaco is a new area for the company.
- EPS grew at a five-year compound annual growth rate of 30% through 2005, and we expect this trend to continue in 2006. Given our view of the company's superior growth metrics, we believe XTO deserves a premium valuation. Our 12-month target price of $52 is based on an enterprise value of 5.3X our 2007 EBITDA estimate.

Qualitative Risk Assessment

LOW	MEDIUM	**HIGH**

XTO operates in a very capital intensive industry that is cyclical and derives value from producing a commodity with a volatile price. Magnifying the inherent risk in this industry, XTO has utilized an aggressive growth through acquisition strategy, and maintains relatively high financial leverage.

Quantitative Evaluations

S&P Quality Ranking B+

D	C	B-	B	**B+**	A-	A	A+

Relative Strength Rank STRONG

76

LOWEST = 1 HIGHEST = 99

Revenue/Earnings Data

Revenue (Million $)

	1Q	2Q	3Q	4Q	Year
2006	1,215	1,066	1,096	--	--
2005	628.9	748.7	964.2	1,177	3,519
2004	394.8	444.8	507.4	600.7	1,948
2003	253.5	282.2	322.1	331.9	1,190
2002	180.0	189.2	201.7	239.3	810.2
2001	249.2	209.0	197.3	183.3	838.8

Earnings Per Share ($)

	1Q	2Q	3Q	4Q	Year
2006	1.26	1.62	0.99	**E**1.07	**E**4.00
2005	0.47	0.60	0.85	1.22	3.15
2004	0.30	0.30	0.40	0.50	1.52
2003	0.23	0.19	0.33	0.20	0.95
2002	0.16	0.12	0.18	0.20	0.66
2001	0.17	0.33	0.25	0.15	1.06

Fiscal year ended Dec. 31. Next earnings report expected: Early February. EPS Estimates based on S&P Operating Earnings; historical GAAP earnings are as reported.

Dividend Data (Dates: mm/dd Payment Date: mm/dd/yy)

Amount ($)	Date Decl.	Ex-Div. Date	Stk. of Record	Payment Date
0.075	02/21	03/29	03/31	04/13/06
0.075	05/16	06/28	06/30	07/14/06
0.075	08/15	09/27	09/29	10/13/06

Dividends have been paid since 1993. Source: Company reports.

Please read the Required Disclosures and Analyst Certification on the last page of this report.

XTO Energy Inc.

Business Summary October 26, 2006

CORPORATE OVERVIEW. XTO Energy (formerly Cross Timbers Oil Co.) produces and markets natural gas, natural gas liquids (NGLs) and crude oil predominantly from its southwestern and central U.S. properties, most of which XTO operates. The company has achieved production and proved reserve growth generally through producing property acquisitions, followed by development. Development activities are usually funded by cash flow from operating activities. Funding sources for acquisitions include proceeds from sales of public equity and debt, bank borrowings, cash flow from operating activities, or a combination of these sources.

As of December 31, 2005, the company's proved oil and gas reserves were up 30%, year to year, to 7.62 trillion cubic feet equivalent (Tcfe), for a reserve-to-production index of 16.3 years. During 2005, XTO replaced 274% of production via extensions, additions and discoveries. Proved natural gas reserves at 2005 year end were up 29% from the level a year earlier, to 6.08 trillion cubic feet (Tcf) (66% developed). Proved crude oil and natural gas liquids (NGL) reserves were 134% higher, at 256 million barrels (bbl.) (80% developed).

PRIMARY BUSINESS DYNAMICS. XTO's addressable market is the North American continent. As a large onshore natural gas producer, XTO competes in a fragmented market that is beginning to rationalize, in our view, with several large onshore players such as Devon Energy (DVN) and Chesapeake Energy (CHK). We believe North America is a relatively mature supply source for hydrocarbons, and natural gas production has been relatively flat over the past seven years. XTO has been one of the most active consolidators of onshore U.S. natural gas assets, having purchased 3.26 Tcfe of reserves for $4.8 billion over the past five years for a per proved acquisition cost of $1.48. XTO has created value through acquisitions by employing so-called unconventional resource recovery techniques, in our opinion. Such unconventional plays include basin-centered tight gas formations, coal-bed methane formations, and fractured shale formations, which are characterized by a low proportion of exploration capital expenditures resulting in relatively low risk resource acquisition capability. In our view, the main driver of value in these resource plays is development of repeatable drilling techniques, increasing productivity organically and moving reserves characterized as probable and possible to the proven category.

Company Financials

Per Share Data ($) Year Ended Dec. 31	2005	2004	2003	2002	2001	2000	1999	1998	1997	1996
Tangible Book Value	11.01	5.62	4.70	3.22	2.98	1.82	1.02	0.67	0.72	0.59
Cash Flow	5.04	2.06	1.90	1.40	1.64	1.58	0.64	0.06	0.36	0.29
Earnings	3.15	1.52	0.95	0.66	1.06	0.46	0.19	-0.33	0.12	0.10
S&P Core Earnings	3.01	1.41	0.91	0.65	0.90	NA	NA	NA	NA	NA
Dividends	0.24	0.09	0.02	0.02	0.02	0.01	0.01	0.02	0.03	0.03
Payout Ratio	8%	6%	3%	3%	2%	2%	7%	NM	25%	27%
Prices:High	47.61	27.66	17.58	11.88	9.78	8.70	3.03	4.23	3.83	2.56
Prices:Low	23.87	15.35	10.21	6.61	5.54	1.51	0.91	1.01	1.97	1.39
P/E Ratio:High	15	18	19	18	9	19	16	NM	32	26
P/E Ratio:Low	8	10	11	10	5	3	5	NM	17	14

Income Statement Analysis (Million $)	2005	2004	2003	2002	2001	2000	1999	1998	1997	1996
Revenue	3,519	1,948	1,190	810	839	601	341	249	201	161
Operating Income	2,198	1,338	801	550	611	398	208	124	114	85.9
Depreciation, Depletion and Amortization	655	407	284	204	154	260	112	83.6	47.7	37.9
Interest Expense	153	93.7	63.8	53.6	55.6	78.9	64.2	52.1	26.7	17.2
Pretax Income	1,810	826	445	287	455	176	70.6	-106	39.2	31.0
Effective Tax Rate	36.4%	38.5%	35.5%	35.1%	35.6%	33.7%	33.9%	NM	34.5%	34.4%
Net Income	1,152	508	287	186	293	117	46.7	-69.8	25.7	20.3
S&P Core Earnings	1,098	476	275	183	249	NA	NA	NA	NA	NA

Balance Sheet & Other Financial Data (Million $)	2005	2004	2003	2002	2001	2000	1999	1998	1997	1996
Cash	2.00	9.70	7.00	15.0	6.81	7.44	5.73	12.3	3.82	3.94
Current Assets	943	437	261	245	239	193	113	138	52.2	51.8
Total Assets	9,857	6,110	3,611	2,648	2,132	1,592	1,477	1,208	788	523
Current Liabilities	884	501	321	286	202	219	74.2	99.6	54.9	52.0
Long Term Debt	3,109	2,043	1,252	1,118	856	769	991	921	539	315
Common Equity	4,209	2,599	1,466	908	821	470	249	149	142	114
Total Capital	7,318	5,398	3,144	2,312	1,876	1,349	1,395	1,105	730	468
Capital Expenditures	1,621	1,905	654	358	225	45.6	270	296	257	114
Cash Flow	1,807	915	571	390	448	375	157	12.0	71.6	57.6
Current Ratio	1.1	0.9	0.8	0.9	1.2	0.9	1.5	1.4	1.0	1.0
% Long Term Debt of Capitalization	42.5	37.8	39.8	48.4	45.6	57.0	71.1	83.3	73.8	67.3
% Return on Assets	14.4	10.4	9.2	7.8	15.8	7.6	3.5	NM	3.9	4.4
% Return on Equity	33.8	25.0	24.1	21.5	45.4	32.0	21.3	NM	18.7	16.2

Data as orig reptd.; bef. results of disc opers/spec. items. Per share data adj. for stk. divs.; EPS diluted. E-Estimated. NA-Not Available. NM-Not Meaningful. NR-Not Ranked. UR-Under Review.

Office: 810 Houston St, Fort Worth, TX 76102.
Telephone: 817-870-2800.
Email: investor_relations@xtoenergy.com
Website: http://www.xtoenergy.com

Chrmn & CEO: B.R. Simpson
Pres: K.A. Hutton
Sr EVP: V.O. Vennerberg, II
EVP & CFO: L.G. Baldwin

Investor Contact: G.D. Simpson
Board of Directors: W. H. Adams, III, L. G. Baldwin, L. G. Collins, K. A. Hutton, P. R. Kevil, T. L. Petrus, J. P. Randall, S. G. Sherman, H. D. Simons, B. R. Simpson, V. O. Vennerberg, II

Founded: 1986
Domicile: Delaware
Employees: 1,680

Yahoo! Inc

STANDARD &POOR'S

S&P Recommendation HOLD ★★★★★

Price $26.34 (as of Oct 31, 2006)

12-Mo. Target Price $28.00

Investment Style Large-Cap Growth

GICS Sector Information Technology
Sub-Industry Internet Software & Services

Comment This company is one of the world's largest providers of online content and services.

Key Stock Statistics (Source S&P, Vickers, company reports)

52-Wk Range	**$43.66–22.65**	S&P Oper. EPS 2006E	**0.47**	P/E on S&P Oper. EPS 2006E	**56.0**	Dividend Rate/Share	**Nil**
Trailing 12-Month EPS	**$0.79**	S&P Oper. EPS 2007E	**0.62**	Common Shares Outstg. (M)	**1,381.2**	Yield (%)	**Nil**
Trailing 12-Month P/E	**33.3**	S&P Core EPS 2006E	**0.47**	Market Capitalization(B)	**$36.380**	Beta	**2.36**
$10K Invested 5 Yrs Ago	**$42,023**	S&P Core EPS 2007E	**0.62**	Institutional Ownership (%)	**77**	S&P Credit Rating	**BBB-**

Price Performance

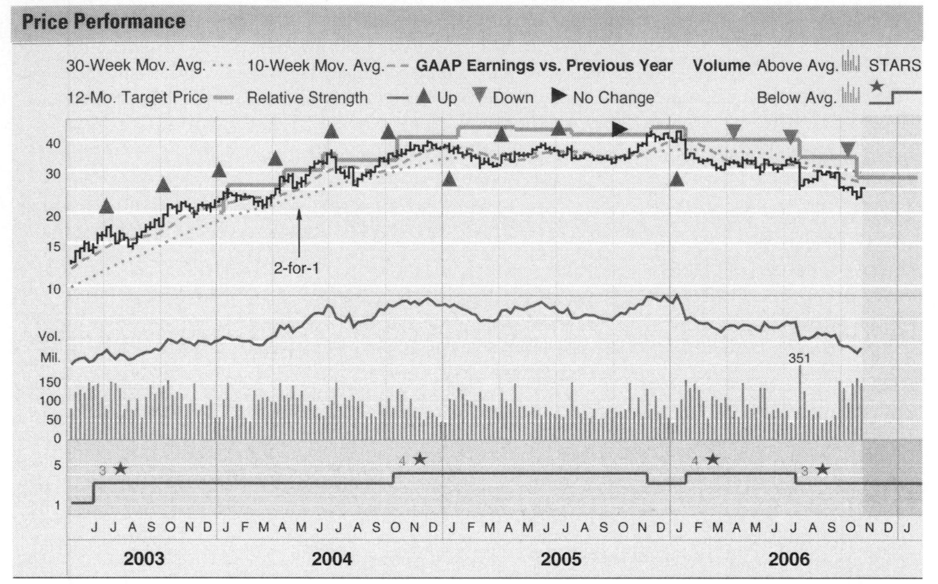

Options: ASE, CBOE, P, Ph

Analysis prepared by **Scott H. Kessler** on October 31, 2006, when the stock traded at **$ 25.95**.

Highlights

- We see revenues, excluding traffic acquisition costs, rising 23% in 2006 and 25% in 2007. We expect YHOO to benefit from increasing online users and usage, connection speeds, and corporate spending on Internet advertising. We believe it will become increasingly focused on, and successful at, combining sales of both display and search advertising, and domestic and international advertising.
- We expect marketing services revenues (87% of 2006 third quarter revenues) to continue to benefit from secular growth in branded and keyword advertising. We think fee revenues (13%) will be bolstered by YHOO's co-branded Internet access services with broadband providers in the U.S., the U.K. and Canada.
- We project that annual EBITDA and net margins will narrow in 2006, reflecting decelerating revenue growth, and notable product and technology investments, and trend higher in 2007. We believe the $3 billion stock repurchase announced in March 2005 will bolster EPS. Notable anticipated stock option expenses are included in our EPS projections.

Investment Rationale/Risk

- We believe growth in online advertising will remain healthy, as marketers likely commit an increasing percentage of their advertising budgets to the Internet. We think YHOO's market leadership and broad international footprint have appeal. However, the prior delayed launch of its search-technology upgrade, and the failure to significantly capitalize on trends such as social networking and online video, have negatively impacted fundamentals, in our view.
- Risks to our recommendation and target price include increasing competition in online advertising and services. As a result of Microsoft's (MSFT: hold, $28) introduction of a search advertising offering, it ended its sponsored search partnership with YHOO in mid-2006.
- Our DCF model's assumptions include a discount rate of 13.6%, annual growth in free cash flow averaging 21% from 2006 to 2010, and a perpetuity growth rate of 3%, and yields an intrinsic value estimate of $22. We believe YHOO's minority stakes in Yahoo Japan, China's Alibaba.com, and South Korea's Gmarket are worth about $8. Accounting for a modest discount, our 12-month target price is $28.

Qualitative Risk Assessment

LOW | MEDIUM | **HIGH**

The company is a large and well capitalized leader in a number of areas related to Internet content and services. However, in our view, the markets in which it participates change rapidly, and have relatively low barriers to entry, which have contributed to the notable competition we have observed.

Quantitative Evaluations

S&P Quality Ranking **B**

D | C | B- | **B** | B+ | A- | A | A+

Relative Strength Rank **MODERATE**

32

LOWEST = 1 HIGHEST = 99

Revenue/Earnings Data

Revenue (Million $)

	1Q	2Q	3Q	4Q	Year
2006	1,567	1,576	1,580	--	--
2005	1,174	1,253	1,330	1,501	5,258
2004	757.8	832.3	906.7	1,078	3,575
2003	283.0	321.4	356.8	663.9	1,625
2002	192.7	225.8	248.8	285.8	953.1
2001	180.2	182.2	166.1	188.9	717.4

Earnings Per Share ($)

2006	0.11	0.11	0.11	E0.13	E0.47
2005	0.14	0.51	0.17	0.46	1.28
2004	0.07	0.08	0.17	0.25	0.58
2003	0.04	0.04	0.05	0.06	0.19
2002	0.01	0.02	0.03	0.04	0.09
2001	-0.01	-0.05	-0.02	-0.01	-0.08

Fiscal year ended Dec. 31. Next earnings report expected: Mid January. EPS Estimates based on S&P Operating Earnings; historical GAAP earnings are as reported.

Dividend Data

No cash dividends have been paid.

Please read the Required Disclosures and Analyst Certification on the last page of this report.

Yahoo! Inc

Business Summary October 31, 2006

CORPORATE OVERVIEW. Yahoo! is one of the world's largest Internet companies, providing offerings in 15 languages in more than 20 countries, regions and territories. Primary categories for its properties and services are Search and Marketplace (focused on areas including search, yellow pages, maps, real estate, shopping, auctions, travel, autos, HotJobs, and small business); Information and Content (The Yahoo! Front Page; My Yahoo!; Yahoo! Toolbar; news and information related to finance, health, sports and entertainment; music; games; and Yahooligans! for kids); and Communications and Consumer Services (premium Internet packages, e-mail, instant messaging, photo-sharing, community services, and dating services). YHOO's worldwide registered users (excluding Yahoo! Japan, Alibaba.com, and Gmarket; as of December 2005, YHOO owned only 34% of Yahoo! Japan and 40% of Alibaba.com, and as of June 2006, it owned 10% of Gmarket) grew to 418 million as of September 2006, from 350 million a year earlier. Active registered users rose to 215 million, from 185 million. Yahoo! China was divested as part of an October 2005 joint venture agreement (as a result, YHOO owns a minority stake in Alibaba).

MARKET PROFILE. Forrester Research estimates that U.S. online advertising and marketing spending will increase from $12.0 billion in 2004 to $26.0 billion in 2010 (average annual growth of 14%). During this period, online advertising and marketing spending is expected to increase from 5% to 8% as a percentage of overall advertising and marketing spending. We believe the U.S. accounts for roughly two-thirds of the market, and will grow to closer to half of it in 2010. That means YHOO's worldwide market opportunity in the category will exceed $50 billion by 2010, in our view. We expect YHOO's Marketing Services segment to account for over 85% of the company's revenues for the foreseeable future.

Company Financials

Per Share Data ($) Year Ended Dec. 31	**2005**	**2004**	**2003**	**2002**	**2001**	**2000**	**1999**	**1998**	**1997**	**1996**
Tangible Book Value	3.59	2.94	1.64	1.47	1.52	1.69	1.11	0.62	0.16	0.16
Cash Flow	1.54	0.79	0.31	0.18	0.03	0.11	0.09	0.04	-0.03	-0.00
Earnings	1.28	0.58	0.19	0.09	-0.08	0.06	0.05	0.03	-0.03	-0.00
S&P Core Earnings	0.56	0.24	0.03	-0.32	-0.85	NA	NA	NA	NA	NA
Dividends	Nil	Nil	Nil	Nil	Nil	Nil	Nil	Nil	Nil	Nil
Payout Ratio	Nil	Nil	Nil	Nil	Nil	Nil	Nil	Nil	Nil	Nil
Prices:High	43.45	39.79	22.74	10.68	21.69	125.03	112.00	35.75	4.44	1.79
Prices:Low	30.30	20.57	8.25	4.47	4.01	12.53	27.50	3.60	0.70	0.54
P/E Ratio:High	34	69	NM	NM	NM	NM	NM	NM	NM	NM
P/E Ratio:Low	24	35	NM	NM	NM	NM	NM	NM	NM	NM

Income Statement Analysis (Million $)	2005	2004	2003	2002	2001	2000	1999	1998	1997	1996
Revenue	5,258	3,575	1,625	953	717	1,110	589	203	67.4	19.1
Operating Income	1,505	1,000	455	198	34.5	390	197	58.4	-0.95	-6.40
Depreciation	397	311	160	109	131	69.1	42.3	10.2	2.55	0.39
Interest Expense	Nil	Nil	Nil	Nil	Nil	Nil	Nil	Nil	Nil	Nil
Pretax Income	2,672	1,280	391	180	-81.1	264	104	43.3	-23.6	-2.30
Effective Tax Rate	28.7%	34.2%	37.6%	39.7%	NM	71.2%	39.0%	41.1%	NM	NM
Net Income	1,896	840	238	107	-92.8	70.8	61.1	25.6	-22.9	-2.30
S&P Core Earnings	840	353	35.5	-377	-966	NA	NA	NA	NA	NA

Balance Sheet & Other Financial Data (Million $)	2005	2004	2003	2002	2001	2000	1999	1998	1997	1996
Cash	2,561	3,512	1,310	774	926	1,120	872	433	156	92.5
Current Assets	3,450	4,090	1,722	970	1,052	1,291	946	467	107	97.6
Total Assets	10,832	9,178	5,932	2,790	2,379	2,270	1,470	622	142	110
Current Liabilities	1,204	1,181	708	412	359	311	192	80.0	23.5	7.70
Long Term Debt	750	750	750	Nil	Nil	Nil	Nil	Nil	Nil	Nil
Common Equity	8,566	7,101	4,363	2,262	1,967	1,897	1,261	536	118	102
Total Capital	9,316	7,896	5,151	2,294	1,997	1,926	1,265	540	118	102
Capital Expenditures	409	246	117	51.6	86.2	94.4	49.5	11.9	6.60	2.40
Cash Flow	2,293	1,151	398	216	37.8	140	103	35.8	-20.3	-1.91
Current Ratio	2.9	3.5	2.4	2.4	2.9	4.1	4.9	5.8	4.6	12.6
% Long Term Debt of Capitalization	8.0	9.5	14.6	Nil	Nil	Nil	Nil	Nil	Nil	Nil
% Net Income of Revenue	36.0	23.5	14.6	11.2	NM	6.4	10.3	12.6	NM	NM
% Return on Assets	18.9	11.1	5.5	4.1	NM	3.7	5.4	6.7	NM	NM
% Return on Equity	24.2	14.6	7.2	5.1	NM	4.5	6.3	7.8	NM	NM

Data as orig reptd.; bef. results of disc opers/spec. items. Per share data adj. for stk. divs.; EPS diluted. E-Estimated. NA-Not Available. NM-Not Meaningful. NR-Not Ranked. UR-Under Review.

Office: 701 First Avenue, Sunnyvale, CA 94089.
Telephone: 408-349-3300.
Email: investor_relations@yahoo-inc.com
Website: http://www.yahoo.com

Chrmn & CEO: T.S. Semel
COO: D. Rosensweig
EVP & CFO: S.L. Decker
EVP & CTO: F. Nazem

SVP & Chief Acctg Officer: M. Murray
Investor Contact: C. La Rocca (408-349-5188)
Board of Directors: R. Bostock, R. W. Burkle, E. Hippeau, V. Joshi, A. Kern, R. Kotick, E. R. Kozel, T. Semel, G. L. Wilson, J. Yang

Founded: 1995
Domicile: Delaware
Employees: 9,800

STANDARD &POOR'S

YUM! Brands Inc.

S&P Recommendation HOLD ★★★★★

Price $58.96 (as of Oct 27, 2006)

12-Mo. Target Price $59.00

Investment Style Large-Cap Growth

GICS Sector Consumer Discretionary
Sub-Industry Restaurants

Comment YUM is the world's largest fast-food business, with more than 34,000 units, including the KFC, Pizza Hut and Taco Bell chains.

Key Stock Statistics (Source S&P, Vickers, company reports)

52-Wk Range	$61.84–44.21	S&P Oper. EPS 2006E	2.96	P/E on S&P Oper. EPS 2006E	19.9	Dividend Rate/Share	$0.60
Trailing 12-Month EPS	$2.87	S&P Oper. EPS 2007E	3.28	Common Shares Outstg. (M)	265.1	Yield (%)	1.02
Trailing 12-Month P/E	20.5	S&P Core EPS 2006E	2.89	Market Capitalization(B)	$15.629	Beta	0.20
$10K Invested 5 Yrs Ago	$24,411	S&P Core EPS 2007E	3.28	Institutional Ownership (%)	81	S&P Credit Rating	BBB

Price Performance

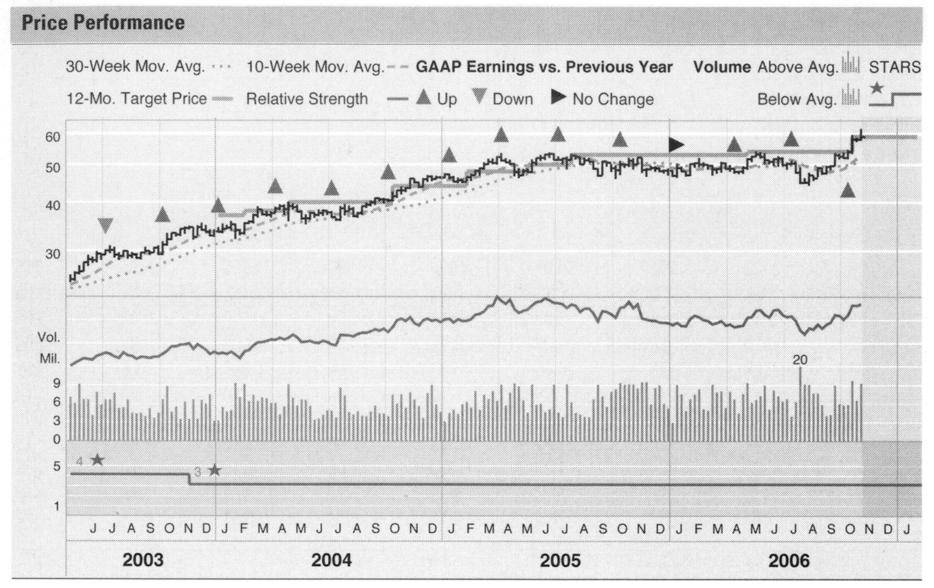

Options: ASE, CBOE, Ph

Highlights

➤ The 12-month target price for YUM has recently been changed to $59.00 from $54.00. The Highlights section of this Stock Report will be updated accordingly.

Investment Rationale/Risk

➤ The Investment Rationale/Risk section of this Stock Report will be updated shortly. For the latest News story on YUM from MarketScope, see below.

➤ 10/12/06 03:38 pm EDT... S&P REITERATES HOLD RECOMMENDATION ON SHARES OF YUM BRANDS (YUM 58.81***): Sep-Q EPS of $0.83 vs. $0.72 before one-time items, is $0.05 above our estimate. Results benefited from international expansion, lower food costs, reduced corporate costs, and significant share buybacks. We are raising our '06 EPS estimate $0.07 to $2.96 and our 12-month target price $5 to $59, to reflect lower projected operating costs and improved profitability of international operations. At nearly 20X our '06 EPS estimate, YUM is trading at a slight premium to fast-food peers. We believe this valuation adequately reflects strong international growth prospects. / D.Milton

Qualitative Risk Assessment

LOW | **MEDIUM** | HIGH

YUM competes in the relatively stable fast food industry, in which its concepts possesses a very strong brand name presence, in our view. However, operating margins can vary widely due to fluctuations in food costs. Furthermore, YUM's profits can be impacted by changing currency exchange rates due to its large international business.

Quantitative Evaluations

S&P Quality Ranking B+

D | C | B- | B | **B+** | A- | A | A+

Relative Strength Rank STRONG

86

LOWEST = 1 HIGHEST = 99

Revenue/Earnings Data

Revenue (Million $)

	1Q	2Q	3Q	4Q	Year
2006	2,085	2,182	2,278	--	--
2005	2,054	2,153	2,243	2,899	9,349
2004	1,970	2,077	2,179	2,785	9,011
2003	1,802	1,936	1,989	2,653	8,380
2002	1,614	1,767	1,915	2,461	7,757
2001	1,506	1,605	1,640	2,202	6,953

Earnings Per Share ($)

2006	0.59	0.68	0.83	E0.86	E2.96
2005	0.50	0.59	0.69	0.77	2.55
2004	0.47	0.58	0.61	0.77	2.42
2003	0.39	0.40	0.53	0.70	2.02
2002	0.40	0.45	0.47	0.56	1.88
2001	0.29	0.38	0.41	0.54	1.62

Fiscal year ended Dec. 31. Next earnings report expected: Early February. EPS Estimates based on S&P Operating Earnings; historical GAAP earnings are as reported.

Dividend Data (Dates: mm/dd Payment Date: mm/dd/yy)

Amount ($)	Date Decl.	Ex-Div. Date	Stk. of Record	Payment Date
0.115	11/18	01/11	01/13	02/03/06
0.115	03/16	04/11	04/14	05/05/06
0.150	05/18	07/12	07/14	08/04/06
0.150	09/14	10/11	10/13	11/03/06

Dividends have been paid since 2004. Source: Company reports.

YUM! Brands Inc.

Business Summary July 24, 2006

Yum! Brands has the world's largest quick service restaurant (QSR) system, with more than 34,000 restaurants in more than 100 countries and territories. The company operates and franchises restaurants under the KFC, Pizza Hut, Taco Bell, Long John Silver's and A&W All American Food concepts. In 2005, the company's brands generated nearly $30.0 billion in systemwide sales and $9.3 billion in worldwide revenues, up 3.8% from 2004.

KFC (originally Kentucky Fried Chicken) is the leader in the U.S. chicken QSR segment, with about a 45% market share. At the end of 2005, it operated 5,443 units in the U.S. and 8,288 units internationally. Systemwide sales totaled approximately $5.2 billion in the U.S. and $13.2 billion worldwide 2005.

Pizza Hut is the world's largest restaurant chain specializing in ready-to-eat pizza products. As of December 2005, it operated 7,566 units in the U.S. and 5,006 units internationally, and led the U.S. pizza QSR segment with about a 15% market share. Systemwide sales totaled $5.3 billion in the U.S. and $9.1 billion worldwide in 2005.

Taco Bell is the leader in the U.S. Mexican food QSR segment, with about a 65% market share. At the end of 2005, it operated 5,845 units in the U.S. and 245 units internationally. Systemwide sales totaled $6.2 billion in the U.S. and $6.4 billion worldwide in 2005.

In each concept, units are operated by the company as well as by independent franchisees, licensees, or unconsolidated affiliates. Over the past several years, YUM rebalanced its system toward increased franchisee ownership, to focus resources on growth opportunities. At the end of 2005, 22% of worldwide units were operated by YUM , 66% by franchisees, 7% by licensees, and 5% by unconsolidated affiliates. Company-owned units accounted for 88% of total revenues in 2005.

In 2005, international operations accounted for 37% of total revenues, up from 36% in 2004. At the end of 2005, the company had 13,805 total units in operation outside the U.S. The company's largest international markets include China, Japan, Great Britain, Canada, Australia, and Korea.

Company Financials

Per Share Data ($) Year Ended Dec. 31	**2005**	**2004**	**2003**	**2002**	**2001**	**2000**	**1999**	**1998**	**1997**	**1996**
Tangible Book Value	2.09	2.40	0.83	NM	NM	NM	NM	NM	NA	NM
Cash Flow	4.13	3.90	3.33	3.07	2.78	2.57	3.17	2.76	1.40	NM
Earnings	2.55	2.42	2.02	1.88	1.62	1.39	1.96	1.42	-0.37	0.43
S&P Core Earnings	2.52	2.30	2.08	1.60	1.37	NA	NA	NA	NA	NA
Dividends	0.43	0.20	Nil	Nil	Nil	Nil	Nil	Nil	Nil	NA
Payout Ratio	17%	8%	Nil	Nil	Nil	Nil	Nil	Nil	Nil	NA
Prices:High	53.79	47.47	35.41	33.17	26.66	19.28	36.94	25.44	18.13	NA
Prices:Low	44.74	32.13	21.54	20.35	15.78	11.78	17.50	12.53	13.94	NA
P/E Ratio:High	21	20	18	18	16	14	19	18	NM	NA
P/E Ratio:Low	18	13	11	11	10	8	9	9	NM	NA
Income Statement Analysis (Million $)										
Revenue	9,349	9,011	8,380	7,757	6,953	7,093	7,822	8,468	9,681	9,838
Operating Income	1,538	1,518	1,471	1,375	1,220	1,217	1,280	1,185	1,198	NA
Depreciation	469	448	401	370	354	354	386	417	536	NA
Interest Expense	127	129	173	172	158	176	202	272	276	NA
Pretax Income	1,026	1,026	886	858	733	684	1,038	756	-35.0	308
Effective Tax Rate	25.7%	27.9%	30.2%	32.1%	32.9%	39.6%	39.6%	41.1%	NM	57.5%
Net Income	762	740	618	583	492	413	627	445	-111	131
S&P Core Earnings	754	704	635	494	416	NA	NA	NA	NA	NA
Balance Sheet & Other Financial Data (Million $)										
Cash	158	62.0	192	130	110	133	89.0	121	268	157
Current Assets	837	747	806	730	547	688	486	625	683	819
Total Assets	5,698	5,696	5,620	5,400	4,388	4,149	3,961	4,531	5,098	5,976
Current Liabilities	1,605	1,376	1,461	1,520	1,805	1,216	1,298	1,473	1,579	1,382
Long Term Debt	1,649	1,731	2,056	2,299	1,552	2,397	2,391	3,436	4,551	4,674
Common Equity	1,449	1,595	1,120	594	104	-322	-560	-1,163	-1,620	-835
Total Capital	3,098	3,326	3,176	2,893	1,656	2,085	1,838	2,338	2,964	4,139
Capital Expenditures	609	645	663	760	636	572	470	460	541	NA
Cash Flow	1,231	1,188	1,019	953	846	767	1,013	862	425	NA
Current Ratio	0.5	0.5	0.6	0.5	0.3	0.6	0.4	0.4	0.4	0.6
% Long Term Debt of Capitalization	53.2	52.0	64.7	79.5	93.7	115.0	130.1	147.0	153.5	113.0
% Net Income of Revenue	8.2	8.2	7.4	7.5	7.1	5.8	8.0	5.3	NM	1.3
% Return on Assets	13.4	13.1	11.2	11.9	11.5	10.2	14.8	9.2	NM	NM
% Return on Equity	50.1	54.5	72.1	167.0	NM	NM	NM	NM	NM	NM

Data as orig reptd.; bef. results of disc opers/spec. items. Per share data adj. for stk. divs.; EPS diluted. E-Estimated. NA-Not Available. NM-Not Meaningful. NR-Not Ranked. UR-Under Review.

Office: 1441 Gardiner Lane, Louisville, KY 40213.
Telephone: 502-874-8300.
Email: yum.investors@yum.com
Website: http://www.yum.com

Chrmn & CEO: D.C. Novak
COO: G. Creed
SVP & CFO: R. Carucci
SVP, Secy & General Counsel: C.L. Campbell

SVP & Cntlr: T.F. Knopf
Investor Contact: Q. Nghe (888-298-6986)
Board of Directors: D. Dorman, M. Ferragamo, J. D. Grissom, B. G. Hill, R. Holland, Jr., K. G. Langone, J. Linen, T. C. Nelson, D. C. Novak, A. E. Pearson, T. M. Ryan, J. Trujillo, R. J. Ulrich

Auditor: KPMG
Founded: 1997
Domicile: North Carolina
Employees: 272,000

Zimmer Holdings Inc.

STANDARD &POOR'S

S&P Recommendation HOLD ★★★★★	**Price** $71.24 (as of Oct 27, 2006)	**12-Mo. Target Price** $70.00	**Investment Style** Large-Cap Growth

GICS Sector Health Care
Sub-Industry Health Care Equipment

Comment This company, spun off by Bristol-Myers Squibb in August 2001, manufactures orthopedic reconstructive implants and fracture management products.

Key Stock Statistics (Source S&P, Vickers, company reports)

52-Wk Range	$73.25–52.20	S&P Oper. EPS 2006E	3.32	P/E on S&P Oper. EPS 2006E	21.5	Dividend Rate/Share	Nil
Trailing 12-Month EPS	$3.19	S&P Oper. EPS 2007E	3.80	Common Shares Outstg. (M)	242.7	Yield (%)	Nil
Trailing 12-Month P/E	22.3	S&P Core EPS 2006E	3.32	Market Capitalization(B)	$17.293	Beta	0.04
$10K Invested 5 Yrs Ago	$24,557	S&P Core EPS 2007E	3.80	Institutional Ownership (%)	74	S&P Credit Rating	BBB+

Price Performance

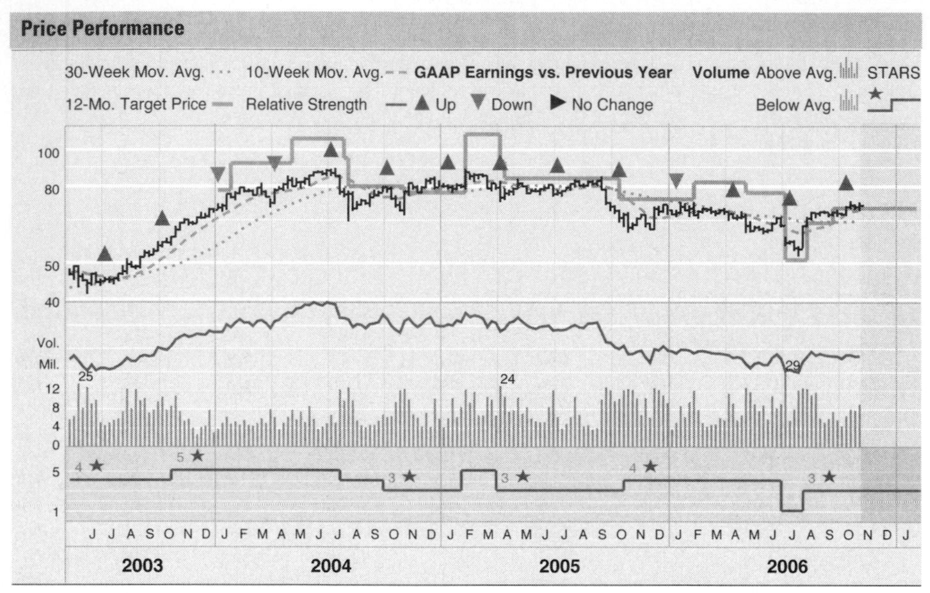

Analysis prepared by **Robert M. Gold** on September 15, 2006, when the stock traded at **$ 68.17**.

Highlights

- We see 2006 revenues approximating $3.5 billion, which assumes an approximate 1% decline in global orthopedic implant pricing and contributions from the expected launch of several new products in the second half of the year. Some of the new product launches envisioned in 2006 include a trabecular metal shoulder implant, revision system and hip stem, a ceramic-on-ceramic hip system, and some new trauma products. Looking to 2007, we think sales will reach $3.9 billion, including significant contributions from a new knee implant designed specifically for women.
- Given pricing pressures we see across many key product categories in 2006, we think ZMH faces challenges on its gross margin line. However, we believe new product launches, if successful, have the potential to drive modestly higher gross margins in the second half. We recently boosted our SG&A spending estimate to account for legal costs incurred from the U.S. Department of Justice (DOJ) investigation.
- We see 2006 operating EPS of $3.34, including $0.25 of estimated stock option costs. For 2007, we project that EPS will reach $3.80, after $0.20 of estimated stock option expense.

Investment Rationale/Risk

- We think pricing in the global orthopedic implant categories will be flat to slightly negative in 2006 and 2007. However, an expanding DOJ investigation into possible anti-competitive practices in the orthopedic device industry could, in our view, potentially result in additional pressure on U.S. unit pricing.
- Risks to our recommendation and target price include unfavorable Medicare reimbursement changes, an adverse outcome to a government investigation and greater-than-expected device reimbursement cuts in key overseas markets.
- Based on recent comments made by Zimmer and other orthopedic device companies in our coverage universe, we believe the highly publicized DOJ investigations may be much more narrow in scope than originally feared. Our 12-month target price is $70, or approximately 18.4X our 2007 EPS estimate and 4.5X estimated 2007 sales per share, slightly discounted to orthopedic device peers, which we believe is justified by a lower projected growth rate. However, we think valuations in the orthopedics area will gain support from reduced investor concerns over the DOJ probes and improving visibility on unit pricing trends.

Qualitative Risk Assessment

LOW | **MEDIUM** | HIGH

Zimmer operates in a highly competitive industry characterized by relatively short product life cycles, thereby requiring a significant number of new product introductions to maintain market share and sustain gross profit margins. Many of the company's customers are reimbursed by the federal government through Medicare, and a more restrictive budgetary environment could, in our view, result in lower prices paid to medical device suppliers such as Zimmer. However, we believe the company stands among the more dominant manufacturers in the orthopedic device industry, with substantial global sales force capabilities and an expansive product line.

Quantitative Evaluations

S&P Quality Ranking **NR**

D | C | B- | B | B+ | A- | A | A+

Relative Strength Rank **MODERATE**

64

LOWEST = 1 HIGHEST = 99

Revenue/Earnings Data

Revenue (Million $)

	1Q	2Q	3Q	4Q	Year
2006	860.4	881.6	819.8	--	--
2005	828.5	846.8	762.5	848.3	3,286
2004	742.2	737.4	700.2	801.1	2,981
2003	390.1	411.1	398.2	701.6	1,901
2002	319.1	345.6	337.5	370.2	1,372
2001	286.0	294.3	286.7	311.6	1,179

Earnings Per Share ($)

2006	0.82	0.81	0.76	E0.93	E3.32
2005	0.70	0.76	0.67	0.80	2.93
2004	0.40	0.47	0.52	0.81	2.19
2003	0.41	0.45	0.43	0.15	1.38
2002	0.28	0.34	0.33	0.37	1.31
2001	0.16	0.22	0.14	0.22	0.77

Fiscal year ended Dec. 31. Next earnings report expected: Late January. EPS Estimates based on S&P Operating Earnings; historical GAAP earnings are as reported.

Dividend Data

No cash dividends have been paid.

Zimmer Holdings Inc.

Business Summary September 15, 2006

CORPORATE OVERVIEW. Zimmer Holdings primarily designs, develops, manufactures and markets orthopedic reconstructive implants and fracture management products. The former division of Bristol-Myers Squibb was spun off to BMY shareholders in August 2001.

Zimmer's reconstructive implants (83% of 2005 sales) are used to restore function lost due to disease or trauma in joints such as knees, hips, shoulders and elbows. The company offers a wide range of products for specialized knee procedures, including The NexGen Complete Knee Solution, NexGen Legacy, NexGen Revision Knee, Innex Total Knee System, M/G Unicompartmental Knee System, and Prolong Highly Crosslinked Polyethylene Articular Surface material. Hip replacement products include the VerSys Hip System, the ZMR Hip System, the Trilogy Acetabular System and a line of specialty hip products. The company also continues to develop a portfolio of minimally invasive hip replacement procedures. ZMH also sells the Coonrad/Morrey product line of elbow replacement implant products, along with a line of restorative dental products.

In the spine/trauma area (10%), the company sells devices used to reattach or stabilize damaged bone and tissue to support the body's natural healing process. The most common stabilization of bone fractures involves the internal fixation of bone fragments, which can involve the use of an assortment of plates, screws, rods, wires and pins. ZMH offers a line of products designed for use in fracture fixation.

ZMH makes and markets other orthopedic surgical products (7%) used by surgeons for orthopedic as well as non-orthopedic procedures. Products include tourniquets, blood management systems, wound debridgement products, powered surgical instruments, pain management devices, and orthopedic soft goods that provide support and/or heat retention and compression for trauma of the knee, ankle, back and upper extremities, including the shoulder, elbow, neck and wrist.

Company Financials

Per Share Data ($) Year Ended Dec. 31	2005	2004	2003	2002	2001	2000	1999	1998	1997	1996
Tangible Book Value	7.94	2.52	0.38	1.88	0.41	NM	NA	NA	NA	NA
Cash Flow	3.68	2.92	1.87	1.43	0.89	0.92	NA	NA	NA	NA
Earnings	2.93	2.19	1.38	1.31	0.77	0.81	NA	NA	NA	NA
S&P Core Earnings	2.73	2.08	1.31	1.24	0.70	NA	NA	NA	NA	NA
Dividends	Nil	Nil	Nil	Nil	Nil	NA	NA	NA	NA	NA
Payout Ratio	Nil	Nil	Nil	Nil	Nil	NA	NA	NA	NA	NA
Prices:High	89.10	89.44	71.85	43.00	33.30	NA	NA	NA	NA	NA
Prices:Low	60.19	64.40	38.02	28.00	24.70	NA	NA	NA	NA	NA
P/E Ratio:High	30	41	52	33	43	NA	NA	NA	NA	NA
P/E Ratio:Low	21	29	28	21	32	NA	NA	NA	NA	NA

Income Statement Analysis (Million $)	2005	2004	2003	2002	2001	2000	1999	1998	1997	1996
Revenue	3,286	2,981	1,901	1,372	1,179	1,041	NA	NA	NA	NA
Operating Income	1,297	1,026	633	426	272	291	NA	NA	NA	NA
Depreciation	186	181	103	25.0	23.4	23.0	NA	NA	NA	NA
Interest Expense	14.0	32.0	13.0	12.0	7.40	29.0	NA	NA	NA	NA
Pretax Income	1,040	732	438	389	241	239	NA	NA	NA	NA
Effective Tax Rate	29.5%	25.9%	33.6%	33.7%	37.8%	34.3%	NA	NA	NA	NA
Net Income	733	542	291	258	150	157	NA	NA	NA	NA
S&P Core Earnings	682	515	277	244	137	NA	NA	NA	NA	NA

Balance Sheet & Other Financial Data (Million $)	2005	2004	2003	2002	2001	2000	1999	1998	1997	1996
Cash	233	155	78.0	16.0	18.4	50.0	NA	NA	NA	NA
Current Assets	1,576	1,561	1,339	612	509	487	NA	NA	NA	NA
Total Assets	5,722	5,696	5,156	859	745	669	NA	NA	NA	NA
Current Liabilities	607	701	645	401	373	217	NA	NA	NA	NA
Long Term Debt	82.0	624	1,008	Nil	214	500	NA	NA	NA	NA
Common Equity	4,683	3,943	3,143	366	78.7	-48.0	NA	NA	NA	NA
Total Capital	4,767	4,574	4,158	366	293	452	NA	NA	NA	NA
Capital Expenditures	105	101	45.0	34.0	54.7	NA	NA	NA	NA	NA
Cash Flow	919	723	394	283	173	180	NA	NA	NA	NA
Current Ratio	2.6	2.2	2.1	1.5	1.4	2.2	NA	NA	NA	NA
% Long Term Debt of Capitalization	1.7	13.6	24.2	Nil	73.0	110.6	NA	NA	NA	NA
% Net Income of Revenue	22.3	18.1	15.3	18.9	12.7	15.1	NA	NA	NA	NA
% Return on Assets	12.8	9.9	9.7	32.1	22.4	NA	NA	NA	NA	NA
% Return on Equity	16.9	15.2	10.6	115.0	NM	NA	NA	NA	NA	NA

Data as orig reptd.; bef. results of disc opers/spec. items. Per share data adj. for stk. divs.; EPS diluted. E-Estimated. NA-Not Available. NM-Not Meaningful. NR-Not Ranked. UR-Under Review.

Office: 345 East Main Street, Warsaw, IN 46580.
Telephone: 574-267-6131.
Email: zimmer.infoperson@zimmer.com
Website: http://www.zimmer.com

Chrmn, Pres & CEO: J.R. Elliott
Investor Contact: S.R. Leno (574-372-4790)
EVP & CFO: S.R. Leno
SVP & CSO: C.R. Blanchard

SVP, Chief Acctg Officer & Cntlr: J.T. Crines
Board of Directors: J. R. Elliott, S. M. Essig, L. C. Glasscock, J. L. McGoldrick, A. A. White, III

Founded: 1927
Domicile: Delaware
Employees: 6,700

Zions BanCorp

STANDARD &POOR'S

S&P Recommendation HOLD ★★★★★

Price $80.08 (as of Oct 27, 2006)

12-Mo. Target Price $88.00

Investment Style Mid-Cap Value

GICS Sector Financials
Sub-Industry Regional Banks

Comment ZION has some 470 full-service banking offices in 10 western states. At December 31, 2005, it had assets of $42.8 billion and deposits of $32.6 billion.

Key Stock Statistics (Source S&P, Vickers, company reports)

52-Wk Range	$85.25–72.39	S&P Oper. EPS 2006E	5.52	P/E on S&P Oper. EPS 2006E	14.5	Dividend Rate/Share	$1.44
Trailing 12-Month EPS	$5.36	S&P Oper. EPS 2007E	6.12	Common Shares Outstg. (M)	106.7	Yield (%)	1.80
Trailing 12-Month P/E	14.9	S&P Core EPS 2006E	5.52	Market Capitalization(B)	$8.543	Beta	0.70
$10K Invested 5 Yrs Ago	$18,062	S&P Core EPS 2007E	6.12	Institutional Ownership (%)	54	S&P Credit Rating	BBB+

Price Performance

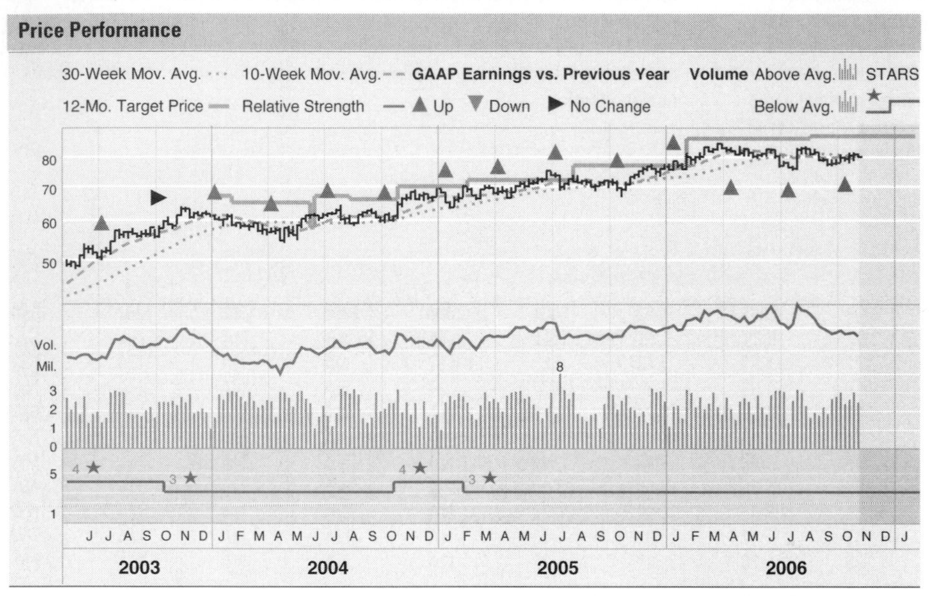

Options: CBOE, Ph

Analysis prepared by **Christopher B. Muir** on August 14, 2006, when the stock traded at **$ 82.00**.

Highlights

- We expect relatively strong loan and fee income growth, in part due to the Amegy acquisition, to drive revenue growth of 28% in 2006. We also expect fewer losses on the sale of securities. Our 2006 estimates include a net interest margin of 4.61% (up from 4.58% in 2005 despite our view of continued pressure from a relatively flat yield curve), average earning asset growth of 28%, and non-interest income growth of 23%.
- We see ZION continuing its focus on expense control. Our 2006 non-interest expense to total revenue forecast of 56.6% is higher than 2005's 55.9%, as we expect the expensing of stock options in 2006 to more than offset efficiency improvements. Asset quality has improved over the past four years. We expect loan loss provisions to increase to about $61 million in 2006, from $43 million in 2005.
- Assuming an effective tax rate of 35.4% and no share repurchases, we project operating EPS of $5.52 in 2006, up 14% from 2005's $4.86. We see 2007 EPS of $6.12, a further increase of 11%.

Investment Rationale/Risk

- As a bank focused on small to mid-sized business lending, the majority of ZION's loans are tied to the prime rate or LIBOR. Combined with what we view as strong growth in loans and low cost deposits, we believe the bank will continue to generate stable net interest margins. Due to strong credit risk management, asset quality does not pose a potential problem in the near term, in our view. Despite a short-term impact to earnings, we see ZION benefiting from its acquisition of Amegy.
- Risks to our opinion and target price include detrimental changes in the slope of the yield curve or operational performance that does not meet our expectations.
- Our 12-month target price of $88 is based on our relative valuation analysis and dividend discount model. Our target price indicates a P/E multiple of 14.4X our 2007 EPS estimate, an 8% premium to ZION's mid-cap regional banking peers, which we believe is warranted by our EPS growth projections. The dividend model, which assumes a discount rate of 8.5% and a terminal growth rate of 4%, estimates an intrinsic value of $88.

Qualitative Risk Assessment

LOW | MEDIUM | HIGH

Our risk assessment reflects the company's mid-cap valuation, strong credit quality of its loan portfolio, and history of profitability. While the company operates in a highly competitive and fragmented industry, companies in the industry tend to produce relatively stable financial results.

Quantitative Evaluations

S&P Quality Ranking **A**

D | C | B- | B | B+ | A- | A | A+

Relative Strength Rank **MODERATE**

35

LOWEST = 1 HIGHEST = 99

Revenue/Earnings Data

Revenue (Million $)

	1Q	2Q	3Q	4Q	Year
2006	768.0	824.4	877.1	--	--
2005	525.8	562.3	594.5	666.5	2,349
2004	457.4	469.8	492.6	503.3	1,923
2003	445.7	454.3	539.6	449.8	1,889
2002	460.8	472.7	441.4	462.2	1,833
2001	518.7	501.3	509.6	481.1	2,011

Earnings Per Share ($)

	1Q	2Q	3Q	4Q	Year
2006	1.28	1.35	1.42	E1.47	E5.52
2005	1.20	1.30	1.34	1.32	5.16
2004	1.10	1.09	1.13	1.15	4.47
2003	0.96	1.02	0.71	1.05	3.74
2002	0.89	0.92	0.71	0.92	3.44
2001	0.80	0.79	0.78	0.78	3.15

Fiscal year ended Dec. 31. Next earnings report expected: Late January. EPS Estimates based on S&P Operating Earnings; historical GAAP earnings are as reported.

Dividend Data (Dates: mm/dd Payment Date: mm/dd/yy)

Amount ($)	Date Decl.	Ex-Div. Date	Stk. of Record	Payment Date
0.360	10/28	11/07	11/09	11/23/05
0.360	01/30	02/06	02/08	02/22/06
0.360	05/01	05/08	05/10	05/24/06
0.360	07/25	08/07	08/09	08/23/06

Dividends have been paid since 1966. Source: Company reports.

Zions BanCorp

Business Summary August 14, 2006

CORPORATE OVERVIEW. ZION is a financial holding company that operates 8 different banks in 10 western states with each bank operating under a different name and management and operating as an individual segment. In addition, the company's Other segment contains the parent company operations, certain nonbank subsidiaries and operating units, The Commerce Bank of Oregon, and eliminations of transactions between segments.

The company's largest bank is Zions First National Bank (ZFNB), which we estimate generated 32% of 2005 revenues (assuming Amegy's revenues for all of 2005 are included) and serves Utah and Idaho. ZFNB also houses the company's capital markets and wealth management operations. California Bank & Trust (25%) serves California and has loan production offices in Arizona, Colorado, Florida, Georgia, Illinois, Michigan, Missouri, Nevada, Ohio, Oregon, and Washington. Amagy Corporation (16%) was acquired in December 2005 and serves Houston and Dallas, Texas. National Bank of Arizona (10%) serves the Phoenix and Tucson metropolitan areas. Nevada State Bank (10%) serves the state of Nevada. Vectra Bank Colorado (6%) serves Colorado. The Commerce Bank of Washington (1%) has one office in the Seattle area serving businesses, executives, and professionals.

The company tries to control risks by maintaining formal loan policies and procedures, independent compliance examinations of adherence to the policies and procedures, performing portfolio risk analysis, using financial instruments to reduce interest rate risk, and by pursuing a loan portfolio diversification strategy.

MARKET PROFILE. ZION's mainly western footprint includes 127 branches in Utah, 94 in California, 83 in Texas, 71 in Nevada, 53 in Arizona, 40 in Colorado, 24 in Idaho, and 4 branches in other states. The projection for deposit weighted average population growth in the company's service territory is 9.7% from 2005 to 2010 according to SNL Financial. The projected national growth rate is 6.3% and the population weighted average growth rate of the states in the company's service territory is 11%.

Company Financials

Per Share Data ($) Year Ended Dec. 31	**2005**	**2004**	**2003**	**2002**	**2001**	**2000**	**1999**	**1998**	**1997**	**1996**
Tangible Book Value	20.45	23.29	20.96	17.21	15.19	13.06	11.61	9.44	7.76	7.98
Earnings	5.16	4.47	3.74	3.44	3.15	1.86	2.20	1.91	1.09	1.71
S&P Core Earnings	5.04	4.33	4.42	3.17	2.42	NA	NA	NA	NA	NA
Dividends	1.44	1.26	1.02	0.80	0.80	0.89	0.86	0.52	0.58	0.32
Payout Ratio	28%	28%	27%	23%	25%	48%	38%	27%	30%	18%
Prices:High	77.67	69.29	63.86	59.65	64.00	62.88	75.88	62.50	46.00	26.00
Prices:Low	63.33	54.08	39.31	34.14	42.30	32.00	48.25	37.88	25.44	16.25
P/E Ratio:High	15	16	17	17	20	34	34	33	24	15
P/E Ratio:Low	12	12	11	10	13	17	21	20	13	10

Income Statement Analysis (Million $)	2005	2004	2003	2002	2001	2000	1999	1998	1997	1996
Net Interest Income	1,301	1,174	1,095	1,035	950	803	741	544	352	260
Tax Equivalent Adjustment	NA	NA	NA	NA	NA	NA	16.2	8.84	6.90	7.10
Non Interest Income	439	425	426	402	388	274	270	199	143	111
Loan Loss Provision	43.0	44.1	69.9	71.9	73.2	31.8	18.0	12.2	6.18	3.54
% Expense/Operating Revenue	56.4%	57.8%	63.7%	59.8%	63.9%	75.9%	66.4%	68.3%	60.9%	56.6%
Pretax Income	742	624	546	401	440	243	309	218	188	153
Effective Tax Rate	35.5%	35.3%	39.1%	34.9%	35.8%	32.8%	35.5%	32.5%	34.8%	34.0%
Net Income	480	406	340	317	290	162	194	147	122	101
% Net Interest Margin	4.58	4.32	4.45	4.56	4.64	4.27	4.31	4.60	4.27	4.56
S&P Core Earnings	469	394	402	292	223	NA	NA	NA	NA	NA

Balance Sheet & Other Financial Data (Million $)	2005	2004	2003	2002	2001	2000	1999	1998	1997	1996
Money Market Assets	667	593	569	543	280	528	525	804	898	648
Investment Securities	6,996	5,786	5,402	4,238	3,463	4,188	4,437	3,488	2,629	1,776
Commercial Loans	23,122	16,337	10,404	13,648	4,110	3,615	3,311	2,905	1,393	944
Other Loans	7,131	6,395	9,613	5,195	13,304	10,843	9,133	7,777	3,521	2,509
Total Assets	42,780	31,470	28,558	26,566	24,304	21,939	20,281	16,649	9,522	6,485
Demand Deposits	9,954	6,822	5,883	5,117	4,481	3,586	3,277	3,170	1,783	1,160
Time Deposits	22,689	16,471	15,014	15,015	13,361	11,484	10,786	8,622	5,071	3,392
Long Term Debt	2,746	1,919	1,843	1,310	781	420	453	511	470	252
Common Equity	4,237	2,790	2,540	2,374	2,281	1,779	1,660	1,014	655	507
% Return on Assets	1.3	2.0	1.2	1.2	1.3	0.8	1.0	1.1	1.5	1.7
% Return on Equity	13.7	15.2	13.8	13.6	14.3	9.4	12.5	17.6	21.0	21.6
% Loan Loss Reserve	1.1	1.2	0.9	1.4	1.5	1.3	1.6	1.9	1.7	2.0
% Loans/Deposits	92.3	97.1	142.6	96.0	97.0	96.6	91.0	79.8	71.1	75.8
% Equity to Assets	9.5	13.3	8.9	9.2	8.8	8.1	8.1	6.4	7.3	7.7

Data as orig reptd.; bef. results of disc opers/spec. items. Per share data adj. for stk. divs.; EPS diluted. E-Estimated. NA-Not Available. NM-Not Meaningful. NR-Not Ranked. UR-Under Review.

Office: 1 South Main Street, Salt Lake City, UT, USA 84111-1904.
Telephone: 801-524-4787.
Website: http://www.zionsbancorporation.com
Chrmn, Pres & CEO: H.H. Simmons

Vice Chrmn & CFO: D. Arnold
Investor Contact: C.B. Hinckley (801-524-4787)
SVP & Cntlr: N.X. Bellon

Board of Directors: D. L. Arnold, J. C. Atkin, R. D. Cash, P. Frobes, J. D. Heaney, R. B. Porter, S. D. Quinn, H. H. Simmons, L. E. Simmons, S. C. Wheelbright, S. T. Williams

Founded: 1961
Domicile: Utah
Employees: 10,102